OFFICIAL TOURIST BOA

B&B

2011

England's quality-assessed guest accommodation

New 36th edition. Brighter, better, easier to use.

Congratulations for making the decision to holiday in England. You've chosen a country of immense diversity with a fascinating history of pageantry, medieval villages, castles and palaces alongside a more modern, sophisticated England with chic urban centres and world-class restaurants and attractions.

Divided into nine distinct regions each with its own unique personality, there is something new to explore in every corner of the country.

From the rolling hills of the Cotswolds and bustling city life of Liverpool, to the charms of sleepy Cornish villages and dramatic coastal splendour of the North East – this is the year to explore England.

Research carried out by VisitEngland has shown that a combination of factors is driving an increased interest in our nation holidaying at home. With an unrivalled calendar of world-class events – from music festivals to Royal Ascot, The Proms to the Chelsea Flower Show – there are plenty of opportunities to enjoy every minute of our precious free time in England.

English destinations have inspired some of the world's greatest authors, musicians, actors, and sporting legends, as well as iconic fictional characters from Harry Potter to James Bond. So whether it's exploring Shakespeare country, Manchester United's Old Trafford, or whizzing down the River Thames in a speedboat 007 style – you can experience England through the eyes of our legends.

With the spotlight firmly on England this year, it's time for us to shine and our accommodation sector has never been more ready for the challenge.

Whatever your destination or budget, there's a limitless range of quality accommodation to choose from in England. For inspiration and information, just browse through this book, produced on our behalf by Heritage House Group. All accommodation included comes complete with VisitEngland's trusted Quality Assurance Rose stamp of approval so you can choose your accommodation with confidence and be sure of a good night's sleep.

Most importantly, enjoy your holiday, however short or long.

Penelope, Viscountess Cobham
Chairman of VisitEngland

Contents

Foreword	2
How to use this Guide	4
Accommodation Entries Explained	5
Key to Symbols	6
A Special Welcome	7
National Accessible Scheme	8
Enjoy England Star Ratings	12
Sustainable Tourism	16
Gold and Silver Awards	17
Enjoy England Awards for Excellence	19
Location Maps	706

Further Information

Advice and Information	723
About Accommodation Entries	726
Getting Around	728
Travel Information	732

Useful Indexes

A full list of indexes, including The National Accessible Scheme	734

Cover image: The Old School, Northumberland
Enjoy England Awards for Excellence 2010
Gold winner - Bed & Breakfast/GA

South West England — 20
Cornwall & Isles of Scilly, Devon, Dorset, Gloucestershire, Somerset, Wiltshire

South East England — 174
Berkshire, Buckinghamshire, Hampshire, Isle of Wight, Kent, Oxfordshire, Surrey, Sussex

London — 292

East of England — 312
Bedfordshire, Cambridgeshire, Essex, Hertfordshire, Norfolk, Suffolk

East Midlands — 386
Derbyshire, Leicestershire & Rutland, Lincolnshire, Northamptonshire, Nottinghamshire

Heart of England — 440
Herefordshire, Shropshire, Staffordshire, Warwickshire, West Midlands, Worcestershire

Yorkshire — 490

North West England — 558
Cheshire, Cumbria, Lancashire, Manchester, Merseyside

North East England — 658
County Durham, Northumberland, Tyne & Wear

How to use this guide

This official **VisitEngland** guide is packed with information from where to stay, to how to get there and what to see. In fact, everything you need to know to enjoy England.

Choose from a wide range of quality-assessed accommodation to suit all budgets and tastes. This guide contains a comprehensive listing of all bed and breakfast establishments participating in the Enjoy England Quality Rose assessment scheme, including guesthouses, farmhouses, inns, hostels and campus accommodation.

Each property has been visited annually by professional assessors who apply nationally agreed standards so that you can book with confidence knowing your accommodation has been checked and rated for quality.

Check out the places to visit in each region, from towns and cities to spectacular coast and countryside, plus historic homes, castles and great family attractions! Maps show accommodation locations, selected destinations and some of the National Cycle Networks. For even more ideas go online at enjoyengland.com

Regional tourism contacts and tourist information centres are listed – contact them for further information. You'll also find events, travel information, maps and useful indexes.

Accommodation entries explained

Each accommodation entry contains detailed information to help you decide if it is right for you. This has been provided by proprietors and our aim is to ensure that it is as objective and factual as possible.

① ② ③ ④ ⑤ ⑥

LAUNCESTON, Cornwall Map ref 1C2   SAT NAV PL15 9PE

Primrose Cottage
Primrose Cottage, Lawhitton, Launceston PL15 9PE
t (01326) 773645   e enquiry@primrosecottagesuites.co.uk
primrosecottagesuites.co.uk   ONLINE MAP

B&B PER ROOM PER NIGHT
S £70.00 – £90.00
D £80.00 – £130.00
EVENING MEAL PER PERSON
£12.00 – £16.00

Discounts on stays of 2 or 3 days. Please see website for details.

Primrose Cottage is set in gardens and woodland leading to the River Tamar. Each luxury suite has its own sitting room, entrance and en suite facilities with beautiful views across the Tamar Valley. Five minutes from the A30 with easy access to both north and south coasts and the moors.

open All year
bedrooms 2 double, 1 twin
bathrooms 3 en suite
payment credit/debit cards, cash, cheques

directions Leave Launceston on the A388 Plymouth road. After 1 mile turn left on B3362 signposted Tavistock. Primrose Cottage is on the left after 2.5 miles.

Room · · · · · General · · · · · Leisure ·

Sample Enhanced Entry

⑦ ⑧ ⑨ ⑩ ⑪ ⑫

1 Listing under town or village with map reference

2 Rating (and/or) Award where applicable

3 Prices per room for bed and breakfast (B&B) and per person for half board (HB) accommodation

4 Establishment name, address, telephone and email

5 Website information

6 Satellite navigation

7 Accessible rating where applicable

8 Walkers, cyclists, pets and families welcome where applicable

9 Indicates when the establishment is open

10 Accommodation details and payment accepted

11 At-a-glance facility symbols

12 Travel directions

At the end of each regional section you will find a listing of all bed & breakfast accommodation in England that has been assessed for quality by Enjoy England.

The information includes brief contact details for each place to stay, together with its star rating, classification and quality award if appropriate. The listing also shows if an establishment has a National Accessible rating or participates in the Welcome schemes:

Cyclists Welcome, Walkers Welcome, Welcome Pets! and Families Welcome (see pg 7 of the guide for further information)

More detailed information on all the properties shown in bold can be found in the main 'Where to Stay' sections (where establishments have paid to have their details included) To find these entries please refer to the property index at the back of this guide.

Key to symbols

Information about many of the accommodation services and facilities is given in the form of symbols.

General

- Children welcome (a number following gives minimum age)
- Cots
- Highchairs
- Parking on site
- Wi-Fi
- Internet access
- Bar
- Evening meals served
- Special diets by arrangement
- Games console available
- Laundry facilities
- Garden/patio
- Pets welcome by arrangement

Businesses displaying this logo have undergone a rigorous verification process to ensure that they are sustainable (green). See page 16 for further information.

Enjoy England's Breakfast Award recognises hotels and B&Bs that offer a quality and choice of breakfast, service and hospitality that exceeds what would be expected at their star rating.

Visitor Attraction Quality Assurance
Participating attractions are visited annually by a professional assessor. High standards in welcome, hospitality, services, presentation; standards of toilets, shop and café, where provided, must be achieved to receive this Enjoy England award.

Rooms

- Bedroom(s) on ground floor
- Four-poster bed(s)
- Telephone in all bedrooms
- TV in all bedrooms
- Satellite/cable channels in all bedrooms
- Tea/coffee facilities in all bedrooms
- Hairdryer in all bedrooms
- Smoking rooms available

Leisure

- Swimming pool – indoor
- Swimming pool – outdoor
- Tennis court(s)
- Riding/pony-trekking nearby
- Fishing nearby
- Access to golf
- Cycle hire nearby

Campus/Hostels

- Cooking facilities available
- Lounge
- Games room

National Accessible Scheme
The National Accessible Scheme includes standards for hearing and visual impairment as well as mobility impairment – see pages 8-9 for further information.

Welcome schemes
Walkers, cyclists, families and pet owners are warmly welcomed where you see these signs – see page 7 for further information.

A special welcome

To help make your selection of accommodation easier VisitEngland has four special Welcome schemes which accommodation in England can be assessed to. Owners participating in these schemes go the extra mile to welcome walkers, cyclists, families or pet owners and provide additional facilities and services to make your stay even more comfortable.

Families Welcome

If you are searching for a great family break look out for the Families Welcome sign. The sign indicates that the proprietor offers additional facilities and services catering for a range of ages and family units. For families with young children, the accommodation will have special facilities such as cots and highchairs, storage for push-chairs and somewhere to heat baby food or milk. Where meals are provided, children's choices will be clearly indicated, with healthy options available. They'll also have information on local walks, attractions, activities or events suitable for children, as well as local child-friendly pubs and restaurants. Not all accommodation is able to cater for all ages or combinations of family units, so do check when you book.

Welcome Pets!

Want to travel with your faithful companion? Look out for accommodation displaying the Welcome Pets! sign. Participants in this scheme go out of their way to meet the needs of guests bringing dogs, cats and/or small birds. In addition to providing water and food bowls, torches or nightlights, spare leads and pet washing facilities, they'll buy in food on request, and offer toys, treats and bedding. They'll also have information on pet-friendly attractions, pubs, restaurants and recreation. Of course, not everyone is able to offer suitable facilities for every pet, so do check if there are any restrictions on the type, size and number of animals when you book.

Walkers Welcome

If walking is your passion seek out accommodation participating in the Walkers Welcome scheme. Facilities include a place for drying clothes and boots, maps and books for reference and a first-aid kit. Packed breakfasts and lunch are available on request in hotels and guesthouses, and you have the option to pre-order basic groceries in self-catering accommodation. A wide range of information is provided including public transport, weather, local restaurants and attractions, details of the nearest bank and all night chemists.

Cyclists Welcome

If you like to explore by bike seek out accommodation displaying the Cyclists Welcome symbol. Facilities include a lockable undercover area and a place to dry outdoor clothing and footwear, an evening meal if there are no eating facilities available within one mile, and a packed breakfast or lunch on request. Information is also provided on cycle hire and cycle repair shops, maps and books for reference, weather and details of the nearest bank and all night chemists and more.

For further information go online at enjoyengland.com/stay/quality-ratings

National Accessible Scheme

Finding suitable accommodation is not always easy, especially if you have to seek out rooms with level entry or large print menus. Use the National Accessible Scheme to help you make your choice.

Proprietors of accommodation taking part in the National Accessible Scheme have gone out of their way to ensure a comfortable stay for guests with special hearing, visual or mobility needs. These exceptional places are full of extra touches to make everyone's visit trouble-free, from handrails, ramps and step-free entrances (ideal for buggies too) to level-access showers and colour contrast in the bathrooms. Members of staff may have attended a disability awareness course and will know what assistance will really be appreciated.

Appropriate National Accessible Scheme symbols are included in the guide entries (shown opposite). If you have additional needs or special requirements we strongly recommend that you make sure these can be met by your chosen establishment before you confirm your reservation. The index at the back of the guide gives a list of accommodation that have received a National Accessible rating.

For the widest possible selection of places to stay OpenBritain 2011 is the new guide to accessible accommodation in Britain. Packed with Hotels, B&B's, Self Catering and Caravan and Camping sites – OpenBritain is the perfect accessible travel planner. Available from all good bookstores or direct from Tourism for All priced £9.99 (plus £4.50 P&P)

England

Mobility Impairment Symbols

The criteria VisitEngland and national/regional tourism organisations have adopted do not necessarily conform to British Standards or to Building Regulations. They reflect what the organisations understand to be acceptable to meet the practical needs of guests with mobility or sensory impairments and encourage the industry to increase access to all.

For tips and advice on holiday travel in England and to search for NAS accredited accommodation, go to: www.enjoyengland.com/access

Additional help and guidance on accessible tourism can be obtained from the national charity Tourism for All:

Tourism for All
Tourism for All c/o Vitalise
Shap Road Industrial Estate
Kendal LA9 6NZ

Information helpline 0845 124 9971
Reservations 0845 124 9973
(lines open 9-5 Mon-Fri)
F 01539 735567
E info@tourismforall.org.uk
W http://www.tourismforall.org.uk

Older and less mobile guests
Typically suitable for a person with sufficient mobility to climb a flight of steps but who would benefit from fixtures and fittings to aid balance.

Part-time wheelchair users
Typically suitable for a person with restricted walking ability and for those who may need to use a wheelchair some of the time and can negotiate a maximum of three steps.

Independent wheelchair users
Typically suitable for a person who depends on the use of a wheelchair and transfers unaided to and from the wheelchair in a seated position. This person may be an independent traveller.

Assisted wheelchair users
Typically suitable for a person who depends on the use of a wheelchair and needs assistance when transferring to and from the wheelchair in a seated position.

Access Exceptional is awarded to establishments that meet the requirements of independent wheelchair users or assisted wheelchair users shown above and also fulfil more demanding requirements with reference to the British Standards BS8300.

Visual Impairment Symbols

Typically provides key additional services and facilities to meet the needs of visually impaired guests.

Typically provides a higher level of additional services and facilities to meet the needs of visually impaired guests.

Hearing Impairment Symbols

Typically provides key additional services and facilities to meet the needs of guests with hearing impairment.

Typically provides a higher level of additional services and facilities to meet the needs of guests with hearing impairment.

THE DEFINITIVE GUIDE TO ACCESSIBLE BRITAIN

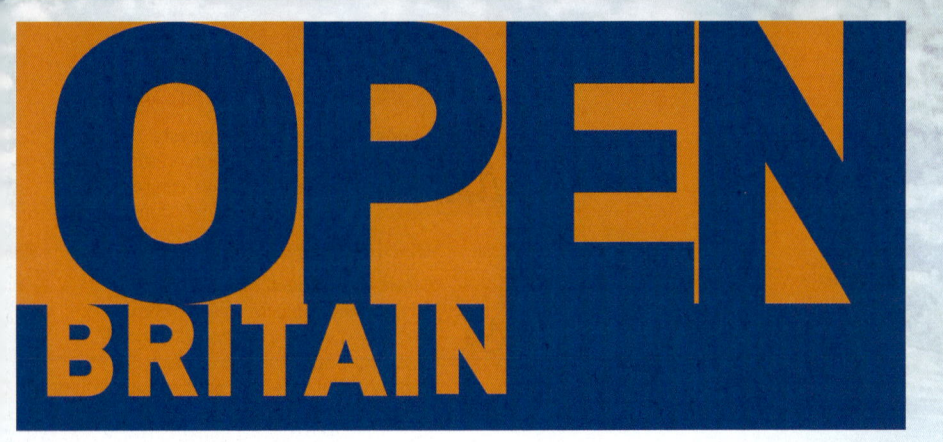

OPEN BRITAIN

THE OPENBRITAIN GUIDE was created by a partnership between Tourism for All UK, and RADAR, with support from the National Federation of Shopmobility, and the backing of the national tourism agencies VisitEngland, VisitScotland, and VisitWales. The partnership has now been joined by DisabledGo, and is backed by a raft of industry bodies including the Automobile Association, the British Hospitality Association, the Historic Houses Association, English Heritage, the National Trust, the Good Food Guide, Hudson's guide, and many more. The 2011 edition contains pages of information for travellers with access needs.

- Where to Go
- Where to Stay
- What to Do ... and much, much more

OPENLONDON is the new guide to accessible London that has been published thanks to the support of the London Development Agency. It contains vital information to ensure that visitors with access needs enjoy London to the full.

- Where to Stay
- Where to Go
- What to Do
- Where to Eat ... and much, much more

Order your copy of **OpenBritain 2011** now!
Online: www.openbritain.net
Bookshops: ISBN 978-0-85101-482-1
Call: 01603 813319

OpenBritain is a project of Tourism for All UK, a national charity No 279169, Regd company no. 01466822 www.tourismforall.org.uk

www.openbritain.net | info@openbritain.net | Call: 01603 813319

THE DEFINITIVE GUIDE TO ACCESSIBLE BRITAIN

OPENBRITAIN
The one-stop-shop to accessible Britain.

OpenBritain for holidays and short breaks or even a day out – you'll find just what you're looking for if you, or a member of your party, has an access need - whether impaired mobility, vision or hearing. If you need a ground floor room because you can't manage stairs, or you have a child in a buggy, or a wheelchair, or if you need staff trained to offer a welcome to all... OpenBritain is the answer.

- Over 1,000 places to stay that have been audited for accessibility
- Ideas for great days out for all
- Travel tips and resources
- All in a handy guide, or on www.openbritain.net with even more easy ways to find us coming soon!
- Share your experiences with others – simply logon to www.openbritain.net and help build this vital resource

THE WEBSITE
www.openbritain.net now contains over 30,000 venues with places to stay and visit. All are assessed, or self-assessed and subject to a random check. The dynamic website will keep you inspired and active, and we are asking for feedback so that you can add your own recommendations to help others with similar needs benefit from your experience.

We are working with specialist partners to create a truly national and exciting platform that meets the needs of all. Watch this space for exciting developments in the year ahead.

Cost: £9.99 plus P&P | Order online: www.openbritain.net

Peace of Mind with Enjoy England Star Ratings

Most bed and breakfast establishments in Britain have a star rating from one of the four assessing bodies – VisitEngland, VisitScotland, Visit Wales or the AA. They all assess to the same national standards so you can expect comparable services, facilities and quality standards at each star rating.

All the accommodation in this guide is checked annually by VisitEngland assessors. An assessment is made every year and an overnight stay takes place at intervals of one to three years (the highest rated properties are visited every year). So when you see the Quality Rose sign showing the star ratings you can be confident that we've checked it out.

The national standards are based on our research of consumer expectations. The independent assessors decide the type (classification) of accommodation – for example if it's a 'bed and breakfast', 'guest accommodation', 'farmhouse', etc – and award a star rating based on the range and quality of facilities offered and as well as, where appropriate, a further special quality award.

Our assessors consider every aspect of your stay such as the warmth of welcome, comfort of furnishings including beds, food quality (with a particular eye on breakfast), cleanliness of rooms and common areas and the level of care and safety offered.

The Quality Rose sign helps you choose with confidence knowing that the accommodation has been thoroughly checked out before you check in.

Accommodation Types

Always look at or ask for the type of accommodation as each offers a very distinct experience. The bed and breakfast types you'll find in this guide are:

Guest Accommodation – wide range of establishments from one-room bed and breakfast to larger properties, which may offer dinner and hold an alcohol licence.

Bed and Breakfast – accommodating generally no more than six people, the owners of these establishments welcome you into their home as a special guest.

Guest House – generally comprising more than three rooms. Dinner may be available (if it is, it will need to be booked in advance). May possibly be licensed.

Farmhouse – bed and breakfast, and sometimes dinner, but always on a farm.

Inn – pubs with rooms, and many with restaurants as well.

Room Only – Accommodation that either does not offer breakfast or, if it does, it will not be served (ie self-service or breakfast pack)

Hostel – safe, budget-priced, short-term accommodation for individuals and groups. The Hostel classification includes Group Hostel, Backpacker and Activity Accommodation (all of which are awarded star ratings).

Campus – Accommodation provided by educational establishments, including university halls of residence and student village complexes. May be offered on a bed and breakfast or sometimes a self-catering basis.

Star ratings you can trust

All bed and breakfast accommodation that is awarded a star rating (from 1 to 5 stars) will assure you of minimum standards so you can be confident that you will find the basic services that you would expect, such as:

- A clear explanation of booking charges, services offered and cancellation terms.
- A full cooked breakfast or substantial continental breakfast.
- At least one bathroom or shower room for every six guests.
- For a stay of more than one night, rooms cleaned and beds made daily.
- Printed advice on how to summon emergency assistance at night.
- All statutory obligations will be met, including Fire Safety.

The more stars, the higher the quality and the greater the range of facilities and level of service.

To achieve higher star ratings, an increasing level of facilities and services are offered. For example, at 3-star, bed and breakfast must offer a guest bathroom which cannot be shared with the owners and bedrooms must have a washbasin if not en suite, and at 4-star, 50% of bedrooms will be en suite or with private bathroom. At 5-star, all rooms must be en suite or with private bathroom.

In order to assess the quality of the bed and breakfast, our assessors stay overnight (in the first year of assessment and regularly thereafter). Every aspect of the experience is assessed, from the comfort of the beds, the standard of the breakfast (and dinner if offered) and, most importantly, the cleanliness. They also score the warmth of welcome and the level of care that each offers its guests.

Star ratings are based on a combination of range of facilities, level of service offered and quality - if a bed and breakfast offers facilities required to achieve a certain star rating but does not achieve the quality score required for that rating, a lower star rating is awarded.

Gold and Silver Awards

How can you find those special places to stay – those that, regardless of the range of facilities and services, achieve top scores for quality (from hospitality and housekeeping, bedrooms and bathrooms, food and cleanliness)? Look for Enjoy England Gold and Silver awards. These awards are given to bed and breakfast offering the highest level of quality within their particular star rating.

Accommodation with a lower star rating may be more suited to your needs: sometimes a bed and breakfast establishment has exceptional bedrooms and bathrooms and offers guests a very special welcome, but cannot achieve a higher star rating because, for example, there are no en suite bedrooms, or it is difficult to put washbasins in the bedrooms (three star). This is sometimes the case with period properties. Look out for accommodation with Gold or Silver Awards which recognise quality rather than specific facilities.

Enjoy England unique Gold and Silver Awards are given in recognition of exceptional quality.

A full list of all Gold and Silver Award winning bed and breakfast accommodation is given on pages 738 to 757.

THE GOOD FOOD GUIDE

The selection of restaurant reviews in this VisitBritain guide has been taken from the highly respected *The Good Food Guide 2011*.

The Good Food Guide 2011 is the 60th anniversary edition of the UK's bestselling and longest-running restaurant guide. It includes in-depth reviews of the best restaurants, pubs and cafés throughout the UK.

Compiled from scratch every year, the Guide is based on reader feedback, and all inspections are carried out anonymously. The Guide does not accept advertising or free meals.

Since 1951, the Guide has pushed the boundaries of the British dining scene and is often the first to spot hidden gems and phenomenal talent. Both a national treasure and a trend forecaster, *The Good Food Guide* is *the* restaurant bible.

Inside the 2011 edition you will find:

✷ Detailed and incisive reviews
✷ Great-value pubs and high-end restaurants
✷ Foodie features and chef interviews
✷ £50 of money-off vouchers to use across the UK

> **The Guide has been instrumental in the evolution and improvement of food and cooking in this country.**
>
> *Heston Blumenthal*

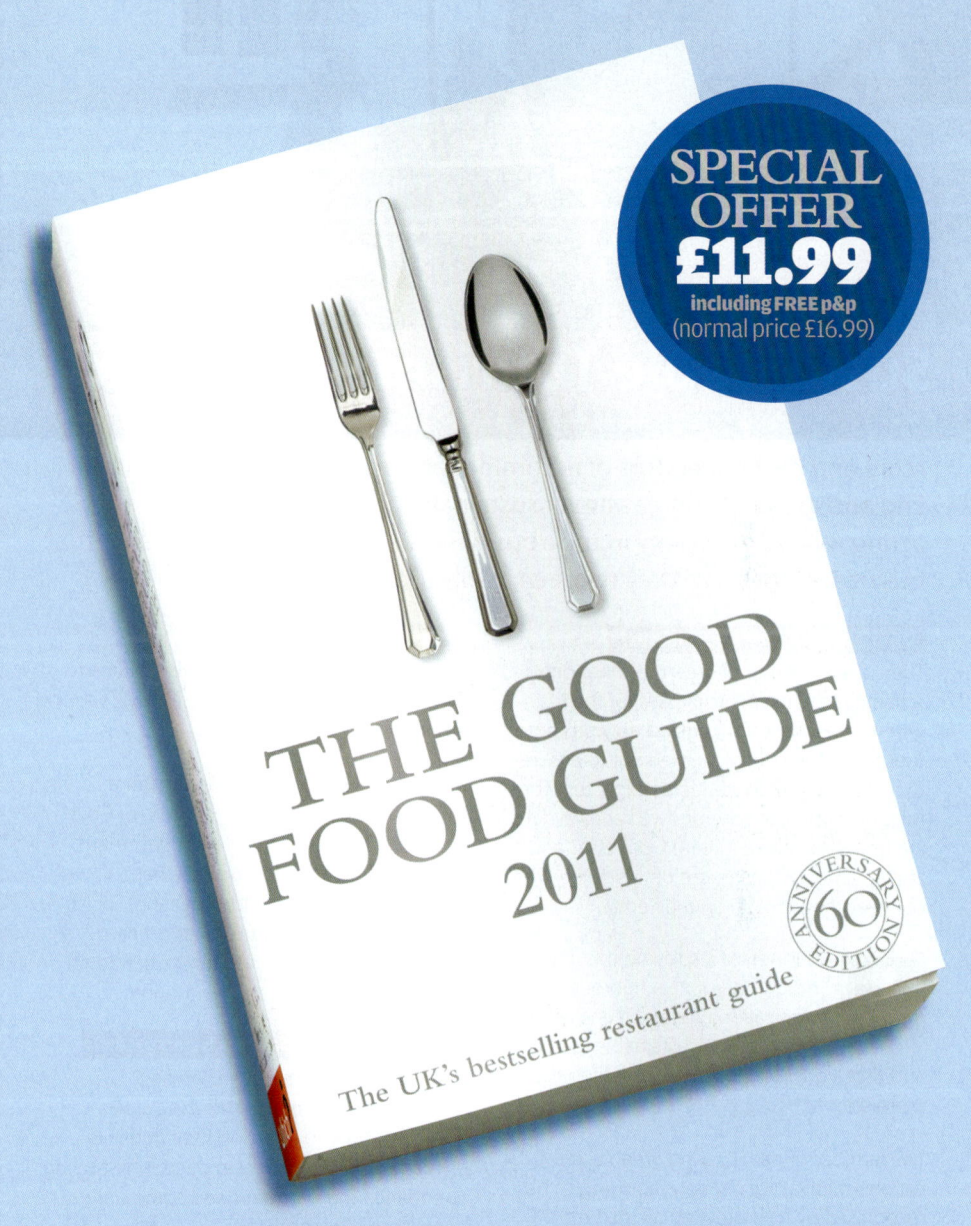

SPECIAL OFFER £11.99 including FREE p&p (normal price £16.99)

THE GOOD FOOD GUIDE 2011

60th Anniversary Edition

The UK's bestselling restaurant guide

To order your copy of *The Good Food Guide 2011* at the special offer price of £11.99 including FREE p&p (normal price £16.99), please call 01992 822800 and quote GFGV11.

Offer is valid to 31 December 2011.

ISBN: 978 1 84490 195 1 | 624 pages | Full colour, including maps for each region

Sustainable Tourism in England

More and more operators of accommodation, attractions and events in England are becoming aware of sustainable or "green" issues and are acting more responsibly in their businesses. But how can you be sure that businesses that 'say' they're green, really are?

Who certifies green businesses?

There are a number of green certification schemes that assess businesses for their green credentials. VisitEngland only promotes those that have been checked out to ensure they reach the high standards expected. The members of those schemes we have validated are truly sustainable (green) businesses and appear amongst the pages of this guide with our heart-flower logo on their entry.

Businesses displaying this logo have undergone a rigorous verification process to ensure that they are sustainable (green) and that a qualified assessor has visited the premises.

The number of participating green certification scheme organisations applying to be recognised by us is growing all the time. At the moment we promote the largest green scheme in the world - Green Tourism Business Scheme (GTBS).

Green Tourism Business Scheme

GTBS recognises places to stay and attractions that are taking action to support the local area and the wider environment. With over 2000 members in the UK it's the largest sustainable (green) scheme to operate globally and assesses hundreds of fantastic places to stay and visit in Britain. From small bed and breakfasts to large visitor attractions and activity holiday providers.

Businesses that meet the standard for a GTBS award receive a Bronze, Silver, or Gold award based on their level of achievement. Businesses are assessed in areas that include Management and Marketing, Social Involvement and Communication, Energy, Water, Purchasing, Waste, Transport, Natural and Cultural Heritage and Innovation.

How are these businesses being green?

Any business that has been certified 'green' will have implemented initiatives that contribute to reducing their negative environmental and social impacts whilst trying to enhance the economic and community benefits to their local area.

Many of these things may be behind the scenes such as energy efficient boilers, insulated lofts or grey water recycling, but there are many fun activities that you can expect to find too. For example, your green business should be able to advise you about traditional activities nearby, the best places to sample local food and buy craft products, or even help you to enjoy a 'car-free' day out.

Gold and Silver Awards

Enjoy England's unique Gold and Silver Awards are given in recognition of exceptional quality in bed and breakfast accommodation.

Enjoy England professional assessors make recommendations for Gold and Silver Awards during assessments. They will look at the quality provided in all areas, in particular housekeeping, hospitality, bedrooms, bathrooms and food, to see if it meets the highest quality for the star level achieved.

While star ratings are based on a combination of quality, range of facilities and level of service offered, Gold and Silver Awards are based solely on quality.

Here we feature bed and breakfast establishments with a Gold Award for which detailed entries are included in the regional pages. Use the property index starting on page 773 to find their page numbers.

An index of all Gold and Silver Award-winning accommodation can be found at the back of this guide.

Gold Award with entries in the regional pages

Anchorage Bed and Breakfast
Amesbury, Wiltshire

The Old Pump House
Aylsham, Norfolk

Mallards
Basingstoke, Hampshire

Cotteswold House
Bibury, Gloucestershire

Number One St Luke's
Blackpool, Lancashire

Farnham Farm House
Blandford Forum, Dorset

Churton Heath Farm Bed & Breakfast
Bruera, Cheshire

Harefield Cottage
Bude, Cornwall

Magnolia House
Canterbury, Kent

Clanville Manor B&B
Castle Cary, Somerset

Beaumont House
Cheltenham, Gloucestershire

Nineveh Farm
Chipping Campden, Gloucestershire

Druid House
Christchurch, Dorset

Trinity Town House
Colchester, Essex

Seven Acres House
Coltishall, Norfolk

Hay Farm House
Cornhill-on-Tweed, Northumberland

Horseshoe Cottage Farm
Cropston, Leicestershire & Rutland

Laurel House
Culgaith, Cumbria

Blackbrook House
Dorking, Surrey

The Victorian Town House
Durham, Co Durham

Harptree Court
East Harptree, Somerset

Brayscroft House
Eastbourne, Sussex

Broom House and Whites (Restaurant)
Egton Bridge, Yorkshire

Flindor Cottage
Framlingham (7 miles), Suffolk

Old School
Friston, Suffolk

The Hill on the Wall
Gilsland, Cumbria

Rickyard Cottage
Great Missenden, Buckinghamshire

Cold Cotes
Harrogate, Yorkshire

Swan House
Hastings, Sussex

Copyhold Hollow Bed & Breakfast
Haywards Heath, Sussex

The Dairy Barns
Hickling, Norfolk

Underleigh House
Hope, Derbyshire

Kilham Hall Country House
Kilham, Yorkshire

Primrose Cottage
Launceston, Cornwall

Lavenham Old Rectory
Lavenham, Suffolk

Little Holtby
Leeming Bar, Yorkshire

Brook Barn
Letcombe Regis, Oxfordshire

Beechwood B&B
Lewes, Sussex

Bucklawren Farm
Looe, Cornwall

DeGreys
Ludlow, Shropshire

The Nurse's Cottage Restaurant with Rooms
Lymington, Hampshire

Lyth Hill House
Lyth Bank, Shropshire

The Old School
Newton-on-The-Moor, Northumberland

Lowe Farm B&B
Pembridge, Herefordshire

The Old Vicarage at Toftly View
Pickering, Yorkshire

Caradoc Court
Ross-on-Wye, Herefordshire

Colton House
Rugeley, Staffordshire

Cote How Organic Guest House
Rydal, Cumbria

Fairacres
Rye, Sussex

Jeake's House
Rye, Sussex

Oaklands
Rye, Sussex

Strand House
Rye, Sussex

The Alexander
Scarborough, Yorkshire

Anchorage House
St Austell, Cornwall

Highland Court Lodge
St Austell, Cornwall

Higher Trevorrick Country House
St Issey, Cornwall

Pentillie Castle & Estate
St Mellion, Cornwall

High Muffles
Stape, Yorkshire

Woodside Bed & Breakfast
Staplecross, Sussex

Locksley, Bed & Breakfast
Stocksfield, Northumberland

Bays Farm
Stowmarket, Suffolk

Folly Farm Cottage
Stratford-upon-Avon, Warwickshire

Carricks at Castle Farm
Swanton Morley, Norfolk

Silver Ridge
Tansley, Derbyshire

Beera Farmhouse
Tavistock, Devon

Tor Cottage
Tavistock, Devon

Haldon Priors
Torquay, Devon

Spanhoe Lodge
Uppingham, Northamptonshire

Yew Tree House
Vowchurch, Herefordshire

Moresby Hall
Whitehaven, Cumbria

The Inn at Whitewell
Whitewell, Lancashire

Meadow View Guest House
Wighton, Norfolk

Giffard House
Winchester, Hampshire

Oakfold House
Windermere, Cumbria

Firwood Country Bed and Breakfast
Wooler, Northumberland

Benson's Guest House
Worthing, Sussex

Witch Hazel
Wymondham, Norfolk

The Hazelwood
York, Yorkshire

picnic **2 HOURS**

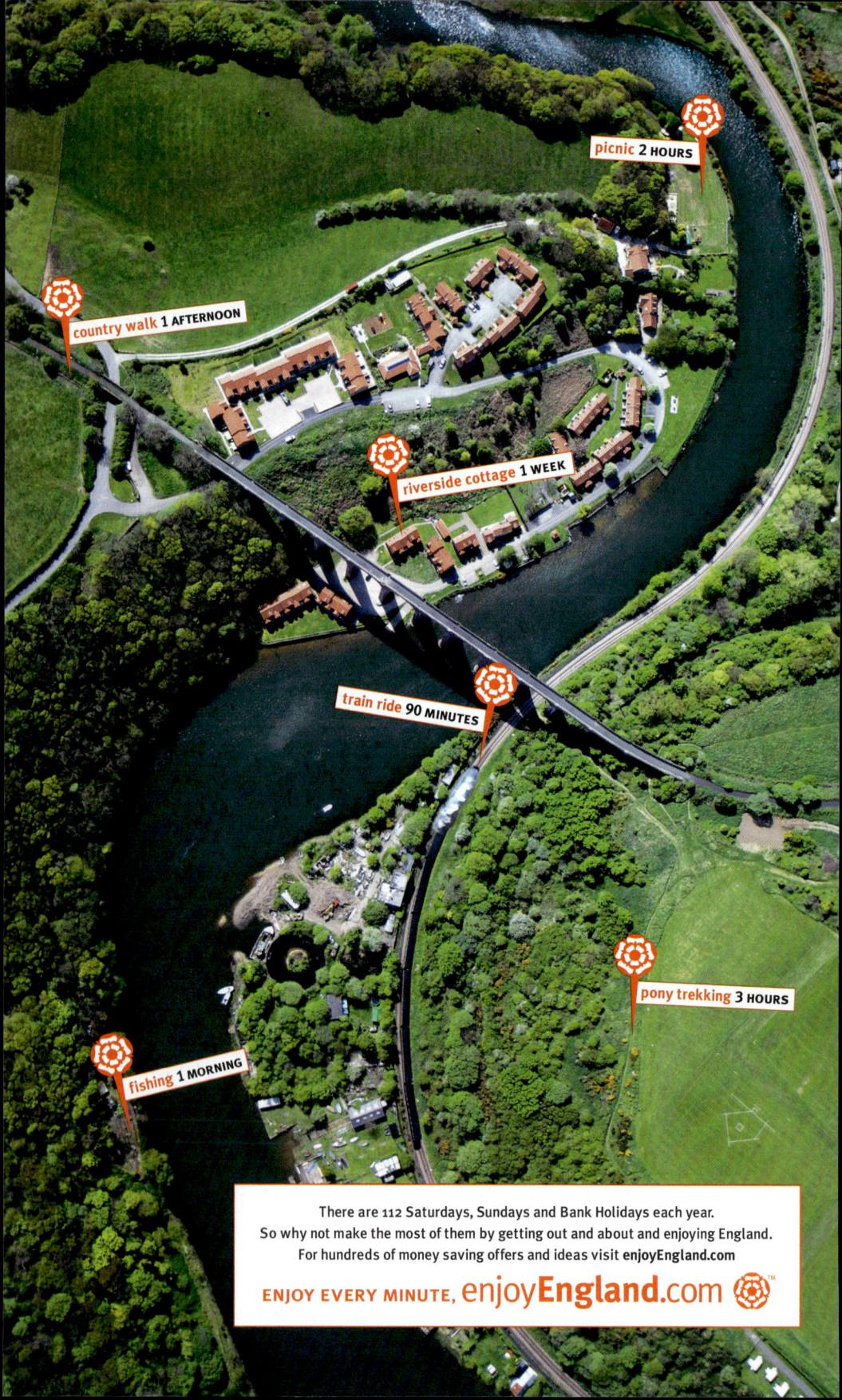

country walk **1 AFTERNOON**

riverside cottage **1 WEEK**

train ride **90 MINUTES**

pony trekking **3 HOURS**

fishing **1 MORNING**

There are 112 Saturdays, Sundays and Bank Holidays each year.
So why not make the most of them by getting out and about and enjoying England.
For hundreds of money saving offers and ideas visit **enjoyEngland.com**

ENJOY EVERY MINUTE, enjoy**England**.com™

Enjoy England Awards for Excellence

Enjoy England awards for Excellence are all about telling the world what a fantastic place England is to visit, whether it's for a day trip, a weekend break or a fortnight's holiday.

Organised by VisitBritain and sponsored by The Caravan Club, The Enjoy England Awards for Excellence are the annual accolades for English tourism, recognizing the best places to stay and visit. Now in their 22nd year, the Awards are known throughout the industry, promoting healthy competition and high standards. Competition is fierce, and entries are submitted to regional tourism organizations across England before being short-listed for the national finals, culminating in an Awards ceremony held in April each year.

There are fifteen categories, from visitor attractions and hotels to self-catering accommodation and caravan parks. This year's winners include a tranquil 18th Century converted school B&B in Northumberland, 200 year old converted self catering barns in the Peak District National Park, a luxury small hotel in Windermere with stunning gardens and views over a private lake and a beautifully landscaped 12 acre Cornish touring park. Seek them out and experience them for yourself – you won't be disappointed.

The complete list of winners can be found online at www.enjoyengland.com.

Gold winner for Bed & Breakfast of the Year is The Old School, an exceptional 5-star B&B set in an 18th Century stone property that nestles in the tranquil conservation village of Newton-on-the-Moor in Northumberland, halfway between the Scottish Borders and Newcastle upon Tyne. Surrounded by woodland, this recently refurbished B&B has superb facilities with plenty of thoughtful touches and home comforts. It boasts lovely south facing gardens and also has one of the finest old coaching inns in Northumberland just a 300 metre walk away. With the bustling market town of Alnwick nearby and only a short drive from the acclaimed Northumberland coastline, designated as an Area of Outstanding Natural Beauty and home to one of Britain's best views - Bamburgh Castle - and other jewels including the Holy Island of Lindisfarne and the Farne Islands, The Old School is a perfectly situated for exploring.

As a member of the Green Tourism Business Scheme, The Old School is committed to sustainable business practices and also actively encourages a varied and beautiful wildlife habitat at the property. Home cooked breakfasts using fresh, locally sourced produce are on the menu and were described by the judges as "outstanding".

Bed & Breakfast of the Year 2010

GOLD WINNER
The Old School, Newton-on-the-Moor, Northumberland ★★★★★

SILVER WINNERS
The Ashton, Lancaster, Lancashire ★★★★★

Underleigh House, Hope Valley, Derbyshire ★★★★★

South West

The region boasts a staggering four UNESCO World Heritage Sites in the Roman city of Bath, Stonehenge and Avebury, the Jurassic Coast, and the Cornwall and West Devon Mining Landscape, each revealing a fascinating past.

There are famous landmarks and places to visit including the Cotswolds - an area of rolling green hills and charming honey-coloured cottages, the one thousand-year-old majestic ruins of Corfe Castle in Dorset, the world famous outdoor Minack theatre in Cornwall, and Brunel's SS Great Britain on Bristol's harbourside - the world's first ocean-going, propeller driven, iron ship.

Lovers of the great outdoors will be in their element in the varied and green natural environment, ideal for leisurely walks or adrenaline fuelled activities. There are two beautiful National Parks in Dartmoor and Exmoor, 14 Areas of Outstanding Natural Beauty, the magical Royal Forest of Dean as well as wonderful countryside with a wealth of prehistoric sites, stone circles, villages with thatched cob cottages and riverside walks past country pubs. Beautiful coastlines offer everything from lively resorts and safe, sandy beaches to dramatic cliffs guarding secluded coves and picturesque fishing villages - the South West Coast Path covers 630 miles of dramatic coastline with every inch available to explore on foot.

Majestic cathedrals grace cities like Salisbury, Gloucester, Wells, Truro and Exeter. The City of Bath boasts elegant Georgian splendour and famous Roman Baths. Maritime history features strongly in Plymouth, the departure port for Sir Francis Drake and the Pilgrim Fathers, and Bristol, the largest city in the South West, offers a unique blend of fascinating history and contemporary culture on the recently

South West

South West

Cornwall & Isles of Scilly, Devon, Dorset,
Gloucestershire, Somerset, Wiltshire

22	**Counties**	**31**	**Where to Eat**
28	**Where to Go**	**38**	**Where to Stay**
30	**Events**		

redeveloped harbourside with a fabulous choice of restaurants, wine bars and shops alongside some unique attractions.

The South West's climate and natural environment provide the perfect conditions for producing an incredible range of food and drink. Top restaurants, featuring celebrity chefs, serve-up mouth watering local produce daily. Food events take place throughout the year with festivals, celebrations, and weekly farmers markets giving locals and visitors alike the chance to taste some of the country's best local produce.

Beautiful historic gardens and stately homes make for great days out. There's the magically reclaimed Lost Gardens of Heligan; the Palladian grandeur at the National Trust Stourhead; the first safari park outside Africa at Longleat House; Westonbirt, The National Arboretum and perhaps the most well known garden - the Eden Project in Cornwall.

South West | Cornwall & Isles of Scilly

Cornwall & Isles of Scilly

Mix a mild, sub-tropical climate with a stunning coastline dotted with stretches of golden sands and secluded coves. Add acres of beautiful countryside and you have the perfect holiday destination. Gorgeous gardens, adrenaline-filled sports, tantalising restaurants, indulgent spas, sublime walks; the list of things to do in Cornwall is endless.

Coasts and Moor

Take your pick from the north coast with its towering cliffs and pounding surf and the gentler south coast which boasts leafy estuaries, traditional fishing villages and vibrant waterfront communities. Or why not enjoy the best of both worlds with a central base, you'll find rugged Moors with wild and beautiful landscapes and ancient monuments on your doorstep just waiting to be explored.

St Ives

Life in this picturesque fishing town with an artistic flair revolves around the scenic harbour which is hugged by a warren of back streets hiding a mixture of galleries, cafes and stylish studios. Meandering visitors will stumble across many working artists taking inspiration from the surroundings as well as the architecturally impressive Tate St Ives which more than lives up to its city counterparts.

Padstow

Nestled in the Camel Estuary, Padstow has become known for its culinary prowess and is overflowing with restaurants offering fine dining and quality local produce. Explore the knot of small streets and delve into the warren of shops selling contemporary home furnishings, local arts & crafts and an abundance of Cornish produce.

Falmouth

Falmouth's natural harbour is the third deepest in the world and regularly plays host to major sailing events and festivals. It provides a picturesque backdrop to the busy main streets where unsurpassed views of Flushing, Falmouth Bay, St Mawes and beyond can be glimpsed between the buildings or from walkways meandering through the town. Falmouth is also home to the world-class National Maritime Museum Cornwall which explores the world of small boats and Cornwall's connection to the sea.

Fowey

The small town of Fowey hugs the natural harbour and offers stunning estuary views as well as sheltered sailing waters. Wander through the cobbled streets taking in the relaxed atmosphere and sample one of the many restaurants or cafes which line the narrow streets. Close by (about 9 miles away) is the historic town of Lostwithiel once the capital of Cornwall. The town is home to the ancient Restormel Castle owned by English Heritage. A little further up the road is the National Trust property Lanhydrock with its extensive parkland and beautiful gardens.

South West | **Devon**

Devon

Known for its breathtaking landscapes, rural heritage and dramatic coastlines, Devon offers a huge variety of attractions and a jam packed calendar of events, from carnivals to concerts and sports to arts, and with two coastlines, two National Parks, miles of beaches, cycling and walking trails, Devon's outdoors offer an unrivalled range activities and landscapes for visitors to discover.

North Devon

From the miles of fabulous golden beaches to the wild moorlands of Exmoor, from tiny villages tucked away in hidden valleys to bustling seaside towns, North Devon has it all. You can follow deep winding lanes through North Devon's beautiful countryside to discover bustling market towns and tranquil villages with picturesque thatched cottages.

South Devon & The English Riviera

South Devon features thirteen historic market towns surrounded by coasts and countryside, each one unique and waiting to be explored. The contrast of river estuaries, rolling hills and lovely old towns combined with long warm summers and mild winters make South Devon the perfect year-round holiday destination.

Stretching along 22 miles of stunning South Devon coastline, the stunning English Riviera has been a popular holiday destination for centuries. Sandy beaches, rocky coves, picturesque harbours and a wonderfully mild climate combine to attract visitors seeking a unique experience.

Exeter & Essential Devon

Exeter & Essential Devon includes the areas of Exeter, Mid Devon, East Devon and parts of South Devon and Dartmoor, encompassing many different landscapes. Exeter and its surrounding areas have much to attract the visitor - a rich and varied landscape, the fascinating rocks and sandy beaches of the Jurassic Coast, plus the vibrant regional cultural capital of Devon, Exeter. From moor to sea, there are a host of things to discover and do, all enriched by Devon's distinctive culture and history.

South West | **Dorset**

Dorset

Dorchester, the county town in southern central Dorset, is deep in the heart of Thomas Hardy's Wessex. Hardy based many of his novels in Dorset and '*Casterbridge*' is based on Hardy's home town of Dorchester.

Christchurch
A beautiful Saxon market town with a magnificent 900 year old Priory Church, situated on the spectacular Dorset coast; close to lively Bournemouth and the tranquillity of the New Forest. Its Saxon charm and fascinating heritage, combined with beautiful floral displays make it an ideal location for a short break, day trip or as a base to discover the hidden treasures of rural Dorset and the New Forest.

Jurassic Coast World Heritage Site
From Studland Bay in Dorset to Orcombe Rocks in Devon the Jurassic Coast gives a unique insight into life in the past through the rocks exposed along the 95 miles of beautiful coastline. 185 million years of Earth history for you to explore. Walk along the coast and walk through time! Discover the Mesozoic Era, a time when dinosaurs ruled the Earth! Marine reptiles continue to be found, including new species. A remarkable new specimen of Scelidosauras dinosaur and many other fossils, often exceptionally preserved, make this coast a world class venue for palaeontology.

Lyme Regis
Lyme Regis is a picturesque seaside town set in an Area of Outstanding Natural Beauty, on the border where Dorset meets Devon. It's a narrow tangle of streets and shops that find their way to the famous 13th century Cobb harbour. The Cobb has been a haven for shipping from the time it was built and is famous for being the landing place of the Duke of Monmouth prior to the Pitchfork Rebellion at Sedgemoor in 1685.

Bournemouth & Poole
Bournemouth and Poole boast 10 miles of stunning golden sands, two historic piers, great nightlife, top accommodation, countless water sports, exciting attractions and superb cuisine.

The resorts have long been a magnet for families and there are acres of open space to explore – beaches, parks, gardens, cycle paths, traffic-free shopping zones and dozens of new play areas.

Bournemouth is the place to learn to surf, bodyboard or paddleboard and Poole Harbour is Europe's largest natural harbour and perfect for every conceivable water sport. Its shallow waters make it ideal for beginners to learn to windsurf, kite-surf or sail. To get adrenaline-junkies' pulses racing, wake-boarding, jetskiing and Rib rides on the open sea are a must.

Bournemouth's parks and award-winning gardens are spectacular year round. Just steps from the beach, the Lower Gardens still boast much of their Victorian character filled with the aroma of pines and packed year-round with colourful floral displays. Alum Chine's tropical gardens and the Italianate gardens at Boscombe are a horticulturalist's dream.

Poole's atmospheric Old Town waits to be explored with an exciting mix of smuggler's passageways and elegant houses built by wealthy merchants in the 17th and 18th centuries. A trail along the Quay and through the old streets and alleys highlights tales of Poole's past from sailors to ghosts.

South West | **Gloucestershire**

Gloucestershire

The region is famed for the breathtaking countryside and picturesque chocolate box villages of the Cotswolds, and the magical fun for all ages in the Forest of Dean. With various activities to enjoy from cycling, walking and adrenaline filled adventure courses, to shopping and eating out in the bustling historic towns.

Gloucester

The magnificent Norman cathedral lies at the heart of the city of Gloucester, monument to the finest craftsmanship with its extraordinary fan-vaulted cloisters. In the historic Gloucester Docks, fifteen Victorian warehouses stand as proud guardians to Britain's most inland port. Gloucester has a lively city centre with a range of shops, restaurants, wine bars, pubs, entertainment and many unique visitor attractions.

Cheltenham

Considered the most complete Regency town in England; the 'town within a park' offers beautiful parks and gardens, tree-lined avenues and colourful floral displays. With a whole range of stylish shopping, fine hotels and a wide variety of restaurants to choose from.

Cheltenham hosts an annual programme of major sporting and cultural events, including internationally acclaimed music and literature festivals, cricket and horse racing, including the famous Cheltenham Gold Cup – the highlight of the National Hunt Festival.

Tewkesbury

Tewkesbury lies at the heart of the Severn vale and is dominated by the beautiful 12th century Abbey. The town is renowned for its wealth of history and also as having one of the best medieval black and white townscapes in the country. Tewkesbury hosts many annual events including their local Food and Drinks Festival and the Spring Arts Festival.

Forest of Dean

The Royal Forest of Dean is one of England's few remaining ancient forests, covering 27,000 acres of woodland. Designated as a National Forest Park in 1938, this 'Queen of Forests' boasts a spectacular range of natural beauty combined with an aura of magic and mystery that has been the inspiration for many great artists and writers including Tolkien and JK Rowling. Here you will find something for all ages to take pleasure in from canoeing and cycling to adventure courses and much more.

Stroud

Built on steep slopes at the junction of five valleys, this busy market town has retained considerable character and is still thriving as a centre for artists and crafts people. Stroud is known for its popular farmers market which takes place every Saturday, with lots of local produce on display.

The Cotswolds, stretching over 100 miles, are a designated Area of Outstanding Natural Beauty, recognised as a unique environment, with some of England's finest countryside. Well known for its honey coloured stone, this beautiful area attracts visitors all year round and is a fascinating place to explore.

There are charming villages, historic towns, impressive churches, rolling countryside and glorious gardens. Often the best views are seen on foot or by cycle.

South West | **Somerset**

Somerset

Taunton, the county capital, lies in the spectacular Vale of Taunton Deane between the Quantock and Blackdown Hills. It combines relics of its dramatic past with the buzz and efficiency of a modern county town. The town has many fine architectural features, attractive back streets, parks and gardens.

Burnham-on-Sea and Minehead

Burnham-on-Sea is a traditional seaside resort, famous for its unique nine-legged lighthouse and seven miles of sandy beach. Burnham has all the ingredients for a traditional English seaside holiday; donkey rides, ice creams, a jetty for launching boats, and pier pavilion. Burnham has a fine esplanade and seafront overlooking Bridgwater Bay and the distant Welsh coast.

Another traditional resort, Minehead has a lively seafront, quieter areas with lime-washed thatched cottages and a harbour. The 630 mile South West Coast Path, the longest of the National Tails, begins in Minehead.

Cheddar and Cheddar Gorge

View the magnificent limestone gorge carved into the southern slopes of the Mendip hills above the village of Cheddar. Reaching 500 feet in places, the sides of the ravine boast the highest inland cliffs in the country and can be viewed from the road running through the base of the gorge or from footpaths along the cliff tops. At the lower end of the gorge you will find riverside walks, tea rooms and gift shops and the famous Showcaves, a series of labyrinthine underground chambers. Cheddar cheese is known throughout the world, its manufacture originating at farms in the region. You can watch traditional Cheddar cheese making at the Cheddar Gorge Cheese Company in the lower Gorge.

Wells

Nestling in the Mendip Hills is Wells, England's smallest city with a beautiful cathedral. Probably the finest national example of early English architecture, Wells Cathedral was largely built between the 12th and 14th centuries, but was itself a successor to a 7th century church, founded by the Saxon King Ina. The cathedral is famed for its magnificent west front, featuring over 300 statues and carvings; the inverted scissor arches of the nave, and one of the oldest working mechanical clocks (dated about 1390). The wells, which gave the city its name are now contained within the grounds of the Bishop's Palace, which is regularly open to the public.

Weston-Super-Mare

Weston-super-Mare is a great seaside resort. The wide sweep of Weston Bay has miles of clean sandy beach, traditional seaside attractions and beautiful countryside and coastline to explore. Despite the devastating fire on the Grand Pier in 2008, a brand new state of the art pavilion has been built and re-opened in 2010. Weston beach has a designated area for kite buggies, small land yachts and kite boards, while jet skiers, power boat users and other boats can launch from Knightstone slipway.

Wookey Hole

Carved out under the limestone Mendip Hills over millions of years by the mysterious River Axe, Wookey Hole Caves have become a popular visitor attraction, featuring magnificent underground chambers and pools, where spectacular light and sound effects bring the caves' natural wonder to life. Cave diving expeditions since 1935 have revealed 25 caverns, but there are surely more that remain unexplored.

South West | **Wiltshire**

Wiltshire

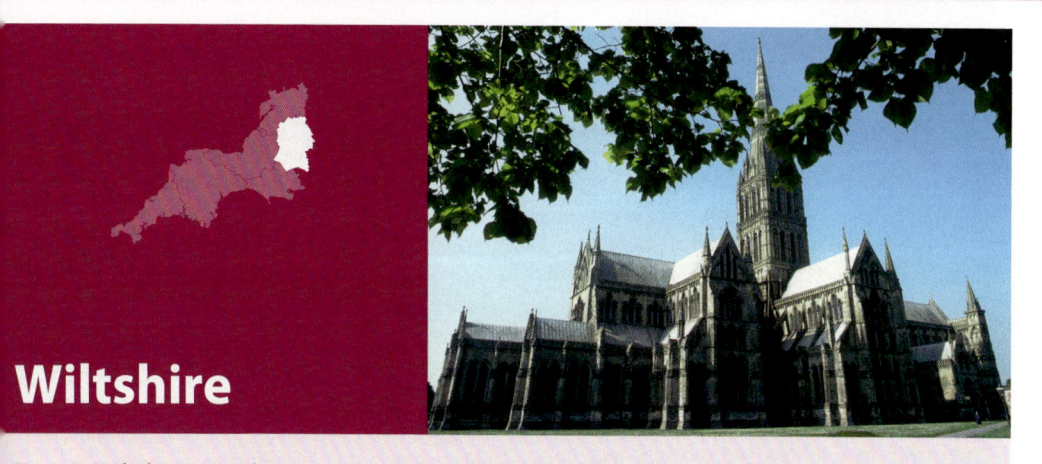

To visit Wiltshire is to discover a land shrouded in mystery, steeped in legend, where history comes alive through its iconic attractions; a land where breathtaking sights combine with picture-perfect villages nestling peacefully amid rolling, unspoiled countryside. Trowbridge, the county town of Wiltshire, is situated on the River Biss in the west of the county

Bradford-on-Avon

Bradford-on-Avon is a bustling market town on the edge of the Cotswolds. The view from the ancient bridge over the River Avon incorporates both the hill above the town, which is dotted with old weaver's cottages, and the river bank, flanked by 19th century former cloth mills. Be sure to visit both the Saxon Church of St Lawrence, and the Tithe Barn at Barton Farm Country Park.

Chippenham

Chippenham, founded over 1000 years ago, was the Royal Hunting Lodge for Alfred the Great from where he pursued his fight against the invading Danes. In the Middle Ages corn mills made way for the prosperous wool trade and famous cheese market. West of Chippenham, are the exquisite "picture postcard" villages of Castle Combe, Lacock and Biddestone, complete with village green and duck pond.

Devizes

Devizes is an historic market town combining a colourful medieval past with a rich heritage of fine Georgian houses. Cobbled alleyways and hidden courtyards are lined with specialist retailers and cafés and the Market Place is home to a bustling Thursday market. Explore the Kennet & Avon Canal, with its impressive flight of 29 locks at Caen Hill.

Malmesbury & Marlborough

As England's oldest borough, with a history dating back over 1,000 years, Malmesbury is rightly called the 'Queen of Hilltop Towns'. Set on a hill, encircled by the River Avon, the skyline is dominated by the imposing Norman Abbey. St Aldhelm founded a monastery here in the 7th century and in the 10th century Athelstan (first King of all England) made Malmesbury his capital.

Marlborough lies in the valley of the River Kennet between the ancient Savernake Forest and the Marlborough Downs. Reputedly one of the widest streets in Britain, Marlborough's High Street is lined with notable buildings, including the splendid Merchant's House, built during the Cromwell period and now restored as a 17th century town house.

Salisbury

Known as 'the city in the countryside' medieval Salisbury is the perfect fusion of ancient and modern, where high street names and modern café culture intermingle with independent shops and traditional English pubs. The awe-inspiring sight of the Cathedral rising up from the water-meadows has been described as 'Britain's best view', while other attractions in and around the city include award-winning museums, an elegant National Trust mansion and the Iron Age hill fort of Old Sarum.

South West | Where to Go

Where to Go

Attractions with this sign participate in the **Visitor Attraction Quality Assurance Scheme** (see page 6) which recognises high standards in all aspects of the visitor experience.

ENTERTAINMENT & CULTURE

City Sightseeing - The Bristol Tour
Central Bristol, Bristol BS1 4AH
0333 3210101
www.citysightseeingbristol.co.uk
Open top bus tours with guides and headphones around the city of Bristol. Service runs daily throughout the Summer months.

Falmouth Art Gallery
Falmouth, Cornwall TR11 2RT
(01326) 313863
www.falmouthartgallery.com
Family friendly exhibitions, internationally acclaimed artists and one of the best collections in the Southwest featuring Pre-Raphaelites and British Impressionists.

Fashion Museum
Bath, Somerset BA1 2QH
(01225) 477173
www.fashionmuseum.co.uk
The story of fashion over the last 400 years is brought alive at the Fashion Museum, the finest museum of fashionable garments in the world.

Roman Baths
Bath, Somerset BA1 1LZ
(01225) 477785
www.romanbaths.co.uk
Visit the heart of the World Heritage Site. Around Britain's only hot spring, the Romans built a magnificent temple and bathing complex that still flows with natural hot water. See the water's source and walk where Romans walked.

STEAM - Museum of the Great Western Railway
Swindon, Wiltshire SN2 2TA
(01793) 466646
www.swindon.gov.uk/steam
Housed in a beautifully restored Grade II railway building in the heart of the former Swindon railway works.

The Jane Austen Centre
Bath, Somerset BA1 2NT
(01225) 443000
www.janeausten.co.uk
Celebrate Bath's most famous resident with this snapshot of the Regency life that inspired her.

Victoria Art Gallery
Bath, Somerset BA2 4AT
(01225) 477232
www.victoriagal.org.uk
Work by Gainsborough, Sickert, Zoffany and many other leading artists from the 15th century to the present day.

Wookey Hole Caves & Papermill
Wells, Somerset BA5 1BB
(01749) 672243
www.wookey.co.uk
Spectacular caves, a working Victorian paper mill, maze and Cave Diving Museum.

FAMILY FUN

At-Bristol
Bristol BS1 5DB
0845 345 1235
www.at-bristol.org.uk
21st century science and technology centre with hands-on activities and the latest multi-media including being able to make your own animation and email it to family and friends.

Cornwall's Crealy Great Adventure Park
Wadebridge, Cornwall PL27 7RA
(01841) 540276
www.crealy.co.uk/cornwall
Maximum magical fun and unforgettable adventures. Discover Cornwall's all-weather family attraction.

FOOD & DRINK

Healey's Cornish Cyder Farm
Truro, Cornwall TR4 9LW
(01872) 573356
www.thecornishcyderfarm.co.uk
Visit a real working cider farm, we produce country wines, Scrumpy, preserves and ciders. Take a guided tour to learn the art of cider making and join us with a trailer ride around our fruit orchards.

Plymouth Gin Distillery
Barbican, Devon PL1 2LQ
(01752) 665292
www.plymouthgin.com
Tour the Black Friars Distillery, England's oldest working gin distillery, where Plymouth Gin has been distilled for over 200 years.

Wadworth Visitor Centre
Devizes, Wiltshire SN10 1JW
(01380) 732277
www.wadworth.co.uk
Sample the delights and discover the history & heritage of Wadworth brewing. Featuring an exhibition of Wadworth brewing memorabilia, an insight into 'a year in the life of a Wadworth Shire Horse' and products created by our Master Cooper

South West | Where to Go

HERITAGE

Avon Valley Railway
Bristol, Gloucestershire
BS30 6HD
(0117) 932 5538
www.avonvalleyrailway.org
More than just a steam train ride, offering a whole new experience for some or a nostalgic memory for others.

Brunel's ss Great Britain
Bristol BS1 6TY
0117) 926 0680
www.ssgreatbritain.org
Visit the world's first great ocean liner.

Dartmouth Castle
Dartmouth, Devon TQ6 0JN
01803) 833588
www.english-heritage.org.uk/dartmouth
One of the most picturesquely-sited fortresses in England. For over six hundred years Dartmouth Castle has guarded the narrow entrance to the Dart Estuary and the busy, vibrant port of Dartmouth.

Gloucester Cathedral
Gloucester, Gloucestershire
GL1 2LR
01452) 528095
www.gloucestercathedral.org.uk
Gloucester Cathedral of honey coloured lime stone is a place of worship and architectural gem with crypt, cloisters.

GWR Gloucestershire Warwickshire Steam Railway
Cheltenham, Gloucestershire
GL54 5DT
01242) 621405
www.gwsr.com
The GWR is an all-volunteer steam and diesel heritage railway in the English Cotswolds.

Number One Royal Crescent
Bath, Somerset BA1 2LR
01225) 428126
www.bath-preservation-trust.org.uk/museums/no1/
The magnificently restored and authentically furnished town house creates a wonderful picture of fashionable life in 18th century Bath.

Oakham Treasures
Bristol, Somerset BS20 7SP
01275) 375236
www.oakhamtreasures.co.uk
Visit a truly historic experience - where the past comes to life! Oakham Treasures is believed to be the largest display of retail and farming history in the UK, and will give any visitor an amazing uplifting trip down memory lane.

Old Sarum
Salisbury, Wiltshire SP1 3SD
(01722) 335398
www.english-heritage.org.uk/oldsarum
The massive Iron Age hill fort of Old Sarum (Old Salisbury) was re-used by the Romans, Saxons and Normans, before growing into one of the most flourishing settlements in medieval England. See the ruins of a castle, cathedral & royal palace.

Old Wardour Castle
Tisbury, Wiltshire SP3 6RR
(01747) 870487
www.english-heritage.org.uk/oldwardour
The unusual hexagonal ruins of Old Wardour Castle stand serenely in their lakeside setting, protected by acres of wood, making a picturesque setting for picnics. But their beguiling scene of rural tranquillity masks a bloodthirsty past.

Portland Castle
Portland, Dorset DT5 1AZ
(01305) 820539
www.english-heritage.org.uk/portland
A well preserved coastal fort built by Henry VIII to defend Weymouth harbour against possible French and Spanish attack. Exhibition: 400 years of the castle's history.

Salisbury Cathedral
Salisbury, Wiltshire SP1 2EJ
(01722) 555120
www.salisburycathedral.org.uk
Britain's finest 13th century cathedral with the tallest spire in Britain. Discover nearly 800 years of history, including the world's best preserved Magna Carta (AD 1215) and Europe's oldest working clock (AD 1386). Also restaurant & shop.

Stonehenge
Amesbury, Wiltshire SP4 7DE
0870 333 1181
www.english-heritage.org.uk/stonehenge
Stonehenge stands impressively as a prehistoric monument of unique importance, a World Heritage Site, surrounded by remains of ceremonial and domestic structures - some older than the monument itself.

Swanage Railway
Swanage, Dorset BH19 1HB
(01929) 425800
www.swanagerailway.co.uk
Enjoy a nostalgic steam-train ride on the Purbeck line. Steam trains run most weekend throughout the year with daily running Apr to Oct.

NATURE & WILDLIFE

Bristol Zoo Gardens
Bristol BS8 3HA
(0117) 974 7399
www.bristolzoo.org.uk
A visit to Bristol Zoo is your passport for a day trip to an amazing world of animals.

Cheddar Caves & Gorge
Cheddar, Somerset BS27 3QF
(01934) 742343
www.cheddarcaves.co.uk
Towering limestone cliffs, underground cathedrals beautifully lit, the secrets of your ancestors - experience this exciting world of nature, culture and adventure.

Dairyland Farm World
Newquay, Cornwall TR8 5AA
(01872) 510246
www.dairylandfarmworld.com
Meets lots of beautiful animals, including lambs, kids, rabbits, donkeys, piglets and Lawrence the Llama. Large indoor play area too!

Hidcote Manor Garden (National Trust)
Chipping Campden, Gloucestershire GL55 6LR
(01386) 438333
www.nationaltrust.org.uk/hidcote
One of England's great gardens, famous for its rare trees and shrubs, outstanding herbaceous borders and unusual plants from all over the world.

Horseworld
Bristol, Somerset BS14 0QJ
(01275) 540173
www.horseworld.org.uk
Meet the rescued horses, ponies, donkeys and support the charity's welfare work. There's lots going on - presentations, meet a furry friend, feeding the animals and fun in the playbarn, straw den and sandpit - plus more!

Living Coasts
Torquay, Devon TQ1 2BG
(01803) 202470
www.livingcoasts.org.uk
Fascinating coastal creatures from loud and loveable penguins to playful fur seals, colourful puffins to waders and sea ducks.

Longleat
Warminster, Wiltshire
BA12 7NW
(01985) 844400
www.longleat.co.uk
Animal Park, Longleat Hedge Maze, Safari Boats, Longleat Railway, Longleat House and much much more...your day at Longleat will never be long enough.

29

South West | Where to Go/Events

Lost Gardens of Heligan
St Austell, Cornwall PL26 6EN
(01726) 845100
www.heligan.com
Unveiled in 1992 after decades of neglect, the Lost Gardens have been restored to their previous splendour. Hailed by The Times as "…the garden restoration of the century". Heligan is a garden for all seasons & well worth a visit at anytime.

Monkey World - Ape Rescue Centre
Wareham, Dorset BH20 6HH
(01929) 462537
www.monkeyworld.org
The internationally-acclaimed ape rescue centre, is home to over 230 rescued and endangered monkeys and apes. Combining fun with conservation, half-hourly talks explain all about man's closest living relative.

Newquay Zoo
Newquay, Cornwall TR7 2LZ
(01637) 873342
www.newquayzoo.org.uk
Calling all wildlife adventurers! Come and visit multi-award winning Newquay Zoo set in sub-tropical lakeside gardens and home to over 130 species of animals - set your passion for animal exploration wild!

Noah's Ark Zoo Farm
Bristol, Somerset BS48 1PG
(01275) 852606
www.noahsarkzoofarm.co.uk
Get hands on and meet a variety of animals including giraffe, rhinos, tigers and lions. Home to the big zoo animals with 12 adventure playgrounds for all the family to enjoy.

Painswick Rococo Garden
Painswick, Gloucestershire GL6 6TH
(01452) 813204
www.rococogarden.org.uk
This unique Garden restoration, situated in a hidden valley, dates from a period when 18th century gentle folk were creating flamboyant pleasure grounds in which to entertain their guests.

Springfields Fun Park & Pony Centre
St Columb, Cornwall TR9 6HU
(01637) 881224
www.springfieldsponycentre.co.uk
If you enjoy an active family day Springfields is the place for you, set in 35 acres the park is in the centre of Cornwall, 7 miles from Newquay off the A39. Have fun with the ponies and other farm animals, explore the new wet woodland walk.

Stourhead House and Garden
Stourton, Wiltshire BA12 6QD
(01747) 841152
www.nationaltrust.org.uk/stourhead
On the Wiltshire-Somerset border is the perfect day out for everyone. A breathtaking 18thC landscape garden with lakeside walks, grottoes and classical temples is only the beginning.

Westonbirt, The National Arboretum
Tetbury, Gloucestershire GL8 8QS
(01666) 880220
www.forestry.gov.uk/westonbirt
600 acres with one of the finest collections of trees in the world. The Arboretum offers beautiful spring flowers, stunning autumn colours and a wide range of events.

Weymouth Sea Life Park and Marine Sanctuary
Weymouth, Dorset DT4 7SX
0871 423 2110
www.sealifeeurope.com/
Weymouth SEA LIFE Adventure Park & Marine Sanctuary is unique among the network of SEA LIFE attractions in that its numerous marine life exhibitions are housed both indoors and out.

Events 2011

Annual Bath Flower Show
www.bathnes.gov.uk/bathspringflowershow
Spring Bank Holiday

Bath Fringe Festival
www.bathfringe.co.uk/
May/June

Bath Literature Festival
www.bathlitfest.org.uk
February/March

Beaminster Festival of Music & Arts
www.beamfest.org.uk
June-July

Bristol International Festival of Kites & Air Creations
www.kite-festival.org.uk
September

Bristol Wine & Food Fair
www.bristolwineandfoodfair.co.uk
July

Chippenham Folk Festival
www.chippfolk.co.uk
Spring Bank Holiday

Christchurch Food Festival
www.christchurchfoodfest.co.uk
May

Dartmoor Classic Cyclosportive
www.dartmoorclassic.co.uk
June

Dartmouth Royal Regatta
www.dartmouthregatta.co.uk
August

International Beach Kite Festival
Weymouth
www.visitweymouth.co.uk
April-May

Jane Austen Festival
Bath
www.janeausten.co.uk/festival/
September

Lyme Regis Jazz Festival
Lyme Regis
www.lymeregis.com/jazz-festival/
July

Plymouth Summer Festival
www.plymouthsummerfestival.com
May - September

Royal International Air Tattoo
www.airtattoo.com
July

Salisbury International Arts Festival
www.salisburyfestival.co.uk
May/June

Spirit of the Sea
Weymouth
www.spiritofthesea.org.uk
July

Swanage Jazz Festival
www.swanagejazz.org.uk
July

Taunton Flower Show
www.tauntonflowershow.co.uk
August

The Bath and West Show
Shepton Mallet
www.bathandwest.co.uk
May

The North Somerset Show
www.nsas.org.uk
May

SOUTH WEST | **Where to Eat**

Where to Eat

The South West England region has great places to eat. The restaurant reviews on these pages are just a small selection from the highly respected *The Good Food Guide 2011*. Please see page 14 for further information on the Guide and details of a Special Offer for our readers.

CORNWALL

Porthminster Beach Café
Funky beach hangout with freewheeling flavours
Porthminster Beach, St Ives TR26 2EB
01736) 795352
www.porthminstercafe.co.uk
Seafood | £35

This striking Art Deco building beneath the slopes of Porthminster Point is the kind of funky beach hangout that would fire up chef/owner Mick Smith's ozone-addicted Aussie mates. It's much more than just a seaside café – fabulous views are a given, but the kitchen also rises to the occasion by offering a world tour of upbeat dishes with a fusion undercurrent and bold, freewheeling flavours. Cornish seafood is the star: Indonesian-style monkfish curry amazed one reader, but the choice extends to spiced black bream fillets with crab noodle salad or baked hake with salt cod croquettes, smoked tomato and langoustine velouté. Meat dishes also stake their claim (perhaps West Country venison with crispy Parma ham and celeriac purée), and desserts are in keeping – especially the 'black berry' tasting plate and showstopping caramelised banana with cinnamon meringues, pistachio ice cream, banana pudding and cinder toffee. A cherry-picked, worldwide wine list starts at £12.95. The same team also runs the seasonal Porthgwidden Beach Café.

Chef/s: Isaac Anderson and Tom Pryce. **Open:** all week L 11 to 5, D 6 to 10. **Meals:** alc (main courses £13 to £20). **Service:** not inc. **Details:** major cards accepted. 80 seats. 80 seats outside. Separate bar. No mobile phones. Wheelchair access. Music. Children welcome.

The View
Outstanding clifftop package
Treninnow Cliff Road, Millbrook PL10 1JY
(01752) 822345
www.theview-restaurant.co.uk
Modern British | £28

'Would that there were more places like it,' enthused one reporter of this clifftop restaurant with its gorgeous coastal views. The décor may be basic, but the overall package is outstanding. Very fresh seafood, mostly from Looe Harbour, makes up the bulk of the menu and is treated with respect and without flamboyance – delicate crab, lime and Parmesan risotto to start, followed, perhaps, by turbot with tiger prawns and ginger. Equal care is taken handling meat: 'very tender and delicious' best end of lamb, for instance. Strawberry jelly and almond biscuits add interest to vanilla mousse. House wine is £13.95.

Chef/s: Matt Corner. **Open:** Wed to Sun L 12 to 2, D 7 to 9. **Closed:** Mon, Tue, Feb. **Meals:** alc (main courses £12 to £19). **Service:** not inc. **Details:** major cards accepted. 45 seats. 30 seats outside. No mobile phones. Music. Children welcome. Car parking.

South West | **Where to Eat**

DEVON

James Duckett at the Old Custom House
Spot-on neighbourhood restaurant
9 The Strand, Barnstaple EX31 1EU
(01271) 370123
www.jamesduckett.co.uk
Modern European | £30

The oldest building on Barnstaple's Strand was indeed once the custom house – before doing duty as a tobacconists and tearoom – but nowadays it's home to James Duckett's passionately run, 'spot-on' neighbourhood restaurant. Local produce is close to his heart, and he wows the punters with everything from creamed Hallwood Farm Jerusalem artichokes with artichoke crisps to daube of West Country beef with wild mushrooms and parsnip purée. Elsewhere, Creedy chicken leg is stuffed with black pudding and served on pearl barley risotto, while a bonanza of local shellfish goes into a saffron-tinged ragoût. To finish, the pyramid of lime parfait with caramelised figs is a showstopper. Keenly priced wines start at £14.50.

Chef/s: James Duckett. **Open:** Tue to Sat L 12 to 2.30, D 7 to 10. **Closed:** Sun, Mon, 26 Dec, first 2 weeks Jan. **Meals:** alc Fri and Sat D (main courses £14 to £24). Set L £12 (2 courses) to £15. Midweek set D £21 to £26. Tasting menu £65. **Service:** not inc. **Details:** major cards accepted. 52 seats. 16 seats outside. No mobile phones. Wheelchair access. Music. Children welcome.

The Seahorse
Tonks comes up trumps
5 South Embankment, Dartmouth TQ6 9BH
(01803) 835147
www.seahorserestaurant.co.uk
Seafood | £45

The main attraction of any waterside restaurant called the Seahorse is likely to be fish, and on that score Mitch Tonks' lively eatery on the Dart waterfront comes up trumps. The menu does not shy away from adventure and may turn up a main course of roasted mackerel with North African spices, or a starter of local cuttlefish braised in Chianti with borlotti beans, but skate roasted with black butter means more traditional treatments are in evidence too. A starter of Bismarck pickled herrings impressed one visitor – 'much more solid than traditional soused herrings' – as did a well-timed sea bream cooked 'al cartoccio' (in paper) with chilli, roasted garlic, rosemary and olive oil. Cornish lamb chops or a single rib of South Devon beef should please meat eaters. For dessert, sticky toffee pudding has been praised yet again. The wine list is packed with good bottles and stretches to some prestigious offerings, including fine Italians. House French from £18.

Chef/s: Mitch Tonks and Mat Prowse. **Open:** Wed to Sat L 12 to 3, Tue to Sat D 6 to 10. **Closed:** Sun, Mon. **Meals:** alc (main courses £15 to £25). Set L £15 (2 courses) to £20. **Service:** not inc. **Details:** major cards accepted. 40 seats. 4 seats outside. Air conditioning. Wheelchair access. Music. Children welcome.

DORSET

Hive Beach Café
Beach Road, Burton Bradstock DT6 4RF
(01308) 897070
www.hivebeachcafe.co.uk
Seafood

Perched on the headland between a scruffy car park and a beach of fine-ground shingle, the Hive Beach is a proper seafood café, open for breakfasts and lunches, plus Friday and Saturday evenings in the spring and summer. Order your food at the counter, and wait for one of the waiting staff to shout your number. Big Martini glasses of crab and crayfish cocktail (£5.95) start you off, while mains run from mackerel fillets in caper cream sauce (£10.95) to grilled half-lobsters with garlic chive butter (£19.95) served with brilliant chunky chips. Wines from £13.50. Open all week.

The Print Room
Popular all-day brasserie
Richmond Hill, Bournemouth BH2 6HH
(01202) 789669
www.theprintroom-bournemouth.co.uk
Modern European | £22

A buzzy atmosphere, friendly service, all-day opening and good-value, flexible menus make this large modern brasserie and bar an understandably popular spot. The repertoire is wide-ranging, taking in starters of wild mushrooms on toasted brioche with duck egg and red onion jam, and main courses of crab linguine, lobster thermidor and roast peppered duck breast with orange marmalade, fondant potato and Swiss chard. Eggs Benedict is a fixture on both the breakfast and afternoon menu, while desserts are variations on old favourites such as pear and praline crumble. Nine wines (from £3.25 a glass, £16.50 a bottle) head the extensive list.

Chef/s: Michael Lecouteur. **Open:** all week 8am to 10pm **Meals:** alc (main courses £8 to £28). Set L £12.50 (2 courses) to £15.50. Sun L £11.95. **Service:** 10% (optional). **Details:** major cards accepted. 145 seats. Separate bar. Wheelchair access. Music. Children welcome.

South West | **Where to Eat**

GLOUCESTERSHIRE

The New Inn
Honest pub food
Main Street, Coln St Aldwyns GL7 5AN
(01285) 750651
www.new-inn.co.uk
British | £30

In one of Gloucestershire's prettiest villages, this creeper-covered sixteenth-century inn really looks the part. In a setting of beams and flagstones you can sample real ales and a workmanlike version of honest pub food – simple stuff for lunch (deli boards of cold meats, fish and chips), a touch more elaboration in the evening. Much of the repertoire has a cosmopolitan feel, say lime-scented crab and chargrilled pepper tian, although more robust game dishes also win votes. Reporters have found it 'costly by local standards', but food is good' and 'service well run'. House wine £14.50.
Chef/s: Oliver Addis. **Open:** all week L 12.30 to 2.30 (3 Sun), D 7 to 9 (9.30 Fri and Sat, 6.30 to 8 Sun). **Meals:** alc main courses £10 to £19). Sun L £15. **Service:** not inc. **Details:** major cards accepted. 50 seats. 80 seats outside. Separate bar. No mobile phones. Wheelchair access. Music. Children welcome. Car parking.

SOMERSET

Greens' Dining Room
Delightful, good-value local eatery
25 Zetland Road, Bristol BS6 7AH
(01179) 246437
www.greensdiningroom.com
Modern British | £28

The green awning and big shopfront windows announce one of Bristol's best-loved neighbourhood restaurants. It's 'always a delight', according to one regular who notes that 'the front-of-house staff are charming and well-informed, and the food punches well above its weight in terms of value and class.' The Green team produces dishes in the modern European vein, with the emphasis on seasonality. A satisfying winter meal proceeded from potato pancakes with sour cream and caviar, through lemon sole with beurre blanc, capers and double-cooked chips, to alight at Seville orange curd tart at the end. The rump of beef with rosemary, served with dauphinoise, is well reported too, while the Set Supper menu looks particularly good value. A single-page wine slate is appealing in every way. Prices are kept on a leash, and there is an imaginative selection of international growers, with Spanish house wines at £13.95.
Chef/s: Andrew and Simon Green. **Open:** Tue to Sat L 12.30 to 3, Tue to Sat D 6.30 to 10.30. **Closed:** Sun, Mon, 23 Dec to 5 Jan, last 2 weeks Aug. **Meals:** alc (main courses £9 to £15). Set L £10 (2 courses). Set D £21.50 (2 courses) to £27.50. **Service:** not inc. **Details:** major cards accepted. 38 seats. 14 seats outside. No mobile phones. Music. Children welcome. No Amex.

Murrays
Top-notch goodies for foodies
87-93 Hill Road, Clevedon BS21 7PN
(01275) 341555
www.murraysofclevedon.co.uk
Italian | £26

This 'light and airy' restaurant, and its first-class deli next door, draws savvy locals and visitors with its civilized, cheerful character and stress on top-quality produce. A seasonally-focused menu is based on local supplies (with a little help from Italy) and manages to push all the right buttons. The very reasonably-priced menu at lunch (and some weekday evenings) offers a couple of daily specials as well as a selection of more standard Italian fare and could include 'very tender and nicely gamey' wood pigeon with potatoes and roast vegetables, and well-timed sea bass fillets with sautéed potatoes and spinach, followed by excellent figs with hazelnut ice cream or Amaretti tart. Otherwise, the carte may produce Umbrian lentil and mushroom tart, followed by osso bucco (from free-range Devon rose veal) or roast wild Mendip hare wrapped in speck with a juniper and redcurrant sauce. Prices on the all-Italian wine list start at £14.50.
Chef/s: Reuben Murray. **Open:** Tue to Sat L 12 to 2, D 6 to 9.30. **Closed:** Sun, Mon, 25 and 26 Dec. **Meals:** alc (main courses £10 to £23). Set L and D £15 (2 courses) to £20. **Service:** not inc. **Details:** major cards accepted. 70 seats. Air conditioning. Separate bar. Wheelchair access. Music. Children welcome.

The Lord Poulett Arms
Atmospheric inn with delightful fare
High Street, Hinton St George TA17 8SE
(01460) 73149
www.lordpoulettarms.com
Gastropub | £24

Part of the draw is that this atmospheric, late seventeenth-century inn still functions as a pub (check out the real ales), including a boule piste and a flag-floored bar with a log fire. The food covers pub-fare bases too – toad in the hole, fish and chips and a first-class local steak with béarnaise and triple-cooked chips – and to find them done so well is a delight. But the menu has wider appeal too and ideas are straightforward yet lively: beef fillet in spicy black bean and ginger sauce followed by venison sausage with roasted garlic crushed potatoes and sundried Morello cherry and port wine gravy with, perhaps, molten Valrhona chocolate cake for dessert. House wines from £13.
Chef/s: Gary Coughlan. **Open:** all week L 12 to 2.30, D 7 to 9.15. **Closed:** 25 and 26 Dec, 1 Jan. **Meals:** alc (main courses £10 to £24). Sun L £16 (2 courses) to £19. **Service:** not inc. **Details:** major cards accepted. 60 seats. 60 seats outside. Separate bar. No music. Wheelchair access. Children welcome. Car parking.

South West | Where to Eat

WILTSHIRE

Red Lion
Startlingly accomplished food worth travelling for
East Chisenbury SN9 6AQ
(01980) 671124
www.redlionfreehouse.com
Modern British | £28

Pack an OS map and programme your SatNav if you're heading out to this welcoming thatched freehouse in the wild reaches of Salisbury Plain south of Upavon. Also persevere, because 'startlingly accomplished' modern food is your reward at the sympathetically spruced-up Red Lion (along with ales from Wiltshire's microbreweries). Guy Manning started out as a sous chef at Chef Bruce, but he and his wife have also done stints with Thomas Keller in New York's Per Se and at Martin Berasategui's self-named restaurant in San Sebastien. Given their pedigree, it's no surprise that the cooking makes you sit up and take notice – roast scallops are partnered by crispy pig's head, parsnip, apple and meat juices, while desserts such as yoghurt tapioca with roasted pineapple and macadamia granola show the couple's instinct for contrasts. The Mannings' daily menus are driven by impressive local sourcing and what they can produce in-house, although many dishes are given a Mediterranean spin. Roast black bream is served with risotto nero, braised squid and chorizo, while stuffed free-range chicken leg might appear with Ibérico croquettes and braised leeks. Elsewhere, mighty 24oz ribeyes (for two) keep traditional company with béarnaise and hand-cut chips. The nifty, 40-bin wine list comes courtesy of the team at Stone, Vine & Sun. Prices start at £14.50.

Chef/s: Guy and Brittany Manning. **Open:** Tues to Sun L 12.30 to 2.30 (3 Sun), Tues to Sat D 6.30 to 9. **Closed:** Mon, 25 Dec, 2 weeks Jan. **Meals:** alc (main courses £13 to £19). **Service:** 10% (optional). **Details:** major cards accepted. 45 seats. 20 seats outside. Separate bar. Wheelchair access. Music. Children welcome. Car parking.

The Somerset Arms
Reborn boozer with heartwarming victuals
Church Street, Maiden Bradley BA12 7HW
(01985) 844207
www.thesomersetarms.co.uk
Gastropub | £26

Pitched idyllically between Longleat and Stourhead, the rejuvenated Somerset Arms has won over readers with its endearing blend of country conviviality, relaxed vibes and heartwarming victuals. The short menu dips its toe into the Med for, say, pan-fried halibut fillet with chorizo and white bean stew, but there are emphatic local flavours too – spot-on steaks from nearby Stourhead Estate, venison cottage pie, and rabbit hotpot with mustard mash, plus puds ranging from rhubarb and custard to treacle tart with marmalade ice cream. Those partial to handmade burgers and Sunday roasts won't be disappointed, either. Wines start at £13.25 (£3.10), and there are some snazzy cocktails too.

Chef/s: Rachel Seed. **Open:** Tue to Sun L 12 to 2 (4 Sun), Tue to Sat D 6.30 to 9. **Closed:** Mon. **Meals:** alc (main courses £8 to £21). **Service:** not inc. **Details:** major cards accepted. 36 seats. 24 seats outside. Separate bar. Wheelchair access. Music. Children welcome. Car parking.

Content brought to you by **The Good Food Guide 2011**. Please see page 14 for further details.

South West

Tourist Information Centres

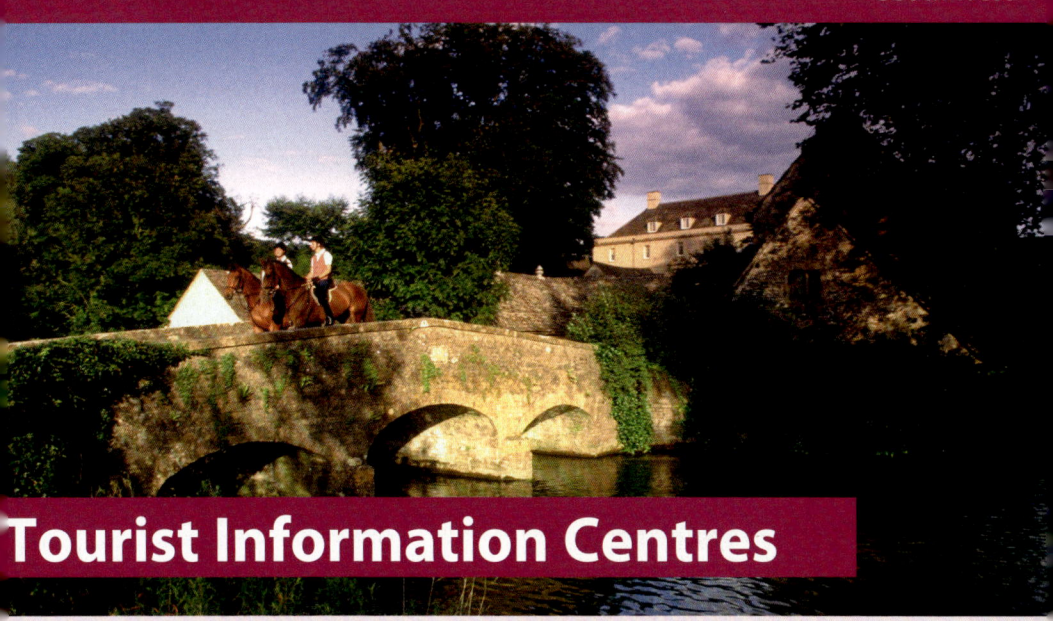

When you arrive at your destination, visit an Official Partner Tourist Information Centre for quality assured help with accommodation and information about local attractions and events, or email your request before you go. To find a Tourist Information Centre by region visit enjoyEngland.com/find-tic.

AVEBURY	Avebury Chapel Centre	01672 539179	all.tics@wiltshire.gov.uk
BATH	Abbey Chambers	0906 711 2000	tourism@bathtourism.co.uk
BODMIN	Shire Hall	01208 76616	bodmintic@visit.org.uk
BOURTON-ON-THE-WATER	Victoria Street	01451 820211	bourtonvic@btconnect.com
BRIDPORT	47 South Street	01308 424901	bridport.tic@westdorset-dc.gov.uk
BRISTOL : HARBOURSIDE	E Shed	0333 321 0101	ticharbourside@destinationbristol.co.uk
BRIXHAM	The Old Market House	01803 211 211	holiday@torbay.gov.uk
BUDE	Bude Visitor Centre	01288 354240	budetic@visitbude.info
BURNHAM-ON-SEA	South Esplanade	01278 787852	burnham.tic@sedgemoor.gov.uk
CAMELFORD	North Cornwall Museum	01840 212954	manager@camelfordtic.eclipse.co.uk
CARTGATE	South Somerset TIC	01935 829333	cartgate.tic@southsomerset.gov.uk
CHARD	The Guildhall	01460 65710	chardtic@chard.gov.uk
CHEDDAR	The Gorge	01934 744071	cheddar.tic@sedgemoor.gov.uk
CHELTENHAM	Municipal Offices	01242 522878	info@cheltenham.gov.uk
CHIPPENHAM	Yelde Hall	01249 665970	tourism@chippenham.gov.uk
CHIPPING CAMPDEN	The Old Police Station	01386 841206	information@visitchippingcampden.com
CHRISTCHURCH	49 High Street	01202 471780	enquiries@christchurchtourism.info
CIRENCESTER	Corn Hall	01285 654180	cirencestervic@cotswold.gov.uk
CORSHAM	Arnold House	01249 714660	enquiries@corshamheritage.org.uk
DEVIZES	Cromwell House	01380 734669	all.tics@wiltshire.gov.uk
DORCHESTER	11 Antelope Walk	01305 267992	dorchester.tic@westdorset-dc.gov.uk
FALMOUTH	11 Market Strand	01326 312300	info@falmouthtic.co.uk
FOWEY	5 South Street	01726 833616	info@fowey.co.uk
FROME	The Round Tower	01373 467271	enquiries@frometouristinfo.co.uk
GLASTONBURY	The Tribunal	01458 832954	glastonbury.tic@ukonline.co.uk

South West

GLOUCESTER	28 Southgate Street	01452 396572	tourism@gloucester.gov.uk
LOOE	The Guildhall	01503 262072	looetic@btconnect.com
LYME REGIS	Guildhall Cottage	01297 442138	lymeregis.tic@westdorset-dc.gov.uk
MALMESBURY	Town Hall	01666 823748	tic@malmesbury.gov.uk
MORETON-IN-MARCH	High Street	01608 650881	moreton@cotswold.gov.uk
PADSTOW & WADEBRIDGE	Red Brick Building	01841 533449	padstowtic@btconnect.com
PAIGNTON	The Esplanade	01803 211 211	holiday@torbay.gov.uk
PENZANCE	Station Road	01736 362207	pztic@penwith.gov.uk
PLYMOUTH	Plymouth Mayflower Centre	01752 306330	barbicantic@plymouth.gov.uk
SALISBURY	Fish Row	01722 334956	visitorinfo@salisbury.gov.uk
SHEPTON MALLET	70 High Street	01749 345258	sheptonmallet.tic@ukonline.co.uk
SHERBORNE	3 Tilton Court	01935 815341	sherborne.tic@westdorset-dc.gov.uk
SOMERSET VISITOR CENTRE	Sedgemoor Services	01934 750833	somersetvisitorcentre@somerset.gov.uk
ST AUSTELL	Southbourne Road	01726 879 500	tic@cornish-riviera.co.uk
ST IVES	The Guildhall	01736 796297	ivtic@penwith.gov.uk
STREET	Clarks Village	01458 447384	street.tic@ukonline.co.uk
STROUD	Subscription Rooms	01453 760960	tic@stroud.gov.uk
SWANAGE	The White House	01929 422885	mail@swanage.gov.uk
SWINDON	37 Regent Street	01793 530328	infocentre@swindon.gov.uk
TAUNTON	The Library	01823 336344	tauntontic@tauntondeane.gov.uk
TETBURY	33 Church Street	01666 503552	tourism@tetbury.org
TEWKESBURY	100 Church Street	01684 855043	tewkesburytic@tewkesburybc.gov.uk
TORQUAY	The Tourist Centre	01803 211 211	holiday@torbay.gov.uk
TRURO	Municipal Building	01872 274555	tic@truro.gov.uk
WAREHAM	Holy Trinity Church	01929 552740	tic@purbeck-dc.gov.uk
WARMINSTER	Central Car Park	01985 218548	visitwarminster@btconnect.com
WELLS	Town Hall	01749 672552	touristinfo@wells.gov.uk
WESTON-SUPER-MARE	Beach Lawns	01934 888800	westontouristinfo@n-somerset.gov.uk
WEYMOUTH	The King's Statue	01305 785747	tic@weymouth.gov.uk
WINCHCOMBE	Town Hall	01242 602925	winchcombetic@tewkesbury.gov.uk
YEOVIL	Hendford	01935 845946/7	yeoviltic@southsomerset.gov.uk

Regional Contacts and Information

For more information on accommodation, attractions, activities, events and holidays in South West England, contact one of the following regional or local tourism organisations. Their websites have a wealth of information and many produce free publications to help you get the most out of your visit.

Visit the following websites for further information on South West England:
- visitsouthwest.co.uk
- swcp.org.uk
- accessiblesouthwest.co.uk

Publications available from South West Tourism:
- The Trencherman's Guide to Top Restaurants in South West England
- Adventure South West
  Your ultimate activity and adventure guide.
- World Heritage Map
  Discover our World Heritage.

BREAKFAST AWARD
enjoyEngland.com

Enjoy England's Breakfast Award, sponsored by Kellogg's, recognises those hotels and B&Bs that offer their guests a quality and choice of breakfast, service and hospitality that exceeds what would be expected at their star rating.

We have indicated the accommodation which has achieved a Breakfast Award... look out for the following symbol **BREAKFAST AWARD** in the entry, and you can find an index to accommodation with a Breakfast Award at the back of this guide.

South West | **Cornwall**

Where to Stay

Entries appear alphabetically by town name in each county. A key to symbols appears on page 6. Maps start on page 706. A listing of all Enjoy England assessed accommodation appears at the end of the region.

BODMIN, Cornwall Map ref 1B2 — SAT NAV PL31 2DX

Bedknobs
Polgwyn, Castle Street, Bodmin, Cornwall PL31 2DX
t (01208) 77553   e gilly@bedknobs.co.uk
w bedknobs.co.uk ONLINE MAP GUEST REVIEWS

B&B PER ROOM PER NIGHT
S £60.00 – £75.00
D £75.00 – £110.00

Elegant, welcoming and award-winning B&B at the cutting edge of sustainable tourism. Spacious rooms overlooking woodland gardens. Choice of bedding. No synthetic chemicals, complimentary organic toiletries and great breakfasts. **directions** From A30 travelling west, take Bodmin turning onto sliproad, right hand lane, first turning right, at end, turn left, 600 metres down hill on left. **open** All year **bedrooms** 2 double, 1 twin **bathrooms** 2 en suite, 1 with private bathroom **payment** credit/debit cards, cash, cheques

Room General Leisure

BOLVENTOR, Cornwall Map ref 1C2 — SAT NAV PL15 7TS

Jamaica Inn
Bolventor, Launceston PL15 7TS
t (01566) 86250 f (01566) 86177 e enquiry@jamaicainn.co.uk
w jamaicainn.co.uk

B&B PER ROOM PER NIGHT
S £65.00 – £80.00
D £70.00 – £100.00
EVENING MEAL PER PERSON
£8.95 – £16.50

Inspiration for Daphne du Maurier's novel. Bars, restaurant, accommodation and gift shop. Whilst here visit Daphne du Maurier's Smugglers at Jamaica Inn. Check our website for our accommodation special offer!! **directions** Between Launceston and Bodmin on the A30. Follow brown signs. **open** All year **bedrooms** 14 double, 2 twin, 1 family **bathrooms** 17 en suite, 17 with private bathroom **payment** credit/debit cards, cash, euros

Room General Leisure

Looking for something else?

You can also buy a copy of our popular guide 'Hotels' including country house and town house hotels, metro and budget hotels, serviced apartments, restaurants with rooms and Spas in England 2011. Now available in good bookshops and online at **visitbritainshop.com**

£10.99

South West | Cornwall

BOSCASTLE, Cornwall Map ref 1B2
SAT NAV PL35 0BN

Home Farm B&B
Home Farm, Boscastle PL35 0BN
t (01840) 250195 **e** homefarm.boscastle@tiscali.co.uk
w homefarm-boscastle.co.uk

B&B PER ROOM PER NIGHT
S £53.00 – £55.00
D £34.00 – £38.00

A warm welcome awaits you at Home Farm, where you can enjoy a friendly stay with traditional farmhouse fare. Sea views and lovely walks to Boscastle and the Valency valley. **directions** Please contact us for directions **open** All year except Xmas and New Year **bedrooms** 2 double, 1 twin **bathrooms** 3 en suite **payment** credit/debit cards, cash, cheques

BREAKFAST AWARD

Room | General | Leisure

BUDE, Cornwall Map ref 1C2
SAT NAV EX23 0AW

Beach House
Marine Drive, Widemouth Bay, Bude, Cornwall EX23 0AW
t (01288) 361256 **e** beachhousebookings@tiscali.co.uk
w beachhousewidemouth.co.uk

B&B PER ROOM PER NIGHT
S £34.00 – £41.00
D £58.00 – £72.00

EVENING MEAL PER PERSON
£14.00

SPECIAL PROMOTIONS
Discounts on bookings of 4 days or more.

The Wilkins family welcome you to their unique site, private access onto Widemouth Beach. All bedrooms are en suite, the majority with sundeck balconies. Sun lounge, new bar lounge, general and wet fish shop, surf shop and hire. Restaurant serving traditional Cornish and seafood menus. Outside dining on decked patios.

open Easter to end of October
bedrooms 1 single, 7 double, 1 twin, 2 family
bathrooms 11 en suite
payment credit/debit cards, cash, cheques

directions From Bude Visitors Centre turn left, follow the road for 3 miles. Beach House sited on the right, on the foreshore to the beach.

Room | General | Leisure

BUDE, Cornwall Map ref 1C2
SAT NAV EX23 0LY

Harefield Cottage
Harefield Cottage, Upton, Bude, Cornwall EX23 0LY
t (01288) 352350 **e** sally@coast-countryside.co.uk
w coast-countryside.co.uk ONLINE MAP GUEST REVIEWS ONLINE BOOKING LAST MINUTE OFFERS

B&B PER ROOM PER NIGHT
S £40.00
D £56.00

EVENING MEAL PER PERSON
£22.00

Luxurious and spacious en suite accommodation with outstanding views situated between Bude and Widemouth Bay. 250 yards from the coastal footpath. Personal attention assured at all times. **directions** From A39 follow signs to Bude. Turn left at mini-roundabout signposted Widemouth, drive for 1 mile take first left-hand turn Harefield on left. **open** All year except Xmas and New Year **bedrooms** 2 double, 2 twin, 1 family **bathrooms** 5 en suite **payment** credit/debit cards, cash, cheques

Room | General | Leisure

For **key to symbols** see page 6

39

South West | Cornwall

BUDE, Cornwall Map ref 1C2
SAT NAV EX23 8RG

Surf Haven Guest House
31 Downs View, Bude EX23 8RG
t (01288) 353923 **e** info@surfhaven.co.uk
w surfhaven.co.uk ONLINE MAP GUEST REVIEWS

B&B PER ROOM PER NIGHT
S £28.00 – £45.00
D £52.00 – £64.00
EVENING MEAL PER PERSON
£12.00 – £19.50

A warm and friendly guest house, overlooks the golf course and is 200m from the beach. A short walk to town. Fresh, locally sourced and organic produce used wherever possible. **directions** From A3072 follow signs to Bude town centre, bear left at the top of the hill and follow signs for Crooklets Beach. **open** All year **bedrooms** 4 double, 2 twin, 2 family **bathrooms** 7 en suite, 1 with private bathroom **payment** credit/debit cards, cash, cheques

Room General Leisure

BUDE, Cornwall Map ref 1C2
SAT NAV EX23 8BY

Tee-Side
2 Burn View, Bude EX23 8BY
t (01288) 352351 **e** rayandjune@tee-side.co.uk
w tee-side.co.uk ONLINE MAP LAST MINUTE OFFERS

B&B PER ROOM PER NIGHT
S £25.00 – £35.00
D £25.00 – £32.00

Overlooking golf course, near town and beaches. High quality en-suite rooms. Delicious full English or buffet style breakfast. Ideal for golfers with reduced green fees. Walkers and cyclists welcome. **directions** From The Strand head to top of town, bear right, signpost Golf Course, and situated first guest house on the right opposite golf club **open** All year **bedrooms** 1 single, 2 double, 2 twin **bathrooms** 5 en suite **payment** credit/debit cards, cash, cheques

Room General Leisure

BUGLE, Cornwall Map ref 1B2
SAT NAV PL26 8PB

The Bugle Inn
57 Fore Street, St Austell PL26 8PB
t (01726) 850307 **f** (01726) 850181 **e** bugleinn@aol.com
w bugleinn.co.uk GUEST REVIEWS

B&B PER ROOM PER NIGHT
S £47.50
D £67.50

Home from home pub. Selection of real ales. Good home cooked food. Very near to Eden Project. **directions** Please contact us for directions **open** All year except Xmas and New Year **bedrooms** 2 double, 2 twin, 1 family **bathrooms** 5 en suite **payment** credit/debit cards, cash, cheques, euros

Room General Leisure

CALLINGTON, Cornwall Map ref 1C2
SAT NAV PL17 8LX

Hampton Manor
Alston, Callington PL17 8LX
t (01579) 370494 **f** (01579) 370494 **e** hamptonmanor@supanet.com
w hamptonmanor.co.uk ONLINE MAP LAST MINUTE OFFERS

B&B PER ROOM PER NIGHT
S £50.00 – £55.00
D £70.00 – £80.00
EVENING MEAL PER PERSON
£12.95 – £24.90

Country House with licensed restaurant, in 2.5 acres in the Tamar Valley. North and South coasts, Dartmoor & Bodmin Moor all within a 1/2 hour drive **directions** A30 to Launceston, then A388 towards Callington. After 7 miles turn left towards Horsebridge. Straight on at two crossroads, then left at sign for Alston/Tutwell. **open** All year **bedrooms** 3 double **bathrooms** 5 en suite, 1 with private bathroom **payment** credit/debit cards, cash, cheques, euros

Room General Leisure

Official tourist board guide Bed & Breakfast

South West | Cornwall

CALLINGTON, Cornwall Map ref 1C2
SAT NAV PL17 8PX

FARMHOUSE

B&B PER ROOM PER NIGHT
S £35.00 – £38.00
D £56.00 – £64.00

Higher Manaton
Callington, Cornwall PL17 8PX
t (01579) 370460 f (01579) 370460 e dtrewin@manaton.fsnet.co.uk
w cornwall-devon-bandb.co.uk ONLINE MAP

From our traditional working farm explore the moors and beaches of Cornwall & Devon, National Trust and English Heritage properties. Within easy reach of Eden Project and Heligan Gardens. **directions** From the A30 at Launceston take the A388 towards Callington. After 8 miles turn right onto the B3257; 450yds turn left into the farm drive. **open** All year except Xmas and New Year **bedrooms** 1 double, 1 twin, 1 family **bathrooms** 2 en suite, 1 with private bathroom **payment** cash, cheques, euros

FALMOUTH, Cornwall Map ref 1B3
SAT NAV TR11 2AN

BED & BREAKFAST

B&B PER ROOM PER NIGHT
S £28.00 – £30.00
D £56.00 – £60.00
EVENING MEAL PER PERSON
£7.00 – £15.00

BREAKFAST AWARD

Anchor House
17 Harbour Terrace, Falmouth TR11 2AN
t (01326) 317006 e tinarange@btinternet.com
w anchorhousebandbfalmouth.co.uk ONLINE MAP

Look no further if you want 180 degree panoramic views of Falmouth harbour. Anchor House is situated in a Victorian terrace, five minutes from the town, beaches and coastal footpath. **directions** Dracaena Avenue, left Kimberley Park Road. Argos on left, Party Zone on right, turn immediately left up Quarry Hill, follow Erisey Terrace to Harbour Terrace. **open** All year **bedrooms** 1 single, 1 double **bathrooms** 1 with private bathroom **payment** cash, cheques

FALMOUTH, Cornwall Map ref 1B3
SAT NAV TR11 4BG

GUEST ACCOMMODATION

B&B PER ROOM PER NIGHT
S £45.00 – £50.00
D £60.00 – £100.00

Chelsea House
2 Emslie Road, Falmouth TR11 4BG
t (01326) 212230 e info@chelseahousehotel.com
w chelseahousehotel.com ONLINE MAP GUEST REVIEWS LAST MINUTE OFFERS

Beautifully furnished en suite rooms with panoramic sea views over Falmouth Bay, some with own balcony. Parking. Short walk to town and two minutes' walk to lovely sandy, Quiet location. **directions** See website **open** All year **bedrooms** 1 single, 5 double, 1 twin, 1 family **bathrooms** 8 en suite **payment** credit/debit cards, cash, cheques

FALMOUTH, Cornwall Map ref 1B3
SAT NAV TR11 3PR

GUEST ACCOMMODATION

B&B PER ROOM PER NIGHT
S £29.00 – £40.00
D £55.00 – £60.00

Engleton Bed & Breakfast
67 Killigrew Street, Falmouth TR11 3PR
t (01326) 372644 f (01326) 330210 e dawnemmerson@aol.com
w falmouth-bandb.co.uk GUEST REVIEWS ONLINE BOOKING

Small friendly B&B located in the heart of Falmouth. 2 mins walk from all the shops & restaurants. En-suite rooms. Single/Double/Twin & Family. All you can eat Breakfasts! **directions** Follow signs Falmouth and beaches. Past police station, straight over lights with Livery Dole garage on left. Next Roundabout turn left into Killigrew Street. **open** All year **bedrooms** 2 single, 3 double, 3 twin, 4 family **bathrooms** 10 en suite **payment** credit/debit cards, cash, cheques

For key to symbols see page 6

41

South West | **Cornwall**

ILLOGAN, Cornwall Map ref 1B3
SAT NAV TR16 4HD

Sonnier
Merritts Hill, Illogan, Redruth, Cornwall TR16 4HD
t (01209) 203934 **e** david.darkin@tesco.net
w cornwall-online.co.uk/activeleisure/Welcome.asp GUEST REVIEWS

B&B PER ROOM PER NIGHT
S £35.00 – £40.00
D £50.00 – £56.00
EVENING MEAL PER PERSON
£14.00 – £16.00

Small friendly family B&B very local for most West Cornwall attractions including The Southwest Coastal Path, National Trust, Properties, Hiking & Biking, Mineral tramways etc. **directions** From A30 Redruth follow signs for Porthtowan North Country. At first crossroads turn left, straight across at next crossroads, take third left into Merritts Hill. **open** All year **bedrooms** 1 suite **bathrooms** 1 with private bathroom **payment** cash, cheques

LAUNCESTON, Cornwall Map ref 1C2
SAT NAV PL15 7JL

Oakside Farm Bungalow
South Petherwin, Launceston, Cornwall PL15 7JL
t (01566) 86733 **e** janetcrossman415@btinternet.com
w oaksidebb.co.uk

B&B PER ROOM PER NIGHT
S £27.50 – £30.00
D £55.00 – £60.00

SPECIAL PROMOTIONS
Looking for comfortable, friendly accommodation in picturesque Cornwall? -You have just found it -welcome to our home.

Panoramic views of Bodmin Moor from farm bungalow, nestling peacefully amongst delightful surroundings, conveniently situated one minute from A30. Ideal base for touring Devon and Cornwall. Twenty-five minutes from Eden Project. English breakfasts a speciality with home-made bread and preserves. Warm welcome awaits. Cosy, well-equipped rooms. Ideal place to relax.

open All year
bedrooms 2 double, 1 twin
bathrooms 2 en suite, 1 with private bathroom
payment cash, cheques

directions A30 into Cornwall. Three miles west of Launceston, underneath A395, still on A30. Slow down, no slip road. Next left, Oakside 1st bungalow on right.

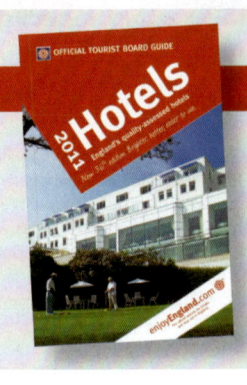

Looking for something else?
You can also buy a copy of our popular guide 'Hotels' including country house and town house hotels, metro and budget hotels, serviced apartments, restaurants with rooms and Spas in England 2011.

Now available in good bookshops and online at
visitbritainshop.com

£10.99

South West | Cornwall

LAUNCESTON, Cornwall Map ref 1C2
SAT NAV PL15 9PE

Primrose Cottage
Primrose Cottage, Lawhitton, Launceston PL15 9PE
t (01566) 773645 e enquiry@primrosecottagesuites.co.uk
w primrosecottagesuites.co.uk ONLINE MAP

B&B PER ROOM PER NIGHT
S £70.00 – £90.00
D £80.00 – £130.00

EVENING MEAL PER PERSON
£12.00 – £16.00

SPECIAL PROMOTIONS
Discounts on stays of 2 or 3 days. Please see website for details.

Primrose Cottage is set in gardens and woodland leading to the River Tamar. Each luxury suite has its own sitting room, entrance and en suite facilities with beautiful views across the Tamar Valley. Five minutes from the A30 with easy access to both north and south coasts and the moors.

open All year except Xmas
bedrooms 2 double, 1 twin
bathrooms 3 en suite
payment credit/debit cards, cash, cheques

directions Leave Launceston on the A388 Plymouth road. After 1 mile turn left on B3362 signposted Tavistock. Primrose Cottage is on the left after 2.5 miles.

LOOE, Cornwall Map ref 1C2
SAT NAV PL13 1LP

Barclay House
Saint Martins Road, Looe PL13 1LP
t (01503) 262929 f (01503) 262632 e info@barclayhouse.co.uk
w barclayhouse.co.uk ONLINE MAP GUEST REVIEWS ONLINE BOOKING LAST MINUTE OFFERS

B&B PER ROOM PER NIGHT
S £55.00 – £95.00
D £105.00 – £175.00

EVENING MEAL PER PERSON
£25.00 – £35.00

SPECIAL PROMOTIONS
Special Dinner, Room and Breakfast breaks of 2 nights or more always available £79.50 pppn. Please call to enquire

High on the hill offering spectacular river views yet just minutes away from the historic fishing port of Looe stands Barclay House. Smart contemporary rooms, 2AA Rosette restaurant, amazing staff, luxury cottages, outdoor pool, gym, sauna, hair salon, 6 acres of beautiful gardens and woodland. We have it all!

open All year
bedrooms 1 single, 8 double, 2 twin, 1 suite
bathrooms 12 en suite
payment credit/debit cards, cash, cheques, euros

directions Leave A38 following signs to Looe. As you approach looe through glorious countryside, you will fine Barclay House on the left by the 30mph sign!

BREAKFAST AWARD

South West | **Cornwall**

LOOE, Cornwall Map ref 1C2   SAT NAV PL13 1NZ

Bucklawren Farm
St Martin by Looe, Looe PL13 1NZ
t (01503) 240738 f 01503 240738 e bucklawren@btopenworld.com
w bucklawren.co.uk ONLINE MAP

B&B PER ROOM PER NIGHT
S £36.00 – £50.00
D £60.00 – £72.00

Delightful farmhouse with spectacular sea views. Quiet location, situated one mile from the beach and coastal path and three miles from the fishing village of Looe. Restaurant on site. **directions** From Looe take B3253 towards Plymouth. After 2 miles turn right for Monkey Sanctuary. After 1 mile turn right to Bucklawren down road past Restaurant **open** March to November **bedrooms** 3 double, 2 twin, 2 family **bathrooms** 7 en suite **payment** credit/debit cards, cash, cheques

LOOE, Cornwall Map ref 1C2   SAT NAV PL13 2LY

Trenderway Farm
Pelynt, Nr Polperro, Looe PL13 2LY
t (01503) 272214 e yaron@trenderwayfarm.com
w trenderwayfarm.co.uk ONLINE MAP GUEST REVIEWS ONLINE BOOKING LAST MINUTE OFFERS

B&B PER ROOM PER NIGHT
S £95.00 – £165.00
D £95.00 – £165.00

SPECIAL PROMOTIONS
Long Weekend (3 nights) and 7 Night special rates are available - Please contact us for details.

Trenderway Farm is set in 200 acres of beautiful farmland bordering Cornwall's Heritage Coastline, a true Cornish haven. Choose from seven luxurious en suite bedrooms and enjoy a sumptuous Trenderway breakfast in the farmhouse conservatory. 25 minutes from Eden Project, Trenderway is an ideal base from which to explore Cornwall.

open All year
bedrooms 5 double, 2 twin
bathrooms 7 en suite
payment credit/debit cards, cash, cheques

directions Trenderway Farm is located between Looe (2.5 miles), Polperro and Pelynt (1 mile), between the A387 and the B3359.

LOSTWITHIEL, Cornwall Map ref 1B2   SAT NAV PL22 0RP

Cross Close House B&B
West Taphouse, Lostwithiel PL22 0RP
t (01579) 320355 e crossclose@alexlister1.plus.com
w cornwall-online.co.uk/cross-close LAST MINUTE OFFERS

B&B PER ROOM PER NIGHT
S £38.00 – £56.00
D £56.00
EVENING MEAL PER PERSON
£10.00 – £15.00

We are a comfortable 4 star B and B with 2 ensuite bedrooms, a guest lounge, and a lovely garden, Nr the Eden Project, Lanhydrock(NT), Lostwithiel and the coast. **directions** West Taphouse in Cornwall on A390 . Come into Cornwall on A38 , then A390 from Dobwalls - signposted to St. Austell - 4 miles **open** All year **bedrooms** 1 double, 1 twin **bathrooms** 2 en suite **payment** credit/debit cards, cash, cheques

44   Official tourist board guide Bed & Breakfast

South West | Cornwall

LOSTWITHIEL, Cornwall Map ref 1B2
SAT NAV PL22 0ER

Hazelmere House
58 Grenville Road, Lostwithiel, Cornwall PL22 0ER
t (01208) 873345 e rth346@aol.com
w hazelmerehouse.co.uk LAST MINUTE OFFERS

B&B PER ROOM PER NIGHT
S £40.00 – £45.00
D £80.00 – £90.00

Situated in the beautiful Fowey Valley, Hazelmere is a comfortable Edwardian House with rural views overlooking the Historic town of Lostwithiel. Richard & Sheila Hanson with 30 years experience in hospitality offer comfortable accomodation in a warm informal atmosphere. Centrally situated close to the Eden Project, Heligan Gardens and many National Trust Properties.

bedrooms 1 single, 1 double, 1 twin
bathrooms 2 en suite, 1 with private bathroom
payment cash, cheques, euros

directions On the A390 East of Lostwithiel. Close to Bodmin Parkway and Lostwithiel Railway Stations

MEVAGISSEY, Cornwall Map ref 1B3
SAT NAV PL26 6RX

Bacchus B&B
Trevarth, Mevagissey PL26 6RX
t (01726) 843173 e susiecannone@yahoo.co.uk
w bacchus-cornwall.co.uk ONLINE MAP GUEST REVIEWS ONLINE BOOKING LAST MINUTE OFFERS

B&B PER ROOM PER NIGHT
S £45.00
D £55.00

A large, elevated modern house with views of the sea & harbour in the popular old fishing village of Mevagissey. **directions** Arrival Mevagissey, you'll see a large car park on your left. Turn right into Trevarth & Ava Estate. Turn immediately right again and follow signs. **bedrooms** 2 double, 2 twin **bathrooms** 4 en suite

MEVAGISSEY, Cornwall Map ref 1B3
SAT NAV PL26 6ER

Corran Farm
St Ewe, Mevagissey PL26 6ER
t (01726) 842159 e info@corranfarm.co.uk
w corranfarm.co.uk ONLINE MAP

B&B PER ROOM PER NIGHT
S £32.00 – £35.00
D £54.00 – £58.00

Quality farmhouse B&B on working farm in open countryside with own farm shop. Farm adjoins Heligan Gardens. Choice of delicious breakfast, beautiful walks, beaches, inns. Ideal for exploring Cornwall. **directions** From St Austell take the B3273 (towards Mevagissey). Follow the signs towards Heligan Gardens/Gorran. Corran Farm is the next turning left after Heligan Gardens. **open** February to November **bedrooms** 2 double, 1 twin **bathrooms** 3 en suite **payment** cash, cheques

For **key to symbols** see page 6

45

South West | Cornwall

MEVAGISSEY, Cornwall Map ref 1B3 SAT NAV PL26 6ND

Tregilgas Farm
Gorran, St Austell PL26 6ND
t (01726) 842342 or 07789 113520   e dclemes88@aol.com
w tregilgasfarmbedandbreakfast.co.uk ONLINE MAP

B&B PER ROOM PER NIGHT
S £30.00 – £40.00
D £50.00 – £60.00
EVENING MEAL PER PERSON
£20.00 – £25.00

Lovely 5-bedroomed detached farmhouse on working farm. Tastefully decorated. Very central for touring Cornwall. Lovely food for breakfast. Friendly welcome awaits you. **directions** Follow signs to Heligan Gardens. Go past gardens, take 4th turning on right, go to crossroads, go straight across. Tregilgas is 1st farm on right. **open** March–September **bedrooms** 2 double, 1 twin **bathrooms** 2 en suite, 1 with private bathroom **payment** cash, cheques, euros

MORWENSTOW, Cornwall Map ref 1C2 SAT NAV EX23 9SR

The Bush Inn
The Bush Inn Crosstown, Morwenstow, Bude EX23 9SR
t (01288) 331242   e coryfarmltd@aol.com
w bushinn-morwenstow.co.uk

B&B PER ROOM PER NIGHT
S £47.50
D £85.00
EVENING MEAL PER PERSON
£8.50 – £17.50

Historic inn situated off South West Coast Path. Sympathetically refurbished rooms with breathtaking views. Delicious meals freshly prepared from seasonal local produce; beef from our farm and locally caught seafood. **directions** Follow sign to Morwenstow from A39. After 2 miles take 2nd right in village, continue 1 mile to Crosstown. The Bush is on your left. **open** All year **bedrooms** 1 double, 2 twin **bathrooms** 3 en suite **payment** credit/debit cards, cash, cheques

NEWQUAY, Cornwall Map ref 1B2 SAT NAV TR7 2LR

Chichester Guest House
14 Bay View Terrace, Newquay, Cornwall TR7 2LR
t (01637) 874216   e sheila.harper@virgin.net
w freespace.virgin.net/sheila.harper ONLINE MAP

B&B PER ROOM PER NIGHT
S £25.00
D £50.00

Friendly, clean, comfortable. Near beaches and shops. Showers and sea views in most bedrooms. Specialist information on walking, nature and heritage, Cornish Archaeology. Microscope room for mineral collectors. Good conversation. **directions** Please contact us for directions **open** March to October **bedrooms** 1 single, 3 double, 2 twin, 1 family **payment** cash, cheques

NEWQUAY, Cornwall Map ref 1B2 SAT NAV TR8 5HY

Degembris Farmhouse
Degembris Major Farm, St Newlyn East, Nr Newquay, Cornwall TR8 5HY
t (01872) 510555   e thefarmhouse@degembris.co.uk
w degembris.co.uk ONLINE MAP

B&B PER ROOM PER NIGHT
S £30.00 – £40.00
D £60.00 – £70.00

Centrally situated in beautiful countryside, yet close to the sea, Degembris is the perfect holiday base. This delightful Grade II listed building and picturesque gardens overlook a peaceful wooded valley. **directions** Exit A30 at junct signed 'Summercourt.' At crossroads turn rt, A3058 towards Newquay. Take 3rd left, signed St Newlyn East. Take 2nd left, signed Degembris. **open** All year except Xmas and New Year **bedrooms** 1 single, 2 double, 1 twin, 1 family **bathrooms** 3 en suite **payment** credit/debit cards, cash, cheques

South West | Cornwall

NEWQUAY, Cornwall Map ref 1B2
SAT NAV TR7 2BH

enjoyEngland.com ★★ BED & BREAKFAST

B&B PER ROOM PER NIGHT
S £35.00 – £60.00
D £50.00 – £70.00

Surfside Stop Guest House
35 Mount Wise, Newquay TR7 2BH
t (01637) 872707 e surfsidehotel@btconnect.com
w surfsidenewquay.co.uk ONLINE MAP GUEST REVIEWS ONLINE BOOKING LAST MINUTE OFFERS

All en suite accommodation, car park, close to town, beaches, restaurants, clubs and bars. Small groups by prior arrangement only. No stag parties. **directions** Directions on website. **open** All year except Xmas **bedrooms** 4 double, 5 twin, 1 family **bathrooms** 10 en suite **payment** credit/debit cards, cash

Room General Leisure

PENZANCE, Cornwall Map ref 1A3
SAT NAV TR18 2HA

enjoyEngland.com ★★★ GUEST ACCOMMODATION

B&B PER ROOM PER NIGHT
S £30.00 – £35.00
D £60.00 – £70.00
EVENING MEAL PER PERSON
£16.50

Cornerways Guest House
5 Leskinnick Street, Penzance TR18 2HA
t (01736) 364645 f (01736) 364645 e enquiries@cornerways-penzance.co.uk
w penzance.co.uk/cornerways ONLINE MAP GUEST REVIEWS

Cornerways is an attractively decorated townhouse, four minutes from car parks, bus/railway stations. Freshly cooked breakfast to order including vegetarian, using organic produce where possible. Touring base. Rooms en suite. **directions** Walk up from rail/bus station towards main road, cross at pedestrian lights. Leskinnick Street is facing you, we are 50 yards on right. **open** All year **bedrooms** 2 single, 1 double, 1 twin **bathrooms** 4 en suite **payment** credit/debit cards, cash, cheques, euros

Room General Leisure

PENZANCE, Cornwall Map ref 1A3
SAT NAV TR18 4BG

enjoyEngland.com ★★★ GUEST ACCOMMODATION

B&B PER ROOM PER NIGHT
D £50.00 – £56.00

Wymering Guest House
15 Regent Square, Penzance TR18 4BG
t (01736) 362126 f (01736) 362126 e pam@wymering.com
w wymering.com ONLINE MAP ONLINE BOOKING LAST MINUTE OFFERS

Small, select guesthouse situated in a peaceful Regency square, just off the beach. Town centre, promenade, bathing pool, bus, coach and train station all nearby. **directions** From railway station along harbour and promanade to Lugger hotel. Turn right two minutes up on right hand side. **open** All year **bedrooms** 2 double, 2 twin, 1 family **bathrooms** 2 en suite, 3 with private bathroom **payment** credit/debit cards, cash, cheques

Room General Leisure

POLZEATH, Cornwall Map ref 1B2
SAT NAV PL27 6TJ

enjoyEngland.com ★★★★ GUEST HOUSE

B&B PER ROOM PER NIGHT
D £63.00 – £78.00

White Heron
Polzeath, Wadebridge PL27 6TJ
t (01208) 863623 e info@whiteheronhotel.co.uk
w whiteheronhotel.co.uk ONLINE MAP GUEST REVIEWS

Family-run, non-smoking, licensed establishment, 500yds from beaches. TV and tea-/coffee-making facilities in bedrooms. All rooms en suite. **directions** Please contact us for directions **open** May to October **bedrooms** 5 double **bathrooms** 5 en suite **payment** credit/debit cards, cash, cheques

Room General

For **key to symbols** see page 6

47

South West | **Cornwall**

PORTHCURNO, Cornwall Map ref 1A3   SAT NAV TR19 6JL

Ardensawah Farm
St Levan, Penzance, Cornwall TR19 6JL
t (01736) 871520 or 07877124550 e ardensawah@btinternet.com
w porthcurnofarmholidays.com ONLINE MAP

B&B PER ROOM PER NIGHT
S £55.00 – £75.00
D £75.00 – £85.00

SPECIAL PROMOTIONS
Special rates for minimum 3 night breaks between Nov – March excluding Christmas.

Discover our delightful Cornish farmhouse in this wonderful area of outstanding natural beauty. A warm welcome, sea views and delicious breakfasts made with our own produce await you. Relax, unwind and enjoy the peace and tranquility of both the countryside and stunning beaches around us. The perfect holiday choice.

open All year except Xmas
bedrooms 2 double, 1 family
bathrooms 2 en suite, 1 with private bathroom
payment credit/debit cards, cash, cheques, euros
directions 2 miles from Lands End. Situated between Porthcurno and Porthgwarra. On the migratory path for birdwatching.

Room
General
Leisure

PORT ISAAC, Cornwall Map ref 1B2   SAT NAV PL30 3HH

Cornish Arms
Pendoggett, Port Isaac PL30 3HH
t (01208) 880263 f (01208) 880335 e info@cornisharms.com
w cornisharms.com ONLINE MAP GUEST REVIEWS LAST MINUTE OFFERS

B&B PER ROOM PER NIGHT
S £55.00 – £75.00
D £70.00 – £110.00
EVENING MEAL PER PERSON
£15.00 – £25.00

Olde Worlde coaching inn near to North Cornish coast, serving fresh, homecooked food, + Authentic Thai. Real ales. Port Isaac a short drive, home to TV program Doc Martin. **directions** Please see our website. **open** All year **bedrooms** 3 double, 2 twin, 3 family **bathrooms** 8 en suite **payment** credit/debit cards, cash

Room General Leisure

PORT ISAAC, Cornwall Map ref 1B2   SAT NAV PL29 3RH

Slipway
The Slipway, The Harbour Front, Port Isaac PL29 3RH
t (01208) 880264 e mark.forbes@tesco.net
w portisaachotel.com ONLINE MAP GUEST REVIEWS ONLINE BOOKING LAST MINUTE OFFERS

B&B PER ROOM PER NIGHT
S £75.00 – £110.00
D £90.00 – £180.00
EVENING MEAL PER PERSON
£12.00 – £35.00

The Slipway is a friendly, family-run inn of great character. Bedrooms are stylishly furnished and many overlook the harbour. Menus are imaginative, utilizing locally sourced fish, meat and produce. **directions** In Port Isaac pass Co-op on right. 100m, turn left down Back Hill and follow road to harbour. **open** All year except Xmas **bedrooms** 7 double, 1 twin, 2 suites **bathrooms** 10 en suite **payment** credit/debit cards, cash, cheques, euros

Room General Leisure

Official tourist board guide Bed & Breakfast

South West | Cornwall

REDRUTH, Cornwall Map ref 1B3   SAT NAV TR16 5DF

Goonearl Cottage
Wheal Rose, Scorrier, Redruth TR16 5DF
t (01209) 891571 f (01209) 891916 e goonearl@tiscali.co.uk
w goonearlcottage.com ONLINE MAP ONLINE BOOKING

enjoyEngland.com ★★★★ GUEST HOUSE
enjoyEngland.com Silver AWARD

B&B PER ROOM PER NIGHT
S £45.00 – £50.00
D £70.00 – £90.00
EVENING MEAL PER PERSON
£12.50 – £15.00

Set in open countryside. Perfectly situated for visiting Cornwall. Within easy reach of golden sandy beaches of the North coast. Our rooms are beautifully decorated providing a relaxing atmosphere.
directions Leave the A30 at the Scorrier/A3047 sign. Turn right at The Plume of Feathers, first left into Wheal Rose. **open** All year **bedrooms** 5 double, 1 twin, 1 family, 1 suite **bathrooms** 5 en suite, 2 with private bathroom **payment** credit/debit cards, cash, cheques

Room / General / Leisure

RUAN HIGH LANES, Cornwall Map ref 1B3   SAT NAV TR2 5JS

Trenona Farm B&B
Ruan High Lanes, Truro TR2 5JS
t (01872) 501339 f (01872) 501253 e info@trenonafarmholidays.co.uk
w trenonafarmholidays.co.uk ONLINE MAP GUEST REVIEWS ONLINE BOOKING LAST MINUTE OFFERS

enjoyEngland.com ★★★ FARMHOUSE

B&B PER ROOM PER NIGHT
S £28.00 – £42.00
D £56.00 – £64.00

SPECIAL PROMOTIONS
Discounts for stays of 4 or more nights for children and for family rooms.

Enjoy a warm welcome and scrumptious Cornish breakfasts in our Victorian farmhouse on a working farm on the beautiful Roseland Peninsula. Our guest bedrooms have en suite or private bathrooms, and we welcome children and pets. Public footpaths lead to Veryan and the south coast (three miles).

open March to November
bedrooms 1 double, 3 family
bathrooms 3 en suite, 1 with private bathroom
payment credit/debit cards, cash, cheques

directions A390 to Truro. At Hewaswater B3287 to Tregony then A3078 to St Mawes. After 2 miles, pass Jet garage. 2nd farm on left-hand side.

Room / General / Leisure

ST AGNES, Cornwall Map ref 1B3   SAT NAV TR5 0XX

Little Trevellas Farm
Trevellas, St Agnes TR5 0XX
t (01872) 552945 f (01872) 552945 e velvetcrystal@xln.co.uk
w stagnesbandb.co.uk ONLINE BOOKING

enjoyEngland.com ★★★ FARMHOUSE

B&B PER ROOM PER NIGHT
S £27.50 – £30.00
D £50.00 – £60.00

A 250-year-old house on a working farm on the B3285 provides a peaceful, comfortable base for a holiday that will appeal to lovers of both coast and countryside. **directions** Please contact us for directions **open** All year **bedrooms** 1 single, 1 double, 1 twin **bathrooms** 3 en suite **payment** cash, cheques

Room / General

For **key to symbols** see page 6   49

South West | Cornwall

ST AUSTELL, Cornwall Map ref 1B3   SAT NAV PL25 3RH

Anchorage House
Nettles Corner, Boscundle, St Austell, Cornwall PL25 3RH
t (01726) 814071 f (01726) 813462 e info@anchoragehouse.co.uk
w anchoragehouse.co.uk ONLINE MAP GUEST REVIEWS ONLINE BOOKING

B&B PER ROOM PER NIGHT
S £75.00 – £115.00
D £95.00 – £135.00

EVENING MEAL PER PERSON
£23.00 – £29.00

SPECIAL PROMOTIONS
(1) Room Only discount of £10 per room. (2) 5% discount for 7 nights or more

Luxurious small, private, national award winning bed and breakfast, and the ultimate in Cornwall, Eden Project and child-free accommodation, offering indulgent bistro suppers, huge beds and bathtubs, indoor swimming pool, small gym, free WiFi and much more. Special attention to detail and flair are evident everywhere.

open March - November
bedrooms 2 double, 1 twin, 2 suites
bathrooms 5 en suite
payment credit/debit cards, cash, cheques

directions 2 miles East of St Austell off the A390. Across from the St Austell Garden Centre, turn left and then immediately left again.

BREAKFAST AWARD

ST AUSTELL, Cornwall Map ref 1B3   SAT NAV PL25 5DU

The Gables Guest House
1 Edgcumbe Road, St Austell, Cornwall PL25 5DU
t 01726 72638 e info@gablesguesthousebnb.co.uk
w gablesguesthousebnb.co.uk ONLINE MAP GUEST REVIEWS ONLINE BOOKING LAST MINUTE OFFERS

B&B PER ROOM PER NIGHT
S £45.00 – £60.00
D £70.00 – £120.00

EVENING MEAL PER PERSON
£17.50 – £25.00

Family run guest-house with good food and relaxed atmosphere. Believed to be 19th century, with solid stone walls, beautiful gardens, feature fish-pond and lovely views of garden and beyond.
directions Please see our website for map and full directions. **open** All year except Xmas **bedrooms** 3 double, 1 twin **bathrooms** 2 en suite, 2 with private bathroom **payment** credit/debit cards, cash

ST AUSTELL, Cornwall Map ref 1B3   SAT NAV PL24 2HW

Highland Court Lodge
Biscovey Road, Biscovey, St Austell PL24 2HW
t (01726) 813320 e enquiries@highlandcourt.co.uk
w highlandcourt.co.uk LAST MINUTE OFFERS

B&B PER ROOM PER NIGHT
S £85.00 – £145.00
D £90.00 – £190.00

EVENING MEAL PER PERSON
£19.00 – £48.00

Award winning luxurious family-run country hotel with stunning views over St Austell Bay. Two acres of beautiful grounds, near Eden Project. Impressively equipped en suite bedrooms, comfortable lounge, terrace with fine views. **directions** From A30 take A391 to St Austell. Turn left onto A390 through St Blazey Gate. Turn right into Biscovey Road. Lodge is 400yds on right. **open** All year **bedrooms** 1 double, 2 twin, 1 family, 1 suite **bathrooms** 5 en suite **payment** credit/debit cards, cash, cheques, euros

BREAKFAST AWARD

Official tourist board guide Bed & Breakfast

South West | Cornwall

ST ISSEY, Cornwall Map ref 1B2
SAT NAV PL27 7QH

Higher Trevorrick Country House
Saint Issey, Nr Padstow, Wadebridge PL27 7QH
t (01841) 540943 e enquiries@higher-trevorrick.co.uk
w higher-trevorrick.co.uk ONLINE MAP GUEST REVIEWS ONLINE BOOKING LAST MINUTE OFFERS

B&B PER ROOM PER NIGHT
S £49.50 – £89.25
D £90.00 – £119.00

EVENING MEAL PER PERSON
£22.50

SPECIAL PROMOTIONS
Telephone for special breaks in February and March. Special offers on 4 day breaks or longer.

Near Padstow. Luxurious Accommodation, brand new rooms. Exclusively for adults. Situated in large garden and grounds between Padstow and Wadebridge overlooking The Camel Estuary and Rock. David and Lorraine Goldsworthy ran a successful Cornish Hotel for twenty years really know how to look after you keeping the same high standards.

open All year except Xmas and New Year
bedrooms 1 double, 2 twin
bathrooms 3 en suite
payment credit/debit cards, cash, cheques

directions A30 – Bodmin – A389 Wadebridge – Padstow – right turn entry of St. Issey village – follow Pickwick Inn – continue 500yards on left

Room
General
Leisure

ST IVES, Cornwall

The Grey Mullet
GUEST HOUSE

One of the best known and friendliest guest houses in the old fishing and artists' quarter of St Ives. Situated only 20 yards from the harbour, beaches, car parks, restaurants, pubs, shops and art galleries including the Tate Gallery and Barbara Hepworth Museum. The house though modernised to a high standard retains its "olde worlde" charm. Some private parking available. All major credit cards accepted.

For brochure please write to:
Ken Weston, 2 Bunkers Hill, St Ives TR26 1LJ
or telephone: (01736) 796635 Email: greymulletguesthouse@lineone.net
www.touristnetuk.com/sw/greymullet

ST IVES, Cornwall Map ref 1B3
SAT NAV TR26 2JN

Chy an Gwedhen
Saint Ives Road, Carbis Bay, Saint Ives, Cornwall TR26 2JN
t (01736) 798684 e info@chyangwedhen.com
w chyangwedhen.com GUEST REVIEWS

B&B PER ROOM PER NIGHT
S £35.00 – £50.00
D £64.00 – £82.00

Gill & Mike welcome you to our family run 4 star award winning establishment. All rooms ensuite, excellent choice of breakfast, Private car park. Coastal path leading to beautiful beaches.
directions Follow main St.Ives Rd to Carbis Bay, approach Island, Tesco on left, straight on, take first right, turn first right (Kew Vean).
open All year except Xmas **bedrooms** 1 single, 3 double, 1 twin
bathrooms 5 en suite **payment** credit/debit cards, cash, cheques

Room General Leisure

or key to symbols see page 6

South West | Cornwall

ST IVES, Cornwall Map ref 1B3
SAT NAV TR26 1QP

abode

1 Fern Glen, St Ives TR26 1QP
t (01736) 799047 e enquiries@abodestives.co.uk
w abodestives.co.uk ONLINE MAP GUEST REVIEWS LAST MINUTE OFFERS

B&B PER ROOM PER NIGHT
D £80.00 – £110.00

abode is a bouchique style bed and breakfast in St Ives, Cornwall. Sleeping 8/10 in 4 bedrooms, with sea views towards Godrevy lighthouse and beyond. Just a short walk from shops, galleries, bars, restaurants and our superb Porthmeor, Porthminster, Porthgwidden and Harbour beaches ... this is abode.

open All year except Xmas
bedrooms 2 double, 1 twin, 1 family
bathrooms 4 en suite
payment credit/debit cards, cash

directions Turn right at Porthminster Hotel. Turn left between the Natwest and the library. Over mini island, 100 metres on the right is abode.

BREAKFAST AWARD

Room
General
Leisure

ST JUST-IN-ROSELAND, Cornwall Map ref 1B3
SAT NAV TR2 5JJ

Roundhouse Barn B&B Holidays

Messack Lane, St Just In Roseland, Near St Mawes TR2 5JJ
t (01872) 580038 e info@roundhousebarnholidays.co.uk
w roundhousebarnholidays.co.uk ONLINE MAP GUEST REVIEWS ONLINE BOOKING LAST MINUTE OFFERS

B&B PER ROOM PER NIGHT
D £95.00 – £135.00

Stunningly converted 17th Century cornish stone barns providing 2 five star ensuite B&B rooms. Beautiful gardens to relax in. Stunning sea views from the top of our driveway. Complimentary home-baked cream tea on arrival. Close to St Mawes, Truro and many of Cornwall's great gardens, including Eden and Heligan.

open All year except Xmas and New Year
bedrooms 1 double, 1 twin
bathrooms 2 en suite
payment credit/debit cards, cash, cheques

directions A3078 to St Just in Roseland. Right turn, B3289, signposted King Harry Ferry. After 1.5 miles turn left at our brown tourist sign.

Room
General
Leisure

South West | Cornwall

ST MAWGAN, Cornwall Map ref 1B2
SAT NAV TR8 4EZ

enjoyEngland.com ★★★★ GUEST ACCOMMODATION

B&B PER ROOM PER NIGHT
S £59.00 – £65.00
D £90.00 – £95.00
EVENING MEAL PER PERSON
£21.00

Dalswinton House
Parsonage Lane, St Mawgan in Pydar, Cornwall TR8 4EZ
t (01637) 860385 **f** (01637) 860385 **e** dalswintonhouse@btconnect.com
w dalswinton.com ONLINE MAP LAST MINUTE OFFERS

A former farmhouse standing in eight acres of grounds, specializing in holidays for dogs and their owners. Dog-friendly beach and coastal path 1.5 miles. Good food cooked with local ingredients. **directions** Printed directions sent out with confirmation. **open** Mid March to Late October **bedrooms** 6 double, 2 twin **bathrooms** 8 en suite **payment** credit/debit cards, cash, cheques

Room General Leisure

ST MELLION, Cornwall Map ref 1C2
SAT NAV PL12 6QD

enjoyEngland.com ★★★★★ GUEST ACCOMMODATION **Gold AWARD**

B&B PER ROOM PER NIGHT
S £120.00 – £200.00
D £120.00 – £200.00
EVENING MEAL PER PERSON
£25.00 – £40.00

Pentillie Castle & Estate
Saint Mellion, Saltash PL12 6QD
t 01579 350044 **f** 01579 212002 **e** contact@pentillie.co.uk
w pentillie.co.uk and www.pentillieweddings.co.uk ONLINE MAP GUEST REVIEWS LAST MINUTE OFFERS

Pentillie Castle boasts a riverside location with views over the Tamar Valley. With nine ensuite bedrooms, available for exclusive hire, weddings or corporate events. **directions** 10 miles from Plymouth on the River Tamar, Off the A388 between Saltash and Callington. **open** All year **bedrooms** 8 double, 1 suite **bathrooms** 9 en suite **payment** credit/debit cards, cash, cheques, euros

Room General Leisure

ST MINVER / POLZEATH, Cornwall Map ref 1B2
SAT NAV PL27 6RG

enjoyEngland.com ★★★ BED & BREAKFAST

B&B PER ROOM PER NIGHT
S £45.00 – £55.00
D £55.00 – £70.00

Tredower Barton
St Minver, Wadebridge, Cornwall PL27 6RG
t (01208) 813501

Tredower Barton is a farm bed and breakfast set in beautiful countryside near the North Cornish coast. Delicious breakfast and relaxing stay guaranteed. Near to local attractions, Padstow, Port Isaac. **directions** 3 miles from Wadebridge on road B3314 to Port Issac. **open** Easter to October **bedrooms** 1 twin, 1 family **bathrooms** 2 en suite **payment** cash, cheques

Room General Leisure

TINTAGEL, Cornwall Map ref 1B2
SAT NAV PL34 0HD

enjoyEngland.com ★★★★ INN

B&B PER ROOM PER NIGHT
S £52.50 – £90.00
D £70.00 – £120.00
EVENING MEAL PER PERSON
£10.00 – £35.00

Mill House
The Mill House, Trebarwith, Tintagel PL34 0HD
t (01840) 770200 **f** (01840) 770647 **e** management@themillhouseinn.co.uk
w themillhouseinn.co.uk ONLINE MAP GUEST REVIEWS ONLINE BOOKING LAST MINUTE OFFERS

The 18thC Mill House is close to Trebarwith Strand surfing beach. It has a traditional bar and large restaurant set alongside the millstream. 8 stylishly furnished bedrooms. Licensed for weddings. **directions** Take the B3263 towards Tintagel from Camelford and turn left just before Trewarmett for Trebarwith Strand and follow the signs. **open** All year except Xmas **bedrooms** 6 double, 1 twin, 1 family **bathrooms** 8 en suite **payment** credit/debit cards, cash, cheques, euros

Room General Leisure

53

South West | Cornwall

TRURO, Cornwall Map ref 1B3
SAT NAV TR2 4PG

Bissick Old Mill
Ladock, Truro TR2 4PG
t (01726) 882557 e enquiries@bissickoldmill.plus.com
w bissickoldmill.co.uk

B&B PER ROOM PER NIGHT
S £50.00 – £60.00
D £70.00 – £90.00

17thC water mill converted to exceptional standards throughout. Top quality beds; Top quality breakfasts. Ideal central base for visiting the Eden Project, Heligan and all of Cornwall's beautiful attractions. **directions** Take B3275 signed from A30 Indian Queens/Fraddon bypass. Bissick Old Mill is in Ladock village. Take the 1st left on entering the village. **open** All year **bedrooms** 1 double, 1 twin, 1 family, 1 suite **bathrooms** 4 en suite **payment** credit/debit cards, cash

TRURO, Cornwall Map ref 1B3
SAT NAV TR1 1TD

Chy Vista
Higher Penair, St Clement, Truro TR1 1TD
t (01872) 270592 e vc_richards@yahoo.co.uk

B&B PER ROOM PER NIGHT
S £40.00 – £45.00
D £60.00 – £65.00

Peaceful rural location with countryside views. Large well equipped bedrooms. WiFi. Delicious breakfasts using local produce. Ideal for both coasts and main attractions. A warm and friendly welcome awaits you. **directions** From A39: 1st left off roundabout up St Clement's Hill. 100m past Penair School, 'Penair' sign on left drive through gateposts. 1st left off drive. **open** March-End October. **bedrooms** 2 double **bathrooms** 1 en suite, 1 with private bathroom **payment** cash, cheques

TRURO, Cornwall Map ref 1B3
SAT NAV TR1 3SY

Tor Vean Bed & Breakfast
Kenwyn Road, Truro TR1 3SY
t (01872) 271766 e heather591@hotmail.com

B&B PER ROOM PER NIGHT
S £50.00 – £55.00
D £65.00

Tor Vean is a Victorian House offering refurbished comfortable and spacious accommodation in the conveniently located and favoured Conservation Area of Kenwyn. Truro City centre, bus stop (opposite Tor Vean and providing hourly service), Railway Station, Kenwyn Church and Victoria Gardens are within close proximity, as is Truro Bowling Club.

open All year
bedrooms 2 double, 1 twin
bathrooms 3 en suite
payment credit/debit cards, cash, cheques, euros

directions On B3284 directly opposite Hendra Hill turning. Car parking: turn into Cyril Road, just before Mountford House entrance take left lane, first carpark on left.

South West | Cornwall

TRURO, Cornwall Map ref 1B3
SAT NAV TR1 2HX

B&B PER ROOM PER NIGHT
D £59.00 – £79.00

Townhouse Rooms
City Centre, 20 Falmouth Road, Truro TR1 2HX
t 00 44 (0)1872 277374 **f** 00 44 (0)1872 241666 **e** info@trurotownhouse.com
w trurotownhouse.com ONLINE MAP GUEST REVIEWS ONLINE BOOKING

The Townhouse is different, relaxed, friendly, flexible, our guests say so! Lovely rooms, fully equipped. Rates include Buffet continental breakfast, walking distance to all amenities. **directions** Please see website for detailed directions **open** All year except Xmas and New Year **bedrooms** 9 double, 3 twin **bathrooms** 12 en suite **payment** credit/debit cards, cash

Room General

WADEBRIDGE (4 MILES), Cornwall Map ref 1B2
SAT NAV PL30 5PG

B&B PER ROOM PER NIGHT
D £61.00 – £65.00
EVENING MEAL PER PERSON
£14.50

Tregolls Farm B&B
Saint Wenn, Bodmin PL30 5PG
t (01208) 812154 **f** (01208) 812154 **e** tregollsfarm@btclick.com
w tregollsfarm.co.uk ONLINE MAP ONLINE BOOKING LAST MINUTE OFFERS

Set in picturesque valley overlooking fields of sheep. Grade II Listed farmhouse with countryside views. Farm trail links to Saints Way footpath. Eden, Heligan, Fowey and Padstow close by. **directions** From A30 take Victoria Interchange exit. Follow signs to Withiel (2 1/2miles) continue down steep hill, take 1st left. Tregolls is one mile on right. **open** All year except Xmas and New Year **bedrooms** 1 double, 1 twin **bathrooms** 2 en suite **payment** credit/debit cards, cash, cheques

Room General Leisure

WEST LOOE, Cornwall Map ref 1C3
SAT NAV PL13 2EX

B&B PER ROOM PER NIGHT
S £25.00 – £35.00
D £46.00 – £56.00

Tidal Court Guest House
Church Street, West Looe, Looe PL13 2EX
t (01503) 263695

Small, family-run guesthouse where a warm welcome is assured. Tidal Court is situated in the centre of West Looe, less than one minute's walk from harbour, quayside and ferry to East Looe. Enjoy the seaside amenities of beaches, coves, boat trips and fishing, or a stunning cliff walk to Polperro.

open All year
bedrooms 1 double, 1 twin, 2 family
bathrooms 4 en suite
payment cash, cheques, euros

directions Please contact us for directions

Room General Leisure

South West | Isles of Scilly

PORTHLOO, Isles of Scilly Map ref 1A3
SAT NAV TR21 0NF

Armeria
Porthloo, St Mary's, Isles of Scilly TR21 0NF
t (01720) 422961 e brian.holt1@mypostoffice.co.uk

B&B PER ROOM PER NIGHT
D £60.00

'Armeria' is enviably situated in a quiet part of the island overlooking a sandy beach at Porthloo, providing safe bathing. Full central heating and a garden with picnic table. **directions** Skybus fixed-wing aeroplane. B.I.H. Helicopters. Scillonian III ferry. **open** All year except Xmas and New Year **bedrooms** 2 twin **payment** cash, cheques

ST MARY'S, Isles of Scilly Map ref 1A3
SAT NAV TR21 0HX

Treboeth Guest House
Buzza Street, Porth Cressa, St Mary's, Isles of Scilly TR21 0HX
t 01720 422 548

B&B PER ROOM PER NIGHT
S £32.00 – £38.00
D £64.00 – £76.00

Very close to Porth Cressa beach, within walking distance of town centre and Quay for Off Islands. Peaceful and tranquil area next to coastal walks. **directions** Please contact us for directions **open** March - November **bedrooms** 1 single, 3 double, 1 family **bathrooms** 4 en suite, 1 with private bathroom **payment** cash, cheques

TRESCO, Isles of Scilly Map ref 1A3
SAT NAV TR24 0QE

The New Inn
Tresco, Isles of Scilly TR24 0QE
t (01720) 422844 f (01720) 423200 e newinn@tresco.co.uk
w tresco.co.uk/holidays/new_inn.asp ONLINE MAP LAST MINUTE OFFERS

B&B PER ROOM PER NIGHT
D £140.00 – £230.00

SPECIAL PROMOTIONS
Please see our website for all special rates and breaks.

The only pub on Tresco. A cosy inn with 16 en suite rooms. Eclectic menu served in three dining areas, with great alfresco garden. Great selection of real ales, wines and spirits. The social centre of the private island of Tresco.

open All year
bedrooms 16 double
bathrooms 16 en suite
payment credit/debit cards, cash, cheques

directions Penzance to Tresco or St Mary's by helicopter or boat. Flights from Southampton, Bristol, Exeter, Newquay and Land's End.

Breakfast Award

South West | Devon

ASHBURTON, Devon Map ref 1C2
SAT NAV TQ13 7LZ

Blackler Barton House
Landscove, Ashburton, Newton Abbot, Devon TQ13 7LZ
t (01803) 762385 e blacklerbarton@btinternet.com
w blacklerbartonhouse.co.uk ONLINE MAP GUEST REVIEWS

B&B PER ROOM PER NIGHT
S £39.00
D £68.00 – £70.00

Attractive listed home in idyllic South Hams countryside. Three rooms, two featuring superkingsize double bed or twin beds. Hearty breakfasts. Ample off-road parking. Great for exploring Dartmoor or the coast. **directions** Situated 2½ miles from A38 Exeter-Plymouth Expressway near Ashburton. Take B3352 Peartree exit to Landscove. Follow sign to Blackler Barton at Victory Hall, Landscove. **open** All year **bedrooms** 2 double, 1 twin **bathrooms** 2 en suite, 1 with private bathroom **payment** cash, cheques, euros

Room General

ASHBURTON, Devon Map ref 1C2
SAT NAV TQ13 7AX

Golden Lion House
58 East Street, Ashburton, Newton Abbot, Devon TQ13 7AX
t 07831 787317 f 08719005232 e info@goldenlionhouse.com
w goldenlionhouse.com ONLINE MAP GUEST REVIEWS

B&B PER ROOM PER NIGHT
S £60.00
D £75.00

SPECIAL PROMOTIONS
Discount for stays of three nights or more.

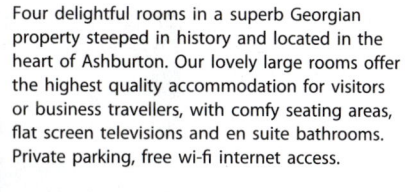

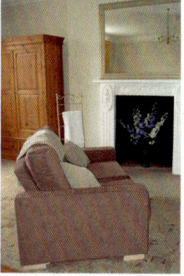

Four delightful rooms in a superb Georgian property steeped in history and located in the heart of Ashburton. Our lovely large rooms offer the highest quality accommodation for visitors or business travellers, with comfy seating areas, flat screen televisions and en suite bathrooms. Private parking, free wi-fi internet access.

open All year except Xmas
bedrooms 3 double, 1 twin
bathrooms 4 en suite
payment credit/debit cards, cash

directions From A38 southbound take first Ashburton exit following signs to town centre. Our house is on the left with a golden lion above the porch.

Room
General

BARNSTAPLE, Devon Map ref 1C1
SAT NAV EX31 4JR

The Spinney Country Guesthouse
Shirwell, Barnstaple EX31 4JR
t (01271) 850282 e thespinneyguesthouse@btconnect.com
w thespinneyshirwell.co.uk ONLINE MAP GUEST REVIEWS

B&B PER ROOM PER NIGHT
S £35.00
D £60.00

A former Georgian rectory, with countryside views towards Exmoor. Delicious breakfasts served during summer months in restored Victorian conservatory. Tastefully decorated rooms. Ensuite facilities. Freesat TV. Internet access. Ample parking. **directions** 3 miles from Barnstaple on main A39 Lynton road. The Spinney is in Shirwell on the left hand side. Satnav EX31 4JR **open** All year **bedrooms** 1 single, 1 double, 1 twin, 2 family **bathrooms** 4 en suite, 1 with private bathroom **payment** credit/debit cards, cash, cheques

Room General

South West | **Devon**

BEAWORTHY, Devon Map ref 1C2
SAT NAV EX21 5EA

enjoyEngland.com ★★★★ FARMHOUSE

B&B PER ROOM PER NIGHT
D £55.00

Greenacres
Virginstow, Beaworthy EX21 5EA
t (01409) 211691 07789901261   e paul@greenacresdevon.co.uk
w greenacresdevon.co.uk ONLINE MAP

Luxury Bed and Breakfast set in 7 acres with private lake. All bedrooms double with ensuite. Dogs and horses welcome. A peaceful retreat idyllically located to explore Devon and Cornwall. **directions** From A30, take the turning to Roadford Lake keep on this road 4 miles at T Junction turn left Greenacres is 2 miles on the left. **open** All year **bedrooms** 3 double **bathrooms** 3 en suite **payment** cash, cheques

Room   General   Leisure

BOWD, Devon Map ref 1D2
SAT NAV EX10 0ND

enjoyEngland.com ★★★★ GUEST HOUSE

B&B PER ROOM PER NIGHT
S £37.50 – £44.00
D £68.00 – £110.00

EVENING MEAL PER PERSON
£13.00 – £19.50

SPECIAL PROMOTIONS
3 Day Christmas Break
£430.00 pp. 2 Night
Valentines £240.00 pp.
Special Occasions/Functions
by arrangement.

The Barn & Pinn Cottage Guest House
Bowd Cross, Sidmouth EX10 0ND
t (01395) 513613   e barnpinncottage@btinternet.com
w thebarnandpinncottage.co.uk ONLINE MAP GUEST REVIEWS

This beautiful 15th Century thatched cottage nestles within two acres of award winning gardens 5 minutes drive from Sidmouth. All en-suite rooms have full central heating, TV, and Tea/Coffee making facilities. Dinner available Thur-Sun. Good home cooking, varied menu, well stocked bar. Comfortable guest lounge, Large private Car Park.

open All year
bedrooms 1 single, 5 double, 2 twin, 2 family
bathrooms 10 en suite
payment credit/debit cards, cash, cheques

directions Located on A3052 12 Miles from Exeter, 15 miles from Lyme Regis. Between Newton Poppleford and Sidford. 5 mins from beach at Sidmouth using B3176

BREAKFAST AWARD

Room   General   Leisure

BRAUNTON, Devon Map ref 1C1
SAT NAV EX33 2JJ

enjoyEngland.com ★★★ INN

B&B PER ROOM PER NIGHT
S £35.00 – £50.00
D £50.00 – £76.00

EVENING MEAL PER PERSON
£5.25 – £17.00

WALKERS CYCLISTS

George Hotel
Exeter Road, Braunton EX33 2JJ
t (01271) 812029   e georgehoteldevon@btconnect.com
w thegeorgehotel-braunton.co.uk ONLINE MAP GUEST REVIEWS ONLINE BOOKING

Central to Barnstaple, Croyde, Saunton, Woolacombe and the Tarka Trail **directions** Following through Barnstaple for 4 miles, heading towards, Ilfracombe, and the coast, you will find us in central Braunton with our own managed car park **open** All year **bedrooms** 1 single, 2 double, 4 twin **bathrooms** 4 en suite **payment** credit/debit cards, cash, cheques

Room   General   Leisure

South West | Devon

BRIXHAM, Devon   Map ref 1D2
SAT NAV TQ5 8HS

enjoyEngland.com ★★★★ GUEST ACCOMMODATION

B&B PER ROOM PER NIGHT
S £26.00 – £30.00
D £48.00 – £52.00

Brioc
11 Prospect Road, Brixham, Devon TQ5 8HS
t 01803 853540   e briochotel@btconnect.com
w briochotel.co.uk   ONLINE MAP

The Brioc is detached south facing with superb views over the harbour and bay. All rooms en-suite, flat screen tv, hospitality tray, Wi-Fi available. Licensed bar. Garage parking. **directions** Map and directions available on website. www.briochotel.co.uk
open All year except Xmas and New Year **bedrooms** 2 single, 4 double, 2 twin **bathrooms** 8 en suite, 4 with private bathroom **payment** cash, cheques, euros

Room   General   Leisure

BRIXTON, Devon   Map ref 1C3
SAT NAV PL8 2AX

enjoyEngland.com ★★★★ GUEST ACCOMMODATION

B&B PER ROOM PER NIGHT
S £45.00
D £60.00 – £75.00

Venn Farm
Brixton, Plymouth PL8 2AX
t (01752) 880378   f (01752) 880378   e info@vennfarm.co.uk
w vennfarm.co.uk   ONLINE MAP

A 300-year-old working farm. Enjoy traditional farmhouse bed and our legendary breakfast made with home made and fresh local produce. Relax in one of the beautiful new self-contained en suite rooms converted from the original stone barns. Central for coast and country. Off-road parking.

open All year
bedrooms 4 double, 1 twin
bathrooms 4 en suite
payment credit/debit cards, cash, cheques

directions Please see our website details.

Room   General   Leisure

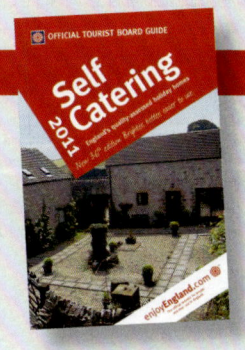

Looking for something else?
You can also buy a copy of our popular guide 'Self Catering' including self-catering holiday homes, approved caravan holiday homes, boat accommodation and holiday cottage agencies in England 2011.

Now available in good bookshops and online at
visitbritainshop.com
£11.99

key to symbols see page 6   59

South West | **Devon**

BUDLEIGH SALTERTON, Devon Map ref 1D2 — SAT NAV EX9 6BY

Hansard House

3 Northview Road, Budleigh Salterton EX9 6BY
t (01395) 442773 f (01935) 442475 e enquiries@hansardhousehotel.co.uk
w hansardhousehotel.co.uk GUEST REVIEWS

B&B PER ROOM PER NIGHT
S £41.00 – £49.00
D £87.00 – £97.00

Adjacent to the World Heritage Coastal Path and only 400yds from East Devon Golf Club, this small, family-run hotel is ideally situated to enjoy the delights of Budleigh Salterton.

open All year
bedrooms 2 single, 3 double, 6 twin, 1 family
bathrooms 12 en suite
payment credit/debit cards, cash, cheques

directions Please contact us for directions

Room
General
Leisure

COMBE MARTIN, Devon Map ref 1C1 — SAT NAV EX34 0DG

Blair Lodge Guest House

Moory Meadow, Combe Martin EX34 0DG
t (01271) 882294 f (01271) 882294 e info@blairlodge.co.uk
w blairlodge.co.uk ONLINE MAP GUEST REVIEWS

B&B PER ROOM PER NIGHT
S £32.50 – £35.00
D £27.50 – £35.00
EVENING MEAL PER PERSON
£12.00 – £14.00

A homely, licensed guesthouse on the South West Coast Path, yards from the beach and Exmoor. Superbly placed for endless walks with fantastic scenery offering homemade meals and sea views. **directions** From Junction 27 on the M5, take A361 towards Barnstaple. Turn right at the roundabout near South Molton onto A399 to Combe Martin. **open** All year **bedrooms** 1 single, 5 double, 2 twin, 1 family **bathrooms** 8 en suite, 1 with private bathroom **payment** credit/debit cards, cash, cheques

Room   General   Leisure

Do you like Camping?

You can also buy a copy of our popular guide 'Camping, Touring & Holiday Parks' including touring parks, camping holidays and holiday parks and villages in Britain 2011.

Now available in good bookshops and online at
visitbritainshop.com

£8.99

South West | Devon

COMBE MARTIN, Devon Map ref 1C1
SAT NAV EX34 0AR

enjoyEngland.com ★★★★ GUEST HOUSE

Mellstock House
Woodlands, Combe Martin EX34 0AR
t (01271) 882592 e enquiries@mellstockhouse.co.uk
w mellstockhouse.co.uk ONLINE MAP GUEST REVIEWS LAST MINUTE OFFERS

B&B PER ROOM PER NIGHT
S £36.00 – £45.00
D £54.00 – £70.00

EVENING MEAL PER PERSON
£7.00 – £10.00

SPECIAL PROMOTIONS
One weeks stay 7 nights for the price of 6 October to April 4 nights for the price of 3

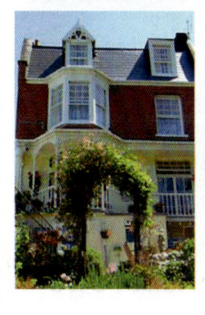

Situated by the North Devon Coastal Path we offer all our guests a very warm welcome with tea and biscuits. Attractive en-suite rooms, licensed bar and delicious home cooked breakfasts and evening meals. Everything you need for that relaxing break.

open All year
bedrooms 3 double, 1 twin, 1 suite
bathrooms 5 en suite
payment credit/debit cards, cash, cheques

directions Leave the M5 at Jnc 27 travel west on the A361. Before reaching Barnstaple turn right onto the A399 to Combe Martin

Room General Leisure

CREDITON, Devon Map ref 1D2
SAT NAV EX17 4LW

enjoyEngland.com ★★★★ INN **Silver AWARD**

The Lamb Inn
The Square, Sandford, Crediton, Devon EX17 4LW
t (01363) 773676 e thelambinn@gmail.com
w lambinnsandford.co.uk ONLINE MAP ONLINE BOOKING LAST MINUTE OFFERS

B&B PER ROOM PER NIGHT
S £59.00 – £95.00
D £69.00 – £95.00

EVENING MEAL PER PERSON
£6.50 – £19.50

WALKERS / CYCLISTS

Award-winning, unspoilt, 16th century pub in attractive Devon village, close to Exeter and Crediton. Stunning contemporary rooms with underfloor heating and all mod cons. Fantastic local food, beautiful garden. Cinema. **directions** M5 follow signs to A30, then A377 to Crediton, then first right and left to Sandford. Go to square at top of hill in Sandford. **open** All year **bedrooms** 5 double, 1 twin **bathrooms** 6 en suite **payment** credit/debit cards, cash, cheques

Room General Leisure

CROYDE, Devon Map ref 1C1
SAT NAV EX33 1NP

enjoyEngland.com ★★★ GUEST ACCOMMODATION

Moorsands
34 Moor Lane, Croyde Bay, Braunton EX33 1NP
t +44(0)1271 890781 e paul@moorsands.co.uk
w croyde-bay.com/moorsands.htm

B&B PER ROOM PER NIGHT
S £41.00 – £47.00
D £62.00 – £74.00

BREAKFAST AWARD

Delightful welcoming comfortable B&B only 6 minutes stroll from Croyde Village or Beach, within Braunton Burrows World Biosphere Reserve. Breakfast Award. Sea views. Surf Board Storage. Car Park. Non Smoking. **directions** M5J27 A361 Braunton, B3231 Croyde. Left turn (Putsborough and Croyde Bay). Up hill, left turn Croyde Bay. Moorsands ½mile on right. **open** All year except Xmas **bedrooms** 2 double, 1 twin, 1 family **bathrooms** 4 en suite **payment** cash, cheques

Room General Leisure

For **key to symbols** see page 6

61

South West | **Devon**

DARTMOUTH, Devon Map ref 1D3　　　　　　　　　　　　　　　　SAT NAV TQ6 9EF

Cladda Bed & Breakfast and Self Catering Apartments
88-90 Victoria Road, and Ford Valley, Dartmouth, Devon TQ6 9EF
t (01803) 835957 or Mob : 07967 060003 e info@cladda-dartmouth.co.uk
w cladda-dartmouth.co.uk ONLINE MAP GUEST REVIEWS LAST MINUTE OFFERS

B&B PER ROOM PER NIGHT
S £50.00 – £65.00
D £65.00 – £85.00

SPECIAL PROMOTIONS
Self Catering some short breaks available please call us.

4* Quality Bed & Breakfast and Self Catering Apartments in Dartmouth Town with On Site Of Road Parking a Stroll from The Embankment Waterfront, Quality Restaurants, Pubs, Shops and Galleries. We have Drying and Deep Freeze facilities and can cater for Walkers, Cyclists, Divers, Golfers and Anglers or just Relaxing.

open All year
bedrooms 2 double, 2 twin, 2 family, 2 suites
bathrooms 8 en suite, 1 with private bathroom
payment credit/debit cards, cash, cheques, euros
directions Dartmouth Town with On Site Off Road Parking a Stroll from the Embankment Waterfront, Quality Restaurants, Pubs, Shops and Galleries.

Room
General
Leisure

DARTMOUTH, Devon Map ref 1D3　　　　　　　　　　　　　　　　SAT NAV TQ6 9DZ

Valley House
46 Victoria Road, Dartmouth, South Devon TQ6 9DZ
t (01803) 834045 e enquiries@valleyhousedartmouth.com
w valleyhousedartmouth.com ONLINE MAP GUEST REVIEWS LAST MINUTE OFFERS

B&B PER ROOM PER NIGHT
S £50.00 – £65.00
D £60.00 – £90.00

Wonderful Bed & Breakfast! Central location, 5 minutes walk to town centre. On-site parking, a particular advantage in Dartmouth. Well-equipped rooms, lovely breakfasts. Britain in Bloom prizewinner last 5 years. **directions** From the end of the M5 at Exeter take A38 (signposted to Plymouth). Leave A38 at Buckfastleigh and follow A384 left to Dartmouth (via Totnes). **open** All year except Xmas **bedrooms** 2 double, 1 twin **bathrooms** 3 en suite **payment** cash, cheques

Room   General   Leisure

DAWLISH, Devon Map ref 1D2　　　　　　　　　　　　　　　　　SAT NAV EX7 0NJ

The Beeches Bed & Breakfast
15a Old Teignmouth Road, Dawlish EX7 0NJ
t (01626) 866345 e enquiries@thebeechesbandb.co.uk
w thebeechesbandb.co.uk

B&B PER ROOM PER NIGHT
S £48.00 – £52.00
D £65.00 – £78.00

We welcome you to our beautiful modern home which offers spacious accommodation. We are located on a quiet road amongst mature trees with lovely sea views to the rear. **directions** From Dawlish proceed towards Teignmouth (A379). Turn left just past hospital signs into Old Teignmouth Road. We can be found 250 metres on the right. **open** All year **bedrooms** 1 double, 1 twin, 1 suite **bathrooms** 2 en suite, 1 with private bathroom **payment** credit/debit cards, cash, cheques

Room   General

62　　　　　　　　　　　　　　　　　　　　　　Official tourist board guide Bed & Breakfast

South West | Devon

DUNKESWELL, Devon Map ref 1D2
SAT NAV EX14 4RW

The Old Kennels
Stentwood, Dunkeswell, nr Honiton, Devon EX14 4RW
t 01823 681138 **f** (01823) 681138 **e** info@theoldkennels.co.uk
w theoldkennels.co.uk ONLINE MAP GUEST REVIEWS

B&B PER ROOM PER NIGHT
S £32.00 – £36.00
D £64.00 – £72.00

Quiet rural setting offering wonderfully comfortable bed & breakfast accommodation, also available as a two bedroom/bathroom suite with lounge, garden and terrace. Optional courses in rural and traditional arts. **directions** We are easily accessible from the M5 or A303, please see our website or call for verbal or written directions. **open** All year except Xmas and New Year **bedrooms** 1 double, 1 twin **bathrooms** 1 en suite, 1 with private bathroom **payment** cash, cheques, euros

Room General Leisure

EXETER, Devon Map ref 1D2
SAT NAV EX4 4HF

Clock Tower Guest House
16-17 New North Road, Exeter EX4 4HF
t (01392) 424545 **f** (01392) 218445 **e** reservations@clocktowerhotel.co.uk
w clocktowerhotel.co.uk

B&B PER ROOM PER NIGHT
S £52.00
D £70.00 – £80.00

Located centrally in Exeter near to Exeter College, University and train stations. Short walk to historic Cathedral green and new shopping precinct. **directions** See website for travel directions. **open** All year except Xmas and New Year **bedrooms** 5 single, 5 double, 5 twin, 3 family **bathrooms** 18 en suite **payment** credit/debit cards, cash

Room General

EXETER, Devon Map ref 1D2
SAT NAV EX5 4EG

Culm Vale Country House
Culm Vale, Stoke Canon, Exeter EX5 4EG
t (01392) 841615 **f** (01392) 841615 **e** culmvale@hotmail.com
w culmvaleaccommodation.co.uk ONLINE MAP GUEST REVIEWS ONLINE BOOKING LAST MINUTE OFFERS

B&B PER ROOM PER NIGHT
S £30.00 – £40.00
D £45.00 – £55.00

Family-run, spacious, comfortable accommodation. Victorian country house set in one acre of garden, 3.5 miles from Exeter city centre. Free parking. Ideal touring base. Convenient for university, moors, coasts. **directions** Travelling down M5, come off at jct 27; go towards Tiverton. Pick up A396 (signed Bickleigh). Stoke Canon is 10 miles from Tiverton on A396. **open** All year **bedrooms** 3 double, 2 twin **bathrooms** 2 en suite **payment** credit/debit cards, cash, cheques, euros

Room General Leisure

EXETER, Devon Map ref 1D2
SAT NAV EX4 7JH

The Grange
Stoke Hill, Exeter EX4 7JH
t (01392) 259723 **e** dudleythegrange@aol.com

B&B PER ROOM PER NIGHT
S £34.00 – £38.00
D £54.00 – £58.00

Country house set in three acres of woodlands, 1.5 miles from the city centre. Ideal for holidays and off-season breaks. All rooms en suite. Off-street parking. **directions** M5 jct 29 for city centre, first roundabout 4th exit Western Way, next roundabout 2nd exit Old Tiverton Road, over next roundabout - Stoke Hill. **open** All year **bedrooms** 1 double, 1 twin **bathrooms** 2 en suite **payment** cash, cheques, euros

Room General

South West | Devon

EXETER, Devon Map ref 1D2

SAT NAV EX4 4LG

Park View
8 Howell Road, Exeter, Devon EX4 4LG
t (01392) 271772 f (01392) 253047 e enquiries@parkviewexeter.co.uk
w parkviewexeter.co.uk ONLINE MAP

B&B PER ROOM PER NIGHT
S £29.00 – £48.00
D £60.00 – £70.00

Grade II Listed Georgian town house in a quiet area overlooking Bury Meadow Park. 5 minutes walk to city centre, Exeter University, bus and rail stations. **directions** M5 junction 29 Following Exeter A3015, City Centre until Clock Tower. Then Elm Grove Rd, left at end into Howell Road. 100 metres on right. **open** All year except Xmas and New Year **bedrooms** 1 single, 6 double, 3 twin, 2 family **bathrooms** 9 en suite, 2 with private bathroom **payment** credit/debit cards, cash, cheques

EXETER, Devon Map ref 1D2

SAT NAV EX5 1LB

Rydon Farm
Rydon Farm, Woodbury, Exeter EX5 1LB
t (01395) 232341 f (01395) 232341 e sallyglanvill@aol.com
w rydonfarmwoodbury.co.uk ONLINE MAP ONLINE BOOKING

B&B PER ROOM PER NIGHT
S £47.00 – £60.00
D £74.00 – £80.00

Renowned for our hospitality, Rydon provides a peaceful and relaxing atmosphere for business and leisure guests. Delicious farmhouse breakfasts using fresh, local produce. Several local pubs and restaurants. Highly recommended. **directions** From M5 J30 take A376 Exmouth Road. At Clyst St George roundabout take B3179 to Woodbury. Turn rt into Rydon Lane just before 30mph signs. **open** All year **bedrooms** 1 double, 1 twin, 1 family **bathrooms** 3 en suite **payment** credit/debit cards, cash, cheques, euros

EXETER, Devon Map ref 1D2

SAT NAV EX2 9UP

South View Farm
Shillingford Saint George, Exeter, Devon EX2 9UP
t 01392 832278 e dorothy@southviewbandb.co.uk
w southviewbandb.co.uk ONLINE MAP

B&B PER ROOM PER NIGHT
S £35.00
D £60.00

4 star quality en suite accommodation, good access Exeter and M5 Peaceful, rural, beautiful views. Guests welcome for business/relaxation. Hospitality tray, breakfast menu, C/H. Coarse fishing lakes. **directions** From M5 take A38 then next exit for Kennford. Follow signs to Clapham then Shillingford. Approx 1 mile South View on left before village. **open** All year **bedrooms** 1 double, 1 twin, 1 family **bathrooms** 2 en suite, 1 with private bathroom **payment** cash, cheques

EXETER, Devon Map ref 1D2

SAT NAV EX4 4QR

University of Exeter
Event Exeter, Reed Hall, Streatham Drive, Exeter EX4 4QR
t (01392) 215566 f (01392) 263512 e holidaylets@exeter.ac.uk
w eventexeter.com ONLINE MAP GUEST REVIEWS ONLINE BOOKING LAST MINUTE OFFERS

B&B PER ROOM PER NIGHT
S £25.60 – £54.95
BED ONLY PER NIGHT
£19.95 – £45.95

The University offers a variety of accommodation spread across two campuses. Both campuses offer a choice of excellent value for money accommodation to suit all budgets. **directions** Please contact us for directions **bedrooms** 282 single, 973 double, 67 twin **bathrooms** 1052 en suite **payment** credit/debit cards, cash

64 Official tourist board guide Bed & Breakfast

South West | Devon

FROGMORE, Devon Map ref 1C3
SAT NAV TQ7 2NR

INN ★★★★

B&B PER ROOM PER NIGHT
S £50.00
D £80.00
EVENING MEAL PER PERSON
£10.00 – £20.00

Globe Inn
Frogmore, Nr Kingsbridge TQ7 2NR
t (01548) 531351   **f** (01548) 531375   **e** info@theglobeinn.co.uk
w theglobeinn.co.uk   ONLINE MAP   GUEST REVIEWS   ONLINE BOOKING   LAST MINUTE OFFERS

The Inn is situated in the pretty village of Frogmore, between Dartmouth and Kingsbridge, in glorious unspoilt South Hams countryside. The pub has undergone a tasteful renovation and now boasts 8 well appointed ensuite bedrooms. We have a fresh look to the restaurant and bars whilst retaining a cosy atmosphere.

open All year
bedrooms 5 double, 2 twin, 1 family
bathrooms 8 en suite
payment credit/debit cards, cash, cheques

directions Via Kingsbridge take the A379 to Dartmouth and Torcross. After 2 miles look out for the Inn on the left as you enter Frogmore.

Room
General
Leisure

KINGSBRIDGE, Devon Map ref 1C3
SAT NAV TQ7 1HB

GUEST ACCOMMODATION ★★★

B&B PER ROOM PER NIGHT
S £35.00 – £45.00
D £60.00 – £70.00

WALKERS / CYCLISTS

Ashleigh House
Ashleigh Road, Kingsbridge TQ7 1HB
t (01548) 852893   **e** reception@ashleigh-house.co.uk
w ashleigh-house.co.uk   ONLINE MAP   GUEST REVIEWS

Attractive Victorian guesthouse, ideal base for exploring beautiful South Devon with amenities of the town a short walk away. All 8 rooms en suite. Some off-road parking, unlimited free nearby.
directions Leave Kingsbridge on A381 going towards Salcombe. After roundabout proceed up hill, Ashleigh Road is 3rd turning on left, brown sign points to Ashleigh House **open** All year **bedrooms** 5 double, 1 twin, 2 family **bathrooms** 8 en suite **payment** credit/debit cards, cash, cheques

Room   General   Leisure

LYNTON, Devon Map ref 1C1
SAT NAV EX35 6AY

RATING APPLIED FOR

B&B PER ROOM PER NIGHT
S £29.00 – £33.00
D £62.00 – £70.00

WALKERS / CYCLISTS

Sinai House
Lynway, Lynton EX35 6AY
t (01598) 753227   **f** (01598) 752633   **e** enquiries@sinaihouse.co.uk
w sinaihouse.co.uk   ONLINE MAP   GUEST REVIEWS   ONLINE BOOKING

An 1850 Victorian house offering magnificent sea views from en suite bedrooms and lounge in a peaceful atmosphere set in half acre terraced gardens. With private Parking. **directions** Enter Lynton via carpark, left into Market Street. Turn left and proceed up Sinaihill 400 metres, sharpe left into Lynway. Car park on left. **open** Mid Feb - Mid Nov **bedrooms** 2 single, 5 double, 1 twin **bathrooms** 6 en suite, 2 with private bathroom **payment** credit/debit cards, cash, cheques, euros

Room   General   Leisure

For key to symbols see page 6

65

South West | Devon

MILTON DAMEREL, Devon Map ref 1C2
SAT NAV EX22 7PB

Buttermoor Farm

FARMHOUSE ★★★★

B&B PER ROOM PER NIGHT
S £32.00 – £34.00
D £64.00 – £68.00

Buttermoor Farm, Milton Damerel, Nr Holsworthy, North Devon EX22 7PB
t (01309) 261314 **e** info@buttermoorfarm.co.uk
w buttermoorfarm.co.uk ONLINE MAP GUEST REVIEWS

Lovely farmhouse with two ensuite bedrooms (twin or double). Fantastic views, large garden, TV/DVD, logfire, large sitting/dining room, private entrance. A family of five can book exclusively. Wheelchair friendly. **directions** Located off the beaten track, close to the Tarka Trail. 10 minutes to Holsworthy market town, easy access to Bude beaches, Bideford and Dartmoor. **open** All year **bedrooms** 2 double **bathrooms** 2 en suite **payment** cash, cheques

Room General Leisure

MORETONHAMPSTEAD, Devon Map ref 1C2
SAT NAV TQ13 8QF

Great Sloncombe Farm

FARMHOUSE ★★★★

B&B PER ROOM PER NIGHT
S £40.00 – £42.00
D £70.00 – £80.00

Great Sloncombe Farm, Moretonhampstead, Dartmoor, Devon TQ13 8QF
t (01647) 440595 **f** (01647) 440595 **e** hmerchant@sloncombe.freeserve.co.uk
w greatsloncombefarm.co.uk

13thC farmhouse in a magical Dartmoor valley. Meadows, woodland, wild flowers and animals. Farmhouse breakfast with freshly baked bread. Everything provided for an enjoyable break. **directions** From Moretonhampstead take A382 towards Chagford. Take left turn (farm signed) up lane, through hamlet, farm is on right. **open** All year **bedrooms** 2 double, 1 twin **bathrooms** 3 en suite **payment** credit/debit cards, cash, cheques

Room General Leisure

MORETONHAMPSTEAD, Devon Map ref 1C2
SAT NAV TQ13 8QA

Great Wooston Farm

GUEST ACCOMMODATION ★★★★

B&B PER ROOM PER NIGHT
S £35.00 – £45.00
D £68.00 – £70.00

Moretonhampstead, Newton Abbot TQ13 8QA
t (01647) 440367 **f** (01647) 440367 **e** info@greatwoostonfarm.com
w greatwoostonfarm.com

Great Wooston is a peaceful haven with views across the moor and walks nearby. Two rooms en suite, one with four-poster. Excellent breakfast. Quality accommodation. **directions** Please contact us for directions **open** All year **bedrooms** 2 double, 1 twin **bathrooms** 2 en suite, 1 with private bathroom **payment** credit/debit cards, cash, cheques

BREAKFAST AWARD

Room General Leisure

Where is my pet welcome?

Some properties welcome well-behaved pets. Look for the 🐾 in the accommodation listings.

You can also buy a copy of our popular guide 'Pets Come Too!' Now available in good bookshops and online at **visitbritainshop.com**

£9.99

South West | Devon

OKEHAMPTON, Devon Map ref 1C2
SAT NAV EX20 4HZ

Week Farm
Bridestowe, Okehampton EX20 4HZ
t (01837) 861221 **f** (01837) 861221 **e** accom@weekfarmonline.com
w weekfarmonline.com

B&B PER ROOM PER NIGHT
S £30.00 – £40.00
D £60.00 – £70.00

SPECIAL PROMOTIONS
Winter Breaks and Fishing weekend breaks. 3 well-stocked coarse-fishing lakes, something for the whole family.

200-acre beef and sheep farm. A warm welcome awaits at this homely 17thC farmhouse in Devonshire countryside and six miles from Okehampton. Three coarse-fishing lakes. Good home cooking assured and every comfort. Ideal touring base Dartmoor and coasts, walking, cycling, pony-trekking, fishing. Outdoor heated swimming pool. Cream tea on arrival. Come and spoil yourselves.

open All year except Xmas
bedrooms 3 double, 1 twin, 1 family
bathrooms 5 en suite
payment credit/debit cards, cash, cheques

directions Pass Okehampton. Leave A30 Sourton Cross. Follow sign towards Bridestowe. Tescott Way and Week, turn right. End of three-lane traffic, follow signs to Week.

PAIGNTON, Devon Map ref 1D2
SAT NAV TQ4 6AT

Ashleigh Guest House
15 Queens Road, Paignton TQ4 6AT
t 01803 558923 **e** info@ashleigh-guesthouse.co.uk
w ashleigh-guesthouse.co.uk ONLINE MAP GUEST REVIEWS ONLINE BOOKING

B&B PER ROOM PER NIGHT
S £25.00 – £29.00
D £50.00 – £58.00

SPECIAL PROMOTIONS
10% discount for Emergency personnel for stays of 3 nights+.

At the Ashleigh you will find a warm and friendly atmosphere awaiting you from Mick and Hazel, we are centally located within a short level walk from the Town Centre, Restaurants, Parks, Rail, Bus and coach stations. All rooms are ensuite with Tea and coffee facilities, toiletries and freeview TVs.

open All year except Xmas and New Year
bedrooms 1 single, 5 double, 2 twin, 1 family
payment credit/debit cards, cash, cheques

directions From Seafront, turn into Adelphi Road by Marine Hotel at end of road turn left into Queens Road, we are first building on the right.

South West | **Devon**

PAIGNTON, Devon Map ref 1D2

SAT NAV TQ4 6AX

Belle Dene Guest House
25 Garfield Road, Paignton TQ4 6AX
t (01803) 559645 f (01803) 557593 e belledeneguesthouse@btconnect.com
w belledeneguesthouse.co.uk ONLINE MAP ONLINE BOOKING LAST MINUTE OFFERS

B&B PER ROOM PER NIGHT
S £22.00 – £30.00
D £42.00 – £52.00

Jennie and Jim offer you a warm friendly welcome to their homely guest house which is ideally located in the popular resort of Paignton close to the sea front and all the tourist attractions. Ample private parking available for the sole use of guests. We look forward to meeting you.

open All year
bedrooms 1 single, 3 double, 1 twin
bathrooms 4 en suite, 1 with private bathroom
payment credit/debit cards, cash

directions Follow signs for seafront Esplanade Road. Turn into Beach Road, right into Garfield Road, Follow the road round and we are situated on the left.

Room / General / Leisure

PAIGNTON, Devon Map ref 1D2

SAT NAV TQ3 2HR

Braedene Lodge
22 Manor Road, Paignton TQ3 2HR
t (01803) 551079 e stay@braedenehotel.co.uk
w braedenehotel.co.uk ONLINE MAP GUEST REVIEWS ONLINE BOOKING LAST MINUTE OFFERS

B&B PER ROOM PER NIGHT
S £20.00 – £24.00
D £40.00 – £54.00

Braedene Lodge is situated on the level 400 yards from the beach and 2 minutes to Pubs and places to eat, easy access to surrounding area via public transport. **directions** Braedene Lodge is on Manor Road which is situated just off Preston Beach and the main road between Paignton and Torquay. **open** All year except Xmas and New Year **bedrooms** 1 single, 5 double, 1 twin, 2 family **bathrooms** 6 en suite **payment** credit/debit cards, cash

Room / General / Leisure

PAIGNTON, Devon Map ref 1D2

SAT NAV TQ4 6AX

Cliveden Guest House
27 Garfield Road, Paignton TQ4 6AX
t (01803) 557461 f (01803) 557461 e enquiries@clivedenguesthouse.co.uk
w clivedenguesthouse.co.uk ONLINE MAP

B&B PER ROOM PER NIGHT
S £22.00 – £26.00
D £44.00 – £52.00
EVENING MEAL PER PERSON
£10.00

Family-run guesthouse close to the sea and town. Six bedrooms. Car park. Substantial breakfast. Evening meals available. Open all year. **directions** Follow the signs for the cinema and the large car park and you will find us on the left after the bend on Garfield Road. **open** All year **bedrooms** 1 single, 3 double, 1 twin, 1 family **bathrooms** 4 en suite, 2 with private bathroom **payment** credit/debit cards, cash, cheques

Room / General / Leisure

Official tourist board guide Bed & Breakfast

South West | Devon

PAIGNTON, Devon Map ref 1D2
SAT NAV TQ4 6HA

enjoyEngland.com ★★★★ GUEST ACCOMMODATION

B&B PER ROOM PER NIGHT
S £25.00 – £33.00
D £50.00 – £69.00
EVENING MEAL PER PERSON
£15.00

Earlston House
31 St Andrews Road, Paignton TQ4 6HA
t (01803) 558355 e stay@earlstonhouse.co.uk
w earlstonhouse.co.uk ONLINE MAP GUEST REVIEWS LAST MINUTE OFFERS

Earlston House is a small Hotel with a big reputation for good home cooked food, comfortable beds and a friendly atmosphere. Ideally situated for the beaches of Goodrington and Paignton. **directions** From Esplanade Road along Paignton sea front, turn right at the roundabout into Sands Road then second turning on the left into St Andrews Road. **open** All year except Xmas and New Year **bedrooms** 5 double, 3 family **bathrooms** 8 en suite **payment** credit/debit cards, cash, cheques

Room General

PLYMOUTH, Devon Map ref 1C2
SAT NAV PL1 2RQ

enjoyEngland.com ★★★★ GUEST ACCOMMODATION

B&B PER ROOM PER NIGHT
S £30.00 – £43.00
D £46.00 – £58.00

Athenaeum Lodge Guest House
4 Athenaeum Street, The Hoe, Plymouth PL1 2RQ
t (01752) 665005 f (01752) 665005 e us@athenaeumlodge.com
w athenaeumlodge.com ONLINE MAP GUEST REVIEWS ONLINE BOOKING LAST MINUTE OFFERS

Elegant, Grade II Listed guesthouse, ideally situated on The Hoe. Centrally located for the Barbican, Theatre Royal, Plymouth Pavilions, Ferry Port and the National Marine Aquarium. City centre and university are a few minutes walk. Diving, sailing and fishing close by. Excellent location for touring Devon. Wi-Fi and free computer use.

open All year except Xmas and New Year
bedrooms 3 double, 2 twin, 3 family
bathrooms 7 en suite, 1 with private bathroom
payment credit/debit cards, cash, cheques

directions From the A38 follow signs to Plymouth City Centre. Take left fork marked THE BARBICAN-THE HOE-THE SEAFRONT. Continue to Walrus pub, turn into Athenaeum Street.

Room
General
Leisure

PLYMOUTH, Devon Map ref 1C2
SAT NAV PL1 3AS

enjoyEngland.com ★★★★ GUEST ACCOMMODATION

B&B PER ROOM PER NIGHT
S £40.00 – £45.00
D £60.00 – £70.00

Berkeleys of St James
4 Saint James Place East, The Hoe, Plymouth PL1 3AS
t (01752) 221654 f (01752) 221654 e enquiry@onthehoe.co.uk
w onthehoe.co.uk ONLINE MAP GUEST REVIEWS ONLINE BOOKING

Victorian town house ideally situated for seafront, Dockyard, Barbican, theatres, touring Devon and Cornwall and Eden Project. Flexible accommodation between double/twin/triple. Excellent breakfast serving free-range, organic produce. **directions** Please contact us for directions **open** All year except Xmas and New Year **bedrooms** 1 single, 3 double, 1 twin **bathrooms** 4 en suite, 1 with private bathroom **payment** credit/debit cards, cash, cheques

Room General Leisure

South West | Devon

PLYMOUTH, Devon Map ref 1C2
SAT NAV PL1 2PU

The Bowling Green
9-10 Osborne Place, Plymouth PL1 2PU
t (01752) 209090 **e** info@thebowlinggreenplymouth.com
w thebowlinggreenplymouth.com ONLINE MAP GUEST REVIEWS ONLINE BOOKING LAST MINUTE OFFERS

B&B PER ROOM PER NIGHT
S £46.00 – £50.00
D £68.00 – £72.00

This elegant Victorian establishment has superbly appointed bedrooms offering all modern facilities. Our friendly staff will make your stay a memorable one. Centrally situated for the Barbican, Theatre and seafront. **directions** Off A38 at Marsh Mills roundabout Follow signs for city centre, then for The Hoe. Right Citadel Road. We are on 1st crossroads on right. **open** All year **bedrooms** 1 single, 8 double, 3 family **bathrooms** 12 en suite **payment** credit/debit cards, cash, cheques

Room General Leisure

PLYMOUTH, Devon Map ref 1C2
SAT NAV PL1 3BS

Caraneal
12-14 Pier Street, West Hoe, Plymouth PL1 3BS
t (01752) 663589 **f** (01752) 663589 **e** caranealhotel@hotmail.com
w caranealplymouth.co.uk ONLINE MAP GUEST REVIEWS ONLINE BOOKING

B&B PER ROOM PER NIGHT
S £30.00 – £40.00
D £50.00 – £60.00

Caraneal is a cosy family-run establishment near the famous Hoe and seafront and within easy walking distance of the city centre and the historic Barbican. **directions** From A38 follow signs for City Centre, then the Hoe and Seafront. On seafront pass Plymouth Dome and turn right at the next mini-roundabout. **open** All year except Xmas and New Year **bedrooms** 8 double, 2 twin **bathrooms** 10 en suite **payment** credit/debit cards, cash, cheques

Room General Leisure

PLYMOUTH, Devon Map ref 1C2
SAT NAV PL9 0AW

Gabber Farm
Gabber Lane, Down Thomas, Plymouth PL9 0AW
t (01752) 862269 **f** (01752) 862269 **e** gabberfarm@tiscali.co.uk
w gabberfarm.co.uk ONLINE MAP

B&B PER ROOM PER NIGHT
S £25.00 – £30.00
D £50.00 – £54.00

A courteous welcome at this farm, near coast and Mount Batten Centre. Lovely walks. Special weekly rates, especially for Senior Citizens and children. Directions provided. **directions** Directions of how to find the farm can be obtained by contacting Margaret directly or by email **open** All year **bedrooms** 1 single, 1 double, 1 twin, 2 family **bathrooms** 3 en suite **payment** credit/debit cards, cash, cheques

Room General Leisure

SEATON, Devon Map ref 1D2
SAT NAV EX12 2QW

Beaumont Guest House
Castle Hill, Seaton EX12 2QW
t (01297) 20832 **e** jane@lymebay.demon.co.uk
w smoothhound.co.uk/hotels/beaumon1.html

B&B PER ROOM PER NIGHT
S £45.00 – £55.00
D £65.00 – £75.00

Select Victorian, seafront guesthouse on World Heritage Coast. Two minutes' walk from town. Excellent walks, country parks, attractions and sporting facilities. Unrivalled views over Lyme Bay and Beer cliffs. **directions** From A3052 Exeter to Lyme Regis road, turn south to Seaton. Continue to sea front. We are next to the clock tower and memorial gardens. **open** All year except Xmas and New Year **bedrooms** 2 double, 2 twin, 1 family **bathrooms** 5 en suite **payment** cash, cheques

Room General Leisure

South West | Devon

SIDMOUTH, Devon Map ref 1D2

SAT NAV EX10 8PX

B&B PER ROOM PER NIGHT
D £60.00 – £72.00

Berwick Guest House
Salcombe Road, Sidmouth, Devon EX10 8PX
t (01395) 513621   e reservations@berwick-house.co.uk
w berwick-house.co.uk   ONLINE MAP GUEST REVIEWS

Berwick is close to all amenities and an 8 minute walk to the sea front and a few minutes walk into the town for a selection of restaurants and pubs. **directions** 12 miles from M5 (Exeter) 10 miles from Honiton (A303) **open** March till November **bedrooms** 4 double, 2 twin **bathrooms** 6 en suite **payment** cash, cheques

SIDMOUTH, Devon Map ref 1D2

SAT NAV EX10 8PR

B&B PER ROOM PER NIGHT
S £29.00 – £37.00
D £58.00 – £74.00
EVENING MEAL PER PERSON
£10.00 – £15.00

Canterbury Guest House
Salcombe Road, Sidmouth, Devon EX10 8PR
t (01395) 513373   e enquiries@canterbury-house.com
w canterbury-house.com

From Canterbury House it is a short stroll into Sidmouth's unspoilt town Centre, where lovely shops, pubs and restaurants await, as well as the beautiful sea front esplanade. **directions** Please contact us for directions **open** All year **bedrooms** 1 single, 4 double, 3 twin **bathrooms** 8 en suite **payment** cash, cheques

SIDMOUTH, Devon Map ref 1D2

SAT NAV EX10 9AW

B&B PER ROOM PER NIGHT
D £76.00 – £85.00

SPECIAL PROMOTIONS
Single person occupancy by arrangement. Car collection service for walkers. Special Winter Breaks. 2 nights minimum stay May to September.

Salcombe Close House
Sid Lane, Sidmouth, Devon EX10 9AW
t 01395 579067   e thebeesleybunch@aol.com
w salcombeclosehouse.com   ONLINE MAP GUEST REVIEWS

Set in a wonderfully quiet location, yet still near the heart of the regency town of Sidmouth, we aim to provide something a little bit special. Two large rooms which can be either spacious twins, or sumptuous super-king doubles, both have luxury ensuite facilities. We look forward to welcoming you.

open All year except Xmas and New Year
bedrooms 1 double, 1 twin
bathrooms 2 en suite
payment cash, cheques

directions Please contact us for directions

South West | **Devon**

STOKE GABRIEL, Devon Map ref 1D2
SAT NAV TQ9 6SX

Stoke Gabriel Lodgings

Badgers Retreat, 2 Orchard Close, Paignton Road, Stoke Gabriel, Totnes, South Devon TQ9 6SX
t 01803 782003 f 01803 782003 e david@stokegabriellodgings.com
w stokegabriellodgings.com ONLINE MAP LAST MINUTE OFFERS

B&B PER ROOM PER NIGHT
S £35.00 – £90.00
D £70.00 – £90.00

SPECIAL PROMOTIONS
Reduced Weekly rates are available and vary according to the time of year. Please telephone for details

Stoke Gabriel Lodgings is a newly-built interior-designed 5* luxury B&B. From an elevated position, bedrooms offer stunning views overlooking the village, church, Mill Pond, River Dart and rolling hills beyond. Each bedroom's patio window opens fully onto a personal private verandah equipped with table and chairs Superb choice Breakfast Menu.

open All year except Xmas
bedrooms 1 double, 1 twin, 1 family
bathrooms 3 en suite
payment cash, cheques, euros

directions Stoke Gabriel's 3miles south of Totnes. In village left onto Paignton Rd after Baptist Chapel on left. 80metres, left up to Orchard Close by public bench.

Room
General
Leisure

TAVISTOCK, Devon Map ref 1C2
SAT NAV PL19 8PL

Beera Farmhouse

Milton Abbot, Tavistock, Devon PL19 8PL
t (01822) 870216 f (01822) 870216 e hilary.tucker@farming.co.uk
w beera-farm.co.uk ONLINE MAP GUEST REVIEWS ONLINE BOOKING

B&B PER ROOM PER NIGHT
S £55.00 – £65.00
D £70.00 – £85.00
EVENING MEAL PER PERSON
£17.00 – £21.00

BREAKFAST AWARD

Beera Farmhouse Bed and Breakfast is in the heart of the beautiful Tamar Valley, on a working farm. Very peaceful. Ideal location for touring Devon and Cornwall. **directions** From Tavistock take B3362 to Milton Abbot, take 1st left signposted Endsleigh, go 2.2 miles and Beera Farm is on the left. **open** All year except Xmas and New Year **bedrooms** 2 double, 1 twin **bathrooms** 3 en suite **payment** credit/debit cards, cash, cheques, euros

Room   General

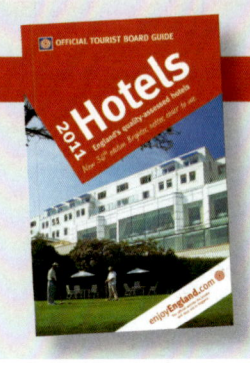

Looking for something else?

You can also buy a copy of our popular guide 'Hotels' including country house and town house hotels, metro and budget hotels, serviced apartments, restaurants with rooms and Spas in England 2011.

Now available in good bookshops and online at
visitbritainshop.com

£10.99

South West | **Devon**

TAVISTOCK, Devon Map ref 1C2

SAT NAV PL16 0JE

Tor Cottage
Chillaton, Lifton PL16 0JE
t (01822) 860248 **f** (01822) 860126 **e** info@torcottage.co.uk
w torcottage.co.uk ONLINE MAP ONLINE BOOKING LAST MINUTE OFFERS

B&B PER ROOM PER NIGHT
S £98.00
D £140.00 – £150.00

SPECIAL PROMOTIONS
Autumn/Spring breaks: 3 nights for 2. Special Valentine Breaks. Picnic Platters available to order. 10% discount on 7-night stay.

Enjoy complete peace and privacy in beautiful ensuite bed-sitting rooms, each with own log-fire and private garden, terrace or conservatory. Streamside setting in hidden valley, 28 acres of wildlife hillsides, beautiful gardens, heated outdoor pool. Adjacent Dartmoor and near Tavistock. Visit Devon/Cornwall coastlines, National Trust properties or the Eden Project.

open All year except Xmas and New Year
bedrooms 3 double, 1 twin, 1 suite
bathrooms 5 en suite
payment credit/debit cards, cash

directions See Website or Brochure

BREAKFAST AWARD

Room
General
Leisure

TEIGNMOUTH, Devon Map ref 1D2

SAT NAV TQ14 8DJ

Dresden House
26 Orchard Gardens, Teignmouth TQ14 8DJ
t (01626) 773465 **e** info@dresdenhouse.com
w dresdenhouse.com

B&B PER ROOM PER NIGHT
S £30.00 – £39.00
D £50.00 – £60.00
EVENING MEAL PER PERSON
£15.00

Town centre location. Home from home, warm friendly family run guest house. Very short walk to beach, shops, pubs and restaurants. All transport systems are close by. **directions** Please contact us for directions **open** All year **bedrooms** 2 single, 3 double, 3 family **bathrooms** 8 en suite **payment** cash, cheques

Room   General   Leisure

TEIGNMOUTH, Devon Map ref 1D2

SAT NAV TQ14 9JZ

Woodside Guest House
17 Hermosa Road, Teignmouth TQ14 9JZ
t (01626) 770681 **f** (01626) 770681 **e** info@woodsideguesthouse.com
w woodsideguesthouse.com ONLINE MAP GUEST REVIEWS LAST MINUTE OFFERS

B&B PER ROOM PER NIGHT
S £40.00 – £45.00
D £55.00 – £60.00

Only 10 minutes from town and beach. Seaviews, private parking, all rooms en-suite. Four poster. You are assured a warm welcome and excellent service in this family run B&B. **directions** From north B3192 footbridge, turn right, Landscore Road, second left, private drive, left. From south, A381, past Shaldon bridge, left Coombevale Road, right private drive. **open** All year except Xmas **bedrooms** 1 double, 1 twin, 3 family **bathrooms** 4 en suite, 1 with private bathroom

Room   General   Leisure

or **key to symbols** see page 6   73

South West | **Devon**

TORQUAY, Devon Map ref 1D2   SAT NAV TQ1 1SU

Abberley Guest House
100 Windsor Road, Babbacombe, Torquay TQ1 1SU
t (01803) 392787   f (01803) 392787   e stay@abberleyguesthouse.co.uk
w abberleyguesthouse.co.uk   ONLINE MAP GUEST REVIEWS ONLINE BOOKING LAST MINUTE OFFERS

B&B PER ROOM PER NIGHT
S £28.00 – £53.00
D £56.00 – £72.00
EVENING MEAL PER PERSON
£7.50 – £10.00

Situated in a quiet residential area. Ideal location for exploring the delights of South Devon. Our delicious full English breakfast will set you up for the day. **directions** Please contact us for directions
open All year **bedrooms** 4 double, 3 twin **bathrooms** 7 en suite
payment credit/debit cards, cash

Room · General · Leisure

TORQUAY, Devon Map ref 1D2   SAT NAV TQ2 5BE

Carlton Court
18 Cleveland Road, Torquay TQ2 5BE
t (01803) 297318   f (01803) 290069   e stay@carlton-court.co.uk
w carlton-court.co.uk   ONLINE MAP ONLINE BOOKING LAST MINUTE OFFERS

B&B PER ROOM PER NIGHT
S £60.00 – £65.00
D £70.00 – £90.00

We offer the highest standards of quality at The Carlton Court in Torquay as reflected in our 5 star guest accommodation with Silver Award from VisitBritain. We have a selection of superior deluxe and guest suites and all our rooms are en suite. Also have a private car park.

bedrooms 2 double, 2 twin, 2 suites
bathrooms 6 en suite
payment credit/debit cards, cash, euros

directions Come into Torquay on the A3022, go past Torre train station, pass CARZ garage first left into Cleveland Road, 600 yards on the right.

Room · General

TORQUAY, Devon Map ref 1D2   SAT NAV TQ2 6QD

Cloudlands
St Agnes Lane, Torquay, Devon TQ2 6QD
t (01803) 606550   e info@cloudlands.co.uk
w cloudlands.co.uk   ONLINE MAP GUEST REVIEWS ONLINE BOOKING LAST MINUTE OFFERS

B&B PER ROOM PER NIGHT
S £34.00 – £42.00
D £60.00 – £86.00

Cloudlands is a delightful Victorian villa set in a peaceful location close to the sea, within walking distance to the town centre, harbour, Conference Centre, Cockington Village, and railway station.
directions A380 to Torquay. At Torre Station take right fork. 2nd set of lights turn right. Turn left into Rousdown Road. Continue to St Agnes Lane. **open** All year except Xmas and New Year
bedrooms 1 single, 5 double, 2 twin, 1 family **bathrooms** 9 en suite **payment** credit/debit cards, cash

Room · General · Leisure

Official tourist board guide Bed & Breakfast

South West | Devon

TORQUAY, Devon Map ref 1D2
SAT NAV TQ1 3LX

Cary Arms Hotel & Restaurant
Babbacombe Beach, Babbacombe, Torquay TQ1 3LX
t 01803 327110 **f** 01803 323221 **e** enquiries@caryarms.co.uk
w caryarms.co.uk ONLINE MAP GUEST REVIEWS ONLINE BOOKING LAST MINUTE OFFERS

B&B PER ROOM PER NIGHT
S £100.00 – £200.00
D £150.00 – £250.00

EVENING MEAL PER PERSON
£15.00 – £30.00

SPECIAL PROMOTIONS
Please visit our website for the latest offers

The charm, personality and fun of a good English pub with all the luxury and style of a boutique hotel. The very best of traditional gastro pub food and real ales. Sheltering in its own unsung part of the South Devon coast. Elemis spa treatment room and holiday cottages.

open All year
bedrooms 6 double, 1 twin, 1 family
bathrooms 8 en suite
payment credit/debit cards, cash, cheques

directions M5 to Exeter, A380 to Torquay. B3192 to Teignmouth. Follow A379 to Torquay and Babbacombe. Turn left Babbacombe Downs, then turn left onto Beach Road.

TORQUAY, Devon Map ref 1D2
SAT NAV TQ1 3LP

Coombe Court
67 Babbacombe Downs Road, Torquay TQ1 3LP
t (01803) 327097 **f** (01803) 327097 **e** enquiries@coombecourthotel.co.uk
w coombecourthotel.co.uk ONLINE MAP

B&B PER ROOM PER NIGHT
S £35.00 – £38.00
D £70.00 – £76.00

EVENING MEAL PER PERSON
£14.00 – £20.00

The Coombe Court is a family run Guest Accommodation. Situated in a level location 50 yards from Babbacombe Downs, Babbacombe Theatre and the Cliff Railway. Easy walking distance to St Mary church and Wells Wood. Traditional Cooking and private car park for all guests. No pets.

open All year except Xmas and New Year
bedrooms 1 single, 10 double, 3 twin, 1 family
bathrooms 15 en suite
payment credit/debit cards, cash, cheques

directions Please contact us for directions

For **key to symbols** see page 6

South West | Devon

TORQUAY, Devon Map ref 1D2
SAT NAV TQ2 5JP

Crimdon Dene
Falkland Road, Torquay TQ2 5JP
t (01803) 294651 f 0845 280 0271 e vbguide@crimdondenehotel.co.uk
w crimdondenehotel.co.uk ONLINE MAP GUEST REVIEWS ONLINE BOOKING LAST MINUTE OFFERS

B&B PER ROOM PER NIGHT
S £23.00 – £35.00
D £46.00 – £70.00

Situated within a short walk to the beach, Torre Abbey, the esplanade, Princess Theatre, Torquay Harbour & the main shopping centre. All our rooms are en-suite & nicely decorated to a good standard, we have a lower ground floor dining room, a licensed bar & an on site car park.

open All year
bedrooms 2 single, 4 double, 2 twin, 2 family
bathrooms 10 en suite
payment credit/debit cards, cash, cheques

directions Take A380 to Torquay, at Torre Station traffic lights bear right, continue along Avenue Road, turn left at second set of lights into Falkland Road.

Room
General
Leisure

TORQUAY, Devon Map ref 1D2
SAT NAV TQ2 5LH

Crown Lodge
83 Avenue Road, Torquay TQ2 5LH
t (01803) 298772 f (01803) 291155 e stay@crownlodgehotel.co.uk
w crownlodgehotel.co.uk GUEST REVIEWS ONLINE BOOKING LAST MINUTE OFFERS

B&B PER ROOM PER NIGHT
D £55.00 – £79.00

EVENING MEAL PER PERSON
£14.95 – £16.95

SPECIAL PROMOTIONS
Price per night varies depending on time of year, length of stay and room variations. Low tariff for late availability

Quality B&B within walking distance of Torquay seafront. Crown Lodge receives fabulous guest reviews in appreciation of the quality, cleanliness and friendly service on offer. Each of the six en suite bedrooms has been recently refurbished to include a very comfortable bed, quality bed linen & a flat screen TV

open All year
bedrooms 5 double, 1 twin
bathrooms 6 en suite
payment credit/debit cards, cash

directions A380 onto A3022. After approx 1.5 miles fork right at lights by Torre Station into Avenue Road. Crown Lodge is 220yds on left.

Room
General
Leisure

South West | Devon

TORQUAY, Devon Map ref 1D2
SAT NAV TQ2 5AY

B&B PER ROOM PER NIGHT
S £40.00 – £50.00
D £60.00 – £70.00

Fleurie House
50 Bampfylde Road, Torquay TQ2 5AY
t (01803) 294869 f (01803) 294869 e fleuriehousemandc@btinternet.com
w fleuriehouse.co.uk

Fleurie House is a 7 bedroom victorian house close to all amenities **directions** within walking distance of the sea, torre abbey, railway and coach stations, theatre and shops **open** All year except Xmas and New Year **bedrooms** 6 double, 1 twin **bathrooms** 7 en suite **payment** cash, cheques

Room General

TORQUAY, Devon Map ref 1D2
SAT NAV TQ1 2LQ

B&B PER ROOM PER NIGHT
S £64.00 – £94.00
D £78.00 – £138.00

Haldon Priors
Meadfoot Sea Road, Torquay TQ1 2LQ
t (01803) 213365 f (01803) 215577 e travelstyle.ltd@talk21.com
w haldonpriors.co.uk ONLINE MAP

Haldon Priors is a beautiful Victorian villa adjacent to Meadfoot Bay, set in exquisite subtropical gardens with heated outdoor pool and sauna. All rooms have everything needed to make your stay memorable, with complimentary refreshments on arrival and all the beauty of Devon on the doorstep. No smoking in hotel.

open Easter to end of September
bedrooms 1 single, 1 double, 1 twin, 1 family, 2 suites
bathrooms 6 en suite, 6 with private bathroom
payment credit/debit cards, cash, cheques

directions Pass Torquay Harbour on your right. Turn left at the clock tower, right at the 1st lights, to Meadfoot Road. On the left just before the beach.

Room General Leisure

TORQUAY, Devon Map ref 1D2
SAT NAV TQ2 5NP

B&B PER ROOM PER NIGHT
S £44.00 – £58.00
D £54.00 – £98.00

Hotel Cimon
82 Abbey Road, Torquay TQ2 5NP
t (01803) 294454 f (01803) 294454 e enquiries@hotelcimon.co.uk
w hotelcimon.co.uk ONLINE MAP GUEST REVIEWS ONLINE BOOKING LAST MINUTE OFFERS

The Cimon is a detached 17 bedroom Victorian Villa, set in its own ground and gardens in the heart of Torquay. Close to town centre. **directions** Please contact us for directions **open** All year except Xmas and New Year **bedrooms** 3 single, 9 double, 3 twin, 2 family **bathrooms** 16 en suite, 1 with private bathroom **payment** credit/debit cards, cash, cheques

Room General Leisure

South West | Devon

TORQUAY, Devon Map ref 1D2
SAT NAV TQ2 5LB

Mount Edgcombe
23 Avenue Road, Torquay TQ2 5LB
t (01803) 292310 f (01803) 292510 e info@mountedgcombe.co.uk
w mountedgcombe.co.uk ONLINE MAP GUEST REVIEWS ONLINE BOOKING LAST MINUTE OFFERS

B&B PER ROOM PER NIGHT
S £40.00 – £50.00
D £50.00 – £60.00

EVENING MEAL PER PERSON
£15.00

Mount Edgcombe is a detached family run hotel situated in a level location, convenient for all local amenities and within easy walking distance of the seafront, Torre Abbey and Gardens. **directions** Please contact us for directions **open** All year **bedrooms** 5 double, 1 twin, 3 family, 1 suite **bathrooms** 10 en suite **payment** credit/debit cards, cash, cheques

Room General Leisure

TORQUAY, Devon Map ref 1D2
SAT NAV TQ2 5BQ

Villa Marina
Tor Park Road, Torquay TQ2 5BQ
t (01803) 292187 f (01803) 231177 e enquiries@villamarina-torquay.co.uk
w villamarina-torquay.co.uk ONLINE MAP GUEST REVIEWS ONLINE BOOKING LAST MINUTE OFFERS

B&B PER ROOM PER NIGHT
S £35.00 – £50.00
D £50.00 – £80.00

SPECIAL PROMOTIONS
Special Offers and Short Break Deals are available all year round. Please visit our website for further details.

Situated in one of the most favoured areas of Torquay, this elegant detached Victorian villa offers high quality accommodation in relaxing and peaceful surroundings. Our individually appointed bedrooms are generously sized, stylishly decorated in soft neutral shades and beautifully furnished. Our delicious breakfasts are freshly prepared using locally sourced produce.

open All year except Xmas
bedrooms 3 double, 2 twin
bathrooms 5 en suite
payment credit/debit cards, cash

directions Easy to access by car from the M5 and A38. Torquay also benefits from good rail and coach links and courtesy collections are available.

Room General Leisure

TORQUAY, Devon Map ref 1D2
SAT NAV TQ2 5PD

Whitburn Guest House
Saint Lukes Road North, Torquay, Devon TQ2 5PD
t 01803296719 e lazenby1210@btinternet.com
w whitburnguesthouse.co.uk ONLINE MAP GUEST REVIEWS ONLINE BOOKING LAST MINUTE OFFERS

B&B PER ROOM PER NIGHT
S £40.00 – £55.00
D £40.00 – £55.00

Ann and Joe warmly welcome you to our clean comfortable guest house, 5 mins walk seafront, town centre. Lovely residential area, no restriction parking. Full cooked breakfast included in price. **directions** At Seafront go up Shedden Hill, take 2nd right into St Lukes Road, 1st left into St Lukes Road North. Whitburn Guest House on left **open** All year **bedrooms** 1 double, 1 twin, 3 family **bathrooms** 4 en suite, 1 with private bathroom **payment** credit/debit cards, cash, cheques

Room General Leisure

Official tourist board guide Bed & Breakfast

South West | **Devon**

TOTNES, Devon Map ref 1D2
SAT NAV TQ9 5AY

enjoyEngland.com
★★★★
GUEST HOUSE

B&B PER ROOM PER NIGHT
S £50.00 – £88.00
D £71.00 – £100.00

The Old Forge
Seymour Place, Totnes TQ9 5AY
t (01803) 862174 e enq@oldforgetotnes.com
w **oldforgetotnes.com**

Delightful, 600 year Old Forge. Close to Totnes town yet peaceful. Excellent breakfasts, walled garden and conservatory with spa bath. Cottage style rooms. Doubles, twins, family and Cottage Suite available. **directions** Detailed directions on request. **open** All year **bedrooms** 5 double, 2 twin, 1 family, 1 suite **bathrooms** 8 en suite, 1 with private bathroom **payment** credit/debit cards, cash, cheques

Room   General   Leisure

WEST DOWN, Devon Map ref 1C1
SAT NAV EX34 8NT

enjoyEngland.com
★★★
GUEST HOUSE

B&B PER ROOM PER NIGHT
S £29.00 – £50.00
D £64.00 – £75.00
EVENING MEAL PER PERSON
£17.50

Sunnymeade Country Hotel
Dean Cross, Woolacombe EX34 8NT
t (01271) 863668 f (01271) 866061 e holidays@sunnymeade.co.uk
w **sunnymeade.co.uk** ONLINE MAP GUEST REVIEWS ONLINE BOOKING LAST MINUTE OFFERS

Comfortable, small family run guesthouse. Homecooked food, homemade bread. Licensed small bar, well appointed rooms including ground floor, dogs welcome. **directions** Leave M5 junction 27 onto A361 to Barnstaple, follow signs to Ilfracombe on the right on the A361. **open** All year **bedrooms** 2 single, 4 double, 6 twin **bathrooms** 10 en suite, 2 with private bathroom **payment** credit/debit cards, cash, cheques, euros

Room   General   Leisure

WESTWARD HO!, Devon Map ref 1C1
SAT NAV EX39 1HX

enjoyEngland.com
★★★★
BED & BREAKFAST

B&B PER ROOM PER NIGHT
S £35.00 – £45.00
D £60.00 – £80.00

Brockenhurst
11 Atlantic Way, Westward Ho!, Bideford EX39 1HX
t (01237) 423346 f (01237) 423346 e info@brockenhurstindevon.co.uk

Comfortable detached house adjoining the village centre (shops, restaurants, pubs). Within sight and sound of the sea. Good walking, cycling and bus service. Vast beach. **directions** M5, junction 27: 45 miles. British Rail, Barnstaple: 10 miles. National Express: 150 yards. Local buses: 100 yards. See our website for details. **open** All year except Xmas and New Year **bedrooms** 2 double, 1 twin **bathrooms** 3 en suite **payment** credit/debit cards, cash, cheques, euros

Room   General   Leisure

WOODLEIGH, Devon Map ref 1C3
SAT NAV TQ7 4DP

enjoyEngland.com
★★★★
FARMHOUSE

B&B PER ROOM PER NIGHT
S £45.00 – £50.00
D £60.00 – £75.00
EVENING MEAL PER PERSON
£15.00 – £20.00

Higher Hendham House
Woodleigh, Kingsbridge TQ7 4DP
t (01548) 550015 e higherhendhamhouse@fsmail.net
w **higherhendhamhouse.com**

Attractive 19thC farmhouse in quiet garden of mature trees and shrubs in glorious South Hams countryside. Three en suite bedrooms, newly refurbished. TV/DVD, beverage tray, delicious breakfasts using local produce. **directions** A381 Totnes to Kingsbridge, turn off right at Halwell, for Moreleigh. After Moreleigh turn left for Preston/Woodleigh. After approx. 2 miles sign on left. **open** All year **bedrooms** 2 double, 1 twin **bathrooms** 3 en suite **payment** cash, cheques

Room   General

For **key to symbols** see page 6

South West | **Devon**

YELVERTON, Devon Map ref 1C2   SAT NAV PL20 6DY

Barnabas House Yelverton

Harrowbeer Lane, Yelverton PL20 6DY
t (01822) 853268 **e** enquiries@barnabas-house.co.uk
w barnabas-house.co.uk ONLINE MAP GUEST REVIEWS ONLINE BOOKING LAST MINUTE OFFERS

B&B PER ROOM PER NIGHT
S £40.00 – £45.00
D £55.00 – £78.00

EVENING MEAL PER PERSON
£12.95 – £15.95

SPECIAL PROMOTIONS
10% off stays of 4 nights or longer - all year round

Ian and Carolyn welcome you to our charming Edwardian residence in a quiet location, most rooms with views over Dartmoor. Come and enjoy our clean spacious rooms with all modern amenities, before waking up to a delicious locally-sourced breakfast. Great location for walking, cycling or just relaxing.

open All year except Xmas
bedrooms 1 single, 2 double, 2 twin, 2 family
bathrooms 6 en suite, 1 with private bathroom
payment credit/debit cards, cash, cheques

directions A386 from Plymouth towards Tavistock. At the Yelverton roundabout, take the Princetown Road, then left into Harrowbeer Lane. We are 100m down on the right.

Room   General   Leisure

YELVERTON, Devon Map ref 1C2   SAT NAV PL20 6EA

Harrabeer Country House

Harrowbeer Lane, Yelverton, Devon PL20 6EA
t (01822) 853302 **e** reception@harrabeer.co.uk
w harrabeer.co.uk ONLINE MAP ONLINE BOOKING

B&B PER ROOM PER NIGHT
S £55.00 – £80.00
D £65.00 – £95.00

EVENING MEAL PER PERSON
£20.00

Delightful, small, quiet, family-run residence offering many services of a small hotel. Close to Dartmoor. Finalist for prestigious Landlady of the Year award. Licensed. Two self-catering suites available. **directions** A386. Yelverton roundabout. Tavistock exit. Brown sign 200 yards LHS. Grange Road. Turn right. Property 300 yards LHS after road narrows. **open** All year except Xmas and New Year **bedrooms** 3 double, 3 twin, 2 suites **bathrooms** 7 en suite, 1 with private bathroom **payment** credit/debit cards, cash, cheques, euros

Room   General   Leisure

Looking for something else?

You can also buy a copy of our popular guide 'Self Catering' including self-catering holiday homes, approved caravan holiday homes, boat accommodation and holiday cottage agencies in England 2011.

Now available in good bookshops and online at
visitbritainshop.com

£11.99

80   Official tourist board guide **Bed & Breakfast**

South West | **Devon/Dorset**

YELVERTON, Devon Map ref 1C2

SAT NAV PL20 7RA

B&B PER ROOM PER NIGHT
S £39.50 – £49.50
D £70.00 – £85.00

Overcombe House

Old Station Road, Horrabridge, Yelverton PL20 7RA
t (01822) 853501 **e** enquiries@overcombehotel.co.uk
w overcombehotel.co.uk ONLINE MAP ONLINE BOOKING

Offering a warm, friendly welcome in relaxed, comfortable surroundings with a substantial breakfast using local and home-made produce. Enjoying beautiful views over the village and Dartmoor. Conveniently located for exploring the varied attractions of both Devon and Cornwall, in particular Dartmoor National Park and the adjacent Tamar Valley.

open All year
bedrooms 1 single, 4 double, 3 twin
bathrooms 8 en suite
payment credit/debit cards, cash

directions Located on the edge of Horrabridge just off the A386 over a mile north west of Yelverton heading towards Tavistock.

BREAKFAST AWARD   Room   General   Leisure

BLANDFORD FORUM, Dorset Map ref 2B3

SAT NAV DT11 8UQ

B&B PER ROOM PER NIGHT
S £80.00 – £85.00
D £105.00 – £125.00

The Anvil Inn

Salisbury Road, Pimperne, Blandford Forum DT11 8UQ
t (01258) 453341 **f** (01258) 480182 **e** theanvil.inn@btconnect.com
w anvilinn.co.uk

Picturesque, family-run, 16thC thatched hotel. Beamed a la carte restaurant, mouth-watering menu, delicious desserts. Tasty bar meals and specials cooked from fresh, fine food. Meals available all day. **directions** On A354 Salisbury road. **open** All year **bedrooms** 2 single, 7 double, 2 twin, 1 suite **bathrooms** 12 en suite **payment** credit/debit cards, cash

Room   General   Leisure

BLANDFORD FORUM, Dorset Map ref 2B3

SAT NAV DT11 8DG

B&B PER ROOM PER NIGHT
S £60.00 – £70.00
D £80.00

Farnham Farm House

Farnham, Blandford Forum DT11 8DG
t (01725) 516254 **f** (01725) 516306 **e** info@farnhamfarmhouse.co.uk
w farnhamfarmhouse.co.uk ONLINE MAP GUEST REVIEWS

Picturesque 19thC farmhouse in secluded, rolling slopes of Cranborne Chase. Flagstone floors, open fires and an acre of tranquil garden. Comfortable, and relaxing, with Sarpenela Treatment Centre offering Natural Therapies. **directions** From Thickthorn crossroads on A354, northwards for 1 mile, left into village, after 1 mile right at signpost to farmhouse. **open** All year except Xmas **bedrooms** 2 double, 1 twin **bathrooms** 3 en suite **payment** credit/debit cards, cash, cheques, euros

Room   General   Leisure

South West | **Dorset**

BOURNEMOUTH, Dorset Map ref 2B3 — SAT NAV BH2 5DP

Cremona B&B

61 St Michaels Road, West Cliff, Bournemouth, Dorset BH2 5DP
t (01202) 290035 **e** enquiries@cremona.co.uk
w cremona.co.uk ONLINE MAP GUEST REVIEWS LAST MINUTE OFFERS

B&B PER ROOM PER NIGHT
S £25.00 – £35.00
D £60.00 – £80.00

SPECIAL PROMOTIONS
Weekday offers, please call or email for details on all offers all year round.

Victorian terraced town house covering three floors, friendly, stylish, clean and comfortable accommodation provides outstanding value, European feel throughout. Good location for the beach, gardens, town centre and Bournemouth International Centre.

open All year
bedrooms 1 single, 4 double, 2 twin, 2 family
bathrooms 8 en suite
payment credit/debit cards, cash, euros

directions By car: We are a few minutes from the Wessex Way, (A338). Follow the signs for the West Cliff and Bournemouth International Centre.

BOURNEMOUTH, Dorset Map ref 2B3 — SAT NAV BH1 3QA

Ingledene Guest House

20 Gardens View, Derby Road, Bournemouth BH1 3QA
t (01202) 291914 **f** 070058 10914 **e** ingledenehouse@yahoo.com
w ingledenehouse.co.uk ONLINE MAP GUEST REVIEWS ONLINE BOOKING LAST MINUTE OFFERS

B&B PER ROOM PER NIGHT
S £35.00 – £55.00
D £44.00 – £65.00
EVENING MEAL PER PERSON
£6.00 – £15.00

Located opposite Knyveton Gardens Bowling greens, adjoining Tennis Courts and conveniently situated 2 minutes walk from Station, 500 metres from beach, 15 minute walk to the centre and nightlife. **directions** 2 Minutes from Central Railway station **open** All year **bedrooms** 2 single, 2 double, 2 twin, 8 family, 1 suite **bathrooms** 12 en suite **payment** credit/debit cards

---

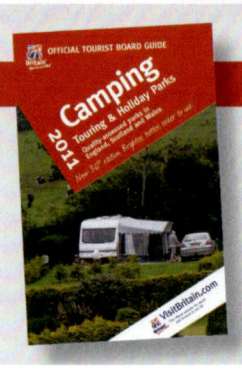

Do you like Camping?

You can also buy a copy of our popular guide 'Camping, Touring & Holiday Parks' including touring parks, camping holidays and holiday parks and villages in Britain 2011.

Now available in good bookshops and online at
visitbritainshop.com

£8.99

South West | Dorset

BOURNEMOUTH, Dorset Map ref 2B3
SAT NAV BH2 5ES

enjoyEngland.com ★★★ GUEST HOUSE

B&B PER ROOM PER NIGHT
S £35.00 – £65.00
D £50.00 – £76.00

EVENING MEAL PER PERSON
£10.00

SPECIAL PROMOTIONS
Weekly stay breakfast & eve meal from £249 pp. Free facility for swimming nearby. Special price breaks upon request.

Kings Langley
1 West Cliff Road, Bournemouth BH2 5ES
t (01202) 557349   f (01202) 789739   e john@kingslangleyhotel.com
w kingslangleyhotel.com   ONLINE MAP   GUEST REVIEWS   LAST MINUTE OFFERS

Warm, friendly, family-run hotel excellent accommodation & traditional home-cooked food. Few minutes walk to beach, shops & entertainment. Free parking. Central heating, tea-making facilities, Sky TV & hairdryers in all bedrooms. Some complimentary leisure facilities use including pools at nearby hotel. Open for Christmas & New Year.

open All year
bedrooms 10 double, 6 twin, 4 family
bathrooms 20 en suite
payment credit/debit cards, cash, cheques

directions Please contact us for directions

Room   General   Leisure

BRIDPORT, Dorset Map ref 2A3
SAT NAV DT6 3DL

enjoyEngland.com ★★★ BED & BREAKFAST

B&B PER ROOM PER NIGHT
S £30.00 – £35.00
D £60.00 – £70.00

The Well
St Andrews Well, Bridport DT6 3DL
t (01308) 424156   e thewellbandb@yahoo.co.uk
w thewellbandb.co.uk

The Well offers high quality, friendly guest accommodation, situated less than one mile from the historic market town of Bridport and two miles from the sea at West Bay. **directions** Located half a mile from Bridport town centre on A3066 towards Beaminster, 400 yards from Co-Op supermarket **open** All year except Xmas **bedrooms** 1 single, 1 double, 1 family **bathrooms** 2 en suite, 1 with private bathroom **payment** cash, cheques

Room   General

BRIDPORT (4 MILES), Dorset Map ref 2A3
SAT NAV DT6 5NR

enjoyEngland.com ★★★ FARMHOUSE

B&B PER ROOM PER NIGHT
S £27.00 – £37.00
D £54.00 – £68.00

Dunster Farm
Broadoak, Bridport DT6 5NR
t (01308) 424626   e dunsterfarm@onebillinternet.co.uk
w dunsterfarm.co.uk

Dunster farm is a working family farm in peaceful marshwood vale. Guests welcome to view or join in. Lyme Regis, Charmouth, Westbay nearby. Excellent restaurants. A warm welcome for all. **directions** Take B3162 Chard. First crossroads turn left. Follow through to Broadoak. Go straight on up hill Dunster farm next right. Up concrete lane to farmhouse. **open** Easter to October **bedrooms** 1 double, 1 twin, 1 family **payment** cash, cheques

Room   General

for key to symbols see page 6

South West | **Dorset**

BRIDPORT - WEST DORSET, Dorset Map ref 2A3   SAT NAV DT6 4PE

Dippers
42 Uploders, Bridport DT6 4PE
t (01308) 485504/07855 344121 (mobile) e liz@dipperswestdorset.co.uk
w dipperswestdorset.co.uk ONLINE MAP LAST MINUTE OFFERS

B&B PER ROOM PER NIGHT
S £25.00 – £35.00
D £60.00 – £70.00

Dippers sits on the banks of the River Asker in the beautiful West Dorset village of Uploders. 2mls from Bridport: a wonderful location for exploring Jurassic Coast and Hardy Country. **directions** Uploders is ½-mile north of the A35, 2 miles east of Bridport. Turn right at the Crown Inn and Dippers is 200m on the left. **open** All year **bedrooms** 1 single, 1 double, 1 twin **bathrooms** 2 en suite, 1 with private bathroom **payment** cash, cheques

Room   General

CHARMINSTER, Dorset Map ref 2B3   SAT NAV DT2 9QT

The Three Compasses
The Square, Charminster, Dorchester DT2 9QT
t (01305) 263618

B&B PER ROOM PER NIGHT
S £30.00
D £70.00
EVENING MEAL PER PERSON
£5.00 – £10.00

Traditional village inn with skittle alley set in village square. Lunch and evening meals provided. **directions** Please contact us for directions **open** All year except Xmas **bedrooms** 1 single, 1 double, 1 twin **bathrooms** 1 en suite **payment** cash, cheques

Room   General   Leisure

CHRISTCHURCH, Dorset Map ref 2B3   SAT NAV BH23 1JE

Druid House
26 Sopers Lane, Christchurch BH23 1JE
t (01202) 485615 f (01202) 473484 e reservations@druid-house.co.uk
w druid-house.co.uk ONLINE MAP GUEST REVIEWS

B&B PER ROOM PER NIGHT
S £35.00 – £70.00
D £60.00 – £96.00

SPECIAL PROMOTIONS
Weekend 3 day breaks £89-£99 pp 3 night stay Weekday breaks available upon request. November - March inc.

Overlooking park, this delightful family-run establishment is just a stroll from the High Street, Priory and Quay. Bedrooms, some with balconies, are modern and very comfortably furnished, with many welcome extras, i-pod docking, flat screen tv with dvd/cd, wi-fi access. Beautiful rear garden, patio and relaxing lounge and bar areas.

open All year
bedrooms 1 single, 4 double, 2 twin, 2 family
bathrooms 8 en suite, 1 with private bathroom
payment credit/debit cards, cash, cheques

directions A35 exit Christchurch main rdbt onto Sopers Lane, establishment on the left. Christchurch train station 10 min walk and Bournemouth International Airport 3 miles.

Breakfast Award

Room   General   Leisure

84   Official tourist board guide Bed & Breakfast

South West | Dorset

COMPTON VALENCE, Dorset Map ref 2A3
SAT NAV DT2 9ES

enjoyEngland.com ★★★★ BED & BREAKFAST

B&B PER ROOM PER NIGHT
S £50.00 – £70.00
D £70.00 – £90.00
EVENING MEAL PER PERSON
£15.00 – £30.00

Manor Farm
Compton Valence, Dorchester, Dorset DT2 9ES
t (01308) 482227 **e** tessa.nrussell@btinternet.com
w manor-farm.uk.com ONLINE MAP

Victorian Farmhouse in stunning secluded location. Forgotton sounds and views of the Dorset countryside. The coast, beautiful walks and good eateries not far away. Relaxed Family Atmosphere. **directions** Grid Reference 596931 SATNAV not always reliable to find us!!! Please look at good map on website or ask **open** All year except Xmas and New Year **bedrooms** 1 double, 1 twin **bathrooms** 1 with private bathroom **payment** cash, cheques, euros

Room General Leisure

CRANBORNE, Dorset Map ref 2B3
SAT NAV BH21 5PR

enjoyEngland.com ★★★★ GUEST ACCOMMODATION

B&B PER ROOM PER NIGHT
S £49.00 – £70.00
D £70.00 – £85.00
EVENING MEAL PER PERSON
£19.95 – £24.95

SPECIAL PROMOTIONS
Dinner, Bed and Breakfast rate Short Break Long term stay

La Fosse at Cranborne
London House, The Square, Cranborne, Wimborne BH21 5PR
t (01725) 517604 **e** lafossemail@gmail.com
w la-fosse.com ONLINE MAP GUEST REVIEWS ONLINE BOOKING LAST MINUTE OFFERS

Mark and Emmanuelle would like to extend a very warm welcome to you and invite you to experience our homely Restaurant with Rooms in this beautiful countryside of Dorset.

open All year except Xmas
bedrooms 3 double, 2 twin, 1 family
bathrooms 6 en suite
payment credit/debit cards, cash, cheques

directions Please contact us for directions

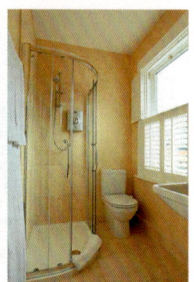

Room General Leisure

DORCHESTER, Dorset Map ref 2B3
SAT NAV DT2 8RW

enjoyEngland.com ★★★★ GUEST ACCOMMODATION

B&B PER ROOM PER NIGHT
S £48.00 – £60.00
D £70.00 – £86.00

Yellowham Farm
Yellowham Wood, Dorchester DT2 8RW
t (01305) 262892 **f** (01305) 848155 **e** mail@yellowham.freeserve.co.uk
w yellowham.co.uk

Situated in heart of Hardy Country on the edge of the idyllic Yellowham Wood in 120 acres of farmland. Excellent base for exploring the Jurassic Coast. Peace and tranquillity guaranteed. **directions** 2 Miles east of Dorchester off the A35 (signpost says Higher/Lower Bockhampton) situated on the edge of Yellowham Wood **open** All year **bedrooms** 2 double, 1 twin, 1 family **bathrooms** 4 en suite **payment** credit/debit cards, cash, cheques, euros

Room General Leisure

For key to symbols see page 6

South West | Dorset

GILLINGHAM, Dorset Map ref 2B3
SAT NAV SP8 5LX

enjoyEngland.com ★★★ BED & BREAKFAST

B&B PER ROOM PER NIGHT
S £30.00 – £35.00
D £60.00

Lyde Hill Farmhouse
Woodville, Stour Provost, Gillingham, Dorset SP8 5LX
t (01747) 838483

17thC stone farmhouse - lovely garden and views, good walking on the Hardy Way and Duncliffe Wood. Comfortable south-facing rooms overlooking garden. Mostly organic food. Vegetarians catered for. **directions** Details on enquiry **open** March to October **bedrooms** 1 double, 1 twin **bathrooms** 1 with private bathroom **payment** cash, cheques

Room / General

PORTLAND, Dorset Map ref 2B3
SAT NAV DT5 1BD

enjoyEngland.com ★★★ GUEST ACCOMMODATION

B&B PER ROOM PER NIGHT
S £19.00 – £40.00
D £30.00 – £80.00

EVENING MEAL PER PERSON
£5.00 – £20.00

The Aqua
Castletown, Portland, Dorset DT5 1BD
t (01305) 860269 **e** reception@hotelaqua.co.uk
w hotelaqua.co.uk ONLINE MAP ONLINE BOOKING LAST MINUTE OFFERS

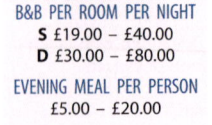

Sheltering beneath Portland's Jurassic coast The Aqua looks east across the whole of Portland Harbour. Just a short walk from the Weymouth and Portland sailing academy, venue of the 2012 sailing events, The Aqua offers 20 en-suite rooms almost all with sea views.

open All year except Xmas and New Year
bedrooms 1 single, 6 double, 4 twin, 7 family, 2 suites
bathrooms 20 en suite
payment credit/debit cards, cash, cheques

directions Taking the A354 from Dorchester through Weymouth to Portland follow signs for Castletown and Portland Port. The Aqua is on the left.

Room / General / Leisure

SHAFTESBURY, Dorset Map ref 2B3
SAT NAV SP7 8AE

enjoyEngland.com ★★★★ GUEST HOUSE   Silver AWARD

B&B PER ROOM PER NIGHT
S £50.00
D £80.00

The Retreat
47 Bell Street, Shaftesbury, Dorset, England SP7 8AE
t 01747850372 **e** info@the-retreat.co.uk
w the-retreat.co.uk

Perfectly positioned in quiet street, this Georgian townhouse has light and airy, individually furnished, en-suite bedrooms with Flat-Screen TV-DVD and complimentary tray. Off-road-parking. Winner of 2005 'Best B&B North Dorset'. **directions** Please contact us for directions **open** All year **bedrooms** 1 single, 4 double, 1 twin, 4 family **bathrooms** 10 en suite **payment** credit/debit cards, cash, cheques

Room / General

Official tourist board guide Bed & Breakfast

South West | Dorset

SHAVE CROSS, Dorset Map ref 1D2
SAT NAV DT6 6HW

The Shave Cross Inn
Shave Cross, Marshwood Vale, Bridport DT6 6HW
t (01308) 868358 **f** (01308) 867064 **e** roy.warburton@virgin.net
w theshavecrossinn.co.uk ONLINE MAP GUEST REVIEWS LAST MINUTE OFFERS

B&B PER ROOM PER NIGHT
S £90.00 – £110.00
D £160.00

EVENING MEAL PER PERSON
£11.95 – £28.00

New luxury boutique hotel and 14thC inn in the Marshwood Vale, West Dorset, three miles from the Jurassic Coast.

open All year
bedrooms 5 double, 1 twin, 1 suite
bathrooms 7 en suite
payment credit/debit cards, cash, cheques

directions Please contact us for directions

Room | General | Leisure

STUDLAND, Dorset Map ref 2B3
SAT NAV BH19 3AS

Shell Bay Cottage
Glebe Estate, Studland, Dorset BH19 3AS
t (01929) 450249 **f** (01929) 450249 **e** shellbayrose@btinternet.com
w shellbaycottage.com ONLINE MAP

B&B PER ROOM PER NIGHT
S £45.00 – £49.50
D £90.00 – £99.00

The house is on a secluded private estate overlooking Studland Bay and is surrounded by National Trust land. **directions** M3 to Bournemouth. Take Sandbanks ferry then 2.5 miles into Studland or A351 Poole to Wareham, A351 to Corfe Castle. At castle B3351 to Studland. **open** All year except Xmas and New Year **bedrooms** 1 double, 1 family **bathrooms** 2 with private bathroom **payment** cash, cheques, euros

BREAKFAST AWARD

Room | General | Leisure

SWANAGE, Dorset Map ref 2B3
SAT NAV BH19 2AA

Clare House
1 Park Road, Swanage BH19 2AA
t (01929) 422855 **e** info@clare-house.com
w clare-house.com ONLINE MAP GUEST REVIEWS ONLINE BOOKING LAST MINUTE OFFERS

B&B PER ROOM PER NIGHT
S £75.00
D £98.00

A five-star guesthouse in one of Swanage's historic buildings. Ideally placed for those wishing to spend time on the beach, the pier, restaurants and bars, only a short walk. **directions** Please refer to the website. **open** All year **bedrooms** 6 double **bathrooms** 6 en suite **payment** credit/debit cards, cash, cheques, euros

Room | General | Leisure

for key to symbols see page 6

87

South West | **Dorset**

SWANAGE, Dorset Map ref 2B3

SAT NAV BH19 1AP

Corner Meadow

24 Victoria Avenue, Swanage BH19 1AP
t (01929) 423493 **e** geogios@hotmail.co.uk
w cornermeadow.co.uk ONLINE MAP GUEST REVIEWS

B&B PER ROOM PER NIGHT
S £42.00 – £47.00
D £56.00 – £62.00

Family run bed and breakfast in Swanage. All you should expect from a VisitBritain four star establishment high quality rooms, facilities and breakfast everyone welcome. **directions** We are situated in Victoria Avenue Swanage opposite the main beach car park. **open** All year except Xmas **bedrooms** 2 double, 1 twin, 1 family, 1 suite **bathrooms** 5 en suite **payment** cash, cheques

Room · General · Leisure

SWANAGE, Dorset Map ref 2B3

SAT NAV BH19 2BY

Taunton House

4 Taunton Road, Swanage BH19 2BY
t (01929) 425440 **e** info@tauntonhouse-swanage.com
w tauntonhouse-swanage.com ONLINE MAP GUEST REVIEWS LAST MINUTE OFFERS

B&B PER ROOM PER NIGHT
S £60.00
D £60.00 – £110.00

SPECIAL PROMOTIONS
£10 reduction after the second and subsequent nights.

Taunton House is a stunning Victorian B&B set in the heart of Swanage, close to the sea, restaurants and pubs. It's full of character with large airy, centrally heated rooms. It has its own car park and a guest lounge. A warm welcome, great hospitality and fabulous food!

open All year
bedrooms 2 double, 1 twin, 4 family
bathrooms 5 en suite, 1 with private bathroom
payment credit/debit cards, cash, cheques, euros

directions Follow the one way system down Station Road and at The Ship Pub turn right int Taunton Road. Taunton House is on the right.

Room
General
Leisure

Where is my pet welcome?

Some properties welcome well-behaved pets. Look for the 🐕 in the accommodation listings.

You can also buy a copy of our popular guide 'Pets Come Too!' Now available in good bookshops and online at **visitbritainshop.com**

£9.99

Official tourist board guide **Bed & Breakfas**

South West | Dorset

WAREHAM, Dorset Map ref 2B3
SAT NAV BH20 4QA

Frome Corner
10 Frome Road, Wareham, Dorset BH20 4QA
t (01929) 551550 e m.bridger2@btinternet.com

B&B PER ROOM PER NIGHT
S £55.00
D £70.00

SPECIAL PROMOTIONS
15% off four nights or more stay

Luxurious, peaceful accommodation, lovely views, twin and double ensuite rooms, refreshment tray, TV, WiFi, own entrance, off road parking. Walking distance to town, restaurants, bars, cinema, swimming pool, sport centre. Golf, Fishing, Swanage, Corfe Castle, Dorchester, Weymouth, Poole and Bournemouth nearby. Good walking, cycling and sailing all around.

open All year except Xmas and New Year
bedrooms 1 double, 1 twin
bathrooms 2 en suite
payment cash, cheques

directions From Wareham central crossroads, proceed ½ mile along West street, after firestation turn left into Stowell Cresent, 10 Frome Road is second on the left

WEYMOUTH, Dorset Map ref 2B3
SAT NAV DT4 7AA

B+B Weymouth
68 The Esplanade, Weymouth, Dorset DT4 7AA
t 01305 761190 e info@bb-weymouth.com
w bb-weymouth.com ONLINE MAP GUEST REVIEWS ONLINE BOOKING

B&B PER ROOM PER NIGHT
S £50.00 – £80.00
D £65.00 – £95.00

Central seafront location; 4* boutique B+B, stunning sea views, 22 ensuite rooms + 1 apartment; modern and contemporary; spacious guest lounge, breakfast room. Tea, coffee, mineral water & wifi included. **directions** From the clock tower on the Esplanade, go towards the Kings Statue; B+B Weymouth is on the right corner by the Kings Statue **open** All year **bedrooms** 5 single, 14 double, 6 twin, 1 suite **bathrooms** 24 en suite, 2 with private bathroom **payment** credit/debit cards, cash, cheques

WEYMOUTH, Dorset Map ref 2B3
SAT NAV DT4 8DN

Beaufort Guesthouse
24 The Esplanade, Weymouth DT4 8DN
t (01305) 782088 f (01305) 782088
w beaufortguesthouse.co.uk

B&B PER ROOM PER NIGHT
D £50.00 – £70.00

Recently refurbished Victorian grade two listed Bed and Breakfast on Jurassic Coast, near shops, harbour, restaurants and sandy beach in the heart of Weymouth. Parking permits. Bar meals. **directions** Along the sea front, then follow the one-way system around Alexandra Gardens until you see us on the left. **open** All year except Xmas and New Year **bedrooms** 4 double, 1 family **bathrooms** 4 en suite, 1 with private bathroom **payment** credit/debit cards, cash, cheques

South West | **Dorset**

WEYMOUTH, Dorset Map ref 2B3
SAT NAV DT3 5EQ

Graingers Guest Accommodation
215 Dorchester Road, Weymouth, Dorset DT3 5EQ
t (01305) 782362 **f** (01305) 786777 **e** info@graingersguesthouse.co.uk
w graingersguesthouse.co.uk GUEST REVIEWS ONLINE BOOKING LAST MINUTE OFFERS

Graingers is a friendly guest house situated within easy reach of Weymouth's Blue Flag beach, Esplanade, picturesque harbour and the Jurassic Coast. With free parking at Graingers, you can safely leave your car behind and either stroll or take a short bus ride to many local attractions.

open All year
bedrooms 2 single, 3 double, 1 twin, 1 family
bathrooms 3 en suite, 3 with private bathroom
payment credit/debit cards, cash

directions From the A35, turn onto the A354. At the roundabout (Approx 4 miles), Proceed straight on. Graingers is 200 metres after the C Spa Pub.

Room
General

WEYMOUTH, Dorset Map ref 2B3
SAT NAV DT4 7QF

Oaklands Edwardian Guest House
1 Glendinning Avenue, Weymouth DT4 7QF
t (01305) 767081 **e** stay@oaklands-guesthouse.co.uk
w oaklands-guesthouse.co.uk ONLINE MAP GUEST REVIEWS LAST MINUTE OFFERS

B&B PER ROOM PER NIGHT
D £50.00 – £90.00

EVENING MEAL PER PERSON
£8.00 – £20.00

SPECIAL PROMOTIONS
Discounts on stays of 3 or more nights. Other special offers available throughout the year - see website for details.

Beautiful Edwardian house set in quiet, yet central location in the picturesque harbour town of Weymouth. All rooms are individually decorated and equipped to the highest standard with modern en suite or private facilities. Doubles, twins, family and a ground-floor room available. Extensive breakfast menu with vegetarian options available. Licensed.

open All year
bedrooms 6 double, 2 twin, 1 family
bathrooms 8 en suite, 1 with private bathroom
payment credit/debit cards, cash, cheques

directions A354 from Dorchester. Straight across 1st roundabout. After 1 mile, right into Carlton Road North. 2nd left into Glendinning Avenue. Oaklands is at far end.

Room
General
Leisure

South West | Dorset/Gloucestershire

WEYMOUTH, Dorset Map ref 2B3
SAT NAV DT4 8TJ

Old Harbour View
12 Trinity Road, Weymouth DT4 8TJ
t (01305) 774633 **f** (01305) 750828 **e** info@oldharbourview.co.uk
w oldharbourviewweymouth.co.uk ONLINE MAP GUEST REVIEWS

B&B PER ROOM PER NIGHT
S £60.00 – £66.00
D £80.00 – £88.00

Idyllic Georgian harbourside town house, offering two charming bedrooms, one double and one twin, both en suite. Restaurants, pubs, sandy beach and ferries to the Channel Islands on the doorstep. **directions** Please contact us for directions **open** All year except Xmas and New Year **bedrooms** 1 double, 1 twin **bathrooms** 2 en suite **payment** credit/debit cards, cash, cheques

Room   General   Leisure

ALDERTON, Gloucestershire Map ref 2B2
SAT NAV GL20 8NH

Corner Cottage
Stow Road, Alderton, Tewkesbury GL20 8NH
t (01242) 620630 **e** cornercottagebb@talk21.com
w cornercottage-bedandbreakfast.co.uk ONLINE MAP GUEST REVIEWS ONLINE BOOKING

B&B PER ROOM PER NIGHT
S £35.00 – £45.00
D £60.00 – £70.00

Easy to find on B4077. Unrestricted parking, family home, cottage style, ensuite bedrooms. Sitting room. Breakfast using local produce. Special diets on request. Village pubs nearby. WiFi. Credit cards accepted. **directions** Jt 9 M5 east on A46 then B4077 2 miles opposite Alderton Garage. Entrance in Willowbank Road. Drive around house to parking **open** All year except Xmas and New Year **bedrooms** 2 double, 1 twin **bathrooms** 3 en suite **payment** credit/debit cards, cash, cheques

Room   General   Leisure

BATH, Gloucestershire Map ref 2B2
SAT NAV BS16 9PG

Fern Cottage Bed & Breakfast
188 Shortwood Hill, Pucklechurch, South Gloucestershire, Nr Bath BS16 9PG
t (0117) 937 4966 **e** sueandpete@ferncottagebedandbreakfast.co.uk
w ferncottagebedandbreakfast.co.uk GUEST REVIEWS ONLINE BOOKING

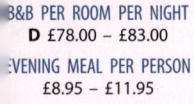

B&B PER ROOM PER NIGHT
D £78.00 – £83.00

EVENING MEAL PER PERSON
£8.95 – £11.95

SPECIAL PROMOTIONS
3 night special offer 2 people including Award Winning breakfast.
Chamomile £235.00
Lavender/Rosemary £230.00
Bergamot £225.00

National Award Winning B&B, recently awarded Bed & Breakfast of the Year 2010. Famous for its homemade and locally sourced food. Panoramic views in 2 acres of delightful countryside, just 15 mins drive from Bath/Bristol. Beautifully furnished accommodation, luxurious bedding in converted stables with own entrance doors, all ground floor.

open All year except Xmas and New Year
bedrooms 4 double
bathrooms 4 en suite

directions We are 10 minutes from Junction 18 of the M4. Just 15 mins drive from Bath. See our website for full directions from various locations.

Room
General
Leisure

key to symbols see page 6

South West | **Gloucestershire**

BIBURY, Gloucestershire Map ref 2B1
SAT NAV GL7 5ND

B&B PER ROOM PER NIGHT
S £50.00 – £55.00
D £68.00 – £75.00

Cotteswold House
Arlington, Bibury, Gloucestershire GL7 5ND
t 01285 740609 f 01285 740609 e enquiries@cotteswoldhouse.net
w cotteswoldhouse.net

Cotteswold House offers high-quality accommodation in a relaxed, friendly atmosphere. An ideal base for touring the Cotswolds and surrounding area. No smoking/pets. Private parking. **directions** As you enter the village of Bibury from Cirencester on the B4425, Cotteswold House is on the left before descending the hill. **open** All year **bedrooms** 2 double, 1 twin **bathrooms** 3 en suite **payment** credit/debit cards, cash, cheques

BOURTON-ON-THE-WATER, Gloucestershire Map ref 2B1
SAT NAV GL54 2AN

B&B PER ROOM PER NIGHT
S £50.00 – £55.00
D £65.00 – £70.00

Chestnuts Bed & Breakfast
High Street, Bourton-on-the-Water, Cheltenham GL54 2AN
t (01451) 820244 e thechestnutsbb@hotmail.co.uk

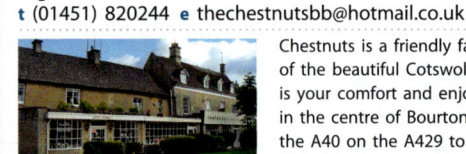

Chestnuts is a friendly family run Bed and Breakfast, in the centre of the beautiful Cotswold village of Bourton-on-the-Water. Our aim is your comfort and enjoyment. **directions** Chestnuts can be found in the centre of Bourton-on-the-Water, which is situated north of the A40 on the A429 to Stow. **open** 1st Feb to 31st Dec **bedrooms** 5 double, 1 twin, 2 family **bathrooms** 8 en suite **payment** credit/debit cards, cash, cheques

BOURTON-ON-THE-WATER, Gloucestershire Map ref 2B1
SAT NAV GL54 2AZ

B&B PER ROOM PER NIGHT
S £35.00
D £50.00

Trevone Bed & Breakfast
Moore Road, Bourton-on-the-Water GL54 2AZ
t 07740 805 250 e admin@trevonebb.co.uk
w trevonebb.co.uk ONLINE MAP ONLINE BOOKING

Cotswold stone house ideally situated for exploring the picturesque and historic delights of the Cotswolds. Within one minute walk from the village centre. **directions** Please contact us for directions **open** All year **bedrooms** 2 double **bathrooms** 2 en suite **payment** credit/debit cards, cash, cheques, euros

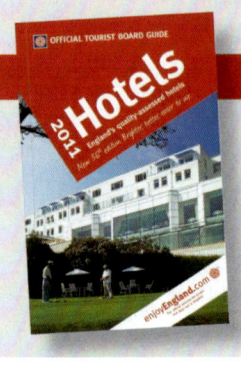

Looking for something else?
You can also buy a copy of our popular guide 'Hotels' including country house and town house hotels, metro and budget hotels, serviced apartments, restaurants with rooms and Spas in England 2011.

Now available in good bookshops and online at
visitbritainshop.com

£10.99

South West | **Gloucestershire**

BRISTOL, Gloucestershire Map ref 2A2

SAT NAV BS13 8AG

The Town & Country Lodge

A38 Bridgwater Road, Bristol BS13 8AG
t (01275) 392441 f (01275) 393362 e reservations@tclodge.co.uk
w tclodge.co.uk ONLINE MAP GUEST REVIEWS LAST MINUTE OFFERS

B&B PER ROOM PER NIGHT
S £62.50 – £70.50
D £62.50 – £87.00

EVENING MEAL PER PERSON
£9.50 – £19.50

SPECIAL PROMOTIONS
Stay Fri and Sat night and get Sunday night free (incl Bank Holiday weekends).

Highly comfortable hotel offering genuine value for money. Splendid, rural location on the A38 only three miles from central Bristol and handy for airport, Bath, Weston and all major, local attractions. Excellent restaurant offering international cuisine with a la carte and bar menus. Ideal for functions, wedding receptions and conferences.

open All year except Xmas
bedrooms 4 single, 11 double, 14 twin, 7 family
bathrooms 36 en suite
payment credit/debit cards, cash

directions Situated on A38 halfway between Airport and city centre. From North M5 exit J18 Avonmouth. A4 Bristol Airport. From South exit M5 J22. A38 Bristol.

Room
General
Leisure

CHELTENHAM, Gloucestershire Map ref 2B1

SAT NAV GL53 0JE

Beaumont House

56 Shurdington Road, Cheltenham GL53 0JE
t (01242) 223311 f (01242) 520044 e reservations@bhhotel.co.uk
w bhhotel.co.uk ONLINE MAP GUEST REVIEWS ONLINE BOOKING LAST MINUTE OFFERS

B&B PER ROOM PER NIGHT
S £68.00 – £125.00
D £90.00 – £175.00

EVENING MEAL PER PERSON
£15.00 – £25.00

SPECIAL PROMOTIONS
Champagne, flowers and chocolates can all be arranged in your room for that special day.

Historic private residence now run as a private boutique style guesthouse. Elegant large lounge with trust bar. Complimentary tea, cappuccino etc. Delicious freshly cooked breakfast. Just 15 minutes walk to the fashionable Montpelier area of Cheltenham with its boutiques, bars and restaurants. Evening room service meals Monday through Thursday nights.

open All year
bedrooms 2 single, 9 double, 3 twin, 1 family, 1 suite
bathrooms 16 en suite
payment credit/debit cards, cash

directions Situated at the Cheltenham end of the A46 Shurdington Road, which is the extension of the A46 Bath Road, just south of Cheltenham town centre.

BREAKFAST AWARD Room General Leisure

or key to symbols see page 6

93

South West | Gloucestershire

CHELTENHAM, Gloucestershire Map ref 2B1   SAT NAV GL52 2BD

Cheltenham Townhouse
12-14 Pittville Lawn, Cheltenham GL52 2BD
t (01242) 221922 f (01242) 244687 e info@cheltenhamtownhouse.com
w cheltenhamtownhouse.com ONLINE MAP GUEST REVIEWS ONLINE BOOKING LAST MINUTE OFFERS

B&B PER ROOM PER NIGHT
S £63.00 – £98.00
D £73.00 – £108.00

Central location, a pleasant walk from the racecourse and Pump Rooms, leafy surroundings, ample parking. Offering excellent value for money, it is the perfect place to relax, sleep and eat. **directions** Head out of Cheltenaham town center towards the racecourse via Evesham Road. Take a right at Wellington Road and Right again at Pittville lawn. **open** All year **bedrooms** 15 double, 4 twin, 2 family 5 suites **bathrooms** 25 en suite, 1 with private bathroom **payment** credit/debit cards, cash

CHELTENHAM, Gloucestershire Map ref 2B1   SAT NAV GL50 2QW

Lypiatt House
Lypiatt Road, Cheltenham GL50 2QW
t (01242) 224994 f (01242) 224996 e stay@lypiatt.co.uk
w lypiatt.co.uk ONLINE MAP LAST MINUTE OFFERS

B&B PER ROOM PER NIGHT
S £75.00 – £90.00
D £80.00 – £120.00

5 star guest accommodation situated in the Montpellier area of Cheltenham. In typical Victorian style with contemporary decor. In its own grounds, parking and just a short walk from town. **directions** Close to A40 & A46 apprx. 3 miles junction 11 M5. Link road between Lansdown Road & Suffolk Road Montpellier/Tivoli area of Cheltenham. **open** All year **bedrooms** 7 double, 3 twin **bathrooms** 10 en suite **payment** credit/debit cards, cash, cheques euros

CHIPPING CAMPDEN, Gloucestershire Map ref 2B1   SAT NAV GL55 6QH

Manor Farm
Weston-sub-Edge, Chipping Campden GL55 6QH
t (01386) 840390 f 08701 640538 e lucy@manorfarmbnb.demon.co.uk
w manorfarmbnb.demon.co.uk GUEST REVIEWS LAST MINUTE OFFERS

B&B PER ROOM PER NIGHT
S £55.00 – £70.00
D £65.00 – £70.00

Perfect location for The Cotswolds & Stratford-upon-Avon. 600 acres, Farmhouse built in 1624! King-size beds, Power Showers. Free Wi-Fi. Sky TV. Free Farm Tours during 3 night stays. Village Pub. **directions** On B4632 - Manor Farm on right hand side as you drive through village. Free pick up from Honeybourne Train Station. **open** All year **bedrooms** 2 double, 1 twin **bathrooms** 3 en suite **payment** credit/debit cards, cash, cheques

CHIPPING CAMPDEN, Gloucestershire Map ref 2B1   SAT NAV GL55 6PS

Nineveh Farm
Campden Road, Mickleton, Chipping Campden GL55 6PS
t (01386) 438923 e stayinthecotswolds@hotmail.co.uk
w stayinthecotswolds.co.uk ONLINE MAP LAST MINUTE OFFERS

B&B PER ROOM PER NIGHT
D £60.00 – £90.00

Ideal for touring North Cotswolds villages, Shakespeare Country, Warwick Castle, Blenheim Palace and Oxford. Several National Trust properties nearby, including the renowned Hidcote Manor Gardens. Free use of cycles. **directions** Please contact us for directions **open** All year **bedrooms** 3 double, 2 twin, 1 family **bathrooms** 5 en suite, 1 with private bathroom **payment** credit/debit cards, cash

BREAKFAST AWARD

94   Official tourist board guide Bed & Breakfast

South West | **Gloucestershire**

CIRENCESTER, Gloucestershire Map ref 2B1

SAT NAV GL7 2LN

Greensleeves

Baunton Lane, Cirencester GL7 2LN
t (01285) 642516 e johnps1@tesco.net
w greensleeves4u.co.uk GUEST REVIEWS

B&B PER ROOM PER NIGHT
S £40.00 – £50.00
D £55.00 – £75.00

Located on the edge of town overlooking the Cotswold Area of Outstanding Natural Beauty. Guests have their own private entrance. **directions** From Cirencester take the old Gloucester road to Stratton. Past Plough Inn take the 2nd next right into Baunton Lane. Last house on the left. **open** All year **bedrooms** 1 single, 2 double **bathrooms** 3 en suite **payment** cash, euros

Room General Leisure

CIRENCESTER, Gloucestershire Map ref 2B1

SAT NAV GL7 1EN

The Ivy House

2 Victoria Road, Cirencester GL7 1EN
t (01285) 656626 e info@ivyhousecotswolds.com
w ivyhousecotswolds.com ONLINE MAP GUEST REVIEWS LAST MINUTE OFFERS

B&B PER ROOM PER NIGHT
S £50.00
D £65.00

Close to town centre. A welcoming atmosphere in this lovely bright and comfortable house with en suite facilities. Bed and breakfast of a high standard. No smoking please. **directions** Travel directions available upon request. **open** All year **bedrooms** 3 double, 1 twin, 1 family **bathrooms** 5 en suite **payment** credit/debit cards, cash, cheques

Room General Leisure

CIRENCESTER, Gloucestershire Map ref 2B1

SAT NAV GL7 1LF

Riverside House

Watermoor, Cirencester GL7 1LF
t (01285) 647642 f (01285) 647615 e riversidehouse@mitsubishi-cars.co.uk
w riversidehouse.org.uk ONLINE MAP GUEST REVIEWS ONLINE BOOKING LAST MINUTE OFFERS

B&B PER ROOM PER NIGHT
S £54.00 – £64.00
D £69.50 – £79.50

EVENING MEAL PER PERSON
£9.00 – £16.50

SPECIAL PROMOTIONS
Special group discounts are available at weekends. Ideal for clubs and societies.

Located 15 minutes walk from the centre of the historic market town of Cirencester with easy access to and from M4/M5 and the Cotswolds. Riverside House is fully licensed and provides superb bed and breakfast for private and corporate guests. Built in the grounds of Mitsubishi UK headquarters.

open All year
bedrooms 15 double, 9 twin
bathrooms 24 en suite
payment credit/debit cards, cash, cheques

directions Located just off A419 opposite the Tesco superstore.

Room
General
Leisure

key to symbols see page 6

95

South West | Gloucestershire

CIRENCESTER, Gloucestershire Map ref 2B1
SAT NAV GL7 6JS

The Royal Agricultural College
Stroud Road, Cirencester GL7 6JS
t (01285) 652531 f (01285) 654214 e commercial.services@rac.ac.uk
w rac.ac.uk ONLINE MAP

B&B PER ROOM PER NIGHT
S £40.00

The Royal Agricultural College is an ideal venue for individual or group Bed & Breakfast. Stay for one night or more, relax and enjoy the beautiful surroundings of the Cotswolds. **directions** M4 Motorway, exit Jnct. 15 (A419) M5 Motorway, exit Jnct. 13 (A419) exit Jnct. 11A (A417) **open** All year except Xmas and New Year **bedrooms** 14 single, 9 double, 2 twin **bathrooms** 25 en suite **payment** credit/debit cards, cash, cheques

Room General Leisure

FAIRFORD, Gloucestershire Map ref 2B1
SAT NAV GL7 4JG

Waiten Hill Farm
Coronation Street, Fairford GL7 4HX
t (01285) 712652 e richard@waiten-hill-farmhouse.com
w waiten-hill-farmhouse.com ONLINE MAP

B&B PER ROOM PER NIGHT
S £30.00 – £35.00
D £40.00 – £50.00

Imposing 19thC farmhouse overlooking River Coln Water Meadow old mill and famous church. Short walk to pubs, shops and restaurants. Ideal for touring the Cotswolds and waterparks. Ample parking. **directions** Entering Fairford on A417 from Cirencester, at first cross roads by Marlborough Arms Pub, turn left we are 300yd on right. **open** All year **bedrooms** 2 double, 1 twin **bathrooms** 2 en suite, 1 with private bathroom **payment** credit/debit cards, cash, cheques

Room General

FORD, Gloucestershire Map ref 2B1
SAT NAV GL54 5RU

The Plough Inn
Ford GL54 5RU
t (01386) 584215 f (01386) 584042 e info@theploughinnatford.co.uk
w theploughinnatford.co.uk

B&B PER ROOM PER NIGHT
S £50.00
D £70.00

EVENING MEAL PER PERSON
£10.00 – £18.00

SPECIAL PROMOTIONS
Bargain Breaks of four nights for the price of three available all year EXCEPT for Cheltenham Races and Bank Holidays

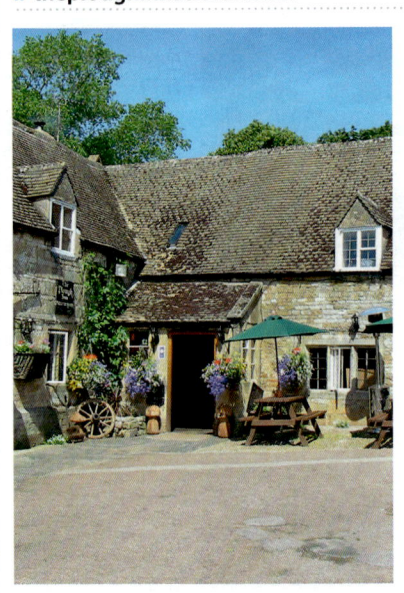

This quaint cobble-stoned building once used a hayloft has now been converted to provide separate, comfortable accommodation. The Plough Inn at Ford makes a perfect base for exploring the Cotswolds.

open All year
bedrooms 1 double, 2 family
bathrooms 3 en suite
payment credit/debit cards, cash, cheques

directions Please contact us for directions

Room
General
Leisure

South West | **Gloucestershire**

FOSSEBRIDGE, Gloucestershire Map ref 2B1

SAT NAV GL54 3JS

The Inn at Fossebridge
Fossebridge, Cheltenham GL54 3JS
t (01285) 720721 e info@fossebridgeinn.co.uk
w fossebridgeinn.co.uk ONLINE MAP GUEST REVIEWS ONLINE BOOKING LAST MINUTE OFFERS

INN ★★★★

B&B PER ROOM PER NIGHT
S £110.00 – £135.00
D £110.00 – £165.00

EVENING MEAL PER PERSON
£30.00 – £50.00

SPECIAL PROMOTIONS
Now partnered with Rob Rees, the Cotswold celebrity chef for cookery breaks. For shortbreak offers see website - www.fossebridgeinn.co.uk

Fully refurbished Georgian Inn, with eight beautiful bedrooms. In four acres of grounds including lake, river, walks. Special Cotswolds short breaks. English-French Cuisine. Near Cirencester.

open All year
bedrooms 4 double, 3 twin, 1 family
bathrooms 8 en suite
payment credit/debit cards, cash, cheques

directions Located between Cirencester and Northleach on A429. Nearest stations Kemble, Moreton-in-Marsh, Cheltenham.

Room
General
Leisure

FRAMPTON-ON-SEVERN, Gloucestershire Map ref 2B1

SAT NAV GL2 7EP

The Bell Inn
The Green, Frampton-on-Severn GL2 7EP
t (01452) 740346 f (01452) 740544 e relax@thebellatframpton.co.uk
w thebellatframpton.co.uk LAST MINUTE OFFERS

INN ★★★★

B&B PER ROOM PER NIGHT
S £40.00 – £50.00
D £60.00 – £90.00

EVENING MEAL PER PERSON
£5.95 – £15.95

SPECIAL PROMOTIONS
Weekend breaks email for latest offer.

Lying at the top of the largest green in England in the centre of the beautiful village of Frampton. The Bell has undergone major refurbishment and transformation and is now a contemporary-designed, welcoming pub and restaurant with gastro food. The rooms are large and well equipped, overlooking the village green.

open All year except Xmas
bedrooms 2 double, 2 suites
bathrooms 4 en suite
payment credit/debit cards, cash, cheques

directions Exit jct 13 M5 onto A38 towards Bristol. Two miles to Frampton-on-Severn.

Room
General
Leisure

or **key to symbols** see page 6

97

South West | **Gloucestershire**

GUITING POWER, Gloucestershire Map ref 2B1   SAT NAV GL54 5TZ

Guiting Guest House
Post Office Lane (formerly Cow Pat Lane), Guiting Power, Gloucestershire GL54 5TZ
t (01451) 850470 e info@guitingguesthouse.com
w guitingguesthouse.com ONLINE MAP GUEST REVIEWS ONLINE BOOKING LAST MINUTE OFFERS

B&B PER ROOM PER NIGHT
S £46.00
D £75.00 – £85.00
EVENING MEAL PER PERSON
£35.00

Converted 16thC Cotswold-stone farmhouse in centre of delightful village. Dining-room with polished elm floor and inglenook fireplace. Some rooms have four-poster beds, all have colour TV and touches of luxury. **directions** See our website for map/directions. **open** All year **bedrooms** 1 single, 5 double, 1 twin **bathrooms** 5 en suite, 2 with private bathroom **payment** credit/debit cards, cash, cheques

GUITING POWER, Gloucestershire Map ref 2B1   SAT NAV GL54 5UX

The Hollow Bottom
Winchcombe Road, Guiting Power GL54 5UX
t (01451) 850392 f (01451) 850945 e hello@hollowbottom.com
w hollowbottom.com ONLINE MAP GUEST REVIEWS ONLINE BOOKING LAST MINUTE OFFERS

B&B PER ROOM PER NIGHT
S £50.00 – £75.00
D £60.00 – £90.00
EVENING MEAL PER PERSON
£9.95 – £19.95

SPECIAL PROMOTIONS
Late room discounts available when booking on line. See website for details.
www.hollowbottom.com

The most beautiful well kept 17th Century stone pub. The Hollow Bottom ensures a warm welcome to all who are kind enough to pass through their doors. With a relaxed atmosphere and emphasis on friendly, first rate service The Hollow Bottom is the perfect place to be. Come, Relax, Enjoy!

open All year
bedrooms 3 double, 2 twin, 1 family
bathrooms 5 en suite, 1 with private bathroom
payment credit/debit cards, cash, cheques

directions M5 jct 11, Cheltenham to Stow A436 turn off, 7 miles from Cheltenham signed Guiting Power. Close proximity to Bourton-on-the-Water and Winchcombe.

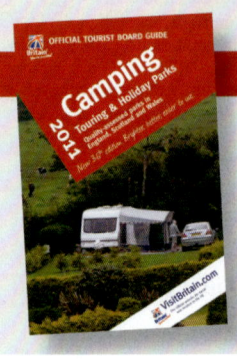

Do you like Camping?
You can also buy a copy of our popular guide 'Camping, Touring & Holiday Parks' including touring parks, camping holidays and holiday parks and villages in Britain 2011.

Now available in good bookshops and online at
visitbritainshop.com
£8.99

98   Official tourist board guide **Bed & Breakfast**

South West | **Gloucestershire**

LECHLADE-ON-THAMES, Gloucestershire Map ref 2B1
SAT NAV GL7 3AY

enjoyEngland.com
★★★★
GUEST ACCOMMODATION

B&B PER ROOM PER NIGHT
S £45.00 – £55.00
D £60.00 – £75.00

Cambrai Lodge
Oak Street, Lechlade-on-Thames GL7 3AY
t (01367) 253173 **e** cambrailodge@btconnect.com
w cambrailodgeguesthouse.co.uk

Friendly, family-run guesthouse, recently modernised and close to River Thames. Ideal base for touring the Cotswolds, working in/visiting Swindon or walking the Thames. Garden and ample off-road parking. **directions** A short distance from the village centre, on the A361 going north (signposted Burford). On the LHS of the road, up a short drive. **open** All year **bedrooms** 3 double, 3 twin **bathrooms** 6 en suite **payment** cash, cheques, euros

Room General Leisure

LECHLADE-ON-THAMES, Gloucestershire Map ref 2B1
SAT NAV GL7 3AB

enjoyEngland.com
★★★
INN

B&B PER ROOM PER NIGHT
S £40.00 – £60.00
D £45.00 – £70.00
EVENING MEAL PER PERSON
£10.00 – £25.00

The New Inn hotel
Market Square, Lechlade GL7 3AB
t (01367) 252296 **f** (01367) 252315 **e** info@newinnhotel.com
w newinnhotel.co.uk

The New Inn Hotel is where 250-year tradition of hospitality blends with 21st century comfort and Cotswold charm. On the banks of the River Thames in the centre of Lechlade. **directions** Please contact us for directions **open** All year except Xmas **bedrooms** 4 single, 10 double, 12 twin, 2 family **bathrooms** 28 en suite **payment** credit/debit cards, cash, cheques, euros

Room General Leisure

MORETON-IN-MARSH, Gloucestershire Map ref 2B1
SAT NAV GL56 9NS

enjoyEngland.com
★★★
FARMHOUSE

B&B PER ROOM PER NIGHT
S £45.00 – £70.00
D £70.00 – £95.00

SPECIAL PROMOTIONS
Discounts available for stays of 3 nights or more. Family room available from £95/night.

Old Farm
Dorn, Moreton in Marsh, Gloucestershire GL56 9NS
t (01608) 650394 **f** (01608) 650394 **e** info@oldfarmdorn.co.uk
w oldfarmdorn.co.uk ONLINE MAP ONLINE BOOKING

'Comfortable beds, friendly hosts and great breakfasts.' A working farm, the house dates back to the 15th century, spacious en-suite bedrooms (including four-poster), guest lounge and large gardens. Local breakfast served with home-produced eggs and Old Spot sausages and bacon. Peaceful, rural location but only one mile from Moreton.

open All year except Xmas
bedrooms 2 double, 1 family
bathrooms 3 en suite
payment credit/debit cards, cash, cheques

directions 1 mile north of Moreton-in-Marsh on A429, turn left at the lay-by for Dorn. Old Farm is 0.25 miles on the left.

Room General Leisure

or **key to symbols** see page 6   99

South West | Gloucestershire

PARKEND, Gloucestershire Map ref 2A1
SAT NAV GL15 4JD

Fountain Inn
Parkend, Lydney, Gloucestershire GL15 4JD
t (01594) 562189 f (01594) 564438 e thefountaininn@aol.com
w thefountaininnandlodge.com

INN

B&B PER ROOM PER NIGHT
S £35.00 – £43.00
D £50.00 – £62.00

EVENING MEAL PER PERSON
£6.80 – £13.30

Situated in the heart of the Royal Forest of Dean, it makes an ideal base for sightseeing, or for exploring some of the many peaceful forest walks nearby. **directions** North, exit M5 at J11, follow signs for Forest, Blakeney, then Parkend. South, exit M48 at J2, follow signs for Forest, Lydney, then Parkend. **open** All year except Xmas **bedrooms** 1 single, 4 double, 1 twin, 2 family **bathrooms** 8 en suite **payment** credit/debit cards, cash, cheques

RUDFORD, Gloucestershire Map ref 2B1
SAT NAV GL2 8DX

The Dark Barn
The Dark Barn Conference & Events Centre, Barbers Bridge, Rudford, Gloucester GL2 8D
t (01452) 790412 f (01452) 358000 e info@barbersbridge.co.uk
w darkbarn.co.uk ONLINE MAP GUEST REVIEWS ONLINE BOOKING LAST MINUTE OFFERS

GUEST ACCOMMODATION

B&B PER ROOM PER NIGHT
S £35.00 – £42.00
D £55.00 – £74.00

EVENING MEAL PER PERSON
£10.00 – £15.00

Four star friendly guest house, all rooms ensuite, only 4 miles from Gloucester city centre. 32 acres of open countryside, free wireless internet, bar, TV lounge, large free park. **directions** M50 jct2, 10 miles south on B4215 towards Gloucester. From Gloucester, take A40 to Ross on Wye, turn right on B4215, 3 miles on right. **open** All year **bedrooms** 16 double, 2 family, 1 suite **bathrooms** 19 en suite, 19 with private bathroom **payment** credit/debit cards, cash, cheques

SLIMBRIDGE, Gloucestershire Map ref 2B1
SAT NAV GL2 7BP

Tudor Arms Lodge and Freehouse
Shepherds Patch, Slimbridge, Gloucester GL2 7BP
t (01453) 890306 f (01453) 890103 e enquiries@thetudorarms.co.uk
w thetudorarms.co.uk ONLINE MAP ONLINE BOOKING

INN

B&B PER ROOM PER NIGHT
S £60.00 – £70.00
D £70.00 – £90.00

EVENING MEAL PER PERSON
£6.50 – £14.00

Real Ales, Real Food, Real Pub with separate Lodge Accommodation refurbished to 4 star quality. Close to Slimbridge WWT. Adjacent to Glos/Sharpness Canal. Ideal for Walking/Cycling. Families welcome. **directions** From M5 Junction 13 or 14 follow the brown duck signs for Slimbridge WWT. **open** All year **bedrooms** 6 double, 5 twin, 1 family **bathrooms** 12 en suite **payment** credit/debit cards, cash, cheques

SOUTHVILLE, Gloucestershire Map ref 2A2
SAT NAV BS3 1DB

The White House Guest Rooms
28-30 Dean Lane, Southville, Bristol BS3 1DB
t (0117) 953 7725 e info@bedandbreakfast_bristol.co.uk
w bedandbreakfast-bristol.co.uk ONLINE BOOKING

GUEST ACCOMMODATION

B&B PER ROOM PER NIGHT
S £35.00 – £40.00
D £50.00

Clean, comfortable guest house five minutes' walk from city centre. Five minute drive to Temple Meads Train Station and 15 minutes to Bristol Airport. Close to harbour and city centre. **directions** Please contact us for directions **open** All year except Xmas and New Year **bedrooms** 1 single, 4 double, 6 twin, 3 family **bathrooms** 13 en suite, 1 with private bathroom **payment** credit/debit cards, cash

South West | **Gloucestershire**

STAUNTON, Gloucestershire Map ref 2A1

SAT NAV GL16 8PD

BED & BREAKFAST ★★★★

B&B PER ROOM PER NIGHT
S £46.00 – £56.00
D £30.00 – £39.00

EVENING MEAL PER PERSON
£14.00 – £19.00

SPECIAL PROMOTIONS
Stay 7 nights for price of 6.
Midweek breaks, minimum
2 nights stay £30-£35pp.
Special offers see website.

Steep Meadow
Staunton, Coleford GL16 8PD
t (01594) 832316 **e** helen@steepmeadow.co.uk
w steepmeadow.co.uk ONLINE MAP GUEST REVIEWS LAST MINUTE OFFERS

Relaxed, friendly atmosphere on Wye Valley smallholding. Ideal walking, sightseeing and cycling. Delicious breakfasts using our OWN eggs, bacon, sausages. Panoramic views from guest lounge. Spacious, comforable, well-equipped bedrooms with ensuite shower rooms. Evening meals by prior arrangement. Many walks from our door. Dog friendly room with own garden.

open All year except Xmas
bedrooms 3 double
bathrooms 3 en suite
payment credit/debit cards, cash

directions A4136 from Monmouth towards Coleford. Right immediately after Staunton 30mph signs. At fork in road (150 yds) right up steep hill; house 1st on left.

BREAKFAST AWARD

Room
General
Leisure

STONEHOUSE, Gloucestershire Map ref 2B1

SAT NAV GL10 2LQ

BED & BREAKFAST ★★

B&B PER ROOM PER NIGHT
S £26.00 – £28.00
D £52.00 – £56.00

Merton Lodge
8 Ebley Road, Stonehouse GL10 2LQ
t (01453) 822018

Former gentleman's residence offering a warm welcome. Non-smoking. Three miles from M5 junction 13, over four roundabouts. Along Ebley Road, under footbridge. **directions** M5 Junction 13. 3 miles from Junction 13. Road B4008. **open** All year **bedrooms** 2 double, 1 suite **bathrooms** 1 en suite, 1 with private bathroom **payment** credit/debit cards, cash, cheques

General

STOW-ON-THE-WOLD, Gloucestershire Map ref 2B1

SAT NAV GL56 0TJ

BED & BREAKFAST ★★★★ **Silver AWARD**

B&B PER ROOM PER NIGHT
D £70.00 – £80.00

Aston House
Broadwell, Near Stow-on-the-Wold, Moreton-in-Marsh GL56 0TJ
t (01451) 830475 **e** fja@astonhouse.net
w astonhouse.net

We welcome guests to our home in quiet village 1.5 miles from Stow-on-the-Wold, central for Cotswolds. Tea-making facilities, bedtime drinks, TV, armchairs, electric blankets. Good breakfast. Pub in walking distance. **directions** A429. Take Right turn 1 mile from Stow-on-the-Wold at Broadwell / Donnington crossroad. Aston House is 1/2 mile, first house on Left **open** Open March to October **bedrooms** 2 double, 1 twin **bathrooms** 2 en suite, 1 with private bathroom **payment** cash, cheques

Room **General**

or key to symbols see page 6

South West | Gloucestershire

STOW-ON-THE-WOLD, Gloucestershire Map ref 2B1
SAT NAV GL54 1AA

Chure House

Sheep Street, Stow-on-the-Wold, Cheltenham GL54 1AA
t (01451) 832 185   e churehouse@googlemail.com
w bedandbreakfast-stowonthewold.co.uk   ONLINE MAP GUEST REVIEWS

B&B PER ROOM PER NIGHT
S £50.00 – £60.00
D £65.00 – £75.00

Quietly located, in the centre of historic Stow-on-the-Wold, this luxury B&B offers rooms furnished to a particulary high standard. Organic/free range produce for breakfast. Sunny, walled garden. **directions** Located between 'The Gallery' (No. 50 Sheep Street) and 'Cream Tea Room' in Sheep Street, on the right-hand side going down Sheep Street. **open** All year **bedrooms** 2 double, 1 family **bathrooms** 3 en suite **payment** credit/debit cards, cash, cheques

Room   General   Leisure

STOW-ON-THE-WOLD, Gloucestershire Map ref 2B1
SAT NAV GL54 1JH

Corsham Field Farmhouse

Bledington Road, Stow-on-the-Wold, Gloucestershire GL54 1JH
t 01451 831750   f 01451 832247   e farmhouse@corshamfield.co.uk
w corshamfield.co.uk   ONLINE MAP LAST MINUTE OFFERS

B&B PER ROOM PER NIGHT
S £40.00 – £45.00
D £50.00 – £65.00

Traditional farmhouse with spectacular views. Peaceful location one mile from Stow. Ideal for Cotswold villages, Stratford, Blenheim and Warwick. Garden. Relaxing lounge. Free WiFi. Excellent pub food five minutes' walk. **directions** A436 from Stow-on-the-Wold for 1 mile, fork right onto B4450 Bledington Road. We are 1st farm on right opposite the Oddington turn. **open** All year except Xmas **bedrooms** 2 double, 2 twin, 4 family **bathrooms** 6 en suite, 2 with private bathroom **payment** cash, cheques, euros

Room   General   Leisure

STROUD, Gloucestershire Map ref 2B1
SAT NAV GL5 5PA

1 Woodchester Lodge

Southfield Road, Woodchester, Stroud GL5 5PA
t (01453) 872586   e anne@woodchesterlodge.co.uk
w woodchesterlodge.co.uk

B&B PER ROOM PER NIGHT
S £40.00 – £45.00
D £60.00 – £65.00

EVENING MEAL PER PERSON
£3.75 – £13.50

SPECIAL PROMOTIONS
Weekly rates on request.

Historic, Victorian timber merchant's property; peaceful village setting near Cotswold Way. Attractive gardens, parking, spacious and comfortable rooms, separate TV lounge/dining room. Meals cooked by qualified chef using our own produce and eggs. Outdoor activities, scenic villages, local attractions, links to main cities: Bristol, Bath, Gloucester, Cheltenham and London.

open All year except Xmas and New Year
bedrooms 2 double, 1 family
bathrooms 1 en suite, 2 with private bathroom
payment credit/debit cards, cash, cheques

directions From Stroud/M5, take A46 towards Bath. Pass the Old Fleece pub. Right into Selsley Road. 2nd left, Southfield Road. 200yds on left-hand side.

Room
General
Leisure

102   Official tourist board guide Bed & Breakfast

South West | Gloucestershire

STROUD, Gloucestershire Map ref 2B1

SAT NAV GL6 7EE

Pretoria Villa

Wells Road, Eastcombe, Stroud GL6 7EE
t (01452) 770435 **f** (01452) 770435 **e** pretoriavilla@btinternet.com
w bedandbreakfast-cotswold.co.uk

B&B PER ROOM PER NIGHT
S £40.00
D £60.00 – £70.00

Enjoy luxurious bed and breakfast in a relaxed family country house, set in peaceful secluded gardens. Spacious bedrooms with many home comforts. Guest lounge with TV. Superb breakfast served at your leisure. An excellent base from which to explore the Cotswolds. Personal service and your comfort guaranteed.

open All year except Xmas
bedrooms 1 double, 2 twin
bathrooms 3 en suite
payment cash, cheques

directions At bottom of village green in Eastcombe take the lane with the red telephone box, at first crossroad very sharp right. 400yds on right.

Room   General   Leisure

TEWKESBURY, Gloucestershire Map ref 2B1

SAT NAV GL20 6DA

Abbots Court Farm

Churchend, Twyning, Tewkesbury GL20 6DA
t (01684) 292515 **f** (01684) 292515 **e** abbotscourt@aol.com

B&B PER ROOM PER NIGHT
S £35.00 – £40.00
D £57.00 – £60.00

Farm of 350 acres situated on the site of a monastic settlement, with private entrance to church, in a small hamlet one mile from M5/M50 junction. Bounded by the river Avon, several coarse and carp lakes available for fishing. Large dining/sitting room, excellent home-cooked food. Pool and table tennis.

open All year except Xmas and New Year
bedrooms 2 double, 1 twin, 1 family
bathrooms 4 en suite
payment cash, cheques, euros

directions Tewkesbury, A38 north, 3 miles, right at Jason Jones Garage, 1st right in Churchend, 20yds right at postbox (Abbots Court Drive), left into Abbots Court.

BREAKFAST AWARD   Room   General   Leisure

or **key to symbols** see page 6

South West | **Gloucestershire/Somerset**

ULEY, Gloucestershire Map ref 2B1

SAT NAV GL11 5SN

INN

B&B PER ROOM PER NIGHT
S £40.00 – £60.00
D £70.00 – £90.00
EVENING MEAL PER PERSON
£4.95 – £13.50

The Old Crown Inn
The Green, Uley, Dursley GL11 5SN
t (01453) 860502 f (01453) 861078 e info@theoldcrownuley.co.uk
w theoldcrownuley.co.uk

Village pub set in the Cotswolds, serving good food and real ales and providing comfortable accommodation. **directions** Please contact us for directions **open** All year except Xmas and New Year **bedrooms** 2 double, 1 twin, 1 suite **bathrooms** 4 en suite **payment** credit/debit cards, cash, cheques

Room General Leisure

BATH, Somerset Map ref 2B2

SAT NAV BA1 2NB

GUEST HOUSE

B&B PER ROOM PER NIGHT
S £45.00 – £85.00
D £70.00 – £105.00

Albany Guest House
24 Crescent Gardens, Upper Bristol Road, Bath BA1 2NB
t (01225) 313339 e stay@albanybath.co.uk
w albanybath.co.uk ONLINE MAP

The Albany offers friendly hospitality in a warm, welcoming atmosphere, with many of our guests returning again and again to enjoy the personal and unpretentious service we offer. **directions** The Albany is ideally placed to enjoy the delights of Bath, close to the Royal Crescent and five minutes level walk from the city centre **open** All year **bedrooms** 2 double, 2 twin, 1 family **bathrooms** 4 en suite, 1 with private bathroom **payment** credit/debit cards, cash cheques

Room General

BATH, Somerset Map ref 2B2

SAT NAV BA2 4HG

GUEST HOUSE

B&B PER ROOM PER NIGHT
S £55.00 – £65.00
D £85.00 – £99.00

Apple Tree Guest House
7 Pulteney Gardens, Bath BA2 4HG
t (01225) 337642 e enquiries@appletreeguesthouse.co.uk
w appletreeguesthouse.co.uk ONLINE MAP GUEST REVIEWS ONLINE BOOKING LAST MINUTE OFFERS

Bath central guest house. Newly renovated, 5 minutes level walk to the city centre attractions. Parking included. Family owned and operated. Spotlessly clean and comfortable. **directions** Please check our website for exact directions, with journey description and mapping details available. **open** All year **bedrooms** 2 single, 3 double, 1 family **bathrooms** 6 en suite **payment** credit/debit cards, cash, cheques

Room General Leisure

BATH, Somerset Map ref 2B2

SAT NAV BA2 3LB

BED & BREAKFAST

B&B PER ROOM PER NIGHT
S £65.00 – £75.00
D £75.00 – £100.00

Beckford House Bed & Breakfast
59 Upper Oldfield Park, Bath BA2 3LB
t (01225) 310005 e info@beckford-house.com
w beckford-house.com GUEST REVIEWS LAST MINUTE OFFERS

A quiet pleasant place to stay with off-street parking; with wi-fi internet access, and open views. Walking distance centre. Excellent fresh wholefood/traditional breakfasts. Single/double/triple en suite accommodation. **directions** Off A36. Turn opposite Skoda Showroom (at Green Park Tavern); then 3rd turning on left. Look for No 59. **open** All year except Xmas and New Year **bedrooms** 2 double **bathrooms** 2 en suite **payment** cash, cheques

Room General Leisure

South West | **Somerset**

BATH, Somerset Map ref 2B2   SAT NAV BA15 2QJ

Church Farm Monkton Farleigh
Monkton Farleigh, Bradford-on-Avon BA15 2QJ
t (01225) 858583 **f** 0871 714 5859 **e** reservations@churchfarmmonktonfarleigh.co.uk
w churchfarmmonktonfarleigh.co.uk ONLINE MAP

B&B PER ROOM PER NIGHT
S £55.00
D £60.00

Converted farmhouse barn with exceptional views in peaceful, idyllic setting. Ten minutes from Bath, ideal base for touring/walking South West England. Families/dogs welcome. **directions** Midway between Bath and Bradford on Avon 1 mile from A363 **open** All year **bedrooms** 2 double, 1 family **bathrooms** 3 en suite **payment** cash, cheques

Room General Leisure

BATH, Somerset Map ref 2B2   SAT NAV BA1 3PU

The Firs
2 Newbridge Hill, Bath BA1 3PU
t (01225) 334575 **e** dawnsandora@gmail.com
w thefirsbath.co.uk ONLINE MAP GUEST REVIEWS

B&B PER ROOM PER NIGHT
S £50.00 – £60.00
D £70.00 – £80.00

Elegant Victorian House renovated to a high standard. Lovely gardens, restaurants nearby, 15 mins walk from centre of Bath with a lovely stroll through Victoria Park and the Royal Crescent. **directions** Please contact us for directions **open** All year **bedrooms** 3 double, 1 family **bathrooms** 3 en suite, 1 with private bathroom **payment** cash, cheques

Room General Leisure

BATH, Somerset Map ref 2B2   SAT NAV BA1 2AP

Griffin Inn
Beauford Square, Bath BA1 2AP
t (01225) 420919 **f** (01225) 789572 **e** bookings@griffinbath.co.uk
w griffinbath.co.uk ONLINE MAP GUEST REVIEWS ONLINE BOOKING LAST MINUTE OFFERS

B&B PER ROOM PER NIGHT
S £59.00 – £79.00
D £99.00 – £129.00

The Griffin Inn boasts four star ensuite accommodation above the traditional bar. The location is central and peaceful by the Theatre Royal and the elegant Queen Square. It is a quaint Georgian Grade II listed inn that was refurbished in 2009. There are 5 double/twin rooms and 2 single rooms.

open All year except Xmas
bedrooms 2 single, 2 double, 3 twin
bathrooms 7 en suite
payment credit/debit cards, cash, cheques

directions Just off the South West corner of Queen Square via Princes Street and to the rear of the Theatre Royal.

Room
General

South West | **Somerset**

BATH, Somerset Map ref 2B2   SAT NAV SN13 8DT

The Hermitage
Bath Road, Box, Corsham SN13 8DT
t (01225) 744187   e hermitagebb@btconnect.com

B&B PER ROOM PER NIGHT
S £37.00 – £45.00
D £60.00 – £70.00

The Hermitage is a charming Georgian style country house, with some parts of it dating back to the 16th Century, set in it's own gardens and grounds. Close to Bath. **directions** Six miles from Bath on A4 to Chippenham, first drive on left by 30mph sign. **open** All year except Xmas and New Year **bedrooms** 4 double, 1 family **bathrooms** 5 en suite **payment** cash, cheques

Room   General   Leisure

BATH, Somerset Map ref 2B2   SAT NAV BA1 2NA

Lamp Post Villa
3 Crescent Gardens, Bath BA1 2NA
t 00441225331221   e lamppostvilla@aol.com
w lamppostvilla.com   ONLINE MAP GUEST REVIEWS ONLINE BOOKING LAST MINUTE OFFERS

B&B PER ROOM PER NIGHT
S £59.00 – £86.00
D £65.00 – £110.00

This beautiful Victorian Villa is ideally situated close to Royal Victoria Park and Royal Crescent. Just 5 mins flat walk into the City centre and attractions, great value! **directions** Bath Spa staion/ bus terminal 12 minutes walk or No.14 bus (to Weston) Nile St. From M4 jct 18 take A46/ A4 Upper Bristol Road. **open** All year **bedrooms** 1 single, 5 double, 1 twin, 2 family **bathrooms** 9 en suite **payment** credit/debit cards, cash, euros

Room   General   Leisure

BATH, Somerset Map ref 2B2   SAT NAV BA2 6XJ

Lindisfarne Guest House
41a Warminster Road, Bathampton, Bath BA2 6XJ
t (01225) 466342 / 07917665001   e lindisfarne-bath@talk21.com
w bath.org/hotel/lindisfarne.htm   LAST MINUTE OFFERS

B&B PER ROOM PER NIGHT
S £50.00 – £60.00
D £75.00 – £85.00

Comfortable en-suite rooms, full English breakfast, friendly hosts. Within walking distance of pubs, restaurants, canal walks. On a regular bus route. Easy drive to university. Private parking. Triple room available. **directions** About 1.5 miles from city centre on A36 to Warminster. Good bus service to Bath. **open** All year except Xmas **bedrooms** 2 double, 1 twin, 1 family **bathrooms** 4 en suite **payment** credit/debit cards, cash, cheques

Room   General   Leisure

BATH, Somerset Map ref 2B2   SAT NAV BA1 2NQ

Marlborough House Guest House
1 Marlborough Lane, Bath BA1 2NQ
t (01225) 318175 f (01225) 466127   e mars@manque.dircon.co.uk
w marlborough-house.net

B&B PER ROOM PER NIGHT
S £75.00 – £110.00
D £85.00 – £140.00

Enchanting Victorian town house in Bath's Georgian centre, exquisitely furnished. Beautiful en suite rooms with four poster or king size beds. Generous and organic breakfast choices. Free parking **directions** M4 take exit 18 to Bath. Head for Bath city centre and follow the road through Queen Square and Monmouth Street to Marlborough Lane. **open** All year except Xmas **bedrooms** 2 double, 2 twin, 2 family **bathrooms** 6 en suite **payment** credit/debit cards, cash, cheques, euros

Room   General   Leisure

Official tourist board guide **Bed & Breakfast**

South West | Somerset

BATH, Somerset Map ref 2B2
SAT NAV BA2 4HJ

Membland Guest House
7 Pulteney Terrace, Pulteney Road, Bath BA2 4HJ
t (01225) 336712 Mobile: 07958 599572 e membland@tiscali.co.uk

B&B PER ROOM PER NIGHT
D £60.00 – £80.00

Warm and friendly accommodation with delicious freshly cooked breakfasts. Great location, only 5 minutes level stroll to the stunning attractions of the city, Thermae Spa, Roman Baths and the magnificent Bath Abbey. Situated below the Kennet & Avon canal with beautiful walks, perfect for exploring the picturesque villages surrounding Bath.

open All year
bedrooms 3 double
bathrooms 3 en suite
payment cash, cheques, euros

directions Membland Guest House is on the corner of Pulteney Terrace and Pulteney Avenue. Under the Railway Bridge of Pulteney Road, opposite the Royal Oak Pub.

Room   General

BATH, Somerset Map ref 2B2
SAT NAV BA2 4HA

Pulteney House
14 Pulteney Road, Bath, Avon BA2 4HA
t (01225) 460991 f (01225) 460991 e pulteney@tinyworld.co.uk
w pulteneyhotel.co.uk ONLINE MAP GUEST REVIEWS ONLINE BOOKING LAST MINUTE OFFERS

B&B PER ROOM PER NIGHT
S £48.00 – £80.00
D £75.00 – £130.00

SPECIAL PROMOTIONS
Reduced rates for stays of 3 nights or more - each booking assessed individually.

Large, elegant, Victorian house in picturesque, south-facing gardens. Large, private car park. 5-10 minutes' walk from city centre. An ideal base for exploring Bath and surrounding areas. All rooms (except one) en suite with hairdryer, TV, tea/coffee facilities and radio/alarm clocks. Free Wi-Fi in most rooms.

open All year
bedrooms 2 single, 7 double, 3 twin, 5 family
bathrooms 16 en suite, 1 with private bathroom
payment credit/debit cards, cash, cheques

directions Hotel situated on A36, which runs through Bath. From M4 follow signs to Bath on A46. Then follow signs to A36, Exeter and Wells.

Room
General

or **key to symbols** see page 6   107

South West | **Somerset**

BATH, Somerset Map ref 2B2   SAT NAV BA1 3PW

enjoyEngland.com
★★★★
GUEST ACCOMMODATION

B&B PER ROOM PER NIGHT
S £40.00 – £50.00
D £60.00 – £75.00

Walton Villa
3 Newbridge Hill, Bath BA1 3PW
t (01225) 482792 f (01225) 313093 e walton.villa@virgin.net
w walton.izest.com ONLINE MAP GUEST REVIEWS

Family-run bed and breakfast, offering pretty en suite/private facilities accommodation. One mile from city centre. Off-street parking and bus service nearby. **directions** Follow A4 towards Bristol - right fork A431 - 100 metres on left. More detailed directions on Web-site **open** All year except Xmas and New Year **bedrooms** 1 single, 2 double, 1 twin **bathrooms** 3 en suite, 1 with private bathroom **payment** credit/debit cards, cash, cheques

Room TV SC General P Leisure

BATH, Somerset Map ref 2B2   SAT NAV BA2 4HG

enjoyEngland.com
★★★
GUEST HOUSE

B&B PER ROOM PER NIGHT
S £40.00 – £45.00
D £55.00 – £70.00

The White Guest House
23 Pulteney Gardens, Bath BA2 4HG
t (01225) 426075 f (01225) 426075 e enquiries@whiteguesthouse.co.uk
w whiteguesthouse.co.uk

Steve and Anna welcome you to their guest house. 7 minute walk to the city centre, Thermae Spa, Train/Coach station, Kennet and Avon canal. Great English or continental breakfast. **directions** From City Centre head across North Parade turn right into Pulteney Rd and 2nd turning on left is Pulteney Gardens. **bedrooms** 1 single, 3 double, 1 twin **bathrooms** 5 en suite **payment** cash, cheques

Room TV SC

BREAN, Somerset Map ref 1D1   SAT NAV TA8 2QT

enjoyEngland.com
★★★★
GUEST ACCOMMODATION

B&B PER ROOM PER NIGHT
S £35.00 – £45.00
D £57.50 – £65.00

Yew Tree House
Hurn Lane, Berrow Nr Brean, Burnham on Sea TA8 2QT
t (01278) 751382 e yewtree@yewtree-house.co.uk
w yewtree-house.co.uk ONLINE MAP GUEST REVIEWS ONLINE BOOKING LAST MINUTE OFFERS

We warmly welcome visitors to our charming old house. We are easy to reach from the motorway and in the perfect location for a short break or holiday. **directions** M5 jct 22. B3140 to Burnham and Berrow. From Berrow follow signs to Brean. 0.5miles after church turn right, we are 300yds on left. **open** All year except Xmas **bedrooms** 2 double, 2 twin, 1 family, 2 suites **bathrooms** 7 en suite **payment** credit/debit cards, cash, cheques

BREAKFAST AWARD

Room TV SC General P Leisure

BURNHAM-ON-SEA, Somerset Map ref 1D1   SAT NAV TA8 1BQ

enjoyEngland.com
★★★
INN

B&B PER ROOM PER NIGHT
S £40.00 – £47.00
D £70.00 – £85.00
EVENING MEAL PER PERSON
£3.50 – £12.50

Royal Clarence Hotel
31 The Esplanade, Burnham-on-Sea TA8 1BQ
t 01278 783138 e graham-townley@supanet.com
w rchotel.co.uk ONLINE MAP GUEST REVIEWS

Established since 1796. Located on the sea front enjoying uninterrupted views over the sea. Bar and Restaurant serving homestyle cooking all day. Sunday Carvery available. 100 metres from High Street. **directions** Please contact us for directions **open** All year **bedrooms** 3 single, 7 double, 3 twin, 2 family **bathrooms** 14 en suite, 1 with private bathroom **payment** credit/debit cards, cash, euros

Room TV SC General P Leisure

108   Official tourist board guide Bed & Breakfast

South West | **Somerset**

CASTLE CARY, Somerset Map ref 2B2
SAT NAV BA7 7PJ

FARMHOUSE
Gold AWARD

B&B PER ROOM PER NIGHT
S £37.50 – £55.00
D £75.00 – £100.00

Clanville Manor B&B
Clanville, Castle Cary BA7 7PJ
t (01963) 350124 **e** info@clanvillemanor.co.uk
w clanvillemanor.co.uk ONLINE MAP GUEST REVIEWS ONLINE BOOKING LAST MINUTE OFFERS

Gold-Award winning Georgian farmhouse. Wonderful locally sourced Aga breakfasts, pool in summer and lots of National Trust properties nearby! Online availability and booking. What more could you want? **directions** 3/4 mile from A371 on B3153, white gate and cattle grid at entrance to drive. Grid ref: ST 6133. **open** All year except Xmas and New Year **bedrooms** 1 single, 2 double, 1 twin **bathrooms** 4 en suite **payment** credit/debit cards, cash, cheques

BREAKFAST AWARD

Room General Leisure

CHARD, Somerset Map ref 1D2
SAT NAV TA20 3AQ

GUEST ACCOMMODATION ★★★★

B&B PER ROOM PER NIGHT
S £70.00
D £95.00

EVENING MEAL PER PERSON
£10.00 – £30.00

SPECIAL PROMOTIONS
Special mid-week breaks available - call for details

Hornsbury Mill
Eleighwater, Chard TA20 3AQ
t (01460) 63317 **f** (01460) 63317 **e** info@hornsburymill.co.uk
w hornsburymill.co.uk ONLINE MAP GUEST REVIEWS

A beautiful 200-year-old working water mill set in four acres of water gardens which provide a tranquil setting. Close to Blackdown Hills and Dorset coast. Cosy en suite rooms and renowned restaurant in the heart of Somerset.

open All year except Xmas and New Year
bedrooms 7 double, 2 twin, 1 suite
bathrooms 10 en suite
payment credit/debit cards, cash, cheques

directions M5 jct 25, take A358 towards Chard (12 miles). Once through village of Donyatt approx 2 miles on A358 on right-hand side.

Room General Leisure

CHEDDAR, Somerset Map ref 1D1
SAT NAV BS27 3RA

GUEST ACCOMMODATION ★★★

B&B PER ROOM PER NIGHT
S £30.00 – £45.00
D £60.00 – £84.00

EVENING MEAL PER PERSON
£18.00 – £25.00

Arundel House
Church Street, Cheddar BS27 3RA
t (01934) 742264 **f** (01934) 741411 **e** enquiries@arundelhousecheddar.co.uk
w arundelhousecheddar.co.uk ONLINE MAP ONLINE BOOKING

Privately owned regency guest house in the heart of Cheddar village, within easy reach of the Gorge. Wells, Glastonbury and Weston-Super-Mare are within 12 miles. Great walking country. **directions** From M5, J22. A38 north, at Cross turn right onto A371. We are on A371 in centre of the village next to the Market Cross. **open** All year except Xmas **bedrooms** 1 single, 2 double, 2 family **bathrooms** 3 en suite **payment** credit/debit cards, cash, cheques

Room General Leisure

or **key to symbols** see page 6

South West | Somerset

CHEDDAR, Somerset Map ref 1D1   SAT NAV BS26 2DP

enjoyEngland.com
BED & BREAKFAST

B&B PER ROOM PER NIGHT
S £25.00 – £30.00
D £50.00 – £70.00

Waterside
Cheddar Road, Cheddar BS26 2DP
t (01934) 743182   e gillianaldridge@hotmail.com
w watersidecheddar.co.uk ONLINE BOOKING

A friendly welcome awaits you. Surrounded by the Mendip hills, ideal for discovering Glastonbury, Wells, Brean, Weston, Wookey Hole, or Cheddar Gorge and show caves. Children and dogs welcome. **directions** Please contact us for directions **open** All year **bedrooms** 1 double, 1 twin, 1 family **bathrooms** 3 en suite **payment** cash, cheques, euros

Room   General   Leisure

CHEDDAR, Somerset Map ref 1D1   SAT NAV BS28 4SN

enjoyEngland.com
BED & BREAKFAST

B&B PER ROOM PER NIGHT
S £35.00 – £40.00
D £30.00 – £64.00
EVENING MEAL PER PERSON
£13.50 – £17.50

Yew Tree Farm
Wells Road, Theale BS28 4SN
t (01934) 712475   f (01934) 712475   e enquiries@yewtreefarmbandb.co.uk
w yewtreefarmbandb.co.uk ONLINE MAP GUEST REVIEWS ONLINE BOOKING LAST MINUTE OFFERS

17th Century farmhouse Nr Cheddar Wells Wookey. Idyllic walks fishing/golf/cycling. Home cooked meals. **directions** From Wells, take B3139 towards Burnham-on-Sea. Drive through Wookey, Henton, Panborough. **open** All year **bedrooms** 1 double, 1 twin, 1 family **bathrooms** 2 en suite, 1 with private bathroom **payment** cash, cheques, euros

Room   General   Leisure

CHEWTON MENDIP, Somerset Map ref 2A2   SAT NAV BA3 4GP

enjoyEngland.com
GUEST ACCOMMODATION

B&B PER ROOM PER NIGHT
S £40.00 – £50.00
D £65.00 – £70.00

Copper Beeches
Lower Street, Chewton Mendip, Wells, Somerset BA3 4GP
t (01761) 241496   e copperbeechesbandb@tiscali.co.uk
w copperbeechesbandb.co.uk

Large house set in landscaped gardens on the edge of Mendip Hills. Village shop and pub a short walk. All rooms ensuite with a great 2 bedroomed family suite. **directions** When you reach Chewton Mendip, come down the hill, turn right at the bottom into Lower Street, we are the 2nd drive on the right. **bedrooms** 1 single, 2 double, 2 twin, 1 family **bathrooms** 6 en suite **payment** credit/debit cards, cash, cheques

Room   General   Leisure

Looking for something else?

You can also buy a copy of our popular guide 'Self Catering' including self-catering holiday homes, approved caravan holiday homes, boat accommodation and holiday cottage agencies in England 2011.

Now available in good bookshops and online at
visitbritainshop.com

£11.99

---

110   Official tourist board guide Bed & Breakfast

South West | Somerset

DUNSTER, Somerset Map ref 1D1
SAT NAV TA24 6SW

Millstream Cottage
2 Mill Lane, Dunster, Exmoor National Park TA24 6SW
t (01643) 821966 **e** stay@millstreamcottagedunster.co.uk
w millstreamcottagedunster.co.uk ONLINE MAP GUEST REVIEWS

B&B PER ROOM PER NIGHT
S £45.00 – £55.00
D £74.00 – £79.00

Dunster is a fascinating medieval village situated in the beautiful Exmoor National Park. Formally the Old Workhouse up until 1843 and now an extremely comfortable, high quality B&B. Full of charm and character it provides luxurious bed and breakfast accommodation with old beams, pine doors, and large fireplaces.

open All year except Xmas and New Year
bedrooms 1 double, 1 twin, 1 family, 1 suite
bathrooms 4 en suite
payment credit/debit cards, cash

directions Millstream Cottage is in the heart of Dunster which lies within the Exmoor National Park.

Room
General
Leisure

EAST BRENT, Somerset Map ref 1D1
SAT NAV TA9 4DA

Burton Row Farmhouse
Burton Row, East Brent TA9 4DA
t (01278) 769252 **f** (01278) 769252 **e** lindaisgrove@btinternet.com
w somersetbandb.co.uk ONLINE MAP GUEST REVIEWS LAST MINUTE OFFERS

B&B PER ROOM PER NIGHT
D £60.00 – £110.00

SPECIAL PROMOTIONS
10% discount on stays of 3 nights or more.

A wisteria clad C17th Somerset longhouse on the Somerset Levels, rural but central to all the delights of Somerset and beyond, beautifully renovated to a high standard. We offer a high quality bed and breakfast experience. Enjoy tea or coffee with homemade cake to refresh you after your journey.

open All year except Xmas and New Year
bedrooms 2 double, 1 suite
bathrooms 3 en suite
payment cash, cheques

directions From M5 Junction 22, at the roundabout A38 north. Next roundabout 1st exit. Traffic lights East Brent turn left. House on the right.

Room
General
Leisure

South West | **Somerset**

EAST HARPTREE, Somerset Map ref 2A2   SAT NAV BS40 6AA

Harptree Court

Whitecross Road, East Harptree, Bristol BS40 6AA
t (01761) 221729   e bandb@harptreecourt.co.uk
w harptreecourt.co.uk   GUEST REVIEWS

B&B PER ROOM PER NIGHT
S £75.00 – £85.00
D £95.00 – £120.00

Harptree Court is a very special family-run B&B in an elegant Georgian setting in amazing gardens. Enjoy a complimentary tea on the lawn or in front of a roaring log-fire. Attention to detail is notable in the bedrooms and guest sitting room, and in the welcome given to guests.

open All year except Xmas
bedrooms 3 double
bathrooms 3 en suite
payment credit/debit cards, cash, cheques

directions From A368 take B3114 for Chewton Mendip. After approx 0.5 miles turn right into drive entrance (straight after crossroad). Turn left at top of drive.

Room
General
Leisure

GLASTONBURY, Somerset Map ref 2A2   SAT NAV BA6 8BZ

Chalice Hill House

Dod Lane, Glastonbury, Somerset BA6 8BZ
t (01458) 830828   e mail@chalicehill.co.uk
w chalicehill.co.uk   ONLINE MAP   GUEST REVIEWS

B&B PER ROOM PER NIGHT
S £75.00
D £100.00 – £120.00

This gracious and elegant Georgian manor house is a luxury en-suite bed and breakfast set in its own grounds in the heart of Glastonbury, the legendary town that is the centre of rural Somerset. Recently refurbished to a high standard it is stylish and comfortable, with welcoming hosts.

open All year except Xmas and New Year
bedrooms 2 double, 1 twin
bathrooms 3 en suite
payment cash, cheques, euros

directions At the top of the High St turn right then second left into Dod Lane. The drive is the second turn on the right.

Room
General

South West | **Somerset**

GLASTONBURY, Somerset Map ref 2A2

SAT NAV BA6 8BG

Little Orchard

Ashwell Lane, Glastonbury BA6 8BG
t (01458) 831620 **e** the.littleorchard@lineone.net
w littleorchardglastonbury.co.uk

B&B PER ROOM PER NIGHT
S £25.00 – £30.00
D £50.00 – £60.00

A warm welcome awaits you at Little Orchard. Our bedrooms are spacious, light and comfortable, all with wash basins. We offer a varied choice of breakfast, traditional English, vegetarian or Continental. The television lounge leads onto the patio and garden where you can take in the views.

open All year
bedrooms 1 single, 1 double, 1 twin, 1 family
payment credit/debit cards, cash, cheques

directions We are situated on the A361 Shepton Mallet road on the slopes of Glastonbury Tor.

GLASTONBURY, Somerset Map ref 2A2

SAT NAV BA6 9SR

Meare Manor

60 St Mary's Road, Meare, Nr Glastonbury BA6 9SR
t (01458) 860449 **f** (01458) 860855 **e** reception@mearemanor.com
w mearemanor.com ONLINE MAP GUEST REVIEWS ONLINE BOOKING LAST MINUTE OFFERS

B&B PER ROOM PER NIGHT
S £60.00 – £105.00
D £80.00 – £150.00
EVENING MEAL PER PERSON
£8.95 – £23.95

4 star Guest House located in the Somerset Levels near historical sites. Comfortable ensuite rooms. Guests with restricted walking ability/children/pets welcome. Good food, special diets and meals by prior arrangement. **directions** At Street take the A39 towards Glastonbury and Wells. At Northload Bridge roundabout Glastonbury) turn left onto the B3151 to Meare. **open** All year except Xmas and New Year **bedrooms** 6 double, 1 twin, 2 family **bathrooms** 9 en suite **payment** credit/debit cards, cash, euros

ILMINSTER, Somerset Map ref 1D2

SAT NAV TA19 0SG

Graden

Graden, Nr Ilminster TA19 0SG
t (01460) 52371 **f** (01460) 52371

B&B PER ROOM PER NIGHT
S £23.00 – £25.00
D £42.00 – £45.00

Everyone welcome, long or short stays. Many local attractions. Nearest beach 20 miles, Taunton 12.5 miles, M5 12 miles, A303 three miles. Television lounge, central heating, fridge and microwave for sole use of guests. **directions** From Southfield's (Ilminster) take Chard A358, go right through village of Donyatt, from Bowling Club on the left take the second left. **open** All year **bedrooms** 2 double, 1 family **payment** cash, cheques

South West | Somerset

LANGPORT, Somerset Map ref 1D1
SAT NAV TA10 0LS

Orchard Barn
Law Lane, Langport TA10 0LS
t (01458) 252310 e ann@orchard-barn.com
w orchard-barn.com ONLINE MAP

B&B PER ROOM PER NIGHT
S £45.00 – £55.00
D £65.00 – £75.00

Comfortable, friendly accommodation in spacious house and gardens, surrounded by the beautiful Somerset Levels. Ideally situated for walking, cycling and many places of interest. Excellent breakfasts, evening meals by arrangement. **directions** Please contact us for directions **open** All year except Xmas and New Year **bedrooms** 2 double, 1 twin **bathrooms** 3 en suite **payment** cash, cheques

Room General Leisure

LOTTISHAM, Somerset Map ref 2A2
SAT NAV BA6 8PF

Lower Farmhouse Bed & Breakfast
Lower Farm, Lottisham, Glastonbury, Somerset BA6 8PF
t (01458) 850206 e dboard51@btinternet.com
w lowerfarmbandb.co.uk

B&B PER ROOM PER NIGHT
S £35.00 – £70.00
D £70.00 – £140.00

A beautiful B&B in the heart of Somerset, a short drive from local attractions such as Glastonbury, Wells and Bath. A family run, friendly newly converted barn, with ensuite facilities. **directions** Please contact us for directions **open** All year except Xmas and New Year **bedrooms** 1 family **bathrooms** 1 en suite **payment** cash, cheques

Room General P

MARTOCK, Somerset Map ref 2A3
SAT NAV TA12 6JQ

The White Hart
East Street, Martock TA12 6JQ
t (01935) 822005 f (01935) 822056 e enquiries@whiteharthotelmartock.co.uk
w whiteharthotelmartock.co.uk ONLINE MAP ONLINE BOOKING

B&B PER ROOM PER NIGHT
S £48.00 – £65.00
D £65.00 – £88.00
EVENING MEAL PER PERSON
£10.00 – £50.00

Pleasant Hamstone, Grade II Listed coaching inn. Centre of Martock seven miles from Yeovil and two miles off the A303. Top-class, fresh food served. Real ales, fine wines. **directions** Please contact us for directions **open** All year except Xmas and New Year **bedrooms** 3 double, 4 twin, 3 family **bathrooms** 6 en suite, 4 with private bathroom **payment** credit/debit cards, cash, cheques

Room General

PORLOCK, Somerset Map ref 1D1
SAT NAV TA24 8PY

Rose Bank Guest House
High Street, Porlock TA24 8PY
t (01643) 862728 f (01643) 862728 e info@rosebankguesthouse.co.uk
w rosebankguesthouse.co.uk

B&B PER ROOM PER NIGHT
S £25.00 – £35.00
D £50.00 – £65.00
EVENING MEAL PER PERSON
£8.00 – £15.00

Restored Victorian house in village high street. Private parking. All rooms en suite, luxury showers. TV, radio, CD and tea-making facilities. Free Wi-Fi. Sea views. Dog friendly. Welcoming hosts. **directions** From Minehead we are at west end of the village on left, elevated from street. From Lynmouth we are on the right after Ship Inn **open** All year **bedrooms** 1 single, 2 double, 2 twin, 1 family **bathrooms** 6 en suite **payment** credit/debit cards, cash, cheques

Room General Leisure

South West | Somerset

SOUTH PETHERTON, Somerset Map ref 1D2
SAT NAV TA13 5DB

enjoyEngland.com ★★★★ GUEST ACCOMMODATION

B&B PER ROOM PER NIGHT
S £65.00
D £90.00

Rock House B&B
5, Palmer Street, South Petherton, Somerset TA13 5DB
t (01460) 240324 **e** enquiries@unwindarockhouse.co.uk
w unwindarockhouse.co.uk ONLINE MAP

Rock House, an unexpected discovery in the heart of South Petherton; an unspoilt Somerset village - a place to unwind. Garden for guests sole use, secure parking. National Trust nearby.
directions See website for accurate directions **open** All year **bedrooms** 2 suites **bathrooms** 2 en suite **payment** credit/debit cards, cash, cheques

Room General

STOGUMBER, Somerset Map ref 1D1
SAT NAV TA4 3SZ

enjoyEngland.com ★★★★ GUEST HOUSE

B&B PER ROOM PER NIGHT
S £35.00 – £50.00
D £70.00 – £80.00

EVENING MEAL PER PERSON
£18.00 – £24.00

Wick House
2 Brook Street, Stogumber, Taunton, Somerset TA4 3SZ
t (01984) 656422 **e** sheila@wickhouse.co.uk
w wickhouse.co.uk ONLINE MAP

Within the picturesque village of Stogumber. Between the Quantock and Brendon Hills of Exmoor National Park. Offering a friendly, high standard of accommodation. Tranquil, perfect for escaping modern world stresses. **directions** From Taunton, take A358 towards Minehead. After approx 11 miles, turn left to Stogumber. After 2 miles turn left at crossroads. Wickhouse 20yds on left. **open** All year **bedrooms** 4 double, 4 twin **bathrooms** 8 en suite **payment** credit/debit cards, cash, cheques

BREAKFAST AWARD Room General Leisure

STOKE ST GREGORY, Somerset Map ref 1D1
SAT NAV TA3 6EW

enjoyEngland.com ★★★ INN

B&B PER ROOM PER NIGHT
S £35.00 – £55.00
D £55.00 – £85.00

EVENING MEAL PER PERSON
£6.50 – £19.95

Rose & Crown
Woodhill, Stoke St Gregory, Taunton TA3 6EW
t (01823) 490296 **e** info@browningpubs.com
w browningpubs.com GUEST REVIEWS ONLINE BOOKING LAST MINUTE OFFERS

Successful, family run business for over 30 years. Take enormous pride in our home cooked food and our dedication to the business. The rooms are all ensuite and recently refurbished. **directions** Please contact us for directions **open** All year **bedrooms** 3 double, 1 family **bathrooms** 3 en suite **payment** credit/debit cards, cash, cheques

WALKERS CYCLISTS FAMILIES Room General Leisure

WELLINGTON, Somerset Map ref 1D1
SAT NAV TA21 0JJ

enjoyEngland.com ★★★★ BED & BREAKFAST

B&B PER ROOM PER NIGHT
S £45.00
D £60.00

Greenham Hall
Greenham, Wellington TA21 0JJ
t (01823) 672603 **e** greenhamhall@btopenworld.com
w greenhamhall.co.uk ONLINE MAP GUEST REVIEWS LAST MINUTE OFFERS

A warm friendly Victorian house complete with a tower set in an idyllic garden. Lovely local walks and good pub/restaurant nearby.
directions Please contact us for directions **bedrooms** 1 double, 1 twin, 1 family **bathrooms** 2 en suite, 1 with private bathroom **payment** credit/debit cards, cash, cheques, euros

Room General Leisure

For key to symbols see page 6

South West | Somerset

WELLINGTON, Somerset Map ref 1D1
SAT NAV TA21 8AR

Mantle B&B
34 Mantle Street, Wellington TA21 8AR
t (01823) 668514   e dalsod@aol.com
w mantlecottage.com   ONLINE MAP

B&B PER ROOM PER NIGHT
S £30.00
D £50.00

Friendly and comfortable cottage bed and breakfast in the attractive town of Wellington on the Somerset/Devon border. **directions** Situated in Mantle Street, a continuation of the High Street - take Junction 26 from M5. Full details on website and map **open** All year except Xmas and New Year **bedrooms** 2 double **bathrooms** 2 en suite **payment** cash, cheques

BREAKFAST AWARD

Room · General · Leisure

WELLS, Somerset Map ref 2A2
SAT NAV BA5 1TH

26 Glastonbury Road
Wells BA5 1TH
t (01749) 675620 or 07759 348342

B&B PER ROOM PER NIGHT
S £30.00 – £45.00
D £50.00 – £65.00

A warm welcome in a cosy home, with two twin en-suite rooms. Secure off-street parking. Full English breakfast. Vegetarians catered for. Fifteen minute flat walk to city centre and cathedral. **directions** No. 26 is found on the A39 south of the city centre. Entrance to the property is via the police station entrance. **open** Closed December 20th–January 2nd **bedrooms** 2 twin **bathrooms** 2 en suite **payment** cash, cheques

Room · General · Leisure

WELLS, Somerset Map ref 2A2
SAT NAV BA5 2UB

Canon Grange
Cathedral Green, Wells BA5 2UB
t (01749) 671800   e canongrange@email.com
w canongrange.co.uk   ONLINE MAP   GUEST REVIEWS   ONLINE BOOKING

B&B PER ROOM PER NIGHT
S £45.00 – £81.00
D £55.00 – £81.00

Enjoy a restful stay in our beautiful bed and breakfast Wells Somerset. Situated on the Cathedral Green and facing the internationally acclaimed medieval statuary of Wells Cathedral Somerset. **directions** We park free alongside the Cathedral Green, beside us. Access via St. Andrew st. which is off Bath road or The East Liberty **open** All year **bedrooms** 1 single, 2 double, 2 twin, 2 family **bathrooms** 5 en suite, 2 with private bathroom **payment** credit/debit cards, cash, cheques

Room · General · Leisure

WELLS, Somerset Map ref 2A2
SAT NAV BA5 1US

Islington Farm
next to The Bishop's Palace, Silver Street, Wells BA5 1US
t (01749) 673445   e islingtonfarm2004@yahoo.co.uk
w islingtonfarmatwells.co.uk

B&B PER ROOM PER NIGHT
S £50.00 – £65.00
D £65.00 – £70.00

Uniquely situated adjacent to the Bishop's Palace, a 300-year-old farmhouse surrounded by fields and parkland. Tranquil setting just a three-minute walk from the city centre. Private parking. **directions** At roundabout on A371 take 3rd exit. Right by Sherston Hotel. Right opposite Full Moon Inn. Enter Silver Street. 200yds on right with white gates. **open** All year except Xmas and New Year **bedrooms** 1 double, 1 twin **bathrooms** 2 en suite **payment** credit/debit cards, cash, cheques

Room · General · Leisure

116   Official tourist board guide Bed & Breakfast

South West | **Somerset**

WESTON-SUPER-MARE, Somerset Map ref 1D1
SAT NAV BS24 7NA

FARMHOUSE

B&B PER ROOM PER NIGHT
S £40.00 – £80.00
D £60.00 – £100.00

Locking Head Farm
Locking Head Drove, Locking, Weston-super-Mare BS24 7NA
t (01934) 820511 **e** lockingheadfarm@btinternet.com
w lockingheadfarm.co.uk ONLINE MAP

A perfect retreat for couples and families seeking a tranquil and peaceful setting minutes from the M5 and town centre. Large spacious period rooms in 18th century farmhouse. **directions** A370 take exit on roundabout to West Wick. Go through small chicane and take first right along Locking Head Drove, B&B at end. **open** All year except Xmas and New Year **bedrooms** 2 double, 1 family **bathrooms** 2 en suite, 1 with private bathroom **payment** cash, cheques

Room   General   Leisure

WESTON-SUPER-MARE, Somerset Map ref 1D1
SAT NAV BS23 2SH

GUEST HOUSE

B&B PER ROOM PER NIGHT
S £49.00 – £60.00
D £66.00 – £72.00

SPECIAL PROMOTIONS
(3-4-2) Book 3 nights and only pay for 2 low season. Short Breaks welcome. Please telephone for details.

Milton Lodge Guest House
15 Milton Road, Weston-super-Mare, Somerset BS23 2SH
t 01934 623161 **f** (01934) 623210 **e** info@milton-lodge.co.uk
w milton-lodge.co.uk ONLINE MAP GUEST REVIEWS ONLINE BOOKING LAST MINUTE OFFERS

Milton Lodge Guest House is a charming Victorian villa, fully and beautifully furnished throughout, conveniently located just a short level stroll to the town centre and seafront. No smoking, No pets No children under 12 years old. So peace and quiet is our aim.

open All year
bedrooms 2 double, 3 twin, 1 family
bathrooms 6 en suite, 2 with private bathroom
payment credit/debit cards, cash, cheques

directions M5 J21 to A370. L(B3440)Town. 2 miles roundabout, Turn R, 300 yards turn L at lights. Milton Rd. 1 mile, lights. MLGH on R.

Room   General 12   Leisure

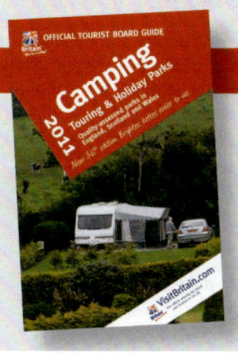

Do you like Camping?

You can also buy a copy of our popular guide 'Camping, Touring & Holiday Parks' including touring parks, camping holidays and holiday parks and villages in Britain 2011.

Now available in good bookshops and online at
visitbritainshop.com

£8.99

South West | **Wiltshire**

ALDERTON, Wiltshire Map ref 2B2

SAT NAV SN14 6NL

Arland House

The Street, Alderton, Chippenham, Wiltshire SN14 6NL
t (01666) 840439 **e** arlandhouse@hotmail.co.uk
w arlandhouse.co.uk

B&B PER ROOM PER NIGHT
S £45.00
D £70.00

Delightful rooms in peaceful setting overlooking duckpond, the house in Cotswold conservation village, is 30mins Bath Cirencester Bristol. Castle Combe, Westonbirt Arboretum 5mins. Malmesbury 7 miles. Walking cyclng riding golfing motor racing nearby. Large area offroad parking, bicycle/drying facilities. Lounge has oak beams open fireplace. Warm welcome guaranteed.

open All year except Xmas and New Year
bedrooms 2 double
bathrooms 2 en suite
payment cash, cheques

directions M4 junction 17, exit north A429, left B4040, Alderton 7 miles. M4 junction 18, exit north A46, right B4040, Alderton 6 miles.

Room   General   Leisure

AMESBURY, Wiltshire Map ref 2B2

SAT NAV SP4 7HH

Anchorage Bed and Breakfast

21 Salisbury Road, Amesbury, Salisbury, SP4 7HH SP4 7HH
t (01980) 555029 **e** sheryll@hotmail.co.uk
w theanchorageamesbury.co.uk GUEST REVIEWS

B&B PER ROOM PER NIGHT
S £50.00 – £55.00
D £70.00 – £90.00

SPECIAL PROMOTIONS
Family or happy to share. Book 1 Double and 1 Twin with private bathroom for £120 inclusive Full English breakfast

A Traditional Bed and Breakfast with quality accommodation awaits you. Friendly home from home atmosphere. Guests have use of a sitting room Breakfast with finest ingredients, cooked to order at a time to suit. Local knowledge of walks to Stonehenge and surrounding area.

open All year
bedrooms 2 double, 1 twin
bathrooms 1 en suite, 1 with private bathroom
payment cash, cheques

directions From Countess roundabout on A303 take A345 towards Salisbury, past bus station and Co-op on your right. We are opposite Wiltshire Fire Station

Room   General   Leisure

118   Official tourist board guide Bed & Breakfa

South West | Wiltshire

BRADFORD-ON-AVON, Wiltshire Map ref 2B2
SAT NAV BA15 2RD

Elbury House Bed & Breakfast
Leigh Road, Bradford-on-Avon BA15 2RD
t (01225) 863336   **e** joy@elburyhouse.co.uk
w elburyhouse.co.uk   GUEST REVIEWS

B&B PER ROOM PER NIGHT
D £90.00

Elbury House is set in six acres of gardens and paddocks offering spacious double rooms, with outstanding views. Our aim is to make your stay a relaxing and pleasurable experience. **directions** Please contact us for directions **open** All year **bedrooms** 1 double, 1 twin **bathrooms** 1 en suite, 1 with private bathroom **payment** cash, cheques

Room General Leisure

BROAD CHALKE, Wiltshire Map ref 2B3
SAT NAV SP5 5LU

Lodge Farmhouse Bed & Breakfast
Lodge Farmhouse, Broad Chalke, Salisbury SP5 5LU
t (01725) 519242   **f** (01725) 519597   **e** mj.roe@virgin.net
w lodge-farmhouse.co.uk   ONLINE MAP GUEST REVIEWS ONLINE BOOKING LAST MINUTE OFFERS

B&B PER ROOM PER NIGHT
S £30.00 – £35.00
D £60.00 – £70.00

SPECIAL PROMOTIONS
For bookings of 3 nights, or more, discount of £5 per person per night.

Peaceful brick-and-flint farmhouse with Wiltshire's most stunning views overlooking 1,000 square miles of Southern England. Comfortable and welcoming, the perfect tour base for Wessex. Lying on the Ox Drove 'green lane', a paradise for walkers. For nature reserves and archaeological sites, plus our Quirky Tours service, see our website.

open All year except Xmas and New Year
bedrooms 2 double, 1 twin
bathrooms 3 en suite
payment credit/debit cards, cash, cheques

directions A354 from Salisbury (8mls) or Blandford (14mls). Turn to Broad Chalke at crossroads on only stretch of dual carriageway on the A354. One mile signposted.

Room General 12 Leisure

CHOLDERTON, Wiltshire Map ref 2B2
SAT NAV SP4 0EW

Cholderton Stonehenge Youth Hostel
Cholderton Charlie's Farm, Amesbury Road, Cholderton, Wiltshire SP4 0EW
t (01980) 629438   **f** (01980) 629594   **e** choldertonstonehenge@yha.org.uk
w choldertoncharliesfarm.com

B&B PER ROOM PER NIGHT
S £19.95 – £22.95
BED ONLY PER NIGHT
£22.95

Situated on a Rare Breeds Farm just outside the small village Cholderton. Join us in tranquil surroundings with animals to pet, feed and plenty of space. **directions** From London, take the A303 and follow the brown signs for Rare Breeds Farm. From Salisbury, A338 and follow brown signs for Rare Breeds Farm. **open** All year except Xmas and New Year **bedrooms** 2 twin **bathrooms** 6 en suite **payment** credit/debit cards, cash

Room General

key to symbols see page 6   119

South West | **Wiltshire**

CHOLDERTON, Wiltshire Map ref 2B2   SAT NAV SP4 0EG

Parkhouse Motel
Cholderton, Salisbury SP4 0EG
t (01980) 629256 f (01980) 629256 e info@parkhousemotel.com

B&B PER ROOM PER NIGHT
S £56.00 – £60.00
D £70.00 – £72.00
EVENING MEAL PER PERSON
£8.95 – £10.95

Attractive, family-run, 17thC former coaching inn, five miles east of Stonehenge, ten miles north of Salisbury and seven miles west of Andover. **directions** Please contact us for directions **open** All year **bedrooms** 4 single, 14 double, 9 twin, 3 family **bathrooms** 27 en suite **payment** credit/debit cards, cash, cheques, euros

Room · General · Leisure

COLLINGBOURNE KINGSTON, Wiltshire Map ref 2B2   SAT NAV SN8 3SD

Manor Farm B&B
Collingbourne Kingston, Nr Marlborough SN8 3SD
t (01264) 850859 f (01264) 850859 e stay@manorfm.com
w **manorfm.com** ONLINE MAP GUEST REVIEWS LAST MINUTE OFFERS

B&B PER ROOM PER NIGHT
S £42.00 – £49.00
D £65.00 – £74.00

SPECIAL PROMOTIONS
Discounted rates for stays of three or more nights.

A warm welcome awaits you at our attractive, Grade II Listed, period village farmhouse on a working family farm. Enjoy the comfortable and spacious rooms (all en suite/private) and a sumptuous traditional, vegetarian or special-diet breakfast. We are surrounded by beautiful countryside with superb walking and cycling from the farm.

open All year
bedrooms 1 double, 1 twin, 1 family
bathrooms 2 en suite, 1 with private bathroom
payment credit/debit cards, cash, cheques, euros

directions Opposite the church in the centre of the small village of Collingbourne Kingston, nine miles south of Marlborough.

Room · General · Leisure

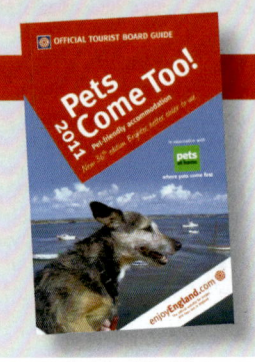

Where is my pet welcome?

Some properties welcome well-behaved pets. Look for the 🛖 in the accommodation listings.

You can also buy a copy of our popular guide 'Pets Come Too!' Now available in good bookshops and online at **visitbritainshop.com**

£9.99

South West | **Wiltshire**

CRICKLADE, Wiltshire Map ref 2B1

SAT NAV SN6 6DD

The Red Lion

74 High Street, Cricklade SN6 6DD
t (01793) 750776 e info@theredlioncricklade.co.uk
w **theredlioncricklade.co.uk** ONLINE MAP GUEST REVIEWS

B&B PER ROOM PER NIGHT
S £75.00
D £85.00

EVENING MEAL PER PERSON
£7.95 – £20.00

SPECIAL PROMOTIONS
Dinner, Bed and Breakfast at £85.00 for single occupancy and £105.00 for double occupancy.

Situated on the Thames path, The Red Lion Inn dates back to the 1600s. Roaring log fires, 9 traditional ales and 40 bottled beers combine with a contemporary restaurant serving homemade and seasonal food, a traditional bar area serving pub classics, a garden and 5 recently built ensuite bedrooms.

open All year
bedrooms 3 double, 2 twin
bathrooms 5 en suite
payment credit/debit cards, cash, cheques

directions Located just off the A419 between Swindon and Cirencester, which is minutes from junction 15 of the M4

Room
General
Leisure

DEVIZES, Wiltshire Map ref 2B2

SAT NAV SN10 1PH

Gables

Bath Road, Devizes, Wiltshire SN10 1PH
t (01380) 723086 e enquiries@thegablesdevizes.co.uk
w **thegablesdevizes.co.uk** ONLINE MAP GUEST REVIEWS

B&B PER ROOM PER NIGHT
S £30.00 – £40.00
D £60.00 – £75.00

Situated at the top of the Caen Hill Flight of locks, we offer a warm welcome and home from home accommodation for our guests.
directions The Gables is situated at the top of the Caen Hill Flight of Locks on the corner of Beauclerc Street on the A361. **open** All year except Xmas and New Year **bedrooms** 1 single, 1 twin, 1 family **bathrooms** 3 en suite **payment** cash, cheques

Room   General

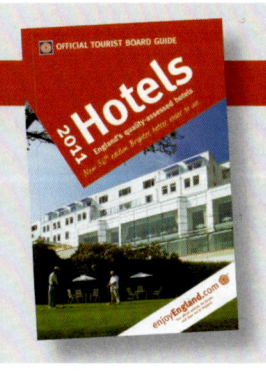

Looking for something else?

You can also buy a copy of our popular guide 'Hotels' including country house and town house hotels, metro and budget hotels, serviced apartments, restaurants with rooms and Spas in England 2011.

Now available in good bookshops and online at
visitbritainshop.com

£10.99

key to symbols see page 6   121

South West | **Wiltshire**

DEVIZES, Wiltshire Map ref 2B2 — SAT NAV SN10 2DS

Rosemundy Cottage

London Road (A361), Devizes, Wiltshire SN10 2DS
t +44 (0)1380 727122 f +44 (0)1380 720495 e info@rosemundycottage.co.uk
w rosemundycottage.co.uk ONLINE MAP GUEST REVIEWS ONLINE BOOKING LAST MINUTE OFFERS

B&B PER ROOM PER NIGHT
S £39.00 – £45.00
D £65.00 – £75.00

SPECIAL PROMOTIONS
Single is Double or twin en-suite at single occupancy rate. Discount for 4 or more consecutive nights.

Canal-side cottage, short walk to market-place. Fully equipped en-suite bedrooms, including four poster and a ground floor room. Sitting room with maps/guides provided. Guest office, free Wi-Fi. Garden with barbecue and heated pool in summer. Wiltshire Breakfast, Green Tourism Gold, Wiltshire Wildlife, Five-star Food Hygiene and Fairtrade Awards. Off-road parking.

open All year
bedrooms 2 double, 1 twin, 1 family
bathrooms 4 en suite
payment credit/debit cards, cash, cheques

directions A361 just north of Devizes centre, towards Avebury. Right just past County Police HQ. On Wessex Ridgeway and bridge 137 on canal routes.

DINTON, Wiltshire Map ref 2B3 — SAT NAV SP3 5ET

Marshwood Farm B&B

Dinton, Salisbury SP3 5ET
t (01722) 716334 e marshwood1@btconnect.com
w marshwoodfarm.co.uk

B&B PER ROOM PER NIGHT
S £45.00 – £60.00
D £60.00 – £70.00

SPECIAL PROMOTIONS
Discount for stays of 2 consecutive nights or more.

Come and enjoy the peace and tranquility of the Wiltshire countryside in one of our spacious rooms. We look forward to welcoming you in our farmhouse dating from 17thC. Within easy reach to explore Stonehenge, Salisbury, Bath, Longleat, English Heritage and National Trust Properties. Walkers and cyclists welcome.

open All year
bedrooms 1 twin, 1 family
bathrooms 2 en suite
payment credit/debit cards, cash, cheques, euros

directions At A303/A36 intersection turn into Wylye, follow the Dinton signs. Marshwood Farm is approx 4 miles.

South West | Wiltshire

HEYTESBURY, Wiltshire Map ref 2B2

SAT NAV BA12 0ED

BED & BREAKFAST ★★★★

B&B PER ROOM PER NIGHT
S £40.00 – £60.00
D £60.00 – £75.00

The Resting Post
67 High Street, Heytesbury, Warminster BA12 0ED
t (01985) 840204 e enquiries@therestingpost.co.uk
w **therestingpost.co.uk** ONLINE MAP

Grade II Listed period house offering friendly, comfortable, en suite accommodation in the centre of a delightful village. There are two pubs in the village serving evening meals. **directions** Just off the A36, 4 miles from Longleat and Warminster. Within easy reach of Bath, Salisbury and Stonehenge **open** All year **bedrooms** 2 double, 1 twin **bathrooms** 3 en suite **payment** cash, cheques

Room General Leisure

MANNINGFORD ABBOTS, Wiltshire Map ref 2B2

SAT NAV SN9 6HZ

FARMHOUSE ★★★

B&B PER ROOM PER NIGHT
S £30.00 – £38.00
D £48.00 – £70.00
EVENING MEAL PER PERSON
£15.00 – £17.00

Huntly's Farmhouse
Manningford Abbots, Pewsey SN9 6HZ
t (01672) 563663 f (01672) 563663 e gimspike@esend.co.uk

Peaceful thatched 17th century farmhouse including horse-stabling/grazing. Good walking country. Heated outdoor swimming pool. Free range and organic food. Twin is also a family room when combined with the single. **directions** Turn off A345 SW of Pewsey signed Manningford Abbotts. Huntlys is 0.5 mile on RHS just past turn to Sharcott. Opposite post box in wall. **open** All year **bedrooms** 1 double, 1 twin **bathrooms** 1 en suite, 1 with private bathroom **payment** cash, cheques

Room General Leisure

MARKET LAVINGTON, Wiltshire Map ref 2B2

SAT NAV SN10 4AG

INN ★★★

B&B PER ROOM PER NIGHT
S £30.00 – £50.00
D £60.00 – £75.00
EVENING MEAL PER PERSON
£6.50 – £20.00

Green Dragon
26-28 High Street, Market Lavington, Devizes, Wiltshire SN10 4AG
t (01380) 813235 f (01380) 813235 e greendragonlavington@tiscali.co.uk
w **greendragonlavington.co.uk** ONLINE MAP GUEST REVIEWS ONLINE BOOKING LAST MINUTE OFFERS

Family-run public house, situated in the heart of the village; comfortable rooms; good home-cooked food. Ideal for walkers and cyclists. Close to Salisbury plain. **directions** Situated in the centre of Market Lavington close to the market place. Approximately 7 miles from Devizes, and halfway between Stonehenge and Avebury **open** All year **bedrooms** 1 single, 1 double, 1 twin **bathrooms** 1 en suite **payment** credit/debit cards, cash, cheques

Room General Leisure

MARLBOROUGH, Wiltshire Map ref 2B2

SAT NAV SN8 3JP

BED & BREAKFAST ★★★★ **Silver AWARD**

B&B PER ROOM PER NIGHT
S £55.00
D £80.00
EVENING MEAL PER PERSON
£20.00 – £25.00

The White House
Little Bedwyn, Marlborough, Wiltshire SN8 3JP
t (01672) 870321 e whitehousebandb@btinternet.com
w **the-white-house-b-and-b.co.uk** ONLINE MAP GUEST REVIEWS

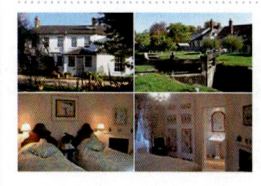

A warm welcome, two luxuriously appointed bedrooms, en-suite. Wholesome, full English breakfasts in delightful rural surroundings on towpath of the Kennet & Avon Canal. Evening meals by prior arrangement only. **directions** 8 miles from Marlborough on A4, after exiting Froxfield turn right. Follow signs to Little Bedwyn, on arrival right towards canal and railway. **open** All year except Xmas and New Year **bedrooms** 1 double, 1 twin **bathrooms** 2 en suite **payment** credit/debit cards, cash, cheques, euros

Room General Leisure

South West | **Wiltshire**

MARLBOROUGH, Wiltshire Map ref 2B2

SAT NAV SN8 3BY

Mayfield
West Grafton, Marlborough SN8 3BY
t (01672) 810339 f (01672) 811158 e countess.an@virgin.net
w **mayfieldbandb.com** ONLINE MAP

B&B PER ROOM PER NIGHT
S £50.00 – £60.00
D £80.00 – £90.00

EVENING MEAL PER PERSON
£20.00 – £25.00

Dating from 15th C and oozing with history, Mayfield is a charming thatched house with swimming-pool and tennis court standing in its own large grounds - a haven of peace and tranquillity. Beautifully decorated with antiques and fine furnishings. Televisions, wireless internet games etc. Breakfast taken in conservatory or dining-room.

open All year except Xmas
bedrooms 1 double, 1 twin
bathrooms 2 en suite
payment cash, cheques, euros

directions From Burbage roundabout take the A338 (Hungerford) for 1 mile. Turn right by telephone box to West Grafton. Mayfield (white sign) is 300yds on right.

Room General Leisure

MONKTON FARLEIGH, Wiltshire Map ref 2B2

SAT NAV BA15 2QH

The Kings Arms
42 Monkton Farleigh, Monkton Farleigh BA15 2QH
t (01225) 858705 e enquiries@kingsarms-bath.co.uk
w **kingsarms-bath.co.uk** ONLINE MAP GUEST REVIEWS LAST MINUTE OFFERS

B&B PER ROOM PER NIGHT
S £75.00 – £90.00
D £90.00 – £160.00

EVENING MEAL PER PERSON
£15.00 – £35.00

Individually styled boutique rooms above a stunning 17th century country pub. Situated in the picturesque village of Monkton Farleigh just 5 miles from Bath. Friendly service, local seasonal food **directions** Junction 18 M4 towards Bath. Just off the A36 Bath to Bradford on Avon road follow signs to Monkton Farleigh Bath Spa Train Station 5m **open** All year **bedrooms** 3 double **bathrooms** 3 en suite, 3 with private bathroom **payment** credit/debit cards, cash

Room General Leisure

ROWDE, Wiltshire Map ref 2B2

SAT NAV SN10 2QB

Vine Cottage Bed & Breakfast
26 Bunnies Lane, Rowde, Devizes, Wiltshire SN10 2QB
t (01380) 728390 e vinecottagebb@btinternet.com
w **vinecottagebb.co.uk** ONLINE MAP GUEST REVIEWS ONLINE BOOKING LAST MINUTE OFFERS

B&B PER ROOM PER NIGHT
S £45.00 – £55.00
D £65.00 – £85.00

Comfortable, quiet accommodation in central Wiltshire. Sauna, Wi-included. 2 pubs in 5 minutes walk serve evening meals. Devizes 2 miles. Walkers, cyclists welcome. Room available for family of 3. **directions** 13 miles south of the M4 junction 17 via Chippenham towards Devizes on A342 and 2 miles north of Devizes on the A342. **open** All year **bedrooms** 2 double, 1 twin **bathrooms** 3 en suite **payment** credit/debit cards, cash, cheques

Room General Leisure

South West | Wiltshire

SALISBURY, Wiltshire Map ref 2B3

SAT NAV SP1 2JA

Alabare House

15 Tollgate Road, Salisbury SP1 2JA
t 07802 631968 **f** (01722) 501586 **e** info@alabare.org
w alabare.org ONLINE MAP ONLINE BOOKING

enjoyEngland.com
GUEST HOUSE ★★★

B&B PER ROOM PER NIGHT
S £40.00 – £55.00
D £60.00 – £80.00

SPECIAL PROMOTIONS
Special rates for extended stays of 3 weeks or more out of season.

This is a small oasis in the heart of Salisbury with ample off-road parking. A family-run B&B, the venue is a good choice for a holiday break. There are many local places of interest, and Salisbury offers a wide variety of restaurants and shops. Online booking available.

open All year except Xmas
bedrooms 2 single, 2 double, 6 twin, 1 family
bathrooms 5 en suite, 1 with private bathroom
payment credit/debit cards, cash, cheques

directions From A36 (Southampton), off Salisbury ringroad take first left into Tollgate Road. After 200 yards Alabare House is opposite you on the lefthand bend.

Room
General
Leisure

SALISBURY, Wiltshire Map ref 2B3

SAT NAV SP5 2RR

Blaxwell Farm

Blaxwell Farm, Whiteparish, Salisbury SP5 2RR
t (01794) 884000 **e** tricia@blaxwellfarm.co.uk
w blaxwellfarm.co.uk LAST MINUTE OFFERS

enjoyEngland.com
BED & BREAKFAST ★★★★

B&B PER ROOM PER NIGHT
S £35.00 – £50.00
D £60.00 – £80.00

SPECIAL PROMOTIONS
Please contact us for special offers.

18th century farmhouse with well appointed en suite rooms. Tranquil pondside setting in 50 acres of meadows with abundant wildlife. 5 minutes walk to village centre with pubs, shops, and church. Excellent walking, borders of New Forest National Park, convenient Salisbury, Stonehenge, Winchester, Bournemouth, Isle of Wight and South Coast.

open All year
bedrooms 2 double, 1 twin
bathrooms 3 en suite
payment cash, cheques

directions Junction 2 M27. A36 to Salisbury. Turn right at A27 (to Romsey). 400m past Whiteparish church turn right into private lane alongside Parish Lantern Pub.

Room
General
Leisure

South West | Wiltshire

SALISBURY, Wiltshire Map ref 2B3
SAT NAV SP2 0EJ

Burcombe Manor

Burcombe Lane, Burcombe, Salisbury SP2 0EJ
t (01722) 744288 f (01722) 744600 e nickatburcombemanor@btinternet.com
w burcombemanor.co.uk

B&B PER ROOM PER NIGHT
S £60.00 – £65.00
D £75.00 – £80.00

SPECIAL PROMOTIONS
Reduction for stays of 3 or more nights.

Burcombe Manor is set in the Nadder Valley, four miles west of Salisbury. The Victorian house with central heated rooms and a sitting room for guests to plan their day trips or relax in. Local base to explore Wilton, Salisbury and the surrounding area.

open All year
bedrooms 1 double, 1 twin
bathrooms 2 en suite
payment credit/debit cards, cash, cheques

directions Come out of Wilton 1 mile on A30. Left to Burcombe. At T-junction, turn right. Burcombe Manor drive is on the left.

SALISBURY, Wiltshire Map ref 2B3
SAT NAV SP2 0EJ

Manor Farm

Burcombe Lane, Burcombe, Salisbury, Wiltshire SP2 0EJ
t (01722) 742177 f (01722) 744600 e suecombes@manorfarmburcombe.fsnet.co.uk
w manorfarmburcombebandb.com

B&B PER ROOM PER NIGHT
D £60.00 – £70.00

Comfortable farmhouse, warm and attractively furnished, on 1,400 acre mixed farm in quiet, pretty village 5 miles west of Salisbury. Ideal for touring. Wilton House, Salisbury and Stonehenge nearby. Wonderful walks. **directions** From Salisbury A36/30 west to Wilton, left at roundabout, A30 for 2 miles, left for 0.25 miles then turn right. 1st house on left. **open** 1 March to 1 December **bedrooms** 1 double, 1 twin **bathrooms** 2 en suite **payment** credit/debit cards, cash, cheques

---

SALISBURY, Wiltshire Map ref 2B3
SAT NAV SP1 3YE

The Old Rectory Bed & Breakfast

75 Belle Vue Road, Salisbury SP1 3YE
t (01722) 502702 e stay@theoldrectory-bb.co.uk
w theoldrectory-bb.co.uk ONLINE MAP GUEST REVIEWS

B&B PER ROOM PER NIGHT
S £40.00 – £55.00
D £55.00 – £80.00

Victorian rectory in quiet street, a short walk from the heart of Salisbury and convenient for all attractions. Warm, welcoming atmosphere and well-appointed rooms. Wi-Fi internet. **directions** See our website for detailed directions. **open** All year except Xmas and New Year **bedrooms** 1 single, 1 double, 1 twin **bathrooms** 2 en suite, 1 with private bathroom **payment** cash, cheques

South West | Wiltshire/Cornwall

WARMINSTER, Wiltshire Map ref 2B2
SAT NAV BA12 7BY

Deverill End
Deverill Road, Sutton Veny, Warminster BA12 7BY
t 01985 840 356
w suttonveny.co.uk

B&B PER ROOM PER NIGHT
S £55.00 – £70.00
D £65.00 – £70.00

Longleat 5mls away, midway between Bath and Salisbury. Our house has spectacular views overlooking Racehorse Gallops. The garden specialises in roses and clematis. Rare bantams and chickens range the orchard. **directions** Please see our website or call for details. **open** Closed December and January **bedrooms** 2 double, 1 twin **bathrooms** 3 en suite **payment** cash, cheques

Room | General | Leisure

WINTERBOURNE STOKE, Wiltshire Map ref 2B2
SAT NAV SP3 4TF

Scotland Lodge Farm
Winterbourne Stoke, Salisbury SP3 4TF
t (01980) 621199 f (01980) 621188 e catherine.lockwood@bigwig.net
w scotlandlodgefarm.co.uk ONLINE MAP GUEST REVIEWS ONLINE BOOKING LAST MINUTE OFFERS

B&B PER ROOM PER NIGHT
S £35.00 – £40.00
D £65.00 – £70.00

Warm welcome at family-run competition yard set in 46 acres. Lovely views. Stonehenge/Salisbury nearby. Conservatory for guests' use. Easy access off A303. Silver/Breakfast Awards. Excellent local pubs. **directions** Entrance just west of Winterbourne Stoke on A303, on right hand side after Scotland Lodge. Follow B & B signs. Park on gravel outside conservatory. **open** All year except Xmas **bedrooms** 2 double, 1 twin **bathrooms** 2 with private bathroom **payment** credit/debit cards, cash, cheques

BREAKFAST AWARD

Room | General | Leisure

All Assessed Accommodation

Cornwall

ALVERTON

nzance Youth Hostel ★★★
stel
tle Horneck, Alverton, Penzance
8 4LP
t (01736) 362666
e penzance@yha.org.uk

BLISLAND, BODMIN

wint Farm ★★★★★
d & Breakfast **GOLD AWARD**
sland, Bodmin
30 4HX
t 07970 835560
e johntipler@btinternet.com

BODMIN

dknobs ★★★★ *Bed & Breakfast*
VER AWARD
gwyn, Castle Street, Bodmin,
nwall
31 2DX
t (01208) 77553
e gilly@bedknobs.co.uk
w bedknobs.co.uk

kiddick Farm ★★★★★
rmhouse **SILVER AWARD**
kiddick, Lanivet, Bodmin
30 5HP
t (01208) 831481
e gillhugo@bokiddickfarm.co.uk
w bokiddickfarm.co.uk

n Grove ★★★ *Bed & Breakfast*
lm Grove, Cardell Road, Bodmin
31 2NJ
t (01208) 74044
w alfatravel.co.uk

Many Views House ★★★
Bed & Breakfast
Launceston Road, Cooksland, Bodmin
PL31 2AR
t (01208) 269991
e chris@manyviewshouse.co.uk
w manyviewshouse.co.uk

Priory Cottage ★★★★
Bed & Breakfast
34 Rhind Street, Bodmin
PL31 2EL
t (01208) 73064
e jackiedingle@yahoo.com
w bodminlive.com

Rocquaine B&B ★★★★
Bed & Breakfast
Westheath Road, Bodmin
PL31 1QQ
t (01208) 72368
e pam@robilliard.freeserve.co.uk

South Tregleath Farm B&B
★★★★ *Bed & Breakfast*
SILVER AWARD
South Tregleath Farm, Washaway, Bodmin
PL30 3AA
t (01208) 72692
e info@south-tregleath.co.uk
w south-tregleath.co.uk

St Benets Abbey ★★★★
Guest Accommodation
Truro Road, Lanivet, Bodmin
PL30 5HF
t (01208) 831352
e st.benetsabbey@btconnect.com
w stbenetsabbey.com

Willowbrook ★★★★
Guest Accommodation
Lamorick, Lanivet, Bodmin
PL30 5HB
t (01208) 831670
e willowbrookbandb@aol.com
w welcomingyou.co.uk/willowbrook

Wooladon *Guest Accommodation*
Waterloo, Blisland, Bodmin
PL30 4JX
t (01208) 850110
e stevepa28@hotmail.co.uk

BOLVENTOR

Jamaica Inn ★★★★ *Inn*
Bolventor, Launceston
PL15 7TS
t (01566) 86250
e enquiry@jamaicainn .co.uk
w jamaicainn.co.uk

BOSCASTLE

Boscastle House ★★★★★
Guest Accommodation
GOLD AWARD
Tintagel Road, Boscastle
PL35 0AS
t (01840) 250654
e relax@boscastlehouse.com
w boscastlehouse.com

Boscastle Youth Hostel ★★★★
Hostel
Palace Stables, The Harbour, Boscastle
PL35 0HD
t 0870 770 5710
e boscastle@yha.org.uk
w yha.org.uk

The Bottreaux ★★★★
Guest Accommodation
Boscastle
PL35 0BG
t (01840) 250231
e info@boscastlecornwall.co.uk
w boscastlecornwall.co.uk

Bridge House Bed & Breakfast
★★★ *Guest Accommodation*
The Bridge, Boscastle
PL35 0HE
t (01840) 250011
e bridgehousebnb@talktalk.net
w cornwall-online.co.uk/bridg ehouse-boscastle

Home Farm B&B ★★★★★
Farmhouse **SILVER AWARD**
Home Farm, Boscastle
PL35 0BN
t (01840) 250195
e homefarm.boscastle@tiscali.co.uk
w homefarm-boscastle.co.uk

Lower Meadows ★★★★
Guest Accommodation
SILVER AWARD
Penally Hill, Boscastle
PL35 0HF
t (01840) 250570
e stay@lowermeadows.co.uk
w lowermeadows.co.uk

Oaklands ★★★★ *Bed & Breakfast*
Tresparrett, Boscastle
PL32 9SX
t (01840) 261302
e daphneiroutly@tiscali.co.uk
w boscastlebedandbreakfast.biz

---

key to symbols see page 6

127

South West | Cornwall

The Old Coach House ★★★★
Guest Accommodation
SILVER AWARD
Tintagel Road, Boscastle
PL35 0AS
t (01840) 250398
e stay@old-coach.co.uk
w old-coach.co.uk

The Old Parsonage ★★★★★
Guest Accommodation
SILVER AWARD
Boscastle
PL35 0DJ
t (01840) 250339
e morag@old-parsonage.com
w old-parsonage.com

The Old Rectory ★★★★★
Guest Accommodation
GOLD AWARD
Boscastle
PL35 0BT
t (01840) 250225
e sally@stjuliot.com
w stjuliot.com

Orchard Lodge ★★★★★
Guest Accommodation
GOLD AWARD
Gunpool Lane, Boscastle
PL35 0AT
t (01840) 250418
e orchardlodge@fsmail.net
w orchardlodgeboscastle.co.uk

Reddivallen Farm ★★★★★
Guest Accommodation
GOLD AWARD
Boscastle
PL35 0EE
t (01840) 250854
e liz@redboscastle.com
w redboscastle.com

The Riverside ★★★★★
Guest Accommodation
The Bridge, Boscastle
PL35 0HE
t (01840) 250216
e reception@hotelriverside.co.uk
w hotelriverside.co.uk

Trefoil Farm ★★★★ Farmhouse
Camelford Road, Boscastle
PL35 0AD
t (01840) 250606
e trefoil.farm@tiscali.co.uk
w boscastle-online.co.uk/trefoilfarm

Tregatherall Farm ★★★★
Guest Accommodation
Minster, Boscastle
PL35 0EQ
t (01840) 250277
e ness7tregatherall@yahoo.co.uk
w boscastlebedandbreakfast.co.uk

Valency Bed & Breakfast ★★★★
Bed & Breakfast **GOLD AWARD**
Penally Hill, Boscastle
PL35 0HF
t (01840) 250397
e tillinghast@btinternet.com
w valencybandb.com

BRYHER

Bank Cottage Guest House
★★★★ Guest House
SILVER AWARD
Bryher
TR23 0PR
t (01720) 422612
e macmace@homecall.co.uk
w bank-cottage.com

Soleil D'or ★★★★ Bed & Breakfast
Bryher
TR23 0PR
t (01720) 422003
e angelabushell@aol.com
w bryher-ios.co.uk/sd

BUDE

Adventure International ★★★
Hostel
Belle Vue, Bude
EX23 8JP
t 0870 777 5111
e info@adventure.uk.com
w adventure.uk.com

Bay View Inn ★★★★ Inn
Marine Drive, Bude
EX23 0AW
t (01288) 361273
e thebayviewinn@aol.com
w bayviewinn.co.uk

Beach House ★★★
Guest Accommodation
Marine Drive, Widemouth Bay,
Bude, Cornwall
EX23 0AW
t (01288) 361256
e beachhousebookings@tiscali.co.uk
w beachhousewidemouth.co.uk

Bossiney House ★★★★
Bed & Breakfast
1 Flexbury Park Road, Flexbury,
Bude
EX23 8HP
t (01288) 353356
e info@bossineyhousebandb.com
w bossineyhousebandb.co.uk

Breakwater House B&B ★★★★★
Bed & Breakfast
3 Breakwater Road, Bude
EX23 8LQ
t (01288) 353137
e ptilzey@hotmail.co.uk
w breakwaterhouse.co.uk

Brendon Arms ★★★ Inn
Vicarage Road, Bude
EX23 8SD
t (01288) 354542
e enquiries@brendonarms.co.uk
w brendonarms.co.uk

Creathorne Farm Bed & Breakfast
★★★★★ Farmhouse
SILVER AWARD
The Granary, Creathorne Farm, Bude
EX23 0NE
t (01288) 361077
e alison@creathornefarm.co.uk
w creathornefarm.co.uk

The Edgcumbe ★★★★
Guest Accommodation
SILVER AWARD
Summerleaze Crescent, Bude
EX23 8HJ
t (01288) 353846
e info@edgcumbe-hotel.co.uk
w edgcumbe-hotel.co.uk

The Elms Guest House ★★★
Bed & Breakfast
37 Lynstone Road, Bude
EX23 8LR
t (01288) 353429
w visitbude.info

The Grosvenor ★★★ Guest House
10 Summerleaze Crescent, Bude
EX23 8HH
t (01288) 352062
e enquiries@thegrosvenor-bude.co.uk
w thegrosvenor-bude.co.uk/

Harefield Cottage ★★★★
Guest House **GOLD AWARD**
Harefield Cottage, Upton, Bude,
Cornwall
EX23 0LY
t (01288) 352350
e sally@coast-countryside.co.uk
w coast-countryside.co.uk

Heatham Farmhouse ★★★★
Farmhouse **GOLD AWARD**
Kilkhampton, Bude
EX23 9RH
t (01288) 321325
e heathamfarm@btconnect.com
w heathamfarm.co.uk

Hillbrook ★★★ Bed & Breakfast
37 Killerton Road, Bude
EX23 8EL
t (01288) 353156
e hillbrookinfo@tiscali.co.uk
w hillbrook-bude.co.uk

Langaton Farm ★★★★ Farmhouse
Whitstone, Bude
EX22 6TS
t (01288) 341215
e langatonfarm@hotmail.com
w langaton-farm-holidays.co.uk

Links Side ★★★★ Guest House
7 Burn View, Bude
EX23 8BY
t (01288) 352410
e linksidebude@hotmail.com
w linkssidebude.co.uk

Little Haven ★★★★
Bed & Breakfast **SILVER AWARD**
Silverton Road, Bude
EX23 8EY
t (01288) 354995
e anne@littlehaven-bude.co.uk
w littlehaven-bude.co.uk

Meadow View ★★★★
Bed & Breakfast
6 Kings Hill Close, Bude
EX23 8RR
t (01288) 355095
e nickyandjohn@hotmail.co.uk
w meadowview-bude.co.uk/

Oak Lodge B&B ★★★★
Bed & Breakfast **SILVER AWARD**
Bude
EX23 9AT
t (01288) 354144
e julie@oaklodgebude.com
w oaklodgebude.com/

Oketon ★★★★ Bed & Breakfast
SILVER AWARD
11 Flexbury Park Road, Bude
EX23 8HR
t (01288) 350614
e orrwilcox@aol.com
w oketon.co.uk

Outdoor Adventure Ltd ★★★
Activity Accommodation
Atlantic Court, Bude
EX23 0DF
t (01288) 361312

Palms Guest House ★★★★
Guest House **SILVER AWARD**
17 Burn View, Bude
EX23 8BY
t (01288) 353962
e palmsguesthouse@tiscali.co.uk
w palms-bude.co.uk

Shorething ★★★★ Bed & Breakfast
GOLD AWARD
Madeira Drive, Bude
EX23 0AJ
t (01288) 361731
e info@shorething-bb-cornwall.co.uk
w shorething-bb-cornwall.co.uk

Strands ★★★★ Bed & Breakfast
Bude
EX23 9HW
t (01288) 353514
e brendadunstanbude@yahoo.co.uk
w strandsatstibb.co.uk

Stratton Gardens House ★★★★
Guest Accommodation
Cot Hill, Bude
EX23 9DN
t (01288) 352500
e moira@stratton-gardens.co.uk
w stratton-gardens.co.uk

Sunrise Guest House ★★★★
Guest House **SILVER AWARD**
6 Burn View, Bude
EX23 8BY
t (01288) 353214
e sunriseguest@btconnect.com
w sunrise-bude.co.uk

Surf Haven Guest House ★★★★
Guest House
31 Downs View, Bude
EX23 8RG
t (01288) 353923
e info@surfhaven.co.uk
w surfhaven.co.uk

Tee-Side ★★★★ Guest House
SILVER AWARD
2 Burn View, Bude
EX23 8BY
t (01288) 352351
e rayandjune@tee-side.co.uk
w tee-side.co.uk

Willow Tree Cottage ★★★★
Bed & Breakfast **GOLD AWARD**
Bude
EX23 9SJ
t (01288) 331100
e willowtreecottage@tiscali.co.uk
w willowtreecottage.co.uk

Wyvern Guest House ★★★★
Guest House
7 Downs View, Bude
EX23 8RF
t (01288) 352205
e eileen@wyvernhouse.co.uk
w wyvernhouse.co.uk

BUGLE

The Bugle Inn ★★★ Inn
57 Fore Street, St Austell
PL26 8PB
t (01726) 850307
e bugleinn@aol.com
w bugleinn.co.uk

BURNGULLOW

Station House ★★★★
Bed & Breakfast
Burngullow Lane, St Austell
PL26 7TQ
t (01726) 67226
e stationhousebb@yahoo.co.uk
w stationhousebb.co.uk

CALLINGTON

Cadson Manor ★★★★★
Farmhouse **GOLD AWARD**
Callington
PL17 7HW
t (01579) 383969
e brenda.crago@btclick.com
w cadsonmanor.co.uk

Hampton Manor ★★★★
Guest House
Alston, Callington
PL17 8LX
t (01579) 370494
e hamptonmanor@supanet.com
w hamptonmanor.co.uk

Higher Manaton ★★★★
Farmhouse
Callington, Cornwall
PL17 8PX
t (01579) 370460
e dtrewin@manaton.fsnet.co.uk
w cornwall-devon-bandb.co.uk

Lower House Guest House ★★★★
Guest House
9 Church Street, Callington
PL17 7AN
t (01579) 383491
e info@lower-house.com
w lower-house.com

Polhilsa Farm ★★★★
Guest Accommodation
Polhilsa, Callington
PL17 8PP
t (01579) 370784
e barriball@polhilsa.free-online.co.uk
w polhilsa.co.uk

South West | Cornwall

CAMBORNE

llingwood ★★★
est Accommodation
unt Whistle Road, South Tehidy,
mborne
14 0JA
t (01209) 714696
e enquiries@accommodation-in-
cornwall.com
w accommodation-in-cornwall.com

scroggan Chapel Guest House
★★ Guest House
scroggan Hill, Roscroggan,
mborne
14 0JA
t (01209) 714696
e enquiries@accommodation-in-
cornwall.com
w visitcornwall.com/site/-p40161

CAMELFORD

gher Trezion ★★★★ *Farmhouse*
esinney, Advent, Camelford
32 9QW
t (01840) 213761
e higher.trezion@btinternet.com
w highertrezion.co.uk

elorne Farmhouse ★★★★★
d & Breakfast SILVER AWARD
melford Station, Camelford
32 9TZ
t (01840) 211301
e jane@melornefarmhouse.com
w melornefarmhouse.com

ndragon Country House
★★★★ *Guest Accommodation*
OLD AWARD
avidstow, Camelford
32 9XR
t (01840) 261131
e enquiries@pendragoncountr
yhouse.com
w pendragoncountryhouse.com

enlea House ★★★
d & Breakfast
ation Road, Camelford
32 9UR
t (01840) 212194
e jandrews04@supanet.com

vermoon ★★★★ *Bed & Breakfast*
ne End, Camelford
32 9LE
t (01840) 213736
e silvermoonbandb@aol.com

armington House ★★★★
d & Breakfast SILVER AWARD
Market Place, Camelford
32 9PD
t (01840) 214961
e enquiries@warmingtonhouse.co.
uk
w warmingtonhouse.co.uk

oolland House ★★★★★
d & Breakfast
efrew Road, Camelford
32 9TP
t (01840) 212342
e l.cornwall1@btinternet.com
w woollandbandbcornwall.co.uk

CARDINHAM

e Old School House ★★★★
d & Breakfast
verys Green, Bodmin
30 4EA
t (01208) 821303
e libby@cardinhambb.co.uk
w cardinhambb.co.uk

CARLYON BAY

ppins ★★★ *Bed & Breakfast*
Beach Road, St Austell
25 3PJ
t (01726) 815491
e douglas.lowings@btinternet.com

Wheelwright's ★★★
Bed & Breakfast
151 Charlestown Road, Charlestown,
St Austell
PL25 3NN
t (01726) 63637
e derek-bates@hotmail.com
w wheelwrightscornwall.co.uk

CARNON DOWNS

Woodsedge ★★★★
Bed & Breakfast
10 Gig Lane, Truro
TR3 6JS
t (01872) 870269
e linda@woodsedgebb.co.uk
w woodsedgebb.co.uk

CHACEWATER

Salem B&B ★★★★
Guest Accommodation
Salem Chapel, Killifreth Hill,
Chacewater
TR4 8NA
t (01872) 560076
e roger@bbsalem.co.uk
w bbsalem.co.uk

CONNOR DOWNS

Nanterrow Farm B&B ★★★
Farmhouse
Gwithian, Hayle
TR27 5BP
t (01209) 712282
e nanterrow@hotmail.com
w nanterrowfarm.co.uk

COOMBE

Little Downderry ★★★★
Bed & Breakfast
St Austell
PL26 7LT
t (01726) 882247
e bill@westenviro.prestel.co.uk

COVERACK

Coverack Youth Hostel ★★★★
Hostel
Parc Behan, School Hill, Helston
TR12 6SA
t (01326) 280687
e coverack@yha.org.uk

DULOE

Tremadart Country House ★★★★
Bed & Breakfast
Tremadart Lane, Duloe
PL14 4PE
t (01503) 262766
e info@tremadart.co.uk
w tremadart.co.uk

EAST LOOE

Bridgeside Guest House ★★★★
Guest House
Fore Street, East Looe
PL13 1HH
t (01503) 263113
w bridgeside.cornwall.uk.net/

Dolphin Guest House ★★★★
Guest House
Station Road, East Looe
PL13 1HL
t (01503) 262578
e dolphinhouse@btconnect.com
w dolphin-house.co.uk

Sea Breeze Guest House ★★★★
Guest House
Lower Chapel Street, East Looe
PL13 1AT
t (01503) 263131
e info@seabreezelooe.com

EAST PORTHOLLAND

Caerhays Castle ★★★★★
Guest Accommodation
GOLD AWARD
East Portholland
PL26 6NA
t (01872) 501059
e info@nicheretreats.co.uk
w nicheretreats.co.uk

FALMOUTH

Anchor House ★★★
Bed & Breakfast
17 Harbour Terrace, Falmouth
TR11 2AN
t (01326) 317006
e tinarange@btinternet.com
w anchorhousebandbfalmouth.co.
uk

An Chy Coth ★★★★
Bed & Breakfast
37 Kersey Road, Flushing, Falmouth
TR11 5TR
t (01326) 377028
e anchycoth@hotmail.com

Avalon Guest House ★★★★
Guest Accommodation
Falmouth
TR11 5HN
t (01326) 250704
e avalon@avalonmaenporth.com
w avalonmaenporth.com

The Beach House ★★★★
Guest Accommodation
SILVER AWARD
1 Boscawen Road, Falmouth
TR11 4EL
t (01326) 210407
e beachhousefalmouth@hotmail.
com
w beachhousefalmouth.co.uk

Camelot Guest House ★★★★
Guest Accommodation
5 Avenue Road, Falmouth
TR11 4AZ
t (01326) 312480
e camelotfalmouth@aol.com
w camelot-guest-house.co.uk

Castleton Guest House ★★★
Guest House
68 Killigrew Street, Falmouth
TR11 3PR
t (01326) 372614
e dawnemmerson@aol.com
w falmouth-bandb.co.uk

Chellowdene ★★★★ *Guest House*
SILVER AWARD
Gyllyngvase Hill, Falmouth
TR11 4DN
t (01326) 314950
e info@chellowdene.co.uk
w chellowdene.co.uk

Chelsea House ★★★★
Guest Accommodation
2 Emslie Road, Falmouth
TR11 4BG
t (01326) 212230
e info@chelseahousehotel.com
w chelseahousehotel.com

Dolvean House ★★★★★
Guest Accommodation
SILVER AWARD
50 Melvill Road, Falmouth
TR11 4DQ
t (01326) 313658
e reservations@dolvean.co.uk
w dolvean.co.uk

Engleton Bed & Breakfast ★★★
Guest Accommodation
67 Killigrew Street, Falmouth
TR11 3PR
t (01326) 372644
e dawnemmerson@aol.com
w falmouth-bandb.co.uk

The Falmouth Townhouse ★★★★
Guest Accommodation
3 Grove Place, Falmouth
TR11 4AL
t (01326) 312009
e info@falmouthtownhouse.co.uk
w falmouthtownhouse.co.uk

The Grove ★★★★
Guest Accommodation
1 Grove Place, Falmouth
TR11 4AU
t (01326) 319577
e grovehotel@btconnect.com
w thegrovehotel.net

The Guest House
Guest Accommodation
7 Malbrough Road, Falmouth
TR11 3LP
t (01326) 314959
e info@guesthousefalmouth.co.uk
w guesthousefalmouth.co.uk

Gyllyngvase House ★★★★
Guest Accommodation
Gyllyngvase Road, Falmouth
TR11 4GH
t (01326) 312956
e info@gyllyngvase.co.uk
w gyllyngvase.co.uk

Hawthorne Dene ★★★★
Guest House SILVER AWARD
12 Pennance Road, Falmouth
TR11 4EA
t (01326) 311427
e enquiries@hawthornedenehotel.
co.uk
w hawthornedenehotel.co.uk

Headlands ★★★★
Guest Accommodation
4 Avenue Road, Falmouth
TR11 4AZ
t (01326) 311141
e headlandsfalmouth@hotmail.co.
uk
w headlandsfalmouth.com

Highcliffe Guest House ★★★★
Guest House SILVER AWARD
22 Melvill Road, Falmouth
TR11 4AR
t (01326) 314466
e info@falmouth-hotel.co.uk
w falmouth-hotel.co.uk

Lugo Rock ★★★★
Guest Accommodation
SILVER AWARD
59 Melvill Road, Falmouth
TR11 4DF
t (01326) 311344
e info@lugorockhotel.co.uk
w lugorockhotel.co.uk

Lyonesse Guest House ★★★
Guest Accommodation
17 Western Terrace, Falmouth
TR11 4QN
t (01326) 313017
e info@lyonessefalmouth.co.uk
w lyonessefalmouth.co.uk

The Mill ★★★★ *Bed & Breakfast*
Brill, Falmouth
TR11 5PZ
t (01326) 340036
e brillmill@hotmail.co.uk
w discoverglobalbookings.com/
themill

The Palms Guest House ★★★★
Guest Accommodation
11 Castle Drive, Falmouth
TR11 4NF
t (01326) 314007
e j_miller99@hotmail.com
w thepalmsguesthouse.co.uk

Poltair ★★★★ *Guest House*
GOLD AWARD
4 Emslie Road, Falmouth
TR11 4BG
t (01326) 313158
e info@poltair.co.uk
w poltair.co.uk

The Red House ★★★★
Guest Accommodation
24 Melvill Road, Falmouth
TR11 4AR
t (01326) 311172
e info@theredhousebandb.co.uk
w theredhousebandb.co.uk

Tregedna Lodge ★★★★ *Hostel*
Falmouth
TR11 5HL
t (01326) 250529
e tregednafarm@btinternet.com
w tregednafarmholidays.co.uk

South West | Cornwall

Tregenna Guest House ★★★★
Guest Accommodation
28 Melvill Road, Falmouth
TR11 4AR
t (01326) 313881
e info@tregennafalmouth.co.uk
w tregennafalmouth.co.uk

Trelawney Guest House ★★★★
Guest Accommodation
6 Melvill Road, Falmouth
TR11 4AS
t (01326) 316607
e trelawney@hotmail.co.uk
w trelawney-guesthouse.co.uk

Trevaylor ★★★★
Guest Accommodation
8 Pennance Road, Falmouth
TR11 4EA
t (01326) 313041
e trevaylorhotel@aol.com
w trevaylorhotel.com

Wellington House ★★★★
Guest Accommodation
26 Melvill Road, Falmouth
TR11 4AR
t (01326) 319947
e wellingtonhousefalmouth@googlemail.com
w wellingtonhousefalmouth.co.uk

The Westcott ★★★★ *Guest House*
Gyllyngvase Hill, Falmouth
TR11 4DN
t (01326) 311309
e westcotthotel@btinternet.com
w westcotthotelfalmouth.co.uk

FOWEY

28a Park Road ★★ *Bed & Breakfast*
Park Road, Fowey
PL23 1ED
t (01726) 832154
e nickjenbancroft@yahoo.co.uk

Artist's House ★★★★
Bed & Breakfast
40 Vicarage Meadow, Fowey
PL23 1EA
t (01726) 833680
e priddypink@macace.co.uk

Austins B&B ★★★★
Guest Accommodation
51 Vicarage Meadow, Fowey
PL23 1EA
t (01726) 833705
e barbara_austin51@hotmail.co.uk

Brents ★★★ *Bed & Breakfast*
19 Station Road, Fowey
PL23 1DF
t (01726) 833592
e barry@bgiles8.wanadoo.co.uk
w foweybandb.wanadoo.co.uk

Coombe Farm B&B ★★★
Farmhouse
Fowey
PL23 1HW
t (01726) 833123
e tessapaull@hotmail.com
w coombefarmbb.co.uk

Dawns B&B ★★★★
Guest Accommodation
59 Tavern Barn, Fowey
PL23 1EG
t (01726) 833232
e dawn@tavernbarn.fslife.co.uk

The Dwelling House at Fowey
★★★★ *Bed & Breakfast*
6 Fore Street, Fowey
PL23 1AQ
t (01726) 833662
e enquiries@thedwellinghouse.co.uk
w thedwellinghouse.co.uk

Fowey Marine Guest House
★★★★ *Guest House*
21-27 Station Road, Fowey
PL23 1DF
t (01726) 833920
e enquiries@foweymarine.com
w foweymarine.com

The Galleon ★★★★ *Inn*
12 Fore Street, Fowey
PL23 1AQ
t (01726) 833014
e info@galleon-inn.co.uk
w galleon-inn.co.uk

Golant Youth Hostel ★★★ *Hostel*
Penquite House, Fowey
PL23 1LA
t (01726) 833507

King of Prussia ★★★★ *Inn*
Town Quay, Fowey
PL23 1AT
t (01726) 833694
e kingofprussiafowey@yahoo.com
w kingofprussiafowey.co.uk

Mazirah ★★★ *Bed & Breakfast*
51 Polvillion Road, Fowey
PL23 1HG
t (01726) 833339

The Old Ferry Inn ★★★★ *Inn*
Bodinnick, Fowey
PL23 1LX
t (01726) 870237
e royce972@aol.com
w oldferryinn.com

Pendower ★★★★ *Bed & Breakfast*
11 Park Road, Fowey
PL23 1EB
t (01726) 833559
e carol.a.d@hotmail.co.uk

Penventinue Manor Farm
★★★★★ *Bed & Breakfast*
SILVER AWARD
Fowey
PL23 1JT
t (01726) 833393
e stay@cornwallholidaysdirect.com
w cornwallholidaysdirect.com

Polmarine B&B ★★★★
Guest Accommodation
West Street, Fowey
PL23 1PL
t (01726) 870459
e polmarine@btopenworld.com
w polmarine.com

River View ★★★★ *Bed & Breakfast*
20 Park Road, Fowey
PL23 1ED
t (01726) 833498
e histgilla@aol.com

Safe Harbour Inn ★★★ *Inn*
58 Lostwithiel Street, Fowey
PL23 1BQ
t (01726) 833379
e info@cornwall-safeharbour.co.uk
w cornwall-safeharbour.co.uk

Terracotta House ★★★★
Bed & Breakfast SILVER AWARD
1 Lankelly Close, Fowey
PL23 1HG
t (01726) 834925
e terracottahouse-fowey@gmx.net
w terracottahouse.co.uk

Trehaida ★★★★ *Farmhouse*
SILVER AWARD
Whitecross, Lanteglos, Fowey
PL23 1NF
t (01726) 870880
e trehaida@btopenworld.com
w trehaida.co.uk

Trekelyn ★★★★ *Bed & Breakfast*
3 Hanson Drive, Fowey
PL23 1ET
t (01726) 833375

The Well House ★★★
Bed & Breakfast
31-35 Fore Street, Fowey
PL23 1AH
t (01726) 833832
e lesleymccartney@btinternet.com
w wellhousefowey.co.uk

GORRAN HAVEN

Boswinger Youth Hostel ★★★
Hostel
Boswinger, St Austell
PL26 6LL
t (01726) 844527

Bumblebees ★★★★
Bed & Breakfast
Foxhole Lane, Gorran Haven
PL26 6JP
t (01726) 842219
e bumblebeesbandb@googlemail.com
w bumblebees.biz

GRAMPOUND

Perran House ★★★
Guest Accommodation
Fore Street, Grampound
TR2 4RS
t (01726) 882066

Resparveth Farm Guesthouse
★★★ *Farmhouse*
Resparveth Farm, Grampound
TR2 4EF
t (01726) 882382
e lisawilley83@hotmail.com

GUNNISLAKE

Bridge House ★★★
Bed & Breakfast GOLD AWARD
4 Alexandra Terrace, Well Park Road, Gunnislake
PL18 9DT
t (01822) 832071
e enquiries@cornwallbedandbreakfast.org
w cornwallbedandbreakfast.org

HAYLE

Bostrase Country Guest House
★★★★ *Guest Accommodation*
Tolroy Farm, Hayle
TR27 6HG
t (01736) 754644
e bostrasecottage@tolroy.wanadoo.co.uk
w bostraseholidays.co.uk

Byways ★★★ *Bed & Breakfast*
22 Steamers Hill, Angarrack, Hayle
TR27 5JB
t (01736) 753463
e bywaysbb@lineone.net
w bywaysbb.co.uk

The Penellen ★★★★
Guest Accommodation
64 Riviere Towans, Phillack, Hayle
TR27 5AF
t (01736) 753777
e penellen@btconnect.com
w bedandbreakfasthotelcornwall.co.uk

HELSTON

Chyheira ★★★★
Guest Accommodation
Ruan Minor, Cadgwith, Helston
TR12 7LQ
t (01326) 290343
e chrissy@chyheira.co.uk
w chyheira.co.uk

Hollow Tree House ★★★★
Bed & Breakfast SILVER AWARD
27 Church Hill, Helston
TR13 8NW
t (01326) 572410
e otg@talktalk.net
w hollowtreehouse.com

Jentone Bed & Breakfast ★★★★
Guest Accommodation
Carnkie, Helston
TR13 0DZ
t (01209) 860883
e johns@jentone.net
w jentone.net

Lyndale Cottage Guest House
★★★★ *Guest House*
4 Greenbank, Meneage Road, Helston
TR13 8JA
t (01326) 561082
e enquiries@lyndalecottage.co.uk
w lyndalecottage.co.uk

Mandeley Guesthouse ★★★★
Guest House SILVER AWARD
Clodgey Lane, Helston
TR13 8PJ
t (01326) 572550
e mandeley@btconnect.com
w mandeley.co.uk

New Thatch B&B ★★★★
Guest Accommodation
SILVER AWARD
New Thatch, Ruan Minor, Helston
TR12 7JN
t (01326) 290257
e newthatch@btinternet.com
w cornwall-online.co.uk/newthatc

Strathallan Guest House ★★★★
Guest Accommodation
6 Monument Road, Helston
TR13 8HF
t (01326) 573683
e strathallangh@aol.com
w connexions.co.uk/strathallan

Tregaddra Farmhouse B&B
★★★★ *Farmhouse* SILVER AWARD
Cury Cross Lanes, Helston
TR12 7BB
t (01326) 240235
e june@tregaddra.co.uk
w tregaddra.co.uk

Tregathenan House B&B ★★★★
Bed & Breakfast
The Old Farmhouse, Tregathenan, Helston
TR13 0RZ
t (01326) 569840
e tregathenan@hotmail.com
w tregathenan.co.uk

Trethvas Farmhouse ★★★★
Farmhouse
The Lizard, Helston
TR12 7AR
t (01326) 290720
e gwen@trethvas.plus.com

HOLSWORTHY

Highbre Crest ★★★★
Guest Accommodation
SILVER AWARD
Whitstone, Holsworthy
EX22 6UF
t (01288) 341002
e lindacole285@btinternet.com
w highbrecrest.co.uk

ILLOGAN

Sonnier ★★★★ *Bed & Breakfast*
Merritts Hill, Illogan, Redruth, Cornwall
TR16 4HD
t (01209) 203934
e david.darkin@tesco.net
w cornwall-online.co.uk/activeleisure/Welcome.asp

ISLES OF SCILLY

Pier House ★★★
Guest Accommodation
The Bank, St Mary's, Isles of Scilly
TR21 0HY
t (01720) 423061
e taniaandpetereynolds@btinternet.com
w pier-house.co.uk

LANDS END

Boswedden House ★★★★
Guest Accommodation
Cape Cornwall, St Just, Lands End
TR19 7NJ
t (01736) 788733
e relax@boswedden.org.uk
w boswedden.org.uk

South West | Cornwall

e Commercial ★★★★
est Accommodation
Market Square, St Just, Lands
d
19 7HE
t (01736) 788455
e enquiries@commercial-hotel.co.
uk
w commercial-hotel.co.uk

LANLIVERY

ngfield House ★★★
d & Breakfast
nlivery
30 5BT
t (01208) 873439

LANREATH-BY-LOOE

caddon Farm ★★★★
d & Breakfast SILVER AWARD
caddon Farm, Lanreath, Looe
13 2PG
t (01503) 220192
e holidays@bocaddon.com
w bocaddon.com

LAUNCESTON

eechgrove ★★★★
est Accommodation
LVER AWARD
a Dunheved Road, Launceston
15 9JF
t (01566) 779455
e enquiries@beechgrovecornwall.
co.uk
w beechgrovecornwall.co.uk

pper Meadow ★★★★
rmhouse GOLD AWARD
ngdons Shop, Launceston
15 7PW
t (01566) 782239
e trevadlock@farming.co.uk
w trevadlock.co.uk

orset Farm ★★★★ *Farmhouse*
yton, Launceston
15 9RF
t (01566) 775772
e jon@dorset-farm.co.uk
w dorset-farm.co.uk

encoe Villa ★★★
est Accommodation
Race Hill, Launceston
15 9BB
t (01566) 775819
e keigil.robinson@virgin.net

ll Park ★★★★ *Bed & Breakfast*
LVER AWARD
loskerry, Launceston
15 8SH
t (01566) 86937
e hill_park@btinternet.com
w hill-park.com

nher Farm ★★★★
d & Breakfast
orth Hill, Launceston
15 7NR
t (01566) 782273
e pam@lynherfarm.fsnet.co.uk
w lynherfarm.co.uk

iddle Tremollett ★★★★
rmhouse SILVER AWARD
ads Green, Launceston
15 7NA
t (01566) 782416
e btrewin@btinternet.com
w tremollett.com

akside Farm Bungalow ★★★★
d & Breakfast
uth Petherwin, Launceston,
ornwall
15 7JL
t (01566) 86733
e janetcrossman415@btinternet.
com
w oaksidebb.co.uk

Primrose Cottage ★★★★★
Bed & Breakfast GOLD AWARD
Primrose Cottage, Lawhitton,
Launceston
PL15 9PE
t (01566) 773645
e enquiry@primrosecottagesuites.
co.uk
w primrosecottagesuites.co.uk

Rezare Farmhouse ★★★★
Guest Accommodation
SILVER AWARD
Rezare, Launceston
PL15 9NX
t (01579) 371214
e info@rezarefarmhouse.co.uk
w rezarefarmhouse.co.uk

Stitch Park ★★★★ *Bed & Breakfast*
SILVER AWARD
Laneast, Launceston
PL15 8PN
t (01566) 86687
e katehandford@btinternet.com

St Leonards House ★★★★
Bed & Breakfast
Polson, Launceston
PL15 9QR
t (01566) 779195
e enquiries@stleonardshouse.co.uk
w stleonardshouse.co.uk

Thornbank B&B ★★
Bed & Breakfast
6 Highfield Park Road, Launceston
PL15 7DY
t (01566) 776136
e bkressinger513@btinternet.com
w launcestonbedandbreakfast.com

Three Quoins ★★★★
Bed & Breakfast
Trevallet, Launceston
PL15 8SJ
t (01566) 86386
e cmheath@btinternet.com
w threequoins.co.uk

Tregood Farm ★★★
Bed & Breakfast
Congdon Shop, Launceston
PL15 7PN
t (01566) 782263

Wheatley Farm ★★★★★
Farmhouse GOLD AWARD
Maxworthy, Launceston
PL15 8LY
t (01566) 781232
e valerie@wheatley-farm.co.uk
w wheatley-farm.co.uk

LEEDSTOWN

Little Pengelly - Farmhouse B&B
★★★★ *Guest Accommodation*
SILVER AWARD
Trenwheal, Leedstown, Hayle
TR27 6BP
t (01736) 850452
e maxine@littlepengelly.co.uk
w littlepengelly.co.uk

LISKEARD

Carglonnon Farm ★★★★
Farmhouse
Duloe, Liskeard
PL14 4QA
t (01579) 320210
e holidays@carglonnon.co.uk

Gillwood ★★★★ *Bed & Breakfast*
Liskeard
PL14 6HR
t (01208) 821648
e cliffnsheila@tiscali.co.uk
w gillwoodbedandbreakfast.com

Higher Trevartha Farm ★★★★
Farmhouse SILVER AWARD
Pengover, Liskeard
PL14 3NJ
t (01579) 343382
e tandksobey@btconnect.com
w highertrevarthafarm.com

Hyvue House ★★★ *Bed & Breakfast*
Endsleigh Terrace, Liskeard
PL14 6BN
t (01579) 348175

Nebula ★★★ *Guest House*
27 Higher Lux Street, Liskeard
PL14 3JU
t (01579) 343989
e info@nebula-hotel.com
w nebula-hotel.com

Penharget Farm ★★★★
Farmhouse SILVER AWARD
Pensilva, Liskeard
PL14 5RJ
t (01579) 362221
e penhargetfarm@ukonline.co.uk
w penharget-farm-cornwall.co.uk

Trecorme Barton ★★★★
Farmhouse SILVER AWARD
Quethiock, Liskeard
PL14 3SH
t (01579) 342646
e david-renfree@btinternet.com
w trecormebarton.co.uk/

Tregondale Manor Farm ★★★★
Farmhouse SILVER AWARD
Menheniot, Liskeard
PL14 3RG
t (01579) 342407
e tregondalefarm@btconnect.com
w tregondalefarm.co.uk

LIZARD

Atlantic House ★★★★★
Guest Accommodation
SILVER AWARD
Pentreath Lane, Lizard
TR12 7NY
t (01326) 290399
e jayne@atlantichouselizard.co.uk
w atlantichouselizard.co.uk

LOOE

Bake Farm ★★★★ *Farmhouse*
Pelynt, Looe
PL13 2QQ
t (01503) 220244
e bakefarm@btopenworld.com
w bakefarm.co.uk

Barclay House ★★★★
Guest Accommodation
SILVER AWARD
Saint Martins Road, Looe
PL13 1LP
t (01503) 262929
e info@barclayhouse.co.uk
w barclayhouse.co.uk

Bucklawren Farm ★★★★
Farmhouse GOLD AWARD
St Martin by Looe, Looe
PL13 1NZ
t (01503) 240738
e bucklawren@btopenworld.com
w bucklawren.co.uk

The Deganwy ★★★★ *Guest House*
Station Road, Looe
PL13 1HL
t (01503) 262984
e enquiries@deganwyhotel.co.uk
w deganwyhotel.co.uk

Dovers House ★★★★ *Guest House*
SILVER AWARD
St Martins, Looe
PL13 1PB
t (01503) 265468
e twhyte@btconnect.com
w doveshouse.co.uk

Driftwood House ★★★★
Guest Accommodation
Portuan Road, Hannafore, Looe
PL13 2ND
t (01503) 262990
e daviddriftwood@googlemail.com
w driftwoodlooe.co.uk

The Gulls ★★★★ *Guest House*
SILVER AWARD
Hannafore Road, Looe
PL13 2DE
t (01503) 262531
e enquiries@gullshotel.co.uk
w gullshotel-looe.co.uk

Hillingdon Guest House ★★★
Guest House
Portuan Road, Looe
PL13 2DW
t (01503) 262906
e info@hillingdonguesthouse.co.uk
w hillingdonguesthouse.co.uk

Lesquite Farm B&B ★★★★
Farmhouse SILVER AWARD
Lesquite, Lansallos, Looe
PL13 2QE
t (01503) 220315
e stay@lesquite.co.uk
w lesquite.co.uk

Little Larnick Farm ★★★★
Farmhouse SILVER AWARD
Looe
PL13 2NB
t (01503) 262837
e littlelarnick@btclick.com
w littlelarnick.co.uk

Meneglaze Bed & Breakfast
★★★★ *Guest House*
Shutta, Looe
PL13 1LU
t (01503) 269227
e meneglaze@tiscali.co.uk
w looebedandbreakfast.com/

Schooner Point B&B ★★★★
Guest Accommodation
1 Trelawney Terrace, Polperro Road,
Looe
PL13 2AG
t (01503) 262670
e enquiries@schoonerpoint.co.uk
w schoonerpoint.co.uk

Seaview ★★★ *Bed & Breakfast*
Portuan Road, Hannafore, Looe
PL13 2DW
t (01503) 265837
e sharon@seaviewlooe.fsworld.co.
uk
w seaview-looe.co.uk

Trelren ★★★ *Bed & Breakfast*
Polperro Road, Looe
PL13 2JS
t (01503) 263918
e enquiries@trelren.co.uk
w trelren.co.uk

Trenderway Farm ★★★★★
Farmhouse SILVER AWARD
Pelynt, Nr Polperro, Looe
PL13 2LY
t (01503) 272214
e yaron@trenderwayfarm.com
w trenderwayfarm.com

The Watermark ★★★★
Guest House SILVER AWARD
Hannafore Road, West Looe, Looe
PL13 2DE
t (01503) 262123
e ash@looe.co.uk
w looe.co.uk

West Kellow Farm ★★★★
Farmhouse SILVER AWARD
Lansallos, Looe
PL13 2QL
t (01503) 272089
e westkellow@aol.com
w westkellow.co.uk

LOSTWITHIEL

Cross Close House B&B ★★★★
Bed & Breakfast
West Taphouse, Lostwithiel
PL22 0RP
t (01579) 320255
e crossclose@alexlister1.plus.com
w cornwall-online.co.uk/cross-close

Hazelmere House ★★★★
Bed & Breakfast SILVER AWARD
58 Grenville Road, Lostwithiel,
Cornwall
PL22 0ER
t (01208) 873315
e rth346@aol.com
w hazelmerehouse.co.uk

South West | Cornwall

The Kings Arms ★★★★ *Inn*
Fore Street, Lostwithiel
PL22 0BL
t (01208) 872383
e info@thekingsarmslostwithiel.co.uk
w thekingsarmslostwithiel.co.uk

The Royal Oak ★★★ *Inn*
Duke Street, Lostwithiel
PL22 0AG
t (01208) 872552
e royaloaklostwithiel@btconnect.com
w royaloaklostwithiel.co.uk

Tremont House ★★★★
Bed & Breakfast
2 The Terrace, Lostwithiel
PL22 0DT
t (01208) 873055
e alorna5@aol.com
w tremonthouse.co.uk

MARAZION

Rosario B&B ★★★★
Guest Accommodation
The Square, Marazion, Penzance
TR17 0BH
t (01736) 711998
e penzancetic@cornwall.gov.uk
w rosario-marazion.co.uk

MAWGAN PORTH

Bre-Pen Farm ★★★★ *Farmhouse*
Mawgan Porth
TR8 4AL
t (01637) 860420
e jill.brake@virgin.net
w bre-penfarm.co.uk

Kernow Trek Lodge ★★★
Guest Accommodation
Trevarrian, Mawgan Porth
TR8 4AQ
t (01637) 860437
e info@activityholidayscornwall.co.uk
w activityholidayscornwall.co.uk

Trevarrian Lodge ★★★
Guest House
Trevarrian, Mawgan Porth
TR8 4AQ
t (01637) 860156
e trevarrian@aol.com
w trevarrianlodge.com

MEVAGISSEY

Bacchus B&B ★★★★
Bed & Breakfast
Trevarth, Mevagissey
PL26 6RX
t (01726) 843473
e susiecannone@yahoo.co.uk
w bacchus-cornwall.co.uk

Buckingham House ★★★
Guest House
17 Tregoney Hill, Mevagissey
PL26 6RD
t (01726) 843375
e andy@buckinghamhousemevagissey.co.uk
w buckinghamhousemevagissey.co.uk

The Cherrypickers ★★★★
Bed & Breakfast
34 Lavorrick Orchards, Mevagissey
PL26 6TL
t (01726) 843321
e lorraineboulter@hotmail.co.uk
w chycor.co.uk/bnb/mevagissey-bed-and-breakfast-cherrypickers/

Corran Farm ★★★★ *Farmhouse*
SILVER AWARD
St Ewe, Mevagissey
PL26 6ER
t (01726) 842159
e info@corranfarm.co.uk
w corranfarm.co.uk

Greystones ★★★★
Guest Accommodation
5 Lower Well Park, Mevagissey
PL26 6UZ
t (01726) 842099
e mike.sundercombe@btopenworld.com
w greystones-mevagissey.co.uk

Honeycombe House ★★★★
Guest House
61 Polkirt Hill, Mevagissey
PL26 6UR
t (01726) 843750
e enquiries@honeycombehouse.co.uk
w honeycombehouse.co.uk

Mandalay ★★★ *Guest House*
School Hill, Mevagissey
PL26 6TQ
t (01726) 842435
e jillconneely@yahoo.com
w mandalaymevagissey.co.uk

The Old Parsonage ★★★
Guest Accommodation
58 Church Street, Mevagissey
PL26 6SR
t (01726) 843709
e reservations@mevagissey-bed-and-breakfast.com
w mevagissey-bed-and-breakfast.com

Portmellon Cove Guest House ★★★★ *Guest House*
SILVER AWARD
121 Portmellon Park, Portmellon, Mevagissey
PL26 6XD
t (01726) 843410
e stay@portmellon-cove.com
w portmellon-cove.com

St Meva ★★★★ *Bed & Breakfast*
Beach Road, Mevagissey
PL26 6TE
t (01726) 843681
e caroline.morgan@virgin.net
w stmeva.co.uk

Tregilgas Farm ★★★★ *Farmhouse*
Gorran, St Austell
PL26 6ND
t (01726) 842342 or 07789 113620
e dclemes88@aol.com
w tregilgasfarmbedandbreakfast.co.uk

Tregoney House ★★★★
Bed & Breakfast
19 Tregoney Hill, Mevagissey
PL26 6RD
t (01726) 842760
e dianne.young@hotmail.co.uk
w tregoneyhouse.co.uk

Tregorran Guest House ★★★★
Guest House SILVER AWARD
Cliff Street, Mevagissey
PL26 6QW
t (01726) 842319
e helen@tregorran.co.uk
w tregorran.co.uk

Trennicks *Guest Accommodation*
Valley Park Lane, Mevagissey
PL26 6RS
t (01726) 842235
e trennicks@btinternet.com
w trennicksguesthouse.co.uk

Wild Air Guest House ★★★★
Bed & Breakfast SILVER AWARD
Polkirt Hill, Mevagissey
PL26 6UX
t (01726) 843302
e clareavent@aol.com
w wildair.co.uk

MORWENSTOW

The Bush Inn ★★★ *Inn*
The Bush Inn Crosstown, Morwenstow, Bude
EX23 9SR
t (01288) 331242
e coryfarmltd@aol.com
w bushinn-morwenstow.co.uk

MOUSEHOLE

Ship Inn ★★★★ *Inn*
South Cliff, Mousehole, Penzance
TR19 6QX
t (01736) 731234
e shipmousehole@staustellbrewery.co.uk
w staustellbrewery.co.uk

NANCEGOLLAN

Little Pengwedna Farm ★★★★
Farmhouse
Nancegollan, Helston
TR13 0AY
t (01736) 850649
e ray@good-holidays.co.uk
w good-holidays.co.uk

NEWQUAY

The Alex Guest House ★★★
Guest House
19 Alexandra Road, Newquay
TR7 3ND
t (01637) 875311
e enquiries@alexguesthouse.co.uk
w alexguesthouse.co.uk

Alicia ★★★★ *Guest House*
136 Henver Road, Newquay
TR7 3EQ
t (01637) 874328
e alicianewquay@googlemail.com
w alicia-guesthouse.co.uk

Breaks ★★★★ *Guest House*
80 Crantock Street, Newquay
TR7 1JW
t (01637) 874641
e info@newquaybreakshotel.co.uk
w newquaybreakshotel.co.uk

The Carlton ★★★★
Guest Accommodation
SILVER AWARD
6 Dane Road, Newquay
TR7 1HL
t (01637) 872658
e enquiries@carltonhotelnewquay.co.uk
w carltonhotelnewquay.co.uk

Chichester Guest House ★★
Guest Accommodation
14 Bay View Terrace, Newquay, Cornwall
TR7 2LR
t (01637) 874216
e sheila.harper@virgin.net
w freespace.virgin.net/sheila.harper

Chynoweth Lodge ★★★★
Guest Accommodation
1 Eliot Gardens, Newquay
TR7 2QE
t (01637) 876684
e chynowethlodge@btconnect.com
w chynowethlodge.co.uk

Degembris Farmhouse ★★★★
Farmhouse
Degembris Major Farm, St Newlyn East, Nr Newquay, Cornwall
TR8 5HY
t (01872) 510555
e thefarmhouse@degembris.co.uk
w degembris.co.uk

The Escape ★★ *Group Hostel*
1 Mount Wise, Newquay, Cornwall
TR7 2BQ
t 01637 851736
e escapebook@yahoo.co.uk
w escape2newquay.co.uk

The Glendeveor ★★★
Guest Accommodation
25 Mount Wise, Newquay
TR7 2BQ
t (01637) 872726
e enquiries@glendeveor.co.uk
w glendeveornewquay.co.uk

Godolphin Arms ★★★ *Inn*
86-88 Henver Road, Newquay
TR7 3BL
t (01637) 872572
e godolphin.arms@btconnect.com
w godolphinarmshotel.co.uk

Goofys ★★★★ *Hostel*
5 Headland Road, Fistral Beach, Newquay
TR7 1HW
t (01637) 872684
e info@goofys.co.uk
w goofys.co.uk

Gratton Lodge ★★★★
Guest House
119 Mount Wise, Newquay
TR7 1QR
t (01637) 877011
e enquiries@grattonlodge.co.uk
w grattonlodge.co.uk

The Harbour ★★★★
Guest Accommodation
SILVER AWARD
North Quay Hill, Newquay
TR7 1HF
t (01637) 873040
e alanburnett@harbourhotel.co.uk
w harbourhotel.co.uk

Harrington Guest House ★★★
Guest House
25 Tolcarne Road, Newquay
TR7 2NQ
t (01637) 873581
e harringtonguesthouse@yahoo.com
w harringtonguesthouse.com

Hepworth ★★★★
Guest Accommodation
27 Edgcumbe Avenue, Newquay
TR7 2NJ
t (01637) 873686
e hepworthnewquay@aol.com
w hepworthnewquay.co.uk

Hillcrest ★★★★ *Hostel*
33 Mount Wise, Newquay
TR7 2BH
t (01637) 875312
e info@hillcresthotelnewquay.co.uk
w hillcresthotelnewquay.co.uk

Lynton House ★★★★ *Guest House*
4 The Crescent, Newquay
TR7 1DT
t (01637) 873048
e info@lyntonhotel.wanadoo.co.uk
w lynton-hotel-newquay.co.uk

Merrymoor Inn ★★★★
Guest Accommodation
Mawgan Porth, Newquay
TR8 4BA
t (01637) 860258
e info@merrymoorinn.com
w merrymoorinn.com

The Metro ★★★
Guest Accommodation
142 Henver Road, Newquay
TR7 3EQ
t (01637) 871638
e info@metronewquay.co.uk
w metronewquay.co.uk

Pengilley Guest House ★★★
Guest House
12 Trebarwith Crescent, Newquay
TR7 1DX
t (01637) 872039
e jan@pengilley-guesthouse.co.uk
w pengilley-guesthouse.co.uk

Pensalda Guest House ★★★★
Guest House
98 Henver Road, Newquay
TR7 3BL
t (01637) 874601
e karen_pensalda@yahoo.co.uk
w pensalda-guesthouse.co.uk

Pine Lodge ★★★★
Guest Accommodation
91 Henver Road, Newquay
TR7 3DJ
t (01637) 850891
e enquiries@pinelodgehotel.co.uk
w pinelodgehotel.co.uk

Porth View ★★★ *Bed & Breakfast*
16 Porth Way, Newquay
TR7 3LP
t (01637) 877801
e sandraporthview@hotmail.co.uk
w porthview.co.uk

South West | Cornwall

ef Surf Lodge ★★★★ *Hostel*
-12 Berry Road, Newquay
7 1AR
(01637) 879058
enquiries@reefsurflodge.com
reefsurflodge.info

ma Guest House ★★★★
est Accommodation
Atlantic Road, Newquay
7 1QJ
(01637) 875085
romaghnewquay@aol.com
romaguesthouse.co.uk

rfside Stop Guest House ★★★
d & Breakfast
Mount Wise, Newquay
7 2BH
(01637) 872707
surfsidehotel@btconnect.com
surfsidenewquay.co.uk

ree Beaches ★★★
est Accommodation
Godolphin Way, Newquay
7 3BU
(01637) 873931
graham@threebeacheshotel.co.uk
threebeacheshotel.co.uk

**Chonaill Guest
ccommodation** ★★★
est Accommodation
6 Mount Wise, Newquay
7 1QP
(01637) 876492
tirchonailhotel@talk21.com
tirchonaill.co.uk

egenna House ★★★★
est House
est Pentire Road, Crantock
8 5RZ
(01637) 830222
info@tregennahouse.co.uk
tregennahouse.co.uk

elinda ★★★
est Accommodation
St Georges Road, Newquay
7 1RD
(01637) 872591
trelindahotel@btinternet.com
trelinda.co.uk

estward B&B ★★★★
est Accommodation
Edgcumbe Avenue, Newquay
7 2NJ
(01637) 871627
westwardnewquay@aol.com
westwardnewquay.co.uk

OTTERHAM

lloden Farmhouse B&B ★★★★
d & Breakfast
Victoria Road, Camelford
32 9XA
(01840) 211128
debbie_balaam@msn.com
cullodenfarmhouse.co.uk

PADSTOW

Caswarth Terrace ★★
d & Breakfast
dstow
28 8EE
(01841) 532025

Church Street ★★★★
d & Breakfast SILVER AWARD
Church Street, Padstow
28 8BG
(01841) 532121
churchstreet50@hotmail.com
50churchstreet.co.uk

thea House ★★★★★
d & Breakfast GOLD AWARD
Church Street, Padstow
28 8BG
(01841) 532579
zooat14@aol.com
altheahouse.co.uk

Althea Library ★★★★★
Guest Accommodation
GOLD AWARD
27 High Street, Padstow
PL28 8BB
t (01841) 532717
e enquiries@althealibrary.co.uk
w althealibrary.co.uk

Arum House Bed & Breakfast
★★★★ *Bed & Breakfast*
3 Grenville Road, Padstow
PL28 8EX
t (01841) 532364
e emmathompson@talktalk.net
w padstow-bed-and-breakfast.com

Cally Croft ★★★★★
Bed & Breakfast SILVER AWARD
26 Raleigh Close, Padstow
PL28 8BQ
t (01841) 533726
e callycroft@btinternet.com
w padstow-callycroft.co.uk

Coswarth House Bed & Breakfast
★★★★★ *Bed & Breakfast*
GOLD AWARD
12 Dennis Road, Padstow
PL28 8DD
t (01841) 534755
e coswarthhouse@btinternet.com
w coswarthhouse.com

Cyntwell ★★★★ *Bed & Breakfast*
4 Cross Street, Padstow
PL28 8AT
t (01841) 533447
e wendy@wgidlow.fsnet.co.uk
w cyntwell.co.uk

Damara House ★★★★
Guest Accommodation
1 Grenville Road, Padstow
PL28 8EX
t (01841) 532653
e sianhowells@btconnect.com
w padstow-accommodation.co.uk

Efflins Farmhouse ★★★★
Guest Accommodation
Bedruthan Steps, Padstow
PL27 7UU
t (01841) 540985
e efflins@yahoo.com

Garslade Guest House ★★★★
Bed & Breakfast
52 Church Street, Padstow
PL28 8BG
t (01841) 533804
e garsladeguest@btconnect.com
w garslade.com

The Harlyn Inn ★★★★ *Inn*
Harlyn Bay, Padstow
PL28 8SB
t (01841) 520207
e mail@harlyn-inn.com
w harlyn-inn.com

Khandalla B&B ★★★
Bed & Breakfast
Sarahs Lane, Padstow
PL28 8EL
t (01841) 533354
e suewalk@btconnect.com
w bedandbreakfastsearcher.co.uk/
detail.asp?id=5542&search=true.
co.uk

Lamorva House ★★★★
Guest Accommodation
3 Sarahs Meadow, Padstow
PL28 8LX
t (01841) 533841
e dplume9705@aol.com
w lamorvapadstow.co.uk

Lellizzick Farm ★★★★ *Farmhouse*
SILVER AWARD
Lellizzick, Padstow
PL28 8HR
t (01841) 532838
e lellizzick1@aol.com
w lellizzick.co.uk

Little Tregonna B&B ★★★★
Bed & Breakfast
Little Petherick, Padstow
PL27 7QT
t (01841) 540446
e jayneclinton@hotmail.com
w littletregonna.co.uk

Molesworth Manor ★★★★
Guest Accommodation
Little Petherick, Padstow
PL27 7QT
t (01841) 540292
e molesworthmanor@aol.com
w molesworthmanor.co.uk

Number Eight ★★★★
Bed & Breakfast
8 Drake Road, Padstow
PL28 8ES
t (01841) 532541
e carol_gidlow@sky.com

The Old Custom House Inn
★★★★ *Inn*
South Quay, Padstow
PL28 8BL
t (01841) 532359
e oldcustomhouse@staustellb
rewery.co.uk
w oldcustomhousepadstow.co.uk

Pendeen House ★★★★
Guest Accommodation
GOLD AWARD
28 Dennis Road, Padstow
PL28 8DE
t (01841) 532724
e enquire@pendeenhousepadstow.
com
w pendeenhousepadstow.com

Petrocstowe ★★★★
Guest Accommodation
SILVER AWARD
30 Treverbyn Road, Padstow
PL28 8DW
t (01841) 532429
e andrearichards@btinternet.com
w stayinpadstow.co.uk

Symply Padstow ★★★★
Bed & Breakfast SILVER AWARD
32 Dennis Road, Padstow
PL28 8DE
t (01841) 532814
e info@symply-padstow.co.uk
w symply-padstow.co.uk

Tamarisk ★★★★ *Bed & Breakfast*
13 Grenville Road, Padstow
PL28 8EX
t (01841) 532272
e king616@btinternet.com
w tamariskpadstow.co.uk

Trealaw Bed & Breakfast ★★★★
Bed & Breakfast
22 Duke Street, Padstow
PL28 8AB
t (01841) 533161
w trealaw.com

Treann House ★★★★★
Bed & Breakfast GOLD AWARD
24 Dennis Road, Padstow
PL28 8DE
t (01841) 533855
e bookings@treannhouse.co.uk
w treannhouse.com

Tregavone Farm ★★★ *Farmhouse*
St Merryn, Padstow
PL28 8JZ
t (01841) 520148
e info@tregavonefarm.co.uk

Tregudda ★★★★★ *Bed & Breakfast*
GOLD AWARD
5 Grenville Road, Padstow
PL28 8EX
t (01841) 533754
e enquiries@tregudda.co.uk
w tregudda.co.uk

Trethillick Farmhouse ★★★★
Farmhouse
Padstow
PL28 8HJ
t (01841) 532352
e mwatsonsmyth@aol.com

Treverbyn House ★★★★
Guest Accommodation
SILVER AWARD
Treverbyn House, Station Road,
Padstow
PL28 8DA
t (01841) 532855
w treverbynhouse.com

Trewithen Farmhouse ★★★★
Guest Accommodation
SILVER AWARD
St Merryn, Padstow
PL28 8JZ
t (01841) 520420
e maystrewithen@aol.com
w trewithenfarmhouse.com

Treyarnon Bay Youth Hostel
★★★ *Hostel*
Tregonnan, Treyarnon, Padstow
PL28 8JR
t 0870 770 6076
e treyarnon@yha.org.uk

West House ★★★★
Bed & Breakfast SILVER AWARD
Grenville Rd, Padstow
PL28 8EX
t (01841) 533479
e info@westhouse-padstow.co.uk
w westhouse-padstow.co.uk

The White Hart ★★★★
Bed & Breakfast SILVER AWARD
1 New Street, Padstow
PL28 8EA
t (01841) 532350
e whitehartpad@aol.com
w whitehartpadstow.co.uk

Woodlands Country House
★★★★★ *Guest Accommodation*
GOLD AWARD
Treator, Padstow
PL28 8RU
t (01841) 532426
e enquiries@woodlands-padstow.
co.uk
w woodlands-padstow.co.uk

PAR

An Skyber ★★★★ *Bed & Breakfast*
SILVER AWARD
The Mount, Par
PL24 2DA
t (01726) 815013
e valeriejobes@tiscali.co.uk
w an-skyber.co.uk

Boslowen ★★★★ *Guest House*
96 Par Green, Par
PL24 2AG
t (01726) 813720
e boslowen@gmail.com
w boslowen.co.uk

Farthings ★★★★ *Bed & Breakfast*
17-19 Polmear, Par
PL24 2AY
t (01726) 816637
e lauraparfitt@talktalk.net

Great Pelean Farm ★★★★
Farmhouse SILVER AWARD
Tywardreath, Par
PL24 2RX
t (01726) 812106
e andyjones74@hotmail.com
w greatpeleanfarm.com

Menabilly Barton ★★★ *Farmhouse*
Menabilly, Par
PL24 2TN
t (01726) 812844
e menabilly155@yahoo.co.uk

Penarwyn House ★★★★★
Guest Accommodation
GOLD AWARD
St Blazey, Par
PL24 2DS
t (01726) 814224
e info@penarwyn.co.uk
w penarwyn.co.uk

r key to symbols see page 6   133

South West | Cornwall

Polbrean House ★★★★
Bed & Breakfast
26 Woodland Avenue, Par
PL24 2PL
t (01726) 812530
e polbreanhouseandb@btinternet.com

Reynards Rest ★★★★
Bed & Breakfast SILVER AWARD
The Mount, Par
PL24 2BZ
t (01726) 815770
e carol@reynardsrest.co.uk
w reynardsrest.co.uk

Royal Inn ★★★★ Inn
66 Eastcliffe Road, Par
PL24 2AJ
t (01726) 815601
e info@royal-inn.co.uk
w royal-inn.co.uk

Tregaminion Farm ★★★★
Farmhouse
Menabilly, Par
PL24 2TL
t (01726) 812442

PELYNT

The Jubilee Inn ★★★★ Inn
Jubilee Hill, Pelynt
PL13 2JZ
t (01503) 220312
e jubileeinnpelynt@hotmail.com
w jubilee-inn.co.uk

PENPILLICK, PAR

Vine Cottage ★★★★
Bed & Breakfast
Penpillick Hill, Par
PL24 2RU
t (01726) 825008
e paula@vinecottagebandb.co.uk
w vinecottagebandb.co.uk

PENRYN

Bay View ★★★ Bed & Breakfast
Busvannah, Penryn
TR10 9LQ
t (01326) 372644
e dawnemmerson@aol.com
w falmouth-bandb.co.uk

PENTEWAN

The Old Post Office ★★★★
Guest Accommodation
19 West End, St Austell
PL26 6BX
t (01726) 844421
e jillbasham@hotmail.com
w the-old-post-office.com

PENWITHICK

Innis Inn ★★★ Inn
Innis Moor, St Austell
PL26 8YH
t (01726) 851162
e innis@tiscali.co.uk
w innis-fly-fishery.co.uk

PENZANCE

Boskenna Home Farm ★★★★★
Guest Accommodation
GOLD AWARD
St Buryan, Penzance
TR19 6DQ
t (01736) 810705
e julia@boskenna.co.uk
w boskenna.co.uk

Carnson House ★★★
Guest Accommodation
2 East Terrace, Penzance
TR18 2TD
t (01736) 365589
e carnsonhouse@btconnect.com
w carnson-house.co.uk

Castallack Farm ★★★★ Farmhouse
SILVER AWARD
Castallack, Lamorna, Penzance
TR19 6NL
t (01736) 731969
e info@castallackfarm.co.uk
w castallackfarm.co.uk

Chiverton House ★★★★
Guest Accommodation
SILVER AWARD
9 Mennaye Road, Penzance
TR18 4NG
t (01736) 332733
e alan.waller@sky.com
w chivertonhousebedandbreakfast.co.uk

Con Amore ★★★★
Guest Accommodation
38 Morrab Road, Penzance
TR18 4EX
t (01736) 363423
e krich30327@aol.com
w con-amore.co.uk

The Corner House ★★★★
Guest Accommodation
20 Marine Terrace, Penzance
TR18 4DL
t (01736) 351324
e info@thecornerhousepenzance.co.uk
w thecornerhousepenzance.co.uk

Cornerways Guest House ★★★
Guest Accommodation
5 Leskinnick Street, Penzance
TR18 2HA
t (01736) 364665
e enquiries@cornerways-penzance.co.uk
w penzance.co.uk/cornerways

**The Dovecote Romantic Retreat
★★★★** Guest Accommodation - Room Only
Kymaurah, Kemyel-Wartha, Penzance
TR19 6XG
t (01736) 732266
e zoeanphil@aol.com
w 2lamorna.co.uk

Glencree House ★★★★
Guest Accommodation
2 Mennaye Road, Penzance
TR18 4NG
t (01736) 362026
e stay@glencreehouse.co.uk
w glencreehouse.co.uk

Halcyon Guest House ★★★★
Guest House
6 Chyandour Square, Penzance
TR18 3LW
t (01736) 366302
e pat+bob@halcyon1.co.uk
w halcyon1.co.uk

Keigwin House ★★★ Guest House
Alexandra Road, Penzance
TR18 4LZ
t (01736) 363930
e fran@keigwinhouse.co.uk
w keigwinhouse.co.uk

Kerris Farm ★★★★ Farmhouse
SILVER AWARD
Kerris, Paul, Penzance
TR19 6UY
t (01736) 731309
e kerrisfarm@btconnect.com
w kerrisfarm.co.uk

Lombard House ★★★★★
Guest Accommodation
SILVER AWARD
16 Regent Terrace, Penzance
TR18 4DW
t (01736) 364897
e lombardhouse@btconnect.com
w lombardhousehotel.com

Menwinnen Farm ★★★ Farmhouse
Ludgvan, Penzance
TR20 8BN
t (01736) 740415
e coramenwidden@tiscali.co.uk

Mzima ★★★ Guest Accommodation
Penlee Close, Praa Sands, Penzance
TR20 9SR
t (01736) 763856
e marianfoy@prussia-cove-holiday.com

Number Nine ★★★
Bed & Breakfast
9 Regent Square, Penzance
TR18 4BG
t (01736) 369715
e janeclayton27@gmail.com
w numberninepenzance.com

The Pendennis ★★★★
Guest Accommodation
Alexandra Road, Penzance
TR18 4LZ
t (01736) 363823
e thependennis@googlemail.com
w thependennis.co.uk

Penrose Guest House ★★★★
Guest House
8 Penrose Terrace, Penzance
TR18 2HQ
t (01736) 362782
e enquiries@penrosegsthse.co.uk
w penrosegsthse.co.uk

**Richmond Lodge Guest House
★★★★** Guest Accommodation
61 Morrab Road, Penzance
TR18 4EP
t (01736) 365560
e info@richmondlodge.net
w richmondlodge.net

Rose Farm ★★★★ Farmhouse
Chyanhal, Buryas Bridge, Penzance
TR19 6AN
t (01736) 731808
e penny@rosefarmcornwall.co.uk
w rosefarmcornwall.co.uk

Rosevidney Manor ★★★★★
Guest Accommodation
SILVER AWARD
Tredrea Lane, Rosevidney, Penzance
TR20 9BX
t (01736) 740811
e enquiries@rosevidneymanor.co.uk
w rosevidneymanor.co.uk

Sea View House ★★★★
Guest Accommodation
The Valley, Porthcurno, Penzance
TR19 6JX
t (01736) 810638
e svhouse@btinternet.com
w seaviewhouseporthcurno.com

Shoreline Guest House ★★★★
Guest Accommodation
17 Marine Terrace, The Promenade, Penzance
TR18 4DL
t (01736) 366821
e enquiries@shoreline-penzance.com
w shoreline-penzance.com

The Summer House ★★★★★
Guest Accommodation
GOLD AWARD
Cornwall Terrace, Penzance
TR18 4HL
t (01736) 363744
e reception@summerhouse-cornwall.com
w summerhouse-cornwall.com

Torwood House ★★★★
Guest House
Alexandra Road, Penzance
TR18 4LZ
t (01736) 360063
e lyndasowerby@aol.com
w torwoodhousehotel.co.uk

Tredinney Farm B&B ★★★★
Crows-An-Wra, St Buryan, Penzance
TR19 6HX
t (01736) 810352
e rosemary.warren@btopenworld.com
w tredinneyfarm.co.uk

Tregiffian Farm ★★★★ Farmhouse
SILVER AWARD
St Buryan, Penzance
TR19 6BG
t (01736) 810243
e vicki@tregiffianfarm.co.uk
w tregiffianfarm.co.uk

Trelew Farm B&B ★★★★
Farmhouse SILVER AWARD
Trelew Farm, St Buryan, Penzance
TR19 6ED
t (01736) 810308
e info@trelew.co.uk
w trelew.co.uk

Tremont ★★★★
Guest Accommodation
SILVER AWARD
Alexandra Road, Penzance
TR18 4LZ
t (01736) 362614
e info@tremonthotel.co.uk
w tremonthotel.co.uk

Treventon ★★ Guest House
Alexandra Place, Penzance
TR18 4NE
t (01736) 363521

Warwick House ★★★★
Guest House SILVER AWARD
17 Regent Terrace, Penzance
TR18 4DW
t (01736) 363881
e bookings.warwickhouse@ntlworld.com
w warwickhousepenzance.co.uk

Woodstock Guest House ★★★★
Guest House
29 Morrab Road, Penzance
TR18 4EZ
t (01736) 369049
e info@woodstockguesthouse.co.uk
w woodstockguesthouse.co.uk

Wymering Guest House ★★★
Guest Accommodation
15 Regent Square, Penzance
TR18 4BG
t (01736) 362126
e pam@wymering.com
w wymering.com

PERRANPORTH

The Perranporth Inn ★★★★ Inn
St Pirans Road, Perranporth
TR6 0BJ
t (01872) 573234
e perranporthinn@btconnect.com
w perranporthinn.co.uk

Perranporth Youth Hostel ★★
Hostel
Droskyn Point, Perranporth
TR6 0GS
t (01872) 573812
e perranporth@yha.org.uk

POLPERRO

Chyavallon ★★★★ Bed & Breakfast
SILVER AWARD
Landaviddy Lane, Polperro
PL13 2RT
t (01503) 272788
e chyavallon@btinternet.com
w chyavallon.co.uk

Old Mill House Inn ★★★ Inn
Mill Hill, Polperro
PL13 2RP
t (01503) 272362
e enquiries@oldmillhouseinn.co.uk
w oldmillhouseinn.co.uk

POLRUAN

Hormond House B&B ★★★★
Bed & Breakfast
Fore Street, Fowey
PL23 1PH
t (01726) 870853
e bella@chrisbella.demon.co.uk
w hormondhouse.co.uk

POLZEATH

White Heron ★★★★ Guest House
Polzeath, Wadebridge
PL27 6TJ
t (01208) 863623
e info@whiteheronhotel.co.uk
w whiteheronhotel.co.uk

South West | Cornwall

PORTHCURNO

ardensawah Farm ★★★★
Farmhouse **SILVER AWARD**
 Levan, Penzance, Cornwall
R19 6JL
t (01736) 871520 or 07877124550
e ardensawah@btinternet.com
w porthcurnofarmholidays.com

PORTHLEVEN

he Copper Kettle ★★★★
Guest Accommodation
LVER AWARD
3 Fore Street, Porthleven
R13 9HQ
t (01326) 565660
e tsue.copperkettle@btinternet.com
w cornishcopperkettle.com

arbour Inn ★★★★ *Inn*
LVER AWARD
ommercial Road, Porthleven
R13 9JB
t (01326) 573876
e harbourinn@taustellbrewery.co.uk
w staustellbrewery.co.uk/hotels/
 harbour-inn---porthleven.html

PORT ISAAC

ornish Arms ★★★ *Inn*
endoggett, Port Isaac
30 3HH
t (01208) 880263
e info@cornisharms.com
w cornisharms.com

ane End Farm B&B ★★★★
ed & Breakfast
ort Isaac
30 3HH
t (01208) 880013
e info@laneendcornwall.co.uk
w laneendcornwall.co.uk

ipway ★★★★ *Inn*
he Slipway, The Harbour Front,
ort Isaac
29 3RH
t (01208) 880264
e mark.forbes@tesco.net
w portisaachotel.com

regellist Farm ★★★★
uest Accommodation
OLD AWARD
regellist, Port Isaac
30 3HG
t (01208) 880537
e mail@tregellistfarm.co.uk
w tregellistfarm.co.uk

relulla ★★★★ *Bed & Breakfast*
relill, Port Isaac
30 3HT
t (01208) 850938
e eileenroberts@trellula.freeserve.
w

estaway ★★★★★
ed & Breakfast **SILVER AWARD**
ort Isaac
29 3TF
t (01208) 881156
e info@westawaycornwall.com
w westawaycornwall.com

REDRUTH

ettyscot at the Coombe ★★★
ed & Breakfast
hurch Coombe, Redruth
R16 6RT
t (01209) 315319
e june.hedley242@btinternet.com
w bettyscot.co.uk

Gooneearl Cottage ★★★★
uest House **SILVER AWARD**
heal Rose, Scorrier, Redruth
R16 5DF
t (01209) 891571
e gooneearl@tiscali.co.uk
w gooneearlcottage.com

Lyndhurst Guest House ★★★
Guest House
80 Agar Road, Redruth
TR15 3NB
t (01209) 215146
e sales@lyndhurst-guesthouse.net
w lyndhurst-guesthouse.net

Solcett ★★★★ *Bed & Breakfast*
SILVER AWARD
West Tolgus, Illogan, Redruth
TR15 3TN
t (01209) 218424
e malcom.dunstan@sky.com
w solcett.co.uk

RELUBBUS

Rowan Barn ★★★★ *Farmhouse*
SILVER AWARD
Bosworgy Road, Townshend
TR27 6ES
t (01736) 851223
e sallyandhuw@hotmail.co.uk
w rowanbarn.co.uk

ROCHE

Victoria Inn & Lodge ★★★★ *Inn*
Victoria, Roche, St Austell
PL26 8LQ
t 0845 241 1133
e reservations@smallandfriendly.co.
 uk
w smallandfriendly.co.uk

ROCK

Tregwormond Grange ★★★★
Farmhouse
Tregwormond Farm, St Minver, Rock
PL27 6RE
t (01208) 869640
e janetsluggett@hotmail.co.uk
w visitcornwall.co.uk

Tzitzikama Lodge ★★★★
Guest Accommodation
Rock Road, Rock
PL26 6NP
t (01208) 862839
e enquiries@tzitzikama.co.uk
w cornwall-accommodation.com

RUAN HIGH LANES

New Gonitor Farm ★★★★
Farmhouse
Ruan High Lanes, Truro
TR2 5LE
t (01872) 501345
e rosemary@newgonitorfarm.
 wanadoo.co.uk

Trenona Farm B&B ★★★
Farmhouse
Ruan High Lanes, Truro
TR2 5JS
t (01872) 501339
e info@trenonafarmholidays.co.uk
w trenonafarmholidays.co.uk

SALTASH

Kilna Guest House ★★★
Guest Accommodation
Tideford, Saltash
PL12 5AD
t (01752) 851236
e kilnahouse01@aol.com
w kilnaguesthouse.co.uk

Lantallack ★★★★
Guest Accommodation
GOLD AWARD
Landrake, Saltash
PL12 5AE
t (01752) 851281
e nickywalker44@tiscali.co.uk
w lantallack.co.uk

Riverview B&B ★★★
Bed & Breakfast
82 North Road, Saltash
PL12 6BE
t (01752) 840141
e dvpeterson@btinternet.com
w riverview-saltash.co.uk

SENNEN COVE

Old Success Inn ★★★★ *Inn*
Sennen Cove
TR19 7DG
t (01736) 871232
e oldsuccess@staustellbrewery.co.
 uk
w staustellbrewery.co.uk/hotels/the-
 old-success-inn---sennen-cove.
 html

ST AGNES

Little Trevellas Farm ★★★
Farmhouse
Trevellas, St Agnes
TR5 0XX
t (01872) 552945
e velvetcrystal@xln.co.uk
w stagnesbandb.co.uk

Penkerris ★★ *Guest House*
Penwinnick Road, St Agnes, Truro
TR5 0PA
t (01872) 552262
e info@penkerris.co.uk
w penkerris.co.uk

**The Whitehouse Inn & Luxury
Lodge** ★★★★ *Inn*
Penhallow, St Agnes
TR4 9LQ
t (01872) 573306
e whitehouseinn@btconnect.com
w whitehousecornwall.co.uk

ST AUSTELL

Alexandra Heights ★★★★
Guest Accommodation
43 Alexandra Road, St Austell,
Cornwall
PL25 4QW
t 0172 661855
e alexandraheights@hotmail.co.uk
w alexandraheights.co.uk

Anchorage House ★★★★★
Guest Accommodation
GOLD AWARD
Nettles Corner, Boscundle, St
Austell, Cornwall
PL25 3RH
t (01726) 814071
e info@anchoragehouse.co.uk
w anchoragehouse.co.uk

Ancient Shipbrokers ★★★★
Bed & Breakfast
1 Higher West End, Pentewan, St
Austell
PL26 6BY
t (01726) 843370
e wendy@shipbrokers.orangehome.
 co.uk
w pentewanbedandbreakfast.com

Bankside B&B ★★★★
Guest Accommodation
40A Bodmin Road, St Austell
PL25 5AF
t (01726) 61479
e heather@banksidebb.co.uk
w banksidebb.co.uk

Beech Tree Guest House ★★★★
Guest Accommodation
SILVER AWARD
23 Beech Road, St Austell
PL25 4TS
t (01726) 77461
e info@thebeechtreeguesthouse.co.
 uk
w thebeechtreeguesthouse.co.uk

Cestria B&B ★★★ *Bed & Breakfast*
19 Trevanion Road, St Austell
PL25 4RZ
t (01726) 71172
e steve@cestriabandb.com
w cestriabandb.com

The Chapel Guest House ★★★★
Guest Accommodation
The Old Chapel, St Austell
PL26 8XG
t (01726) 851602
e bookings@thechapelguesthouse.
 co.uk
w thechapelguesthouse.co.uk

Cherry Eden House ★★★
Guest Accommodation
3 Elm Terrace, North Street, St
Austell
PL25 5QF
t (01726) 68466
e info@cherryedenhouse.co.uk
w cherryedenhouse.co.uk

Chy An Gwel ★★
Guest Accommodation
33 Cooperage Road, St Austell
PL25 5SJ
t (01726) 63462
e shyangwel@tiscali.co.uk

Cooperage ★★★★ *Bed & Breakfast*
37 Cooperage Road, Trewoon,
Staustell
PL25 5SJ
t (01726) 70497
e lcooperage@tiscali.co.uk
w cooperagebb.co.uk

Cornerways Guest House ★★★
Guest Accommodation
Penwinnick Road, St Austell
PL25 5DS
t (01726) 61579
e nwsurveys@aol.com

The Cove ★★★
Guest Accommodation
The Square, Pentewan, St Austell
PL26 6DA
t (01726) 843781
e thecove@virgin.net
w pentewanbandb.co.uk

Crossways ★★★★
Guest Accommodation
6 Cromwell Road, St Austell
PL25 4PS
t (01726) 74670
e crossways@sky.com
w crosswaysaccommodation.co.uk

Dowgas House B&B ★★★
Guest Accommodation
Great Dowgas, St Austell
PL26 7LU
t (01726) 883213
e eresdor@aol.com

Duke of Cornwall ★★★ *Inn*
98 Victoria Road, Mount Charles, St
Austell
PL25 4QD
t (01726) 72031
e info@dukeofcornwall.co.uk
w dukeofcornwall.co.uk

The Gables Guest House ★★★★
Guest House
1 Edgcumbe Road, St Austell,
Cornwall
PL25 5DU
t 01726 72638
e info@gablesguesthousebnb.co.uk
w gablesguesthousebnb.co.uk

Gemstones ★★★★
Guest Accommodation
5 Roche Road, St Austell
PL26 8SY
t (01726) 850041
e simon@gemstonesbandb.co.uk
w gemstonesbandb.co.uk

Gwyndra House ★★★
Bed & Breakfast
7 Kings Avenue, St Austell
PL25 4TT
t (01726) 73870
e gwyndrahouse@btconnect.com
w gwyndrahouse.co.uk

Highland Court Lodge ★★★★★
Guest Accommodation
GOLD AWARD
Biscovey Road, Biscovey, St Austell
PL24 2HW
t (01726) 813320
e enquiries@highlandcourt.co.uk
w highlandcourt.co.uk

135

South West | Cornwall

Hillside House Guest House ★★★★
Bed & Breakfast
SILVER AWARD
14 Hillside Road, St Austell
PL25 4DW
t (01726) 64210
e stay@hillside-guesthouse.com
w hillside-guesthouse.com

Holly House ★★★★
Bed & Breakfast
84 Truro Road, St Austell
PL25 5JS
t (01726) 70022
e penny@hollyhousecornwall.co.uk
w hollyhousecornwall.co.uk

Hunter's Moon ★★★★
Guest House **SILVER AWARD**
Chapel Hill, St Austell
PL26 7BU
t (01726) 66445
e enquiries@huntersmooncornwall.co.uk
w huntersmooncornwall.co.uk

Little Grey Cottage ★★★★
Bed & Breakfast
Garker Road, St Austell
PL26 8YD
t (01726) 850486
e info@littlegreycottagebb.co.uk
w littlegreycottagebb.co.uk

Locksley ★★★ *Bed & Breakfast*
Church Road, St Austell
PL25 3NS
t (01726) 72613
e gallowayj265@aol.com

Lowarn ★★★★ *Bed & Breakfast*
16 Poltair Road, St Austell
PL25 4LT
t (01726) 61669
e lowarne@aol.com

Lowarth Gwyth ★★★
Guest Accommodation
80 Truro Road, St Austell
PL25 5JS
t (01726) 70513
e lowarthgwyth@tiscali.co.uk
w lowarthgwyth.co.uk

Lower Barn ★★★★★ *Guest House*
SILVER AWARD
Bosue, St Ewe, St Austell
PL26 6EU
t (01726) 844881
e janie@bosue.co.uk
w bosue.co.uk

Pen Star House ★★★★
Bed & Breakfast **SILVER AWARD**
20 Cromwell Road, St Austell,
Cornwall
PL25 4PS
t (01726) 61367
e pen.star@btinternet.com
w penstarguesthouse.co.uk

Poltarrow Farmhouse ★★★★
Farmhouse **SILVER AWARD**
St Mewan, St Austell
PL26 7DR
t (01726) 67111
e enquire@poltarrow.co.uk
w poltarrow.co.uk

Rashleigh Arms ★★★★ *Inn*
SILVER AWARD
Quay Road, Charlestown
PL25 3NJ
t (01726) 73105
e rashleigh@staustellbrewery.co.uk
w staustellbrewery.co.uk/hotels/rashleigh-arms---st-austell.html

Rescorla Farmhouse ★★★★
Guest Accommodation
Rescorla, St Austell
PL26 8YT
t (01726) 851669
e rescorlafarmhouse@googlemail.com
w rescorlafarmhouse.co.uk

Tall Ships ★★★★★
Bed & Breakfast **SILVER AWARD**
2 Eleven Doors, Charlestown, St Austell
PL25 3NZ
t (01726) 871095
e tallshipscharlestown@tiscali.co.uk
w tallshipscharlestown.com

Trevelyan ★★★★ *Bed & Breakfast*
Porthpean Beach Road, St Austell
PL26 6AU
t (01726) 61201
e info@trevelyanbedandbreakfast.co.uk
w trevelyanbedandbreakfast.co.uk

Yazumez ★★★ *Bed & Breakfast*
Rescorla, St Austell
PL25 8YT
t (01726) 852043
e yazumez@talk21.com
w guest-house-eden-project.com

ST BURYAN

Downs Barn Farm ★★★★★
Farmhouse **GOLD AWARD**
St Buryan
TR19 6DG
t (01736) 810295
e stay@downsbarnfarm.co.uk

Tregurnow Farm ★★★
Guest Accommodation
St Buryan, Penzance
TR19 6BL
t (01736) 810255
e tregurnow@lamorna.biz
w lamorna.biz

ST COLUMB MAJOR

Pennatillie Farm ★★★★★
Farmhouse **SILVER AWARD**
Talskiddy, Nr St Columb Major
TR9 6EF
t (01637) 880280
e angelacolgrove@btconnect.com
w cornish-riviera.co.uk/pennatilliefarm.htm

ST ISSEY

Higher Trevorrick Country House
★★★★★ *Guest Accommodation*
GOLD AWARD
Saint Issey, Nr Padstow, Wadebridge
PL27 7QH
t (01841) 540943
e enquiries@higher-trevorrick.co.uk
w higher-trevorrick.co.uk

ST IVES

abode ★★★★★
Guest Accommodation
SILVER AWARD
1 Fern Glen, St Ives
TR26 1QP
t (01736) 799047
e enquiries@abodestives.co.uk
w abodestives.co.uk

Amie ★★★ *Bed & Breakfast*
Spernen Close, Carbis Bay, St Ives
TR26 2QT
t (01736) 797643
e mrobinson42@googlemail.com
w accommodationstives.com

Beechwood ★★★★
Guest Accommodation
St Ives Road, Carbis Bay, St Ives
TR26 2SX
t (01736) 795170
e beechwood@carbisbay.wanadoo.co.uk
w visitcornwall.com/site/places-to-stay/beechwood-p41223

Blue Hayes ★★★★★
Guest Accommodation
GOLD AWARD
Trelyon Avenue, St Ives
TR26 2AD
t (01736) 797129
e info@bluehayes.co.uk
w bluehayes.co.uk

Carlill Guesthouse ★★★★
Guest House
9 Porthminster Terrace, St Ives
TR26 2DQ
t (01736) 796738
e carlillguesthouse@hotmail.co.uk
w carlillguesthouse.co.uk

Carlyon Guest House ★★★
Guest House
18 The Terrace, St Ives
TR26 2BP
t (01736) 795317
e andrea.papworth@btinternet.com
w carlyon-stives.co.uk

Chy an Gwedhen ★★★★
Guest Accommodation
SILVER AWARD
Saint Ives Road, Carbis Bay, Saint Ives, Cornwall
TR26 2JN
t (01736) 798684
e info@chyangwedhen.com
w chyangwedhen.com

The Chy Morvah ★★★★
Guest Accommodation
The Belyars, St Ives
TR26 2DB
t (01736) 796314

Cornerways ★★★ *Guest House*
1 Bethesda Place, St Ives
TR26 1PA
t (01736) 796706
e cornerwaysstives@aol.com
w cornerwaysstives.com

Dean Court ★★★★★
Guest Accommodation
SILVER AWARD
Trelyon Avenue, St Ives
TR26 2AD
t (01736) 796023
e info@deancourt.vispa.com
w deancourthotel.com

Grey Mullet Guest House ★★★★
Guest Accommodation
2 Bunkers Hill, St Ives
TR26 1LJ
t (01736) 796635
e greymulletguesthouse@lineone.net
w touristnetuk.com/sw/greymullet

Harbour View Guest House ★★★
Guest Accommodation
6 Parc Avenue, St Ives
TR26 2DN
t (01736) 796102
e robfox@fsmail.net
w stives-harbourview.co.uk

The Light House Bed & Breakfast
★★★★★ *Bed & Breakfast*
GOLD AWARD
Pannier Lane, Carbis Bay, St Ives
TR26 2RF
t (01736) 793830
e info@thelighthousebedandbreakfast.co.uk
w thelighthousebedandbreakfast.co.uk

Monterey ★★★★
Guest Accommodation
7 Clodgy View, St Ives
TR26 1JG
t (01736) 794248
e info@monterey-stives.fsnet.co.uk
w monterey-stives.co.uk

The Olive Branch Guest House
★★★★ *Guest Accommodation*
6 Porthminster Terrace, St Ives
TR26 2DQ
t (01736) 795363
e info@theolivebranchstives.co.uk
w theolivebranchstives.co.uk

Panalba ★★★★ *Bed & Breakfast*
8 Belmont Terrace, St Ives
TR26 1DZ
t (01736) 795915
e panalba@btconnect.com
w panalba.co.uk

Salt House ★★★★★
Guest Accommodation
GOLD AWARD
Venton Road, St Ives
TR26 2AQ
t (01736) 791857
e stay@salthousestives.co.uk
w salthousestives.co.uk

Sea Breeze ★★★★
Guest Accommodation
SILVER AWARD
5 Higher Trewidden Road, The Belyars, St Ives
TR26 2DP
t (01736) 797549
e jill.yelling@tiscali.co.uk
w seabreeze-stives.co.uk

Shun Lee House: Luxury Guest Accommodation ★★★★★
Bed & Breakfast **GOLD AWARD**
Trelyon Avenue, St Ives
TR26 2AD
t +44 (01736) 796777
e terry@shunleehotel.co.uk
w shunleehotel.co.uk

Tradewinds ★★★★★
Guest Accommodation
GOLD AWARD
Pannier Lane, Carbis Bay, St Ives
TR26 2RF
t (01736) 799114
e enquiries@tradewindsstives.co.u
w tradewindsstives.co.uk

Tregony Guest House ★★★★
Guest Accommodation
1 Clodgy View, St Ives
TR26 1JG
t (01736) 795884
e info@tregony.com
w tregony.com

Westcliff ★★★
Guest Accommodation
Beach Road, St Ives
TR26 1JY
t (01736) 797708
e westcliff.stives@btinternet.com
w guesthouse-stives.co.uk

ST JUST

Bosavern House ★★★★
Guest House
Bosavern, St Just, Lands End
TR19 7RD
t (01736) 788301
e info@bosavern.com
w bosavern.com

Land's End YHA ★★ *Hostel*
Letcha Vean, Cot Valley, St Just-in-Penwith
TR19 7NT
t (01736) 788437

ST JUST-IN-ROSELAND

Roundhouse Barn B&B Holidays
★★★★★ *Bed & Breakfast*
SILVER AWARD
Messack Lane, St Just In Roseland, Near St Mawes
TR2 5JJ
t (01872) 580038
e info@roundhousebarnholidays.co.uk
w roundhousebarnholidays.co.uk

ST MABYN

Treglown House ★★★★
Farmhouse
Haywood Farm, St Mabyn, Wadebridge
PL30 3BU
t (01208) 841896
e enquiries@treglownhouse.co.uk
w treglownhouse.co.uk

South West | Cornwall

ST MARTIN

ndermere House ★★★
d & Breakfast
Martin, Looe
13 1NX
(01503) 262035
enquiries@windermerehouse.co.uk
uk
windermerehouse.co.uk

ST MARTIN'S

lreath Guest House ★★★★
d & Breakfast
gher Town, St Martin's
25 0QL
(01720) 422046
sjpolreath@aol.com
polreath.com

ST MARY'S

anet B&B ★★★★ Bed & Breakfast
LVER AWARD
rthloo, St Mary's
21 0NF
(01720) 422441
annetcottage@tiscali.co.uk
annet-cottage.co.uk

ril Cottage ★★★★
d & Breakfast SILVER AWARD
urch Road, St Mary's
21 0NA
(01720) 422279
louisehicks@btinternet.com
scillybandb.com

riga Guest House ★★★★
est Accommodation
rthcrassa Road, St Mary's
21 0JL
(01720) 422637
aurigascilly@aol.com

achfield House ★★★★
est House
rthloo, St Mary's
21 0NE
(01720) 422463
whomersley@supanet.com

elmont ★★★★ Guest House
urch Road, St Mary's
21 0NA
(01720) 423154
enquiries@the-belmont.co.uk
the-belmont.co.uk

owarth ★★★ Bed & Breakfast
ms Valley, St Mary's
21 0JX
(01720) 422353
rachaelsmalley@aol.com

uckingham House ★★★
est House
e Bank, St Mary's
21 0HY
(01720) 422543

ylet ★★★ Guest House
urch Road, St Mary's
21 0NA
(01720) 422479
thebylet@bushinternet.com
byletholidays.com

arn Ithen ★★★★ Bed & Breakfast
LVER AWARD
ench Lane, Old Town, St Mary's
21 0PA
(01720) 422917
roz-allen@carn-ithen.fsnet.co.uk
carnithen.co.uk

arntop Guest House ★★★★
est House SILVER AWARD
urch Road, St Mary's
21 0NA
(01720) 423763
jenkins@carntop.co.uk
carntop.co.uk

olossus ★★★★ Bed & Breakfast
lot's Retreat, St Mary's
21 0PB
(01720) 423361
enquiries@colossus-scilly.co.uk
colossus-scilly.co.uk

Covean Cottage ★★★ Guest House
St Agnes
TR22 0PL
t (01720) 422620
e stay@coveancottage.com
w coveancottage.com

Crebinick House ★★★★
Guest House SILVER AWARD
Church Street, St Mary's
TR21 0JT
t (01720) 422968
e enquiries@crebinick.co.uk
w crebinick.co.uk

Demelza Bed & Breakfast ★★★★
Bed & Breakfast
Demelza, Jackson's Hill, St Mary's
TR21 0JZ
t (01720) 422803
e sibleysonscilly@tiscali.com

Eastbank ★★★★ Bed & Breakfast
Porthloo, St Mary's
TR21 0NE
t (01720) 423695
e enquiries@scilly-holidays.co.uk

**Evergreen Cottage Guest House
★★★★** Guest House
The Parade, Hugh Town, St Mary's
TR21 0LP
t (01720) 422711
e evergreen.scilly@btinternet.com
w evergreencottageguesthouse.co.uk

Freesia Guesthouse ★★★★
Guest House
The Parade, St Mary's
TR21 0LP
t (01720) 423676
e freesiaguesthouse@hotmail.com
w scillyfreesia.co.uk

The Greenlaws ★★★★
Bed & Breakfast
Old Town, St Mary's
TR21 0NH
t (01720) 422045

Hellweathers Guest House ★★★★
Bed & Breakfast
St Agnes
TR22 0PL
t (01720) 422430

**Isles of Scilly Country Guest
House ★★★** Guest House
Sage House, High Lanes, St Mary's
TR21 0NW
t (01720) 422440
e scillyguesthouse@hotmail.com
w scillyguesthouse.co.uk

Kistvaen ★★★★ Bed & Breakfast
Sally Port, St Mary's
TR21 0JE
t (01720) 422002
e chivy002@yahoo.com
w kistvaen.co.uk

The Lookout ★★★★
Bed & Breakfast
Porthcressa, St Mary's
TR21 0JQ
t (01720) 422132
e thelookout@sky.com
w thelookoutbandb.co.uk

Lynwood ★★★★ Bed & Breakfast
Church Street, St Mary's
TR21 0JT
t (01720) 423313
e d-parr@sky.com

Lyonnesse Guest House ★★★
Guest House
Lower Strand, St Mary's
TR21 0PS
t (01720) 422458
e lyonnesse-scilly@tiscali.co.uk

Mincarlo ★★★ Guest House
Strand, Carn Thomas, St Mary's
TR21 0PT
t (01720) 422513
e manager@mincarlo-ios.co.uk
w mincarlo-ios.co.uk

Nundeeps ★★★★
Guest Accommodation
Rams Valley, St Mary's
TR21 0JX
t (01720) 422517
e hawkins@nundeeps.co.uk
w nundeeps.co.uk

The Old Town Inn ★★★★ Inn
The Old Town Inn, Old Town, St Mary's
TR21 0NN
t (01720) 422301
e oldtowninn@hotmail.co.uk
w oldtowninn.co.uk

Pelistry Cottage ★★★★
Bed & Breakfast SILVER AWARD
Pelistry Cottage, The Parade, St Mary's
TR21 0LP
t (01720) 422506
e scillyhols@hotmail.com
w scillyholidays.com

Rose Cottage ★★★★
Bed & Breakfast SILVER AWARD
Strand, St Mary's
TR21 0PT
t (01720) 422078
e jeremy@scillyrose.co.uk
w scillyrose.co.uk

Santa Maria ★★★★ Guest House
Sallyport, St Mary's
TR21 0JE
t (01720) 422687

**Shamrock Bed & Breakfast
★★★★** Bed & Breakfast
High Lanes, St Mary's
TR21 0NW
t (01720) 423269
e scillyhorse@hotmail.com

Shearwater Guest House ★★★
Guest House
The Parade, St Mary's
TR21 0LP
t (01720) 422402
e shearwater2010@hotmail.com
w shearwater-guest-house.co.uk

St Hellena ★★★★ Bed & Breakfast
13 Garrison Lane, St Mary's
TR21 0JD
t (01720) 423231
e mcguinness@st-hellena.fsnet.co.uk
w sthellenascilly.co.uk

Sylina Guesthouse ★★★★
Guest House SILVER AWARD
McFarlands Downs, St Mary's
TR21 0NS
t (01720) 422129
e enquiries@sylina.co.uk
w sylina.co.uk

Tolman House ★★★★
Guest Accommodation
SILVER AWARD
Old Town, St Mary's
TR21 0NH
t (01720) 422967
e tolmanhouse@hotmail.co.uk
w tolmanhouse-scilly.co.uk

Trelawney ★★★★ Guest House
Church Street, St Mary's
TR21 0JT
t (01720) 422377
e jharlin@hotmail.com
w trelawney-ios.co.uk

Veronica Lodge ★★★
Bed & Breakfast
The Garrison, St Mary's
TR21 0LS
t (01720) 422585
e veronicalodge@freenetname.co.uk

Westford House ★★★★
Guest House
Church Street, St Mary's
TR21 0JT
t (01720) 422510
e westfordhouse@aol.com
w westfordhouse.com

The Wheelhouse ★★★★
Guest House
Little Porth, St Mary's
TR21 0JG
t (01720) 422719

Wingletang Guest House ★★★
Guest House
The Parade, St Mary's
TR21 0LP
t (01720) 422381
e enquiries@wingletangguesthouse.co.uk
w wingletangguesthouse.co.uk

ST MAWES

Gwelesmor ★★★ Bed & Breakfast
Gwelesmor House, 18 Polvarth Road, St Mawes
TR2 5AT
t (01326) 270731
e phyllismichell@supanet.com
w gwelesmorhouse.co.uk

Nearwater Guest Accommodation
Polvarth Road, St Mawes
TR2 5AY
t (01326) 279278
e info@nearwaterstmawes.co.uk
w nearwaterstmawes.co.uk

The Rising Sun Hotel ★★★★ Inn
The Square, St Mawes
TR2 5DJ
t (01326) 270233
e therisingsun@btclick.com
w risingsunstmawes.co.uk

The Rosevine ★★★★★
Guest Accommodation
GOLD AWARD
Porthcurnick Beach, St Mawes
TR2 5EW
t (01872) 580206
e info@rosevine.co.uk
w rosevine.co.uk

Trenestral Farm ★★★ Farmhouse
St Mawes
TR2 5LX
t (01872) 501259
e ann@trenestral5.plus.com
w trenestralfarm.co.uk

Trewithian Farm B&B ★★★★
Guest Accommodation
Trewithian, St Mawes
TR2 5EJ
t (01872) 580293
e enquiries@trewithian-farm.co.uk
w trewithian-farm.co.uk

ST MAWGAN

Dalswinton House ★★★★
Guest Accommodation
Parsonage Lane, St Mawgan in Pydar, Cornwall
TR8 4EZ
t (01637) 860385
e dalswintonhouse@btconnect.com
w dalswinton.com

ST MELLION

Pentillie Castle & Estate ★★★★★
Guest Accommodation
GOLD AWARD
Saint Mellion, Saltash
PL12 6QD
t 01579 350044
e contact@pentillie.co.uk
w pentillie.co.uk and www.pentillieweddings.co.uk

ST MERRYN

Greenacres ★★★★ Bed & Breakfast
Tregavone Farm, St Merryn
PL28 8JZ
t (01841) 520478
e kelly@kellylynden.orangehome.co.uk

South West | Cornwall

ST MINVER / POLZEATH
Tredower Barton ★★★
Bed & Breakfast
St Minver, Wadebridge, Cornwall
PL27 6RG
t (01208) 813501

ST NEOT
Colliford Tavern ★★★★ *Inn*
Colliford Lake, St Neot
PL14 6PZ
t (01208) 821335
e info@colliford.com
w colliford.com

Lampen Farm ★★★★ *Farmhouse*
St Neot
PL14 6PB
t (01579) 320284
e joan@lampenfarm.fsnet.co.uk
w lampen-farm.co.uk

ST NEOT, LISKEARD
Higher Searles Down ★★★★
Bed & Breakfast **SILVER AWARD**
Liskeard
PL14 6QA
t (01208) 821412
e glen@hsdown.go-plus.net
w hsdown.go-plus.net

ST NEWLYN EAST
Chy-An-Eglos *Guest Accommodation*
5 Churchtown, St Newlyn East
TR8 5LQ
t (01872) 519170
e info@chy-an-eglos-bb.co.uk
w chy-an-eglos-bb.co.uk

ST TEATH
Path's End ★★★★ *Bed & Breakfast*
North Road, St Teath
PL30 3JZ
t (01208) 850441
e btg65@hotmail.com

THE LIZARD
Lizard Point Youth Hostel ★★★★
Hostel
Lizard
TR12 7NT
t 0870 770 6120

The Top House Inn ★★★★ *Inn*
The Lizard
TR12 7NQ
t (01326) 290974
e clarejulier@tiscali.co.uk
w thetophouselizard.co.uk

TINTAGEL
The Avalon ★★★★★ *Guest House*
SILVER AWARD
Atlantic Road, Tintagel
PL34 0DD
t (01840) 770116
e avalontintagel@googlemail.com
w tintagelbedbreakfast.co.uk/

The Bluff Centre ★★★★
Guest House
Tintagel
PL34 0EP
t (01840) 770033
e book@bluffcentre.co.uk
w bluffcentre.co.uk

Bosayne Guest House ★★★★
Guest Accommodation
Atlantic Road, Tintagel
PL34 0DE
t (01840) 770514
e enquiries@bosayne.co.uk
w bosayne.co.uk

The Cottage Teashop ★★★★
Bed & Breakfast
Bossiney Road, Tintagel
PL34 0AH
t (01840) 770639

Four Winds ★★★★ *Bed & Breakfast*
Knight's Close, Atlantic Road, Tintagel
PL34 0DR
t (01840) 770300
e kay4windsaccom@aol.com

King Arthur's Arms Inn ★★★★
Inn
Fore Street, Tintagel
PL34 0DA
t (01840) 770831
e kingarthurs.pub@btconnect.com
w kingarthursarms.co.uk

Lan-Y-Mor ★★★★ *Bed & Breakfast*
3 Knights Close, Tintagel
PL34 0DR
t (01840) 770933
e dave@dowen20.eclipse.co.uk
w watersedgeholidaylet.vpweb.co.uk

Melrosa ★★★★ *Bed & Breakfast*
Tintagel
PL34 0ES
t (01840) 770360
e valerie.stephens@btinternet.com

Mill House ★★★★ *Inn*
The Mill House, Trebarwith, Tintagel
PL34 0HD
t (01840) 770200
e management@themillhouseinn.co.uk
w themillhouseinn.co.uk

The Penallick ★★★ *Guest House*
Tintagel
PL34 0EJ
t (01840) 770296
e jason.haynes@talk21.com
w tintagelbedandbreakfast.co.uk

Reevescott ★★★★ *Bed & Breakfast*
Tintagel
PL34 0BG
t (01840) 770533
e john.pen@talktalk.net

Tintagel Youth Hostel ★★ *Hostel*
Dunderhole Point, Tintagel
PL34 0DW
t (01840) 770334
e tintagel@yha.org.uk

Trevenna Lodge ★★★★
Guest House
Castle Heights, Atlantic Road, Tintagel
PL34 0DE
t (01840) 770264
e trevennalodge.com

Westcote House B&B ★★★★
Bed & Breakfast
Bossiney Road, Tintagel
PL34 0AX
t (01840) 779194
e nevchamberlain@btinternet.com
w westcote-house.co.uk

TOLGUS MOUNT
Tumblydown Farm ★★★
Bed & Breakfast
Tolgus Mount, Redruth
TR15 3TA
t (01209) 211191
w tumblydownfarm.co.uk

TORPOINT
Cambridge House ★★★★
Guest Accommodation
Wellington Street, Torpoint
PL11 2DG
t (01752) 813062
e milton.hussey@virgin.net
w cam-house.co.uk

TREBARWITH STRAND
The Port William ★★★★ *Inn*
Trebarwith Strand, Tintagel
PL34 0HB
t (01840) 770230
e theportwilliam@btinternet.com
w theportwilliam.com

TREGONY
Tregonan ★★★★
Guest Accommodation
SILVER AWARD
Tregony
TR2 5SN
t (01872) 530249
e sandra@tregonan.co.uk
w tregonan.co.uk

TRELOWTH, ST AUSTELL
Polgreen ★★★★ *Bed & Breakfast*
Trelowth, St Austell
PL26 7DZ
t (01726) 64546
e office@polgreenguesthouse.co.uk
w polgreenguesthouse.co.uk

TRURO
Bissick Old Mill ★★★★
Guest House
Ladock, Truro
TR2 4PG
t (01726) 882557
e enquiries@bissickoldmill.plus.com
w bissickoldmill.co.uk

Chycara ★★★★ *Bed & Breakfast*
Chycara House, Chyreen Lane, Truro
TR3 6LG
t (01872) 865447
e info@chycara.co.uk
w chycara.co.uk

Chy Vista ★★★★ *Bed & Breakfast*
Higher Penair, St Clement, Truro
TR1 1TD
t (01872) 270592
e vc_richards@yahoo.co.uk

Come-To-Good Farm ★★★★
Farmhouse
Come-to-Good, Feock, Truro
TR3 6QS
t (01872) 863828
e info@cometogoodfarm.co.uk
w cometogoodfarm.co.uk

Hazelnut Cottage ★★★★
Bed & Breakfast
Perranwell Station, Truro
TR3 7PU
t (01872) 865082
e tic@truro.gov.uk

Highfield House ★★★★
Bed & Breakfast
1 Newmills Close, Truro
TR1 3EY
t (01872) 277725
e angela@highfield4u.com
w highfield4u.com

Homestead Farm B&B ★★★★
Bed & Breakfast
Homestead Farm, Penhallow, Truro
TR4 9LT
t (01872) 572583
e julieharrod@btinternet.com
w homesteadfarmcornwall.co.uk

Killagorden Cottage ★★
Bed & Breakfast
Idless, Truro
TR4 9QP
t (01872) 272840
e bb@cornwallgetaway.com
w cornwallgetaway.com

Lambriggan Court ★★★★
Guest Accommodation
Lambriggan, Penhallow, Truro
TR4 9LU
t (01872) 571636
e lynn@lambriggancourt.com
w lambriggancourt.com

Palm Tree House ★★★★
Bed & Breakfast
8 Parkins Terrace, Truro
TR1 1EJ
t (01872) 270100
e bodybusiness@btconnect.com

The Rowan Tree ★★★
Bed & Breakfast
3 Parkvedras Terrace, Truro
TR1 3DF
t (01872) 277928
e christinecartlidge101@googlemail.com
w rowantreetruro.co.uk

Stanton House ★★ *Bed & Breakfast*
11 Ferris Town, Truro
TR1 3JG
t (01872) 223666
e iris@stantons.eclipse.co.uk

Tor Vean Bed & Breakfast ★★★
Bed & Breakfast
Kenwyn Road, Truro
TR1 3SY
t (01872) 271766
e heather591@hotmail.com

Townhouse Rooms ★★★★
Guest Accommodation
City Centre, 20 Falmouth Road, Truro
TR1 2HX
t 00 44 (0)1872 277374
e info@trurotownhouse.com
w trurotownhouse.com

Treswithian Barn ★★★★
Bed & Breakfast
Truro
TR2 5JT
t (01872) 501274

Woodland Valley Farm ★★★★
Group Hostel
Truro
TR2 4PT
t (01726) 884127
e enquiries@woodlandvalley.co.uk
w woodlandvalley.co.uk

VERYAN
Treverbyn House ★★★★
Bed & Breakfast
Pendower Road, Veryan, Truro, Cornwall
TR2 5QL
t (01872) 501201
e info@treverbyn.co.uk
w treverbyn.co.uk

WADEBRIDGE
Brookdale B&B ★★★★
Bed & Breakfast **SILVER AWARD**
Trevanion Road, Wadebridge
PL27 7PA
t (01208) 815425
e enquiries@brookdalebandb.co.uk
w brookdalebandb.co.uk

Burlawn Farm ★★★★ *Farmhouse*
Burlawn Farm, Higher Pengelly Cross, Wadebridge
PL27 7LA
t (01208) 815548
e burlawnfarm@tiscali.co.uk

Cannalidgey Villa Farm ★★★★
Farmhouse **SILVER AWARD**
St Issey, Wadebridge
PL27 7RB
t (01208) 812276
e info@cannalidgeycottages.co.uk
w cannalidgeycottages.co.uk

Pawton Stream ★★★★
Bed & Breakfast **SILVER AWARD**
St Breock, Wadebridge
PL27 7LN
t (01208) 814845
e jon.bristow@btopenworld.com

Pengelly Farmhouse ★★★★
Bed & Breakfast **SILVER AWARD**
Burlawn, Wadebridge
PL27 7LA
t (01208) 814217
e hodgepete@hotmail.com
w pengellyfarm.co.uk

Spring Gardens ★★★
Bed & Breakfast
Bradfords Quay, Wadebridge
PL27 6DB
t (01208) 813771
e springjen1@aol.com
w spring-garden.co.uk

South West | Cornwall/Isles of Scilly/Devon

Giles Cottage ★★★★
Bed & Breakfast
Bonvena Hill, Wadebridge
PL27 6DP
t (01208) 813695
e info@stgilescottage.co.uk
w stgilescottage.co.uk

Trevanger Farm ★★★★
Farmhouse
Minver, Wadebridge
PL27 6QR
t (01208) 869092
e trevanger@hotmail.co.uk

Trevorrick Farm ★★★★
Wadebridge
PL27 7QH
t (01841) 540574
e info@trevorrick.co.uk
w trevorrick.co.uk

WADEBRIDGE (4 MILES)

Tregolls Farm B&B ★★★★
Guest Accommodation
Saint Wenn, Bodmin
PL30 5PG
t (01208) 812154
e tregollsfarm@btclick.com
w tregollsfarm.co.uk

WEST LOOE

Calico Guest House ★★★★
Guest Accommodation
Marine Drive, West Looe
PL13 2DH
t (01503) 262160
e enquiries@calicoguesthouse.co.uk
w calicoguesthouse.co.uk

The Old Bridge House ★★★★
Guest House SILVER AWARD
The Quay, West Looe, Looe
PL13 2BU
t (01503) 263159
e mail@theoldbridgehousehotel.co.uk
w theoldbridgehousehotel.co.uk

Tidal Court Guest House ★★★
Guest House
Church Street, West Looe, Looe
PL13 2EX
t (01503) 263695

WHITSTONE

Whiteleigh Cottage ★★★★
Bed & Breakfast
Whitstone, Holsworthy
EX22 6LB
t (01288) 341082
e whiteleighcot@hotmail.com
w whiteleighcottage.co.uk

WIDEGATES

Coombe Farm ★★★★
Guest Accommodation
Widegates, Looe
PL13 1QN
t (01503) 240223
e coombe_farm@hotmail.com
w coombefarmhotel.co.uk

Isles of Scilly

PORTHLOO

Armeria ★★ Bed & Breakfast
Porthloo, St Mary's, Isles of Scilly
TR21 0NF
t (01720) 422961
e brian.holt1@mypostoffice.co.uk

ST MARY'S

Anjeric Guest House ★★★
Guest House
The Strand, St Mary's
TR21 0PS
t (01720) 422700
e judyarcher@yahoo.co.uk
w scillyonline.co.uk

Treebooth Guest House ★★★
Guest Accommodation
Buzza Street, Porth Cressa, St Mary's, Isles of Scilly
TR21 0HX
t 01720 422 548

TRESCO

The New Inn ★★★★ Inn
SILVER AWARD
Tresco, Isles of Scilly
TR24 0QE
t (01720) 422844
e newinn@tresco.co.uk
w tresco.co.uk/holidays/new_inn.asp

Devon

APPLEDORE

West Farm ★★★★★
Bed & Breakfast SILVER AWARD
Irsha Street, Appledore, Bideford
EX39 1RY
t (01237) 425269
e gail@appledore-devon.co.uk
w appledore-devon.co.uk

ASHBURTON

Blackler Barton House ★★★★★
Bed & Breakfast SILVER AWARD
Landscove, Ashburton, Newton Abbot, Devon
TQ13 7LZ
t (01364) 762385
e blacklerbarton@btinternet.com
w blacklerbartonhouse.co.uk

Golden Lion House ★★★★★
Guest House
58 East Street, Ashburton, Newton Abbot, Devon
TQ13 7AX
t 07831 787837
e info@goldenlionhouse.com
w goldenlionhouse.com

ASH MILL

Kerscott Farm ★★★★★ Farmhouse
GOLD AWARD
Ash Mill, Bishops Nympton, South Molton
EX36 4QG
t (01769) 550262
e kerscott.farm@virgin.net
w devon-bandb.co.uk

AXMINSTER

Hedgehog Corner ★★★★
Guest Accommodation
SILVER AWARD
Lyme Road, Axminster
EX13 5SU
t (01297) 32036
e info@hedgehogcorner.co.uk
w hedgehogcorner.co.uk

Kerrington House ★★★★★
Guest Accommodation
GOLD AWARD
Musbury Road, Axminster
EX13 5JR
t (01297) 35333
e ja.reaney@kerringtonhouse.com
w kerringtonhouse.com

Prestoller House ★★★★
Guest Accommodation
Beavor Lane, Axminster
EX13 5EQ
t (01297) 33659
e prestollerhouse@btinternet.com
w prestollerbedandbreakfast.co.uk

AYLESBEARE

Livermore Farm ★★★★ Farmhouse
Aylesbeare, Exeter
EX5 2DH
t (01395) 232351
e stevesmith@livermorefarm.co.uk
w livermorefarm.co.uk

BARBROOK

Culdoon ★★★★ Bed & Breakfast
Cherrybridge, Barbrook, Lynton
EX35 6PE
t (01598) 752335
e info@culdoon.co.uk
w culdoon.co.uk

BARNSTAPLE

Huxtable Farm ★★★★ Farmhouse
SILVER AWARD
West Buckland, Barnstaple
EX32 0SR
t (01598) 760254
e jackie@huxtablefarm.co.uk
w huxtablefarm.co.uk

Kimbland Farm ★★★ Farmhouse
Brayford, Barnstaple
EX32 7PS
t (01598) 710352
e info@kimblandfarmholidays.co.uk
w kimblandfarmholidays.co.uk

Lower Yelland Farm ★★★★
Guest Accommodation
Fremington, Barnstaple
EX31 3EN
t (01271) 860101
e peterday@loweryellandfarm.co.uk
w loweryellandfarm.co.uk

Sheltercombe Cottage ★★★★
Bed & Breakfast
Bratton Fleming, Barnstaple
EX32 7JL
t (01598) 710513
e enquiries@sheltercombecottage.co.uk
w sheltercombecottage.co.uk

The Spinney Country Guesthouse
★★★★ Guest House
Shirwell, Barnstaple
EX31 4JR
t (01271) 850282
e thespinneyguesthouse@btconnect.com
w thespinneyshirwell.co.uk

Twitchen Farm ★★★★ Farmhouse
Challacombe, Barnstaple
EX31 4TT
t (01598) 763568
e holidays@twitchen.co.uk
w twitchen.co.uk

BATTISBOROUGH CROSS

Bugle Rocks ★★★★
Bed & Breakfast
Battisborough Cross, Plymouth
PL8 1JX
t (01752) 830422
e stay@buglerocks.co.uk
w buglerocks.co.uk

BEAWORTHY

Greenacres ★★★★ Farmhouse
Virginstow, Beaworthy
EX21 5EA
t (01409) 211691 07789901261
e paul@greenacresdevon.co.uk
w greenacresdevon.co.uk

BEER

Belmont House B&B ★★★★
Guest Accommodation
Gordon Terrace, Clapps Lane, Beer
EX12 3EN
t (01297) 24415
e simongooch12345@aol.com
w belmonthousebedandbreakfast.co.uk

YHA Beer ★★★★ Hostel
Bovey Combe, Townsend, Seaton
EX12 3LL
t 0870 770 5690
e beer@yha.org.uk
w yha.org.uk

BERRYNARBOR

The Lodge ★★★★
Guest Accommodation
Pitt Hill, Ilfracombe
EX34 9SG
t (01271) 883246
e philbridle@aol.com
w lodge-country-house-hotel.co.uk

BERRY POMEROY

Berry Farm ★★★★ Farmhouse
Berry Pomeroy, Totnes
TQ9 6LG
t (01803) 863231

BIDEFORD

Great Court Farm ★★★★
Farmhouse SILVER AWARD
Weston Lane, Totnes
TQ9 6LB
t (01803) 862326
e janet.hooper3@btinternet.com
w greatcourt-totnes.co.uk

Bulworthy Cottage ★★★★
Guest House SILVER AWARD
Stony Cross, Alverdiscott, Bideford
EX39 4PY
t (01271) 858441
e bulworthy@aol.com
w bulworthycottage.co.uk

Elmscott Farm ★★★★ Farmhouse
Hartland, Bideford
EX39 6ES
t (01237) 441276
e info@elmscott.org.uk
w elmscott.org.uk

The Mount ★★★★ Guest House
SILVER AWARD
Northdown Road, Bideford
EX39 3LP
t (01237) 473748
e andrew@themountbideford.fsnet.co.uk
w themountbideford.co.uk

BLACKAWTON

Middle Wadstray Farm ★★★
Farmhouse
Middle Wadstray, Blackawton, Totnes
TQ9 7DD
t (01803) 712346
e stella.buckpitt1@btopenworld.com
w middle-wadstray-farm.com

Washwalk Mill ★★★★
Bed & Breakfast SILVER AWARD
Blackawton, Totnes
TQ9 7AE
t (01803) 712217
e enquiries@washwalkmill.co.uk
w washwalkmill.co.uk

BOVEY TRACEY

Brookfield House ★★★★★
Bed & Breakfast GOLD AWARD
Challabrook Lane, Bovey Tracey
TQ13 9DF
t (01626) 836181
e enquiries@brookfield-house.com
w brookfield-house.com

Oaklands ★★★★ Bed & Breakfast
SILVER AWARD
Challabrook Lane, Bovey Tracey
TQ13 9DF
t (01626) 832602
e oaklandsbedandbreakfast@sky.com
w oaklandsholidaysdevon.co.uk

BOWD

The Barn & Pinn Cottage Guest House ★★★★ Guest House
Bowd Cross, Sidmouth
EX10 0ND
t (01395) 513613
e barnpinncottage@btinternet.com
w thebarnandpinncottage.co.uk

BRADFORD

Bason Farm ★★★★ Farmhouse
Bradford, Holsworthy
EX22 7AW
t (01409) 281277
e info@basonfarmholidays.co.uk
w basonfarmholidays.co.uk

BRADWORTHY

Lew Barn ★★★ Bed & Breakfast
Bradworthy, Holsworthy, North Devon
EX22 7SQ
t (01409) 241964
e mail@lewbarn.co.uk
w lewbarn.co.uk

139

South West | Devon

BRATTON CLOVELLY

Eversfield Lodge ★★★★
Guest Accommodation
Ellacott Barton, Bratton Clovelly, Okehampton
EX20 4LB
t (01837) 871480
e bookings@eversfieldlodge.co.uk
w eversfieldlodge.co.uk/

BRATTON FLEMING

Haxton Down Farm ★★★★
Farmhouse
Bratton Fleming, Barnstaple
EX32 7JL
t (01598) 710275
e haxtondownfarm@btconnect.com
w haxton-down-farm-holidays.co.uk

BRAUNTON

Combas Farm ★★★★ *Farmhouse*
Putsborough, Croyde, Braunton
EX33 1PH
t (01271) 890398
e combasfarm@hotmail.co.uk
w combasfarm.co.uk

George Hotel ★★★ *Inn*
Exeter Road, Braunton
EX33 2JJ
t (01271) 812029
e georgehoteldevon@btconnect.com
w thegeorgehotel-braunton.co.uk

BRENDON

Brendon House ★★★★
Guest House
Brendon, Exmoor, Lynton
EX35 6PS
t (01598) 741206
e brendonhouse4u@aol.com
w brendonhouse4u.com

BRIDESTOWE

Knole Farm ★★★★★ *Farmhouse*
SILVER AWARD
Bridestowe, Okehampton
EX20 4HA
t (01837) 861241
e mavis.bickle@btconnect.com
w knolefarm-dartmoor-holidays.co.uk

BRIXHAM

Brioc ★★★★ *Guest Accommodation*
11 Prospect Road, Brixham, Devon
TQ5 8HS
t 01803 853540
e briochotel@btconnect.com
w briochotel.co.uk

Brixham House ★★★★
Guest House
130 New Road, Brixham
TQ5 8DA
t (01803) 853954
e stay@brixhamhouse.co.uk
w brixhamhouse.co.uk

Brookside Guest House ★★★★★
Guest Accommodation
SILVER AWARD
160 New Road, Brixham
TQ5 8DA
t (01803) 858858
e info@brooksidebrixham.co.uk
w brooksidebrixham.co.uk

Churston Way Lodge ★★★★
Guest Accommodation
2 Churston Way, Brixham
TQ5 8DD
t (01803) 853315
e info@churchstonwaylodge.co.uk
w churstonwaylodge.co.uk

Fair Winds ★★★★ *Guest House*
SILVER AWARD
166 New Road, Brixham
TQ5 8DA
t (01803) 857537
e stay@fairwindsbrixham.co.uk
w fairwindsbrixham.co.uk

Melville Guesthouse ★★★★
Guest House
45 New Road, Brixham
TQ5 8NL
t (01803) 852033
e info@themelville.co.uk
w themelville.co.uk

Midhurst Bed & Breakfast ★★★★
Guest Accommodation
132 New Road, Brixham
TQ5 8DA
t (01803) 857331
e l.goodwill@homecall.co.uk
w midhurstbnb.co.uk

Ranscombe House ★★★★
Guest Accommodation
Ranscombe Road, Brixham
TQ5 9UP
t (01803) 882337
e ranscombe@lineone.net
w ranscombehousehotel.co.uk

Redlands ★★★★ *Guest House*
136 New Road, Brixham
TQ5 8DA
t (01803) 853813
e redlandsbrixham@aol.com
w redlandsbrixham.co.uk

Sampford House ★★★
Guest Accommodation
57-59 King Street, Brixham
TQ5 9TH
t (01803) 857761
e sampfordhouse@yahoo.co.uk
w sampfordhouse.co.uk

Sea Tang Guest House ★★★★
Guest House
67 Berry Head Road, Brixham
TQ5 9AA
t (01803) 854651
e seatang@btconnect.com
w seatang.guesthouse.co.uk

The Shoalstone ★★★
Guest Accommodation
105 Berry Head Road, Brixham
TQ5 9AG
t (01803) 857919

Sunnybrook Guest House ★★★
Guest House
156 New Road, Brixham
TQ5 8DA
t (01803) 854386
e info@sunnybrook.co.uk
w sunnybrook.co.uk

Thirty *Bed & Breakfast*
30 Penpethy Close, Brixham
TQ5 8NP
t (01803) 858499
e thirty30@btinternet.com
w thirty-bed-and-breakfast.co.uk

Trefoil Guest House ★★★★
Guest House
134 New Road, Brixham
TQ5 8DA
t (01803) 855266
e david.harmer@virgin.net
w trefoilguesthouse.co.uk

Westbury Guest House ★★★★
Guest House
51 New Road, Brixham
TQ5 8NL
t (01803) 851684
e info@westburyguesthouse.co.uk
w westburyguesthouse.co.uk

Woodlands Guest House ★★★★
Guest House
Parkham Road, Brixham
TQ5 9BU
t (01803) 852040
e woodlandsbrixham@btinternet.com
w woodlandsdevon.co.uk

BRIXTON

Venn Farm ★★★★
Guest Accommodation
Brixton, Plymouth
PL8 2AX
t (01752) 880378
e info@vennfarm.co.uk
w vennfarm.co.uk

BROADCLYST

Heath Gardens ★★★★
Bed & Breakfast
Broadclyst, Exeter
EX5 3HL
t (01392) 462311
e info@heathgardens.co.uk
w heathgardens.co.uk

BROADHEMBURY

Stafford Barton Farm ★★★★
Farmhouse
Broadhembury, Honiton
EX14 3LU
t (01404) 841403
e jeanwalters1@tesco.net

BUCKERELL

Broadlands ★★★★ *Bed & Breakfast*
Buckerell, Honiton
EX14 3EP
t (01404) 850894

BUDLEIGH SALTERTON

Hansard House ★★★★
Guest Accommodation
SILVER AWARD
3 Northview Road, Budleigh Salterton
EX9 6BY
t (01395) 442773
e enquiries@hansardhousehotel.co.uk
w hansardhousehotel.co.uk

Heath Close Bed & Breakfast ★★★★★ *Bed & Breakfast*
GOLD AWARD
Lansdowne Road, Budleigh Salterton
EX9 6AH
t (01395) 444337
e info@heathclose.com
w heathclose.com

CHERITON FITZPAINE

Devon Wine School ★★★★★
Bed & Breakfast GOLD AWARD
Redyeates Farm, Cheriton Fitzpaine, Crediton
EX17 4HG
t (01363) 866742
e alastair@devonwineschool.co.uk
w devonwineschool.co.uk/index.html

CHILSWORTHY

Thorne Park ★★★★ *Farmhouse*
Thorne Park, Holsworthy
EX22 7BL
t (01409) 253339
e thornepark@farming.co.uk
w thornepark-devon.co.uk

CHITTLEHAMPTON

Higher Biddacott Farm ★★★★
Farmhouse
Chittlehampton, Umberleigh
EX37 9PY
t (01769) 540222
e waterers.@sosi.net
w heavyhorses.net

CHRISTOW

Hyner Farm ★★★★
Guest Accommodation
Christow, Exeter
EX6 7NT
t (01647) 252923
e preston916@btinternet.com

CHURSTON FERRERS

White Horse Guesthouse ★★★★
Guest House
Dartmouth Road, Churston Ferrers, Brixham
TQ5 0LL
t (01803) 842381
e bookings@thewhitehorsehotel.co.uk
w thewhitehorsehotel.co.uk

CLOVELLY

Fuchsia Cottage ★★★★
Bed & Breakfast
Burscott, Clovelly, Bideford
EX39 5RR
t (01237) 431398
e tom@clovelly-holidays.co.uk
w clovelly-holidays.co.uk

COLYFORD

Swan Hill House ★★★★★
Guest House SILVER AWARD
Swan Hill Road, Colyford, Colyton
EX24 6QQ
t (01297) 553387
e hello@swanhillhouse.com
w swanhillhouse.co.uk

COLYTON

The Old Bakehouse ★★★★
Bed & Breakfast SILVER AWARD
Lower Church Street, Colyton
EX24 6ND
t (01297) 552518
e france.bakehouse@hotmail.co.uk
w theoldbakehousebandb.co.uk

Smallicombe Farm ★★★★
Guest Accommodation
SILVER AWARD
Northleigh, Colyton
EX24 6BU
t (01404) 831310
e maggie_todd@yahoo.com
w smallicombe.com

COMBE MARTIN

Acorns Guest House ★★★★
Guest Accommodation
2 Woodlands, Combe Martin
EX34 0AT
t (01271) 882769
e info@acorns-guesthouse.co.uk
w acorns-guesthouse.co.uk

Blair Lodge Guest House ★★★★
Guest House
Moory Meadow, Combe Martin
EX34 0DG
t (01271) 882294
e info@blairlodge.co.uk
w blairlodge.co.uk

Channel Vista ★★★ *Guest House*
4 Woodlands, Combe Martin
EX34 0AT
t (01271) 883514
e channelvista@btconnect.com
w channelvista.co.uk

Langleigh Guest House ★★★★
Guest Accommodation
The Village, Berrynarbor, Combe Martin
EX34 9SG
t (01271) 883410
e relax@langleighguesthouse.co.uk
w langleighguesthouse.co.uk

Mellstock House ★★★★
Guest House
Woodlands, Combe Martin
EX34 0AR
t (01271) 882592
e enquiries@mellstockhouse.co.uk
w mellstockhouse.co.uk

COPPLESTONE

Harebell ★★★★
Guest Accommodation
SILVER AWARD
Harebell, Copplestone, Crediton
EX17 5LA
t (01363) 84771
e kenjwarren@aol.com
w harebellbandb.co.uk

South West | Devon

COUNTISBURY

Coombe Farm ★★★ *Farmhouse*
Countisbury, Lynton
EX35 6NF
t (01598) 741236
e coombefarm@freeuk.com
w brendonvalley.co.uk/
coombe_farm.htm

CREDITON

The Lamb Inn ★★★★ *Inn*
SILVER AWARD
The Square, Sandford, Crediton, Devon
EX17 4LW
t (01363) 773676
e thelambinn@gmail.com
w lambinnsandford.co.uk

Thelbridge Cross Inn ★★★★ *Inn*
Thelbridge, Crediton
EX17 4SQ
t (01884) 860316
e admin@thethelbridgexinn.co.uk
w thelbridgexinn.co.uk

CROYDE

Denham House ★★★★
Guest House
North Buckland, Croyde
EX33 1HY
t (01271) 890297
e info@denhamhouse.co.uk
w denhamhouse.co.uk

Moorsands ★★★
Guest Accommodation
4 Moor Lane, Croyde Bay, Braunton
EX33 1NP
t +44(0)1271 890781
e paul@moorsands.co.uk
w croyde-bay.co.uk/moorsands.htm

CULLOMPTON

Newcourt Barton ★★★★
Farmhouse **SILVER AWARD**
Langford, Cullompton
EX15 1SE
t (01884) 277326
e newcourtbarton@btinternet.com
w newcourtbarton-devon.co.uk

DARTMOOR

Cherrybrook ★★★ *Guest House*
Two Bridges, Dartmoor
PL20 6SP
t (01822) 880260
e info@thecherrybrook.co.uk
w thecherrybrook.co.uk

DARTMOUTH

Anchor House ★★★★
Bed & Breakfast
4 Victoria Road, Dartmouth
TQ6 9DZ
t (01803) 833274
e anchorhousedartmouth@yahoo.co.uk
w anchorhouse.info

Capritia Guest House ★★★
Bed & Breakfast
10 Victoria Road, Dartmouth
TQ6 9RX
t (01803) 833419
e kenjohnston@btinternet.com
w capritia.com

Cladda Bed & Breakfast and Self Catering Apartments ★★★★
Guest Accommodation
SILVER AWARD
88-90 Victoria Road, and Ford Valley, Dartmouth, Devon
TQ6 9EF
t (01803) 835957 or Mob: 07967 060003
e info@cladda-dartmouth.co.uk
w cladda-dartmouth.co.uk

Crow's Nest ★★★★
Guest Accommodation - Room Only
The Crow's Nest, 5A Lower Street, Dartmouth
TQ6 9AJ
t (01803) 834323
e info@crowsnestdartmouth.co.uk
w crowsnestdartmouth.co.uk

Frogwell Bed & Breakfast ★★★★
Guest Accommodation
SILVER AWARD
Strete, Dartmouth
TQ6 0RH
t (01803) 770273
e frogwell@talktalk.net
w frogwell.net/

Hill View House ★★★★
Guest Accommodation
GOLD AWARD
76 Victoria Road, Dartmouth
TQ6 9DZ
t (01803) 839372
e enquiries@hillviewdartmouth.co.uk
w hillviewdartmouth.co.uk

The Maitland ★★★
Bed & Breakfast
28 Victoria Road, Dartmouth
TQ6 9SA
t (01803) 835854
e enquiries@themaitland.co.uk
w themaitland.co.uk

Melverley House ★★★★
Bed & Breakfast **SILVER AWARD**
Townstal Pathfields, Dartmouth
TQ6 9HL
t (01803) 835756
e hils@hhm.myzen.co.uk
w melverleyhouse.co.uk

Mounthaven ★★★★★
Guest Accommodation
SILVER AWARD
Mount Boone, Dartmouth
TQ6 9PB
t (01803) 839061
e enquiries@mounthavendartmouth.co.uk
w mounthavendartmouth.co.uk

Orleans ★★★★
Guest Accommodation
South Town, Dartmouth
TQ6 9BX
t (01803) 835450
e julieandgeoff@orleans-guest-house-dartmouth.co.uk
w orleans-guesthouse-dartmouth.co.uk

Paper Moon Bed & Breakfast ★★★★ *Guest Accommodation*
SILVER AWARD
107 Victoria Road, Dartmouth
TQ6 9DY
t (01803) 833943
e lyon@eclipse.co.uk
w papermoon-bed-and-breakfast.co.uk

Valley House ★★★★
Bed & Breakfast
46 Victoria Road, Dartmouth, South Devon
TQ6 9DZ
t (01803) 834045
e enquiries@valleyhousedartmouth.com
w valleyhousedartmouth.co.uk

The Victorian House ★★★★★
Guest Accommodation
SILVER AWARD
1 Vicarage Hill, Dartmouth
TQ6 9EW
t (01803) 832766
e sue@victorianhouse.org.uk
w victorianhouse.org.uk

Westbourne House ★★★★★
Bed & Breakfast **SILVER AWARD**
4 Vicarage Hill, Dartmouth
TQ6 9EW
t (01803) 832213
e peterwalton@westbourne-house.co.uk
w westbourne-house.co.uk

DAWLISH

**The Beeches Bed & Breakfast
★★★★** *Bed & Breakfast*
15a Old Teignmouth Road, Dawlish
EX7 0NJ
t (01626) 866345
e enquiries@thebeechesbandb.co.uk
w thebeechesbandb.co.uk

Channel View Guest House ★★★★ *Guest House*
SILVER AWARD
14 Teignmouth Hill, Westcliff, Dawlish
EX7 9DN
t (01626) 866973
e channelviewguesthouse@fsmail.net
w channelviewguesthouse.co.uk

Lammas Park House ★★★★★
Guest Accommodation
GOLD AWARD
3 Priory Road, Dawlish
EX7 9JF
t (01626) 888064
e lammaspark@hotmail.com
w lammasparkhouse.co.uk

Lockwood House ★★★★
Bed & Breakfast
Exeter Road, Dawlish
EX7 0NU
t (01626) 867645
e karenlipscombe@hotmail.com
w lockwoodhouseholidays.co.uk

Lyme Bay House ★★★★
Guest House
West Cliff, Dawlish
EX7 9DN
t (01626) 864211
e enquiries@lymebaydawlish.co.uk
w lymebaydawlish.co.uk

Sandays Bed & Breakfast ★★★★ *Bed & Breakfast*
Warren Road, Dawlish Warren, Dawlish
EX7 0PQ
t (01626) 888973

Sealawn Lodge ★★★ *Guest House*
Exeter Road, Dawlish
EX7 0AB
t (01626) 865998
e sealawnlodge@tiscali.co.uk

DOLTON

Rams Head Inn ★★★ *Inn*
South Street, Dolton, Winkleigh, Devon
EX19 8QS
t (01805) 804255
e ramsheadinn@btinternet.com
w ramsheadinn.co.uk

DUNKESWELL

The Old Kennels ★★★★
Guest Accommodation
Stentwood, Dunkeswell, nr Honiton, Devon
EX14 4RW
t 01823 681138
e info@theoldkennels.co.uk
w theoldkennels.co.uk

EAST CHARLETON

The Barley House ★★★★
Bed & Breakfast
The Barley House, Home Farm Barns, East Charleton, Kingsbridge
TQ7 2AR
t (01548) 531882
e stay@thebarleyhouse.co.uk
w thebarleyhouse.co.uk

EXETER

The Bendene ★★★★
Guest Accommodation
15-16 Richmond Road, Exeter
EX4 4JA
t (01392) 213526
e reservations@bendene.co.uk
w bendene.co.uk

Braeside Guest House ★★★★
Guest House
21 New North Road, Exeter
EX4 4HF
t (01392) 256875
e reception@braeside.biz
w braeside.biz

Clock Tower Guest House ★★★★
Guest Accommodation
16-17 New North Road, Exeter
EX4 4HF
t (01392) 424545
e reservations@clocktowerhotel.co.uk
w clocktowerhotel.co.uk

Culm Vale Country House ★★★
Bed & Breakfast
Culm Vale, Stoke Canon, Exeter
EX5 4EG
t (01392) 841615
e culmvale@hotmail.com
w culmvaleaccommodation.co.uk

Exeter YHA ★★★ *Hostel*
47 Countess Wear Road, Exeter
EX2 6LR
t (01392) 873329
e exeter@yha.org.uk
w yha.org.uk

The Georgian Lodge ★★★★
Guest Accommodation
5 Bystock Terrace, Exeter
EX4 4HY
t (01392) 213079
e reservations@georgianlodge.co.uk
w georgianlodge.com

The Grange ★★★★
Guest Accommodation
Stoke Hill, Exeter
EX4 7JH
t (01392) 259723
e dudleythegrange@aol.com

Higher Southbrook Farm ★★★★
Farmhouse **SILVER AWARD**
Southbrook Lane, Whimple, Exeter
EX5 2PG
t (01404) 823000
e val.hsf@googlemail.com
w southbrook-farm-devon.co.uk

Home Farm ★★★★ *Farmhouse*
Farringdon, Exeter
EX5 2HY
t (01395) 232293
e rupert_thompson@hotmail.com

Jades Guest House ★★★
Guest House
65 St Davids Hill, Exeter
EX4 4DW
t (01392) 435610
e jllbkrb@aol.com
w a1tourism.com/uk/jades.html

Larkbeare Grange ★★★★★
Bed & Breakfast **GOLD AWARD**
Larkbeare, Talaton, Exeter
EX5 2RY
t (01404) 822069
e stay@larkbeare.net
w larkbeare.net

The Old Rectory ★★★★★
Bed & Breakfast **SILVER AWARD**
Clyst House, Clyst Honiton, Exeter
EX5 2LZ
t (01392) 364330
e info@oldrectory-bandb.co.uk
w oldrectory-bandb.co.uk

South West | Devon

Park View ★★★
Guest Accommodation
8 Howell Road, Exeter, Devon
EX4 4LG
t (01392) 271772
e enquiries@parkviewexeter.co.uk
w parkviewexeter.co.uk

Radnor ★★★
Guest Accommodation
79 St Davids Hill, Exeter
EX4 4DW
t (01392) 272004
e ddweeks@radnorhotel.eclipse.co.uk
w radnorhotel.net

Raffles ★★★★
Guest Accommodation
11 Blackall Road, Exeter
EX4 4HD
t (01392) 270200
e raffleshtl@btinternet.com
w raffles-exeter.co.uk

Roselands ★★★ *Bed & Breakfast*
1 Stuart Road, Heavitree, Exeter
EX1 2SZ
t (01392) 410430
e bb@exeteraccommodation.co.uk
w exeteraccommodation.co.uk

Rydon Farm ★★★★ *Farmhouse*
SILVER AWARD
Rydon Farm, Woodbury, Exeter
EX5 1LB
t (01395) 232341
e sallyglanvill@aol.com
w rydonfarmwoodbury.co.uk

Silversprings ★★★★
Guest Accommodation
GOLD AWARD
12 Richmond Road, St Davids, Exeter
EX4 4JA
t (01392) 494040
e juliet@silversprings.co.uk
w silversprings.co.uk

South View Farm ★★★★
Farmhouse
Shillingford Saint George, Exeter, Devon
EX2 9UP
t 01392 832278
e dorothy@southviewbandb.co.uk
w southviewbandb.co.uk

Strete Ralegh Farm ★★★★
Bed & Breakfast SILVER AWARD
Whimple, Exeter
EX5 2PP
t (01404) 822464
e info@streteraleghfarm.co.uk
w streteraleghfarm.co.uk

The Telstar ★★★★ *Guest House*
75-77 St Davids Hill, Exeter
EX4 4DW
t (01392) 272466
e reception@telstar-hotel.co.uk
w telstar-hotel.co.uk

Three Tuns Inn ★★★ *Inn*
14 Exeter Road, Silverton, Exeter
EX5 4HX
t (01392) 860352
e info@threetunsinn.com
w thethreetunsinn.com

University of Exeter ★★★★
Campus
Event Exeter, Reed Hall, Streatham Drive, Exeter
EX4 4QR
t (01392) 215566
e holidaylets@exeter.ac.uk
w eventexeter.com

Woodbine Guesthouse ★★★★
Guest House
1 Woodbine Terrace, Exeter
EX4 4LJ
t (01392) 203302
e info@woodbineguesthouse.co.uk
w woodbineguesthouse.co.uk

Yeo's Farm ★★★★ *Farmhouse*
Dunchideock, Exeter
EX2 9UJ
t (01392) 883927
e killinger.legg@tiscali.co.uk
w yeos-farm-exeter.co.uk

EXMOUTH

The Devoncourt ★★★★
Guest Accommodation
Douglas Avenue, Exmouth
EX8 2EX
t (01395) 272277
e enquiries@devoncourt.com
w devoncourt.com

The Swallows ★★★★
Guest Accommodation
11 Carlton Hill, Exmouth
EX8 2AJ
t (01395) 263937
e p.russo@btclick.com
w swallowsguesthouse.co.uk

FROGMORE

Globe Inn ★★★★ *Inn*
Frogmore, Nr Kingsbridge
TQ7 2NR
t (01548) 531351
e info@theglobeinn.co.uk
w theglobeinn.co.uk

HALWELL

Orchard House ★★★★★
Bed & Breakfast SILVER AWARD
Horner, Hallwell, Totnes
TQ9 7LB
t (01548) 821448
e helen@orchard-house-halwell.co.uk
w orchard-house-halwell.co.uk

HARBERTON

Foales Leigh ★★★★★
Guest Accommodation
GOLD AWARD
Harberton, Totnes
TQ9 7SS
t (01803) 862365

HARBERTONFORD

Pound Court Cottage ★★★★
Bed & Breakfast
Old Road, Harbertonford, Totnes
TQ9 7TA
t (01803) 732441
e poundcourtcottage@tiscali.co.uk
w poundcourtcottage.co.uk

HARTLAND

Elmscott YHA ★★★ *Hostel*
Elmscott, Hartland, Bideford
EX39 6ES
t (01237) 441367
e reservation@yha.org.uk
w yha.org.uk

Gawlish Farm ★★★★ *Farmhouse*
Hartland, Bideford
EX39 6AT
t (01237) 441320

Golden Park ★★★★★
Bed & Breakfast GOLD AWARD
Bideford
EX39 6EP
t (01237) 441254
e lynda@goldenpark.co.uk
w goldenpark.co.uk

Trutrese ★★★
Guest Accommodation
Harton Cross, Hartland, Bideford
EX39 6AE
t (01237) 441274
e trutrese@hotmail.co.uk
w trutrese.co.uk

HAYTOR

Moorlands House ★★★★
Guest Accommodation
Moorlands House, Haytor, Newton Abbot
TQ13 9XT
t (020) 8511 1534

HEMYOCK

Pounds Farm ★★★★ *Farmhouse*
Hemyock, Nr Cullompton
EX15 3QS
t (01823) 680802
e diana@poundsfarm.co.uk
w poundsfarm.co.uk

HILLHEAD

Raddicombe Lodge ★★★★
Guest House
Kingswear Road, Brixham
TQ5 0EX
t (01803) 882125
e stay@raddicombelodge.co.uk
w raddicombelodge.co.uk

HOLCOMBE

Ashlawn Cottage ★★★
Bed & Breakfast
Holcombe Road, Holcombe, Dawlish
EX7 0JB
t (01626) 863622

Manor Farm ★★★★ *Farmhouse*
Holcombe Village, Holcombe, Dawlish
EX7 0JT
t (01626) 863020
e humphreyclem@aol.com
w farmaccom.com

HOLSWORTHY

Oak Tree Farm ★★★★ *Farmhouse*
Burnards House, Holsworthy
EX22 7JA
t (01409) 254870
e colinvalerie.stevens@oaktreelleyns.co.uk
w oaktreelleyns.co.uk

South Worden B&B ★★★★★
Bed & Breakfast GOLD AWARD
West Putford, Holsworthy
EX22 7LG
t (01409) 261448
e mike@southworden.co.uk
w southworden.co.uk

HONITON

Wessington Farm ★★★★
Guest Accommodation
SILVER AWARD
Awliscombe, Honiton
EX14 3NU
t (01404) 42280
e bandb@lre9.com
w eastdevon.com/bedandbreakfast

HOPE COVE

The Hope & Anchor ★★★★ *Inn*
Hope Cove, Kingsbridge
TQ7 3HQ
t (01548) 561294

Sand Pebbles ★★★★
Guest Accommodation
Hope Cove, Kingsbridge
TQ7 3HF
t (01548) 561673
e info@sandpebbles.co.uk
w sandpebbles.co.uk

IDE

Drakes Farmhouse ★★★★
Bed & Breakfast
Ide, Exeter
EX2 9RQ
t (01392) 256814
e drakesfarm@hotmail.com
w drakesfarm-devon.co.uk

ILFRACOMBE

Burnside Guest House ★★★★
Bed & Breakfast
34 St Brannocks Road, Ilfracombe
EX34 8EQ
t (01271) 863097
e san-dave@meekb.freeserve.co.uk
w burnside-ilfracombe.co.uk

Cairn House ★★★
Guest Accommodation
43 St Brannocks Road, Ilfracombe
EX34 8EH
t (01271) 863911
e info@cairnhousehotel.co.uk
w cairnhousehotel.co.uk

Combe Lodge ★★★ *Guest House*
Chambercombe Park Road, Ilfracombe
EX34 9QW
t (01271) 864518
e combelodgehotel@tinyworld.co.uk
w combe-lodge.co.uk

The Graystoke ★★★★ *Guest House*
58 St Brannocks Road, Ilfracombe
EX34 8EQ
t (01271) 862328
e info@thegraystoke.co.uk
w thegraystoke.co.uk

Lyncott House ★★★★
Guest Accommodation
56 St Brannocks Road, Ilfracombe
EX34 8EQ
t (01271) 862425
e heffpete@hotmail.co.uk
w lyncotthouse.co.uk

Saffron House ★★★
Guest Accommodation
King Street, Combe Martin, Ilfracombe
EX34 0BX
t (01271) 883521
e stay@saffronhousehotel.co.uk
w saffronhousehotel.co.uk

The Sherborne Lodge ★★
Guest Accommodation
Torrs Park, Ilfracombe
EX34 8AY
t (01271) 862297
e visit@sherborne-lodge.co.uk
w sherborne-lodge.co.uk

Varley House ★★★★
Guest Accommodation
Chambercombe Park, Ilfracombe
EX34 9QW
t (01271) 863927
e info@varleyhouse.co.uk

The Woodlands ★★★★
Guest Accommodation
Torrs Park, Ilfracombe
EX34 8AZ
t (01271) 863098
e info@woodlandsdevon.com

IVYBRIDGE

Weeke Farm ★★★★ *Farmhouse*
Modbury, Ivybridge
PL21 0TT
t (01548) 830219

KENN

Lower Thornton Farm ★★★★
Farmhouse SILVER AWARD
Kenn, Exeter
EX6 7XH
t (01392) 833434
e alison@lowerthorntonfarm.co.uk
w lowerthorntonfarm.co.uk

KINGSBRIDGE

Ashleigh House ★★★
Guest Accommodation
Ashleigh Road, Kingsbridge
TQ7 1HB
t (01548) 852893
e reception@ashleigh-house.co.uk
w ashleigh-house.co.uk

Down Farm ★★★ *Farmhouse*
Start Point, Kingsbridge
TQ7 2NQ
t (01548) 511234
e downfarm@btinternet.com
w downfarm.co.uk

South West | Devon

ountain Water Experience ★★
Activity Accommodation
ourtlands, Kingsbridge
Q7 4BN
t (01548) 550675
e mwe@mountainwaterexp.demon.co.uk
w mountainwaterexperience.com

ollards Combe Farm ★★★
Guest Accommodation
apton, Kingsbridge
Q7 2QG
t (01548) 580339
e pollardscombe@hotmail.co.uk
w pollardscombefarm.co.uk

KINGSKERSWELL

arewood Guesthouse ★★★
Guest House
7 Torquay Road, Kingskerswell, ewton Abbot
Q12 5HH
t (01803) 872228
e correneandbill1@blueyonder.co.uk
w harewoodguesthouse.pwp.blueyonder.co.uk

KNOWSTONE

est Bowden Farm ★★★★
Farmhouse
howstone, South Molton
X36 4RP
t (01398) 341224
e west.bowden@ukf.net
w westbowden.ukf.net

LANDKEY

cland Barton ★★★ Farmhouse
cland Road, Landkey, Barnstaple
X32 0LD
t (01271) 830253

LANGFORD

angford Court North ★★★★
Farmhouse
angford, Cullompton
X15 1SQ
t (01884) 277234
e tchattey@yahoo.co.uk

LYDFORD

ydford Country House ★★★★★
Guest House SILVER AWARD
kehampton
X20 4AU
t (01822) 820347
e info@lydfordhouse.com
w lydfordhouse.com

LYNMOUTH

orna Doone House ★★★★
Guest House SILVER AWARD
Tors Park, Lynmouth
X35 6ET
t (01598) 753354
e info@lornadoonehouse.co.uk
w lornadoonehouse.co.uk

LYNTON

astle Hill Guest House ★★★★
Guest House
astle Hill, Lynton
X35 6JA
t (01598) 752291
e info@castlehillhotel.co.uk
w castlehillhotel.co.uk

roft House ★★★★
Guest Accommodation
ydiate Lane, Lynton
X35 6HE
t (01598) 752391
e stay@lyntonbandb.co.uk
w lyntonbandb.co.uk

enes ★★★★ Guest House
SILVER AWARD
5 Longmead, Lynton
X35 6DQ
t (01598) 753573
e enquiries@thedenes.com
w thedenes.com

Gable Lodge Guest House ★★★★
Guest House
35 Lee Road, Lynton
EX35 6BS
t (01598) 752367
e gablelodge@btconnect.com
w gablelodgelynton.co.uk

Highcliffe House ★★★★★
Guest Accommodation
GOLD AWARD
Sinai Hill, Lynton
EX35 6AR
t (01598) 752235
e info@highcliffehouse.co.uk
w highcliffehouse.co.uk

Ingleside ★★★★
Guest Accommodation
SILVER AWARD
Lee Road, Lynton
EX35 6HW
t (01598) 752223
e keithdiana@supanet.com
w ingleside-hotel.co.uk

Kingford House ★★★★
Guest Accommodation
SILVER AWARD
Longmead, Lynton
EX35 6DQ
t (01598) 752361
e patriciakingford@.aol.com
w kingfordhouse.co.uk

Lee House ★★★★
Guest Accommodation
27-28 Lee Road, Lynton
EX35 6BP
t (01598) 752364
e info@leehouselynton.co.uk
w leehouselynton.co.uk

Longmead House ★★★★
Guest Accommodation
9 Longmead, Lynton
EX35 6DQ
t (01598) 752523
e info@longmeadhouse.co.uk
w longmeadhouse.co.uk

Rockvale ★★★
Guest Accommodation
Lee Road, Lynton
EX35 6HW
t (01598) 752279
e rockvalehouse@hotmail.com
w rockvalehotel.co.uk

Sinai House Guest House
Lynway, Lynton
EX35 6AY
t (01598) 753227
e enquiries@sinaihouse.co.uk
w sinaihouse.co.uk

Southcliffe ★★★★
Guest Accommodation
SILVER AWARD
34 Lee Road, Lynton
EX35 6BS
t (01598) 753328
e info@southcliffe.co.uk
w southcliffe.co.uk

South View Guest House ★★★★
Guest Accommodation
23 Lee Road, Lynton
EX35 6BP
t (01598) 752289
e maureenroper@hotmail.com
w southview-lynton.co.uk

Waterloo House ★★★★
Guest House
Lydiate Lane, Lynton
EX35 6AJ
t (01598) 753391
e relax@waterloohousehotel.com
w waterloohousehotel.com

Wilsham Farm Farmhouse
Countisbury, Lynton
EX35 6NF
t (01598) 741289
e info@wilshamfarm.co.uk
w wilshamfarm.co.uk

MARSH

The Cottage ★★★★
Guest Accommodation
Marsh, Honiton
EX14 9AJ
t (01460) 234240
e buttonstephens@btopenworld.com
w cottagemarsh.co.uk

MAYPOOL

Maypool YHA ★★ Hostel
Maypool, Brixham
TQ5 0ET
t (01803) 842444
e maypool@yha.org.uk
w yha.org.uk

MILTON DAMEREL

Buttermoor Farm ★★★★
Farmhouse
Buttermoor Farm, Milton Damerel, Nr Holsworthy, North Devon
EX22 7PB
t (01409) 261314
e info@buttermoorfarm.co.uk
w buttermoorfarm.co.uk

MOLLAND

West Lee Farm ★★★★ Farmhouse
Molland, South Molton
EX36 3NJ
t (01398) 341751
e maggi.woodward@googlemail.com
w westleefarm.co.uk

MORETONHAMPSTEAD

Great Sloncombe Farm ★★★★
Farmhouse
Great Sloncombe Farm, Moretonhampstead, Dartmoor, Devon
TQ13 8QF
t (01647) 440595
e hmerchant@sloncombe.freeserve.co.uk
w greatsloncombefarm.co.uk

Great Wooston Farm ★★★★
Guest Accommodation
Moretonhampstead, Newton Abbot
TQ13 8QA
t (01647) 440367
e info@greatwoostonfarm.com
w greatwoostonfarm.com

Little Wooston Farm ★★★
Farmhouse
Moretonhampstead, Newton Abbot
TQ13 8QA
t (01647) 440551
e jeannecuming@tesco.net

MUDDIFORD

Broomhill Farm ★★★★ Farmhouse
Muddiford, Barnstaple
EX31 4EX
t (01271) 850676

Field House ★★★★
Bed & Breakfast
Muddiford, Barnstaple
EX31 4ET
t (01271) 376205
e fieldhouse@adslexpress.co.uk

NEWTON ABBOT

Rock House Bed & Breakfast
★★★★★ Bed & Breakfast
SILVER AWARD
Maddacombe Road, Kingskerswell, Newton Abbot
TQ12 5LF
t (01803) 404990
e alison.rockhouse@blueyonder.co.uk
w rockhouse-cottage.co.uk

OAKFORD

Harton Farm ★★★ Farmhouse
Oakford, Tiverton
EX16 9HH
t (01398) 351209
e lindy@hartonfarm.co.uk
w hartonfarm.co.uk

OKEHAMPTON

Adventure Okehampton ★★★
Activity Accommodation
Klondyke Road, Okehampton
EX20 1EW
t (01837) 53916
e okehampton@yha.org.uk
w adventureokehampton.com

Fairway Lodge ★★★★
Guest House
Thorndon Cross, Okehampton
EX20 4NE
t (01837) 55122
e info@fairway-lodge.co.uk
w fairway-lodge.co.uk

Lower Trecott Farm ★★★★
Bed & Breakfast SILVER AWARD
Wellsprings Lane, Okehampton
EX20 2TD
t (01837) 880118
e lowertrecott@btinternet.com
w lowertrecottfarm.co.uk

The Oxenham Arms ★★★★ Inn
South Zeal, Okehampton
EX20 2JT
t (01837) 840244
e relax@theoxenhamarms.co.uk
w theoxenhamarms.co.uk

Week Farm ★★★★ Farmhouse
Bridestowe, Okehampton
EX20 4HZ
t (01837) 861221
e accom@weekfarmonline.com
w weekfarmonline.com

OTTERY ST MARY

Pitt Farm ★★★★ Farmhouse
Coombelake, Ottery St Mary
EX11 1NL
t (01404) 812439
e pittfarm@tiscali.co.uk
w pitt-farm-devon.co.uk

PAIGNTON

Amber House ★★★★
Guest Accommodation
SILVER AWARD
6 Roundham Road, Paignton
TQ4 6EZ
t (01803) 558372
e enquiries@amberhousehotel.co.uk
w amberhousehotel.co.uk

Ashleigh Guest House ★★★
Guest House
15 Queens Road, Paignton
TQ4 6AT
t 01803 558923
e info@ashleigh-guesthouse.co.uk
w ashleigh-guesthouse.co.uk

The Baildon Royd ★★★★
Guest House
4 Marine Park, Paignton
TQ3 2NW
t (01803) 400096
e stay@baildonroyd.co.uk
w baildonroyd.co.uk

The Bay Sands ★★★
Guest Accommodation
14 Colin Road, Paignton
TQ3 2NR
t (01803) 524877
e enquiries@baysands.co.uk
w baysands.co.uk

Beach House ★★★★
Guest Accommodation
39 Garfield Road, Paignton
TQ4 6AX
t (01803) 525742
e karen-l@btconnect.com

South West | Devon

Beecroft Lodge ★★★★
Guest Accommodation
10 St Andrews Road, Paignton
TQ4 6HA
t (01803) 558702
e stay@beecroftlodge.co.uk
w beecroftlodge.co.uk

Bella Vista Guest House ★★★
Guest Accommodation
Berry Square, Paignton
TQ4 6AZ
t (01803) 558122
e bellavista@berrysquare.fsbusiness.co.uk
w english-riviera.co.uk/accommodation/guest-houses/bella-vista/index.htm

Belle Dene Guest House ★★★★
Guest House
25 Garfield Road, Paignton
TQ4 6AX
t (01803) 559645
e belledeneguesthouse@btconnect.com
w belledeneguesthouse.co.uk

Benbows Guest House ★★★
Guest House
1 Alta Vista Road, Roundham, Paignton
TQ4 6DB
t (01803) 558128
e benbowshotel@btinternet.com
w benbowshotel.co.uk

The Beresford ★★★★
Guest Accommodation
5 Adelphi Road, Paignton
TQ4 6AW
t (01803) 551560
e info@beresfordhotel.co.uk
w beresfordhotel.co.uk

Birchwood House ★★★★
Guest House
33 St Andrews Road, Paignton
TQ4 6HA
t (01803) 551323
e birchwoodhouse@aol.com
w birchwoodhouse.co.uk

Birklands Guest House ★★★★
Guest House
33 Garfield Road, Paignton
TQ4 6AX
t (01803) 556970
e trevor@trevor27.freeserve.co.uk
w birklands.co.uk

Blueberry House ★★★★
Guest House SILVER AWARD
34 Garfield Road, Paignton
TQ4 6AX
t (01803) 552211
e horsepost@hotmail.com
w blueberryhouse.co.uk

Blue Waters Lodge ★★★★
Guest Accommodation
4 Leighon Road, Paignton
TQ3 2BQ
t (01803) 557749
e bluewaters.lodge@virgin.net
w bluewaterslodge.co.uk

Braedene Lodge ★★★
Guest House
22 Manor Road, Paignton
TQ3 2HR
t (01803) 551079
e stay@braedenehotel.co.uk
w braedenehotel.co.uk

Briars ★★★★
Guest Accommodation
26 Sands Road, Paignton
TQ4 6EJ
t (01803) 557729
e enquiries@briarshotel.com
w briarshotel.com

Bristol House ★★ *Guest House*
Garfield Road, Paignton
TQ4 6AU
t (01803) 558282
e info@bristolhousehotel.com
w bristolhousehotel.com

Carrington Guest House ★★★
Guest House
10 Beach Road, Paignton
TQ4 6AY
t (01803) 558785
e info@carringtonguesthouse.co.uk
w carringtonguesthouse.co.uk

The Cherra ★★★
Guest Accommodation
15 Roundham Road, Paignton
TQ4 6DN
t (01803) 550723
e info@cherrahotel.co.uk
w cherrahotel.co.uk

Cleve Court Hotel ★★★
Guest Accommodation
3 Cleveland Road, Paignton
TQ4 6EN
t (01803) 551444
e info@clevecourthotel.co.uk
w clevecourthotel.co.uk

Cliveden Guest House ★★★★
Guest House
27 Garfield Road, Paignton
TQ4 6AX
t (01803) 557461
e enquiries@clivedenguesthouse.co.uk
w clivedenguesthouse.co.uk

Colin House ★★★★
Guest Accommodation
2 Colin Road, Paignton
TQ3 2NR
t (01803) 550609
e karen@colinhouse.co.uk
w colinhouse.co.uk

Collerton Lodge ★★★★
Bed & Breakfast
332 Totnes Road, Paignton
TQ4 7HD
t (01803) 554018
e sandra.singleton@sky.com
w collertonlodge.co.uk

The Cosmopolitan ★★★★
Guest Accommodation
2 Kernou Road, Paignton
TQ4 6BA
t (01803) 523118
e mail@paignton-cosmopolitan.com
w paignton-cosmopolitan.com

Craigmore Guest House ★★★★
Guest House
54 Dartmouth Road, Paignton
TQ4 5AN
t (01803) 557373
e craigmore-guesthouse@hotmail.co.uk

Culverden Guest House ★★★★
Guest Accommodation
4 Colin Road, Preston, Paignton
TQ3 2NR
t (01803) 559786
e info@culverdenhotel.co.uk
w culverdenhotel.co.uk

Earlston House ★★★★
Guest Accommodation
31 St Andrews Road, Paignton
TQ4 6HA
t (01803) 558355
e stay@earlstonhouse.co.uk
w earlstonhouse.co.uk

Easton Court ★★★★ *Guest House*
5 St Andrews Road, Paignton
TQ4 6HA
t (01803) 555810
e info@eastoncourt.co.uk
w eastoncourt.co.uk

Harbour Lodge ★★★
Guest Accommodation
4 Cleveland Road, Paignton
TQ4 6EN
t (01803) 556932
e enquiries@harbourlodge.co.uk
w harbourlodge.co.uk

The Mayfield ★★★★
Guest Accommodation
8 Queens Road, Paignton
TQ4 6AT
t (01803) 556802
e info@themayfield.co.uk
w themayfield.co.uk

Norbreck ★★★ *Guest House*
35 New Street, Paignton
TQ3 3HL
t (01803) 558033
e norbreckguesthouse@hotmail.com
w norbreck.com

Paignton Court ★★★
Guest Accommodation
17-19 Sands Road, Paignton
TQ4 6EG
t 01803 553111
e enquiries@paigntoncourt.co.uk
w paigntoncourt.co.uk

The Park Lodge ★★★ *Guest House*
16-18 Adelphi Road, Paignton
TQ4 6AW
t (01803) 551232
e sal@parklodgepaignton.co.uk
w parklodgepaignton.co.uk

Richmond Guest House ★★★
Guest House
19 Norman Road, Paignton
TQ3 2BE
t (01803) 550978
e info@richmondgh.co.uk
w richmondgh.co.uk

Rockview Guest House ★★★
Guest House
13 Queens Road, Paignton
TQ4 6AT
t (01803) 556702
e rockview@blueyonder.co.uk
w rockview.co.uk

Rosemead Guest House ★★★
Guest Accommodation
22 Garfield Road, Paignton
TQ4 6AX
t (01803) 557944
e rosemeadhotel@aol.com
w rosemeadpaignton.co.uk

Roundham Lodge ★★★★★
Guest Accommodation
SILVER AWARD
16 Roundham Road, Paignton
TQ4 6DN
t (01803) 558485
e enquiries@roundham-lodge.co.uk
w roundham-lodge.co.uk

Rowcroft Hotel ★★★★
Guest Accommodation
14 Youngs Park Road, Paignton
TQ4 6BU
t (01803) 559420
e enquiries@rowcroft-hotel.com
w rowcroft-hotel.com

San Brelade ★★★ *Guest House*
3 Alta Vista Road, Paignton
TQ4 6DB
t (01803) 553725
e info@sanbrelade.co.uk
w sanbrelade.co.uk

The Sands ★★★★
Guest Accommodation
32 Sands Road, Paignton
TQ4 6EJ
t (01803) 551282
e hotel.sands@virgin.net
w hotelsands.co.uk

Seaford Sands ★★★
Guest Accommodation
17 Roundham Road, Paignton
TQ4 6DN
t (01803) 557722
e leeseaford@aol.com
w seafordsandshotel.co.uk

Sea Spray House ★★★
Guest House
1 Beach Road, Paignton
TQ4 6AY
t (01803) 553141
e mail@seasprayhotel.co.uk
w seasprayhotel.co.uk

Seaways ★★★
Guest Accommodation
30 Sands Road, Paignton
TQ4 6EJ
t (01803) 551093
e seawayshotel@aol.com
w seawayshotel.co.uk

Sonachan House ★★★★
Guest Accommodation
35 St Andrews Road, Paignton
TQ4 6HA
t (01803) 558021
e info@sonachan.co.uk
w sonachan.co.uk

St Edmunds House ★★★
Guest House
25 Sands Road, Paignton
TQ4 6EG
t (01803) 558756
e stedmundshouse@googlemail.com
w stedmundshotel.com

St Marguerite Guesthouse ★★★★
Guest House
3 The Riviera, Paignton
TQ4 5EX
t (01803) 698376
e info@stmarguerite.co.uk
w stmarguerite.co.uk

The Sundale ★★
Guest Accommodation
10 Queens Road, Paignton
TQ4 6AT
t (01803) 557431
e sundalehotel@tiscali.co.uk
w sundalehotelpaignton.co.uk

Three Palms ★★★
Guest Accommodation
21 Sands Road, Paignton
TQ4 6EG
t (01803) 551340
e enquiries@threepalmshotel.co.u
w threepalmshotel.co.uk

The Torland ★★★ *Guest House*
24 Sands Road, Paignton
TQ4 6EJ
t (01803) 558755
e torlandhotel@hotmail.com
w torlandhotel.co.uk

Two Beaches ★★★★
Guest Accommodation
27 St Andrews Road, Paignton
TQ4 6HA
t (01803) 522164
e stay@twobeaches.co.uk
w twobeaches.co.uk

PARRACOMBE

Higher Bodley Farm ★★★★
Farmhouse SILVER AWARD
Higher Bodley Farm, Parracombe
EX31 4QN
t (01598) 763798
e higherbodley@hotmail.co.uk
w higherbodleyfarm.co.uk

Moorlands ★★★★
Guest Accommodation
Woody Bay, Parracombe, Lynton
EX31 4RA
t (01598) 763224
e info@moorlandshotel.co.uk
w moorlandshotel.co.uk

PAYHEMBURY

Luton Barn ★★★★ *Bed & Breakfa*
Luton, Payhembury, Honiton
EX14 3HZ
t (01404) 841498
e lutonbarn@talktalk.net
w lutonbarn.co.uk

Yellingham Farm ★★★★
Farmhouse SILVER AWARD
Payhembury, Honiton
EX14 3HE
t (01404) 850272
e janeteast@yellinghamfarm.co.uk
w yellinghamfarm.co.uk

South West | Devon

PINN

ower Pinn Farm ★★★★
armhouse
eak Hill, Sidmouth
X10 0NN
t (01395) 513733
e liz@lowerpinnfarm.co.uk
w lowerpinnfarm.co.uk

inn Barton Farm ★★★★
armhouse
eak Hill, Pinn, Sidmouth
X10 0NN
t (01395) 514004
e betty@pinnbartonfarm.co.uk
w pinnbartonfarm.co.uk

PLYMOUTH

thenaeum Lodge Guest House
★★★ *Guest Accommodation*
Athenaeum Street, The Hoe,
ymouth
L1 2RQ
t (01752) 665005
e us@athenaeumlodge.com
w athenaeumlodge.com

erkeleys of St James ★★★★
uest Accommodation
Saint James Place East, The Hoe,
ymouth
L1 3AS
t (01752) 221654
e enquiry@onthehoe.co.uk
w onthehoe.co.uk

he Bowling Green ★★★★
uest Accommodation
-10 Osborne Place, Plymouth
L1 2PU
t (01752) 209090
e info@thebowlinggreenplymouth.com
w thebowlinggreenplymouth.com

rittany Guest House ★★★★
uest Accommodation
3 Athenaeum Street, The Hoe,
ymouth
L1 2RQ
t (01752) 262247
e thebrittanyguesthouse@btconnect.com
w brittanyguesthouse.co.uk

araneal ★★★★
2-14 Pier Street, West Hoe,
ymouth
L1 3BS
t (01752) 663589
e caranealhotel@hotmail.com
w caranealplymouth.co.uk

itadel House ★★ *Guest House*
5 Citadel Rd, The Hoe, Plymouth
L1 3AU
t (01752) 661712
w citadelhouse.co.uk

our Seasons ★★★ *Guest House*
07 Citadel Road East, The Hoe,
ymouth
L1 2JF
t (01752) 223591
f.seasons@btconnect.com
w fourseasonsguesthouse.co.uk

abber Farm ★★★ *Farmhouse*
abber Lane, Down Thomas,
ymouth
L9 0AW
t (01752) 862269
e gabberfarm@tiscali.co.uk
w gabberfarm.co.uk

he George Guest House ★★★
uest House
61 Citadel Road, The Hoe,
ymouth
L1 2HU
t (01752) 661517
e georgeguesthouse@btconnect.com
w accommodationplymouth.co.uk

Hotspur Guest House ★★★★
Guest House
108 North Road East, Plymouth
PL4 6AW
t (01752) 663928
e info@hotspurguesthouse.co.uk
w hotspurguesthouse.co.uk

The Imperial ★★★★★
Guest Accommodation
Lockyer Street, The Hoe, Plymouth
PL1 2QD
t (01752) 227311
e info@imperialplymouth.co.uk
w imperialplymouth.co.uk

Kynance Guest House ★★
Guest Accommodation
113 Citadel Road, The Hoe,
Plymouth
PL1 2RN
t (01752) 266821
e info@kynancehotel.co.uk
w kynancehotel.co.uk

Mariners Guest House ★★★★
Guest House
11 Pier Street, West Hoe, Plymouth
PL1 3BS
t (01752) 261778
e marinersguesthouse@blueyonder.co.uk
w marinersguesthouse.co.uk

The Moorings Guest House ★★★
Guest Accommodation
4 Garden Crescent, West Hoe,
Plymouth
PL1 3DA
t (01752) 250128
e enquiries@themooringsguesthouseplymouth.com
w themooringsguesthouseplymouth.com

Phantele Guest House ★★★★
Guest House
176 Devonport Road, Stoke,
Plymouth
PL1 5RD
t (01752) 561506
e bookings@thephantele.co.uk
w thephantele.co.uk

Poppy's Guest House ★★★
Guest House
4 Alfred Street, The Hoe, Plymouth
PL1 2RP
t (01752) 670452
e bookings@poppysguesthouse.co.uk
w smothhound.co.uk/hotels

Seymour Guest House ★★★★
Guest House
211 North Road East, The Hoe,
Plymouth
PL1 2JF
t (01752) 667002
e karen_ray_cooke@yahoo.co.uk
w seymourguesthouse.co.uk

Squires Guest House ★★★★
Guest House
7 St James Place East, Plymouth
PL1 3AS
t (01752) 261459
e info@squiresguesthouse.co.uk
w squiresguesthouse.com

Sydney Guest House ★★
Guest House
181 North Road West, Plymouth
PL1 5DE
t (01752) 266541

University of Plymouth ★★★
Campus
Drake Circus, Plymouth
PL4 8AA
t 01752 588559
e summeraccommodation@plymouth.ac.uk
w plymouth.ac.uk/summeraccommodation

POSTBRIDGE

Bellever YHA ★★ *Hostel*
Bellever, Postbridge
PL20 6TU
t (01822) 880227
e bellever@yha.org.uk
w yha.org.uk

PRINCETOWN

The Forest Inn ★★★ *Inn*
Hexworthy, Princetown
PL20 6SD
t (01364) 631211
e info@theforestinn.co.uk
w theforestinn.co.uk

SALCOMBE

**Burton Farmhouse & Garden
Room Restaurant** ★★★★
Farmhouse
Burton Farmhouse, Galmpton,
Kingsbridge, Devon
TQ7 3EY
t (01548) 561210
e anne@burtonfarm.co.uk
w burtonfarmhouse.co.uk

Salcombe YHA ★★★ *Hostel*
Overbecks, Sharpitor, Salcombe
TQ8 8LW
t (01548) 842856
e salcombe@yha.org.uk
w yha.org.uk

SAMPFORD PEVERELL

**Leonardmoor Farm House Bed &
Breakfast** ★★★★ *Farmhouse*
Leonard Moor, Sampford Peverell,
Tiverton
EX16 7EL
t (01884) 820881
e sue.quick1@btinternet.com
w leonardhousebbaccommodation.com

SANDFORD

Ashridge Farm ★★★★
Bed & Breakfast
Ashridge Farm, Sandford, Crediton
EX17 4EN
t (01363) 774292
e info@ashridgefarm.co.uk
w ashridgefarm.co.uk/

SEATON

Beaumont Guest House ★★★★
Guest House
Castle Hill, Seaton
EX12 2QW
t (01297) 20832
e jane@lymebay.demon.co.uk
w smoothhound.co.uk/hotels/beaumon1.html

Gatcombe Farm ★★★★
Farmhouse SILVER AWARD
Gatcombe Farm, Seaton
EX12 3AA
t (01297) 21235
e bedandbreakfast@gatcombefarm.co.uk
w gatcombe-farm-devon.co.uk

Holmleigh House Bed & Breakfast
★★★★ *Guest Accommodation*
SILVER AWARD
Holmleigh House, Sea Hill, Seaton
EX12 2QT
t (01297) 625671
e gaynorjones_8@hotmail.com
w holmleighhouse.co.uk

The Mariners ★★★★
Guest Accommodation
SILVER AWARD
East Walk, Seaton
EX12 2NP
t (01297) 20560
e marinershotel@aol.com
w marinershotelseaton.co.uk

Pebbles ★★★★
Guest Accommodation
GOLD AWARD
Sea Hill, Seaton
EX12 2QU
t (01297) 22678
e enquiries@pebbleshouse.co.uk
w pebbleshouse.co.uk

SHALDON

Farthings ★★★★ *Bed & Breakfast*
102 Ringmore Road, Shaldon
TQ14 0ET
t (01626) 872860
e farthings_bb@btinternet.com

SHILLINGFORD

Barleycorn House B&B ★★★★
Guest Accommodation
Shillingford, Tiverton
EX16 9AZ
t (01398) 332026
e contact@barleycornhouse.co.uk
w barleycornhouse.co.uk

SIDBURY

Burscombe Farm ★★★ *Farmhouse*
Burscombe, Sidbury, Sidmouth
EX10 0QB
t (01395) 597648
e burscombefarm@fwi.co.uk
w burscombefarm-devon.co.uk

Rose Cottage Guest House
★★★★ *Guest Accommodation*
SILVER AWARD
Greenhead, Sidbury
EX10 0RH
t (01395) 597357
e roz.kendall@btinternet.com
w rosecottagesidbury.co.uk

SIDMOUTH

108 Alexandria Road
Guest Accommodation
Sidmouth
EX10 9HG
t (01395) 515968
e t.silversides@btopenworld.com

Berwick Guest House ★★★★
Guest Accommodation
Salcombe Road, Sidmouth, Devon
EX10 8PX
t (01395) 513621
e reservations@berwick-house.co.uk
w berwick-house.co.uk

Canterbury Guest House ★★★★
Guest Accommodation
Salcombe Road, Sidmouth, Devon
EX10 8PR
t (01395) 513373
e enquiries@canterbury-house.com
w canterbury-house.com

Cheriton Guest House ★★★★
Guest House
Vicarage Road, Sidmouth
EX10 8UQ
t (01395) 513810
e sara.land1@virgin.net
w smoothhound.co.uk/hotels/cheritong.html

Coombe Bank Guest House
★★★★ *Guest House*
SILVER AWARD
86 Alexandria Road, Sidmouth
EX10 9HG
t (01395) 514843
e info@coombebank.co.uk
w coombebank.co.uk

Dukes ★★★★ *Inn*
The Esplanade, Sidmouth
EX10 8AR
t (01395) 513320
e dukes@hotels-sidmouth.co.uk
w hotels-sidmouth.co.uk

Higher Coombe Farm ★★★
Farmhouse
Tipton St John, Sidmouth
EX10 0AX
t (01404) 813385
e kerstinfarmer@farming.co.uk
w smoothhound.co.uk/hotels/higherco.html

South West | Devon

Hollies Guest House ★★★★
Guest House **SILVER AWARD**
Salcombe Road, Sidmouth
EX10 8PU
t (01395) 514580
e enquiries@holliesguesthouse.co.uk
w holliesguesthouse.co.uk

Kyneton Lodge ★★★★
Bed & Breakfast
87 Alexandria Road, Sidmouth
EX10 9HG
t (01395) 513213
e info@kyneton.co.uk
w kyneton.co.uk

Larkstone House ★★
Bed & Breakfast
22 Connaught Road, Sidmouth
EX10 8TT
t (01395) 514345

Lavenders Blue ★★★★
Guest House **GOLD AWARD**
33 Sidford High Street, Sidford, Sidmouth
EX10 9SN
t (01395) 576656
e info@lavendersbluesidmouth.com
w lavendersbluesidmouth.com

The Longhouse ★★★★★
Bed & Breakfast **SILVER AWARD**
Salcombe Hill Road, Sidmouth
EX10 0NY
t (01395) 577973
e pvcia@aol.com
w holidaysinsidmouth.co.uk

Lynstead ★★★★ *Guest House*
Vicarage Road, Sidmouth
EX10 8UQ
t (01395) 514635
e info@lynsteadguesthouse.co.uk
w lynsteadguesthouse.co.uk

Ryton Guest House ★★★
Guest House
52-54 Winslade Road, Sidmouth
EX10 9EX
t (01395) 513981
e info@ryton-guest-house.co.uk
w ryton-guest-house.co.uk

Salcombe Close House ★★★★★
Bed & Breakfast **SILVER AWARD**
Sid Lane, Sidmouth, Devon
EX10 9AW
t 01395 579067
e thebeesleybunch@aol.com
w salcombeclosehouse.com

Southcombe Guesthouse ★★★★
Guest House
Vicarage Road, Sidmouth
EX10 8UQ
t (01395) 513861
e southcombeguesthouse@googlemail.com
w smoothhound.co.uk/hotels/south.html

Southcroft ★★★★
Guest Accommodation
Arcot Road, Sidmouth
EX10 9ES
t (01395) 516903
e southcroft_sidmouth@yahoo.com
w southcroftsidmouth.co.uk

Southern Cross Guest House
★★★ *Guest House*
High Street, Newton Poppleford, Sidmouth
EX10 0DU
t (01395) 568439
e timothy.flaher@btconnect.com
w southerncrossdevon.co.uk

Tyrone ★★★★ *Bed & Breakfast*
Sid Road, Sidmouth
EX10 9AL
t (01395) 516753
e owner@tyrone-bedandbreakfast.co.uk
w tyrone-bedandbreakfast.co.uk

The Willow Bridge ★★★★
Guest House
Millford Road, Sidmouth
EX10 8DR
t (01395) 513599
e willowbridge@hotmail.com
w willowbridge-sidmouth.co.uk

SOUTH ALLINGTON

South Allington House ★★★★
Farmhouse
Chivelstone, Kingsbridge
TQ7 2NB
t (01548) 511272
e barbara@southallingtonhouse.co.uk
w southallingtonhouse.co.uk

SOUTH BRENT

The Pack Horse Inn ★★★
Guest Accommodation
1 Plymouth Road, South Brent, Devon
TQ10 9BH
t (01364) 72283
e info@thepackhorse.co.uk
w thepackhorse.co.uk

The Royal Oak ★★★★ *Inn*
Station Road, South Brent
TQ10 9BE
t (01364) 72133
e info@royaloaksouthbrent.co.uk
w oakonline.net

SOUTH MOLTON

Townhouse Barton ★★★
Farmhouse
Nadder Lane, South Molton
EX36 4HR
t (01769) 572467

SPREYTON

The Tom Cobley Tavern ★★★★
Inn
Spreyton, Okehampton
EX17 5AL
t (01647) 231314

STARCROSS

The Croft Guest House ★★★★
Guest Accommodation
Cockwood Harbour, Starcross, Exeter
EX6 8QY
t (01626) 890282
e croftcockwood@aol.com
w thecroftcockwood.com

STAVERTON

Kingston House ★★★★★
Guest Accommodation
GOLD AWARD
Staverton, Totnes
TQ9 6AR
t (01803) 762235
e info@kingston-estate.co.uk
w kingston-estate.co.uk

The Sea Trout Inn ★★★★ *Inn*
SILVER AWARD
Staverton, Totnes
TQ9 6PA
t (01803) 762274
e enquiries@seatroutinn.com
w seatroutinn.com

STOKE FLEMING

Fairholme ★★★★ *Bed & Breakfast*
Bay View Estate, Stoke Fleming, Dartmouth
TQ6 0QX
t (01803) 770356
e stay@fairholmedartmouth.co.uk
w fairholmedartmouth.co.uk

Southfield House ★★★★
Bed & Breakfast **GOLD AWARD**
Stoke Fleming, Dartmouth
TQ6 0NR
t (01803) 770359
e info@southfieldhouse.co.uk
w southfieldhouse.co.uk

STOKE GABRIEL

Stoke Gabriel Lodgings ★★★★★
Guest Accommodation
SILVER AWARD
Badgers Retreat, 2 Orchard Close, Paignton Road, Stoke Gabriel, Totnes, South Devon
TQ9 6SX
t 01803 782003
e david@stokegabriellodgings.com
w stokegabriellodgings.com

SYDENHAM DAMEREL

Higher Woodley Farm ★★★★
Farmhouse **SILVER AWARD**
Lamerton, Tavistock
PL19 8QU
t (01822) 832374
e info@woodleybandb.co.uk
w woodleybandb.co.uk

TAVISTOCK

Beera Farmhouse ★★★★
Farmhouse **GOLD AWARD**
Milton Abbot, Tavistock, Devon
PL19 8PL
t (01822) 870216
e hilary.tucker@farming.co.uk
w beera-farm.co.uk

Burnville Farm ★★★★★
Farmhouse **GOLD AWARD**
Tavistock
PL19 0NE
t (01822) 820443
e burnvillef@aol.com
w burnville.co.uk

Colcharton Farm ★★★★
Farmhouse **SILVER AWARD**
Gulworthy, Tavistock
PL19 8HU
t (01822) 616435
e colchartonfarm@agriplus.net
w visit-dartmoor.co.uk

Mallards ★★★★ *Guest House*
48 Plymouth Road, Tavistock
PL19 8BU
t (01822) 615171
e mallards-guest-house@tiscali.co.uk
w mallardsoftavistock.co.uk

Rubbytown Farm ★★★★
Farmhouse
Gulworthy, Tavistock
PL19 8PA
t (01822) 832493
e mary@dartmoor-bb.co.uk
w dartmoor-bb.co.uk

Tor Cottage ★★★★★
Guest Accommodation
GOLD AWARD
Chillaton, Lifton
PL16 0JE
t (01822) 860248
e info@torcottage.co.uk
w torcottage.co.uk

TEDBURN ST MARY

Great Cummins Farm ★★★★
Farmhouse **SILVER AWARD**
Tedburn St Mary, Exeter
EX6 6BJ
t (01647) 61278
e greatcumminsfarm@yahoo.com
w greatcumminsfarm.co.uk

TEIGNMOUTH

Coombe Bank ★★★ *Guest House*
Landscore Road, Teignmouth
TQ14 9JL
t (01626) 772369
e dianne.loach@btopenworld.com
w coombebankhotel.net

The Craigs ★★★★ *Bed & Breakfast*
Landscore Road, Teignmouth
TQ14 9JL
t (01626) 778003
e thecraigsbandb@btinternet.com

Dresden House ★★★★
Guest House
26 Orchard Gardens, Teignmouth
TQ14 8DJ
t (01626) 773465
e info@dresdenhouse.com
w dresdenhouse.com

Higher Holcombe ★★★
Bed & Breakfast
Holcombe Down Road, Teignmouth
TQ14 9NU
t (01626) 777144

Higher Rixdale Farm ★★★★
Farmhouse
Luton, Chudleigh, Teignmouth
TQ13 0BW
t (01626) 867980
e info@higher-rixdale-farm.com
w higher-rixdale-farm.com

Lynton House ★★
Guest Accommodation
7 Powderham Terrace, Sea Front, Teignmouth
TQ14 8BL
t (01626) 774349
e stay@lyntonhouseteignmouth.com
w lyntonhouseteignmouth.com/

Meran House ★★★★
Bed & Breakfast
Third Drive, Landscore Road, Teignmouth
TQ14 9JT
t (01626) 778828

The Moorings B&B ★★★★★
Guest Accommodation
SILVER AWARD
33 Teignmouth Road, Teignmouth
TQ14 8UR
t (01626) 770400
e mickywaters@aol.com
w themooringsteignmouth.co.uk

Seascape ★★★★ *Bed & Breakfast*
Oak Hill Cross Road, Teignmouth
TQ14 8TN
t (01626) 772766
e annie.tester@hotmail.com
w freewebs.com/annsea

Thomas Luny House ★★★★★
Guest Accommodation
GOLD AWARD
Teign Street, Teignmouth, Devon
TQ14 8EG
t (01626) 772976
e alisonandjohn@thomas-luny-house.co.uk
w thomas-luny-house.co.uk

The Thornhill ★★★★
Guest Accommodation
Mere Lane, Seafront, Teignmouth
TQ14 8TA
t (01626) 773460
e thornhillhotel@aol.com
w thornhillhotelteignmouth.co.uk

Woodside Guest House ★★★★
Guest House
17 Hermosa Road, Teignmouth
TQ14 9JZ
t (01626) 770681
e info@woodsideguesthouse.com
w woodsideguesthouse.com

THORNBURY

Forda Farm ★★★★ *Farmhouse*
Thornbury, Holsworthy
EX22 7BS
t (01409) 261369

TIVERTON

Bridge Guest House ★★★
Guest House
23 Angel Hill, Tiverton
EX16 6PE
t (01884) 252804
w smoothhound.co.uk/hotels/bridgegh.html

South West | Devon

TORBRYAN

ld Church House Inn ★★★ *Inn*
orbryan, Newton Abbot
Q12 5UR
t (01803) 812372
e info@oldchurchhouseinn.co.uk
w oldchurchhouseinn.co.uk

TORQUAY

bberley Guest House ★★★
uest House
00 Windsor Road, Babbacombe,
orquay
Q1 1SU
t (01803) 392787
e stay@abberleyguesthouse.co.uk
w abberleyguesthouse.co.uk

he Abbeyfield ★★★★
uest Accommodation
idge Road, Torquay
Q2 5AX
t (01803) 294268
e abbeyfieldinfo@btconnect.com
w theabbeyfieldtorquay.co.uk

corn Lodge ★★★ *Guest House*
8 Bridge Road, Torquay
Q2 5BA
t (01803) 296939
e enquiries@bnbtorquay.co.uk
w bnbtorquay.co.uk

shleigh House ★★★★
uest Accommodation
1 Meadfoot Lane, Torquay
Q1 2BP
t (01803) 294660
e dawnsmale@btinternet.com
w ashleighhousetorquay.co.uk

shurst Lodge ★★★
uest Accommodation
4 St Efrides Road, Torquay
Q2 5SG
t (01803) 292132
e n.hutch@btopenworld.com
w ashurstlodgehotel.co.uk

shwood Grange ★★★★
uest Accommodation
8 Newton Road, Torquay
Q2 5BZ
t (01803) 212619
e stay@ashwoodgrangehotel.co.uk
w ashwoodgrangehotel.co.uk

vron House ★★★★
1 Windsor Road, Babbacombe,
orquay
Q1 1SZ
t (01803) 294182
e avronhouse@blueyonder.co.uk
w avronhouse.co.uk

abbacombe Guest House ★★★★
uest House
5 Babbacombe Road, Torquay
Q1 3SN
t (01803) 328071
e info@babbacombeguesthouse.com
w babbacombeguesthouse.com

abbacombe Palms ★★★★
uest Accommodation
 York Road, Babbacombe, Torquay
Q1 3SG
t (01803) 327087
e reception@babbacombepalms.com
w babbacombepalms.com

he Baytree ★★★★
uest Accommodation
ILVER AWARD
8 Bridge Road, Torquay
Q2 5BA
t (01803) 293718
e enquiries@thebaytreehotel.com
w thebaytreehotel.com

The Belmont ★★★★
Guest Accommodation
66 Belgrave Road, Torquay
TQ2 5HY
t (01803) 295028
e enquiries@belmonthoteltorquay.co.uk
w belmonthoteltorquay.co.uk

Bentley Lodge ★★★★
Guest Accommodation
SILVER AWARD
Tor Park Road, Torquay
TQ2 5BQ
t (01803) 290698
e cj@bentleylodge.co.uk
w bentleylodge.co.uk

The Berburry ★★★★★
Guest Accommodation
GOLD AWARD
64 Bampfylde Road, Torquay
TQ2 5AY
t (01803) 297494
e stay@berburry.co.uk
w berburry.co.uk

The Brandize ★★★★
Guest Accommodation
19 Avenue Road, Torquay
TQ2 5LB
t (01803) 297798
e stay@brandize.co.uk
w brandize.co.uk

Brocklehurst Guest House ★★★★
Guest House
Rathmore Road, Chelston, Torquay
TQ2 6NZ
t (01803) 390883
e enquiries@brocklehursthotel.co.uk
w brocklehursthotel.co.uk

Buckingham Lodge ★★★★
Guest Accommodation
Falkland Road, Torquay
TQ2 5JP
t (01803) 293538
e stay@buckinghamlodge.co.uk
w buckinghamlodge.co.uk

The Capri ★★★★
Guest Accommodation
12 Torbay Road, Torquay
TQ2 6RG
t (01803) 293158
e stay@caprihoteltorquay.co.uk
w caprihotelltorquay.co.uk

Carlton Court ★★★★★
Guest Accommodation
SILVER AWARD
18 Cleveland Road, Torquay
TQ2 5BE
t (01803) 297318
e stay@carlton-court.co.uk
w carlton-court.co.uk

Cary Arms Hotel & Restaurant
★★★★★ *Inn* **SILVER AWARD**
Babbacombe Beach, Babbacombe,
Torquay
TQ1 3LX
t 01803 327110
e enquiries@caryarms.co.uk
w caryarms.co.uk

The Charterhouse ★★★★
Guest Accommodation
Cockington Lane, Torquay
TQ2 6QT
t (01803) 605804
e charterhousehtl@btconnect.com
w charterhouse-hotel.co.uk

Chesterfield ★★★★
Guest Accommodation
62 Belgrave Road, Torquay
TQ2 5HY
t (01803) 292318
e enquiries@chesterfieldhoteltorquay.co.uk
w chesterfieldhoteltorquay.co.uk

The Cleveland ★★★★
Guest Accommodation
SILVER AWARD
7 Cleveland Road, Torquay
TQ2 5BD
t (01803) 297522
e wjennings@hotmail.co.uk
w theclevelandtorquay.co.uk/

Cloudlands ★★★★
Guest Accommodation
St Agnes Lane, Torquay, Devon
TQ2 6QD
t (01803) 606550
e info@cloudlands.co.uk
w cloudlands.co.uk

Coombe Court ★★★★
Guest Accommodation
67 Babbacombe Downs Road, Torquay
TQ1 3LP
t (01803) 327097
e enquiries@coombecourthotel.co.uk
w coombecourthotel.co.uk

Crimdon Dene ★★★★ *Guest House*
Falkland Road, Torquay
TQ2 5JP
t (01803) 294651
e vbguide@crimdondenehotel.co.uk
w crimdondenehotel.co.uk

Crown Lodge ★★★★
Guest Accommodation
83 Avenue Road, Torquay
TQ2 5LH
t (01803) 298772
e stay@crownlodgehotel.co.uk
w crownlodgehotel.co.uk

The Daylesford ★★★★
Guest Accommodation
SILVER AWARD
60 Bampfylde Road, Torquay
TQ2 5AY
t (01803) 294435
e info@daylesfordhotel.com
w daylesfordhotel.com

The Downs ★★★★
Guest Accommodation
41-43 Babbacombe Downs Road,
Babbacombe, Torquay
TQ1 3LN
t (01803) 34543
e manager@downshotel.co.uk
w downshotel.co.uk

The Elmdene ★★★★
Guest Accommodation
Rathmore Road, Torquay
TQ2 6NZ
t (01803) 294940
e enquiries@elmdenehotel.co.uk
w elmdenehotel.co.uk

Emlea ★★★★
Guest Accommodation
91 Windor Road, Babbacombe,
Torquay
TQ1 1SU
t (01803) 323471
e info@emlea.co.uk
w emlea.co.uk

Exton House ★★★★
Guest Accommodation
12 Bridge Road, Torquay
TQ2 5BA
t (01803) 293561
e enquiries@extonhotel.co.uk
w extonhotel.co.uk

Fairways ★★★★
Guest Accommodation
SILVER AWARD
72 Avenue Road, Torquay
TQ2 5LF
t (01803) 298471
e cgallachersmith@yahoo.co.uk
w fairwaystorbay.co.uk

Ferndale Lodge ★★★
Guest Accommodation
22 St Marychurch Road, Torquay
TQ1 3HY
t (01803) 295311
e info@ferndalehotel.co.uk
w ferndalehotel.co.uk

Fleurie House ★★★★
Guest Accommodation
50 Bampfylde Road, Torquay
TQ2 5AY
t (01803) 294869
e fleuriehouseandc@btinternet.com
w fleuriehouse.co.uk

The Garlieston Guest House ★★★
Guest Accommodation
Bridge Road, Torquay
TQ2 5BA
t (01803) 294050
e enquiries@thegarlieston.com
w thegarlieston.com

Garway Lodge Guest House
★★★★ *Guest House*
SILVER AWARD
79 Avenue Road, Torquay
TQ2 5LL
t (01803) 293126
e garwaylodge@hotmail.com
w garwaylodgetorquay.co.uk

Glendower ★★★★
Guest Accommodation
Falkland Road, Torquay
TQ2 5JP
t (01803) 299988
e pete@hoteltorquay.co.uk
w hoteltorquay.co.uk

The Glenross ★★★★
Guest Accommodation
SILVER AWARD
25 Avenue Road, Torquay
TQ2 5LB
t (01803) 297517
e jan@glenross-hotel.co.uk
w glenross-hotel.co.uk

The Glenwood ★★★★
Guest Accommodation
Rowdens Road, Torquay
TQ2 5AZ
t (01803) 296318
e enquiries@glenwood-hotel.co.uk
w glenwood-hotel.co.uk

Grosvenor House ★★★★
Guest Accommodation
Falkland Road, Torquay
TQ2 5JP
t (01803) 294110
e etc@grosvenorhousehotel.co.uk
w grosvenorhousehotel.co.uk

Haldon Priors ★★★★★
Guest Accommodation
GOLD AWARD
Meadfoot Sea Road, Torquay
TQ1 2LQ
t (01803) 213365
e travelstyle.ltd@talk21.com
w haldonpriors.com

Haute Epine Guest House ★★★
Guest House
36 Bampfylde Road, Torquay
TQ2 5AR
t (01803) 296359
e gerryhauteepine@tiscali.co.uk
w haute-epineguesthouse.co.uk

Haven House ★★★★ *Guest House*
11 Scarborough Road, Torquay
TQ2 5UJ
t (01803) 293390
e enquiries@havenhotel.biz
w havenhotel.biz

Heathcliff House ★★★★
Guest Accommodation
16 Newton Road, Torquay
TQ2 5BZ
t (01803) 211580
e heathcliffhouse@btconnect.com
w heathcliffhousehotel.co.uk

The Hillcroft ★★★★
Guest Accommodation
GOLD AWARD
Matlock Terrace, 9 St Lukes Road,
Torquay
TQ2 5NY
t (01803) 297247
e info@thehillcroft.co.uk
w thehillcroft.co.uk

South West | Devon

Hotel Cimon ★★★★
Guest Accommodation
82 Abbey Road, Torquay
TQ2 5NP
t (01803) 294454
e enquiries@hotelcimon.co.uk
w hotelcimon.co.uk

Jesmond Dene ★★
Guest Accommodation
85 Abbey Road, Torquay
TQ2 5NN
t (01803) 293062

Kethla House ★★★★
Guest Accommodation
33 Belgrave Road, Torquay
TQ2 5HX
t (01803) 294995
e stay@kethlahouse.co.uk
w kethlahouse.co.uk

Kings Lodge ★★★★
Guest Accommodation
44 Bampfylde Road, Torquay
TQ2 5AY
t (01803) 293108
e enquiries@kingshotel-torquay.co.uk
w kingshotel-torquay.co.uk

Kingston House ★★★★★
Guest Accommodation
SILVER AWARD
75 Avenue Road, Torquay
TQ2 5LL
t (01803) 212760
e stay@kingstonhousehotel.co.uk
w kingstonhousehotel.co.uk

Kingsway Lodge Guest House
★★★★ *Guest House*
95 Avenue Road, Torquay
TQ2 5LH
t (01803) 295288
e kingswaylodge@hotmail.co.uk
w kingswaylodgeguesthouse.co.uk

Lanscombe House ★★★★
Guest Accommodation
SILVER AWARD
Cockington Village, Torquay
TQ2 6XA
t (01803) 606938
e stay@lanscombehouse.co.uk
w lanscombehouse.co.uk

Lawnswood Guest House ★★★★
Guest House
6 Scarborough Road, Torquay
TQ2 5UJ
t (01803) 292595
e info@lawnswoodguesthouse.com
w lawnswoodguesthousetorquay.co.uk

Lindum Lodge ★★★★
Guest Accommodation
105 Abbey Road, Torquay
TQ2 5NP
t (01803) 292795
e enquiries@lindum-hotel.co.uk
w lindum-hotel.co.uk

Melba House *Guest House*
62 Bampfylde Road, Torquay
TQ2 5AY
t (01803) 213167
e stay@melbahouse.co.uk
w melbahouse.co.uk

Mount Edgcombe ★★★★
Guest Accommodation
23 Avenue Road, Torquay
TQ2 5LB
t (01803) 292310
e info@mountedgcombe.co.uk
w mountedgcombe.co.uk

Mount Nessing ★★★★
Guest Accommodation
St Lukes Road North, Torquay
TQ2 5PD
t (01803) 294259
e stay@mountnessinghotel.co.uk
w mountnessinghotel.co.uk

The Netley ★★★
Guest Accommodation
52 Bampfylde Road, Torquay
TQ2 5AY
t (01803) 295109
e thenetley@btconnect.com
w thenetleyhotel.co.uk

The Norwood ★★★★
Guest Accommodation
60 Belgrave Road, Torquay
TQ2 5HY
t (01803) 294236
e enquiries@norwoodhoteltorquay.co.uk
w norwoodhoteltorquay.co.uk

The Parks ★★★★
Guest Accommodation
Rathmore Road, Torquay
TQ2 6NZ
t (01803) 292420
e enquiries@parks-hotel.co.uk
w parks-hotel.co.uk

The Patricia ★★★★
Guest Accommodation
64 Belgrave Road, Torquay
TQ2 5HY
t (01803) 293339
e info@hotel-patricia.co.uk
w hotel-patricia.co.uk

Richwood Hotel ★★★
Guest Accommodation
20 Newton Road, Torquay
TQ2 5BZ
t (01803) 293729
e enq@richwoodhotel.co.uk
w richwood-hotel-torquay.co.uk

Robin Hill Guest House ★★★
Guest Accommodation
74 Braddons Hill Road East, Torquay
TQ1 1HF
t (01803) 214518
e stay@robinhillhotel.co.uk
w robinhillhotel.co.uk

Rutland Lodge ★★★★
Guest House
448 Babbacombe Road, Torquay
TQ1 1HW
t (01803) 213972
e rutlandlodge@mac.com
w web.mac.com/rutlandlodge

The Sandpiper ★★★★
Guest House
Rowdens Road, Torquay
TQ2 5AZ
t (01803) 292779
e sandpiper57@home13859.fsnet.co.uk
w sandpiper-hotel.co.uk

Sandway House ★★★★
Guest Accommodation
72 Belgrave Road, Torquay
TQ2 5HY
t (01803) 298499
e info@sandwayhouse.co.uk
w sandwayhouse.co.uk

Sea Point ★★★
Guest Accommodation
Clifton Grove, Old Torwood Road, Torquay
TQ1 1PR
t (01803) 211808
e seapointhotel@hotmail.com
w seapointhotel.co.uk

The Shirley ★★★★
Guest Accommodation
Braddons Hill Road East, Torquay
TQ1 1HF
t (01803) 293016
e enquiries@shirley-hotel.co.uk
w shirley-hotel.co.uk

The Somerville ★★★★★
Guest Accommodation
GOLD AWARD
515 Babbacombe Road, Torquay
TQ1 1HJ
t (01803) 294755
e stay@somervillehotel.co.uk
w somervillehotel.co.uk

The Southbank ★★★★
Guest Accommodation
15-17 Belgrave Road, Torquay
TQ2 5HU
t (01803) 296701
e stay@southbankhotel.co.uk
w southbankhotel.co.uk

South View ★★★★
Guest Accommodation
12 Scarborough Road, Torquay
TQ2 5UJ
t (01803) 296029
e stay@thesouthview.com
w thesouthview.com

Torbay Star Guest House ★★★★
Guest House
73 Avenue Road, Torquay
TQ2 5LL
t (01803) 293998
e torbaystar@btinternet.com
w torbaystarguesthouse.co.uk

Tor Dean ★★★★
Guest Accommodation
27 Bampfylde Road, Torquay
TQ2 5AY
t (01803) 294669
e stay@tordeanhotel.com
w tordeanhotel.com

Tower Hall ★★★★
Guest Accommodation
Solsbro Road, Torquay
TQ2 6PF
t (01803) 605292
e john@towerhallhotel.co.uk
w towerhallhotel.co.uk

Trouville ★★★★ *Guest House*
70 Belgrave Road, Torquay
TQ2 5HY
t (01803) 294979
e info@trouvillehoteltorquay.co.uk
w trouvillehoteltorquay.co.uk

Villa Marina ★★★★
Guest Accommodation
SILVER AWARD
Tor Park Road, Torquay
TQ2 5BQ
t (01803) 292187
e enquiries@villamarina-torquay.co.uk
w villamarina-torquay.co.uk

Walnut Lodge ★★★★
Guest Accommodation
SILVER AWARD
48 Bampfylde Road, Torquay
TQ2 5AY
t (01803) 200471
e stay@walnutlodgetorquay.co.uk
w walnutlodgetorquay.co.uk

The Wellsway ★★★★
Guest Accommodation
56 Bampfylde Road, Torquay
TQ2 5AY
t (01803) 215588
e info@wellsway-hotel.co.uk
w wellsway-hotel.co.uk

The Westbank ★★★★
Guest Accommodation
SILVER AWARD
54 Bampfylde Road, Torquay
TQ2 5AY
t (01803) 295271
e enquiries@thewestbank.co.uk
w thewestbank.co.uk

The Westbourne ★★★★
Guest Accommodation
106 Avenue Road, Torquay
TQ2 5LQ
t (01803) 292927
e enquiries@westbournehotel torquay.co.uk
w westbournehoteltorquay.co.uk

The Westbrook ★★★★
Guest House
15 Scarborough Road, Torquay
TQ2 5UJ
t (01803) 292559
e westbrookhotel@tesco.net
w westbrookhotel.net

The Westgate ★★★★
Guest Accommodation
SILVER AWARD
Falkland Road, Torquay
TQ2 5JP
t (01803) 295350
e stay@westgatehotel.co.uk
w westgatehotel.co.uk

Whitburn Guest House ★★★
Guest House
Saint Lukes Road North, Torquay, Devon
TQ2 5PD
t 01803296719
e lazenby1210@btinternet.com
w whitburnguesthouse.co.uk

Wilsbrook Guest House ★★★
Guest House
77 Avenue Road, Torquay
TQ2 5LL
t (01803) 298413
e thewilsbrook@talktalk.net
w wilsbrook.co.uk

TORRINGTON

Locksbeam Farm ★★★★
Farmhouse
Locksbeam Farm, Torrington
EX38 7EZ
t (01805) 623213
e tracey@locksbeamfarm.co.uk
w locksbeamfarm.co.uk

TOTNES

The Elbow Room ★★★★★
Guest Accommodation
SILVER AWARD
North Street, Totnes
TQ9 5NZ
t (01803) 863480
e r.savin@btinternet.com
w theelbowroomtotnes.co.uk

Four Seasons Guest House
★★★★ *Guest House*
13 Bridgetown, Totnes
TQ9 5AB
t (01803) 862146
e info@fourseasonstotnes.co.uk
w fourseasonstotnes.co.uk

The Great Grubb B&B ★★★★
Guest House **SILVER AWARD**
Fallowfields, Plymouth Road, Totnes
TQ9 5LX
t (01803) 849071
e accommodation@thegreatgrubb.co.uk
w thegreatgrubb.co.uk

The Old Forge ★★★★ *Guest House*
Seymour Place, Totnes
TQ9 5AY
t (01803) 862174
e enq@oldforgetotnes.com
w oldforgetotnes.com

Steam Packet Inn ★★★★ *Inn*
4 St Peters Quay, Totnes
TQ9 5EW
t (01803) 863880
e steampacket@buccaneer.com
w steampacketinn.co.uk

UGBOROUGH

Higher Coarsewell Farm ★★★★
Bed & Breakfast
Ugborough, Ivybridge
PL21 0HP
t (01548) 821560
e sue@highercoarsewellfarm.co.uk
w highercoarsewellfarm.co.uk

Hillhead Farm ★★★★ *Farmhouse*
SILVER AWARD
Ugborough, Ivybridge
PL21 0HQ
t (01752) 892674
e info@hillhead-farm.co.uk
w hillhead-farm.co.uk

South West | Devon/Dorset

UPOTTERY

wer Luxton Farm ★★★
wer Luxton Farm, Upottery
14 9PB
t (01823) 601269
e lwrluxtonfm@hotmail.com
w lowerluxtonfarm.co.uk

VIRGINSTOWE

akcroft Farm Holidays ★★★★
rmhouse
rginstow, Beaworthy
21 5EA
t (01409) 211019
e rogers@oakcroftfarmholidays.co.uk
w oakcroftfarmholidays.co.uk

WATERROW

andley Farm Accommodation
★★★★ Farmhouse
OLD AWARD
aterrow, Taunton
4 2BE
t (01398) 361516
e info@handleyfarm.co.uk
w handleyfarm.co.uk

WEST DOWN

nnymeade Country Hotel ★★★
est House
ean Cross, Woolacombe
34 8NT
t (01271) 863668
e holidays@sunnymeade.co.uk
w sunnymeade.co.uk

WESTWARD HO!

ockenhurst ★★★★
& Breakfast
Atlantic Way, Westward Ho!,
deford
39 1HX
t (01237) 423346
e info@brockenhurstindevon.co.uk

WESTWARD HO

e Village Inn ★★★★ Inn
ungaton Road, Westward Ho!,
deford
39 1HU
t (01237) 477331
e info@villageinndevon.co.uk
w villageinndevon.co.uk

WHITESTONE

ayne Barton Milverton Country Holidays ★★★ Bed & Breakfast
hitestone, Exeter
4 2JN
t (01392) 811268
e g_milverton@haynebarton.demon.co.uk
w milvertoncountryholidays.com

WINKLEIGH

e Old Parsonage ★★★★
est Accommodation
urt Walk, Winkleigh
19 8JA
t (01837) 83772
e tony@lymingtonarms.co.uk
w lymingtonarms.co.uk

rsonage Farm ★★★★
rmhouse **SILVER AWARD**
desleigh, Winkleigh
19 8SN
t (01837) 810318
e roseward01@yahoo.co.uk
w parsonage-farm-devon.co.uk

WITHLEIGH

eat Bradley Farmhouse ★★★★
rmhouse **SILVER AWARD**
eat Bradley Farm, Withleigh,
verton
16 8JL
t (01884) 256946
e hann@agriplus.net
w greatbradleyfarm-devon.co.uk

WOODLEIGH

Higher Hendham House ★★★★
Farmhouse
Woodleigh, Kingsbridge
TQ7 4DP
t (01548) 550015
e higherhendhamhouse@fsmail.net
w higherhendhamhouse.com

WOOLACOMBE

Castle ★★★★
Guest Accommodation
The Esplanade, Woolacombe
EX34 7DJ
t (01271) 870788

Ossaborough House ★★★★
Guest Accommodation
Ossaborough Lane, Woolacombe
EX34 7HJ
t (01271) 870297
e info@ossaboroughhouse.co.uk
w ossaboroughhouse.co.uk

Sandunes ★★★★ Guest House
SILVER AWARD
Beach Road, Woolacombe, N. Devon
EX34 7BT
t (01271) 870661
e info@sandwool.fsnet.co.uk
w sandunesbedandbreakfast.co.uk

YELVERTON

Barnabas House Yelverton ★★★★
Guest Accommodation
Harrowbeer Lane, Yelverton
PL20 6DY
t (01822) 853268
e enquiries@barnabas-house.co.uk
w barnabas-house.co.uk

Callisham Farm ★★★★ Farmhouse
Meavy, Yelverton
PL20 6PS
t (01822) 853901
e esme@callisham.co.uk
w callisham.co.uk

Harrabeer Country House ★★★★
Guest Accommodation
Harrowbeer Lane, Yelverton, Devon
PL20 6EA
t (01822) 853302
e reception@harrabeer.co.uk
w harrabeer.co.uk

Overcombe House ★★★★
Guest Accommodation
Old Station Road, Horrabridge,
Yelverton
PL20 7RA
t (01822) 853501
e enquiries@overcombehotel.co.uk
w overcombehotel.co.uk

Dorset

ALTON PANCRAS

Whiteways Farmhouse Accommodation ★★★★
Bed & Breakfast **SILVER AWARD**
Bookham, Alton Pancras, Dorchester
DT2 7RP
t (01300) 345511
e andy.foot1@btinternet.com
w bookhamcourt.co.uk

ATHELHAMPTON

White Cottage ★★★★
Bed & Breakfast **GOLD AWARD**
Athelhampton, Dorchester
DT2 7LG
t (01305) 848622 Mobile- 07778 987906
e bookings@white-cottage-bandb.co.uk
w white-cottage-bandb.co.uk

BEAMINSTER

Kitwhistle Farm ★★★ Farmhouse
Beaminster Down, Beaminster
DT8 3SG
t (01308) 862458

North Buckham Farm ★★★★
Farmhouse
North Buckham Farm, Beaminster
DT8 3SH
t (01308) 863054
e trish@northbuckham.fsnet.co.uk
w northbuckhamfarm.co.uk

BINNEGAR

Holmebridge House ★★★★
Bed & Breakfast
Holmebridge, Wareham
BH20 6AF
t (01929) 550599
e holmebridge@googlemail.com
w holmebridgehouse.co.uk

BLANDFORD FORUM

The Anvil Inn ★★★★ Inn
Salisbury Road, Pimperne, Blandford Forum
DT11 8UQ
t (01258) 453431
e theanvil.inn@btconnect.com
w anvilinn.co.uk

Cashmoor House ★★★★
Farmhouse
Cashmoor, Blandford Forum
DT11 8DN
t (01725) 552339
e mary@cashmoorhouse.co.uk
w cashmoorhouse.co.uk

Farnham Farm House ★★★★★
Guest Accommodation
GOLD AWARD
Farnham, Blandford Forum
DT11 8DG
t (01725) 516254
e info@farnhamfarmhouse.co.uk
w farnhamfarmhouse.co.uk

St Leonards Farmhouse ★★★★
Bed & Breakfast
Wimborne Road, Blandford Forum
DT11 7SB
t (01258) 456635
e info.stleonardsfarmhouse@fsmail.net
w stleonardsfarmhouse.com

BOURNEMOUTH

Alexander Lodge ★★★★
Guest House
21 Southern Road, Southbourne,
Bournemouth
BH6 3SR
t (01202) 421662
e alexanderlodge@yahoo.com
w alexanderlodgehotel.co.uk

Aloha Wyvern Hotel ★★★★
Guest House
24 Glen Road, Bournemouth
BH5 1HR
t (01202) 397543
e mail@wyvernhotel.co.uk
w wyvernhotel.co.uk

Balincourt ★★★★★
Guest Accommodation
SILVER AWARD
58 Christchurch Road, Bournemouth
BH1 3PF
t (01202) 552962
e reservations@balincourt.co.uk
w balincourt.co.uk

Beach Lodge ★★★★
Guest Accommodation
61 Grand Avenue, Southbourne,
Bournemouth
BH6 3TA
t (01202) 423396
e stay@beach-lodge.co.uk
w beach-lodge.co.uk

Beech Grove Lodge ★★★★
Guest Accommodation
1 Beech Avenue, Southbourne,
Bournemouth
BH6 3ST
t (01202) 421769
e p.layburn@btconnect.com
w beechgrovelodgebournemouth.co.uk

Blue Palms ★★★★
Guest Accommodation
26 Tregonwell Road, Bournemouth
BH2 5NS
t (01202) 554968
e bluepalmshotel@btopenworld.com
w bluepalmshotel.com

The Cavendish ★★★★
Guest Accommodation
20 Durley Chine Road, West Cliff,
Bournemouth
BH2 5LF
t (01202) 290489
e info@thecavendishhotel.co.uk

The Charlesworth ★★★
Guest Accommodation
35 Tregonwell Road, Bournemouth
BH2 5NT
t (01202) 779177
e enquiries@charlesworthhotel.net
w charlesworthhotel.net

The Claremont ★★★★
Guest Accommodation
89 St Michael's Road, Bournemouth
BH2 5DR
t (01202) 290875
e info@claremonthotelbournemouth.co.uk

Cransley ★★★★
Guest Accommodation
SILVER AWARD
11 Knyveton Road, East Cliff,
Bournemouth
BH1 3QG
t (01202) 290067
e info@cransley.com
w cransley.com

Cremona B&B ★★★
Guest Accommodation
61 St Michaels Road, West Cliff,
Bournemouth, Dorset
BH2 5DP
t (01202) 290035
e enquiries@cremona.co.uk
w cremona.co.uk

Dean Park Inn ★★★ Inn
41 Wimbourne Road, Bournemouth
BH2 6NB
t (01202) 552941
e deanpark@wadworth.co.uk

Denewood ★★★
Guest Accommodation
40 Sea Road, Bournemouth
BH5 1BQ
t (01202) 394493
e info@denewood.co.uk
w denewood.co.uk

Earlham Lodge ★★★★
Guest House
91 Alumhurst Road, Alum Chine,
Bournemouth
BH4 8HR
t (01202) 761943
e earlhamlodge@hotmail.com
w earlhamlodge.com

Fielden Court ★★★★ Guest House
20 Southern Road, Southbourne,
Bournemouth
BH6 3SR
t (01202) 427459
e enquiries@fieldencourthotel.co.uk
w fieldencourthotel.co.uk

The Fircliff ★★★★ Guest House
SILVER AWARD
Studland Road, Bournemouth
BH4 8HZ
t (01202) 765307
e coastl@tiscali.co.uk

Ingledene Guest House ★★
Guest House
20 Gardens View, Derby Road,
Bournemouth
BH1 3QA
t (01202) 291914
e ingledenehouse@yahoo.com
w ingledenehouse.co.uk

149

South West | Dorset

Kings Langley ★★★ *Guest House*
1 West Cliff Road, Bournemouth
BH2 5ES
t (01202) 557349
e john@kingslangleyhotel.com
w kingslangleyhotel.com

Marlins ★★★★
Guest Accommodation
2 West Cliff Road, West Cliff,
Bournemouth
BH2 5EY
t (01202) 299645
e reservations@marlinshotel.com
w marlinshotel.com

Mount Lodge Guest Accommodation ★★★ *Guest House*
19 Beaulieu Road, Alum Chine,
Bournemouth
BH4 8HY
t (01202) 761173
e mountlodgehotel@yahoo.com
w mountlodge.co.uk

Ocean Breeze ★★★ *Guest House*
5 Westby Road, Boscombe Spa,
Bournemouth
BH5 1HA
t (01202) 394791
e oceanbreeze@btconnect.com
w oceanbreezeboscombe.com

The Silver How ★★★
Guest Accommodation
4-5 West Cliff Gardens, West Cliff,
Bournemouth
BH2 5HN
t (01202) 551537
e reservations@silverhowhotel.co.uk
w silverhowhotel.co.uk

Southernhay Guest House ★★★
Guest Accommodation
42 Alum Chine Road, Westbourne,
Bournemouth
BH4 8DX
t (01202) 761251
e enquiries@southernhayhotel.co.uk
w southernhayhotel.co.uk

Wenrose ★★★★
Guest Accommodation
23 Drummond Road, Boscombe,
Bournemouth
BH1 4DP
t (01202) 396451
e wendyruth-bradford@tiscali.co.uk
w bournemouthbedandbreakfast.com

Winter Dene ★★★★
Guest Accommodation
11 Durley Road South, West Cliff,
Bournemouth
BH2 5JH
t (01202) 554150
e info@winterdenehotel.com
w winterdenehotel.com

Wood Lodge ★★★★
Guest Accommodation
10 Manor Road, East Cliff,
Bournemouth
BH1 3EY
t (01302) 290891
e enquiries@woodlodgehotel.co.uk
w woodlodgehotel.co.uk

BRADPOLE

Orchard Barn ★★★★★
Guest Accommodation
GOLD AWARD
off Lee Lane, Bradpole, Bridport
DT6 4AR
t (01308) 455655
e reservations@lodgeatorchardbarn.co.uk
w lodgeatorchardbarn.co.uk

Spray Copse Farm ★★★★
Bed & Breakfast
Spray Copse Farm, Lee Lane,
Bridport
DT6 4AP
t (01308) 458510
e helen.mcreavie@zen.co.uk

BRIDPORT

The Barn ★★★
Guest Accommodation
39a South Street, Bridport
DT6 3NY
t (01308) 459323
e pjharmony2004@yahoo.co.uk

Britmead House ★★★★
Guest Accommodation
SILVER AWARD
West Bay Road, Bridport
DT6 4EG
t (01308) 422941
e britmead@talk21.com
w britmeadhouse.co.uk

Cardsmill Farmhouse ★★★★
Farmhouse
Whitchurch Canonicorum, Bridport
DT6 6RP
t (01297) 489375
e cardsmill@aol.com
w farmhousedorset.com

Colly Farm *Farmhouse*
Dottery, Bridport
DT6 5PU
t (01308) 422978
e john_dean@hotmail.co.uk
w collyfarmbridport.co.uk

Eypeleaze ★★★★ *Bed & Breakfast*
117 West Bay Road, Bridport
DT6 4EQ
t (01308) 423363
e enquiries@eypeleaze.co.uk
w eypeleaze.co.uk

The Gables ★★★★ *Bed & Breakfast*
SILVER AWARD
West Allington, Bridport
DT6 5BH
t (01308) 459963
e donaldbroadley@hotmail.com
w thegablesbridport.co.uk

Gerrards Farm ★★★★ *Farmhouse*
SILVER AWARD
Pilsdon, Bridport
DT6 5PA
t (01308) 867474
e chrisrabbetts@btinternet.com
w gerrardsfarm.co.uk

Heatherbell Cottage ★★★★
Guest Accommodation
Hill Close, West Cliff, Bridport
DT6 4HW
t (01308) 422998
e info@cu4bnb.com
w cu4bnb.com

Highway Farm ★★★★
Guest Accommodation
SILVER AWARD
West Road, Bridport
DT6 6AE
t (01308) 424321
e bale@highwayfarm.co.uk
w highwayfarm.co.uk

New House Farm ★★★★
Farmhouse
Mangerton Lane, Bradpole, Bridport
DT6 3SF
t (01308) 422884
e mangertonlake@btconnect.com
w mangertonlake.co.uk

The Roundham House ★★★★★
Guest Accommodation
SILVER AWARD
Roundham Gardens, West Bay Road,
Bridport
DT6 4BD
t (01308) 422753
e cyprencom@compuserve.com
w roundhamhouse.co.uk

The Tiger Inn ★★★ *Inn*
14-16 Barrack Street, Bridport
DT6 3LY
t (01308) 427543
e jacquie@tigerinnbridport.co.uk
w tigerinnbridport.co.uk

The Well ★★★ *Bed & Breakfast*
St Andrews Well, Bridport
DT6 3DL
t (01308) 424156
e thewellbandb@yahoo.co.uk
w thewellbandb.co.uk

The White House ★★★★
Bed & Breakfast
90 West Bay Road, Bridport
DT6 4AX
t (01308) 458708
e enquiries@thewhitehousebb.co.uk
w thewhitehousebb.co.uk

Wisteria Cottage ★★★★
Guest Accommodation
SILVER AWARD
Taylors Lane, Morcombelake,
Bridport
DT6 6ED
t (01297) 489019
e dave@dorsetcottage.org.uk
w dorsetcottage.org.uk

BRIDPORT (4 MILES)

Dunster Farm ★★★ *Farmhouse*
Broadoak, Bridport
DT6 5NR
t (01308) 424626
e dunsterfarm@onebillinternet.co.uk
w dunsterfarm.co.uk

BRIDPORT - WEST DORSET

Dippers ★★★★ *Bed & Breakfast*
42 Uplopers, Bridport
DT6 4PE
t (01308) 485504/07855 344121 (mobile)
e liz@dipperswestdorset.co.uk
w dipperswestdorset.co.uk

BROADSTONE

Honey Lodge ★★★★
Bed & Breakfast **SILVER AWARD**
41 Dunyeats Road, Broadstone,
Poole
BH18 8AB
t (01202) 694247
e honey_lodge41@hotmail.com
w honeylodge.co.uk

Tarven ★★ *Bed & Breakfast*
Corfe Lodge Road, Broadstone
BH18 9NF
t (01202) 694338
e browning@tarvencorfe.fsnet.co.uk
w tarven.co.uk/

Weston Cottage ★★★★
Bed & Breakfast
6 Macaulay Road, Broadstone, Poole
BH18 8AR
t (01202) 699638
e westoncot@aol.com
w westoncottage.org.uk

BROADWINDSOR

Cross Keys House ★★★★★
Bed & Breakfast **SILVER AWARD**
High Street, Broadwindsor,
Beaminster
DT8 3QP
t (01308) 868063
e robin.adeney@care4free.net
w crosskeyshouse.com

BUCKLAND NEWTON

Rew Cottage ★★★★
Bed & Breakfast
Buckland Newton, Dorchester
DT2 7DN
t (01300) 345467

BURTON BRADSTOCK

Chesil Beach Lodge ★★★★
Guest House
Coast Road, Burton Bradstock,
Bridport
DT6 4RJ
t (01308) 897428
e enquiries@chesilbeachlodge.co.uk
w chesilbeachlodge.co.uk

Norburton Hall ★★★★★
Guest Accommodation
GOLD AWARD
Shipton Lane, Burton Bradstock,
Bridport
DT6 4NQ
t (01308) 897007
e info@norburtonhall.com
w norburtonhall.com

CHARMINSTER

The Three Compasses ★★★ *Inn*
The Square, Charminster, Dorchester
DT2 9QT
t (01305) 263618

CHARMOUTH

Befferlands Farm B&B ★★★★
Bed & Breakfast
Befferlands Farm, Charmouth,
Bridport
DT6 6RD
t (01297) 560203
e bob@befferlands.freeserve.co.uk
w befferlands.co.uk

Cliffend ★★★★
Guest Accommodation
Higher Sea Lane, Charmouth,
Bridport
DT6 6BD
t (01297) 561047
e janicemuller@tesco.net
w cliffend.org.uk

Cliff House ★★★
Guest Accommodation - Room Only
Old Lyme Road, Charmouth
DT6 6BW
t (01297) 561493
e wendyknee@hotmail.com
w charmouthroomwithaview.com

CHIDEOCK

Bay Tree House ★★★★
Bed & Breakfast **SILVER AWARD**
Duck Street, Chideock, Bridport
DT6 6JW
t (01297) 489336
e sally@baytreechideock.co.uk
w baytreechideock.co.uk

CHILD OKEFORD

Manor Barn Bed & Breakfast ★★★★★ *Bed & Breakfast*
SILVER AWARD
Upper Street, Child Okeford,
Blandford Forum
DT11 8EF
t (01258) 860638
e carisorby@btinternet.com
w manorbarnbedandbreakfast.co.uk

CHRISTCHURCH

10 Brook Way ★★ *Bed & Breakfast*
10 Brook Way, Fiars Cliff,
Christchurch
BH23 4HA
t (01425) 276738
e midgefinn@hotmail.com

Beechcroft Place ★★★★
Bed & Breakfast **SILVER AWARD**
106 Lymington Road, Christchurch
BH23 4JX
t (01425) 277171
e info@beachmeetsforest.co.uk
w beachmeetsforest.co.uk

Bure Lodge ★★★★ *Guest House*
18 Bure Haven Drive, Christchurch
BH23 4BS
t (01425) 277260
e burelodge@yahoo.co.uk
w burelodge.co.uk

Castle Lodge ★★★★ *Guest House*
SILVER AWARD
173 Lymington Road, Christchurch
BH23 4JS
t (01425) 275170
e sharon@castlelodge-highcliffe.co.uk
w castlelodge-highcliffe.co.uk

South West | Dorset

ewton Edge ★★★
d & Breakfast
7 Ringwood Road, Walkford,
ristchurch
23 5RB
t (01425) 271430
e nealchewtonedge@btinternet.com
w chewtonedge.co.uk

uid House ★★★★★
est Accommodation
OLD AWARD
Sopers Lane, Christchurch
23 1JE
t (01202) 485615
e reservations@druid-house.co.uk
w druid-house.co.uk

e Fisherman's Haunt Inn ★★★ *Inn*
lisbury Road, Christchurch
23 7AS
t (01202) 477283
e fishermanshaunt@fullers.co.uk
w fullershotels.co.uk

lmon's Reach Guest House ★★ *Guest Accommodation*
Stanpit, Christchurch
23 3LZ
t (01202) 477315
e info@salmonsreach.com
w salmonsreach.com

a Corner ★★★★ *Guest House*
7 Waterford Road, Christchurch
23 5JN
t (01425) 272731
e kevin.seacorner@hotmail.co.uk
w seacorner-guesthouse.co.uk

apoint ★★★
est Accommodation
1 Mudeford, Christchurch
23 4AF
t (01425) 279541
e seapointb-b@tiscali.co.uk
w seapointb-b.com

our Lodge Guest House ★★★★
est House
Stour Road, Christchurch
23 1LW
t (01202) 486902
e enquiries@stourlodge.co.uk
w stourlodge.co.uk

COMPTON VALENCE

anor Farm ★★★★
d & Breakfast
mpton Valence, Dorchester,
orset
2 9ES
t (01308) 482227
e tessa.nrussell@btinternet.com
w manor-farm.uk.com

CORFE CASTLE

orden House ★★★★
est Accommodation
orden, Corfe Castle, Wareham
20 5DS
t (01929) 480177
e nordenhouse@fsmail.net
w nordenhouse.com

estaway ★★★★ *Bed & Breakfast*
West Street, Corfe Castle,
areham
20 5HE
t (01929) 480188
e info@westaway-corfecastle.co.uk
w westaway-corfecastle.co.uk

CORFE MULLEN

ms Lodge ★★★★
d & Breakfast **GOLD AWARD**
Cogdean Way, Corfe Mullen,
mborne, Dorset
21 3XD
t (01202) 699669
e elmslodge@hotmail.com
w elmslodge.co.uk

CRANBORNE

La Fosse at Cranborne ★★★★
Guest Accommodation
London House, The Square,
Cranborne, Wimborne
BH21 5PR
t (01725) 517604
e lafossemail@gmail.com
w la-fosse.com

DORCHESTER

Aquila Heights Guest House
★★★★ *Guest Accommodation*
SILVER AWARD
44 Maiden Castle Road, Dorchester
DT1 2ES
t (01305) 267145
e aquila.heights@tiscali.co.uk
w aquilaheights.co.uk

Bay Tree House B&B ★★★★
Bed & Breakfast **SILVER AWARD**
4 Athelstan Road, Dorchester
DT1 1NR
t (01305) 263696
e info@baytreedorchester.com
w bandbdorchester.co.uk

Dalkeith B&B ★★★★
Bed & Breakfast
8 Poplar Drive, Charlton Down,
Dorchester
DT2 9XY
t (01305) 250808
e denise.addison@dorset-bandb.co.uk
w dorset-bandb.co.uk

Hazel Cottage ★★★★
Bed & Breakfast **SILVER AWARD**
1 Waterside Walk, Sydling St
Nicholas, Dorchester
DT2 9PJ
t (01300) 341618
e charlescordy@hazelcottage.ndo.co.uk
w hazelcottagedorset.co.uk

Hembury House ★★★
Guest Accommodation
Askerswell, Dorchester
DT2 9EN
t (01308) 485297
e peter.richards17@btopenworld.com
w hembury.house.co.uk

Magiston Farm ★★ *Farmhouse*
Sydling St Nicholas, Dorchester
DT2 9NR
t (01300) 320295

The Old Ship Inn ★★★ *Inn*
High West Street, Dorchester
DT1 1UW
t (01305) 264455
e info@orbitecnica.com
w bestpubindorchester.com

The Poachers Inn ★★★★ *Inn*
Piddletrenthide, Dorchester
DT2 7QX
t (01300) 348358
e info@thepoachersinn.co.uk
w thepoachersinn.co.uk

Slades Farm ★★★★
Bed & Breakfast
North Street, Charminster,
Dorchester
DT2 9QZ
t (01305) 264032
e info@bandbdorset.org.uk
w bandbdorset.org.uk

Sunrise Guest House ★★★
Guest House
34 London Road, Dorchester
DT1 1NE
t (01305) 262425
e info@sunriseguesthousedorchester.com
w sunriseguesthousedorchester.com

Tarkaville ★★★ *Bed & Breakfast*
30 Shaston Crescent, Dorchester
DT1 2EB
t (01305) 266253
e tarkaville@lineone.net
w tarkaville.co.uk

Westwood House ★★★★
Guest House **SILVER AWARD**
29 High West Street, Dorchester
DT1 1UP
t (01305) 268018
e reservations@westwoodhouse.co.uk
w westwoodhouse.co.uk

The White House ★★★
Bed & Breakfast
9 Queens Avenue, Dorchester
DT1 2EW
t (01305) 266714
e sandratwh@yahoo.co.uk
w whbandb.co.uk

Yellowham Farm ★★★★
Guest Accommodation
Yellowham Wood, Dorchester
DT2 8RW
t (01305) 262892
e mail@yellowham.freeserve.co.uk
w yellowham.co.uk

EAST STOUR

Aysgarth ★★★★ *Bed & Breakfast*
SILVER AWARD
Back Street, East Stour, Gillingham
SP8 5JY
t (01747) 838351
e aysgarth@lineone.net
w website.lineone.net/~aysgarth

FERNDOWN

Carey ★★★★ *Bed & Breakfast*
11 Southern Avenue, West Moors,
Ferndown
BH22 0BJ
t (01202) 861159
e russell@lesmor.fsnet.co.uk

FIFEHEAD ST QUINTIN

Lower Fifehead Farm ★★★
Farmhouse
Fifehead St Quintin, Sturminster
Newton
DT10 2AP
t (01258) 817335
e lowerfifeheadfarm@googlemail.com
w lowerfifeheadfarm.co.uk

FRIAR WADDON

Corton Farm ★★★★
Bed & Breakfast
Friar Waddon, Weymouth
DT3 4EP
t (01305) 815784
e hollylasseter@corton.org

Pump Cottage ★★★
Bed & Breakfast
Friar Waddon Road, Upwey,
Weymouth
DT3 4EW
t (01305) 816002
e ronjamsden@hotmail.com
w pumpcottagebedandbreakfast.com

FROME WHITFIELD

Yalbury Park ★★★★ *Farmhouse*
Frome Whitfield Farm, Frome
Whitfield, Dorchester
DT2 7SE
t (01305) 250336
e yalburypark@tesco.net

GILLINGHAM

Lyde Hill Farmhouse ★★★
Bed & Breakfast
Woodville, Stour Provost,
Gillingham, Dorset
SP8 5LY
t (01747) 838483

HALSTOCK

Quiet Woman House ★★★★
Bed & Breakfast
Halstock, Yeovil
BA22 9RX
t (01935) 891218
e enquiry@qwhdorset.co.uk
w qwhdorset.co.uk

HIGHCLIFFE

The Beech Tree ★★★★
Guest House
2 Stuart Road, Highcliffe,
Christchurch
BH23 5JS
t (01425) 272038
e hkowalski@beechtree.info
w beechtree.info

HOOKE

Water Meadow House ★★★★★
Farmhouse **SILVER AWARD**
Bridge Farm, Hooke, Beaminster
DT8 3PD
t (01308) 862619
e enquiries@watermeadowhouse.co.uk
w watermeadowhouse.co.uk

HURN

Avon Causeway Inn ★★★★ *Inn*
Hurn, Christchurch
BH23 6AS
t (01202) 482714
e avoncauseway@wadworth.co.uk
w avoncauseway.co.uk

IWERNE MINSTER

The Talbot ★★★★ *Inn*
SILVER AWARD
Blandford Road, Iwerne Minster,
Blandford Forum
DT11 8QN
t (01747) 811269
e enquiries@the-talbot.com
w the-talbot.com

KIMMERIDGE

Kimmeridge Farmhouse ★★★★★
Farmhouse **SILVER AWARD**
Kimmeridge, Wareham
BH20 5PE
t (01929) 480990
e kimmeridgefarmhouse@hotmail.com
w kimmeridgefarmhouse.co.uk

LITTON CHENEY

Litton Cheney YHA ★★★ *Hostel*
Litton Cheney, Dorchester
DT2 9AT
t (01308) 482340

LOWER BRYANSTON

Lower Bryanston Farm B&B
★★★★ *Farmhouse*
Lower Bryanston Farm, Blandford
Forum
DT11 0LS
t (01258) 452009
e andrea@bryanstonfarm.co.uk
w brylow.co.uk

LOWER WRAXALL

Lower Wraxhall Farmhouse
★★★★ *Bed & Breakfast*
Lower Wraxall, Dorchester
DT2 0HL
t (01935) 83218
e judy-thompson@beeb.net

LULWORTH COVE

Seavale Bed & Breakfast ★★★★
Bed & Breakfast **SILVER AWARD**
Main Road, Lulworth Cove, West
Lulworth
BH20 5RJ
t 07517†540045
e seavale@hotmail.co.uk
w lulworthcove-seavale.co.uk

r key to symbols see page 6

151

South West | Dorset

LYME REGIS

Charnwood Guest House ★★★★
Guest Accommodation
21 Woodmead Road, Lyme Regis
DT7 3AD
t (01297) 445281
e enquiries@lymeregisaccommodation.com
w lymeregisaccommodation.com

Clappentail House ★★★★★
Bed & Breakfast **SILVER AWARD**
Uplyme Road, Lyme Regis
DT7 3LP
t (01297) 445739
e info@clappentailhouse.com
w clappentailhouse.co.uk

Coombe House ★★★
Bed & Breakfast
41 Coombe Street, Lyme Regis
DT7 3PY
t (01297) 443849
e dymps@coombe-house.co.uk
w coombe-house.co.uk

Devonia Guest House ★★★★
Guest House **SILVER AWARD**
2 Woodmead Road, Lyme Regis
DT7 3AB
t (01297) 442869
e bookings@devoniaguest.co.uk
w devoniaguest.co.uk

Dorset House *Bed & Breakfast*
Pound Road, Lyme Regis
DT7 3HX
t (01297) 442482
e dorset@eclipse.co.uk
w lymeregis.com/dorset-house

Hensleigh House ★★★★
Guest Accommodation
SILVER AWARD
Lower Sea Lane, Charmouth, Lyme Regis
DT6 6LW
t (01297) 560830
e info@hensleighhotel.co.uk
w hensleighhotel.co.uk

Kersbrook Guest Accommodation
★★★ *Guest Accommodation*
Pound Road, Lyme Regis
DT7 3HX
t (01297) 442596
e alex@kersbrook.co.uk
w kersbrook.co.uk

The London Guesthouse ★★★★
Guest Accommodation
40 Church Street, Lyme Regis
DT7 3DA
t (01297) 442083
e info@londonlymeregis.co.uk
w londonlymeregis.co.uk

Lucerne ★★★★
Guest Accommodation
View Road, Lyme Regis
DT7 3AA
t (01297) 443752
e lucernelyme@btopenworld.com
w lymeregis.com/lucerne

Manaton ★★★★
Guest Accommodation
Hill Road, Lyme Regis
DT7 3PE
t (01297) 445138
e info@manatonlymeregis.co.uk
w manatonlymeregis.co.uk

Rotherfield ★★★★
Guest Accommodation
View Road, Lyme Regis
DT7 3AA
t (01297) 445585
e rotherfield@lymeregis.com
w rotherfieldguesthouse.com

Southernhaye ★★★
Bed & Breakfast
Pound Road, Lyme Regis
DT7 3HX
t (01297) 443077
e info@southernhaye.co.uk
w southernhaye.co.uk

Springfield ★★★★
Guest Accommodation
Woodmead Road, Lyme Regis
DT7 3LJ
t (01297) 443409
e springfield@lymeregis.com
w lymeregis.com/springfield

Thatch ★★★★ *Bed & Breakfast*
Uplyme Road, Lyme Regis
DT7 3LP
t (01297) 442212
e thatchbb@btinternet.com
w thatchatlymeregis.co.uk

LYONS GATE

Purbeck Lodge ★★★★
Bed & Breakfast
Lyons Gate, Dorchester
DT2 7AZ
t (01300) 345584

MOTCOMBE

The Coppleridge Inn ★★★ *Inn*
Motcombe, Shaftesbury
SP7 9HW
t (01747) 851980
e thecoppleridgeinn@btinternet.com
w coppleridge.com

NETHERBURY

Parnham Farm ★★★★ *Farmhouse*
Crook Hill, Netherbury, Bridport
DT6 5LY
t (01308) 488214
e rbbowditch@btconnect.com
w parnhamfarm.co.uk

OKEFORD FITZPAINE

Okeapple House ★★★★
Bed & Breakfast
Okeford Fitzpaine, Blandford Forum
DT11 0RS
t (01258) 861126
e 51fairmount@tiscali.co.uk
w okeapplebandb.co.uk

PIDDLETRENTHIDE

Kingsmead ★★★★ *Bed & Breakfast*
Piddletrenthide, Dorchester
DT2 7QX
t (01300) 348234
e mikehtkingsmead@aol.com

POOLE

Alice Sea Guest House B&B ★★★
Bed & Breakfast
17 Burngate Road, Hamworthy, Poole
BH15 4HS
t (01202) 679840
e reginald.coker@ntlworld.com

Corkers Restaurant & Cafe Bar with Guest Rooms ★★★★
Guest Accommodation
SILVER AWARD
1 High Street, Poole
BH15 1AB
t (01202) 681393
e corkers@corkers.co.uk
w corkers.co.uk

Cranborne House ★★★★
Guest Accommodation
SILVER AWARD
45 Shaftesbury Road, Poole
BH15 2LU
t (01202) 685200
w cranborne-house.co.uk

Danecourt Lodge ★★★★
Bed & Breakfast **GOLD AWARD**
58 Danecourt Road, Poole
BH14 0PQ
t (01202) 730957
e pat@danecourtlodge.co.uk
w danecourtlodge.co.uk

Fleetwater Guest House ★★★★
Guest House
161 Longfleet Road, Poole
BH15 2HS
t (01202) 682509
e fleetwater161@yahoo.co.uk
w fleetwaterguesthouse.co.uk

Foxes B&B ★★★★★
Bed & Breakfast **SILVER AWARD**
13 Sandbanks Road, Poole
BH14 8AG
t (01202) 269633
e sue.fox@foxesbandb.co.uk
w foxesbandb.co.uk

Grovefield Manor Guesthouse
★★★★★ *Guest Accommodation*
GOLD AWARD
18 Pinewood Road, Branksome Park, Poole
BH13 6JS
t (01202) 766798
e info@grovefieldmanor.co.uk
w grovefieldmanor.co.uk

Harbourside Guest House ★★
Guest House
195 Blandford Road, Poole
BH15 4AX
t (01202) 673053
e harboursideguesthouse@gmail.com

Harlequins B&B ★★★★
Bed & Breakfast **SILVER AWARD**
134 Ringwood Road, Poole
BH14 0RP
t (01202) 677624
e gill@harlequinsbb.co.uk
w harlequinsbb.co.uk

Heathwood Guest House ★★★
Guest House
266 Wimborne Road, Oakdale, Poole
BH15 3EF
t (01202) 679176
e enquiries@heathwood.biz
w heathwoodhotel.co.uk

Holes Bay B&B ★★ *Bed & Breakfast*
365 Blandford Road, Poole
BH15 4JL
t (01202) 672069
e maggie.dixon1@ntlworld.com

Jessimine B&B ★★★
Bed & Breakfast
77 Lake Road, Hamworthy, Poole
BH15 4LF
t (01202) 257726
e anita.saville@ntlworld.com

Mariners Guest House ★★★★
Guest House
26 Sandbanks Road, Poole
BH14 8AQ
t (01202) 247218
e admin@themarinersguesthouse.co.uk
w themarinersguesthouse.co.uk

Oakborne ★★★★ *Bed & Breakfast*
SILVER AWARD
116 Ringwood Road, Poole
BH14 0RW
t (01202) 678211
e absmurrey@aol.com
w oakborne.co.uk

Pine Ridge ★★★★ *Guest House*
SILVER AWARD
2b Lower Golf Links Road, Broadstone, Poole
BH18 8BG
t (01202) 694216
e jill@pineridgebedandbreakfast.co.uk
w pineridgebedandbreakfast.co.uk

Quayside B&B ★★★
Guest Accommodation
9 High Street, Poole
BH15 1AB
t (01202) 683733
w poolequayside.co.uk

The Saltings ★★★★
Bed & Breakfast **GOLD AWARD**
5 Salterns Way, Poole
BH14 8JR
t (01202) 707349
e saltings_poole@yahoo.co.uk
w the-saltings.com

Sarnia Cherie ★★★★
Bed & Breakfast
375 Blandford Road, Hamworthy, Poole
BH15 4JL
t (01202) 679470
e criscollier@aol.com
w sarniacherie.co.uk

Seashells ★★★ *Bed & Breakfast*
4 Lake Road, Hamworthy, Poole
BH15 4LH
t (01202) 671921
e chris.tony@ntlworld.com
w 4seashells.co.uk

Vernon ★★★ *Bed & Breakfast*
96 Blandford Road North, Beacon Hill, Poole
BH16 6AD
t (01202) 625185
e vernonbnb@googlemail.com
w vernonguesthouse.co.uk

Viewpoint Guest House ★★★★
Guest House **SILVER AWARD**
11 Constitution Hill Road, Parkstone, Poole
BH14 0QB
t (01202) 733586
e enquiry@viewpoint-gh.co.uk
w viewpoint-gh.co.uk

PORTLAND

Alessandria ★★
Guest Accommodation
71 Wakeham, Easton, Portland
DT5 1HW
t (01305) 822217
w alessandriahotel.co.uk

Aqua, The ★★★
Guest Accommodation
Castletown, Portland, Dorset
DT5 1BD
t (01305) 860269
e reception@hotelaqua.co.uk
w hotelaqua.co.uk

Brackenbury House ★★★
Bed & Breakfast
Fortuneswell, Portland
DT5 1LP
t (01305) 826509
e enquiries@brackenburyhouse.co.uk
w brackenburyhouse.co.uk

Leam House ★★★★
Guest Accommodation
13 Wakeham, Portland
DT5 1HW
t (01305) 824255
e janelyle@btinternet.com
w leamhouse.co.uk

Lobster Farmhouse ★★★
Guest Accommodation
Portland Bill, Portland
DT5 2JT
t (01305) 861253

Sea View ★★★★ *Bed & Breakfast*
151 Weston Street, Portland
DT5 2DG
t (01305) 821573
e stay@seaviewbandb.co.uk
w seaviewbandb.co.uk

YHA Portland ★★★ *Hostel*
Hardy House, Portland
DT5 1AU
t 0870 770 6000
e portland@yha.org.uk
w yha.org.uk

POUNDBURY

Poundbury Village B&B ★★★
Bed & Breakfast
7 Pendruffle Lane, Dorchester
DT1 3WJ
t (01305) 265591
e bridget.trotman@virgin.net
w poundburyvillagebandb.co.uk

South West | Dorset

RINGWOOD

[Li]ttle Paddock ★★★★
[Bed] & Breakfast **SILVER AWARD**
[3] Hurn Road, Matchams,
[Ring]wood
[BH]24 2BT
t (01425) 470889
e enquiries@little-paddock.com
w little-paddock.com

SANDFORD ORCAS

[Th]e Alders ★★★★ *Bed & Breakfast*
[Sa]ndford Orcas, Sherborne
[DT]9 4SB
t (01963) 220666
e jonsue@thealdersbb.com
w thealdersbb.com

SHAFTESBURY

[Gl]ebe Farm ★★★★★
[Bed] & Breakfast **GOLD AWARD**
[Hig]h Street, Ashmore, Shaftesbury
[SP]5 5AE
t (01747) 811994
e stay@glebefarmbandb.co.uk
w glebefarmbandb.co.uk

[Th]e Retreat ★★★★ *Guest House*
[SIL]VER AWARD
[40] Bell Street, Shaftesbury, Dorset,
[Eng]land
[SP]7 8AE
t 01747850372
e info@the-retreat.co.uk
w the-retreat.co.uk

[Ro]semary House B&B ★★★★
[Bed] & Breakfast
[40] Street, Motcombe, Shaftesbury,
[Dor]set
[SP]7 9LU
t (01747) 855700
e phtm@btinternet.com
w rosemaryhousebandb.com

SHAVE CROSS

[The] Shave Cross Inn ★★★★★ *Inn*
[SIL]VER AWARD
[Sh]ave Cross, Marshwood Vale,
[Brid]port
[DT]6 6HW
t (01308) 868358
e roy.warburton@virgin.net
w theshavecrossinn.co.uk

SHERBORNE

[Bri]dleways ★★★ *Bed & Breakfast*
[Ho]rne Road, Sherborne
[DT]9 3RX
t (01935) 814716
e bridleways@tiscali.co.uk

[Ch]etnole Inn ★★★★ *Inn*
[SIL]VER AWARD
[Ch]etnole, Sherborne
[DT]9 6NY
t (01935) 872337
e enquiries@thechetnoleinn.co.uk
w thechetnoleinn.co.uk

[Cum]berland House ★★★★
[Bed] & Breakfast **SILVER AWARD**
[Gre]en Hill, Sherborne
[DT]9 4EP
t (01935) 817554
e sandie@bandbdorset.co.uk
w bandbdorset.co.uk

[Gle]be House *Guest Accommodation*
[Oa]ke, Sherborne
[DT]9 5HP
t (01963) 210337
e glebe.house@hotmail.com
w glebehouse-dorset.co.uk

[Ho]neycombe View ★★★★
[Bed] & Breakfast
[Lo]wer Clatcombe, Sherborne
[DT]9 4RH
t (01935) 814644
e honeycombeview@talktalk.net

[The] Pheasants B&B ★★★★
[Bed] & Breakfast
[Gre]enhill, Sherborne
[DT]9 4EW
t (01935) 815252
e louise.weston@thepheasants.com
w thepheasants.com

Stoneleigh Barn ★★★★
Bed & Breakfast **SILVER AWARD**
North Wootton, Sherborne
DT9 5JW
t (01929) 815964
e stoneleighbarn@aol.com
w stoneleighbarn.com

SHILLINGSTONE

Cedar Lodge ★★★ *Bed & Breakfast*
Knapps, Shillingstone, Blandford Forum
DT11 0RA
t (01258) 863771
e mkennarduk@aol.com

SIXPENNY HANDLEY

Chase House ★★★★
Bed & Breakfast
Deanland, Sixpenny Handley
SP5 5PD
t (01725) 552829
e chasehouse1@gmail.com

STOUR ROW

Woodville Farm ★★★★
Bed & Breakfast
Green Lane, Stour Row, Shaftesbury
SP7 0QD
t (01747) 838241
e woodvillefarm@btconnect.com
w stonebank-chickerell.com

STUDLAND

The Bankes Arms Inn ★★★ *Inn*
Manor Road, Studland, Swanage
BH19 3AU
t (01929) 450225

Shell Bay Cottage ★★★★
Guest Accommodation
SILVER AWARD
Glebe Estate, Studland, Dorset
BH19 3AS
t (01929) 450249
e shellbayrose@btinternet.com
w shellbaycottage.com

STURMINSTER NEWTON

Blackmore Farm Cottage ★★★★
Guest Accommodation
Lydlinch, Sturminster Newton
DT10 2HZ
t (01258) 471624
e blackmorefarmcottagebnb@yahoo.co.uk
w bfcbednbreakfast.co.uk

Hazeldean Bed & Breakfast
★★★★ *Bed & Breakfast*
Bath Road, Sturminster Newton
DT10 1DS
t (01258) 472224
e sarah_grounds@hotmail.com
w hazeldeanbnb.co.uk

Manston Guest House ★★★★
Guest House **SILVER AWARD**
2 Northwood Cottages, Manston, Sturminster Newton
DT10 1HD
t (01258) 472666
e info@manstonguesthouse.co.uk
w manstonguesthouse.co.uk

SWANAGE

A Great Escape Guest House
★★★★ *Guest House*
SILVER AWARD
6 Argyle Road, Swanage
BH19 1HZ
t (01929) 475853
e stay@agreatescapeguesthouse.co.uk
w agreatescapeguesthouse.co.uk/

A Little Gem ★★★ *Guest House*
4 Cecil Road, Swanage, Dorset
BH19 1JJ
t (01929) 427904
e mary@littlegemguesthouse.co.uk
w littlegemguesthouse.co.uk

Amberlea ★★★ *Guest House*
36 Victoria Avenue, Swanage
BH19 1AP
t (01929) 426213
e stay@amberleahotel-swanage.co.uk
w amberleahotel-swanage.co.uk

Amberlodge ★★★ *Guest House*
34 Victoria Avenue, Swanage
BH19 1AP
t (01929) 426446
e stay@amberlodge-swanage.co.uk
w amberlodge-swanage.co.uk

Arbour House ★★★★ *Guest House*
19 Walrond Road, Swanage
BH19 1PB
t (01929) 426237
e info@arbourhouseswanage.co.uk
w arbourhouseswanage.co.uk

Bella Vista ★★★★ *Guest House*
SILVER AWARD
14 Burlington Road, Swanage
BH19 1LS
t (01929) 422873
e mail@bellavista-swanage.co.uk
w bellavista-swanage.co.uk

The Castleton ★★★★
Guest Accommodation
SILVER AWARD
1 Highcliffe Road, Swanage
BH19 1LW
t (01929) 423972
e stay@thecastleton.co.uk
w thecastleton.co.uk

Caythorpe House ★★★
Guest House
7 Rempstone Road, Swanage
BH19 1DN
t (01929) 422892
e enquiries@caythorpehouse.co.uk
w caythorpehouse.co.uk

Chiltern Lodge ★★ *Bed & Breakfast*
8 Newfoundland Close, Worth Matravers, Swanage
BH19 3LX
t (01929) 439337
e densor@btopenworld.com
w chilternlodge.co.uk

Clare House ★★★★★ *Guest House*
SILVER AWARD
1 Park Road, Swanage
BH19 2AA
t (01929) 422855
e info@clare-house.com
w clare-house.com

Corner Meadow ★★★★
Bed & Breakfast
24 Victoria Avenue, Swanage
BH19 1AP
t (01929) 423493
e geogios@hotmail.com
w cornermeadow.co.uk

Danesfort ★★★ *Guest House*
Highcliffe Road, Swanage
BH19 1LW
t (01929) 424224
e reception@danesforthotel.co.uk
w danesforthotel.co.uk

Easter Cottage ★★★★
Bed & Breakfast **SILVER AWARD**
9 Eldon Terrace, Swanage
BH19 1HA
t (01929) 427782
e info@eastercottage.co.uk
w eastercottage.co.uk

The Fairway ★★ *Bed & Breakfast*
De Moulham Road, Swanage
BH19 1NR
t (01929) 423367
e rita@ritawaller.plus.com
w swanagefairway.co.uk

Fiftyeight ★★★★ *Bed & Breakfast*
58 Queens Road, Swanage
BH19 2EU
t (01929) 426815
e info@fiftyeightswanage.co.uk
w fiftyeightswanage.co.uk

Glenlee Guest House ★★★★
Guest House
6 Cauldon Avenue, Swanage
BH19 1PQ
t (01929) 425794
e info@glenleehotel.co.uk
w glenleehotel.co.uk

Goodwyns ★★★★ *Bed & Breakfast*
2 Walrond Road, Swanage
BH19 1PB
t (01929) 421088
e knapman104@btinternet.com

Grace Gardens Guest House
★★★★ *Guest House*
28 Victoria Avenue, Swanage
BH19 1AP
t (01929) 422502
e enquiries@gracegardens.co.uk
w gracegardens.co.uk

Knollsea ★★★
Guest Accommodation
8 Moor Road, Swanage
BH19 1RG
t 07805 882008
w knollsea.co.uk

Meadow View ★★★★
Bed & Breakfast
40 Victoria Avenue, Swanage
BH19 1AP
t (01929) 427016
e fernscott99@hotmail.com
w meadowviewswanage.co.uk/

Millbrook Guest House ★★★
Guest House
56 Kings Road West, Swanage
BH19 1HR
t (01929) 423443
e info@millbrookswanage.com
w millbrookswanage.com

The Oxford House ★★★
Guest House
5 Park Road, Swanage
BH19 2AA
t (01929) 422247
e enquiries@theoxfordswanage.co.uk
w theoxfordswanage.co.uk

Sandhaven Guest House ★★★
Guest Accommodation
5 Ulwell Road, Swanage
BH19 1LE
t (01929) 422322
e mail@sandhaven-guest-house.co.uk
w sandhaven-guest-house.co.uk

St Michaels ★★★★ *Guest House*
31 Kings Road West, Swanage
BH19 1HF
t (01929) 422064
w stmichaelsguesthouse.org.uk

Tall Trees ★★★★ *Bed & Breakfast*
Ulwell, Swanage
BH19 3DG
t (01929) 422164
e jml@markluty.com
w talltreesswanage.co.uk

Taunton House ★★★ *Guest House*
4 Taunton Road, Swanage
BH19 2BY
t (01929) 425440
e info@tauntonhouse-swanage.com
w tauntonhouse-swanage.com

Town Hall Lodge ★★★★
Bed & Breakfast
Town Hall Lane, Swanage
BH19 1EX
t (01929) 421027
e admin@town-hall-lodge.co.uk
w town-hall-lodge.co.uk

YHA Swanage ★★★ *Hostel*
Cluny Crescent, Swanage
BH19 2BS
t (01929) 422113
e swanage@yha.org.uk
w yha.org.uk

South West | Dorset

TARRANT LAUNCESTON

Launceston Farmhouse ★★★★★
Farmhouse SILVER AWARD
Tarrant Launceston, Blandford
Forum
DT11 8BY
t (01258) 830528
e info@launcestonfarm.co.uk
w launcestonfarm.co.uk

THREE LEGGED CROSS

South View Guest House ★★★★
Bed & Breakfast
Ringwood Road, Three Legged
Cross, Wimborne
BH21 6QY
t (01202) 813746
e southveiw.guesthouse@btintern et.com
w southview-guest-house.co.uk

Thatch Cottage ★★★★
Guest House
Ringwood Road, Three Legged
Cross, Wimborne
BH21 6QY
t (01202) 822042
e dthatchcottage@aol.com
w thatch-cottage.co.uk

TOLLER PORCORUM

Colesmoor Farm ★★★★
Farmhouse
Toller Porcorum, Dorchester
DT2 0DU
t (01300) 320812
e rachael@colesmoorfarm.co.uk
w colesmoorfarm.co.uk

Higher Kingcombe Lodge ★★★
Guest Accommodation
Higher Kingcombe, Toller Porcorum,
Dorchester
DT2 0EH
t (01300) 320537
e info@higherkingcombelodge.co. uk
w higherkingcombelodge.co.uk

The Kingcombe Centre ★★★
Guest Accommodation
Lower Kingcombe, Toller Porcorum,
Dorchester
DT2 0EQ
t (01300) 320684
e office@kingcombecentre.org.uk
w kingcombecentre.org.uk

WAREHAM

Anglebury House ★★★
Guest Accommodation
15-17 North Street, Wareham
BH20 4AB
t (01929) 552988
e info@anglebuyhouse.co.uk
w anglebuyhouse.co.uk

Ashcroft ★★★★ *Bed & Breakfast*
64 Furzebrook Road, Wareham
BH20 5AX
t (01929) 552392
e cake@ashcroft-bb.co.uk
w ashcroft-bb.co.uk

Beryl's B&B ★★★ *Bed & Breakfast*
2 Heath Cottages, Sandford Road,
Wareham
BH20 7DF
t (01929) 550138
e beryle@homecall.co.uk

Bradle Farmhouse ★★★★
Farmhouse GOLD AWARD
Bradle Farm, Church Knowle,
Wareham
BH20 5NU
t (01929) 480712
e info@bradlefarmhouse.co.uk
w bradlefarmhouse.co.uk

The Dorset Golf Lodge ★★★★
Guest Accommodation
The Dorset Golf & Country Club,
Hyde, Wareham
BH20 7NT
t (01929) 472245
e admin@dorsetgolfresort.com
w dorsetgolfresort.com

Frome Corner ★★★
Bed & Breakfast
10 Frome Road, Wareham, Dorset
BH20 4QA
t (01929) 551550
e m.bridger2@btinternet.com

Kingston Country Courtyard
★★★★ *Guest Accommodation*
Langton Road, Kingston,, Wareham
BH20 5LR
t (01929) 481066
e enquiries@kingstoncountry courtyard.com
w kingstoncountrycourtyard.com

Spurwing Guest House ★★★★
Guest House
10 Sandford Road, Wareham
BH20 4DH
t (01929) 553869
e spencers@spurwing.info
w spurwing.info

The Withies ★★★ *Bed & Breakfast*
16 Colliers Lane, Wool, Wareham
BH20 6DL
t (01929) 405339
e pazwold@btinternet.com
w atthewithies.co.uk

WEST BAY

Beachcroft ★★★★ *Bed & Breakfast*
SILVER AWARD
23 Forty Foot Way, West Bay,
Bridport
DT6 4HD
t (01308) 423604
e sue_marks@sky.com
w beachcroftbedandbreakfast.co.uk

Bridport Arms ★★★★ *Inn*
SILVER AWARD
West Bay, West Bay
DT6 4EN
t (01308) 422994
e reservations@bridportarms.com
w bridportarms.com

Durbeyfield Guest House ★★★
Guest Accommodation
10 West Bay, Bridport
DT6 4EL
t (01308) 423307
e manager@durbeyfield.co.uk
w durbeyfield.co.uk

Seacroft ★★★★ *Bed & Breakfast*
24 Forty Foot Way, West Bay,
Bridport
DT6 4HD
t (01308) 423407
e seacroft24@btinternet.com
w seacroftbandb.co.uk

WEST LULWORTH

Gatton House ★★★★ *Guest House*
SILVER AWARD
Main Road, Lulworth Cove, West
Lulworth
BH20 5RL
t (01929) 400252
e avril@gattonhouse.co.uk
w lulworthcovebedandbreakfast. com

Lulworth Cove Inn ★★★ *Inn*
Main Road, West Lulworth
BH20 5RQ
t (01929) 400333
e hotel@lulworth-cove.com
w lulworth-cove.com

Lulworth Cove YHA ★★ *Hostel*
School Lane, West Lulworth
BH20 5SA
t (01929) 400564
e lulworth@yha.org.uk
w yha.org.uk

The Old Barn ★★★★
Guest Accommodation
Main Road, West Lulworth
BH20 5RL
t (01929) 400305

WEYMOUTH

Aaran House ★★★ *Guest House*
2 The Esplanade, Weymouth
DT4 8EA
t (01305) 766669
e denise.groves@sky.com
w aaranhouse.co.uk

A Knight's Rest Guest House
★★★ *Guest House*
93 Dorchester Road, Weymouth
DT4 7JY
t (01305) 839005
e enquiries@aknightsrest.co.uk
w aknightsrest.co.uk

Albern House ★★★ *Guest House*
13 Holland Road, Weymouth
DT4 0AL
t (01305) 783951
w albern.tk

Arcadia Guest House ★★★
Guest House
7 Waterloo Place, Weymouth
DT4 7PA
t (01305) 782458
e stay@arcadiaguesthouse.com
w arcadiaguesthouse.com

Ashmira ★★★★
Guest Accommodation
3 Westerhall Road, Weymouth
DT4 7SZ
t (01305) 768584
e ashmirahotel@btconnect.com
w ashmirahotel.co.uk

B+B Weymouth ★★★★
Guest Accommodation
68 The Esplanade, Weymouth,
Dorset
DT4 7AA
t 01305 761190
e info@bb-weymouth.com
w bb-weymouth.com

The Bakehouse ★★★★★
Guest Accommodation
27 East Street, Weymouth
DT4 8BN
t 07768 568057
e pennypiggin@hotmail.com
w harbourandbeach.com

The Bay Guest House ★★★★
Guest House
10 Waterloo Place, Weymouth
DT4 7PE
t (01305) 786289
e harrisbay@aol.com
w thebayguesthouse.co.uk

Beach Guest House ★★★
Guest House
34 Lennox Street, Weymouth
DT4 7HD
t (01305) 779212
e beachguesthouse@btinternet. com
w beachguesthouse.net

The Beach House ★★★
Guest Accommodation
2 Brunswick Terrace, Weymouth
DT4 7RR
t (01305) 789353
e stay@thebeachhouseweymouth. co.uk
w thebeachhouseweymouth.co.uk

Beach View Guest House ★★★
Guest House
3 The Esplanade, Weymouth
DT4 8EA
t (01305) 786528
e beachviewweymouth@hotmail. com
w beachviewguesthouse.com

Beaufort Guesthouse ★★★
Guest Accommodation
24 The Esplanade, Weymouth
DT4 8DN
t (01305) 782088
w beaufortguesthouse.co.uk

The Bourneville ★★★ *Guest House*
31-32 The Esplanade, Weymouth
DT4 8DJ
t (01305) 784784
e enquiries@bournevillehotel.co.uk
w bournevillehotel.co.uk

Brierley Guest House ★★★
Guest House
6 Lennox Street, Weymouth
DT4 7HD
t (01305) 782050

Brunswick Guest House ★★★
Guest Accommodation
9 Brunswick Terrace, Weymouth
DT4 7RW
t (01305) 785408
e info@brunswickweymouth.co.u
w brunswickweymouth.co.uk

Chandlers ★★★★ *Guest House*
SILVER AWARD
4 Westerhall Road, Weymouth
DT4 7SZ
t (01305) 771341
e info@chandlershotel.com
w chandlershotel.com

The Channel Guest House ★★★
Guest Accommodation
93 The Esplanade, Weymouth
DT4 7AY
t (01305) 785405
e stay@channelhotel.co.uk
w channelhotel.co.uk

The Chatsworth ★★★
Guest Accommodation
14 The Esplanade, Weymouth
DT4 8EB
t (01305) 785012
e david@thechatsworth.co.uk
w thechatsworth.co.uk

The Clarence ★★★★
Guest Accommodation
SILVER AWARD
20 The Esplanade, Weymouth
DT4 8DN
t (01305) 787573
e clarence.hotel1@btconnect.cor
w theclarenceweymouth.co.uk

Corfe Gate House ★★★★
Bed & Breakfast SILVER AWARD
Coryates, Portesham, Weymouth
DT3 4HW
t (01305) 871483
e corfegatehouse@aol.com
w corfegatehouse.co.uk

The Cottage ★★★★
Bed & Breakfast
Puddledock Lane, Sutton Poyntz,
Weymouth
DT3 6LZ
t (01305) 834729
e mark.thecottage@tiscali.co.uk
w thecottageweymouth.co.uk

Cowleaze Cottage ★★★★★
Bed & Breakfast
Coryates, Weymouth
DT3 4HW
t (01305) 871535
e cowleazecottage@yahoo.co.uk
w cowleazecottage.co.uk/

Crofton Guest House ★★
Guest Accommodation
36 Lennox Street, Weymouth
DT4 7HD
t (01305) 785903
e croftonguesthouse@btconnect com
w croftonguesthouse.co.uk

The Cumberland ★★★★
Guest House
95 The Esplanade, Weymouth
DT4 7AT
t (01305) 785644
e simon_reid@yahoo.co.uk
w cumberlandhotelweymouth.co

The Cunard Guest House ★★★
Guest Accommodation
45-46 Lennox Street, Weymouth
DT4 7HB
t (01305) 771546
e harrisweymouth@aol.com
w cunardguesthouse.co.uk

South West | Dorset/Gloucestershire

tney ★★★★ *Guest House*
Longfield Road, Weymouth
4 8RQ
(01305) 771682
e eastneyhotel@aol.com
w eastneyhotel.co.uk

atstones Guest House ★★★
st House
Carlton Road South, Weymouth
4 7PJ
(01305) 784153
abs1@weymouth.gov.uk

rian Guest House ★★★★
st Accommodation
Abbotsbury Road, Weymouth
4 0AQ
(01305) 773836
e enquiryflorian@aol.com
w florianguesthouse.co.uk

sters Guest House ★★★
st Accommodation
nox Street, Weymouth
4 7HB
(01305) 771685
e spencer-j3@sky.com

nthorne Castle Cove ★★★★
d & Breakfast **SILVER AWARD**
Old Castle Road, Weymouth
4 8QB
(01305) 777281
e info@glenthorne-holidays.co.uk
w glenthorne-holidays.co.uk

ucester House ★★★★
st Accommodation
The Esplanade, Weymouth
4 7AT
(01305) 785191
e gloucesterwey@aol.com
w gloucesterhouseweymouth.co.uk

aingers Guest Accommodation ★★★★
Dorchester Road, Weymouth,
rset
3 5EQ
(01305) 782362
e info@graingersguesthouse.co.uk
w graingersguesthouse.co.uk

een Gables ★★★★
st House
Carlton Road South, Weymouth
4 7PJ
(01305) 774808
e paula@greengablesweymouth.co.uk
w greengablesweymouth.co.uk

e Gresham ★★ *Guest House*
) The Esplanade, Weymouth
4 7EW
(01305) 785897
e stuart.june@btconnect.com
w greshamhotel-weymouth.co.uk

rbour Lights ★★★★
st Accommodation
Buxton Road, Weymouth
4 9PJ
(01305) 783273
e harbourlights@btconnect.com
w harbourlights-weymouth.co.uk

**rlequin Guest House
ymouth ★★★★** *Guest House*
VER AWARD
Carlton Road South, Weymouth
4 7PL
(01305) 785598
e mike_evans9999@yahoo.com
w harlequin-guest-house.co.uk

tel Concorde ★★★ *Guest House*
The Esplanade, Weymouth
4 7EY
(01305) 776900
e info@hotel-weymouth.co.uk
w theconcordehotel.co.uk

lston Guest House ★★★
st Accommodation
Lennox Street, Weymouth
4 7HB
(01305) 780692
e stay@kelstonguesthouse.co.uk
w kelstonguesthouse.co.uk

The Kinley ★★★ *Guest House*
98 The Esplanade, Weymouth
DT4 7AT
t (01305) 782264
e hotelkinley@hotmail.com
w hotelkinley.com

Lacey's Guest House ★★★
Guest House
12 Holland Road, Weymouth
DT4 0AL
t (01305) 760587
e laceysweymouth@googlemail.com
w laceysweymouth.co.uk

The Langham ★★★
Guest Accommodation
130 The Esplanade, Weymouth
DT4 7EX
t (01305) 782530
e enquiries@langham-hotel.com
w langham-hotel.com

Letterbox House ★★★★
Guest House
22 The Esplanade, Weymouth
DT4 8DN
t 07768 568057
e pennypiggin@hotmail.com

Lichfield House ★★★ *Guest House*
8 Brunswick Terrace, Weymouth
DT4 7RW
t (01305) 784112
e lich.house@virgin.net
w lichfieldhouse.co.uk

Lilac Villa Guest House ★★★★
Guest House
124 Dorchester Road, Weymouth
DT4 7LG
t (01305) 782670
e lilacvilla@ukonline.co.uk

The Lugger Inn ★★★ *Inn*
30 West Street, Chickerell,
Weymouth
DT3 4DY
t (01305) 766611
e john@theluggerinn.co.uk
w theluggerinn.co.uk

Marina Court ★★★
Guest Accommodation
142 The Esplanade, Weymouth
DT4 7PB
t (01305) 782146
e marion@vassie.fsnet.co.uk
w marinacourt.co.uk

Mar June Guest House ★★★
Guest House
32 Lennox Street, Weymouth
DT4 7HD
t (01305) 761320
e marjuneweymouth@hotmail.co.uk

The Mayfair ★★★
Guest Accommodation
99 The Esplanade, Weymouth
DT4 7BE
t (01305) 782094
e info@mayfairweymouth@gmail.com
w mayfairhotelweymouth.com

Morven House ★★★★
Guest Accommodation
2 Westerhall Road, Weymouth
DT4 7SZ
t (01305) 785075
e enquiries@morvenweymouth.co.uk
w morvenweymouth.co.uk

**Oaklands Edwardian Guest House
★★★★** *Guest Accommodation*
1 Glendinning Avenue, Weymouth
DT4 7QF
t (01305) 767081
e stay@oaklands-guesthouse.co.uk
w oaklands-guesthouse.co.uk

Old Harbour View ★★★★
Bed & Breakfast
12 Trinity Road, Weymouth
DT4 8TJ
t (01305) 774633
e info@oldharbourview.co.uk
w oldharbourviewweymouth.co.uk

The Pebbles ★★★★ *Guest House*
SILVER AWARD
18 Kirtleton Avenue, Weymouth
DT4 7PT
t (01305) 784331
e info@thepebbles.co.uk
w thepebbles.co.uk

Seacrest Guest House ★★★
Guest House
4 Esplanade, Weymouth
DT4 8EA
t (01305) 784759

Seaham ★★★★ *Guest House*
3 Waterloo Place, Weymouth
DT4 7NU
t (01305) 782010
e stay@theseahamweymouth.co.uk
w theseahamweymouth.co.uk

Sou'West Lodge ★★★
Guest Accommodation
Rodwell Road, Weymouth
DT4 8QT
t (01305) 783749
e enquiry@souwestlodge.co.uk
w souwestlodge.co.uk

Spindrift Guest House ★★★
Guest House
11 Brunswick Terrace, Weymouth
DT4 7RW
t (01305) 773625
e stay@spindriftguesthouse.co.uk
w spindriftguesthouse.co.uk

Sunbay Guest House ★★★
Guest House
12 Brunswick Terrace, Weymouth
DT4 7RW
t (01305) 785992
e info@sunbayguesthouse.co.uk
w sunbayguesthouse.co.uk

Valentine Guest House ★★★
Guest House
1 Waterloo Place, Weymouth
DT4 7NS
t (01305) 774000
e stay@valentineweymouth.co.uk
w valentineweymouth.co.uk

Warwick Court ★★★ *Guest House*
20 Abbotsbury Road, Weymouth
DT4 0AE
t (01305) 783261
e warwickcourtweymouth@hotmail.co.uk
w thewarwickcourt.com

Weymouth Sands ★★★
Guest House
5 The Esplanade, Weymouth
DT4 8EA
t (01305) 839022
e enquiries@weymouthsands.co.uk
w weymouthsands.co.uk

Wilton Guest House ★★★
Guest House
5 Gloucester Street, Weymouth
DT4 7AP
t (01305) 782820
e enq@wiltonguesthouse.co.uk
w thewiltonguesthouse.co.uk

WIMBORNE

Homestay ★★★ *Bed & Breakfast*
22 West Borough, Wimborne
BH21 1NF
t (01202) 849015
e julie@gribble.com

Linden Lea ★★★★ *Bed & Breakfast*
Higher Merley Lane, Corfe Mullen, Wimborne
BH21 3EG
t (01202) 886215
e enquiry@linden-lea.co.uk
w linden-lea.co.uk

Long Lane Farmhouse ★★★★
Bed & Breakfast **SILVER AWARD**
Long Lane, Colehill, Wimborne
BH21 7AQ
t (01202) 887829
e patricksmyth@btinternet.com
w longlanefarmhouse.co.uk

The Old George ★★★★
Bed & Breakfast **SILVER AWARD**
2 Corn Market, Wimborne
BH21 1JL
t (01202) 888510
e chrissie_oldgeorge@yahoo.co.uk
w theoldgeorge.net

WINFRITH NEWBURGH

Wynards Farm ★★★★
Bed & Breakfast
Chaldon Road, Winfrith Newburgh
DT2 8DQ
t (01305) 852660
e enquiries@wynardsfarm.co.uk
w wynardsfarm.co.uk

WINTERBORNE ZELSTON

Brook Farm ★★★ *Farmhouse*
Winterborne Zelston, Blandford Forum
DT11 9EU
t (01929) 459284/267
e rosebrookfarm@hotmail.com
w brookfarmdorset.co.uk

WINTERBOURNE ABBAS

Churchview Guest House ★★★★
Guest House
Winterbourne Abbas, Dorchester
DT2 9LS
t (01305) 889186
e stay@churchview.co.uk
w churchview.co.uk

WOOL

East Burton House ★★★★
Guest Accommodation
East Burton Road, Wool
BH20 6HE
t (01929) 462083
e info@eastburtonhouse.com
w eastburtonhouse.com

Frome Dale ★★★★
Bed & Breakfast
East Burton Road, Wool
BH20 6HF
t (01929) 405075
e debcharliebrown@yahoo.com
w fromedalebedandbreakfast.co.uk

Gloucestershire
ALDERTON

Corner Cottage ★★★★
Bed & Breakfast
Stow Road, Alderton, Tewkesbury
GL20 8NH
t (01242) 620630
e cornercottagebb@talk21.com
w cornercottage-bedandbreakfast.co.uk

AMBERLEY (STROUD 4 MILES)

High Tumps ★★★ *Bed & Breakfast*
St Chloe Green, Amberley, Stroud
GL5 5AR
t (01453) 873584
e dakavic@btinternet.com

ARLINGHAM

Red Lion Inn ★★★ *Inn*
The Cross, High Street, Arlington
GL2 7JH
t (01452) 740700

AYLBURTON

Millingbrook Lodge ★★★★ *Inn*
George Inn, High Street, Aylburton, Lydney
GL15 6DE
t (01594) 845522
e jackicollie@aol.com
w millingbrooklodge.com

---

key to symbols see page 6

155

South West | Gloucestershire

BATH

Fern Cottage Bed & Breakfast
★★★★ *Farmhouse* **SILVER AWARD**
188 Shortwood Hill, Pucklechurch,
South Gloucestershire, Nr Bath
BS16 9PG
t (0117) 937 4966
e sueandpete@ferncottagebeda
ndbreakfast.co.uk
w ferncottagebedandbreakfast.co.
uk

BERRY HILL

Berry Hill House ★★★
Bed & Breakfast
Park Road, Berry Hill, Coleford
GL16 7AG
t (01594) 832325
e glynis@berryhillhouse.co.uk
w berryhillhouse.co.uk

BIBURY

Cotteswold House ★★★★
Bed & Breakfast **GOLD AWARD**
Arlington, Bibury, Gloucestershire
GL7 5ND
t 01285 740609
e enquiries@cotteswoldhouse.net
w cotteswoldhouse.net

**The William Morris Bed &
Breakfast** ★★★★ *Bed & Breakfast*
SILVER AWARD
11 The Street, Bibury
GL7 5NP
t (01285) 740555
e ian.howard8.wanadoo.co.uk
w thewilliammorris.com

BIRDWOOD

Birdwood Villa Farm ★★★
Farmhouse
Main Road, Birdwood, Gloucester
GL19 3EQ
t (01452) 750451
e birdwood.villafarm@virgin.net
w birdwoodvillafarm.co.uk

Kings Head Inn ★★★ *Inn*
Birdwood, Gloucester
GL19 3EF
t (01452) 750348
e enquiries@kingsheadbirdwood.
co.uk
w kingsheadbirdwood.co.uk

BLAKENEY

The Cock Inn ★★★ *Inn*
Nibley Hill, Blakeney
GL15 4DB
t (01594) 510239
e info@thecockinnblakeney.com
w thecockinnblakeney.com

The Old Tump House ★★★
Bed & Breakfast
New Road, Blakeney
GL15 4DG
t (01594) 517333
e georgiandangelo@btinternet.com
w oldtumphouse.co.uk

BLEDINGTON

Kings Head Inn & Restaurant
★★★★ *Inn* **SILVER AWARD**
The Green, Bledington
OX7 6XQ
t (01608) 658365
e info@kingsheadinn.net
w kingsheadinn.net

BOURTON-ON-THE-WATER

Aylworth Manor ★★★★
Bed & Breakfast
Naunton, Bourton-on-the-Water
GL54 3AH
t (01451) 850850
e jeaireland@aol.com
w aylworthmanor.co.uk

Bella Dorma ★★★★
Bed & Breakfast
Station Road, Bourton-on-the-Water
GL54 2EN
t (01451) 810489
e email@belladorma.co.uk
w belladorma.co.uk

Broadlands Guest House ★★★★
Guest Accommodation
Clapton Row, Bourton-on-the-Water
GL54 2DN
t (01451) 822002
e marco@broadlands-guest-house.
co.uk
w broadlands-guest-house.co.uk

Chestnuts Bed & Breakfast
★★★★ *Guest House*
High Street, Bourton-on-the-Water,
Cheltenham
GL54 2AN
t (01451) 820244
e thechestnutsbb@hotmail.co.uk

Coombe House ★★★★
Guest Accommodation
GOLD AWARD
Rissington Road, Bourton-on-the-
Water
GL54 2DT
t (01451) 821966
e info@coombehouse.net
w coombehouse.net

Cranbourne House ★★★★
Guest Accommodation
SILVER AWARD
Moore Road, Bourton-on-the-Water
GL54 2AZ
t (01451) 821883
e info@cranbournehousebandb.co.
uk
w cranbournehousebandb.co.uk

Elvington Bed & Breakfast ★★★★
Bed & Breakfast
Rissington Road, Bourton-on-the-
Water
GL54 2DX
t (01451) 822026
e the@tuckwells.freeserve.co.uk
w bandb.fsnet.co.uk

Fieldways ★★★★ *Bed & Breakfast*
Cold Aston, Bourton-on-the-Water
GL54 3BJ
t (01451) 810659
e cascadegroup@aol.com
w fieldways.com

Holly House ★★★★
Guest Accommodation
SILVER AWARD
Station Road, Bourton-on-the-Water
GL54 2ER
t (01451) 821302
e paula@hollyhousebourton.co.uk
w hollyhousebourton.co.uk

Lansdowne Villa Guest House
★★★★ *Guest House*
Lansdowne, Bourton-on-the-Water
GL54 2AR
t (01451) 820673
e enquiries@lansdownevilla.co.uk
w lansdownevilla.co.uk

Manor Close ★★★★
Guest Accommodation
High Street, Bourton-on-the-Water
GL54 2AP
t (01451) 820339
e sheenamanorclose@aol.com
w manorclosebandb.co.uk

Meadow Rise Guest House
★★★★ *Bed & Breakfast*
GOLD AWARD
Pock Hill Lane, Bourton-on-the-
Water
GL54 2DD
t (01451) 821860
e info@meadow-rise.co.uk
w meadow-rise.co.uk

The Old New Inn ★★★ *Inn*
Bourton-on-the-Water
GL54 2AF
t (01451) 820467
e reception@theoldnewinn.co.uk
w theoldnewinn.co.uk

The Old Station ★★★★
Bed & Breakfast
Westfield, Notgrove, Bourton-on-
the-Water
GL54 3BU
t (01451) 850305

The Ridge Guesthouse ★★★★
Guest Accommodation
SILVER AWARD
Whiteshoots Hill, Bourton-on-the-
Water
GL54 2LE
t (01451) 820660
e info@theridge-guesthouse.co.uk
w theridge-guesthouse.co.uk

Southlands ★★★★
Guest Accommodation
Rissington Road, Bourton-on-the-
Water
GL54 2DT
t (01451) 821987
e christine.hutchman@o2.co.uk
w southlands-bb.co.uk

Touchstone ★★★★
Bed & Breakfast
Little Rissington, Bourton-on-the-
Water
GL54 2ND
t (01451) 822481
e touchstone.bb@lineone.net
w website.lineone.net/~touchstone.
bb

Trevone Bed & Breakfast ★★★
Bed & Breakfast
Moore Road, Bourton-on-the-Water
GL54 2AZ
t 07740 805 250
e admin@trevonebb.co.uk
w trevonebb.co.uk

BREAM

Lindum House ★★★
Bed & Breakfast
Oakwood Road, Bream, Lydney
GL15 6HS
t (01594) 560378
e lynne@lindumhouse.fsworld.co.uk
w lindum-house.co.uk

BRIMSCOMBE

The Yew Tree Bed & Breakfast
★★★★ *Bed & Breakfast*
Walls Quarry, Brimscombe
GL5 2PA
t (01453) 887980
e info@theyewtreestroud.co.uk
w theyewtreestroud.co.uk

BRISTOL

Arches House ★★★
Guest Accommodation
132 Cotham Brow, Bristol
BS6 6AE
t (0117) 924 7398
e ml@arches-hotel.co.uk
w arches-hotel.co.uk

Basca House ★★★ *Guest House*
19 Broadway Road, Bishopston,
Bristol
BS7 8ES
t (0117) 942 2182

Bristol YHA ★★★★ *Hostel*
14 Narrow Quay, Bristol
BS1 4QA
t (0117) 922 1659
e bristol@yha.org.uk
w yha.org.uk

The Coach House ★★★
Guest Accommodation
Bristol Road, Hambrook, Bristol
BS16 1RY
t (0117) 956 9601
e info@bristolcoachhouse.co.uk
w bristolcoachhouse.co.uk

Downs View Guest House ★★★★
Guest House
38 Upper Belgrave Road, Bristol
BS8 2XN
t (0117) 973 7046
e bookings@downsviewg
uesthouse.co.uk
w downsviewguesthouse.co.uk

The Greenhouse ★★★★
Bed & Breakfast
61 Greenbank Road, Southville,
Bristol
BS3 1RJ
t (0117) 902 9166
e kathy@thegreenhousebristol.co.
uk
w thegreenhousebristol.co.uk

North Green Lodge ★★★★
Guest Accommodation
North Green Street, Hotwells, Bristol
BS8 4NE
t (0117) 927 2167
e northgreenlodge@hotmail.co.uk
w desinationbristol.com

Toghill House Farm ★★★★
Farmhouse
Freezing Hill, Wick, Bristol
BS30 5RT
t (01225) 891261
e accommodation@toghillhou
sefarm.co.uk
w toghillhousefarm.co.uk

The Town & Country Lodge ★★
Guest Accommodation
A38 Bridgwater Road, Bristol
BS13 8AG
t (01275) 392441
e reservations@tclodge.co.uk
w tclodge.co.uk

Tyndall's Park ★★
Guest Accommodation
4 Tyndall's Park Road, Clifton, Bristol
BS8 1PG
t (0117) 973 5407
e contactus@tyndallsparkhotel.co.uk
w tyndallsparkhotel.co.uk

Wesley College ★★ *Campus*
College Park Drive, Henbury Road,
Bristol
BS10 7QD
t (0117) 959 1200
e rogers@wesley-college-bristol.a
uk
w wesley-college-bristol.ac.uk

Westfield House ★★★★
Guest Accommodation
SILVER AWARD
37 Stoke Hill, Sneyd Park, Bristol
BS9 1LQ
t (0117) 962 6119
e guest@westfieldhouse.net
w westfieldhouse.net

Woodstock Guest House ★★★★
Guest House
534 Bath Road, Brislington, Bristol
BS4 3JZ
t (0117) 987 1613
e woodstock@blueyonder.co.uk
w woodstockguesthouse.org

BROADWELL

The White House ★★★
Bed & Breakfast
2 South Road, Broadwell, Coleford
GL16 7BH
t (01594) 837069
e whitehousebroadwell@yahoo.c
uk
w whitehousebroadwell.co.uk

BUCKLAND

Burhill Farm ★★★★★ *Farmhouse*
SILVER AWARD
Buckland, Broadway
WR12 7LY
t (01386) 858171
e burhillfarm@yahoo.co.uk
w burhillfarm.co.uk

South West | Gloucestershire

BULLO PILL

ove Farm ★★★★ *Farmhouse*
lo Pill, Newnham
4 1DZ
(01594) 516304
davidandpennyhill@btopenworld.com
grovefarm-uk.com

CAM

resters ★★★★ *Bed & Breakfast*
apel Street, Cam, Dursley
1 5NX
(01453) 549996
foresters@freeuk.com

CERNEY WICK

verley Cottage B&B ★★★★
d & Breakfast **SILVER AWARD**
urch Lane, Cerney Wick
7 5QJ
(01793) 752629
jeannieadam003@aol.com

CHALFORD

e House *Bed & Breakfast*
h Street, Chalford
5 8NN
(01453) 886771
mandy@valehouse.net
valehouse.net

CHELTENHAM

Montpellier ★★★★
est Accommodation
Montpellier Terrace, Cheltenham
50 1UX
(01242) 526009
montpellierhotel@btopenworld.com
montpellier-hotel.co.uk/

e Abbey ★★★★
est Accommodation
16 Bath Parade, Cheltenham
53 7HN
(01242) 516053
office@abbeyhotel-cheltenham.com
abbeyhotel-cheltenham.com

ce Guest House
est Accommodation
I Swindon Road, Cheltenham
51 9EW
0789 680 4924
peyker65@hotmail.com

aumont House ★★★★★
est Accommodation
LD AWARD
Shurdington Road, Cheltenham
53 0JE
(01242) 223311
reservations@bhhotel.co.uk
bhhotel.co.uk

ntons Guest House ★★★
est Accommodation
Bath Road, Cheltenham
53 7LH
01242 517417
lucy.benton@btconnect.com
bentons-guesthouse.co.uk

nnan Guest House ★★★
est Accommodation
St Lukes Road, Cheltenham
53 7JF
(01242) 525904
colintaylor@blueyonder.co.uk

dge House ★★★★
est Accommodation
Lansdown Road, Cheltenham
51 6QR
(01242) 583599
bridgehouse@freeuk.com
bridgehouse88.co.uk

Burlington House ★★★★
Guest Accommodation
SILVER AWARD
418 Gloucester Road, Cheltenham
GL51 7TB
t (01242) 526665
e info@burlingtonhouse.net
w burlingtonhouse.net

Butlers ★★★★
Guest Accommodation
GOLD AWARD
Western Road, Cheltenham
GL50 3RN
t (01242) 570771
e info@butlers-hotel.co.uk
w butlers-hotel.co.uk

Cheltenham Lawn & Pittville Gallery ★★★★
Guest Accommodation
5 Pittville Lawn, Cheltenham
GL52 2BE
t (01242) 526638
e anthea.millier@cheltenhamlawn.co.uk
w cheltenhamlawn.co.uk

Cheltenham Townhouse ★★★★
Guest Accommodation
12-14 Pittville Lawn, Cheltenham
GL52 2BD
t (01242) 221922
e info@cheltenhamtownhouse.com
w cheltenhamtownhouse.com

Crossways Guest House ★★★★
Guest Accommodation
Oriel Place, 57 Bath Road, Cheltenham
GL53 7HL
t (01242) 527683
e cross.ways@btinternet.com
w crosswaysguesthouse.com

Detmore House ★★★★
Guest Accommodation
SILVER AWARD
London Road, Charlton Kings, Cheltenham
GL52 6UT
t (01242) 582868
e enquiries@detmorehouse.com
w detmorehouse.com

Garden House ★★★★
Guest Accommodation
SILVER AWARD
24a Christ Church Road, Cheltenham
GL50 2PL
t (01242) 522525
e miggilorraine@hotmail.co.uk
w gardenhousebb.co.uk

Hannafords ★★★★
Guest Accommodation
20 Evesham Road, Cheltenham
GL52 2AB
t (01242) 515181
e sue@hannafords.icom43.net
w hannafords-hotel.co.uk

Hanover House ★★★★★
Bed & Breakfast **GOLD AWARD**
65 St George's Road, Cheltenham
GL50 3DU
t (01242) 541297
e info@hanoverhouse.org
w hanoverhouse.org

Harrington House
Guest Accommodation
Bourton-on-the-Water, Cheltenham
GL54 2BY
t (01451) 821213

Hilden Lodge ★★★★
Guest Accommodation
271 London Road, Charlton Kings, Cheltenham
GL52 6YG
t (01242) 583242
e info@hildenlodge.co.uk
w hildenlodge.co.uk/

Homelands Bed & Breakfast
Bed & Breakfast
Butts Lane, Woodmancote, Cheltenham
GL52 9QH
t (01242) 677227
e erikburger@hotmail.co.uk
w cotswoldsaccommodation.net/

Laurel House ★★★★
Bed & Breakfast
143 Hewlett Road, Cheltenham
GL52 6TS
t (01242) 269968
e family.barton@btinternet.com
w bedandbreakfastcheltenham.com

Lypiatt House ★★★★★
Guest Accommodation
Lypiatt Road, Cheltenham
GL50 2QW
t (01242) 224994
e stay@lypiatt.co.uk
w lypiatt.co.uk

Malvern View ★★★★
Guest Accommodation
Cleeve Hill, Cheltenham
GL52 3PR
t (01242) 672017
e info@malvernview.com
w malvernview.com

Manor Cottage Guest House
★★★ *Guest Accommodation*
41 Station Road, Bishops Cleeve, Cheltenham
GL52 8HH
t (01242) 673537
e richardtorpy@sky.com

Moorend Park Hotel ★★★
Guest Accommodation
Moorend Park Road, Cheltenham
GL53 0LA
t (01242) 224441
e elvira@themoorendpark.co.uk
w moorend.park.freeuk.com

The Prestbury House ★★★★
Guest Accommodation
The Burgage, Prestbury, Cheltenham
GL52 3DN
t (01242) 529533
e enquiries@prestburyhouse.co.uk
w prestburyhouse.co.uk

Staverton House ★★★★
Bed & Breakfast
Church Lane, Cheltenham
GL51 0TW
t (01242) 680886

Strayleaves ★★★ *Guest House*
282 Gloucester Road, Cheltenham
GL51 7AG
t (01242) 572303
e strayleaves@live.co.uk

Whalley Farm House ★★★★
Farmhouse **SILVER AWARD**
Whalley Farm, Whittington, Cheltenham
GL54 4HA
t (01242) 820213
e rowefarms@farmline.com
w whalleyfarm.co.uk

Whittington Lodge Farm ★★★★
Farmhouse **SILVER AWARD**
Whittington, Cheltenham
GL54 4HB
t (01242) 820603
e stay@whittingtonlodgefarm.com
w whittingtonlodgefarm.com

The Wyastone Hotel ★★★★★
Guest Accommodation
SILVER AWARD
Parabola Road, Cheltenham
GL50 3BG
t (01242) 245549
e reservations@wyastonehotel.co.uk
w wyastonehotel.co.uk

CHELTENHAM (1 MILE)

Cotswold Studio ★★★
Bed & Breakfast
22 Ledmore Road, Charlton Kings, Cheltenham
GL53 8RA
t (01242) 526957
e geraldine.white@btinternet.com
w cotswoldstudio.co.uk

CHIPPING CAMPDEN

Arreton House ★★★★
Bed & Breakfast **SILVER AWARD**
Station Road, Blockley, Chipping Campden
GL56 9DT
t (01386) 701077
e bandb@arreton.demon.co.uk
w arreton.demon.co.uk

Brymbo B&B ★★★★
Guest Accommodation
Honeybourne Lane, Mickleton, Chipping Campden
GL55 6PU
t (01386) 438890
e enquiries@brymbo.com
w brymbo.com

Dragon House ★★★★
Bed & Breakfast
High Street, Chipping Campden
GL55 6AG
t (01386) 840734
e valatdragonhouse@btinternet.com
w dragonhouse-chipping-campden.com

The Eight Bells ★★★★ *Inn*
Church Street, Chipping Campden
GL55 6JG
t (01386) 840371
e neilhargreaves@bellinn.fsnet.co.uk
w eightbellsinn.co.uk

Home Farm Bed & Breakfast
★★★★ *Farmhouse* **SILVER AWARD**
Ebrington, Chipping Campden
GL55 6NL
t (01386) 593309
e willstanley@farmersweekly.net
w homefarminthecotswolds.htm

Little Gidding ★★★★
Bed & Breakfast **SILVER AWARD**
Ebrington, Chipping Campden
GL55 6NL
t (01386) 593302
e bookings@ebrington.com
w ebrington.com

The Malins ★★★★ *Bed & Breakfast*
21 Station Road, Blockley, Chipping Campden
GL56 9ED
t (01386) 700402
e malinsblockley@btinternet.com
w chippingcampden.co.uk/themalins.htm

Manor Farm ★★★★ *Farmhouse*
Weston-sub-Edge, Chipping Campden
GL55 6QH
t (01386) 840390
e lucy@manorfarmbnb.demon.co.uk
w manorfarmbnb.demon.co.uk

Nineveh Farm ★★★★★
Guest Accommodation
GOLD AWARD
Campden Road, Mickleton, Chipping Campden
GL55 6PS
t (01386) 438923
e stayinthecotswolds@hotmail.co.uk
w stayinthecotswolds.co.uk

Sandalwood House ★★★★
Bed & Breakfast **SILVER AWARD**
Back Ends, Chipping Campden
GL55 6AU
t (01386) 840091
e sandalwoodhouse@hotmail.com

r key to symbols see page 6

157

South West | Gloucestershire

Taplins ★★★★ *Bed & Breakfast*
5 Aston Road, Chipping Campden
GL55 6HR
t (01386) 840927
e info@cotswoldstay.co.uk
w cotswoldstay.co.uk

CINDERFORD, FOREST OF DEAN

Victoria House B&B ★★★
Guest Accommodation
56 Victoria Street, Cinderford,
Gloucestershire
GL14 2HR
t 01594 822734
e victoriahouse56@googlemail.com
w victoriahousebnb.co.uk

CIRENCESTER

Abbeymead Guest House ★★★★
Guest House
Victoria Road, Cirencester
GL7 1ES
t (01285) 653740
e land0603@aol.com
w abbeymeadguesthouse.com

Apsley Villa ★★★ *Guest House*
Victoria Road, Cirencester
GL7 1ES
t (01285) 653489
e natalie-nash@sky.com
w apsleyvilla.co.uk

Brooklands Farm ★★ *Farmhouse*
Ewen, Cirencester
GL7 6BU
t (01285) 770487
w glosfarmhols.co.uk

Columbrae ★★★★ *Bed & Breakfast*
3 School Hill, Stratton, Cirencester
GL7 2LS
t (01285) 653114
e margaret@columbrae.co.uk
w columbrae.co.uk

Dix's Barn ★★★★ *Bed & Breakfast*
Duntisbourne Abbots, Cirencester
GL7 7JN
t (01285) 821249
e wilcoxr@hotmail.com

Forge House ★★★★
Bed & Breakfast
Kemble, Cirencester
GL7 6AD
t (01285) 771157
e info@forgehousekemble.co.uk
w forgehousekemble.co.uk

Greensleeves ★★★★
Bed & Breakfast **SILVER AWARD**
Baunton Lane, Cirencester
GL7 2LN
t (01285) 642516
e johnps1@tesco.net
w greensleeves4u.co.uk

The Ivy House ★★★★ *Guest House*
2 Victoria Road, Cirencester
GL7 1EN
t (01285) 656626
e info@ivyhousecotswolds.com
w ivyhousecotswolds.com

The Leauses ★★★★
Guest Accommodation
GOLD AWARD
101 Victoria Road, Cirencester
GL7 1EU
t (01285) 653643
e info@theleauses.co.uk
w theleauses.co.uk

The Old Brewhouse ★★★★
Guest Accommodation
7 London Road, Cirencester
GL7 2PU
t (01285) 656099
e info@theoldbrewhouse.com
w theoldbrewhouse.com

The Old Bungalow Guest House
★★★★ *Guest Accommodation*
SILVER AWARD
93 Victoria Road, Cirencester
GL7 1ES
t (01285) 654179
e info@bandbcirencester.co.uk
w bandbcirencester.co.uk

Riverside House ★★★★
Guest Accommodation
Watermoor, Cirencester
GL7 1LF
t (01285) 647642
e riversidehouse@mitsubishi-cars.co.uk
w riversidehouse.org.uk

The Royal Agricultural College
★★★ *Campus*
Stroud Road, Cirencester
GL7 6JS
t (01285) 652531
e commercial.services@rac.ac.uk
w rac.ac.uk

Springfield Country House ★★★★
Bed & Breakfast
Rendcomb, Cirencester
GL7 7HD
t (01285) 831130
e j.m.timmins@hotmail.co.uk
w springfieldcountryhouse.co.uk

The Talbot Inn ★★★★ *Inn*
14 Victoria Road, Cirencester
GL7 1EN
t (01285) 653760
e info@talbotinncotswolds.co.uk
w talbotinncotswolds.co.uk

COBERLEY VILLAGE

The Old Post Office ★★★★
Bed & Breakfast
Coberley Village
GL53 9QZ
t (01242) 870694
e pjcarlton@btinternet.com
w cotswoldbb.co.uk

COLEFORD

Forest House ★★★★
Guest Accommodation
Cinderhill, Coleford
GL16 8HQ
t (01594) 832424
e suesparkes@tumphouse.fsnet.co.uk
w forest-house-hotel.co.uk

COLESBOURNE

Colesbourne Inn ★★★★ *Inn*
Colesbourne, Colesbourne
GL53 9NP
t (01242) 870376
e info@thecolesbourneinn.co.uk
w thecolesbourneinn.co.uk

COOMBE DINGLE

Treborough ★★ *Bed & Breakfast*
3 Grove Road, Coombe Dingle,
Bristol
BS9 2RQ
t (0117) 968 2712

CORSE

Kilmorie Small Holding ★★★★
Guest Accommodation
Gloucester Road, Corse, Gloucester
GL19 3RQ
t (01452) 840224
e sheila-barnfield@supanet.com
w smoothhound.co.uk/hotels/kilmorie.html

DEERHURST

Deerhurst Bed & Breakfast
★★★★ *Farmhouse*
Deerhurst Priory, Deerhurst
GL19 4BX
t (01684) 293358
e timandcate@aol.com
w deerhurstbandb.co.uk

Odda's Barn ★★★★
Bed & Breakfast **SILVER AWARD**
Deerhurst
GL19 4BX
t 07786 256016
e kimfound@aol.com
w oddasbarn.co.uk

DIDMARTON

The Kings Arms at Didmarton
★★★★ *Inn*
The Street, Didmarton, Badminton
GL9 1DT
t (01454) 238245
e bookings@kingsarmsdidmarton.co.uk
w kingsarmsdidmarton.co.uk

DOWN HATHERLEY

**Newbridge House Bed &
Breakfast** ★★★★★
Guest Accommodation
SILVER AWARD
Down Hatherley
GL2 9QB
t (01452) 730404
e info@newbridgehouse.co.uk
w newbridgehouse.co.uk

DURSLEY

Waterend Farm ★★★★ *Farmhouse*
Coaley, Dursley
GL11 5DR
t (01453) 899141
e enquiries@waterendfarm.co.uk
w waterendfarm.co.uk

EBRINGTON

Kissing Gate ★★★★
Bed & Breakfast
Coldicott Leys, Ebrington, Chipping
Campden
GL55 6NZ
t (01386) 593934
e anne.bulger@virgin.net
w kissinggate.net

EWEN

Well Cottage Bed & Breakfast
★★★★ *Bed & Breakfast*
Ewen, Cirencester, Gloucestershire
GL7 6BU
t (01285) 770212
e info@wellcottagebandb.co.uk
w wellcottagebandb.co.uk

FAIRFORD

Hathaway ★★★★ *Bed & Breakfast*
SILVER AWARD
London Road, Fairford
GL7 4AR
t (01285) 712715
e lizian.spurway@btinternet.com
w mini-webs.com/hathaway

Waiten Hill Farm ★★★
Bed & Breakfast
Coronation Street, Fairford
GL7 4HX
t (01285) 712652
e richard@waiten-hill-farmhouse.com
w waiten-hill-farmhouse.com

FORD

The Plough Inn ★★★★ *Inn*
Ford
GL54 5RU
t (01386) 584215
e info@theploughinnatford.co.uk
w theploughinnatford.co.uk

FOSSEBRIDGE

The Inn at Fossebridge ★★★★
Inn
Fossebridge, Cheltenham
GL54 3JS
t (01285) 720721
e info@fossebridgeinn.co.uk
w fossebridgeinn.co.uk

FRAMPTON-ON-SEVERN

The Bell Inn ★★★★ *Inn*
The Green, Frampton-on-Severn
GL2 7EP
t (01452) 740346
e relax@thebellframpton.co.uk
w thebellframpton.co.uk

GLOUCESTER

The Albert House ★★★
Guest Accommodation
56 Worcester Street, Gloucester
GL1 3AG
t (01452) 502081
e enquiries@alberthotel.com
w alberthotel.com

Brawn Farm ★★★★ *Farmhouse*
SILVER AWARD
Sandhurst Lane, Sandhurst,
Gloucester
GL2 9NR
t (01452) 731010
e brawnfarm@yahoo.co.uk
w brawnfarmbandb.co.uk/

Brookthorpe Lodge ★★★
Guest House
Stroud Road, Brookthorpe,
Gloucester
GL4 0UQ
t (01452) 812645
e enq@brookthorpelodge.demon.co.uk
w brookthorpelodge.demon.co.uk

Centre Lodge Guest House ★★
Guest Accommodation - Room Only
12 Arthur Street, Gloucester
GL1 1QY
t (01452) 522243
e jens_eberhardt_uk@hotmail.co
w centrelodgeguesthouse.co.uk

City Lodge Guesthouse ★★
Guest Accommodation - Room Only
72 Weston Road, Gloucester
GL1 5AX
t (01452) 522243
e jens_eberhardt_uk@hotmail.co
w citylodgeguesthouse.co.uk

Crickley Court ★★★★
Guest Accommodation
SILVER AWARD
Dog Lane, Witcombe, Gloucester
GL3 4UF
t (01452) 863634
e lispilgrimmorris@yahoo.co.uk
w crickleycourt.co.uk

Longford Lodge ★★★
Guest Accommodation - Room Only
68 Tewkesbury Road, Longford,
Gloucester
GL2 9EH
t (01452) 526380
e jens_eberhardt_uk@hotmail.co
w longfordlodge.co.uk

Lulworth ★★★
Guest Accommodation
12 Midland Road, Gloucester
GL1 4UF
t (01452) 521881
e lulworthgh@hotmail.co.uk

The Mulberry House ★★★
Bed & Breakfast
2a Heathville Road, Gloucester
GL1 3DP
t (01452) 720079
e themulberryhouse@hotmail.co
w the-mulberry-house.co.uk/

Nicki's Guesthouse & Taverna ★
Guest House
105-107 Westgate Street, Gloucester
GL1 2PG
t (01452) 301359

Notley House & Coach House
★★★ *Guest Accommodation*
93 Hucclecote Road, Gloucester
GL3 3TR
t (01452) 611584
e notleyhouse@blueyonder.co.uk
w notleyhouse.co.uk

Spalite Hotel ★★★ *Guest House*
121 Southgate Street, Gloucester
GL1 1XQ
t (01452) 380828
e marsh@spalitehotel.fsnet.co.uk
w spalitehotel.com

South West | Gloucestershire

wn Street Farm ★★★
mhouse
vn Street, Tirley, Gloucester
l9 4HG
t (01452) 780442
e townstreetfarm@hotmail.com
w townstreetfarm.co.uk

GUITING POWER

hill ★★★★
est Accommodation
VER AWARD
w Road, Naunton, Guiting Power
54 5RL
t (01451) 850496
w smoothhound.co.uk/hotels/foxhi
llnaunton

iting Guest House ★★★★
est House SILVER AWARD
st Office Lane (formerly Cow Pat
e), Guiting Power,
ucestershire
54 5TZ
t (01451) 850470
e info@guitingguesthouse.com
w guitingguesthouse.com

e Hollow Bottom ★★★★ Inn
nchcombe Road, Guiting Power
54 5UX
t (01451) 850392
e hello@hollowbottom.com
w hollowbottom.com

HORFIELD

rfolk House ★★★
est Accommodation
7 Gloucester Road, Bristol
0 0BW
t (0117) 951 3191
e 577norfolk@blueyonder.co.uk

HORTON

ttage Courtyard ★★★
est Accommodation
ter Oak Farm, Little Sodbury
d, Horton
87 6QG
t 07544 274696
e ellewilliams@live.co.uk
w cottagecourtyard.co.uk

KILCOT

thyland Heights ★★★★
mhouse
avans Hill, Kilcot, Newent,
ucestershire
18 1PG
t (01989) 720582
e katrina@withylandheights.co.uk
w withylandheights.co.uk

KINGS STANLEY

se Nook B&B ★★★★
& Breakfast
ddleyard, King's Stanley, Stroud
10 3PP
t (01453) 791697
e richard@rosenook.plus.com
w rosenook.plus.com

lley Views ★★★★
& Breakfast SILVER AWARD
Orchard Close, Middleyard,
nehouse
10 3QA
t (01453) 827458
e enquiries@valley-views.com
w valley-views.com

LECHLADE

verside Pub ★★★ Guest House
k End Wharf, Lechlade
7 3AQ
t (01367) 252534
e info@theriverside-lechlade.co.uk
w theriverside-lechlade.co.uk

LECHLADE-ON-THAMES

mbrai Lodge ★★★★
est Accommodation
k Street, Lechlade- on -Thames
7 3AY
t (01367) 253173
e cambrai@btconnect.com
w cambrailodgeguesthouse.co.uk

The New Inn hotel ★★★ Inn
Market Square, Lechlade
GL7 3AB
t (01367) 252296
e info@newinnhotel.com
w newinnhotel.co.uk

LONGHOPE

The Farmers Boy Inn ★★★ Inn
Ross Road, Longhope
GL17 0LP
t (01452) 831300
e info@thefarmersboyinn.co.uk
w thefarmersboyinn.co.uk

MINCHINHAMPTON

Forwood Farm ★★★★
Bed & Breakfast SILVER AWARD
Well Hill, Forwood, Minchinhampton
GL6 9AB
t (01453) 731620
e rose@forwoodfarm.com
w forwoodfarm.com

MORETON-IN-MARSH

Acacia ★★ Guest Accommodation
New Road, Moreton-in-Marsh
GL56 0AS
t (01608) 650130
e acacia.guesthouse@tiscali.co.uk
w acaciathecotswolds.co.uk/default.
aspx

Bran Mill Cottage ★★★
Bed & Breakfast
Near Aston Magna, Moreton-in-
Marsh
GL56 9QW
t (01386) 593517
e enquiries@branmillcottage.co.uk
w branmillcottage.co.uk

Fosseway Farm B&B ★★★★
Guest Accommodation
Stow Road, Moreton-in-Marsh
GL56 0DS
t (01608) 650503
e fosewayfarmbandb@hotmail.com

Old Farm ★★★ Farmhouse
Dorn, Moreton in Marsh,
Gloucestershire
GL56 9NS
t (01608) 650394
e info@oldfarmdorn.co.uk
w oldfarmdorn.co.uk

Snowshill Hill Estate B&B ★★★★
★ Farmhouse
SILVER AWARD
Snowshill Hill, Moreton-in-Marsh
GL56 9TH
t (01386) 853959
e snowshillhill@aol.com
w broadway-cotswolds.co.uk/snows
hillhill.html

Treetops ★★★★ Guest House
London Road, Moreton-in-Marsh
GL56 0HE
t (01608) 651036
e Treetops1@talk21.com
w treetopscotswolds.co.uk

NEWENT

The George ★★★ Inn
Church Street, Newent
GL18 1PU
t (01531) 820203
e enquiries@georgehotel.uk.com
w georgehotel.uk.com

Newent Golf Club & Lodges ★★★
Guest Accommodation
Cold Harbour Lane, Newent
GL18 1DJ
t (01531) 820478
e newentgolf@btconnect.com
w newentgolf.co.uk

Sandyway Nurseries Countryside
B&B ★★★★ Bed & Breakfast
Redmarley Road, Newent
GL18 1DR
t (01531) 820693
e jean@sandy.f9.co.uk

Three Ashes House ★★★★
Bed & Breakfast SILVER AWARD
Ledbury Road, Newent
GL18 1DE
t (01531) 820226
e judith@threeasheshouse.co.uk

NEWLAND

Tan House Farm ★★★
Bed & Breakfast
Laundry Lane, Newland, Coleford
GL16 8NQ
t (01594) 832222
e christiearno@talktalk.net
w tanhousefarm.org.uk

NEWNHAM

The Old House Bed & Breakfast
★★★ Bed & Breakfast
High Street, Newnham
GL14 1BW
t (01594) 510944
e griffiths6@btinternet.com
w theoldhousenewnham.co.uk

NORTH CERNEY

The Bathurst Arms ★★★★ Inn
The Bathurst Arms, North Cerney,
Cirencester
GL7 7BZ
t (01285) 831281
e james@bathurstarms.com
w bathurstarms.com

PAINSWICK

Cardynham House ★★★★
Guest Accommodation
Tibbiwell Street, Painswick
GL6 6XX
t (01452) 814006
e info@cardynham.co.uk
w cardynham.co.uk

Hambutts Mynd ★★★
Guest Accommodation
Edge Road, Painswick
GL6 6UP
t (01452) 812352
e ewarland@supanet.com
w accommodation.uk.net/hambutts.
htm

Thorne ★★★ Bed & Breakfast
Friday Street, Painswick
GL6 6QJ
t (01452) 812476
w painswick.co.uk/thorne

Tibbiwell Lodge Bed & Breakfast
Tibbiwell Lane, Painswick
GL6 6YA
t (01452) 812748
e lovell_richard@hotmail.com
w tibbiwelllodgepainswick.webs.
com

Troy House ★★★★ Bed & Breakfast
Gloucester Street, Painswick, Stroud
GL6 6QN
t (01452) 812339
e simonnefrissen@microdia.com
w troy-house.co.uk

PAMINGTON

Pamington Court Farm ★★★★
Farmhouse SILVER AWARD
Pamington, Ashchurch, Tewkesbury
GL20 8LY
t (01684) 772301
e mhill@uwclub.net
w pamingtoncourtfarm.com

PARKEND

Deanfield ★★★★
Guest Accommodation
Folly Road, Parkend, Lydney
GL15 4JF
t (01594) 562256
e deanfieldbb@aol.com
w deanfield.org.uk

Fountain Inn ★★★ Inn
Parkend, Lydney, Gloucestershire
GL15 4JD
t (01594) 562189
e thefountaininn@aol.com
w thefountaininnandlodge.co.uk

PITCHCOMBE

Gable End ★★★ Bed & Breakfast
Pitchcombe
GL6 6LN
t (01452) 812166

RUDFORD

The Dark Barn ★★★★
Guest Accommodation
The Dark Barn Conference & Events
Centre, Barbers Bridge, Rudford,
Gloucester
GL2 8DX
t (01452) 790412
e info@barbersbridge.co.uk
w darkbarn.co.uk

SELSLEY

Little Owl Cottage ★★★★
Bed & Breakfast SILVER AWARD
Selsey Hill, Selsley, Stroud
GL5 5LN
t (01453) 757050
e littleowlcottage@sky.com
w littleowlcottagebedandbreakfast.
co.uk

SLIMBRIDGE

Tudor Arms Lodge and Freehouse
★★★★ Inn
Shepherds Patch, Slimbridge,
Gloucester
GL2 7BP
t (01453) 890306
e enquiries@thetudorarms.co.uk
w thetudorarms.co.uk

SOUDLEY

White Horse Inn ★★★ Inn
Church Road, Soudley, Cinderford
GL14 2UA
t (01594) 825968

SOUTH CERNEY

Mallin Bed & Breakfast ★★
Bed & Breakfast
49 Meadow Way, South Cerney,
Cirencester
GL7 6HY
t (01285) 869080
e linda@lcs-mcm.co.uk
w mallinbandb.co.uk

SOUTHVILLE

The White House Guest Rooms
★★★ Guest Accommodation
28-30 Dean Lane, Southville, Bristol
BS3 1DB
t (0117) 953 7725
e info@bedandbreakfast_bristol.co.
uk
w bedandbreakfast-bristol.co.uk

STAUNTON

Steep Meadow ★★★★
Bed & Breakfast
Staunton, Coleford
GL16 8PD
t (01594) 832316
e helen@steepmeadow.co.uk
w steepmeadow.co.uk

ST BRIAVELS

St Briavels Castle YHA ★★ Hostel
Church Street, St Briavels, Lydney
GL15 6RG
t 0845 371 9042
e stbriavels@yha.org.uk
w yha.org.uk

STONEHOUSE

Merton Lodge ★★ Bed & Breakfast
8 Ebley Road, Stonehouse
GL10 2LQ
t (01453) 822018

159

South West | Gloucestershire/Somerset

STOW-ON-THE-WOLD

Aston House ★★★★
Bed & Breakfast **SILVER AWARD**
Broadwell, Near Stow-on-the-Wold,
Moreton-in-Marsh
GL56 0TJ
t (01451) 830475
e fja@astonhouse.net
w astonhouse.net

Chure House ★★★★
Bed & Breakfast **SILVER AWARD**
Sheep Street, Stow-on-the-Wold,
Cheltenham
GL54 1AA
t (01451) 832 185
e churehouse@googlemail.com
w bedandbreakfast-stowonthewold.co.uk

Corsham Field Farmhouse ★★★
Farmhouse
Bledington Road, Stow-on-the-Wold,
Gloucestershire
GL54 1JH
t 01451 831750
e farmhouse@corshamfield.co.uk
w corshamfield.co.uk

Cross Keys Cottage ★★★
Bed & Breakfast
Park Street, Stow-on-the-Wold
GL54 1AQ
t (01451) 831128
e rogxmag@hotmail.com

Number Nine ★★★★
Bed & Breakfast **SILVER AWARD**
Park Street, Stow-on-the-Wold
GL54 1AQ
t (01451) 870333
e enquiries@number-nine.info
w number-nine.info

South Hill Farmhouse ★★★★
Guest House
Station Road, Stow-on-the-Wold
GL54 1JU
t (01451) 831888
e info@southhill.co.uk
w southhill.co.uk

Windy Ridge House ★★★★★
Bed & Breakfast **SILVER AWARD**
The Crook, Longborough, Stow-on-the-Wold
GL56 0QY
t (01451) 830465
e nick@windy-ridge.co.uk
w windy-ridge.co.uk

Wren House ★★★★
Bed & Breakfast
Donnington, Stow-on-the-Wold
GL56 0XZ
t (01451) 831787
e enquiries@wrenhouse.net
w wrenhouse.net

YHA Stow on the Wold ★★★★
Hostel
The Square, Stow-on-the-Wold
GL54 1AF
t (01451) 830497
e stow@yha.org.uk
w yha.org.uk

STROUD

1 Woodchester Lodge ★★★★
Bed & Breakfast **SILVER AWARD**
Southfield Road, Woodchester,
Stroud
GL5 5PA
t (01453) 872586
e anne@woodchesterlodge.co.uk
w woodchesterlodge.co.uk

The Clothiers Arms ★★★ Inn
1 Bath Road, Stroud
GL5 3JJ
t (01453) 763101
e harry.counsell@btconnect.com
w clothiersarms.co.uk

Coach House B&B ★★★★
Bed & Breakfast
Highfield Way, Stroud
GL6 8LZ
t (01453) 887529
e info@coachhousebnb.co.uk
w coachhousebnb.co.uk

Hollingham House
Guest Accommodation
Hollingham Lane, Horsley, Stroud
GL6 0NZ
t (01453) 832497
e a.r.marchand@talk21.com

Meadowcote ★★★★
Bed & Breakfast
Stroud Road, Painswick, Stroud
GL6 6UT
t (01452) 813565
e lockmeadowcote@talktalk.net

Pretoria Villa ★★★★
Bed & Breakfast **SILVER AWARD**
Wells Road, Eastcombe, Stroud
GL6 7EE
t (01452) 770435
e pretoriavilla@btinternet.com
w bedandbreakfast-cotswold.co.uk

Upper Doreys Mill ★★★
Bed & Breakfast
Edge, Painswick, Stroud
GL6 6NF
t (01452) 812459
e sylvia@doreys.co.uk
w doreys.co.uk

The Withyholt ★★★★
Bed & Breakfast
Paul Mead, Edge, Stroud
GL6 6PG
t (01452) 813618

TETBURY

Lyncombe House B&B ★★★★
Bed & Breakfast **SILVER AWARD**
Silver Street, Tetbury
GL8 8DH
t (01666) 503807
e josieprice@googlemail.com

One Market Place ★★★★
Bed & Breakfast
1 Market Place, Tetbury
GL8 8DA
t (01666) 504334
e onemarketplace@tiscali.co.uk

TEWKESBURY

Abbots Court Farm ★★★
Farmhouse
Churchend, Twyning, Tewkesbury
GL20 6DA
t (01684) 292515
e abbotscourt@aol.com

Astalleigh House ★★★★
Bed & Breakfast
Ripple, Tewkesbury, Gloucestershire
GL20 6EU
t 01684 593740
e jewers@jewers.freeserve.co.uk
w astalleighhouse.co.uk

Gantier ★★★★ Bed & Breakfast
SILVER AWARD
12 Church Road, Alderton,
Tewkesbury
GL20 8NR
t (01242) 620343
e johnandsueparry@yahoo.co.uk
w gantier.co.uk

Jessop House ★★★★
Guest Accommodation
65 Church Street, Tewkesbury
GL20 5RZ
t (01684) 292017
e bookings@jessophousehotel.com
w jessophousehotel.com

Malvern View Guest House ★★★
Guest Accommodation
1 St Marys Road, Tewkesbury
GL20 5SE
t (01684) 292776
e helengracey900@btinternet.com

Tudor House Guest Accommodation
High Street, Tewkesbury
GL20 5BH
t (01684) 297755

TIBBERTON

The Laurels ★★
Guest Accommodation
Bovone Lane, Tibberton, Gloucester
GL2 8EA
t (01452) 790300
e henryandchris.rivers@btinternet.com
w newentbedandbreakfast.co.uk

ULEY

The Old Crown Inn ★★★ Inn
The Green, Uley, Dursley
GL11 5SN
t (01453) 860502
e info@theoldcrownuley.co.uk
w theoldcrownuley.co.uk

UPPER LYDBROOK

Ferndale House Bed & Breakfast
★★★ Bed & Breakfast
Ferndale House, Upper Lydbrook,
Lydbrook
GL17 9LQ
t (01594) 861294
e ferndalehouse@hotmail.co.uk
w ferndale-house.co.uk

WELSH BICKNOR

Welsh Bicknor Youth Hostel ★★
Hostel
Welsh Bicknor, Ross-on-Wye
HR9 6JJ
t 0870 770 6086
e welshbicknor@yha.org.uk
w yha.org.uk

WHITECROFT

Edale House ★★★★ Guest House
Folly Road, Parkend, Lydney
GL15 4JP
t (01594) 562835
e enquiry@edalehouse.co.uk
w edalehouse.co.uk

WHITMINSTER

The Whitminster Inn ★★★★ Inn
Bristol Rd, Whitminster
GL2 7NY
t (01452) 740234
e info@whitminsterinn.co.uk
w whitminsterinn.co.uk/

WINCHCOMBE

Cleevely ★★★★ Bed & Breakfast
Wadfield Farm, Corndean Lane,
Winchcombe
GL54 5AL
t (01242) 602059
e cleevelybxb@hotmail.com

North Farmcote Bed & Breakfast
★★★★ Farmhouse
North Farmcote, Winchcombe
GL54 5AU
t (01242) 602304
e davideayrs@yahoo.co.uk
w northfarmcote.co.uk

Parks Farm ★★★★ Farmhouse
Sudeley, Winchcombe
GL54 5JB
t (01242) 603874
e parksfarmbandb@googlemail.com
w parksfarm.co.uk

Postlip Hall Farm ★★★★
Farmhouse **GOLD AWARD**
Winchcombe, Cheltenham
GL54 5AQ
t (01242) 603351
e postliphallfarm@tiscali.co.uk
w smoothhound.co.uk/hotels/postlip

YORKLEY

Silverdeane ★★★★
Bed & Breakfast
Lower Road, Yorkley, Lydney
GL15 4TQ
t (01594) 560262
e enquiries@silverdeane.co.uk
w silverdeane.co.uk

Somerset

ALFORD

The Coach House ★★★★
Farmhouse **SILVER AWARD**
Alford, Castle Cary
BA7 7PN
t (01963) 240315
e liz@alfordcoachhouse.co.uk
w alfordcoachhouse.co.uk

ASHBRITTLE

Lower Westcott Farm ★★★★
Farmhouse
Ashbrittle, Wellington
TA21 0HZ
t (01398) 361296
e lowerwestcott@aol.com
w lowerwestcottfarm.co.uk

ASHCOTT

Hillview Cottage ★★★★
Bed & Breakfast
6 Berhill, Ashcot, Bridgewater
TA7 9QN
t (01458) 210621
e liz@hillviewcottage.org.uk
w hillviewcottage.org.uk

Sunnyside ★★★★ Bed & Breakfast
SILVER AWARD
34 Taunton Road, Pedwell
TA7 9BG
t (01458) 210097
e sheila@sunnyside-pedwell.co.uk
w sunnyside-pedwell.co.uk

ASHWICK

Springfield Farm ★★★★
Farmhouse
Ashwick, Dulverton
TA22 9QD
t (01398) 323722
e stay@springfieldfarms.co.uk
w springfieldfarms.co.uk

AVON

Pennsylvania Farm B&B ★★★★
Farmhouse
Newton St Loe, Avon
BA2 9DP
t (01225) 314912
e info@pennsylvaniafarm.co.uk
w pennsylvaniafarm.co.uk

AXBRIDGE

Reservoir View Motel ★★★
Guest Accommodation - Room Only
Cheddar Road, Axbridge
BS26 2DL
t (01934) 732180
e reservoirviewmotel@fsmail.net
w reservoirviewmotel.co.uk

BARWICK

Barwick Farm House ★★★
Farmhouse
Rexs Lane, Barwick
BA22 9TD
t (01935) 410779
e info@barwickfarmhouse.co.uk
w barwickfarmhouse.co.uk

BATCOMBE

Romsey Cottage ★★★
Bed & Breakfast
Kale Street, Shepton Mallet
BA4 6AB
t (01749) 850207
e loumarnic@yahoo.com
w prcubed.co.uk

South West | Somerset

lley View Farm ★★★★
est Accommodation
ncombe Hill, Batcombe
4 6AJ
t (01749) 850302
e valleyviewfarm@lineone.co.uk
w valleyview-farm.co.uk

BATH

a North Road B&B ★★★★★
d & Breakfast **SILVER AWARD**
a North Road, Combe Down, Bath
2 5DF
t (01225) 835593
e info@55anorthroad.co.uk
w 55anorthroad.co.uk

bey Rise ★★★★
est Accommodation
Wells Road, Bath
2 3AN
t (01225) 316177
e stay@abbeyrise.co.uk
w abbeyrise.co.uk

banny Guest House ★★★
est House
Crescent Gardens, Upper Bristol
ad, Bath
1 2NB
t (01225) 313339
e stay@albanybath.co.uk
w albanybath.co.uk

nabelle's Guest House ★★
est House
Manvers Street, Bath
1 1JQ
t (01225) 330133
e nathy.anabelles@gmail.com
w anabellesguesthouse.co.uk

ple Tree Guest House ★★★★
est House
Pulteney Gardens, Bath
2 4HG
t (01225) 337642
e enquiries@appletreeguesthouse.co.uk
w appletreeguesthouse.co.uk

quae Sulis ★★★★
est Accommodation
4-176 Newbridge Road, Bath
1 3LE
t (01225) 420061
e enquiries@aquaesulishotel.co.uk
w aquaesulishotel.co.uk

hgrove Guest House ★★
est House
Bathwick Street, Bath
2 6PA
t (01225) 421911
e traceyjayne71@hotmail.com
w ashgroveguesthouse.co.uk

shley Villa ★★★★ *Guest House*
Newbridge Road, Bath
1 3JZ
t (01225) 421683
e reservations@ashleyvilla.co.uk
w ashleyvilla.co.uk

stor House ★★★★ *Guest House*
Oldfield Road, Bath
2 3ND
t (01225) 429134
e astorhouse.visitus@virgin.net
w visitus.co.uk

hole Guest House ★★★★★
est House **GOLD AWARD**
Upper Oldfield Park, Bath
2 3JX
t (01225) 320000
e info@atholehouse.co.uk
w atholehouse.co.uk

von Guest House ★★★
est House
Pulteney Gardens, Bath
2 4HG
t (01225) 313009
e julie@avonguesthousebath.co.uk
w avonguesthousebath.co.uk

The Ayrlington ★★★★★
Guest Accommodation
24-25 Pulteney Road, Bath
BA2 4EZ
t (01225) 425495
e mail@ayrlington.com
w ayrlington.com

Badminton Villa ★★★★
Guest House **SILVER AWARD**
10 Upper Oldfield Park, Bath
BA2 3JZ
t (01225) 426347
e badmintonvilla@blueyonder.co.uk
w badmintonvilla.co.uk

The Bath Courtyard ★★★★
Bed & Breakfast
38 Vellore Lane, Bath
BA2 6JQ
t (01225) 424741
e michaelnwilson@gmail.com
w thebathcourtyard.co.uk

The Bathwick Townhouse ★★★★
Bed & Breakfast
15 Daniel Street, Bath
BA2 6NB
t (01225) 420499
e justinereid1@aol.com
w thebathwicktownhouse.com/

Bath YHA ★★★ *Hostel*
Bathwick Hill, Bath
BA2 6JZ
t (01225) 465674
e bath@yha.org.uk
w yha.org.uk

Bath YMCA *Hostel*
International House, Broad Street Place, Bath
BA1 5LH
t (01225) 325900
e stay@bathymca.co.uk
w bathymca.co.uk

Bay Tree House ★★ *Guest House*
12 Crescent Gardens, Bath
BA1 2NA
t (01225) 483699
e stay@baytreehousebath.co.uk
w baytreehousebath.co.uk/vbath

Beckford House Bed & Breakfast ★★★★ *Bed & Breakfast*
59 Upper Oldfield Park, Bath
BA2 3LB
t (01225) 310005
e info@beckford-house.com
w beckford-house.com

Belmont The ★★★
Guest Accommodation
7 Belmont, Lansdown Road, Bath
BA1 5DZ
t 01225 423082
e archie_watson@hotmail.com
w belmontbath.co.uk

Belvedere Bed & Breakfast ★★★
Guest Accommodation
25 Belvedere, Lansdown Road, Bath
BA1 5ED
t (01225) 330264
e info@belvederewinevaults.com

Bloomfield House ★★★★
Guest House
146 Bloomfield Road, Bath
BA2 2AS
t (01225) 420105
e karibarnard@hotmail.com
w ecobloomfield.co.uk

Bodhi House ★★★★
Guest Accommodation
31A Englishcombe Lane, Bath
BA2 2EE
t (01225) 461990
e stay@bodhihouse.co.uk
w bodhihouse.co.uk

Braemar Guest House ★★★★
Bed & Breakfast
43 Wellsway, Bath
BA2 4RS
t (01225) 422743
e info@bathbraemar.co.uk
w bathbraemar.co.uk

Chestnuts House ★★★★★
Guest Accommodation
16 Henrietta Road, Bathwick, Bath
BA2 6LY
t (01225) 334279
e bookings.chestnuthouse@siteminder.co.uk
w chestnutshouse.co.uk

Church Farm Monkton Farleigh ★★★ *Farmhouse*
Monkton Farleigh, Bradford-on-Avon
BA15 2QJ
t (01225) 858583
e reservations@churchfarmmonktonfarleigh.co.uk
w churchfarmmonktonfarleigh.co.uk

Crescent Guest House ★★★★
Guest House
21 Crescent Gardens, Bath
BA1 2NA
t (01225) 425945
e info@crescentbath.co.uk
w crescentbath.co.uk

The Edgar Townhouse ★★★
Guest Accommodation
64 Great Pulteney Street, Bath
BA2 4DN
t (01225) 420619
e edgar-hotel@btconnect.com
w edgar-townhouse.co.uk

Eleven Belgrave ★★
Bed & Breakfast
11 Belgrave Crescent, Bath
BA1 5JU
t 07852 148065
e info@elevenbelgrave.co.uk
w elevenbelgrave.co.uk

The Firs ★★★★ *Bed & Breakfast*
2 Newbridge Hill, Bath
BA1 3PU
t (01225) 334575
e dawnsandora@gmail.com
w thefirsbath.co.uk

Friary Dene *Bed & Breakfast*
The A36 Frome Road, Hinton Charter House, Bath
BA2 7TE
t (01225) 720020
e info@friarydene.co.uk
w friarydene.co.uk

Friary Wood ★★★★
Guest Accommodation
A36 Frome Road, Hinton Charterhouse, Bath
BA2 7TE
t (01225) 723023
e info@friarywood.co.uk
w friarywood.co.uk

The Garden House ★★★★
Bed & Breakfast
Adelaide Place, Bath
BA2 6BU
t 07769 658453
e caroline@gardenhousebath.co.uk

Griffin Inn ★★★★ *Inn*
Beauford Square, Bath
BA1 2AP
t (01225) 420919
e bookings@griffinbath.co.uk
w griffinbath.co.uk

The Henry ★★★ *Guest House*
6 Henry Street, Bath
BA1 1JT
t (01225) 424052
e stay@thehenry.com
w thehenry.com

The Hermitage ★★
Guest Accommodation
Bath Road, Box, Corsham
SN13 8DT
t (01225) 744187
e hermitagebb@btconnect.com

High Beeches ★★★★
Guest Accommodation
156 Midford Road, Combe Down, Bath
BA2 5SE
t (01225) 830518
e info@high-beeches.com
w high-beeches.com

Highways House ★★★★
Guest Accommodation
143 Wells Road, Bath
BA2 3AL
t (01225) 421238
e reservations@highwayshouse.co.uk
w highwayshouse.co.uk

Lamp Post Villa ★★★
Guest Accommodation
3 Crescent Gardens, Bath
BA1 2NA
t 004412253312 21
e lamppostvilla@aol.com
w lamppostvilla.com

Lavender House ★★★★★
Guest Accommodation
GOLD AWARD
17 Bloomfield Park, Bath
BA2 2BY
t (01225) 314500
e bookings.lavenderhouse0710@siteminder.co.uk
w lavenderhouse-bath.com

Lindisfarne Guest House ★★★★
Guest House
41a Warminster Road, Bathampton, Bath
BA2 6XJ
t (01225) 466342 / 07917665001
e lindisfarne-bath@talk21.com
w bath.org/hotel/lindisfarne.htm

Marisha's Guest House ★★★
Guest House
68 Newbridge Hill, Bath
BA1 3QA
t (01225) 446881
e marishasguesthouse@tiscali.co.uk
w marishasinbath.com

Marlborough House Guest House ★★★★ *Guest Accommodation*
1 Marlborough Lane, Bath
BA1 2NQ
t (01225) 318175
e mars@manque.dircon.co.uk
w marlborough-house.net

Membland Guest House ★★★
Bed & Breakfast
7 Pulteney Terrace, Pulteney Road, Bath
BA2 4HJ
t (01225) 336712 Mobile: 07958 599572
e membland@tiscali.co.uk

Milton House ★★★★ *Guest House*
75 Wellsway, Bear Flat, Bath
BA2 4RU
t (01225) 335632
e info@milton-house.co.uk
w milton-house.co.uk

Parkside ★★★★ *Guest House*
11 Marlborough Lane, Bath
BA1 2NQ
t (01225) 429444
e post@parksidebandb.co.uk
w parksidebandb.co.uk

Pulteney House ★★★
Guest Accommodation
14 Pulteney Road, Bath, Avon
BA2 4HA
t (01225) 460991
e pulteney@tinyworld.co.uk
w pulteneyhotel.co.uk

Queen Charlottes Orangery ★★★★ *Bed & Breakfast*
93a Sydney Place, Bath
BA2 6NE
t (01225) 427373
e deniseoneill425@aol.com
w queencharlottesorangery.com

Radnor Guest House ★★★★
Guest House
9 Pulteney Terrace, Pulteney Road, Bath
BA2 4HJ
t (01225) 316159
e info@radnorguesthouse.co.uk
w radnorguesthouse.co.uk

South West | Somerset

Ramscombe Cottage ★★★
Bed & Breakfast
Vivienne Rogers, Ramscombe Lane, Bath
BA1 8EP
t (01225) 859808
e ramscombe@yahoo.co.uk
w ramscombe.co.uk

Ravenscroft ★★★★
Bed & Breakfast SILVER AWARD
Sydney Road, Bath
BA2 6NT
t (01225) 469267
e rav.bath@ukonline.co.uk

Roban House ★★★★
Bed & Breakfast
26 Lower Oldfield Park, Bath
BA2 3HP
t (01225) 445390
e info@robanhouse.co.uk
w robanhouse.co.uk

Royal Park Guest House ★★★★
Guest House SILVER AWARD
16 Crescent Gardens, Bath
BA1 2NA
t (01225) 317651
e info@royalparkbath.co.uk
w royalparkbath.co.uk

Tasburgh House
Guest Accommodation
Warminster Road, Bath
BA2 6SH
t (01225) 425096
e hotel@bathtasburgh.co.uk
w bathtasburgh.co.uk

Three Abbey Green ★★★★
Guest House SILVER AWARD
3 Abbey Green, Bath
BA1 1NW
t (01225) 428558
e stay@threeabbeygreen.com
w threeabbeygreen.com

The Villa Magdala ★★★★★
Guest Accommodation
SILVER AWARD
Henrietta Road, Bath
BA2 6LX
t (01225) 466329
e office@villamagdala.co.uk
w villamagdala.co.uk

Walton Villa ★★★★
Guest Accommodation
3 Newbridge Hill, Bath
BA1 3PW
t (01225) 482792
e walton.villa@virgin.net
w walton.izest.com

Wellsway Guest House ★★
Guest Accommodation
51 Wellsway, Bath
BA2 4RS
t (01225) 423434

The White Guest House ★★★
Guest House
23 Pulteney Gardens, Bath
BA2 4HG
t (01225) 426075
e enquiries@whiteguesthouse.co.uk
w whiteguesthouse.co.uk

The Windsor ★★★★★ *Guest House*
69 Great Pulteney Street, Bath
BA2 4DL
t (01225) 422100
e sales@bathwindsorguesthouse.com
w bathwindsorguesthouse.com

BATHEALTON

Hagley Bridge Farm ★★★★
Farmhouse
Ridge Highway, Bathealton
TA4 2BQ
t (01984) 629026
e info@hagleybridgefarm.co.uk
w hagleybridgefarm.co.uk

BATHWICK

14 Raby Place ★★★★
Guest Accommodation
14 Raby Place, Bath
BA2 4EH
t (01225) 465120

Greenways ★★★
Guest Accommodation
1 Forester Road, Bathwick
BA2 6QF
t (01225) 310132

BAWDRIP

Kings Farm ★★ *Farmhouse*
10 Eastside Lane, Bawdrip
TA7 8QB
t (01278) 683233

BEAMBRIDGE

The Beambridge Inn ★★★★ *Inn*
Beam Bridge, Wellington
TA21 0HB
t (01823) 672223

BECKINGTON

Arundel ★★★★ *Bed & Breakfast*
SILVER AWARD
7 Bath Road, Beckington, Frome
BA11 6SW
t (01373) 831856
e arundel07@hotmail.com
w arundel-house.moonfruit.com

Eden Vale Farm ★★★ *Farmhouse*
Mill Lane, Beckington, Frome
BA11 6SN
t (01373) 830371
e bandb@edenvalefarm.co.uk
w edenvalefarm.co.uk

Seymours Court ★★★★
Farmhouse SILVER AWARD
Green Park Lane, Frome
BA11 6TT
t (01373) 830466
e seymourscourt@btinternet.com
w seymourscourt.co.uk

BILBROOK

Steps Farmhouse ★★★★
Guest Accommodation
Bilbrook
TA24 6HE
t (01984) 640974
e stay@stepsfarmhouse.co.uk
w stepsfarmhouse.co.uk

The Wayside B&B ★★★★
Guest Accommodation
SILVER AWARD
The Wayside, Bilbrook
TA24 6HE
t (01984) 641669
e thewayside@tiscali.co.uk
w thewayside.co.uk

BINEGAR

Mansfield House ★★★★
Guest Accommodation
SILVER AWARD
Mansfield House, Binegar
BA3 4UG
t (01749) 840568
e mansfield-house@aol.com
w mansfield-house.com

BISHOPS HULL

The Old Mill ★★★★★
Bed & Breakfast SILVER AWARD
Netherclay, Bishops Hull
TA1 5AB
t (01823) 289732
w theoldmillbandb.co.uk

BISHOPS LYDEARD

Four Seasons B&B ★★★★
Bed & Breakfast
Seven Ash, Bishops Lydeard
TA4 3EX
t (01823) 430337
e info@fourseasonsbedbreakfast.co.uk
w fourseasonsbedbreakfast.co.uk

Pound Farm ★★★★
Bed & Breakfast
Pound Lane, Bishops Lydeard
TA4 3DN
t (01823) 433443
e poundfarm04@fsmail.net
w poundfarm.co.uk

West View ★★★★
Guest Accommodation
Minehead Road, Bishops Lydeard
TA4 3BS
t (01823) 432223
e info@westviewbandb.co.uk
w westviewbandb.co.uk

BLATCHBRIDGE

Granados ★★★ *Bed & Breakfast*
East Woodland Road, Frome
BA11 5EL
t (01373) 465317
e granadosbandb@aol.com

Windwistle Cottage ★★★★
Bed & Breakfast
42 Blatchbridge, Frome
BA11 5EL
t (01373) 463643
e ajchant42@btinternet.com
w windwistle.co.uk

BLUE ANCHOR

Camelot House ★★★★
Guest Accommodation
SILVER AWARD
Carhampton Road, Minehead
TA24 6LB
t (01643) 821118
e stay@camelothousebandb.co.uk
w camelothousebandb.co.uk

The Langbury ★★★★
Guest Accommodation
SILVER AWARD
Carhampton Road, Blue Anchor
TA24 6LB
t (01643) 821375
e post@langbury.co.uk
w langbury.co.uk

BOWLISH (WELLS 4 MILES)

Bowlish Grange ★★★★
Bed & Breakfast
Forum Lane, Bowlish, Shepton Mallet
BA4 5JL
t (01749) 344212

BREAN

The Old Rectory Motel ★★★★
Guest Accommodation
Church Road, Brean
TA8 2SF
t (01278) 751447
e helen@old-rectory.fsbusiness.co.uk
w oldrectorybrean.co.uk

Yew Tree House ★★★★
Guest Accommodation
Hurn Lane, Berrow Nr Brean, Burnham on Sea
TA8 2QT
t (01278) 751382
e yewtree@yewtree-house.co.uk
w yewtree-house.co.uk

BRIDGWATER

Apple View ★★★★ *Farmhouse*
SILVER AWARD
Temple Farm, Bridgwater
TA7 8QR
t (01278) 423201
e temple_farm@hotmail.com
w apple-view.co.uk

The Boat & Anchor Inn ★★★ *Inn*
Meads Crossing, Huntworth, Bridgwater
TA7 0AQ
t (01278) 662473
e andrea@theboatandanchor.co.uk
w theboatandanchor.co.uk

Buzzard Heights B&B ★★★
Guest Accommodation
Aethandune, Tower Hill Road, Bridgwater
TA7 9AJ
t (01278) 722743
e teresa@buzzardheights.co.uk
w buzzardheights.co.uk

Hill View ★★★★ *Bed & Breakfast*
SILVER AWARD
55 Liney Road, Westonzoyland
TA7 0EU
t (01278) 699027
e denise@westonzoyland.fsbusiness.co.uk
w visit-hillview.co.uk

The Old Mill ★★★★
Bed & Breakfast
A39, Kilve, Bridgwater
TA5 1EB
t (01278) 741571

BRISTOL

The Carpenters Arms ★★★★ *Inn*
Stanton Wick, Pensford, Bristol
BS39 4BX
t (01761) 490202
e carpenters@buccaneer.co.uk
w the-carpenters-arms.co.uk

Greenditch Farm B&B
Guest Accommodation
Greenditch Farm, Dundry Lane, Dundry, Bristol
BS41 8JQ
t (01275) 472854
e enquiries@greenditchfarmbandb.co.uk
w greenditchfarmbandb

Leigh Farm ★★ *Farmhouse*
Old Road, Pensford, Bristol
BS39 4BA
t (01761) 490281
w leighfarmholidays.co.uk

BROMPTON REGIS

The George Inn ★★★ *Inn*
The George Inn, Dulverton
TA22 9NL
t (01398) 371273
e thegeorgeexmoor@btconnect.com
w thegeorgeexmoor.co.uk

BROOMFIELD

Manor Farm ★★★ *Farmhouse*
Waterpits, Broomfield
TA5 1AT
t (01823) 451266
e sue@manorfarmbreaks.co.uk
w manorfarmbreaks.co.uk

BRUSHFORD

Three Acres Country House
★★★★★ *Guest Accommodation*
GOLD AWARD
Brushford, Dulverton
TA22 9AR
t (01398) 323730
e enquiries@threeacrescountryhouse.co.uk
w threeacrescountryhouse.co.uk

BRUTON

Redlynch Farmhouse ★★★★
Bed & Breakfast
B3081, Bruton
BA10 0NH
t (01749) 812795
e angelafroud@hotmail.com

BURCOTT

Burcott Mill Guesthouse ★★★
Guest Accommodation
Wookey, Wells
BA5 1NJ
t (01749) 673118
e enquiries@burcottmill.com
w burcottmill.com

South West | Somerset

BURNHAM-ON-SEA

hbourne House ★★★★
est House
Berrow Road, Burnham-on-Sea
8 2EY
t (01278) 783217
e ashbourne.house@btinternet.com
w ashbournehouse.biz

oisters ★★★
est Accommodation
Berrow Road, Burnham-on-Sea
8 2HN
t (01278) 789280

ights Rest ★★★ Bed & Breakfast
Dunstan Road, Burnham-on-Sea
8 1ER
t (01278) 782318
e enquiries@knightsrest.uk.net
w knightsrest.uk.net/

gnolia House ★★★★
est House
Manor Road, Burnham-on-Sea
8 2AS
t (01278) 792460
e enquiries@magnoliahouse.gb.com
w magnoliahouse.gb.com

yal Clarence Hotel ★★★ Inn
The Esplanade, Burnham-on-Sea
8 1BQ
t 01278 783138
e graham-townley@supanet.com
w rchotel.co.uk

ndhills Guest House ★★★
est House
Poplar Road, Burnham-on-Sea
8 2HD
t (01278) 781208

alimar Guest House ★★★
est House
4 Berrow Road, Burnham-on-Sea
8 2JE
t (01278) 785898
e info@shalimarguesthouse.co.uk
w shalimarguesthouse.co.uk

Aubyns ★★★★ Guest House
Berrow Road, Burnham-on-Sea
8 2ET
t (01278) 773769
e markhowes@stevejefferies.fsnet.co.uk
w staubyns-guesthouse.co.uk

ctoria Hotel ★★★
est Accommodation
rnham-on-Sea
8 1EQ
t (01278) 783085
w the-victoria-hotel.co.uk

alton House ★★★★
est Accommodation
8 Berrow Road, Burnham-on-Sea
8 2PN
t (01278) 780034
e waltonhousebnb@aol.com
w waltonhousebnb.co.uk

e Warren Guest House ★★★★
est House SILVER AWARD
Berrow Road, Burnham-on-Sea
8 2EZ
t (01278) 786726
e info@thewarrenguesthouse.co.uk
w thewarrenguesthouse.co.uk

BUTCOMBE

oodbarn Farm Bed & Breakfast
★★ Farmhouse
nny Lane, Chew Magna, Bristol
40 8SZ
t (01275) 332599
e woodbarnfarm@hotmail.com
w smoothhound.co.uk/hotels/woodbarn1.html

CANNARDS GRAVE

rnt House Farm ★★★★
rmhouse
ndsor Hill, Shepton Mallet
4 4JQ
t (01749) 840185
e ehparry@btinternet.com
w burnthousedrove.co.uk

CANNINGTON

Gurney Manor Mill ★★★★
Guest Accommodation
SILVER AWARD
Gurney Street, Cannington
TA5 2HW
t (01278) 653582
e gurneymill@yahoo.co.uk
w gurneymill.co.uk

CARY FITZPAINE

Cary Fitzpaine Farmhouse ★★★★
Farmhouse
Cary Fitzpaine, Yeovil
BA22 8JB
t (01458) 223250
e acrang@aol.com
w caryfitzpaine.com

CASTLE CARY

Clanville Manor B&B ★★★★
Farmhouse GOLD AWARD
Clanville, Castle Cary
BA7 7PJ
t (01963) 350124
e info@clanvillemanor.co.uk
w clanvillemanor.co.uk

The Pilgrims at Lovington ★★★★
Inn SILVER AWARD
Lovington, Castle Cary
BA7 7PT
t (01963) 240597
e jools@thepilgrimsatlovington.co.uk
w thepilgrimsatlovington.co.uk

CHAPMANSLADE

Little Orchard B&B Bed & Breakfast
Little Orchard, 34 Lodge Hill, Chapmanslade, Westbury
BA13 4AR
t (01373) 832893
e hallhouse@hazelcliff.co.uk

CHARD

Ammonite Lodge ★★★★
Guest House
43 High Street, Chard
TA20 1QL
t (01460) 63839
e info@ammonitelodge.co.uk
w ammonitelodge.co.uk

Home Farm ★★★
Guest Accommodation
Hornsbury Hill, Chard
TA20 3DB
t (01460) 63731

Hornsbury Mill ★★★★
Guest Accommodation
Eleighwater, Chard
TA20 3AQ
t (01460) 63317
e info@hornsburymill.co.uk
w hornsburymill.co.uk

Wambrook Farm ★★★★
Farmhouse
Wambrook, Chard
TA20 3DF
t (01460) 62371
e wambrookfarm@aol.com
w wambrookfarm.co.uk

CHEDDAR

Arundel House ★★★
Guest Accommodation
Church Street, Cheddar
BS27 3RA
t (01934) 742264
e enquiries@arundelhousecheddar.co.uk
w arundelhousecheddar.co.uk

Cheddar YHA ★★★ Hostel
Hillfield, Cheddar
BS27 3HN
t (01934) 742494
e cheddar@yha.org.uk
w yha.org.uk/find-accommodation/south-west-england/hostels/cheddar/index.aspx

Chedwell Cottage ★★★★
Guest Accommodation
59 Redcliffe Street, Cheddar
BS27 3PF
t (01934) 743268
e info@chedwellcottage.co.uk

Constantine ★★★
Guest Accommodation
Lower New Road, Cheddar
BS27 3DY
t (01934) 741339

Gordon's ★★★
Guest Accommodation
Cliff Street, Cheddar
BS27 3PT
t (01934) 742497
e info@gordonshotel.co.uk
w gordonshotel.co.uk

Neuholme ★★★★
Guest Accommodation
The Barrows, Cheddar
BS27 3BG
t (01934) 742841
w neuholme.co.uk

Wassells House ★★★★
Guest Accommodation
Upper New Road, Cheddar
BS27 3DW
t (01934) 744317
e enquiries@wassellshouse.co.uk
w wassellshouse.co.uk

Waterside ★★★ Bed & Breakfast
Cheddar Road, Cheddar
BS26 2DP
t (01934) 743182
e gillianaldridge@hotmail.com
w watersidecheddar.co.uk

Yew Tree Farm ★★★
Bed & Breakfast
Wells Road, Theale
BS28 4SN
t (01934) 712475
e enquiries@yewtreefarmbandb.co.uk
w yewtreefarmbandb.co.uk

CHELYNCH

The Old Stables ★★★★
Bed & Breakfast
Chelynch Road, Shepton Mallet
BA4 4PY
t (01749) 880098
e maureenkeevil@live.co.uk
w the-oldstables.co.uk

CHEW STOKE

Orchard House ★★★
Guest Accommodation
Bristol Road, Chew Stoke, near Bristol
BS40 8UB
t (01275) 333143
e orchardhse@ukgateway.net
w orchardhouse-chewstoke.co.uk

CHEWTON MENDIP

Copper Beeches ★★★★
Guest Accommodation
Lower Street, Chewton Mendip, Wells, Somerset
BA3 4GP
t (01761) 241496
e copperbeechesbandb@tiscali.co.uk
w copperbeechesbandb.co.uk

CLAVERTON DOWN

University of Bath ★★★ - ★★★★
Campus
The Avenue, Claverton Down, Bath
BA2 7AY
t (01225) 386622
e acc-bathtourism@rt.bath.ac.uk
w haatbath.com

COMBE DOWN

Beech Wood ★★★★
Bed & Breakfast
Shaft Road, Combe Down, Bath
BA2 7HP
t (01225) 832242
e beechwoodbath@talktalk.net
w beechwoodbath.ihoststudio.com/

Grey Lodge ★★★★
Bed & Breakfast SILVER AWARD
Summer Lane, Combe Down, Bath
BA2 7EU
t (01225) 832069
e greylodge@surfree.co.uk
w greylodge.co.uk

COMPTON DUNDON

The Yew Tree @ Church Farm
★★★★ Bed & Breakfast
School Lane, Compton Dundon, Somerton
TA11 6TE
t (01458) 274891
e info@yewtreebnb.co.uk
w yewtreebnb.co.uk

CORSTON

Corston Fields Farm ★★★★
Farmhouse
Corston, Bath
BA2 9EZ
t (01225) 873305
e corston.fields@btinternet.com
w corstonfields.com

COSSINGTON

Brookhayes Farm ★★★★
Farmhouse
Bell Lane, Cossington
TA7 8LR
t (01278) 722559
e brookhayesfarm@tiscali.co.uk

CREWKERNE

Barn Cottage Bed & Breakfast
★★★★ Bed & Breakfast
SILVER AWARD
Barn Cottage, Crewkerne
TA18 8QP
t (01460) 75313
e bandbbarncottage@aol.com
w smoothhound.co.uk/hotels/barncottage

Hollowell Cottage ★★★★
Bed & Breakfast
West chinnock, Crewkerne
TA18 7PR
t (01935) 881099
e info@hollowellcottage.co.uk
w hollowellcottage.co.uk

CROSS

The Old Manor House ★★★★
Guest Accommodation
SILVER AWARD
Cross Lane, Axbridge
BS26 2ED
t (01934) 733164
e sue@theoldmanorhousebb.co.uk
w theoldmanorhousebb.co.uk

DARSHILL

Mulberry House ★★★★
Bed & Breakfast
Darshill, Shepton Mallet
BA4 5HZ
t (01749) 344598
e hilsac@talktalk.net

DITCHEAT

Longhill Farm Bed & Breakfast
★★★★ Bed & Breakfast
Longhill Farm, Shepton Mallet
BA4 6QR
t (01749) 860189
e info@longhillfarm.co.uk
w longhillfarm.co.uk

163

South West | Somerset

DOULTING

Temple House Farm ★★★★
Farmhouse
Chelynch Rd, Shepton Mallet
BA4 4RQ
t (01749) 880294
e reakesbedbugs@aol.com
w templehousefarm.co.uk

DULVERTON

Ashwick Manor Farm ★★★★
Farmhouse
Ashwick Manor Farm, Dulverton
TA22 9QE
t (01398) 323371
e ashwickmanorfarm@tiscali.co.uk
w ashwickmanorfarm.co.uk

The Copse ★★★★ Bed & Breakfast
Brushford, Dulverton
TA22 9AH
t (01398) 323376
e enquiries@thecopsebrushford.co.uk
w thecopsebrushford.co.uk

Streamcombe Farm ★★★★
Bed & Breakfast SILVER AWARD
Streamcombe Farm, Dulverton
TA22 9SA
t (01398) 323775
e karen@streamcombefarm.co.uk
w streamcombefarm.co.uk

Town Mills ★★★★
Guest Accommodation
SILVER AWARD
High Street, Dulverton
TA22 9HB
t (01398) 323124
e townmillsdulverton@btinternet.com
w townmillsdulverton.co.uk

Winsbere House ★★★★
Bed & Breakfast
64 Battleton, Dulverton
TA22 9HU
t (01398) 323278
e info@winsbere.co.uk
w winsbere.co.uk

DUNSTER

The Dunster Castle Hotel ★★★★
Inn SILVER AWARD
High Street, Minehead
TA24 6SF
t (01643) 823030
e info@thedunstercastlehotel.co.uk
w thedunstercastlehotel.co.uk

Exmoor House Dunster ★★★★
Guest Accommodation
SILVER AWARD
12 West Street, Dunster, Somerset
TA24 6SN
t (01643) 821268
e stay@exmoorhousedunster.co.uk
w exmoorhousedunster.co.uk

Millstream Cottage ★★★★
Bed & Breakfast SILVER AWARD
2 Mill Lane, Dunster, Exmoor National Park
TA24 6SW
t (01643) 821966
e stay@millstreamcottagedunster.co.uk
w millstreamcottagedunster.co.uk

Spears Cross ★★★★★
Guest Accommodation
GOLD AWARD
1 West Street, Dunster
TA24 6SN
t (01643) 821439
e visit@spearscross.demon.co.uk
w spearscross.co.uk

EAST BRENT

Burton Row Farmhouse ★★★★★
Bed & Breakfast SILVER AWARD
Burton Row, East Brent
TA9 4DA
t (01278) 769252
e lindaisgrove@btinternet.com
w somersetbandb.co.uk

EAST CHINNOCK

Barrows Farmhouse ★★★★
Bed & Breakfast
Weston Street, East Chinnock, Yeovil
BA22 9EJ
t (01935) 864576
e barrowsfarmhouse@aol.com
w barrowsfarmhouse.com

Gables Guest House ★★★
Guest House
High Street, East Chinnock, Nr Yeovil
BA22 9DR
t (01935) 862237
e tands.whitehead@btinternet.com
w thegablesyeovil.co.uk

EAST HARPTREE

Harptree Court ★★★★★
Guest Accommodation
GOLD AWARD
Whitecross Road, East Harptree, Bristol
BS40 6AA
t (01761) 221729
e bandb@harptreecourt.co.uk
w harptreecourt.co.uk

EVERCREECH

The Old Dairy Rooms ★★★★
Farmhouse
Rodmoor Farm, Evercreech
BA4 6DW
t (01749) 830531
w olddairyrooms.co.uk

EXFORD

Exford YHA ★★★ Hostel
Exe Mead, Exford
TA24 7PU
t (01643) 831288
e exford@yha.org.uk
w yha.org.uk/find-accommodation/south-west-england/hostels/exford/index.aspx

Exmoor Lodge Guest House ★★★★
Guest House
Chapel Street, Exford
TA24 7PY
t (01643) 831694
e exmoor-lodge@talktalk.net
w exmoor-lodge.co.uk

Newland House ★★★★★
Bed & Breakfast
Newland House, Minehead
TA24 7NF
t (01643) 831199
e info@newlandhouse-exmoor.co.uk
w newlandhouse-exmoor.co.uk

FARRINGTON GURNEY

The Croft Bed & Breakfast ★★★★
Bed & Breakfast
The Croft, Bristol Road, Farrington Gurney, Bristol
BS39 6TJ
t (01761) 453479
w thecroftbandb.com

FELTHAM

Lower Grange Farm ★★★★
Farmhouse
Feltham, Feltham, Frome
BA11 5LL
t (01373) 452938
e bandb@thelowergrangefarm.fsnet.co.uk

FROME

Broadgrove House ★★★★
Bed & Breakfast
Leighton, Frome
BA11 4PP
t (01373) 836396
e broadgrove836@tiscali.co.uk
w broadgrovehouse.co.uk

GLASTONBURY

Apple ★★ Bed & Breakfast
25 Norbins Road, Glastonbury
BA6 9JF
t (01458) 834547
e applebnb@ukonline.co.uk
w apple-glastonbury.co.uk

Chalice Hill House ★★★★
Bed & Breakfast SILVER AWARD
Dod Lane, Glastonbury, Somerset
BA6 8BZ
t (01458) 830828
e mail@chalicehill.co.uk
w chalicehill.co.uk

Cherrywood ★★★★
Bed & Breakfast
11 Rowley Road, Glastonbury
BA6 8HU
t (01458) 833115

Chestnuts Boutique Bed & Breakfast ★★★★ Bed & Breakfast
SILVER AWARD
Bove Town, Glastonbury
BA6 8JG
t (01458) 830562
e jane@glastonburyaccommodation.com
w glastonburyaccommodation.com

Chindit House ★★★★
Bed & Breakfast SILVER AWARD
23 Wells Road, Glastonbury
BA6 9DN
t (01458) 830404
e enquiries@chindit-house.co.uk
w cottagesdirect.co.uk/

Coxwithy House B&B ★★★★
Bed & Breakfast
Coxwithy Lane, Edgarley, Glastonbury
BA6 8LA
t (01458) 833021
e jo@coxwithyhouse.co.uk
w coxwithyhouse.co.uk

Daisy Centre Retreat ★★
Guest Accommodation
6 Church Lane, Glastonbury
BA6 9JQ
t (01458) 834587
e info@daisycentres.com
w daisycentres.com

Divine Light Bed & Breakfast ★★★ Bed & Breakfast
16a Magdalene Street, Glastonbury
BA6 9EH
t (01458) 835909
e glastonburyrose@lineone.net
w divinelightcentre.co.uk

Havyatt Cottage ★★★
Guest Accommodation
2 Havyatt, Havyatt
BA6 8LF
t (01458) 832520
e christinahavyatt@hotmail.co.uk
w havyattcottage.co.uk

Little Orchard ★★★
Guest Accommodation
Ashwell Lane, Glastonbury
BA6 8BG
t (01458) 831620
e the.littleorchard@lineone.net
w littleorchardglastonbury.co.uk

Magdalene House B&B ★★★★
Guest Accommodation
SILVER AWARD
Magdalene Street, Glastonbury
BA6 9EJ
t (01458) 830202
e contact@magdalenehouseglastonbury.com
w magdalenehouseglastonbury.com

Meare Manor ★★★★
Guest Accommodation
60 St Mary's Road, Meare, Nr Glastonbury
BA6 9SR
t (01458) 860449
e reception@mearemanor.com
w mearemanor.com

New House Farm ★★★★
Farmhouse SILVER AWARD
Burtle Road, Glastonbury
BA6 9TT
t (01458) 860238
e bell-bell@btconnect.com
w newhousefarmbandb.co.uk

Pippin Bed & Breakfast ★★★
Bed & Breakfast
4 Ridgeway Gardens, Glastonbury
BA6 8ER
t (01458) 834262
e daphne.slater@talktalk.net
w smoothhound.co.uk/hotels/pippin.html

Tordown B&B & Healing Centre ★★★★ Guest Accommodation
5 Ashwell Lane, Glastonbury
BA6 8BG
t (01458) 832287
e info@tordown.com
w tordown.com

Who'd A Thought It Inn ★★★ Inn
17 Northload Street, Glastonbury
BA6 9JJ
t (01458) 834460
e enquiries@whodathoughtit.co.uk
w whodathoughtit.co.uk

HALSE

Rock House ★★★★
Bed & Breakfast SILVER AWARD
Main Road, Halse
TA4 3AF
t (01823) 432956
e dwolverson@rockhousesomerset.co.uk
w rockhousesomerset.co.uk

HAWKRIDGE

Parsonage Farm Guesthouse ★★★★ Farmhouse
Hawkridge, Dulverton
TA22 9QP
t (01643) 831503
e guests@parsonagefarm.info
w parsonagefarm.info

HENLADE

Barn Close Bed & Breakfast ★★
Guest Accommodation
Stoke Road, Henlade
TA3 5DH
t (01823) 443507
e jujuat66@hotmail.co.uk

HENSTRIDGE

Bridge House ★★
Guest Accommodation
Shaftesbury Road, Templecombe
BA8 0PT
t (01963) 362028
e chrisbrady@hotmail.co.uk

HIGHBRIDGE

Burnt House Farm ★★★
Guest Accommodation
Yarrow Road, Highbridge
TA9 4LR
t (01278) 641280
e carmenburnthouse@yahoo.co.uk
w burnthouse.org

Ilex House ★★★★ Bed & Breakfast
SILVER AWARD
102 Main Road, West Huntspill, Highbridge
TA9 3QZ
t (01278) 783801
e enquiries@ilexhouse.co.uk
w ilexhouse.co.uk

HORSINGTON

Half Moon Inn ★★★ Inn
off Higher Road, Horsington, Nr Templecombe
BA8 0EF
t (01963) 370140
e halfmoon@horsington.co.uk
w horsington.co.uk

South West | Somerset

HUTTON
oorlands Country House ★★★
uest House
Main Road, Hutton, Weston-per-Mare
24 9QH
t (01934) 812283
e margaret-holt@hotmail.co.uk
w smoothhound.co.uk/hotels/moorlandscountrygh.html

ILCHESTER
e Ilchester Arms ★★★★ *Inn*
urch Street, Ilchester, Yeovil
A22 8LN
t (01935) 840220
e mail@ilchesterarms.com
w ilchesterarms.com

ILMINSTER
llington House ★★★★★
mpus
Bay Hill, Ilminster
19 9DT
t (01460) 258648
e ccrocker@somerset.gov.uk
w somerset.gov.uk/personnel/dh/

aden ★★★ Bed & Breakfast
aden, Nr Ilminster
19 0SG
t (01460) 52371

oodleigh Bed & Breakfast
★★★ Bed & Breakfast
Station Road, Ilminster
19 9BD
t (01460) 57267
e woodleigh@yahoo.co.uk
w woodleigh-ilminster.co.uk

LANGPORT
nberley ★★★★
est Accommodation
artock Road, Long Load, Langport
10 9LD
t (01458) 241542
e jean.atamberley@talk21.com
w amberleybandb.co.uk

erry Orchard Cottage ★★★★★
d & Breakfast **GOLD AWARD**
wnsend, Langport
10 0HT
t (01458) 252545
e reservations@cherryorchardcottage.com
w cherryorchardcottage.com

uchelney Ham Farm ★★★★
rmhouse
uchelney Ham, Langport
10 0DL
t (01458) 250737
e muchelneyhamfarm.co.uk

rchard Barn ★★★★
d & Breakfast
w Lane, Langport
10 0LS
t (01458) 252575
e ann@orchard-barn.com
w orchard-barn.com

LANSDOWN
e Blathwayt ★★★★ *Inn*
nsdown, Bath
1 9BT
t (01225) 421995
e info@theblathwayt-bath.co.uk
w theblathwayt-bath.co.uk

LOTTISHAM
wer Farmhouse Bed &
eakfast ★★★★ *Farmhouse*
wer Farm, Lottisham, Glastonbury,
merset
6 8PF
t (01458) 850206
e dboard51@btinternet.com
w lowerfarmbandb.co.uk

LOWER GODNEY
Double-Gate Farm ★★★★
Farmhouse **GOLD AWARD**
Double-Gate Farm, Godney
BA5 1RX
t (01458) 832217
e doublegate@aol.com
w doublegatefarm.com

LOWER RUDGE
The Full Moon ★★★ *Inn*
Rudge Lane, Frome
BA11 2QF
t (01373) 830936
e info@thefullmoon.co.uk
w thefullmoon.co.uk

LYDEARD ST LAWRENCE
Fitzhead Court ★★★
Bed & Breakfast
Fitzhead Court, Taunton
TA4 3JP
t (01823) 400923
e kilpatrick@eclipse.co.uk
w fitzheadcourt.eclipse.co.uk

MARSTON BIGOT
Home Farm House ★★★★
Farmhouse
Marston Bigot, Frome
BA11 5DE
t (01373) 836116
e info@homefarm-house.co.uk
w homefarm-house.co.uk

MARTOCK
The Rockery Bed & Breakfast
Bed & Breakfast
The Rockery, Back Lane, Martock
TA12 6LJ
t (01935) 829566
e nicholasfricker@btinternet.com
w bedandbreakfastattherockery.web247.net

The White Hart ★★★★ *Inn*
East Street, Martock
TA12 6JQ
t (01935) 822005
e enquiries@whitehartholtelmartock.co.uk
w whitehartholtelmartock.co.uk

MIDDLE LAMBROOK
Burnt House Farm ★★★
Bed & Breakfast
Middle Lambrook, South Petherton
TA13 5HE
t (01460) 241779
e caroline@avonbulbs.co.uk
w avonbulbs.co.uk/bed-and-breakfast_98.htm

MINEHEAD
Bethany Guest House ★★★
Guest House
10 Townsend Road, Minehead
TA24 5RG
t (01643) 704289
e info@mineheadguesthouse.co.uk
w mineheadguesthouse.co.uk

Beverleigh ★★★★ *Bed & Breakfast*
Beacon Road, Minehead
TA24 5SE
t (01643) 708450

Buckley Lodge ★★★★
Bed & Breakfast
Bossington, Minehead
TA24 8HQ
t (01643) 862521
e buckloduk@yahoo.co.uk

Dunkery Lodge ★★★★
Guest Accommodation
Townsend Road, Minehead
TA24 5RQ
t (01643) 607160
e stay@dunkery-lodge.co.uk
w dunkery-lodge.co.uk

The Gables ★★★★
Guest Accommodation
Doverhay, Minehead
TA24 8LG
t (01643) 863432
e info@thegablesporlock.co.uk
w thegablesporlock.co.uk

Glendower House ★★★★
Guest House **SILVER AWARD**
30-32 Tregonwell Road, Minehead
TA24 5DU
t (01643) 707144
e info@glendower-house.co.uk
w glendower-house.co.uk

Holnicote House
Guest Accommodation
Selworthy, Minehead
TA24 8TJ
t (01643) 862013

Marston Lodge ★★★★
Guest Accommodation
St Michaels Road, Minehead
TA24 5JP
t (01643) 702510
e marstonlodge@aol.com
w marstonlodgehotel.co.uk

Montrose Guest House ★★★★
Guest House
14 Tregonwell Road, Minehead
TA24 5DU
t (01643) 706473
e montroseminehead@btinternet.com
w montroseminehead.co.uk

Oakfield Guest House ★★★★★
Guest Accommodation
SILVER AWARD
Northfield Road, Minehead
TA24 5QH
t (01643) 704911
e oakfieldminehead@yahoo.com
w oakfieldminehead.co.uk

The Parks ★★★★ *Guest House*
SILVER AWARD
26 The Parks, Minehead
TA24 8BT
t (01643) 703547
e info@parksguesthouse.co.uk
w parksguesthouse.co.uk

Pilgrim Corner ★★★★
Bed & Breakfast
Church Steps, Vicarage Road,
Minehead
TA24 5JT
t (01643) 703236
e pilgrimcorner@hotmail.com

Promenade ★★★★
Guest Accommodation
The Esplanade, Minehead
TA24 5QS
t (01643) 702572
e jgph@globalnet.co.uk

Stockleigh Lodge ★★★★
Guest Accommodation
B3224, Exford, Exmoor, Minehead
TA24 7PZ
t (01643) 831500
e stay@stockleighexford.co.uk
w stockleighexford.co.uk

Sunfield ★★★★
Guest Accommodation
83 Summerland Avenue, Minehead
TA24 5BW
t (01643) 703565
e stay@sunfieldminehead.co.uk
w sunfieldminehead.co.uk

Townsend Farmhouse B&B
★★★★ *Guest Accommodation*
Main Road, Carhampton, Minehead
TA24 6NH
t (01643) 822313
e mgarrity@hotmail.com
w townsendfarmhouse.co.uk

Tranmere House ★★★★
Guest Accommodation
24 Tregonwell Road, Minehead
TA24 5DU
t (01643) 702647
e info@tranmereguesthouse.orangehome.co.uk
w tranmereguesthouse.co.uk

Tregonwell House ★★★
Guest House
1 Tregonwell Road, Minehead
TA24 5DT
t (01643) 709287
e info@tregonwellhouse.co.uk
w tregonwellhouse.co.uk

YHA Minehead ★★★ *Hostel*
Manor Road, Minehead
TA24 6EW
t (01643) 702595
e minehead@yha.org.uk
w yha.org.uk

MONKTON COMBE
Wheelwrights Arms ★★★★ *Inn*
SILVER AWARD
Monkton Combe, Bath
BA2 7HB
t (01225) 722287
e bookings@wheelwrightsarms.co.uk
w wheelwrightsarms.co.uk/

MONTACUTE
Carents House ★★★★
Bed & Breakfast
7A Middle Street, Montacute
TA15 6UZ
t (01935) 824914
e dianasloan@talktalk.net
w carentshouse.co.uk

Montacute Country Tearooms
★★★ *Bed & Breakfast*
1 South Street, Montacute
TA15 6XD
t (01935) 823024
e info@montacutemuseum.co.uk
w montacutemuseum.co.uk/default.aspx?contentid=3

MUCHELNEY
The Parsonage ★★★★★
Guest Accommodation
GOLD AWARD
Silver Street, Muchelney,
Langport,Somerset
TA10 0DL
t 01458 259058
e valerie@parsonagesomerset.co.uk
w parsonagesomerset.co.uk

NETHER STOWEY
Castle of Comfort Country House
★★★★★ *Guest Accommodation*
SILVER AWARD
A39, Dodington
TA5 1LE
t (01278) 741264
e reception@castle-of-comfort.co.uk
w castle-of-comfort.co.uk

The Old Cider House ★★★★
Guest Accommodation
25 Castle Street, Nether Stowey
TA5 1LN
t (01278) 732228
e info@theoldciderhouse.co.uk
w theoldciderhouse.co.uk

The Old House ★★★★
Bed & Breakfast **SILVER AWARD**
St Mary Street, Nether Stowey,
Bridgwater
TA5 1LJ
t (01278) 732392
e scourfieldfam@yahoo.co.uk
w theoldhouse-quantocks.co.uk

South West | Somerset

NORTH CADBURY

Ashlea House ★★★★
Guest Accommodation
SILVER AWARD
High Street, North Cadbury, Wincanton
BA22 7DP
t (01963) 440891
e ashlea@btinternet.com
w ashlea.btinternet.co.uk/

NORTON FITZWARREN

Old Rectory ★★★★
Bed & Breakfast
Rectory Road, Norton Fitzwarren
TA2 6SE
t (01823) 330081
e jw@oldrectorynorton.net
w oldrectorynorton.net

NORTON ST PHILIP

George Inn ★★★★ *Inn*
SILVER AWARD
High Street, Norton St Philip, Bath
BA2 7LH
t (01373) 834224
e info@thegeorgeinn-nsp.co.uk

The Plaine ★★★★
Guest Accommodation
Bell Hill, Norton St Philip, Bath
BA2 7LT
t (01373) 834723
e enquiries@theplaine.co.uk
w theplaine.com

NORTON SUB HAMDON

Bagnell Cottage ★★★★
Bed & Breakfast
Bagnell Cottage, Little Norton, Norton sub Hamdon
TA14 6TF
t (01935) 862802
e eileenbagnellcottage@btinternet.com
w bagnellcottage.com

OLD CLEEVE

Cedar House ★★★★
Guest Accommodation
SILVER AWARD
Minehead
TA24 6HH
t (01984) 640437
e millship@btinternet.com
w cedarhousesomerset.co.uk

OVER STRATTON

New Farm Restaurant ★★★★
Guest Accommodation
New Farm, Over Stratton, South Petherton
TA13 5LQ
t (01460) 240584
e dine@newfarmrestaurant.co.uk

PANBOROUGH

Garden End Farm ★★★ *Farmhouse*
Wells Road, Panborough
BA5 1PN
t (01934) 712414
e sheila@gardenendfarm.freeserve.co.uk
w gardenendfarm.freeserve.co.uk

PEDWELL

Polden Vale ★★★★
Bed & Breakfast
20 Taunton Road, Pedwell
TA7 9BG
t (01458) 211114
e paul.malabar@onetel.net

PENDOMER

Pendomer House ★★★
Bed & Breakfast
Pendomer House, Pendomer, Yeovil, Somerset BA22 9PB
BA22 9PB
t (01935) 862785
e enquiries@pendomerhouse.co.uk
w pendomerhouse.co.uk

PENSFORD

Greenacres ★★
Guest Accommodation
Stanton Wick, Bristol
BS39 4BX
t (01761) 490397

PILTON

Bowermead House ★★★★★
Bed & Breakfast **SILVER AWARD**
Whitstone Hill, Pilton
BA4 4DT
t (01749) 890744
e w.southcombe@btopenworld.com
w bowermeadhouse.co.uk

PORLOCK

Exmoor House ★★★★★
Guest Accommodation
SILVER AWARD
Minehead Road, Porlock
TA24 8EY
t (01643) 863599
e ann@exmoor-house.co.uk
w exmoor-house.co.uk

Glen Lodge ★★★★
Guest Accommodation
SILVER AWARD
Hawkcombe, Porlock
TA24 8LN
t (01643) 863371
e glenlodge@gmail.com
w glenlodge.net

Myrtle Cottage ★★★
Bed & Breakfast
High Street, Porlock
TA24 8PU
t (01643) 862978
e bob.steer@virgin.net
w myrtleporlock.co.uk

Rose Bank Guest House ★★★★
Guest House **SILVER AWARD**
High Street, Porlock
TA24 8PY
t (01643) 862728
e info@rosebankguesthouse.co.uk
w rosebankguesthouse.co.uk

Sea View ★★★★ *Bed & Breakfast*
High Bank, Porlock
TA24 8NP
t (01643) 863456
e seaview.porlock@btconnect.com
w seaviewporlock.co.uk

RADSTOCK

The Post House *Bed & Breakfast*
Bathway, Chewton Mendip, Radstock
BA3 4NS
t (01761) 241704
e info@theposthouseandb.co.uk
w theposthouseandb.co.uk

REDHILL

Hailstones Farm ★★★★
Farmhouse
Hailstones Farm, Redhill, Bristol
BS40 5TG
t (01934) 861178
e info@hailstonesfarmbandb.co.uk

SAMPFORD ARUNDEL

Selby House ★★★★
Bed & Breakfast **SILVER AWARD**
Sampford Arundel, Wellington
TA21 9QE
t (01823) 667384
e enquiries@selbyhouse.co.uk
w selbyhouse.co.uk

SHEPTON MALLET

At Higher Farm
Guest Accommodation
Higher Farm, Gunnings Lane, Upton Noble, Shepton Mallet
BA4 6AR
t (01749) 850131

Belfield House ★★★
Guest Accommodation
34 Charlton Road, Shepton Mallet
BA4 5PA
t (01749) 344353
e info@belfieldhouse.com
w belfieldhouse.com

The Dusthole ★★ *Inn*
The Kings Arms-The Dusthole, Garston Street, Shepton Mallet
BA4 5LN
t (01749) 343781
e aanthony622@aol.co.uk
w thedusthole.co.uk

Maplestone ★★★★
Guest Accommodation
Quarr, Shepton Mallet
BA4 5NP
t (01749) 347979
e info@maplestonehall.co.uk
w maplestonehall.co.uk

Middleton House ★★★★
Guest Accommodation
68 Compton Road, Shepton Mallet
BA4 5QT
t (01749) 343720
e lynandbob@shepton.freeserve.co.uk

Primrose Hill B&B ★★★★
Guest Accommodation
Knowle Farm Bungalow, Shepton Mallet
BA4 4PD
t (01749) 899279
e mail@primrosehillbb.co.uk
w primrosehillbb.co.uk

SIMONSBATH

Emmetts Grange ★★★★
Guest Accommodation
Simonsbath, Simonsbath
TA24 7LD
t (01643) 831138
e mail@emmettsgrange.co.uk
w emmettsgrange.co.uk

Exmoor Forest Inn ★★★★ *Inn*
Simonsbath, Simonsbath
TA24 7SH
t (01643) 831341
e info@exmoorforestinn.co.uk
w exmoorforestinn.co.uk

SOMERTON

Lower Farm ★★★★ *Farmhouse*
SILVER AWARD
High Street, Somerton
TA11 6BA
t (01458) 223237
e lowerfarm@btconnect.com
w lowerfarm.net

Mill House ★★★★★
Bed & Breakfast **SILVER AWARD**
Mill Road, Somerton
TA11 6DF
t (01458) 851215
e b&b@millhousebarton.co.uk
w millhousebarton.co.uk

SOUTH PETHERTON

Rock House B&B ★★★★
Guest Accommodation
5, Palmer Street, South Petherton, Somerset
TA13 5DB
t (01460) 240324
e enquiries@unwindatrockhouse.co.uk
w unwindatrockhouse.co.uk

STANTON DREW

Valley Farm ★★★★
Bed & Breakfast
Sandy Lane, Stanton Drew, Bristol
BS39 4EL
t (01275) 332723
e valleyfarm2000@tiscali.co.uk
w smoothhound.com

STAPLEY

Thatched Country Cottage & Garden B&B ★★★ *Bed & Breakfast*
Pear Tree Cottage, Taunton
TA3 7QA
t (01823) 601224
e colvin.parry@virgin.net
w smoothhound.co.uk/hotels/thatch.html

STOGUMBER

The White Horse Inn ★★★ *Inn*
High Street, Stogumber
TA4 3TA
t (01984) 656277
e info@whitehorsestogumber.co.uk
w whitehorsestogumber.co.uk

Wick House ★★★★ *Guest House*
2 Brook Street, Stogumber, Taunton
Somerset
TA4 3SZ
t (01984) 656422
e sheila@wickhouse.co.uk
w wickhouse.co.uk

STOKE-SUB-HAMDON

Castle Farm ★★★★ *Farmhouse*
North Street, Stoke-sub-Hamdon
TA14 6QS
t (01935) 822231
e karen@castlefarmaccomodation.com
w castlefarmaccomodation.com

STOKE ST GREGORY

Rose & Crown ★★★ *Inn*
Woodhill, Stoke St Gregory, Taunton
TA3 6EW
t (01823) 490296
e info@browningpubs.com
w browningpubs.com

STONEY STRATTON

Stratton Farm ★★★★ *Farmhouse*
High Street, Shepton Mallet
BA4 6DY
t (01749) 830830
w strattonfarm.co.uk

STRATTON-ON-THE-FOSSE

Oval House ★★ *Bed & Breakfast*
Fosse Road, Stratton-on-the-Fosse
BA3 4RB
t (01761) 232183
e mellotte@metronet.co.uk
w mellotte.clara.co.uk

STREET

Marshalls Elm Farm ★★★
Farmhouse
B3151, Street
BA16 0TZ
t (01458) 442878

Old Orchard House ★★★★
Bed & Breakfast **SILVER AWARD**
Middle Brooks, Street
BA16 0TU
t (01458) 442212
e old.orchard.house@amserve.com
w oldorchardhouse.co.uk

Rickham House ★★★★ *Farmhouse*
Compton Dundon, Street
TA11 6QA
t (01458) 445056
e rickham.house@btconnect.com
w rickhamhouse.co.uk

Street YHA ★ *Hostel*
The Chalet, Ivythorn Hill, Street
BA16 0TZ
t 0870 770 6056
e street@yha.org.uk
w yha.org.uk

TAUNTON

Acorn Lodge ★★★
Guest Accommodation
22 Wellington Road, Taunton
TA1 4EQ
t (01823) 337613

South West | Somerset

artletts Farm ★★★★ *Farmhouse*
e Brewers, Taunton
A3 6QN
t (01460) 281423
e sandjpeach@tesco.net
w bartletts-farm.co.uk/

anonsgrove Farm ★★★
armhouse
ull, Taunton
A3 7PD
t (01823) 279720
e c.ralph57@btinternet.com
w canonsgrovefarm.co.uk

auseway Cottage ★★★★
ed & Breakfast
arbers Lane, West Buckland
A21 9JZ
t (01823) 663458
e causewaybb@talktalk.net
w causewaycottage.co.uk

ulford Grange ★★★★★
ed & Breakfast **GOLD AWARD**
ngston St Mary, Taunton
A2 8AJ
t (01823) 451206
e enquiries@fulfordgrange.co.uk
w fulfordgrange.co.uk

eathercroft ★★★ *Guest House*
8 Wellington Road, Taunton
A1 5LA
t (01823) 275516
e info@heathercroft-guesthouse.co.uk
w heathercroft-guesthouse.co.uk

ndale Bed & Breakfast ★★★★
ed & Breakfast
Mount Street, Taunton
A1 3QE
t (01823) 257204
e rudramvet@tiscali.co.uk
w lyndalebandb.com

yngford House ★★★★
uest Accommodation
elworthy Road, Taunton
A2 8HD
t (01823) 284649
e reservations@lyngford-house.nhs.uk
w lyngford-house.co.uk

eare Green Farm ★★★★
armhouse
eare Green, Stoke St Gregory,
aunton
A3 6HT
t (01823) 490759
e jane.pine2@btinternet.com
w mearegreenfarm.com

e Mount ★★★★ *Bed & Breakfast*
Mount Street, Taunton
A4 3AN
t (01823) 431897
e b+bthemount@talktalk.net
w themount-accommodation.co.uk

yrland Farm ★★★★ *Farmhouse*
heddon Road, Taunton
A2 7QX
t (01823) 334148
e contactus@pyrlandfarm.co.uk
w pyrlandfarm.co.uk

oringfield House ★★★★
uest Accommodation
alford Cross, Taunton
A2 8QW
t (01823) 412116
e tina.ridout@btopenworld.com
w springfieldhse.co.uk

taplegrove Lodge ★★★★
ed & Breakfast **SILVER AWARD**
aplegrove, Taunton
A2 6PX
t (01823) 331115
e staplegrovelodge@onetel.com
w staplegrovelodge.co.uk

Yallands Farmhouse ★★★★
Guest Accommodation
SILVER AWARD
Staplegrove, Taunton
TA2 6PZ
t (01823) 278979
e mail@yallands.co.uk
w yallands.co.uk

TICKENHAM

Elm Tree Cottage ★★★★
Guest Accommodation
Jacklands Bridge, Tickenham
BS21 6SQ
t (01275) 866484
e info@aspecialplacetostay.co.uk
w aspecialplacetostay.co.uk

TIMSBURY

Pitfour House ★★★★★
Guest Accommodation
SILVER AWARD
High Street, Timsbury, Bath
BA2 0HT
t (01761) 479554
e pitfourhouse@btinternet.com

TRUDOXHILL

Trudox Mead Country B&B ★★★
Bed & Breakfast
Foghamshire Lane, Trudoxhill
BA11 5DR
t (01373) 836387
e careWprices@greenbee.net
w trudoxmead.co.uk

TYTHERINGTON

Lighthouse Guest House ★★★★
Guest Accommodation
Tytherington, Frome
BA11 5BW
t (01373) 453585
e contact@lighthouse-uk.com
w lighthouse-uk.com

UPTON NOBLE

Crosselm ★★★★ *Farmhouse*
Crosselm, Shepton Mallet
BA4 6AX
t (01749) 850201

WADEFORD

The Haymaker Inn ★★★★ *Inn*
Main Road, Chard
TA20 3AP
t (01460) 64161
e stevetingle11@hotmail.com

WASHFORD

Monkscider House ★★★★
Guest Accommodation
SILVER AWARD
Main Road, Washford
TA23 0NS
t (01984) 641055
e david@netgates.co.uk
w monksciderhouse.com

WATCHET

Raleghs Cross Inn ★★★★ *Inn*
Brendon Hill, Watchet
TA23 0LN
t (01984) 640343
e info@raleghscross.co.uk
w raleghscross.co.uk

WELLINGTON

Backways Farmhouse ★★★★
Bed & Breakfast
Backways Farmhouse, Wellington
TA21 9RN
t (01823) 660712
e info@backways.co.uk
w backways.co.uk

Greenham Hall ★★★★
Bed & Breakfast
Greenham, Wellington
TA21 0JJ
t (01823) 672603
e greenhamhall@btopenworld.com
w greenhamhall.co.uk

Mantle B&B ★★★ *Bed & Breakfast*
34 Mantle Street, Wellington
TA21 8AR
t (01823) 668514
e dalsod@aol.com
w mantlecottage.com

Old Vicarage ★★★★
Bed & Breakfast
8 Exeter Road, Rockwell Green,
Wellington, Somerset
TA21 9DH
t (01823) 661376 or
  0797 1243 026
e sarah@theoldvicarage-rockwellgreen.co.uk
w theoldvicarage-rockwellgreen.co.uk

WELLS

26 Glastonbury Road ★★★
Bed & Breakfast
Wells
BA5 1TH
t (01749) 675620 or 07759 348342

Ashford House ★★★★
Guest Accommodation
SILVER AWARD
109 Portway, Wells
BA5 2BR
t (01749) 673087
e info@ashfordhousewells.co.uk
w ashfordhousewells.co.uk

Baytree House ★★★★
Guest Accommodation
85 Portway, Wells
BA5 2BJ
t (01749) 677933
e stay@baytree-house.co.uk
w baytree-house.co.uk

Beryl ★★★★★
Guest Accommodation
off Hawkers Lane, Wells
BA5 3JP
t (01749) 678738
e stay@beryl-wells.co.uk
w beryl-wells.co.uk

Cadgwith House ★★★★
Bed & Breakfast
Hawkers Lane, Wells
BA5 3JH
t (01749) 677799
e cadgwith.house@yahoo.co.uk
w cadgwithhouse.co.uk

Canon Grange ★★★★
Guest Accommodation
Cathedral Green, Wells
BA5 2UB
t (01749) 671800
e canongrange@email.com
w canongrange.co.uk

The Crown at Wells & Anton's Bistrot ★★★★ *Inn*
Market Place, Wells
BA5 2RP
t (01749) 673457
e stay@crownatwells.co.uk
w crownatwells.co.uk

Dapa House ★★★★
Bed & Breakfast
62 Bath Road, Wells
BA5 3LQ
t (01749) 689248
e enquiries@dapahouse.co.uk
w dapahouse.co.uk

Islington Farm ★★★★
Bed & Breakfast
next to The Bishop's Palace, Silver Street, Wells
BA5 1US
t (01749) 673445
e islingtonfarm2004@yahoo.co.uk
w islingtonfarmatwells.co.uk

Mary Road ★★★
Guest Accommodation
30 Mary Road, Wells
BA5 2NF
t (01749) 674031
e triciabailey30@hotmail.com

Mendip House ★★★
Guest Accommodation
46 Portway, Wells
BA5 2BN
t (01749) 679719
e info@mendiphousewells.co.uk
w mendiphousewells.co.uk

No 23 ★★★★ *Bed & Breakfast*
Glastonbury Road, Wells
BA5 1TW
t (01749) 677648
e info@bedandbreakfastinwells.co.uk
w bedandbreakfastinwells.co.uk

Paradise House ★★★
Bed & Breakfast
Long Street, Croscombe, Wells
BA5 3QH
t (01749) 343502
e paradisehouse@talktalk.net
w paradisecroscombe.co.uk

WEST LYDFORD

Fosse House Farm ★★★★
Guest Accommodation
A37, Somerton
TA11 7DW
t (01963) 240268
e stay@fossehousefarm.co.uk
w fossehousefarm.co.uk

WESTON

Weston Lawn ★★★★
Guest Accommodation
Lucklands Road, Weston
BA1 4AY
t (01225) 421362
e reservations@westonlawn.co.uk
w westonlawn.co.uk

WESTON-SUPER-MARE

9 The Park ★★★★★
Bed & Breakfast **SILVER AWARD**
Ellenborough Park Road, Weston-super-Mare
BS23 1XJ
t (01934) 415244
e info@9theparkbandb.co.uk
w 9theparkbandb.co.uk

Albany Lodge Guest House ★★★
Guest House
9 Clevedon Road, Weston-super-Mare
BS23 1DA
t (01934) 629936
e d.longdon123@btinternet.com
w albanylodgeguesthouse.co.uk

Cornerways ★★★ *Bed & Breakfast*
14 Whitecross Road, Weston-super-Mare
BS23 1EW
t (01934) 623708
e cornerwaysgh@aol.com
w cornerwaysweston.com

Flora Glen Guest House ★★★
Guest House
130 Locking Road, Weston-super-Mare
BS23 3HF
t (01934) 620592
e info@floraglenguesthouse.com
w floraglenguesthouse.com

Grove Lodge ★★★ *Guest House*
1 Bristol Road Lower, Weston-super-Mare
BS23 2PL
t (01934) 620494
e thegrovelodge@aol.com
w grovelodge.info

Harmony Poynt ★★★★
Guest Accommodation
4 Park Place, Weston-super-Mare
BS23 2BA
t (01934) 620258
e enquiries@harmonypoynthotel.co.uk
w harmonypoynt.co.uk/

167

South West | Somerset/Wiltshire

Lewinsdale Lodge ★★★
Guest House
5-7 Clevedon Road, Weston-super-Mare
BS23 1DA
t (01934) 632501
e info@lewinsdalelodge.co.uk
w lewinsdale-hotel.co.uk

Locking Head Farm ★★★★
Farmhouse
Locking Head Drove, Locking, Weston-super-Mare
BS24 7NA
t (01934) 820511
e lockingheadfarm@btinternet.com
w lockingheadfarm.co.uk

Milton Lodge Guest House ★★★★ *Guest House*
15 Milton Road, Weston-super-Mare, Somerset
BS23 2SH
t 01934 623161
e info@milton-lodge.co.uk
w milton-lodge.co.uk

Orchard House ★★★★★
Bed & Breakfast **SILVER AWARD**
Summer Lane, West Wick, Weston-super-Mare
BS24 7TF
t (01934) 520948
e orchardhousewsm@yahoo.com

Richmond ★★★
Guest Accommodation
14 Park Place, Weston-super-Mare
BS23 2BA
t (01934) 644722
e info@richmond-hotel.co.uk
w richmond-hotel.co.uk

Rosita ★★★ *Guest Accommodation*
30 Upper Church Road, Weston-super-Mare
BS23 2DX
t (01934) 620823

Saxonia Guest House ★★★
Guest House
95 Locking Road, Weston-super-Mare
BS23 3EW
t (01934) 424850
e stay@saxoniaguesthouse.com
w saxoniaguesthouse.co.uk

Soraya ★★ *Guest House*
34 Upper Church Road, Weston-super-Mare
BS23 2DX
t (01934) 629043
e ivor.skidmore@sky.com

Spreyton Guest House ★★★
Guest House
72 Locking Road, Weston-super-Mare
BS23 3EN
t (01934) 416887
e info@spreytonguesthouse.com
w spreytonguesthouse.com

Welbeck ★★ *Guest Accommodation*
Knightsone Road, Marine Parade, Weston-super-Mare
BS23 2BB
t (01934) 621258
e welbeckhotel@aol.com
w weston-welbeck.com

WHEDDON CROSS

Exmoor House ★★★★
Guest Accommodation
SILVER AWARD
Wheddon Cross
TA24 7DU
t (01643) 841432
e info@exmoorhouse.com
w exmoorhouse.com

Little Brendon Hill Farm ★★★★★
Guest Accommodation
SILVER AWARD
Summerway, Wheddon Cross
TA24 7BG
t (01643) 841556
e info@exmoorheaven.co.uk
w exmoorheaven.co.uk

Sundial House ★★★★
Guest Accommodation
SILVER AWARD
Sundial House, Wheddon Cross
TA24 7DP
t (01643) 841188
e info@sundialhouse.co.uk
w exmoor-bed-breakfast.co.uk

WILLITON

Arden Cottage ★★★★
Bed & Breakfast **SILVER AWARD**
33 Long Street, Williton, Somerset
TA4 4QU
t 01984 634090
e enquiries@ardencottagewilliton.co.uk
w ardencottagewilliton.co.uk

Hartnells B&B ★★★★
Bed & Breakfast
28 Long Street, Williton
TA4 4QU
t (01984) 634777
e stay@hartnellsbandb.co.uk
w hartnellsbandb.co.uk

Stilegate Bed & Breakfast
★★★★★ *Guest Accommodation*
SILVER AWARD
Staple Close, Williton
TA4 4DN
t (01984) 639119
e stilegate@aol.com
w stilegate.co.uk

Woodford House ★★★★
Guest Accommodation
Woodford, Williton
TA4 4HR
t (01984) 641621
e anna@woodfordhouse.com
w woodfordhouse.com

WINSHAM

Fulwood House ★★★★
Bed & Breakfast
Ebben Lane, Chard
TA20 4QU
t (01460) 30163
e liz.earl@virgin.net
w fulwoodhouse.co.uk

WITHAM FRIARY

Higher West Barn Farm ★★★★
Farmhouse **SILVER AWARD**
Bindon Lane, Frome
BA11 5HH
t (01749) 850819
e enquiry@higherwestbarnfarm.co.uk
w higherwestbarnfarm.co.uk

WIVELISCOMBE

North Down Farm ★★★★
Farmhouse **SILVER AWARD**
Pyncombe Lane, Wiveliscombe
TA4 2BL
t (01984) 623730
e jennycope@btinternet.com
w north-down-farm.co.uk

WOOTTON COURTENAY

Dunkery Beacon Country House Accommodation ★★★★
Guest House
Dunkery Beacon, Wootton Courtenay
TA24 8RH
t (01643) 841241
e info@dunkerybeaconaccommodation.co.uk
w dunkerybeaconaccommodation.co.uk

WRAXALL

Roses Farm ★★★★ *Farmhouse*
Wraxall, Shepton Mallet
BA4 6RQ
t (01749) 860261
e info@rosesfarm.com
w rosesfarm.com

YEOVIL

Courtry Farm ★★★ *Farmhouse*
Yeovil
BA22 8HF
t (01935) 840327
e courtryfarm@hotmail.com

Dairy Court ★★★★
Bed & Breakfast
Dairy Court, Yeovil
BA22 7PA
t (01935) 850003
e enquiries@dairycourt.com
w dairycourt.com

Greystones Court ★★★★
Guest Accommodation
152 Hendford Hill, Yeovil
BA20 2RG
t (01935) 426124
e peterandsimone.adlam@btopenworld.com
w greystonescourt.com

Hawk House ★★★★
Guest Accommodation
Camel Cross, West Camel, Yeovil
BA22 7RA
t (01935) 851804
e mail@hawk-house.co.uk
w hawk-house.co.uk

Number 29 B&B ★★★★
Bed & Breakfast
29 The Park, Yeovil
BA20 1DG
t (01935) 420046
e info@number29.biz
w number29.biz

Wiltshire
ALDERTON

Arland House ★★★★
Guest Accommodation
The Street, Alderton, Chippenham, Wiltshire
SN14 6NL
t (01666) 840439
e arlandhouse@hotmail.com
w arlandhouse.co.uk

AMESBURY

Anchorage Bed and Breakfast
★★★★★ *Bed & Breakfast*
GOLD AWARD
21 Salisbury Road, Amesbury, Salisbury, SP4 7HH
SP4 7HH
t (01980) 555029
e sheryll@hotmail.co.uk
w theanchorageamesbury.co.uk

The Dovecot ★★★★★
Bed & Breakfast **GOLD AWARD**
Watergate Lane, Bulford, Amesbury
SP4 9DY
t (01980) 632625
e bandb@thedovecot.com
w thedovecot.com

Fairlawn House ★★★★
Guest House
42 High Street, Amesbury, Salisbury
SP4 7DL
t (01980) 622103
e fairlawnhotel@hotmail.com
w fairlawnhouse.co.uk

The George Hotel ★★★ *Inn*
High Street, Amesbury, Salisbury
SP4 7ET
t (01980) 622108

ASHTON KEYNES

Wheatleys Farm ★★★★
Farmhouse **SILVER AWARD**
High Road, Ashton Keynes, Swindon
SN6 6NX
t (01285) 861310
e gill@wheatleysfarm.co.uk
w wheatleysfarm.co.uk

AVEBURY

Manor Farm ★★★★
Bed & Breakfast
High Street, Avebury
SN8 1RF
t (01672) 539294
w manorfarmavebury.com

BOTTLESFORD

The Seven Stars Inn ★★★ *Inn*
Bottlesford, Pewsey
SN9 6LW
t (01672) 851325
e info@thesevenstars.co.uk
w thesevenstars.co.uk

BOWOOD

Queenwood Lodge ★★★★★
Guest Accommodation
GOLD AWARD
Bowood Hotel, Spa & Golf Resort, Derry Hill, Calne
SN11 9PQ
t (01249) 822228
e queenwood@bowood.org
w bowood.org

BOX

Lorne House ★★★★
Guest Accommodation
SILVER AWARD
London Road, Box, Corsham
SN13 8NA
t (01225) 742597
e info@lornehousebox.co.uk
w lornehousebox.co.uk

Saltbox Farm ★★★★ *Farmhouse*
Box
SN13 8PT
t (01225) 742608
e bbsaltboxfarm@yahoo.co.uk
w saltboxfarm.verypretty.co.uk

BRADFORD-ON-AVON

Beeches Farmhouse Bed & Breakfast ★★★★ *Farmhouse*
Holt Road, Bradford-on-Avon
BA15 1TS
t (01225) 865170
e beeches-farmhouse@netgates.co.uk
w beeches-farmhouse.co.uk/farmhouse.htm

Clifton House ★★★★★
Guest Accommodation
GOLD AWARD
Bath Road, Bradford-on-Avon
BA15 1SL
t (01225) 309399
e info@cliftonhouse-boa.co.uk
w cliftonhouse-boa.co.uk

Elbury House Bed & Breakfast
★★★★ *Bed & Breakfast*
Leigh Road, Bradford-on-Avon
BA15 2RD
t (01225) 863336
e joy@elburyhouse.co.uk
w elburyhouse.co.uk

The Georgian Lodge ★★
Guest Accommodation
25 Bridge Street, Bradford-on-Avon
BA15 1BY
t (01225) 862268
e georgianlodge@btconnect.com
w georgianlodgehotel.com

Great Ashley Farm ★★★★
Bed & Breakfast **SILVER AWARD**
Great Ashley, Bradford-on-Avon
BA15 2PP
t (01225) 8645630
e info@greatashley.co.uk
w greatashley.co.uk

South West | Wiltshire

Springfields ★★★★
Guest Accommodation
Great Ashley, Bradford-on-Avon
BA15 2PP
t (01225) 866125
e springfieldsbnb@talktalk.net
w springfieldsbnb.co.uk

Stillmeadow ★★★★★
Bed & Breakfast
3 Bradford Road, Bradford-on-Avon
BA15 2HW
t (01225) 722119
e sue.gilby@btinternet.com
w stillmeadow.co.uk

BRITFORD

Bridge Farm ★★★★ Farmhouse
SILVER AWARD
Lower Road, Britford, Salisbury
SP5 4DY
t (01722) 332376
e mail@bridgefarmbb.co.uk
w bridgefarmbb.co.uk

BROAD CHALKE

Lodge Farmhouse Bed & Breakfast ★★★★ Bed & Breakfast
Lodge Farmhouse, Broad Chalke, Salisbury
SP5 5LU
t (01725) 519242
e mj.roe@virgin.net
w lodge-farmhouse.co.uk

Old Stoke B&B ★★★★
Bed & Breakfast
Stoke Farthing, Broad Chalke, Salisbury
SP5 5ED
t (01722) 780513
e stay@oldstoke.co.uk
w oldstoke.co.uk

BROUGHTON GIFFORD

Honeysuckle Cottage ★★★★
Bed & Breakfast SILVER AWARD
5 The Common, Broughton Gifford, Melksham
SN12 8ND
t (01225) 782463
e info@honeysuckle-cottage.org.uk
w honeysuckle-cottage.org.uk

CHIPPENHAM

Arch House ★★★★
Bed & Breakfast
Manor Close, Kington St Michael, Chippenham
SN14 6JA
t (01249) 758377
e christinejago@btinternet.com
w archhousebandb.co.uk

Barnbridge ★★ Bed & Breakfast
East Tytherton, Chippenham
SN15 4LT
t (01249) 740280
e bgiffard@aol.com
w barnbridge.co.uk

Beanhill Farm ★★★ Farmhouse
Main Road, Christian Malford, Chippenham
SN15 4BS
t 07775 660000
e bandb@beanhillfarm.orangehome.co.uk
w beanhillfarm.co.uk

Damson Cottage ★★
Bed & Breakfast
Greybridge, Lacock, Chippenham
SN15 2PF
t (01249) 730274
e dillycampbell@hotmail.com
w damsoncottage.2day.ws

Glebe House ★★★★
Bed & Breakfast SILVER AWARD
Chittoe, Chippenham
SN15 2EL
t (01380) 850864
e gscrope@aol.com
w glebehouse-chittoe.co.uk

King John's Hunting Lodge
★★★★ Bed & Breakfast
SILVER AWARD
21 Church Street, Lacock, Chippenham
SN15 2LB
t (01249) 730313
e info@kingjohns.co.uk
w kingjohns.2day.ws

Lacock Pottery Bed & Breakfast
★★★★ Bed & Breakfast
1 The Tanyard, Church Street, Chippenham
SN15 2LB
t (01249) 730266
e simone@lacockbedandbreakfast.com
w lacockbedandbreakfast.com

Lanhill Stables ★★★★
Bed & Breakfast SILVER AWARD
Lanhill, Chippenham
SN14 6LY
t (01249) 661344
e info@lanhillstablesbedandbreakfast.co.uk
w lanhillstablesbedandbreakfast.co.uk

Lovett Farm ★★★★ Farmhouse
Little Somerford, Chippenham
SN15 5BP
t (01666) 823268
e sue@lovettfarm.co.uk
w lovettfarm.co.uk

Lower Lodge ★★★ Bed & Breakfast
35 Bowden Hill, Chippenham
SN15 2PP
t (01249) 730711
e duboulaylowerlodge@hotmail.co.uk
w lowerlodge.2day.ws

Manor Farm ★★★ Farmhouse
Slaughterford, Chippenham
SN14 8RE
t (01249) 782243
e janmanorfm@hotmail.co.uk

Manor Farm Grittleton ★★
Farmhouse
Alderton Road, Grittleton, Chippenham
SN14 6AN
t (01249) 782403
e bruntbrothers@btconnect.com

The Moors ★★ Bed & Breakfast
Malmesbury Road, Kington Langley, Chippenham
SN14 6HT
t (01249) 750288
e carolinetayler@hotmail.com

New Road Guest House ★★★
Guest House
31 New Road, Chippenham
SN15 1HP
t (01249) 657259
e mail@newroadguesthouse.co.uk
w newroadguesthouse.co.uk

Number 35 B&B ★★★★
Bed & Breakfast
35 Marshfield Road, Chippenham
SN15 1JT
t (01249) 660691
e jenny@numberthirtyfive.co.uk
w numberthirtyfive.co.uk

The Old Rectory ★★★★
Guest Accommodation
Cantax Hill, Lacock, Chippenham
SN15 2JZ
t (01249) 730335
e sexton.oldrectorylacock.co.uk
w oldrectorylacock.co.uk

Red Box Guest House ★★
Bed & Breakfast
35 Buckingham Road, Pewsham, Chippenham
SN15 3TE
t (01249) 444988
e julieann@redboxguesthouse.co.uk
w redboxguesthouse.co.uk

Red Lion ★★★★ Inn
SILVER AWARD
1 High Street, Lacock, Chippenham
SN15 2LQ
t (01249) 730456
e redlionlacock@wadworth.co.uk

Serendipity Bed & Breakfast
★★★★ Bed & Breakfast
15 The Street, Hullavington, Chippenham
SN14 6EF
t (01666) 837661
e alison.reed@serendipitybedandbreakfast.co.uk

Thorngrove Cottage ★★★★
Bed & Breakfast
Summer Lane, Castle Combe, Chippenham
SN14 7NG
t (01249) 782607
e chrisdalene@btinternet.com

CHOLDERTON

Cholderton Stonehenge Youth Hostel ★★★★ Hostel
Cholderton Charlie's Farm, Amesbury Road, Cholderton, Wiltshire
SP4 0EW
t (01980) 629438
e choldertonstonehenge@yha.org.uk
w choldertoncharliesfarm.com

Parkhouse Motel ★★★★
Guest Accommodation
Cholderton, Salisbury
SP4 0EG
t (01980) 629256
e info@parkhousemotel.com

CODFORD

Glebe Cottage ★★★★
Bed & Breakfast
Church Lane, Codford, Warminster
BA12 0PJ
t (01985) 850565
e bob.ra@woolrych.net
w glebecottagecodford.co.uk

COLERNE

Trimnells House ★★★★
Guest Accommodation
Trimnells, Bath
SN14 8EP
t (01225) 742239
e stay@trimnellshouse.com
w trimnellshouse.com

COLLINGBOURNE KINGSTON

Manor Farm B&B ★★★★
Farmhouse
Collingbourne Kingston, Nr Marlborough
SN8 3SD
t (01264) 850859
e stay@manorfm.com
w manorfm.com

CORSHAM

Guyers House ★★★★
Guest Accommodation
Pickwick, Corsham
SN13 0PS
t (01249) 713399
e enquiries@guyershouse.com
w guyershouse.com

Hatt Farm Bed & Breakfast
★★★★ Farmhouse
Hatt Farm, Old Jockey, Corsham
SN13 8DJ
t (01225) 742989
e bb@hattfarm.co.uk
w hattfarm.co.uk

The Hollies ★★★★
Guest Accommodation
6 Bradford Road, Corsham
SN13 0QR
t (01249) 716498
e enquiries@holliesbandb.co.uk
w holliesbandb.co.uk

Mead Lodge B&B ★★★★
Bed & Breakfast SILVER AWARD
21 Ludmead Road, Corsham, Wiltshire
SN13 9AS
t (01249) 715091
e info@meadlodge.com
w meadlodge.com

Norbin Farm ★★★★ Farmhouse
Norbin, Box, Corsham
SN13 8JJ
t (01225) 866907
e gillhillier@yahoo.co.uk
w norbin-farm.co.uk

Park Farm Barn ★★★★ Farmhouse
SILVER AWARD
Westrop, Corsham
SN13 9QF
t (01249) 715911
e parkfarmbarn@btinternet.com
w parkfarmbarn.co.uk

Pickwick Lodge Farm ★★★★
Farmhouse SILVER AWARD
Guyers Lane, Corsham
SN13 0PS
t (01249) 712207
e bandb@pickwickfarm.co.uk
w pickwickfarm.co.uk

CRICKLADE

The Red Lion ★★★★
Guest Accommodation
74 High Street, Cricklade
SN6 6DD
t (01793) 750776
e info@theredlioncricklade.co.uk
w theredlioncricklade.co.uk

DEVIZES

Asta B&B ★★ Bed & Breakfast
66 Downlands Road, Devizes
SN10 5EF
t (01380) 722546
e astabedandbreakfast@tiscali.co.uk

The Bell Inn ★★★★ Inn
57 High Street, Great Cheverell, Devizes
SN10 5TH
t (01380) 813277
e gary06weston@aol.com
w thebellgreatcheverell.co.uk

Bramley House ★★★★
Bed & Breakfast SILVER AWARD
5 The Breach, Devizes
SN10 5BJ
t (01380) 729444
e margaret@bhdevizes.com
w bhdevizes.com

Byde a Whyle ★★★
Bed & Breakfast
29 Roundway Park, Devizes
SN10 2ED
t (01380) 723288
e robert@arbyde.wanadoo.co.uk
w byde-a-whyle.co.uk

Eastleigh House ★★★★
Bed & Breakfast
3 Eastleigh Road, Devizes
SN10 3EE
t (01380) 726918
e barbara@eastleighhouse.co.uk
w eastleighhouse.co.uk

Embrea ★★★★ Bed & Breakfast
Devizes Road, Rowde, Devizes
SN10 2LU
t (01380) 728189
e info@embrea.co.uk
w embrea.co.uk

Gables ★★★★ Bed & Breakfast
Bath Road, Devizes, Wiltshire
SN10 1PH
t (01380) 723086
e enquiries@thegablesdevizes.co.uk
w thegablesdevizes.co.uk

South West | Wiltshire

The Gatehouse Bed & Breakfast ★★★ *Bed & Breakfast*
Wick Lane, Devizes
SN10 5DW
t (01380) 725283
e info@visitdevizes.co.uk
w visitdevizes.co.uk

The Old Manor ★★★★
Bed & Breakfast
The Street, Chirton, Devizes
SN10 3QS
t (01380) 840777
e bandb@theoldmanor.biz
w theoldmanor.biz

Rosemundy Cottage ★★★★
Guest Accommodation
London Road (A361), Devizes, Wiltshire
SN10 2DS
t +44 (0)1380 727122
e info@rosemundycottage.co.uk
w rosemundycottage.co.uk

Southdown/White Horse Walking Holidays ★★★★ *Bed & Breakfast*
Southdown, Roundway Village, Devizes, Wiltshire
SN10 2HY
t 01380 726 830
e info@whitehorsewalking.co.uk
w whitehorsewalking.co.uk

Summerhayes ★★★★★
Bed & Breakfast **GOLD AWARD**
143 High Street, Littleton Panell, Devizes
SN10 4EU
t (01380) 813521
e summerhayesbandb@ukonline.co.uk
w summerhayesbandb.co.uk

DILTON MARSH

Angel Cottage ★★★★
Bed & Breakfast
High Street, Dilton Marsh, Westbury
BA13 4DR
t (01373) 825480
w angel-cottage.co.uk

DINTON

Marshwood Farm B&B ★★★★
Bed & Breakfast
Dinton, Salisbury
SP3 5ET
t (01722) 716334
e marshwood1@btconnect.com
w marshwoodfarm.co.uk

DONHEAD ST MARY

Cedar Lodge ★★★ *Bed & Breakfast*
5 Deweys Place, Donhead St Mary, Shaftesbury
SP7 9LW
t (01747) 829240
e cedarlodge@onetel.com
w cedarlodge.org.uk

DOWNTON

Casterbridge House Bed & Breakfast ★★★★ *Bed & Breakfast*
140 The Borough, Downton
SP5 3LT
t (01725) 513270
e info@casterbridgehouse.co.uk
w casterbridgehouse.co.uk

FROXFIELD

The Pelican Inn ★★★ *Inn*
Bath Road, Froxfield
SN8 3JY
t (01488) 682479

GRITTLETON

The Neeld Arms Inn ★★★ *Inn*
The Street, Grittleton, Chippenham
SN14 6AP
t (01249) 782470
e info@neeldarms.co.uk
w neeldarms.co.uk

HARTHAM

Church Farm ★★★★ *Farmhouse*
Hartham, Corsham
SN13 0PU
t (01249) 715180
e churchfarmbandb@hotmail.com
w churchfarmbandb.com

HEYTESBURY

The Red Lion ★★★★
Guest Accommodation
42a High Street, Heytesbury, Warminster
BA12 0EA
t (01985) 840315
e donna.pease@btinternet.com
w theredlion-heytesbury.co.uk

The Resting Post ★★★★
Bed & Breakfast
67 High Street, Heytesbury, Warminster
BA12 0ED
t (01985) 840204
e enquiries@therestingpost.co.uk
w therestingpost.co.uk

HEYWOOD

Redwood Lodge ★★★★
Guest Accommodation
The Ham, Westbury
BA13 4HD
t (01373) 823949
w redwoodlodgeuk.com

HORTON

Partacre ★★ *Bed & Breakfast*
Horton, Devizes
SN10 3NB
t (01380) 860261

KINGSDOWN

Ashley Wood Farm ★★★★
Farmhouse **SILVER AWARD**
Ashley Wood Farm, Kingsdown
SN13 8BG
t (01225) 742288
e ashleywoodfarm@hotmail.com
w ashleywoodfarm.co.uk

KINGTON LANGLEY

Gate Farm ★★★★ *Bed & Breakfast*
Swindon Road, Kington Langley, Chippenham
SN15 5NB
t (01249) 758374
e rebeccarenny@btinternet.com
w gatefarmwiltshire.co.uk/

LONGBRIDGE DEVERILL

The George Inn ★★★★ *Inn*
Longbridge Deverill, Warminster
BA12 7DG
t (01985) 840396
e thegeorgeinnlongbridgedeverill.co.uk

MALMESBURY

Manor Farm ★★★★ *Farmhouse*
Corston, Malmesbury
SN16 0HF
t (01666) 822148
e ross@johneavis.wanadoo.co.uk
w manorfarmbandb.co.uk

Marsh Farmhouse ★★★
Guest House
Crudwell Road, Malmesbury
SN16 9JL
t (01666) 822208

Oakwood Farm ★★ *Bed & Breakfast*
Upper Minety, Malmesbury
SN16 9PY
t (01666) 860286
e katiegallop@btinternet.com

MANNINGFORD ABBOTS

Huntly's Farmhouse ★★★★
Farmhouse
Manningford Abbots, Pewsey
SN9 6HZ
t (01672) 563663
e gimspike@esend.co.uk

MARKET LAVINGTON

Green Dragon ★★★ *Inn*
26-28 High Street, Market Lavington, Devizes, Wiltshire
SN10 4AG
t (01380) 813235
e greendragonlavington@tiscali.co.uk
w greendragonlavington.co.uk

MARLBOROUGH

Crofton Lodge ★★★★
Bed & Breakfast **SILVER AWARD**
Crofton, Marlborough
SN8 3DW
t (01672) 870328
e ali@croftonlodge.co.uk
w croftonlodge.co.uk

The Crown & Anchor ★★★
Guest Accommodation - Room Only
1 Crowood Lane, Marlborough
SN8 2PT
t (01672) 520335
e crown.ramsbury@btconnect.com

Mayfield ★★★★ *Bed & Breakfast*
SILVER AWARD
West Grafton, Marlborough
SN8 3BY
t (01672) 810339
e countess.an@virgin.net
w mayfieldbandb.com

The Merlin ★★★
Guest Accommodation
36-39 High Street, Marlborough
SN8 1LW
t (01672) 512151
e bookings@merlin-bed-and-breakfast-marlborough.co.uk
w merlin-bed-and-breakfast-marlborough.co.uk

Monks Rest Lodge ★★★★
Bed & Breakfast
Salisbury Road, Marlborough
SN8 4AE
t (01672) 512169
e stay@monksrest.co.uk
w monksrest.co.uk

The Old Forge ★★★★
Bed & Breakfast **SILVER AWARD**
East Kennett, Marlborough
SN8 4EY
t (01672) 861686
e laura@feeleyfamily.fsnet.co.uk
w theoldforge-avebury.co.uk

Orchard Close ★★★★
Bed & Breakfast
Wye Lane, London Road, Marlborough
SN8 1PJ
t (01672) 513210
e orchardclosebandb@googlemail.com
w orchardclose-bb.com

Poulton Grange ★★★★★
Farmhouse **GOLD AWARD**
Poulton Farm Estate, Poulton, Marlborough
SN8 2LN
t (01672) 516888
e sheppard@poultongrange.com
w poultongrange.com

The Royal Oak ★★ *Inn*
Wootton Rivers, Marlborough
SN8 4NQ
t (01672) 810322
e royaloak35@hotmail.com
w wiltshire-pubs.com

The Sanctuary ★★★★
Bed & Breakfast
Ogbourne St George, Marlborough
SN8 1SQ
t (01672) 841473
e rebecca.macdonald@core-support.co.uk
w the-sanctuary.biz

Teal Cottage ★★★★
Bed & Breakfast **SILVER AWARD**
High Street, Manton, Marlborough
SN8 4HH
t (01672) 513904
e tealcottagebandb@yahoo.co.uk
w tealcottage.co.uk

The White House ★★★★
Bed & Breakfast **SILVER AWARD**
Little Bedwyn, Marlborough, Wiltshire
SN8 3JP
t (01672) 870321
e whitehousebandb@btinternet.com
w the-white-house-b-and-b.co.uk

MELKSHAM

Church Farm ★★★★ *Farmhouse*
Church Street, Atworth, Melksham
SN12 8JA
t (01225) 702215
e churchfarm@tinyonline.co.uk
w churchfarm-atworth.freeserve.co.uk/

Rew Farm ★★★ *Farmhouse*
Seend Cleeve, Melksham
SN12 6PS
t (01380) 828289
e enquiries@rewfarm.com
w rewfarm.com

MERE

Castleton House ★★★★
Bed & Breakfast
Castle Street, Mere
BA12 6JE
t (01747) 860446
e info@castletonhouse.com
w castletonhouse.com

MONKTON FARLEIGH

The Kings Arms ★★★★ *Inn*
SILVER AWARD
42 Monkton Farleigh, Monkton Farleigh
BA15 2QH
t (01225) 858705
e enquiries@kingsarms-bath.co.uk
w kingsarms-bath.co.uk

NETTLETON

Fosse Farmhouse ★★★★
Bed & Breakfast **SILVER AWARD**
Nettleton Shrub, Nettleton
SN14 7NJ
t (01249) 782286
e caroncooper@fossefarmhouse.com
w fossefarmhouse.com

OGBOURNE ST GEORGE

The Inn with the Well ★★★ *Inn*
Marlborough Road, Ogbourne St George
SN8 1SQ
t (01672) 841445
e info@theinnwiththewell.co.uk
w theinnwiththewell.co.uk

PEWSEY

Follets B&B ★★★★
Guest Accommodation
SILVER AWARD
Easton Royal, Pewsey
SN9 5LZ
t (01672) 810619
e margaretlandless@talk21.com
w folletsbb.com

Well Cottage ★★★ *Bed & Breakfast*
Honeystreet, Woodborough, Pewsey
SN9 5PS
t (01672) 851577
e booking@well-cottage.org.uk
w well-cottage.org.uk

South West | Wiltshire

REDLYNCH

Forest Edge Bed & Breakfast ★★★ *Bed & Breakfast*
SILVER AWARD
Lower Windyeats Cottage, Forest Road, Redlynch
SP5 2PU
t (01725) 511516
e forestedge@hotmail.com
w newforestholidayaccommodation.co.uk

RODBOURNE

The Manor House Bed & Breakfast ★★★★ *Bed & Breakfast*
SILVER AWARD
Rodbourne, Malmesbury
SN16 0EX
t (01666) 823837
e miranda@manorhouserodbourne.com
w manorhouserodbourne.com

ROWDE

Vine Cottage Bed & Breakfast ★★★ *Bed & Breakfast*
36 Bunnies Lane, Rowde, Devizes, Wiltshire
SN10 2QB
t (01380) 728360
e vinecottagebb@btinternet.com
w vinecottagebb.co.uk

RUSHALL

Chestnuts Cottage ★★★★ *Bed & Breakfast*
Church Lane, Rushall, Pewsey
SN9 6EH
t (01980) 630976
e richard@chestnuts-cot.co.uk

The Cottage Rushall ★★★★ *Bed & Breakfast*
Devizes Road, Rushall
SN9 6ET
t (01980) 635391
e info@thecottagerushall.co.uk
w thecottagerushall.co.uk

Little Thatch ★★★★
Rushall, Pewsey
SN9 6EN
t (01980) 635282
e littlethatch42@talktalk.net

SALISBURY

10 Potters Way ★★★ *Bed & Breakfast*
Laverstock, Salisbury
SP1 1PY
t (01722) 335031

8 Belle Vue Road ★★ *Bed & Breakfast*
Salisbury
SP1 3YD
t (01722) 329477

Alabare House ★★★ *Guest House*
25 Tollgate Road, Salisbury
SP1 2JA
t 07802 631968
e info@alabare.org
w alabare.org

Ballantynes ★★ *Bed & Breakfast*
114 Netherhampton Road, Salisbury
SP2 8LZ
t (01722) 325743
e info@ballantynesbandb.com
w ballantynesbandb.com

Blaxwell Farm ★★★★ *Bed & Breakfast*
Blaxwell Farm, Whiteparish, Salisbury
SP5 2RR
t (01794) 884000
e tricia@blaxwellfarm.co.uk
w blaxwellfarm.co.uk

Burcombe Manor ★★★
Bed & Breakfast
Burcombe Lane, Burcombe, Salisbury
SP2 0EJ
t (01722) 744288
e nickatburcombemanor@btinternet.com
w burcombemanor.co.uk

Byways House ★★★ *Guest House*
31 Fowlers Road, Salisbury
SP1 2QP
t (01722) 328364
e info@bywayshouse.co.uk
w bywayshouse.co.uk

Carp Cottage ★★★ *Bed & Breakfast*
Stratford Road, Stratford sub Castle, Salisbury
SP1 3LH
t (01722) 327219
e carp-cottage@dsl.pipex.com

Cawden Cottage ★★★
Bed & Breakfast
Stratford Tony, Salisbury
SP5 4AT
t (01722) 718463
e cawdencottage@yahoo.co.uk
w cawdencottage.co.uk

Edwardian Lodge ★★★★
Guest House
59 Castle Road, Salisbury
SP1 3RH
t (01722) 413329
e enquiries@edwardianlodge.co.uk
w edwardianlodge.co.uk

Evening Hill ★★ *Bed & Breakfast*
Blandford Road, Coombe Bissett, Salisbury
SP5 4LH
t (01722) 718561
e henrys@eveninghill.com
w eveninghill.com

Farthings ★★★ *Bed & Breakfast*
9 Swaynes Close, Salisbury
SP1 3AE
t (01722) 330749
e gill.rodwell@tiscali.co.uk
w farthingsbandb.co.uk

Greenbank B&B ★★★★
Bed & Breakfast
Church Street, Bowerchalke, Salisbury
SP5 5BE
t (01722) 780350
e suelee@greenbank101.com
w greenbank101.com

Hillcroft ★★★
Guest Accommodation
Merrick Avenue, Salisbury
SP2 8ED
t (01722) 330271
e jumarriott@hotmail.co.uk
w hillcroftbandb.co.uk

Kinvara House ★★★
Bed & Breakfast
28 Castle Road, Salisbury
SP1 3RJ
t (01722) 325233
e kinvarahouse@btinternet.com
w kinvarahouse.co.uk

Leena's Guest House ★★★
Guest House
50 Castle Road, Salisbury
SP1 3RL
t (01722) 335419

Little Hazels ★★★★
Bed & Breakfast
Monmouth Road, Tuckingmill, Salisbury
SP3 6NR
t (01747) 870906
e keeblings@yahoo.com
w littlehazels.co.uk

Manor Farm ★★★★ *Farmhouse*
Burcombe Lane, Burcombe, Salisbury, Wiltshire
SP2 0EJ
t (01722) 742177
e suecombes@manorfarmburcombe.fsnet.co.uk
w manorfarmburcombebandb.com

Merivale House ★★★★
Bed & Breakfast
The Green, Laverstock, Salisbury
SP1 1QS
t 07748 978190
e merivale.house@btinternet.com

The Old Police House ★★★★
Bed & Breakfast
North Street, Mere, Salisbury
BA12 6HH
t (01747) 861768
e gilly.gristwood@btopenworld.com
w theoldpolicehouse.org.uk

The Old Rectory Bed & Breakfast
★★★★ *Bed & Breakfast*
75 Belle Vue Road, Salisbury
SP1 3YE
t (01722) 502702
e stay@theoldrectory-bb.co.uk
w theoldrectory-bb.co.uk

The Rokeby Guest House ★★★★
Guest House SILVER AWARD
3 Wain-A-Long Road, Salisbury
SP1 1LJ
t (01722) 329800
e karenrogers@rokebyguesthouse.co.uk
w rokebyguesthouse.co.uk

Salisbury Old Mill House ★★★★
Bed & Breakfast SILVER AWARD
Warminster Road, South Newton, Salisbury
SP2 0QD
t (01722) 742458
e salisburymill@yahoo.com
w salisburymill.co.uk

Salisbury Youth Hostel Association ★★★ *Hostel*
Milford Hill House, Milford Hill, Salisbury
SP1 2QW
t (01722) 327572
e salisbury@yha.org.uk
w yha.org.uk/salisbury

Scotland Lodge ★★★
Guest Accommodation
Winterbourne Stoke, Salisbury
SP3 4TF
t (01980) 620943
e enquiries@scotlandlodge.co.uk
w scotlandlodge.co.uk

Spire House ★★★★
Guest Accommodation
SILVER AWARD
84 Exeter Street, Salisbury
SP1 2SE
t (01722) 339213
e spire.enquiries@btinternet.com
w salisbury-bedandbreakfast.com

Swan Inn ★★★★ *Inn*
Warminster Road, Stoford, Salisbury
SP2 0PR
t (01722) 790236
e info@theswanatstoford.co.uk
w theswanatstoford.co.uk

Swaynes Firs Farm ★★★
Farmhouse
Grimsdyke, Coombe Bissett, Salisbury
SP5 5RF
t (01725) 519240
e swaynes.firs@virgin.net
w swaynesfirs.co.uk

Victoria Lodge Guest House ★★★
Guest House
61 Castle Road, Salisbury
SP1 3RH
t (01722) 320586
e info@victoria-guest-house.co.uk
w viclodge.co.uk

Walsworth House ★★★★★
Bed & Breakfast SILVER AWARD
31 Albany Road, Salisbury
SP1 3YQ
t (01722) 504074
e tkenny@thetalentmanager.co.uk
w walsworthhouse.webeden.co.uk

The Wheatsheaf ★★★ *Inn*
1 King Street, Wilton, Salisbury
SP20AX
t (01722) 742267
e mail@thewheatsheafwilton.co.uk
w thewheatsheafwilton.co.uk

Willow Springs Riverside Bed & Breakfast ★★★★ *Bed & Breakfast*
Willow Springs, The Ham, Salisbury
SP4 8HW
t (01980) 555151
e gail.sims@tiscali.co.uk
w willowsprings.co.uk

Woodfalls Inn ★★★ *Inn*
The Ridge, Redlynch, Salisbury
SP5 2LN
t (01725) 513222
e enquiries@woodfallsinnhotel.co.uk
w woodfallsinn.co.uk

Wyndham Park Lodge ★★★★
Guest Accommodation
51 Wyndham Road, Salisbury
SP1 3AB
t (01722) 416517
e enquiries@wyndhamparklodge.co.uk
w wyndhamparklodge.co.uk

SHERSTON

Carriers Farm ★★★
Bed & Breakfast
Luckington Road, Malmesbury
SN16 0QA
t (01666) 841445
e cotswoldbandb@yahoo.com
w carriersfarmbandb.com

SWINDON

Cheney Thatch ★★★
Bed & Breakfast
Oxon Place, Bishopstone, Swindon
SN6 8PS
t (01793) 790508

Courtleigh House *Bed & Breakfast*
40 Draycott Road, Chiseldon, Swindon
SN4 0LS
t (01793) 740246
e courtleighhouse@yahoo.co.uk

Jessamine Cottage B&B ★★★★
Bed & Breakfast
156 Drove Road, Swindon
SN1 3AG
t (01793) 345654
e enquiries@jessaminecottage.net
w jessaminecottage.net

The Lodge ★★★★
Guest Accommodation
1 Hunt Street, Swindon
SN1 3HW
t (01793) 526952
e info@thelodgeswindon.co.uk
w thelodgeswindon.co.uk

Park Farm ★★★★ *Farmhouse*
Hook Street, Lydiard Tregoze, Swindon
SN5 3NY
t (01793) 853608
w parkfarmguesthouse.com

Rossendale ★★★★
Guest Accommodation
44a Station Road, Chiseldon, Swindon
SN4 0PW
t (01793) 740726
e anneward333@btinternet.com

The Swandown ★★★
Guest Accommodation
36-37 Victoria Road, Old Town, Swindon
SN1 3AS
t (01793) 536695
e swandownhotel@gmail.com
w s-h-systems.co.uk/hotels/swandown

The Village Apartment ★★★★
Guest Accommodation - Room Only
SILVER AWARD
4 Church Farm Lane, Swindon
SN3 4SR
t (01793) 828441

For key to symbols see page 6

171

South West | Wiltshire

Waterhay Farm ★★★★ *Farmhouse*
Waterhay, Leigh, Swindon
SN6 6QY
t (01285) 861253

TROWBRIDGE

49a Church Lane ★★★★
Bed & Breakfast
North Bradley, Trowbridge
BA14 0TA
t (01225) 762558
e marilyn@d-wise.co.uk

Church Farm Steeple Ashton ★★
Farmhouse
5 High Street, Steeple Ashton, Trowbridge
BA14 6EL
t (01380) 870518
e susan.churchfarm@tesco.net

Longs Arms Inn ★★★ *Inn*
High Street, Steeple Ashton, Trowbridge
BA14 6EU
t (01380) 870245
e carolinequartley@hotmail.com
w thelongsarms.co.uk/

Newhouse Farm ★★★★
Bed & Breakfast
Littleton, Semington, Trowbridge
BA14 6LF
t (01380) 870349
e stay@newhousefarmwilts.co.uk
w newhousefarmwilts.co.uk

Paxcroft Cottages ★★★★
Bed & Breakfast
62B Devizes Road, Hilperton, Trowbridge
BA14 6JB
t (01225) 765838
e paxcroftcottages@hotmail.com
w paxcroftcottages.pwp.blueyonder.co.uk

Watergardens ★★★★
Guest Accommodation
131 Yarnbrook Road, West Ashton, Trowbridge
BA14 6AF
t (01225) 766539
e watergardens@btinternet.com
w watergardens-stay.co.uk

WARMINSTER

The Carriers *Guest Accommodation*
Stockton, Warminster
BA12 0SQ
t (01985) 850653
e kathy@thecarriers.co.uk
w thecarriers.co.uk

Deverill End ★★★★
Bed & Breakfast
Deverill Road, Sutton Veny, Warminster
BA12 7BY
t 01985 840 356
w suttonveny.co.uk

Home Farm ★★★★ *Farmhouse*
221 Boreham Road, Warminster
BA12 9HF
t (01985) 213266
e enquiries@homefarmboreham.co.uk
w homefarmboreham.co.uk

WESTBURY

Black Dog Farm ★★★★
Farmhouse
Chapmanslade, Westbury
BA13 4AE
t (01373) 832858
e blackdogfarmills@aol.com
w blackdogfarm.co.uk

WINGFIELD

Stowford Manor Farm ★★★
Farmhouse
Wingfield, Trowbridge
BA14 9LH
t (01225) 781318
e stowford1@supanet.com
w stowfordmanorfarm.co.uk

WINTERBOURNE STOKE

Scotland Lodge Farm ★★★★
Bed & Breakfast **SILVER AWARD**
Winterbourne Stoke, Salisbury
SP3 4TF
t (01980) 621199
e catherine.lockwood@bigwig.net
w scotlandlodgefarm.co.uk

Looking for something else?

You can also buy a copy of our popular guide 'Hotels' including country house and town house hotels, metro and budget hotels, serviced apartments, restaurants with rooms and Spas in England 2011.

Now available in good bookshops and online at **visitbritainshop.com**

£10.99

So much to see, so little time - how do you choose?

enjoyEngland.com
QUALITY ASSURED VISITOR ATTRACTION

Make the most of your leisure time; look for attractions with the Quality Marque.

VisitEngland operates the Enjoy England Visitor Attraction Quality Assurance Scheme.

Annual assessments by trained impartial assessors test all aspects of the customer experience so you can visit with confidence.

For ideas and inspiration visit www.enjoyengland.com/attractions

South East

South East England is a region rich in experiences with coast and countryside. It has something to offer every age group. Visit the historic houses and marvel at the wonderful interiors. Relax in the tranquil settings of some of the most beautiful gardens and parks. Stroll through the streets, villages, towns and cities and experience the splendid architectural heritage on offer.

Buckinghamshire has The Chiltern Hills, River Thames and some of the finest stately homes and heritage sites. Berkshire is a great destination providing something to keep the whole family entertained, Legoland Windsor, Ascot Racecourse, and the royal residence, Windsor Castle.

South East

South East

Berkshire, Buckinghamshire, Hampshire, Isle of Wight, Kent, Oxfordshire, Surrey, Sussex

176 Counties
184 Where to Go
187 Events
188 Where to Eat
196 Where to Stay

The rolling hills and riverside walks of Hampshire are waiting to be discovered, whilst the Isle of Wight has all the elements needed for a perfect break. Often referred to as 'The Garden of England', Kent has rolling hills, green valleys and miles of open landscape; perfect English countryside! Or you could enjoy the charm of the Oxfordshire Cotswolds, with its breathtaking scenery, chocolate box villages and busy market towns. Oxford, the 'city of dreaming spires' has much to inspire!

Just 16 miles from London, Surrey is an interesting yet relaxing escape, steeped in history, with market towns and an excellent range of attractions. Sussex offers a diverse variety of destinations from vibrant and colourful Brighton in the East to chic Chichester in the West.

The South East Region really does have everything to suit all tastes and budgets.

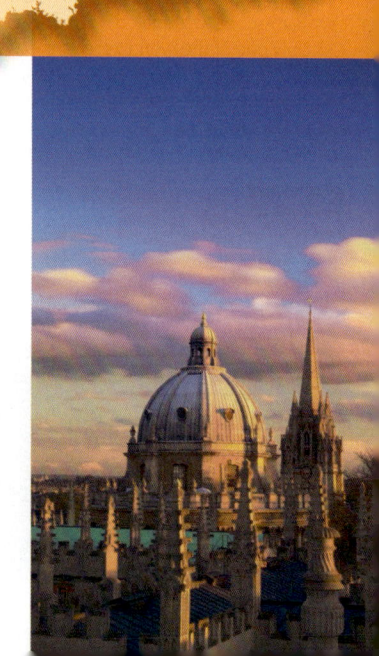

South East | Berkshire

Berkshire

In a county that boasts several of the UK's top attractions, the hardest part is knowing where to begin. You could put on your best outfit for a day at Ascot Racecourse, take the family to LEGOLAND® Windsor for adventure rides or visit the stunning Windsor Castle – the largest occupied castle in the world.

Windsor
Windsor Castle is the main attraction, but don't miss tranquil Savill Gardens, or family-friendly Legoland nearby. Set amidst the grandeur of the refurbished Victorian railway station a short walk from Windsor Castle is Windsor Royal Shopping with over 40 shops, restaurants and bars and craft boutiques. A must is a trip on the Royal Windsor Wheel which (March to November) soars over 50 metres above historic Windsor to give you a breathtaking view of Windsor Castle, the River Thames and the surrounding countryside.

Ascot
Though a pretty Berkshire town in its own right, it's fair to say that Ascot is dominated by its spectacular racecourse. Certainly one of the world's greatest and most historic racecourses, Ascot comes alive every summer in a kaleidoscope of hats, dresses, jackets and jodhpurs. There are meets throughout the year, but the highlight of the racing calendar is Royal Ascot, held for one week in June.

Reading
Reading is an appealing combination of excellent shopping facilities and historic buildings set around the confluence of the River Thames and the River Kennet. Those looking for a little retail therapy should head straight for The Oracle Shopping Centre - one of the best shopping destinations in South East England. Reading is a place with a fascinating heritage. As well as the town where Oscar Wilde wrote his famous Ballad of Reading Gaol. Reading has a 12th century ruined Abbey, and even a huge replica of the Bayeux Tapestry. Today it's also the site of one of the biggest and longest running music festivals in the UK - The Reading Festival.

Cookham
Charming and friendly Cookham is one of the most popular Thameside resorts with its many superb restaurants and inns, including Bel and the Dragon dating from 1417 and reputedly one of the oldest licensed houses in England. The name of Cookham today is closely associated with Sir Stanley Spencer, who lived in the village until his death in 1959 and who used its scenery as the background to many of his paintings. Another famous former resident was Kenneth Grahame, author of 'The Wind in the Willows'. He lived with his grandmother at 'The Mount' in Cookham Dean. It is thought this is where he wrote the book and it is certainly accepted that the river scenes between Cookham and Henley inspired the work along with Winter Hill above it.

Newbury
Set along the banks of the River Kennet and the Kennet & Avon Canal, Newbury has a fresh, rural atmosphere combined with great shopping facilities and new attractions. The 17th century architecture and cobbled streets host farmer's markets and annual festivals. The remains of Donnington Castle overlook the town, having sustained a lot of damage during the English Civil War. You'll find plenty of restaurants and pubs along the canal side and in the centre. The Corn Exchange Theatre offers superb programme of theatre and entertainment.

South East | **Buckinghamshire**

Buckinghamshire

Inspiring, serene and beautiful, Buckinghamshire is one the UK's finest counties. You can take an invigorating walk through the fresh green Chiltern Hills, float down the River Thames on a sunset cruise, or tuck into a cosy country pub in one of dozens of perfect little English villages.

West Wycombe

The small traditional village of West Wycombe is owned by the National Trust and its one main street is lined with buildings dating from the 17th and 18th centuries. West Wycombe also boasts several unique attractions such as the Hell Fire Caves, reputed to have hosted the Hell-Fire Club, and the Golden Ball in the Church of St. Lawrence.

Great Missenden

Once home to much-loved children's author Roald Dahl, Great Missenden is a pleasant village with a long curving High Street of half timbered and Georgian shops with many original features and a number of traditional pubs. The village is home to the Roald Dahl Museum and Story Centre, a museum dedicated to the famous author and his works.

Milton Keynes

Visitors will love the excellent shopping facilities, with over 300 shops, including one of the longest indoor shopping centres in Europe at thecentre:mk. Milton Keynes has also become an extreme sports hotspot. You can water-ski, wakeboard and more on Willen Lake, or head to Xscape for the UK's longest indoor real-snow ski and boarding slope, as well as some of the best indoor climbing facilities in the south. For more sedate pursuits, Milton Keynes offers one of the best theatres outside of London, excellent free art exhibitions at the Milton Keynes Gallery and dozens of regular free festivals and events.

High Wycombe

The largest town in Buckinghamshire and one time "Furniture Capital of England", High Wycombe is today a lively, modern location with plenty of attractions. The town centre has some beautiful Georgian architecture, including the Little Market House, and the stunning Guildhall. There has been a market in the high street since medieval times and you'll still find farmer's produce and goods for sale. For peace and quiet head for the beautiful and serene Chilterns Countryside which surrounds the town.

Buckingham

Once the county town of Buckinghamshire, as granted by Alfred the Great, Buckingham has had an abundance of historical references throughout the centuries. The town is characterised by its fine array of Georgian buildings and the Old Gaol and Town Hall. The Old Gaol was one of the first purpose-built county gaols in England but today it houses a museum telling the complete history of Buckingham. The tightly interwoven streets of the town are perfect for a gentle stroll to discover the many specialist shops, pubs and restaurants they contain.

South East | **Hampshire**

Hampshire

From the lively coastal cities of Portsmouth and Southampton, to the picturesque rolling hills of the North Wessex Downs, Hampshire offers a fantastic range of attractions for the whole family. The New Forest stretches across 140,000 acres of shaded ancient woodland and unspoilt grassland. It's one of the most beautiful national parks in the UK and home to dozens of fascinating historic villages.

Southampton

A short break in Southampton means time for serious shopping in the West Quay Shopping Centre, a look at classic and cutting edge art in the Southampton City Art Gallery, or taking in a show at the Mayflower Theatre. Southampton also has a rich history to explore. Wander the medieval city walls, built to protect the city from French invaders, or discover the tragic tale of the Titanic in the Southampton Maritime Museum.

Portsmouth

With a rich maritime and naval history, Portsmouth's fortunes have long been intimately tied to the sea. Even today, many of Portsmouth's most stunning features and most popular attractions are found near the harbour. From the imposing Spinnaker Tower, to the historic ship HMS Victory, you'll find a huge range of things to see and do. Portsmouth Historic Dockyard is home to some of the most impressive historic ships in the world – with the remains of Henry VIII's Mary Rose and HMS Warrior 1860 both here. Take a break from the historical attractions to indulge in a little shopping. The bustling Gunwharf Quays is one of the best shopping locations in the south, with dozens of big brands and stores to choose from (not to mention bowling alleys, cinemas and nightclubs).

Winchester

Winchester, Hampshire's historic cathedral city, is one of the oldest settlements in Britain and the ancient capital of the Kingdom of England. Today Winchester is a fascinating mix of legend, myth, history, and heritage. As for ancient constructions, the city is dominated by the imposing spire of Winchester Cathedral. In the north aisle of the nave you'll find the grave of Jane Austen. King Arthur (whose statue stands in central Winchester) is another of the city's most iconic figures. A 13th century version of the King's legendary Round Table can be found in Winchester Cast The castle, built by William the Conqueror in 1067, was a but destroyed through the centuries. However, Henry VII impressive Great Hall addition still stands today.

New Forest

Recently designated National Park status, the New Forest is home to some of South East England's most picturesque countryside and is filled with a great variety of things to do and places to stay. With shaded paths meandering through ancient woodland, picturesque villages dotted amongst the landscape, stunning coastal routes and dozens of unique attractions, The New Forest is one of the UK's best loved outdoor treasures. The New Forest is an absolute paradise for walkers, campers and cyclists. As an added bonus for bike riders, the region is mainly hill-free! You'll also find family adventures at Paultons Park and attractions such as the vintage car experience of Beaulieu.

South East | Isle of Wight

Isle of Wight

From coloured sands and smugglers coves, to racing yachts and dinosaur bones – the Isle of Wight is full of amazing things to discover. Everything is within easy reach of each other, and all just a short ferry ride from mainland UK. The coastal towns are filled with unique attractions and offer relaxed seaside activities.

Ventnor

Sheltered from the winds by high cliffs and a southerly aspect, Ventnor is a picture-perfect seaside town and home to the stunning Ventnor Botanic Gardens. Different in character from the other seaside towns, Ventnor on the Isle of Wight is built on a series of terraces that zig-zag down to the sun-trap seafront with part sand, part shingle beach. Ventnor Botanic Garden occupies the site of the former Royal National Hospital. Exhibitions at the heritage centre provide glimpses of the town's past and you may find your own interesting pieces of history in the many local shops of antiques and collectables.

Cowes

At the mouth of the Medina River, Cowes is the island's chief port and a place rich in maritime heritage. Cowes on the Isle of Wight is a Mecca for yachtsman and hosts many national and international events. Each year Cowes plays host to Cowes Week and is the start point of the Round the Island Race. The narrow pedestrianised High Street is bursting with interesting boutiques, antique shop, chandlers, delicatessens, restaurants and lively pubs.

Shanklin

Shanklin is a resort of great charm whose popular seaside attractions include a sandy beach, with excellent swimming and sunbathing opportunities. The seafront Esplanade is lined with small hotels, cafes and amusements including crazy golf, arcades, indoor children's play area and fun fair. A cliff lift links the town with the Esplanade and a road train operates between the seafront, town centre and the Old Village. Shanklin Chine, with its unique microclimate is home to unusual plants.

Newport

Right in the heart of the island, Newport is one of the more lively towns with great shopping, pubs and restaurants. Newport on the Isle of Wight has two elegant squares and many fine Georgian and Victorian town houses. Shopping in Newport is a pleasure, with a variety of exclusive small shops, coffee shops and cafes all within easy walking distance. Newport Harbour is just a short walk from the town centre, with facilities for visiting yachtsman. Museums, crafts studios and the Quay Arts Centre are housed in former warehouses.

Brading

Standing on the western bank of the River Yar in the east of the Isle of Wight, the ancient little town of Brading is pleasantly built on a hillside below Brading Down within an Area of Outstanding Natural Beauty. One of the oldest towns on the island, reputedly founded by King Alfred in the 7th century, Brading's history goes back thousands of years to before the Iron age. Brading's 3rd century Roman Villa still survives and is one of the best preserved, with some magnificent mosaics on show. The surrounding landscape is as much of a highlight, with rolling green hills dropping down towards the sea, breathtaking views from Brading Down, numerous footpaths and bridleways and a variety of special wildlife, including the birds at the Brading Marshes RSPB Reserve.

How To Get There

Wightlink and Red Funnel Isle of Wight Ferries operate the ferry service between the England mainland and the Isle of Wight, sailing the Southampton to Cowes, Portsmouth to Fishbourne, Lymington to Yarmouth and Portsmouth to Ryde routes.

South East | **Kent**

Kent

The famous "Garden of England", Kent is one of the most beautiful areas of the South East. In Kent, you can spend time in historic villages, roam unspoilt countryside and discover traditional harbour towns. Yet with so much to see and do in Kent, you're only ever a short train ride from London or an hour or two from France!

Canterbury

The World Heritage Site of Canterbury in Kent is home to some of the most historic buildings in Britain - from the ancient 6th century St. Martin's Church to the towering Canterbury Cathedral. You can find a Roman city wall (rebuilt in the 14th century), the oldest school in England (The King's School) and ancient preserved mosaics. Take the city wall trail and it will lead you past dozens of historic buildings and ruins. Canterbury also offers a great range of modern attractions, from excellent shops and restaurants, to lively bars and is a great base for touring the surrounding countryside too.

Whitstable

Know as the "Pearl of Kent", Whitstable is famed for its delicious, fresh oysters and is a charming seaside town on the north coast of Kent. Everything about Whitstable speaks of its 2000 year love affair with the sea – from the bustling harbour, to the fishing artefacts and first ever diving helmets in the Whitstable Museum and Gallery. Whitstable is also a place that values tradition. May Day involves processions from the castle into the town, accompanied by Morris Dancers and the ancient woodland spirit of Jack in the Green. Every July, Whitstable's Oyster Festival celebrates the town's famous produce. You can join in the fun and hear live music, see local art – and of course tuck in to some of the freshest oysters available anywhere in the UK.

Broadstairs

Broadstairs is a beautiful town on the Kent coast – celebrated by the likes of the artist William Turner for its stunning skies and sunsets. A promenade amble reveals charming gardens, great for relaxing in with a delicious homemade ice cream, whilst a clifftop stroll uncovers seven beautiful beaches and bays, each a little different.

The resorts main beach, Viking Bay, has a small harbour, children's amusements and garden on the sands! Joss Bay is more rural and offers great surfing opportunities, while Botany Bay is quieter and more secluded and can feel a million miles from anywhere – absolute bliss when you want to laze around and recharge your batteries.

Royal Tunbridge Wells

A magnet for royalty and the gentry, Tunbridge Wells was one of the most fashionable destinations of Georgian England - ever since the discovery of the Chalybeate Spring over 400 years ago. The elegance and atmosphere of this bygone era still remain today in this, the only spa town in South East England. The Pantiles - the famous colonnaded walkway where the aristocracy once promenaded - is now home to a wonderful selection of high quality boutiques, antiques shops, bars and cafés.

Rochester

The ancient cathedral city of Rochester, with its Norman castle was a place cherished by the Victorian novelist, Charles Dickens, who lived in the area as a child and returned as a successful author. Explore the stunning Rochester Cathedral, founded in 604 and the second oldest in England. Enjoy the breathtaking views from the top of one of the tallest keeps in the country at the magnificent Rochester Castle. Built on the highest part of Rochester's Roman city wall, to defend the crossing of the River Medway.

South East | **Oxfordshire**

Oxfordshire

Elegant, unspoilt and historic – Oxfordshire is one of the UK's most picturesque and beloved counties. From the fresh green hills of the Cotswolds to the City of Dreaming Spires, Oxfordshire offers endless opportunities for memorable short breaks and holidays.

Oxfordshire Cotswolds

Picturesque villages, old market towns and rolling countryside, all this and more are waiting for you in the Oxfordshire Cotswolds. Burford, is one of the iconic sleepy villages you'll find in the Cotswolds. You'll feel yourself slow down as you explore honey-coloured villages like Ingham, Shipton under Wychwood and Churchill. The Cotswolds are an Area of Outstanding Natural Beauty full of stately homes, ancient churches and fascinating museums to enjoy.

Oxford

The world-famous City of Dreaming Spires, Oxford is a picture-perfect historic site set in the heart of the Oxfordshire countryside. For the best view of this magnificent city and the Oxford University buildings, climb the 99 steps of Carfax Tower and gaze over the rooftops below. While history echoes through every street and alley in Oxford, it also has its fair share of modern attractions and lively arts and entertainment too. The large student population means that there are plenty of cinemas, art cafés and live music venues to choose from – including the excellent Sheldonian Theatre.

You may want to indulge in a timeless Oxford classic – punting along the serene Cherwell on a bright summer's day. You can also book river cruises along a beautiful stretch of the River Thames.

Bicester

Bicester is one of Oxfordshire's most attractive market towns. Every Friday, the charming 16th century market still turns into Bicester's bustling, focal point (with delicious locally-sourced produce available from the monthly farmer's market).

Bicester is also ideally located as a base for exploring the stunning North Oxfordshire countryside. Those looking for a little retail therapy are spoilt for choice in Bicester Shopping Village – a huge open-air outlet mall home to dozens of discount brands.

Woodstock

A fine Georgian town with a distinct Royal heritage, containing many attractive period buildings: including the 17th century Fletcher's House, home to the excellent Oxfordshire Museum and the Visitor Information Centre; the 18th century Town Hall; the Church of St Mary Magdalene with its Norman doorway, early English windows and a musical clock, which plays tunes hourly. Woodstock is renowned for its antique shops but also has an interesting selection of other shops and galleries, as well as some excellent pubs and restaurants. Sir Winston Churchill was born at Blenheim Palace and his grave is in Bladon.

Henley on Thames

Henley is inextricably linked with the Royal River Thames. The town is overlooked by beautiful Chiltern landscape of wooded hills and green fields. Just a few strides from the riverbank is the very heart of Henley with its historic church, town hall and market square, the latter bustling with busy stall-holders and shoppers on market days. They also enjoy browsing the town's many boutiques. Visitors can enjoy a boat trip down the regatta course, either in one of the commercial boats that operate along this stretch or, rather more energetically, in a rowing boat. Afterwards they can relax in the well-maintained Mill Meadows public park.

South East | Surrey

Surrey

For a county that sits just 16 miles from London, Surrey is remarkably green, unspoilt and enchanting. You'll find picturesque villages and historic towns, fun theme parks and immaculate public gardens, ancient buildings and shiny new shopping centres. From the cobbled streets of Guildford to the thrills and spills of Mercedes Benz World, there's something in Surrey for everyone.

Weybridge

The famous Brooklands racing track at Weybridge was the world's first purpose built racing circuit and portions of its banked track are still in evidence. The aerodrome on the site also saw the development of the World War Two Wellington bomber and contributed to the design and manufacture of the supersonic Concorde. Brooklands Museum features a fine collection of racing and sports cars, and aeroplanes including the first production Concorde built in Britain.

Farnham

An old English market town with narrow streets lined with some of the finest Georgian architecture in the south of England, with a parish church and castle dating back to the 12th century. Farnham has been an important site for thousands of years, the Romans used its plentiful clay to make pottery and the Saxons gave it its name. Walking through its streets you can sense its history and when you meet Castle Street (described as one of the finest streets in England) with its sweep up to the Castle, you can appreciate this is indeed, a distinctive and attractive town.

Guildford

With cobbled streets and ancient alleys, historic buildings and lively festivals, Guildford is one of the most popular towns in the South. Set around the River Wey, Guildford was historically an important trade point between Portsmouth and London. Today you can amble along the riverside or take a gentle cruise in a riverboat. Guildford is also a hugely popular shopping destination. The cobbled streets and historic alleys are home to hundreds of shops – from high-street favourites to independent craft, book and clothing stores.

Dorking

Set between the Greensand Hills and the North Downs (an Area of Outstanding Natural Beauty), Dorking is a market town that offers wonderful opportunities for walking, cycling and discovering the great outdoors. The town provides a mixture of architectural styles from picturesque medieval houses to robust Victorian properties. As well as a fantastic variety of shops including the largest concentration of antique dealers in the county, the town also provides great eateries and a Museum.

Surrey Hills

This nationally treasured landscape stretches across a quarter of the county of Surrey and includes the chalk slopes of the North Downs from Farnham in the west to Oxted in the east and extends south to the deeply wooded Greensand Hills which rise in Haslemere. The Surrey Hills is not only rich in wildlife, woodland, attractive market towns and villages but also provides some of the best walking in southern England.

South East | **Sussex**

Sussex

Miles of pristine coastline, protected natural habitats, historic cities and fairytale castles, Sussex catches the imagination of all that visit. Relax on perfect sandy beaches at the Witterings, tour the 950-year-old Chichester Cathedral, explore the vibrant city of Brighton or admire elegance of Glyndebourne. In Sussex there is something for everyone.

Arundel

You can't help being impressed in Arundel. From exploring the magnificent Arundel Castle to pottering on the River Arun, it's an almost fairytale destination. There's much history in Arundel, all of it dominated by the castle. Standing proudly on a hill, Arundel Castle has been the home of the Dukes of Norfolk for more than 850 years. Inside, suits of armour, guard rooms hung with wonderful paintings and a grand yet cosy library. Shopping is equally tempting with lots of antique shops, studios and gift shops. Or take a boat on the River Arun and potter down to Littlehampton. On the west bank of the River Arun is Arundel Cathedral, an imposing Gothic building.

Chichester

One of the most charming and stylish cities on the South East, Chichester combines all the attractions of a thriving urban centre with the rural delights of West Sussex. Chichester is ideally placed for exploring the glorious coastline and the stunning surrounding countryside of the South Downs. The 600-year-old spire of Chichester Cathedral, rising above the peaceful streets below, can be seen from miles out at sea. Adding to Chichester's atmosphere of elegance and sophistication is Goodwood Racecourse. One of the world's great racecourses, with expansive views across the Downs towards the Solent, Goodwood is a picturesque gem.

Hastings

Hastings has long had a close relationship with the ocean, and although its fishing industry has declined, it still has Europe's largest beach-launched fishing fleet. As for the Norman Conquests, Hastings is not the actual location of the famous battle in 1066. That exact spot is just a few miles down the road at Battle Abbey. However, its legacy still colours the entire town. The remains of William the Conqueror's first English castle still stand today, though centuries of warfare and erosion have taken their toll. Hastings also boasts a lively (and growing) arts scene.

Brighton

Quirky, colourful – and never boring – Brighton is one of the UK's most vibrant destinations. Brighton offers an incredible range of attractions for every taste and every age group. Visit the Royal Pavilion. King George IV's India-inspired palace is a masterpiece of over-the-top architecture. Brighton is also a shopper's paradise. The winding, historic lanes are full of unique jewellery makers and specialist boutiques. From bohemian bars and arty clubs, to high-class restaurants and traditional pubs, there's something for everyone.

Seven Sisters

The Seven Sisters are part of a magnificent stretch of coastline between Seaford and Eastbourne, including Beachy Head beauty spot. The area is designated and protected as a 'Heritage Coast' and is the finest example of unprotected chalk cliffs in Britain. Part of the South Downs Way long distance footpath, passes over the Seven Sisters on its way from Eastbourne to Seaford. Seaford is an original Victorian seaside town with an unspoiled coastline, stunning scenery and surrounded by the Sussex Downs Area of Outstanding Natural Beauty.

183

South East | Where to Go

Where to Go

Attractions with this sign participate in the **Visitor Attraction Quality Assurance Scheme** (see page 6) which recognises high standards in all aspects of the visitor experience.

ENTERTAINMENT & CULTURE

Canterbury Tales
Canterbury, Kent CT1 2TG
(01227) 479227
www.canterburytales.org.uk
Step into medieval Canterbury and accompany Geoffrey Chaucer and his colourful characters on their magical pilgrimage from London to the shrine of St Thomas Becket in Canterbury Cathedral.

Dinosaur Isle
Sandown, Isle of Wight PO36 8QA
(01983) 404344
www.dinosaurisle.com
In a spectacular pterosaur shaped building on Sandown's blue flag beach walk back through fossilised time and meet life sized replica dinosaurs.

National Motor Museum Beaulieu
Brockenhurst, Hampshire SO42 7ZN
(01590) 612345
www.beaulieu.co.uk
In the heart of the New Forest, Beaulieu is a magical place, combining the charm of an ancient Abbey, the grace of a classical stately home and the celebrated National Motor Museum, all presented as a modern visitor attraction.

Roald Dahl Museum and Story Centre
Great Missenden, Buckinghamshire HP16 0AL
(01494) 892192
www.roalddahlmuseum.org
Is in Great Missenden where Roald Dahl (1916-1990) lived and wrote many of his well-loved books.

The Hop Farm Family Park
Paddock Wood, Kent TN12 6PY
(01622) 872068
www.thehopfarm.co.uk
A collection of well-preserved Victorian oast houses, home to the Hop Story Museum and the famous grey and black shire horses. Indoor adventure playground and nature trail.

Weald & Downland Open Air Museum
Chichester, West Sussex PO18 0EU
(01243) 811348
www.wealddown.co.uk
Home to over 45 original buildings which have been rescued from destruction & rebuilt in a beautiful 50 acre setting in the heart of the South Downs National Park.

FAMILY FUN

Go Ape! High Wire Forest Adventure - Alice Holt
Farnham, Hampshire GU10 4LS
0845 094 8739
www.goape.co.uk
Take to the trees and experience an exhilarating course of rope bridges, tarzan swings and zip slides...all set high above the forest floor.

INTECH Science Centre & Planetarium
Winchester, Hampshire SO21 1HX
(01962) 863791
www.intech-uk.com
A family attraction with 90 interactive science exhibits. Holiday activities, monthly science shows, education service, birthday parties, venue hire.

LEGOLAND® Windsor
Windsor, Berkshire SL4 4AY
0870 504 0404
www.legoland.co.uk
Experience over 50 interactive rides and attractions.

Paultons Park
Romsey, Hampshire SO51 6AL
(023) 8081 4442
www.paultonspark.co.uk
The theme park for families with over 50 fantastic rides and attractions, play areas, a water splash park, exotic birds and animals all set in over 140 acres of landscaped parkland.

The Look Out Discovery Centre
Bracknell, Berkshire RG12 7QW
(01344) 354400
www.bracknell-forest.gov.uk/be
A hands-on, interactive science exhibition with over 80 exhibits, set in 1,000 hectares of Crown woodland. Ideal for school and family visits.

Thorpe Park
Chertsey, Surrey KT16 8PN
0870 444 4466
www.thorpepark.com
One of UK's most thrilling theme parks, boasting Stealth, Europe's fastest rollercoaster, launching from 0-80mph in 2 seconds.

FOOD & DRINK

Denbies Wine Estate
Dorking, Surrey RH5 6AA
(01306) 876616
www.denbiesvineyard.co.uk
Established in 1986, Denbies Wine Estate is England's largest single estate vineyard with 265 acres of vines.

South East | Where to Go

HERITAGE

1066 Battle Abbey and Battlefield
Battle, East Sussex TN33 0AD
(01424) 773792
www.english-heritage.org.uk
An abbey founded by William the Conqueror on the site of the Battle of Hastings. Battlefield views and new visitor centre with film and interactive exhibition.

Anne of Cleves House
Lewes, East Sussex BN7 1JA
(01273) 487460
www.sussexpast.co.uk
Anne of Cleves House formed part of her divorce settlement from Henry VIII in 1541, although she never actually lived there.

Blenheim Palace
Woodstock, Oxfordshire
OX20 1PX
(01993) 811091
www.blenheimpalace.com
Birthplace of Sir Winston Churchill and home to the Duke of Marlborough, Blenheim Palace, one of the finest Baroque houses in England, is set in over 2,000 acres of landscaped gardens.

Chichester Cathedral
Chichester, West Sussex
PO19 1RP
(01243) 782595
www.chichestercathedral.org.uk
In the heart of Chichester, a magnificent Cathedral with treasures ranging from medieval stone carvings to world famous 20th Century artworks. Free entry and free guided tours. Exhibitions, concerts and special events for children.

Didcot Railway Centre
Didcot, Oxfordshire OX11 7NJ
(01235) 817200
www.didcotrailwaycentre.org.uk
A living museum recreating the golden age of the Great Western Railway. Steam locomotives and trains, Brunel's broad gauge railway, engine shed and small relics museum.

Gardens and Grounds of Herstmonceux Castle
Hailsham, East Sussex BN27 1RN
(01323) 833816
www.herstmonceux-castle.com
Herstmonceux is renowned for its magnificent moated castle, set in 550 acres of glorious parkland and superb Elizabethan gardens.

Hever Castle and Gardens
Edenbridge, Kent TN8 7NG
(01732) 865224
www.hevercastle.co.uk
Romantic 13th century moated castle, once Anne Boleyn's childhood home. Magnificently furnished interiors, spectacular award winning gardens. Miniature Model House Exhibition, Yew Maze, unique Splashing Water Maze.

Loseley Park
Guildford, Surrey GU3 1HS
(01483) 405112
www.loseley-park.com
Loseley House, a beautiful Elizabethan mansion, is set in stunning gardens and parkland. Built in 1562 it has a fascinating history and contains a wealth of treasures.

Mapledurham House
Mapledurham, Oxfordshire
RG4 7TR
(0118) 972 3350
www.mapledurham.co.uk
An Elizabethan manor house alongside the River Thames, containing paintings, oak staircases, and moulded ceilings. Home to the Blount family for over 500 years.

Mid-Hants Railway 'Watercress Line'
Alresford, Hampshire SO24 9JG
(01962) 733810
www.watercressline.co.uk
Experience 'More than just a Train Ride' at the Mid Hants Railway 'Watercress Line'. Travel by Steam or Heritage Diesel train through 10 miles of beautiful Hampshire countryside between Alresford and Alton stations.

Osborne House
East Cowes, Isle of Wight
PO32 6JX
(01983) 200022
www.english-heritage.org.uk/osbornehouse
Step into Queen Victoria's favourite country home and experience a world unchanged since the country's longest reigning monarch died here just over 100 years ago.

Oxford Castle Unlocked
Oxford, Oxfordshire OX1 1AY
(01865) 260666
www.oxfordcastleunlocked.co.uk
For the first time in 1000 years, the secrets of Oxford Castle have been 'unlocked', revealing episodes of violence, executions, great escapes, betrayal and even romance. Visit Oxford Castle and uncover the secrets for yourself.

Petworth House & Park
Petworth, West Sussex
GU28 0AE
(01798) 342207
www.nationaltrust.org.uk/petworth
Discover the National Trust's finest art collection displayed in a magnificent 17th century mansion within a beautiful 700-acre park. Petworth House contains works by artists such as Van Dyck, Reynolds and Turner.

Spinnaker Tower
Portsmouth, Hampshire
PO1 3TT
(023) 9285 7520
www.spinnakertower.co.uk
The Spinnaker Tower is a new national icon. It is a striking viewing tower on the south coast offering the public spectacular views from 3 platforms.

The Historic Dockyard Chatham
Chatham, Kent ME4 4TZ
(01634) 823807
www.thedockyard.co.uk
Costumed guides bring this spectacular maritime heritage site alive! Who do YOU want to meet today? Discover over 400 years of maritime history as you explore the world's most complete dockyard of the Age of Sail.

Waddesdon Manor
Aylesbury, Buckinghamshire
HP18 0JH
(01296) 653226
www.waddesdon.org.uk
This National Trust property houses the Rothschild Collection of art treasures and wine cellars. It also features spectacular grounds with an aviary, parterre and woodland playground, licensed restaurants, gift and wine shops.

Winchester Cathedral
Winchester, Hampshire
SO23 9LS
(01962) 857200
www.winchester-cathedral.org.uk
Now over 900 years old, a priceless jewel in a scarcely less precious setting. See the tombs of Jane Austen and Izaak Walton, the Chantry Chapels and hear how the diver saved the Cathedral in 1906.

Windsor Castle
Windsor, Berkshire SL4 1NJ
(020) 7766 7304
www.royalcollection.org.uk
The oldest and largest inhabited castle in the world and The Queen's favourite weekend home.

South East | Where to Go

NATURE & WILDLIFE

Ashdown Forest Llama Park
Forest Row, East Sussex
RH18 5JN
(01825) 712040
www.llamapark.co.uk
Llamas, alpacas. Picnic area, farm trail, museum. Coffee shop and shop selling 'llamarabilia' and alpaca knitwear. 'Walking with Llamas' - booking essential.

Beale Park
Reading, Berkshire RG8 9NH
0844 826 1761
www.bealepark.co.uk
Located on the banks of the River Thames in Berkshire, Beale Park is home to a unique collection of rare and endangered birds, animals favourites including monkeys, prairie dogs, meerkats and wallabies.

Borde Hill Garden
Haywards Heath, West Sussex
RH16 1XP
(01444) 450326
www.bordehill.co.uk
Set within 200 acres of spectacular parkland, the garden is a series of 'rooms' - each with its own particular atmosphere, form and planting design. Glorious heritage and collectors' garden.

Botanical Garden
Oxford, Oxfordshire OX1 4AZ
(01865) 286690
www.botanic-garden.ox.ac.uk
The oldest botanic garden in the UK displays over 7,000 different species in a grade 1 listed garden with exotic glasshouses, water & rock gardens and beautiful boarders. The garden has events for all ages throughout the year.

Cotswold Wildlife Park & Gardens
Burford, Oxfordshire OX18 4JW
(01993) 823006
www.cotswoldwildlifepark.co.uk
Wildlife park in 200 acres of gardens and woodland - variety of animals from all over the world.

Exbury Gardens and Steam Railway
Exbury, Hampshire SO45 1AZ
(023) 8089 1203
www.exbury.co.uk
A spectacular 200-acre woodland garden showcasing the world famous Rothschild Collection of rhododendrons, azaleas and camellias plus enchanting Steam Railway.

Groombridge Place and The Enchanted Forest
Royal Tunbridge Wells, Kent
TN3 9QG
(01892) 861444
www.groombridge.co.uk
Experience magic and mystery, history and romance at these beautiful award winning gardens - such as an unusual mix of traditional 17th century walled gardens with the excitement, challenge and contemporary landscaping of the Enchanted Forest.

High Beeches Gardens
Haywards Heath, West Sussex
RH17 6HQ
(01444) 400589
www.highbeeches.com
Conservation trust. Quality assured visitor attraction. 27 acres of magical and beautiful landscaped woodland and water gardens. Especially lovely in Spring and in Autumn. Many rare plants, natural Wildflower Meadows and much more!

Marwell Wildlife
Winchester, Hampshire
SO21 1JH
(01962) 777407
www.marwell.org.uk
A visit to Marwell Wildlife is a chance to get close to the wonders of the natural world – and play a big part in helping to save them.

Painshill Park
Cobham, Surrey KT11 1JE
(01932) 868113
www.painshill.co.uk
Discover a magnificent 18th century Georgian landscape with lake, crystal Grotto, Vineyard and interesting follies.

Port Lympne Wild Animal Park
Ashford, Kent CT21 4LR
0844 842 4647
www.totallywild.net
Port Lympne Wild Animal Park, set in 600 acres, has something for everyone, whether you're interested in animals, historic houses, elegant gardens or magnificent scenery, you'll have a totally wild day out!

RHS Garden Wisley
Woking, Surrey GU23 6QB
0845 260 9000
www.rhs.org.uk/wisley
Stretching over 240 acres of glorious garden, Wisley demonstrates the best in British gardening practices, whatever the season. Plant centre, gift shop and restaurant.

Stowe Landscape Gardens
Buckingham, Buckinghamshire
MK18 5DQ
(01280) 822850
www.nationaltrust.org.uk
Over forty temples and monuments, laid out against an inspiring backdrop of lakes and valleys. Onsite facilities include a Visitor Centre, gift shop and tea-room.

The Living Rainforest
Newbury, Berkshire RG18 0TN
(01635) 202444
www.livingrainforest.org
Wander beneath the canopy of this living rainforest recreation and watch for free roaming butterflies and birds. A perfect all weather family attraction.

The Savill Garden
Egham, Surrey TW20 0UU
(01784) 435544
www.theroyallandscape.co.uk
Woodland garden set in spectacular landscape with year-round colour. Award-winning visitor centre with floating grid-shell roof.

Ventnor Botanic Gardens
St Lawrence, Isle of Wight
PO38 1UL
(01983) 855397
www.botanic.co.uk
The Botanic Garden on the Isle of Wight is a place where the pleasure of plants can be enjoyed to the fullest.

OUTDOOR ACTIVITIES

French Brothers Ltd
Windsor, Berkshire SL4 5JH
(01753) 851900
www.boat-trips.co.uk
Large range of public trips on weather-proof vessels from Windsor, Runnymede and Maidenhead.

Hobbs of Henley Ltd
Henley-on-Thames, Oxfordshire
RG9 1AZ
(01491) 572035
www.hobbsofhenley.com
Self-drive boat hire available 10:00-17:00. Charter available for weddings, parties and corporate events.

RELAXING & PAMPERING

Xscape
Milton Keynes, Buckinghamshire
MK9 3XS
(01908) 680813
www.xscape.co.uk/
Xscape, Milton Keynes offers a unique combination of extreme sports and leisure activities for all ages.

Events 2011

anbury and District Show
www.banbury.gov.uk
ne

attle of Hastings re-enactment
ttle
www.1066country.com
tober

ighton Festival
www.brightonfestival.org
ay

itish Science Festival
uildford
www.britishsciencefestival.org
- 10 September (TBC)

ckens Festival
chester
www.medway.gov.uk/tourism
ne

stbourne Beer Festival
ww.eastbournebeerfestival.co.uk
tober

stbourne International Airshow
ww.eastbourneairshow.com/
gust

stival of Corpus Christi
undel
www.arundelcathedral.org/
ne

oodwood Festival of Speed
ichester
www.goodwood.co.uk
5 July (TBC)

oodwood Rivival Festival
ichester
www.goodwood.co.uk
ptember

eat Gardening Show
Loseley Park
uildford
www.greatgardeningshow.co.uk
ly

Guildford Summer Festival
www.guildfordsummerfestival.co.uk
01 May - 30 September (TBC)

Hampshire Food Festival
www.hampshirefare.co.uk/
July

Henley Royal Regatta
www.hrr.co.uk
1 - 5 July (TBC)

Isle of Wight Walking Festival
www.isleofwightwalkingfestival.co.uk
May

Kent County Show
Maidstone
www.kentshowground.co.uk
17 - 19 July (TBC)

Littlehampton Bonfire Celebrations
www.lbs.me.uk
29 October

MAD 2011
Aylesbury
www.madaboutwaddesdon.com
June

Marlow Town Regatta & Festival
www.marlowtownregatta.org.uk
13 - 14 June (TBC)

Medieval Spectacular at Appuldurcombe House
Ventnor
www.appuldurcombe.co.uk
25 - 26 July (TBC)

Medway Festival of Steam
Chatham
www.thedockyard.co.uk
April

New Forest and Hampshire Show
Brockenhurst
www.newforestshow.co.uk
28 - 30 July (TBC)

Oxford Jazz Festival
www.oxfordjazzfestival.com
April

Oxford Literary Festival
www.oxfordliteraryfestival.com/
March

Reading Festival
www.readingfestival.com
26-28 August

Royal Windsor Horse Show
www.royal-windsor-horse-show.co.uk
May

Surrey County Show
Guildford
www.surreycountyshow.co.uk
Spring Bank Holiday

Tenterden Folk Festival
www.tenterdenfolkfestival.org.uk/
Sept

The Henley Food Festival
www.henleyfoodfestival.co.uk
16 - 17 May (TBC)

Uckfield Festival
www.uckfieldfestival.co.uk/
July (TBC)

Weyfest at The Rural Life Centre
Farnham
www.rural-life.org.uk
05 - 06 September (TBC)

Winchester Hat Fair
www.hatfair.co.uk
02 - 05 July (TBC)

Windsor Castle Royal Tattoo
www.windsortattoo.com
13 - 16 May (TBC)

Worthing International Birdman competition
www.worthingbirdman.co.uk/
August

South East | **Where to Eat**

Where to Eat

The South East England region has great places to eat. The restaurant reviews on these pages are just a small selection from the highly respected *The Good Food Guide 2011*. Please see page 14 for further information on the Guide and details of a Special Offer for our readers.

BERKSHIRE

Boulters Restaurant & Bar
Ambitous restaurant on an island
Boulters Lock Island, Maidenhead SL6 8PE
(01628) 621291
www.boultersrestaurant.co.uk
Modern British | £35

Set on an island commanding idyllic views of the Thames, Boulter's restaurant is light, airy and tastefully decorated, with well-spaced tables and luxuriously upholstered chairs. Daniel Woodhouse's cooking successfully combines classical French techniques with bold innovations, such as brandade soup with slow-poached egg and beef cheek ravioli with snails. Perfectly timed sea bream fillet and breast of black-leg chicken show sensitive handling of fish and meat dishes. Although pastry needs a lighter touch, other desserts such as sticky toffee soufflé with Earl Grey ice cream are well executed. Wines start £15.75 a bottle (£5.10 a glass).

Chef/s: Daniel Woodhouse. **Open:** Wed to Sun L 12 to 3, Wed to Sat D 7 to 10. **Meals:** alc (main courses £13 to £20) Set L £14.95 (2 courses) to £19.95. Sun L £29.95. Tasting menu £65. **Service:** 12.5% (optional). **Details:** major cards accepted. 150 seats. 75 seats outside. Air conditioning. Separate bar. Wheelchair access. Music. Children welcome. Car parking.

London Street Brasserie
Generous, comforting food and good-value lunches
2-4 London Street, Reading RG1 4SE
(01189) 505036
www.londonstbrasserie.co.uk
Modern European | £29

'Consistently good local restaurant with strong client base and excellent service', is one regular's fond verdict on this fixture of the Reading restaurant scene. Paul Clerehugh is not about to rock an exceedingly steady ship, and his food remains true to the spirit of generosity, wholesome flavour and comfort. His menus are a mixed bag of contemporary European ideas: fish soup or partridge and ham hock terrine could be followed by a well-reported sea bass with garlic king shrimp skewer, Mediterranean vegetable and salsa verde or rabbit saddle baked in pancetta and served with a potato cake and light cider cream. Desserts might feature an excellent hot chocolate fondant with vanilla ice cream. Lunchtime menus are very good value. Wines from a wide ranging list start at £18.

Chef/s: Paul Clerehugh. **Open:** all week L 12 to 6, D 6 to 10.30 (11 Fri and Sat, 10 Sun and Mon). **Closed:** 25 Dec. **Meals:** alc (main courses £12 to £22). Set L and D £14.95 (2 courses) to £18.90. **Service:** not inc. **Details:** major cards accepted. 80 seats. 24 seats outside. Separate bar. Wheelchair access. Music. Children welcome.

South East | **Where to Eat**

BUCKINGHAMSHIRE

The Crooked Billet
Cheery artisan pub with stupendous wine
Westbrook End, Newton Longville
MK17 0DF
(01908) 373936
www.thebillet.co.uk
Modern British | £28

Newton Longville's allotment holders provide a bumper crop for this thatched hostelry, which has evolved into a cheery landmark dedicated to artisan produce: the Gilchrists buy wisely, smoke bacon and hams, make preserves and bake impressively. They also know how to procure from abroad – witness a gorgeous starter of Serrano ham with shaved two-year Gouda, celeriac rémoulade and truffled honey, although more intricately worked dishes can be let down by the details: sea bream with sweet hams, beetroot purée and lemon beurre blanc has been marred by 'leaden, unseasoned' olive oil mash. Spicy homemade gingerbread with caramelised apples is a moreish dessert, and the cheese trolley is unrivalled in these parts. The Billet is also recommended as a lunchtime pit-stop for, say, chimney-smoked duck sausages and mash with a pint of ale. Pride of place, however, goes to the stupendous 200-bin wine list – a treasure for curious imbibers, with almost everything available by the glass and friendly prices from £13.75.
Chef/s: Emma Gilchrist. **Open:** Tue to Sun L 12 to 2 (4 Sun), Mon to Sat D 7 to 9.30 (10 Fri and Sat). **Meals:** alc (main courses £14 to £28). Set L £16.75 (2 courses) to £21. Set D £18.75 (2 courses) to £23. Sun L £24.75. Tasting menu £45. **Service:** not inc. **Details:** major cards accepted. 60 seats. 50 seats outside. Separate bar. No music. Wheelchair access. Children welcome. Car parking.

The Hand & Flowers
A beacon of quality
126 West Street, Marlow SL7 2BP
(01628) 482277
www.thehandandflowers.co.uk
Modern British | £35

Tom and Beth Kerridge opened this roadside inn, with rooms a little way along the road, in 2005 and have achieved remarkable results in a very short time. Unsuspecting visitors who know nothing of its reputation come away in a state of breathless excitement, while to those in the know it has become one of Buckinghamshire's beacons of quality. It all looks so unassuming, and yet the calibre of the materials lifts the place to another level. Tom Kerridge's skill has something to do with it too, of course, witnessed in dishes such as a memorable slow-cooked shoulder and rump of lamb with smoked aubergine. Meals might begin enterprisingly with Cornish mackerel tartare with avruga, radish and black pepper toast, or

with something as apparently straightforward as an omelette, but all lushed up with smoked haddock and Parmesan. It's the accuracy of cooking and the sheer impact on the palate that impress readers, as when sea bass fillet is partnered with belly pork, cockles, pickled apple and honey gravy. The lavender pannacotta with whisky jelly and honeycomb continues to be mentioned in dispatches. A good spread of house wines comes by the glass (from £3.95), carafe (£7.90) or bottle (£15.50).
Chef/s: Tom Kerridge. **Open:** all week L 12 to 2.30 (3.30 Sun), Mon to Sat D 6.30 to 9. **Closed:** 24 to 26 Dec. **Meals:** alc (main courses £16 to £25). **Service:** not inc. **Details:** major cards accepted. 50 seats. 25 seats outside. Music. Children welcome. Car parking.

HAMPSHIRE

Pebble Beach
Glorious clifftop eatery where fish stars
Marine Drive, Barton on Sea BH25 7DZ
(01425) 627777
www.pebblebeach-uk.com
French | £30

Given such a glorious clifftop location overlooking the Isle of Wight at the Needles, it is perhaps no surprise that fish has the most important role to play on the menu. Scallops, langoustine, crab and lobster are star turns, the latter served either cold, thermidor or cooked in garlic butter, but there is much more besides. Breton-style fish soup is a robust version, crispy onion rings and mashed potato accompany skate wing with black butter, capers and lemon. Meat dishes include duck braised in red wine with blackcurrants, and a veal cutlet with morel mushrooms and roasted shallots. Finish with lemon parfait filled with hot raspberries and topped with crunchy meringue. Service is 'first class and very friendly'. House wine is £15.
Chef/s: Pierre Chevillard. **Open:** all week L 11 to 2.30 (12 to 3 Sun), D 6 to 11 (6.30 to 10.30 Sun). **Closed:** 1 Jan. **Meals:** alc (main courses £13 to £34). **Service:** not inc. **Details:** major cards accepted. 90 seats. 36 seats outside. Air conditioning. Separate bar. No mobile phones. Wheelchair access. Music. Children welcome. Car parking.

The Black Rat
Surprisingly charming, with quality not frippery
88 Chesil Street, Winchester SO23 0HX
(01962) 844465
www.theblackrat.co.uk
Modern British | £32

At first glance you might be forgiven for thinking this was a run-of-the-mill city boozer, with its rather unkempt look and busy roadside location. In reality, this early eighteenth-century building is a charming restaurant with cheerful, idiosyncratic décor creating

189

South East | Where to Eat

a contemporary feel. Simple table settings indicate that the focus is on the quality of what you eat rather than unnecessary frippery. Menus could open with a good bouillabaisse and finish with a Welsh rarebit made with local ale. Along the way, expect braised duck hearts with confit potatoes and sorrel, roast partridge with Jerusalem artichoke, kale and sloe gin, as well as desserts like home-baked madeleines with butterscotch sauce. The wide-roaming wine list is realistically priced with house wine at £16.50.

Chef/s: Chris Bailey. **Open:** Sat and Sun L 12 to 2, all week D 7 to 9.30. **Closed:** 23 Dec to 8 Jan, 2 weeks Easter, 2 weeks end Oct/Nov. **Meals:** alc (main courses £17 to £22). Set L £19.50 (2 courses) to £23.50. **Service:** not inc. **Details:** major cards accepted. 60 seats. 18 seats outside. Separate bar. Music. Children allowed for Sat and Sun L. Use of car park after 6pm.

KENT

Age & Sons
Making waves
Charlotte Court, Ramsgate CT11 8HE
(01843) 851515
www.ageandsons.co.uk
Modern British | £24

This one-time wine warehouse was originally called Page & Sons, but the 'P' dropped off the sign and current incumbent Toby Leigh decided to run with the truncated name. Since then, Age & Sons has been making waves, with much attention focused on the vaulted top-floor restaurant. Here visitors can delve into a sharp seasonal menu that favours local ingredients. Fish fans could drift towards, say, herring roes with rhubarb, cucumber and capers, or brill with purple sprouting broccoli and brown shrimps. Meat-eaters might prefer pigeon breast salad followed by pig's face with prune sauce, mash and Savoy cabbage. After that, rice pudding with milk jam and blackberries sounds suitably comforting. Light bites are served in the ground-floor café, and there's a funky basement bar for cocktails. Wines start at £14.50 (£4 a glass).

Chef/s: Toby Leigh. **Open:** Tue to Sun L 12 to 3, Tue to Sat D 6.30 to 9.30. **Closed:** Mon, 25 to 28 Dec. **Meals:** alc (main courses £10 to £17). Set L £12 (2 courses) to £15. Set D £19 (2 courses) to £25. Sun L £18. **Service:** not inc. **Details:** major cards accepted. 60 seats. 40 seats outside. Separate bar. Music. Children welcome.

The Allotment
Mightily satisfying urban bistro
9 High Street, Dover CT16 1DP
(01304) 214467
www.theallotmentdover.com
Modern British | £24

David Flynn's urban bistro has certainly kick-started Dover's restaurant scene. Menus change from day to day, and feature some well-wrought, internationally influenced dishes. Spicy pork casserole with couscous and Andalucian lamb with dauphinois potatoes left one pair of diners feeling mightily satisfied. Local ingredients receive a fair outing, whether it is Dungeness mackerel with grain mustard dressing, or slow-roasted shoulder of Canterbury lamb. Puddings, in the shape of baked blueberry cheesecake or lemon posset, will prove hard to resist. Some have found the front-of-house approach a little distracting, but we have received many plaudits too. A spread of wines sold at the uniform price of £17 (or £4 a glass) – a nice idea.

Chef/s: David Flynn. **Open:** Tue to Sat 8.30am to 11pm. **Closed:** Sun, Mon, 24 Dec to 11 Jan. **Meals:** alc (main courses £8 to £16). **Service:** not inc. **Details:** major cards accepted. 26 seats. 26 seats outside. Wheelchair access. Music. Children welcome.

OXFORDSHIRE

The Kings Head Inn
Shining ingredients in an idyllic spot
The Green, Bledington OX7 6XQ
(01608) 658365
www.thekingsheadinn.net
Modern British | £25

The setting is as attractive as ever: a honey-hued sixteenth-century former cider house overlooking Bledington's green. It's no backwoods watering hole, however, but a strongly rooted enterprise, a combination of pub and serious restaurant. Raw materials are consistently good (meat comes from the family farm at Fifield) and unflashy elements, such as chicken liver parfait or Baltic-cured sea trout with beetroot relish and sour cream, are allowed to shine. Straightforward main courses bring whole baked lemon sole with brown shrimp dressing or free-range chicken breast with chorizo and leek tartiflette, with caramelised rhubarb and custard with rhubarb schnapps to finish. House wine is £14.

Chef/s: Charlie Loader. **Open:** all week L 12 to 2 (2.30 Sat and Sun), D 7 to 9 (9.30 Fri and Sat). **Closed:** 25 and 26 Dec. **Meals:** alc (main courses £10 to £20). Sun L £13. **Service:** not inc. **Details:** major cards accepted. 76 seats. 44 seats outside. Separate bar. Wheelchair access. Music. Children welcome. Car parking.

The White Hart
Quality cooking with a Mediterranean touch
Main Road, Fyfield OX13 5LW
(01865) 390585
www.whitehart-fyfield.com
Modern British | £27

The fifteenth-century White Hart is an immaculately maintained pub with a kitchen that cares about the provenance of its supplies, so much so that the owner have developed a large kitchen garden. Mediterranea

South East | **Where to Eat**

...fluences loom large on the daily changing menus, as a neat starter of sautéed baby squid with couscous and gremolata. The quality also shows in dishes like ...ow-roasted belly of pork with celeriac purée, cider jus and the crispiest of crackling or braised lamb shoulder ...th dauphinoise potatoes, Savoy cabbage, beer and ...con. To finish, there are desserts like apple and ...lvados mousse with cinnamon shortbread. The wine ...t provides fair back-up at prices starting from £16. **...ef/s:** Mark Chandler. **Open:** Tue to Sun L 12 to 2.30 (3.30 ...n), Tue to Sat D 6.45 to 9.30. **Closed:** Mon. **Meals:** alc ...ain courses £12 to £20). Set L £15 (2 courses) to £18. Sun ...17 (2 courses) to £20. **Service:** not inc. **Details:** major ...rds accepted. 45 seats. 50 seats outside. Separate bar. ...usic. Children welcome. Car parking.

SURREY

Drake's Restaurant
...tting-edge, big-attitude food
...e Clock House, High Street, Ripley GU23 6AQ
...483) 224777
...ww.drakesrestaurant.co.uk
...odern British | £46

...eve Drake's restaurant occupies a clock-fronted ...orgian house in a suitably timeless Surrey village. ...od local artworks help create an air of relaxed ...inement in the low-ceilinged dining room, where ...rvice is 'unobtrusively attentive' and there is a ...refied and hushed air' to proceedings. The food is ...tting-edge, the fixed-price menus offering artfully ...mposed pile-ups of ingredients that are big on ...titude. A plump and immaculately timed roast scallop ...ght turn up with a portion of braised pig cheek ...d ceps, dressed with pear and saffron relish, while ...ared duck foie gras is accompanied by peppered ...neapple. Choose from main course listings such as ...ll, cauliflower, cucumber and turmeric, or venison, ...rusalem artichoke, beans, marrow and crackers. If ...ere is a note of doubt, as there was for one reporter, ...ies in the determinedly dinky dimensions of dishes, ...t the technical wizardry is so great that we should ...rhaps trust the chef's judgement on that. A voyage of discovery at dessert stage might take in the beautifully juxtaposed flavours of beetroot parfait with mandarin sorbet, chocolate crumbs and a gel of star anise. An opulent wine list opens with small glasses from £5.50.
Chef/s: Steve Drake. **Open:** Tue to Fri L 12 to 1.30, Tue to Sat D 7 to 9 (9.30 Fri and Sat). **Closed:** Sun, Mon, 2 weeks Jan, 2 weeks Aug, bank hols (exc Good Friday). **Meals:** Set L £21 (2 courses) to £26. Set D £38.50 (2 courses) to £46. Tasting menu £60. **Service:** not inc. **Details:** major cards accepted. 40 seats. Children welcome. Car parking.

La Luna
Inventive Italian food and sensational wine
10-14 Wharf Street, Godalming GU7 1NN
(01483) 414155
www.lalunarestaurant.co.uk
Italian | £26

La Luna celebrates 10 years at Godalming in 2011. From the start it gained plaudits – and a devoted loyal following – for its modern setting and for serving Italian food to an appreciated formula: a concise menu that follows the Italian style (four courses with pasta or risotto for the second) and juxtaposes classics like gnocchi with gorgonzola, and minestrone with trendier offerings including poached duck egg with baby spinach, crispy root vegetables and horseradish dressing, and mackerel with squid casserole and crushed parsley potato. Elsewhere there could be wild mushroom and butternut squash risotto or Sicilian casarecce (pasta) with fennel seed and pork sausage and sprouting broccoli, and mains of calf's liver with sautéed curly kale and parsnip purée. Efficient staff work the tables with consummate skill, uncorking bottles from the sensational all-Italian list that opens in Sicily at £13, goes on to a carefully selected choice under £30 and includes some real gems elsewhere.
Chef/s: Valentino Gentile. **Open:** Tue to Sat L 12 to 2, D 7 to 10. **Closed:** Sun, Mon. **Meals:** alc (main courses £10 to £19). Set L £11.95 to £14.50. **Service:** not inc.
Details: major cards accepted. 50 seats. Air conditioning. Music. Children welcome.

SUSSEX

Gingerman
Impressive bistro cooking
21A Norfolk Square, Brighton BN1 2PD
(01273) 326688
www.gingermanrestaurants.com
Modern European | £30

This was the first of Ben McKellar's ever-growing group of restaurants and pubs and for many it's still the most intimately agreeable. It's a smallish, low-ceilinged room in the centre of town, with an intelligently chatty service approach and some impressive cooking. A fashionably urban dish offers plaice goujons with a pea

191

South East | Where to Eat

shooter, and caper and nori hash, perhaps followed by fillet of local beef with celeriac gratin, broccoli purée, salsify crisps and red wine sauce, or a multi-layered vegetarian rösti dish. Desserts relax into slightly more classic bistro mould with Drambuie chocolate mousse and almond shortbread, or rhubarb gratin with pecan crumble ice cream. Ridgeview Sussex sparklers crop up among the fizzes on a quality list that starts at £14.
Chef/s: Simon Neville-Jones and Ben McKellar. **Open:** Tue to Sun L 12.30 to 1.30, D 7 to 9.15. **Closed:** Mon, 2 weeks Jan. **Meals:** Set L £15 (2 courses) to £18. Set D £26 (2 courses) to £30. **Service:** not inc. **Details:** major cards accepted. 32 seats. Air conditioning. Music. Children welcome.

Terre à Terre
Funky veggie maverick
71 East Street, Brighton BN1 1HQ
(01273) 729051
www.terreaterre.co.uk
Vegetarian | £28

In recent times, this rule-breaking veggie has reined in some of its maverick global tendencies, but it still knows how to assault the taste buds and challenge preconceptions about flesh-free food. Smoked sakuri soba (a chilled Japanese collation involving noodles, umeboshi plums, smoked tofu, white miso, pomegranate 'beads', wasabi cashews) is a typically full-on starter, likewise a main called Sodden Socca (hot chickpea pancakes with piquant caponata, marmara tapenade, thyme, saffron and orange dressing). For a sweet hit, finish with Bum (a little sheep's cheesecake with sambuca-soaked raisins, rosemary lemon syrup, black grapes, fennel, orange zest and almond biscotti). The mood is pure Brighton (offbeat, extrovert, funky, colourful), kids do well and the organically inclined wine list is totally in tune with the restaurant's philosophy. Prices start at £12.95 a carafe, £17.50 a bottle.
Chef/s: Dino Pavledis. **Open:** Tue to Sun L 12 to 4.30, D 5 to 10.30 (11 Sat, 10 Sun). **Closed:** Mon (exc bank hols), 25 and 26 Dec. **Meals:** alc (main courses £11 to £15). **Service:** 10% (optional). **Details:** major cards accepted. 100 seats. 15 seats outside. Air conditioning. Wheelchair access. Music. Children welcome.

The Earl of March
Inspirational views and terrific food
Lavant PO18 0BQ
(01243) 533993
www.theearlofmarch.com
Modern British | £30

As you gaze out towards Goodwood, over the lovely prospect of the South Downs, it's easy to see why William Blake was inspired to pen Jerusalem here. A lot has changed since 1803, but the views are still inspirational and the Earl of March has a new-found reputation as a hostelry with terrific food. Main man

Giles Thompson earned his stripes as executive chef at The Ritz, before decamping to Sussex and filling his larder with regional produce. The result is an inviting checklist of finely honed, seasonal dishes: grilled Sussex haloumi is paired with Tangmere red pepper mousse, steaks are from beasts reared in the Rother Valley and Southdown lamb cutlets are fired up with devil sauce. Fish is also handled with exemplary flair, witness diver caught scallops with white bean purée, black pudding and truffle oil. Desserts could usher in lemon and goat curd tart with pear caramel. Lunch bites are served in the bar, and the well-spread wine list starts at £16.50.
Chef/s: Giles Thompson and Mattie Thumshirn.
Open: all week L 12 to 2.30 (4 Sun), Mon to Sat D 5.30 to 9.30. **Meals:** alc (main courses £12 to £20). Set L and early D £17.95 (2 courses) to £22.95. **Service:** not inc.
Details: major cards accepted. 60 seats. 40 seats outside. Separate bar. Wheelchair access. Music. Children welcome. Car parking.

The Ginger Fox
Convivial country pub star
Muddleswood Road, Albourne BN6 9EA
(01273) 857888
www.gingermanrestaurants.com
Modern British | £25

'A country inn with "city restaurant" standards', is how one reader summed up this West Sussex branch of Ben McKellar's little empire (see also Gingerman in Brighton). Originally called Shaves Thatch, the building now sports a tidy new roof (complete with an effigy of our vulpine friend stalking a pheasant) and an interior that has been tricked out for maximum country-loving conviviality – 'it really works', added another fan. The scenery is great, service is bright as a button, and the cooking derives from a natural-born instinct for local flavours, without fuss or contrivance. Rye Bay scallops with Seville orange and fennel could be followed by haunch of venison with Puy lentils, Jerusalem artichokes and Banyuls vinegar. The kitchen isn't slavishly patriotic, though – hence the presence of sesame beef and spiced enoki mushroom salad, roast monkfish with harissa potatoes, and toffee banana cornetto with espresso ice cream. Real ales do duty at the bar, and quaffable wines start at £14 (£3.70 a glass).
Chef/s: David Keats and Ben McKellar. **Open:** all week L 12 to 2 (12.30 to 4 Sat and Sun), D 6 to 10 (6.30 Sat and Sun). **Closed:** 25 Dec. **Meals:** alc (main courses £9 to £20). Set L £10 (2 courses). **Service:** not inc. **Details:** major cards accepted. 55 seats. 90 seats outside. Separate bar. Wheelchair access. Music. Children welcome. Car parking.

Content brought to you by **The Good Food Guide 2011.** Please see page 14 for further details.

South East

Tourist Information Centres

When you arrive at your destination, visit an Official Partner Tourist Information Centre for quality assured help with accommodation and information about local attractions and events, or email your request before you go. To find a Tourist Information Centre by region visit enjoyEngland.com/find-tic.

ASHFORD	18 The Churchyard	01233 629165	tourism@ashford.gov.uk
AYLESBURY	The Kings Head	01296 330559	tic@aylesburyvaledc.gov.uk
BANBURY	Spiceball Park Road	01295 259855	banbury.tic@cherwell-dc.gov.uk
BICESTER	Bicester Visitor Centre	01869 369055	bicester.vc@cherwell-dc.gov.uk
BRIGHTON	Royal Pavilion Shop	0906 711 2255	brighton-tourism@brighton-hove.gov.uk
BURFORD	The Brewery	01993 823558	burford.vic@westoxon.gov.uk
CANTERBURY	12/13 Sun Street	01227 378100	canterburyinformation@canterbury.gov.uk
CHICHESTER	29a South Street	01243 775888	chitic@chichester.gov.uk
COWES	9 The Arcade	01983 813818	info@islandbreaks.co.uk
CROYDON	Croydon Clocktower	020 8253 1009	tic@croydon.gov.uk
DOVER	The Old Town Gaol	01304 205108	tic@doveruk.com
GRAVESEND	Towncentric	01474 337600	info@towncentric.co.uk
HASTINGS	Queens Square	01424 781111	hic@hastings.gov.uk
LEWES	187 High Street	01273 483448	lewes.tic@lewes.gov.uk
MAIDSTONE	Town Hall, Middle Row	01622 602169	tourism@maidstone.gov.uk
MARGATE	12-13 The Parade	0870 2646111	margate.tic@visitor-centre.net
MARLOW	31 High Street	01628 483597	tourism_enquiries@wycombe.gov.uk
NEWBURY	The Wharf	01635 30267	tourism@westberks.gov.uk
NEWPORT	The Guildhall	01983 813818	info@islandbreaks.co.uk
OXFORD	Oxford Information Centre	01865 252200	tic@oxford.gov.uk
PORTSMOUTH	Clarence Esplanade	023 9282 6722	vis@portsmouthcc.gov.uk
PORTSMOUTH (THE HARD)	The Hard	023 9282 6722	vis@portsmouthcc.gov.uk
RAMSGATE	17 Albert Court	0870 2646111	ramsgate.tic@visitor-centre.net
RICHMOND	Old Town Hall	020 8940 9125	info@visitrichmond.co.uk
ROCHESTER	95 High Street	01634 843666	visitor.centre@medway.gov.uk

South East

ROMSEY	Heritage & Visitor Centre	01794 512987	romseytic@testvalley.gov.uk
ROYAL TUNBRIDGE WELLS	The Old Fish Market	01892 515675	touristinformationcentre@tunbridgewells.gov.uk
RYDE	81-83 Union Street	01983 813818	info@islandbreaks.co.uk
SANDOWN	8 High Street	01983 813818	info@islandbreaks.co.uk
SHANKLIN	67 High Street	01983 813818	info@islandbreaks.co.uk
SOUTHAMPTON	9 Civic Centre Road	023 8083 3333	tourist.information@southampton.gov.uk
SWANLEY	Swanley Library	01322 614660	touristinfo@swanley.org.uk
WINCHESTER	Guildhall	01962 840500	tourism@winchester.gov.uk
WINDSOR	Royal Windsor Shopping Centre	01753 743900	windsor.tic@rbwm.gov.uk
WITNEY	26A Market Square	01993 775802	witney.vic@westoxon.gov.uk
WOODSTOCK	Oxfordshire Museum	01993 813276	woodstock.vic@westoxon.gov.uk
WORTHING	Marine Parade	01903 221066	tic@worthing.gov.uk
YARMOUTH	The Quay	01983 813818	info@islandbreaks.co.uk

Regional Contacts and Information

For more information on accommodation, attractions, activities, events and holidays in South East England, contact the regional or local tourism organisations. Their websites have a wealth of information and many produce free publications to help you get the most out of your visit.

The following publications are available from Tourism South East by logging on to www.visitsoutheastengland.com or by calling (023) 8062 5300.

E-Brochures
Family Fun
Time for Us

South East England – We know just the place...

Be part of our story

Britain™
You're invited

Whitby Abbey, North Yorkshire

GREAT BRITISH HERITAGE PASS

Enjoy the magic of Britain with the
Great British Heritage Pass

- Entry to over 570 top heritage attractions
- Castles, stately homes, historic houses, gardens
- The more you see, the more you save!

Buy online at: **visitbritain.com/heritagepass**

or at the Britain & London Visitor Centre, 1 Regent Street, London SW1Y 4XT (Tube: Piccadilly Circus)

Not available to British residents or groups of more than 10 people.

South East | **Berkshire**

Where to Stay

Entries appear alphabetically by town name in each county. A key to symbols appears on page 6. Maps start on page 706. A listing of all Enjoy England assessed accommodation appears at the end of the region.

BRACKNELL, Berkshire Map ref 2C2   SAT NAV RG42 1PB

★★★★ GUEST ACCOMMODATION

B&B PER ROOM PER NIGHT
S £55.00 – £95.00
D £65.00 – £95.00

Elizabeth House
Rounds Hill, Wokingham Road, Bracknell RG42 1PB
t (01344) 868480 f (01344) 648453 e res@lizhotel.co.uk
w lizhotel.co.uk

Everything is to make your stay as comfortable and enjoyable as possible, finest linens and toiletries with attention to finishing touches in our individually styled rooms. **directions** See website for map and directions. **open** All year **bedrooms** 4 single, 8 double, 4 twin, 1 family **bathrooms** 15 en suite, 2 with private bathroom **payment** credit/debit cards, cash, cheques, euros

Room   General

Looking for something else?

You can also buy a copy of our popular guide 'Self Catering' including self-catering holiday homes, approved caravan holiday homes, boat accommodation and holiday cottage agencies in England 2011.

Now available in good bookshops and online at **visitbritainshop.com**

£11.99

South East | Berkshire

BRACKNELL, Berkshire Map ref 2C2
SAT NAV RG12 2JR

Holly House
Goughs Lane, Bracknell RG12 2JR
t (01344) 411340 **f** (01344) 411340 **e** reservations@hollyhousebracknell.co.uk
w hollyhousebracknell.co.uk ONLINE MAP GUEST REVIEWS

B&B PER ROOM PER NIGHT
S £60.00 – £75.00
D £80.00 – £135.00

SPECIAL PROMOTIONS
Weekend Breaks £110-£200 for 2 night stays, Friday and Saturday. Complimentary drink of choice on arrival.

An elegant charming house with a beautiful garden in a quiet leafy lane offering exceptional yet affordable bed and breakfast in a warm and relaxing atmoshphere. Comfort and cleanliness are our bywords. Close to Windsor, Ascot, Henley, Marlow and Reading with London and Gatwick airport an hour away.

open All year except Xmas and New Year
bedrooms 1 single, 2 double, 1 twin
bathrooms 4 en suite
payment credit/debit cards, cash, cheques

directions Once along Warfield Road (A3095) turn right by pedestrian traffic lights into Holly Spring Lane then left into Goughs Lane. 350 yards on left entrance.

Room
General
Leisure

KINTBURY, Berkshire Map ref 2C2
SAT NAV RG17 9UT

Dundas Arms
Station Road, Kintbury, Hungerford RG17 9UT
t (01488) 658263 **f** (01488) 658568 **e** info@dundasarms.co.uk
w dundasarms.co.uk ONLINE MAP

B&B PER ROOM PER NIGHT
S £80.00 – £90.00
D £90.00 – £100.00

EVENING MEAL PER PERSON
£8.00 – £18.00

Canal and riverside pub selling good food, real ale beers and wine in both bar and restaurant, with hotel rooms overlooking the river.
directions Please contact us for directions **open** All year except Xmas and New Year **bedrooms** 3 double, 2 twin **bathrooms** 5 en suite **payment** credit/debit cards, cash

Room General Leisure

NEWBURY, Berkshire Map ref 2C2
SAT NAV RG18 0TD

Manor Farm House
Church Street, Hampstead Norreys, Thatcham, Berkshire RG18 0TD
t (01635) 201346 **e** bettsbedandbreakfast@hotmail.com
w bettsbedandbreakfast.co.uk ONLINE MAP GUEST REVIEWS

B&B PER ROOM PER NIGHT
S £40.00 – £47.00
D £65.00 – £76.00

Superbly comfortable 17thC house on working farm in centre of peaceful village. Whirlpool bath, self-contained ground-floor apartment. Wi-Fi. Pub two minutes' stroll. Labrador dogs available for longer walks. **directions** From E: M4 jct 12, through Bradfield and Yattendon to Hampstead Norreys. From other directions: A34/M4 jct 13 to Hermitage, then B4009 to Hampstead Norreys. **open** All year **bedrooms** 1 double, 1 twin, 1 suite **bathrooms** 3 en suite **payment** credit/debit cards, cash, cheques, euros

BREAKFAST AWARD

Room General

197

South East | Berkshire

NEWBURY, Berkshire Map ref 2C2
SAT NAV RG20 8TN

★★★★ BED & BREAKFAST

B&B PER ROOM PER NIGHT
S £45.00 – £55.00
D £80.00 – £85.00

The Old Farmhouse
Down End Lane, Chieveley, Newbury, Berkshire RG20 8TN
t (01635) 248361 e palletts@aol.com
w mychieveley.co.uk/info/theoldfarmhouse

Period farmhouse within 2 miles of M4/A34 junction 13. Ground-floor annexe comprising hall, kitchenette, sitting room, double bedroom, bathroom. Large gardens. Oxford, Bath, Windsor and Heathrow Airport within easy reach. **directions** A34/M4 jct 13 take Chieveley exit. At junction, left to Chieveley then right towards Beedon. 2nd left into Downend Lane. House on right **open** All year **bedrooms** 1 suite **bathrooms** 1 en suite **payment** cash, cheques

Room General

OAKLEY GREEN, Berkshire Map ref 2C2
SAT NAV SL4 5UL

★★★★ GUEST ACCOMMODATION
Silver AWARD

B&B PER ROOM PER NIGHT
S £65.00 – £90.00
D £85.00 – £95.00

Rainworth House
Oakley Green Road, Oakley Green, Windsor SL4 5UL
t (01753) 856749 f (01753) 859192 e info@rainworthhouse.com
w rainworthhouse.com

Rainworth House is a large spacious country house that provides a peaceful and relaxed atmosphere. Guests can be assured of excellent accommodation, traditional comforts and warm hospitality. **directions** Turn off the Windsor to Maidenhead Road (A308) into Oakley Green Road. Rainworth House is first on the left (One mile from Windsor Racecourse) **open** All year **bedrooms** 2 double, 2 twin, 2 family **bathrooms** 5 en suite, 1 with private bathroom **payment** credit/debit cards, cash, cheques, euros

Room General

WINDSOR, Berkshire Map ref 2D2
SAT NAV SL4 5EQ

★★★★ BED & BREAKFAST

B&B PER ROOM PER NIGHT
S £55.00
D £70.00

Barbara's Bed & Breakfast
16 Maidenhead Road, Windsor SL4 5EQ
t 0044 (0)1753 840273 e bbandbwindsor@btinternet.com
w bbandbwindsor.com ONLINE MAP

Conveniently located B&B 25 minutes from Heathrow, mile from M and 10 minutes walk from Windsor Castle. Victorian house with many original features, which also provides modern facilities for guests. **directions** From M4 follow signs to Windsor, first exit, left toward the town centre, 100 metres on left opposite Windsor Boys School **open** All year except Xmas **bedrooms** 2 double, 1 twin **bathrooms** 1 en suite, 2 with private bathroom **payment** cash, cheques, euros

Room General

Do you like Camping?

You can also buy a copy of our popular guide 'Camping, Touring & Holiday Parks' including touring parks, camping holidays and holiday parks and villages in Britain 2011.

Now available in good bookshops and online at
visitbritainshop.com

£8.99

South East | Berkshire/Buckinghamshire

WINDSOR, Berkshire Map ref 2D2
SAT NAV SL4 5AE

Clarence Hotel
9 Clarence Road, Windsor SL4 5AE
t (01753) 864436 f (01753) 857060 e clarence.hotel@btconnect.com
w clarence-hotel.co.uk ONLINE MAP LAST MINUTE OFFERS

GUEST HOUSE

B&B PER ROOM PER NIGHT
S £45.00 – £75.00
D £55.00 – £86.00

SPECIAL PROMOTIONS
Special Winter weekend rates available on request

Recently upgraded and located in town centre and short walk from Windsor Castle, Eton College and River Thames. Licensed bar and steam-sauna. All rooms with en suite bathroom, TV, tea/coffee makers, hairdryer and radio-alarm. Free Wi-Fi and guest Internet. Convenient for Legoland, Heathrow Airport and trains to London.

open All year except Xmas
bedrooms 4 single, 4 double, 6 twin, 6 family
bathrooms 20 en suite
payment credit/debit cards, cash, cheques

directions Exit M4 at jct 6 to Windsor. Stay on dual carriageway and turn left at the roundabout onto Clarence Road.

Room General

AYLESBURY, Buckinghamshire Map ref 2C1
SAT NAV HP17 8SH

Tanamera
37 Bishopstone Village, Bishopstone, Aylesbury HP17 8SH
t (01296) 748551 e mary.purdy01@btinterenet.com

BED & BREAKFAST / **Silver AWARD**

B&B PER ROOM PER NIGHT
S £40.00
D £60.00 – £70.00

Warm welcome, owner's personal attention. Quality English breakfast, large, attractive, en suite, twin or king-size double, TV, tea/coffee. Central location, village pub, historic houses (Waddesdon Manor, Chequers), private parking. **directions** From the M1 motorway, 25 miles using the A43 - A413 & A418 roads. From the M40 motorway, 14 miles on the A418 road. **open** All year except Xmas and New Year **bedrooms** 1 double **bathrooms** 1 en suite **payment** cash, cheques, euros

BREAKFAST AWARD Room General

BUCKINGHAM, Buckinghamshire Map ref 2C1
SAT NAV MK18 5ND

Huntsmill Farm B&B
Huntsmill Farm, Shalstone, Nr. Buckingham MK18 5ND
t (01280) 704852 f (01280) 704852 e fiona@huntsmill.com
w huntsmill.com

BED & BREAKFAST

B&B PER ROOM PER NIGHT
S £40.00
D £60.00

Home-made bread and preserves welcome you at Huntsmill Farm. Comfortable, en suite rooms adjacent to farmhouse, in stone courtyard. Quiet location, views over open countryside. Close to National Trust properties and Silverstone. **directions** Midway between Buckingham and Brackley on A422. South side, signposted 'Finmere & Mixbury', 1/3mile on the left. **open** All year except Xmas **bedrooms** 1 double, 2 twin **bathrooms** 3 en suite **payment** credit/debit cards, cash, cheques, euros

Room General Leisure

or key to symbols see page 6

199

South East | Buckinghamshire

GREAT MISSENDEN, Buckinghamshire Map ref 2C1 — SAT NAV HP16 0AX

Forge House
Forge House, 10 Church Street, Great Missenden HP16 0AX
t (01494) 867347

B&B PER ROOM PER NIGHT
S £31.33
D £62.66

Set in the wooded Chiltern Hills, quiet village location - a charming 18thC beamed house traditionally refurbished with three en suite double bedrooms. English/continental breakfast included. Chiltern Line to Marylebone 35 minutes. Car access to Waddesdon Manor, Hughendon Manor, West Wycombe Park and caves, Milton's Cottage, Bekonscot Model Village. Walking/cycling The Ridgeway, Chiltern Way. **directions** Please contact us for directions **open** All year **bedrooms** 2 double, 1 twin **bathrooms** 3 en suite **payment** cash, cheques

Room General Leisure

GREAT MISSENDEN, Buckinghamshire Map ref 2C1 — SAT NAV HP16 0HZ

Rickyard Cottage
Rickyard Cottage, Denner Hill, Great Missenden HP16 0HZ
t (01494) 488388 e richard@rickyard.plus.com
w rickyardcottage.co.uk ONLINE MAP

B&B PER ROOM PER NIGHT
S £55.00 – £60.00
D £75.00 – £85.00
EVENING MEAL PER PERSON
£10.00 – £15.00

BREAKFAST AWARD

Exclusive luxury accommodation and farmhouse hospitality in quiet beautiful Chiltern Hills. Own barn with garden, view, beside historic cottage. Generous award-winning breakfast, WiFi, Midsomer Murders country, ideal pleasure or business **directions** Denner Hill is in the Chiltern Hills, 5 miles North of High Wycombe, 3 miles west of Great Missenden, 6 miles from M40, Junction 4. **open** All year **bedrooms** 1 double **bathrooms** 1 en suite **payment** cash, cheques, euros

Room General Leisure

HENLEY-ON-THAMES, Buckinghamshire Map ref 2C2 — SAT NAV RG9 6TD

The Old Bakery
The Old Bakery, Henley-on-Thames RG9 6TD
t (01491) 638309 f (01491) 638086 e lizzroach@aol.com
w bedbreakfasthenley.co.uk ONLINE MAP

B&B PER ROOM PER NIGHT
D £70.00 – £80.00

The Old Bakery is in the beautiful Hambleden valley with countryside views. 7 miles from Henley. A large welcoming family house within walking distance from excellent pub/restaurant. **directions** Please contact us for directions **open** All year **bedrooms** 2 double, 1 twin **bathrooms** 1 en suite, 1 with private bathroom **payment** cash, cheques

Room General Leisure

HIGH WYCOMBE, Buckinghamshire Map ref 2C2 — SAT NAV HP13 6PQ

Amersham Hill Guest House
52 Amersham Hill, High Wycombe HP13 6PQ
t (01494) 520365 e amershamhillguesthouse@btconnect.com

B&B PER ROOM PER NIGHT
S £35.00 – £45.00
D £58.00 – £68.00

Conveniently located five minutes from High Wycombe station. Easy access to M40 and M4. All rooms have colour TV, radio alarm, tea-/coffee-making facilities. Full English breakfast included. Ample parking. Wi-Fi. **directions** 5 minutes from High Wycombe rail station. 2 miles from junction 4 off M40 and 7 miles from M4. 35 minutes by rail to London. **open** All year **bedrooms** 4 single, 2 double, 1 twin **bathrooms** 2 en suite **payment** cash, cheques

Room General

Official tourist board guide **Bed & Breakfast**

South East | **Buckinghamshire/Hampshire**

MARLOW, Buckinghamshire Map ref 2C2

SAT NAV SL7 2BP

The Hand & Flowers
The Hand & Flowers, West Street, Marlow SL7 2BP
t (01628) 482277 e theoffice@thehandandflowers.co.uk
w thehandandflowers.co.uk ONLINE MAP LAST MINUTE OFFERS

B&B PER ROOM PER NIGHT
D £140.00 – £190.00
EVENING MEAL PER PERSON
£31.00 – £44.00

Cottages are described as quirky and luxurious, perfect for a romantic weekend or as an escape from the city. Enjoy a short walk to the river or relax in the spa. Have breakfast in bed or full English in our pub.

open All year except Xmas
bedrooms 4 double
bathrooms 4 en suite
payment credit/debit cards, cash

directions M4 jct 9, A404 north, into Marlow, A4155 direction Henley. On edge of town on right.

ALRESFORD, Hampshire Map ref 2C2

SAT NAV SO24 9LJ

Haygarth
82 Jacklyns Lane, Alresford SO24 9LJ
t (01962) 732715 / 07986 372895 e valramshaw@aol.com

B&B PER ROOM PER NIGHT
S £35.00
D £65.00

A pleasant welcome awaits visitors to Haygarth. Close to town centre and golf course. Convenient for Winchester, Salisbury, New Forest, Watercress Line and Wayfarers Walk. Relax and unwind in the heart of Hampshire. Guest annexe includes separate entrance, lounge, kitchen, en suite bedrooms. Sky TV. **directions** From Winchester take A31 towards Alton. Turn off at B3047 (Alresford), at Running Horse public house next rt (B3046 to Cheriton). House 0.5 miles on right. **open** All year **bedrooms** 3 double **bathrooms** 2 en suite, 1 with private bathroom **payment** cash, cheques

ALTON, Hampshire Map ref 2C2

SAT NAV GU34 4NP

Neatham Barn Self Catering & Bed & Breakfast
Neatham, Holybourne, Alton GU34 4NP
t (01420) 544 215 e alastair@neathamcottage.com
w neathambarn.com

B&B PER ROOM PER NIGHT
S £53.00 – £59.00
D £70.00 – £78.00

Situated up a quiet country lane, this detached 'oak' framed barn annexe enjoys a lovely setting and views over Hampshire countryside. Long term 'lets' are welcomed. Please enquire for prices. **directions** Through Holybourne towards Binsted, under A31, right after river, up lane, Neatham Barn on left through wooden gate. Press button on gate post to open. **open** All year **bedrooms** 1 double **bathrooms** 1 en suite **payment** cash, cheques, euros

key to symbols see page 6

201

South East | **Hampshire**

ANDOVER, Hampshire Map ref 2C2 — SAT NAV SP11 8LZ

May Cottage
Thruxton, Andover SP11 8LZ
t (01264) 771241 **f** (01264) 771770 **e** info@maycottage-thruxton.co.uk
w maycottage-thruxton.co.uk

B&B PER ROOM PER NIGHT
S £40.00 – £55.00
D £65.00 – £90.00

Dating back to 1740, May Cottage is situated in the heart of this picturesque Village. All rooms en-suite/private bathroom. Guests' own sitting/dining room. Secluded garden. Historic attractions nearby. Non-smoking. **directions** From Andover take A303 towards Exeter, then take turning for Thruxton (village only). Left at T-junction. May Cottage is on right opposite The George Inn. **open** All year **bedrooms** 2 double, 1 twin **bathrooms** 3 en suite, 1 with private bathroom **payment** cash, cheques

BASINGSTOKE, Hampshire Map ref 2C2 — SAT NAV RG25 3JZ

Mallards
3 Trims Court, Overton, Nr Basingstoke, Hampshire RG25 3JZ
t (01256) 770039 **e** mallards@test-the-water.co.uk
w test-the-water.co.uk ONLINE MAP

B&B PER ROOM PER NIGHT
S £50.00 – £60.00
D £65.00 – £75.00

BREAKFAST AWARD

Luxury Bed and Breakfast Accommodation set in beautiful riverfront location on the River Test. Peace and tranquility, yet only 50 metres from charming village centre. Beautifully appointed en-suite bedrooms. **directions** Mallards is located to the right of the converted Cornstore in Trims Court, off Overton High Street on the B3400 Basingstoke to Whitchurch Road **open** All year **bedrooms** 2 double **bathrooms** 2 en suite **payment** credit/debit cards, cash, cheques

BURLEY, Hampshire Map ref 2B3 — SAT NAV BH24 4EA

Wayside Cottage
Garden Road, Burley BH24 4EA
t (01425) 403414 **e** jwest@wayside-cottage.co.uk
w wayside-cottage.co.uk LAST MINUTE OFFERS

B&B PER ROOM PER NIGHT
S £35.00 – £50.00
D £60.00 – £75.00
EVENING MEAL PER PERSON
£18.00 – £24.00

Enchanting and peaceful wisteria-covered Edwardian cottage. Full of antique furniture, ideal for walking, cycling or exploring the forest and coast. Local produce cooked by ex-professional chef. Dinners by arrangement. **directions** Leave A31 Picket Post services east of Ringwood. Through Burley Street to Burley. Rt onto Garden Rd, opposite Burley Manor, 200yds on left. **open** open except for winter annual holidays **bedrooms** 3 double, 2 twin, 1 family **bathrooms** 5 en suite, 1 with private bathroom **payment** cash, cheques

---

Where is my pet welcome?

Some properties welcome well-behaved pets. Look for the 🐕 in the accommodation listings.

You can also buy a copy of our popular guide 'Pets Come Too!' Now available in good bookshops and online at **visitbritainshop.com**

£9.99

South East | Hampshire

CADNAM, Hampshire Map ref 2C3

SAT NAV SO40 2NQ

Twin Oaks Guest House
Southampton Road, Cadnam SO40 2NQ
t (023) 8081 2345 e carol.gerrett2@tiscali.co.uk
w twinoaks-guesthouse.co.uk ONLINE MAP GUEST REVIEWS ONLINE BOOKING LAST MINUTE OFFERS

B&B PER ROOM PER NIGHT
S £35.00 – £50.00
D £75.00 – £83.00

SPECIAL PROMOTIONS
Hamper for special occasions, 2 nights minimum stay – special price £20 – includes champagne, chocolates, roses and strawberries.

A warm welcome awaits at Twin Oaks Guest House. Situated in the New Forest and National Park, it is a perfect base to explore the area and places of interest. Two excellent restaurants – minutes' walk away. Plenty of off road parking. Rail and airport links 15 minutes by car.

open All year except Xmas and New Year
bedrooms 1 single, 3 double, 1 twin, 1 family
bathrooms 6 en suite
payment credit/debit cards, cash, cheques, euros

directions M27 westbound – junction 1: take sign for Cadnam, then follow brown directional signs for Twin Oaks Guest House.

Room   General   Leisure

CHINEHAM, Hampshire Map ref 2C2

SAT NAV RG24 8LT

Ashfields
51a Reading Road, Chineham, Basingstoke RG24 8LT
t (01256) 324629 / 07974641705 f (01256) 336125

B&B PER ROOM PER NIGHT
S £30.00
D £50.00

Friendly family-run bungalow within walking distance of Chineham and business park. Pubs and restaurants close by. Outskirts of Basingstoke. Suitable bus/train services for area. **directions** Approximately 4 miles from Basingstoke town centre and well positioned for M3 & M4 motorways. **open** All year except Xmas and New Year **bedrooms** 2 double, 1 twin **bathrooms** 2 en suite, 1 with private bathroom **payment** cash, cheques, euros

Room   General   Leisure

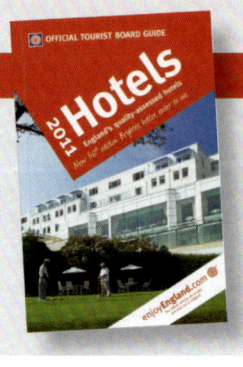

Looking for something else?

You can also buy a copy of our popular guide 'Hotels' including country house and town house hotels, metro and budget hotels, serviced apartments, restaurants with rooms and Spas in England 2011.

Now available in good bookshops and online at
visitbritainshop.com

£10.99

South East | **Hampshire**

DIBDEN PURLIEU, Hampshire Map ref 2C3
SAT NAV SO45 4PW

enjoyEngland.com RATING APPLIED FOR

B&B PER ROOM PER NIGHT
D £70.00

Heatherdene B&B
Beaulieu Road, Dibden Purlieu, Southampton SO45 4PW
t (023) 8084 6485 **e** heatherdene.995@btinternet.com
w heatherdenebandb.co.uk ONLINE MAP GUEST REVIEWS

Heatherdene is situated within a short walk of The New Forest, 3 miles from the popular village of Beaulieu. We also have the Solent and the coast within a few miles. We offer comfortable accommodation in a homely environment where you can relax and enjoy this beautiful area.

open All year
bedrooms 2 double
bathrooms 2 en suite
payment cash, cheques

directions Leave the M27 at junction 2 and follow the heritage brown signs for Beaulieu. At the 8th roundabout take the 2nd exit to Dibden Purlieu.

Room [icons]
General [icons]
Leisure [icons]

EAST TYTHERLEY, Hampshire Map ref 2C3
SAT NAV SP5 1LF

enjoyEngland.com ★★★ BED & BREAKFAST

B&B PER ROOM PER NIGHT
S £35.00 – £50.00
D £45.00 – £65.00

Nursery Cottage
The Avenue, East Tytherley, Romsey SP5 1LF
t (01794) 341060 **e** nursery-cottage@waitrose.com
w nursery-cottage.com ONLINE MAP

Located in this quiet Test Valley hamlet this traditional victorian cottage offers you a peaceful and relaxing break in very comfortable accomodation. A great location for many outdoor activities. **directions** 15 minutes drive from Romsey. Please see website for full directions **open** All year except Xmas and New Year **bedrooms** 2 double, 1 twin, 1 suite **bathrooms** 2 en suite, 2 with private bathroom **payment** cash, cheques

Room [icons] General [icons] Leisure [icons]

FAREHAM, Hampshire Map ref 2C3
SAT NAV PO14 1NS

enjoyEngland.com ★★★★ GUEST ACCOMMODATION

B&B PER ROOM PER NIGHT
S £60.00 – £75.00
D £65.00 – £90.00

Travelrest Solent Gateway
22 The Avenue, Fareham PO14 1NS
t (01329) 232175 **f** (01329) 232196 **e** solentreservations@travelrest.co.uk
w travelrest.co.uk/fareham ONLINE MAP GUEST REVIEWS ONLINE BOOKING LAST MINUTE OFFERS

Recently refurbished, comfortable accommodation, in landscaped gardens. Free car park and within walking distance of town-centre bars, restaurants and railway station. Ideal location on A27 between Southampton and Portsmouth. **directions** located on A27 west of Town Centre, approx 1/4 mile from station. Take M27 jnc 9 or 11. Follow signs for Fareham A27/Station. **open** All year **bedrooms** 13 double, 5 twin, 3 family **bathrooms** 21 en suite **payment** credit/debit cards, cash, euros

Room [icons] General [icons]

South East | Hampshire

LYMINGTON, Hampshire Map ref 2C3
SAT NAV SO41 8LR

Gorse Meadow Guest House
Sway Road, Pennington, Lymington SO41 8LR
t (01590) 673354 f (01590) 673336 e gorsemeadow@btconnect.com
w gorsemeadowguesthouse.co.uk ONLINE MAP

B&B PER ROOM PER NIGHT
S £45.00 – £55.00
D £90.00 – £120.00
EVENING MEAL PER PERSON
£30.00

Beautiful Edwardian residence in 16 acres, close to New Forest. Licensed. Use of Spa and Leisure Facilities nearby. Landscaped grounds with fish pond. Mushroom Seminars available during the autumn. **directions** From M27 west, A337 to Brockenhurst, over level crossing towards Lymington. Go under railway bridge, over mini-roundabout, turn right, then 1.25 miles on right. **open** All year
bedrooms 3 double, 1 twin, 2 family **bathrooms** 6 en suite
payment credit/debit cards, cash, cheques

LYMINGTON, Hampshire Map ref 2C3
SAT NAV SO41 0ND

Ha'penny House
16 Whitby Road, Milford-on-Sea, Lymington, Hants SO41 0ND
t (01590) 641210 e info@hapennyhouse.co.uk
w hapennyhouse.co.uk/ ONLINE MAP GUEST REVIEWS

B&B PER ROOM PER NIGHT
S £48.00 – £55.00
D £70.00 – £85.00

A delightful character house with a warm friendly atmosphere set in a quiet area of this unspoilt village, very close to the sea. Perfect for visiting the New Forest, Lymington, Isle of Wight and much more. Beautifully decorated rooms and excellent breakfasts. Your comfort and enjoyment are paramount.

open All year
bedrooms 1 single, 2 double, 1 twin
bathrooms 4 en suite
payment credit/debit cards, cash, cheques

directions From Lymington follow A337/B3058 through Milford village onto cliff top. Turn right into Cornwallis Road and right into Whitby Road. Ha'Penny House on left.

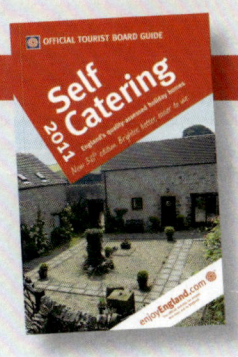

Looking for something else?
You can also buy a copy of our popular guide 'Self Catering' including self-catering holiday homes, approved caravan holiday homes, boat accommodation and holiday cottage agencies in England 2011.

Now available in good bookshops and online at
visitbritainshop.com
£11.99

or **key to symbols** see page 6

205

South East | Hampshire

LYMINGTON, Hampshire Map ref 2C3
SAT NAV SO41 6BA

The Nurse's Cottage Restaurant with Rooms
Station Road, Sway, Lymington, Hampshire SO41 6BA
t 01590 683402   e stay@nursescottage.co.uk
w nursescottage.co.uk ONLINE MAP GUEST REVIEWS ONLINE BOOKING LAST MINUTE OFFERS

SPECIAL PROMOTIONS
Half-board per person packages from £92.50 (to March 2011), £97.50 (April-October 2011). Reduced rate Bargain Breaks for 3+ night stays.

One of the New Forest National Park's most highly acclaimed places to unwind and be pampered. Over two decades, The Nurse's Cottage has secured a reputation for top-notch hospitality, excellent service, fine food and wines. Advance booking is strongly advised, as this firm Forest favourite is often over-subscribed months ahead.

open Closed 3 weeks November/ December and March
bedrooms 2 single, 2 double, 1 twin
bathrooms 5 en suite
payment credit/debit cards, cash, euros
directions M27 jct 1 follow A337 to Lyndhurst, then Brockenhurst and B3055 to Sway. The Nurse's Cottage is in the village centre, close to shops.

BREAKFAST AWARD

MILFORD ON SEA, Hampshire Map ref 2C3
SAT NAV SO41 0RH

Alma Mater Guest House
4 Knowland Drive, Milford-on-Sea, Lymington SO41 0RH
t (01590) 642811   f (01590) 642811   e almamaterguesthouse@googlemail.com
w almamaternewforest.co.uk

B&B PER ROOM PER NIGHT
S £40.00 – £50.00
D £70.00 – £80.00

Detached, quiet, spacious, non-smoking chalet bungalow with en suite bedrooms overlooking lovely garden. Quiet residential area close to village, beaches, New Forest, Keyhaven, Milford beach and cliffs. Secure, off-road parking. **directions** From Lymington follow New Milton/the West 2 miles, left B3058 Milford on Sea. After South Lawns Hotel, right Manor Road, first left Knowland Drive.
open All year **bedrooms** 2 double, 1 twin **bathrooms** 3 en suite
payment cash, cheques

NEW FOREST – BROCKENHURST, Hampshire Map ref 2C3
SAT NAV SO42 7RF

Goldenhayes
9 Chestnut Road, Brockenhurst, Hants SO42 7RF
t (01590) 623743   e briangeorgecurtis@fsmail.net

B&B PER ROOM PER NIGHT
S £25.00 – £28.00
D £45.00 – £56.00

Single-storey, owner-occupied home, in central but quiet situation. Close to village, station and open forest. Large garden. **directions** Take the A337 from Lyndhurst and turn right into Grigg Lane. Chestnut Road is the first turning to the left. **open** All year
bedrooms 1 family **payment** cash, cheques, euros

206

Official tourist board guide Bed & Breakfast

South East | Hampshire

PETERSFIELD, Hampshire Map ref 2C3
SAT NAV GU32 3JZ

enjoyEngland.com
★★★★
BED & BREAKFAST

B&B PER ROOM PER NIGHT
S £45.00 – £48.00
D £66.00 – £70.00

1 The Spain
Petersfield, Hampshire GU32 3JZ
t (01730) 263261 **e** allantarver@ntlworld.com
w 1thespain.com

18thC house with charming walled garden, in conservation area of Petersfield. Good eating places nearby, lovely walks, plenty to see and do. **directions** 100 yards down Sheep Street running from the southwest corner of the Square **open** All year **bedrooms** 2 double, 1 twin **bathrooms** 2 en suite, 1 with private bathroom **payment** cash, cheques, euros

Room General Leisure

PORTSMOUTH, Hampshire Map ref 2C3
SAT NAV PO9 3PJ

enjoyEngland.com
★★★★
BED & BREAKFAST

Silver AWARD

B&B PER ROOM PER NIGHT
S £40.00 – £45.00
D £60.00 – £65.00

SPECIAL PROMOTIONS
Except Goodwood - minimum 2 nights stay, Glorious Goodwood and The Festival of Speed.

Cherry Trees
23 Parkside, Bedhampton, Havant PO9 3PJ
t (023) 9248 2480 **e** diana.patrick@talk21.com

Situated just outside the city of Portsmouth in the residential area of Bedhampton, this detached house is beautifully presented and offers a high degree of comfort and hospitality. With the extra touches that make this a silver award home we hope to provide a stay that is enjoyable and memorable.

open All year
bedrooms 1 double, 1 twin
bathrooms 1 en suite, 1 with private bathroom
payment credit/debit cards, cash, cheques

directions Leave A27 at M3 London jct following signs for local traffic on B2177.

Room
General
Leisure

SOUTHAMPTON, Hampshire Map ref 2C3
SAT NAV SO15 5AF

enjoyEngland.com
★★★
GUEST ACCOMMODATION

B&B PER ROOM PER NIGHT
S £35.00 – £46.00
D £55.00 – £66.00

Madison House
137 Hill Lane, Southampton SO15 5AF
t (023) 8033 3374 **e** foley@madisonhouse.co.uk
w madisonhouse.co.uk ONLINE MAP LAST MINUTE OFFERS

Beautiful Victorian house with modern facilities offers spacious ensuite rooms and a home cooked breakfast. Good location with easy access to Centre, University, Docks and cruise terminals. Very friendly establishment. **directions** Hill Lane is just off A35 Winchester Road. See www.madisonhouse.co.uk
open All year except Xmas and New Year **bedrooms** 2 single, 3 double, 4 twin **bathrooms** 9 en suite, 9 with private bathroom **payment** credit/debit cards, cash

Room General

South East | Hampshire

SOUTHAMPTON, Hampshire Map ref 2C3
SAT NAV SO15 0LU

Trenerry House Bed and Breakfast

66 Redbridge Road, Redbridge, Southampton, SO15 0LU SO15 0LU
t (023) 8077 5273 f 02380 775273 e diana.gange@hotmail.com
w trenerryhouse.co.uk

B&B PER ROOM PER NIGHT
S £30.00
D £60.00

Trenerry House B & B Southampton historical city, university, West Quay shopping, cruise terminals parking whilst on your cruise, general hospital, 6 mins to New Forest **directions** Turn left, off the M271 onto the A35 towards Southampton drive half a mile, just past the School, we are the 4th house. **open** All year **bedrooms** 1 single, 1 double, 1 twin **bathrooms** 1 en suite **payment** cash, cheques

Room General

WINCHESTER, Hampshire Map ref 2C3
SAT NAV SO23 9SR

12 Christchurch Road

12 Christchurch Road, Winchester SO23 9SR
t (01962) 854272 / 0787 985 0076 e pjspatton@yahoo.co.uk

B&B PER ROOM PER NIGHT
S £40.00 – £50.00
D £50.00 – £60.00

Elegant Victorian house furnished with style. Easy, pleasant walk to city centre, cathedral and water meadows. Breakfast in conservatory, overlooking beautiful gardens, features home-made bread, preserves and local produce. **directions** Please contact us for directions **open** All year except Xmas and New Year **bedrooms** 1 double, 1 twin **payment** cash, cheques

Room General

WINCHESTER, Hampshire Map ref 2C3
SAT NAV SO23 9SU

Giffard House

50 Christchurch Road, St Cross, Winchester SO23 9SU
t (01962) 852628 f (01962) 856722 e giffardhotel@aol.com
w giffardhotel.co.uk ONLINE MAP GUEST REVIEWS

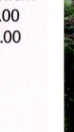

B&B PER ROOM PER NIGHT
S £69.00 – £109.00
D £89.00 – £135.00

A warm welcome awaits those who visit this stunning Victorian house, recently refurbished to the highest standard. Relax in crisp, white bed linen and in luxurious, en suite bathrooms. Start the day with a traditional breakfast in our elegant dining room. Ten minutes' walk to town centre.

open All year except Xmas
bedrooms 4 single, 6 double, 2 twin, 1 family
bathrooms 13 en suite, 13 with private bathroom
payment credit/debit cards, cash, cheques, euros

directions From M3 jct 11, follow signs to Winchester travelling St Cross Road. After BP garage, take 1st left (Ranelagh), 2nd right (Christchurch). Hotel opposite Grafton.

Room General Leisure

South East | **Isle of Wight**

BEMBRIDGE, Isle of Wight Map ref 2C3
SAT NAV PO35 5PJ

Ivar Cottage "Summer House"
Hillway Road, Bembridge PO35 5PJ
t 07969 647914 e contact@ivarcottagesummerhouse.co.uk
w **ivarcottagesummerhouse.co.uk** GUEST REVIEWS

B&B PER ROOM PER NIGHT
D £100.00

Luxury accommodation on outskirts of Bembridge, stunning views, private lounge, bar, bathroom. Short walk to beautiful beach, woodland walks, Bembridge Airport, "Whitecliff-Bay". Ideal retreat for professional and discerning couples. **directions** PO35 5PJ. **open** All year **bedrooms** 1 double **bathrooms** 1 with private bathroom **payment** cash, cheques

Room

BONCHURCH, Isle of Wight Map ref 2C3
SAT NAV PO38 1RF

The Lake
Shore Road, Bonchurch PO38 1RF
t (01983) 852613 f (01983) 852613 e enquiries@lakehotel.co.uk
w **lakehotel.co.uk** GUEST REVIEWS

B&B PER ROOM PER NIGHT
S £37.00 – £67.00
D £78.00 – £96.00

Charming country-house in two acres of beautiful gardens. 400 Yards from Sea in Bonchurch village. Same family for over 45 years, offering good value accommodation on our beautiful island. **directions** Car ferry breaks available. Public transport directions on our website. **open** All year except Xmas and New Year **bedrooms** 1 single, 10 double, 5 twin, 4 family **bathrooms** 20 en suite **payment** credit/debit cards, cash, cheques, euros

Room General Leisure

BRIGHSTONE, Isle of Wight Map ref 2C3
SAT NAV PO30 4ED

Mottistone Manor Farmhouse
Mottistone, Near Brighstone, South West Wight PO30 4ED
t (01983) 740207 e bookings@bolthols.co.uk
w **bolthols.co.uk** ONLINE MAP

B&B PER ROOM PER NIGHT
S £35.00 – £49.00
D £64.00 – £80.00

Tranquil 17th/18thC farmhouse B&B in beautiful setting in AONB. Rural views to the sea; ideal for walking, cycling, beaches, sightseeing. On bus route. Pubs, village shops etc nearby. **directions** From West - 150 yards past Mottistone Church. From East - On right opposite Mottistone village sign. **open** All year except Xmas **bedrooms** 3 double, 1 twin **bathrooms** 3 en suite, 1 with private bathroom **payment** credit/debit cards, cash, cheques

Room General Leisure

BRIGHSTONE, Isle of Wight Map ref 2C3
SAT NAV PO30 4AH

Seven Bed & Breakfast
Main Road, Brighstone PO30 4AH
t (01983) 740370 e bookings@visitseven.co.uk
w **visitseven.co.uk** ONLINE MAP GUEST REVIEWS ONLINE BOOKING LAST MINUTE OFFERS

B&B PER ROOM PER NIGHT
S £40.00 – £45.00
D £60.00 – £70.00
EVENING MEAL PER PERSON
£10.00 – £20.00

Guest accommodation furnished to VisitBritain standard. Restaurant and licensed bar on site, picturesque West Wight village with all facilities and amazing walking by coast and countryside. **directions** Centre of Brighstone villiage opposite church of St Mary , 7 miles from Newport. **open** All year **bedrooms** 3 double, 1 twin **bathrooms** 4 en suite **payment** credit/debit cards, cash, cheques

Room General Leisure

South East | Isle of Wight

FRESHWATER, Isle of Wight Map ref 2C3
SAT NAV PO40 9ED

The Orchards
Princes Road, Freshwater PO40 9ED
t (01983) 753795 e paulaattheorchards@googlemail.com
w theorchardsbandb.co.uk

B&B PER ROOM PER NIGHT
S £27.50 – £42.50
D £55.00 – £85.00

EVENING MEAL PER PERSON
£12.00 – £15.00

Enjoy a warm welcome, comfortable stay, located in Freshwater village. Near Yarmouth ferry, local walks, beaches and amenities. Locally-sourced food when available. Off-road parking and secure bicycle storage. **directions** Please contact us for directions **open** All year **bedrooms** 2 single, 1 double, 1 family **bathrooms** 3 en suite, 1 with private bathroom **payment** cash, cheques

FRESHWATER, Isle of Wight Map ref 2C3
SAT NAV PO40 9PP

Seahorses
Victoria Road, Freshwater, Isle-of-Wight PO40 9PP
t (01983) 752574 f (01983) 752574 e seahorses-iow@tiscali.co.uk
w seahorsesisleofwight.com ONLINE MAP ONLINE BOOKING

B&B PER ROOM PER NIGHT
S £33.00 – £38.00
D £66.00 – £76.00

A charming early-19thC rectory, standing in 2.5 acres of lovely gardens with direct footpath access to Yarmouth and Freshwater Bay. Art courses available in our studio. Pets welcome. **directions** From the Freshwater Co-op (large), go up Stroud Road becoming Victoria Road, just past St. Andrews Village Hall, turn left into our driveway. Ample parking. **open** All year **bedrooms** 1 double, 2 twin, 2 family **bathrooms** 5 en suite **payment** cash, cheques

LAKE, Isle of Wight Map ref 2C3
SAT NAV PO36 8PA

Cliff Lodge Guest House
13 Cliff Path, Lake PO36 8PL
t 01983 402963 e clifflodge@uwclub.net
w cliff-lodge-isle-of-wight.co.uk

B&B PER ROOM PER NIGHT
S £21.50 – £27.00
D £43.00 – £54.00

EVENING MEAL PER PERSON
£10.00 – £12.50

SPECIAL PROMOTIONS
Stay 6 nights get the 7th night free at all times.

Situated between Sandown and Shanklin Bay, access to beach close by. Local produce used, car park available, close to station, sports centre and pool. Garden available for guests use, access available all day, any day bookings and any length of stay.

open All year except Xmas and New Year
bedrooms 2 single, 4 double, 1 twin, 2 family
bathrooms 8 en suite, 1 with private bathroom
payment cash, cheques
directions Off Lake Hill, turn down Brownlow Road and follow road along to unadopted part and we are first big house on left.

South East | **Isle of Wight**

LAKE, Isle of Wight Map ref 2C3

SAT NAV PO36 9JX

&B PER ROOM PER NIGHT
S £27.00 – £29.00
D £44.00 – £60.00

SPECIAL PROMOTIONS
Discount for 2-6 or 7 nights.
Reduced ferry fares.

Osterley Lodge
62 Sandown Road, Lake PO36 9JX
t (01983) 402017 **e** osterleylodgeiw@aol.com
w wightstay.co.uk/basic/osterley.html ONLINE MAP

Between Sandown and Shanklin, near Cliff Path, buses and train station. Suite available with sitting room, de-luxe and ground floor rooms. Licensed. Choice of breakfast menu. Secure storage for bicycles. Guests have access at all times. Private parking and garden. No children under 5, or pets. Reduced ferry fares offered.

open All year except Xmas and New Year **bedrooms** 5 double, 1 twin, 1 suite **bathrooms** 6 en suite, 1 with private bathroom **payment** credit/debit cards, cash, cheques

directions On A3055 between Sandown and Shanklin.

Room
General
Leisure

NEWPORT (3 MILES), Isle of Wight Map ref 2C3

SAT NAV PO30 3EQ

&B PER ROOM PER NIGHT
D £72.00

Freewaters
New Barn Lane, Gatcombe, NR Newport PO30 3EQ
t (01983) 721339 **e** john@pitstopmodels.demon.co.uk
w colourpointdesign.co.uk/freewaters ONLINE MAP

Renovated farmhouse in area of outstanding natural beauty. Centrally located, ideal for exploring this idyllic island. Walkers, cyclists paradise. Newport 3 Miles. **directions** Please contact us for directions **open** All year except Xmas and New Year **bedrooms** 1 double, 1 twin **bathrooms** 2 en suite **payment** cash, cheques

Room   General

RYDE, Isle of Wight Map ref 2C3

SAT NAV PO33 2NW

&B PER ROOM PER NIGHT
S £25.00
D £45.00 – £50.00

Fern Cottage
8 West Street, Ryde PO33 2NW
t (01983) 565856 **f** (01983) 565856 **e** sandra@psdferguson.freeserve.co.uk

Fern Cottage is a family-run, non-smoking guest house, close to the beach, shops, ferries and golf course. With a warm welcome on arrival with a tray of tea and biscuits. **directions** Fern Cottage is 10 minutes walk from passenger ferry and 15 minutes drive from car ferry. Email me for further details. **open** All year except Xmas **bedrooms** 3 twin **bathrooms** 1 en suite **payment** cash, cheques

Room   General   Leisure

key to symbols see page 6

South East | Isle of Wight

SANDOWN, Isle of Wight Map ref 2C3
SAT NAV PO36 9BY

B&B PER ROOM PER NIGHT
S £36.00 – £40.00
D £72.00 – £80.00

Beaufort House
30 Broadway, Sandown PO36 9BY
t (01983) 403672 f (01983) 403672 e web@thebeaufortsandown.co.uk
w thebeaufortsandown.co.uk ONLINE MAP GUEST REVIEWS ONLINE BOOKING LAST MINUTE OFFERS

Family-run, family friendly guesthouse situated just 5 minutes wal[k] from Sandowns' beautiful sandy beach. Close to restaurants, train station and bus stops. Licensed bar, childrens' playroom and quie[t] lounge. **directions** Please contact us for directions **open** All year **bedrooms** 1 single, 5 double, 2 twin, 3 family **bathrooms** 11 en suite **payment** credit/debit cards, cash, cheques

Room   General

SANDOWN, Isle of Wight Map ref 2C3
SAT NAV PO36 9BW

B&B PER ROOM PER NIGHT
S £33.00 – £36.00
D £66.00 – £72.00

The Fernside
30 Station Avenue, Sandown PO36 9BW
t (01983) 402356 f (01983) 407527 e enquiries@thefernside.co.uk
w thefernside.co.uk LAST MINUTE OFFERS

The Fernside is a licensed family run guest house ideally located i[n] the resort of Sandown. Local shops and excellent restaurants are nearby. Bar snacks available. **directions** Close to the station and only a short walk from the town centre & beach. See website. **op**[en] Open February to end November **bedrooms** 2 single, 5 double, 2 twin, 1 family **bathrooms** 10 en suite **payment** credit/debit cards, cash, cheques

Room   General

SANDOWN, Isle of Wight Map ref 2C3
SAT NAV PO36 8JR

B&B PER ROOM PER NIGHT
S £27.00 – £33.00
D £54.00 – £66.00

The Montpelier
5 Pier Street, Sandown PO36 8JR
t (01983) 403964 f 070922 12734 e steve@themontpelier.co.uk
w themontpelier.co.uk ONLINE MAP GUEST REVIEWS LAST MINUTE OFFERS

The Montpelier is situated opposite the pier and beaches with th[e] high street just around the corner. We offer B&B, room-only and ferry-inclusive packages. Sea views available. **directions** Please contact us for directions **open** All year **bedrooms** 1 single, 3 double, 2 twin, 2 family **bathrooms** 8 en suite **payment** credit/debit cards, cash

Room   General   Leisure

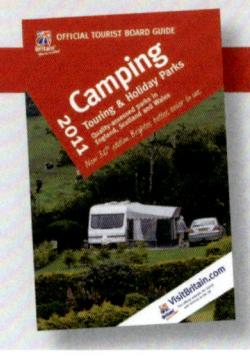

Do you like Camping?
You can also buy a copy of our popular guide 'Camping, Touring & Holiday Parks' including touring parks, camping holidays and holiday parks and villages in Britain 2011.

Now available in good bookshops and online at
visitbritainshop.com

£8.99

South East | Isle of Wight

SANDOWN, Isle of Wight Map ref 2C3

SAT NAV PO36 9DB

The Sandhill
6 Hill Street, Sandown PO36 9DB
t (01983) 403635 f (01983) 403695 e sandhillsandown@aol.com
w sandhill-hotel.co.uk ONLINE MAP LAST MINUTE OFFERS

B&B PER ROOM PER NIGHT
S £27.00 – £37.00
D £54.00 – £74.00

EVENING MEAL PER PERSON
£5.65 – £16.00

SPECIAL PROMOTIONS
Car Ferry inclusive packages available all year round, details on website or by phone for best prices

Situated in quiet residential area, close to Railway and Bus services. The beautiful Sandy Beach and Town Centre are less than 10 minutes walk. Very family oriented. With 5 star food hygiene rating the restaurant is open every evening as is the well stocked bar.

open All year
bedrooms 1 single, 6 double, 3 twin, 6 family
bathrooms 16 en suite
payment credit/debit cards, cash, cheques, euros

directions Located in quiet residential area, just of the main Broadway at the top of Leed Street, 100 yds from Railway Station

SHANKLIN, Isle of Wight Map ref 2C3

SAT NAV PO37 6AA

Bedford Lodge
Eastcliff Road, Shanklin PO37 6AA
t (01983) 862416 f (01983) 868704 e info@bedfordlodge.co.uk
w bedfordlodge.co.uk ONLINE MAP GUEST REVIEWS ONLINE BOOKING LAST MINUTE OFFERS

B&B PER ROOM PER NIGHT
S £27.00 – £47.00
D £25.00 – £50.00

SPECIAL PROMOTIONS
We run many special price breaks between November and March. Please contact us or check the website for details

Nestling in Shanklin Old Village, we're ideally placed for a relaxing break within walking distance of excellent restaurants and thatched pubs. With the beach at the end of the road, walking and cycling trails close to hand and bus routes on the doorstep it's easy to explore from the Lodge.

open All year
bedrooms 3 single, 7 double, 3 twin, 1 family
bathrooms 14 en suite
payment credit/debit cards, cash

directions Our car park is accessed via Eastcliff Road, which is a dead end road. Our drive is half way down on the right hand side.

BREAKFAST AWARD

South East | **Isle of Wight**

SHANKLIN, Isle of Wight Map ref 2C3
SAT NAV PO37 6NN

The Birkdale
5 Grange Road, Shanklin PO37 6NN
t (01983) 862949 f (01983) 862949 e birkdale-iow@hotmail.co.uk
w birkdalehotel.com ONLINE MAP GUEST REVIEWS ONLINE BOOKING

B&B PER ROOM PER NIGHT
D £58.00 – £76.00

The Birkdale is situated in a quiet position, a short stroll from the beach, picturesque Shanklin Old Village, Theatre, Chine and Rylstone Gardens. **directions** We are located in the heart of Shanklin Old Village, Grange Road is opposite the famous Crab In just a few yards up the hill. **open** All year except Xmas and New Year **bedrooms** 5 double, 2 twin **bathrooms** 7 en suite **payment** credit/debit cards, cash, cheques

Room   General

SHANKLIN, Isle of Wight Map ref 2C3
SAT NAV PO37 6AW

Heatherleigh Guest House
17 Queens Road, Shanklin PO37 6AW
t (01983) 862503 e enquiries@heatherleigh.co.uk
w heatherleigh.co.uk ONLINE MAP GUEST REVIEWS ONLINE BOOKING

B&B PER ROOM PER NIGHT
S £35.00 – £60.00
D £56.00 – £70.00

Heatherleigh Guest House is family-run and ideally situated minutes from beach, shops, restaurants, Old Village and Chine, with a friendly family atmosphere. Extensive breakfast menu. Doggies welcome. No grumpy people! **directions** Directions on web site. **open** All year except Xmas and New Year **bedrooms** 4 double, 2 family **bathrooms** 6 en suite **payment** credit/debit cards, cash, cheques, euros

Room   General

SHANKLIN, Isle of Wight Map ref 2C3
SAT NAV PO37 6AZ

The Parkway
6 Park Road, Shanklin PO37 6AZ
t (01983) 862740 e info@parkwayhotelshanklin.co.uk
w parkwayhotelshanklin.co.uk ONLINE MAP GUEST REVIEWS LAST MINUTE OFFERS

B&B PER ROOM PER NIGHT
S £33.00 – £35.00
D £33.00 – £35.00
EVENING MEAL PER PERSON
£15.00 – £17.00

Situated close to beach town and old village The Parkway is a family run converted victorian residence. we have a residents bar, evening meals are also available. **directions** Please contact us for directions **open** All year except Xmas and New Year **bedrooms** 2 single, 2 double, 1 twin, 3 family, 4 suites **bathrooms** 12 en suite **payment** cash, cheques

Room   General   Leisure

Where is my pet welcome?
Some properties welcome well-behaved pets. Look for the 🐕 in the accommodation listings.

You can also buy a copy of our popular guide 'Pets Come Too!' Now available in good bookshops and online at **visitbritainshop.com**

£9.99

South East | Isle of Wight

SHANKLIN, Isle of Wight Map ref 2C3

SAT NAV PO37 6BA

Swiss Cottage

10 St Georges Road, Shanklin PO37 6BA
t (01983) 862333   e info@swiss-cottage.co.uk
w swiss-cottage.co.uk   ONLINE MAP   LAST MINUTE OFFERS

B&B PER ROOM PER NIGHT
S £22.50 – £37.00
D £45.00 – £75.00

EVENING MEAL PER PERSON
£12.00 – £14.00

SPECIAL PROMOTIONS
7 Nights for the price of 6 on H/B & B/B. Reduced Rates for Senior Citizens Discounted Car Ferry Bookings

Swiss Cottage was built in 1866 and is an attractive, 4 Star, friendly traditional non smoking seaside accommodation, under the personal supervision of Keith & Christine Beckett, where we cater for all your needs on Half Board and B & B. Where guests meet as strangers and leave as friends.

open All year except Xmas and New Year
bedrooms 5 double, 3 twin, 3 family
bathrooms 10 en suite, 1 with private bathroom
payment cash, cheques

directions Please look at our website for full driving instructions from all ferry terminals. Total Journey time to us is approx 30 minutes, 12 miles

Room
General
Leisure

SHANKLIN, Isle of Wight Map ref 2C3

SAT NAV PO37 6AF

Victoria Lodge

5 Alexandra Road, Shanklin PO37 6AF
t (01983) 862361   e info@victorialodgehotel.com
w victorialodgehotel.com   GUEST REVIEWS   ONLINE BOOKING

B&B PER ROOM PER NIGHT
S £33.00 – £39.00
D £66.00 – £78.00

EVENING MEAL PER PERSON
£10.00

SPECIAL PROMOTIONS
Any-day to any-day bookings (minimum 2 nights), ferry inclusive special deals available. Ferry can be arranged at preferential prices.

Family run with a warm personal service assured. Situated in own grounds in Shanklin's premier peaceful position. Close to Cliff Path, beaches, Chine and beautiful Old Village. Relax in the spacious lounge which has delightful sea views, as do several of the bedrooms. Half board available some weeks throughout the season.

open March-October and Christmas
bedrooms 1 single, 11 double, 6 twin, 1 family
bathrooms 19 en suite
payment credit/debit cards, cash, cheques

directions Rail to Portsmouth, Fastcat to Ryde and train to Shanklin. Then 10-minute walk or taxi. Car: drive to Shanklin, Prospect Road last on right.

Room
General
Leisure

key to symbols see page 6

215

South East | **Isle of Wight/Kent**

YARMOUTH, Isle of Wight Map ref 2C3
SAT NAV PO41 0RH

Medlars
Halletts Shute, Yarmouth PO41 0RH
t (01923) 761541 f (01923) 761541 e e.grey855@btinternet.com
w milford.co.uk/go/medlars.html ONLINE MAP ONLINE BOOKING

B&B PER ROOM PER NIGHT
S £45.00
D £70.00

Medlars is an attractive, stone-built converted barn in a quiet, rural location within easy walking distance of Yarmouth and walking routes. Dogs welcome by arrangement and off-road parking is available. **directions** From Yarmouth, cross harbour swing bridge continue up Halletts Shute. Turn left after sign for Norton between stone pillars. Medlars is second house. **open** All year except Xmas **bedrooms** 1 double, 1 twin **bathrooms** 1 en suite, 1 with private bathroom **payment** cash, cheques

Room General Leisure

ASHFORD, Kent Map ref 3B4
SAT NAV TN27 0HG

Bowl Inn
Egg Hill Road, Charing, Ashford, Kent TN27 0HG
t 01233 712256 e roomsvb@bowl-inn.co.uk
w bowl-inn.co.uk ONLINE MAP ONLINE BOOKING

B&B PER ROOM PER NIGHT
S £50.00 – £60.00
D £60.00 – £75.00
EVENING MEAL PER PERSON
£5.00 – £10.00

Traditional rural 16th Century inn on top of North Downs in AONB with great accommodation. Kentish produce used when possible. Canterbury, Leeds Castle, Dover, Tunnel, all within 30 minutes **directions** Leave M20 J8 eastbound, J9 westbound. Take A20 to Charing. Signed from A20 Maidstone - Ashford and from A252 Charing - Canterbury **open** All year **bedrooms** 3 double, 2 twin **bathrooms** 5 en suite **payment** credit/debit cards, cash, euros

Room General Leisure

ASHFORD (5 MILES), Kent Map ref 3B4
SAT NAV TN25 4NH

Dean Court
Challock Lane, Westwell, Ashford TN25 4NH
t (01233) 712924

B&B PER ROOM PER NIGHT
S £35.00 – £40.00
D £60.00 – £65.00
EVENING MEAL PER PERSON
£12.00 – £15.00

Period farmhouse on working farm with modern amenities. Magnificent views in quiet valley. Comfortable accommodation with separate sitting room for guests. Central for Channel Ports, Channel Tunnel and touring Kent.

open All year except Xmas and New Year
bedrooms 1 double, 1 twin, 1 family
bathrooms 1 en suite
payment cash, cheques

directions M20 motorway to Junction 9 (Ashford). Take A20 west 1 mile then Westwell signposted. Property 1 mile north of Wheel Public House.

Room
General

South East | Kent

BIDDENDEN, Kent Map ref 3B4

SAT NAV TN27 8HH

Heron Cottage
Biddenden, Ashford TN27 8HH
t (01580) 291358 e susantwort@hotmail.com
w heroncottage.info

B&B PER ROOM PER NIGHT
S £45.00 – £60.00
D £55.00 – £70.00

EVENING MEAL PER PERSON
£17.50 – £19.50

Set in five acres, surrounded by farmland, between historic Biddenden and Sissinghurst Castle. Thoughtfully-equipped bedrooms. Breakfast in smart dining room, cosy lounge with open fire. One room with wheelchair access. **directions** 1 mile north-west of Biddenden. A262 west from Biddenden, first right, 0.25 mile across sharp left bend, through stone pillars, left onto unmade road. **open** February to December **bedrooms** 2 double, 2 twin, 2 family **bathrooms** 6 en suite **payment** cash, cheques

BLADBEAN, Kent Map ref 3B4

SAT NAV CT4 6LU

Molehills
Bladbean, Canterbury CT4 6LU
t (01303) 840051 e molehills84@hotmail.com
w molehillsbedbreakfast.co.uk ONLINE MAP

B&B PER ROOM PER NIGHT
S £35.00 – £40.00
D £50.00 – £60.00

EVENING MEAL PER PERSON
£8.00 – £12.00

SPECIAL PROMOTIONS
B&B Price for Family Room £60-£90 per night. Can sleep 2 adults and up to 3 children.

The house, in large gardens, is in a peaceful hamlet within the beautiful Elham Valley. We are within easy reach of Canterbury and the Channel terminals. We produce home-grown vegetables and excellent home cooking. Our comfortable accommodation includes ground floor bedrooms, sitting room with woodburning stove and conservatory.

open All year except Xmas
bedrooms 1 double, 1 twin, 1 family
bathrooms 3 en suite
payment cash, cheques, euros

directions Leave A2 for Barham. Beyond Barham pass Elham Valley Vineyard. Take right turn at crossroads. Continue over second crossroads. Molehills is 3rd house on right.

BRENCHLEY, Kent Map ref 3B4

SAT NAV TN12 7BJ

Hononton Cottage
Palmers Green Lane, Nr Brenchley, Tonbridge, Kent TN12 7BJ
t (01892) 722483 e stay@honontoncottage.co.uk
w honontoncottage.co.uk ONLINE MAP

B&B PER ROOM PER NIGHT
S £50.00 – £65.00
D £75.00 – £90.00

BREAKFAST AWARD

Picturesque 16th C Listed farmhouse, with superb views. On quiet lane in Kent apple orchards. Ideal base for golfers, walking and touring with NT properties and gardens nearby. **directions** A21 south of Tunbridge Wells, B2160 to Matfield. Right at crossroads to Brenchley. Turn left signed Castle Hill. Right into Palmers Green Lane. **open** All year **bedrooms** 2 double, 1 twin **bathrooms** 2 en suite, 1 with private bathroom **payment** cash, cheques, euros

key to symbols see page 6   217

South East | **Kent**

BROADSTAIRS, Kent Map ref 3C3 — SAT NAV CT10 1DR

Bay Tree Broadstairs
12 Eastern Esplanade, Broadstairs CT10 1DR
t (01843) 862502 f (01843) 860589

B&B PER ROOM PER NIGHT
S £44.00 – £69.00
D £88.00 – £98.00

The Eastern Esplanade overlooking Stone Bay, with panoramic sea views across the Channel. Close to the town centre and sandy beaches. A warm welcome awaits at this family-run establishment. **directions** By Road: M2 - A2 - A299, via Birchington and Margate via Ramsgate By Rail: London to Broadstairs then taxi or half mile walk. **open** All year except Xmas and New Year **bedrooms** 1 single, 7 double, 2 twin **bathrooms** 10 en suite, 10 with private bathroom **payment** credit/debit cards, cash, cheques

Room General 10 P

CANTERBURY, Kent Map ref 3B3 — SAT NAV CT1 3TY

Carena House
250 Wincheap, Canterbury CT1 3TY
t (01227) 765630 f (01227) 765630 e carena.house@btconnect.com
w **carenaguesthouse.co.uk** ONLINE MAP

B&B PER ROOM PER NIGHT
S £35.00 – £50.00
D £55.00 – £70.00

A welcoming guest-house offering homely accommodation. En suite, TV, WiFi, tea coffee making facilities. Carena House is ten minute walk into the city where the Cathedral is located. Free parking. **directions** Map as on website at present. **open** All year **bedrooms** 1 single, 2 double, 1 twin, 1 family **bathrooms** 5 en suite **payment** credit/debit cards, cash

Room General P Leisure

CANTERBURY, Kent Map ref 3B3 — SAT NAV CT4 6JD

Hornbeams
Jesses Hill, Kingston, Canterbury CT4 6JD
t (01227) 830119 e bandb@hornbeams.co.uk
w **hornbeams.co.uk** ONLINE MAP

B&B PER ROOM PER NIGHT
S £45.00 – £55.00
D £75.00 – £85.00
EVENING MEAL PER PERSON
£20.00 – £25.00

Rolling hills, woodland, long views over luscious Kent, and lovely garden. Full English breakfast. Idyllic place to stay, yet near town and historical landmarks. Private parking. Well-behaved pets welcome. **directions** From A2 (Canterbury to Dover), right to Kingston. Right, bottom of hill into The Street. Top of hill, right for 1st left, left into farm. **open** All year except Xmas **bedrooms** 1 single, 1 double, 1 twin **bathrooms** 1 en suite, 1 with private bathroom **payment** cash, cheques

Room General P Leisure

CANTERBURY, Kent Map ref 3B3 — SAT NAV CT1 3JT

Kipps Independent Hostel
40 Nunnery Fields, Canterbury CT1 3JT
t (01227) 786121 e kippshostel@gmail.com
w **kipps-hostel.com** ONLINE MAP GUEST REVIEWS ONLINE BOOKING LAST MINUTE OFFERS

BED ONLY PER NIGHT
£15.00 – £19.50

Self-catering hostel only a short walk from cathedral and city centre. Group catering available for 10+ persons. Private rooms to dormitories available, excellent facilities. **directions** Go to our website www.kipps-hostel.com **open** All year **payment** credit/debit cards, cash, euros

Room General P Leisure

218 Official tourist board guide **Bed & Breakfast**

South East | Kent

CANTERBURY, Kent Map ref 3B3

SAT NAV CT4 7BE

Iffin Farmhouse
Iffin Lane, Canterbury, Kent CT4 7BE
t (01227) 462776 **e** info@iffin.co.uk
w iffinfarmhouse.co.uk ONLINE MAP GUEST REVIEWS ONLINE BOOKING LAST MINUTE OFFERS

B&B PER ROOM PER NIGHT
S £67.00 – £87.00
D £87.00 – £135.00

EVENING MEAL PER PERSON
£19.70 – £27.90

SPECIAL PROMOTIONS
Special Promotions are available for accommodation, meals, and other events including creative workshops and groups. Please enquire.

A home from home. "The accommodation was lovely, the food great and the service even better. We will certainly recommend you to anyone we know intending to visit Canterbury". "What a blessing to stay in a haven of peace and beauty". Please enquire for self-catering, special offers, homemade meals.

open All year
bedrooms 2 double, 1 twin, 1 family
bathrooms 4 en suite
payment credit/debit cards, cash, cheques, euros

directions 2 miles from the centre of Canterbury, yet in the heart of the countryside, between the B2068 and A28, South West of Canterbury

Room
General
Leisure

CANTERBURY, Kent Map ref 3B3

SAT NAV CT2 8AX

Magnolia House
36 St Dunstans Terrace, Canterbury CT2 8AX
t (01227) 765121 **f** (01227) 765121 **e** info@magnoliahousecanterbury.co.uk
w magnoliahousecanterbury.co.uk ONLINE MAP ONLINE BOOKING LAST MINUTE OFFERS

B&B PER ROOM PER NIGHT
S £55.00 – £65.00
D £95.00 – £125.00

EVENING MEAL PER PERSON
£35.00 – £45.00

Charming, late-Georgian house, quiet residential street, ten-minutes from city centre. Every facility for an enjoyable stay. Breakfasts are served overlooking attractive walled garden. Evening meals served Nov–Feb by arrangement. **directions** Please contact us for directions **open** All year except Xmas **bedrooms** 1 single, 5 double, 1 twin **bathrooms** 7 en suite **payment** credit/debit cards, cash

Room   General   Leisure

CANTERBURY, Kent Map ref 3B3

SAT NAV CT2 8LF

Yorke Lodge
50 London Road, Canterbury CT2 8LF
t (01227) 451243 **f** (01227) 462006 **e** info@yorkelodge.com
w yorkelodge.com ONLINE MAP

B&B PER ROOM PER NIGHT
S £55.00 – £70.00
D £90.00 – £120.00

Charming Victorian villa offering distinctive, well appointed en suite bedrooms and high quality home-cooked Aga breakfast. A relaxing place to stay. Close to city centre, universities and public schools. **directions** From London via M2 and A2, take 1st exit signposted Canterbury. At 1st roundabout turn left into London Road, we are 100m on the left. **open** All year **bedrooms** 1 single, 5 double, 1 twin, 1 family **bathrooms** 8 en suite **payment** credit/debit cards, cash, cheques

Room   General   Leisure

key to symbols see page 6

South East | **Kent**

CHARING, Kent Map ref 3B4   SAT NAV TN27 0HU

Oak
High Street, Charing, Ashford TN27 0HU
t (01233) 712612 e info@theoakcharing.co.uk
w **theoakcharing.co.uk** ONLINE MAP GUEST REVIEWS ONLINE BOOKING

B&B PER ROOM PER NIGHT
S £65.00
D £75.00 – £85.00
EVENING MEAL PER PERSON
£6.00 – £30.00

Situated in the heart of historic Charing, nestled at the foot of the North Downs. The Oak has 8 stylishly refurbished bedrooms, all with en suite facilities. The bar and restaurant provide a warm and relaxing atmosphere, serving great food made from locally sourced produce.

open All year except Xmas and New Year
bedrooms 1 single, 5 double, 1 twin, 1 family
bathrooms 8 en suite
payment credit/debit cards, cash, cheques

directions Exit M20 at junction 8. follow A20 direction of Ashford. Turn left into Charing High Street from the A20. Pub 30metres on left.

Room General Leisure

DETLING, Kent Map ref 3B3   SAT NAV ME14 3JY

Wealden Hall
Pilgrims Way, Detling, Maidstone ME14 3JY
t (01622) 739622 e johnwatson@wealdenhall.net
w **wealdenhall.co.uk** ONLINE MAP LAST MINUTE OFFERS

B&B PER ROOM PER NIGHT
S £50.00 – £55.00
D £65.00 – £70.00

Wealden Hall offers spacious fully equipped en suite rooms, rural setting, stunning views. Situated near Maidstone. Secure parking, gardens and heated swimming pool. Quality breakfasts using own produce. **directions** Exit M20 Junct 7, A249 towards Sheerness. Turn right into Detling. Turn right opposite Cock Horse pub into Pilgrims Way; take 2nd drive on left. **open** All year except Xmas and New Year **bedrooms** 1 double, 1 twin **bathrooms** 2 en suite **payment** credit/debit cards, cash, cheques, euros

Room General Leisure

DOVER, Kent Map ref 3C4   SAT NAV CT16 1QW

Castle House
Castle Hill Road, Dover CT16 1QW
t (01304) 201656 e dimechr@aol.com
w **castle-guesthouse.co.uk** GUEST REVIEWS

B&B PER ROOM PER NIGHT
S £36.00 – £40.00
D £58.00 – £70.00

Ideally located below Dover Castle, close to town centre, seafront and port. Genuine hospitality from Rodney and Elizabeth, and an excellent breakfast available from 6.00 a.m. Off street parking. **directions** Approaching from A20, pass 4 roundabouts, turn left at lights past petrol station, then 1st right into Castle Hill Road. From A2, right onto A258 **open** All year except Xmas **bedrooms** 2 single, 1 double, 1 twin, 2 family **bathrooms** 6 en suite **payment** credit/debit cards, cash, cheques

Room General

220   Official tourist board guide Bed & Breakfast

South East | Kent

DOVER, Kent Map ref 3C4
SAT NAV CT16 1RU

Maison Dieu Guest House
89 Maison Dieu Road, Dover CT16 1RU
t (01304) 204033 **f** (01304) 242816 **e** info@maisondieu.co.uk
w maisondieu.com

B&B PER ROOM PER NIGHT
S £30.00 – £38.00
D £56.00

SPECIAL PROMOTIONS
Special Offer for Families—
2 free childs breakfasts
(under 13yrs) per family
Bed & Breakfast (excl.
School, Bank & Public
Holidays)

Elegant, comfortable & extremely welcoming - our Silver Award Guest Accommodation is offered with genuine English warmth & hospitality. Central for shops & restaurants, minutes from ferry & Cruise Terminals, providing parking & Wi-Fi, maps and information - our personal attention ensures the very best is made of your stay

open All year except Xmas
bedrooms 2 single, 1 double, 1 twin, 3 family
bathrooms 4 en suite, 1 with private bathroom
payment credit/debit cards, cash, cheques

directions A20/Townhall Street, turn into York Street, at roundabout take 2nd exit (Priory Road). At lights turn right (Ladywell). At lights turn right (Maison Dieu Road).

Room
General
Leisure

FAVERSHAM, Kent Map ref 3B3
SAT NAV ME13 9JG

Barnsfield
Fostall, Hernhill, Faversham ME13 9JG
t (01227) 750973 **f** (01227) 273098 **e** barnsfield@mac.com
w barnsfield.co.uk ONLINE MAP

B&B PER ROOM PER NIGHT
S £28.00 – £48.00
D £54.00 – £72.00

Grade II Listed country cottage accommodation, just off A299, in three acres of orchards, six miles from Canterbury. Convenient for ports and touring. Close to Whitstable **directions** M2 runs onto A299, continue for 1 mile, take slip road signed Fostall, follow signs into village, turn left, approx 200yds on right. **open** All year except Xmas and New Year **bedrooms** 1 double, 1 twin **bathrooms** 1 with private bathroom **payment** cash, cheques

Room General Leisure

FAVERSHAM, Kent Map ref 3B3
SAT NAV ME13 8NH

Fairlea Bed & Breakfast
27 Preston Avenue, Faversham ME13 8NH
t (01795) 539610 **e** info@fairleabandb.co.uk
w fairleabandb.co.uk ONLINE MAP GUEST REVIEWS

B&B PER ROOM PER NIGHT
S £40.00
D £70.00

Accommodation comprises a double, twin and single bedrooms, all en suite. All bedrooms include individually controlled heating, colour TV, clock alarms and coffee/tea making facilities and free wi-fi. **directions** Please contact us for directions **open** All year except Xmas and New Year **bedrooms** 1 single, 1 double, 1 twin **bathrooms** 3 en suite **payment** cash, cheques, euros

Room General Leisure

key to symbols see page 6

221

South East | **Kent**

FAVERSHAM, Kent Map ref 3B3
SAT NAV ME9 0AU

HOSTEL

B&B PER ROOM PER NIGHT
S £22.00 – £100.00

Palace Farm Hostel
Down Court Road, Doddington, Sittingbourne, Kent ME9 0AU
t (01795) 886200 **e** info@palacefarm.com
w palacefarm.com ONLINE MAP GUEST REVIEWS ONLINE BOOKING LAST MINUTE OFFERS

Clean, friendly, warm, easy to use accommodation with kitchen in six private en suite rooms. Double beds and bunks make this idea for all with rooms sleeping 1 - 8. **directions** In central Kent North Downs AONB. Please ask when booking or see website. **open** All year **bedrooms** 1 single, 2 double, 1 twin **bathrooms** 6 en suite **payment** credit/debit cards, cash

Room General Leisure

FOLKESTONE, Kent Map ref 3B4
SAT NAV CT19 6NH

GUEST HOUSE

B&B PER ROOM PER NIGHT
S £32.00 – £45.00
D £46.00 – £62.00

The Rob Roy Guest House
227 Dover Road, Folkestone, Kent CT19 6NH
t (01303) 253341 **f** (01303) 770060 **e** robroy.folkestone@ntlworld.com
w therobroyguesthouse.co.uk ONLINE MAP GUEST REVIEWS ONLINE BOOKING LAST MINUTE OFFERS

Comfortable accomodation & tasty breakfast. Ideal for exploring East Kent. 4 minutes drive to town centre & beach, 10 to Channel Tunnel and 20 to Dover ferries or Eurostar Ashford. **directions** Ex M20 jct 13. (4 roundabouts) A259 towards Folkestone harbour the A260 Hill Rd until Dover Road. The Rob Roy is halfway down on right. **open** All year except Xmas and New Year **bedrooms** 3 double, 3 twin, 1 family **bathrooms** 3 en suite **payment** credit/debit cards, cash, cheques, euros

Room General Leisure

FOLKESTONE (2 MILES), Kent Map ref 3B4
SAT NAV CT18 7AA

★★★★ GUEST ACCOMMODATION

B&B PER ROOM PER NIGHT
S £50.00 – £55.00
D £72.00 – £80.00

Crete Down
Crete Road West, Folkestone CT18 7AA
t (01303) 892392 **f** (01303) 760733 **e** enquiries@crete-down.co.uk
w crete-down.co.uk ONLINE MAP GUEST REVIEWS ONLINE BOOKING LAST MINUTE OFFERS

Crete Down is on the Northdowns Way. Channel tunnel, ferry por at Dover and Eurostar at Ashford short distance away. All rooms have stunning views of the sea and garden. **directions** From London: Follow M20 towards Folkestone. Continue to A20 (Dover, Canterbury). Take next exit (A260), turn left for folkestone. Crete Road West first on right. **open** All year except Xmas and New Yea **bedrooms** 1 double, 1 twin, 1 suite **bathrooms** 2 en suite, 1 with private bathroom **payment** cash, cheques, euros

Room General Leisure

GILLINGHAM, Kent Map ref 3B3
SAT NAV ME7 4NT

GUEST HOUSE

B&B PER ROOM PER NIGHT
S £22.00 – £34.00
D £25.00 – £44.00

The Balmoral
57 - 59 Balmoral Road, Gillingham, Kent ME7 4NT
t (01634) 853682 **e** bookings@thebalmoral-guesthouse.co.uk
w thebalmoral-guesthouse.co.uk/ ONLINE MAP ONLINE BOOKING LAST MINUTE OFFERS

In the heart of Medway, we offer great accommodation at extremely affordable prices. Weekly stay rates ideal for work/leisu Excellent access to all London & South East attractions. **directions** Across from Gillingham Train station. High speed rail link to Lond & Kent Coast. Easy access to A2/M2, Chatham docks, Medway University and Hospital **open** All year **bedrooms** 4 single, 6 doub 6 twin, 2 family **bathrooms** 18 en suite **payment** credit/debit cards, cash

Room General

222 Official tourist board guide **Bed & Breakf**

South East | Kent

HERNE BAY, Kent Map ref 3B3

SAT NAV CT6 8TZ

Seahaven
64 Linden Avenue, Herne Bay CT6 8TZ
t 01227 366582   e marilynbudd@hotmail.co.uk
w hernebayseahaven.com   ONLINE MAP

B&B PER ROOM PER NIGHT
S £40.00
D £60.00

Offering two first floor double en-suite rooms, a single room which may be used in addition to one of the doubles as family accommodation or as a single en-suite room. **directions** Seahaven is a 5 minute walk from the sea front, high street and railway staion. **open** All year except Xmas **bedrooms** 1 single, 2 double **bathrooms** 2 en suite **payment** cash, cheques

Room   General   Leisure

HERNHILL, Kent Map ref 3B3

SAT NAV ME13 9JW

Church Oast
Church Oast, Hernhill, Faversham ME13 9JW
t (01227) 750974   e jill@geliot.plus.com
w churchoast.co.uk   ONLINE MAP

B&B PER ROOM PER NIGHT
S £35.00 – £50.00
D £55.00 – £90.00

SPECIAL PROMOTIONS
Winter break offers 1st December - 1st March

A warm welcome and luxury accommodation in converted Oast House in quiet picturesque village. Lovely garden with views over orchards. Varied breakfast menu using local produce. Guest lounge with TV and real fire. Special winter breaks. Evening meals available in nearby pub. Close to Canterbury, Whitstable, Faversham and Channel ports.

open All year except Xmas
bedrooms 1 double, 1 twin, 1 family
bathrooms 2 en suite, 1 with private bathroom
payment cash, cheques, euros

directions From London M2 then A299 Margate first exit and follow signs to Hernhill. From Dover A2 to M2 roundabout 4th exit A299 then as above.

BREAKFAST AWARD   Room   General   Leisure

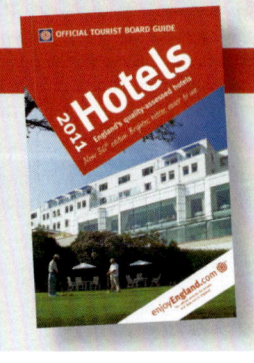

Looking for something else?

You can also buy a copy of our popular guide 'Hotels' including country house and town house hotels, metro and budget hotels, serviced apartments, restaurants with rooms and Spas in England 2011.

Now available in good bookshops and online at
visitbritainshop.com

£10.99

South East | Kent

MAIDSTONE, Kent Map ref 3B3   SAT NAV ME14 5JT

Grove House
Grove Green Road, Maidstone ME14 5JT
t (01622) 738441

B&B PER ROOM PER NIGHT
S £35.00 – £40.00
D £65.00 – £70.00

Attractive comfortable detached house in quiet road. Off-street parking. Close to Leeds Castle, pubs, restaurants, M20 and M2 motorways, for access to Channel Tunnel. Prices include full English breakfast.

open All year
bedrooms 1 double, 1 twin
bathrooms 1 en suite, 1 with private bathroom
payment credit/debit cards, cash, cheques

directions Leave M20 jct 7. Follow signs to TV studios, left into Grovewood Drive. Past Tesco, 2nd left at mini-roundabout. 1st left Grove Green Road.

Room
General
Leisure

MAIDSTONE, KENT, Kent Map ref 3B4   SAT NAV ME17 1RQ

Ash Cottage
Penfold Hill, Leeds Village, Nr Maidstone, Kent ME17 1RQ
t (01622) 863142 e rayne@ashcottagekent.co.uk
w ashcottagekent.co.uk ONLINE MAP GUEST REVIEWS LAST MINUTE OFFERS

B&B PER ROOM PER NIGHT
S £40.00 – £60.00
D £60.00 – £90.00

SPECIAL PROMOTIONS
Long stay discount available. Anniversary, birthday, special occasion packages offered i.e. wine, flowers etc.

A historic Grade II listed building being formerly part of the Leeds Castle estate. Heavily beamed with inglenook fireplaces and set in a lovely cottage garden, this property boasts stunning winter castle views. Leave your car snug and secure, castle gates (0.6 miles) and fine pubs within walking distance.

open All year except Xmas and New Year
bedrooms 2 double, 1 twin
bathrooms 2 en suite, 1 with private bathroom
payment cash, cheques

directions At M20 Junction 8 follow sign for Leeds Castle. Pass castle entrance, Ash Cottage on right after bridge and 30 mph sign before bend.

Room   General   Leisure

South East | Kent

MARGATE, Kent Map ref 3C3
SAT NAV CT9 5JP

Hussar
219 Canterbury Road, Margate CT9 5JP
t (01843) 836296 e rdobbs@ukgateway.net
w hussarhotel.co.uk ONLINE BOOKING

B&B PER ROOM PER NIGHT
S £50.00
D £60.00
EVENING MEAL PER PERSON
£6.00 – £12.00

Recently undergone major refurbishment programme. All rooms contemporary design with full en suite facilities. Warm welcome and friendly atmosphere. Evening meals available. On the A28 on the outskirts of Margate. **directions** The Hussar is situated on the A28 about a mile before arriving in Margate. Margate main line station is 3/4 of a mile away. **open** All year **bedrooms** 1 single, 3 double, 1 twin, 1 family **bathrooms** 6 en suite **payment** credit/debit cards, cash, cheques

Room General Leisure

MINSTER, Kent Map ref 3C3
SAT NAV CT12 4HD

Durlock Lodge
Durlock, Minster, Ramsgate CT12 4HD
t (01843) 821219 f (01843)825722 e david@durlocklodge.co.uk
w durlocklodge.co.uk ONLINE MAP GUEST REVIEWS ONLINE BOOKING LAST MINUTE OFFERS

Relaxing village location in 18th century lodge with renowned Bell Inn, a five minute stroll. Within 6 miles of: Broadstairs (beach), Sandwich (Cinque Port & Pfizers), Ramsgate (Airport & marina) **directions** Turn off the A299 to Minster Village. We are at the bottom of the village 500 m past the church and opposite the abbey. **open** All year except Xmas and New Year **bedrooms** 2 double, 1 twin **bathrooms** 3 en suite **payment** credit/debit cards, cash, cheques

Leisure

NEW ROMNEY, Kent Map ref 3B4
SAT NAV TN28 8DR

Broadacre
North Street, New Romney, Kent TN28 8DR
t (01797) 362381 f (01797) 362381 e info@broadacrehotel.co.uk
w broadacrehotel.co.uk ONLINE MAP

B&B PER ROOM PER NIGHT
S £50.00 – £60.00
D £65.00 – £85.00

Family run and quietly situated in the Historic Cinque Port Town of New Romney on the Romney Marsh. Nr Channel ports & Rye. **directions** M20 Junction 10 then A2070 to Brenzett, left at roundabout onto A259. Proceed to New Romney High Street, left into Rome Road for 100mts. **open** All year except Xmas and New Year **bedrooms** 3 single, 4 double, 2 twin **bathrooms** 9 en suite **payment** credit/debit cards, cash, cheques

Room General Leisure

Looking for something else?
You can also buy a copy of our popular guide 'Self Catering' including self-catering holiday homes, approved caravan holiday homes, boat accommodation and holiday cottage agencies in England 2011.

Now available in good bookshops and online at
visitbritainshop.com

£11.99

South East | **Kent**

PLUCKLEY, Kent Map ref 3B4
SAT NAV TN27 0SU

Elvey Farm
Elvey Lane, Ashford TN27 0SU
t (01233) 840442 e bookings@elveyfarm.co.uk
w elveyfarm.co.uk ONLINE MAP GUEST REVIEWS ONLINE BOOKING LAST MINUTE OFFERS

B&B PER ROOM PER NIGHT
S £80.00 – £120.00
D £100.00 – £200.00
EVENING MEAL PER PERSON
£23.95 – £27.95

Medieval farmstead set in 75 acres in the heart of Darling Buds of May country. Suites in Stable Block, 16th century barn, and Oast House, packed with period features and stylish, contemporary en suites. Private entrances and living rooms. Stunning Kentish restaurant.

open All year
bedrooms 3 double, 2 family, 4 suites
bathrooms 9 en suite
payment credit/debit cards, cash, cheques

directions Take the M20 to jct 8. Follow A20 towards Lenham. At Charing roundabout, head towards Ashford. Turn right at lights, towards Pluckley.

BREAKFAST AWARD

Room
General
Leisure

RAMSGATE, Kent Map ref 3C3
SAT NAV CT11 8DB

Glendevon Guest House
8 Truro Road, Ramsgate CT11 8DB
t 0800 035 2110 f (01843) 570909 e info@glendevonguesthouse.co.uk
w glendevonguesthouse.co.uk GUEST REVIEWS

B&B PER ROOM PER NIGHT
S £35.00 – £50.00
D £60.00 – £70.00

Victorian house near beach, harbour and town. All rooms have en suite, modern kitchen/dining area. Free Wi-fi TV/VCR/Freeview, Fairtrade tea, coffee & hot chocolate. Excellent full English breakfast. **directions** Please contact us for directions **open** All year **bedrooms** 3 double, 1 twin, 2 family **bathrooms** 6 en suite, 6 with private bathroom **payment** credit/debit cards, cash, cheques

Room   General   Leisure

ROYAL TUNBRIDGE WELLS, Kent Map ref 2D2
SAT NAV TN4 9UP

Great Oaks
163 St Johns Road, Royal Tunbridge Wells TN4 9UP
t (01892) 529992 e greatoaks163@tiscali.co.uk

B&B PER ROOM PER NIGHT
S £30.00
D £50.00

Detached family home, off road parking for five cars, large back garden, easy to find. Bedrooms - one double, one single, one bathroom and one separate toilet. **directions** Approximately one mile from the centre of town and one and a half miles from the railway station. **open** All year except Xmas **bedrooms** 1 single, 1 double, 1 twin **payment** cash, cheques

Room   General

226   Official tourist board guide Bed & Breakfast

South East | **Kent**

ROYAL TUNBRIDGE WELLS, Kent Map ref 2D2   SAT NAV TN3 9AD

B&B PER ROOM PER NIGHT
D £50.00 – £60.00

Hawkenbury Farm Bed & Breakfast
Hawkenbury Road, Royal Tunbridge Wells TN3 9AD
t (01892) 536977 f (01892) 536200 e rhwright1@aol.com

Accommodation on small working farm, set in quiet location 1.5 miles south east of Tunbridge Wells. Unlimited parking, views and walks. **directions** Please contact us for directions **open** All year except Xmas and New Year **bedrooms** 2 double, 1 twin **bathrooms** 3 en suite **payment** credit/debit cards, cash, cheques, euros

Room   General   Leisure

ROYAL TUNBRIDGE WELLS, Kent Map ref 2D2   SAT NAV TN3 9TB

B&B PER ROOM PER NIGHT
S £28.00 – £45.00
D £56.00 – £66.00

SPECIAL PROMOTIONS
Reductions for longer stays.
Reductions for children.

Manor Court Farm Bed & Breakfast
Ashurst Road, Ashurst TN3 9TB
t (01892) 740279 f (01892) 740919 e jsoyke@jsoyke.freeserve.co.uk
w manorcourtfarm.co.uk

Georgian farmhouse with friendly atmosphere, spacious rooms and lovely views of Medway Valley. Mixed 350-acre farm, many animals. Good base for walking. Penshurst Place, Hever Castle, Chartwell, Sissinghurst etc all within easy reach by car. Excellent camping facilities. Good train service to London from Ashurst station (two minutes away).

open All year except Xmas
bedrooms 2 twin, 1 family
payment cash, cheques, euros

directions On A264 road 5 miles west of Tunbridge Wells, towards East Grinstead/Gatwick etc. $\frac{1}{2}$ mile east of Ashurst village, in hamlet of Stone Cross.

Room   General   Leisure

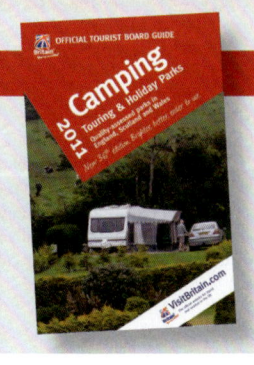

Do you like Camping?

You can also buy a copy of our popular guide 'Camping, Touring & Holiday Parks' including touring parks, camping holidays and holiday parks and villages in Britain 2011.

Now available in good bookshops and online at
visitbritainshop.com

£8.99

key to symbols see page 6

South East | **Kent**

SHEERNESS, Kent Map ref 3B3 — SAT NAV ME12 4BQ

Ferry House Inn
Harty Ferry Road, Sheerness, Kent ME12 4BQ
t 01795 510214 e info@theferryhouseinn.co.uk
w **theferryhouseinn.co.uk** ONLINE MAP GUEST REVIEWS LAST MINUTE OFFERS

B&B PER ROOM PER NIGHT
S £50.00 – £70.00
D £85.00 – £95.00

EVENING MEAL PER PERSON
£8.50 – £25.00

SPECIAL PROMOTIONS
Stay 3 nights, get 3rd night half price (excl Bank Holidays). Themed evenings. See our website for more details.

Traditional 16th Century inn. Rural location overlooking the Swale Estuary. Great for walking, birdwatching or just relaxing. Oak Barn Restaurant using locally sourced and farmed produce, specialising in game, steak and fresh fish.

open All year except Xmas
bedrooms 3 double, 1 twin
bathrooms 4 en suite
payment credit/debit cards, cash, cheques

directions M20 jct 7 or M2 jct 5. A249 onto Is of Sheppey. Follow signs to Leysdown B2231. After Eastchurch turn right into Harty Ferry Rd

Room General Leisure

SISSINGHURST, Kent Map ref 3B4 — SAT NAV TN17 4AL

Tollgate Farm B&B
Tollgate Farm, Golford, Sissinghurst, Cranbrook TN17 4AL
t (01580) 712864 e enquiry@tollgate-farm.co.uk
w **tollgate-farm.co.uk** ONLINE MAP GUEST REVIEWS ONLINE BOOKING

B&B PER ROOM PER NIGHT
S £45.00
D £60.00 – £65.00

Tollgate farm is situated in the High Weald within an orchard and bluebell wood. Close to Sissinghurst Castle, Scotney Castle garden and Hemsted forest golf course. **directions** Tollgate Farm is 1 mile south of the village of Sissinghurst heading towards Benenden **open** All year except Xmas and New Year **bedrooms** 1 double, 1 family **bathrooms** 2 en suite **payment** cash, cheques

Room General Leisure

STELLING MINNIS, Kent Map ref 3B4 — SAT NAV CT4 6DE

Great Field Farm B&B
Misling Lane, Stelling Minnis, Canterbury CT4 6DE
t (01227) 709217 f (01227) 709209 e greatfieldfarm@aol.com
w **great-field-farm.co.uk** ONLINE MAP GUEST REVIEWS

B&B PER ROOM PER NIGHT
S £35.00 – £65.00
D £70.00 – £90.00

Delightful farmhouse set amidst lovely gardens and countryside. Spacious, private suites; B&B or self-catering. Hearty breakfasts with home-grown fruits and eggs. Ten minutes to Canterbury/Channel Tunnel. **directions** From M20 exit J11 onto B2068 to Canterbury. Look out for brown B & B signs after about 6 miles. **open** All year **bedrooms** 3 double, 2 twin **bathrooms** 5 en suite **payment** credit, debit cards, cash, cheques, euros

BREAKFAST AWARD   Room General Leisure

South East | **Kent**

SWANLEY, Kent Map ref 2D2   SAT NAV BR8 8HT

Greenacre
15 Greenacre Close, Swanley BR8 8HT
t (01322) 613656 **e** pauline.snow1@btinternet.com
w **greenacrebandb.co.uk**

B&B PER ROOM PER NIGHT
S £42.00 – £50.00
D £80.00 – £95.00

Quality ground-floor annexe, double and twin rooms with private bathroom and private garden, fridge and private conservatory. Four miles Brands Hatch, close Bluewater shopping centre. Choice of breakfast menu. **directions** Leave M25 junction 3 take B2173 Swanley first roundabout first exit Goldsel Road third right Azalea Drive first left Greenacre Close left last house right **open** All year **bedrooms** 1 double, 1 twin **bathrooms** 1 with private bathroom **payment** cash, cheques, euros

Room General

TENTERDEN, Kent Map ref 3B4   SAT NAV TN30 6RL

Collina House
5 East Hill, Tenterden TN30 6RL
t (01580) 764852 **f** (01580) 762224 **e** enquiries@collinahousehotel.co.uk
w **collinahousehotel.co.uk** ONLINE MAP

B&B PER ROOM PER NIGHT
S £45.00 – £60.00
D £75.00 – £95.00
EVENING MEAL PER PERSON
£22.50 – £25.00

Attractive Edwardian house set in peaceful location only a few minutes walk from town centre. Smart, spacious, well equipped en suite bedrooms. Bar serving renowned local wines. Restaurant offering imaginative home-made dishes. **directions** Off High Street east onto B2067 Oaks Road, leads into East Hill and the property is on the left opposite an orchard. **open** All year except Xmas and New Year **bedrooms** 2 single, 9 double, 2 twin, 2 family **bathrooms** 15 en suite **payment** credit/debit cards, cash, cheques

Room General

TUNBRIDGE WELLS, Kent Map ref 2D2   SAT NAV TN1 1JY

40 York Road
40 York Road, Royal Tunbridge Wells TN1 1JY
t (01892) 531342 **f** (01892) 531342 **e** yorkrd@uwclub.net
w **yorkroad.co.uk** ONLINE MAP GUEST REVIEWS

B&B PER ROOM PER NIGHT
S £42.00 – £45.00
D £36.00 – £38.00
EVENING MEAL PER PERSON
£13.00 – £25.00

Comfortable house situated in the centre of town close to shops and restaurants. Ideal for Castle and Garden visits in Kent. Near rail station, London 50 minutes. Good breakfast choices. **directions** From M25, junction 5, A21, then A26 to T.Wells. Access York Rd (one way) from London Rd. See website for more. **open** All year except Xmas and New Year **bedrooms** 1 double, 1 twin **bathrooms** 2 en suite **payment** credit/debit cards, cash, cheques

Room General

Where is my pet welcome?

Some properties welcome well-behaved pets. Look for the 🐕 in the accommodation listings.

You can also buy a copy of our popular guide 'Pets Come Too!' Now available in good bookshops and online at **visitbritainshop.com**

£9.99

key to symbols see page 6

South East | **Kent**

WALMER, Kent Map ref 3C4
SAT NAV CT14 8AW

Hardicot Guest House
Kingsdown Road, Walmer, Deal CT14 8AW
t (01304) 373867 **f** (01304) 389234 **e** guestboss@btopenworld.com
w hardicot-guest-house.co.uk ONLINE MAP GUEST REVIEWS ONLINE BOOKING

B&B PER ROOM PER NIGHT
S £35.00 – £40.00
D £70.00 – £80.00

SPECIAL PROMOTIONS
7 nights for the price of 6.
4 or 5 nights 5% reduction.
6 nights 10% reduction.

Large, quiet, detached Victorian house with Channel views and secluded garden, situated 100yds from the beach. Guests have unrestricted access to rooms. Close to three championship golf courses, ferries and the Channel Tunnel. Ideal centre for cliff walks and exploring Canterbury and the castles and gardens of East Kent.

open All year except Xmas
bedrooms 1 double, 2 twin
bathrooms 2 en suite, 1 with private bathroom
payment cash, cheques, euros

directions From Dover take A258 direction Deal. At Ringwould turn right signed Kingsdown. Continue 1.5 miles through village. Hardicot is 100m past Rising Sun pub.

Room
General
Leisure

WEST BRABOURNE, Kent Map ref 3B4
SAT NAV TN25 5NB

Bulltown Farmhouse Bed & Breakfast
Bulltown Lane, West Brabourne, Ashford TN25 5NB
t (01233) 813505 **f** (01227) 709544 **e** lily.wilton@bulltown.co.uk

B&B PER ROOM PER NIGHT
S £40.00 – £45.00
D £70.00 – £80.00

Stunning 15th century timber framed farmhouse with a wealth of beams surrounded by cottage garden in area of outstanding natural beauty. Rooms have unspoilt views. Guest lounge with large inglenook fireplace **directions** See website for directions but under 4 miles from Junction 10 M20 **bedrooms** 1 double, 1 twin, 1 family **bathrooms** 3 en suite **payment** cash, cheques, euros

Room   General   Leisure

WESTERHAM, Kent Map ref 2D2
SAT NAV TN16 2HW

Old Farmhouse
430 Main Road, Westerham Hill, Westerham TN16 2HW
t (01959) 571003 **e** potsnpots@aol.com
w theoldfarmhousewesterham.co.uk ONLINE MAP GUEST REVIEWS

B&B PER ROOM PER NIGHT
S £58.00 – £70.00
D £77.00 – £94.00

Beautiful 16th century farmhouse overlooking North Downs. Antique furniture, large inglenook fireplace, guest lounge, home cooking, large garden, off street parking. Personal service in cosy surroundings. Chartwell, Hever, Down etc. **directions** Situated on A233 between M25 junctions 5 and 6. **open** All year except Xmas **bedrooms** 3 double, 1 twin **bathrooms** 1 en suite **payment** credit, debit cards, cash, cheques

BREAKFAST AWARD   Room   General   Leisure

230   Official tourist board guide Bed & Breakfast

South East | **Kent**

WORTH, Kent Map ref 3C3   SAT NAV CT14 0DF

B&B PER ROOM PER NIGHT
S £50.00 – £70.00
D £65.00 – £70.00

EVENING MEAL PER PERSON
£3.95 – £16.00

St Crispin Inn
The Street, Worth, Deal CT14 0DF
t (01304) 612081 f (01304) 614838 e info@stcrispininn.com
w stcrispininn.com ONLINE MAP GUEST REVIEWS ONLINE BOOKING LAST MINUTE OFFERS

The St Crispin Inn is a 15th century traditional pub in the small country village of Word in Worth, close to the mediaeval cinque port of Sandwich and not far from Deal and Dover. Enjoy traditional beers, continental lagers and tasty home cooked food for all the family.

open All year
bedrooms 1 double, 2 twin, 3 family
bathrooms 6 en suite
payment credit/debit cards, cash, cheques

directions Please contact us for directions

Room   General   Leisure

WYE, Kent Map ref 3B4   SAT NAV TN25 5BH

B&B PER ROOM PER NIGHT
S £30.00
D £60.00

Mistral
3 Oxenturn Road, Wye, Ashford TN25 5BH
t (01233) 813011 f (01233) 813011 e geoff@chapman.invictanet.co.uk
w chapman.invictanet.co.uk ONLINE BOOKING

Small bed and breakfast offering high-quality food and facilities in a central but secluded part of Wye village. Parking is available by arrangement. **directions** Please contact us for directions **open** All year except Xmas **bedrooms** 1 single, 1 twin **bathrooms** 1 with private bathroom **payment** cash, cheques

Room   General

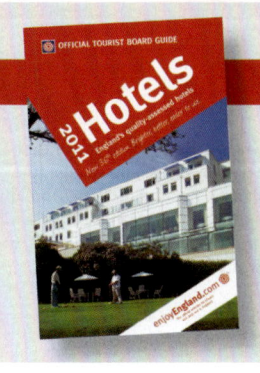

Looking for something else?

You can also buy a copy of our popular guide 'Hotels' including country house and town house hotels, metro and budget hotels, serviced apartments, restaurants with rooms and Spas in England 2011.

Now available in good bookshops and online at
visitbritainshop.com

£10.99

South East | **Oxfordshire**

ADDERBURY, Oxfordshire Map ref 2C1
SAT NAV OX17 3LS

★★★ INN

B&B PER ROOM PER NIGHT
S £45.00 – £60.00
D £60.00 – £90.00

EVENING MEAL PER PERSON
£6.00 – £15.00

SPECIAL PROMOTIONS
Midweek (Mon-Thur) prices from £40 - room only rates also available, please contact us for up to date prices

The Bell Inn
High Street, Adderbury, Oxon OX17 3LS
t (01295) 810338 e info@the-bell.com
w the-bell.com

Traditional English inn serving award-winning ales and home-cooked food. With its striking inglenook fireplace, the Bell offers a warm and friendly welcome to customers old and new. Quiet location, pretty village on the edge of th Cotswolds. Regular folk and quiz nights. Traditional pub games including 'Aunt Sally'!

open All year
bedrooms 1 double, 1 twin
bathrooms 1 en suite, 1 with private bathroom
payment credit/debit cards, cash, cheques

directions M40 jct 11 straight through Banbury (A4260). Once in Twyford, turn right after traffic lights, signposted West Adderbury. Bell situated on left down by church.

Room
General
Leisure

BADGEMORE, Oxfordshire Map ref 2C2
SAT NAV RG9 4NR

★★★★ GUEST ACCOMMODATION

B&B PER ROOM PER NIGHT
S £75.00
D £75.00

Badgemore Park Golf Club
Badgemore, Henley on Thames RG9 4NR
t (01491) 637300 f (01491) 637301 e info@badgemorepark.com
w badgemorepark.com GUEST REVIEWS ONLINE BOOKING LAST MINUTE OFFERS

Badgemore Park is set amongst the scenic Oxfordshire Countryside Located less than 1 mile from the historic centre of Henley on Thames, the ideal base for a weekend away. **directions** Less than mile from the River Thames and Henley town centre, easily accessible from the M4 & M40 **open** All year **bedrooms** 3 double, family **bathrooms** 4 en suite, 1 with private bathroom **payment** credit/debit cards, cash, cheques, euros

Room   General   Leisure

BAMPTON, Oxfordshire Map ref 2C1
SAT NAV OX18 2DN

RATING APPLIED FOR

B&B PER ROOM PER NIGHT
S £65.00
D £75.00

EVENING MEAL PER PERSON
£12.00 – £20.00

Manor Farm Barn B&B
Bull Street, Aston, Bampton OX18 2DN
t (01993) 852907 e enquiries@manorfarmbarn.net
w manorfarmbarn.net ONLINE MAP GUEST REVIEWS ONLINE BOOKING

Located in the village of Aston, Manor Farm Barn is close to the River Thames and conveniently placed for visits to Burford, the Cotswolds, Oxford and Stratford upon Avon. **directions** Turn off Bull Street from the centre of the village and Manor Farm Barn is 400 meters on the left hand side. **open** All year **bedrooms** 1 twin **bathrooms** 1 en suite **payment** cash, cheques, euros

Room   General   Leisure

232   Official tourist board guide **Bed & Breakfa**

South East | **Oxfordshire**

BLACK BOURTON, Oxfordshire Map ref 2C1
SAT NAV OX18 2PF

enjoyEngland.com ★★★★ INN

B&B PER ROOM PER NIGHT
S £65.00 – £70.00
D £95.00 – £120.00
EVENING MEAL PER PERSON
£15.00 – £28.00

The Vines
Burford Road, Black Bourton, Bampton OX18 2PF
t (01993) 843559   e info@vineshotel.com
w **vineshotel.com**   GUEST REVIEWS   LAST MINUTE OFFERS

Renowned for fine dining in elegant surroundings and with eighteen en suite bedrooms. Rooms are well furnished. Most have king sized beds and wet rooms. All have internet access. **directions** Signposted from A4095 Faringdon to Witney. Also be reached from A40 Cheltenham to Witney road. Telephone or see website for map. **open** All year **bedrooms** 2 single, 8 double, 4 twin, 4 family **bathrooms** 18 en suite **payment** credit/debit cards, cash, cheques

Room   General   Leisure

BRIZE NORTON, Oxfordshire Map ref 2C1
SAT NAV OX18 3NA

enjoyEngland.com ★★★ GUEST ACCOMMODATION

B&B PER ROOM PER NIGHT
S £35.00
D £55.00

The Priory
Manor Farm, Manor Road, Brize Norton OX18 3NA
t (01993) 843062   f (01993) 843062   e priorymanor@uwclub.net
w **priorymanor.co.uk**

Situated in Brize Norton Village near Burford, a comfortable natural stone character house in 0.75 acres of beautiful gardens. Ample parking, comfortable rooms some self-catering with all facilities **directions** Located within the Cotswold's - approximately 14-miles west of Oxford. 4-miles from Burford and 10-miles from Bourton-on-the-Water, 10 miles Blenheim Palace. **open** All year **bedrooms** 2 double, 1 twin, 1 family, 2 suites **bathrooms** 5 en suite, 1 with private bathroom **payment** cash, cheques, euros

Room   General   Leisure

CULHAM, Oxfordshire Map ref 2C2
SAT NAV OX14 3BS

enjoyEngland.com ★★★★ FARMHOUSE

B&B PER ROOM PER NIGHT
S £70.00 – £75.00
D £80.00 – £85.00

Zouch Farm B&B
Culham, Abingdon, Oxon OX14 3BS
t (01235) 521777   f (01235) 532928   e selina_wallis@hotmail.co.uk
w **zouchfarm.co.uk**   ONLINE MAP   GUEST REVIEWS

Zouch Farm B&B has beautiful views and a tranquil setting. Our three spacious bedrooms are comfortable and inviting, included with Egyptian Cotton bedding, HDTV's, toiletries, and an indulgent breakfast. **directions** We are opposite Culham train station, which is the London-Oxford route. Near us there is Oxford, Blenheim, The Cotswolds, Burford and Bicester. **open** All year **bedrooms** 3 double **bathrooms** 3 en suite **payment** cash, cheques

Room   General   Leisure

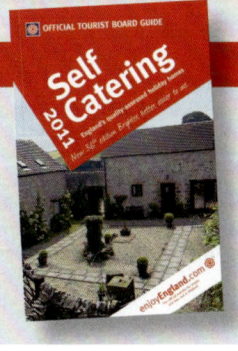

Looking for something else?
You can also buy a copy of our popular guide 'Self Catering' including self-catering holiday homes, approved caravan holiday homes, boat accommodation and holiday cottage agencies in England 2011.

Now available in good bookshops and online at
visitbritainshop.com

£11.99

South East | Oxfordshire

EWELME, Oxfordshire Map ref 2C2
SAT NAV OX10 6HU

Fords Farm
Ewelme, Wallingford OX10 6HU
t (01491) 839272 e fordsfarm@callnetuk.com
w fordsfarm.co.uk ONLINE MAP

B&B PER ROOM PER NIGHT
S £45.00 – £60.00
D £70.00 – £75.00

A warm welcome awaits you at Fords Farm. Located in an idyllic location steeped in history and offers peace and tranquility. Wonderful walks, near the Ridgeway and the Thames Path and plenty of good pubs and restaurants nearby. Within easy reach of London, Heathrow, Windsor, Henley, Reading and Oxford.

open All year
bedrooms 1 double, 1 twin
bathrooms 2 with private bathroom
payment cash, cheques

directions Please contact us for directions

Room
General
Leisure

HENLEY-ON-THAMES, Oxfordshire Map ref 2C2
SAT NAV RG9 6HS

Bank Farm
The Old Road, Pishill, Henley-on-Thames RG9 6HS
t (01491) 638601 Mobile 07791 665643 f (01491) 638601 e e.f.lakey@btinternet.com
w stayatbankfarm.co.uk

B&B PER ROOM PER NIGHT
S £28.00
D £56.00

Peaceful listed farmhouse in an Area of Outstanding Natural Beauty. Good for walking, birdwatching, reading. Ideal for visiting London and Thameside towns from Oxford to Windsor. **directions** Please contact us for directions **open** All year except Xmas **bedrooms** 2 double, 1 twin **bathrooms** 1 with private bathroom **payment** cash, cheques

Room   General

HENLEY-ON-THAMES, Oxfordshire Map ref 2C2
SAT NAV RG9 1QU

The Old Wood
197 Greys Road, Henley-on-Thames RG9 1QU
t (01491) 573930 e janice@janicejones.co.uk

B&B PER ROOM PER NIGHT
S £45.00 – £60.00
D £65.00 – £75.00

Secluded location set in half acre garden half mile from Henley centre/ station/ river. Easy access Oxford/ Windsor/ London. Ground floor rooms. Off street parking. Warm welcome assured. Children welcome. **directions** From Henley Bridge, continue up Hart St; over traffic lights; at Town Hall turn left thro car park; turn right into Greys Road. **open** All year except Xmas **bedrooms** 1 double, 1 family **bathrooms** 1 en suite, 1 with private bathroom **payment** cash, cheques, euros

Room   General

234

Official tourist board guide Bed & Breakfast

South East | **Oxfordshire**

HENLEY-ON-THAMES, Oxfordshire Map ref 2C2

SAT NAV RG9 3NY

The Baskerville
Station Road, Lower Shiplake, Henley-on-Thames RG9 3NY
t (0118) 940 3332 **f** (0118) 940 4735 **e** enquiries@thebaskerville.com
w thebaskerville.com ONLINE MAP

B&B PER ROOM PER NIGHT
S £75.00
D £85.00

EVENING MEAL PER PERSON
£10.00 – £25.00

A small village pub close to the River Thames and just minutes from Henley-on-Thames. Good Pub Guide County Dining Pub of the Year 2007, excellent wine list, cosy, comfortable bar with a good choice of cask-conditioned ales. 50 cover restaurant and a garden with seating for 100.

open All year
bedrooms 2 double, 1 twin, 1 family
bathrooms 4 en suite
payment credit/debit cards, cash, cheques

directions From Henley-on-Thames, take Reading road for 2 miles, turn left down Station Road.

Room   General

HENLEY-ON-THAMES, Oxfordshire Map ref 2C2

SAT NAV RG9 6AG

Orchard Dene Cottage
Lower Assendon, Henley-on-Thames RG9 6AG
t (01491) 575490 **f** (01491) 575490 **e** orcharddenecottage@btinternet.com
w orcharddenecottage.co.uk ONLINE MAP

B&B PER ROOM PER NIGHT
S £35.00
D £60.00

Two miles from Henley in beautiful Chilterns countryside. Comfortable and friendly old family home, with interesting garden and log fires. Full English breakfasts all year. Excellent meals in nearby restaurant. **directions** Follow A4130 (Wallingford) through Henley; after 1 mile, fork right to Assendons, then after 150yds fork left (narrow lane). Cottage 150yds on left. **open** All year **bedrooms** 1 single, 1 double **bathrooms** 1 with private bathroom **payment** cash, cheques, euros

BREAKFAST AWARD

Room   General   Leisure

Do you like Camping?

You can also buy a copy of our popular guide 'Camping, Touring & Holiday Parks' including touring parks, camping holidays and holiday parks and villages in Britain 2011.

Now available in good bookshops and online at
visitbritainshop.com

£8.99

for key to symbols see page 6

South East | Oxfordshire

LETCOMBE REGIS, Oxfordshire Map ref 2C2
SAT NAV OX12 9JD

Brook Barn
Letcombe Regis, Wantage OX12 9JD
t (01325) 766502 f (0118) 3290452 e info@brookbarn.com
w brookbarn.com ONLINE MAP GUEST REVIEWS ONLINE BOOKING

B&B PER ROOM PER NIGHT
S £85.00 – £140.00
D £100.00 – £210.00

EVENING MEAL PER PERSON
£15.00 – £35.00

Brook Barn is luxurious, relaxing and extremely comfortable. Enjoy our award winning breakfast and dinners and a delicious afternoon tea. The house is set in an acre of gardens which include a wild flower meadow and a chalk stream. We are in easy reach of Oxford and the Cotswolds.

open All year
bedrooms 1 single, 2 double, 1 twin, 1 suite
bathrooms 4 en suite, 1 with private bathroom
payment credit/debit cards, cash, cheques, euros

directions We are about 2 miles from Wantage on the outskirts of Letcombe Regis. Take the B4507 from Wantage.

BREAKFAST AWARD

MILTON-UNDER-WYCHWOOD, Oxfordshire Map ref 2B1
SAT NAV OX7 6JH

Hillborough House
The Green, Shipton Road, Burford OX7 6JH
t (01993) 832352 f (01993) 832352 e hillboroughhouse@btinternet.com

B&B PER ROOM PER NIGHT
S £40.00 – £55.00
D £70.00 – £80.00

A Victorian village house with spacious ensuite rooms overlooking the green with views to distant hills. You will be assured of a warm welcome and a great breakfast. **directions** Please contact us for directions **bedrooms** 1 double, 1 twin, 1 family **bathrooms** 3 en suite **payment** credit/debit cards, cash, cheques

OXFORD, Oxfordshire Map ref 2C1
SAT NAV OX1 3AP

The Buttery
11 Broad Street, Oxford OX1 3AP
t (01865) 811950 e enquiries@thebutteryhotel.co.uk
w thebutteryhotel.co.uk ONLINE MAP GUEST REVIEWS ONLINE BOOKING

B&B PER ROOM PER NIGHT
S £55.00 – £90.00
D £95.00 – £130.00

Set on Broad Street, surrounded by historic Oxford colleges and museums, The Buttery welcomes you to explore the wonders of Oxford from its central location. Spacious well-furnished en suite rooms. **directions** Please contact us for directions **open** All year **bedrooms** 1 single, 10 double, 2 twin, 3 family **bathrooms** 16 en suite **payment** credit/debit cards, cash, cheques

South East | **Oxfordshire**

OXFORD, Oxfordshire Map ref 2C1

SAT NAV OX2 8DX

Arden Lodge
34 Sunderland Avenue, Oxford OX2 8DX
t (01865) 552076 f (01865) 512265

B&B PER ROOM PER NIGHT
S £35.00 – £40.00
D £56.00 – £60.00

Modern detached house, in select part of Oxford, easy reach to Oxford City Centre. Excellent position for Blenheim Palace, Cotswolds, Stratford, Warwick, London etc. Close to parks, golf course and River. The famous Trout Inn in Wolvercote is a short drive away.

open All year except Xmas
bedrooms 1 single, 1 double, 1 twin
bathrooms 1 en suite, 2 with private bathroom
payment cash, cheques

directions Please contact us for directions

Room General P Leisure

OXFORD, Oxfordshire Map ref 2C1

SAT NAV OX1 5DZ

Broomhill Bed and Breakfast
Broomhill, Lincombe Lane, Boars Hill, Oxford OX1 5DZ
t (01865) 735339 e sara@broomhill-oxford.co.uk
w broomhill-oxford.co.uk

B&B PER ROOM PER NIGHT
S £40.00 – £50.00
D £65.00 – £80.00

Broomhill Bed and Breakfast is situated five minutes from Oxford. Heathrow 45 minutes. Large house in family environment in extensive grounds. Large double and single rooms, all en suite. Excellent pub five minutes walk, serving good, all-day food. See website or email for more information.

open All year
bedrooms 2 single, 2 double, 1 twin
bathrooms 4 en suite
payment cash, cheques, euros

directions From North, leave A34 at Hinksey Hill interchange. Go over A34 and up hill. At top turn right. Continue 1 mile. Lincombe Lane on left.

BREAKFAST AWARD

Room General P Leisure

South East | **Oxfordshire**

OXFORD, Oxfordshire Map ref 2C1
SAT NAV OX2 7PL

Cotswold House
363 Banbury Road, Oxford OX2 7PL
t (01865) 310558 f (01865) 310558 e d.r.walker@talk21.com
w cotswoldhouse.co.uk ONLINE MAP ONLINE BOOKING

B&B PER ROOM PER NIGHT
S £55.00 – £65.00
D £85.00 – £95.00

A well-situated and elegant property, offering excellent accommodation and service. Cotswold House is in a most desirable part of Oxford. **directions** Exit Oxford ring road on North side, following sign to Summertown. We are half a mile on right as you head towards city centre. **open** All year **bedrooms** 2 single, 2 double, 1 twin, 2 family **bathrooms** 7 en suite **payment** credit/debit cards, cash, cheques

Room   General   P

OXFORD, Oxfordshire Map ref 2C1
SAT NAV OX1 4PL

Newton House Guest House B&B Oxford
82-84 Abingdon Road, Oxford OX1 4PL
t (01865) 240561 f (01865) 244547 e newton.house@btinternet.com
w oxfordcity.co.uk/accom/newton ONLINE MAP GUEST REVIEWS ONLINE BOOKING LAST MINUTE OFFERS

B&B PER ROOM PER NIGHT
S £46.00 – £76.00
D £59.00 – £84.00

SPECIAL PROMOTIONS
Ask about special offers

Close to Oxford's city centre, on foot, bus, coach, train or car a perfect opportunity to visit Oxford's university central city attractions, research facilities, museums, hospitals. Family run with a personal touch free wifi car park English traditional breakfast, vegetarian and continental special diets catered for.

open All year
bedrooms 7 double, 2 twin, 4 family
bathrooms 13 en suite, 13 with private bathroom
payment credit/debit cards, cash, cheques

directions Situated on A4144 (OX1 4PL) Postal code 1/2 mile (800 mtrs) from the city centre 10 to 15 min walk see us on google maps.

Room
General   P
Leisure

OXFORD, Oxfordshire Map ref 2C1
SAT NAV OX2 6EH

Park House
7 St Bernards Road, Oxford OX2 6EH
t (01865) 310824 e krynpark@hotmail.com

B&B PER ROOM PER NIGHT
S £40.00
D £60.00

Traditional Victorian terraced house in north Oxford, five minutes walk from city centre and within easy reach of all amenities. Friendly and relaxed atmosphere. **directions** Please contact us for directions **open** All year except Xmas **bedrooms** 1 single, 1 double **payment** cash, cheques, euros

Room   General   P   Leisure

South East | **Oxfordshire**

OXFORD, Oxfordshire Map ref 2C1
SAT NAV OX3 7SP

Pickwick's Guest House
15-17 London Road, Headington, Oxford OX3 7SP
t (01865) 750487 f (01865) 742208 e pickwicks@tiscali.co.uk
w pickwicksguesthouse.co.uk ONLINE MAP

★★★★ GUEST HOUSE

B&B PER ROOM PER NIGHT
S £30.00 – £55.00
D £70.00 – £90.00

Guest house within easy reach of Oxford's universities and hospitals. Nearby bus stop to London, Heathrow, Gatwick and Stansted Airports. Contact us for family room rates. **directions** Oxford Ring Road to the Green Road roundabout (A40), then A420 into Headington. We are at the junction of London/Sandfield Road.
open All year except Xmas and New Year **bedrooms** 4 single, 4 double, 3 twin, 4 family **bathrooms** 13 en suite **payment** credit/debit cards, cash, cheques

SHILLINGFORD, Oxfordshire Map ref 2C2
SAT NAV OX10 7ER

Marsh House
7 Court Drive, Shillingford, Wallingford OX10 7ER
t (01865) 858496 f (01865) 595204 e marsh.house@talk21.com
w marshhousebandb.co.uk ONLINE MAP GUEST REVIEWS

★★★★ BED & BREAKFAST

B&B PER ROOM PER NIGHT
S £40.00 – £50.00
D £65.00 – £70.00

Treat yourself to a stay at this large family house set in a peaceful private road. Tastfully furnished with all modern comforts. Delicious breakfasts served with tranquil garden views. **directions** From the A4074, Oxford to Reading turn right at Shillingford roundabout. After approximately 300yds turn right into Court Drive. We are third house on left. **open** All year except Xmas **bedrooms** 1 single, 1 double, 1 twin **bathrooms** 3 en suite **payment** cash, cheques

WALLINGFORD, Oxfordshire Map ref 2C2
SAT NAV OX10 8BG

B&B @ Little Gables
166 Crowmarsh Hill, Crowmarsh Gifford, Wallingford, Oxfordshire OX10 8BG
t (01491) 837834 e mail@littlegables.co.uk
w littlegables.co.uk ONLINE MAP GUEST REVIEWS ONLINE BOOKING

★★★★ BED & BREAKFAST

B&B PER ROOM PER NIGHT
S £55.00 – £70.00
D £70.00 – £90.00

Boutique B&B recently fully refurbished FlatScreen TV's, WAN, Kingsize Beds and luxurious breakfasts. Garden seating, off-road parking, bike storage. Near M4/M40, Henley, Oxford, Reading, Heathrow and London **directions** On the Ridgeway and Thames Path footpaths. Oxford & Henley 15 mins drive. Windsor Castle, Heathrow, Reading station and London within one hours drive.
open All year **bedrooms** 1 single, 1 double, 1 twin, 1 family **bathrooms** 3 en suite **payment** cash, cheques, euros

WANTAGE, Oxfordshire Map ref 2C2
SAT NAV OX12 7AL

B&B in Wantage
50 Foliat Drive, Wantage OX12 7AL
t (01235) 760495 e eleanor@eaturner.freeserve.co.uk
w geocities.com/bandbinwantage

★★★★ BED & BREAKFAST

B&B PER ROOM PER NIGHT
S £26.00 – £30.00
D £40.00 – £48.00

B&B in Wantage is a clean, comfortable and quiet establishment within easy walking distance of the town centre and buses. **directions** From M4 East, J13, A34 North, exit on A4185, A417 from M4 West J14, A338 from A34 North, A4130, A417 No.32 bus from Didcot **open** All year **bedrooms** 2 double, 1 twin **bathrooms** 2 en suite, 1 with private bathroom **payment** cash, cheques

or key to symbols see page 6

South East | **Oxfordshire/Surrey**

WANTAGE, Oxfordshire Map ref 2C2
SAT NAV OX12 8ER

Regis Guest House
12 Charlton Road, Wantage OX12 8ER
t (01235) 762860 e millie_rastall@hotmail.com
w regisguesthouse.com ONLINE MAP GUEST REVIEWS ONLINE BOOKING LAST MINUTE OFFERS

B&B PER ROOM PER NIGHT
S £45.00 – £50.00
D £70.00 – £75.00

EVENING MEAL PER PERSON
£15.00 – £25.00

SPECIAL PROMOTIONS
Weekend breaks £65-£70 per person for two sharing an ensuite room for 2 night minimum stay. Offer excludes Bank Holidays.

A warm and friendly welcome assured. Our aim is to ensure that your stay in our comfortable Edwardian Home (whether an overnight visit, a weekend or much longer) will be a comfortable and memorable experience. Ensuite rooms, colour flat screen tv, tea/coffee, free WiFi, off street parking evening meals.

open All year
bedrooms 2 double, 2 twin
bathrooms 3 en suite, 1 with private bathroom
payment credit/debit cards, cash, cheques, euros

directions M40-A34 Botley Road exit towards Swindon on A420. Turn left on A338 for Wantage. M4-A34 (Junction 13 north) towards Oxford. Take A417 towards Wantage.

BREAKFAST AWARD

Room
General
Leisure

WOODSTOCK, Oxfordshire Map ref 2C1
SAT NAV OX29 8HQ

Shepherds Hall
Witney Road, Freeland, Witney OX29 8HQ
t (01993) 881256 f (01993) 883455
w shepherdshall.co.uk

B&B PER ROOM PER NIGHT
S £35.50 – £38.50
D £60.00 – £70.00

Well-appointed licensed guest house offering good food and accommodation. All rooms en suite. Ideally situated for Oxford, Woodstock, Blenheim Palace and the Cotswolds. **directions** About 18 miles north west of Oxford on the A4095 Woodstock to Witney road, just outside the village of Long Hanborough. **open** All year except Xmas **bedrooms** 1 single, 2 double, 2 twin **bathrooms** 5 en suite, 5 with private bathroom **payment** credit/debit cards, cash, cheques

Room   General

CAPEL, Surrey Map ref 2D2
SAT NAV RH5 5HE

Nightless Copse
Rusper Road, Capel, Dorking, Surrey RH5 5HE
t (01306) 713247 f (01306) 711765 e bb@nightlesscopse.co.uk
w nightlesscopse.co.uk

B&B PER ROOM PER NIGHT
S £42.00 – £45.00
D £70.00 – £75.00

Nightless Copse is a family home set in 20 acres of ancient bluebell woods on the outskirts of the Surrey Hills (AONB). Many National Trust properties and country pubs nearby. **directions** From the Clark's Green roundabout on the A24 south of Capel, take the Rusper Road. We are half a mile along on the left. **open** All year **bedrooms** 1 double, 1 twin **bathrooms** 2 en suite **payment** credit, debit cards, cash, cheques

Room   General

South East | Surrey

DORKING, Surrey Map ref 2D2
SAT NAV RH5 4DS

B&B PER ROOM PER NIGHT
S £55.00 – £65.00
D £85.00

Blackbrook House
Blackbrook House, Blackbrook, Dorking RH5 4DS
t (01306) 888898 e blackbrookbb@btinternet.com
w blackbrookhouse.org.uk ONLINE MAP

In the heart of a peaceful hamlet, Blackbrook House is a substantial and comfortable family home surrounded by National Trust woodlands. **directions** Please contact us for directions **open** Closed from December 20th - January 10th. **bedrooms** 2 double **bathrooms** 2 en suite **payment** cash, cheques

BREAKFAST AWARD Room General Leisure

DORKING, Surrey Map ref 2D2
SAT NAV RH4 3QQ

B&B PER ROOM PER NIGHT
S £42.00 – £45.00
D £60.00 – £65.00

Broomhill
15 Broomfield Park, Westcott RH4 3QQ
t (01306) 885565 f (01306) 881457 e suzannewillis15@googlemail.com
w broomhillbandb.co.uk ONLINE MAP GUEST REVIEWS ONLINE BOOKING

Spacious house, walking distance of Westcott village. Dorking 1.5 miles. Two double/family rooms, shared bathroom, TV/DVD, coffee/tea. Magnificent views, safe parking. Gatwick 30 mins, M25 15 mins (junctions 8/9), London, train 40 mins. Fabulous walking countryside (North Downs and Greensand Way). Singles, Children and pets welcome.

open All year except Xmas and New Year
bedrooms 1 double, 1 family
payment cash, cheques

directions From centre of Dorking, take A25 towards Guildford into Westcott village, turn left, immediately after Crown Inn, into Broomfield Park.

Room
General
Leisure

DORKING, Surrey Map ref 2D2
SAT NAV RH5 5JA

B&B PER ROOM PER NIGHT
S £42.00 – £50.00
D £70.00 – £90.00

Stylehurst Farm
Weare Street, Capel, Dorking RH5 5JA
t (01306) 711259 e rosemary.goddard@virgin.net
w stylehurstfarm.com

Stylehurst Farm set in the beautiful Surrey countryside. The house, recently converted from old farm buildings, provides comfortable accommodation. There is an attractive garden and many places of interest nearby. **directions** Five miles south of Dorking on A24. At Clarks Green roundabout take 4th exit. 200yds left to Ockley Station. After station, left into Weare Street. **open** All year except Xmas and New Year **bedrooms** 1 double, 2 twin **bathrooms** 3 en suite **payment** cash, cheques

BREAKFAST AWARD Room General

South East | **Surrey**

FARNHAM, Surrey Map ref 2C2
SAT NAV GU10 5RP

Mill Lane Lodge
Mill Lane, Crondall, Farnham, Surrey GU10 5RP
t 01252 850230 e milllanelodge@googlemail.com

B&B PER ROOM PER NIGHT
S £27.50 – £35.00
D £65.00 – £85.00

A 300-year-old beamed house, in secluded gardens in quiet count setting within the hamlet of Mill Lane. Friendly atmosphere, spacious and comfortable accommodation, breakfast served in cos beamed dining room. **directions** Four miles from M3 motor way junction 5 on the A287. 25 miles from Heathrow. Four miles from Farnham, Fleet and Farnborough. **open** All year except Xmas and New Year **bedrooms** 1 single, 1 double, 1 family **bathrooms** 2 en suite, 1 with private bathroom **payment** cash, cheques, euros

Room   General   Leisure

GODALMING, Surrey Map ref 2D2
SAT NAV GU8 4XR

Combe Ridge
Pook Hill, Chiddingfold, Godalming GU8 4XR
t (01428) 682607 f (01428) 682607 e brendaessex@btinternet.com

B&B PER ROOM PER NIGHT
S £35.00 – £40.00
D £70.00 – £80.00

Combe Ridge lies in peaceful unspoilt countryside with grazing sheep and views of gently wooded hills. London an hour away by train, Heathrow & Gatwick airports an hour by car. **directions** M25 exit jct 10. A3 to A283. At Wormley, right to Combe Lane/Witley Station. Right to Haslemere. Left Pook Hill. After 500m left to hous **open** All year except Xmas and New Year **bedrooms** 1 single, 2 double **bathrooms** 1 en suite, 1 with private bathroom **payment** cash, cheques

Room   General   Leisure

GODALMING, Surrey Map ref 2D2
SAT NAV GU8 6NW

Heath Hall Farm
Bowlhead Green, Godalming GU8 6NW
t (01428) 682808 f (01428) 684025 e heathhallfarm@btinternet.com
w heathhallfarm.co.uk GUEST REVIEWS

B&B PER ROOM PER NIGHT
S £35.00 – £40.00
D £65.00 – £70.00

Secluded farmhouse, converted stable courtyard in own farm. Free-range fowl. Tennis court. Relaxed atmosphere. Ground-floor accommodation. Sitting room for guests with fridge and micro wave. Ample parking. Wonderful walking. Green Sand Way and National Nature Reserve. Easy access to A3.

open All year
bedrooms 1 single, 1 double, 1 twin, 1 family
bathrooms 3 en suite, 1 with private bathroom
payment credit/debit cards, cash, cheques, euros

directions A3, south Guildford. Bypass Milford. Take 2nd turning on left signed Bowlhead Green. Follow signs Bowlhead Green. Second sharp corner drive (half mile) on left.

Room   General   Leisure

South East | **Surrey**

GUILDFORD, Surrey Map ref 2D2

SAT NAV GU3 3HJ

FARMHOUSE

B&B PER ROOM PER NIGHT
S £50.00
D £70.00

Littlefield Manor
Littlefield Common, Guildford GU3 3HJ
t (01483) 233068 **f** (01483) 233686 **e** john@littlefieldmanor.co.uk
w littlefieldmanor.co.uk

A 17thC listed manor house with Tudor origins set in large walled garden surrounded by farmland. **directions** Please refer to website. **open** All year except Xmas **bedrooms** 2 double, 1 twin **bathrooms** 1 en suite, 2 with private bathroom **payment** credit/debit cards, cash, cheques

Room General Leisure

GUILDFORD, Surrey Map ref 2D2

SAT NAV GU1 1ET

GUEST HOUSE

B&B PER ROOM PER NIGHT
S £35.00 – £37.00
D £57.00 – £59.00

Stoke House
113 Stoke Road, Guildford GU1 1ET
t (01483) 453025 **f** (01483) 453023 **e** bookings@stokehouse.net
w stokehouse.net

Friendly family-run guest house close to town centre. Tea/coffee-making facilities and TV in all rooms. En suite rooms available. **directions** Please contact us for directions **open** All year except Xmas and New Year **bedrooms** 2 single, 2 double, 2 twin **bathrooms** 2 en suite **payment** credit/debit cards, cash, cheques

Room General

HASLEMERE, Surrey Map ref 2C2

SAT NAV GU27 3BU

BED & BREAKFAST

B&B PER ROOM PER NIGHT
S £40.00 – £45.00
D £60.00 – £65.00

EVENING MEAL PER PERSON
£8.00 – £14.00

SPECIAL PROMOTIONS
10% discount on three nights or more.

Deerfell
Blackdown, Haslemere GU27 3BU
t (01428) 653409 **f** (01428) 656106 **e** deerfell@tesco.net
w deerfell.co.uk ONLINE MAP LAST MINUTE OFFERS

Delightful country house four miles from Haslemere and set in glorious open countryside with many superb walks on the doorstep. Spacious, comfortable, quiet en suite rooms with TV and tea/coffee. Locally sourced breakfasts with home-made jams/marmalade. Choice of excellent pubs nearby with good seasonal menus.

open All year except Xmas and New Year
bedrooms 1 double, 1 twin
bathrooms 2 en suite
payment cash, cheques

directions Take A286 Midhurst/Haslemere. After Border sign, left into Fernden Lane. At 2.6 miles bear right Blackdown Park sign, automatic gate. Deerfell 1st house on left.

Room General

key to symbols see page 6

243

South East | **Surrey**

HASLEMERE, Surrey Map ref 2C2   SAT NAV GU27 2DE

The Wheatsheaf Inn
Grayswood Road, Haslemere GU27 2DE
t (01428) 644440 f (01428) 641285 e ken@thewheatsheafgrayswood.co.uk
w Thewheatsheafgrayswood.co.uk

B&B PER ROOM PER NIGHT
S £55.00
D £75.00

A delightful building in wooded area. Award-winning menu. Comfortable en suite rooms. All has a bright and airy non-smoking conservatory. Ideal location for meeting friends, walking and central for the coast, London, Surrey Hills and The Downs. PS, great food!

open All year
bedrooms 2 single, 4 double, 1 twin
bathrooms 7 en suite
payment credit/debit cards, cash, cheques

directions Can be reached from the A3 at Milford Junction. The A3 is junction 10 on M25

Room
General
Leisure

HOLMBURY ST MARY, Surrey Map ref 2D2   SAT NAV RH5 6LG

Bulmer Farm Bed & Breakfast
Holmbury St Mary, Pasturewood Road, Dorking RH5 6LG
t (01306) 731871 e enquiries@bulmerfarm.co.uk
w bulmerfarm.co.uk GUEST REVIEWS

B&B PER ROOM PER NIGHT
S £50.00
D £70.00

Sympathetic barn conversion of 5 Bedrooms, all with direct courtyard access and recently refurbished ensuite showers. Breakfast provided in beamed dining room using local produce where possible. Good pubs locally **directions** Take B2126 from Abinger Hammer into village. Turn left onto Pasturewood road and our drive is first on the left. **open** All year **bedrooms** 2 double, 2 twin, 1 family **bathrooms** 5 en suite **payment** credit/debit cards, cash, cheques

Room   General   Leisure

LOWER BOURNE, Surrey Map ref 2C2   SAT NAV GU10 3LR

Kiln Farm Bed & Breakfast
8 Kiln Lane, Lower Bourne, Farnham, Surrey GU10 3LR
t (01252) 726083 e raphe_palmer@tiscali.co.uk
w kilnfarm.plus.com ONLINE MAP

B&B PER ROOM PER NIGHT
S £55.00
D £69.00

In a beautiful tranquil former farmyard with parking, Kiln Farm offers 3 double rooms all with ensuites, 2 of which are in independent units, one offering disabled facilities. **directions** 1.5 miles South of Farnham, and Farnham is on the A31 12 miles West of Guildford. Easy access from M3, M25 and Farnham Mainline railway. **open** All year **bedrooms** 3 double **bathrooms** 3 en suite **payment** credit/debit cards, cash, cheques

Room   General

244   Official tourist board guide **Bed & Breakfast**

South East | Surrey

WEYBRIDGE, Surrey Map ref 2D2
SAT NAV KT13 0RD

The Clock House
242 Brooklands Road, Weybridge KT13 0RD
t (01932) 859595 e julie@sunshinelink.com
w theclockhouseweybridge.com ONLINE MAP GUEST REVIEWS

B&B PER ROOM PER NIGHT
S £69.00
D £85.00

Newly refurbished to high standard. Luxury you would expect from a first class hotel. 5 minutes walk from Weybridge Station. 30 minutes from London. Heathrow (15 mins) Gatwick (40 mins). **directions** From M25 exit junction 10 onto A3 towards London. 1st exit towards Woking. Right at the roundabout Brooklands Road. We are situated past Brooklands Museum. **open** All year **bedrooms** 1 single, 3 double, 1 suite **bathrooms** 5 en suite **payment** credit/debit cards, cash, cheques

Room General ≥12 Leisure

WOKING, Surrey Map ref 2D2
SAT NAV GU21 6NU

Fenton House
19 Kingsway, Woking GU21 6NU
t 01483 828 225 e fentonhouse19@googlemail.com
w fentonhousebandb.co.uk ONLINE MAP

B&B PER ROOM PER NIGHT
S £60.00
D £80.00

Elegant attractive and comfortable Edwardian house, next to the Surrey history centre, within easy walking distance of Woking town centre, with it's many shops, theatres, cinemas, restaurants and railway station. **directions** Please contact us for directions **open** All year except Xmas and New Year **bedrooms** 4 double, 1 twin, 1 family **bathrooms** 2 en suite, 2 with private bathroom **payment** cash, cheques

Room General ≥4 Leisure

WOKING, Surrey Map ref 2D2
SAT NAV GU22 8AB

Saint Columba's House
Maybury Hill, Woking GU22 8AB
t (01483) 766498 e retreats@stcolumbashouse.org.uk
w stcolumbashouse.org.uk ONLINE MAP LAST MINUTE OFFERS

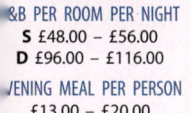

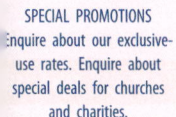

B&B PER ROOM PER NIGHT
S £48.00 – £56.00
D £96.00 – £116.00

EVENING MEAL PER PERSON
£13.00 – £20.00

SPECIAL PROMOTIONS
Enquire about our exclusive-use rates. Enquire about special deals for churches and charities.

A quiet retreat house and conference centre with 21stC facilities for business, leisure, and spiritual renewal. We welcome individuals and groups from all over the world and provide a range of meeting and catering facilities for groups of up to 50, whether for business or leisure.

open All year except Easter, Christmas and New Year
bedrooms 22 single, 5 twin
bathrooms 26 en suite, 26 with private bathroom
payment cash, cheques

directions Car: M3 (jct 2), M25 (jcts 10, 11), and A3 15mins. Rail: London Waterloo to Woking 30mins. Air: London Gatwick 50mins; London Heathrow 40mins.

Room General ≥7 Leisure

key to symbols see page 6 245

South East | Sussex

AMBERSTONE, Sussex Map ref 3B4   SAT NAV BN27 1PJ

Waldernheath Country House
Hailsham Road, Amberstone, Hailsham BN27 1PJ
t (01323) 442259 f (01323) 440553 e l.j.g@waldernheath.com
w visitsussex.org/waldernheathcountryhouse

RATING APPLIED FOR

B&B PER ROOM PER NIGHT
S £45.00
D £65.00

Charming 15th century house, 5 acres gardens/paddocks, heart of 1066 country views over South Downs restaurants/pubs. National Trust Glyndebourne nearby, 10 miles sea, one hour channel ports and Gatwick. **directions** From A22 Boship roundabout follow A27 (Bexhill Road) for 2.2 miles Waldernheath is situated on left large car park house position back from road. **bedrooms** 3 double, 2 twin, 1 family **bathrooms** 1 en suite, 5 with private bathroom **payment** cash, cheques

Room   General

ARUNDEL, Sussex Map ref 2D3   SAT NAV PO20 3SJ

Eastmere House B&B
Eastergate Lane, Eastergate, Arundel, Nr Chichester PO20 3SJ
t (01243) 544204 e bernardlane@hotmail.com
w eastmere.com ONLINE MAP

BED & BREAKFAST ★★★★

B&B PER ROOM PER NIGHT
S £35.00 – £40.00
D £60.00 – £70.00

In a quiet location Jean and Bernard offer: Double bedroom en-suite (adjoining single room can create private family suite). Twin ground-floor room (roomy private facilities includes large walk-shower, appreciated by less-able visitors. Refrigerator in bedrooms. A healthy cooked breakfast using local produce, plus home-made preserves. Guest lounge and gardens.

bedrooms 1 double, 1 twin, 1 family
bathrooms 1 en suite, 1 with private bathroom
payment cash, cheques

directions A27 East Chichester to Fontwell Racecourse roundabout. Take A29 South. 2nd left Eastergate Lane. 1/3 mile on left is Eastmere with hanging nameplate and flagpole

Room   General

BEXHILL-ON-SEA, Sussex Map ref 3B4   SAT NAV TN40 1SB

English Rose
16 Magdalen Road, Bexhill-on-Sea TN40 1SB
t (01424) 218969 e enquiries@englishrosebexhill.com
w englishrosebexhill.com ONLINE MAP GUEST REVIEWS LAST MINUTE OFFERS

BED & BREAKFAST ★★★★

B&B PER ROOM PER NIGHT
S £30.00 – £35.00
D £65.00

The English Rose B&B is one of the oldest buildings in Bexhill offering you period and modern living. Conveniently situated 300 from Bexhill railway station & the town center, seafront. **directions** Please contact us for directions **open** All year **bedrooms** 2 single, double, 1 twin **bathrooms** 2 en suite **payment** cash, cheques

Room   General   Leisure

246   Official tourist board guide Bed & Breakfast

South East | **Sussex**

BOGNOR REGIS, Sussex Map ref 2C3

SAT NAV PO22 7EJ

★★★★ BED & BREAKFAST

B&B PER ROOM PER NIGHT
S £35.00 – £40.00
D £60.00 – £80.00

Hayleys Corner
14 Limmer Lane, Bognor Regis PO22 7EJ
t (01243) 826139 mobile 07854814728 e hayleyscornerbandb@yahoo.co.uk
w hayleyscorner.co.uk ONLINE MAP GUEST REVIEWS

A character Edwardian house with delightful south facing walled garden. In the heart of Felpham village, a quiet, peaceful place to stay, comfortable and friendly. All amenities close by. **directions** See website for google map. **open** All year **bedrooms** 3 double, 2 twin **bathrooms** 3 en suite, 2 with private bathroom **payment** cash, cheques

Room General Leisure

BOGNOR REGIS, Sussex Map ref 2C3

SAT NAV PO21 1NU

★★★ GUEST ACCOMMODATION

B&B PER ROOM PER NIGHT
S £25.00 – £50.00
D £50.00 – £100.00

Jubilee Guest House
5 Gloucester Road, Bognor Regis PO21 1NU
t (01243) 863016 f (01243) 868017 e jubileeguesthouse@tiscali.co.uk
w jubileeguesthouse.com

Family-run business, 75yds from seafront and beach. Ideal for visiting Butlins family entertainment resort, Chichester, Goodwood, Fontwell, Arundel, Portsmouth and the Isle of Wight. **directions** Please contact us for directions **open** All year except Xmas and New Year **bedrooms** 2 single, 1 double, 3 family **bathrooms** 2 en suite, 2 with private bathroom **payment** credit/debit cards, cash

Room General Leisure

BOGNOR REGIS, Sussex Map ref 2C3

SAT NAV PO21 2DZ

★★★ GUEST HOUSE

B&B PER ROOM PER NIGHT
S £35.00 – £45.00
D £55.00 – £65.00
EVENING MEAL PER PERSON
£12.00 – £15.00

Selwood Lodge
93 Victoria Drive, Bognor Regis PO21 2DZ
t (01243) 865071 f (01243) 865071 e mail@selwoodlodge.com
w selwoodlodge.com

Friendly, family run guesthouse, recently refurbished. Short walk to the north of Town Centre convenient for shops, cinema, railway station, beach etc. Access at all times. Open all year. **directions** From A29 and A259 entering Bognor Regis meeting at large roundabout, Victoria Drive is off this, signposted Aldwick. Selwood Lodge on right just before roundabout. **open** All year **bedrooms** 1 single, 1 double, 1 twin, 2 family **bathrooms** 4 en suite, 1 with private bathroom **payment** credit/debit cards, cash

Room General Leisure

Where is my pet welcome?

Some properties welcome well-behaved pets. Look for the 🐕 in the accommodation listings.

You can also buy a copy of our popular guide 'Pets Come Too!' Now available in good bookshops and online at **visitbritainshop.com**

£9.99

key to symbols see page 6

247

South East | **Sussex**

BOGNOR REGIS, Sussex Map ref 2C3 — SAT NAV PO22 7AH

White Horses Felpham

Clyde Road, Felpham, Bognor Regis, West Sussex PO22 7AH
t (01243) 824320 f (01243) 824320 e whitehorsesbandb@btinternet.com
w whitehorsesfelpham.co.uk ONLINE MAP LAST MINUTE OFFERS

B&B PER ROOM PER NIGHT
S £45.00 – £50.00
D £75.00 – £90.00

SPECIAL PROMOTIONS
3 nights or more qualify for reduced rate.

White Horses is located in a quiet cul-de-sac 20yds from Felpham beach. It has recently been refurbished and offers high-quality accommodation in a friendly environment. A three-mile promenade close to the entrance provides easy seaside walking with a variety of amenities for all ages.

open All year
bedrooms 3 double, 1 twin, 1 family
bathrooms 5 en suite, 1 with private bathroom
payment credit/debit cards, cash, cheques, euros

directions From Butlins Roundabout just outside Bognor Regis (A259 towards Littlehampton) take turning for Felpham Village then first turning on right and second turning on left

BOSHAM (CHICHESTER 3 MILES), Sussex Map ref 2C3 — SAT NAV PO18 8QL

Benbow

Shore Road, Bosham, Chichester, West Sussex PO18 8QL
t 01243 572 127 e bb@benbowbosham.co.uk
w benbowbosham.co.uk ONLINE MAP LAST MINUTE OFFERS

B&B PER ROOM PER NIGHT
S £55.00 – £80.00
D £80.00 – £140.00

Bosham's sole waterfront B&B, a beautifully restored Grade II Listed house, stunning views across the harbour, welcoming and friendly hosts: if that's what you're looking for, then look no further! **directions** A259 Bosham roundabout, signs to Bosham church, T-junction turn left. First right into Taylors Lane, 3rd right into Stumps Lane, over hump, 2nd house. **open** All year except Xmas and New Year **bedrooms** 2 double **bathrooms** 2 en suite **payment** cash, cheques, euros

BREDE, Sussex Map ref 3B4 — SAT NAV TN31 6DX

Little Garth Bed & Breakfast

Little Garth, Cackle Street, Rye TN31 6DX
t (01424) 882093 e info@littlegarthbrede.co.uk
w littlegarthbrede.co.uk ONLINE MAP GUEST REVIEWS

B&B PER ROOM PER NIGHT
S £45.00
D £60.00 – £70.00

Little Garth Bed and Breakfast is near the historc town of Rye, central to 1066 country. We have two guest rooms one family room ensuite and double room with ensuite. **directions** Little Garth can be found on the A28 in the village of Brede, we are 7 miles inland from the coast. **open** All year **bedrooms** 1 double, 1 family **bathrooms** 2 en suite **payment** cash, cheques

248 Official tourist board guide Bed & Breakfast

South East | **Sussex**

BRIGHTON & HOVE, Sussex Map ref 2D3
SAT NAV BN2 9JA

Kipps Brighton
76 Grand Parade, Brighton BN2 9JA
t 01273 604182 **e** kippshostelbrighton@gmail.com
w kipps-brighton.com ONLINE MAP GUEST REVIEWS ONLINE BOOKING LAST MINUTE OFFERS

BED ONLY PER NIGHT
£15.00 – £40.00

Small friendly quirky hostel in the heart of Brighton. Excellent facilities, clean and well maintained. Outside terrace and views overlooking the historic Royal Pavillion. **directions** We are situated in the Centre of Brighton, Visit our website to print off a map **open** All year **bedrooms** 1 single, 6 double, 1 twin **bathrooms** 4 en suite **payment** credit/debit cards, cash, euros

Room General Leisure

BRIGHTON & HOVE, Sussex Map ref 2D3
SAT NAV BN3 1FE

Lansdowne Guest House
Hove BN3 1FE
t 07803 484715 **e** lansdowneguesthouse@hotmail.co.uk
w lansdowneguesthouseonline.com ONLINE MAP GUEST REVIEWS

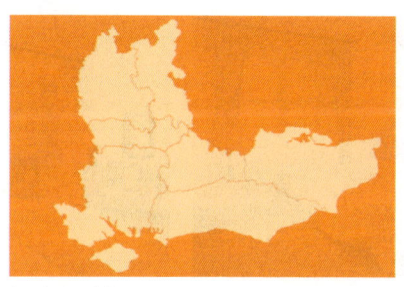

&B PER ROOM PER NIGHT
S £75.00 – £95.00
D £85.00 – £95.00

A substantial property set in its own grounds, providing a very peaceful and pleasant environment and good location only a few minute's walk from the sea-front and town centre. The guest accommodation is new and modern. Picnic hampers available on request.

open All year except Xmas and New Year
bedrooms 1 double, 1 twin
bathrooms 1 en suite, 1 with private bathroom
payment credit/debit cards, cash, cheques

directions Please contact us for directions

Room General Leisure

CHELWOOD GATE, Sussex Map ref 2D3
SAT NAV RH17 7LF

Holly House
Beaconsfield Road, Chelwood Gate, Haywards Heath, West Sussex RH17 7LF
t (01825) 740344 **e** db@hollyhousebnb.demon.co.uk
w hollyhousebnb.demon.co.uk ONLINE MAP

&B PER ROOM PER NIGHT
S £35.00
D £70.00

On Ashdown Forest, the ideal location from which to explore Sussex, our comfortable old forest farmhouse offers a warm welcome, inviting lounge, comfortable beds and memorable breakfasts. Dogs by arrangement. **directions** From M25, A22 through East Grinstead to Wych Cross. Left on A275 1 mile, left into Beaconsfield Road. 800yds on right opposite village hall. **open** All year **bedrooms** 1 single, 2 double, 2 twin **bathrooms** 3 en suite **payment** cash, cheques

Room General Leisure

South East | **Sussex**

CHELWOOD GATE, EAST GRINSTEAD, Sussex Map ref 2D3   SAT NAV RH17 7LU

Laurel Cottage
Baxters Lane, Chelwood Gate, Haywards Heath RH17 7LU
t (01825) 740547 f (01825) 740057 e smartin@chelwood.fsnet.co.uk

B&B PER ROOM PER NIGHT
S £35.00
D £60.00

A warm, light, sunny, quiet village house with comfortable rooms offering TV, tea/coffee-making facilities and fantastic home cooked breakfasts. With Coach and Horses pub only 4 minutes walk. **directions** Close to Ashdown Forest between A22 and A275. Bluebell Railway within 3 miles and close to Pooh Bear country. **open** All year **bedrooms** 1 single, 1 double **bathrooms** 2 with private bathroom **payment** cash, cheques

Room General Leisure

CHICHESTER, Sussex Map ref 2C3   SAT NAV PO19 1PX

George Bell House
4 Canon Lane, Chichester, West Sussex PO19 1PX
t (01243) 813586 e bookings@chichestercathedral.org.uk
w chichestercathedral.org.uk

B&B PER ROOM PER NIGHT
S £79.00
D £138.00

EVENING MEAL PER PERSON
£22.00

8 bedrooms superbly finished with tea /coffee making facilities, all rooms are en suite with colour TV available. Situated in the heart of the city of Chichester, surrounded by the iconic historic Cathedral, we offer evening meals and a taste of Sussex breakfast. Limited parking available for our guests.

open All year
bedrooms 1 single, 7 double
bathrooms 8 en suite

directions Please contact us for directions

Room General

CHICHESTER, Sussex Map ref 2C3   SAT NAV PO18 8RT

Kia-ora
Main Road, Nutbourne, Chichester PO18 8RT
t (01243) 572858 e ruthiefp@tiscali.co.uk

B&B PER ROOM PER NIGHT
S £32.50
D £65.00

Views to Chichester Harbour. Warm welcome in comfortable family house. Large garden. Restaurants and country pubs within walking distance. Closed Christmas. **directions** Please contact us for directions **open** All year except Xmas and New Year **bedrooms** 1 double **bathrooms** 1 en suite **payment** cash, cheques, euros

Room General

South East | Sussex

CHICHESTER, Sussex Map ref 2C3
SAT NAV PO19 7SJ

The Nags Head
3 St Pancras, Chichester PO19 7SJ
t (01243) 785823 e nagsheadhotel@aol.com
w **thenagshotel.co.uk** ONLINE MAP GUEST REVIEWS

B&B PER ROOM PER NIGHT
S £55.00 – £70.00
D £70.00 – £90.00

EVENING MEAL PER PERSON
£5.00 – £24.00

The Nags has ten individually designed bedrooms. All are en-suite with colour television and coffee and tea making facilities. Breakfast included in the price. **directions** Please contact us for directions **open** All year except Xmas and New Year **bedrooms** 5 double, 5 twin **bathrooms** 10 en suite **payment** credit/debit cards, cash, euros

Room General Leisure

CROWBOROUGH, Sussex Map ref 2D3
SAT NAV TN6 2EA

Yew House Bed & Breakfast
Crowborough Hill, Crowborough, East Sussex TN6 2EA
t (01892) 610522 & (07789) 993982 e yewhouse@yewhouse.com
w **yewhouse.com** ONLINE MAP GUEST REVIEWS LAST MINUTE OFFERS

B&B PER ROOM PER NIGHT
S £45.00
D £70.00 – £80.00

EVENING MEAL PER PERSON
£15.00 – £20.00

Two ensuite rooms, 1 four-poster bed, double shower. Double room use of bathroom. Single/twin room use of shower. Close to shops, station and parking. Quiet location. Gold awarded for green. **directions** Please contact us for directions **open** All year except Christmas Day **bedrooms** 1 single, 3 double, 1 twin **bathrooms** 2 en suite, 2 with private bathroom **payment** credit/debit cards, cash, cheques

Room General Leisure

EAST ASHLING (CHICHESTER 3 MILES), Sussex Map ref 2C3
SAT NAV PO18 9AX

Horse & Groom
East Ashling, Chichester PO18 9AX
t (01243) 575339 f (01243) 575560 e info@thehorseandgroomchichester.co.uk
w **thehorseandgroomchichester.co.uk** ONLINE MAP GUEST REVIEWS

B&B PER ROOM PER NIGHT
S £45.00 – £55.00
D £70.00 – £80.00

A traditional 17thC inn with en suite accommodation. Friendly, with fine cuisine, real ales and cast-iron range. Plenty of parking. Close to Goodwood. All rooms can function as single/double. **directions** B2178 between Chichester and Funtington, 3 miles Chichester **open** All year **bedrooms** 5 double, 6 twin **bathrooms** 11 en suite **payment** credit/debit cards, cash, cheques

Room General Leisure

EASTBOURNE, Sussex Map ref 3B4
SAT NAV BN20 7AH

Brayscroft House
13 South Cliff Avenue, Eastbourne BN20 7AH
t (01323) 647005 f (01323) 720705 e brayscroft@hotmail.com
w **brayscrofthotel.co.uk** GUEST REVIEWS ONLINE BOOKING

B&B PER ROOM PER NIGHT
S £36.00 – £40.00
D £72.00 – £80.00

EVENING MEAL PER PERSON
£15.00 – £18.00

Elegant guest house, in the 2010 Michelin guide with a coveted bib award, only one in Eastbourne for 'outstanding accommodation and hospitality'. Superb position. **directions** Please contact us for directions **open** All year except Xmas and New Year **bedrooms** 1 single, 3 double, 2 twin **bathrooms** 6 en suite **payment** credit/debit cards, cash, cheques, euros

Room General Leisure

key to symbols see page 6

251

South East | **Sussex**

EASTBOURNE, Sussex Map ref 3B4   SAT NAV BN20 7AJ

The Cherry Tree Guest House
15 Silverdale Road, Lower Meads, Eastbourne BN20 7AJ
t (01323) 722406 **e** carol@cherrytree-eastbourne.co.uk
w cherrytree-eastbourne.co.uk ONLINE MAP GUEST REVIEWS ONLINE BOOKING

B&B PER ROOM PER NIGHT
S £35.00 – £45.00
D £70.00 – £90.00

The Cherry Tree is a friendly, family run guest house offering quiet relaxed accommodation. Close to the beach, a short walk to the Eastbourne theatres, town centre and Beachy Head. **directions** Please contact us for directions **open** All year **bedrooms** 3 single, double, 2 twin, 1 family **bathrooms** 9 en suite **payment** credit/debit cards, cash, cheques

Room   General

EASTBOURNE, Sussex Map ref 3B4   SAT NAV BN22 7BS

Eastbourne Reymar
2-4 Cambridge Road, Eastbourne BN22 7BS
t (01323) 724649 **e** info@eastbournereymarhotel.co.uk
w eastbournereymarhotel.co.uk ONLINE MAP GUEST REVIEWS ONLINE BOOKING LAST MINUTE OFFERS

B&B PER ROOM PER NIGHT
S £27.00 – £50.00
D £50.00 – £70.00

EVENING MEAL PER PERSON
£12.00 – £15.00

A warm and friendly welcome always awaits you at the Eastbourne Reymar where we endeavour to make your stay a happy one. All bedrooms are attractively decorated and comfortably furnished, all with en suite facilities. 30m from seafront, ground floor and family rooms available. Private parking.

open All year
bedrooms 3 single, 5 double, 5 twin, 2 family
bathrooms 15 en suite
payment credit/debit cards, cash, cheques

directions Please contact us for directions

BREAKFAST AWARD

Room
General
Leisure

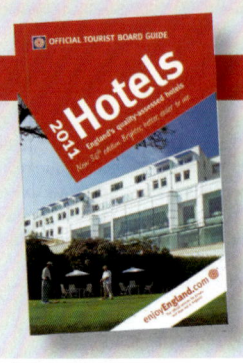

Looking for something else?
You can also buy a copy of our popular guide 'Hotels' including country house and town house hotels, metro and budget hotels, serviced apartments, restaurants with rooms and Spas in England 2011.

Now available in good bookshops and online at
visitbritainshop.com

£10.99

South East | Sussex

EAST WITTERING, Sussex Map ref 2C3
SAT NAV PO20 8NU

Racing Sea Horses
95 Stocks Lane, East Wittering, Chichester PO20 8NU
t 01243 672157/07932163079 e jacqui&tony@racingseahorses.com
w racingseahorses.com ONLINE MAP GUEST REVIEWS LAST MINUTE OFFERS

B&B PER ROOM PER NIGHT
S £29.99 – £55.00
D £50.00 – £95.00

SPECIAL PROMOTIONS
winter break Mon to Thur
£200.00 Fri to Sun £130 not Christmas & New Year week supplement for Goodwood events

Few minutes from the beach, beautiful views of the southdowns, stroll to the village plenty of places to eat & drink. Ground floor double en-suite, first floor double with bath seperate shower both en-suite. We will do our best to make your stay a pleasure.

open All year
bathrooms 3 en suite
payment cash, cheques

directions From A27 drive along the A286 to Bracklesham turn down beside the Lively Lady pub to East Wittering, just a few minuets on the right.

Room
General
Leisure

GATWICK, Sussex Map ref 2D2
SAT NAV RH6 7DF

The Lawn Guest House
30 Massetts Road, Gatwick RH6 7DF
t (01293) 775751 f (01293) 821803 e info@lawnguesthouse.co.uk
w lawnguesthouse.com ONLINE MAP GUEST REVIEWS

B&B PER ROOM PER NIGHT
S £40.00 – £50.00
D £55.00 – £60.00

Imposing Victorian house set in pretty gardens. Five minutes from Gatwick airport. All bedrooms are en suite. Full English breakfast available. Guests' ice machine. Overnight/long-term holiday parking. Airport transfers included. **directions** M23 jct9 (Gatwick). First two roundabouts A23 (Redhill). Third roundabout, petrol station on left - 3rd exit. 300yds right, Massetts Road. 500yds on left. **open** All year **bedrooms** 3 single, 3 double, 3 twin, 3 family **bathrooms** 12 en suite **payment** credit/debit cards, cash, cheques

Room General Leisure

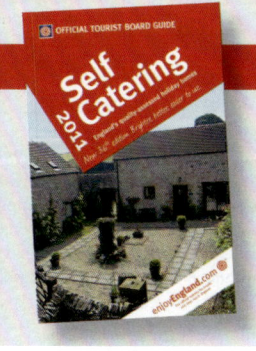

Looking for something else?
You can also buy a copy of our popular guide 'Self Catering' including self-catering holiday homes, approved caravan holiday homes, boat accommodation and holiday cottage agencies in England 2011.

Now available in good bookshops and online at
visitbritainshop.com

£11.99

key to symbols see page 6   253

South East | **Sussex**

GATWICK, Sussex Map ref 2D2
SAT NAV RH6 7DS

Southbourne Guest House Gatwick
34 Massetts Road, Horley RH6 7DS
t (01293) 771991 f (01293) 820112 e reservations@southbournegatwick.com
w southbournegatwick.com ONLINE MAP GUEST REVIEWS ONLINE BOOKING LAST MINUTE OFFERS

B&B PER ROOM PER NIGHT
S £45.00 – £50.00
D £59.00 – £65.00

A warm welcome awaits you in our family-run guesthouse. Ideally located for Gatwick Airport and exploring Surrey, Sussex and London. Five minutes walk from Horley train station, restaurants, shops and pubs and 30 minutes by train from London. Five minutes drive from Gatwick with free courtesy transport from 0930 2130.

open All year
bedrooms 2 single, 3 double, 3 twin, 4 family
bathrooms 12 en suite
payment credit/debit cards, cash, cheques

directions M23 jct 9, follow the A23 through 3 roundabouts. At 3rd roundabout take 3rd exit and continue to the 2nd right-hand turn into Massetts Road.

Room
General

HASTINGS, Sussex Map ref 3B4
SAT NAV TN34 3EN

Gallery 53
53 High Street, Old Town, Hastings TN34 3EN
t (01424) 433486 e jane_edmonds@hotmail.com
w hastingsbedandbreakfast.co.uk/gallery-53.htm ONLINE BOOKING

B&B PER ROOM PER NIGHT
S £45.00 – £50.00
D £70.00 – £85.00

Homely B&B, quality double rooms, en-suite bathrooms, (roll-top baths). We're a family art gallery in heart of old town hastings, walking distance to sea, restaurants and beautiful countryside.
directions On the high street, old town, steeped in history, opposite museum, amongst charming shops and mins from beach and fishing fleet. **open** All year **bedrooms** 2 double, 1 family **bathrooms** 3 en suite, 3 with private bathroom **payment** credit/debit cards, cash

Room   General   Leisure

HASTINGS, Sussex Map ref 3B4
SAT NAV TN37 6DB

Seaspray Bed and Breakfast
54 Eversfield Place, St. Leonards-on-Sea, Hastings TN37 6DB
t 01424 436581 e jo@seaspraybb.co.uk
w seaspraybb.co.uk ONLINE MAP GUEST REVIEWS ONLINE BOOKING LAST MINUTE OFFERS

B&B PER ROOM PER NIGHT
S £30.00 – £45.00
D £60.00 – £75.00

Seafront extra special home from home. High standard refurbishment. Quiet location 5mins to amenities. Superking, Wi-Fi plasma Freeview, fridge. Complimentary parking. Extensive breakfast menu, all diets catered. Silver award. **directions** M25 jct 5 onto A Hastings. Follow signs to seafront to A259. Located on promenade 100m west of pier. **open** All year except Xmas **bedrooms** 3 single, 3 double, 3 twin, 1 family **bathrooms** 8 en suite **payment** cash, cheques

Room   General   Leisure

254   Official tourist board guide Bed & Breakfast

South East | **Sussex**

HASTINGS, Sussex Map ref 3B4

SAT NAV TN34 3HU

Swan House
1 Hill Street, Old Town, Hastings TN34 3HU
t (01424) 430014 **f** (01424) 234696 **e** res@swanhousehastings.co.uk
w swanhousehastings.co.uk ONLINE MAP GUEST REVIEWS ONLINE BOOKING LAST MINUTE OFFERS

B&B PER ROOM PER NIGHT
S £70.00 – £95.00
D £115.00 – £145.00

EVENING MEAL PER PERSON
£9.00 – £24.00

SPECIAL PROMOTIONS
Check our website for special offers

Tourism South East B&B of the Year 2009, five star Swan House continues to receive widespread glowing press recognition. More than just a guest-house, we offer luxury and relaxation unprecedented in Hastings Old Town. Guests enjoy a locally-sourced breakfast menu, spacious guest lounge, broadband internet and a landscaped patio garden.

open All year except Xmas
bedrooms 2 double, 1 twin, 1 suite
bathrooms 4 en suite
payment credit/debit cards, cash, cheques, euros

directions Please contact us for directions

BREAKFAST AWARD Room General Leisure

HAYWARDS HEATH, Sussex Map ref 2D3

SAT NAV RH16 1XU

Copyhold Hollow Bed & Breakfast
Copyhold Lane, Lindfield, Haywards Heath RH16 1XU
t (01444) 413245 **e** vb@copyholdhollow.co.uk
w copyholdhollow.co.uk

B&B PER ROOM PER NIGHT
S £55.00
D £100.00

Grade II listed 16th century home with Victorian addition, oak beams and inglenook fireplace in guests' sitting room. Enjoy the spectacular 2 acre woodland garden, 1,000 year old box hedge and treehouse, surrounded by countryside. Maps for nearby walks. London 45 mins by train. Glyndebourne 40 mins by car.

open All year
bedrooms 1 single, 1 double, 1 twin
bathrooms 3 en suite
payment cash, cheques

directions Follow signs for Borde Hill Gardens, leave entrance on your left, after quarter mile turn right, signposted Ardingly. Copyhold Hollow half mile on right.

BREAKFAST AWARD
Room
General
Leisure

key to symbols see page 6

South East | **Sussex**

HAYWARDS HEATH, Sussex Map ref 2D3
SAT NAV RH16 1JH

B&B PER ROOM PER NIGHT
S £35.00 – £40.00
D £55.00 – £70.00

The Old Forge
16 Lucastes Avenue, Haywards Heath RH16 1JH
t (01444) 451905 f (01444) 451905

The Old Forge is a charming, late-Victorian home set in a delightf conservation area within easy reach of the mainline station. Frien owners, warm welcome. Delicious cooked breakfast. Centrally heated rooms. **directions** Please contact us for directions **open** A year except Xmas **bedrooms** 2 double **bathrooms** 1 en suite, 1 with private bathroom **payment** cash, cheques

Room General

HENFIELD, Sussex Map ref 2D3
SAT NAV BN5 9RQ

B&B PER ROOM PER NIGHT
S £35.00 – £40.00
D £65.00

1 The Laurels
Martyn Close, Henfield BN5 9RQ
t (01273) 493518 e malc.harrington@lineone.net
w no1thelaurels.co.uk ONLINE MAP

A detached house faced with traditional knapped Sussex flint stones. Comfortable rooms, a warm welcome, easy access to Brighton. Many places of interest nearby. **directions** Please refer t website. **open** All year **bedrooms** 1 single, 2 double, 1 twin **bathrooms** 3 en suite **payment** credit/debit cards, cash, cheques

Room General Leisure

HERSTMONCEUX, Sussex Map ref 3B4
SAT NAV BN27 1RG

B&B PER ROOM PER NIGHT
S £50.00 – £60.00
D £60.00 – £100.00

Sandhurst
Church Road, Herstmonceux, Hailsham BN27 1RG
t (01323) 833088 or 07808144799 f (01323) 833088 e junealanruss@aol.com
w herstmonceuxbandb.com

Large bungalow with plenty of off-road parking. Within walking distance of Herstmonceux village and close to Herstmonceux Cas Twenty minutes drive to sea. No smoking. **directions** turn into church road off the A271 towards Herstmoncuux church and we will be found just around the bend in the road on the right **oper** All year except Xmas **bedrooms** 2 double, 1 family **bathrooms** 2 en suite, 1 with private bathroom **payment** cash, cheques

Room General

LEWES, Sussex Map ref 2D3
SAT NAV BN8 6PS

B&B PER ROOM PER NIGHT
S £49.00 – £69.00
D £85.00

Gold AWARD

Beechwood B&B
Eastbourne Road, Halland, Lewes BN8 6PS
t (01825) 840937 e chyland1956@aol.com
w beechwoodbandb.co.uk ONLINE MAP LAST MINUTE OFFERS

Within village of Halland in the heart of Sussex in one-acre of mature-gardens. Ideally located for East Sussex National Golf Club Glyndebourne Opera House. **directions** Please contact us for directions **open** All year **bedrooms** 1 single, 2 double, 1 twin **bathrooms** 2 en suite, 1 with private bathroom **payment** credit/ debit cards, cash, cheques, euros

Room General Leisure

256 — Official tourist board guide **Bed & Breakf**

South East | Sussex

LEWES, Sussex Map ref 2D3
SAT NAV BN7 3QD

The Blacksmiths Arms
Offham, Lewes BN7 3QD
t (01273) 472971 **e** blacksmithsarms@shineadsl.co.uk
w theblacksmithsarms-offham.co.uk

B&B PER ROOM PER NIGHT
D £65.00 – £90.00
EVENING MEAL PER PERSON
£10.00 – £25.00

18thC village inn close to South Downs Way on main A275. Close to historic town of Lewes. Convenient for Sussex University and Glyndebourne. Mentioned in Good Pub Guide. **directions** Please contact us for directions **open** All year **bedrooms** 4 double **bathrooms** 4 en suite **payment** credit/debit cards, cash, cheques

Room General Leisure

LEWES, Sussex Map ref 2D3
SAT NAV BN7 2RD

The Dorset
22 Malling Street, Lewes BN7 2RD
t (01273) 474823 **e** info@thedorsetlewes.com
w thedorsetlewes.com

B&B PER ROOM PER NIGHT
S £55.00 – £70.00
D £75.00 – £110.00
EVENING MEAL PER PERSON
£8.00 – £25.00

Friendly pub-restaurant with rooms in central Lewes. Six well-equipped en-suite B&B rooms, including family room; extensive breakfast menu. Excellent restaurant with emphasis on seafood and local produce. **directions** Easy access from A27 and A26. See our website for detailed directions or enquire when booking. **open** All year except Xmas **bedrooms** 4 double, 2 family **payment** credit/debit cards, cash, cheques

Room General Leisure

LEWES, Sussex Map ref 2D3
SAT NAV BN7 1EQ

Lill Stugan
33 Houndean Rise, Lewes BN7 1EQ
t (01273) 483580 **f** (01273) 483580 **e** araikes@gotadsl.co.uk

B&B PER ROOM PER NIGHT
S £65.00
D £90.00

Modern self-contained garden flat, in Swedish house backing on to Downs and National Park. Own access to flat and patio area. Kitchen/diner, breakfast foods supplied. Parking. Use of beach hut. **directions** Coming from Brighton direction on the A27 turn left at the roundabout as you approach Lewes. Buses and taxis from Lewes Station. **open** All year **bedrooms** 1 single, 1 double **bathrooms** 1 en suite **payment** cash, cheques

Room General Leisure

LITTLEHAMPTON, Sussex Map ref 2D3
SAT NAV BN17 5DD

Arun View Inn
Wharf Road, Littlehampton BN17 5DD
t (01903) 722335 **f** (01903) 722335 **e** info@thearunview.co.uk
w thearunview.co.uk ONLINE MAP ONLINE BOOKING

B&B PER ROOM PER NIGHT
S £27.50 – £35.00
D £42.50 – £50.00
EVENING MEAL PER PERSON
£6.95 – £25.00

A pleasant riverside pub, offering a good range of home-cooked food and a selection of drinks in a friendly atmosphere. Open for breakfasts, lunch and dinner Mon-Sat and all-day Sundays. **directions** 2 minute walk from Littlehampton Train Station, turn right as you walk out of station and we are 100 metres down the road **open** All year except Xmas **bedrooms** 1 double, 4 twin **payment** credit/debit cards, cash, cheques

BREAKFAST AWARD

Room General Leisure

key to symbols see page 6

South East | **Sussex**

NEWHAVEN, Sussex Map ref 2D3   SAT NAV BN9 9NB

★★★ GUEST HOUSE

B&B PER ROOM PER NIGHT
S £29.00 – £35.00
D £54.00 – £64.00

Newhaven Lodge
12 Brighton Road, Newhaven BN9 9NB
t (01273) 513736 f (01273) 734619 e info@newhavenlodge.co.uk
w **newhavenlodge.com** ONLINE MAP GUEST REVIEWS

A comfortable, bright, family-run establishment located close to the Newhaven/Dieppe ferry terminal. Brighton, Lewes and South Downs nearby. The establishment motto is 'Arrive as a guest and leave as a friend'. **directions** Please contact us for directions **open** All year **bedrooms** 2 single, 1 double, 3 family **bathrooms** 4 en suite **payment** credit/debit cards, cash, cheques, euros

Room General Leisure

PETWORTH, Sussex Map ref 2D3   SAT NAV RH20 1EZ

★★★★ BED & BREAKFAST

B&B PER ROOM PER NIGHT
S £45.00
D £70.00 – £75.00

Eedes Cottage
Bignor Park Road, Bury Gate, Pulborough RH20 1EZ
t (01798) 831438 e eedes.bandb@btinternet.com

Quiet country house surrounded by farmland. Convenient for main roads to Arundel, Chichester and Brighton. Dogs and children welcome. All bedrooms large and comfortable. **directions** Eedes is situated on the B2138 - half a mile from its junction with the A29. Fittleworth is 1½ miles away. **open** All year **bedrooms** 2 double, 2 twin **bathrooms** 2 en suite **payment** cash, cheques, euros

Room General Leisure

PULBOROUGH, Sussex Map ref 2D3   SAT NAV RH20 2BS

★★★★ BED & BREAKFAST

B&B PER ROOM PER NIGHT
S £40.00 – £45.00
D £60.00 – £70.00

Barn House Lodge
Barn House Lane, Pulborough, West Sussex RH20 2BS
t (01798) 872682 e sue@barnhouselodge.co.uk
w **barnhouselodge.co.uk**

Lovely family house, very well maintained with well kept gardens in rural village environment with panoramic view across the meadows to the South Downs. **directions** Take the A29 to Pulborough. Turn left onto A283 for approximately ¼ mile. Londis on right, take small lane down side, first house on right **open** All year **bedrooms** 1 double, 1 twin **bathrooms** 1 en suite, 1 with private bathroom **payment** cash, cheques, euros

Room General Leisure

PULBOROUGH, Sussex Map ref 2D3   SAT NAV RH20 1LF

★★★★ INN

B&B PER ROOM PER NIGHT
S £55.00 – £65.00
D £90.00 – £120.00
EVENING MEAL PER PERSON
£6.95 – £17.95

The Labouring Man
Old London Road, Coldwaltham, Pulborough RH20 1LF
t (01798) 872215 e philip.beckett@btconnect.com
w **thelabouringman.co.uk** ONLINE MAP GUEST REVIEWS LAST MINUTE OFFERS

Pub/restaurant with five luxury bed and breakfast rooms. Car park, home-cooked food, real ales Camra recommended, log fire. Walkers, Shooting Parties, game & clays, welcome. **directions** On Line Map **open** All year **bedrooms** 4 double, 1 twin **bathrooms** 5 en suite, with private bathroom **payment** credit/debit cards, cash, cheques

Room General Leisure

258 Official tourist board guide **Bed & Breakfast**

South East | Sussex

RINGMER, Sussex Map ref 2D3
SAT NAV BN8 5RU

B&B PER ROOM PER NIGHT
S £50.00 – £70.00
D £65.00 – £75.00

Bryn Clai
Uckfield Road (A26), Ringmer, Lewes BN8 5RU
t (01273) 814042 **e** daphne@brynclai.co.uk
w brynclai.co.uk ONLINE MAP GUEST REVIEWS ONLINE BOOKING

Set in seven acres with beautiful garden, parking. Comfortable interior. Large, bedrooms (ground-floor rooms) views over farmland. Walking distance country pub with excellent food. Glyndebourne, South Downs and Brighton nearby. **directions** From A26, 2 miles north of Lewes, 5 miles south of Uckfield. **open** All year **bedrooms** 1 double, 1 twin, 2 family **bathrooms** 2 en suite, 2 with private bathroom **payment** credit/debit cards, cash, cheques

Room General Leisure

RODMELL, Sussex Map ref 2D3
SAT NAV BN7 3HS

B&B PER ROOM PER NIGHT
S £35.00
D £60.00

Garden Cottage
Garden Studio, Mill Lane, Rodmell, Lewes BN7 3HS
t (01273) 476715 / 07518 617604

Self-contained studio flat on South Downs Way. Twin beds, bed-settee, own kitchen, breakfast supplied. Close to Glyndebourne, Brighton, port of Newhaven. Use of garden. Popular village inn. **directions** Please contact us for directions **open** All year **bedrooms** 1 twin **bathrooms** 1 en suite **payment** cash, cheques

Room General Leisure

RUSTINGTON, Sussex Map ref 2D3
SAT NAV BN16 2JP

B&B PER ROOM PER NIGHT
D £70.00 – £130.00

Mallondene
47 Mallon Dene, Rustington, Littlehampton BN16 2JP
t (01903) 775383 mobile 07970 845 689 **e** jenny@mallondene.co.uk
w mallondene.co.uk GUEST REVIEWS

Beautiful home/garden, quiet location, 2 minutes to beach. Village shops/cafes 10 mins walk. Chichester, Arundel, Worthing and Brighton easily reached by car/rail. Large en suite rooms. Excellent English breakfast. **directions** Please contact us for directions **open** All year **bedrooms** 1 double, 1 twin **bathrooms** 2 en suite **payment** cash, cheques

Room General Leisure

RYE, Sussex Map ref 3B4
SAT NAV TN31 7DB

B&B PER ROOM PER NIGHT
S £60.00 – £79.00
D £79.00 – £115.00

Old Borough Arms
The Strand, Rye, East Sussex TN31 7DB
t 01797 222 128 **e** info@oldboroughams.co.uk
w oldboroughams.co.uk ONLINE MAP

All nine rooms at the Old Borough Arms guest house are en suite, and have been recently decorated. All of the rooms are equipped with the usual facilities including free Wi-Fi. **directions** Please contact us for directions **open** All year **bedrooms** 1 single, 6 double, 2 family **bathrooms** 9 en suite **payment** credit/debit cards, cash

Room General Leisure

key to symbols see page 6

South East | **Sussex**

RYE, Sussex Map ref 3B4
SAT NAV TN31 6DG

Fairacres
Fairacres, Udimore Road, Broad Oak, Rye, East Sussex TN31 6DG
t (01424) 883236 f (01424) 883236 e info@fairacresrye.co.uk
w **fairacresrye.co.uk** ONLINE MAP GUEST REVIEWS

B&B PER ROOM PER NIGHT
S £48.00 – £100.00
D £80.00 – £100.00

SPECIAL PROMOTIONS
20% discount for a three night stay, Oct-Mar (excl Christmas, New Year and Easter).

John and Shelagh welcome you to their multi award winning 17th century listed house where attention to detail and guests comfort is paramount. All rooms en-suite and beautifully furnished with many unexpected extras and a truly sumptuous breakfast. With a delightful garden and secure parking. A warm welcome awaits you.

open All year except Xmas and New Year
bedrooms 2 double, 1 twin
bathrooms 3 en suite
payment cash, cheques, euros

directions On the Udimore Road 400 yards on the left from the junction of the A28 and B2089 at the Broad Oak Cross Roads.

BREAKFAST AWARD Room General ☒12 P Leisure

RYE, Sussex Map ref 3B4
SAT NAV TN31 7ET

Jeake's House
Jeake's House, Mermaid Street, Rye TN31 7ET
t (01797) 222828 f (01797) 222623 e stay@jeakeshouse.com
w **jeakeshouse.com** ONLINE MAP LAST MINUTE OFFERS

B&B PER ROOM PER NIGHT
S £70.00 – £79.00
D £90.00 – £138.00

SPECIAL PROMOTIONS
20% Mid-week Winter Special. Jan/Feb Offer available.

Ideally located historic house on winding, cobbled street in the heart of ancient medieval town. Individually restored rooms provide traditional luxury combined with all modern facilities. Book-lined bar, cosy parlours, extensive breakfast menu to suit all tastes. Easy walking distance to restaurants and shops. Private car park.

open All year
bedrooms 7 double, 3 twin, 1 suite
bathrooms 10 en suite, 1 with private bathroom
payment credit/debit cards, cash, cheques

directions Within the cobbled medieval town centre, approached either from the High Street via West Street or from The Strand Quay, A259.

BREAKFAST AWARD
Room
General ☒5
Leisure

South East | Sussex

RYE, Sussex Map ref 3B4

SAT NAV TN31 6AB

Oaklands

Udimore Road, Rye, East Sussex TN31 6AB
t (01797) 229734 f (01797) 229734 e info@oaklands-rye.co.uk
w **oaklands-rye.co.uk** ONLINE MAP

B&B PER ROOM PER NIGHT
D £90.00 – £110.00

Edwardian country house with stunning views to the sea and surrounding countryside. Located within an 'Area of Outstanding Natural Beauty'. Luxurious en suite rooms with thoughtful extras. Hearty breakfasts with home-made bread and preserves. Great for walking, cycling, birdwatching and relaxing. Ample off-road parking. A great break!

open All year
bedrooms 2 double, 1 twin
bathrooms 3 en suite
payment credit/debit cards, cash, euros

directions From Rye, B2089 for 1.3 miles. Oaklands is on the right. Broad Oak - Rye, B2089 after 5 miles Oaklands on left.

BREAKFAST AWARD

Room
General
Leisure

RYE, Sussex Map ref 3B4

SAT NAV TN36 4JT

Strand House

Strand House, Tanyards Lane, Winchelsea, nr Rye TN36 4JT
t (01797) 226276 f (01797) 224806 e info@thestrandhouse.co.uk
w **thestrandhouse.co.uk** ONLINE MAP GUEST REVIEWS ONLINE BOOKING LAST MINUTE OFFERS

B&B PER ROOM PER NIGHT
S £55.00 – £120.00
D £65.00 – £135.00

EVENING MEAL PER PERSON
£15.00 – £29.50

SPECIAL PROMOTIONS
Christmas and New Year house party. Dinner, bed and breakfast packages. Special offers throughout the year. Licensed for weddings.

A Tudor house with character rooms and an inglenook fireplace in the lounge. Food is the heart of the house with Sussex breakfast, tea on the lawn and evening dinner. Explore the many castles, houses and gardens in the area. A house of calm to while away the hours.

open All year
bedrooms 7 double, 1 twin, 2 family
bathrooms 9 en suite, 1 with private bathroom
payment credit/debit cards, cash, cheques, euros

directions Follow A259 from Rye in direction of Hastings for two miles. Strand House is clearly seen on the left at bottom of Winchelsea hill.

BREAKFAST AWARD

Room   General   Leisure

261

South East | **Sussex**

SEAFORD, Sussex Map ref 2D3   SAT NAV BN25 1RH

The Silverdale
21 Sutton Park Road, Seaford BN25 1RH
t (01323) 491849   e info@silverdaleseaford.co.uk
w silverdaleseaford.co.uk ONLINE MAP GUEST REVIEWS LAST MINUTE OFFERS

B&B PER ROOM PER NIGHT
S £45.00 – £55.00
D £60.00 – £80.00

Edwardian guest house in the centre of Seaford. A few minutes walk to beach, Seven Sisters country park and many friendly pubs and restaurants in Seaford. **directions** On A259 in centre of Seaford. **open** All year except Xmas and New Year **bedrooms** 2 double, 1 family, 1 suite **bathrooms** 4 en suite **payment** credit/debit cards, cash, cheques

Room   General   Leisure

STAPLECROSS, Sussex Map ref 3B4   SAT NAV TN32 5SG

Woodside Bed & Breakfast
Woodside, Junction Road, Robertsbridge, Nr Rye and Battle TN32 5SG
t (01580) 830903   f 0844 804 0390   e reservations@woodsidebandb.com
w woodsidebandb.com ONLINE MAP GUEST REVIEWS LAST MINUTE OFFERS

B&B PER ROOM PER NIGHT
S £55.00 – £75.00
D £80.00 – £110.00

EVENING MEAL PER PERSON
£20.00 – £34.00

SPECIAL PROMOTIONS
Use of Health Suite £10pp;
70 minute Massage £50.
See website for current promotions please

Luxury B&B set in 10 acres of gardens, paddoc & ancient bluebell woods. WOW factor suites/bathrooms. Health Suite. Air Hockey, Home Cinema (9ft screen). A la Carte dining. Licensed Our aim: to pamper our guests. In an AONB ne National Trust/English Heritage properties. Nea the coast.

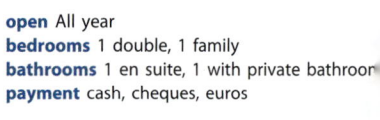

open All year
bedrooms 1 double, 1 family
bathrooms 1 en suite, 1 with private bathroor
payment cash, cheques, euros

directions Please see our website which will produce a bespoke route and map from your home.

BREAKFAST AWARD

Room
General
Leisure

STEYNING, Sussex Map ref 2D3   SAT NAV BN44 3GG

Springwells
9 High Street, Steyning, West Sussex BN44 3GG
t (01903) 812446   e contact@springwells.co.uk
w springwells.co.uk ONLINE MAP GUEST REVIEWS LAST MINUTE OFFERS

B&B PER ROOM PER NIGHT
S £43.00 – £65.00
D £72.00 – £120.00

Once a Georgian merchant's town house now an elegant 11 bedroom bed and breakfast hotel. Lovely walled gardens. Victorian style conservatory. Outdoor swimming pool. Two four poster beds **directions** Please contact us for directions **bedrooms** 2 single, 6 double, 2 twin, 1 suite **bathrooms** 9 en suite **payment** credit/deb cards, cash, cheques

Room   General   Leisure

262   Official tourist board guide **Bed & Breakfa**

South East | Sussex/Berkshire

WORTHING, Sussex Map ref 2D3
SAT NAV BN11 2EU

Benson's Guest House
143 Brighton Road, Worthing, West Sussex BN11 2EU
t (01903) 206323   e bensonsguesthouse@btinternet.com
w bensonstheguesthouse.co.uk ONLINE MAP GUEST REVIEWS

B&B PER ROOM PER NIGHT
S £50.00 – £60.00
D £80.00 – £90.00

Ten minute walk from Worthing shopping centre, theatres and the pier. All rooms en suite and contain a fridge, TV, hairdryer. Tea & coffee making facilities. Gold Award for Quality. **directions** Please contact us for directions **open** All year **bedrooms** 2 double, 1 twin **bathrooms** 3 en suite, 1 with private bathroom **payment** credit/debit cards, cash, cheques

Room General

WORTHING, Sussex Map ref 2D3
SAT NAV BN11 2DX

Glenhill Guest House
21 Alexandra Road, Worthing BN11 2DX
t (01903) 202756   e filmersankeylinda@yahoo.co.uk
w glenhillguesthouse.co.uk ONLINE MAP GUEST REVIEWS

B&B PER ROOM PER NIGHT
S £26.00 – £30.00
D £56.00 – £60.00

An Edwardian House on a quiet street. Close to beach, theatres and restaurants. Brighton 20 minutes drive and the lovely south downs also close by. **directions** Just 100 yards from beach and ten minutes walk to all amenetities **open** All year **bedrooms** 2 single, 2 double, 1 twin **payment** credit/debit cards, cash, cheques

Room General Leisure

All Assessed Accommodation

Berkshire

ALDERMASTON

The Hinds Head ★★★★ Inn
Bed & Breakfast
asing Lane, Aldermaston
7 4LX
(0118) 971 2194
hindshead@fullers.co.uk
fullershotels.co.uk

ALDWORTH

eldview Cottage ★★★★
d & Breakfast
dworth, Reading
8 9SB
(01635) 578964
haroldhunt@btinternet.com

ASCOT

aufort House ★★★★
d & Breakfast
oomfield Park, Ascot
5 0JT
(01344) 622991
jenny@beaufort-house.com
beaufort-house.co.uk

nglewood ★★★ Bed & Breakfast
nglewood Birch Lane, Long Hill
ad Chavey Down, Ascot
5 8RF
(01344) 882528
beer.tanglewood@btinternet.com
tanglewood-ascot.co.uk/index.html

n Cottage ★★★★
d & Breakfast SILVER AWARD
ckhurst Road, Ascot
5 7QE
(01344) 873073
info@tuncottage.co.uk
tuncottage.co.uk

BRACKNELL

Elizabeth House ★★★★
Guest Accommodation
Rounds Hill, Wokingham Road, Bracknell
RG42 1PB
t (01344) 868480
e res@lizhotel.co.uk
w lizhotel.co.uk

Holly House ★★★★
Bed & Breakfast SILVER AWARD
Goughs Lane, Bracknell
RG12 2JR
t (01344) 411750
e reservations@hollyhousebracknell.co.uk
w hollyhousebracknell.co.uk

CHIEVELEY

Thatched House B&B ★★★★
Bed & Breakfast SILVER AWARD
High Street, Chieveley, Newbury
RG20 8TE
t (01635) 248295
e s.malty@btinternet.com
w mychieveley.co.uk/info/thatchedhousebandb

Ye Olde Red Lion ★★★★ Inn
SILVER AWARD
Green Lane, Chieveley, Newbury
RG20 8XB
t (01635) 248379
e redlion@toucansurf.com
w yeolderedlion.com

COLD ASH

2 Woodside ★★★★
Bed & Breakfast SILVER AWARD
Woodside, Cold Ash, Thatcham
RG18 9JF
t (01635) 860028
e anita.rhiggs@which.net

COOKHAM DEAN

Riverbank Cottage ★★★★
Bed & Breakfast SILVER AWARD
Spade Oak Reach, Cookham Dean
SL6 9RQ
t (01628) 530662
e ianberrido@mac.com
w riverbankcookham.co.uk

FIFIELD

Victoria Cottage ★★
Bed & Breakfast
2 Victoria Cottages, Fifield Road, Fifield, Maidenhead
SL6 2NZ
t (01628) 623564

HURLEY

Meadow View ★★★★★
Bed & Breakfast SILVER AWARD
Henley Road, Hurley, Maidenhead
SL6 5LW
t (01628) 829764
e lin.meadowview@tiscali.co.uk
w meadowviewbedandbreakfast.co.uk

KINTBURY

Dundas Arms ★★★ Inn
Station Road, Kintbury, Hungerford
RG17 9UT
t (01488) 658263
e info@dundasarms.co.uk
w dundasarms.co.uk

LECKHAMPSTEAD

Bow River House ★★★★★
Guest House SILVER AWARD
Leckhampstead, Newbury, Berkshire
RG20 8QY
t (01488) 639776
e bookings@bowriver.co.uk
w bowriver.co.uk

MAIDENHEAD

Braywick Grange ★★★★
Bed & Breakfast
100 Braywick Road, Maidenhead
SL6 1DJ
t (01628) 625915
e admin@braywickgrange.co.uk

Clifton Guest House ★★★
Guest House
21 Craufurd Rise, Maidenhead
SL6 7LR
t (01628) 620086
e reservation@cliftonguesthouse.co.uk
w cliftonguesthouse.co.uk

Gables End ★★ Bed & Breakfast
4 Gables End, Maidenhead
SL6 8QD
t (01628) 639630
e christablight@onetel.com

Sunny Cottage ★★★★
Guest House SILVER AWARD
Manor Lane, Maidenhead
SL6 2QW
t (01628) 770731
e beadvr@aol.com
w sunnycottagebb.co.uk

MARLOW

Riverdale ★★★★ Bed & Breakfast
Marlow Bridge Lane, Marlow
SL7 1RH
t (01628) 485206
e christopherrawlings@talktalk.net
w bed-breakfast-marlow.co.uk

MIDGHAM

The Paddock ★★ Bed & Breakfast
Midgham Green, Midgham, Reading
RG7 5TT
t (0118) 971 3098
e enquiries@midghamgreen.co.uk
w midghamgreen.co.uk

263

South East | Berkshire/Buckinghamshire

NEWBURY

The Bell at Boxford ★★★ *Inn*
Lambourn Road, Newbury, Berkshire
RG20 8DD
t (01488) 608721
e helen@bellatboxford.com
w bellatboxford.com

The Chase Guest House ★★★★
Bed & Breakfast SILVER AWARD
Wash Water, Newbury
RG20 0LZ
t (01635) 231141
e chaseguesthouse@btconnect.com
w thechaseguesthouse.com

Ingledene Bed & Breakfast
★★★★ *Guest Accommodation*
225 Andover Road, Newbury
RG14 6NG
t 07770 876840
e info@ingledenebnb.co.uk
w ingledenebnb.co.uk

Manor Farm House ★★★★
Farmhouse SILVER AWARD
Church Street, Hampstead Norreys,
Thatcham, Berkshire
RG18 0TD
t (01635) 201276
e bettsbedandbreakfast@hotmail.com
w bettsbedandbreakfast.co.uk

The Old Farmhouse ★★★★
Bed & Breakfast
Down End Lane, Chieveley,
Newbury, Berkshire
RG20 8TN
t (01635) 248361
e palletts@aol.com
w mychieveley.co.uk/info/theoldfarmhouse

NEWBURY.

160 Craven Road ★★
Bed & Breakfast
Newbury.
RG14 5NR
t (01635) 40522

OAKLEY GREEN

Rainworth House ★★★★
Guest Accommodation
SILVER AWARD
Oakley Green Road, Oakley Green,
Windsor
SL4 5UL
t (01753) 856749
e info@rainworthhouse.com
w rainworthhouse.com

OLD WINDSOR

The Union Inn ★★★★ *Inn*
17 Crimp Hill, Old Windsor, Windsor
SL4 2QY
t (01753) 861955
w unioninnwindsor.co.uk

READING

Bird In Hand ★★★★ *Inn*
Bath Road, Knowl Hill, Reading
RG10 9UP
t (01628) 826622
e sthebirdinhand@aol.com
w birdinhand.co.uk

Caversham Lodge ★★
Guest Accommodation - Room Only
133a Caversham Road, Reading
RG1 8AS
t (0118) 961 2110
e raj.roy@hotmail.co.uk

Eastfield ★★★ *Bed & Breakfast*
Birds Lane, Midgham, Reading
RG7 5UL
t (0118) 971 3160

Great Expectations ★★★ *Inn*
33 London Street, Reading
RG1 4PS
t (0118) 950 3925
e greatexpectations@thechapmansgroup.co.uk
w great-expectations.hotel-rv.com

SANDHURST

The Wellington Arms ★★★ *Inn*
203 Yorktown Road, Sandhurst
GU47 9BN
t (01252) 872408
e info@thewellingtonarms.co.uk
w thewellingtonarms.co.uk

SLOUGH

Furnival Lodge ★★★★
Guest House
53-55 Furnival Avenue, Slough
SL2 1DH
t (01753) 570333
e info@furnival-lodge.co.uk
w furnival-lodge.co.uk

SONNING

The Bull Inn ★★★★ *Inn*
SILVER AWARD
High Street, Sonning, Reading
RG4 6UP
t (0118) 969 3901
e bullinn@fullers.co.uk
w fullershotels.co.uk

STAINES

The Oast Barn ★★★★
Bed & Breakfast
Staines Road, Wraysbury Village,
Staines
TW19 5BS
t (01784) 481598
e bandb@oastbarn.com
w oastbarn.com

STREATLEY

Streatley On Thames YHA ★★★
Hostel
Hill House, Reading Road, Streatley,
Reading
RG8 9JJ
t (01491) 872378
e streatley@yha.org.uk
w yhastreatley.org.uk

THATCHAM

One Church Lane ★★★★
Bed & Breakfast
One Church Lane, Thatcham
RG19 3LQ
t (01635) 869098
e johnhousemaster@aol.com

WINDSOR

3 York Road ★★★★ *Bed & Breakfast*
3 York Road, Windsor
SL4 3NX
t (01753) 861741
e kerrin@tiscali.co.uk

76 Duke Street ★★★★
Bed & Breakfast SILVER AWARD
76 Duke Street, Windsor
SL4 1SQ
t (01753) 620636
e admin@76dukestreet.co.uk
w 76dukestreet.co.uk

Alma Lodge ★★★ *Guest House*
58 Alma Road, Windsor
SL4 3HA
t (01753) 855620
e info@almalodge.co.uk
w almalodge.co.uk

Barbara's Bed & Breakfast ★★★★
Bed & Breakfast
16 Maidenhead Road, Windsor
SL4 5EQ
t 0044 (0)1753 840273
e bbandbwindsor@btinternet.com
w bbandbwindsor.com

Bluebell House ★★★★
Guest Accommodation
Lovel Lane, Woodside, Windsor,
Berkshire
SL4 2DG
t (01344) 886828
e registrations@bluebellhousehotel.co.uk
w bluebellhousehotel.com

Clarence Hotel ★★★ *Guest House*
9 Clarence Road, Windsor
SL4 5AE
t (01753) 864436
e clarence.hotel@btconnect.com
w clarence-hotel.co.uk

Cumberland Lodge *Campus*
The Great Park, Windsor
SL4 2HP
t (01784) 432316
e reception@cumberlandlodge.ac.uk
w cumberlandlodge.ac.uk

Frances Lodge ★★★★
Guest Accommodation
53 Frances Road, Windsor
SL4 3AQ
t (01753) 832019
e reservations@franceslodge.co.uk
w franceslodge.co.uk

Langton House ★★★★
Guest Accommodation
46 Alma Road, Windsor
SL4 3HA
t (01753) 858299
e paul@langtonhouse.co.uk
w langtonhouse.co.uk

The Old Farmhouse ★★★★
Bed & Breakfast
Dedworth Road, Oakley Green,
Windsor
SL4 4LH
t (01753) 850411
e debbie@theoldfarmhousewindsor.com
w theoldfarmhousewindsor.com

Rutlands ★★★★ *Bed & Breakfast*
102 St Leonards Road, Windsor
SL4 3DA
t (01753) 859533
e eileen.fahri@hotmail.co.uk
w rutlandsbandb.com

Windsor Edwardian ★★★
Bed & Breakfast
21 Osborne Road, Windsor
SL4 3EG
t (01753) 858995
e info@windsoredwardian.co.uk

The Windsor Trooper ★★★ *Inn*
97 St Leonard's Road, Windsor
SL4 3BZ
t (01753) 670123
e thewindsortrooper@live.co.uk
w thewindsortrooper.com

WINKFIELD

The Cottage Inn ★★★★ *Inn*
Winkfield Street, Winkfield, Windsor
SL4 4SW
t (01344) 882242
e cottage@btconnect.com
w cottage-inn.co.uk

Buckinghamshire

ADSTOCK

Folly Farm ★★★★ *Farmhouse*
Buckingham Road, Adstock,
Buckingham
MK18 2HS
t (01296) 712413

ASTON ABBOTTS

Windmill Hill Barns ★★★★
Bed & Breakfast
Moat Lane, Aston Abbotts,
Aylesbury
HP22 4NF
t (01296) 681714

AYLESBURY

Bay Lodge Guest House ★★
Guest Accommodation
47 Tring Road, Aylesbury
HP20 1LD
t (01296) 331404
e blodge47@hotmail.com
w bay-lodge.co.uk

Dinton Cottage ★★★
Guest Accommodation
Biggs Lane, Dinton, Aylesbury
HP17 8UH
t (01296) 748270
e lesley@dintoncottage.co.uk
w dintoncottage.co.uk

Dunsmore Edge ★★★★
Bed & Breakfast
Dunsmore Lane, London Road,
Wendover, Aylesbury
HP22 6PN
t (01296) 623080
e drackford@btinternet.com

The Old Forge Barn ★★★
Bed & Breakfast
Ridings Way, Cublington, Leighton
Buzzard
LU7 0LW
t (01296) 681194
e waples@ukonline.co.uk

Tanamera ★★★★ *Bed & Breakfast*
SILVER AWARD
37 Bishopstone Village, Bishopstone
Aylesbury
HP17 8SH
t (01296) 748551
e mary.purdy01@btinterenet.com

Town House ★★★ *Guest House*
35 Tring Road, Aylesbury
HP20 1LD
t (01296) 395295
w thetownhousebandb.co.uk

BEACONSFIELD

Jordans Youth Hostel ★ *Hostel*
Jordans Youth Hostel, Welders Lane
Beaconsfield
HP9 2SN
t 0870 770 5886
e jordans@yha.org.uk
w yha.org.uk

BISHOPSTONE

Standalls Farm ★★★
Bed & Breakfast
Bishopstone, Aylesbury
HP17 8SL
t (01296) 612687
e roger.goodchild@tesco.net

BOARSTALL

New Farm ★★ *Farmhouse*
Oxford Road, Oakley, Oxford
HP18 9UR
t (01844) 237360

BOURNE END

Hollands Farm ★★★★ *Farmhouse*
Hollands Farm, Hedsor Road,
Bourne End
SL8 5EE
t (01628) 520423
e info@hollands-farm.co.uk
w hollands-farm.co.uk

Lower Martins ★★★★
Bed & Breakfast
Lower Martins, Coldmoorholme
Lane, Bourne End
SL8 5PS
t (01628) 521730
e marianiwills@supanet.com
w marianiwills.supanet.com

BRADWELL

YHA Bradwell Village ★★ *Hostel*
Manor Farm, Vicarage Road, Milton
Keynes
MK13 9AG
t (01908) 227477
e bradwellvillage@yha.org.uk
w yha.org.uk

BUCKINGHAM

Churchwell ★★ *Bed & Breakfast*
23 Church Street, Buckingham
MK18 1BY
t (01280) 815415
w churchwell.co.uk

South East | Buckinghamshire

Huntsmill Farm B&B ★★★★
Bed & Breakfast
Huntsmill Farm, Shalstone, Nr. Buckingham
MK18 5ND
t (01280) 704852
e fiona@huntsmill.com
w huntsmill.com

CASTLETHORPE

Village B&B ★★
Guest Accommodation
Manor Farm House, South Street, Milton Keynes
MK19 7EL
t (01908) 510216
e reservations@manorfarmhouse.org
w mkweb.co.uk

CHALFONT ST GILES

The Ivy House ★★★★ Inn
The Ivy House, London Road, Chalfont St Giles
HP8 4RS
t (01494) 872184
e ivyhouse@fullers.co.uk
w fullershotels.com

CHESHAM

Katsina ★★ Bed & Breakfast
Katsina, Broomstick Lane, Chesham
HP5 1XU
t (01494) 773110
e pat.jeffrey@virgin.net
w katsina.co.uk

CUBLINGTON

Manor Farm B&B ★★★★
Bed & Breakfast
Whitchurch Road, Cublington, Leighton Buzzard
LU7 0LP
t (01296) 681107
e honor.vale@tesco.net

DENHAM

The Falcon Inn & Brasserie ★★★★ Inn
Village Road, Denham Village
UB9 5BG
t (01895) 832125
e mail@falcondenham.com
w falcondenham.com

EDGCOTT AYLESBURY

Perry Manor Farm ★★ Farmhouse
Perry Hill, Edgcott, Aylesbury, Buckinghamshire
HP18 0TS
t (01296) 770257
e perrymanorfarm@btconnect.com
w perrymanorfarm.co.uk

GREAT MISSENDEN

George House ★★★ Bed & Breakfast
George House, 10 Church Street, Great Missenden
HP16 0AX
t (01494) 867347

Lower Bassibones Farm B&B ★★★★ Guest Accommodation
SILVER AWARD
Lower Bassibones Farm, Ballinger Road, Great Missenden
HP16 9LA
t (01494) 837798
e lowerbassibones@yahoo.co.uk
w discover-real-england.com

Rickyard Cottage ★★★★
Bed & Breakfast GOLD AWARD
Rickyard Cottage, Denner Hill, Great Missenden
HP16 0HZ
t (01494) 488388
e richard@rickyard.plus.com
w rickyardcottage.co.uk

GRENDON UNDERWOOD

Shakespeare House ★★★★★
Guest Accommodation
GOLD AWARD
Main Street, Grendon Underwood
HP18 0ST
t (01296) 770776
e shakespearehouse@msn.com
w shakespeare-house.co.uk

HANSLOPE

Spinney Lodge Farm ★★★
Farmhouse
Forest Road, Hanslope, Milton Keynes
MK19 7DE
t (01908) 510267

Woad Farm ★★★ Farmhouse
Tathall End, Hanslope, Milton Keynes
MK19 7NE
t (01908) 510985
e s.stacey@btconnect.com

HENLEY-ON-THAMES

The Old Bakery ★★★★
Bed & Breakfast
The Old Bakery, Henley-on-Thames
RG9 6TD
t (01491) 638309
e lizzroach@aol.com
w bedbreakfasthenley.co.uk

HIGH WYCOMBE

9 Green Road ★★★★
Bed & Breakfast SILVER AWARD
9 Green Road, High Wycombe
HP13 5BD
t (01494) 437022
w lovetostayat9.co.uk

Amersham Hill Guest House ★★★
Guest House
52 Amersham Hill, High Wycombe
HP13 6PQ
t (01494) 520635
e amershamhillguesthouse@btconnect.com

Georgian House B&B ★★★
Bed & Breakfast
9 Sandford Gardens, Daws Hill, High Wycombe
HP11 1QT
t (01494) 441723

Longforgan ★★★★
Bed & Breakfast SILVER AWARD
Magpie Lane, Flackwell Heath, High Wycombe
HP10 9EA
t (01628) 525178
e bedbreakfasthighwycombe@hotmail.co.uk
w bedandbreakfasthighwycombe.co.uk

Malvern House ★★★★
Guest Accommodation
Malvern House, Fernie Fields, High Wycombe
HP12 4SP
t 07792 815846
e krysmaddocks@hotmail.com
w malvernguesthouse.co.uk

**Old Meadows Bed & Breakfast
★★★★** Bed & Breakfast
SILVER AWARD
10 Chapman Lane, Flackwell Heath, High Wycombe
HP10 9AZ
t (01628) 522177
e bobpearce1@btinternet.com
w bedbreakfast-highwycombe.co.uk

Rosling House ★★★★
Bed & Breakfast SILVER AWARD
Rosling House, Radnage Common Road, High Wycombe
HP14 4DD
t (01494) 482724
e carol.wheeler1@googlemail.com
w roslinghouse.co.uk

LECKHAMPSTEAD

Weatherhead Farm ★★★★
Farmhouse
Leckhampstead, Buckingham
MK18 5NP
t (01280) 860502
e weatherheadfarm@aol.com

MAIDENHEAD

**Bridge Cottage Guest House
★★★** Guest House
Bridge Cottage Guest House, Bath Road, Maidenhead
SL6 0AR
t (01628) 626805
e bridgecottagebb@btconnect.com
w bridgecottagebb.co.uk

MARLOW

31 Institute Road ★★
Bed & Breakfast
31 Institute Road, Marlow
SL7 1BJ
t (01628) 485662

Bullen's B&B ★★★★
Bed & Breakfast
18 Rookery Court, Marlow
SL7 3HR
t (01628) 486451
e gillbullen@rookerycourt.fsnet.co.uk
w bandb-marlow.co.uk

Granny Anne's ★★★★
Bed & Breakfast SILVER AWARD
Granny Anne's, 54 Seymour Park Road, Marlow
SL7 3EP
t (01628) 473086
e roger@grannyannes.com
w marlowbedbreakfast.co.uk

The Hand & Flowers ★★★★★ Inn
The Hand & Flowers, West Street, Marlow
SL7 2BP
t (01628) 482277
e theoffice@thehandandflowers.co.uk
w thehandandflowers.co.uk

Hazeldene ★★ Bed & Breakfast
Hazeldene, 53 Stapleton Close, Marlow
SL7 1TZ
t (01628) 482183
e hazeldenebandb@gmail.com

Oak Tree B&B ★★★
Bed & Breakfast
76 Oak Tree Road, Marlow
SL7 3EX
t (01628) 475340
e sheila.budd@btinternet.com
w oaktreebandb.org.uk

Red Barn Farm ★★★ Farmhouse
Red Barn Farm, Marlow Road, Marlow
SL7 3DQ
t (01494) 882820
e redbarnfarm@btinternet.com
w redbarn-farm.co.uk

**Sue Simmons Bed & Breakfast
★★** Bed & Breakfast
61 Hill Farm Road, Marlow Bottom, Marlow
SL7 3LX
t (01628) 475145
e suesimmons@accommodationmarlow.com
w accommodationmarlow.com

Swiss Cottage B&B ★★★★
Bed & Breakfast SILVER AWARD
22 New Road, Marlow
SL7 3NG
t 07752 032407
e swisscottagebb@hotmail.com
w swisscottagemarlow.com

MILTON KEYNES

Chantry Farm ★★★ Farmhouse
Pindon End, Hanslope, Milton Keynes
MK19 7HL
t (01908) 510269
e chuff.wake@tiscali.co.uk

MOULSOE

The Old Stables ★★★★
Guest House
Newport Road, Moulsoe, Newport Pagnell
MK16 0HR
t (01908) 217766
e liz@oldstablesmoulsoe.com
w oldstablesmoulsoe.com

OLNEY

Colchester House ★★★★
Guest Accommodation
SILVER AWARD
26 High Street, Olney
MK46 4BB
t (01234) 712602
e peter.blenkinsop@btopenworld.com
w olneybucks.co.uk

The Lindens ★★★★
Guest Accommodation
30A High Street, Olney
MK46 4BB
t (01234) 712891
e accommodation@thelindens.com
w thelindens.com

OVING

The Cottage B&B ★★★★
Bed & Breakfast
Pitchcott Road, Oving, Aylesbury
HP22 4HP
t (01296) 641891
e figeorge@btinternet.com

PRINCES RISBOROUGH

Drifters Lodge ★★★★
Bed & Breakfast
60 Picts Lane, Princes Risborough
HP27 9DX
t (01844) 274773
e info@drifterslodge.co.uk
w drifterslodge.co.uk

RADCLIVE

Radclive Dairy Farm ★★★★
Farmhouse
Radclive Road, Buckingham
MK18 4AA
t (01280) 813433
e rosalind.fisher@radclivedairyfarm.co.uk
w radclivedairyfarm.co.uk

SHERINGTON

The White Hart ★★★★ Inn
1 Gun Lane, Sherington, Newport Pagnell
MK16 9PE
t (01908) 611953
e whitehartresort@aol.com
w whitehartsherington.com

WADDESDON

The Lion ★★★★ Inn
70a High Street, Waddesdon
HP18 0JD
t (01296) 651227
e info@thelionwaddesdon.co.uk
w thelionwaddesdon.co.uk

The Old Dairy ★★★
Bed & Breakfast
4 High Street, Waddesdon
HP18 0JA
t (01296) 658627
e hconyard@tesco.net
w theolddairywaddesdon.co.uk

WATER STRATFORD

The Rolling Acres ★★★★
Bed & Breakfast
Water Stratford, Buckingham
MK18 5DX
t (01280) 847302
e amanda@rolling-acres.co.uk
w rolling-acres.co.uk

South East | Buckinghamshire/Hampshire

WOBURN SANDS

The Old Stables ★★★★
Guest House
Bow Brickhill Road, Woburn Sands,
Milton Keynes
MK17 8DE
t (01908) 281340
e info@oldstables.co.uk
w oldstables.co.uk

Woodley's Cottage ★★★★
Bed & Breakfast
2 The Granary, Bow Brickhill Road,
Milton Keynes
MK17 8DE
t (01908) 281460
e info@woodleyscottage.co.uk
w woodleyscottage.co.uk

WORMINGHALL

Crabtree Barn ★★★★ Farmhouse
Menmarsh Road, Worminghall,
Aylesbury
HP18 9JY
t (01844) 339719
e issy@crabtreebarn.co.uk
w crabtreebarn.co.uk

Hampshire

ALRESFORD

Haygarth ★★★ Bed & Breakfast
82 Jacklyns Lane, Alresford
SO24 9LJ
t (01962) 732715 / 07986 372895
e valramshaw@aol.com

Old Kennetts Cottage ★★★★
Bed & Breakfast SILVER AWARD
Cheriton, Alresford
SO24 0PX
t (01962) 771863
e dglssmith@aol.com

ALTON

Boundary House ★★★★
Bed & Breakfast SILVER AWARD
Gosport Road, Lower Farringdon,
Alton
GU34 3DH
t (01420) 587076
e boundarys@messages.co.uk
w boundaryhouse.co.uk

Halketts ★★★★ Bed & Breakfast
72 Kings Hill, Beech, Alton
GU34 4AN
t (01420) 562258
e halketts_bandb@btinternet.com
w halketts.co.uk

**Neatham Barn Self Catering &
Bed & Breakfast ★★★★**
Bed & Breakfast
Neatham, Holybourne, Alton
GU34 4NP
t (01420) 544 215
e alastair@neathamcottage.com
w neathambarn.com

St Mary's Hall ★★★★
Bed & Breakfast SILVER AWARD
18 Albert Road, Alton
GU34 1LP
t (01420) 88269
e joanmossop@stmaryshall.com
w stmaryshall.com

The Threshing Barn ★★★★★
Bed & Breakfast SILVER AWARD
Stocks Lane, Privett, Alton
GU34 3NZ
t (01730) 828383
e emma@thethreshingbarn.co.uk
w thethreshingbarn.co.uk

**Upper Neatham Mill Farm Guest
House ★★★★**
Guest Accommodation
SILVER AWARD
Upper Neatham Mill Lane,
Holybourne, Alton
GU34 4EP
t (01420) 542908
e upperneatham@btinternet.com
w upperneatham.co.uk

AMPORT

Amport Inn ★★ Inn
Amport, Andover
SP11 8AE
t (01264) 710371
e info@amportinn.co.uk

ANDOVER

The Bourne Valley Inn ★★ Inn
Upper Link, St Mary Bourne,
Andover
SP11 6BT
t (01264) 738361
e enquiries@thebournevalleyinn.
com
w bournevalleyinn.com

Church Mews Guest House ★★★
Guest House
2 Chantry Street, Andover
SP10 1DE
t (01264) 324323
e edmund@churchmews.co.uk

May Cottage ★★★★
Bed & Breakfast SILVER AWARD
Thruxton, Andover
SP11 8LZ
t (01264) 771241
e info@maycottage-thruxton.co.uk
w maycottage-thruxton.co.uk

**Salisbury Road Bed & Breakfast
★★★★** Bed & Breakfast
99 Salisbury Road, Andover
SP10 2LN
t (01264) 362638
e jenny@andoveraccommodation.
co.uk
w andoveraccommodation.co.uk

Staggs Cottage ★★★★
Bed & Breakfast
Windmill Hill, Ibthorpe, Andover
SP11 0BP
t (01264) 736235
e staggscottage@aol.com
w staggscottage.co.uk

The Station Hotel ★★★★ Inn
SILVER AWARD
Bridge Street, Andover
SP10 1BY
t (01264) 336585
e romanab@btinternet.com
w stationhotelandover.co.uk

Upton Cottage ★★★
Bed & Breakfast
Vernham Dean, Andover
SP11 0JY
t (01264) 737640
e upton.cottage@hotmail.com
w upton-cottage.co.uk

**Yew Cottage Bed & Breakfast
★★★** Bed & Breakfast
Longparish, Andover
SP11 6QE
t (01264) 720325
e rosie@yewcottagelongparish.com
w yewcottagelongparish.com

ASHURST

Forest Gate Lodge ★★★
Guest Accommodation
161 Lyndhurst Road, Ashurst,
Lyndhurst
SO40 7AW
t (023) 8029 3026
e forestgatelodge161@hotmail.co.
uk
w forestgatelodge.co.uk

BASINGSTOKE

Mallards ★★★★★ Bed & Breakfast
GOLD AWARD
3 Trims Court, Overton, Nr
Basingstoke, Hampshire
RG25 3JZ
t (01256) 770039
e mallards@test-the-water.co.uk
w test-the-water.co.uk

Manor Farm Stables ★★★★
Bed & Breakfast SILVER AWARD
Vyne Road, Sherborne St John,
Basingstoke
RG24 9HX
t (01256) 851324

The Old Rectory ★★★
Bed & Breakfast
Freefolk, Overton, Basingstoke
RG28 7NW
t (01256) 895408
e sue.etridge@oldrectoryfreefolk.co.
uk
w oldrectoryfreefolk.co.uk

Wessex House ★★★
Guest Accommodation
120 Winchester Road, Basingstoke
RG21 8YW
t (01256) 325202
e wessexhouse@gmail.com
w wessexhouseandbb.co.uk

BEAULIEU

Dale Farm House ★★★★
Farmhouse SILVER AWARD
Manor Road, Dibden, Southampton,
Hampshire
SO45 5TJ
t (023) 8084 9632
e chris@dalefarmhouse.co.uk
w dalefarmhouse.co.uk

BENTLEY

Pittersfield ★★★★ Bed & Breakfast
Hole Lane, Bentley, Farnham
GU10 5LT
t (01420) 22414
e m.coulton1@btinternet.com

BLACKFIELD

Lakeside ★★★★ Bed & Breakfast
West Common, Blackfield, New
Forest
SO45 1XJ
t (023) 8089 8926
e tonycavell@aol.com
w lakesidebandb.net

BLASHFORD

Fraser House ★★★★ Guest House
Salisbury Road, Blashford, Ringwood
BH24 3PB
t (01425) 473958
e mail@fraserhouse.net
w fraserhouse.net

BORDON

Groomes ★★★★
Guest Accommodation
GOLD AWARD
Frith End, Bordon
GU35 0QR
t (01420) 489858
e pete@groomes.co.uk
w groomes.co.uk

Spring Cottage ★★
Bed & Breakfast
Main Road, Kingsley, Bordon
GU35 9NA
t (01420) 472703
e paulineansell@aol.com

BRAMSHAW

Wych Green Cottage ★★★★
Bed & Breakfast SILVER AWARD
Bramshaw, Lyndhurst
SO43 7JF
t (023) 8081 2561
e suniverseone@aol.com
w newforest-uk.com

BURLEY

The Burley Inn ★★★ Inn
The Cross, Burley
BH24 4AB
t (01425) 403448
e info@theburleyinn.co.uk
w theburleyinn.co.uk

Burley YHA ★★ Hostel
Cottesmore House, Cott Lane,
Ringwood
BH24 4BB
t (01425) 403233

Wayside Cottage ★★★★
Bed & Breakfast
Garden Road, Burley
BH24 4EA
t (01425) 403414
e jwest@wayside-cottage.co.uk
w wayside-cottage.co.uk

The White Buck Inn ★★★★ Inn
Bisterne Close, Burley, Ringwood
BH24 4AT
t (01425) 402264
e whitebuck@fullers.co.uk
w fullershotels.co.uk

BURSLEDON

Heather Gables ★★★★
Bed & Breakfast SILVER AWARD
Dodwell Lane, Bursledon,
Southampton
SO31 1DJ
t (023) 8040 4925
e heather.gables@talktalk.net
w heathergables.co.uk

CADNAM

Kingsbridge House ★★★★
Guest Accommodation
SILVER AWARD
Southampton Road, Cadnam
SO40 2NH
t (023) 8081 1161
e linda@kingsbridgehouse.plus.com
w kingsbridge-house.co.uk

Twin Oaks Guest House ★★★★
Guest House SILVER AWARD
Southampton Road, Cadnam
SO40 2NQ
t (023) 8081 2305
e carol.gerrett2@tiscali.co.uk
w twinoaks-guesthouse.co.uk

CATHERINGTON

Flowerdown ★★★ Bed & Breakfast
82 Downhouse Road, Catherington
PO8 0TY
t (023) 9259 8029
e madeingb1@googlemail.com

CHINEHAM

Ashfields ★★★★
Guest Accommodation
51a Reading Road, Chineham,
Basingstoke
RG24 8LT
t (01256) 324629 / 07974641705

DIBDEN PURLIEU

Heatherdene B&B Bed & Breakfast
Beaulieu Road, Dibden Purlieu,
Southampton
SO45 4PW
t (023) 8084 6485
e heatherdene.995@btinternet.com
w heatherdenebandb.co.uk

EASTLEIGH

Carinya B&B ★★★ Bed & Breakfast
38 Sovereign Way, Eastleigh
SO50 4SA
t (023) 8061 3128
e carinya38@talktalk.net

EAST TYTHERLEY

Nursery Cottage ★★★
Bed & Breakfast
The Avenue, East Tytherley, Romsey
SP5 1LF
t (01794) 341060
e nursery-cottage@waitrose.com
w nursery-cottage.com

FAREHAM

**Catisfield Cottage Guest House
★★** Guest Accommodation
1 Catisfield Lane, Fareham
PO15 5NW
t (01329) 843301
e neale.hesselmann@ntlworld.com

South East | Hampshire

even Sevens Guest House ★★★
Guest Accommodation
6 Hill Head Road, Hill Head,
areham
O14 3JL
t (01329) 662408
e red.reed77@amserve.com

rafalgar Guest House ★★★
Guest Accommodation
3 High Street, Fareham
O16 7BG
t (01329) 235010
e enquiries@trafalgarguesthouse.
co.uk
w trafalgarguesthouse.co.uk

ravelrest Solent Gateway ★★★★
Guest Accommodation
2 The Avenue, Fareham
O14 1NS
t (01329) 232175
e solentreservations@travelrest.co.
uk
w travelrest.co.uk/fareham

FAWLEY

Valcot House ★★★★
Guest House SILVER AWARD
lackfield Road, Fawley, Beaulieu
O45 1ED
t (023) 8089 1344
e stephenjbrown@tiscali.co.uk
w walcothousehotel.com

FLEET

quirrels Leap Coach House
★★★★ Guest House
ueen Mary Close, Fleet
U51 4QR
t (01252) 616746
e info@squirrels-leap.co.uk
w squirrels-leap.co.uk

FORDINGBRIDGE

ottage Crest ★★★★★
ed & Breakfast SILVER AWARD
astle Hill, Woodgreen,
ordingbridge
P6 2AX
t (01725) 512009
e lupita_cadman@yahoo.co.uk
w cottage-crest.co.uk

nowtalia Lodge ★★★
ed & Breakfast
ingwood Road, Fordingbridge
P6 2EY
t (01425) 655114
e bookings@snowtalialodge.co.uk
w snowtalialodge.co.uk

FORTON

he Barn House B&B ★★★★★
ed & Breakfast GOLD AWARD
orton, Andover
P11 6NU
t (01264) 720544
e hello@thebarnhousebandb.co.uk
w thebarnhousebandb.co.uk

GODSHILL

roft Cottage ★★★
ed & Breakfast
outhampton Road, Godshill,
ordingbridge
P6 2LE
t (01425) 657955
e croftcottage@btopenworld.com
w croftcottagenewforest.co.uk

HAVANT

igh Towers ★★★ Bed & Breakfast
4 Portsdown Hill Road,
edhampton, Havant
O9 3JY
t (023) 9247 1748
e hightowers14@aol.com
w hightowers.co.uk

HAYLING ISLAND

6 Charleston Close ★★
ayling Island
O11 0JY
t (023) 9246 2527

Ann's Cottage ★★ Bed & Breakfast
45 St Andrews Road, Hayling Island
PO11 9JN
t (023) 9246 7048
e ann.jay@virgin.net

Copsewood House ★★★★
Bed & Breakfast SILVER AWARD
Copse Lane, Hayling Island
PO11 0QD
t (023) 9246 9294
e jillgoulding@hotmail.com
w copsewoodhouse.piczo.com

White House ★★★★
Bed & Breakfast
250 Havant Road, Hayling Island
PO11 0LN
t (023) 9246 3464
e info@whitehousehayling.co.uk
w whitehousehayling.co.uk/

HIGHCLERE

Highclere Farm ★★★★
Bed & Breakfast
Highclere Street, Highclere,
Newbury
RG20 9PY
t (01635) 255013
e walshhighclere@newburyweb.net
w highclerefarmnewbury.co.uk

HOOK

The Jolly Miller ★★★ Inn
Hook Road, North Warnborough,
Hook
RG29 1ET
t (01256) 702085
e enquiries@the-jollymiller.co.uk
w the-jollymiller.co.uk

HORNDEAN

The Ship & Bell ★★★ Inn
6 London Road, Horndean,
Waterlooville
PO8 0BZ
t (023) 9259 2107
e shipandbell@fullers.co.uk
w fullershotels.co.uk

IBTHORPE

Ibthorpe Manor Farm ★★★★★
Bed & Breakfast SILVER AWARD
Horse Shoe Lane, Ibthorpe, Andover
SP11 0BZ
t (01264) 736672
e info@ibthorpemanorfarm.com
w ibthorpemanorfarm.com

KILMESTON

Dean Farm ★★★★ Farmhouse
Kilmeston, Alresford
SO24 0NL
t (01962) 771286
e warrdeanfarm@btinternet.com
w warrdeanfarm.btinternet.co.uk

KINGSLEY

The Granary ★★★★ Farmhouse
GOLD AWARD
Stubbs Farm, South Hay, Kingsley
GU35 9NR
t (01420) 474906
e info@stubbsfarm.co.uk
w stubbsfarm.co.uk

LEE-ON-THE-SOLENT

Avon Manor Guest House ★★★
Guest Accommodation
12 South Place, Lee-on-the-Solent
PO13 9AS
t (023) 9255 2773
e karen@avonmanor.co.uk
w avonmanor.co.uk

Chester Lodge ★★★★
Bed & Breakfast
20 Chester Crescent, Lee-on-the-Solent
PO13 9BH
t (023) 9255 0894
e chesterlodgebandb@yahoo.co.uk
w chesterlodge.com

Leeward House B&B ★★★★
Bed & Breakfast SILVER AWARD
18 Russell Road, Lee-on-the-Solent
PO13 9HP
t (023) 9255 6090
e enq@leewardhouse.co.uk
w leewardhouse.co.uk

Milvil Corner ★★★★★
Guest Accommodation
SILVER AWARD
41 Milvil Road, Lee-on-the-Solent
PO13 9LU
t (023) 9255 3489
e enquiries@milvilcorner.co.uk
w milvilcorner.co.uk

LINWOOD

High Corner Inn ★★★★ Inn
Linwood, Ringwood
BH24 3QY
t (01425) 473973

LISS

Glendale ★★★★ Bed & Breakfast
Hatch Lane, Liss
GU33 7NJ
t (01730) 893451
e carol.browse@btinternet.com
w bedandbreakfastglendale.co.uk

LYMINGTON

Bluebird Restaurant & B&B ★★★
Bed & Breakfast
4-5 Quay Street, Lymington
SO41 3AS
t (01590) 676908
e bluebird.restaurant@yahoo.co.uk
w bluebirdrestaurant.co.uk

Britannia House ★★★★★
Guest Accommodation
SILVER AWARD
Station Street, Lymington
SO41 3BA
t (01590) 672091
e enquiries@britannia-house.com
w britannia-house.com

Durlston House ★★★
Guest Accommodation
Gosport Street, Lymington
SO41 9EG
t (01590) 677364
e durlstonhouse@aol.com
w durlstonhouse.co.uk

Glenhurst B&B ★★★★
Bed & Breakfast
86 Wainsford Road, Everton,
Lymington
SO41 0UD
t (01590) 644256
e a.rose@virgin.net
w newforest-bedbreakfast.co.uk

Gorse Meadow Guest House
★★★★ Guest House
Sway Road, Pennington, Lymington
SO41 8LR
t (01590) 673354
e gorsemeadow@btconnect.com
w gorsemeadowguesthouse.co.uk

Greenacre B&B
Guest Accommodation
Silver Street, Sway, Lymington
SO41 6DJ
t (01590) 682365
e sidcrowton@yahoo.com

Ha'penny House ★★★★★
Guest Accommodation
SILVER AWARD
16 Whitby Road, Milford-on-Sea,
Lymington, Hants
SO41 0ND
t (01590) 641210
e info@hapennyhouse.co.uk
w hapennyhouse.co.uk/

Inglemere B&B ★★★★
Bed & Breakfast SILVER AWARD
182 Everton Road, Hordle,
Lymington
SO41 0HB
t (01425) 610782
e inglemerebandb@btinternet.com
w inglemerebandb.yolasite.com

Moonraker Cottage ★★★★
Bed & Breakfast
62 Milford Road, Lymington
SO41 8DU
t (01590) 678677
e moonraker62@tiscali.co.uk

The Nurse's Cottage Restaurant with Rooms ★★★★
Guest Accommodation
GOLD AWARD
Station Road, Sway, Lymington,
Hampshire
SO41 6BA
t 01590 683402
e stay@nursescottage.co.uk
w nursescottage.co.uk

LYNDHURST

Acorns of Lyndhurst ★★★★
Bed & Breakfast SILVER AWARD
31 Romsey Road, Lyndhurst
SO43 7AR
t (023) 8028 4559
e enquiries@acornsoflyndhurst.co.
uk
w acornsoflyndhurst.co.uk

Burwood Lodge ★★★★
Guest Accommodation
27 Romsey Road, Lyndhurst
SO43 7AA
t (023) 8028 2445
e burwood.1@ukonline.co.uk
w burwoodlodge.co.uk

Hurst End ★★★★ Bed & Breakfast
Clayhill, Lyndhurst
SO43 7DE
t (023) 8028 2606
e hurst.end@btinternet.com
w hurstend.co.uk

Kingswood Cottage ★★★★
Bed & Breakfast SILVER AWARD
10 Woodlands Road, Ashurst,
Lyndhurst
SO40 7AD
t (023) 8029 2582
e kingswoodcottage@yahoo.co.uk
w kingswoodcottage.co.uk

Okeover ★★★★ Bed & Breakfast
12 Forest Gardens, Lyndhurst
SO43 7AF
t (023) 8028 2406
e okeover12@btinternet.com
w okeoveraccommodation.co.uk

Rosedale Bed & Breakfast ★★★★
Bed & Breakfast
24 Shaggs Meadow, Lyndhurst
SO43 7BN
t (023) 8028 3793
e rosedalebandb@btinternet.com
w rosedalebedandbreakfast.co.uk

MICHELDEVER

Willow Cottage ★★★★
Bed & Breakfast
Duke Street, Micheldever,
Winchester
SO21 3DF
t (01962) 774520
e willcott@globalnet.co.uk
w winchesterbedandbreakfast.co.uk

MILFORD-ON-SEA

The Bay Trees Bed & Breakfast
★★★★ Bed & Breakfast
GOLD AWARD
8 High Street, Milford-on-Sea,
Lymington
SO41 0QD
t (01590) 642186
e rp.fry@virgin.net
w baytreebedandbreakfast.co.uk

MILFORD ON SEA

Alma Mater Guest House ★★★★
Bed & Breakfast
4 Knowland Drive, Milford-on-Sea,
Lymington
SO41 0RH
t (01590) 642811
e almamaterguesthouse@googl
email.com
w almamaternewforest.co.uk

South East | Hampshire

NEW FOREST – BROCKENHURST

Goldenhayes ★★ *Bed & Breakfast*
9 Chestnut Road, Brockenhurst, Hants
SO42 7RF
t (01590) 623743
e briangeorgecurtis@fsmail.net

NEW MILTON

Taverners Cottage ★★★★
Bed & Breakfast **SILVER AWARD**
Bashley Cross Road, Bashley, New Milton
BH25 5SZ
t (01425) 615403
e judith@tavernerscottage.co.uk
w tavernerscottage.co.uk

Willy's Well ★★★★
Bed & Breakfast
Bashley Common Road, Bashley, New Milton
BH25 5SF
t (01425) 616834
e moyramac2@hotmail.com

Woodlands ★★★★ *Bed & Breakfast*
Ashley Lane, New Milton
BH25 5AQ
t (01425) 616425
e bealwoodlands@yahoo.co.uk
w newforest-bed-and-breakfast.co.uk/default.asp

OGDENS

Broomy ★★★★ *Bed & Breakfast*
Broomy, Ogdens, Fordingbridge
SP6 2PY
t (01425) 653264

OLD BASING

Arundel ★★ *Bed & Breakfast*
25 Linden Avenue, Old Basing
RG24 7HS
t (01256) 327282
e mjcole1@sky.com

The Haven ★★★★ *Bed & Breakfast*
8 Newnham Lane, Old Basing, Basingstoke
RG24 7AT
t (01256) 462892

Millfield House ★★★★
Guest Accommodation
SILVER AWARD
1A Little Basing, Bartons Lane, Basingstoke
RG24 8AX
t (01256) 474513
e info@millfieldhouse.co.uk
w millfieldhouse.co.uk

PETERSFIELD

1 The Spain ★★★★
Bed & Breakfast
Petersfield, Hampshire
GU32 3JZ
t (01730) 263261
e allantarver@ntlworld.com
w 1thespain.com

22 Church Path ★★★
Bed & Breakfast
The Square, Petersfield
GU32 3HS
t 07957 438666
e coffeeinthesquare@me.com

80 Rushes Road ★★★
Bed & Breakfast
80 Rushes Road, Petersfield
GU32 3BP
t (01730) 261638
e collinstudor@waitrose.com
w rushes-road.co.uk

Border Cottage ★★★★
Bed & Breakfast **SILVER AWARD**
4 Heath Road, Petersfield
GU31 4DU
t (01730) 263179
e lawrence@bordercottage.co.uk
w bordercottage.com

Downsview ★★★★ *Bed & Breakfast*
SILVER AWARD
58 Heath Road, Petersfield
GU31 4EJ
t (01730) 264171
e info@downsview58.co.uk
w downsview58.co.uk

Heath Farmhouse ★★★★
Bed & Breakfast
Heath Farmhouse, Sussex Road, Petersfield
GU31 4HU
t (01730) 264709
e info@heathfarmhouse.co.uk
w heathfarmhouse.co.uk

The Holt ★★★★ *Bed & Breakfast*
60 Heath Road, Petersfield
GU31 4EJ
t (01730) 262836

Upper Parsonage Farm ★★★★
Farmhouse **SILVER AWARD**
Harvesting Lane, East Meon, Petersfield
GU32 1QR
t (01730) 823490
e sue@atko.demon.co.uk
w upperparsonagefarm.co.uk

Yew Tree Farm House ★★★
Bed & Breakfast
Langrish, Petersfield
GU32 1RB
t (01730) 264959
e jane.sprinks@tesco.net

PORTSMOUTH

Albatross Guest House ★★★
Guest Accommodation
51 Waverley Road, Portsmouth
PO5 2PJ
t (023) 9282 8325
w albatrossguesthouse.co.uk

Arden Guest House ★★★★
Guest Accommodation
14 Herbert Road, Portsmouth
PO4 0QA
t (023) 9282 6409
e crichard240@aol.com

Bembell Court ★★★
Guest Accommodation
69 Festing Road, Portsmouth
PO4 0NQ
t (023) 9273 5915
e keith@bembell.co.uk
w bembell.co.uk

Birchwood Guest House ★★★★
Guest Accommodation
44 Waverley Road, Portsmouth
PO5 2PP
t (023) 9281 1337
e enquiries@birchwood.uk.com
w birchwood.uk.com

Cecil Cottage ★★★★
Bed & Breakfast
45 Broad Street, Portsmouth
PO1 2JD
t 07894 072253
e malcolm@cecilcottage.co.uk
w cecilcottage.co.uk

Cherry Trees ★★★★
Bed & Breakfast **SILVER AWARD**
23 Parkside, Bedhampton, Havant
PO9 3PJ
t (023) 9248 2480
e diana.patrick@talk21.com

Esk Vale Guest House ★★★
Guest Accommodation
39 Granada Road, Portsmouth
PO4 0RD
t (023) 9286 2639
e enquiries@eskvaleguesthouse.co.uk
w eskvaleguesthouse.co.uk

Everley Guest House ★★★
Guest House
33 Festing Road, Portsmouth
PO4 0NG
t (023) 9273 1001
e everleyguesthouse@ntlworld.com
w smoothhound.co.uk/hotels/everleyguesthouse.html

The Ferryman Guest House ★★★
Guest Accommodation
16 Victoria Road South, Portsmouth
PO5 2BZ
t (023) 9287 5824
e theferrymanhotel@hotmail.com
w ferryman-hotel.co.uk

Fortitude Cottage ★★★★
Guest Accommodation
SILVER AWARD
51 Broad Street, Spice Island, Portsmouth
PO1 2JD
t (023) 9282 3748
e info@fortitudecottage.co.uk
w fortitudecottage.co.uk

Gainsborough House ★★★
Guest Accommodation
9 Malvern Road, Portsmouth
PO5 2LZ
t (023) 9282 2604
e enquiries@gainsboroughhouse.co.uk
w gainsboroughhouse.co.uk

Hamilton House Bed & Breakfast
★★★★ *Guest Accommodation*
95 Victoria Road North, Portsmouth, Hants
PO5 1PS
t (023) 9282 3502
e sandra@hamiltonhouse.co.uk
w hamiltonhouse.co.uk

Homestead Guest House ★★★
Guest Accommodation
11 Bembridge Crescent, Portsmouth
PO4 0QT
t (023) 9273 2362
e b.currie1@ntlworld.com
w homesteadguesthouse-southsea.co.uk

Lamorna Guest House ★★
Guest Accommodation
23 Victoria Road South, Portsmouth
PO5 2BX
t (023) 9281 1157
e merry_kerry2003@yahoo.co.uk
w lamornaguesthouse.co.uk

Stattons ★★★★★
Guest Accommodation
6 Florence Road, Portsmouth
PO5 2NE
t (023) 9282 3409
e woodvillehotel@boltblue.com

Waverley Park Lodge Guest House ★★★ *Guest Accommodation*
99 Waverley Road, Portsmouth
PO5 2PL
t (023) 9273 0402
e waverleyparklodge@yahoo.co.uk
w waverleyparklodge.co.uk

RINGWOOD

Auld Kennels ★★★★
Bed & Breakfast
215 Christchurch Road, Ringwood
BH24 3AN
t (01425) 475170
e auldkennels@aol.com
w auldkennels.co.uk

Avonmead House ★★★★
Bed & Breakfast **SILVER AWARD**
16 Salisbury Road, Ringwood
BH24 1AS
t (01425) 475531
e chrissie.peckham@talktalk.net
w avonmeadhouse.co.uk

Moortown Lodge ★★★★
Guest Accommodation
SILVER AWARD
244 Christchurch Road, Ringwood
BH24 3AS
t (01425) 471404
e enquiries@moortownlodge.co.uk
w moortownlodge.co.uk

Torre Avon ★★★★ *Bed & Breakfast*
SILVER AWARD
21 Salisbury Road, Ringwood
BH24 1AS
t (01425) 472769
e b&b@torreavon.freeserve.co.uk
w torreavon.freeserve.co.uk

ROCKBOURNE

Ducks Nest B&B ★★★★★
Guest Accommodation - Room Only
SILVER AWARD
Ducks Nest, Tenantry Farm, Rockbourne, Hampshire
SP6 3PA
t 01725 518 657
e treborlodge@btinternet.com
w bnb-ducksnest.co.uk

ROMSEY

The Chalet Guest House ★★★
Bed & Breakfast
105 Botley Road, Whitenap, Romsey
SO51 5RQ
t (01794) 517299
e thechalet@ntlworld.com

The Dairy at Packridge Farm
★★★★ *Bed & Breakfast*
SILVER AWARD
Packridge Lane, Toothill, Romsey
SO51 9LL
t (023) 8073 3073
e thedairy@packridgeestate.com
w packridgeestate.com

Pauncefoot House ★★★★
Bed & Breakfast
Pauncefoot Hill, Romsey
SO51 6AA
t (01794) 513139
e pauncefootbandb@aol.com
w pauncefoothouse.co.uk

Pyesmead Farm ★★★★
Farmhouse
Plaitford, Romsey
SO51 6EE
t (01794) 323386
e pyesmead@talk21.com
w pyesmeadfarm.co.uk

Ranvilles Farm House ★★★★★
Bed & Breakfast
Pauncefoot Hill, Romsey
SO51 6AA
t (023) 8081 4481
e info@ranvilles.com
w ranvilles.com

The Shoe Inn ★★★★ *Inn*
SILVER AWARD
Salisbury Road, Romsey
SO51 6EE
t (01794) 322397
e bookings@theshoeinn.co.uk
w theshoeinn.co.uk

Stoneymarsh Bed & Breakfast
★★★ *Bed & Breakfast*
Stoneymarsh Cottage, Stoneymarsh, Michelmersh, Romsey
SO51 0LB
t (01794) 368867
e mail@stoneymarshcottage.co.uk
w stoneymarshcottage.co.uk

The Sun Inn ★★★★ *Inn*
Winchester Road, Romsey
SO51 7JG
t (01794) 512255
e paulwilson121@btinternet.com

SELBORNE

Ivanhoe ★★★★ *Bed & Breakfast*
Oakhanger, Selborne
GU35 9JG
t (01420) 473464
w ivanhoe-bnb.co.uk

Thatched Barn House ★★★★
Bed & Breakfast
Gracious Street, Selborne, Alton
GU34 3JG
t (01420) 511007
e b&b@selborne.eu
w selborne.eu

SOUTHAMPTON

Alcantara Guest House ★★★★
Guest Accommodation
20 Howard Road, Shirley, Southampton
SO15 5BN
t (023) 8033 2966
e alcantaraguesthouse@sky.com
w alcantaraguesthouse.co.uk

South East | Hampshire

mberley Guest House ★★★★
uest Accommodation
 Howard Road, Shirley,
outhampton
O15 5BB
t (023) 8022 3789
e contact@amberleyguesthouse.co.uk
w amberleyguesthouse.co.uk

rgyle Lodge Guest House
★★★ Guest Accommodation
3 Landguard Road, Shirley,
outhampton
O15 5DL
t (023) 8022 4063
e judith@higgs1236.freeserve.co.uk
w argylelodge.com

sturias House ★★★★
uest Accommodation - Room Only
2 Howard Road, Southampton
O15 5BN
t (023) 8022 3372
e enquiries@asturiashouse.co.uk
w asturiashouse.co.uk

he Avenue Bed & Breakfast
★★ Bed & Breakfast
SILVER AWARD
9 The Avenue, Southampton
O17 1XF
t (023) 8022 1450
e theavenuebandb@aol.com
w southamptonbandb.co.uk/

anister Guest House ★★★★
uest Accommodation
1 Brighton Road, Southampton
O15 2JJ
t (023) 8022 1279
e info@banisterhotel.co.uk
w banisterhotel.co.uk

runswick Lodge ★★★★
uest Accommodation
00 Anglesea Road, Shirley,
outhampton
O15 5QS
t (023) 8077 4777
e brunswick.lodge@btconnect.com
w brunswicklodge.co.uk

aton Court ★★★
uest Accommodation
2 Hill Lane, Southampton
O15 5AY
t (023) 8022 3081
e ecourthot@aol.com
w eatoncourtsouthampton.co.uk

lenborough House ★★★
uest Accommodation
72 Hill Lane, Southampton
O15 5DB
t (023) 8022 1716
e ellenborough.house@googlemail.com
w ellenboroughhouse.co.uk

enland Guest House ★★★
uest Accommodation
9 Hill Lane, Southampton
O15 5AD
t (023) 8022 0360
e fenland@btconnect.com
w fenlandguesthouse.co.uk

azmina Place
uest Accommodation
pham Street, Southampton
O32 1JA
t (01489) 861240

andguard House Guest House
★★★ Guest House
4 Landguard Road, Southampton
O15 5DP
t (023) 8022 9708
e enquiries@landguardhouse.co.uk
w landguardhouse.co.uk

inden Guest House ★★★
Guest House
1-53 The Polygon, Southampton
O15 2BP
t (023) 8022 5653
e trisha@lindenguesthouse.net
w lindenguesthouse.net

Madison House ★★★
Guest Accommodation
137 Hill Lane, Southampton
SO15 5AF
t (023) 8033 3374
e foley@madisonhouse.co.uk
w madisonhouse.co.uk

Mayfair Guest House ★★★★
Guest House
11 Landguard Road, Southampton
SO15 5DL
t (023) 8022 9861
e info@themayfairguesthouse.co.uk
w themayfairguesthouse.co.uk

Mayview Guest House ★★
Guest Accommodation
30 The Polygon, Southampton
SO15 2BN
t (023) 8022 0907
e info@mayview.co.uk
w mayview.co.uk

Netley Village Bed & Breakfast
★★★ Guest Accommodation
New Road, Netley Abbey,
Southampton
SO31 5BS
t (023) 8045 2414
e netleyvillage.bandb@ntlworld.com
w netleyvillagebandb.com

Pilgrim Inn ★★★★★ Inn
SILVER AWARD
Hythe Road, Marchwood,
Southampton
SO40 4WU
t (023) 8086 7752
e pilgrim.inn@fullers.co.uk
w fullershotels.com

Rivendell Guest House ★★★★
Guest Accommodation
19 Landguard Road, Hill Lane,
Southampton
SO15 5DL
t (023) 8022 3240
e rivendelllalley@talktalkbusiness.net
w rivendellguesthousesouthampton.co.uk/

Trenerry House Bed and Breakfast ★★★ Bed & Breakfast
66 Redbridge Road, Redbridge,
Southampton, SO15 0LU
SO15 0LU
t (023) 8077 5273
e diana.gange@hotmail.com
w trenerryhouse.co.uk

SOUTHSEA

Abbey Lodge ★★★ Guest House
30 Waverley Road, Southsea
PO5 2PW
t (023) 9282 8285
e linda@abbeylodge.co.uk
w abbeylodge.co.uk

The Retreat ★★★★ Guest House
GOLD AWARD
35 Grove Road South, Portsmouth
PO5 3QS
t (023) 9235 3701
e theretreatguesthouse@yahoo.co.uk
w theretreatguesthouse.co.uk

University of Portsmouth Conference & Lettings ★★★
Guest Accommodation
Queen Elizabeth the Queen Mother Hall, Furze Lane, Portsmouth
PO4 8LW
t (023) 9284 4567

SPARSHOLT

The Wessex Centre ★★★
Guest Accommodation
Sparsholt, Winchester
SO21 2NF
t (01962) 797259
e info@thewessexcentre.co.uk
w thewessexcentre.co.uk

STOCKBRIDGE

The White Hart Inn ★★★★ Inn
SILVER AWARD
High Street, Stockbridge
SO20 6HF
t (01264) 810663
e whitehart.stockbridge@fullers.co.uk
w fullershotels.co.uk

SWAY

Manor Farm ★★★ Farmhouse
Manor Farm, Coombe Lane, Sway
SO41 6BP
t (01590) 683542

Tiverton ★★★★ Bed & Breakfast
SILVER AWARD
9 Cruse Close, Sway, Lymington
SO41 6AY
t (01590) 683092
e ronrowe@talk21.com
w tivertonnewforest.co.uk

UPPER FARRINGDON

Old Timbers ★★★★
Bed & Breakfast
1 Crows Lane, Farringdon, Alton
GU34 3ED
t (01420) 588449
e info@oldtimberscottage.co.uk
w oldtimberscottage.co.uk

Tangley Hall ★★★★
Bed & Breakfast
The Street, Upper Farringdon, Alton
GU34 3DT
t (01420) 588105
e elizabeth@tangleyhall.co.uk
w tangleyhall.co.uk

UPPER FROYLE

West End Farm ★★★★ Farmhouse
Upper Froyle, Alton
GU34 4JG
t (01420) 22130
e westend@hampshirebedandbreakfast.co.uk
w hampshirebedandbreakfast.co.uk

WATERLOOVILLE

Fairways ★★★★ Bed & Breakfast
SILVER AWARD
98A The Brow, Waterlooville
PO7 5DA
t (023) 9271 1711
e info@fairwaysbedandbreakfast.co.uk
w fairwaysbedandbreakfast.co.uk

The Hampshire Hog ★★★★★ Inn
Gravel Hill, Waterlooville
PO8 0QD
t (023) 9259 1083
e hampshirehog@fullers.co.uk
w fullershotels.com

Newhaven Bed & Breakfast ★★★
Bed & Breakfast
193 London Road, Waterlooville
PO7 7RN
t (023) 9226 8559
e newhavenbnb@sky.com.
w smoothhound.co.uk/hotels/newhavenbedandbreakfast.html

WHITCHURCH

Peak House Farm ★★★ Farmhouse
Cole Henley, Whitchurch
RG28 7QJ
t (01256) 892052
e peakhouse.farm@btinternet.com
w peakhousefarm.co.uk

WINCHESTER

5 Clifton Terrace ★★★★
Bed & Breakfast SILVER AWARD
5 Clifton Terrace, Winchester
SO22 5BJ
t (01962) 890053
e cliftonterrace@hotmail.co.uk

12 Christchurch Road ★★★
Bed & Breakfast
12 Christchurch Road, Winchester
SO23 9SR
t (01962) 854272 / 0787 985 0076
e pjspatton@yahoo.co.uk

53a Parchment Street ★★★
Bed & Breakfast
Winchester
SO23 8BA
t (01962) 849962

58 Hyde Street ★★★
Bed & Breakfast
Hyde Street, Winchester
SO23 7DY
t (01962) 854646
e gj.harvey@ntlworld.com
w 58hydestreet.co.uk

152 Teg Down Meads ★★★
Bed & Breakfast
Winchester
SO22 5NS
t (01962) 862628
e l.chalk4@ntlworld.com

Cheriton House ★★★
Bed & Breakfast
61 Cheriton Road, Winchester
SO22 5AY
t (01962) 620374
e cheritonhouse@hotmail.com

City Guest House ★★
Bed & Breakfast
6 Moss Road, Winchester
SO23 8DP
t (01962) 867026
e lynndurling@o2oo.freeserve.co.uk

Complyns B&B ★★★★
Bed & Breakfast
Chilcomb, Winchester
SO21 1HT
t (01962) 861600
w complyns.co.uk

Dawn Cottage ★★★★★
Bed & Breakfast SILVER AWARD
99 Romsey Road, Winchester
SO22 5PQ
t (01962) 869956
e dawncottage@hotmail.com

Dolphin House Studios ★★★★
Guest Accommodation - Room Only
SILVER AWARD
3 Compton Road, Winchester
SO23 9SL
t (01962) 853284
e bookings@dolphinhousestudios.co.uk
w dolphinhousestudios.co.uk

Giffard House ★★★★★
Guest Accommodation
GOLD AWARD
50 Christchurch Road, St Cross,
Winchester
SO23 9SU
t (01962) 852628
e giffardhotel@aol.com
w giffardhotel.co.uk

Hatch End ★★★★ Bed & Breakfast
Main Road, Itchen Abbas,
Winchester
SO21 1AT
t (01962) 779279
e info@hatchendbandb.co.uk
w hatchendbandb.co.uk

Highfield Cottage ★★★★
Bed & Breakfast
Old Rectory Lane, Twyford,
Winchester
SO21 1NR
t (01962) 712921
e highfieldcottage@gmail.com
w smoothhound.co.uk/hotels/highfieldcott.html

The King Alfred Public House ★★★★ Inn
11 Saxon Road, Hyde, Winchester
SO23 7DJ
t (01962) 854370
e thekingalfredpub@yahoo.co.uk
w thekingalfred.co.uk

Lainston ★★★ Bed & Breakfast
Lainston Close, Winchester
SO22 5LJ
t (01962) 866072
e j.carlick@btinternet.com
w lainston.co.uk

South East | Hampshire/Isle of Wight

The Lilacs ★★ *Bed & Breakfast*
1 Harestock Close, Winchester
SO22 6NP
t (01962) 884122
e susanm.pell@ntlworld.com
w smoothhound.co.uk/hotels/lilacs.html

Little Mead ★★★★ *Bed & Breakfast*
Home Lane, Sparsholt, Winchester
SO21 2NN
t (01962) 776204
e stay@little-mead.com
w little-mead.com

Orchard House ★★★
Bed & Breakfast
Manor Farm, Twyford, Winchester
SO21 1RJ
t (01962) 712087
e smflemons@googlemail.com
w orchardhousetwyford.co.uk

R J & V J Weller ★★★
Bed & Breakfast
63 Upper Brook Street, Winchester
SO23 8DG
t (01962) 620367
e robert.weller55@googlemail.com

Staddle Stones ★★★★
Bed & Breakfast SILVER AWARD
15b Bereweeke Avenue, Winchester
SO22 6BH
t (01962) 877883
e staddle-stones@hotmail.co.uk
w staddle-stones.co.uk

St John's Croft ★★★
Bed & Breakfast
St Johns Street, Winchester
SO23 0HF
t (01962) 859976
e dottyfraser@gmail.com

St Margaret's ★★★
Bed & Breakfast
St Margaret's, 3 St Michael's Road, Winchester
SO23 9JE
t (01962) 861450
e brigid@bbrett.f2s.com
w stmargaretsbandb.com

Twyford House ★★★★
Bed & Breakfast
High Street, Twyford, Winchester
SO21 1NJ
t (01962) 713114
e crchtwyho@aol.com
w twyfordhousebnb.co.uk

Windy Ridge ★★★ *Bed & Breakfast*
GOLD AWARD
99 Andover Road, Winchester
SO22 6AX
t (01962) 882527
e angela.westall@virgin.net

The Wykeham Arms ★★★★ *Inn*
75 Kingsgate Street, Winchester
SO23 9PE
t (01962) 853834
e wykeham.arms@fullers.co.uk
w fullershotels.co.uk

Isle of Wight

ARRETON

Arreton Manor ★★★★★
Bed & Breakfast GOLD AWARD
Main Road, Arreton
PO30 3AA
t (01983) 522604
e arreton@arretonmanor.co.uk
w arretonmanor.co.uk

BEMBRIDGE

Breakfast at Tiffany's ★★★★
Bed & Breakfast
40 Forelands Road, Bembridge
PO35 5XW
t (01983) 874665
e tiffanyrichardbandb@hotmail.com
w tiffanysbandb.com

Ivar Cottage "Summer House" ★★★★ *Guest Accommodation*
Hillway Road, Bembridge
PO35 5PJ
t 07969 647914
e contact@ivarcottagesummerhouse.co.uk
w ivarcottagesummerhouse.co.uk

St Veronica's ★★★★★
Guest Accommodation
Lane End Road, Bembridge
PO35 5TB
t (01983) 872872
e theresa@stveronicasiow.co.uk
w stveronicasiow.co.uk

BINSTEAD

Newnham Farm ★★★★★
Farmhouse SILVER AWARD
Newnham Lane, Binstead
PO33 4ED
t (01983) 882423
e di@newnhamfarm.co.uk
w newnhamfarm.co.uk

Sillwood Acre ★★★★
Bed & Breakfast SILVER AWARD
Church Road, Binstead
PO33 3TB
t (01983) 563553
e debbie@sillwood-acre.co.uk
w sillwood-acre.co.uk

BONCHURCH

The Lake ★★★★
Guest Accommodation
Shore Road, Bonchurch
PO38 1RF
t (01983) 852613
e enquiries@lakehotel.co.uk
w lakehotel.co.uk

Westfield House ★★★★
Bed & Breakfast
Shore Road, Bonchurch
PO38 1RF
t (01983) 853232
e garethhughesiow@hotmail.co.uk

Winterbourne Country House ★★★★★ *Guest House*
GOLD AWARD
Bonchurch Village Road, Bonchurch
PO38 1RQ
t (01983) 852535
e info@winterbournehouse.co.uk
w winterbournehouse.co.uk

BRIGHSTONE

Chilton Farm B&B ★★★★
Farmhouse
Chilton Farm, Chilton Lane, Brighstone
PO30 4DS
t (01983) 740338
e info@chiltonfarm.co.uk
w chiltonfarm.co.uk

The Lodge Brighstone ★★★★
Guest Accommodation
Main Road, Brighstone
PO30 4DJ
t (01983) 741272
e paul@thelodgebrighstone.com
w thelodgebrighstone.com

Mottistone Manor Farmhouse
★★★★ *Guest Accommodation*
Mottistone, Near Brighstone, South West Wight
PO30 4ED
t (01983) 740207
e bookings@bolthols.co.uk
w bolthols.co.uk

Seven Bed & Breakfast ★★★
Guest Accommodation
Main Road, Brighstone
PO30 4AH
t (01983) 740370
e bookings@visitseven.co.uk
w visitseven.co.uk

CARISBROOKE

Alvington Manor Farm ★★★
Guest Accommodation
Manor Farm Lane, Carisbrooke
PO30 5SP
t (01983) 523463
e info@islandbreaks.co.uk

Idlecombe Farm ★★★ *Farmhouse*
Bowcombe Road, Carisbrooke
PO30 3JB
t (01983) 522593
e rosemariesmith65@hotmail.co.uk

CHALE

Sunacre B&B ★★ *Bed & Breakfast*
The Terrace, Chale
PO38 2HL
t (01983) 731611
e butterfly@paraglide.uk.com
w paraglide.uk.com

COWES

Endeavour House ★★★★
Bed & Breakfast
47 Mill Hill Road, West Cowes
PO31 7EG
t (01983) 297406
e enquiries@endeavourhousecowes.co.uk
w endeavourhousecowes.co.uk

Hillbrow House ★★★★
Guest Accommodation
Tuttons Hill, Cowes
PO31 8JA
t (01983) 297240
e hill-brow@btconnect.com

EAST COWES

Crossways House ★★★★
Guest Accommodation
SILVER AWARD
Crossways Road, East Cowes
PO32 6LJ
t (01983) 298282
e enquiries@bedbreakfast-cowes.co.uk
w bedbreakfast-cowes.co.uk

Wisteria House ★★★★
Bed & Breakfast
191 York Avenue, East Cowes
PO32 6BE
t (01983) 295999
e philgillan@hotmail.co.uk

FRESHWATER

Braewood ★★★★ *Bed & Breakfast*
Afton Road, Freshwater
PO40 9TP
t (01983) 759910
e enquiries@braewood-iow.co.uk
w braewood-iow.co.uk

Freshwater Bay House ★★★★
Guest Accommodation
Freshwater Bay House, Freshwater Bay, Freshwater
PO40 9RB
t (020) 8511 1534

The Orchards ★★★★
Bed & Breakfast
Princes Road, Freshwater
PO40 9ED
t (01983) 753795
e paulaattheorchards@googlemail.com
w theorchardsbandb.co.uk

Rockstone Cottage ★★★★
Guest House
Colwell Chine Road, Freshwater
PO40 9NR
t (01983) 753723
e enquiries@rockstonecottage.co.uk
w rockstonecottage.co.uk

Seahorses ★★★★
Guest Accommodation
Victoria Road, Freshwater, Isle-of-Wight
PO40 9PP
t (01983) 752574
e seahorses-iow@tiscali.co.uk
w seahorsesisleofwight.com

Sunnyside B&B ★★
Bed & Breakfast
119 School Green Road, Freshwate
PO40 9AZ
t (01983) 752451
e ctjmurph@hotmail.com

FRESHWATER BAY

Heather Cottage B&B ★★★★
Bed & Breakfast
Afton Road, Freshwater Bay
PO40 9TP
t (01983) 754319
e heathercottbb@aol.com

GURNARD

The Woodvale ★★★★ *Inn*
1 Princes Esplanade, Gurnard
PO31 8LE
t (01983) 292037
e info@the-woodvale.co.uk
w the-woodvale.co.uk

HULVERSTONE

The Elms ★★★★ *Bed & Breakfast*
The Elms, Hulverstone
PO30 4EH
t (01983) 741528
e theelmsbnb@aol.com
w theelmsbnb.com

LAKE

Cliff Lodge Guest House ★★★★
Guest House
13 Cliff Path, Lake
PO36 8PL
t 01983 402963
e clifflodge@uwclub.net
w cliff-lodge-isle-of-wight.co.uk

Haytor Lodge ★★★★
Guest Accommodation
16 Cliff Path, Lake
PO36 8PL
t (01983) 402969
e info@islandbreaks.co.uk

Osterley Lodge ★★★★
Guest Accommodation
62 Sandown Road, Lake
PO36 9JX
t (01983) 402017
e osterleylodgeiw@aol.com
w wightstay.co.uk/basic/osterley.html

NEWCHURCH

Rosemary Cottage ★★★★
Bed & Breakfast SILVER AWARD
Langbridge, Newchurch
PO36 0NP
t (01983) 867735
e info@rosemarycottagebreaks.co.uk
w rosemarycottagebreaks.co.uk

NEWPORT

Forest View B&B ★★★★
Bed & Breakfast
1 Forest View, Marks Corner, Newport
PO30 5UD
t (01983) 295578
e janet@forestviewbb.co.uk
w forestviewbb.co.uk

The Meadows B&B ★★★★
Bed & Breakfast
57 Mountbatten Drive, Newport
PO30 5SJ
t 07896 844649
e themeadows.isleofwight@googlemail.com
w themeadowsnewport.com

Newport Quay ★★★★
Guest Accommodation
41 Quay Street, Newport
PO30 5BA
t (01983) 528544
e enquiries@newportquayhotel.co.uk
w newportquayhotel.co.uk

South East | Isle of Wight

NEWPORT (3 MILES)

reewaters ★★★★
Guest Accommodation
ILVER AWARD
ew Barn Lane, Gatcombe, NR
ewport
O30 3EQ
t (01983) 721439
e john@pitstopmodels.demon.co.uk
 colourpointdesign.co.uk/freew
aters

NITON

he Enchanted Manor ★★★★★
Guest Accommodation
GOLD AWARD
t Catherine's Point, Sandrock Road,
liton
O38 2NG
t (01983) 730215
e info@enchantedmanor.co.uk
 enchantedmanor.co.uk

PORCHFIELD

oungwoods Farm ★★★
armhouse
hitehouse Road, Porchfield
O30 4LJ
t (01983) 522170
e judith@youngwoods.com
 youngwoods.com

ROOKLEY

ennerley House - B&B ★★★★
Bed & Breakfast **SILVER AWARD**
ain Road, Rookley
O38 3NB
t (01983) 842001
e carolfoote@btinternet.com
 kennerleyhouse.com

RYDE

bingdon Lodge *Bed & Breakfast*
9-20 West Street, Ryde
O33 2QQ
t (01983) 564537
e abingdonlodge@aol.com
 abingdonlodge.co.uk

laverton House Bed & Breakfast
★★★★ *Bed & Breakfast*
laverton House, 12 The Strand,
yde
O33 1JE
t (01983) 613015
e clavertonhouse@aol.com
 clavertonhouse.co.uk

orset House ★★★
Guest Accommodation
1 Dover Street, Ryde
O33 2BW
t (01983) 564327
e hoteldorset@aol.com
 thedorsethotel.co.uk

ern Cottage ★★ *Bed & Breakfast*
West Street, Ryde
O33 2NW
t (01983) 565856
e sandra@psdferguson.freeserve.co.uk

encombe House ★★★★
Bed & Breakfast
ewnham Road, Ryde
O33 3TH
t (01983) 567910

ea View B&B ★★★★
Bed & Breakfast
Dover Street, Ryde
O33 2AQ
t (01983) 810976
e seaviewbandbinryde@hotmail.com

SANDFORD

he Barn ★★★★ *Farmhouse*
ILVER AWARD
ound Farm, Shanklin Road,
andford
O38 3AW
t (01983) 840047
e barnpoundfarm@barnpoundfarm.free-online.co.uk
 sites.google.com/site/isleo
fwight2010/home

SANDOWN

Ashleigh House ★★★★
Guest Accommodation
81 Sandown Road, Lake, Sandown
PO36 9LE
t (01983) 402340
e richard@ashleighhousehotel.com
w ashleighhousehotel.com

Beaufort House ★★★★
Guest House
30 Broadway, Sandown
PO36 9BY
t (01983) 403672
e web@thebeaufortsandown.co.uk
w thebeaufortsandown.co.uk

The Belmore ★★★★ *Guest House*
101 Station Avenue, Sandown
PO36 8HD
t (01983) 404189
e belmorebandb@aol.com
w thebelmore.co.uk

Bernay ★★★★
Guest Accommodation
24 Victoria Road, Sandown
PO36 8AL
t (01983) 402205
e info@thebernayhotel.co.uk
w thebernayhotel.co.uk

The Caprera ★★★★ *Guest House*
Melville Street, Sandown
PO36 8LE
t (01983) 402482
e info@caprerahotel.com
w caprerahotel.com

Copperfield Lodge ★★★★
Bed & Breakfast **SILVER AWARD**
Newport Road, Apse Heath,
Sandown
PO36 9PJ
t 07733 262889
e copperfieldlodge@aol.com

The Denewood ★★★★
Guest Accommodation
7-9 Victoria Road, Sandown
PO36 8AL
t (01983) 402980
e holidays@denewoodhotel.co.uk
w denewood-hotel.co.uk

The Fernside ★★★★ *Guest House*
30 Station Avenue, Sandown
PO36 9BW
t (01983) 402356
e enquiries@thefernside.co.uk
w thefernside.co.uk

Inglewood Guest House ★★★★
Guest House
15 Avenue Road, Sandown
PO36 8BN
t (01983) 403485
e inglewooduk@yahoo.com
w inglewoodguesthouse-iow.co.uk

The Montpelier ★★★
Guest Accommodation
5 Pier Street, Sandown
PO36 8JR
t (01983) 403964
e steve@themontpelier.co.uk
w themontpelier.co.uk

The Philomel Guest House ★★★
Guest House
21 Carter Street, Sandown
PO36 8BL
t (01983) 406413
e enquiries@philomel-hotel.co.uk
w philomel-hotel.co.uk

Piers View Guest House ★★★★
Guest Accommodation
20 Cliff Path, Lake
PO36 8PL
t (01983) 404646
e info@islandbreaks.co.uk

Rooftree ★★★★ *Guest House*
26 The Broadway, Sandown
PO36 9BY
t (01983) 403175
e rooftree@btconnect.com
w rooftree-hotel.co.uk

The Sandhill ★★★
Guest Accommodation
6 Hill Street, Sandown
PO36 9DB
t (01983) 403635
e sandhillsandown@aol.com
w sandhill-hotel.co.uk

Sandown Manor ★★★
Guest House
Yaverland Road, Sandown
PO36 8QP
t (01983) 402266
e sandownmanor@yahoo.co.uk
w sandownmanor.co.uk

Southwood House ★★★
Guest Accommodation
26 Albert Road, Sandown
PO36 8AW
t (01983) 407297
e southwoodhouse@aol.com
w southwoodhouse.co.uk

St Catherines ★★★★
Guest Accommodation
1 Winchester Park Road, Sandown
PO36 8HJ
t (01983) 402392
e info@stcatherines-hotel.co.uk
w stcatherines-hotel.co.uk

St Michaels ★★★★
Guest Accommodation
33 Leed Street, Sandown
PO36 8JE
t (01983) 403636
e stmichaelsiow@btconnect.com
w stmichaelsiow.com

Treval Guest House ★★★★
Bed & Breakfast **SILVER AWARD**
46 Culver Way, Yaverland, Sandown
PO36 8QJ
t (01983) 407910
e valnewton@talktalk.net
w treval-sandown.co.uk

SEAVIEW

1 Cluniac Cottages ★★★
Bed & Breakfast **SILVER AWARD**
Priory Road, Seaview
PO34 5BU
t (01983) 812119
e bill.elfenjay@virgin.net
w cluniaccottages.co.uk

Clover Ridge ★★★★
Bed & Breakfast **SILVER AWARD**
18 Horestone Rise, Seaview
PO34 5DB
t (01983) 617377
e cloverridge.seaviewiow@virgin.net
w cloverridge.co.uk

SHANKLIN

The Appley ★★★★ *Guest House*
13 Queens Road, Shanklin
PO37 6AW
t (01983) 862666
e rod.folds@virgin.net
w theappley.com

Bedford Lodge ★★★★
Guest Accommodation
SILVER AWARD
Eastcliff Road, Shanklin
PO37 6AA
t (01983) 862416
e info@bedfordlodge.co.uk
w bedfordlodge.co.uk

The Birkdale ★★★★ *Guest House*
SILVER AWARD
5 Grange Road, Shanklin
PO37 6NN
t (01983) 862949
e birkdale-iow@hotmail.com
w birkdalehotel.com

Brooke House ★★★ *Guest House*
2 St Pauls Avenue, Shanklin
PO37 7AL
t (01983) 863162
e brookehouse@btconnect.com
w brookehousehotel.co.uk

The Chestnuts ★★★★ *Guest House*
4 Hope Road, Shanklin
PO37 6EA
t (01983) 862162
e info@thechestnutsshanklin.co.uk
w thechestnutsshanklin.co.uk

Claremont Guest House ★★★★
Guest House
4 Eastmount Road, Shanklin
PO37 6DN
t (01983) 862083
e claremont@dsl.pipex.com
w claremontshanklin.co.uk

Clarence House B&B ★★★★
Guest Accommodation
2 Clarence Gardens, Shanklin, Isle of Wight
PO37 6HA
t 01983 865090
e graeme.sheridan-wallis@fsmail.net
w clarencehousebb.co.uk

Cliftonville Guest House ★★★
Guest House
6 Hope Road, Shanklin
PO37 6EA
t (01983) 862197
e info@cliftonvillehotel.wanadoo.co.uk
w cliftonvilleguesthouse.co.uk

The Edgecliffe ★★★★
Guest Accommodation
7 Clarence Gardens, Shanklin
PO37 6HA
t (01983) 866199
e edgecliffehtl@aol.com
w wightonline.co.uk/edgecliffehotel

The Fawley Guest House ★★★★
Guest House
12 Hope Road, Shanklin
PO37 6EA
t (01983) 868898
e enquiries@the-fawley.co.uk
w the-fawley.co.uk

Foxhills ★★★★★
Guest Accommodation
GOLD AWARD
30 Victoria Avenue, Shanklin
PO37 6LS
t (01983) 862329
e info@foxhillsofshanklin.co.uk
w foxhillsofshanklin.co.uk

Grange Bank House ★★★★
Guest Accommodation
SILVER AWARD
Grange Road, Shanklin
PO37 6NN
t (01983) 862337
e grangebank@btinternet.com
w grangebank.co.uk

The Havelock ★★★★
Guest Accommodation
SILVER AWARD
2 Queens Road, Shanklin
PO37 6AN
t (01983) 862747
e info@havelockhotel.co.uk
w havelockhotel.co.uk

The Hazelwood ★★★ *Guest House*
14 Clarence Road, Shanklin
PO37 7BH
t (01983) 862824
e hazelwoodiow@aol.com
w hazelwoodiow.co.uk

Heatherleigh Guest House ★★★★
Guest House **SILVER AWARD**
17 Queens Road, Shanklin
PO37 6AW
t (01983) 862503
e enquiries@heatherleigh.co.uk
w heatherleigh.co.uk

Holly Lodge ★★★★
Guest Accommodation
29 Queens Road, Shanklin
PO37 6DQ
t (01983) 863604
e hollylodge.iow@btinternet.com
w hollylodge-iow.co.uk

or **key to symbols** see page 6

271

South East | Isle of Wight/Kent

The Kenbury ★★★★
Guest Accommodation
SILVER AWARD
Clarence Road, Shanklin
PO37 7BH
t (01983) 862085
e kenbury@isleofwighthotel.co.uk
w isleofwighthotel.co.uk

The Lincoln ★★★★ *Guest House*
30 Littlestairs Road, Shanklin
PO37 6HS
t (01983) 861171
e bookings@thelincoln.org.uk
w thelincoln.org.uk

The Miclaran ★★★★ *Guest House*
37 Littlestairs Road, Shanklin
PO37 6HS
t (01983) 862726
e miclaran@btinternet.com
w miclaran.co.uk

Mount House ★★★ *Guest House*
20 Arthurs Hill, Shanklin
PO37 6EE
t (01983) 862556
e graham.mounthouse@btopenworld.com
w wightstay.co.uk/mount.html

Overstrand ★★★★
Guest Accommodation
5 Howard Road, Shanklin
PO37 6HD
t (01983) 862100
e enquiries@overstrandhotel.co.uk
w overstrandhotel.co.uk

Palmerston ★★★
Guest Accommodation
Palmerston Road, Shanklin
PO37 6AS
t (01983) 865547
e info@palmerston-hotel.co.uk
w palmerston-hotel.co.uk

The Parkway ★★★★ *Guest House*
6 Park Road, Shanklin
PO37 6AZ
t (01983) 862740
e info@parkwayhotelshanklin.co.uk
w parkwayhotelshanklin.co.uk

Rosemary B&B ★★★★
Bed & Breakfast **SILVER AWARD**
87 Victoria Avenue, Shanklin
PO37 6QN
t (01983) 861440
e nod@rosemaryb-b.co.uk
w rosemaryb-b.co.uk

The Royson ★★★★ *Guest House*
26 Littlestairs Road, Shanklin
PO37 6HS
t (01983) 862163
e info@theroyson.co.uk
w theroyson.co.uk

The Ryedale ★★★
Guest Accommodation
3 Atherley Road, Shanklin
PO37 7AT
t (01983) 862375
e hayley@ryedale-hotel.co.uk
w ryedale-hotel.co.uk

Snowdon House ★★★★
Guest Accommodation
SILVER AWARD
19 Queens Road, Shanklin
PO37 6AW
t (01983) 862853
e info@snowdonhotel.fsnet.co.uk
w thesnowdonhotel.co.uk

Somerville ★★★★
Guest Accommodation
14 St Georges Road, Shanklin
PO37 6BA
t (01983) 862821
e somerville@fsmail.net

Steamer Inn - Quayside Leisure ★★★★ *Inn*
18 The Esplanade, Shanklin
PO37 6BS
t (01983) 862641
e info@thesteamer.co.uk
w thesteamer.co.uk

The St Leonards ★★★★
Guest Accommodation
SILVER AWARD
22 Queens Road, Shanklin
PO37 6AW
t (01983) 862121
e info@thestleonards.co.uk
w thestleonards.co.uk

Swiss Cottage ★★★★
Guest Accommodation
SILVER AWARD
10 St Georges Road, Shanklin
PO37 6BA
t (01983) 862333
e info@swiss-cottage.co.uk
w swiss-cottage.co.uk

The Triton ★★★ *Guest House*
23 Atherley Road, Shanklin
PO37 7AU
t (01983) 862494
e jackie@iow-accommodation.com
w iow-accommodation.com

Victoria Lodge ★★★★
Guest Accommodation
5 Alexandra Road, Shanklin
PO37 6AF
t (01983) 862361
e info@victorialodgehotel.com
w victorialodgehotel.com

Westbury Lodge ★★★★
Guest Accommodation
SILVER AWARD
25 Queens Road, Shanklin
PO37 6AW
t (01983) 864926
e enquiries@westburylodge.co.uk
w westburylodge.co.uk

YMCA Winchester House ★★★
Group Hostel
Sandown Road, Shanklin
PO37 6HT
t (01983) 862411
e winchesterhouse@ymca-fg.org
w ymca-fg.org/winchesterhouse

SHORWELL

Northcourt ★★★★
Guest Accommodation
Northcourt, Main Road, Shorwell
PO30 3JG
t (01983) 740415
e enquiries@northcourt.info
w northcourt.info

Westcourt Farm ★★★★
Farmhouse **SILVER AWARD**
Limerstone Road, Shorwell
PO30 3LA
t (01983) 740233
e julie@westcourt-farm.co.uk
w westcourt-farm.co.uk

ST LAWRENCE

Lisle Combe ★★★
Guest Accommodation
Bank End Farm, Undercliff Drive, St Lawrence
PO38 1UW
t (01983) 852582
e lislecombe@yahoo.com
w lislecombe.co.uk

Little Orchard ★★★★
Guest Accommodation
Undercliff Drive, St Lawrence
PO38 1YA
t (01983) 731106
e info@islandbreaks.co.uk

TOTLAND

Chart House ★★★★
Guest Accommodation
SILVER AWARD
Madeira Road, Totland Bay, Totland
PO39 0BJ
t (01983) 755091
e info@islandbreaks.co.uk

TOTLAND BAY

Clifton House ★★★★
Guest Accommodation
Colwell Common Road, Totland Bay
PO39 0DD
t (01983) 753237
e clifton.house@btinternet.com
w cliftonhouse-iow.co.uk

The Granville ★★★★
Bed & Breakfast **SILVER AWARD**
Granville Road, Totland Bay, Isle of Wight
PO39 0AZ
t (01983) 756030
e granvilleiow@googlemail.com
w the-granville.co.uk

Littledene Lodge ★★★
Guest House
Granville Road, Totland Bay
PO39 0AX
t (01983) 752411
e littledenehotel@aol.com

Totland Bay YHA ★★★ *Hostel*
Hurst Hill, Totland Bay
PO39 0HD
t (01983) 752165
e totland@yha.org.uk
w yha.org.uk

VENTNOR

Brunswick House ★★★★
Guest House
Victoria Street, Ventnor
PO38 1ET
t (01983) 852656
e enquiries@brunswickhouse-web.co.uk
w brunswickhouse-web.co.uk

The Hermitage Country House ★★★★★ *Guest Accommodation*
GOLD AWARD
St Catherines Down, Ventnor
PO38 2PD
t (01983) 730010
e enquiries@hermitage-iow.co.uk
w hermitage-iow.co.uk

The Leconfield ★★★★★
Guest Accommodation
GOLD AWARD
85 Leeson Road, Upper Bonchurch, Ventnor
PO38 1PU
t (01983) 852196
e enquiries@leconfieldhotel.com
w leconfieldhotel.com

Windsor Carlton ★★★★
Guest Accommodation
SILVER AWARD
5 Alexandra Gardens, Ventnor
PO38 1EE
t (01983) 852543
e windsorcarlton@btinternet.com
w windsorcarltonhotel.co.uk

WEST COWES

UKSA ★★★ *Hostel*
Arctic Road, West Cowes
PO31 7PQ
t (01983) 294941
e info@uksa.org
w uksa.org

Windward House ★★★★
Guest Accommodation
69 Mill Hill Road, West Cowes
PO31 7EQ
t (01983) 280940
e info@islandbreaks.co.uk

WOOTTON

Grange Farm B&B ★★★★
Farmhouse **SILVER AWARD**
Grange Farm, Staplers Road, Wootton
PO33 4RW
t (01983) 882147
e info@grange-farm-holidays.co.uk
w grange-farm-holidays.co.uk

YARMOUTH

Ivy Cottage ★★★★
Guest Accommodation
SILVER AWARD
St James Street, Yarmouth
PO41 0NU
t (01983) 760117
e veronicaativycottage@btinternet.com
w ivycottageyarmouth.co.uk

Medlars ★★★ *Bed & Breakfast*
Halletts Shute, Yarmouth
PO41 0RH
t (01983) 761541
e e.grey855@btinternet.com
w milford.co.uk/go/medlars.html

Kent

ALDINGTON

Hogben Farm ★★★★ *Farmhouse*
Church Lane, Aldington, Ashford
TN25 7EH
t (01233) 720219
e ros@hogbenfarm.co.uk
w hogbenfarm.co.uk

ALKHAM

Alkham Court Farmhouse ★★★★★ *Farmhouse*
GOLD AWARD
Meggett Lane, South Alkham, Dover
CT15 7DG
t (01303) 892056
e wendy.burrows@alkhamcourt.co.uk
w alkhamcourt.co.uk

ASH

Molland House B&B ★★★★★
Guest Accommodation
GOLD AWARD
Molland Lane, Ash, Sandwich
CT3 2JB
t (01304) 814210
e tracy@mollandhouse.co.uk
w mollandhouse.co.uk

ASHFORD

Bishopsdale Oast *Bed & Breakfast*
Biddenden, Ashford
TN27 8DR
t (01580) 291027
e drysdale@bishopsdaleoast.co.uk
w bishopsdaleoast.co.uk

Bowl Inn ★★★★ *Inn*
Egg Hill Road, Charing, Ashford, Kent
TN27 0HG
t 01233 712256
e roomsvb@bowl-inn.co.uk
w bowl-inn.co.uk

Culvers ★★★★ *Bed & Breakfast*
Ball Lane, Kennington, Ashford
TN25 4EB
t (01233) 633018
e robinwm@btinternet.com

Curtis Farm ★★★★ *Farmhouse*
Waterman Quarter, Headcorn, Ashford
TN27 9JJ
t (01622) 890393
e curtis.farm@btopenworld.com
w curtis-farm-kent.co.uk

Downsview Guest House ★★★★
Guest Accommodation
Willesborough Road, Kennington, Ashford
TN24 9QP
t (01233) 621391
e downsviewguesthouse@msn.com
w ashforddownsview.co.uk

The New Flying Horse ★★★★ *Inn*
Upper Bridge Street, Wye, Ashford
TN25 5AN
t (01233) 812297
e newflyhorse@shepherdneame.co.uk
w newflyinghorsewye.co.uk

South East | Kent

ap Mill ★★★★
est Accommodation
LVER AWARD
nden Road, Smarden, Ashford
27 8RB
t (01233) 770333
e snapmill@aol.com
w snapmill.co.uk

e & Jim's Bed & Breakfast ★★
est Accommodation
Birling Road, Ashford
24 8BD
t (01233) 643069
e susan.mclaren1@ntlworld.com
w sueandjimsbandb.co.uk

ASHFORD (5 MILES)

an Court ★★★
est Accommodation
allock Lane, Westwell, Ashford
25 4NH
t (01233) 712924

AYLESFORD

ckham Lodge ★★★★★
est Accommodation
LD AWARD
h Street, Aylesford
20 7AY
t (01622) 717267
e wickhamlodge@aol.com
w wickhamlodge.co.uk

BETHERSDEN

derson Potters Farm ★★★
d & Breakfast
ssenden Lane, Bethersden,
hford
26 3JX
t (01233) 820341
e pottersfarms@aol.com
w pottersfarm.co.uk

e Old Stables ★★★★
est Accommodation
VER AWARD
ssenden, Bethersden, Ashford
26 3EL
t (01233) 820597
e pennygillespie@theoldstables.co.uk
w theoldstables.co.uk

BIDDENDEN

on Cottage ★★★★
est Accommodation
ldenden, Ashford
27 8HH
t (01580) 291358
e susantwort@hotmail.com
w heroncottage.info

hitfield Farm ★★★★
est Accommodation
VER AWARD
shmonden Lane, Biddenden,
hford
27 8BZ
t +44 (0) 1580 291092
e enquiries@whitfieldfarm.co.uk
w whitfieldfarm.co.uk

BLADBEAN

olehills ★★★★
est Accommodation
dbean, Canterbury
4 6LU
t (01303) 840051
e molehills84@hotmail.com
w molehillsbedbreakfast.co.uk

BOUGHTON-UNDER-BLEAN

d Stable *Hostel*
enley Farm, Brenley Lane,
versham
E13 9LY
t (01227) 751203

White Horse Inn ★★★★
Guest Accommodation
The Street, Boughton-under-Blean,
Faversham
ME13 9AX
t (01227) 751700
e whitehorse@shepherd-neame.co.uk
w shepherd-neame.co.uk

BOUGHTON MONCHELSEA

The Granary ★★★★
Bed & Breakfast
Lower Farm Road, Boughton
Monchelsea, Maidstone
ME17 4DD
t (01622) 743532
e sue@granarybandb.co.uk
w granarybandb.co.uk

BRASTED

The Mount House ★★★★
Bed & Breakfast
Brasted, Westerham
TN16 1JB
t (01959) 563617
e diana@themounthouse.com
w themounthouse.com

BRASTED CHART

The Orchard House ★★
Bed & Breakfast
Brasted Chart, Westerham
TN16 1LR
t (01959) 563702
e david.godsal@tesco.net

BRENCHLEY

Hononton Cottage ★★★★★
Bed & Breakfast **SILVER AWARD**
Palmers Green Lane, Nr Brenchley,
Tonbridge, Kent
TN12 7BJ
t (01892) 722483
e stay@hononcottage.co.uk
w hononcottage.co.uk

BROADSTAIRS

Anchor House ★★★★ *Guest House*
10 Chandos Road, Broadstairs
CT10 1QP
t (01843) 863347
e stay@anchorhouse.net
w anchorhouse.net

Anchor Lodge ★★★★
Bed & Breakfast **GOLD AWARD**
57 Dumpton Park Drive, Broadstairs
CT10 1RH
t (01843) 602564
e enquiries@anchorlodge.net
w anchorlodge.net

Aria House Bed & Breakfast
★★★★ *Guest Accommodation*
SILVER AWARD
110a Pierremont Avenue,
Broadstairs
CT10 1NT
t (01843) 862692
e ariahouse@googlemail.com
w ariahouse.co.uk

Bay Tree Broadstairs ★★★★
Guest Accommodation
12 Eastern Esplanade, Broadstairs
CT10 1DR
t (01843) 862502

Belvidere Place
Guest Accommodation
43 Belvedere Road, Broadstairs
CT10 1PF
t 07900 823374

Burrow House ★★★★★
Guest Accommodation
GOLD AWARD
Granville Road, Broadstairs
CT10 1QD
t (01843) 601817
e gavincox@aol.com
w burrowhouse.com

Cintra ★★★ *Guest Accommodation*
24 Victoria Parade, Broadstairs
CT10 1QL
t (01843) 862253
e visit@cintrabb.com
w cintrabb.com

Cloonlara ★★★★
Guest Accommodation
SILVER AWARD
5 Ramsgate Road, Broadstairs
CT10 1QQ
t 05602 538238
e info@cloonlarabedandbreakfast.com
w cloonlarabedandbreakfast.com

Copperfields Guest House ★★★★
Guest House **SILVER AWARD**
Queens Road, Broadstairs
CT10 1NU
t (01843) 601247
e copperfieldsbb@btinternet.com
w copperfieldsbb.co.uk

The Devonhurst ★★★★
Guest Accommodation
SILVER AWARD
Eastern Esplanade, Broadstairs
CT10 1DR
t (01843) 863010
e info@devonhurst.co.uk
w devonhurst.co.uk

East Horndon ★★★★
Guest Accommodation
SILVER AWARD
4 Eastern Esplanade, Broadstairs
CT10 1DP
t (01843) 868306
e easthorndon@hotmail.com
w easthorndonhotel.com

The Hanson ★★★
Guest Accommodation
41 Belvedere Road, Broadstairs
CT10 1PF
t (01843) 868936
e hotelhanson@tiscali.co.uk
w hansonhotel.co.uk

Merriland ★★★★ *Guest House*
13 The Vale, Broadstairs
CT10 1RB
t (01843) 861064
e merrilandhotel@aol.com

Number 68 ★★★★
Guest Accommodation
SILVER AWARD
68 West Cliff Road, Broadstairs
CT10 1PY
t (01843) 609459
e number68@btinternet.com
w number68.co.uk

South Lodge Guest House ★★★★
Guest House **SILVER AWARD**
19 The Vale, Broadstairs
CT10 1RB
t (01843) 600478
e reservations@visitsouthlodge.co.uk
w visitsouthlodge.co.uk

Torwood House ★★★★★
Bed & Breakfast **SILVER AWARD**
41 West Cliff Road, Broadstairs
CT10 1PU
t (01843) 863953
e enquiries@torwoodhouse.co.uk
w torwoodhouse.co.uk

The Victoria Bed & Breakfast
★★★★ *Bed & Breakfast*
SILVER AWARD
23 Victoria Parade, Broadstairs
CT10 1QL
t (01843) 871010
e helen@thevictoriabroadstairs.co.uk
w thevictoriabroadstairs.co.uk

Viking Guest House ★★★★
Guest Accommodation
SILVER AWARD
West Cliff Avenue, Broadstairs
CT10 1QA
t (01843) 862375
e bookings@viking-guesthouse.co.uk
w viking-guesthouse.co.uk

BROOKLAND

The Royal Oak ★★★★ *Inn*
High Street, Brookland, Romney
Marsh
TN29 9QR
t (01797) 344215
e dzrj@btinternet.com
w royaloakbrookland.co.uk

BURMARSH

Stable Cottage ★★★★
Bed & Breakfast
The Sheiling, Donkey Street,
Burmarsh, Romney Marsh
TN29 0JN
t (01303) 872335
e eric777@tiscali.co.uk
w stablecottageburmarsh.co.uk

CANTERBURY

Acacia Lodge & Tanglewood
★★★★ *Guest Accommodation*
39-40 London Road, Canterbury
CT2 8LF
t (01227) 769955

Alexandra House ★★★★
Guest Accommodation
1 Roper Road, Canterbury
CT2 7EH
t (01227) 786617
e alexandrahouse2@aol.com
w alexandrahouse.net

Alicante Guest House ★★★★
Guest House
4 Roper Road, Canterbury
CT2 7EH
t (01227) 766277
e alicanteguesthouse@googlemail.com
w alicanteguesthouse.co.uk

Ann's House ★★★ *Guest House*
63 London Road, Canterbury
CT2 8JZ
t (01227) 768767
e info@annshousecanterbury.co.uk
w annshousecanterbury.co.uk

Ashley Guest House ★★
Bed & Breakfast
9 London Road, Canterbury
CT2 8LR
t (01227) 455863

Bluebells Guest House ★★★★
Guest Accommodation
248 Wincheap, Canterbury
CT1 3TY
t (01227) 478842
e canterburybluebells@yahoo.co.uk
w canterburybluebells.com

Bower Farm House ★★★★
Bed & Breakfast **SILVER AWARD**
Bossingham Road, Stelling Minnis,
Canterbury
CT4 6BB
t (01227) 709430
e nick@bowerbb.freeserve.co.uk
w bowerfarmhouse.co.uk

Canterbury Cathedral Lodge
★★★ *Guest Accommodation*
The Precincts, Canterbury
CT1 2EH
t (01227) 865350
e stay@canterbury-cathedral.org
w canterburycathedrallodge.org

Canterbury YHA ★★ *Hostel*
54 New Dover Road, Canterbury
CT1 3DT
t (01227) 462911
e canterbury@yha.org.uk
w yha.org.uk/canterbury

Carena House ★★★★ *Guest House*
250 Wincheap, Canterbury
CT1 3TY
t (01227) 765630
e carena.house@btconnect.com
w carenaguesthouse.co.uk

273

South East | Kent

The City Of Canterbury ★★★★
Guest Accommodation
27 St Thomas Hill, Canterbury
CT2 8HW
t (01227) 457455
e t.mills@talktalk.net
w thecityofcanterbury.co.uk

Clare Ellen Guest House
Guest House
9 Victoria Road, Canterbury
CT1 3SG
t (01227) 760205
e enquiry@clareellenguesthouse.co.uk
w clareellenguesthouse.co.uk

The Duke of Cumberland ★★★★
Inn
The Street, Barham, Canterbury
CT4 6NY
t (01227) 831396

Four Seasons Guest Accommodation ★★★★
Guest Accommodation
77 Sturry Road, Canterbury
CT1 1BU
t (01227) 787078
e bookingenquiries@aol.com
w fourseasonsbookings.co.uk

Harriet House ★★★★ Guest House
3 Broad Oak Road, Canterbury
CT2 7PL
t (01227) 457363
e enquiries@harriethouse.co.uk
w harriethouse.co.uk

Hornbeams ★★★★ Farmhouse
Jesses Hill, Kingston, Canterbury
CT4 6JD
t (01227) 830119
e bandb@hornbeams.co.uk
w hornbeams.co.uk

Iffin Farmhouse ★★★★
Guest Accommodation
Iffin Lane, Canterbury, Kent
CT4 7BE
t (01227) 462776
e info@iffin.co.uk
w iffinfarmhouse.co.uk

Kings Head ★★★ Inn
204 Wincheap, Canterbury
CT1 3RY
t (01227) 462885
e thekingshead@wincheap.wanadoo.co.uk
w smoothhound.co.uk/hotels/thekingshead.html

Kipps Independent Hostel ★★★
Backpackers
40 Nunnery Fields, Canterbury
CT1 3JT
t (01227) 786121
e kippshostel@gmail.com
w kipps-hostel.com

Magnolia House ★★★★★
Guest Accommodation
GOLD AWARD
36 St Dunstans Terrace, Canterbury
CT2 8AX
t (01227) 765121
e info@magnoliahousecanterbury.co.uk
w magnoliahousecanterbury.co.uk

The Millers Arms ★★★★ Inn
2 Mill Lane, St Radigunds, Canterbury
CT1 2AW
t (01227) 456057
e millersarms@shepherdneame.co.uk
w millerscanterbury.co.uk

Oak Cottage ★★★★
Guest Accommodation
Elmsted, Ashford
TN25 5JT
t (01233) 750272 - Mobile 07775843743
e oakcottage@invictanet.co.uk
w oakcottage-elmsted.co.uk

Tudor House ★★★ Guest House
6 Best Lane, Canterbury
CT1 2JB
t (01227) 765650
e info@tudorhousecanterbury.co.uk
w tudorhousecanterbury.co.uk

University of Kent ★★★★ - ★★★★★
Campus
Kent Hospitality, Tanglewood, The University, Giles Lane, Canterbury
CT2 7LX
t (01227) 828000
e hospitality-enquiry@kent.ac.uk
w kent.ac.uk/holidays/

Wincheap Guest House ★★★
Guest House
94 Wincheap, Canterbury
CT1 3RS
t (01227) 762309
e wincheapguesthouse@tiscali.co.uk
w wincheapguesthouse.co.uk

Woodchip B&B
Guest Accommodation
Maidstone Road, Chilham, Canterbury
CT4 8DD
t (01227) 730386
e woodchiphouse@aol.com
w woodchiphouse.co.uk

Yorke Lodge ★★★★★
Guest Accommodation
SILVER AWARD
50 London Road, Canterbury
CT2 8LF
t (01227) 451243
e info@yorkelodge.com
w yorkelodge.com

CHARCOTT

Charcott Farmhouse ★★★★
Bed & Breakfast
Charcott, Penshurst
TN11 8LG
t (01892) 870024
e charcottfarmhouse@btinternet.com
w smoothound.co.uk/hotels/charcott

CHARING

Oak ★★★★ Inn SILVER AWARD
High Street, Charing, Ashford
TN27 0HU
t (01233) 712612
e info@theoakcharing.co.uk
w theoakcharing.co.uk

CHART SUTTON

Chart Hill Cottage ★★★★
Bed & Breakfast GOLD AWARD
Chart Road, Chart Sutton, Maidstone
ME17 3RG
t (01622) 844397
e maggiet@gotadsl.co.uk
w charthillcottage.co.uk

White House Farm ★★★★
Farmhouse SILVER AWARD
Green Lane, Chart Sutton
ME17 3ES
t (01622) 842490
e info@whitehousefarm-kent.co.uk
w whitehousefarm-kent.co.uk

CHATHAM

College Road B&B ★★★★★
Bed & Breakfast GOLD AWARD
7 College Road, The Historic Dockyard, Chatham
ME4 4QX
t (01634) 828436
e gmchambers@btopenworld.com

Normandy House ★★★
Bed & Breakfast
Maidstone Road, Chatham
ME4 6JE
t (01634) 843047
e david.rands@blueyonder.co.uk
w bedandbreakfastchatham.co.uk

Ship & Trades ★★★
Guest Accommodation
Maritime Way, St Marys Island, Chatham
ME4 3ER
t (01634) 895200
e ship&trades@shepherd-neame.co.uk
w shepherd-neame.co.uk

CHESTFIELD

Cherries B&B ★★★★
Bed & Breakfast
25 Cherry Orchard, Chestfield, Whitstable
CT5 3NH
t (01227) 792600
e info@thecherries.net
w thecherries.net

CHILHAM

Castle Cottage Chilham Bed & Breakfast ★★★★ Bed & Breakfast
School Hill, Chilham, Canterbury
CT4 8DE
t (01227) 730330
e l.frankel@btinternet.com
w castlecottagechilham.co.uk

The Woolpack Inn ★★★★ Inn
The Street, Chilham, Canterbury
CT4 8DL
t (01227) 730351
e woolpack@shepherdneame.co.uk

CHIPSTEAD

Windmill Farm ★★★★
Guest Accommodation
Chevening Road, Sevenoaks
TN13 2SA
t (01732) 452054

CLIFTONVILLE

House Of Many Stairs
Guest Accommodation
A part of Florence Rose Tearoom, 8 First Avenue, Cliftonville, Margate
CT9 2LF
t (01843) 224005

The Malvern Guest House & Blues Grill ★★★ Guest House
29 Eastern Esplanade, Cliftonville, Margate
CT9 2HL
t (01843) 290192
e themalvern@aol.com
w malvernhotelmargate.co.uk

COWDEN

Southernwood House ★★★★
Bed & Breakfast
Church Street, Hever
TN8 7JE
t (01342) 850880
e info@southernwoodhouse.org.uk

CRANBROOK

1 Maytham Cottages
Guest Accommodation
Frogs Lane, Rolvenden Layne, Cranbrook
TN17 4NH
t (01580) 241484
e jobeddows@aol.com

Bargate House ★★★★
Guest Accommodation
SILVER AWARD
Angley Road, Cranbrook
TN17 2PQ
t (01580) 714254
e pennylane@bargatehouse.co.uk
w bargatehouse.co.uk

Beacon Hall House ★★★★
Bed & Breakfast SILVER AWARD
Rolvenden Road, Benenden, Cranbrook
TN17 4BU
t (01580) 240434
e julie.jex@btconnect.com

Bull Farm Oast ★★★★
Bed & Breakfast
Corner Bishops Lane, Glassonbur Road, Cranbrook
TN17 2ST
t (01580) 714140
e b+b@bullfarmoast.co.uk
w bullfarmoast.co.uk

Guernsey Cottage ★★★
Guest Accommodation
Wilsley Green, Cranbrook
TN17 2LG
t (01580) 712542
e grahamstarkey@mac.com

Hallwood Farm Oast ★★★★★
Farmhouse SILVER AWARD
Hallwood Farm, Hawkhurst Road, Cranbrook
TN17 2SP
t (01580) 712416
e email@hallwoodfarm.co.uk
w hallwoodfarm.co.uk

Orchard Way Guest Accommoda
Heartenoak Road, Hawkhurst, Cranbrook
TN18 5EU
t (01580) 755684
e orchard.way@hotmail.com
w orchardwaybandb.co.uk

Tilsden House ★★★★
Bed & Breakfast
Tilsden Lane, Cranbrook
TN17 3PJ
t (01580) 714226
e pauldean67@aol.com
w tilsdenhouse.co.uk

Waters End ★★★★★
Bed & Breakfast
Standen Street, Iden Green, Cranbrook
TN17 4LA
t (01580) 850731
e jill@watersendfarm.co.uk
w watersendfarm.co.uk

CROCKHAM HILL

Pootings Oast ★★★
Bed & Breakfast
Pootings Road, Crockham Hill, Edenbridge
TN8 6SD
t (01732) 866235
e alanwhitlock@hotmail.com

DEAL

Beachbrow ★★★
Guest Accommodation
29 Beach Street, Deal
CT14 6HY
t (01304) 374338
e info@beachbow-hotel.com
w beachbow-hotel.com

By the Beach ★★★★
Bed & Breakfast
55 The Beach, Deal
CT14 6NP
t (01304) 366511
e info@bythebeachindeal.co.uk
w bythebeachindeal.co.uk

Kings Head Public House ★★★
Inn
9 Beach Street, Deal
CT14 7AH
t (01304) 368194
e bookings@kingsheaddeal.co.uk
w kingsheaddeal.co.uk

The Malvern ★★★ Guest House
5-7 Ranelagh Road, Deal
CT14 7BG
t (01304) 372944
e reception@themalvernguesthouse.com
w themalvernguesthouse.com

Number One B&B ★★★★
Guest Accommodation
GOLD AWARD
1 Ranelagh Road, Deal
CT14 7BG
t (01304) 364459
e enquiries@numberonebandb.co.uk
w numberonebandb.co.uk

South East | Kent

DENSOLE

den Lodge Guest House & taurant ★★★★
Guest Accommodation
Canterbury Road, Densole,
estone
8 7BB
(01303) 893147
stay@garden-lodge.com
garden-lodge.com

DETLING

alden Hall ★★★★
& Breakfast
rims Way, Detling, Maidstone
4 3JY
(01622) 739622
johnwatson@wealdenhall.net
wealdenhall.co.uk

DODDINGTON

ace Farmhouse ★★★
Guest Accommodation
equers Hill, Doddington,
ngbourne, Kent
9 0AU
(01795) 886820

DOVER

anda Guest House ★★★
est House
arold Street, Dover
6 1SF
(01304) 201711
amandaguesthouse@hotmail.com
amandaguesthouse.com

kes of Dover ★★★★
est Accommodation
Castle Street, Dover
6 1PJ
(01304) 202194
blakesofdover.com

tle House ★★★★ *Guest House*
tle Hill Road, Dover
6 1QW
(01304) 201656
dimechr@aol.com
castle-guesthouse.co.uk

urchill Guest House ★★★★
est House
astle Hill Road, Dover
6 1QN
(01304) 204622
coastofdover@gmail.com
churchillhouse.homestead.com

re House ★★★ *Guest House*
Folkestone Road, Dover
7 9SJ
(01304) 204553
stay@clarehouse-dover.co.uk
clarehouse-dover.co.uk

t Lee Guest House ★★★★
est House **SILVER AWARD**
Maison Dieu Road, Dover
6 1RT
(01304) 210176
elgh@eclipse.co.uk
eastlee.co.uk

ather's Woodlands ★★★
est Accommodation
London Road, River, Dover
7 0SF
(01304) 823695
heatherswoodlands@hotmail.co.
uk

bert House Guesthouse ★★★★
est House **GOLD AWARD**
astle Hill Road, Dover
6 1QW
(01304) 202253
stay@huberthouse.co.uk
huberthouse.co.uk

ddington House ★★★★
est Accommodation
East Cliff, Dover
6 1LX
(01304) 201947
loddingtonhotel@btconnect.com
loddingtonhousehotel.co.uk

Longfield Guest House ★★★
Guest Accommodation
203 Folkestone Road, Dover
CT17 9SL
t (01304) 204716
e res@longfieldguesthouse.com
w longfieldguesthouse.co.uk

Maison Dieu Guest House ★★★★
Guest House **SILVER AWARD**
89 Maison Dieu Road, Dover
CT16 1RU
t (01304) 204033
e info@maisondieu.com
w maisondieu.com

The Norman Guest House ★★★
Guest House
75 Folkestone Road, Dover
CT17 9RZ
t (01304) 207803
e the.norman@btconnect.com
w thenorman-guesthouse.co.uk

Number One Guest House ★★★★
Guest House
1 Castle Street, Dover
CT16 1QH
t (01304) 202007
e res@number1guesthouse.com
w number1guesthouse.co.uk

Number Twenty-Four Bed & Breakfast ★★★★ *Bed & Breakfast*
24 East Cliff, Marine Parade, Dover
CT16 1LU
t (01304) 330549
e number24dover@aol.com

Sandown Guesthouse ★★
Bed & Breakfast
229 Folkestone Road, Dover
CT17 9SL
t (01304) 226 807

Victoria Guest House ★★★★
Guest House
1 Laureston Place, Dover
CT16 1QX
t (01304) 205140
e wham101496@aol.com
w dover-victoria-guest-house.co.uk

Westbank Guest House ★★★★
Guest House
239-241 Folkestone Road, Dover
CT17 9LL
t (01304) 201061
e thewestbank@btconnect.com
w westbankguesthouse.co.uk

DYMCHURCH

Waterside Guest House ★★★★
Guest House
15 Hythe Road, Dymchurch,
Romney Marsh
TN29 0LN
t (01303) 872253

EASTCHURCH

Dunmow House ★★★★
Guest Accommodation
9 Church Road, Eastchurch,
Sheerness
ME12 4DQ
t (01795) 880576
e mep4@btinternet.com

EDENBRIDGE

Becketts ★★★★ *Bed & Breakfast*
SILVER AWARD
Pylegate Farm, Hartfield Road,
Cowden, Edenbridge
TN8 7HE
t (01342) 850514
e jacqui@becketts-bandb.co.uk
w becketts-bandb.co.uk

Mowshurst Farm House ★★★★
Bed & Breakfast **SILVER AWARD**
Swan Lane, Edenbridge
TN8 6AH
t (01732) 862064
w mowshurstfarmhouse.co.uk

EGERTON

Frasers ★★★★★
Guest Accommodation
GOLD AWARD
Coldharbour Farm, Barhams Mill
Road, Ashford
TN27 9DD
t (01233) 756548
e lisa@frasers-events.co.uk
w frasers-events.co.uk

ELHAM

The Rose & Crown ★★★★ *Inn*
High Street, Elham
CT4 6TD
t (01303) 840226
e info@roseandcrown.co.uk
w roseandcrown.co.uk

ELMSTED

Elmsted Court Farm ★★★★
Farmhouse **SILVER AWARD**
Elmsted Court farm, Elmsted,
Ashford
TN25 5JN
t (01233) 750269
e carol@elmsted-court-farm.co.uk
w elmsted-court-farm.co.uk

FAVERSHAM

Barnsfield ★★ *Farmhouse*
Fostall, Hernhill, Faversham
ME13 9JG
t (01227) 750973
e barnsfield@mac.com
w barnsfield.co.uk

Brenley Farm House ★★★★
Farmhouse
Brenley Lane, Boughton-under-
Blean, Faversham
ME13 9LY
t (01227) 751203
e info@brenley-farm.co.uk
w brenley-farm.co.uk

Fairlea Bed & Breakfast ★★★★
Bed & Breakfast **SILVER AWARD**
27 Preston Avenue, Faversham
ME13 8NH
t (01795) 539610
e info@fairleabandb.co.uk
w fairleabandb.co.uk

Gladstone House ★★★★
Guest Accommodation
SILVER AWARD
60 Newton Road, Faversham
ME13 8DZ
t (01795) 536432
e maryjmackay@hotmail.com
w gladstoneguesthouse.com

March Cottage Bed & Breakfast
★★★ *Guest Accommodation*
5 Preston Avenue, Faversham
ME13 8NH
t (01795) 536514
e sarah@marchcottagebandb.co.uk
w marchcottagebandb.co.uk

Palace Farm Hostel ★★★ *Hostel*
Down Court Road, Doddington,
Sittingbourne, Kent
ME9 0AU
t (01795) 886200
e info@palacefarm.com
w palacefarm.com

The Railway Hotel ★★★★ *Inn*
Preston Street, Faversham
ME13 8PE
t (01795) 533173
w shepherdneame.co.uk

The Sun Inn ★★★ *Inn*
10 West Street, Faversham
ME13 7JE
t (01795) 535098
w shepherdneame.co.uk

FAWKHAM

The Rising Sun Inn ★★★ *Inn*
Fawkham Green, Fawkham,
Longfield
DA3 8NL
t (01474) 872291

FOLKESTONE

Kentmere Guest House ★★★
Guest House
76 Cheriton Road, Folkestone
CT20 1DG
t (01303) 259661
e enquiries@kentmere-guesthouse.
co.uk
w kentmere-guesthouse.co.uk

The Rob Roy Guest House ★★★
Guest House
227 Dover Road, Folkestone, Kent
CT19 6NH
t (01303) 253341
e robroy.folkestone@ntlworld.com
w therobroyguesthouse.co.uk

Seacliffe ★★★
Guest Accommodation
3 Wear Bay Road, Folkestone
CT19 6AT
t (01303) 254592
e sheila_foot@yahoo.com

Windsor Hotel ★★
Guest Accommodation
5-6 Langhorne Gardens, Folkestone
CT20 2EA
t (01303) 251348
e windsorhotel_folkestone@
hotmail.com

FOLKESTONE (2 MILES)

Crete Down ★★★★
Guest Accommodation
Crete Road West, Folkestone
CT18 7AA
t (01303) 892392
e enquiries@crete-down.co.uk
w crete-down.co.uk

FRITTENDEN

Tolehurst Barn ★★★★
Guest Accommodation
Cranbrook Road, Frittenden,
Cranbrook
TN17 2BP
t (01580) 714385
e info@tolehurstbarn.co.uk
w tolehurstbarn.co.uk

GILLINGHAM

Abigails ★★★
Guest Accommodation
17 The Maltings, Rainham,
Gillingham
ME8 8JL
t (01634) 365427
e davidjpenfold@btopenworld.com

The Balmoral ★★★ *Guest House*
57 - 59 Balmoral Road, Gillingham,
Kent
ME7 4NT
t (01634) 853682
e bookings@thebalmoral-guest
house.co.uk
w thebalmoral-guesthouse.co.uk/

Medway YHA ★★★ *Hostel*
351 Capstone Road, Gillingham
ME7 3JE
t (01634) 400788
e medway@yha.org.uk
w yha.org.uk

Ramsey House ★★★★
Guest Accommodation
228A Barnsole Road, Gillingham
ME7 4JB
t (01634) 854193

FAWKHAM

TENTERDEN

Tenterden House ★★★
Guest Accommodation
209 The Street, Boughton,
Faversham
ME13 9BL
t (01227) 751593
e platham@tesco.net
w faversham.org/tenterdenhouse

South East | Kent

GRAFTY GREEN

Bramley Knowle Farm ★★★★
Farmhouse
Eastwood Road, Ulcombe
ME17 1ET
t (01622) 858878
e diane@bramleyknowlefarm.co.uk
w bramleyknowlefarm.co.uk

Foxes Earth Bed & Breakfast
★★★★ *Guest Accommodation*
GOLD AWARD
Headcorn Road, Grafty Green,
Maidstone
ME17 2AP
t (01622) 858350
e foxesearth@btinternet.com
w foxesearthbedandbreakfast.co.uk

GRAVESEND

Briars Court B&B ★★★★
Bed & Breakfast
90 Windmill Street, Gravesend
DA12 1LH
t (01474) 363788
e bandb@briarscourt.co.uk
w briarscourt.co.uk

Eastcourt Oast ★★★
Guest Accommodation
SILVER AWARD
Church Lane, Gravesend
DA12 2NL
t (01474) 823937
e mary@eastcourtoast.co.uk
w eastcourtoast.co.uk

Thames House ★★★★
Bed & Breakfast
29 Royal Pier Road, Graves End
DA12 2BD
t 0780 547 7973
e clairefiona.brown@virgin.net

GREATSTONE-ON-SEA

White Horses Cottage ★★★★★
Guest Accommodation
SILVER AWARD
180 The Parade, Greatstone on Sea,
Romney Marsh
TN28 8RS
t (01797) 366626
e whitehorses@tesco.net
w white-horses-cottage.co.uk

HADLOW

Fieldswood Bed & Breakfast
★★★★ *Bed & Breakfast*
SILVER AWARD
Hadlow Park, Hadlow
TN11 0HZ
t (01732) 851433
e info@fieldswood.co.uk
w fieldswood.co.uk

HAWKENBURY

The White Cottage ★★★★
Bed & Breakfast **SILVER AWARD**
Headcorn Road, Hawkenbury,
Staplehurst
TN12 0DU
t (01580) 891480
e john.batten@mac.com
w the-whitecottage.co.uk

HAWKHURST

Royal Oak ★★★ *Inn*
Rye Road, Hawkhurst
TN18 4EP
t (01580) 755782
e sean.gallen@hotmail.com

HEADCORN

Four Oaks ★★★★
Guest Accommodation
Four Oaks Road, Headcorn
TN27 9PB
t (01622) 891224
e info@fouroaks.uk.com
w fouroaks.uk.com

Headcorn Lodge ★★★
Guest Accommodation
Weald of Kent, Maidstone Road,
Maidstone
TN27 9PT
t (01622) 891671
e info@headcorn-lodge-hotel.co.uk
w headcorn-lodge-hotel.co.uk

Wilderness Bed & Breakfast
★★★★ *Bed & Breakfast*
Waterman Quarter, Headcorn,
Maidstone
TN27 9JJ
t (01622) 891757
e vhonychurch@toucansurf.com
w wildernessbandb.co.uk

HERNE BAY

Evening Tide Bed & Breakfast
★★★★ *Guest House*
97 Central Parade, Herne Bay
CT6 5JJ
t (01227) 365014
e info@eveningtide.co.uk
w eveningtide.co.uk

Priory B&B ★★★★
Guest Accommodation
203 Canterbury Road, Herne Bay
CT6 5UG
t (01227) 366670
e stephen@theprioryandb.co.uk
w theprioryandb.co.uk

Seahaven ★★★★ *Bed & Breakfast*
64 Linden Avenue, Herne Bay
CT6 8TZ
t 01227 366582
e marilynbudd@hotmail.co.uk
w hernebayseahaven.com

Summerhouse ★★★★
Bed & Breakfast
15 Glenbervie Drive, Beltinge, Herne
Bay
CT66QL
t (01227) 363192
e john.pye1@talktalk.net
w beltingesummerhouse.co.uk

**Westgrange House Bed &
Breakfast ★★★★** *Bed & Breakfast*
42 Busheyfield Road, Herne Bay
CT6 7LJ
t (01227) 740663

HERNHILL

Church Oast ★★★★
Bed & Breakfast **SILVER AWARD**
Church Oast, Hernhill, Faversham
ME13 9JW
t (01227) 750974
e jill@geliot.plus.com
w churchoast.co.uk

HIGHAM

Field View ★★ *Bed & Breakfast*
SILVER AWARD
32 Walmers Avenue, Rochester
ME3 7EH
t (01474) 822330
e hazelbigwood@hotmail.co.uk
w field-view.co.uk

HIGH HALDEN

Durrants Court ★★★★
Bed & Breakfast
High Halden Tenterden, Ashford
TN26 3BS
t (01233) 850027/07729378496
e jennifer.gentle@durrants-court.co.uk
w durrants-court.co.uk

IGHTHAM

The Studio At Double Dance
★★★★ *Guest Accommodation -
Room Only* **SILVER AWARD**
Penny Cracknell, Double Dance,
Bates Hill, Ightham
TN15 9AT
t (01732) 884198
e pennycracknell@doubledance.co.uk
w doubledance.co.uk

KEMSING

Upthedowns ★★★★
Bed & Breakfast
23 Northdown Road, Kemsing,
Sevenoaks
TN15 6SD
t (01959) 526869
e upthedowns@btinternet.com
w upthedowns.com

KENNINGTON

The Conningbrook Hotel ★★★★
Guest Accommodation
Canterbury Road, Kennington,
Ashford
TN24 9QR
t (01233) 636863
e conningbrook@shepherdneame.co.uk
w conningbrookashford.co.uk

KINGSDOWN

The Gardeners Rest ★★★★★
Guest Accommodation
GOLD AWARD
Nemesis, Queensdown Road,
Kingsdown, Deal
CT14 8EF
t (01304) 371449
e sandra@gardenersrest.me.uk
w gardenersrest.me.uk

Sparrow Court ★★★
Bed & Breakfast
Chalk Hill Road, Kingsdown, Deal
CT14 8DP
t (01304) 389253
e gmaude@waitrose.com

LADDINGFORD

Chequers Inn ★★★★ *Inn*
Near Yalding, Laddingford
ME18 6BP
t (01622) 871266

LANGLEY

Orchard House ★★★★
Bed & Breakfast
Sutton Road, Maidstone
ME17 3LZ
t (01622) 862694
e orchard_house2004@yahoo.com

LEAVELAND

Leaveland Court ★★★★
Guest Accommodation
SILVER AWARD
Leaveland, Faversham
ME13 0NP
t (01233) 740596
e info@leavelandcourt.co.uk
w leavelandcourt.co.uk

LEEDS

Further Fields ★★★★
Bed & Breakfast
Caring Lane, Leeds
ME17 1TJ
t (01622) 861288
e furtherfields@aol.com
w furtherfields.co.uk

West Forge ★★★
Guest Accommodation
Back Street, Leeds
ME17 1TF
t (01622) 861428
e e.wiesbauer@btinternet.com
w westforge.co.uk

LENHAM

The Dog & Bear Hotel ★★★★ *Inn*
The Square, Lenham, Maidstone
ME17 2PG
t (01622) 858219
e dogbear@shepherd-neame.co.uk
w shepherd-neame.co.uk

LITTLEBOURNE

The Evenhill ★★★★ *Inn*
62 The Hill, Littlebourne, Canterbury
CT3 1TA
t (01227) 728073
w shepherdneame.co.uk

The Pilgrims Rest ★★★★
Guest Accommodation
48-50 High Street, Littlebourne,
Canterbury
CT3 1ST
t (01227) 721341
e info@thepilgrimsrest.biz
w thepilgrimsrest.biz

LOWER UPNOR

Arethusa Venture Centre ★★★
Activity Accommodation
Arethusa Venture Centre, Lower
Upnor
ME2 4XB
t (01634) 719933
e lwright@shaftesbury.org.uk
w arethusa.org.uk

LYMINGE

Roundwood Hall Bed & Breakfast
★★★★ *Bed & Breakfast*
SILVER AWARD
Stone Street, Lyminge, Folkestone
CT18 8DJ
t (01303) 862260
e bnb@roundwoodhall.co.uk
w roundwoodhall.co.uk

MAIDSTONE

At Home ★★ *Bed & Breakfast*
SILVER AWARD
39 Marston Drive, Vinters Park,
Maidstone
ME14 5NE
t (01622) 202196
e steveandlesley@steleybrown.freeserve.co.uk

The Black Horse Inn ★★★★ *Inn*
Pilgrims Way, Thurnham, Maidstone
ME14 3LD
t (01622) 737185
e info@wellieboot.net
w wellieboot.net

Calgary ★★★ *Bed & Breakfast*
18 Bower Mount Road, Maidstone
ME16 8AU
t (01622) 208963
e jandpt@blueyonder.co.uk
w calgarybedandbreakfast.co.uk

Grove House ★★★★
Bed & Breakfast **SILVER AWARD**
Grove Green Road, Maidstone
ME14 5JT
t (01622) 738441

The Hazels ★★★★ *Bed & Breakfast*
13 Yeoman Way, Bearsted,
Maidstone
ME15 8PQ
t (01622) 737943
e carolbuse@hotmail.com
w the-hazels.co.uk

The Limes ★★
Guest Accommodation
118 Boxley Road, Maidstone
ME14 2BD
t (01622) 750629
w thelimesmaidstone.co.uk

Maidstone Lodge ★★★
Guest Accommodation
22-24 London Road, Maidstone
ME16 8QL
t (01622) 758778
e maidstonelodge@btinternet.com
w maidstonelodge.co.uk

Oakwood House ★★★★
Guest Accommodation
Oakwood Park, Maidstone
ME16 8AE
t (01622) 626600
e oakwoodhouse@kent.gov.uk
w oakwoodhouse-kcc.co.uk

Roslin Villa ★★★★ *Guest House*
11 St Michaels Road, Maidstone
ME16 8BS
t (01622) 758301
e brian.ff@btinternet.com
w roslinvilla.com

South East | Kent

MAIDSTONE, KENT

...Cottage ★★★★★
...Bed & Breakfast **SILVER AWARD**
...fold Hill, Leeds Village, Nr
...dstone, Kent
...7 1RQ
t (01622) 863142
e ...ayne@ashcottagekent.co.uk
w ...ashcottagekent.co.uk

MARDEN

...hainhurst Cottages ★★★★
...& Breakfast **SILVER AWARD**
...y Lane, Marden
...2 9SU
t (01622) 820483
e ...heatherscott@waitrose.com
w ...hainhurstcottages.co.uk

...hard Retreat ★★★★★
...& Breakfast
...mmerhill Farmhouse, St Ann's
...en Lane, Marden
...2 9AQ
t (01622) 831908
e ...gazebou@hotmail.com
w ...orchardretreat.co.uk

...ner House ★★★★ *Farmhouse*
...ner Farm, Goudhurst Road,
...den, Tonbridge
...2 9ND
t (01622) 831214
e ...enquiries@tannerfarmpark.co.uk
w ...tannerfarmpark.co.uk

MARGATE

...ssar ★★★★ *Inn*
...Canterbury Road, Margate
...5JP
t (01843) 836296
e ...dobbs@ukgateway.net
w ...hussarhotel.co.uk

...rgate YHA Youth Hostel ★★
...tel
...Beachcomber, 3-4 Royal
...lanade, Margate
...5DL
t (01843) 221616
e ...margate.yha.org.uk
w ...yha.org.uk

...Reading Rooms
...st Accommodation
...Hawley Square, Margate
...1PH
t (01843) 225166
e ...info@thereadingroomsmargate.
...co.uk
w ...thereadingroomsmargate.co.uk

MARSHBOROUGH

...thside ★★★★ *Bed & Breakfast*
...shborough Road, Marshborough,
...dwich
...3 0PQ
t (01304) 812 802
e ...reservations.southsidebandb@
...yahoo.co.uk
w ...southsidebandb.co.uk

MARSH GREEN

...rborough Manor ★★★★★
...st Accommodation
...LD AWARD
...sh Green Road, Marsh Green,
...nbridge
...5QY
t (01732) 862152
e ...lynn@starboroughmanor.co.uk
w ...starboroughmanor.co.uk

MERSHAM

...be Place ★★★★
...d & Breakfast
... Street, Mersham, Ashford
...25 6ND
t (01233) 500174
e ...bedandbreakfast@glebeplace
...inkent.co.uk
w ...glebeplaceinkent.co.uk

Stone Green Farm ★★★★★
Bed & Breakfast **SILVER AWARD**
Mersham, Ashford
TN25 7HE
t (01233) 720365
e info@stonegreenfarm.co.uk
w stonegreenfarm.co.uk

MINSTER

Durlock Lodge ★★★
Guest Accommodation - Room Only
Durlock, Minster, Ramsgate
CT12 4HD
t (01843) 821219
e david@durlocklodge.co.uk
w durlocklodge.co.uk

Hoo Farmhouse ★★★★★
Bed & Breakfast **GOLD AWARD**
147 Monkton Road, Minster,
Ramsgate
CT12 4JB
t (01843) 821322
e stay@hoofarmhouse.com
w hoofarmhouse.com

NETTLESTEAD

Rock Farm Cottage ★★★★
Guest Accommodation
Rock Farm, Gibbs Hill, Nettlestead
ME18 5HT
t (01622) 812244
w rockfarmhousebandb.co.uk

NEW ROMNEY

Broadacre ★★★★
Guest Accommodation
North Street, New Romney, Kent
TN28 8DR
t (01797) 362381
e info@broadacrehotel.co.uk
w broadacrehotel.co.uk

NONINGTON

Farthingales Bed & Breakfast
★★★★ *Bed & Breakfast*
SILVER AWARD
Old Court Hill, Nonington, Dover
CT15 4LQ
t 07599 303494
e farthingalesbandb@yahoo.co.uk
w farthingales.co.uk

OFFHAM

Little Quintain ★★★★
Bed & Breakfast
Teston Road, Offham, West Malling
ME19 5NR
t (01732) 871618
e m.homard@oefs.co.uk
w littlequintain.co.uk

OSPRINGE

The Lodge ★★★★ *Bed & Breakfast*
SILVER AWARD
Syndale Park, London Road, Kent
ME13 0RH
t (01795) 531488
e sallyfarley18@yahoo.com

OTTINGE

Bridge Cottage Bed & Breakfast
★★ *Bed & Breakfast*
Shuttlesfield Lane, Ottinge,
Canterbury
CT4 6XJ
t (01303) 862933
e chris@cjelly.plus.com
w elham.co.uk

PADDOCK WOOD

The Annexe, Pinto ★★★★
Bed & Breakfast
Chantlers Hill, Brenchley
TN12 6LX
t (01892) 836254
e janemoor@supanet.com
w kentbedbreakfast.com

PEMBURY

Camden Arms Hotel ★★★★ *Inn*
SILVER AWARD
High Street, Pembury, Tunbridge
Wells
TN2 4PH
t (01892) 822012
e food@camdenarms.co.uk
w camdenarms.co.uk

PENENDEN HEATH

Penenden Heath Lodge ★★★★
Guest Accommodation
2 Penenden Heath Road, Penenden
Heath, Maidstone
ME14 2DA
t (01622) 672562
e penendenheathlodge@blueyonder.co.uk
w penendenheathlodge.com

PETHAM

South Wootton House ★★★
Farmhouse
Capel Lane, Petham, Canterbury
CT4 5RG
t (01227) 700643
e mountfrances@farming.co.uk

PLUCKLEY

Elvey Farm ★★★★
Guest Accommodation
SILVER AWARD
Elvey Lane, Ashford
TN27 0SU
t (01233) 840442
e bookings@elveyfarm.co.uk
w elveyfarm.co.uk

RAMSGATE

Abbeygail Guest House ★★★★
Guest House
17 Penshurst Road, Ramsgate
CT11 8EG
t (01843) 594154
e abbeygail2004@aol.com
w abbeygail.co.uk

Belvidere Guest House ★★★
Guest House
26 Augusta Road, Ramsgate
CT11 8JS
t (01843) 588809

Glendevon Guest House ★★★★
Guest House
8 Truro Road, Ramsgate
CT11 8DB
t 0800 035 2110
e info@glendevonguesthouse.co.uk
w glendevonguesthouse.co.uk

The Royale Guest House ★★★
Guest Accommodation
7 Royal Road, Ramsgate
CT11 9LE
t (01843) 594712
e sylvbarry@aol.com
w theroyaleguesthouse.co.uk

Spencer Court ★★★
Guest Accommodation
37 Spencer Square, Ramsgate
CT11 9LD
t (01843) 594582
e glendaanken@hotmail.com
w smoothhound.co.uk/hotels/spencer.html

RINGWOULD

**Rippledown Environmental
Education** ★★★ *Group Hostel*
Ripple Down House, Dover Road,
Deal
CT14 8HE
t (01304) 364854
e office@rippledown.com
w rippledown.com

ROCHESTER

Churchfields B&B ★★
Bed & Breakfast **SILVER AWARD**
6 Churchfields Terrace, St Margaret's
Street, Rochester
ME1 1TQ
t (01634) 400679
e info@churchfieldsbandb.co.uk
w churchfieldsbandb.co.uk

The Cottage ★★★★
Bed & Breakfast **SILVER AWARD**
66 Borstal Road, Rochester
ME1 3BD
t (01634) 403888

Greystones ★★★★
Guest Accommodation
25 Watts Avenue, Rochester
ME1 1RX
t (01634) 409565
e greystonesrochester@googlemail.com
w greystonesbandb.org.uk

Guinea Lodge ★★★
Guest Accommodation
435 Maidstone Road, Rochester
ME1 3PQ
t (01634) 306716

The Horseshoe & Castle ★★★★
Inn
Main Road, Cooling, Rochester
ME3 8DJ
t (01634) 221691
e horseshoe.castle@btconnect.com
w horseshoeandcastle.co.uk

North Downs Barn ★★★★
Bed & Breakfast
Bush Road, Cuxton, Rochester
ME2 1HF
t (01634) 296829
e alisonevans14@btinternet.com
w northdownsbarn.co.uk

Orchard Cottage ★★★★
Guest Accommodation
SILVER AWARD
11 View Road, Cliffe Woods,
Rochester
ME3 8JQ
t (01634) 222780
e enquiries@orchardcottagekent.co.uk
w orchardcottagekent.co.uk

Riverview Lodge ★★ *Guest House*
88 Borstal Road, Rochester
ME1 3BD
t (01634) 842241
e riverviewlodgerochester@googlemail.com
w riverviewlodge-rochester.co.uk

Salisbury House ★★★★
Bed & Breakfast
29 Watts Avenue, Rochester
ME1 1RX
t (01634) 400182

The Sundial ★★ *Bed & Breakfast*
18 Ranscombe Close, Strood,
Rochester
ME2 2PB
t (01634) 721831
e sean@company8234.freeserve.co.uk

The White Cottage ★★★★
Bed & Breakfast
41 Rede Court Road, Rochester
ME2 3SP
t (01634) 719988

ROLVENDEN

Duck & Drake Cottage ★★★
Bed & Breakfast
Sandhurst Lane, Rolvenden,
Cranbrook
TN17 4PQ
t (01580) 241533
e duckanddrake@supanet.com

key to symbols see page 6

277

South East | Kent

ROLVENDEN LAYNE

Thornden Oaks ★★★★
Bed & Breakfast
Thornden Lane, Rolvenden Layne,
Cranbrook
TN17 4PS
t (01580) 241157
e john@jwasurveyors.co.uk

ROUND GREEN

Cordons ★★★ *Bed & Breakfast*
Round Green Lane, Colliers Green,
Cranbrook
TN17 2NB
t (01580) 211633
e ajdjals@hotmail.com
w cordonsbandb.co.uk

ROYAL TUNBRIDGE WELLS

A & A Studley Cottage ★★★★
Guest Accommodation
GOLD AWARD
Bishop's Down Park Road, Royal
Tunbridge Wells
TN4 8XX
t (01892) 539854
e cook@studleycottage.co.uk
w studleycottage.co.uk

Alconbury Guest House ★★★★★
Bed & Breakfast **GOLD AWARD**
41 Molyneux Park Road, Royal
Tunbridge Wells
TN4 8DX
t (01892) 511279
e camilla.robinson@live.co.uk
w alconburyguesthouse.com

The Beacon ★★★★ *Inn*
Tea Garden Lane, Royal Tunbridge
Wells
TN3 9JH
t (01892) 524252
e beaconhotel@btopenworld.com
w the-beacon.co.uk

Cedar House *Bed & Breakfast*
185 Forest Road, Royal Tunbridge
Wells
TN2 5JA
t (01892) 538504
e jodobson@gmail.com
w cedarhousebandb.co.uk

Danehurst House ★★★★★
Bed & Breakfast **GOLD AWARD**
41 Lower Green Road, Royal
Tunbridge Wells
TN4 8TW
t (01892) 527739
e info@danehurst.net
w danehurst.net

Great Oaks ★★ *Bed & Breakfast*
163 St Johns Road, Royal Tunbridge
Wells
TN4 9UP
t (01892) 529992
e greatoaks163@tiscali.co.uk

**Hawkenbury Farm Bed &
Breakfast** ★★★ *Bed & Breakfast*
Hawkenbury Road, Royal Tunbridge
Wells
TN3 9AD
t (01892) 536977
e rhwright1@aol.com

**Manor Court Farm Bed &
Breakfast** ★★★ *Farmhouse*
Ashurst Road, Ashurst
TN3 9TB
t (01892) 740279
e jsoyke@jsoyke.freeserve.co.uk
w manorcourtfarm.co.uk

Rosnaree ★★★ *Bed & Breakfast*
189 Upper Grosvenor Road, Royal
Tunbridge Wells
TN1 2EF
t (01892) 524017
e davidann.rosnaree@yahoo.co.uk

SANDHURST

Lamberden Cottage ★★★★
Bed & Breakfast
Rye Road, Sandhurst
TN18 5PH
t (01580) 850743
e thewalledgarden@lamberdenc
ottage.co.uk
w lamberdencottage.co.uk

Lamberden House ★★★★
Bed & Breakfast **SILVER AWARD**
Rye Road, Sandhurst
TN18 5PH
t (01580) 850968
e margie@lamberdenhouse.co.uk
w lamberdenhouse.co.uk

SANDWICH

White Rose Lodge ★★★★
Bed & Breakfast **SILVER AWARD**
88 St George's Road, Sandwich
CT13 9LE
t (01304) 620406
w whiteroselodge.co.uk

SEVENOAKS

40 Robyns Way ★★
Bed & Breakfast
Sevenoaks
TN13 3EB
t (01732) 452401
e ingram7oaks@onetel.com
w web.onetel.com/~ingram7oaks/

Darenth Dene ★★★
Bed & Breakfast
Shoreham Road, Otford, Sevenoaks
TN14 5RP
t (01959) 522293
e sandnreid@waitrose.com

Old Timbertop Cottage ★★★★
Bed & Breakfast **SILVER AWARD**
4 Old Timbertop Cottages, Bethel
Road, Sevenoaks
TN3 3UE
t (01732) 460506
e timbertopcottage@tiscali.co.uk
w timbertopcottage.co.uk

SHEERNESS

Ferry House Inn ★★★★ *Inn*
SILVER AWARD
Harty Ferry Road, Sheerness, Kent
ME12 4BQ
t 01795 510214
e info@theferryhouseinn.co.uk
w theferryhouseinn.co.uk

Invicta Guest House ★★★
Guest House
6 Marine Parade, Sheerness
ME12 2AL
t (01795) 661731
w invictaguesthouse.co.uk

SISSINGHURST

Sissinghurst Castle Farmhouse
★★★★★ *Farmhouse*
SILVER AWARD
Biddenden Road, Sissinghurst,
TN17 2AB
t (01580) 720992
e info@sissinghurstcastlefa
rmhouse.com
w sissinghurstcastlefarmhouse.com

Tollgate Farm B&B ★★★★
Bed & Breakfast
Tollgate Farm, Golford, Sissinghurst,
Cranbrook
TN17 4AL
t (01580) 712864
e enquiry@tollgate-farm.co.uk
w tollgate-farm.co.uk

SITTINGBOURNE

The Black Lion ★★★★★
Guest Accommodation - Room Only
The Black Lion, Lynsted,
Sittingbourne
ME9 0RJ
t (01795) 521 229

Holly House Bed & Breakfast
★★★★ *Bed & Breakfast*
SILVER AWARD
Holly House, Wises Lane, Borden,
Sittingbourne
ME9 8LR
t (01795) 426953
e jane.lee-frost@talktalk.net
w hollyhousebandb.org.uk

Woodstock Guesthouse ★★★★
Bed & Breakfast **SILVER AWARD**
25 Woodstock Road, Sittingbourne
ME10 4HJ
t (01795) 421516
w woodstockguesthouse.com

SMARDEN

Hereford Oast ★★★★
Bed & Breakfast **SILVER AWARD**
Smarden Bell Road, Smarden,
Ashford
TN27 8PA
t (01233) 770541
e suzy@herefordoast.fsnet.co.uk
w herefordoast.co.uk

STAPLEHURST

Tudorhurst B&B ★★★★
Bed & Breakfast
Pagehurst Road, Staplehurst
TN12 0JA
t (01580) 891564
e lonetta@lwilliams.wanadoo.co.uk

STELLING MINNIS

Great Field Farm B&B ★★★★
Farmhouse
Misling Lane, Stelling Minnis,
Canterbury
CT4 6DE
t (01227) 709223
e greatfieldfarm@aol.com
w great-field-farm.co.uk

ST MARGARET'S BAY

Small Acre ★★★★
Guest Accommodation
SILVER AWARD
Sea View Road, St Margarets Bay,
Dover
CT15 6EE
t (01304) 851840
e marion@smallacre.co.uk
w smallacre.co.uk

ST MARGARETS BAY

Lenox House ★★★★
Bed & Breakfast **SILVER AWARD**
27 Granville Road, St Margarets Bay,
Dover
CT15 6DS
t (01304) 853253
e sheena_lenox@hotmail.co.uk

STONE

Tighe Farmhouse ★★★★
Farmhouse
Stone-in-Oxney, Tenterden
TN30 7JU
t (01233) 758251
e robin.kingsley@ndierct.co.uk
w accommodationrye.co.uk

SWANLEY

Greenacre ★★★★ *Bed & Breakfast*
SILVER AWARD
15 Greenacre Close, Swanley
BR8 8HT
t (01322) 613656
e pauline.snow1@btinternet.com
w greenacrebandb.co.uk

SWINGFIELD

The Old Kent Barn ★★★★★
Bed & Breakfast **GOLD AWARD**
Smersole Farm, Swingfield, Dover
CT15 7HF
t (01303) 844270
e hilaryjanesimmons@zoom.co.uk

TENTERDEN

Barclay Farmhouse ★★★★★
Bed & Breakfast **GOLD AWARD**
Woolpack Corner, Biddenden,
Tenterden
TN27 8BQ
t (01580) 292626
e info@barclayfarmhouse.co.uk
w barclayfarmhouse.co.uk

Brook Farm ★★★★★
Bed & Breakfast **GOLD AWARD**
Brook Street, Woodchurch, Nr
Tenterden, Kent
TN26 3SR
t (01233) 860444
e reservations@BrookFarmBandB
.co.uk
w BrookFarmBandB.co.uk

Collina House ★★★★
Guest Accommodation
5 East Hill, Tenterden
TN30 6RL
t (01580) 764852
e enquiries@collinahousehotel.co.
uk
w collinahousehotel.co.uk

Kench Hill Centre ★★★
Group Hostel
Appledore Road, Tenterden
TN30 7DG
t (01580) 762073
e admin@kenchhill.co.uk
w kenchhill.co.uk

Rosings Bed & Breakfast ★★★
Bed & Breakfast **GOLD AWARD**
Rosings, Cranbrook Road, Tenter
TN30 6UJ
t (01580) 766750
e bb@rosings.co.uk
w rosings.co.uk

Signal Cottage B&B ★★★★
Bed & Breakfast
3 Rogersmead, Tenterden
TN30 6LF
t (01580) 761806

The Tower House ★★★★★
Bed & Breakfast **SILVER AWARD**
27 Ashford Road, Tenterden
TN30 6LL
t (01580) 761920
e pippa@towerhouse.biz
w towerhouse.biz

The White Cottage ★★★
Bed & Breakfast
London Beach, Ashford Road,
Tenterden
TN30 6SR
t (01233) 850583
e ruth@thewhitecottagebedan
dbreakfast.co.uk
w thewhitecottagebedandbreak
.co.uk

The White Lion Hotel ★★★★
57 High Street, Tenterden
TN30 6BD
t (01580) 765077
e whitelion.tenterden@marstons
.uk
w marstons.co.uk

TUNBRIDGE WELLS

40 York Road ★★★★
Bed & Breakfast
40 York Road, Royal Tunbridge
Wells
TN1 1JY
t (01892) 531342
e yorkrd@uwclub.net
w yorkroad.co.uk

Ash Tree Cottage ★★★★
Bed & Breakfast **SILVER AWARD**
7 Eden Road, Royal Tunbridge W
TN1 1TS
t (01892) 541317
e info@ashtreekent.co.uk
w ashtreekent.co.uk

South East | Kent/Oxfordshire

gers End ★★ *Bed & Breakfast*
hirlmere Road, Royal Tunbridge
s
9SS
01892) 533176

ndeston ★★★★
st *Accommodation*
n Road, Royal Tunbridge Wells
1TS
01892) 513030
laysblundeston@excite.com

Brick House ★★★★
& Breakfast SILVER AWARD
Mount Ephraim Road, Royal
bridge Wells
1EN
01892) 516517
ulia_cassel@yahoo.co.uk
hebrickhousebandb.co.uk

adwater ★★★★
& Breakfast
Clarendon Way, Royal Tunbridge
s
5LD
01892) 528161
avid.thompson4@which.net

ken Guest House ★★
st *House*
rant Road, Royal Tunbridge
s
5LH
01892) 533397
uekench@hotmail.com

elwood House ★★★★
& Breakfast SILVER AWARD
op's Down Park Road, Royal
bridge Wells
8XS
01892) 545924
udith.hurcomb@googlemail.com
azelwoodhouse.org

th & Western ★★★★
st *Accommodation*
en Park Road, Royal Tunbridge
s
5QL
01892) 550750
unbridgewells@smith-western.
o.uk
mith-western.co.uk

n Cottage ★★★★
& Breakfast
Warwick Road, Royal Tunbridge
s
1YL
01892) 525910
wancot@btinternet.com
wancottage.co.uk

WALMER

dicot Guest House ★★★★
& Breakfast
sdown Road, Walmer, Deal
4 8AW
01304) 373867
guestboss@btopenworld.com
ardicot-guest-house.co.uk

WEST BRABOURNE

town Farmhouse Bed &
akfast ★★★★
st *Accommodation*
town Lane, West Brabourne,
ford
5 5NB
01233) 813505
ily.wilton@bulltown.co.uk

WESTERHAM

Farmhouse ★★
& Breakfast SILVER AWARD
Main Road, Westerham Hill,
sterham
6 2HW
01959) 571003
ootsnpots@aol.com
theoldfarmhousewesterham.co.uk

WESTGATE-ON-SEA

White Lodge Guest House ★★★★
Guest House
12 Domneva Road, Westgate-on-Sea
CT8 8PE
t (01843) 831828
e heather@whitelodge.co.uk
w whitelodge.co.uk

WEST KINGSDOWN

Greenacres ★★★★ *Bed & Breakfast*
Hollywood Lane, West Kingsdown,
Sevenoaks
TN15 6JG
t (01474) 853660
e valcella1@aol.com
w greenacres-bedandbreakfast.co.uk

WEST MALLING

Appledene ★★★★
Guest Accommodation
SILVER AWARD
164 Norman Road, West Malling
ME19 6RW
t (01732) 842071
e appledene@westmalling.
freeserve.co.uk
w smoothhound.co.uk/hotelsappl
edene

WHITFIELD

Rolles Court ★★★★
Guest Accommodation
Church Whitfield Road, Whitfield,
Dover
CT16 3HY
t (01304) 827487
e enquiries@rollescourt.co.uk
w rollescourt.co.uk

WHITSTABLE

Alliston House ★★★★
Bed & Breakfast SILVER AWARD
1 Joy Lane, Whitstable
CT5 4LS
t (01227) 779066
e bobgough57@aol.com
w stayinwhitstable.co.uk

The Captain's House ★★★★
Bed & Breakfast
56 Harbour Street, Whitstable
CT5 1AQ
t (01227) 275156
w thecaptainshouse.org.uk

Copeland House ★★★★
Guest House
4 Island Wall, Whitstable
CT5 1EP
t (01227) 266207
e mail@copelandhouse.co.uk
w copelandhouse.co.uk

The Duke of Cumberland ★★★
Inn
High Street, Whitstable
CT5 1AP
t (01227) 280617
e enquiries@thedukeinwhitstable.
co.uk
w thedukeinwhitstable.co.uk

Victoria Villa ★★★★
Guest Accommodation
GOLD AWARD
Victoria Street, Whitstable
CT5 1JB
t (01227) 779191
e victoria.villa@virgin.net
w victoria-villa.i12.com

Windy Ridge ★★★★
Bed & Breakfast
Wraik Hill, Whitstable
CT5 3BY
t (01227) 263506
e hawkins@windyridgewhitstable.
com
w windyridgewhitstable.co.uk

WILLESBOROUGH

Boys Hall ★★★★★
Guest Accommodation
Boys Hall Road, Willesborough,
Ashford
TN24 0LA
t (01233) 633772
e enquiries@boyshall.co.uk
w boyshall.co.uk

WINGHAM

Twitham Barn ★★★★★
Bed & Breakfast
Twitham Court Farm, Staple Road,
Canterbury
CT3 1LP
t (01227) 728607
e twithamcourtbarn@tiscali.co.uk
w twithambarn-bedandbreakfast.co.uk

WORTH

Ilex Cottage ★★★★
Guest Accommodation
Temple Way, Worth, Deal
CT14 0DA
t (01304) 617206
e info@ilexcottage.co.uk
w ilexcottage.co.uk

Solley Farm House ★★★★★
Bed & Breakfast GOLD AWARD
The Street, Worth, Sandwich
CT14 0DG
t (01304) 613701
e solleyfarmhouse@tiscali.co.uk
w solleyfarmhouse.co.uk

St Crispin Inn ★★★★ *Inn*
The Street, Worth, Deal
CT14 0DF
t (01304) 612081
e info@stcrispininn.com
w stcrispininn.com

WYE

Mistral ★★★★ *Bed & Breakfast*
3 Oxenturn Road, Wye, Ashford
TN25 5BH
t (01233) 813011
e geoff@chapman.invictanet.co.uk
w chapman.invictanet.co.uk

Oxfordshire

ABINGDON

Abbey Guest House ★★★★
Guest House SILVER AWARD
136 Oxford Road, Abingdon
OX14 2AG
t (01235) 537020
e info@abbeyguest.com
w abbeyguest.com

The Grange ★★★ *Bed & Breakfast*
High Street, Abingdon
OX14 4QH
t (01865) 407808
e grahamneil@grangebb.co.uk
w brangebb.com

Kingfisher Barn ★★★★
Guest Accommodation
Rye Farm, Abingdon
OX14 3NN
t (01235) 537538
e info@kingfisherbarn.com
w kingfisherbarn.com

The Railway Inn ★★★ *Inn*
Station Road, Culham, Abingdon
OX14 3BT
t (01235) 528046
e info@railwayinnculham.co.uk
w railwayinnculham.co.uk

Sherwood ★★★★★
Bed & Breakfast
Oxford Road, Frilford Heath,
Abingdon
OX13 5NW
t (01865) 390660
e mortezaee5@aol.com

Tethers End ★★★ *Bed & Breakfast*
Abingdon Road, Abingdon
OX13 6RW
t (01235) 834015
e peterdmiller@btinternet.com
w millerbandb.co.uk

The White House ★★
Bed & Breakfast
Faringdon Road, Shippon, Abingdon
OX13 6LW
t (01235) 521998
e judymccairns@hotmail.co.uk

ADDERBURY

The Bell Inn ★★★ *Inn*
High Street, Adderbury, Oxon
OX17 3LS
t (01295) 810338
e info@the-bell.com
w the-bell.com

ARDLEY

The Old Post Office ★★★
Bed & Breakfast
Church Road, Ardley, Bicester
OX27 7NP
t (01869) 345958
e mail@theoldpostofficeardley.co.uk
w theoldpostofficeardley.co.uk

ASCOTT-UNDER-WYCHWOOD

College Farm ★★★★ *Farmhouse*
Ascott-under-Wychwood
OX7 6AL
t (01993) 831900
e sally@college-farm.com

Meadowbank House ★★★★
Bed & Breakfast
Shipton Road, Ascott-under-
Wychwood
OX7 6AG
t (01993) 830612
e ingrid@meadowbank-ascott.co.uk
w meadowbank-ascott.co.uk

The Swan at Ascott ★★★★ *Inn*
4 Shipton Road, Ascott-under-
Wychwood
OX7 6AY
t (01993) 832332
e ricky@swanatascott.com
w swanatascott.com/

BADGEMORE

Badgemore Park Golf Club
★★★★ *Guest Accommodation*
Badgemore, Henley on Thames
RG9 4NR
t (01491) 637300
e info@badgemorepark.com
w badgemorepark.com

BAMPTON

The Coach House ★★★★
Bed & Breakfast SILVER AWARD
College Farm, Bridge Street,
Bampton
OX18 2HG
t (01993) 851041
e info@thecoachhousebampton.co.uk
w thecoachhousebampton.co.uk

Manor Farm Barn B&B ★★★★
Guest Accommodation
Bull Street, Aston, Bampton
OX18 2DN
t (01993) 852907
e enquiries@manorfarmbarn.net
w manorfarmbarn.net

Wheelgate House B&B ★★★★
Bed & Breakfast
Market Square, Bampton,
Oxfordshire
OX18 2JH
t (01993) 851151
e enquiries@wheelgatehouse.co.uk
w wheelgatehouse.co.uk

key to symbols see page 6

South East | Oxfordshire

BANBURY

Ark Guesthouse ★★★ *Guest House*
Warwick Road, Banbury
OX16 2AN
t (01295) 254498

Ashlea Guesthouse ★★
Guest Accommodation
58 Oxford Road, Banbury
OX16 9AN
t (01295) 250539
e billyboland@tiscali.co.uk
w ashleaguesthouse.co.uk

Avonlea Guesthouse ★★★
Guest Accommodation
41 Southam Road, Banbury
OX16 7EP
t (01295) 267837
e whitforddebbie@hotmail.com
w avonleaguesthouse.co.uk

Banbury Cross B&B ★★★★
Guest House SILVER AWARD
1 Broughton Road, Banbury
OX16 9QB
t (01295) 266048
e mscarsbrook@btconnect.com
w banburycrossbandb.co.uk

Easington House ★★★★
Guest House
50 Oxford Road, Banbury
OX16 9AN
t (01295) 270181
e enquiries@easingtonhouse.co.uk
w easingtonhouse.co.uk

Hanwell House ★★★★
Bed & Breakfast
2 Lapsley Drive, Banbury
OX16 1EJ
t (01295) 263001
e hanwell.house@googlemail.com
w hanwellhouse.com

Pretty Bush Barn ★★★★
Bed & Breakfast
Wigginton
OX15 4LD
t (01608) 738262
e trev@prettybushbarn.fsnet.co.uk

Prospect House ★★★
Guest Accommodation
70 Oxford Road, Banbury
OX16 9AN
t (01295) 268749
e info@prospecthousebanbury.co.uk
w prospecthousebanbury.co.uk

Treetops Guest House ★★★★
Guest Accommodation
28 Dashwood Road, Banbury
OX16 5HD
t (01295) 254444
e enquiries@treetopsbanbury.co.uk
w treetopsbanbury.co.uk

White Cross House ★★★★
Bed & Breakfast
7 Broughton Road, Banbury
OX16 9QB
t (01295) 277932
e whitecrosshouse@googlemail.com

BENSON

Brookside ★★★★ *Bed & Breakfast*
Brook Street, Benson, Wallingford
OX10 6LJ
t (01491) 838289
e clivefolley@btinternet.com

Fyfield Manor ★★★★
Bed & Breakfast GOLD AWARD
Benson, Wallingford
OX10 6HA
t (01491) 835184
e chris_fyfield@hotmail.co.uk
w fyfieldmanor.co.uk

BICESTER

Ava House B&B ★★★
Guest Accommodation
23 Churchill Road, Bicester
OX26 4TR
t (01869) 345958
e mail@ava-house.co.uk
w ava-house.co.uk

Westfield Court House B&B
★★★★ *Bed & Breakfast*
North Lane, Weston-on-the-Green, Bicester
OX25 3RG
t (01869) 350777
e jbrownwest@aol.com
w westfieldcourthouse.co.uk

BLACK BOURTON

The Vines ★★★★ *Inn*
Burford Road, Black Bourton, Bampton
OX18 2PF
t (01993) 843559
e info@vineshotel.com
w vineshotel.com

BLACKTHORN

Lime Trees Farm ★★★★
Farmhouse
Lower Road, Blackthorn
OX25 1TG
t (01869) 248435
e caroline@limetreesfarm.co.uk
w limetreesfarm.co.uk

BLADON

Park House Tearoom ★★★★
Bed & Breakfast
26 Park Street, Bladon
OX20 1RW
t (01993) 813888
e info@parkhouseantiques.co.uk
w parkhouseantiques.co.uk/bandb

BRIZE NORTON

The Priory ★★★
Guest Accommodation
Manor Farm, Manor Road, Brize Norton
OX18 3NA
t (01993) 843062
e priorymanor@uwclub.net
w priorymanor.co.uk

BURFORD

Cotland House ★★★★
Guest Accommodation
Fulbrook Hill, Fulbrook, Burford
OX18 4BH
t (01993) 822382
e info@cotlandhouse.com
w cotlandhouse.com

Maytime Inn ★★★★ *Inn*
Asthall, Burford
OX18 4HW
t (01993) 822068
e info@themaytime.com
w themaytime.com/

Star Cottage ★★★★
Bed & Breakfast SILVER AWARD
Meadow Lane, Burford
OX18 4BW
t (01993) 822032
e enquiries@burfordbedandbreakfast.co.uk
w burfordbedandbreakfast.co.uk/

Westview House ★★★★
Bed & Breakfast GOLD AWARD
151 The Hill, Burford
OX18 4RE
t (01993) 824373
e titcombe@aol.com
w westview-house.co.uk

CARTERTON

The Jays ★★★★ *Bed & Breakfast*
23 The Crescent, Carterton
OX18 3SJ
t (01993) 843301
e info@thejays-carterton.co.uk
w thejays-carterton.co.uk

CHARLBURY

Banbury Hill Farm ★★★★
Guest Accommodation
Enstone Road, Charlbury
OX7 3JH
t (01608) 810314
e info@gfwiddows.co.uk
w charlburyoxfordaccom.co.uk

Bull Inn ★★★★ *Inn*
Sheep Street, Charlbury
OX7 3RR
t (01608) 810689
e info@bullinn-charlbury.com
w bullinn-charlbury.com

CHINNOR

The Croft ★★★★ *Bed & Breakfast*
Chinnor Hill, Chinnor
OX39 4BS
t (01844) 353654
e beth@acornhomesltd.co.uk
w bethatthecroft.co.uk

CHIPPING NORTON

Hackers End ★★★★
Bed & Breakfast SILVER AWARD
Hackers Lane, Churchill, Chipping Norton
OX7 6NL
t (01608) 659959
e hackers.end@btinternet.com
w hackersend.co.uk

Wild Thyme Restaurant with Rooms *Guest Accommodation*
10 New Street, Chipping Norton
OX7 5LJ
t (01608) 645060
e enquiries@wildthymerestaurant.co.uk
w wildthymerestaurant.co.uk

CHURCHILL

The Forge ★★★★
Guest Accommodation
SILVER AWARD
Church Road, Chipping Norton
OX7 6NJ
t (01608) 658173
e enquiries@cotswolds-accommodation.com
w cotswolds-accommodation.com

CULHAM

Zouch Farm B&B ★★★★
Farmhouse
Culham, Abingdon, Oxon
OX14 3BS
t (01235) 521777
e selina_wallis@hotmail.co.uk
w zouchfarm.co.uk

DEDDINGTON

Hill Barn ★★★ *Bed & Breakfast*
Banbury Road, Deddington
OX15 0TS
t (01869) 338631
e hillbarn-bb@supanet.com
w hillbarn-bb.co.uk

DIDCOT

Hagbourne Mill Farm ★★
Bed & Breakfast
Blewbury Road, Didcot
OX11 9EA
t (01235) 813140
e corderoy@hagmill.freeserve.co.uk

Prospect House ★★★
Bed & Breakfast
Upton, Didcot
OX11 9HU
t (01235) 850268

DUCKLINGTON

Ducklington Farm ★★★
Farmhouse
Course Hill Lane, Ducklington, Witney
OX29 7YL
t (01993) 772175
e strainge@ducklingtonfarm.co.uk
w countryaccom.co.uk/ducklington-farm

EWELME

Fords Farm ★★★★ *Farmhouse*
SILVER AWARD
Ewelme, Wallingford
OX10 6HU
t (01491) 839272
e fordsfarm@callnetuk.com
w fordsfarm.co.uk

EYNSHAM

Talbot Inn ★★★ *Inn*
Oxford Road, Eynsham
OX29 4BT
t (01865) 881348
e enquiries@talbot-oxford.co.uk
w talbot-oxford.co.uk

FARINGDON

Cox's Hall ★★★★ *Bed & Breakfast*
60 High Street, Stanford-In-the-Vale, Faringdon
SN7 8NQ
t (01367) 710248
e coxshall@gotadsl.co.uk

Weston Farm ★★★★ *Farmhouse*
Buscot Wick, Faringdon
SN7 8DJ
t (01367) 252222
e andrewwoof@btconnect.com
w country-accom.co.uk/weston-f

GREAT TEW

Falkland Arms ★★★★ *Inn*
Great Tew, Chipping Norton
OX7 4DB
t (01608) 683653
e falklandarms@wadworth.co.uk
w falklandarms.org.uk

HAILEY

Hunters Close Farm ★★★★
Bed & Breakfast
Middletown, Witney
OX29 9UB
t (01993) 772332
e huntersclose@yahoo.co.uk
w huntersclosefarm.co.uk

HAMPTON POYLE

The Bell at Hampton Poyle
★★★★★ *Inn* SILVER AWARD
11 Oxford Road, Hampton Poyle
OX5 2QD
t (01865) 376242
e info@thebellathamptonpoyle.co.uk
w thebellathamptonpoyle.co.uk

HARPSDEN

Apple Ash ★★★★ *Bed & Breakfast*
SILVER AWARD
Woodlands Road, Harpsden Wood, Henley-on-Thames
RG9 4AB
t (01491) 574198
e appleash@fsnet.net
w appleashbandb.co.uk

HEADINGTON

Dial House ★★★★ *Guest House*
25 London Road, Headington, Oxford
OX3 7RE
t (01865) 425100
e dialhouse@ntlworld.com
w dialhouseoxford.co.uk

Mount Pleasant ★★★
Guest Accommodation
76 London Road, Headington, Oxford
OX3 9AJ
t (01865) 762749
e mount.pleasant@ukonline.co.uk
w mountpleasanthotel.org

Mulberry Guest House ★★★
Guest Accommodation
265 London Road, Headington, Oxford
OX3 9EH
t (01865) 767114
e stay@mulberryguesthouse.co.uk
w mulberryguesthouse.co.uk

South East | Oxfordshire

HENLEY-ON-THAMES

Alushta ★★★★
Guest Accommodation
SILVER AWARD
9 Queen Street, Henley-on-Thames
RG9 1AR
t (01491) 636041
e sdr@alushta.co.uk
w alushta.co.uk

Lanchris ★★★★ Bed & Breakfast
Baronsmead, Henley-on-Thames
RG9 2DL
t (01491) 578044
e pamelajstuart@aol.com
w amanchris.co.uk

Alea House ★★★★
Guest Accommodation
Deanfield Road, Henley-on-Thames
RG9 1UU
t (01491) 576407
e massey@globalnet.co.uk
w azaleahouse.co.uk

Bank Farm ★★ Farmhouse
Old Road, Pishill, Henley-on-Thames
RG9 6HS
t (01491) 638601 Mobile
07791 665643
e e.f.lakey@btinternet.com
w stayatbankfarm.co.uk

The Baskerville ★★★★ Inn
SILVER AWARD
Station Road, Lower Shiplake,
Henley-on-Thames
RG9 3NY
t (0118) 940 3332
e enquiries@thebaskerville.com
w thebaskerville.com

Coldharbour House ★★★★
Bed & Breakfast
Coldharbour Close, Henley-on-Thames
RG9 1QF
t (01491) 575229
e coldharbourhouse@aol.com
w coldharbourhouse.com

Denmark House ★★★★
Bed & Breakfast SILVER AWARD
Northfield End, Henley-on-Thames
RG9 2HN
t (01491) 572028
e ds.hutchings@virgin.net
w denmark-house.net

Falaise House ★★★★★
Guest Accommodation
GOLD AWARD
Market Place, Henley-on-Thames
RG9 2AA
t (01491) 573388
e jane@falaisehouse.com
w falaisehouse.net

Garden View ★★★ Bed & Breakfast
Greys Road, Henley-on-Thames
RG9 1TF
t (01491) 579010
e carolplocka@aol.com
w gardenview.org.uk

Bell House ★★★
Bed & Breakfast
Northfield End, Henley-on-Thames
RG9 2JG
t (01491) 574350
e antony@antonydesign.co.uk

The Old Wood ★★★
Bed & Breakfast
Greys Road, Henley-on-Thames
RG9 1QU
t (01491) 573930
e janice@janicejones.co.uk

Orchard Dene Cottage ★★★
Bed & Breakfast
Lower Assendon, Henley-on-Thames
RG9 6AG
t (01491) 575490
e orcharddenecottage@btinternet.com
w orcharddenecottage.co.uk

Robhill ★★★★ Bed & Breakfast
267 Greys Road, Henley-on-Thames
RG9 1QS
t (01491) 577391
e jill@robhill.info
w robhillbandb.com

The Walled Garden ★★★★
Bed & Breakfast
Bell Lane, Henley-on-Thames
RG9 2HR
t (01491) 573142
e walledgard@aol.com

HENTON

Manor Farm Cottage ★★★★
Bed & Breakfast SILVER AWARD
Manor Farm Cottage, Henton,
Chinnor
OX39 4AE
t (01844) 353301
e dixonhenton@aol.com
w manorfarmcottage.info

HIGH COGGES

**Springhill Farm Bed & Breakfast
★★★★** Farmhouse
Cogges, Witney
OX29 6UL
t (01993) 704919
e jan@strainge.fsnet.co.uk

HOLTON

Home Farm House ★★★★
Bed & Breakfast SILVER AWARD
Holton, Oxford
OX33 1QA
t (01865) 872334
e sonja.barter@tiscali.co.uk
w homefarmholton.co.uk

KIDLINGTON

Warsborough House ★★★★
Bed & Breakfast
52 Mill Street, Kidlington
OX5 2EF
t (01865) 370316
e warsboroughhouse@gmail.com
w warsboroughhouse.co.uk

LETCOMBE REGIS

Brook Barn ★★★★★
Guest Accommodation
GOLD AWARD
Letcombe Regis, Wantage
OX12 9JD
t (01235) 766502
e info@brookbarn.com
w brookbarn.com

LITTLE COMPTON

The Old School ★★★★★
Guest Accommodation
SILVER AWARD
Little Compton, Moreton-in-Marsh
GL56 0SL
t (01608) 674588
e wendy@theoldschoolbedandbreakfast.com
w theoldschoolbedandbreakfast.com

LONG HANBOROUGH

Old Farmhouse ★★★★
Bed & Breakfast
Station Hill, Long Hanborough,
Woodstock
OX29 8JZ
t (01993) 882097
e rvmaundrell@btinternet.com
w countryaccom.co.uk/old-farmhouse

LONG WITTENHAM

Wittas Ham Cottage ★★★★
Bed & Breakfast SILVER AWARD
High Street, Abingdon
OX14 4QH
t (01865) 407686
e bandb@wittenham.com

LOWER TADMARTON

**Grange Farm Bed & Breakfast
★★★★** Farmhouse
Swalcliffe Grange, Banbury
OX15 5EX
t (01295) 780206
e taylor@swalcliffe-grange.freeserve.co.uk
w swalcliffegrange.com

The Horse & Groom Inn ★★★★
Inn
Milcombe
OX15 4RS
t (01295) 722142
e argyles@swalcliffe.net
w horseandgroom.biz

MILTON-UNDER-WYCHWOOD

Hillborough House ★★★★
Bed & Breakfast
The Green, Shipton Road, Burford
OX7 6JH
t (01993) 832352
e hillboroughhouse@btinternet.com

MILTON COMMON

Byways ★★★★ Bed & Breakfast
SILVER AWARD
Old London Road, Milton Common,
Thame
OX9 2JR
t (01844) 279386
e byways.mott@tiscali.co.uk
w bywaysbedandbreakfast.co.uk

MINSTER LOVELL

Hill Grove Farmhouse ★★★★
Farmhouse
Crawley Dry Lane, Witney
OX29 0NA
t (01993) 703120
e katharinemcbrown@btinternet.com
w countryaccom.co.uk/hill-grove-farm/

NEWINGTON

Hill Farm ★★★ Farmhouse
Newington, Wallingford
OX10 7AL
t (01865) 891173

NORTH MORETON

North Moreton House ★★★★★
Guest Accommodation
SILVER AWARD
High Street, North Moreton, Didcot
OX11 9AT
t (01235) 813283
e katie@northmoretonhouse.co.uk
w northmoretonhouse.co.uk

NORTH NEWINGTON

**The Blinking Owl Country Inn
★★★** Inn
Main Street, North Newington,
Banbury
OX15 6AE
t (01295) 730650

OXFORD

Adams Guest House ★★
Guest Accommodation
302 Banbury Road, Oxford
OX2 7ED
t (01865) 556118
e oxfordadamsguesthouse@hotmail.com

Arden Lodge ★★★
Guest Accommodation
34 Sunderland Avenue, Oxford
OX2 8DX
t (01865) 552076

Becket House ★★
Guest Accommodation
5 Becket Street, Oxford
OX1 1PP
t (01865) 724675
e becketguesthouse@yahoo.co.uk

Brenal Guest House ★★★
Guest House
307 Iffley Road, Oxford
OX4 4AG
t (01865) 721561
e brenalguesthouse@hotmail.co.uk
w oxfordcity.co.uk/accom/brenal

**Broomhill Bed and Breakfast
★★★★** Bed & Breakfast
SILVER AWARD
Broomhill, Lincombe Lane, Boars
Hill, Oxford
OX1 5DZ
t (01865) 735339
e sara@broomhill-oxford.co.uk
w broomhill-oxford.co.uk

Brown's Guest House ★★★
Guest Accommodation
281 Iffley Road, Oxford
OX4 4AQ
t (01865) 246822
e brownsgh@hotmail.com
w brownsguesthouse.co.uk

The Bungalow ★★★
Guest Accommodation
Mill Lane, Marston, Oxford
OX3 0QF
t (01865) 557171
e ros.bungalowbb@btinternet.com
w cherwellfarm-oxford-accom.co.uk

The Buttery ★★★★ Guest House
11 Broad Street, Oxford
OX1 3AP
t (01865) 811950
e enquiries@thebutteryhotel.co.uk
w thebutteryhotel.co.uk

Central Backpackers Oxford ★★
Backpackers
13 Park End Street, Oxford
OX1 1HH
t (01865) 242288
e oxford@centralbackpackers.co.uk
w centralbackpackers.co.uk

Chestnuts ★★★★ Bed & Breakfast
Cumnor Hill, Oxford
OX2 9HU
t (01865) 863602
e fmjones@phonecoop.coop

Cornerways Guest House ★★★★
Guest Accommodation
282 Abingdon Road, Oxford
OX1 4TA
t (01865) 240135
e jeakings@btopenworld.com
w oxfordcity.co.uk/accom/cornerways

Cotswold House ★★★★
Guest Accommodation
363 Banbury Road, Oxford
OX2 7PL
t (01865) 310558
e d.r.walker@talk21.com
w cotswoldhouse.co.uk

Falcon Guest House ★★★
Guest Accommodation
88-90 Abingdon Road, Oxford
OX1 4PX
t (01865) 511122
e stay@falconoxford.co.uk
w falconoxford.co.uk

Five Mile View Guest House ★★★
Guest House
528 Banbury Road, Oxford
OX2 8EG
t (01865) 558747
e stay@5mileview.com
w 5mileview.com

Gables ★★★★
Guest Accommodation
SILVER AWARD
6 Cumnor Hill, Oxford
OX2 9HA
t (01865) 862153
e stay@gables-oxford.co.uk
w gables-guesthouse.co.uk

key to symbols see page 6

281

South East | Oxfordshire

Head of the River ★★★★ Inn
Folly Bridge, St Aldates, Oxford
OX1 4LB
t (01865) 721600
e headoftheriver@fullers.co.uk
w fullershotels.co.uk

Isis Guest House ★★ Guest House
45-53 Iffley Road, Oxford
OX4 1ED
t (01865) 613700
e isis@herald.ox.ac.uk
w isisguesthouse.com

Lakeside Guest House ★★★★
Guest Accommodation
118 Abingdon Road, Oxford
OX1 4PZ
t (01865) 244725
e daniella.s@ntlworld.com
w oxfordcity.co.uk/accom/lakeside/

Lonsdale Guest House ★★★
Guest House
312 Banbury Road, Summertown, Oxford
OX2 7ED
t (01865) 554872
e info@lonsdale-guesthouse.co.uk
w lonsdale-guesthouse.co.uk

Milka's Guest House ★★★
Guest Accommodation
379 Iffley Road, Oxford
OX4 4DP
t (01865) 778458
e info@milkas.co.uk
w milkas.co.uk

Newton House Guest House B&B Oxford ★★★ Guest Accommodation
82-84 Abingdon Road, Oxford
OX1 4PL
t (01865) 240561
e newton.house@btinternet.com
w oxfordcity.co.uk/accom/newton

The Old Black Horse ★★★★ Inn
102 St Clements, Oxford
OX4 1AR
t (01865) 244691
e oldblackhorse@googlemail.com
w theoldblackhorsehoteloxford.co.uk

Park House ★★ Bed & Breakfast
7 St Bernards Road, Oxford
OX2 6EH
t (01865) 310824
e krynpark@hotmail.com

Parklands ★★★★
Guest Accommodation
100 Banbury Road, Oxford
OX2 6JU
t (01865) 554374
e stay@parklandsoxford.co.uk
w parklandsoxford.co.uk

Pickwick's Guest House ★★★★
Guest House
15-17 London Road, Headington, Oxford
OX3 7SP
t (01865) 750487
e pickwicks@tiscali.co.uk
w pickwicksguesthouse.co.uk

Remont ★★★★
Guest Accommodation
SILVER AWARD
367 Banbury Road, Summertown, Oxford
OX2 7PL
t (01865) 311020
e info@remont-oxford.co.uk
w remont-oxford.co.uk

Rewley House ★★★ Campus
1 Wellington Square, Oxford
OX1 2JA
t (01865) 270362
e res-ctr@conted.ox.ac.uk
w conted.ox.ac.uk

Sportsview Guest House ★★★
Guest Accommodation
106-110 Abingdon Road, Oxford
OX1 4PX
t (01865) 244268
e stay@sportsviewguesthouse.co.uk
w sportsviewguesthouse.co.uk

The Talkhouse ★★★
Guest Accommodation
Wheatley Road, Stanton St John, Oxford
OX33 1EX
t (01865) 351648
e talkhouse@fullers.co.uk
w fullershotels.com

Tilbury Lodge ★★★★
Guest Accommodation
SILVER AWARD
5 Tilbury Lane, Botley, Oxford
OX2 9NB
t (01865) 862138
e tilburylodge@yahoo.co.uk
w oxfordcity.co.uk/hotels/tilbury

The Westgate ★★
Guest Accommodation
1 Botley Road, Oxford
OX2 0AA
t (01865) 726721
e westgatehotel.2@btopenworld.com
w westgatehoteloxford.co.uk

Whitehouse View Guest House ★★★ Guest House
9 Whitehouse Road, Grandpont, Oxford
OX1 4PA
t (01865) 721626 Mobile (07831) 201259
e sramdoo@aol.com
w whitehouseviewguesthouse.co.uk

YHA Oxford ★★★★ Hostel
2A Botley Road, Oxford
OX2 0AB
t (01865) 727275
e oxford@yha.org.uk
w yha.org.uk/find-accommodation/heart-of-england/hostels/oxford/index.aspx

ROTHERFIELD PEPPARD

Slaters Farm ★★★ Bed & Breakfast
Church Lane, Rotherfield Peppard, Henley-on-Thames
RG9 5JL
t (01491) 628675
e stay@slatersfarm.co.uk

RUSSELLS WATER

Brackenhurst ★★★★
Bed & Breakfast
Brackenhurst, Russells Water, Henley-on-Thames
RG9 6EU
t (01491) 642399
e info@foolonthehill.co.uk
w foolonthehill.co.uk

SHILLINGFORD

Alouette Bed & Breakfast ★★★★
Bed & Breakfast SILVER AWARD
2 Caldicot Close, Shillingford, Wallingford
OX10 7HF
t (01865) 858600
e wendy@alouettebandb.co.uk
w alouettebandb.co.uk

The Kingfisher Inn ★★★★ Inn
27 Henley Road, Shillingford, Wallingford
OX10 7EL
t (01865) 858595
e enquiries@kingfisher-inn.co.uk
w kingfisher-inn.co.uk

Marsh House ★★★★
Bed & Breakfast
7 Court Drive, Shillingford, Wallingford
OX10 7ER
t (01865) 858496
e marsh.house@talk21.com
w marshhousebandb.co.uk

SHIPTON-UNDER-WYCHWOOD

Court Farm ★★★★ Bed & Breakfast
Mawles Lane, Shipton-under-Wychwood
OX7 6DA
t (01993) 831515
e enquiries@courtfarmbb.com
w courtfarmbb.com

Courtlands B&B ★★★★
Bed & Breakfast
6 Courtlands Road, Shipton-under-Wychwood
OX7 6DF
t (01993) 830551
e jeanandjohn@cotswoldsbandb.com
w cotswoldsbandb.com

Garden Cottage ★★★
Bed & Breakfast
Fiddlers Hill, Shipton-under-Wychwood
OX7 6DR
t (01993) 830640
e cw@gardencott.co.uk

Lodge Cottage ★★★
Bed & Breakfast
High Street, Shipton-under-Wychwood
OX7 6DG
t (01993) 830811
e helen-savill@tiscali.co.uk

SOULDERN

Tower Fields ★★★ Farmhouse
Souldern, Bicester
OX27 7HY
t (01869) 346554
e toddyclive@towerfields.com
w towerfields.com

STANDLAKE

The Cottage ★★★★
Bed & Breakfast SILVER AWARD
Witney Road, Brighthampton, Standlake
OX29 7QQ
t (01865) 300891
e info@cottagebedandbreakfaststwitney.co.uk
w cottagebedandbreakfastwitney.co.uk

STEVENTON

Cherry Tree ★★★ Inn
33 High Street, Steventon, Abingdon
OX13 6RZ
t (01235) 831222
e cherrytree@wadworth.co.uk

STOKE ROW

The Cherry Tree Inn ★★★★ Inn
Stoke Row, Henley-on-Thames
RG9 5QA
t (01491) 680430
e info@thecherrytreeinn.com
w thecherrytreeinn.com

THAME

Elm Tree Farmhouse ★★★★
Farmhouse
Moreton, Thame
OX9 2HR
t (01844) 213692
e wendyvonbergen@btinternet.com
w elmtreefarmhouse.co.uk

UFFINGTON

Norton House ★★★★
Bed & Breakfast SILVER AWARD
Broad Street, Uffington, Faringdon, Oxfordshire
SN7 7RA
t (01367) 820230
e carloberman@aol.com
w smoothhound.co.uk/hotels/nortonfaringdon

WALLINGFORD

B&B @ Little Gables ★★★★
Bed & Breakfast
166 Crowmarsh Hill, Crowmarsh Gifford, Wallingford, Oxfordshire
OX10 8BG
t (01491) 837834
e mail@littlegables.co.uk
w littlegables.co.uk

WANTAGE

A Monk's Court ★★★
Bed & Breakfast
Newbury Road, East Hendred, Wantage
OX12 8LG
t (01235) 833797
e udsl@udg.org.uk
w monkscourt.co.uk

B&B in Wantage ★★★★
Bed & Breakfast
50 Foliat Drive, Wantage
OX12 7AL
t (01235) 760495
e eleanor@eaturner.freeserve.co.
w geocities.com/bandbinwantage

Regis Guest House ★★★★
Guest House SILVER AWARD
12 Charlton Road, Wantage
OX12 8ER
t (01235) 762860
e millie_rastall@hotmail.com
w regisguesthouse.com

WESTON-ON-THE-GREEN

Weston Grounds Farm ★★★
Farmhouse
Northampton Road, Bicester
OX25 3QX
t (01869) 351168
e westongroundsbb@aol.com

WITNEY

Crofters Guest House ★★★★
Guest Accommodation
29 Oxford Hill, Witney
OX28 3JU
t (01993) 778165
e crofters.ghouse@virgin.net

The Laurels ★★★ Guest House
53 Burford Road, Witney
OX28 6DR
t (01993) 702193
e info@thelaurelsguesthouse.co.uk
w thelaurelsguesthouse.co.uk

Quarrydene ★★
Guest Accommodation
17 Dene Rise, Witney
OX28 6LU
t (01993) 772152
e jeanniemarshall@quarrydene.fswrol.co.uk

The Witney ★★★
Guest Accommodation
7 Church Green, Witney
OX28 4AZ
t (01993) 702137
e reservations@thewitneyhotel.co.uk
w thewitneyhotel.co.uk

WOODSTOCK

Blenheim Guest House & Tearooms ★★★★ Guest House
17 Park Street, Woodstock
OX20 1SJ
t (01993) 813814
e theblenheim@aol.com
w theblenheim.com

The Close Guest House ★★★
Guest House
Witney Road, Long Hanborough, Woodstock
OX29 8HF
t (01993) 882485

The Duke of Marlborough ★★★★
Inn
A44 Woodleys, Woodstock
OX20 1HT
t (01993) 811460
e sales@dukeofmarlborough.co.uk
w dukeofmarlborough.co.uk

Elbie House ★★★★
Bed & Breakfast SILVER AWARD
East End, Woodstock
OX29 6PX
t (01993) 880166
e mandy@cotswoldbreak.co.uk
w cotswoldbreak.co.uk

South East | Oxfordshire/Surrey

rselands Hall ★★★★
est Accommodation
VER AWARD
ddington Lane, Woodstock
29 6PU
t (01993) 882292
e hamilton@gorselandshall.com
w gorselandshall.com

pe House ★★★★★
d & Breakfast GOLD AWARD
Oxford Street, Woodstock
20 1TS
t (01993) 815990
e stay@hopehousewoodstock.co.uk
w hopehousewoodstock.co.uk

ephards Hall ★★★ Guest House
ney Road, Freeland, Witney
29 8HQ
t (01993) 881256
w shepherdshall.co.uk

WOODSTOCK (3 MILES)

rleigh Farm ★★★★ Farmhouse
leigh Road, Cassington,
ordshire
29 4DZ
t (01865) 881352
e cook_jane@btconnect.com
w oxfordcity.co.uk/accom/burle ighfarm

Surrey
BOOKHAM

worthy ★★ Bed & Breakfast
) Lower Road, Bookham,
otherhead
23 4DW
t (01372) 453952
e bnb.selworthy@btinternet.com
w selworthybnb.co.uk

CAPEL

htless Copse ★★★★
d & Breakfast
sper Road, Capel, Dorking, Surrey
5 5HE
t (01306) 713247
e bb@nightlesscopse.co.uk
w nightlesscopse.co.uk

CHARLWOOD

mbles Guest House ★★★★
est Accommodation
n Hill, Charlwood, Horley
6 0EP
t (01293) 863418
e stay@trumbles.co.uk
w trumbles.co.uk

CHERTSEY

ndsors ★★★★
est Accommodation
ndsor Street, Chertsey
16 8AY
t (01932) 560745
e admin@windsorshotel.com
w windsorshotel.com

DORKING

ckbrook House ★★★★★
d & Breakfast GOLD AWARD
ckbrook House, Blackbrook,
rking
5 4DS
t (01306) 888898
e blackbrookbb@internet.com
w blackbrookhouse.org.uk

oomhill ★★★ Bed & Breakfast
Broomfield Park, Westcott
4 3QQ
t (01306) 885565
e suzannewillis15@googlemail.com
w broomhillbandb.co.uk

remont Cottage ★★★★
d & Breakfast
se Hill, Dorking
4 2ED
t (01306) 885487
e claremontcott@btinternet.com
w claremontcott.co.uk

Denbies Farmhouse ★★★★
Farmhouse SILVER AWARD
Denbies Wine Estate, London Road,
Dorking
RH5 6AA
t (01306) 876777
e bandb@denbiesvineyard.co.uk
w denbiesvineyard.co.uk

Fairdene Guest House ★★★
Guest Accommodation
Moores Road, Dorking
RH4 2BG
t (01306) 888337
e zoe.richardson@ntlworld.com

Holmbury Farm ★★★★
Bed & Breakfast
Holmbury St Mary, Dorking
RH5 6NB
t (01306) 621443
e virginia@holmsburysheep.co.uk
w smoothhound.co.uk/hotels/ holmbury.html

The Kings Arms Inn ★★★★ Inn
Stane Street, Ockley, Dorking
RH5 5TS
t (01306) 711224
e enquiries@thekingsarmsockley.co. uk
w thekingsarmsockley.co.uk

Leylands Farm ★★★★
Guest Accommodation - Room Only
Leylands Lane, Abinger Common,
Dorking
RH5 6JU
t (01306) 730115
e annieblf@btopenworld.com
w leylandsfarm.co.uk

Stylehurst Farm ★★★★
Bed & Breakfast SILVER AWARD
Weare Street, Capel, Dorking
RH5 5JA
t (01306) 711259
e rosemary.goddard@virgin.net
w stylehurstfarm.com

Tanners Hatch YHA ★ Hostel
off Ranmore Road, Dorking
RH5 6BE
t (01306) 877964
e tanners@yha.org.uk
w yha.org.uk

EGHAM

Royal Holloway University of
London ★★★ - ★★★★ Campus
Egham Hill, Egham
TW20 0EX
t (01784) 443045
e sales-office@rhul.ac.uk
w rhul.ac.uk/fm

ENGLEFIELD GREEN

Bulkeley House ★★
Guest Accommodation
Englefield Green, Egham
TW20 0JU
t (01784) 431287
e bfagerstro@aol.com
w bulkeleyhouse.co.uk

EWHURST

Long Copse ★★★
Guest Accommodation
Pitch Hill, Ewhurst, Cranleigh
GU6 7NN
t (01483) 277458
e shhandley@btinternet.com

Rumbeams Cottage ★★★
Bed & Breakfast
The Green, Ewhurst, Cranleigh
GU6 7RR
t (01483) 268627
e joanna@joannacadman.com

FARNHAM

High Wray ★★★ Bed & Breakfast
73 Lodge Hill Road, Lower Bourne,
Farnham
GU10 3RB
t (01252) 715589
e alexine@highwray73.co.uk
w highwray73.co.uk

Mill Lane Lodge ★★★
Bed & Breakfast
Mill Lane, Crondall, Farnham, Surrey
GU10 5RP
t 01252 850230
e milllanelodge@googlemail.com

Princess Royal Lodge ★★★★ Inn
Guildford Road, Runfold, Farnham
GU10 1NX
t (01252) 782243
e princessroyal@fullers.co.uk
w fullershotels.co.uk

GODALMING

Combe Ridge ★★★
Bed & Breakfast
Pook Hill, Chiddingfold, Godalming
GU8 4XR
t (01428) 682607
e brendaessex@btinternet.com

Heath Hall Farm ★★★ Farmhouse
Bowlhead Green, Godalming
GU8 6NW
t (01428) 682808
e heathhallfarm@btinternet.com
w heathhallfarm.co.uk

Heath House ★★★★★
Bed & Breakfast GOLD AWARD
Alldens Lane, Godalming
GU8 4AP
t (01483) 416961
e info@heathhouse.eu
w heathhouse.eu

Highview ★★ Bed & Breakfast
SILVER AWARD
39 Nightingale Road, Godalming
GU7 2HU
t (01483) 861974
e highview@which.net
w highview-Bedbreakfast.co.uk

Hindhead YHA ★ Hostel
Punch Bowl Lane, Thursley,
Godalming
GU8 6NS
t (01428) 604285
w yha.org.uk

Lavender's ★★★ Bed & Breakfast
129 Binscombe, Godalming
GU7 3QL
t (01483) 415261
e colingardner@btinternet.com

No 24 ★★★ Guest Accommodation
24 Croft Road, Godalming
GU7 1BY
t (01483) 429982
e mandy@no24croftroad.co.uk

GUILDFORD

Abeille House ★★★★
Bed & Breakfast
119 Stoke Road, Guildford
GU1 1ET
t (01483) 532200
e abeille.house119@ntlworld.com
w abeillehouse.co.uk

Barn Cottage ★★★★
Bed & Breakfast
Farley Green, Albury, Guildford
GU5 9DN
t (01483) 202571
e bookings@barn-cottage.com
w barn-cottage.com

Bluebells ★★★ Bed & Breakfast
21 Coltsfoot Drive, Guildford
GU1 1YH
t (01483) 826124
e hughes.a@ntlworld.com
w bluebellsbedandbreakfast.co.uk

East Woodhay ★★★★
Bed & Breakfast
86a Epsom Road, Guildford
GU1 2DH
t (01483) 575986
e eastwoodhay@yahoo.co.uk

Field Villa ★★ Bed & Breakfast
Liddington New Road, Guildford
GU3 3AH
t (01483) 233961

Guildford YMCA ★★★★ Hostel
Bridge Street, Guildford
GU1 4SB
t (01483) 532555
e accom@guildfordymca.org.uk
w guildfordymca.org.uk

The Homestead BNB ★★
Bed & Breakfast
75 Bray Road, Guildford
GU2 7LJ
t (01483) 828663
w thehomesteadbnb.co.uk

Littlefield Manor ★★★ Farmhouse
Littlefield Common, Guildford
GU3 3HJ
t (01483) 233068
e john@littlefieldmanor.co.uk
w littlefieldmanor.co.uk

Matchams ★★ Bed & Breakfast
35 Boxgrove Avenue, Guildford
GU1 1XQ
t (01483) 567643

Patcham ★★ Bed & Breakfast
44 Farnham Road, Guildford
GU2 4LS
t (01483) 570789

Plaegan House ★★★★
Bed & Breakfast
96 Wodeland Avenue, Guildford
GU2 4LD
t (01483) 822181
e froxanphillips@yahoo.co.uk
w plaeganhouse.co.uk

Silkmore ★★★★ Bed & Breakfast
Silkmore Lane, West Horsley,
Guildford
KT24 6JQ
t (01483) 284109
e info@silkmorehouse.com
w silkmorehouse.com

Stoke House ★★★ Guest House
113 Stoke Road, Guildford
GU1 1ET
t (01483) 453025
e bookings@stokehouse.net
w stokehouse.net

HASLEMERE

Deerfell ★★★★ Bed & Breakfast
Blackdown, Haslemere
GU27 3BU
t (01428) 653409
e deerfell@tesco.net
w deerfell.co.uk

Langhams Cottage B&B ★★★★
Bed & Breakfast SILVER AWARD
Petworth Road, Haslemere
GU27 3BG
t (01428) 643052
e enquiries@langhamscottage.com
w langhamscottage.com

Strathire ★★★★ Bed & Breakfast
Grayswood Road, Haslemere
GU27 2BW
t (01428) 642466
e joyce.malcolm.harris@hotmail.co. uk
w strathire.co.uk

The Wheatsheaf Inn ★★★ Inn
Grayswood Road, Haslemere
GU27 2DE
t (01428) 644440
e ken@thewheatsheafgrayswood. co.uk
w Thewheatsheafgrayswood.co.uk

HOLMBURY ST MARY

Bulmer Farm Bed & Breakfast
★★★★ Guest Accommodation
Holmbury St Mary, Pasturewood
Road, Dorking
RH5 6LG
t (01306) 731871
e enquiries@bulmerfarm.co.uk
w bulmerfarm.co.uk

key to symbols see page 6

South East | Surrey/Sussex

Holmbury St Mary YHA ★★ *Hostel*
Radnor Lane, Dorking
RH5 6NW
t (01306) 730777
e holmbury@yha.org.uk
w yha.org.uk

HORLEY

Berrens Guest House ★★★
Guest House
62 Massetts Road, Horley
RH6 7DS
t (01293) 430800

Melville Lodge Guest House ★★★
Guest House
15 Brighton Road, Horley
RH6 7HH
t (01293) 784951
e melvillelodge.guesthouse@tesco.net
w melvillelodgegatwick.co.uk

Rosemead Guest House ★★★★
Guest House SILVER AWARD
19 Church Road, Horley
RH6 7EY
t (01293) 784965
e info@rosemeadguesthouse.co.uk
w rosemeadguesthouse.co.uk

The Turret Guest House ★★★
Guest Accommodation
48 Massetts Road, Horley
RH6 7DS
t (01293) 782490
e info@theturret.com
w theturret.com

LOWER BOURNE

Kiln Farm Bed & Breakfast
★★★★ *Bed & Breakfast*
8 Kiln Lane, Lower Bourne,
Farnham, Surrey
GU10 3LR
t (01252) 726083
e raphe_palmer@tiscali.co.uk
w kilnfarm.plus.com

St Gallen ★★★★ *Bed & Breakfast*
Old Frensham Road, Lower Bourne,
Farnham
GU10 3PT
t (01252) 793412
e cary_wilkins@cw1999.freeserve.co.uk

PEASLAKE

The Garden Room ★★★★
Guest Accommodation
Crest Hill, Peaslake, Guildford
GU5 9PE
t (01306) 730547
e coltsfoot@btinternet.com
w gardenroom.btng.uk

Woodhouse Farm
Guest Accommodation
The Old Stables, Rad Lane, Peaslake
GU5 9PB
t (01306) 731760
e info@woodhousefarm.net

RIPLEY

Four Oaks Cottage ★★★
Bed & Breakfast
Polesden Lane, Ripley, Woking
GU23 6DX
t (01483) 225151
e fouroaksbb@aol.com
w fouroaksbb.co.uk

ROWLEDGE

Rosebarton ★★★★ *Bed & Breakfast*
Cherry Tree Walk, Rowledge,
Farnham
GU10 4AD
t (01252) 793580
e rosebarton@btinternet.com

RUDGWICK

Linacre Lodge ★★★★
Bed & Breakfast GOLD AWARD
Baynards, Rudgwick, Horsham
RH12 3AD
t (01403) 823522
e chrisandlauraanstead@mac.com

SHALFORD

2 Northfield ★★★ *Bed & Breakfast*
off Summersbury Drive, Shalford,
Guildford
GU4 8JN
t (01483) 570431
e themordens@tiscali.co.uk
w northfieldbnb.net

The Laurels ★★★ *Bed & Breakfast*
23 Dagden Road, Shalford,
Guildford
GU4 8DD
t (01483) 565753

SHERE

Lockhurst Hatch Farm ★★★★
Farmhouse
Lockhurst Hatch Lane, Shere,
Guildford
GU5 9JN
t (01483) 202689
e gill@lockhurst-hatch-farm.co.uk
w users.waitrose.com/~gmgellatly

STAINES

The Swan ★★★★ *Inn*
The Hythe, Staines
TW18 3JB
t (01784) 452494
e swan.hotel@fullers.co.uk
w fullershotels.co.uk

SURBITON

Ditton Lodge ★★★★
Guest Accommodation
47 Lovelace Road, Long Ditton,
Kingston-upon-Thames
KT6 6NA
t (020) 8399 7482
e info@dittonlodge.co.uk

VIRGINIA WATER

Savannah Bed & Breakfast
★★★★ *Bed & Breakfast*
Luddington Avenue, Virginia Water
GU25 4DF
t (01344) 843579
e helen@savannah-bandb.co.uk
w savannah-bandb.co.uk

WALTON-ON-THAMES

Bricklayers Arms ★★★★ *Inn*
6 Queens Road, Walton-on-Thames
KT12 5LS
t (01932) 220936
e ff@bricklayers-arms.fsworld.co.uk

WEST CLANDON

The Oaks ★★ *Bed & Breakfast*
Highcotts Lane, West Clandon,
Guildford
GU4 7XA
t (01483) 222531
e kate_broad@yahoo.co.uk

WEYBRIDGE

The Clock House ★★★★
Guest House SILVER AWARD
242 Brooklands Road, Weybridge
KT13 0RD
t (01932) 859595
e julie@sunshinelink.com
w theclockhouseweybridge.com

WOKING

Fenton House ★★★★
Bed & Breakfast
19 Kingsway, Woking
GU21 6NU
t 01483 828 225
e fentonhouse19@googlemail.com
w fentonhousebandb.co.uk

Grantchester ★★ *Bed & Breakfast*
Boughton Hall Avenue, Send,
Woking
GU23 7DF
t (01483) 225383
e info@bandb-bandb.co.uk
w bandb-bandb.co.uk

Saint Columba's House ★★★
Guest Accommodation
Maybury Hill, Woking
GU22 8AB
t (01483) 766498
e retreats@stcolumbashouse.org.uk
w stcolumbashouse.org.uk

WONERSH

Woodyers Farm ★★★★
Bed & Breakfast
Barnett Lane, Wonersh, Guildford
GU5 0RX
t (01483) 892862
e woodyersfarm@hotmail.co.uk

Sussex

ALFRISTON

Rose Cottage ★★★★
Bed & Breakfast SILVER AWARD
North Street, Alfriston
BN26 5UQ
t (01323) 871534
e hd.rosecottage@btinternet.com
w rosecott.uk.com

AMBERLEY

The Thatched House ★★★★
Guest Accommodation
SILVER AWARD
Hog Lane, Amberley, Arundel
BN18 9NS
t (01798) 831329
e ma.leonard@tiscali.co.uk
w thatchedhouseamberley.co.uk

AMBERSTONE

Waldernheath Country House
Bed & Breakfast
Hailsham Road, Amberstone,
Hailsham
BN27 1PJ
t (01323) 442259
e l.j.g@waldernheath.com
w visitsussex.org/waldernheathcountryhouse

ANSTY

Highbridge Mill ★★★★
Bed & Breakfast GOLD AWARD
Cuckfield Road, Ansty, Cuckfield,
Haywards Heath
RH17 5AE
t (01444) 450881
w highbridgemill.com

ARUNDEL

April Cottage ★★★★
Bed & Breakfast GOLD AWARD
Crossbush Lane, Arundel
BN18 9PQ
t (01903) 885401
e april.cott@btinternet.com
w april-cottage.co.uk

Brook Green, Amberley ★★
Bed & Breakfast
Hog Lane, Amberley, Arundel
BN18 9NQ
t (01798) 831275

Burpham Country House ★★★★
Guest House SILVER AWARD
(formerly The Old Parsonage), The
Street, Arundel
BN18 9RJ
t (01903) 882160
e info@burphamcountryhouse.com
w burphamcountryhouse.com

Eastmere House B&B ★★★★
Bed & Breakfast
Eastergate Lane, Eastergate,
Arundel, Nr Chichester
PO20 3SJ
t (01243) 544204
e bernardlane@hotmail.com
w eastmere.co.uk

Furzetor ★★★★ *Bed & Breakfast*
SILVER AWARD
Clay Lane, Warningcamp, Arundel
BN18 9QN
t (01903) 882974
e furzetor@hotmail.com
w furzetorbedandbreakfast.co.uk

Longacre ★★★★ *Bed & Breakfast*
The Street, Walberton, Arundel
BN18 0PY
t (01243) 543542
e longacrebandb@tinyworld.co.u
w visitsussex.org/site/where-to-st
longacre-p22261

Swan Hotel, Arundel ★★★★ *In*
27-29 High Street, Arundel
BN18 9AG
t (01903) 882314
e swanhotel.arundel@fullers.co.u
w fullershotels.com

Woodacre ★★★★
Guest Accommodation
Arundel Road, Fontwell, Arundel
BN18 0QP
t (01243) 814301
e wacrebb@aol.com
w woodacre.co.uk

Woodpeckers ★★★★
Bed & Breakfast
15 Dalloway Road, Arundel
BN18 9HJ
t (01903) 883948
e arundel.vic@arun.gov.uk

BALCOMBE

Rocks Lane Cottage ★★★★
Bed & Breakfast
Rocks Lane, Balcombe, Haywards
Heath
RH17 6JG
t (01444) 811245
e angelaparry@talktalk.net

BARNHAM

The Chicken Shed ★★★★
Bed & Breakfast
Highground Barn, Highground La
Bognor Regis
PO22 0BU
t (01243) 553817
e family@bedford52.plus.com
w thechickenshed.englishhome.c

Downhills ★★ *Bed & Breakfast*
87 Barnham Road, Barnham, Bog
Regis
PO22 0EQ
t (01243) 553104

BATTLE

The Annex Cottage ★★★★
Bed & Breakfast
Whatlington, Battle
TN33 0NN
t (01424) 870342

Battle Golf Club ★★★
Guest Accommodation
Netherfield Hill, Battle
TN33 0LH
t (01424) 775677
e clare@battlegolfclub.com
w battlegolfclub.com

The Bull Inn ★★★ *Inn*
27 High Street, Battle
TN33 0EA
t (01424) 775171
w bullinbattle.eu

Forge House ★★★★
Bed & Breakfast
The Green, Sedlescombe, Battle
TN33 0QA
t (01424) 870054

Tollgate Farm House ★★★★
Guest Accommodation
SILVER AWARD
59 North Trade Road, Battle
TN33 0HS
t (01424) 777436
e christinemhowe@hotmail.com
w tollgatefarmhouse.co.uk

South East | Sussex

dor House ★★★★
& Breakfast
Mount Street, Battle
33 0EG
(01424) 775386
stan@stanrosenthal.com
stanrosenthal.com

BEXHILL

e's Bed & Breakfast ★★★★
est Accommodation
Hastings Road, Bexhill
40 2HH
(01424) 733268
evesbandb@googlemail.com
evesbandb.com

BEXHILL-ON-SEA

any House ★★★★
& Breakfast **SILVER AWARD**
Albany Road, Bexhill-on-Sea
40 1BY
(01424) 217151
albanyhouse@fsmail.net

den House ★★★★
& Breakfast **SILVER AWARD**
Manor Road, Bexhill-on-Sea
40 1SP
(01424) 225068
info@ardenhousebexhill.co.uk
ardenhousebexhill.co.uk

osa ★★★★
est Accommodation
Albert Road, Bexhill-on-Sea
40 1DG
(01424) 212574
info@arosahotel.co.uk
arosahotel.co.uk

rrington ★★★★
est Accommodation
Wilton Road, Bexhill-on-Sea
40 1HY
(01424) 210250

khill Bed & Breakfast ★★★★
& Breakfast
field, 21 Glyne Ascent, Bexhill-Sea
40 2NX
(01424) 222323
bexhillbedandbreakfast@yahoo.
bedbreakfastbexhill.co.uk

ast B&B ★★★★ *Bed & Breakfast*
VER AWARD
Sea Road, Bexhill-on-Sea
40 1JP
(01424) 225260
info@coastbexhill.co.uk
coastbexhill.co.uk

bwebs ★★★★
est Accommodation
Collington Avenue, Bexhill-on-
39 3QA
(01424) 213464
kobwebs@waitrose.com
cobwebsbexhill.co.uk

llington Lodge ★★★★
est House
Collington Avenue, Bexhill-on-
39 3PX
(01424) 210024
enquiries@collingtonlodge.co.uk
collingtonlodge.co.uk

nselma ★★★★
est Accommodation
VER AWARD
nselma, 25 Marina, Bexhill-on-Sea
40 1BP
(01424) 734144
stay@dunselma.co.uk
dunselma.co.uk

glish Rose ★★★★
d & Breakfast
Magdalen Road, Bexhill-on-Sea
40 1SB
(01424) 218969
enquiries@englishrosebexhill.com
englishrosebexhill.co.uk

Highwoods Farm B&B ★★★★★
Bed & Breakfast **SILVER AWARD**
Whydown Road, Bexhill-on-Sea
TN39 4RB
t (01424) 846835
e highwoodsbandb@hotmail.co.uk
w highwoodsfarmbandb.co.uk

Manor Barn Ensuite Chalets ★★★
Bed & Breakfast
Ninfield Road, Lunsford Cross,
Bexhill-on-Sea
TN39 5JJ
t (01424) 893018
e bsgillingham@yahoo.co.uk

The Old Manse ★★★★★
Bed & Breakfast **GOLD AWARD**
18 Terminus Avenue, Bexhill-on-Sea
TN39 3LS
t (01424) 216151
e debbie.march@virgin.net
w theoldmansebexhill.co.uk

The Old Vicarage ★★★★★
Bed & Breakfast **GOLD AWARD**
5 Brassey Road, Bexhill-on-Sea
TN40 1LD
t (01424) 213498
e oldvicaragebexhill@hotmail.com

Park Lodge ★★★★
Guest Accommodation
16 Egerton Road, Bexhill-on-Sea
TN39 3HH
t (01424) 216547
e info@parklodgehotel.co.uk
w parklodgehotel.co.uk

The Wiltons ★★★★
Guest Accommodation
33 Wilton Road, Bexhill-on-Sea
TN40 1HX
t (01424) 212748
e email@the-wiltons.com
w the-wiltons.com

BIGNOR

Stane House ★★★★
Guest Accommodation
SILVER AWARD
Bignor, Pulborough, Petworth
RH20 1PQ
t (01798) 869454
e angie@stanehouse.co.uk
w stanehouse.co.uk

BIRDHAM

Croftside Cottage ★★★★
Bed & Breakfast **SILVER AWARD**
Main Road, Birdham, Chichester
PO20 7HS
t (01243) 512864
e croftside@btinternet.com
w croftsidebandb.com

BLACKBOYS

Rangers Cottage ★★★★
Bed & Breakfast
Terminus Road, Blackboys, Uckfield
TN22 5LX
t (01825) 890463
e rangers.cottage@btinternet.com
w rangerscottage.co.uk

BOGNOR REGIS

The Aldwick ★★★★
Guest Accommodation
25 Princess Avenue, Aldwick,
Bognor Regis
PO21 2QU
t (01243) 821945
e careyjane99@yahoo.co.uk
w thealdwickroomsandrestaurant.
co.uk

Bognor Regis Campus ★★ - ★★★
Campus
University College Chichester, Upper
Bognor Road, Bognor Regis
PO21 1HR
t (01243) 812140
e conference@ucc.ac.uk
w chi.ac.uk/conference/index.cfm

Hayleys Corner ★★★★
Bed & Breakfast
14 Limmer Lane, Bognor Regis
PO22 7EJ
t (01243) 826139 mobile
07854814728
e hayleyscornerbandb@yahoo.co.uk
w hayleyscorner.co.uk

Homestead Guest House ★★★
Guest House
90 Aldwick Road, Bognor Regis
PO21 2PD
t (01243) 823443
e the_homestead@hotmail.co.uk
w homesteadbognor.com

Jubilee Guest House ★★★
Guest Accommodation
5 Gloucester Road, Bognor Regis
PO21 1NU
t (01243) 863016
e jubileeguesthouse@tiscali.co.uk
w jubileeguesthouse.com

Margee's B&B ★★★★
Guest Accommodation
62 Downview Road, Bognor Regis
PO22 8JA
t (01243) 864173
e margeesbbfelpham@uwclub.net
w margeesfelpham.co.uk

Sea Crest ★★★
Guest Accommodation
19 Nyewood Lane, Aldwick, Bognor
Regis
PO21 2QB
t (01243) 821438
e seacrest.19@btinternet.com
w seacrestguesthouse.co.uk

Selwood Lodge ★★★ *Guest House*
93 Victoria Drive, Bognor Regis
PO21 2DZ
t (01243) 865071
e mail@selwoodlodge.com
w selwoodlodge.com

Swan Guest House ★★★★
Guest House
17 Nyewood Lane, Aldwick, Bognor
Regis
PO21 2QB
t (01243) 826880
e swanhse@globalnet.co.uk
w swanguesthousebognor.co.uk

Trevali Guest House ★★★★
Guest Accommodation
Belmont Street, Bognor Regis
PO21 1LE
t (01243) 862203
e info@trevaliguesthouse.co.uk
w trevaliguesthouse.co.uk

Tudor Cottage Guest House ★★★
Bed & Breakfast
194 Chichester Road, Bognor Regis
PO21 5BJ
t (01243) 821826
e tudorcottage@supernet.com

White Horses Felpham ★★★★
Bed & Breakfast
Clyde Road, Felpham, Bognor Regis,
West Sussex
PO22 7AH
t (01243) 824320
e whitehorsesbandb@btinternet.
com
w whitehorsesfelpham.co.uk

Willow Rise ★★★★
Bed & Breakfast **SILVER AWARD**
131 North Bersted Street, Bognor
Regis
PO22 9AG
t (01243) 829544
e gillboon@aol.com
w visitsussex.org/willowrise

BOLNEY

Bramble Cottage ★★★★
Bed & Breakfast
The Street, Bolney, Haywards Heath
RH17 5PG
t (01444) 881643
e enquiries@bramblecottagebb.co.
uk
w bramblecottagebb.co.uk

Broxmead Paddock ★★★★
Bed & Breakfast **SILVER AWARD**
Broxmead Lane, Bolney, Haywards
Heath
RH17 5RG
t (01444) 881458
e broxmeadpaddock@hotmail.com
w broxmeadpaddock.eclipse.co.uk

BOSHAM

Good Hope ★★★★ *Bed & Breakfast*
SILVER AWARD
Delling Lane, Bosham, Chichester
PO18 8NR
t (01243) 572487
e goodhope_bosham@yahoo.co.uk
w visitsussex.org/goodhope

BOSHAM (CHICHESTER 3 MILES)

Benbow ★★★★ *Inn*
Shore Road, Bosham, Chichester,
West Sussex
PO18 8QL
t 01243 572 127
e bb@benbowbosham.co.uk
w benbowbosham.co.uk

BOXGROVE

Brufords ★★★★
Guest Accommodation
66-66A The Street, Boxgrove,
Chichester
PO18 0EE
t (01243) 774085
e room4me@brufords.org
w brufords.org

BREDE

2 Stonelink Cottages ★★
Bed & Breakfast
Stubb Lane, Brede, Rye
TN31 6BL
t (01424) 882943/07802 573612
e stonelinkC@aol.com

Little Garth Bed & Breakfast
★★★★ *Bed & Breakfast*
SILVER AWARD
Little Garth, Cackle Street, Rye
TN31 6DX
t (01424) 882093
e info@littlegarthbrede.co.uk
w littlegarthbrede.co.uk

BRIGHTON

Amblecliff ★★★
Guest Accommodation
35 Upper Rock Gardens, Brighton
BN2 1QF
t (01273) 681161
e reservations@amblecliff.co.uk
w amblecliff.co.uk

Andorra Guest Accommodation
★★★ *Guest Accommodation*
15-16 Oriental Place, Brighton
BN1 2LJ
t (01273) 321787
e andorrahotel@hotmail.com
w andorrahotelbrighton.co.uk

Artist Residence ★★★ *Guest House*
33 Regency Square, Brighton
BN1 2GG
t (01273) 324302
e info@artistresidence.co.uk
w artistresidence.co.uk

Atlantic Seafront ★★★★
Guest Accommodation
16 Marine Parade, Brighton
BN2 1TL
t (01273) 695944
e majanatlantic@hotmail.com
w atlantichotelbrighton.co.uk

Blanch House ★★★★
Guest Accommodation
17 Atlingworth Street, Brighton
BN2 1PL
t (01273) 603504
e info@blanchhouse.co.uk
w blanchhouse.co.uk

key to symbols *see page 6*

285

South East | Sussex

brightonwave ★★★★
Guest Accommodation
SILVER AWARD
10 Madeira Place, Brighton
BN2 1TN
t (01273) 676794
e info@brightonwave.co.uk
w brightonwave.co.uk

The Cavalaire ★★★★
Guest Accommodation
GOLD AWARD
34 Upper Rock Gardens, Brighton
BN2 1QF
t (01273) 696899
e welcome@cavalaire.co.uk
w cavalaire.co.uk

Christina Guest House ★★★
Guest House
20 St Georges Terrace, Brighton
BN2 1JH
t (01273) 690862
e christinaguesthouse@yahoo.co.uk
w christinaguesthousebrighton.co.uk

Hudsons ★★★★
Guest Accommodation
22 Devonshire Place, Brighton
BN2 1QA
t (01273) 683642
e info@hudsonshotel.com
w hudsonsinbrighton.co.uk

Kemp Townhouse ★★★★★
Guest Accommodation
SILVER AWARD
21 Atlingworth Street, Brighton
BN2 1PL
t (01273) 681400
e reservations@kemptownhouse.com
w kemptownhousebrighton.com

Lanes Hotel ★★★
Guest Accommodation
70-72 Marine Parade, Brighton
BN2 1AE
t (01273) 674131
e enquiries@laneshotel.co.uk
w laneshotel.co.uk

Leona House ★★★★
Guest Accommodation
SILVER AWARD
74 Middle Street, Brighton
BN1 1AL
t (01273) 327109
e hazel.eastman@btconnect.com
w leonahousebrighton.com

The Neo ★★★★
Guest Accommodation
SILVER AWARD
19 Oriental Place, Brighton
BN1 2LL
t (01273) 711104
e info@neohotel.com
w neohotel.com

New Madeira ★★★★
Guest Accommodation
19-23 Marine Parade, Brighton
BN2 1TL
t (01273) 698331
e info@newmadeirahotel.com
w newmadeirahotel.com

One Broad Street ★★★★
Guest Accommodation
1 Broad Street, Brighton
BN2 1TJ
t (01273) 699227
e info@onebroadstreet.com
w onebroadstreet.com

Russell Guest House ★★★
Guest Accommodation
19 Russell Square, Brighton
BN1 2EE
t (01273) 327122
e info@therussell.co.uk
w therussell.co.uk

Sandpiper Guest House ★★★
Guest House
11 Russell Square, Brighton
BN1 2EE
t (01273) 328202
e sandpiper@brighton.co.uk

Sea Breeze ★★★★ *Guest House*
SILVER AWARD
13 Upper Rock Gardens, Brighton
BN2 1QE
t 0844 736 1847
e info@seabreezebrighton.com
w seabreezebrighton.com

Sea Spray ★★★★
Guest Accommodation
SILVER AWARD
25 New Steine, Brighton
BN2 1PD
t (01273) 680332
e seaspray@brighton.co.uk
w seaspraybrighton.co.uk

St Christophers & Belushi's ★★
Hostel
10-12 Grand Junction Road, Brighton
BN1 1PN
t (01273) 202035
e chris.spence@st-christophers.co.uk
w st-christophers.co.uk

University of Brighton ★★ - ★★★
Campus
Conference Office, Exion 27, Brighton
BN1 8AF
t (01273) 643167
e conferences@brighton.ac.uk
w brighton.ac.uk/conferences

Whitburn Lodge ★★★★
Guest House
12 Montpelier Road, Brighton
BN1 2LQ
t (01273) 729005
e info@whitburnlodge.com
w whitburnlodge.com

BRIGHTON & HOVE

Adelaide House ★★★★
Guest Accommodation
51 Regency Square, Brighton
BN1 2FF
t (01273) 205286
e info@adelaide-house.co.uk
w adelaide-house.co.uk

Kipps Brighton ★★ *Hostel*
76 Grand Parade, Brighton
BN2 9JA
t 01273 604182
e kippshostelbrighton@gmail.com
w kipps-brighton.com

Lansdowne Guest House ★★★★
Guest Accommodation
SILVER AWARD
Hove
BN3 1FE
t 07803 484775
e lansdowneguesthouse@hotmail.co.uk
w lansdowneguesthouseonline.com

The Twenty One ★★★★
Guest Accommodation
GOLD AWARD
21 Charlotte Street, Brighton, East Sussex
BN2 1AG
t 01273 686450
e enquiries@thetwentyone.co.uk
w thetwentyone.co.uk

BROAD OAK

Hazelhurst ★★★★
Guest Accommodation
SILVER AWARD
Hazelhurst, Chitcombe Road, Broad Oak, Rye, East Sussex
TN31 6EU
t (01424) 883411
e bookings@hazelhurstbroadoak.co.uk
w hazelhurstbroadoak.co.uk

BURGESS HILL

Daisy Lodge ★★★
Guest Accommodation
Royal George Road, Burgess Hill
RH15 9SE
t (01444) 870570
e stay@daisylodge.co.uk

Meadows ★★★★ *Bed & Breakfast*
87 Meadow Lane, Burgess Hill
RH15 9JD
t (01444) 248421
e bsayers@hotmail.co.uk

St Owens ★★★★ *Bed & Breakfast*
SILVER AWARD
11 Silverdale Road, Burgess Hill
RH15 0ED
t (01444) 236435
e nevillebaker@btinternet.com
w visitsussex.org/stowens

Wellhouse ★★★★
Guest Accommodation
SILVER AWARD
Wellhouse Lane, Burgess Hill
RH15 0BN
t (01444) 233231
e amhallen@onetel.com
w visitsussex.org/wellhouse

BURY

The Barn at Penfolds ★★★★
Bed & Breakfast **GOLD AWARD**
The Street, Bury, Pulborough
RH20 1PA
t (01798) 831496
e susiemacnamara@hotmail.co.uk
w thebarnatpenfolds.co.uk

CARTERS CORNER

Windesworth ★★★★
Bed & Breakfast
Carters Corner, Hailsham
BN27 4HT
t (01323) 847178
e windesworth.bedandbreakfast@virgin.net
w visitsussex.org/windesworth

CHARLTON

Fox Goes Free ★★★★ *Inn*
Charlton, Chichester
PO18 0HU
t (01243) 811461
e thefoxgoesfree.always@virgin.net
w thefoxgoesfree.com

Woodstock House ★★★★
Guest Accommodation
SILVER AWARD
Charlton, Chichester
PO18 0HU
t (01243) 811666
e info@woodstockhotel.co.uk
w woodstockhousehotel.co.uk

CHELWOOD GATE

Holly House ★★★★ *Guest House*
SILVER AWARD
Beaconsfield Road, Chelwood Gate, Haywards Heath, West Sussex
RH17 7LF
t (01825) 740484
e db@hollyhousebnb.demon.co.uk
w hollyhousebnb.demon.co.uk

CHELWOOD GATE, EAST GRINSTEAD

Laurel Cottage ★★★
Bed & Breakfast
Baxters Lane, Chelwood Gate, Haywards Heath
RH17 7LU
t (01825) 740547
e smartin@chelwood.fsnet.co.uk

CHICHESTER

5a Little London ★★★
Bed & Breakfast
Little London, Chichester
PO19 1PH
t (01243) 788405

21 Brandyhole Lane ★★
Guest Accommodation
Brandy Hole Lane, Chichester
PO19 5RL
t (01243) 528201
e anne@anneparry.me.uk

Anna's ★★★★ *Bed & Breakfast*
SILVER AWARD
27 Westhampnett Road, Chichester
PO19 7HW
t (01243) 788522
e judiths@fsmail.net
w annasofchichester.co.uk

Cherry End ★★★★ *Bed & Breakfast*
3 Clydesdale Avenue, Chichester
PO19 7PW
t (01243) 531397
e cherryendbb@yahoo.co.uk
w cherryend.com

The Cottage ★★★ *Bed & Breakfast*
22B Westhampnett Road, Chichester
PO19 7HW
t (01243) 774979
e mbc.technical@virgin.net

The Cottage ★★★★
Bed & Breakfast **SILVER AWARD**
Church Road, North Mundham, Chichester
PO20 1JU
t (01243) 784586
e lambrinudi-bandb@supanet.com
w the-thatched-cottage.co.uk

The Dairy Farm ★★★★
Bed & Breakfast **SILVER AWARD**
East Ashling, Chichester
PO18 9AR
t (01243) 575544
e d.a.ash@btinternet.com

Field View ★★★★ *Bed & Breakfast*
SILVER AWARD
Nyton Road, Chichester
PO20 3TX
t (01243) 543784
e info@fieldviewbedandbreakfast.co.uk
w fieldviewbedandbreakfast.co.uk

George Bell House ★★★★★
Guest House
4 Canon Lane, Chichester, West Sussex
PO19 1PX
t (01243) 813586
e bookings@chichestercathedral.org.uk
w chichestercathedral.org.uk

Kia-ora ★★★ *Bed & Breakfast*
Main Road, Nutbourne, Chichester
PO18 8RT
t (01243) 572858
e ruthiefp@tiscali.co.uk

Limmer Pond Cottage ★★★
Bed & Breakfast
Church Road, Aldingbourne, Chichester
PO20 3TX
t (01243) 543210

Mount Pleasant House ★★★★
Bed & Breakfast
Level Mare Lane, Eastergate, Chichester
PO20 3SB
t (01243) 545368
e gforsyth1@btinternet.com
w mountpleasant-bedandbreakfast.co.uk

The Nags Head ★★★★ *Inn*
3 St Pancras, Chichester
PO19 7SJ
t (01243) 785823
e nagshedhotel@aol.com
w thenagshotel.co.uk

Pen Cottage ★★★★
Bed & Breakfast
The Drive, Summersdale, Chichester
PO19 5QA
t (01243) 783667
e monicaandcolinkaye@talktalk.net
w pencottage.co.uk

Spooners ★★★★ *Bed & Breakfast*
SILVER AWARD
1 Maplehurst Road, Chichester
PO19 6QL
t (01243) 528467
e sue-spooner@tiscali.co.uk

South East | Sussex

bcroft Farm ★★★
& Breakfast **SILVER AWARD**
bcroft Lane, East Wittering,
chester
20 8PJ
t (01243) 671469
e mail@stubcroft.com
w stubcroft.com

e Studio B&B Birdham ★★★★
est Accommodation - Room Only
VER AWARD
r Timbers, Main Road, Birdham,
chester
20 7HS
t (01243) 512736
e contact@thestudiobirdham.co.uk
w thestudiobirdham.co.uk

ngmere House ★★★★
& Breakfast
gmere Road, Tangmere,
chester
20 2HB
t (01243) 773276
e info@tangmerehouse.co.uk
w tangmerehouse.co.uk

st Dean College ★★★
est Accommodation
st Dean Park, Chichester
18 0QZ
t (01243) 818258
e kathy.williams@westdean.org.uk
w westdean.org.uk

lowbrook Riding Centre ★★
& Breakfast
mbrook Hill South, Hambrook,
chester
18 8UJ
t (01243) 572683
e willowbrookrc@btconnect.com
w willowbrook-stables.co.uk

CHIDDINGLY

e Farm House ★★★★
est Accommodation
VER AWARD
e Green, Chiddingly, Lewes
3 6HQ
t (01825) 872619
e s.burrough@virgin.net
w halefarmhouse.co.uk

CHILGROVE

lgrove Farm ★★★★
& Breakfast
lgrove, Chichester
18 9HU
t (01243) 519436
e simonrenwick@aol.com
w chilgrovefarmbedandbreakfast.co.uk

CLIMPING

ld Place ★★★★
est Accommodation
rch Lane, Climping, West Sussex
17 5RR
t (01903) 723 200
e oldcherfold@aol.com
w fieldplace.org.uk

COPSALE

chwood ★★★★
est Accommodation
adwater Lane, Copsale, Horsham
13 6QW
t (01403) 731313
e wendy@copsale.fsnet.co.uk

COWDEN

ite Horse Inn ★★★ *Inn*
tye, Cowden, Edenbridge
3 7ED
t (01342) 850640
e admin@twhilive.com
w twhilive.com

CROWBOROUGH

hurst ★★★★ *Bed & Breakfast*
Iden Road, Crowborough
5 1TR
t (01892) 665476
e annslender1@hotmail.com

Braemore ★★★★ *Bed & Breakfast*
SILVER AWARD
Eridge Road, Crowborough
TN6 2SS
t (01892) 665700
e triciafogg@tiscali.co.uk

Rose Cottage ★★★★
Bed & Breakfast
Mill Lane, Mark Cross, Crowborough
TN6 3PJ
t (01892) 852592
e johnandsoniacooper@hotmail.co.uk

Yew House Bed & Breakfast
★★★★ *Guest Accommodation*
SILVER AWARD
Crowborough Hill, Crowborough,
East Sussex
TN6 2EA
t (01892) 610522 &
(07789) 993982
e yewhouse@yewhouse.com
w yewhouse.com

EARNLEY

Millstone ★★★★ *Bed & Breakfast*
GOLD AWARD
Clappers Lane, Earnley, Chichester
PO20 7JJ
t (01243) 670116
e m.harrington193@btinternet.com
w visitsussex.org/millstone

EAST ASHLING (CHICHESTER 3 MILES)

Horse & Groom ★★★★ *Inn*
East Ashling, Chichester
PO18 9AX
t (01243) 575339
e info@thehorseandgroomchichester.co.uk
w thehorseandgroomchichester.co.uk

EASTBOURNE

Albert & Victoria ★★★★★
Guest House **SILVER AWARD**
19 St Aubyns Road, Eastbourne
BN22 7AS
t (01323) 730948
e albertandvictoria@fsmail.net
w albertandvictoria.com

Bramble Guest House ★★★★
Guest House
16 Lewes Road, Eastbourne
BN21 2BT
t (01323) 722343
e bramble@eastbourneguesthouse.co.uk
w brambleguesthouse.co.uk

Brayscroft House ★★★★
Guest House **GOLD AWARD**
13 South Cliff Avenue, Eastbourne
BN20 7AH
t (01323) 647005
e brayscroft@hotmail.com
w brayscrofthotel.co.uk

Cambridge House ★★★
Guest House
6 Cambridge Road, Eastbourne
BN22 7BS
t (01323) 721100
e rochester11@btinternet.com
w cambridgehouseeastbourne.co.uk

The Cherry Tree Guest House
★★★★ *Guest House*
15 Silverdale Road, Lower Meads,
Eastbourne
BN20 7AJ
t (01323) 722406
e carol@cherrytree-eastbourne.co.uk
w cherrytree-eastbourne.co.uk

Coast Guest Accommodation
★★★★ *Guest Accommodation*
84 Royal Parade, Eastbourne
BN22 7AE
t (01323) 431399
e info@coasteastbourne.co.uk
w coasteastbourne.co.uk

Cromwell House ★★★★
Guest House
23 Cavendish Place, Eastbourne
BN21 3EJ
t (01323) 725288
e info@cromwell-house.co.uk
w cromwell-house.co.uk

Devonia ★★★★
Guest Accommodation
74 Royal Parade, Eastbourne
BN22 7AQ
t (01323) 720059
e cj.devonia@btconnect.com
w devoniaeastbourne.com

Eastbourne Reymar ★★★
Guest Accommodation
SILVER AWARD
2-4 Cambridge Road, Eastbourne
BN22 7BS
t (01323) 724649
e info@eastbournereymarhotel.co.uk
w eastbournereymarhotel.co.uk

Eastbourne YHA ★★★★ *Hostel*
East Dean Road, Eastbourne
BN20 8ES
t 0845 371 9316

The Guesthouse East ★★★★
Guest House **SILVER AWARD**
13 Hartington Place, Eastbourne
BN21 3BS
t (01323) 722774
e book@theguesthouseeast.co.uk
w theguesthouseeast.co.uk

Loriston Guest House ★★★★★
Guest Accommodation
SILVER AWARD
17 Saint Aubyn's Road, Eastbourne
BN22 7AS
t (01323) 726193
e loriston@btconnect.com
w loriston.co.uk

The New England ★★★★
Guest Accommodation
GOLD AWARD
60 Royal Parade, Eastbourne
BN22 7AQ
t (01323) 736988
e info@thenewengland.org
w thenewengland.org

The Nirvana ★★★ *Guest House*
32 Redoubt Road, Eastbourne
BN22 7DL
t (01323) 722603
e eastbournenirvana@btinternet.com

Ocklynge Manor ★★★★★
Bed & Breakfast **GOLD AWARD**
Mill Road, Eastbourne
BN21 2PG
t (01323) 734121
e ocklyngemanor@hotmail.com
w ocklyngemanor.co.uk

Southcroft ★★★★ *Guest House*
SILVER AWARD
15 South Cliff Avenue, Eastbourne
BN20 7AH
t (01323) 729071
e mail@southcrofthotel.co.uk
w southcrofthotel.co.uk

Welkin Halls of Residence ★★★★
Campus
Servite Houses, Gaudick Road,
Eastbourne
BN20 7SH
t (01323) 431698

EAST DEAN

Rubens Barn ★★★★★
Guest Accommodation
SILVER AWARD
Droke Lane, East Dean, West Sussex
PO18 0JJ
t 01243 818187
e info@rubensbarn.co.uk
w rubensbarn.co.uk

EAST GRINSTEAD

Gothic House ★★★★
Guest Accommodation
55 High Street, East Grinstead
RH19 3DD
t (01342) 301910
e charlie@cjs-coffeebar.com
w gothichouse55.com

EAST WITTERING

Racing Sea Horses ★★★★
Guest Accommodation
95 Stocks Lane, East Wittering,
Chichester
PO20 8NU
t 01243 672157/07932163079
e jacqui&tony@racingseahorses.com
w racingseahorses.com

ELSTED

The Elsted Inn ★★★ *Inn*
Elsted, Midhurst
GU29 0JT
t (01730) 813662
e danyclaire88@yahoo.co.uk
w theelstedinn.co.uk

EWHURST GREEN

Clouds Bed & Breakfast ★★★★★
Bed & Breakfast **SILVER AWARD**
9 Dagg Lane, BODIAM, Ewhurst Green
TN32 5RD
t (01580) 830677
e jandfwouters@aol.com
w cloudsbedandbreakfast.co.uk

FAIRLIGHT

Fairlight Cottage ★★★★
Guest Accommodation
Warren Road, Fairlight, Hastings
TN35 4AG
t (01424) 812545
e fairlightcottage@supanet.com
w fairlightcottage.co.uk

FERNHURST

Colliers Farm ★★★★★
Bed & Breakfast **SILVER AWARD**
Midhurst Road, Fernhurst,
Haslemere
GU27 3EX
t (01428) 652265
e marina.allan@yahoo.co.uk

FITTLEWORTH

Lyon Cottage ★★ *Bed & Breakfast*
Bury Gate, Pulborough
RH20 1EY
t (01798) 865295

FOREST ROW

West Meadows ★★★★
Bed & Breakfast **SILVER AWARD**
Bell Lane, Nutley, Forest Row
TN22 3PD
t (01825) 712434
e west.meadows@virgin.net
w westmeadows.co.uk

GATWICK

The Lawn Guest House ★★★★
Guest House
30 Massetts Road, Gatwick
RH6 7DF
t (01293) 775751
e info@lawnguesthouse.co.uk
w lawnguesthouse.com

Southbourne Guest House Gatwick ★★★★ *Guest House*
SILVER AWARD
34 Massetts Road, Horley
RH6 7DS
t (01293) 771991
e reservations@southbournegatwick.com
w southbournegatwick.com

key to symbols see page 6

South East | Sussex

GRAFFHAM

Little Hoyle ★★★★
Bed & Breakfast **SILVER AWARD**
Hoyle Lane, Heyshott, Midhurst
GU29 0DX
t (01798) 867359
e ralphs.littlehoyle@btinternet.com
w smoothhound.co.uk/hotels/littl
ehoyle

Withy ★★★★★ *Bed & Breakfast*
GOLD AWARD
Graffham, Petworth
GU28 0PY
t (01798) 867000
e jacquelinewoods@hotmail.com
w withy.uk.com

GUESTLING

Mount Pleasant Farm ★★★★
Bed & Breakfast
White Hart Hill, Guestling, Hastings
TN35 4LR
t (01424) 813108
e angelajohn@mountpleasantfarm.fsbusiness.co.uk
w mountpleasantfarm.fsbusiness.co.uk

HAILSHAM

Longleys Farm Cottage ★★★★
Guest Accommodation
Harebeating Lane, Hailsham
BN27 1ER
t (01323) 841227
e longleysfarmcottagebb@dsl.pipex.com
w longleysfarmcottage.co.uk

The Stud Farm ★★★ *Farmhouse*
Bodle Street Green, Hailsham
BN27 4RJ
t (01323) 832647
e timkatemills@aol.com
w studfarmsussex.co.uk

HALLAND

Tamberry Hall ★★★★★
Guest Accommodation
GOLD AWARD
Eastbourne Road, Halland, Lewes
BN8 6PS
t (01825) 880090
e rosi@tamberryhall.co.uk
w tamberryhall.co.uk

HALNAKER

Old Store Guest House ★★★★
Guest House **SILVER AWARD**
Stane Street, Halnaker, Chichester
PO18 0QL
t (01243) 531977
e theoldstore4@aol.com
w theoldstoreguesthouse.com

HARTFIELD

The Hay Waggon Inn ★★★ *Inn*
High Street, Hartfield
TN7 4AB
t (01892) 770252
e michelleorawe@yahoo.com
w haywaggon.co.uk

HASLEMERE

Sheps Hollow ★★★
Bed & Breakfast
Henley Common, Henley, Haslemere
GU27 3HB
t (01428) 653120
e bizzielizziebee@msn.com
w shepshollow.co.uk

HASTINGS

Alexander's ★★★★
Guest Accommodation
2 Carlisle Parade, Hastings
TN34 1JG
t (01424) 717329
e keith@alexandershotelhastings.co.uk
w alexandershotelhastings.co.uk

Black Rock House ★★★★★
Guest Accommodation
GOLD AWARD
10 Stanley Road, Hastings
TN34 1UE
t (01424) 438448
e enquiries@black-rock-hastings.co.uk
w black-rock-hastings.co.uk

Churchills ★★★
Guest Accommodation
3 St Helens Crescent, Hastings
TN34 2EN
t (01424) 439359
e enquiries@churchillshotel
hastings.co.uk
w churchillshotelhastings.co.uk

The Elms ★★★ *Bed & Breakfast*
9 St Helens Park Road, Hastings
TN34 2ER
t (01424) 429979
e jmktbriggs@tiscali.co.uk

Gallery 53 ★★★★ *Bed & Breakfast*
53 High Street, Old Town, Hastings
TN34 3EN
t (01424) 433486
e jane_edmonds@hotmail.com
w hastingsbedandbreakfast.co.uk/gallery-53.htm

Hastings House ★★★★★
Guest Accommodation
GOLD AWARD
9 Warrior Square, St Leonards on Sea, Hastings
TN37 6BA
t (01424) 422709
e sengloy@btconnect.com
w hastingshouse.co.uk

Lavender & Lace ★★★★
Bed & Breakfast **SILVER AWARD**
106 All Saints Street, Hastings
TN34 3BE
t (01424) 716290
e lavenderlace1066@btinternet.com
w lavenderlace1066.co.uk

The Lindum ★★★★
Guest Accommodation - Room Only
1A Carlisle Parade, Hastings
TN34 1JG
t (01424) 434070
e bookingslindum@aol.com
w thelindum.co.uk

Minstrel's Rest ★★★★
Bed & Breakfast **SILVER AWARD**
21 Greville Road, Hastings
TN35 5AL
t (01424) 443500
e minstrelsrest@hotmail.com
w minstrelsrest.co.uk

Seaspray Bed and Breakfast
★★★★ *Guest Accommodation*
SILVER AWARD
54 Eversfield Place, St. Leonards-on-Sea, Hastings
TN37 6DB
t 01424 436583
e jo@seaspraybb.co.uk
w seaspraybb.co.uk

South Riding Guest House ★★★
Guest House
96 Milward Road, Hastings
TN34 3RT
t (01424) 420345

Summerfields House ★★★★
Guest Accommodation
SILVER AWARD
Bohemia Road, Hastings
TN34 1EX
t (01424) 718142
e liz.summerfields@btinternet.com
w summerfieldshouse.co.uk

Swan House ★★★★★
Guest Accommodation
GOLD AWARD
1 Hill Street, Old Town, Hastings
TN34 3HU
t (01424) 430014
e res@swanhousehastings.co.uk
w swanhousehastings.co.uk

The White House ★★★★★
Guest Accommodation
SILVER AWARD
12 Godwin Road, Hastings
TN35 5JR
t (01424) 722744
e suzieatthewhitehouse@gmail.com
w thewhitehousehastings.co.uk

HAYWARDS HEATH

Copyhold Hollow Bed & Breakfast
★★★★ *Bed & Breakfast*
GOLD AWARD
Copyhold Lane, Lindfield, Haywards Heath
RH16 1XU
t (01444) 413265
e vb@copyholdhollow.co.uk
w copyholdhollow.co.uk

Oakfield Cottage ★★★★
Guest Accommodation
SILVER AWARD
Brantridge Lane, Staplefield, Haywards Heath
RH17 6JR
t (01444) 401121
e joydougoakfield@btinternet.com
w smoothhound.co.uk/hotels/oakfieldcottage.html

The Old Forge ★★★★
Bed & Breakfast
16 Lucastes Avenue, Haywards Heath
RH16 1JH
t (01444) 451905

HEATHFIELD

Iwood Bed & Breakfast ★★★★
Guest Accommodation
GOLD AWARD
Mutton Hall Lane, Heathfield
TN21 8NR
t (01435) 863918
e iwoodbb@aol.com
w iwoodbb.com

HENFIELD

1 The Laurels ★★★★
Bed & Breakfast
Martyn Close, Henfield
BN5 9RQ
t (01273) 493518
e malc.harrington@lineone.net
w no1thelaurels.co.uk

HERSTMONCEUX

Sandhurst ★★★★
Guest Accommodation
Church Road, Herstmonceux, Hailsham
BN27 1RG
t (01323) 833088 or 07808144799
e junealanruss@aol.com
w herstmonceuxbandb.com

HILL BROW

The Jolly Drover ★★★★ *Inn*
SILVER AWARD
London Road, Hill Brow, Liss
GU33 7QL
t (01730) 893137
e thejollydrover@googlemail.com
w thejollydrover.co.uk

HORSHAM

Goffslands Farm B&B ★★★★
Farmhouse **SILVER AWARD**
Shipley, Horsham
RH13 9BQ
t (01403) 730434
e david.l@farmersweekly.net

Mucky Duck Inn ★★★★ *Inn*
Tismans Common, Loxwood Road, Horsham
RH12 3BW
t (01403) 822300
e mucky_duck_pub@msn.com
w mucky-duck-inn.co.uk

Nowhere House ★★★★
Bed & Breakfast
Dorking Road, Durfold Hill, Horsh
RH12 3RZ
t (01306) 627272

Pound Cottage ★★★
Bed & Breakfast
Mill Lane, Littleworth, Horsham
RH13 8JU
t (01403) 710218
e thegeo@poundcott.freeserve.c
uk

The Wirrals ★★ *Bed & Breakfast*
1 Downsview Road, Horsham
RH12 4PF
t (01403) 269400
e thewirralsarchibald@btinternet.com
w visitsussex.org/thewirrals

HOVE

Aymer Guest House ★★★★
Guest Accommodation
13 Aymer Road, Hove
BN3 4GB
t (01273) 271165
e michelle@aymerguesthouse.co
w aymerguesthouse.co.uk

Chatsworth House ★★
Guest House
9 Salisbury Road, Hove
BN3 3AB
t (01273) 737360

The Claremont ★★★★★
Guest Accommodation
SILVER AWARD
13 Second Avenue, Hove, Brighto
BN3 2LL
t (01273) 735161
e info@theclaremont.eu
w theclaremont.eu

Lichfield House ★★★★
Guest Accommodation
30 Waterloo Street, Hove
BN3 1AN
t (01273) 777740
e bookings@fieldhousehotels.co
w fieldhousehotels.co.uk

Seafield House ★★★★
Guest Accommodation
23 Seafield Road, Hove
BN3 2TP
t (01273) 777740
e enquiries@fieldhousehotels.co
w fieldhousehotels.co.uk

HUNSTON

Spire Cottage ★★★★
Guest Accommodation
SILVER AWARD
Church Lane, Hunston, Chichester
PO20 1AJ
t (01243) 778937
e jan@spirecottage.co.uk
w spirecottage.co.uk

HURST

Copper Beeches ★★★
Bed & Breakfast
Torberry Farm, Hurst, Petersfield
GU31 5RG
t (01730) 826662
e info@copperbeeches.net
w copperbeeches.net

HURST GREEN

The Old Courthouse B&B ★★★
Bed & Breakfast **SILVER AWARD**
46-48 London Road, Hurst Green
TN19 7QP
t (01580) 860080
e stay@oldcourthousebandb.co.uk
w oldcourthousebandb.co.uk

South East | Sussex

HURSTPIERPOINT

ckham Place ★★★★
est Accommodation
VER AWARD
ckham Drive, Hurstpierpoint,
ssocks
6 9AP
t (01273) 832172
e accommodation@wickham-place.
 co.uk
w wickhamplace.co.uk

LAMBERHURST

oodpecker Barn ★★★★★
d & Breakfast GOLD AWARD
ckhurst Farm, Bartley Mill Road,
nberhurst, Wadhurst
3 8BH
t (01892) 891958
e info@woodpeckerbarn.co.uk
w woodpeckerbarn.co.uk

LAVANT

nt Cottage ★★★★
d & Breakfast
Mid Lavant, Lavant, Chichester
18 0AA
t (01243) 785883
e info@flintcottagebedandbr
 eakfast.co.uk
w smoothhound.co.uk/hotels/flint.
 html

nters Lodge ★★★★
est Accommodation
dhurst Road, Lavant, Chichester
18 0DA
t (01243) 532415
e allyb0708@msn.com
w home2.btconnect.com/hunte
 rslodgebandb/

est Faldie ★★★★
d & Breakfast SILVER AWARD
vant, Chichester
18 0BW
t (01243) 527450
e hilary@mitten.fsnet.co.uk
w west-faldie.com

LEWES

echwood B&B ★★★★★
est Accommodation
LD AWARD
stbourne Road, Halland, Lewes
8 6PS
t (01825) 840937
e chyland1956@aol.com
w beechwoodbandb.co.uk

rkeley House ★★★★
est Accommodation
Albion Street, Lewes
7 2ND
t (01273) 476057
e enquiries@berkeleyhouselewes.
 co.uk
w berkeleyhouselewes.co.uk

thany ★★ Bed & Breakfast
Ballard Drive, Ringmer, Lewes
8 5NH
t (01273) 812025
e dimeadows@rockuk.net

e Blacksmiths Arms ★★★★ Inn
ham, Lewes
7 3QD
VER AWARD
t (01273) 472971
e blacksmitharms@shineadsl.co.uk
w theblacksmithsarms-offham.co.uk

amble Barn ★★★★
d & Breakfast
utherham, Lewes
8 6JN
t (01273) 474924

e Dorset ★★★★ Inn
Malling Street, Lewes
7 2RD
t (01273) 474823
e info@thedorsetlewes.com
w thedorsetlewes.com

Langtons House ★★★★
Guest Accommodation
SILVER AWARD
143b High Street, Lewes
BN7 1XT
t (01273) 476644
e info@langtonshouse.com
w langtonshouse.com

Lill Stugan ★★★★
Guest Accommodation
33 Houndean Rise, Lewes
BN7 1EQ
t (01273) 483580
e araikes@gotadsl.co.uk

Millers ★★★★ Bed & Breakfast
SILVER AWARD
134 High Street, Lewes
BN7 1XS
t (01273) 475631
e millers134@aol.com
w hometown.aol.com/millers134

Montys ★★★★ Bed & Breakfast
4 Albion Street, Lewes
BN7 2ND
t (01273) 474095
e montysplace4@googlemail.com

The Old Wash House ★★★★
Guest Accommodation
Mill Laine Farm, Offham, Lewes
BN7 3QB
t (01273) 475473
e harmer@farming.co.uk
w milllainebarns.co.uk

LINDFIELD

Little Lywood ★★★★
Bed & Breakfast
Ardingly Road, Lindfield, Haywards Heath
RH16 2QX
t (01444) 892571
e nick@nleadsom.plus.com

LITTLEHAMPTON

Arun Sands ★★★
Guest Accommodation
84 South Terrace, Littlehampton
BN17 5LJ
t (01903) 732489
e info@arun-sands.co.uk
w arun-sands.co.uk

Arun View Inn ★★ Inn
Wharf Road, Littlehampton
BN17 5DD
t (01903) 722335
e info@thearunview.co.uk
w thearunview.co.uk

East Beach Guest House ★★★
Guest Accommodation
South Terrace, Littlehampton
BN17 5LQ
t (01903) 714270
e info@eastbeachguesthouse.co.uk
w eastbeachguesthouse.co.uk

Littlehampton Youth Hostel ★★★★ Hostel
63 Surrey Street, Littlehampton
BN17 5AW
t 0870 770 6114
e littlehampton@yha.org.uk
w yha.org.uk/hostel/hostelpages/
 866.html

Racing Greens (B&B) ★★★★
Bed & Breakfast SILVER AWARD
70 South Terrace, Littlehampton
BN17 5LQ
t (01903) 732972
e racingreens@aol.com
w littlehampton-racing-greens.co.uk

Sandfield House ★★★
Bed & Breakfast
Lyminster Road, Wick, Littlehampton
BN17 7PG
t (01903) 724129
e francesfarrerbrown@btconnect.
 com
w visitsussex.org/sandfieldhouse

Selborne House ★★★
Bed & Breakfast
21 Selborne Road, Littlehampton
BN17 5LZ
t (01903) 726064
e fipickett@hotmail.com
w selbornehouse.net

LODSWORTH

Halfway Bridge Inn ★★★★★ Inn
GOLD AWARD
Halfway Bridge, Lodsworth, Petworth
GU28 9BP
t (01798) 861281
e enquiries@halfwaybridge.co.uk
w halfwaybridge.co.uk

MIDHURST

18 Pretoria Avenue ★★★
Bed & Breakfast
Pretoria Avenue, Midhurst
GU29 9PP
t (01730) 814868
e ericstratford@uwclub.net

20 Guillards Oak ★★★★
Bed & Breakfast
Midhurst
GU29 9JZ
t (01730) 812550
e coljenmidhurst@tiscali.co.uk
w guillards-oak-midhurst-bed-
 breakfast.co.uk

Carrondune ★★★ Bed & Breakfast
Carron Lane, Midhurst
GU29 9LD
t (01730) 813558

Oakhurst Cottage ★★
Bed & Breakfast
Carron Lane, Midhurst
GU29 9LF
t (01730) 813523

Orchard House ★★★★
Bed & Breakfast SILVER AWARD
Mill Lane, Trotton, Midhurst
GU31 5JT
t (01730) 812530
e orchardhouse.trotton@btinternet.
 com
w orchardhouse.cabanova.com

Pear Tree Cottage ★★★
Guest Accommodation - Room Only
Lamberts Lane, Midhurst
GU29 9EF
t (01730) 817216

Sunnyside ★★★ Bed & Breakfast
Cocking Causeway, Midhurst
GU29 9QH
t (01730) 814370

NEWHAVEN

Newhaven Lodge ★★★
Guest House
12 Brighton Road, Newhaven
BN9 9NB
t (01273) 513736
e info@newhavenlodge.co.uk
w newhavenlodge.com

TelscombeYouth Hostel ★★ Hostel
Bank Cottages, Telscombe Village, Newhaven
BN7 3HZ
t (01273) 301357
e reservations@yha.org.uk
w yha.org.uk

NEWICK

Holly Lodge ★★★★
Bed & Breakfast SILVER AWARD
Oxbottom Lane, Newick, Lewes
BN8 4RA
t (01825) 722738
e lallie@waitrose.com

PETT

The Lookout ★★★★
Bed & Breakfast GOLD AWARD
Chick Hill, Pett
TN35 4EQ
t (01424) 812070
e busby@btinternet.com
w lookoutbb.co.uk

PETWORTH

Brook Barn ★★★★ Bed & Breakfast
SILVER AWARD
Selham Road, Graffham, Petworth
GU28 0PU
t (01798) 867356
e brookbarn@hotmail.com
w visitsussex.org/brookbarn

Eedes Cottage ★★★★
Bed & Breakfast
Bignor Park Road, Bury Gate, Pulborough
RH20 1EZ
t (01798) 831438
e eedes.bandb@btinternet.com

Old Railway Station ★★★★
Guest Accommodation
Station Road, Petworth
GU28 0JF
t (01798) 342346
e info@old-station.co.uk
w old-station.co.uk

Willow Barns Bed & Breakfast
Guest House
Heyshott Road, Graffham, Petworth
GU28 0NU
t (01798) 867291
e godmandorington@aol.com
w willowbarns.co.uk

PEVENSEY

The Bay ★★★ Inn
Eastbourne Road, Pevensey Bay, Pevensey
BN24 6EJ
t (01323) 768645
w thechapmangroup.co.uk

POLEGATE

Alfriston Youth Hostel ★★ Hostel
Frog Firle, Alfriston, Polegate
BN26 5SD
t 0870 770 5666
e alfriston@yha.org.uk
w yha.org.uk

PULBOROUGH

Barn House Lodge ★★★★
Bed & Breakfast
Barn House Lane, Pulborough, West Sussex
RH20 2BS
t (01798) 872682
e sue@barnhouselodge.co.uk
w barnhouselodge.co.uk

The Labouring Man ★★★★ Inn
Old London Road, Coldwaltham, Pulborough
RH20 1LF
t (01798) 872215
e philip.beckett@btconnect.com
w thelabouringman.co.uk

St Cleather ★★★★ Bed & Breakfast
SILVER AWARD
Rectory Lane, Pulborough
RH20 2AD
t (01798) 873038
e enquiries@stcleather.me.uk
w stcleather.me.uk

RINGMER

Bryn Clai ★★★★
Guest Accommodation
Uckfield Road (A26), Ringmer, Lewes
BN8 5RU
t (01273) 814042
e daphne@brynclai.co.uk
w brynclai.co.uk

RIPE

Hall Court Farm ★★★★★
Bed & Breakfast GOLD AWARD
Ripe, Lewes
BN8 6AY
t (01323) 811496
e johnhecks@btconnect.com
w hallcourtfarm.co.uk

South East | Sussex

ROBERTSBRIDGE

Glenferness ★★★★
Bed & Breakfast
Brightling Road, Robertsbridge
TN32 5DP
t (01580) 881841
e info@glenferness.co.uk
w glenferness.co.uk

Slides Farm B&B ★★★★★
Bed & Breakfast SILVER AWARD
Silverhill, Robertsbridge
TN32 5PA
t (01580) 880106
e slides.farm@btinternet.com
w slidesfarm.com

RODMELL

Garden Cottage ★★★★
Guest Accommodation
Garden Studio, Mill Lane, Rodmell, Lewes
BN7 3HS
t (01273) 476715 / 07518 617606

RUDGWICK

Alliblaster House ★★★★★
Bed & Breakfast GOLD AWARD
Hillbrook Lane, Rudgwick, Horsham
RH12 3BD
t (01403) 822860
e info@alliblasterhouse.com
w alliblasterhouse.com

RUSTINGTON

Mallondene ★★★★
Bed & Breakfast SILVER AWARD
47 Mallon Dene, Rustington, Littlehampton
BN16 2JP
t (01903) 775383 mobile 07970 845 689
e jenny@mallondene.co.uk
w mallondene.co.uk

RYE

At Wisteria Corner ★★★★
Bed & Breakfast
At Wisteria Corner, 47 Ferry Road, Rye
TN31 7DJ
t (01797) 225011
e info@wisteriacorner.co.uk
w wisteriacorner.co.uk

Brede Court Country House
★★★★ Guest House
Brede Hill, Brede, Rye
TN31 6EJ
t (01424) 883105
e bredecrt@globalnet.co.uk
w bredecourt.co.uk

The Corner House ★★★★
Guest Accommodation
Rye Road, Rye
TN31 7UL
t (01797) 280439
e yvonne@the-corner-house.com
w the-corner-house.com

Fairacres ★★★★★ Bed & Breakfast
GOLD AWARD
Fairacres, Udimore Road, Broad Oak, Rye, East Sussex
TN31 6DG
t (01424) 883236
e info@fairacresrye.co.uk
w fairacresrye.co.uk

Four Seasons ★★★★
Bed & Breakfast
96 Udimore Road, Rye
TN31 7DY
t (01797) 224305
e coxsam@btinternet.com

The Hare & Hounds ★★★★ Inn
Rye Road, Rye
TN31 7ST
t (01797) 230483
e mail@hare-hounds.info
w hare-hounds.info

Haydens ★★★★★
Guest Accommodation
SILVER AWARD
108 High Street, Rye
TN31 7JE
t (01797) 224501
e haydens_in_rye@mac.com
w haydensinrye.co.uk

Jeake's House ★★★★★
Guest Accommodation
GOLD AWARD
Jeake's House, Mermaid Street, Rye
TN31 7ET
t (01797) 222828
e stay@jeakeshouse.com
w jeakeshouse.com

The Mill House ★★★★
Bed & Breakfast SILVER AWARD
The Mill House, Pottery Lane, Rye
TN31 6EA
t (01424) 883096
e michaeltay@tiscali.co.uk
w themillhousebandb.co.uk

Oaklands ★★★★★
Guest Accommodation
GOLD AWARD
Udimore Road, Rye, East Sussex
TN31 7DB
t (01797) 229734
e info@oaklands-rye.co.uk
w oaklands-rye.co.uk

Old Borough Arms ★★★★
Guest House
The Strand, Rye, East Sussex
TN31 7DB
t 01797 222 128
e info@oldboroughams.co.uk
w oldboroughams.co.uk

Playden Oasts Inn ★★★ Inn
Rye Road, Playden, Rye
TN31 7UL
t (01797) 223502
e playdenoasts@btinternet.com
w playdenoast.co.uk

Ranters' Rest ★★★★
Bed & Breakfast SILVER AWARD
The Jays, Float Lane, Rye
TN31 6BY
t (01797) 224625
e gilly.little1@btinternet.com
w rantersrest.co.uk

Regent Motel ★★★
Guest Accommodation - Room Only
42 Cinque Ports Street, Rye
TN31 7AN
t (01797) 225884
e enquiries@regentmotel.co.uk
w regentmotel.co.uk

The Rise ★★★★★ Bed & Breakfast
GOLD AWARD
82 Udimore Road, Rye
TN31 7DY
t (01797) 222285
e theriserye@aol.com
w therise-rye.co.uk

Saltcote Place ★★★★★
Guest Accommodation
GOLD AWARD
Saltcote Lane, Rye
TN31 7NR
t (01797) 222220
e stay@saltcote.co.uk
w saltcote.co.uk

Simmons of Rye ★★★★★
Guest House GOLD AWARD
68-69 The Mint, Rye
TN31 7EW
t (01797) 226032
e info@simmonsofrye.co.uk
w simmonsofrye.co.uk

Strand House ★★★★
Guest Accommodation
GOLD AWARD
Strand House, Tanyards Lane, Winchelsea, nr Rye
TN36 4JT
t (01797) 226276
e info@thestrandhouse.co.uk
w thestrandhouse.co.uk

Top o' The Hill at Rye ★★★ Inn
Rye Hill, Rye
TN31 7NH
t (01797) 223284
e jmanklow@aol.com

Treetops ★★★★
Guest Accommodation
Love Lane, Rye
TN31 7NE
t (01797) 227141
e wendy.wright@treetops-rye.co.uk
w treetops-rye.co.uk

Willow Tree House ★★★★★
Guest Accommodation
GOLD AWARD
Winchelsea Road, Rye
TN31 7EL
t (01797) 227820
e info@willow-tree-house.com
w willow-tree-house.com

SEAFORD

Cornerways ★★★
Guest Accommodation
10 The Covers, Seaford
BN25 1DF
t (01323) 492400

Florence House ★★★★
Guest Accommodation
Southdown Road, Seaford
BN25 4JS
t (01323) 873700
e info@florencehouse.co.uk
w florencehouse.co.uk

Malvern House ★★★
Bed & Breakfast
Alfriston Road, Seaford
BN25 3QG
t (01323) 492058
e malvernbandb@aol.com
w malvernhouse.gb.com

The Silverdale ★★★★ Guest House
21 Sutton Park Road, Seaford
BN25 1RH
t (01323) 491849
e info@silverdaleseaford.co.uk
w silverdaleseaford.co.uk

SELSEY

Greenacre Bed & Breakfast
★★★★ Guest Accommodation
Manor Farm Court, Selsey
PO20 0LY
t (01243) 602912
e green.acre4@btinternet.com
w visitsussex.org/greenacre

Keston House ★★★★
Bed & Breakfast SILVER AWARD
16 Beacon Drive, Selsey
PO20 0TW
t (01243) 604513
e mrt@mercedes553.wanadoo.co.uk
w kestonhouseselsey.co.uk

Norton Lea Guest House ★★★
Bed & Breakfast
Chichester Road, Selsey, Chichester
PO20 9EA
t (01243) 605454
e nortonlea@aol.com
w nortonlea.com

St Andrews Lodge ★★★★
Guest Accommodation
Chichester Road, Selsey
PO20 0LX
t (01243) 606899
e info@standrewslodge.co.uk
w standrewslodge.co.uk

Vincent Lodge ★★★★
Bed & Breakfast
Vincent Road, Selsey
PO20 9DJ
t (01243) 602985
e info@vincentlodge.co.uk
w vincentlodge.co.uk

SHARPTHORNE

Coach House ★★★ Bed & Breakfast
Courtlands, Chilling Street, East Grinstead
RH19 4JF
t (01342) 810512
e friends@mmarshall.vispa.com
w visitsussex.org/coachhousesharpthorne

Courtlands Nurseries ★★★★
Bed & Breakfast
Chilling Street, Sharpthorne, East Grinstead
RH19 4JF
t (01342) 810780
e lindsay.shurvell@virgin.net
w courtlandsnurseries.co.uk

SHOREHAM-BY-SEA

Truleigh Hill Youth Hostel ★★
Hostel
Truleigh Hill, Shoreham-by-Sea
BN43 5FB
t (01903) 813419

SIDLESHAM

Landseer House ★★★★★
Guest Accommodation
GOLD AWARD
Cow Lane, Sidlesham, Chichester
PO20 7LN
t (01243) 641525
e enq@landseerhouse.co.uk
w landseerhouse.co.uk

SIDLESHAM COMMON

Brimfast House ★★★
Bed & Breakfast
Brimfast Lane, Sidlesham Common, Chichester
PO20 7PZ
t (01243) 641841
e bookings@brimfastbandb.co.uk
w brimfastbandb.co.uk

SINGLETON

1 Rose Cottage ★★★★
Guest Accommodation
SILVER AWARD
Singleton, Chichester
PO18 0HP
t (01243) 811607
e rosecottagesingleton@yahoo.co.uk
w 1rosecottage.com

SLAUGHAM

Slaugham Place Farm ★★★★
Bed & Breakfast SILVER AWARD
Staplefield Road, Slaugham, Haywards Heath
RH17 6AL
t (01444) 400414
e slaughambandb@btconnect.com
w slaughamplacefarm.co.uk

SLINFOLD

Magpies ★★★★ Bed & Breakfast
Stane Street, Slinfold, Horsham
RH13 0QX
t (01403) 790764

SOUTH HARTING

South Gardens Cottage ★★★
Bed & Breakfast
South Harting, Petersfield
GU31 5QJ
t (01730) 825040
e julia@randjholmes.plus.com

South East | Sussex

SOUTHWATER

chwood House ★★★★★
d & Breakfast
ws Lane, Southwater, Horsham
13 9BX
t (01403) 731949
e nickie@birchingand.co.uk
w birchwoodlodge.co.uk

STAPLECROSS

oodside Bed & Breakfast ★★★★ Bed & Breakfast
LD AWARD
oodside, Junction Road,
ertsbridge, Nr Rye and Battle
32 5SG
t (01580) 830903
e reservations@woodsidebandb.com
w woodsidebandb.com

STEYNING

sh Manor ★★★★
est Accommodation
LD AWARD
rsham Road, Steyning
44 3AA
t (01903) 814988
e info@nashmanor.co.uk
w nashmanor.co.uk

ringwells ★★★ Guest House
ligh Street, Steyning, West
sex
44 3GG
t (01903) 812446
e contact@springwells.co.uk
w springwells.co.uk

ST LEONARDS-ON-SEA

llington Croft ★★★
& Breakfast
Battle Road, St Leonards-on-Sea
37 7BA
t (01424) 851795

rina Lodge ★★★ Guest House
Marina, St Leonards-on-Sea
38 0BN
t (01424) 715067
e marinalodge@talktalk.net
w marinalodge.co.uk

tland ★★★★ Guest House
Grosvenor Crescent, St Leonards-
-Sea
38 0AA
t (01424) 714720
e carol@rutlandguesthouse.co.uk
w rutlandguesthouse.co.uk

Sea Spirit Guest House ★★★ Guest House
Tower Road West, St Leonards
-Sea
38 0RJ
t (01424) 729518
e lorraineedwards@btinternet.com
w sea-spirit-guesthouse.co.uk

erwood Guest House ★★★★
est House
Grosvenor Crescent, St Leonards-
-Sea
38 0AA
t (01424) 433331
e jimandjeanette@btinternet.com
w sherwoodhastings.co.uk

wer House 1066 ★★★★
est Accommodation
VER AWARD
Tower Road West, St Leonards
38 0RG
t (01424) 427117
e reservations@towerhouse1066.co.uk
w towerhouse1066.co.uk

TELSCOMBE

d Farm House ★★★★
mhouse
scombe, Lewes
7 3HZ
t (01273) 302486
e ninaamour5@yahoo.co.uk

THAKEHAM

Abingworth Hall ★★★★
Guest Accommodation
Storrington Road, Thakeham,
Pulborough
RH20 3EF
t (020) 8511 1534
e vladi@hfholidays.co.uk
w hfholidays.co.uk

UCKFIELD

Beggars Barn ★★★★
Guest Accommodation
SILVER AWARD
Barn Lane, Framfield, Uckfield
TN22 5RX
t (01825) 890868
e caroline@beggarsbarn.co.uk
w beggarsbarn.co.uk

Blackboys Youth Hostel ★★
Group Accommodation
Gun Road, Blackboys, Uckfield
TN22 5HU
t (01825) 890607
e blackboys@yha.org.uk

South Paddock ★★★★★
Bed & Breakfast **SILVER AWARD**
The Drive, Maresfield Park,
Maresfield, Uckfield
TN22 2HA
t (01825) 762335

VINES CROSS

Brookside Farm ★★★★
Bed & Breakfast
Laundry Lane, Vines Cross,
Heathfield
TN21 9ED
t (01435) 813391
e kernahanv@tinyworld.co.uk

WADHURST

Church House Bed & Breakfast ★★★★ Bed & Breakfast
SILVER AWARD
Church Street, Wadhurst
TN5 6AR
t (01892) 782845
e cbtkbell@tiscali.co.uk
w wadhurstbandb.co.uk

Forest Edge Motel ★★★
Guest Accommodation
London Road, Flimwell, Wadhurst
TN5 7PL
t (01580) 879222
e info@forestedgemotel.co.uk
w forestedgemotel.co.uk

Spring Cottage ★★★
Bed & Breakfast
Best Beech Hill, Wadhurst
TN5 6JH
t (01892) 783896
e penny@southerncrosstravel.co.uk

WARNINGCAMP

Arundel Youth Hostel ★★★ Hostel
Warningcamp, Arundel
BN18 9QY
t (01903) 882204
e arundel@yha.org.uk
w yha.org.uk/hostel/hostelpages/154.html

WEST BROYLE

Longmeadow ★★ Bed & Breakfast
Pine Grove, Chichester
PO19 3PN
t (01243) 782063
e bbeeching@lineone.net
w longmeadow-bandb-chichester.co.uk

WEST CHILTINGTON

Old Oaks ★★★★
Guest Accommodation
SILVER AWARD
Spinney Lane, West Chiltington,
West Sussex
RH20 2NX
t 01798 817284
e aduke123@btinternet.com
w oldoaksbedandbreakfast.co.uk

The Old School House ★★★★★
Bed & Breakfast **SILVER AWARD**
Church Street, West Chiltington,
Pulborough
RH20 2JW
t (01798) 812585
e enquiries@theoldschoolhousebandb.com
w theoldschoolhousebandb.com

WESTFIELD

Four Winds ★★★★ Bed & Breakfast
Parsonage Lane, Westfield, Hastings
TN35 4SH
t (01424) 752585
e judy@4-winds.org
w 4-winds.org

WEST HARTING

Three Quebec ★★★★
Bed & Breakfast
West Harting, Midhurst
GU31 5PG
t (01730) 825386
e patriciastevens@threequebec.co.uk
w threequebec.co.uk

WINCHELSEA

West View B&B ★★★
Bed & Breakfast
Station Road, Winchelsea
TN36 4JU
t (01797) 226351
e westviewbandb@btinternet.com
w westview-winchelsea.co.uk

Winchelsea Lodge Motel ★★★★
Guest Accommodation
Hastings Road, Winchelsea
TN36 4AD
t (01797) 226211
e julie.hannah@1066motels.co.uk
w thelodgeatwinchelsea.co.uk

WITHYHAM

Dorset House ★★★
Bed & Breakfast
Withyham, Hartfield
TN7 4BD
t (01892) 770035
e meg@rosneathengineering.co.uk
w dorset-house.co.uk

WITTERINGS

The Beach House ★★★★
Guest House
Rookwood Road, West Wittering,
Witterings
PO20 8LT
t (01243) 514800
e info@beachhse.co.uk
w beachhse.co.uk

WORTHING

Benson's Guest House ★★★★
Bed & Breakfast **GOLD AWARD**
143 Brighton Road, Worthing, West
Sussex
BN11 2EU
t (01903) 206623
e bensonsguesthouse@btinternet.com
w bensonstheguesthouse.co.uk

Blair House ★★★★ Guest House
St Georges Road, Worthing
BN11 2DS
t (01903) 234071
e stay@blairhousehotel.co.uk
w blairhousehotel.co.uk

Brunswick ★★ Inn
Thorn Road, Worthing
BN11 3ND
t (01903) 202141
e pavilion_inns@hotmail.com
w thebrunswick.co.uk

Camelot House ★★★★
Guest Accommodation
20 Gannon Road, Worthing
BN11 2DT
t (01903) 204334
e stay@camelothouse.co.uk
w camelothouse.co.uk

Edwardian Dreams ★★★★
Guest Accommodation
SILVER AWARD
77 Manor Road, Worthing
BN11 4SL
t (01903) 218565
e info@edwardiandreams.co.uk
w edwardiandreams.co.uk

Glenhill Guest House ★★★
Guest Accommodation
21 Alexandra Road, Worthing
BN11 2DX
t (01903) 202756
e filmersankeylinda@yahoo.co.uk
w glenhillguesthouse.co.uk

The Grand Victorian ★★★
Guest Accommodation
27 Railway Approach, Worthing
BN11 1UR
t (01903) 230690
e grandvictorian@thechapmansgroup.co.uk
w chapmansgroup.co.uk

Haytor Guest House ★★
Bed & Breakfast
5 Salisbury Road, Worthing
BN11 1RB
t (01903) 235287
e lindashipley379@btinternet.com

Heenefields Guest House ★★★★
Guest Accommodation
98 Heene Road, Worthing
BN11 3RE
t (01903) 538780
e info@heenefields.co.uk
w heenefields.com

High Trees Guest House ★★★
Guest Accommodation
2 Warwick Gardens, Worthing
BN11 1PE
t (01903) 236668
e bill@hightreesguesthouse.co.uk
w hightreesguesthouse.co.uk

Marine View ★★★
Guest Accommodation
111 Marine Parade, Worthing
BN11 3QG
t (01903) 238413
e reservations@marineviewhotel.co.uk
w marineviewhotel.co.uk

Merton House ★★★★ Guest House
SILVER AWARD
96 Broadwater Road, Worthing
BN14 8AW
t (01903) 238222
e stay@mertonhouse.co.uk
w mertonhouse.co.uk

Moorings ★★★★
Guest Accommodation
4 Selden Road, Worthing
BN11 2LL
t (01903) 208882
e themooringsworthing@hotmail.co.uk
w mooringsworthing.co.uk

The Old Guard House ★★★★
Bed & Breakfast **SILVER AWARD**
55 Poulters Lane, Worthing
BN14 7ST
t (01903) 527470
e karen@oldguardhouse.co.uk
w oldguardhouse.co.uk

Pebble Beach ★★★
Bed & Breakfast
281 Brighton Road, Worthing
BN11 2HG
t (01903) 210766
e pebblebeach281@aol.com
w pebblebeach-worthing.co.uk

Tamara Guest House ★★★★
Bed & Breakfast
19 Alexandra Road, Worthing
BN11 2DX
t (01903) 520332
e cd.mcgaw@ntlworld.com
w tamara-worthing.co.uk

London

There is nowhere in the world quite like London. The capital of England and Britain, and the biggest city in the EU, London is a vibrant, multi-cultural, 24-hour city.

Culture and Heritage

There is a stimulating blend of old and new, the buzz of the city and the tranquility of its many open spaces which make London unique for both visitors and locals alike. Over 300 languages are spoken in London, contributing to the city's own fascinating culture, making it a fantastic place to visit and experience cultures from all over the world.

There is always something new to see or do in London. At the same time, the city retains its fantastic historical features, such as the Royal Botanic Gardens, Tower of London, Westminster Palace, Westminster Abbey & St Margaret's Church and, to the south east, Maritime Greenwich – all are UNESCO World Heritage Sites.

Attractions

London has the greatest concentration of major attractions in Britain. There are 238 attractions which are free to enter, and there is nowhere else in the world where you can see so much for so little. If modern art is your thing then the world's most visited modern art gallery, Tate Modern (which is free except for major exhibitions) is a must. There are also many paying attractions, the Merlin Entertainments London Eye with its fabulous views of the city, is an experience you cannot afford to miss.

Shopping

If its shopping you want, you will never get bored in London with over 30,000 shops to choose from and a respected reputation in the fashion world. Oxford Street is Europe's biggest shopping area, Bond Street is designer label paradise, and the street markets of Camden, Portobello Road and Brick Lane are perfect for vintage hunters.

Sport

Football is the most popular sport in London and is home to several of England's leading football clubs. London boasts 13 professional teams – more than any other city in the world. London also has four rugby union teams and is home to two test cricket grounds (Lords and The Oval) as well as Wimbledon, home to the only Grand Slam tennis event still played on grass. London has been chosen to host the 201

London

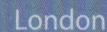

London

294	Where to Go	297	Where to Eat
296	Events	300	Where to Stay

...ympic Games and Paralympic Games, making it the first city in the world to ...st the Summer Olympics three times.

Food and Drink

...ndon is a world-class destination for food-lovers. With its smart restaurants, ...ormal gastropubs, superb delis and buzzing cafes, there really is something to ...it all tastes and budgets. And the choice is staggering – you'll find cuisine from ...er 70 countries and over 6,000 restaurants from which to choose: 48 of which ...e Michelin-starred (2010).

Music and Nightlife

...ndon's music scene and heritage is truly spectacular. There are 400 live music ...nues catering for everything from opera and jazz to rock and hip hop. All over ...e city you will find famous musical landmarks and reminders of some of the ...pital's biggest music stars. Summer is a great time for live music in London ...you can enjoy everything from pop and rock festivals to the world's largest ...assical musical festival – the Proms.

...may have been 1777 when Samuel Johnson famously declared 'When a man is ...ed of London, he is tired of life; for there is in London all that life can afford.' But ...s still true today.

London | Where to Go

Where to Go

Attractions with this sign participate in the **Visitor Attraction Quality Assurance Scheme** (see page 6) which recognises high standards in all aspects of the visitor experience.

ENTERTAINMENT & CULTURE

Apsley House
Westminster W1J 7NT
(020) 7499 5676
www.english-heritage.org.uk
Former residence of the first Duke of Wellington. This great 18th century town house pays homage to the Duke's dazzling military career, which culminated in his victory at Waterloo in 1815.

BBC Television Centre Tours
Hammersmith and Fulham W12 7RJ
0370 9011227
www.bbc.co.uk/tours
On the award-winning tour of BBC Television Centre you will see what happens inside the most famous TV headquarters in the world!

British Museum
Camden WC1B 3DG
(020) 7323 8299
www.thebritishmuseum.ac.uk
Founded in 1753, the British Museum's remarkable collections span over two million years of human history and culture, all under one roof. Experience collections from Africa, Asia, Europe, the Americas and the Ancient World.

Discover
Newham E15 4BG
(020) 8536 5555
www.discover.org.uk
Discover is a magical place in Stratford, East London for children aged 2-7 and their families, carers, friends and teachers to make stories together.

Estorick Collection of Modern Italian Art
Islington N1 2AN
(020) 7704 9522
www.estorickcollection.com
World-famous collection of Italian Futurists, Modigliani, Morandi and others in a beautiful Georgian house.

Greenwich Heritage Centre
Greenwich SE18 4DX
(020) 8854 2452
www.greenwich.gov.uk
Local history museum with displays of archaeology, natural history and geology. Also temporary exhibitions, schools service, sales point and Saturday club.

Imperial War Museum
Southwark SE1 6HZ
(020) 7416 5320
www.iwm.org.uk
This award-winning museum tells the story of conflict involving Britain and the Commonwealth since 1914. See thousands of imaginatively displayed exhibits, from art to aircraft, utility clothes to U-boats.

London Glassblowing & Glass Art Gallery
Southwark SE1 3ER
(020) 7403 2800
www.londonglassblowing.co.uk
Peter Layton's London Glassblowing is a hot glass studio focused on the creation and display of contemporary glass art. It has a reputation as one of Europe's leading workshops with a flair for the use of colour, form and texture.

London's Transport Museum
Westminster WC2E 7BB
(020) 7379 6344
www.ltmuseum.co.uk
The history of transport for everyone, from spectacular vehicles, special exhibitions, actors and guided tours to film shows, gallery talks and children's craft workshops.

Lord's Tour (MCC)
Westminster NW8 8QN
(020) 7616 8595
lords.org/history/tours-of-lords
Guided tour of Lord's Cricket Ground including the Long Room, MCC Museum, Real Tennis Court, Mound Stand and Indoor School.

Museum of London
City of London EC2Y 5HN
0870 444 3852
www.museumoflondon.org.uk
Step inside Museum of London for an unforgettable journey through the capital's turbulent past.

National Gallery
Westminster WC2N 5DN
(020) 7747 2888
www.nationalgallery.org.uk
The National Gallery houses one of the greatest collections of Western European painting in the world. Discover inspiring art by Botticelli, Caravaggio, Leonardo da Vinci, Monet, Raphael, Rembrandt, Titian, Vermeer and Van Gogh.

London | Where to Go

ational Maritime useum
reenwich SE10 9NF
20) 8858 4422
ww.nmm.ac.uk
tain's seafaring history housed in an pressive modern museum. Themes clude exploration, Nelson, trade and pire, passenger shipping, luxury ers, maritime London, costume, t and the sea, the future and vironmental issues.

ational Portrait Gallery
estminster WC2H 0HE
20) 7306 0055
ww.npg.org.uk
uses the world's largest collection portraits. Visitors come face to face th the people who have shaped tish history from Elizabeth I to David ckham.

atural History Museum
ensington and Chelsea
W7 5BD
20) 7942 5000
ww.nhm.ac.uk
e Natural History Museum reveals w the jigsaw of life fits together. imal, vegetable or mineral, the best our planet's most amazing treasures e here for you to see.

oyal Air Force Museum endon
arnet NW9 5LL
20) 8205 2266
ww.rafmuseum.org
ke off to the Royal Air Force Museum d flypast the history of aviation th an exciting display of suspended craft, touch screen technology, ulator rides, hands-on section, film ows, licensed restaurant.

oyal London Hospital rchives and Museum
wer Hamlets E1 2AA
20) 7377 7608
ww.brlcf.org.uk
chives and museum housed in the pt of a fine 19thC Gothic church ere the story of the Royal London spital (founded 1740) is told.

outhbank Centre
mbeth SE1 8XX
71 663 2501
ww.southbankcentre.co.uk
uthbank Centre is a unique arts ntre with 21 acres of creative space, cluding the Royal Festival Hall, Queen zabeth Hall and The Hayward.

St Bartholomew's Hospital Archives and Museum
City of London EC1A 7BE
(020) 7601 8152
www.bartsandthelondon.nhs.uk/aboutus/st_bartholomews_hospital.asp
The museum tells the inspiring story of Bart's Hospital. Founded nearly 9 centuries ago, it is one of the oldest hospitals in Britain.

Tate Britain
Westminster SW1P 4RG
(020) 7887 8888
www.tate.org.uk
Tate Britain presents the world's greatest collection of British art in a dynamic series of new displays and exhibitions.

Tate Modern
Southwark SE1 9TG
(020) 7887 8888
www.tate.org.uk/modern
The national gallery of international modern art and is one of London's top free attractions. It's packed with challenging modern art and is housed within a disused power station on the south bank of the River Thames.

The Museum of Domestic Design and Architecture
Barnet EN4 8HT
(020) 8411 5244
www.moda.mdx.ac.uk
A place of inspiration and enjoyment for visitors of all ages who are interested in the history of design for the home.

The Original London Sightseeing Tour
Westminster SW18 1TB
(020) 8877 1722
www.theoriginaltour.com
London's 'The Original Tour' offers guests a hop-on, hop-off tour including live and digitally recorded commentaries, a free river cruise and a unique Kid's Club.

Tower Bridge Exhibition
Southwark SE1 2UP
(020) 7403 3761
www.towerbridge.org.uk
Inside Tower Bridge Exhibition you will travel up to the high-level walkways, located 140 feet above the Thames and witness stunning panoramic views of London before visiting the Victorian Engine Rooms. See the original machinery in action.

Victoria and Albert Museum
Kensington and Chelsea SW7 2RL
(020) 7942 2000
www.vam.ac.uk
The V&A is the world's greatest museum of art and design, with collections unrivalled in their scope and diversity.

Wallace Collection
Westminster W1U 3BN
(020) 7563 9551
www.wallacecollection.org
The Wallace Collection is a national museum, displaying superb works of art in an historic London town house.

Wimbledon Lawn Tennis Museum
Merton SW19 5AE
(020) 8944 1066
www.wimbledon.org
A fantastic collection of memorabilia dating from 1555, including Championship Trophies. Art Gallery, 220-degree cinema and special exhibitions, reflecting the game and championships of today.

FAMILY FUN

Chessington World of Adventures
Kingston upon Thames KT9 2NE
0870 444 7777
www.chessington.com
Explore Chessington - it's a whole world of adventures! Soar on the Vampire rollercoaster or discover the mystery of Tomb Blaster. Take a walk on the wild side in the Trails of the Kings or visit the park's own SEA LIFE Centre.

London Eye
Lambeth SE1 7PB
0870 500 0600
www.londoneye.com/
A top London attraction and the world's largest observation wheel. Located by Westminster on the River Thames, the Eye gives you spectacular 360-degree views of London's most famous landmarks.

HERITAGE

Chiswick House
Hounslow W4 2RP
(020) 8995 0508
www.english-heritage.org.uk
The celebrated villa of Lord Burlington with impressive grounds featuring Italianate garden with statues, temples, obelisks and urns.

London | Where to Go/Events

Churchill Museum and Cabinet War Rooms
Westminster SW1A 2AQ
(020) 7930 6961
www.iwm.org.uk
Learn more about the man who inspired Britain's finest hour at the highly interactive and innovative Churchill Museum, the world's first major museum dedicated to life of the 'greatest Briton'.

Eltham Palace
Greenwich SE9 5QE
(020) 8294 2548
www.elthampalace.org.uk/
A spectacular fusion of 1930s Art Deco villa and magnificent 15th century Great Hall. Surrounded by period gardens.

Hampton Court Palace
Richmond upon Thames KT8 9AU
0870 752 7777
www.hrp.org.uk
This magnificent palace set in delightful gardens was famously one of Henry VIII's favourite palaces. Explore his State Apartments and those of King William III where history is brought to life with costumed guides.

HMS Belfast
Southwark SE1 2JH
(020) 7940 6300
www.iwm.org.uk
Launched 1938, served throughout WWII, played a leading part in the destruction of the German battle cruiser Scharnhorst and in the Normandy Landings.

Kensington Palace State Apartments
Kensington and Chelsea W8 4PX
0870 751 5170
www.hrp.org.uk
Home to the Royal Ceremonial Dress Collection, which includes some of Queen Elizabeth II's dresses worn throughout her reign, as well as 14 of Diana, Princess of Wales' evening dresses.

Kenwood House
Camden NW3 7JR
(020) 8348 1286
www.english-heritage.org.uk
Beautiful 18th century villa with fine interiors, and a world-class collection of paintings. Fabulous landscaped gardens and an award-winning restaurant.

Somerset House
Westminster WC2R 1LA
(020) 7845 4670
www.somerset-house.org.uk
Somerset House is a place for enjoyment, refreshment, arts and learning. This magnificent 18thC building houses the celebrated collections of the Courtauld Institute of Art Gallery, Gilbert Collection and Hermitage Rooms.

Southwark Cathedral
Southwark SE1 9DA
(020) 7367 6700
www.southwark.anglican.org/cathedral
Oldest Gothic church in London (c1220) with memorials connected with the Elizabethan theatres of Bankside.

Tower of London
Tower Hamlets EC3N 4AB
0870 756 6060
www.hrp.org.uk
Spanning over 900 years of British history. Fortress, palace, prison, arsenal and garrison, one of the most famous fortified buildings in the world, and houses the Crown Jewels, armouries, Yeoman Warders and ravens.

NATURE & WILDLIFE

London Wetland Centre
Richmond upon Thames SW13 9WT
(020) 8409 4400
www.wwt.org.uk
A unique wildlife visitor attraction just 25 minutes from central London. Run by the Wildfowl and Wetlands Trust (WWT), it is acclaimed as the best urban site in Europe to watch wildlife.

OUTDOOR ACTIVITIES

Bateaux London Restaurant Cruisers
Westminster WC2N 6NU
(020) 7695 1800
www.bateauxlondon.com
Lunch/dinner cruises, combining luxury dining, world-class live entertainment and five-star customer care.

London Eye River Cruise Experience
Lambeth SE1 7PB
0870 500 0600
www.londoneye.com
Take a London Eye River Cruise and see London from a different perspective.

Events 2011

Chelsea Flower Show
London
www.rhs.org.uk
May

Daily Mail Ideal Home Show
London
www.idealhomeshow.co.uk/
11 - 27 March

London Marathon
London
www.virginlondonmarathon.com/
17 April

London Open House Weekend
London
www.londonopenhouse.org
September

Mayor's Thames Festival
London
www.thamesfestival.org/
September

New Year's Day Parade
London
www.londonparade.co.uk/
01 January

Notting Hill Carnival
London
www.rbkc.gov.uk
28 - 30 August

State Opening of Parliament
London
www.parliament.uk
October - November

The BBC Proms
London
www.bbc.co.uk/proms/
July/September

The Lord Mayor's Show
London
www.lordmayorsshow.org/
November

University Boat Race
London
www.theboatrace.org
26 March

Wimbledon Tennis Championships
London
www.wimbledon.org
June/July

London | **Where to Eat**

Where to Eat

London has great places to eat. The restaurant reviews on these pages are just a small selection from the highly respected *The Good Food Guide 2011*. Please see page 14 for further information on the Guide and details of a Special Offer for our readers.

ARCHWAY

500 Restaurant
Genuine neighbourhood Italian
782 Holloway Road, Archway N19 3JH
(020) 7272 3406
www.500restaurant.co.uk
Italian | £25

The welcome is friendly and service attentive at this genuine neighbourhood Italian. The décor is agreeably understated: wooden floors, blue-grey walls and a lack of napery help crank up the volume and lend an informal air to proceedings. In the kitchen co-owner Mario Magli cooks with an earthy straightforwardness. Simple dishes such as risotto with smoked eel and parsley or oven-baked rabbit served with pistachios, black olives and sun-dried tomatoes are capably done, and a delicate mint-flavoured pannacotta with strawberry sauce is an appealing dessert. The all-Italian wines include some interesting bottles and prices are fair. House wines from £12.50.
Chef/s: Mario Magli. **Open:** Tue to Sat L 12 to 3, Tue to Sun D 5.30 to 10. **Closed:** Mon, 2 weeks Christmas. **Meals:** alc (main courses £9 to £15). **Service:** not inc. **Details:** major cards accepted. 30 seats. Wheelchair access. Music. Children welcome.

BLOOMSBURY

Cigala
Good classic tapas and fascinating wine
54 Lamb's Conduit Street, Bloomsbury WC1N 3LW
(020) 7405 1717
www.cigala.co.uk
Spanish | £28

Spanish cooking based on good raw materials has proved a winning formula here for 10 years. The room hasn't changed either; the large windows give views of the bustle on the street and simple, white-clad tables add to the sense of light and space. You can graze your way through an extensive menu of classic tapas ranging from chargrilled chorizo and Jamón de Teruel to clams with white wine, garlic and parsley and pastel de bacalao (salt cod and potato fritters) with aïoli, or opt for something more substantial, say grilled veal chop or a parillada of fish and shellfish. The fascinating all-Spanish wine list opens at £16.50.
Chef/s: Jake Hodges. **Open:** Mon to Fri 12 to 10.45, Sat 12.30 to 10.45, Sun 12.30 to 9.30. **Closed:** 24 to 26 Dec, Good Fri to Easter Mon. **Meals:** alc (main courses £12 to £19). Set L £16 (2 courses) to £18. **Service:** 12.5% (optional). **Details:** major cards accepted. 60 seats. 16 seats outside. Air conditioning. Separate bar. No music. Children welcome.

CROYDON

Fish & Grill
A wonderful surprise, with great ingredients
48-50 South End, Croydon CR0 1DP
(020) 8774 4060
www.fishandgrill.co.uk
Modern British | £23

This is the third restaurant opened by Malcom John following the success of nearby Le Cassoulet and Le Vacherin in Chiswick and it's proved 'a wonderful surprise for a Croydon-located restaurant'. This is true of both the relaxed and unpretentious atmosphere and the cooking. The emphasis is on fresh fish and grilled meats, with starters such as scallops and spinach gratin, shellfish bisque and Montgomery cheddar and leek tart being praised in reports this year. Careful sourcing means that meat dishes, for instance, are a cut above

297

the norm – excellent steaks, veal chop and burgers – and there's been warm approval for the monkfish tail, grilled sea bass, bread-and-butter pudding and sherry trifle. House wine is £15.50.

Chef/s: Jason Nott. **Open:** all week 12 to 11. **Closed:** 25 Dec. **Meals:** alc (main courses £12 to £32). Set L £11.95 (2 courses) to £14.95. Sun L £15.95. **Service:** 12.5% (optional). **Details:** major cards accepted. 70 seats. 6 seats outside. Air conditioning. Separate bar. Wheelchair access. Music. Children welcome. No Diners Club.

MAYFAIR
El Pirata of Mayfair
Traditional tapas at rock-bottom prices
5-6 Down Street, Mayfair W1J 7AQ
(020) 7491 3810
www.elpirata.co.uk
Spanish | £20

El Pirata deserves a rousing cheer and some celebratory olés for dishing up traditional tapas at rock-bottom prices in the moneyed enclaves of Mayfair. The congenial 'family atmosphere' (with the occasional celeb thrown in) wins everyone over, and it's perfect if you fancy grazing through some grilled wild asparagus, octopus with olive oil and paprika, or marinated chicken skewers with chorizo. If you're ravenous and are out to impress, there are also two sorts of paella for sharing. Spain reigns on the wine list, with prices from £15.95.

Chef/s: Rosendo Gimbana. **Open:** Mon to Fri 12 to 11.30, Sat D 6 to 11.30. **Closed:** Sun, Easter and bank hols. **Meals:** alc (main courses £13 to £18). Set L £9.95 (2 courses). Set L and D tapas £14.95 to £19.50. **Service:** 10% (optional). **Details:** major cards accepted. 110 seats. 16 seats outside. Air conditioning. Separate bar. Wheelchair access. Music. Children welcome.

RICHMOND
Tangawizi
Colourful, classy Indian cooking
406 Richmond Road, Richmond TW1 2EB
(020) 8891 3737
www.tangawizi.co.uk
Indian | £25

Hard by Richmond Bridge on the fringes of East Twickenham, Tangawizi strikes a colourful pose with its lilac frontage and multi-hued interiors – all saffron, purple and gold tones. The cooking aims a notch or two higher than your average suburban curry house, and the kitchen shows ambition by adding a mango dressing to grilled marinated paneer, cooking lamb with mustard seeds, curry leaves and coconut milk, and dishing up grilled fillet of sea bream with spiced potatoes. Otherwise, expect classy renditions of the usual suspects including vegetable samosas, chicken jalfrezi and prawn masala. House wine is £11.95. Plans are afoot to expand and take over the premises next door.

Chef/s: Surat Singh Rana. **Open:** all week D only 6 to 11 (10.30 Sun). **Closed:** 25 and 26 Dec, 1 Jan. **Meals:** alc (main courses £7 to £13). **Service:** not inc. **Details:** major cards accepted. 50 seats. Air conditioning. Wheelchair access. Music. Children welcome.

SOUTHALL
Madhu's
Stylish favourite with pitch-perfect food
39 South Road, Southall UB1 1SW
(020) 8574 1897
www.madhus.co.uk
Indian | £20

Madhu's is run by the Anand family with genuine confidence and style. Following a high-gloss makeover, the interior now oozes contemporary chic – although the kitchen has resolutely resisted any temptation to emulate its flashy new-wave cousins in the capital. What it offers is pitch-perfect food that scales heights few other local curry houses can dream of. Dishes are generous to a fault, expertly spiced and zingingly fresh, whether you plump for one of the Southall staples (tandoori lamb chops, butter chicken, masala fish) or something from the family's East African back catalogue – perhaps nyamah choma (a Masai warrior's dish of chargrilled marinated ribs). Veggies also do well, with unusual specialities such as karela gourd with potatoes and pomegranate. Beer and lassi suit the chilli-spiked food, although wines start at a very affordable £9.

Chef/s: Rakesh Verma. **Open:** Mon and Wed to Fri L 12.30 to 3, Wed to Mon D 6 to 11.30. **Closed:** Tue. **Meals:** alc (main courses £5 to £11). Set L and D £18 (2 courses) to £20. **Service:** not inc. **Details:** major cards accepted. 105 seats. Air conditioning. Wheelchair access. Music. Children welcome.

Content brought to you by **The Good Food Guide 2011**. Please see page 14 for further details.

London

Tourist Information Centres

When you arrive at your destination, visit an Official Partner Tourist Information Centre for quality assured help with accommodation and information about local attractions and events, or email your request before you go. To find a Tourist Information Centre by region visit enjoyEngland.com/find-tic.

CITY OF LONDON	St Paul's Churchyard	020 7606 3030	greig.oldbury@cityoflondon.gov.uk
GREENWICH	46 Greenwich Church Street	0870 608 2000	tic@greenwich.gov.uk
LEWISHAM	Lewisham Library	020 8297 8317	tic@lewisham.gov.uk
BRITAIN & LONDON VISITOR CENTRE	1 Regent Street	0870 1566366	london@responseuk.co.uk

Regional Contacts and Information

For more information on accommodation, attractions, activities, events and holidays in London, contact Visit London. When you arrive at your destination, visit an Official Partner Tourist Information Centre for quality assured help, or email your request before you go.

The publications listed are available from the following organisations:

Go to **visitlondon.com** for all you need to know about London. Look for inspirational itineraries with great ideas for weekends and short breaks.

Or call 0870 1 LONDON (0870 1 566 366) for:

• A London visitor information pack

Visitor information on London
Speak to an expert for information and advice on museums, galleries, attractions, riverboat trips, sightseeing tours, theatre, shopping, eating out and much more! Or simply go to visitlondon.com

• Accommodation reservations

London | **Inner London**

Where to Stay

Entries appear alphabetically by town name in each county. A key to symbols appears on page 6. Maps start on page 706. A listing of all Enjoy England assessed accommodation appears at the end of the region.

LONDON

at Home in London
Bed and breakfast in London homes

Tel 020 8748 1943
www.athomeinlondon.co.uk

enjoyEngland.com ★★★★ BED & BREAKFAST

At Home in London offers good quality, affordable Bed & Breakfast accommodation in some of the capital's most charming homes.

- Up-market locations: Knightsbridge, Belgravia, Kensington, Westminster
- 4 star homes assessed and star rated by Visit Britain
- The only Gold Award B&B in London
- Hosts include architects, designers, lawyers, teachers and writers
- En suite/private facilities
- Own keys to come and go as you please.
- Awarded Silver & Bronze by Green Tourism for promoting eco-friendly tourism
- Subscribe free to Grapevine, our monthly insider's guide
- Established 1986.

At Home in London, 70 Black Lion Lane, London W6 9BE
Tel 020 8748 1943   www.athomeinlondon.co.uk

Do you like Camping?

You can also buy a copy of our popular guide 'Camping, Touring & Holiday Parks' including touring parks, camping holidays and holiday parks and villages in Britain 2011. Now available in good bookshops and online at **visitbritainshop.com**

£8.99

London | **Inner London**

LONDON E8, Inner London
SAT NAV E8 1EN

The Old Ship
2 Sylvester Path, London E8 1EN
t (020) 8986 1641 **e** oldship@urbaninns.co.uk
w urbaninns.co.uk ONLINE MAP GUEST REVIEWS ONLINE BOOKING LAST MINUTE OFFERS

B&B PER ROOM PER NIGHT
S £79.95
D £99.95 – £129.95

EVENING MEAL PER PERSON
£8.95 – £14.95

SPECIAL PROMOTIONS
Weekend rates from £69.95 per room.

The Old Ship is a modern boutique hotel located in the heart of Hackney directly adjacent to the Hackney Empire. 10 beautifully appointed rooms, relaxing bar area and fantastic British cuisine in a friendly contemporary interior combined with the welcoming warmth of a classic British Inn, without the inflated prices.

bedrooms 6 single, 2 double, 2 family
bathrooms 10 en suite
payment credit/debit cards, cash

directions Please contact us for directions

Room General Leisure

LONDON E15, Inner London
SAT NAV E15 1DB

The Railway Tavern
131 Angel Lane, Stratford, London E15 1DB
t (020) 8534 3123 Fax (020) 8519 0564 **e** therailwaytavern@btconnect.com
w railwaytavernhotel.co.uk ONLINE MAP

B&B PER ROOM PER NIGHT
S £65.00 – £99.00
D £65.00 – £99.00

EVENING MEAL PER PERSON
£6.95

SPECIAL PROMOTIONS
Weekend breaks £99 per room, 2 nights minimum stay.

Family run inn, providing quality accommodation easy access of Stratford regional & mainline stations, DLR, Central & Jubilee Lines. Conveniently placed for London and Canary Wharf. Directly opposite the Olympic site, ideal for tourists visiting the area and well placed for London attractions, East End Hospitality ... West End Style.

open All year
bedrooms 3 double, 6 twin
bathrooms 9 en suite
payment credit/debit cards, cash, cheques

directions By road A112. National Coaches from Stansted. Central, Jubilee, DLR lines to Stratford regional station. Five minute walk from Stratford station.

Room General

London | Inner London

LONDON N1, Inner London
SAT NAV N1 3NW

Kandara Guest House
68 Ockendon Road, Islington, London N1 3NW
t (020) 7226 5721 f (020) 7226 3379 e admin@kandara.co.uk
w kandara.co.uk

B&B PER ROOM PER NIGHT
S £49.00 – £63.00
D £69.00 – £83.00

Family-run guesthouse near the Angel, Islington. All bedrooms and bathrooms have recently been decorated. Excellent public transport with 11 bus routes and 4 stations nearby. Free overnight street parking. **directions** From A1, Highbury Corner roundabout take St Paul's Road for 0.5 mile. Turn right onto Essex Road. Ockendon Road is 5th on the left. **open** All year except Xmas **bedrooms** 4 single, 3 double, 1 twin, 4 family **payment** credit/debit cards, cash, cheques, euros

Room   General

LONDON N10, Inner London
SAT NAV N10 3HT

The Muswell Hill
73 Muswell Hill Road, London N10 3HT
t (020) 8883 6447 f (020) 8883 5158 e reception@muswellhillhotel.co.uk
w muswellhillhotel.co.uk ONLINE MAP

B&B PER ROOM PER NIGHT
S £55.00
D £70.00

A comfortable, three-storey, Edwardian corner property, close to Muswell Hill and Alexandra Palace, offering a warm, friendly service. **directions** Please contact us for directions **open** All year except Xmas **bedrooms** 4 single, 3 double, 4 twin, 3 family **bathrooms** 10 en suite **payment** credit/debit cards, cash, cheques

Room   General   Leisure ▶

LONDON SE3, Inner London
SAT NAV SE3 9EN

59A Lee Road
59A Lee Road, Blackheath, London SE3 9EN
t (020) 8318 7244 (07780 925402) e ac@blackheath318.freeserve.co.uk

B&B PER ROOM PER NIGHT
S £50.00
D £75.00

Charming accommodation in leafy location. Minutes from amenities of Blackheath village. Extremely convenient for historic Greenwich, central London and Docklands Light Railway. Free off-road parking. Minimum two nights' stay. **directions** Please contact us for directions **open** All year except Xmas and New Year **bedrooms** 1 double **payment** cash, cheques

Room   General

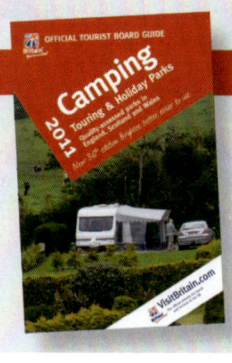

Do you like Camping?

You can also buy a copy of our popular guide 'Camping, Touring & Holiday Parks' including touring parks, camping holidays and holiday parks and villages in Britain 2011.

Now available in good bookshops and online at
visitbritainshop.com

£8.99

302   Official tourist board guide Bed & Breakfast

London | **Inner London**

LONDON SE3, Inner London
SAT NAV SE3 7DH

onesixtwo
162 Westcombe Hill, Near Blackheath, London SE3 7DH
t 020 8465 5344 e bookings@onesixtwo.co.uk
w **onesixtwo.co.uk** ONLINE BOOKING

B&B PER ROOM PER NIGHT
S £69.00 – £110.00
D £79.00 – £120.00

onesixtwo is a high quality contemporary Guest House with a boutique hotel feel. The stylish rooms include comfortable quality hotel beds, Egyptian cotton bedding, free Wi-Fi and laptop loan, mini fridge and flat screen TV. Within 10 minutes of historic Greenwich, Blackheath and O2 arena.

open All year
bedrooms 9 double, 1 twin
bathrooms 10 en suite
payment credit/debit cards, cash, cheques

directions 2 min drive from Sun and Sands roundabout at A2/A102 junction. Nearest train - Westcombe Park. Nearest tube - North Greenwich. Bus routes 108/422/286.

Room
General 12

LONDON SE6, Inner London
SAT NAV SE6 1JD

Heathers Guest House
71 Verdant Lane, Catford, Lewisham, London SE6 1JD
t 44(0)20 8698 8340 e berylheath@yahoo.co.uk
w **theheathersbb.com** GUEST REVIEWS

B&B PER ROOM PER NIGHT
S £35.00 – £40.00
D £55.00 – £60.00

The Heathers is a warm and comfortable Home from Home and we want you to enjoy your stay. Tea and Coffee TV. Radio, Hairdryers. Roomy bathroom/power shower. Guests fridge. **directions** Train from Charing Cross or London Bridge to Hither Green Station. Directions from airport on request. Free On Road parking. **open** All year **bedrooms** 2 twin **bathrooms** 1 with private bathroom **payment** cash, cheques

Room General 5

LONDON SE20, Inner London
SAT NAV SE20 7LY

Melrose House
89 Lennard Road, London SE20 7LY
t (020) 8776 8884 f (020) 8778 6366 e melrose.hotel@virgin.net
w **guesthouseaccommodation.co.uk** ONLINE MAP GUEST REVIEWS

B&B PER ROOM PER NIGHT
S £40.00 – £50.00
D £65.00 – £70.00

Superb accommodation in Victorian house with spacious, en suite bedrooms. Easy access to West End. Quiet, respectable, friendly and welcoming. Ground floor rooms opening onto the lovely garden. **directions** 15 minutes by train to the centre of London, the train runs every 15 minutes and the station is a 5 minute walk. **open** All year **bedrooms** 1 single, 4 double, 2 twin, 2 family **bathrooms** 8 en suite, 1 with private bathroom **payment** credit/debit cards, cash, euros

Room General 8 P

London | **Inner London**

LONDON SW1, Inner London
SAT NAV SW1V 1RG

Dover
44 Belgrave Road, London SW1V 1RG
t (020) 7821 9385 f (020) 7834 6525 e reception@dover-hotel.co.uk
w **dover-hotel.co.uk** ONLINE MAP GUEST REVIEWS ONLINE BOOKING LAST MINUTE OFFERS

B&B PER ROOM PER NIGHT
S £40.00 – £65.00
D £50.00 – £75.00

Friendly bed & breakfast hotel, very near Victoria Station and Gatwick Express. Rooms with satellite TV, shower/wc, telephone, hairdryer. Free Wi-Fi. Near Buckingham Palace, Big Ben and London Eye. **directions** Nearest Underground/Rail/Coach Station is Victoria Station. From Vauxhall Bridge Road (A202) turn into Warwick Way and then turn right into Belgrave Road **open** All year **bedrooms** 5 single, 13 double, 7 twin, 8 family **bathrooms** 29 en suite **payment** credit/debit cards, cash, cheques, euros

Room   General

LONDON SW5, Inner London
SAT NAV SW5 9SU

Mowbray Court
28-32 Penywern Road, London SW5 9SU
t (020) 7370 2316 or (020) 7373 8285 f (020) 7370 5693 e mowbraycrthot@hotmail.com
w **mowbraycourthotel.co.uk**

B&B PER ROOM PER NIGHT
S £50.00 – £70.00
D £70.00 – £86.00

Close to Earls Court underground and West Brompton Station with links to Heathrow and Gatwick airports. **directions** Please contact us for directions **open** All year **bedrooms** 30 single, 20 double, 10 twin, 10 family **bathrooms** 70 with private bathroom **payment** credit/debit cards, cash, cheques

Room   General   Leisure

LONDON W1, Inner London
SAT NAV W1U 8HY

Lincoln House - Central
33 Gloucester Place, Marble Arch, London W1U 8HY
t (020) 7486 7630 f (020) 7486 0166 e reservations@lincoln-house-hotel.co.uk
w **lincoln-house-hotel.co.uk** ONLINE MAP GUEST REVIEWS ONLINE BOOKING LAST MINUTE OFFERS

B&B PER ROOM PER NIGHT
S £59.00 – £79.00
D £69.00 – £89.00

SPECIAL PROMOTIONS
Long-stay discounts on request. Most Sundays discounted. For latest long-stay and other special offers visit our website.

A Georgian guest house with period character and nautical theme throughout offering English and vegetarian breakfast. En suite rooms with free Wi-Fi internet. Most rooms air-conditioned. Located in the heart of London near to Oxford Street shopping, theatres, museums and exhibitions. Next to airbus stop for most airports.

open All year
bedrooms 6 single, 6 double, 4 twin, 7 family
bathrooms 23 en suite
payment credit/debit cards, cash, cheques

directions Upon reaching Baker Street Station, left into Baker Street. Fourth set of lights, right into George Street. First set of lights turn into Gloucester Place.

Room   General   Leisure

London | **Inner London/Outer London**

LONDON W1, Inner London
SAT NAV W1H 5QR

Marble Arch Inn
49-50 Upper Berkeley Street, London W1H 5QR
t (020) 7723 7888 f (020) 7723 6060 e sales@marblearch-inn.co.uk
w **marblearch-inn.co.uk** ONLINE MAP GUEST REVIEWS ONLINE BOOKING LAST MINUTE OFFERS

B&B PER ROOM PER NIGHT
S £35.00 – £75.00
D £35.00 – £85.00

Friendly bed and breakfast hotel within minutes of Hyde Park, Oxford Street, Heathrow Express. Most rooms with satellite TV, shower/wc, telephone, hairdryer. Free Wi-Fi. Very competitive prices. **directions** Near Marble Arch Underground and Paddington Rail Station. From Edgware Road (A5) near Marble Arch, turn into Upper Berkeley Street. **open** All year **bedrooms** 2 single, 11 double, 7 twin, 9 family **bathrooms** 23 en suite **payment** credit/debit cards, cash, cheques, euros

LONDON W2, Inner London
SAT NAV W2 2TP

Barry House
12 Sussex Place, Hyde Park, London W2 2TP
t (020) 7723 7340 f (020) 7723 9775 e hotel@barryhouse.co.uk
w **barryhouse.co.uk** ONLINE MAP GUEST REVIEWS ONLINE BOOKING

B&B PER ROOM PER NIGHT
S £44.00 – £65.00
D £72.00 – £99.00

Family-run Barry House offers warm hospitality in a Victorian town house. Comfortable en suite rooms, English breakfast served. Located close to West End. Paddington Station, Hyde Park just three minutes' walk. **directions** From A40 take Paddington exit and follow the road, then turn left into Sussex Gardens, then 1st right into Sussex Place. **open** All year **bedrooms** 3 single, 4 double, 4 twin, 6 family **bathrooms** 14 en suite, 3 with private bathroom **payment** credit/debit cards, cash

LONDON W2, Inner London
SAT NAV W2 2RX

Kingsway Park Guest Accommodation
139 Sussex Gardens, London W2 2RX
t (020) 7723 5677 f (020) 7402 4352 e info@kingswaypark-hotel.com
w **kingswaypark-hotel.com** ONLINE MAP ONLINE BOOKING

B&B PER ROOM PER NIGHT
S £50.00 – £75.00
D £70.00 – £95.00

Elegant, Victorian, Grade II Listed building beautifully refurbished. Three minutes' walk from Paddington Station and Heathrow Express, five minutes from Hyde Park, Ten minutes to Oxford Street and Marble Arch. **directions** Please contact us for directions **open** All year **bedrooms** 4 single, 6 double, 7 twin, 5 family **bathrooms** 22 en suite **payment** credit/debit cards, cash, cheques

CROYDON, Outer London
SAT NAV CR0 1JR

Woodstock Guest House
30 Woodstock Road, Croydon CR0 1JR
t (020) 8680 1489 f (020) 8667 1229 e woodstockhotel@tiscali.co.uk
w **woodstockhotel.co.uk**

B&B PER ROOM PER NIGHT
S £40.00 – £45.00
D £70.00

Located in a quiet residential area, only five minutes' walk to town centre and East Croydon Railway Station. Well-appointed and spacious rooms. High standard of housekeeping and homely atmosphere. **directions** From East Croydon Station via George Street turn left into Park Lane. At roundabout exit into A212. Woodstock Road is 2nd left off Park Lane. **open** All year except Xmas **bedrooms** 4 single, 2 twin, 2 family **bathrooms** 2 en suite, 4 with private bathroom **payment** credit/debit cards, cash

London | Outer London

RICHMOND, Outer London
SAT NAV TW10 6UL

Hobart Hall Guest House
43-47 Petersham Road, Richmond TW10 6UL
t (020) 8940 0435 f (020) 8332 2996 e hobarthall@aol.com
w hobarthall.net ONLINE MAP LAST MINUTE OFFERS

B&B PER ROOM PER NIGHT
S £45.00 – £75.00
D £100.00 – £105.00

SPECIAL PROMOTIONS
Special deals for late bookers subject to availability.

Built c1690. Past occupants include the Countess of Buckinghamshire and William IV. Historic setting overlooking River Thames, 200yds from Richmond Bridge. Heritage, cultural and business centres in near proximity. Heathrow, M3, M4 15 minutes. Over ground and underground trains: Waterloo 20 minutes, West End 25 minutes.

open All year
directions see our website
bedrooms 13 single, 9 double, 5 twin, 5 family, 1 suite
bathrooms 26 en suite
payment credit/debit cards, cash, cheques

RICHMOND, Outer London
SAT NAV TW10 5LA

Ivy Cottage
Upper Ham Road, Ham Common, Richmond TW10 5LA
t (020) 8940 8601 e taylor@dbta.freeserve.co.uk
w dbta.freeserve.co.uk

B&B PER ROOM PER NIGHT
S £35.00 – £40.00
D £70.00 – £80.00

Charming, wisteria-clad Georgian home offering exceptional views over Ham Common. Period features dating from 1760. Garden. Se catering an option. Good bus route and parking. **directions** Please contact us for directions **open** All year **bedrooms** 1 single, 1 double, 1 twin, 1 family **bathrooms** 4 with private bathroom **payment** cash, cheques, euros

RICHMOND, Outer London
SAT NAV TW9 1YJ

The Red Cow
59 Sheen Road, Richmond TW9 1YJ
t (020) 8940 2511 f (020) 8940 2581 e tom@redcowpub.com
w redcowpub.com ONLINE MAP

B&B PER ROOM PER NIGHT
S £60.00 – £75.00
D £70.00 – £95.00
EVENING MEAL PER PERSON
£7.95 – £14.95

Traditional Victorian inn retaining lovely original features. A short walk from Richmond town centre, river, royal parks and rail links t London. Nearby, Heathrow Airport, Twickenham RFU, Hampton Court and Windsor. **directions** Five-minute walk from Richmond town centre and train station. Easily accessed from M25, M4 and M3. **open** All year **bedrooms** 2 double, 1 twin, 1 family **bathroom** 4 en suite **payment** credit/debit cards, cash, cheques, euros

London | Outer London

SUTTON, Outer London
SAT NAV SM2 7PE

enjoyEngland.com
GUEST HOUSE

B&B PER ROOM PER NIGHT
S £25.00 – £35.00
D £40.00 – £45.00

St Margarets Guest House
31 Devon Road, Sutton SM2 7PE
t (020) 8643 0164 **f** (020) 8643 0517 **e** margarettrotman@hotmail.com
w stmargaretsbandb.co.uk ONLINE MAP

Family-run, established over 20 years. Detached house in a quiet residential area. Long-term stays welcomed. Washing machines, fridges and microwaves available for own use. **directions** Cheam station on Victoria line is 10 minutes walk from us. Will collect by prior arrangement. Exit 8 from M25 onto A217. **open** All year **bedrooms** 2 single, 2 twin **bathrooms** 1 en suite **payment** cash, cheques

Room General Leisure

TWICKENHAM, Outer London
SAT NAV TW1 3EG

enjoyEngland.com
ROOM ONLY

B&B PER ROOM PER NIGHT
D £68.00 – £135.00

The Old Stables
1 Bridle Lane, Twickenham TW1 3EG
t 07966 549515 **f** (020) 8892 9503 **e** jenny@oldstables.com
w oldstables.com

Luxurious accommodation in the heart of St Margarets' village. A two-minute walk to bus and rail connections. St Margarets' best-kept secret. **directions** Please contact us for directions **open** All year **bedrooms** 2 double, 1 twin, 1 family **bathrooms** 4 en suite **payment** cash, cheques

Room General

UXBRIDGE, Outer London
SAT NAV UB8 3AE

enjoyEngland.com
GUEST ACCOMMODATION

B&B PER ROOM PER NIGHT
S £35.00 – £45.00
D £50.00 – £60.00

Oakdene Guest House
17 Orchard Drive, Cowley UB8 3AE
t (01895) 237338 **e** albie@uxbridge-guesthouse.com
w uxbridge-guesthouse.com ONLINE MAP

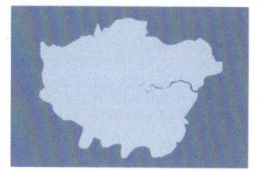

Quiet location approx one mile from Uxbridge town centre, there are local buses to town and underground to London. www.uxbridge-guesthouse.com **directions** One mile from Uxbridge, M25, M4 and M40. **open** All year **bedrooms** 1 single, 3 double, 2 twin, 1 family **bathrooms** 3 en suite, 3 with private bathroom **payment** cash, cheques, euros

Room General Leisure

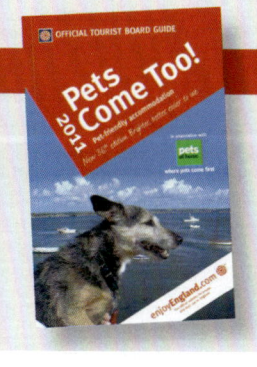

Where is my pet welcome?

Some properties welcome well-behaved pets. Look for the 🐕 in the accommodation listings.

You can also buy a copy of our popular guide 'Pets Come Too!' Now available in good bookshops and online at **visitbritainshop.com**

£9.99

key to symbols see page 6   307

London | Inner London

All Assessed Accommodation

Inner London
LONDON E1

Queen Mary, University of London ★★★ *Campus*
Mile End Road, London
E1 4NS
t (020) 7882 3642
e holiday@qmul.ac.uk
w qmul.ac.uk/conferences

LONDON E8

The Old Ship ★★★★ *Inn*
2 Sylvester Path, London
E8 1EN
t (020) 8986 1641
e oldship@urbaninns.co.uk
w urbaninns.co.uk

LONDON E15

The Railway Tavern ★★★★ *Inn*
131 Angel Lane, Stratford, London
E15 1DB
t (020) 8534 3123 Fax
   (020) 8519 0864
e therailwaytavern@btconnect.com
w railwaytavernhotel.co.uk

LONDON EC4

City of London YHA ★★★ *Hostel*
36 Carter Lane, London
EC4V 5AB
t (020) 7236 4965
e city@yha.org.uk
w yha.org.uk

LONDON N1

Kandara Guest House ★★★
Guest House
68 Ockendon Road, Islington, London
N1 3NW
t (020) 7226 5721
e admin@kandara.co.uk
w kandara.co.uk

University of Westminster-Alexander Fleming Halls of Residence ★★★ *Campus*
3 Hoxton Market, London
N1 6HG
t (020) 7911 5181
e summeraccommodation@westminster.ac.uk
w westminster.ac.uk/business/summer-accommodation

LONDON N7

Europa ★★★ *Guest Accommodation*
62 Anson Road, London
N7 0AA
t (020) 7607 5935
e info@europahotellondon.co.uk
w europahotellondon.co.uk

LONDON N8

Homestead Crouch End London ★
Guest Accommodation
141 Ferme Park Road, Crouch End, London
N8 9SE
t (020) 8347 8768
e homlon@btconnect.com

White Lodge ★★★
Guest Accommodation
1 Church Lane, London
N8 7BU
t (020) 8348 9765
e info@whitelodgehornsey.co.uk
w whitelodgehornsey.co.uk

LONDON N10

The Muswell Hill ★★★
Guest House
73 Muswell Hill Road, London
N10 3HT
t (020) 8883 6447
e reception@muswellhillhotel.co.uk
w muswellhillhotel.co.uk

LONDON N11

Bay Tree House B&B ★★★★
Guest Accommodation
59 Brookdale, New Southgate, London
N11 1BS
t (020) 8351 2836
e j.monaghan@blueyonder.co.uk
w baytreehouse@blueyonder.co.uk

LONDON NW1

MIC Conferences & Accommodation ★★★★
Guest Accommodation
81-103 Euston Street, London
NW1 2EZ
t (020) 7380 0001

St Pancras YHA ★★★★ *Hostel*
79-81 Euston Road, London
NW1 2QS
t (020) 7388 9998
e stpancras@yha.org.uk
w yha.org.uk

University of Westminster-Marylebone Hall of Residence ★★★★ *Campus*
35 Marylebone Road, London
NW1 5LS
t (020) 7911 5181
e summeraccommodation@westminster.ac.uk
w westminster.ac.uk/summeraccommodation

LONDON NW3

Dillons ★★★ *Guest Accommodation*
21 Belsize Park, London
NW3 4DU
t (020) 7794 3360
e desk@dillonshotel.com
w dillonshotel.com

LONDON NW8

The New Inn ★★★ *Inn*
2 Allitsen Road, St John's Wood, London
NW8 6LA
t (020) 7722 0726
e thenewinnlondon@aol.com
w newinnlondon.co.uk

LONDON NW11

Anchor House ★★★ *Guest House*
10 West Heath Drive, London
NW11 7QH
t (020) 8458 8764
e enquir@anchor-hotel.co.uk
w anchorhousehotel.co.uk

Martel Guest House ★★★
Guest House
27 The Ridgeway, Golders Green, London
NW11 8QP
t +44 (0)20 8455 1802
e reservations@martelguesthouse.co.uk
w martelguesthouse.co.uk

LONDON SE1

Great Dover Street Apartments ★★★ *Campus*
165 Great Dover Street, London
SE1 4XA
t (020) 7407 0069
e vacations.at.kings@kcl.ac.uk
w kcl.ac.uk/kcvb

St Christopher's Village ★★
Backpackers
161-165 Borough High Street, London
SE1 1HR
t (020) 7407 1856
e bookings@st-christophers.co.uk
w st-christophers.co.uk

University of Westminster-International House ★★ *Campus*
1-5 Lambeth Road, London
SE1 6HU
t (020) 7911 5181
e summeraccommodation@westminster.ac.uk
w westminster.ac.uk/business/summer-accommodation

LONDON SE3

59A Lee Road ★★ *Bed & Breakfast*
59A Lee Road, Blackheath, London
SE3 9EN
t (020) 8318 7244 (07780 925402)
e ac@blackheath318.freeserve.co.uk

Greenland Villa ★★★★
Guest Accommodation
9 Charlton Road, London
SE3 7EU
t (020) 8858 4175
e bookings@greenlandvilla.com
w greenlandvilla.com

onesixtwo ★★★★
Guest Accommodation
162 Westcombe Hill, Near Blackheath, London
SE3 7DH
t 020 8465 5444
e bookings@onesixtwo.co.uk
w onesixtwo.co.uk

LONDON SE4

Crofton Park Holdenby
Bed & Breakfast
28 Holdenby Road, London
SE4 2DA
t (020) 8694 0011
e savitri.gaines@totalise.co.uk
w ukhomestay.net

LONDON SE6

Heathers Guest House ★★
Bed & Breakfast
71 Verdant Lane, Catford, Lewisham, London
SE6 1JD
t 44(0)20 8698 8340
e berylheath@yahoo.co.uk
w theheathersbb.com

LONDON SE8

McMillan Student Village ★★★★
Campus
Creek Road, Greenwich, London
SE8 3BU
t (020) 8691 8996
e roberta@opalgroup.com

LONDON SE9

Boru House ★★ *Bed & Breakfast*
70 Dunvegan Road, London
SE9 1SB
t (020) 8850 0584

Michelle's Guest House ★★
Guest Accommodation
54 Gourock Road, London
SE9 1HY
t 077651 35604
e mlogica@hotmail.co.uk

LONDON SE10

16 St Alfeges ★★★★
Bed & Breakfast
16 St Alfege Passage, London
SE10 9JS
t (020) 8853 4337
e nicmesure@yahoo.co.uk
w st-alfeges.co.uk

Captains Retreat ★★★★
Bed & Breakfast **SILVER AWARD**
37 Crosslet Vale, Greenwich, London
SE10 8DH
t (020) 8694 2827
e captmcdonnell@gmail.com

The Corner House ★★★★
Guest Accommodation
28 Royal Hill, London
SE10 8RT
t (020) 8692 3023
e joannacourtney@aol.com

Number 37 ★★★
Guest Accommodation
37 Burney Street, Greenwich, London
SE10 8EX
t (020) 8265 2623
e info@burney.org.uk
w burney.org.uk

Pilot Inn ★★★★ *Inn*
68 River Way, London
SE10 0BE
t (020) 8858 5910
e pilotgreenwich@fullers.co.uk
w fullershotels.co.uk

LONDON SE13

24 Wellmeadow Road ★★
Bed & Breakfast
Hither Green, Greenwich, London
SE13 6TB
t 07949 933249
e violet_deller@hotmail.com

Manna House ★★★
Bed & Breakfast
320 Hither Green Lane, London
SE13 6TS
t (020) 8461 5984
e lynne@mannahouse.co.uk
w mannahouse.co.uk

LONDON SE16

YHA London Thameside ★★
Hostel
20 Salter Road, London
SE16 5PR
t 0870 770 6010
e thameside@yha.org.uk
w yha.org.uk

LONDON SE18

Cherish Lodge ★ *Bed & Breakfast*
Vicarage Road, London
SE18 7SP
t (020) 8855 8638
e cherishlodge@btinternet.com
w cherishlodge.com

Ebenezer Lodge ★★
Bed & Breakfast
St Mary Street, London
SE18 5AN
t (020) 8855 3051
e ebenezerlodge@btconnect.com
w ebenezerlodge.co.uk

LONDON SE20

Melrose House ★★★★
Guest Accommodation
89 Lennard Road, London
SE20 7LY
t (020) 8776 8884
e melrose.hotel@virgin.net
w guesthouseaccommodation.co.uk

LONDON SW1

Astors ★★★★
Guest Accommodation
Ebury Street, London
SW1W 9QD
t (020) 7730 0158
e info@astorshotelvictoria.co.uk
w astorshotelvictoria.co.uk

Caswell ★★ *Guest Accommodation*
25 Gloucester Street, London
SW1V 2DB
t (020) 7834 6345
e manager@hotellondon.co.uk
w hotellondon.co.uk

Central House ★★★
Guest Accommodation
37-41 Belgrave Road, London
SW1V 2BB
t (020) 7834 8036
e info@centralhousehotel.co.uk

Dover ★★ *Guest Accommodation*
44 Belgrave Road, London
SW1V 1RG
t (020) 7821 9085
e reception@dover-hotel.co.uk
w dover-hotel.co.uk

London | Inner London

...abeth ★★★
...st Accommodation
...Eccleston Square, London
...1V 1PB
...(020) 7828 6812
...info@elizabethhotel.com
...elizabethhotel.com

...orgian House ★★★
...st Accommodation
...St Georges Drive, London
...1V 4DG
...(020) 7834 1438
...reception@georgianhousehotel.
...co.uk
...georgianhousehotel.co.uk

...ly House ★
...st Accommodation
...Hugh Street, Victoria, London
...1V 1RP
...(020) 7834 5671
...hhhotel@ukgateway.net
...hollyhousehotel.co.uk

...ttons ★★★
...Belgrave Road, London
...1V 2BB
...(020) 7834 3726

...Lord Milner ★★★★★
...st Accommodation
...VER AWARD
...Ebury Street, London
...1W 9QU
...(020) 7881 9880
...info@lordmilner.com
...lordmilner.com

...a Simone Guest House ★★★★
...st House
...Belgrave Road, London
...1V 2BB
...(020) 7834 5897

...ita House ★★★
...st Accommodation
...Charlwood Street, London
...V 2DU
...(020) 7828 0471
...reserve@melitahotel.com
...melitahotel.com

...nley House ★★
...st Accommodation
...21 Belgrave Road, London
...1V 1RB
...(020) 7834 5042
...cmahotel@aol.com
...londonbudgethotels.co.uk

...versity of Westminster-Wigram
...use ★★ Campus
...99 Ashley Gardens, Thirleby
...d, London
...1P 1HG
...(020) 7911 5181
...summeraccommodation@westm
...nster.ac.uk
...westminster.ac.uk/business/
...summer-accommodation

...don House ★★★
...st Accommodation
...andon Street, London
...H 0AH
...(020) 7799 6780
...info@vandonhouse.com
...vandonhouse.com

...tor ★★★ Guest Accommodation
...Belgrave Road, London
...V 2BB
...(020) 7592 9853
...victorhotel.co.uk

...Victoria Inn London ★★★
...57 Belgrave Road, London
...V 2BG
...(020) 7834 6721
...welcome@victoriainn.co.uk
...victoriainn.co.uk

...Windermere ★★★★
...st Accommodation
...VER AWARD
...-144 Warwick Way, London
...V 4JE
...(020) 7834 5163
...reservations@windermere-hotel.
...co.uk
...windermere-hotel.co.uk

LONDON SW5

base2stay Kensington ★★★★★
Guest Accommodation - Room Only
GOLD AWARD
25 Courtfield Gardens, London
SW5 0PG
t (020) 7244 2255
w base2stay.com

Beaver ★★ *Guest Accommodation*
57-59 Philbeach Gardens, London
SW5 9ED
t (020) 7373 4553
e hotelbeaver@hotmail.com
w beaverhotel.co.uk

Best Western The Boltons ★★★★
Guest Accommodation
19-21 Penywern Road, London
SW5 9TT
t (020) 7373 8900
e rasool@rasool.demon.co.uk
w rasoolcourthotel.com

Earls Court ★ *Guest House*
28 Warwick Road, London
SW5 9UD
t (020) 7373 7079
e info@hotelearlscourt.com
w hotelearlscourt.com

Lord Jim ★★ *Guest House*
25 Penywern Road, London
SW5 9TT
t (020) 7370 6071
e ljh@lgh-hotels.com
w lgh-hotels.com

Mowbray Court ★★
Guest Accommodation
28-32 Penywern Road, London
SW5 9SU
t (020) 7370 2316 or
  (020) 7373 8285
e mowbraycrthot@hotmail.com
w mowbraycourthotel.com

YHA Earl's Court ★★★★ *Hostel*
38 Bolton Gardens, London
SW5 0AQ
t (020) 7373 7083
e earlscourt@yha.org.uk
w yha.org.uk

LONDON SW7

**Imperial College London ★★★ -
★★★★** *Campus*
South Kensington Campus, London
SW7 2AZ
t (020) 7594 9507
e reservations@imperial.ac.uk
w imperial-accommodationlink.com

**Meininger City Hostel & Hotel
London ★★★★** *Hostel*
65-67 Queen's Gate, London
SW7 5JS
t (020) 3051 8173
e welcome@meininger-hostels.com
w meininger-hostels.com

LONDON SW9

Belgrave Oval ★★★★
Guest Accommodation
9-13 Clapham Road, London
SW9 0JD
t (020) 7793 0142
e enquiries@belgravehotel.net

LONDON SW11

Lavender Guest House ★★★
Guest House
18 Lavender Sweep, London
SW11 1HA
t (020) 7585 2767
w thelavenderguesthouse.com

LONDON SW16

The Konyots ★ *Bed & Breakfast*
95 Pollards Hill South, London
SW16 4LS
t (020) 8764 0075

LONDON SW18

Grosvenor Arms *Inn*
204 Garratt Lane, Wandsworth,
London
SW18 4ED
t (020) 8874 2709

LONDON W1

The Hallam ★★★
Guest Accommodation
12 Hallam Street, London
W1W 6JF
t (020) 7580 1166
e hallam-hotel@hotmail.com
w hallamhotel.com

**International Students House
★★★** *Hostel*
229 Great Portland Street, Regent's
Park, London
W1N 5HD
t (020) 7631 8300
e accom@ish.org.uk
w ish.org.uk

Lincoln House - Central ★★★
Guest Accommodation
33 Gloucester Place, Marble Arch,
London
W1U 8HY
t (020) 7486 7630
e reservations@lincoln-house-hotel.
co.uk
w lincoln-house-hotel.co.uk

Marble Arch Inn ★★
Guest Accommodation
49-50 Upper Berkeley Street,
London
W1H 5QR
t (020) 7723 7888
e sales@marblearch-inn.co.uk
w marblearch-inn.co.uk

Oxford Street YHA ★★★ *Hostel*
14 Noel Street, London
W1F 8GJ
t (020) 7734 1618
e oxfordst@yha.org.uk
w yha.org.uk

YHA London Central ★★★★
Hostel
104-108 Bolsover Street, London
W1W 6AB
t (01629) 592633

LONDON W2

The Abbey Court ★★★★
Guest Accommodation
20 Pembridge Gardens, London
W2 4DU
t (020) 7221 7518
e info@abbeycourthotel.co.uk
w abbeycourthotel.com

Abbey Court & Westpoint ★★★
Guest Accommodation
174 Sussex Gardens, London
W2 1TP
t (020) 7402 0281
e info@abbeycourt.com
w abbeycourthotel.com

Albro House Hotel ★★
Guest Accommodation
155 Sussex Gardens, London
W2 2RY
t (020) 7706 8153
e joe@albrohotel.freeserve.co.uk
w albrohotel.co.uk

Alexandra ★★★
Guest Accommodation
159-161 Sussex Gardens, London
W2 2RY
t (020) 7402 6471
e hotels.leventis-group@virgin.net
w hotels-leventis-group.com

Barry House ★★★
Guest Accommodation
12 Sussex Place, Hyde Park, London
W2 2TP
t (020) 7723 7340
e hotel@barryhouse.co.uk
w barryhouse.co.uk

Cardiff ★★★ *Guest Accommodation*
5-9 Norfolk Square, London
W2 1RU
t (020) 7723 9068
e stay@cardiff-hotel.com
w cardiff-hotel.com

Elysee ★★★★
Guest Accommodation
25-26 Craven Terrace, London
W2 3EL
t (020) 7402 7633
e info@hotelelysee.co.uk
w hotelelysee.co.uk

Hyde Park Radnor ★★★★
Guest Accommodation
7-9 Sussex Place, London
W2 2SX
t (020) 7723 5969
e hydeparkradnor@btconnect.com
w hydeparkradnor.co.uk

**Kingsway Park Guest
Accommodation ★★★**
Guest Accommodation
139 Sussex Gardens, London
W2 2RX
t (020) 7723 5677
e info@kingswaypark-hotel.com
w kingswaypark-hotel.com

Nayland ★★★★
Guest Accommodation
132-134 Sussex Gardens, London
W2 1UB
t (020) 7723 4615
e info@naylandhotel.com
w naylandhotel.com

Rhodes House Hotel ★★★
Guest Accommodation
195 Sussex Gardens, London
W2 2RJ
t (020) 7262 5617
e chris@rhodeshotel.com
w rhodeshotel.com

St David's & Norfolk Court ★★
Guest Accommodation
16 Norfolk Square, London
W2 1RS
t (020) 7723 3856
e info@stdavidshotels.com
w stdavidshotels.com

LONDON W3

Park Lodge ★★★★ *Guest House*
335 Uxbridge Road, London
W3 9RA
t (020) 8992 7874
w parklodge.com

LONDON W5

Grange Lodge ★★ *Guest House*
48-50 Grange Road, London
W5 5BX
t (020) 8567 1049
e enquiries@londonlodgehotels.
com
w londonlodgehotels.com

LONDON W6

**At Home in London: South
Kensington Ref 30 ★★**
Bed & Breakfast
South Kensington, London
W6 9BE
t (020) 8748 1943
e info@athomeinlondon.co.uk
w athomeinlondon.co.uk

**At Home in London: Westminster
Ref 5 ★★** *Guest Accommodation*
GOLD AWARD
Westminster, London
W6 9BE
t (020) 8748 1943
e info@athomeinlondon.co.uk
w athomeinlondon.co.uk

Temple Lodge Club Ltd ★★★
Guest Accommodation
Temple Lodge, 51 Queen Caroline
Street, Hammersmith
W6 9QL
t (020) 8748 8388
e templelodgeclub@btconnect.com
w templelodgeclub.com

London | Inner London/Outer London

LONDON W8

Holland House YHA ★★ *Hostel*
Holland Walk, Kensington, London
W8 7QN
t (020) 7937 0748
e hollandhouse@yha.org.uk
w yha.org.uk

LONDON W14

Ace Hotel ★★★ *Hostel*
16-22 Gunterstone Road, West
Kensington, London
W14 9BX
t (020) 7602 6600
e reception@ace-hotel.co.uk
w ace-hotel.co.uk

LONDON WC1

Comfort Inn Kings Cross ★★★★
Guest Accommodation
2-5 St Chad's Street, London
WC1H 8BD
t (020) 7837 1940
e info@comfortinnkingscross.co.uk
w comfortinnkingscross.co.uk

Generator ★★★ *Backpackers*
London
WC1N 9SE
t (020) 7388 7666
e info@the-generator.co.uk
w the-generator.co.uk

Goodenough Club ★★★★
Guest Accommodation
23 Mecklenburgh Square, London
WC1N 2AB
t (020) 7837 8831
e club@goodenough.ac.uk
w club.goodenough.ac.uk

Guilford House ★★★ *Guest House*
6 Guilford Street, London
WC1N 1DR
t (020) 7430 2504
e guilford-hotel@lineone.net
w guilford-hotel.co.uk

LONDON WC2

LSE Grosvenor House Studios
★★★ *Campus*
141-143 Drury Lane, London
WC2B 5TB
t (020) 7107 5950
e grosvenor@lse.ac.uk
w lsevacations.co.uk

LSE Northumberland House ★★★
Campus
8a Northumberland Avenue,
London
WC2N 5BY
t (020) 7107 5603
e northumberland-house@lse.ac.uk
w lse.ac.uk/vacations

Outer London

BEXLEY

66 Arcadian Avenue ★★★
Bed & Breakfast
66 Arcadian Avenue, Bexley
DA5 1JW
t (020) 8303 5732

Blendon Lodge ★★★★
Bed & Breakfast
30 Blendon Road, Bexley
DA5 1BW
t (020) 8303 2571

BRENTFORD

Kings Arms ★★★ *Inn*
19 Boston Manor Road, Brentford
TW8 8EA
t (020) 8560 5860
w kingsarmsbrentjord.co.uk

BROMLEY

Glendevon House ★★★
Guest Accommodation
80 Southborough Road, Bromley
BR1 2EN
t (020) 8467 2183
w glendevonhotel.co.uk

CHISLEHURST

The Crown Inn ★★★ *Inn*
School Road, Chislehurst
BR7 5PQ
t (020) 8467 7326
e crownchislehurst@shepherdneame.co.uk
w crownchislehurst.co.uk

CROYDON

Bramley ★★★ *Bed & Breakfast*
7 Greencourt Avenue, Croydon
CR0 7LD
t (020) 8654 6776

Woodstock Guest House ★★★
Guest House
30 Woodstock Road, Croydon
CR0 1JR
t (020) 8680 1489
e woodstockhotel@tiscali.co.uk
w woodstockhotel.co.uk

HAMPTON

The Chestnuts ★★★★
Bed & Breakfast
16 Chestnut Avenue, Hampton
TW12 2NU
t (020) 8979 8314
e thechestnuts_16@fsmail.net

Houseboat Riverine ★★★
Guest Accommodation
Riverine, Taggs Island, Hampton
TW12 2HA
t (020) 8979 2266
e malcolm@feedtheducks.com
w feedtheducks.com

HARROW

Rhondda House ★★★ *Guest House*
16 Harrow View, Harrow
HA1 1RG
t (020) 8427 5009
w rhonddahouse.com

Tara's London Bed & Breakfast
★★★ *Bed & Breakfast*
8 Argyle Road, North Harrow
HA2 7AJ
t (020) 8248 4039
e tara.e.muldoon@gmail.com
w taraslondonbandb.com

**University of Westminster-Harrow
Hall of Residence** ★★★ - ★★★★
Campus
Watford Road, Harrow
HA1 3TP
t (020) 7911 5181
e summeraccommodation@westminster.ac.uk
w westminster.ac.uk/business/summer-accommodation

West London B&B ★★★
Bed & Breakfast
15 Beaumont Avenue, Harrow
HA2 7AT
t (020) 8723 3890
e westlondonbandb@msn.com
w westlondonbandb.com

KINGSTON-UPON-THAMES

40 The Bittoms ★★
Bed & Breakfast
40 The Bittoms, Kingston-upon-Thames
KT1 2AP
t (020) 8541 3171

Walkden Hall of Residence ★★★
Campus
Kingston Hill Campus, Kingston Hill,
Kingston-upon-Thames
KT2 7LB
t (020) 8417 5519
e kucel@kingston.ac.uk
w kucel.co.uk

NEW MALDEN

Beamsley House ★★
Bed & Breakfast
30 Presburg Road, New Malden
KT3 5AH
t (020) 8949 4910
e angela_evans@btinternet.com

PINNER

Delcon ★★★ *Bed & Breakfast*
468 Pinner Road, Pinner
HA5 5RR
t (020) 8863 1054
e delcon@homecall.co.uk

PURLEY

Ardra Guest House ★★★★
Guest Accommodation
108 Foxley Lane, Purley
CR8 3NB
t (020) 8668 4483
e jillsturgess@yahoo.com

The Maple House ★★★★
Bed & Breakfast
174 Foxley Lane, Purley
CR8 3NF
t (020) 8407 5123
e trevbrgg@aol.com

RICHMOND

Hobart Hall Guest House ★★★
Guest House
43-47 Petersham Road, Richmond
TW10 6UL
t (020) 8940 0435
e hobarthall@aol.com
w hobarthall.net

Ivy Cottage ★★★ *Bed & Breakfast*
Upper Ham Road, Ham Common,
Richmond
TW10 5LA
t (020) 8940 8601
e taylor@dbta.freeserve.co.uk
w dbta.freeserve.co.uk

Melbury ★★ *Guest House*
33 Marksbury Avenue, Richmond
TW9 4JE
t (020) 8876 3930
e jennieallen@mac.com
w accommodation-kew-richmond.co.uk

Pro Kew Gardens B&B ★★
Bed & Breakfast
15 Pensford Avenue, Richmond
TW9 4HR
t (020) 8876 3354
e info@prokewbandb.demon.co.uk
w prokewbandb.demon.co.uk

The Red Cow ★★★ *Inn*
59 Sheen Road, Richmond
TW9 1YJ
t (020) 8940 2511
e tom@redcowpub.com
w redcowpub.com

Richmond Inn ★★★★
Guest Accommodation
50-56 Sheen Road, Richmond
TW9 1UG
t (020) 8940 0171
w richmondinnhotel.com

Riverside ★★★
Guest Accommodation
23 Petersham Road, Richmond
TW10 6UH
t (020) 8940 1339
e riversidehotel@yahoo.com
w riversiderichmond.co.uk

West Lodge ★★★ *Bed & Breakfast*
179 Mortlake Road, Richmond
TW9 4AW
t (020) 8876 0584
e westlodge@thakria.demon.co.uk

West Park Gardens ★★★
Bed & Breakfast
105 Mortlake Road, Kew, Richmond
TW9 4AA
t (020) 8876 6842
e nj.edwards@ukonline.co.uk

SIDCUP

Hilbert House ★★★★
Guest Accommodation
Halfway Street, Sidcup
DA15 8DE
t (020) 8300 0549
e annandeddie@talktalk.net

SOUTH CROYDON

Owlets ★★★ *Bed & Breakfast*
112 Arundel Avenue, South
Croydon
CR2 8BH
t (020) 8657 5213

SURBITON

The Broadway Lodge ★★
Guest House
41 The Broadway, Tolworth,
Surbiton
KT6 7DJ
t (020) 8399 6555
e info@broadwaylodge.co.uk

SUTTON

St Margarets Guest House ★★
Guest House
31 Devon Road, Sutton
SM2 7PE
t (020) 8643 0164
e margarettrotman@hotmail.cor
w stmargaretsbandb.co.uk

TEDDINGTON

King Edwards Grove ★★★
Bed & Breakfast
King Edwards Grove, Teddington
TW11 9LY
t (020) 8977 7251
e peter.midgley@blueyonder.co

Ladywood ★★ *Bed & Breakfast*
Ladywood, Teddington
TW11 8AP
t (020) 8977 6066
e lyndano@hotmail.com
w visitrichmond.co.uk/thedms.asp?dms=2&pid=3500156&
startday=14&month=9&nd=1

Middle Cottage ★★★★
Bed & Breakfast **GOLD AWARD**
Ferry Road, Teddington
TW11 9NN
t 0777 5803 664
e sarah@middlecottage.org
w middlecottage.org

THORNTON HEATH

Croydon Court ★★★
Guest Accommodation
597-603 London Road, Thornton
Heath
CR7 6AY
t (020) 8684 3947
e bookings@croydencourthotel.uk

TWICKENHAM

11 Spencer Road ★★★
Bed & Breakfast
Strawberry Hill, Twickenham
TW2 5TH
t (020) 8894 5271
e bruceduff@hotmail.com

136 London Road ★★★
Bed & Breakfast
136 London Road, Twickenham
TW1 1HD
t (020) 8892 3158
e jenniferjfinnerty@hotmail.com
w accommodation-in-twickenha.co.uk/

**Byrnes Twickenham
Accommodation** ★★★★
Guest Accommodation
35 Grange Avenue, Strawberry H
Twickenham
TW2 5TW
t (020) 8744 8150
e pjbjak@talktalk.net
w byrnestwickenhamaccommodation.co.uk

The Old Stables ★★★★
Guest Accommodation - Room Or
1 Bridle Lane, Twickenham
TW1 3EG
t 07966 549515
e jenny@oldstables.org
w oldstables.org

London | Outer London/London

UPMINSTER

ner Farm ★★
st Accommodation
Lane, North Ockendon,
ninster
4 3RB
01708) 851310
corner-farm.co.uk

UXBRIDGE

nel University ★★★ -
★★★ Campus
nel Conference Services, Brunel
versity, Kingston Lane, UXBRIDGE
3PH
01895 238353
conference@brunel.ac.uk
brunelconferenceservices.co.uk

dene Guest House ★★★
st Accommodation
Orchard Drive, Cowley
3AE
01895) 237838
lbie@uxbridge-guesthouse.com
uxbridge-guesthouse.com

London

LONDON

**Home in London: Bayswater
172** ★★★★ Bed & Breakfast
don
020) 8748 1943
nfo@athomeinlondon.co.uk
thomeinlondon.co.uk

**Home in London: Bayswater
211** ★★★★ Bed & Breakfast
don
020) 8748 1943
nfo@athomeinlondon.co.uk
thomeinlondon.co.uk

Home in London: Belgravia
★★★★ Bed & Breakfast
X
020) 8748 1943
nfo@athomeinlondon.co.uk
thomeinlondon.co.uk

Home in London: Chelsea Ref
★★★★ Bed & Breakfast
020) 8748 1943
nfo@athomeinlondon.co.uk
thomeinlondon.co.uk

Home in London: Chiswick Ref
★★★★ Bed & Breakfast
ER AWARD
don
020) 8748 1943
nfo@athomeinlondon.co.uk
thomeinlondon.co.uk

Home in London: Chiswick Ref
★★★★ Bed & Breakfast
ER AWARD
don
020) 8748 1943
nfo@athomeinlondon.co.uk
thomeinlondon.co.uk

At Home in London: Clapham
★★★★ Bed & Breakfast
London
SW4
t (020) 8748 1943
e info@athomeinlondon.co.uk
w athomeinlondon.co.uk

At Home in London: Ealing 288
★★★★ Bed & Breakfast
London
W5
t (020) 8748 1943
e info@athomeinlondon.co.uk
w athomeinlondon.co.uk

At Home in London: Ealing 301
★★★★ Bed & Breakfast
London
W5
t (020) 8748 1943
e info@athomeinlondon.co.uk
w athomeinlondon.co.uk

At Home in London: Fulham 300
★★★★ Bed & Breakfast
London
SW6
t (020) 8748 1943
e info@athomeinlondon.co.uk
w athomeinlondon.co.uk

**At Home in London:
Hammersmith Ref 62** ★★★★
Bed & Breakfast
London
W6
t (020) 8748 1943
e info@athomeinlondon.co.uk
w athomeinlondon.co.uk

**At Home in London: Holland Park
236** ★★★★ Bed & Breakfast
London
W11
t (020) 8748 1943
e info@athomeinlondon.co.uk
w athomeinlondon.co.uk

**At Home in London: Holland Park
Ref 114** ★★★★ Bed & Breakfast
London
W11
t (020) 8748 1943
e info@athomeinlondon.co.uk
w athomeinlondon.co.uk

**At Home in London: Holland Park
Ref 248** ★★★★ Bed & Breakfast
London
W11
t (020) 8748 1943
e info@athomeinlondon.co.uk
w athomeinlondon.co.uk

**At Home in London: Parsons
Green 296** ★★★★ Bed & Breakfast
London
SW6
t (020) 8748 1943
e info@athomeinlondon.co.uk
w athomeinlondon.co.uk

**At Home in London: Parsons
Green Ref 36** Guest Accommodation
London
SW6
t (020) 8748 1943
e info@athomeinlondon.co.uk
w athomeinlondon.co.uk

At Home in London: Putney 352
★★★★ Bed & Breakfast
London
SW15
t (020) 8748 1943
e info@athomeinlondon.co.uk
w athomeinlondon.co.uk

**At Home in London: Vauxhall Ref
134** ★★★★ Bed & Breakfast
London
SW8
t (020) 8748 1943
e info@athomeinlondon.co.uk
w athomeinlondon.co.uk

**At Home in London: Victoria Ref
3** ★★★★ Bed & Breakfast
Victoria, London
SW1P
t (020) 8748 1943
e info@athomeinlondon.co.uk
w athomeinlondon.co.uk

**At Home in London: Victoria Ref
14** Guest Accommodation
London
SW1V
t (020) 8748 1943
e info@athomeinlondon.co.uk
w athomeinlondon.co.uk

**At Home in London: West
Kensington Ref 77** ★★★
Bed & Breakfast
London
W14
t (020) 8748 1943
e info@athomeinlondon.co.uk
w athomeinlondon.co.uk

**At Home in London: Westminster
292** ★★★★ Guest Accommodation -
Room Only
London
SW1P
t (020) 8748 1943
e info@athomeinlondon.co.uk
w athomeinlondon.co.uk

**Uptown Reservations: Barons
Court Ref BC1** ★★★★
Guest Accommodation
London
SW1P
t (020) 7937 2001
e inquiries@uptownres.co.uk
w uptownres.co.uk

**Uptown Reservations: Chelsea Ref
C1** ★★★★ Guest Accommodation
London
SW1P
t (020) 7937 2001
e inquiries@uptownres.co.uk
w uptownres.co.uk

**Uptown Reservations: Fulham Ref
F1** ★★★★ Guest Accommodation
London
SW1P
t (020) 7937 2001
e inquiries@uptownres.co.uk
w uptownres.co.uk

**Uptown Reservations: Kensington
Ref. K2** Guest Accommodation
London
SW1P
t (020) 7937 2001
e inquiries@uptownres.co.uk
w uptownres.co.uk

**Uptown Reservations: Kensington
Ref. K3** Guest Accommodation
London
SW1P
t (020) 7937 2001
e inquiries@uptownres.co.uk
w uptownres.co.uk

**Uptown Reservations: Kensington
Ref. K4** Guest Accommodation
London
SW1P
t (020) 7937 2001
e inquiries@uptownres.co.uk
w uptownres.co.uk

**Uptown Reservations: Kensington
Ref. K5** Guest Accommodation
London
SW1P
t (020) 7937 2001
e inquiries@uptownres.co.uk
w uptownres.co.uk

**Uptown Reservations: Kensington
Ref K1** ★★★★
Guest Accommodation
London
SW1P
t (020) 7937 2001
e inquiries@uptownres.co.uk
w uptownres.co.uk

**Uptown Reservations:
Knightsbridge Ref KN1** ★★★★
Bed & Breakfast
London
SW1P
t (020) 7937 2001
e inquiries@uptownres.co.uk
w uptownres.co.uk

**Uptown Reservations:
Knightsbridge Ref KN2** ★★★★
Guest Accommodation
London
SW1P
t (020) 7937 2001
e inquiries@uptownres.co.uk
w uptownres.co.uk

**Uptown Reservations: Marble
Arch Ref MA1** ★★★★
Guest Accommodation
London
SW1P
t (020) 7937 2001
e inquiries@uptownres.co.uk
w uptownres.co.uk

**Uptown Reservations: South
Kensington Ref SK1** ★★★★
Guest Accommodation
London
SW1P
t (020) 7937 2001
e inquiries@uptownres.co.uk
w uptownres.co.uk

**Uptown Reservations: West End
Ref WE1** ★★★★
Guest Accommodation
London
SW1P
t (020) 7937 2001
e inquiries@uptownres.co.uk
w uptownres.co.uk

**Uptown Reservations:
Westminster Ref. WM3**
Guest Accommodation
London
SW1P
t (020) 7937 2001
e inquiries@uptownres.co.uk
w uptownres.co.uk

**Uptown Reservations:
Westminster Ref WM2** ★★★★
Guest Accommodation
London
SW1P
t (020) 7937 2001
e inquiries@uptownres.co.uk
w uptownres.co.uk

East of England

Based around the ancient kingdom of East Anglia, the East of England is a region where tradition is a way of life, eccentric customs are commonplace and people take the time to offer the warmest of welcomes.

Beautiful timber-framed villages, traditional market towns, gently rolling countryside and unspoilt coastline – this is England as you always thought it should be – right on London's doorstep.

The region covers 7,380 square miles stretching approximately 109 miles from north to south; and 108 miles east to west. Perfect for touring.

The Broads are Britain's largest nationally protected wetland. Stretching out from The Wash, The Fens a noted for their dramatic skies and sweeping vistas. the west of the region, the rolling Dunstable Down offer chalk life flora and fauna. All offer fantastic wildlife-spotting, the region is one of the UK's best places for birdwatching.

The coastline comprises unspoilt sandy beaches, ti fishing villages, crumbling cliffs, estuaries, shingle spits and Britain's best mudflats and salt marshes. Here smugglers inns nestle close to the waters whe Lord Nelson learnt to sail. Enjoy the fun-packed family resorts of Great Yarmouth and Southend contrasted by the quieter idyllic coastal towns such as Southwold and Cromer.

East of England

East of England

Bedfordshire, Cambridgeshire, Essex, Hertfordshire, Norfolk, Suffolk

- **314** Counties
- **320** Where to Go
- **322** Events
- **324** Where to Eat
- **330** Where to Stay

...land, explore the inspirational landscapes of artists, authors and films such as Constable Country, where Britain's greatest landscape painter, John Constable, was born and worked. Whilst picturesque Lavenham in Suffolk is England's best preserved medieval town, from 14th to 16th century it was a major wool and cloth making centre.

Cycling is a great way to get around and explore quiet rural lanes, country pubs and a superb collection of churches. Look out as well for scrumptious culinary delights. The area is the 'Food Basket of Britain' – delicious hams, fine ales and wine, prize-winning jams, seafood treats and fresh fruit and vegetables.

Discover the spectacular colours and delicate fragrances of some of Britain's finest gardens, and magnificent treasure houses such as Woburn Abbey, Hatfield House, Blickling Hall and Royal Sandringham - alongside ancient castles, steam trains, intriguing museums and a rich aviation and maritime heritage.

East of England | Bedfordshire

Bedfordshire

Explore the historic county town of Bedford, which dates back to before Saxon times. Fine buildings, museums and mound of Norman castle. The Embankment is one of the country's finest river settings, with tree-lined walkways, gardens, bandstand and elegant suspension bridge. Connections to preacher and author John Bunyan.

Ampthill
The picturesque, narrow streets are lined with fine Georgian buildings and quaint antique shops. Ampthill Park was once home to a 15th century castle, where Henry VIII stayed. It was also here that his wife, Katherine of Aragon, was kept during their divorce proceedings. A stone cross now marks the spot.

Dunstable Downs
The Dunstable Downs are one of the highest points in the East of England, providing superb views over Bedfordshire and the Vale of Aylesbury. The chalk grassland is rich in flora and fauna. Take a walk, and spot the gliders soaring overhead. This is a great place for a picnic and kite flying - and you can buy them from the Chilterns Gateway Centre.

Luton
Situated on the edge of The Chilterns, Luton is a thriving town with one of the most vibrant multi-cultural communities in the country. From the 17th century it was noted for its straw plait and hat-making industries. The Mall Arndale shopping centre, museums, excellent entertainment/leisure facilities and several landscaped parks are other key attractions. Luton holds Britain's biggest one day carnival.

Leighton Buzzard
Situated on the Grand Union Canal, the town has always been famous for its sand. Fine Georgian buildings line the wide High Street, alongside a medieval market cross, 19th century former moot hall and charming mews. The 13th century parish church is noted for its 191 feet high spire. Adjoining Linslade is popular with boaters and walkers.

Woburn
Surrounded by wooded countryside, Woburn is acknowledged as one of Britain's most beautifully preserved Georgian towns. This is a great place for antiques and collectables - with 18/19th century houses and period shop-fronts lining the High Street. Close by is the famous Abbey, the 18th century palatial mansion home of the Dukes of Bedford. The treasures on view are acknowledged as one of the finest private collections in the country. The estate is also home of the award-winning safari park with its drive-through game reserve and leisure areas.

314

East of England | Cambridgeshire

Cambridgeshire

The famous University city of Cambridge is noted for its ancient colleges and historic churches. The crowning glory is King's College Chapel. Enjoy a walking tour of the medieval streets, or take a trip along the River Cam aboard a punt. Great shopping, theatres, galleries, museums, pubs, restaurants and lovely parks in which to relax.

Ely

The city of Ely is rich in history, charm and beauty, and the jewel in the crown of The Fens. Dominating the skyline is one of England's most beautiful and largest cathedrals. Known locally as the 'Ship of the Fens', the cathedral is also home to the only national museum dedicated to stained glass. Ely's most famous resident and former MP, Oliver Cromwell, lived in Ely for many years before becoming Lord Protector of England. His home is open to the public throughout the year and visitors can learn more about him in specially restored rooms and exhibits about 17th century life. The city has a splendid array of historic buildings with a beautiful waterside area where you can enjoy a boat trip, riverside walk or explore the many cafes and antiques shops.

The Fens

Nearly a million acres of beautiful black soil and wildlife rich water, perfect for birdwatching, boating and fishing. Over the centuries the land has been drained by man to create some of the most fertile soil in Britain; growing flowers, fruit and vegetables. Criss-crossed by waterways they offer stunning skyscapes and unforgettable sunsets, plus some of Britain's most important nature reserves. Because it is so flat, it's ideal walking or cycling country.

Huntingdon

Historic market town, the birthplace (1599) of Oliver Cromwell. The former grammar school which he attended is now the Cromwell Museum. Huntingdon grew up around an important crossing of the River Great Ouse, and from the 16-18th century prospered as a coaching stop on the Great North Road. The old stone river crossing is one of England's finest medieval bridges. Close by is the Hinchingbrooke Country Park and horse-racing course.

Peterborough

Originally founded around a Saxon abbey, Peterborough has developed into a vibrant modern city - with a rich and ancient heritage. One of the UK's top shopping destinations, the centre is dominated by its magnificent Norman Cathedral (noted for its breath-taking west front and painted wooden ceiling). Green open spaces include the Nene Park, with its lakes, cycle trails and steam train rides. Good nightlife, theatres, sporting venues and special events (East of England Showground).

Wisbech

The 'Capital of the Fens' - this busy market town grew up around its port, trading from medieval times. After the Fen drainage, it became a wealthy agricultural centre, evident today in some of the finest Georgian street architecture in Britain (such as The Brinks, The Crescent and Museum Square). Brewery and annual Rose Fair. The town remains at the heart of a fruit and flower growing area. Birthplace of social reformer and National Trust co-founder Octavia Hill.

East of England | Essex

Essex

Chelmsford was granted its market charter by King John in 1199. It is internationally known as the birthplace of broadcasting - Guglielmo Marconi building the world's first radio factory here in 1899. The 15th century parish church is England's second smallest cathedral. Enjoy shopping, special events and a vibrant cultural scene.

Clacton-on-Sea

Clacton is a popular seaside town with tree-lined streets, sand/shingle beaches and beautiful clifftop gardens. The fun-packed 19th century pier offers fairground rides and sea fishing. Try out a range of watersports, or take a pleasure flight from the Clacton Aero Club. Enjoy an evening out at the Princes and West Cliff Theatres - venues for spectacular shows, attracting a host of top showbiz names.

Colchester

Bold, energetic and contrasting - Colchester is more than Britain's oldest recorded town. Discover important Roman remains, alongside Europe's biggest Norman castle keep (now an award-winning museum), impressive 19th century Town Hall and 'Jumbo' the water tower. Great shopping, gardens/parks and special events. Enjoy vibrant culture and nightlife, such as bars, restaurants and theatre - alongside the new inspirational 'firstsite' contemporary art gallery (opening spring 2011).

Maldon

An ancient hilltop town, port and sailing centre - at the head of the Blackwater Estuary. Famed for its sea salt production and majestic Thames Sailing Barges. See them moored beside the Hythe Quay. The great-great-grandfather of first US President George Washington is buried at All Saints' Church, with its unusual triangular tower. Edwardian Promenade Park (with ornamental lake), 15th century Moot Hall and The Plume Library with its fine collection of 16/17th century books.

Saffron Walden

An ancient market town, which takes its name from the Saffron Crocus which grew here in the 16th century. The wealth of this industry is reflected in the lovely timber-framed buildings which line the medieval streets today - some decorated with elaborate pargetting (such as the Sun Inn). The parish church (with its elegant spire) is the largest in Essex. Enjoy the flowers, trees and traditional hedge maze at idyllic Bridge End Gardens. Explore Norman Castle ruins in the grounds of the museum.

Southend-on-Sea

Bright, vibrant and exciting – Southend offers a glorious seven mile stretch of coastline. Award-winning beaches, beautiful parks and gardens, family fun attractions, museums, art galleries and exhilarating watersports. Take a walk along the world's longest pleasure pier (stretching 1.33 miles in the Thames estuary) or ride the little train to the end.

East of England | **Hertfordshire**

Hertfordshire

Hertford is an historic county town, set at the confluence of four rivers and a royal borough for more than 1,000 years. The castle stands in delightful gardens, whilst the town is largely a conservation area. There are many Georgian shop-fronts, delightful old pubs, and antique shops, especially along St. Andrew Street.

Berkhamsted

A thriving town steeped in history where William the Conqueror received the crown of England at the castle in 1066. Berkhamsted enjoys a beautiful setting on the banks of the River Bulbourne and the Grand Union Canal, making it an ideal base to explore the glorious Chiltern Hills and West Hertfordshire Downs either by foot or aboard a brightly painted narrowboat. Discover the literary links with Geoffrey Chaucer, Graham Greene and J.M Barrie. The characterful 16th century architecture is not lost on the large number of unique retailers and restaurateurs who provide the thriving picturesque town with a fashionable buzz.

Bishop's Stortford

The ancient market town of Bishop's Stortford is superbly situated in rural Hertfordshire. It is a modern lively town with a long and varied history. There is much to see in the town - a rich collection of 16th and 17th century buildings in the centre, including several of the old inns made famous when the town was an important staging post on the route between London and both Newmarket and Cambridge. The River Stort, running through the town centre, provides leisurely activities and is popular with walkers, anglers and visiting narrow-boats.

Letchworth Garden City

Wide tree-lined streets and distinctive early 20th century buildings mark Letchworth Garden City as somewhere special. It was here, in the heart of the wholesome countryside, that Ebenezer Howard founded the world's first garden city in 1903. Highlights include the Art Deco cinema, two museums and a range of individual shops, restaurants and cafes.

St. Albans

An historic city shaped by 2,000 years of history. First built as Verulamium by the Romans, the city was renamed St. Albans after the first British Christian martyr. The magnificent Cathedral dominates the skyline. Take a walk in Verulamium Park, leading to the best preserved Roman theatre in Britain. The city boasts a wide range of attractions, including the Roman artefacts of the Verulamium Museum. Shopping includes high street names, alongside many specialist shops offering antiques and books. There is also a bustling street market. Enjoy a range of restaurants, historic pubs and inns for that well-deserved refreshment break.

Tring

The market town of Tring lies at the edge of the Chiltern Hills. It remains unspoilt, with the peaceful Grand Union Canal on its doorstep. Tring was once home of the Rothschild banking family. Passionate about wildlife - it was Walter Rothschild who founded the Natural History Museum in the town. The high street offers specialist shopping. Take a walk in the 300 acre Tring Park, or at the nearby Tring Reservoirs, great for bird-watching.

East of England | Norfolk

Norfolk

Norwich is the most complete medieval city in Britain, with its ancient buildings, winding streets and city wall remains. Dominated by its magnificent cathedral and impressive 12th century castle, it has a lively cultural scene with museums, galleries, theatres, restaurants and pubs. Norwich is one of the top 10 places to shop in the UK.

The Broads

A unique and fascinating place, so timeless and natural that its hard to believe that this landscape is man made. The Broads were formed in medieval times, when old peat diggings were gradually filled in with water creating shallow lakes or 'broads'. Today they are Britain's largest nationally protected wetland. There are around 60 broads, connected by the area's six rivers - making up to 125 miles (200 kilometres) of lock-free navigable waterways. The best way to see them is by boat - enjoy regular excursions, or hire craft for day trips, short breaks or longer holidays. Of course - the waterways and their surrounding fens, woodland, marshes and estuary habitats are a haven for some of Britain's rarest flora and fauna, such as the swallowtail - the country's largest butterfly.

Cromer

Dominated by the tower of its parish church (the tallest in the county), this sedate seaside town stands on a cliff top, with beaches of sand and shingle running down to the sea. Cromer is famous for its catch of common crabs caught by its little fishing boats which still work from the beach. The pier (built in 1901) is noted for its traditional seaside theatre and RNLI lifeboat station.

Great Yarmouth

Great Yarmouth, with 15 miles of glorious sandy beaches is one of the UK's most popular seaside resorts, with an enviable mix of attractions, entertainment and heritage, with quality accommodation. Behind the glitter and bright lights, lies a charming town that is steeped in history. Discover one of the most complete medieval town walls in England, the historic South Quay and Nelson's 'other' column.

King's Lynn

King's Lynn is more than just a medieval port. The town is now a treasure trove for history lovers with narrow streets and handsome merchant houses in the old town. See the only surviving Hanseatic warehouse in the country and plenty of fascinating visitor attractions to help bring the 'olden days' alive. Down by the river, you can take a ferry over to the west bank and take in the outstanding view of King's Lynn's townscape. There is a vibrant mix of theatre, cinemas, arts festivals, exhibitions, museums, pubs, stylish café bars and restaurants.

Hunstanton

The only west facing resort on the east coast of England - there are two sides to Hunstanton. The elegant old Victorian town with its Esplanade Gardens and rather sedate air of days gone by... and the lively buzzing family centre with a large sandy beach, pony rides, amusements and summer season theatre. Old Hunstanton has more of a village feel, with its beach (including rock pools) backed by famous red and white striped cliffs.

East of England | **Suffolk**

Suffolk

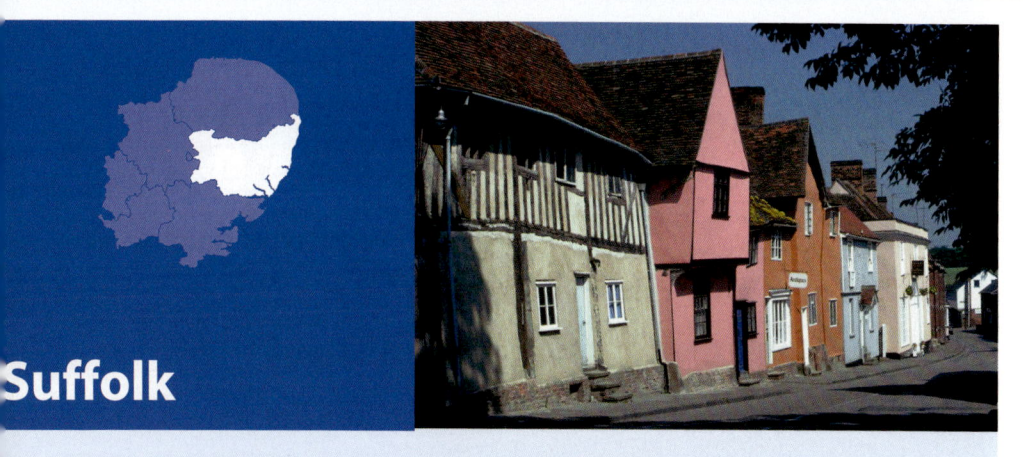

Ipswich is England's oldest continuously settled Anglo-Saxon town. Historic buildings include twelve medieval churches, and the Ancient House, with its fine pargetting. Tudor Christchurch Mansion boasts the best collection of Constable and Gainsborough works outside London. Stroll along the waterfront, with its marina, restaurants and river cruises. Good shopping and green open spaces.

of East Anglia. During medieval times, a powerful abbey grew up - the remains can be admired in the award-winning Abbey Gardens. The cathedral dates back to 1503, complete with its stunning new Millennium Tower. Flourishing market, art galleries, museums, Britain's smallest pub 'The Nutshell' and a rare Regency theatre.

Lavenham
England's best preserved medieval town. From the 14-16th century it was a major wool and cloth making centre. The wealth generated has left a beautiful legacy of timber-framed houses set along narrow streets, such as the Guildhall and Swan Hotel. The 13th century church is noted for its 141 feet high tower. Gift, craft and tea shops.

Newmarket
Busy market town, set amongst rolling chalk heathland - and internationally renowned for being the historic home of horseracing. 2,500 horses, numerous stable yards, training gallops, the horseracing museum and National Stud. Take an equine tour then spend the afternoon at the races.

Southwold
This seaside town is famous for being quintessentially English. Its simplicity in character and charm means you will find the perfect haven from the demands of modern society. With its Quality Coast Award beach, promenade of stylish beach chalets, lighthouse overlooking the town and classical award-winning pier - it is no wonder that visitors fall in love with this resort. Take to the waves on Coastal Voyager, look out for the Punch and Judy show and make sure you visit the harbour to sample the local catch of the day - wash it down with a pint of Adnams Bitter.

Aldeburgh
Charming, traditional seaside town that harks back to an earlier age. There is a traditional boating lake for model yachts, a local museum, and historic 16th century Moot Hall. The fishermen still draw their boats up on to the shore and sell fish from the beach. Aldeburgh was one of the leading ports on the East Coast and its shipbuilding was renowned. Sir Francis Drake's ships "Pelican" and "Greyhound" were built locally. The industry declined as the river Alde silted up.

Bury St. Edmunds
Ancient market town - which for more than five centuries was visited by pilgrims from all over the world, coming to worship at the shrine of the martyred Edmund, King

East of England | Where to Go

Where to Go

Attractions with this sign participate in the **Visitor Attraction Quality Assurance Scheme** (see page 6) which recognises high standards in all aspects of the vistor experience.

ENTERTAINMENT & CULTURE

Bedford Museum
Bedford, Bedfordshire MK40 3XD
(01234) 353123
www.bedfordmuseum.org
Housed in the former Higgins and Sons Brewery, the Museum is situated within the gardens of bygone Bedford Castle.

Christchurch Mansion
Ipswich, Suffolk IP4 2BE
(01473) 433554
www.ipswich.gov.uk/museums
Discover 500 years of history in beautiful Christchurch Mansion. Period rooms from the 16th-19th century.

Colchester Castle Museum
Colchester, Essex CO1 1YG
(01206) 282939
www.colchestermuseums.org.uk
The largest Norman Keep in Europe. Superb Roman displays, hands-on activities and tours. An award winning experience of 2000 years of history.

Imperial War Museum Duxford
Cambridge, Cambridgeshire CB22 4QR
(01223) 835000
www.iwm.org.uk/duxford
With its air shows, unique history and atmosphere, nowhere else combines the sights, sounds and power of aircraft quite like Duxford.

Royal Gunpowder Mills
Waltham Abbey, Essex EN9 1JY
(01992) 707370
www.royalgunpowdermills.com
A spectacular 170-acre location for a day of family fun.

The Shuttleworth Collection
Biggleswade, Bedfordshire SG18 9EP
(01767) 627970
www.shuttleworth.org
Aircraft from a 1909 Bleriot to a 1942 Spitfire in flying condition, and cars dating from an 1898.

Verulamium Museum
St Albans, Hertfordshire AL3 4SW
(01727) 751810
www.stalbansmuseums.org.uk
The museum of everyday life in Roman Britain. Award-winning displays of re-created Roman rooms and hands-on areas.

Wroxham Barns
Wroxham, Norfolk NR12 8QU
(01603) 783762
www.wroxhambarns.co.uk
Craft centre with 12 resident craftsmen, restaurant-cafe and various shops. Junior Farm and children's funfair.

FAMILY FUN

Adventure Island
Southend-on-Sea, Essex SS1 1EE
(01702) 443400
www.adventureisland.co.uk
One of the best value 'theme parks' in the South East with over 60 great rides and attractions for all ages.

BeWILDerwood
Norwich, Norfolk NR12 8JW
(01603) 783900
www.bewilderwood.co.uk
A huge forest of wild family fun and adventure. Treehouse, zip wires, jungle bridges, Crocklebogs, boat trips, marsh walks and really yummy food.

Bodyflight Bedford
Clapham, Bedfordshire MK41 6AE
0845 200 2960
www.bodyflight.co.uk
Indoor Skydiving! Learn to fly like a skydiver on a vertical column of air! Offering lessons for all abilities.

Go Ape! - Thetford
Brandon, Suffolk IP27 0AF
(01284) 852218
www.goape.co.uk
Take to the trees and experience an exhilarating course of rope bridges, tarzan swings and zip slides...all set high above the forest floor.

Pleasurewood Hills
Lowestoft, Suffolk NR32 5DZ
(01502) 586000
www.pleasurewoodhills.com
Don't let the year slip by without planning a visit to East Anglia's largest pay once attraction. Set in 50 acres of coastal parkland with rides & attractions for all the family.

The National Stud
Newmarket, Cambridgeshire CB8 0
(01638) 663464
www.nationalstud.co.uk
Guided tours giving an insight into the day to day running of a stud farm.

HERITAGE

Audley End House and Gardens
Saffron Walden, Essex CB11 4JF
(01799) 522399
www.english-heritage.org.uk/audleyend
Built by Thomas Howard, Earl of Suffol to entertain King James.

320

East of England | **Where to Go**

Cathedral and Abbey Church of St Alban
St Albans, Hertfordshire AL1 1BY
(01727) 860780
www.stalbanscathedral.org
Britain's first Christian martyr and the cathedral, with its shrine, is its oldest place of continuous worship.

Framlingham Castle
Woodbridge, Suffolk IP13 9BP
(01223) 582700
www.english-heritage.org.uk/framlingham
A magnificent castle with 12thC curtain walls, 13 towers, Tudor brick chimneys and a wall walk, built by the Bigods, the Earls of Norfolk. The home of Mary Tudor in 1553.

Hatfield House
Hatfield, Hertfordshire AL9 5NQ
(01707) 287010
www.hatfield-house.co.uk
Splendid Jacobean House and Garden in a spectacular countryside setting. Childhood home of Elizabeth I.

Holkham Hall
Wells-next-the-Sea, Norfolk NR23 1AB
(01328) 710227
www.holkham.co.uk
Magnificent Palladian hall. Rolling parkland. A wealth of wildlife. Attractions and events. The best beach in England.

Hylands House and Estate
Chelmsford, Essex CM2 8WQ
(01245) 605500
www.chelmsford.gov.uk/hylands
Hylands House is a beautiful Grade II* listed neo-classical villa set in over 500 acres of Repton landscaped parkland and gardens. Diary of special events available. Pre-booked guided tours of house and garden available.

Ickworth House, Park and Gardens
Bury St Edmunds, Suffolk IP29 5QE
(01284) 735270
www.nationaltrust.org.uk/ickworth
An extraordinary oval house with flanking wings, begun in 1795. Fine paintings, a beautiful collection of Georgian silver, an Italian garden and stunning parkland.

Kings College Chapel
Cambridge, Cambridgeshire CB2 1ST
(01223) 331212
www.kings.cam.ac.uk/chapel
King's College Chapel is a masterpiece of English craftsmanship & the most recognisable building in Cambridge.

Sandringham
King's Lynn, Norfolk PE35 6EN
(01553) 612908
www.sandringhamestate.co.uk
The country retreat of H.M. The Queen. A fascinating house, an intriguing museum and the best of the Royal gardens. Restaurant and shops.

Somerleyton Hall and Gardens
Lowestoft, Suffolk NR32 5QQ
(01502) 730224
www.somerleyton.co.uk
Early Victorian stately mansion in Anglo-Italian style. Beautiful 12 acre gardens, with historic Yew hedge maze.

NATURE & WILDLIFE

Africa Alive - African Animal Adventure
Lowestoft, Suffolk NR33 7TL
(01502) 740291
www.africa-alive.co.uk
Take your family on a walking safari at one of the UK's largest and most exciting wildlife attractions.

Banham Zoo
Norwich, Norfolk NR16 2HE
(01953) 887771
www.banhamzoo.co.uk
Experience tigers, leopards and zebra plus some of the world's most exotic, rare and endangered animals.

Colchester Zoo
Colchester, Essex CO3 0SL
(01206) 331292
www.colchester-zoo.co.uk
Award winning zoo, one of Europe's finest. Feed elephants/giraffes, touch a snake or watch a bird of prey show.

Mead Open Farm
Leighton Buzzard, Bedfordshire LU7 9JH
(01525) 852954
www.meadopenfarm.co.uk
Farm Park with hands-on animal activities, Shaggy's 13,000 sq ft indoor Play World, go karts, crazy golf and in season sheep racing and tractor rides.

RHS Garden Hyde Hall
Chelmsford, Essex CM3 8AT
(01245) 400256
www.rhs.org.uk/hydehall
A garden of inspiration beauty with an eclectic range of horticultural styles from traditional to modern providing year round interest.

RSPB Minsmere Nature Reserve
Saxmundham, Suffolk IP17 3BY
(01728) 648281
www.rspb.org.uk/minsmere
One of the UK's premier nature reserves.

Southend Sea Life Adventure
Southend-on-Sea, Essex SS1 2ER
(01702) 442211
www.sealifeadventure.co.uk
Displays bring you close to the wonders of marine life. Various talks throughout the day. Also "Little Tykes" indoor play activity centre and restaurant.

The Raptor Foundation
Huntingdon, Cambridgeshire PE28 3BT
(01487) 741140
www.raptorfoundation.org.uk
Bird of prey centre, offering 3 daily flying displays with audience participation, gift shop, Silent Wings tearoom, Raptor crafts shop.

Welney Wetland Centre
Wisbech, Norfolk PE14 9TN
(01353) 860711
www.wwt.org.uk/welney
A wetland nature reserve of 1,000 acres attracting large numbers of ducks and swans in winter and waders in spring and summer plus a range of wild plants and butterflies.

Wild Britain
Bedford, Bedfordshire MK44 2PX
(01234) 772770
www.wild-britain.co.uk
Discover one wild day out! Safari spot in the butterfly jungle, follow the hedgehog play trail, meet creepy crawlies and more!

Willows Farm Village
St Albans, Hertfordshire AL4 0PF
0870 129 9718
www.willowsfarmvillage.com
At the unique Willows Farm Village families discover their true animal instincts, roaming free in the countryside and running wild with the adventure activities.

Wrest Park
Bedford, Bedfordshire MK45 4HS
(01223) 582700
www.english-heritage.org.uk/wrestpark
One hundred and fifty years of English gardens laid out in the early 18th century including painted pavilion, Chinese bridge, lakes, classical temple, orangery and bath house.

OUTDOOR ACTIVITIES

Broads Tours
Wroxham, Norfolk NR12 8RX
(01603) 782207
www.broads.co.uk
Discover the beautiful Norfolk Broads by joining Broads Tours for a scheduled river trip, or hire a self drive day-launch.

321

Events 2011

Aldeburgh Festival of Music and the Arts
Saxmundham
www.aldeburgh.co.uk
June

Bedford International Kite Festival
www.bedfordevents.co.uk
June

Cambridge Folk Festival
Cherry Hinton
www.cambridgefolkfestival.co.uk
July/August

Clacton Airshow
Clacton-on-Sea
www.tendringdc.gov.uk
August

Eel Day
Ely
visitely.eastcambs.gov.uk
May

Essex Book Festival
www.essexbookfestival.org.uk
March

Essex Country Show
Billericay
www.essexcountryshow.co.uk
September

Flying Legends
Cambridge
www.iwm.org.uk/duxford
July

Great Annual Re-creation of Tudor Life
Sudbury
www.kentwell.co.uk
June/July

Great Yarmouth Maritime Festival
Great Yarmouth
www.maritime-festival.co.uk
September

Harpenden Highland Gathering
www.harpenden-lions.co.uk
July

Hatfield House Country Show
www.hatfield-house.co.uk
August

Hertfordshire County Show
www.hertsshow.com
May

Latitude Festival
Beccles
www.latitudefestival.co.uk
July

Lowestoft Seafront Air Festival
Lowestoft
www.lowestoftairfestival.co.uk
August

Luton International Carnival
Luton
www.lutoncarnival.co.uk
Spring Bank Holiday - May

Norfolk and Norwich Festival
Norwich
www.nnfestival.org.uk
2 weeks in May

Norfolk Food Festival
Norwich
www.norfolkfoodfestival.co.uk
September/October

Rhythms of the World
Hitchin
www.rotw.org.uk
July

Royal Norfolk Show
Norwich
www.royalnorfolkshow.co.uk
Early July

Southend Festival of the Air
Southend-on-Sea
www.southendairshow.com
May

St. Albans Festival
St. Albans
www.stalbansfestival.co.uk
June

St. George's Day Festival
Bedford
www.english-heritage.org.uk/wrestpark
April

Stilton Cheese Rolling Contest
Peterborough
www.stilton.org
May

Suffolk Show
Ipswich
www.suffolkshow.co.uk
Early June

The East of England Show
Peterborough
www.eastofengland.org.uk
June

Twinwood Festival
Bedford
www.twinwoodevents.com
August

V Festival
Chelmsford
www.vfestival.com
20-21 August

Woburn Oyster Festival
Milton Keynes
www.woburnoysterfestival.co.uk
September

World Snail Racing Championships
Congham
www.snailracing.net
July

There are hundreds of "Green" places to stay and visit in England from small bed and breakfasts to large visitor attractions and activity holiday providers. Businesses displaying this logo have undergone a rigorous verification process to ensure that they are sustainable (green) and that a qualified assessor has visited the premises.

We have indicated the accommodation which has achieved a Green award... look out for the 🌱 symbol in the entry.

East of England | **Where to Eat**

Where to Eat

The East of England region has great places to eat. The restaurant reviews on these pages are just a small selection from the highly respected *The Good Food Guide 2011*. Please see page 14 for further information on the Guide and details of a Special Offer for our readers.

BEDFORDSHIRE

Chez Jerome
26 Church Street, Dunstable LU5 4RU
(01582) 603310
www.chezjerome.co.uk
French

A genuine local 'pick-me-up', this sociable bistro comes complete with stuccoed walls, brick arches and cosy little alcoves. The neighbourly vibe is matched by generous cooking that makes a good fist of top-notch raw materials ('gigantic, sublimely sweet' scallops have been a standout). Starters of moules marinière or goats' cheese soufflé with sun-dried tomatoes (£6.15) could be followed by calf's liver with pomme purée, onions and 'boozy' Bordeaux jus (£14.95) or grilled sea bass fillet with basil dressing. Desserts such as crème brûlée (£4.25) are an afterthought. House wine is £12.50. Closed Sun D and Mon.

CAMBRIDGESHIRE

The Old Bridge Hotel
Menus with a taste of the Med
1 High Street, Huntingdon PE29 3TQ
(01480) 424300
www.huntsbridge.com
Modern British | £30

Overlooking the River Ouse, the Old Bridge is a tastefully extended, ivy-clad eighteenth-century building. At its heart is the Terrace, an easy-on-the-eye conservatory restaurant with white-clothed tables and a breezy, modern feel. The kitchen brings touches of the Mediterranean to menus that offer fine fresh seafood, perhaps in a salad of Dorset crab with fennel, red pepper and pomegranate dressing. Properly choosy buying of main course meats brings saddle of Denham Castle lamb with a mini lamb suet pudding, and slow-roast pork belly with sesame, spring greens,

East of England | **Where to Eat**

piced parsnip purée and pork dim sum. A passion for ine shows in winning selections from all regions, and uitable for all pockets, including some mature bottles. he changing house line-up of a dozen or so by the ass or bottle (from £14.95) offers good value. **hef/s:** Simon Cadge. **Open:** all week L 12 to 2.15 (2.30 un), D 6 to 10. **Meals:** alc (main courses £13 to £25). Set L 5 (2 courses) to £19.50. **Service:** not inc. **Details:** major rds accepted. 80 seats. 25 seats outside. Air conditioning. eparate bar. No music. No mobile phones. Wheelchair ccess. Children welcome. Car parking.

he Pheasant
oodie thatched pub
llage Loop Road, Keyston PE28 0RE
1832) 710241
ww.thepheasant-keyston.co.uk
astropub | £28

may have a thatched roof, beams and an open fire, ut this is no unchanging olde-worlde pub. A nicely dged mix of unpretentious modern British and editerranean ideas inform the menus, say boudin oir with caramelised apple, and brill with pappardelle, uttlefish, gremolata and brown shrimps. Reports is year have differed quite markedly, suggesting me inconsistencies in standards (perhaps due to ressure, since the Pheasant was runner-up in Gordon amsay's *F Word* search for the best independent local staurant), but at its best the cooking is simple and ffective. Wines are arranged by style, making it easy to d one's way around the high-class modern offerings. dozen classy, affordable house wines come by the ottle (from £15.50) and glass (from £4). **hef/s:** Jay Scrimshaw and Liam Goodwill. **Open:** all week 12 to 2.30, Mon to Sat D 6.30 to 9.30. **Meals:** alc (main urses £15 to £21). Set L and D £14.50 (2 courses) to 19.50. Sun L £15.50 (2 courses) to £19.50. **Service:** not inc. etails:** major cards accepted. 80 seats. 61 seats outside. eparate bar. Music. Children welcome. Car parking.

ESSEX

he Sun Inn
odern Med classics with Italian accent
igh Street, Dedham CO7 6DF
1206) 323351
ww.thesuninndedham.com
editerranean | £23

s you drive through the pretty Constable-country illage, you can't miss this sunny yellow fifteenth-entury inn. There's a congenial bar, a large timbered nd beamed dining room and a spacious patio, but enus are rather more cutting edge than you might xpect to find in a country pub. Local and regional uppliers play a role, their produce worked into a odern version of Mediterranean classics with a trong Italian accent. Among successes have been red mullet with curly kale, chickpeas and mint, and grilled Tuscan-style sausages with spinach and soft polenta. Desserts have ranged from apple, lemon and almond tart to rhubarb and ice cream. Excellent drinking is to be had by the glass and carafe on a list with interesting Mediterranean emphasis; bottles from £13.50.
Chef/s: Ugo Simonelli. **Open:** all week L 12 to 2.30 (3 Sat and Sun), D 6.30 to 9.30 (10 Fri and Sat, 9 Sun). **Closed:** 25 and 26 Dec. **Meals:** alc (main courses £9 to £18). Set L and D £10.50 (2 courses) to £13.50. **Service:** not inc.
Details: major cards accepted. 60 seats. 60 seats outside. Music. Children welcome. Car parking.

The Pier at Harwich, Harbourside Restaurant
Classic seafood and fine estuary views
The Quay, Harwich CO12 3HH
(01255) 241212
www.milsomhotels.com
Seafood | £28

There's a traditional look to the menu at this long-standing first-floor seafooder with fine views over the Stour and Orwell estuaries. The classic approach brings lobster bisque with cream and brandy or an impeccably timed local Dover sole. There are some foreign forays, too, like Thai-flavoured salmon cake served with home-smoked salmon, tomato and coriander salsa and tzatziki and a couple of meat options for those who must, perhaps a straightforward Dedham Vale sirloin steak served with fat chips. Tables are sensibly spaced, there are crisp white cloths and service from 'friendly young staff' is good. House wine is £16.
Chef/s: Chris Oakley. **Open:** all week L 12 to 2, D 6 to 9.30. **Meals:** alc (main courses £15 to £35). Set L £19.50 (2 courses) to £25. Sun L £27. **Service:** 10%. **Details:** major cards accepted. 70 seats. 40 seats outside. Air conditioning. Separate bar. No mobile phones. Music. Children welcome. Car parking.

East of England | Where to Eat

HERTFORDSHIRE

The Sun at Northaw
Splendid package from a local champion
1 Judges Hill, Northaw EN6 4NL
(01707) 655507
www.thesunatnorthaw.co.uk
Gastropub | £25

Artisan provisions, 'field fare' and sustainable fish loom large at this jolly champion of produce from England's eastern counties, which has been tricked out in fashionably folksy style with boxes of veg, cookbooks and reclaimed tables. Oliver Smith arrived here armed with a natural-born appetite for seasonal food and a rallying cry of 'Ingredients! Ingredients! Ingredients!' A 'wondrous' starter of Jerusalem artichokes, pickled walnuts, soft goats' cheese and crisp red radishes in a tangle of thyme typifies his ingenious way of doing things; elsewhere venison comes with an incisive sauce of sea buckthorn berries, and whole flounder is scattered with sweet cockles and alexanders. Moreish nibbles include crispy sweetbreads with green sauce, free-range Label Anglais chicken (from Essex) is a revelation and heaps of fresh-as-a-daisy vegetables are a given. Handmade cheeses, hand-pulled ales and handpicked wines (from £14.50) complete a splendid package.
Chef/s: Oliver Smith. **Open:** Tue to Sun L 12 to 3 (4 Sat, 5 Sun), Tue to Sat D 6 to 10. **Closed:** Mon. **Meals:** alc (main courses £12 to £19). Sun L £22 (2 courses) to £28. **Service:** not inc. **Details:** major cards accepted. 90 seats. 60 seats outside. Separate bar. Wheelchair access. Music. Children welcome. Car parking.

Lussmanns
Chic brasserie dining
Waxhouse Gate, Off High Street, St Albans
AL3 4EW
(01727) 851941
www.lussmanns.com
International | £22

One of Andrei Lussmann's group of chic Hertfordshire brasseries (also in Hertford and Bishop's Stortford). Like its relatives, the menu races through starters (grilled squid with fresh chilli and rocket), salads, pasta (rabbit and chestnut mushroom linguine), fish, steaks and burgers. There are also specials like venison with mash and leek crisp, and a few puddings including warm chocolate and walnut brownie. Menus are keen to promote provenance and seasonality, service 'is second to none' and a short global wine list opens at £14.25.
Chef/s: Kevin Lee. **Open:** all week 12 to 10 (10.30 Fri and Sat, 9.30 Sun). **Closed:** 25 and 26 Dec. **Meals:** alc (main courses £7 to £17). Set L and D £10.95 (2 courses) to £13.95. **Service:** not inc. **Details:** major cards accepted. 100 seats. 10 seats outside. Air conditioning. Wheelchair access. Music. Children welcome.

NORFOLK

Seafood Restaurant
A seaside jewel
85 North Quay, Great Yarmouth NR30 1JF
(01493) 856009
www.theseafood.co.uk
Seafood | £35

'Great Yarmouth is not renowned for its eating places and this is a real jewel', noted one visitor to Christopher and Miriam Kikis' welcoming seafood restaurant, which is now in its thirty-second year. With its comfortable, safe and well-tried style, the kitchen goes in for starters such as pan-fried scallops with bacon, and crab claws with garlic butter, and mains ranging from grilled skate with black butter to scampi provençale with rice. What gets the show off to a cracking start is the high-quality materials and the kitchen's sheer consistency. Sensibly, the wine list is two-thirds white, with bottles starting at £16.50.
Chef/s: Christopher Kikis. **Open:** Mon to Fri L 12 to 1.45, Mon to Sat D 6.30 to 10.30. **Closed:** Sun, 2 weeks Christmas, 2 weeks May, bank hols. **Meals:** alc (main courses £11 to £30). **Service:** not inc. **Details:** major cards accepted. 40 seats. Air conditioning. Separate bar. No mobile phones. Wheelchair access. Music. Car parking.

The Neptune
Seriously good food
85 Old Hunstanton Road, Old Hunstanton
PE36 6HZ
(01485) 532122
www.theneptune.co.uk
Modern British | £42

Swapping the Isle of Wight for the flat expanses of the Norfolk coast seems to have paid dividends for Kevin and Jacki Mangeolles, who have transformed this seventeenth-century inn into a cool restaurant-with-rooms, noted for its mellow vibes and seriously good food. Local fishermen play their part by providing maritime pickings, and customers reap the benefit in the form of some startlingly vivid ideas – say grilled mackerel and crab salad fashionably dovetailed with slivers of watermelon, or a 'magnificent' exceptionally fresh piece of turbot accompanied by avocado mousse, with a poached oyster topped with baby leeks adding extra depth to the dish. Norfolk's farmers also make a valuable contribution – loin of Courtyard Farm pork comes to the table in good company with wild mushrooms, Savoy cabbage and creamed potatoes, while a duo of pan-fried ribeye and braised beef is dressed up with Binham Blue cheese butter, shiitake mushrooms and pumpkin seeds. To finish, reporters have praised the sublime cinnamon bavarois on a bed of apple sponge with poached figs and a sorbet of walnut and yoghurt. Jackie Mangeolles gives a winning 'professional performance' out front,

East of England | **Where to Eat**

s well as tending to the well-constructed wine list; xpect a broad global spread with a page of house elections from £17.50 (£5 a glass).
hef/s: Kevin Mangeolles. **Open:** Sun L 12 to 2, Tue to Sun 7 to 9. **Closed:** Mon, 2 weeks Nov, 3 weeks Jan.
eals: Set L £20.50 (2 courses) to £25. Sun L £25 courses). **Service:** not inc. **Details:** major cards ccepted. 24 seats. Separate bar. No mobile phones. Music. ar parking. No Amex. No children under 10 years.

SUFFOLK

he Great House
evitalised French favourite
larket Place, Lavenham CO10 9QZ
01787) 247431
ww.greathouse.co.uk
lodern French | £32
eteran supporters of the timber-framed Great ouse still remember it as a genuine 'French country estaurant' dishing up bourgeois food in surroundings at were as Gallic as a pack of Gauloises. A serious akeover in 2008 changed all that, although the wners have managed to preserve much of the venue's ivilised charm amid all the new-found, clean-lined odernity. The food has also taken a quantum leap orward, and readers have been quick to applaud the bsolutely exquisite' dishes emanating from Regis répy's kitchen. Contemporary flavours now define he repertoire, from carpaccio of hand-dived scallops arinated in Cabernet Sauvignon to a praline and omage blanc tartlet with verbena sorbet. In between, idigenous Suffolk ingredients also pop up regularly perhaps grilled Woodbridge pigeon breasts on red abbage stew with beetroot sauce – and local fish is ensitively handled (steamed fillet of turbot marinated n olive oil with black truffle and rosemary, say). Suffolk eers line up alongside a hefty, French-led wine list ith house selections from £13.20.
hef/s: Regis Crépy. **Open:** Wed to Sun L 12 to 2.30, Tue to Sat D 7 to 9 (9.30 Fri and Sat). **Closed:** Mon, Jan, 2 weeks summer. **Meals:** alc (main courses £15 to £24). Set L £16.95 (2 courses) to £19.95. Set D £31.95. Sun L £31.95.
Service: not inc. **Details:** major cards accepted. 50 seats. 24 seats outside. No mobile phones. Wheelchair access. Music. Children welcome. Car parking.

The Swan Inn
Globetrotting gastropub food
The Street, Monks Eleigh IP7 7AU
(01449) 741391
www.monkseleigh.com
Gastropub | £22
Polished wood floors and subtle sage tones may suggest a trendy modern eatery, but the medieval Swan Inn is still a local watering hole, complete with a thatched roof and real ales on tap. Carol and Nigel Ramsbottom run the place as a double act – she greets everyone as if they were old friends, while he mans the stoves. British, Mediterranean and oriental influences bed happily together on the blackboard menu, and East Anglian fish is always a strong suit – perhaps dressed Cromer crab or whole roast sea bass with ginger and coriander butter. The kitchen also sends out emphatically flavoured dishes ranging from spicy Thai pork to braised lamb knuckle with Puy lentil sauce or Italian-style sweet and sour duck leg. Close the show with, say, hot caramelised fig tart. House wine is £13.50.
Chef/s: Nigel Ramsbottom. **Open:** Tue to Sun L 12 to 2, Tue to Sat D 7 to 9. **Closed:** Mon, 25 and 26 Dec, 2 weeks school summer hols. **Meals:** alc (main courses £9 to £20). Set L and D £13.75 (2 courses) to £17.75. **Service:** not inc. **Details:** major cards accepted. 40 seats. 24 seats outside. No music. Children welcome. Car parking.

Content brought to you by **The Good Food Guide 2011.** Please see page 14 for further details.

East of England

Tourist Information Centres

When you arrive at your destination, visit an Official Partner Tourist Information Centre for quality assured help with accommodation and information about local attractions and events, or email your request before you go. To find a Tourist Information Centre by region visit enjoyEngland.com/find-tic.

ALDEBURGH	152 High Street	01728 453637	atic@suffolkcoastal.gov.uk
BEDFORD	St Pauls Square	01234 221712	TouristInfo@bedford.gov.uk
BISHOP'S STORTFORD	The Old Monastery	01279 655831	tic@bishopsstortford.org
BRAINTREE	Town Hall Centre	01376 550066	tic@braintree.gov.uk
BURY ST EDMUNDS	6 Angel Hill	01284 764667	tic@stedsbc.gov.uk
CAMBRIDGE	Wheeler Street	0871 226 8006	tourism@cambridge.gov.uk
COLCHESTER	Tymperleys Clock Museum	01206 282920	vic@colchester.gov.uk
DISS	Meres Mouth	01379 650523	dtic@s-norfolk.gov.uk
ELY	Oliver Cromwell's House	01353 662062	tic@eastcambs.gov.uk
FELIXSTOWE	91 Undercliff Road West	01394 276770	ftic@suffolkcoastal.gov.uk
GREAT YARMOUTH	25 Marine Parade	01493 846345	tourism@great-yarmouth.gov.uk
HARWICH	Iconfield Park	01255 506139	harwichtic@btconnect.com
HUNSTANTON	Town Hall	01485 532610	hunstanton.tic@west-norfolk.gov.uk
IPSWICH	St Stephens Church	01473 258070	tourist@ipswich.gov.uk
KING'S LYNN	The Custom House	01553 763044	kings-lynn.tic@west-norfolk.gov.uk
LAVENHAM	Lady Street	01787 248207	lavenhamtic@babergh.gov.uk
LETCHWORTH GARDEN CITY	33-35 Station Road	01462 487868	tic@letchworth.com
LOWESTOFT	East Point Pavilion	01502 533600	touristinfo@waveney.gov.uk
LUTON	Luton Central Library	01582 401579	tourist.information@luton.gov.uk
MALDON	Coach Lane	01621 856503	tic@maldon.gov.uk
NEWMARKET	Palace House	01638 667200	tic.newmarket@forest-heath.gov.uk
NORWICH	The Forum	01603 727927	tourism@norwich.gov.uk

East of England

ETERBOROUGH	3-5 Minster Precincts	01733 452336	tic@peterborough.gov.uk
AFFRON WALDEN	1 The Market Place	01799 524002	tourism@saffronwalden.gov.uk
OUTHEND-ON-SEA	Pier Entrance	01702 215620	vic@southend.gov.uk
OUTHWOLD	69 High Street	01502 724729	southwold.tic@waveney.gov.uk
T ALBANS	Town Hall	01727 864511	tic@stalbans.gov.uk
TOWMARKET	The Museum of East Anglian Life	01449 676800	tic@midsuffolk.gov.uk
UDBURY	Town Hall	01787 881320	sudburytic@babergh.gov.uk
ITHAM	61 Newland Street	01376 502674	ticwitham@braintree.gov.uk
OODBRIDGE	Station Buildings	01394 382240	wtic@suffolkcoastal.gov.uk

Regional Contacts and Information

For more information on accommodation, attractions, activities, events and holidays in Eastern England, contact the regional or local tourism organisations. Their websites have a wealth of information and many produce free publications to help you get the most out of your visit.

East of England Tourism
Tel: (01284) 727470
Email: info@eet.org.uk
Web: www.visiteastofengland.com

The comprehensive website is updated daily. Online brochures and information sheets can be downloaded including Whats's New; Major Events; Stars and Stripes (connections with the USA) and a range of Discovery Tours around the region.

East of England | **Bedfordshire**

Where to Stay

Entries appear alphabetically by town name in each county. A key to symbols appears on page 6. Maps start on page 706. A listing of all Enjoy England assessed accommodation appears at the end of the region.

BEDFORD, Bedfordshire Map ref 2D1   SAT NAV MK40 3PD

B&B PER ROOM PER NIGHT
S £85.00 – £90.00
D £85.00 – £90.00

The Embankment
6 The Embankment, Bedford MK40 3PD
t (01234) 261332 **e** embankment@peachpubs.com
w embankmentbedford.co.uk ONLINE MAP GUEST REVIEWS ONLINE BOOKING LAST MINUTE OFFERS

An imposing mock-Tudor pub with rooms in the heart of Bedford with wonderful views out over the River Great Ouse. **directions** visit our website at www.embankmentbedford.co.uk for directions. **open** Closed Christmas Day only **bathrooms** 20 en suite **payment** credit/debit cards, cash, cheques

Room   General

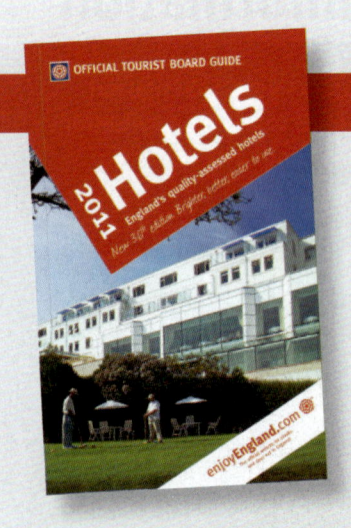

Looking for something else?

You can also buy a copy of our popular guide 'Hotels' including country house and town house hotels, metro and budget hotels, serviced apartments, restaurants with rooms and Spas in England 2011.

Now available in good bookshops and online at **visitbritainshop.com**

£10.99

East of England | **Bedfordshire/Cambridgeshire**

EAST HYDE, Bedfordshire Map ref 2D1

SAT NAV LU2 9PX

B&B PER ROOM PER NIGHT
S £50.00 – £60.00
D £60.00 – £85.00

Hyde Mill
Lower Luton Road, East Hyde, Luton, Bedfordshire LU2 9PX
t (01582) 712641 e info@hydemill.co.uk
w hydemill.co.uk ONLINE MAP

Hyde Mill offers unique and luxurious bed and breakfast accommodation on the outskirts of Harpenden on the banks of the River Lea. A warm and friendly welcome awaits you at this beautiful water mill. An ideal location for both business and leisure guests.

open All year
bedrooms 4 double, 1 twin
bathrooms 5 with private bathroom
payment credit/debit cards, cash, cheques

directions Junction 10 of M1 turn right towards Harpenden, 2nd left Thrales End Lane. T junction turn right we are on the right after 1/4 mile.

Room
General
Leisure

CAMBRIDGE, Cambridgeshire Map ref 2D1

SAT NAV CB1 3JS

B&B PER ROOM PER NIGHT
S £35.00 – £50.00
D £60.00 – £75.00

Allenbell
517a Coldham Lane, Cambridge CB1 3JS
t (01223) 210353 e enquiries@allenbell.co.uk
w allenbell.co.uk ONLINE MAP

Warm, friendly bed and breakfast providing newly furnished, en suite, comfortable accommodation. Quality breakfast served in light, spacious dining room. Easy access from A14/M11, close to city centre. **directions** Please contact us for directions **bedrooms** 1 double, 1 twin **bathrooms** 2 en suite **payment** credit/debit cards, cash, cheques

Room   General   Leisure

CAMBRIDGE, Cambridgeshire Map ref 2D1

SAT NAV CB2 8RJ

B&B PER ROOM PER NIGHT
S £45.00 – £60.00
D £65.00 – £80.00

Bridge Guest House
151 Hills Road, Cambridge CB2 8RJ
t (01223) 247942 f (01223) 416585 e bghouse@gmail.com
w bridgeguesthouse.co.uk

Ensuite rooms. Free parking/internet/WiFi. Walking distance: Historic City centre, Addenbrookes, Homerton College, Botanic Gardens, Railway/Bus station, Cambridge Leisure Park, cinema & restaurants. **directions** Close to railway and bus stations. M11 (2 miles), Stansted (35 minutes). Historic town centre and university colleges a 15 minute walk away. **open** All year except Xmas and New Year **bedrooms** 2 single, 2 double, 2 twin, 1 family **bathrooms** 7 en suite **payment** credit/debit cards, cash, cheques, euros

Room   General   Leisure

East of England | Cambridgeshire

CAMBRIDGE, Cambridgeshire Map ref 2D1
SAT NAV CB4 1DH

Fifty One
51 Saint Andrews Road, Cambridge CB4 1DH
t 07885 942544 e anna@bedandbreakfast51.co.uk
w bedandbreakfastfiftyone.co.uk/ ONLINE MAP GUEST REVIEWS ONLINE BOOKING

RATING APPLIED FOR

B&B PER ROOM PER NIGHT
S £50.00
D £75.00
EVENING MEAL PER PERSON
£25.00

Situated in Chesterton and within 20 minutes walk via the River Cam and Midsummer Common to the historic city centre of Cambridge. Super-king sized bed and plenty of off-street parking!
directions Please contact us for directions **open** All year **bedroom** 1 double, 1 twin, 1 family **bathrooms** 2 en suite, 2 with private bathroom **payment** cash, cheques, euros

Room General Leisure

CAMBRIDGE, Cambridgeshire Map ref 2D1
SAT NAV CB4 1LA

Home From Home
78-80 Milton Road, Cambridge CB4 1LA
t (01223) 323555 f (01223) 277705 e homefromhome2@btconnect.com
w homefromhomeguesthouse-cambridge.co.uk ONLINE MAP ONLINE BOOKING

★★★★ BED & BREAKFAST
Silver AWARD

B&B PER ROOM PER NIGHT
S £40.00 – £70.00
D £60.00 – £85.00

SPECIAL PROMOTIONS
2 night minimum stay at weekends

We offer comfortable rooms, a high level of housekeeping and a delicious home cooked breakfast to order from our extensive menu. You can be assured of a warm welcome, pleasant stay, and helpful assistance at the Home from Home bed and breakfast.

open All year
bedrooms 2 double, 2 family
bathrooms 3 en suite, 1 with private bathroom
payment credit/debit cards, cash, cheques, euros

directions From A14 exit at Jct 33 to Cambridge A1309. Go straight over at the roundabout and before the traffic lights we are on the left.

Room
General

CAMBRIDGE, Cambridgeshire Map ref 2D1
SAT NAV CB4 1DA

Lantern House
174 Chesterton Road, Cambridge CB4 1DA
t (01223) 359980 f (01223) 525682 e lanternhouse@msn.com
w guesthousecambridge.net ONLINE MAP LAST MINUTE OFFERS

★★★ GUEST HOUSE

B&B PER ROOM PER NIGHT
S £40.00
D £60.00 – £65.00

Lantern House offers good value for money, clean comfortable accommodation. Breakfast is great, atmosphere is friendly and the location is close to the centre of the beautiful city of Cambridge.
directions See our website for details **bedrooms** 2 single, 3 double, 2 twin **bathrooms** 7 en suite **payment** credit/debit cards, cash

Room General Leisure

332 Official tourist board guide Bed & Breakfast

East of England | **Cambridgeshire**

CAMBRIDGE, Cambridgeshire Map ref 2D1 — SAT NAV CB4 1DE

Southampton Guest House
7 Elizabeth Way, Cambridge CB4 1DE
t (01223) 357310 f (01223) 314297 e southamptonhouse@btinternet.com
w southamptonguesthouse.com

B&B PER ROOM PER NIGHT
S £35.00 – £45.00
D £48.00 – £58.00

Victorian property with friendly atmosphere, only 15 minutes walk along riverside to city centre, colleges and shopping mall.
directions Please contact us for directions **open** All year **bedrooms** 1 single, 1 double, 3 family **bathrooms** 5 en suite **payment** cash, cheques, euros

Room / General

CAMBRIDGE, Cambridgeshire Map ref 2D1 — SAT NAV CB4 3HS

Tudor Cottage
292 Histon Road, Cambridge CB4 3HS
t 01223565212 f 01954251117 e email@tudor-cottage.net
w tudorcottageguesthouse.co.uk ONLINE MAP ONLINE BOOKING

B&B PER ROOM PER NIGHT
S £30.00 – £50.00
D £50.00 – £65.00

Comfortable, friendly, Tudor-style cottage situated within 30 minutes walking distance of city centre. En suite or shared facilities, central heating, colour Freeview TV, wi-fi, tea/coffee-making facilities. Excellent food and friendly, personal service. Off-street parking. Easy access to A14/M11. 5* Health and Hygiene rating.

open All year
bedrooms 2 single, 2 double, 1 twin
bathrooms 3 en suite
payment cash, cheques, euros

directions Close to A14 and M11. For further details please refer to website.

Room / General

CAMBRIDGE, Cambridgeshire Map ref 2D1 — SAT NAV CB4 1DA

Worth House
152 Chesterton Road, Cambridge CB4 1DA
t (01223) 316074 f (01223) 316074 e enquiry@worth-house.co.uk
w worth-house.co.uk ONLINE MAP GUEST REVIEWS LAST MINUTE OFFERS

B&B PER ROOM PER NIGHT
S £49.00 – £65.00
D £60.00 – £85.00

Worth House offers quiet, comfortable and spacious accommodation in this Victorian home. Within easy reach of the city centre. 'Which?' recommended. **directions** Please contact us for directions **open** All year **bedrooms** 4 suites **bathrooms** 4 en suite **payment** credit/debit cards, cash, cheques, euros

Room / General / Leisure

for key to symbols see page 6

East of England | Cambridgeshire

CAMBRIDGE (12 MILES), Cambridgeshire Map ref 2D1
SAT NAV CB21 4PW

enjoyEngland.com ★★★★ INN

B&B PER ROOM PER NIGHT
S £55.00
D £55.00

EVENING MEAL PER PERSON
£6.95 – £11.95

SPECIAL PROMOTIONS
Special rates available for week-day breaks. Minimum two nights.

Three Hills
Ashdon Road, Bartlow, Cambridge CB21 4PW
t (01223) 891259 **e** threehills@rhubarb-inns.co.uk
w rhubarb-inns.co.uk ONLINE MAP GUEST REVIEWS

In beautiful walking countryside 12 miles from Cambridge and 6 miles from Saffron Walden. Delightful 17th century freehouse Inn with clean and modern en-suite rooms in traditional building alongside. Excellent food and real ales. Ideal base for visitors or business travellers with easy access to M11, A11 & A14.

open All year
bedrooms 2 double, 2 twin
bathrooms 4 en suite
payment credit/debit cards, cash, cheques

directions From A1307 Cambridge to Haverhill, through Linton, take turning to Bartlow on right. Turn right at cross roads, Three Hills is on left.

Room
General
Leisure

ELLINGTON THORPE, Cambridgeshire Map ref 3A2
SAT NAV PE28 0AP

enjoyEngland.com ★★★★ FARMHOUSE

B&B PER ROOM PER NIGHT
S £38.00
D £70.00

Thorpe Lodge Farm B&B
Ellington, Huntingdon, Cambridgeshire PE28 0AP
t (01480) 810244 **e** tl.farm@tiscali.co.uk
w thorpe-lodge-farm.co.uk GUEST REVIEWS ONLINE BOOKING

A warm welcome to our farmhouse B&B with fantastic views overlooking open countryside from all our en-suite guest rooms each offering digital TV, courtesy tray. Traditional english breakfast offered. **directions** Junction 20 off A14 follow directions to Grafham water. Come into Ellington Thorpe, round a sharp bend and farm drive is on the right. **open** All year **bedrooms** 1 double, 2 twin, 1 family **bathrooms** 4 en suite **payment** credit/debit cards, cash, cheques

Room   General   Leisure

ELY, Cambridgeshire Map ref 3A2
SAT NAV CB6 2DB

enjoyEngland.com ★★★★ BED & BREAKFAST

B&B PER ROOM PER NIGHT
S £36.00 – £40.00
D £60.00 – £66.00

EVENING MEAL PER PERSON
£10.00 – £25.00

The Old School B&B
The Old School, School Lane, Coveney, Ely CB6 2DB
t (01353) 777087 07802-174541 **f** (01353) 777091 **e** info@TheOldSchoolBandB.co.uk
w TheOldSchoolBandB.co.uk ONLINE MAP GUEST REVIEWS ONLINE BOOKING LAST MINUTE OFFERS

Quality accommodation in former village school, quiet location 3 miles from Ely. Set in gardens with views onto Ely Cathedral. Ground-floor bedrooms. Wir sprechen Deutsch. Nous parlons français ici. **directions** Please refer to website www.TheOldSchoolBandB.co.uk
open All year **bedrooms** 1 double, 1 suite **bathrooms** 1 en suite, with private bathroom **payment** credit/debit cards, cash, cheques, euros

Room   General   Leisure

East of England | **Cambridgeshire**

GUYHIRN, Cambridgeshire Map ref 3A1

SAT NAV PE13 4EA

INN ★★★★

B&B PER ROOM PER NIGHT
S £59.00
D £80.00

EVENING MEAL PER PERSON
£7.95 – £18.95

Oliver Twist Country Inn

High Road, Guyhirn, Wisbech, Cambridgeshire PE13 4EA
t (01945) 450523 **f** (01945) 450009 **e** enquiries@theolivertwist.com
w theolivertwist.com ONLINE MAP ONLINE BOOKING

The Oliver Twist Country Inn are proud of their four star accommodation, all six rooms are en-suite with freeview television in comfortable, quiet bedrooms. A function room, which is ideal for meetings and/or fine dining is available where an extensive and varied menu of high quality food is offered.

open All year except Xmas
bedrooms 3 double, 3 twin
bathrooms 6 en suite
payment credit/debit cards, cash

directions Roundabout junction with the A47/A141, proceed to Peterborough, 100m after bridge turn right. At T-junction turn right. We are on the left after 350m.

Room
General
Leisure

HUNTINGDON, Cambridgeshire Map ref 3A2

SAT NAV PE28 2AZ

BED & BREAKFAST ★★★★★
Silver AWARD

B&B PER ROOM PER NIGHT
S £68.00 – £75.00
D £75.00 – £90.00

Cheriton House

Mill Street, Houghton, Huntingdon PE28 2AZ
t (01480) 464004 **f** (01480) 496960 **e** sales@cheritonhousecambs.co.uk
w cheritonhousecambs.co.uk ONLINE MAP GUEST REVIEWS ONLINE BOOKING LAST MINUTE OFFERS

Large garden, picturesque riverside village. Homemade breads, jams, etc. 20/25 minutes from Cambridge, Ely and RAF Duxford. Enjoy country walks, good food, local pubs with winter fires and summer gardens. Free wifi. **directions** From A1/M1/A14 West take A141 towards March then A1123 to St Ives. From M11/A14 East take Jct 26 A1096 to St Ives then A1123 . **open** All year **bedrooms** 4 double, 1 twin **bathrooms** 5 en suite **payment** credit/debit cards, cash, cheques

Room   General   Leisure

NEWMARKET (4 MILES), Cambridgeshire Map ref 3B2

SAT NAV CB25 0HB

GUEST ACCOMMODATION ★★★★

B&B PER ROOM PER NIGHT
S £35.00 – £40.00
D £35.00

The Meadow House B&B

2a High Street, Burwell, Cambridge CB25 0HB
t (01638) 741926 **f** (01638) 741861 **e** bookings@themeadowhouse.co.uk
w themeadowhouse.co.uk

Magnificent modern house set in 2 acres of wooded grounds. King size beds, large rooms, plenty of parking, generous breakfasts. Self catering also available. **directions** Leave A14 at Stow-cum-Quy. Follow B1102 via the Swaffhams to Burwell. Larger house on right as you enter village, before you get to the church. **open** All year **bedrooms** 2 double, 1 twin, 3 family, 1 suite **bathrooms** 4 en suite, 3 with private bathroom **payment** cash, cheques, euros

Room   General

key to symbols see page 6

335

East of England | Cambridgeshire/Essex

PIDLEY, Cambridgeshire Map ref 3A2
SAT NAV PE28 3DF

Lakeside Lodge Golf Centre
Fen Road, Pidley, Huntingdon, Cambs PE28 3DF
t (01487) 740540 f (01487) 740852 e jane@lakeside-lodge.co.uk
w lakeside-lodge.co.uk ONLINE MAP

enjoyEngland.com GUEST ACCOMMODATION

B&B PER ROOM PER NIGHT
S £48.00
D £76.00

EVENING MEAL PER PERSON
£12.00 – £22.00

SPECIAL PROMOTIONS
Special Golf Break promotions available for groups and individuals throughout the year

Lakeside Lodge offers 4 Golf Courses, a Driving Range and large Golf Shop, Tenpin Bowling, Conference facilities, Wedding/Civil Ceremonies, a superbly equipped Health Club and a welcoming Bar/Restaurant offering A La Carte/Snacks. The 64 en-suite comfortable bedrooms are mostly in spacious Lodges which are ideal for family or corporate groups.

open All year except Xmas
bedrooms 2 single, 4 double, 30 twin, 28 family
bathrooms 64 en suite, 64 with private bathroom
payment credit/debit cards, cash, cheques
directions From Cambridge leave the A1 at St Ives taking the B1040 to Pidley. From Huntingdon take the A141 to Warboys following the brown tourist signs.

Room
General
Leisure

WITCHFORD, Cambridgeshire Map ref 3A2
SAT NAV CB6 2HQ

The Village Inn
80 Main Street, Witchford, Ely CB6 2HQ
t (01353) 663763 e claire.parsons@virgin.net
w thevillageinnely.com LAST MINUTE OFFERS

enjoyEngland.com INN

B&B PER ROOM PER NIGHT
S £50.00
D £65.00

EVENING MEAL PER PERSON
£5.00 – £10.00

Luxury accommodation in clean comfortable surroundings ideally situated for Cambridge and Ely. We offer an extensive menu catering for all tastes, with friendly, welcoming staff, and a great atmosphere. **directions** Please contact us for directions **open** All year **bedrooms** 2 double **payment** credit/debit cards, cash, cheques

Room General Leisure

BRIGHTLINGSEA, Essex Map ref 3B3
SAT NAV CO7 0HG

Hurst Green Bed and Breakfast
1 Hurst Green, Brightlingsea, Essex CO7 0HG
t 01206 308 819 (07842193070) e info@hurstgreenbedandbreakfast.co.uk
w hurstgreenbedandbreakfast.co.uk

enjoyEngland.com BED & BREAKFAST | Silver AWARD

B&B PER ROOM PER NIGHT
S £40.00
D £60.00

400 year-old listed house in conservation area where guests can relax in our pleasant garden. We specialise in offering comfortable accommodation and delicious food. **directions** Easily accessible from A12 via A120. By bus we are 9 miles from Colchester where there is a mainline station. **open** All year **bedrooms** 1 double, 1 twin **bathrooms** 1 en suite, 1 with private bathroom **payment** cash, cheques, euros

Room General Leisure

336 Official tourist board guide Bed & Breakfast

East of England | **Essex**

CLACTON-ON-SEA, Essex Map ref 3B3

SAT NAV CO15 1RA

Chudleigh
Agate Road, Marine Parade West, Clacton-on-Sea, Essex CO15 1RA
t (01255) 425347 f (01255) 470280 e chudleighhotel@btconnect.com
w chudleighhotel.com ONLINE MAP GUEST REVIEWS ONLINE BOOKING LAST MINUTE OFFERS

B&B PER ROOM PER NIGHT
S £48.00 – £50.00
D £75.00 – £80.00

An oasis in a town centre location, 200m from seafront gardens, near pier and main shops. Ideal for the business visitor, the tourist and for overnight stays. Free parking. **directions** From A12 follow sign to Clacton. At seafront turn right. After pier traffic lights, with sea on your left, turn right into Agate Road. **open** All year **bedrooms** 2 single, 4 double, 2 twin, 2 family **bathrooms** 10 en suite, 3 with private bathroom **payment** credit/debit cards, cash, cheques, euros

CLAVERING, Essex Map ref 2D1

SAT NAV CB11 4QT

Cricketers, The
Wicken Road, Clavering, Saffron Walden CB11 4QT
t (01799) 550442 f (01799) 550882 e info@thecricketers.co.uk
w thecricketers.co.uk ONLINE MAP

B&B PER ROOM PER NIGHT
S £65.00 – £75.00
D £90.00 – £110.00

A delightful 16th century country Inn with award winning food and accommodation. Very popular for business and pleasure alike, good food being a core ingredient of a stay at The Cricketers. Owners' son, Jamie Oliver, grew up here and supplies vegetables, leaves and herbs from his nearby certifed organic garden.

open All year except Xmas
bedrooms 11 double, 3 twin
bathrooms 14 en suite
payment credit/debit cards, cash

directions M11 jct 8. A120 west and B1383 to Newport. B1038 to Clavering.

COLCHESTER, Essex Map ref 3B2

SAT NAV CO6 4BU

Knowles Barn
London Road, Great Horkesley, Colchester, Essex CO6 4BU
t (01206) 271110 e ContactUs@knowlesbarn.com
w knowlesbarn.com ONLINE MAP

B&B PER ROOM PER NIGHT
S £40.00
D £75.00

Knowles Barn, built around 1650, was converted in 2006 to provide a modern family house retaining many of its traditional features. It is set in 10 acres of paddocks/gardens **directions** Please contact us for directions **open** All year **bedrooms** 2 double, 1 twin **bathrooms** 3 en suite **payment** cash, cheques, euros

For **key to symbols** see page 6   337

East of England | Essex

COLCHESTER, Essex Map ref 3B2
SAT NAV CO1 1JN

Trinity Town House
6 Trinity Street, Colchester CO1 1JN
t (01206) 575955 e info@trinitytownhouse.co.uk
w **trinitytownhouse.co.uk** ONLINE MAP GUEST REVIEWS ONLINE BOOKING

B&B PER ROOM PER NIGHT
S £60.00 – £95.00
D £75.00 – £100.00

This Four Star Gold and Grade II listed Tudor house offers modern luxury bedrooms and bathrooms providing affordable accommodation in the heart of Colchester. The price includes full English breakfast. **directions** Trinity Townhouse is located in central Colchester, off Head Street via West Culver Street, or by foot from the High Street via Pelhams Lane. **open** February to November **bedrooms** 5 double **bathrooms** 4 en suite, 1 with private bathroom **payment** credit/debit cards, cash, cheques

BREAKFAST AWARD

COLCHESTER (5 MILES), Essex Map ref 3B2
SAT NAV CO6 3PH

Caterpillar Cottage
Ford Street, Aldham, Colchester CO6 3PH
t (01206) 240456 f (01206) 240456 e bandbcaterpillar@tiscali.co.uk
w **smoothhound.co.uk/hotels/caterpillar**

B&B PER ROOM PER NIGHT
S £35.00 – £45.00
D £65.00 – £75.00

Newly built house in 'traditional' style in conservation area and grounds of listed building. Quiet location well back from road, ample secure parking. Three pubs nearby, family home, friendly atmosphere. **directions** On A1124 opposite Old Queens Head in Ford Street. Gate shared with Old House. **open** All year **bedrooms** 1 double, 1 family **bathrooms** 1 en suite, 1 with private bathroom **payment** cash, cheques

DUNMOW, Essex Map ref 3B2
SAT NAV CM6 1AY

Mallards
Star Lane, Dunmow, Great Dunmow, essex CM6 1AY
t (01371) 872641 e bookings@mallardsdunmow.co.uk
w **mallardsdunmow.co.uk**

B&B PER ROOM PER NIGHT
S £40.00
D £60.00 – £80.00

Mallards, a charming detached house in a tranquil country lane, in the centre of a quaint market town. Comfortably furnished, friendly atmosphere, two minutes walk from good restaurants, cosy pubs. **directions** From High Street - Market Place - Starr Restaurant, Star Lane is to the left hand side, Mallards is 50yds down on the left. **open** All year **bedrooms** 1 twin, 1 family **bathrooms** 1 en suite, 1 with private bathroom **payment** cash, cheques, euros

EARLS COLNE, Essex Map ref 3B2
SAT NAV CO6 2PH

Riverside Lodge
40 Lower Holt Street, Earls Colne, Colchester CO6 2PH
t (01787) 223387 f (01787) 223387 e bandb@riversidelodge-uk.com
w **riversidelodge-uk.com**

B&B PER ROOM PER NIGHT
S £50.00 – £53.00
D £58.00 – £64.00

En suite chalets on banks of River Colne. Restaurants, pubs and village amenities within walking distance. Fine country walks from lodge. All rooms on ground level. **directions** On A1124 Colchester Halstead road by bridge over river Colne. Post code CO6 2PH. **open** All year **bedrooms** 2 double, 3 twin **bathrooms** 5 en suite **payment** credit/debit cards, cash, cheques

East of England | Essex

MANNINGTREE, Essex Map ref 3B2

SAT NAV CO11 2UP

Curlews
Station Road, Bradfield, Manningtree, Essex CO11 2UP
t (01255) 870890   e margherita@curlewsaccommodation.co.uk
w curlewsacccommodation.co.uk ONLINE MAP

B&B PER ROOM PER NIGHT
S £50.00 – £60.00
D £60.00 – £80.00

SPECIAL PROMOTIONS
Single-let discounts, internet all rooms, laundry and drying facilities, self-catering family and disabled suites

Curlews is a superb property situated on the outskirts of Bradfield village offering luxury bed and breakfast and self-catering accommodation including facilities for the disabled. Located approximately 30m above sea level, most bedrooms provide stunning elevated panoramic views over farmland and the Stour Estuary.

open All year
bedrooms 3 double, 5 twin, 1 family, 1 suite
bathrooms 10 en suite
payment credit/debit cards, cash, cheques

directions B1035 from A120 towards Manningtree for 1.5 miles, turn right at radio mast for further 1.6 miles, Location on the right past Strangers Home pub.

Room   General   Leisure

ORSETT, Essex Map ref 3B3

SAT NAV RM16 3LJ

Jays Lodge
Chapel Farm, Baker Street, Orsett, Grays RM16 3LJ
t (01375) 891663   e info@jayslodge.co.uk
w jayslodge.co.uk ONLINE MAP

B&B PER ROOM PER NIGHT
S £33.00 – £38.00
D £48.00

Barn conversion to provide twelve rooms all with en suite, mini kitchen and colour television. Ample, free and secure parking available. **directions** Please contact us for directions **open** All year **bedrooms** 2 single, 2 double, 8 twin **bathrooms** 12 en suite **payment** credit/debit cards, cash, cheques, euros

Room   General   Leisure

SAFFRON WALDEN, Essex Map ref 2D1

SAT NAV CB10 2LP

Redgates Farmhouse
Redgates Lane, Sewards End, Saffron Walden CB10 2LP
t (01799) 516166   e info@redgates.eu
w redgates.eu

B&B PER ROOM PER NIGHT
S £35.00
D £60.00

Redgates is set in pretty countryside 1 1/2 miles from Saffron Walden, it is a renovated farm house with ample parking, Pets welcome by arrangement. **directions** Please contact us for directions **open** All year except Xmas and New Year **bedrooms** 1 double, 1 twin, 1 family **bathrooms** 1 en suite, 1 with private bathroom **payment** cash, cheques

Room   General   Leisure

key to symbols see page 6

East of England | **Essex**

SOUTHEND-ON-SEA, Essex Map ref 3B3   SAT NAV SS1 3AA

The Moorings B&B
172 Eastern Esplanade, Southend-on-Sea SS1 3AA
t (01702) 587575 e mail@themooringsbedandbreakfast.com
w themooringsbedandbreakfast.com ONLINE MAP GUEST REVIEWS

B&B PER ROOM PER NIGHT
S £35.00 – £45.00
D £50.00 – £60.00

The Moorings is a home away from home, by the sea. With our clean cosy rooms, hearty breakfasts and seafront postition, we're sure you'll agree. **directions** M25 take the A127 into Southend. Follow signs to the seafront and turn East. The B&B is past the Ocean Beach restaurant on the seaside. **open** All year **bedrooms** 2 double, 1 twin **bathrooms** 3 en suite **payment** cash, cheques, euros

STANSTED, Essex Map ref 2D1   SAT NAV CM23 5QA

The Cottage
71 Birchanger Lane, Bishop's Stortford CM23 5QA
t (01279) 812349 f (01279) 815045 e bookings@thecottagebirchanger.co.uk
w thecottagebirchanger.co.uk ONLINE MAP ONLINE BOOKING

B&B PER ROOM PER NIGHT
S £40.00 – £60.00
D £70.00 – £85.00

17thC listed house. Breakfast room overlooks mature garden. Quiet village near M11 jct8, Stansted Airport (4mls). Ample off-road parking. Rooms furnished in cottage style with Free Wi-Fi Internet. Village Pub. **directions** M11 jct8 take A120 signed Hertford. After 1 mile turn rt, B1383 signed Newport. Next rt into Birchanger Lane. **open** All year except Xmas and New Year **bedrooms** 2 single, 8 double, 3 twin, 1 family **bathrooms** 13 en suite, 1 with private bathroom **payment** credit/debit cards, cash, cheques

STANSTED, Essex Map ref 2D1   SAT NAV CM22 6NR

White House
Smiths Green, Takeley CM22 6NR
t (01279) 870257 f (01279) 870423 e enquiries@whitehousestansted.co.uk
w whitehousestansted.co.uk ONLINE MAP GUEST REVIEWS ONLINE BOOKING LAST MINUTE OFFERS

B&B PER ROOM PER NIGHT
S £60.00
D £65.00

EVENING MEAL PER PERSON
£7.50 – £20.00

SPECIAL PROMOTIONS
All rooms can be made into triples, doubles and quad rooms on request.

A 15thC manor house set in one acre with ample parking. Two miles from Stansted Airport (but not on flight path). Beautifully renovated. Modern, en suite facilities in a traditional family environment. Evening meal available at nearby Lion and Lamb pub/restaurant, which is also owned by Mike and Linda.

open All year except Xmas and New Year
bedrooms 1 single, 1 double, 1 twin
bathrooms 2 en suite, 1 with private bathroom
payment credit/debit cards, cash, cheques, euros

directions Exit M11 jct 8. On roundabout take B1256 Takeley. The White House is 400yds past the traffic lights on the left, opposite the carpet shop.

East of England | Essex

WALTON-ON-THE-NAZE, Essex Map ref 3C2
SAT NAV CO14 8HJ

Bufo Villae Guest House
31 Beatrice Road, Walton-on-the-Naze, Frinton-on-Sea CO14 8HJ
t (01255) 672644   e bufovillae@btinternet.com
w bufovillae.co.uk   ONLINE MAP   GUEST REVIEWS

B&B PER ROOM PER NIGHT
S £27.00 – £29.00
D £54.00 – £58.00

Close to seafront in quiet area of Walton. Two rooms have sea views, all rooms en suite with tea/coffee-making facilities. Colour television, parking, downstairs room for those with mobility difficulties. **directions** By road, details on booking. Hourly rail service from London Liverpool Street to Walton - approx. 1½ hrs. About 12 miles drive from Harwich port. **open** All year **bedrooms** 1 single, 1 double, 1 twin **bathrooms** 3 en suite **payment** cash, cheques

Room   General   Leisure

WESTCLIFF-ON-SEA, Essex Map ref 3B3
SAT NAV SS0 7SR

Rose House
21-23 Manor Road, Westcliff-on-Sea SS0 7SR
t (01702) 341959   f (01702) 342663
w rosehousehotel.co.uk   ONLINE MAP

B&B PER ROOM PER NIGHT
S £30.00
D £50.00 – £70.00

A Victorian hotel by sea front opposite Westcliff Station with professional but friendly service. We are renowned for giving excellent value for money with many of our guests returning frequently. **directions** Please contact us for directions **bedrooms** 10 single, 5 double, 2 twin, 2 family **bathrooms** 15 en suite **payment** credit/debit cards, cash, cheques

Room   General   Leisure

WEST MERSEA, Essex Map ref 3B3
SAT NAV CO5 8LS

The Victory at Mersea
92 Coast Road, Mersea Island, Colchester CO5 8LS
t (01206) 382907   e info@victoryatmersea.com
w victoryatmersea.com   ONLINE MAP   GUEST REVIEWS   ONLINE BOOKING   LAST MINUTE OFFERS

B&B PER ROOM PER NIGHT
S £67.00 – £85.00
D £73.00 – £90.00
EVENING MEAL PER PERSON
£8.00 – £20.00

The Victory is situated on the Mersea waterfront. We have 3 really comfortable, superior quality rooms, individually decorated with a personal touch and all with fantastic estuary views. **directions** Mersea is clearly signposted from the A12 and you'll find us on the outskirts of the village centre, right on the waterfront. **open** All year **bedrooms** 2 double, 1 family **bathrooms** 3 en suite **payment** credit/debit cards, cash, cheques

Room   General   Leisure

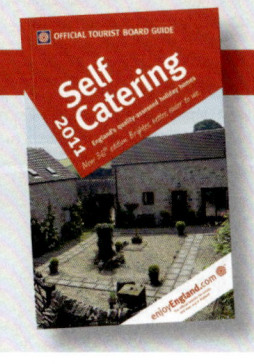

Looking for something else?
You can also buy a copy of our popular guide 'Self Catering' including self-catering holiday homes, approved caravan holiday homes, boat accommodation and holiday cottage agencies in England 2011.

Now available in good bookshops and online at
visitbritainshop.com

£11.99

East of England | **Hertfordshire**

ASHWELL, Hertfordshire Map ref 2D1
SAT NAV SG7 5NL

Three Tuns Hotel
6 High Street, Ashwell, Nr Baldock, Hertfordshire SG7 5NL
t (01462) 742 107   e info@threetunshotel.co.uk
w **threetunshotel.co.uk** ONLINE MAP ONLINE BOOKING

B&B PER ROOM PER NIGHT
S £39.00 – £53.00
D £62.00 – £79.00

EVENING MEAL PER PERSON
£9.45 – £18.95

This traditional country hotel dates back to 17
built in the reign of Queen Anne, the last of th
Stuart monarchs and was converted into a
popular hostelry from 1806. Major refurbishme
in both 1998 and 2009 have created a wonder
English hotel combining old fashioned dignity
with modern comfort.

open All year
bedrooms 1 single, 4 double, 1 twin
bathrooms 4 en suite, 2 with private bathroom
payment credit/debit cards, cash, cheques

directions Please contact us for directions

Room
General
Leisure

AYOT ST LAWRENCE, Hertfordshire Map ref 2D1
SAT NAV AL6 9BT

The Brocket Arms
Ayot St Lawrence, Welwyn AL6 9BT
t (01438) 820250   e bookings@brocketarms.com
w **www.brocketarms.com** ONLINE MAP ONLINE BOOKING LAST MINUTE OFFERS

B&B PER ROOM PER NIGHT
S £85.00
D £85.00 – £120.00

EVENING MEAL PER PERSON
£16.95 – £19.95

Typical English Inn dating from the 14th
Century. Oak beams and huge inglenook
fireplaces create a warm and friendly
atmosphere. Set in one of the most beautiful
Hertfordshire villages where George Bernard
Shaw lived for most of his life. Real ales bar
snacks and an excellent restaurant.

open All year
bedrooms 5 double, 1 twin
bathrooms 5 en suite, 1 with private bathroom
payment credit/debit cards, cash, cheques,
euros

directions From A1M follow signs to
Wheathampstead, then signs for Shaws Corner.
The Brocket Arms is located past Shaws Corner
on the right hand side.

Room
General
Leisure

East of England | Hertfordshire/Norfolk

HEMEL HEMPSTEAD, Hertfordshire Map ref 2D1
SAT NAV HP2 6HA

Marsh Farm
Ledgemore Lane, Great Gaddesden HP2 6HA
t (01442) 252517 **f** (01442) 232023 **e** nicky@bennett-baggs.com
w marshfarm.org.uk ONLINE MAP GUEST REVIEWS

B&B PER ROOM PER NIGHT
S £55.00
D £65.00

On the private Gaddesden Estate, Marsh Farm is a beautiful farmhouse in a rural location. Excellent local pubs, wonderful country walks from our front door. Comfortable, well-appointed room, good breakfasts. **directions** From Gt Gaddesden (Berkhamsted 4 miles, Hemel Hempsted 4 miles) cross A4146 onto Ledgemore Lane. Take first right onto track, then left at barns.

open All year except Xmas and New Year **bedrooms** 1 twin
bathrooms 1 en suite **payment** cash, cheques

ALDBOROUGH NEAR CROMER, Norfolk Map ref 3C1
SAT NAV NR11 7AA

Butterfly Cottage B&B
The Green, Aldborough, Cromer, Norfolk NR11 7AA
t (01263) 768198 (01263) 761689 **f** (01263) 768198 **e** butterflycottage@btinternet.com
w butterflycottage.com ONLINE MAP LAST MINUTE OFFERS

B&B PER ROOM PER NIGHT
S £32.50 – £35.00
D £65.00 – £75.00
EVENING MEAL PER PERSON
£13.00 – £15.00

On the Weavers Way. Comfortable, cottage-style, well equipped, friendly atmosphere. Rooms overlook large garden or village green. Each has TV/DVD player, fridge and own entrance. Car parking. **directions** Approximately one and a half miles off the A140 half way between Aylsham and Cromer. **open** All year **bedrooms** 1 single, 1 double, 1 twin, 1 family, 1 suite **bathrooms** 4 en suite, 1 with private bathroom **payment** cash, cheques

AYLSHAM, Norfolk Map ref 3B1
SAT NAV NR11 6BY

The Old Pump House
Holman Road, Aylsham, Norwich NR11 6BY
t (01263) 733789 **f** (01263) 733789 **e** theoldpumphouse@btconnect.com
w theoldpumphouse.com ONLINE MAP

B&B PER ROOM PER NIGHT
S £75.00 – £95.00
D £95.00 – £115.00
EVENING MEAL PER PERSON
£25.00 – £30.00

SPECIAL PROMOTIONS
Seven nights for the price of six.

A luxurious Georgian home, near the market place, with five tastefully furnished, comfortable bedrooms. Lavish breakfasts are served in the elegant Georgian room, overlooking the peaceful garden. The house is within easy reach of Blickling Hall, other stately homes, the north Norfolk coast and the cathedral city of Norwich.

open All year except Xmas and New Year
bedrooms 2 double, 1 twin, 2 family
bathrooms 5 en suite
payment credit/debit cards, cash, cheques

directions Please contact us for directions

BREAKFAST AWARD

key to symbols see page 6

343

East of England | Norfolk

BLICKLING, Norfolk Map ref 3B1
SAT NAV NR11 6NF

Buckinghamshire Arms
Blickling, Aylsham NR11 6NF
t (01263) 732133 e bucksarms@tiscali.co.uk
w bucks-arms.co.uk ONLINE MAP

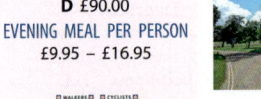

INN

B&B PER ROOM PER NIGHT
S £60.00 – £90.00
D £90.00
EVENING MEAL PER PERSON
£9.95 – £16.95

The Bucks is a place to relax and unwind with woodburning stove food served 7 days a week including traditional Sunday lunch all freshly prepared using locally sourced produce. **directions** Please contact us for directions **open** All year except Xmas **bedrooms** 3 double **bathrooms** 3 en suite **payment** credit/debit cards, cash, cheques

Room General Leisure

BRUNDALL, Norfolk Map ref 3C1
SAT NAV NR13 5PA

Breckland B&B
12 Strumpshaw Road, Brundall, Norwich NR13 5PA
t (01603) 712122 e brecklandbandb@hotmail.co.uk
w breckland-bandb.co.uk ONLINE MAP

BED & BREAKFAST
Silver AWARD

B&B PER ROOM PER NIGHT
S £40.00
D £60.00

At Breckland B&B in Brundall, David and Tina Ward have two superior self-contained bedrooms with en suite facilities. Convenient for Strumpshaw RSPB, the Broads and Norwich. Walkers and cyclists welcome. **directions** Please refer to website. **open** All year except Xmas and New Year **bedrooms** 1 double, 1 twin **bathrooms** 2 en suite **payment** cash, cheques, euros

Room General Leisure

BURNHAM THORPE, Norfolk Map ref 3B1
SAT NAV PE31 8HN

Whitehall Farm
Burnham Thorpe, Norfolk PE31 8HN
t (01328) 738416 e barrysoutherland@aol.com
w whitehallfarm-accommodation.com

FARMHOUSE
Silver AWARD

B&B PER ROOM PER NIGHT
S £45.00 – £80.00
D £75.00 – £80.00

Barry and Valerie welcome you for a quiet, relaxed stay in North Norfolk, two miles from the coast. 2 Double, 1 Flexi room with full facilities in 16thC farmhouse. **directions** Please contact us for directions **open** All year except Xmas **bedrooms** 2 double, 1 twin **bathrooms** 3 en suite **payment** credit/debit cards, cash, cheques, euros

BREAKFAST AWARD Room General Leisure

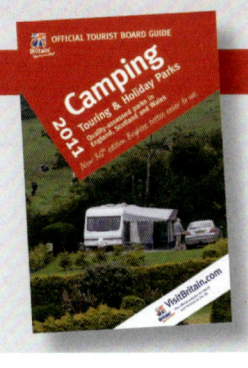

Do you like Camping?

You can also buy a copy of our popular guide 'Camping, Touring & Holiday Parks' including touring parks, camping holidays and holiday parks and villages in Britain 2011.

Now available in good bookshops and online at
visitbritainshop.com

£8.99

East of England | **Norfolk**

COLTISHALL, Norfolk Map ref 3C1
SAT NAV NR12 7JZ

Seven Acres House
Great Hautbois, Coltishall, Norwich NR12 7JZ
t (01603) 736737 e info@hautbois.plus.com
w norfolkbroadsbandb.com

B&B PER ROOM PER NIGHT
S £58.00
D £82.00 – £98.00

SPECIAL PROMOTIONS
10% reduction for 3 or more nights' stay.

Edwardian Seven Acres House is surrounded by extensive grounds in a peaceful rural location, close to village amenities. Easy access to Broads, Norwich, NT properties and coast. Two spacious well equipped, beautifully furnished south-facing bedrooms. A delicious cooked breakfast is served in the bright morning room leading onto terrace.

open All year except Xmas and New Year
bedrooms 1 double, 1 twin
bathrooms 2 en suite
payment credit/debit cards, cash, cheques, euros

directions From Norwich, take the B1150 to Coltishall. Seven Acres is about 0.5 miles from the High Street just off Hautbois Road.

Room General Leisure

CROMER, Norfolk Map ref 3C1
SAT NAV NR27 0AA

Shrublands Farm Guesthouse
Church Street, Northrepps, Cromer NR27 0AA
t (01263) 579297 e youngman@farming.co.uk
w shrublandsfarm.com ONLINE MAP

B&B PER ROOM PER NIGHT
S £43.00 – £47.00
D £66.00 – £74.00

Shrublands Farm situated close to coast in north Norfolk. National trust properties nearby and wonderful walks by the sea or in the countryside. 4 star silver and breakfast awards. **directions** Two miles south of Cromer, turn off A149 to Northrepps, 1 mile to Foundry Arms pub. We are 50m passed pub on left. **open** All year except Xmas **bedrooms** 1 double, 1 twin **bathrooms** 1 en suite, 1 with private bathroom **payment** credit/debit cards, cash, cheques, euros

BREAKFAST AWARD Room General 12 P Leisure

DEREHAM, Norfolk Map ref 3B1
SAT NAV NR20 4JU

Hunters Hall
Park Farm, Swanton Morley, Dereham NR20 4JU
t (01362) 637457 f (01362) 637987 e office@huntershall.com
w huntershall.com GUEST REVIEWS

B&B PER ROOM PER NIGHT
S £40.00 – £60.00
D £60.00 – £80.00

A traditional working farm offering accommodation, function and conference facilities in a conservation area. **directions** A47 Dereham, B1147 Swanton Morley. In village of Swanton Morley right at Darby's Pub into Elsing Road. 0.5 miles on the right down long drive. **open** All year **bedrooms** 4 double, 5 twin, 2 family **bathrooms** 7 en suite **payment** credit/debit cards, cash, cheques

Room General Leisure

key to symbols see page 6   345

East of England | **Norfolk**

DERSINGHAM, Norfolk Map ref 3B1   SAT NAV PE31 6PP

Barn House Bed & Breakfast
14 Station Road, Dersingham, King's Lynn PE31 6PP
t (01485) 543086 e barnhousebnb@gmail.com
w smoothhound.co.uk/hotels/barnho GUEST REVIEWS LAST MINUTE OFFERS

B&B PER ROOM PER NIGHT
S £40.00 – £65.00
D £65.00 – £80.00

Barn conversion offering spacious, warm, comfortable, ensuite character accommodation with home comforts, sofa etc. Easy walking to Sandringham and RSPB. Drying room. Cycle facilities. Extensive beach, woodland and countryside walks. **directions** Sev miles N of King's Lynn, at Dersingham roundabout, take B1440 int village. Left at lights into Station Road. Barn House 100m on right **open** All year **bedrooms** 1 double, 1 twin **bathrooms** 2 en suite **payment** cash, cheques

Room General Leisure

DOWNHAM MARKET, Norfolk Map ref 3B1   SAT NAV PE38 9EB

Dial House B&B
12 Railway Road, Downham Market, Norfolk PE38 9EB
t 01366 385775 e robert.shrimpton@btopenworld.com
w dialhousbnb.com GUEST REVIEWS

B&B PER ROOM PER NIGHT
S £40.00
D £60.00

Stay at our 18th century listed home where our double en suite rooms feature shuttered windows. **directions** By train - turn left o of Downham Railway station easy 10 minute walk towards town centre, on left hand side opposite The Green. **open** All year **bedrooms** 2 double **bathrooms** 2 en suite **payment** cash, cheques, euros

Room General Leisure

ELSING, Norfolk Map ref 3B1   SAT NAV NR20 3EA

Bartles Lodge
Church Street, Elsing, Dereham, Norfolk NR20 3EA
t (01362) 637177 e bartleslodge@yahoo.co.uk
w bartleslodge.co.uk ONLINE MAP

B&B PER ROOM PER NIGHT
S £50.00 – £67.00
D £62.00 – £67.00

Located in the sleepy village of Elsing. We offer comfortable bed breakfast accommodation in a converted dairy in 11 acres of beautiful grounds of lakes and mature countryside. **directions** Leave A47 at North Tuddenham exit. Follow signs for Elsing. We a next door to Mermaid ph and opposite church. **open** All year **bedrooms** 3 double, 3 twin **bathrooms** 6 en suite **payment** cash cheques

Room Leisure

FAKENHAM, Norfolk Map ref 3B1   SAT NAV NR21 0AW

Abbott Farm B&B
Walsingham Road, Binham, Fakenham NR21 0AW
t (01328) 830519 e abbot.farm@btinternet.com
w abbottfarm.co.uk ONLINE MAP

B&B PER ROOM PER NIGHT
S £26.00 – £30.00
D £52.00 – £60.00

A 190-acre arable farm. Rural views of North Norfolk including the historic Binham Priory. Liz and Alan offer a warm welcome to the guest house. **directions** Please refer to website. **open** All year except Xmas **bedrooms** 1 double, 2 twin **bathrooms** 3 en suite **payment** cash, cheques, euros

Room General Leisure

Official tourist board guide **Bed & Breakf**

East of England | **Norfolk**

GREAT YARMOUTH, Norfolk Map ref 3C1
SAT NAV NR30 1EX

The Chimes
48 Wellesley Road, Great Yarmouth NR30 1EX
t (01493) 844610 **e** veronica.mardle@ntlworld.com
w thechimes.co.uk ONLINE MAP ONLINE BOOKING LAST MINUTE OFFERS

B&B PER ROOM PER NIGHT
S £22.50 – £25.00
D £45.00 – £50.00

Quality Bed and Breakfast in peaceful location, two minutes walk from beach. Non-smoking throughout. Rooms are en-suite, designed for comfort. Private car park. Restaurants, shows, shops and bars close by. **directions** See website. **open** All year **bedrooms** 1 single, 3 double, 1 twin, 2 family **bathrooms** 7 en suite **payment** credit/debit cards, cash, cheques, euros

Room General Leisure

GREAT YARMOUTH, Norfolk Map ref 3C1
SAT NAV NR30 2LD

Merivon Guest House
6 Trafalgar Road, Great Yarmouth NR30 2LD
t (01493) 844419 **e** reception@merivon.co.uk
w merivonguesthouse.co.uk GUEST REVIEWS ONLINE BOOKING

B&B PER ROOM PER NIGHT
S £35.00 – £45.00
D £25.00 – £80.00

If you are visiting Great Yarmouth as a tourist or business you can be assured of a warm welcome and that your stay will be a comfortable and enjoyable one. **directions** Please contact us for directions **open** All year except Xmas and New Year **bedrooms** 1 single, 2 double, 1 twin, 2 family **bathrooms** 6 en suite **payment** credit/debit cards, cash, cheques

Room General

GREAT YARMOUTH, Norfolk Map ref 3C1
SAT NAV NR30 2NF

The Weatherdene
2 St Johns Terrace, Great Yarmouth NR30 2NF
t (01493) 843058 **e** theweatherdene@yahoo.com
w theweatherdene.co.uk ONLINE BOOKING

B&B PER ROOM PER NIGHT
S £22.50 – £24.00
D £45.00 – £48.00

Rooms are bright & airy, some with views over the traditional flint knapped St John's Church. Early or late arrivals catered for, breakfast is served up until 10am. **directions** Please contact us for directions **open** All year **bedrooms** 5 double, 3 twin, 1 family **bathrooms** 9 en suite, 1 with private bathroom **payment** credit/debit cards, cash, cheques

Room General Leisure

HICKLING, Norfolk Map ref 3C1
SAT NAV NR12 0BE

The Dairy Barns
Lound Farm, Hickling Lane, Hickling, Norwich NR12 0BE
t (01692) 598123 **e** enquiries@dairybarns.co.uk
w dairybarns.co.uk ONLINE MAP GUEST REVIEWS LAST MINUTE OFFERS

B&B PER ROOM PER NIGHT
S £50.00
D £60.00 – £70.00
EVENING MEAL PER PERSON
£12.00

Winner of Best Bed and Breakfast in Norfolk Beautiful accommodation in self-contained barns. Fabulous Fantastic and Faultless just one of many visitor comments. Excellent farmhouse cooking. Spacious en suite rooms. **directions** Full directions available from our website. Located on Hickling lane between the villages of Hickling and Sea Palling. **open** All year except Xmas and New Year **bedrooms** 3 double, 3 twin **bathrooms** 6 en suite **payment** credit/debit cards, cash

BREAKFAST AWARD

Room General Leisure

key to symbols see page 6

East of England | **Norfolk**

HOLT, Norfolk Map ref 3B1
SAT NAV NR25 6DY

Holm Oaks
83a Cromer Road, Holt NR25 6DY
t (01263) 711061 e holmoaks@talktalk.net

B&B PER ROOM PER NIGHT
S £50.00
D £70.00

SPECIAL PROMOTIONS
Out of season offers available, please call for details.

Holm Oaks is located a 5 minute walk from Holt centre offering 3 twin / double ground floor en suite rooms and private car parking. Close to the Poppy Line. Private entrance to all rooms. Ideal accomodation for bird watchers.

open All year
bedrooms 1 double, 1 twin, 1 family
bathrooms 3 en suite
payment cash, cheques

directions Please contact us for directions

Room | General | Leisure

HUNSTANTON, Norfolk Map ref 3B1
SAT NAV PE36 5HW

Ellinbrook House
37 Avenue Road, Hunstanton PE36 5HW
t (01485) 532022 e enquiries@ellinbrookhouse.com
w ellinbrookhouse.com ONLINE MAP GUEST REVIEWS

B&B PER ROOM PER NIGHT
S £40.00 – £45.00
D £60.00 – £79.00

Ellinbrook Guest House, situated in Hunstanton, is the perfect base to explore the Norfolk countryside. Close to beach and town centre. Offering B&B, off-street parking and secure bicycle storage.
directions Take A149 from Kings Lynn (approx 17 miles). Ellinbrook House on junction of Sandringham and Avenue Rd. Parking at rear on Sandringham Rd. **open** All year except Xmas and New Year
bedrooms 3 double, 1 twin, 2 family **bathrooms** 6 en suite
payment cash, cheques

Room | General

HUNSTANTON, Norfolk Map ref 3B1
SAT NAV PE36 5LU

The King William IV, Country Inn & Restaurant
Heacham Road, Sedgeford, Hunstanton PE36 5LU
t (01285) 571765 f (01485) 571743 e info@thekingwilliamsedgeford.co.uk
w thekingwilliamsedgeford.co.uk ONLINE MAP GUEST REVIEWS LAST MINUTE OFFERS

B&B PER ROOM PER NIGHT
S £55.00 – £65.00
D £85.00 – £100.00
EVENING MEAL PER PERSON
£9.00 – £19.95

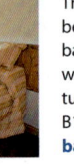

Traditional country inn. Near Peddars Way, RSPB reserves, golf and beaches. Luxury accommodation, excellent menus, 3 restaurants, bar (free house), garden and alfresco dining area. Delightful escape whatever the season. **directions** Follow the A149 to Hunstanton, turn right at Norfolk Lavender onto the B1454 into village. Follow B1454 from Fakenham/Docking. **open** All year **bedrooms** 9 double **bathrooms** 9 en suite **payment** credit/debit cards, cash, cheques

BREAKFAST AWARD   Room | General | Leisure

348 Official tourist board guide Bed & Breakfast

East of England | **Norfolk**

KING'S LYNN, Norfolk Map ref 3B1
SAT NAV PE31 6DJ

The Coppice
Fakenham Road, Hillington, King's Lynn PE31 6DJ
t (01485) 600413 **e** info@thecoppicehillington.co.uk
w thecoppicehillington.co.uk ONLINE MAP

B&B PER ROOM PER NIGHT
S £35.00
D £55.00

Situated about seven miles from King's Lynn, three from Sandringham and within 30 minutes of the North Norfolk coast, The Coppice is ideally placed for walkers, tourists and bird-watchers alike. **directions** Continue through the village, into the 50-mile zone, look for our green sign on the right, just after the B1153 on the left to Flitcham. **open** Open all year except December and January **bedrooms** 1 double, 1 twin **bathrooms** 1 en suite, 1 with private bathroom **payment** cash, cheques

Room General

LONG STRATTON, Norfolk Map ref 3B1
SAT NAV NR15 2RR

Greenacres Farmhouse
Wood Green, Long Stratton, Norwich NR15 2RR
t (01508) 530261 **f** (01508) 530261 **e** greenacresfarm@tinyworld.co.uk

B&B PER ROOM PER NIGHT
S £40.00 – £47.00
D £60.00 – £75.00

SPECIAL PROMOTIONS
Reduced rates for two or more nights.

17thC farmhouse on 30-acre common with ponds and wildlife (ten miles south of Norwich). Bedrooms tastefully furnished. Tea/coffee facilities, TV. Beams and inglenooks create a relaxing atmosphere. Jo can offer therapeutic massage/reflexology and Pilates sessions to guests. Come and enjoy the peace and tranquillity of our home.

open All year
bedrooms 2 double, 1 twin
bathrooms 2 en suite, 1 with private bathroom
payment cash, cheques

directions A140 Norwich to Long Stratton. Left at Hall Lane. 1.5 miles. Right to Bush Green (after Mayfield Farm). First right. First property on right.

Room
General
Leisure

NORWICH, Norfolk Map ref 3C1
SAT NAV NR1 1SL

3 Chalk Hill Road B&B
3 Chalk Hill Road, Norwich NR1 1SL
t (01603) 619188 **e** moira@beauvillage.com
w beauvillage.com/b&b.html ONLINE MAP LAST MINUTE OFFERS

B&B PER ROOM PER NIGHT
S £25.00 – £35.00
D £45.00 – £55.00

Receive a warm and friendly welcome in this comfortable home-from-home B&B. Good facilities in all the rooms with most being en-suite. A substantial continental breakfast is included in the price. **directions** Two minutes from the Station and bus links, 5 minutes from the Riverside restaurants and bars. Just 10 minutes to city centre, castle and cathedral. **bedrooms** 1 single, 1 double, 1 twin, 1 family **bathrooms** 2 en suite, 2 with private bathroom **payment** cash, euros

Room General Leisure

key to symbols see page 6 349

East of England | **Norfolk**

NORWICH, Norfolk Map ref 3C1
SAT NAV NR10 3A

Becklands
105 Holt Road, Horsford, Norwich NR10 3AB
t (01603) 898582 f (01603) 755010 e becklands@aol.com
w becklands.com

B&B PER ROOM PER NIGHT
S £35.00 – £45.00
D £55.00 – £65.00

Quietly located modern house overlooking open countryside five miles north of Norwich. Central for the Broads and coastal areas. **directions** Follow directions to Norwich Airport - follow signs to A140 roundabout - follow signs to B1449 to Horsford. **open** All y **bedrooms** 2 single, 3 double, 2 twin, 1 family **bathrooms** 8 en suite **payment** credit/debit cards, cash, cheques

Room ... General ... Leisure ...

NORWICH, Norfolk Map ref 3C1
SAT NAV NR6 7H

Catton Old Hall
Lodge Lane, Old Catton, Norwich, Norfolk NR6 7HG
t (01603) 419379 f (01603) 400339 e enquiries@catton-hall.co.uk
w **catton-hall.co.uk** ONLINE MAP GUEST REVIEWS ONLINE BOOKING LAST MINUTE OFFERS

B&B PER ROOM PER NIGHT
S £75.00 – £95.00
D £75.00 – £150.00

Charming, quirky historic 17th century house nr Norwich. Spaciou comfortable rooms, good local food, friendly relaxed atmosphere. Perfect for city breaks or Norfolk touring base. Free parking. Wor seeking out. **directions** From ring road A140, take Spixworth Roa to left and at traffic lights, left into Lodge Lane and Catton Old H is on right. **open** All year **bedrooms** 7 double **bathrooms** 7 en suite **payment** credit/debit cards, cash

Room ... General ... Leisure ...

NORWICH, Norfolk Map ref 3C1
SAT NAV NR2 3D

Edmar Lodge
64 Earlham Road, Norwich NR2 3DF
t (01603) 615599 f (01603) 495599 e mail@edmarlodge.co.uk
w **edmarlodge.co.uk** ONLINE MAP GUEST REVIEWS

B&B PER ROOM PER NIGHT
S £38.00 – £43.00
D £45.00 – £50.00

Edmar Lodge is a family-run guest house whe you will receive a warm welcome from Ray an Sue. We are situated only 10 minutes walk fro the city centre. All rooms have en suite faciliti We are well known for our excellent breakfast that set you up for the day.

open All year
bedrooms 3 double, 1 twin, 1 family
bathrooms 5 en suite
payment credit/debit cards, cash, cheques

directions On the B1108. Off the Norwich rin road.

BREAKFAST AWARD

Room ...
General ...

East of England | **Norfolk**

NORWICH, Norfolk Map ref 3C1
SAT NAV NR13 4DE

Hall Paddock
Hall Road, Blofield Heath, Norwich, Norfolk NR13 4DE
t 01603 211854 e stay@hallpaddock.com
w hallpaddock.com ONLINE MAP GUEST REVIEWS ONLINE BOOKING LAST MINUTE OFFERS

B&B PER ROOM PER NIGHT
S £45.00 – £70.00
D £60.00 – £90.00

Hall Paddock provides a tranquil setting to unwind and relax. Ideally located for the Norfolk Broads, coast and Norwich. 3 twin/double spacious ground floor rooms. **directions** On A47 east of Norwich take 'Blofield Heath' exit, turn right into Shack Lane, third left into Hall Road, Hall Paddock is 1/2 mile. **open** Open all year but for room only at Christmas and new year **bedrooms** 2 double, 1 twin **bathrooms** 2 en suite, 1 with private bathroom **payment** credit/debit cards, cash, cheques, euros

NORWICH, Norfolk Map ref 3C1
SAT NAV NR13 6NN

Manor Barn House
7 Back Lane, Rackheath, Norwich NR13 6NN
t (01603) 783543 e jane.roger@manorbarnhouse.co.uk
w manorbarnhouse.co.uk ONLINE MAP LAST MINUTE OFFERS

B&B PER ROOM PER NIGHT
S £28.00 – £35.00
D £58.00 – £62.00

Norfolk barn conversion in quiet rural setting, 5 miles north-east of the historic cathedral city of Norwich. Locally produced and home-cooked foods. Very convenient for Broads and coast. Ample parking. **directions** Please visit our website for full directions on how to find us. **open** All year **bedrooms** 3 double, 2 twin **bathrooms** 4 en suite, 1 with private bathroom **payment** cash, cheques, euros

NORWICH, Norfolk Map ref 3C1
SAT NAV NR10 5NP

Marsham Arms Inn
Holt Road, Hevingham, Norwich NR10 5NP
t (01603) 754268 f (01603) 754839 e nigelbradley@marshamarms.co.uk
w marshamarms.co.uk ONLINE MAP LAST MINUTE OFFERS

B&B PER ROOM PER NIGHT
S £55.00 – £70.00
D £60.00 – £100.00

EVENING MEAL PER PERSON
£10.00 – £25.00

SPECIAL PROMOTIONS
See website for our special room deals. Enjoy our monthly jazz evenings or attend our informal wine tastings.

Country inn on B1149 north of Horsford. Extensive menu using fresh local produce. Real ales, comprehensive wine list. Restaurant and function room for weddings, private parties and training courses. Heated patio area, breeze house and large garden to enjoy. 4 miles from Norwich International Airport. 20 minutes to coast, Norfolk Broads or city of Norwich.

open All year
bedrooms 4 double, 4 twin, 3 family
bathrooms 11 en suite
payment credit/debit cards, cash, cheques

directions 2 miles north of Horsford on B1149. 4 miles from Norwich International Airport.

East of England | Norfolk

NORWICH, Norfolk Map ref 3C1
SAT NAV NR3 1B

number 17
17 Colegate, Norwich NR3 1BN
t (01603) 764386   e enquiries@number17norwich.co.uk
w **number17norwich.co.uk** GUEST REVIEWS ONLINE BOOKING

B&B PER ROOM PER NIGHT
S £49.00
D £75.00

This contemporary styled, family run bed and breakfast is close to Norwich city centre making it an ideal location whether your stay for business or pleasure. **directions** number 17 is located about a 15 minute walk from both Norwich railway station or the bus station and about 10 miles from Norwich airport. **open** All year except Xmas and New Year **bedrooms** 1 single, 2 double, 3 twin family **bathrooms** 8 en suite **payment** credit/debit cards, cash

PENTNEY, Norfolk Map ref 3B1
SAT NAV PE32 1J

Little Abbey Farm
Low Road, Pentney, King's Lynn PE32 1JF
t (01760) 337348   e enquiries@littleabbeyfarm.co.uk
w **littleabbeyfarm.co.uk**

B&B PER ROOM PER NIGHT
S £40.00 – £45.00
D £60.00 – £70.00
EVENING MEAL PER PERSON
£10.00 – £18.00

Farmhouse, ensuite bed and breakfast on family run working farm, all meats eggs, produced on the farm. lounge for guests use, with wood burning stove. **directions** Please contact us for directions **open** All year **bedrooms** 3 double, 1 twin **bathrooms** 4 en suite **payment** credit/debit cards, cash, cheques

SHERINGHAM, Norfolk Map ref 3B1
SAT NAV NR26 8D

Alverstone B&B
33 The Avenue, Sheringham NR26 8DG
t (01263) 825527 / 07766151903
w **alverstone-sheringham.co.uk**

B&B PER ROOM PER NIGHT
D £27.50 – £32.00

Family run bed and breakfast. Comfortable and modern, tasteful decorated en-suite rooms. Close to town and beach. Central Heating, lovely breakfast! (no pets, non smoking) **directions** At roundabout into Sheringham. Turn right to Cromer for 1/4 mile. left turn down Beeston road. Under bridge. The Avenue is second on right. **open** All year except Xmas and New Year **bedrooms** 3 double **bathrooms** 2 en suite, 1 with private bathroom **payment** cash, cheques

SHERINGHAM, Norfolk Map ref 3B1
SAT NAV NR26 8L

Cleat House
7 Montague Road, Sheringham NR26 8LN
t (01263) 822765   e stay@cleathouse.co.uk
w **cleathouse.co.uk** ONLINE MAP GUEST REVIEWS

B&B PER ROOM PER NIGHT
S £75.00 – £110.00
D £85.00 – £125.00

We offer quality luxury accommodation in a relaxed friendly Edwardian home. Situated quiet town centre, 5 minutes walk to coast, shops, pubs and restaurants. Sitting room with internet and freeview. **directions** A148 to Sheringham. In Sheringham turn left on A149. first right to town, first left at church. turn left into No. st. and Montague rd. **open** All year except Xmas and New Year **bedrooms** 3 double **bathrooms** 2 en suite, 1 with private bathroom **payment** credit/debit cards, cash

352

Official tourist board guide Bed & Breakfast

East of England | Norfolk

SNETTISHAM, Norfolk Map ref 3B1
SAT NAV PE31 7LW

The Queen Victoria
19 Lynn Road, Snettisham, King's Lynn PE31 7LW
t (01485) 541344 **e** bobwarburton@talk21.com
w queenvictoriasnettisham.co.uk ONLINE MAP GUEST REVIEWS ONLINE BOOKING

INN

B&B PER ROOM PER NIGHT
S £50.00
D £75.00

EVENING MEAL PER PERSON
£7.50 – £15.00

The Queen Victoria is a traditional pub situated in the pretty village of Snettisham. It is the perfect place to enjoy superb home cooked food in an idyllic location. **directions** Please contact us for directions **open** All year **bedrooms** 2 double, 1 twin, 2 family **bathrooms** 5 en suite **payment** credit/debit cards, cash, cheques

Room General Leisure

SOUTH CREAKE, Norfolk Map ref 3B1
SAT NAV NR21 9PG

Valentine Studio
62 Back Street, South Creake, Walsingham NR21 9PG
t (01328) 823413 **e** ros@valentinehouse.fsnet.co.uk
w valentinehouse.co.uk LAST MINUTE OFFERS

GUEST ACCOMMODATION

B&B PER ROOM PER NIGHT
S £65.00 – £80.00
D £60.00 – £80.00

Charming 18thC former inn set in attractive, cottage-style garden. Ideal for families with connecting bedrooms, travel cot, high chair, fridge, microwave and black-out blinds. **directions** From Fakenham, B1355 Burnham Market. At South Creake, left past village green. Studio entrance will be found on left-hand side past the old brewery building. **open** All year except Xmas **bedrooms** 1 suite **bathrooms** 1 en suite **payment** cash, cheques

Room General

SOUTH WALSHAM, Norfolk Map ref 3C1
SAT NAV NR13 6DS

Old Hall Farm
3 Newport Road, South Walsham, Norwich, Norfolk NR13 6DS
t (01603) 270271 **f** (01603) 270017 **e** veronica@oldhallfarm.co.uk
w oldhallfarm.co.uk ONLINE MAP ONLINE BOOKING

GUEST ACCOMMODATION / Silver AWARD

B&B PER ROOM PER NIGHT
S £35.00 – £40.00
D £55.00 – £60.00

17thC thatched farmhouse with large garden on edge of Broadland village. Within walking distance of Fairhaven Watergardens. Wide choice of cooked breakfasts. Packed lunches, Afternoon teas and simple suppers available. **directions** Two miles from A47, turning signposted South Walsham. Turn right and then immediately right again. **open** April to October **bedrooms** 2 double, 1 twin **bathrooms** 3 en suite **payment** cash, cheques

Room General Leisure

STRATTON STRAWLESS, Norfolk Map ref 3B1
SAT NAV

Woodmans Farm
Cromer Road, Stratton Strawless, Norwich NR10 5LU
t (01603) 754658 **e** janice@woodmansfarm.com
w woodmansfarm.com

BED & BREAKFAST / Silver AWARD

B&B PER ROOM PER NIGHT
S £40.00 – £45.00
D £60.00

In 12 acres of grounds, this delightful farmhouse offers a warm welcome, comfortable B&B and peace from the outside world. Our indoor heated pool is a plus during the summer. **directions** A140 toward Cromer. Pass Stratton Strawless Hall - 200 metres beyond the junction with Parish/Shorthorn Road, turn right into the woods (signed Woodmans Farm). **bedrooms** 1 double, 2 twin **bathrooms** 3 en suite **payment** cash, cheques

key to symbols see page 6   353

East of England | **Norfolk**

SWANTON MORLEY, Norfolk Map ref 3B1

SAT NAV NR20 4JT

Carricks at Castle Farm

Castle Farm, Elsing Road, Swanton Morley, Dereham NR20 4JT
t (01362) 638302 **f** 01362 637227 **e** jean@castlefarm-swanton.co.uk
w carricksatcastlefarm.co.uk ONLINE MAP GUEST REVIEWS

B&B PER ROOM PER NIGHT
S £55.00
D £85.00

EVENING MEAL PER PERSON
£20.00

SPECIAL PROMOTIONS
Special promotions per request. Evenings meals are served by arrangement.

Carricks at Castle Farm is the family home of the Carrick family and is a large Victorian farmhouse surrounded by beautiful gardens on the banks of the River Wensum where the peace and quiet is only interrupted by the bird song.

open All year
bedrooms 2 double, 1 twin
bathrooms 2 en suite, 1 with private bathroom
payment credit/debit cards, cash, cheques, euros

directions A47 Dereham, B1147 Swanton Morley (don't go into Dereham). In Swanton Morley right at Darby's pub into Elsing Road. 0.5 miles left into Farm Drive.

BREAKFAST AWARD

Room
General
Leisure

THETFORD, Norfolk Map ref 3B2

SAT NAV IP26 5HU

Colveston Manor

Mundford, Thetford, Norfolk IP26 5HU
t (01842) 878218 **e** mail@colveston-manor.co.uk
w colveston-manor.co.uk ONLINE MAP GUEST REVIEWS LAST MINUTE OFFERS

B&B PER ROOM PER NIGHT
S £35.00 – £37.50
D £60.00 – £75.00

EVENING MEAL PER PERSON
£20.00

Colveston Manor set in the heart of Breckland birdwatcher's paradise, quiet and peaceful. Delicious Norfolk breakfasts. National Trust properties, cathedrals, gardens and coast within easy reach true countryside experience **directions** Please refer to website or phone. Sat navs do not know where we live and take you into the forest! **open** All year except Xmas and New Year **bedrooms** 1 single, 2 double, 1 twin **bathrooms** 1 en suite, 2 with private bathroom **payment** cash, cheques, euros

BREAKFAST AWARD

Room General Leisure

Where is my pet welcome?

Some properties welcome well-behaved pets. Look for the 🐕 in the accommodation listings.

You can also buy a copy of our popular guide 'Pets Come Too!' Now available in good bookshops and online at **visitbritainshop.com**

£9.99

354

Official tourist board guide **Bed & Breakfast**

East of England | **Norfolk**

THOMPSON, Norfolk Map ref 3B1
SAT NAV IP24 1PX

Chequers Inn
Griston Road, Thompson IP24 1PX
t (01953) 483360 f (01953) 488092 e richard@thompsonchequers.co.uk
w thompsonchequers.co.uk ONLINE MAP GUEST REVIEWS LAST MINUTE OFFERS

B&B PER ROOM PER NIGHT
S £45.00
D £65.00

EVENING MEAL PER PERSON
£6.00 – £25.00

SPECIAL PROMOTIONS
Special promotions upon request.

The Chequers is a 16thC village inn with a thatched roof, still retaining all of its original character. A true country retreat, in the heart of Breckland. Local produce, fresh fish a speciality. Local real ales include Breckland Gold, Wolf, Wherry, Adnams and Greene King IPA to name a few.

open All year
bedrooms 2 double, 1 twin
bathrooms 3 en suite
payment credit/debit cards, cash, cheques

directions Twelve miles north east of Thetford, just off the A1075. Snetterton Race Track just a short drive away.

Room
General
Leisure

WALSINGHAM, Norfolk Map ref 3B1
SAT NAV NR22 6DA

St Felix
2A Knight Street, Walsingham NR22 6DA
t (01328) 820117 e th@paston.co.uk
w 3B1

B&B PER ROOM PER NIGHT
S £35.00 – £65.00
D £45.00 – £75.00

St Felix is a newly refurbished period cottage in the much sought after village of Little Walsingham, renowned as the home of the Shrine of Our Lady of Walsingham. The cottage is situated adjacent to the Shrine, but also just five miles from the sea at Wells.

open All year except Xmas
bedrooms 1 double, 1 twin
bathrooms 2 en suite
payment cash, cheques

directions Please contact us for directions

General   Leisure

key to symbols see page 6

355

East of England | **Norfolk**

WELLS-NEXT-THE-SEA, Norfolk Map ref 3B1   SAT NAV NR23 1DB

Arch House Bed + Breakfast
Arch House, 50 Mill Road, Wells-next-the-Sea NR23 1DB
t (01328) 710112 e enquiries@archhouse.co.uk
w archhouse.co.uk ONLINE MAP GUEST REVIEWS

B&B PER ROOM PER NIGHT
S £50.00 – £75.00
D £65.00 – £110.00

Arch House is a distinguished Grade II Listed B&B, just a short wal from the quay and town centre. Rooms on ground and first floors garden rooms with sun deck. **directions** Please contact us for directions **open** All year **bedrooms** 9 double, 1 twin **bathrooms** en suite, 1 with private bathroom **payment** credit/debit cards, cas

Room General Leisure

WIGHTON, Norfolk Map ref 3B1   SAT NAV NR23 1PF

Meadow View Guest House
53 High Street, Wighton, Wells-next-the-Sea, Norfolk NR23 1PF
t (01328) 821527 f (01328) 821527 e booking@meadow-view.net
w meadow-view.net ONLINE MAP ONLINE BOOKING

B&B PER ROOM PER NIGHT
D £40.00

Guest house just 3 miles from the coast, 1 double, 1 Twin, 3 Suites all with seating area, Bath robes, slippers. Flat screen TV and iPod docking Stations. Breakfast in or out side, Hot Tub in the Garden. Beautiful house.

open All year
bedrooms 1 double, 1 twin, 3 suites
bathrooms 5 en suite

directions From B1105 Wighton is situated jus off the B1105, accessible from the A149 coast road.

BREAKFAST AWARD

Room
General
Leisure

WROXHAM, Norfolk Map ref 3C1   SAT NAV NR12 8SA

Wroxham Park Lodge Guest House
142 Norwich Road, Wroxham NR12 8SA
t (01603) 782991 e parklodge@computer-assist.net
w wroxhamparklodge.com ONLINE MAP LAST MINUTE OFFERS

B&B PER ROOM PER NIGHT
S £42.00 – £46.00
D £62.00 – £66.00

Warm welcome in comfortable Victorian house. Tastefully furnishe ensuite rooms all with TV and tea/coffee . Hearty freshly cooked breakfast, large garden, patio and car park. Situated in Norfolk Broads. **directions** Situated on A1151 8 miles north of Norwich **open** All year **bedrooms** 2 double, 1 twin **bathrooms** 3 en suite **payment** cash, cheques

Room General P Leisure

East of England | **Norfolk/Suffolk**

WYMONDHAM, Norfolk Map ref 3B1

SAT NAV NR18 9QH

B&B PER ROOM PER NIGHT
D £56.00 – £60.00

EVENING MEAL PER PERSON
£15.00 – £18.00

Witch Hazel

55 Church Lane, Wicklewood, Wymondham, Norfolk NR18 9QH
t (01953) 602347 e witchhazel@tiscali.co.uk
w witchhazel-norfolk.co.uk GUEST REVIEWS

Witch Hazel is set with views over open countryside and our en-suite bedrooms are well equipped with your comfort our priority. Wicklewood is an ideal touring base. **directions** Please contact us for directions **open** All year **bedrooms** 2 double, 1 twin **bathrooms** 3 en suite **payment** credit/debit cards, cash, cheques

BREAKFAST AWARD

BAWDSEY, Suffolk Map ref 3C2

SAT NAV IP12 3AZ

B&B PER ROOM PER NIGHT
S £95.00
D £95.00

EVENING MEAL PER PERSON
£15.00 – £25.00

Bawdsey Manor

Bawdsey Manor, Bawdsey, Nr Woodbridge, Suffolk IP12 3AZ
t (01394) 412396 e info@bawdseymanor.co.uk
w bawdseymanor.co.uk ONLINE MAP

Bawdsey Manor, the home of RADAR, offers guest accommodation with breathtaking views of the sea and River Deben. Set in 120 acres of historic parkland, ideal for birdwatching, sailing, cycling and walking. The Manor has an alcohol licence and serves food to pre-booked groups using seasonal Suffolk produce.

open All year
bedrooms 2 double
bathrooms 2 en suite
payment credit/debit cards, cash, cheques, euros

directions Do not rely on Sat Nav but take the B1083 from Melton, north of Woodbridge, and drive through Bawdsey village to our entrance on Bawdsey-Quay.

BECCLES, Suffolk Map ref 3C1

SAT NAV NR34 7DQ

B&B PER ROOM PER NIGHT
S £50.00 – £45.00
D £60.00 – £55.00

Pinetrees

Park Drive, Beccles, Suffolk NR34 7DQ
t (01502) 470796 e info@pinetrees.net
w pinetrees.net ONLINE MAP GUEST REVIEWS

Pinetrees is a B&B with a difference—eco-friendly, contemporary attractive wooden house set in 6.25 acres of the peaceful Waveney Valley—an oasis of tranquility in a hectic world! **directions** On the Beccles / Worlingham border just 10 miles off the coast in the lovely Waveney Valley, East Anglia **open** All year **bedrooms** 3 double **bathrooms** 3 en suite **payment** cash, cheques

BREAKFAST AWARD

key to symbols see page 6

357

East of England | **Suffolk**

BURY ST EDMUNDS, Suffolk Map ref 3B2
SAT NAV IP33 1SZ

St Edmunds Guesthouse
35 St Andrews Street North, Bury St Edmunds IP33 1SZ
t (01284) 700144 **e** info@stedmundsguesthouse.net
w stedmundsguesthouse.net ONLINE MAP GUEST REVIEWS ONLINE BOOKING

B&B PER ROOM PER NIGHT
S £40.00 – £45.00
D £65.00

St Edmunds Guest house offers 9 fully equipped luxury rooms furnished to the highest of standards, with oak furniture and pow showers amongst some of the many features. Keyless Entry
directions Please contact us for directions **open** All year **bedroom** 1 single, 3 double, 5 twin **bathrooms** 9 en suite **payment** credit/debit cards, cash, cheques

BURY ST EDMUNDS (6 MILES), Suffolk Map ref 3B2
SAT NAV IP30 0HE

The Old Manse Barn
Chapel Road, Cockfield, Bury St Edmunds IP30 0HE
t (01284) 828120 **e** bookings@theoldmansebarn.co.uk
w theoldmansebarn.co.uk ONLINE MAP GUEST REVIEWS

B&B PER ROOM PER NIGHT
S £70.00 – £80.00
D £70.00 – £80.00

Secluded self contained barn loft apartment modern contemporar approach. Private luxury retreat, extensive views. Own entrance, drive. Openplan kitchen/dining/lounge area. Great choice continental breakfast in apartment. Walkers & cyclists welcome
directions A134 Bury St. Edmunds to Sudbury. 5 miles left A1141 to Lavenham. 1.4 miles turn left Cockfield/Stowmarket. 1.2 miles The Old Manse Barn on right **open** All year **bedrooms** 1 suite
bathrooms 1 en suite **payment** cash, cheques

CREETING ST MARY, Suffolk Map ref 3B2
SAT NAV IP6 8PR

Creeting House
All Saints Road, Creeting Saint Mary, Ipswich, Suffolk IP6 8PR
t (01449) 720988 **f** (01449) 726067 **e** diana@creetinghouse.com
w creetinghouse.com ONLINE MAP GUEST REVIEWS LAST MINUTE OFFERS

B&B PER ROOM PER NIGHT
S £45.00 – £65.00
D £70.00 – £90.00
EVENING MEAL PER PERSON
£15.00 – £25.00

Former rectory set in 9 acres convenient for A14. Relaxed country house hospitality with modern facilities, fully licensed, flexible accommodation. Weddings, conferences and celebrations catered.
directions Turn off A14 at junction 51 towards Needham Market. Take the second right into Flordon Road, turn right into All Saints Road. Opposite the Church. **open** All year **bedrooms** 1 single, 2 double, 1 twin, 1 family, 1 suite **bathrooms** 4 en suite, 2 with private bathroom **payment** credit/debit cards, cash, cheques, euro

ELMSWELL, Suffolk Map ref 3B2
SAT NAV IP30 9QR

Kiln Farm Guest House
Kiln Lane, Elmswell, Bury St Edmunds IP30 9QR
t (01359) 240442 **e** davejankilnfarm@btinternet.com

B&B PER ROOM PER NIGHT
S £40.00 – £50.00
D £80.00 – £100.00
EVENING MEAL PER PERSON
£12.50

Welcoming Victorian farmhouse with courtyard of converted barns set in secluded location just off A14. Licensed bar with conservato for breakfasts and pre-booked evening meals. Ideally placed for exploring Suffolk. **directions** A14 jct47. Travelling east Kiln Lane is right off exit slip road. From west, turn right over to roundabout, third exit. 50yds on left. **open** All year **bedrooms** 4 double, 2 twin 2 family **bathrooms** 8 en suite, 4 with private bathroom **payment** credit/debit cards, cash, cheques, euros

BREAKFAST AWARD

East of England | **Suffolk**

FRAMLINGHAM, Suffolk Map ref 3C2
SAT NAV IP13 9NU

★★★★ BED & BREAKFAST (enjoyEngland.com)

B&B PER ROOM PER NIGHT
S £35.00 – £50.00
D £70.00 – £80.00

Boundary Farm
off Saxmundham Road, Framlingham, Woodbridge IP13 9NU
t (01728) 723401 **e** info@boundaryfarm.biz
w boundaryfarm.biz ONLINE MAP GUEST REVIEWS

A traditional 17thC Suffolk farmhouse located in open countryside with magnificent views of farmland in all directions. Extremely quiet & peaceful and the perfect retreat for a short break. **directions** From Framlingham on the B1119 towards Saxmundham. 1.5 miles turn left at crossroads signposted Cransford & Badingham. We are situated past first bend on left. **open** All year **bedrooms** 3 double, 1 twin **bathrooms** 2 en suite, 1 with private bathroom **payment** cash, cheques

Room General

FRAMLINGHAM, Suffolk Map ref 3C2
SAT NAV IP13 9PD

★★★★ FARMHOUSE (enjoyEngland.com)

B&B PER ROOM PER NIGHT
S £46.00 – £60.00
D £60.00 – £95.00

High House Farm
Cransford, Woodbridge, Suffolk IP13 9PD
t (01728) 663461 **e** info@highhousefarm.co.uk
w highhousefarm.co.uk ONLINE MAP LAST MINUTE OFFERS

A warm welcome awaits you in our beautifully restored 15thC farmhouse, featuring exposed beams, inglenook fireplaces and attractive gardens. Situated midway between Framlingham and Saxmundham. **directions** Please refer to website address. **open** All year **bedrooms** 1 double, 1 family **bathrooms** 1 en suite, 1 with private bathroom **payment** cash, cheques

Room General Leisure

FRAMLINGHAM (7 MILES), Suffolk Map ref 3C2
SAT NAV IP14 6HG

★★★★★ BED & BREAKFAST (enjoyEngland.com) **Gold AWARD**

B&B PER ROOM PER NIGHT
S £70.00 – £85.00
D £80.00 – £100.00

EVENING MEAL PER PERSON
£20.00 – £30.00

Flindor Cottage
The Street, Framsden, Near Stowmarket, Suffolk IP14 6HG
t 01473 890058 **e** tanya@flindor.com
w flindorcottage.co.uk ONLINE MAP

C17th cottage in quiet village setting. Totally private accommodation in adjoining barn. A wealth of beams and antique furniture help provide warmth and character in the very spacious suite. Situated just off A1120 tourist route so numerous and varied attractions nearby. Licensed. Superb wine list.

open All year except Xmas and New Year
bedrooms 1 suite
bathrooms 1 en suite
payment cash, cheques

directions Situated in The Street, just off the B1077 Ipswich Road, less than 1 mile from A1120 Tourist Route.

Room General Leisure

East of England | **Suffolk**

FRISTON, Suffolk Map ref 3C2
SAT NAV IP17 1NP

B&B PER ROOM PER NIGHT
S £60.00
D £68.00 – £70.00

Old School
Aldeburgh Road, Friston, Nr. Saxmundham IP17 1NP
t (01728) 688173 e fristonoldschool@btinternet.com
w fristonoldschool.co.uk ONLINE MAP GUEST REVIEWS

The house is a converted former victorian village school offering comfortable en suite accommodation. It is situated in a peaceful location, three miles from Aldeburgh. Large garden with countryside views. **directions** A12 - A1094 to Aldeburgh SECOND left off A1094 to Friston signposted The Old school with brown tourist sign. Entrance gate is on left -1/4mile. **open** All year except Xmas **bedrooms** 1 double, 2 twin **bathrooms** 3 en suite **payment** cash, cheques

Room General Leisure

HINTLESHAM, Suffolk Map ref 3B2
SAT NAV IP8 3NT

B&B PER ROOM PER NIGHT
S £40.00 – £45.00
D £62.00 – £72.00

College Farm Bed & Breakfast
College Farm, Hintlesham, Ipswich, Suffolk IP8 3NT
t 01473 652253 f (01473) 652253 e bandb@collegefarm.plus.com
w collegefarm.net ONLINE MAP

Peaceful 500-year-old beamed house on an arable farm west of Ipswich (6 miles). Well-appointed comfortable rooms. Good food locally. Convenient for Constable Country, Sutton Hoo (NT) and the coast. **directions** From Ipswich take A1071 towards Hadleigh. Go through Hintlesham, the farm is half a mile on towards Hadleigh. On left on z-bend, well signposted. **open** All year except Xmas and New Year **bedrooms** 2 double, 1 twin **bathrooms** 2 en suite, 1 with private bathroom **payment** cash, cheques

Room General 12 Leisure

HONINGTON, Suffolk Map ref 3B2
SAT NAV IP31 1RE

B&B PER ROOM PER NIGHT
S £25.00
D £50.00

North View Guest House
Malting Road, Honington, Bury St Edmunds, Suffolk IP31 1RE
t (01359) 269423 f (01359) 269423

North View Guest House is situated in the village of Honington opposite the church. Close to Thetford and Bury St Edmunds stations. Hearty English breakfast. **directions** A14 to Bury St Edmunds. Head for A1088, Honington village. **open** All year **bedrooms** 1 single, 1 double, 1 family **payment** cash, cheques

Room General Leisure

IPSWICH, Suffolk Map ref 3B2
SAT NAV IP4 4EP

B&B PER ROOM PER NIGHT
S £49.00 – £59.00
D £69.00

Lattice Lodge Guest House
499 Woodbridge Road, Ipswich IP4 4EP
t (01473) 712474 f 0871 528 9751 e info@latticelodge.co.uk
w latticelodge.co.uk GUEST REVIEWS ONLINE BOOKING LAST MINUTE OFFERS

Lattice Lodge is a large Edwardian Property built in 1908 as a doctors surgery and residence, and has been completely renovated throughout and extended in keeping with the original style. **directions** We are located on the Eastern side of Ipswich, and are superbly situated as a base for exploring Suffolk, by car or public transport. **open** All year **bedrooms** 2 single, 4 double, 4 twin, 1 family **bathrooms** 11 en suite **payment** credit/debit cards, cash, cheques

Room General Leisure

360 Official tourist board guide Bed & Breakfa

East of England | **Suffolk**

KETTLEBURGH, Suffolk Map ref 3C2
SAT NAV IP13 7LF

Church Farm
Church Road, Kettleburgh, Woodbridge IP13 7LF
t (01728) 723532 e jbater@suffolkonline.net
w **churchfarmkettleburgh.co.uk** ONLINE BOOKING

B&B PER ROOM PER NIGHT
S £30.00 – £35.00
D £60.00 – £70.00

EVENING MEAL PER PERSON
£17.00

Oak-beamed, 400-year-old farmhouse on a working farm. Bedrooms with lovely views and every comfort. Excellent food from home-grown produce. **directions** A12 North to Wickham Market, Easton, Kettleburgh A14, A1120 to Earl Soham, Brandeston, Kettleburgh **open** All year **bedrooms** 2 double, 2 twin **bathrooms** 2 en suite, 2 with private bathroom **payment** cash, cheques

Room   General   Leisure

LAVENHAM, Suffolk Map ref 3B2
SAT NAV CO10 9PG

Brett Farm
The Common, Lavenham, Sudbury CO10 9PG
t (01787) 248533 e brettfarmbandb@aol.com
w **brettfarm.com**

B&B PER ROOM PER NIGHT
S £45.00 – £65.00
D £70.00

Riverside bungalow set in rural surroundings within walking distance of Lavenham high street. Comfortable bedrooms, with either en suite or private bathroom. Stabling available. **directions** Please contact us for directions **open** All year **bedrooms** 1 double, 1 twin, 1 family **bathrooms** 2 en suite, 1 with private bathroom **payment** cash, cheques

Room   General   Leisure

LAVENHAM, Suffolk Map ref 3B2
SAT NAV CO10 9SA

Lavenham Old Rectory
Church Street, Lavenham, Suffolk CO10 9SA
t (01787) 247572 e info@lavenhamoldrectory.co.uk
w **lavenham-old-rectory.com** ONLINE MAP GUEST REVIEWS LAST MINUTE OFFERS

B&B PER ROOM PER NIGHT
S £130.00 – £150.00
D £155.00 – £190.00

EVENING MEAL PER PERSON
£15.00 – £50.00

SPECIAL PROMOTIONS
Enjoy our romantic week end break; champagne breakfast, afternoon tea and dinner at one of our partner restaurants

The Lavenham Old Rectory is a stunning boutique residence offering 5-star quality accomodation in its three expansive and award winning rooms. All rooms are en-suite and offer luxurious linens, robes, slippers, plasma TV, DVD, tea and coffee, newspapers and those little touches that make such a difference.

open All year except Xmas
bedrooms 2 double, 1 twin
bathrooms 3 en suite
payment credit/debit cards, cash

directions Lavenham can be accessed from either the M11 from junction 8A or the A12 at Colchester. Head for Sudbury and Lavenham is well signposted

Room   General   Leisure

or **key to symbols** see page 6

361

East of England | **Suffolk**

LONG MELFORD, Suffolk Map ref 3B2
SAT NAV CO10 9BD

High Street Farmhouse
High Street, Long Melford, Sudbury CO10 9BD
t (01787) 375765   e mail@gallopingchef.co.uk
w highstreetfarmhouse.co.uk

B&B PER ROOM PER NIGHT
S £30.00 – £60.00
D £50.00 – £70.00

EVENING MEAL PER PERSON
£7.00 – £15.00

Be assured of the friendliest of welcomes, the cosiest of rooms, the tastiest of breakfasts, the charm of an historic English village in the beautiful county of Suffolk. **directions** The farmhouse is the last house on the right in the High Street prior to the A134 junction. **open** All year **bedrooms** 2 double, 1 twin **bathrooms** 3 en suite **payment** cash, cheques

Room   General   Leisure

SIBTON, Suffolk Map ref 3C2
SAT NAV IP17 2JB

Eben-Ezer
Abbey Road, Sibton, Saxmundham IP17 2JB
t (01728) 660236   e dianaallen@btinternet.com

B&B PER ROOM PER NIGHT
S £35.00 – £45.00
D £70.00 – £75.00

EVENING MEAL PER PERSON
£10.00 – £15.00

Modern Bungalow offering comfortable, relaxed breaks. Quiet location. Lovely Garden. Good local food. White Horse Pub up the road. Close to Darsham Cycling Centre. Snape Maltings, coast, Minsmere 10 miles. **directions** Approach from A12 Yoxford Jubilee Seat. Turn onto A1120 Stowmarket direction. Sibton 2½ miles on entry turn right at Nursery School. Second bungalow. **open** All yea except Xmas **bedrooms** 1 double **bathrooms** 1 with private bathroom **payment** cash, cheques

Room   General P   Leisure

SIBTON, Suffolk Map ref 3C2
SAT NAV IP17 2JJ

Sibton White Horse Inn
Halesworth Road, Sibton, Saxmundham IP17 2JJ
t (01728) 660337   e info@sibtonwhitehorseinn.co.uk
w sibtonwhitehorseinn.co.uk   ONLINE MAP GUEST REVIEWS ONLINE BOOKING LAST MINUTE OFFERS

B&B PER ROOM PER NIGHT
S £60.00 – £65.00
D £80.00 – £90.00

EVENING MEAL PER PERSON
£20.00 – £30.00

SPECIAL PROMOTIONS
Low season special deals often available. Telephone or see website for further details.

Off the beaten track with the sound of bird song rather than traffic and a somewhat feeling of time standing still, the White Horse is the perfect place to drink, eat or stay. Multiple award winning food embraced by friendly attentive service within charming and relaxed atmosphere.

open All year except Xmas
bedrooms 1 single, 4 double, 1 twin
bathrooms 6 en suite
payment credit/debit cards, cash, cheques

directions A12 at Yoxford, turn onto A1120, proceed for 3 miles until reaching Peasenhall. Turn right into Pouy Street opposite Creaseys butchers. White Horse 600m ahead.

Room   General   Leisure

East of England | **Suffolk**

SOUTHWOLD, Suffolk Map ref 3C2
SAT NAV NR34 7JA

Poplar Hall

Frostenden Corner, Frostenden, Southwold, Suffolk NR34 7JA
t (01502) 578349   **e** poplarhall@tiscali.co.uk
w poplarhallsouthwold.com   ONLINE MAP   GUEST REVIEWS   ONLINE BOOKING   LAST MINUTE OFFERS

B&B PER ROOM PER NIGHT
S £50.00 – £70.00
D £80.00 – £90.00

SPECIAL PROMOTIONS
7 nights for the price of 6 (weekly). Please contact regarding self-catering cottages.

Peaceful and quiet, yet only minutes from the lovely seaside town of Southwold, Poplar Hall is a 16thC thatched house in a 1.5-acre garden. Enjoy our famed breakfasts of fresh fruit, local fish, sausage, bacon and home-made preserves. Luxury accommodation. Also available, two self catering cottages within the grounds.

open All year except Xmas and New Year
bedrooms 1 single, 1 double, 1 suite
bathrooms 1 en suite, 2 with private bathroom
payment cash, cheques

directions From A12 Wangford, Plough Inn on left. Right at Frostenden/South Cove sign. left fork, we are on the left just past the green.

Room General Leisure

STOWMARKET, Suffolk Map ref 3B2
SAT NAV IP14 5HU

Bays Farm

Forward Green, Stowmarket IP14 5HU
t (01449) 711286   **e** info@baysfarmsuffolk.co.uk
w baysfarmsuffolk.co.uk

B&B PER ROOM PER NIGHT
S £65.00 – £100.00
D £75.00 – £110.00

Bays Farm has the ambiance of a small luxury hotel with the intimacy of a country home. With luxurious bedrooms, stylish and modern en suite facilities and a cooked breakfast to delight all, our guests feel completely at home and totally spoiled.

open All year
bedrooms 4 double
bathrooms 4 en suite
payment credit/debit cards, cash, cheques, euros

directions Please contact us for directions

BREAKFAST AWARD   Room   General   Leisure

East of England | **Suffolk**

STOWMARKET, Suffolk Map ref 3B2   SAT NAV IP14 5EU

enjoyEngland.com ★★★★ GUEST ACCOMMODATION

B&B PER ROOM PER NIGHT
S £25.00

Three Bears Cottage
Mulberry Tree Farm, Middlewood Green, Stowmarket IP14 5EU
t (01449) 711707 **f** (01449) 711707 **e** gbeckett01@aol.com
w aristoclassics.com

Self-contained converted barn offering comfort, privacy, country views, lounges with satellite TV. kitchen, breakfast bar. Continental breakfast provided. Ground floor shower/bathroom. Sleeps 6. Indoor swimming pool. June-September arrangement only. **directions** A14 exit A1120 tourist route through Stowupland turning into Saxham Street first right 1mile at left-hand bend turn right Blacksmiths Lane, 3 Bears on left. **open** All year **bedrooms** 1 double, 1 family **payment** cash, cheques

Room   General   Leisure

THORNHAM MAGNA, Suffolk Map ref 3B2   SAT NAV IP23 8HD

enjoyEngland.com ★★★★ INN

B&B PER ROOM PER NIGHT
S £45.00
D £65.00

The Four Horseshoes
Wickham Road, Thornham Magna, Eye IP23 8HD
t (01379) 678777 **e** thefourhorseshoes@btconnect.com
w thefourhorseshoes.org

A family run, 12C inn, serving home cooked food prepared with fresh local ingredients. We have B&B accommodation, a large car park and two function rooms. Come and visit Suffolk's oldest inn!

open All year
bedrooms 2 single, 5 double, 1 family, 1 suite
bathrooms 7 en suite
payment credit/debit cards, cash

directions Just off the A140 at Stoke Ash, set in the beautiful Suffolk countryside.

Room   General   Leisure

WALDRINGFIELD, Suffolk Map ref 3C2   SAT NAV IP12 4PW

enjoyEngland.com ★★★★ BED & BREAKFAST

B&B PER ROOM PER NIGHT
D £76.00 – £96.00

Thatched Farm Bed & Breakfast
Woodbridge Road, Waldringfield, Woodbridge, Suffolk IP12 4PW
t (01473) 811755 **e** mailus@thatchedfarm.co.uk
w thatchedfarm.co.uk

Between Woodbridge and Waldringfield, Thatched Farm is surrounded by woods, fields and footpaths. 5 minutes from the A12, pubs and shops. Each room has its own breakfast, sitting, TV area. **directions** Please contact us for directions **open** All year **bedrooms** 2 double **bathrooms** 1 en suite, 1 with private bathroom **payment** cash, cheques

WALKERS WELCOME / CYCLISTS WELCOME

Room   General   Leisure

364   Official tourist board guide Bed & Breakfast

East of England | **Suffolk**

WANGFORD, Suffolk Map ref 3C2

SAT NAV NR34 8RL

The Angel Inn

High Street, Wangford, Nr Southwold NR34 8RL
t (01502) 578636 e info@angelinnwangford.co.uk
w angelinnwangford.co.uk ONLINE MAP GUEST REVIEWS ONLINE BOOKING LAST MINUTE OFFERS

B&B PER ROOM PER NIGHT
S £75.00 – £65.00
D £80.00 – £90.00
EVENING MEAL PER PERSON
£20.00 – £50.00

A former 16th Century coaching inn set in the picturesque village of Wangford, Suffolk, the Angel Inn is a seven bedroom hotel, with a friendly bar and restaurant. **directions** Conveniently located three miles inland from Southwold, at the edge of the Suffolk Coast and Heaths Area of Outstanding Natural Beauty. **open** All year **bedrooms** 4 double, 1 twin, 1 family, 1 suite **bathrooms** 7 en suite, 6 with private bathroom **payment** credit/debit cards, cash, cheques

Room   General   Leisure

WESTHORPE, Suffolk Map ref 3B2

SAT NAV IP14 4SZ

Moat Hill Farm B&B

Church Road, Westhorpe, Stowmarket IP14 4SZ
t (01449) 780165 e info@moathillfarm.co.uk
w moathillfarm.co.uk ONLINE MAP GUEST REVIEWS

B&B PER ROOM PER NIGHT
S £50.00
D £60.00

SPECIAL PROMOTIONS
Stays of 4 - 9 nights attract a 10% discount on advertised prices. 10+ nights attract a 15% discount.

Moat Hill Farm (not a working farm) is set in peaceful Suffolk countryside offering guests a quiet, relaxing stay in clean, comfortable, well appointed en-suite accommodation & guest lounge. Steve & Gilly Christian assure you a very warm welcome and unobtrusive but attentive service.

open All year
bedrooms 1 double, 1 twin
bathrooms 2 en suite
payment cash, cheques, euros

directions Westhorpe is located 10m north of Stowmarket. Take B1113 from Stowmarket to Finningham, turn left at Finningham White Horse PH crossroads for 1.5m

BREAKFAST AWARD

Room
General
Leisure

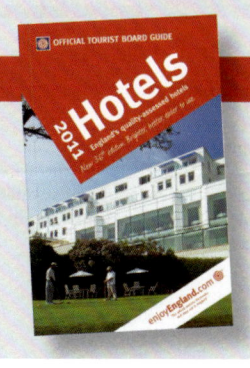

Looking for something else?

You can also buy a copy of our popular guide 'Hotels' including country house and town house hotels, metro and budget hotels, serviced apartments, restaurants with rooms and Spas in England 2011.

Now available in good bookshops and online at
visitbritainshop.com

£10.99

or key to symbols see page 6   365

East of England | **Suffolk**

WINGFIELD, Suffolk Map ref 3B2
SAT NAV IP21 5RH

Gables Farm
Wingfield, Diss IP21 5RH
t (01379) 586355 (07824 445 464) **f** (01379) 586355 **e** enquiries@gablesfarm.co.uk
w gablesfarm.co.uk ONLINE MAP GUEST REVIEWS

B&B PER ROOM PER NIGHT
S £40.00 – £50.00
D £68.00 – £80.00

SPECIAL PROMOTIONS
Special promotions available upon request.

A 16thC timbered farmhouse in moated gardens. Wingfield is a quiet village in the centre of East Anglia, central to everywhere and in the middle of nowhere!

open All year except Xmas and New Year
bedrooms 2 double, 1 twin
bathrooms 3 en suite
payment cash, cheques, euros

directions See website for details of how to find us.

Room   General   Leisure

WOODBRIDGE, Suffolk Map ref 3C2
SAT NAV IP12 4LJ

Grove House Hotel
39 Grove Road, Woodbridge IP12 4LJ
t (01394) 382202 **e** reception@thegrovehousehotel.ltd.co.uk
w grovehousehotel.ltd.uk ONLINE MAP GUEST REVIEWS LAST MINUTE OFFERS

B&B PER ROOM PER NIGHT
S £55.00
D £70.00
EVENING MEAL PER PERSON
£7.95 – £10.95

Grove House Hotel run with the aim of being a 'home from home'. It consists of 10 en suite bedrooms. Each room has tea and coffee making facilities. **directions** Once in Woodbridge. The road turns into a dual carriageway. Near the roundabout you will pass a Shell petrol station. We are the terracotta building. **open** All year **bedrooms** 1 single, 6 double, 2 twin, 1 family **bathrooms** 10 en suite **payment** credit/debit cards, cash, cheques

Room   General

WOOLPIT, Suffolk Map ref 3B2
SAT NAV IP30 9SA

Bull Inn & Restaurant
The Street, Woolpit, Bury St Edmunds IP30 9SA
t (01359) 240393 **f** (01359) 240393 **e** info@bullinnwoolpit.co.uk
w bullinnwoolpit.co.uk

B&B PER ROOM PER NIGHT
S £40.00 – £45.00
D £75.00 – £80.00
EVENING MEAL PER PERSON
£4.75 – £20.00

Public house and restaurant offering good accommodation in centre of pretty village. Large garden, ample parking. Ideal base for touring Suffolk. **directions** Please contact us for directions **open** All year **bedrooms** 2 single, 4 double, 1 twin, 1 family **bathrooms** 8 en suite **payment** credit/debit cards, cash, cheques

Room   General   Leisure

Official tourist board guide **Bed & Breakfast**

East of England | **Suffolk**

WORTHAM, Suffolk Map ref 3B2

SAT NAV IP22 1RB

FARMHOUSE ★★★★
Silver AWARD

Rookery Farm
Old Bury Road, Wortham, Diss IP22 1RB
t (01379) 783236 **f** (01379) 783236 **e** maureen@therookeryfarm.co.uk
w therookeryfarm.co.uk ONLINE MAP

B&B PER ROOM PER NIGHT
S £35.00 – £45.00
D £55.00 – £70.00

A warm welcome awaits at this comfortable Georgian farmhouse with its spacious, tastefully decorated, fully en suite rooms. Enjoy a traditional farmhouse breakfast made from fresh local produce wherever possible.

open All year except Xmas and New Year   **directions** Please contact us for directions
bedrooms 2 double, 1 twin
bathrooms 3 en suite
payment cash, cheques

BREAKFAST AWARD   Room   General

WRENTHAM, Suffolk Map ref 3C2

SAT NAV NR34 7JF

INN ★★★

Five Bells
Southwold Road, Wrentham NR34 7JF
t (01502) 675249 **f** (01502) 676127 **e** victoriapub@aol.com
w five-bells.com

B&B PER ROOM PER NIGHT
S £65.00 – £70.00
D £75.00 – £90.00

Traditional country inn set in a rural location. Close to Southwold. **directions** Leaving the A12 at Wrentham, head towards Southwold on the B1127. **open** All year except Xmas **bedrooms** 1 double, 3 twin, 1 family **bathrooms** 5 en suite **payment** credit/debit cards, cash, cheques

Room   General   Leisure

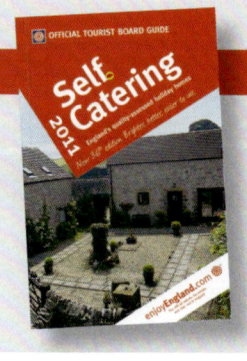

Looking for something else?

You can also buy a copy of our popular guide 'Self Catering' including self-catering holiday homes, approved caravan holiday homes, boat accommodation and holiday cottage agencies in England 2011.

Now available in good bookshops and online at
visitbritainshop.com

£11.99

or **key to symbols** see page 6   367

East of England | Bedfordshire/Cambridgeshire

All Assessed Accommodation

Bedfordshire

BEDFORD

Bourne End Farm ★★★★★
Farmhouse **SILVER AWARD**
Bourne End Lane, Bletsoe, Bedford
MK44 1QS
t (01234) 783184
e bourneendbandb@btconnect.com
w bourneendfarm.co.uk

The Embankment ★★★★
Guest Accommodation
6 The Embankment, Bedford
MK40 3PD
t (01234) 261332
e embankment@peachpubs.com
w embankmentbedford.co.uk

The Victoria Guesthouse ★★★
Guest House
26 De Parys Avenue, Bedford
MK40 2TW
t (01234) 359219
e info@bedandbreakfastbedford.com
w bedandbreakfastbedford.com

BIGGLESWADE – 3 MILES

Old Warden Guesthouse ★★★
Bed & Breakfast
The Clock House, Old Warden,
Biggleswade
SG18 9HQ
t (01767) 627201
e owgh@idnet.co.uk

BLETSOE

North End Barns ★★★★
Farmhouse
North End Barns, Bletsoe, Bedford
MK44 1QT
t (01234) 781320
w northendbarns.co.uk

BOLNHURST

Old School House ★★★★
Bed & Breakfast **SILVER AWARD**
School Lane, Bolnhurst, Bedford
MK44 2EN
t (01234) 376754
e enquiries@breakfastinbeds.co.uk
w breakfastinbeds.co.uk

CLAPHAM

Narly Oak Lodge ★★★★
Bed & Breakfast
The Baulk, Green Lane, Bedford
MK41 6AA
t (01234) 350353
e mollie.foster07@btinternet.com
w narlyoaklodge.com

DUNSTABLE

Cherish End ★★★★
Guest Accommodation
21 Barton Avenue, Dunstable
LU5 4DF
t (01582) 606266
e cherishend@hotmail.co.uk
w cherishend.co.uk

EAST HYDE

Hyde Mill ★★★★ *Bed & Breakfast*
Lower Luton Road, East Hyde,
Luton, Bedfordshire
LU2 9PX
t (01582) 712641
e info@hydemill.co.uk
w hydemill.co.uk

LITTLE STAUGHTON

Robins Reach ★★★★
Bed & Breakfast
Top End, Little Staughton, Bedford
MK44 2BY
t (01234) 376889
e bnb@robinsreach.co.uk
w robinsreach.co.uk

LUTON

Pat & Doreens B&B ★★
Guest Accommodation
32 Blundell Road, Unitary Authority,
Luton
LU3 1SH
t (01582) 651689
e patrick.hayes.4.@ntlworld.com

MARSTON MORETAINE

The White Cottage ★★★★
Guest House
Marston Hill, Marston Moretaine,
Bedford
MK43 0QJ
t (01234) 751766
e stay@thewhitecottage.frbusiness.co.uk
w thewhitecottage.net

MEPPERSHALL

Old Joe's ★★ *Bed & Breakfast*
90 Fildyke Road, Meppershall,
Shefford
SG17 5LU
t (01462) 815585
e cih@freenet.co.uk
w oldjoes.co.uk

MILTON BRYAN

Town Farm ★★★★ *Farmhouse*
South End, Milton Bryan, Woburn
MK17 9HS
t (01525) 210001
e townfarm@tesco.net

RENHOLD

Aldwyck Wood ★★★★
Bed & Breakfast **SILVER AWARD**
2 Green End, Renhold, Bedford
MK41 0LL
t (01234) 871614
e enquiries@aldwyckwood.co.uk
w aldwyckwood.co.uk

ROXTON

Church Farm ★★★★
Bed & Breakfast **SILVER AWARD**
High Street, Bedford
MK44 3EB
t (01234) 870234
e churchfarm@amserve.net

SANDY

Highfield Farm ★★★★★
Farmhouse **SILVER AWARD**
Tempsford Road, Sandy,
Bedfordshire
SG19 2AQ
t (01767) 682352
e margaret@highfield-farm.co.uk
w highfield-farm.co.uk

THURLEIGH

The Windmill ★★★★
Bed & Breakfast
Milton Road, Thurleigh, Bedford
MK44 2DF
t (01234) 771016
e wendy.armitage1@talk21.com
w thewindmill.uk.com

Cambridgeshire

ALCONBURY

The Manor House ★★★ *Inn*
20 Chapel Street, Alconbury,
Huntingdon
PE28 4DY
t (01480) 890423
e annjones2@btconnect.com
w manorhousealconbury.com

BARHAM

Ye Olde Globe & Chequers
★★★★ *Guest Accommodation*
Main Street, Barham, Huntingdon
PE28 5AB
t (01480) 890247
e cheryllgroveprice@btinternet.com
w globeandchequers.co.uk

BARNACK

Rowan House ★★★★
Bed & Breakfast **SILVER AWARD**
Station Road, Barnack, Stamford
PE9 3DW
t (01780) 740705
e rowanbarnack@aol.com
w bedandbreakfaststamford.co.uk

BARTLOW

Westoe Farm ★★★★
Bed & Breakfast **SILVER AWARD**
Bartlow, Cambridge
CB21 4PR
t (01223) 892731
e enquire@bartlow.u-net.com
w westoefarm.co.uk

BURWELL

Chestnut House ★★★★
Bed & Breakfast
14A High Street, Burwell,
Cambridge
CB25 0HB
t (01638) 742996

CAMBRIDGE

A & B Guesthouse ★★★★
Guest House
124 Tenison Road, Cambridge
CB1 2DP
t 01223 315 702
e stay@aandbguesthouse.co.uk
w aandbguesthouse.co.uk

Acorn Guesthouse ★★★★
Guest House
154 Chesterton Road, Cambridge
CB4 1DA
t (01223) 353888
e info@acornguesthouse.co.uk
w acornguesthouse.co.uk

Alexander Bed & Breakfast
★★★★ *Bed & Breakfast*
56 St Alexander Bed and Breakfast
Barnaba, Cambridge
CB1 2DE
t (01223) 525725
e enquiries@beesley-schuster.co.uk
w beesley-schuster.co.uk

Allenbell ★★★★ *Bed & Breakfast*
517a Coldham Lane, Cambridge
CB1 3JS
t (01223) 210353
e enquiries@allenbell.co.uk
w allenbell.co.uk

Alpha Milton Guesthouse ★★★
Guest House
61-63 Milton Road, Cambridge
CB4 1XA
t (01223) 311625
e info@alphamilton.com
w alphamilton.com

The Arbury ★★★
Guest Accommodation
54 Arbury Road, Cambridge
CB4 2JE
t (01223) 359697
e djenkins100@hotmail.com

Arbury Lodge Guesthouse ★★★★
Guest House
82 Arbury Road, Cambridge
CB4 2JE
t (01223) 364319
e arbury-lodge@btconnect.com
w arburylodgeguesthouse.co.uk

Archway House ★★★★
Bed & Breakfast **SILVER AWARD**
52 Gilbert Road, Cambridge
CB4 3PE
t (01223) 575314
e archway52@ntlworld.com
w archwayhousebandb.co.uk

At Woodhaven ★★★★
Bed & Breakfast
245 Milton Road, Cambridge
CB4 1XQ
t (01223) 226108
e woodhavencambridge@btinternet.com
w stayatwoodhaven.co.uk

Autumn House ★★★★
Bed & Breakfast
710 Newmarket Road, Cambridge
CB5 8RS
t (01223) 575122
e us@autumnhousecambridge.co.uk
w autumnhousecambridge.co.uk

Avalon ★★★★ *Bed & Breakfast*
SILVER AWARD
62 Gilbert Road, Cambridge
CB4 3PD
t (01223) 353071
e avalonbandb@hotmail.com
w avaloncambridge.co.uk

Aylesbray Lodge Guesthouse
★★★★ *Guest House*
5 Mowbray Road, Cambridge
CB1 7SR
t (01223) 240089
e stay@aylesbray.com
w aylesbray.com

Beech Farm Bed & Breakfast
★★★★ *Guest Accommodation*
SILVER AWARD
Beech Farm, 34 Church Street,
Cambridge
CB22 7NR
t (01223) 871563
e accommodation@beechfarm.demon.co.uk
w beechfarmcambridge.com

Bridge Guest House ★★★
Guest House
151 Hills Road, Cambridge
CB2 8RJ
t (01223) 247942
e bghouse@gmail.com
w bridgeguesthouse.co.uk

Cambridge YHA ★★ *Hostel*
97 Tenison Road, Cambridge
CB1 2DN
t (01223) 354601

Cam Guesthouse ★★★★
Guest House
17 Elizabeth Way, Cambridge
CB4 1DD
t (01223) 354512
e camguesthouse@btinternet.com
w camguesthouse.co.uk

Canterbury House ★★★★
Bed & Breakfast
69 Canterbury Street, Cambridge
CB4 3QG
t (01223) 300053
w canterburyhouse.co.uk

Carlton Lodge ★★★ *Guest House*
245 Chesterton Road, Cambridge
CB4 1AS
t (01223) 367792
e info@carltonlodge.co.uk
w carltonlodge.co.uk

Carolina B&B ★★★★
Bed & Breakfast
138 Perne Road, Cambridge
CB1 3NX
t (01223) 247015
e carolina.amabile@tesco.net
w carolinaguesthouse.co.uk

City Centre North Bed & Breakfast ★★ *Bed & Breakfast*
328A Histon Road, Cambridge
CB4 3HT
t (01223) 312843
e gscambs@tiscali.co.uk
w citycentrenorth.co.uk

The Conifers ★★★★
Bed & Breakfast **SILVER AWARD**
213 Histon Road, Cambridge
CB4 3HL
t (01223) 311784
e enquiry@the-conifers.net
w the-conifers.net

East of England | Cambridgeshire

ty One *Guest Accommodation*
Saint Andrews Road, Cambridge
4 1DH
07885 942544
e anna@bedandbreakfast51.co.uk
w bedandbreakfastfiftyone.co.uk/

anta House ★★★
d & Breakfast
Eltisley Avenue, Newnham,
mbridge
3 9JQ
t (01223) 560466
e tj.dathan@ntlworld.com

milton Lodge ★★★ *Guest House*
5 Chesterton Road, Cambridge
4 1DA
t (01223) 365664
e hamiltonhotel@talk21.com
w hamiltonhotelcambridge.co.uk/

rrys Bed & Breakfast ★★★★
est House SILVER AWARD
Milton Road, Cambridge
4 1XA
t (01223) 503866
e cjmadden@ntlworld.com
w welcometoharrys.co.uk

wthorn House ★★★★
d & Breakfast
Hawthorn Way, Cambridge
4 1AX
t (01223) 364483
e hawthornhouse@hotmail.co.uk

bsons House ★★★
d & Breakfast
Barton Road, Cambridge
3 9LH
t (01223) 304906
w hilltout.vpweb.co.uk

me From Home ★★★★
d & Breakfast SILVER AWARD
-80 Milton Road, Cambridge
4 1LA
t (01223) 323555
e homefromhome2@btconnect.com
w homefromhomeguesthouse-cambridge.co.uk

ni House Bed & Breakfast
★★★ *Guest House*
1 Coleridge Road, Cambridge
1 3PN
t (01223) 708967
e paragon.holdings@ntlworld.com
w icenihouse.co.uk

ne's Bed & Breakfast ★★★★
d & Breakfast
Arbury Road, Cambridge
4 2JE
t (01223) 572034
e j.nayar1@ntlworld.com

rkwood Guesthouse ★★★
est House
rkwood Guesthouse, Cambridge
4 1DA
t (01223) 306283
e info@kirkwoodhouse.co.uk
w kirkwoodhouse.co.uk

ntern House ★★★ *Guest House*
4 Chesterton Road, Cambridge
4 1DA
t (01223) 359980
e lanternhouse@msn.com
w guesthousecambridge.net

verton House ★★★★
est House
2-734 Newmarket Road,
mbridge
5 8RS
t (01223) 292094
e wendy.ison@ntlworld.com
w levertonhouse.co.uk

adingley Hall University of ambridge *Campus*
adingley Hall, Madingley,
mbridge
325 9HD
t (01223) 745222
e enquiry@madingleyhall.co.uk

The Old Rosemary Branch ★★
Bed & Breakfast
67 Church End, Cherry Hinton,
Cambridge
CB1 3LF
t (01223) 247161
e saa30@cam.ac.uk
w theoldrosemarybranch.co.uk

Railway Lodge Guest House ★★★
Guest House
150 Tenison Road, Cambridge
CB1 2DP
t (01223) 467688
e railwaylodge@cambridge-guest-house-accommodation.co.uk
w cambridge-guesthouse-accommodation.co.uk

Robinson College ★★★★ *Campus*
Grange Road, Cambridge
CB3 9AN
t (01223) 332859
e bandb@robinson.cam.ac.uk
w robinson.cam.ac.uk/conferences/bedbreakfast.php

Rosa's Bed & Breakfast ★★★★
Bed & Breakfast
53 Roseford Road, Cambridge
CB4 2HA
t (01223) 512596
e rosadscott@lycos.com

Somerset House ★★★
Bed & Breakfast
Somerset House, Cambridge
CB4 1XE
t (01223) 505131
e somersetbedandbreakfast@msn.com
w bedandbreakfastcambridge.net

Southampton Guest House ★★★
Guest House
7 Elizabeth Way, Cambridge
CB4 1DE
t (01223) 357780
e southamptonhouse@btinternet.com
w southamptonguesthouse.com

Tudor Cottage ★★★★
Bed & Breakfast
292 Histon Road, Cambridge
CB4 3HS
t 01223565212
e email@tudor-cottage.net
w tudorcottageguesthouse.com

Vicarage ★★★ *Bed & Breakfast*
15 St Pauls Road, Cambridge
CB1 2EZ
t (01223) 315832
e debbie.beckett2@googlemail.com

Victoria House ★★★★
Guest House
57 Arbury Road, Cambridge
CB4 2JB
t (01223) 350086
e info@victoria-guesthouse.co.uk
w victoria-guesthouse.co.uk

Warkworth House ★★★★
Guest House
Warkworth Terrace, Cambridge
CB1 1EE
t (01223) 363682
e enquiries@warkworthhouse.co.uk
w warkworthhouse.co.uk

Worth House ★★★★ *Guest House*
SILVER AWARD
152 Chesterton Road, Cambridge
CB4 1DA
t (01223) 316074
e enquire@worth-house.co.uk
w worth-house.co.uk

CAMBRIDGE (12 MILES)

Three Hills ★★★★ *Inn*
Ashdon Road, Bartlow, Cambridge
CB21 4PW
t (01223) 891259
e threehills@rhubarb-inns.com
w rhubarb-inns.co.uk

CHEVELEY

1eleven Bed & Breakfast ★★★★
Bed & Breakfast SILVER AWARD
111 High Street, Cheveley,
Newmarket
CB8 9DG
t (01638) 731177
e richard@1elevenbandb.co.uk
w 1elevenbandb.co.uk

The Old Farmhouse ★★★★
Bed & Breakfast
165 High Street, Cheveley,
Newmarket
CB8 9DG
t (01638) 730771
e amrobinson@clara.co.uk
w cheveleybandb.co.uk

COTON

Woodfield House ★★★★
Bed & Breakfast
Madingley Road, Coton, Cambridge
CB23 7PH
t (01954) 210265
e wendy-john@wsadler.freeserve.co.uk

DODDINGTON

Fenview Lodge ★★★★
Guest Accommodation
SILVER AWARD
15 Brickmakers Arms Lane,
Doddington, March
PE15 0TR
t (01354) 740103
e info@fenviewlodge.co.uk
w fenviewlodge.co.uk

DUXFORD

The John Barleycorn ★★★★ *Inn*
3 Moorfield Road, Duxford,
Cambridge
CB22 4PP
t (01223) 832699
e info@johnbarleycorn.co.uk
w johnbarleycorn.co.uk

ELLINGTON THORPE

Thorpe Lodge Farm B&B ★★★★
Farmhouse
Ellington, Huntingdon,
Cambridgeshire
PE28 0AP
t (01480) 810266
e tl.farm@tiscali.co.uk
w thorpe-lodge-farm.co.uk

ELY

9 Willow Walk ★★★★
Bed & Breakfast
9 Willow Walk, Ely
CB7 4AT
t (01353) 664205

29 Waterside ★★★★
Bed & Breakfast
Ely, Ely
CB7 4AU
t (01353) 614329
e info@29waterside.org.uk
w 29waterside.org.uk

57 Lynn Road ★★★★
Bed & Breakfast SILVER AWARD
57 Lynn Road, Ely
CB6 1DD
t (01353) 663685
e marting7vgh@aol.com

96 Lynn Road ★★★★
Guest Accommodation
SILVER AWARD
96 Lynn Road, Ely
CB6 1DE
t (01353) 665044

B&B @ 1A ★★★★ *Bed & Breakfast*
SILVER AWARD
1A Little Lane, Ely
CB6 1AZ
t (01353) 659724
e bandbat1a@googlemail.com
w elybedandbreakfastat1a.co.uk

Bowmount House ★★★★
Bed & Breakfast SILVER AWARD
Bowmount House, Ely
CB6 3WP
t (01353) 669943
e pauljacton@hotmail.com

Cathedral House ★★★★
Bed & Breakfast
17 St Mary's Street, Ely
CB7 4ER
t (01353) 662124
e farndale@cathedralhouse.co.uk
w cathedralhouse.co.uk

Harvest House ★★★★
Bed & Breakfast
122B St Johns Road, Ely
CB6 3BW
t (01353) 663517
e chrisbarnes2@hotmail.com

The Nyton ★★★★
Guest Accommodation
7 Barton Road, Ely
CB7 4HZ
t (01353) 662459
e nytonhotel@yahoo.co.uk
w thenytonhotel.co.uk

The Old School B&B ★★★★
Bed & Breakfast
The Old School, School Lane,
Coveney, Ely
CB6 2DB
t (01353) 777087 07802-174541
e info@TheOldSchoolBandB.co.uk
w TheOldSchoolBandB.co.uk

Post House ★★ *Bed & Breakfast*
12a Egremont Street, Ely
CB6 1AE
t (01353) 667184
e info@posthouse-ely.co.uk
w posthouse-ely.co.uk

Riverside Inn ★★★★ *Guest House*
SILVER AWARD
8 Annesdale, Ely
CB7 4BN
t (01353) 661677
e info@riversideinn-ely.co.uk
w riversideinn-ely.co.uk

Sycamore House ★★★★
Guest Accommodation
91 Cambridge Road, Ely
CB7 4HX
t (01353) 662139
e info@sycamorehouse.gb.com
w sycamorehouse.gb.com

Walnut House ★★★★
Bed & Breakfast SILVER AWARD
Walnut House, 1 Houghton
Gardens, Ely
CB7 4JN
t (01353) 661793
e walnuthouse1@aol.com
w walnuthouse-ely.co.uk

FORDHAM

Annes Bed & Breakfast ★★★★
Bed & Breakfast
158 Mildenhall Road, Fordham, Ely
CB7 5NS
t (01638) 720514
e annes.bnb@btinternet.com

The Willows B&B ★★★★
Bed & Breakfast
78 Mill Lane, Fordham, Newmarket
CB7 5NQ
t (01638) 720561
e suzanne@thewillowsbedandbreakfast.co.uk
w thewillowsbedandbreakfast.co.uk

GIRTON

Finches Bed & Breakfast ★★★★
Bed & Breakfast SILVER AWARD
144 Thornton Road, Girton,
Cambridge
CB3 0ND
t (01223) 276653
e enquiry@finches-bnb.com
w finches-bnb.com

East of England | Cambridgeshire

GOREFIELD

The Old Vicarage Bed & Breakfast ★★★★
Guest Accommodation
SILVER AWARD
Goat Lane, Gorefield, Wisbech
PE13 4NJ
t (01945) 871144
e info@wisbechbedandbreakfast.co.uk
w wisbechbedandbreakfast.co.uk

GREAT CHISHILL

Hall Farm ★★★★ *Farmhouse*
110 Hall Lane, Great Chishill, Royston
SG8 8SH
t (01763) 838263
e wisehall@tiscali.co.uk
w hallfarmbb.co.uk

GREAT WILBRAHAM

Kettles Cottage ★★★★
Bed & Breakfast **SILVER AWARD**
30 High Street, Great Wilbraham, Cambridge
CB21 5JD
t (01223) 880801
e enquiries@kettlescottage.co.uk
w kettlescottage.co.uk

GUYHIRN

Oliver Twist Country Inn ★★★★
Inn
High Road, Guyhirn, Wisbech, Cambridgeshire
PE13 4EA
t (01945) 450523
e enquiries@theolivertwist.com
w theolivertwist.com

HEMINGFORD ABBOTS

Riverside House ★★★
Bed & Breakfast
Common Lane, Hemingford Abbots, Huntingdon
PE28 9AN
t (01480) 468993
e caroline@carolinecatering.co.uk
w carolinecatering.co.uk

HEYDON

The End Cottage ★★★★
Guest Accommodation
Fowlmere Road, Heydon, Cambridge
SG8 8PZ
t (01763) 838212
e diana.macfadyen@virgin.net

Greenhill B&B ★★★★
Bed & Breakfast
Greenhill, Chishill Road, Heydon, Cambridge
SG8 8PN
t (01763) 837170
e mitchellgreenhill@btinternet.com

HIGHFIELDS CALDECOTE

Avondale ★★★ *Bed & Breakfast*
35 Highfields Road, Caldecote, Cambridge
CB23 7NX
t (01954) 210746
e avondalecambs@amserve.com

The Poplars ★★★★
Bed & Breakfast
12 East Drive, Highfields Caldecote, Cambridge
CB23 7NZ
t (01954) 210396
e thepoplars@onetel.com

HILDERSHAM

The Pear Tree Inn ★★★★ *Inn*
High Street, Hildersham, Cambridge
CB21 6BU
t (01223) 891680
e peartreeinn@btconnect.com
w peartreecambridge-bb.co.uk

HUNTINGDON

Bramble Corner ★★★
Guest Accommodation
9 Rectory Road, Bluntisham, Huntingdon
PE28 3LN
t (01487) 842646
e info@bramblecorner.co.uk
w bramblecorner.co.uk

Cheriton House ★★★★★
Bed & Breakfast **SILVER AWARD**
Mill Street, Houghton, Huntingdon
PE28 2AZ
t (01480) 464004
e sales@cheritonhousecambs.co.uk
w cheritonhousecambs.co.uk

Coach & Horses Guest House ★★
Guest Accommodation
54-56 Ermine Street, Huntingdon
PE29 3EJ
t (01480) 458619
e guesthousehuntingdon@gmail.com

ICKLETON

Chestnuts ★★★ *Bed & Breakfast*
22 Abbey Street, Ickleton, Saffron Walden
CB10 1SS
t (01799) 530152
e stella@ickletonchestnuts.co.uk
w ickletonchestnuts.co.uk

Shepherds Cottage ★★★★
Bed & Breakfast
Grange Road, Ickleton, Saffron Walden
CB10 1TA
t (01799) 531171
e jackie.fishhut@btinternet.com
w shepherdscottage.weebly.com

ISLEHAM

The Old Vicarage ★★★★
Bed & Breakfast
7 Church Street, Isleham, Ely
CB7 5RY
t (01638) 780095
e gill@pedersen.co.uk

LITTLE DOWNHAM

Bury House Bed & Breakfast
★★★★ *Bed & Breakfast*
SILVER AWARD
11 Main Street, Little Downham, Ely
CB6 2ST
t (01353) 698645
e emma.beeney@googlemail.com
w buryhouse.com

Wood Fen Lodge ★★★★
Guest Accommodation
Wood Fen Lodge, 6 Black Bank Road, Little Downham, Ely
CB6 2UA
t (01353) 862495
e info@woodfenlodge.co.uk
w woodfenlodge.co.uk

LITTLEPORT

Glebe House ★★★★
Bed & Breakfast **SILVER AWARD**
Glebe House, Littleport, Ely
CB6 1RG
t (01353) 862924
e info@glebehouseuk.co.uk
w glebehouseuk.co.uk

Killiney House ★★★★★
Bed & Breakfast **GOLD AWARD**
18 Barkhams Lane, Littleport, Ely
CB6 1NN
t (01353) 860404
e enquiries@killineyhouse.co.uk
w killineyhouse.co.uk

LITTLE SHELFORD

Dorset House ★★★★
Guest Accommodation
Dorset House, 35 Newton road, Cambridge
CB2 5HL
t (01223) 844440
e dorsethouse@btopenworld.com

MARCH

Causeway Guest House ★★★
Guest House
6 The Causeway, March
PE15 9NT
t (01354) 650823
e brentmorris@btconnect.com
w causewayguesthouse.co.uk

MILTON

Ambassador Lodge ★★★★
Guest Accommodation
37 High Street, Milton, Cambridge
CB24 6DF
t (01223) 860168
e ambassadorlodge@yahoo.com
w ambassadorlodge.co.uk

NEWMARKET (4 MILES)

The Meadow House B&B ★★★★
Guest Accommodation
2a High Street, Burwell, Cambridge
CB25 0HB
t (01638) 741926
e bookings@themeadowhouse.co.uk
w themeadowhouse.co.uk

PERRY

West Perry B&B ★★★★
Bed & Breakfast
38 West Perry, Perry, Huntingdon
PE28 0BX
t (01480) 810225
e dianahickling@tesco.net
w westperrybandb.co.uk

PETERBOROUGH

Aragon House ★★★ *Guest House*
75-77 London Road, Peterborough
PE2 9BS
t (01733) 563718
e aragonhouse@tiscali.co.uk
w aragonhouse.co.uk

The Brandon ★★★
Guest Accommodation
161 Lincoln Road, Peterborough
PE1 2PW
t (01733) 568631
e enquiries@brandonhotel.co.uk

Graham Guesthouse ★★★
Guest House
296 Oundle Road, Peterborough
PE2 9QA
t (01733) 567824
e grahamguesthouse@btinternet.com

PIDLEY

Lakeside Lodge Golf Centre ★★★
Guest Accommodation
Fen Road, Pidley, Huntingdon, Cambs
PE28 3DF
t (01487) 740540
e jane@lakeside-lodge.co.uk
w lakeside-lodge.co.uk

The Old Grain Store ★★★★
Guest Accommodation
Fen Road, Pidley, Huntingdon
PE28 3DF
t (01487) 840627
e louise@theoldgrainstore.co.uk
w theoldgrainstore.co.uk

SAWTRY

Redwings Lodge ★★★
Guest Accommodation
Old Great North Road, Sawtry, Huntingdon
PE28 5XP
t (01487) 830100
e sales@redwingslodge.co.uk
w redwingslodge.co.uk

STAPLEFORD

Vine Farm ★★★ *Bed & Breakfast*
38 Church Street, Stapleford, Cambridge
CB22 5DS
t (01223) 524821
e jayneransom@hotmail.com
w vinefarm.co.uk

STUNTNEY

The Old Hall ★★★★★
Bed & Breakfast **GOLD AWARD**
Stuntney, Ely
CB7 5TR
t (01353) 663275
e stay@theoldhallely.co.uk
w theoldhallely.co.uk

SUTTON

The Grove ★★★★ *Bed & Breakfast*
GOLD AWARD
Bury Lane, Sutton Gault, Ely
CB6 2BD
t (01353) 777196
e stella.f.anderson@btopenworld.com

Grove Barn Guest Rooms ★★★
Guest Accommodation
Grove Barn, Bury Lane, Sutton Gault, Ely
CB6 2BD
t (01353) 778311
e info@grovebarncambridgeshire.com
w grovebarncambridgeshire.com

SWAFFHAM BULBECK

B&B at Martin House ★★★★
Bed & Breakfast **SILVER AWARD**
1 Station Road, Swaffham Bulbeck, Cambridge
CB25 0NB
t (01223) 813115
e sally@martinhousebb.co.uk
w martinhousebb.co.uk

THORNEY

The Jester ★★★ *Inn*
116 Station Road, Odsey, Baldock
SG7 5RS
t (01462) 742011
e enquires@thejesterhotel.co.uk
w thejesterhotel.co.uk

TOFT

Meadowview ★★★★
Bed & Breakfast
3 Brookside, Toft, Cambridge
CB23 2RJ
t (01223) 263395
e carol@meadowview.co.uk
w meadowview.co.uk

WANSFORD

Stoneacre Guest House ★★★
Guest Accommodation - Room Only
Elton Road, Wansford, Peterborough
PE8 6JT
t (01780) 783283
w stoneacreguesthouse.co.uk

WENNINGTON

Wennington Lodge Bed & Breakfast ★★ *Farmhouse*
Abbots Ripton, Huntingdon
PE28 2LP
t (01487) 773276
e tom.moore2@btopenworld.com
w wennington-lodge.co.uk

WENTWORTH

Desiderata ★★★ *Bed & Breakfast*
44 Main Street, Wentworth, Ely
CB6 3QG
t (01353) 776131
e chips.1@virgin.net
w mgraham.net

WEST WICKHAM

Chequer Cottage ★★★★
Bed & Breakfast **SILVER AWARD**
43 Streetly End, Horseheath, Cambridge
CB21 4RP
t (01223) 891522
e stay@chequercottage.com
w chequercottage.com

East of England | Cambridgeshire/Essex

WHITTLESEY

Whitmore House ★★★★
Bed & Breakfast
Whitmore Street, Whittlesey, Peterborough
PE7 1HE
t (01733) 203088
w whitmore-house.co.uk

WISBECH

Union Place ★★★
Bed & Breakfast
Wisbech, Wisbech
PE13 1HB
t (01945) 588160

Marmion House ★★★
Guest Accommodation
19 Lynn Road, Wisbech
PE13 3DD
t (01945) 582822
e kbunton@btinternet.com
w a1tourism.com/uk/marmionhouse.html

WISTOW

Manor Farm B&B ★★★★
Farmhouse
Manor Street, Wistow, Ramsey
PE28 2QB
t (01487) 822622
e lizzie.thomas@btopenworld.com
w manorfarmwistow.co.uk

Pointers Guest House ★★★★
Farmhouse SILVER AWARD
Pointers, Wistow, Huntingdon
PE28 2QH
t (01487) 822366
e view@pointers-guest-house.co.uk
w pointers-guest-house.co.uk

WITCHFORD

The Village Inn ★★★ Inn
Main Street, Witchford, Ely
CB6 2HQ
t (01353) 663763
e claire.parsons@virgin.net
w thevillageinnely.com

The Woodlands ★★★★
Guest House
Grunty Fen Road, Witchford, Ely
CB6 2JE
t (01353) 663746
e info@woodlandsbandb.co.uk
w woodlandsbandb.co.uk

WOODHURST

Fullards Farm ★★★★ Farmhouse
SILVER AWARD
South Street, Woodhurst, Huntingdon
PE28 3BW
t (01487) 824356
e fullards@btopenworld.com
w fullardsfarm.co.uk

The Raptor Foundation ★★★
Guest Accommodation
The Heath, St Ives Road, Woodhurst, St Ives
PE28 3BT
t (01487) 741140
e theleowl@aol.com
w raptorfoundation.org.uk

WOOLLEY

New Manor Farm ★★★★
Farmhouse
Kimbolton Road, Woolley, Huntingdon
PE28 5BH
t (01480) 890092
e newmanor.farm@virgin.net
w new-manor-farm.co.uk

WYTON

Magdalene House ★★★★★
Guest Accommodation - Room Only
GOLD AWARD
Huntingdon Road, Wyton, Huntingdon
PE28 2AD
t (01480) 465011
e magdalenehouse@btinternet.com
w magdalene-house.co.uk

Essex

ARDLEIGH

Old Shields Farm ★★★★
Bed & Breakfast
Waterhouse Lane, Ardleigh, Colchester
CO7 7NE
t (01206) 230251 mobile 07831 278036
e ruthemarshall@btinternet.com
w oldshieldsbedandbreakfast.co.uk

Park Cottage ★★★★
Bed & Breakfast SILVER AWARD
Bromley Road, Ardleigh, Colchester
CO7 7SJ
t (01206) 230170
e mrs.j.alder@googlemail.com
w parkcottage.org

ARKESDEN

Parsonage Farm ★★★★
Guest Accommodation
Parsonage Farm, Arkesden, Saffron Walden
CB11 4HB
t (01799) 550306
e danijaud@aol.com

AYTHORPE RODING

Westpoint ★★★ Bed & Breakfast
Aythorpe Roding, Dunmow, Great Dunmow
CM6 1PU
t (01279) 876462
e barbara@westpointbandb.co.uk
w westpointbandb.co.uk

BATTLESBRIDGE

Frasers ★★★★
Guest Accommodation
5 Maltings Road, Battlesbridge, Wickford
SS11 7RF
t 07876 717353
e accommodation@battlesbridge.com
w battlesbridge.com/guesthouse.php

BIRCH

Woodview B&B ★★★★
Bed & Breakfast
Lynch Cottage, Mill Lane, Birch, Colchester
CO2 0NH
t (01206) 331956
e lynchcottage@fsmail.net

BLACKHEATH

Fridaywood Farm ★★★★
Farmhouse SILVER AWARD
Bounstead Road, Colchester
CO2 0DF
t (01206) 573595
e lochorem8@aol.com
w fridaywoodfarm.co.uk

BRAINTREE

Fennes View ★★★★
Bed & Breakfast
131 Church Street, Bocking, Braintree
CM7 5LF
t (01376) 326080

Hare & Hounds ★★★★ Inn
104 High Garrett, Braintree
CM7 5NT
t (01376) 324430
e handhpub@hotmail.com
w hare-and-hounds.com

The Old House ★★★ Guest House
The Old House, Braintree
CM7 9AS
t (01376) 550457
e old_house@talk21.com
w theoldhousebraintree.co.uk

BRENTWOOD

Brentwood Guesthouse ★★★
Guest Accommodation
Rose Valley, Brentwood
CM14 4HJ
t (01277) 262713
e info@brentwoodguesthouse.com
w brentwoodguesthouse.com

BRIGHTLINGSEA

Hurst Green Bed and Breakfast
★★★★ Bed & Breakfast
SILVER AWARD
1 Hurst Green, Brightlingsea, Essex
CO7 0HG
t 01206 308 819 (07842193070)
e info@hurstgreenbedandbreakfast.co.uk
w hurstgreenbedandbreakfast.co.uk

Paxton Dene ★★★★
Bed & Breakfast SILVER AWARD
Church Road, Brightlingsea, Colchester
CO7 0QT
t (01206) 304560
e holben@btinternet.com
w paxtondenebedandbreakfast.co.uk

BURNHAM-ON-CROUCH

Mangapp Manor ★★★★
Bed & Breakfast SILVER AWARD
Southminster Road, Burnham-on-Crouch
CM0 8QQ
t 07769 676735
e kewilsdon@yahoo.co.uk
w mangappmanor.co.uk

The Oyster Smack Inn ★★★★ Inn
112 Station Road, Burnham-on-Crouch
CM0 8HR
t (01621) 782141
e trevor@theoystersmackinn.co.uk
w theoystersmackinn.co.uk

The Railway ★★★★ Inn
SILVER AWARD
12 Station Road, Burnham-on-Crouch
CM0 8BQ
t (01621) 786868
w therailwayhotelburnham.co.uk

CHELMSFORD

Sherwood ★★★ Bed & Breakfast
Cedar Avenue West, Chelmsford
CM1 2XA
t (01245) 257981
e jeremy.salter@btclick.com

CLACTON-ON-SEA

Adelaide Guesthouse ★★★
Guest House
24 Wellesley Road, Clacton-on-Sea
CO15 3PP
t (01255) 435628
e adelaide_guesthouse@yahoo.co.uk
w adelaide-guesthouse.co.uk

Beam Guest House ★★★★
Guest House
26 Nelson Road, Clacton-on-Sea
CO15 1LU
t (01255) 433992
e beamguesthouse@talk21.com
w clacton-on-sea.net

Chudleigh ★★★★
Guest Accommodation
SILVER AWARD
Agate Road, Marine Parade West, Clacton-on-Sea, Essex
CO15 1RA
t (01255) 425407
e chudleighhotel@btconnect.com
w chudleighhotel.com

Pond House ★★★★ Farmhouse
GOLD AWARD
Earls Hall Farm, St Osyth, Clacton-on-Sea
CO16 8BP
t (01255) 820458
e brenda_lord@farming.co.uk
w earlshallfarm.info

CLAVERING

Cricketers, The ★★★★ Inn
SILVER AWARD
Wicken Road, Clavering, Saffron Walden
CB11 4QT
t (01799) 550442
e info@thecricketers.co.uk
w thecricketers.co.uk

COLCHESTER

17 Roman Road ★★★★
Bed & Breakfast
17 Roman Road, Colchester
CO1 1UR
t (01206) 768898
e marianne.gilbert@btinternet.com
w 17romanroad.co.uk

Apple Blossom House ★★★★
Guest Accommodation
8 Guildford Road, Colchester
CO1 2YL
t (01206) 512303
e patricia.appleblossom@virgin.net

Armoury Guest House ★★★
Bed & Breakfast
Armoury Road, West Bergholt, Colchester
CO6 3JP
t 01206 241740
e johnthearmoury@aol.com
w thearmoury.org

Beacon Guest House ★★
Guest House
12 Berrimans Close, Colchester
CO4 3XF
t (01206) 794501
e hannahmulvey@aol.com

Charlie Brown's ★★★★
Bed & Breakfast SILVER AWARD
60 East Street, Colchester
CO1 2TS
t (01206) 517541
e info@charliebrownsbedandbreakfast.co.uk
w charliebrownsbedandbreakfast.co.uk

Corner House ★★★
Bed & Breakfast
36 West Stockwell Street, Colchester
CO1 1HS
t 07737 533879
e anneminns@googlemail.com
w cornerhouse-bb.co.uk

Four Sevens Guest House ★★★★
Guest Accommodation
28 Inglis Road, Colchester
CO3 3HU
t (01206) 546093
e calypso.demetri@gmail.com
w foursevens.co.uk

Greenview House ★★★★
Bed & Breakfast
6 St Johns Green, Colchester
CO2 7HA
t (01206) 570847
e greenviewhouse@btinternet.com
w greenviewhouse.co.uk

Knowles Barn ★★★★
Bed & Breakfast
London Road, Great Horkesley, Colchester, Essex
CO6 4BU
t (01206) 271110
e ContactUs@knowlesbarn.com
w knowlesbarn.com

key to symbols see page 6

371

East of England | Essex

Myland Pear Tree B&B ★★★
Bed & Breakfast
53 Mile End Rd, Colchester
CO4 5BU
t 07957 358757
e elizabeth.kelly@mylandpeartree.co.uk
w mylandpeartree.co.uk

Scheregate Guesthouse ★★
Guest House
Osborne Street, Colchester
CO2 7DB
t (01206) 573034

Trinity Town House ★★★★
Guest Accommodation
GOLD AWARD
6 Trinity Street, Colchester
CO1 1JN
t (01206) 575955
e info@trinitytownhouse.co.uk
w trinitytownhouse.co.uk

University of Essex ★★★ *Campus*
Wivenhoe Park, Colchester
CO4 3SQ
t (01206) 872358
e venues@essex.ac.uk
w essex.ac.uk/venue-essex

COLCHESTER (5 MILES)

Caterpillar Cottage ★★★★
Bed & Breakfast
Ford Street, Aldham, Colchester
CO6 3PH
t (01206) 240456
e bandbcaterpillar@tiscali.co.uk
w smoothhound.co.uk/hotels/caterpillar

DUDDENHOE END

Rockells Farm ★★★★ *Farmhouse*
Duddenhoe End, Saffron Walden
CB11 4UY
t (01763) 838053
e evert.westerhuis@tiscali.co.uk

DUNMOW

Harwood Guest House ★★★★
Guest House
52 Stortford Road, Great Dunmow
CM6 1DN
t (01371) 874627
e info@harwoodguesthouse.com
w harwoodguesthouse.com

Homelye Farm ★★★★
Guest Accommodation
Homelye Chase, Braintree Road, Great Dunmow
CM6 3AW
t (01371) 872127
e homelyebandb@btconnect.com
w homelyefarm.co.uk

Mallards ★★★★ *Bed & Breakfast*
Star Lane, Dunmow, Great Dunmow, essex
CM6 1AY
t (01371) 872641
e bookings@mallardsdunmow.co.uk
w mallardsdunmow.co.uk

Puttocks Farm B&B ★★★★
Farmhouse
Philpot End, Great Dunmow
CM6 1JQ
t (01371) 872377
e roger@puttocksfarm.com
w puttocksfarm.com

EARLS COLNE

Greenlands Farm ★★★★
Bed & Breakfast **GOLD AWARD**
Lamberts Lane, Earls Colne, Colchester
CO6 2LE
t (01787) 224895
e david@greenlandsfarm.freeserve.co.uk
w greenlandsfarm.co.uk

Riverside Lodge ★★★
Guest Accommodation
40 Lower Holt Street, Earls Colne, Colchester
CO6 2PH
t (01787) 223487
e bandb@riversidelodge-uk.com
w riversidelodge-uk.com

ELMSTEAD

Pheasant Lodge ★★★★★
Bed & Breakfast **GOLD AWARD**
Balls Farm, Tye Road, Elmstead Market, Colchester
CO7 7BB
t 07952 799646
e pheasantlodge@btinternet.com
w ballsfarm.net

FEERING

Old Wills Farm ★★★★ *Farmhouse*
SILVER AWARD
Little Tey Road, Feering, Colchester
CO5 9RP
t (01376) 570259
e janecrayston@btconnect.com

FRINTON-ON-SEA

Uplands Guesthouse ★★★
Guest Accommodation
41 Hadleigh Road, Frinton-on-Sea
CO13 9HQ
t (01255) 674889
e info@uplandsguesthouse.co.uk
w uplandsguesthouse.com

GOLDHANGER

Longwick Farm ★★★★
Bed & Breakfast **SILVER AWARD**
Joyces Chase, Maldon
CM9 8AQ
t (01621) 788233
e longwick.farm@virgin.net
w longwickfarm.co.uk

GREAT BADDOW

Homecroft ★★★ *Bed & Breakfast*
Southend Road, Great Baddow, Chelmsford
CM2 7AD
t (01245) 475070
e jesse@pryke.fsbusiness.co.uk

GREAT BROMLEY

Old Courthouse Inn ★★★★ *Inn*
Harwich Road, Great Bromley, Colchester
CO7 7JG
t (01206) 250322
e info@theoldcourthouseinn.co.uk
w theoldcourthouseinn.co.uk

GREAT EASTON

The Swan Inn ★★★★ *Inn*
SILVER AWARD
The Endway, Great Easton, Great Dunmow
CM6 2HG
t (01371) 870359
e theswangreateaston@tiscali.co.uk
w swangreateaston.co.uk

GREAT OAKLEY

Zig Zag Cottage ★★★★★
Bed & Breakfast
8 Queen Street, Great Oakley, Harwich
CO12 5AS
t (01255) 880968
e ziza.lifestyle@zigzagcottage.com
w zigzagcottage.com

HARLOW

Harlow International Hostel ★★
Hostel
13 School Lane, Harlow
CM20 2QD
t (01279) 421702
e mail@h-i-h.co.uk
w h-i-h.co.uk

HARWICH

The Hive Bed & Breakfast ★★★★
Bed & Breakfast
81 Parkeston Road, Dovercourt Bay, Harwich
CO12 4HE
t (01255) 503316
e bumbles.debbie@virgin.net
w thehiveharwich.co.uk

Stingray Freehouse ★★★ *Inn*
56 Church Street, Harwich
CO12 3DS
t (01255) 503507
e enquiries@thestingray.co.uk
w thestingray.co.uk

HATFIELD BROAD OAK

Bury House ★★★ *Bed & Breakfast*
High Street, Hatfield Broad Oak, Bishops Stortford
CM22 7HQ
t (01279) 718259
e bswan@buryhouse.wanadoo.co.uk
w tiscover.co.uk/gb/guide/5gb,en/objectid,acc16187gb/home.html

The Cottage ★★ *Bed & Breakfast*
Dunmow Road, Hatfield Broad Oak, Bishop's Stortford
CM22 7JJ
t (01279) 718230
e elizabeth.britton@virgin.net

HATFIELD HEATH

Friars Farm ★★★★ *Farmhouse*
SILVER AWARD
Friars Lane, Hatfield Heath, Bishop's Stortford
CM22 7AP
t (01279) 730244
e enquiries@friarsfarmbedandbreakfast.co.uk
w friarsfarmbedandbreakfast.co.uk

Oaklands ★★★ *Bed & Breakfast*
Hatfield Heath, Bishop's Stortford
CM22 7AD
t (01279) 730240
e bob.pam@easykey.com

HIGHWOOD

Wards Farm ★★ *Bed & Breakfast*
Loves Green, Highwood Road, Chelmsford
CM1 3QJ
t (01245) 248812
e alsnbrtn@aol.com

KELVEDON

Highfields Farm ★★★★ *Farmhouse*
Highfields Lane, Kelvedon
CO5 9BJ
t (01376) 570334
e highfieldsfarm@tiscali.co.uk
w highfieldsfarm.co.uk

Swan House ★★★★
Bed & Breakfast
3 Swan Street, Kelvedon
CO5 9NG
t (01376) 573768
e dnspiers@lineone.net
w swan-house.co.uk

LANGHAM

Oak Apple Farm ★★★★
Bed & Breakfast
Greyhound Hill, Langham, Colchester
CO4 5QF
t (01206) 272234
e oak_apple_farm@btinternet.com
w smoothhound.co.uk/hotels/oak.html

LATCHINGDON

Crouch Valley Lodge ★★★
Guest Accommodation
Burnham Road, Latchingdon, Chelmsford
CM3 6EX
t (01621) 740770
e info@crouchvalley.com
w crouchvalley.com

LAYER-DE-LA-HAYE

Rye Farm ★★★★ *Farmhouse*
Rye Lane, Layer-de-La-Haye, Colchester
CO2 0JL
t (01206) 734350
e peterbunting@btconnect.com
w ryefarm.org.uk

LITTLEBURY

Riverside Cottage ★★★
Bed & Breakfast
Walden Road, Littlebury, Saffron Walden
CB11 4TA
t (01799) 522554
e woodward724@btconnect.com

LITTLE HALLINGBURY

Sway ★★★★ *Bed & Breakfast*
Wrights Green, Little Hallingbury, Bishop's Stortford
CM22 7RH
t (01279) 723572
e caroleedwards112@aol.com

LITTLE SAMPFORD

Bush Farm ★★★★
Guest Accommodation
SILVER AWARD
Bush Lane, Little Sampford, Saffron Walden
CB10 2RY
t (01799) 586636
e angelabushfarm@yahoo.com

LITTLE WALTHAM

Channels Lodge ★★★★
Guest Accommodation
GOLD AWARD
Belsteads Farm Lane, Little Waltham, Chelmsford
CM3 3PT
t (01245) 441547
e info@channelslodge.co.uk
w channelslodge.co.uk

LOUGHTON

9 Garden Way ★★ *Bed & Breakfast*
9 Garden Way, Loughton
IG10 2SF
t (020) 8508 6134

Forest Edge ★★★★ *Bed & Breakfast*
61 York Hill, Loughton
IG10 1HZ
t (020) 8508 9834
e arthur@catterallarthur.fsnet.co.uk

MALDON

Anchor Guesthouse ★★★
Guest House
7 Church Street, Maldon
CM9 5HW
t (01621) 853711

Hanson House ★★★★
Bed & Breakfast
2 Conyer Close, Maldon, Essex
CM9 6XN
t 01621 857788
e johnhanson2@btconnect.com

Home Farm Accommodation
★★★★ *Farmhouse* **SILVER AWARD**
Broad Street Green Road, Great Totham, Maldon, Essex
CM9 8NU
t 01621 891137/07785 773320/07832 263649
e info@homefarmaccommodation.com
w homefarmaccommodation.com

Limburn House ★★★★
Bed & Breakfast
Wycke Hill, Maldon
CM9 6SH
t (01621) 851392
e carol_cozens_40@hotmail.co.uk
w limburnhouse.co.uk

East of England | Essex

e Limes Guesthouse ★★★★
est House
Market Hill, Maldon
9 4PZ
t (01621) 850350
e info@thelimesguesthouse.com
w thelimesguesthouse.com

Star House Bed & Breakfast ★★ *Bed & Breakfast*
Wantz Road, Maldon
9 5DE
t 07789 113954
e starhouse@btinternet.com

oi Bed & Breakfast ★★★★
& Breakfast
Acacia Drive, Maldon
9 6AW
t (01621) 853841
e diana.rogers2@btinternet.com

MANNINGTREE

rlews ★★★ *Bed & Breakfast*
VER AWARD
tion Road, Bradfield,
nningtree, Essex
11 2UP
t (01255) 870890
e margherita@curlewsaccommodation.co.uk
w curlewsaccommodation.co.uk

Dock ★★★★ *Bed & Breakfast*
ay Street, Manningtree
11 1AU
t (01206) 392620
e tedforshort@hotmail.com

sworth House ★★★★
& Breakfast
p Hill, Station Road, Bradfield,
nningtree, Essex
11 2UP
t (01255) 870860
e emsworthhouse@hotmail.com
w emsworthhouse.co.uk

NORTH FAMBRIDGE

ry Boat Inn ★★★ *Inn*
ry Road, North Fambridge,
elmsford
3 6LR
t (01621) 740208
e enquiries@ferryboatinn.net
w ferryboatinn.net

ORSETT

s Lodge ★★★★
est Accommodation
apel Farm, Baker Street, Orsett,
ays
16 3LJ
t (01375) 891663
e info@jayslodge.co.uk
w jayslodge.co.uk

PENTLOW

hool Barn Farm ★★★★
& Breakfast **SILVER AWARD**
ntlow, Sudbury
10 7JN
t (01787) 282556
e janesouthin@aol.com
w schoolbarnfarm.com

PLESHEY

ry Farm ★★★★ *Bed & Breakfast*
VER AWARD
ry Road, Pleshey, Chelmsford
3 1HB
t (01245) 237234
e anne@oates.u-net.com
w burybarncottage.com

RIDGEWELL

e White Horse Inn ★★★★ *Inn*
l Road, Ridgewell, Halstead
9 4SG
t (01440) 785132
e enquiries@ridgewellwhitehorse.com
w ridgewellwhitehorse.com

ROYDON

Riverside Guesthouse ★★★★
Guest Accommodation - Room Only
218 High Street, Roydon, Harlow
CM19 5EQ
t (01279) 792332
e info@riversideguesthouse.biz
w riversideguesthouse.biz

SAFFRON WALDEN

Ashleigh House ★★★
Guest Accommodation
7 Farmadine Grove, Saffron Walden
CB11 3DR
t (01799) 513611
e info@ashleighhouse.dabsol.co.uk
w ashleighhouse.net

Bell House ★★★★ *Bed & Breakfast*
Castle Street, Saffron Walden
CB10 1BD
t (01799) 527857

Chapmans ★★ *Bed & Breakfast*
30 Lambert Cross, Saffron Walden
CB10 2DP
t (01799) 527287

The Limes *Bed & Breakfast*
Park Road, Great Chesterford,
Saffron Walden
CB10 1RL
t (01799) 532053
e lindsey@thelimes-bedandbreakfast.co.uk
w thelimes-bedandbreakfast.co.uk

Redgates Farmhouse ★★★★
Bed & Breakfast
Redgates Lane, Sewards End,
Saffron Walden
CB10 2LP
t (01799) 516166
e info@redgates.eu
w redgates.eu

Saffron Walden Yha ★★ *Hostel*
2 Myddylton Place, Saffron Walden
CB10 1BB
t (01799) 523117
e saffron@yha.org.uk
w yha.org.uk

Victoria House ★★ *Bed & Breakfast*
10 Victoria Avenue, Saffron Walden
CB11 3AE
t (01799) 525923

SHALFORD

Lynton House ★★★
Bed & Breakfast **SILVER AWARD**
Lynton, Church End, Braintree
CM7 5EZ
t (01371) 850975
e lynton-house@hotmail.co.uk
w lynton-house.co.uk

SHEERING

Shrubbs Farm B&B ★★★★
Farmhouse
Sheering Road, Hatfield Heath,
Bishop's Stortford
CM22 7LL
t (01279) 730332
e jennylidell@yahoo.co.uk

SIBLE HEDINGHAM

The Limes B&B ★★★★
Bed & Breakfast
100 Swan Street, Sible Hedingham,
Halstead
CO9 3HP
t (01787) 460360
e patricia@patriciapatterson.wanadoo.co.uk
w thelimeshedingham.co.uk

SOUTHEND-ON-SEA

Arosa Guesthouse ★★★
Guest House
184 Eastern Esplanade, Thorpe Bay,
Southend-on-Sea
SS1 3AA
t (01702) 585416
e sam_arosa@yahoo.co.uk
w arosaguesthouse.co.uk

Beaches ★★★★ *Guest House*
SILVER AWARD
192 Eastern Esplanade, Thorpe Bay,
Southend-on-Sea
SS1 3AA
t (01702) 586124
e mark@beachesguesthouse.co.uk
w beachesguesthouse.co.uk

The Moorings B&B ★★★
Bed & Breakfast
172 Eastern Esplanade, Southend-on-Sea
SS1 3AA
t (01702) 587575
e mail@themooringsbedandbreakfast.com
w themooringsbedandbreakfast.com

Pebbles Guesthouse ★★★★
Guest House
190 Eastern Esplanade, Thorpe Bay,
Southend-on-Sea
SS1 3AA
t (01702) 582329
e res@mypebbles.co.uk
w mypebbles.co.uk

Pier View ★★★★
Guest Accommodation
SILVER AWARD
5 Royal Terrace, Southend-on-Sea
SS1 1DY
t (01702) 437900
e info@pierviewguesthouse.co.uk
w pierviewguesthouse.co.uk

The Waverley Guesthouse ★★★
Guest House
191 Eastern Esplanade, Thorpe Bay,
Southend-on-Sea
SS1 3AA
t (01702) 585212
e waverleyguesthouse@hotmail.com
w waverleyguesthouse.co.uk

STANSTED

Chimneys ★★★★ *Guest House*
SILVER AWARD
44 Lower Street, Stansted
Mountfitchet, Stansted
CM24 8LR
t (01279) 813388
e info@chimneysguesthouse.co.uk
w chimneysguesthouse.co.uk

The Cottage ★★★★
Guest Accommodation
SILVER AWARD
71 Birchanger Lane, Bishop's
Stortford
CM23 5QA
t (01279) 812349
e bookings@thecottagebirchanger.co.uk
w thecottagebirchanger.co.uk

White House ★★★★
Bed & Breakfast **SILVER AWARD**
Smiths Green, Takeley
CM22 6NR
t (01279) 870257
e enquiries@whitehousestansted.co.uk
w whitehousestansted.co.uk

STANWAY

The Loft ★★★ *Bed & Breakfast*
Frederick House, New Road,
Stanway, Colchester
CO3 0HU
t (01206) 516006
e theloft@frederickhouse.co.uk

STEBBING

Motts Cottage ★★★★
Bed & Breakfast
High Street, Stebbing, Great
Dunmow
CM6 3SE
t (01371) 856633
e dianekittow@hotmail.com
w mottsbedandbreakfast.co.uk

ST OSYTH

Park Hall Country House
★★★★★ *Guest Accommodation*
GOLD AWARD
Park Chase, St Osyth, Clacton-on-Sea
CO16 8HG
t (01255) 820922
e trish@parkhall.info
w parkhall.info

TAKELEY

High Trees Farm ★★
Bed & Breakfast
Parsonage Road, Takeley, Bishop's
Stortford
CM22 6QX
t (01279) 871306
e jeanhightrees@aol.com
w stansted-bandb.co.uk

Jan Smiths Bandb ★★★★
Bed & Breakfast
The Cottage, Jacks Lane, Bishop's
Stortford
CM22 6NT
t (01279) 870603
e smiths-residence@fsmail.net
w thecottagebnbjackslane.co.uk

Little Bullocks Farm ★★★★
Guest Accommodation
Bullocks Lane, Hope End, Bishop's
Stortford
CM22 6TA
t (01279) 870464
e julie@waterman-farm.fsnet.co.uk
w littlebullocksfarm.co.uk

Oak Lodge Bed & Breakfast
★★★★ *Bed & Breakfast*
SILVER AWARD
Oak Lodge, Jacks Lane, Takeley,
Bishop's Stortford
CM22 6NT
t (01279) 871667
e oaklodgebb@aol.com
w oaklodgebb.com

Pussy Willow ★★★★
Bed & Breakfast **SILVER AWARD**
Mill House, The Street, Bishop's
Stortford
CM22 6QR
t (01279) 871609
e enquiries@thepussywillow.co.uk
w thepussywillow.co.uk

Taphall ★★★ *Bed & Breakfast*
15 The Street, Bishop's Stortford
CM22 6QS
t (01279) 871035
e carolking.taphall@hotmail.com
w taphall.com

THAXTED

Crossways Guesthouse ★★★★
Bed & Breakfast **SILVER AWARD**
32 Town Street, Thaxted
CM6 2LA
t (01371) 830348
e info@crosswaysthaxted.co.uk
w crosswaysthaxted.co.uk

TOLLESBURY

Fernleigh ★★★ *Bed & Breakfast*
16 Woodrolfe Farm Lane,
Tollesbury, Maldon
CM9 8SX
t (01621) 868345
e lesgill69@live.co.uk

TOLLESHUNT MAJOR

Wicks Manor Farm ★★★★
Farmhouse
Witham Road, Tolleshunt Major,
Maldon
CM9 8JU
t (01621) 860629
e rhowie@aspects.net
w wicksmanor.co.uk

East of England | Essex/Hertfordshire

WAKES COLNE

Rosebank ★★★★ *Bed & Breakfast*
Station Road, Wakes Colne,
Colchester
CO6 2DS
t (01787) 223552
e barbaralynn@btconnect.com

WALTON-ON-THE-NAZE

Bufo Villae Guest House ★★★★
Guest Accommodation
31 Beatrice Road, Walton-on-the-Naze, Frinton-on-Sea
CO14 8HJ
t (01255) 672644
e bufovillae@btinternet.com
w bufovillae.co.uk

WESTCLIFF-ON-SEA

The Pavilion ★★ *Guest House*
1 Trinity Avenue, Westcliff-on-Sea
SS0 7PU
t (01702) 332767
e pavilion.hotel@btconnect.com
w pavhot.com

Rose House ★★★ *Guest House*
21-23 Manor Road, Westcliff-on-Sea
SS0 7SR
t (01702) 341959
w rosehousehotel.co.uk

WEST MERSEA

The Victory at Mersea ★★★★ *Inn*
92 Coast Road, Mersea Island,
Colchester
CO5 8LS
t (01206) 382907
e info@victoryatmersea.com
w victoryatmersea.com

WETHERSFIELD

Brook Farm ★★★★ *Farmhouse*
Braintree Road, Wethersfield,
Braintree
CM7 4BX
t (01371) 850284
e abutlerbrookfarm@aol.com
w brookfarmwethersfield.co.uk

Church Hill House ★★★★
Bed & Breakfast **GOLD AWARD**
High Street, Wethersfield, Braintree
CM7 4BY
t (01371) 850342
e clubley@churchhillhouse.co.uk
w churchhillhouse.co.uk

The Green ★★★★ *Bed & Breakfast*
SILVER AWARD
The Green, Wethersfield, Braintree
CM7 4BU
t (01371) 851643
e pedro.harris@btinternet.com
w thegreen-wethersfield.co.uk

WHITE NOTLEY

Elms Farm ★★★★ *Bed & Breakfast*
Green Lane, White Notley, Witham
CM8 1RB
t (01376) 321559

WIMBISH

Newdegate House ★★★★
Guest Accommodation
SILVER AWARD
Howlett End, Wimbish, Saffron
Walden
CB10 2XW
t (01799) 599748
e jacky@newdegate.co.uk

WITHAM

Chestnuts ★★★ *Bed & Breakfast*
8 Octavia Drive, Witham Lodge,
Witham
CM8 1HQ
t (01376) 515990
e janetmoya@aol.com

WOODHAM MORTIMER

Chase Farm Bed & Breakfast
★★★ *Bed & Breakfast*
Hyde Chase, Woodham Mortimer,
Maldon
CM9 6TN
t (01245) 223268
e info@chasefarmbnb.uk
w chasefarmbnb.co.uk

Hertfordshire

ANSTEY

Anstey Grove Barn ★★★★
Farmhouse **SILVER AWARD**
The Grove, Anstey, Buntingford
SG9 0BJ
t (01763) 848828
e enquiries@ansteygrovebarn.co.uk
w ansteygrovebarn.co.uk

ASHWELL

Three Tuns Hotel ★★★ *Inn*
6 High Street, Ashwell, Nr Baldock,
Hertfordshire
SG7 5NL
t (01462) 742 107
e info@threetunshotel.co.uk
w threetunshotel.co.uk

AYOT ST LAWRENCE

The Brocket Arms ★★★★
Guest Accommodation
Ayot St Lawrence, Welwyn
AL6 9BT
t (01438) 820250
e bookings@brocketarms.com
w ww.brocketarms.com

BISHOP'S STORTFORD

Acer Cottage ★★★ *Bed & Breakfast*
17 Windhill, Bishop's Stortford
CM23 2NE
t (01279) 834797
e info@acercottage.co.uk
w acercottage.co.uk

AJ Bed & Breakfast ★★
Bed & Breakfast
5 Ascot Close, Bishop's Stortford
CM23 5BP
t (01279) 652228
e aandjbnb@tesco.net
w aandjbandb.co.uk

Ascot B&B ★★★ *Bed & Breakfast*
6 Ascot Close, Bishop's Stortford
CM23 5BP
t (01279) 651027
e derek@derekfox1.wanadoo.co.uk
w ascot-bandb.co.uk

Avery House ★★★★
Bed & Breakfast
52 Thorley Hill, Bishop's Stortford
CM23 3NA
t (01279) 658311
e jacki-ross.accommodation@virgin.net
w averyhouse.co.uk

Coral's B&B ★★★★
Bed & Breakfast
Shire House, 14 Cannons Mill Lane,
Bishop's Stortford
CM23 2BN
t (01279) 508544
e shirehouse@coralsbnb.co.uk
w coralsbnb.co.uk

Phoenix Lodge ★★★ *Guest House*
91 Dunmow Road, Bishop's
Stortford
CM23 5HF
t (01279) 659780
e phoenixlodge@ntlworld.com
w phoenixlodge.co.uk

BRAMFIELD

The Kings' House ★★★
Bed & Breakfast
1 Holly Grove Road, Bramfield,
Hertford
SG14 2QH
t (01992) 551678
e jillyking@eprimus.co.uk

BROOKMANS PARK

Stewards Cottage ★★★★
Farmhouse
60 Bell Lane, Bell Bar, Hatfield
AL9 7AY
t (01707) 642091
e info@stewardscottagebandb.co.uk
w stewardscottagebandb.co.uk

CHESHUNT

YHA Lee Valley Village ★★★★
Hostel
Windmill Lane, Cheshunt, Waltham
Cross
EN8 9AJ
t (01992) 628392
e leevalley@yha.org.uk
w yha.org.uk

CHORLEYWOOD

Ashburton Country House
★★★★★ *Bed & Breakfast*
GOLD AWARD
48 Berks Hill, Chorleywood,
Rickmansworth
WD3 5AH
t (01923) 285510
e info@ashburtonhouse.co.uk
w ashburtonhouse.co.uk

EPPING GREEN

Mulberry Lodge ★★★★
Guest Accommodation
Newgate Street, Epping Green,
Hertford
SG13 8NQ
t (01707) 879652
e boookings@mulberrylodge.org.uk
w mulberrylodge.org.uk

FROGMORE

Riverside ★★★★ *Bed & Breakfast*
SILVER AWARD
24 Minister Court, St Albans
AL2 2NF
t (01727) 758780
e ellispatriciam@ntlworld.com

GREAT HORMEAD

**Brick House Farm Bed &
Breakfast** ★★★★ *Farmhouse*
SILVER AWARD
Great Hormead, Buntingford
SG9 0PB
t (01763) 289356
e helen@brickhousefarm.net
w brickhousefarm.net

HATFIELD

**University of Hertfordshire de
Havilland** ★★★ *Campus*
Fielder Centre, Hatfield Business
Park, Hatfield
AL10 9FL
t (01707) 284841

HEMEL HEMPSTEAD

47 Crescent Road ★★
Bed & Breakfast
47 Crescent Road, Hemel
Hempstead
HP2 4AY
t (01442) 255137

Marsh Farm ★★★★
Bed & Breakfast
Ledgemore Lane, Great Gaddesden
HP2 6HA
t (01442) 252517
e nicky@bennett-baggs.com
w marshfarm.org.uk

HERTFORD

Boutique B&B ★★★★
Bed & Breakfast
10 Cowbridge, Hertford
SG14 1PQ
t (01992) 300717
e info@hertfordbandb.com
w hertfordbandb.com

Castle Moat House ★★★★
Bed & Breakfast
25 Castle Street, Hertford
SG14 1HH
t (01992) 584004
e castlemoathouse@gmail.com
w castlemoathouse.com

MUCH HADHAM

Wheatcroft ★★★★ *Bed & Break*
Hadham Cross, Much Hadham
SG10 6AP
t (01279) 842206
e hope@wheatcroft.freeserve.co
w wheatcroftbedandbreakfast.co

OFFLEY

Honeysuckle Cottage ★★
Bed & Breakfast
25 High Street, Great Offley, Hitc
SG5 3AP
t (01462) 768050

SAWBRIDGEWORTH

2 Bursteads Cottages ★★★★
Bed & Breakfast
Spellbrook Lane West,
Sawbridgeworth
CM21 0NB
t 07789 214127
e mileswade640@btinternet.com
w 2bursteadscottages.com

7 Church Walk ★★ *Bed & Break*
7 Church Walk, Sawbridgeworth
CM21 9BJ
t (01279) 723233
e kent@sawbridgeworth.co.uk
w ourbedandbreakfast.co.uk

ST ALBANS

2 The Limes ★★ *Bed & Breakfast*
Spencer Gate, St Albans
AL1 4AT
t (01727) 831080
e hunter.mitchell@virgin.net

5 Approach Road ★★★
Bed & Breakfast
5 Approach Road, St Albans
AL1 1SP
t (07944) 837533
e eileenvkent@aol.com

7 Marlborough Gate ★★★
Bed & Breakfast
7 Marlborough Gate, St Albans
AL1 3TX
t (01727) 865498
e michael.jameson@btinternet.co

22 Ardens Way ★★★★
Bed & Breakfast
Marshalswick, St Albans
AL4 9UJ
t (01727) 861986
e beteddickens@btinternet.com

36 Potters Field ★★
Bed & Breakfast
36 Potters Field, St Albans
AL3 6LJ
t (01727) 766840
e manners-smith@ntlworld.com

178 London Road ★★★
Bed & Breakfast **SILVER AWARD**
178 London Road, St Albans
AL1 1PL
t (01727) 846726
e bookings_178londonroad@btconnect.com
w 178londonroad.co.uk

Braemar House ★★★★
Bed & Breakfast
89 Salisbury Avenue, St Albans
AL1 4TY
t (01727) 839641
e slatersbraemar@btinternet.com
w braemar-st-albans.co.uk

Carousel Guest House ★★★
Bed & Breakfast
122 Hatfield Road, St Albans
AL1 4HY
t (01727) 850004
e sandra.woodland@ntlworld.com

East of England | Hertfordshire/Norfolk

n Cottage ★★★★
& Breakfast
Old London Road, St Albans
1PU
01727) 834200
ookinginfo@ferncottage.uk.net
erncottage.uk.net

uchary House ★★★★
st Accommodation
VER AWARD
pper Lattimore Road, St Albans
3UD
01727) 766764
inda@fleucharyhouse.freeserve.
o.uk
leucharyhouse.com

Greens ★★★★ *Bed & Breakfast*
andpit Lane, St Albans
4BW
01727) 856799
vonnegreen@talktalk.net

er Red Lion ★★ *Inn*
Fishpool Street, St Albans
4RX
01727) 855669
contact@lowerredlion.co.uk

tree House ★★★★
& Breakfast
Hatfield Road, St Albans
0SX
01727) 857521

k House ★★ *Bed & Breakfast*
The Park, St Albans
4RY
01727) 811910
nora@parkhouseonline.co.uk
parkhouseonline.co.uk

sco ★★★ *Bed & Breakfast*
Clarence Road, St Albans
4NG
01727) 864880
pat_leggatt@hotmail.com
trescohouse.co.uk

ite House ★★ *Bed & Breakfast*
Salisbury Avenue, St Albans
4TU
01727) 861017

TEWIN

bells ★★★★ *Bed & Breakfast*
Firs Walk, Tewin Wood, Welwyn
0NZ
01438) 798412

WARE

baras B&B ★★
st Accommodation - Room Only
igh Oak Road, Ware
2 7PG
01920) 484796
ruttb@aol.com

Norfolk

ACLE

e Bed & Breakfast
& Breakfast
letcher Way, Acle
13 3RQ
01493) 754166
dkimpark@aol.com
aclebedandbreakfast.co.uk

e Kings Head Inn ★★★ *Inn*
Street, Acle, Norwich
13 3DY
01493) 750204
info@kingsheadinnacle.co.uk
kingsheadinnacle.co.uk

ALDBOROUGH NEAR CROMER

tterfly Cottage B&B ★★★★
est House
e Green, Aldborough, Cromer,
rfolk
1 7AA
01263) 768198 (01263) 761689
butterflycottage@btinternet.com
butterflycottage.com

ALDEBY

The Old Vicarage ★★★
Bed & Breakfast
Rectory Road, Beccles
NR34 0BJ
t (01502) 678229
e dorothybutler832@btinternet.com

AYLMERTON

Driftway Guest House ★★★★
Bed & Breakfast **SILVER AWARD**
Driftway, The Close, Aylmerton, Cromer
NR11 8PX
t (01263) 838589
e dawn@sparrowsnorfolkholidaycottages.co.uk
w sparrowsnorfolkholidaycottages.co.uk

AYLSHAM

Deepdale Backpackers Hostel ★★★★ *Hostel*
Main Road, Burnham Deepdale, King's Lynn
NR11 6AL
t (01485) 210256
e info@deepdalebackpackers.co.uk
w deepdalebackpackers.co.uk

The Old Pump House ★★★★★
Guest Accommodation
GOLD AWARD
Holman Road, Aylsham, Norwich
NR11 6BY
t (01263) 733789
e theoldpumphouse@btconnect.com
w theoldpumphouse.com

BARNEY

The Old Brick Kilns Guesthouse ★★★★ *Bed & Breakfast*
SILVER AWARD
Little Barney Lane, Barney, Fakenham
NR21 0NL
t (01328) 878305
e enquiries@old-brick-kilns.co.uk
w old-brick-kilns.co.uk

BAWBURGH

The Old Lodge ★★★★
Bed & Breakfast **SILVER AWARD**
The Old Lodge, New Road, Norwich
NR9 3LZ
t (01603) 742318
e theoldlodge@tiscali.co.uk
w theoldlodge.co.uk

BEESTON

Holmdene Farm ★★★ *Farmhouse*
Syers Lane, Beeston, King's Lynn
PE32 2NJ
t (01328) 701284
e holmdenefarm@farmersweekly.net
w holmdenefarm.co.uk

BERGH APTON

Hillside Farm ★★★★ *Farmhouse*
Welbeck Road, Brooke, Norwich
NR15 1AU
t (01508) 550260
e carrie.holl@btconnect.com
w hillside-farm.co.uk

BLAKENEY

Cornfield Bed & Breakfast ★★★
Bed & Breakfast
32 The Cornfield, Langham, Blakeney
NR25 7DQ
t (01328) 830939
e cornfieldbandb@googlemail.com
w cornfieldbandb.co.uk

Navestock Bed & Breakfast ★★★★ *Bed & Breakfast*
Cley Road, Blakeney
NR25 7NL
t (01263) 740998
e johnmander@tiscali.co.uk
w glavenvalley.co.uk/navestock

BLICKLING

Buckinghamshire Arms ★★★★
Inn
Blickling, Aylsham
NR11 6NF
t (01263) 732133
e bucksarms@tiscali.co.uk
w bucks-arms.co.uk

BRANTHILL

Branthill Farm ★★★ *Farmhouse*
Wells-next-the-Sea
NR23 1SB
t (01263) 710246
e branthill.farms@unicombox.co.uk
w therealaleshop.co.uk/norfolk

BRESSINGHAM

Hazel Barn ★★★★ *Bed & Breakfast*
Lodge Lane, Bressingham, Diss
IP22 2BE
t (01379) 644396
e info@hazelbarn.com
w hazelbarn.com

BROOKE

The Old Vicarage ★★★★
Bed & Breakfast **SILVER AWARD**
48 The Street, Brooke, Norwich
NR15 1JU
t (01508) 558329

BRUNDALL

Braydeston House ★★★★
Bed & Breakfast
9 The Street, Brundall, Norwich
NR13 5JY
t (01603) 713123
e ann@braydeston.freeserve.co.uk
w braydestonhouse.co.uk

Breckland B&B ★★★★
Bed & Breakfast **SILVER AWARD**
12 Strumpshaw Road, Brundall, Norwich
NR13 5PA
t (01603) 712122
e brecklandbandb@hotmail.com
w breckland-bandb.co.uk

BUNWELL

The Cottage ★★★★
Guest Accommodation
SILVER AWARD
Rectory Lane, Bunwell, Norwich
NR16 1QU
t (01953) 789226
w thecottagenorfolk.co.uk

BURNHAM DEEPDALE

Deepdale Granary Group Hostel ★★★ *Group Hostel*
Deepdale Farms, Main Road, King's Lynn
PE31 8DD
t (01485) 210256
e info@deepdalebackpackers.co.uk
w deepdalebackpackers.co.uk

BURNHAM MARKET

Wood Lodge ★★★★
Bed & Breakfast **SILVER AWARD**
Millwood, Herring's Lane, King's Lynn
PE31 8DP
t (01328) 730152
e philip.roll@btinternet.com

BURNHAM THORPE

Whitehall Farm ★★★★ *Farmhouse*
SILVER AWARD
Burnham Thorpe, Norfolk
PE31 8HN
t (01328) 738416
e barrysoutherland@aol.com
w whitehallfarm-accommodation.com

CASTLE ACRE

Church Gate Tea Room & Bed & Breakfast ★★★★
Guest Accommodation
Willow Cottage, Stocks Green, Castle Acre, Swaffham
PE32 2AE
t (01760) 755551
e info@churchgatecastleacre.co.uk
w churchgatecastleacre.co.uk

CATFIELD

The Limes ★★★★ *Bed & Breakfast*
SILVER AWARD
Limes Road, Catfield, Norfolk Broads
NR29 5DG
t (01692) 581221
e info@thelimesatcatfield.com
w thelimesatcatfield.com

CHEDGRAVE

Chedgrave House B&B ★★★★
Bed & Breakfast
2 Norwich Road, Chedgrave, Loddon, Norwich, Norfolk
NR14 6HB
t 01508 521095
e june@chedgrave-house.freeserve.co.uk
w chedgrave-house.co.uk

Little Willows ★★★★
Bed & Breakfast **SILVER AWARD**
Willow Cottage, Nursery Road, Chedgrave, Loddon
NR14 6BF
t (01508) 528525
e info@littlewillows.co.uk
w littlewillows.co.uk

CLENCHWARTON

Kismet Lodge Bed & Breakfast ★★★★ *Bed & Breakfast*
SILVER AWARD
15 Willow Drive, Clenchwarton, King's Lynn
PE34 4EN
t (01553) 761409
e francesgoodwin@hotmail.com
w bed-and-breakfast-kismet-lodge.co.uk

COLTISHALL

Bridge House ★★★★ *Guest House*
Bridge House, Coltishall, Norwich
NR12 7AA
t (01603) 737323
e bhbookings@talktalk.net
w bridgehouse-coltishall.co.uk

Hedges Guesthouse ★★★★
Guest Accommodation
Tunstead Road, Coltishall
NR12 7AL
t (01603) 738361
e info@hedgesbandb.co.uk
w hedgesbandb.co.uk

Seven Acres House ★★★★★
Bed & Breakfast **GOLD AWARD**
Great Hautbois, Coltishall, Norwich
NR12 7JZ
t (01603) 736737
e info@hautbois.plus.com
w norfolkbroadsbandb.com

CROMER

Albury House ★★★★ *Guest House*
20 Alfred Road, Cromer
NR27 9AN
t (01263) 515011
e vicky@albury-house.co.uk
w albury-house.co.uk

key to symbols see page 6

375

East of England | Norfolk

Cambridge House ★★★★
Guest Accommodation
Sea Front, East Cliff, Cromer
NR27 9HD
t (01263) 512085
e elizabeth.wass@btconnect.com
w cambridgecromer.co.uk

Cliff Cottage ★★★★
Bed & Breakfast
18 High Street, Overstrand, Cromer
NR27 0AB
t (01263) 578179
e roymin@btinternet.com
w cliffcottagebandb.com

Cromer House B&B ★★★★
Guest Accommodation
10 Alfred Road, Cromer
NR27 9AN
t (01263) 510923
e peterscarbrow@tiscali.co.uk
w cromerhouse.co.uk

The Grove ★★★★
Guest Accommodation
95 Overstrand Road, Cromer
NR27 0DJ
t (01263) 512412
e thegrovecromer@btopenworld.com
w thegrovecromer.co.uk

Knoll Guest House ★★★
Guest Accommodation
23 Alfred Road, Cromer
NR27 9AN
t (01263) 512753
e arnold_p@btconnect.com
w knollguesthouse.co.uk

No 4 ★★★★ *Bed & Breakfast*
4 Vicarage Road, Cromer
NR27 9DQ
t (01263) 510116
e debrahparry06@aol.com
w 4bedandbreakfast.com

The Old Barn ★★★★
Bed & Breakfast SILVER AWARD
Cromer Road, West Runton, Cromer
NR27 9QT
t (01263) 838285
e mkelliot2@aol.com
w theoldbarnnorfolk.co.uk

Shrublands Farm Guesthouse
★★★★ *Farmhouse* SILVER AWARD
Church Street, Northrepps, Cromer
NR27 0AA
t (01263) 579297
e youngman@farming.co.uk
w shrublandsfarm.com

DENVER

Westhall Cottages ★★★
Bed & Breakfast
20-22 Sluice Road, Downham Market
PE38 0DY
t (01366) 382987

DEOPHAM

Park Farm Bed & Breakfast
★★★★ *Farmhouse* SILVER AWARD
Park Lane, Deopham, Wymondham
NR18 9HL
t (01953) 602289
e parkfarmbb@yahoo.co.uk
w parkfarmbandb.co.uk

DEREHAM

Hunters Hall ★★★★ *Farmhouse*
Park Farm, Swanton Morley, Dereham
NR20 4JU
t (01362) 637457
e office@huntershall.com
w huntershall.com

DERSINGHAM

Ashdene House ★★★★
Guest Accommodation
SILVER AWARD
60 Hunstanton Road, Dersingham, King's Lynn
PE31 6HQ
t (01485) 540395
e mail@ashdene-house.co.uk
w ashdene-house.co.uk

Barn House Bed & Breakfast
★★★★ *Guest Accommodation*
SILVER AWARD
14 Station Road, Dersingham, King's Lynn
PE31 6PP
t (01485) 543086
e barnhousebnb@gmail.com
w smoothhound.co.uk/hotels/barnho

The Corner House ★★★★
Bed & Breakfast GOLD AWARD
2 Sandringham Road, Dersingham, King's Lynn
PE31 6LL
t (01485) 543532
e the_corner_house@btinternet.com

Holkham Cottage ★★★★
Guest Accommodation
34 Hunstanton Road, Dersingham, King's Lynn
PE31 6HQ
t (01485) 544562
e holkham.cottage@btinternet.co.uk
w holkhamcottage.co.uk

Tall Trees ★★★★ *Bed & Breakfast*
7 Centre Vale, Dersingham, King's Lynn
PE31 6JR
t (01485) 542638
e frostytrees@tiscali.co.uk
w talltrees-norfolk.co.uk

The White House ★★★★
Guest House SILVER AWARD
44 Hunstanton Road, Dersingham, King's Lynn
PE31 6HQ
t (01485) 541895
e aaquapure@talktalk.net

DICKLEBURGH

Dickleburgh Hall Country House
★★★★★ *Bed & Breakfast*
GOLD AWARD
Semere Green Lane, Dickleburgh, Diss
IP21 4NT
t (01379) 741259
e johntaylor05@btinternet.com
w dickhall.co.uk

Moor View ★★★★ *Bed & Breakfast*
Semere Green Lane, Dickleburgh, Diss
IP21 4NT
t (01379) 741401
e vehooper@aol.com
w moor-view.com

DISS

Cobwebs ★★★ *Bed & Breakfast*
6 Riverside, Denmark Street, Diss
IP22 4BE
t (01379) 641388
e cobwebsbandb@yahoo.co.uk
w cobwebsbandb.co.uk

DOCKING, BURNHAM MARKET (6 MILES)

Jubilee Lodge ★★★★
Guest Accommodation
Station Road, Docking, King's Lynn
PE31 8LS
t (01328) 518473
e eghoward62@hotmail.com
w jubilee-lodge.com

DOWNHAM MARKET

Chestnut Villa ★★★
Guest Accommodation
44 Railway Road, Downham Market
PE38 9EB
t (01366) 384099
e chestnutvilla@talk21.com
w chestnutvilla-downham.com

Dial House B&B ★★★★
Bed & Breakfast
12 Railway Road, Downham Market, Norfolk
PE38 9EB
t 01366 385775
e robert.shrimpton@btopenworld.com
w dialhousbnb.com

Station Villa ★★★★
Bed & Breakfast
11 Bennett Street, Downham Market
PE38 9EE
t (01366) 386663
e downhampost4@tiscali.co.uk
w archiesholidays.com

EARSHAM

Earsham Park Farm ★★★★
Farmhouse GOLD AWARD
Harleston Road, Bungay
NR35 2AN
t (01986) 892180
e bobbie@earsham-parkfarm.co.uk
w earsham-parkfarm.co.uk

EAST RUDHAM

The Close ★★★★★
Bed & Breakfast GOLD AWARD
East Rudham, King's Lynn
PE31 8SU
t (01485) 528925
e rorymcgouran@hotmail.com
w closenorfolk.com

EAST RUNTON

Incleborough House ★★★★★
Bed & Breakfast GOLD AWARD
Lower Common, East Runton, Cromer
NR27 9PG
t (01263) 515939
e enquiries@incleboroughhouse.co.uk
w incleboroughhouse.com

EDINGTHORPE

Church Farm Barn ★★★★★
Bed & Breakfast GOLD AWARD
Rectory Road, Edingthorpe, North Walsham
NR28 9TN
t (01692) 651014
e andywkerr@tiscali.co.uk
w churchfarmbarn.com

ELSING

Bartles Lodge ★★★★ *Guest House*
Church Street, Elsing, Dereham, Norfolk
NR20 3EA
t (01362) 637177
e bartleslodge@yahoo.co.uk
w bartleslodge.co.uk

FAKENHAM

Abbott Farm B&B ★★★
Farmhouse
Walsingham Road, Binham, Fakenham
NR21 0AW
t (01328) 830519
e abbot.farm@btinternet.com
w abbottfarm.co.uk

Erika's Bed & Breakfast ★★★★
Guest Accommodation
3 Gladstone Road, Fakenham
NR21 9BZ
t (01328) 863059
w erikasbedandbreakfast.co.uk

Holly Lodge ★★★★★
Bed & Breakfast GOLD AWARD
The Street, Thursford Green, Fakenham
NR21 0AS
t (01328) 878465
e info@hollyguestlodge.co.uk
w hollylodgeguesthouse.co.uk

White Rose Lodge ★★★★★
Bed & Breakfast GOLD AWARD
Green Farm Lane, Thursford, Fakenham
NR21 0RX
t (01328) 878995
e whiterose.lodge@btinternet.co
w whiteroselodgethursford.co.uk

FERSFIELD

Strenneth ★★★★
Guest Accommodation
SILVER AWARD
Strenneth, Airfield Road, Diss
IP22 2BP
t (01379) 688182
e pdavey@strenneth.co.uk
w strenneth.co.uk

FOULDEN

The White Hart Inn ★★★
Guest Accommodation
White Hart Street, Foulden, Thetf
IP26 5AW
t (01366) 328638
e hartpub@yahoo.co.uk

FRITTON

Decoy Barn Bed & Breakfast
★★★★ *Guest Accommodation*
SILVER AWARD
Beccles Road, Fritton, Great Yarmouth
NR31 9AB
t (01493) 488222
e karenwilder9@aol.com
w decoybarn.co.uk

GARBOLDISHAM

Ingleneuk Lodge ★★★★
Guest House
Hopton Road, Garboldisham, Diss
IP22 2RQ
t (01953) 681541
e info@ingleneuklodge.co.uk
w ingleneuk-lodge.co.uk

GAYTON

Bridge House ★★★★ *Guest Hou*
SILVER AWARD
Winch Road, Gayton, King's Lynn
PE32 1QP
t (01553) 636756
e info@bridgehouseholidays.co.u
w bridgehouseholidays.co.uk

GREAT CRESSINGHAM

The Olde Windmill Inn ★★★★
Water End, Great Cressingham, Thetford
IP25 6NN
t (01760) 756232
e halls232@aol.com

The Vines ★★★★
Guest Accommodation
The Street, Great Cressingham, Thetford
IP25 6NL
t (01760) 756303
e stay@thevinesbedandbreakfast.co.uk
w thevines.fsbusiness.co.uk

GREAT MOULTON

South Norfolk Guest House ★★
Guest Accommodation
Oakbrook House, Frith Way, Norwich
NR15 2HE
t (01379) 677359
e oakbrookhouse@btinternet.co
w oakbrookhouse.co.uk

East of England | Norfolk

GREAT SNORING

p Farm ★★★★ *Farmhouse*
ursford Road, Great Snoring,
enham
21 0HW
t (01328) 820351
e davidperowne@aol.com
w topfambandb.co.uk

e Park Cottage ★★★★
mhouse **SILVER AWARD**
ursford Road, Great Snoring,
enham
21 0PF
t (01328) 821016
e rita@vineparkcottagebandb.co.uk
w vineparkcottagebandb.co.uk

GREAT YARMOUTH

glia House ★★★ *Guest House*
Wellesley Road, Great Yarmouth
30 1EX
t (01493) 844395
e angliahouse@aol.com

rnard House ★★★★
& Breakfast **SILVER AWARD**
arnard Crescent, Great Yarmouth
30 4DR
t (01493) 855139
e enq@barnardhouse.com
w barnardhouse.com

ons Court ★★★★
st Accommodation
lorfolk Square, Great Yarmouth
30 1EE
t (01493) 843987
e info@baronscourthotel.co.uk
w baronscourthotel.co.uk

ach House *Guest Accommodation*
Wellesley Road, Great Yarmouth
30 2AR
t (01493) 843 977

aumont House ★★★★
est House **SILVER AWARD**
Wellesley Road, Great Yarmouth
30 1EX
t (01493) 843957
e info@beaumonthousehotel.com
w beaumonthousehotel.com

vedere Guest House ★★★
est House
North Denes Road, Great
mouth
30 4LW
t (01493) 844200
e info@stayatbelvedere.co.uk
w stayatbelvedere.co.uk

e Bromley ★★★★ *Guest House*
VER AWARD
Apsley Road, Great Yarmouth
30 2HG
t (01493) 842321
e info@thebromleyhotel.co.uk
w bromleyhotel.co.uk

vendish House ★★★
est Accommodation
20 Princes Road, Great Yarmouth
30 2DG
t (01493) 843148
e cavendishhousehotel@yahoo.co.uk
w cavendishhousehotel.com

e Chateau ★★★★
est Accommodation
lorth Drive, Great Yarmouth
30 1ED
t (01493) 859052
e info@chateau-gy.fsbusiness.co.uk
w chateau-gy.fsbusiness.co.uk

e Chatsworth ★★★
est Accommodation
Wellesley Road, Great Yarmouth
30 1EU
t (01493) 842890
e roger@chatsworthfamilyhotel.co.uk
w chatsworthfamilyhotel.com

The Chimes ★★★★ *Guest House*
48 Wellesley Road, Great Yarmouth
NR30 1EX
t (01493) 844610
e veronica.mardle@ntlworld.com
w thechimes.co.uk

Cleasewood ★★★ *Guest House*
55 Wellesley Road, Great Yarmouth
NR30 1EX
t (01493) 843960
e enquiries@thecleasewood.co.uk
w thecleasewood.co.uk

Copperfields Guesthouse ★★★
Guest House
16 Trafalgar Road, Great Yarmouth
NR30 2LD
t (01493) 856679
e bauervrnn@aol.com
w copperfieldsguesthouse.com

Dene House ★★★★ *Guest House*
89 North Denes Road, Great
Yarmouth
NR30 4LW
t (01493) 844181
e denehouse@btinternet.com
w denehouse-greatyarmouth.co.uk

The Fjaerland ★★★★
Guest Accommodation
24-25 Trafalgar Road, Great
Yarmouth
NR30 2LD
t (01493) 856339
w smoothhound.co.uk/hotels/fjaerland

The Kensington ★★★★
Guest Accommodation
29 North Drive, Great Yarmouth
NR30 4EW
t (01493) 844145
e frontdesk@kensington-hotel.co.uk
w kensington-hotel.co.uk

Kentville Guest House ★★★
Guest House
5 Kent Square, Great Yarmouth
NR30 2EX
t (01493) 844783
e info@kentville.co.uk
w kentville.co.uk

Kilbrannan Guest House ★★★★
Guest House
14 Trafalgar Road, Great Yarmouth
NR30 2LD
t (01493) 850383
e enquiries@kilbrannanguesthouse.co.uk
w kilbrannanguesthouse.co.uk

Lea Hurst Guesthouse ★★★
Guest House
117 Wellesley Road, Great Yarmouth
NR30 2AP
t (01493) 843063
e info@theleahurst.co.uk
w theleahurst.co.uk

The Little Emily ★★★ *Guest House*
18 Princes Road, Great Yarmouth
NR30 2DG
t (01493) 842515
e little-emily@hotmail.co.uk
w littleemily.co.uk

Maluth Lodge ★★★★
Guest Accommodation
40 North Denes Road, Great
Yarmouth
NR30 4LU
t (01493) 304652
e enquiries@maluthlodge.co.uk
w maluthlodge.co.uk

The Maryland ★★★★ *Guest House*
The Maryland, Great Yarmouth
NR30 1EX
t (01493) 844409
e lucy@themaryland.co.uk
w themaryland.co.uk

Merivon Guest House ★★★★
Guest Accommodation
SILVER AWARD
6 Trafalgar Road, Great Yarmouth
NR30 2LD
t (01493) 844419
e reception@merivon.co.uk
w merivonguesthouse.co.uk

Royston House ★★★ *Guest House*
Royston House, Great Yarmouth
NR30 1DY
t (01493) 844680
e enquiries@roystonhouse.com
w roystonhouse.com

The Ryecroft ★★★ *Guest House*
91 North Denes Road, Great
Yarmouth
NR30 4LW
t (01493) 844015
e info@ryecroftguesthouse.co.uk
w ryecroftguesthouse.co.uk

Saffrons ★★★★ *Guest House*
SILVER AWARD
102 Wellesley Road, Great Yarmouth
NR30 2AR
t (01493) 844693
e enquiries@saffronsguesthouse.co.uk
w saffronsguesthouse.co.uk

Sandy Acres ★★★★
Guest Accommodation
80-81 Salisbury Road, Great
Yarmouth
NR30 4LB
t (01493) 856553
e enquiries@sandyacres.co.uk
w sandyacres.co.uk

Seashells ★★★ *Guest House*
57 Nelson Road North, Great
Yarmouth
NR30 2AT
t (01493) 859492
e enquiries@seashellsguesthouse.co.uk
w seashellsguesthouse.co.uk

**The Shrewsbury Guest House
★★★★** *Guest Accommodation*
SILVER AWARD
9 Trafalgar Road, Great Yarmouth
NR30 2LD
t (01493) 844788
e shrewsbury.guesthouse@virgin.net
w shrewsburyguesthouse.co.uk

Silverstone House ★★★
Guest Accommodation
29 Wellesley Road, Great Yarmouth
NR30 1EU
t (01493) 844862
e silverstonehouse@yahoo.co.uk
w silverstone-house.co.uk

The Southern ★★★★
Guest Accommodation
46 Queens Road, Great Yarmouth
NR30 3JR
t (01493) 843313
e sally@southernhotel.co.uk
w southernhotel.co.uk

Spindrift Guest House ★★★★
Guest House
36 Wellesley Road, Great Yarmouth
NR30 1EU
t (01493) 843772
e enquiries@spindriftbandb.co.uk
w spindriftbandb.co.uk

Sunnydene ★★★★ *Guest House*
83-84 North Denes Road, Great
Yarmouth
NR30 4LW
t (01493) 843554
e info@sunnydenehotel.co.uk
w sunnydenehotel.co.uk

Trevi Guest House ★★★
Guest House
57 Wellesley Road, Great Yarmouth
NR30 1EX
t (01493) 854473
e button594@btinternet.com
w treviguesthouse.com

Trotwood ★★★★
Guest Accommodation
2 North Drive, Great Yarmouth
NR30 1ED
t (01493) 843971
e ian.irons@btconnect.com
w thetrotwood.co.uk

Tudor House ★★★★ *Guest House*
11 Trafalgar Road, Great Yarmouth
NR30 2LD
t (01493) 855415
e info@tudor-house.co.uk
w tudor-house.co.uk

The Weatherdene ★★★
Guest House
2 St Johns Terrace, Great Yarmouth
NR30 2NF
t (01493) 843058
e theweatherdene@yahoo.com
w theweatherdene.co.uk

Woods End ★★★ *Guest House*
49 Wellesley Road, Great Yarmouth
NR30 1EX
t (01493) 842229
w woodsendhotel.co.uk

GRIMSTON

The Old Bell Guesthouse ★★★★
Guest House
1 Gayton Road, Grimston, King's
Lynn
PE32 1BG
t (01485) 601156
e sjwood1@sky.com
w theoldbellgrimston.co.uk

HARLESTON

The Swan Hotel ★★★ *Inn*
The Thoroughfare, Harleston
IP20 9AS
t (01379) 852221

HEACHAM

Holly House ★★★★
Guest Accommodation
3 Broadway, Heacham
PE31 7DF
t (01485) 572935
e enquiries@hollyhouseheacham.co.uk
w hollyhouseheacham.co.uk

Saint Annes Guest House ★★★★
Guest House **SILVER AWARD**
53 Neville Road, Heacham
PE31 7HB
t (01485) 570021
e elaine@stannesguesthouse.co.uk
w stannesguesthouse.co.uk

HELHOUGHTON

Woodfarm House ★★★★★
Bed & Breakfast **GOLD AWARD**
Near Helhoughton, Fakenham
NR21 7BT
t (01485) 528586
e booking@woodfarm-house.com
w woodfarm-house.com

HEVINGHAM

Primrose Lodge ★★★
Guest Accommodation - Room Only
Bingles Turn, Hevingham, Norwich
NR10 5NF
t (01603) 754888
e jamie-mcleod@hotmail.co.uk

HICKLING

The Dairy Barns ★★★★
Farmhouse **GOLD AWARD**
Lound Farm, Hickling Lane, Hickling,
Norwich
NR12 0BE
t (01692) 598243
e enquiries@dairybarns.co.uk
w dairybarns.co.uk

HINDRINGHAM

Field House ★★★★★
Bed & Breakfast **GOLD AWARD**
Moorgate Road, Hindringham,
Walsingham
NR21 0PT
t (01328) 878726
e stay@fieldhousehindringham.co.uk
w fieldhousehindringham.co.uk

East of England | Norfolk

HOLT

Byfords ★★★★★
Guest Accommodation
GOLD AWARD
1-3 Shirehall Plain, Holt, Holt
NR25 6BG
t (01263) 711400
e queries@byfords.org.uk
w byfords.org.uk

Hempstead Hall ★★★★
Farmhouse
Holt, Holt
NR25 6TN
t (01263) 712224

Holm Oaks ★★★★ *Bed & Breakfast*
83a Cromer Road, Holt
NR25 6JY
t (01263) 711061
e holmoaks@talktalk.net

Three Corners ★★ *Bed & Breakfast*
12 Kelling Close, Holt
NR25 6RU
t (01263) 713389
e ronvcox@aol.com

HORNING

The Moorhen ★★★★
Bed & Breakfast **SILVER AWARD**
45 Lower Street, Horning, Norwich
NR12 8AA
t (01692) 631444
e themoorhenhorning@tiscali.co.uk
w themoorhenhorning.co.uk

HORSFORD

Church Farm Guesthouse ★★★★
Guest Accommodation
Church Street, Horsford, Norwich
NR10 3DB
t (01603) 898020
e churchfarm.guesthouse@btinternet.com
w btinternet.com

HOVETON

The Vineries Bed & Breakfast
★★★★ *Guest Accommodation*
SILVER AWARD
72 Stalham Road, Hoveton, Wroxham
NR12 8DU
t (01603) 782514
e enquiries@thevineries.com
w thevineries.com

HUNSTANTON

Ashleigh Lodge ★★★★
Guest House
14 Austin Street, Hunstanton
PE36 6AL
t (01485) 533247
e enquiries@ashleighlodge.co.uk
w ashleighlodge.co.uk

The Bays Guest House ★★★★★
Guest House **GOLD AWARD**
31 Avenue Road, Hunstanton
PE36 5BW
t (01485) 532079
e enquiries@thebays.co.uk
w thebays.co.uk

Belgrave House ★★★★
Guest Accommodation
SILVER AWARD
49 Northgate, Hunstanton
PE36 6DS
t (01485) 533007
e belgrave-house@btconnect.com
w belgrave-housebb.co.uk

The Burleigh ★★★★
Guest Accommodation
SILVER AWARD
7 Cliff Terrace, Hunstanton
PE36 6DY
t (01485) 533080
e reservations@theburleigh.com
w theburleigh.com

Burlington House ★★★★
Bed & Breakfast **GOLD AWARD**
3 Austin Street, Hunstanton
PE36 6AJ
t (01485) 533366
e enquiries@burlingtonhouse.info
w burlingtonhouse.info

Cori House Bed & Breakfast
★★★★ *Bed & Breakfast*
SILVER AWARD
9 Church Street, Hunstanton
PE36 5HA
t (01485) 533034
e corihousebandb@yahoo.co.uk
w corihouse.co.uk

Deepdene House ★★★★
Guest House **SILVER AWARD**
29 Avenue Road, Hunstanton
PE36 5BW
t (01485) 532460
e deepdenehouse@btopenworld.com
w deepdenehouse.co.uk

Ellinbrook House ★★★★
Guest Accommodation
37 Avenue Road, Hunstanton
PE36 5HW
t (01485) 532022
e enquiries@ellinbrookhouse.com
w ellinbrookhouse.com

Forget-Me-Not ★★★★
Guest House
35 Glebe Avenue, Hunstanton
PE36 6BS
t (01485) 534431

The Gables ★★★★
Guest Accommodation
28 Austin Street, Hunstanton
PE36 6AW
t (01485) 532514
e bbatthegables@aol.com
w thegableshunstanton.co.uk

Garganey House ★★★★
Guest House
46 Northgate, Hunstanton
PE36 6DR
t (01485) 533269
e garganey1.@f.s.net.co.uk
w garganeyhouse.co.uk

Gate Lodge Guest House ★★★★
Guest Accommodation
GOLD AWARD
Gate Lodge, 2 Westgate, Hunstanton
PE36 5AL
t (01485) 533549
e lynn@gatelodge-guesthouse.co.uk
w gatelodge-guesthouse.co.uk

Glenberis Bed & Breakfast ★★★★
Bed & Breakfast **SILVER AWARD**
6 St Edmunds Avenue, Hunstanton
PE36 6AY
t (01485) 533663
e enquiries@glenberis.co.uk
w glenberis.co.uk

Hunstanton YHA ★★★ *Hostel*
15 Avenue Road, Hunstanton
PE36 5BW
t (01485) 532061
e hunstanton@yha.org.uk
w yha.org.uk

Kingfisher B&B ★★★★
Guest Accommodation
SILVER AWARD
16 Peddars Drive, Hunstanton
PE36 6HF
t (01485) 532776
e enquiries@kingfisherbedandbreakfast.com
w kingfisherbedandbreakfast.co.uk

The King William IV, Country Inn & Restaurant ★★★★ *Inn*
SILVER AWARD
Heacham Road, Sedgeford, Hunstanton
PE36 5LU
t (01485) 571765
e info@thekingwilliamsedgeford.co.uk
w thekingwilliamsedgeford.co.uk

Lakeside ★★★★
Guest Accommodation
Waterworks Road, Old Hunstanton, Hunstanton
PE36 6JE
t (01485) 533763
w oldwaterworks.co.uk

Linksway Country House ★★★★
Guest Accommodation
SILVER AWARD
Golf Course Road, Old Hunstanton, Hunstanton
PE36 6JE
t (01485) 532209
w linksway-hotel@totalise.co.uk
w linkswayhotel.com

The Lodge ★★★★ *Inn*
SILVER AWARD
Old Hunstanton Road, Hunstanton
PE36 6HX
t (01485) 532896
e info@thelodgehunstanton.co.uk
w thelodgehunstanton.co.uk

Miramar Guesthouse ★★★★
Guest House
7 Boston Square, Hunstanton
PE36 6DT
t (01485) 532902

Peacock House ★★★★
Guest Accommodation
GOLD AWARD
28 Park Road, Hunstanton
PE36 5BY
t (01485) 534551
e angie@peacockhouse-hunstanton.co.uk
w peacockhouse-hunstanton.co.uk

Queensbury House ★★★
Bed & Breakfast
Glebe Avenue, Hunstanton
PE36 6BS
t (01485) 534320

Rosamaly Guesthouse ★★★★
Guest Accommodation
14 Glebe Avenue, Hunstanton
PE36 6BS
t (01485) 534187
e vacancies@rosamaly.co.uk
w rosamaly.co.uk

Rose Fitt House ★★★★
Guest Accommodation
GOLD AWARD
40 Northgate, Hunstanton
PE36 6DR
t (01485) 534776
e andrea.rosefitt@btinternet.com
w rose-fitt-house-hunstanton.co.uk

The Shellbrooke ★★★★
Guest House
9 Cliff Terrace, Hunstanton
PE36 6DY
t (01485) 532289
e info@theshellbrooke.co.uk
w theshellbrooke.co.uk

INGOLDISTHORPE

Pencob House ★★★★
Bed & Breakfast **SILVER AWARD**
56 Hill Road, Ingoldisthorpe, King's Lynn
PE31 6NZ
t (01485) 543882
e pencob@supanet.com
w swanholidays.co.uk

KING'S LYNN

Beeches Guesthouse ★★★★
Guest Accommodation
2 Guanock Terrace, King's Lynn
PE30 5QT
t (01553) 766577
e kelvin.sellers@btconnect.com
w beechesguesthouse.co.uk

The Coppice ★★★★
Bed & Breakfast
Fakenham Road, Hillington, King's Lynn
PE31 6DJ
t (01485) 600413
e info@thecoppicehillington.co.uk
w thecoppicehillington.co.uk

Fairlight Lodge ★★★★
Guest Accommodation
SILVER AWARD
79 Goodwins Road, King's Lynn
PE30 5PE
t (01553) 762234
e enquiries@fairlightlodge.co.uk
w fairlightlodge.co.uk

Maranatha Guesthouse ★★★★
Guest House
115-117 Gaywood Road, King's Lynn
PE30 2PU
t (01553) 774596
e maranathaguesthouse@yahoo.co.uk
w maranathaguesthouse.co.uk

Old Rectory ★★★★
Guest Accommodation
33 Goodwins Road, King's Lynn
PE30 5QX
t (01553) 768544
e clive@theoldrectory-kingslynn.com
w theoldrectory-kingslynn.co.uk

The Ostrich Inn ★★★★ *Inn*
Stocks Green, Castle Acre, King's Lynn
PE32 2AE
t (01553) 777865
e info@ostrichcastleacre.com
w ostrichcastleacre.com

KIRBY BEDON

Hall Park Bed & Breakfast ★★★★
Bed & Breakfast **SILVER AWARD**
Kirby Road, Kirby Bedon, Norwich
NR14 7DU
t (01508) 495567
e enquiries@hallparknorfolk.co.uk
w hallparknorfolk.co.uk

KIRBY CANE

Butterley House ★★★★
Bed & Breakfast
Leet Hill Farm, Kirby Cane, Bungay
NR35 2HJ
t (01508) 518301

LANGHAM

Home Close ★★★★
Guest Accommodation
Langham, Holt, Blakeney
NR25 7DG
t (01328) 830348
e patallen@lineone.net
w homecloselangham.co.uk

LARLING

Angel Inn ★★★★ *Inn*
Larling, Norwich
NR16 2QU
t (01953) 717963
w larlingangel.co.uk

LINGWOOD

Station House ★★★★
Bed & Breakfast
26 Station Road, Norwich
NR13 4AZ
t (01603) 715872
e rosalyn.meo@btconnect.com
w stationhouse.line.co.uk

East of England | Norfolk

LITTLE CRESSINGHAM
amore House B&B ★★★★
est Accommodation
amore House, Little
ssingham, Thetford
5 6NE
(01953) 881887
j.wittridge@btinternet.com

LITTLE SNORING
: Farm B&B ★★★★ *Farmhouse*
VER AWARD
ursford Road, Little Snoring,
ham
21 0JJ
(01328) 878257
farmerstephen@jexfarm.
wanadoo.co.uk
jexfarm.co.uk

LODDON
l Green Farm B&B ★★★★
& Breakfast SILVER AWARD
ton Road, Loddon
14 6DT
(01508) 522039

LONG STRATTON
enacres Farmhouse ★★★★
& Breakfast
od Green, Long Stratton,
wich
5 2RR
(01508) 530261
greenacresfarm@tinyworld.net

LUDHAM
adland Bed & Breakfast
★★★ *Bed & Breakfast*
VER AWARD
st End Lodge, Norwich Road, The
ads
29 5PB
(01692) 678420
info@bedbreakfast-norfolkbroads.
co.uk
bedbreakfast-norfolkbroads.co.uk

MARSHAM
e Plough Inn ★★★★ *Inn*
l Norwich Road, Aylsham,
wich
0 5PS
(01263) 735000
enq@ploughinnmarsham.co.uk
ploughinnmarsham.co.uk

MUNDESLEY
e Durdans ★★★★
est Accommodation
VER AWARD
e Durdans, 36 Trunch Road,
ndesley
1 8JX
(01263) 722225
info@thedurdans.co.uk
thedurdans.co.uk

ercliff Lodge ★★★★
est House
Cromer Road, Mundesley
1 8DB
(01263) 720016
enquiries@overclifflodge.co.uk
overclifflodge.co.uk

MUNDHAM
ange Farm Cottage ★★★★
d & Breakfast
ange Road., Mundham, Norwich
14 6EP
(01508) 550027

NARBOROUGH
l View Rooms ★★★★
d & Breakfast
in Road, Narborough, King's Lynn
32 1TE
(01760) 338005
narfish@supanet.com
narfish.com

NEAR DISS
Pansthorne Bed & Breakfast
★★★★ *Guest House*
Pansthorne Farm, Redgrave Road,
South Lopham, Near Diss, Norfolk
IP22 2HL
t 01379 688 096
e enquiries@pansthorne.co.uk
w pansthorne.co.uk

NEATISHEAD
Regency Guesthouse ★★★★
Guest House SILVER AWARD
The Street, Neatishead, Norwich
NR12 8AD
t (01692) 630233
e regencywrigley@btinternet.com
w regencyguesthouse.com

NORTH LOPHAM
Church Farm House ★★★★★
Guest Accommodation
GOLD AWARD
Church Road, North Lopham, Diss
IP22 2LP
t (01379) 687270
e hosts@bassetts.demon.co.uk
w churchfarmhouse.org

NORTH WALSHAM
Bradfield House ★★★★
Bed & Breakfast
19 Station Road, North Walsham
NR28 0DZ
t (01692) 404352
e info@bradfieldhouse.com
w bradfieldhouse.com

NORTH WOOTTON
Red Cat ★★★ *Inn*
Station Road, North Wootton, King's
Lynn
PE30 3QH
t (01553) 631244
e enquiries@redcathotel.com
w redcathotel.com

NORWICH
3 Chalk Hill Road B&B ★★★
Bed & Breakfast
3 Chalk Hill Road, Norwich
NR1 1SL
t (01603) 619188
e moira@beauvillage.com
w beauvillage.com/b&b.html

38 St Giles B&B ★★★★★
Guest Accommodation
GOLD AWARD
38 St Giles, Norwich
NR2 1LL
t (01603) 662944
e cheeseman695@aol.com
w 38stgiles.co.uk

All Seasons Bed & Breakfast ★★
Bed & Breakfast
32 Wroxham Road, Sprowston,
Norwich
NR7 8TY
t (01603) 426069
e allseasonsbnb@talktalkbusiness.
net
w norwichbedbreakfast.co.uk

Arbor Linden Lodge ★★★★
Guest House
Linden House, 557 Earlham Road,
Norwich
NR4 7HW
t (01603) 462308
e info@guesthousenorwich.com
w guesthousenorwich.com

Arrandale Lodge ★★★★
Guest House SILVER AWARD
431 Earlham Road, Norwich
NR4 7HL
t (01603) 250150
e info@arrandalelodge.co.uk
w arrandalelodge.co.uk

Aylwyne House ★★★
Bed & Breakfast
59 Aylsham Road, Norwich
NR3 2HF
t (01603) 665798
e daniel@listedescape.com
w listedescape.com

Beaufort Lodge ★★★★
Bed & Breakfast SILVER AWARD
62 Earlham Road, Norwich
NR2 3DF
t (01603) 627928
e beaufortlodge@aol.com
w beaufortlodge.com

Becklands ★★★★ *Guest House*
105 Holt Road, Horsford, Norwich
NR10 3AB
t (01603) 898582
e becklands@aol.com
w becklands.com

The Beeches Bed & Breakfast
Guest Accommodation
Coltishall Road, Buxton, Norwich
NR10 5JD
t (01603) 279771
e beechesbedandbreakfast@live.co.
uk
w thebeechesbuxtonnorfolk.co.uk

The Blue Boar Inn ★★★★ *Inn*
259 Wroxham Road, Sprowston,
Norwich
NR7 8RL
t (01603) 426802
e blueboar@btconnect.com
w blueboarnorwich.co.uk

Blue Cedar Lodge Guesthouse
★★★ *Guest House*
391 Earlham Road, Norwich
NR2 3RQ
t (01603) 458331
e irenbrister@aol.com

Cairdean ★★★★ *Bed & Breakfast*
71 Middletons Lane, Hellesdon,
Norwich
NR6 5NS
t (01603) 419041
e info@cairdean.co.uk
w cairdean.co.uk

Catton Old Hall ★★★★★
Guest Accommodation
SILVER AWARD
Lodge Lane, Old Catton, Norwich,
Norfolk
NR6 7HG
t (01603) 419379
e enquiries@catton-hall.co.uk
w catton-hall.co.uk

Chestnut Grove ★★★★
Guest House
129 Newmarket Road, Norwich
NR4 6SZ
t (01603) 451932
e bookings@chestnutgrovebb.co.uk

Copperfields Guesthouse ★★★
Guest House
113 Constitution Hill, Old Catton,
Norwich
NR6 7RN
t (01603) 410098
e dukl2000@yahoo.com
w copperfieldsguesthouses.co.uk

Driftwood Lodge ★★★★
Bed & Breakfast
102 Wroxham Road, Sprowston,
Norwich
NR7 8EX
t (01603) 444908
e info@driftwoodlodge.co.uk
w driftwoodlodge.co.uk

Earlham Guesthouse ★★★
Guest House
147 Earlham Road, Norwich
NR2 3RG
t (01603) 454169
e info@earlham-guesthouse.co.uk
w earlham-guesthouse.co.uk

Edmar Lodge ★★★
Guest Accommodation
64 Earlham Road, Norwich
NR2 3DF
t (01603) 615599
e mail@edmarlodge.co.uk
w edmarlodge.co.uk

Flint Barn *Bed & Breakfast*
The Green, North Burlingham,
Norwich
NR13 4SZ
t (01603) 270976
e flintbarn@googlemail.com
w flint-barn.com

Gilman Lodge Guest House
★★★★★ *Guest House*
SILVER AWARD
221 Sprowston Road, Norwich
NR3 4HZ
t (01603) 447716
e gilman.lodge@ntlworld.com
w gilmanlodge.co.uk

The Grove ★★★★★
Bed & Breakfast SILVER AWARD
59 Bracondale, Norwich, Norfolk
NR1 2AT
t 01603 622053
e thegrovenorwich@live.com
w thegrovenorwich.co.uk

Hall Paddock ★★★★
Bed & Breakfast
Hall Road, Blofield Heath, Norwich,
Norfolk
NR13 4DE
t 01603 211854
e stay@hallpaddock.com
w hallpaddock.com

Hill House Guest House ★★★★
Bed & Breakfast
2 Hillside Road, Norwich
NR7 0QG
t (01603) 432165
e jeannie.peachey@btconnect.com

Hotel Belmonte ★★★
Guest Accommodation
60-62 Prince of Wales Road,
Norwich
NR1 1LT
t (01603) 622533
e info@hotelbelmonte.co.uk
w hotelbelmonte.co.uk

Ivy Dene ★★★ *Guest House*
12 Earlham Road, Norwich
NR2 3DB
t (01603) 762567
e theivydene@hotmail.com

Manor Barn House ★★★★
Guest Accommodation
7 Back Lane, Rackheath, Norwich
NR13 6NN
t (01603) 783543
e jane.roger@manorbarnhouse.co.
uk
w manorbarnhouse.co.uk

Marlborough House ★★★
Guest Accommodation
22 Stracey Road, Norwich
NR1 1EZ
t (01603) 628005
e marlbhouse@btconnect.com
w themarlboroughhouse.co.uk

Marsham Arms Inn ★★★★ *Inn*
Holt Road, Hevingham, Norwich
NR10 5NP
t (01603) 754268
e nigelbradley@marshamarms.co.uk
w marshamarms.co.uk

number 17 ★★★★ *Guest House*
17 Colegate, Norwich
NR3 1BN
t (01603) 764486
e enquiries@number17norwich.co.
uk
w number17norwich.co.uk

East of England | Norfolk

The Old Corner Shop Guesthouse ★★★ *Bed & Breakfast*
26 Cromer Road, Norwich
NR6 6LZ
t (01603) 419000
e info@theoldcornershopguesthouse.co.uk
w theoldcornershopguesthouse.co.uk

Tamarix Bed & Breakfast ★★★★
Bed & Breakfast
37 Burnt Street, Wells-next-the-Sea
NR3 1HN
t (01328) 710388
e rodneycrafer@talktalk.net
w thehoneystore.co.uk/tamarix/index.html

UEA Broadview Lodge ★★★
Campus
University of East Anglia, Norwich
NR4 7TJ
t (01603) 591918
e broadviewlodge@uea.ac.uk
w broadviewlodge.co.uk

Wedgewood House ★★★★
Guest Accommodation
42 St Stephens Road, Norwich
NR1 3RE
t (01603) 625730
e stay@wedgewoodhouse.co.uk
w wedgewoodhouse.co.uk

Wensum Guest House ★★★★
Guest House
225 Dereham Road, Norwich
NR2 3TF
t (01603) 621069
e info@wensumguesthouse.co.uk
w wensumguesthouse.co.uk

OVERSTRAND

Danum House ★★★
Guest Accommodation
22 Pauls Lane, Overstrand, Cromer
NR27 0PE
t (01263) 579127
e sim920@btinternet.com
w rococoatthecrown.co.uk

PENTNEY

Little Abbey Farm ★★★★
Farmhouse SILVER AWARD
Low Road, Pentney, King's Lynn
PE32 1JF
t (01760) 337348
e enquiries@littleabbeyfarm.co.uk
w littleabbeyfarm.co.uk

PULHAM MARKET

The Old Bakery ★★★★★
Guest Accommodation
SILVER AWARD
Church Walk, Pulham Market, Diss
IP21 4SL
t (01379) 676492
e info@theoldbakery.net
w theoldbakery.net

RACKHEATH

Barn Court ★★★★
Guest Accommodation
6 Back Lane, Rackheath, Norwich
NR13 6NN
t (01603) 782536
e barncourtbb@hotmail.com

Green Haven Lodge ★★★★
Bed & Breakfast
46 Green Lane West, Rackheath, Norwich
NR13 6PG
t (01603) 721418
e greenhavenbnb@aol.com
w greenhavenbnb.co.uk

Hill Farm Lodge ★★★★
Bed & Breakfast
Wroxham Road, Rackheath, Norwich
NR13 6NE
t (01603) 720093
e patandclivemarshall@btinternet.com
w hillfarmlodge.co.uk

SCULTHORPE

Manor Farm Bed & Breakfast ★★★★ *Farmhouse* SILVER AWARD
Manor Farm, Sculthorpe, Fakenham
NR21 9NJ
t (01328) 862185
e carol@manorfarmbandb.fsworld.co.uk
w manorfarmbandb.com

Sculthorpe Mill ★★★★ *Inn*
Lynn Road, Fakenham
NR21 9QG
t (01328) 853549
e elainesbarnett@hotmail.com
w sculthorpemill.co.uk

SHERINGHAM

Alverstone B&B ★★★★
Bed & Breakfast
33 The Avenue, Sheringham
NR26 8DG
t (01263) 825527 / 07766151903
w alverstone-sheringham.co.uk

Augusta House ★★★★
Bed & Breakfast SILVER AWARD
8 The Boulevard, Sheringham
NR26 8LJ
t (01263) 820173
e info@augustahouse.co.uk
w augustahouse.co.uk

Brook House Bed & Breakfast ★★★★ *Bed & Breakfast*
SILVER AWARD
Brook House, Brook Road, Sheringham, Norfolk
NR26 8QE
t 01263 824 827
e jacquie.ogrady@btinternet.com
w brookhousebandb.com

The Burlington Lodge ★★★
Guest Accommodation
5 St Nicholas Place, Sheringham
NR26 8LF
t (01263) 820931
e r.mcdermott0@btinternet.com

Camberley House ★★★★
Guest Accommodation
62 Cliff Road, Sheringham
NR26 8BJ
t (01263) 823101
e admin@camberleyhouse.co.uk
w camberleyhouse.co.uk

Claremont ★★★★ *Bed & Breakfast*
49 Holway Road, Sheringham
NR26 8HP
t (01263) 821889
e claremontbb@googlemail.com
w claremont-sheringham.co.uk

Cleat House ★★★★★
Bed & Breakfast SILVER AWARD
7 Montague Road, Sheringham
NR26 8LN
t (01263) 822765
e stay@cleathouse.co.uk
w cleathouse.co.uk

The Melrose ★★★ *Guest House*
9 Holway Road, Sheringham
NR26 8HN
t (01263) 823299
e john.parsonage@btconnect.com
w themelrosesheringham.co.uk

Myrtle House ★★★★
Bed & Breakfast
29 Nelson Road, Sheringham
NR26 8BU
t 01263 823889
e enquiries@myrtlehouse-sheringham.co.uk
w myrtlehouse-sheringham.co.uk

Olivedale Guest House ★★★★
Guest Accommodation
GOLD AWARD
20 Augusta Street, Sheringham
NR26 8LA
t (01263) 825871
e olivedale@btinternet.com
w olivedale.co.uk

Pentland Lodge ★★★★
Guest Accommodation
51 The Avenue, Sheringham
NR26 8DQ
t (01263) 823533
e janejeffpentland@msn.com
w pentland-lodge.co.uk

Sheringham Lodge ★★★★
Guest House
50 Cromer Road, Sheringham
NR26 8RS
t (01263) 821954
e mikewalker19@hotmail.com

Sheringham View Cottage ★★★★
Bed & Breakfast SILVER AWARD
Cromer Road, Sheringham
NR26 8RX
t (01263) 820300
e info@sheringhamview.co.uk
w sheringhamview.co.uk

Sheringham YHA ★★★ *Hostel*
1 Cremers Drift, Sheringham
NR26 8HX
t 0870 770 6024
e sheringham@yha.org.uk
w yha.org.uk

The Sun Deck ★★★★
Bed & Breakfast
10 Holway Road, Sheringham
NR26 8HN
t (01263) 823489
e andrewparish@tiscali.co.uk
w thesundeck.co.uk

Sunrays Bed & Breakfast ★★★★
Bed & Breakfast SILVER AWARD
29 Holt Road, Sheringham
NR26 8NB
t (01263) 822663
e elainesunrays@btinternet.com
w sunrays-sheringham.co.uk

Viburnham House Bed & Breakfast ★★★★
Guest Accommodation
SILVER AWARD
Augusta Street, Sheringham
NR26 8LB
t (01263) 822528
e viburnhamhouse@aol.com
w viburnhamhouse.co.uk

SNETTERTON

Holly House Guest House ★★★★★ *Guest House*
GOLD AWARD
Holly House, Snetterton, Norwich
NR16 2LG
t (01953) 498051
e jeffstonell@aol.com
w hollyhouse-guesthouse.co.uk

SNETTISHAM

The Queen Victoria ★★★★ *Inn*
19 Lynn Road, Snettisham, King's Lynn
PE31 7LW
t (01485) 541344
e bobwarburton@talk21.com
w queenvictoriasnettisham.co.uk

Twitchers Retreat ★★★★
Bed & Breakfast GOLD AWARD
9 Beach Road, Snettisham, King's Lynn
PE31 7RA
t (01485) 543581
e twitchers.retreat@googlemail.com
w twitchers-retreat.co.uk

SOUTH CREAKE

Valentine Studio ★★★★
Guest Accommodation
62 Back Street, South Creake, Walsingham
NR21 9PG
t (01328) 823413
e ros@valentinehouse.fsnet.co.uk
w valentinehouse.co.uk

SOUTH WALSHAM

Leeward Bed & Breakfast ★★★
Bed & Breakfast SILVER AWARD
5 Broad Lane, South Walsham, Norwich
NR13 6EE
t (01603) 270491
e angela.horsfield@btinternet.com
w leewardbedandbreakfast.co.uk

Old Hall Farm ★★★★
Guest Accommodation
SILVER AWARD
3 Newport Road, South Walsham
Norwich, Norfolk
NR13 6DS
t (01603) 270271
e veronica@oldhallfarm.co.uk
w oldhallfarm.co.uk

SPIXWORTH

Moorsticks B&B ★★★★
Bed & Breakfast
Buxton Road, Spixworth, Norwich
NR12 7BJ
t (01603) 488808
e moorsticksaccommodation@yahoo.co.uk
w moorsticksaccommodation.com

SPORLE

Corfield House ★★★★
Guest Accommodation
SILVER AWARD
Sporle, Swaffham
PE32 2EA
t (01760) 723636
e info@corfieldhouse.co.uk
w corfieldhouse.co.uk

STIFFKEY

Stiffkey Bed & Breakfast ★★★★
Bed & Breakfast SILVER AWARD
10 Greenway, Stiffkey, Wells-next-the-Sea
NR23 1QF
t (01328) 830494
e isabeltipple888@btinternet.com
w stiffkeybedandbreakfast.com

STOKE HOLY CROSS

Highfields Farm ★★★
Bed & Breakfast
Chandler Road, Upper Stoke Holy Cross, Norwich
NR14 8RQ
t (01508) 493247
e stay@highfields-farm.co.uk
w highfields-farm.co.uk

Salamanca Farm ★★★ *Farmhouse*
118 Norwich Road, Norwich
NR14 8QJ
t (01508) 492322

STRATTON STRAWLESS

Woodmans Farm ★★★★
Bed & Breakfast SILVER AWARD
Cromer Road, Stratton Strawless, Norwich
NR10 5LU
t (01603) 754658
e janice@woodmansfarm.com
w woodmansfarm.com

SURLINGHAM

Pottles Barn ★★★ *Bed & Breakfast*
Ferry Road, Surlingham, Norwich
NR14 7AR
t (01508) 538117
e hilary.bond@virgin.net
w britainsfinest.co.uk

East of England | Norfolk/Suffolk

SWAFFHAM

ney House ★★★★ *Guest House*
rwich Road, Swaffham
7 7QS
(01760) 723355
rooms@lydney-house.demon.co.uk
lydney-house.demon.co.uk

pton House ★★★★
d & Breakfast **SILVER AWARD**
Oaks Drive, Swaffham
7 7DR
(01760) 336399
booking@reptonhouse.com
reptonhouse.com

SWANTON MORLEY

rricks at Castle Farm ★★★★★
est Accommodation
LD AWARD
stle Farm, Elsing Road, Swanton
rley, Dereham
20 4JT
(01362) 638302
jean@castlefarm-swanton.co.uk
carricksatcastlefarm.co.uk

gs Hall Farm ★★★★★
est Accommodation
VER AWARD
gs Hall Lane, Woodgate,
anton Morley, Dereham
20 4NX
(01362) 638355
mail@frogshallfarm.co.uk
frogshallfarm.co.uk

TERRINGTON ST JOHN

e White House ★★★★
d & Breakfast **SILVER AWARD**
in Road, Terrington St John,
sbech
4 7RR
(01945) 880741
fieldcarol@hotmail.com
thewhitehousebnb.co.uk

THETFORD

lveston Manor ★★★★
rmhouse
ndford, Thetford, Norfolk
6 5HU
(01842) 878218
mail@colveston-manor.co.uk
colveston-manor.co.uk

wereham House ★★★★
est Accommodation
White Hart Street, Thetford
4 1AD
(01842) 761956
mail@werehamhouse.co.uk
werehamhouse.co.uk

THOMPSON

equers Inn ★★★★ *Inn*
ston Road, Thompson
4 1PX
(01953) 483360
richard@thompsonchequers.co.uk
thompsonchequers.co.uk

THORNHAM

shmeadow ★★★★
d & Breakfast **SILVER AWARD**
in Road, Thornham, Hunstanton
36 6LZ
(01485) 512372
rushmeadow@sky.com
rushmeadow.com

THORPE MARKET

anorwood ★★★★
d & Breakfast
urch Road, Thorpe Market,
mer
11 8UA
(01263) 834938
manorwooddoc@hotmail.com
manorwoodnorfolk.co.uk

TUNSTALL

Manor House ★★★★ *Farmhouse*
SILVER AWARD
Tunstall Road, Halvergate, Norwich
NR13 3PS
t (01493) 700279
e smore@fsmail.net
w manorhousenorfolk.com

UPPER SHERINGHAM

Lodge Cottage ★★★★
Guest Accommodation
SILVER AWARD
Lodge Hill, Upper Sheringham,
Sheringham
NR26 8TJ
t (01263) 821445
e stay@visitlodgecottage.com
w lodgecottage.co.uk

WACTON

Le Grys Barn ★★★★
Bed & Breakfast
Wacton Common, Wacton, Norwich
NR15 2UR
t (01508) 531576
e jm.franklin@virgin.net
w legrys-barn.co.uk

WALSINGHAM

**The Old Bakehouse Tea Room &
Guesthouse** ★★★★ *Guest House*
33 High Street, Little Walsingham,
Walsingham
NR22 6BZ
t (01328) 820454
e theoldbakehouseguesthouse@
yahoo.co.uk
w glavenvalley.co.uk/oldbakehouse

St Felix ★★★★ *Bed & Breakfast*
2A Knight Street, Walsingham
NR22 6DA
t (01328) 820117
e th@paston.co.uk
w 3B1

WATERDEN

The Old Rectory ★★★★
Bed & Breakfast
Waterden, Walsingham
NR22 6AT
t (01328) 823298
w theoldrectory.waterden.co.uk

WEASENHAM

The Wheatcroft Bed & Breakfast
★★★★ *Bed & Breakfast*
Dodma Road, Weasenham All
Saints, King's Lynn
PE32 2SW
t (01328) 838651
e thewheatcroft@talktalk.net
w thewheatcroft.com

WELLS-NEXT-THE-SEA

Admiral House ★★★★
Bed & Breakfast **SILVER AWARD**
6 Southgate Close, Wells-next-the-
Sea
NR23 1HG
t (01328) 711669
e info@admiralhouse-wells.co.uk
w admiralhouse-wells.co.uk

Arch House Bed + Breakfast
★★★★ *Guest Accommodation*
Arch House, 50 Mill Road, Wells-
next-the-Sea
NR23 1DB
t (01328) 710112
e enquiries@archhouse.co.uk
w archhouse.co.uk

Boxwood Guest House ★★★★
Guest House **SILVER AWARD**
Northfield Lane, Wells-next-the-Sea
NR23 1JZ
t (01328) 711493
e info@boxwood-guesthouse.co.uk
w boxwood-guesthouse.com

The Cobblers' Guest House
★★★★ *Guest House*
Standard Road, Wells-next-the-Sea
NR23 1JU
t (01328) 710155
e info@cobblers.co.uk
w cobblers.co.uk

Glebe Barn ★★★★ *Bed & Breakfast*
7A Glebe Road, Wells-next-the-Sea
NR23 1AZ
t (01328) 711809
e glebebarn@aol.com

The Globe Inn ★★★★ *Inn*
SILVER AWARD
The Buttlands, Wells-next-the-Sea
NR23 1EU
t (01328) 710206
e globe@holkham.co.uk
w globeatwells.com

Machrimore ★★★★
Bed & Breakfast **GOLD AWARD**
Burnt Street, Wells-next-theSea,
Wells-next-the-Sea
NR23 1HS
t (01328) 711653
e enquiries@machrimore.co.uk
w machrimore.co.uk

The Normans ★★★★★
Guest Accommodation
GOLD AWARD
Invaders Court, Standard Road,
Wells-next-the-Sea
NR23 1JW
t (01328) 710657
e gwatthen0rmans@btconnect.com
w thenormansatwells.co.uk

The Old Custom House ★★★★
Guest Accommodation
East Quay, Wells-next-the-Sea
NR23 1LD
t (01328) 711463
e bb@eastquay.co.uk
w eastquay.co.uk

Wells-next-the-Sea YHA ★★★★
Hostel
Church Plain, Wells-next-the-Sea
NR23 1EQ
t (01328) 711748
e wellsnorfolk@yha.org.uk
w yha.org.uk

WENDLING

Greenbanks ★★★★
Guest Accommodation
Greenbanks, Wendling, Dereham
NR19 2AB
t (01362) 687742
e jenny@greenbankshotel.co.uk
w greenbankshotel.co.uk

WEST RAYNHAM

Rosemary Cottage ★★★
Guest Accommodation
13 The Street, West Raynham,
Fakenham
NR21 7AD
t (01328) 838318
e francoisew@btinternet.com

WEST RUDHAM

Oyster House ★★★★
Bed & Breakfast **SILVER AWARD**
Lynn Road, West Rudham,
Walsingham
PE31 8RW
t (01485) 528327
e oyster-house@tiscali.co.uk
w oysterhouse.co.uk

WHITTINGTON

The Old Rectory ★★★★
Guest Accommodation
The Old Rectory, Ferry Road,
Oxborough, King's Lynn
PE33 9PT
t (01366) 328962
e info@morethangoodmanners.
com
w morethangoodmanners.com

WICKMERE

Pink House Bed & Breakfast
★★★★ *Bed & Breakfast*
SILVER AWARD
Pink House Bed & Breakfast,
Wickmere, Norwich
NR11 7AL
t (01263) 577678
e info@pinkhousebb.co.uk
w pinkhousebb.co.uk

WIGHTON

Meadow View Guest House
★★★★★ *Guest Accommodation*
GOLD AWARD
53 High Street, Wighton, Wells-next-
the-Sea, Norfolk
NR23 1PF
t (01328) 821527
e booking@meadow-view.net
w meadow-view.net

WROXHAM

58 Norwich Road ★★★★
Bed & Breakfast
Wroxham, Norwich
NR12 8RX
t (01603) 783998

Coach House ★★★★
Bed & Breakfast **SILVER AWARD**
96 Norwich Road, Wroxham
NR12 8RY
t (01603) 784376
e bishop@worldonline.co.uk
w coachhousewroxham.co.uk

**Wroxham Park Lodge Guest
House** ★★★★ *Bed & Breakfast*
142 Norwich Road, Wroxham
NR12 8SA
t (01603) 782991
e parklodge@computer-assist.net
w wroxhamparklodge.com

WYMONDHAM

Elm Lodge B&B ★★★★
Bed & Breakfast
Downham Grove, Wymondham
NR18 0SN
t (01953) 607501

Witch Hazel ★★★★
Bed & Breakfast **GOLD AWARD**
55 Church Lane, Wicklewood,
Wymondham, Norfolk
NR18 9QH
t (01953) 602247
e witchhazel@tiscali.co.uk
w witchhazel-norfolk.co.uk

Suffolk

ACTON

Barbies ★★ *Bed & Breakfast*
25 Clay Hall Place, Acton, Sudbury
CO10 0BT
t (01787) 373702

ALDEBURGH

Oak ★★★★ *Bed & Breakfast*
111 Saxmundham Road, Aldeburgh
IP15 5JF
t (01728) 453503
e info@ppasletting.co.uk
w ppasletting.co.uk

The Toll House ★★★★
Guest House
50 Victoria Road, Aldeburgh
IP15 5EJ
t (01728) 453239
e tollhouse@fsmail.net
w tollhouse.travelbugged.com

BADINGHAM

Colston Hall ★★★★ *Farmhouse*
SILVER AWARD
Badingham, Woodbridge
IP13 8LB
t (01728) 638375
e enquiries@colstonhall.com
w colstonhall.com

key to symbols see page 6

East of England | Suffolk

BADWELL ASH

Old Guildhall Bed & Breakfast ★★★★ *Bed & Breakfast*
Old Guildhall, The Street, Badwell Ash, Bury St Edmunds
IP31 3DP
t (01359) 259610
e di.males@btinternet.com

BARNBY

Salmon's Leap ★★★★ *Bed & Breakfast* SILVER AWARD
Beccles Road, Barnby, Oulton Broad
NR34 7QY
t (01502) 476756
e cullabine@btinternet.com
w salmonsleap.co.uk

BAWDSEY

Bawdsey Manor ★★★★ *Guest Accommodation*
Bawdsey Manor, Bawdsey, Nr Woodbridge, Suffolk
IP12 3AZ
t (01394) 412396
e info@bawdseymanor.co.uk
w bawdseymanor.co.uk

BECCLES

Buckland House B&B ★★★★ *Bed & Breakfast*
Buckland House B&B, Halesworth Road, Beccles
NR34 8LB
t (01986) 781413
e info@buckland-house.co.uk
w buckland-house.co.uk

Catherine House ★★★★ *Guest Accommodation*
2 Ringsfield Road, Beccles
NR34 9PQ
t (01502) 716428
e karenrenilson@hotmail.com
w catherinehouse.net

Eveleigh House B&B ★★★★ *Bed & Breakfast* SILVER AWARD
49 London Road, Beccles
NR34 9YR
t (01502) 715214
e bookings@eveleighhouse.com
w eveleighhouse.com

Pinetrees ★★★★ *Guest Accommodation*
Park Drive, Beccles, Suffolk
NR34 7DQ
t (01502) 470796
e info@pinetrees.net
w pinetrees.net

Saltgate House ★★★★ *Guest Accommodation*
5 Saltgate, Beccles
NR34 9AN
t (01502) 710889
e cazjohns@aol.com
w saltgatehouse.co.uk

BENHALL

Honeypot Lodge ★★★★ *Bed & Breakfast*
Aldecar Lane, Benhall Green, Saxmundham
IP17 1HN
t (01728) 602449
e enquiries@honeypotlodge.co.uk
w saxmundham.info

BEYTON

Manorhouse ★★★★★ *Bed & Breakfast* GOLD AWARD
The Green, Beyton, Bury St Edmunds
IP30 9AF
t (01359) 270960
e manorhouse@beyton.com
w beyton.com

BILDESTON

Silwood Barns ★★★★ *Bed & Breakfast* SILVER AWARD
Consent Lane, Bildeston, Ipswich
IP7 7SB
t (01449) 741370
e neilashwell@aol.com
w lalaproducts.com

BLAXHALL

Blaxhall YHA ★★★ *Hostel*
Heath Walk, Blaxhall, Woodbridge
IP12 2EA
t (01728) 688206
e blaxhall@yha.org.uk
w yha.org.uk

BRADFIELD COMBUST

Church Farm Bed & Breakfast ★★★★ *Farmhouse*
Bradfield Combust, Bury St Edmunds
IP30 0LW
t (01284) 386333
e ruth@churchfarm-bandb.co.uk
w churchfarm-bandb.co.uk

BRADFIELD ST GEORGE

Laurel Farmhouse ★★★★★ *Bed & Breakfast*
Felsham Road, Bradfield St George, Bury St Edmunds
IP30 0AD
t (01284) 386988
e ml_lml@btinternet.com
w laurelfarmhouse.co.uk

BREDFIELD

Moat Barn ★★★ *Bed & Breakfast*
Dallinghoo Road, Bredfield, Woodbridge
IP13 6BD
t (01473) 737520
w moatbarn.co.uk

BURY ST EDMUNDS

Dunston Guesthouse ★★★ *Guest House*
8 Springfield Road, Bury St Edmunds
IP33 3AN
t (01284) 767981
e anndakin@btconnet.com
w dunstonguesthouse.co.uk

The Glen B&B ★★★★ *Guest House*
84 Eastgate Street, Bury St Edmunds
IP33 1YR
t (01284) 755490
e rallov@yahoo.com
w smoothhound.co.uk/hotels/theglen.html

Hilltop ★★ *Bed & Breakfast*
Hilltop, 22 Bronyon Close, Bury St Edmunds
IP33 3XB
t (01284) 767066
e bandb@hilltop22br.freeserve.co.uk
w hilltop22br.freeserve.co.uk

Ounce House ★★★★★ *Guest Accommodation* SILVER AWARD
Northgate Street, Bury St Edmunds
IP33 1HP
t (01284) 761779
e enquiries@ouncehouse.co.uk
w ouncehouse.co.uk

Regency House ★★★★ *Guest Accommodation*
3 Looms Lane, Bury St Edmunds
IP33 1HE
t (01284) 764376

Sanctuary B&B ★★★★ *Bed & Breakfast* SILVER AWARD
1 Kings Road, Bury St Edmunds
IP33 3DE
t 07756 940372
e allison814@btinternet.com

St Edmunds Guesthouse ★★★★ *Guest House* SILVER AWARD
35 St Andrews Street North, Bury St Edmunds
IP33 1SZ
t (01284) 700144
e info@stedmundsguesthouse.net
w stedmundsguesthouse.net

Sycamore House ★★★★★ *Guest Accommodation*
23 Northgate Street, Bury St Edmunds
IP33 1HP
t (01284) 755828
e me.chalkley@btinternet.com
w sycamorehouse.net

Westbank House B&B ★★ *Guest Accommodation*
Westbank Place, 116A Westley Road, Bury St Edmunds
IP33 3SD
t (01284) 753874
e grahampaske@tiscali.co.uk
w westbank-house.co.uk

BURY ST EDMUNDS (6 MILES)

The Old Manse Barn ★★★★★ *Guest Accommodation* SILVER AWARD
Chapel Road, Cockfield, Bury St Edmunds
IP30 0HE
t (01284) 828120
e bookings@theoldmansebarn.co.uk
w theoldmansebarn.co.uk

CAMPSEA ASHE

The Dog & Duck ★★★ *Inn*
Station Road, Campsea Ashe, Woodbridge
IP13 0PT
t (01728) 748439

CARLTON

Moat House Farm ★★★★ *Bed & Breakfast* GOLD AWARD
Rendham Road, Carlton, Saxmundham
IP17 2QN
t (01728) 602228
e sally@goodacres.com
w goodacres.com

Willow Tree Cottage ★★★★ *Bed & Breakfast*
3 Belvedere Close, Kelsale, Saxmundham
IP17 2RS
t (01728) 602161

CLARE

The Bell ★★★★ *Inn*
Market Hill, Clare, Sudbury
CO10 8NN
t (01787) 277741
w thebellhotel-clare.com

COLCHESTER (7 MILES)

Stratford House ★★★★ *Bed & Breakfast*
Stubbins Lane, Holton St Mary, Colchester
CO7 6NT
t (01206) 298246
e fselleck@uwclub.net
w accomsuffolk.co.uk

COPDOCK

Poplar Farm House ★★★★ *Bed & Breakfast*
Poplar Lane, Sproughton, Ipswich
IP8 3HL
t (01473) 601211
e sparrowsally@aol.com

CREETING ST MARY

Creeting House ★★★★ *Guest House*
All Saints Road, Creeting Saint Mary, Ipswich, Suffolk
IP6 8PR
t (01449) 720988
e diana@creetinghouse.com
w creetinghouse.com

Hungercut Hall Bed & Breakfast ★★★★ *Guest Accommodation*
Coddenham Road, Creeting St Mary, Ipswich
IP6 8NX
t (01449) 721323
e info@hungercuthall.co.uk
w hungercuthall.co.uk

CULFORD

47 Benyon Gardens ★★ *Bed & Breakfast*
Culford, Bury-St-Edmunds, Bury St Edmunds
IP28 6EA
t (01284) 728763

DARSHAM

White House Farm ★★ *Farmhouse*
Main Road, Darsham, Saxmundham
IP17 3PP
t (01728) 668632
e elainewhf@aol.com
w whitehousefarmdarsham.co.uk

EARL SOHAM

Bridge House ★★★★ *Guest Accommodation* SILVER AWARD
Earl Soham, Framlingham, Woodbridge
IP13 7RT
t (01728) 685473
e bridgehouse@suffolkonline.net
w bridgehouseuk.com

EAST BERGHOLT

Granary ★★★ *Guest Accommodation*
Flatford, East Bergholt, Colchester
CO7 6UL
t (01206) 298111
e b&b@derektripp.plus.com
w granaryflatford.co.uk

Rosemary ★★★ *Guest Accommodation*
Rectory Hill, East Bergholt, Colchester
CO7 6TH
t (01206) 298241
w rosemarybnb.co.uk

West Lodge Bed & Breakfast ★★★★ *Bed & Breakfast*
The Street, East Bergholt, Colchester
CO7 6TF
t (01206) 299808
e westlodgebandb@talktalk.net
w westlodge.uk.com

ELMSWELL

Elmswell Hall B&B ★★★★ *Farmhouse* SILVER AWARD
Elmswell Hall, Bury St Edmunds
IP30 9EN
t (01359) 240215
e kate@elmswellhall.freeserve.co.uk
w elmswellhall.co.uk

Kiln Farm Guest House ★★★★ *Guest House* SILVER AWARD
Kiln Lane, Elmswell, Bury St Edmunds
IP30 9QR
t (01359) 240442
e davejankilnfarm@btinternet.com

Mulberry Farm ★★★★ *Farmhouse* GOLD AWARD
Ashfield Road, Elmswell, Bury St Edmunds
IP30 9HG
t (01359) 244244
e mulberryfarm@tesco.net

382

Official tourist board guide Bed & Breakfast

East of England | Suffolk

ELVEDEN

**be Country House Bed &
eakfast** ★★★★
est Accommodation
VER AWARD
be Country House Bed &
akfast, Elveden, Thetford
4 3TL
t (01842) 890027
e deirdre@jrudderham.freeserve.co.
uk
w glebecountryhouse.co.uk

EXNING

rraton B&B ★★★★
d & Breakfast
ucks Lane, Exning, Newmarket
3 7HQ
t (01638) 615550
e stay@harraton.co.uk
w harraton.co.uk

e Rosery ★★★★
est Accommodation
Church Street, Exning,
wmarket
3 7EH
t (01638) 577312
e rosery99@yahoo.co.uk
w roseryhotel.co.uk

FELIXSTOWE

rlington House ★★★
est Accommodation
each Road West, Felixstowe
2 2BH
t (01394) 282051

stle Lodge ★★★★ *Guest House*
VER AWARD
evalier Road, Felixstowe
1 7EY
t (01394) 282149
e info@castlelodgefelixstowe.co.uk
w castlelodgefelixstowe.co.uk

rincourt Guesthouse ★★★
est House
dercliff Road West, Felixstowe
2AH
t (01394) 270447
e info@dorincourt.co.uk
w dorincourt.t83.net

e Grafton Guesthouse ★★★★
est Accommodation
Sea Road, Felixstowe
2BB
t (01394) 284881
e info@grafton-house.com
w grafton-house.com

e Norfolk Guest House ★★★★
est House **SILVER AWARD**
Holland Road, Felixstowe
2BA
t (01394) 283160
e thenorfolk@btconnect.com
w thenorfolk.com

nevale ★★★★ *Bed & Breakfast*
Ranelagh Road, Felixstowe
7HU
t (01394) 270001
e joy.s@btclick.com

FRAMLINGHAM

undary Farm ★★★★
d & Breakfast
Saxmundham Road,
mlingham, Woodbridge
3 9NU
t (01728) 723401
e info@boundaryfarm.biz
w boundaryfarm.biz

gh House Farm ★★★★
rmhouse
ansford, Woodbridge, Suffolk
3 9PD
t (01728) 663461
e info@highhousefarm.co.uk
w highhousefarm.co.uk

FRAMLINGHAM (7 MILES)

Flindor Cottage ★★★★★
Bed & Breakfast **GOLD AWARD**
The Street, Framsden, Near
Stowmarket, Suffolk
IP14 6HG
t 01473 890058
e tanya@flindor.com
w flindorcottage.co.uk

FRECKENHAM

The Golden Boar Inn ★★★★ *Inn*
The Street, Freckenham, Newmarket
IP28 8HZ
t (01638) 723000
e thegoldenboar@hotmail.com
w goldenboar.co.uk

FRISTON

Old School ★★★★ *Bed & Breakfast*
GOLD AWARD
Aldeburgh Road, Friston, Nr.
Saxmundham
IP17 1NP
t (01728) 688173
e fristonoldschool@btinternet.com
w fristonoldschool.co.uk

GREAT BARTON

The Wallow ★★★★
Bed & Breakfast **SILVER AWARD**
Mount Road, Bury St Edmunds
IP31 2QU
t (01284) 788055
e info@thewallow.co.uk
w thewallow.co.uk

GREAT BEALINGS

Apple Tree Cottage ★★★
Bed & Breakfast
Boot Street, Great Bealings,
Woodbridge
IP13 6PB
t (01473) 738997
e appletreebb@btinternet.com
w appletreebedandbreakfast.co.uk

GREAT BRICETT

Riverside Cottage ★★★★
Bed & Breakfast
The Street, Great Bricett, Ipswich
IP7 7DQ
t (01473) 658266
e chasmhorne@aol.com
w riversidecottagebandb.co.uk

HADLEIGH

Edge Hall ★★★★★
Guest Accommodation
SILVER AWARD
2 High Street, Hadleigh, Ipswich
IP7 5AP
t (01473) 822458
e r.rolfe@edgehall.co.uk
w edgehall.co.uk

HALESWORTH

The Angel Hotel ★★★★ *Inn*
Thoroughfare, Halesworth
IP19 8AH
t (01986) 873365
e hotel@angel-halesworth.co.uk
w angel-halesworth.co.uk

Fen Way Guest House ★★★★
Bed & Breakfast
Fen-Way, School Lane, Halesworth
IP19 8BW
t (01986) 873574
e tiscover.co.uk

Wissett Lodge B&B ★★★★
Farmhouse **SILVER AWARD**
Wissett Lodge, Lodge Lane,
Halesworth
IP19 0JU
t (01986) 873173
e mail@wissettlodge.co.uk
w wissettlodge.co.uk

HAUGHLEY

Haughley House ★★★★★
Guest Accommodation
GOLD AWARD
Haughley, Stowmarket
IP14 3NS
t (01449) 673398
e bowden@keme.co.uk
w haughleyhouse.co.uk

HAUGHLEY, NR STOWMARKET (3 MILES)

Red House Farm ★★★★
Farmhouse
Station Road, Haughley, Stowmarket
IP14 3QP
t (01449) 673323
e enquiries@redhousefarmhau
ghley.co.uk
w redhousefarmhaughley.co.uk/

HINTLESHAM

College Farm Bed & Breakfast
★★★★ *Farmhouse* **SILVER AWARD**
College Farm, Hintlesham, Ipswich,
Suffolk
IP8 3NT
t 01473 652253
e bandb@collegefarm.plus.com
w collegefarm.net

HITCHAM

Box Tree Farm ★★★★ *Farmhouse*
SILVER AWARD
Box Tree Farm, Kettlebaston,
Ipswich
IP7 7PZ
t (01449) 741318
e junecarpenter@btinternet.com
w boxtreefarm.350.com

The White Horse Inn ★★★★ *Inn*
The Street, Hitcham, Ipswich
IP7 7NQ
t (01449) 740981
e lewis@thewhitehorse.wanadoo.
co.uk
w thewhitehorsehitcham.co.uk

HONINGTON

North View Guest House ★★
Guest Accommodation
Malting Road, Honington, Bury St
Edmunds, Suffolk
IP31 1RE
t (01359) 269423

Willow Bed & Breakfast ★★★★
Bed & Breakfast
Ixworth Road, Honington, Bury St
Edmunds
IP31 1QY
t (01359) 269600
e celialawrence@talk21.com
w honingtonwillow.com

HOPTON

The Old Rectory Hopton ★★★★★
Bed & Breakfast **GOLD AWARD**
The Old Rectory, Hopton, Diss
IP22 2QX
t (01953) 688135
e llewellyn.hopton@btinternet.com
w theoldrectoryhopton.com

HUNDON

The Plough Inn ★★★★ *Inn*
Brockley Green, Hundon, Sudbury
CO10 8DT
t (01440) 786789
e info@theploughhundon.co.uk
w theploughhundon.co.uk

IPSWICH

Lattice Lodge Guest House
★★★★ *Guest House*
SILVER AWARD
499 Woodbridge Road, Ipswich
IP4 4EP
t (01473) 712474
e info@latticelodge.co.uk
w latticelodge.co.uk

Melverley Heights Guest House
★★★★ *Guest House*
SILVER AWARD
62 Tuddenham Road, Ipswich
IP4 2SP
t (01473) 253524
e enquiries@melverleyheights.co.uk
w melverleyheights.co.uk

Queenscliffe Bed & Breakfast
★★★★ *Bed & Breakfast*
2 Queenscliffe Road, Ipswich
IP2 9AS
t (01473) 686810
e queenscliffe2@ymail.com

Sidegate Guesthouse ★★★★
Guest House **GOLD AWARD**
121 Sidegate Lane, Ipswich
IP4 4JB
t (01473) 728714
e bookings@sidegateguesthouse.
co.uk
w sidegateguesthouse.co.uk

KESSINGLAND

The Old Rectory ★★★★★
Bed & Breakfast **GOLD AWARD**
157 Church Road, Kessingland
NR33 7SQ
t (01502) 742188
e theoldrectory_kessingland@
hotmail.co.uk
w bandblowestoft.co.uk

KETTLEBURGH

Chequers Inn ★★★★ *Inn*
The Street, Kettleburgh,
Framlingham
IP13 7JT
t (01728) 723760
e debbie@thechequers.net
w thechequers.net

Church Farm ★★★★ *Farmhouse*
Church Road, Kettleburgh,
Woodbridge
IP13 7LF
t (01728) 723532
e jbater@suffolkonline.net
w churchfarmkettleburgh.co.uk

LAVENHAM

Angel Gallery ★★★★
Bed & Breakfast **SILVER AWARD**
17 Market Place, Lavenham,
Sudbury
CO10 9QZ
t (01787) 248417
e angel-gallery@gofornet.co.uk
w lavenham.co.uk

Brett Farm ★★★★ *Bed & Breakfast*
The Common, Lavenham, Sudbury
CO10 9PG
t (01787) 248533
e brettfarmbandb@aol.com
w brettfarm.com

Erindor ★★★★ *Bed & Breakfast*
36 High Street, Lavenham, Sudbury
CO10 9PY
t (01787) 249198
e erindor.co.uk

Guinea House Bed & Breakfast
★★★★ *Bed & Breakfast*
SILVER AWARD
16 Bolton Street, Lavenham,
Sudbury
CO10 9RG
t (01787) 249046
e gdelucy@aol.com
w guineahouse.co.uk

Lavenham Old Rectory ★★★★★
Bed & Breakfast **GOLD AWARD**
Church Street, Lavenham, Suffolk
CO10 9SA
t (01787) 247572
e info@lavenhamoldrectory.co.uk
w lavenham-old-rectory.com

Lavenham Priory ★★★★★
Bed & Breakfast **GOLD AWARD**
Water Street, Lavenham
CO10 9RW
t (01787) 247404
e mail@lavenhampriory.co.uk
w lavenhampriory.co.uk

East of England | Suffolk

LAVENHAM (6 MILES)

Stanstead Hall ★★★★ *Farmhouse*
Hares Road, Hitcham, Ipswich
IP7 7NY
t (01449) 740270
e stanstead@btinternet.com
w stansteadcamping.co.uk

LAWSHALL

Brighthouse Farm ★★★★
Farmhouse
Melford Road, Lawshall, Bury St Edmunds
IP29 4PX
t (01284) 830385
e info@brighthousefarm.co.uk
w brighthousefarm.co.uk

LEISTON

Field End ★★★★ *Guest House* **SILVER AWARD**
1 Kings Road, Leiston
IP16 4DA
t (01728) 833527
e herbert@herbertwood.wanadoo.co.uk
w fieldendbedandbreakfast.co.uk

LEVINGTON

Lilac Cottage ★★★★
Bed & Breakfast
Levington Green, Levington, Ipswich
IP10 0LE
t (01473) 659509
e lenandjo.wenham@btinternet.com

LONG MELFORD

Denmark House ★★★★
Bed & Breakfast
Hall Street, Long Melford, Sudbury
CO10 9JD
t (01787) 378798
e info@denmarkhousebb.co.uk
w denmarkhousebb.co.uk

High Street Farmhouse ★★★★
Bed & Breakfast **SILVER AWARD**
High Street, Long Melford, Sudbury
CO10 9BD
t (01787) 375765
e mail@gallopingchef.co.uk
w highstreetfarmhouse.co.uk

LOWESTOFT

Britten House ★★★★★
Guest Accommodation
SILVER AWARD
21 Kirkley Cliff Road, Lowestoft
NR33 0DB
t (01502) 573950
e info@brittenhouse.co.uk
w brittenhouse.co.uk

Fairways Bed & Breakfast ★★★★
Bed & Breakfast **SILVER AWARD**
288 Normanston Drive, Oulton Broad
NR32 2PS
t (01502) 582756
e info@fairwaysbb.co.uk
w fairwaysbb.co.uk

Homelea Guest House ★★★
Guest House
33 Marine Parade, Lowestoft
NR33 0QN
t (01502) 511640
e info@homeleaguesthouse.co.uk
w homeleaguesthouse.co.uk

Lorne Guest House ★★★
Guest House
4 Pakefield Road, Lowestoft
NR33 0HS
t (01502) 568972

The Sandcastle ★★★★
Guest House **SILVER AWARD**
35 Marine Parde, Lowestoft
NR33 0QN
t (01502) 511799
e susie@thesandcastle.co.uk
w thesandcastle.co.uk

Winelodge ★★★
Guest Accommodation
1 Victoria Terrace, Lowestoft
NR33 0QJ
t (01502) 512777
w winelodge.co.uk

MONK SOHAM

The Firs Farmhouse ★★★★
Bed & Breakfast **SILVER AWARD**
Monk Soham, Woodbridge, Framlingham
IP13 7HD
t (01728) 627969
e jean.richardson2@btopenworld.com
w thefirsfarmhouse.co.uk

MOULTON

37 Newmarket Road ★★★★
Bed & Breakfast **SILVER AWARD**
Newmarket Road, Moulton, Newmarket
CB8 8QP
t (01638) 750362
e dkbowes@waitrose.com

NAYLAND

The Steam Mill House ★★★★
Guest Accommodation
SILVER AWARD
1 Fen Street, Nayland, Colchester
CO6 4HT
t (01206) 262818
e brendaassing@tiscali.co.uk
w thesteammillhouse.com

NEWMARKET

Birdcage Walk ★★★★
Guest Accommodation
GOLD AWARD
2 Birdcage Walk, Newmarket
CB8 0NE
t (01638) 669456
e patmerry@btinternet.com
w birdcagewalk.co.uk

Sandhurst ★★★ *Bed & Breakfast*
14 Cardigan Street, Newmarket
CB8 8HZ
t (01638) 667483
e crighton@rousnewmarket.freeserve.co.uk
w sandhurstbandb.mysite.orange.co.uk

OULTON

The Courtyard ★★★★ *Farmhouse*
SILVER AWARD
Laurel Farm, Hall Lane, Lowestoft
NR32 5DL
t (01502) 568724
e kevin@laurelfarm.co.uk
w laurelfarm.co.uk

OULTON BROAD

The Mill House Bed & Breakfast
★★★★ *Guest House*
SILVER AWARD
53 Bridge Road, Lowestoft, Oulton Broad
NR32 3LN
t (01502) 565038
e penny@themillhousebedandbreakfast.co.uk
w themillhousebedandbreakfast.co.uk

PAKENHAM

Fen House Bed & Breakfast
★★★★ *Bed & Breakfast*
SILVER AWARD
Fen Road, Pakenham, Bury St Edmunds
IP31 2LP
t (01359) 234968
e fen.house@hotmail.com
w fenhouse.net

POLSTEAD

Polstead Lodge ★★★★
Bed & Breakfast
Mill Street, Polstead, Colchester
CO6 5AD
t (01206) 262196
e howards@polsteadlodge.freeserve.co.uk
w polsteadlodge.com

RENDHAM

Rendham Hall ★★★ *Farmhouse*
Rendham Hall, Rendham, Saxmundham
IP17 2AW
t (01728) 663440
e colette@marybelle.co.uk
w farmstayanglia.co.uk/database/page.php?farmno=nsfh65

REYDON

Newlands Country House ★★★★
Guest Accommodation
SILVER AWARD
72 Halesworth Road, Southwold
IP18 6NS
t (01502) 722164
e info@newlandsofsouthwold.co.uk
w newlandsofsouthwold.co.uk

Ridge Bed & Breakfast ★★★★
Bed & Breakfast
14 Halesworth Road, Reydon, Southwold
IP18 6NH
t (01502) 724855
e ridgebandb@btinternet.com
w southwold.ws/ridge

RISBY

Brambles Lodge ★★★★
Bed & Breakfast **SILVER AWARD**
Welham Lane, Risby, Bury St Edmunds
IP28 6QS
t (01284) 810701
e brambleslodge.bandb@homecall.co.uk

ROUGHAM

Oak Farm Barn ★★★★
Bed & Breakfast **GOLD AWARD**
Moat Lane, Rougham, Bury St Edmunds
IP30 9JU
t (01359) 270014
e oakfarmbarn@tiscali.co.uk
w oakfarmbarn.co.uk

SAXMUNDHAM

The Cowshed *Bed & Breakfast*
Cowshed Holidays, The Cowshed, Walnut Tree Farm, Thorington, Saxmundham
IP17 3QP
t (01502) 478065

Pattles Farm ★★★★
Bed & Breakfast
Grove Road, Knodishall, Saxmundham
IP17 1TJ
t (01728) 604640
e sue@pattlesfarmsuffolk.co.uk

SHOTLEY

Hill House Farm Bed & Breakfast
★★★★ *Farmhouse* **SILVER AWARD**
Wades Lane, Shotley, Ipswich
IP9 1EW
t (01473) 787318
e hazel@wrinchfarmstay.co.uk
w wrinchfarmstay.co.uk

SIBTON

Eben-Ezer ★★★★ *Bed & Breakfast*
Abbey Road, Sibton, Saxmundham
IP17 2JB
t (01728) 660236
e dianaallen@btinternet.com

Sibton White Horse Inn ★★★★
Inn **SILVER AWARD**
Halesworth Road, Sibton, Saxmundham
IP17 2JJ
t (01728) 660337
e info@sibtonwhitehorseinn.co.uk
w sibtonwhitehorseinn.co.uk

SOUTHWOLD

Brenda's ★★★ *Bed & Breakfast*
3 Strickland Place, Southwold
IP18 6HN
t (01502) 722403

The Plough Inn ★★★★ *Inn*
London Road, Wangford, Southwold
NR34 8AZ
t (01502) 578239

Poplar Hall ★★★★ *Bed & Breakfast*
Frostenden Corner, Frostenden, Southwold, Suffolk
NR34 7JA
t (01502) 578549
e poplarhall@tiscali.co.uk
w poplarhallsouthwold.com

St Catherines House ★★★
Bed & Breakfast
186 Denmark Road, Lowestoft
NR32 2EL
t (01502) 500951

Sunset House ★★★★
Bed & Breakfast
27 The Old School Drive, Reydon, Southwold
IP18 6JZ
t (01502) 722931

SPEXHALL

St Peter's House B&B ★★★★
Bed & Breakfast
Wash Lane, Halesworth
IP19 0RQ
t (01986) 874275
e steve@stevemurray.demon.co.uk
w stpetersspexhall.co.uk

SPROUGHTON

Finjaro ★★★★ *Guest House*
SILVER AWARD
Valley Farm Drive, Hadleigh Road, Sproughton, Ipswich
IP8 3EL
t (01473) 652581
e jan@finjaro.freeserve.co.uk
w s-h-systems.co.uk/hotels/finjaro.html

ST CROSS SOUTH ELMHAM

South Elmham Hall ★★★★★
Guest Accommodation
SILVER AWARD
St Cross, Harleston
IP20 0PZ
t (01986) 782526
e info@southelmham.co.uk
w southelmham.co.uk

STOWMARKET

Bays Farm ★★★★★
Bed & Breakfast **GOLD AWARD**
Forward Green, Stowmarket
IP14 5HU
t (01449) 711286
e info@baysfarmsuffolk.co.uk
w baysfarmsuffolk.co.uk

Three Bears Cottage ★★★★
Guest Accommodation
Mulberry Tree Farm, Middlewood Green, Stowmarket
IP14 5EU
t (01449) 711707
e gbeckett01@aol.com
w aristoclassics.com

Verandah House ★★★★
Guest House
29 Ipswich Road, Stowmarket
IP14 1BD
t (01449) 676104
e info@verandahhouse.co.uk
w verandahhouse.co.uk

East of England | Suffolk

SUDBURY

l Lodge ★★★
est Accommodation
lewton Road, Sudbury
10 2RL
 (01787) 377568
e enquiries@hilllodgehotel.co.uk
w hilllodgehotel.co.uk

e Bull Guest House ★★★
est House
urch Street, Ballingford, Sudbury
10 2BL
 (01787) 374120
e theoldebulhotel@aol.com
w theoldebulhotel.co.uk

David's Hall ★★★★
d & Breakfast SILVER AWARD
 Friars Street, Sudbury
10 2AG
 (01787) 373044
e stdavidshall@tiscali.co.uk

THEBERTON

ders ★★★ Bed & Breakfast
ters Street, Theberton, Leiston
6 4RL
 (01728) 831790

pin Cottage ★★★
d & Breakfast
urch Road, Theberton, Leiston
6 4SF
 (01728) 830531
e elis.pehkonen@mypostoffice.co.
uk

THORINGTON

rk Farm ★★★★ Farmhouse
LVER AWARD
xford Road, Sibton, Saxmundham
7 2LZ
 (01728) 668324
e mail@sibtonparkfarm.co.uk
w sibtonparkfarm.co.uk

THORNDON

at Farm ★★★★ Farmhouse
LD AWARD
orndon, Eye
3 7LX
 (01379) 678437
e bookings@moatfarm.co.uk
w moatfarm.co.uk

THORNHAM MAGNA

e Four Horseshoes ★★★★ Inn
ckham Road, Thornham Magna,
e
3 8HD
 (01379) 678777
e thefourhorseshoes@btconnect.
com
w thefourhorseshoes.org

ornham Hall ★★★★★
est Accommodation
LVER AWARD
ornham Magna, Eye
3 8HA
 (01379) 783314
e thornhamhall@aol.com
w thornhamhall.com

THORPENESS

Dolphin Inn ★★★★ Inn
Old Homes Road, Thorpeness
IP16 4NA
t (01728) 454994
e dolphininn@hotmail.co.uk
w thorpenessdolphin.com

THURSTON

The Fox & Hounds ★★★★ Inn
SILVER AWARD
Barton Road, Thurston, Bury St
Edmunds
IP31 3QT
t (01359) 232228
e thurstonfox@btinternet.com
w thurstonfoxandhounds.co.uk

UFFORD

Strawberry Hill ★★★★
Bed & Breakfast
Loudham Lane, Lower Ufford,
Woodbridge
IP13 6ED
t (01394) 460252
e strawberryhilly@yahoo.co.uk
w smoothhound.co.uk/hotels/
strawber.html

UGGESHALL

Bankside Bed & Breakfast ★★★★
Bed & Breakfast SILVER AWARD
The Hills, Uggeshall, Southwold
NR34 8EN
t (01502) 578047
e liz@bankside19.fsnet.co.uk
w banksidebandb.co.uk

WALBERSWICK

Troy ★★★★ Bed & Breakfast
Church Field, Walberswick,
Southwold
IP18 6TG
t (01502) 723387
w visit.walberswick.com

WALDRINGFIELD

Thatched Farm Bed & Breakfast
★★★★ Bed & Breakfast
Woodbridge Road, Waldringfield,
Woodbridge, Suffolk
IP12 4PW
t (01473) 811755
e mailus@thatchedfarm.co.uk
w thatchedfarm.co.uk

WANGFORD

The Angel Inn ★★★★ Inn
High Street, Wangford, Nr
Southwold
NR34 8RL
t (01502) 578636
e info@angelinnwangford.co.uk
w angelinnwangford.co.uk

Fluff Cottage ★★★★
Bed & Breakfast
1 High Street, Wangford, Beccles
NR34 8RL
t (01502) 578997

WESTHORPE

Moat Hill Farm B&B ★★★★
Bed & Breakfast SILVER AWARD
Church Road, Westhorpe,
Stowmarket
IP14 4SZ
t (01449) 780165
e info@moathillfarm.co.uk
w moathillfarm.co.uk

WEYBREAD

Mill Lane Farm B&B ★★★★★
Farmhouse GOLD AWARD
Mill Lane, Weybread, Harleston
IP21 5TP
t (01379) 588141
e info@milllanefarm.co.uk
w milllanefarm.co.uk

WHEPSTEAD

The Old Pear Tree ★★★★
Bed & Breakfast SILVER AWARD
Whepstead, Bury St Edmunds
IP29 4UD
t (01284) 850470
e jenny@theoldpeartree.co.uk
w theoldpeartree.itgo.com

WINGFIELD

Gables Farm ★★★★
Bed & Breakfast SILVER AWARD
Wingfield, Diss
IP21 5RH
t (01379) 586355 (07824 445 464)
e enquiries@gablesfarm.co.uk
w gablesfarm.co.uk

WOODBRIDGE

2 St Anne's School House ★★★★
Bed & Breakfast SILVER AWARD
Crown Place, Woodbridge
IP12 1BU
t (01394) 386942
e lesley@st-annesbandb.co.uk
w st-annesbandb.co.uk

Cherry Tree Inn ★★★★
Guest Accommodation
73 Cumberland Street, Woodbridge
IP12 4AG
t (01394) 384627
e info@thecherrytreepub.co.uk
w thecherrytreepub.co.uk

The Coach House ★★★★
Bed & Breakfast SILVER AWARD
121 Ipswich Road, Woodbridge
IP12 4BY
t (01394) 385918
e rita@thecoachhouse-woodbridge.
co.uk
w thecoachhouse-woodbridge.co.uk

Fir Tree Lodge ★★★★
Bed & Breakfast SILVER AWARD
25 Moorfield Road, Woodbridge
IP12 4JN
t 07968 346029
e nights@debenaccom.com
w debenaccom.com

Grove House Hotel ★★★
Guest House
39 Grove Road, Woodbridge
IP12 4LJ
t (01394) 382202
e reception@thegrovehousehotel.
ltd.co.uk
w grovehousehotel.ltd.uk

Hill House ★★★★ Bed & Breakfast
30 Market Hill, Woodbridge
IP12 4LU
t (01394) 383890
e sarenkaknight@tiscali.co.uk
w hillhousewoodbridge.com

Mill View House ★★★
Bed & Breakfast
33 Mill View Close, Woodbridge
IP12 4HR
t (01394) 383010
e millview.house@btinternet.com
w mill-view.com

WOOLPIT

Bull Inn & Restaurant ★★★ Inn
The Street, Woolpit, Bury St
Edmunds
IP30 9SA
t (01359) 240393
e info@bullinnwoolpit.co.uk
w bullinnwoolpit.co.uk

Grange Farm ★★★★ Farmhouse
Grange Farm, Woolpit, Bury St
Edmunds
IP30 9RG
t (01359) 241143
e grangefarm@btinternet.com
w farmstayanglia.co.uk/grangefarm

WORTHAM

Rookery Farm ★★★★ Farmhouse
SILVER AWARD
Old Bury Road, Wortham, Diss
IP22 1RB
t (01379) 783256
e maureen@therookeryfarm.co.uk
w therookeryfarm.co.uk

WRENTHAM

Five Bells ★★★ Inn
Southwold Road, Wrentham
NR34 7JF
t (01502) 675249
e victoriapub@aol.com
w five-bells.com

YOXFORD

Chapel Cottage ★★★★
Bed & Breakfast SILVER AWARD
High Street, Yoxford, Saxmundham
IP17 3HP
t (01728) 667096
e info@chapelcottage-yoxford.co.uk
w chapelcottage-yoxford.co.uk

Sans Souci B&B ★★★★
Bed & Breakfast SILVER AWARD
Yoxford, Saxmundham
IP17 3EX
t (01728) 668827
e sue.norris3@btinternet.com
w sanssoucibandb.co.uk

Looking for something else?

You can also buy a copy of our popular guide 'Hotels' including country house and town house hotels, metro and budget hotels, serviced apartments, restaurants with rooms and Spas in England 2011. Now available in good bookshops and online at **visitbritainshop.com**

£10.99

East Midlands

No matter what your interests the East Midlands has something for everyone. If you're looking for adventure in the great outdoors then visit the rugged landscape of the Peak District and Derbyshire, with beautiful moorland, stunning valleys and acres of woodland.

You could also visit the rolling hills of the Lincolnshire Wolds or take a walk through Nottingham's Sherwood Forest where Robin Hood and his band of outlaws once lived. Whether it's walking, cycling, horse riding or rock climbing you can do it all in the East Midlands.

For those who prefer a little history the region boasts an astounding array of castles, old English gardens and impressive stately homes. Visit Chatsworth House in Derbyshire used as the backdrop for a number of Hollywood blockbusters such as The Duchess and Pride and Prejudice, and see the stunning collections of artwork or enjoy the picturesque grounds and gardens.

Travel to Lincoln's cathedral quarter and visit Lincoln Cathedral as featured in 'The Da Vinci Code' and Lincoln Castle, home to the Magna Carta one of only four surviving originals sealed by King John, and take a stroll down the aptly named 'Steep Hill' with it's cobbled street and quaint little shops.

For art lovers the region is home to a number of fantastic galleries and museums, from Nottingham Contemporary to the Curve in Leicester, or why not visit the visually astounding 78 Derngate in Northamptonshire, a stunning piece of Charles Rennie Mackintosh history.

East Midlands

East Midlands

Derbyshire, Leicestershire & Rutland,
Lincolnshire, Northamptonshire,
Nottinghamshire

388	Counties	396	Where to Eat
393	Where to Go	400	Where to Stay
395	Events		

The East Midlands has a wonderful coastline, running from The Wash in the south to the Humber Estuary in the north of Lincolnshire. There's also an abundance of wildlife to be seen along the coastline, and Gibraltar Point is a birdwatchers paradise. With miles of award winning beaches and a great choice of family resorts it is the hidden gem of the region.

If you prefer a livelier atmosphere then the cities of the region could have just what you're looking for, visit Nottingham, Derby, Leicester and Lincoln and enjoy some fantastic shopping and experience the great nightlife. For sports enthusiasts there's thrills and spills of motor racing at Donington and Silverstone or the favourite English sport of cricket at the world famous Trent Bridge.

From coastline to culture and history to adventure visit the East Midlands for an experience you'll never forget!

East Midlands | Derbyshire

Derbyshire

Derbyshire offers visitors a mix of quintessential English villages situated in and around the beautiful landscape of the Peak District National Park. It is also home to some of the UK's most famous and impressive stately homes.

Buxton
Based at the heart of the Peak District and blessed with stunning scenery, magnificent architecture, a wealth of shops, and a thriving arts scene. Coupled with its world-famous spa water, Buxton has plenty to offer any visitor. There is a splendid Crescent, ornamental gardens, an Opera House and the largest unsupported dome in the country.

Bakewell
The beautiful market town of Bakewell is typical of the stunning original market towns of Derbyshire. There's lots to see and do including visiting the Rutland Arms' where Jane Austen once stayed and included in her novel Pride and Prejudice and where the Bakewell Pudding was invented by a chef of 1859 who made a mistake that has made this beautiful little town world famous.

Castleton
Castleton is an outstandingly pretty village situated at the head of the lovely Vale of Hope, in the heart of the Derbyshire Peak District National Park. Castleton is surrounded by steep hills and the mighty bulk of Mam Tor. On a hill, overlooking Castleton, is the ancient Peveril Castle.

Castleton has four underground show caves, all worth a visit. These are Blue John Cavern, Speedwell Cavern, Treak Cliff Cavern and Peak Cavern. Blue John Cavern and Treak Cliff contain the treasured, pretty blue and yellow stone called Blue John.

Peak District National Park
The southern portion of the park, called White Peak, is filled with limestone hills, tiny villages, old stone walls, and hidden valleys. In the northern Dark Peaks the scenery changes to rugged moors and deep gullies. The beautiful heathers of the Dark Peak were popularly written about by Emily Bronte and the park was used as the stunning backdrop to Pride and Prejudice starring Keira Knightly. Those who visit can experience stunning views, extensive walks and the chance to see some of England's beautiful wildlife.

Matlock
Matlock Bath in Derbyshire, became an instant tourist resort for the wealthy and influential, when warm springs at a constant temperature of 68 degrees fahrenheit, were discovered back in 1698. Situated at a sharp bend in the River Derwent, where it turns south to carve its way through the ridge of limestone which bars its route towards Derby, Matlock offers local shops and stunning scenery.

East Midlands | **Leicestershire & Rutland**

Leicestershire & Rutland

Notable attractions include 'Leicester Cathedral', 'The National Space Centre', the UK's largest attraction dedicated to space science and astronomy, 'New Walk Museum and Art Gallery'. Leicestershire has beautiful countryside and interesting towns and villages.

Melton Mowbray

The market town of Melton Mowbray has a long established association with foxhunting, pork pies and Stilton cheese. It is a popular and lively place to visit, especially on market days and has a rich and varied heritage. Melton's history is still evident today, the cathedral-sized St Mary's Church dates from 1170. Known as the stateliest and most impressive of all Leicestershire churches, its 100-foot tower dominates the town.

National Forest

The National Forest is one of Britain's boldest environmental projects creating a new forest for the nation across 200 square miles and embracing parts of Leicestershire and Derbyshire. There are plenty of beautiful walks and cycle routes throughout the forest and also a number of bridleways so everyone can enjoy the forest.

Ashby de la Zouch

Ashby de la Zouch is a beautiful market town with Georgian architecture offering a delightful look at a traditional English town. Ashby Castle can also be visited and although now in ruins offers an insight into the great history of the region.

Vale of Belvoir

The Vale of Belvoir (pronounced "Beaver") borders the three counties of Leicestershire, Nottinghamshire and Lincolnshire but is officially located in the county of Leicestershire. With beautiful views and traditional stone villages Belvoir provides a real sense of old England. With the Stunning Belvoir Castle at its heart which to this day serves as the family home to the Duke and Duchess of Rutland.

The Grand Union Canal

The Grand Union is a 1920s marriage of historic waterways. The attractive 137-mile main line has many branches to towns along the way. The longest of these, the Leicester Line, runs to Leicester, from where the River Soar continues to Nottingham.

Rutland

The smallest county in England, full of enchanting villages and picturesque countryside, plus being home to Rutland Water, one of the largest man-made reservoirs with watersports, nature reserves, outdoor adventure centre, cycling & walking.

There are over 50 pretty villages to explore in Rutland, all of which are well kept, charming and unspoilt. Oakham, the county town, is a pretty, traditional English market town, bustling with activity and packed with heritage. It is also ideal for a unique shopping experience from the finest handmade jewellery to the most desirable fashion labels. There is also a fantastic monthly farmers market. Uppingham is charming, full of honey coloured buildings and blessed with a range of speciality and antique shops, many of which are still family owned and run.

East Midlands | Lincolnshire

Lincolnshire

On a trip to Lincoln city you can explore history and heritage around the cobbled streets of the magnificent Cathedral and Castle, take part in the city's lively events programme or enjoy a spot of shopping in boutiques, outlets and high street stores.

Skegness, Mablethorpe & The Coast
With over 50 miles of award winning beaches the Lincolnshire coast has something for everyone. In the north, Cleethorpes offers tranquil boating lakes and promenade walks; Mablethorpe's quiet charm has been attracting visitors for generations; and the illuminations and attractions of the UK's most renowned coastal resorts – Skegness – remains a firm family favourite all year round.

Stamford & The Vales
The Vales offer a rich landscape of green fields and stone built towns which keep visitors returning year on year. Stamford is one such town and offers magnificent Georgian town-houses, churches and cobbled streets. A 10 min drive will take you to Burghley House, one of the finest stately homes from the Elizabethan age.

Louth & The Wolds
The Lincolnshire Wolds are an Area of Outstanding Natural Beauty and home to one of the county's tastiest Market Towns – Louth. Whether driving through rural hamlets, exploring the rolling landscape on foot or bike, don't miss a visit to Louth's butchers, bakers and local food producers. A visit to the Wolds will dispel any myths that Lincolnshire is flat.

Boston & The Fens
The criss-cross of waterways is paradise for anyone who enjoys water activities. Spalding and Boston remain the areas key market towns. Look out for St Botolph's church locally nicked named 'The Stump' or take part in the Spalding Flower Festival each May which sees floats, circuses and other delights set the town alight.

East Midlands | **Northamptonshire**

Northamptonshire

Northamptonshire is a vibrant county full of places to go and hidden beauties to explore to suit all tastes. Whether you are looking for relaxation or adventure, history or beautiful landscapes, Northamptonshire has it all. Once famous around the world as `shoe town`, Northamptonshire still celebrates its Leather Heritage today and is one of the few places in Europe offering courses in Leather Technology; it is also the home of various tanneries and leather businesses.

Brackley

Brackley marketplace is surrounded by Georgian and Victorian buildings, housing a delightful selection of shops and cafes. The impressive baroque Town Hall, built in 1706, still dominates the town centre today. Brackley Antique Cellar has a range of treasures from furniture to china. Close by is Silverstone for some Formula One, or Whittlebury Hall Luxury Spa for some relaxation. There is also National Trust Canons Ashby (16th Century manor house) and Evenley Wood Gardens.

Brixworth

Brixworth is home to one of England's largest and finest surviving Anglo-Saxon Churches, built around 680 A.D. Nearby are super walks at Brampton Valley Way and garden visits to Coton Manor Gardens, Holdenby House and Cottesbrooke Hall & Gardens. Althorp, owned by Earl Spencer is a few miles away where you can visit the exhibition celebrating the life of Diana, Princess of Wales. Historic houses Kelmarsh Hall and Lamport Hall are also close by.

Oundle

Situated beside a meander in the River Nene the ancient market town of Oundle is edged by water meadows, popular with anglers, walkers and artists it also provides a wonderful spot for wildlife spotting. Oundle is also famous for its public school with many buildings of outstanding architectural and historical interest in the town.

Weekley

The roads in the village have no name plates, with mail being delivered by house number. With its twenty thatched cottages, Weekley has remained largely unchanged over the last 250 years, and still remains a fabulous 'postcard' picture, with many visitors pausing for a photo. To help protect its historic character, it is now designated a Conservation Area. Nearby attractions include Boughton House, Rushton Hall and Rushton Triangular Lodge, as well as a fantastic tea room, the Dovecote Buttery at Newton.

East Midlands | Nottinghamshire

Nottinghamshire

Nottingham Old Market Square is the biggest market square in Britain and holds an annual Goose Fair, one of Europe's largest travelling fairs dating back to 1541. The oldest pub in England is also to be found here, The Jerusalem Inn dating back to 1189 AD

Sherwood Forest

Sherwood Forest is an historic royal forest located in the North and is world famous as the legendary home of Robin Hood. Ancient oak trees are still to be found in some portions of the forest, especially in the area known as the Dukeries, which used to contain five ducal residences in proximity to one another. The forest's vast landscape of woodland, heath, farms and settlement is home to some of Europe's greatest trees and lowland heathland that is as rare as rainforest.

Retford

The ancient market town of Retford was granted its first charter (the right to hold a fair) by Henry III in 1246. This was extended by Edward I in 1275 to holding a Saturday market; a tradition that continues today. The town features fine Georgian buildings, a spacious square, and two theatres. It also played a remarkable part in the story of the Pilgrim Fathers, who fled to America in 1620 after being persecuted for their religious beliefs. Explore their story on the Mayflower Trail, a circular tour starting at nearby Babworth.

Eastwood

The birthplace of D.H. Lawrence who changed English literature for ever with his novel 'Lady Chatterley's Lover'. In the 20th century, when Lawrence was growing up, the area was dominated by the coal mining industry. The house is a tiny terrace but is a glimpse into the author's early life and works. A short walk is Durban House which offers a look into the past of the Barber Walker Mining Company.

Newark

Newark is a picturesque town situated on the banks of the River Trent. The Georgian Town Hall overlooks the market place but the town is famous for six annual antique fairs held at Newark County Showground. Thousands of international antique hunters descend on thousands of stalls in search of a bargain! The town is home to Newark Air Museum with 65 aircraft. But for relaxation nearby North Clifton is home to a meditation centre and Japanese garden.

Southwell

Famous for the Minster church which boasts some of the best medieval stone carving in England, Southwell is a prosperous small town with many elegant Regency houses. Southwell Minster is thought by many to be the 'best kept secret' among all English cathedrals. Outside the town is the best-preserved workhouse in England, owned by The National Trust it offers a chance to explore the workshops and dormitories of an early 'welfare' institution. There are interactive displays charting poverty through the ages.

East Midlands | Where to Go

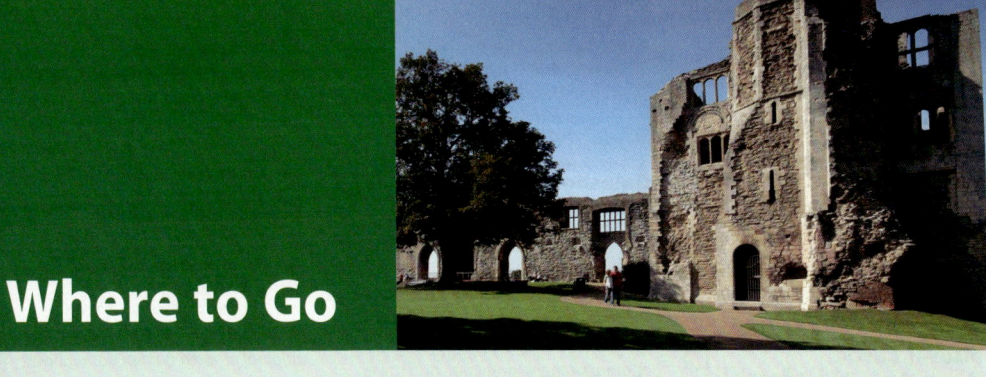

Where to Go

Attractions with this sign participate in the **Visitor Attraction Quality Assurance Scheme** (see page 6) which recognises high standards in all aspects of the visitor experience.

ENTERTAINMENT & CULTURE

Battle of Britain Memorial Flight Centre
Coningsby, Lincolnshire
LN4 4SY
(01526) 344041
www.lincolnshire.gov.uk/bbmf
The Battle of Britain Memorial Flight operates a Lancaster, five Spitfires, two Hurricanes, two Chipmunks, and a Dakota. In 1986 it became possible to view these historic aircraft at their base at RAF Coningsby.

Conkers Discovery Centre
Ashby-de-la-Zouch,
Leicestershire DE12 6GA
(01283) 216633
www.visitconkers.com
Conkers, the award winning attraction at the heart of the National Forest. A unique mix of indoor and outdoor experiences.

Crich Tramway Village
Matlock, Derbyshire DE4 5DP
(01773) 854321
www.tramway.co.uk
Situated in the heart of the Derbyshire countryside is a world from a bygone age, where vintage trams transport visitors along cobbled streets, past enchanting buildings, and into breathtaking scenery.

Newark Castle and Conflict
Newark, Nottinghamshire
NG24 1BG
(01636) 655765
www.newark-sherwood.gov.uk
Has been at the heart of the town for many centuries and has played an important role in historical events.

Rockingham Motor Racing Circuit
Corby, Northamptonshire
NN17 5AF
(01536) 500500
www.rockingham.co.uk
Rockingham is the ultimate entertainment venue. Home to the SCSA racing series and host to a variety of driving experiences.

Silverstone Circuit
Silverstone, Northamptonshire
NN12 8TN
0844 372 8200
www.silverstone.co.uk
Silverstone is recognised as the Home of British Motor Racing.

Snibston
Coalville, Leicestershire
LE67 3LN
(01530) 278444
www.leics.gov.uk
Visit Snibston, the award-winning hands-on museum for the whole family.

FAMILY FUN

Foxton Locks
Market Harborough,
Leicestershire LE16 7RA
(01908) 302500
www.foxtonlocks.com
Fascinating ten lock 'staircase' climbing a 75ft hill. The museum explores Britain's canal development.

National Space Centre
Leicester, Leicestershire LE4 5NS
0845 605 2001
www.spacecentre.co.uk
The award winning National Space Centre is the UK's largest attraction dedicated to space.

Twinlakes Park
Melton Mowbray, Leicestershire
LE14 4SB
(01664) 567777
www.twinlakespark.co.uk
Twinlakes Park is a family day out with rides for all the family. All year, all weather, plus falconry centre and animal farm.

HERITAGE

78 Derngate
Northampton,
Northamptonshire NN1 1UH
(01604) 603407
www.78derngate.org.uk
Charles Rennie Mackintosh transformed a typical terraced house into a startlingly modern house for local model maker W.J. Bassett-Lowke. It was his last major commission and his only work in England.

Alford Manor House
Alford, Lincolnshire LN13 9HT
(01507) 463073
www.alfordmanorhouse.co.uk
Reputedly the largest thatched manor house in the country, Alford Manor House was built in 1611.

Althorp
Northampton,
Northamptonshire NN7 4HQ
(01604) 770107
www.althorp.com
Experience 500 years of history at the Spencer family home. Diana exhibition and magnificent treasures.

393

East Midlands | Where to Go

Belton House
Belton (South Kesteven), Lincolnshire NG32 2LS
(01476) 566116
www.nationaltrust.org.uk
Belton, as a perfect example of an English Country House, welcomes the visitor.

Belvoir Castle
Melton Mowbray, Leicestershire NG32 1PE
(01476) 871002
www.belvoircastle.com
Home to the Duke and Duchess of Rutland, Belvoir Castle offers stunning views of the Vale of Belvoir.

Bolsover Castle
Bolsover, Derbyshire S44 6PR
(01246) 822844
www.english-heritage.org.uk/bolsover
Built by Sir Charles Cavendish in 1612 and completed by his son William. Marvel at the outstanding craftsmanship everywhere - the rich panelling, elaborate fireplaces and painted ceilings.

Bosworth Battlefield Heritage Centre
Market Bosworth, Leicestershire CV13 0AD
(01455) 290429
www.bosworthbattlefield.com
Visit the site of Bosworth Battlefield 1485, the battle that ended the War of the Roses and began the dynasty of the Tudors.

Canons Ashby House
Canons Ashby, Northamptonshire NN11 3SD
(01327) 860044
www.nationaltrust.org.uk
Elizabethan Manor House largely unaltered since 1710. 18thC gardens, parkland, church, tearoom and shop.

Clumber Park
Worksop, Nottinghamshire S80 3AZ
(01909) 544917
www.nationaltrust.org.uk/clumberpark
Theres so much to do at Clumber Park throughout the year, whether you like walking or cycling, eating in the restaurant or joining in with one of our many events.

Creswell Crags
Bolsover, Derbyshire S80 3LH
(01909) 720378
www.creswell-crags.org.uk
Creswell Crags is a world famous archaeological site, home to Britain's only known Ice Age cave art.

Doddington Hall
Lincoln, Lincolnshire LN6 4RU
(01522) 694308
www.doddingtonhall.com
A superb Elizabethan mansion by the renowned architect Robert Smythson. The hall stands today as it was completed in 1600 with walled courtyards, turrets and gatehouse.

Gainsborough Old Hall
Gainsborough, Lincolnshire DN21 2NB
(01427) 612669
www.lincolnshire.gov.uk/gainsborougholdhall
A magnificent medieval manor house in the centre of Gainsborough with original kitchens, great hall and tower.

Great Central Railway
Leicester, Leicestershire LE11 1RW
(01509) 230726
www.gcrailway.co.uk
The Great Central Railway is Britain's only double track main line steam railway. Why not treat yourself to a three course meal whilst riding in style?

Grimsthorpe Castle, Park and Gardens
Grimsthorpe, Lincolnshire PE10 0LY
(01778) 591205
www.grimsthorpe.co.uk
The castle covers 4 periods of architecture with a collection of portraits and furniture which are mainly 18thC.

Haddon Hall
Bakewell, Derbyshire DE45 1LA
(01629) 812855
www.haddonhall.co.uk
Haddon Hall is conveniently located between Bakewell and Matlock, Derbyshire.

Hardwick Hall
Chesterfield, Derbyshire S44 5QJ
(01246) 850430
www.nationaltrust.org.uk/hardwick
Owned by the National Trust the Estate includes Hardwick Hall, Stainsby Mill and a Park. The Hall is one of Britain's greatest Elizabethan houses, the water-powered Mill is fully functioning, the Park has a fishing lake and circular walks.

Lincoln Castle
Lincoln, Lincolnshire LN1 3AA
(01522) 511068
www.lincolnshire.gov.uk/lincolncastle
Lincoln Castle is located in the heart of historic City of Lincoln.

Lincoln Cathedral
Lincoln, Lincolnshire LN2 1PX
(01522) 561600
www.lincolncathedral.com
Lincoln Cathedral is one of the finest medieval buildings in Europe. High on its hill overlooking the ancient city of Lincoln and dominating the skyline for many miles, it has a visual impact which is nothing less than startling.

Lyveden New Bield
Peterborough, Northamptonshire PE8 5AT
(01832) 205358
www.nationaltrust.org.uk/lyveden
An intriguing Elizabethan Lodge and original moated garden dating back to 1600.

Newstead Abbey
Nottingham, Nottinghamshire NG15 8NA
(01623) 455900
www.nottinghamcity.gov.uk/newsteadabbey
A beautiful historic house set in a glorious landscape of gardens and parkland within the heart of Nottinghamshire.

Peveril Castle
Hope Valley, Derbyshire S33 8WQ
(01433) 620613
www.english-heritage.org.uk
Wonder at the inspiring views afforded from the remains of Peveril Castle - a spectacular view of the Peak District. Made famous by Scott's 'Peveril'.

Rockingham Castle
Market Harborough, Northamptonshire LE16 8TH
(01536) 770240
www.rockinghamcastle.com
Rockingham Castle stands on the edge of an escarpment giving dramatic views over five counties and the Welland Valley below. Built by William the Conqueror, the Castle was a royal residence for 450 years.

Rufford Abbey & Country Park
Newark, Nottinghamshire NG22 9DF
(01623) 821338
www.nottinghamshire.gov.uk/ruffordcp
Located near Ollerton, on the edge of historic Sherwood Forest, this 150 acre park is one of Nottinghamshire's most popular visitor attractions. At the heart of the park are the picturesque remains of a 12th century Cistercian monastery.

East Midlands | Where to Go/Events

St Botolph's Church
Boston, Lincolnshire PE21 6NP
(01205) 362864
www.parish-of-boston.org.uk
Described by Pevsner as a 'giant among English parish churches' St Botolph's Church has always been a landmark to both seafarers and people travelling across the flat fenland that surrounds the market town of Boston.

Sulgrave Manor
Sulgrave, Northamptonshire OX17 2SD
(01295) 760205
www.sulgravemanor.org.uk
A Tudor manor house and garden, the ancestral home of George Washington's family with authentic furniture shown by friendly guides.

Tattershall Castle
Tattershall, Lincolnshire LN4 4LR
(01526) 342543
www.nationaltrust.org.uk/tattershall
Tattershall Castle was built in the 15th Century to impress and dominate by Ralph Cromwell, one of the most powerful men in England. The castle is a dramatic red brick tower.

NATURE & WILDLIFE

Bradgate Country Park
Leicester, Leicestershire LE6 0HE
(0116) 236 2713
Bradgate park is a 340 hectare ancient deer park which was the home of Lady Jane Grey, 9 day Queen of England (1553).

Castle Ashby Gardens
Castle Ashby, Northamptonshire NN7 1LQ
(01604) 695200
www.castleashbygardens.co.uk
Castle Ashby Gardens are a haven of tranquility and beauty in the heart of Northamptonshire. Take your time to explore these beautiful gardens and enjoy the fascinating attractions from the rare breed farmyard to the historic orangery.

Rutland Water Nature Reserve
Oakham, Rutland LE15 8PX
(01572) 770651
www.rutlandwater.u-net.com
The nature reserve consists of a narrow strip of land stretching for 7 miles covering an area of 350 acres.

Salcey Forest
Hartwell, Northamptonshire NN17 3BB
(01780) 444920
www.forestry.gov.uk/salceyforest
Salcey Forest; get a birds eye view of this wonderful woodland on the tremendous Tree Top Way.

Sherwood Forest Country Park
Mansfield, Nottinghamshire NG21 9HN
(01623) 823202
www.nottinghamshire.gov.uk/sherwoodforestcp
Once part of a royal hunting forest, Sherwood Forest Country Park covers 450 acres and incorporates some truly ancient areas of native woodland.

Twycross Zoo
Hinckley, Leicestershire CV9 3PX
(01827) 880250
www.twycrosszoo.com
Twycross Zoo opened in 1963 on a site in Leicestershire. Initially a comparatively modest collection, it has become one of the major British zoos, attracting over 450,000 visitors a year. It is famous for its collection of primates.

Events 2011

Althorp Literary Festival
Northampton
www.althorp.com
June

Buxton Festival
www.buxtonfestival.co.uk/
July

CAMRA Summer Beer Festival
Derby
www.derbycamra.org.uk
July

Chatsworth Country Fair
www.countryfairoffice.co.uk
September

Churches Festival
Gainsborough
www.churchesfestival.com/
May

Crick Boat Show
www.crickboatshow.com/
May

DH Lawrence Festival
Eastwood
www.broxtowe.gov.uk/festival
August - September

Goose Fair
Nottingham
www.nottinghamcity.gov.uk/goosefair/
October

Holdenby Food Show
www.stonehouse-events.co.uk
August

Lincoln Christmas Market
christmasmarket.lincoln.gov.uk/
December

Lincolnshire Show
www.lincolnshireshowground.co.uk
June

Lincolnshire Wolds Walking Festival
www.woldswalkingfestival.co.uk
May/June

Lustre
Nottingham
www.lakesidearts.org.uk
November

Newark Jazz Festival
www.newarkjazz.co.uk/
May

Peak District Walking Festival
Derby
www.visitpeakdistrict.com
April/May

Robin Hood Festival
Nottingham
www.robinhood.org.uk/rhf.htm
July/August

Silverstone Classic
www.silverstoneclassic.com/
July

Splendour Music Festival
Nottingham
www.splendourfestival.com/
July

Summer Sundae Music Festival
Leicester
www.summersundae.com/
August

Waddington Air Show
www.waddingtonairshow.co.uk
July

Wirksworth Festival
www.wirksworthfestival.co.uk/
September

395

East Midlands | Where to Eat

Where to Eat

The East Midlands region has great places to eat. The restaurant reviews on these pages are just a small selection from the highly respected *The Good Food Guide 2011*. Please see page 14 for further information on the Guide and details of a Special Offer for our readers.

DERBYSHIRE

Callow Hall
Imposing Peak District pile
Mappleton Road, Ashbourne DE6 2AA
(01335) 300900
www.callowhall.co.uk
Modern British | £42

A fine Victorian pile resting in 34 acres of garden, fields and woodland, Callow Hall is what most people would expect a country house hotel to be. It is now owned by Von Essen Hotels, but Anthony Spencer, son of the former owners, continues to head the kitchen and at its best his cooking exudes and inspires quiet confidence. Chicken liver terrine with fig and orange chutney could start a lunch, followed by grilled fillet of salmon with thyme-scented slow-roast courgettes and peppers, puréed potatoes and white wine fumé, with sticky toffee chocolate pudding to finish. House wine is £18.95. As we went to press, Von Essen was planning a 'full refurbishment' of the hotel.

Chef/s: Anthony Spencer. **Open:** all week L 12 to 2, D 7.15 to 9. **Meals:** alc (main courses £17 to £22). Set L £16.95 (2 courses) to £19.95. Set D £29.95 (2 courses) to £42. Sun L £28.95. **Service:** not inc. **Details:** major cards accepted. 70 seats. 20 seats outside. Separate bar. No mobile phones. Wheelchair access. Music. Children welcome. Car parking.

LEICESTERSHIRE

Entropy
Appealing all-day food, good weekend breakfasts
42 Hinckley Road, Leicester LE3 0RB
(0116) 2259650
www.entropylife.com
Modern British | £25

Tom Cockerill pitched his camp in this Leicester suburb a decade ago and over time has reworked both the premises and his own cooking style. What he and his wife Cassandra are offering is very much in tune with modern times, at least for those who don't expect three lots of appetisers and a pre-dessert with their dinner. It's two shops knocked together, both of which have been simply decorated with lots of pale wood and an on-view kitchen. The food has broad appeal, not least because it is offered all day. Sensible, unfussy dishes include game broth with root vegetable and pearl barley or ox heart served with ratte potatoes, red chard and chilli oil, followed by Dexter steak and smoked oyster pie or roast free-range chicken. Equally well-handled desserts have included duck egg crème brûlée with peanut butter cookies. Good weekend breakfasts, too. The short, modern wine list starts at £13.95.

Chef/s: Tom Cockerill. **Open:** all week 10.30 to 10 (9.30am to 10pm Sat, 9.30am to 7pm Sun). **Closed:** 25 and 26 Dec, 1 Jan. **Meals:** alc (main courses £9 to £24). **Service:** not inc. **Details:** major cards accepted. 62 seats. 32 seats outside. Air conditioning. Music. Children welcome.

East Midlands | **Where to Eat**

LINCOLNSHIRE

Winteringham Fields
Unique charm and culinary finesse
Silver Street, Winteringham DN15 9ND
(01724) 733096
www.winteringhamfields.com
Modern European | £75

The beguiling restaurant-with-rooms that famously put Lincolnshire on the foodie map seems to have finally regained some of its stature and equilibrium. Germain and Annie Schwab were always going to be a hard act to follow, but supporters reckon that Winteringham can still deliver 'unique charm' and culinary finesse – witness a euphorically reported lunch that yielded an exquisite amuse-bouche of anchovy tuile with 'revelatory' tarragon ice cream on a sweetcorn base, wickedly luxurious seared scallops on scrambled egg with caviar and truffles ('possibly the best starter I have ever eaten'), and near-perfect belly pork with apple rémoulade and tempura squid. Those who come for dinner have even more high-calibre strokes to consider – perhaps Cornish halibut (cooked at 50°C) with truffle mousse, Puy lentils, langoustine crêpes and artichoke barigoule, or a dessert of dark chocolate coulant with parsnip ice cream and raspberries. The whole experience is crowned by service that has that magic blend of formality and friendliness. If you are staying over, take time to wallow in the wine list, which is packed with distinguished names from around the globe – whether you are after a top-end Mersault, a South African Sumaridge Merlot or Tasmanian Pinot Grigio. Prices start at £24.
Chef/s: Colin McGurran. **Open:** Tue to Sat L 12 to 3, D 7 to 10. **Closed:** Sun, Mon, 2 weeks Dec/Jan, 3 weeks Aug. **Meals:** Set L £35 (2 courses) to £39.95. Set D £65 (2 courses) to £75. **Service:** not inc. **Details:** major cards accepted. 60 seats. Air conditioning. Separate bar. No music. No mobile phones. Wheelchair access. Children welcome. Car parking.

NORTHAMPTONSHIRE

The Vine House
Lively cooking with an army of fans
100 High Street, Paulerspury NN12 7NA
(01327) 811267
www.vinehousehotel.com
Modern British | £30

A 300-year-old limestone house in an unruffled Northants village, the Vine House has a loyal army of followers. The place is an especial delight in fine weather, when a table inside a kind of summerhouse in the garden comes into its own. Marcus Springett's cooking is lively modern British, with Mediterranean and east Asian influences used to good effect. Home-smoked Loch Duart salmon dressed in toasted sesame seeds and wasabi is a typical way to start. One reporter found no fault with a meal that progressed from wild garlic and rocket gnocchi to saddle of lamb with

crushed peas and salsa verde. The determination to make an impact is sustained through to desserts such as passion-fruit jelly with dark chocolate sauce. Wines start at £16.95.
Chef/s: Marcus Springett. **Open:** Tue to Sat L 12 to 1.30, Mon to Sat D 7 to 9. **Closed:** Sun. **Meals:** Set L and D £26.95 (2 courses) to £29.95. **Service:** 12.5%. **Details:** major cards accepted. 33 seats. No music. No mobile phones. Wheelchair access. Children welcome. Car parking.

NOTTINGHAMSHIRE

French Living
A patriotic foodie package
27 King Street, Nottingham NG1 2AY
(0115) 9585885
www.frenchliving.co.uk
French | £20

The traditional English take on a French city bistro is alive and well in this bustling red-brick eatery in the basement of a well-stocked deli/café. The main menu, supplemented by blackboard set deals, combines basic crowd-pleasers (gratinée à l'oignon, moules), with classic regional dishes (tartiflette, cassoulet Toulousain). There's also onglet (steak) with shallot and veal sauce and wild boar casserole in a rich red wine sauce, with tartelette au chocolat or excellent unpasteurised French cheeses to finish. House French is £10.50.
Chef/s: Jeremy Tourne. **Open:** Tue to Sat L 12 to 2 (2.30 Sat), D 6 to 10. **Closed:** Sun, Mon, 25 Dec to 1 Jan. **Meals:** alc (main courses £12 to £17). Set L £8.50 (2 courses) to £10.50. Pre theatre set D £7.90 (1 course) to £12.50. Set D £21.50. **Service:** not inc. **Details:** major cards accepted. 40 seats. Air conditioning. Music. Children welcome.

> Content brought to you by **The Good Food Guide 2011**. Please see page 14 for further details.

397

East Midlands

Tourist Information Centres

When you arrive at your destination, visit an Official Partner Tourist Information Centre for quality assured help with accommodation and information about local attractions and events, or email your request before you go. To find a Tourist Information Centre by region visit enjoyEngland.com/find-tic.

ASHBOURNE	13 Market Place	01335 343666	ashbourneinfo@derbyshiredales.gov.uk
ASHBY-DE-LA-ZOUCH	North Street	01530 411767	ashby.tic@nwleicestershire.gov.uk
BAKEWELL	Old Market Hall	01629 813227	bakewell@peakdistrict-npa.gov.uk
BRIGG	The Buttercross	01652 657053	brigg.tic@northlincs.gov.uk
BUXTON	The Crescent	01298 25106	tourism@highpeak.gov.uk
CASTLETON	Buxton Road	01433 620679	castleton@peakdistrict-npa.gov.uk
CHESTERFIELD	Rykneld Square	01246 345777	tourism@chesterfield.gov.uk
CLEETHORPES	42-43 Alexandra Road	01472 323111	cleetic@nelincs.gov.uk
DERBY	Assembly Rooms	01332 255802	tourism@derby.gov.uk
LEICESTER	7/9 Every Street	0844 888 5181	info@goleicestershire.com
LINCOLN CASTLE HILL	9 Castle Hill	01522 873213	tourism@lincoln.gov.uk
MATLOCK	Crown Square	01629 583388	matlockinfo@derbyshiredales.gov.uk
NEWARK	The Gilstrap Centre	01636 655765	gilstrap@nsdc.info
NORTHAMPTON	Northampton Visitor Centre	01604 838800	northampton.tic@northamptonshireenterprise.ltd.uk
NOTTINGHAM CITY	1-4 Smithy Row	08444 775 678	tourist.information@nottinghamcity.gov.uk
OLLERTON	Tourist Information Centre	01623 824545	sherwoodheath@nsdc.info
SLEAFORD	Advice Centre, Money's Yard,	01529 414294	tic@n-kesteven.gov.uk
SWADLINCOTE	Sharpe's Pottery Museum	01283 222848	Jo@sharpespotterymuseum.org.uk

East Midlands

Regional Contacts and Information

The publications listed are available from the following organisations:

East Midlands Tourism
Web: www.discovereastmidlands.com
Discover East Midlands

Experience Nottinghamshire
Tel: 0844 477 5678
Web: www.visitnotts.com
Nottinghamshire Essential Guide, Where to Stay Guide, City Breaks, The City Guide, Robin Hood Breaks

Peak District and Derbyshire
Web: www.visitpeakdistrict.com
Peak District and Derbyshire Visitor Guide
Well Dressing
Camping and Caravanning Guide
Walking Festivals Guide and Visitor Guide

Discover Rutland
Tel: (01572) 720924
Web: www.discover-rutland.co.uk
Discover Rutland, Eat drink Rutland, Attractions, Uppingham, Oakham, Oakham Heritage Trail

Lincolnshire
Tel: (01522) 545458
Web: www.visitlincolnshire.com
Visit Lincolnshire – Destination Guide, Great Days Out, Good Taste
Keep up with the flow

Explore Northamptonshire
Tel: (01604) 609393
Web: www.explorenorthamptonshire.co.uk
Northamptonshire Visitor Guide,
Northamptonshire presents Britain on show
County Map

Leicestershire
Tel: 0844 888 5181
Web: www.goleicestershire.com
Leicestershire City Guide
Stay, Play, Explore
Great Days Out in Leicestershire

399

East Midlands | Derbyshire

Where to Stay

Entries appear alphabetically by town name in each county. A key to symbols appears on page 6. Maps start on page 706. A listing of all Enjoy England assessed accommodation appears at the end of the region.

ASHBOURNE, Derbyshire Map ref 4B2
SAT NAV DE6 1QU

enjoyEngland.com
★★★ GUEST ACCOMMODATION

B&B PER ROOM PER NIGHT
D £59.00 – £88.00

EVENING MEAL PER PERSON
£5.00 – £12.95

SPECIAL PROMOTIONS
Stay Sunday - Thursday night (5 nights) and pay for 4.

Peak District Spa
Buxton Road, Nr Alsop-en-le-Dale, Ashbourne DE6 1QU
t (01335) 310100 f (01335) 310100 e PeakDistrictSpa@rivendalecaravanpark.co.uk
w peakdistrictspa.co.uk ONLINE BOOKING LAST MINUTE OFFERS

Occupying a secluded location on part of Rivendale's 37 acre site with its own parking, terrace and garden with superb views over Eaton Dale. Ideal for cycling, walking & outdoor pursuits. Convenient Chatsworth, Alton Towers, Carsington Water. All rooms with en suites, oak or travertine floors, under floor heating.

open All year except closed Sunday after New Years day until 1st Friday in February.
bedrooms 2 double, 2 twin
bathrooms 4 en suite
payment credit/debit cards, cash, cheques

directions Travelling north from Ashbourne towards Buxton on the A515, find Rivendale on the RHS.

Room
General
Leisure

Looking for something else?

You can also buy a copy of our popular guide 'Hotels' including country house and town house hotels, metro and budget hotels, serviced apartments, restaurants with rooms and Spas in England 2011. Now available in good bookshops and online at **visitbritainshop.com**
£10.99

400 Official tourist board guide Bed & Breakfa

East Midlands | Derbyshire

ASHBOURNE, Derbyshire Map ref 4B2
SAT NAV DE6 3AT

Shirley Hall
Shirley, Ashbourne, Derbyshire DE6 3AT
t (01335) 360820/07799 762624 f (01335) 360346 e ian@iancrabtree.wanadoo.co.uk
w shirleyhallfarm.com

B&B PER ROOM PER NIGHT
S £45.00 – £50.00
D £33.00 – £40.00

Wonderful Tudor manor house with spacious ensuite rooms set in lawned gardens on our farm nr to pretty village. Excellent meals at local pub within walking distance. Self-catering cottage available. **directions** Take A52 from Derby towards Ashbourne. Approx 8 miles take left to Shirley. 1 mile on right before the village. Phone if lost. **open** All year except Xmas and New Year **bedrooms** 1 double, 1 twin **bathrooms** 2 en suite **payment** cash, cheques, euros

ASHBOURNE, Derbyshire Map ref 4B2
SAT NAV DE6 2BL

Stone Cottage
Green Lane, Clifton, Ashbourne DE6 2BL
t (01335) 343377 f (01335) 34117 e info@stone-cottage.fsnet.co.uk
w stone-cottage.fsnet.co.uk

B&B PER ROOM PER NIGHT
S £28.00 – £45.00
D £50.00 – £72.00

A charming cottage in the parish of Clifton 1 mile from the market town of Ashbourne. Each bedroom is furnished to a high standard with en-suite TV and welcome tray **directions** 1 mile west of Ashbourne just of the A52 **open** All year **bedrooms** 1 double, 1 family **bathrooms** 2 en suite **payment** credit/debit cards, cash, cheques, euros

BAKEWELL, Derbyshire Map ref 4B2
SAT NAV DE45 1AA

Castle Hill Farm House
Castle Mount Crescent, Baslow Road, Bakewell DE45 1AA
t (01629) 813168 e christine@castlehillfarmhouse.co.uk
w castlehillfarmhouse.co.uk ONLINE MAP GUEST REVIEWS ONLINE BOOKING LAST MINUTE OFFERS

B&B PER ROOM PER NIGHT
S £70.00
D £75.00 – £80.00

Delightful C17th Farmhouse, overlooking River Wye. Peaceful location a few minutes walk from the town centre. Ideally situated for Chatsworth House & Haddon Hall. Comfortable rooms, delicious food, Friendly atmosphere. **directions** See website. **open** All year **bedrooms** 2 double **bathrooms** 2 with private bathroom **payment** cash, cheques

Do you like Camping?

You can also buy a copy of our popular guide 'Camping, Touring & Holiday Parks' including touring parks, camping holidays and holiday parks and villages in Britain 2011.

Now available in good bookshops and online at
visitbritainshop.com

£8.99

East Midlands | Derbyshire

BAKEWELL, Derbyshire Map ref 4B2
SAT NAV S32 5QB

Housley Cottage
Foolow, Hope Valley S32 5QB
t (01433) 631505 e kevin@housleycottages.co.uk
w housleycottages.co.uk ONLINE MAP ONLINE BOOKING LAST MINUTE OFFERS

B&B PER ROOM PER NIGHT
S £45.00
D £62.00

SPECIAL PROMOTIONS
Family room (sleeps 4): children half price. 10% reduction when booking 3 or more nights. See website for latest offers.

A 16thC farm cottage set in open countryside but within ten minutes' walk of the Bulls Head pu in Foolow village. Public footpaths pass our garden gate to Millers Dale, Chatsworth House, Eyan and Castleton. All rooms en suite with views over open countryside. Full English breakfast or vegetarian.

open March to Oct
bedrooms 2 double, 1 twin, 1 family
bathrooms 4 en suite
payment credit/debit cards, cash, cheques, euros

directions Buxton A6, A623, junction to Foolo we are opposite on right-hand side. Chesterfie A619/A623; 300m past Housley sign on left-hand side.

Room   General   P   Leisure

BAMFORD, Derbyshire Map ref 4B2
SAT NAV S33 0BN

Pioneer House
Station Road, Bamford, Hope Valley S33 0BN
t (01433) 650638 e pioneerhouse@yahoo.co.uk
w pioneerhouse.co.uk ONLINE MAP GUEST REVIEWS LAST MINUTE OFFERS

B&B PER ROOM PER NIGHT
S £40.00 – £60.00
D £60.00 – £70.00

Pioneer House is set in the stunning Hope Valley between Hathersage, Hope & Castleton. An ideal base for exploring this beautiful and interesting area, whether walking, climbing or sightseeing. **directions** Pioneer House is in the beautiful Hope Valley, on the A6013, linking the A6187 to the A57, or is accessibl by rail via Bamford Station **open** All year **bedrooms** 2 double, 1 twin **bathrooms** 2 en suite, 1 with private bathroom **payment** credit/debit cards, cash, cheques

Room   General 12   P   Leisure

Where is my pet welcome?
Some properties welcome well-behaved pets. Look for the 🐕 in the accommodation listings.

You can also buy a copy of our popular guide 'Pets Come Too!' Now available in good bookshops and online at **visitbritainshop.com**

£9.99

402   Official tourist board guide Bed & Breakfa

East Midlands | **Derbyshire**

BAMFORD, Derbyshire   Map ref 4B2

SAT NAV S33 0AZ

Yorkshire Bridge Inn

Ashopton Road, Bamford, Hope Valley S33 0AZ
t (01433) 651361   **f** (01433) 651361   **e** info@yorkshire-bridge.co.uk
w yorkshire-bridge.co.uk   ONLINE MAP   GUEST REVIEWS   ONLINE BOOKING

B&B PER ROOM PER NIGHT
S £60.00 – £65.00
D £76.00 – £120.00

EVENING MEAL PER PERSON
£8.95 – £16.95

SPECIAL PROMOTIONS
Special breaks available - 3 nights or more; Bank Holiday Special Breaks; New Year Breaks

This famous inn enjoys an idyllic setting near the beautiful reservoirs of Ladybower, Derwent and Howden in the Peak District, and was voted one of the top six freehouses of the year for all-year-round excellence. Superb, en suite rooms, lovely bar and dining areas offering excellent cuisine. Brochure available.

open All year except Xmas
bedrooms 10 double, 2 twin, 2 family
bathrooms 14 en suite
payment credit/debit cards, cash, cheques

directions M1 jct 29, Chesterfield - Baslow - Calver - Hathersage - Bamford. A6013 through Bamford. After 0.5 miles on left-hand side.

Room   General   Leisure

BARLBOROUGH, Derbyshire   Map ref 4C2

SAT NAV S43 4ER

Stone Croft

15 Church Street, Barlborough, Chesterfield, Derbyshire S43 4ER
t (01246) 810974   **f** (01246) 810974   **e** enquiries.stone-croft@live.co.uk
w stone-croft.co.uk   ONLINE MAP

B&B PER ROOM PER NIGHT
S £30.00 – £35.00
D £40.00 – £45.00

Stone Croft offers a refreshing getaway in a grade 2 listed home; with an all inclusive 4 star full English breakfast on offer and ample secure parking. **directions** Please contact us for directions **open** All year **bedrooms** 1 double, 1 family **bathrooms** 1 en suite, 2 with private bathroom **payment** cash, cheques

Room   General   Leisure

BRADWELL, Derbyshire   Map ref 4B2

SAT NAV S33 9HG

Travellers Rest

Brough Lane End, Brough, Hope Valley S33 9HG
t (01433) 620343   **f** (01433) 623338   **e** info@travellers-rest.net
w travellers-rest.net

B&B PER ROOM PER NIGHT
S £40.00 – £49.00
D £60.00 – £85.00

EVENING MEAL PER PERSON
£6.95 – £13.95

Country inn set in the picturesque Hope Valley Derbyshire in the Peak District. Friendly, with great food and beer. **directions** On the T Junction of the A6187 and the B6049 please see google maps for details. **open** All year except Xmas **bedrooms** 3 double, 2 twin **bathrooms** 5 en suite **payment** credit/debit cards, cash, cheques

Room   General   Leisure

key to symbols see page 6   403

East Midlands | **Derbyshire**

BUXTON, Derbyshire Map ref 4B2   SAT NAV SK17 0BS

FARMHOUSE ★★★★ **Silver AWARD**

B&B PER ROOM PER NIGHT
S £45.00 – £55.00
D £72.00 – £80.00

Fernydale Farm
Earl Sterndale, Buxton SK17 0BS
t (01298) 83236   e wjnadin@btconnect.com
w fernydalefarmbandb.co.uk ONLINE MAP GUEST REVIEWS ONLINE BOOKING LAST MINUTE OFFERS

A working farm nestling in the Peaks with stunning views. Attractive bedrooms, modern bathrooms, spacious conservatory and garden to relax in. Excellent breakfast. Buxton, Bakewell, Ashbourn and numerous attractions/walks. **directions** From Buxton A515. At Country Bookstore right onto B5053 to Longnor. At small crossroads turn left (Earl Sterndale). **open** All year **bedrooms** 1 double, 1 twin, 1 family **bathrooms** 3 en suite **payment** credit/debit cards, cash, cheques, euros

BUXTON, Derbyshire Map ref 4B2   SAT NAV SK17 9DP

GUEST HOUSE ★★★★ **Silver AWARD**

B&B PER ROOM PER NIGHT
S £35.00 – £45.00
D £60.00 – £80.00

Kingscroft Guest House
10 Green Lane, Buxton, Derbyshire SK17 9DP
t (01298) 22757   f (01298) 27858   e kingscroftbuxton1@btinternet.com

Late-Victorian luxury guesthouse, in central yet quiet position in the heart of the Peak District. Comfortable surroundings with period decor. Enjoy our hearty, delicious, home-cooked full English or continental breakfasts. **directions** Kingscroft is situated only 5 minutes walk from the town's shopping centre, pubs and restaurants, and easy reach at both railway and bus stations. **open** All year **bedrooms** 1 single, 6 double, 1 twin **bathrooms** 8 en suite **payment** cash, cheques

BUXTON, Derbyshire Map ref 4B2   SAT NAV SK17 9AL

GUEST HOUSE ★★★★

B&B PER ROOM PER NIGHT
D £70.00 – £80.00

Lakenham Guest House
11 Burlington Road, Buxton SK17 9AL
t (01298) 79209   e enquiries@lakenhambuxton.co.uk
w lakenhambuxton.co.uk ONLINE MAP GUEST REVIEWS

Sample Victorian elegance in one of Buxton's finest guest houses. Lakenham offers all modern facilities yet retains its Victorian character. Period furniture and antiques. Superb quiet central location overlooking picturesque Pavilion Gardens. Spacious, tastefully furnished bedrooms with TV and hospitality tray. First-class, personal service in a friendly, relaxed atmosphere.

open All year
bedrooms 4 double, 3 twin
bathrooms 5 en suite, 2 with private bathroom
payment credit/debit cards, cash, cheques

directions Lakenham is located opposite the Pavilion Gardens on Burlington Road. Burlington Road is situated between St Johns Road (A54) and Macclesfield Road/West Road.

404   Official tourist board guide **Bed & Breakf**

East Midlands | Derbyshire

CASTLETON, Derbyshire Map ref 4B2

SAT NAV S33 8WJ

Swiss House
How Lane, Castleton, Hope Valley, Derbyshire S33 8WJ
t (01433) 621098 **e** info@swiss-house.co.uk
w swiss-house.co.uk ONLINE MAP GUEST REVIEWS ONLINE BOOKING LAST MINUTE OFFERS

B&B PER ROOM PER NIGHT
S £40.00 – £70.00
D £60.00 – £83.00

Family run B&B with a difference. Quality service, warm, clean and friendly. Excellent, plentiful full English breakfast using lots of local and home-made produce. **directions** Please contact us for directions **open** All year **bedrooms** 5 double, 1 twin, 2 family **bathrooms** 8 en suite **payment** credit/debit cards, cash, cheques

Room   General   Leisure

CHESTERFIELD, Derbyshire Map ref 4B2

SAT NAV S40 4EE

Abigail's Guest House
62 Brockwell Lane, Chesterfield S40 4EE
t (01246) 279341 **f** (01246) 854468 **e** gail@abigails.fsnet.co.uk
w abigailsguesthouse.co.uk ONLINE MAP

B&B PER ROOM PER NIGHT
S £38.00
D £52.00

Relax taking breakfast in the conservatory overlooking Chesterfield and surrounding moorlands. Garden with pond, private car park. Best B&B winners 2000. Free Wi-Fi Access. **directions** Please contact us for directions **open** All year **bedrooms** 2 single, 3 double, 2 twin **bathrooms** 7 en suite **payment** credit/debit cards, cash, cheques

Room   General   Leisure

CHESTERFIELD, Derbyshire Map ref 4B2

SAT NAV S43 3TL

Old Rectory Guest House
8 Church Street, Staveley, Chesterfield, derbyshire S43 3TL
t (01246) 473307 **e** billcooneyb@aol.com
w oldrectoryguesthouse.com ONLINE MAP GUEST REVIEWS ONLINE BOOKING LAST MINUTE OFFERS

B&B PER ROOM PER NIGHT
S £25.00
D £40.00

Grade 2 listed building built in 1719 situated in the centre of Staveley. Once home of William Gisborn the then Rector of Staveley. Now a well established guest house for 25 yrs run by your host Mrs Briony Cooney.

open All year except Xmas and New Year
bedrooms 2 single, 2 twin
bathrooms 2 en suite
payment credit/debit cards, cash, cheques

directions M1 j30 take A619 to Chesterfield, approx 2 miles you enter Staveley, small chevron roundabout turn left, the mini roundabout turn right, church on right.

Room   General   Leisure

East Midlands | Derbyshire

CRESSBROOK, Derbyshire Map ref 4B2
SAT NAV SK17 8SY

enjoyEngland ★★★★ GUEST ACCOMMODATION

B&B PER ROOM PER NIGHT
S £50.00 – £75.00
D £100.00 – £120.00

Cressbrook Hall
Cressbrook, Buxton SK17 8SY
t (01298) 871289 f (01298) 871845 e stay@cressbrookhall.co.uk
w cressbrookhall.co.uk

Accommodation with a difference. Enjoy this magnificent family home built in 1835, set in 23 acres, with spectacular views around the compass. Elegance, simplicity, peace and quiet. Formal garden by Edward Kemp. **directions** Please contact us for directions **open** All year except Xmas and New Year **bedrooms** 2 double, 1 suite **bathrooms** 3 en suite **payment** credit/debit cards, cash, cheques

Room · General · Leisure

DERBY, Derbyshire Map ref 4B2
SAT NAV DE3 0DN

enjoyEngland ★★★ BED & BREAKFAST

B&B PER ROOM PER NIGHT
S £30.00 – £32.00
D £55.00 – £60.00

Bonehill Farm
Etwall Road, Mickleover, Derby DE3 0DN
t (01332) 513553 e bonehillfarm@hotmail.com
w bonehillfarm.co.uk

A 120-acre mixed farm. Comfortable Georgian farmhouse in rural setting, three miles from Derby. Alton Towers, Peak District, historic houses all within easy reach. Peaceful location. Full fire certificate. **directions** On A516 between Mickleover and Etwall **open** All year except Xmas and New Year **bedrooms** 1 double, 1 twin, 1 family **bathrooms** 2 en suite, 1 with private bathroom **payment** cash, cheques

Room · General

DERBY, Derbyshire Map ref 4B2
SAT NAV DE65 5FZ

enjoyEngland ★★★★★ FARMHOUSE · Silver AWARD

B&B PER ROOM PER NIGHT
S £58.00 – £75.00
D £75.00 – £90.00

The Lavender Patch
Hall Croft Farm, Uttoxeter Road, Hilton, Derby, Derbyshire DE65 5FZ
t 01283 732303/ 07815956026 e info@thelavenderpatch.com
w thelavenderpatch.com LAST MINUTE OFFERS

Georgian farmhouse at Derbyshire's only lavender garden. Enormous en suite bedroom with king size or twin beds, private sitting room with log burner. Delicious breakfasts. Nr historic houses, Alton Towers. **directions** Access off A50 junction 5, through Hilton village on main street and Farm drive is located on right hand side, just before T-junction. **open** All year **bedrooms** 1 double **bathrooms** 1 en suite **payment** credit/debit cards, cash, cheques

Room · General · Leisure

GREAT LONGSTONE, Derbyshire Map ref 4B2
SAT NAV DE45 1TF

enjoyEngland ★★★★★ BED & BREAKFAST · Silver AWARD

B&B PER ROOM PER NIGHT
D £90.00

The Forge House
Main Street, Great Longstone, Nr Bakewell, Derbyshire DE45 1TF
t (01629) 640375 e emma@theforgehouse.co.uk

The Forge House has excellent modern facilities including luxury prestine bathrooms and flat screen TV in bedroom and bathroom. Close to Chatsworth House, Haddon Hall, Heights of Abraham and Bakewell. **directions** Please contact us for directions **bedrooms** 2 double **bathrooms** 2 en suite **payment** cash, cheques, euros

Room · General · Leisure

406 Official tourist board guide Bed & Breakfast

East Midlands | Derbyshire

HIGHAM, Derbyshire Map ref 4B2   SAT NAV DE55 6EF

Bramble Cottage

22-23 Main Road, Higham, Alfreton DE55 6EF
t (01773) 830298 e enquiries@bramblecottagebandb.com
w bramblecottagebandb.com GUEST REVIEWS LAST MINUTE OFFERS

B PER ROOM PER NIGHT
S £25.00 – £50.00
D £60.00 – £90.00

Bramble Cottage, full of Elizabethan charm and original beams, has had a sympathetic refurbishment. Surrounded by beautiful Peak Park (Matlock 6, Bakewell 9 miles approx). A warm welcome is assured.

open All year
bedrooms 3 double
bathrooms 2 en suite, 1 with private bathroom
payment credit/debit cards, cash, cheques

directions Please contact us or use google maps

Room General Leisure

HOPE, Derbyshire Map ref 4B2   SAT NAV S33 6AF

Underleigh House

Lose Hill Lane, Off Edale Road, Hope, Hope Valley S33 6AF
t (01433) 621372 f (01433) 621324 e info@underleighhouse.co.uk
w underleighhouse.co.uk ONLINE MAP GUEST REVIEWS ONLINE BOOKING

B PER ROOM PER NIGHT
S £62.00 – £82.00
D £82.00 – £102.00

BREAKFAST AWARD

Award-winning and secluded cottage/barn conversion with magnificent countryside views. Ideal for walking and exploring the Peak District. Delicious breakfasts, featuring local and home-made specialities, served in flagstoned dining hall. **directions** From Hope, take Edale Road (opp church) for 0.6 mls. Turn left at de-restriction sign and take Lose Hill Lane for 0.3 mls. **open** All Year Except Christmas, New Year and January **bedrooms** 3 double, 2 suites **bathrooms** 5 en suite **payment** credit/debit cards, cash, cheques

Room General 12 Leisure

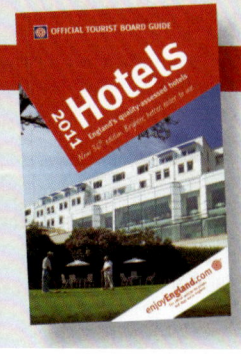

Looking for something else?

You can also buy a copy of our popular guide 'Hotels' including country house and town house hotels, metro and budget hotels, serviced apartments, restaurants with rooms and Spas in England 2011.

Now available in good bookshops and online at
visitbritainshop.com

£10.99

key to symbols see page 6   407

East Midlands | Derbyshire

HOPE, Derbyshire Map ref 4B2

SAT NAV S33 6RD

Woodbine B&B

18 Castleton Road, Hope, Hope Valley S33 6RD
t 07778 113882

B&B PER ROOM PER NIGHT
S £40.00
D £60.00 – £80.00

SPECIAL PROMOTIONS
3 night weekend break – third night half price. Two nights midweek stay for 2 people £99.

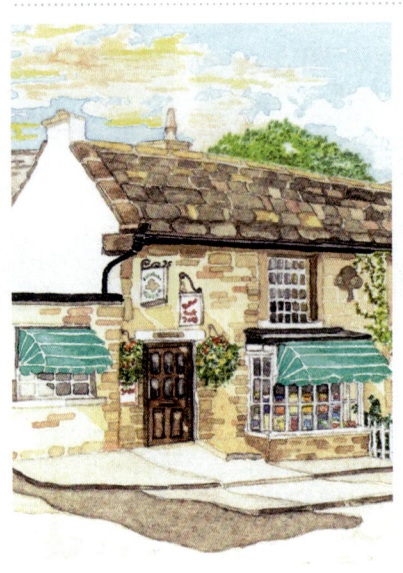

Comfortable, friendly B&B and tearoom (famous homemade cakes) in 16th century Blacksmiths cottages popular with walkers, cyclists and visitors to the Peak District National Park.

open All year except Xmas
bedrooms 4 double, 5 twin
bathrooms 9 en suite
payment cash, cheques

directions Please contact us for directions

Room
General
Leisure

LEA BRIDGE, Derbyshire Map ref 4B2

SAT NAV DE4 5JN

Pear Tree Farm Guest House

Pear Tree Farm, Lea Main Road, Matlock, Derbyshire DE4 5JN
t (01629) 534215 e sue@derbyshirearts.co.uk
w derbyshirearts.co.uk ONLINE MAP GUEST REVIEWS ONLINE BOOKING LAST MINUTE OFFERS

B&B PER ROOM PER NIGHT
S £50.00 – £60.00
D £70.00 – £80.00

EVENING MEAL PER PERSON
£15.00 – £25.00

SPECIAL PROMOTIONS
Mid-week price – £30-£35 pppn (£15 single supplement. 3+ night stay - £30-£35 pppn

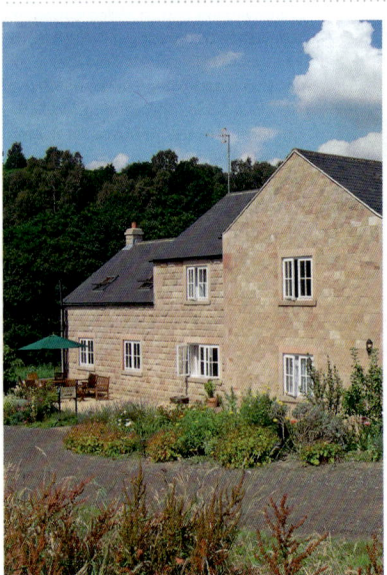

Friendly, traditional 4 star B&B accommodation in the heart of Derbyshire, Nr Matlock. With the Peak District National Park on the doorstep, Pear Tree Farm is the perfect base for walking, cycling, sight-seeing, or simply relaxing! We also host residential and day art courses in our purpose built studio.

open All year
bedrooms 4 double, 4 twin, 1 family
bathrooms 9 en suite
payment credit/debit cards, cash, cheques

directions By Car - 25mins from M1, Junction 28. By Train - 5mins from Cromford Station. By Air - 45mins from East Midlands Airport.

Room
General
Leisure

408 Official tourist board guide Bed & Breakfast

East Midlands | Derbyshire

MATLOCK BATH, Derbyshire Map ref 4B2
SAT NAV DE4 3NS

B&B PER ROOM PER NIGHT
S £35.00 – £45.00
D £60.00 – £70.00

Ashdale Guest House
92 North Parade, Matlock Bath, Matlock DE4 3NS
t (01629) 57826 e ashdale@matlockbath.fsnet.co.uk
w ashdaleguesthouse.co.uk ONLINE MAP LAST MINUTE OFFERS

A Grade II Listed Victorian villa situated in the centre of Matlock Bath. Large, comfortable rooms, level walking to restaurants, pubs, museums and station. Home-made bread and marmalade. **directions** Centre of Matlock Bath, opposite The Jubilee Bridge. **open** All year **bedrooms** 1 double, 1 twin, 2 family **bathrooms** 4 en suite **payment** credit/debit cards, cash, cheques, euros

BREAKFAST AWARD

TANSLEY, Derbyshire Map ref 4B2
SAT NAV DE4 5LF

B&B PER ROOM PER NIGHT
S £60.00
D £75.00 – £95.00

Silver Ridge
Foxholes Lane, Tansley, Matlock, Derbyshire DE4 5LF
t (01629) 55071 e pcspaul@hotmail.com
w silverridgetansley.co.uk ONLINE MAP GUEST REVIEWS ONLINE BOOKING LAST MINUTE OFFERS

Luxury accommodation, surrounded by mature gardens. Offering peace and tranquility. Separate guests dining room and entrance. Quality home cooking, using home made and local produce, a truly memorable stay. **directions** Please contact us for directions **open** All year **bedrooms** 1 double, 1 twin, 1 family **bathrooms** 3 en suite **payment** cash, cheques

BREAKFAST AWARD

TISSINGTON, Derbyshire Map ref 4B2
SAT NAV DE6 1RD

B&B PER ROOM PER NIGHT
S £40.00 – £50.00
D £70.00 – £80.00

Bassett Wood Farm
Tissington, Ashbourne DE6 1RD
t (01335) 350254 e janet@bassettwood.freeserve.co.uk
w bassettwoodfarm.co.uk ONLINE MAP

A working Dairy Farm. Indulge yourself in the Tea Room and from the breakfast window, enjoy a unique viewing of cows and newly born calves. A play Area. **directions** Enter Tissington off the A515 over cattle grid. Keep duck pond and Trail entrance on your right. Exit village. Sign in field. Turn right. **open** All year **bedrooms** 1 double, 1 twin, 1 family **bathrooms** 3 en suite **payment** credit/debit cards, cheques

WESSINGTON, Derbyshire Map ref 4B2
SAT NAV DE55 6DU

B&B PER ROOM PER NIGHT
S £30.00 – £35.00
D £60.00 – £70.00

Crich Lane Farm
Moorwood Moor Lane, Wessington, Alfreton, Derbyshire DE55 6DU
t (01773) 835186/07930 553219 e crichlanefarm@w3z.co.uk
w crichlanefarm.co.uk

Stone Farmhouse set in beautiful countryside, a perfect setting for a relaxing break in peaceful surroundings, families very welcome. Meals are served in the village pubs within walking distance. **directions** M1 junc 28, A38 towards Derby 3mls, A615 Matlock to Wessington 3 mls, turn opposite church in Wessington, 400yds down lane on lefthand side **open** All year **bedrooms** 2 single, 2 double, 1 twin, 2 family **bathrooms** 5 en suite **payment** cash, cheques

East Midlands | Leicestershire & Rutland

CROPSTON, Leicestershire & Rutland Map ref 4C3
SAT NAV LE7 7HQ

Horseshoe Cottage Farm
Hallgates, Roecliffe Road, Cropston, Leicester LE7 7HQ
t (0116) 235 0038 e lindajee@ljee.freeserve.co.uk
w horseshoecottagefarm.com ONLINE MAP GUEST REVIEWS

B&B PER ROOM PER NIGHT
S £62.50
D £95.00
EVENING MEAL PER PERSON
£20.00 – £25.00

Luxury, award winning barn conversion located midway between Leicester and Loughborough. Situated in countryside, opposite to Bradgate Park. Homecooked, locally sourced food for breakfast and dinner. A warm welcome awaits. **directions** Please see our website for full and easy to follow directions **open** All year **bedrooms** 2 double, 1 twin **bathrooms** 3 en suite **payment** credit/debit cards, cash, cheques, euros

BREAKFAST AWARD Room   General   Leisure

EYE KETTLEBY, Leicestershire & Rutland Map ref 4C3
SAT NAV LE14 2TS

Old Guadaloupe B&B
Old Guadaloupe, Kirby Lane, Eye Kettleby, Melton Mowbray LE14 2TS
t 07989 960588 e sue@suelomas.orangehome.co.uk
w oldguadaloupecottage.co.uk

B&B PER ROOM PER NIGHT
S £30.00 – £35.00
D £50.00 – £80.00

500-year-old farmhouse. Rooms fitted to a high standard with Freeview TV and DVD tea/coffee, hair dryer. Doubles have 5ft bed all en-suite Bathrooms. Own lounge. Near Melton Mowbray. **directions** Off A607 Leicester Road, turn for Great Dalby, 200yds turn left, 3rd right. When drive forks, take right-hand fork. **open** All year **bedrooms** 1 double, 1 twin, 1 family **bathrooms** 3 en suite **payment** cash, cheques

Room   General   Leisure

LEICESTER, Leicestershire & Rutland Map ref 4C3
SAT NAV LE3 0TF

Abinger Guest House
175 Hinckley Road, Leicester LE3 0TF
t (0116) 255 4674 e abinger@btinternet.com
w leicesterguest.co.uk ONLINE MAP GUEST REVIEWS ONLINE BOOKING

B&B PER ROOM PER NIGHT
S £28.00 – £32.00
D £41.00 – £49.00

Extensively modernised guesthouse situated 0.8 miles from Leicester city centre. Friendly staff, great breakfasts and extremely comfortable beds. Freeview TV in every room, and free Wi-Fi internet throughout. **directions** From M1. Jn 21 take A5460 toward Leicester. Left on to Hinckley Road after 2.4 miles. 500 yards up on right **open** All year except Xmas and New Year **bedrooms** 1 single, 2 double, 3 twin, 2 family **bathrooms** 1 en suite, 1 with private bathroom **payment** credit/debit cards, cash, cheques, euros

Room   General

Looking for something else?

You can also buy a copy of our popular guide 'Self Catering' including self-catering holiday homes, approved caravan holiday homes, boat accommodation and holiday cottage agencies in England 2011.

Now available in good bookshops and online at
visitbritainshop.com

£11.99

East Midlands | **Leicestershire & Rutland**

LEICESTER, Leicestershire & Rutland Map ref 4C3

SAT NAV LE6 0AE

Wondai B&B

47-49 Main Street, Newtown Linford, Leicester LE6 0AE
t (01530) 242728 **e** rmwarrillow@googlemail.com

B&B PER ROOM PER NIGHT
S £30.00 – £35.00
D £45.00 – £50.00

SPECIAL PROMOTIONS
Weekend breaks £40 per room based on 2 people sharing, 2 nights minimum, off-peak.

Our bed and breakfast is located in the village just a short walk from Bradgate Deer Park which was home to Lady Jane Grey, Queen of England for nine days in 1553. Great Central Railway, the only twin-track mainline steam train in England, is a short drive away.

open All year except Xmas
bedrooms 1 twin, 1 family
bathrooms 2 en suite
payment credit/debit cards, cash, cheques

directions Via the M1, take Junction 22 - Follow signs to Markfield, Fieldhead.

Room General Leisure

LOUGHBOROUGH, Leicestershire & Rutland Map ref 4C3

SAT NAV LE11 2AQ

Highbury Guest House

146 Leicester Road, Loughborough LE11 2AQ
t (01509) 230545 **f** (01509) 233086 **e** irene@thehighburyguesthouse.co.uk
w highburyguesthouse.co.uk ONLINE MAP GUEST REVIEWS ONLINE BOOKING LAST MINUTE OFFERS

B&B PER ROOM PER NIGHT
S £35.00 – £40.00
D £58.00 – £65.00

EVENING MEAL PER PERSON
£8.00 – £20.00

High quality is not achieved by chance. It is always the outcome of planning, care and attention to detail. In short a genuine concern for the needs of the client. **directions** On the main A6 going north into Loughborough just past the BP petrol station on the right. **open** All year except Xmas and New Year **bedrooms** 3 single, 4 double, 3 twin, 6 family **bathrooms** 16 en suite, 1 with private bathroom **payment** credit/debit cards, cash, cheques

Room General

MORCOTT, Leicestershire & Rutland Map ref 3A1

SAT NAV LE15 9EB

Redoak Bed and Breakfast

Seaton Road, Morcott, Oakham, Rutland LE15 9EB
t (01572) 747842 **f** (01572) 747842 **e** redoakbb@googlemail.com
w redoakonline.co.uk ONLINE MAP GUEST REVIEWS

B&B PER ROOM PER NIGHT
S £30.00
D £50.00

EVENING MEAL PER PERSON
£12.00 – £15.00

A warm and friendly welcome guaranteed! 6 miles from Rutland Water, private sitting room, use of 3 acre garden and summerhouse, evening meals and lunches **directions** 4 Miles from Uppingham 6 miles from Rutland Water 10 miles from Oakham & Stamford Just off the A47 at Morcott **open** All year except Xmas and New Year **bedrooms** 1 twin **bathrooms** 1 en suite **payment** cash, cheques, euros

BREAKFAST AWARD Room General Leisure

key to symbols see page 6

411

East Midlands | **Leicestershire & Rutland**

OAKHAM, Leicestershire & Rutland Map ref 4C3   SAT NAV LE15 6QR

17 Northgate
Oakham, Rutland LE15 6QR
t (01572) 759271   f (01572) 759271   e dane@danegould.wanadoo.co.uk
w **17northgate.co.uk** ONLINE MAP

B&B PER ROOM PER NIGHT
S £50.00 – £60.00
D £75.00 – £85.00

SPECIAL PROMOTIONS
Discounts are available for stays of 3 or more nights.

A recently renovated, 300-year-old thatched farmhouse in the centre of Oakham close to Rutland Water, the church, railway station and the excellent pubs and restaurants. The two en suite rooms are newly built, with their own patios and private entrance from the drive, where off-road parking is available.

open All year except Xmas and New Year
bedrooms 1 double, 1 twin
bathrooms 2 en suite
payment credit/debit cards, cash, cheques, euros

directions Northgate is in the centre of Oakham, off Church Street and opposite the church. Number 17 is 250m along on right, away from church.

BREAKFAST AWARD

OAKHAM, Leicestershire & Rutland Map ref 4C3   SAT NAV LE15 6JD

Dial House
18 Uppingham Road, Oakham, Rutland LE15 6JD
t (01572) 771685   e info@dialhouse.eu
w **dialhouse.eu** ONLINE MAP

B&B PER ROOM PER NIGHT
S £35.00 – £45.00
D £70.00

EVENING MEAL PER PERSON
£15.00 – £20.00

Detached house in quiet residential road quarter mile from town centre. High standard of decor and furnishing. Comfortable sitting room with TV for guests. Local produce used where available.
directions Please contact us for directions **open** All year except Xmas and New Year **bedrooms** 1 single, 1 double, 1 twin **bathrooms** 3 en suite **payment** cash, cheques, euros

Do you like Camping?
You can also buy a copy of our popular guide 'Camping, Touring & Holiday Parks' including touring parks, camping holidays and holiday parks and villages in Britain 2011.

Now available in good bookshops and online at **visitbritainshop.com**

£8.99

412   Official tourist board guide Bed & Breakfast

East Midlands | **Leicestershire & Rutland/Lincolnshire**

RIDLINGTON, Leicestershire & Rutland Map ref 4C3

SAT NAV LE15 9AX

BED & BREAKFAST

B&B PER ROOM PER NIGHT
S £50.00
D £75.00 – £95.00

EVENING MEAL PER PERSON
£20.00 – £25.00

SPECIAL PROMOTIONS
On a 3 night stay, the 3rd night is discounted by 10%.

Post Cottage
5 Top Road, Ridlington, Oakham LE15 9AX
t (01572) 823112   e bm.best@virgin.net
w bedandbreakfast-rutland.co.uk/bed-and-breakfast-rutland.htm ONLINE MAP
GUEST REVIEWS

Set upon a ridge and overlooking open countryside, Post Cottage is situated in one of the loveliest villages in Rutland. We offer excellent B&B accommodation and we are ideally situated just 2 miles from the A47 at Uppingham, 6 from Oakham and 12 from Stamford. Comfortable rooms and wonderful food!

open All year except Xmas and New Year
bedrooms 1 double, 1 twin, 1 suite
bathrooms 1 en suite, 2 with private bathroom
payment cash, cheques

directions From A47 at the Uppingham roundabout, take turning to Ayston. Through village to T-Junction, turn left, after 200 yards turn left into Ridlington.

Room
General
Leisure

BARKSTON, Lincolnshire Map ref 3A1

SAT NAV NG32 2NL

BED & BREAKFAST

B&B PER ROOM PER NIGHT
S £35.00 – £47.50
D £70.00 – £85.00

EVENING MEAL PER PERSON
£7.50 – £25.00

Kelling House
17 West Street, Barkston, Nr Grantham NG32 2NL
t +44(0)1400 251440   f +44 (0)7771 761251   e sue@kellinghouse.co.uk
w kellinghouse.co.uk ONLINE MAP

In quiet conservation village. 18thC cottage, large South facing garden. Serving freshly prepared food. Perfectly placed to explore the Lincoln Wolds, Belton House, Belvoir Castle, Lincoln Cathedral etc. **directions** A1/Grantham train station 4 miles. **open** All year **bedrooms** 1 single, 1 double, 1 twin **bathrooms** 1 en suite, 1 with private bathroom **payment** cash, cheques, euros

Room   General   Leisure

CRANWELL, Lincolnshire Map ref 3A1

SAT NAV NG34 8EY

BED & BREAKFAST

B&B PER ROOM PER NIGHT
S £25.00
D £50.00

EVENING MEAL PER PERSON
£15.00

Byards Leap Bed & Breakfast
Byards Leap Cottage, Cranwell NG34 8EY
t (01400) 261537   f (01400) 261537   e ml.wood@btopenworld.com
w byardsleapcottage.co.uk ONLINE MAP

Comfortable cottage in beautiful gardens, on Viking Way long distance footpath. Good home cooking using local and home grown produce. Convenient for Lincoln, Grantham, Sleaford and RAF Cranwell. **directions** Situated off A17 opposite junction with B6403. If using SAT navigation please phone for final advice **open** All year except Xmas **bedrooms** 1 double, 1 twin **payment** cash, cheques

Room   General

key to symbols see page 6

413

East Midlands | Lincolnshire

CRANWELL, Lincolnshire Map ref 3A1
SAT NAV NG34 8EY

B&B PER ROOM PER NIGHT
S £55.00 – £60.00
D £63.00 – £68.50

Byards Leap Lodge
Byards Leap, Cranwell NG34 8EY
t (01304) 261375 f (01304) 261375 e byards.leap@virgin.net
w byards-leap-lodge.co.uk ONLINE MAP GUEST REVIEWS ONLINE BOOKING LAST MINUTE OFFERS

Whether on leisure or business, you will find the hospitality of our Country Kitchen and Lodge just as warm as it was in the times of Bayard and Old Meg. **directions** Please contact us for directions **open** All year except Xmas and New Year **bedrooms** 3 double, 2 twin **bathrooms** 5 en suite **payment** credit/debit cards, cash, cheques

Room   General   Leisure

GAINSBOROUGH (4 MILES), Lincolnshire Map ref 4C2
SAT NAV DN21 5PJ

B&B PER ROOM PER NIGHT
S £27.00 – £30.00
D £48.00 – £52.00

The Grange
Kexby, Gainsborough DN21 5PJ
t (01427) 788265

650-acre mixed farm. Victorian farmhouse offering warm welcome Four miles from Gainsborough. Convenient for Lincoln, Hemswell Antique Centre and Wolds. Both rooms have private bathrooms. **directions** Situated on B1241 half a mile from Kexby village. **open** All year except Xmas and New Year **bedrooms** 1 double, 1 twin **bathrooms** 2 with private bathroom **payment** cash, cheques

Room   General   Leisure

GRANTHAM, Lincolnshire Map ref 3A1
SAT NAV NG32 1DL

B&B PER ROOM PER NIGHT
S £35.00
D £60.00

EVENING MEAL PER PERSON
£15.00

The Cedars
Low Road, Barrowby, Grantham, Lincolnshire NG32 1DL
t (01476) 563400 e pbcbennett@mac.com

Enjoy the relaxed atmosphere of this Grade II Listed farmhouse and gardens. Delicious breakfasts, and evening meals if required, using our own, and local fresh produce. Italian cuisine a speciality. Five minute drive from A1 motorway, two miles from Grantham mainline station. French and Italian spoken.

open All year except Xmas and New Year
bedrooms 1 double, 1 twin
bathrooms 2 with private bathroom
payment cash, cheques, euros

directions A1 North Sign says Nottingham A52 Barrowby. A1 South sign Grantham A52 Barrowby take Low Road Cedars on right free standing Farm House Gravelled Yard

Room
General
Leisure

414   Official tourist board guide Bed & Breakfast

East Midlands | Lincolnshire

HANTHORPE, Lincolnshire Map ref 3A1

SAT NAV PE10 0RB

Maycroft Cottage

6 Edenham Road, Hanthorpe, Bourne PE10 0RB
t (01778) 571689 e enquiries@maycroftcottage.co.uk
w maycroftcottage.co.uk ONLINE MAP GUEST REVIEWS

B&B PER ROOM PER NIGHT
S £24.00 – £32.00
D £46.00 – £54.00

Ideally situated for Grimsthorpe Castle, Bourne, Stamford, Burghley Horse Trials, Spalding Flower Festival, Shakespeare at Tolthorpe Hall, The Deepings, Peterborough, Rutland Water, The BBMF, and many other events and attractions. **directions** Please visit our website for directions **open** All year except Xmas and New Year **bedrooms** 1 double, 1 twin **bathrooms** 2 with private bathroom **payment** cash, cheques

LINCOLN, Lincolnshire Map ref 4C2

SAT NAV LN2 2SL

The Old Vicarage Bed & Breakfast

East Street, Nettleham LN2 2SL
t (01522) 750819 f (01522) 750819 e susan@oldvic.net
w oldvic.net ONLINE MAP

B&B PER ROOM PER NIGHT
S £50.00
D £70.00

Our Listed Georgian farmhouse is a couple of minutes walk from the centre of this attractive, award winning village with traditional Village Green and Beck. A warm welcome, tastefully furnished rooms and excellent location make us an ideal base when visiting historic Lincoln and surrounding counties.

open All year
bedrooms 1 double, 1 twin
bathrooms 1 en suite, 1 with private bathroom
payment credit/debit cards, cash, cheques

directions Follow A46 from Lincoln towards Grimsby, take 2nd right turn to Nettleham, entrance is on the right-hand side.

BREAKFAST AWARD

LINCOLN, Lincolnshire Map ref 4C2

SAT NAV LN6 9PF

Welbeck Cottage Bed and Breakfast

19 Meadow Lane, South Hykeham, Lincoln LN6 9PF
t (01522) 692669 e maggied@hotmail.co.uk
w welbeckcottagelincoln.co.uk ONLINE BOOKING

B&B PER ROOM PER NIGHT
S £30.00
D £55.00
EVENING MEAL PER PERSON
£10.00

We offer a warm welcome to our home set in a quiet village location, with access to Lincoln, Newark and many local attractions. Children and pet friendly. Evening meal available. **directions** Map and directions supplied on request. **open** All year except Xmas and New Year **bedrooms** 2 double, 1 twin **bathrooms** 3 en suite **payment** cash, cheques

key to symbols see page 6

415

East Midlands | Lincolnshire

MUMBY, Lincolnshire Map ref 4D2
SAT NAV LN13 9JU

B&B PER ROOM PER NIGHT
S £25.00 – £30.00
D £25.00 – £30.00
EVENING MEAL PER PERSON
£3.95 – £8.00

Brambles
Occupation Lane, Mumby, Alford LN13 9JU
t (01507) 490174 e suescrimshaw@btinternet.com

Newly built rural bungalow, quiet scenic setting, close to the coastal resorts. Two en suite double rooms for bed and breakfast.

open All year
bedrooms 2 double
bathrooms 2 en suite
payment cash, cheques

directions Between Skegness and Mablethorpe on the A52 down Thrumber Marsh Lane, keep left on to Occupation Lane.

Room General Leisure

NORTHORPE, Lincolnshire Map ref 4C2
SAT NAV DN21 4AN

B&B PER ROOM PER NIGHT
S £55.00
D £70.00

Grayingham Lodge
Gainsborough Road, Northorpe, Gainsborough, Lincs DN21 4AN
t (01652) 648544 e janesummers@btinternet.com
w grayinghamlodge.co.uk ONLINE MAP

A 5 Star Silver award winning property, situated in a quiet yet easily accessible area of Lincolnshire. Our aim is to provide guests with all the comforts of modern living. **directions** Grayingham Lodge is situated two miles west from the B1205 junction of the A15, 9 miles from Gainsborough, Brigg and Scunthorpe, 18 miles from Lincoln. **open** All year except Xmas and New Year **bedrooms** 1 double, 1 twin **bathrooms** 2 en suite **payment** credit/debit card, cash, cheques

Room General Leisure

RUSKINGTON, Lincolnshire Map ref 3A1
SAT NAV NG34 9AH

B&B PER ROOM PER NIGHT
S £28.00
D £56.00

Sunnyside Farm Bed & Breakfast
Leasingham Lane, Ruskington NG34 9AH
t (01526) 833010 e sunnyside_farm@btinternet.com
w sunnysidefarm.co.uk

A family-run farmhouse with en suite guest bedrooms. Warm, friendly welcome. Local golf courses. Coast 40 miles. Boston, Grantham, Lincoln, Newark all within easy reach. **directions** From A17, A153 towards Ruskington, B1188 into village. Left at roundabout, 400m turn left into Leasingham Lane, follow road 500m to Sunnyside Farm. **open** All year **bedrooms** 1 double, 1 tw **bathrooms** 2 en suite **payment** cash, cheques

BREAKFAST AWARD

Room General Leisure

416 Official tourist board guide Bed & Breakfast

East Midlands | Lincolnshire

SKEGNESS, Lincolnshire Map ref 4D2
SAT NAV PE25 2UB

Chatsworth
15/16 North Parade, Skegness PE25 2UB
t (01754) 764177 f (01754) 761173 e info@chatsworthskegness.co.uk
w chatsworthskegness.co.uk ONLINE MAP GUEST REVIEWS

B&B PER ROOM PER NIGHT
S £30.00 – £47.00
D £60.00 – £90.00
EVENING MEAL PER PERSON
£11.50 – £15.00

The Chatsworth is centrally situated close to many of the main attractions. Delicious home-made food, friendly staff, passenger lift, comfortable beds and an outstanding position overlooking the seafront. directions Please refer to website. open March to December bedrooms 10 single, 14 double, 15 twin, 1 family bathrooms 40 en suite payment credit/debit cards, cash, euros

Room   General   Leisure

SKEGNESS, Lincolnshire Map ref 4D2
SAT NAV PE25 3JS

The Fountaindale Skegness
69 Sandbeck Avenue, Skegness PE25 3JS
t (01754) 762731 e info@fountaindale-hotel.co.uk
w fountaindale-hotel.co.uk ONLINE MAP GUEST REVIEWS ONLINE BOOKING LAST MINUTE OFFERS

B&B PER ROOM PER NIGHT
S £30.00 – £35.00
D £48.00 – £55.00
EVENING MEAL PER PERSON
£12.00

The Fountaindale, is a 4 Star Silver Accolade property in Skegness, it nestles in the heart of this fantastic east coast seaside resort, and offers visitors a truly wonderful visit. directions We are ideally situated only minutes from the coach and train stations, the town centre and seafront amenities. open All year except Xmas bedrooms 1 single, 4 double, 3 twin bathrooms 8 en suite payment credit/debit cards, cash, cheques

Room   General   Leisure

SKEGNESS, Lincolnshire Map ref 4D2
SAT NAV PE25 3JS

Stoneleigh
67 Sandbeck Avenue, Skegness PE25 3JS
t (01754) 769138 f (01754) 769138 e janrog&hotelinskegness.co.uk
w stoneleigh-hotel.com ONLINE MAP GUEST REVIEWS

B&B PER ROOM PER NIGHT
S £35.00 – £45.00
D £45.00 – £65.00
EVENING MEAL PER PERSON
£10.00

Welcome to Stoneleigh. 4 star silver accolade. Fully en suite. Ground floor room for the elderly or less mobile. On site parking. Short walking distance from seafront and town centre. directions Please contact us for directions open All year except Xmas bedrooms 5 double, 2 twin bathrooms 7 en suite payment credit/debit cards, cash, cheques

Room   General   Leisure

SKEGNESS, Lincolnshire Map ref 4D2
SAT NAV PE25 3HP

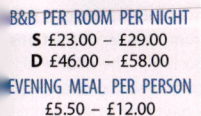

Woodthorpe Guest House
64 South Parade, Skegness, Lincolnshire PE25 3HP
t 01754 763452 f 01754 763452 e info@woodthorpeskegness.co.uk
w woodthorpeskegness.co.uk GUEST REVIEWS

B&B PER ROOM PER NIGHT
S £23.00 – £29.00
D £46.00 – £58.00
EVENING MEAL PER PERSON
£5.50 – £12.00

Lovely Spacious rooms four poster beds available. Tastefully decorated. 1 ground floor twin room. Own front door key, no restrictions. Off road parking, town centre 2 mins walk. directions Sea front location, lovely uninterrupted views of the sea, boating lake, bowling greens & gardens. Town centre 2 mins walk. open All year except Xmas bedrooms 1 single, 4 double, 3 twin bathrooms 8 en suite payment cash

Room   General   Leisure

East Midlands | Lincolnshire

SOUTH COCKERINGTON, Lincolnshire Map ref 4D2 — SAT NAV LN11 7ED

B&B PER ROOM PER NIGHT
S £45.00 – £50.00
D £65.00 – £75.00

West View Bed & Breakfast
West View, South View Lane, South Cockerington, Louth LN11 7ED
t (01507) 327209   e enquiries@west-view.co.uk
w west-view.co.uk   ONLINE MAP   GUEST REVIEWS   ONLINE BOOKING   LAST MINUTE OFFERS

Single-storey barn conversion with old-world charm. All bedrooms en suite. Beamed ceilings, disabled facilities, newly painted and furnished, broadband wireless internet access. **directions** Take the A157, go onto the B1200 signposted Manby. In 2 miles at lights le through Grimoldby, at South Cockerington left into South View Lane. **open** All year except Xmas **bedrooms** 2 double, 1 twin **bathrooms** 3 en suite **payment** cash, cheques

BREAKFAST AWARD

SWINESHEAD, Lincolnshire Map ref 3A1 — SAT NAV PE20 3LJ

B&B PER ROOM PER NIGHT
S £35.00 – £40.00
D £40.00 – £50.00
EVENING MEAL PER PERSON
£5.00 – £25.00

The Wheatsheaf
Market Place, Swineshead, Boston, Lincolnshire PE20 3LJ
t 01205 820349   f 01205 820316   e info@smoke-screen.co.uk
w wheatsheafhotel.co.uk   ONLINE MAP   GUEST REVIEWS

A 300-year-old Coaching Inn offering modern en suite accommodation, excellent restaurant, quality food, a choice of fine wines and real ales. **directions** Located at the intersection of A52 and A17. Convenient for visitors to Boston, Spalding, Sleaford and Lincoln. **open** All year **bedrooms** 2 double, 1 twin, 1 family **bathrooms** 4 en suite **payment** credit/debit cards, cash, cheques, euros

THORNTON CURTIS, Lincolnshire Map ref 4C1 — SAT NAV DN39 6XW

B&B PER ROOM PER NIGHT
S £41.99 – £44.99
D £65.99 – £69.99
EVENING MEAL PER PERSON
£7.99 – £15.99

Thornton Hunt Inn
17 Main Street, Thornton Curtis, Near Ulceby, North Lincolnshire DN39 6XW
t (01469) 531252   f (01469) 531252   e thorntonhuntinn@thorntoncurtis.net
w thornton-inn.co.uk

Grade II Listed building serving traditional homemade bar meals. Previous winner of 'Taste of Excellence' and 'Tastes of Lincolnshire' awards. Extensive garden. Children welcome. Convenient for airpor and M180. **directions** M180 East, Junction 5, to airport, take B1211 to Ulceby, then Thornton Curtis. A15 over Humber Bridge to Barto on Humber A1077, then Thornton Curtis **open** All year except Xma and New Year **bedrooms** 1 single, 5 double **bathrooms** 6 en suite **payment** credit/debit cards, cash, cheques

WAINFLEET, Lincolnshire Map ref 4D2 — SAT NAV PE24 4QH

B&B PER ROOM PER NIGHT
S £25.00
D £50.00 – £60.00
EVENING MEAL PER PERSON
£5.00 – £7.00

Willow Farm
Thorpe Fendykes, Wainfleet, Skegness, Lincolnshire PE24 4QH
t (01754) 830316   e willowfarmhols@aol.com
w willowfarmholidays.co.uk   ONLINE MAP   LAST MINUTE OFFERS

Comfortable ensuite bed and breakfast on a Lincolnshire family farm with ponies, goats, free range hens and ducks. A quiet hamle abundant in wildlife, yet only 10-15mins from Skegness **directions** 10mins Spilsby/15mins Skegness/20mins Boston in the middle of nowhere! Ring for directions or check map on website! **open** All year **bedrooms** 1 double, 1 twin, 1 family **payment** cash, cheques

Official tourist board guide Bed & Breakfa

East Midlands | Lincolnshire

WOODHALL SPA, Lincolnshire Map ref 4D2
SAT NAV LN4 3QT

Chaplin House
92 High Street, Martin, Lincolnshire LN4 3QT
t (01526) 378745 f (01526) 378745 e info@chaplin-house.co.uk
w chaplin-house.co.uk ONLINE MAP GUEST REVIEWS ONLINE BOOKING LAST MINUTE OFFERS

B&B PER ROOM PER NIGHT
S £50.00
D £65.00

EVENING MEAL PER PERSON
£20.00

Award-winning accommodation in the heart of Lincolnshire countryside. Barn conversion with 3 spacious en suite rooms and guest lounge; one en suite room in house. Locally sourced, free-range, organic produce. **directions** We are in the village of Martin on B1191 between Metheringham and Woodhall Spa. **open** All year except Xmas and New Year **bedrooms** 2 double, 1 twin, 1 family **bathrooms** 4 en suite **payment** credit/debit cards, cash, cheques

BREAKFAST AWARD

Room General Leisure

WOODHALL SPA, Lincolnshire Map ref 4D2
SAT NAV LN10 6UQ

Kirkstead Old Mill Cottage
Tattershall Road, Woodhall Spa, Lincolnshire LN10 6UQ
t (01526) 35 36 37 / 07970 04 04 01 e barbara@woodhallspa.com
w woodhallspa.com ONLINE MAP GUEST REVIEWS LAST MINUTE OFFERS

B&B PER ROOM PER NIGHT
S £50.00 – £60.00
D £65.00 – £75.00

EVENING MEAL PER PERSON
£10.00 – £15.00

Kirkstead Old Mill Cottage, a warm, welcoming, tranquil home beside the River Witham, offers three en-suite guest bedrooms in an oasis of nature, away from the hurly-burly of modern life. **directions** One mile outside of Woodhall Spa on the B1192, heading towards Coningsby, look on your right for signs at the end of our mile-long track. **open** All year except Xmas **bedrooms** 1 double, 2 twin **bathrooms** 3 en suite **payment** credit/debit cards, cash, cheques, euros

BREAKFAST AWARD

Room General Leisure

WOODHALL SPA, Lincolnshire Map ref 4D2
SAT NAV LN10 6TW

The Limes
The Limes, Tattershall Road, Woodhall Spa LN10 6TW
t (01526) 352219

B&B PER ROOM PER NIGHT
D £55.00

A warm welcome assured in this elegant Edwardian house, set in the leafy village of Woodhall Spa. Convenient for the golf course and all the amenities in Woodhall Spa. **directions** Please contact us for directions. **open** All year except Xmas and New Year **bedrooms** 2 double **payment** cash, cheques

Room General Leisure

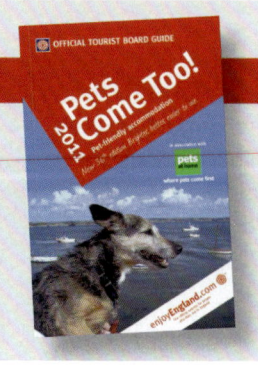

Where is my pet welcome?

Some properties welcome well-behaved pets. Look for the 🐾 in the accommodation listings.

You can also buy a copy of our popular guide 'Pets Come Too!' Now available in good bookshops and online at **visitbritainshop.com**

£9.99

key to symbols see page 6   419

East Midlands | Lincolnshire/Northamptonshire

WOODHALL SPA, Lincolnshire Map ref 4D2   SAT NAV LN10 6UJ

Village Limits Country Pub, Restaurant & Motel
Stixwould Road, Woodhall Spa LN10 6UJ
t (01526) 353312   e info@villagelimits.co.uk
w villagelimits.co.uk   ONLINE MAP LAST MINUTE OFFERS

B&B PER ROOM PER NIGHT
S £40.00 – £50.00
D £60.00 – £75.00

SPECIAL PROMOTIONS
10% discount for 4 nights or more. Special offers off season

Tastes of Lincolnshire Award Winners 2006-09 for food & accommodation. Serving homemade food from local produce. All accommodation refurbished in 2010. All rooms en-suite with Freeview, free WiFi & hairdryers. Food daily 1130-1400 and 1830-2100. Sunday/Monday evening food at owners discretion please confirm when booking. Free parking.

open All year except Xmas
bedrooms 8 twin
bathrooms 8 en suite
payment credit/debit cards, cash, cheques

directions Located 1 mile from the centre of Woodhall Spa. We are on Stixwould Road, 500 past Jubilee Park on the right-hand side.

Room   General

BYFIELD, Northamptonshire Map ref 4C3   SAT NAV NN11 6XN

Glebe Farm Bed & Breakfast
Glebe Farm Church Street, Byfield, Daventry NN11 6XN
t (01327) 260512   f (01327) 260512

B&B PER ROOM PER NIGHT
S £35.00 – £45.00
D £60.00 – £75.00

Join the family for a farmhouse breakfast whilst enjoying panoram views over the Northamptonshire countryside. Close to M1, M40, M6, Silverstone, Stratford upon Avon and the Cotswolds. Ground floor accomodation **directions** Situated in the village of Byfield, ju off the A361 between Daventry and Banbury with easy access to M1 and M40 **open** All year except Xmas and New Year **bedrooms** 1 double, 1 family **bathrooms** 1 en suite, 1 with private bathroom **payment** cash, cheques

Room   General   Leisure

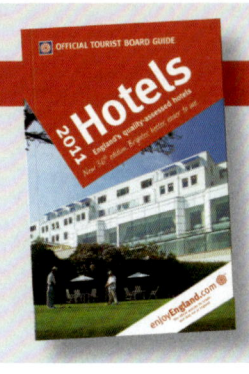

Looking for something else?
You can also buy a copy of our popular guide 'Hotels' including country house and town house hotels, metro and budget hotels, serviced apartments, restaurants with rooms and Spas in England 2011.

Now available in good bookshops and online at
visitbritainshop.com
£10.99

East Midlands | **Northamptonshire**

DAVENTRY, Northamptonshire Map ref 2C1   SAT NAV NN11 3BL

Threeways House

Threeways House, Everdon, Daventry, Northamptonshire NN11 3BL
t (01327) 361631, 07774 428242 **e** threewayshouse@googlemail.com
w threewayshouse.com   ONLINE MAP GUEST REVIEWS

B&B PER ROOM PER NIGHT
S £30.00 – £50.00
D £50.00 – £75.00

SPECIAL PROMOTIONS
Please enquire for Silverstone Grand Prix weekend special rates.

Threeways House stands on Everdon's peaceful village green. Very comfortable, quiet, ensuite rooms are in a separate coachhouse, come and go as you please!! Delicious English breakfasts served in a comfortable dining room overlooking the garden. Excellent evening meals within easy walking distance. Convenient M1/J16 and M40/J11. Free Wi-Fi. Freeview.

open All year
bedrooms 1 single, 2 double, 1 twin, 1 family
bathrooms 5 en suite
payment cash, cheques, euros

directions From M1/J16 take A45-Daventry. After Weedon, 1st left to Everdon. From M40/J11 take A361-Daventry. After Charwelton, 2nd right Fawsley. Over crossroads to Everdon.

EYDON, Northamptonshire Map ref 2C1   SAT NAV NN11 3QA

Crockwell Farm

Crockwell Farm, Eydon, Daventry NN11 3QA
t (01327) 361358 **f** (01327) 361573 **e** info@crockwellfarm.co.uk
w crockwellfarm.co.uk   ONLINE MAP GUEST REVIEWS

B&B PER ROOM PER NIGHT
S £44.00 – £49.00
D £78.00 – £88.00

Beautiful 18thC ironstone farmhouse and self-contained cottages in idyllic rural setting. Delicious breakfasts served in the farmhouse. Ideal base for local attractions & walking. Great pub approximately one mile away. **directions** South Northamptonshire halfway between villages of Canons Ashby & Eydon. See website for detailed directions. **open** All year **bedrooms** 3 twin, 4 family **bathrooms** 7 en suite **payment** credit/debit cards, cash, cheques

KETTERING, Northamptonshire Map ref 3A2   SAT NAV NN14 4AQ

Dairy Farm

Cranford St Andrew, Kettering NN14 4AQ
t (01536) 330273

B&B PER ROOM PER NIGHT
S £30.00 – £40.00
D £60.00 – £80.00

EVENING MEAL PER PERSON
£18.00

17thC thatched farmhouse in lovely Northamptonshire village just off the A14. Large garden containing ancient dovecote and summerhouse. Good food, friendly welcome. Safe off-road parking. Many places of interest nearby. **directions** Please contact us for directions **open** All year except Xmas and New Year **bedrooms** 2 double, 1 twin **bathrooms** 2 en suite, 1 with private bathroom **payment** cash, cheques

East Midlands | Northamptonshire

LONG BUCKBY, Northamptonshire Map ref 4C3   SAT NAV NN6 7QR

Murcott Mill

Murcott Mill, Murcott, Long Buckby NN6 7QR
t (01327) 842236   f (01327) 842236   e carrie.murcottmill@virgin.net
w murcottmill.com   ONLINE MAP   GUEST REVIEWS   ONLINE BOOKING   LAST MINUTE OFFERS

B&B PER ROOM PER NIGHT
S £35.00 – £40.00
D £65.00 – £70.00
EVENING MEAL PER PERSON
£8.00 – £10.00

A beautiful Georgian mill house with views over open countryside on the outskirts of Long Buckby. All en suite rooms and high standard of accommodation and facilities. Off road parking.
directions Close to M1, A14, M6, A5 and A428. Situated on B5385 on the outskirts of Long Buckby. Down a drive. **open** All year
bedrooms 1 double, 2 twin, 1 family   **bathrooms** 3 en suite
payment credit/debit cards, cash, cheques, euros

Room | General | Leisure

TOWCESTER, Northamptonshire Map ref 2C1   SAT NAV NN12 8PF

Slapton Manor Bed & Breakfast

Slapton Manor, Slapton NN12 8PF
t (01327) 860344   f (01327) 860758   e accommodation@slaptonmanor.co.uk
w slaptonmanor.co.uk   ONLINE MAP

B&B PER ROOM PER NIGHT
S £25.00 – £45.00
D £50.00 – £65.00

En suite rooms within stable/hay loft conversion and self-catering studios adjoining village 12thC manor house on working farm.
directions From M1, take A43 South. Towcester South roundabout by McDonalds, 3rd exit for Abthorpe. Through Abthorpe, after 0.5 miles right turn, 1st left in village. **open** All year **bedrooms** 1 double, 1 twin, 1 family **bathrooms** 3 en suite **payment** credit/debit cards, cash, cheques, euros

Room | General | Leisure

UPPINGHAM, Northamptonshire Map ref 4C3   SAT NAV NN17 3AT

Spanhoe Lodge

Laxton Road, Harringworth, (Near Corby) NN17 3AT
t (01780) 450328   f (01780) 450546   e jennie.spanhoe@virgin.net
w spanhoelodge.co.uk   ONLINE MAP   GUEST REVIEWS   ONLINE BOOKING   LAST MINUTE OFFERS

B&B PER ROOM PER NIGHT
S £80.00 – £90.00
D £95.00 – £100.00
EVENING MEAL PER PERSON
£12.00 – £18.00

SPECIAL PROMOTIONS
Weekend breaks & short stays available - please ring or visit www.spanhoelodge.co.uk for details of offers.

A warm, friendly welcome awaits you at this gold-awarded establishment in the heart of Rockingham Forest. Luxuriously appointed, en suite accommodation, wide choice of gourmet breakfasts, light bites, licensed bar, conferencing. Ideally situated for Stamford, Corby, Uppingham, Oundle, Oakham, Rutland Water and Rockingham Motor Speedway. You will not be disappointed.

open All year
bedrooms 4 double, 2 twin, 2 family
bathrooms 8 en suite
payment credit/debit cards, cash, cheques

directions Just off A43 between Corby and Stamford. Take signpost to Laxton, travel through village to open countryside. Spanhoe Lodge is half a mile on right.

BREAKFAST AWARD   Room | General | Leisure

East Midlands | Northamptonshire/Nottinghamshire

WOODNEWTON, Northamptonshire Map ref 3A1
SAT NAV PE8 5EG

B&B PER ROOM PER NIGHT
S £40.00
D £80.00

Bridge Cottage Bed and Breakfast
Oundle Road, Woodnewton, Peterborough PE8 5EG
t 01780470779 (07979 644864) e enquiries@bridgecottage.net
w bridgecottage.net ONLINE MAP GUEST REVIEWS LAST MINUTE OFFERS

Bridge Cottage is a pretty Bed and Breakfast situated on the edge of Woodnewton by the Willowbrook. Children and dogs welcome – under supervision! **directions** Bridge Cottage is approximately 4 miles from Oundle, Northamptonshire, 10 miles down the A1 from Stamford, Lincolnshire, 8 miles from the centre of Peterborough, Cambridgeshire. **open** All year except Xmas **bedrooms** 2 double, 2 twin **bathrooms** 2 en suite, 2 with private bathroom **payment** cash, cheques, euros

Room General Leisure

LANGWITH, Nottinghamshire Map ref 4C2
SAT NAV NG20 9JD

B&B PER ROOM PER NIGHT
S £30.00 – £32.00
D £60.00 – £64.00

Blue Barn Farm
Langwith, Mansfield NG20 9JD
t (01623) 742348 f (01623) 742248 e bluebarnfarm@supanet.com
w bluebarnfarm-notts.co.uk

Family run 450 acre arable farm near Sherwood Forest in Robin Hood country. Interesting places catering for all tastes only short car journey away. Suitable for the business traveller. **directions** 6 miles from the M1 junction 30 off the A616 between Creswell and Cuckney. Also 6 miles from the A1 Worksop junction. **open** All year except Xmas and New Year **bedrooms** 1 double, 1 twin, 1 family **bathrooms** 1 en suite **payment** cash, cheques

Room General Leisure

LAXTON, Nottinghamshire Map ref 4C2
SAT NAV NG22 0SX

B&B PER ROOM PER NIGHT
S £55.00
D £68.00

Crosshill House Bed & Breakfast
Crosshill, Laxton, Newark, Notts NG22 0SX
t (01777) 871953 e roberta@crosshillhouse.com
w crosshillhouse.com ONLINE MAP GUEST REVIEWS LAST MINUTE OFFERS

Crosshill house is situated in the historical village of laxton in the heart of Robin Hood country. The house is elevated and looks over the village with unspoilt views. There are picturesque walking routes in abundance. Warm friendly surroundings with a log fire burning in the winter.

open All year
bedrooms 4 double, 1 family
bathrooms 4 en suite, 1 with private bathroom
payment credit/debit cards, cash, euros

directions very clear directions on our website but please contact us if necessary.

Room General Leisure

key to symbols see page 6

East Midlands | Nottinghamshire

NEWARK, Nottinghamshire Map ref 4C2   SAT NAV NG23 6LZ

Brecks Cottage B&B
Green Lane, Moorhouse, Newark NG23 6LZ
t (01636) 822445   e bandb@breckscottage.co.uk
w breckscottage.co.uk ONLINE MAP GUEST REVIEWS

B&B PER ROOM PER NIGHT
S £48.00
D £62.00

Beautiful 17th Century chocolate box cottage, oak beams and inglenook fires. Rooms are en-suite, choose from our award winning breakfast to ensure you of a relaxed and comfortable sta **directions** From Newark, A1 north, exit at Carlton junction. Left towards Kneesall, into Ossington village. Right into Moorhouse Road, left to Laxton. Brecks Cottage on right. **open** All year excep Xmas and New Year **bedrooms** 2 double, 2 family **bathrooms** 4 suite **payment** credit/debit cards, cash, cheques

BREAKFAST AWARD Room   General   Leisure

NOTTINGHAM, Nottinghamshire Map ref 4C2   SAT NAV NG13 0HQ

Belvoir B & B at Woodside Farm
Long Lane, Nr. Barkestone le vale, Nottingham, Nottinghamshire NG13 0HQ
t 01476 870336 (07703 299291)   e hickling-woodside@supanet.com
w woodsidebandb.co.uk ONLINE MAP GUEST REVIEWS LAST MINUTE OFFERS

B&B PER ROOM PER NIGHT
S £48.00 – £58.00
D £68.00 – £75.00

Delightful countryside retreat nr. Belvoir Castle. Excellent hospitali delicious breakfasts with good local pubs nearby. Footpaths/wildli in abundance and unspoilt views. Wifi. Secure parking. Cycle storage. Perfect halfway stop A1/M1. **directions** From A52 at Bottesford exit towards Harby and Belvoir Castle. After passing crossroads lane leading to Woodside Farm, 0.7 miles on left. **oper** All year except Xmas **bedrooms** 1 double, 1 twin, 1 family **bathrooms** 2 en suite **payment** cash, cheques

BREAKFAST AWARD Room   General   Leisure

WEST BRIDGFORD, Nottinghamshire Map ref 4C2   SAT NAV NG2 5HH

Firs Guesthouse
96 Radcliffe Road, West Brigford NG2 5HH
t (0115) 981 0199   f (01582) 767829   e firs.hotel@btinternet.com
w firshotelnottingham.co.uk ONLINE MAP

B&B PER ROOM PER NIGHT
S £25.00 – £29.00
D £35.00 – £40.00

High-quality Victorian establishment, well maintained with reasonable rates. Guest lounge with pool table and Sky TV. Close Trent Bridge, Nottingham Forest FC, watersports and all amenities Good city accessibility. **directions** Please contact us for directions **open** All year except Xmas **bedrooms** 3 twin, 6 family **bathroom** 2 en suite **payment** credit/debit cards, cash

Room   General   Leisure

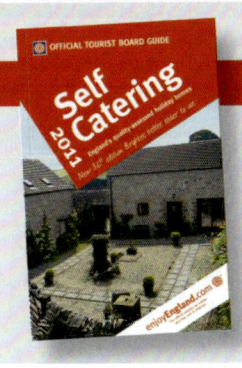

Looking for something else?

You can also buy a copy of our popular guide 'Self Catering' including self-catering holiday homes, approved caravan holiday homes, boat accommodation and holiday cottage agencies in England 2011.

Now available in good bookshops and online at
visitbritainshop.com

£11.99

424   Official tourist board guide Bed & Breakf

East Midlands | Derbyshire

All Assessed Accommodation

Derbyshire
ALVASTON

Brace Guest House ★★
Guest Accommodation - Room Only
1063 London Road, Alvaston, Derby
DE24 8PZ
t (01332) 571051

The Maryland B&B ★★★
Guest House
1083 London Road, Alvaston, Derby
DE24 8PZ
t (01332) 754892
e themaryland7@yahoo.co.uk
w derbybedandbreakfast.com

AMBERGATE

The Lord Nelson Inn ★★★ Inn
Bullbridge, Ambergate, Ripley
DE56 2EW
t (01773) 852037
e bob@lordnelsonbelper.co.uk
w lordnelsonbelper.co.uk

ASHBOURNE

Cross Farm ★★★★ Bed & Breakfast
Main Road, Ellastone, Ashbourne
DE6 2GZ
t (01335) 324668
e info@cross-farm.co.uk
w cross-farm.co.uk

The Lilacs ★★★★
Guest Accommodation
Mayfield Road, Ashbourne
DE6 2BJ
t (01335) 343749

Newton House ★★★
Guest Accommodation
Buxton Road, Ashbourne
DE6 1EX
t (020) 8511 1534

Peak District Spa ★★★
Guest Accommodation
Buxton Road, Nr Alsop-en-le-Dale,
Ashbourne
DE6 1QU
t (01335) 310100
e PeakDistrictSpa@rivendalecaravanpark.co.uk
w peakdistrictspa.co.uk

Shirley Hall ★★★★ Farmhouse
SILVER AWARD
Shirley, Ashbourne, Derbyshire
DE6 3AT
t (01335) 360820/07799 762624
e ian@iancrabtree.wanadoo.co.uk
w shirleyhallfarm.com

Stone Cottage ★★★
Bed & Breakfast
Green Lane, Clifton, Ashbourne
DE6 2BL
t (01335) 343377
e info@stone-cottage.fsnet.co.uk
w stone-cottage.fsnet.co.uk

Weaver View ★★★
Guest Accommodation
5 Spencer Close, Ashbourne
DE6 1BU
t (01335) 343718
e annburton1bu@hotmail.com

ASHFORD-IN-THE-WATER

The Ashford Arms ★★★★ Inn
Church Street, Ashford-in-the-Water, Bakewell
DE45 1QB
t (01629) 812725
e enquiries@ashford-arms.co.uk

A Woodland View ★★★★
Bed & Breakfast
John Bank Lane, Ashford-in-the-Water, Bakewell
DE45 1PY
t (01629) 813008
e woodview@neilellis.free-online.co.uk
w woodlandviewbandb.co.uk

Chy-an-Dour ★★★★
Guest Accommodation
SILVER AWARD
Vicarage Lane, Ashford-in-the-Water, Bakewell
DE45 1QN
t (01629) 813162
w smoothhound.co.uk/hotels/chyandour.html

River Cottage ★★★★★
Guest Accommodation
SILVER AWARD
The Duke's Drive, Ashford-in-the-Water, Bakewell
DE45 1QP
t (01629) 813327
e info@rivercottageashford.co.uk
w rivercottageashford.co.uk

ASHOVER

Old School Farm ★★★★
Farmhouse
Uppertown, Ashover, Chesterfield
S45 0JF
t (01246) 590813
e jonty19@btinternet.com

BAKEWELL

2 Lumford Cottages ★★★
Bed & Breakfast
off Holme Lane, Bakewell
DE45 1GG
t (01629) 813273

Applegate House ★★★★
Bed & Breakfast
Church Lane, Bakewell
DE45 1DE
t (01629) 812001
e pam@applegatehouse.co.uk
w applegatehouse.co.uk

Castle Cliffe ★★★★
Bed & Breakfast SILVER AWARD
Monsal Head, Bakewell
DE45 1NL
t (01629) 640358
e relax@castle-cliffe.com
w castle-cliffe.com

Castle Hill Farm House ★★★★
Bed & Breakfast SILVER AWARD
Castle Mount Crescent, Baslow Road, Bakewell
DE45 1AA
t (01629) 813168
e christine@castlehillfarmhouse.co.uk
w castlehillfarmhouse.co.uk

Dale View ★★★★
Guest Accommodation
Ashford Road, Bakewell
DE45 1GL
t (01629) 813832
e enquiries@dale-view.com
w dale-view.com/

The Garden Room ★★★★
Bed & Breakfast SILVER AWARD
1 Park Road, Bakewell
DE45 1AX
t (01629) 814299
e the.garden.room@talk21.com
w smoothhound.co.uk/hotels/thegarden

The Haven ★★★★
Guest Accommodation
Haddon Road, Bakewell
DE45 1AW
t (01629) 812113
e contact@visitbakewell.com
w visitbakewell.com

Housley Cottage ★★★★
Bed & Breakfast
Foolow, Hope Valley
S32 5QB
t (01433) 631505
e kevin@housleycottages.co.uk
w housleycottages.co.uk

Meadow View ★★★★
Bed & Breakfast
Coombs Road, Bakewell
DE45 1AQ
t (01629) 812961

Melbourne House & Easthorpe ★★★★ Guest Accommodation
Buxton Road, Bakewell
DE45 1DA
t (01629) 815357
e enquiries@bakewell-accommodation.co.uk
w bakewell-accommodation.co.uk

Normanhurst B&B ★★★★
Bed & Breakfast
Normanhurst, Ashford Road, Bakewell
DE45 1GL
t (01629) 812317
e info@normanhurstbandb.co.uk
w normanhurstbandb.co.uk

River Walk Bed & Breakfast ★★★★ Bed & Breakfast
3 New Lumford, Bakewell
DE45 1GH
t (01629) 812459
e jean.davies22@btinternet.com
w riverwalkbedandbreakfast.co.uk

Tannery House Bed & Breakfast
Matlock Street, Bakewell
DE45 1EE
t (01629) 815011
e jphilcrosby@yahoo.co.uk
w tannery.co.uk

Treetops Bed And Breakfast ★★★★ Guest Accommodation
Treetops, Coombs Road, Bakewell, Derbyshire
DE45 1AQ
t (01629) 812200
e info@treetopsofbakewell.co.uk
w treetopsofbakewell.co.uk

West Lawn ★★★★ Bed & Breakfast
Aldern Way, Bakewell
DE45 1AJ
t (01629) 812243
e couplandallan@hotmail.com
w westlawn.co.uk

Westmorland House ★★★★
Guest Accommodation
Park Road, Bakewell
DE45 1AX
t (01629) 812932
e lesley@westmorlandhouse.co.uk
w westmorlandhouse.co.uk

Wilmadah ★★★★ Bed & Breakfast
The Square, Middleton-by-Youlgreave, Bakewell
DE45 1LS
t (01629) 636303

BAMFORD

Pioneer House ★★★★
Bed & Breakfast SILVER AWARD
Station Road, Bamford, Hope Valley
S33 0BN
t (01433) 650638
e pioneerhouse@yahoo.co.uk
w pioneerhouse.co.uk

The Rising Sun ★★★★ Inn
SILVER AWARD
Thornhill Moor, Bamford, Hope Valley
S33 0AL
t (01433) 651323
e info@the-rising-sun.org
w the-rising-sun.org

Yorkshire Bridge Inn ★★★★ Inn
SILVER AWARD
Ashopton Road, Bamford, Hope Valley
S33 0AZ
t (01433) 651361
e info@yorkshire-bridge.co.uk
w yorkshire-bridge.co.uk

BARLBOROUGH

Dusty Miller Inn ★★★ Inn
Sheffield Road, Barlborough, Chesterfield
S43 4TW
t (01246) 810507
e adrian.fazakerley@virgin.net
w dustymillerbarlborough.co.uk

Stone Croft ★★★★
Bed & Breakfast
15 Church Street, Barlborough, Chesterfield, Derbyshire
S43 4ER
t (01246) 810974
e enquiries.stone-croft@live.co.uk
w stone-croft.co.uk

BARLOW

Nesfield Cottage ★★★★
Bed & Breakfast
Nesfield, Barlow, Dronfield
S18 7TB
t (01246) 559786
e nesfieldcottage@tiscali.co.uk
w nesfieldcottage.co.uk

BARROW-ON-TRENT

5 Nook Cottages ★★★★
Bed & Breakfast SILVER AWARD
The Nook, Barrow-upon-Trent, Derby
DE73 7NA
t (01332) 702050
e nookcottage@nookcottage.co.uk
w nookcottage.co.uk

BASLOW

Bubnell Cliff Farm ★★★★
Farmhouse
Wheatlands Lane, Baslow, Bakewell
DE45 1RF
t (01246) 582454
e c.k.mills@btinternet.com
w bubnellcliff.co.uk

BELPER

The Cedars ★★★★
Guest Accommodation
Field Lane, Belper
DE56 1DD
t (01773) 824157
e cedars@derbyshire-holidays.com
w derbyshire-holidays.com/cedars

BIRCHOVER

Poppy Cottage ★★★★
Bed & Breakfast
Main Street, Birchover, Matlock
DE4 2BN
t (01629) 650847
e alison@poppycottagebandb.co.uk
w poppycottagebandb.co.uk

BLACKWELL

The Old Bake & Brewhouse, Blackwell Hall ★★★★ Farmhouse
Blackwell in the Peak, Taddington, Buxton
SK17 9TQ
t (01298) 85271
e christine.gregory@btinternet.com
w peakdistrictfarmhols.co.uk

BONSALL

Cascades Gardens ★★★★★
Guest Accommodation
SILVER AWARD
Clatterway Hill, Bonsall, Matlock
DE4 2AH
t (01629) 822464
e info@cascadesgardens.com
w cascadesgardens.com

The Old Schoolhouse ★★★
Bed & Breakfast
The Dale, Bonsall, Matlock
DE4 2AY
t (01629) 826017
e lydia.art@btinternet.com
w oldschoolhousebonsall.co.uk

East Midlands | Derbyshire

Town Head Farmhouse ★★★★
Guest House **SILVER AWARD**
70 High Street, Bonsall, Matlock
DE4 2AR
t (01629) 823762
w townheadfarmhouse.co.uk

BRADLEY

Holly Meadow Farm ★★★★
Farmhouse **SILVER AWARD**
Pinfold Lane, Bradley, Ashbourne
DE6 1PN
t (01335) 370261
e babette_lawton@yahoo.com
w hollymeadowfarm.co.uk

Yeldersley Old Hall Farm ★★★★
Farmhouse **SILVER AWARD**
Yeldersley Lane, Bradley, Ashbourne
DE6 1PH
t (01335) 344504
e janethindsfarm@yahoo.co.uk
w yeldersleyoldhallfarm.co.uk

BRADWELL

Travellers Rest ★★★ *Inn*
Brough Lane End, Brough, Hope Valley
S33 9HG
t (01433) 620363
e info@travellers-rest.net
w travellers-rest.net

BURTON-ON-TRENT

DoveVale.co.uk ★★★★
Guest Accommodation
20 Station Road, Hatton, Burton-on-Trent
DE65 5EL
t (01283) 815996
e rodandberyl@dovevale.co.uk
w dovevale.co.uk

BUXTON

9 Green Lane B&B ★★★★
Guest Accommodation
SILVER AWARD
Green Lane, Buxton
SK17 9DP
t (01298) 73731
e book@9greenlane.co.uk
w 9greenlane.co.uk

Braemar ★★★★
Guest Accommodation
10 Compton Road, Buxton
SK17 9DN
t (01298) 78050
e buxtonbraemar@supanet.com
w cressbrook.co.uk/buxton/braemar

Buxton Hilbre ★★★
Bed & Breakfast
8 White Knowle Road, Buxton
SK17 9NH
t (01298) 22358
e min.hilbre@virgin.net
w buxtonhilbre.co.uk

The Church Inn ★★★★ *Inn*
Chelmorton, Buxton
SK17 9SL
t (01298) 85319
e justinsatur@tiscali.co.uk
w thechurchinn.co.uk

Compton House Guest House
★★★ *Guest House*
4 Compton Road, Buxton
SK17 9DN
t (01298) 26926
e bill@comptonhouse.plus.com
w cressbrook.co.uk/buxton/compton

Corbar Bank ★★★★
Guest Accommodation
20 Corbar Road, Buxton
SK17 6RQ
t (01298) 22664
e the.crabs@virgin.net
w corbarbank.co.uk

Devonshire Lodge Guest House
★★★★ *Guest Accommodation*
SILVER AWARD
2 Manchester Road, Buxton
SK17 6SB
t (01298) 71487
e enquiries@devonshirelodgeguesthouse.co.uk
w devonshirelodgeguesthouse.co.uk

Fairhaven Guest House ★★★
Guest Accommodation
1 Dale Terrace, Buxton
SK17 6LU
t (01298) 24481
e fairhavenguesthouse@btconnect.com

Fernydale Farm ★★★★ *Farmhouse*
SILVER AWARD
Earl Sterndale, Buxton
SK17 0BS
t (01298) 83236
e wjnadin@btconnect.com
w fernydalefarmbandb.co.uk

Grendon Guest House ★★★★★
Guest House **GOLD AWARD**
Grendon Guest House, Bishops Lane, Buxton
SK17 6UN
t (01298) 78831
e grendonguesthouse@hotmail.com
w grendonguesthouse.co.uk

Grosvenor House ★★★★
Guest House **SILVER AWARD**
Broad Walk, Buxton
SK17 6JE
t (01298) 72439
e grosvenor.buxton@btopenworld.com
w grosvenorbuxton.co.uk

Kingscroft Guest House ★★★★
Guest House **SILVER AWARD**
10 Green Lane, Buxton, Derbyshire
SK17 9DP
t (01298) 22757
e kingscroftbuxton1@btinternet.com

Lakenham Guest House ★★★★
Guest House
11 Burlington Road, Buxton
SK17 9AL
t (01298) 79209
e enquiries@lakenhambuxton.co.uk
w lakenhambuxton.co.uk

Lowther Guest House ★★★★
Guest Accommodation
7 Hardwick Square West, Buxton
SK17 6PX
t (01298) 71479
e enquiries@lowtherguesthouse.co.uk
w lowtherguesthouse.co.uk

Netherdale Guest House ★★★★
Guest House
16 Green Lane, Buxton
SK17 9DP
t (01298) 23896
w smoothhound.co.uk/hotels/netherdale

The Old Manse ★★★★
Guest Accommodation **SILVER AWARD**
6 Clifton Road, Buxton
SK17 6QL
t (01298) 25638
e info@oldmanse.co.uk
w oldmanse.co.uk

Roseleigh ★★★★ *Guest House*
SILVER AWARD
19 Broad Walk, Buxton
SK17 6JR
t (01298) 24904
e enquiries@roseleighhotel.co.uk
w roseleighhotel.co.uk

Southmead ★★★★
Guest Accommodation
GOLD AWARD
Bishops Lane, Buxton
SK17 6UN
t (01298) 24029
e hardie@southmead-guesthouse.co.uk
w southmead-guesthouse.co.uk

Stoneridge Guest House ★★★★
Guest Accommodation
SILVER AWARD
9 Park Road, Buxton
SK17 6SG
t (01298) 26120
e duncan@stoneridge.co.uk
w stoneridge.co.uk

Westlands ★★★★★
Guest Accommodation
SILVER AWARD
Bishops Lane, Burbage, Buxton
SK17 6UN
t (01298) 71122
e enquiries@westlandshouse.co.uk
w westlandshouse.co.uk

CALVER

The Chequers Inn ★★★★ *Inn*
SILVER AWARD
Froggatt Edge, Hope Valley
S32 3ZJ
t (01433) 630231
e info@chequers-froggatt.com
w chequers-froggatt.com

Valley View Guest House ★★★★
Guest House **SILVER AWARD**
Smithy Knoll Road, Calver, Hope Valley
S32 3XW
t (01433) 631407
e sue@a-place-2-stay.co.uk
w a-place-2-stay.co.uk

CARSINGTON

Breach Farm ★★★★ *Farmhouse*
Carsington, Wirksworth
DE4 4DD
t (01629) 540265
w breachfarm.co.uk

CASTLETON

Bargate Cottage B&B ★★★★
Bed & Breakfast
Market Place, Castleton, Hope Valley
S33 8WQ
t (01433) 620201
e info@bargatecottage.co.uk
w bargatecottage.co.uk

Causeway House B&B ★★★
Bed & Breakfast
Back Street, Castleton, Hope Valley
S33 8WE
t (01433) 623291
e steynberg@btinternet.com
w causewayhouse.co.uk

Cheshire House ★★★
Bed & Breakfast
How Lane, Castleton, Hope Valley
S33 8WJ
t (01433) 623225
e sue_cheshirehouse@btinternet.com
w cheshire-house.co.uk

Cheshire Mews ★★★★
Guest Accommodation
How Lane, Castleton, Hope Valley
S33 8WJ
t 07977 998881
e kslack@btconnect.com
w cheshiremews-castleton.co.uk

Denewood ★★★★
Guest Accommodation - Room Only
Buxton Road, Castleton
S33 8WP
t (01433) 621595
e denewood.bandb@gmail.com
w denewood.me.uk

Dunscar Farm Bed & Breakfast
★★★★ *Guest Accommodation*
Castleton, Hope Valley
S33 8WA
t (01433) 620483
e janet@dunscarfarm.co.uk
w dunscarfarm.co.uk

Hillside House ★★★★
Bed & Breakfast
Hillside House, Pindale Road, Hope Valley
S33 8WU
t (01433) 620312
e r.l.webster@hotmail.com
w perfectpetalsgallery.co.uk/painting_holidays.html

Swiss House ★★★★
Guest Accommodation
How Lane, Castleton, Hope Valley, Derbyshire
S33 8WJ
t (01433) 621098
e info@swiss-house.co.uk
w swiss-house.co.uk

Ye Olde Nags Head ★★★★ *Inn*
Cross Street, Castleton, Hope Valley
S33 8WH
t (01433) 620248
e info@yeoldenagshead.co.uk
w yeoldenagshead.co.uk

YHA Castleton Hall ★★★ *Hostel*
Castle Street, Castleton, Hope Valley
S33 8WG
t (01433) 620235
e castleton@yha.org.uk
w yha.org.uk

CHADDESDEN

Green Gables ★★★ *Guest House*
19 Highfield Lane, Chaddesden, Derby
DE21 6PG
t (01332) 672298
e enquiries@greengablesuk.co.uk
w greengablesuk.co.uk

CHAPEL-EN-LE-FRITH

Forest Lodge ★★★★
Bed & Breakfast
58 Manchester Road, Chapel-en-le-Frith, High Peak
SK23 9TH
t (01298) 812854
e noreen@forestlodge.org.uk
w forestlodge.org.uk

High Croft Guest House ★★★★★
Bed & Breakfast **GOLD AWARD**
Manchester Road, Chapel-en-le-Frith, High Peak
SK23 9UH
t (01298) 814843
e elaine@highcroft-guesthouse.co.uk
w highcroft-guesthouse.co.uk

Roebuck Inn ★★★ *Inn*
Market Place, Chapel-en-le-Frith, High Peak
SK23 0EN
t (01298) 812274
e jillbob@hotmail.co.uk

Rushup Hall B&B ★★★★
Farmhouse **SILVER AWARD**
Rushup Lane, Rushup, High Peak
SK23 0QT
t (01298) 813323
e neil@rushophall.com
w rushophall.com

Slack Hall Farm ★★★★ *Farmhouse*
Castleton Road, Chapel-en-le-Frith, High Peak
SK23 0QS
t (01298) 812845
e slackhallfarm@btconnect.com
w slackhallfarm.co.uk

East Midlands | Derbyshire

CHESTERFIELD

Abigail's Guest House ★★★
Guest House
2 Brockwell Lane, Chesterfield
S40 4EE
- t (01246) 279391
- e gail@abigails.fsnet.co.uk
- w abigailsguesthouse.co.uk

Acorns Guest House ★★★★
Guest House
76 Sheffield Road, Chesterfield
S41 7LS
- t (01246) 233602

Anis Louise Guest House ★★★★
Guest House SILVER AWARD
34 Clarence Road, Chesterfield
S40 1LN
- t (01246) 235412
- e anislouise@gmail.com
- w anislouiseguesthouse.co.uk

Clarendon Guest House ★★★
Guest Accommodation
32 Clarence Road, Chesterfield
S40 1LN
- t (01246) 235004
- e info@clarendonguesthouse.com
- w clarendonguesthouse.com

Old Rectory Guest House
Guest Accommodation
1 Church Street, Staveley,
Chesterfield, derbyshire
S43 3TL
- t (01246) 473307
- e billcooneyb@aol.com
- w oldrectoryguesthouse.com

CHINLEY

Moseley House Farm ★★★
Farmhouse
Maynestone Road, Chinley, High Peak
SK23 6AH
- t (01663) 750240
- e moseleyhouse@supanet.com
- w smoothhound.co.uk/hotels/moseleyhouse.html

CLAY CROSS

Blanches Guesthouse ★★★★
Bed & Breakfast
72 Market Street, Clay Cross, Chesterfield
S45 9LY
- t (01246) 861163
- e info@blanchesguesthouse.co.uk
- w blanchesguesthouse.co.uk

COTON-IN-THE-ELMS

Fern Cottage ★★★★
Bed & Breakfast
Mill Street, Coton in the Elms, Swadlincote
DE12 8ES
- t (01283) 763306
- e heather@ferncottagebb.co.uk
- w ferncottagebb.co.uk

Manor Farm ★★★★ Farmhouse
Coton in the Elms, Swadlincote
DE12 8EP
- t (01283) 760340
- e paul@pryanet.com
- w manorfarmbb.co.uk

CRESSBROOK

Cressbrook Hall ★★★★
Guest Accommodation
Cressbrook, Buxton
SK17 8SY
- t (01298) 871289
- e stay@cressbrookhall.co.uk
- w cressbrookhall.co.uk

The Old Hay Barn ★★★★★
Bed & Breakfast SILVER AWARD
The Barns, Cressbrook, Buxton
SK17 8SY
- t (01298) 873503
- e dcmacb@aol.com
- w theoldhaybarn.com

CROWDEN

YHA Crowden ★★★★ Hostel
Crowden-in-Longdendale, Glossop
SK13 1HZ
- t (01629) 592600
- e crowden@yha.org.uk
- w yha.org.uk/find-accommodation/peak-district-sherwood/hostels/crowden/index.aspx

CUTTHORPE

Cowclose Farm ★★★★
Bed & Breakfast
Overgreen, Cutthorpe, Chesterfield
S42 7BA
- t (01246) 272948
- e cowclosebarn@hotmail.co.uk
- w cowclosebarn.com

DARLEY ABBEY

The Coach House ★★★
Guest Accommodation
185a Duffield Road, Darley Abbey, Derby
DE22 1JB
- t (01332) 551795
- e carolcoachousederby@tiscali.co.uk

DARLEY BRIDGE

Square & Compass ★★★★ Inn
Station Road, Darley Dale, Matlock
DE4 2EQ
- t (01629) 733255
- e info@thesquareandcompass.co.uk
- w thesquareandcompass.co.uk

DERBY

Bonehill Farm ★★★
Bed & Breakfast
Etwall Road, Mickleover, Derby
DE3 0DN
- t (01332) 513553
- e bonehillfarm@hotmail.com
- w bonehillfarm.co.uk

Chuckles Guest House ★★★
Bed & Breakfast
48 Crompton Street, Derby
DE1 1NX
- t (01332) 367193
- e enquiries@chucklesguesthouse.co.uk
- w chucklesguesthouse.co.uk

The Lavender Patch ★★★★★
Farmhouse SILVER AWARD
Hall Croft Farm, Uttoxeter Road,
Hilton, Derby, Derbyshire
DE65 5FZ
- t 01283 732303/ 07815956626
- e info@thelavenderpatch.com
- w thelavenderpatch.com

The Mackworth ★★★ Inn
Ashbourne Road, Mackwoth, Derby
DE22 4LY
- t (01332) 824324
- e mackworthhotel.derby@marstons.co.uk
- w themackworth.co.uk

Thornhill Lodge Guest House ★★★★ Guest House SILVER AWARD
Thornhill Lodge, Derby
DE22 3LX
- t (01332) 345318
- e info@thornhill-lodge.com
- w thornhill-lodge.com

DETHICK

The Manor Farm House ★★★★
Bed & Breakfast
Dethick, Matlock
DE4 5GG
- t (01629) 534302
- e gilly.groom@virgin.net
- w manorfarmdethick.com

DOVERIDGE

Ashmore Bed & Breakfast ★★★★
Guest Accommodation
Derby Road, Doveridge, Ashbourne
DE6 5JU
- t (01889) 569620
- e ashmorecottage@btinternet.com
- w ashmorecottage.co.uk

EDALE

Edale YHA ★★ Hostel
Rowland Cote, Nether Booth, Hope Valley
S33 7ZH
- t 0870 770 5808

Stonecroft Country Guest House ★★★★ Bed & Breakfast
GOLD AWARD
Stonecroft, Grindsbrook, Hope Valley
S33 7ZA
- t (01433) 670262
- e stonecroftedale@btconnect.com
- w stonecroftguesthouse.co.uk

ELTON

Elton Guest House ★★★★
Bed & Breakfast
Moor Lane, Elton, Matlock
DE4 2DA
- t (01629) 650217
- e jenny.hirst@w3z.co.uk
- w eltonholidays.com

Hawthorn Cottage ★★★★★
Guest Accommodation
SILVER AWARD
Well Street, Elton, Bakewell
DE4 2BY
- t (01629) 650372
- w hawthorncottage-elton.co.uk

Homestead Farm B&B ★★★★
Farmhouse
Main Street, Elton, Matlock
DE4 2BW
- t (01629) 650359
- e jeanniecarson@hotmail.co.uk

ETWALL

The Barn Retreat ★★★
Guest Accommodation
Tara Centre, Ashe Hall, Derby
DE65 6HT
- t 07875 250716
- e relax@thebarnretreat.co.uk
- w thebarnretreat.co.uk

EYAM

Bretton Cottage ★★★★★
Bed & Breakfast GOLD AWARD
Bretton, Eyam, Hope Valley
S32 5QD
- t (01433) 631076
- e andrew@metcalfeandco.co.uk
- w peakholidayhomes.com

Crown Cottage ★★★★
Bed & Breakfast
Main Road, Eyam, Hope Valley
S32 5QW
- t (01433) 630858
- e janet@eatonfold.demon.co.uk
- w crown-cottage.co.uk

YHA Eyam ★★★ Hostel
Hawkhill Road, Eyam, Hope Valley
S32 5QP
- t (01433) 630335
- e eyam@yha.org.uk
- w yha.org.uk

FAIRFIELD

Barms Farm ★★★★★
Bed & Breakfast SILVER AWARD
Fairfield Common, Buxton
SK17 7HW
- t (01298) 77723
- e enquiries@barmsfarm.co.uk
- w barmsfarm.co.uk

FENNY BENTLEY

Bentley Brook Inn ★★★ Inn
Fenny Bentley, Ashbourne
DE6 1LF
- t (01335) 350278
- e all@bentleybrookinn.co.uk
- w bentleybrookinn.co.uk

Cairn Grove ★★★★
Guest Accommodation
Ashes Lane, Fenny Bentley, Ashbourne
DE6 1LD
- t (01335) 350538
- e cairngrove@supanet.com
- w cairngrove.co.uk

Millfields ★★★ Bed & Breakfast
Fenny Bentley, Ashbourne
DE6 1LA
- t (01335) 350454
- e millfieldsbandb@hotmail.com
- w millfieldsbandb.co.uk

FLAGG

Knotlow Farm B&B ★★★★
Farmhouse
Flagg, Buxton
SK17 9QP
- t (01298) 85313
- e enquiries@knotlowfarm.co.uk
- w knotlowfarm.co.uk

GLOSSOP

Avondale ★★★★ Guest House
28 Woodhead Road, Glossop
SK13 7RH
- t (01457) 853132
- e margaret@avondale28.plus.com
- w avondale-guesthouse.co.uk

Norfolk Arms ★★★★
Guest Accommodation
Norfolk Square, Glossop
SK13 8BP
- t (01457) 851940

Windy Harbour Farm ★★★★
Guest Accommodation
Woodhead Road, Glossop
SK13 7QE
- t (01457) 853107
- e enquiries@peakdistrict-hotel.co.uk
- w peakdistrict-hotel.co.uk

GRANGE MILL

Avondale Farm ★★★★
Bed & Breakfast SILVER AWARD
Grangemill, Matlock
DE4 4HT
- t (01629) 650820
- e avondale@tinyworld.co.uk
- w avondalefarm.co.uk

GREAT LONGSTONE

The Forge House ★★★★★
Bed & Breakfast SILVER AWARD
Main Street, Great Longstone, Nr Bakewell, Derbyshire
DE45 1TF
- t (01629) 640735
- e emma@theforgehouse.com

HARDSTOFT

Whitton Lodge ★★★★
Guest Accommodation
Chesterfield Road, Hardstoft
S45 8AX
- t (01773) 875614
- e pjohnthestud@aol.com
- w whittonlodge.co.uk

HARTINGTON

Cotesfield Farm B&B ★★
Farmhouse
Parsley Hay, Buxton
SK17 0BD
- t (01298) 83256

427

East Midlands | Derbyshire

The Hayloft ★★★★
Guest Accommodation
Church Street, Hartington, Buxton
SK17 0AW
t (01298) 84358
e jane.bassett1@tiscali.co.uk
w hartingtonhayloft.co.uk

YHA Hartington Hall ★★★★
Hostel
Hartington, Buxton
SK17 0AT
t 0870 770 5848
w yha.org.uk

HATHERSAGE

Cannon Croft ★★★★
Bed & Breakfast **GOLD AWARD**
Cannonfields, Hathersage, Hope Valley
S32 1AG
t (01433) 650005
e sandra@cannoncroftbedandbreakfast.co.uk
w cannoncroftbedandbreakfast.co.uk

The Plough Inn ★★★★ *Inn*
SILVER AWARD
Leadmill Bridge, Hathersage, Hope Valley
S32 1BA
t (01433) 650319

YHA Hathersage ★★ *Hostel*
The Hollies, Castleton Road, Hope Valley
S32 1EH
t 0870 770 5852
w yha.org.uk

HEATH

Stainsby Mill Farm ★★★
Farmhouse
Stainsby, Heath, Chesterfield
S44 5RW
t (01246) 850288
e charlotte.e.hitch@royalmail.com

HIGHAM

Bramble Cottage ★★★★
Guest Accommodation
22-23 Main Road, Higham, Alfreton
DE55 6EF
t (01773) 830298
e enquiries@bramblecottagebandb.com
w bramblecottagebandb.com

The Crown Inn ★★ *Inn*
Main Road, Higham, Alfreton
DE55 6EH
t (01773) 832310
e crownathigham@aol.com

HIGH PEAK

The Old Hall Inn ★★★★ *Inn*
Whitehough, Chinley, High Peak
SK23 6EJ
t (01663) 750529
e info@old-hall-inn.co.uk
w old-hall-inn.co.uk

Pack Horse Inn ★★★★ *Inn*
SILVER AWARD
Mellor Road, New Mills, High Peak
SK22 4QQ
t (01663) 742365
e info@packhorseinn.co.uk
w packhorseinn.co.uk

Springbank Guest House ★★★★
Guest House **SILVER AWARD**
3 Reservoir Road, Whaley Bridge, High Peak
SK23 7BL
t (01663) 732119
e margot@whaleyspringbank.co.uk
w whaleyspringbank.co.uk

HOLLINGTON

Reevsmoor ★★★★ *Bed & Breakfast*
Hoargate Lane, Hollington, Ashbourne
DE6 3AG
t (01335) 330318
w smoothhound.co.uk

HOLLINSCLOUGH

Stoop Farm Bed & Breakfast
★★★★ *Farmhouse*
Hollinsclough, Buxton
SK17 0RW
t (01298) 23618
e stoop.farm@btinternet.com
w stoopfarm.co.uk

HOLMESFIELD

Cordwell House ★★★★
Bed & Breakfast
Cordwell Lane, Millthorpe, Dronfield
S18 7WH
t (0114) 289 0271

HOPE

Poachers Arms ★★★★ *Inn*
SILVER AWARD
Castleton Road, Hope Valley
S33 6SB
t (01433) 620380
e btissington95@aol.com
w poachersarms.co.uk

Underleigh House ★★★★★
Guest Accommodation
GOLD AWARD
Lose Hill Lane, Off Edale Road, Hope, Hope Valley
S33 6AF
t (01433) 621372
e info@underleighhouse.co.uk
w underleighhouse.co.uk

Woodbine B&B ★★★ *Guest House*
18 Castleton Road, Hope, Hope Valley
S33 6RH
t 07778 113882

HOPE VALLEY

Polly's B&B ★★★★ *Bed & Breakfast*
Moorview Cottage, Cannonfields, Hope Valley
S32 1AG
t (01433) 650110
e pollybandb@moorviewcottage.plus.com
w cressbrook.co.uk

Ramblers Rest ★★★ *Guest House*
Mill Bridge, Hope Valley
S33 8WR
t (01433) 620125
e enquiries@ramblersrest-castleton.co.uk
w ramblersrest-castleton.co.uk

Ye Olde Cheshire Cheese Inn
★★★ *Inn*
How Lane, Castleton, Hope Valley
S33 8WJ
t (01433) 620330
e info@cheshirecheeseinn.co.uk
w cheshirecheeseinn.co.uk

IDRIDGEHAY

Millbank House ★★★
Guest Accommodation
Idridgehay, Wirksworth
DE56 2SH
t (01629) 823161
e cmjones123@hotmail.co.uk
w millbankhousebandb.co.uk

LEA BRIDGE

Pear Tree Farm Guest House
★★★★ *Guest Accommodation*
Pear Tree Farm, Lea Main Road, Matlock, Derbyshire
DE4 5JN
t (01629) 534215
e sue@derbyshirearts.co.uk
w derbyshirearts.co.uk

LITTLE HAYFIELD

Lantern Pike Inn ★★★ *Inn*
45 Glossop Road, Little Hayfield, High Peak
SK22 2NG
t (01663) 747590
e sales@lanternpikeinn.co.uk
w lanternpikeinn.co.uk

LITTON

Ashleigh ★★★★ *Bed & Breakfast*
Ashleigh, Buxton
SK17 8QU
t (01298) 873135
e peterbrown459@hotmail.com

Beacon House ★★★★
Bed & Breakfast
Litton, Buxton
SK17 8QP
t (01298) 871752
e rjp1949@hotmail.co.uk
w beaconhse.co.uk

Hall Farm House ★★★★
Bed & Breakfast **SILVER AWARD**
Litton, Buxton
SK17 8QP
t (01298) 872172
e jfscott@waitrose.com
w users.waitrose.com/~jfscott

MARSH LANE

Ravencar Farm ★★★★
Bed & Breakfast
Main Road, Marsh Lane, Dronfield
S21 5RH
t (01246) 433717
e helenmrshcfish@aol.com
w ravencarfarmbedandbreakfast.co.uk

MATLOCK

The Cables ★★★★ *Bed & Breakfast*
182 Dale Road, Matlock Bath, Matlock
DE4 3PS
t (01629) 583629
e info@thecablesmatlockbath.com
w thecablesmatlockbath.com

Ellen House ★★★★
Bed & Breakfast **SILVER AWARD**
37 Snitterton Road, Matlock
DE4 3LZ
t (01629) 55584
e anne.ellenhouse@w3z.co.uk
w ellenhousebandbmatlock.co.uk

Riverbank House ★★★★
Guest House **SILVER AWARD**
Derwent Avenue, Matlock
DE4 3LX
t (01629) 582593
e bookings@riverbankhouse.co.uk
w riverbankhouse.co.uk

Robertswood Country House
★★★★★ *Guest Accommodation*
SILVER AWARD
Farley Hill, Matlock
DE4 3LL
t (01629) 55642
e robertswoodhouse@aol.com
w robertswood.co.uk

Rosegarth ★★★★ *Bed & Breakfast*
57 Dimple Road, Matlock
DE4 3JX
t (01629) 56294
e john@crich.ndo.co.uk
w rosegarthmatlock.co.uk

Sheriff Lodge ★★★★ *Guest House*
GOLD AWARD
Dimple Road, Matlock
DE4 3JX
t (01629) 760760
e info@sherifflodge.co.uk
w sherifflodge.co.uk

MATLOCK BATH

Ashdale Guest House ★★★
Guest Accommodation
92 North Parade, Matlock Bath, Matlock
DE4 3NS
t (01629) 57826
e ashdale@matlockbath.fsnet.co.uk
w ashdaleguesthouse.co.uk

Fountain Villa ★★★★
Guest Accommodation
86 North Parade, Matlock Bath, Matlock
DE4 3NS
t (01629) 56195
e enquiries@fountainvilla.co.uk
w fountainvilla.co.uk

Sunnybank B&B ★★★★
Bed & Breakfast **GOLD AWARD**
37 Clifton Road, Matlock Bath, Matlock
DE4 3PW
t (01629) 584621

MIDDLETON-BY-YOULGRAVE

Castle Farm ★★★★ *Farmhouse*
Middleton-by-Youlgreave, Bakewell
DE45 1LS
t (01629) 636746

Smerrill Grange Farm ★★★
Farmhouse
Middleton-by-Youlgreave, Bakewell
DE45 1LQ
t (01629) 636232
e alisonyates267@btinternet.com

MILLERS DALE

YHA Ravenstor ★★★ *Hostel*
Millers Dale, Buxton
SK17 8SS
t 0870 770 6008
e ravenstor@yha.org.uk
w yha.org.uk

NETHERSEAL

Campville Cottage ★★★★
Bed & Breakfast
Clifton Road, Netherseal, Swadlincote
DE12 8BS
t (01283) 760265
e petetheshirt@aol.com

NEWHAVEN

The Kings at Ivy House ★★★★★
Guest Accommodation
GOLD AWARD
Biggin-by-Hartington, Newhaven, Buxton
SK17 0DT
t (01298) 84709
e kings.ivyhouse@lineone.net
w thekingsativyhouse.co.uk

PEAK FOREST

Devonshire Arms ★★★ *Inn*
Hernstone Lane, Peak Forest, Buxton
SK17 8EJ
t (01298) 23875
e lesleywoodward@tiscali.co.uk
w devarms.com

PENTRICH

Coney Grey Farm ★★ *Farmhouse*
Chesterfield Road, Pentrich, Ripley
DE5 3RJ
t (01773) 833179

PRIESTCLIFFE

Highfield B&B ★★★★
Bed & Breakfast
Highfield, Priestcliffe, Buxton
SK17 9TN
t (01298) 85740
e theslackies@btinternet.com
w highfieldbedandbreakfast@wordpress.com

East Midlands | Derbyshire/Leicestershire & Rutland

RIPLEY

B&B at The Latte Lounge ★★
Guest Accommodation
Church Street, Ripley
DE5 3BU
t (01773) 512000
e misscagarner@hotmail.com

Hartshay Village School ★★
Guest Accommodation
Hartshay Village School, Main Road,
Lower Hartshay, Ripley
DE5 3RP
t (01773) 748746

ROWSLEY

The Old Station House ★★★★
Bed & Breakfast
Chatsworth Road, Rowsley,
Bakewell
DE4 2EJ
t (01629) 732987
e enquiries@oldstationhousebandb.
   org.uk
w oldstationhousebandb.org.uk

SMISBY

Forest Court Accommodation ★★
Guest Accommodation - Room Only
Annwell Lane, Smisby, Ashby-de-la-
Zouch
LE65 2TA
t (01530) 413604
e info@taphouse-smisby.co.uk
w forestcourtashby.co.uk

SNELSTON

Oldfield House ★★★★★
Guest Accommodation
GOLD AWARD
Snelston, Ashborne
DE6 2EP
t (01335) 324510
e s-jarvis@tiscali.co.uk
w oldfieldhouse.uk.com

STANTON-IN-THE-PEAK

Congreave Farm ★★★★
Farmhouse **GOLD AWARD**
Congreave, Bakewell
DE4 2NF
t (01629) 732063
e deborah@matsam16.orang
   ehome.co.uk
w derbyshire-farm-accommodation.
   co.uk

TANSLEY

B&B Yew Tree Cottage ★★★★
Bed & Breakfast **SILVER AWARD**
The Knoll, Tansley, Matlock
DE4 5FP
t (01629) 583862
e enquiries@yewtreecottagebb.co.
   uk
w yewtreecottagebb.co.uk

Packhorse Farm Bungalow
★★★★ *Bed & Breakfast*
Foxholes Lane, Tansley, Matlock
DE4 5LF
t (01629) 582781

Silver Ridge ★★★★★
Bed & Breakfast **GOLD AWARD**
Foxholes Lane, Tansley, Matlock,
Derbyshire
DE4 5LF
t (01629) 55071
e pcspaul@hotmail.com
w silverridgetansley.co.uk

THORPE

Hillcrest House ★★★★
Guest House
Dovedale, Thorpe, Ashbourne
DE6 2AW
t (01335) 350436
e info@hillcresthousedovedale.co.
   uk
w hillcresthousedovedale.co.uk

TIBSHELF

Rosvern House ★★ *Bed & Breakfast*
High Street, Tibshelf, Alfreton
DE55 5NY
t (01773) 874800
e sara.byard@orange.net

TICKNALL

The Staff of Life ★★★★
Guest Accommodation
7 High Street, Ticknall, Derby
DE73 7JH
t (01332) 862479
e reservations@thestaffoflife.co.uk
w thestaffoflife.co.uk

TIDESWELL

Bankfield Stable ★★★★
Guest Accommodation
Bankfield House, Buxton Road,
Buxton
SK17 8PG
t (01298) 872656
e bankfieldstable@tiscali.co.uk
w bankfieldstable.co.uk

Jaret House ★★★★
Guest Accommodation
Queen Street, Tideswell, Buxton
SK17 8JZ
t (01298) 872470
e info@jarethouse.co.uk
w jarethouse.co.uk

Merman Barn B&B ★★★★
Bed & Breakfast **SILVER AWARD**
Alma Road, Tideswell, Buxton
SK17 8LS
t (01298) 872033
e mermanbarn@yahoo.co.uk
w mermanbarn.co.uk

TISSINGTON

Bassett Wood Farm ★★★★
Farmhouse
Tissington, Ashbourne
DE6 1RD
t (01335) 350254
e janet@bassettwood.freeserve.co.
   uk
w bassettwoodfarm.co.uk

Overfield Farm ★★★★ *Farmhouse*
Tissington, Ashbourne
DE6 1RA
t (01335) 390285
e info@overfieldfarm.co.uk
w overfieldfarm.co.uk

WADSHELF

Temperance House Farm ★★★★
Guest Accommodation
SILVER AWARD
Bradshaw Lane, Wadshelf,
Chesterfield
S42 7BT
t (01246) 566416
e info@temperancehousefarm.co.uk
w temperancehousefarm.co.uk

WESSINGTON

Crich Lane Farm ★★★★
Farmhouse
Moorwood Moor Lane, Wessington,
Alfreton, Derbyshire
DE55 6DU
t (01773) 835186/07930 553219
e crichlanefarm@w3z.co.uk
w crichlanefarm.co.uk

WESTON-ON-TRENT

The Willows ★★★★
Guest Accommodation
SILVER AWARD
Trent Lane, Weston-on-Trent, Derby
DE72 2BT
t (01332) 702525
e stay@willowsinweston.co.uk
w willowsinweston.co.uk

WHATSTANDWELL

Riverdale Guest House ★★★★
Bed & Breakfast
Middle Lane, Crich Carr, Matlock
DE4 5EG
t (01773) 853905
e riverdale@clara.co.uk
w riverdaleguesthouse.co.uk

WINSTER

Brae Cottage ★★★★
Guest Accommodation
SILVER AWARD
East Bank, Winster, Matlock
DE4 2DT
t (01629) 650375

WIRKSWORTH

The Glenorchy Centre ★★★
Group Hostel
West Derbyshire United Reformed
Church, Coldwell Street, Wirksworth
DE4 4FB
t (01629) 824323
w glenorchycentre.org.uk

The Old Lock-Up ★★★★★
Guest Accommodation
GOLD AWARD
North End, Wirksworth
DE4 4FG
t (01629) 826272
e wheeler@theoldlockup.co.uk
w theoldlockup.co.uk

YOULGRAVE

Farmyard Inn ★★★
Guest Accommodation
Main Street, Youlgrave, Bakewell
DE45 1UW
t (01629) 636221
e sjg.healey@zen.co.uk
w farmyardinn.co.uk

YHA Youlgreave ★★★ *Hostel*
Fountain Square, Youlgrave,
Bakewell
DE45 1UR
t (01629) 636518
w yha.org.uk

YOULGREAVE

The Old Bakery ★★★
Bed & Breakfast
Church Street, Youlgrave, Bakewell
DE45 1UR
t (01629) 636887

Leicestershire & Rutland

APPLEBY MAGNA

Ferne Cottage ★★★ *Bed & Breakfast*
5 Black Horse Hill, Appleby Magna,
Ashby-de-la-Zouch
DE12 7AQ
t (01530) 271772
e gbirdappplebymag@aol.com
w fernecottagebandb.co.uk

ASFORDBY

Dairy Farm ★★★ *Farmhouse*
8 Burrough End, Great Dalby,
Melton Mowbray
LE14 2EW
t (01664) 562783
e info@dairy-farm.co.uk
w dairy-farm.co.uk

ASHBY-DE-LA-ZOUCH

Clockmakers House B&B ★★★★
Guest Accommodation
8 Lower Church Street, Ashby-de-la-
Zouch
LE65 1AB
t (01530) 417974
e mike@clockmakershouse.com
w clockmakershouse.com

BARLEYTHORPE

Barleythorpe Conference Centre
★★★ *Guest Accommodation*
Barleythorpe, Barleythorpe
LE15 7ED
t (01572) 725318
e ccarter@eef.org.uk
w barleythorpe.com

BARROW-UPON-SOAR

The Hunting Lodge ★★★★ *Inn*
38 South Street, Barrow upon Soar,
Loughborough
LE12 8LZ
t (01509) 412337
w probablythebestpubsintheworld.
   co.uk/huntinglodge/hunti
   nglodge.aspx

BELTON-IN-RUTLAND

**Belton Old Rectory Bed &
Breakfast** ★★★
Guest Accommodation
4 New Road, Belton-in-Rutland
LE15 9LE
t (01572) 717279
e bb@iepuk.com
w theoldrectorybelton.co.uk

BRAUNSTON

Gable Cottage ★★★★
Bed & Breakfast
3 Ratts Lane, Braunston-in-Rutland
LE15 8QW
t (01572) 723382
e fiona@rutlandbedandbreakfast.co.
   uk
w rutlandbedandbreakfast.co.uk

BREEDON-ON-THE-HILL

Underhill Cottage ★★
Bed & Breakfast
9-11 Main Street, Breedon-on-the-
Hill, Castle Donington
DE73 8AN
t (01332) 865630
e benicebep@aol.com
w t-multimedia.co.uk/underhillc
   ottage

CADEBY

Bosworth Firs ★★★
Bed & Breakfast
Bosworth Road, Market Bosworth
CV13 0DW
t (01455) 290727
e bosworthfirs1.accommodation@
   yahoo.co.uk

CALDECOTT

Meadow Farm ★★ *Farmhouse*
The Green, Caldecott
LE16 8RR
t (01536) 770343
e meadowfarm5@hotmail.com
w meadowfarmcaldecott.co.uk

The Old Plough ★★★★
Guest Accommodation
41 Main Street, Caldecott
LE16 8RS
t (01536) 772031
e comfort@oldplough-rutland.co.uk
w oldplough-rutland.co.uk

CASTLE DONINGTON

Castletown House ★★★★
Guest House
4 High Street, Castle Donington
DE74 2PP
t (01332) 812018
e info@castletownhouse.fsnet.co.uk
w castletownhouse.com

Scot's Corner Guest House ★★★
Bed & Breakfast
82 Park Lane, Castle Donington
DE74 2JG
t (01332) 811226
e linda.deary@ntlworld.com
w scots-corner.com

East Midlands | Leicestershire & Rutland

Spring Cottage ★★★★
Bed & Breakfast
79 High Street, Castle Donington
DE74 2PQ
t (01332) 814289
e madge.stic@btinternet.com
w springcottagebb.co.uk

COTTESMORE

The Tithe Barn ★★★★
Guest Accommodation
Clatterpot Lane, Cottesmore
LE15 7DW
t (01572) 813591
e jpryke@thetithebarn.co.uk
w tithebarn-rutland.co.uk

CROPSTON

Horseshoe Cottage Farm
★★★★★ *Bed & Breakfast*
GOLD AWARD
Hallgates, Roecliffe Road, Cropston, Leicester
LE7 7HQ
t (0116) 235 0038
e lindajee@ljee.freeserve.co.uk
w horseshoecottagefarm.com

DADLINGTON

Apple Orchard Farm ★★★★
Farmhouse
Fenn Lane, Dadlington, Hinckley
CV13 6DR
t (01455) 213186
e appleorchardfarm@btinternet.com
w appleorchardfarm.co.uk

DISEWORTH

Lady Gate Guest House ★★★★
Guest House **SILVER AWARD**
47 The Green, Diseworth, Castle Donington
DE74 2QN
t (01332) 811565
e ladygateguesthouse@tiscali.co.uk
w ladygateguesthouse.co.uk

EAST LANGTON

West Langton Lodge ★★★
Guest Accommodation - Room Only
Melton Road, East Langton, Market Harborough
LE16 7TG
t (01858) 545450
e lindsay@westlangtonlodge.co.uk
w westlangtonlodge.co.uk

ELMESTHORPE

Badgers Mount ★★★★
Guest Accommodation
6 Station Road, Elmesthorpe, Hinckley
LE9 7SG
t (01455) 848161
e info@badgersmount.com
w badgersmount.com

EMPINGHAM

Onne House ★★★★
Bed & Breakfast
4 Whitwell Road, Empingham
LE15 8PX
t (01780) 460106
e johnannarcher@ukonline.co.uk

Shacklewell Lodge ★★★★
Bed & Breakfast
Shacklewell Lodge, Empingham
LE15 8QQ
t (01780) 460646
e shacklewell@hotmail.com
w rutnet.co.uk/pp/business/bronze.asp?id=20417

EYE KETTLEBY

Old Guadaloupe B&B ★★★★
Farmhouse
Old Guadaloupe, Kirby Lane, Eye Kettleby, Melton Mowbray
LE14 2TS
t 07989 960588
e sue@suelomas.orangehome.co.uk
w oldguadaloupecottage.co.uk

GILMORTON

Holt Farm Guest House ★★★★
Guest House
Ullesthorpe, Gilmorton, Lutterworth
LE17 5PD
t (01455) 558008
e stay@holtfarmguesthouse.co.uk
w holtfarmguesthouse.co.uk

GOADBY

The Hollies ★★★ *Bed & Breakfast*
Goadby, Leicester, Market Harborough
LE7 9EE
t (0116) 259 8301
e j.parr@btinternet.com

GREAT BOWDEN

Langton Brook Farm ★★★★
Farmhouse
Langton Road, Great Bowden, Market Harborough
LE16 7EZ
t (01858) 545730
e mervyn@langtonbrookfarm.freeserve.co.uk
w langtonbrookfarm.com

HAMBLETON

Dove Cottage ★★★★
Bed & Breakfast
Ketton Road, Hambleton
LE15 8TH
t (01572) 757264
e dovecottagehambleton@hotmail.co.uk
w dovecottagehambleton.com

Finches Arms ★★★★ *Inn*
Oakham Road, Hambleton, Oakham
LE15 8TL
t (01572) 756575
e finchsarms@talk21.com

HATHERN

Leys Guest House ★★★
Guest House
Loughborough Road, Hathern, Loughborough
LE12 5JB
t (01509) 844373
e leysab2@msn.com

HIGHAM-ON-THE-HILL

Bed & Breakfast at Vale Farm
★★★★ *Farmhouse*
Stoke Lane, Higham-on-The-Hill, Hinckley
CV13 6ES
t 07077 915272
e valefarm@gmail.com
w valefarm-bed-and-breakfast.co.uk

HINCKLEY

Elsted House ★★★★ *Guest House*
101 Derby Road, Hinckley
LE10 1QE
t (01530) 220556
e elstedhouse@ntlworld.com
w elstedhouse.co.uk

HOLWELL

Hall Farm ★★★★ *Farmhouse*
1 Main Street, Holwell, Melton Mowbray
LE14 4SZ
t (01664) 444275
e enquiries@hallfarmholwell.co.uk
w hallfarmholwell.co.uk

HUSBANDS BOSWORTH

Honeypot Lane Bed & Breakfast
★★★★ *Bed & Breakfast*
SILVER AWARD
32 Honeypot Lane, Husbands Bosworth, Lutterworth
LE17 6LY
t (01858) 880836
e bandb@honeypotlane.co.uk
w honeypotlane.co.uk

KIRKBY MALLORY

Oaks Lodge ★★★
Guest Accommodation - Room Only
Stapleton Lane, Kirkby Mallory, Hinckley
LE9 7QJ
t (01455) 848125
e gpenney49@googlemail.com
w oakslodge.co.uk

KNAPTOFT

Bruntingthorpe Farmhouse B&B
★★★★ *Farmhouse* **SILVER AWARD**
Knaptoft House Farm, Bruntingthorpe Road, Lutterworth
LE17 6PR
t (0116) 247 8388
e info@knaptofthousefarm.co.uk
w knaptoft.co.uk

LEICESTER

Abinger Guest House ★★★
Guest House
175 Hinckley Road, Leicester
LE3 0TF
t (0116) 255 4674
e abinger@btinternet.com
w leicesterguest.co.uk

Campbells ★★ *Guest House*
17-19 Westleigh Road, Leicester
LE3 0HH
t (0116) 254 6875
e desk@campbellshotel.com
w campbellshotel.com

Croft Hotel ★★★ *Guest House*
3 Stanley Road, Leicester
LE2 1RF
t (0116) 270 3220
e crofthotel@montessorigroup.com

Glenfield Lodge *Bed & Breakfast*
4 Glenfield Road, Leicester
LE3 6AP
t (0116) 262 7554
e r.w.brown@live.com
w glenfieldlodge.co.uk

The Haynes ★★★★ *Guest House*
185 Uppingham Road, Leicester
LE5 4BQ
t (0116) 276 8973
e hayneshotel@yahoo.co.uk

South Fork Guest House ★★
Guest House
464-466 Narborough Road, Leicester
LE3 2FT
t (0116) 299 9960
e southforkhotel@ntlworld.com
w southforkguesthouse.co.uk

University of Leicester ★★★
Campus
Stoughton Drive South, Leicester, Oadby
LE2 2ND
t (0116) 271 9933
e conferences@le.ac.uk
w leicesterconferences.co.uk

Wondai B&B ★★★ *Bed & Breakfast*
47-49 Main Street, Newtown Linford, Leicester
LE6 0AE
t (01530) 242728
e rmwarrillow@googlemail.com

LITTLE CASTERTON

4 Camphill Cottages ★★★★
Bed & Breakfast **SILVER AWARD**
Little Casterton, Stamford
PE9 4BE
t (01780) 763661
e anna.martin@tesco.net

LONG CLAWSON

Elms Farm ★★★★ *Bed & Breakfast*
52 East End, Long Clawson, Melton Mowbray
LE14 4NG
t (01664) 822395
e elmsfarm@whittard.net
w whittard.net

LOUGHBOROUGH

Charnwood Lodge ★★★★
Guest House
136 Leicester Road, Loughborough
LE11 2AQ
t (01509) 211120
e reservations@charnwoodlodge.com
w charnwoodlodge.com

Forest Rise ★★★
Guest Accommodation
55-57 Forest Road, Loughborough
LE11 3NW
t (01509) 215928
e reception@forestrise.co.uk
w forestrise.co.uk

Garendon Park ★★★ *Guest House*
92 Leicester Road, Loughborough
LE11 2AQ
t (01509) 236557
e info@garendonparkhotel.co.uk
w hotelsloughborough.co.uk

Highbury Guest House ★★★★
Guest House
146 Leicester Road, Loughborough
LE11 2AQ
t (01509) 230545
e irene@thehighburyguesthouse.co.uk
w highburyguesthouse.co.uk

Lane End Cottage ★★★★
Bed & Breakfast **SILVER AWARD**
School Lane, Woodhouse, Loughborough
LE12 8UJ
t (01509) 890706
e maryj.hudson@btinternet.com

New Life Guest House ★★★★
Guest House
121 Ashby Road, Loughborough
LE11 3AB
t (01509) 216699
e accommodation@newlife-guest house.co.uk
w newlife-guesthouse.co.uk

MANTON

Broccoli Bottom ★★★★
Bed & Breakfast **SILVER AWARD**
Wing Road, Manton, Oakham
LE15 8SZ
t 07702 437102
e sally@udale.wanadoo.co.uk
w broccolibottom.website.orange.co.uk

MARKET BOSWORTH

Mythe Farm B&B ★★★★ *Farmhouse*
Mythe Farm Pinwall Lane, Atherstone, Market Bosworth
CV9 3PF
t (01827) 722123
e info@mythefarm.co.uk
w mythefarm.co.uk

MEASHAM

Measham House Farm ★★★★
Bed & Breakfast
Gallows Lane, Measham, Ashby-de-la-Zouch
DE12 7HD
t (01530) 270465
e dilovett@meashamhouse.freeserve.co.uk
w meashamhouse.co.uk

East Midlands | Leicestershire & Rutland/Lincolnshire

MEDBOURNE

Homestead House ★★★★
Bed & Breakfast SILVER AWARD
Ashley Road, Medbourne, Market Harborough
LE16 8DL
t (01858) 565724
e june@homesteadhouse.co.uk
w homesteadhouse.co.uk

MELTON MOWBRAY

Beckmill Guest House Guest House
4 Kings Road, Melton Mowbray
LE13 1QF
t (01664) 852881
e lesleyfarrow476@btinternet.com
w beckmill.co.uk

Hillside House ★★★★
Bed & Breakfast
7 Melton Road, Burton Lazars, Melton Mowbray
LE14 2UR
t (01664) 566312
e hillhs27@aol.com
w hillside-house.co.uk

Shoby Lodge Farmhouse ★★★★
Farmhouse SILVER AWARD
Shoby, Melton Mowbray
LE14 3PF
t (01664) 812156

MOIRA

YHA National Forest ★★★★
Hostel
48 Bath Lane, Moira, Ashby-de-la-Zouch
DE12 6BD
t 0870 770 6141
e nationalforest@yha.org.uk
w yha.org.uk

MORCOTT

Redoak Bed and Breakfast ★★★
Bed & Breakfast
Beaton Road, Morcott, Oakham, Rutland
LE15 9EB
t (01572) 747862
e redoakbb@googlemail.com
w redoakonline.co.uk

MOUNTSORREL

The Mountsorrel ★★★★
Guest House
217 Loughborough Road, Mountsorrel, Loughborough
LE12 7AR
t (01509) 412627
e info@mountsorrel-guesthouse.co.uk
w mountsorrel-guesthouse.co.uk

NEWBOLD VERDON

Sunshine Cottage ★★★★
Bed & Breakfast
Main Street, Newbold Verdon, Leicester
LE9 9NN
t (01455) 828582
e sue@sunshinecottage41.co.uk
w sunshinecottage41.co.uk

NORTH KILWORTH

Old Rectory ★★★★
Bed & Breakfast SILVER AWARD
Church Street, North Kilworth, Lutterworth
LE17 6EZ
t (01858) 881130
e info@oldrectorybandb.co.uk
w oldrectorybandb.co.uk

OAKHAM

17 Northgate ★★★★
Bed & Breakfast SILVER AWARD
Oakham, Rutland
LE15 6QR
t (01572) 759271
e dane@danegould.wanadoo.co.uk
w 17northgate.co.uk

The Coach House Inn ★★★★ Inn
3 Stamford Road, South Luffenham
LE15 6DX
t (01780) 720166
e thecoachhouse123@aol.com
w coachhouserutland.co.uk

Dial House ★★★★ Bed & Breakfast
18 Uppingham Road, Oakham, Rutland
LE15 6JD
t (01572) 771685
e info@dialhouse.eu
w dialhouse.eu

Lakeside B&B ★★★★
Guest Accommodation
The Lodge, Barnsdale, North Shore, Rutland Water, Oakham
LE15 8AB
t (01572) 722422
e robwaddington@onetel.com
w thelodgebarnsdale.co.uk

Mayfield B&B ★★★★
Bed & Breakfast SILVER AWARD
19 Ashwell Road, Oakham
LE15 6QG
t (01572) 756656
e sgbruce@onetel.com

RATCLIFFE CULEY

Manor Farm Bed & Breakfast ★★
Farmhouse
Main Road, Ratcliffe Culey, Hinckley
CV9 3NY
t (01827) 712269
e janetrivett@btinternet.com

REARSBY

Manor Farm ★★★★ Farmhouse
40 Brookside, Rearsby, Melton Mowbray
LE7 4YB
t (01664) 424239
e manorfarmb.b@hotmail.co.uk
w farmstayuk.co.uk

REDMILE

Peacock Inn ★★★★ Inn
Church Corner, Main Street, Redmile, Melton Mowbray
NG13 0GA
t (01949) 842554
e reservations@thepeacockinnredmile.co.uk
w thepeacockinnredmile.co.uk

RIDLINGTON

Post Cottage ★★★★
Bed & Breakfast
5 Top Road, Ridlington, Oakham
LE15 9AX
t (01572) 823112
e bm.best@virgin.net
w bedandbreakfast-rutland.co.uk/bed-and-breakfast-rutland.htm

SCALFORD

The Lodge ★★★★ Bed & Breakfast
Melton Road, Scalford, Melton Mowbray
LE14 4UB
t (01664) 444205
e rchfel@aol.com

SHENTON

Top House Farm ★★★★
Farmhouse
Top House Farm, Shenton, Market Bosworth
CV13 6DP
t (01455) 212200
e eileen_clarke@btconnect.com

SHEPSHED

Croft Guest House ★★★
Guest House
21 Hall Croft, Shepshed, Loughborough
LE12 9AN
t (01509) 505637
e js@croftguesthouse.demon.co.uk
w croftguesthouse.demon.co.uk

GRANGE COURTYARD

Grange Courtyard ★★★★★
Guest Accommodation
SILVER AWARD
Forest Street, Shepshed, Loughborough
LE12 9DA
t (01509) 600189
e info@thegrangecourtyard.co.uk
w thegrangecourtyard.co.uk

SWANNINGTON

Hillfield House ★★★★
Bed & Breakfast
Station Hill, Swannington, Coalville
LE67 8RH
t (01530) 837414
e molly@hillfieldhouse.co.uk
w hillfieldhouse.co.uk

THURMASTON

Aaron Lodge ★★★
Guest Accommodation
3 Coppice Court, Thurmaston, Leicester
LE4 8PJ
t (0116) 269 4494
e info@aaronlodgeguesthouse.co.uk
w aaronlodgeguesthouse.co.uk

TINWELL

The Old Village Hall ★★★★
Bed & Breakfast
Main Road, Tinwell, Stamford
PE9 3UD
t (01780) 763900
e theoldvillagehall@hotmail.com

UPPINGHAM

Crown Coaching Inn ★★★ Inn
19 High Street East, Uppingham
LE15 9PY
t (01572) 822302
e thecrownrutland@aol.com

Meadowsweet Lodge ★★★
Bed & Breakfast
South View, Uppingham
LE15 9TU
t (01572) 822504

Rutland House ★★★
Guest Accommodation - Room Only
61a High Street East, Uppingham
LE15 9PY
t (01572) 822497
e rutland.house@virgin.net
w rutlandbedbreakfast.co.uk

WITHERLEY

The Old House Bed & Breakfast ★★★★ Guest House
SILVER AWARD
Watling Street, Witherley, Hinckley
CV9 1RD
t (01827) 715634
e enquiries@theoldhousebandb.co.uk
w theoldhousebandb.co.uk

Lincolnshire

ALFORD

Alford Bed & Breakfast ★★★
Bed & Breakfast
27 Chauntry Road, Alford
LN13 9HH
t (01507) 462751
e nick.ofarrell@virgin.net
w lincolnshire-isntboring.com

Old Mill House ★★★★
Guest Accommodation
SILVER AWARD
Main Road, Maltby le Marsh, Alford
LN13 0JP
t (01507) 450504
e pwbreeds@onetel.net
w oldmillmaltby.co.uk

Westbrook House B&B ★★★★
Bed & Breakfast
Westbrook House, Gayton-le-Marsh, Alford
LN13 0NW
t (01507) 450624
e info@bestbookwestbrook.co.uk
w bestbookwestbrook.co.uk

ATTERBY

East Farm Farmhouse Bed & Breakfast ★★★★ Bed & Breakfast
East Farm, Atterby, Bishop Norton
LN8 2BJ
t (01673) 818917
e info@eastfarm.me.uk

BARDNEY

The Black Horse ★★★ Guest House
16, Wragby Road, Bardney
LN3 5XL
t (01526) 398900
e jgandmr@btinternet.com
w blackhorsebardney.co.uk

BARKSTON

Kelling House ★★★★
Bed & Breakfast
17 West Street, Barkston, Nr Grantham
NG32 2NL
t +44(0)1400 251140
e sue@kellinghouse.co.uk
w kellinghouse.co.uk

BARNETBY

Holcombe Guest House ★★★★
Guest House
34 Victoria Road, Barnetby
DN38 6JR
t (01652) 680655
e holcombe.house@virgin.net

Whistle & Flute ★★★★
Guest Accommodation
Railway Street, Barnetby
DN38 6DG
t (01652) 688238
e styles@whisteandflute.net
w whisteandflute.net

BARTON UPON HUMBER

West Wold Farmhouse ★★★★
Guest House
Deepdale, Barton-upon-Humber, North Lincolnshire
DN18 6ED
t (01652) 633293
e pam@westwoldfarmhouse.co.uk
w westwoldfarmhouse.co.uk

BILLINGHAY

Mayfield Bed & Breakfast ★★★★
Bed & Breakfast
119 Walcott Road, Billinghay
LN4 4EW
t (01526) 861661
e chuckiesue@btinternet.com
w mayfield-bb.co.uk

Old Mill Crafts B&B ★★★
Bed & Breakfast
8 Mill Lane, Billinghay
LN4 4ES
t (01526) 861996
e info@old-mill-crafts.co.uk
w old-mill-crafts.co.uk

BLYTON

Blyton (Sunnyside) Ponds ★★★
Bed & Breakfast
Sunnyside Farm, Station Road, Blyton, Gainsborough
DN21 3LE
t (01427) 628240
e blytonponds@msn.com
w blytonponds.co.uk

BOSTON

Bramley Guest House ★★★
Guest House
267 Sleaford Road, Boston
PE21 7PQ
t (01205) 354538
w bramleyguesthouse.co.uk/

Haven Guest House ★★★★
Guest Accommodation
49 Robin Hood's Walk, Boston
PE21 9EX
t (01205) 364076

for key to symbols see page 6   431

East Midlands | Lincolnshire

Park Lea Guest House ★★★
Guest Accommodation
85 Norfolk Street, Boston
PE21 6PE
t (01205) 356309
e parklea.info@googlemail.com
w park-lea.co.uk/

Plummers Place Guest House
★★★★ *Guest Accommodation*
Plummers Place, Freiston Shore, Boston
PE22 0LY
t (01205) 761490
e frei24@btopenworld.com
w plummersplace.com

Y-Not Guesthouse ★★★
Guest Accommodation
10-12 Langrick Road, Boston
PE21 8HT
t (01205) 367422
e margaret.mcgarry@homecall.co.uk

BOURNE

Mill House ★★★★ *Bed & Breakfast*
64 North Road, Bourne
PE10 9BU
t (01778) 422278
e pat.stratford@googlemail.com
w millhousebnb.co.uk

BRANSTON

73 Station Road ★★★
Bed & Breakfast
73 Station Road, Branston, Lincoln
LN4 1LG
t (01522) 828658

The Waggon & Horses ★★ *Inn*
High Street, Branston
LN4 1NB
t (01522) 791356
e andrew.neall@btconnect.com
w branstonwaggon.co.uk

BRIGG

Albert House ★★★★
Guest Accommodation
23 Bigby Street, Brigg
DN20 8ED
t (01652) 658081
e jeancwalker@yahoo.co.uk
w albert-house.co.uk

Beldon House ★★★★
Guest Accommodation
Wrawby Road, Brigg
DN20 8DL
t (01652) 653517
e info@beldonhouse.co.uk

CADNEY

Old Barn Bed & Breakfast
Guest Accommodation
Old Barn, Main Street, Cadney, Brigg
DN20 9HR
t (01652) 678612
e enquiries@theoldbarn-bnb.co.uk
w theoldbarn-bnb.co.uk

CAENBY CORNER

Ermine Lodge Bed & Breakfast
★★★★ *Bed & Breakfast*
SILVER AWARD
Ermine Lodge, Caenby Corner
LN8 2AR
t (01673) 878152
e info@erminelodgebandb.com
w erminelodgebandb.com

CAMMERINGHAM

Field View B&B ★★★★
Bed & Breakfast
Back Lane, Cammeringham
LN1 2SH
t (01522) 730193
e info@fieldviewbandb.com
w fieldvwbandb.com

Groom's Cottage ★★★★
Farmhouse
Lincoln Road, Cammeringham
LN1 2SH
t (01522) 730788
e jbarker08@btinternet.com
w cammeringham-estate.co.uk

CLAXBY

Swallows Barn ★★★★
Bed & Breakfast
St Mary's Lane, Claxby
LN8 3YX
t (01673) 828626
e swallowsbarn@btinternet.com
w swallowsbarn.co.uk

CLEETHORPES

The 77 ★★★ *Guest Accommodation*
77 Kingsway, Cleethorpes
DN35 0AB
t (01472) 692035
e hotel77@25.fsbusiness.co.uk

Arlana Guest House & Therapy Centre ★★★★ *Guest House*
53 Princes Road, Cleethorpes
DN35 8AW
t (01472) 699689
e info@arlana.co.uk
w arlana.co.uk

Ginnie's Guest House ★★★
Guest House
27 Queen's Parade, Cleethorpes
DN35 0DF
t (01472) 694997
e enquiries@ginnies.co.uk
w ginnies.co.uk

Gladson Guest House ★★★
Guest Accommodation
43 Isaacs Hill, Cleethorpes
DN35 8AD
t (01472) 694858
e enquiries@gladsonguesthouse.co.uk
w gladsonguesthouse.co.uk

Tudor Terrace Guest House
★★★★ *Guest House*
11 Bradford Avenue, Cleethorpes
DN35 0BB
t (01472) 600800
e tudor.terrace@ntlworld.com
w tudorterrace.co.uk

The Vines B&B ★★★
Guest Accommodation
15 Isaacs Hill, Cleethorpes
DN35 8JU
t (01472) 690524
e stevhw3@aol.com

COLSTERWORTH

The Stables ★★★★ *Guest House*
SILVER AWARD
Stainby Road, Colsterworth
NG33 5JB
t (01476) 861057
e thestablesbb@aol.com
w stablesbandb.co.uk

York House B&B ★★★★
Bed & Breakfast SILVER AWARD
Bourne Road, Colsterworth
NG33 5JE
t (01476) 861955
e reservations@yorkhousebnb.co.uk
w yorkhousebnb.co.uk/

CONISHOLME

Wickham House ★★★★
Guest Accommodation
SILVER AWARD
Church Lane, Conisholme
LN11 7LX
t (01507) 358465
e cizekann@hotmail.com
w wickham-house.co.uk

CORRINGHAM

The Beckett Arms ★★★ *Inn*
25 High Street, Corringham
DN21 5QP
t (01427) 838201

CRANWELL

Byards Leap Bed & Breakfast
★★★ *Bed & Breakfast*
Byards Leap Cottage, Cranwell
NG34 8EY
t (01400) 261537
e ml.wood@btopenworld.com
w byardsleapcottage.co.uk

Byards Leap Lodge ★★★★
Guest Accommodation
SILVER AWARD
Byards Leap, Cranwell
NG34 8EY
t (01400) 261375
e byards.leap@virgin.net
w byards-leap-lodge.co.uk

CROFT

The Cottage Restaurant ★★★★
Guest Accommodation
Croft Bank, Wainfleet Road, Skegness
PE24 4RE
t (01234) 123456
w thecottageatcroft.co.uk

CROWLAND

The Abbey ★★★ *Inn*
21 East Street, Crowland
PE6 0EN
t (01733) 210200
e bruce.upson@btopenworld.com

CROXTON

Croxton House ★★★
Guest Accommodation
Croxton House, Croxton
DN39 6YD
t (01652) 688306
e info@croxtonhousebedandbreakfast.co.uk
w croxtonhousebedandbreakfast.com

CUMBERWORTH

Muffins ★★★★ *Bed & Breakfast*
Willloughby Road, Cumberworth
LN13 9LF
t (01507) 490068
e jean.robert@btopenworld.com
w muffins-cumberworth.co.uk/

DEEPING ST NICHOLAS

St Nicholas House ★★★★★
Guest Accommodation
SILVER AWARD
Main Road, Deeping St Nicholas
PE11 3HA
t (01775) 630484
e stnicholashouse@f2s.com
w stnicholashouse.co.uk

DIGBY

Digby Manor Bed & Breakfast
★★★★ *Bed & Breakfast*
SILVER AWARD
The Manor, North Street, Digby
LN4 3LY
t (01526) 322064
e gill@digbymanor.com
w digbymanor.com

Woodend Bed & Breakfast ★★
Bed & Breakfast
Woodend Farm, The Lodge, Digby
LN4 3NG
t (01526) 860347

DONINGTON

Browntoft House ★★★★
Guest Accommodation
SILVER AWARD
Browntoft Lane, Donington
PE11 4TQ
t (01775) 822091
e finchedward@hotmail.com
w browntofthouse.co.uk

EAST BARKWITH

The Grange ★★★★ *Farmhouse*
SILVER AWARD
Torrington Lane, East Barkwith, Market Rasen, Lincoln
LN8 5RY
t (01673) 858670
e sarahstamp@farmersweekly.net
w thegrange-lincolnshire.co.uk

FOLKINGHAM

The Barn ★★★★ *Bed & Breakfast*
SILVER AWARD
Spring Lane, Folkingham, Sleaford
NG34 0SJ
t (01529) 497199
e sjwright@farming.co.uk
w thebarnspringlane.co.uk

GAINSBOROUGH (4 MILES)

The Grange ★★★★ *Farmhouse*
Kexby, Gainsborough
DN21 5PJ
t (01427) 788265

GOULCEBY

Thorngate Bed & Breakfast
★★★★ *Bed & Breakfast*
Watery Lane, Goulceby, Louth
LN11 9UR
t (01507) 343270
e johnhamp@waitrose.com
w thorngatebb.co.uk

GRANTHAM

Belvoir Vale Cottage ★★★★
Bed & Breakfast SILVER AWARD
Woolsthorpe-by-Belvoir, Barrowby Stenwith, Grantham
NG32 2HE
t (01949) 842434
e reservations@belvoirvale-cottage.co.uk
w belvoirvale-cottage.co.uk

The Cedars ★★★★ *Bed & Breakfast*
Low Road, Barrowby, Grantham, Lincolnshire
NG32 1DL
t (01476) 563400
e pbcbennett@mac.com

The Red House ★★★★
Guest House
74 North Parade, Grantham
NG31 8AN
t (01476) 579869
e enquiry@red-house.com
w red-house.com/

GRASBY

Little Hen Bed & Breakfast
★★★★ *Bed & Breakfast*
Brocklesby Hilltop Cottage, Brigg Road, Grasby
DN38 6AQ
t (01652) 629005
e polly@littlehen.co.uk
w littlehen.co.uk

HACKTHORN

Honeyholes ★★ *Farmhouse*
South Farm, Hackthorn
LN2 3PW
t (01673) 861868
e dgreen8234@aol.com

HADDINGTON

Wheelwright's Cottage B&B
★★★★ *Bed & Breakfast*
Wheelwright's Cottage, Haddington
LN5 9EF
t (01522) 788154
e dawn.dunning2@btopenworld.com
w wheelwrightsbnb.co.uk

East Midlands | Lincolnshire

HANTHORPE

aycroft Cottage ★★★★
uest Accommodation
LVER AWARD
Edenham Road, Hanthorpe,
urne
10 0RB
t (01778) 571689
e enquiries@maycroftcottage.co.uk
w maycroftcottage.co.uk

HAXEY

e Loco ★★★★ Inn
-33 Church Street, Haxey
N9 2HY
t (01427) 752879
e info@thelocohaxey.co.uk
w thelocohaxey.co.uk

HOLBEACH

ackle Hill House ★★★★
d & Breakfast SILVER AWARD
ackle Hill Lane, Holbeach
12 8BS
t (01406) 426721
e cacklehillhouse@farming.co.uk

HORNCASTLE

**ank Cottage B & B & Self
atering ★★★★** Guest House
Bank Street, Horncastle
N9 5BW
t (01507) 526666
e horncastleinfo@e-lindsey.gov.uk
w bankcottage-guesthouse.com

ilestone Cottage B&B ★★★
d & Breakfast
North Street, Horncastle
N9 5DX
t (01507) 522238

izpah Villa B&B ★★★★
d & Breakfast
izpah Villa, 9 Low Toynton Road,
orncastle
N9 5LL
t (01507) 523917
e mizpahvilla@googlemail.co.uk
w stayatmizpah.co.uk

ak House ★★★★ Bed & Breakfast
Harrison Close, Horncastle
N9 5ER
t (01507) 522096
e info@garnersuffolksheep.co.uk

KIRKBY-ON-BAIN

ose Cottage ★★★★
uest Accommodation
harf Lane, Kirkby-on-Bain
N10 6YW
t (01526) 354932
e info@rosecottagebandb.net
w rosecottagebandb.net

KIRMINGTON

**ink Bonny Bed & Breakfast
★★** Guest House
imsby Road, Kirmington
N39 6YQ
t (01652) 680610
e info@blinkbonnybedandbrea
kfast.com
w blinkbonnybedandbreakfast.co.uk

KIRTON LINDSEY

**he George Quality
ccommodation
uest Accommodation ★★★★**
High Street, Kirton-in-Lindsey,
ainsborough
N21 4LX
t (01652) 640600
e enquiry@thegeorgekirton.co.uk
w thegeorgekirton.co.uk

LANGWORTH

he Blackbirds ★★★ Guest House
ragby Road, Langworth
N3 5DH
t (01522) 754404
e bbenterprise@fsmail.net
w theblackbirds.co.uk

LINCOLN

202 Guesthouse ★★★★
Guest Accommodation
202 West Parade, Lincoln
LN2 1RN
t (01522) 878642
e enquiries@202guesthouse.co.uk
w 202guesthouse.co.uk

Aaron Whisby Guest House ★★★
Guest House
262 West Parade, Lincoln
LN1 1LY
t (01522) 526930
e aaron-whisby@hotmail.co.uk
w aaron-whisby.webeden.co.uk

Brant House ★★★★★
Bed & Breakfast SILVER AWARD
Stragglethorpe, Lincoln
LN5 0QZ
t (01400) 272626
e branthouse@aol.com
w branthouse.co.uk

**Canal View Bed & Breakfast
★★★★** Bed & Breakfast
Lincoln Road, Saxilby, Lincoln
LN1 2NF
t (01522) 704475
e stay@canal-view.co.uk
w canal-view.co.uk

**Creston Villa Guest House
★★★★★** Guest House
GOLD AWARD
27 St Catherines, Lincoln
LN5 8LW
t (01522) 872511
e info@crestonvilla.co.uk
w crestonvilla.co.uk

Crossfell Bed & Breakfast ★★★★
Bed & Breakfast SILVER AWARD
16 Worcester Close, Doddington
Park, Lincoln
LN6 3LW
t (01522) 683538
e crossfellbandb@yahoo.co.uk

Damon's Motel ★★★★
Guest Accommodation
997 Doddington Road, Lincoln
LN6 3SE
t (01522) 887733
e motel@damons.co.uk
w damons.co.uk

Goodlane B&B ★★★
Guest Accommodation
31 Good Lane, Lincoln
LN1 3EH
t (01522) 542994
e sue@goodlane.co.uk
w goodlane.co.uk

Hamiltons ★★★ Guest House
2 Hamilton Road, Lincoln
LN5 8ED
t (01522) 528243
e enquiries@hamiltonhotel.co.uk
w hamiltonhotel.co.uk

Ivory Guest House ★★★★
Guest Accommodation
258 West Parade, Lincoln
LN1 1LY
t (01522) 887868
e ivoryguesthouse@hotmail.co.uk
w ivoryguesthouse.co.uk

Old Rectory Guest House ★★★
Guest House
19 Newport, Lincoln
LN1 3DQ
t (01522) 514774
w theoldrectorylincoln.co.uk

**The Old Tannery at Diamond
House ★★★★** Bed & Breakfast
Ferry Road, Fiskerton, Lincoln
LN3 4HU
t (01522) 595356
e oldtannerydiamondhouse@btint
ernet.com

**The Old Vicarage Bed & Breakfast
★★★★** Guest Accommodation
SILVER AWARD
East Street, Nettleham
LN2 2SL
t (01522) 750819
e susan@oldvic.net
w oldvic.net

**Robindale Bed & Breakfast
★★★★** Bed & Breakfast
Back Lane, Brattleby, Lincoln
LN1 2SQ
t (01522) 730712
w robindale.co.uk

**Rose Cottage Bed & Breakfast
★★★★** Bed & Breakfast
Rose Cottage, Main Street,
Hackthorn, Lincoln
LN2 3PF
t (01673) 861821
e annie_wardy@yahoo.co.uk
w rosecottagehackthorn.co.uk

Savill Guest House ★★★★
Guest Accommodation
203 Yarborough Road, Lincoln
LN1 3NQ
t (01522) 523261
e info@savillguesthouse.co.uk
w savillguesthouse.co.uk

**Welbeck Cottage Bed and
Breakfast ★★★★** Bed & Breakfast
19 Meadow Lane, South Hykeham,
Lincoln
LN6 9PF
t (01522) 692669
e maggied@hotmail.co.uk
w welbeckcottagelincoln.co.uk

LOUTH

**Nutty Cottage Guest House
★★★★** Bed & Breakfast
Legbourne Road, Legbourne, Louth
LN11 8LQ
t (01507) 601766
e janeandmike23@tiscali.co.uk
w nuttycottage.co.uk

**The Old Rectory at Stewton
★★★★** Bed & Breakfast
SILVER AWARD
Stewton, Louth, Lincolnshire
LN11 8SF
t (01507) 328063
e ajp100@postmaster.co.uk
w louthbedandbreakfast.co.uk

**The Paddock at Scamblesby
★★★★** Bed & Breakfast
SILVER AWARD
Old Main Road, Scamblesby, Louth
LN11 9XG
t 07787 998906
e steve@thepaddockatscamblesby.
co.uk
w thepaddockatscamblesby.co.uk

**The Royal Oak Inn - The Splash
★★★★** Inn
Watery Lane, Little Cawthorpe,
Louth
LN11 8LZ
t (01507) 600750
e info@royaloaksplash.co.uk
w royaloaksplash.co.uk

**The Travellers Bed & Breakfast
★★★★** Guest Accommodation
The Travellers Hotel, Upgate, Louth
LN11 9HG
t (01507) 602765
e cj.sowter@btinternet.com
w the-travellers.we.bs/

Woody's Top Youth Hostel ★★★
Hostel
Woody's Top, Ruckland, Louth
LN11 8RQ
t 0870 770 8868
e woodystop@yha.org.uk
w yha.org.uk

MABLETHORPE

Angel's Retreat ★★★★
Guest Accommodation
8 The Strand, Mablethorpe
LN12 1BQ
t (01507) 478474
e angelretrat@googlemail.com

The Cannon Guest House ★★★
Guest House
7 Waterloo Road, Mablethorpe
LN12 1JR
t (01507) 473148
e info@cannon-guesthouse.co.uk
w cannon-guesthouse.co.uk

Colours Guest House ★★★★
Guest House
Queens Park Close, Mablethorpe
LN12 2AS
t (01507) 473427
e info@coloursguesthouse.co.uk
w coloursguesthouse.co.uk

The Cross Guest House ★★★★
Guest Accommodation
Alford Road, Mablethorpe
LN12 1PX
t (01507) 477708
e reception@thecrossguesthouse.
co.uk
w thecrossguesthouse.co.uk

**Grange Farmhouse Bed &
Breakfast ★★★** Farmhouse
Grange Farm, Maltby le Marsh,
Mablethorpe
LN13 0JP
t (01507) 450267
e anngraves@btinternet.com
w grange-farmhouse.co.uk

Leicester Guest House ★★★
Guest Accommodation
61 Victoria Road, Mablethorpe
LN12 2AF
t (01507) 477741
e karenn222@aol.com
w leicesterguesthouse.co.uk

Myrtle Lodge ★★★ Guest House
60 Victoria Road, Mablethorpe
LN12 2AJ
t (01507) 472228
e info@myrtlelodge.co.uk
w myrtlelodge.co.uk

**The Ramblers Guest House
★★★★** Guest House
Sutton Road, Trusthorpe,
Mablethorpe
LN12 2PY
t (01507) 441171
e theramblers@hotmail.co.uk
w theramblers.info

MARKET RASEN

Beechwood Guest House ★★★★
Guest House
54 Willingham Road, Market Rasen
LN8 3DX
t (01673) 844043
e beechwoodgh@aol.com
w beechwoodguesthouse.co.uk

Glebe Farm ★★★★ Farmhouse
SILVER AWARD
Church Lane, Benniworth, Market
Rasen
LN8 6JP
t (01507) 313231
e info@glebe-farm.com
w glebe-farm.com

Hoe Hill House ★★★★
Bed & Breakfast SILVER AWARD
Swinhope, Market Rasen
LN8 6HX
t (01472) 399366
e hoehill@hotmail.co.uk
w hoehill.co.uk

Kingthorpe Manor Farm ★★★★
Bed & Breakfast
Kingthorpe, Market Rasen
LN8 5JF
t (01673) 857270
e patrickbritton@mac.com
w kingthorpemanorfarm.com

433

East Midlands | Lincolnshire

Redhurst B&B ★★★★
Bed & Breakfast
Redhurst, Holton cum Beckering, Market Rasen
LN8 5NG
t (01673) 857927
e vivienne@redhurstbandb.com
w redhurstbandb.co.uk

Waveney Cottage Bed & Breakfast ★★★★ *Bed & Breakfast*
Willingham Road, Market Rasen
LN8 3DN
t (01673) 843236
e vacancies@waveneycottage.co.uk
w waveneycottage.co.uk

MARSHCHAPEL

Duckthorpe Grange B&B ★★★★
Bed & Breakfast
Duckthorpe Grange, West End Lane, Marshchapel
DN36 5TN
t (01472) 388367
e duckthorpegrange@live.com
w duckthorpegrangebandb.co.uk

MARTIN

Stables Studio ★★★★
Guest Accommodation
94 High Street, Martin
LN4 3QT
t (01526) 378528
e stablesstudio@homecall.co.uk
w stablesstudio.co.uk

MUMBY

Brambles ★★★★
Guest Accommodation
Occupation Lane, Mumby, Alford
LN13 9JU
t (01507) 490174
e suescrimshaw@btinternet.com

NETTLETON

Nettleton Lodge Inn ★★★
Guest Accommodation - Room Only
off Moortown Road (B1205), Nettleton
LN7 6HX
t (01472) 851829
e pubinthewood@btinternet.com
w nettletonlodgeinn.co.uk

NEWARK

The Old Tavern ★★★★
Bed & Breakfast SILVER AWARD
Bakers Lane, Westborough, Newark
NG23 5HL
t (01400) 281071
e enquiries@theoldtavern.co.uk
w theoldtavern.co.uk

NEW WALTHAM

Peaks Top Farm ★★★★
Farmhouse
Hewitts Avenue, New Waltham, Grimsby
DN36 4RS
t (01472) 812941
e lmclayton@tinyworld.co.uk

NORTH HYKEHAM

The Gables Guest House ★★★★
Guest House SILVER AWARD
546 Newark Road, North Hykeham, Lincoln
LN6 9NG
t (01522) 829102
e info@gablesguesthouse.com
w gablesguesthouse.com

NORTH KYME

Old Coach House Motel ★★★★
Guest Accommodation
1 Church Lane, North Kyme
LN4 4DJ
t (01526) 861465
e barbara@motel-plus.co.uk
w motel-plus.co.uk

NORTHORPE

Grayingham Lodge ★★★★★
Bed & Breakfast SILVER AWARD
Gainsborough Road, Northorpe, Gainsborough, Lincs
DN21 4AN
t (01652) 648544
e janesummers@btinternet.com
w grayinghamlodge.co.uk

NORTH OWERSBY

Little Owls ★★★★ *Farmhouse*
North End Farm, Thornton Road, North Owersby, Market Rasen
LN8 3PP
t (01673) 828116
e askus@littleowls.com
w littleowls.com

NORTON DISNEY

Brills Farm ★★★★ *Farmhouse*
SILVER AWARD
Brills Hill, Norton Disney
LN6 9JN
t (01636) 892311
e admin@brillsfarm-bedandbreakfast.co.uk
w brillsfarm-bedandbreakfast.co.uk

Norton Lodge Hotel & Conference Centre ★★★★
Guest Accommodation
Old Harbour Farm, Newark Road, Norton Disney
LN6 9JR
t (01522) 789111
e norton.lodge@virgin.net
w nortonlodge.co.uk

OASBY

The Pinomar ★★★★
Bed & Breakfast
Mill Lane, Oasby
NG32 3ND
t (01529) 455400
e joturner@pinomar.fsnet.co.uk

OSBOURNBY

Barn Gallery ★★★★
Bed & Breakfast SILVER AWARD
18 West Street, Osbournby
NG34 0DS
t (01529) 455631
e enquiries@barngallery.co.uk
w barngallery.co.uk

RUSKINGTON

Sunnyside Farm Bed & Breakfast ★★★ *Farmhouse*
Leasingham Lane, Ruskington
NG34 9AH
t (01526) 833010
e sunnyside_farm@btinternet.com
w sunnysidefarm.co.uk

SANDILANDS

Sunnycroft Bed & Breakfast ★★★★ *Bed & Breakfast*
Sea Lane, Sandilands, Sutton-on-Sea
LN12 2RA
t 07890 892816
e keithmeagan@aol.com
w sunnycroft.biz

SAXILBY

Orchard Cottage ★★★★
Bed & Breakfast SILVER AWARD
3 Orchard Lane,, Saxilby
LN1 2HT
t (01522) 703192
e margaretallen@orchardcottage.org.uk
w smoothhound.co.uk/hotels/orchardcot.html

SCOTTER

Ivy Lodge ★★★★
Guest Accommodation
4 Messingham Road, Scotter
DN21 3UQ
t (01724) 763723
e bandb@ivylodgehotel.co.uk
w ivylodgehotel.co.uk

SCUNTHORPE

Cosgrove Guest House ★★★
Guest House
33-35 Wells Street, Scunthorpe
DN15 6HL
t (01724) 279405
e b.pridgeon@btconnect.com
w cosgrovehotel.co.uk

Kirks Korner Motel ★★
Guest Accommodation
12 Scotter Road, Scunthorpe
DN15 8DR
t (01724) 855344

The Normanby ★★★ *Guest House*
9-11 Normanby Road, Scunthorpe
DN15 6NU
t (01724) 289982
e jnormanby@ntlworld.com
w normanbyhotel.co.uk/

SILK WILLOUGHBY

Willoughby Lodge Guest House ★★★★ *Bed & Breakfast*
12 London Road, Silk Willoughby
NG34 8PB
t (01529) 304273
e info@willoughbylodge.co.uk
w willoughbylodge.co.uk

SKEGNESS

Balmoral ★★★ *Guest House*
28 South Parade, Skegness
PE25 3HW
t (01754) 764222
e p1uhs@hotmail.com
w balmoralhotel.net

Beachlands Quality Guest Accommodation ★★★
Guest Accommodation
58 Scarborough Avenue, Skegness
PE25 2TB
t (01754) 764106
e beachlandshotel@aol.com

Belle View ★★★ *Guest House*
12 South Parade, Skegness
PE25 3HW
t (01754) 765274
e debra.rear@virgin.net
w belleview-hotel.co.uk

Belmont Guest House ★★
Guest House
30 Grosvenor Road, Skegness
PE25 2DB
t (01754) 765439
e info@belmont-guesthouse.co.uk
w belmont-guesthouse.co.uk

The Carmelle ★★★ *Guest House*
16 Castleton Boulevard, Skegness
PE25 2TY
t (01754) 764587
e mad-mom@hotmail.co.uk
w carmelle.co.uk

Caxton House ★★★ *Guest House*
Caxton House, Trafalgar Avenue, Skegness
PE25 3EU
t (01754) 764328
e info@caxton-house.com
w caxton-house.com

The Chalfonts ★★★
Guest Accommodation
41 Beresford Avenue, Skegness
PE25 3JF
t (01754) 766374
e info@chalfontshotel.com
w chalfontshotel.com

Chatsworth ★★★
Guest Accommodation
15/16 North Parade, Skegness
PE25 2UB
t (01754) 764177
e info@chatsworthskegness.co.uk
w chatsworthskegness.co.uk

Clarence House ★★★★
Guest House
32 South Parade, Skegness
PE25 3HW
t (01754) 765588
e colin-rita@lineone.net
w clarence-house-hotel.co.uk

The Craigside ★★★
Guest Accommodation
26 Scarborough Avenue, Skegness
PE25 2SY
t (01754) 763307
e info@craigside-hotel.co.uk
w craigside-hotel.co.uk

The Eastleigh ★★★★ *Guest House*
60 Scarborough Avenue, Skegness
PE25 2TB
t (01754) 764605
e info@eastleigh-skegness.co.uk
w eastleigh-skegness.co.uk

Englemere Guest House ★★★
Guest House
52 Algitha Road, Skegness
PE25 2AJ
t (01754) 763036
e englemere1@yahoo.co.uk
w englemere-skegness.co.uk

The Fairfax ★★★★
Guest Accommodation
36 Drummond road, Skegness
PE25 3EB
t (01754) 763690
w fairfax-hotel.com

The Fountaindale Skegness ★★★★ *Guest Accommodation*
SILVER AWARD
69 Sandbeck Avenue, Skegness
PE25 3JS
t (01754) 762731
e info@fountaindale-hotel.co.uk
w fountaindale-hotel.co.uk

The Grafton ★★★
Guest Accommodation
15 Seaview Road, Skegness
PE25 1BW
t (01754) 766158
e thegraftonhotelskegness@fsmail.net
w grafton-skegness.co.uk

Hoylake Guest House ★★★
Guest House
23 Hoylake Drive, Skegness
PE25 1AB
t (01754) 765695
e chazsmith@supanet.com
w hoylakeguesthouse.co.uk

Ivernia Hotel ★★★
Guest Accommodation
7 Saxby Avenue, Skegness
PE25 3JZ
t (01754) 764107
w ivernia.net

The Karema ★★★★
Guest Accommodation
17 Sunningdale Drive, Skegness
PE25 1BB
t (01754) 764440
e info@karema.co.uk
w karema.co.uk

The Kildare ★★★★
Guest Accommodation
80 Sandbeck Avenue, Skegness
PE25 3JS
t (01754) 762935
e info@kildare-hotel.co.uk
w kildare-hotel.co.uk

Knighton Lodge ★★★ *Guest House*
9 Trafalgar Avenue, Skegness
PE25 3EY
t (01754) 764354
e info@knighton-lodge.co.uk
w knighton-lodge.co.uk

Linroy Guesthouse ★★★
Guest House
26 Lumley Avenue, Skegness
PE25 2AT
t (01754) 763924
e info@linroy.co.uk
w linroy.co.uk

East Midlands | Lincolnshire

e Lyndsay Guest House ★★★★
st House
Scarborough Avenue, Skegness
25 2SZ
t (01754) 765565
e lindagjones@btinternet.com
w lyndsayguesthouse.co.uk

e Mayfair ★★★
est Accommodation
Saxby Avenue, Skegness
25 3JZ
t (01754) 764687
e info@mayfair-skegness.co.uk
w mayfair-skegness.co.uk

ckleton Guest House ★★★
est House
North Parade Extension, Skegness
25 1BX
t (01754) 763862
e mickleton-guesthouse.co.uk

e Monsell ★★★ *Guest House*
irbeck Avenue, Skegness
25 3JY
t (01754) 898374
e enquiries@monsell-hotel.co.uk
w monsell-hotel.co.uk

e Northdale ★★★
est Accommodation
Firbeck Avenue, Skegness
25 3JY
t (01754) 610554
e info@northdale-hotel.co.uk
w northdale-hotel.co.uk

rth Parade Seafront
commodation ★★★
est Accommodation
North Parade, Skegness
25 2UB
t (01754) 762309
e juleebunce@aol.com
w north-parade-hotel.co.uk

m Court ★★★
est Accommodation
South Parade, Skegness
25 3HP
t (01754) 767711
e palmcourtskegness@yahoo.com
w palmcourtskegness.co.uk

lmar Guest House ★★★
est House
Sunningdale Drive, Skegness
25 1AZ
t (01754) 762781
e info@skegnessguesthouses.co.uk
w skegnessguesthouses.co.uk

e Queen's ★★★★
est Accommodation
Scarborough Avenue, Skegness
25 2TD
t (01754) 762073
e northsouthent@aol.com
w thequeenshotelskegness.co.uk

e Quorn ★★★
est Accommodation
North Parade, Skegness
25 2UB
t (01754) 763508
e reservations@quornhotel.net
w quornhotel.net

osevelt Lodge ★★★
est Accommodation
Drummond Road, Skegness
25 3EQ
t (01754) 766548

e Rufford ★★★
est Accommodation
fford Hotel, 5 Saxby Avenue,
gness
25 3JZ
t (01754) 763428
e steve@srain.wanadoo.co.uk
w rufford-skegness.co.uk

e Sandgate ★★★ *Guest House*
Drummond Road, Skegness
25 3EB
t (01754) 762667
e info@sandgate-hotel.co.uk
w sandgate-hotel.co.uk

Sherwood Lodge ★★★
Guest House
100 Drummond Road, Skegness
PE25 3EH
t (01754) 762548
e info@sherwood-skegness.co.uk
w sherwood-skegness.co.uk

The Singlecote ★★★ *Guest House*
34 Drummond Road, Skegness
PE25 3EB
t (01754) 764698
e mark87evans@yahoo.co.uk
w singlecotehotel.com

Southwold ★★★ *Guest House*
16 Sea View Road, Skegness
PE25 1BW
t (01754) 611335
e info@southwold-hotel.co.uk
w southwold-hotel.co.uk

Stoneleigh ★★★★ *Guest House*
SILVER AWARD
67 Sandbeck Avenue, Skegness
PE25 3JS
t (01754) 769138
e janrog&hotelinskegness.co.uk
w stoneleigh-hotel.com

The Sunningdale ★★★
Guest Accommodation
19 Seaview Road, Skegness
PE25 1BW
t (01754) 766220
e info@sunningdalehotel.net
w sunningdalehotel.net

Thisledome Guest House ★★★
Guest House
5 Glentworth Crescent, Skegness
PE25 2TG
t (01754) 612212
e info@thisledome.com
w thisledome.com

Tudor Lodge Guest House ★★★
Guest House
61-63 Drummond Road, Skegness
PE25 3EQ
t (01754) 766487
e info@thetudorlodge.co.uk
w thetudorlodge.co.uk

Westdene ★★★ *Guest House*
1 Trafalgar Avenue, Skegness
PE25 3EU
t (01754) 765168
e reservations@westdenehotel.co.
uk
w westdenehotel.co.uk

The White Lodge ★★★★
Guest Accommodation
129 Drummond Road, Skegness
PE25 3DW
t (01754) 764120
e info@white-lodge.co.uk
w white-lodge.co.uk

Woodthorpe Guest House ★★★
Guest House
64 South Parade, Skegness,
Lincolnshire
PE25 3HP
t 01754 763452
e info@woodthorpeskegness.co.uk
w woodthorpeskegness.co.uk

SOUTH COCKERINGTON

West View Bed & Breakfast
★★★★ *Bed & Breakfast*
SILVER AWARD
West View, South View Lane, South
Cockerington, Louth
LN11 7ED
t (01507) 327209
e enquiries@west-view.co.uk
w west-view.co.uk

SOUTH HYKEHAM

Hall Farm House ★★★★
Farmhouse
Meadow Lane, South Hykeham
LN6 9PF
t (01522) 686432
e info@hallfarmhouselincoln.co.uk
w hallfarmhouselincoln.co.uk

SOUTH WILLINGHAM

The Old Rectory ★★★★
Bed & Breakfast
The Old Rectory, South Willingham
LN8 6NG
t (01507) 313584
e paul&maureen@the-old-rectory.
info
w uniquevenues.org.uk

SOUTH WITHAM

Blue Cow Inn & Brewery ★★★ *Inn*
29 High St, South Witham
NG33 5QB
t (01572) 768432
e richard@thirlwell.fslife.co.uk
w bluecowinn.co.uk

SPALDING

The Beeches Bed & Breakfast
★★★★ *Guest Accommodation*
The Beeches, Austendyke Road,
Weston Hills, Spalding
PE12 6BZ
t (01406) 370345
e marierawlings@compuserve.com
w beechesspalding.co.uk

White Lodge Guest House
★★★★★ *Guest House*
SILVER AWARD
10 Helmergate, Spalding
PE11 2DR
t (01775) 719002
e whitelodge@lincmail.co.uk
w whitelodge-guesthouse.com

SPANBY

Mareham House B&B ★★★★
Bed & Breakfast
Mareham House, Mareham Lane,
Spanby
NG34 0AS
t (01529) 305266
e dean.reddish@btinternet.com
w marehamhouse.com

SPILSBY

Red Lion Inn ★★★★ *Inn*
Skegness Road, Partney, Spilsby
PE23 4PG
t (01790) 752271
e chrishurrell@btconnect.com
w redlioninnpartney.co.uk

Spye House ★★★★
Bed & Breakfast **SILVER AWARD**
Main Road, Spilsby
PE23 4BE
t (01790) 752102
e spye.house@btinternet.com
w spilsby.info

STAMFORD

5 Rock Terrace ★★★★
Bed & Breakfast
Scotgate, Stamford
PE9 2YJ
t (01780) 755475
e mandtaverdieck@btinternet.com

30 Casewick Lane ★★★
Bed & Breakfast
Uffington, Stamford
PE9 4SX
t (01780) 757392
e denisea@talktalk.net

Elm Guest House B&B ★★★★
Guest Accommodation
New Cross Road, Stamford
PE9 1AJ
t (01780) 764210
e info@elmguesthouse.co.uk
w elmguesthouse.co.uk

Gwynne House ★★★
Bed & Breakfast
Kings Road, Stamford
PE9 1HD
t (01780) 762210
e john@johng.demon.co.uk
w gwynnehouse.co.uk

Park Farm ★★★★ *Bed & Breakfast*
SILVER AWARD
Park Farm, Careby, Stamford
PE9 4EA
t (01780) 410515
e enquiries@parkfarmcareby.co.uk
w parkfarmcareby.co.uk

Parkgate House B&B ★★★
Bed & Breakfast
Water Street, Stamford
PE9 2NJ
t (01780) 751446
e info@parkgatehouseandb.co.uk
w parkgatehouseandb.co.uk

Rock Lodge ★★★★★
Guest Accommodation
GOLD AWARD
1 Empingham Road, Stamford
PE9 2RH
t (01780) 481758
e philipsagar@innpro.co.uk
w rock-lodge.co.uk

Stamford Lodge Guest House
★★★★ *Guest House*
66 Scotgate, Stamford
PE9 2YB
t (01780) 482932
e info@stamfordlodge.co.uk
w stamfordlodge.co.uk

The Willoughby Arms ★★★★ *Inn*
Station Road, Little Bytham,
Stamford
NG33 4RA
t (01780) 410276
e lkulme@tiscali.co.uk
w willoughbyarms.co.uk

STOW

Belle Vue Farm ★★★★
Bed & Breakfast
21 Church Road, Stow
LN1 2DE
t (01427) 788981
e patriciaclaxton@btinternet.com

SUTTON-ON-SEA

Bacchus ★★★★ *Inn*
17 High Street, Sutton-on-Sea
LN12 2EY
t (01507) 441204
e enquiries@bacchushotel.co.uk
w bacchushotel.co.uk

SWINESHEAD

The Wheatsheaf ★★★ *Inn*
Market Place, Swineshead, Boston,
Lincolnshire
PE20 3LJ
t 01205 820349
e info@smoke-screen.co.uk
w wheatsheafhotel.co.uk

TATTERSHALL

Castle Lodge Bed & Breakfast
★★★★ *Bed & Breakfast*
11 Sleaford Road, Tattershall
LN4 4LR
t (01526) 343293
e peter.hopkin@virgin.net
w castlelodge.net

TETFORD

Tetford Country Cottages ★★★
Bed & Breakfast
Manor Farm, East Road, Tetford
LN9 6QQ
t (01507) 533276
e contact@tetfordcountrycottages.
co.uk
w tetfordcountrycottages.co.uk

THORNTON CURTIS

Pine Lodge Bed & Breakfast
★★★★ *Bed & Breakfast*
SILVER AWARD
Laurel Lane, Thornton Curtis
DN39 6XJ
t 07880 601476

East Midlands | Lincolnshire/Northamptonshire

Thornton Hunt Inn ★★★★ *Inn*
17 Main Street, Thornton Curtis,
Near Ulceby, North Lincolnshire
DN39 6XW
t (01469) 531252
e thorntonhuntinn@thorntoncurtis.net
w thornton-inn.co.uk

THURLBY

6 The Pingles ★★★★
Guest Accommodation
SILVER AWARD
6 The Pingles, Thurlby
PE10 0EX
t (01778) 394517

Thurlby YHA ★★★ *Hostel*
16 High Street, Thurlby, Bourne
PE10 0EE
t (01778) 425588
e thurlby@yha.org.uk

ULCEBY

Gillingham Court ★★★★
Bed & Breakfast
Spruce Lane, Ulceby
DN39 6UL
t (01469) 588427
e gillinghamrest@supanet.com
w gillinghamcourt.co.uk

WADDINGTON

Carnforth Guest House ★★★★
Guest House
Carnforth, Tinkers Lane, Waddington
LN5 9RU
t (01522) 722492
e christinecroxton@hotmail.com
w carnforthguesthouse.co.uk

WAINFLEET

Willow Farm ★★★ *Farmhouse*
Thorpe Fendykes, Wainfleet,
Skegness, Lincolnshire
PE24 4QH
t (01754) 830316
e willowfarmhols@aol.com
w willowfarmholidays.co.uk

WOODHALL SPA

Chaplin House ★★★★
Guest Accommodation
SILVER AWARD
92 High Street, Martin, Lincolnshire
LN4 3QT
t (01526) 378795
e info@chaplin-house.co.uk
w chaplin-house.co.uk

Kirkstead Old Mill Cottage
★★★★ *Guest Accommodation*
SILVER AWARD
Tattershall Road, Woodhall Spa,
Lincolnshire
LN10 6UQ
t (01526) 35 36 37 / 07970 04 04 01
e barbara@woodhallspa.com
w woodhallspa.com

The Limes ★★★★ *Bed & Breakfast*
The Limes, Tattershall Road,
Woodhall Spa
LN10 6TW
t (01526) 352219

Newlands Guest House ★★★★
Bed & Breakfast
56 Woodland Drive, Woodhall Spa
LN10 6YG
t (01526) 352881
e chrisramsay@aol.com

Oglee Guest House ★★★★
Guest Accommodation
16 Stanhope Avenue, Woodhall Spa
LN10 6SP
t (01526) 353512
e ogleeguesthouse@gmail.com

Pitchaway ★★★ *Guest House*
The Broadway, Woodhall Spa
LN10 6SQ
t (01526) 352969
e info@pitchaway.co.uk
w pitchaway.co.uk

The Vale ★★★ *Bed & Breakfast*
50 Tor-O-Moor Road, Woodhall Spa
LN10 6SB
t (01526) 353022
e margot.mills@hotmail.co.uk

Village Limits Country Pub, Restaurant & Motel ★★★★
Guest Accommodation
Stixwould Road, Woodhall Spa
LN10 6UJ
t (01526) 353312
e info@villagelimits.co.uk
w villagelimits.co.uk

WRAWBY

Mowden House ★★★★
Guest Accommodation
Barton Road, Wrawby
DN20 8SQ
t (01652) 652145
e dr@prabhakaran.fsnet.co.uk

Northamptonshire

ALDERTON

Magnolia ★★★★ *Bed & Breakfast*
Magnolia, Church Lane, Alderton
NN12 7LP
t (01327) 811479
e bandb@magnolia.me.uk
w magnolia.me.uk

ALDWINCLE

Pear Tree Farm ★★★★ *Farmhouse*
Aldwincle, Aldwincle
NN14 3EL
t (01832) 720614
e beverley@peartreefarm.net
w peartreefarm.net

BADBY

Meadows Farm ★★★★ *Farmhouse*
Meadows Farm, Newnham Lane,
Badby
NN11 3AA
t (01327) 703302

BANBURY, 8 MILES

B&B at Stone Court ★★★★
Bed & Breakfast
Helmdon Road, Sulgrave, Banbury
OX17 2SQ
t 07771524566 or 01295 760818
e ronnie@ronnielg.co.uk
w stonecourtsulgrave.co.uk

BRACKLEY

Floral Hall ★★★ *Bed & Breakfast*
50 Valley Road, Brackley
NN13 7DQ
t (01280) 702950

Hill Farm ★★★★ *Farmhouse*
Halse, Brackley
NN13 6DY
t (01280) 703300
e j.g.robinson@btconnect.com
w hillfarmbrackley.co.uk

The Old Surgery ★★★★
Bed & Breakfast **SILVER AWARD**
Pebble Lane, Brackley
NN13 7DA
t (01280) 705090
w theoldsurgerybedandbreakfast.co.uk

Two Hoots ★★★★ *Bed & Breakfast*
SILVER AWARD
The Green, Hinton-in-the-Hedges,
Brackley
NN13 5NG
t (01280) 701220
e louise.withers@talktalk.net
w twohootsbrackley.co.uk

Yew Tree House ★★★★
Bed & Breakfast
The Green, Hinton-in-the-Hedges,
Brackley
NN13 5NG
t (01280) 700547
e pamelasprason@hotmail.com
w yewtreehousebedandbreakfast.co.uk

BRAUNSTON

The Old Workshop ★★★★
Bed & Breakfast
The Old Workshop, The Wharf,
Braunston
NN11 7JQ
t (01788) 891421
e info@the-old-workshop.com
w the-old-workshop.com

BRIXWORTH

Coach & Horses Brixworth ★★★★
Inn
Harborough Road, Brixworth
NN6 9BX
t (01604) 880329
e info@coachandhorsesbrixworth.co.uk
w coachandhorsesbrixworth.co.uk

Lake House Bed & Breakfast
★★★★ *Bed & Breakfast*
SILVER AWARD
Brixworth Hall Park, Brixworth
NN6 9DE
t (01604) 880280
e rosemarytuckley@talktalk.net
w brixworthlakehouse.com

BYFIELD

Glebe Farm Bed & Breakfast
★★★ *Farmhouse*
Glebe Farm Church Street, Byfield,
Daventry
NN11 6XN
t (01327) 260512

CALDECOTE

Home Farm ★★★★
Guest Accommodation
Caldecote, Towcester
NN12 8AG
t (01327) 352651
e gisela@giselasbedandbreakfast.com
w giselasbedandbreakfast.com

CATESBY

Long Furlong Farm ★★★
Farmhouse
Catesby, Daventry
NN11 6LW
t (01327) 264770
e haighfamily@waitrose.com
w catesby.net

CHELVESTON

Sunburrow ★★★★ *Bed & Breakfast*
15 Hill Side, Chelveston
NN9 6AQ
t (01933) 624383
e baxter941@btinternet.com
w sunburrow.moonfruit.com

CHIPPING WARDEN

Cool Contours ★★★★
Guest Accommodation - Room Only
Warden Hill, Chipping Warden,
Banbury
OX17 1AJ
t (01295) 660755
e heather@coolcontours.co.uk
w coolcontours.co.uk

CORBY

Home Farm Barn ★★★
Guest Accommodation - Room Only
Home Farm House, Main Street,
Sudborough, Kettering
NN14 3BX
t (01832) 730488
e bandbhomefarmsud@aol.com
w homefarmsudborough.co.uk

Manor Farm Guest House ★★★★
Guest Accommodation
Station Road, Rushton, Kettering
NN14 1RL
t (01536) 710305
w rushtonmanorfarm.com

COSGROVE

Elm Tree Farm B&B ★★★
Guest Accommodation
Thrupp Wharf, Cosgrove
MK19 7BE
t (01908) 542437
e info@elmtreefarmbandb.co.uk
w elmtreefarmbandb.co.uk

CREATON

Highgate House ★★★★
Guest Accommodation
Grooms Lane, Creaton
NN6 8NN
t (01604) 731999
e highgate@sundialgroup.com
w sundialgroup.com/highgatehouse

DAVENTRY

Drayton Lodge ★★★★ *Farmhouse*
Staverton Road, Daventry
NN11 4NL
t (01327) 702449
e ann.spicer@farming.co.uk
w draytonlodge.com

Threeways House ★★★★
Bed & Breakfast
Threeways House, Everdon,
Daventry, Northamptonshire
NN11 3BL
t (01327) 361631, 07774 428242
e threewayshouse@googlemail.com
w threewayshouse.com

EAST HADDON

East Haddon Lodge ★★★
Farmhouse
Main Street, East Haddon,
Northampton
NN6 8BU
t (01604) 770240

EVERDON

Everdon Activity Centre ★★
Group Hostel
The Old School, Everdon, Daventry
NN11 3BL
t (01327) 361384
w northamptonshire.gov.uk/everdononexperience

EYDON

Crockwell Farm ★★★★ *Farmhouse*
SILVER AWARD
Crockwell Farm, Eydon, Daventry
NN11 3QA
t (01327) 361358
e info@crockwellfarm.co.uk
w crockwellfarm.co.uk

FOTHERINGHAY

Castle Farm Guesthouse ★★★★
Guest House
Castle Farm Guest House,
Fotheringhay
PE8 5HZ
t (01832) 226200
e castle_farm_bnb@hotmail.com

GUILSBOROUGH

Coton Lodge ★★★★★
Bed & Breakfast **SILVER AWARD**
West Haddon Road, Guilsborough
NN6 8QE
t (01604) 740215
e jo@cotonlodge.co.uk
w cotonlodge.co.uk

HARRINGTON

Church Farm Lodge ★★★★
Guest Accommodation
Church Farm Lodge, Harrington
NN6 9NU
t (01536) 713320
e info@churchfarmlodge.com
w churchfarmlodge.com

HELMDON

Astwell Mill ★★★★ *Farmhouse*
Astwell, Helmdon
NN13 5QU
t (01295) 760507
w astwellmill.co.uk

East Midlands | Northamptonshire/Nottinghamshire

KETTERING

ry Farm ★★★ *Farmhouse*
nford St Andrew, Kettering
14 4AQ
(01536) 330273

KING'S CLIFFE

g John Hunting Lodge/19
st St ★★★★ *Bed & Breakfast*
West Street, King's Cliffe
6XB
(01780) 470365
kjhl_dixon@hotmail.com
kingjohnhuntinglodge.co.uk

KISLINGBURY

e Nook ★★ *Farmhouse*
he Green, Northampton
7 4AS
(01604) 830326

LITTLE BRINGTON

e Saracens Head ★★★★ *Inn*
n Street, Little Brington,
thampton
7 4HS
(01604) 770640
info@yeoldesaracenshead.co.uk
yeoldesaracenshead.co.uk

LONG BUCKBY

rcott Mill ★★★★ *Farmhouse*
rcott Mill, Murcott, Long Buckby
5 7QR
(01327) 842086
carrie.murcottmill@virgin.net
murcottmill.com

MIDDLETON CHENEY

e House Bed & Breakfast
★★ *Bed & Breakfast*
e House, 65 Main Road,
ddleton Cheney, Banbury
7 2LU
(01295) 711723
info@gatehousemc.com
gatehousemc.com

MORETON PINKNEY

ne Farm ★★★★
 & *Breakfast* SILVER AWARD
ne Farm, Upper Green, Moreton
kney
11 3SG
(01295) 760382
wendy.lainchbury@btinternet.
com
home-farm-bandb.co.uk

MOULTON

e Poplars Hotel ★★★★
st Accommodation
VER AWARD
Cross Street, Moulton,
thampton
3 7RZ
(01604) 643983
info@thepoplarshotel.com
thepoplarshotel.com

NASSINGTON

rlands ★★★★ *Bed & Breakfast*
Church Street, Nassington
6QG
(01780) 783603
enquiries@fairlandsbandb.co.uk
fairlandsbandb.co.uk

OLD

ld Farm ★★★★ *Farmhouse*
VER AWARD
ld Farm, Harrington Road, Old
5 9RJ
(01604) 781258
woldfarm.co.uk

OLD STRATFORD

tho Manor Farm ★★★
nhouse
thampton Road, Old Stratford,
ton Keynes
19 6NR
(01908) 542139
furtho@talktalk.net
furthomanorfarm.co.uk

OUNDLE

2 Benefield Road ★★★
Bed & Breakfast
2 Benefield Road, Oundle
PE8 4ET
t (01832) 273953

Lilford Lodge Farm ★★★★
Farmhouse
Barnwell, Oundle
PE8 5SA
t (01832) 272230
e trudy@lilford-lodge.demon.co.uk
w lilford-lodge.demon.co.uk

Rowan House ★★★★
Bed & Breakfast SILVER AWARD
45 Hillfield Road, Oundle,
Peterborough
PE8 4QR
t (01832) 273252
e angie.fowles@yahoo.com

PETERBOROUGH

Lodge Lawn Cottage ★★★★
Bed & Breakfast
Lodge Lawn, Fotheringhay,
Peterborough
PE8 5HZ
t (01832) 226101
e sallyloveday@aol.com

SCALDWELL

The Old House Bed & Breakfast
★★★★ *Bed & Breakfast*
SILVER AWARD
East End, Scaldwell
NN6 9LB
t (01604) 880359
e mrsv2@aol.com
w the-oldhouse.co.uk

SILVERSTONE

Pembury House ★★★★
Bed & Breakfast
6 Brackley Road, Silverstone
NN12 8UA
t (01327) 858743
e joyce@pembury.f2s.com
w pembury.f2s.com

Silverstone Bed & Breakfast
Guest Accommodation
The Chantry Coach House, Brackley
Road, Silverstone
NN12 8UA
t (01327) 857458
e elaine@silverstone.biz
w silverstone.biz

Silverstone Guest House ★★★★
Bed & Breakfast SILVER AWARD
Silver Blades, Blackmires Lane,
Silverstone
NN12 8UZ
t (01327) 858611
e s_m@silverstoneguesthouse.co.uk
w silverstoneguesthouse.co.uk

SPRATTON

Dale House ★★★★ *Bed & Breakfast*
Dale House, Yew Tree Lane,
Spratton
NN6 8HL
t (01604) 846458
e cjcatdalehouse@aol.com

TOWCESTER

The Old Barn at The Old Mint
House ★★★★ *Bed & Breakfast*
GOLD AWARD
The Old Mint House, 21 Park Street,
Towcester
NN12 6DQ
t (01327) 351359
e enquiries@theoldminthouse.co.uk
w theoldminthouse.co.uk

Potcote Bed & Breakfast ★★★★★
Guest Accommodation
SILVER AWARD
Between Towcester & Weedon,
Towcester
NN12 8LP
t (01327) 830224
w potcote.co.uk

Rignall Farm Barns ★★★
Guest Accommodation - Room Only
Handley Park, Abthorpe Road,
Towcester
NN12 8PA
t (01327) 350766
e ray@silson.go-plus.net

Slapton Manor Bed & Breakfast
★★★★ *Farmhouse* SILVER AWARD
Slapton Manor, Slapton
NN12 8PF
t (01327) 860344
e accommodation@slaptonmanor.
co.uk
w slaptonmanor.co.uk

UPPER BENEFIELD

Benefield Wheatsheaf Hotel *Inn*
Main Street, Upper Benefield,
Oundle
PE8 5AN
t (01832) 205400

UPPINGHAM

Spanhoe Lodge ★★★★★
Guest Accommodation
GOLD AWARD
Laxton Road, Harringworth, (Near
Corby)
NN17 3AT
t (01780) 450328
e jennie.spanhoe@virgin.net
w spanhoelodge.co.uk

WELDON

Thatches on the Green ★★★★
Bed & Breakfast SILVER AWARD
9 School Lane, Weldon, Corby
NN17 3JN
t (01536) 266681
e tom@thatches-on-the-green.fsnet.
co.uk
w thatches-on-the-green.fsnet.co.uk

WELLINGBOROUGH

Middle Farm Villa ★★★★
Bed & Breakfast
The Green, Chelveston,
Wellingborough
NN9 6AJ
t (01933) 625541
e middlefarmvilla@aol.com

Oak House Hotel ★★★
Guest Accommodation
Broad Green, 8-9 High Street,
Wellingborough
NN8 4LE
t (01933) 271133
e gayle.osullivan@uwclub.net

WEST FARNDON

The Mill House ★★★★
Bed & Breakfast
The Mill House, West Farndon
NN11 3TX
t (01327) 261727
e jcblincoln@hotmail.com
w millhousebandb.co.uk

WEST HADDON

Shepherds Row Bed & Breakfast
★★★★ *Bed & Breakfast*
19-21 West End, West Haddon,
Northampton
NN6 7AY
t (01788) 510503
e jane@shepherdsrow.co.uk
w shepherdsrow.co.uk

WHITFIELD

Chestnut View ★★ *Bed & Breakfast*
Mill Road, Whitfield, Brackley
NN13 5TQ
t (01280) 850246

WHITTLEBURY

Linden Cottage Guest House
★★★★ *Guest Accommodation*
12 High Street, Whittlebury,
Northants
NN12 8XJ
t (01327) 857862
e thomasthomas99@aol.com
w lindencottagewhittlebury.co.uk

WOODNEWTON

Bridge Cottage Bed and Breakfast
★★★★ *Bed & Breakfast*
Oundle Road, Woodnewton,
Peterborough
PE8 5EG
t 01780470779 (07979 644864)
e enquiries@bridgecottage.net
w bridgecottage.net

Nottinghamshire

BESTHORPE

Lord Nelson Inn ★★★★ *Inn*
Main Road, Besthorpe, Newark-on-
Trent, Nottinghamshire
NG23 7HR
t (01636) 892265
e enquiries@thelordnelsoninn.plus.
com
w thelordnelsoninn.com

COTGRAVE

Primrose House ★★★★ *Farmhouse*
Scrimshire Lane, Cotgrave,
Nottingham
NG12 3JD
t (0115) 989 9189
w primrose-house.co.uk

CROPWELL BISHOP

Highbury House ★★★★
Guest Accommodation
11 Cropwell Butler Road, Cropwell
Bishop
NG12 3DD
t (0115) 989 2315
e info@highbury-house.co.uk
w highbury-house.co.uk

GRINGLEY-ON-THE-HILL

Gringley Hall ★★★★
Guest Accommodation
Mill Road, Gringley-on-the-Hill
DN10 4QT
t (01777) 817262
e dulce@gringleyhall.fsnet.co.uk

LANGWITH

Blue Barn Farm ★★★ *Farmhouse*
Langwith, Mansfield
NG20 9JD
t (01623) 742248
e bluebarnfarm@supanet.com
w bluebarnfarm-notts.co.uk

LAXTON

Crosshill House Bed & Breakfast
★★★★ *Guest Accommodation*
SILVER AWARD
Crosshill, Laxton, Newark, Notts
NG22 0SX
t (01777) 871953
e roberta@crosshillhouse.com
w crosshillhouse.com

Lilac Farm ★★★ *Guest House*
Laxton, Newark
NG22 0NX
t (01777) 870376
e na@na.com

MANSFIELD

Marion's Manor ★★★
Bed & Breakfast
Ollerton Road, Edwinstowe,
Mansfield
NG21 9QF
t (01623) 822135
e marionsmanor@hotmail.com
w marionsmanor.co.uk

key to symbols see page 6   437

East Midlands | Nottinghamshire

Sherwood Forest Youth Hostel ★★
Hostel
Forest Corner, Edwinstowe, Mansfield
NG21 9RN
t 0870 770 6026
e sherwood@yha.org.uk
w yha.org.uk

MORTON

Barns Country Guest House ★★★★ *Guest House*
Morton Farm, Babworth, Retford
DN22 8HA
t (01777) 706336
e enquiries@thebarns.co.uk
w thebarns.co.uk

NEWARK

Brecks Cottage B&B ★★★★
Guest Accommodation
Green Lane, Moorhouse, Newark
NG23 6LZ
t (01636) 822445
e bandb@breckscottage.co.uk
w breckscottage.co.uk

Bridge House ★★★★
Guest Accommodation
SILVER AWARD
4 London Road, New Balderton, Newark
NG24 3AJ
t (01636) 674663
e info@arnoldsbandb.co.uk
w arnoldsbandb.co.uk

The Georgian Townhouse
★★★★★ *Guest Accommodation*
SILVER AWARD
19 Baldertongate, Newark
NG24 1RY
t (01636) 605343
e gthnewark@fsmail.net
w wwwthegeorgiantownhousenewark.co.uk

Greystones Guest Accommodation ★★★★
Bed & Breakfast SILVER AWARD
Main Street, South Scarle, Newark
NG23 7JH
t (01636) 893969
e sheenafowkes@greystonesguests.co.uk
w greystonesguests.co.uk

The Hollies ★★★★ *Bed & Breakfast*
SILVER AWARD
41 Victoria Street, Newark
NG24 4UU
t (01636) 676533
e pamela@theholliesnewark.co.uk
w theholliesnewark.co.uk

Ivy Farm B&B ★★★ *Farmhouse*
Newark Road, Barnby-in-the-Willows, Newark
NG24 2SL
t (01636) 672568
e clare@ivyfarmnewark.co.uk
w ivyfarmnewark.co.uk

Newark Lodge Guest House
★★★★★ *Guest House*
GOLD AWARD
5 Bullpit Road, Balderton, Newark
NG24 3PT
t (01636) 703999
e coolspratt@aol.com

Nicholson House ★★★★
Bed & Breakfast
39 London Road, Newark
NG24 1RZ
t (01636) 610933
e godfreycozens@hotmail.com

The Vicarage ★★★★
Bed & Breakfast
107 Main Street, Balderton, Newark
NG24 3NN
t (01636) 707934
e linda4607@googlemail.com
w vicarage-bedbreakfast.co.uk

Wisteria House ★★★
Bed & Breakfast
71 Harcourt Street, Newark
NG24 1RG
t (01636) 706333
e murieldyson71@hotmail.com
w wisteriahousenewark.co.uk

NOTTINGHAM

4 Poplar Avenue ★★
Guest Accommodation
4 Poplar Avenue, Sherwood, Nottingham
NG5 1DJ
t (0115) 962 2307

Andrews Guest House ★★★
Guest Accommodation
310 Queens Road, Beeston, Nottingham
NG9 1JA
t (0115) 925 4902
e andrews.hotel@ntlworld.com
w andrewshotelnottingham.com

Belvoir B & B at Woodside Farm
★★★★ *Farmhouse*
Long Lane, Nr. Barkestone le vale, Nottingham, Nottinghamshire
NG13 0HQ
t 01476 870336 (07703 299291)
e hickling-woodside@supanet.com
w woodsidebandb.co.uk

Cotswold Hotel ★★★
Guest Accommodation
330-332 Mansfield Road, Sherwood, Nottingham
NG5 2EF
t (0115) 955 1070
e cotswoldhotel@btinternet.com
w cotswold-hotel.co.uk

Elm Bank Lodge ★★★
Bed & Breakfast
9 Elm Bank, Mapperley Park, Nottingham
NG3 5AJ
t (0115) 962 5493
e elmbanklodge@aol.com

Greenwood Lodge City Guest House ★★★★★ *Guest House*
GOLD AWARD
5 Third Avenue, Sherwood Rise, Nottingham
NG7 6JH
t (0115) 962 1206
e pdouglas71@aol.com
w greenwoodlodgecityguesthouse.co.uk

Hylands ★★★ *Guest House*
Beeston, Nottingham
NG9 1JB
t (0115) 925 5678
e hyland.hotel@btconnect.com
w hylandshotel.co.uk

Igloo Backpackers Hostel ★★★
Hostel
110 Mansfield Road, Nottingham
NG1 3HL
t (0115) 947 5250
e reception@igloohostel.co.uk
w igloohostel.co.uk

The Old Post Office B & B ★★★
Bed & Breakfast
Annesley Cutting, Annesley Village, Nottingham
NG15 0AJ
t 01623 750958
e lisa6519@hotmail.com
w rose6519.googlepages.com

Olive Tree (by the Castle) ★★
Guest Accommodation
9-11 St James Terrace, Nottingham
NG1 6FW
t (0115) 941 1997
e olivetree.hotel@ntlworld.com

P & J Hotel ★★★
Guest Accommodation
277-279 Derby Road, Nottingham
NG7 2DP
t (0115) 978 3998
e enquiries@pj-hotel.co.uk
w pj-hotel.co.uk

Park Hotel ★★★
Guest Accommodation
5-7 Waverley Street, Nottingham
NG7 4HF
t (0115) 978 6299
e info@parkhotelnottingham.co.uk
w parkhotelcitycentre.co.uk

Vine Lodge ★★★★ *Bed & Breakfast*
8 Highbury Road, Keyworth, Nottingham
NG12 5JB
t (0115) 937 3944
e enquiries@vine-lodge.co.uk
w vine-lodge.co.uk

OLLERTON

Maun River Cottage ★★★
Bed & Breakfast
Main Street, Ollerton Village, Newark
NG22 9AD
t (01623) 824746
e dms@discovernottinghamshire.co.uk

OXTON

Far Baulker Farm ★★★★
Farmhouse
Old Rufford Road, Oxton, Southwell
NG25 0RQ
t (01623) 882375
e j.esam@virgin.net
w farbaulkerfarm.info

PAPPLEWICK

Forest Farm ★★ *Farmhouse*
Mansfield Road, Papplewick
NG15 8FL
t (0115) 963 2310
e dms@discovernottingham.co.uk

RAVENSHEAD

Oak House B&B ★★★★
Guest Accommodation
SILVER AWARD
3 Church Drive, Ravenshead
NG15 9FG
t (01623) 792723
e cooke@oakhouseravenshead.co.uk
w oakhouseravenshead.co.uk

RETFORD

Bolham Manor ★★★★
Bed & Breakfast SILVER AWARD
off Tiln Lane, Retford
DN22 9JG
t (01777) 703528
e pamandbutch@bolham-manor.com
w bolham-manor.com/

TROWELL

Orchard Cottage ★★★★
Bed & Breakfast
Orchard Cottage, Trowell Moor, Nottingham
NG9 3PQ
t (0115) 928 0933
e orchardcottage.bandb@virgin.
w orchardcottages.com

WEST BRIDGFORD

County Hotel ★★★
Guest Accommodation
6 Millicent Road, West Bridgford
NG2 7LD
t (0115) 981 6004
e countyhotel-nottingham.co.uk

Firs Guesthouse ★★★ *Guest House*
96 Radcliffe Road, West Brigford
NG2 5HH
t (0115) 981 0199
e firs.hotel@btinternet.com
w firshotelnottingham.co.uk

Grantham Hotel ★★★ *Guest House*
24-26 Radcliffe Road, West Brigford
NG2 5FW
t (0115) 981 1373

WHATTON

Aslockton Grange Barn ★★★★
Bed & Breakfast
Grantham Road, Whatton
NG13 9AJ
t (01949) 851836
e sinclair@kersey1412.freeserve.uk

The Vale of Belvoir Inn & Hotel
★★★ *Inn*
Grantham Road, Whatton-in-the-Vale
NG13 9EU
t (01949) 850800
e info@valeofbelvoirhotel.co.uk
w valeofbelvoirhotel.co.uk

WORKSOP

Browns ★★★★★ *Bed & Breakfast*
GOLD AWARD
The Old Orchard Cottage, Holbeck, Worksop
S80 3NF
t (01909) 720659
e browns.holbeck@btconnect.co
w brownsholbeck.co.uk

Looking for something else?

You can also buy a copy of our popular guide 'Self Catering' including self-catering holiday homes, approved caravan holiday homes, boat accommodation and holiday cottage agencies in England 2011. Now available in good bookshops and online at **visitbritainshop.com**

£11.99

Walkers and cyclists welcome

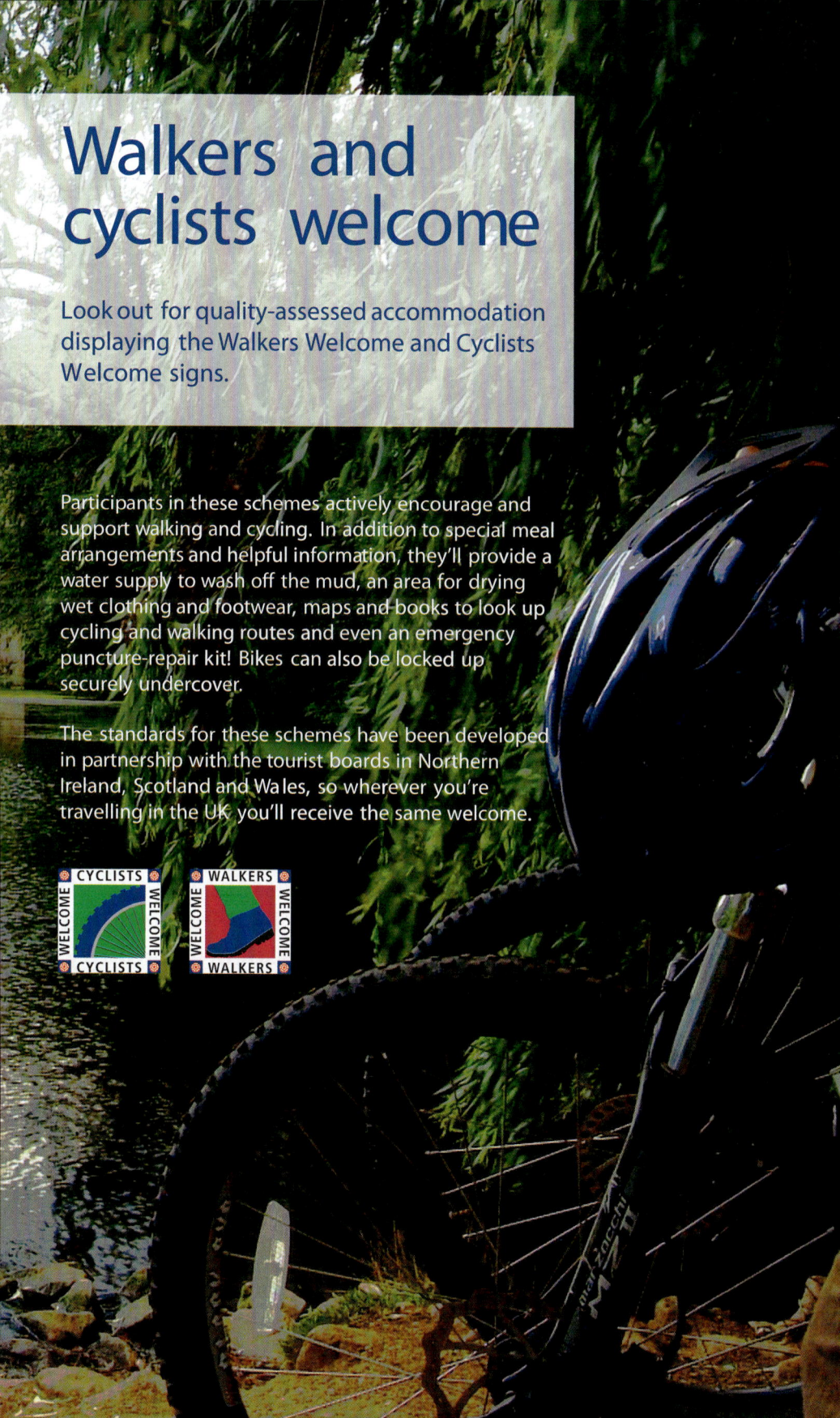

Look out for quality-assessed accommodation displaying the Walkers Welcome and Cyclists Welcome signs.

Participants in these schemes actively encourage and support walking and cycling. In addition to special meal arrangements and helpful information, they'll provide a water supply to wash off the mud, an area for drying wet clothing and footwear, maps and books to look up cycling and walking routes and even an emergency puncture-repair kit! Bikes can also be locked up securely undercover.

The standards for these schemes have been developed in partnership with the tourist boards in Northern Ireland, Scotland and Wales, so wherever you're travelling in the UK you'll receive the same welcome.

Heart of England

The Heart of England, the West Midlands region, is the real core of the country. It's the place where you'll find what make England tick, where you'll discover the essence of everything English. And we have a lot to thank The Heart of England for; the Industrial Revolution, William Shakespeare, Cadbury and Charles Darwin being just some of its famous products.

Birmingham, the Black Country, Coventry and Warwickshire, Herefordshire, Shakespeare Country, Ironbridge, Shropshire, Worcestershire and Staffordshire make up the West Midlands, or what is affectionately known as The Heart of England. So, make sure you leave time to experience the eight fascinating counties, all of which boast their own unique heritage and special attractions.

Birmingham is firmly on the culinary map as three of the city's chefs have been awarded Michelin stars. The city is also home to the world-famous Balti Triangle which is packed with irresistible award-winning Asian restaurants.

Ludlow in Shropshire is similarly famous for its Michelin Stars (at La Becasse) and for being the very epicentre of the UK's Slow Food movement. Its sumptuous local produce fills the busy markets and delicatessens; and the excellent fayre now filters into every aspect of dining, from picnic to pub lunch to candlelit dinner.

The Heart of England is also renowned for its annual food festivals including Flavours of Herefordshire (October), Blossomtime (May), Ludlow Marches Food and Drink Festival (September) and the Stratford Food Festival (September).

The region is steeped in heritage and history with plenty of fascinating attractions such as the Wedgwood Visitor

Heart of England

Heart of England

Herefordshire, Shropshire, Staffordshire, Warwickshire, West Midlands, Worcestershire

442	Counties	451	Where to Eat
448	Where to Go	456	Where to Stay
450	Events		

...entre and Museum, Stoke-on-Trent - the home of fine pottery. Here visitors can listen to the story of Josiah Wedgwood before heading to the visitor centre for demonstrations.

Alternatively take your pick from more medieval masterpieces such as Kenilworth and Warwick Castles.

Don't forget too that Stratford-on-Avon was the birthplace of William Shakespeare and many of the buildings where he once wrote, lived and loved, are beautifully preserved and open to the public. The hop-on hop-off sightseeing bus is a great way to take in these Shakespearean sights.

The region is famed for its festivals in particular its music festivals. Highlights include the annual jazz festival in Upton and Moseley Folk Festival. And on a larger scale The Big Chill and V Festival attract revellers from across the world.

With so much to see and do there really is a lot to love about the Heart of England.

Heart of England | Herefordshire

Herefordshire

An ancient city on the banks of the River Wye, Hereford is the commercial and artistic heart of the county. Don't be surprised to find historic buildings housing modern shops and modern buildings holding historic treasures. The Left Bank Village, graces the banks of the beautiful River Wye.

Eastnor

Mainly known for Eastnor Castle, Eastnor is in the centre of the county, between the Cotswolds and the Welsh Marches. In the dramatic setting of the Malvern Hills and surrounded by a beautiful deer park, arboretum and lake, the fairy-tale castle is the home of the Hervey-Bathurst family. Eastnor has undergone a triumphant renaissance in recent years and many of the castle's treasures are now displayed for the first time in richly decorated splendour.

Leominster

Located in the heart of the beautiful border countryside, where England and Wales nudge each other back and forth along Offa's Dyke, lays Leominster, an historic market town. Leominster (pronounced 'Lemster') dates back to the 7th century and is named after Earl Leofric, the husband of Lady Godiva who famously rode naked through the streets of Coventry on horseback. The town possesses some fine examples of architecture throughout the ages. See medieval overhangs in Drapers Lane and School Lane, and Georgian splendour on Broad Street. The town-centre has recently become semi-pedestrianised, recreating the bustling atmosphere of a market town; a market is still held each Friday in Corn Square.

Ross-on-Wye

Perched on a sandstone cliff high above a broad loop of the magnificent River Wye, the dramatic setting of Ross-on-Wye belies the friendliness of a town that has restored the spirits of world-weary travellers for centuries. A striking 17th century market hall dominates the town centre and while the upper storey is now a fascinating heritage centre, the lower level still shelters twice-weekly markets. There is also an excellent range of shops from antiques and craft specialists to some of the more familiar high street names.

Symonds Yat

The river has carved a dramatic gorge through towering limestone cliffs that are home to a myriad of birds including the rare peregrine falcon. The two settlements nestling in the depths of the gorge, offer a variety of attractions and are connected, during the day and when conditions allow, by an unusual man-powered rope ferry. The rope ferry offers a tranquil way to cross from Symonds Yat East to Symonds Yat West. The watery thoroughfare of the River Wye provides endless opportunities for leisure and relaxation. Renowned the world over for the quality of its salmon, the river is loved by fishermen. Walkers enjoy the rich wildlife along the banks and canoeists can paddle for miles through magnificent scenery.

Heart of England | Shropshire

Shropshire

Shropshire is one of England's last remaining rural idylls, unspoilt yet full of history. Medieval Shrewsbury was also Charles Darwin's home, Ludlow once the seat of warring kings, and the World Heritage Site of Ironbridge gave rise to the industrial revolution. Shropshire may well come as a surprise to visitors.

Shrewsbury

The medieval town of Shrewsbury may be full of black and white buildings, historic shuts and passages but this no museum - it is a vibrant market town, with cafes, art galleries, festivals and events as well as plenty of unique independent shops to discover.

Almost entirely surrounded by the River Severn, Shrewsbury is easy to walk around, although the beautiful Ingle Park, the castle and numerous museums may distract you on your way.

Charles Darwin, Shrewsbury's most famous son, was born and educated here before he left on his voyage of discovery. The International Cartoon Festival is fast becoming a regular fixture in the Shrewsbury event calendar and Shrewsbury is also host to one of the longest running flower shows in the country, justifiably earning its title 'Town of Flowers'.

Ironbridge

Ironbridge sits in the beautiful Severn Valley and is home to the world's first iron bridge. This little market town simply changed everything and gave the world the industrial revolution. Now a World Heritage Site there are 'hands on' museums including the award-winning Blist's Hill Victorian Town to explain it all. Here, even the Queen still has to pay to cross the bridge as she did when she visited a few years back.

Ludlow & South Shropshire

Ludlow is rightly Shropshire's gastronomic capital - with more Michelin-stars than anywhere else outside London, a sausage trail, a regional food festival and numerous award-winning pubs, restaurants and food shops it's easy to see why.

Built around a magnificent castle, Ludlow was once the seat of the kings, and home of princes. Medieval buildings sit beside Georgian grandeur. Ludlow has been declared the prettiest town in England.

Much Wenlock

It is a little known fact that the pretty little town of Much Wenlock in Shropshire is actually the birthplace of the modern Olympic Games, for it was here in 1850 that Doctor Penny Brookes introduced the first Wenlock Olympian Games which went on to inspire Baron De Coubertin to create the Olympics we know today. The town still holds its own annual Olympiad in July.

Oswestry and North Shropshire

Shropshire has plenty of award-winning gardens and national collections to provide horticultural sanctuary. There are plants-man's gardens at Wollerton Old Hall and the unique and magical Hawkstone Park & Follies - the world's first theme park which opened in 748 (not a roller coaster in sight). Ellesmere, situated by the largest lake in Shropshire, is the hub of some 70 miles of beautiful canals, which lead to the World Heritage Site at The Pontcysyllte Aqueduct. The canals also take in the border town of Oswestry and Whittington Castle on their way. Whittington was home to Dick who became the Mayor of London and Oswestry was also home to the real King Arthur and his lady Guinevere so legends naturally abound in this area. Enchanting.

443

Heart of England | Staffordshire

Staffordshire

As well as being home to the recently discovered 'Staffordshire Hoard', the county is full of national treasures, from great expanses of glorious countryside, historic forest and more miles of canal than any other shire county, to celebrated museums and castles, world renowned theme parks and the UK's only monkey forest.

Staffordshire Peaks

To the north east lies the Staffordshire Peak District, part of Britain's first National Park. With dramatic peaks, moors and crags to conquer, its spectacular scenery attracts visitors from all over the world looking to find peace, tranquility and adventure and experience some of England's finest climbing, caving, walking and cycling. The county is also home to the UK's most famous theme park, Alton Towers Resort. Enjoy a mind-blowing mix of fantastic rides and attractions for kids of all ages, families and thrill seekers.

Stoke-on-Trent

Staffordshire's unique ceramic heritage comes to life with a visit to The Potteries in Stoke-on-Trent, a unique British city made up of six separate towns - it's the World Capital of Ceramics. There are more than 20 pottery factory shops to choose from including the world renowned brands of Royal Doulton, Wedgwood, Portmeirion, Spode and Moorcroft. Nearby, The Trentham Estate offers something for everyone – formal gardens and fountains, woodland and lakeside walks, adventure playground, retail village, restaurants and the fascinating Monkey Forest.

Stafford

Staffordshire is home to a myriad of museums, ancient monuments, magnificent country estates and art galleries, many of which can be found in and around the county town of Stafford. The Ancient High House is the tallest Elizabethan town house in England, Stafford Castle provides a dramatic backdrop to the Shakespearian productions hosted during the annual Stafford Festival. At Shugborough visitors can leave the 21st century behind and step into the real working environments of The Complete Working Historic Estate.

Cannock Chase

Designated as an Area of Outstanding Natural Beauty, Cannock Chase is the largest surviving area of lowland heathland in the Midlands. Miles of heather hills and quiet forests offer the perfect place for walking, cycling, horse-riding and picnicking and are also home to Britain's large herd of fallow deer, which roam free.

Lichfield

Home to Dr Samuel Johnson, compiler of the first English dictionary, Lichfield, is Staffordshire's premier heritage city. With stunning architecture, including the magnificent three-spired Cathedral, every building has a tale to tell.

Set in 150 acres of wooded parkland, the National Memorial Arboretum in Alrewas is not so much a garden as a national focus of remembrance in memory of those who have died on duty or as a result of terrorist action since the end of the Second World War, designed to provide a haven of peace and contemplation.

Heart of England | Warwickshire

Warwickshire

The historic county of Warwickshire boasts stunning countryside with quaint market towns running through it. There is so much to see and do in this region which encompasses the magnificent Warwick Castle which towers over the banks of the river Avon, chic and elegant shopping destinations and famed for being the home county of William Shakespeare.

Stratford-upon-Avon

Discover the town in which Shakespeare was born and grew up, where he gained inspiration for his work and even where he used to poach deer! A stroll along the River Avon will lead you to Holy Trinity Church – Shakespeare's final resting place. Stratford has many other attractions including Guide Friday, The Butterfly Farm and Cox's Yard. For the visitor, the area offers the best of town and country – not one but two world renowned motor museums, Britain's national organic garden and a living Roman fort, canals and country churches, great houses and battlefields. The surrounding countryside has six fascinating and historical National Trust houses and gardens including Hidcote Manor and Charlecote Park.

Rugby

Home to the game of Rugby Football; where the sport began in 1823. Enthusiasts from all over the world visit to see the statue of William Webb Ellis and read the famous words on the commemoration plaque at Rugby School Close. Rugby School itself dominates much of the centre and south of the town. It was the subject of the famous Thomas Hughes novel 'Tom Brown's School Days'.

Kenilworth

Discover the ruined glory of Elizabethan England amid the red sandstone ruins of Kenilworth Castle. Hear of lovers' trysts, bloody battles and water pageants. Visit Leicester's Gatehouse, reopened following a £2.5m restoration project. The gatehouse includes a major exhibition exploring the connections between Kenilworth and Elizabeth I. From the castle, stroll through Abbey Fields with its lake, remains of an historic Abbey, swimming pool (both indoors and outdoors) and children's play area. See the cottages of 'Little Virginia' where Sir Walter Raleigh planted England's first potatoes.

Royal Leamington Spa

A fashionable and elegant regency town in the heart of South Warwickshire. Georgian and Victorian architecture, tree lined avenues and squares, stunning parks and gardens, it offers a unique shopping, dining and cultural experience. The magnificent Royal Pump Rooms house the elegant Assembly Rooms, a traditional café and the town's art gallery and museum. See displays on the historic use of the Pump Rooms and spa treatments. You can even sample the spa water! Opposite the Royal Pump Rooms lie the Jephson Gardens, perfect for a gentle stroll. These Grade II listed gardens of horticultural excellence have undergone a £4.3 million restoration project and include a sensory garden, temperate glasshouse, refurbished boathouse and children's play area.

Warwick

The historic town of Warwick is a magical place for a short break. Warwick Castle lies at the heart of the town. Visit the State Rooms, scale the towers and ramparts and descend into the dark dungeon. Other architecture of note is Lord Leycester Hospital. This beautiful collection of 14th century timber-framed buildings, house a chapel, Great Hall, galleried courtyard and Regimental Museum of the Queen's Own Hussars. Hidden at the back of the Hospital discover one of the oldest gardens in Warwick, the Master's Garden, a tranquil oasis in the midst of the town. Discover a wealth of other historic treasures in Warwick including the Great Fire of 1694 at the Market Hall Museum.

Heart of England | West Midlands

West Midlands

The West Midlands is a region with a strong historical heritage combined with a tradition for innovation and contemporary thinking which makes it an exciting destination for arts, culture, entertainment, shopping, dining and quality family attractions.

Birmingham

Birmingham is a city that surprises at every turn. The city's world class cultural scene is a must for all visitors and includes the Birmingham Royal Ballet, City of Birmingham Symphony Orchestra, Birmingham Museum & Art Gallery and a never ending range of fantastic festivals. Birmingham also offers a range of visitor attractions that's sure to please from the Thinktank, a science and technology museum with over 200 hands-on exhibitions, to Cadbury World where chocoholics of all ages can indulge in a little of the nations favourite chocolate. Then let's not forget a huge range of shopping from all your high street favourites to chic designers like Hugo Boss, Prada, Polo Ralph Lauren and Emporio Armani. Perfect for lunch and dinner is the city's range of award-winning restaurants with a wealth of choice which is sure to get those taste buds tingling.

Coventry

A city of heritage and innovation, famous for Lady Godiva and pioneering the motoring industry. It is the ideal visitor destination with fantastic shopping facilities, a range of bars, restaurants and breathtaking historical buildings. Discover the city that is re-inventing itself. Coventry is home to heritage and culture right in the heart of the city. From the Medieval St Mary's Guildhall, Coventry Cathedral and the Cathedral Ruins as well as the old alms houses of Fords and Bonds Hospitals to the modern Priory Gardens, Lady Herbert's Garden and the Garden of International Friendship. The city also has a variety of visitor attractions including the world class Transport Museum and the Herbert Art Gallery and Museum. Well worth a visit. Order a new visitor guide now by emailing tic@cvone.co.uk

The Black Country

Tour the Black Country and you travel a trail through time from a primeval shallow sea, to the birth of the Industrial Revolution, to the modern day. A visit to The Black Country reveals a rich seam of art, crafts, tradition and culture set amidst historic towns and inviting green countryside. Just thirty minutes by bus or train from Birmingham International Airport you can watch Black Country artisans in authentic 18th/19th century workshops busy at their crafts. Well worth a visit are the leatherworks at Walsall, the Red House Cone and Broadfield House glassmaking museums at Dudley and the enamelling workshops at Bilston. Alternatively, visit the Black Country Living Museum at Dudley, where you will see the reconstructed buildings and cross the portal into Victorian times. Prepare to be amazed by the colourful flotillas of narrowboats and myriad of canals that twine through the towns and countryside. Perhaps you prefer to walk along quiet nature trails or through green countryside where you can see historic castles and stately homes. Or spend time at Sandwell Valley Country Park, home to rare, native farm breeds like the Tamworth pig.

Wolverhampton

The city has a vibrant and multi-cultural offering for the tourist ranging from a visit to Wightwick Manor to view William Morris originals to a day out at the races at Wolverhampton's all weather race-course. Then end your day with an evening at the Grand Theatre or one of the many concerts at the Civic Halls. Other award-winning attractions such as Bantock House and Park, Moseley Old Hall, Wolverhampton Art Gallery, Bilston Craft Gallery & Museum only enhance the city further.

Heart of England | Worcestershire

Worcestershire

Situated on the banks of the River Severn the city of Worcester has a rich and varied heritage to explore from the 11th century cathedral to Royal Worcester porcelain factory with its museum and visitor centre. Apart from historical interests there are a variety of other attractions including riverside walks, boat trips and excellent high street and speciality shopping.

Broadway

Broadway is reputed to be one of the most beautiful villages in the country; the honey-coloured stone of the houses have attracted visitors for centuries. The village stands at the foot of the Cotswold Hills immediately adjacent to the base of the 1026ft high Fish Hill which is the highest point of the northern end of the hills. The superb skyline is dominated by Broadway Tower, a folly built by the sixth Earl of Coventry in the 18th century. It is situated in a 30-acre country park and from the top of the 65ft tower spectacular views can be enjoyed over 12 counties.

Droitwich

Unique among the spa towns of Britain, Droitwich achieved fame and recognition as a Brine Spa. The natural brine contains 2.5 lbs of salt per gallon – ten times stronger than sea water and only rivalled by the Dead Sea. Visitors do not drink the waters at Droitwich, but experience the therapeutic and remedial benefits by floating weightless in the warm brine of the bathing pool. Surrounded by beautiful Worcestershire countryside, Droitwich is a town of great charm and character, offering its visitors plenty to see and enjoy.

Evesham

The town witnessed the Battle of Evesham in 1265 when Simon de Montfort, known as the father of the English Parliament, was brutally killed. His remains were brought by the monks from the battlefield, (Greenhill at the north of the town) and solemnly buried in front of the High Altar in the Abbey Church. A modest stone memorial in the park marks the spot where the burial took place.

The Malverns

The Malverns are the centre piece of a wonderful region stretching from lowland, riverside Upton upon Severn to Malvern itself, and up the River Teme's winding course through northwest Worcestershire's hills to delightful Tenbury Wells. The pure water of the Malvern Hills springs made Malvern a 19th century spa with the elegance to become a place of culture, attracting people like Sir Edward Elgar and George Bernard Shaw. From the hills you will see some of England's grandest views, eastwards towards the Cotswolds, northwards to Shropshire and westward to the misty mountains of Wales.

Upton upon Severn

Located in the south of Worcestershire, the pretty town of Upton upon Severn is a haven for boat enthusiasts. It was an important coaching stop and the many Georgian Inns are a testament to this, notably the White Lion, which is said to be the model for parts of Henry Fielding's 'Tom Jones'.

Heart of England | Where to Go

Where to Go

Attractions with this sign participate in the **Visitor Attraction Quality Assurance Scheme** (see page 6) which recognises high standards in all aspects of the visitor experience.

ENTERTAINMENT & CULTURE

Avoncroft Museum of Historic Buildings
Bromsgrove, Worcestershire
B60 4JR
(01527) 831363
www.avoncroft.org.uk
Avoncroft Museum is a unique home for historic buildings which have been rescued from demolition and rebuilt in a beautiful corner of Worcestershire's rural countryside.

Black Country Living Museum
Dudley, West Midlands DY1 4SQ
(0121) 557 9643
www.bclm.co.uk
A warm welcome awaits you at Britain's friendliest open-air museum. Wander around original shops and houses, ride on fair attractions, take a look down the underground coalmine.

Blists Hill Victorian Town
Telford, Shropshire TF7 5DU
(01952) 884391
www.ironbridge.org.uk
Watch the world go by over 100 years ago.

Compton Verney
Stratford-upon-Avon,
Warwickshire CV35 9HZ
(01926) 645500
www.comptonverney.org.uk
Award-winning art gallery housed in a grade I listed Robert Adam mansion. Explore artworks from around the world and relax in 'Capability' Brown parkland.

Coventry Transport Museum
Coventry, West Midlands
CV1 1JD
(024) 7623 4270
www.transport-museum.com
The world's largest collection of British road transport located in the birthplace of British transport. Offering everything from 'bone shaking' cycles to land speed record cars.

Heritage Motor Centre
Stratford-upon-Avon,
Warwickshire CV35 0BJ
(01926) 641188
www.heritage-motor-centre.co.uk
Uncover the story of the British motor industry with the exciting and interactive exhibitions. Home to the world's largest collection of historic British cars.

Royal Air Force Museum Cosford
Telford, Shropshire TF11 8UP
(01902) 376200
www.rafmuseum.org
Transport, Research; Development, Warplanes, Missiles and Aero-Engine collections. Art gallery, temporary exhibition gallery and interactives in our Fun 'n' Flight area.

The Worcester Porcelain Museum
Worcester, Worcestershire
WR1 2ND
(01905) 617 827
www.worcesterporcelainmuseum.org.uk/friendssociety/
Learn about the talented workforce and everyday life as you travel through the Georgian, Victorian and 20thC galleries. Free audio tour with entry.

FAMILY FUN

Go Ape! Highwire Forest Adventure - Cannock Forest
Rugeley, Staffordshire
WS15 2UQ
0845 643 9215
www.goape.co.uk
Experience an exhilarating course of rope bridges, tarzan swings and zip slides...all set high above the forest floor

Wedgwood Visitor Centre
Stoke-on-Trent, Staffordshire
ST12 9ER
(01782) 282986
www.wedgwoodvisitorcentre.com
The Wedgwood Visitor Centre offers a unique chance to immerse yourself in the heritage of Britain's greatest ceramics company.

HERITAGE

Aston Hall
Birmingham, West Midlands
B6 6JD
0121 675 4722
www.bmag.org.uk
Built by Sir Thomas Holte between 161 and 1635. Noted for its great staircase, long gallery and plasterwork ceilings.

Attingham Park
Shrewsbury, Shropshire SY4 4TP
(01743) 708123
www.nationaltrust.org.uk/attinghampark
For a meagre sum you may have the house and grounds to enjoy for a whole day. You'll see a late 18thC house commanding views over 500 acres of wonderful parkland.

448

Heart of England | Where to Go

akesley Hall
rmingham, West Midlands
25 8RN
(121) 464 2193
ww.bmag.org.uk
delightfully restored, handsome, mber-framed Yeoman farmer's use built around 1590 by Richard nallbrook and furnished to an ventory of 1684. Set in landscaped ounds including herb gardens, the e has a new visitor centre.

oventry Cathedral - St lichael's
oventry, West Midlands
1 5AB
24) 7652 1257
ww.coventrycathedral.org.uk
orious 20th century Cathedral, with nning 1950's art & architecture, ing above the stark ruins of the edieval Cathedral destroyed by rman air raids in 1940.

awkstone Historic Park nd Follies
rewsbury, Shropshire
4 5UY
948) 841700
ww.hawkstone.co.uk
awkstone Historic Park; Follies is nique place. Created in the 18th ntury by the Hill family (Sir Rowland d his son Richard), Hawkstone came one of the greatest historic rklands in Europe.

enilworth Castle & izabethan Garden
enilworth, Warwickshire
8 1NE
1926) 852078
ww.english-heritage.org.uk/server/ ow/nav.16880
e of the most spectacular castle ns in England, Kenilworth is a werful reminder of great leaders and ents.

chfield Cathedral
chfield, Staffordshire
S13 7LD
1543) 306100
ww.lichfield-cathedral.org
edieval Cathedral with 3 spires in e heart of an historic City set in its n serene Close.

udlow Castle
dlow, Shropshire SY8 1AY
1584) 873355
ww.ludlowcastle.com
nstruction of Ludlow Castle began the late 11th Century as the border ronghold of one of the Marcher Lords, ger De Lacy.

National Memorial Arboretum
Lichfield, Staffordshire
DE13 7AR
(01283) 792333
www.thenma.org.uk
150 acres of trees and memorials, planted as a living tribute to those who have served, died or suffered in the service of their Country. Chapel, Visitor Centre, Cafe & Shop.

Red House Glass Cone
Stourbridge, West Midlands
DY8 4AZ
(01384) 812750
www.redhousecone.co.uk
Late 18thC Glass Cone, one of four surviving in the UK. Facilities include audio tour around the tunnels and furnace, changing displays and craft studios.

Royal Pump Rooms
Leamington Spa, Warwickshire
CV32 4AA
(01926) 742700
www.warwickdc.gov.uk/ royalpumprooms
The historic Royal Pump Rooms have been redeveloped to create a cultural complex worthy of the 21st century. The multi-million pound restoration houses the art gallery & museum, assembly rooms, cafe, tourist information centre and library.

Selly Manor Museum
Birmingham, West Midlands
B30 2AE
(0121) 472 0199
www.bvt.org.uk/sellymanor
Thirteenth-century cruck house and 14th to 16thC half-timbered house with period furniture and fittings and authentic Tudor garden.

Severn Valley Railway
Bewdley, Worcestershire
DY12 1BG
(01299) 403816
www.svr.co.uk
Steam-hauled trains running along the beautiful Severn Valley. Special events throughout the year appeal to all ages.

Shakespeare's Birthplace
Stratford-upon-Avon, Warwickshire CV37 6QW
(01789) 204016
www.shakespeare.org.uk
Step into the house where William Shakespeare was born in 1564 and re-enter the Tudor world. Newly refurbished, the house now offers visitors a fascinating insight into life as it was when Shakespeare was a child.

Soho House Museum
Handsworth, West Midlands
B18 5LB
(0121) 554 9122
www.bmag.org.uk
Historic house with period rooms and visitor centre. Displays on Matthew Boulton his business interests and the Lunar Society. Tearoom, temporary exhibition gallery.

Stokesay Castle
Craven Arms, Shropshire
SY7 9AH
(01588) 672544
www.english-heritage.org.uk/ stokesaycastle
Stokesay Castle, near Craven Arms, nestles in peaceful South Shropshire countryside near the Welsh Border. It is one of more than a dozen English Heritage properties in the county.

The Morgan Motor Company
Malvern, Worcestershire
WR14 2LL
(01684) 573104
www.morgan-motor.co.uk
Morgan Motor Company, over 100 years of Driving Passion! Guided Factory Tours - Be amazed at hand craftsmanship, Museum and Shop.

Warwick Castle
Warwick, Warwickshire
CV34 4QU
0871 265 2000
www.warwick-castle.co.uk
Imagine a totally electrifying, full day out at Britain's ultimate castle.

Weston Park
Stafford, Staffordshire TF11 8LE
(01952) 852100
www.weston-park.com
Stately home and gardens with events held throughout the year.

Whittington Castle
Oswestry, Shropshire SY11 4DF
(01691) 662397
www.whittingtoncastle.co.uk
Whittington Castle is very impressive and picturesque, situated in the heart of Whittington village.

Witley Court & Gardens (English Heritage)
Worcester, Worcestershire
WR6 6JT
(01299) 896636
www.english-heritage.org.uk/server. php?show=nav.16927
Step back in time to a bygone age of great wealth when the house played host to royal parties. Enjoy beautiful gardens & lake, woodland walks, fountains - a magical world for children to explore.

449

Heart of England | Where to Go/Events

Worcester Cathedral
Worcester, Worcestershire WR1 2LA
(01905) 732900
www.worcestercathedral.co.uk
One of England's most magnificent and inspiring buildings, a place of prayer and worship for fourteen centuries.

NATURE & WILDLIFE

Acton Scott Historic Working Farm
Church Stretton, Shropshire
SY6 6QN
(01694) 781307
www.actonscottmuseum.com
Near Church Stretton, demonstrates life on a Shropshire upland farm at the turn of the last century.

Croome Park (National Trust)
Severn Stoke, Worcestershire
WR8 9JS
(01905) 371006
www.nationaltrust.org.uk
The first complete landscape design by 'Capability' Brown, restoration has been ongoing since 1996.

Hatton Farm Village at Hatton Country World
Warwick, Warwickshire CV35 8XA
(01926) 843411
www.hattonworld.com
Come and join us for Farm Village entertainment or to treat yourself to a little retail therapy.

Park Farm
Stafford, Staffordshire ST17 0XB
0845 459 8900
www.shugborough.org.uk
Experience the beautiful sights, evocative sounds, real smells and true taste of The Complete Working Historic Estate. Set on the banks of the beautiful River Sow, and on the northern wooded fringes of Cannock Chase.

Stratford-upon-Avon Butterfly Farm
Stratford-upon-Avon,
Warwickshire CV37 7LS
(01789) 299288
www.butterflyfarm.co.uk
The UK's largest tropical butterfly paradise! Rain or shine, discover many of the world's most beautiful butterflies.

The Trentham Estate
Stoke-on-Trent, Staffordshire
ST4 8AX
(01782) 646646
www.trenthamleisure.co.uk
One of the most important historic gardens in Britain, which along with the Barefoot Walk, Adventure Trail, Shopping Village and Garden Centre make it ideal for everyone. Nearby, you will also find the Aerial Extreme and the Monkey Forest.

West Midland Safari & Leisure Park
Bewdley, Worcestershire DY12 1
(01299) 402114
www.wmsp.co.uk
A great line up of fantastic family entertainment.

Wollerton Old Hall Garden
Market Drayton, Shropshire
TF9 3NA
(01630) 685760
www.wollertonoldhallgarden.com
An example of horticultural excellence set in the Shropshire countryside, about 1 hour travelling from Manchester.

Events 2011

Artsfest
Birmingham
www.birmingham.gov.uk
10-12 September

Birmingham International Dance Festival
www.idfb.co.uk
19 April-15 May

British Asparagus Festival
Evesham
www.britishasparagusfestival.org/
April-June

Flavours of Herefordshire Food Festival
Hereford
www.visitherefordshire.co.uk/
October

Herefordshire Walking Festival
www.visitherefordshire.co.uk
June

Kenilworth Festival
Kenilworth
www.kenilworthfestival.co.uk/
May

Lichfield Festival
Lichfield
www.lichfieldfestival.org
July

Lord's Mayor Show
Birmingham
www.birmingham.gov.uk
31st May

Ludlow Food Festival
www.foodfestival.co.uk
September

Midlands Grand National
Uttoxeter
www.uttoxeter-racecourse.co.uk
March

RAF Cosford Air Show
Shifnal
www.cosfordairshow.co.uk
June

Scarefest
Alton Towers area
www.altontowers.com
October

Severn Valley Railway
Bewdley
www.svr.co.uk
Various

Shakespeare Birthday celebrations
Stratford-upon-Avon
www.shakespeare.org.uk/
22-25 April

Shrewsbury Flower Show
www.shrewsburyflowershow.org.
August

St Patrick's Parade
Birmingham
www.stpatricksbirmingham.com
14th March

Stone Food & Drink Festival
Stone
stonefooddrink.org.uk/
October

Stratford Literary Festival
Stratford-upon-Avon
www.stratfordliteraryfestival.co.uk
April–May

The Great British Weekend - summer concerts at Warwick Castle
www.warwick-castle.co.uk/events
summer_concerts.asp
15th-18th July

V Festival
Stafford
www.vfestival.com
August

Warwick Folk Festival
www.warwickfolkfestival.co.uk
23-25 July

Heart of England | Where to Eat

Where to Eat

The Heart of England region has great places to eat. The restaurant reviews on these pages are just a small selection from the highly respected *The Good Food Guide 2011*. Please see page 14 for further information on the Guide and details of a Special Offer for our readers.

HEREFORDSHIRE

The Stagg Inn
Home-grown cooking with flair
Titley HR5 3RL
(01544) 230221
www.thestagg.co.uk
Modern British | £29

Steve and Nicola Reynolds are now into their second decade as custodians of this Herefordshire inn. Industrious home production and keen sourcing are at the heart of the whole enterprise: Steve bakes his own bread, cures chorizo and makes black pudding (perhaps served with a poached duck egg from his mum's brood of Khaki Campbells. Her Middle White pigs also live in the village (hunks of their belly meat might appear on the plate with apple and brawn salad), and Steve's larder is bulked out with vegetables from smallholdings and locally bagged game. But this isn't simply homespun rusticity and honest endeavour for its own sake: the cooking has sharpness and flair when it's required – as in a rump of Byton lamb with slow-cooked shoulder and fennel purée. Seafood takes a back seat. Desserts offer chocolate meringue with satsuma cream, or blackcurrant compote, blood orange sorbet and citrus syrup. A stupendous wood-boarded trolley loaded with 20 regional cheeses gets rave reviews. There is an exemplary wine list: growers and grape varieties have been chosen with unfailing intelligence, and prices (from £13.50) are ungreedy to a fault.

Chef/s: Steve Reynolds. **Open:** Tue to Sun L 12 to 2, Tue to Sat D 6.30 to 9 (9.30 Sat). **Closed:** Mon, 2 weeks Jan/Feb, first 2 weeks Nov, 25 and 26 Dec. **Meals:** alc (main courses £15 to £19). **Service:** not inc. **Details:** major cards accepted. 70 seats. 20 seats outside. Separate bar. No music. No mobile phones. Children welcome. Car parking.

The Wellington
Good value, heart-on-sleeve cooking
Wellington HR4 8AT
(01432) 830367
www.wellingtonpub.co.uk
Gastropub | £27

Reporters continue to applaud Ross Williams' rustic pub, singling out for praise the 'excellent value for money' and 'charming service'. Don't expect refined cuisine here: direct, earthy, heart-on-sleeve dishes are the order of the day, and it's all fuelled by a dedication to well-sourced local and seasonal produce. Rabbit ravioli with grain mustard and cream sauce won over one reporter. Fillet of sea bass is served with wild mushroom and Puy lentil salad, while calf's liver comes with crispy pancetta, buttered mash and sage butter. Cheeses are from Herefordshire and desserts are uncomplicated offerings

451

Heart of England | Where to Eat

like pannacotta with poached fig. Wines start at £13.
Chef/s: Ross Williams. **Open:** Tue to Sun L 12 to 2 (12.30 Sun), Mon to Sat D 7 to 9. **Closed:** 25 and 26 Dec. **Meals:** alc (main courses £12 to £18). Sun L £12.50 (1 course) to £17.50. **Service:** not inc. **Details:** major cards accepted. 70 seats. 20 seats outside. Separate bar. Music. Children welcome. Car parking.

STAFFORDSHIRE

The George
Idyllic village pub
Alstonefield   DE6 2FX
(01335) 310205
www.thegeorgeatalstonefield.com
Gastropub | £25

Perched above Dovedale in the heart of the Peak District national park, the George is an eighteenth-century former coaching inn that remains a true village hostelry. A reader lucky enough to live in a neighbouring village returns regularly for dishes such as scallops on borlotti bean and chestnut purée, and fillet steak of local beef with fondant potatoes, wild mushrooms and horseradish butter. Dishes don't shy away from piling up the layers, but always to good effect, as when sea bass comes with braised lettuce, a galette of potato, peas and fennel and a white wine and tarragon sauce. Reporters' favourite desserts include the matching lemon duo of posset and sorbet – 'light, stacked full of lemony flavour and very refreshing'. A compact wine list starts with house French at £12 a bottle.
Chef/s: Chris Rooney. **Open:** all week L 12 to 2.30, D 7 to 9 (6.30 to 8 Sun). **Closed:** 25 Dec. **Meals:** alc (main courses £8 to £20). **Service:** not inc. **Details:** major cards accepted. 44 seats. 60 seats outside. Separate bar. No music. No mobile phones. Wheelchair access. Children welcome. Car parking.

WARWICKSHIRE

Restaurant Bosquet
Ever-popular Gallic charmer
97a Warwick Road, Kenilworth   CV8 1HP
(01926) 852463
www.restaurantbosquet.co.uk
French | £32

Bernard and Jane Lignier have been charming everyone since 1981, and their cosily intimate converted house is 'all the better for being resolutely French', according to one reporter. They run things with great personal affection and irreproachable devotion to duty, adding a generous helping of bonhomie and never bowing to stiff-collared formality. Bernard's cooking takes its inspiration from the kitchens of his native south-west France: earthy richness and generosity are his watchwords, game and foie gras have their say, and his chips are fried in goose fat.

Menus follow the seasons, with wintery offerings including game pâté en croûte with walnut salad or roast partridge on truffled polenta with mandarin sauce, giving way to spring lamb, basil confit and provençale vegetables, or boneless saddle of rabbit with crayfish tails in a sherry-laced sauce. Desserts are mostly standards such as lemon tart, and the patriotically French wine list heads south for some prime pickings. Prices start at £16.50.
Chef/s: Bernard Lignier. **Open:** Tue to Fri L 12 to 1.15, Tue to Sat D 7 to 9.15. **Closed:** Sun, Mon. **Meals:** alc (main courses £20 to £22). Set L and D Tue to Fri £31.50. **Service:** not inc. **Details:** major cards accepted. 26 seats. No music. No mobile phones. Children welcome.

The Bluebell
Comfort classics and cooking with care
93 High Street, Henley-in-Arden   B95 5AT
(01564) 793049
www.bluebellhenley.co.uk
Gastropub | £25

'It appears to be the place to be seen locally,' noted a reader of the Taylors' 500-year-old former coaching inn on the Tudor high street. Oodles of original features contribute to the cheering atmosphere, and it's run with great aplomb. Much of the kitchen produce comes from the owners' expanding allotment, and the pick of local suppliers provides the rest. On a cold night, one reporter was glad to be served with a hearty winter vegetable soup swirled with pesto, followed by braised lamb shank with dauphinoise, accompanied by devilled kidneys. Whisky-jellied oranges and blood orange sorbet made for an impeccably refreshing conclusion. Great care is taken over these dishes, as also with fish cookery, and there is a listing of pies and 'comfort classics', as befits the pub ethos. A short wine list offers a good geographical spread, with most things available by the glass (from £3.85).
Chef/s: Rob Round. **Open:** Tue to Sun L 12 to 2.30 (3.30 Sun), Tue to Sat D 6 to 9.30. **Closed:** Mon. **Meals:** alc (main courses £10 to £25). **Service:** not inc. **Details:** major cards accepted. 50 seats. 50 seats outside. Wheelchair access. Music. Children welcome. Car parking.

Heart of England | Where to Eat

WEST MIDLANDS

Simpsons
City high-flier with flair
20 Highfield Road, Edgbaston, Birmingham
B15 3DU
(0121) 4543434
www.simpsonsrestaurant.co.uk
Modern French | £45

Some serious competitors are staking their gastronomic claims in Birmingham, but Andreas Antona's high-flying restaurant-with-rooms has cemented its reputation as one of the top players in a city that is on the up. The setting is a classically proportioned Georgian mansion in leafy Edgbaston, with a lovely conservatory overlooking a riot of rhododendrons. It's the kind of place where polish and courtesy come with the territory. Contemporary French cuisine is the kitchen's business, shored up by generally impeccable technique, oodles of subtlety and a flair for creating unexpected mixed marriages on the plate. Seared Scottish scallops appear with Avruga caviar, orzo pasta and seaweed butter, home-salted cod is exotically paired with coconut basmati rice, coriander and cauliflower salad, while the meaty tones of milk-fed Pyrenean lamb, with couscous, semi-dried apricots, aubergine caviar and ras-el-hanout seem to have wafted over on a southerly wind. Stiff Gallic breezes also blow through slow-cooked belly of suckling pig with Agen prunes and a meaty combo of braised beef cheek and fillet with parsley roots and red wine sauce. To finish, exquisite ice creams point up many of the cleverly crafted desserts – a star anise version with aromatic roasted pear, for example. Five-star French names dominate the majestic wine list, although there is plenty of room for high-strength Super Tuscans and glistering Aussie reds. For best value, visit La Petite Cave – a collection of bottles priced around £30.

Chef/s: Luke Tipping. **Open:** all week L 12 to 2 (2.30 Sat and Sun), Mon to Sat D 7 to 9.30 (10 Fri and Sat). **Closed:** bank hols. **Meals:** alc (main courses £20 to £27). Set L £30. Set D £32.50. Tasting menu £70. **Service:** 12.5% (optional). **Details:** major cards accepted. 70 seats. 10 seats outside. Air conditioning. No music. No mobile phones. Children welcome. Car parking.

WORCESTERSHIRE

Grafton Manor
Country cooking with a spicy twist
Grafton Lane, Bromsgrove B61 7HA
(01527) 579007
www.graftonmanorhotel.co.uk
Modern British | £29

The original manor house was built in the sixteenth century by an Earl of Shrewsbury and played centre-stage in the hatching of the Gunpowder Plot. Now a high-end country hotel, it enjoys a tranquil setting, a refined tone and a chef who loves Indian food. So the country cooking often has a spicy twist – and there are sometimes special all-Indian menus to celebrate festivals. The usual fixed-price menus feature the likes of seared scallops with spiced pear, pork fillet wrapped in pancetta with champ mash, braised red cabbage and Madeira, and chocolate tart with caramel ice cream to finish. That Indian touch might influence the dessert menu too, so don't be surprised to see Hyderabadi apricots with mango and coriander sorbet. A French-led wine list opens with nine house wines, including Ardèche blends at £13.95.

Chef/s: Tim Waldron and Adam Harrison. **Open:** Sun to Fri L 12 to 2.30, Mon to Sat D 7 to 9. **Closed:** 30 Dec to 1 Jan. **Meals:** Set L £22.50. Set D £28.95 to £33.75 (4 courses). **Service:** not inc. **Details:** major cards accepted. 50 seats. Separate bar. No music. No mobile phones. Wheelchair access. Children welcome. Car parking.

Russell's
Boutique brasserie with panache
20 High Street, Broadway WR12 7DT
(01386) 853555
www.russellsofbroadway.co.uk
Modern British | £27

Once home to celebrated furniture designer Gordon Russell, this painstakingly restored Georgian building now plies its trade as a boutique restaurant-with-rooms. The stylish contemporary dining room occupies the ground floor, with glass doors opening onto a secluded courtyard for alfresco meals. Chef Matthew Laughton cooks with panache and an open mind, happily reinventing prawn cocktail, dressing Caesar salads and offering tapas 'slates' to share, as well as pulling some unexpected brasserie strokes along the way. Home-cured gravlax is given a perky lift with pickled vegetable salad, and pan-fried lamb's liver is plated up with haggis mash and roasted beetroot, while dried fruit couscous, butternut squash, olives and mint yoghurt relish add some warm Middle Eastern tones to grilled Barnsley chop. To finish there are British cheeses and inviting desserts ranging from chocolate mousse with mulled berries to coffee pannacotta with espresso ice cream. The commendable 50-bin wine list includes 11 house recommendations at £18.50 (£4.75 a glass).

Chef/s: Matthew Laughton. **Open:** all week L 12 to 2.30, Mon to Sat D 6 to 9.30 (6.30 Sat). **Meals:** alc (main courses £12 to £22). Set L and D £12 (2 courses) to £15. Sun L £22.95. **Service:** not inc. **Details:** major cards accepted. 60 seats. 30 seats outside. Air conditioning. Wheelchair access. Music. Children welcome. Car parking.

Content brought to you by **The Good Food Guide 2011**. Please see page 14 for further details.

453

Tourist Information Centres

When you arrive at your destination, visit an Official Partner Tourist Information Centre for quality assured help with accommodation and information about local attractions and events, or email your request before you go. To find a Tourist Information Centre by region visit enjoyEngland.com/find-tic.

BEWDLEY	Load Street	01299 404740	bewdleytic@wyreforestdc.gov.uk
BIRMINGHAM Rotunda	The Rotunda	0844 888 3883	callcentre@marketingbirmingham.com
BRIDGNORTH	The Library	01746 763257	bridgnorth.tourism@shropshire.gov.uk
CHURCH STRETTON	Church Street	01694 723133	churchstretton.scf@shropshire.gov.uk
COVENTRY CATHEDRAL	Coventry Cathedral	024 7622 5616	tic@cvone.co.uk
COVENTRY TRANSPORT MUSEUM	Millenium Place	024 7622 5616	tic@cvone.co.uk
HEREFORD	1 King Street	01432 268430	tic-hereford@herefordshire.gov.uk
IRONBRIDGE	Ironbridge Gorge Museum Trust	01952 884391	tic@ironbridge.org.uk
LEEK	Stockwell Street	01538 483741	tourism.services@staffsmoorlands.gov.uk
LICHFIELD	Lichfield Garrick	01543 412112	info@visitlichfield.com
LUDLOW	Castle Street	01584 875053	ludlow.tourism@shropshire.gov.uk
MALVERN	21 Church Street	01684 892289	malvern.tic@malvernhills.gov.uk
OSWESTRY (MILE END)	Mile End	01691 662488	oswestrytourism@shropshire.gov.uk
ROSS-ON-WYE	Swan House	01989 562768	tic-ross@herefordshire.gov.uk
RUGBY	Rugby Visitor Centre	01788 533217	visitor.centre@rugby.gov.uk
SHREWSBURY	The Music Hall	01743 281200	visitorinfo@shrewsbury.gov.uk
SOLIHULL	Central Library	0121 704 6130	artscomplex@solihull.gov.uk
STAFFORD	Stafford Gatehouse Theatre	01785 619619	tic@staffordbc.gov.uk
STOKE-ON-TRENT	Victoria Hall, Bagnall Street	01782 236000	stoke.tic@stoke.gov.uk
TAMWORTH	Tamworth Information Centre	01827 709581	tic@tamworth.gov.uk
WARWICK	The Court House	01926 492212	touristinfo@warwick-uk.co.uk
WORCESTER	The Guildhall	01905 728787	touristinfo@cityofworcester.gov.uk

Heart of England

Regional Contacts and Information

Marketing Birmingham
Tel: (0121) 202 5115
Web: www.visitbirmingham.com

Visit Coventy & Warwickshire
Tel: (024) 7622 5616
Web: www.visitcoventryandwarwickshire.co.uk

Visit Herefordshire
Tel: (01432) 260621
Web: www.visitherefordshire.co.uk

Shakespeare Country
Tel: 0870 160 7930
Web: www.shakespeare-country.co.uk

Shropshire Tourism
Tel: (01743) 261919
Web: www.shropshiretourism.co.uk

Destination Staffordshire
Tel: 0870 500 4444
Web: www.enjoystaffordshire.com

Stoke-on-Trent
Tel: (01782) 236000
Web: www.visitstoke.co.uk

Destination Worcestershire
Tel: (01905) 728787
Web: www.visitworcestershire.org

Heart of England | Gloucestershire/Herefordshire

Where to Stay

Entries appear alphabetically by town name in each county. A key to symbols appears on page 6. Maps start on page 706. A listing of all Enjoy England assessed accommodation appears at the end of the region.

KILCOT, Gloucestershire Map ref 2B1   SAT NAV GL18 1PG

FARMHOUSE ★★★★

B&B PER ROOM PER NIGHT
S £35.00
D £56.00

Withyland Heights
Beavans Hill, Kilcot, Newent, Gloucestershire GL18 1PG
t (01989) 720582 f (01989) 720238 e katrina@withylandheights.co.uk
w **withylandheights.co.uk** GUEST REVIEWS

Our working dairy farm boasts stunning views and easy access to M50. Rooms are spacious and attractively furnished. Hearty breakfasts and relaxed atmosphere. **directions** In Gorsley turn off B4221 at 'The Roadmaker' pub. Follow to T-junction, turn left. Straight over crossroads to T-junction, turn right. Withyland Heights on left. **open** All year **bedrooms** 1 twin, 1 family **bathrooms** 2 en suite **payment** cash, cheques

Room | General | Leisure

HAY-ON-WYE, Herefordshire Map ref 2A1   SAT NAV HR3 6EU

INN ★★★★

B&B PER ROOM PER NIGHT
S £47.50
D £95.00
EVENING MEAL PER PERSON
£20.00 – £35.00

Rhydspence Inn
Whitney-on-Wye, Near Hay-on-Wye HR3 6EU
t (01497) 831262 f (01497) 831751 e info@rhydspence-inn.co.uk
w **rhydspence-inn.co.uk** ONLINE MAP

14thC drovers' inn, in superb Wye Valley, serving top-quality local produce in comfortable surroundings. Beautiful en suite bedrooms and oak-beamed bars. **directions** Please refer to website. 1 and ha miles on the A438 West of Whitney-On-Wye **open** All year except Xmas **bedrooms** 1 single, 4 double, 2 twin **bathrooms** 7 en suite **payment** credit/debit cards, cash, cheques

Room | General | Leisure

Looking for something else?

You can also buy a copy of our popular guide 'Self Catering' including self-catering holiday homes, approved caravan holiday homes, boat accommodation and holiday cottage agencies in England 2011. Now available in good bookshops and online at **visitbritainshop.com**

£11.99

Heart of England | Herefordshire

LEDBURY, Herefordshire Map ref 2B1
SAT NAV HR8 1EG

Bluebell Lodge
Massington Lodge, Old Pumping Station, Eastnor, Ledbury HR8 1EG
t (01531) 636524   e massingtonlodge@hotmail.co.uk
w massingtonlodge.webeden.co.uk

B&B PER ROOM PER NIGHT
S £38.50
D £75.00

This private and self contained lodge is situated within 2.5 acres of grounds and woodland. Has ensuite shower, compact kitchenette, tea and coffee facilities and a continental breakfast is provided. **directions** Located a mile from historic Ledbury and within walking distance of Eastnor Castle. Only a short drive away from British Camp and the Malverns. **open** All year **bedrooms** 1 double **bathrooms** 1 en suite **payment** cash

Room   General

LEINTWARDINE, Herefordshire Map ref 4A3
SAT NAV SY7 0NF

Lower House
Adforton, Leintwardine, Ludlow SY7 0NF
t (01568) 770223   e reservations@sy7.com
w sy7.com ONLINE MAP

B&B PER ROOM PER NIGHT
S £32.00 – £37.00
D £64.00 – £74.00
EVENING MEAL PER PERSON
£12.50 – £20.00

Inglenooks, log fires and Aga cooking! A delightfully comfortable C17th country house set in two acres of beautiful gardens. Great walking countryside and a superb base to sample local delights. **directions** From the north proceed through Leintwardine on A4113. Take 2nd right signed Knighton then 1st left (unmarked road) **open** All year **bedrooms** 1 double, 3 twin, 2 family **bathrooms** 3 en suite, 3 with private bathroom **payment** cash, cheques

Room   General   Leisure

MUCH BIRCH, Herefordshire Map ref 2A1
SAT NAV HR2 8HJ

The Old School
Much Birch, Hereford HR2 8HJ
t (01981) 541317   e carolannedixon@btinternet.com
w oldschoolbb.co.uk ONLINE MAP

B&B PER ROOM PER NIGHT
S £30.00 – £35.00
D £50.00 – £60.00

The Old School was converted to a house in 1960. We are situated on the A49 between Hereford and Ross. Local food used where possible. Come and see us! **directions** 5 miles from Hereford, 7 miles from Ross on A49 **open** All year except Xmas **bedrooms** 2 double, 1 twin **bathrooms** 3 en suite **payment** cash, cheques, euros

Room   General   Leisure

Where is my pet welcome?
Some properties welcome well-behaved pets. Look for the 🐕 in the accommodation listings.

You can also buy a copy of our popular guide 'Pets Come Too!' Now available in good bookshops and online at **visitbritainshop.com**

£9.99

key to symbols see page 6

Heart of England | Herefordshire

PEMBRIDGE, Herefordshire Map ref 2A1
SAT NAV HR6 9JD

Lowe Farm B&B

Lowe Farm, Pembridge, Leominster, Herefordshire HR6 9JD
t (01544) 388395   e Juliet@lowe-farm.co.uk
w lowe-farm.co.uk   GUEST REVIEWS

B&B PER ROOM PER NIGHT
S £38.00 – £55.00
D £64.00 – £110.00

EVENING MEAL PER PERSON
£23.00 – £24.00

SPECIAL PROMOTIONS
Three nights plus £64 prpn
Free hot tub and one gents one ladies cycles free of charge.

Gold Winner 2009/10 Excellence Awards Servicemark. Juliet and Clive offer stress-free living, relaxation, late breakfast 8-10, Hot Tub. Farm Produce, ingredients, unrivalled taste, texture but it's not the veg alone, healthy exercise in rural Herefordshire or just relax any time of year. See website and Trip Adviser for Guests comments.

open All year except Xmas and New Year
bedrooms 1 single, 2 double, 2 twin
bathrooms 5 en suite
payment credit/debit cards, cash, cheques

directions Leominster A44 through Pembridge, 2 miles out village, turn right Marston, carry on through to next T-junction turn right 1/4 mile right, sign, tree.

BREAKFAST AWARD

Room
General
Leisure

ROSS-ON-WYE, Herefordshire Map ref 2A1
SAT NAV HR9 6LS

Caradoc Court

Sellack, Ross-on-Wye HR9 6LS
t (01989) 730257   e kathy@caradoccourt.co.uk
w caradoccourt.co.uk

B&B PER ROOM PER NIGHT
S £75.00 – £90.00
D £95.00 – £120.00

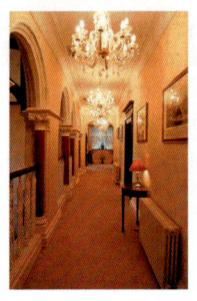

A magnificent historic Jacobean manor house, set in its own beautiful grounds above the River Wye, which has recently been meticulously restored to its former splendour. The bedrooms are extremely spacious and fitted out to a very high standard. A warm welcome awaits guests to this lovely home.

open All year except Xmas and New Year
bedrooms 2 double, 1 twin
bathrooms 3 en suite
payment credit/debit cards, cash

directions Turn right for Sellack off the A49 one mile north of Ross-on-Wye. Follow this lane for miles. Entrance on right opposite Lough Pool inn.

BREAKFAST AWARD

Room
General
Leisure

458   Official tourist board guide Bed & Breakfast

Heart of England | Herefordshire/Shropshire

VOWCHURCH, Herefordshire Map ref 2A1
SAT NAV HR2 9PF

Yew Tree House
Bacho Hill, Vowchurch, Golden Valley, Hereford HR2 9PF
t (01981) 251195 **e** enquiries@yewtreehouse-hereford.co.uk
w yewtreehouse-hereford.co.uk ONLINE MAP

B&B PER ROOM PER NIGHT
S £35.00 – £50.00
D £70.00 – £85.00
EVENING MEAL PER PERSON
£15.00 – £25.00

Two-hundred-year-old house with magnificent views of the Golden Valley, offering luxurious accommodation in an extremely comfortable family home. **directions** Please refer to website. **open** All year **bedrooms** 1 double, 1 twin, 1 family **bathrooms** 3 en suite **payment** cash, cheques, euros

BREAKFAST AWARD

Room General Leisure

BRIDGNORTH, Shropshire Map ref 4A3
SAT NAV WV16 6BA

Bulls Head Inn
Chelmarsh, Bridgnorth WV16 6BA
t (01746) 861469 **f** (01746) 861469 **e** bull_chelmarsh@btconnect.com
w bullsheadchelmarsh.co.uk ONLINE MAP LAST MINUTE OFFERS

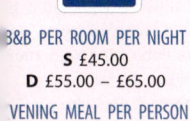

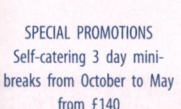

B&B PER ROOM PER NIGHT
S £45.00
D £55.00 – £65.00
EVENING MEAL PER PERSON
£6.95 – £16.00

SPECIAL PROMOTIONS
Self-catering 3 day mini-breaks from October to May from £140

Family owned 18thC country inn offering excellent accommodation and food, approximately four miles from Bridgnorth. All bedrooms are en suite with tea-/coffee-making facilities. Three ground-floor bedrooms for people with disabilities. Choice of cottages/apartments for self-catering or bed and breakfast. Fishing parties welcome.

open All year
bedrooms 1 single, 6 double, 2 twin, 3 family
bathrooms 12 en suite
payment credit/debit cards, cash, cheques

directions From Bridgnorth take the B4363 signposted Cleobury Mortimer & Highley, then an immediate left turn onto the B4555 Highley & Chelmarsh road for 3 miles.

Room General Leisure

BRIDGNORTH, Shropshire Map ref 4A3
SAT NAV WV16 4DW

The Croft
10/11 St Mary's Street, Bridgnorth WV16 4DW
t (01746) 762416 **f** (01746) 767431 **e** thecrofthotelbridgnorth@yahoo.co.uk
w crofthotelbridgnorth.co.uk ONLINE MAP GUEST REVIEWS

B&B PER ROOM PER NIGHT
S £36.00 – £51.50
D £64.25 – £85.00

Grade 2 listed with olde world charm, oak beams, inglenook fireplaces and comfortable lounge. Individually styled, well furnished bedrooms. Centrally located in town centre within a quiet conservation area. **directions** Please contact us for directions **open** All year **bedrooms** 3 single, 7 double, 1 twin, 1 family **bathrooms** 10 en suite **payment** credit/debit cards, cash, cheques

Room General Leisure

Heart of England | Shropshire

BROSELEY, Shropshire Map ref 4A3
SAT NAV TF12 5EW

Enjoy England ★★★★ Guest House – Silver Award

B&B PER ROOM PER NIGHT
S £45.00 – £55.00
D £35.00 – £45.00

Broseley House
1 The Square, Broseley, Ironbridge TF12 5EW
t (01952) 882043   e info@broseleyhouse.co.uk
w broseleyhouse.co.uk   ONLINE MAP   GUEST REVIEWS   LAST MINUTE OFFERS

Period townhouse, quality accomodation in the heart of a small historic town one mile from World Heritage Site Ironbridge. Walkers, cyclists welcome. Unique style bedrooms with many extra touches. **directions** Refer to the website or call for directions. **open** All year **bedrooms** 1 single, 3 double, 2 twin, 1 family **bathrooms** 7 en suite **payment** credit/debit cards, cash, cheques, euros

BREAKFAST AWARD

Room   General   Leisure

CLUN, Shropshire Map ref 4A3
SAT NAV SY7 8JA

Enjoy England ★★★ Inn

B&B PER ROOM PER NIGHT
S £32.50 – £40.00
D £55.00 – £70.00
EVENING MEAL PER PERSON
£5.25 – £15.00

The White Horse Inn
The Square, Clun SY7 8JA
t (01588) 640305   f (01588) 640305   e room@whi-clun.co.uk
w whi-clun.co.uk

Small, friendly, Good-Beer-Guide-listed pub with well-appointed, en suite family bedrooms in traditional style. Wide-ranging menu available in dining room. CAMRA Shropshire Pub of the Year 2007. **directions** Please contact us for directions **open** All year except Xmas **bedrooms** 1 double, 3 family **bathrooms** 4 en suite **payment** credit/debit cards, cash, cheques

WALKERS WELCOME   CYCLISTS WELCOME

Room   General   Leisure

ELLESMERE (3 MILES), Shropshire Map ref 4A2
SAT NAV SY12 9BB

Enjoy England ★★★★ Bed & Breakfast

B&B PER ROOM PER NIGHT
S £30.00 – £35.00
D £60.00 – £65.00

Hordley Hall
Hordley, Ellesmere SY12 9BB
t (01691) 622772   e hazel@hordleyhall.co.uk
w hordleyhall.co.uk

Spacious Georgian house in very peaceful unspoilt location, Shropshire's Lake District. Large attractive garden with parking and cycle storage. Ideal for walking, cycling or touring with easy access to A5. **directions** A5 Shrewsbury to Oswestry. Leave A5 at Queen's Head junction. Past the 'Queen's Head', turn left down the side of the canal. Hordley 4 miles. **open** All year **bedrooms** 1 single, 2 double, 1 twin **bathrooms** 2 en suite, 2 with private bathroom **payment** cash, cheques

WALKERS WELCOME   CYCLISTS WELCOME

Room   General

LUDLOW, Shropshire Map ref 4A3
SAT NAV SY8 1LR

Enjoy England ★★★ Guest House

B&B PER ROOM PER NIGHT
S £27.00 – £47.00
D £68.00 – £74.00
EVENING MEAL PER PERSON
£18.00

Cecil Guest House
Sheet Road, Ludlow SY8 1LR
t (01584) 872442   f (01584) 872442
w cecil-ludlow.co.uk

Attractive guesthouse 15 minutes' walk from town centre and station. Freshly cooked food from local produce. Residents' bar and lounge. Off-street parking. **directions** From A49 north, right at 2nd roundabout. From A49 south, left at first roundabout, guest house 300 yards on left. **open** All year **bedrooms** 2 single, 3 double, 3 twin, 1 family **bathrooms** 7 en suite **payment** cash, cheques

Room   General   Leisure

460   Official tourist board guide Bed & Breakfast

Heart of England | Shropshire

LUDLOW, Shropshire Map ref 4A3
SAT NAV SY8 1PQ

Bromley Court
18–20 Lower Broad Street, Ludlow SY8 1PQ
t (01584) 876996 e bromley.court18@btinternet.com
w ludlowhotels.com LAST MINUTE OFFERS

SPECIAL PROMOTIONS
Special promotions available out of season.

Tudor cottages of great charm, in Ludlow town. Each cottage forms a delightful, individually furnished suite - for total privacy and relaxation. Within walking distance of everything in Ludlow.

open All year
bedrooms 3 suites
bathrooms 3 en suite
payment credit/debit cards, cash, cheques

directions From north, fork left on B4361 through town. Right at lights, 100m on right. From south, fork left on B4361 over bridge, 100m on right.

Leisure

LUDLOW, Shropshire Map ref 4A3
SAT NAV SY8 1NG

DeGreys
5-6 Broad Street, Ludlow, Shropshire SY8 1NG
t (01584) 872764 f (01584) 879764 e degreys@btopenworld.com
w degreys.co.uk ONLINE MAP LAST MINUTE OFFERS

B&B PER ROOM PER NIGHT
S £60.00 – £130.00
D £80.00 – £190.00

SPECIAL PROMOTIONS
For last-minute offers please check our website. Weekday breaks from £200-£385. Weekend breaks from £220-£445

An irresistible fusion of the past and present is how one would describe our nine bedrooms and suites. Each with its own individual charm, they ensure a feeling of luxury and comfort. All the rooms have en-suite facilities and some feature stunning bathrooms with roll-top baths and large, powerful showers.

open All year except Xmas and New Year
bedrooms 5 double, 3 twin, 1 suite
bathrooms 9 en suite
payment credit/debit cards, cash, cheques

directions Off the A49, into the town centre, 50yds beyond the clock tower in Broad Street. Black and white Tudor building.

BREAKFAST AWARD Room General

key to symbols see page 6

461

Heart of England | **Shropshire**

LYTH BANK, Shropshire Map ref 4A3
SAT NAV SY3 0BP

Lyth Hill House
28 Old Coppice, Lyth Hill, Shrewsbury SY3 0BP
t (01743) 874660 **e** bnb@lythhillhouse.com
w lythhillhouse.com GUEST REVIEWS

B&B PER ROOM PER NIGHT
S £40.00 – £56.00
D £60.00 – £96.00

SPECIAL PROMOTIONS
Exclusive use of our facilities for families or friends wanting to enjoy a really special break together: maximum six people.

A luxury 5-Star Gold Award B & B in the heart of the Shropshire countryside, four miles from Shrewsbury. Beautifully appointed, comfortable bedrooms, with Egyptian cotton linen. Enjoy a swim, or stroll in our beautiful gardens - panoramic views of 30 miles. A warm welcome, comfort, peace and tranquility awaits.

open All year except Xmas and New Year
bedrooms 1 single, 1 double, 2 twin
bathrooms 3 en suite, 1 with private bathroom
payment credit/debit cards, cash, cheques, euros
directions Between Shrewsbury and Church Stretton, 3 miles south of A5 and 3 miles west of A49. Directions provided on request and with each booking confirmation.

BREAKFAST AWARD

Room
General
Leisure

OSWESTRY, Shropshire Map ref 4A3
SAT NAV SY11 4PB

Yew Tree House
Lower Frankton, Nr Oswestry SY11 4PB
t 01691 622126 **e** info@yewtreebandb.co.uk
w YewTreeBandB.co.uk ONLINE MAP

B&B PER ROOM PER NIGHT
S £59.00 – £70.00
D £79.00 – £90.00

Yew Tree House has two stylish, en-suite rooms which are contemporary, luxuriously equipped, full of original artworks and have their own entrance and terrace with seating area. All rooms groundfloor **directions** From Oswestry take A495 Whitchurch, 2.5 miles past Whittington enter Welsh Frankton; immediately before church turn right signed Lower Frankton. House 1.5 miles on right.
open All year **bedrooms** 1 double, 1 twin **bathrooms** 2 en suite
payment credit/debit cards, cash

Room   General   Leisure

SHIFNAL, Shropshire Map ref 4A3
SAT NAV TF11 9AU

Odfellows Wine Bar
Market Place, Shifnal TF11 9AU
t (01952) 461517 **e** reservations@odley.co.uk
w odleyinns.co.uk/odfellows

B&B PER ROOM PER NIGHT
S £35.00 – £48.00
D £40.00 – £55.00
EVENING MEAL PER PERSON
£8.95 – £28.00

Comfortable bedrooms upstairs, with lively winebar downstairs. Modern British food, intelligently assembled wine list and draught-beer range. The cooked breakfast from 10.30, early birds are amply served the continental. **directions** M54 J4, Direction Shifnal. 1st roundabout take 3rd exit. Follow road under railway bridge. Odfellows is on the left just after the bridge. **open** All year
bedrooms 6 double, 1 family **bathrooms** 7 en suite **payment** credit/debit cards, cash, cheques

Room   General

462

Heart of England | Shropshire

SHREWSBURY, Shropshire Map ref 4A3

SAT NAV SY5 6LE

Brompton Farmhouse

Cross Houses, Shrewsbury SY5 6LE
t (01743) 761629 f (01743) 761679 e info@bromptonfarmhouse.co.uk
w bromptonfarmhouse.co.uk ONLINE MAP GUEST REVIEWS ONLINE BOOKING LAST MINUTE OFFERS

B&B PER ROOM PER NIGHT
S £45.00 – £65.00
D £70.00 – £95.00

EVENING MEAL PER PERSON
£20.00 – £35.00

SPECIAL PROMOTIONS
Cookery school in converted barn, courses to suit all.
www.bromptoncookeryschool.co.uk

Our delightful Georgian farmhouse, set in extensive lawns and gardens, is a haven of peace, comfort and tranquility. We are part of the Attingham Park a stunning National Trust estate. We are three miles from Shrewsbury and 6 miles from Ironbridge and Telford - ideally situated to explore Shropshire.

open All year
bedrooms 2 double, 1 twin, 1 family
bathrooms 4 en suite
payment credit/debit cards, cash, cheques

directions B4380 at Atcham take turn to X-Houses. Follow signs to Brompton.

TELFORD, Shropshire Map ref 4A3

SAT NAV TF6 6BE

The Mill House

Shrewsbury Road, High Ercall, Telford TF6 6BE
t (01952) 770394 e judy@ercallmill.co.uk
w ercallmill.co.uk ONLINE MAP

B&B PER ROOM PER NIGHT
S £39.00 – £45.00
D £55.00 – £65.00

Beautiful, Grade II Listed, converted water mill (no machinery) beside River Roden. Rural setting. All rooms en suite, TV, Freeview and DVD. Working smallholding. Ideal for Ironbridge, Telford, Shrewsbury, mid-Wales. **directions** From M54 jct 6. One mile south of High Ercall on B5062. **open** All year **bedrooms** 1 double, 1 twin, 1 family **bathrooms** 3 en suite **payment** cash, cheques

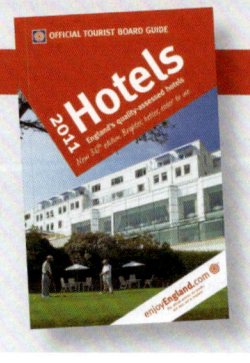

Looking for something else?

You can also buy a copy of our popular guide 'Hotels' including country house and town house hotels, metro and budget hotels, serviced apartments, restaurants with rooms and Spas in England 2011.

Now available in good bookshops and online at
visitbritainshop.com

£10.99

Heart of England | Shropshire/Staffordshire

TELFORD, Shropshire Map ref 4A3
SAT NAV TF1 2HA

enjoyEngland.com ★★★★★ INN
enjoyEngland.com Silver AWARD

B&B PER ROOM PER NIGHT
S £65.00 – £98.00
D £65.00 – £128.00

EVENING MEAL PER PERSON
£12.00 – £35.00

SPECIAL PROMOTIONS
Stay&Eat offer (DBB for £125 per couple) Wrekin Weekend (3 nights DBB plus extras £325).

Old Orleton Inn
Holyhead Road, Wellington, Shropshire TF1 2HA
t (01952) 255011 **e** info@theoldorleton.com
w theoldorleton.com ONLINE MAP GUEST REVIEWS ONLINE BOOKING LAST MINUTE OFFERS

Contemporary restyled 17thC Coaching Inn facing the famous Wrekin Hill. A charming retreat for both work and pleasure. With ten boutique-style bedrooms, each unique in design and character. A comprehensive selection of freshly prepared vegetarian, fish and meat dishes are served using fresh, quality, local produce.

open Closed for two weeks in January
bedrooms 1 single, 8 double, 1 twin
bathrooms 10 en suite
payment credit/debit cards, cash, cheques

directions 7 miles from Shrewsbury, 4 miles from Ironbridge, M54 (exit 7), 400yds on the left towards Wellington.

Room
General
Leisure

ALREWAS, Staffordshire Map ref 4B3
SAT NAV DE13 7DL

enjoyEngland.com RATING APPLIED FOR

B&B PER ROOM PER NIGHT
S £85.00
D £120.00 – £170.00

Alrewas Hayes
Alrewas Hayes, Burton-on-Trent DE13 7DL
t (01283) 791625 **f** 01283791625 **e** info@alrewashayes.com
w alrewashayes.com

Alrewas Hayes is an elegant Queen Anne residence in the heart of rural Staffordshire. All rooms are fully equiped with televisions, tea/coffee making facilities, power showers and complimentary toiletries. **directions** Exit A38 at Alrewas, at Orgeave turn left towards Fradley junction, about 3/4 mile turn right into Alrewas Hayes. **open** All year **bedrooms** 6 double **bathrooms** 6 en suite **payment** credit/debit cards, cash, cheques

Room   **General**

ALTON, Staffordshire Map ref 4B2
SAT NAV ST14 5HP

enjoyEngland.com ★★★★ GUEST HOUSE

B&B PER ROOM PER NIGHT
S £35.00
D £60.00

Windy Arbour
Hollis Lane, Denstone, Uttoxeter ST14 5HP
t (01889) 591013 **f** (01889) 591054 **e** stay@windyarbour.co.uk
w windyarbour.co.uk ONLINE MAP GUEST REVIEWS ONLINE BOOKING LAST MINUTE OFFERS

Windy Arbour farmhouse is a peaceful haven graced with superb views. A warm country welcome is guaranteed. Alton Towers, the Peak District and Derbyshire Dales all within easy reach. **directions** From A50 follow Alton Towers. Left into Denstone, following signs for Denstone College. Ahead is Hollis Lane, leading to the hilltop farm. **open** All year except Xmas and New Year **bedrooms** 1 double, 1 twin, 2 family, 2 suites **bathrooms** 5 en suite, 1 with private bathroom **payment** credit/debit cards, cash, cheques

Room   **General**

FAMILIES

Heart of England | Staffordshire

ALTON, Staffordshire Map ref 4B2
SAT NAV ST10 4QZ

enjoyEngland.com ★★★★ BED & BREAKFAST

B&B PER ROOM PER NIGHT
S £33.00 – £37.00
D £45.00 – £51.00

EVENING MEAL PER PERSON
£9.00 – £19.00

Fields Farm
Chapel Lane, Threapwood Alton, Staffs ST10 4QZ
t (01538) 752721 Mobile 07850310381 e pat.massey@fieldsfarmbb.co.uk
w fieldsfarmbb.co.uk

Traditional farmhouse hospitality and comfort in the picturesque Churnet Valley area. Ten-minutes from Alton-Towers. Near Peak District National Park, potteries, Uttoxeter race-course, stately-homes and many more local attractions. Barbecue area. Stabling available (situated on Sabrina Way). Ideal for walking, cycling and riding. Family rooms. Children £15 each sharing with adult.

open All year except Xmas
bedrooms 1 double, 1 twin, 1 family
bathrooms 2 en suite, 1 with private bathroom
payment cash, cheques

directions Detailed directions available on request.

Room · General · Leisure

ASHBOURNE (1.25 MILES), Staffordshire Map ref 4B2
SAT NAV DE6 2HN

enjoyEngland.com ★ RATING APPLIED FOR

B&B PER ROOM PER NIGHT
S £29.50
D £55.00 – £60.00

Dove House B&B
Bridge Hill, Mayfield, Ashbourne DE6 2HN
t (01335) 343329

A comfortable detached Victorian house with garden and off road parking. Nearby is the attractive Georgian town of Ashbourne. The Peak District, Chatsworth House and Alton Towers are within reach. **directions** Please contact us for directions **open** All year except Xmas and New Year **bedrooms** 1 double **bathrooms** 1 en suite **payment** cash, cheques

Room · General P · Leisure

CHEADLE, Staffordshire Map ref 4B2
SAT NAV ST10 1RA

enjoyEngland.com ★★★★ FARMHOUSE

B&B PER ROOM PER NIGHT
S £25.00
D £50.00

Rakeway House Farm B&B
Rakeway Road, Cheadle, Alton Towers Area ST10 1RA
t (01538) 755345 e rakewayhousefarm@btinternet.com
w rakewayhousefarm.com

Charming farmhouse, beautiful gardens. Fantastic views over Cheadle and surrounding countryside. Alton Towers 15 minutes' drive. Good base for Peak District and Potteries. First-class accommodation, excellent menu, superb hospitality. **directions** Please contact us for directions **open** All year **bedrooms** 1 double, 1 twin, 1 family **bathrooms** 3 en suite **payment** cash, cheques

Room · General · Leisure

for key to symbols see page 6

465

Heart of England | Staffordshire

LICHFIELD, Staffordshire Map ref 4B3
SAT NAV WS14 0BG

Copper's End Guest House
Walsall Road, Muckley Corner, Lichfield WS14 0BG
t (01543) 372910 f (01543) 360423 e info@coppersendguesthouse.co.uk
w coppersendguesthouse.co.uk ONLINE MAP ONLINE BOOKING

B&B PER ROOM PER NIGHT
S £35.00 – £42.00
D £52.00 – £64.00

SPECIAL PROMOTIONS
Special Promotions Per Request. Freeview In All Rooms.

Detached guesthouse, character and charm in own grounds. Conservatory dining room, large walled garden with patio, guests' lounge. Vegetarians catered for. Parking, safes in rooms, luggage racks. Access M6, M42 and M1, Lichfie[ld], Walsall, Birmingham. Sixteen miles to NEC, six miles Whittington Barracks. Motorcyclist, cyclist, walker friendly.

open All year except Xmas and New Year
bedrooms 3 double, 3 twin
bathrooms 4 en suite
payment credit/debit cards, cash, cheques

directions 100yds from Muckley Corner roundabout off the A5, 3 miles south of Lichfield, Walsall 5 miles. Ordnance Survey ref. SK083067.

Room
General
Leisure

MODDERSHALL, Staffordshire Map ref 4B2
SAT NAV ST15 8TG

Moddershall Oaks Spa Restaurant Suites
Moddershall, Nr Stone, Staffordshire ST15 8TG
t 01782 399000 f 01782 399662 e enquiries@moddershalloaks.com
w moddershalloaks.com ONLINE MAP GUEST REVIEWS LAST MINUTE OFFERS

B&B PER ROOM PER NIGHT
S £105.00 – £115.00
D £140.00 – £160.00

EVENING MEAL PER PERSON
£25.00 – £35.00

SPECIAL PROMOTIONS
Fantastic offers available - please check online at www.moddershalloaks.com for our latest offers.

Located in the heart of Staffordshire & set in 7[0] acres of picturesque grounds, Moddershall Oak[s] is a magnificent setting for an adult friendly sp[a] restaurant and suites facility. Facilities include 5[0] accommodation, spa, relaxation lounge, hair salon, award winning restaurant, woodland wal[k], gym, tennis court & bicycle hire.

open All year
bedrooms 10 double
bathrooms 10 en suite
payment credit/debit cards

directions Motorway: J14 or J15 of the M6 - 10 miles Major road: A50 - 4 miles Main station: Stoke on Trent - 8 miles

Room
General
Leisure

466 Official tourist board guide Bed & Breakfa[st]

Heart of England | Staffordshire

RUGELEY, Staffordshire Map ref 4B3
SAT NAV WS15 3LL

Colton House
Bellamour Way, Colton, Rugeley, Staffs. WS15 3LL
t (01889) 578580 **f** (01889) 578580 **e** mail@coltonhouse.com
w coltonhouse.com ONLINE MAP

B&B PER ROOM PER NIGHT
S £55.00 – £79.00
D £72.00 – £106.00

EVENING MEAL PER PERSON
£9.00 – £12.50

Pretty, peaceful village, winner of Best B&B in our region, Georgian licensed boutique accommodation, views across 1.5-acre garden to Cannock Chase. All rooms ensuite, individually designed with comfort in mind. **directions** M6 Toll Jct 7, A460 to Rugeley then B5013 towards Uttoxeter, after 2 miles, right into Colton. Colton House is 0.25 miles on the right. **open** All year **bedrooms** 5 double, 1 twin **bathrooms** 6 en suite **payment** credit/debit cards, cash, cheques

Room General

STAFFORD, Staffordshire Map ref 4B3
SAT NAV ST18 0BA

Rooks Nest Farm
Weston Bank, Weston, Stafford ST18 0BA
t (01889) 270624 **e** info@rooksnest.co.uk
w rooksnest.co.uk ONLINE MAP

B&B PER ROOM PER NIGHT
S £35.00
D £55.00

Modern farmhouse on working farm, with far-reaching views over the Trent valley. Close to Weston Hall and County Showground, easy access to all Staffordshire attractions. **directions** Please Refer To Website. **open** All year **bedrooms** 1 double, 1 twin **bathrooms** 2 en suite **payment** cash, cheques

Room General Leisure

STAFFORD, Staffordshire Map ref 4B3
SAT NAV ST16 3LQ

Wyndale Guest House
199 Corporation Street, Stafford ST16 3LQ
t (01785) 223069 **e** wyndale@aol.com
w wyndaleguesthouse.co.uk ONLINE MAP GUEST REVIEWS LAST MINUTE OFFERS

B&B PER ROOM PER NIGHT
S £35.00 – £48.00
D £60.00 – £68.00

EVENING MEAL PER PERSON
£8.00 – £18.00

SPECIAL PROMOTIONS
Please phone for offers that may be available.

The Wyndale is a comfortable Victorian house conveniently situated 0.25-miles from the town centre, less to the records office. We are on route to county show ground, hospitals & business parks. Easy access to the M6. Local attractions, including Shugborough, Trentham Gardens, & Amerton Farm. Enjoy our home made preserves.

open All year except Xmas
bedrooms 2 single, 2 double, 2 twin, 2 family
bathrooms 5 en suite, 1 with private bathroom
payment credit/debit cards, cash, cheques, euros

directions Please go to our web site where we have full direction & maps.
www.wyndaleguesthouse.co.uk

Room General

Heart of England | Staffordshire/Warwickshire

STOKE-ON-TRENT, Staffordshire Map ref 4B2   SAT NAV ST1 3JY

Verdon Guest House
44 Charles Street, Hanley, Stoke-on-Trent, Staffordshire ST1 3JY
t (01782) 264244 f (01782) 264244
w verdonguesthouse.co.uk ONLINE MAP

B&B PER ROOM PER NIGHT
S £25.00 – £28.00
D £40.00 – £44.00

Large, friendly, newly renovated, city centre guesthouse. Alton Towers 20 minutes. All rooms: large flat-screen tv with 50 Freeview channels and DVDs. Free wireless internet. Quality and value guaranteed. **directions** M6 Jct15 or Jct16. Follow signs to Hanley City Centre and Cultural Quarter (A5006). Turn right on sharp bend in Birch Terrace (near Bus Station). **open** All year **bedrooms** 1 single, 4 double, 3 twin, 5 family **bathrooms** 5 en suite, 5 with private bathroom **payment** credit/debit cards, cash, cheques

LEAMINGTON SPA, Warwickshire Map ref 4B3   SAT NAV CV33 9NE

Braeside Bed & Breakfast
26 Temple End, Harbury, Leamington Spa CV33 9NE
t (01926) 613402 e rosemary@braesidebb.co.uk
w braesidebb.co.uk

B&B PER ROOM PER NIGHT
S £30.00 – £35.00
D £55.00 – £65.00

Comfortable accommodation in Warwickshire village, close to historic Warwick. Within reach of Stratford-upon-Avon, the Cotswolds, Kenilworth, Coventry, Oxford, NEC, Stoneleigh Park, Gaydon Heritage Centre and the M40. **directions** Close to junction 12 off M40 and Fosse Way. Near Warwick. **open** All year except Xmas **bedrooms** 1 double, 1 twin **bathrooms** 1 en suite, 1 with private bathroom **payment** cash, cheques

LEAMINGTON SPA, Warwickshire Map ref 4B3   SAT NAV CV31 3PW

Victoria Park Lodge
12 Adelaide Road, Royal Leamington Spa, Warwick CV31 3PW
t (01926) 424195 f (01926) 421521 e info@victoriaparkhotelleamingtonspa.co.uk
w victoriaparkhotelleamingtonspa.co.uk ONLINE BOOKING

B&B PER ROOM PER NIGHT
S £55.00
D £70.00 – £75.00

With 29 en-suite bedrooms and a spacious serviced apartment nearby for short/long stays. 4 mins walk from the town centre and 5 mins drive from Warwick Castle. **directions** Please contact us for directions **open** All year except Xmas and New Year **bedrooms** 8 single, 10 double, 2 twin, 9 family **bathrooms** 29 en suite **payment** credit/debit cards, cash, cheques

LONG COMPTON, Warwickshire Map ref 2B1   SAT NAV CV36 5JZ

Butlers Road Farm
Long Compton, Shipston-on-Stour CV36 5JZ
t (01608) 684262 f (01608) 684262 e eileen@butlersroadfarm.com
w butlersroadfarm.co.uk

B&B PER ROOM PER NIGHT
S £35.00
D £50.00

120-acre stock farm. Listed Cotswold-stone farmhouse adjacent to A3400 between Oxford and Stratford-upon-Avon. Home comforts. Local pub nearby. Rooms also function as family rooms. **directions** Midway between Stratford-upon-Avon and Oxford on A3400 **open** All year **bedrooms** 1 double, 1 twin **payment** cash, cheques

BREAKFAST AWARD

Heart of England | **Warwickshire**

STRATFORD-UPON-AVON, Warwickshire Map ref 2B1   SAT NAV CV35 8PQ

enjoyEngland.com ★★★★ BED & BREAKFAST

B&B PER ROOM PER NIGHT
S £45.00 – £55.00
D £65.00 – £90.00

Austons Down
Saddle Bow Lane, Claverdon, Stratford-upon-Avon CV35 8PQ
t (01926) 842068 f (01926) 842068 e lmh@austonsdown.com
w austonsdown.com ONLINE MAP

Queen Anne-style home in a rural setting. Ten minutes drive to Stratford-upon-Avon and Warwick Castle, 25 minutes to the NEC. A warm welcome is offered to all. **directions** Directions on web site www.austonsdown.com
open All year except Xmas and New Year **bedrooms** 2 double, 1 twin **bathrooms** 3 en suite **payment** cash, cheques, euros

Room General Leisure

STRATFORD-UPON-AVON, Warwickshire Map ref 2B1   SAT NAV CV37 7LN

enjoyEngland.com ★★★★ GUEST HOUSE

B&B PER ROOM PER NIGHT
S £30.00 – £40.00
D £60.00 – £74.00

SPECIAL PROMOTIONS
3 nights for the price of 2
from Oct–March.

Avonlea
47 Shipston Road, Stratford-upon-Avon CV37 7LN
t (01789) 205940 e enquiries@avonlea-stratford.co.uk
w avonlea-stratford.co.uk ONLINE MAP GUEST REVIEWS

Stylish Victorian town house situated only five minutes' walk from the theatre and Stratford town centre. All rooms are en suite and furnished to the highest quality. Our guests are assured of a warm welcome and friendly atmosphere. On site parking.

open All year except Xmas
bedrooms 1 single, 4 double, 2 twin, 1 family
bathrooms 7 en suite, 1 with private bathroom
payment credit/debit cards, cash, cheques, euros

directions A3400 Shipston Road, 100m from Clopton Bridge

Room General Leisure

STRATFORD-UPON-AVON, Warwickshire Map ref 2B1   SAT NAV CV37 9RA

enjoyEngland.com ★★★★ BED & BREAKFAST

B&B PER ROOM PER NIGHT
S £35.00
D £58.00

Larkrise Cottage
Upper Billesley, Stratford-upon-Avon CV37 9RA
t (01789) 268618 e alanbailey17@googlemail.com
w larkrisecottage.co.uk ONLINE MAP

Larkrise Cottage provides quality fare in a tranquil rural location. It is within easy reach of the theatres of Stratford and the charm of the Cotswolds. **directions** Please Refer To Website. **open** All year except Xmas and New Year **bedrooms** 1 double, 1 twin **bathrooms** 2 with private bathroom **payment** cash, cheques, euros

Room General

or key to symbols see page 6   469

Heart of England | **Warwickshire**

STRATFORD-UPON-AVON, Warwickshire Map ref 2B1 — SAT NAV CV36 4LJ

Folly Farm Cottage

Back Street, Ilmington, Stratford-upon-Avon CV36 4LJ
t (01608) 682425   e bruceandpam@follyfarm.co.uk
w follyfarm.co.uk   ONLINE MAP   GUEST REVIEWS   LAST MINUTE OFFERS

B&B PER ROOM PER NIGHT
S £55.00 – £65.00
D £68.00 – £84.00

EVENING MEAL PER PERSON
£15.00 – £18.50

SPECIAL PROMOTIONS
Discounts on stays of 3 nights or more. Call for further details.

Old-world country cottage accommodation. Double or king-size four-poster rooms, en suite bathroom with bath and shower or whirlpool, hospitality tray, clock/radio, TV, DVD, free DVD library. Home cooking is our speciality. Ideal for exploring the Cotswolds and nearby Stratford. A warm welcome guaranteed.

open All year
bedrooms 3 double
bathrooms 3 en suite
payment credit/debit cards, cash, cheques

directions M40 jct 15. A429 to Cirencester. 10 miles to Halford, turn right to Ilmington. Enter Ilmington, turn right, then left and left again.

BREAKFAST AWARD   Room   General   Leisure

STRATFORD-UPON-AVON, Warwickshire Map ref 2B1 — SAT NAV CV37 6HT

Quilt & Croissants

33 Evesham Place, Stratford-upon-Avon CV37 6HT
t (01789) 267629   f (01789) 550181   e rooms@quilt-croissants.demon.co.uk
w quiltcroissants.co.uk   ONLINE MAP   GUEST REVIEWS   LAST MINUTE OFFERS

B&B PER ROOM PER NIGHT
S £28.00 – £50.00
D £60.00 – £70.00

EVENING MEAL PER PERSON
£10.00 – £15.00

SPECIAL PROMOTIONS
We are happy to offer Group rates for Schools and University groups as well as private family occasions.

With the Shakespeare Centre & Birthplace five minutes walk away, Holy Trinity Church and RSC Theatres just as close by foot. We are happy to answer any queries once you've arrived about where to go, what to do or how to get there - just ask.

open All year except Xmas
bedrooms 3 single, 2 double, 1 twin, 1 family
bathrooms 5 en suite
payment cash, cheques

directions Situated on A4390. From the train station head towards town, turn right at traffic lights. Quilt and Croissants on the left after the pelican crossing.

BREAKFAST AWARD
Room
General
Leisure

Official tourist board guide **Bed & Breakfast**

Heart of England | Warwickshire/West Midlands

WARWICK, Warwickshire Map ref 2B1
SAT NAV CV34 4NP

B&B PER ROOM PER NIGHT
S £40.00 – £55.00
D £60.00 – £78.00

Agincourt Lodge
36 Coten End, Warwick CV34 4NP
t (01926) 499399 **f** (01926) 499399 **e** enquiries@agincourtlodge.co.uk
w agincourtlodge.co.uk ONLINE MAP GUEST REVIEWS LAST MINUTE OFFERS

Mike and Marisa welcome you to their Victorian family run guest house, just 5 minutes from Warwick Castle, Warwick train station, and easy proximity to Leamington Spa and Stratford. **directions** Located on the A445 Warwick to Leamington Spa. We are ideally situated for those travelling by car, bus or train. Come off J15 on M40. **open** All year except Xmas and New Year **bedrooms** 5 double, 1 family **bathrooms** 5 en suite, 1 with private bathroom **payment** credit/debit cards, cash, cheques, euros

Room General Leisure

WISHAW, Warwickshire Map ref 4B3
SAT NAV B76 9QB

B&B PER ROOM PER NIGHT
S £38.00 – £45.00
D £50.00 – £60.00

Ash House
The Gravel, Wishaw, Sutton Coldfield B76 9QB
t (01675) 475782 **f** (01675) 475782 **e** kate@rectory80.freeserve.co.uk

Former rectory with lovely views. Minutes walk from Belfry Golf and Leisure Hotel. 0.50 miles M42, ten minutes drive from Birmingham Airport/NEC. Drayton Manor Park and zoo five miles. **directions** Junction 9 on the M42, Take A446 Litchfield, 1st Left Signposted Wishaw, 2nd Left Into Church Lane, 1st Right Is The Gravel (On The Corner) **open** All year except Xmas and New Year **bedrooms** 1 double, 1 twin, 1 family **bathrooms** 3 en suite **payment** cash, cheques

Room General P Leisure

COVENTRY, West Midlands Map ref 4B3
SAT NAV CV6 3BU

B&B PER ROOM PER NIGHT
S £20.00 – £30.00
D £35.00 – £55.00

Bede Guest House
250 Radford Road, Radford, Coventry CV6 3BU
t (024) 7659 7837 **f** (024) 7660 1413 **e** bedehouse@aol.com
w bedeguesthouse.co.uk ONLINE MAP LAST MINUTE OFFERS

Based near the city centre. Most rooms en suite, all rooms have TVs, tea/coffee facilities. Rooms changed daily and guests have the added peace of mind of secure parking. **directions** Please Refer To Website. **open** All year **bedrooms** 1 single, 1 double, 1 twin **bathrooms** 2 with private bathroom **payment** credit/debit cards, cash, cheques

Room General

COVENTRY, West Midlands Map ref 4B3
SAT NAV CV1 4AQ

B&B PER ROOM PER NIGHT
S £22.00 – £32.00
D £38.00 – £48.00

EVENING MEAL PER PERSON
£5.00

Highcroft Guest House
65 Barras Lane, Coundon, Coventry CV1 4AQ
t (024) 7622 8157 **f** (024) 7663 1609 **e** info@highcroftguesthouse.com
w highcroftguesthouse.com ONLINE MAP LAST MINUTE OFFERS

Large, detached guesthouse close to city centre. A family-run business that endeavours to make guests feel at home. Discounts available. Good transport to airports, train stations and motorways. **directions** Please contact us for directions **open** All year **bedrooms** 1 single, 2 double, 2 twin, 2 family, 3 suites **bathrooms** 3 en suite, 3 with private bathroom **payment** cash, cheques

Room General

key to symbols see page 6

Heart of England | West Midlands/Worcestershire

MERIDEN, West Midlands Map ref 4B3
SAT NAV CV7 7LB

Bonnifinglas Guest House
3 Berkswell Road, Meriden, Solihull, Nr Coventry CV7 7LB
t (01676) 523193 **f** (01676) 523193 **e** Bookings@Bonnifinglas.co.uk
w bonnifinglas.co.uk ONLINE MAP

★★★ GUEST HOUSE

B&B PER ROOM PER NIGHT
S £25.00
D £45.00

Country house, all rooms en suite with TV. Several pubs and restaurants within walking distance. Fire certificate. Large, off-road car park. Five minutes NEC. Free Wi-Fi internet. **directions** Please Refer To Website. **open** All year except Xmas and New Year **bedrooms** 2 single, 2 double, 3 twin, 1 family **bathrooms** 8 en suite **payment** credit/debit cards, cash, cheques

Room General Leisure

SOLIHULL, West Midlands Map ref 4B3
SAT NAV B91 2DJ

Acorn Guest House
29 Links Drive, Solihull B91 2DJ
t (0121) 705 5241 **e** acorn.wood@btinternet.com

★★★ GUEST HOUSE Silver AWARD

B&B PER ROOM PER NIGHT
S £25.00 – £30.00
D £50.00 – £60.00

Homely service in a superb, quiet, family home. All rooms have wash basin, fridge, microwave, hairdryer, hospitality tray. Walk to Solihull centre. Three miles to NEC, Rail, Airport. Parking. **directions** M42, jct 5. A41 Birmingham. After 1.5 miles turn right at 3rd set of lights (Lode Lane). 1st left (Buryfield), then 1st right. **open** All year except Xmas **bedrooms** 2 single, 1 double, 2 twin **bathrooms** 1 er suite **payment** cash, cheques

BREAKFAST AWARD

Room General

BROADWAY, Worcestershire Map ref 2B1
SAT NAV WR12 7PJ

The Bell at Willersey
Main Street, Willersey, Broadway WR12 7PJ
t (01386) 858405 **f** (01386) 853563 **e** enq@bellatwillersey.fsnet.co.uk
w the-bell-willersey.com ONLINE MAP LAST MINUTE OFFERS

★★★★ INN

B&B PER ROOM PER NIGHT
S £66.50 – £75.00
D £80.00 – £85.00
EVENING MEAL PER PERSON
£10.50 – £14.95

17thC inn overlooking the village green and duck pond. 1-mile from Broadway, a perfect location for touring. Enjoys a high reputation for home-produced food. Restaurant open lunchtime and evenings. **directions** From the A44, take the B4632 (signposted Willersey). A full map is on our website. **open** All year **bedrooms** 2 double, 1 twin, 2 suites **bathrooms** 5 en suite **payment** credit/debit cards, cash, cheques

Room General Leisure

BROADWAY, Worcestershire Map ref 2B1
SAT NAV WR12 7DE

Brook House
Station Road, Broadway WR12 7DE
t (01386) 852313 **e** brookhousebb@googlemail.com
w brookhousebandb.co.uk GUEST REVIEWS ONLINE BOOKING

★★★★ GUEST ACCOMMODATION

B&B PER ROOM PER NIGHT
S £40.00 – £60.00
D £70.00 – £90.00

The proprietor established this friendly and successful business 28 years ago in her late Victorian villa. Only 5 minutes level walk to the Cotswolds beautiful village of Broadway. **directions** A44 Evesham to Morton in Marsh. Through Wickhamford first roundabout, third turning. Half mile on left. Call for alternative directions. **bedrooms** 1 single, 3 double, 1 family **bathrooms** 3 en suite **payment** cash, cheques, euros

Room General Leisure

472 Official tourist board guide Bed & Breakfast

Heart of England | Worcestershire

BROADWAY, Worcestershire Map ref 2B1   SAT NAV WR11 7HF

Lowerfield Farm
Willersey, Broadway WR11 7HF
t (01386) 858273 f (01386) 854608 e info@lowerfieldfarm.com
w lowerfieldfarm.com ONLINE MAP GUEST REVIEWS ONLINE BOOKING LAST MINUTE OFFERS

B&B PER ROOM PER NIGHT
S £50.00 – £66.00
D £62.00 – £88.00

EVENING MEAL PER PERSON
£19.50 – £25.00

SPECIAL PROMOTIONS
Off-season & weekday discounts. Please see website.

A largely 17thC farmhouse just outside Broadway, with wonderful views of the Cotswold escarpment. All rooms en suite, beautifully furnished and with digital TV and DVD players. Doubles have king-size beds. We offer a varied and high quality breakfast menu, and farmhouse dinner by request. Licensed premises; Wi-Fi internet available.

open All year
bedrooms 1 single, 3 double, 1 twin, 2 family
bathrooms 7 en suite
payment credit/debit cards, cash, cheques

directions From A44 at Broadway, head for village of Willersey. At roundabout go downhill under railway bridge. Guesthouse 0.5 miles on right - large sign outside.

BREAKFAST AWARD

BROMSGROVE, Worcestershire Map ref 4B3   SAT NAV B61 9HE

Manor Hill House Guest House
Swan Lane, Upton Warren, Bromsgrove B61 9HE
t (01527) 861200 e info@manorhillhouse.co.uk
w manorhillhouse.co.uk ONLINE MAP GUEST REVIEWS

B&B PER ROOM PER NIGHT
S £42.00 – £49.00
D £70.00 – £75.00

Comfortable 4* contemporary country house. Light spacious refurbished rooms with designer ensuites. Large sitting room. Rural views. Good walks. Local country pubs. Convenient for M5/M42, Bromsgrove, Droitwich, Worcester & NEC. **directions** From M5/J5 take A38 Bromsgrove. Turn left at Swan Inn after Webbs Garden Centre. Proceed over motorway to last property at end of Swan Lane. **open** All year except Xmas **bedrooms** 2 double, 1 twin **bathrooms** 3 en suite **payment** credit/debit cards, cash, cheques, euros

---

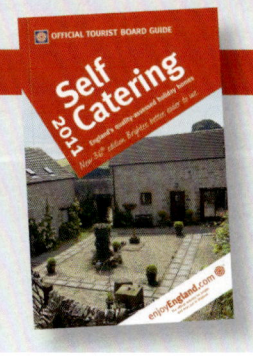

Looking for something else?

You can also buy a copy of our popular guide 'Self Catering' including self-catering holiday homes, approved caravan holiday homes, boat accommodation and holiday cottage agencies in England 2011.

Now available in good bookshops and online at
visitbritainshop.com

£11.99

key to symbols see page 6   473

Heart of England | Worcestershire

HANLEY SWAN, Worcestershire Map ref 2B1
SAT NAV WR8 0DX

B&B PER ROOM PER NIGHT
S £40.00 – £50.00
D £75.00 – £85.00

SPECIAL PROMOTIONS
For mid-week bookings Sunday - Thursday of more than two nights i.e. 3+ nights we offer a 10% discount.

Kingfisher Bed & Breakfast
Kingfisher Barn, Merebrook Farm, Malvern WR8 0DX
t (01684) 311922 e info@kingfisher-barn.co.uk
w kingfisher-barn.co.uk

Stunning views of the Malvern Hills, close to the Three Counties Showground, ideally situated for exploring the scenic beauty of the surrounding area. Sympathetically converted with a unique combination of traditional oak timbers, perfectly offset against the contemporary interior design. 17th-Century charm with 21st Century comfort and style.

open All year
bedrooms 1 single, 2 double, 1 family
bathrooms 3 en suite, 1 with private bathroom
payment credit/debit cards, cash, cheques

directions On B4209, 0.5 miles from the Three Counties Showground. Nearest motorway junctions: M5 jct 7 and M50 jct 1.

Room
General
Leisure

KIDDERMINSTER, Worcestershire Map ref 4B3
SAT NAV DY11 6BS

B&B PER ROOM PER NIGHT
S £35.00
D £60.00

Bewdley Hill Guest House
8 Bewdley Hill, Kidderminster DY11 6BS
t (01562) 60473 f 0871 236 1608 e info@bewdleyhillhouse.co.uk
w bewdleyhillhouse.co.uk ONLINE MAP GUEST REVIEWS

Attractive, en suite accommodation, colour TVs, tea/coffee facilities. Noted for full English breakfasts. Cosy surroundings, warm welcome and off-road parking. Wi-Fi internet. **directions** Please contact us for directions **open** All year except Xmas and New Year **bedrooms** 2 double, 2 twin, 2 family **bathrooms** 6 en suite **payment** credit/debit cards, cash, cheques

Room   General   Leisure

MALVERN, Worcestershire Map ref 2B1
SAT NAV WR14 4AZ

B&B PER ROOM PER NIGHT
S £32.50 – £40.00
D £55.00 – £65.00

Harmony House Malvern
184 West Malvern Road, West Malvern WR14 4AZ
t (01684) 891650 e catherineinharmony@hotmail.com
w harmonyhousemalvern.com ONLINE MAP GUEST REVIEWS

A warm and spacious home set on the western slopes of the Malvern Hills. Close to footpaths and bus routes. Wonderful views. Double/twin bed option. Organic/local food. **directions** Please refer to website. **open** All year **bedrooms** 1 double, 1 twin, 1 family **bathrooms** 3 en suite **payment** cash, cheques

Room   General   Leisure

474   Official tourist board guide Bed & Breakfast

Heart of England | Worcestershire

MALVERN, Worcestershire Map ref 2B1
SAT NAV WR6 5AH

Hidelow House
Acton Green, Acton Beauchamp, Worcester WR6 5AH
t (01886) 884547 f (01886) 884658 e visit@hidelow.co.uk
w hidelow.co.uk ONLINE MAP GUEST REVIEWS ONLINE BOOKING

B&B PER ROOM PER NIGHT
S £45.00 – £75.00
D £75.00 – £105.00

SPECIAL PROMOTIONS
For special occasions: champagne and roses Four-poster suite available (3 nights minimum).

Small country house in peaceful pastureland. Central for many places of historical interest, walking/golf. En suite rooms, magnificent residents' lounge with grand piano and sun terrace overlooking extensive landscaped gardens, fish pool, waterfall and stunning views across unspoilt countryside. Breakfasts using local produce. Accessible graded accommodation in adjacent cottages.

open All year
bedrooms 2 double, 1 twin
bathrooms 3 en suite
payment credit/debit cards, cash, cheques, euros

directions Leave M5 jct 7, take A4103 from Worcester towards Hereford. Turn right at B4220, signposted Bromyard. Hidelow House is 2 miles on the left.

MALVERN, Worcestershire Map ref 2B1
SAT NAV WR14 3LW

Puddle Lane
54 Barnards Green Road, Malvern, Worcestershire WR14 3LW
t 01684 572 720 e puddlelanemalvern@hotmail.co.uk
w puddlelanemalvern.co.uk ONLINE MAP

B&B PER ROOM PER NIGHT
S £45.00 – £50.00
D £70.00 – £80.00

Ground Floor, disabled friendly ensuite rooms. Close to all amenities, railway, Great Malvern town centre and the Malvern Hills and the Three Counties Showground. Theatre trips and qualified babysitting available. **directions** Please contact us for directions
open All year except Xmas **bedrooms** 2 double, 1 twin **bathrooms** 3 en suite **payment** cash, cheques, euros

BREAKFAST AWARD

PERSHORE, Worcestershire Map ref 2B1
SAT NAV WR10 2HU

Arbour House
Main Road, Wyre Piddle, Pershore WR10 2HU
t (01386) 555833 f (01386) 555833 e liz@arbour-house.com
w arbour-house.com ONLINE MAP LAST MINUTE OFFERS

B&B PER ROOM PER NIGHT
S £35.00 – £50.00
D £65.00 – £75.00

A fine Grade II Listed character home overlooking Bredon Hill and close to the River Avon. Private car park. An ideal base for visiting the Cotswolds, Stratford, Worcester and Malvern. **directions** Wyre Piddle is signposted off A44 between M5 Jct 6 and Evesham. Arbour House is situated on the left just behind the village green.
open All year **bedrooms** 2 double, 2 twin **bathrooms** 3 en suite, 1 with private bathroom **payment** cash, cheques

key to symbols see page 6

475

Heart of England | Worcestershire/Gloucestershire/Herefordshire

WORCESTER, Worcestershire Map ref 2B1

SAT NAV WR5 2JT

Holland House
210 London Road, Worcester WR5 2JT
t (01905) 353939   f (01905) 353939   e beds@holland-house.me.uk
w holland-house.me.uk ONLINE MAP ONLINE BOOKING

B&B PER ROOM PER NIGHT
S £42.00
D £52.50 – £56.00
EVENING MEAL PER PERSON
£7.00 – £10.00

A warm welcome awaits you at this Victorian mid-terrace house, situated within walking distance of the cathedral. It retains many original features and offers fully en suite rooms throughout. **directions** We are situated on A44 approximately half way between M5/J7 and the cathedral. **open** All year **bedrooms** 2 double, 1 tw **bathrooms** 3 en suite **payment** credit/debit cards, cash

Room   General

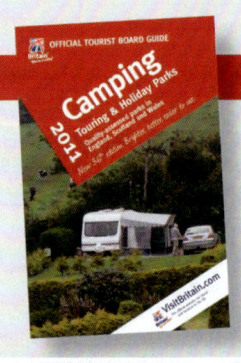

Do you like Camping?

You can also buy a copy of our popular guide 'Camping, Touring & Holiday Parks' including touring parks, camping holidays and holiday parks and villages in Britain 2011.

Now available in good bookshops and online at
visitbritainshop.com

£8.99

All Assessed Accommodation

Gloucestershire

KILCOT

Withyland Heights ★★★★
Farmhouse
Beavans Hill, Kilcot, Newent, Gloucestershire
GL18 1PG
t (01989) 720582
e katrina@withylandheights.co.uk
w withylandheights.co.uk

Herefordshire

AYMESTREY

The Farmhouse ★★★★
Bed & Breakfast
Aymestrey
HR6 9ST
t (01568) 708075
e farmbreakfasts@tesco.net

BARONS CROSS

Lavender House ★★★★
Bed & Breakfast **SILVER AWARD**
1 Richmond Villas, Barons Cross Road, Leominster
HR6 8RS
t (01568) 617559
e lavenderhouse@fsmail.net
w lavenderhouse.012webpages.com

BELMONT

Hedley Lodge ★★★★
Guest Accommodation
Belmont Abbey, Abergavenny Road, Hereford
HR2 9RZ
t (01432) 374147
e hedley@belmontabbey.org.uk
w hedleylodge.com

BRAMPTON ABBOTTS

Brampton Cottage ★★★
Bed & Breakfast
Brampton Abbotts, Ross-on-Wye
HR9 7JD
t (01989) 562459
e caroline-keen@btconnect.com

BRIMFIELD

Mill Hill House B&B ★★
Bed & Breakfast
Wyson Lane, Ludlow
SY8 4NW
t (01584) 711509
e info@millhillhouseludlow.co.uk
w millhillhouseludlow.co.uk

BROBURY

Brobury House & Gardens ★★★★
Bed & Breakfast **SILVER AWARD**
Brobury, By Bredwardine, Hereford
HR3 6BS
t (01981) 500229
e enquiries@broburyhouse.co.uk
w broburyhouse.co.uk

BROMSASH

Eastview Bed & Breakfast ★★★★
Bed & Breakfast **SILVER AWARD**
Bromsash, Ross-on-Wye
HR9 7PN
t (01989) 750508
e eastviewselfcatering@tiscali.co.uk
w eastviewselfcatering.co.uk

BURGHILL

Heron House ★★★ *Bed & Breakfast*
Canon Pyon Road, Portway, Hereford
HR4 8NG
t (01432) 761111
e info@theheronhouse.com
w theheronhouse.com

BYFORD

Old Rectory ★★★★
Guest Accommodation
SILVER AWARD
Byford, Hereford
HR4 7LD
t (01981) 590218
e info@cm-ltd.com
w smoothhound.co.uk/hotels/oldrectory2.html

CLEHONGER

The Old Vicarage ★★★★
Guest House **SILVER AWARD**
Church Road, Old Clehonger, Hereford
HR2 9SE
t (01432) 371343
e info@theoldvicarage.uk.com
w theoldvicarage.uk.com

CRADLEY

The Old Rectory ★★★★
Guest Accommodation
SILVER AWARD
Cradley, Malvern
WR13 5LQ
t (01886) 880109
e oldrectorycradley@btinternet.com
w oldrectorycradley.com

DILWYN

Sollars Barn ★★★★
Bed & Breakfast
Dilwyn, Leominster
HR4 8JJ
t (01544) 388260

DORSTONE

Cottage Farm ★★ *Bed & Breakfa*
Middlewood, Golden Valley
HR3 5SX
t (01497) 831496
e cottagefarm@fsmail.net
w cottagefarmmiddlewood.com

Highfield ★★★★ *Farmhouse*
SILVER AWARD
The Bage, Dorstone, Golden Valle
HR3 5SU
t (01497) 831431
e book@highfieldbandb.com
w highfieldbandb.com

DUNFIELD

Dunfield House & Stables ★★★
Group Hostel
Kington
HR5 3NN
t (01544) 230653
e info@dunfieldhouse.org.uk
w dunfieldhouse.org.uk

EARDISLAND

Lawton Bury Farm B&B ★★★★
Farmhouse **SILVER AWARD**
Lawton, Leominster
HR6 9AX
t (01568) 709285
e enquiries@visitlawtonbury.co.uk
w visitlawtonbury.co.uk

476   Official tourist board guide Bed & Breakf

Heart of England | Herefordshire

EWYAS HAROLD COMMON

e Cider Barn
est Accommodation
cks Pitch, Ewyas Harold Common
2 0JF
t (01981) 240565
e ciderbarnsarah@hotmail.com

FOWNHOPE

rk Cottage ★★★★
d & Breakfast
wnhope, Hereford
1 4PE
t (01432) 860344
e arthur@wyeleisure.com

HAY-ON-WYE

e Hayloft@The Granary ★★★★
d & Breakfast
eston Barns, Bredwardine, Hay-on-
ye
3 6DD
t (01981) 500014
e chez.turner@googlemail.com

ydspence Inn ★★★★ Inn
itney-on-Wye, Near Hay-on-Wye
3 6EU
t (01497) 831262
e info@rhydspence-inn.co.uk
w rhydspence-inn.co.uk

HEREFORD

berta Guest House ★★★
est House
3 Newtown Road, Hereford
4 9LH
t (01432) 270313
e albertaguesthouse@amserve.com
w thealbertaguesthouse.co.uk

dar Guest House ★★★
d & Breakfast
3 Whitecross Road, Whitecross,
reford
4 0LS
t 01432 267235
e info@cedarguesthouse.com
w cedarguesthouse.com

arades ★★★★ Guest House
Southbank Road, Hereford
1 2TJ
t (01432) 269444
e stay@charadeshereford.co.uk
w charadeshereford.co.uk

aiseley House ★★★★
d & Breakfast
0 Whitecross Road, Hereford
4 0DJ
t (01432) 358289
e janespearpoint@yahoo.co.uk
w graiseleyhouse.co.uk

pbine House ★★★ Guest House
man Road, Hereford
1 1LE
t (01432) 268722
e info@hopbine.com
w hopbine.com

ree Park Street ★★★
d & Breakfast
ark Street, Hereford
1 2RB
t (01432) 356003
e threeparkstreet@yahoo.co.uk
w threeparkstreet.com

HOARWITHY

e Old Mill ★★★★
d & Breakfast
arwithy, Hereford
2 6QH
t (01432) 840602
e carol.probert@virgin.net

HOW CAPLE

e Falcon House ★★★★
est Accommodation
w Caple, Hereford, Ross-on-Wye
1 4TF
t (01989) 740223
e falcon.house@gmail.com
w thefalconhouse.co.uk

KERNE BRIDGE

Lumleys B&B ★★★★
Bed & Breakfast SILVER AWARD
Kerne Bridge, Bishop Wood, Ross-on-Wye
HR9 5TQ
t (01600) 890040
e helen@lumleys.force9.co.uk
w lumleys.force9.co.uk

KIMBOLTON

Lower Bache House ★★★★
Bed & Breakfast SILVER AWARD
Kimbolton, Leominster
HR6 0ER
t (01568) 750304
e leslie.wiles@care4free.net
w smoothhound.co.uk/hotels/lower bache

KINGS CAPLE

Ruxton Farm ★★★★ Farmhouse
Kings Caple, Hereford
HR1 4TX
t (01432) 840493

KINGSLAND

The Corners Inn ★★★★ Inn
Kingsland, Leominster
HR6 9RY
t (01568) 708385
w cornersinn.co.uk

The Old House ★★★★
Bed & Breakfast
Kingsland, Leominster
HR6 9QS
t (01568) 709120
e andrea@teacosy.nl
w teacosy.nl

KINGSTHORNE

Pullastone ★★★★ Bed & Breakfast
SILVER AWARD
Kingsthorn, Hereford, Hereford
HR2 8AQ
t (01981) 540450
e info@pullastone.com
w pullastone.com

KINGTON

Arrowbank Lodge ★★★★
Bed & Breakfast
Tanyard Lane,, Bridge Street, Kington
HR5 3DX
t (01544) 231115
e jmpw@mac.com
w arrowbanklodge.co.uk

Arrow Weir House ★★★★
Bed & Breakfast
Kingswood Road, Kington
HR5 3HD
t (01544) 231780
e info@arrowweirhouse.co.uk
w arrowweirhouse.co.uk

Kington Youth Hostel ★★★★
Hostel
Victoria Road, Kington
HR5 3BX
t (01544) 232745
e kington@yha.org.uk
w yha.org.uk

LEDBURY

Bluebell Lodge ★★★
Guest Accommodation
Massington Lodge, Old Pumping Station, Eastnor, Ledbury
HR8 1EG
t (01531) 636524
e massingtonlodge@hotmail.co.uk
w massingtonlodge.webeden.co.uk

Orchard Cottage ★★★
Bed & Breakfast
Bromyard Road, Ledbury
HR8 1LG
t (01531) 635107

Pridewood ★★★
Guest Accommodation
Ashperton, Ledbury
HR8 2SF
t (01531) 670416
e julia@pridewoodbandb.co.uk
w pridewoodbandb.co.uk

Redlands ★★★ Bed & Breakfast
Newbury Park, Ledbury
HR8 1AU
t (01531) 634803
e sallywoodrobinson@hotmail.com
w ledburybandb.com

Russet House ★★★★
Guest Accommodation
Belle Orchard, Ledbury
HR8 1DD
t (01531) 630060
e info@russethousebnb.co.uk
w russethousebnb.co.uk

The Talbot ★★★ Inn
New Street, Ledbury
HR8 2DX
t (01531) 632963
e talbot@wadworth.co.uk
w talbotinnledbury.co.uk

LEINTHALL STARKES

Marlbrook Hall ★★★★ Farmhouse
Elton, Ludlow
SY8 2HR
t (01568) 770230
e valemorgan@hotmail.com
w marlbrookhall.co.uk

LEINTWARDINE

Lower Buckton Country House
★★★★ Bed & Breakfast
SILVER AWARD
Buckton, Leintwardine, Leintwardine
SY7 0JU
t (01547) 540532
e carolyn@lowerbuckton.co.uk
w lowerbuckton.co.uk

Lower House ★★★★
Guest Accommodation
Adforton, Leintwardine, Ludlow
SY7 0NF
t (01568) 770223
e reservations@sy7.com
w sy7.com

Upper Buckton ★★★★★
Farmhouse GOLD AWARD
Leintwardine, Ludlow
SY7 0JU
t (01547) 540634

Walford Court ★★★★ Farmhouse
SILVER AWARD
Walford, Leintwardine, Leintwardine
SY7 0JT
t (01547) 540570
e enquiries@romanticbreak.com
w romanticbreak.com

LEOMINSTER

Copper Hall ★★★★
Bed & Breakfast
134 South Street, Leominster
HR6 8JN
t (01568) 611622
e copperhall@hotmail.com
w smoothhound.co.uk/hotels/copper

Grove Farm ★★★ Farmhouse
Kimbolton, Leominster
HR6 0HE
t (01568) 613425
e info@grovefarmdirect.co.uk
w grovefarmdirect.co.uk

Highgate House ★★★★
Bed & Breakfast
29 Hereford Road, Leominster
HR6 8JS
t (01568) 614562
e cyrilmerriman@btinternet.com
w highgate-house.co.uk

Moat Edge ★★★★ Bed & Breakfast
6 St Mary's Walk, Eardisland, Leominster
HR6 9BB
t (01544) 388097
e moatedge@btinternet.com
w moatedge.co.uk

YHA Leominster ★★★★ Hostel
The Priory, Leominster
HR6 8EQ
t (01568) 620517
e leominster@yha.org.uk
w yha.org.uk

LOWER WILLEY

Willey Lane Farm B&B ★★★★
Farmhouse
Lower Willey, Presteigne
LD8 2LU
t (01544) 267148
e juliamurray@willeylane.co.uk
w willeylane.co.uk

LUGWARDINE

Steppes ★★★★ Bed & Breakfast
Hemhill, Lumber Lane, Lugwardine, Hereford
HR1 4AL
t 07974 960 956
e lin@thesteppeshereford.co.uk
w thesteppeshereford.co.uk

LYONSHALL

Penrhos Farm ★★★★
Guest Accommodation
SILVER AWARD
Lyonshall, Kington
HR5 3LH
t (01544) 231467
e sallyatpenrhos@aol.com
w penrhosfarm.co.uk

MADLEY

Shenmore Cottage ★★★★
Guest Accommodation
Upper Shenmore, Madley, Hereford
HR2 9NX
t (01981) 250507
e shenmorecottage@talktalk.net
w shenmorecottage.co.uk

MALVERN

Little Kings Hill ★★★★
Bed & Breakfast SILVER AWARD
Walwyn Road,, Upper Colwall, Malvern
WR13 6PL
t (01684) 540589
e littlekingshill@xln.co.uk
w malvernbreaks.co.uk

MICHAELCHURCH ESCLEY

The Grove Farm ★★★★
Farmhouse
Michaelchurch Escley, Golden Valley
HR2 0PT
t (01981) 510229
e lyn229@hotmail.com

MONNINGTON-ON-WYE

Dairy House Farm ★★★★
Farmhouse
Monnington-on-Wye, Golden Valley
HR4 7NL
t (01981) 500143
e pearson-greg@clara.co.uk
w dairyhousefarm.org

MORTIMER COUNTRY

Pear Tree Farm ★★★★
Guest Accommodation
GOLD AWARD
Wigmore
HR6 9UR
t (01568) 770140
e info@peartree-farm.co.uk
w peartree-farm.co.uk

key to symbols see page 6

477

Heart of England | Herefordshire/Shropshire

MUCH BIRCH

The Old School ★★★★
Bed & Breakfast
Much Birch, Hereford
HR2 8HJ
t (01981) 541317
e carolannedixon@btinternet.com
w oldschoolbb.co.uk

MUCH MARCLE

Bodenham Farm Bed & Breakfast
Farmhouse
Much Marcle, Ledbury
HR8 2NJ
t (01531) 660222
e bodenhamfarm@lineone.net
w bodenhamfarm.co.uk

Little Acre ★★★★ Bed & Breakfast
SILVER AWARD
Much Marcle, Ledbury
HR8 2PQ
t (01989) 740600
e stay@littleacre.co.uk
w littleacre.co.uk

NEWTON ST MARGARETS

Marises Barn ★★★★
Guest Accommodation
Newton St Margarets, Golden Valley
HR2 0QG
t (01981) 510101
e marisesbandb@aol.com
w s-h-systems.co.uk/hotels/marises

ORLETON

Rosecroft ★★★★★ Bed & Breakfast
SILVER AWARD
Orleton, Ludlow
SY8 4HN
t (01568) 780565
e gailanddavid@rosecroftorleton.freeserve.co.uk

PEMBRIDGE

Lowe Farm B&B ★★★★
Farmhouse GOLD AWARD
Lowe Farm, Pembridge, Leominster, Herefordshire
HR6 9JD
t (01544) 388395
e Juliet@lowe-farm.co.uk
w lowe-farm.co.uk

PETERSTOW

Broome Farm ★★★★
Bed & Breakfast
Peterstow, Ross-on-Wye
HR9 6QG
t (01989) 562824
e broomefarm@tesco.net
w broomefarmhouse.co.uk

REDHILL

Brandon Lodge ★★★★
Guest Accommodation
SILVER AWARD
Ross Road, Grafton, Hereford
HR2 8BH
t (01432) 355621
e info@brandonlodge.co.uk
w brandonlodge.co.uk

RICHARDS CASTLE

Longlands ★★★★ Farmhouse
Woodhouse Lane, Richards Castle, Ludlow
SY8 4EU
t (01584) 831136
e iankemsley@aol.com

ROSS-ON-WYE

Caradoc Court ★★★★
Bed & Breakfast GOLD AWARD
Sellack, Ross-on-Wye
HR9 6LS
t (01989) 730257
e kathy@caradoccourt.co.uk
w caradoccourt.co.uk

Linden House ★★★ Guest House
14 Church Street, Ross-on-Wye
HR9 5HN
t (01989) 565373
e pat@lindenguesthouse.com
w lindenguesthouse.com

Norton House ★★★★
Bed & Breakfast GOLD AWARD
Norton House, Whitchurch, Ross-on-Wye
HR9 6DJ
t (01600) 890046
e enquiries@norton-house.com
w norton-house.com

Sunnymount ★★★★
Guest Accommodation
Ryefield Road, Ross-on-Wye
HR9 5LU
t (01989) 563880
e sunnymount@tinyworld.co.uk

RYELANDS

Ryelands ★★★★★ Bed & Breakfast
GOLD AWARD
Ryelands Road, Leominster
HR6 8QB
t (01568) 617575
e info@ryelandsbandb.co.uk
w ryelandsbandb.co.uk

STAUNTON-ON-WYE

Portway Inn ★★★ Inn
Staunton-on-Wye, Hereford
HR4 7NH
t (01981) 500474
e portwayinn@googlemail.com
w theportwayinnhotel.co.uk

ST OWENS CROSS

Little Treaddow Farmhouse
★★★★ Farmhouse
St Owen's Cross, Ross-on-Wye
HR2 8LQ
t (01989) 730353
e sleep@treaddow.co.uk
w treaddow.co.uk

The New Inn ★★★★ Inn
St Owens Cross, Ross-on-Wye
HR2 8LQ
t (01989) 730274
e info@newinn.biz
w newinn.biz

SYMONDS YAT

Walnut Tree Cottage ★★★★
Guest House
Symonds Yat West, Ross-on-Wye, Symonds Yat
HR9 6BN
t (01600) 890828
e enquiries@walnuttreehotel.co.uk
w walnuttreehotel.co.uk

TARRINGTON

Swan House ★★★★
Guest Accommodation
Tarrington, Ledbury
HR1 4EU
t (01432) 890203
e parrylizzy@aol.com
w swanhousetarrington.co.uk

UPTON BISHOP

May Hill View ★★★★
Bed & Breakfast
Lower Rylands, Upton Bishop, Ross-on-Wye
HR9 7UA
t 07745 568431
e elaine@mayhillview.co.uk
w mayhillview.co.uk

VOWCHURCH

New Barns Farm ★★★★
Farmhouse
Vowchurch, Golden Valley
HR2 0QA
t (01981) 250250
e lloydnewbarns@tiscali.co.uk
w golden-valley.co.uk/newbarns

Yew Tree House ★★★★
Bed & Breakfast GOLD AWARD
Bacho Hill, Vowchurch, Golden Valley, Hereford
HR2 9PF
t (01981) 251195
e enquiries@yewtreehouse-hereford.co.uk
w yewtreehouse-hereford.co.uk

WALFORD

Inn-On-The-Wye ★★★ Inn
Kerne Bridge, Goodrich, Ross-on-Wye
HR9 5QS
t (01600) 890872
e info@thewyeinn.co.uk
w thewyeinn.co.uk

WIGMORE

Abbots Lodge B&B ★★★★
Bed & Breakfast SILVER AWARD
School Lane, Wigmore, Leominster
HR6 9UD
t (01568) 770036
e john@abbotslodgebandb.co.uk
w abbotslodgebandb.co.uk

WILTON

Benhall Farmhouse ★★★★
Bed & Breakfast SILVER AWARD
Wilton, Ross-on-Wye
HR9 6AG
t (01989) 563900
e info@benhallfarm.co.uk
w benhallfarm.co.uk

WOODEND

Woodend Farm ★★★★
Bed & Breakfast
Woodend, Nr. Ledbury, Ledbury
HR8 2RS
t (01432) 890227
e enquiry@bed-breakfast-herefordshire.co.uk
w woodendfarmhouse.co.uk

WORMELOW

Lyston Villa ★★★ Bed & Breakfast
Wormelow, Hereford
HR2 8EL
t (01981) 540130
e sue@lystonvilla.co.uk
w lystonvilla.co.uk

Shropshire

ACTON SCOTT

Acton Scott Farm B&B ★★★
Farmhouse
Acton Scott, Church Stretton
SY6 6QN
t (01694) 781260
e shrops@actonscottfarm.co.uk
w actonscottfarm.co.uk

ALBRIGHTON

Boningale Manor ★★★★
Bed & Breakfast
Holyhead Road, Boningale, Albrighton
WV7 3AT
t (01902) 373376
e boningalemanor@aol.com
w boningalemanor.com

ALL STRETTON

Jinlye Guest House ★★★★★
Guest House GOLD AWARD
Castle Hill, All Stretton, Church Stretton
SY6 6JP
t (01694) 723243
e info@jinlye.co.uk
w jinlye.co.uk

Juniper Cottage ★★★★
Bed & Breakfast SILVER AWARD
All Stretton, Church Stretton
SY6 6HG
t (01694) 723427
e colinmcintyre@ukonline.co.uk

ASH

Ash Hall Bed & Breakfast ★★
Bed & Breakfast
Ash Magna, Whitchurch
SY13 4DL
t (01948) 663151
w stmem.com/ashhall/

ASHFORD BOWDLER

Orchard House ★★★★
Bed & Breakfast SILVER AWARD
Ashford Bowdler, Ludlow
SY8 4DJ
t (01584) 831270
e judith@orchard-barn.co.uk
w orchard-barn.co.uk

ASTON MUNSLOW

Chadstone ★★★★ Guest House
SILVER AWARD
Aston Munslow, Craven Arms
SY7 9ER
t (01584) 841675
e chadstone.lee@btinternet.com
w chadstonebandb.co.uk

BAGLEY

The Poplars Farm B&B ★★★
Farmhouse
Bagley, Ellesmere
SY12 9BY
t (01939) 270273
e info@thebandb.co.uk
w thebandb.co.uk

BAYSTON HILL

Chatford House ★★★★
Bed & Breakfast SILVER AWARD
Chatford, Bayston Hill, Shrewsbury
SY3 0AY
t (01743) 718301
e b&b@chatfordhouse.co.uk
w chatfordhouse.co.uk

BENTHALL

Hilltop House ★★★★ Guest House
Bridge Road, Benthall, Ironbridge
TF12 5RB
t (01952) 884441
e info@hilltop-house.co.uk
w hilltop-house.co.uk

BICTON

The Isle Estate Bed & Breakfast
★★★★ Bed & Breakfast
SILVER AWARD
Isle Lane, Bicton, Shrewsbury
SY3 8EE
t (01743) 851218
e ros@isleestate.co.uk

BISHOP'S CASTLE

Inn on the Green ★★★★ Inn
Wentnor, Bishop's Castle
SY9 5EF
t (01588) 650105
e sempleaj@aol.com
w theinnonthegreen.net

BISHOPS CASTLE

Magnolia ★★★★ Bed & Breakfast
GOLD AWARD
3 Montgomery Road, Bishop's Castle
SY9 5EZ
t (01588) 638098
e magnoliabishopscastle@yahoo.uk
w magnoliabishopscastle.co.uk

BOMERE HEATH

The Old Station ★★★★
Guest House SILVER AWARD
Leaton, Bomere Heath, Shrewsbury
SY4 3AP
t (01939) 290905
e langley.cm@virgin.net
w theoldstationshropshire.co.uk

Heart of England | Shropshire

BRIDGNORTH

ulls Head Inn ★★★★ *Inn*
helmarsh, Bridgnorth
V16 6BA
t (01746) 861469
e bull_chelmarsh@btconnect.com
w bullsheadchelmarsh.co.uk

hurchdown House ★★★★★
d & Breakfast SILVER AWARD
East Castle Street, Bridgnorth
V16 4AL
t (01746) 761236
e churchdownhouse@tiscali.co.uk
w churchdownhouse.co.uk

he Croft ★★★★
uest Accommodation
LVER AWARD
/11 St Mary's Street, Bridgnorth
V16 4DW
t (01746) 762016
e thecrofthotelbridgnorth@yahoo.co.uk
w crofthotelbridgnorth.co.uk

he Golden Lion ★★★
uest Accommodation
High Street, Bridgnorth
V16 4DS
t (01746) 762016
e jeff@goldenlionbridgnorth.co.uk
w goldenlionbridgnorth.co.uk

he Old House ★★★★
d & Breakfast
lton, Bridgnorth
V15 5PJ
t (01746) 716560
e enquiries@oldhousehilton.co.uk
w oldhousehilton.co.uk

he Old Rectory *Bed & Breakfast*
e Old Rectory, Wheathill,
dgnorth
V16 6QT
t (01746) 787110
e enquiries@theoldrectorywheathill.com

he Severn Arms ★★★★
uest Accommodation
Underhill Street, Bridgnorth
V16 4BB
t (01746) 764616
e thesevernarms@aol.com

he Swan ★★★ *Inn*
owle Sands, Bridgnorth
V16 5JL
t (01746) 763424

BROCKTON

d Quarry Cottage ★★★★
d & Breakfast SILVER AWARD
d Quarry Cottage, Brockton, Much
enlock
13 6JR
t (01746) 785596
e triciawebb@oldquarrycottage.co.uk
w oldquarrycottage.co.uk

BROSELEY

roseley House ★★★★
uest House SILVER AWARD
The Square, Broseley, Ironbridge
12 5EW
t (01952) 882043
e info@broseleyhouse.co.uk
w broseleyhouse.co.uk

alport YHA ★★★ *Hostel*
o John Rose Building, High Street,
elford
8 7HT
t 0870 770 5882
e ironbridge@yha.org.uk
w yha.org.uk

Rock Dell ★★★★
Guest Accommodation
SILVER AWARD
30 Ironbridge Road, Broseley
TF12 5AJ
t (01952) 883054
e rockdell@ukgateway.net
w rock-dell.co.uk

BURWARTON

Peace Haven ★★★★
Guest Accommodation
The Old School, Burwarton,
Bridgnorth
WV16 6QG
t (01746) 787566
e kw.ukla@virgin.net
w findpeacehaven.co.uk

CARDINGTON

Woodside Farm ★★★★ *Farmhouse*
Cardington, Church Stretton
SY6 7LB
t (01694) 771314
w virtual-shropshire.co.uk/woodside-farm

CHELMARSH

Dinney Farm ★★★★ *Farmhouse*
Chelmarsh, Bridgnorth
WV16 6AU
t (01746) 861070
e info@thedinney.co.uk
w thedinney.co.uk

CHETWYND

Lane End Farm ★★★★
Bed & Breakfast
Chetwynd, Newport
TF10 8BN
t (01952) 550337
e janicepark854@aol.com
w stmem.com/laneendfarm

CHURCH STRETTON

Brookfields Guest House ★★★★★
Guest House SILVER AWARD
Watling Street North, Church
Stretton
SY6 7AR
t (01694) 722314
e paulangie@brookfields51.fsnet.co.uk
w churchstretton-guesthouse.co.uk

Highcliffe ★★★ *Bed & Breakfast*
Madeira Walk, Church Stretton
SY6 6JQ
t (01694) 722908
w stmem.com/highcliffe

Highlands Bed & Breakfast
★★★★ *Bed & Breakfast*
Hazler Road, Church Stretton
SY6 7AF
t (01694) 723737
e info@highlandsbandb.co.uk
w highlandsbandb.co.uk

Victoria House ★★★★
Guest Accommodation
SILVER AWARD
48 High Street, Church Stretton
SY6 6BX
t (01694) 723823
e victoriahouse@fsmail.net
w bedandbreakfast-shropshire.co.uk

CLEEDOWNTON

Stone Barn ★★★★ *Bed & Breakfast*
West Farm, Cleedownton, Ludlow
SY8 3EH
t (01584) 823511
e helenscott3@btinternet.com
w stonebarnshropshire.com

CLEE STANTON

Timberstone B&B ★★★★
Guest House
Clee Stanton, Ludlow
SY8 3EL
t (01584) 823519
e enquiry@timberstone.co.uk
w timberstoneludlow.co.uk

CLEOBURY MORTIMER

Broome Park Farm ★★★★
Farmhouse
Catherton Road, Cleobury Mortimer
DY14 0LB
t (01299) 270647
e catherine@broomeparkfarm.co.uk
w broomeparkfarm.co.uk

Woodview B&B ★★★★★
Guest Accommodation
SILVER AWARD
Mawley Oak, Cleobury Mortimer
DY14 9BA
t (01299) 271422
w woodviewbedandbreakfast.co.uk

CLUN

Clun Mill Youth Hostel ★★★
Hostel
The Mill, Clun, Craven Arms
SY7 8NY
t (01588) 640582
e reservations@yha.org.uk
w yha.org.uk

Llanhedric Farm ★★★★
Farmhouse
Clun, Craven Arms
SY7 8NG
t (01588) 640203
e llanhedric@btconnect.com
w llanhedricfarm.co.uk

New House Farm ★★★★★
Farmhouse GOLD AWARD
Clun, Craven Arms
SY7 8NJ
t (01588) 638314
e sarah@bishopscastle.co.uk
w new-house-clun.co.uk

The Old Farmhouse ★★★★
Bed & Breakfast
Woodside, Clun
SY7 0JB
t (01588) 640695
e helen@vuan1.freeserve.co.uk
w theoldfarmhousebandb.co.uk

Thomas Cottage ★★★★
Bed & Breakfast
Church Bank, Clun
SY7 8LP
t (01588) 640029
e info@thomascottageclun.co.uk
w thomascottageclun.co.uk

The White Horse Inn ★★★ *Inn*
The Square, Clun
SY7 8JA
t (01588) 640305
e room@whi-clun.co.uk
w whi-clun.co.uk

CLUNTON

Bush Farm ★★★★ *Farmhouse*
Clunton, Craven Arms
SY7 0HU
t (01588) 660330
e enquiries@bushfarmbandb.co.uk
w bushfarmbandb.co.uk

COALBROOKDALE

Coalbrookdale Villa Guest House
★★★★ *Guest Accommodation*
SILVER AWARD
Paradise, Coalbrookdale, Telford
TF8 7NR
t (01952) 433450
e coalbrookdalevilla@currantbun.com
w coalbrookdale.f9.co.uk

Springhill B&B ★★★★
Guest Accommodation
SILVER AWARD
2 School Road, Coalbrookdale,
Ironbridge
TF8 7DY
t (01952) 433225
e info@springhillbandb.co.uk
w springhillbandb.co.uk

COALPORT

Ironbridge Youth Hostel ★★★
Group Hostel
John Rose Building, High Street,
Telford
TF8 7HT
t (01952) 588755
e ironbridge@yha.org.uk
w yha.org.uk

The Shakespeare Inn ★★★★ *Inn*
High Street, Coalport, Ironbridge
TF8 7HT
t (01952) 580675
w shakespeare-inn.co.uk

CROSS HOUSES

North Farm Bed & Breakfast
★★★★ *Farmhouse*
Eaton Mascot, Shrewsbury
SY5 6HF
t (01743) 761031
e northfarm@btinternet.com
w northfarm.co.uk

DAWLEY

Hartfield Guest House ★★★★
Guest Accommodation
SILVER AWARD
Pool Hill Road, Horsehay, Telford
TF4 3AS
t (01952) 505626
e enquiries@hartfieldguesthouse.co.uk
w hartfieldguesthouse.co.uk

DORRINGTON

Meadowlands ★★★
Bed & Breakfast
Lodge Lane, Frodesley, Shrewsbury
SY5 7HD
t (01694) 731350
e meadowlands.t21@btinternet.com
w meadowlands.co.uk

Upper Shadymoor Farm ★★★★
Farmhouse
Stapleton, Shrewsbury
SY5 7LB
t (01743) 718670
e kevan@shadymoor.co.uk
w shadymoor.co.uk

EASTHOPE WOOD

Easthope Wood Farm ★★★★
Bed & Breakfast SILVER AWARD
Easthope Wood, Much Wenlock
TF13 6DL
t (01694) 771562
e easthopewood@talktalk.net
w easthopewoodfarm.co.uk

ELLESMERE

Red Lion Coaching Inn ★★★ *Inn*
18 Church Street, Ellesmere
SY12 0HP
t (01691) 622632
e mike-loftus@tiscali.co.uk
w ellesmere.info/redlion

ELLESMERE (3 MILES)

Hordley Hall ★★★★
Bed & Breakfast
Hordley, Ellesmere
SY12 9BB
t (01691) 622772
e hazel@hordleyhall.co.uk
w hordleyhall.co.uk

479

Heart of England | Shropshire

FISHMORE
Acorn Place ★★★★
Bed & Breakfast **SILVER AWARD**
Fishmore Road, Ludlow
SY8 3DP
t (01584) 875295
e info@acornplace.plus.com
w acornplace.co.uk

HAMPTON LOADE
The Unicorn Inn ★★ *Inn*
Hampton Loade, Chelmarsh,
Bridgnorth
WV16 6BN
t (01746) 861515
e kenunicorninn@aol.com
w freespace.virginnet.co.uk/unico rninn.bridgnorth

HANWOOD
Caer-Urfa ★★★★ *Bed & Breakfast*
46 Woodlands Avenue, Hanwood,
Shrewsbury
SY5 8NG
t (01743) 861120
e caer-urfa@hotmail.co.uk
w caer-urfa.co.uk

HILL TOP
Wenlock Edge Inn ★★★ *Inn*
Hilltop, Wenlock Edge, Much
Wenlock
TF13 6DJ
t (01746) 785678
e chefryder@hotmail.co.uk
w wenlockedgeinn.co.uk

HOPE BOWDLER
Sayang House ★★★★
Bed & Breakfast **SILVER AWARD**
Hope Bowdler, Church Stretton
SY6 7DD
t (01694) 723981
e madegan@aol.com
w sayanghouse.co.uk

HOPTON HEATH
Hopton House ★★★★★
Bed & Breakfast **GOLD AWARD**
Hopton Heath, Craven Arms
SY7 0QD
t (01547) 530885
e info@shropshirebreakfast.co.uk
w shropshirebreakfast.co.uk

IRONBRIDGE
Golden Ball Inn ★★★★ *Inn*
1 Newbridge Road, Ironbridge,
Telford
TF8 7BA
t (01952) 432179
e info@goldenballinn.com
w goldenballinn.co.uk

The Library House ★★★★★
Guest Accommodation
GOLD AWARD
11 Severn Bank, Ironbridge
TF8 7AN
t (01952) 432299
e info@libraryhouse.com
w libraryhouse.co.uk

The Meadow Inn ★★★★ *Inn*
29 Buildwas Road, Telford
TF8 7BZ
t (020) 8777 3636
e reservations@meadowinn.net
w meadowinn.net

The Old Rectory at Broseley
★★★★★ *Guest House*
SILVER AWARD
46 Ironbridge Road, Broseley
TF12 5AF
t (01952) 883199
e info@theoldrectoryatbroseley.co.uk
w theoldrectoryatbroseley.co.uk

Tontine ★★★ *Inn*
The Square, Ironbridge, Telford
TF8 7AL
t (01952) 432127
e tontinehotel@tiscali.co.uk
w tontine-hotel.com

Wharfage Cottage ★★★
Bed & Breakfast
17 The Wharfage, Ironbridge
TF8 7AW
t (01952) 432721
e info@wharfagecottage.co.uk
w wharfagecottage.co.uk

JACKFIELD
The Calcutts House ★★★★
Guest Accommodation
Calcutts Road, Jackfield, Ironbridge,
Telford
TF8 7LH
t (01952) 882631
e info@calcuttshouse.co.uk
w calcuttshouse.co.uk

LAWLEY VILLAGE
The Stanage ★★★★
Bed & Breakfast **SILVER AWARD**
Dawley Road, Lawley Village, Telford
TF4 2PG
t (01952) 507742
e hazelbexon@yahoo.co.uk
w bedandbreakfastintelford.co.uk

LEDWYCHE
Mill House ★★★★ *Bed & Breakfast*
Squirrel Lane, Lower Ledwyche,
Ludlow
SY8 4JX
t (01584) 872837
e millhousebnb@btopenworld.com
w virtual-shropshire.co.uk/mill

LILLESHALL
Lilleshall National Sports Centre
★★★ *Campus*
Lilleshall Hall, Lilleshall, Newport
TF10 9AT
t (01952) 603003
e enquiries@lilleshall.co.uk
w lilleshallnsc.co.uk

LITTLE BOLAS
Potford House ★★★
Bed & Breakfast
Little Bolas, Telford
TF6 6PS
t (01952) 541362
e d.sadler@uwclub.net
w shropshirebedandbreakfast.com

LITTLE NESS
Hollies Farm ★★★ *Bed & Breakfast*
Valeswood, Little Ness, Shrewsbury
SY4 2LH
t (01939) 261046
e janetwakefield@btinternet.com
w holliesfarm.co.uk

LITTLE STRETTON
Mynd House ★★★★ *Guest House*
SILVER AWARD
Little Stretton, Church Stretton
SY6 6RB
t (01694) 722212
e info@myndhouse.co.uk
w myndhouse.co.uk

LLANYMYNECH
The Cross Keys ★★ *Inn*
North Road, Llanmynech
SY22 6EA
t (01691) 831585
e reservations@crosskeyshotel.info
w crosskeyshotel.info

LONGVILLE
Wilderhope Manor YHA ★★ *Hostel*
The John Cadbury Memorial Hostel,
Much Wenlock
TF13 6EG
t 0870 770 6090
e wilderhope@yha.org.uk
w yha.org.uk

LUDLOW
Bromley Court ★★★★
Guest Accommodation - Room Only
SILVER AWARD
18–20 Lower Broad Street, Ludlow
SY8 1PQ
t (01584) 876996
e bromley.court18@btinternet.com
w ludlowhotels.com

Cecil Guest House ★★★
Guest House
Sheet Road, Ludlow
SY8 1LR
t (01584) 872442
w cecil-ludlow.co.uk

The Church Inn ★★★★ *Inn*
The Buttercross, Ludlow
SY8 1AW
t (01584) 872174
e reception@thechurchinn.com
w thechurchinn.com

DeGreys ★★★★★
Guest Accommodation
GOLD AWARD
5-6 Broad Street, Ludlow, Shropshire
SY8 1NG
t (01584) 872764
e degreys@btopenworld.com
w degreys.co.uk

Elm Lodge B&B ★★★★
Bed & Breakfast **SILVER AWARD**
Elm Lodge, Fishmore, Ludlow
SY8 3DP
t (01584) 872308
e info@elm-lodge.org.uk
w elm-lodge.org.uk

Hen & Chickens Guest House
★★★★ *Guest House*
103 Old Street, Ludlow
SY8 1NU
t (01584) 874318
e charlotte@henandchickensgh.biz
w henandchickensgh.biz

Henwick House ★★★★
Bed & Breakfast
Gravel Hill, Ludlow
SY8 1QU
t (01584) 873338
e info@henwickhouse.co.uk
w henwickhouse.co.uk

The Mount Guest House ★★★★
Guest House
61 Gravel Hill, Ludlow
SY8 1QS
t (01584) 874084
e rooms@themountludlow.co.uk
w themountludlow.co.uk

LYTH BANK
Lyth Hill House ★★★★★
Bed & Breakfast **GOLD AWARD**
28 Old Coppice, Lyth Hill,
Shrewsbury
SY3 0BP
t (01743) 874660
e bnb@lythhillhouse.com
w lythhillhouse.com

MAESBURY MARSH
**White House Vegetarian Bed &
Breakfast** ★★★★ *Bed & Breakfast*
Maesbury Marsh, Oswestry
SY10 8JA
t (01691) 658524
e whitehouse@maesburymarsh.co.uk
w maesburymarsh.co.uk

MARKET DRAYTON
Brooklands B&B ★★★★★
Bed & Breakfast
Adderley Road, Market Drayton
TF9 3SW
t (01630) 695988
e brooklandsdirect@btinternet.co

The Hermitage ★★★ *Guest House*
44 Stafford Street, Market Drayton
TF9 1JB
t (01630) 658508
e info@thehermitagebb.co.uk
w thehermitagebb.co.uk

MARTON
Lowfield Inn ★★★★ *Inn*
Marton, Welshpool
SY21 8JX
t (01743) 891313
e lowfieldinn@tiscali.co.uk
w lowfieldinn.com

MILSON
Clod Hall ★★ *Bed & Breakfast*
Clod Hall, Milson, Cleobury
Mortimer
DY14 0BJ
t (01584) 781421
w stmem.com/clod-hall

MONTGOMERY
Broughton Farm B&B ★★★
Farmhouse
Broughton Farm, Bishop's Castle
SY15 6SZ
t (01588) 638393
e lbrfarm@fastmail.co.uk
w broughtonfarm.org.uk

MUCH WENLOCK
Carnewydd ★★★★ *Bed & Breakfast*
Farley Road, Much Wenlock
TF13 6NB
t (01952) 728418
e cliveandlucyship@hotmail.co.uk

Danywenallt ★★★ *Bed & Breakfast*
Farley Road, Much Wenlock
TF13 6NB
t 07974 081618
e merlibobs@tiscali.co.uk
w stmem.com/danywenallt

Talbot Inn ★★★ *Inn*
High Street, Much Wenlock
TF13 6AA
t (01952) 727077
e the_talbot_inn@hotmail.com
w the-talbot-inn.com

Wenlock Pottery & Craft Centre
★★★★ *Bed & Breakfast*
Shineton Street, Much Wenlock
TF13 6HT
t (01952) 727600
e wenlockpots@btopenworld.com
w wenlockpottery.co.uk

NEWCASTLE
Springhill Farm ★★★ *Farmhouse*
Clun, Craven Arms
SY7 8PE
t (01588) 640337
e info.springhillfarm@gmail.com
w springhill-farm.org.uk

OSWESTRY
Harthill ★★★ *Bed & Breakfast*
80 Welsh Walls, Oswestry
SY11 1RW
t (01691) 679024
e josh@catmur.net
w welshwalls.co.uk

Yew Tree House ★★★★
Bed & Breakfast **SILVER AWARD**
Lower Frankton, Nr Oswestry
SY11 4PB
t 01691 622126
e info@yewtreebandb.co.uk
w YewTreeBandB.co.uk

Heart of England | Shropshire/Staffordshire

RATLINGHOPE

dges Youth Hostel (Long nd) ★★★ *Hostel*
tlinghope, Shrewsbury
5 0SP
t (01588) 650656
w yha.org.uk

ROCK GREEN

lson Cottage ★★★★
d & Bed & Breakfast
cks Green, Ludlow
8 2DS
t (01584) 878108
e info@ludlow.uk.com
w ludlow.uk.com

SAMBROOK

mbrook Manor ★★★★
rmhouse
mbrook, Newport
10 8AL
t (01952) 550256
e sambrookmanor@btconnect.com
w sambrookmanor.co.uk

SELATTYN

e Old Rectory Selattyn ★★★
est Accommodation
yn Road, Selattyn, Oswestry
10 7DH
t (01691) 659708
e maggie.barnes.b@btinternet.com

SHIFNAL

fellows Wine Bar ★★★ *Inn*
arket Place, Shifnal
11 9AU
t (01952) 461517
e reservations@odley.co.uk
w odleyinns.co.uk/odfellows

SHREWSBURY

bey Court Guest House ★★★★
est House
4 Abbey Foregate, Shrewsbury
2 6AU
t (01743) 364416
e info@abbeycourt.biz
w abbeycourt.biz

ton Guest House ★★★★
d & Breakfast
Canon Street, Cherry Orchard,
rewsbury
2 5HG
t (01743) 359275
e antonguesthouse@btconnect.com
w antonhouse.com

ompton Farmhouse ★★★★
d & Breakfast **SILVER AWARD**
oss Houses, Shrewsbury
5 6LE
t (01743) 761629
e info@bromptonfarmhouse.co.uk
w bromptonfarmhouse.co.uk

stlecote Guest House ★★★
uest Accommodation
Monkmoor Road, Shrewsbury
2 5AT
t (01743) 245473
e soniataplin@yahoo.co.uk
w castlecote.co.uk

stlegates House ★★★★★
d & Breakfast **GOLD AWARD**
stle Gates, Shrewsbury
1 2AT
t (01743) 362395
e rachel-castlegates@hotmail.com

arnwood ★★★★ *Bed & Breakfast*
0 London Road, Shrewsbury
2 6PP
t (01743) 359196
e charnwoodguesthouse@tiscali.co.uk
w charnwoodguesthouse.co.uk

College Hill Guest House ★★★
Guest Accommodation
11 College Hill, Shrewsbury
SY1 1LZ
t (01743) 365744
e collegehillguesthouse@yahoo.co.uk
w stmem.com/collegehillhouse

Ferndell B&B ★★★★
Bed & Breakfast
14 Underdale Road, Abbey
Foregate, Shrewsbury
SY2 5DL
t (01743) 344949
e ferndell@tiscali.co.uk
w ferndellbandb.co.uk

Grove Farm House ★★★★★
Guest Accommodation
SILVER AWARD
Condover, Shrewsbury
SY5 7BH
t (01743) 718544
e liz@grovefarmhouse.com
w grovefarmhouse.com

Kingsland Bed & Breakfast ★★★
Bed & Breakfast
47 Kennedy Road, Shrewsbury
SY3 7AA
t (01743) 355990
e kate@kingslandbandb.com
w kingslandbandb.com

Sandford House ★★★★
Guest Accommodation
St Julians Friars, Shrewsbury
SY1 1XL
t (01743) 343829
e sandfordhouse@lineone.net
w sandfordhouse.co.uk

Trevellion House Bed & Breakfast
★★★★ *Bed & Breakfast*
1 Bradford Street, Monkmoor,
Shrewsbury
SY2 5DP
t (01743) 249582
e soniataplin@yahoo.co.uk
w castlecote.co.uk

Ye Olde Bucks Head Inn ★★★ *Inn*
Frankwell, Shrewsbury
SY3 8JR
t (01743) 369392
e adminbuckshead inn@tesco.net
w bucksheadinn.co.uk

ST GEORGES

Grove House Bed & Breakfast
★★★★ *Guest Accommodation*
1 Stafford Street, St Georges,
Telford
TF2 9JW
t (01952) 616140
w virtual-shropshire.co.uk/birchesmih

STOTTESDON

Cox's Barn ★★★★ *Farmhouse*
Bagginswood, Cleobury Mortimer
DY14 8LS
t (01746) 718415
e iain.thompson12@btopenworld.com
w stmem.com/coxs-barn

Hardwicke Farm Bed & Breakfast
★★★★ *Farmhouse* **SILVER AWARD**
Stottesdon, Cleobury Mortimer
DY14 8TN
t (01746) 718220
e hardwickefarm@btinternet.com
w hardwickefarm.co.uk

TELFORD

The Mill House ★★★★
Bed & Breakfast
Shrewsbury Road, High Ercall,
Telford
TF6 6BE
t (01952) 770394
e judy@ercallmill.co.uk
w ercallmill.co.uk

Old Orleton Inn ★★★★★ *Inn*
SILVER AWARD
Holyhead Road, Wellington,
Shropshire
TF1 2HA
t (01952) 255011
e info@theoldorleton.com
w theoldorleton.com

Stone House ★★★★
Guest Accommodation
Shifnal Road, Priorslee, Telford
TF2 9NN
t (01952) 290119
e stonehousegh@aol.com
w stonehouseguesthouse.co.uk

THE DOWN

The Down Inn ★★★★ *Inn*
SILVER AWARD
Ludlow Road, Bridgnorth
WV16 6UA
t (01746) 789539
e info@thedowninn.co.uk
w thedowninn.co.uk

TREFONEN

Lynstead Lodge ★★★★
Bed & Breakfast
Bellan Lane, Trefonen, Oswestry
SY10 9DQ
t (01691) 657452
e ddoyle951@btinternet.com
w lynsteadlodge.trefonen

TRENCH

Furnace House ★★★
Guest Accommodation
64 Furnace Lane, Trench, Telford
TF2 7JE
t (01952) 603917
e info@furnacehouse.co.uk
w furnacehouse.co.uk

WELLINGTON

Clairmont ★★★★
Guest Accommodation
54 Haygate Road, Wellington
TF1 1QN
t (01952) 414214
e info@clairmontguesthouse.co.uk
w clairmontguesthouse.co.uk

WHITCHURCH

Sedgeford House ★★★★
Bed & Breakfast
Sedgeford, Whitchurch
SY13 1EX
t (01948) 665598
e sedgefordhousebandb@tesco.net
w sedgefordhouse.com

WHITTINGTON

Fitzwarine House ★★★★
Bed & Breakfast
Castle Street, Whittington
SY11 4DF
t (01691) 680882
e fitzwarinehouse@supanet.com
w fitzwarinehouse.co.uk

WISTANSWICK

Marsh Farm Bed & Breakfast
★★★★ *Bed & Breakfast*
SILVER AWARD
Marsh Farm, Wistanswick, Market
Drayton
TF9 2BB
t (01630) 638520
e wiz.light@talk21.com
w marshfarmbandb.com

WOOFFERTON

Ravenscourt Manor ★★★★★
Bed & Breakfast **GOLD AWARD**
Woofferton, Ludlow
SY8 4AL
t (01584) 711905
e elizabeth@ravenscourtmanor.plus.com
w smoothhound.co.uk/hotels/ravenscourt.html

WROCKWARDINE

Church Farm Guest House ★★★★
Guest Accommodation
Wrockwardine Village, Wellington,
Telford
TF6 5DG
t (01952) 251927
e info@churchfarm-shropshire.co.uk
w churchfarm-shropshire.co.uk

Staffordshire

ALREWAS

Alrewas Hayes
Guest Accommodation
Alrewas Hayes, Burton-on-Trent
DE13 7DL
t (01283) 791625
e info@alrewashayes.com
w alrewashayes.com

ALSTONEFIELD

Alstonefield YHA ★★★ *Hostel*
Overdale, Lode Lane, Ashbourne
DE6 2FZ
t (01335) 310206
w yha.org.uk

ALTON

Alverton Motel ★★★
Guest Accommodation
Denstone Lane, Alton, Alton Towers
Area
ST10 4AX
t (01538) 702265
e enquiries@alvertonmotel.co.uk

Bank House ★★★★
Guest Accommodation
Smithy Bank, Alton, Alton Towers
Area
ST10 4AD
t (01538) 702524
e altonbandb@aol.com
w alton-bandb.co.uk

Bulls Head Inn ★★★ *Inn*
High Street, Alton, Alton Towers
Area
ST10 4AQ
t (01538) 702307
e janet@thebullsheadinn.freeserve.co.uk
w thebullsheadinn.freeserve.co.uk

Fields Farm ★★★★
Bed & Breakfast
Chapel Lane, Threapwood Alton,
Staffs
ST10 4QZ
t (01538) 752721 Mobile 07850310381
e pat.massey@fieldsfarmbb.co.uk
w fieldsfarmbb.co.uk

Hillside Farm ★★★ *Bed & Breakfast*
Alton Road, Denstone, Uttoxeter
ST14 5HG
t (01889) 590760
w smoothhound.co.uk/hotels/hillside.html

Peakstones Inn ★★★ *Inn*
Cheadle Road, Alton, Alton Towers
Area, Staffordshire
ST10 4DH
t (01538) 755776
e info@peakstones-inn.co.uk
w peakstones-inn.co.uk

Tythe Barn House ★★★
Guest Accommodation
Tythe Barn House, Denstone Lane,
Alton Towers Area
ST10 4AX
t (01538) 702852
w tythebarnhouse.co.uk

The Warren ★★★★
Guest Accommodation
SILVER AWARD
The Warren, Battlesteads, Alton
Towers Area
ST10 4BG
t (01538) 702493
e annettebas@tinyworld.co.uk
w thewarren-bb.com

or key to symbols see page 6   481

Heart of England | Staffordshire

Windy Arbour ★★★★ *Guest House*
Hollis Lane, Denstone, Uttoxeter
ST14 5HP
t (01889) 591013
e stay@windyarbour.co.uk
w windyarbour.co.uk

ALTON TOWERS AREA

The Malthouse ★★★★
Guest Accommodation
Malthouse Road, Alton, Alton Towers Area
ST10 4AG
t (01538) 703273
e enquiries@the-malthouse.com

AMERTON

Amerton Farm ★★★ *Farmhouse*
Amerton, Stowe by Chartley, Stafford
ST18 0LA
t (01889) 272 777
w amertonfarm.co.uk

ASHBOURNE

Stanshope Hall ★★★★
Guest Accommodation
Stanshope, Ashbourne
DE6 2AD
t (01335) 310278
e naomi@stanshope.demon.co.uk
w stanshope.net

Throwley Hall Farm ★★★★
Farmhouse
Ilam, Ashbourne
DE6 2BB
t (01538) 308202
e throwleyhall@btinternet.com
w throwleyhallfarm.co.uk

ASHBOURNE (1.25 MILES)

Dove House B&B *Bed & Breakfast*
Bridge Hill, Mayfield, Ashbourne
DE6 2HN
t (01335) 343329

BARTON-UNDER-NEEDWOOD

Shoulder of Mutton ★★★ *Inn*
16 Main Street, Barton under Needwood, Burton on Trent, Staffordshire
DE13 8AA
t (01283) 712568
e info@shoulderofmutton.com
w shoulderofmutton.com

BIDDULPH

Chapel Croft Guest House ★★★★
Guest House
Newtown Road, Biddulph Park, Stoke-on-Trent
ST8 7SW
t (01782) 511013
e chapelcroft@hotmail.co.uk
w chapelcroft.com

BOBBINGTON

Red Lion Inn ★★★★ *Inn*
Six Ashes Road, Bobbington, Stourbridge
DY7 5DU
t (01384) 221237
e bookings@redlioninn.co.uk
w redlioninn.co.uk

BRADNOP

Middle Farm ★★★
Guest Accommodation
Apesford, Bradnop, Leek
ST13 7EX
t (01538) 382839
e pgrowbottom@hotmail.com
w middlefarmbandb.co.uk

BRAMSHALL

Bowmore House ★★★★
Farmhouse
Stone Road, Bramshall, Uttoxeter
ST14 8SH
t (01889) 564352
e enquiries@bowmorehouse.com

BURNTWOOD

Davolls Cottage ★★★★
Bed & Breakfast
Davolls Cottage, 156 Woodhouses Road, Burntwood
WS7 9EL
t (01543) 671250

BURTON-ON-TRENT

Redmoor Accommodation ★★
Bed & Breakfast
6 Redmoor Close, Winshill, Burton-on-Trent
DE15 0HZ
t (01283) 531977
e petervyze@btinternet.com

BUTTERTON

Coxon Green Farm ★★★★
Farmhouse SILVER AWARD
Butterton, Leek
ST13 7TA
t (01538) 304221
e jtomkinson@coxongreenfarm.co.uk
w coxongreenfarm.co.uk

Stoop House Farm ★★★★★
Bed & Breakfast SILVER AWARD
Butterton, Leek
ST13 7SY
t (01538) 304486
e bnfrench@yahoo.co.uk
w stoophousefarm.co.uk

BUXTON

The Manifold Inn ★★★★ *Inn*
Hulme End, Buxton
SK17 0EX
t (01298) 84537
e enquiries@themanifoldinn.com
w themanifoldinn.co.uk

CHEADLE

Ley Fields Farm ★★★★ *Farmhouse*
SILVER AWARD
Leek Road, Cheadle, Alton Towers Area
ST10 2EF
t (01538) 752875
e leyfieldsfarm@aol.com
w leyfieldsfarm.co.uk

The Manor ★★★★ *Guest House*
Watt Place, Cheadle, Alton Towers Area
ST10 1NZ
t (01538) 753450
e info@themanorcheadle.co.uk
w themanorcheadle.co.uk

Park View Guest House ★★★
Guest House
15 Mill Road, Cheadle, Alton Towers Area
ST10 1NG
t (01538) 755412
e kjillsandford@fsmail.net
w parkviewguesthouse.net

Rakeway House Farm B&B ★★★★
Farmhouse
Rakeway Road, Cheadle, Alton Towers Area
ST10 1RA
t (01538) 755295
e rakewayhousefarm@btinternet.com
w rakewayhousefarm.com

CHEDDLETON

Brook House Farm ★★★
Farmhouse
Brookhouse Lane, Cheddleton, Leek
ST13 7DF
t (01538) 360296

The Garden House ★★★★
Bed & Breakfast
150 Cheadle Road, Cheddleton, Leek
ST13 7BD
t (01538) 361449
e pearl@garden-house.org
w garden-house.org

COTTON

The Mousehole ★★★★
Bed & Breakfast
Cotton Lane, Cotton, Alton Towers Area
ST10 3DS
t (01538) 703351
w themouseholebandb.co.uk

DENSTONE

The Riddings Bed & Breakfast
★★★★ *Farmhouse*
The Riddings, Denstone, Uttoxeter
ST14 5HW
t (01889) 590008
e caroline@theriddingsfarm.co.uk
w theriddingsfarm.co.uk

Rowan Lodge ★★★★
Guest Accommodation
Stubwood Lane, Denstone, Alton Towers Area
ST14 5HU
t (01889) 590913
e rowanlodge@hotmail.com
w rowanlodge.co.uk

ECCLESHALL

Cobblers Cottage ★★★★
Guest Accommodation
Kerry Lane, Eccleshall, Stafford
ST21 6EJ
t (01785) 850116

The George Inn ★ *Inn*
Castle Street, Eccleshall, Stafford
ST21 6DF
t (01785) 850300
e information@thegeorgeinn.freeserve.co.uk
w thegeorgeinn.freeserve.co.uk

ENDON

Hollinhurst Farm ★★★ *Farmhouse*
Park Lane, Endon, Stoke-on-Trent
ST9 9JB
t (01782) 502633
e joan.hollinhurst@btconnect.com
w smoothhound.co.uk/hotels/hollinhurst.html

FAZELEY

Hollies Guest House ★★★
Guest House
Atherstone Road, Fazeley, Tamworth
B78 3RF
t (01827) 283550
e thehollies-tamworth@hotmail.co.uk
w thehollies-tamworth.com

FORTON

The Swan at Forton ★★★ *Inn*
Eccleshall Road, Forton, Newport
TF10 8BY
t (01952) 812169

FOXT

Shawgate Farm Guest House
★★★★ *Guest House*
Shay Lane, Foxt, Alton Towers Area
ST10 2HN
t (01538) 266590
e ken@shawgatefarm.co.uk
w shawgatefarm.co.uk

GNOSALL

Leys House ★★★★ *Bed & Breakfast*
Quarry Lane, Gnosall, Stafford
ST20 0BZ
t (01785) 822532
e proffitt.gnosall@virgin.net

GRINDON

Summerhill Farm Bed & Breakfast
★★★ *Farmhouse*
Grindon, Leek
ST13 7TT
t (01538) 304264
e info@summerhillfarm.co.uk
w summerhillfarm.co.uk

HARLASTON

Harlaston Post Office B&B ★★
Guest House
Harlaston Post Office, Main Road, Lichfield
B79 9JU
t (01827) 383324
e info@harlastonpostoffice.co.uk
w harlastonpostoffice.co.uk

HARTINGTON

Bank Top Farm ★★★ *Farmhouse*
Pilsbury Lane, Hartington, Buxton
SK17 0AD
t (01298) 84205
e janepilkington@btinternet.com
w peak-district-bed-breakfast.co.uk

HULME END

Raikes Farm ★★★★ *Farmhouse*
Hulme End, Buxton
SK17 0HJ
t (01298) 84344

ILAM

Beechenhill Farm ★★★★
Farmhouse
Ilam, Ashbourne
DE6 2BD
t (01335) 310274
e beechenhill@btinternet.com
w beechenhill.co.uk

YHA Ilam Hall ★★★★ *Hostel*
Ilam, Ashbourne
DE6 2AZ
t 0870 770 5876
e ilam@yha.org.uk
w yha.org.uk

LEEK

The Green Man ★★★
Guest Accommodation
38 Compton, Leek
ST13 5NH
t (01538) 388084
e diannemoir@btconnect.com
w greenman-guesthouse.co.uk

The Hatcheries ★★★
Bed & Breakfast
Church Lane, Leek
ST13 5EX
t (01538) 399552
e jan@l33k.wanadoo.co.uk
w thehatcheries.co.uk

Peak Weavers Rooms & Restaurant ★★★★
Guest Accommodation
21 King Street, Leek
ST13 5NW
t (01538) 383729
e info@peakweavershotel.co.uk
w peakweavershotel.co.uk

White Hart ★★★★
Guest Accommodation
1 & 3 Stockwell Street, Leek
ST13 6DH
t (01538) 372122
e info@whitehearttearoom.co.uk
w whiteharttearoom.co.uk

LICHFIELD

32 Beacon Street ★★★★
Bed & Breakfast
Lichfield, Lichfield
WS13 7AJ
t (01543) 262378

Altair House ★★ *Bed & Breakfast*
21 Shakespeare Avenue, Lichfield
WS14 9BE
t (01543) 252900

Bogey Hole ★★★★ *Guest House*
21-23 Dam Street, Lichfield
WS13 6AE
t (01543) 264303

Heart of England | Staffordshire/Warwickshire

pper's End Guest House
★★ *Guest House*
Isall Road, Muckley Corner,
hfield
14 0BG
(01543) 372910
info@coppersendguesthouse.co.uk
coppersendguesthouse.co.uk

lly Tree Cottage ★★
d & Breakfast
Daisy Lane, Alrewas, Lichfield
13 7EW
(01283) 791120
hollytreecottage.alrewas@gmail.com

e Maples ★★ *Bed & Breakfast*
Balmoral Close, Lichfield
14 9SP
(01543) 255645
javincen@tiscali.co.uk

de Peculiar ★★★★ *Inn*
e Green, Handsacre, Lichfield
15 4DP
(01543) 491891
corinne.odonnell@ntlworld.com
theoldepeculiar.co.uk

el Farm Bed & Breakfast
★★ *Farmhouse*
herwick Road, Whittington,
hfield
14 9LJ
(01543) 433461
accommodation@peelfarm.co.uk
peelfarm.co.uk

res View ★★★ *Bed & Breakfast*
riary Road, Lichfield
13 6QL
(01543) 306424
tarra@spiresviewbnb.co.uk
spiresviewbnb.co.uk

LONGNOR

ring Cottage ★★★★
est Accommodation
ek Road, Longnor, Buxton
17 0PA
(01298) 83101
garry.roe1@btopenworld.com

MADELEY

e Old Hall Country House
★★★★ *Guest Accommodation*
VER AWARD
olside, Madeley, Newcastle
/3 9DX
(01782) 752543
garywhite@theoldhallatmadeley.com
theoldhallatmadeley.com

MARCHINGTON

rest Hills Guest House ★★★★
est Accommodation
isty Lane, Marchington, Uttoxeter
14 8JY
(01283) 820447

MAVESYN RIDWARE

d Rectory ★★★★
d & Breakfast GOLD AWARD
vesyn Ridware, Lichfield
515 3QE
(01543) 490792
sandra@oldrectory-mavesyn.co.uk
oldrectory-mavesyn.co.uk

MAYFIELD

ona Villas Bed & Breakfast
★★★ *Bed & Breakfast*
Mona Villas, Church Lane,
ayfield, Ashbourne
6 2JS
(01335) 343773
info@moan-villas.fsnet.co.uk
mona-villas.fsnet.co.uk

MODDERSHALL

Moddershall Oaks Spa Restaurant Suites ★★★★★
Guest Accommodation
SILVER AWARD
Moddershall, Nr Stone, Staffordshire
ST15 8TG
t 01782 399000
e enquiries@moddershalloaks.com
w moddershalloaks.com

NEWCASTLE

Graythwaite Guest House ★★★★
Guest Accommodation
106 Lancaster Road, Newcastle-under-Lyme, Newcastle
ST5 1DS
t (01782) 612875
e info@thegraythwaite.co.uk
w thegraythwaite.co.uk

OAKAMOOR

Ribden Farm ★★★ *Farmhouse*
Three Lows, Oakamoor, Alton Towers Area
ST10 3BW
t (01538) 702830
e ribdenfarm@aol.com
w ribdenfarm.com

Trough Ivy House ★★★★
Bed & Breakfast
Longshaw Lane, Farley, Alton Towers Area
ST10 3BQ
t (01538) 702683
e info@troughivyhouse.co.uk
w troughivyhouse.co.uk

YHA Dimmingsdale ★★★ *Hostel*
Oakamoor, Stoke-on-Trent, Alton Towers Area
ST10 3AS
t (01629) 592600
e dimmingsdale@yha.org.uk
w yha.org.uk/find-accommodation/peak-district-sherwood/hostels/dimmingsdale/index.aspx

PRESTWOOD

Manor House Farm ★★★★
Farmhouse **SILVER AWARD**
Quixhill Lane, Prestwood, Uttoxeter
ST14 5DD
t (01889) 590415
e cm_ball@yahoo.com
w 4posteraccom.com

QUARNFORD

Gradbach Mill YHA ★★★ *Hostel*
Gradbach, Buxton
SK17 0SU
t (01260) 227625
e gradbachmill@yha.org.uk
w yha.org.uk

YHA Gradbach Farmhouse ★★★★
Group Hostel
Quarnford
SK17 0SU
t (01269) 592633

RILEY HILL

Common Farm Bed & Breakfast
★★★★ *Bed & Breakfast*
Bromley Hayes, Lichfield
WS13 8JE
t (01543) 472228
e hazel@common-farm.co.uk
w common-farm.co.uk

RUGELEY

Colton House ★★★★★
Guest House **GOLD AWARD**
Bellamour Way, Colton, Rugeley, Staffs.
WS15 3LL
t (01889) 578580
e mail@coltonhouse.com
w coltonhouse.com

Park Farm ★★ *Farmhouse*
Hawksyard, Armitage Lane, Rugeley
WS15 1ED
t (01889) 583477

RUSHTON SPENCER

Heaton House Farm ★★★★
Farmhouse
Rushton Spencer, Macclesfield
SK11 0RD
t (01260) 226203
e weddings@heatonhouse.co.uk
w heatonhousefarm.co.uk

STAFFORD

Cedarwood ★★★★ *Bed & Breakfast*
SILVER AWARD
46 Weeping Cross, Stafford
ST17 0DS
t (01785) 662981

Littywood Manor ★★★★
Bed & Breakfast
Bradley, Stafford
ST18 9DW
t (01785) 780234
e a.bradshaw@btinternet.com
w littywood.co.uk

Park Farm ★★★ *Farmhouse*
Weston Road, Stafford
ST18 0BD
t (01785) 240257
e parkfarm12@hotmail.com
w parkfarmstafford.com

Rooks Nest Farm ★★★ *Farmhouse*
Weston Bank, Weston, Stafford
ST18 0BA
t (01889) 270624
e info@rooksnest.co.uk
w rooksnest.co.uk

Wyndale Guest House ★★★
Guest House
199 Corporation Street, Stafford
ST16 3LQ
t (01785) 223069
e wyndale@aol.com
w wyndaleguesthouse.co.uk

STAPENHILL

Wendy's Bed & Breakfast ★★★★
Guest Accommodation
22 Yarrow Close, Brizlincote Valley, Burton-on-Trent
DE15 9JT
t 07929 075298
e wendyenion@hotmail.com

STOKE-ON-TRENT

Cedar Tree Cottage ★★★★
Bed & Breakfast **SILVER AWARD**
41 Longton Road, Trentham, Stoke-on-Trent
ST4 8ND
t (01782) 644751
e n.portas@btinternet.com

The Northwood Guest House ★★★
Guest Accommodation
146 Keelings Road, Northwood, Stoke-on-Trent
ST1 6QA
t (01782) 279729
e northwoodhotel@tiscali.co.uk
w cityhotels.org.uk

Reynolds Hey ★★★★
Guest Accommodation
Park Lane, Endon, Stoke-on-Trent
ST9 9JB
t (01782) 502717 (07851972863)
e reynoldshey@hotmail.com
w reynoldshey.co.uk

Verdon Guest House ★★
Guest House
44 Charles Street, Hanley, Stoke-on-Trent, Staffordshire
ST1 3JY
t (01782) 264244
w verdonguesthouse.co.uk

STONE

Mayfield House ★★★
Bed & Breakfast
112 Newcastle Road, Stone
ST15 8LG
t (01785) 811446

TAMWORTH

Belmont Guest House ★★★★
Guest House
56 Upper Gungate, Tamworth
B79 8AA
t (01827) 62585

The Peel Aldergate ★★★★
Guest Accommodation
13-14 Aldergate, Tamworth
B79 7DL
t (01827) 67676
w thepeelaldergate.co.uk

Villa Marie ★★★★ *Bed & Breakfast*
63 Quarry Hill, Wilnecote, Tamworth
B77 5BW
t (01827) 250966

TEAN

Granary Room ★★★
Guest Accommodation
Blythe Farm House, Riverside Road, Tean, Stoke-on-Trent
ST10 4JW
t (01538) 724061
e irene@blythefarmhouse.co.uk
w blythefarmhouse.co.uk

Teanford B&B ★★★★
Guest Accommodation
Beech Farm, Teanford, Alton Towers Area
ST104ES
t (01538) 723886
w teanfordbandb.host-ed.net

UPPERHULME

Hen Cloud Cottage ★★★★
Bed & Breakfast
Upperhulme
ST13 8TZ
t (01538) 300086
e lornabarlow@btinternet.com

WATERHOUSES

Leehouse Farm ★★★★
Bed & Breakfast **SILVER AWARD**
Leek Road, Waterhouses, Leek
ST10 3HW
t (01538) 308439
w leehousefarmbandb.co.uk

WETTON

The Old Chapel ★★★★
Guest Accommodation
SILVER AWARD
The Old Chapel, Wetton, Ashbourne
DE6 2AF
t (01335) 310450
e lynne.imeson@tiscali.co.uk

WYCHNOR

St Leonards House ★★
Guest Accommodation
Wychnor, Burton-on-Trent
DE13 8BY
t (01283) 791 077

Warwickshire

ALVESTON

YHA Hemmingford House ★★★★
Hostel
Alveston, Stratford-upon-Avon
CV37 7RG
t 0870 770 6052
e stratford@yha.org.uk
w yha.org.uk/find-accommodation/heart-of-england/hostels/stratford-upon-avon/index.aspx

ARMSCOTE

Willow Corner *Bed & Breakfast*
Armscote, Stratford-upon-Avon
CV37 8DE
t (01608) 682391
e trishandalan@willowcorner.co.uk
w willowcorner.co.uk

Heart of England | Warwickshire

ASTON CANTLOW

Tudor Rose Cottage ★★★★
Bed & Breakfast
29 Chapel Lane, Aston Cantlow,
Stratford-upon-Avon
B95 6HU
t (01789) 488315
e robandwendydean@btinternet.com
w tudor-rose-cottage.co.uk

BANBURY

Wormleighton Hall ★★★★
Farmhouse GOLD AWARD
Wormleighton, Southam, Banbury
CV47 2XQ
t (01295) 770234
e bookings@wormleightonhall.co.uk
w wormleightonhall.com

BARFORD

Ingsley Bank House ★★★★
Bed & Breakfast
2 Westham Lane, Barford, Warwick
CV35 8DP
t (01926) 624929
e enquiries@ingsleybank.co.uk
w inglseybank.co.uk

Machado Gallery ★★★★
Bed & Breakfast
9 Wellesbourne Road, Barford,
Warwick
CV35 8EL
t (01926) 624061
e machadogallery@barford.org.uk
w machadogallery.co.uk

BIDFORD-ON-AVON

Buckle House ★★★★
Guest Accommodation
SILVER AWARD
Honeybourne Road, Bidford-on-
Avon, Stratford-upon-Avon
B50 4PD
t (01789) 778183
e rowav@hotmail.co.uk
w bucklehouse.com

Fosbroke House ★★★★
Guest House
4 High Street, Bidford-on-Avon,
Stratford-upon-Avon
B50 4BU
t (01789) 772327
e mark@swiftvilla.fsnet.co.uk
w smoothhound.co.uk/hotels/fosbroke.html

The Harbour ★★★★
Bed & Breakfast
20 Salford Road, Bidford-on-Avon,
Stratford-upon-Avon
B50 4EN
t (01789) 772975
e peter@theharbour-gh.co.uk
w theharbour-gh.com

BIRMINGHAM

Merrimoles Bed & Breakfast
★★★★ Bed & Breakfast
Back Lane, Shustoke, Coleshill,
Birmingham
B46 2AW
t (01675) 481158
e stella@merrimoles.co.uk
w merrimoles.co.uk

The Railway Guest House ★★★
Guest Accommodation
25 Station Road, Whitacre Heath,
Birmingham Nec
B46 2JA
t (01675) 463909
e railwayguesthouse@btinternet.com
w therailwayguesthouse.co.uk

Ye Olde Station Guest House
★★★ Guest House
Church Road, Shustoke, Coleshill,
Birmingham
B46 2AX
t (01675) 481736
e patr@freeuk.com

COLESHILL

Springfield Guest House ★★★★
Guest House
69 Coventry Road, Coleshill,
Birmingham
B46 3EA
t (01675) 465695
e springfldhouse@aol.com
w springfield-guest-house.co.uk

COUGHTON

Coughton Lodge ★★★★
Guest House
Coughton, Alcester
B49 5HU
t (01789) 764600
e enquiries@coughtonlodge.co.uk
w coughtonlodge.co.uk

CUBBINGTON

Bakers Cottage ★★★★
Bed & Breakfast
52-54 Queen Street, Cubbington,
Leamington Spa
CV32 7NA
t (01926) 772146

Mill House ★★★★ Farmhouse
SILVER AWARD
Offchurch Lane, Offchurch,
Leamington Spa
CV33 9AP
t (01926) 427296
e info@millhouse-offchurch.co.uk
w millhouse-offchurch.co.uk

CURDWORTH

The Old School House Guest Accommodation ★★★★
Guest House
Kingsbury Road, Curdworth, Sutton
Coldfield
B76 9DR
t (01675) 470177
e info@oldschoolhousehotel.co.uk
w oldschoolhousehotel.co.uk

Reindeer Park Lodge ★★★★
Guest House
Kingsbury Road, Curdworth, Sutton
Coldfield
B76 0DE
t (01675) 470811
e enquiries@reindeerpark.co.uk
w reindeerpark.co.uk

DUNCHURCH

Courtyard ★★★★ Guest House
Toft House, Toft, Rugby
CV22 6NR
t (01788) 810540

The Old Thatched Cottage of Dunchurch ★★★★
Guest Accommodation
Southam Road, Dunchurch, Rugby
CV22 6NG
t (01788) 810417

ETTINGTON

Drybank Farm ★★★★ Farmhouse
SILVER AWARD
Fosseway, Ettington, Stratford-upon-Avon
CV37 7PD
t (01675) 740476
e drybank@btinternet.com
w drybank.co.uk

FENNY COMPTON

The Grange ★★★ Farmhouse
The Slade, Fenny Compton,
Southam, Warwickshire
CV47 2YB
t 01295770590
e mikkel.squire@farmline.com

FILLONGLEY

Grooms Cottage ★★★★
Farmhouse SILVER AWARD
Manor House Farm, Green End
Road, Fillongley, Coventry
CV7 8DS
t (01676) 540256

GREAT WOLFORD

The Old Coach House ★★★★
Bed & Breakfast
Great Wolford, Shipston-on-Stour,
Moreton-in-Marsh
CV36 5NQ
t (01608) 674152
e info@oldcoachhouse.org.uk
w oldcoachhouse.org.uk

GRENDON

Chestnuts Country Guest House
★★★★ Guest House
SILVER AWARD
Watling Street, Grendon, Atherstone
CV9 2PZ
t (01827) 331355
e ccltd@aol.com
w thechestnutshotel.com

HASELEY KNOB

Croft Guest House ★★★★
Guest House
Haseley Knob, Warwick
CV35 7NL
t (01926) 484447
e david@croftguesthouse.co.uk
w croftguesthouse.co.uk

HATTON

Shrewley Pools Farm ★★★★
Farmhouse SILVER AWARD
Haseley, Warwick
CV35 7HB
t (01926) 484315
e cathydodd@hotmail.com
w s-h-systems.co.uk/hotels/shrewley.html

KENILWORTH

Aaron Quince House ★★★★
Bed & Breakfast
29 Moseley Road, Kenilworth
CV8 2AR
t (01926) 858652
e enquiries@aaronquince.co.uk
w aaronquince.co.uk

Abbey Guest House ★★★★
Guest House
41 Station Road, Kenilworth
CV8 1JD
t (01926) 512707
e enquiries@abbeyguesthouse.com
w abbeyguesthouse.com

Avondale B&B ★★★★
Bed & Breakfast
18 Moseley Road, Kenilworth
CV8 2AQ
t (01926) 859072
e latimerhigham@aol.com
w avondalebandb.co.uk

Castle Laurels Guest House
★★★★ Guest House
22 Castle Road, Kenilworth,
Warwickshire
CV8 1NG
t (01926) 856179
e reception@castlelaurels.co.uk
w castlelaurels.co.uk

Enderley Guest House ★★★★
Guest House
20 Queens Road, Kenilworth
CV8 1JQ
t (01926) 855388
e enderleyguesthouse@supanet.com
w enderleyguesthouse.com

Ferndale House ★★★★
Guest House
45 Priory Road, Kenilworth
CV8 1LL
t (01926) 853214
e info@kenilworth-guesthouse-accommodation.com
w kenilworth-guesthouse-accommodation.com

Hilltop B&B ★★★ Bed & Breakfast
5 Holmewood Close, Kenilworth
CV8 2JE
t (01926) 856224
e maggi@hilltopbandbkenilworth.co.uk
w hilltopbandbkenilworth.co.uk

Loweridge Guest House ★★★★
Guest House GOLD AWARD
Hawkesworth Drive, Kenilworth
CV8 2GP
t (01926) 859522
e info@loweridgeguesthouse.co.uk
w loweridgeguesthouse.co.uk

Victoria Lodge ★★★★
Guest Accommodation
SILVER AWARD
180 Warwick Road, Kenilworth
CV8 1HU
t (01926) 512020
e info@victorialodgekenilworth.co.uk
w victorialodgekenilworth.co.uk

LAWFORD HEATH

Lawford Hill Farm ★★★★
Farmhouse SILVER AWARD
Lawford Heath Lane, Rugby
CV23 9HG
t (01788) 542001
e www.lawford.hill@talk21.com
w lawfordhill.co.uk

LEAMINGTON SPA

Braeside Bed & Breakfast ★★★
Bed & Breakfast
26 Temple End, Harbury,
Leamington Spa
CV33 9NE
t (01926) 613402
e rosemary@braesidebb.co.uk
w braesidebb.co.uk

Buckland Lodge ★★★ Guest House
35 Avenue Road, Leamington Spa
CV31 3PG
t (01926) 423843
e info@buckland-lodge.co.uk
w buckland-lodge.co.uk

Bungalow Farm ★★★★
Bed & Breakfast
Windmill Hill, Cubbington,
Leamington Spa
CV32 7LW
t (01926) 423276
e sheila@bungalowfarm.co.uk
w bungalowfarm.co.uk

Charnwood Guest House ★★★
Guest House
47 Avenue Road, Leamington Spa
CV31 3PF
t (01926) 831074
e ray@charnwoodguesthouse.com
w charnwoodguesthouse.com

The Coach House ★★★★
Farmhouse SILVER AWARD
Snowford Hall Farm, Hunningham
Leamington Spa
CV33 9ES
t (01926) 632297
e the_coach_house@lineone.net
w website.lineone.net/~the_coach_house

Hedley Villa Guest House ★★★
Guest House
31 Russell Terrace, Leamington Spa
CV31 1EZ
t (01926) 424504
e hedley_villa@hotmail.com
w hedleyvillaguesthouse.co.uk

Hill Cottage ★★★ Guest House
78 Southam Road, Radford Semele
Leamington Spa
CV31 1UA
t (01926) 427636
e hillcott78@aol.com
w leamingtonbedbreakfast.co.uk

No 8 Clarendon Crescent ★★★★
Bed & Breakfast SILVER AWARD
Royal Leamington Spa,
Warwickshire, Leamington Spa
CV32 5NY
t (01926) 429840
e lawson@lawson71.fsnet.co.uk
w 8clarendoncrescent.co.uk

484 Official tourist board guide Bed & Breakfast

Heart of England | Warwickshire

ctoria Park Lodge ★★★★
uest House
Adelaide Road, Royal
amington Spa, Warwick
V31 3PW
t (01926) 424195
e info@victoriaparkhotelleamingt
onspa.co.uk
w victoriaparkhotelleamingtonspa.
co.uk

**oodland Grange Conference
entre ★★★★**
uest Accommodation
d Milverton Lane, Leamington
oa
V32 6RN
t (01926) 336621
e conferencehire@wgrange.com
w woodlandgrange.com

ork House Guest House ★★★★
uest House
York Road, Leamington Spa
V31 3PR
t (01926) 424671
e reservations@yorkhousehotel.biz
w yorkhousehotel.biz

LIGHTHORNE

hurch Hill Farm B&B ★★★★
rmhouse SILVER AWARD
ghthorne, Warwick
V35 0AR
t (01926) 651251
e sue@churchillfarm.co.uk
w churchhillfarm.co.uk

LONG COMPTON

utlers Road Farm ★★★
rmhouse
ng Compton, Shipston-on-Stour
V36 5JZ
t (01608) 684262
e eileen@butlersroadfarm.com
w butlersroadfarm.co.uk

LONG MARSTON

hurch Farm B&B ★★★★
d & Breakfast
urch Farm, Long Marston,
ratford-upon-Avon
V37 8RH
t (01789) 720275
e timchurchfarm@hotmail.com
w churchfarmhouse.co.uk

LOXLEY

oxley Guest House ★★★★
uest House SILVER AWARD
ratford Road, Loxley, Stratford-
pon-Avon
V35 9JN
t (01789) 470607
e enquiries@loxleyguesthouse.co.
uk
w loxleyguesthouse.co.uk

MIDDLETON

iddleton House Farm ★★★★
uest Accommodation
ILVER AWARD
amworth Road, Middleton,
amworth
78 2BD
t (01827) 873474
e contact@middletonhousefarm.co.
uk
w middletonhousefarm.co.uk/

NUNEATON

**ll House Country Guest House
★★★** *Guest House*
f Mancetter Road, Nuneaton
V10 0RS
t (024) 7639 6685

OXHILL

able Croft ★★★★
ed & Breakfast
een Lane, Oxhill, Warwick
V35 0RB
t (01295) 680055
e pam@stablecroft.co.uk
w stablecroft.co.uk

PRIORS HARDWICK

Hill Farm ★★★ *Farmhouse*
Lower End, Priors Hardwick,
Southam
CV47 7SP
t 07740 853085
e simon@hillfarm.me.uk
w stayathillfarm.co.uk

RUGBY

The Carlton ★★★★
Guest Accommodation
130 Railway Terrace, Rugby
CV21 3HE
t (01788) 560211
e stay@thecarltonrugby.co.uk
w thecarltonrugby.co.uk

Diamond House ★★★ *Guest House*
28-30 Hillmorton Road, Rugby
CV22 5AA
t (01788) 572701
e diamondhouse2830@aol.com
w diamondhousehotel.co.uk

Green Cottage ★★★
Guest Accommodation
Brookside, Rugby
CV22 6AH
t 07802 982157
e philgodden@btinternet.com
w greencottagebandb.com

SHILTON

Barnacle Hall ★★★★★
Bed & Breakfast GOLD AWARD
Shilton Lane, Shilton, Coventry
CV7 9LH
t (024) 7661 2629
e rose@barnaclehall.co.uk
w barnaclehall.co.uk

SHIPSTON-ON-STOUR

The Howard Arms ★★★★★ *Inn*
SILVER AWARD
Lower Green, Ilmington, Shipston-
on-Stour
CV36 4LT
t (01608) 682226
e info@howardarms.com
w howardarms.com

SNITTERFIELD

Shakespeare's View ★★★★★
Bed & Breakfast GOLD AWARD
Kings Lane, Snitterfield, Stratford-
upon-Avon
CV37 0QB
t (01789) 731824
e shakespeares.view@btinternet.
com
w shakespeares.view.btinternet.co.
uk

SOLIHULL

The Limes Country Lodge ★★★
Guest House
Forshaw Heath Road, Earlswood,
Solihull
B94 5JZ
t (0121) 744 4800
e info@thelimes.biz
w thelimes.biz

STRATFORD-UPON-AVON

Adelphi Guest House ★★★★
Guest House SILVER AWARD
39 Grove Road, Stratford-upon-Avon
CV37 6PB
t (01789) 204469
e info@adelphi-guesthouse.com
w adelphi-guesthouse.com

Aidan Guest House ★★★★
Guest House
11 Evesham Place, Stratford-upon-
Avon
CV37 6HT
t (01789) 292824
e enquiries@aidanhouse.com
w aidanhouse.com

Ambleside Guest House ★★★★
Guest House SILVER AWARD
41 Grove Road, Stratford-upon-Avon
CV37 6PB
t (01789) 297239
e ruth@amblesideguesthouse.com
w amblesideguesthouse.com

Arden Park Guest House ★★★★
Guest House
6 Arden Street, Stratford-upon-Avon
CV37 6PA
t (01789) 262126
e mark@ardenparkhotel.co.uk
w ardenparkhotel.co.uk

Arrandale Guest House ★★★
Bed & Breakfast
208 Evesham Road, Stratford-upon-
Avon
CV37 9AS
t (01789) 267112
e arrandale.netfirms.com

Ashgrove House ★★★★
Guest House
37 Grove Road, Stratford-upon-Avon
CV37 6PB
t (01789) 297278
e info@ashgrovehousestratford.co.
uk
w ashgrovehousestratford.co.uk

Austons Down ★★★★
Bed & Breakfast
Saddle Bow Lane, Claverdon,
Stratford-upon-Avon
CV35 8PQ
t (01926) 842068
e lmh@austonsdown.com
w austonsdown.com

Avonlea ★★★★ *Guest House*
47 Shipston Road, Stratford-upon-
Avon
CV37 7LN
t (01789) 205940
e enquiries@avonlea-stratford.co.uk
w avonlea-stratford.co.uk

Avonpark House ★★★★
Guest House
123 Shipston Road, Stratford-upon-
Avon
CV37 7LW
t (01789) 417722
e avonparkhouse@sky.com
w avonparkhouse.com

Bradbourne House ★★★★
Guest House
44 Shipston Road, Stratford-upon-
Avon
CV37 7LP
t (01789) 204178
e ian@bradbournehouse.com
w bradbourne-house.co.uk

Broadlands Guest House ★★★★
Guest House SILVER AWARD
23 Evesham Place, Stratford-upon-
Avon
CV37 6HT
t (01789) 299181
e enquiries@broadlandsguest
house.co.uk
w broadlandsguesthouse.co.uk

**Brookleys Bed & Breakfast
★★★★** *Bed & Breakfast*
Honeybourne Road, Bidford-on-
Avon, Stratford-upon-Avon
B50 4PD
t (01789) 772785
e brookleyschris@aol.com
w brookleys.co.uk

Brook Lodge Guest House ★★★★
Guest House SILVER AWARD
192 Alcester Road, Stratford-upon-
Avon
CV37 9DR
t (01789) 295988
e brooklodgeguesthouse@btint
ernet.com
w brook-lodge.co.uk

Caterham House ★★★★
Guest House
58-59 Rother Street, Stratford-upon-
Avon
CV37 6LT
t (01789) 267309
e caterhamsoa@btconnect.com
w caterhamhouse.co.uk

Church Farm ★★★ *Farmhouse*
Dorsington, Stratford-upon-Avon
CV37 8AX
t (01789) 720471
e chfarmdorsington@aol.com
w churchfarmstratford.co.uk

Courtland ★★★★ *Guest House*
SILVER AWARD
12 Guild Street, Stratford-upon-
Avon
CV37 6RE
t (01789) 292401
e info@courtlandhotel.com
w courtlandhotel.co.uk

Craig Cleeve House ★★★★
Guest House
67-69 Shipston Road, Stratford-
upon-Avon
CV37 7LW
t (01789) 296573
e craigcleeve@aol.com
w craigcleeve.com

Cymbeline House ★★★
Guest House
24 Evesham Place, Stratford-upon-
Avon
CV37 6HT
t (01789) 292958
e linda@cymbelineguesthouse.co.
uk
w cymbelinehouse.co.uk

The Emsley Guest House ★★★★
Guest House
4 Arden Street, Stratford-upon-Avon
CV37 6PA
t (01789) 299557
e val@theemsley.co.uk
w theemsley.co.uk

Faviere Guest House ★★★★
Guest House
127 Shipston Road, Stratford-upon-
Avon
CV37 7LW
t (01789) 293764
e reservations@faviere.com
w faviere.com

Folly Farm Cottage ★★★★
Bed & Breakfast GOLD AWARD
Back Street, Ilmington, Stratford-
upon-Avon
CV36 4LJ
t (01608) 682425
e bruceandpam@follyfarm.co.uk
w follyfarm.co.uk

Green Gables ★★★
Bed & Breakfast
47 Banbury Road, Stratford-upon-
Avon
CV37 7HW
t (01789) 205557
e jke985@aol.com
w stratford-upon-avon.co.uk/green
gables.htm

Green Haven ★★★★ *Guest House*
217 Evesham Road, Stratford-upon-
Avon
CV37 9AS
t (01789) 297874
e info@green-haven.co.uk
w green-haven.co.uk

Halford Bridge Inn ★★★★ *Inn*
Fosseway, Halford, Stratford-upon-
Avon
CV36 5BN
t (01789) 748217
e su@thehalfordbridge.co.uk
w thehalfordbridge.co.uk

485

Heart of England | Warwickshire

Hampton Lodge Guest House ★★★ *Guest Accommodation*
38 Shipston Road, Stratford-upon-Avon
CV37 7LP
t (01789) 299374
e hamptonlodge.info@btopenworld.com
w hamptonlodge.co.uk

Heron Lodge ★★★★ *Guest Accommodation*
260 Alcester Road, Stratford-upon-Avon
CV37 9JQ
t (01789) 299169
e info@heronlodge.com
w heronlodge.com

The Houndshill ★★★ *Inn*
Banbury Road, Stratford-upon-Avon
CV37 7NS
t (01789) 740167

The Hunters Moon Guest House ★★★ *Guest House*
150 Alcester Road, Stratford-upon-Avon
CV37 9DR
t (01789) 292888
e thehuntersmoon@ntlworld.com
w huntersmoonguesthouse.com

Ingon Bank Farm ★★★
Bed & Breakfast
Warwick Road, Stratford-upon-Avon
CV37 0NY
t (01789) 292642
e ingonbankfarmbandb@tiscali.co.uk
w ingonbankfarmbandb.co.uk

Larkrise Cottage ★★★★
Bed & Breakfast
Upper Billesley, Stratford-upon-Avon
CV37 9RA
t (01789) 268618
e alanbailey17@googlemail.com
w larkrisecottage.co.uk

Linhill Guest House ★★★ *Guest House*
35 Evesham Place, Stratford-upon-Avon
CV37 6HT
t (01789) 292879
e linhill@bigwig.net
w linhillguesthouse.co.uk

Melita ★★★★
Guest Accommodation
37 Shipston Road, Stratford-upon-Avon
CV37 7LN
t (01789) 292432
e info@melitaguesthouse.co.uk
w melitaguesthouse.co.uk

Midway Guest House ★★★ *Guest House*
182 Evesham Road, Stratford-upon-Avon
CV37 9BS
t (01789) 204154
e midwayguesthouse@btinternet.com
w stratford-upon-avon.co.uk/midway.htm

Mil-Mar ★★★★ *Guest House*
96 Alcester Road, Stratford-upon-Avon
CV37 9DP
t (01789) 267095
e milmar@btinternet.com
w mil-mar.co.uk

Minola Guest House ★★★ *Guest House*
25 Evesham Place, Stratford-upon-Avon
CV37 6HT
t (01789) 293573

Penryn Guest House ★★★★
Guest House **SILVER AWARD**
126 Alcester Road, Stratford-upon-Avon
CV37 9DP
t (01789) 293718
e penrynhouse@btinternet.com
w penrynguesthouse.co.uk

The Poplars ★★★★ *Farmhouse*
Mansell Farm, Newbold-on-Stour, Stratford-upon-Avon
CV37 8BZ
t (01789) 450540
e judith@poplars-farmhouse.co.uk
w poplars-farmhouse.co.uk

Quilt & Croissants ★★★ *Guest House*
33 Evesham Place, Stratford-upon-Avon
CV37 6HT
t (01789) 267629
e rooms@quilt-croissants.demon.co.uk
w quiltcroissants.co.uk

Salamander Guest House ★★★ *Guest House*
40 Grove Road, Stratford-upon-Avon
CV37 6PB
t (01789) 205728
e p.delin@btinternet.com
w salamanderguesthouse.co.uk

Sunnydale Guest House ★★★★ *Guest House*
64 Shipston Road, Stratford-upon-Avon
CV37 7LP
t (01789) 295166
e kimhelena@ymail.com
w sunny-dale.co.uk

Victoria Spa Lodge ★★★★
Guest House **SILVER AWARD**
Bishopton Lane, Bishopton, Stratford-upon-Avon
CV37 9QY
t (01789) 267985
e ptozer@victoriaspalodge.demon.co.uk
w victoriaspa.co.uk

Virginia Lodge ★★★★ *Guest House*
12 Evesham Place, Stratford-upon-Avon
CV37 6HT
t (01789) 292157
e enquiries@virginialodge.co.uk
w virginialodge.co.uk

White-Sails ★★★★★ *Guest House*
GOLD AWARD
85 Evesham Place, Stratford-upon-Avon
CV37 9BE
t (01789) 264326
e jan@white-sails.co.uk
w white-sails.co.uk

Woodstock Guest House ★★★★ *Guest House*
30 Grove Road, Stratford-upon-Avon
CV37 6PB
t (01789) 299881
e jackie@woodstock-house.co.uk
w woodstock-house.co.uk

STRETTON-ON-DUNSMORE

Home Farm ★★★★
Bed & Breakfast **SILVER AWARD**
152 London Road, Stretton-on-Dunsmore, Rugby
CV23 9HZ
t (024) 7654 1211
e info@homefarma45.co.uk
w homefarma45.co.uk

STRETTON-ON-FOSSE

Jasmine Cottage ★★★
Bed & Breakfast
Stretton-on-Fosse, Moreton-in-Marsh
GL56 9SA
t (01608) 661972
e ann@jasminecottage.wanadoo.co.uk
w jasminecottagebandb.co.uk

STUDLEY

Sambourne Hall Farm ★★★★
Farmhouse
Wike Lane, Sambourne, Studley
B96 6NZ
t (01527) 852151

TANWORTH-IN-ARDEN

Grange Farm ★★★★ *Farmhouse*
GOLD AWARD
Forde Hall Lane, Tanworth-in-Arden, Solihull
B94 5AX
t (01564) 742911
e enquiries@grange-farm.com
w grange-farm.com

UPTON

Uplands House ★★★★★
Bed & Breakfast **GOLD AWARD**
Upton, Banbury, Stratford-upon-Avon
OX15 6HJ
t (01295) 678663
e poppy@cotswolds-uplands.co.uk
w cotswolds-uplands.co.uk

WARMINGTON

Springfield House ★★★★
Bed & Breakfast
School Lane, Warmington, Banbury
OX17 1DD
t (01295) 690286
e jenny.handscombe@virgin.net
w stayatspringfield.co.uk

WARWICK

76 Westham ★★★ *Guest House*
76 Emscote Road, Warwick
CV34 5QG
t (01926) 491756
e westham.house@ntlworld.com
w westhambedandbreakfast.co.uk

Agincourt Lodge ★★★★
Guest House **SILVER AWARD**
36 Coten End, Warwick
CV34 4NP
t (01926) 499399
e enquiries@agincourtlodge.co.uk
w agincourtlodge.co.uk

Ashburton Guest House ★★★ *Guest House*
74 Emscote Road, Warwick, Warwickshire
CV34 5QG
t (01926) 499133
e ashburton@uwclub.net
w smoothhound.co.uk/hotels/ashburton.html

Avon Guest House ★★★★ *Guest House*
7 Emscote Road, Warwick
CV34 4PH
t (01926) 491367
e info@avonguesthouse.co.uk
w avonguesthouse.co.uk

Cambridge Villa ★★★ *Guest House*
20A-B Emscote Road, Warwick
CV34 4PP
t (01926) 491169
e cambridgevilla_warwick@yahoo.co.uk

Chesterfields Guest House ★★★ *Guest House*
84 Emscote Road, Warwick
CV34 5QT
t (01926) 774864
e john@chesterfields-guest-house.co.uk
w smoothhound.co.uk

Jersey Villa Guest House ★★★ *Guest House*
69 Emscote Road, Warwick
CV34 5QR
t (01926) 730336
e info@jerseyvillaguesthouse.co.uk
w jerseyvillaguesthouse.co.uk

Longbridge Farm ★★★★
Bed & Breakfast
Longbridge, Warwick
CV34 6RB
t (01926) 401857
e paul.preston@longbridge.demon.co.uk

The Old Fourpenny Shop Hotel ★★★★ *Guest Accommodation*
27-29 Crompton Street, Warwick
CV34 6HJ
t (01926) 491360
e info@4pennyhotel.com
w fourpennyshophotel.co.uk

Park Cottage ★★★★
Guest Accommodation
GOLD AWARD
113 West Street, Warwick
CV34 6AH
t (01926) 410319
e janet@parkcottagewarwick.co.uk
w parkcottagewarwick.co.uk

Peacock Lodge ★★★
Bed & Breakfast
97 West Street, Warwick
CV34 6AH
t (01926) 419480

The Seven Stars Guest Accommodation ★★★★
Bed & Breakfast **SILVER AWARD**
Friars Street, Warwick
CV34 6HD
t (01926) 492658
e thesevenstars@btinternet.com

Warwick Lodge ★★ *Guest House*
82 Emscote Road, Warwick
CV34 5QJ
t (01926) 492927

Westham House B&B ★★★★
Bed & Breakfast **SILVER AWARD**
Westham Lane, Barford, Warwick
CV35 8DP
t (01926) 624148
e westhamhouse@gmail.com
w westhamhouse.co.uk

WELFORD-ON-AVON

Bridgend Guest House ★★★★
Bed & Breakfast
Binton Road, Welford-on-Avon, Stratford-upon-Avon
CV37 8PW
t (01789) 750900
e bridgendhouse@aol.com
w stratford-upon-avon.co.uk/bridgend.htm

WELLESBOURNE

Apothecary's Bed & Breakfast ★★★★ *Bed & Breakfast*
The Old Dispensary, Stratford-upon-Avon
CV35 9RN
t (01789) 470060
e bandbapothecary@aol.com
w apothecarysbandb.co.uk

Meadow Cottage ★★★
Bed & Breakfast
36 Church Walk, Wellesbourne, Warwick
CV35 9QT
t (01789) 840220
e thomas.harland@virgin.net
w meadowcottagebandb.co.uk

WESTON-UNDER-WETHERLEY

Wethele Manor Farm ★★★★★
Guest Accommodation
Weston-under-Wetherley, Leamington Spa
CV33 9BZ
t (01926) 831772
e simonmoreton@wethelemanor.com
w wethelemanor.com

WISHAW

Ash House ★★★★ *Bed & Breakfast*
The Gravel, Wishaw, Sutton Coldfield
B76 9QB
t (01675) 475782
e kate@rectory80.freeserve.co.uk

Heart of England | Warwickshire/West Midlands/Worcestershire

WOLSTON

rds Hill Farm, Farmhouse B&B
★★★ *Farmhouse*
rds Hill Farm, Coalpit Lane,
8 3GB
(024) 7654 4430
jane@lordshillfarm.co.uk
lordshillfarm.co.uk

West Midlands
BALSALL COMMON

mp Farm ★★★ *Bed & Breakfast*
ob Lane, Balsall Common,
ventry
7 7GX
(01676) 533804

&G B&B ★★★★ *Bed & Breakfast*
Needlers End Lane, Balsall
mmon, Coventry
7 7AB
(01676) 532847
gillymatthew68@hotmail.com
gillyandgrant.co.uk

illow House ★★★★
d & Breakfast
Needlers End Lane, Balsall
mmon, Coventry
7 7AB
(01676) 533901
christine@glowbox.demon.co.uk
glowbox.demon.co.uk/willo
whouse.htm

BIRMINGHAM

e Conference Park ★★★★
est Accommodation
iversity of Birmingham, 48
gbaston Park Road, Birmingham
5 2RA
(0121) 415 8400
conferenceoffice@bham.ac.uk
conferences.bham.ac.uk

COVENTRY

cacia Guest House ★★★★
est House
Park Road, Coventry
1 2LE
(024) 7663 3622
acaciaguesthouse@hotmail.com
acaciaguesthousecoventry.co.uk

shdowns Guest House ★★★
est House
Regent Street, Coventry
1 3EP
(024) 7622 9280

shleigh Guest House ★★★
est House
Park Road, Coventry
1 2LE
(024) 7622 3804

ede Guest House ★★★
d & Breakfast
0 Radford Road, Radford,
ventry
6 3BU
(024) 7659 7837
bedehouse@aol.com
bedeguesthouse.co.uk

ighcroft Guest House ★★★
est House
Barras Lane, Coundon, Coventry
1 4AQ
(024) 7622 8157
info@highcroftguesthouse.com
highcroftguesthouse.com

erlyn Guest House ★★★
est House
5 Holyhead Road, Coundon,
ventry
1 3AD
(024) 7622 2800
info@merlynguesthouse.co.uk
merlynguesthouse.co.uk

Mount Guest House ★★★
Guest House
9 Coundon Road, Coventry
CV1 4AR
t (024) 7622 5998
e enquiries@guesthousecoventry.com
w guesthousecoventry.com

Spire View Guest House ★★★
Guest House
36 Park Road, Coventry
CV1 2LD
t (024) 7625 1602
e bookings@spireviewguesthouse.co.uk
w spireviewguesthouse.co.uk

HAMPTON-IN-ARDEN

Chelsea Lodge ★★★★
Bed & Breakfast SILVER AWARD
Chelsea Lodge, 48 Meriden Road,
Hampton-in-Arden
B92 0BT
t (01675) 442408
e chelsealodgebnb@aol.com

HOCKLEY HEATH

Eden End Bed & Breakfast ★★★★
Guest House
Eden End, Stratford Road, Hockley
Heath, Solihull
B94 6NN
t (01564) 783372
e bedandbreakfast@edenend.com
w edenend.com

Illshaw Heath Farm ★★★★
Farmhouse
Kineton Lane, Hockley Health
B94 6RX
t (01564) 782214
e janetandtony@amserve.com

KNOWLE

Ivy House Guest House ★★★
Guest House
Warwick Road, Heronfield, Knowle,
Solihull
B93 0EB
t (01564) 770247
e john@ivy-guest-house.freeserve.co.uk
w ivyhouseguesthouse.co.uk

MERIDEN

Barnacle Farm ★★★★ *Farmhouse*
Back Lane, Meriden, Coventry
CV7 7LD
t (024) 7646 8875

Bonninglas Guest House ★★★
Guest House
3 Berkswell Road, Meriden, Solihull,
Nr Coventry
CV7 7LB
t (01676) 523193
e Bookings@Bonninglas.co.uk
w bonninglas.co.uk

SHIRLEY

Baltimore House ★★
Bed & Breakfast
12 Brampton Crescent, Shirley,
Solihull
B90 3SY
t (0121) 744 9100
e egeeborall@aol.com
w baltimorehouse.co.uk

SOLIHULL

Acorn Guest House ★★★
Guest House SILVER AWARD
29 Links Drive, Solihull
B91 2DJ
t (0121) 705 5241
e acorn.wood@btinternet.com

Blythe Orchard ★★★★
Bed & Breakfast
Blythe Way, Solihull
B91 3EY
t 07522 480834
e bookings@blytheorchard.co.uk
w blytheorchard.co.uk

No 6 Gillott Close ★★★★
Bed & Breakfast
Gillott Close, Solihull
B91 2QY
t (0121) 709 2279
e tcsolihull@blueyonder.co.uk

Ravenhurst Guest House ★★★
Guest House
56 Lode Lane, Solihull
B91 2AW
t (0121) 705 5754
e ravenhurstaccom@aol.com

STOURBRIDGE

The Willows B&B ★★★
Bed & Breakfast
4 Brook Road, Stourbridge
DY8 1NH
t (01384) 396964
e trickard@blueyonder.co.uk

WALSALL

Lyndon House Hotel ★★★ *Inn*
Upper Rushall Street, Walsall
WS1 2HA
t (01922) 612511
e bookings@lyndonhousehotel.co.uk
w lyndonhousehotel.com

YARDLEY

Central Guest House ★★★
Guest House
1637 Coventry Road, Yardley,
Birmingham
B26 1DD
t (0121) 706 7757
e stay@centralguesthouse.com
w centralguesthouse.com

Worcestershire
ALVECHURCH

Woodlands Bed & Breakfast
★★★★ *Bed & Breakfast*
SILVER AWARD
Coopers Hill, Alvechurch, Nr
Bromsgrove
B48 7BX
t (0121) 445 6774
e john.impey@gmail.com
w woodlandsbedandbreakfast.com

ARLEY

Tudor Barn ★★★★ *Bed & Breakfast*
GOLD AWARD
Nib Green, Arley, Bewdley
DY12 3LY
t (01299) 400129
e tudor.barn@btinternet.com
w tudor-barn.co.uk

ASTLEY

Woodhampton House ★★★★
Bed & Breakfast
Weather Lane, Astley, Nr Stourport-on-Severn
DY13 0SF
t (01299) 826510
e pete-a@sally-a.freeserve.co.uk
w woodhamptonhouse.co.uk

BADSEY

Orchard House ★★
Guest Accommodation
99 Bretforton Road, Badsey,
Evesham
WR11 7XQ
t (01386) 831245

BEWDLEY

Kateshill House ★★★★★
Bed & Breakfast GOLD AWARD
Red Hill, Bewdley
DY12 2DR
t (01299) 401563
e info@kateshillhouse.com
w kateshillhouse.co.uk

The Old Town Hall ★★★★
Bed & Breakfast
Wyre Hill, Bewdley
DY12 2UE
t (01299) 409465
e theoldtownhall@btinternet.com
w bewdley-oldtownhall-bandb.co.uk

Woodcolliers Arms ★★★ *Inn*
76 Welch Gate, Bewdley
DY12 2AU
t (01299) 400589
e roger@woodcolliers.co.uk
w woodcolliers.co.uk

BIRTSMORTON

The Birches ★★★★
Bed & Breakfast
Birts Street, Birtsmorton, Malvern
WR13 6AW
t (01684) 833821
e katherine-thebirches@hotmail.co.uk

Brook House ★★★★
Bed & Breakfast
Birtsmorton, Malvern
WR13 6AF
t (01531) 650664
e marydowding@onetel.com
w brookhousemalvern.co.uk

BREDONS NORTON

Home Farm *Guest Accommodation*
Bredons Norton, Tewkesbury
GL20 7HA
t (01684) 772322

BRICKLEHAMPTON

Oaklands Farmhouse ★★★★★
Bed & Breakfast GOLD AWARD
Bricklehampton, Pershore
WR10 3JT
t (01386) 861716
e barbara-stewart@lineone.net
w oaklandsfarmhouse.co.uk

BROAD HEATH

Tally Ho Inn ★★★ *Inn*
Bell Lane, Broadheath, Nr Tenbury
Wells
WR15 8QX
t (01886) 853241
e mike.fazakarley@btconnect.com
w tallyhorestaurant.co.uk

BROADWAY

The Bell at Willersey ★★★★ *Inn*
Main Street, Willersey, Broadway
WR12 7LJ
t (01386) 858405
e enq@bellatwillersey.fsnet.co.uk
w the-bell-willersey.com

Brook House ★★★★
Guest Accommodation
Station Road, Broadway
WR12 7DE
t (01386) 852313
e brookhousebb@googlemail.com
w brookhousebandb.co.uk

Farncombe Estate Centre ★★★★
Guest Accommodation
Farncombe Estate, Broadway
WR12 7LJ
t (01386) 854100
e enquiries@farncombeestate.co.uk
w farncombeestate.co.uk

Lowerfield Farm ★★★★
Farmhouse SILVER AWARD
Willersey, Broadway
WR11 7HF
t (01386) 858273
e info@lowerfieldfarm.com
w lowerfieldfarm.com

The Old Stationhouse ★★★★
Guest House SILVER AWARD
Station Drive, Broadway
WR12 7DF
t (01386) 852659
e oldstationhouse@eastbankbroadway.fsnet.co.uk
w broadway-cotswolds.co.uk/oldstationhouse.html

Heart of England | Worcestershire

The Olive Branch Guest House ★★★★ *Guest House*
SILVER AWARD
78 High Street, Broadway
WR12 7AJ
t (01386) 853440
e davidpam@theolivebranch-broadway.com
w theolivebranch-broadway.com

Sheepscombe House ★★★★
Bed & Breakfast GOLD AWARD
Snowshill, Broadway
WR12 7JU
t (01386) 853769
e reservations@snowshill-broadway.co.uk
w broadway-cotswolds.co.uk/sheepscombe.html

Small Talk Lodge ★★★★
Guest House
32 High Street, Broadway
WR12 7DP
t (01386) 858953
e bookings@smalltalklodge.co.uk
w smalltalklodge.co.uk

Southwold House ★★★★
Guest House SILVER AWARD
Station Road, Broadway
WR12 7DE
t (01386) 853681
e alyson@cotswolds-broadway-southwold.co.uk
w cotswolds-broadway-southwold.co.uk

Windrush House ★★★★
Guest House GOLD AWARD
Station Road, Broadway
WR12 7DE
t (01386) 853577
e evan@broadway-windrush.co.uk
w broadway-windrush.co.uk

BROMSGROVE

Alcott Farm ★★★ *Farmhouse*
Icknield Street, Weatheroak, Bromsgrove
B48 7EH
t (01564) 824051
e alcottfarm@btinternet.com
w alcottfarm.co.uk

Avoncroft Guest House ★★★★
Guest House
77 Redditch Road, Bromsgrove
B60 4JP
t (01527) 832819
e reservations@avoncroftguesthouse.co.uk
w avoncroftguesthouse.co.uk

The Durrance ★★★★ *Farmhouse*
SILVER AWARD
Berry Lane, Upton Warren, Bromsgrove
B61 9EL
t (01562) 777533
e helenhirons@thedurrance.co.uk
w thedurrance.co.uk

Manor Hill House Guest House ★★★★ *Bed & Breakfast*
Swan Lane, Upton Warren, Bromsgrove
B61 9HE
t (01527) 861200
e info@manorhillhouse.co.uk
w manorhillhouse.co.uk

Wellington Lodge Luxury Bed & Breakfast ★★★★
Guest Accommodation
49 Wellington Road, Bromsgrove
B60 2AX
t (01527) 570433
e info@wellington-lodge.co.uk
w wellington-lodge.co.uk

CASTLEMORTON

Myrtleberry House ★★★
Guest Accommodation
New Road, Castlemorton, Malvern
WR13 6BY
t (01684) 833648
e malvern@kumoncentre.co.uk

CHADDESLEY CORBETT

The Brook House ★★★★
Bed & Breakfast SILVER AWARD
Hemming Way, Chaddesley Corbett, Kidderminster
DY10 4SF
t (01562) 777453
e enquiries@thebrookhouse.co.uk
w thebrookhouse.co.uk

CLEVELODE

Severnside Bed & Breakfast ★★★★ *Bed & Breakfast*
SILVER AWARD
Clevelode, Malvern
WR13 6PD
t (01684) 311894
e info@severn-side.co.uk
w severn-side.co.uk

CLOWS TOP

Colliers Hill Guest House & Conference Centre ★★★★
Bed & Breakfast
Colliers Hill, Bayton
DY14 9NZ
t (01299) 832247
e info@collliershill.co.uk
w colliershill.co.uk

CRADLEY

Cowleigh Park Farm ★★★★
Bed & Breakfast
Cowleigh Road, Malvern
WR13 5HJ
t (01684) 566750
e info@cowleighparkfarm.co.uk
w cowleighparkfarm.co.uk

CROWLE

Green Farm ★★★★ *Farmhouse*
Crowle Green, Worcester
WR7 4AB
t (01905) 381807
e thegreenfarm@btinternet.com
w thegreenfarm.co.uk

DROITWICH SPA

Foxbrook ★★★
Guest Accommodation
238A Worcester Road, Droitwich Spa
WR9 8AY
t (01905) 772414

The Hayloft ★★★★
Bed & Breakfast
Upper Hall, Hampton Lovett, Droitwich Spa
WR9 0PA
t (01905) 772819
e maureen@hayloftbandb.com
w hayloftbandb.com

ECKINGTON

Harrowfields Bed & Breakfast ★★★★ *Bed & Breakfast*
SILVER AWARD
Harrowfields, Cotheridge Lane, Eckington
WR10 3BA
t (01386) 751053
e susie@harrowfields.co.uk
w harrowfields.co.uk

Lower End House ★★★★★
Guest Accommodation
GOLD AWARD
Manor Farm, Manor Road, Pershore
WR10 3BH
t (01386) 751600
e info@lowerendhouse.co.uk
w lowerendhouse.co.uk

Myrtle Cottage ★★★★
Bed & Breakfast SILVER AWARD
Jarvis Street, Eckington, Pershore
WR10 3AS
t (01386) 750893
e veronica@myrtle-cottage.com
w myrtle-cottage.com

EVESHAM

Longacres Bed & Breakfast ★★★
Bed & Breakfast
Longdon Hill, Wickhamford, Evesham
WR11 7RP
t (01386) 442575
e eveshambandb@tiscali.co.uk

FERNHILL HEATH

Dilmore House ★★★★
Bed & Breakfast SILVER AWARD
254 Droitwich Road, Fernhill Heath, Worcester
WR3 7UL
t (01905) 451543
e enquiries@dilmorehouse.co.uk
w dilmorehouse.co.uk

Heathside ★★★★ *Guest House*
SILVER AWARD
172 Droitwich Road, Fernhill Heath, Worcester
WR3 7UA
t (01905) 458245
e info@heathsideguesthouse.co.uk
w heathsideguesthouse.co.uk

GREAT WITLEY

Camp Farm Bed & Breakfast ★★★★ *Bed & Breakfast*
Camp Lane, Great Witley, Worcester
WR6 6JQ
t (01299) 896126
e info@worcestershirebandb.co.uk
w worcestershirebandb.co.uk

HADLEY HEATH

The Old Farmhouse ★★★★★
Guest Accommodation
SILVER AWARD
Hadley Heath, Ombersley, Droitwich Spa
WR9 0AR
t (01905) 620837
e judylambe@theoldfarmhouse.com
w theoldfarmhouse.uk.com

HANLEY CASTLE

The Chestnuts ★★★★
Bed & Breakfast SILVER AWARD
Gilberts End, Hanley Castle, Upton-upon-Severn
WR8 0AS
t (01684) 311219
e heather@chestnutshp.co.uk
w chestnutshp.co.uk

Gilberts End Farm B&B ★★★★
Bed & Breakfast
Gilberts End, Hanley Castle, Upton-upon-Severn
WR8 0AR
t (01684) 311392
e chrissy.bacon@onetel.net
w gilbertsendfarm.co.uk

HANLEY SWAN

Blackmore Gardens ★★★★
Guest Accommodation
Hanley Swan, Worcester
WR8 0EF
t (01684) 311931
e stay@blackmore-gardens.co.uk
w blackmore-gardens.co.uk

Kingfisher Bed & Breakfast ★★★★ *Bed & Breakfast*
Kingfisher Barn, Merebrook Farm, Malvern
WR8 0DX
t (01684) 311922
e info@kingfisher-barn.co.uk
w kingfisher-barn.co.uk

KIDDERMINSTER

Bewdley Hill Guest House ★★★★
Guest House
8 Bewdley Hill, Kidderminster
DY11 6BS
t (01562) 60473
e info@bewdleyhillhouse.co.uk
w bewdleyhillhouse.co.uk

Collingdale ★★★ *Guest House*
197 Comberton Road, Kidderminster
DY10 1UE
t (01562) 515460
e collingdalehotel@hotmail.com

KNIGHTWICK

The Talbot ★★★★ *Inn*
Bromyard Road, Knightwick, Worcester
WR6 5PH
t (01886) 821235
e info@the-talbot.co.uk
w the-talbot.co.uk

LEIGH SINTON

Chirkenhill Farm ★★★★
Farmhouse
Sherridge Road, Leigh Sinton, Malvern
WR13 5DE
t (01886) 832205
e chirkenhillbandb@tiscali.co.uk
w chirkenhill.co.uk

MALVERN

The Brambles ★★★★
Guest Accommodation
SILVER AWARD
173 Wells Road, Malvern Wells
WR14 4HE
t (01684) 572994
e bren.lawler@talk21.com
w thebramblesmalvern.com

Cannara Guest House ★★★★
Guest House SILVER AWARD
147 Barnards Green Road, Malvern
WR14 3LT
t (01684) 564418
e info@cannara.co.uk
w cannara.co.uk

Clevelands ★★★ *Bed & Breakfast*
SILVER AWARD
41 Alexandra Road, Malvern
WR14 1HE
t (01684) 572164
e jonmargstocks@aol.com
w malvernbandbconsortium.co.uk

Como House ★★★
Guest Accommodation
Como Road, Malvern
WR14 2TH
t (01684) 561486
e kevin@comohouse.co.uk
w comohouse.co.uk

Copper Beech House ★★★★
Guest House
32 Avenue Road, Malvern
WR14 3BJ
t (01684) 565013
e enquiries@copperbeechhouse.co.uk
w copperbeechhouse.co.uk

Edgeworth ★★★ *Bed & Breakfast*
4 Carlton Road, Malvern
WR14 1HH
t (01684) 572565
e garlandsidney@yahoo.co.uk

The Elms ★★★ *Bed & Breakfast*
52 Guarlford Road, Malvern
WR14 3QP
t (01684) 573466
e jili_holland@yahoo.co.uk

Grassendale House ★★★
Guest Accommodation
3 Victoria Road, Malvern
WR14 2TD
t (01684) 893348
e hilarymurray@hotmail.co.uk

Guarlford Grange ★★★
Bed & Breakfast SILVER AWARD
11 Guarlford Road, Malvern
WR14 3QW
t (01684) 575996
e guarlfordgrange@msn.com
w malvern-hills.co.uk/gg

Heart of England | Worcestershire

rmony House Malvern ★★★
d & Breakfast
4 West Malvern Road, West
alvern
R14 4AZ
t (01684) 891650
e catherineinharmony@hotmail.com
w harmonyhousemalvern.com

delow House ★★★★
d & Breakfast **SILVER AWARD**
ton Green, Acton Beauchamp,
rcester
R6 5AH
t (01886) 884547
e visit@hidelow.co.uk
w hidelow.co.uk

ontrose House ★★★
est Accommodation
Graham Road, Malvern
R14 4HD
t (01684) 572335
e info@themontrosehotel.co.uk
w themontrosehotel.co.uk

e Old Coach House ★★★★
d & Breakfast
8 Wells Road, Malvern Wells,
alvern
R14 4HD
t (01684) 564382
w coachhousemalvern.co.uk

e Old Croque ★★★★
d & Breakfast **SILVER AWARD**
1 Wells Road, Malvern
R14 4HF
t (01684) 564522
e griffiths@theoldcroque.co.uk
w theoldcroque.co.uk

chid House ★★★★
d & Breakfast **SILVER AWARD**
St Wulstans Drive, Upper
elland, Malvern
R14 4JA
t (01684) 568717
e sally@oml.demon.co.uk
w orchidmalvern.co.uk

plar Cottage Bed & Breakfast
★★★ *Guest Accommodation*
d Worcester Road, Newland,
alvern
R13 5AY
t (01886) 832397
e info@poplarcottage.co.uk
w poplarcottage.co.uk

ddle Lane ★★★ *Bed & Breakfast*
LVER AWARD
Barnards Green Road, Malvern,
rcestershire
R14 3LW
t 01684 572 720
e puddlelanemalvern@hotmail.co.uk
w puddlelanemalvern.co.uk

sendale Bed & Breakfast
★★★ *Bed & Breakfast*
sendale The View, 66 Worcester
ad, Malvern
R14 1NU
t (01684) 566159

ornbury House ★★★★
est House
Avenue Road, Great Malvern
R14 3AR
t (01684) 572278
e thornburyhousehotel@compuserve.com
w thornburyhouse-hotel.co.uk

Treherne House & The Malvern Retreat ★★★★ *Bed & Breakfast*
SILVER AWARD
54 Guarlford Road, Malvern
WR14 3QP
t (01684) 572445
e relax@trehernehouse.co.uk
w trehernehouse.co.uk

PERSHORE

Anchor Inn & Restaurant ★★★
Inn
Cotheridge Lane, Eckington, Nr
Pershore, Worcestershire
WR10 3BA
t (01386) 750356
e anchoreck@aol.com
w anchoreckington.co.uk

Arbour House ★★★★
Bed & Breakfast **SILVER AWARD**
Main Road, Wyre Piddle, Pershore
WR10 2HU
t (01386) 555833
e liz@arbour-house.com
w arbour-house.com

Cropvale Farm Bed & Breakfast
★★★★ *Farmhouse* **GOLD AWARD**
Smokey Lane, Cropthorne, Pershore
WR10 3NF
t (01386) 861925
e cropvale@hotmail.com
w cropvalefarm.co.uk

PHEPSON

Phepson Farm ★★★★
Guest Accommodation
Phepson Farm, Himbleton,
Droitwich Spa
WR9 7JZ
t (01905) 391205
e info@phepsonfarm.co.uk
w phepsonfarm.co.uk

REDDITCH

The Steps ★★★★ *Bed & Breakfast*
6 High Street, Feckenham, Redditch
B96 6HS
t (01527) 892678
e jenny@thesteps.co.uk
w thesteps.co.uk

White Hart Inn ★★★
Guest Accommodation
157 Evesham Road, Headless Cross,
Redditch
B97 5EJ
t (01527) 545442
e enquiries@whitehartredditch.co.uk
w whitehartredditch.co.uk

SALWARPE

Middleton Grange ★★★★
Guest Accommodation
SILVER AWARD
Ladywood Road, Salwarpe,
Droitwich Spa
WR9 0AH
t (01905) 451678
e salli@middletongrange.com
w middletongrange.com

SEVERN STOKE

Roseland Bed & Breakfast ★★★★
Bed & Breakfast
Clifton, Severn Stoke, Worcester
WR8 9JF
t (01905) 371463
e guy@roselandworcs.demon.co.uk
w roselandworcs.demon.co.uk

STOULTON

Sunbrae Bed & Breakfast ★★★★
Bed & Breakfast **GOLD AWARD**
Wadborough Road, Stoulton,
Worcester
WR7 4RF
t (01905) 841129
e rita@sunbrae.co.uk
w sunbrae.co.uk

STOURBRIDGE

Tall Trees Cottage ★★★★
Bed & Breakfast
Thicknall Lane, Clent, Stourbridge,
West Midlands
DY9 0HN
t (01562) 883883
e talltreescottage@btconnect.com
w talltreescottage.co.uk

STOURPORT-ON-SEVERN

Baldwin House ★★★★
Guest House
8 Lichfield Street, Stourport-on-Severn
DY13 9EU
t (01299) 877221
e philpam@dialstart.net
w smoothhound.co.uk

Victoria Villa Bed & Breakfast
★★★★ *Guest House*
SILVER AWARD
4 Lion Hill, Stourport-on-Severn
DY13 9HD
t (01299) 824017
e bookings@victoriavilla.co.uk
w victoriavilla.co.uk

TEWKESBURY

Ivydene House Bed & Breakfast
★★★★★ *Bed & Breakfast*
SILVER AWARD
Ivydene House, Uckinghall,
Tewkesbury
GL20 6ES
t (01684) 592453
e rosemaryg@fsmail.net
w ivydenehouse.net

UPTON-UPON-SEVERN

Tiltridge Farm & Vineyard ★★★★
Farmhouse **SILVER AWARD**
Upper Hook Road, Upton-upon-Severn
WR8 0SA
t (01684) 592906
e sandy@tiltridge.com
w tiltridge.com

UPTON SNODSBURY

Bants ★★★★ *Inn*
Worcester Road, Upton Snodsbury
WR7 4NN
t (01905) 381282
e info@bants.co.uk
w bants.co.uk

UPTON WARREN

Overwood ★★★★ *Bed & Breakfast*
SILVER AWARD
Woodcote Lane, Bromsgrove
B61 9EE
t (01562) 777193
e info@overwood.net
w overwood.net

WORCESTER

De-Bury House ★★★★
Bed & Breakfast
3 The Bullring, St Johns, Worcester
WR2 5AA
t (01905) 425532
w de-bury.co.uk

Henwick House Bed & Breakfast
★★★ *Bed & Breakfast*
Jennett Tree Lane, Callow End,
Worcester, Worcestershire
WR2 4UB
t 01905 831736
e henwickhouse@hotmail.com
w henwickhouse.com

Hill Farm House ★★★★
Bed & Breakfast **SILVER AWARD**
Dormston Lane, Inkberrow, Nr
Worcester
WR7 4JS
t (01386) 793159
e james@hillfarmhouse.co.uk
w hillfarmhouse.co.uk

Holland House ★★★
Bed & Breakfast
210 London Road, Worcester
WR5 2JT
t (01905) 353939
e beds@holland-house.me.uk
w holland-house.me.uk

Laburnum Villa ★★★★
Bed & Breakfast
243 Ombersley Road, Worcester
WR3 7BY
t (01905) 755572
e laburnumvilla@tiscali.co.uk
w laburnumvilla.com

The Manor Coach House ★★★★
Guest Accommodation
Hindlip Lane, Hindlip, Worcester
WR3 8SJ
t (01905) 456457
e info@manorcoachhouse.co.uk
w manorcoachhouse.co.uk

Osborne House ★★★
Guest Accommodation
17 Chestnut Walk, Worcester
WR1 1PR
t (01905) 22296
e enquiries@osborne-house.co.uk
w osborne-house.co.uk

Perrymill Farm ★★★
Bed & Breakfast
Little Inkberrow, Worcester
WR7 4JQ
t (01386) 792177
e alexander@perrymill.com

Shrubbery Guest House ★★★
Guest House
38 Barbourne Road, Worcester
WR1 1HU
t (01905) 24871
e shrubberyguesthouse@hotmail.com

University of Worcester ★★ -
★★★★ *Campus*
Henwick Grove, Worcester
WR2 6AJ
t (01905) 542121
e conferencing@worc.ac.uk
w worcester.ac.uk

r key to symbols see page 6   489

Yorkshire

Rhubarb and real ale, vibrant cities and culture, golden sand and sea, stunning walks and waterfalls. This is Yorkshire. With an abundance of places to stay, from boutique hotels to eco lodges and even yurts, this is an exciting and diverse destination for all budgets.

South Yorkshire

Encompasses Sheffield, Rotherham, Doncaster and Barnsley, and has an abundance of heritage, gardens and open spaces, bustling nightlife and cultural events, sports and outdoor activities along with traditional rural villages and market towns. You'll be spoilt for choice with so many inspiring ideas and fresh new places to visit.

East Yorkshire

Offers a diverse visitor experience, combining spectacular countryside, coastline and city. Hull is a vibrant waterfront city which manages to combine a vibrant mix of culture, shopping and nightlife with a rich maritime heritage. Less than an hour away, discover the relaxing Yorkshire Wolds and family friendly seaside resorts.

Yorkshire Wolds

A range of low, rolling hills which rise from the River Humber at Hessle and culminate in the east with the dramatic cliffs of Flamborough Head and Bempton, north of Bridlington. The Yorkshire Wolds are an area of great beauty with much to see and do in picturesque villages and lively market towns. The gentle hills make it an ideal area for both walking and cycling. The 79-mile Wolds Way National Trail leads to ancient sites, unspoilt villages and beauty spots. Country parks and nature reserves provide wonderful opportunities for bird watching and photography.

East Coast

With extensive wildlife and smugglers coves, explore miles of sandy beaches surrounded by the sparkling North Sea. Discover family seaside resorts dotted along the coastline.

Yorkshire

Yorkshire

492	Where to Go	495	Where to Eat
494	Events	498	Where to Stay

retty Hornsea is a small seaside town with an award-winning promenade and ntriguing folk museum. Or for a larger resort Bridlington makes the perfect oliday destination as well as a fun filled day out. With its own unique character nd charm this is a destination that appeals to all ages.

North Yorkshire Moors and Coast

 region of stunning contrasts. The unique scenery and special nature of the rea has been recognised with the establishment of the North York Moors lational Park which extends from Scarborough, Whitby, Staithes and Saltburn n the coast, to the charming towns of Pickering, Helmsley and Thirsk inland, via tunning moorland and perfect walking country. The market town of Helmsley ffers a great choice of local produce with a number of independent stores and n award winning ice cream shop.

The Dales

re a favourite destination for walkers, cyclists, artists and writers. The National ark is crossed by several long-distance routes including the Pennine Way, the)ales Way, the Coast to Coast Path and the Pennine Bridleway. This stunning rea features the market and spa towns of Hawes, Skipton, Ilkley and Harrogate. ake a tour through the rural splendours of Swaledale, Wharfdale or Ribblesdale /here you will cross brooks and discover gushing waterfalls.

Yorkshire | Where to Go

Where to Go

Attractions with this sign participate in the **Visitor Attraction Quality Assurance Scheme** (see page 6) which recognises high standards in all aspects of the vistor experience.

ENTERTAINMENT & CULTURE

Clifton Park Museum
Rotherham, South Yorkshire S65 2AA
(01709) 336633
www.rotherham.gov.uk/graphics/learning/museums/edscliftonparkmuseum.htm
Local pottery and antiquities, natural and social history. Restored period kitchen. Major collection of Rockingham porcelain. Temporary exhibitions.

DIG
York, North Yorkshire YO1 8NN
(01904) 615505
www.digyork.co.uk
Grab a trowel and dig to see what you can find in DIG's specially designed excavation pits. Rediscover some of the finds that archaeologists have uncovered under the streets of York.

Dinostar - The Dinosaur Experience
Hull, East Riding of Yorkshire HU1 1TH
(01482) 320424
www.dinostar.co.uk
Dinostar is Hull's Dinostar Experience featuring a fascinating interactive exhibition of dinosaurs and fossils from around the world.

Eureka! The National Children's Museum
Halifax, West Yorkshire HX1 2NE
(01422) 330069
www.eureka.org.uk
A magical place where children play to learn and grown-ups learn to play. Eureka! is the leading children's museum in the UK and gives children aged 0-11 a fun-packed day out.

Ferens Art Gallery
Hull, East Riding of Yorkshire HU1 3RA
(01482) 613902
www.hullcc.gov.uk/museums
Opened in 1927, the award winning Ferens Art Gallery combines internationally renowned permanent collections with a thriving programme of temporary exhibitions.

Hands On History Museum
Hull, East Riding of Yorkshire HU1 1RR
(01482) 613902
www.hullcc.gov.uk/museums
Hull's oldest secular building c1583, used as a grammar school and merchants hall. Restored 1985-88. The story of Hull and its people. Victorian, ancient Egypt and Britain.

Museums Sheffield: Millennium Gallery
Sheffield, South Yorkshire S1 2PP
(0114) 278 2600
www.museums-sheffield.org.uk
One of modern Sheffield's landmark public spaces. Whether you're in town or just passing through, the Gallery always has something new to offer. Home to the city's Ruskin Collection.

Museums Sheffield: Weston Park
Sheffield, South Yorkshire S10 2TP
(0114) 278 2600
www.museums-sheffield.org.uk
The collections of beautiful, varied & unusual treasures are brought to life through fascinating histories; incredible facts; hands-on interactives - wind the children up and let them go! Discover the real story of Sheffield

National Coal Mining Museum for England
Wakefield, West Yorkshire WF4 4RH
(01924) 848806
An exciting and enjoyable insight into the working lives of miners through the ages.

National Media Museum
Bradford, West Yorkshire BD1 1NQ
0870 701 0200
www.nationalmediamuseum.org.uk
Seven floors devoted to film, photography, television, radio and the web, plus a giant screen IMAX.

National Railway Museum
York, North Yorkshire YO26 4XJ
0844 815 3139
www.nrm.org.uk
Largest Railway Museum in the world.

Streetlife Museum
Hull, East Riding of Yorkshire HU1 1PS
(01482) 613902
www.hullcc.gov.uk/museums
You can see over 200 years of transport with period scenes, sound and smells, to recreate a thrilling journey back in time.

Withernsea Lighthouse Museum
Withernsea, East Riding of Yorkshire HU19 2DY
(01964) 614834
Magnificent view of Withernsea from top of the 127ft-high lighthouse. Local history museum and the Kay Kendall Memorial Museum. HM Coastguard and RNLI collection.

Yorkshire | Where to Go

World of James Herriot
Thirsk, North Yorkshire YO7 1PL
(01845) 524234
www.worldofjamesherriot.org
Explore the home and surgery of James Herriot in 1950's themed rooms. Experience hands on activities and fun in the visible farm. Try your hand in the TV studios. Investigate the variety of veterinary equipment.

FAMILY FUN

Magna Science Adventure Centre
Rotherham, South Yorkshire S60 1DX
(01709) 720002
www.visitmagna.co.uk
Magna is the UK's 1st Science Adventure Centre set in the vast Templeborough steelworks in Rotherham. Fun is unavoidable here with giant interactives.

HERITAGE

Beverley Guildhall
Beverley, East Riding of Yorkshire HU17 9XX
(01482) 392783
www.eastriding.gov.uk
Beverley Guildhall is a Grade 1 listed building, originally late medieval, remodelled in 17th and 18th C. Impressive Georgian courtroom with ornate plasterwork ceiling. Original 17th C furniture. Also houses Beverley's Community Museum.

Brodsworth Hall and Gardens
Doncaster, South Yorkshire DN5 7XJ
(01302) 722598
www.english-heritage.org.uk
One of England's most complete surviving Victorian houses. Inside many of the original fixtures & fittings are still in place, although faded with time. Outside the 15 acres of woodland & gardens have been restored to their 1860's heyday.

Castle Howard
Malton, North Yorkshire YO60 7DA
(01653) 648444
www.castlehoward.co.uk
Magnificent 18th Century historic house and Stable Courtyard within 1,000 acres of breathtaking gardens. Located just 15 miles North East of York.

Fountains Abbey
Ripon, North Yorkshire HG4 3DY
(01765) 608888
www.fountainsabbey.org.uk
This magnificent world heritage site provides a fantastic day out.

Harewood House
Leeds, West Yorkshire LS17 9LG
(0113) 218 1010
www.harewood.org
Harewood House, Bird Garden, Grounds and Adventure Playground.

JORVIK Viking Centre
York, North Yorkshire YO1 9WT
(01904) 615505
www.jorvik-viking-centre.co.uk
Travel back 1000 years on board your time machine through the backyards and houses to the bustling streets of Jorvik.

Temple Newsam House and Farm
Leeds, West Yorkshire LS15 0AD
(0113) 264 5535
Home Farm has 400 head of stock including some of the most endangered British breeds.

Whitby Abbey
Whitby, North Yorkshire YO22 4JT
(01947) 603568
www.english-heritage.org.uk/whitbyabbey
The ruins of Whitby Abbey have drawn successive generations – from Saints to Dracula - to this site of settlement, religious devotion and literary inspiration.

Yorkshire Sculpture Park
Wakefield, West Yorkshire WF4 4LG
(01924) 832631
www.ysp.co.uk/
A place that sets out to challenge, inspire, inform and delight. With 4 indoor galleries and 500 acres of 18th century parkland.

NATURE & WILDLIFE

RSPB Bempton Cliffs Reserve
Bridlington, East Riding of Yorkshire YO15 1JF
(01262) 851179
www.rspb.org.uk
One of England's top wildlife attractions. Over 200,000 nesting seabirds, including gannets and puffins, from April - September. Visitor Centre, shop, refreshments, toilets, nature trail and spectacular cliff top walks.

RSPB Old Moor Nature Reserve
Barnsley, South Yorkshire S73 0YF
(01226) 751593
www.rspb.org.uk
Get close to the wildlife on your doorstep. This friendly nature reserve with visitor centre, shop cafe and playground has plenty for the whole family to enjoy.

Sheffield Botanical Gardens
Sheffield, South Yorkshire S10 2LN
(0114) 267 1115
www.sbg.org.uk
Extensive gardens with over 5,500 species of plants, Grade II Listed garden pavillion. Fully restored and containing a temperate plant collection. The Curators House provides a welcome refreshment stop in this wonderful oasis.

The Deep
Hull, East Riding of Yorkshire HU1 4DP
(01482) 381000
www.thedeep.co.uk
The Deep is Hull's £53million Millennium Commission Lottery Project. Full with over 3500 fish and more than 40 sharks, it tells the story of the world's oceans using live animals and the latest hands on interactives.

The Forbidden Corner
Leyburn, North Yorkshire DL8 4TJ
(01969) 640638
www.theforbiddencorner.co.uk
A unique labyrinth of tunnels, chambers, follies and surprises in the heart of the Yorkshire Dales.

Tropical Butterfly House
Rotherham, South Yorkshire S25 4EQ
(01909) 569416
www.butterflyhouse.co.uk
Discover a wild family day out, catch a glimpse of a far-away world and make friends with creatures great and small.

Wentworth Castle Gardens
Barnsley, South Yorkshire S75 3ET
(01226) 776040
www.wentworthcastle.org
This magnificent 600 acre Parkland estate features over 26 listed monuments as well as a 60-acre Garden which cares for National Plant Collections of Rhododendrons, Camellias and Magnolias.

Yorkshire Wildlife Park
Doncaster, South Yorkshire DN3 3NH
(01302) 535057
www.yorkshirewildlifepark.co.uk
Brand new wildlife attraction just off the M18 (J3) near Doncaster, offering a fabulous fun day and animal experience. Walk through 'Lemar Woods' and meet these mischievous primates, or come face to face with the wallabies in Wallaby Walk.

Events 2011

Barnsley Original Music
Barnsley
www.bomfest.com
July

Beverley Early Music
Beverley
www.realyorkshire.co.uk
May

Bradfield Festival of Music
Bradfield
www.bradfieldfestivalofmusic.co.uk
June

Bradford International Film Festival
www.bradfordfilmfestival.org.uk
March

Bradford Mela
www.bradfordmela.org.uk
June

Burton Agnes Jazz & Blues Festival
Burton Agnes
www.burtonagnes.com/Display.aspx?iid=831
August

Cliffhanger
Sheffield
www.cliff-hanger.co.uk
July

Coastival
Scarborough
www.coastival.com/
18 - 20 February

Great Yorkshire Show
Harrogate
www.greatyorkshireshow.co.uk
12 - 14 July

Harrogate International
www.harrogate-festival.org.uk/
22 - 30 July

Huddersfield Contemporary Music
www.hcmf.co.uk
November

Hull Freedom Festival
www.hullcc.gov.uk
9 - 11 Spetember

Humber Mouth - Hull Literature Festival
www.humbermouth.org.uk/
Late June/Early July

Ilkley Literature Festival
www.ilkleyliteraturefestival.org.uk
October

Illunminating York
York
www.illuminatingyork.org.uk/
October

Rotherham Show
Rotherham
September

Saltaire Festival
Saltaire
www.saltairefestival.co.uk
8 - 18 September

St Leger
Doncaster
www.doncaster-racecourse.co.uk
September

UCI Mountain Bike World Cup
Pickering
April

Whitby Gothic Weekends
Whitby
wgw.topmum.co.uk
Last weekends in April and October

Yorkshire | **Where to Eat**

Where to Eat

Yorkshire has great places to eat. The restaurant reviews on this page are just a small selection from the highly respected **The Good Food Guide 2011**. Please see page 14 for further information on the Guide and details of a Special Offer for our readers.

ARKENGARTHDALE

The Charles Bathurst Inn
Plain surroundings, surprisingly good food
Langthwaite, Arkengarthdale DL11 6EN
01748) 884567
www.cbinn.co.uk
Gastropub | £23

There's no pretension at this roadside Dales pub, just scrubbed wooden tables, bare boards and the menu written on a huge mirror over an open fire. But make no mistake, the dishes coming out of the kitchen belie the humble surroundings. Goats' cheese pannacotta with beetroot carpaccio is carefully judged, and wild salmon tart delivers perfect pastry. Chicken with wild rice has pleasing depth of flavour, and the accompanying black bean spring roll has a shock chilli finish. House wine starts at £12.50.
Chef/s: Gareth Bottomley. **Open:** all week L 12 to 2, D 6.30 to 9. **Closed:** 25 Dec. **Meals:** alc (main courses £10 to £20). Sun L £10. **Service:** not inc. **Details:** major cards accepted. 50 seats. Air conditioning. Separate bar. Music. Children welcome. Car parking.

MASHAM

Vennell's
Imaginative food from excellent ingredients
7 Silver Street, Masham HG4 4DX
01765) 689000
www.vennellsrestaurant.co.uk
Modern British | £23

Six years on, there's a lot to be said for Jon Vennell's restaurant just off Masham's picturesque square. Reporters have emerged full of praise for 'imaginative and well prepared' food and for the 'congenial atmosphere'. It is all neat, uncluttered and unshowy, with neutral colours and white linen the backdrop to a short (four choices per course) seasonal menu built around excellent raw materials. A refreshing lack of undue fuss characterises dishes such as seared mackerel with celeriac rémoulade and sardine dressing or a main course of roasted roe deer with wilted spinach, cep risotto and port jus. Egg and bacon salad, comprising crisp pancetta, soft poached egg, croûtons and dressed leaves, might be served as a starter, while cod is poached to make an earthy main course with cassoulet. Desserts such as warm ginger pudding with gingerbread ice cream or a dark chocolate trio – warm brownie, mousse, and chocolate and hazelnut ice cream – round things off with style. Tasting notes point the way on a wine list that's arranged by style; eight house bottles at £14.95 open proceedings.
Chef/s: Jon Vennell. **Open:** Sun L 12 to 4, Tue to Sun D 7.15 to 11. **Closed:** Mon, 2 weeks Jan. **Meals:** Set D £19.50 (2 courses) to £26. Sun L £19.95. **Service:** not inc. **Details:** major cards accepted. 28 seats. Separate bar. No mobile phones. Music. Children welcome.

Content brought to you by **The Good Food Guide 2011**. Please see page 14 for further details.

Yorkshire

Tourist Information Centres

When you arrive at your destination, visit an Official Partner Tourist Information Centre for quality assured help with accommodation and information about local attractions and events, or email your request before you go. To find a Tourist Information Centre by region visit enjoyEngland.com/find-tic.

AYSGARTH FALLS	Aysgarth Falls National Park Centre	01969 662910	aysgarth@ytbtic.co.uk
BEVERLEY	34 Butcher Row	01482 391672	beverley.tic@eastriding.gov.uk
BRADFORD	City Hall	01274 433678	tourist.information@bradford.gov.uk
BRIDLINGTON	25 Prince Street	01262 673474	bridlington.tic@eastriding.gov.uk
DANBY	The Moors Centre, Danby Lodge	01439 772737	moorscentre@northyorkmoors-npa.gov.uk
DONCASTER	Blue Building	01302 734309	tourist.information@doncaster.gov.uk
FILEY	Filey TIC	01723 383637	fileytic@scarborough.gov.uk
GRASSINGTON	National Park Centre	01756 751690	grassington@ytbtic.co.uk
GUISBOROUGH	Priory Grounds	01287 633801	guisborough_tic@redcar-cleveland.gov.uk
HALIFAX	Piece Hall	01422 368725	halifax@ytbtic.co.uk
HARROGATE	Royal Baths	01423 537300	tic@harrogate.gov.uk
HAWES	Dales Countryside Museum	01969 666210	hawes@ytbtic.co.uk
HAWORTH	2/4 West Lane	01535 642329	haworth@ytbtic.co.uk
HEBDEN BRIDGE	Visitor and Canal Centre	01422 843831	hebdenbridge@ytbtic.co.uk
HELMSLEY	The Visitor Centre, Helmsley Castle	01439 770173	helmsley@ytbtic.co.uk
HOLMFIRTH	49-51 Huddersfield Road	01484 222444	holmfirth.tic@kirklees.gov.uk
HORNSEA	120 Newbegin	01964 536404	hornsea.tic@eastriding.gov.uk
HULL	1 Paragon Street	01482 223559	tourist.information@hullcc.gov.uk
HUMBER BRIDGE	North Bank Viewing Area	01482 640852	humberbridge.tic@eastriding.gov.uk
ILKLEY	Town Hall	01943 602319	ilkley@ytbtic.co.uk
KNARESBOROUGH	9 Castle Courtyard	0845 389 0177	kntic@harrogate.gov.uk
LEEDS	Leeds Visitor Centre	0113 242 5242	tourinfo@leeds.gov.uk
LEEMING BAR	The Great North Road	01677 424262	leeming@ytbtic.co.uk
LEYBURN	4 Central Chambers	01748 828747	leyburn@ytbtic.co.uk
MALHAM	National Park Centre	01969 652380	malham@ytbtic.co.uk
MALTON	Malton Museum	01653 600048	maltontic@btconnect.com

Yorkshire

TLEY	Otley Library	01943 462485	otleytic@leedslearning.net
ATELEY BRIDGE	18 High Street	0845 389 0177	pbtic@harrogate.gov.uk
ICKERING	Ropery House	01751 473791	pickering@ytbtic.co.uk
EETH	Hudson House, The Green	01748 884059	reeth@ytbtic.co.uk
ICHMOND	Friary Gardens	01748 828742	richmond@ytbtic.co.uk
IPON	Minster Road	01765 604625	ripontic@harrogate.gov.uk
OTHERHAM	40 Bridgegate	01709 835904	tic@rotherham.gov.uk
CARBOROUGH	Brunswick Shopping Centre	01723 383636	tourismbureau@scarborough.gov.uk
CARBOROUGH	Harbourside TIC	01723 383636	harboursidetic@scarborough.gov.uk
ETTLE	Town Hall	01729 825192	settle@ytbtic.co.uk
HEFFIELD	Visitor Information Point	0114 2211900	visitor@yorkshiresouth.com
KIPTON	35 Coach Street	01756 792809	skipton@ytbtic.co.uk
UTTON BANK	Sutton Bank Visitor Centre	01845 597426	suttonbank@ytbtic.co.uk
HIRSK	Thirsk Tourist Information Centre	01845 522755	thirsktic@hambleton.gov.uk
ODMORDEN	15 Burnley Road	01706 818181	todmorden@ytbtic.co.uk
VAKEFIELD	9 The Bull Ring	0845 601 8353	tic@wakefield.gov.uk
VETHERBY	Wetherby Library & Tourist Info. Centre	01937 582151	wetherbytic@leedslearning.net
VHITBY	Langborne Road	01723 383637	whitbytic@scarborough.gov.uk
VITHERNSEA	131 Queen Street	01964 615683	withernsea.tic@eastriding.gov.uk
ORK (DE GREY ROOMS)	The De Grey Rooms	01904 550099	info@visityork.org

Regional Contacts and Information

For more information on accommodation, attractions, activities, events and holidays in Yorkshire, contact the regional tourism organisation. Their website has a wealth of information and produces many free publications to help you get the most out of your visit.

The following publications are available from the Yorkshire Tourist Board by logging on to www.yorkshire.com or calling 0844 888 5123

This is Y Magazine

Yorkshire

Where to Stay

Entries appear alphabetically by town name in each county. A key to symbols appears on page 6. Maps start on page 706. A listing of all Enjoy England assessed accommodation appears at the end of the region.

AIRTON, Yorkshire Map ref 5B3

SAT NAV BD23 4BE

★★★ GUEST HOUSE (enjoyEngland.com)

Lindon House

Airton, Skipton BD23 4BE
t (01729) 830418 **e** lindonguesthouse@googlemail.com
w yorkshirenet.co.uk/stayat/lindonguesthouse ONLINE MAP

B&B PER ROOM PER NIGHT
S £35.00 – £45.00
D £50.00 – £65.00

EVENING MEAL PER PERSON
£18.75

SPECIAL PROMOTIONS
Special rates available Nov to Feb £25 pppn

A friendly, family-run guest house converted from an old barn and set in the beautiful Dales National Park. Fantastic panoramic limestone views, ideal for touring and walking. The accommodation is very comfortable, and retains all its character with oak beams. All meals cooked using fresh local produce.

open All year except Xmas
bedrooms 3 double, 1 twin
bathrooms 4 en suite
payment credit/debit cards, cash, cheques

directions Lindon Guest House is situated on the Malham road, just leaving the village of Airton on the left-hand side.

Room
General
Leisure

Do you like Camping?

You can also buy a copy of our popular guide 'Camping, Touring & Holiday Parks' including touring parks, camping holidays and holiday parks and villages in Britain 2011. Now available in good bookshops and online at **visitbritainshop.com**

£8.99

Yorkshire

BEDALE, Yorkshire Map ref 5C3
SAT NAV DL8 2TB

Castle Arms Inn
Snape, Bedale DL8 2TB
t (01677) 470270 f (01677) 470837 e castlearms@aol.com
w castlearmsinn.com LAST MINUTE OFFERS

B&B PER ROOM PER NIGHT
S £55.00 – £65.00
D £75.00 – £85.00

A family run inn with twin and double en suite bedrooms furnished to an exceptional standard. A warm welcome awaits you, with open fires, traditional ales and real home cooking. **directions** From A1 Leeming Bar take A684 to Bedale. Follow B6268 to Masham 2 miles. Turn left to Arboretum after one mile turn left to Snape. **open** All year **bedrooms** 6 double, 3 twin **bathrooms** 9 en suite **payment** credit/debit cards, cash, cheques

Room General Leisure

BEDALE, Yorkshire Map ref 5C3
SAT NAV DL8 1NE

Elmfield House
Arrathorne, Bedale DL8 1NE
t (01677) 450558 f (01677) 450557 e stay@elmfieldhouse.co.uk
w elmfieldhouse.co.uk ONLINE BOOKING LAST MINUTE OFFERS

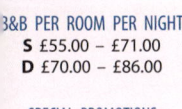

B&B PER ROOM PER NIGHT
S £55.00 – £71.00
D £70.00 – £86.00

SPECIAL PROMOTIONS
Seasonal offers on website.
Packages for group bookings – please enquire.

A family run guesthouse in lovely rural Dales location. A warm welcome awaits with tea and homemade cake or a glass of wine. Relax in peaceful surroundings, sleep in spacious, comfy, en-suite rooms and start your day by tucking into a hearty, locally sourced breakfast. Good pubs/restaurants nearby for dinner.

open All year
bedrooms 4 double, 2 twin, 1 family
bathrooms 7 en suite
payment credit/debit cards, cash, cheques

directions A684 from Bedale to Leyburn. Turn right at crossroads past church at Patrick Brompton. 1.5 miles on right after turn-off to Hunton.

Room
General
Leisure

Where is my pet welcome?

Some properties welcome well-behaved pets. Look for the 🐕 in the accommodation listings.

You can also buy a copy of our popular guide 'Pets Come Too!' Now available in good bookshops and online at **visitbritainshop.com**

£9.99

499

Yorkshire

BEVERLEY, Yorkshire Map ref 4C1
SAT NAV HU17 0DR

GUEST ACCOMMODATION ★★★★

B&B PER ROOM PER NIGHT
S £25.00 – £55.00
D £50.00 – £85.00

SPECIAL PROMOTIONS
Stay 7 nights pay for 6 (not in conjunction with other offers).

Eastgate Guest House
7 Eastgate, Beverley, East Yorkshire HU17 0DR
t (01482) 868464 **f** (01482) 871899 **e** eastgateguesthouse@live.co.uk
w eastgateguesthouse.com LAST MINUTE OFFERS

Eastgate is a Victorian 16 bedroom family run Guest House. Situated perfectly in the heart of Beverley. Only a minute walk from Beverley Minster, town centre, railway station and only fifteen minutes from Hull. Julie and Ray will assure you a comfortable and pleasant stay, including a hearty cooked breakfast.

open All year
bedrooms 4 single, 8 double, 2 twin, 2 family
bathrooms 8 en suite
payment cash, cheques

directions Follow signs for Beverley Minster. Turn left on to Eastgate, our Guest House is approximately 100yds from the Minster on the right hand side.

Room
General
Leisure

BISHOP WILTON, Yorkshire Map ref 4C1
SAT NAV YO42 1SB

FARMHOUSE ★★★

B&B PER ROOM PER NIGHT
S £30.00
D £25.00

EVENING MEAL PER PERSON
£15.00

High Belthorpe
Belthorpe Lane, Bishop Wilton YO42 1SB
t (01759) 368238 **f** 07786923330 **e** meg@highbelthorpe.co.uk
w highbelthorpe.co.uk ONLINE MAP

Victorian farmhouse on an ancient site, with large, comfortable bedrooms giving panoramic views of the Yorkshire Wolds. Own private fishing lake and access to fabulous country walks. York 12 miles. **directions** A166 from York towards Bridlington. After 10 miles take right turn to Bishop Wilton. In village, turn right before pub, continue straight for 1.5 miles. **open** All year except Xmas
bedrooms 1 double, 2 family **bathrooms** 2 en suite, 1 with private bathroom **payment** cash, cheques, euros

Room   General   Leisure

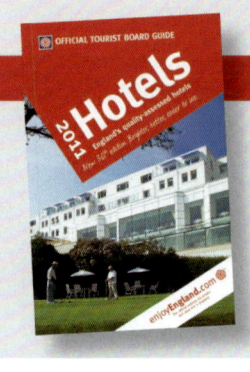

Looking for something else?

You can also buy a copy of our popular guide 'Hotels' including country house and town house hotels, metro and budget hotels, serviced apartments, restaurants with rooms and Spas in England 2011.

Now available in good bookshops and online at
visitbritainshop.com

£10.99

500 Official tourist board guide Bed & Breakfast

Yorkshire

BRIDLINGTON, Yorkshire Map ref 5D3

SAT NAV YO15 2EZ

Kilburn Guest House

25 Trinity Road, Bridlington YO15 2EZ
t (01262) 679724   **e** enquiries@thekilburn.co.uk
w thekilburn.co.uk   ONLINE MAP   GUEST REVIEWS

B&B PER ROOM PER NIGHT
S £24.00 – £25.00
D £28.00 – £32.00

EVENING MEAL PER PERSON
£7.50 – £10.50

SPECIAL PROMOTIONS
2 nights minimum stay,
O.A.P special Mon to Fri, 7 nights stay for the price of 6

Welcome to the Kilburn in the lovely East Yorkshire town of Bridlington. We are a family run guest house with a warm, friendly and relaxing atmosphere. The town centre, north beach, local amenities and the award winning Spa Complex are only a short walk away.

open All year
bedrooms 1 single, 4 double, 1 twin, 1 family, 1 suite
bathrooms 7 en suite, 1 with private bathroom

directions We are sutuated north side of Bridlington close to beach, Leisure World and town centre. A map is available on the website.

CASTLE HOWARD, Yorkshire Map ref 5C3

SAT NAV YO60 6QD

Gate Farm

Ganthorpe, Castle Howard, York, Malton YO60 6QD
t (01653) 648269   **f** (01653) 648269   **e** millgate001@msn.com
w ganthorpegatefarm.co.uk   ONLINE MAP   ONLINE BOOKING   LAST MINUTE OFFERS

B&B PER ROOM PER NIGHT
S £35.00 – £40.00
D £70.00 – £80.00

EVENING MEAL PER PERSON
£20.00 – £25.00

BREAKFAST AWARD

Working dairy farm in quiet hamlet near to Castle Howard, offering friendly, traditional, Yorkshire hospitality. 5 star breakfasts, breakfast award. Convenient for the Moors, east coast and York. **directions** Close to Castle Howard, Yorkshire Lavender, Eden Camp, FlamingoLand, Coast and Moors, York. www.ganthorpegatefarm.co.uk has map of area. **open** All year **bedrooms** 2 double, 2 twin, 1 family **bathrooms** 4 en suite, 1 with private bathroom **payment** credit/debit cards, cash, cheques, euros

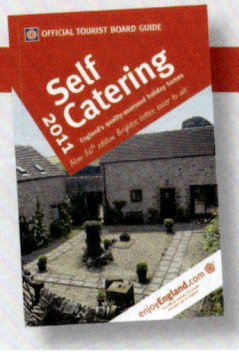

Looking for something else?

You can also buy a copy of our popular guide 'Self Catering' including self-catering holiday homes, approved caravan holiday homes, boat accommodation and holiday cottage agencies in England 2011.

Now available in good bookshops and online at
visitbritainshop.com

£11.99

key to symbols see page 6

Yorkshire

CLAPHAM, Yorkshire Map ref 5B3

SAT NAV LA2 8HH

New Inn

Old Road, Clapham, via Lancaster LA2 8HH
t (01524) 251203 f (01524) 251824 e info@newinn-clapham.co.uk
w newinn-clapham.co.uk ONLINE MAP GUEST REVIEWS LAST MINUTE OFFERS

B&B PER ROOM PER NIGHT
S £45.00 – £60.00
D £90.00 – £120.00

EVENING MEAL PER PERSON
£7.95 – £30.00

SPECIAL PROMOTIONS
5 night Dinner Bed and Breakfast (Sunday to Thursday) from £179.00 per person.

Nestling beneath Ingleborough, the beautiful village straddles either side of Clapham Beck, linked by three bridges. The church is at the top, the New Inn is at the bottom. This family run inn is set amidst a geological wonderland of limestone, cavern and fell country.

open All year
bedrooms 13 double, 6 twin
bathrooms 19 en suite, 19 with private bathroom
payment credit/debit cards, cash, cheques

directions We are located in the village of Clapham on the A65 between Settle and Ingleton, 19 miles east of M6 Junction 34.

BREAKFAST AWARD

Room
General
Leisure

CLOUGHTON, Yorkshire Map ref 5D3

SAT NAV YO13 0AR

Cober Hill

Newlands Road, Cloughton, Scarborough YO13 0AR
t (01723) 870310 f (01723) 870271 e enquiries@coberhill.co.uk
w coberhill.co.uk LAST MINUTE OFFERS

B&B PER ROOM PER NIGHT
S £32.00 – £58.00
D £64.00 – £116.00

EVENING MEAL PER PERSON
£13.00

SPECIAL PROMOTIONS
Weekend breaks, midweek breaks, themed holidays, group bookings welcome. Summer holidays, Xmas and New Year with entertainment programme.

Impressive Edwardian building, with new annexes, set in a beautiful, peaceful and tranquil location between Scarborough and Whitby, in the North York Moors National Park and overlooking the Heritage Coast.

open All year
bedrooms 22 single, 6 double, 25 twin, 10 family
bathrooms 63 en suite
payment credit/debit cards, cash, cheques

directions 6 miles north of Scarborough and 1 miles south of Whitby 100 yards off the A171 Scarborough to Whitby road.

Room
General
Leisure

Yorkshire

COTTINGHAM, Yorkshire Map ref 4C1

SAT NAV HU16 5SW

Woodhill Bed and Breakfast

Woodhill Way, Cottingham HU16 5SW
t 01482 843512 e lucy@woodhillbandb.co.uk
w woodhillbandb.co.uk ONLINE MAP

B&B PER ROOM PER NIGHT
S £40.00
D £65.00

Friendly family run guesthouse situated in the grounds of Skidby Lakes Golf Club in East Yorkshire. Immaculate, comfortable accommodation in a newly renovated house, ideal for both business or pleasure. **directions** Please contact us for directions **open** All year **bedrooms** 2 double, 1 twin, 1 family **bathrooms** 4 en suite **payment** credit/debit cards, cash

Room General Leisure

CRAYKE, Yorkshire Map ref 5C3

SAT NAV YO61 4TD

The Hermitage

Mill Lane, Crayke, Easingwold YO61 4TD
t (01347) 821635

B&B PER ROOM PER NIGHT
S £34.00 – £36.00
D £68.00 – £72.00

Peaceful location with panoramic views. Overlooking our own farm and the Howardian Hills. Offering a warm and friendly welcome at our comfortable modern farmhouse. Hot tub on patio. **directions** Please contact us for directions **open** All year except Xmas **bedrooms** 1 double, 2 twin **bathrooms** 1 en suite **payment** cash, cheques

Room General

DALBY, Yorkshire Map ref 5C3

SAT NAV YO13 0LW

South Moor Farm

Dalby Forest Drive, Pickering YO13 0LW
t 01751 460285 e gol@southmoorfarm.co.uk
w southmoorfarm.co.uk ONLINE MAP ONLINE BOOKING

B&B PER ROOM PER NIGHT
S £30.00 – £40.00
D £60.00 – £80.00

EVENING MEAL PER PERSON
£12.00 – £20.00

SPECIAL PROMOTIONS
Reduced rates for children under 14 years. Discounts on stays of 3 nights or more.

Quiet rural location on Dalby Forest Drive between Pickering and Scarborough. An excellent base to explore Dalby Forest on foot, bike or horse after a full English breakfast. Packed lunches and evening meals by arrangement. Children's play area, orienteering courses, Go Ape, Ability Outdoors and astronomy in Dalby Forest.

open All year
bedrooms 1 single, 1 double, 1 twin, 1 family
bathrooms 3 en suite, 1 with private bathroom
payment credit/debit cards, cash, cheques

directions Follow Dalby Forest Drive (look for brown tourism signs). We are 10 miles from Thornton-le-Dale, 3.5 miles from Langdale End. Grid Ref SE905905.

Room General Leisure

for key to symbols see page 6

503

Yorkshire

DANBY, Yorkshire Map ref 5C3
SAT NAV YO21 2LD

Fox & Hounds Inn
45 Brook Lane, Ainthorpe, Whitby YO21 2LD
t (01287) 660218 f (01287) 660030 e info@foxandhounds-ainthorpe.com
w foxandhounds-ainthorpe.com

B&B PER ROOM PER NIGHT
S £48.00 – £70.00
D £82.00 – £95.00

16thC former coaching inn, now a high-quality residential country inn and restaurant in the beautiful North York Moors National Park. Enjoy freshly prepared dishes, cask ales and quality wines.
directions Turn off A171 Guisborough to Whitby road. Follow sign to Castleton or Danby, then Ainthorpe. **open** All year **bedrooms** 3 double, 3 twin, 1 family **bathrooms** 7 en suite **payment** credit/debit cards, cash, cheques, euros

DONCASTER, Yorkshire Map ref 4C1
SAT NAV DN2 5BH

Balmoral Guesthouse
129 Thorne Road, Doncaster DN2 5BH
t (01302) 364385 f (01302) 364385 e info@thebalmoralguesthouse.co.uk
w thebalmoralguesthouse.co.uk ONLINE MAP

B&B PER ROOM PER NIGHT
S £25.00 – £45.00
D £40.00 – £55.00
EVENING MEAL PER PERSON
£8.50 – £12.50

The Balmoral is close to the town center, Racecourse and Royal Infirmary. This elegantly furnished family-run hotel offers comfortable accommodation with choice of facilities combined with true Yorkshire hospitality. **directions** M18-Jct3, follow Racecourse signs, straight on at R/about, 2nd-left (at lights) to top of road, left, guesthouse on right. From A1 follow Royal Infirmary sign **open** All year **bedrooms** 3 single, 4 double, 1 twin **bathrooms** 3 en suite, 3 with private bathroom **payment** credit/debit cards, cash, cheques, euros

DONCASTER, Yorkshire Map ref 4C1
SAT NAV DN5 7BT

Rock Farm
Hooton Pagnell, Doncaster DN5 7BT
t (01977) 642200 or 07785916186 f (01977) 642200 e info@rockfarm.info
w rockfarm.info

B&B PER ROOM PER NIGHT
S £28.00 – £36.00
D £50.00 – £60.00

A warm welcome awaits you at our Grade II stone farmhouse. In the picturesque village of Hooton Pagnell, six miles north-west of Doncaster. Five minutes A1 and Brodsworth Hall. **directions** A1 junction 38 take A638 towards Wakefield, approx 1 mile turn left up Hampole Field Lane, left again, left into Hooton Pagnell. First on right. **open** All year **bedrooms** 1 double, 1 twin, 1 family **bathrooms** 1 en suite **payment** cash, cheques, euros

DRAX, Yorkshire Map ref 4C1
SAT NAV YO8 8NY

Dove Cottage
Back Lane, Drax, Selby, North Yorkshire YO8 8NY
t (01757) 617103. Mobile. 07885205693. e lthorn@btinternet.com

B&B PER ROOM PER NIGHT
S £35.00
D £50.00

Dove Cottage is a new bungalow, with private car parking to rear, 2 double rooms both en-suite. We overlook our paddock, beyond that there is a wooded walk and fields **directions** M62 Junction 36 left A614 to roundabout 2nd exit A645 to Roundabout 3rd exit main street Drax 800Mtrs left we are 20mtrs on the left **open** All year **bedrooms** 2 double **bathrooms** 2 en suite **payment** cash, cheques

Yorkshire

EGTON BRIDGE, Yorkshire Map ref 5D3

SAT NAV YO21 1XD

Broom House and Whites (Restaurant)
Broom House Lane, Egton Bridge, Whitby YO21 1XD
t (01947) 895279 f (01947) 895657 e mw@broom-house.co.uk
w egton-bridge.co.uk ONLINE MAP GUEST REVIEWS ONLINE BOOKING LAST MINUTE OFFERS

B&B PER ROOM PER NIGHT
S £60.00
D £86.00 – £126.00

Beautiful National Park Countryside, Moorland and coast line combined to offer the ultimate luxury hideaway. This delightful setting is an ideal base for walking, fishing, bird watching etc. **directions** Please Refer To Website **open** All year except Xmas **bedrooms** 1 single, 4 double, 1 twin, 2 suites **bathrooms** 8 en suite **payment** credit/debit cards, cash, cheques, euros

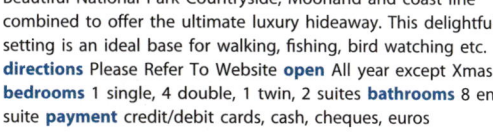

BREAKFAST AWARD

GREAT AYTON, Yorkshire Map ref 5C3

SAT NAV TS9 6QR

The Kings Head at Newton Under Roseberry
The Green, Newton Under Rosebery, Near Great Ayton TS9 6QR
t 01642 722318 f 01642 724750 e info@kingsheadhotel.co.uk
w kingsheadhotel.co.uk ONLINE MAP GUEST REVIEWS ONLINE BOOKING LAST MINUTE OFFERS

B&B PER ROOM PER NIGHT
S £60.00 – £87.50
D £77.50 – £115.00

EVENING MEAL PER PERSON
£8.95 – £35.00

Tourism North East Bed and Breakfast of the Year. Delightful family-owned hotel and restaurant. Individually designed, en suite bedrooms from two adjoining 18th Century cottages oozing character and charm. **directions** We are situated in the village of Newton Under Roseberry in between Guisborough and Great Ayton on the A173. Sat Nav Ref: TS9 6QR. **open** All year except Xmas and New Year **bedrooms** 1 single, 4 double, 2 twin, 1 family **bathrooms** 8 en suite **payment** credit/debit cards, cash, cheques

HAROME, Yorkshire Map ref 4C1

SAT NAV YO62 5JA

Bramble Cottage B&B
Harome, York YO62 5JA
t 01439 771158 e lizbetts@hotmail.com
w bramble-cottage-harome.co.uk

B&B PER ROOM PER NIGHT
S £65.00 – £70.00
D £80.00 – £95.00

Thatched cottage overlooking open countryside in the village of Harome. Comfortable en suite rooms and spacious lounge opening onto cottage garden. This detached house is near Helmsley and Yorkshire Moors. **directions** From A1 take A168 to Thirsk then A170 signposted Scarborough. After passing through Helmsley turn right towards Harome then phone us for assistance. **open** All year **bedrooms** 3 double **bathrooms** 2 en suite, 1 with private bathroom **payment** cash, cheques

BREAKFAST AWARD

HARROGATE, Yorkshire Map ref 4B1

SAT NAV HG3 2LW

Cold Cotes
Cold Cotes Road, Felliscliffe, Harrogate HG3 2LW
t (01423) 770937 e info@coldcotes.com
w coldcotes.com ONLINE MAP GUEST REVIEWS LAST MINUTE OFFERS

B&B PER ROOM PER NIGHT
S £60.00 – £95.00
D £70.00 – £95.00

EVENING MEAL PER PERSON
£7.50

On the edge of Nidderdale in the picturesque Yorkshire Dales. Guests say, - a special place to stay, tranquil setting, beautiful and comfortable rooms, excellent food with an inspiring garden. **directions** A59 west of Harrogate for 7 miles to Black Bull pub. Turn right after the pub onto Cold Cotes Road then third entrance on right. **open** All year **bedrooms** 4 double, 1 twin, 1 suite **bathrooms** 6 en suite **payment** credit/debit cards, cash, cheques

key to symbols see page 6   505

Yorkshire

HAWES, Yorkshire Map ref 5B3

SAT NAV DL8 3NL

B&B PER ROOM PER NIGHT
S £40.00
D £60.00 – £70.00

Old Station House
Hardraw Road, Hawes, North Yorkshire DL8 3NL
t (01969) 666912   e oldstationhouse@ymail.com
w oldstationhousehawes.co.uk ONLINE MAP GUEST REVIEWS

Old Station House, a charming stone built house with modern facilities required by today's tourists conveniently situated minutes from the centre of Hawes in Upper Wensleydale. Private parking. Ensuite bedrooms. **directions** 2 minutes walk away from Hawes Centre in Upper Wensleydale. **open** All year except Xmas and New Year **bathrooms** 3 en suite **payment** credit/debit cards, cash, cheques

BREAKFAST AWARD

Room   General   Leisure

HAWES, Yorkshire Map ref 5B3

SAT NAV DL8 3LP

B&B PER ROOM PER NIGHT
D £60.00 – £70.00

SPECIAL PROMOTIONS
Winter short breaks available

Pry House Farm B&B
Hawes DL8 3LP
t (01969) 667241   e pryhousefarm@hotmail.com
w pryhousefarm.co.uk ONLINE MAP GUEST REVIEWS LAST MINUTE OFFERS

Would you like to Escape to Wensleydale. Wake to the sound of wild bird song or the occasional bleating sheep. Pick your own free range egg from the nest to eat at breakfast. Spacious accommodation in a peaceful setting surrounded by stunning views. A walkers paradise.

open March to November
bedrooms 2 double
bathrooms 1 en suite, 1 with private bathroom
payment cash, cheques, euros

directions One mile west from Hawes on the A684 Sedbergh road we are on the right hand side just past the village of Appersett.

Room   General   Leisure

HAWORTH, Yorkshire Map ref 4B1

SAT NAV BD22 8QQ

B&B PER ROOM PER NIGHT
S £40.00 – £45.00
D £80.00 – £85.00

Rosebud Cottage Guest House
1 Belle Isle Road, Haworth BD22 8QQ
t (01535) 640321 f (01535) 646720 e info@rosebudcottage.co.uk
w rosebudcottage.co.uk ONLINE MAP GUEST REVIEWS ONLINE BOOKING LAST MINUTE OFFERS

Traditional Yorkshire-stone cottage, c1752 with many fine features All rooms en suite with added luxury of four-poster beds. LCD televisions with DVD player. Vaulted guest Lounge, conservatory and private garden. **directions** Please Refer To Website. **open** All year except Xmas **bedrooms** 1 single, 3 double, 1 twin **bathrooms** 5 en suite **payment** credit/debit cards, cash, cheques

Room   General   Leisure

506 Official tourist board guide Bed & Breakfast

Yorkshire

HAWORTH, Yorkshire Map ref 4B1

SAT NAV BD22 8DP

enjoyEngland.com ★★★ GUEST HOUSE

The Apothecary Guest House
86 Main Street, Haworth BD22 8DP
t (01535) 643642 f (01535) 643642 e nicholasapt@aol.com
w theapothecaryguesthouse.co.uk

B&B PER ROOM PER NIGHT
S £35.00 – £40.00
D £60.00 – £65.00

SPECIAL PROMOTIONS
Stay three nights or more and receive 10% discount. Special offers available all year round, please ask.

Friendly, family-run guest house at the top of Haworth Main Street, opposite the famous Brontë church. We are one minutes' walk from the Brontë Parsonage, and ten minutes' walk from the KWV Railway. Enjoy the views from our dining room and terraced gardens. Relax in our sauna. Free wifi.

open All year
bedrooms 1 single, 3 double, 2 twin, 2 family
bathrooms 7 en suite, 1 with private bathroom
payment credit/debit cards, cash, cheques

directions Take the A629 Keighley–Halifax road, turn right at the village of Cross Roads, follow signs to Haworth (approx 1 mile).

Room / General / Leisure

HAWORTH, Yorkshire Map ref 4B1

SAT NAV BD22 8DU

enjoyEngland.com ★★★★ INN

Old White Lion Hotel
Main Street, Haworth BD22 8DU
t (01535) 642313 f (01535) 646222 e enquiries@oldwhitelionhotel.com
w oldwhitelionhotel.com ONLINE MAP

B&B PER ROOM PER NIGHT
S £65.25 – £75.25
D £90.50 – £100.50

SPECIAL PROMOTIONS
Special bargain breaks available. Great value and good food in old-world surroundings.

Family-run, centuries-old coaching inn situated at the top of the charming cobbled Main Street. Most en suite rooms command spectacular views of surrounding countryside or village. Candlelit, a la carte restaurant, oak-beamed bars serving traditional ales and home-cooked food. Wi-Fi Internet is available in all bedrooms.

open All year
bedrooms 3 single, 8 double, 1 twin, 2 family
bathrooms 14 en suite
payment credit/debit cards, cash, cheques

directions Turn off Halifax-Keighley A629 at Crossroads onto B6142. Hotel adjoining Haworth Visitor Centre at top of cobbled Main Street, 0.5 miles past Haworth Railway Station.

Room / General / Leisure

Yorkshire

HEBDEN, Yorkshire Map ref 5B3
SAT NAV BD23 5DX

enjoyEngland.com
★★★
B&B BED & BREAKFAST

B&B PER ROOM PER NIGHT
S £35.00 – £40.00
D £30.00 – £40.00

Court Croft
Church Lane, Hebden, Skipton BD23 5DX
t (01756) 753406 **f** 07808 597815

Five-hundred-acre livestock farm. Farmhouse in village location close to the Dales Way. Ideal for touring the Dales, Nidderdale and Ribblesdale. **directions** Please contact us for directions **open** All year **bedrooms** 3 twin **bathrooms** 2 en suite, 1 with private bathroom **payment** cash, cheques

Room General Leisure

HEBDEN BRIDGE, Yorkshire Map ref 4B1
SAT NAV HX7 8EH

enjoyEngland.com
★★★★
GUEST ACCOMMODATION

B&B PER ROOM PER NIGHT
S £49.00 – £59.00
D £79.00 – £109.00

EVENING MEAL PER PERSON
£5.95 – £15.00

SPECIAL PROMOTIONS
Midweek promotions available.

b@r place
10 Crown Street, Hebden Bridge HX7 8EH
t (01422) 842814 **e** intouch@barplace.co.uk
w barplace.co.uk ONLINE MAP GUEST REVIEWS ONLINE BOOKING LAST MINUTE OFFERS

Bar and bistro with modern en-suite accommodation of an excellent standard. Eight rooms available on b&b basis. Town centre location, family friendly, great customer service and warm welcome. LCD TV/DVD, Wi-Fi throughout.

open All year
bedrooms 1 single, 5 double, 1 twin, 1 family
bathrooms 8 en suite, 8 with private bathroom
payment credit/debit cards, cash, cheques

directions Centre of town, 5 minutes walk from train station.

Room
General

HEBDEN BRIDGE, Yorkshire Map ref 4B1
SAT NAV HX7 8AD

enjoyEngland.com
★★★★★
B&B BED & BREAKFAST

Silver AWARD

B&B PER ROOM PER NIGHT
S £60.00 – £70.00
D £70.00 – £90.00

Holme House
New Road, Hebden Bridge HX7 8AD
t (01283) 847588 **f** (01422) 847354 **e** mail@holmehousehebdenbridge.co.uk
w holmehousehebdenbridge.co.uk ONLINE MAP GUEST REVIEWS ONLINE BOOKING

Magnificent Georgian house situated in the centre of Hebden Bridge. All bedrooms en suite. Close to shops and restaurants. Efficient, friendly service. Extensive breakfast menu. Private car park **directions** Please refer to website. **open** All year **bedrooms** 2 double, 1 twin **bathrooms** 3 en suite **payment** credit/debit cards, cash, cheques

Room General Leisure

Yorkshire

HELMSLEY, Yorkshire Map ref 5C3
SAT NAV YO62 5NB

Laskill Grange
Mrs Sue Smith, Laskill Grange, Nr Hawnby, Helmsley, York YO62 5NB
t (01439) 798268 or (01439) 798265 **e** laskillgrange@tiscali.co.uk
w laskillgrange.co.uk ONLINE MAP GUEST REVIEWS LAST MINUTE OFFERS

B&B PER ROOM PER NIGHT
S £40.00 – £50.00
D £80.00 – £90.00

EVENING MEAL PER PERSON
£15.00 – £25.00

Peaceful, idyllic setting in North Yorkshire Moors. Luxury accommodation in beautiful grounds, lake, swans, peacocks. Attention to detail, personal service. Recommended on BBC Holiday Programme. Own spring water. Hot tub. **directions** From York, take A19 to Thirsk, A170 to Helmsley, then B1257. 6miles north of Helmsley on left at Laskill, see our sign on B1257. **open** All year **bedrooms** 1 single, 1 double, 1 twin **bathrooms** 2 en suite, 1 with private bathroom **payment** credit/debit cards, cash, cheques

Room · General · Leisure

HUDDERSFIELD, Yorkshire Map ref 4B1
SAT NAV HD1 5BS

Cambridge Lodge
4 Clare Hill, Huddersfield HD1 5BS
t (01484) 519892 **f** (01484) 534534 **e** info@cambridgelodge.co.uk
w cambridgelodge.co.uk ONLINE MAP GUEST REVIEWS ONLINE BOOKING LAST MINUTE OFFERS

B&B PER ROOM PER NIGHT
S £35.00 – £40.00
D £50.00 – £75.00

Thirty-four en suite rooms with tea/coffee making facilities, telephones, colour TV. Free parking. Less than 0.5 miles from train/bus station. Easy to find on Clare Hill off St Johns Road. **directions** Please contact us for directions **open** All year **bedrooms** 12 single, 10 double, 9 twin, 3 family **bathrooms** 34 en suite **payment** credit/debit cards, cash, cheques, euros

Room · General

INGLETON, Yorkshire Map ref 5B3
SAT NAV LA2 7AN

New Butts Farm
New Butts Farm, High Bentham, Ingleton LA2 7AN
t (01524) 241238 **e** jeanandterry@googlemail.com
w newbutts.co.uk

B&B PER ROOM PER NIGHT
S £25.50 – £28.50
D £50.00 – £52.00

EVENING MEAL PER PERSON
£13.50 – £15.50

We are situated in beautiful part of the Dales, with easy access to many other local attractions, e.g. Waterfalls at Ingleton, Lake District. Suitable for sightseeing or walking. **directions** 2 miles off A65 on the B6480 Clapham to Bentham road. **open** All year except Xmas **bedrooms** 1 single, 2 double, 2 twin, 2 family **bathrooms** 5 en suite **payment** cash, cheques

Room · General

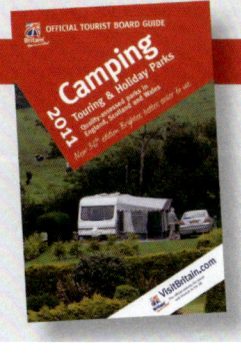

Do you like Camping?

You can also buy a copy of our popular guide 'Camping, Touring & Holiday Parks' including touring parks, camping holidays and holiday parks and villages in Britain 2011.

Now available in good bookshops and online at
visitbritainshop.com

£8.99

key to symbols see page 6

509

Yorkshire

KILHAM, Yorkshire Map ref 5C3
SAT NAV YO25 4SP

Kilham Hall Country House
Driffield Road, Kilham, Driffield YO25 4SP
t (01262) 420466 e enquiries@kilhamhall.co.uk
w kilhamhall.co.uk ONLINE MAP GUEST REVIEWS ONLINE BOOKING LAST MINUTE OFFERS

B&B PER ROOM PER NIGHT
S £95.00 – £120.00
D £110.00 – £170.00

EVENING MEAL PER PERSON
£32.50

SPECIAL PROMOTIONS
Spring/Autumn Mid-Week Breaks 3 night for 2

Luxurious Country House offering elegant and exquisitely furnished accommodation fusing old world charm with contemporary chic. Delicious award winning breakfasts with daily homemade bread. Peaceful location, beautiful gardens with outdoor heated swimming pool & tennis court. Winner of Conde Nast Johansens most excellent small hotel in UK & Ireland 2010.

open 1st February to 5th November
bedrooms 2 double, 1 suite
bathrooms 3 en suite
payment credit/debit cards, cash, cheques

directions From York take the A166 Bridlington and follow approx 30 miles. Turn left for Kilham. Follow 1½ miles, first house on the right.

BREAKFAST AWARD

KILNWICK PERCY, Yorkshire Map ref 4C1
SAT NAV YO42 1UF

The Wolds Retreat
Kilnwick Percy Hall, Kilnwick Percy, Pocklington YO42 1UF
t (01759) 305968 f (01759) 305962 e info@thewoldsretreat.co.uk
w TheWoldsRetreat.co.uk ONLINE MAP GUEST REVIEWS ONLINE BOOKING

B&B PER ROOM PER NIGHT
S £35.00 – £60.00
D £60.00

The Wolds Retreat is run by Madhyamaka Buddhist Centre and set in the heart of the beautiful Yorkshire Wolds. Wonderfully set in 4 acres of gardens lakes and woodland this is the perfect place to stay for a quiet break.

open All year
bedrooms 2 single, 2 double, 1 twin
bathrooms 3 en suite
payment credit/debit cards, cash, cheques

directions Please contact us for directions

Yorkshire

KIRKBY MALZEARD, Yorkshire Map ref 5C3
SAT NAV HG4 3SE

Cowscot House
Back Lane, Kirkby Malzeard, Ripon, N. Yorkshire HG4 3SE
t 01765 658181 **e** liz@cowscothouse.co.uk
w cowscothouse.co.uk ONLINE MAP

B&B PER ROOM PER NIGHT
S £55.00 – £62.50
D £70.00 – £85.00

Sympathetically converted stone barn and stables on the edge of a popular village. Welcoming and extremely comfortable. Providing an excellent base for touring and exploring the Yorkshire Moors or Dales. **directions** From Ripon direction enter Kirkby Malzeard and continue down Main Street. Take right turn just after Highside Butchers turning immediately left into Back Lane. **open** All year except Xmas and New Year **bedrooms** 3 double, 1 twin **bathrooms** 4 en suite **payment** credit/debit cards, cash, cheques

Room   General   Leisure

KIRKBYMOORSIDE, Yorkshire Map ref 5C3
SAT NAV YO62 6NP

The Cornmill
Kirby Mills, Kirkbymoorside YO62 6NP
t (01751) 432000 **e** cornmill@kirbymills.co.uk
w kirbymills.demon.co.uk LAST MINUTE OFFERS

B&B PER ROOM PER NIGHT
S £55.00 – £67.50
D £75.00 – £110.00

EVENING MEAL PER PERSON
£27.50 – £32.50

Converted 18thC watermill and Victorian farmhouse providing well-appointed bed and breakfast accommodation. Bedrooms (one with four-poster), lounge, wood-burning stove and bootroom are in the farmhouse. Sumptuous breakfasts and pre-booked group dinners are served in the mill, with viewing panel in the floor.

open All year
bedrooms 4 double, 1 twin
bathrooms 5 en suite
payment credit/debit cards, cash, cheques

directions From Thirsk, A170 to Scarborough. 1km after Kirkbymoorside roundabout take left turn into Kirby Mills. Entrance to car park is 20m up on right.

Room   General   Leisure

Where is my pet welcome?
Some properties welcome well-behaved pets. Look for the 🐕 in the accommodation listings.

You can also buy a copy of our popular guide 'Pets Come Too!' Now available in good bookshops and online at **visitbritainshop.com**

£9.99

Yorkshire

KIRKBYMOORSIDE, Yorkshire Map ref 5C3
SAT NAV YO62 7LF

The Feversham Arms Inn
Church Houses, Farndale, Kirkbymoorside YO62 7LF
t (01751) 433206 e rrmurray2@aol.com
w feversham armsinn.co.uk

B&B PER ROOM PER NIGHT
D £65.00

The Feversham Arms is a traditional Yorkshire Inn. Hidden in the remote valley of Farndale which is famous for wild daffodils. The inn is referred as the most remote in North Yorkshire Moors. The location is ideal for walkers, cyclists, horse rider's, artists and for people to enjoy the area.

open All year
bedrooms 2 double, 1 family
bathrooms 3 en suite
payment credit/debit cards, cash, cheques

directions To access Church Houses travel on the moors road between Castleton and Hutton le Hole & follow the signs. Sat Nav YO62 7LF

Room General Leisure

LANGTOFT, Yorkshire Map ref 5D3
SAT NAV YO25 3BQ

The Old Mill Hotel & Restaurant
Mill Lane, Langtoft, Driffield YO25 3BQ
t (01377) 267284 f (01377) 267383 e enquiries@old-mill-hotel.co.uk
w old-mill-hotel.co.uk ONLINE MAP GUEST REVIEWS ONLINE BOOKING LAST MINUTE OFFERS

B&B PER ROOM PER NIGHT
S £58.00
D £85.00
EVENING MEAL PER PERSON
£8.95 – £32.95

BREAKFAST AWARD

Family run countryhouse hotel set in Yorkshire wolds. Superb restaurant, cosy licenced bar serving cask ales. Ideal for luxury break or business stopover. Licenced for weddings/civil ceremonies. Pets welcome **directions** Situated on B1249 Driffield to Scarborough road north of Langtoft. From M62 take jn 37 follow A614/613 towards Bridlington. B1249 is signed from Driffield. **open** All year **bedrooms** 5 double, 3 twin, 1 family **bathrooms** 9 en suite, 9 with private bathroom **payment** credit/debit cards, cash, cheques, euro

Room General Leisure

LEEDS, Yorkshire Map ref 4B1
SAT NAV LS2 9LZ

Avalon Guest House
132 Woodsley Road, Leeds LS2 9LZ
t (0113) 243 2545 f (0113) 242 0549 e info@woodsleyroad.com
w avalonguesthouseleeds.co.uk ONLINE MAP

B&B PER ROOM PER NIGHT
S £27.00 – £40.00
D £40.00 – £50.00

Superbly decorated Victorian establishment close to the university and Leeds General Infirmary. Less than one mile from the city centre. Most of the rooms have en suite facilities. **directions** Please contact us for directions **open** All year **bedrooms** 8 single, 6 double, 6 twin, 2 family **bathrooms** 20 en suite, 20 with private bathroom **payment** credit/debit cards, cash, cheques, euros

Room General

Official tourist board guide **Bed & Breakfast**

Yorkshire

LEEDS, Yorkshire Map ref 4B1
SAT NAV LS2 9LZ

*** GUEST HOUSE (enjoyEngland.com)

B&B PER ROOM PER NIGHT
S £27.00 – £40.00
D £40.00 – £50.00

Glengarth Guest House
162 Woodsley Road, Leeds LS2 9LZ
t (0113) 245 7940 **f** (0113) 216 8033 **e** info@woodsleyroad.com
w glengarthhotel.co.uk

Attractive, clean, family-run hotel close to city centre, university and city hospital. 20 minutes from Leeds City Airport. Most of the rooms have en suite facilities **directions** Please contact us for directions **open** All year **bedrooms** 6 single, 4 double, 2 twin, 3 family **bathrooms** 9 en suite, 9 with private bathroom **payment** credit/debit cards, cash, cheques, euros

Room · General · P

LEEMING BAR, Yorkshire Map ref 5C3
SAT NAV DL7 9LH

**** BED & BREAKFAST (enjoyEngland.com) / Gold AWARD

B&B PER ROOM PER NIGHT
S £45.00
D £75.00 – £80.00

Little Holtby
Leeming Bar, Northallerton, Bedale DL7 9LH
t (01609) 748762 **f** (01609) 748822 **e** littleholtby@yahoo.co.uk
w littleholtby.co.uk ONLINE MAP GUEST REVIEWS

Lovely period house with outstanding views. We hope to provide you with everything for your comfort. Log fires, comfy beds, upmarket toiletries, amazing breakfasts. Come and indulge. **directions** From A1 northbound, 2miles above junction A684 Bedale to Northallerton. **open** All year except Xmas and New Year **bedrooms** 2 double, 1 twin **bathrooms** 2 en suite, 1 with private bathroom **payment** cash, cheques

Room · General · P · Leisure

MALTON, Yorkshire Map ref 5D3
SAT NAV YO17 7EG

**** GUEST ACCOMMODATION (enjoyEngland.com)

B&B PER ROOM PER NIGHT
S £70.00 – £85.00
D £110.00 – £150.00
EVENING MEAL PER PERSON
£20.00

Old Lodge Malton
Old Maltongate, Malton YO17 7EG
t (01653) 690570 **f** (01653) 690652 **e** info@theoldlodgemalton.com
w theoldlodgemalton.com ONLINE BOOKING LAST MINUTE OFFERS

Tudor mansion with luxurious four-poster bedrooms. Great restaurant serving freshly prepared, locally-sourced food. All-day Yorkshire Sunday lunch. All-day tea, coffee and clotted cream scones. Super gardens. **directions** Take the Malton exit from the A64. We are approx. 250 yards from the town centre, towards Old Malton. We're behind a big, old wall. **open** All year **bedrooms** 14 double, 3 twin, family 2 **bathrooms** 20 en suite, 20 with private bathroom **payment** credit/debit cards, cash, cheques

Room · General · Leisure

MASHAM, Yorkshire Map ref 5C3
SAT NAV HG4 4EN

***** INN (enjoyEngland.com)

B&B PER ROOM PER NIGHT
S £95.00 – £175.00
D £95.00 – £175.00
EVENING MEAL PER PERSON
£12.00 – £25.00

WALKERS / CYCLISTS

The White Bear Hotel
Wellgarth, Masham HG4 4EN
t (01765) 689319 **e** sue@whitebearmasham.co.uk
w whitebearmasham.co.uk ONLINE MAP GUEST REVIEWS

The White Bear Hotel is a five star Inn of great character with a stong reputation for, freshly prepared locally sourced food, an atmospheric locals bar and superb bedroom accommodation **directions** Situated just north of Ripon, from the A1, take the B6267 to Masham. Once in Masham, follow the brown signs **open** All year **bedrooms** 4 double, 7 twin, 2 family, 1 suite **bathrooms** 14 en suite, 14 with private bathroom **payment** credit/debit cards, cash, cheques

Room · General · Leisure

Yorkshire

NORTHALLERTON, Yorkshire Map ref 5C3
SAT NAV DL6 2PB

★★★★ FARMHOUSE
Silver AWARD

B&B PER ROOM PER NIGHT
S £40.00 – £50.00
D £70.00 – £110.00
EVENING MEAL PER PERSON
£17.50 – £23.00

Lovesome Hill Farm
Lovesome Hill Farm, Lovesome Hill, Northallerton, North Yorkshire DL6 2PB
t (01609) 772311 f (01609) 774515 e lovesomehillfarm@btinternet.com
w lovesomehillfarm.co.uk ONLINE MAP LAST MINUTE OFFERS

Relax over tea and home-made biscuits. Savour our award winning breakfast using fresh farm produce. Family occasion, break or business, ideally placed near Northallerton the heart of North Yorkshire. **directions** Four miles North of Northallerton on the A1 towards Darlington, situated on the right hand side. **open** All year except Xmas and New Year **bedrooms** 1 single, 2 double, 1 twin, family **bathrooms** 5 en suite **payment** credit/debit cards, cash, cheques, euros

Room General Leisure

OSGOODBY, Yorkshire Map ref 5C3
SAT NAV YO7 2AL

★★★★ FARMHOUSE

B&B PER ROOM PER NIGHT
S £55.00
D £70.00 – £80.00

Low Osgoodby Grange
Low Osgoodby Grange, Bagby, Thirsk YO7 2AL
t (01845) 597241 e lowosgoodbygrange@googlemail.com

A warm welcome awaits at this 4 Star Silver Family B&B situated below Hambleton Hills. Ensuite rooms, high standard with breakfast using Local produce. Many attractions and good restaurants nearby. **directions** Situated 5 miles out of Thirsk off the A170 between the villages of Bagby and Kilburn. **bedrooms** 2 double, 1 family **bathrooms** 3 en suite, 3 with private bathroom **payment** cash, cheques

Room General Leisure

PICKERING, Yorkshire Map ref 5D3
SAT NAV YO18 8BA

★★★★ BED & BREAKFAST
Silver AWARD

B&B PER ROOM PER NIGHT
S £40.00 – £55.00
D £60.00 – £75.00

Eleven Westgate
Eden House, 11 Westgate, Pickering YO18 8BA
t (01751) 475111 e info@elevenwestgate.co.uk
w elevenwestgate.co.uk ONLINE MAP GUEST REVIEWS LAST MINUTE OFFERS

Elegant Victorian townhouse, luxury spacious ensuite accommodation, three minutes' walk from Pickering town centre. Lovely garden. Aga-cooked breakfast. Ideal for North Yorkshire and steam railway. Also run mountain biking holidays. **directions** On Westgate, a tree-lined road into Pickering on the A170 towards Scarborough. You will find us on the rt-hand side. **open** All year except Xmas **bedrooms** 3 double, 3 twin **bathrooms** 2 en suite, 1 with private bathroom **payment** credit/debit cards, cash, cheques

Room General Leisure

PICKERING, Yorkshire Map ref 5D3
SAT NAV YO18 8PB

★★★★ BED & BREAKFAST
Silver AWARD

B&B PER ROOM PER NIGHT
S £40.00 – £45.00
D £70.00 – £80.00
EVENING MEAL PER PERSON
£15.00 – £20.00

The Hawthornes
High Back Side, Middleton, Nr Pickering YO18 8PB
t (01751) 474755 f (01751) 474755 e paulaappleby@btinternet.com
w thehawthornes.co.uk ONLINE MAP

The Hawthornes offers comfortable accommodation in three generous-sized rooms, two on ground floor. Aga-cooked breakfast, home-baked bread. Tea and fresh baked scones on arrival. Ample parking. **directions** One and a half miles from Pickering. **open** All year except Xmas **bedrooms** 2 double, 1 twin **bathrooms** 3 en suite **payment** cash, cheques

BREAKFAST AWARD

Room General Leisure

514 Official tourist board guide **Bed & Breakfast**

Yorkshire

PICKERING, Yorkshire Map ref 5D3
SAT NAV YO18 8AP

Laurel Bank
Swainsea Lane, Pickering, North Yorkshire YO18 8AP
t 01751 476 399 mob 07766495071 e brenda.devine@btinternet.com
w laurelbankpickering.co.uk ONLINE MAP GUEST REVIEWS LAST MINUTE OFFERS

B&B PER ROOM PER NIGHT
S £40.00
D £70.00

Edwardian House. Warm welcome. Home cooking, local farm/fair trade produce. Quiet tree lined, off road parking. 10 minutes walk Pickering steam railway, excellent restaurants, North Yorkshire moors, coast, forest **directions** At roundabout A169 left Thirsk A170. Right traffic lights. First left before station. Follow road into Middleton Rd. Laurel Bank right 25m after Junior School. **open** All year except Xmas **bedrooms** 1 double, 1 twin **bathrooms** 1 en suite, 1 with private bathroom **payment** cash, cheques

Room General Leisure

PICKERING, Yorkshire Map ref 5D3
SAT NAV YO18 8QD

The Old Vicarage at Toftly View
The Old Vicarage, Toftly View, Pickering YO18 8QD
t (01751) 476126 f (01751) 477585 e oldvic@toftlyview.co.uk
w toftlyview.co.uk ONLINE MAP

B&B PER ROOM PER NIGHT
S £65.00 – £105.00
D £80.00 – £120.00

On the edge of The North Yorkshire Moors National Park, The Old Vicarage offers stylish accommodation with glorious views. We welcome guests with a blend of tradition and contemporary comforts. **directions** On entering Newton upon Rawcliffe from Pickering. Turn right into the gravel drive directly before the Church. The Old Vicarage is behind the Church. **open** March to October **bedrooms** 4 double **bathrooms** 4 en suite **payment** credit/debit cards, cash, cheques

BREAKFAST AWARD

Room General Leisure

PICKERING (4 MILES), Yorkshire Map ref 5D3
SAT NAV YO18 7JY

The Old Forge Bed & Breakfast
Wilton, North Yorkshire., Pickering YO18 7JY
t (01751) 477399 e theoldforge1@aol.com
w forgecottages.co.uk ONLINE MAP GUEST REVIEWS LAST MINUTE OFFERS

B&B PER ROOM PER NIGHT
S £43.00
D £68.00

Dating from 1701. Comfortable, quality, Bed and Breakfast. Private parking. Near Pickering Steam Railway, Dalby Forest, Yorkshire Moors, Eden Camp, Fishing. Cyclists Welcome. Close to Thornton-le-Dale. Excellent public transport. **directions** Follow the A170 Pickering–Scarborough road. Turn left in Wilton, just after the bus stop. Park in courtyard behind The Old Forge. Sign on building. **open** All year **bedrooms** 2 double, 1 twin **bathrooms** 3 en suite **payment** cash, cheques

Room General Leisure

RIPON, Yorkshire Map ref 5C3
SAT NAV HG4 1EN

Crescent Lodge Guest House
42 North Street, Ripon, North Yorkshire, United Kingdom HG4 1EN
t (01765) 609589 e jacksonp@datec.uk.com
w crescent-lodge.com ONLINE MAP GUEST REVIEWS

B&B PER ROOM PER NIGHT
S £50.00
D £65.00

Georgian Grade II listed building. You're assured a warm and friendly welcome to a Family run Guest House. Ideally located for local attractions, Yorkshire Dales and Moors. Exceptional breakfast choice. **directions** On North Street near to Ripon Police Station - directly opposite BP Fuel Station. 5 mins walk to City centre. Easy access to/from A1. **open** All year except Xmas and New Year **bedrooms** 1 single, 2 double, 1 twin, 1 family **bathrooms** 5 en suite **payment** credit/debit cards, cash, cheques, euros

Room General Leisure

Yorkshire

ROBIN HOODS BAY, Yorkshire Map ref 5D3
SAT NAV YO22 4RL

★★★ GUEST HOUSE (enjoyEngland.com)

B&B PER ROOM PER NIGHT
S £50.00
D £70.00

SPECIAL PROMOTIONS
Winter deals - 3 nights for the price of 2 from 1st November till 31st March.

Devon House
Station Road, Robin Hood's Bay, Whitby, North Yorkshire YO22 4RL
t (01947) 880197 e devonhouse.rhb@virgin.net
w devonhouserhb.co.uk ONLINE MAP LAST MINUTE OFFERS

Spectacular views of Ravenscar and the surrounding countryside can be enjoyed from the sun terrace of Devon House. All rooms are en-suite and have satellite TV, hot and cold drinks tray, fresh towels, toiletries and hair dry. Rooms are cleaned daily and vegetarian option is available for breakfast.

open All year except Xmas
bedrooms 1 single, 2 double, 1 twin
bathrooms 4 en suite
payment cash, cheques

directions From the A171 Whitby to Scarborough Road, Follow the signs for Robin Hood's Bay. Devon House overlooks the Bay opposite the small car park.

Room General Leisure

RUNSWICK BAY, Yorkshire Map ref 5D3
SAT NAV TS13 5HR

★★★★ GUEST HOUSE (enjoyEngland.com)

B&B PER ROOM PER NIGHT
S £48.00
D £77.00
EVENING MEAL PER PERSON
£24.50

Firs Guesthouse
Hinderwell Lane, Runswick Bay, Whitby TS13 5HR
t (01947) 840433 f (01947) 841616 e mandy.shackleton@talk21.com
w the-firs.co.uk ONLINE MAP

In a coastal village, eight miles north of Whitby. All rooms en suite with colour TV, tea/coffee facilities. Private parking. Children and dogs welcome. **directions** Please contact us for directions **open** April to October **bedrooms** 1 single, 3 double, 2 twin, 4 family **bathrooms** 10 en suite **payment** cash, cheques, euros

Room General Leisure

RUNSWICK BAY, Yorkshire Map ref 5D3
SAT NAV TS13 5HR

★★★ INN (enjoyEngland.com)

B&B PER ROOM PER NIGHT
S £52.00 – £60.00
D £62.00 – £70.00
EVENING MEAL PER PERSON
£7.25 – £13.75

Runswick Bay
2 Hinderwell Lane, Runswick Bay, North Yorkshire TS13 5HR
t (01947) 841010 f (01947) 841337 e info@therunswickbay.co.uk
w therunswickbay.co.uk ONLINE MAP GUEST REVIEWS LAST MINUTE OFFERS

A traditional coastal Inn, offering comfortable all year round accommodation, serving delicious seasonal menus including many specials. We are a popular choice for walkers, and welcome well-behaved pets. **directions** Follow signs off The A174 **open** All year **bedrooms** 4 double, 1 twin, 1 family **bathrooms** 6 en suite **payment** credit/debit cards, cash

Room General Leisure

516 Official tourist board guide Bed & Breakfa

Yorkshire

SALTBURN-BY-THE-SEA, Yorkshire Map ref 5C3

SAT NAV TS12 2QX

The Arches

Low Farm, Brotton, Saltburn-by-the-Sea, North Yorkshire TS12 2QX
t (01287) 677512 **f** (01287) 677150 **e** mail@gorallyschool.co.uk
w thearcheshotel.co.uk ONLINE MAP LAST MINUTE OFFERS

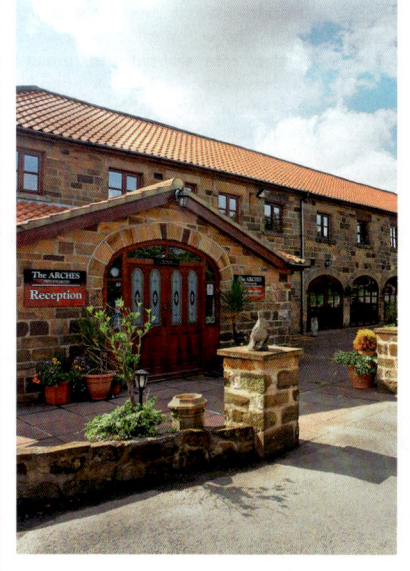

B&B PER ROOM PER NIGHT
S £35.00 – £40.00
D £60.00 – £100.00

SPECIAL PROMOTIONS
Special Promotions Upon Request.

The Arches offers a relaxing environment and overlooks spectacular views of cliffs and golf course. All the rooms are individually furnished with en suite bathrooms.

open All year
bedrooms 4 double, 4 twin, 3 family
bathrooms 11 en suite
payment credit/debit cards, cash, cheques

directions Please Refer To Website.

Room
General
Leisure

SCARBOROUGH, Yorkshire Map ref 5D3

SAT NAV YO12 6PG

The Alexander

33 Burniston Road, Scarborough YO12 6PG
t (01723) 363178 **e** enquiries@alexanderhotelscarborough.co.uk
w alexanderhotelscarborough.co.uk GUEST REVIEWS ONLINE BOOKING LAST MINUTE OFFERS

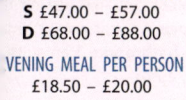

B&B PER ROOM PER NIGHT
S £47.00 – £57.00
D £68.00 – £88.00

EVENING MEAL PER PERSON
£18.50 – £20.00

SPECIAL PROMOTIONS
Special discount breaks for spring and autumn. Contact direct for best prices.

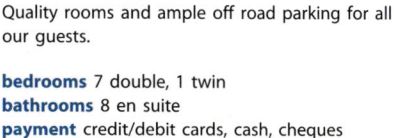

A detached friendly hotel, exclusively for adults. We specialise in comfort and quality, conveniently situated for visiting Whitby, Yorkshire Moors and only five minutes walk from the main Scarborough beach. Our food is excellent, prepared by our professional Chef. Quality rooms and ample off road parking for all our guests.

bedrooms 7 double, 1 twin
bathrooms 8 en suite
payment credit/debit cards, cash, cheques

directions On entering Scarborough head for North Bay. At North Bay take roundabout at Peasholm Park, head up hill towards Burniston. Property then 300m on left.

Room
General
Leisure

key to symbols see page 6   517

Yorkshire

SCARBOROUGH, Yorkshire Map ref 5D3
SAT NAV YO11 1NR

Blands Cliff Lodge
Blands Cliff, Scarborough YO11 1NR
t (01723) 351747 or 363653 **f** (01723) 363653 **e** stayinscarborough@gmail.com
w yorkshire-coast.co.uk/blandscliff LAST MINUTE OFFERS

enjoyEngland.com ★★★ GUEST HOUSE

B&B PER ROOM PER NIGHT
S £25.00 – £45.00
D £50.00 – £62.00

Our family run, town-centre guest house is within easy walking distance of seafront, shops, cafes & nightlife. Families and respectful small groups welcome. B&B or room only option available. **directions** From seafront road, turn at the Lifeboat station traffic lights into Eastborough, 3rd left into Blands Cliff (opposite Argos). **open** February to November **bedrooms** 3 single, 5 double, 4 twin, 4 family **bathrooms** 11 en suite, 5 with private bathroom **payment** credit/debit cards, cash, cheques

Room General Leisure

SCARBOROUGH, Yorkshire Map ref 5D3
SAT NAV YO12 7HU

Howdale
121 Queen's Parade, Scarborough YO12 7HU
t (01723) 372696 **e** mail@howdalehotel.co.uk
w howdalehotel.co.uk ONLINE MAP GUEST REVIEWS ONLINE BOOKING

enjoyEngland.com ★★★★ GUEST HOUSE

B&B PER ROOM PER NIGHT
S £25.00 – £28.00
D £52.00 – £68.00

Beautifully situated overlooking the North Bay and Scarborough Castle, yet close to town. We are renowned for our cleanliness and the friendly, efficient service we provide in a comfortable atmosphere. **directions** At traffic lights opposite railway station turn left. Next traffic lights turn right. At 1st roundabout turn left. Property is 0.5 miles on the right. **open** March to October **bedrooms** 1 single, 10 double, 2 twin, 2 family **bathrooms** 13 en suite **payment** credit/debit cards, cash

Room General

SCARBOROUGH, Yorkshire Map ref 5D3
SAT NAV YO11 3TP

Killerby Cottage Farm
Killerby Cottage Farm, Killerby Lane, Cayton, Scarborough YO11 3TP
t (01723) 581236 **f** (01723) 585465 **e** val@stainedglasscentre.co.uk
w killerbycottagefarm.co.uk ONLINE BOOKING LAST MINUTE OFFERS

enjoyEngland.com ★★★★ BED & BREAKFAST **Silver AWARD**

B&B PER ROOM PER NIGHT
S £45.00 – £50.00
D £60.00 – £80.00
EVENING MEAL PER PERSON
£15.00

Situated between Scarborough and Filey, 1.5 miles from Cayton Bay. Farmhouse of character adjacent to Stained-Glass Centre. Good food, lovely garden, warm welcome. **directions** Situated just off the B1261 between Cayton and Lebberston. **open** All year except Xmas and New Year **bedrooms** 2 double, 1 twin **bathrooms** 3 en suite **payment** credit/debit cards, cash, cheques, euros

Room General

SCARBOROUGH, Yorkshire Map ref 5D3
SAT NAV YO12 7QZ

Robyn's Guest House
139 Columbus Ravine, Scarborough YO12 7QZ
t (01723) 374217 **e** info@robynsguesthouse.co.uk
w robynsguesthouse.co.uk ONLINE MAP GUEST REVIEWS LAST MINUTE OFFERS

enjoyEngland.com ★★★★ GUEST HOUSE

B&B PER ROOM PER NIGHT
S £35.00 – £40.00
D £52.00 – £56.00
EVENING MEAL PER PERSON
£12.00 – £14.00

Robyn's Guest House offers you the very best in comfortable, luxury accommodation at affordable rates in the heart of Yorkshire's premier seaside resort. **directions** See website. **open** All year **bedrooms** 3 double, 3 family **bathrooms** 6 en suite **payment** credit/debit cards, cash, cheques

Room General Leisure

Yorkshire

SCARBOROUGH, Yorkshire Map ref 5D3
SAT NAV YO12 7HJ

★★★★ GUEST HOUSE

B&B PER ROOM PER NIGHT
S £30.00
D £27.00 – £30.00

Sylvern House
25 New Queen Street, Scarborough, North Yorkshire YO12 7HJ
t (01723) 360952 **e** richardandvicki@sylvernhouse.com
w sylvernhouse.com ONLINE MAP GUEST REVIEWS ONLINE BOOKING LAST MINUTE OFFERS

Enjoy a warm welcome, good home cooking and a friendly atmosphere with Vicki and Richard at Sylvern House. Situated close to both bays and town centre. Children and pets welcome. **directions** Directions to the hotel will be included with your booking acknowledgement. **open** All year **bedrooms** 2 single, 4 double, 1 twin, 2 family **bathrooms** 9 en suite **payment** credit/debit cards, cash, cheques

Room General Leisure

SCARBOROUGH, Yorkshire Map ref 5D3
SAT NAV YO12 7EY

★★★ GUEST HOUSE

B&B PER ROOM PER NIGHT
S £20.00 – £22.00
D £22.00 – £24.50

EVENING MEAL PER PERSON
£6.00 – £11.00

The Thoresby
53 North Marine Road, Scarborough YO12 7EY
t (01723) 365715

Small family-run guesthouse. Warm welcome on arrival. Recently refurbished to high standard. Close to all facilities, open air theatre opened summer 2010. Comfortable lounge to relax with colour TV. **directions** Please contact us for directions **open** All year **bedrooms** 2 single, 2 double, 2 twin, 3 family **bathrooms** 8 en suite, 1 with private bathroom **payment** credit/debit cards, cash, cheques

Room General Leisure

SCARBOROUGH, Yorkshire Map ref 5D3
SAT NAV YO12 7HY

★★★★ GUEST ACCOMMODATION

B&B PER ROOM PER NIGHT
S £33.50 – £35.00
D £55.00 – £66.00

SPECIAL PROMOTIONS
Oct-May inclusive (excl Bank Holidays): reduction of £1.50pppn when staying 2 nights or more.

The Whiteley
99-101 Queens Parade, Scarborough YO12 7HY
t (01723) 373514 **f** (01723) 373007 **e** whiteleyhotel@bigfoot.com
w yorkshirecoast.co.uk/whiteley

Small, family-run, non-smoking, licensed guest accommodation located in an elevated position overlooking the North Bay, close to the town centre and ideally situated for all amenities. The bedrooms are well co-ordinated and equipped with useful extras, many with sea views. Good home cooking is served in the traditional dining room.

open February to November
bedrooms 7 double, 3 family
bathrooms 10 en suite
payment credit/debit cards, cash, cheques

directions Left at traffic lights near railway station, right at next lights, Castle Road to roundabout. Left onto North Marine Road. 2nd right onto Queens Parade.

Room General

---

key to symbols see page 6   519

Yorkshire

SETTLE, Yorkshire Map ref 5B3

SAT NAV BD23 4PH

★★★★ INN

B&B PER ROOM PER NIGHT
S £42.00 – £60.00
D £75.00 – £85.00

EVENING MEAL PER PERSON
£8.75 – £13.95

SPECIAL PROMOTIONS
Special promotions available on request. Midweek and winter breaks available - please telephone for details.

Maypole Inn
Long Preston, Skipton, Nr Settle BD23 4PH
t 01729 840219 e robert@maypole.co.uk
w maypole.co.uk ONLINE MAP GUEST REVIEWS ONLINE BOOKING LAST MINUTE OFFERS

Traditional 17thC village inn on Maypole Green. Awarded regional CAMRA pub of the year 2010. Good base for walking, cycling and exploring the Dales. Homemade food available all day, every day. Selection of real ales and ciders. Open fires, Beer garden and ample parking.

open All year
bedrooms 1 single, 2 double, 3 family
bathrooms 6 en suite
payment credit/debit cards, cash, cheques, euros

directions We are situated on the A65, 10 miles North of Skipton or 4 miles South of Settle.

Room
General
Leisure

SKIPTON, Yorkshire Map ref 4B1

SAT NAV BD20 8LJ

★★★★★ BED & BREAKFAST **Silver AWARD**

B&B PER ROOM PER NIGHT
S £50.00 – £55.00
D £80.00 – £90.00

SPECIAL PROMOTIONS
Stays of 3 nights or more only £40pp (based on 2 people sharing). Children aged 3 and under - free.

Cononley Hall Bed & Breakfast
Main Street, Cononley, Skipton BD20 8LJ
t (01535) 633923 f (01535) 630200 e cononleyhall@madasafish.com
w cononleyhall.co.uk ONLINE MAP GUEST REVIEWS LAST MINUTE OFFERS

Grade II Listed Georgian house in unspoilt village, near to Skipton. Cononley Hall is ideally located for those wishing to explore the picturesque Yorkshire Dales or the Brontë countryside and attractions. All rooms en-suite and offer excellent facilities. Breakfast consists of local produce, including free-range eggs from Cononley hens.

open All year except Xmas and New Year
bedrooms 2 double, 1 twin
bathrooms 3 en suite
payment credit/debit cards, cash, cheques

directions From A629, follow sign for Cononley station. Across level crossing, up Main Street. New Inn on right. We are 25yds further up on left.

Room
General
Leisure

Yorkshire

SKIPTON, Yorkshire Map ref 4B1
SAT NAV BD23 3NT

Newton Grange
Bank Newton, Gargrave, Skipton BD23 3NT
t (01756) 796016 f (01756) 796016 e bookings@banknewton.fsnet.co.uk
w cravencountryconnections.co.uk GUEST REVIEWS

B&B PER ROOM PER NIGHT
S £39.00 – £49.00
D £78.00

A Grade II Listed Georgian farmhouse in rolling countryside, suitable for walking, cycling, horse-riding or touring. Rooms en suite or with private bathroom. Eating places nearby. **directions** A65 to Gargrave. Take Left over river. At Masons Arms pub turn Right for 1.5mls. In Banknewton left over steam for .5mls **open** All year **bedrooms** 2 double, 1 twin **bathrooms** 2 en suite, 1 with private bathroom **payment** cash, cheques

Room General Leisure

SKIPTON, Yorkshire Map ref 4B1
SAT NAV BD23 3BY

Poppy Cottage Guest House
Ivy Cottage Farm, Main Street, Carleton in Craven, Skipton, North Yorkshire BD23 3BY
t (01756) 792874 e steve@poppycottageguesthouse.co.uk
w poppycottageguesthouse.co.uk ONLINE MAP GUEST REVIEWS LAST MINUTE OFFERS

B&B PER ROOM PER NIGHT
S £55.00 – £60.00
D £75.00 – £85.00

Traditional Dales longhouse in quiet village location just 2 miles from Skipton. Lovely public footpath route into town crossing the River Aire. Original farmhouse features, private lounge, gardens and parking. **directions** On entering the village from Skipton, Poppy Cottage Guest House is on the left of Main Street with green sign to the front. **open** All year except Xmas **bedrooms** 2 double, 1 twin **bathrooms** 3 en suite **payment** credit/debit cards, cash, cheques

Room General Leisure

SOUTH KILVINGTON, Yorkshire Map ref 5C3
SAT NAV YO7 2NY

Manor House Cottage
Hag Lane, South Kilvington, Thirsk YO7 2NY
t (01845) 527712 e info@manor-house-cottage.co.uk
w manor-house-cottage.co.uk ONLINE BOOKING

B&B PER ROOM PER NIGHT
S £40.00 – £45.00
D £50.00 – £70.00

EVENING MEAL PER PERSON
£12.95 – £15.95

SPECIAL PROMOTIONS
October to April we offer 3 nights for the price of 2 and 7 nights for the price of 5

Manor house cottage is set in an idyllic location with many local attractions been close at hand including the Yorkshire Dales, national moors and parks. Harrogate and York are also very close at hand.

open All year
bedrooms 2 double, 1 twin
bathrooms 2 en suite, 1 with private bathroom
payment cash, cheques

directions Please contact us for directions

Room
General
Leisure

or key to symbols see page 6

521

Yorkshire

STAITHES, Yorkshire Map ref 5C3

SAT NAV TS13 5BG

Brooklyn Bed & Breakfast

Browns Terrace, Staithes, North Yorkshire TS13 5BG
t (01947) 841396   e m.heald@tiscali.co.uk
w brooklynuk.co.uk LAST MINUTE OFFERS

B&B PER ROOM PER NIGHT
S £35.00
D £60.00

Sea-captain's house in picturesque, historic fishing village. Comfortable, individually decorated rooms with view of Cowbar cliffs. Pets and children welcome. Generous breakfasts. Vegetarians welcome.

open All year except Xmas
bedrooms 2 double, 1 twin
payment cash, cheques

directions Please refer to the website www.brooklynuk.co.uk

Room
General
Leisure

STAPE, Yorkshire Map ref 5D3

SAT NAV YO18 8HP

High Muffles

High Muffles, Stape, Pickering YO18 8HP
t (01751) 417966   e candrew840@aol.com
w highmuffles.co.uk ONLINE MAP

B&B PER ROOM PER NIGHT
S £46.00 – £50.00
D £79.00 – £85.00
EVENING MEAL PER PERSON
£14.95 – £24.95

Beautifully renovated farmhouse accommodation with en suite bathrooms. Situated within Cropton Forest, North Yorkshire National Park. Perfect for walking and cycling. Ground floor annex rooms.
directions Please contact us for directions **open** All year except Xmas and New Year **bedrooms** 2 double **bathrooms** 2 en suite
payment cash, cheques

Room   General 14   Leisure

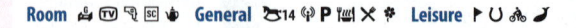

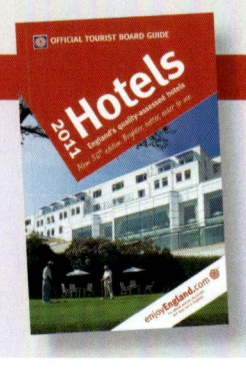

Looking for something else?

You can also buy a copy of our popular guide 'Hotels' including country house and town house hotels, metro and budget hotels, serviced apartments, restaurants with rooms and Spas in England 2011.

Now available in good bookshops and online at
visitbritainshop.com

£10.99

522   Official tourist board guide Bed & Breakfast

Yorkshire

STIRTON, Yorkshire Map ref 4B1

SAT NAV BD23 3LQ

Tarn House Country Inn

Stirton, Nr Skipton BD23 3LQ
t (01756) 794891 f (01756) 799040 e reception@tarnhouse.net
w partingtons.com ONLINE BOOKING

B&B PER ROOM PER NIGHT
S £52.00 – £55.00
D £60.00 – £68.00

Victorian country house built in a Gothic style and set in 2 acres of lawned gardens with magnificent views. Newly refurbished Dining Room & Function Room.

open All year except Xmas and New Year
bedrooms 1 single, 4 double, 4 twin, 1 family
bathrooms 10 en suite
payment credit/debit cards, cash, cheques
directions Please contact us for directions

Room General Leisure

THIRSK, Yorkshire Map ref 5C3

SAT NAV YO7 4AW

Borrowby Mill Bed & Breakfast

Borrowby, Thirsk YO7 4AW
t (01845) 537717 e markandvickipadfield@btinternet.com
w borrowbymill.co.uk ONLINE MAP

B&B PER ROOM PER NIGHT
S £47.50 – £49.50
D £73.00 – £76.00
EVENING MEAL PER PERSON
£21.50 – £22.50

Converted 18thC flour-mill in a secluded location between Thirsk and Northallerton. Convenient for touring Yorkshire Moors-Dales. Excellent breakfasts, dinners prepared by chef-proprietor. Drawing room with library or explore woodland gardens. **directions** From A19 trunk road take turn for Borrowby. The mill is situated just before turning into the village. **open** All year except Xmas and New Year **bedrooms** 1 double, 2 twin **bathrooms** 3 en suite **payment** credit/debit cards, cash, cheques

Room General Leisure

THIRSK, Yorkshire Map ref 5C3

SAT NAV YO7 2HJ

Garbutt Farm

Cold Kirby, Thirsk, North Yorkshire YO7 2HJ
t 01845 597 966 e lloyd.sallie@gmail.com
w garbuttfarm.co.uk ONLINE MAP

B&B PER ROOM PER NIGHT
S £40.00
D £80.00

Situated at the top of Sutton Bank and borders the Cleveland Way. Access to the Cleveland Way is direct from the farm for hikers, bikers and riders alike. **directions** Please contact us for directions **open** All year **bedrooms** 1 double, 1 twin **bathrooms** 2 en suite **payment** credit/debit cards, cash, cheques

Room General

523

Yorkshire

THIRSK, Yorkshire Map ref 5C3

SAT NAV YO7 2DY

Town Pasture Farm
Boltby, Thirsk YO7 2DY
t (01845) 537298
w townpasturefarm.co.uk

B&B PER ROOM PER NIGHT
S £35.00 – £40.00
D £60.00 – £65.00

Comfortable farmhouse in Boltby village within the North York Moors National Park. Views of the Hambleton Hills. Excellent walks. Horse-riding available in village. Great for touring. Colour TV in lounge. **directions** Leave Thirsk on A170 Scarborough Road. 1mile. Turn left for Boltby. At the far end of the village on right. Signposted Farmhouse Bed & Breakfast. **open** All year except Xmas **bedrooms** 1 twin, 1 family **bathrooms** 2 en suite **payment** cash, cheques

Room   General   Leisure

THIXENDALE, Yorkshire Map ref 4C1

SAT NAV YO17 9TG

The Cross Keys
The Cross Keys, Thixendale, Malton YO17 9TG
t (01377) 288372   e xkmairs@aol.com

B&B PER ROOM PER NIGHT
S £30.00
D £60.00

Family-run, award-winning, small village pub nestling in the valleys of the Yorkshire Wolds. Well situated on four major and several short, circular walks. Single occupancy available. **directions** Please contact us for directions **open** All year except Xmas and New Year **bedrooms** 1 double, 2 twin **bathrooms** 3 en suite **payment** credit debit cards, cash, cheques

Room   General

TRIANGLE (SOWERBY BRIDGE), Yorkshire Map ref 4B1

SAT NAV HX6 3EA

The Dene
Triangle, Sowerby Bridge HX6 3EA
t (01422) 823562   e thedene.triangle@gmail.com

B&B PER ROOM PER NIGHT
S £30.00
D £55.00
EVENING MEAL PER PERSON
£15.00

A Grade II Listed building. A mill owner's house with interesting courtyard setting and walled garden. Built in 1828. Quiet location but easy access to M62 and local towns. **directions** From A58 turn up hill at Triangle towards Millbank. Left on Sandy Dyke Lane. House on left just past double garage doors. **open** All year **bedrooms** 1 double, 1 twin, 1 family **bathrooms** 3 en suite **payment** cash, cheques

Room   General

WAKEFIELD, Yorkshire Map ref 4B1

SAT NAV WF1 1EH

The Bank House Hotel
11 Bank Street, Westgate, Wakefield WF1 1EH
t (01924) 368248   f (01924) 363724   e manager@thebankhousehotelandrestaurant.com

B&B PER ROOM PER NIGHT
S £40.00
D £50.00
EVENING MEAL PER PERSON
£5.00 – £10.00

City-centre licensed hotel run by professional staff. All rooms have en suite facilities, Sky Digital, telephones, tea/coffee facilities, restaurant facilities and room service. **directions** City central, 2 minutes walk away from Westgate's railway station and main bus depo. Close to all the main shops, restaurants, bars and Theatre. **open** All year **bedrooms** 3 single, 6 double, 3 twin, 1 family **bathrooms** 13 en suite **payment** credit/debit cards, cash, cheques

Room   General   Leisure

Yorkshire

WALKINGTON, Yorkshire Map ref 4C1
SAT NAV HU17 8RX

The Ferguson Fawsitt Arms
East End, Walkington, Beverley HU17 8RX
t (01482) 882665 f 01482882665 e info@fergusonfawsitt.com
w fergusonfawsitt.co.uk   ONLINE MAP   ONLINE BOOKING

B&B PER ROOM PER NIGHT
S £50.00 – £70.00
D £56.00 – £75.00

EVENING MEAL PER PERSON
£6.95 – £10.95

SPECIAL PROMOTIONS
Special rates are available for long stays or repeat stays. Please telephone for availability and rates.

The Ferguson Fawsitt Arms is set in the middle of the picturesque village of Walkington. We are just 3 miles from the market town of Beverely and Beverley racecourse. The Lodge is seperate from the main building in a quiet setting. All the rooms are modern and comfortable.

open All year
bedrooms 6 double, 4 twin
bathrooms 10 en suite
payment credit/debit cards, cash, cheques

directions We are in the centre of the village of Walkington on the B1230 Beverley to South Cave Road. The M62 is some 8 miles away.

WEST WITTON, Yorkshire Map ref 5B3
SAT NAV DL8 4LU

The Old Star
Main Street, West Witton, Leyburn DL8 4LU
t (01969) 622949 e enquiries@theoldstar.com
w theoldstar.com

B&B PER ROOM PER NIGHT
S £27.00 – £40.00
D £46.00 – £56.00

SPECIAL PROMOTIONS
Price reduction for stays of 3 or more nights and a further reduction for a week or more.

A seventeenth-century, stone-built former coaching inn set in the Yorkshire Dales National Park with views of Wensleydale from the rear of the property. Oak beams, log fire, cottage garden and a friendly atmosphere. An excellent centre for exploring the Dales with two nearby pubs for good food.

open All year except Xmas
bedrooms 4 double, 1 twin, 2 family
bathrooms 5 en suite
payment cash, cheques, euros

directions West Witton is on the A684, 4 miles west of Leyburn. Northallerton is our nearest station, there is a bus from Northallerton to West Witton.

key to symbols see page 6   525

Yorkshire

WHITBY, Yorkshire Map ref 5D3

SAT NAV YO21 3EG

The Middleham

3 Church Square, Whitby, North Yorkshire YO21 3EG
t 01947 603423 e themiddleham@btinternet.com
w themiddleham.com ONLINE MAP

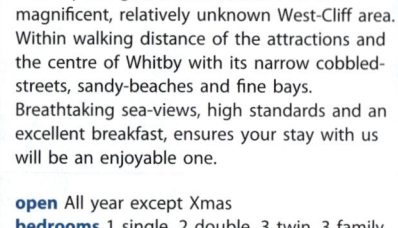

B&B PER ROOM PER NIGHT
S £32.00 – £34.00
D £64.00 – £76.00

A family-run guesthouse situated on the magnificent, relatively unknown West-Cliff area. Within walking distance of the attractions and the centre of Whitby with its narrow cobbled-streets, sandy-beaches and fine bays. Breathtaking sea-views, high standards and an excellent breakfast, ensures your stay with us will be an enjoyable one.

open All year except Xmas
bedrooms 1 single, 2 double, 3 twin, 3 family
bathrooms 8 en suite, 1 with private bathroom
payment credit/debit cards, cash, cheques

directions From A171 turn into Crescent Avenue then left at St Hilda's Church into Church Square.

Room
General
Leisure

WHITBY, Yorkshire Map ref 5D3

SAT NAV YO21 1QE

Prospect Villa Guest House

13 Prospect Hill, Whitby YO21 1QE
t (01947) 603118 f (01947) 825445 e prospectvillawhitby@hotmail.com
w prospectvillawhitby.co.uk ONLINE MAP ONLINE BOOKING LAST MINUTE OFFERS

B&B PER ROOM PER NIGHT
S £35.00
D £55.00 – £65.00

SPECIAL PROMOTIONS
3 night midweek break - £83 pp inlcuding Fish and Chip supper. Not available July or August.

Friendly, welcoming well established guest house in the heart of Whitby. Short walk from attractions and centre. Private parking and ground floor rooms available. Secure bike store. Mid victorian house, music themed breakfast room, comfortable bedrooms including family rooms.

open All year except Xmas
bedrooms 2 single, 2 double, 1 twin, 2 family
bathrooms 4 en suite
payment credit/debit cards, cash, cheques

directions Please contact us for directions

Room
General
Leisure

Yorkshire

WHITBY, Yorkshire Map ref 5D3

SAT NAV YO21 3QN

enjoyEngland.com
★★★★ GUEST ACCOMMODATION

B&B PER ROOM PER NIGHT
S £38.00
D £76.00

EVENING MEAL PER PERSON
£8.50

SPECIAL PROMOTIONS
November - March - 3 nights for the price of two. Disabled access available.

Sneaton Castle Centre
Sneaton Castle Centre, Whitby YO21 3QN
t (01947) 600051 f (01947) 603490 e reception@sneatoncastle.co.uk
w sneatoncastle.co.uk ONLINE MAP

St Francis House, set in stunning grounds of Sneaton Castle, on outskirts of Whitby and edge of the North York Moors. High quality en suite accommodation. Excellent breakfast. Ample parking.

open All year except Xmas and New Year
bedrooms 9 twin, 3 family
bathrooms 12 en suite
payment credit/debit cards, cash, cheques

directions Please refer to website.

Room
General
Leisure

WHITBY, Yorkshire Map ref 5D3

SAT NAV YO21 3EP

enjoyEngland.com
★★★ GUEST HOUSE

B&B PER ROOM PER NIGHT
S £25.00 – £30.00
D £29.00 – £35.00

EVENING MEAL PER PERSON
£15.00

Wentworth Guest House
27 Hudson Street, Whitby YO21 3EP
t (01947) 602433 e info@whitbywentworth.co.uk
w whitbywentworth.co.uk ONLINE MAP GUEST REVIEWS ONLINE BOOKING

Small, friendly family-run guesthouse. Pets welcome. Central location for beach, town pubs, restaurant and all the facilities of the North York coast and moors. **directions** Centre of West Cliff part of town, one street behind Royal Crescent. **open** All year **bedrooms** 1 single, 2 double, 1 twin, 3 family **bathrooms** 6 en suite, 1 with private bathroom **payment** cash, cheques

Room General Leisure

YORK, Yorkshire Map ref 4C1

SAT NAV YO24 1DE

enjoyEngland.com
★★★★ GUEST HOUSE

B&B PER ROOM PER NIGHT
S £55.00
D £60.00 – £90.00

The Acer Guest House
52 Scarcroft Hill, York YO24 1DE
t (01904) 653839 f (01904) 677017 e info@acerhotel.co.uk
w acerhotel.co.uk ONLINE MAP GUEST REVIEWS ONLINE BOOKING LAST MINUTE OFFERS

Licenced four star award winning B&B with parking, located on a quiet residential street only 10 minutes walk from the city and 15 minutes walk from the station. **directions** From South A1, A64, A1036(City), The Mount, Scarcroft Rd, Scarcroft Hill. From North A1, A59(York), Dalton Terrace, Albemarle Rd, Scarcroft Hill. **open** All year except Xmas **bedrooms** 3 double, 1 twin, 1 family **bathrooms** 5 en suite **payment** credit/debit cards, cash, cheques, euros

Room General Leisure

For **key to symbols** see page 6

527

Yorkshire

YORK, Yorkshire Map ref 4C1   SAT NAV YO30 7DD

23 Saint Marys Guesthouse
23, Saint Marys, Bootham, York YO30 7DD
t (01904) 622738   f (01904) 628802   e stmarys23@hotmail.com
w **23stmarys.co.uk**   ONLINE MAP   GUEST REVIEWS   ONLINE BOOKING   LAST MINUTE OFFERS

B&B PER ROOM PER NIGHT
S £45.00 – £55.00
D £75.00 – £95.00

SPECIAL PROMOTIONS
3rd night at 50% reduction
(excl peak periods).

Large Victorian terraced house peacefully set within five minutes' stroll of city centre. Spacious rooms, antique furnishings, en suite bedrooms of different sizes and character. Extensive breakfast menu in elegant surroundings. Julie and Chris will offer you a warm welcome to their home.

open All year except Xmas
bedrooms 1 single, 6 double, 1 twin, 1 family
bathrooms 9 en suite
payment credit/debit cards, cash, cheques, euros

directions Please contact us for directions

Room
General
Leisure

YORK, Yorkshire Map ref 4C1   SAT NAV YO31 7YH

Ascot House
80 East Parade, York YO31 7YH
t (01904) 426826   f (01904) 431077   e admin@ascothouseyork.com
w **ascothouseyork.com**   ONLINE MAP   GUEST REVIEWS   ONLINE BOOKING   LAST MINUTE OFFERS

B&B PER ROOM PER NIGHT
S £55.00 – £70.00
D £70.00 – £80.00

A family-run Victorian villa, built in 1869, with en suite rooms of character and many four-poster or canopy beds. Delicious English, continental and vegetarian breakfasts served. Fifteen minutes' walk to historic walled city centre, castle museum or York Minster. Residential licence and residents' lounge. Private enclosed car park.

open All year except Xmas
bedrooms 8 double, 2 twin, 3 family
bathrooms 12 en suite, 1 with private bathroom
payment credit/debit cards, cash, cheques

directions From M1 take A64 then A1036 from EAST into York. 100yds past 30mph signs, take 2nd exit off roundabout. Right at lights into East Parade.

Room
General

528   Official tourist board guide **Bed & Breakfast**

Yorkshire

YORK, Yorkshire Map ref 4C1
SAT NAV YO24 1AX

Ashberry
103 The Mount, York YO24 1AX
t (01904) 647339 **f** (01904) 733698 **e** steveandsara@theashberry.co.uk
w theashberry.co.uk GUEST REVIEWS ONLINE BOOKING LAST MINUTE OFFERS

B&B PER ROOM PER NIGHT
S £45.00 – £60.00
D £60.00 – £90.00

The Ashberry is a charming 4 star bed and breakfast accommodation in a Victorian townhouse close to York city centre, the racecourse and 10-15 mins walk from the railway station. **directions** From A64 take A1036. After 1 mile racecourse is on right. Up slight hill through lights. The Ashberry is on the right after 50 metres **open** All year except Xmas **bedrooms** 3 double, 1 twin, 1 family **bathrooms** 5 en suite **payment** credit/debit cards, cash, cheques

Room   General

YORK, Yorkshire Map ref 4C1
SAT NAV YO10 5AA

Barbican House
20 Barbican Road, York YO10 5AA
t (01904) 627617 **f** (01904) 647140 **e** info@barbicanhouse.co.uk
w barbicanhouse.co.uk ONLINE MAP GUEST REVIEWS ONLINE BOOKING LAST MINUTE OFFERS

B&B PER ROOM PER NIGHT
S £66.00 – £92.00
D £82.00 – £96.00

SPECIAL PROMOTIONS
Discount on stays of 3 or more days (excl Fri and Sat). See Barbican House own website for details.

Welcome to our wonderful restored Victorian villa overlooking York Minster and medieval city walls. 500 yards to City Centre. Delightful bedrooms, each individually decorated to complement the charm and character of the period. All rooms are en suite. Full English breakfast using local, free-range produce. Free parking.

open All year
bedrooms 6 double, 1 twin, 1 family
bathrooms 8 en suite
payment credit/debit cards, cash, cheques

directions From A64 proceed north on A19 through Fulford then follow sign for York Hospital. This will take you to Barbican Road. Barbican House on right.

Room
General 10
Leisure

YORK, Yorkshire Map ref 4C1
SAT NAV YO31 8HS

Cumbria House
2 Vyner Street, Haxby Road, York YO31 8HS
t (01904) 636817 **e** candj@cumbriahouse.freeserve.co.uk
w cumbriahouse.com ONLINE MAP LAST MINUTE OFFERS

B&B PER ROOM PER NIGHT
S £28.00 – £32.00
D £54.00 – £65.00

Family-run guesthouse, warm welcome assured, 12 minutes' walk from York Minster, City Centre and major attractions. En suites available. Easily located from ring road. Private car park. Special offers available. **directions** See online map and directions. **open** All year **bedrooms** 1 single, 3 double, 2 family **bathrooms** 2 en suite **payment** credit/debit cards, cash, cheques

Room   General

Yorkshire

YORK, Yorkshire Map ref 4C1   SAT NAV YO24 4DF

Bishops

135 Holgate Road, York YO24 4DF
t (01904) 628000 f (01904) 628181 e enquiries@bishopsyork.co.uk
w bishopsyork.co.uk ONLINE MAP ONLINE BOOKING LAST MINUTE OFFERS

B&B PER ROOM PER NIGHT
S £40.00 – £50.00
D £70.00 – £120.00

SPECIAL PROMOTIONS
Celebration Package of flowers, chocolates and champagne. Business-traveller and off-peak, mid-week, short-break rates available Sun-Thu.

Elegant Victorian villa, peaceful yet near to city. Spacious, comfortable interior, individually styled suites and bedrooms all en suite. Hearty breakfast using fresh, local produce. Fully licensed establishment with a friendly family atmosphere and off-road parking. Ideal base for exploring our beautiful Roman city and the Yorkshire countryside. 5% surcharge on credit cards.

open All year except Xmas
bedrooms 1 single, 2 double, 1 twin, 3 family, 6 suites
bathrooms 13 en suite
payment credit/debit cards, cash

directions Take the A59 from the A1. This becomes Holgate Road where the establishme is situated. Or a 15-minute walk from the railway station.

Room   General   Leisure

YORK, Yorkshire Map ref 4C1   SAT NAV YO31 1ES

Blakeney House & Restaurant

180 Stockton Lane, York YO31 1ES
t (01904) 422786 e reception@blakeneyhotel-york.co.uk
w blakeneyhotel-york.co.uk ONLINE MAP GUEST REVIEWS ONLINE BOOKING LAST MINUTE OFFERS

B&B PER ROOM PER NIGHT
S £38.00 – £51.00
D £58.00 – £82.00

EVENING MEAL PER PERSON
£16.00 – £21.00

SPECIAL PROMOTIONS
Special B&B rates for stays of 2, 3-6 or 7 nights. Special dinner inclusive rates for 2 nights or more.

We offer a warm welcome, free parking, comfortable en-suite rooms, lounge, bar, spacious restaurant, hearty English breakfasts, fine evening dining and pleasant friendly service. Ideally located within 20 minutes' walk or 7 minutes bus ride of historic city centre. No smoking throughout. Free Wi-Fi access.

open All year except Xmas
bedrooms 3 single, 5 double, 3 twin, 6 family
bathrooms 15 en suite, 2 with private bathroom
payment credit/debit cards, cash, cheques, euros

directions A64 York East, take 1st left exits at roundabouts (A1036). Turn left onto Hopgrove Lane South. Right at T-junction. Blakeney on le 1.5 miles.

Room   General   Leisure

530   Official tourist board guide Bed & Breakfa

Yorkshire

YORK, Yorkshire Map ref 4C1
SAT NAV YO30 6AE

Blossoms York
28 Clifton, York YO30 6AE
t (01904) 652391 **f** (01904) 652492 **e** reception@blossomsyork.co.uk
w blossomsyork.co.uk ONLINE MAP GUEST REVIEWS ONLINE BOOKING LAST MINUTE OFFERS

B&B PER ROOM PER NIGHT
S £39.00 – £85.00
D £45.00 – £97.50

EVENING MEAL PER PERSON
£2.50 – £8.50

SPECIAL PROMOTIONS
Free Wi-Fi. Special midweek rates. Discounts for 3+ nights stays.

Centrally located in a Georgian townhouse on a tree-lined avenue, only minutes' walk from the Minster, with shops, restaurants and bars nearby. Free parking; large family rooms; fresh local breakfasts; bar snacks; friendly welcome; laundry service; maps & local information.

open All year
bedrooms 6 double, 2 twin, 8 family
bathrooms 16 en suite
payment credit/debit cards, cash

directions Located on the A19; 15 minutes walk or £6 taxi from the train station. See website or call for full directions.

Room
General
Leisure

YORK, Yorkshire Map ref 4C1
SAT NAV YO24 1QG

Curzon Lodge & Stable Cottages
23 Tadcaster Road, York YO24 1QG
t (01904) 703157 **f** (01904) 703157 **e** admin@curzonlodge.com
w smoothhound.co.uk/hotels/curzon ONLINE MAP

B&B PER ROOM PER NIGHT
S £49.50 – £58.00
D £65.00 – £85.00

Charming 17thC house and converted stables, once home to the Terry 'chocolate' family. Comfortable rooms and freshly prepared choice of breakfasts. Conveniently situated. Parking in grounds. Restaurants nearby. **directions** From A64 bypass, take A1036 (York west exit), follow City Centre signs. 2 miles on right between York Holiday Inn and Marriott hotels. **open** All year except Xmas and New Year **bedrooms** 1 single, 6 double, 2 twin, 1 family **bathrooms** 10 en suite **payment** credit/debit cards, cash, cheques

Room   General   Leisure

YORK, Yorkshire Map ref 4C1
SAT NAV YO23 1ND

Dairy Guest House
3 Scarcroft Road, York YO23 1ND
t (01904) 639367 **e** stay@dairyguesthouse.co.uk
w dairyguesthouse.co.uk ONLINE MAP ONLINE BOOKING

B&B PER ROOM PER NIGHT
S £50.00 – £65.00
D £60.00 – £85.00

A lovingly restored and upgraded Victorian town house with original features, situated just 300yds from the medieval city walls and within an easy stroll of York's many attractions and museums. **directions** Please contact us for directions **open** All year **bedrooms** 4 double, 1 twin, 1 family **bathrooms** 6 en suite **payment** credit/debit cards, cash

Room   General

---

key to symbols see page 6   531

Yorkshire

YORK, Yorkshire Map ref 4C1
SAT NAV YO30 7AH

Grange Lodge Guest House
52 Bootham Crescent, York YO30 7AH
t (01904) 621137 e grange-lodge@btconnect.com
w grange-lodge.com ONLINE MAP GUEST REVIEWS

B&B PER ROOM PER NIGHT
S £35.00 – £45.00
D £70.00 – £95.00

Attractive, tastefully furnished Victorian townhouse with a friendly atmosphere. Special emphasis is given to food, cleanliness and hospitality. Very close to York City Centre. All rooms have ensuite facilities. **directions** Please contact us for directions **open** All year **bedrooms** 1 single, 4 double, 1 twin, 2 family **bathrooms** 8 en suite **payment** credit/debit cards, cash, cheques

Room General

YORK, Yorkshire Map ref 4C1
SAT NAV YO31 7EH

The Hazelwood
24-25 Portland Street, York YO31 7EH
t (01904) 626548 f (01904) 628032 e reservations@thehazelwoodyork.com
w thehazelwoodyork.com ONLINE MAP ONLINE BOOKING LAST MINUTE OFFERS

B&B PER ROOM PER NIGHT
S £55.00 – £105.00
D £80.00 – £125.00

SPECIAL PROMOTIONS
33% reduction Nov-Easter min 3 nights. See web site for full details.

Situated in the very heart of York only 400yds from York Minster in an extremely quiet residential area. An elegant Victorian townhouse with private car park providing high-quality accommodation in tastefully furnished and individually styled en-suite bedrooms. Choice of breakfasts including vegetarian all prepared using quality ingredients. Completely non-smoking. Licensed.

open All year
bedrooms 1 single, 7 double, 3 twin, 2 family
bathrooms 13 en suite
payment credit/debit cards, cash, cheques

directions Situated in city centre 400yards from York Minster in side street off inner ring road (Gillygate). Best approached from the north on the A19.

Room General Leisure

YORK, Yorkshire Map ref 4C1
SAT NAV YO10 4HE

Limes
135 Fulford Road, York YO10 4HE
t (01904) 624548 f (01904) 624944 e queries@limeshotel.co.uk
w limeshotel.co.uk LAST MINUTE OFFERS

B&B PER ROOM PER NIGHT
S £55.00 – £80.00
D £70.00 – £95.00

Friendly guest house, near city, racecourse, university and golf course. Licensed Bar. Private car park. Ensuite rooms,welcome tray,colour TV, clock/alarm radio,ipod docking station, hairdryer, heated towel rails,toiletries. Superb breakfast. **directions** From A1, take A64 to York. A64 becomes the outer ring road of York. Take slip road for York Centre, A19 (Selby). **open** All year except Xmas **bedrooms** 4 double, 3 twin, 1 family **bathrooms** 8 en suite **payment** credit/debit cards, cash, cheques, euros

BREAKFAST AWARD

Room General

Yorkshire

YORK, Yorkshire Map ref 4C1

SAT NAV YO31 7TQ

Heworth Court B&B and Lamplight Restaurant

76-78 Heworth Green, York YO31 7TQ
t (01904) 425156 **f** (01904) 415290 **e** hotel@heworth.co.uk
w **heworth.co.uk** ONLINE MAP GUEST REVIEWS ONLINE BOOKING LAST MINUTE OFFERS

B&B PER ROOM PER NIGHT
S £40.50 – £75.00
D £59.00 – £99.00

EVENING MEAL PER PERSON
£12.95 – £19.95

SPECIAL PROMOTIONS
www.heworth.co.uk
click Roombasket for special offers. Example:special rates dbb rates from £39.50-£54.50pppn in Standard Room.

Offering bed and full English breakfast. Lamplight Restaurant open Tuesday to Saturday 6pm-8.30pm (last orders 8pm). Twelve minutes from York Minster. Free parking. 'Minster Bells' bar features over 30 malt whiskies, draught beers and soft drinks. Superking-size, king-size with Rolltop Bath, Four-poster, Executive, VIP Chandelier and Standard rooms.

open All year except Xmas and New Year
bedrooms 2 single, 19 double, 5 twin, 2 family
bathrooms 28 en suite
payment credit/debit cards, cash

directions Drive around York Outer Ring Road (bypass A64 or A1237) until reaching double roundabout on east side of York. Exit York A1036, hotel on left.

Room General Leisure

YORK, Yorkshire Map ref 4C1

SAT NAV YO30 2AY

The Manor House

Main Street, Linton-on-Ouse, York YO30 2AY
t (01347) 848391 **e** manorguesthouse@tiscali.co.uk
w **manorguesthouse.co.uk** ONLINE MAP GUEST REVIEWS ONLINE BOOKING LAST MINUTE OFFERS

B&B PER ROOM PER NIGHT
S £45.00 – £55.00
D £68.00 – £76.00

EVENING MEAL PER PERSON
£14.00 – £25.00

SPECIAL PROMOTIONS
Book full week and pay for 6 nights. Various seasonal and midweek offers. Excellent dinners available on request from £14.00.

Relax in a beautiful listed Georgian Manor House with award winning spacious comfortable rooms and ground-floor suite. Lovely gardens, private parking. Set in a lovely village with riverside walks and 3 nearby pubs with restaurants. 10 minute drive to York park and ride and ideal for Dales and Moors.

open All year except Xmas and New Year
bedrooms 1 single, 2 double, 2 twin, 1 family, 1 suite
bathrooms 7 en suite
payment credit/debit cards, cash, cheques, euros

directions From bypass/A1237 roundabout north onto A19. 2 miles turn left at Shipton. 2 miles turn left and follow to Linton. Last house on right.

BREAKFAST AWARD Room General Leisure

Yorkshire

YORK, Yorkshire Map ref 4C1   SAT NAV YO31 8RB

enjoyEngland.com ★★★ GUEST ACCOMMODATION

B&B PER ROOM PER NIGHT
D £66.00 – £68.00

SPECIAL PROMOTIONS
7 Nights Bed and Breakfast £205pp Children £70 under14 sharing 2 adults to May 2011.Tel for weekly rate summer 2011.

Palm Court
17 Huntington Road, York YO31 8RB
t (01904) 639387 **f** (01904) 639387 **e** helencoll_2000@hotmail.com
w thepalmcourt.org.uk ONLINE MAP

A very warm welcome awaits you at our elega[nt] Victorian family run guest accommodation. Offering excellent value for money. Overlookin[g] River Foss, a pleasant five minute walk to Minster. Tastefully decorated spacious double, twin and family en-suite rooms with welcome tray, TV and central heating. Free private parking.

open All year except Xmas and New Year
bedrooms 2 double, 2 twin, 4 family
bathrooms 8 en suite
payment cash, cheques

directions Please see at www.thepalmcourt.org.uk

Room
General

YORK, Yorkshire Map ref 4C1   SAT NAV YO23 1EN

enjoyEngland.com ★★★ GUEST ACCOMMODATION

B&B PER ROOM PER NIGHT
S £38.00 – £50.00
D £76.00 – £106.00

Tyburn Guest House
11 Albemarle Road, The Mount, York YO23 1EN
t (01904) 655069 **f** (01904) 655069 **e** info@tyburnguesthouse.co.uk
w tyburnguesthouse.co.uk

Family-owned and -run guesthouse overlooking the racecourse. In quiet and beautiful area, close to the city centre and railway station. **directions** Please contact us for directions **open** Easter to November **bedrooms** 2 single, 3 double, 1 twin, 7 family **bathrooms** 12 en suite, 1 with private bathroom **payment** cash, cheques

Room   General

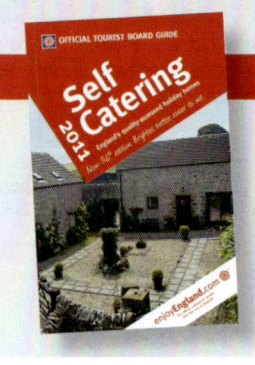

Looking for something else?

You can also buy a copy of our popular guide 'Self Catering' including self-catering holiday homes, approved caravan holiday homes, boat accommodation and holiday cottage agencies in England 2011.

Now available in good bookshops and online at
visitbritainshop.com

£11.99

Yorkshire

YORK, Yorkshire Map ref 4C1

SAT NAV YO31 7TQ

York House

62 Heworth Green, York YO31 7TQ
t (01904) 427070 f (01904) 427070 e yorkhouse.bandb@tiscali.co.uk
w yorkhouseyork.co.uk ONLINE MAP GUEST REVIEWS

B&B PER ROOM PER NIGHT
S £31.00 – £35.00
D £62.00 – £72.00

SPECIAL PROMOTIONS
Four-poster rooms £35.50 – £40.50 pppn.

Located a short stroll from the heart of one of Europe's most historic cities, York House is the perfect base for a visit to York or the surrounding area. A Georgian house with later additions, rooms feature all the modern conveniences you could possibly need for a relaxing, enjoyable stay.

open All year except Xmas and New Year
bedrooms 1 single, 5 double, 1 twin, 1 family
bathrooms 7 en suite, 1 with private bathroom
payment credit/debit cards, cash

directions North east of York, A1036 signed City Centre. Straight over roundabouts and 2 sets traffic lights, next mini-roundabout 3rd exit. York House 300yds on left.

Room   General

All Assessed Accommodation

Yorkshire

ACKLAM

ut Pond Barn ★★★★
mhouse
ut Pond Barn, Acklam Malton,
lton
17 9RG
t (01653) 693088
e mandg.tpb@gmail.com
w troutpondbarn.co.uk

ADDINGHAM

ck House Farm ★★★★
d & Breakfast SILVER AWARD
orside Lane, Addingham, Ilkley
29 9JX
t (01943) 830397
e cathandave@tiscali.co.uk
w beckhousefarm.co.uk

mb Beck Farmhouse Bed & eakfast ★★★★ *Bed & Breakfast*
LD AWARD
orside Lane, Addingham
orside, Ilkley
29 9JX
t (01943) 830400
e croft-lumbbeck@tiscali.co.uk

AINDERBY MIERS

nderby Myers Farm ★★★
mhouse
dale, North Yorkshire, Bedale
8 1PF
t (01609) 748668

AINTHORPE

Rowantree Farm ★★★★
Farmhouse
Fryup Road, Ainthorpe, Whitby
YO21 2LE
t (01287) 660396
e krbsatindall@aol.com
w rowantreefarm.co.uk

AIRTON

Lindon House ★★★ *Guest House*
Airton, Skipton
BD23 4BE
t (01729) 830418
e lindonguesthouse@googlemail.com
w yorkshirenet.co.uk/stayat/lindonguesthouse

ALDBROUGH

Wentworth House ★★★★
Guest House
12 Seaside Road, Aldbrough,
Hornsea
HU11 4RX
t (01964) 527246
e enquiry@wentworthhousehotel.com
w wentworthhousehotel.com

West Carlton Country Guest House ★★★★ *Guest House*
SILVER AWARD
Carlton Road, Aldbrough, Hornsea
HU11 4RB
t (01964) 527324
e caroline@west-carlton.co.uk
w west-carlton.co.uk

ALDFIELD

Bay Tree Farm ★★★★ *Farmhouse*
GOLD AWARD
Aldfield, Ripon
HG4 3BE
t (01765) 620394
e val@btfarm.entadsl.com
w baytreefarm.co.uk

ALLERSTON

**Rains Farm Bed & Breakfast
★★★★** *Farmhouse* SILVER AWARD
Rains Farm, Allerston, Pickering
YO18 7PQ
t (01723) 859333
e rainsholidays@btconnect.com
w rains-farm-holidays.co.uk

AMOTHERBY

Cherry Tree B&B ★★★★
Bed & Breakfast
4 Cherry Tree Walk, Amotherby,
Malton
YO17 6TR
t (01653) 690825
e cherrytreeamotherby@googlemail.com
w 4cherrytree.googlepages.com

AMPLEFORTH

Carr House Farm ★★★ *Farmhouse*
Ampleforth, North Yorkshire,
Helmsley
YO62 4ED
t (01347) 868526
e anna@carrhousefarm.co.uk
w carrhousefarm.co.uk

Daleside ★★★★★ *Bed & Breakfast*
GOLD AWARD
East End, Ampleforth, Helmsley
YO62 4DA
t (01439) 788266
e paul.williams266@btinternet.com

Shallowdale House ★★★★★
Guest Accommodation
GOLD AWARD
West End, Ampleforth, Helmsley
YO62 4DY
t (01439) 788325
e phillip@shallowdalehouse.co.uk
w shallowdalehouse.co.uk

APPLETON-LE-MOORS

The Moors Inn ★★★ *Inn*
Appleton-le-Moors, York
YO62 6TF
t (01751) 417435
e enquiries@moorsinn.co.uk
w moorsinn.co.uk

APPLETON-LE-STREET

Cresswell Arms ★★★★ *Inn*
Cresswell Arms, Appleton-le-Street,
Malton
YO17 6PG
t (01653) 693647
e tombrisbane@aol.com
w cresswellarms.co.uk

ARKENGARTHDALE

Chapel Farmhouse ★★★★
Bed & Breakfast
Whaw, Arkengarthdale, Reeth
DL11 6RT
t (01748) 884062
e info@chapelfarmhouse.co.uk
w yorkshirenet.co.uk/stayat/chapelfarm

The Charles Bathurst Inn ★★★★
Inn
The Charles Bathurst Inn,
Arkengarthdale, Reeth
DL11 6EN
t (01748) 884567
e info@cbinn.co.uk
w cbinn.co.uk

---

key to symbols see page 6   535

Yorkshire

ASKRIGG

Apothecary's House ★★★★
Guest Accommodation
SILVER AWARD
Main Street, Askrigg, Leyburn
DL8 3HT
t (01969) 650626
e bookings@apothecaryhouse.co.uk
w apothecaryhouse.co.uk

Bottom Chapel ★★★★
Bed & Breakfast
Station Road, Askrigg, Leyburn
DL8 3HZ
t (01969) 650180/ 07866 118315
e ianandbetsy@bottomchapel.co.uk
w bottomchapel.co.uk

Home Farm ★★★★ Farmhouse
Stalling Busk, Askrigg, Leyburn
DL8 3DH
t (01969) 650360
w wensleydale.org/premier/15/index.html

Milton House ★★★★
Guest Accommodation
Leyburn Road, Askrigg, Leyburn
DL8 3HJ
t (01969) 650217
e stay_miltonhouse@btinternet.com
w a1tourism.com/uk/milton.house.html

AUSTWICK

The Dalesbridge Centre ★★★
Group Accommodation
The Dalesbridge Centre, Austwick, Settle
LA2 8AZ
t (01524) 251021
e info@dalesbridge.co.uk
w dalesbridge.co.uk

Pengarth ★★★★ Bed & Breakfast
Pengarth, Austwick, Settle
LA2 8BD
t (01524) 251073
e jishreid@austwick.org
w pengarth.co.uk

Scar Close Farmhouse ★★★★
Guest House
Feizor, Austwick, Settle
LA2 8DF
t (01729) 823496
e yeadonjohn@yahoo.com
w scarclosefarmhouse.co.uk

Wood View ★★★★ Guest House
SILVER AWARD
The Green, Austwick, Settle
LA2 8BB
t (01524) 251190
e woodview@austwick.org
w woodviewbandb.co.uk

AYSGARTH

Cornlee ★★★★ Guest House
SILVER AWARD
Aysgarth, Leyburn, Aysgarth Falls
DL8 3AE
t (01969) 663779
e cornlee.aysgarth@btinternet.com
w cornlee.co.uk

Field House ★★★★
Bed & Breakfast SILVER AWARD
East End, Aysgarth, Aysgarth Falls
DL8 3AB
t (01969) 663556
e rosfieldhouse@btinternet.com
w fieldhouse-aysgarth.co.uk

Heather Cottage Guesthouse ★★★★ Bed & Breakfast
SILVER AWARD
Heather Cottage, Aysgarth, Leyburn
DL8 3AH
t (01969) 663129
e hcind@btinternet.com
w heathercottage.com

ASKRIGG

Wensleydale Farmhouse ★★★★
Guest Accommodation
Wensleydale Farmhouse, Aysgarth, Aysgarth Falls
DL8 3SR
t (01969) 663534
e stay@wensleydale-farmhouse.co.uk
w wensleydale-farmhouse.co.uk

Yoredale House ★★★★
Guest House
Aysgarth, Leyburn, Aysgarth Falls
DL8 3AE
t (01969) 663423
e info@yoredalehouse.com
w yoredalehouse.com

BAILDON

Ford House Farm Bed & Breakfast ★★★★ Guest Accommodation
SILVER AWARD
Ford House, Buck Lane, Shipley
BD17 7RW
t (01274) 584489
e info@fordhousefarmbedandbreakfast.co.uk
w fordhousefarmbedandbreakfast.co.uk

Langbar House ★★★★
Bed & Breakfast
Langbar House, 8 Temple Rhydding Drive, Bradford
BD17 5PU
t (01274) 599900
e enquiry@langbarhouse.co.uk
w langbarhouse.co.uk

BAINTON

Wolds Village Luxury Guest Accommodation ★★★★
Guest Accommodation
SILVER AWARD
Manor Farm, Bainton, Driffield
YO25 9EF
t (01377) 217698
e sally@woldsvillage.co.uk
w woldsvillage.co.uk

BARLOW

Berewick House ★★★★
Guest House SILVER AWARD
Park Lane, Barlow, Selby
YO8 8EW
t (01757) 617051
e wilson.guesthouse@berewick.co.uk
w berewick.co.uk

BARMBY MOOR

Alder Carr House ★★★
Bed & Breakfast
York Road, Barmby Moor, York
YO42 4HU
t (01759) 380566

Mohair Farm ★★★ Bed & Breakfast
York Road, Barmby Moor, York
YO42 4HU
t (01759) 380308

BARNBY DUN

The Lodge ★★★★
Guest Accommodation
Station Road, Barnby Dun, Doncaster
DN3 1HA
t (01302) 881251
e thelodge@olivetreepub.co.uk
w olivetreepub.co.uk

BECKWITHSHAW

Central House Farm ★★★★
Farmhouse SILVER AWARD
Haverah Park, Beckwithshaw, Harrogate
HG3 1SQ
t (01423) 566050
e jayne@centralhousefarm.freeserve.co.uk
w centralhousefarm.co.uk

BEDALE

Castle Arms Inn ★★★★ Inn
Snape, Bedale
DL8 2TB
t (01677) 470270
e castlearms@aol.com
w castlearmsinn.com

Elmfield House ★★★★
Guest House SILVER AWARD
Arrathorne, Bedale
DL8 1NE
t (01677) 450558
e stay@elmfieldhouse.co.uk
w elmfieldhouse.co.uk

BEIGHTON

Beighton Bed & Breakfast ★★★
Guest Accommodation - Room Only
48-50 High Street, Beighton, Sheffield
S20 1EA
t (0114) 269 2004
e beightonbandb@aol.com

BELL BUSK

Tudor House ★★★★ Guest House
Bell Busk, Nr. Malham, Skipton
BD23 4DT
t (01729) 830301
e tudorhousebb@gmail.com
w tudorbellbusk.co.uk

BELLERBY

Grove House ★★★ Guest House
8 Grove Square, Leyburn
DL8 5AE
t (01969) 622569
e info@grove-hotel.com
w grove-hotel.com

Westfield Farm ★★★★
Guest Accommodation
Westfields Farm, Moor Road, Bellerby, Leyburn
DL8 5QX
t (01969) 622047
e stay@westfieldsfarmbandb.co.uk
w westfieldsfarmbandb.co.uk

BENTHAM

Halsteads Barn ★★★★★
Bed & Breakfast SILVER AWARD
Mewith, Bentham, Settle
LA2 7AR
t (01524) 262641
e info@halsteadsbarn.co.uk
w halsteadsbarn.co.uk

BEVERLEY

Beck View Guest House ★★★★
Guest Accommodation
1A Blucher Lane, Beverley
HU17 0PT
t (01482) 866446
e beckviewhouse@aol.com
w beckviewguesthouse.co.uk

Beverley Friary YHA ★★★ Hostel
Friar's Lane, Beverley
HU17 0DF
t 0870 770 5696
e beverleyfriary@yha.org.uk
w yha.org.uk

Eastgate Guest House ★★★★
Guest Accommodation
7 Eastgate, Beverley, East Yorkshire
HU17 0DR
t (01482) 868464
e eastgateguesthouse@live.com
w eastgateguesthouse.co.uk

Farah's Guest House ★★★★
Bed & Breakfast
8 Newbegin, Beverley
HU17 8EG
t (01482) 888625
e joekhan786@hotmail.com

The Inn on the Bar ★★★
Guest House
8 North Bar Without, Beverley
HU17 7AA
t (01482) 868137
e dave@bignell.karoo.co.uk

Minster Garth Guest House ★★★★ Guest House
2 Keldgate, Beverley
HU17 8HY
t (01482) 882402
e minstergarth@yahoo.co.uk
w beverleybedandbreakfast.co.uk

Newbegin B&B ★★★★
Bed & Breakfast
Newbegin House, 10 Newbegin, Beverley
HU17 8EG
t (01482) 888880
e wsweeney@wsweeney.karoo.co.uk

Number One ★★★ Bed & Breakfast
1 Woodlands, Beverley
HU17 8BT
t (01482) 862752
e neilandsarah@mansle.karoo.co.uk
w number-one-bedandbreakfast-beverley.co.uk

Potts of Flemingate Guest Accommodation ★★★
Bed & Breakfast
18 Flemingate, Beverley
HU17 0NR
t (01482) 862586
e pottsofflemingate@hotmail.com
w pottsofflemingate.co.uk

Trinity Guest House ★★★★
Guest House
Trinity Lane, Beverley
HU17 0AR
t (01482) 869537
e trinity_house@hotmail.com
w trinityguesthouse.com

Westfield Bed & Breakfast ★★★
Bed & Breakfast
13 Westfield Avenue, Beverley
HU17 7HA
t (01482) 860212

BISHOP THORNTON

Bowes Green Farm ★★★★
Farmhouse SILVER AWARD
Colber Lane, Bishop Thornton, Harrogate
HG3 3JX
t (01423) 770114

Dukes Place ★★★★
Guest Accommodation
Fountains Abbey Road, Bishop Thornton, Harrogate
HG3 3JY
t (01765) 620229
e jakimoorhouse@aol.com
w dukesplace-courtyard.co.uk

BISHOP WILTON

High Belthorpe ★★★ Farmhouse
Belthorpe Lane, Bishop Wilton
YO42 1SB
t (01759) 368238
e meg@highbelthorpe.co.uk
w highbelthorpe.co.uk

BLAXTON

Barnside Cottage ★★★
Bed & Breakfast
Mosham Road, Blaxton, Doncaster
DN9 3AZ
t (01302) 770315
e info@barnside.net
w barnside.net

Beech Grove Lodge ★★★★
Guest Accommodation - Room Only
SILVER AWARD
Station Road, Blaxton, Doncaster
DN9 3AF
t (01302) 771771
e enquiries@beechgrovelodge.co.uk
w beechgrovelodge.co.uk

536 Official tourist board guide Bed & Breakfast

Yorkshire

BLUBBERHOUSES

Scaife Hall Farm ★★★★
Farmhouse **GOLD AWARD**
Kirdisty Hill, Blubberhouses, Harrogate
HG21 2PL
t (01943) 880354
e christine.a.ryder@btinternet.com
w scaifehallfarm.co.uk

BOLTBY

Willow Tree Cottage Bed & Breakfast ★★★★
Guest Accommodation
Boltby, Thirsk
YO7 2DY
t (01845) 537406
e townsend.sce@virgin.net

BRADFIELD

Rickett Field Guest Accommodation
Guest Accommodation
Bingworth, Sidling Hollow, Bradfield
S6 6HA
t (0114) 285 1218
e info@rickettfieldfarm.co.uk
w rickettfieldfarm.co.uk

The Royal ★★★★ Inn
Main Road, Dungworth, Bradfield, Sheffield
S6 6HF
t (0114) 285 1213
e joanne@royalhotel-dungworth.co.uk
w royalhotel-dungworth.co.uk

BRADFORD

Ivy Guest House ★ Guest House
5 Melbourne Place, Bradford
BD5 0HZ
t (01274) 727060
e enquiries@ivyguesthousebradford.com
w ivyguesthousebradford.com

New Beehive Inn ★★★
Guest Accommodation
169-171 Westgate, Bradford
BD1 3AA
t (01274) 721784
e newbeehiveinn.t21@btinternet.com
w newbeehiveinn.co.uk

Norland Guest House ★★★
Guest Accommodation
105 Great Horton Road, Bradford
BD7 4DU
t (01274) 571698
e norlandguesthouse@yahoo.co.uk
w norlandguesthouse.gbr.cc

BRIDLINGTON

Balmoral House ★★★★
Guest Accommodation
1 Marshall Avenue, Bridlington
YO15 2DT
t (01262) 676678
e enquiry@thebalmoralhouse.co.uk
w thebalmoralhouse.co.uk

The Bay Court ★★★★
Guest Accommodation
SILVER AWARD
6a Sands Lane, Bridlington
YO15 2JG
t (01262) 676288
e bay.court@virgin.net
w baycourt.co.uk

Bay Ridge ★★★★
Guest Accommodation
11-13 Summerfield Road, Bridlington
YO15 3LF
t (01262) 673425
e bayridgehotel@aol.com
w bayridgehotel.co.uk

Blantyre House ★★★ Guest House
3 Pembroke Terrace, Bridlington
YO15 3BX
t (01262) 400660
e info@blantyreguesthouse.com
w blantyreguesthouse.co.uk

Bluebell Guest House ★★★
Guest House
3 St Annes Road, Bridlington
YO15 2JB
t (01262) 675163
e linda@thebluebellguesthouse.co.uk
w thebluebellguesthouse.co.uk

Bradfield House ★★★★
Guest House
Horsforth Avenue, Bridlington
YO15 3DF
t (01262) 672457

Brentwood House ★★★
Guest House
42 Princess Street, Bridlington
YO15 2RB
t (01262) 608739
e info@brentwoodhouse.co.uk
w brentwoodhouse.co.uk

Broadfield Guest House ★★★★
Guest Accommodation
18 Shaftesbury Road, Bridlington
YO15 3NW
t (01262) 677379
e broadfieldhotel@talktalk.net
w broadfieldbridlington.co.uk

The Brockton ★★★★ Guest House
4 Shaftesbury Road, Bridlington
YO15 3NP
t (01262) 673967
e info@thebrocktonhotelbridlington.co.uk
w thebrocktonhotelbridlington.co.uk

Charleston Guest House ★★★
Guest House
12 Vernon Road, Bridlington
YO15 2HQ
t (01262) 676228
e charlestongh@aol.com

Chatley Court ★★★
Guest Accommodation
54-56 Windsor Crescent, Bridlington
YO15 3JA
t (01262) 674666
e chatlycourt@aol.com
w chatleycourt.com

The Chimes ★★★
Guest Accommodation
9 Wellington Road, Bridlington
YO15 2BA
t (01262) 401659
e sandisbb@aol.com
w smoothhound.co.uk/hotels/chimesgu.html

The Crescent ★★★ Guest House
12 The Crescent, Bridlington
YO15 2NX
t (01262) 401015

Cromer Guest House ★★★
Guest House
78 Trinity Road, Bridlington
YO15 2HF
t (01262) 679452
w cromerguesthouse.co.uk

Doriam Guest House ★★★
Guest Accommodation
35 Windsor Crescent, Bridlington
YO15 3HX
t (01262) 672513

Glen Alan Guest House ★★★★
Guest House
21 Flamborough Road, Bridlington
YO15 2HU
t (01262) 674650
e enquiries@glenalanhotel.co.uk
w glenalanhotel.co.uk

The Grantlea Guest House ★★★
Guest House
2 South Street, Bridlington
YO15 3BY
t (01262) 400190
e enquiries@grantlea-guest-house.co.uk
w grantlea-guest-house.co.uk

Harmony Guesthouse ★★★
Guest House
38 Marshall Avenue, Bridlington
YO15 2DS
t (01262) 603 867
e enquiries@harmonyguesthouse.co.uk
w harmonyguesthouse.co.uk

Ivanhoe Guest House ★★★
Guest House
63 Cardigan Road, Bridlington
YO15 3JS
t (01262) 675983
e enquiries@ivanhoeguesthouse.co.uk
w ivanhoeguesthouse.co.uk

The Jasmine Guest House ★★★
Guest House
27-29 Richmond Street, Bridlington
YO15 3DL
t (01262) 676608
e jasmineguesthouse@btinternet.com
w jasmineguesthouse.com

Kilburn Guest House ★★★★
Guest Accommodation
25 Trinity Road, Bridlington
YO15 2EZ
t (01262) 679724
e enquiries@thekilburn.co.uk
w thekilburn.co.uk

Lansdowne Lodge Guest House
★★★ Guest House
14 Lansdowne Crescent, Bridlington
YO15 2QR
t (01262) 676307

Leeds House ★★★ Guest House
40 Windsor Crescent, Bridlington
YO15 3HY
t (01262) 674227
e info@leedshousebridlington.co.uk
w leedshousebridlington.co.uk

Lincoln House ★★★★
Bed & Breakfast
43 Wellington Road, Bridlington
YO15 2AX
t (01262) 679595
e lincolnhousebrid@fsmail.net
w lincolnhousebridlington.co.uk

The London Guest House ★★★★
Guest Accommodation
1 Royal Crescent, York Road, Bridlington
YO15 2PF
t (01262) 675377
e londonhotelbrid@yahoo.co.uk
w londonhotelbrid.co.uk

Longcroft Lodge ★★★★
Guest House
100 Trinity Road, Bridlington
YO15 2HF
t (01262) 672180
e longcroft_hotel@hotmail.com

Malvern Guest House ★★★
Guest Accommodation
15 Wellington Road, Bridlington
YO15 2BA
t (01262) 679695
e surat@talktalk.net
w malvernguesthouse1.co.uk

The Marina ★★★★ Guest House
8 Summerfield Road, Bridlington
YO15 3LF
t 0800 970 0591
e themarina8@hotmail.com
w themarina-bridlington.com

Mont Millais ★★★★
Guest Accommodation
64 Trinity Road, Bridlington
YO15 2HF
t (01262) 601890
w montmillais.co.uk

The Mount ★★★★
Guest Accommodation
2 Roundhay Road, Bridlington
YO15 3JY
t (01262) 672306
e mounthotel01@btconnect.com
w mounthotelbridlington.com

Number 7 Guest House ★★★★
Guest Accommodation
SILVER AWARD
7 South Street, Bridlington
YO15 3BY
t (01262) 601249
e gjswhite@hotmail.com
w numbersevenguesthouse.com

Oakwell Aparthotel ★★★
Guest Accommodation
31-33, 43 Horsforth Avenue, Bridlington
YO15 3DG
t (01262) 403666
e oakwellholidays@aol.com

Oakwell Guest House ★★★
Guest House
84 Windsor Crescent, Bridlington
YO15 3JA
t (01262) 674238
e info@oakwell-guesthouse-bridlington.co.uk
w oakwell-guesthouse-bridlington.co.uk

Park View ★★★★
Guest Accommodation
9-11 Tennyson Avenue, Bridlington
YO15 2EU
t (01262) 672140
e info@park-view-bridlington.co.uk
w park-view-bridlington.co.uk

The Promenade ★★★★
Guest Accommodation
121 Promenade, Bridlington
YO15 2QN
t (01262) 602949
e info@thepromenadehotel.co.uk
w thepromenadehotel.co.uk

Providence Place ★★★★
Guest House
11 North View Terrace, Bridlington
YO15 2QP
t (01262) 603840
e enquiries@providenceplace.info
w providenceplace.info

Ridings Guest House ★★★
Guest House
100 Windsor Crescent, Bridlington
YO15 3JA
t (01262) 671744
e susan.potter7@tesco.net
w ridingsguesthouse.co.uk

Rivendell Guest House ★★★★
Guest Accommodation
19 Sands Lane, Bridlington
YO15 2JG
t (01262) 679189
e rivendellhoteld@hotmail.co.uk
w rivendellhotel.net

Rosebery House ★★★★
Guest Accommodation
1 Belle Vue, Tennyson Ave, Bridlington
YO15 2ET
t (01262) 670336
e info@rosebery-house.com
w rosebery-house.com

Sandringham House ★★★
Guest House
11 The Crescent, Bridlington
YO15 2NX
t (01262) 672064
e sandringham-hotel@talk21.com

The Sandsend ★★★ Guest House
8 Sands Lane, Bridlington
YO15 2JE
t (01262) 673265

The Seacourt ★★★★
Guest Accommodation
76 South Marine Drive, Bridlington
YO15 3NS
t (01262) 400872
e seacourt.hotel@tiscali.co.uk

Sea View House ★★★★
Guest House **SILVER AWARD**
54 South Marine Drive, Bridlington
YO15 3JN
t (01262) 677775
e judybebber@hotmail.com

Yorkshire

Seawinds Guest House ★★★
Guest Accommodation
48 Horsforth Avenue, Bridlington
YO15 3DF
t (01262) 676330
e alan@seawinds.co.uk
w seawinds.co.uk

Shearwater ★★★
Guest Accommodation
22 Vernon Road, Bridlington
YO15 2HE
t (01262) 679883
e shearwaterhotel@amserve.com
w shearwaterhotel.co.uk

Southdowne ★★★★ *Guest House*
78 South Marine Drive, Bridlington
YO15 3NS
t (01262) 673270

Spinnaker House ★★★★
Guest Accommodation
19-20 Pembroke Terrace, Bridlington
YO15 3BX
t (01262) 678440
e spinnaker-hotel@btconnect.com

Stonmar Guest House ★★★★
Guest House
15 Flamborough Road, Bridlington
YO15 2HU
t (01262) 674580
e info@stonmar.co.uk
w stonmar.co.uk

The Trinity ★★★
Guest Accommodation
9 Trinity Road, Bridlington
YO15 2EZ
t (01262) 670444
e davcazz@aol.com
w bridlingtontrinityhotel.co.uk

Vernon Villa ★★★★
Guest Accommodation
2 Vernon Road, Bridlington
YO15 2HQ
t (01262) 670661
e vernonvillaguesthouse@yahoo.co.uk

Victoria House ★★★
Guest Accommodation
25-27 Victoria Road, Bridlington
YO15 2AT
t (01262) 673871
e contact@victoriahotelbridlington.co.uk
w victoriahotelbridlington.co.uk

White Lodge Guest House ★★★
Guest Accommodation
9 Neptune Terrace, Neptune Street, Bridlington
YO15 3DE
t (01262) 670903
e caitlyn.greene@btinternet.com
w whitelodgeguesthouse.co.uk

Winston House ★★★
Guest Accommodation
5-6 South Street, Bridlington
YO15 3BY
t (01262) 670216
e winstonhouse@tiscali.co.uk

BRIGGSWATH

The Lawns ★★★★★
Guest Accommodation
GOLD AWARD
73 Carr Hill Lane, Briggswath, Whitby
YO21 1RS
t (01947) 810310
e lorton@onetel.com
w thelawnsbedandbreakfastwhitby.co.uk

BRIGHOUSE

Elder Lea House ★★★★★
Guest Accommodation
GOLD AWARD
Clough Lane, Rastrick, Halifax
HD6 3QH
t (01484) 717832
e elderleahouse@blueyonder.co.uk
w elderleahouse.com

The Lodge @ Birkby Hall ★★★★
Bed & Breakfast **SILVER AWARD**
Birkby Hall, Birkby Lane, Brighouse
HD6 4JJ
t (01484) 400321
e thelodge@birkbyhall.co.uk
w birkbyhall.co.uk

BUCKDEN

Low Raisgill ★★★★
Bed & Breakfast
Buckden, Skipton
BD23 5JQ
t (01756) 760351
w lowraisgill.co.uk

Nethergill Farm ★★★★ *Farmhouse*
SILVER AWARD
Oughtershaw, Buckden, Nr. Skipton, North Yorkshire
BD23 5JS
t (01756) 761126
e fiona.clark@nethergill.co.uk
w nethergill.co.uk

BURNISTON

Harmony Country Lodge ★★★★
Guest House
80 Limestone Road, Burniston, Scarborough
YO13 0DG
t 0800 298 5840
e tony@harmonylodge.net
w harmonycountrylodge.co.uk

BURNT YATES

High Winsley Farm ★★★★
Farmhouse
Brimham Rocks Road, Burnt Yates, Harrogate
HG3 3EP
t (01423) 770376
e highwinsley@aol.com

The New Inn ★★★★ *Inn*
Pateley Bridge Road, Burnt Yates, Harrogate
HG3 3EG
t (01423) 771070
e newinnharrogate@btconnect.com
w thenewinnburntyates.co.uk

BURYTHORPE

Low Penhowe ★★★★★
Bed & Breakfast **GOLD AWARD**
Low Penhowe, Burythorpe, Malton
YO17 9LU
t (01653) 658336
e lowpenhowe@btinternet.com
w bedandbreakfastyorkshire.co.uk

CALTON

Newfield Hall ★★★★
Guest Accommodation
Newfield Hall, Calton, Skipton
BD23 4AA
t (020) 8511 1534

CARLTON

Abbots Thorn ★★★★
Guest Accommodation
Carlton in Coverdale, Leyburn
DL8 4AY
t (01969) 640620
e abbots.thorn@virgin.net
w abbotsthorn.co.uk

The Foresters Arms ★★★★ *Inn*
The Foresters Arms, Carleton in Coverdale, Leyburn
DL8 4BB
t (01969) 640272
e cjchambers100@hotmail.com
w forestersarms-carlton.co.uk

CARLTON MINIOTT

The Poplars ★★★★ *Guest House*
SILVER AWARD
Carlton Miniott, Thirsk
YO7 4LX
t (01845) 522712
e amanda@thepoplarsthirsk.com
w thepoplarsthirsk.com

CARPERBY

Wheatsheaf Inn ★★★ *Inn*
Main Street, Carperby, Leyburn
DL8 4DF
t (01969) 663216
e info@wheatsheafinwensleydale.co.uk
w wheatsheafinwensleydale.co.uk

CASTLE HOWARD

Gate Farm ★★★ *Farmhouse*
Ganthorpe, Castle Howard, York, Malton
YO60 6QD
t (01653) 648269
e millgate001@msn.com
w ganthorpegatefarm.co.uk

CATTERICK BRIDGE

St Giles Farm ★★★★ *Farmhouse*
St Giles Farm, Catterick Bridge, Richmond
DL10 7PH
t (01748) 811372
e janethor@aol.com

CHAPEL-LE-DALE

Croft Gate ★★★★ *Bed & Breakfast*
SILVER AWARD
Chapel-le-Dale, Ingleton
LA6 3JG
t (01524) 242664
e stay@croft-gate.co.uk
w croft-gate.co.uk

CHERRY BURTON

Burton Mount Country House
★★★★★ *Guest Accommodation*
GOLD AWARD
Malton Road, Cherry Burton, Beverley
HU17 7RA
t (01964) 550541
e pg@burtonmount.co.uk
w burtonmount.co.uk

CLAPHAM

New Inn ★★★ *Inn*
Old Road, Clapham, via Lancaster
LA2 8HH
t (01524) 251203
e info@newinn-clapham.co.uk
w newinn-clapham.co.uk

Turnerford Fold ★★★★
Bed & Breakfast **GOLD AWARD**
Keasden, Clapham, Lancaster
LA2 8EX
t (01524) 251731
e enquiries@turnerfordfold.com

CLOUGHTON

Cober Hill ★★★
Guest Accommodation
Newlands Road, Cloughton, Scarborough
YO13 0AR
t (01723) 870310
e enquiries@coberhill.co.uk
w coberhill.co.uk

COLDEN

Riverdene House ★★★★
Bed & Breakfast **SILVER AWARD**
Smithy Lane, Colden, Hebden Bridge
HX7 7HN
t (01422) 847447

COLTON

Walnut Lodge - Ye Old Sun Inn
★★★★ *Inn*
Colton, Tadcaster
LS24 8EP
t (01904) 744261
e kelly.mccarthy@btconnect.com
w yeoldsuninn.co.uk

COTTINGHAM

Kenwood House ★★★
Bed & Breakfast
7 Newgate Street, Cottingham, Hull
HU16 4DY
t (01482) 847558

Newholme Guest House ★★★
Guest House
47 Thwaite Street, Cottingham, Hull
HU16 4QX
t (01482) 849879
e lorraine.headley@hotmail.com

Woodhill Bed and Breakfast
★★★★ *Bed & Breakfast*
Woodhill Way, Cottingham
HU16 5SW
t 01482 843512
e lucy@woodhillbandb.co.uk
w woodhillbandb.co.uk

COXWOLD

The Fauconberg Arms ★★★ *Inn*
Coxwold, York
YO61 4AD
t (01347) 868214
e simon@fauconbergarms.com
w fauconbergarms.co.uk

CRAYKE

Hazelwood Farm Bed & Breakfast
★★★★ *Farmhouse* **SILVER AWARD**
Mosswood Lane, Crayke, York
YO61 4TQ
t (01347) 824654
e sleep@hazelwoodfarm.net
w hazelwoodfarm.net

The Hermitage ★★★
Bed & Breakfast
Mill Lane, Crayke, Easingwold
YO61 4TD
t (01347) 821635

CROFT-ON-TEES

Clow-Beck House ★★★★★
Guest Accommodation
GOLD AWARD
Monk End, Croft on Tees, Darlington
DL2 2SW
t (01325) 721075
e heather@clowbeckhouse.co.uk
w clowbeckhouse.co.uk

CROFTON

Redbeck Motel Ltd ★★★
Guest Accommodation
Doncaster Road, Crofton, Wakefield
WF4 1RR
t (01924) 862730
e enquiries@redbeckmotel.co.uk
w redbeckmotel.co.uk

CROPTON

High Farm Bed & Breakfast
★★★★ *Farmhouse* **SILVER AWARD**
High Farm, Cropton, Pickering
YO18 8HL
t (01751) 417461
e highfarmcropton@aol.com
w hhml.com/bb/highfarmcropton.htm

New Inn & Cropton Brewery
★★★ *Inn*
New Inn and Cropton Brewery, Cropton, Pickering
YO18 8HH
t (01751) 417330
e info@croptonbrewery.co.uk
w croptonbrewery.com

CROW EDGE

The Dog & Partridge Inn ★★★★ *Inn*
Bord Hill, Flouch, Barnsley
S36 4HH
t (01226) 763173
e info@dogandpartridgeinn.co.uk
w dogandpartridgeinn.co.uk

CULLINGWORTH

Manor Guest House ★★★★★
Guest House **GOLD AWARD**
The Manor, Sutton Drive, Bradford
BD13 5BQ
t (01535) 274374
e info@cullingworthmanor.co.uk
w cullingworthmanor.co.uk

Yorkshire

CUNDALL

ndall Lodge Farm ★★★★★
rmhouse **GOLD AWARD**
ndall Lodge Farm,
roughbridge, Ripon
061 2RN
t (01423) 360203
e info@lodgefarmbb.co.uk
w cundall-lodgefarm.co.uk

DACRE BANKS

ate Eel Bed & Breakfast ★★★★
uest House
ate Eel Farm, Dacre Banks, Pateley
idge
G3 4ED
t (01423) 781707
e diandpeterdriver@aol.com
w gateeelfarmhouse.com

DALBY

uth Moor Farm ★★★★
rmhouse
alby Forest Drive, Pickering
O13 0LW
t 01751 460285
e gol@southmoorfarm.co.uk
w southmoorfarm.co.uk

DANBY

uke of Wellington Inn ★★★★
n
est Lane, Danby
O21 2LY
t (01287) 660351
e landlord@danby-dukeofwell
ington.co.uk
w danby-dukeofwellington.co.uk

x & Hounds Inn ★★★★ Inn
Brook Lane, Ainthorpe, Whitby
O21 2LD
t (01287) 660218
e info@foxandhounds-ainthorpe.
com
w foxandhounds-ainthorpe.co.uk

reat Fryupdale Outdoorcentre
★★ Group Hostel
anby, Whitby
O21 2NP
t (01947) 893333
e enquiries@eastbarnby.co.uk
w eastbarnby.co.uk

DARLEY

ellington Inn ★★★ Inn
ellington Inn, Darley, Harrogate
G3 2QQ
t (01423) 780362
e enquiries@wellington-inn.co.uk
w wellington-inn.co.uk

DEIGHTON

rimston House ★★★★
uest Accommodation
eighton House, York
O19 6HB
t (01904) 728328
e pat_wright@btinternet.com
w grimstonhouse.com

ush Farm ★★★
uest Accommodation
rk Road, Deighton, York
O19 6HQ
t (01904) 728459
e david@rushfarm.co.uk
w rushfarm.co.uk

DINNINGTON

hroapham House Bed &
reakfast ★★★★★
uest Accommodation
OLD AWARD
ldcotes Road, Throapham,
nnington S25, Rotherham
25 2QS
t (01909) 562208
e enquiries@throapham-house.co.
uk
w throapham-house.co.uk

DONCASTER

Balmoral Guesthouse ★★★
Guest Accommodation
129 Thorne Road, Doncaster
DN2 5BH
t (01302) 364385
e info@thebalmoralguesthouse.co.
uk
w thebalmoralguesthouse.co.uk

The Caribbean ★★★
Guest Accommodation
87-89 Thorne Road, Doncaster
DN1 2ES
t (01302) 364605
e dene@caribbean-hotel.co.uk
w caribbean-hotel.co.uk

Earlsmere Guest House ★★★
Guest House
84 Thorne Road, Doncaster
DN2 5BL
t (01302) 368532

The Lyntone Guest House ★★★
Guest Accommodation
24 Avenue Road, Wheatley,
Doncaster
DN2 4AQ
t (01302) 361586

Oaklands Guest House ★★
Guest House
36 Christ Church Road, Doncaster
DN1 2QL
t (01302) 369875
e patsywillis@hotmail.co.uk
w oaklandsguesthouse.co.uk

Park Inn ★★★ Inn
232 Carrhouse Road, Doncaster
DN4 5DS
t (01302) 364008
e theparkhotel@hotmail.com

Rock Farm ★★★ Farmhouse
Hooton Pagnell, Doncaster
DN5 7BT
t (01977) 642200 or 07785916186
e info@rockfarm.info
w rockfarm.info

Windsor House ★★★★
Guest Accommodation
7 Windsor Road, Town Moor,
Doncaster
DN2 5BS
t (01302) 768768
e ianmgell@aol.com
w windsorhousedoncaster.com

The Woodenborough ★★★
Guest Accommodation
2 Belle-Vue Avenue, Belle-Vue,
Doncaster
DN4 5DX
t (01302) 361381
e mail@woodboroughhotel.co.uk
w woodboroughhotel.co.uk

DRAX

Dove Cottage ★★★★
Bed & Breakfast
Back Lane, Drax, Selby, North
Yorkshire
YO8 8NY
t (01757) 617103. Mobile.
07885205693.
e lthorn@btinternet.com

DREWTON

Rudstone Walk Country B&B
★★★★ Guest Accommodation
South Cave, Brough, Beverley
HU15 2AH
t (01430) 422230
e rooms@rudstone-walk.co.uk
w rudstone-walk.co.uk

DRIFFIELD

Burnside Bed & Breakfast ★★★★
Bed & Breakfast
Burnside, 25 Middle Street North,
Driffield
YO25 6SW
t 07900 032194
e richard@burnsidemsn.freeserve.
co.uk

DRINGHOUSES

The Racecourse Centre ★★★★
Group Hostel
Tadcaster Road, Dringhouses, York
YO24 1QG
t (01904) 620911
e info@racecoursecentre.co.uk
w racecoursecentre.co.uk

DUNNINGTON

The Windmill ★★★★ Inn
Hull Road, Dunnington, York
YO19 5LP
t (01904) 481898
e j.saggers@btopenworld.com
w thewindmilldunnington.com

DUNSWELL

The Ship's Quarters ★★★★
Guest Accommodation - Room Only
Beverley High Road, Dunswell, Hull
HU6 0AJ
t (01482) 859160
e theshipinn@theshipinn.karoo.co.
uk
w theshipsquarters.co.uk

EARSWICK

Oaklands Guest House ★★★★
Guest Accommodation
351 Strensall Road, Earswick, York
YO32 9SW
t (01904) 768443
e mavmo@oaklands5.fsnet.co.uk

EASINGWOLD

The Old Vicarage ★★★★
Guest Accommodation
SILVER AWARD
Market Place, Easingwold
YO61 3AL
t (01347) 821015
e info@oldvicarage-easingwold.co.
uk
w oldvicarage-easingwold.co.uk

Thornton Lodge Farm ★★★★
Farmhouse
Thornton Hill, Easingwold
YO61 3QA
t (01347) 821306
e enquiries@thorntonlodgefarm.co.
uk
w thorntonlodgefarm.co.uk

EASTBY

Bondcroft Farm ★★★★ Farmhouse
Bondcroft Farm, Skipton
BD23 6SF
t (01756) 793371
e bondcroftfarm@bondcroftfarm.
yorks.net
w bondcroft.yorks.net

EAST HESLERTON

Manor Farm ★★★ Farmhouse
Manor Farm, East Heslerton, Malton
YO17 8RN
t (01944) 728268
e info@manorfarmonline.co.uk
w manorfarmonline.co.uk

EBBERSTON

Chestnut Cottage B&B ★★★★
Bed & Breakfast
Ebberston, Scarborough
YO13 9PA
t (01723) 859416
e david.jordan11@tiscali.co.uk
w chestnutcottagebandb.co.uk

Studley House Farm ★★★★
Bed & Breakfast
67 Main Street, Ebberston, Pickering
YO13 9NR
t (01723) 859285
e brenda@yorkshireancestors.com
w studleyhousefarm.co.uk

EGTON BRIDGE

Broom House and Whites
(Restaurant) ★★★★ Guest House
GOLD AWARD
Broom House Lane, Egton Bridge,
Whitby
YO21 1XD
t (01947) 895279
e mw@broom-house.co.uk
w egton-bridge.co.uk

ELLERBY

Ellerby Residential Country Inn
★★★★ Inn **SILVER AWARD**
Ellerby Hotel, Ellerby, Saltburn-by-
the-Sea
TS13 5LP
t (01947) 840342
e relax@ellerbyhotel.co.uk

ELLINGSTRING

Hollybreen ★★★★
Guest Accommodation
Ellingstring, Masham
HG4 4PW
t (01677) 460216
e dales.accommodation@virgin.net
w dalesaccommodation.org.uk

ESCRICK

Glade Farm ★★★★
Bed & Breakfast
Riccall Road, Escrick, Selby
YO19 6ED
t (01904) 728098
e victorialeaf@hotmail.com
w glade-farm.co.uk

FEARBY

The Black Swan ★★★★ Inn
Fearby, Masham
HG4 4NF
t (01765) 689477
e info@blackswan-masham.co.uk
w blackswan-masham.co.uk

FELLISCLIFFE

Knabbs Ash ★★★★ Farmhouse
GOLD AWARD
Skipton Road, Kettlesing, Felliscliffe,
Harrogate
HG3 2LT
t (01423) 771040
e sheila@knabbsash.co.uk
w knabbsash.co.uk

FILEY

Abbot's Leigh Guest House
★★★★ Guest House
7 Rutland Street, Filey
YO14 9JA
t (01723) 513334
e abbots.leigh@btinternet.com
w fileybedandbreakfast.com

All Seasons Guesthouse ★★★★
Guest House **SILVER AWARD**
11 Rutland Street, Filey
YO14 9JA
t (01723) 515321
e lesley@allseasonsfiley.co.uk
w allseasonsfiley.co.uk

Binton Guest House ★★★★
Guest House
25 West Avenue, Filey
YO14 9AX
t (01723) 513753
e jag25@tiscali.co.uk
w bintonguesthouse.co.uk

Cherries ★★★★ Guest House
59 West Avenue, Filey
YO14 9AX
t (01723) 513299
e cherriesfiley@talktalk.net
w cherriesfiley.co.uk

or key to symbols see page 6

539

Yorkshire

The Edwardian Guest House
★★★★ *Guest Accommodation*
2 Brooklands, Filey
YO14 9BA
t (01723) 514557
e the.edwardian@btinternet.com
w edwardianfiley.co.uk

The Forge Guest House ★★★★
Guest Accommodation
SILVER AWARD
23 Rutland Street, Filey
YO14 9JA
t (01723) 512379
e theforge2@btinternet.com
w theforgefiley.com

Sea Brink ★★★
Guest Accommodation
3 The Beach, Filey
YO14 9LA
t (01723) 513257
e anntindall@aol.com
w seabrinkhotel.co.uk

The Seafield ★★★★
Guest Accommodation
SILVER AWARD
9 Rutland Street, Filey
YO14 9JA
t (01723) 513715
e seafield1@btconnect.com
w seafieldguesthouse.co.uk

FIMBER

Fimber Gate Bed & Breakfast
Guest Accommodation
Beverley Road, Driffield, Fimber
YO25 3HA
t (01377) 236042
e stay@fimbergate.co.uk
w fimbergate.co.uk

FLAMBOROUGH

Crab Pot Cottage ★★★★
Guest Accommodation
10 High Street, Flamborough, Bridlington
YO15 1JX
t (01262) 850555
e stay@crabpotcottage.com
w crabpotcottage.com

FLAXBY

Herons Keep B&B ★★
Bed & Breakfast
Shortsill Lane, Flaxby, Knaresborough
HG5 0RT
t (01423) 860353
e buck_kath@yahoo.co.uk

FLAXTON

The Blacksmiths Arms ★★★★ *Inn*
The Blacksmiths Arms, Flaxton, Malton
YO60 7RJ
t (01904) 468210
e ritchieflaxton@btinternet.com
w blacksmithsarmsflaxton.co.uk

Claxton Hall Cottage Guest House
★★★★ *Bed & Breakfast*
SILVER AWARD
Malton Road, York
YO60 7RE
t (01904) 468697
e claxcott@aol.com
w claxtonhallcottage.com

FREMINGTON

Dales Bike Centre Bunk Barn
★★★★ *Hostel*
Parks Barn, Fremington, Richmond
DL11 6AW
t (01748) 884908
e enquiries@dalesbikecentre.co.uk
w dalesbikecentre.co.uk

FRYUP

Crossley Side Farm ★★★★
Farmhouse
Crossley Side Farm, Fryup, Whitby
YO21 2NR
t (01287) 660313
e fryupruth@aol.com
w crossley-side-farm.co.uk

Furnace Farm ★★★★ *Farmhouse*
Fryup, Whitby
YO21 2AP
t (01947) 897271
e furnacefarm@hotmail.com
w furnacefarm.co.uk

FULFORD

Pinfold Cottage B&B ★★★★
Guest House
145-147 Main Street, Fulford, York
YO10 4PR
t (01904) 634683
e pinfoldcottage@aol.com
w pinfoldcottageyork.co.uk

FYLINGTHORPE

Boggle Hole YHA ★★★ *Hostel*
Mill Beck, Fylingthorpe, Whitby
YO22 4UQ
t 0870 770 5704
e bogglehole@yha.org.uk
w yha.org.uk

GARFORTH

Myrtle House ★★★ *Guest House*
31 Wakefield Road, Garforth, Leeds
LS25 1AH
t (0113) 286 6445

GARGRAVE

The Masons Arms ★★★★ *Inn*
Marton Road, Gargrave, Skipton
BD23 3NL
t (01756) 749304

GAYLE

East House ★★★★
Guest Accommodation
East House, Gayle, Hawes
DL8 3RZ
t (01969) 667405
e lornaward@lineone.net
w easthouse-hawes.com

GIGGLESWICK

The Black Horse ★★★★ *Inn*
Church Street, Giggleswick, Settle
BD24 0BE
t (01729) 822506

Harts Head Inn ★★★★ *Inn*
Belle Hill, Giggleswick, Settle
BD24 0BA
t (01729) 822086
e info@hartsheadinn.co.uk
w hartsheadinn.co.uk

Tipperthwaite Barn ★★★★
Bed & Breakfast **SILVER AWARD**
Paley Green Lane, Giggleswick, Settle
BD24 0DZ
t (01729) 823146
e stay@tipperthwaitebarn.co.uk
w tipperthwaitebarn.co.uk

GILLAMOOR

Manor Farm ★★★ *Farmhouse*
Main Street, Gillamoor, Kirkbymoorside
YO62 7HX
t (01751) 432695
e gibson.manorfarm@btopenworld.com
w manorfarmgillamoor.co.uk

Royal Oak Inn ★★★★ *Inn*
Main Street, Gillamoor, Kirkbymoorside
YO62 7HX
t (01751) 431414
e mcgill473@btinternet.com

GILLING EAST

The Fairfax Arms ★★★★ *Inn*
Main Street, Gilling East, Helmsley
YO62 4JH
t (01439) 788212
e info@fairfax.plus.com
w thefairfaxarms-gilling.co.uk

GLAISDALE

Beggar's Bridge Bed & Breakfast
★★★★ *Bed & Breakfast*
Station House, Glaisdale, Whitby
YO21 2QL
t (01947) 897409
e info@beggarsbridge.co.uk
w beggarsbridge.co.uk

Egton Banks Farm ★★★★
Farmhouse
Glaisdale, Whitby
YO21 2QP
t (01947) 897289
e egtonbanksfarm@btconnect.com
w egtonbanksfarm.agriplus.net

GOATHLAND

The Beacon Guest House ★★★★
Guest House
Goathland, Whitby
YO22 5AN
t (01947) 896409
e thebeacongoathland@live.co.uk
w thebeaconguesthouse.co.uk

Fairhaven Country Guest House
★★★★ *Guest House*
The Common, Goathland, Whitby
YO22 5AN
t (01947) 896361
e enquiries@fairhavencountryguesthouse.co.uk
w fairhavencountryguesthouse.co.uk

Heatherdene ★★★★★
Guest House
Goathland, Whitby
YO22 5AN
t (01947) 896334
e info@heatherdenehotel.com
w heatherdenehotel.com

GOOLE

The Briarcroft ★★★★ *Guest House*
51 Clifton Gardens, Goole
DN14 6AR
t (01405) 763024
e briarcrofthotel@aol.com
w briarcrofthotel.co.uk

Carlton Towers
Guest Accommodation
Carlton, Goole
DN14 9LZ
t (01405) 861662
e info@carltontowers.co.uk
w carltontowers.co.uk

GRASSINGTON

Foresters Arms ★★★ *Inn*
20 Main Street, Grassington, Skipton
BD23 5AA
t (01756) 752349
e theforesters@totalise.co.uk
w forestersarmsgrassington.co.uk/

Grassington Lodge ★★★★★
Guest Accommodation
GOLD AWARD
8 Wood Lane, Grassington
BD23 5LU
t (01756) 752518
e relax@grassingtonlodge.co.uk
w grassingtonlodge.co.uk

Grove House ★★★★
Bed & Breakfast
1 Moor Lane, Grassington
BD23 5BD
t (01756) 753364
e fraser.turner@btinternet.com
w grovehousegrassington.co.uk

New Laithe House ★★★★
Guest Accommodation
Wood Lane, Grassington
BD23 5LU
t (01756) 752764
e enquiries@newlaithehouse.co.uk
w newlaithehouse.co.uk

Raines Close Guest House ★★★★
Guest Accommodation
13 Station Road, Grassington
BD23 5LS
t (01756) 752678
e raines.close@btinternet.com
w rainesclose.co.uk

Scar Croft ★★★★ *Bed & Breakfast*
Chapel Street, Grassington
BD23 5BE
t (01756) 752455
e dianemackridge@gmail.com
w scarcroft.net

Springroyd House ★★★★
Guest Accommodation
8A Station Road, Grassington, Skipton
BD23 5NQ
t (01756) 752473
e springroydhouse@hotmail.com
w springroydhouse.co.uk

Yew Tree House ★★★★
Bed & Breakfast **GOLD AWARD**
Scar Street, Grassington
BD23 5AS
t (01756) 753075
e julie@badgergate.com
w yewtreehouse.org

GREAT AYTON

Bridge Guest House ★★
Guest House
Bridge Street, Great Ayton, Stokesley
TS9 6NP
t (01642) 725236
e enquiries@greataytonaccmodation.co.uk
w greataytonaccommodation.co.uk

The Kings Head at Newton Und Roseberry ★★★★
Guest Accommodation
SILVER AWARD
The Green, Newton Under Rosebe Near Great Ayton
TS9 6QR
t 01642 722318
e info@kingsheadhotel.co.uk
w kingsheadhotel.co.uk

Royal Oak ★★★ *Inn*
123 High Street, Great Ayton, Stokesley
TS9 6BW
t (01642) 722361
e info@royaloak-hotel.co.uk
w royaloak-hotel.co.uk

Susie D's B&B ★★★
Guest Accommodation
Crossways, 116 Newton Road, Guisborough
TS9 6DL
t (01642) 724351
e info@susieds.com
w susieds.com

Travellers Rest ★★★★
Bed & Breakfast **SILVER AWARD**
97 High Street, Great Ayton, Stokesley
TS9 6NF
t (01642) 724523
w travellersrest.info

GRINTON

The Bridge Inn ★★★ *Inn*
Grinton, North Yorkshire
DL11 6HH
t (01748) 884224
e atkinbridge@btinternet.com
w bridgeinngrinton.co.uk

Yorkshire

inton Lodge YHA ★★★★ Hostel
inton Lodge YHA, Grinton,
hmond
11 6HS
(01748) 884206
grinton@yha.org.uk
yha.org.uk

GUISBOROUGH

x Inn ★★★ Inn
w Street, Guisborough
14 6BP
(01287) 632958

GUISELEY

ndhurst ★★★★ Bed & Breakfast
ford Road, Guiseley, Leeds
20 9AB
(01943) 879985
guisley.co.uk/lyndhurst

HALIFAX

oughcroft Cottage ★★★★
est Accommodation
Ploughcroft Lane, Halifax
3 6TX
(01422) 341205
ploughcroft.cottage@care4free.net
ploughcroftcottage.com

avis Guest House ★★★
est Accommodation
West Parade, Halifax
1 2TA
(01422) 365727

HAMBLETON

e Owl ★★★★ Inn
5 Main Road, Selby
8 9JH
(01757) 228374
owlhotel.selby@marstons.co.uk
marstonsinns.co.uk

HAMPSTHWAITE

Peckfield Close ★★★
est Accommodation
Peckfield Close, Hampsthwaite, rrogate
3 2ES
(01423) 770765

HARMBY

nnyridge ★★★ Farmhouse
gill Farm, Harmby, Leyburn
8 5HQ
(01969) 622478
hilary@safarm.co.uk
sunnyridgeargillfarm.co.uk

HAROME

amble Cottage B&B ★★★★
d & Breakfast
arome, York
62 5JA
01439 771158
lizbetts@hotmail.com
bramble-cottage-harome.co.uk

HARROGATE

corn Lodge ★★★★
est Accommodation
Studley Road, Harrogate
1 5JU
(01423) 525630
info@acornlodgehotel.com
acornlodgehotel.com

amah Guest House ★★★★
est House
Kings Road, Harrogate
1 5JX
(01423) 502187
alamahguesthouse@btconnect.com
alamah.co.uk

derside Guest House ★★★
d & Breakfast
Belmont Road, Harrogate
2 0LR
(01423) 529400
alderside.harrogate@gmail.com

Alvera Court ★★★★
Guest Accommodation
76 Kings Road, Harrogate
HG1 5JX
t (01423) 505735
e reception@alvera.co.uk
w alvera.co.uk

Applewood House ★★★★
Guest Accommodation
GOLD AWARD
55 St Georges Road, Harrogate
HG2 9BP
t (01423) 544549
e applewood@teamknight.com
w applewoodhouse.co.uk

Arden House ★★★★
Guest Accommodation
69-71 Franklin Road, Harrogate
HG1 5EH
t (01423) 509224
e enquiries@ardenhousehotel.co.uk
w ardenhousehotel.co.uk

Ashbrooke House ★★★★
Guest Accommodation
140 Valley Drive, Harrogate
HG2 0JS
t (01423) 564478
e ashbrooke@harrogate.com
w harrogate.com/ashbrooke

Ash Grove Guest House ★★★★
Guest Accommodation
72 Kings Road, Harrogate
HG1 5JR
t (01423) 569970
e admin@ash-grove.co.uk
w ash-grove.co.uk

Aston ★★ Guest Accommodation
7-9 Franklin Road, Harrogate
HG1 5EJ
t (01423) 564262
e astonhotel@btinternet.com
w hotel-harrogate.com

Barkers Guest House ★★★
Guest Accommodation
204 Kings Road, Harrogate
HG1 5JG
t (01423) 568494
e eebarkeruk@yahoo.co.uk
w barkersguesthouse.co.uk/

Baytree House ★★★★
Guest House
98 Franklin Road, Harrogate
HG1 5EN
t (01423) 564493
e info@baytreeharrogate.co.uk
w baytreeharrogate.co.uk

Belmont Guest House ★★★★
Guest House
86 Kings Road, Harrogate
HG1 5JX
t (01423) 528086
e belmontharrogate@btinternet.com
w belmont-harrogate.co.uk

The Bijou ★★★★★
Guest Accommodation
SILVER AWARD
17 Ripon Road, Harrogate
HG1 2JL
t (01423) 567974
e info@thebijou.co.uk
w thebijou.co.uk

Brookfield House ★★★★★
Guest House SILVER AWARD
5 Alexandra Road, Harrogate
HG1 5JS
t (01423) 506646
e office@brookfieldhotel.co.uk
w brookfieldhousehotel.co.uk

The Cavendish ★★★★
Guest House
3-5 Valley Drive, Harrogate
HG2 0JJ
t (01423) 509637
e cavendishhotel@gmail.com
w cavendishhotelharrogate.co.uk

Cold Cotes ★★★★★
Guest Accommodation
GOLD AWARD
Cold Cotes Road, Felliscliffe, Harrogate
HG3 2LW
t (01423) 770937
e info@coldcotes.com
w coldcotes.com

Conference View Guest House
★★★ Guest Accommodation
74 Kings Road, Harrogate
HG1 5JR
t (01423) 563075
e admin@conferenceview.co.uk
w conferenceview.co.uk

Coppice Guest House ★★★★
Guest House
9 Studley Road, Harrogate
HG1 5JU
t (01423) 569626
e coppice@harrogate.com
w harrogate.com/coppice

Dragon House ★★★★ Guest House
6 Dragon Parade, Harrogate
HG1 5DA
t (01423) 569888
e marie@dragonhousehotel.com
w dragonhousehotel.com

Franklin View ★★★★
Guest Accommodation
SILVER AWARD
19 Grove Road, Harrogate
HG1 5EW
t (01423) 541388
e jennifer@franklinview.com
w franklinview.com

Garden House ★★★★
Guest Accommodation
14 Harlow Moor Drive, Harrogate
HG2 0JX
t (01423) 503059
e gardenhouse@harrogate.com
w gardenhouseharrogate.co.uk

Geminian Guest House ★★★★
Guest House
11-13 Franklin Road, Harrogate
HG1 5ED
t (01423) 523347
e enquiries@geminian.org.uk
w geminian.org.uk

Glenayr ★★★
Guest Accommodation
19 Franklin Mount, Harrogate
HG1 5EJ
t (01423) 504259
e liz-glenayr@boltblue.com
w glenayr.co.uk

The Harrogate Arms ★★★ Inn
Crag Lane, Harrogate
HG3 1QA
t (01423) 567950
e info@theharrogatearms.com
w theharrogatearms.com

Harrogate Motel ★★★
Guest Accommodation
Brackentwaite Lane, Burnbridge, Harrogate
HG3 1PW
t (01423) 871894
e bookings@harrogatemotel.co.uk
w harrogatemotel.co.uk

Hollins House ★★★ Guest House
17 Hollins Road, Harrogate
HG1 2JF
t (01423) 503646
e hollinshouse@tiscali.co.uk
w hollinshouse.co.uk

Lamont House ★★★★
Guest Accommodation
12 St Marys Walk, Harrogate
HG2 0LW
t (01423) 567143
e lamonthouse@btinternet.com
w lamont-house.co.uk

Murray House ★★★★
Guest Accommodation
67 Franklin Road, Harrogate
HG1 5EH
t (01423) 505857
e enquiries@murray-house.com
w murrayhouse.yorkwebsites.co.uk

Park Parade ★★★★★
Bed & Breakfast SILVER AWARD
18 Park Parade, Harrogate
HG1 5AF
t (01423) 563800
e hhy@globalnet.co.uk
w parkparade.co.uk

Sherwood ★★★★
Guest Accommodation
7 Studley Road, Harrogate
HG1 5JU
t (01423) 503033
e sherwood@harrogate.com
w sherwood-hotel.com

Spring Lodge ★★★ Guest House
22 Spring Mount, Harrogate
HG1 2HX
t (01423) 506036
e spring_lodge@btinternet.com
w spring-lodge.co.uk

The Welford ★★★★ Guest House
27 Franklin Road, Harrogate
HG1 5ED
t (01423) 566041
e judith.mudd@btopenworld.com
w the-welford.co.uk

Ye Olde Coach House ★★★★
Guest Accommodation
SILVER AWARD
2 Strawberry Dale Terrace, Harrogate
HG1 5EQ
t (01423) 500302
e yeoldecoachhouse@btinternet.com
w yeoldecoachhouse.com

HARWOOD DALE

The Grainary ★★★★ Farmhouse
The Grainary, Harwood Dale, Scarborough
YO13 0DT
t (01723) 870026
e grainary@btopenworld.com
w grainary.co.uk

HAWES

Cocketts 1688 ★★★★
Guest Accommodation
Market Place, Hawes
DL8 3RD
t (01969) 667312
e enquiries@cocketts.co.uk
w cocketts.co.uk

Crosby House ★★★★
Bed & Breakfast
Burtersett Road, Hawes
DL8 3NP
t (01969) 667322
e waluda@btinternet.com
w crosbyhousehawes.co.uk

Ebor House ★★★★
Guest Accommodation
Burtersett Road, Hawes
DL8 3NT
t (01969) 667337
e eborhousehawes@yahoo.co.uk
w eborhouse.co.uk

FairView House ★★★★
Guest House SILVER AWARD
Burtersett Road, Hawes
DL8 3NP
t (01969) 667348
e info@fairview-hawes.co.uk
w fairview-hawes.co.uk

Hawes YHA ★★★ Hostel
Lancaster Terrace, Hawes
DL8 3LQ
t (01969) 667368
e hawes@yha.org.uk
w yha.org.uk

Yorkshire

Herriots ★★★★
Guest Accommodation
Main Street, Hawes
DL8 3QW
t (01969) 667536
e info@herriotsinhawes.co.uk
w herriotsinhawes.co.uk

Laburnum House ★★★
Guest House
The Holme, Hawes
DL8 3QR
t (01969) 667717
e info@stayatlaburnumhouse.co.uk
w stayatlaburnumhouse.co.uk

The Old Dairy Farm ★★★★★
Guest Accommodation
SILVER AWARD
Widdale, Hawes
DL8 3LX
t (01969) 667070
w olddairyfarm.co.uk

Old Station House ★★★★
Bed & Breakfast SILVER AWARD
Hardraw Road, Hawes, North Yorkshire
DL8 3NL
t (01969) 666912
e oldstationhouse@ymail.com
w oldstationhousehawes.co.uk

Pry House Farm B&B ★★★★
Bed & Breakfast
Hawes
DL8 3LP
t (01969) 667241
e pryhousefarm@hotmail.com
w pryhousefarm.co.uk

South View ★★★ *Bed & Breakfast*
Gayle Lane, Hawes
DL8 3RW
t (01969) 667447
e carolsouthview@btinternet.com
w go-bedandbreakfast.co.uk/southview/

Springbank House ★★★
Guest Accommodation
Town Foot, Hawes
DL8 3NW
t (01969) 667376
e springbankhouse@aol.com

Thorney Mire Barn B&B ★★★★★
Guest Accommodation
GOLD AWARD
Thorney Mire Barn B&B, Appersett, Hawes
DL8 3LU
t (01969) 666122
e stay@thorneymirebarn.co.uk
w thorneymirebarn.co.uk

Thorney Mire House ★★★★
Bed & Breakfast
Thorney Mire House, Appersett, Hawes
DL8 3LU
t (01969) 667159
e sylvia.turner2@virgin.net
w thorneymirehouse.co.uk

Thornsgill House ★★★★
Guest Accommodation
SILVER AWARD
Moor Road, Askrigg, Hawes
DL8 3HH
t (01969) 650617
e stay@thornsgill.co.uk
w thornsgill.co.uk

White Hart Inn ★★ *Inn*
Main Street, Hawes
DL8 3QL
t (01969) 667259
e info@whitehartawes.co.uk
w whitehartawes.co.uk

HAWKSWICK

Warren House B&B ★★★★
Bed & Breakfast
Arncliffe Road, Hawkswick, Skipton
BD23 5PU
t (01756) 770375
e info@warren-house.net
w warren-house.net

HAWNBY

Easterside Farm ★★★★
Farmhouse
Hawnby, Helmsley
YO62 5QT
t (01439) 798277
e info@eastersidefarm.co.uk
w eastersidefarm.co.uk

The Inn at Hawnby ★★★★ *Inn*
Hill Top, Hawnby, Helmsley
YO62 5QS
t (01439) 798202
e info@innathawnby.co.uk
w innathawnby.co.uk

HAWORTH

Aitches Guest House ★★★
Guest House
11 West Lane, Haworth
BD22 8DU
t (01535) 642501
e aitches@talk21.com
w aitches.co.uk

The Apothecary Guest House ★★★ *Guest House*
86 Main Street, Haworth
BD22 8DP
t (01535) 643642
e nicholasapt@aol.com
w theapothecaryguesthouse.co.uk

Ashmount Country House ★★★★★ *Guest House*
GOLD AWARD
Mytholmes Lane, Haworth
BD22 8EZ
t (01535) 645726
e info@ashmounthaworth.co.uk
w ashmounthaworth.co.uk

Bridge House B&B ★★★
Bed & Breakfast
Bridge House, Bridgehouse Lane, Haworth
BD22 8PA
t (01535) 642372
e claire@bridgehouselane.co.uk
w bridgehouselane.co.uk

The Bronte ★★★
Guest Accommodation
Lees Lane, Haworth
BD22 8RA
t (01535) 644112
e brontehotel@btconnect.com
w bronte-hotel.co.uk

The Fleece Inn ★★★★ *Inn*
67 Main Street, Haworth
BD22 8DA
t (01535) 642172
e nickhindle1@yahoo.co.uk
w fleece-inn.co.uk

Haworth Old Hall Inn ★★★★ *Inn*
Sun Street, Haworth
BD22 8BP
t (01535) 642709
e haworth.oldhall@virgin.net
w haworthoidhall.co.uk

Haworth Tea Rooms & Guest House ★★★ *Guest House*
68 Main Street, Haworth
BD22 8DP
t (01535) 644278
e haworthtearooms.co.uk

Haworth YHA ★★★ *Hostel*
Longlands Drive, Lees Lane, Haworth
BD22 8RT
t (01535) 642234
e haworth@yha.org.uk
w yha.org.uk

Heathfield Bed & Breakfast ★★★★ *Guest Accommodation*
1 Bronte Street, Haworth
BD22 8EE
t (01535) 640606
e ray.trudy@heathfield-haworth.co.uk
w heathfield-haworth.co.uk

Kings Arms ★★★ *Inn*
Main Street, Haworth
BD22 8DR
t (01535) 647302
e mail@thekingsarmshaworth.com
w thekingsarmshaworth.com

The Old Registry ★★★★
Guest Accommodation
SILVER AWARD
2-4 Main Street, Haworth
BD22 8DA
t (01535) 646503
e enquiries@theoldregistryhaworth.co.uk
w theoldregistryhaworth.co.uk

Old Sun ★★★ *Inn*
79 West Lane, Haworth
BD22 8EL
t (01535) 642780
e mail@oldsunhaworth.com
w oldsunhaworth.com

Old White Lion Hotel ★★★★ *Inn*
Main Street, Haworth
BD22 8DU
t (01535) 642313
e enquiries@oldwhitelionhotel.com
w oldwhitelionhotel.com

Park Top House ★★★★
Guest Accommodation
1 Rawdon Road, Haworth
BD22 8DX
t (01535) 646102
e vannessa@parktophouse.co.uk
w parktophouse.co.uk

Rosebud Cottage Guest House ★★★★ *Guest Accommodation*
1 Belle Isle Road, Haworth
BD22 8QQ
t (01535) 640321
e info@rosebudcottage.co.uk
w rosebudcottage.co.uk

The Thyme House ★★★★
Guest Accommodation
GOLD AWARD
The Thyme House, 90 West Lane, Haworth
BD22 8EN
t (01535) 211860
e info@thethymehouse.co.uk
w thethymehouse.co.uk

HEBDEN

Court Croft ★★★ *Bed & Breakfast*
Church Lane, Hebden, Skipton
BD23 5DX
t (01756) 753406

HEBDEN BRIDGE

b@r place ★★★★
Guest Accommodation
10 Crown Street, Hebden Bridge
HX7 8EH
t (01422) 842814
e intouch@barplace.co.uk
w barplace.co.uk

Holme House ★★★★★
Bed & Breakfast SILVER AWARD
New Road, Hebden Bridge
HX7 8AD
t (01422) 847588
e mail@holmehousehebdenbridge.co.uk
w holmehousehebdenbridge.co.uk

HELLIFIELD

Chapel Farm B&B ★★★★
Bed & Breakfast SILVER AWARD
Gisburn Road, Hellifield, Settle
BD23 4LA
t (01729) 851158
e info@chapelfarmbandb.com
w chapelfarmbandb.com

HELMSLEY

Carlton Lodge ★★★★ *Guest House*
SILVER AWARD
Bondgate, Helmsley
YO62 5EY
t (01439) 770557
e admin@carlton-lodge.co.uk
w carlton-lodge.co.uk

The Crown Inn ★★★ *Inn*
21 Market Place, Helmsley
YO62 5BJ
t (01439) 770297
e info@tchh.co.uk
w tchh.co.uk

The Feathers ★★★ *Inn*
Market Place, Helmsley
YO62 5BH
t (01439) 770275
e reservations@feathershotelhelmsley.co.uk
w feathershotelhelmsley.co.uk

Helmsley YHA ★★★★ *Hostel*
Carlton Lane, Helmsley
YO62 5HB
t (01439) 770433
e helmsley@yha.org.uk
w yha.org.uk

Laskill Grange ★★★★
Guest Accommodation
Mrs Sue Smith, Laskill Grange, Nr Hawnby, Helmsley, York
YO62 5NB
t (01439) 798268 or
  (01439) 798265
e laskillgrange@tiscali.co.uk
w laskillgrange.co.uk

No 54 ★★★★★ *Guest House*
54 Bondgate, Helmsley
YO62 5EZ
t (01439) 771533
e lizzie@no54.co.uk
w no54.co.uk

Stilworth House ★★★★
Bed & Breakfast SILVER AWARD
1 Church Street, Helmsley
YO62 5AD
t (01439) 771072
e carol@stilworth.co.uk
w stilworth.co.uk

HEPWORTH

Uppergate Farm B&B ★★★★
Guest Accommodation
SILVER AWARD
Uppergate, Hepworth, Holmfirth
HD9 1TG
t (01484) 681369
e info@uppergatefarm.co.uk
w uppergatefarm.co.uk

HIGH CATTON

High Catton Grange ★★★★
Farmhouse SILVER AWARD
High Catton, Stamford Bridge, Yor
YO41 1EP
t (01759) 371374
e foster-s@sky.com
w highcattongrange.co.uk

HINDERWELL

Saultz Bistro ★★★★
Bed & Breakfast
16 High Street, Hinderwell, Saltburn-by-the-Sea
TS13 5JH
t (01947) 841555
e sharon.sault@btinternet.com
w saultzbistro.co.uk

HOLLYM

Plough Inn ★★★ *Inn*
Northside Road, Hollym, Withernse
HU19 2RS
t (01964) 612049
e the.plough.inn@btconnect.com
w theploughinnhollym.co.uk

HOLMBRIDGE

Corn Loft House B&B ★★★
Guest Accommodation
146 Woodhead Road, Holmbridge, Holmfirth
HD9 2NL
t (01484) 683147

Yorkshire

HOLMFIRTH

sh House B&B ★★★
d & Breakfast
0 Dunford Road, Holmfirth
09 2SJ
- t (01484) 688244
- e accommodation@swcch.co.uk
- w ash-house-holmfirth.co.uk

ephant & Castle ★★★
uest Accommodation
ollowgate, Holmfirth
09 2DG
- t (01484) 683178

e Huntsman Inn ★★★★
uest Accommodation
eenfield Road, Holmfirth
09 3XF
- t (01484) 850705
- e kempsterpk@aol.com
- w the-huntsman-inn.com

nnybank Guesthouse ★★★★★
uest Accommodation
OLD AWARD
pperthong Lane, Holmfirth
09 3BQ
- t (01484) 684857
- e info@sunnybankguesthouse.co.uk
- w sunnybankguesthouse.co.uk

HOLMPTON

m Tree Farm ★★★
d & Breakfast
olmpton, Withernsea
U19 2QR
- t (01964) 630957
- e cft-mcox@supanet.com
- w bandbatelmtreefarm.com

ysome Garth ★★★★
uest Accommodation
ysome Garth, Holmpton,
ithernsea
U19 2QR
- t (01964) 631248
- e amandapannett@neoeon.com
- w rysome-longhorns.co.uk

HORNSEA

arlham House Guest House
★★★ *Bed & Breakfast*
OLD AWARD
A Eastgate, Hornsea
U18 1NB
- t (01964) 537809
- e info@earlhamhouse.com
- w earlhamhouse.com

HORSFORTH

rinity & All Saints College ★★★
ampus
rownberrie Lane, Horsforth, Leeds
18 5HD
- t (0113) 283 7120
- e j.cressey@leedstrinity.ac.uk
- w tasc.ac.uk

HORTON-IN-RIBBLESDALE

road Croft House ★★★★
d & Breakfast **SILVER AWARD**
chool Lane, Horton-in-Ribblesdale,
ettle, North Yorkshire
D24 0EX
- t 01729 860302
- e info@broadcroft.co.uk
- w broadcroft.co.uk

HUBBERHOLME

hurch Farm ★★★★ *Farmhouse*
ubberholme, Skipton
D23 5JE
- t (01756) 760240
- e gillhuck@hubberholme.fsnet.co.uk
- w churchfarmhubberholme.co.uk

HUDDERSFIELD

ambridge Guest House ★★★
uest House
5 New North Road, Huddersfield
D1 5NE
- t (01484) 423995
- e cambridge-lodge-hudds@btconnect.com
- w cambridgelodge.co.uk

Cambridge Lodge ★★★
Guest Accommodation
4 Clare Hill, Huddersfield
HD1 5BS
- t (01484) 519892
- e info@cambridgelodge.co.uk
- w cambridgelodge.co.uk

Castle View Guest House
★★★★ *Guest Accommodation*
GOLD AWARD
148 Ashes Lane, Castle Hill,
Huddersfield
HD4 6TE
- t (01484) 307460
- e info@castleviewyorkshire.co.uk
- w castleviewyorkshire.co.uk

Elm Crest ★★★★ *Guest House*
SILVER AWARD
2 Queens Road, Huddersfield
HD2 2AG
- t (01484) 530990
- e ginette@elmcrest.biz
- w elmcrest.biz

Huddersfield Central Lodge
★★★★ *Guest Accommodation*
SILVER AWARD
11-15 Beast Market, Huddersfield
HD1 1QF
- t (01484) 515551
- e enquiries@centrallodge.com
- w centrallodge.com

Thornes Farm Bed & Breakfast
★★★★★ *Bed & Breakfast*
SILVER AWARD
Thornes Farm, Knotty Lane,
Huddersfield
HD8 0ND
- t (01484) 604024
- e janet.woodhead@googlemail.com
- w thornesfarm.com

Weirside Bed & Breakfast ★★★★
Guest Accommodation
SILVER AWARD
Weirside Bungalow, Weirside
Marsden, Huddersfield
HD8 0ND
- t (01484) 842214
- e david.elder3@btinternet.com
- w marsdenbedandbreakfast.com

Woods End Bed & Breakfast
★★★★ *Guest Accommodation*
46 Inglewood Avenue, Huddersfield
HD2 2DS
- t (01484) 513580
- e jmsm2306@hotmail.com
- w the-woods-end.co.uk

HUGGATE

Greenwick Farm Bed & Breakfast
★★★★ *Farmhouse* **SILVER AWARD**
Greenwick Farm, Huggate, Driffield
YO42 1YR
- t (01377) 288122
- e greenwickfarm@hotmail.com
- w greenwickfarm.co.uk

HULL

Acorn Guest House ★★★★
Guest House
719 Beverley Road, Hull
HU6 7JN
- t (01482) 853248
- e janet_the_acorn@yahoo.com
- w acornguesthousehull.co.uk

The Admiral Guest House ★★
Bed & Breakfast
234 The Boulevard, Hull
HU3 3ED
- t (01482) 329664

Cornerbrook Guest House ★★★★
Guest House **SILVER AWARD**
1 Desmond Avenue, Beverley Road,
Hull
HU6 7JY
- t (01482) 474377
- e cornerbrookhouse@cornerbrookhouse.karoo.co.uk

The Earlsmere Guest House ★★★
Guest House
76-78 Sunny Bank, Hull
HU3 1LQ
- t (01482) 341977
- e su@earlsmerehotel.karoo.co.uk
- w earlsmerehotel.co.uk

The Endsleigh Centre ★★★
Guest Accommodation
481 Beverley Road, Hull
HU6 7LJ
- t (01482) 342779
- e endsleigh@endsleigh.karoo.co.uk
- w endsleighcentre.org.uk

Whittington & Cat ★★★★ *Inn*
Commercial Road, Hull
HU1 2SA
- t (01482) 327786

HUTTON-LE-HOLE

Burnley House ★★★★
Guest House **SILVER AWARD**
Hutton-le-Hole, Kirkbymoorside
YO62 6UA
- t (01751) 417548
- e info@burnleyhouse.co.uk
- w burnleyhouse.co.uk

ILKLEY

Denton View ★★★ *Bed & Breakfast*
10 Manley Road, Ilkley
LS29 8QS
- t (01943) 430373
- e dentonview@hotmail.com
- w dentonview.co.uk

Moorland View Bed & Breakfast
★★★★ *Bed & Breakfast*
4 Manor Rise, Ilkley
LS29 8QL
- t (01943) 816483
- e bandb@moorlandviewilkley.co.uk
- w moorlandviewilkley.co.uk

One Tivoli Place ★★★★
Guest Accommodation
1 Tivoli Place, Ilkley
LS29 8SU
- t (01943) 600328
- e enquiries@tivoliplace.co.uk
- w tivoliplace.co.uk

INGLETON

The Dales Guest House ★★★
Guest House
Main Street, Ingleton
LA6 3HH
- t (01524) 241401
- e dalesgh@hotmail.com
- w dalesguesthouse.co.uk

Gatehouse Farm ★★★★
Farmhouse
Westhouse, Ingleton
LA6 3NR
- t (01524) 241458
- e gatehousefarm@ktdinternet.com
- w yorkshirenet.co.uk/stayat/gatehousefarm/

Ingleborough View Guest House
★★★★ *Guest House*
Main Street, Ingleton
LA6 3HH
- t (01524) 241523
- e sue@ingleboroughview.com
- w ingleboroughview.com

Inglenook Guest House ★★★★
Guest Accommodation
20 Main Street, Ingleton
LA6 3HJ
- t (01524) 241270
- e inglenook20@hotmail.com
- w inglenookguesthouse.com

Ingleton YHA ★★★★ *Hostel*
Greta Tower, Sammy Lane, Ingleton
LA6 3EG
- t (01524) 241444
- w yha.org.uk

New Butts Farm ★★★ *Guest House*
New Butts Farm, High Bentham,
Ingleton
LA2 7AN
- t (01524) 241238
- e jeanandterry@googlemail.com
- w newbutts.co.uk

The Pines Country House ★★★★
Guest House
New Road, Ingleton
LA6 3HN
- t (01524) 241252
- e pinesingleton@aol.com
- w pinesingleton.com

Riverside Lodge ★★★★
Guest House **SILVER AWARD**
24 Main Street, Ingleton
LA6 3HJ
- t (01524) 241359
- e info@riversideingleton.co.uk
- w riversideingleton.co.uk

Springfield Country Guest House
★★★★ *Guest Accommodation*
26 Main Street, Ingleton
LA6 3HJ
- t (01524) 241280
- w ingleton.co.uk

Thorngarth Country Guest House
★★★★ *Guest House*
SILVER AWARD
New Road, Ingleton
LA6 3HN
- t (01524) 241295
- e davidegregory@btopenworld.com
- w thorngarth.co.uk

JERVAULX

Park House ★★★★★
Guest Accommodation
SILVER AWARD
Jervaulx, Ripon
HG4 4PH
- t (01677) 460184
- e ba123@btopenworld.com
- w jervaulxabbey.com/parkhouse.php

KEIGHLEY

Golden View Guest House ★★★
Guest Accommodation
21 Golden View Drive, Keighley,
Haworth
BD21 4SN
- t (01535) 662138
- e info@goldenview.supanet.com

KELLINGTON

The Old Vicarage ★★★★
Guest Accommodation
Main Street, Kellington, Selby
DN14 0NE
- t (01977) 661119
- e enquiries@theoldvicarageyorkshire.co.uk
- w theoldvicarageyorkshire.co.uk

KETTLEWELL

Kettlewell YHA ★★★ *Hostel*
Whernside House, Westgate,
Skipton
BD23 5QU
- t (01756) 760232
- e kettlewell@yha.org.uk
- w yha.org.uk

Littlebeck ★★★★
Guest Accommodation
SILVER AWARD
Littlebeck, Kettlewell, Skipton
BD23 5RD
- t (01756) 760378
- e stay@little-beck.co.uk
- w little-beck.co.uk

Yorkshire

KILBURN

Church Farm ★★★ *Farmhouse*
Church Farm, Kilburn, Thirsk
YO61 4AH
t (01347) 868318
e churchfarmkilburn@yahoo.com

The Forresters Arms ★★★ *Inn*
The Square, Kilburn, Thirsk
YO61 4AH
t (01347) 868386
e admin@forrestersarms.com
w forrestersarms.com

KILHAM

Blacksmiths Cottage Country Guest House ★★★★ *Guest House*
Driffield Road, Kilham, Driffield
YO25 4SN
t (01262) 420624
e rob@blacksmiths.orangehome.co.uk
w blacksmithscottage.org.uk

Kilham Hall Country House ★★★★★ *Guest Accommodation*
GOLD AWARD
Driffield Road, Kilham, Driffield
YO25 4SP
t (01262) 420466
e enquiries@kilhamhall.com
w kilhamhall.com

KILNSEA

Westmere Farm ★★★ *Farmhouse*
Westmere Farm, Kilnsea Road, Withernsea
HU12 0UB
t (01964) 650258
e westmerefarm@btconnect.com
w westmerefarm.com

KILNWICK PERCY

The Wolds Retreat ★★★★
Guest Accommodation
Kilnwick Percy Hall, Kilnwick Percy, Pocklington
YO42 1UF
t (01759) 305968
e info@thewoldsretreat.co.uk
w TheWoldsRetreat.co.uk

KIRBY HILL

Shoulder of Mutton ★★★ *Inn*
Shoulder of Mutton, Kirby Hill, Reeth
DL11 7JH
t (01748) 822772
e info@shoulderofmutton.net
w shoulderofmutton.net

KIRBY MISPERTON

Beansheaf ★★★★ *Inn*
Malton Road, Kirby Misperton, Malton
YO17 6UE
t (01653) 668114
e enquiries@beansheafhotel.com
w beansheafhotel.com

KIRBURTON

Manor Mill Cottage ★★★★
Bed & Breakfast
21 Linfit Lane, Kirkburton, Huddersfield
HD8 0TY
t (01484) 604109
e d.askham@btinternet.com
w manormillcottage.co.uk

Storthes Hall Park ★★★ *Campus*
Storthes Hall Park, Storthes Hall Lane, Kirkburton, Huddersfield
HD8 0WA
t (01484) 488820
e info@stortheshall.co.uk
w stortheshall.co.uk

The Woodman Inn ★★★★ *Inn*
Thunderbridge Lane, Kirkburton, Huddersfield
HD8 0PX
t (01484) 605778
e thewoodman@connectfree.co.uk
w woodman-inn.co.uk

KIRKBY-IN-CLEVELAND

Dromonby Grange Farm ★★★★
Farmhouse
Busby Lane, Kirkby-in-Cleveland, Stokesley
TS9 7AR
t (01642) 712227
e jeanhugill@dromonbygrangefarm.co.uk
w dromonbygrangefarm.co.uk

Dromonby Hall Farm ★★★
Bed & Breakfast
Busby Lane, Kirkby-in-Cleveland, Stokesley
TS9 7AP
t (01642) 712312
e pat@dromonby.co.uk
w dromonby.co.uk

KIRKBY MALZEARD

Cowscot House ★★★★
Bed & Breakfast
Back Lane, Kirkby Malzeard, Ripon, N. Yorkshire
HG4 3SE
t 01765 658181
e liz@cowscothouse.co.uk
w cowscothouse.co.uk

KIRKBYMOORSIDE

Brickfields Farm ★★★★
Farmhouse SILVER AWARD
Kirkby Mills, Kirkbymoorside
YO62 6NS
t (01751) 433074
e janet@brickfieldsfarm.co.uk
w brickfieldsfarm.co.uk

The Cornmill ★★★★ *Guest House*
SILVER AWARD
Kirby Mills, Kirkbymoorside
YO62 6NP
t (01751) 432000
e cornmill@kirbymills.co.uk
w kirbymills.demon.co.uk

The Feversham Arms Inn ★★★★
Inn
Church Houses, Farndale, Kirkbymoorside
YO62 7LF
t (01751) 433206
e rrmurray2@aol.com
w fevershamarmsinn.co.uk

George & Dragon ★★★★ *Inn*
Market Place, Kirkbymoorside
YO62 6AA
t (01751) 433334
e reception@georgeanddragon.net
w georgeanddragon.net

KNARESBOROUGH

Ebor Mount ★★★ *Guest House*
18 York Place, Knaresborough
HG5 0AA
t (01423) 863315
e info@ebormount.co.uk
w ebormount.co.uk

Gallon House ★★★★★
Guest House SILVER AWARD
47 Kirkgate, Knaresborough
HG5 8BZ
t (01423) 862102
e gallon-house@ntlworld.com
w gallon-house.co.uk

The Mitre ★★★★★ *Inn*
SILVER AWARD
4 Station Road, Knaresborough
HG5 9AA
t (01423) 868948
e office@themitreinn.co.uk
w themitreinn.co.uk

The Old Royal Oak ★★★★ *Inn*
7 Market Place, Knaresborough
HG5 8AL
t (01423) 865880
e thebarns@theroyaloak.demon.net
w theoldroyaloak-knaresborough.co.uk

KNOTTINGLEY

Wentvale Court ★★★★
Guest Accommodation
Great North Road, Knottingley, Pontefract
WF11 8PF
t (01977) 676714
e wentvale1@btconnect.com
w wentvalecourt.co.uk

LANGTOFT

The Old Mill Hotel & Restaurant ★★★ *Inn*
Mill Lane, Langtoft, Driffield
YO25 3BQ
t (01377) 267284
e enquiries@old-mill-hotel.co.uk
w old-mill-hotel.co.uk

LEALHOLM

High Park Farm ★★★★ *Farmhouse*
High Park Farm, Lealholm, Whitby
YO21 2AQ
t (01947) 897416
e highparkfarm@btinternet.com
w highparklealholm.co.uk

LEEDS

Abbey Guest House ★★★★
Guest House
44 Vesper Road, Leeds
LS5 3NX
t (0113) 278 5580
e enquiries@abbeyguesthouseleeds.co.uk
w abbeyguesthouseleeds.co.uk

Avalon Guest House ★★★★
Guest House
132 Woodsley Road, Leeds
LS2 9LZ
t (0113) 243 2545
e info@woodsleyroad.com
w avalonguesthouseleeds.co.uk

Cliff Lawn ★★★★
Guest Accommodation
44-45 Cliff Road, Headingley, Leeds
LS6 2ET
t (0113) 278 5442
e enquiries@clifflawn-hotel.co.uk
w clifflawn-hotel.co.uk

Glengarth Guest House ★★★
Guest House
162 Woodsley Road, Leeds
LS2 9LZ
t (0113) 245 7940
e info@woodsleyroad.com
w glengarthhotel.co.uk

Green House ★★★ *Bed & Breakfast*
5 Bank View, Chapel Allerton, Leeds
LS7 2EX
t (0113) 268 1380

Headingley Lodge ★★★★
Guest Accommodation - Room Only
Headingley Stadium, St Michael's Lane, Leeds
LS6 3BR
t (0113) 278 5323
e reservations@headingleylodge.co.uk
w headingleylodge.co.uk

Hinsley Hall ★★★
Guest Accommodation
62 Headingley Lane, Leeds
LS6 2BX
t (0113) 261 8000
e info@hinsley-hall.co.uk
w hinsley-hall.co.uk

The Moorlea ★★★
Guest Accommodation
146 Woodsley Road, Leeds
LS2 9LZ
t (0113) 243 2653
e themoorleahotel@aol.com
w moorleahotel.co.uk

Oak Villa ★★★
Guest Accommodation
55-57 Cardigan Road, Leeds
LS6 1DW
t (0113) 275 8439
e oakvillahotel@msn.com
w oakvillahotel.com

University of Leeds ★★★ *Campus*
Conference Office, University House, University of Leeds, Leeds
LS2 9JT
t (0113) 233 6100
e david@universallyleeds.co.uk
w leeds.ac.uk/conference

LEEMING BAR

Little Holtby ★★★★
Bed & Breakfast GOLD AWARD
Leeming Bar, Northallerton, Bedale
DL7 9LH
t (01609) 748762
e littleholtby@yahoo.co.uk
w littleholtby.co.uk

LEVISHAM

The Horseshoe Inn ★★★★ *Inn*
Main Street, Levisham, Pickering
YO18 7NL
t (01751) 460240
e info@horseshoelevisham.co.uk
w horseshoeinn-levisham.co.uk

The Moorlands Country House ★★★★★ *Guest House*
GOLD AWARD
Main Street, Levisham, Pickering
YO18 7NL
t (01751) 460229
e ronaldoleonardo@aol.com
w moorlandslevisham.co.uk

LEYBURN

Clyde House ★★★★
Guest Accommodation
SILVER AWARD
5 Railway Street, Leyburn
DL8 5AY
t (01969) 623941
e lucia.fisher1@btinternet.com
w clydehouseleyburn.co.uk

Dales Haven Guest House ★★★
Guest House
Market Place, Leyburn
DL8 5BJ
t (01969) 623814
e info@daleshaven.co.uk
w daleshaven.co.uk

Eastfield Lodge ★★★★
Guest House
1 St Matthews Terrace, Leyburn
DL8 5EL
t (01969) 623196
e paula@eastfieldlodge.co.uk
w eastfieldlodge.co.uk

Greenhills ★★★★ *Bed & Breakfast*
SILVER AWARD
5 Middleham Road, Leyburn
DL8 5EY
t (01969) 623859
e susan@greenhillsleyburn.co.uk
w greenhillsleyburn.co.uk

Holmedale Bed & Breakfast ★★★★ *Bed & Breakfast*
SILVER AWARD
Main Street, Leyburn
DL8 3HT
t (01969) 650910
e enquiries@holmedale-askrigg.com
w holmedale-askrigg.com

Stow House ★★★★
Guest Accommodation
SILVER AWARD
Aysgarth Falls, Aysgarth, Leyburn
DL8 3SR
t (01969) 663635
e info@stowhouse.co.uk
w stowhouse.co.uk

LINTON

Linton Laithe ★★★★★ *Farmhouse*
SILVER AWARD
The Grange, Linton-in-Craven, Skipton
BD23 5HH
t (01756) 752230
e stay@lintonlaithe.co.uk
w lintonlaithe.co.uk

Yorkshire

LITTLE CRAKEHALL

rakehall Watermill ★★★★
ed & Breakfast **SILVER AWARD**
rakehall Watermill, Little Crakehall,
edale
8 1HU
t (01677) 423240
e stay@crakehallwatermill.co.uk
w crakehallwatermill.co.uk

LOCKTON

arfields Farmhouse ★★★★
armhouse
arfields Farmhouse, Lockton,
ckering
18 7NQ
t (01751) 460239
e stay@farfieldsfarm.co.uk
w farfieldsfarm.co.uk

HA Lockton ★★★★ *Hostel*
e Old School, Lockton, Unknown
18 7PY
t (01751) 460376
e lockton@yha.org.uk
w yha.org.uk

LOFTHOUSE

udfold Farm Activity Centre
★★ *Group Hostel*
udfold Farm, Lofthouse, Pateley
idge
G3 5SG
t (01423) 755399
e enquiries@studfoldfarm.co.uk
w studfoldfarm.co.uk

LONDONDERRY

atton Lodge ★★★ *Guest House*
ondonderry, Northallerton, Bedale
L7 9NF
t (01677) 422222
e enquiries@tattonlodge.co.uk
w tattonlodge.co.uk

LOW ROW

he Old Dairy ★★★★
Guest Accommodation
ILVER AWARD
he Old Dairy, Low Row, Reeth
L11 6PE
t (01748) 886215
e theolddairy@swaledale.org
w theolddairy-swaledale.co.uk

owleth End Guest House ★★★★
uest House **SILVER AWARD**
w Row - Gunnerside, Upper
waledale, Reeth
L11 6PY
t (01748) 886327
e stay@upperswale.co.uk
w upperswale.co.uk

ummer Lodge ★★★★ *Farmhouse*
ummer Lodge Farm, Low Row,
chmond
L11 6NP
t (01748) 886504
w summerlodgefarm.co.uk

LOXLEY

arnfield House ★★★★
uest Accommodation
ILVER AWARD
oxley Road, Loxley, Sheffield
6 6RW
t (0114) 233 6265
e enquiries@barnfieldhouse.com
w barnfieldhouse.com

LUDDENDENFOOT

ockcliffe West ★★★★
ed & Breakfast
urnley Road, Luddendenfoot,
alifax
X2 6HL
t (01422) 882151
e rockcliffe.b.b@virgin.net
w rockcliffewest.co.uk

MALHAM

Malham YHA ★★★ *Hostel*
Malham YHA, Malham, Skipton
BD23 4DE
t (01729) 830321
e malham@yha.org.uk
w yha.org.uk

Miresfield Farm ★★★ *Guest House*
Miresfield Farm, Malham
BD23 4DA
t (01729) 830414
e info@miresfield-farm.com
w miresfield-farm.com

MALTON

Old Lodge Malton ★★★★
Guest Accommodation
Old Maltongate, Malton
YO17 7EG
t (01653) 690570
e info@theoldlodgemalton.com
w theoldlodgemalton.com

MAPPLEWELL

The Grange ★★★ *Guest House*
29 Spark Lane, Mapplewell, Barnsley
S75 6AA
t (01226) 380078
e hwje454@aol.com

MARKET WEIGHTON

Towthorpe Grange ★★
Guest Accommodation
Towthorpe Lane, Londesborough,
Driffield
YO43 3LB
t (01430) 873814
e towthorpegrange@hotmail.com

MARRICK

Marrick Moor B&B ★★★★
Bed & Breakfast
Marrick Moor House, Marrick,
Richmond
DL11 7LF
t (01748) 884065
e info@marrickmoorbedandbreakfast.co.uk
w marrickmoorbedandbreakfast.co.uk

MARSH

Croppers Arms ★★★★
Guest Accommodation
136 Westbourne Road, Huddersfield
HD1 4LF
t (01484) 421522
e enquiries@greystone.co.uk
w croppersarms.co.uk

MASHAM

Garden House ★★★★
Guest Accommodation
1 Park Street, Masham, Ripon
HG4 4HN
t (01765) 689989
e suefurbymasham@gmail.com
w gardenhousemasham.co.uk

Glasshouse B&B (Uredale Glass)
★★★★ *Guest Accommodation*
42 Market Place, Masham, Ripon
HG4 4EF
t (01765) 689780
e info@uredale.co.uk

Warren House Farm ★★★★
Farmhouse
High Ellington, Masham
HG4 4PP
t (01677) 460244
e cathebroadley@msn.com

The White Bear Hotel ★★★★★
Inn
Wellgarth, Masham
HG4 4EN
t (01765) 689319
e sue@whitebearmasham.co.uk
w whitebearmasham.co.uk

MELMERBY

West Close Farmhouse ★★★★
Guest Accommodation
Melmerby in Coverdale, Leyburn
DL8 4TW
t (01969) 640275
e westclosefarmhouse@btinternet.com
w westclosefarmhouse.co.uk

MENSTON

Chevin End Guest House ★★★
Guest House
West Chevin Road, Menston, Ilkley
LS29 6BE
t (01943) 876845
e chevinendguesthouse.co.uk

MIDDLEHAM

The Priory ★★★★ *Guest House*
SILVER AWARD
West End, Middleham, Leyburn
DL8 4QG
t (01969) 623279
e priory.guesthouse@virgin.net
w prioryguesthouse.co.uk

MIDDLETON TYAS

Vintage ★★ *Inn*
Scotch Corner, Middleton Tyas,
Richmond
DL10 6NP
t (01748) 824424
e thevintagescotchcorner@btopenworld.com
w thevintagehotel.co.uk

MIDGLEY

Midgley Lodge Motel ★★★★
Guest Accommodation
Bar Lane, Midgley, Wakefield
WF4 4JJ
t (01924) 830069
e midgleylodgemotel@tiscali.co.uk
w midgleylodgemotel.co.uk

MILLINGTON

Laburnum Cottage B&B ★★★
Bed & Breakfast
Millington, York Near Pocklington
YO42 1TX
t (01759) 303055
e mdykesbb@googlemail.com
w millingtonbandb.co.uk

MORLEY

End Lea ★★
Guest Accommodation - Room Only
39 Town Street, Gildersome, Leeds
LS27 7AX
t 07830 470200
e pat_mcbride@talktalk.net
w endleaguesthouse.com

MUKER

Muker Village Stores & Tea Shop
★★★★ *Bed & Breakfast*
The Village Stores, Muker, Richmond
DL11 6QG
t (01748) 886409
e mukerteashop@btinternet.com
w mukervillage.co.uk

NEWBIGGIN

Street Head Inn ★★★★ *Inn*
Newbiggin-in-Bishopdale, Leyburn
DL8 3TE
t (01969) 663282
e joanne.fawcett@virgin.net
w streetheadinn.co.uk

NEWBRIDGE

Lowther House ★★★★
Bed & Breakfast
Newbridge, Pickering
YO18 8JL
t (01751) 467157
e phil@lowtherhouse.com
w lowtherhouse.com

NEWBY WISKE

Well House ★★★★
Guest Accommodation
Newby Wiske, Northallerton, Thirsk
DL7 9EX
t (01609) 772253
e info@wellhouse-newbywiske.co.uk
w wellhouse-newbywiske.co.uk

NEWHOLM

Beehive Inne ★★★★ *Inn*
GOLD AWARD
Newholm, Whitby
YO21 3QY
t (01947) 602703
w thebeehiveinne.co.uk

NEWTON-ON-RAWCLIFFE

Elm House Farm ★★★★
Farmhouse
Newton-on-Rawcliffe, Pickering
YO18 8QA
t (01751) 473223
e elmhousefarm.co.uk

NORTHALLERTON

Alverton Guest House ★★★
Guest House
26 South Parade, Northallerton
DL7 8SG
t (01609) 776207
e alvertonguesthse@btconnect.com
w alvertonguesthouse.com

Bridge End ★★★ *Bed & Breakfast*
159 Chantry Road, Northallerton
DL7 8JJ
t (01609) 772655

Elmscott ★★★★ *Bed & Breakfast*
SILVER AWARD
10 Hatfield Road, Northallerton
DL7 8QX
t (01609) 760575
e elmscott@btinternet.com
w elmscottbedandbreakfast.co.uk

Lovesome Hill Farm ★★★★
Farmhouse **SILVER AWARD**
Lovesome Hill Farm, Lovesome Hill,
Northallerton, North Yorkshire
DL6 2PB
t (01609) 772311
e lovesomehillfarm@btinternet.com
w lovesomehillfarm.co.uk

Masham House Bed & Breakfast
★★★★ *Bed & Breakfast*
18 South Parade, Northallerton
DL7 8SG
t (01609) 779198
e info@bandbnorthallerton.co.uk
w bandbnorthallerton.co.uk

Victoria House B&B ★★★★
Bed & Breakfast
Victoria House, 36 South Parade,
Northallerton
DL7 8SG
t (01609) 776367
e heslopgill@btinternet.com

NORTH CLIFFE

Red House ★★★★
Guest Accommodation
North Cliffe, Market Weighton,
Beverley
YO43 4XB
t (01430) 827652
e simon.lyn@virgin.net
w redhousenorthcliffe.co.uk

NORTON

Brambling Fields B&B ★★★★
Bed & Breakfast
Brambling Fields, Scarborough
Road, Malton
YO17 8EE
t (01653) 698510
e info@bramblingfields.co.uk
w bramblingfields.co.uk

Yorkshire

NUNNINGTON

Sunley Court ★★★ *Farmhouse*
Muscoates, Nunnington, Helmsley
YO62 5XQ
t (01439) 748233
e sunleycourt@tiscali.co.uk

OLD BYLAND

Barn Close Farm ★★★★
Farmhouse
Barn Close Farm, Old Byland, Helmsley
YO62 5LH
t (01439) 798321
e joanmilburn2@tesco.net

OLDSTEAD

Oldstead Grange ★★★★★
Guest Accommodation
GOLD AWARD
Oldstead, Coxwold, York
YO61 4BL
t (01347) 868634
e enquiries@oldsteadgrange.co.uk
w oldsteadgrange.co.uk

OSGOODBY

Low Osgoodby Grange ★★★★
Farmhouse
Low Osgoodby Grange, Bagby, Thirsk
YO7 2AL
t (01845) 597241
e lowosgoodbygrange@googlemail.com

OSMOTHERLEY

Osmotherley YHA ★★★ *Hostel*
Cote Ghyll, Osmotherley, Northallerton
DL6 3AH
t (01609) 883575
e osmotherley@yha.org.uk
w yha.org.uk

Vane House ★★★★
Guest Accommodation
11A North End, Osmotherley, Northallerton
DL6 3BA
t (01609) 883448
e allan@vanehouse.co.uk
w coast2coast.co.uk/vanehouse

OTLEY

The Timble Inn
Guest Accommodation
Timble, Otley
LS21 2NN
t (01943) 880530
e info@thetimbleinn.co.uk
w thetimbleinn.co.uk

OULTON

New Masons Arms ★★★ *Inn*
26 Aberford Road, Leeds
LS26 8JR
t (0113) 282 2334

OVER SILTON

Greystone Farm ★★★★
Farmhouse
Over Silton, Thirsk
YO7 2LH
t (01609) 883468
e info@greystonefarm-bedandbreakfast.co.uk
w greystonefarm-bedandbreakfast.co.uk

OXENHOPE

Springfield Guest House ★★★★
Guest House
Springfield, Shaw Lane, Haworth
BD22 9QL
t (01535) 643951
e springfieldguesthouse@hotmail.com
w springfield-guesthouse@hotmail.com

PARKGATE

Fitzwilliam Arms ★★★
Guest Accommodation
Taylors Lane, Parkgate, Rotherham
S62 6EE
t (01709) 522744
w fitzwilliam-arms-hotel.co.uk

PATELEY BRIDGE

Bewerley Hall Farm ★★★
Farmhouse
Bewerley Hall Farm, Bewerley, Pateley Bridge
HG3 5JA
t (01423) 711636
e bewerleyhallfarm@yahoo.co.uk
w bewerleyhallfarm.co.uk

High Green Farm ★★★★★
Bed & Breakfast **SILVER AWARD**
Wath Road, Wath, Pateley Bridge
HG3 5PJ
t (01423) 715958
e info@highgreen-nidderdale.co.uk
w highgreen-nidderdale.co.uk

Lyndale Guest House ★★★
Guest House
King Street, Pateley Bridge
HG3 5AT
t (01423) 712657
e lyndale.guesthouse@talktalk.net
w lyndaleguesthouse.com

Nidderdale Lodge Farm ★★★
Farmhouse
Fellbeck, Ripon Road, Pateley Bridge
HG3 5DR
t (01423) 711677
e nidderdalelodgefarm.co.uk/

PATRICK BROMPTON

Mill Close Farm ★★★★★
Farmhouse **GOLD AWARD**
Patrick Brompton, Bedale
DL8 1JY
t (01677) 450257
e pat@millclose.co.uk
w millclose.co.uk

Neesham Cottage ★★★★
Bed & Breakfast
Patrick Brompton, Bedale
DL8 1LN
t (01677) 450271
e info@neeshamcottage.co.uk
w neeshamcottage.co.uk

PENISTONE

Cubley Hall Inn ★★★★ *Inn*
SILVER AWARD
Mortimer Road, Penistone, Barnsley
S36 9DF
t (01226) 766086
e info@cubleyhall.co.uk
w cubleyhall.co.uk

PICKERING

Ashfield House Bed & Breakfast
★★★★ *Bed & Breakfast*
SILVER AWARD
Ashfield House, Ruffa Lane, Pickering
YO18 7HN
t (01751) 477429
e info@ashfield-house.co.uk
w ashfield-house.co.uk

Barker Stakes Farm ★★★★
Farmhouse
Lendals Lane, Pickering
YO18 8EE
t (01751) 476759
e info@barkerstakesfarm.com
w barkerstakesfarm.com

Bramwood Guest House ★★★★
Guest House **SILVER AWARD**
19 Hallgarth, Pickering
YO18 7AW
t (01751) 474066
e enquiries@bramwoodguesthouse.co.uk
w bramwoodguesthouse.co.uk

Bridge House ★★★★
Bed & Breakfast **SILVER AWARD**
8 Bridge Street, Pickering
YO18 8DT
t (01751) 477234
e kgbridgehouse@tiscali.co.uk
w bridgehousepickering.com

Cawthorne House ★★★★
Bed & Breakfast **SILVER AWARD**
42 Eastgate, Pickering
YO18 7DU
t (01751) 477364
e info@cawthornehouse.com
w cawthornehouse.com

Eleven Westgate ★★★★
Bed & Breakfast **SILVER AWARD**
Eden House, 11 Westgate, Pickering
YO18 8BA
t (01751) 475111
e info@elevenwestgate.co.uk
w elevenwestgate.co.uk

Grindale House ★★★★
Guest Accommodation
SILVER AWARD
123 Eastgate, Pickering
YO18 7DW
t (01751) 476636
e info@grindalehouse.co.uk
w grindalehouse.com

The Hawthornes ★★★★
Bed & Breakfast **SILVER AWARD**
High Back Side, Middleton, Nr Pickering
YO18 8PB
t (01751) 474755
e paulaappleby@btinternet.com
w thehawthornes.co.uk

Kirkham Garth Bed & Breakfast
★★★ *Bed & Breakfast*
Kirkham Garth, Whitby Road, Pickering
YO18 7AT
t (01751) 474931
e kirkhamgarth@hotmail.com
w kirkhamgarth.co.uk

Laurel Bank ★★★ *Bed & Breakfast*
Swainsea Lane, Pickering, North Yorkshire
YO18 8AP
t 01751 476 399 mob 07766495071
e brenda.devine@btinternet.com
w laurelbankpickering.co.uk

No 9 luxury B&B ★★★★
Bed & Breakfast **SILVER AWARD**
9 Thornton Road, Pickering
YO18 7HZ
t (01751) 476533
e info@no9pickering.co.uk
w no9pickering.co.uk

Number 17 Burgate ★★★★★
Guest Accommodation
GOLD AWARD
17 Burgate, Pickering
YO18 7AU
t (01751) 473463
e info@17burgate.co.uk
w 17burgate.co.uk

The Old Vicarage at Toftly View
★★★★★ *Guest Accommodation*
GOLD AWARD
The Old Vicarage, Toftly View, Pickering
YO18 8QD
t (01751) 476126
e oldvic@toftlyview.co.uk
w toftlyview.co.uk

Sevenford House ★★★★
Guest Accommodation
SILVER AWARD
Sevenford House, Rosedale Abbey, Pickering
YO18 8SE
t (01751) 417283
e sevenford@aol.com
w sevenford.com

Vivers Mill ★★★★ *Guest House*
Mill Lane, Pickering
YO18 8DJ
t (01751) 473640
e viversmill@talk21.com
w viversmill.co.uk

PICKERING (4 MILES)

The Old Forge Bed & Breakfast
★★★★ *Bed & Breakfast*
Wilton, North Yorkshire., Pickering
YO18 7JY
t (01751) 477399
e theoldforge1@aol.com
w forgecottages.co.uk

PIERCEBRIDGE

Holme House ★★★ *Farmhouse*
Piercebridge, Darlington
DL2 3SY
t (01325) 374280
e graham.holmehouse@gmail.com
w holmehouse.com

POCKLEY

West View Cottage ★★★★
Bed & Breakfast **GOLD AWARD**
West View Cottage, Pockley, Helmsley
YO62 7TE
t (01439) 770526
e westviewcottage@tiscali.co.uk
w westviewcottage.info

PONTEFRACT

Tower House Executive Guest House ★★★★★ *Guest House*
GOLD AWARD
21 Bondgate, Pontefract
WF8 2JP
t (01977) 699988
e info@towerhouseguesthouse.com
w towerhouseguesthouse.com

PRESTON

Little Weghill Farm ★★★★
Farmhouse **SILVER AWARD**
Weghill Road, Preston, Hull
HU12 8SX
t (01482) 897650
e info@littleweghillfarm.co.uk
w littleweghillfarm.co.uk

PRESTON-UNDER-SCAR

Hawthorn Cottage ★★★★
Bed & Breakfast **SILVER AWARD**
Preston-under-Scar, Leyburn
DL8 4AQ
t (01969) 624492
e helen@ricduffield.com
w hawthorn-wensleydale.com

The Old School Barn ★★★★★
Guest Accommodation
SILVER AWARD
Somerset House, Preston-under-Scar, Leyburn
DL8 4AH
t (01969) 625425
e janjchris@aol.com
w theoldschoolbarn.co.uk

PUDSEY

Lynnwood House ★★★
Guest House
18 Alexandra Road, Uppermoor, Leeds
LS28 8BY
t (0113) 257 1117
e lynnwoodhouse.co.uk

RASKELF

Old Black Bull Inn ★★★ *Inn*
Raskelf, Easingwold
YO61 3LF
t (01347) 821431
e info@northyorkshotel.co.uk
w northyorkshotel.co.uk

The Old Farmhouse ★★★★
Bed & Breakfast
North End, Raskelf, Easingwold
YO61 3LF
t (01347) 821491
e oldfarmhouse4bb@aol.com
w theoldfarmhouseraskelfyork.co.uk

546   Official tourist board guide **Bed & Breakfa**

Yorkshire

RATHMELL

ittlebank Guest House ★★★★★
est House **SILVER AWARD**
tlebank, Rathmell, Settle
024 0AJ
t (01729) 822330
e richardlord495@hotmail.com
w littlebankcountryhouse.co.uk

RAVENSCAR

nugglers Rock Country House
★★★ *Guest House*
aintondale Road, Ravenscar,
arborough
013 0ER
t (01723) 870044
e info@smugglersrock.co.uk
w smugglersrock.co.uk

REDCAR

rmada Guest House ★★★
uest House
-30 Henry Street, Redcar
10 1BJ
t (01642) 471710
e info@armadaguesthouse.co.uk
w armadaguesthouse.co.uk

REDMIRE

**he Old Town Hall Guest House
& Tea Room** ★★★★★
est Accommodation
OLD AWARD
e Old Town Hall Guest House &
a Room, Redmire, Aysgarth Falls
8 4ED
t (01969) 625641
e enquiries@theoldtownhall.co.uk
w theoldtownhall.co.uk

REETH

rkleside Country Guest House
★★★ *Guest House*
kleside Hotel, Reeth
11 6SG
t (01748) 884200
e arkleside@supanet.com
w arklesidehotel.co.uk

ambridge House ★★★★★
est House **SILVER AWARD**
kengarthdale Road, Reeth
11 6QX
t (01748) 884633
e info@cambridgehousereeth.co.uk
w cambridgehousereeth.co.uk

y Cottage ★★★
est Accommodation
e Green, Reeth
11 6SF
t (01748) 884418
e ivycottagereeth@supanet.com
w ivycottagereeth.co.uk

ddings Farm ★★★★ *Farmhouse*
ddings Farm, Reeth
11 6UR
t (01748) 884267

RICCALL

airymans of Riccall ★★★★
uest Accommodation
4 Kelfield Road, Riccall, York
O19 6PG
t (01757) 248532
e bookings@dairymansriccall.co.uk
w dairymansriccall.co.uk

outh Newlands Farm ★★★
armhouse
elby Road, Riccall, York
O19 6QR
t (01757) 248203
e southnewlandsfarm@yahoo.co.uk
w southnewlandsfarm.co.uk

hite Rose Villa ★★★★
ed & Breakfast
3 York Road, Riccall, York
O19 6QG
t (01757) 248115
e whiterosevilla@btinternet.com
w whiterosevilla-info.com

RICHMOND

Arandale Guest House ★★★★
Guest Accommodation
27 Queens road, Richmond
DL10 4AL
t (01748) 821282
e stay@arandaleguesthouse.co.uk
w arandaleguesthouse.co.uk

Beechfield Bed & Breakfast
★★★★ *Bed & Breakfast*
16 Beechfield Road, Richmond
DL10 4PN
t (01748) 824060
e enquiries@beechfieldrichmond.
co.uk
w beechfieldrichmond.co.uk

Bridgedown House B&B ★★★
Bed & Breakfast
Station Cottages, Richmond
DL10 4LB
t (01748) 821233
e jenn260982@hotmail.co.uk
w bridgedownhouse.com

The Buck Inn ★★★ *Inn*
27-29 Newbiggin, Richmond, North
Yorkshire
DL10 4DX
t 01748 822259
e garymay90@hotmail.com
w thebuckhotelrichmond.co.uk

Frenchgate Guest House ★★★★
Guest Accommodation
66 Frenchgate, Richmond
DL10 7AG
t (01748) 823421
e info@66frenchgate.co.uk
w 66frenchgate.co.uk

Nuns Cottage ★★★★
Guest Accommodation
5 Hurgill Road, Richmond
DL10 4AR
t (01748) 822809
e the.flints@ukgateway.net
w nunscottage.co.uk

The Old Brewery Guest House
★★★ *Guest House*
29 The Green, Richmond
DL10 4RG
t (01748) 822460
e info@oldbreweryguesthouse.com
w oldbreweryguesthouse.com

Pottergate Guest House ★★★
Guest House
4 Pottergate, Richmond
DL10 4AB
t (01748) 823826

River View B&B ★★★
Guest Accommodation
Park Wynd, Millgate, Richmond
DL10 4JS
t (01748) 824774
e riverview_richmond@yahoo.com

Rosedale Bed & Breakfast ★★★★
Guest House **SILVER AWARD**
2 Pottergate, Richmond
DL10 4AB
t (01748) 823926
e info@richmondbedandbreakfast.
co.uk
w richmondbedandbreakfast.co.uk

Victoria House ★★★★
Guest Accommodation
SILVER AWARD
3 Linden Close, Richmond
DL10 7AL
t (01748) 824830
e info@victoria-house-richmond.co.
uk
w victoria-house-richmond.co.uk

West End Guest House ★★★★
Guest House
45 Reeth Road, Richmond
DL10 4EX
t (01748) 824783
e guesthouse@stayatwestend.co.uk
w stayatwestend.co.uk

RIPON

The White House ★★★★
Bed & Breakfast
Gilling Road, Richmond
DL10 5AA
t (01748) 825491
e dorothyclarkin@aol.com
w richmond.org/stayat/thewh
itehouse/index.html

Willance House ★★★★
Guest House **SILVER AWARD**
24 Frenchgate, Richmond
DL10 7AG
t (01748) 824467
e willancehouse@hotmail.co.uk
w willancehouse.com

RIPON

Bishopton Grove House ★★★
Guest Accommodation
Bishopton, Ripon
HG4 2QL
t (01765) 600888
e bgh@ripon.org
w bishoptongrovehouse.co.uk

Box Tree Cottages ★★★★
Guest House
Coltsgate Hill, Ripon
HG4 2AB
t (01765) 698006
e boxtreecottages@gmail.com
w boxtreecottages.com

Crescent Lodge Guest House
★★★★ *Guest Accommodation*
42 North Street, Ripon, North
Yorkshire, United Kingdom
HG4 1EN
t (01765) 609589
e jacksonp@datec.uk.com
w crescent-lodge.com

Fountain Guest House ★★★★
Guest Accommodation
25 North Road, Ripon
HG4 1JP
t (01765) 606012
e reservations@fountainhouseripon.
co.uk
w fountainhouseripon.co.uk

Lavender House ★★★★
Guest Accommodation
SILVER AWARD
28 College Road, Ripon
HG4 2HA
t (01765) 605469
e bcr47@hotmail.com
w lavendersbluedillydilly.com

The Moorhouse
Guest Accommodation
Dallowgill, Kirkby Malzeard, Ripon
HG4 3RH
t (01765) 658371
e enquiries@moorhousebnb.co.uk
w moorhousebnb.co.uk

The Old Coach House ★★★★★
Guest Accommodation
SILVER AWARD
2 Stable Cottages, North Stainley,
Ripon
HG4 3HT
t (01765) 634900
e enquiries@oldcoachhouse.info
w oldcoachhouse.info

Ravencroft B&B ★★★★
Bed & Breakfast
Moorside Avenue, Ripon
HG4 1TA
t 07736 328958
e enquiries@ravencroftbandb.com
w ravencroftbandb.com

The Royal Oak ★★★★ *Inn*
36 Kirkgate, Ripon
HG4 1PB
t (01765) 602284
e info@royaloakripon.co.uk
w royaloakripon.co.uk

The Ship ★★★
Guest Accommodation - Room Only
Bondgate, Ripon
HG4 1QE
t (01765) 603254
e patriciamarieship@googlemail.
com
w theshipripon.co.uk

The White Horse ★★★ *Inn*
61 North Street, Ripon
HG4 1EN
t (01765) 603622
e david.bate13@btopenworld.com
w white-horse-ripon.co.uk

RIPPONDEN

Thurst House Farm ★★★★
Guest Accommodation
Ripponden, Sowerby Bridge
HX6 4NN
t (01422) 822820
e thursthousefarm@bushinternet.
com

ROBIN HOODS BAY

Devon House ★★★ *Guest House*
Station Road, Robin Hood's Bay,
Whitby, North Yorkshire
YO22 4RL
t (01947) 880197
e devonhouse.rhb@virgin.net
w devonhouserhb.co.uk

Lee-Side ★★★★ *Bed & Breakfast*
SILVER AWARD
Mount Pleasant South, Robin Hoods
Bay, Whitby
YO22 4RQ
t (01947) 881143
e lee-side@rhbay.co.uk
w lee-side.rhbay.co.uk

ROSEDALE ABBEY

Five Acre View ★★★★ *Farmhouse*
Rosedale Abbey, North Yorkshire,
Pickering
YO18 8RE
t (01751) 417830
e fiveacreview@aol.com
w fiveacreview.co.uk

ROSEDALE EAST

Ann's Cottage ★★★★
Bed & Breakfast **SILVER AWARD**
Hill Yard Cottage, Rosedale East,
Pickering
YO18 8RH
t (01751) 417646
e ann@annscottagerosedale.co.uk
w annscottagerosedale.co.uk

August Guest House ★★★★
Guest House
3 Plane Trees, Rosedale, Pickering
YO18 8RF
t (01751) 417328
e mary@augustguesthouse.co.uk
w augustguesthouse.co.uk

The Orange Tree ★★★
Guest House
Rosedale East, Pickering
YO18 8RH
t (01751) 417219
e relax@theorangetree.com
w theorangetree.com

RUDSTON

Bosville Arms Country Inn ★★★
Inn
High Street, Rudston, Bridlington
YO25 4UB
t (01262) 420259
e bosvillearms@aol.com
w thebosvillearms.co.uk

RUFFORTH

Wellgarth House ★★★
Guest Accommodation
Wetherby Road, Rufforth, York
YO23 3QB
t (01904) 738592
w wellgarthhouse.co.uk

Yorkshire

RUNSWICK BAY

Firs Guesthouse ★★★★
Guest House
Hinderwell Lane, Runswick Bay,
Whitby
TS13 5HR
t (01947) 840433
e mandy.shackleton@talk21.com
w the-firs.co.uk

Runswick Bay ★★★ *Inn*
2 Hinderwell Lane, Runswick Bay,
North Yorkshire
TS13 5HR
t (01947) 841010
e info@therunswickbay.co.uk
w therunswickbay.co.uk

RUSWARP

Esk View Cottage ★★★★
Bed & Breakfast
The Carrs, Ruswarp, Whitby
YO21 1RL
t (01947) 605658
e enquiries@eskviewcottage.co.uk
w eskviewcottage.com

Ruswarp Hall ★★★
Guest Accommodation
4-6 High Street, Ruswarp, Whitby
YO21 1NH
t (01947) 602801
e colinscarth@btconnect.com
w ruswarphallhotel.co.uk

SALTBURN-BY-THE-SEA

The Arches ★★★★
Guest Accommodation
Low Farm, Brotton, Saltburn-by-the-
Sea, North Yorkshire
TS12 2QX
t (01287) 677512
e mail@gorallyschool.co.uk
w thearcheshotel.co.uk

SALTMARSHE

The Dairy Farm ★★★★
Guest Accommodation
SILVER AWARD
Saltmarshe, Howden, Goole
DN14 7RX
t (01430) 430677
e vivienne.sweeting@btinternet.com
w appletree-cottages.co.uk

SANCTON

Orchard Lodge B&B ★★★★
Guest Accommodation
King Street, Sancton
YO43 4QP
t (01430) 828831
e orchardlodge@live.co.uk
w orchardlodge.biz

SAWDON

Foxholm B&B ★★★★
Bed & Breakfast SILVER AWARD
Foxholm, Main Street, Sawdon,
Scarborough
YO13 9DY
t (01723) 859743
e info@foxholmsawdon.co.uk
w foxholmsawdon.co.uk

SCARBOROUGH

Aartswood Guest House ★★★
Guest House
27 Trafalgar Square, Scarborough
YO12 7PZ
t (01723) 360689
e aartswood@aol.com
w aartswood.com

Abbeydale Guest House ★★★★
Guest House
8a West Square, Scarborough
YO11 1TW
t (01723) 352334

The Ainsley ★★★
Guest Accommodation
4 Rutland Terrace, Queens Parade,
Scarborough
YO12 7JB
t (01723) 364832
e info@theainsleyhotel.co.uk
w theainsleyhotel.co.uk

Ainsley Court Guest House
★★★★ *Guest House*
112 North Marine Road,
Scarborough
YO12 7JA
t (01723) 500352
e lynn@ainsleycourt.co.uk
w ainsleycourt.co.uk

The Alexander ★★★★
Guest Accommodation
GOLD AWARD
33 Burniston Road, Scarborough
YO12 6PG
t (01723) 363178
e enquiries@alexanderhotelscarborough.co.uk
w alexanderhotelscarborough.co.uk

Alexandra House ★★★★
Guest House
21 West Street, Scarborough
YO11 2QR
t (01723) 503205
e info@scarborough-alexandra.co.uk
w scarborough-alexandra.co.uk

The Almar ★★★ *Guest House*
116 Columbus Ravine, Scarborough
YO12 7QZ
t (01723) 372887
e bevandphill@rendellp.fsnet.co.uk
w thealmar.co.uk

Amrock Guest House ★★★★
Guest House
11 Victoria Park Avenue,
Scarborough
YO12 7TR
t (01723) 374423
e info@amrock.co.uk
w amrock.com

Ashburton ★★★★
Guest Accommodation
43 Valley Road, Scarborough
YO11 2LX
t (01723) 374382
e stay@ashburtonhotel.co.uk
w ashburtonhotel.co.uk

Atlanta ★★★★
Guest Accommodation
60-62 Columbus Ravine,
Scarborough
YO12 7QU
t (01723) 360996
e info@atlanta-hotel.com
w atlanta-hotel.co.uk

Blacksmiths Arms ★★★★ *Inn*
High Street, Cloughton,
Scarborough
YO13 0AE
t (01723) 870244
e enquiries@blacksmithsarmsinn.co.uk
w blacksmithsarmsinn.co.uk

Blands Cliff Lodge ★★★
Guest House
Blands Cliff, Scarborough
YO11 1NR
t (01723) 351747 or 363653
e stayinscarborough@gmail.com
w yorkshire-coast.co.uk/blandscliff

Brambles Lodge ★★★
Guest Accommodation
156-158 Filey Road, Scarborough
YO11 3AA
t (01723) 374613
e nightingales22@aol.com
w accommodation.uk.net/brambleslodge.htm

Breece ★★★ *Guest Accommodation - Room Only*
7 West Street, Scarborough
YO11 2QL
t 07515 060044

Brontes Guest House ★★★
Guest House
135 Columbus Ravine, Scarborough
YO12 7QZ
t (01723) 362934
e ericwatson@talktalk.net
w brontesguesthouse.co.uk

The Castle by the Sea ★★★★
Guest House
Mulgrave Place, Scarborough
YO11 1HZ
t (01723) 365166
e john.cresswell@btconnect.com
w thecastlebythesea.co.uk

Catania ★★★★ *Guest House*
141 Queens Parade, Scarborough
YO12 7HU
t (01723) 364516
e catania@yorkshire.net
w hotelcatania.co.uk

The Cavendish ★★★★
Guest House
53 Esplanade Road, Scarborough
YO11 2AT
t (01723) 362108
e anne@cavendishscarborough.co.uk
w cavendishscarborough.co.uk

The Clarence Gardens ★★★
Guest Accommodation
4-5 Blenheim Terrace, Scarborough
YO12 7HF
t (01723) 374884
e enquiries@clarencegardens.force9.co.uk
w clarencegardenshotel.net

Cliffside ★★★★ *Guest House*
79-81 Queens Parade, Scarborough
YO12 7HH
t (01723) 361087
e info@cliffsidehotel.co.uk
w cliffsidehotel.co.uk

The Cordelia ★★★★
Guest Accommodation
51 Esplanade Road, Scarborough
YO11 2AT
t (01723) 363393
e melanie.watson@btconnect.com
w cordeliahotel.co.uk

The Croft ★★★
Guest Accommodation
87 Queens Parade, Scarborough
YO12 7HY
t (01723) 373904
e information@crofthotel.co.uk
w crofthotel.co.uk

Dene Lea ★★★ *Guest House*
7 Rutland Terrace, Queens Parade,
Scarborough
YO12 7JB
t (01723) 361495

Derwent House ★★★ *Guest House*
6 Rutland Terrace, Queens Parade,
Scarborough
YO12 7JB
t (01723) 373880
e info@derwenthousehotel.co.uk
w derwenthousehotel.co.uk

Dolphin Guest House ★★★
Guest House
151 Columbus Ravine, Scarborough
YO12 7QZ
t (01723) 341914
e dolphinguesthouse@btinternet.com
w thedolphin.info

Douglas Guest House ★★★
Guest House
153 Columbus Ravine, Scarborough
YO12 7QZ
t (01723) 371311
e stay@douglasguesthouse.co.uk
w douglasguesthouse.co.uk

The Ellenby ★★★★ *Guest House*
95-97 Queens Parade, Scarborough
YO12 7HY
t (01723) 372916
e johnfail@aol.com
w theellenby.co.uk

The Empire ★★★ *Guest House*
39 Albemarle Crescent, Scarborough
YO11 1XX
t (01723) 373564
e gillian@empire1939.wanadoo.co.uk
w empireguesthouse.co.uk

Esplanade Gardens Guest House
★★★ *Guest Accommodation*
24 Esplanade Gardens, Scarborough
YO12 2AP
t (01723) 360728
e dekquy@aol.com
w esplanadegardensscarborough.co.uk

The Gordon ★★★★ *Guest House*
24 Ryndleside, Scarborough
YO12 6AD
t (01723) 362177
e sales@gordonhotel.co.uk
w gordonhotel.co.uk

Green Gables ★★★ *Guest House*
West Bank, Scarborough
YO12 4DX
t (01723) 361005
e info@greengablesscarborough.co.uk
w greengablesscarborough.co.uk

Greno Seafront Guest House
★★★★ *Guest House*
25 Blenheim Terrace, Queens
Parade, Scarborough
YO12 7HD
t (01723) 375705
e mk@regalguesthouse.demon.co.uk
w thegrenoseafronthotel.co.uk

The Headlands ★★★★
Guest House
16 Weydale Avenue, Scarborough
YO12 6AX
t (01723) 373717
e info@theheadlandshotel.co.uk
w theheadlandshotel.co.uk

The Helaina ★★★★★
Guest Accommodation
14 Blenheim Terrace, Scarborough
YO12 7HF
t (01723) 375191
e info@hotelhelaina.co.uk
w hotelhelaina.co.uk

Home Farm ★★★★
Bed & Breakfast
3 Green Lane, Lebberston,
Scarborough
YO11 3PF
t 07821 473445
e hjyankee@aol.com

Howdale ★★★★ *Guest House*
121 Queen's Parade, Scarborough
YO12 7HU
t (01723) 372696
e mail@howdalehotel.co.uk
w howdalehotel.co.uk

Island House ★★★★ *Farmhouse*
SILVER AWARD
Staintondale, Scarborough
YO13 0EB
t (01723) 870249
e roryc@tinyworld.co.uk
w islandhousefarm.co.uk

Jadellas ★★★ *Guest House*
72 Columbus Ravine, Scarborough
YO12 7QU
t (01723) 378811
e john@johnhowe.wanadoo.co.uk
w jadellashotelscarborough.co.uk

The Kensington ★★★★
Guest House
66 Columbus Ravine, Scarborough
YO12 7QU
t (01723) 368117
e info@kensingtonguesthouse.co.uk
w kensingtonguesthouse.co.uk

Kenways Guest House ★★★
Guest House
9 Victoria Park Avenue, Scarborough
YO12 7TR
t (01723) 365757
e info@kenwaysguesthouse.co.uk
w kenwaysguesthouse.co.uk

Yorkshire

llerby Cottage Farm ★★★★
d & Breakfast **SILVER AWARD**
llerby Cottage Farm, Killerby Lane,
yton, Scarborough
011 3TP
t (01723) 581236
e val@stainedglasscentre.co.uk
w killerbycottagefarm.co.uk

e Kimberley ★★★★ *Guest House*
1 Queens Parade, Scarborough
012 7HY
t (01723) 372734
e kimberleyhotel@hotmail.com
w kimberleyseafronthotel.co.uk

e Kingsway ★★★★ *Guest House*
Columbus Ravine, Scarborough
012 7QU
t (01723) 372948
e info@kingswayhotelscarborough.
 co.uk
w kingswayhotelscarborough.co.uk

evante ★★★ *Guest House*
8 Columbus Ravine, Scarborough
012 7QZ
t (01723) 372366

e Lincoln ★★★ *Guest House*
2 Columbus Ravine, Scarborough
012 7QZ
t (01723) 500897
e enquiries@lincoln-hotel.net
w lincoln-hotel.net

onsdale Villa ★★★★
uest Accommodation
nsdale Road, Scarborough
011 2QY
t (01723) 363383
e enquiries@lonsdalevilla.com
w lonsdalevilla.com

yness Guest House ★★★
uest House
5 Columbus Ravine, Scarborough
012 7QZ
t (01723) 375952
e info@thelyness.co.uk
w thelyness.co.uk

e Lysander ★★★★ *Guest House*
 Weydale Avenue, Scarborough
012 6AX
t (01723) 373369
e info@lysanderhotel.co.uk
w lysanderhotel.co.uk

ajestic ★★★★
uest Accommodation
 Northstead Manor Drive,
 carborough
012 6AG
t (01723) 363806
e ingrid@majestichotel.co.uk
w hotelmajestic.co.uk

ansion House Scarborough
★★★★ *Guest Accommodation*
 Esplanade, South Cliff,
 carborough, North Yorkshire
011 2AY
t (01723) 373930
e mansionhouse45@aol.com
w mansionhousehotel.com

arine View Guest House ★★★
uest House
 Blenheim Terrace, Scarborough
012 7HD
t (01723) 361864
e info@marineview.co.uk
w marineview.co.uk

e Maynard ★★★ *Guest House*
 Esplanade Gardens, Scarborough
011 2AW
t (01723) 372289
e info@maynardscarborough.co.uk
w maynardscarborough.co.uk

e Meltham ★★★★ *Guest House*
 Victoria Park Avenue, Scarborough
012 7TR
t (01723) 370663
e themeltham@talktalk.net
w themeltham.co.uk

Monico ★★★★ *Guest House*
74 Columbus Ravine, Scarborough
YO12 7QU
t (01723) 365159
e ian@ijones63.wanadoo.co.uk
w monicoscarborough.co.uk

Moseley Lodge ★★★★
Guest House
26 Avenue Victoria, South Cliff,
Scarborough
YO11 2QT
t (01723) 360564
e holidays@moseleylodge.co.uk
w moseleylodge.co.uk

The Mount House ★★★★
Guest Accommodation
33 Trinity Road, South Cliff,
Scarborough
YO11 2TD
t (01723) 362967
e bookings@mounthouse-hotel.co.
 uk
w mounthouse-hotel.co.uk

The Mountview ★★★★
Guest House
32 West Street, Scarborough
YO11 2QP
t (01723) 500608
e info@mountview-hotel.co.uk
w mountview-hotel.co.uk

The Newlands ★★★ *Guest House*
80 Columbus Ravine, Scarborough
YO12 7QU
t (01723) 367261
e newlandshotel@btconnect.com
w thenewlandshotel.co.uk

The Norlands ★★★★
Guest Accommodation
10 Weydale Avenue, Scarborough
YO12 6BA
t (01723) 362606
e info@norlandshotel.co.uk
w norlandshotel.co.uk

The Outlook ★★★★
Guest Accommodation
18 Ryndleside, Scarborough
YO12 6AD
t (01723) 364900
e outlook18@hotmail.com

The Philmore ★★★★ *Guest House*
126 Columbus Ravine, Scarborough
YO12 7QZ
t (01723) 361516
e info@philmorehotel.com
w philmorehotel.co.uk

Phoenix Court ★★★★ *Guest House*
8-9 Rutland Terrace, Queens Parade,
Scarborough
YO12 7JB
t (01723) 501150
e info@hotel-phoenix.co.uk
w hotel-phoenix.co.uk

The Phoenix Guest House ★★★★
Guest House
157 Columbus Ravine, Scarborough
YO12 7QZ
t (01723) 368319

Powys Lodge Guest House
★★★★ *Guest House*
2 Westbourne Road, South Cliff,
Scarborough
YO11 2SP
t (01723) 374019
e info@powyslodge.co.uk
w powyslodge.co.uk

Princess Court Guest House
★★★★ *Guest House*
11 Princess Royal Terrace,
Scarborough
YO11 2RP
t (01723) 501922
e irvin@princesscourt.co.uk
w princesscourt.co.uk

Raincliffe ★★★★ *Guest House*
SILVER AWARD
21 Valley Road, Scarborough
YO11 2LY
t (01723) 373541
e enquiries@raincliffehotel.co.uk
w raincliffehotel.com

The Redcliffe ★★★★
Guest Accommodation
18 Prince of Wales Terrace, South
Bay, Scarborough
YO11 2AL
t (01723) 372310
e b.m.bean@daisybroadband.com
w theredcliffehotel.com

Riviera Town House ★★★★
Guest Accommodation
SILVER AWARD
St Nicholas Cliff, Scarborough
YO11 2ES
t (01723) 372277
e info@riviera-scarborough.co.uk
w riviera-scarborough.co.uk

Robyn's Guest House ★★★★
Guest House
139 Columbus Ravine, Scarborough
YO12 7QZ
t (01723) 374217
e info@robynsguesthouse.co.uk
w robynsguesthouse.co.uk

Rose Dene ★★★ *Guest House*
106 Columbus Ravine, Scarborough
YO12 7QZ
t (01723) 374252
e sandra@rose-denehotel.co.uk
w rosedenehotel.co.uk

The Russell ★★★★ *Guest House*
22 Ryndleside, Scarborough
YO12 6AD
t (01723) 365453
e info@russellhotel.net
w russellhotel.net

Sawdon Heights ★★★★
Farmhouse **SILVER AWARD**
Sawdon Heights, Sawdon,
Scarborough
YO13 9EB
t (01723) 859321
e info@sawdonheights.com
w sawdonheights.com

Scalby Hayes B&B ★★★★
Bed & Breakfast **SILVER AWARD**
1 Scalby Hayes, Barmoor Lane,
Scalby, Scarborough
YO13 0PG
t (01723) 362588
e ktulley@scalby.plus.com
w scalbyhayes.co.uk

**The Scarborough Travel &
Holiday Lodge** ★★★
Guest Accommodation
33 Valley Road, Scarborough
YO11 2LX
t (01723) 363537
e enquiries@scarborough-lodge.co.
 uk
w scarborough-lodge.co.uk

Scarborough YHA ★★★ *Hostel*
The White House, Burniston Road,
Scarborough
YO13 0DA
t 0870 770 6022
e scarborough@yha.org.uk
w yha.org.uk

Selomar ★★★★ *Guest House*
23 Blenheim Terrace, Scarborough
YO12 7HD
t (01723) 364964
e info@selomarhotel.co.uk
w selomarhotel.co.uk

The Sheridan ★★★
Guest Accommodation
108 Columbus Ravine, Scarborough
YO12 7QZ
t (01723) 372094
e kimarfhoteljp@aol.com
w thesheridanhotel.co.uk

The Stuart House ★★★★
Guest House
1 & 2 Rutland Terrace, Queens
Parade, Scarborough
YO12 7JB
t (01723) 373768
e h.graham@btconnect.com
w thestuarthousehotel.com

Sunningdale ★★★★ *Guest House*
105 Peasholm Drive, Scarborough
YO12 7NB
t (01723) 372041
e sunningdale@yorkshire.net
w scarboroughguesthouse.com

Sylvern House ★★★★ *Guest House*
25 New Queen Street, Scarborough,
North Yorkshire
YO12 7HJ
t (01723) 360952
e richardandvicki@sylvernhouse.
 com
w sylvernhouse.com

Tall Storeys ★★★★
Guest Accommodation
SILVER AWARD
Old Town, 131 Longwestgate,
Scarborough
YO11 1RQ
t (01723) 373696
e gordon@gordonking.demon.co.
 uk
w tallstoreyshotel.co.uk

The Terrace ★★ *Guest House*
69 Westborough, Scarborough
YO11 1TS
t (01723) 374937
e theterracehotel@btinternet.com
w smoothhound.co.uk/a13751.html

The Thoresby ★★★ *Guest House*
53 North Marine Road, Scarborough
YO12 7EY
t (01723) 365715

Toulson Court ★★★★ *Guest House*
100 Columbus Ravine, Scarborough
YO12 7QZ
t (01723) 503218
e info@toulsoncourtscarborough.
 co.uk
w toulsoncourtscarborough.co.uk

Victoria Seaview ★★★
Guest Accommodation
125-129 Queens Parade,
Scarborough
YO12 7HY
t (01723) 362164
e info@victoriaseaviewhotel.co.uk
w victoriaseaviewhotel.co.uk

Villa Marina ★★★★ *Guest House*
59 Northstead Manor Drive,
Scarborough
YO12 6AF
t (01723) 361088

The Waves ★★★★ *Guest House*
SILVER AWARD
39 Esplanade Road, Scarborough
YO11 2AT
t (01723) 373658
e enquiries@scarboroughwaves.co.
 uk
w scarboroughwaves.co.uk

West Lodge ★★ *Guest House*
38 West Street, Scarborough
YO11 2QP
t (01723) 500754
e westlodge@live.co.uk
w accommodationscarborough.co.
 uk

The Wharncliffe ★★★★
Guest Accommodation
26 Blenheim Terrace, Scarborough
YO12 7HD
t (01723) 374635
e info@thewharncliffescarborough.
 co.uk
w thewharncliffescarborough.co.uk

Yorkshire

The Whiteley ★★★★
Guest Accommodation
99-101 Queens Parade, Scarborough
YO12 7HY
t (01723) 373514
e whiteleyhotel@bigfoot.com
w yorkshirecoast.co.uk/whiteley

White Rails ★★★★ *Guest House*
128 Columbus Ravine, Scarborough
YO12 7QZ
t (01723) 362800
e info@whiterailshotel.co.uk
w whiterailshotel.co.uk

Willow Dene ★★★★ *Guest House*
110 Columbus Ravine, Scarborough
YO12 7QZ
t (01723) 365173
e andy@willowdenehotel.com

SELBY

Hazeldene Guest House ★★★
Guest House
32-34 Brook Street, Selby
YO8 4AR
t (01757) 704809
e info@hazeldene-selby.co.uk
w hazeldene-selby.co.uk

SETTLE

Austwick Hall ★★★★★
Guest Accommodation
GOLD AWARD
Austwick Hall, Austwick, Settle
LA2 8BS
t (01524) 251794
e austwickhall@austwick.org
w austwickhall.co.uk

Maypole Inn ★★★★ *Inn*
Long Preston, Skipton, Nr Settle
BD23 4PH
t 01729 840219
e robert@maypole.co.uk
w maypole.co.uk

Oast Guest House ★★★
Guest House
5 Penyghent View, Settle
BD24 9JJ
t (01729) 822989
e stay@oastguesthouse.co.uk
w oastguesthouse.co.uk/

Settle Lodge ★★★★ *Guest House*
SILVER AWARD
Duke Street, Settle
BD24 9AS
t (01729) 823258
e book@settlelodge.co.uk
w settlelodge.co.uk

Whitefriars Country Guest House
★★★★ *Guest Accommodation*
Church Street, Settle
BD24 9JD
t (01729) 823753
e info@whitefriars-settle.co.uk
w whitefriars-settle.co.uk

SEWERBY

The Poplars Motel ★★★
Guest Accommodation
45 Jewison Lane, Sewerby,
Bridlington
YO15 1DX
t (01262) 677251
w the-poplars.co.uk

SHAROW

Sharow Cross House ★★★★★
Guest House **GOLD AWARD**
Dishforth Road, Sharow, Ripon
HG4 5BQ
t (01765) 609866
e sharowcrosshouse@btconnect.com
w sharowcrosshouse.com

SHEFFIELD

Coniston Guest House ★★★
Guest House
90 Beechwood Road, Hillsborough,
Sheffield
S6 4LQ
t (0114) 233 9680
e reservations@conistongu
esthouse.co.uk
w conistonguesthouse.co.uk

Etruria House ★★★ *Guest House*
91 Crookes Road, Sheffield
S10 5BD
t (0114) 266 2241
e etruria@waitrose.com

Gulliver's Bed & Breakfast ★★★
Guest Accommodation
167 Ecclesall Road South, Sheffield
S11 9PN
t (0114) 262 0729

Ivory House ★★★
Guest Accommodation
34 Wostenholm Road, Sheffield
S7 1LJ
t (0114) 255 1853
e ivoryhousehotel@amserve.com

The Noose & Gibbet ★ *Inn*
97 Broughton Lane, Attercliffe,
Sheffield
S9 2DE
t (0114) 261 7182

The Norfolk Arms Ringinglow
★★★★ *Inn*
2 Ringinglow Village, Sheffield
S11 7TS
t (0114) 230 2197
e info@norfolkarms.com
w norfolkarms.com

Primrose Cottages *Hostel*
170-172 Queens Road,, Beighton,
Sheffield
S20 1DX
t (0114) 254 0770
e keyline1@tiscali.co.uk

Psalter House ★★★★
Bed & Breakfast
17 Clifford Road, Sheffield
S11 9AQ
t (0114) 255 7758
w smoothhound.co.uk/hotels/
psalter.html

Tyndale ★★★
Guest Accommodation
164 Millhouses Lane, Sheffield
S7 2HE
t (0114) 236 1660

SHELF

Woodlands Guest House ★★★★
Guest Accommodation
2 The Grove, Shelf, Halifax
HX3 7PD
t (01274) 677533
e suewood45@hotmail.com
w woodlands-yorkshire.com

SHIPTON-BY-BENINGBROUGH

Wood Farm ★★★★ *Farmhouse*
SILVER AWARD
Wood Farm, Shipton-by-
Beningbrough, York
YO30 1BU
t (01904) 470333
e email@woodfarmbedandb
reakfast.co.uk
w woodfarmbedandbreakfast.co.uk

SILSDEN

Pickersgill Manor Farm ★★★★
Farmhouse **SILVER AWARD**
Low Lane, Silsden, Ilkley
BD20 9JH
t (01535) 655228
e pickersgillmanorfarm@tiscali.co.
uk
w dalesfarmhouse.co.uk

SINNINGTON

Fox & Hounds ★★★★ *Inn*
SILVER AWARD
Main Street, Sinnington,
Kirkbymoorside
YO62 6SQ
t (01751) 431577
e foxhoundsinn@easynet.co.uk
w thefoxandhoundsinn.co.uk

SKEEBY

Ewden House ★★★★
Guest Accommodation
SILVER AWARD
Sedbury Lane, Skeeby, Richmond
DL10 5ED
t (01748) 824473
e bb@ewdenhouse.com
w bedandbreakfast-directory.co.uk/
info.asp?id=33080

New Skeeby Grange ★★★★★
Bed & Breakfast **SILVER AWARD**
Sedbury Lane, Skeeby, Richmond
DL10 5ED
t (01748) 822276
e gandmf@tiscali.co.uk
w newskeebygrange.co.uk

SKELTON

Skelton Grange Farmhouse
★★★★ *Guest Accommodation*
Orchard View, Skelton, York
YO30 1YQ
t (01904) 470780
e skelton.yorkbnb@hotmail.com
w skelton-farm.co.uk

SKIPSEA

Village Farm ★★★★
Guest Accommodation
SILVER AWARD
Back Street, Skipsea, Driffield
YO25 8SW
t (01262) 468479
e info@villagefarmskipsea.co.uk
w villagefarmskipsea.co.uk

SKIPTON

Carlton House ★★★★
Guest Accommodation
46 Keighley Road, Skipton
BD23 2NB
t (01756) 700921
e carltonhouse@rapidial.co.uk
w carltonhouse.rapidial.co.uk

Chinthurst ★★★★★ *Guest House*
SILVER AWARD
Otley Road, Skipton
BD23 1EX
t (01756) 799264
e info@chinthurst.co.uk
w chinthurst.co.uk

Cononley Hall Bed & Breakfast
★★★★★ *Bed & Breakfast*
SILVER AWARD
Main Street, Cononley, Skipton
BD20 8LJ
t (01535) 633923
e cononleyhall@madasafish.com
w cononleyhall.co.uk

Cravendale Guest House ★★★
Guest House
57 Keighley Road, Skipton
BD23 2LX
t (01756) 795129
w yorkshirenet.co.uk/stayat/crave
ndale/

Craven Heifer Inn ★★★ *Inn*
Grassington Road, Skipton
BD23 3LA
t (01756) 792521
e john@cravenheifer.co.uk
w cravenheifer.co.uk

Dalesgate Lodge ★★★★
Guest Accommodation
69 Gargrave Road, Skipton
BD23 1QN
t (01756) 790672
e dalesgatelodge@hotmail.com
w dalesgatelodge.co.uk

Highfield House Guest House
★★★★ *Guest Accommodation*
58 Keighley Road, Skipton
BD23 2NB
t (01756) 793182
e highfield.skipton@fsmail.net
w highfieldguesthouse.co.uk

Keld Barn ★★★★ *Bed & Breakfast*
Buckden, Skipton
BD23 5JA
t (01756) 761019
e keldbarn@tiscali.co.uk

Newton Grange ★★★★
Bed & Breakfast
Bank Newton, Gargrave, Skipton
BD23 3NT
t (01756) 796016
e bookings@banknewton.fsnet.co.
uk
w cravencountryconnections.co.uk

Pennycroft Guest House ★★★★
Guest House
Far Lane, Kettlewell, Skipton
BD23 5QY
t (01756) 760845
e pennycroft123@tiscali.co.uk
w pennycroft.co.uk

Poppy Cottage Guest House
★★★★ *Guest House*
Ivy Cottage Farm, Main Street,
Carleton in Craven, Skipton, North
Yorkshire
BD23 3BY
t (01756) 792874
e steve@poppycottageguesthous
co.uk
w poppycottageguesthouse.co.uk

Skipton Park Guest'otel Ltd
★★★★ *Guest House*
2 Salisbury Street, Skipton
BD23 1NQ
t (01756) 700640
e skiptonpark@btconnect.com
w skiptonpark.co.uk

The Woolly Sheep ★★★ *Inn*
38 Sheep Street, Skipton
BD23 1HY
t (01756) 700966
e woolly.sheep@btconnect.com
w woollysheepinn.co.uk

SLEDMERE

The Triton Inn ★★★★ *Inn*
The Triton Inn, Sledmere,
Bridlington
YO25 2XQ
t (01377) 236078
e tritoninn@aol.com
w thetritoninn.co.uk

SLEIGHTS

Hedgefield Guest House ★★★★
Guest House **SILVER AWARD**
47 Coach Road, Sleights, Whitby
YO22 5AA
t (01947) 810647
e hedgefieldguesthouse@tiscali.co.
uk
w hedgefieldguesthouse.co.uk

Netherby House ★★★★
Guest Accommodation
SILVER AWARD
90 Coach Road, Sleights, Whitby
YO22 5EQ
t (01947) 810211
e info@netherby-house.co.uk
w netherby-house.co.uk

The Salmon Leap ★★ *Inn*
Coach Road, Sleights, Whitby
YO22 5AA
t (01947) 810233
e adrianmee@ukonline.co.uk
w salmonleaphotel.com

Yorkshire

SLINGSBY

wry's Restaurant & Bed & eakfast ★★★ Guest House
alton Road, Slingsby, Malton
062 4AF
t (01653) 628417
e dgwilliams@onetel.com

SNEATON

e Wilson Arms ★★★ Inn
acon Way, Whitby
022 5HS
t (01947) 602552
e thewilsonarms200@aol.com
w thewilsonarms.co.uk/accom
modation.htm

SOUTH KILVINGTON

anor House Cottage ★★★★
uest Accommodation
ag Lane, South Kilvington, Thirsk
07 2NY
t (01845) 527712
e info@manor-house-cottage.co.uk
w manor-house-cottage.co.uk

SOWERBY

burnum House Bed & Breakfast
Topcliffe Road, Sowerby, Thirsk
07 1RX
t (01845) 524120
e ronturnbull38@aol.com
w smoothhound.co.uk/hotels/labur
numhse.html

**ng Acre Bed & Breakfast
★★★** Bed & Breakfast
a Topcliffe Road, Sowerby, Thirsk
07 1RY
t (01845) 522360
e dawsonlongacre@aol.com
w longacrethirsk.co.uk

STAITHES

rooklyn Bed & Breakfast ★★★
d & Breakfast
owns Terrace, Staithes, North
orkshire
S13 5BG
t (01947) 841396
e m.heald@tiscali.co.uk
w brooklynuk.co.uk

STANBURY

ld Silent Inn ★★★ Inn
ob Lane, Stanbury, Haworth
D22 0HW
t (01535) 647437
e info@old-silent-inn.co.uk
w old-silent-inn.co.uk

onden Guest House ★★★★
uest House
onden House, Stanbury, Haworth
D22 0HR
t (01535) 644154
e brenda.taylor@pondenhouse.co.
uk
w pondenhouse.co.uk

STANNINGTON

oadbrook Cottages B&B ★★★★
d & Breakfast SILVER AWARD
ame Lane, Loadbrook, Sheffield
6 6GT
t (0114) 231 1619
e alisoncolver@hotmail.com
w loadbrook.co.uk

obin Hood Inn ★★★★ Inn
LVER AWARD
reaves Lane, Little Matlock,
heffield
6 6BG
t (0114) 234 4565
e enquiries@robinhoodloxley.co.uk
w robin-hood-loxley.co.uk

STAPE

**Flamborough Rigg Cottage
★★★★★** Bed & Breakfast
GOLD AWARD
Flamborough Rigg Cottage,
Middlehead Road, Pickering
YO18 8HR
t (01751) 475263
e enquiries@flamboroughrigg
cottage.co.uk
w flamboroughriggcottage.co.uk

High Muffles ★★★★
Bed & Breakfast **GOLD AWARD**
High Muffles, Stape, Pickering
YO18 8HP
t (01751) 417966
e candrew840@aol.com
w highmuffles.co.uk

Rawcliffe House Farm ★★★★
Farmhouse **SILVER AWARD**
Rawcliffe House Farm, Stape,
Pickering
YO18 8JA
t (01751) 473292
e stay@rawcliffehousefarm.co.uk
w rawcliffehousefarm.co.uk

Seavy Slack ★★★★ Farmhouse
SILVER AWARD
Seavy Slack, Stape, Pickering
YO18 8HZ
t (01751) 473131
e seavyslack@btconnect.com

STILLINGFLEET

Harmony House ★★★★
Guest Accommodation
The Green, Stillingfleet, York
YO19 6SH
t (01904) 720933
e harmony.house@virgin.net
w harmonyhouseyork.com

STIRTON

Tarn House Country Inn ★★★★
Guest Accommodation
Stirton, Nr Skipton
BD23 3LQ
t (01756) 794891
e reception@tarnhouse.net
w partingtons.com

STOCKTON-ON-THE-FOREST

Orillia House ★★★
Guest Accommodation
89 The Village, Stockton-on-Forest,
York
YO32 9UP
t (01904) 400600
e orillia@globalnet.co.uk
w orilliahouse.co.uk

STOKESLEY

Willow Cottage ★★★★
Bed & Breakfast **SILVER AWARD**
67 Levenside, Stokesley
TS9 5BH
t (01642) 710795
e sue@willowcottagestokesley.co.
uk
w willowcottagestokesley.co.uk

SWINITHWAITE

Temple Farmhouse B&B ★★★★
Farmhouse
Temple Farm, Aysgarth, Aysgarth
Falls
DL8 4UJ
t (01969) 663246
e stay@templefarmhouse.co.uk
w templefarmhouse.co.uk

THIRSK

**Borrowby Mill Bed & Breakfast
★★★★** Bed & Breakfast
SILVER AWARD
Borrowby, Thirsk
YO7 4AW
t (01845) 537717
e markandvickipadfield@btinternet.
com
w borrowbymill.co.uk

The Gallery ★★★★
Bed & Breakfast
18 Kirkgate, Thirsk
YO7 1PQ
t (01845) 523767
e kathryn@gallerybedandbreakfast.
co.uk
w gallerybedandbreakfast.co.uk

Garbutt Farm ★★★ Farmhouse
Cold Kirby, Thirsk, North Yorkshire
YO7 2HJ
t 01845 597 966
e lloyd.sallie@gmail.com
w garbuttfarm.co.uk

Station House ★★★
Guest Accommodation
Station Road, Thirsk
YO7 4LS
t (01845) 522063
e stationhousejones@tiscali.co.uk

St James House B&B ★★★★
Guest Accommodation
35-37 St James Green, Thirsk
YO7 1AQ
t (01845) 526565
e barry@stjameshousethirsk.co.uk
w stjameshousethirsk.co.uk

Town Pasture Farm ★★★★
Farmhouse
Boltby, Thirsk
YO7 2DY
t (01845) 537298
e townpasturefarm.co.uk

THIXENDALE

The Cross Keys ★★★ Inn
The Cross Keys, Thixendale, Malton
YO17 9TG
t (01377) 288272
e xkmairs@aol.com

THORALBY

The George Inn ★★★★ Inn
SILVER AWARD
Thorably, Leyburn
DL8 3SU
t (01969) 663256
e chm@thegeorge.tv
w thegeorge.tv

The Old Barn ★★★★
Guest Accommodation
SILVER AWARD
Thoralby, Leyburn
DL8 3SZ
t (01969) 663590
e holidays@dalesbarn.co.uk
w dalesbarn.co.uk

Pen View ★★★
Guest Accommodation
Pen View, Thoralby, Leyburn
DL8 3SU
t (01969) 663319
e cliffbailey1@btinternet.com

THORNE

**Thorne Central Guest House
★★★** Guest House
11a Queen Street, Thorne,
Doncaster
DN8 5AA
t (01405) 818358
e tcgh@sky.com
w thornecentralguesthouse.co.uk

THORNTON

Ann's Farmhouse ★★★ Farmhouse
New Farm, Thornton Road, Bradford
BD13 3QE
t (01274) 833214
e yorkshirefarmer@hotmail.co.uk

THORNTON DALE

Banavie ★★★★ Bed & Breakfast
Roxby Road, Thornton Dale,
Pickering
YO18 7SX
t (01751) 474616
e info@banavie.uk.com
w banavie.uk.com

Kirkby House ★★★★
Bed & Breakfast **SILVER AWARD**
Priestmans Lane, Thornton Dale,
Pickering
YO18 7RT
t (01751) 475181

New Inn ★★★★ Inn
Maltongate, Thornton-le-Dale, Near
Pickering
YO18 7LF
t (01751) 474226
e enquires@the-new-inn.com
w the-new-inn.com

Tangalwood ★★★★
Bed & Breakfast
Roxby Road, Thornton Dale,
Pickering
YO18 7SX
t (01751) 474688

THORNTON LE MOOR

The Black Swan ★★★★ Inn
Main Street, Thornton le Moor,
Northallerton
DL7 9DN
t (01609) 774444
e woodys@thornton-le-moor.co.uk

THORNTON RUST

Thornton Lodge ★★★★★
Guest Accommodation
GOLD AWARD
Thornton Rust, Leyburn
DL8 3AP
t (01969) 663375
e enquiries@thorntonlodgenorthyo
rkshire.co.uk
w thorntonlodgenorthyorkshire.co.
uk

THORNTON WATLASS

The Buck Inn ★★★
Thornton Watlass, Bedale
HG4 4AH
t (01677) 422461
e innwatlass1@btconnect.com
w buckwatlass.co.uk

THRESHFIELD

Craiglands Guest House ★★★★
Bed & Breakfast
Brooklyn, Threshfield, Skipton
BD23 5ER
t (01756) 752093
e craiglands@talk21.com
w craiglandsguesthouse.co.uk

Station House ★★★
Bed & Breakfast
Station Road, Threshfield,
Grassington
BD23 5ES
t (01756) 752667
e info@stationhousegrassington.co.
uk
w yorkshirenet.co.uk/stayat/stati
onhouse

THRUSCROSS

West End Outdoor Centre ★★★
Group Hostel
West End, Summerbridge, Harrogate
HG3 4BA
t (01943) 880207
e m.verity@virgin.net
w westendoutdoorcentre.co.uk

THURSTONLAND

Ackroyd House ★★★★★
Bed & Breakfast **SILVER AWARD**
13 Top of the Bank, Thurstonland,
Holmfirth
HD4 6XZ
t (01484) 660169
e enquiries@ackroydhouse.co.uk
w ackroydhouse.co.uk

The Old Co-Op ★★★★★
Bed & Breakfast **SILVER AWARD**
96 The Village, Thurstonland,
Holmfirth
HD4 6XF
t (01484) 663621
e contact@theoldco-op.com
w theoldco-op.com

Yorkshire

TICKHILL

Hannah's Guest House ★★★
Guest House
72 Sunderland Street, Tickhill, Doncaster
DN11 9EG
t (01302) 752233
e hannahsguesthouse@tiscali.co.uk
w hannahsguesthouse.com

TODMORDEN

Bentfield Howe ★★
Guest Accommodation
Bentfield Howe, 4 Stoney Drive, Todmorden
OL14 7UR
t (01706) 818288
e bentfield.howe@btinternet.com

Birks Clough ★★★ *Guest House*
Hollingworth Lane, Todmorden
OL14 6QX
t (01706) 814438
e mstorah@mwfree.net

Kilnhurst Old Hall ★★★★★
Guest Accommodation
SILVER AWARD
Kilnhurst Lane, Todmorden
OL14 6AX
t (01706) 814289
e kilnhurst@aol.com
w kilnhurstoldhall.co.uk

Mankinholes YHA ★★★ *Hostel*
Mankinholes YHA, Mankinholes, Todmorden
OL14 6HR
t (01706) 812340
e mankinholes@yha.org.uk
w yha.org.uk

Woodleigh Hall ★★★★
Bed & Breakfast
Ewood Lane, Todmorden
OL14 7DF
t (01706) 814664
e mauricerheath@onetel.net

TOLLERTON

Angel Inn House ★★★★
Bed & Breakfast **SILVER AWARD**
York Road, Tollerton, York
YO61 1QZ
t (01347) 833019
e enquiries@angelinnhouse.co.uk
w angelinnhouse.co.uk

TRENHOLME BAR

Swan House ★★★★
Guest Accommodation
Hutton Rudby, Northallerton
DL6 3JY
t (01642) 700555
e swan100@btinternet.com
w swanhouse.webs.com

TRIANGLE (SOWERBY BRIDGE)

The Dene ★★★★
Guest Accommodation
Triangle, Sowerby Bridge
HX6 3EA
t (01422) 823562
e thedene.triangle@gmail.com

WADSWORTH

Mount Skip Bed & Breakfast
★★★★ *Bed & Breakfast*
1 Mount Road, Wadsworth, Hebden Bridge
HX7 8PH
t (01422) 842903
e mountskipbandb@hotmail.com

WAKEFIELD

The Bank House Hotel ★★
Guest Accommodation
11 Bank Street, Westgate, Wakefield
WF1 1EH
t (01924) 368243
e manager@thebankhousehotelandrestaurant.com

Fieldview ★★★★ *Bed & Breakfast*
13 Ouzlewell Green, Lofthouse, Wakefield, West Yorkshire
WF3 3QR
t 0113 2829583/0777 7637327
e helki197@btinternet.com
w fieldview.vpweb.co.uk

WALKINGTON

The Barn House ★★★★★
Guest Accommodation
SILVER AWARD
18a East End, Walkington, Beverley
HU17 8RY
t (01482) 880542
e info@barnhousewalkington.co.uk
w barnhousewalkington.co.uk

The Ferguson Fawsitt Arms
★★★★ *Inn*
East End, Walkington, Beverley
HU17 8RX
t (01482) 882665
e info@fergusonfawsitt.com
w fergusonfawsitt.co.uk

WARTHILL

Snowball Plantation ★★
Group Accommodation
Stockton-on-Forest, York
YO19 5XS
t (01904) 410084
w snowballplantation.org.uk

WEETON

Arthington Lodge ★★★★
Farmhouse
Wescoe Hill, Weeton, Harrogate
LS17 0EZ
t (01423) 734102
e arthingtonlodge@btinternet.com

WELBURN

Welburn Lodge ★★★★
Bed & Breakfast **SILVER AWARD**
Castle Howard Station Road, Welburn, York
YO60 7EW
t (01653) 618885
e stay@welburnlodge.com
w welburnlodge.com

WELTON

Green Dragon ★★★★ *Inn*
Cowgate, Welton, Hull
HU15 1NB
t (01482) 666700
e greendragon.welton@marstons.co.uk
w marstonsinns.co.uk/home/hotels/hotel-welton/green-dragon

WENSLEY

Wensley House ★★★★
Guest House
Wensley, Leyburn
DL8 4HL
t (01969) 624866
e lindamaloney768@btinternet.com
w yorkshirenet.co.uk/stayat/wensleyhouse/index.htm

WEST WITTON

Ivy Dene Guesthouse ★★★
Guest House
Main Street, West Witton, Leyburn
DL8 4LP
t (01969) 622785
e info@ivydeneguesthouse.co.uk
w ivydeneguesthouse.co.uk

The Old Star ★★★
Guest Accommodation
Main Street, West Witton, Leyburn
DL8 4LU
t (01969) 622949
e enquiries@theoldstar.com
w theoldstar.net

The Old Vicarage ★★★★
Guest House
Main Street, West Witton, Leyburn
DL8 4LX
t (01969) 622108
e grant.chumphreys@btinternet.com
w dalesbreaks.co.uk

WETHERBY

Linton Close ★★★★
Bed & Breakfast **SILVER AWARD**
2 Wharfe Grove, Wetherby
LS22 6HA
t (01937) 582711

Swan Guest House ★★★★
Guest House
38 North Street, Wetherby
LS22 6NN
t (01937) 582381
e info@swanguesthouse.co.uk
w swanguesthouse.co.uk

WETWANG

Life Hill Farm B&B ★★★★
Farmhouse **SILVER AWARD**
Sledmere, Driffield
YO25 3EY
t (01377) 236224
e info@lifehillfarm.co.uk
w lifehillfarm.co.uk

WHASHTON

Mount Pleasant Farm ★★★★
Farmhouse **SILVER AWARD**
Mount Pleasant Farm, Whashton, Richmond
DL11 7JP
t (01748) 822784
e info@mountpleasantfarmhouse.co.uk
w mountpleasantfarmhouse.co.uk

Whashton Springs Farm ★★★★
Farmhouse **SILVER AWARD**
Whashton Springs Farm, Whashton, Richmond
DL11 7JS
t (01748) 822884
e whashtonsprings@btconnect.com
w whashtonsprings.co.uk

WHITBY

Arches Guest House ★★★★
Guest House
The Arches, 8 Havelock Place, (On Hudson Street), Whitby
YO21 3ER
t 0800 915 4256
e archeswhitby@freeola.com
w whitbyguesthouses.co.uk

Argyle House ★★★★
Guest Accommodation
18 Hudson Street, West Cliff, Whitby
YO21 3EP
t (01947) 602733
e bill@argyle-house.co.uk
w argyle-house.co.uk

Autumn Leaves ★★★★
Bed & Breakfast **SILVER AWARD**
4 Chubb Hill Road, Whitby
YO21 1JP
t (01947) 821241
e anthony.fairclough@virgin.net
w autumnleaveswhitby.co.uk

Blencathra House
Guest Accommodation
13 Crescent Avenue, Whitby
YO21 3ED
t (01947) 603706

Boulmer Guest House ★★★★
Guest House
23 Crescent Avenue, Whitby
YO21 3ED
t (01947) 604284
e boulmerguesthouse@tiscali.co.uk
w boulmerguesthouse.co.uk

Bramblewick ★★★★ *Guest House*
3 Havelock Place, Whitby
YO21 3ER
t (01947) 604504
e bramblewick@havelockplace.wanadoo.co.uk
w bramblewick.co.uk

The Captain's Lodge ★★★★
Guest House
3 Crescent Avenue, Whitby
YO21 3EF
t (01947) 601178

Corner Guest House ★★★★
Guest House
3-4 Crescent Place, Whitby
YO21 3HE
t (01947) 602444
e awpicknett@yahoo.co.uk
w thecornerguesthouse.com

Crescent Lodge ★★★★
Guest House
27 Crescent Avenue, Whitby
YO21 3EW
t (01947) 820073
e carol@carolyates.wanadoo.co.uk

Croft Farm ★★★★ *Farmhouse*
Fylingthorpe, Whitby
YO22 4PW
t (01947) 880231
e croftfarmbb@aol.com
w croft-farm.com

Dillons of Whitby ★★★★
Guest House **GOLD AWARD**
14 Chubb Hill Road, Whitby, North Yorkshire
YO21 1JU
t 01947 600290
e info@dillonsofwhitby.co.uk
w dillonsofwhitby.co.uk

Discovery Accommodation
★★★★ *Guest Accommodation*
11 Silver Street, Whitby
YO21 3JS
t (01947) 821598
e enquiries@discoveryaccommodation.com
w discoveryaccommodation.com

Elford House ★★★★
Guest Accommodation - Room Only
10 Prospect Hill, Whitby
YO21 1QE
t (01947) 820730
e elford@oneuk.com
w elfordguesthouse.co.uk

Ellie's Guest House ★★★★
Guest House
4 Langdale Terrace, Whitby
YO21 3EE
t (01947) 600022
e info@elliesguesthouse.co.uk
w elliesguesthouse.co.uk

Esklet Guest House ★★★★
Guest House
22 Crescent Avenue, Whitby
YO21 3ED
t (01947) 605663
e esklet@axis-connect.com
w esklet.com

The Florence Guest House ★★★
Guest House
4 Broomfield Terrace, Whitby
YO21 1QP
t (01947) 605083
e enquiries@florence-guesthouse.co.uk
w florence-guesthouse.co.uk

The Full English ★★★★
Guest House
9 John Street, Whitby
YO21 3ET
t (01947) 604021
e garybevang@aol.com
w thefullenglishwhitby.com

Glendale Guest House ★★★★
Guest House
16 Crescent Avenue, Whitby
YO21 3ED
t (01947) 604242
e mickpelling1@msn.com
w glendalewhitby.co.uk

Glenora ★★★★ *Guest House*
8 Upgang Lane, Whitby
YO21 3EA
t (01947) 605363
e glenora.whitby@btopenworld.com
w glenora.users.btopenworld.com

Yorkshire

amarye Suites B&B ★★★★★
d & Breakfast SILVER AWARD
Coach Road, Sleights, Whitby,
rth Yorks
22 5AA
t (01947) 811656
e gramaryesuites@btinternet.com
w gramaryesuites.co.uk

antley House ★★★★
est House
Hudson Street, Whitby
21 3EP
t (01947) 600895
e request@grantleyhouse.co.uk
w grantleyhouse.com

e Grove ★★★★ Guest House
Bagdale, Whitby
21 1QL
t (01947) 603551
e angela@thegrovewhitby.co.uk
w thegrovewhitby.co.uk

ailwood House ★★★★
est House
A Crescent Avenue, Whitby
21 3ED
t (01947) 602704
e hailwoodhouse@yahoo.co.uk
w hailwoodhousewhitby.co.uk

aven Crest ★★★★
est Accommodation
LVER AWARD
7 Upgang Lane, Whitby
21 3JW
t (01947) 605187
e enquiries@havencrest.co.uk
w havencrest.co.uk

e Haven Guest House ★★★★
est House
East Crescent, Whitby
21 3HD
t (01947) 603842
e info@thehavenwhitby.co.uk
w thehavenwhitby.co.uk

eathfield ★★★★ Bed & Breakfast
Prospect Hill, Whitby
21 1QD
t (01947) 605407
e heathfieldlinda@aol.com
w bedandbreakfast-whitby.co.uk

gh Tor Guest House ★★★★
est House
Normanby Terrace, Whitby
21 3ES
t (01947) 602507
e hightorguesthouse@hotmail.com
w hightorguesthousewhitby.co.uk

llcrest Guest House ★★★★
est House
Prospect Hill, Whitby
21 1QE
t (01947) 606604
e hillcrestgh@btinternet.com
w hillcrestguesthouse.org.uk

e Langley ★★★★★
est Accommodation
LVER AWARD
yal Crescent, West Cliff, Whitby
21 3EJ
t (01947) 604250
e langleyhotel@hotmail.com
w langleyhotel.com

rpool Hall ★★★★
est Accommodation
rpool Drive, Whitby
22 4ND
t 0845 470 7558
e reservations@hfholidays.co.uk
w hfholidays.co.uk

unceston Villa ★★★★
d & Breakfast
Prospect Hill, Whitby
21 1QD
t (01947) 821213
e launcestonvilla@btinternet.com
w launcestonvillawhitby.co.uk

avinia House ★★★★ Guest House
East Crescent, Whitby
21 3HD
t (01947) 602945
e info@laviniahouse.co.uk
w laviniahouse.co.uk

The Leeway ★★★★ Guest House
SILVER AWARD
1 Havelock Place, Whitby
YO21 3ER
t (01947) 602604
e enquiries@theleeway.co.uk
w theleeway.co.uk

Mayfields ★★★★ Bed & Breakfast
30 Mayfield Road, Whitby
YO21 1LX
t (01947) 603228
e mayfield30@btconnect.com
w bandbwhitby.co.uk

The Middleham ★★★★
Guest House
3 Church Square, Whitby, North Yorkshire
YO21 3EG
t 01947 603423
e themiddleham@btinternet.com
w themiddleham.com

Number Five ★★★★ Guest House
5 Havelock Place, Whitby
YO21 3ER
t (01947) 606361

Number Seven Guest House ★★★★ Guest House
7 East Crescent, Whitby
YO21 3HD
t (01947) 606019
e number7.whitbytown@btinternet.com
w numbersevenwhitby.co.uk

Pannett House ★★★★
Guest House
14 Normanby Terrace, Whitby
YO21 3ES
t (01947) 603261
e info@pannetthouse.co.uk
w pannetthouse.co.uk

Prospect House ★★★
Bed & Breakfast
23 Prospect Hill, Whitby
YO21 1QD
t (01947) 601638
e truman.wendy@yahoo.co.uk
w prospecthouse-whitby.co.uk

Prospect Villa Guest House ★★★
Guest House
13 Prospect Hill, Whitby
YO21 1QE
t (01947) 603118
e prospectvillawhitby@hotmail.com
w prospectvillawhitby.co.uk

Queensland ★★★★
Guest Accommodation
2 Crescent Avenue, Whitby
YO21 3ED
t (01947) 604262
e info@queensland.co.uk
w queensland.co.uk

Riviera ★★★★ Guest House
4 Crescent Terrace, West Cliff, Whitby
YO21 3EL
t (01947) 602533
e info@rivierawhitby.com
w rivierawhitby.com

The Rothbury ★★★★
Bed & Breakfast
2 Ocean Road, Whitby
YO21 3HY
t (01947) 606282
e therothbury@f2s.com
w therothbury.co.uk

The Seacliffe ★★★★
Guest Accommodation
12 North Promenade, Whitby
YO21 3JX
t (01947) 603139
e stay@seacliffehotel.com
w seacliffehotel.com

Seacrest Guest House ★★★★
Guest House
10 Crescent Avenue, Whitby
YO21 3ED
t (01947) 605541
e axby18@dsl.pipex.com
w seacrest.org.uk

Sneaton Castle Centre ★★★★
Hostel
Sneaton Castle Centre, Whitby
YO21 3QN
t (01947) 600051
e reception@sneatoncastle.co.uk
w sneatoncastle.co.uk

Sneaton Castle Centre ★★★★
Guest Accommodation
Sneaton Castle Centre, Whitby
YO21 3QN
t (01947) 600051
e reception@sneatoncastle.co.uk
w sneatoncastle.co.uk

Storrbeck Guest House ★★★★
Bed & Breakfast SILVER AWARD
9 Crescent Avenue, Whitby
YO21 3ED
t (01947) 605468
e info@storrbeckguesthouse.co.uk
w storrbeckguesthouse.co.uk

Sunnyvale House ★★★★
Guest House
12 Normanby Terrace, Whitby
YO21 3ES
t (01947) 820389
e sunnyvalehouse@hotmail.co.uk
w sunnyvalehouse.co.uk

Wentworth Guest House ★★★
Guest House
27 Hudson Street, Whitby
YO21 3EP
t (01947) 602433
e info@whitbywentworth.co.uk
w whitbywentworth.co.uk

The Wheeldale ★★★★
Guest House
11 North Promenade, Whitby
YO21 3JX
t (01947) 602365
e enquiries@wheeldale-hotel.co.uk
w wheeldalewhitby.co.uk

Whitby YHA ★★★★ Hostel
East Cliff, Whitby
YO22 4JT
t (01947) 602878

White Linen Guest House ★★★★
Guest House
24 Bagdale, Whitby
YO21 1QS
t (01947) 603635
e info@whitelinenguesthouse.co.uk
w whitelinenguesthouse.co.uk

The Willows ★★★★ Guest House
35 Bagdale, Whitby
YO21 1QL
t (01947) 600288
e thewillows35@hotmail.co.uk
w thewillowsguesthouse.co.uk

York House ★★★★ Guest House
3 Back Lane, High Hawsker, Whitby
YO22 4LW
t (01947) 880314
e admin@york-house-hotel.co.uk
w york-house-hotel.co.uk

WIGGLESWORTH

Cowper Cottage ★★★★
Bed & Breakfast SILVER AWARD
Cowper Terrace, Wigglesworth, Settle
BD23 4RP
t (01729) 840598
e info@cowpercottage.co.uk
w yorkshirenet.co.uk/stayat/cowper/

WOLD NEWTON

The Wold Cottage ★★★★★
Guest Accommodation
GOLD AWARD
The Wold Cottage, Wold Newton, Driffield
YO25 3HL
t (01262) 470696
e katrina@woldcottage.com
w woldcottage.com

WOMBLETON

Rockery Cottage ★★★★
Bed & Breakfast SILVER AWARD
Main Street, Wombleton, Helmsley
YO62 7RX
t (01751) 432257
e enquiries@rockerycottage.co.uk
w rockerycottage.co.uk

WORTLEY

Wortley Hall ★★★★
Guest Accommodation
Wortley Village, Sheffield, Barnsley
S35 7DB
t (0114) 288 2100
e info@wortleyhall.com
w wortleyhall.com

WORTON

Stoney End ★★★★★
Guest Accommodation
GOLD AWARD
Worton, Leyburn
DL8 3ET
t (01969) 650652
e pmh@stoneyend.co.uk
w stoneyend.co.uk

WYKEHAM

Downe Arms ★★★ Inn
Main Road, Wykeham, Scarborough
YO13 9QB
t (01723) 862471
e info@downearmshotel.co.uk
w downearmshotel.co.uk

YEADON

Willow Cottage B&B ★★★★
Guest Accommodation
Willow Cottage, Ivegate, Yeadon, Leeds
LS19 7RE
t (0113) 250 1189
e info@willowcottage.org.uk
w willowcottage.org.uk

YORK

23 Saint Marys guesthouse
★★★★ Guest House
SILVER AWARD
23,saint marys, bootham, York
YO30 7DD
t (01904) 622738
e stmarys23@hotmail.com
w 23stmarys.co.uk

Aaron Guest House Guest House
42 Bootham Crescent, Bootham, York
YO30 7AH
t (01904) 625927
e sofiac21@yahoo.co.uk
w aaronyork.co.uk

Abbeyfields Guest House ★★★★
Guest Accommodation
19 Bootham Terrace, York
YO30 7DH
t (01904) 636471
e enquire@abbeyfields.co.uk
w abbeyfields.co.uk

Abbey Guest House ★★★★
Guest House SILVER AWARD
14 Earlsborough Terrace, Marygate, York
YO30 7BQ
t (01904) 627782
e info@abbeyghyork.co.uk
w abbeyghyork.co.uk

Abbingdon Guest House ★★★
Guest House
60 Bootham Crescent, York
YO30 7AH
t (01904) 621761
e info@abbingdonyork.co.uk
w abbingdonyork.co.uk

The Acer Guest House ★★★★
Guest House
52 Scarcroft Hill, York
YO24 1DE
t (01904) 653839
e info@acerhotel.co.uk
w acerhotel.co.uk

553

Yorkshire

Acres Dene Guest House ★★★
Guest House
87 Fulford Road, York
YO10 4BD
t (01904) 647482
e stay@acresdene.co.uk
w acresdene.co.uk

Airden House ★★★★ *Guest House*
1 St Mary's, Bootham, York
YO30 7DD
t (01904) 638915
e info@airdenhouse.co.uk
w airdenhouse.co.uk

Alexander House ★★★★★
Guest Accommodation
GOLD AWARD
94 Bishopthorpe Road, York
YO23 1JS
t (01904) 625016
e info@alexanderhouseyork.co.uk
w alexanderhouseyork.co.uk

Amber House ★★★★
Bed & Breakfast
36 Bootham Crescent, Bootham, York
YO30 7AH
t (01904) 620275
e amberhouseyork@hotmail.com
w amberhouse-york.co.uk

Ambleside Guest House ★★★
Guest House
62 Bootham Crescent, York
YO30 7AH
t (01904) 637165
e ambles@globalnet.co.uk
w ambleside-gh.co.uk

The Apple House ★★★★
Guest House
74-76 Holgate Road, York
YO24 4AB
t (01904) 625081
e pamelageorge1@yahoo.co.uk
w applehouseyork.co.uk

Ardmore Guest House ★★★
Guest House
31 Claremont Terrace, Gillygate, York
YO31 7EJ
t (01904) 622562
w ardmoreyork.co.uk

Arnot House ★★★★★
Bed & Breakfast **GOLD AWARD**
17 Grosvenor Terrace, Bootham, York
YO30 7AG
t (01904) 641966
e kim.robbins@virgin.net
w arnothouseyork.co.uk

Ascot House ★★★★
Guest Accommodation
SILVER AWARD
80 East Parade, York
YO31 7YH
t (01904) 426826
e admin@ascothouseyork.com
w ascothouseyork.com

Ascot Lodge ★★★★
Guest Accommodation
112 Acomb Road, York
YO24 4EY
t (01904) 798134
e info@ascotlodge.com
w ascotlodge.com

Ashberry ★★★★ *Guest House*
103 The Mount, York
YO24 1AX
t (01904) 647339
e steveandsara@theashberry.co.uk
w theashberry.co.uk

Avondale Guest House ★★★
Guest Accommodation
61 Bishopthorpe Road, York
YO23 1NX
t (01904) 633989
e kaleda@avondaleguesthouse.co.uk
w avondaleguesthouse.co.uk

Barbican House ★★★★
Guest Accommodation
SILVER AWARD
20 Barbican Road, York
YO10 5AA
t (01904) 627617
e info@barbicanhouse.co.uk
w barbicanhouse.co.uk

Bar Convent ★★★
Guest Accommodation
17 Blossom Street, York
YO24 1AQ
t (01904) 643238
e info@bar-convent.org.uk
w bar-convent.org.uk

The Barn Hotel & Tea Rooms
★★★★ *Guest House*
Hutton-le-Hole, York
YO62 6UA
t (01751) 417311

Barrington House ★★★★
Guest Accommodation
15 Nunthorpe Avenue, Scarcroft Road, York
YO23 1PF
t (01904) 634539
e info@barringtonhouse.net
w barringtonhouse.net

Bay Tree Guest House ★★★★
Guest House
92 Bishopthorpe Road, York
YO1 6HQ
t (01904) 659462
e info@baytree-york.co.uk
w baytree-york.co.uk

Beckett Guest House ★★★
Guest Accommodation
58 Bootham Crescent, York
YO30 7AH
t (01904) 644728
e info@becketthotel.co.uk
w becketthotel.co.uk

Beech House ★★★★
Guest Accommodation
SILVER AWARD
6-7 Longfield Terrace, Bootham, York
YO30 7DJ
t (01904) 634581
e beechhouse-york@hotmail.co.uk
w beechhouse-york.co.uk

The Bentley Guest House ★★★★
Guest Accommodation
25 Grosvenor Terrace, Bootham, York
YO30 7AG
t (01904) 644313
e enquiries@bentleyofyork.com
w bentleyofyork.com

Bishopgarth Guest House ★★★
Guest House
3 Southlands Road, York
YO23 1NP
t (01904) 635220
e bishopgarth@btconnect.com
w bishopgarth.co.uk

Bishops ★★★★★
Guest Accommodation
SILVER AWARD
135 Holgate Road, York
YO24 4DF
t (01904) 628000
e enquiries@bishopsyork.co.uk
w bishopsyork.co.uk

Blakeney House & Restaurant
★★★★ *Guest Accommodation*
180 Stockton Lane, York
YO31 1ES
t (01904) 422786
e reception@blakeneyhotel-york.co.uk
w blakeneyhotel-york.co.uk

The Bloomsbury ★★★★
Guest House **SILVER AWARD**
127 Clifton, York
YO30 6BL
t (01904) 634031
e info@bloomsburyhotel.co.uk
w bloomsburyhotel.co.uk

Blossoms York ★★★ *Guest House*
28 Clifton, York
YO30 6AE
t (01904) 652391
e reception@blossomsyork.co.uk
w blossomsyork.co.uk

The Blue Bridge ★★★
Guest Accommodation
Fishergate, York
YO10 4AP
t (01904) 621193
e info@bluebridgehotel.co.uk
w bluebridgehotel.co.uk

Bootham Gardens Guesthouse
★★★★ *Guest House*
47 Bootham Crescent, York
YO30 7AJ
t 07722 856181
e guesthouse@hotmail.co.uk
w bootham-gardens-guesthouse.co.uk

Bootham Guest House ★★★★
Guest Accommodation
56 Bootham Crescent, York
YO30 7AH
t (01904) 672123
e boothamguesthouse1@hotmail.com
w boothamguesthouse.com

Bootham Park ★★★★
Guest Accommodation
9 Grosvenor Terrace, Bootham, York
YO30 7AG
t (01904) 644262
e boothampark@aol.com
w boothamparkhotel.co.uk

Bootham Tavern ★★★
Guest Accommodation - Room Only
29 Bootham, York
YO30 7BW
t (01904) 631093
w boothamtavern.co.uk

Bowen House ★★★★
Guest Accommodation
4 Gladstone St, Huntington Road, York
YO31 8RF
t (01904) 636881
e info@bowenhouseyork.com
w bowenhouseyork.com

Bowmans Guest House ★★★★
Guest House **SILVER AWARD**
33 Grosvenor Terrace, York
YO30 7AG
t (01904) 622204
e info@bowmansguesthouse.co.uk
w bowmansguesthouse.co.uk

The Brentwood ★★★★
Guest Accommodation
54 Bootham Crescent, York
YO30 7AH
t (01904) 636419
e thebrentwood@york.uk.net
w thebrentwoodofyork.com

Briar Lea Guest House ★★★
Guest Accommodation
8 Longfield Terrace, Bootham, York
YO30 7DJ
t (01904) 635061
e briarleahouse@msn.com
w briarlea.co.uk

Bronte Guest House ★★★★
Guest Accommodation
SILVER AWARD
22 Grosvenor Terrace, Bootham, York
YO30 7AG
t (01904) 621066
e enquiries@bronte-guesthouse.com
w bronte-guesthouse.com

Bull Lodge Guest House ★★★
Guest House
37 Bull Lane, Lawrence Street, York
YO10 3EN
t (01904) 415522
e stay@bulllodge.co.uk
w bulllodge.co.uk

Carlton House ★★★★
Guest Accommodation
134 The Mount, York
YO24 1AS
t (01904) 622265
e mail@carltonhouse.co.uk
w carltonhouse.co.uk

Carousel Guest House ★★
Guest House
83 Eldon Street, York
YO31 7NH
t (01904) 646709
e service@yorkcarousel.co.uk
w yorkcarousel.co.uk

The Cavalier ★★★ *Guest House*
39 Monkgate, York
YO3 17PB
t (01904) 636615
e julia@cavalierhotel.co.uk
w cavalierhotel.co.uk

Chelmsford Place Guest House
★★★ *Guest House*
85 Fulford Road, York
YO10 4BD
t (01904) 624491
e chelmsfordplace@btinternet.com
w chelmsfordplace.co.uk

City Guest House ★★★★
Guest Accommodation
68 Monkgate, York
YO31 7PF
t (01904) 622483
e info@cityguesthouse.co.uk
w cityguesthouse.co.uk

Crescent Guest House ★★★
Guest House
77 Bootham, York
YO30 7DQ
t (01904) 623216
w crescentguesthouseyork.co.uk

Crook Lodge ★★★★
Guest Accommodation
SILVER AWARD
26 St Marys, Bootham, York
YO30 7DD
t (01904) 655614
e crooklodge@hotmail.com
w crooklodge.co.uk

Crossways Guest House ★★★★
Guest House
23 Wigginton Road, York
YO31 8HJ
t (01904) 637250
e enquiries@crossways-york.co.uk
w crossways-york.co.uk

Cumbria House ★★★ *Guest House*
2 Vyner Street, Haxby Road, York
YO31 8HS
t (01904) 636817
e candj@cumbriahouse.freeserve.co.uk
w cumbriahouse.com

Curzon Lodge & Stable Cottages
★★★★ *Guest House*
23 Tadcaster Road, York
YO24 1QG
t (01904) 703157
e admin@curzonlodge.com
w smoothhound.co.uk/hotels/curzon

D'Oyly's *Guest Accommodation*
North House, Bolton Percy, York
YO23 7AN
t (01904) 744354
e henreyhouseman@yahoo.co.uk
w doylys.co.uk

Dairy Guest House ★★★★
Guest House
3 Scarcroft Road, York
YO23 1ND
t (01904) 639367
e stay@dairyguesthouse.co.uk
w dairyguesthouse.co.uk

Elliotts ★★★★ *Guest House*
2 Sycamore Place, Bootham, York
YO30 7DW
t (01904) 623333
e elliotshotel@aol.com
w elliottshotel.co.uk

Yorkshire

arthings Guest House ★★★★
uest House
Nunthorpe Avenue, York
023 1PF
 (01904) 653545
 stay@farthingsyork.co.uk
 farthingsyork.co.uk

eversham Lodge ★★★★
uest Accommodation
ILVER AWARD
Feversham Crescent, York
031 8HQ
 (01904) 623882
 bookings@fevershamlodge.co.uk
 fevershamlodge.co.uk

oss Bank Guest House ★★★★
uest House
 Huntington Road, York
031 8RB
 (01904) 635548
 info@fossbank.co.uk
 fossbank.co.uk

ourposter Lodge ★★★
uest House
8-70 Heslington road, York
010 5AU
 (01904) 651170
 fourposter.lodge@virgin.net
 fourposterlodge.co.uk

ur Seasons ★★★★★
uest Accommodation
OLD AWARD
 St Peters Grove, Bootham, York
030 6AQ
 (01904) 622621
 roe@fourseasons.supanet.com
 fourseasons-hotel.co.uk

riars Rest Guest House ★★★
uest House
 Fulford Road, York
010 4BD
 (01904) 629823
 friarsrest@btinternet.com
 friarsrest.co.uk

altres Lodge ★★
uest Accommodation
4 Low Petergate, York
01 7HZ
 (01904) 622478
 info@galtreslodgehotel.co.uk
 galtreslodgehotel.co.uk

eorgian House ★★
uest Accommodation
5 Bootham, York
030 7BT
 (01904) 622874
 york1e45@aol.com
 georgianhouse.co.uk

oldsmiths Guest House ★★★★
uest Accommodation
3 Longfield Terrace, York
030 7DJ
 (01904) 655738
 susan@goldsmith18.freeserve.co.uk
 goldsmithsguesthouse.co.uk

range Lodge Guest House ★★★
uest Accommodation
2 Bootham Crescent, York
030 7AH
 (01904) 621137
 grange-lodge@btconnect.com
 grange-lodge.com

reenside ★★★ Guest House
24 Clifton, York
030 6BQ
 (01904) 623631
 greenside@onebillnet.co.uk
 greensideguesthouse.co.uk

regory's ★★★★
uest Accommodation
ILVER AWARD
60 Bishopthorpe Road, York
023 1LF
 (01904) 627521
 gregorys.york@virgin.net
 gregorysofyork.co.uk

The Groves ★★★★ Guest House
15 St Peters Grove, York
YO30 6AQ
t (01904) 559777
e info@thegrovesyork.co.uk
w thegrovesyork.co.uk

The Hazelwood ★★★★
Guest Accommodation
GOLD AWARD
24-25 Portland Street, York
YO31 7EH
t (01904) 626548
e reservations@thehazelwoodyork.com
w thehazelwoodyork.com

Heworth Court B&B and Lamplight Restaurant ★★★★
Guest Accommodation
76-78 Heworth Green, York
YO31 7TQ
t (01904) 425156
e hotel@heworth.co.uk
w heworth.co.uk

Heworth Guest House ★★★★
Guest House
126 East Parade, Heworth, York
YO31 7YG
t (01904) 426384
e chris@yorkcity.co.uk
w yorkbandb.co.uk

Hillcrest Guest House ★★★
Guest House
110 Bishopthorpe Road, York
YO23 1JX
t (01904) 653160
e info@hillcrest-guest-house.co.uk
w hillcrest-guest-house.co.uk

Holgate Bridge ★★★
Guest Accommodation
106 Holgate Rd, York
YO24 4BD
t (01904) 635971
e info@holgatebridge.co.uk
w holgatebridge.co.uk

The Hollies Guest House ★★★★
Guest House
141 Fulford Road, York
YO10 4HG
t (01904) 634279
e hayleycarlyle@hotmail.com
w holliesguesthouse.yorkwebsites.co.uk

Holly Cottage B&B ★★★★
Bed & Breakfast
194 Malton Road, York
YO32 9TD
t (01904) 424223
e carol@carolz.plus.com
w hollycottageyork.co.uk

Hollylodge Guesthouse ★★★★
Guest Accommodation
204-206 Fulford Road, York
YO10 4DD
t (01904) 646005
e geoff@thehollylodge.co.uk
w thehollylodge.co.uk

Holme - Lea - Manor ★★★★
Guest House **SILVER AWARD**
18 St Peters Grove, Clifton, York
YO30 6AQ
t (01904) 623529
e holmelea@btclick.net
w holmelea.co.uk

Huntington House ★★★
Group Hostel
18 Huntington Road, York
YO31 8RB
t (01904) 622755
e pp@huntingtonhouse.demon.co.uk
w huntingtonhouse.demon.co.uk

The Lighthorseman ★★★★ Inn
124 Fulford Road, Fulford, York
YO10 4BE
t (01904) 624818
e janine@lighthorseman.co.uk
w lighthorseman.co.uk

Limekiln House Bed & Breakfast
Limekiln Farmhouse, Coneysthorpe, York
YO60 7DD
t (01653) 648213
e gillianharris-slt@yahoo.co.uk

Limes ★★★★ Guest House
SILVER AWARD
135 Fulford Road, York
YO10 4HE
t (01904) 624548
e queries@limeshotel.co.uk
w limeshotel.co.uk

Linden Lodge ★★★★
Guest Accommodation
6 Nunthorpe Avenue, York
YO23 1PF
t (01904) 620107
e lindenlodgehotel@btinternet.com
w lindenlodgehotel.co.uk

The Manor House ★★★★
Guest House **SILVER AWARD**
Main Street, Linton-on-Ouse, York
YO30 2AY
t (01347) 848391
e manorguesthouse@tiscali.co.uk
w manorguesthouse.co.uk

Midway House ★★★★
Guest Accommodation
145 Fulford Road, York
YO10 4HG
t (01904) 659272
e info@midwayhouseyork.co.uk
w midwayhouseyork.co.uk

Minster View Guest House ★★★★
Guest House
2 Grosvenor Terrace, Bootham, York
YO30 7AG
t (01904) 655034
e julie.holborn@btconnect.com
w minsterview-york.co.uk

Monkgate Guest House ★★★
Guest House
65 Monkgate, York
YO32 7PA
t (01904) 655947
e 65monkgate@btconnect.com
w monkgateguesthouse.co.uk

Mont-Clare Guest House ★★★★
Guest House
32 Claremont Terrace, Gillygate, York
YO31 7EJ
t (01904) 651011
e info@mont-clare.co.uk
w mont-clare.co.uk

Moorgarth Guest House ★★★
Guest House
158 Fulford Road, York
YO10 4DA
t (01904) 636768
e info@moorgarth.co.uk
w moorgarthyork.co.uk

Moorland House ★★★
Guest Accommodation
1A Moorland Road, Fulford, York
YO10 4HF
t (01904) 629354
e g.metcalfe@tesco.net
w moorlandhouseyork.co.uk

Mowbray House ★★★
Bed & Breakfast
34 Haxby Road, York
YO31 8JX
t (01904) 637710
e carol@mowbrayhouse.co.uk
w mowbrayhouse.co.uk

Northolme Guest House ★★★
Guest House
114 Shipton Road, Rawcliffe, York
YO30 5RN
t (01904) 639132
e g.liddle@tesco.com
w northolmeguesthouse.co.uk

Palm Court ★★★★
Guest Accommodation
17 Huntington Road, York
YO31 8RB
t (01904) 639387
e helencoll_2000@hotmail.com
w thepalmcourt.org.uk

Park View ★★★★ Guest House
34 Grosvenor Terrace, Bootham, York
YO30 7AG
t (01904) 620437
e theparkviewyork@tiscali.co.uk
w theparkviewyork.co.uk

Queen Annes Guest House ★★★
Guest Accommodation
24 Queen Annes Road, Bootham, York
YO30 7AA
t (01904) 629389
e info@queen-annes-guesthouse.co.uk
w queen-annes-guesthouse.co.uk

Southlands Guest House ★★★★
Guest Accommodation
69 Nunmill Street, York
YO23 1NT
t (01904) 675966
w southlands-guesthouse.co.uk

Stanley House ★★★ Guest House
Stanley Street, York
YO31 8NW
t (01904) 637111
e stanleyhouseyork@hotmail.com
w stanleyhouseyork.co.uk

Staymor Guest House ★★★★
Guest House
2 Southlands Road, York
YO23 1NP
t (01904) 626935
e kathwilson@lineone.net
w staymorguesthouse.co.uk

St George's ★★★
Guest Accommodation
6 St Georges Place, York
YO24 1DR
t (01904) 625056
e sixstgeorg@aol.com
w stgeorgesyork.com

St Marys Guest House ★★★★
Guest Accommodation
17 Longfield Terrace, Bootham, York
YO30 7DJ
t (01904) 626972
e stmaryshotel@talk21.com
w stmaryshotel.co.uk

St Paul's Lodge ★★★★ Guest House
120 Holgate Road, York
YO24 4BB
t (01904) 611514
e julie@stpauls.wanadoo.co.uk
w stpaulslodge.co.uk

St Raphael Guesthouse ★★★★
Guest Accommodation
SILVER AWARD
44 Queen Annes Road, York
YO30 7AF
t (01904) 645028
e info@straphaelguesthouse.co.uk
w straphaelguesthouse.co.uk

Sycamore Guest House ★★★★
Guest House
19 Sycamore Place, Bootham, York, North Yorkshire.
YO30 7DW
t (01904) 624712
e mail@thesycamore.co.uk
w guesthousesyork.co.uk

Tower Guest House
Guest Accommodation
2 Feversham Crescent, York
YO31 8HQ
t (01904) 655571
e reservations@towerguesthouse.fsnet.co.uk
w towerguesthouseyork.com

Tree Tops ★★★ Guest House
21 St Marys, Bootham, York
YO30 7DD
t (01904) 629494
e treetopsguesthouseyork@yahoo.co.uk
w treetopsguesthouse.co.uk

Yorkshire

Turnberry House ★★★★
Guest House
143 Fulford Road, York
YO10 4HG
t (01904) 658435
e turnberryhouse@tiscali.co.uk
w turnberryhouse.com

Tyburn Guest House ★★★
Guest Accommodation
11 Albemarle Road, The Mount, York
YO23 1EN
t (01904) 655069
e info@tyburnguesthouse.co.uk
w tyburnguesthouse.co.uk

Waggon & Horses ★★★ *Inn*
19 Lawrence Street, York
YO10 3BP
t (01904) 637478
e info@waggonandhorsesyork.co.uk
w waggonandhorsesyork.co.uk

Warrens ★★★★
Guest Accommodation
30 -32 Scarcroft Road, York
YO23 1NF
t (01904) 643139
e info@warrensguesthouse.co.uk
w warrensguesthouse.co.uk

YHA York International ★★★
Hostel
42 Water End, Clifton, York
YO30 6LP
t (01904) 653147
e york@yha.org.uk
w yha.org.uk

York Backpackers *Hostel*
88-90 Micklegate, York
YO1 6JX
t (01904) 627720
e mail@yorkbackpackers.co.uk
w yorkbackpackers.co.uk

York House ★★★★
Guest Accommodation
62 Heworth Green, York
YO31 7TQ
t (01904) 427070
e yorkhouse.bandb@tiscali.co.uk
w yorkhouseyork.co.uk

York Lodge Guest House ★★★
Guest Accommodation
64 Bootham Crescent, Bootham, York
YO30 7AH
t (01904) 654289
e yorkldg@aol.com
w york-lodge.com

The York Priory ★★★★
Guest House
126 Fulford Road, York
YO10 4BE
t (01904) 819025
e stay@yorkpriory.com
w priory-guest-house-hotel-york.com

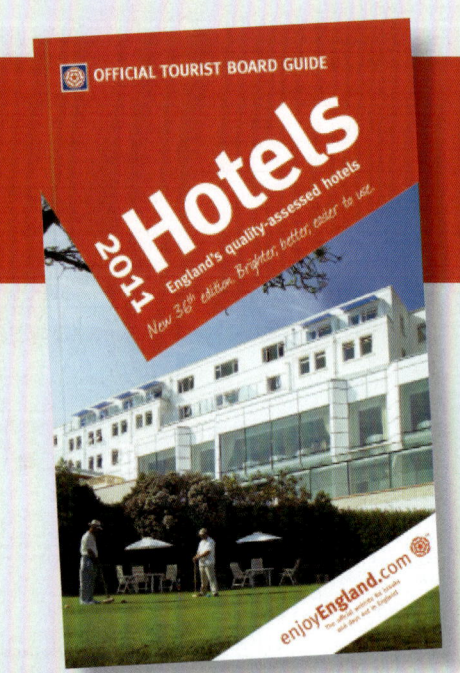

Looking for something else?

You can also buy a copy of our popular guide 'Hotels' including country house and town house hotels, metro and budget hotels, serviced apartments, restaurants with rooms and Spas in England 2011.

£10.99

Now available in good bookshops and online at
visitbritainshop.com

Help before you go

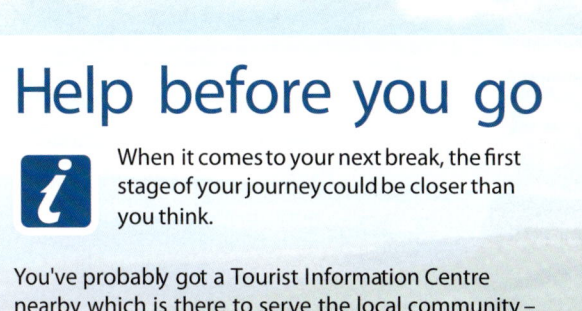

i When it comes to your next break, the first stage of your journey could be closer than you think.

You've probably got a Tourist Information Centre nearby which is there to serve the local community – as well as visitors. Knowledgeable staff will be happy to help you, wherever you're heading.

Many Tourist Information Centres can provide you with maps and guides, and it's often possible to book accommodation and travel tickets too.

You'll find the address of your nearest centre in your local phone book, or look in the regional sections in this guide for a list of Tourist Information Centres.

North West

An exciting and dynamic region, England's Northwest is full of striking landscapes and vibrant cityscapes. From the elegant and ancient city of Chester to the inspirational vistas of the Lake District, and from the award winning industrial heritage of Manchester to the outstanding cultural attractions of Liverpool there's so much to see and do in England's Northwest.

Add to these a spectacular coastline with Britain's favourite seaside resorts, and the delightfully undiscovered countryside of Lancashire, and you're spoilt for choice.

The Roman city of Chester is full of sumptuous 21st century delights. Its unique two-tiered shopping galleries are the perfect place to indulge in some seriously sophisticated retail therapy, whilst Cheshire's gardens promise a kaleidoscope of colour whatever time you visit. In Cumbria – the Lake District you'll be treated to stunning scenery, enticing attractions, exciting activities, and mouth-watering local produce; whether you're stress-busting or adrenaline-pumping there's nowhere better.

Sophisticated and stylish, Manchester is the original 24-hour party city. From fine dining and chic hotels to cutting-edge clubs and bars and the world's most progressive music scene, Manchester is always buzzing. The shopping here is legendary, too. Liverpool is a striking and exciting city, with world-class architecture and a cultural scene to match. Packed with museums, galleries, theatres and concert halls, not to mention a heritage that covers everything from maritime to Mersey Beat, you won't know where to start.

North West

North West

Cheshire, Cumbria, Lancashire, Manchester, Merseyside

560 Counties
564 Where to Go
566 Events
568 Where to Eat
574 Where to Stay

With two Areas of Outstanding Natural Beauty full of dramatic scenery and quiet lanes, Lancashire offers the perfect country escape. This ancient county is a royal duchy full of castles, picturesque stone-built villages and some of the country's favourite seaside resorts, including Blackpool - Europe's biggest and brightest.

It's with good reason that the coastline of England's Northwest is known as 'England's Golf Coast'; here you'll find some of the finest championship golf in the world. Extending from Cumbria in the north down to Wirral in the south, it embraces three Open Championship venues, plus several other courses inextricably linked with the rich history of the English game.

England's Northwest has a rich sporting heritage; from the world-famous Grand National to eight Premiership football teams. And with a host of exhilarating events, both indoor and out, there's always a buzz in England's Northwest.

North West | **Cheshire**

Cheshire

Chester and Cheshire – picturesque and worldly. Well stocked with great places to eat and drink, indulgent shops and fantastic golf courses - it can all be found in one of Britain's most diverse regions. The region is well connected with the rest of the country, but when you need to disappear off the radar for a while, Cheshire is wonderfully full of fascinating hiding places!

Chester
The Roman city of Chester is full of sumptuous 21st century delights. The unique two-tiered shopping galleries are the perfect place to indulge in some seriously sophisticated retail therapy, and when you've 'shopped til you're about to drop', there's a range of hotels to suit your pocket. Add Cheshire's gardens to your short break and you'll enjoy a kaleidoscope of colour with a relaxing twist, whatever time you visit.

Knutsford
Knutsford is said to derive its name from the Danish King Canute who supposedly 'forded' the River Lily in 1016. Elizabeth Gaskell, the famous novelist spent most of her life in Knutsford. Her novel 'Cranford' is set in Victorian Knutsford, and the house where she grew up is situated on what is now Gaskell Avenue. Hip Knutsford becomes even more popular in July, when the glorious RHS Show Tatton Park comes to town.

Macclesfield
Macclesfield became the centre of Britain's silk industry during the Industrial Revolution. There are many attractive Georgian mills, houses, inns, churches and chapels. Cobbled streets and quaint old buildings stand side-by-side with modern shops and three markets. The town is the western gateway to the Peak District, with many beautiful walks on its doorstep and stunning views of the surrounding countryside.

Alderley Edge
Alderley Edge is a picturesque town, which takes its name from the wooded escarpment towering above the Cheshire plain, with fine views and walks. The town of Alderley Edge has excellent shops, restaurants and bars and entertains many premiership footballers and members of the 'Cheshire Set'. There are many historic buildings including Chorley Old Hall - the oldest surviving manor house in Cheshire.

Malpas
Malpas is one of the oldest towns in Cheshire with good timber-framed, old brick buildings. Set in the quiet winding lanes of South Cheshire, there are good opportunities for gentle country walks and cycle rides. Nearby Cholmondeley Castle overlooks 800 acres of parkland and water gardens. Particularly attractive is the Temple Garden with its rockery, lake and islands.

North West | Cumbria

Cumbria

Explore the breathtaking landscape of dramatic mountains, sparkling lakes and a changing coastline. As the country's biggest outdoor playground, the Lake District is full of adventures. Visit market towns, country houses, art galleries and heritage sites. Join in with local festivals or hide away at premium spas then retreat to an unrivalled choice of quality accommodation.

Lake District National Park

From Windermere in the south to Keswick in the north; Ullswater in the east to Ravenglass on the west, the Lake District National Park is England's largest national park. At the centre of this picturesque area is Lake Windermere. On the shores of Windermere lies the bustling town of Bowness-on-Windermere from where you can board one of the lake steamers, taking in spectacular mountain scenery while you discover magical islands and bays.

Enjoy a visit to Ambleside, encircled with fells – the ideal place for a rural break and a good place to get kitted out with the latest outdoor gear. Just a mile up the road is Rydal Mount, much loved home of William Wordsworth. The lovely village of Grasmere is where you'll find Wordsworth's inspirational home, Dove Cottage.

Keswick

The impressive array of mountains, valleys and lakes in close proximity are the obvious attraction to the many visitors but Keswick is also a bustling market town with pedestrianised square and magnificent Moot Hall building as well as the acclaimed Theatre by the Lake. Enjoy a rich variety of visitor attractions and activities and explore pretty public parks, cafes, galleries and shops.

Carlisle

In its 2000 year history, Carlisle has seen Celts, Romans, warring families and invading armies leave a legacy for you to explore. In Carlisle's Historic Quarter, you will find a castle, cathedral and museums in a compact area, crisscrossed with ancient thoroughfares. Within its confines, you can learn about the past, away from the hustle and bustle of city life.

Eden Valley

From mysterious Neolithic sites to imaginative modern sculptures, Eden has it all. The exhilarating mix of vibrant towns and stirring landscapes will be sure to ignite a spark of inspiration. Modern art has also made its mark. The Eden Benchmarks are one such example, great carved stone sculptures were inspired by the local landscape and are located along the River Eden.

Ullswater

Ullswater is set against a breathtaking backdrop of mountain scenery and inspired William Wordsworth, who wrote his famous poem after he discovered multitudes of wild daffodils along the lakeshore. This stunning landscape also makes it an ideal location for walking, mountain biking, skiing and rock climbing adventures.

Western Lake District

As well as being home to Britain's Favourite View at Wastwater, the Western Lake district has an amazing coastline, with stunning views. Visit bird-watching sites and nature reserves along the Solway Coast Area of Outstanding Natural Beauty. Catch the Egremont Castle illuminations, enjoy the acclaimed Maryport Blues Festival, Solfest and the new Lakes Alive programme.

North West | Lancashire

Lancashire

Lancashire is the perfect place for escaping it all. Delve into the Forest of Bowland to discover outstanding natural beauty as it stretches out before you. Wander the winding lanes of historic Lancaster and uncover the secrets of its past. Let the fresh sea air invigorate your senses as you race along Blackpool's famous seafront.

Forest of Bowland
Delve into the Forest of Bowland and discover outstanding natural beauty as lush countryside stretches out for miles in front of you. Explore this beautiful landscape with magical forests and rolling hills. Renowned for its stunning views, make sure you don't miss out, and take a few moments to pause at the side of the River Hodder as it flows under Dunsop Bridge or at the top of a climb up Jeffery Hill. Breathtaking.

Lancaster
As you approach Lancaster on the M6, you can tell by the dramatic change in landscape that you are arriving somewhere special. The air softens, the terrain gives way to rolling hills and an impressive city skyline opens at your side. Head straight for the castle to hear chilling tales of the past, then discover quirky independent shops that rub shoulders with museums and monuments, bars and restaurants. An early evening jaunt up to Williamson Park at the top of the city will be well worth it, as you're greeted with a stunning sunset across Morecambe Bay.

Blackpool
Think you know Blackpool already? Think again. There's far more to this fabulous beach resort than deckchairs and donkeys. Scratch beneath the surface and you'll discover a world of excitement and entertainment you never realised was there. The perfect playground for all the family, you'll be spoilt for choice for ways to fill your days come rain or shine! Mix days at the beach with events across the resort. You'll be amazed how Blackpool is ready to entertain you all season long.

Pennine Lancashire
Pennine Lancashire is a land of breathtaking wild beauty and the birthplace of the Industrial Revolution. Step out and discover the stunning countryside above Burnley whith views over to iconic Pendle Hill, dominating the skyline. Then head east to Rossendale for some exhilarating outdoor activities. Discover a landscape of vivid contrasts in the towns of Blackburn and Accrington where rich history and heritage combines with modern 21st century landscapes.

Heart of Lancashire
The heart of Lancashire is a true area of contrasts, from the open landscape of the west to the vibrant city of Preston, which holds hidden delights at every turn. From the striking Ribble Coast and Wetlands marshes and estuary, it's a bird spotters dream. Take some time to uncover fascinating tales of ghosts and industrial revolutionaries at the many historic houses and museums in the area. Stop off and discover the true hub of Lancashire's charm.

North West | **Manchester & Merseyside**

Manchester & Merseyside

Two 'hip' destinations with something for everybody. Manchester has been transformed from the world's first industrial city to a leisure destination. Liverpool with its strong maritime history is enjoying a stylish and vibrant renaissance since it was nominated European Capital of Culture in 2008.

Manchester

A vibrant and innovative city-region, Manchester boasts stunning architecture, world-class events, great shopping, excellent restaurants and fantastic nightlife.

But Manchester is also a cultural city and it is not hard to spot its past. The magnificent Royal Exchange Theatre, once the Cotton Exchange is now the world's largest theatre-in-the-round whilst Central Library (inspired by the Pantheon in Rome) is the largest municipal library in the world.

There are over 90 attractions, museums and galleries in the region, many are free entry. The stunning landmark Urbis building will re-open in 2011 as the National Football Museum where you will be able to relive legendary moments in football history, see iconic objects and have hands-on football fun for all the family! Don't miss the Imperial War Museum North or the award-winning Lowry a spectacular waterside building at Pier 8 which houses the largest public collection of works by the artist LS Lowry; theatres, restaurants and a Tourist Information Centre.

Manchester is certainly the place for a 'Shopping Spree' from High Street heaven on Market Street via small unusual shops and outlets in the Northern Quarter to prestigious retail therapy on King Street and just around the corner Harvey Nicols and Selfridges on Exchange Street. You may shop 'til you drop but the shopping areas are within in walking distance from each other.

Manchester is the perfect place for a short break but with so much to do you could stay longer!

Merseyside

A city of astonishing beauty and stunning architecture! See the world famous Royal Liverpool Philharmonic, the legendary Everyman Theatre and two majestically different cathedrals, the Anglican Cathedral and the Metropolitan Cathedral. Visit the ornate Philharmonic pub, where the Beatles used to meet. Enjoy fabulous hotels, exceptional shopping, and some of the finest restaurants.

A UNESCO World Heritage city with a big reputation - It's the centre of a vast area of beauty, culture and entertainment that deserves exploration. The Three Graces, Albert Dock and Pier Head are as iconic as they are dramatic, and delving into their history in the city's museums is an enlightening experience. Here you will find Tate Liverpool and Merseyside Maritime Museum and retrace the steps of the Fab Four at the Beatles Story.

For a little peace and quiet, visit the award winning beaches and coastal walks at Sefton and Wirral Peninsula. There are pretty villages such as Brimstage with Hall Courtyard full of arts and crafts shops or Port Sunlight, a Victorian village built by Lord Level for the workers in his soap factory.

There are plenty of sporting choices with horseracing at Aintree or Haydock, football at Everton or Liverpool or rugby league at St Helens. There is also a calendar of running events throughout the city including the Liverpool Half Marathon in Spring the summer Liverpool Triathlon.

Liverpool truly is a fabulous journey of discovery in a city bursting with culture and creativity.

North West | Where to Go

Where to Go

Attractions with this sign participate in the **Visitor Attraction Quality Assurance Scheme** (see page 6) which recognises high standards in all aspects of the visitor experience.

ENTERTAINMENT & CULTURE

Beatles Story
Liverpool, Merseyside L3 4AD
(0151) 709 1963
www.beatlesstory.com
Located within Liverpool's historic Albert Dock, the Beatles Story is a unique visitor attraction that transports you on an enlightening and atmospheric journey into the life, times, culture and music of the Beatles.

Harris Museum and Art Gallery
Preston, Lancashire PR1 2PP
(01772) 258248
www.harrismuseum.org.uk
Offers the best of Preston's heritage in a beautiful Grade 1 listed building.

Imperial War Museum North
Manchester, Greater Manchester
M17 1TZ
(0161) 836 4000
www.iwm.org.uk/north/
The award-winning Imperial War Museum North is located at The Quays and offers dynamic display techniques to reflect on how people's lives are shaped by war.

John Rylands Library
Manchester, Greater Manchester
M3 3EH
(0161) 306 0555
www.library.manchester.ac.uk/
For those who set eyes on Deansgate's John Rylands Library for the first time, 'library' might not be the first word that comes to mind. This masterpiece of Victorian Gothic architecture looks more like a castle or cathedral.

Liverpool Football Club
Liverpool, Merseyside L4 0TH
(0151) 260 6677
www.liverpoolfc.tv
The new LFC Stadium Tour has more availability than ever. Meet an LFC Legend; get your photograph with one of our many trophies or indulge yourself in one of our award winning Experience Days.

Lowry
Salford, Greater Manchester
M50 3AZ
(0161) 876 2020
www.thelowry.com
Salford's answer to the Sydney Opera House and the Guggenheim rolled into one. See LS Lowry's works and other outstanding exhibitions or take in a performance. There's also a rather divine restaurant plus shop and cafe.

Manchester Art Gallery
Manchester, Greater Manchester
M2 3JL
(0161) 235 8888
www.manchestergalleries.org
Houses one of the country's finest art collections in spectacular Victorian and Contemporary surroundings. Also changing exhibitions and a programme of events.

Manchester Museum
Manchester, Greater Manchester
M13 9PL
(0161) 275 2648
www.manchester.ac.uk/museum
Explore the world at the Manchester Museum with it's 4 floors of displays and exhibitions in 15 galleries featuring collections from all over the world.

Museum of Science and Industry (MOSI)
Manchester, Greater Manchester
M3 4FP
(0161) 832 2244
www.mosi.org.uk
This huge 7.5 acre site has 5 historic buildings packed with exciting exhibitions, stimulating hands-on galleries, historic working machinery and superb Special Exhibitions.

Tate Liverpool
Liverpool, Merseyside L3 4BB
(0151) 702 7400
www.tate.org.uk/liverpool
Tate Liverpool presents displays and international exhibitions of modern and contemporary art in beautiful light filled galleries. A wide range of events are also on offer to accompany exhibitions.

The Rheged Centre
Cumbria CA11 0DQ
(01768) 868000
www.rheged.com
International award-winning The Rheged Centre, Europe's largest grass covered building, home to a giant cinema screen showing epic movies daily. Regular events.

The World of Glass
St Helens, Merseyside
WA10 1BX
(01744) 22766
www.worldofglass.com
The World of Glass is a great day out for everyone, young or old. Live glass blowing demonstrations, amazing special effects film show, museum galleries, cafe, ship and art gallery.

North West | Where to Go

The Yellow Duckmarine
Liverpool, Merseyside L3 4AS
(0151) 708 7799
www.theyellowduckmarine.co.uk
Our hour long tour, half on land and half in the water takes in the city's historical sights and attractions and the docklands maritime history with an live commentary.

Tullie House Museum and Art Gallery
Cumbria CA3 8TP
(01228) 618718
www.tulliehouse.co.uk
An excellent choice for a great day.

Whitworth Art Gallery
Manchester, Greater Manchester M15 6ER
(0161) 275 7450
www.whitworth.manchester.ac.uk/
Home to an internationally-famous collection of British watercolours, textiles and wallpapers.

FAMILY FUN

Go Ape! Hire Wire Forest Adventure - Delamere, Northwich Cheshire
CW8 2JD
0845 643 9215
www.goape.co.uk
Experience an exhilarating course of rope bridges, tarzan swings and zip rides...all set high above the forest floor.

Gullivers World Theme Park
Warrington, Cheshire WA5 9YZ
(01925) 444888
www.gulliversfun.co.uk
Designed for the whole family.

Pleasure Beach Resort
Blackpool, Lancashire FY4 1EZ
0871 222 1234
www.pleasurebeachblackpool.com
Something for everyone at Pleasure Beach, Blackpool. Over 125 rides and attractions plus spectacular shows.

Sandcastle Waterpark
Blackpool, Lancashire FY4 1BB
(01253) 343602
www.sandcastle-waterpark.co.uk
The UK's Largest Indoor Waterpark and with 18 slides and attractions it is easy to see why Sandcastle Waterpark continues to make a splash.

Whinlatter Forest Park
Keswick, Cumbria CA12 5TW
(01768) 778469
www.forestry.gov.uk/whinlatterforestpark
England's only true mountain forest. Rising to 790 metres above sea level Whinlatter offers spectacular views of the Lake District and into Scotland.

HERITAGE

Beeston Castle
Tarporley, Cheshire CW6 9TX
(01829) 260464
www.visitcheshire.com/site/beeston
Will you find the legendary treasure of Richard II at magical Beeston?

Birdoswald Roman Fort
Cumbria CA8 7DD
(01697) 747602
www.english-heritage.org.uk
This fort is beside excellent stretches of Hadrian's Wall. Good interpretation of Roman History.

Blackpool Tower & Circus
Blackpool, Lancashire FY1 4BJ
(01253) 622242
www.theblackpooltower.co.uk
Entertainment for all ages, night and day at the world famous Blackpool Tower and Circus.

Chester Cathedral
Chester, Cheshire CH1 2HU
(01244) 324756
www.chestercathedral.com
A must see for Chester, a beautiful cathedral with a fascinating history.

Clitheroe Castle & Museum
Clitheroe, Lancashire BB7 1BA
(01200) 424568
www.lancashire.gov.uk/museums
A day of exploration for all the family. Galleries that will take you on a journey through 350 million years of history, heritage and geology of the local area.

Helmshore Mills Textile Museum
Helmshore, Lancashire BB4 4NP
(01706) 226459
www.lancashire.gov.uk/museums
Explore the true story of the Lancashire Textile Industry from the 18thC to the present day. A memorable atmosphere of these majestic mills and discover textile treasures from famous inventors.

Hoghton Tower
Preston, Lancashire PR5 0SH
(01254) 852986
www.hoghtontower.co.uk
An historic house with magnificent state apartments, banqueting hall, ballroom, grounds and dolls' houses on display. Underground passages and dungeons.

Jodrell Bank Visitor Centre & 3D Theatre
Holmes Chapel, Cheshire SK11 9DL
(01477) 571339
www.jb.man.ac.uk
The Jodrell Bank Visitor Centre is the visitor centre for the world famous Lovell Radio Telescope.

Muncaster Experience
Cumbria CA18 1RQ
(01229) 717614
www.muncaster.co.uk
Historic haunted Castle home to the Pennington family for 800 years. A 70-acre garden famous for its collection of rhododendrons and azaleas.. World Owl Centre home to over 40 species.

Sefton Park Palm House Preservation Trust
Liverpool, Merseyside L17 1AP
(0151) 726 2415
www.palmhouse.org.uk
Sefton Park Palm House is a grade II* listed Victorian glasshouse. it is an octagonal 3 tiered structure, showcasing the Liverpool Botanical collection.

Tatton Park
Knutsford, Cheshire WA16 6QN
(01625) 374400
www.tattonpark.org.uk
Tatton Park is often quoted as England's most complete historic estate, with its fine Neo-Classical mansion full of art treasures and original furnishings.

NATURE & WILDLIFE

Blackpool Zoo
Blackpool, Lancashire FY3 8PP
(01253) 830830
www.blackpoolzoo.org.uk
Set amid 32 acres of mature parkland and lakes, the award winning Blackpool Zoo is home to over 1500 beautiful, rare and exotic animals from all around the world.

Chester Zoo
Chester, Cheshire CH2 1LH
(01244) 380280
www.chesterzoo.org
Chester Zoo is the UK's no 1 charity zoo. Packed with 7,000 rare, exotic and endangered animals in 110 acres of award-winning gardens.

Farmer Ted's Farm Park
Ormskirk, Lancashire L39 7HW
(0151) 526 0002
www.farmerteds.com
Farmer Ted's is a brand new farm park - a safe environment for families with children 0-12 yrs, with older children also welcome.

565

North West | Where to Go/Events

South Lakes Wild Animal Park
Cumbria LA15 8JR
(01229) 466086
www.wildanimalpark.co.uk
Interactive animal experience with Rhinos, giraffes, lions, tigers, bears, lemurs, penguins, kangaroos and more. Get close to wildlife at Cumbria's top tourist attraction.

WWT Martin Mere Wetland Centre
Ormskirk, Lancashire L40 0TA
(01704) 895181
www.wwt.org.uk
Home to over 100 species of rare and endangered ducks, geese, swans, cranes, flamingos and now a beaver enclosure.

OUTDOOR ACTIVITIES

Anderton Boat Lift - Lift Trips
Northwich, Cheshire CW9 6FW
(01606) 786777
www.andertonboatlift.co.uk
Enjoy a 30 minute boat trip, as the magnificent Victorian Boat Lift towers above you.

Ullswater 'Steamers'
Ullswater, Cumbria CA11 0US
(01768) 482229
www.ullswater-steamers.co.uk
The 'Steamers' create the perfect opportunity to combine a cruise with some of the most famous and spectacular walks in the lake District

Windermere Lake Cruises, Lakeside
Cumbria LA12 8AS
(015394) 43360
www.windermere-lakecruises.co.uk
Steamers and launches sail daily between Ambleside, Bowness and Lakeside. Additional summer routes. Timetabled services.

RELAXING & PAMPERING

Liverpool ONE
Liverpool, Merseyside L1 8JQ
(0151) 232 3100
www.liverpool-one.com
More than 160 famous high street stores, ultra-hip fashion brands, cool independent boutiques, cafés and restaurants to the city centre.

Events 2011

Africa Oye
Liverpool
www.africaoye.com/
Mid June

Blackpool Armed Forces and Veterans' Week
www.armedforcesday.co.uk
June

Blackpool Dance Festival
www.blackpooldancefestival.com
May

Blackpool's Annual Airshow - Red Arrows
www.visitblackpool.com
August

Caribbean Carnival
Preston
www.prestoncarnival.co.uk
Spring Bank Holiday - May

Chester Food and Drink Festival
www.chesterfoodanddrink.com/
Easter weekend

Chester Races
www.chester-races.co.uk
May - September

Cholmondeley Pageant of Power
Malpas
www.pageantofpower.com
July

Creamfields
www.creamfields.com/
27-28 August

Garstang Walking Festival
www.wyrebc.gov.uk
May

Great British Rhthym and Blues Festival
Colne
August

Great North Swim
www.greatswim.org
September

Hungry Pigeon
Manchester
www.hungrypigeon.com
May

Irish Festival
Manchester
www.manchesteririshfestival.co.uk
March

Jazz Festival
Manchester
www.manchesterjazz.com
July

John Smith's Grand National
Liverpool
www.aintree.co.uk/
7-9 April

Kendal Mountain Festival
www.breweryarts.co.uk
November

Liverpool Summer Pops Festival
www.summerpops.com/
July - August

Manchester International Festival
www.mif.co.uk
July

Manchester Pride
www.manchesterpride.com
August

Mathew Street Festival
Liverpool
www.mathewstreetfestival.org/
End August

Pendle Walking Festival
Nelson
www.pendle.gov.uk/walking
September

Pennine Lancashire Festival of Food & Culture
Blackburn
www.penninelancashirefestivals.com
August

RHS Flower Show at Tatton Park
Knutsford
www.tattonpark.org.uk
July

Southport Flower Show
Southport
www.southportflowershow.co.uk
Mid August

Theatre Festival
Manchester
www.247theatrefestival.co.uk
July-August

Tractor Pulling Championships
Great Eccleston
www.nwtpc.co.uk
August

Viva' Spanish and Latin American Film Festival
Manchester
www.vivafilmfestival.com
March

BRITAIN – The official magazine
HALF PRICE

Exclusive OFFER!

1 Year (6 Issues) ~~£30~~ £15

BRITAIN magazine tells the story of our island nation, from 1066 and beyond right through to the present day.

If you enjoy finding out more about our country's rich history, then you'll love BRITAIN magazine. Learn more about our kings and queens, heroes and villains, castles and cathedrals, stately homes and gardens, countryside and coastline … and so much more besides.

A copy of BRITAIN makes the perfect companion whether you like to travel the highways and byways by train, coach or car – or simply prefer to explore our glorious country from the comfort of your own armchair!

SPECIAL OFFER
1 year for JUST £15 (usually £30 -HALF PRICE)
Overseas rate £17.50 (usually £35 - HALF PRICE)

SUBSCRIBE NOW
Call: +44 (0)1858 438878 (quote code VB1G)

Visit: www.subscription.co.uk/britain/VB1G

Post: Send a cheque with your name, address and phone number to

Britain, Tower House, Sovereign Park, Market Harborough, LE16 9EF, UK

North West | Where to Eat

Where to Eat

The North West England region has great places to eat. The restaurant reviews on these pages are just a small selection from the highly respected *The Good Food Guide 2011*. Please see page 14 for further information on the Guide and details of a Special Offer for our readers.

CHESHIRE

Pecks
Seriously impressive stuff
Newcastle Road, Moreton CW12 4SB
(01260) 275161
www.pecksrest.co.uk
Modern British | £35

A long-established village restaurant not far from local landmark Mow Cop Castle, Pecks takes an idiosyncratic approach. Dinner is served at 7.30 for 8, and the drill is a five-course menu, with choice at each stage, of dishes that are paraded before you in theatrical display. April diners might have progressed from smoked haddock, leek and potato soup, through wild boar and mushroom pâté with cheese shortbreads and ginger compote, to shin of Hereford beef with spring onion mash in red wine jus, before being offered a dessert selection and then cheeses. It's a thoroughly affable experience, with friendly service and an international list of reasonably priced wines (from £14.50) to match. **Chef/s:** Les Wassall. **Open:** Tue to Sun L 12 to 2 (3 Sun), Tue to Sat D 7.30 for 8 (1 sitting). **Closed:** Mon, 25 to 30 Dec. **Meals:** alc (main courses £9 to £23). Set L £14.95 (2 courses) to £17.95. Set D Tue and Wed £36.50 (5 courses) Thur and Fri £39.95 (7 courses), Sat £44.95 (7 courses). Sun L £18.25. **Service:** not inc. **Details:** major cards accepted. 110 seats. Air conditioning. Separate bar. Wheelchair access. Music. Children welcome. Car parking.

CUMBRIA

George and Dragon
Estate pub with a landmark restaurant
Clifton, Penrith CA10 2ER
(01768) 865381
www.georgeanddragonclifton.co.uk
Gastropub | £23

The low-roofed, whitewashed pub sits in the heart of the owner's estate, which supplies many fresh ingredients to the kitchen. It is both a village hostelry and a landmark restaurant and has a loyal local following which warmly appreciates the kitchen's achievements. A richly savoury twice-baked soufflé starter is a technically impressive feat, or there may be fried mackerel in a tomato stew with crisp-cooked onions. There are blackboard specials as well as the main menu, which offers a superior burger of shorthorn beef, or perhaps hake in mussel and saffron broth with mash, before favourite desserts like sticky toffee pudding and fudge sauce, or apple and cinnamon crumble. A fine, stylistically sorted wine list kicks off with house Italian at £13.

North West | **Where to Eat**

...hef/s: Paul McKinnon. **Open:** all week L 12 to 2.30 (3 Sun), ...6 to 9.30 (9 Sun). **Closed:** 26 Dec. **Meals:** alc (main courses ...to £19). Sun L £10.95. **Service:** not inc. **Details:** major ...rds accepted. 90 seats. 40 seats outside. Separate bar. ...heelchair access. Music. Children welcome. Car parking.

...he Jumble Room
...g-hearted global flavours and good vibes
...ngdale Road, Grasmere LA22 9SU
...15394) 35188
...ww.thejumbleroom.co.uk
...lobal | £30

...dy and Chrissy Hill have certainly imbued their laid-...ack restaurant-with-rooms with bags of 'feel-good' ...ersonality: fun-filled, arty decoration adds to the good ...orations (check out the LP-covered loos) and Andy ...reckoned to be the 'best front-of-house manager ... Cumbria'. In the kitchen, things are equally upbeat, ...ith big-hearted global flavours stuffed into a lively ...enu that might backpack from Herdwick lamb loin ...th a jamboree of aromatic Lebanese inflections to ...uth African dithoise chicken with roasted pumpkin, ...cky beets and chilli jam, by way of smoked haddock ...ufflé and locally reared steak with Madeira sauce. The ...wners' organic allegiances extend to the worldwide ...ne list, which opens at £11.95.

...hef/s: David and Trudy Clay. **Open:** Sat and Sun L 12 to 3, ...ed to Mon D 5 to 11. **Closed:** Tue, 20 to 26 Dec. **Meals:** alc ...ain courses £13 to £24). **Service:** not inc. **Details:** major ...rds accepted. 48 seats. 8 seats outside. No mobile phones. ...heelchair access. Music. Children welcome.

LANCASHIRE

...ood by Breda Murphy
...ood, simple food and top puds
...bbots Court, 41 Station Road, Whalley BB7 9RH
...1254) 823446
...ww.foodbybredamurphy.com
...odern British | £22

...cked in beside the railway arches in an attractive Ribble ...alley village, Breda Murphy's restaurant and deli is a ...aytime venue, with fortnightly themed evenings on ...idays and Saturdays. The cooking is appealingly simple, ...sing quality ingredients for dishes such as prosciutto-...rapped chicken and leek terrine with spiced pears, ...d fish pie made with haddock, salmon and prawns ...der a topping of champ potato and Lancashire cheese. ...esserts such as baked chocolate cheesecake with ...range caramel sauce will prove hard to resist, as may ...eeses from the deli counter. A short list opens with ...ines by the glass from £2.75.

...hef/s: Gareth Bevan. **Open:** Tue to Sat L 10 to 6, Fri and ...t D 7 to 9.30 (themed nights, twice monthly). **Closed:** ...n, Mon, 25 Dec to 6 Jan. **Meals:** alc (main courses £7 to ...4). Set D £42.50 (5 courses). **Service:** not inc. **Details:** ...ajor cards accepted. 50 seats. 20 seats outside. No mobile ...ones. Wheelchair access. Music. Children welcome. Car ...arking.

The Inn at Whitewell
Modern cooking that's a satisfying prospect
Whitewell BB7 3AT
(01200) 448222
www.innatwhitewell.com
Modern British | £28

The fourteenth-century manor house was transformed in the 1700s into a coaching inn, and remains today every inch the welcoming village hostelry, albeit a fairly grand one. Eat in the bar or restaurant. Either way, the modern British cooking of Jamie Cadman presents a satisfying prospect. A crab salad with pickled cucumber, seasoned with coriander seed and mint, offered a nice balance of sweetness and acidity for one reporter. Main courses of duck breast with black pudding mash, pancetta and redcurrant sauce, and seared tuna with a beansprout and mangetout salad in sesame, ginger and soy dressing impressed too, even though the tuna was a few shades further on than the requested rare. Finish with a trio of well-kept British and Irish cheeses. The wine list has some very flash bottles, but starts comfortably enough at £12.99.

Chef/s: Jamie Cadman. **Open:** all week L 12 to 2, D 7.30 to 9.30. **Meals:** alc (main courses £15 to £25). **Service:** not inc. **Details:** major cards accepted. 70 seats. 30 seats outside. Separate bar. No music. Wheelchair access. Children welcome. Car parking.

North West | **Where to Eat**

MANCHESTER

Aumbry
Gem with good cooking at its heart
2 Church Lane, Prestwich M25 1AJ
(0161) 7985841
www.aumbryrestaurant.co.uk
British | £26

Readers describe Aumbry as a little gem. Its unassuming North Manchester location certainly allows for it to become, in time, a diamond in the rough. Co-owner and chef Mary-Ellen McTague has form locally (at ramsons) and nationally (at The Fat Duck), and Aumbry feels like exactly what it is: a small, tentative first project, done on a modest budget and with good cooking at its heart. Portions have, wisely, been boosted since the early days, and plans include an extended wine list (a limited choice presently runs from £12.95) and more facilities upstairs. The open kitchen at the back of a cottagey dining room sends forth limited amounts of excellent bread, interesting starters such as mini black pudding-clad Scotch eggs ('a triumph' with mushroom relish) and main courses garnished with silky vegetable purées. Roast mallard comes with the pumpkin version and a parcel of braised leg, for example. It's to be hoped that the rather brief menu will grow as Aumbry flourishes. House wine from £13.50.

Chef/s: Laurence Tottingham and Mary-Ellen McTague. **Open:** Wed to Sun L 12 to 3 (4 Sun), Wed to Sat D 7 to 9.30. **Closed:** Mon, Tues, first 2 weeks Jan. **Meals:** alc (main courses £12 to £19). Sun L £18.50 (2 courses) to £22.50. Tasting menu £45. **Service:** not inc. **Details:** major cards accepted. 26 seats. Separate bar. Wheelchair access. Music. Children welcome.

Sanmini's
Homespun South Indian flavours
Carrbank Lodge, Ramsbottom Lane, Ramsbottom BL0 9DJ
(01706) 821831
www.sanminis.com
Indian | £26

Run by a husband-and-wife medic team – with their grown-up kids on hand to serve – Sanmini's is a true family affair. This amenable eatery occupies a good-looking Victorian gatehouse, and the food has all-roun appeal for carnivores and veggies alike. The owners have distilled their love of homespun South Indian cooking into a modest menu of distinctive, subtly spiced dishes: starters of crispy cashew and spinach pakoras or fish vadai (tuna and lentil cakes) could give way to equally vivid mains from Chennai potato masala to Chettinad chicken. Also check out Mini's 'tiffi specialities' – vibrant street snacks including dosas,

North West | Where to Eat

...happam and steamed idli with sambar. Lunch for a ...nner is a bargain. The only downsides seem to be an ...changing menu and the difficulty of getting a table. ...ouse wine is £13.95.

Chef/s: Sundara Moorthy and Balraj. **Open:** Tue to Sun ...2 to 2 (2.30 Sat and Sun), D 6.30 to 9.30 (10.30 Fri to ...n). **Closed:** Mon. **Meals:** alc (main courses £8 to £13). ...t L Tue to Fri £10. Thalis £20. **Service:** not inc. **Details:** major cards accepted. 30 seats. Separate bar. ...heelchair access. Music. Children welcome.

Second Floor
Stylish city food and rooftop views

Harvey Nichols, 21 New Cathedral Street,
Manchester M1 1AD
(0161) 8288898
www.harveynichols.com
Modern European | £35

Second Floor, with its beguiling views of rooftops and the Wheel of Manchester, is a stylish designer-led dining room tucked behind a lively bar-brasserie. A black-and-white colour scheme and a huge expanse of window set the trendy tone, while well-spaced, impeccably dressed tables and attentive, formal service give notice of the level of ambition in the kitchen. Stuart Thomson has settled in well. His modern European-biased menus are based on superior ingredients and there is plenty that appeals. Manx scallops with saffron risotto and pickled trompettes, for example, was a vibrant and colourful starter at inspection, the star main course a perfectly timed wild sea bass served with crab, black olive, potatoes and sauce vierge. Others have enjoyed slow-cooked beef, saddle of rabbit wrapped in Parma ham and served with some good choucroute and a smear of fig purée, and roasted peanut parfait with rice crispy crunch and Guanaja chocolate. House wine is £18.

Chef/s: Stuart Thomson. **Open:** all week L 12 to 3 (4 Sun), ...e to Sat D 6 to 10. **Closed:** 25 Dec, 1 Jan. **Meals:** alc (main courses £16 to £23). Set L £25. **Service:** 10% (optional). **Details:** major cards accepted. 35 seats. Air conditioning. Separate bar. No mobile phones. Wheelchair access. Music. Children welcome.

MERSEYSIDE

Bistrot Vérité
Rustic food with big flavours

7 Liverpool Road, Birkdale, Southport PR8 4AR
(01704) 564199
French | £25

This small, lively bistro, a white-fronted venue with a few tables outside, is in photogenic Birkdale village and is dedicated to rustic French cooking. Daily-changing menus (chalked on the board in the evenings) offer inspired choice, from pissaladière topped with red onion, tomatoes and Brie to a pairing of boudin noir and smoked morteau with caramelised apple. The food delivers plenty of flavour without pretension, for instance roasted leg of corn-fed chicken in creamy mushroom and tarragon sauce, or chateaubriand for two with béarnaise, the sorts of dishes that once sustained many a village bistro the length and breadth of France. Finish with caramelised banana and rum crêpes. House wines are £14.95 on a short, unadventurous list.

Chef/s: Marc Vérité. **Open:** Tue to Sat L 12 to 1.30, D 5.30 to 9.30. **Closed:** Sun, Mon, 25 and 26 Dec, 1 week Feb, 1 week Aug. **Meals:** alc (main courses £9 to £16). **Service:** not inc. **Details:** major cards accepted. 45 seats. 16 seats outside. Air conditioning. Music. Children welcome.

Panoramic
Foodie button-pusher, with views

34th Floor, West Tower, Brook Street,
Liverpool L3 9PJ
(0151) 2365534
www.panoramicliverpool.com
Modern European | £48

If you're turned on by 'dining in widescreen', ascend to the rarefied reaches of Liverpool's West Tower for a 360-degree window on the world (well, five counties anyway). Currently the UK's 'tallest restaurant', Panoramic delivers what it promises, with the bonus of sleek surrounds and a menu that pushes lots of foodie buttons – albeit with lofty prices. Pithy dish descriptions spell out the trendy details – say 'scallops' (suckling pig tortellini, apple pannacotta) ahead of 'beef fillet' (blade, pak choi, violet potato, caper and raisin sauce). After that, a confection of sweet potato cheesecake with tonka bean ice cream and lemon jelly might catch the eye. Global wines start at £17.50.

Chef/s: Chris Marshall. **Open:** all week L 12 to 2.30, D 6 to 10. **Closed:** bank hols (exc Good Friday). **Meals:** alc (main courses £18 to £32). Set L £20. **Service:** 10% (optional). **Details:** major cards accepted. 52 seats. Air conditioning. Separate bar. No mobile phones. Wheelchair access. Music. Children welcome.

Content brought to you by **The Good Food Guide 2011**. Please see page 14 for further details.

North West

Tourist Information Centres

When you arrive at your destination, visit an Official Partner Tourist Information Centre for quality assured help with accommodation and information about local attractions and events, or email your request before you go. To find a Tourist Information Centre by region visit enjoyEngland.com/find-tic.

ACCRINGTON	Town Hall	01254 380293	tourism@hyndburnbc.gov.uk
ALTRINCHAM	20 Stamford New Road	0161 912 5931	tourist.information@trafford.gov.uk
AMBLESIDE	Central Buildings	015394 32582	amblesidetic@southlakeland.gov.uk
ASHTON-UNDER-LYNE	Council Offices	0161 343 4343	tourist.information@tameside.gov.uk
BARNOLDSWICK	The Council Shop	01282 666704	tourist.info@pendle.gov.uk
BARROW-IN-FURNESS	Forum 28	01229 876505	touristinfo@barrowbc.gov.uk
BLACKBURN	50-54 Church Street	0125 468 8040	visit@blackburn.gov.uk
BLACKPOOL	1 Clifton Street	01253 478222	tic@blackpool.gov.uk
BOLTON	Central Library Foyer	01204 334321	tourist.info@bolton.gov.uk
BOWNESS	Glebe Road	015394 42895	bownesstic@lake-district.gov.uk
BURNLEY	Burnley Bus Station	01282 664421	tic@burnley.gov.uk
BURY	The Met Arts Centre	0161 253 5111	touristinformation@bury.gov.uk
CARLISLE	Old Town Hall	01228 625600	tourism@carlisle-city.gov.uk
CHESTER (TOWN HALL)	Town Hall	01244 402111	welcome@visitchesterandcheshire.co.uk
CLEVELEYS	Victoria Square	01253 853378	cleveleystic@wyrebc.gov.uk
CLITHEROE	Ribble Valley Borough Council	01200 425566	tourism@ribblevalley.gov.uk
CONGLETON	Town Hall	01260 271095	congletontic@cheshireeast.gov.uk
CONISTON	Ruskin Avenue	015394 41533	mail@conistontic.org
DISCOVER PENDLE CENTRE	Boundary Mill Sores	01282 856186	discoverpendle@pendle.gov.uk
ELLESMERE PORT	McArthur Glen Outlet Village	0151 356 7879	cheshireoaks.cc@visitor-centre.net
FLEETWOOD	Old Ferry Office	01253 773953	fleetwoodtic@wyrebc.gov.uk
GARSTANG	Council Offices, Discovery Centre	01995 602125	garstangtic@wyrebc.gov.uk
KENDAL	Town Hall	01539 797516	kendaltic@southlakeland.gov.uk
KESWICK	Moot Hall	017687 72645	keswicktic@lake-district.gov.uk
KNUTSFORD	Council Offices	01565 632611	knutsfordtic@cheshireeast.gov.uk
LANCASTER	The Storey Creative Industries Centre	01524 582394	lancastervic@lancaster.gov.uk
LIVERPOOL 08 PLACE	Whitechapel	0151 233 2008	info@08place.gov.uk
LIVERPOOL ALBERT DOCK	Anchor Courtyard	0151 233 2008	info@08place.gov.uk
LIVERPOOL JOHN LENNON AIRPORT	Arrivals Hall, South Terminal	0151 907 1058	info@08place.gov.uk

North West

THAM ST ANNES	c/o Town Hall	01253 725610	touristinformation@fylde.gov.uk
ACCLESFIELD	Macclesfield	01625 504114	macclesfieldtic@cheshireeast.gov.uk
ANCHESTER	Manchester Visitor Centre	0871 222 8223	touristinformation@marketing-manchester.co.uk
ORECAMBE	Old Station Buildings	01524 582808	morecambetic@lancaster.gov.uk
ANTWICH	Civic Hall	01270 537359	touristi@crewe-nantwich.gov.uk
ORTHWICH	Information Centre	01606 353534	infocentrenorthwich@cheshirewestandchester.gov.uk
DHAM	Gallery Oldham	0161 7703064	tourist@oldham.gov.uk
NDLE HERITAGE CENTRE	Park Hill	01282 661701	heritage.centre@pendle.gov.uk
NRITH	Middlegate	01768 867466	pen.tic@eden.gov.uk
RESTON	The Guildhall	01772 253731	tourism@preston.gov.uk
HEGED	Rheged Tourist Information Centre	01768 860034	tic@rheged.com
OCHDALE	Touchstones	01706 924928	tic@link4life.org
ALFORD	The Lowry, Pier 8	0161 848 8601	tic@salford.gov.uk
OUTHPORT	112 Lord Street	01704 533333	info@visitsouthport.com
OUTHWAITE	M6 Service Area	016974 73445	southwaitetic@visitscotland.com
HELENS	The World of Glass	01744 755150	info@sthelenstic.com
OCKPORT	Staircase House	0161 474 4444	tourist.information@stockport.gov.uk
LSWATER	Main Car Park	017684 82414	ullswatertic@lake-district.gov.uk
VERSTON	Coronation Hall	01229 587120	ulverstontic@southlakeland.gov.uk
ARRINGTON	The Market Hall	01925 428585	informationcentre@warrington.gov.uk
HITEHAVEN	Market Hall	01946 598914	tic@copelandbc.gov.uk
IGAN	62 Wallgate	01942 825677	tic@wlct.org
ILMSLOW	The Information Centre	01625 522275	wilmslowtic@cheshireeast.gov.uk
INDERMERE	Victoria Street	015394 46499	windermeretic@southlakeland.gov.uk

Regional Contacts and Information

There are various publications and guides about England's North West available from the following Tourist Boards or by logging on to www.visitenglandsnorthwest.com or calling 0845 600 6040:

Visit Chester and Cheshire
Chester Railway Station, 1st Floor, West Wing Offices, Station Road, Chester, CH1 3NT
Tel: (01244) 405600
Tel: 0845 073 1324 (accommodation booking)
Email: info@visitchesterandcheshire.co.uk
Web: www.visitchester.com or www.visitcheshire.com

Cumbria Tourism
Windermere Road, Staveley, Kendal, LA8 9PL
Tel: (015398) 22222
Email: info@cumbriatourism.org
Web: www.golakes.co.uk

The Lancashire and Blackpool Tourist Board
St. George's House, St. George's Street, Chorley, PR7 2AA
Tel: (01257) 226600 (Brochure request)
Email: info@visitlancashire.com
Web: www.visitlancashire.com

Visit Manchester – The Tourist Board For Greater Manchester
Town Hall Extension
Lloyd Street
Manchester
M60 2LA
Tel: 0871 222 8223
Email: touristinformation@visitmanchester.com
Web: www.visitmanchester.com

The Mersey Partnership – The Tourist Board for Liverpool City Region
12 Princes Parade, Liverpool, L3 1BG
Tel: (0151) 233 2008 (information enquiries)
Tel: 0844 870 0123 (accommodation booking)
Email: info@visitliverpool.com
(accommodation enquiries)
Email: liverpoolvisitorcentre@liverpool.gov.uk
(information enquiries)
Web: www.visitliverpool.com

North West | Cheshire

Where to Stay

Entries appear alphabetically by town name in each county. A key to symbols appears on page 6. Maps start on page 706. A listing of all Enjoy England assessed accommodation appears at the end of the region.

ALTRINCHAM (3 MILES), Cheshire Map ref 4A2

SAT NAV WA14 4TJ

B&B PER ROOM PER NIGHT
S £30.00
D £60.00

Bollington Hall Farm
Park Lane, Little Bollington, Altrincham WA14 4TJ
t (0161) 928 1760

18thC Georgian farmhouse, family-run, comfortable rooms with exceptional views overlooking Dunham Hall, superb, quiet location, outstanding hospitality and good food. Pub within five minutes' walk for evening meals. **directions** M56 Junction 7. M56 Manchester Airport 4 miles. **open** All year except Xmas and New Year **bedrooms** 1 single, 1 twin, 1 family **bathrooms** 1 with private bathroom **payment** cash, cheques, euros

Room   General   Leisure

BARTON, Cheshire Map ref 5B3

SAT NAV SY14 7HU

B&B PER ROOM PER NIGHT
S £45.00 – £65.00
D £70.00 – £130.00

Higher Farm Bed & Breakfast
Higher Farm, Barton, Malpas SY14 7HU
t (01829) 782422 e info@higherfarm.co.uk
w higherfarm.co.uk ONLINE MAP GUEST REVIEWS ONLINE BOOKING

Higher Farm has 5 luxury en suite bedrooms located in a picturesque farm building offering outstanding views. Guests enjoy delicious breakfasts of locally sourced food cooked traditionally. **directions** Please see website for comprehensive directions **open** All year **bedrooms** 3 double, 1 twin, 1 family **bathrooms** 5 en suite **payment** credit/debit cards, cash, cheques

Room   General   Leisure

Where is my pet welcome?

Some properties welcome well-behaved pets. Look for the 🐕 in the accommodation listings. You can also buy a copy of our popular guide 'Pets Come Too!' Now available in good bookshops and online at **visitbritainshop.com**

£9.99

North West | Cheshire

BRUERA, Cheshire Map ref 4A2

SAT NAV CH3 6EW

Churton Heath Farm Bed & Breakfast

Churton Heath Farm, Chapel Lane, Chester CH3 6EW
t (01244) 620420 f (01244) 620411 e info@churtonheathfarm.co.uk
w churtonheathfarm.co.uk ONLINE MAP GUEST REVIEWS ONLINE BOOKING LAST MINUTE OFFERS

B&B PER ROOM PER NIGHT
S £55.00
D £80.00

4 Star Gold Luxury Farmhouse situated 4 miles from Chester City Centre. Two ensuite bedrooms, spacious and luxurious, Super King sized beds, scrumptious welcome tray and all modern facilities. **directions** 4 miles south Chester. A41 from Chester to Whitchurch, continue for 2/3 miles, turn right before Black Dog pub. Situated 2.5miles on this road. **open** All year **bedrooms** 2 single, 2 double, 2 twin, 2 family **bathrooms** 2 en suite **payment** credit/debit cards, cash, cheques

BREAKFAST AWARD

CHESTER, Cheshire Map ref 4A2

SAT NAV CH2 3RB

Chester Brooklands

8 Newton Lane, Chester CH2 3RB
t (01244) 348856 f 0871 236 9308 e bookings@chester-bandb.co.uk
w chester-bandb.co.uk ONLINE MAP GUEST REVIEWS ONLINE BOOKING LAST MINUTE OFFERS

B&B PER ROOM PER NIGHT
S £45.00 – £60.00
D £56.00 – £120.00

SPECIAL PROMOTIONS
Stay Friday and Saturday in a Double for £125 total or stay Saturday and Sunday for £115 total. Races excluded.

10 minutes walk to City, Free Wifi, Free Car parking, Traditional English Breakfast, other diets catered, Garden dining weather permitting, Large ensuite cubicles, designer toiletries, Freeview TV and hairdryer to all rooms. Discounts to restaurants, Chester Zoo and Cheshire Oaks. Super King Sized, doubles, twins and single beds.

open All year except Xmas and New Year **bedrooms** 2 double, 1 twin, 2 family **bathrooms** 5 en suite, 5 with private bathroom **payment** credit/debit cards, cash

directions M6 jct 19 to M56 (Chester), then jct 12 onto A56 to Chester. Turn right at All Saints Church. We are on right hand side.

CHESTER, Cheshire Map ref 4A2

SAT NAV CH3 7PG

Cotton Farm

Cotton Edmunds, Chester CH3 7PG
t 01244 336616 e echill@btinernet.com
w cottonfarm.co.uk/ ONLINE MAP LAST MINUTE OFFERS

B&B PER ROOM PER NIGHT
S £50.00
D £75.00

Beautiful farmhouse at the heart of 250 acres offering complete peace and quiet but only 4 miles from Chester. Large bedrooms with great attention to detail. Excellent breakfasts. **directions** Leave Chester on A51 heading East. Appx 2 miles from city outskirts take right turn signed Cotton Edmunds. Follow B&B signs for 1½ miles **open** All year **bedrooms** 2 double, 1 twin **bathrooms** 3 en suite **payment** cash, cheques, euros

key to symbols see page 6

575

North West | Cheshire

CHESTER, Cheshire Map ref 4A2
SAT NAV CH2 3NL

Craigleith Lodge
56 Hoole Road, Chester CH2 3NL
t (01244) 318740 e welcome@craigleithlodge.co.uk
w craigleithlodge.co.uk GUEST REVIEWS LAST MINUTE OFFERS

B&B PER ROOM PER NIGHT
S £35.00 – £75.00
D £35.00 – £75.00

A Victorian family-run bed and breakfast within a mile of Chester city centre, with courtyard rooms. **directions** Please contact us for directions **bedrooms** 1 single, 10 double, 1 twin **bathrooms** 12 en suite **payment** credit/debit cards, cash, cheques

CHESTER, Cheshire Map ref 4A2
SAT NAV CH4 8JQ

Mitchell's of Chester Guest House
28 Hough Green, Chester CH4 8JQ
t (01244) 679004 f (01244) 659567 e mitoches@dialstart.net
w mitchellsofchester.com ONLINE MAP ONLINE BOOKING LAST MINUTE OFFERS

B&B PER ROOM PER NIGHT
S £40.00 – £50.00
D £65.00 – £90.00

Highly recommended by good guides. Relax in this tastefully restored Victorian residence with rooms having hospitality tray, radio, TV, radio broadband, hairdryer and many other comforts. Easy walking to city. **directions** Leave south side of Chester on A483, turning right to A5104 (Saltney). This is Hough Green, and are 300m along on the right. **open** All year except Xmas **bedrooms** 1 single, 2 double, 1 twin, 1 family, 2 suites **bathrooms** 5 en suite, 2 with private bathroom **payment** credit/debit cards, cash, cheques

MACCLESFIELD, Cheshire Map ref 4B2
SAT NAV SK10 4TA

Astle Farm East Bed & Breakfast
Astle Farm, Chelford SK10 4TA
t (01625) 861270 f (01625) 861270 e gill.farmhouse@virgin.net
w astlefarmeast.co.uk ONLINE MAP

B&B PER ROOM PER NIGHT
S £30.00 – £40.00
D £65.00 – £70.00

A warm and friendly welcome awaits you on our picturesque arable farm, where we can offer you a quiet stay in an idyllic setting. Farm walks available. **directions** Take the A537 out of Chelford toward Macclesfield. We are on the right a half mile from the roundabout. **open** All year **bedrooms** 2 double, 1 family **bathrooms** 2 en suite **payment** credit/debit cards, cash, cheques

BREAKFAST AWARD

NORTH RODE, Cheshire Map ref 4B2
SAT NAV CW12 2PH

Ladderstile Retreat
Twin Oaks, Ladderstile Farm, North Rode, Nr Congleton, Cheshire CW12 2PH
t (01260) 223338 f 01260223055 e enquiries@ladderstileretreat.co.uk
w ladderstileretreat.co.uk ONLINE MAP

B&B PER ROOM PER NIGHT
S £45.00 – £55.00
D £80.00 – £90.00
EVENING MEAL PER PERSON
£5.00 – £15.00

Retreat to the countryside and relax in our luxurious ground floor suite reserved exclusively for you. A warm welcome, peace, tranquillity and breathtaking views from every window await you. **directions** Ladderstile Retreat is situated midway between the market towns of Macclesfield and Congleton, setback from the A54. **open** All year except Xmas and New Year **bedrooms** 1 suite **bathrooms** 1 en suite **payment** cash, cheques

576 Official tourist board guide Bed & Breakfast

North West | Cheshire/Cumbria

NORTHWICH, Cheshire Map ref 4A2

SAT NAV CW8 3QE

Wall Hill Farm Guest House

Acton Lane, Acton Bridge, Northwich, Cheshire CW8 3QE
t 01606 852 654 e info@wallhillfarmguesthouse.co.uk
w wallhillfarmguesthouse.co.uk ONLINE MAP GUEST REVIEWS ONLINE BOOKING LAST MINUTE OFFERS

B&B PER ROOM PER NIGHT
S £45.00
D £68.00

7-bedroomed guesthouse offering luxury accommodation in a Grade II listed building within rural setting. Individually designed rooms each with a different theme. Centrally located in Mid-Cheshire. **directions** Please contact us for directions **open** All year **bedrooms** 3 double, 4 twin **bathrooms** 7 en suite **payment** credit/debit cards, cash, cheques

Room   General   Leisure

TATTENHALL, Cheshire Map ref 4A2

SAT NAV CH3 9AQ

Fernlea Cottage Bed & Breakfast

Chester Road, Hatton Heath, Tattenhall CH3 9AQ
t (01829) 770817 e stevegb1@btinternet.com
w fernleacottage.co.uk ONLINE MAP GUEST REVIEWS ONLINE BOOKING

B&B PER ROOM PER NIGHT
S £40.00 – £45.00
D £65.00 – £75.00

Fernlea Cottage is set in the Cheshire countryside 4 miles south of Chester. Comfortable bedrooms overlook the gardens and fields. Locally sourced, freshly cooked breakfasts. Guest lounge and private parking. **directions** 4 miles south of Chester on A41. Fernlea Cottage is the first house on the right-hand side on Chester Road towards Tattenhall. **open** All year **bedrooms** 2 double **bathrooms** 1 en suite, 1 with private bathroom **payment** cash, cheques, euros

Room   General   Leisure

ALSTON, Cumbria Map ref 5B2

SAT NAV CA9 3HX

Cumberland Inn

Townfoot, Alston, Cumbria CA9 3HX
t (01434) 381875 e stay@cumberlandinnalston.com
w cumberlandinnalston.com ONLINE MAP GUEST REVIEWS ONLINE BOOKING

B&B PER ROOM PER NIGHT
S £38.00 – £45.00
D £64.00 – £80.00

EVENING MEAL PER PERSON
£12.00 – £18.00

SPECIAL PROMOTIONS
£45-£55 per person dinner bed and breakfast

Stay at the Cumberland Inn for real ales, real fires and a real family welcome. Our homemade, hearty food is perfect after a busy day out. We welcome muddy boots, dogs and bikes. Local CAMRA pub of the year 2009 and again in 2010.

open All year except Xmas
bedrooms 2 double, 2 twin, 1 family
bathrooms 5 en suite
payment credit/debit cards, cash, cheques

directions On A686 from north or south. Location roadside in Alston, next to Henderson's garage

Room
General
Leisure

577

North West | **Cumbria**

ALSTON, Cumbria Map ref 5B2   SAT NAV CA9 3PF

INN

B&B PER ROOM PER NIGHT
S £35.00
D £70.00

The Miners Arms
Nenthead, Alston, Cumbria CA9 3PF
t (01434) 381427 mobile 07817615417 **e** theminersarms2@googlemail.com
w **nenthead.com** ONLINE MAP GUEST REVIEWS ONLINE BOOKING LAST MINUTE OFFERS

If you like excellent food, great beer the warm feel of wood-burning fires and friendly family hospitality or you just like drinkin at altitude you must try The Miners Arms. **directions** We are situated on the A689 Brampton to Durham Road, Between Killhop and Alston. **open** All year **bedrooms** 1 twin, 1 family **bathrooms** en suite **payment** credit/debit cards, cash, cheques

Room   General   Leisure

AMBLESIDE, Cumbria Map ref 5A3   SAT NAV LA22 9DL

★★★★ GUEST HOUSE

B&B PER ROOM PER NIGHT
S £30.00 – £40.00
D £70.00 – £85.00

2 Cambridge Villas
Church Street, Ambleside LA22 9DL
t (01539) 432142 **f** 01539 432755 **e** charles@black475.fsnet.co.uk
w **2cambridgevillas.co.uk**

Family run Bed & Breakfast accomodation in the centre of Ambleside. Ideally situated for access to fells & all local attractions **directions** Entering Ambleside on the A591 on to Rothay Road. Keep in the right lane to Kelsick Road then left & left again to Church Street **open** All year except Xmas **bedrooms** 3 double, 2 family **bathrooms** 5 en suite **payment** credit/debit cards, cash, cheques

Room   General   Leisure

AMBLESIDE, Cumbria Map ref 5A3   SAT NAV LA22 9DL

★★★★ GUEST HOUSE

B&B PER ROOM PER NIGHT
S £30.00 – £35.00
D £65.00 – £84.00

3 Cambridge Villas
Church Street, Ambleside LA22 9DL
t (01539) 432307 **e** cambridgevillas3@aol.com
w **3cambridgevillas.co.uk** ONLINE MAP

Friendly family run guesthouse in the heart of the lake district ide location for walking & cycling close to all amenities. **directions** Please contact us for directions **open** All year except Xmas **bedrooms** 2 single, 4 double, 1 twin **bathrooms** 6 en suite, 1 wit private bathroom **payment** credit/debit cards, cash

Room   General   Leisure

AMBLESIDE, Cumbria Map ref 5A3   SAT NAV LA22 0EE

★★★★ GUEST ACCOMMODATION

B&B PER ROOM PER NIGHT
D £70.00 – £150.00

Brathay Lodge
Rothay Road, Ambleside LA22 0EE
t (01539) 432000 **e** info@brathay-lodge.co.uk
w **brathay-lodge.co.uk**

Situated close to the centre of Ambleside offering bed and breakfast accommodation to a high standard. Ample private off road parking. Ground floor rooms available. Family and pet friendl **directions** On entering Ambleside from Windermere take the righ hand lane of the one way system Brathay Lodge is opposite the tennis courts/putting green **open** All year except Xmas **bedrooms** 7 double, 6 twin, 6 family **bathrooms** 19 en suite **payment** credit, debit cards, cash, cheques

Room   General   Leisure

578   Official tourist board guide **Bed & Breakfa**

North West | Cumbria

AMBLESIDE, Cumbria Map ref 5A3
SAT NAV LA22 0DB

Elder Grove
Lake Road, Ambleside LA22 0DB
t (01539) 432504 e info@eldergrove.co.uk
w eldergrove.co.uk ONLINE MAP GUEST REVIEWS

enjoyengland.com ★★★★ GUEST ACCOMMODATION
enjoyEngland.com Silver AWARD

B&B PER ROOM PER NIGHT
S £45.00 – £50.00
D £90.00 – £100.00

Quality accommodation and service, relaxing bar & lounge, with complimentary tea/coffee served all day. Choose a hearty Cumbrian breakfast or a lighter bite, served in our Lakeland greenstone dining room **directions** On the south side of Ambleside nr the junction of Wansfell Rd and Lake Road opposite the filling station **open** All year except Xmas **bedrooms** 2 single, 6 double, 1 twin, 1 family **bathrooms** 10 en suite **payment** credit/debit cards, cash, cheques

BREAKFAST AWARD

Room ... General ... Leisure ...

AMBLESIDE, Cumbria Map ref 5A3
SAT NAV LA22 0DB

Ferndale Lodge
Lake Road, Ambleside LA22 0DB
t (01539) 432207 e stay@ferndalelodge.co.uk
w ferndalelodge.co.uk

enjoyEngland.com ★★★ GUEST HOUSE

B&B PER ROOM PER NIGHT
S £25.00 – £35.00
D £50.00 – £70.00

Small, family-run guesthouse close to the centre of Ambleside offering excellent accommodation at realistic prices. Superb breakfasts and a friendly welcome assured. Private car park. An ideal walking base. **directions** Please contact us for directions **open** All year **bedrooms** 1 single, 7 double, 2 twin **bathrooms** 10 en suite **payment** credit/debit cards, cash, cheques

Room ... General ... Leisure ...

AMBLESIDE, Cumbria Map ref 5A3
SAT NAV LA22 9BA

Meadowbank
Rydal Road, Ambleside LA22 9BA
t (01539) 432710 f (01539) 432710 e enquiries@meadowbank.org.uk

enjoyEngland.com ★★★ GUEST ACCOMMODATION

B&B PER ROOM PER NIGHT
S £30.00 – £37.00
D £60.00 – £74.00

Country house in private grounds with ample parking. Overlooking meadowland and fells with an easy walk into Ambleside. Good walking and cycling base. **directions** On the A591 (main Road through) on the Northern edge of town. **open** All year except Xmas **bedrooms** 1 single, 3 double, 2 twin, 1 family **bathrooms** 6 en suite, 1 with private bathroom **payment** credit/debit cards, cash, cheques

Room ... General ... Leisure ...

AMBLESIDE, Cumbria Map ref 5A3
SAT NAV LA22 0EG

Red Bank
Wansfell Road, Ambleside LA22 0EG
t (01539) 434637 f (01539) 434637 e info@red-bank.co.uk
w red-bank.co.uk ONLINE MAP ONLINE BOOKING LAST MINUTE OFFERS

enjoyengland.com ★★★★★ BED & BREAKFAST
enjoyEngland.com Silver AWARD

B&B PER ROOM PER NIGHT
S £60.00 – £80.00
D £70.00 – £90.00

Elegant, traditional Lakeland house in Ambleside. Three en suite rooms offering spacious, de luxe accommodation. We will endeavour to make your stay as relaxing and comfortable as possible. Private parking. **directions** M6 jct 36, follow A591 to Windermere/Ambleside. On passing Waterhead, straight ahead at lights, left at BP station. Red Bank last house on left. **open** All year **bedrooms** 2 double, 1 twin **bathrooms** 3 en suite, 1 with private bathroom **payment** cash, cheques

Room ... General ... Leisure ...

For key to symbols see page 6

579

North West | Cumbria

AMBLESIDE, Cumbria Map ref 5A3
SAT NAV LA22 9DJ

Park House Guest House
Compston Road, Ambleside LA22 9DJ
t (015394) 31107 e mail@loughrigg.plus.com
w parkhouseguesthouse.co.uk ONLINE MAP GUEST REVIEWS ONLINE BOOKING

B&B PER ROOM PER NIGHT
S £30.00
D £45.00

Parkhouse is a fine Victorian residence, which has been carefully upgraded and modernised. is warm, comfortable and has an elegant interi to a high standard. Ideally situated in the town centre, uninterrupted views across parklands a fells beyond. Private parking for all rooms.

open All year
bedrooms 2 single, 4 double
bathrooms 4 en suite, 2 with private bathroom
payment credit/debit cards, cash

directions As you reach the one way system - putting green and church on left. Left hand la road bends to left, on RHS.

Room
General
Leisure

AMBLESIDE, Cumbria Map ref 5A3
SAT NAV LA22 0EE

Rothay Garth
Rothay Road, Ambleside LA22 0EE
t (015394) 32217 f (015394) 34400 e book@rothay-garth.co.uk
w rothay-garth.co.uk ONLINE MAP GUEST REVIEWS ONLINE BOOKING LAST MINUTE OFFERS

B&B PER ROOM PER NIGHT
D £76.00 – £120.00

Rothay Garth is a beautiful Victorian Lakeland slate building in a superb position. Glorious mountain views, perfect base in the Lake District. All rooms en suite, Large private car park. **directions** Pleas contact us for directions **open** All year except Xmas **bedrooms** 11 double, 3 twin, 1 suite **bathrooms** 15 en suite **payment** credit/ debit cards, cash, cheques

Room General Leisure

AMBLESIDE, Cumbria Map ref 5A3
SAT NAV LA22 0EE

Rothay House
Rothay Road, Ambleside LA22 0EE
t (015394) 32434 f (015394) 32434 e email@rothay-house.com
w rothay-house.com ONLINE MAP

B&B PER ROOM PER NIGHT
S £37.00 – £42.00
D £60.00 – £74.00

Enjoy the relaxed atmosphere of Rothay House, a family run quali guest house in Ambleside, in the heart of the lake district. **directions** Please contact us for directions **open** All year except Xmas **bedrooms** 5 double, 1 twin **bathrooms** 6 en suite **paymen** credit/debit cards, cash, cheques

Room General

North West | **Cumbria**

AMBLESIDE, Cumbria   Map ref 5A3

SAT NAV LA22 9DJ

Smallwood House
Compston Road, Ambleside LA22 9DJ
t (015394) 32330   f (015394) 33764   e enq@smallwoodhotel.co.uk
w **smallwoodhotel.co.uk** ONLINE BOOKING LAST MINUTE OFFERS

B&B PER ROOM PER NIGHT
S £30.00 – £55.00
D £60.00 – £110.00

EVENING MEAL PER PERSON
£23.50

In the centre of Ambleside, close to bus stops, putting green, tennis, lakes, walking, park. Just a few minutes walk to pubs & restaurants. Quiet, relaxing & comfortable. **directions** From south, M6 jct 36 then follow A591 to Ambleside, Compston Road is part of this road. We are situated on right-hand side. **open** All year except Xmas **bedrooms** 2 single, 4 double, 3 twin, 3 family **bathrooms** 12 en suite **payment** credit/debit cards, cash, cheques, euros

BREAKFAST AWARD

Room   General   Leisure

AMBLESIDE, Cumbria   Map ref 5A3

SAT NAV LA22 0EP

Wateredge Inn
Waterhead Bay, Ambleside LA22 0EP
t (01539) 432332   f (01539) 431878   e stay@wateredgeinn.co.uk
w **wateredgeinn.co.uk** ONLINE MAP

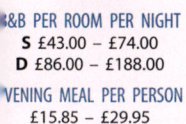

B&B PER ROOM PER NIGHT
S £43.00 – £74.00
D £86.00 – £188.00

EVENING MEAL PER PERSON
£15.85 – £29.95

SPECIAL PROMOTIONS
3-night midweek breaks from £99pp.

Delightfully situated family-run inn on the shores of Windermere at Waterhead Bay. Enjoy country-inn-style dining, freshly prepared bar food, real ales and fine wines, all served overlooking the lake. Pretty bedrooms, many with lake views, and some with balconies or patios.

open All year except Xmas
bedrooms 3 single, 9 double, 6 twin, 3 family, 1 suite
bathrooms 22 en suite
payment credit/debit cards, cash, cheques

directions From M6 jct 36 follow A591 through to Ambleside. At Waterhead bear left at traffic lights. Wateredge is on left at end of promenade.

Room   General   Leisure

Do you like Camping?

You can also buy a copy of our popular guide 'Camping, Touring & Holiday Parks' including touring parks, camping holidays and holiday parks and villages in Britain 2011.

Now available in good bookshops and online at
visitbritainshop.com

£8.99

North West | Cumbria

AMBLESIDE, Cumbria Map ref 5A3
SAT NAV LA22 0DB

Wordsworths Guest House
Lake Road, Ambleside LA22 0DB
t (01539) 432095 **e** anna@wordsworthsguesthouse.co.uk
w wordsworthsguesthouse.co.uk ONLINE MAP LAST MINUTE OFFERS

B&B PER ROOM PER NIGHT
S £40.00 – £45.00
D £60.00 – £90.00

SPECIAL PROMOTIONS
Free passes to Langdale Country Club: swimming pool, steam room, Turkish sauna, gymnasium, beautiful restaurant. Winter/spring breaks, fabulous offers!

An elegant Victorian house with quality en suite accommodation. Level walk to village and Lake Windermere. Wonderful Lakeland fell walks from the front door. Hearty Cumbrian breakfasts. Relax in our beautiful award-winning garden, surrounded by stunning views. Free Wi-Fi access. Private car park. Home from home!

open All year
bedrooms 1 single, 2 double, 1 twin, 1 family
bathrooms 5 en suite
payment credit/debit cards, cash, cheques

directions From north/south, leave M6 at jct 3. Follow A590-A591 Windermere/Ambleside. Turn right on Wansfell Road, first right to private road.

APPLEBY-IN-WESTMORLAND, Cumbria Map ref 5B3
SAT NAV CA16 6UE

Bongate House
Bongate, Appleby-in-Westmorland, Cumbria CA16 6UE
t (01768) 351245 **e** stay@bongatehouse.co.uk
w bongatehouse.co.uk ONLINE MAP GUEST REVIEWS

B&B PER ROOM PER NIGHT
S £30.00 – £45.00
D £35.00
EVENING MEAL PER PERSON
£10.00 – £20.00

Bongate House is large Georgian house in two acres of gardens. We are ideally situated for the Yorkshire Dales, Scotland and Borders, and Lake District. We welcome walkers, cyclist, bikers.
directions Junction 38 of M6 sign post Appleby. From Scotch Corner about 30 mins. Left to Appleby town. From Penrith turn left to Appleby of A66. **open** All year **bedrooms** 1 single, 4 double, 3 twin, 1 family **bathrooms** 6 en suite, 3 with private bathroom **payment** credit/debit cards, cash, cheques

ASPATRIA, Cumbria Map ref 5A2
SAT NAV CA7 2JU

Castlemont
Aspatria, Wigton, Cumbria CA7 2JU
t (016973) 20205 **f** (016973) 20205 **e** castlemont@tesco.net
w britainsfinest.co.uk

B&B PER ROOM PER NIGHT
S £25.00 – £30.00
D £54.00 – £68.00

Castlemont is a large Victorian residence, set in two acres of gardens, giving unrestricted views of lakes, sea and mountains. Extensive breakfast menu. Spacious, warm, comfortable, relaxing.
directions A596, through Aspatria (west) towards Maryport. Brown and white tourist board signs, (Castlemont B&B). Large house on right amongst trees, large offroad parking space. **open** All year **bedrooms** 1 single, 1 double, 1 twin, 1 family **bathrooms** 1 en suite, 2 with private bathroom **payment** cash, cheques, euros

North West | Cumbria

BANKS, Cumbria Map ref 5B2
SAT NAV CA8 2JH

★★★★ BED & BREAKFAST

B&B PER ROOM PER NIGHT
S £35.00 – £40.00
D £60.00 – £65.00

Quarry Side
Banks, Brampton CA8 2JH
t (01697) 72538 e elizabeth.harding@btinternet.com

Situated on the line of Hadrian's wall with the vallum running through the garden. Outstanding views. Ideal touring base for Northumberland, Scotland and the Lakes. A warm welcome awaits you. **directions** A69 to Brampton - follow signs for Lancaster, Banks and Hadrian's wall. **open** All year except Xmas and New Year **bedrooms** 2 double, 1 twin **bathrooms** 1 en suite **payment** cash, cheques

Room   General   Leisure

BARROW-IN-FURNESS, Cumbria Map ref 5A3
SAT NAV LA13 9AD

★★★ GUEST HOUSE

B&B PER ROOM PER NIGHT
S £30.00 – £35.00
D £60.00 – £70.00

East Mount House
55 East Mount, Barrow-in-Furness LA13 9AD
t (01229) 871003 e info@eastmounthouse.co.uk
w eastmounthouse.co.uk ONLINE MAP

We are a delightful 7 bedroomed guest house situated on the lovely tree lined Abbey Road 1 mile from town centre and Furness Abbey within walking distance is the park also the leisure centre.

open All year
bedrooms 2 single, 2 double, 2 twin, 1 family
bathrooms 7 en suite
payment credit/debit cards, cash, cheques

directions google map and directions by road and rail are on web page

Room
General

Where is my pet welcome?

Some properties welcome well-behaved pets. Look for the 🐕 in the accommodation listings.

You can also buy a copy of our popular guide 'Pets Come Too!' Now available in good bookshops and online at **visitbritainshop.com**

£9.99

key to symbols see page 6

North West | Cumbria

BASSENTHWAITE, Cumbria Map ref 5A2
SAT NAV CA13 9YD

Enjoy England ★★★★ GUEST HOUSE
Enjoy England Silver AWARD

B&B PER ROOM PER NIGHT
S £40.00
D £60.00 – £90.00

EVENING MEAL PER PERSON
£17.00 – £20.00

SPECIAL PROMOTIONS
Special offers available for 3 or more nights

Ouse Bridge House
Bassenthwaite Lake, Dubwath, Bassenthwaite CA13 9YD
t (01768) 776322 f (01768) 776350 e enquiries@ousebridge.com
w **ousebridge.com** ONLINE MAP GUEST REVIEWS ONLINE BOOKING LAST MINUTE OFFERS

Friendly guest house with beautiful views over Bassenthwaite Lake and Skiddaw. Delicious breakfasts and dinners using local produce, comfortable well-equipped rooms, great views, walks and attractions close-by, honesty bar and parking. We offer a relaxed atmosphere, excellent service and delicious food in a stunning and peaceful location.

open All year except Xmas
bedrooms 2 single, 6 double, 1 twin, 2 family
bathrooms 9 en suite, 2 with private bathroom
payment credit/debit cards, cash, cheques
directions A66 westbound. Bypass Keswick. Right turn signposted B5291 and Castle Inn. Turn immediately right again and the hotel is 50yds on the left.

Room General Leisure

BLACKFORD, Cumbria Map ref 5A2
SAT NAV CA6 4ER

Enjoy England ★★★★ FARMHOUSE

B&B PER ROOM PER NIGHT
S £35.00
D £25.00 – £35.00

Mount Farm Bed & Breakfast
Blackford, Carlisle CA6 4ER
t (01228) 674641 e judith.wilson11@btinternet.com
w **mount-farm.co.uk** ONLINE MAP

Small working farm. Local activities, walk, horseriding, golf, fishing, birdwatching and cycling. Touring base for Carlisle City, Lake District, Scottish Borders, Hadrian's Wall, Alston Moor, Maryport, Whitehaven, Silloth and Gretna. **directions** Detailed directions on request. **bedrooms** 2 twin **bathrooms** 2 en suite **payment** cash, cheques

Room General Leisure

BOWNESS-ON-WINDERMERE, Cumbria Map ref 5A3
SAT NAV LA23 3EW

Enjoy England ★★★ BED & BREAKFAST

B&B PER ROOM PER NIGHT
S £45.00 – £70.00
D £35.00 – £45.00

May Cottage B&B
Kendal Road, Bowness-on-Windermere LA23 3EW
t (015394) 46378 e bnb@maycottagebowness.co.uk
w **maycottagebowness.co.uk** ONLINE MAP GUEST REVIEWS LAST MINUTE OFFERS

Welcoming, comfortable, light, clean rooms; High-spec en-suites. Superb location 2 mins walk to Lake, shops, restaurants. Healthy breakfast, free Wi-Fi, carpark, leisure facilities; Bike secure, great value! Local information/Drives/Walks. **directions** - Clear travel details can be found on our website. Private car park. West Coast Train Line - Oxenholme/Windermere. We can meet/greet you. **open** All year **bedrooms** 1 double, 1 twin, 1 family **bathrooms** 3 en suite **payment** credit/debit cards, cash, cheques, euros

WALKERS CYCLISTS

Room General Leisure

584 Official tourist board guide Bed & Breakfast

North West | Cumbria

BOWNESS-ON-WINDERMERE, Cumbria Map ref 5A3
SAT NAV LA23 3JD

Storrs Gate House
Longtail Hill, Bowness-on-Windermere, Windermere LA23 3JD
t (015394) 43272 **e** enquiries@storrsgatehouse.co.uk
w storrsgatehouse.co.uk GUEST REVIEWS ONLINE BOOKING

B&B PER ROOM PER NIGHT
D £84.00 – £150.00

SPECIAL PROMOTIONS
Contact us direct for midweek discounts for 3+ nights during mid and low season.

Bed & Breakfast of the Year 2009 - Cumbria Tourism Awards. Five Stars with a Silver Award for Excellence. Luxury family run guest house opposite Lake Windermere. Superb accommodation with sumptuous suites, king-size four posters, ground floor en-suites and wheelchair access. Personal service, wonderful breakfasts, ample parking and romantic gardens.

open All year except Xmas and New Year
bedrooms 2 double, 1 twin, 3 suites
bathrooms 6 en suite
payment credit/debit cards, cash, cheques
directions M6 J36. Signed Windermere to Bowness. From Bowness piers join A592 south to Newby Bridge. Travel 0.5m. On junction (left) after sign to car ferry.

Room   General

BRAMPTON, Cumbria Map ref 5B2
SAT NAV CA8 2QU

Scarrow Hill Guest House
Denton Mill, Scarrow Hill, Brampton CA8 2QU
t (01697) 746759 **e** lindamac@scarrowhillhouse.co.uk
w scarrowhillhouse.co.uk ONLINE MAP GUEST REVIEWS

B&B PER ROOM PER NIGHT
S £45.00 – £60.00
D £75.00 – £90.00
EVENING MEAL PER PERSON
£20.00 – £25.00

BREAKFAST AWARD

A Victorian gamekeeper's dwelling set in secluded grounds . First-class accommodation and food, fine hospitality and relaxation in extensive gardens. Close to Hadrian's Wall, and great for exploring. **directions** 2 miles E of Brampton on A69 to Newcastle, turn left after Naworth/Hallbankgate X-roads down private road marked Denton Mill. **open** All year except Xmas and New Year **bedrooms** 1 double, 1 twin **bathrooms** 2 en suite **payment** credit/debit cards, cash, cheques, euros

Room   General   Leisure

BROUGHTON IN FURNESS, Cumbria Map ref 5A3
SAT NAV LA17 7TR

Low Hall Farm
Kirkby-in-Furness, Broughton-in-Furness LA17 7TR
t (01229) 889220 **f** (01229) 889868 **e** enquiries@low-hall.co.uk
w low-hall.co.uk

B&B PER ROOM PER NIGHT
S £33.00 – £35.00
D £60.00 – £65.00

Low Hall is a working farm with stunning views across Duddon estuary and Lakeland fells. A warm, friendly welcome awaits. High quality accommodation and a traditional farmhouse breakfast our speciality. **directions** M6 jct 36, follow A590 towards Barrow, through Ulverston until roundabout signposted A595 Workington and Whitehaven, through Askam for approx 2.5miles. Turn right 'Low Hall'. **open** All year **bedrooms** 1 double, 1 twin, 1 family **bathrooms** 3 en suite **payment** credit/debit cards, cash, cheques

Room   General   Leisure

For **key to symbols** see page 6

585

North West | Cumbria

BUTTERMERE, Cumbria Map ref 5A3
SAT NAV CA13 9XA

Fish Inn
Buttermere, Nr Cockermouth CA13 9XA
t 017687 70253 f 017687 70287 e info@fishinnbuttermere.co.uk
w fishinnbuttermere.co.uk ONLINE MAP

RATING APPLIED FOR

B&B PER ROOM PER NIGHT
S £45.00 – £58.00
D £35.00 – £53.00
EVENING MEAL PER PERSON
£6.75 – £14.50

Set in unbeatable surroundings a short stroll from Buttermere and Crummock waters. The Inn is comfortable and informal serving traditional food alongside local real ales, assuring a warm welcome **directions** At jct 40 on M6 take A66 to Keswick continue towards Cockermouth, 9 miles after Keswick roundabout turn left following signs B5289 Lorton and Buttermere. **open** open at New Year **bedrooms** 7 double, 2 twin, 1 family **bathrooms** 10 en suite, 10 with private bathroom **payment** credit/debit cards, cash, cheques

Room General Leisure

CALDBECK, Cumbria Map ref 5A2
SAT NAV CA7 8HQ

Swaledale Watch
Whelpo, Caldbeck CA7 8HQ
t (01697) 478409 f (01697) 478409 e nan.savage@talk21.com
w swaledale-watch.co.uk ONLINE MAP

4 star GUEST ACCOMMODATION
Silver AWARD

B&B PER ROOM PER NIGHT
S £25.00 – £33.00
D £50.00 – £60.00

Great comfort, excellent food and a warm welcome amidst peaceful, unspoilt countryside. Central for touring, walking or discovering the northern fells. A memorable walk is through 'The-Howk' a limestone gorge. **directions** On B5299 1 mile west of Caldbeck village. **open** All year except Xmas **bedrooms** 2 double, 1 twin, 2 family **bathrooms** 4 en suite, 1 with private bathroom **payment** credit/debit cards, cash, cheques

Room General Leisure

CARLISLE, Cumbria Map ref 5A2
SAT NAV CA1 1JU

East View Guest House
110 Warwick Road, Carlisle CA1 1JU
t (01228) 522112 f (01228) 522112 e eastviewgh@hotmail.co.uk
w eastviewguesthouse.co.uk GUEST REVIEWS

4 star GUEST ACCOMMODATION

B&B PER ROOM PER NIGHT
S £35.00 – £45.00
D £65.00 – £70.00

City centre location Hadrians Wall, castle, theatre and restaurants nearby. Fully en-suite guest house, comfortable rooms and tasty breakfasts. Digital televisions in all rooms, welcome trays, towels and toiletries provided. **directions** Leave M6 at junction 43(A69) into Warwick road, house 1.25 miles on left. 6 mins walk to bus station 10 mins to railway. **open** All year except Xmas and New Year **bedrooms** 1 single, 4 double, 1 twin, 2 family **bathrooms** 8 en suite **payment** credit/debit cards, cash

Room General Leisure

CARLISLE, Cumbria Map ref 5A2
SAT NAV CA1 1HR

Langleigh House
6 Howard Place, Carlisle CA1 1HR
t (01228) 530440 f N/A e langleighhouse@aol.com
w langleighhouse.co.uk ONLINE MAP GUEST REVIEWS

4 star GUEST HOUSE

B&B PER ROOM PER NIGHT
S £35.00
D £70.00
EVENING MEAL PER PERSON
£5.00 – £25.00

Highly recommended. Victorian house, comfortably furnished situated in a quiet conservation area with Private car park, just five minutes walk from the city centre. **directions** Junction 43 off the M6. Drive along Warwick Road and we are the third turning on the right after St. Aidans church. **open** All year **payment** credit/debit cards, cash, cheques

Room General Leisure

Official tourist board guide **Bed & Breakfast**

North West | Cumbria

CONISTON, Cumbria Map ref 5A3
SAT NAV LA21 8DX

★★★★ GUEST ACCOMMODATION

B&B PER ROOM PER NIGHT
S £30.00 – £35.00
D £60.00 – £70.00

Oaklands Guest House
Yewdale Road, Coniston, Cumbria LA21 8DX
t (01539) 441245 f (01539) 441245 e judithzeke@oaklandsguesthouse.fsnet.co.uk
w oaklandsconiston.co.uk ONLINE MAP LAST MINUTE OFFERS

Spacious 100-year-old Lakeland house, village location, mountain views. Quality breakfast, all rooms with superb pocket sprung beds and high quality furnishings. Parking and garden. **directions** Please refer to website. **open** All year **bedrooms** 1 single, 2 double, 1 twin **bathrooms** 2 en suite, 1 with private bathroom **payment** cash, cheques, euros

CONISTON, Cumbria Map ref 5A3
SAT NAV LA21 8DU

★★★★ BED & BREAKFAST

B&B PER ROOM PER NIGHT
S £35.00 – £42.00
D £56.00 – £74.00

Orchard Cottage
18 Yewdale Road, Coniston LA21 8DU
t (01539) 441319 f (01539) 441373 e enquiries@conistonholidays.co.uk
w conistonholidays.co.uk ONLINE BOOKING

Orchard Cottage centrally situated in Coniston village. Excellent accommodation with three attractive en suite rooms all on ground level. Tea and coffee facilities. Guest lounge with television, separate dining room. **directions** Situated the A593 as you enter Coniston village. **open** All year except Xmas and New Year **bedrooms** 2 double, 1 twin **bathrooms** 3 en suite **payment** credit/debit cards, cash, cheques

CONISTON, Cumbria Map ref 5A3
SAT NAV LA21 8HQ

★★★★ INN

B&B PER ROOM PER NIGHT
S £45.00 – £50.00
D £95.00 – £110.00
EVENING MEAL PER PERSON
£6.50 – £18.00

The Sun, Coniston
The Sun, Coniston LA21 8HQ
t (01539) 441248 f (01539) 441219 e info@thesunconiston.com
w thesunconiston.com ONLINE MAP

Classic Lakeland pub: comfortable, informal, four star inn, diner and great bar with 8 hand-pulls. Freshly prepared food using locally sourced ingredients. The 8 en-suite bedrooms enjoy superb panoramic views. **directions** M6 Junction 36, follow signs for Barrow A590. Turn off at Greenodd. Follow signs for Coniston. On entering the village, turn left (signposted) before bridge. **open** All year except Xmas **bedrooms** 4 double, 2 twin, 1 family, 1 suite **bathrooms** 8 en suite **payment** credit/debit cards, cash, cheques

CONISTON, Cumbria Map ref 5A3
SAT NAV LA21 8DU

★★★ INN

B&B PER ROOM PER NIGHT
S £35.00 – £60.00
D £75.00 – £95.00
EVENING MEAL PER PERSON
£7.50 – £15.00

Yewdale Inn
Yewdale Road, Coniston LA21 8DU
t (01539) 441280 e mail@yewdalehotel.com
w yewdalehotel.com ONLINE MAP GUEST REVIEWS LAST MINUTE OFFERS

Small, family run inn situated in the centre of Coniston, within walking distance of the lake. Ideally positioned for walkers and cyclists. Children and pets welcome. **directions** Please contact us for directions **open** All year **bedrooms** 4 double, 4 family **bathrooms** 8 en suite **payment** credit/debit cards, cash, cheques

For **key to symbols** see page 6

North West | Cumbria

CULGAITH, Cumbria Map ref 5B2
SAT NAV CA10 1QL

Laurel House
Culgaith, Penrith CA10 1QL
t (01768) 886380 f (01768) 886380 e laurelhouse@fsmail.net
w laurelhousecumbria.co.uk GUEST REVIEWS ONLINE BOOKING

B&B PER ROOM PER NIGHT
S £60.00
D £85.00
EVENING MEAL PER PERSON
£17.50 – £30.00

Laurel House is an 18th-century farmhouse, completely refurbished to a modern standard with three luxuriously appointed double rooms, situated in the beautiful Eden Valley. VisitBritain Breakfast Award 2010. **directions** Culgaith is situated 10 minutes drive along the A66, from J40 of the M6, and 40 minutes from Scotch Corner on the A1. **open** All year **bedrooms** 3 double **bathrooms** 3 en suite **payment** credit/debit cards, cash, cheques

BREAKFAST AWARD

Room General Leisure

DOCKRAY, Cumbria Map ref 5A3
SAT NAV CA11 0JY

Royal Hotel
Dockray, Penrith, Ullswater CA11 0JY
t (01768) 482356 f (01768) 482033 e info@the-royal-dockray.co.uk
w the-royal-dockray.co.uk ONLINE MAP GUEST REVIEWS ONLINE BOOKING LAST MINUTE OFFERS

B&B PER ROOM PER NIGHT
S £45.00 – £70.00
D £50.00 – £95.00
EVENING MEAL PER PERSON
£7.50 – £18.95

SPECIAL PROMOTIONS
Pay for three nights and get an extra night free. Offer excludes weekends.

The Hotel nestles peacefully amongst the Lake District Fells and is situated about one mile from the shores of Ullswater and Aira Force. The Helvellyn and High Street Mountain ranges are right on the doorstep which makes the Royal Hotel an ideal and comfortable base for walkers

open All year
bedrooms 7 double, 1 twin, 2 family
bathrooms 10 en suite
payment credit/debit cards, cash

directions M6 North follow signs for A66 Keswick. Continue on the A66, turn left on the A5091. Follow this road until the village of Dockray.

Room General Leisure

DUFTON, Cumbria Map ref 5B3
SAT NAV CA16 6DF

Brow Farm Bed & Breakfast
Dufton, Appleby-in-Westmorland, Cumbria CA16 6DF
t (01768) 352865 f (01768) 352865 e stay@browfarm.com
w browfarm.com

B&B PER ROOM PER NIGHT
S £34.00 – £36.00
D £64.00 – £72.00

Situated on the edge of the Pennines, with superb views from every room. Tasteful barn conversion offers rest and relaxation. Also self-catering cottages - see website for details www.browfarm.com **directions** From Appleby take Dufton road for 3 miles. Farm is on right. From Penrith (A66) take Dufton road. Travel through village. Farm on left. **open** All year except Xmas **bedrooms** 2 double, 1 twin **bathrooms** 3 en suite **payment** credit/debit cards, cash, cheques

Room General

North West | Cumbria

GILSLAND, Cumbria Map ref 5B2
SAT NAV CA8 7AF

Bush Nook Guest House
Upper Denton, Gilsland, Brampton CA8 7AF
t (01697) 747194 **f** (01697) 747194 **e** info@bushnook.co.uk
w bushnook.co.uk   ONLINE MAP GUEST REVIEWS ONLINE BOOKING LAST MINUTE OFFERS

B&B PER ROOM PER NIGHT
S £35.00 – £40.00
D £70.00 – £80.00

EVENING MEAL PER PERSON
£12.00 – £18.00

SPECIAL PROMOTIONS
Seasonal special breaks available, telephone or check website for details.

Bush Nook is a traditional farm house tastefully converted to a comfortable country guest house. Situated in open country, approximately 1 mile from Gilsland on Hadrian's Wall, with expansive views to the Scottish Lowlands, Keilder Forest and Northumberland.

open All year except Xmas
bedrooms 1 single, 4 double, 2 twin
bathrooms 7 en suite, 4 with private bathroom
payment credit/debit cards, cash, cheques, euros
directions Travelling from Newcastle or Carlisle follow the A69 turning of at the RAF Spadeadam/Gilsland junction. Bush Nook is approximately 800 yards on the right.

GILSLAND, Cumbria Map ref 5B2
SAT NAV CA8 7DA

The Hill on the Wall
Gilsland, Brampton CA8 7DA
t (01697) 747214 **f** (01697) 747214 **e** info@hadrians-wallbedandbreakfast.com
w hadrians-wallbedandbreakfast.com   ONLINE MAP GUEST REVIEWS ONLINE BOOKING

B&B PER ROOM PER NIGHT
S £50.00 – £62.50
D £75.00 – £85.00

In one acre of land, The Hill is a fascinating 16thC fortified farmhouse. It overlooks Hadrian's Wall and the beautiful Irthing Valley. **directions** Leave A69 at Brampton, take turning for Lanercost and Hadrian's Wall. Past Tourist Centre (Birdoswald), right at T-junction, approximately 0.5 miles. **open** All year **bedrooms** 1 double, 2 twin **bathrooms** 2 en suite, 1 with private bathroom **payment** cash, cheques

---

HAWKSHEAD, Cumbria Map ref 5A3
SAT NAV LA12 8JU

Crosslands Farm
Rusland, Hawkshead, Nr Ulverston, Cumbria LA12 8JU
t (01229) 860242 **f** no fax machine **e** enquiries@crosslandsfarm.co.uk
w crosslandsfarm.co.uk   ONLINE MAP

B&B PER ROOM PER NIGHT
S £39.00 – £43.00
D £32.00 – £37.00

EVENING MEAL PER PERSON
£16.00

17thC farmhouse with original features, in unspoilt valley of Rusland near the lakeland hills. Perfect for walking & cycling. Near Hawkshead & Grizedale Forest. Great breakfast. Lovely views. **directions** Crosslands farm is situated 4miles from the A590 which leads from the M6, 4 miles from Grizedale Visitors centre and 5 miles south of Hawkshead **open** All year except Xmas **bedrooms** 2 double, 1 twin **bathrooms** 2 en suite, 1 with private bathroom **payment** credit/debit cards, cash

For **key to symbols** see page 6

589

North West | **Cumbria**

HAWKSHEAD HILL, Cumbria Map ref 5A3

SAT NAV LA22 0PR

Yewfield Vegetarian Guest House

Hawkshead Hill, Hawkshead, Ambleside LA22 0PR
t 01539 436765 f 01539 436096 e derek.yewfield@btinternet.com
w yewfield.co.uk ONLINE MAP GUEST REVIEWS LAST MINUTE OFFERS

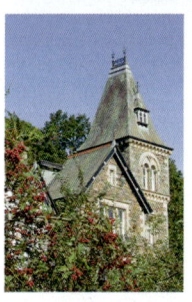

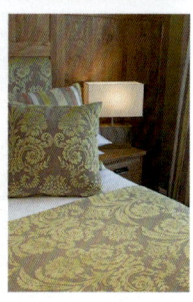

B&B PER ROOM PER NIGHT
S £48.00 – £58.00
D £96.00 – £120.00

SPECIAL PROMOTIONS
Classical concerts throughout the year. See website for dates. also Wild Flower study Weekend

Yewfield is an impressive country house set in over 30 acres of private grounds, a peaceful and quiet retreat with lovely walks straight from the grounds. Following recent refurbishments, Yewfield was awarded a 5 stars silver VisitBritain award.

open All year except Xmas and New Year
bedrooms 6 double, 4 twin
bathrooms 10 en suite
payment credit/debit cards, cash, cheques

directions One mile from Hawkshead, 4 miles from Ambleside, 2 miles past The Drunken Duck. See website for map.

Room
General
Leisure

HEADS NOOK, Cumbria Map ref 5B2

SAT NAV CA8 9DH

Croft House

Newbiggin, Brampton, Carlisle CA8 9DH
t (01768) 896695 e info@crofthousecumbria.co.uk
w crofthousecumbria.co.uk

B&B PER ROOM PER NIGHT
S £39.00 – £45.00
D £74.00 – £85.00

EVENING MEAL PER PERSON
£20.00 – £25.00

A warm Cumbrian welcome with a taste of luxury. Situated in the north west of England in the Eden Valley, between Lake District and the foot of the Pennine Hills in Cumbria.

open All year
bedrooms 1 single, 1 double, 1 family
bathrooms 3 en suite
payment cash, cheques

directions Please contact us for directions

Room   General   Leisure

590   Official tourist board guide **Bed & Breakfast**

North West | Cumbria

HEADS NOOK, Cumbria Map ref 5B2
SAT NAV CA8 9EG

String of Horses Inn
Faugh, Heads Nook, Brampton, Carlisle CA8 9EG
t (01228) 670297 e info@stringofhorses.com
w stringofhorses.com ONLINE MAP GUEST REVIEWS ONLINE BOOKING

B&B PER ROOM PER NIGHT
S £45.00 – £55.00
D £60.00 – £100.00

EVENING MEAL PER PERSON
£7.95 – £15.95

Dating from 1659, this traditional coaching inn is set in a quiet country village only 10 minutes from Carlisle and Junction 43 of the M6 motorway. Near Hadrian's Wall and The Lake District. With great food, oak beams and panelling, real ales, log fires, free Wi-Fi and all rooms ensuite.

open All year
bedrooms 9 double, 1 twin, 1 family
bathrooms 11 en suite, 11 with private bathroom
payment credit/debit cards, cash

directions A69 from J43 M6-Newcastle. 5 miles turn right at Lights Corby Hill/Warwick Bridge at BP Station. 1 mile through Heads Nook, turn left into Faugh.

HESKET NEWMARKET, Cumbria Map ref 5A2
SAT NAV CA7 8HR

Daffodil
Banks Farm, Hesket Newmarket, Penrith CA7 8HR
t 01697478137 e banksfarm@mac.com
w daffodilbanksfarm.co.uk ONLINE BOOKING LAST MINUTE OFFERS

B&B PER ROOM PER NIGHT
S £110.00
D £150.00

EVENING MEAL PER PERSON
£15.00 – £25.00

SPECIAL PROMOTIONS
Stay for more than 3 nights and get 10% reduction in price.

Luxurious, contemporary, boutique style accommodation with great home cooked food. Magnificent views form the garden with eco friendly wood fired hot tub and pizza oven.

open All year
bedrooms 2 suites
bathrooms 2 en suite
payment credit/debit cards, cash, cheques

directions M6 to j41. B5305 to Wigton. 7 miles left. Take 2nd right. Pass Bank End at brow of hill turn right into Banks Farm.

For key to symbols see page 6

North West | Cumbria

HESKET NEWMARKET, Cumbria Map ref 5A2
SAT NAV CA7 8JG

B&B PER ROOM PER NIGHT
S £31.00 – £37.00
D £31.00 – £34.00

Denton House
Hesket Newmarket, Caldbeck CA7 8JG
t (01697) 478415 **e** dentonhnm@aol.com
w dentonhouseguesthouse.co.uk

A large 17th century house modernised to 20th century comforts, set in the centre of Hesket Newmarket, an ideal base for touring the lakes and walking the northern fells **directions** Please contact us for directions **open** All year **bedrooms** 3 double, 3 family **bathrooms** 5 en suite, 1 with private bathroom **payment** cash, cheques

Room General

KENDAL, Cumbria Map ref 5B3
SAT NAV LA9 4LD

B&B PER ROOM PER NIGHT
S £60.00 – £75.00
D £80.00 – £100.00

Beech House
40 Greenside, Kendal LA9 4LD
t (01539) 720385 **f** (01539) 724082 **e** stay@beechhouse-kendal.co.uk
w beechhouse-kendal.co.uk ONLINE MAP

Friendly and stylish 5 star B&B, close to the centre of Kendal, in lovely conservation area, a delightful place to relax and return. 6 bedrooms individually designed with free parking and WiFi. At the southern edge of The Lake District, Kendal is a great centre with superb restaurants and walks.

open All year except Xmas
bedrooms 6 double
bathrooms 6 en suite
payment credit/debit cards, cash, cheques

directions Eight miles from M6 junction 36, follow signs to Kendal, at 2nd set of traffic light turn left, up Gillinggate, Beech House facing crossroad.

Room General Leisure

KENDAL, Cumbria Map ref 5B3
SAT NAV LA9 7AD

B&B PER ROOM PER NIGHT
S £40.00 – £50.00
D £70.00 – £80.00

Bridge House
65 Castle Street, Kendal LA9 7AD
t (015397) 22041 **e** sheila@bridgehouse-kendal.co.uk
w bridgehouse-kendal.co.uk ONLINE MAP GUEST REVIEWS

A Georgian 'listed' building near to the town centre, Kendal castle and river Kent. Guests enjoy our 'secret garden' cyclists and walkers welcomed. Home-made bread and preserves a speciality. **directions** Leave M6 at junction 37. Follow A684 for 5 miles. Bridge House on the right after passing under the railway bridge. **open** All year except Xmas **bedrooms** 1 double, 1 twin **bathrooms** 2 en suite **payment** cash, cheques

Room General Leisure

592 Official tourist board guide **Bed & Breakfast**

North West | Cumbria

KENDAL, Cumbria Map ref 5B3
SAT NAV LA9 7RF

GUEST HOUSE ★★★★

B&B PER ROOM PER NIGHT
S £35.00 – £45.00
D £60.00 – £82.00

The Glen
Oxenholme, Kendal LA9 7RF
t (01539) 726386   e greenintheglen@btinternet.com
w glen-kendal.co.uk ONLINE MAP GUEST REVIEWS

The Glen in a quiet location, under the Helm (local walk and view point), within walking distance of inn and restaurant. Relax in the hot tub after a day's touring! **directions** We are 300 m up the hill on the right from Oxenholme Lake District railway station. **open** All year **bedrooms** 1 single, 2 double, 1 twin, 1 family, 1 suite **bathrooms** 6 en suite **payment** credit/debit cards, cash, cheques

Room   General   Leisure

KESWICK, Cumbria Map ref 5A3
SAT NAV CA12 5ER

GUEST HOUSE ★★★★

B&B PER ROOM PER NIGHT
S £35.00 – £40.00
D £60.00 – £75.00

Appletrees
The Heads, Keswick CA12 5ER
t (01768) 780400   e info@appletreeskeswick.com
w appletreeskeswick.com LAST MINUTE OFFERS

Appletrees offers comfort, quiet and spectacular views south across Crow Park, Borrowdale Valley and Derwentwater, plus north towards Skiddaw and Latrigg. We provide Full English and vegetarian breakfasts, drying room, limited parking and WIFI. Ideal location for town, bus station, lake, parks and theatre. Theatre Discount Vouchers available.

open All year except Xmas
bedrooms 1 single, 5 double, 1 twin
bathrooms 7 en suite
payment credit/debit cards, cash, cheques

directions M6 jct 40, A66 to Keswick. Follow signs to Keswick. Left at mini-roundabout. 4th right turn into The Heads. Appletrees is 200yds on right.

Room
General
Leisure

KESWICK, Cumbria Map ref 5A3
SAT NAV CA12 4LJ

BED & BREAKFAST ★★★★

B&B PER ROOM PER NIGHT
D £50.00 – £70.00

Ash Tree House
Penrith Road, Keswick CA12 4LJ
t (01768) 772303   e peterredfearn@aol.com
w ashtreehouse.co.uk LAST MINUTE OFFERS

Family run Bed and Breakfast in a former farm house built in 1841 with large garden. Comfortable en suite rooms and full English breakfast. Plenty of off road parking. **directions** 15 minute walk from town centre and a good base for all Lake District attractions. Detailed directions on our web site www.ashtreehouse.co.uk **open** All year except Xmas **bedrooms** 1 double, 1 twin **bathrooms** 2 en suite **payment** cash, cheques

Room   General   Leisure

or **key to symbols** see page 6

593

North West | **Cumbria**

KESWICK, Cumbria Map ref 5A3   SAT NAV CA12 5JU

Badgers Wood
30 Stanger Street, Keswick CA12 5JU
t (01768) 772621 e enquiries@badgers-wood.co.uk
w badgers-wood.co.uk

B&B PER ROOM PER NIGHT
S £37.00 – £42.00
D £70.00 – £80.00

Award-winning, restored Victorian guest house in quiet cul-de-sac two-minutes' walk from heart of town/bus station. Totally refurbished bedrooms, colour TVs, tea/coffee facilities and views of fells. Special diets catered for. **directions** From junction 40 M6 exit A66 at the Crosthwaite roundabout(A591)towards Keswick. Turn left at T-junction, over mini-roundabout and first left into Stanger Street. **open** All year except Xmas **bedrooms** 2 single, 3 double, 1 twin **bathrooms** 6 en suite **payment** cash, cheques

Room   General   Leisure

KESWICK, Cumbria Map ref 5A3   SAT NAV CA12 4NL

Briar Rigg House
Brundholme Road, Keswick CA12 4NL
t 0784 985 9391 e accomm@briarrigghouse.co.uk
w briarrigghouse.co.uk ONLINE MAP LAST MINUTE OFFERS

B&B PER ROOM PER NIGHT
S £70.00 – £85.00
D £130.00 – £160.00

SPECIAL PROMOTIONS
Special seasonal breaks available - please contact us for further information. 2 nights minimum stay.

Unique house set within 2 acres of gardens. Beautiful calm environment with luxury of your own sitting room with stunning views across the garden to the hills. Secure parking. Treat yourself - the finest organic bedlinen, top quality local bath products, cooked-to-order breakfast using homemade/local Cumbrian food.

open All year except Xmas
bedrooms 1 double
bathrooms 1 with private bathroom
payment cash, cheques, euros

directions 5 minutes walk from the centre of Keswick yet feels very rural. Very easy to find. Please see our website for directions.

Room   General   Leisure

KESWICK, Cumbria Map ref 5A3   SAT NAV CA12 5ER

Burleigh Mead
The Heads, Keswick CA12 5ER
t (01768) 775935 e info@burleighmead.co.uk
w burleighmead.co.uk ONLINE MAP

B&B PER ROOM PER NIGHT
D £67.00 – £95.00

Conveniently situated between town centre and Derwentwater, our charming Victorian house offers excellent accommodation with outstanding views of surrounding fells. **directions** Once in Keswick follow signs for Lake and Borrowdale. The Heads is across from Central Car Park, we are 100 yards up road on right. **open** February to December **bedrooms** 4 double, 1 twin, 2 family **bathrooms** 7 en suite **payment** cash, cheques

Room   General   Leisure

594   Official tourist board guide **Bed & Breakfast**

North West | Cumbria

KESWICK, Cumbria Map ref 5A3

SAT NAV CA12 4DH

Charnwood Guest House
6 Eskin Street, Keswick CA12 4DH
t (01768) 774111 e sue.banister@googlemail.com

B&B PER ROOM PER NIGHT
S £45.00
D £32.00 – £40.00

Elegant listed building. Close to lake and fells and in a quiet street. A warm welcome and really good food can be found at Charnwood. We cater for vegetarians. **directions** From A66 join the A591 to town centre and before the traffic lights turn left into Greta Street which leads to Eskin Street. **open** All year except Xmas **bedrooms** 2 double, 3 family **payment** credit/debit cards, cash, cheques

Room General

KESWICK, Cumbria Map ref 5A3

SAT NAV CA12 4HL

Easedale House
1 Southey Street, Keswick CA12 4HL
t (01768) 772710 f (01768) 771127 e info@easedalehouse.com
w easedalehouse.com GUEST REVIEWS LAST MINUTE OFFERS

B&B PER ROOM PER NIGHT
D £62.00 – £80.00

SPECIAL PROMOTIONS
Discounts for short breaks, children (up to 14 years) half usual adult rate. See our website for seasonal offers.

High quality, friendly guest house/B & B ideally situated in central Keswick, 10 minutes walk to Derwentwater. Lovely, newly refurbished dining room, serving great breakfasts. Comfortable, spacious en-suite bedrooms, including superior doubles with baths, standard doubles, twins or family rooms; and a relaxing guest lounge. Warm welcome guaranteed.

open All year except Xmas
bedrooms 5 double, 2 twin, 2 family
bathrooms 9 en suite, 9 with private bathroom
payment credit/debit cards, cash, cheques

directions A66 West from junction 40 of M6. Turn right at A591 to Keswick. 1st traffic lights, turn sharp left into Southey Street.

Room
General

KESWICK, Cumbria Map ref 5A3

SAT NAV CA12 4DX

Harvington House
19 Church Street, Keswick CA12 4DX
t (01768) 775582 e info@harvingtonhouse.co.uk
w harvingtonhouse.co.uk GUEST REVIEWS

B&B PER ROOM PER NIGHT
S £28.00 – £32.50
D £60.00 – £65.00

A warm welcome awaits you at Harvington House. Clean comfortable and homely bed and breakfast. Double, twin or single rooms available. For an ideal base give us a call. **directions** Please contact us for directions **open** All year except Xmas **bedrooms** 2 single, 3 double, 1 twin **bathrooms** 4 en suite **payment** credit/debit cards, cash, cheques

Room General Leisure

key to symbols see page 6

595

North West | **Cumbria**

KESWICK, Cumbria Map ref 5A3   SAT NAV CA12 4DG

B&B PER ROOM PER NIGHT
D £38.00 – £40.00

Hawcliffe House
30 Eskin Street, Keswick CA12 4DG
t (01768) 773250 e diane@hawcliffehouse.co.uk
w hawcliffehouse.co.uk

Small family run bed and breakfast. Close to town centre. Ideal base for sightseeing or walking. Early breakfasts available on request. Packed lunches available. **directions** Please contact us for directions **open** All year except Xmas **bedrooms** 3 double, 1 twin **bathrooms** 4 en suite **payment** credit/debit cards, cash

Room   General

KESWICK, Cumbria Map ref 5A3   SAT NAV CA12 4LJ

B&B PER ROOM PER NIGHT
S £35.00 – £60.00
D £58.00 – £80.00

Laurel Bank B&B
Penrith Road, Keswick CA12 4LJ
t (01768) 773006 f (01768) 773006 e info@laurelbankkeswick.co.uk
w laurelbankkeswick.co.uk ONLINE MAP GUEST REVIEWS ONLINE BOOKING

Situated close to Keswick town centre shops, bars, restaurants, parks, leisure facilities and Castlerigg Stone Circle. All rooms en suite, with views towards Grisedale Pike or Latrigg. Private car park and cycle storage. Families, walkers and Pets welcome. En route Stagecoach buses connecting Penrith, Windermere, Keswick, Cockermouth and Workington.

open All year except Xmas
bedrooms 1 double, 2 twin, 2 family
bathrooms 5 en suite
payment credit/debit cards, cash

directions Check our directions page at www.laurelbankkeswick.co.uk

Room
General
Leisure

KESWICK, Cumbria Map ref 5A3   SAT NAV CA12 4DG

B&B PER ROOM PER NIGHT
D £60.00 – £70.00

Littlefield
32 Eskin Street, Keswick CA12 4DG
t (01768) 772949 e info@littlefieldguesthouse.co.uk
w littlefieldguesthouse.co.uk ONLINE MAP ONLINE BOOKING

A small, friendly lakeland home convenient for shops, lake and many lovely walks. Early breakfast and packed lunches available. We pride ourselves on our warm hospitality and attention to detail. **directions** Please contact us for directions **open** All year except Xmas **bedrooms** 3 double, 1 twin **bathrooms** 4 en suite **payment** credit/debit cards, cash, cheques

Room   General   Leisure

North West | **Cumbria**

KESWICK, Cumbria Map ref 5A3   SAT NAV CA12 5ES

Parkfield Guest House
The Heads, Keswick CA12 5ES
t (01768) 772328 e enquiries@parkfieldkeswick.co.uk
w parkfield-keswick.co.uk ONLINE MAP GUEST REVIEWS

B&B PER ROOM PER NIGHT
D £75.00 – £95.00

Parkfield is set in the picturesque market town of Keswick, surrounded by the tranquil mountains of the English Lake District. We are ideally situated for any walking or leisure holiday.
directions Please contact us for directions **open** All year **bedrooms** 4 double, 2 twin **bathrooms** 6 en suite **payment** credit/debit cards, cash, cheques

Room General Leisure

KESWICK, Cumbria Map ref 5A3   SAT NAV CA12 5DQ

Rooms36
36 Lake Road, Keswick CA12 5DQ
t (0800) 056 6401 f (017687) 80527 e andy042195@aol.com
w Rooms36.co.uk ONLINE MAP GUEST REVIEWS ONLINE BOOKING

B&B PER ROOM PER NIGHT
S £60.00 – £65.00
D £90.00 – £110.00

SPECIAL PROMOTIONS
7 nights £620.00 per night double room

Rooms36 (Seymour House) is set midway between Keswick town centre and Derwentwater, just a few minutes flat walk away from theatre by the lake.

open Closed 24th 25th and 26th December
bedrooms 1 single, 4 double, 2 twin, 2 family
bathrooms 9 en suite
payment credit/debit cards, cash, cheques

directions Follow the sign to Borrowdale and the Lake take the Heads Road on your left Rooms36 (seymour-house) is the last property on your left

Room General Leisure

KESWICK, Cumbria Map ref 5A3   SAT NAV CA12 4EG

Sandon Guest House
Southey Street, Keswick CA12 4EG
t (01768) 773648 e enquiries@sandonguesthouse.com
w sandonguesthouse.com

B&B PER ROOM PER NIGHT
S £30.00 – £36.00
D £60.00 – £72.00

Charming Lakeland-stone Victorian guest house, conveniently situated for town, theatre or lake. Friendly, comfortable accommodation. Ideal base for walking or cycling holidays. Superb English breakfast. **directions** Please contact us for directions **open** All year except Xmas **bedrooms** 2 single, 3 double, 1 twin **bathrooms** 5 en suite, 1 with private bathroom **payment** credit/debit cards, cash, cheques

Room General Leisure

597

North West | **Cumbria**

KESWICK, Cumbria Map ref 5A3
SAT NAV CA12 5JZ

Swiss Court Guest House
25 Bank Street, Keswick, Cumbria CA12 5JZ
t (017687) 72637   e enquiries@swisscourt.co.uk
w swisscourt.co.uk ONLINE MAP

B&B PER ROOM PER NIGHT
S £34.00 – £44.00
D £34.00 – £44.00

Maria and Mary welcome you to Swiss Court Guest House, with its excellent views of surrounding Lakeland fells. Ideally located in the heart of Keswick, within easy distance of all amenities. A clean and comfortable quality four star guest house, renowned for its mouth-watering breakfasts and convenient Lake District position.

open All year except Xmas
bedrooms 2 single, 3 double, 1 twin, 1 family
bathrooms 7 en suite
payment credit/debit cards, cash

directions At Penrith take A66 Keswick 18 miles. Take first turn for Keswick follow for town centre, after traffic lights Swiss Court 200 metres on right.

Room
General
Leisure

KESWICK, Cumbria Map ref 5A3
SAT NAV CA12 5ES

West View Guest House
The Heads, Keswick CA12 5ES
t (01768) 773638   e info@westviewkeswick.co.uk
w westviewkeswick.co.uk ONLINE MAP ONLINE BOOKING

B&B PER ROOM PER NIGHT
S £50.00
D £75.00

Victorian guest house offering the highest of standards. Three minutes' walk from Derwentwater, Keswick town centre and Theatre by the Lake. Massive tasty breakfast. All day Lounge facing the hills. **directions** In Keswick town centre follow signs for Borrowdale. The Heads is opposite the main car park. **open** All year except Xmas **bedrooms** 6 double, 1 twin **bathrooms** 7 en suite **payment** credit/debit cards, cash, euros

Room   General   Leisure

KESWICK, Cumbria Map ref 5A3
SAT NAV CA12 4LJ

Woodside
Penrith Road, Keswick, Cumbria CA12 4LJ
t (01768) 773522   e info@woodsideguesthouse.co.uk
w woodsideguesthouse.co.uk ONLINE MAP

B&B PER ROOM PER NIGHT
D £70.00 – £80.00

Family-friendly B&B in beautiful Lakeland town of Keswick. Our extensive gardens are open to guests, so you can relax and plan your days in beautiful surroundings. **directions** Woodside is situated on the junction of Chestnut Hill and Penrith Road on the east side of Keswick. **open** All year except Xmas **bedrooms** 3 double, 1 twin, 1 family **bathrooms** 5 en suite **payment** credit/debit cards, cash

Room   General   Leisure

North West | Cumbria

KESWICK (5 MILES), Cumbria Map ref 5A3
SAT NAV CA12 5TU

Littletown Farm
Newlands, Keswick, Cumbria CA12 5TU
t (01768) 778353 f (01768) 778437 e info@littletownfarm.co.uk
w littletownfarm.co.uk

B&B PER ROOM PER NIGHT
S £40.00 – £50.00
D £76.00 – £84.00

A 150-acre mixed farm in beautiful, unspoilt Newlands Valley. Perfect for hard or leisurely walking, relaxing round Lakes Derwent and Buttermere, or strolling around market towns of Keswick and Cockermouth. **directions** Leave M6 jct 40, A66 west bypass Keswick, left through Portinscale. Follow Swinside, Stair. Take middle road past phone box. Littletown 1 mile on rt. **open** All year except Xmas **bedrooms** 4 double, 2 twin, 2 family **bathrooms** 6 en suite, 2 with private bathroom **payment** credit/debit cards, cash, cheques

KESWICK (7.5 MILES), Cumbria Map ref 5A3
SAT NAV CA11 0SY

Lane Head Farm Country Guest House
Troutbeck, Nr Keswick, Cumbria CA11 0SY
t 01768 779220 e info@laneheadfarm.co.uk
w laneheadfarm.co.uk ONLINE MAP

B&B PER ROOM PER NIGHT
S £47.50 – £95.00
D £72.00 – £95.00

EVENING MEAL PER PERSON
£18.00 – £22.00

SPECIAL PROMOTIONS
Offers available, please see our website for details.

Located in the Lake District National Park close to Keswick, Penrith and Ullswater this 18th century converted farmhouse has a peaceful location with magnificent views. Four poster, double or twin rooms available – all en-suite. Evening meals are served in our licensed dining room. A great base to explore from.

open All year except Xmas
bedrooms 6 double, 1 twin
bathrooms 7 en suite
payment credit/debit cards, cash

directions Leave M6 at Jct 40, follow A66 towards Keswick. We are located on the left, 1 mile passed the turning for Troutbeck and Ullswater.

KIRKBY LONSDALE, Cumbria Map ref 5B3
SAT NAV LA6 2AU

Copper Kettle Restaurant & Guest House
3-5 Market Street, Kirkby Lonsdale LA6 2AU
t (01524) 271714 f (01524) 271714

B&B PER ROOM PER NIGHT
S £30.00
D £22.50 – £27.50

EVENING MEAL PER PERSON
£8.00 – £10.00

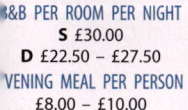

5 comfortable bedrooms in busy market town. **directions** M6, exit 36, follow road for 5½ miles. Turn into Kirkby Lonsdale on Market Street. **open** All year **bedrooms** 2 single, 3 double, 3 twin, 2 family **bathrooms** 3 en suite, 2 with private bathroom **payment** credit/debit cards, cash, cheques, euros

North West | Cumbria

KIRKBY LONSDALE, Cumbria Map ref 5B3
SAT NAV LA6 2NA

enjoyEngland ★★★★ FARMHOUSE
Silver Award

B&B PER ROOM PER NIGHT
S £35.00 – £40.00
D £54.00 – £60.00

High Green Farm
Middleton-in-Lonsdale, Carnforth, Kirkby Lonsdale, Cumbria LA6 2NA
t (01524) 276256 Mobile 07920072790 e nora@highgreenfarm.com
w highgreenfarm.com

Quality ensuite accommodation on working farm in the beautiful Lune valley. An idyllic rural setting midway between lakes and dales, only 10 minutes from M6. Lovely walks, golf, pubs nearby.
directions Situated midway between Kirkby Lonsdale and Sedbergh on A683. 4 miles from M6 Junction 37. **open** March to November **bedrooms** 2 double **bathrooms** 2 en suite **payment** cash, cheque

Room ... General ... Leisure ...

KIRKBY LONSDALE, Cumbria Map ref 5B3
SAT NAV LA6 2LZ

enjoyEngland ★★★★ FARMHOUSE

B&B PER ROOM PER NIGHT
S £30.00 – £35.00
D £54.00 – £60.00

SPECIAL PROMOTIONS
Special promotions on request.

Ullathorns Farm
Middleton, Kirkby Lonsdale LA6 2LZ
t (01524) 276214 Mob: 07800990689 e pauline@ullathorns.co.uk
w ullathorns.co.uk ONLINE MAP LAST MINUTE OFFERS

A warm welcome awaits you at Ullathorns, a working farm situated in the unspoilt Lune Valley midway between Sedbergh and Kirkby Lonsdale. An ideal touring base for lakes and dales. Good overnight stopping-off point, situated between junctions of the M6. Refreshments served upon arrival. Individual breakfast tables.

open March to end of October
bedrooms 1 double, 1 family
bathrooms 2 en suite
payment cash, cheques, euros

directions Ullathorns is set midway between Sedbergh and Kirkby Lonsdale just off the A68

Room ... General ... Leisure ...

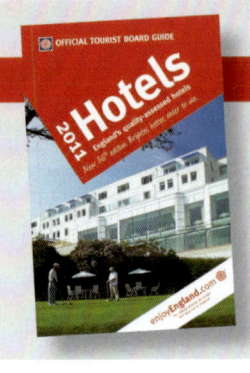

Looking for something else?
You can also buy a copy of our popular guide 'Hotels' including country house and town house hotels, metro and budget hotels, serviced apartments, restaurants with rooms and Spas in England 2011.

Now available in good bookshops and online at
visitbritainshop.com

£10.99

North West | Cumbria

LINDALE, Cumbria Map ref 5A3
SAT NAV LA11 6LP

Greenacres Country Guesthouse
Lindale, Grange-over-Sands LA11 6LP
t (01539) 534578 **e** greenacres.lindale@googlemail.com
w greenacres-lindale.co.uk ONLINE MAP ONLINE BOOKING

B&B PER ROOM PER NIGHT
S £53.00
D £74.00 – £82.00

SPECIAL PROMOTIONS
Reductions for 2/3 nights. Refer to website for further details.

Warm hospitality. Greenacres, in the Lakes National Park, is 10 minutes from the M6, easy access to Morecambe Bay and the Dales. Grange over Sands, (1.5 miles) is an old-fashioned seaside resort, with promenade and impressive ornamental gardens. Windermere, (6 miles). Many museums, castles and stately homes. Excellent food locally.

open All year
bedrooms 2 double, 2 twin, 1 family
bathrooms 5 en suite
payment credit/debit cards, cash, cheques, euros

directions J36/M6 take A590(Barrow). After 3 miles, down to roundabout, A590(Barrow). After 6 miles, roundabout, 1st exit B5277(Grange), Lindale village boundary sign, Greenacres 250m on right.

Room
General
Leisure

MOSEDALE, Cumbria Map ref 5A2
SAT NAV CA11 0XQ

Mosedale End Farm
Mosedale, Penrith, Cumbria CA11 0XQ
t (01768) 779605 **e** enquiries@mosedaleendfarm.co.uk
w mosedaleendfarm.co.uk ONLINE MAP GUEST REVIEWS

B&B PER ROOM PER NIGHT
S £30.00
D £65.00

A 200 acre family run livestock farm in the shadow of Carrock Fell. Double and Family rooms with outstanding views, homemade cakes and locality sourced farmhouse breakfast. Visit the quieter, peacefully relaxing side of the Lakes, halfway between Penrith and Keswick. Walk Wainwright's stunning Northern Fells from the doorstep.

open All year except Xmas
bedrooms 1 double, 1 twin, 1 family
bathrooms 3 en suite
payment cash, cheques

directions From M6-J40 take A66/Keswick for 10 miles. Turn right (Mungrisdale) travel 4 miles to Mosedale, Mosedale End Farm is through the village on the Left.

Room **General** **Leisure**

North West | Cumbria

MUNCASTER, Cumbria Map ref 5A3
SAT NAV CA18 1RQ

enjoyEngland.com ★★★★ GUEST ACCOMMODATION

B&B PER ROOM PER NIGHT
S £60.00
D £80.00 – £100.00

Muncaster Coachman's Quarters
Muncaster Castle, Muncaster, Ravenglass CA18 1RQ
t (01229) 717614 f (01229) 717010 e info@muncaster.co.uk
w muncaster.co.uk ONLINE MAP ONLINE BOOKING LAST MINUTE OFFERS

The Coachman's Quarters are within the magnificent Muncaster Gardens. One room has facilities for people with disabilities. The Granary is a large bedroom with lounge area and kitchenette. Tariff includes admission to the Gardens, World Owl Centre, Meadow Vole Maze, Darkest Muncaster when operational, reduced entry to the Castle.

open All year
bedrooms 4 double, 4 twin, 2 family
bathrooms 9 en suite
payment credit/debit cards, cash, cheques

directions 1 mile south Ravenglass on A595. Jct 36 of M6 follow Brown Western Lake District signs. From north: from Carlisle follow A595 Cockermouth, Whitehaven, Ravenglass.

Room
General
Leisure

PENRITH, Cumbria Map ref 5B2
SAT NAV CA10 1JA

enjoyEngland.com ★★★★ BED & BREAKFAST

B&B PER ROOM PER NIGHT
S £40.00 – £50.00
D £60.00 – £80.00

Addingham View B&B
Addingham View, Gamblesby, Penrith, Cumbria CA10 1JA
t (01768) 881477 e addinghamviewbandb@gmail.com
w addinghamviewbandb.co.uk ONLINE MAP ONLINE BOOKING

1860s sandstone house, quiet rural Eden Valley village. Lake District Pennine views. Walkers, cyclists, photographers, tourers, relaxers welcome. Locally sourced or homemade food at breakfast wherever possible. **directions** M6 to Junction 40; A66 to Scotch Corner; A686 to Alston. Drive to Langwathby-Melmerby-Gamblesby. OR: A66 to Temple Sowerby, Langwathby etc. **open** April 1 to October 31 **bedrooms** 1 double, 1 twin, 1 suite **bathrooms** 2 en suite, 1 with private bathroom **payment** credit/debit cards, cash, cheques, euros

Room General Leisure

PENRITH, Cumbria Map ref 5B2
SAT NAV CA11 9LE

enjoyEngland.com ★★★★ GUEST ACCOMMODATION

B&B PER ROOM PER NIGHT
S £49.00 – £56.00
D £68.00 – £80.00

Bank House
Graham Street, Penrith CA11 9LE
t (01768) 868714 e info@bankhousepenrith.co.uk
w bankhousepenrith.co.uk ONLINE MAP GUEST REVIEWS ONLINE BOOKING

A beautiful period house with elegant rooms large terraced garden located in a quiet part of Penrith. Breakfast using local quality produce. Private parking and storage for bikes. **directions** Bank House is found 3/4 of the way up Graham street on the right just before the first bend. **open** All year **bedrooms** 2 double, 1 twin, 1 family **bathrooms** 4 en suite **payment** credit/debit cards, cash

Room General

North West | Cumbria

PENRITH, Cumbria Map ref 5B2

SAT NAV CA11 7QN

GUEST HOUSE ★★★★★

B&B PER ROOM PER NIGHT
S £40.00 – £60.00
D £75.00 – £85.00

Brooklands Guest House
2 Portland Place, Penrith, cumbria CA11 7QN
t (01768) 863395 f (01768) 863395 e enquiries@brooklandsguesthouse.com
w brooklandsguesthouse.com ONLINE MAP GUEST REVIEWS

If you're looking for the perfect escape, combining elegant accommodation with a touch of luxury, then Brooklands Guest House is the guest house for you. Situated in the bustling market town of Penrith, Brooklands Guest House is one of the Lake Districts most popular guest houses.

open All year except Xmas and New Year
bedrooms 1 single, 4 double, 1 twin
bathrooms 6 en suite
payment credit/debit cards, cash, cheques
directions M6 jct 40 take the first exit for Penrith. Follow for town centre, turn left at town hall, into Portland Place Brooklands 50m on left.

BREAKFAST AWARD Room General Leisure

PENRITH, Cumbria Map ref 5B2

SAT NAV CA11 0TQ

BED & BREAKFAST ★★★★

B&B PER ROOM PER NIGHT
S £35.00 – £50.00
D £80.00 – £90.00

Stafford House Guest House
Greystoke, Penrith CA11 0TQ
t (01768) 483558 f (01768) 483558 e hazel.knight@btconnect.com
w stafford-house.co.uk ONLINE MAP GUEST REVIEWS ONLINE BOOKING LAST MINUTE OFFERS

An enchanting Grade II Listed Folly within easy reach of the M6 and Lake District. Traditional yet full of charm and character, a warm welcome awaits all of our guests. **directions** Please contact us for directions **open** All year **bedrooms** 2 double, 1 twin **bathrooms** 1 en suite, 2 with private bathroom **payment** credit/debit cards, cash, cheques

Room General Leisure

PENTON, Cumbria Map ref 5A2

SAT NAV CA6 5QP

FARMHOUSE ★★★★

B&B PER ROOM PER NIGHT
S £45.00 – £50.00
D £70.00 – £80.00
EVENING MEAL PER PERSON
£11.00 – £23.00

Craigburn Farmhouse
Penton, Longtown CA6 5QP
t (01228) 577214 f (01228) 577014 e louiselawson@hotmail.com
w criagburnfarmhouse.com

Family run farmhouse in quite rural setting, homemade food using local produce, licensed, ideal stop over or for a longer break. **directions** M6 junction 44 A7 to Longtown turn right at Bush Hotel - 6 miles turn right Bridge Inn - 2 miles Catlowdy turn right at sign. **open** All year except Xmas and New Year **bedrooms** 4 double, 2 twin **bathrooms** 6 en suite **payment** credit/debit cards, cash, cheques

Room General Leisure

North West | Cumbria

POOLEY BRIDGE, Cumbria Map ref 5A3
SAT NAV CA10 2NH

Elm House
High Street, Pooley Bridge, Ullswater CA10 2NH
t (01768) 486334 e enquiries@stayullswater.co.uk
w stayullswater.co.uk ONLINE MAP GUEST REVIEWS ONLINE BOOKING LAST MINUTE OFFERS

GUEST HOUSE ★★★★

B&B PER ROOM PER NIGHT
S £50.00 – £70.00
D £70.00 – £100.00

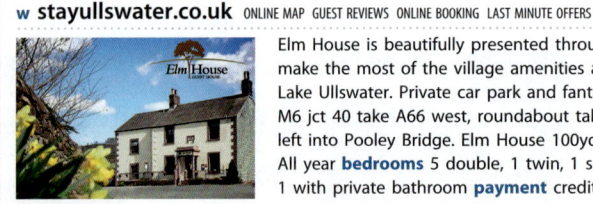

Elm House is beautifully presented throughout, perfectly located to make the most of the village amenities and just a short stroll from Lake Ullswater. Private car park and fantastic breakfasts. **directions** M6 jct 40 take A66 west, roundabout take A592 Ullswater, 4 miles left into Pooley Bridge. Elm House 100yds after The Sun Inn. **open** All year **bedrooms** 5 double, 1 twin, 1 suite **bathrooms** 6 en suite, 1 with private bathroom **payment** credit/debit cards, cash, cheque

Room General Leisure

RYDAL, Cumbria Map ref 5A3
SAT NAV LA22 9LW

Cote How Organic Guest House
Rydal, Ambleside LA22 9LW
t (01539) 432765 e info@cotehow.co.uk
w cotehow.co.uk ONLINE MAP GUEST REVIEWS ONLINE BOOKING LAST MINUTE OFFERS

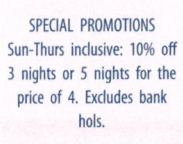

GUEST HOUSE ★★★★ **Gold AWARD**

B&B PER ROOM PER NIGHT
S £88.00 – £150.00
D £108.00 – £160.00

SPECIAL PROMOTIONS
Sun-Thurs inclusive: 10% off 3 nights or 5 nights for the price of 4. Excludes bank hols.

One of only 3 Soil Association licensed Organic guest houses in UK, Cote How is a splendid C16th historic home offering luxury accommodation and quality locally sourced food including Vegetarian/Vegan options. A picturesque rural location between Ambleside & Grasmere, only 300m from Rydal Water and surrounded by stunning natural beauty.

open All year except Xmas
bedrooms 3 family
bathrooms 2 en suite, 1 with private bathroom
payment credit/debit cards, cash

directions A591 north of Ambleside for 1 mile. Turn left over hump back bridge then immediately right. Up lane and first house on RHS.

BREAKFAST AWARD

Room
General
Leisure

SAWREY, Cumbria Map ref 5A3
SAT NAV LA22 0LF

Buckle Yeat Guest House
Nr Sawrey, Hawkshead, Ambleside, Cumbria LA22 0LF
t (01539) 436446 Mob 07703654219 e info@buckle-yeat.co.uk
w buckle-yeat.co.uk

GUEST HOUSE ★★★★ **Silver AWARD**

B&B PER ROOM PER NIGHT
S £40.00 – £45.00
D £80.00 – £90.00

17thC oak-beamed cottage, famous for its connections with Beatrix Potter, provides a warm, friendly and centrally located base, and excellent value for money. **directions** Situated on the western side of Windermere on the road between Hawkshead and the ferry **open** All year **bedrooms** 1 single, 4 double, 2 twin **bathrooms** 6 en suite, 1 with private bathroom **payment** credit/debit cards, cash, cheques

Room General Leisure

604 Official tourist board guide Bed & Breakfast

North West | Cumbria

SEDBERGH, Cumbria Map ref 5B3

SAT NAV LA10 5BA

HOSTEL

BED ONLY PER NIGHT
£15.60 – £26.00

Howgills Bunk Barn

Castlehaw Farm, Castlehaw Lane, Sedbergh, Cumbria LA10 5BA
t (01539) 621990 **e** cobblesedbergh@yahoo.co.uk
w howgillsbunkbarn.co.uk ONLINE MAP GUEST REVIEWS ONLINE BOOKING LAST MINUTE OFFERS

Centrally situated for Sedbergh and travel to Yorkshire Dales and Lakes National Parks. Quality self-catering development in own grounds, nestling at the foot of Howgills Fells. 8 en suite bedrooms sleeping 4-6 each. Superb modern accommodation for groups or families. Once visited, you will want to return like others.

open All year
bathrooms 8 en suite
payment credit/debit cards, cash, cheques, euros

directions M6 J37. To Sedbergh. Through Main Street of Sedbergh to meet Main Road again at Westwoods Books. Drive 400 metres up Castlehaw Lane to left.

Room General Leisure

SHAP, Cumbria Map ref 5B3

SAT NAV CA10 3PW

INN

B&B PER ROOM PER NIGHT
S £45.00 – £50.00
D £70.00 – £100.00

EVENING MEAL PER PERSON
£4.00 – £18.00

SPECIAL PROMOTIONS
3 Nights for the price of two from Nov to March when you quote VisitBritain on booking

Greyhound Hotel

Main Street, Shap, Penrith CA10 3PW
t (01931) 716474 **e** robertfurber@btconnect.com
w greyhoundshap.co.uk ONLINE MAP GUEST REVIEWS

A friendly 17th-century pub close to the M6 and in great walking country included in Wainwright's Coast-to-Coast with 12 well-appointed rooms. Traditional Cumbrian Cuisine to a high standard accompanied by 8 local and national ales. Open fires and a great homely atmosphere.

open All day every day
bedrooms 1 single, 4 double, 6 twin, 1 family
bathrooms 12 en suite, 12 with private bathroom
payment credit/debit cards, cash, cheques, euros

directions Junction 39 off the M6 onto the A6 for one mile into Shap, first pub on the right. On A6 between Kendal and Penrith

Room General Leisure

North West | **Cumbria**

THE GREEN, Cumbria Map ref 5A3   SAT NAV LA18 5JU

FARMHOUSE ★★★★
Silver AWARD

B&B PER ROOM PER NIGHT
S £45.00
D £75.00

rooms @ bank house farm
Broadgate, Hallthwaites, Nr.Broughton-in-Furness, Cumbria LA18 5JU
t (01229) 777193/07795032163 e karen@wforrester.plus.com
w bank-house-farm.co.uk

Two beautiful self contained suites in a converted barn Stunning panoramic scenery. Idyllic and rural in the western Lake district national park. Walks from your door. Masses of extra touches.
directions On the A595 in the western Lake district National Park. High on the cumbrian fell overlooking Duddon Estuary. Stunning panoramic views. Nestled under Black Combe. **open** All year
bedrooms 2 suites **bathrooms** 2 en suite **payment** cash, cheques

Room General Leisure

THRELKELD, Cumbria Map ref 5A3   SAT NAV CA12 4SQ

enjoyEngland.com ★★★ INN

B&B PER ROOM PER NIGHT
S £35.00 – £50.00
D £70.00 – £100.00

EVENING MEAL PER PERSON
£7.50 – £16.50

SPECIAL PROMOTIONS
Dinner Bed & Breakfast Packages From £45.00 exc Weekends. June Offer 4 Nights £220.00 Dinner Bed Breakfast

Horse & Farrier Inn
Threlkeld, Keswick CA12 4SQ
t (01768) 779688 f (01768) 779823 e info@horseandfarrier.com
w horseandfarrier.com ONLINE MAP GUEST REVIEWS ONLINE BOOKING LAST MINUTE OFFERS

This award-winning inn is situated beneath Blencathra and is ideally located for walking or touring the Lake District. All nine bedrooms are en suite with TV, tea-/coffee-making facilities ar hair dryer. Our Head Chef won the Cumbria Tourist Board's Most Inspiring Chef of the Year. Numerous guide book recommendations.

open All year
bedrooms 10 double, 1 twin
bathrooms 9 en suite, 9 with private bathroom
payment credit/debit cards, cash, cheques

directions From the Motorway leave at Junctio Penrith and take the A66 for Keswick and Mort Lakes. We are located four miles before Keswick

Room
General
Leisure

Looking for something else?

You can also buy a copy of our popular guide 'Self Catering' including self-catering holiday homes, approved caravan holiday homes, boat accommodation and holiday cottage agencies in England 2011.

Now available in good bookshops and online at
visitbritainshop.com

£11.99

North West | Cumbria

TROUTBECK, Cumbria Map ref 5A2

SAT NAV CA11 0SJ

The Troutbeck Inn
Troutbeck, Penrith CA11 0SJ
t (01768) 483635 f (01768) 483639 e info@thetroutbeckinn.co.uk
w thetroutbeckinn.co.uk ONLINE BOOKING

enjoyEngland.com ★★★★ INN

B&B PER ROOM PER NIGHT
S £40.00 – £50.00
D £50.00 – £80.00

EVENING MEAL PER PERSON
£14.00 – £32.50

SPECIAL PROMOTIONS
Winter offers are promoted on our website.

A welcoming country inn recently refurbished & with open fire, bar, lounge & restaurant offering quality food, select wines & real ales. Dogs are welcome to stay in all of our bedrooms & our three self catering cottages. Located close to Penrith, Keswick and Ullswater.

open All year
bedrooms 1 single, 4 double, 1 twin, 1 family
bathrooms 7 en suite
payment credit/debit cards, cash, cheques

directions From J40 on M6 travel west towards Keswick. After 8 miles exit onto the A5091 to Ullswater. Troutbeck Inn is on the left.

Room
General
Leisure

ULLSWATER, Cumbria Map ref 5A3

SAT NAV CA11 0JN

Knotts Mill Country Lodge
Watermillock, Ullswater CA11 0JN
t (01768) 486699 f (01768) 486699 e relax@knottsmill.com
w knottsmill.com ONLINE MAP ONLINE BOOKING

enjoyEngland.com ★★★ GUEST HOUSE

B&B PER ROOM PER NIGHT
S £45.00 – £80.00
D £72.00 – £80.00

SPECIAL PROMOTIONS
2 Nights minimum stay at weekends during school holidays

A country lodge offering quality, serviced accommodation and big breakfasts. In private grounds, set in magnificent scenery around Ullswater with stunning views of the surrounding hills. Ideal for walking, touring, bird-watching and sailing. Relaxed, welcoming atmosphere in a peaceful setting, yet only ten minutes from the M6. Pets by arrangement.

open All year except Xmas
bedrooms 4 double, 2 twin, 3 family
bathrooms 9 en suite
payment credit/debit cards, cash, cheques, euros

directions Please contact us for directions

Room
General
Leisure

key to symbols see page 6

North West | Cumbria

WHITEHAVEN, Cumbria Map ref 5A3
SAT NAV CA28 6PJ

Moresby Hall
Moresby, Whitehaven, Cumbria CA28 6PJ
t (01946) 696317 f (01946) 694385 e info@moresbyhall.co.uk
w moresbyhall.co.uk GUEST REVIEWS ONLINE BOOKING LAST MINUTE OFFERS

B&B PER ROOM PER NIGHT
S £90.00 – £105.00
D £110.00 – £150.00

EVENING MEAL PER PERSON
£22.50 – £29.50

SPECIAL PROMOTIONS
Book 2 nights for complimentary champagne on arrival (value 29.00). Book 3 nights for complimentary dinner one night (value 59.00).

Grade I Listed building (circa 1620) - one of the most historic residences in Cumbria. Six stunning rooms, including four-poster rooms with hydromassage power shower, sauna or jacuzzi bath & TileVision colour TV. Delicious breakfasts and imaginative dinners. Semi-rural location, walled gardens, good parking. Near Whitehaven, a Georgian harbour town.

open All year
bedrooms 1 double, 1 twin, 4 suites
bathrooms 6 en suite
payment credit/debit cards, cash, cheques, euros
directions M6 jct 40 onto A66. Then A595 Whitehaven along new by-pass. Take next right signed for Lowca/Parton. Moresby Hall is 50yds on right.

WINDERMERE, Cumbria Map ref 5A3
SAT NAV LA23 2AF

Beaumont House
Holly Road, Windermere LA23 2AF
t (01539) 447075 f (01539) 488311 e enquiries@lakesbeaumont.co.uk
w lakesbeaumont.co.uk ONLINE BOOKING LAST MINUTE OFFERS

B&B PER ROOM PER NIGHT
D £80.00 – £150.00

Beaumont House, an elegant Victorian property occupying an enviable position close to all amenities of Windermere/Bowness, providing superb quality bed and breakfast. Ideal base from which to tour Lakeland. **directions** Head for Windermere town centre, pass through one-way traffic system and then take 2nd left into Ellerthwaite Road. Holly Road is the 1st left turn. **open** All year except Xmas **bedrooms** 9 double, 1 twin **bathrooms** 10 en suite **payment** credit/debit cards, cash, euros

WINDERMERE, Cumbria Map ref 5A3
SAT NAV LA23 3JY

Bowfell Cottage
Middle Entrance Drive, Storrs Park, Bowness-on-Windermere LA23 3JY
t (01539) 444835 e annetomlinson45@btinternet.com

B&B PER ROOM PER NIGHT
S £30.00 – £33.00
D £50.00 – £60.00

EVENING MEAL PER PERSON
£14.50

Cottage in a delightful setting, about 1ml south of Bowness off A5074, offering traditional Lakeland hospitality with comfortable accommodation and good home-cooking. Secluded parking in own grounds surrounding the property. **directions** Please contact us for directions **open** All year **bedrooms** 1 double, 1 twin, 1 family **bathrooms** 1 en suite **payment** cash, cheques

608 Official tourist board guide Bed & Breakfast

North West | **Cumbria**

WINDERMERE, Cumbria Map ref 5A3
SAT NAV LA23 2AH

Brook House
30 Ellerthwaite Road, Windermere LA23 2AH
t (01539) 444932 e stay@brookhouselakes.co.uk
w brookhouselakes.co.uk

B&B PER ROOM PER NIGHT
S £30.00
D £54.00

Lakeland stone Victorian Guest house with 5 en-suite bedrooms offering Bed and freshly cooked Breakfast. Located in a quiet part of Windermere with private car park. Close to all amenities. **directions** Brook House is located on Ellerthwaite Road just 10 minutes walk from Windermere Rail and Bus station. **open** All year except Xmas **bedrooms** 1 single, 3 double, 1 family **bathrooms** 5 en suite **payment** cash, cheques, euros

Room General Leisure

WINDERMERE, Cumbria Map ref 5A3
SAT NAV LA23 2JP

Elim Lodge
Biskey Howe Road, Bowness-on-Windermere, Windermere LA23 2JP
t (01539) 447299 e enquiries@elimlodge.co.uk
w elimlodge.co.uk ONLINE BOOKING LAST MINUTE OFFERS

B&B PER ROOM PER NIGHT
S £25.00 – £35.00
D £48.00 – £80.00

Family-run B&B five minutes' walk from Lake Windermere. Clean, smart accommodation with private parking and garden in quiet, pretty part of Bowness village. Superb breakfasts, local ingredients, Fairtrade tea/coffee. Gay-friendly. **directions** M6 jct 36. A590/591 to Windermere. Down hill to Bowness, 2nd road left after police station. **open** All year except Xmas **bedrooms** 2 double, 1 twin, 2 family **bathrooms** 3 en suite, 2 with private bathroom **payment** credit/debit cards, cash, cheques

BREAKFAST AWARD

Room General Leisure

WINDERMERE, Cumbria Map ref 5A3
SAT NAV LA23 3AE

Fairfield House & Gardens
Brantfell Road, Bowness Bay, Windermere LA23 3AE
t (01539) 446565 f (01539) 446565 e relax@the-fairfield.co.uk
w the-fairfield.co.uk ONLINE MAP GUEST REVIEWS ONLINE BOOKING LAST MINUTE OFFERS

B&B PER ROOM PER NIGHT
S £55.00 – £60.00
D £78.00 – £170.00

SPECIAL PROMOTIONS
Reduced prices for 3 nights or more weekdays. (Single occupancy Sunday to Thursdays only). For weekly promotions see website.

Secluded Georgian house in own grounds with beautiful garden and private car park. Informally run B&B with exceptional breakfasts. King-size, four-poster and spa-bath rooms available. All rooms en suite. Guest lounge, licensed with internet and Wi-Fi access. Located central Bowness - Nr to Lake Windermere, restaurants, shops and pubs.

open All year except Xmas
bedrooms 5 double, 1 twin, 1 family, 3 suites
bathrooms 10 en suite
payment credit/debit cards, cash, cheques, euros

directions M6 jct 36. Follow signs Kendal, Windermere. Through Windermere town to Bowness. 1st left after roundabout and left in front of Spinnery restaurant.

Room
General
Leisure

key to symbols see page 6

609

North West | Cumbria

WINDERMERE, Cumbria Map ref 5A3   SAT NAV LA23 3JB

B&B PER ROOM PER NIGHT
S £40.00 – £55.00
D £64.00 – £88.00

Fair Rigg
Ferry View, Bowness-on-Windermere, Windermere LA23 3JB
t (01539) 443941 e stay@fairrigg.co.uk
w fairrigg.co.uk

Fine Victorian house with superb views, in rural setting on edge of Bowness. Lovely rooms, plenty of space to relax and unwind. High standards assured. **directions** M6 jct 36, A590/591 Windermere, Kendal/South Lakes. At roundabout north of Kendal left B5284, Hawkshead via the ferry. 10 minutes T-junction, Fair Rigg on left. **open** All year except Xmas **bedrooms** 5 double, 1 twin **bathrooms** 6 en suite **payment** credit/debit cards, cash, cheques

Room | General | Leisure

WINDERMERE, Cumbria Map ref 5A3   SAT NAV LA23 2EQ

B&B PER ROOM PER NIGHT
S £45.00 – £60.00
D £68.00 – £96.00

Fir Trees
Lake Road, Windermere LA23 2EQ
t (01539) 442272 f (01539) 442512 e enquiries@fir-trees.co.uk
w fir-trees.co.uk ONLINE MAP GUEST REVIEWS ONLINE BOOKING LAST MINUTE OFFERS

Beautiful Victorian house, full of character. All rooms comfortable & spotlessly clean. Breakfasts cooked to order using all local produce. Off road parking. Close to all amenities. **directions** Mid way between Bowness & Windermere. A 10 min, walk to both villages. Railway Station is a 10 min, walk. **open** All year **bedrooms** 5 double, 2 twin, 2 family **bathrooms** 9 en suite **payment** credit/debit cards, cash, cheques

Room | General | Leisure

WINDERMERE, Cumbria Map ref 5A3   SAT NAV LA23 1EG

B&B PER ROOM PER NIGHT
D £60.00 – £80.00

Heatherbank
13 Birch Street, Windermere LA23 1EG
t (015394) 46503 f (015394) 46503 e heatherbank@btinternet.com
w heatherbank.com

Heatherbank is a quiet and comfortable guest house. It is within 5 minutes walk of the station. All rooms have en suite facilities, TV and tea and coffee making facilities. **directions** Off at J36 (M6) take A590 then A591. Turn left on Windermere Town Centre, about 2 minutes turn left at post office. **open** All year **bedrooms** 2 double, 1 twin, 2 family **bathrooms** 5 en suite **payment** cash, cheques

Room | General

WINDERMERE, Cumbria Map ref 5A3   SAT NAV LA23 1BX

B&B PER ROOM PER NIGHT
S £35.00 – £40.00
D £60.00 – £80.00

Holly Lodge
6 College Road, Windermere LA23 1BX
t (01539) 443873 f (01539) 443873 e enquiries@hollylodge20.co.uk
w hollylodge20.co.uk LAST MINUTE OFFERS

Traditional Lakeland, family-run guest house in a quiet location close to shops, restaurants, buses and trains. Friendly atmosphere, hearty English breakfast and each bedroom individually furnished. **directions** M6 junction 36 (Kendal) A592, becomes A591 Windermere. Ignore first left by train station, next left Elleray Road for 50-60m, first right into College Road. **open** All year except Xmas **bedrooms** 1 single, 4 double, 4 family **bathrooms** 9 en suite **payment** credit/debit cards, cash, cheques

Room | General | Leisure

North West | **Cumbria**

WINDERMERE, Cumbria Map ref 5A3

SAT NAV LA23 3AX

Langdale View Guest House

114 Craig Walk, off Helm Road, Bowness-on-Windermere, Cumbria LA23 3AX
t 01539 444076 e enquiries@langdaleview.co.uk
w langdaleview.co.uk ONLINE MAP GUEST REVIEWS ONLINE BOOKING

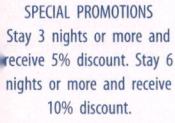

B&B PER ROOM PER NIGHT
S £38.00 – £57.00
D £76.00 – £84.00

SPECIAL PROMOTIONS
Stay 3 nights or more and receive 5% discount. Stay 6 nights or more and receive 10% discount.

Langdale View Guest House has a private car park, garden and is only a few minutes walk from the town centre and shores of Lake Windermere. Our en-suite rooms have everything to make your stay as comfortable as possible and our extensive breakfast menu will cater for all diets.

open All year except Xmas
bedrooms 4 double, 1 twin
bathrooms 5 en suite
payment credit/debit cards, cash

directions From Windermere drive south on the A5074 towards the Lake. Turn opposite the Co-op onto Helm Road then left into Craig Walk.

Room 📺 ☕ General 🛏10 ♿ P 🍴 ♨ Leisure ▶ 🚴 🎣

WINDERMERE, Cumbria Map ref 5A3

SAT NAV LA23 2EN

Lindisfarne Guest House

Sunny Bank Road, Windermere LA23 2EN
t (01539) 446295 e enquiries@lindisfarne-house.co.uk
w lindisfarne-house.co.uk

B&B PER ROOM PER NIGHT
D £50.00 – £90.00

Detached Lakeland-stone house built in 1881. Quiet area within easy walk of Windermere centre, shops, restaurants, pubs, scenic walks, Bowness and Lake Windermere. Home-cooked English breakfasts. Non-smoking. Garage for bicycles/motorbikes. **directions** M6 jct 33, A591 into Windermere. Take directions from the Tourist Info Centre near the station or ring when close to Windermere.
open All year **bedrooms** 2 double, 1 twin, 1 family **bathrooms** 3 en suite, 1 with private bathroom **payment** cash, cheques

Room 📺 ☕ General 🛏5 P 🍴 ♨ Leisure 🚴

WINDERMERE, Cumbria Map ref 5A3

SAT NAV LA23 3EZ

Lingwood Lodge

Birkett Hill, Bowness-on-Windermere, Windermere LA23 3EZ
t (01539) 444680 f (01539) 448154 e stay@lingwoodlodge.co.uk
w lingwoodlodge.co.uk ONLINE MAP GUEST REVIEWS ONLINE BOOKING

B&B PER ROOM PER NIGHT
S £55.00 – £60.00
D £78.00 – £90.00

A contemporary guest house set in own grounds in a peaceful location yet only 400m from the steamer piers on Lake Windermere and shops, restaurants and attractions of Bowness. Parking.
directions In Bowness follow signs to Steamers piers & pass on right. Stay on A592 for 400m. Lingwood Lodge on left hand side after Burnside Hotel. **open** All year except Xmas **bedrooms** 4 double, 2 family **bathrooms** 6 en suite **payment** credit/debit cards, cash, cheques

Room 📺 ☕ General 🛏 ♿ P 🍴 ♨ Leisure 🚴

For key to symbols see page 6

North West | Cumbria

WINDERMERE, Cumbria Map ref 5A3   SAT NAV LA23 3DJ

New Hall Bank

Fallbarrow Road, Bowness-on-Windermere, Windermere LA23 3DJ
t (01539) 443558 f (01539) 443558 e info@newhallbank.co.uk
w newhallbank.co.uk LAST MINUTE OFFERS

B&B PER ROOM PER NIGHT
D £70.00 – £90.00

SPECIAL PROMOTIONS
Seasonal specials - please see our website for details. Discounts on stays of 3 nights or longer.

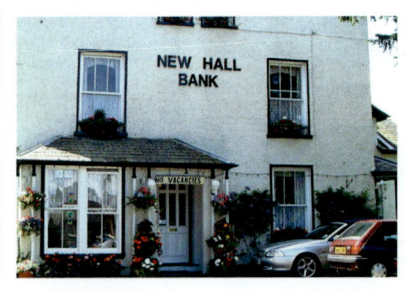

Wonderful Victorian guest house standing in o of the most envied positions in Bowness overlooking the lake! Comfortable en suite rooms, many with lake views, contain all you require for a relaxing stay in the heart of the Lake District. English or vegetarian breakfasts provided, on-site car parking, personal attentio

open All year
bedrooms 9 double, 1 twin, 2 family
bathrooms 10 en suite, 2 with private bathroo
payment credit/debit cards, cash, cheques

directions Leave M6 at jct 36, follow signs to Windermere. Left into Windermere onto mini roundabout, turn right, Rayrigg Road, 200yds sharp left, straight on 200yds

Room / General / Leisure

WINDERMERE, Cumbria Map ref 5A3   SAT NAV LA23 2JG

Oakfold House

Beresford Road, Bowness LA23 2JG
t (01539) 443239 e oakfoldhouse@fsmail.net
w oakfoldhouse.co.uk ONLINE MAP GUEST REVIEWS ONLINE BOOKING LAST MINUTE OFFERS

B&B PER ROOM PER NIGHT
S £25.00 – £45.00
D £30.00 – £48.00

Victorian Guest House, totally refurbished, with prestigious VisitBritain Gold Award for excellence. Individually designed bedrooms. Close to Lake, shops and restaurants. Beautiful garden, Private car park. Free Wi Fi. **directions** Quietly located on the edg of Bowness village yet convenient for shops restaurants, lake cruis and local transport. One mile from Windermere rail station. **open** All year **bedrooms** 1 single, 4 double, 1 twin, 2 family **bathrooms** 8 en suite **payment** credit/debit cards, cash, cheques, euros

Room / General / Leisure

WINDERMERE, Cumbria Map ref 5A3   SAT NAV LA23 2EQ

St John's Lodge

Lake Road, Windermere LA23 2EQ
t (01539) 443078 f (01539) 488054 e mail@st-johns-lodge.co.uk
w st-johns-lodge.co.uk ONLINE MAP GUEST REVIEWS ONLINE BOOKING LAST MINUTE OFFERS

B&B PER ROOM PER NIGHT
S £35.00 – £50.00
D £55.00 – £110.00

BREAKFAST AWARD

Ideal location between Windermere and Lake and close to all amenities. Serving award winning breakfasts including traditional English, veggie/vegan and gluten-free. Free Wi-Fi and use of near leisure club. **directions** A591 to Windermere Village, follow signs Bowness and lake. Leave Windermere on New Road which becom Lake Road. Destination 100m after Catholic Church on left. **open** A year except Xmas **bedrooms** 1 single, 9 double, 1 twin, 1 family **bathrooms** 12 en suite **payment** credit/debit cards, cash, euros

Room / General / Leisure

612   Official tourist board guide Bed & Breakfa

North West | Cumbria

WINDERMERE, Cumbria Map ref 5A3
SAT NAV LA23 1BN

enjoyEngland.com ★★★★ BED & BREAKFAST

Stockghyll Cottage
Rayrigg Road, Bowness-on-Windermere, Bowness LA23 1BN
t (015394) 43246   e stay@stockghyllcottage.co.uk
w stockghyllcottage.co.uk   ONLINE MAP GUEST REVIEWS ONLINE BOOKING

B&B PER ROOM PER NIGHT
S £50.00 – £70.00
D £60.00 – £80.00

Lovely Lakeland stone cottage & gardens surrounded by woodland, with its own waterfall & stream. Situated within a 5 min walk of Bowness village & Lakeside attractions. **directions** Travelling North M6 Junction 36 follow signs to Windermere. Travelling South Juntion 40 follow signs to Windermere. We are located opposite the Steam Boat Museum. **open** All year **bedrooms** 2 double, 1 twin **bathrooms** 3 en suite **payment** credit/debit cards, cash, cheques, euros

Room   General   Leisure

WINSTER, Cumbria Map ref 5A3
SAT NAV LA23 3NR

enjoyEngland.com ★★★★ GUEST ACCOMMODATION

The Brown Horse Inn
Winster, Bowness-on-Windermere, Windermere LA23 3NR
t (01539) 443443   f n/a   e steve@thebrownhorseinn.co.uk
w thebrownhorseinn.co.uk   ONLINE MAP LAST MINUTE OFFERS

B&B PER ROOM PER NIGHT
S £55.00 – £65.00
D £75.00 – £100.00

EVENING MEAL PER PERSON
£11.00 – £25.00

SPECIAL PROMOTIONS
midweek specials sun - thursday 2 night minimum. £60.00 pp pernight dinner B+B. 3 night break £170.00 dinner B+B pp

The Brown Horse is set admist the splender of the winster valley. serving traditional home grown & reared food. Serving traditional ales from our very own brewery. Children are welcome and we have a menu to suit there developing taste buds. We also have 9 newly refurbished bed rooms.

open All year except Xmas
bedrooms 8 double, 1 family
bathrooms 9 en suite, 9 with private bathroom
payment credit/debit cards, cash, cheques

directions We are situated 1 1/2 miles from Bowness-on-Windermere on the A5074 heading south.

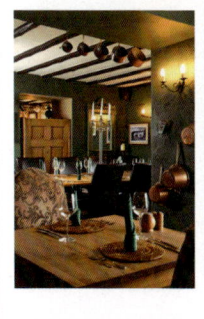

Room
General
Leisure

WORKINGTON, Cumbria Map ref 5A2
SAT NAV CA14 1TS

enjoyEngland.com ★★★★ INN

Old Ginn House Inn
Moor Road, Great Clifton, Workington CA14 1TS
t (01900) 64616   f (01900) 873484   e enquiries@oldginnhouse.co.uk
w oldginnhouse.co.uk   LAST MINUTE OFFERS

B&B PER ROOM PER NIGHT
S £60.00 – £70.00
D £75.00 – £110.00

Old Ginn House has been converted from a 17thC farm into a charming village inn, quality accommodation, great food and a warm welcome. Ideal for exploring the Western Lake District. **directions** Situated in Great Clifton, just off the A66, 5 miles west of Cockermouth 2 miles east of Workington **open** All year except Xmas and New Year **bedrooms** 11 double, 3 twin, 4 family, 1 suite **bathrooms** 19 en suite **payment** credit/debit cards, cash, cheques

Room   General   Leisure

for key to symbols see page 6   613

North West | **Lancashire**

ABBEYSTEAD, Lancashire Map ref 4A1   SAT NAV LA2 9BA

Greenbank Farmhouse
Abbeystead, Lancaster LA2 9BA
t (01524) 792063 e sally@greenbankfarmhouse.co.uk
w greenbankfarmhouse.co.uk LAST MINUTE OFFERS

B&B PER ROOM PER NIGHT
S £30.00
D £55.00

Set in peaceful countryside with a panoramic view of the fells yet still handy for J33 of M6 and Lancaster's University and City, Lakes & dales. Ample parking space. **directions** Leave M6 at J33. Follow the signs for Abbeystead On the R.H.S. about half a mile outside Dolphinholme. **open** All year **bedrooms** 3 double **bathrooms** 3 e suite **payment** cash, cheques

Room General Leisure

BLACKPOOL, Lancashire Map ref 4A1   SAT NAV FY1 4PR

The Allendale
104 Albert Road, Blackpool FY1 4PR
t (01253) 623268 f (01253) 317533 e the-allendale@btconnect.com
w allendalehotelblackpool.co.uk

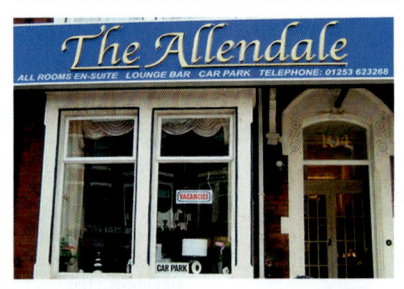

B&B PER ROOM PER NIGHT
S £20.00 – £30.00
D £40.00 – £60.00

EVENING MEAL PER PERSON
£8.00

SPECIAL PROMOTIONS
monday to friday special rates B+B £62-£80PP
monday to friday special rates BBev £85-£108PP

We are situated in the heart of Blackpool, very close to the Winter Gardens and the famous Blackpool Tower. The Allendale offers guests th very best in a family run guest accommodatior where your comfort and pleasure is our prime concern.

open All year except Xmas and New Year
bedrooms 9 double, 3 twin, 3 family
bathrooms 15 en suite
payment credit/debit cards, cash, cheques

directions Exit M55, Yeadon Way towards Blackpool central through car parks,Central Dri stay right lane then in the left hand lane after you pass McDonalds,then staight.

Room General

BLACKPOOL, Lancashire Map ref 4A1   SAT NAV FY1 4QJ

Argyll
53 Hornby Road, Blackpool FY1 4QJ
t (01253) 624677 e info@argyllhotelblackpool.co.uk
w argyllhotelblackpool.co.uk/ GUEST REVIEWS LAST MINUTE OFFERS

B&B PER ROOM PER NIGHT
S £23.00 – £25.00
D £46.00 – £50.00
EVENING MEAL PER PERSON
£7.50

Quality home cooked meals. Clean, comfortable ensuite rooms. Relaxing and quiet atmosphere (no bar. Excellent location for shops, Tower and theatres. Call us for free brochure and special offers. **directions** From promenade opposite central pier turn inland(chapel st). Go to end & at traffic lights turn left, 2nd right is Hornby road. **open** All year **bedrooms** 3 single, 2 double, 1 twin, family **bathrooms** 7 en suite **payment** cash, cheques

Room General Leisure

614   Official tourist board guide Bed & Breakfa

North West | Lancashire

BLACKPOOL, Lancashire Map ref 4A1
SAT NAV FY1 4PR

Arabella
102 Albert Road, Blackpool FY1 4PR
t (01253) 623189   e graham.waters3@virgin.net
w thearabella.co.uk   ONLINE MAP   LAST MINUTE OFFERS

B&B PER ROOM PER NIGHT
S £23.00 – £30.00
D £46.00 – £60.00

EVENING MEAL PER PERSON
£8.00

SPECIAL PROMOTIONS
Mon-Fri B&B two sharing £126-£142. Mon-Fri BB&EM two sharing £174-£180. Bank holidays and Illuminations do not apply.

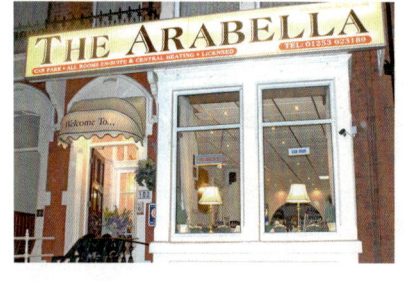

We provide clean and comfortable accommodation within a family friendly atmosphere. Home cooking, dietary needs catered for, rooms are serviced daily, walking distances 5 minutes from the winter gardens, 10 minutes from the Tower and sea front. WE DO NOT TAKE STAG OR HEN PARTIES.

open All year
bedrooms 1 single, 2 double, 2 twin, 9 family
bathrooms 14 en suite, 1 with private bathroom
payment credit/debit cards, cash, cheques

directions Contact our website for google map directions

BLACKPOOL, Lancashire Map ref 4A1
SAT NAV FY1 4JG

Ash Lodge
131 Hornby Road, Blackpool FY1 4JG
t (01253) 627637   e admin@ashlodgehotel.co.uk
w ashlodgehotel.co.uk   ONLINE MAP   ONLINE BOOKING

B&B PER ROOM PER NIGHT
S £25.00 – £27.00
D £50.00 – £68.00

Ash Lodge central Blackpool is situated in quiet residential area. It is a late Victorian house with many original features but with modern facilities, onsite car park and residential licence. **directions** M55 jct4. Take 3rd left onto A583. Travel approx 3 miles. At 10th set of lights turn right onto Hornby Road. Hotel on right. **open** All year except Xmas **bedrooms** 3 single, 1 double, 2 twin, 2 family **bathrooms** 7 en suite, 1 with private bathroom **payment** credit/debit cards, cash, cheques

BLACKPOOL, Lancashire Map ref 4A1
SAT NAV FY1 4PN

Astoria
118-120 Albert Road, Blackpool FY1 4PN
t (01253) 621321   e enquiries@astoria-hotel.co.uk
w astoria-hotel.co.uk

B&B PER ROOM PER NIGHT
S £23.00 – £30.00
D £23.00 – £30.00

A warm welcome awaits you from our family run hotel, all 27 bedrooms are ensuite, we have four poster bedrooms available for that special weekend. **directions** Close to winter gardens, tower Debenhams shopping centre, all amenities and promenade. **bedrooms** 4 single, 10 double, 6 twin, 7 family **bathrooms** 26 en suite **payment** euros

615

North West | Lancashire

BLACKPOOL, Lancashire Map ref 4A1   SAT NAV FY1 5DL

Blenheim Mount Hotel

207 Promenade, Blackpool FY1 5DL
t (01253) 625867 f (01253) 297511 e bmhotel@hotmail.com
w blenheimmounthotel.com ONLINE MAP GUEST REVIEWS ONLINE BOOKING LAST MINUTE OFFERS

B&B PER ROOM PER NIGHT
S £25.00 – £35.00
D £50.00 – £70.00

EVENING MEAL PER PERSON
£7.00 – £9.00

SPECIAL PROMOTIONS
Special Midweeks (selected dates), OAP discounted prices, Single parent discount prices, Tinsel & Turkey, out of season group bookings.

Central seafront location overlooking the Irish Sea, where you can sit on our front patio with drink from our fully stocked bar taking in our magnificent view/sunsets. We are a friendly family owned hotel with an easy going atmosphere, perfect for your family holidays so come and join us!

open All year
bedrooms 3 single, 14 double, 3 twin, 10 famil
bathrooms 30 en suite
payment credit/debit cards, cash, cheques

directions Follow Yeadon Way, straight across both roundabouts, 2nd left at 3rd roundabout, take left then turn right at lights onto seafront, hotel on right hand side.

BLACKPOOL, Lancashire Map ref 4A1   SAT NAV FY1 4QG

Cameo

30 Hornby Road, Blackpool FY1 4QG
t (01253) 626144 f (01253) 296048 e enquiries@blackpool-cameo.com
w blackpool-cameo.com ONLINE MAP GUEST REVIEWS ONLINE BOOKING LAST MINUTE OFFERS

B&B PER ROOM PER NIGHT
S £22.00 – £25.00
D £44.00 – £50.00

EVENING MEAL PER PERSON
£7.00 – £8.00

SPECIAL PROMOTIONS
Reductions for 5 or more nights. 10% loyalty discount. 5% 'Tell a Friend' discount.

The Cameo is a family run guesthouse in the popular central area of Blackpool. An ideal base for families, couples, singles, conference delegates, contractors, special interest groups and small groups of friends. Whatever your reason for visiting Blackpool, we offer a friendly welcome and a comfortable stay.

open All year
bedrooms 3 single, 4 double, 1 twin, 2 family
bathrooms 10 en suite
payment credit/debit cards, cash, cheques, euros

directions Central location, ideal for all major attractions. Less than five minutes walking distance to Tower, Winter Gardens, Houndshill Shopping Centre and Promenade.

North West | Lancashire

BLACKPOOL, Lancashire Map ref 4A1   SAT NAV FY1 6BP

Clovelly
22 Saint Chads Road, Blackpool FY1 6BP
t (01253) 346087   e info@clovellyhotel.com
w clovellyhotel.com   ONLINE MAP GUEST REVIEWS ONLINE BOOKING LAST MINUTE OFFERS

B&B PER ROOM PER NIGHT
S £22.00 – £28.00
D £25.00 – £30.00
EVENING MEAL PER PERSON
£5.00 – £10.00

Licensed 12 bed all en-suite Nr to Blackpool Tower, Pleasure Beach, Casino, airport, train station, Piers and other premier venues. In-house breakfast/dining menu early check in/late checkout option.
directions M55 right hand lane over Yeadon Way 2nd roundabout 2nd exit, stay in Left lane through lights roundabout 3rd exit Lytham Road 7th left StChads **open** All year **bedrooms** 2 single, 7 double, 1 twin, 2 family **bathrooms** 12 en suite **payment** credit/debit cards, cash, cheques, euros

Room   General   Leisure

BLACKPOOL, Lancashire Map ref 4A1   SAT NAV FY1 2DA

The Dragonfly
75 Lord Street, Blackpool FY1 2DA
t (01253) 623204   e queries@dragonflyhotel.com
w dragonflyhotel.com   ONLINE MAP GUEST REVIEWS ONLINE BOOKING LAST MINUTE OFFERS

B&B PER ROOM PER NIGHT
S £25.00 – £45.00
D £55.00 – £99.00
EVENING MEAL PER PERSON
£10.00 – £15.00

The Dragonfly offers 4 star, quality, hotel style accommodation, with a variety of room options available. Located right in the heart of Blackpool only 2 minutes from the beach, close to North Pier, Blackpool Tower and many other attractions.

open All year except Xmas
bedrooms 3 single, 4 double, 1 twin, 1 family
bathrooms 9 en suite
payment credit/debit cards, cash

directions Arrive in Blackpool, follow signs for Railway Station North. Pass Wilkinsons, continue along Dickson Road, turn right Banks Street, turn left into Lord Street.

Room   General   Leisure

BLACKPOOL, Lancashire Map ref 4A1   SAT NAV FY1 6AP

Everglades
14 Barton Avenue, Blackpool FY1 6AP
t (01253) 343093   e info@evergladesblackpool.co.uk
w evergladesblackpool.co.uk

B&B PER ROOM PER NIGHT
S £23.00 – £27.00
D £46.00 – £54.00
EVENING MEAL PER PERSON
£8.00 – £10.00

Adele and Graham welcome you to our family run 3 star guest house. 10 en-suite rooms with TV's DVD's Hairdryers, straighteners and Hospitality trays. Licensed bar and seperate restaraunt.
directions Ideally located, 5 min walk from Central pier towards the pleasure beach. Turn off the promenade into Barton Avenue. 50 yards down on the left. **bedrooms** 1 single, 3 double, 1 twin, 5 family **bathrooms** 10 en suite

Room   General   Leisure

or **key to symbols** see page 6   617

North West | Lancashire

BLACKPOOL, Lancashire Map ref 4A1

SAT NAV FY1 4QB

Fairway

34-36 Hull Road, Blackpool FY1 4QB
t (01253) 623777 f (01253) 297970 e impulsedh@aol.com
w fairwayhotelblackpool.co.uk ONLINE MAP GUEST REVIEWS ONLINE BOOKING

B&B PER ROOM PER NIGHT
S £25.00 – £45.00
D £44.00 – £60.00

EVENING MEAL PER PERSON
£8.00 – £12.00

SPECIAL PROMOTIONS
Great Discounts available by calling us direct on 01253 623777

A very clean and comfortable hotel in the heart of town. Late bar, late keys, pool table, and games. All rooms en-suite with Digital Freeview TV, tea/coffee, phone, iron & ironing board. Free wireless internet access. Free local airport pickup (up to 5 people).

open All year
bedrooms 5 single, 10 double, 10 twin, 10 family
bathrooms 35 en suite, 32 with private bathroom
payment credit/debit cards, cash, cheques, euros

directions FY1 4QB 34

Room
General
Leisure

BLACKPOOL, Lancashire Map ref 4A1

SAT NAV FY2 9TE

Fern Royd

35 Holmfield Road, Blackpool FY2 9TE
t (01253) 351066 e fernroyd@btconnect.com
w thefernroyd.co.uk

B&B PER ROOM PER NIGHT
S £25.00 – £27.00
D £50.00 – £54.00

EVENING MEAL PER PERSON
£9.00

SPECIAL PROMOTIONS
Special offers Mon-Fri all year including Illuminations. weekend breaks £66-£75. per person 3 nights B&B Mon-Fri BB&EM £120.

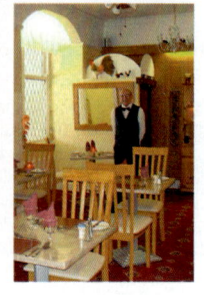

Margaret & Michael offer you a Memorable holiday with 'A Touch of Class'. Spacious en-suit rooms including a ground floor suite. Breakfast cooked to order & Evening Dinner serve daily B.Y.O. drinks, we provide the glasses. The Fern Royd has car parking for eight cars.

bedrooms 2 single, 5 double, 2 twin, 1 family, 1 suite
bathrooms 11 en suite
payment credit/debit cards, cash

directions After Gynn Square on Queens promanade turn 2nd right into King Edward Ave go to the cross roads The Fern Royd is on the left.

Room
General

North West | Lancashire

BLACKPOOL, Lancashire Map ref 4A1   SAT NAV FY1 4PW

enjoyEngland.com
★★★★ GUEST ACCOMMODATION

B&B PER ROOM PER NIGHT
S £25.00 – £31.00
D £25.00 – £31.00

Gleneagles
75 Albert Road, Blackpool FY1 4PW
t (01253) 295266/07818272886 **e** gleneaglesblackpool@tiscali.co.uk
w gleneagles-hotel.com LAST MINUTE OFFERS

Ideally situated close to Tower, Winter Gardens, theatres, promenade and main shopping-centre. All rooms have en-suite facilities, hospitality trays and central-heating. We cater for couples, families and senior citizens only. **directions** M55 follow red central signs onto central car park. Exit onto Central Drive through to Albert Rd through traffic lights we are on the right **open** Summer season through to November and some winter week-ends **bedrooms** 3 single, 9 double, 3 family **bathrooms** 15 en suite **payment** cash, cheques

Room   General

BLACKPOOL, Lancashire Map ref 4A1   SAT NAV FY1 6AP

enjoyEngland.com
★★★★ GUEST HOUSE

B&B PER ROOM PER NIGHT
S £37.00
D £60.00
EVENING MEAL PER PERSON
£10.00

Holmside House
24 Barton Avenue, Blackpool, Lancs FY1 6AP
t (01253) 346045 **e** blackpoolholmsidehouse@talktalk.net
w blackpoolholmsidehouse.co.uk ONLINE MAP ONLINE BOOKING

60 yards from the prom. All the facilities. Within an hour Manchester, Liverpool, the Lakes. Relax in the bar or outside with a brew. **directions** M55, Yeaden Way, Travelodge traffic lodge left. Traffic lights turn right, Nelson Rd left first Right. Holmside on the right. **open** All year except Xmas **bedrooms** 6 double, 1 twin, 3 family **bathrooms** 10 en suite, 10 with private bathroom **payment** cash, cheques

Room   General   Leisure

BLACKPOOL, Lancashire Map ref 4A1   SAT NAV FY1 2HE

enjoyEngland.com
★★★★ GUEST ACCOMMODATION

B&B PER ROOM PER NIGHT
S £20.00 – £55.00
D £25.00 – £120.00
EVENING MEAL PER PERSON
£12.50

SPECIAL PROMOTIONS
Evening meal available on a Friday & Saturday Discounts available for Midweek Breaks We accept groups, rates on request

Homecliffe
5-6 Wilton Parade, Blackpool FY1 2HE
t (01253) 625147 **f** (01253) 292667 **e** enquiry@homecliffehotel.com
w homecliffehotel.com ONLINE MAP GUEST REVIEWS ONLINE BOOKING LAST MINUTE OFFERS

The Award Winning Homecliffe, Blackpool's Best Kept Secret. Refurbished in 2009, we boast some of the most stylish rooms in town. Only a short stroll to the Attractions & Theatres, you can enjoy a fun-packed day before heading back for a relaxing drink & our 4-star Guest Accommodation.

open All year
bedrooms 2 single, 12 double, 5 twin, 1 family, 2 suites
bathrooms 22 en suite
payment credit/debit cards, cash

directions Road: M6/32 - M55/4 Train Station: Blackpool North (Taxi approx. 4 pounds) Airport: Blackpool International Airport (Taxi approx. 10 pounds)

Room
General

619

North West | Lancashire

BLACKPOOL, Lancashire Map ref 4A1
SAT NAV FY1 2LD

B&B PER ROOM PER NIGHT
S £25.00 – £27.00
D £50.00 – £54.00

The Kimberley
25 Gynn Avenue, Blackpool FY1 2LD
t (01253) 352264 e thekimberley@btconnect.com
w kimberleyguesthouse.com ONLINE MAP GUEST REVIEWS ONLINE BOOKING

If you want to stay in Blackpool and relax in a warm and friendly atmosphere we provide quality comfort in peaceful surroundings. Gwyn's cooking is second to none! **directions** Please see our website for full directions. **open** All year except Xmas and New Year **bedrooms** 2 double, 2 twin, 2 family **bathrooms** 4 en suite, 2 with private bathroom **payment** cash, cheques

Room General Leisure

BLACKPOOL, Lancashire Map ref 4A1
SAT NAV FY1 4QB

B&B PER ROOM PER NIGHT
S £20.00 – £25.00
D £36.00 – £50.00
EVENING MEAL PER PERSON
£8.00 – £10.00

Kirkstall House
25 Hull Road, Blackpool FY1 4QB
t (01253) 623077 e rooms@kirkstallhotel.co.uk
w kirkstallhotel.co.uk ONLINE MAP GUEST REVIEWS

Family run hotel in the heart of Blackpool, all rooms en-suite good food and warm welcome are guaranteed. **directions** We are in the town centre 2 minutes walk from the Tower and the Promenade ideally located for all amenities. **open** All year **bedrooms** 1 single, 2 double, 3 twin, 4 family **bathrooms** 10 en suite **payment** credit/debit cards, cash, cheques, euros

Room General

BLACKPOOL, Lancashire Map ref 4A1
SAT NAV FY2 9TA

B&B PER ROOM PER NIGHT
S £75.00 – £95.00
D £95.00 – £125.00

Langtrys
36 King Edward Avenue, North Shore, Blackpool FY2 9TA
t (01253) 352031 e info@langtrysblackpool.co.uk
w langtrysblackpool.co.uk ONLINE MAP GUEST REVIEWS ONLINE BOOKING

Langtrys is a contemporary designed bed and breakfast offering guests a luxurious stay. The spacious bedrooms are elegantly decorated, creating a warm and comfortable atmosphere whilst featuring the latest technology. **directions** Please contact us for directions **open** All year except Xmas **bedrooms** 5 double, 1 twin **bathrooms** 6 en suite **payment** credit/debit cards, cash

Room General

BLACKPOOL, Lancashire Map ref 4A1
SAT NAV FY1 4QD

B&B PER ROOM PER NIGHT
S £25.00 – £40.00
D £50.00 – £70.00
EVENING MEAL PER PERSON
£8.00 – £10.00

Lynbar Guesthouse
32 Vance Road, Blackpool, Lancashire FY1 4QD
t (01253) 294504 f (01253) 294504 e enquiries@lynbarhotel.co.uk
w lynbarhotel.co.uk ONLINE MAP GUEST REVIEWS ONLINE BOOKING LAST MINUTE OFFERS

Clean, friendly and run by resident proprietors Lionel & Sara. Ideally situated in Central Blackpool Nr Blackpool Tower, Winter Gardens, Grand Theatre, Beach, Opera House, Empress Ballroom, The Golden Mile. **directions** From Central Car Park turn left onto Central Drive, take 2nd right into Vance Road. We are on the left hand side. **open** All year **bedrooms** 4 single, 2 double, 1 twin, 2 family **bathrooms** 6 en suite, 1 with private bathroom **payment** credit/debit cards, cash

Room General

North West | Lancashire

BLACKPOOL, Lancashire Map ref 4A1
SAT NAV FY1 6BS

Lyndene Guest House
37 Crystal Road, South Shore, Blackpool FY1 6BS
t (01253) 346662 **mob** 07595919972 **e** geraintgoddard@yahoo.co.uk
w lyndene.org.uk ONLINE MAP LAST MINUTE OFFERS

★★★ GUEST HOUSE

B&B PER ROOM PER NIGHT
S £20.00 – £25.00
D £40.00 – £50.00
EVENING MEAL PER PERSON
£8.00 – £10.00

We would like to welcome you to the Lyndene Guest House Blackpool, where you will receive a warm welcome when you come and stay with us. **directions** M55 follow the signs for Blackpool South Shore, leading you to the Promenade. Heading towards the Tower, turn right beside royal carlton into Crystal Road. **open** All year except Xmas **bedrooms** 3 double, 1 twin, 2 family **bathrooms** 6 en suite **payment** credit/debit cards, cash, cheques

Room General

BLACKPOOL, Lancashire Map ref 4A1
SAT NAV FY2 9SU

Norville House
44 Warbreck Hill Road, Blackpool FY2 9SU
t (01253) 352714 **e** norvillehouse@btconnect.com
w norvillehousehotel.co.uk ONLINE MAP LAST MINUTE OFFERS

★★★ GUEST ACCOMMODATION

B&B PER ROOM PER NIGHT
S £25.00 – £30.00
D £50.00 – £60.00
EVENING MEAL PER PERSON
£10.00

Norville House is a small, recently refurbished Guest-house with the highest standards of cleanliness assured. Evening meal is available Monday to Friday. Special diets catered for with prior notice. **directions** On Blackpool promenade follow signs for North Shore. Take second exit from the Gynn roundabout. Norville House is on the left after the small roundabout. **open** All year except Xmas and New Year **bedrooms** 2 single, 3 double, 3 twin, 1 family **bathrooms** 9 en suite **payment** cash, cheques

Room General Leisure

BLACKPOOL, Lancashire Map ref 4A1
SAT NAV FY1 4QG

Novello
11 Hornby Road, Blackpool FY1 4QG
t (01253) 293474 **f** (01253) 297774 **e** enquiry@novellohotel.co.uk
w novellohotel.co.uk ONLINE MAP GUEST REVIEWS ONLINE BOOKING LAST MINUTE OFFERS

★★★ GUEST ACCOMMODATION

B&B PER ROOM PER NIGHT
S £22.50 – £32.50
D £45.00 – £65.00
EVENING MEAL PER PERSON
£8.50 – £35.00

Blackpool town centre, less than five minutes from most entertainment: Coral Island, Tower, Seafront, Grand Theatre, Wintergardens, Shopping centre. Cleanliness, friendly, good food, welcoming are keywords. **directions** From M55 follow Centre, On Park Road turn into Reads Avenue, at the bottom right, second street right: first hotel on your right. **open** All year **bedrooms** 6 single, 3 double, 6 twin **bathrooms** 15 en suite **payment** credit/debit cards, cash, cheques, euros

Room General Leisure

BLACKPOOL, Lancashire Map ref 4A1
SAT NAV FY4 1BP

The Old Coach House
50 Dean Street, Blackpool FY4 1BP
t (01253) 347657 **f** 0871 522 7917 **e** info@theoldcoachhouse.co.uk
w theoldcoachhouse.co.uk ONLINE MAP GUEST REVIEWS ONLINE BOOKING LAST MINUTE OFFERS

★★★★ GUEST ACCOMMODATION

B&B PER ROOM PER NIGHT
D £77.00 – £97.00

The Old Coach House is a Tudor style boutique establishment with an illustrious history dating back to its contruction in 1851. A warm welcome is bestowed upon everyone who visits! **directions** The Old Coach House is located within the south shore area of Blackpool, close to the promenade and south pier. **open** All year except Xmas **bedrooms** 9 double, 2 twin **bathrooms** 11 en suite, 4 with private bathroom **payment** credit/debit cards, cash

Room General Leisure

For **key to symbols** see page 6

621

North West | **Lancashire**

BLACKPOOL, Lancashire Map ref 4A1 — SAT NAV FY4 2EL

Number One St Luke's

1 St Lukes Road, Blackpool FY4 2EL
t (01253) 343901 f (01253) 343901 e info@numberoneblackpool.com
w numberoneblackpool.com ONLINE MAP GUEST REVIEWS LAST MINUTE OFFERS

B&B PER ROOM PER NIGHT
S £70.00 – £100.00
D £100.00 – £140.00

SPECIAL PROMOTIONS
Discounts for stays of two nights or more!

Car park, gardens, putting green. Stylishly appointed rooms each with king-size bed, 42-inch plasma TV, Freeview, DVD, CD, PlayStation2 Wi-Fi, remote lighting, full bathroom en suite with Whirlpool bath, SplashTV, power shower and music system. Number One is the ultimate boutique B&B experience! VisitBritain's B&B of the Year 2007/2008.

open All year
bedrooms 3 double
bathrooms 3 en suite
payment credit/debit cards, cash, cheques

directions M6, M55. At roundabout go left following signs to Airport. At Airport lights, right to next lights, continue straight, St Luke's is third right.

BREAKFAST AWARD

Room
General
Leisure

BLACKPOOL, Lancashire Map ref 4A1 — SAT NAV FY1 4QJ

The Raffles Guest Accommodation

73-77 Hornby Road, Blackpool FY1 4QJ
t (01253) 294713 f (01253) 294240 e enquiries@raffleshotelblackpool.fsworld.co.uk
w raffleshotelblackpool.co.uk GUEST REVIEWS ONLINE BOOKING

B&B PER ROOM PER NIGHT
S £34.00 – £39.00
D £68.00 – £78.00

EVENING MEAL PER PERSON
£8.95 – £12.95

SPECIAL PROMOTIONS
3 nights for the price of 2, Mon-Fri (excl Bank Holidays), Jan-Aug.

Excellent central location for promenade, shopping centre, Winter Gardens, theatres. All rooms en suite. Licensed bar, English tea rooms, parking and daily housekeeping. Imaginative choice of menus. Listed in the Good Hotel Guide and the Which? Guide to Good Hotels. Four new luxury apartments each sleeping up to four people.

open All year
bedrooms 2 single, 12 double, 3 twin, 1 family, 4 suites
bathrooms 22 en suite, 22 with private bathroom
payment credit/debit cards, cash, cheques

directions Follow signs for central car park. Exit onto Central Drive, left then right onto Hornby Road. Through 1st set of lights, on the right.

Room
General

622 Official tourist board guide Bed & Breakfast

North West | Lancashire

BLACKPOOL, Lancashire Map ref 4A1   SAT NAV FY1 4QJ

★★★★ GUEST HOUSE

Rencliffe
66 Hornby Road, Blackpool FY1 4QJ
t 0800 4320328 e rencliffehotel@aol.com
w rencliffe.co.uk ONLINE MAP LAST MINUTE OFFERS

B&B PER ROOM PER NIGHT
S £25.00
D £40.00 – £50.00

EVENING MEAL PER PERSON
£6.00 – £8.00

SPECIAL PROMOTIONS
Early bird midweek offers available for seniors, please call for details.

The comfort of our guests is paramount here at the Rencliffe. All bedrooms are en-suite, tastefully decorated with free view tv nd hospitality trays. Rooms serviced on a daily basis ensuring highest standards Comfortable bar lounge, with large screen TV. Good home cooking. Centrally Located. Free on-site parking.

open Open March to December
bedrooms 2 single, 4 double, 1 twin, 1 family
bathrooms 80 en suite
payment credit/debit cards, cash, cheques, euros
directions Map & full directions available on our website and brochure.

General

BLACKPOOL, Lancashire Map ref 4A1   SAT NAV FY4 1HE

★★★ GUEST ACCOMMODATION

Rio Rita
49 Withnell Road, Blackpool FY4 1HE
t (01253) 345203 e rioritahotel@btconnect.com
w riorita.co.uk ONLINE MAP GUEST REVIEWS ONLINE BOOKING

B&B PER ROOM PER NIGHT
S £38.00 – £40.00
D £48.00 – £55.00

EVENING MEAL PER PERSON
£10.00

Family run B&B, friendly and good home cooking, families and couples welcome. 200 yds to Beach, Pleasure Beach, Sandcastle & South Pier. Limited car parking. Licensed bar. Good transport links.
directions From M55 continue straight to Yeadon way. At second roundabout turn right. Next roundabout turn left, then left on next roundabout. Then 4th on right. **open** All year except Xmas and New Year **bedrooms** 4 double, 1 twin, 5 family **bathrooms** 10 en suite **payment** credit/debit cards, cash

Room General Leisure

BLACKPOOL, Lancashire Map ref 4A1   SAT NAV FY1 4PW

★★★ GUEST ACCOMMODATION

Roselea
67 Albert Road, Blackpool FY1 4PW
t (01253) 622032 f (01253) 622371 e info@roseleahotel.com
w roseleahotel.com ONLINE MAP GUEST REVIEWS LAST MINUTE OFFERS

B&B PER ROOM PER NIGHT
S £25.00 – £35.00
D £50.00 – £60.00

EVENING MEAL PER PERSON
£7.00

The Roselea is a friendly, family-run hotel with an enviable reputation for its quality accommodation, good food and efficient cheerful service, where you can relax and enjoy your holiday.
directions Please contact us for directions **open** All year **bedrooms** 2 single, 7 double, 7 twin, 3 family **bathrooms** 19 en suite **payment** credit/debit cards, cash, cheques

Room General Leisure

For **key to symbols** see page 6   623

North West | Lancashire

BLACKPOOL, Lancashire Map ref 4A1   SAT NAV FY1 6BJ

enjoyEngland.com ★★★ GUEST ACCOMMODATION

B&B PER ROOM PER NIGHT
S £25.00 – £40.00
D £45.00 – £60.00
EVENING MEAL PER PERSON
£5.00 – £12.00

Sandford Promenade
353 Promenade, Blackpool FY1 6BJ
t (01253) 343041 **e** rbac_mallorca@hotmail.com
w sandfordhotel.co.uk ONLINE MAP GUEST REVIEWS ONLINE BOOKING LAST MINUTE OFFERS

Ideally situated on the famous central promenade. Easy walking distance of the Pleasure Beach and Blackpool Tower. All modern ensuite rooms, sea views. Licenced bar. Wi-Fi. **directions** From motorway, turn for Pleasure Beach, when on seafront you will see hotel 500m heading towards Tower. Fantastic central Promenade position close to all amenities. **open** All year **bedrooms** 2 single, 8 double, 2 twin, 3 family **bathrooms** 15 en suite **payment** credit/debit cards, cash, euros

Room General Leisure

BLACKPOOL, Lancashire Map ref 4A1   SAT NAV FY1 5DH

enjoyEngland.com ★★★ GUEST ACCOMMODATION

B&B PER ROOM PER NIGHT
S £18.00 – £29.95
D £36.00 – £59.90
EVENING MEAL PER PERSON
£8.00 – £12.00

The Shores
29-31 Tyldsley Road, Blackpool FY1 5DH
t (01253) 620064 **e** theshoreshotel@hotmail.co.uk
w shoreshotelblackpool.com ONLINE MAP GUEST REVIEWS ONLINE BOOKING LAST MINUTE OFFERS

Central Family Run Guesthouse. Close to all amenities and promenade. All rooms en-suite with digital TV/DVD, tea/coffee making facilities and central heating. Wireless connection available within the bar area. **directions** 120 metres from Central Pier 200 meters from the Tower 10 minutes walk from the Winter Gardens and town centre. **open** All year except Xmas **bedrooms** 1 single, 3 double, 4 twin, 5 family, 2 suites **bathrooms** 15 en suite **payment** credit/debit cards, cash

Room General Leisure

BLACKPOOL, Lancashire Map ref 4A1   SAT NAV FY1 6BJ

enjoyEngland.com ★★★ GUEST ACCOMMODATION

B&B PER ROOM PER NIGHT
S £25.00 – £50.00
D £40.00 – £80.00
EVENING MEAL PER PERSON
£3.50 – £15.00

South Beach Seafront
365 & 367 Promenade, Blackpool, Lancashire FY1 6BJ
t (01253) 342250 **e** info@southbeachhotel.co.uk
w southbeachhotel.co.uk ONLINE MAP GUEST REVIEWS ONLINE BOOKING LAST MINUTE OFFERS

South Beach is in the best location Blackpool has to offer. 3 star family run accommodation with spectacular sea views and a sea view lounge bar with pool table. **directions** SAT NAV FY1 6BJ. **open** All year except Xmas **bedrooms** 2 single, 10 double, 4 twin, 12 family **bathrooms** 28 en suite **payment** credit/debit cards, cash, euros

Room General Leisure

BLACKPOOL, Lancashire Map ref 4A1   SAT NAV FY1 4PN

enjoyEngland.com ★★ GUEST ACCOMMODATION

B&B PER ROOM PER NIGHT
S £28.00 – £35.00
D £40.00 – £70.00
EVENING MEAL PER PERSON
£8.00 – £10.00

The Southview
122 Albert Road, Blackpool FY1 4PN
t (01253) 624163 **e** info@thesouthviewhotel.net
w thesouthviewhotel.net ONLINE MAP GUEST REVIEWS ONLINE BOOKING LAST MINUTE OFFERS

The Southview is centrally situated near to the Promenade, Winter Gardens, Houndshill shopping centre and car parks, with easy access from the Railway and Central Bus Stations. **directions** Stay on M55 to end, follow signs for Central Car Parks. Turn left from car park into one way system which leads to Albert Rd. **open** All year **bedrooms** 1 single, 8 double, 1 twin, 4 family **bathrooms** 14 en suite **payment** credit/debit cards, cash, cheques

Room General Leisure

North West | Lancashire

BLACKPOOL, Lancashire Map ref 4A1
SAT NAV FY4 1HQ

Sunnyside
84 Osborne Road, Blackpool FY4 1HQ
t (01253) 343840 **e** doreenandtrevor@tiscali.co.uk
w thesunnysidehotel.co.uk ONLINE MAP GUEST REVIEWS LAST MINUTE OFFERS

B&B PER ROOM PER NIGHT
S £20.00 – £25.00
D £40.00 – £50.00

We are a 9 bedroom family hotel close to the pleasure beach and water world, and a tram ride away from the town **directions** m55 to pleasure beach 2mins from pleasure beach **open** All year **bedrooms** 2 single, 4 double, 3 family **bathrooms** 9 en suite **payment** credit/debit cards, cash, cheques, euros

Room General Leisure

BLACKPOOL, Lancashire Map ref 4A1
SAT NAV FY1 2JA

Sussex
14-16 Pleasant Street, North Shore, Blackpool FY1 2JA
t 01253 627824 **e** sussexhotel.blackpool@virgin.net
w sussexhotelblackpool.com GUEST REVIEWS ONLINE BOOKING

B&B PER ROOM PER NIGHT
S £22.00 – £28.00
D £44.00 – £56.00
EVENING MEAL PER PERSON
£12.00

Hotel situated close to both North Shore Rail and Talbot Road Coach Stations. 55 yards from sea front, within walking distance from town centre. No children or stag and hen. **directions** From the main promenade, 5th street on the right after the North Pier. At junction turn right then left. The sixth hotel on your left. **open** All year **bedrooms** 3 single, 10 double, 7 twin **bathrooms** 20 en suite **payment** credit/debit cards, cash

Room General

BLACKPOOL, Lancashire Map ref 4A1
SAT NAV FY1 2AT

The Valentine
35 Dickson Road, Blackpool FY1 2AT
t (01253) 622775 **f** (01253) 753745 **e** anthony@anthonypalmer.orangehome.co.uk
w valentinehotelblackpool.co.uk ONLINE MAP GUEST REVIEWS ONLINE BOOKING LAST MINUTE OFFERS

B&B PER ROOM PER NIGHT
S £25.00 – £30.00
D £55.00 – £60.00
EVENING MEAL PER PERSON
£8.00

SPECIAL PROMOTIONS
Two night minimum stay from June to November. Special midweek breaks available. Weekly rates available.

We provide a quiet haven in central blackpool 5 minutes walk from North Pier, Tower, railway and bus stations. All rooms are ensuite with flatscreen televisions, complimentary toiletries and serviced daily. Full english breakfast served at 08.30. Four course evening dinner available when booked at least 48 hours ahead.

open Open from March to November
bedrooms 1 single, 9 double, 1 twin, 2 family
bathrooms 13 en suite
payment credit/debit cards, cash

directions M55 to Blackpool. Head for promenade, and turn right. Pass North Pier, and take second on right onto Banks Street. First right onto Dickson Road.

Room
General

or **key to symbols** see page 6

625

North West | Lancashire

BOLTON-BY-BOWLAND, Lancashire Map ref 4B1
SAT NAV BB7 4NY

Middle Flass Lodge
Forest Becks Brow, Settle Road, Clitheroe BB7 4NY
t (01295) 447259 f (01295) 447300 e middleflasslodge@btconnect.com
w middleflasslodge.co.uk ONLINE MAP ONLINE BOOKING

B&B PER ROOM PER NIGHT
S £45.00 – £50.00
D £64.00 – £75.00
EVENING MEAL PER PERSON
£25.00 – £35.00

Tastefully converted barn, idyllic countryside Forest of Bowland. Lancashire/Yorkshire border. Personal, professional attention, neat, cosy bedrooms. Lounge with stove, dining room, chef-prepared cuisine. Licensed. Gardens, ample parking. **directions** Clitheroe - Skipton A59. Sawley turning. Follow Bolton-by-Bowland. Just befor village take signpost for Settle. Two miles on the right. **open** All year **bedrooms** 4 double, 2 twin, 1 family **bathrooms** 7 en suite **payment** credit/debit cards, cash, cheques

Room General Leisure

BURNLEY, Lancashire Map ref 4B1
SAT NAV BB11 3QW

Ormerod
123 Ormerod Road, Burnley BB11 3QW
t (01282) 423255

B&B PER ROOM PER NIGHT
S £29.00 – £32.00
D £45.00 – £47.00

The Ormerod is a 10 bedroomed bed & breakfast accommodation. It is walking distance from the town centre, & located in a residential area opposite Queens park. All rooms are en suite, with TV & tea making facilities. Waitress served full English breakfast is included.

open All year
bedrooms 4 single, 2 double, 2 twin, 2 family
bathrooms 10 en suite
payment cash, cheques

directions Junction 10 M65 follow signs for Tur Moor when approaching football club turn left on to A6114 proceed 400 yards turn left opposite Fire station.

Room
General

CHIPPING, Lancashire Map ref 4A1
SAT NAV PR3 2QD

Town End Farm
Longridge Road, Chipping, Forest of Bowland, Lancashire PR3 2QD
t (01995) 61550 e wendy.foot@virgin.net

B&B PER ROOM PER NIGHT
S £30.00 – £40.00
D £60.00 – £80.00

One double bedroom, ensuite shower room, private sitting room with views of the garden. Home cooked breakfast with local ingredients. Walking distance to pubs, shop, cafe, gallery and village hall. **directions** Junction 31A on M6. Chipping village opposite the 30 limit. Look for the white sink by the gate. Parking by the gate. **open** All year **bedrooms** 1 double **bathrooms** 1 en suite **payment** cash

Room General Leisure

626 Official tourist board guide Bed & Breakfast

North West | Lancashire

CHORLEY, Lancashire Map ref 4A1
SAT NAV PR7 5SL

enjoyEngland ★★★★ GUEST HOUSE

B&B PER ROOM PER NIGHT
S £40.00 – £50.00
D £70.00 – £80.00

Parr Hall Farm
Parr Lane, Eccleston, Chorley, Lancashire PR7 5SL
t (01257) 451917 f (01257) 453749 e enquiries@parrhallfarm.com
w parrhallfarm.com ONLINE MAP

Georgian farmhouse built in 1721. Rural location within easy walking distance of public houses, restaurants and village amenities. Conveniently situated for Lancashire coast and countryside. Manchester/Liverpool Airports 45 minutes. **directions** M6 Junction 27, A5209 to Parbold, turn immediately onto B5250 to Eccleston. Parr Lane is on right after 4.8 miles. Parr Hall Farm on left. **open** All year **bedrooms** 6 double, 2 twin, 1 suite **bathrooms** 9 en suite **payment** credit/debit cards, cash, cheques

Room   General   Leisure

CLITHEROE, Lancashire Map ref 4A1
SAT NAV BB7 2HE

enjoyEngland ★★★★ BED & BREAKFAST

B&B PER ROOM PER NIGHT
S £45.00
D £60.00
EVENING MEAL PER PERSON
£7.00 – £15.00

Rowan Tree
10 Railway View Road, Clitheroe BB7 2HE
t (01200) 427115 e query@the-rowan-tree.org.uk
w the-rowan-tree.org.uk ONLINE MAP

Luxurious en suite double / twin / family room, in a welcoming, well-appointed Victorian home. Ideally situated for town and country pursuits. Evening meal by arrangement. **directions** Please contact us for directions **open** All year **bedrooms** 1 double **bathrooms** 1 en suite **payment** cash, cheques

Room   General   Leisure

COLNE, Lancashire Map ref 4B1
SAT NAV BB8 0QD

enjoyEngland ★★ INN

B&B PER ROOM PER NIGHT
S £32.50
D £60.00
EVENING MEAL PER PERSON
£4.50 – £12.00

The Crown
94 Albert Road, Colne BB8 0QD
t (01282) 863580 f (01282) 863580 e crownhotel94@aol.com
w crownhotelcolne.co.uk ONLINE MAP

We are a small friendly inn, situated in the Lancashire hills, in the heart of the Pendle Witch country. An ideal place for exploring the Yorkshire dales and local canals, we offer a warm welcome to all our guests. An extensive homecooked menu is available 7 days a week.

open All year
bedrooms 1 single, 2 double, 7 twin
bathrooms 7 en suite, 7 with private bathroom
payment credit/debit cards, cash

directions Situated near the end of the M65 motorway.

Room   General   Leisure

for key to symbols see page 6

627

North West | **Lancashire**

EARBY, Lancashire Map ref 4B1
SAT NAV BB18 6JL

Grange Fell
Skipton Road, Earby, Barnoldswick BB18 6JL
t (01282) 844991 f (01282) 844991 e info@grangefell.com
w grangefell.com ONLINE MAP GUEST REVIEWS

B&B PER ROOM PER NIGHT
S £25.00
D £25.00 – £30.00

Grange Fell is ideally situated at the gateway to the dales for visitors who wish to visit both Lancashire and Yorkshire. We provide a warm welcome and locally produced food. **directions** Located at the edge of the village on the A56, we are easily accessible being only 5 miles from Skipton and 6 miles from Colne. **open** All year except Xmas and New Year **bedrooms** 2 double **bathrooms** 2 with private bathroom **payment** cash, cheques, euros

Room General Leisure

GARSTANG, Lancashire Map ref 4A1
SAT NAV PR3 1UR

Broadgate Farm B & B
Bleasdale Lane, Bleasdale, Garstang, Preston PR3 1UR
t (01995) 602402 e anneclark_71@hotmail.com
w broadgatefarm.co.uk ONLINE MAP ONLINE BOOKING

B&B PER ROOM PER NIGHT
S £35.00 – £45.00
D £60.00 – £70.00

Forest of Bowland, easy access from M6/A6. Newly converted luxury bedrooms with central heating, sitting room with wood-burning stove and dining room serving Traditional English Breakfast. Splendid views. **directions** Please look on www.broadgatefarm.co.uk for directions **open** All year **bedrooms** 1 single, 1 double, 1 twin **bathrooms** 2 en suite, 1 with private bathroom **payment** cash, cheques

Room General Leisure

MORECAMBE, Lancashire Map ref 5A3
SAT NAV LA4 5AH

Ashley Guest House
371 Marine Road East, Morecambe LA4 5AH
t (01524) 412034 f 0845 527 9931 e info@ashleyhotel.co.uk
w ashleyhotel.co.uk ONLINE MAP GUEST REVIEWS ONLINE BOOKING

B&B PER ROOM PER NIGHT
S £30.00 – £35.00
D £58.00 – £67.00

Situated in a prominent position on the Morecambe seafront. The views over Morecambe Bay and the Lake District are breathtaking. Highest quality accommodation and food, and a relaxed friendly atmosphere. **directions** The Ashley is located on Morecambe's East promenade. Close to Lancaster and well placed to explore the Lake District, Yorkshire Dales and the local coastline. **open** All year **bedrooms** 2 single, 5 double, 2 twin, 1 family **bathrooms** 10 en suite, 10 with private bathroom **payment** credit/debit cards, cash

Room General Leisure

MORECAMBE, Lancashire Map ref 5A3
SAT NAV LA4 4DJ

Sea Crest
9-13 West End Road, Morecambe LA4 4DJ
t (01524) 411006 e seacrest-hotel@tiscali.co.uk
w seacrest-hotel.co.uk/seacreasthotel.co.uk ONLINE MAP

B&B PER ROOM PER NIGHT
S £28.00 – £32.00
D £56.00 – £64.00
EVENING MEAL PER PERSON
£10.00 – £15.00

Sea Crest is a family-run establishment, close to Morecambe seafront where you can enjoy a friendly atmosphere, spacious dining, traditional home cooking & resident bar. **directions** From the South, M6 Junction 33/34 head for Lancaster follow the signs to Morecambe. From the North M6 Junction 35 A5105 coastal road into Morecambe. **open** All year **bedrooms** 6 single, 6 double, 3 twin, 16 family **bathrooms** 31 en suite **payment** credit/debit cards, cash, cheques

Room General Leisure

628 Official tourist board guide Bed & Breakfast

North West | Lancashire

PREESALL, Lancashire Map ref 4A1
SAT NAV FY6 0NS

Grassendale
Green Lane, Preesall, Poulton-Le-Fylde FY6 0NS
t (01253) 812331 e rondeyo@aol.com

B&B PER ROOM PER NIGHT
S £20.00 – £30.00
D £40.00 – £60.00

Family home in a quiet location offering bed and breakfast. Three rooms available, ample parking and pets welcome. Only one hour from Southern Lakes and 30 minutes from Blackpool. **directions** Please send 10% deposit and I will send directions to you **open** All year **bedrooms** 1 double, 1 twin, 1 family **bathrooms** 2 en suite, 1 with private bathroom **payment** cash, cheques

Room General

PRESTON, Lancashire Map ref 4A1
SAT NAV PR4 0BD

Home Barn
Hollowforth Lane, Woodplumpton, Preston PR4 0BD
t 01772 691101 e m.sherdley@sky.com
w homebarngranary.co.uk ONLINE MAP

B&B PER ROOM PER NIGHT
S £39.99
D £70.00

Bed & Breakfast accommodation in a grade II listed barn. Spacious double-bedroom with en suite and built in sound system and comfortable lounge-dining room with wood-burning stove overlooking farm land. **directions** Please contact us for directions **open** All year except Xmas **bedrooms** 1 double **bathrooms** 1 en suite **payment** cash, cheques, euros

Room General Leisure

SCORTON, Lancashire Map ref 4A1
SAT NAV PR3 1AU

The Priory Inn, Scorton
The Square, Scorton, Preston PR3 1AU
t (01524) 791255 f (01524) 793563 e collinsonjulie@aol.com
w theprioryscorton.co.uk

B&B PER ROOM PER NIGHT
S £40.00 – £45.00
D £80.00 – £85.00
EVENING MEAL PER PERSON
£6.00 – £26.00

Set in the picturesque village of Scorton serving fine food and local ales with a real Lancashire Welcome. It is an ideal location for exploring The Forest of Bowland. **directions** From the South J32 off M6 follow A6 North past Garstang follow Scorton signs. From the North J33 off M6 follow A6 South follow Scorton. **open** All year except Xmas **bedrooms** 1 single, 5 double, 1 twin, 1 family **bathrooms** 8 en suite **payment** credit/debit cards, cash, cheques

Room General Leisure

WHITEWELL, Lancashire Map ref 4A1
SAT NAV BB7 3AT

The Inn at Whitewell
Dunsop Road, Whitewell, Nr Clitheroe BB7 3AT
t (01200) 448222 f (01200) 448298 e reception@innatwhitewell.com
w innatwhitewell.com ONLINE MAP

B&B PER ROOM PER NIGHT
S £83.00 – £177.00
D £113.00 – £218.00

Award-winning inn with superb restaurant, own wine merchant and very individual bedrooms. Residential fishing. **directions** Please refer to website **open** All year **bedrooms** 18 double, 4 twin, 1 suite **bathrooms** 23 en suite **payment** credit/debit cards, cash, cheques

Room General Leisure

or key to symbols see page 6   629

North West | Greater Manchester

MANCHESTER, Greater Manchester Map ref 4B1   SAT NAV M3 7DB

B&B PER ROOM PER NIGHT
S £55.00 – £60.00
D £62.95 – £72.95
EVENING MEAL PER PERSON
£5.00 – £14.00

Stay Inn Hotel
55 Blackfriars Road, Salford, Manchester M3 7DB
t (0161) 907 2277 f (0161) 907 2266 e info@stayinn.co.uk
w stayinn.co.uk ONLINE MAP GUEST REVIEWS ONLINE BOOKING

Modern, purpose-built hotel offering excellent value for money. Free car parking, city-centre location, close to railway station. Five minutes' walk from the MEN Arena, and further five minutes from GMEX and MICC. Residents' bar open until 0100. Breakfast from £5.95 to £7.25 for a full English.

open All year
bedrooms 41 double, 12 twin, 12 family
bathrooms 65 en suite
payment credit/debit cards, cash, euros

directions Piccadilly and Victoria train stations are both 10 minutes away from the hotel.

Room   General

SALE, Greater Manchester Map ref 4A2   SAT NAV M33 2AE

B&B PER ROOM PER NIGHT
S £30.00 – £44.95
D £49.95 – £55.00
EVENING MEAL PER PERSON
£4.95 – £12.95

Belforte House
7-9 Broad Road, Sale, Manchester M33 2AE
t (0161) 973 8779 f (0161) 973 8779 e belfortehotel@aol.com
w belfortehousehotel.co.uk/ LAST MINUTE OFFERS

Privately owned hotel with a personal, friendly approach. Ideally located for Manchester Airport, the Metrolink and the city centre. Situated directly opposite Sale Leisure Centre. **directions** 1 mile from Junction 6 M60. 200 metres from Tram Station. **open** All year except Xmas and New Year **bedrooms** 14 single, 4 double, 2 twin, 3 family **bathrooms** 17 en suite, 2 with private bathroom **payment** credit/debit cards, cash, cheques

Room   General   Leisure

SALE, Greater Manchester Map ref 4A2   SAT NAV M33 5AN

B&B PER ROOM PER NIGHT
S £39.95 – £49.95
D £49.95 – £59.95
EVENING MEAL PER PERSON
£6.95 – £15.45

Eskdale Lodge
35 Harboro Road, Sale M33 5AN
t (0161) 973 6770 f (0161) 976 4534 e garvan.smith@eskdalelodge.co.uk
w eskdalelodge.co.uk ONLINE MAP LAST MINUTE OFFERS

Family run establishment comprising of nine ensuite letting bedrooms, two bars and a restaurant. Perfectly located for the motorway network, Metrolink, Manchester Airport, city centre, Trafford Centre and Chill Factor. **directions** We are 1 mile from Junction 8 M60. We are 5 miles from Juction 7 M56. We are 9 miles from Junction 19 M6 **open** All year **bedrooms** 4 double, 4 twin, 1 family **bathrooms** 9 en suite **payment** credit/debit cards, cash, cheques

Room   General   Leisure

North West | Greater Manchester/Merseyside

WEST TIMPERLEY, Greater Manchester Map ref 4A2
SAT NAV WA14 5NH

B&B PER ROOM PER NIGHT
S £47.99 – £51.98
D £51.98 – £61.98

Altrincham Lodge
350 Manchester Road, West Timperley, Altrincham WA14 5NH
t (0161) 962 9000 f (0161) 962 9111 e rooms@altrinchamlodge.co.uk
w altrinchamlodge.co.uk ONLINE MAP GUEST REVIEWS ONLINE BOOKING LAST MINUTE OFFERS

The Altrincham Lodge offers good quality accommodation in an ideal location, close to Old Trafford and Manchester. Recently refurbished with 48 ensuite double, twin and family rooms. **directions** From the North exit M60 Jct7, follow A56 to Altrincham. From the South exit M6 Jct19, follow A556 to Altrincham, then A56 to Sale. **bedrooms** 22 double, 22 twin, 4 family **bathrooms** 48 en suite

Room General

LIVERPOOL, Merseyside Map ref 4A2
SAT NAV L1 9JG

BED ONLY PER NIGHT
£43.00

Cocoon @ International Inn
4 South Hunter Street, Off Hardman Street, Liverpool L1 9JG
t 0151 7098135 e info@internationalinn.co.uk
w cocoonliverpool.co.uk ONLINE MAP GUEST REVIEWS ONLINE BOOKING

Central Liverpool budget boutique pod hotel rooms. Great value and stylish run by award winning International Inn. Internal cabins, king size beds, en suite bathrooms, LCDTV's, Wi-fi, i-pod stations. **directions** Please contact us for directions **open** All year **bedrooms** 2 single, 27 double, 3 twin **bathrooms** 32 en suite **payment** credit/debit cards, cash

Room General Leisure

LIVERPOOL, Merseyside Map ref 4A2
SAT NAV L15 2HG

B&B PER ROOM PER NIGHT
S £21.00 – £28.00
D £39.00 – £48.00

Holmeleigh Guest House
93 Woodcroft Road, Wavertree, Liverpool L15 2HG
t (0151) 734 2216 f (0151) 222 1400 e info@holmeleigh.com
w holmeleigh.com ONLINE MAP GUEST REVIEWS ONLINE BOOKING LAST MINUTE OFFERS

Victorian, red-brick, three-storey corner guest house, just 2.5 miles from city centre, two miles from M62 and close to Sefton Park. **directions** Please refer to website. **open** All year **bedrooms** 2 single, 3 double, 6 twin, 3 family **bathrooms** 14 en suite **payment** credit/debit cards, cash, cheques

Room General Leisure

LIVERPOOL, Merseyside Map ref 4A2
SAT NAV L16 0JH

B&B PER ROOM PER NIGHT
S £35.00
D £70.00

Real McCoy Guest House
126 Childwall Park Avenue, Childwall, Liverpool L16 0JH
t 07971 161542 / (0151) 722 7116 f (0151) 722 7116 e ann557@btinternet.com

Situated in the Childwall area of Liverpool, good transport links into the city centre. Perfect for viewing what Liverpool and surrounding districts have to offer. 5 mins away from M62. **directions** Please contact us for directions **open** All year **bedrooms** 1 single, 3 double, 1 family **bathrooms** 1 en suite, 1 with private bathroom **payment** cash, cheques, euros

Room General Leisure

key to symbols see page 6

631

North West | Merseyside

SOUTHPORT, Merseyside Map ref 4A1
SAT NAV PR9 0NB

The Carleton House
17 Alexandra Road, Southport PR9 0NB
t (01704) 538035 **f** (01772) 816051 **e** enquiries@thecarleton.co.uk

B&B PER ROOM PER NIGHT
S £47.50 – £60.00
D £85.00 – £120.00

Carleton House is an elegant 4 star guest house with restored Victorian features. Situated in a peace location only 5 mins from Lord Street boulevard. Self catering accomodation also available. **directions** Please contact us for directions **open** All year **bedrooms** 3 single, 5 double, 2 twin, 2 family **bathrooms** 12 en suite **payment** credit/debit cards, cash, cheques

Room | General | Leisure

SOUTHPORT, Merseyside Map ref 4A1
SAT NAV PR9 0DP

Crescent House
27 Bath Street, Southport PR9 0DP
t (01704) 530339 **f** (01704) 530339 **e** enquiries@crescenthousehotel.co.uk
w crescenthousehotel.co.uk/index.htm ONLINE MAP GUEST REVIEWS ONLINE BOOKING LAST MINUTE OFFERS

B&B PER ROOM PER NIGHT
S £25.00 – £35.00
D £54.00 – £60.00
EVENING MEAL PER PERSON
£12.00

Warm and welcoming. Centrally situated to facilities, shops, restaurants, the Conference Centre and Theatre. All ensuite, tastefully refurbished rooms with tea and coffee facilities and Freeview television. 24hour entry **directions** Central southport location between the Prom and Lord Street. **open** All year **bedrooms** 1 single, 2 double, 2 twin, 2 family **bathrooms** 7 en suite, 7 with private bathroom **payment** credit/debit cards, cash, cheques

Room | General | Leisure

SOUTHPORT, Merseyside Map ref 4A1
SAT NAV PR8 5LR

Sandy Brook Farm
Wyke Cop Road, Scarisbrick, Southport PR8 5LR
t (01704) 880337 **f** (01704) 880337 **e** sandybrookfarm@gmail.com
w sandybrookfarm.co.uk ONLINE MAP

B&B PER ROOM PER NIGHT
S £35.00
D £55.00

Twenty-seven-acre arable farm. Comfortable accommodation in converted farm buildings in rural area of Scarisbrick, 3.5 miles from Southport. Special facilities for disabled guests. **directions** M6 Motorway 10 miles 1/2 Mile from A570 Ormskirk/Southport Road **open** All year except Xmas and New Year **bedrooms** 1 single, 1 double, 2 twin, 2 family **bathrooms** 6 en suite **payment** cash, cheques

Room | General | Leisure

WALLASEY, Merseyside Map ref 4A2
SAT NAV CH45 2ND

Sherwood Guest House
55 Wellington Road, New Brighton, Wirral CH45 2ND
t (0151) 639 5198 **e** info@sherwoodguesthouse.com
w sherwoodguesthouse.com ONLINE MAP GUEST REVIEWS

B&B PER ROOM PER NIGHT
S £35.00
D £50.00 – £55.00

A family guest house situated facing New Brighton promenade and the Irish Sea. **directions** Please see our website for full details. **open** All year except Xmas **bedrooms** 2 double, 2 twin, 2 family **bathrooms** 6 en suite **payment** cash, cheques

Room | General | Leisure

North West | Merseyside/Cheshire

WEST KIRBY, Merseyside Map ref 4A2
SAT NAV CH48 1PP

At Peel Hey
Frankby Road, Frankby, Nr Liverpool, Wirral CH48 1PP
t (0151) 677 9077 **f** (0151) 604 1999 **e** enquiries@peelhey.co.uk
w peelhey.co.uk ONLINE BOOKING LAST MINUTE OFFERS

B&B PER ROOM PER NIGHT
S £75.00
D £105.00

SPECIAL PROMOTIONS
Winter weekend breaks available.

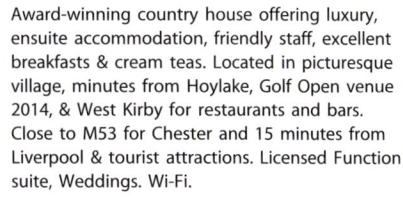

Award-winning country house offering luxury, ensuite accommodation, friendly staff, excellent breakfasts & cream teas. Located in picturesque village, minutes from Hoylake, Golf Open venue 2014, & West Kirby for restaurants and bars. Close to M53 for Chester and 15 minutes from Liverpool & tourist attractions. Licensed Function suite, Weddings. Wi-Fi.

open All year
bedrooms 1 single, 4 double, 2 twin, 2 family
bathrooms 9 en suite
payment credit/debit cards, cash, cheques

directions M53 jct 2. B5139 to Frankby.

BREAKFAST AWARD

Room
General
Leisure

All Assessed Accommodation

Cheshire

ACTON BRIDGE

Ash House Farm Bed & Breakfast ★★★ *Farmhouse*
Chapel Lane, Acton Bridge
CW8 3QS
t (01606) 852717
e enquiries@ashhousefarm.com
w ashhousefarm.com

ALDERLEY EDGE

Mayfield Bed & Breakfast @ Sheila's ★★★ *Bed & Breakfast*
Wilmslow Road, Alderley Edge
SK9 7QW
t (01625) 583991/07703 289663

ALTRINCHAM (3 MILES)

Bollington Hall Farm ★★ *Bed & Breakfast*
Park Lane, Little Bollington, Altrincham
WA14 4TJ
t (0161) 928 1760

BARTON

Higher Farm Bed & Breakfast ★★★ *Guest Accommodation*
SILVER AWARD
Higher Farm, Barton, Malpas
SY14 7HU
t (01829) 782422
e info@higherfarm.co.uk
w higherfarm.co.uk

BETCHTON

Yew Tree Farm Bed & Breakfast ★★★ *Bed & Breakfast*
Love Lane, Betchton, Sandbach
CW11 4TD
t (01477) 500626
e jshollinshead@btinternet.com

BOLLINGTON

Red Oaks Farm ★★★★ *Farmhouse*
SILVER AWARD
Charter Road, Bollington
SK10 5NU
t (01625) 574280
e bb@redoaksfarm.co.uk
w redoaksfarm.co.uk

BRERETON

Bagmere Bank Farm Luxury Bed & Breakfast ★★★★
Bed & Breakfast SILVER AWARD
Brereton Park, Brereton, Sandbach
CW11 1RX
t (01477) 537503

BRUERA

Churton Heath Farm Bed & Breakfast ★★★★ *Bed & Breakfast*
GOLD AWARD
Churton Heath Farm, Chapel Lane, Chester
CH3 6EW
t (01244) 620420
e info@churtonheathfarm.co.uk
w churtonheathfarm.co.uk

CHESTER

Ba Ba Guest House ★★★★
Guest Accommodation
65 Hoole Road, Hoole, Chester
CH2 3NJ
t (01244) 315047
e reservations@babaguesthouse.co.uk
w babaguesthouse.co.uk

Bawn Lodge ★★★ *Guest House*
10 Hoole Road, Hoole, Chester
CH2 3NH
t (01244) 324971
e info@bawnlodge.co.uk
w bawnlodge.co.uk

Bowman Lodge ★★★
Guest Accommodation
52 Hoole Road, Chester
CH2 3NL
t (01244) 342208
e info@bowmanlodge.co.uk
w bowmanlodge.co.uk

Buckingham House ★★★★
Guest Accommodation
SILVER AWARD
38 Hough Green, Chester
CH4 8JQ
t (01244) 681600
e info@buckinghamhousechester.co.uk
w buckinghamhousechester.co.uk

Chester Backpackers ★★
Backpackers
67 Boughton, Chester
CH3 5AF
t (01244) 400185

Chester Brooklands ★★★★
Guest Accommodation
8 Newton Lane, Chester
CH2 3RB
t (01244) 348556
e bookings@chester-bandb.co.uk
w chester-bandb.co.uk

Chester Town House ★★★★
Guest House
23 King Street, Chester
CH1 2AH
t (01244) 350021
e davidbellis@chestertownhouse.co.uk
w chestertownhouse.co.uk

Cotton Farm ★★★★
Guest Accommodation
Cotton Edmunds, Chester
CH3 7PG
t 01244 336616
e echill@btinternet.com
w cottonfarm.co.uk/

Craigleith Lodge ★★★★
Guest Accommodation
56 Hoole Road, Chester
CH2 3NL
t (01244) 318740
e welcome@craigleithlodge.co.uk
w craigleithlodge.co.uk

Derry Raghan Lodge ★★★★
Guest Accommodation
54 Hoole Road, Chester
CH2 3NL
t (01244) 318740
e welcome@derryraghanlodge.co.uk
w derryraghanlodge.co.uk

The Golden Eagle ★★★ *Inn*
Castle Street, Chester
CH1 2DS
t (01244) 321098
e pipadee1@btinternet.com

Grosvenor Place ★★★
Guest Accommodation
2 Grosvenor Place, Chester
CH1 2DE
t (01244) 324455
e info@grosvenorplacechester.co.uk
w grosvenorplacechester.co.uk

Grove Villa ★★★★ *Bed & Breakfast*
18 The Groves, Chester
CH1 1SD
t (01244) 349713
e grovevilla18@btinternet.com
w grovevillachester.com

633

North West | Cheshire

Halcyon Guest House ★★★
Guest House
18 Eaton Road, Handbridge, Chester
CH4 7EN
t (01244) 676159
e eric.owen@tiscali.co.uk

Hameldaeus ★★★
Guest Accommodation
9 Lorne Street, Chester
CH1 4AE
t (01244) 374913
e joyce_brunton@tiscali.co.uk

Hamilton Court ★★★★
Guest Accommodation
5/7 Hamilton Street, Hoole, Chester
CH2 3JG
t (01244) 345387
e hamiltoncourth@aol.com
w hamiltoncourtchester.co.uk

Higher Huxley Hall ★★★★★
Guest Accommodation
SILVER AWARD
Red Lane, Huxley, Chester
CH3 9BZ
t (01829) 781484
e enquiries@huxleyhall.co.uk
w huxleyhall.co.uk

Holly House Guest House ★★★★
Guest House
1 Stone Place, Hoole, Chester
CH2 3NR
t (01244) 328967
e marinacassidy@yahoo.com
w hollyhouseguesthouse.com

Homeleigh Guest House ★★★
Guest Accommodation
14 Hough Green, Chester
CH4 8JG
t (01244) 676761
e colin-judy@tiscali.co.uk
w homeleighchester.co.uk

Kilmorey Lodge ★★★
Guest Accommodation
50 Hoole Road, Chester
CH2 3NL
t (01244) 324306
e kilmoreylodge@aol.com
w smoothhound.co.uk/hotels/kilmorey.html

Kings Guest House ★★★★
Guest House
14 Eaton Road, Handbridge, Chester
CH4 7EN
t (01244) 671249
e kings@kingsguesthouse.co.uk
w kingsguesthouse.co.uk/

Laburnum House ★★★
Guest House
2 St Anne Street, Chester
CH1 3HS
t (01244) 380113
e info@laburnumhousechester.co.uk
w laburnumhousechester.co.uk

Latymer House ★★★
Guest Accommodation
82 Hough Green, Chester
CH4 8JW
t (01244) 675074
e info@latymerhotel.com
w latymerhotel.com

Laurels ★★★★ *Bed & Breakfast*
14 Selkirk Road, Curzon Park, Chester
CH4 8AH
t (01244) 679682
e halandpam@talktalk.net
w visitchester.com/site/accommodation/bookonline?product=761

Lavender Lodge Bed & Breakfast
★★★★ *Guest Accommodation*
46 Hoole Road, Chester
CH2 3NL
t (01244) 323204
e bookings@lavenderlodgechester.co.uk
w lavenderlodgechester.co.uk

The Limes ★★★★
Guest Accommodation
12 Hoole Road, Chester
CH2 3NJ
t (01244) 328239
e bookings@limes-chester.co.uk
w limes-chester.co.uk

Manderley ★★★★ *Bed & Breakfast*
17 Victoria Park, Queens Park, Chester
CH4 7AX
t (01244) 675426
e info@manderleychester.co.uk
w manderleychester.co.uk/b&b/index.htm

Manor Farm Bed & Breakfast
★★★★ *Farmhouse* SILVER AWARD
Egerton, Cholmondeley, Chester
SY14 8AW
t (01829) 720261
e manorfarmbandb@btconnect.com
w egertonmanorfarm.co.uk

Mitchell's of Chester Guest House
★★★★★ *Guest House*
SILVER AWARD
28 Hough Green, Chester
CH4 8JQ
t (01244) 679004
e mitoches@dialstart.net
w mitchellsofchester.com

Newton Hall Farm Bed & Breakfast ★★★★ *Farmhouse*
SILVER AWARD
Tattenhall, Chester
CH3 9NE
t (01829) 770153
e saarden@btinternet.com
w newtonhallfarm.co.uk

Recorder House ★★★★
Guest Accommodation
19 City Walls, Chester
CH1 1SB
t (01244) 326580
e reservations@recorderhotel.co.uk
w recorderhotel.co.uk

Roseville Bed & Breakfast
★★★★★ *Bed & Breakfast*
SILVER AWARD
Roseville, Belle Vue Lane, Chester
CH3 7EJ
t (01244) 300602
e tracyandjerry@tiscali.co.uk
w rosevillechester.co.uk/

Rowland House ★★★★
Bed & Breakfast
21 Walpole Street, Chester
CH1 4HG
t (01244) 390967
e enquiries@rowlandhousechester.co.uk
w rowlandhousechester.co.uk/

Strathearn Bed & Breakfast ★★★
Guest Accommodation
38 Hoole Road, Chester
CH2 3NL
t (01244) 321522
e strathearn.chester@gmail.com
w chesteraccomodation.biz

Sycamore House Bed & Breakfast
★★★★ *Bed & Breakfast*
8 Queens Park Road, Chester
CH4 7AD
t (01244) 675417
e sycamore_house@btinternet.com
w visitchester.com/site/where-to-stay/sycamore-house-bed-and-breakfast-p1951

Tentry Heys ★★★ *Bed & Breakfast*
Queens Park Road, Chester
CH4 7AD
t (01244) 677857
e barbaraarthur1@btinternet.com
w tentryheys.co.uk/index.html

Tower House ★★★★
Bed & Breakfast
14 Dee Hills Park, Chester
CH3 5AR
t (01244) 341396
e sueheather62@hotmail.com

CONGLETON

HP Bed & Breakfast ★★
Bed & Breakfast
1 Norfolk Road, Lower Heath, Congleton
CW12 1NY
t (01260) 279887
e hpbedandbreakfast@hotmail.com

Sandhole Farm Bed & Breakfast
★★★★ *Guest Accommodation*
Manchester Road (A34), Hulme Walfield, Congleton
CW12 2JH
t (01260) 224419
e veronica@sandholefarm.co.uk
w sandholefarm.co.uk

Yew Tree Farm Bed & Breakfast
★★★★ *Farmhouse*
North Rode, Congleton
CW12 2PF
t (01260) 223569
e yewtreebb@hotmail.com
w yewtreebb.co.uk

CROWTON

The Poplars Bed & Breakfast
★★★★ *Farmhouse*
Norley Lane, Crowton, Northwich
CW8 2RR
t (01928) 788083
e thepoplarsbandb@aol.com
w the-poplarsbandb.co.uk/

CUDDINGTON

Acorn House Bed & Breakfast
★★★ *Bed & Breakfast*
34 Forest Close, Cuddington, Northwich
CW8 2EE
t (01606) 881714
e alanbridge02@live.co.uk

DISLEY

The Grey Cottage ★★★★
Bed & Breakfast
20 Jackson's Edge Road, Disley
SK12 2JE
t (01663) 763286
e contact@greycottagedisley.co.uk
w greycottagedisley.co.uk

GOOSTREY

Goostrey Bed & Breakfast ★★★★
Bed & Breakfast
Church Cottage, 10 Station Road, Goostrey
CW4 8PJ
t (01477) 534314
e craggsdavid@sky.com
w goostreybedbreakfast.co.uk

HALE VILLAGE

The Cottage B&B ★★★★
Bed & Breakfast
2 Town Lane, Hale Village, Liverpool
L24 4AG
t (0151) 425 3188
e thecottagebandb@btinternet.com

HAMPTON

Hamilton House Bed & Breakfast
★★★ *Bed & Breakfast*
Station Road, Hampton Heath, Malpas
SY14 8JF
t (01948) 820421
e hamiltonhouse5@hotmail.com
w hamiltonhousecheshire.co.uk

HATTON HEATH

Golborne Manor ★★★★
Bed & Breakfast
Platts Lane, Hatton Heath, Chester
CH3 9AN
t (01829) 770310
e info@golbornemanor.co.uk
w golbornemanor.co.uk

HOLMES CHAPEL

Bridge Farm Bed & Breakfast
★★★★ *Farmhouse*
Blackden, Holmes Chapel
CW4 8BX
t (01477) 571202
e stay@bridgefarm.com
w bridgefarm.com

Padgate Guest House ★★★★
Bed & Breakfast SILVER AWARD
Twemlow Lane, Cranage, Holmes Chapel
CW4 8EX
t (01477) 534291
e lyndaboagmunroe@yahoo.co.uk
w padgateguesthouse.co.uk

KERMINCHAM

The Fields Farm ★★★★
Farmhouse SILVER AWARD
Forty Acre Lane, Kermincham, Crewe
CW4 8DY
t (01477) 571224

KNUTSFORD

Moat Hall Motel ★★★
Guest Accommodation
Chelford Road, Marthall, Knutsford
WA16 8SU
t (01625) 860367
e moathall121@fsmail.net
w moat-hall-motel.co.uk

Pickmere Country Guest House
★★★ *Guest House*
Park Lane, Pickmere, Knutsford
WA16 0JX
t (01565) 733433
e info@pickmerehouse.co.uk
w pickmerehouse.co.uk

LITTLE BUDWORTH

Akesmere Farm Bed & Breakfast
★★★★ *Farmhouse*
Chester Road, Little Budworth, Tarporley
CW6 9ER
t (01829) 760348
e dianne@akesmerefarm.co.uk
w akesmerefarm.co.uk

LOWER PEOVER

Moss Farm Bed & Breakfast
★★★★ *Bed & Breakfast*
SILVER AWARD
Cheadle Lane, Lower Peover, Knutsford
WA16 9SW
t (01565) 722915
e rachel@moss-farm.com
w moss-farm.com

LOWER WITHINGTON

Chapel Cottage ★★★★
Bed & Breakfast
Dicklow Cob, Lower Withington, Holmes Chapel
SK11 9EA
t (01477) 571489
e wilbar2@tiscali.co.uk
w website. www.Chapelcottage.net

MACCLESFIELD

Artizana Suite ★★★★★
Bed & Breakfast SILVER AWARD
The Village, Prestbury, Macclesfield
SK10 4DG
t (01625) 827582
e enquiries@artizana.co.uk
w artizana.co.uk/suite

Astle Farm East Bed & Breakfast
★★ *Farmhouse*
Astle Farm, Chelford
SK10 4TA
t (01625) 861270
e gill.farmhouse@virgin.net
w astlefarmeast.co.uk

North West | Cheshire/Cumbria

rtles Farm Bed & Breakfast
★★ *Bed & Breakfast*
hley Road, Ashley, Macclesfield
A14 3QH
t (0161) 928 0458
e birtlesfarm@btinternet.com

arrop Fold Farm Bed &
eakfast ★★★★★ *Farmhouse*
OLD AWARD
acclesfield Road, Rainow,
acclesfield
K10 5UU
t (01625) 560085
e stay@harropfoldfarm.co.uk
w harropfoldfarm.co.uk

ll Top Farm Bed & Breakfast
★★★ *Farmhouse*
incle, Macclesfield
K11 0QH
t (01260) 227257
e hilltopfarm_bb@hotmail.co.uk
w hill-top-farm.co.uk/welcome-to-hill-top-farm-b-b/

ower Harebarrow Farm Bed &
eakfast ★★ *Bed & Breakfast*
derley Road, Over Alderley,
acclesfield
K10 4SW
t (01625) 829882
w lowerharebarrowfarm.co.uk

oorhayes House ★★★
uest Accommodation
7 Manchester Road, Tytherington,
acclesfield
K10 2JJ
t (01625) 433228
e helen@moorhayes.co.uk
w moorhayes.co.uk/

he Ryles Arms ★★★★ *Inn*
ollin Lane, Higher Sutton,
acclesfield
K11 0NN
t (01260) 252244
e info@rylesarms.com
w rylesarms.com

he Stanley Arms Bed &
reakfast ★★★★ *Inn*
LVER AWARD
acclesfield Forest, Macclesfield
K11 0AR
t (01260) 252414
e thestanleyarms@btconnet.com
w stanleyarms.com

MINSHULL VERNON

igher Elms Farm Bed &
reakfast ★★★ *Farmhouse*
ross Lane, Minshull Vernon, Crewe
W1 4RG
t (01270) 522252

MOTTRAM ST ANDREW

oose Green Farm Bed &
eakfast ★★★★ *Farmhouse*
ak Road, Mottram St Andrew
K10 4RA
t (01625) 828814
e info@goosegreenfarm.com
w goosegreenfarm.com

MOW COP

he Woodlands ★★★★
uest Accommodation
uarry Wood Farm, Wood Street,
ow Cop
T7 3PF
t (01782) 518877

NANTWICH

oole Hall Farm Bed & Breakfast
★★★ *Farmhouse* SILVER AWARD
oole Lane, Coole Pilate, Nantwich
W5 8AU
t (01270) 811232
w coolehallfarm.co.uk

Outlanes Farmhouse Bed &
Breakfast ★★★
Guest Accommodation
The Outlanes, Church Minshull,
Nantwich
CW5 6DX
t (01270) 522284
e robert.parton@theoutlanes.com
w theoutlanes.com

Reaseheath College ★★★ *Campus*
Reaseheath, Nantwich
CW5 6DF
t (01270) 613219
e jennya@reaeheath.ac.uk
w reaseheath.ac.uk

NORTH RODE

Ladderstile Retreat ★★★★★
Farmhouse SILVER AWARD
Twin Oaks, Ladderstile Farm, North
Rode, Nr Congleton, Cheshire
CW12 2PH
t (01260) 223338
e enquiries@ladderstileretreat.co.uk
w ladderstileretreat.co.uk

NORTHWICH

Melvin Holme Farm Bed &
Breakfast ★★ *Bed & Breakfast*
Pennys Lane, Lach Dennis,
Northwich
CW9 7SJ
t (01606) 330008

Parkdale Guest House ★★★
Guest Accommodation
140 Middlewich Road, Rudheath,
Northwich
CW9 7DS
t (01606) 45328
e srb7@btinternet.com

Wall Hill Farm Guest House
★★★★★ *Guest Accommodation*
Acton Lane, Acton Bridge,
Northwich, Cheshire
CW8 3QE
t 01606 852 654
e info@wallhillfarmguesthouse.co.uk
w wallhillfarmguesthouse.co.uk

OVER PEOVER

15 Stocks Lane ★★
Bed & Breakfast
Over Peover, Knutsford
WA16 9HF
t (01565) 723089
e carol.frith@tiscali.co.uk

The Dog Inn ★★★★ *Inn*
Well Bank Lane, Over Peover,
Knutsford
WA16 8UP
t (01625) 861421
e info@doginn-overpeover.com
w doginn-overpeover.com

PRESTBURY

The White House Manor Hotel
★★★★ *Guest Accommodation*
SILVER AWARD
The Village, Prestbury
SK10 4HP
t (01625) 829376
e info@thewhitehousemanor.co.uk
w thewhitehousemanor.co.uk

SALTNEY

Garden Gate Guest House ★★
Guest Accommodation
8 Chester Street, Chester
CH4 8BJ
t (01244) 682306
e dollywal@msn.com
w gardengateguesthouse.co.uk

SANDBACH

Hollybank B&B ★★★★
Bed & Breakfast
Davenport Lane, Brereton, Sandbach
CW11 2SR
t (01477) 500550
e kimray@supanet.com

SIDDINGTON

Golden Cross Farm Bed &
Breakfast ★★★ *Farmhouse*
Siddington, Macclesfield
SK11 9JP
t (01260) 224358

TARPORLEY

Foresters Arms ★★★ *Inn*
92 High Street, Tarporley
CW6 0AX
t (01829) 733151
e foresters-arms@btconnect.com
w theforesters.co.uk

Hill House Farm Bed & Breakfast
★★★★ *Farmhouse* SILVER AWARD
Rushton, Tarporley
CW6 9AU
t (01829) 732238
e info@hillhousefarm-cheshire.com
w hillhousefarm-cheshire.co.uk/

TARVIN

Willow Run Bed & Breakfast
★★★★ *Bed & Breakfast*
SILVER AWARD
Barrow Lane, Tarvin Sands, Tarvin
CH3 8JF
t (01829) 749142
e willowrun@btconnect.com
w willowrun.co.uk

TATTENHALL

Carriages ★★★ *Inn*
New Russia Hall, Chester Road,
Tattenhall
CH3 9AH
t (01829) 770958

Fernlea Cottage Bed & Breakfast
★★★★ *Bed & Breakfast*
Chester Road, Hatton Heath,
Tattenhall
CH3 9AQ
t (01829) 770807
e stevegb1@btinternet.com
w fernleacottage.co.uk

Ford Farm Bed & Breakfast ★★★
Farmhouse
Newton Lane, Tattenhall, Chester
CH3 9NE
t (01829) 770307
e fordfarmcheshire.co.uk

UTKINTON

Yew Tree Farm Bed & Breakfast
★★ *Farmhouse*
Fishers Green, Utkinton, Tarporley
CW6 0JG
t (01829) 732441

WARRINGTON

Happy Guests Lodge ★★★
Guest Accommodation
Tarporley Road, Dutton, Warrington
WA4 4EZ
t (01928) 790824
e ask@happyguestslodge.co.uk
w happyguestslodge.co.uk

WHITEGATE

Beechtree Farm Bed & Breakfast
★★★ *Bed & Breakfast*
Daleford Lane, Whitegate,
Northwich
CW8 2BW
t (01606) 301140
e marylspann@btinternet.com
w cheshire.homestay.googlepages.com/home

WIMBOLDSLEY

The Harvest Store B&B ★★★
Guest Accommodation
(formerly Hopley House),
Wimboldsley, Middlewich
CW10 0LN
t (01270) 526292
e mail@harveststore.co.uk
w harveststore.co.uk/

WINSFORD

Elm Cottage Bed & Breakfast
★★★ *Guest Accommodation*
Chester Lane, Winsford
CW7 2QJ
t (01829) 760544
e chris@elmcottagecp.co.uk
w elmcottagecp.co.uk

Cumbria

AINSTABLE

Heather Glen Country House
★★★ *Guest Accommodation*
Ainstable, Carlisle
CA4 9QQ
t (01768) 896219
e enquiries@heatherglencountryhouse.com
w heatherglencountryhouse.co.uk

ALSTON

Cumberland Inn ★★★ *Inn*
Townfoot, Alston, Cumbria
CA9 3HX
t (01434) 381875
e stay@cumberlandinnalston.com
w cumberlandinnalston.com

The Miners Arms ★★★ *Inn*
Nenthead, Alston, Cumbria
CA9 3PF
t (01434) 381427 mobile
07817615417
e theminersarms2@googlemail.com
w nenthead.com

YHA Alston ★★★ *Hostel*
The Firs, Alston
CA9 3RW
t (01434) 381509

AMBLESIDE

2 Cambridge Villas ★★★★
Guest House
Church Street, Ambleside
LA22 9DL
t (01539) 432142
e charles@black475.fsnet.co.uk
w 2cambridgevillas.co.uk

3 Cambridge Villas ★★★★
Guest House
Church Street, Ambleside
LA22 9DL
t (01539) 432307
e cambridgevillas3@aol.com
w 3cambridgevillas.co.uk

Ambleside Backpackers ★★
Backpackers
Iveing Cottage, Old Lake Road,
Ambleside
LA22 0DJ
t (01539) 432340
e enquiries@englishlakesbackpackers.co.uk
w englishlakesbackpackers.co.uk

Ambleside Central ★★★★
Guest Accommodation - Room Only
10 Lake Road, Ambleside
LA22 0AD
t 07732 440814
e ambleside@central.co.uk
w amblesidecentral.co.uk

Amboseli Lodge ★★★★
Bed & Breakfast SILVER AWARD
Rothay Road, Ambleside
LA22 0EE
t (015394) 31110
e enquiries@amboselilodge.co.uk
w amboselilodge.co.uk

Barnes Fell Guest House ★★★★
Guest House GOLD AWARD
Low Gale, Ambleside
LA22 0BB
t (015394) 33311
e info@barnesfell.co.uk
w barnesfell.co.uk

635

North West | Cumbria

Brantfell House ★★★★
Guest House SILVER AWARD
Rothay Road, Ambleside
LA22 0EE
t (015394) 32239
e stay@brantfell.co.uk
w brantfell.co.uk

Brantholme Guest House ★★★
Guest Accommodation
Millans Park, Ambleside
LA22 9AG
t (015394) 32034
e brantholme1@aol.com
w brantholme.co.uk

Brathay Lodge ★★★★
Guest Accommodation
Rothay Road, Ambleside
LA22 0EE
t (015394) 432000
e info@brathay-lodge.co.uk
w brathay-lodge.co.uk

Chapel House ★★★ *Guest House*
Kirkstone Road, Ambleside
LA22 9DZ
t (015394) 33143
e info@chapelhouse-ambleside.co.uk
w chapelhouse-ambleside.co.uk

Churchill Inn ★★★★ *Inn*
33 Lake Road, Ambleside
LA22 0BH
t (015394) 33192
w churchillhotel.uk.com

Claremont House ★★★★
Guest Accommodation
Compston Road, Ambleside
LA22 9DJ
t (015394) 33448
e enquiries@claremontambleside.co.uk
w claremontambleside.co.uk

Compston House American-Style B&B ★★★★ *Guest House*
Compston Road, Ambleside
LA22 9DJ
t (015394) 32305
e stay@compstonhouse.co.uk
w compstonhouse.co.uk

Crow How Country Guest House
★★★★ *Guest Accommodation*
SILVER AWARD
Rydal Road, Ambleside
LA22 9PN
t (015394) 32193
e stay@crowhow.co.uk
w crowhow.co.uk

Dower House ★★★★
Bed & Breakfast
Wray Castle, Low Wray, Ambleside
LA22 0JA
t (015394) 433211
e margaret@riggs.orangehome.co.uk
w dowerhouselakes.co.uk

Easedale Lodge Guest House
★★★★ *Guest House* GOLD AWARD
Compston Road, Ambleside
LA22 9DJ
t (015394) 32112
e enquiries@easedaleambleside.co.uk
w easedaleambleside.co.uk

Elder Grove ★★★★
Guest Accommodation
SILVER AWARD
Lake Road, Ambleside
LA22 0DB
t (015394) 432504
e info@eldergrove.co.uk
w eldergrove.co.uk

Far Nook ★★★★ *Bed & Breakfast*
GOLD AWARD
Rydal Road, Ambleside
LA22 9BA
t (015394) 31605
e stay@farnook.co.uk
w farnook.co.uk

Fell View ★★★ *Bed & Breakfast*
Cambridge House, Church Street, Ambleside
LA22 0BT
t (015394) 31343
e fellview@sky.com
w fellviewambleside.co.uk

Ferndale Lodge ★★★ *Guest House*
Lake Road, Ambleside
LA22 0DB
t (01539) 432207
e stay@ferndalelodge.co.uk
w ferndalelodge.co.uk

Fisherbeck ★★★★
Guest Accommodation
SILVER AWARD
Lake Road, Ambleside
LA22 0DH
t (015394) 33215
e email@fisherbeckhotel.co.uk
w fisherbeckhotel.co.uk

Foxghyll ★★★ *Bed & Breakfast*
Under Loughrigg, Ambleside, Cumbria
LA22 9LL
t (01539) 433292
e foxghyll@hotmail.com
w foxghyll.co.uk

Freshfields Guest House ★★★★
Guest House SILVER AWARD
Wansfell Road, Ambleside
LA22 0EG
t (015394) 34469
e info@freshfieldsguesthouse.co.uk
w freshfieldsguesthouse.co.uk

The Gables ★★★★
Guest Accommodation
Church Walk, Ambleside
LA22 9DJ
t (015394) 33272
e info@thegables-ambleside.co.uk
w thegables-ambleside.co.uk

Glenside ★★★★ *Bed & Breakfast*
SILVER AWARD
Old Lake Road, Ambleside
LA22 0DP
t (015394) 32635
e enquiries@glenside-ambleside.co.uk
w glenside-ambleside.co.uk

Highfield Bed & Breakfast ★★★★
Bed & Breakfast
Lake Road, Ambleside
LA22 0DB
t (015394) 32671
e info@highfield-ambleside.co.uk
w highfield-ambleside.co.uk

Hillsdale in Ambleside ★★★★
Guest Accommodation
Church Street, Ambleside
LA22 0BT
t (015394) 33174
e stay@hillsdaleambleside.co.uk
w hillsdaleambleside.co.uk

Holme Lea Guest House ★★★
Guest House
Church Street, Ambleside
LA22 0BT
t (015394) 32114
e enquiries@holmeleaguesthouse.co.uk
w holmeleaguesthouse.co.uk

Kingswood 'Bee & Bee' ★★★★
Guest House GOLD AWARD
Old Lake Road, Ambleside
LA22 0AE
t (015394) 34081
e info@kingswood-guesthouse.co.uk
w kingswood-guesthouse.co.uk

Lacet House ★★★★ *Guest House*
Kelsick Road, Ambleside
LA22 0EA
t (015394) 34342
e lacethouse@aol.com
w lacethouse.co.uk

Lattendales Guest House ★★★★
Guest House
Compston Road, Ambleside
LA22 9DJ
t (015394) 32368
e info@lattendales.co.uk
w lattendales.co.uk

Lyndale Guest House ★★★
Guest Accommodation
Low Fold, Lake Road, Ambleside
LA22 0DN
t (01539) 434244
e alison@lyndale-guesthouse.co.uk
w lyndale-guesthouse.co.uk

Meadowbank ★★★
Guest Accommodation
Rydal Road, Ambleside
LA22 9BA
t (01539) 432710
e enquiries@meadowbank.org.uk

Melrose Guest House ★★★★
Guest Accommodation
SILVER AWARD
Church Street, Ambleside
LA22 0BT
t (015394) 32500
e relax@melrose-guesthouse.co.uk
w melrose-guesthouse.co.uk

Nab Cottage ★★★ *Guest House*
Rydal, Grasmere, Ambleside
LA22 9SD
t (015394) 35311
e tim@nabcottage.com
w rydalwater.com

Norwood House ★★★★
Guest Accommodation
SILVER AWARD
Church Street, Ambleside
LA22 0BT
t (015394) 33349
e mail@norwoodhouse.net
w norwoodhouse.net

The Old Vicarage ★★★★
Guest Accommodation
Vicarage Road, Ambleside
LA22 9DH
t (015394) 33364
e info@oldvicarageambleside.co.uk
w oldvicarageambleside.co.uk

Park House Guest House ★★★★
Guest House SILVER AWARD
Compston Road, Ambleside
LA22 9DJ
t (015394) 31107
e mail@loughrigg.plus.com
w parkhouseguesthouse.co.uk

Red Bank ★★★★★ *Bed & Breakfast*
SILVER AWARD
Wansfell Road, Ambleside
LA22 0EG
t (01539) 434637
e info@red-bank.co.uk
w red-bank.co.uk

Riverside ★★★★ *Guest House*
GOLD AWARD
Under Loughrigg, Rothay Bridge, Ambleside
LA22 9LJ
t (015394) 32395
e info@riverside-at-ambleside.co.uk
w riverside-at-ambleside.co.uk

Rothay Garth ★★★★
Guest Accommodation
Rothay Road, Ambleside
LA22 0EE
t (015394) 32217
e book@rothay-garth.co.uk
w rothay-garth.co.uk

Rothay House ★★★
Guest Accommodation
Rothay Road, Ambleside
LA22 0EE
t (015394) 32434
e email@rothay-house.com
w rothay-house.com

Rysdale Guest House ★★★★
Guest Accommodation
SILVER AWARD
Rothay Road, Ambleside
LA22 0EE
t (015394) 32140
e info@rysdalehotel.co.uk
w rysdalehotel.co.uk

Smallwood House ★★★★
Guest Accommodation
Compston Road, Ambleside
LA22 9DJ
t (015394) 32330
e enq@smallwoodhotel.co.uk
w smallwoodhotel.co.uk

Thorneyfield Guest House ★★★
Guest House
Compston Road, Ambleside
LA22 9DJ
t (015394) 32464
e info@thorneyfield.co.uk
w thorneyfield.co.uk

Walmar ★★★★ *Guest House*
Lake Road, Ambleside
LA22 0DB
t (015394) 32454
e walmar.ambleside@tiscali.co.uk
w walmar-ambleside.co.uk

Wateredge Inn ★★★★ *Inn*
Waterhead Bay, Ambleside
LA22 0EP
t (015394) 432332
e stay@wateredginn.co.uk
w wateredginn.co.uk

Waterwheel Guesthouse ★★★★
Bed & Breakfast SILVER AWARD
3 Bridge Street, Ambleside
LA22 9DU
t (015394) 33286
e info@waterwheelambleside.co.uk
w waterwheelambleside.co.uk

Wordsworths Guest House
★★★★ *Guest Accommodation*
Lake Road, Ambleside
LA22 0DB
t (01539) 432095
e anna@wordsworthsguesthouse.co.uk
w wordsworthsguesthouse.co.uk

Wynford Guest House ★★★★
Bed & Breakfast
Nook Lane, Ambleside
LA22 9BH
t (015394) 32294
e wynfordgh@aol.com
w wynfordguesthouse.co.uk

ANTHORN

Kings Arms ★★ *Inn*
Bowness-on-Solway
CA7 5AS
t (01697) 351426
e info@kingsarmsbowness.co.uk
w kingsarmsbowness.co.uk

APPLEBY-IN-WESTMORLAND

Bank End House ★★★★
Bed & Breakfast
Cumbria, Appleby-in-Westmorland
CA16 6LH
t (01768) 352050
e stay@bankendhouse.co.uk
w bankendhouse.co.uk

Bongate House ★★★
Guest Accommodation
Bongate, Appleby-in-Westmorland, Cumbria
CA16 6UE
t (01768) 351245
e stay@bongatehouse.co.uk
w bongatehouse.co.uk

North West | Cumbria

oyal Oak Appleby ★★★★ Inn
Bongate, Appleby-in-
estmorland
A16 6UN
t (01768) 351463
e jan@royaloakappleby.co.uk
w royaloakappleby.co.uk

ARNSIDE

umber 43 ★★★★★
uest Accommodation
GOLD AWARD
e Promenade, Arnside
A5 0AA
t (01524) 762761
e lesley@no43.org.uk
w no43.org.uk

he Willowfield ★★★★
uest Accommodation
The Promenade, Arnside
A5 0AD
t (01524) 761354
e info@thewillowfield.co.uk
w thewillowfield.co.uk

HA Arnside ★★★ Hostel
akfield Lodge, Redhills Road,
rnside
A5 0AT
t (01524) 761781
e arnside@yha.org.uk
w yha.org.uk

ASPATRIA

astlemont ★★★ Bed & Breakfast
spatria, Wigton, Cumbria
A7 2JU
t (016973) 20205
e castlemont@tesco.net
w britainsfinest.co.uk

BAMPTON

ardale Inn @ St Patricks Well
★★★ Inn
St Patrick's Well, Bampton,
A10 2RQ
t (01931) 713244
e info@mardaleinn.co.uk
w mardaleinn.co.uk

BAMPTON GRANGE

rown & Mitre Inn ★★★★ Inn
ampton Grange, Penrith
A10 2QR
t (01931) 713225
e info@crown-and-mitre.co.uk
w crown-and-mitre.co.uk

BANKS

uarry Side ★★★★
ed & Breakfast
anks, Brampton
A8 2JH
t (01697) 72538
e elizabeth.harding@btinternet.com

BARNGATES

he Drunken Duck Inn ★★★★★
n GOLD AWARD
arngates, Hawkshead, Ambleside
A22 0NG
t (015394) 36347
e info@drunkenduckinn.co.uk
w drunkenduckinn.co.uk

BARROW-IN-FURNESS

ast Mount House ★★★
uest House
5 East Mount, Barrow-in-Furness
A13 9AD
t (01229) 871063
e info@eastmounthouse.co.uk
w eastmounthouse.co.uk

November House ★★★★
Bed & Breakfast SILVER AWARD
3 Hawcoat Lane, Barrow-in-Furness
LA14 4HE
t (01229) 827247
e november-house@tiscali.co.uk
w novemberhouse.co.uk

BASSENTHWAITE

Highside Farm ★★★★ Farmhouse
SILVER AWARD
Bassenthwaite, Keswick
CA12 4QG
t (01768) 776952
e info@highside.co.uk
w highside.co.uk

Ouse Bridge House ★★★★
Guest House SILVER AWARD
Bassenthwaite Lake, Dubwath,
Bassenthwaite
CA13 9YD
t (01768) 776322
e enquiries@ousebridge.com
w ousebridge.com

BASSENTHWAITE LAKE

Lakeside Country Guest House
★★★★ Guest Accommodation
SILVER AWARD
Bassenthwaite Lake, Dubwath,
Keswick
CA13 9YD
t (01768) 776358
e info@lakesidebassenthwaite.co.uk
w lakesidebassenthwaite.co.uk

Link House by Bassenthwaite
Lake ★★★★ Guest House
Bassenthwaite Lake, Keswick,
Cockermouth
CA13 9YD
t (01768) 776291
e info@link-house.co.uk
w link-house.co.uk

BEETHAM

Barn Close/North West Birds
★★★ Bed & Breakfast
Barn Close, Beetham, Milnthorpe
LA7 7AL
t (015395) 63191
e anne@nwbirds.co.uk
w nwbirds.co.uk/bcindex.htm

BERRIER

Whitbarrow Farm ★★★★
Farmhouse SILVER AWARD
Berrier, Penrith
CA11 0XB
t (01768) 483366
e mary@whitbarrowfarm.co.uk
w whitbarrowfarm.co.uk

BLACKFORD

Mount Farm Bed & Breakfast
★★★★ Farmhouse
Blackford, Carlisle
CA6 4ER
t (01228) 674641
e judith.wilson11@btinternet.com
w mount-farm.co.uk

BOLTON

Tarka House ★★★★
Guest Accommodation
Bolton, Appleby-in-Westmorland
CA16 6AW
t (01768) 361422

BOLTONGATE

Boltongate Old Rectory ★★★★★
Guest Accommodation
GOLD AWARD
The Old Rectory, Boltongate,
Bassenthwaite
CA7 1DA
t (01697) 371647
e boltongate@talk21.com
w boltongateoldrectory.com

BOOT

Eskdale YHA ★★★ Hostel
Holmrook, Boot, Eskdale
CA19 1TH
t (01946) 723219

BORROWDALE

Ashness Farm ★★★★ Farmhouse
Keswick, Borrowdale
CA12 5UN
t (01768) 777361
e enquiries@ashnessfarm.co.uk
w ashnessfarm.co.uk

Derwentwater YHA ★★★ Hostel
Barrow House, Borrowdale, Keswick
CA12 5UR
t (01768) 777246
e derwentwater@yha.org.uk
w yha.org.uk/find-accommodation/
the-lake-district/hostels/derwe
ntwater/index.aspx

Hazel Bank Country House
★★★★★ Guest House
GOLD AWARD
Rosthwaite, Borrowdale, Keswick
CA12 5XB
t (01768) 777248
e info@hazelbankhotel.co.uk
w hazelbankhotel.co.uk

BOWNESS-ON-SOLWAY

The Old Chapel ★★★
Bed & Breakfast
Wigton, Bowness-on-Solway
CA7 5BL
t (01697) 351126
e oldchapelbowness@hotmail.com
w oldchapelbownessonsolway.co.uk

Shore Gate House ★★★
Guest Accommodation
Wigton, Bowness-on-Solway
CA7 5BH
t (01697) 351308
e bookings@shoregatehouse.co.uk
w shoregatehouse.co.uk

Wallsend House, The Old Rectory
★★★★ Guest Accommodation
Church Lane, Bowness-on-Solway
CA7 5AF
t (01697) 351055
e bandb@wallsend.net
w wallsend.net

BOWNESS-ON-WINDERMERE

Belsfield House ★★★★
Guest House
Kendal Road, Bowness-on-
Windermere, Bowness
LA23 3EQ
t (015394) 45823
e enquiries@belsfieldhouse.co.uk
w belsfieldhouse.co.uk

Brooklands ★★★
Guest Accommodation
Ferry View, Bowness-on-
Windermere, Windermere
LA23 3JB
t (015394) 42344
e enquiries@brooklandsguest
house.net
w brooklandsguesthouse.net

The Cranleigh ★★★★★
Guest House GOLD AWARD
Kendal Road, Bowness-on-
Windermere, Bowness
LA23 3EW
t (015394) 43293
e enquiries@thecranleigh.com
w thecranleigh.com

Eastbourne Guest House ★★★★
Guest House SILVER AWARD
Biskey Howe Road, Bowness-on-
Windermere, Bowness
LA23 2JR
t (015394) 88657
e stay@eastbourne-windermere.co.
uk
w eastbourne-windermere.co.uk

Holmlea Guest House ★★★
Guest House
Kendal Road, Bowness-on-
Windermere, Bowness
LA23 3EW
t (015394) 42597
e info@holmleaguesthouse.co.uk
w holmleaguesthouse.co.uk

Laurel Cottage Bowness ★★★★
Guest House
Kendal Road, Bowness-on-
Windermere, Bowness
LA23 3EF
t (015394) 45594
e enquiries@laurelcottage-bnb.co.
uk
w laurelcottage-bnb.co.uk

May Cottage B&B ★★★
Bed & Breakfast
Kendal Road, Bowness-on-
Windermere
LA23 3EW
t (015394) 46478
e bnb@maycottagebowness.co.uk
w maycottagebowness.co.uk

Melbourne Guest House ★★★
Guest Accommodation
2-3 Biskey Howe Road, Bowness-on-
Windermere, Windermere
LA23 2JP
t (015394) 43475
e info@melbournecottage.co.uk
w melbournecottage.co.uk

The Royal Oak Inn ★★★ Inn
Brantfell Road, Bowness-on-
Windermere, Bowness
LA23 3EG
t (015394) 43970
e info@royaloak-windermere.co.uk
w royaloak-windermere.co.uk

Storrs Gate House ★★★★★
Guest House SILVER AWARD
Longtail Hill, Bowness-on-
Windermere, Windermere
LA23 3JD
t (015394) 43272
e enquiries@storrsgatehouse.co.uk
w storrsgatehouse.co.uk

The Westbourne ★★★★
Guest House SILVER AWARD
Biskey Howe Road, Bowness-on-
Windermere, Bowness
LA23 2JR
t (015394) 43625
e info@westbourne-lakes.co.uk
w westbourne-lakes.co.uk

BRAITHWAITE

Hermiston ★★★★ Guest House
SILVER AWARD
Braithwaite, Keswick
CA12 5RY
t (01768) 778190
e tracy.rostron@tiscali.co.uk
w hermiston-keswick.co.uk

Howe View ★★★★ Bed & Breakfast
Braithwaite, Keswick
CA12 5SZ
t (01768) 778593
e info@howeview.co.uk
w howeview.co.uk

Maple Bank ★★★★ Guest House
Braithwaite, Keswick
CA12 5RY
t (01768) 778229
e enquiries@maplebank.co.uk
w maplebank.co.uk

637

North West | Cumbria

Middle Ruddings ★★★ *Inn*
Braithwaite, Keswick
CA12 5RY
t (01768) 778436
e middleruddings@btconnect.com
w middle-ruddings.co.uk

BRAMPTON

Scarrow Hill Guest House ★★★★
Bed & Breakfast **SILVER AWARD**
Denton Mill, Scarrow Hill, Brampton
CA8 2QU
t (01697) 746759
e lindamac@scarrowhillhouse.co.uk
w scarrowhillhouse.co.uk

Walltown Lodge B&B ★★★★
Bed & Breakfast
Green Head, Brampton
CA8 7JD
t 01697 747514
e diane@walltownlodge.com
w walltownlodge.com

BRIGHAM

Dufton House ★★★★
Guest Accommodation
114 High Brigham, Brigham, Cockermouth
CA13 9TJ
t (01900) 827047
e dutonhouse@btinternet.com
w duftonhouse.co.uk

BRIGSTEER

Plumtree House ★★★
Bed & Breakfast
Brigsteer, Kendal
LA8 8AR
t (015395) 68774
e stay@plumtreehouse.co.uk
w plumtreehouse.co.uk

BRISCO

Crossroads House ★★★★
Bed & Breakfast **GOLD AWARD**
Brisco, Carlisle
CA4 0QZ
t (01228) 528994
e viv@crossroadshouse.co.uk
w crossroadshouse.co.uk

BROUGH

Augill Castle ★★★★★
Guest Accommodation
EXCELLENCE AWARD
Brough, Kirkby Stephen
CA17 4DE
t (01768) 341937
e enquiries@stayinacastle.com
w stayinacastle.co.uk

Ing Hill Lodge ★★★★
Bed & Breakfast
Mallerstang Dale, Kirkby Stephen
CA17 4JT
t (01768) 371153
e tony.sawyer@ing-hill-lodge.co.uk
w ing-hill-lodge.co.uk

River View ★★★★ *Bed & Breakfast*
Kirkby Stephen, Brough
CA17 4BZ
t (01768) 341894
e riverviewbb@btinternet.com
w riverviewbb.co.uk

BROUGHTON IN FURNESS

Low Hall Farm ★★★★ *Farmhouse*
Kirkby-in-Furness, Broughton-in-Furness
LA17 7TR
t (01229) 889120
e enquiries@low-hall.co.uk
w low-hall.co.uk

BURGH-BY-SANDS

Highfield Farm ★★★★ *Farmhouse*
Boustead Hill,, Burgh-by-Sands, Carlisle
CA5 6AA
t (01228) 576060
e info@highfield-holidays.co.uk
w highfield-holidays.co.uk

Hillside Farm ★★★ *Bed & Breakfast*
Boustead Hill, Burgh-by-Sands, Carlisle
CA5 6AA
t (01228) 576398
e ruddshillside1@btinternet.com
w hadrianswalkbnb.co.uk

Rosemount Cottage ★★★★
Guest Accommodation
GOLD AWARD
Rosemount, Burgh-by-Sands, Carlisle
CA5 6AN
t (01228) 576440
e tweentown@aol.com
w rosemountcottage.co.uk

BUTTERMERE

Buttermere YHA ★★★ *Hostel*
King George VI Memorial Hostel, Cockermouth
CA13 9XA
t (01768) 770245

Fish Inn *Inn*
Buttermere, Nr Cockermouth
CA13 9XA
t 017687 70253
e info@fishinnbuttermere.co.uk
w fishinnbuttermere.co.uk

CALDBECK

Swaledale Watch ★★★★
Guest Accommodation
SILVER AWARD
Whelpo, Caldbeck
CA7 8HQ
t (01697) 478409
e nan.savage@talk21.com
w swaledale-watch.co.uk

YHA Caldbeck ★★★ *Group Hostel*
Fellside Centre, Fellside, Witon
CA7 8HA
t (01768) 772816

CARLISLE

Abberley House ★★★★
Bed & Breakfast
33 Victoria Place, Carlisle
CA1 1HP
t (01228) 521645
e booking@abberleyhouse.co.uk
w abberleyhouse.co.uk

Abbey Court ★★★★
Guest Accommodation
24 London Road, Carlisle
CA1 2EL
t (01228) 528696
e abbeycourtguesthouse.co.uk

Ashbourne House ★★★
Guest House
11 Lazonby Terrace, Carlisle
CA1 2PZ
t (01228) 523500
w ashbourneguesthouse.com

Ashleigh Guest House ★★★★
Guest House
46 Victoria Place, Carlisle
CA1 1EX
t (01228) 521631
e ashleighhouse@hotmail.com
w ashleighbedandbreakfast.co.uk

Bessiestown Farm Country Guesthouse ★★★★★
Guest Accommodation
GOLD AWARD
Catlowdy, Longtown, Carlisle
CA6 5QP
t (01228) 577219
e info@bessiestown.co.uk
w bessiestown.co.uk

Cartref Guest House ★★★★
Guest House **GOLD AWARD**
44 Victoria Place, Carlisle
CA1 1EX
t (01228) 522077
e cartref1@sky.com

Cherry Grove ★★★★
Guest Accommodation
87 Petteril Street, Carlisle
CA1 2AW
t (01228) 541942
e cherrygroveguesthouse.co.uk

Cornerways Guest House ★★★★
Guest Accommodation
107 Warwick Road, Carlisle, Cumbria
CA1 1EA
t 01228 521733
e info@cornerwaysbandb.co.uk
w cornerwaysbandb.co.uk

Courtfield Guest House ★★★★
Guest House **SILVER AWARD**
169 Warwick Road, Carlisle
CA1 1LP
t (01228) 522767
e mdawes@courtfieldhouse.fsnet.co.uk
w a1tourism.com/uk/a9469.html

East View Guest House ★★★★
Guest Accommodation
110 Warwick Road, Carlisle
CA1 1JU
t (01228) 522112
e eastviewgh@hotmail.co.uk
w eastviewguesthouse.co.uk

Fernlee Guest House ★★★★
Guest House **SILVER AWARD**
9 St Aidans Road, Carlisle
CA1 1LT
t (01228) 511930
e enquiries@fernlee-guest-house.co.uk

Howard Lodge Guest House
★★★★ *Guest Accommodation*
90 Warwick Road, Carlisle
CA1 1JU
t (01228) 529842
e chrltdavi@aol.com
w howard-lodge.co.uk

Kate's Guest House ★★★
Guest House
6 Lazonby Terrace, London Road, Harraby Green, Carlisle
CA1 2PZ
t 01228 539577
e katesguesthouse@hotmail.co.uk

Knockupworth Hall ★★★★
Bed & Breakfast
Burgh Road, Carlisle
CA2 7RF
t (01228) 523531
e knockupworthdi@aol.com
w knockupworthdi.co.uk

Langleigh House ★★★★
Guest House
6 Howard Place, Carlisle
CA1 1HR
t (01228) 530440
e langleighhouse@aol.com
w langleighhouse.co.uk

Number Thirty One ★★★★★
Guest House **GOLD AWARD**
31 Howard Place, Carlisle
CA1 1HR
t (01228) 597080
e pruirving@aol.com
w number31.co.uk

Old Brewery Residences ★★★
Hostel
Bridge Lane, Caldewgate, Carlisle
CA2 5SR
t (01228) 597352
e deec@impacthousing.org.uk
w impacthousing.org.uk

Townhouse B&B ★★★★
Guest Accommodation
153 Warwick Road, Carlisle
CA1 1LU
t (01228) 598782
e townhouse@christine60.freesereve.co.uk
w townhousebandb.com

University of Cumbria - Carlisle
★★★★ *Campus*
Fusehill Street, Carlisle
CA1 2HH
t (01228) 616317
e andrew.smith@cumbria.ac.uk
w conferencescumbria.co.uk

Vallum House ★★★ *Guest House*
73 Burgh Road, Carlisle
CA2 7NB
t (01228) 521860
e denmar39@tiscali.co.uk
w vallumhousehotel.co.uk

Warren Guest House
Guest Accommodation
368 Warwick Road, Carlisle
CA1 2RU
t (01228) 533663

White Lea Guest House ★★★★
Bed & Breakfast
191 Warwick Road, Carlisle
CA1 1LP
t (01228) 533139

CARTMEL

Cavendish Arms ★★★ *Inn*
Cavendish Street, Cartmel
LA11 6QA
t (015395) 36240
e info@thecavendisharms.co.uk
w thecavendisharms.co.uk

CASTERTON

The Pheasant Inn ★★★★ *Inn*
Casterton, Kirkby Lonsdale
LA6 2RX
t (01524) 271230
e info@pheasantinn.co.uk
w pheasantinn.co.uk

CATTERLEN

The Ginney Country Guest House
★★★★ *Farmhouse*
Low Dyke, Catterlen, Penrith
CA11 0BQ
t (01768) 890789
e linda@theginneycatterlen.co.uk
w theginneycatterlen.co.uk

CAUTLEY

St Mark's ★★★★
Guest Accommodation
Cautley, Sedbergh
LA10 5LZ
t (01539) 620287
e saint.marks@btinternet.com
w saintmarks.uk.com

CLIFTON

George & Dragon ★★★★ *Inn*
George and Dragon, Clifton, Penrith
CA10 2ER
t (01768) 865381
e enquiries@georgeanddragonclifton.co.uk
w georgeanddragonclifton.co.uk

The White House Experience
Guest House ★★★★
Guest Accommodation
Clifton, Penrith
CA10 2EL
t (01768) 865115
e info@thewhitehouseexperience.co.uk
w thewhitehouseexperience.co.uk

COCKERMOUTH

Cockermouth YHA ★★ *Hostel*
Double Mills, Fern Bank Road, Cockermouth
CA13 0DS
t (01900) 822561
e cockermouth@yha.org.uk

North West | Cumbria

raysonside ★★★★
uest Accommodation
OLD AWARD
rton Road, Cockermouth
A13 9TQ
t (01900) 822351
e stay@graysonside.co.uk
w graysonside.co.uk

he Old Homestead ★★★★
uest House
umbria, Cockermouth
A13 9TW
t (01900) 822223
e info@byresteads.co.uk
w byresteads.co.uk

ose Cottage ★★★★ *Guest House*
LVER AWARD
rton Road, Cockermouth
A13 9DX
t (01900) 822189
e bookings@rosecottageguest.co.uk
w rosecottageguest.co.uk

COLBY

he Limes ★★★★ *Bed & Breakfast*
LVER AWARD
olby, Appleby-in-Westmorland
A16 6BD
t (01768) 351605
e info@orangesatthelimes.co.uk
w orangesatthelimes.co.uk

CONISTON

eech Tree House ★★★★
uest House
ewdale Road, Coniston
A21 8DX
t (015394) 41717

oniston Coppermines YHA ★★★
ostel
oniston Coppermines,
oppermines House, Coniston
A21 8HP
t (015394) 41261
e coppermines@yha.org.uk
w yha.org.uk

oniston YHA ★★★ *Hostel*
olly How, Far End, Coniston
A21 8DD
t (01539) 441323

rown Inn ★★★★ *Inn*
lberthwaite Avenue, Coniston
A21 8ED
t (01539) 441243
e info@crowninnconiston.com
w crowninnconiston.com

akeland House ★★★★
uest Accommodation
lberthwaite Avenue, Coniston
A21 8ED
t (01539) 41303
e hollsbcb@lakelandhouse.com
w lakelandhouse.com

aklands Guest House ★★★★
uest Accommodation
ewdale Road, Coniston, Cumbria
A21 8DX
t (01539) 441245
e judithzelea@oaklandsguesthouse.fsnet.co.uk
w oaklandsconiston.co.uk

rchard Cottage ★★★★
ed & Breakfast
8 Yewdale Road, Coniston
A21 8DU
t (01539) 441319
e enquiries@conistonholidays.co.uk
w conistonholidays.co.uk

he Sun, Coniston ★★★★ *Inn*
he Sun, Coniston
A21 8HQ
t (01539) 441248
e info@thesunconiston.com
w thesunconiston.com

Thwaite Cottage ★★★★
Bed & Breakfast
Waterhead, Coniston
LA21 8AJ
t (015394) 41367
e info@thwaitecottage.co.uk
w thwaitecottage.co.uk

Yewdale Inn ★★★ *Inn*
Yewdale Road, Coniston
LA21 8DU
t (01539) 441280
e mail@yewdalehotel.com
w yewdalehotel.com

Yew Tree Farm ★★★★★
Farmhouse GOLD AWARD
Cumbria, Coniston
LA21 8DP
t (015394) 41433
e info@yewtree-farm.com
w yewtree-farm.com

CONISTONWATER

Monk Coniston
Guest Accommodation
Coniston, Conistonwater
LA21 8AQ
t (015394) 41566

COTEHILL

The Green ★★★★ *Bed & Breakfast*
The Green, Cotehill, Carlisle
CA4 0EA
t (01228) 561824
e thegreenbb@uwclub.net
w thegreenbandb.com

CROOK

Gilpin Mill ★★★★★ *Farmhouse*
Crook, Kendal, Bowness
LA8 8LN
t (015395) 68405
e info@gilpinmill.co.uk
w gilpinmill.co.uk

CROSBY RAVENSWORTH

Crake Trees Manor ★★★★
Farmhouse GOLD AWARD
Crosby Ravensworth, Penrith,
Appleby-in-Westmorland
CA10 3JG
t (01931) 715205
e ruth@craketreesmanor.co.uk
w craketreesmanor.co.uk

CULGAITH

Laurel House ★★★★
Bed & Breakfast GOLD AWARD
Culgaith, Penrith
CA10 1QL
t (01768) 886380
e laurelhouse@fsmail.net
w laurelhousecumbria.co.uk

Shepherds Croft ★★★★
Bed & Breakfast
Shepherds Croft, Culgaith, Penrith
CA10 1QW
t (01768) 88484
e bandb@shepherdscroft-culgaith.co.uk
w shepherdscroft-culgaith.co.uk

DENT

The George & Dragon ★★★ *Inn*
Main Street, Dent, Sedbergh
LA10 5QL
t (015396) 25356
e mail@thegeorgeanddragondent.co.uk
w thegeorgeanddragondent.co.uk

DOCKRAY

Royal Hotel ★★★★ *Inn*
Dockray, Penrith, Ullswater
CA11 0JY
t (01768) 482356
e info@the-royal-dockray.co.uk
w the-royal-dockray.co.uk

DUDDON BRIDGE

Dower House ★★★
Guest Accommodation
High Duddon, Duddon Bridge,
Broughton-in-Furness
LA20 6ET
t (01229) 716279
e rozanne.nichols@ukgateway.net
w dowerhouse.biz

DUFTON

Brow Farm Bed & Breakfast
★★★★ *Farmhouse* SILVER AWARD
Dufton, Appleby-in-Westmorland,
Cumbria
CA16 6DF
t (01768) 352865
e stay@browfarm.com
w browfarm.com

YHA Dufton ★★★★ *Hostel*
Redstones, Dufton, Appleby-in-Westmorland
CA16 6DB
t (01768) 351236
e dufton@yha.org.uk
w yha.org.uk

ELTERWATER

Britannia Inn ★★★ *Inn*
Elterwater, Langdale
LA22 9HP
t (015394) 37210
e info@britinn.co.uk
w britinn.co.uk

The Eltermere Inn ★★★★ *Inn*
Elterwater, Langdale Valley,
Langdale
LA22 9HY
t (015394) 37207
e info@eltermere.co.uk
w eltermere.co.uk

Elterwater YHA ★★★ *Hostel*
Elterwater, Ambleside
LA22 9HX
t 0870 770 5816
e elterwater@yha.org.uk
w yha.org.uk

ENNERDALE

YHA Black Sail ★ *Hostel*
High Gillerthwaite, Ennerdale,
Cockermouth
CA23 3AX
t 0845 371 9680
e blacksail@yha.org.uk
w blacksail@yha.org.uk

YHA Ennerdale ★★★★ *Hostel*
Cat Crag, Ennerdale, Cockermouth
CA23 3AX
t 0845 770 5820
e ennerdale@yha.org.uk
w yha.org.uk

FAR SAWREY

West Vale Country House
★★★★★ *Guest Accommodation*
GOLD AWARD
Far Sawrey, Hawkshead
LA22 0LQ
t (015394) 42817
e enquiries@westvalecountryhouse.co.uk
w westvalecountryhouse.co.uk

GILSLAND

Birdoswald YHA ★★★★ *Hostel*
Birdoswald Roman Fort, Gilsland,
Brampton
CA8 7DD
t 0870 770 8868

Bush Nook Guest House ★★★★
Guest House
Upper Denton, Gilsland, Brampton
CA8 7AF
t (01697) 747194
e info@bushnook.co.uk
w bushnook.co.uk

Gilsland Spa ★★★★
Guest Accommodation
Gilsland, Brampton
CA8 7AR
t (01697) 747203
e reception@gilslandspahotel.fsnet.co.uk
w gilslandspa.co.uk

Hadrian's Wall Residential Study Centre *Group Hostel*
Birdoswald Roman Fort, Gilsland,
Brampton
CA8 7DD
t (01697) 747602
e birdoswald.romanfort@english-heritage.org.uk
w english-heritage.org.uk

The Hill on the Wall ★★★★★
Guest Accommodation
GOLD AWARD
Gilsland, Brampton
CA8 7DA
t (01697) 747214
e info@hadrians-wallbedandbreakfast.com
w hadrians-wallbedandbreakfast.com

GLENRIDDING

Helvellyn YHA ★★ *Hostel*
Greenside, Glenridding, Ullswater
CA11 0QR
t (01768) 482269
e helvellyn@yha.org.uk
w yha.org.uk

Mosscrag Guest House ★★★
Guest House
Glenridding, Penrith, Ullswater
CA11 0PA
t (01768) 482500
e info@mosscrag.co.uk
w mosscrag.co.uk

GRANGE-OVER-SANDS

Elton Guest House ★★★★
Guest House
Windermere Road, Grange-over-Sands
LA11 6EQ
t (015395) 32838
e info@eltonprivatehotel.co.uk
w eltonprivatehotel.co.uk

GRASMERE

Beck Allans Guest House ★★★★
Guest House SILVER AWARD
Beck Allans Guest House, College Street, Grasmere
LA22 9SZ
t (015394) 35563
e mail@beckallans.com
w beckallans.com/guesthouse.html

Dunmail House ★★★★★
Bed & Breakfast SILVER AWARD
Keswick Road, Grasmere
LA22 9RE
t (015394) 35256
e info@dunmailhouse.com
w dunmailhouse.com

Grasmere Butharlyp Howe YHA
★★★★ *Hostel*
Easdale Road, Grasmere
LA22 9QG
t 0870 770 5836
e grasmere@yha.org.uk
w yha.org.uk

Grasmere Independent Hostel
★★★★ *Hostel*
Broadrayne Farm, Grasmere
LA22 9RU
t (015394) 35055
e bev@grasmerehostel.co.uk
w grasmerehostel.co.uk

639

North West | Cumbria

Heron Beck Guest House ★★★★
Guest Accommodation
GOLD AWARD
Cumbria, Grasmere
LA22 9RB
t (015394) 35272
e info@heronbeck.com
w heronbeck.com

How Foot Lodge ★★★
Guest House
Town End, Grasmere
LA22 9SQ
t (015394) 35366
e enquiries@howfoot.co.uk
w howfoot.co.uk

Lake View Country House ★★★★
Guest House **GOLD AWARD**
Lake View Drive, Grasmere
LA22 9TD
t (015394) 35384
e info@lakeview-grasmere.com
w lakeview-grasmere.com

Stonegarth ★★★★★
Guest Accommodation
Lake View Drive, Grasmere
LA22 9TD
t (015394) 35458
e info@stonegarth-guesthouse.co.uk
w stonegarth-guesthouse.co.uk

The Travellers Rest Inn ★★★ *Inn*
Cumbria, Grasmere
LA22 9RR
t 05006 00725
e stay@lakedistrictinns.co.uk
w lakedistrictinns.co.uk/travellers_welcome.cfm

YHA Grasmere (Thorney How) ★
Hostel
Easedale Road, Ambleside
LA22 9QG
t (015394) 435316

GREAT STRICKLAND

The Strickland Arms ★★★ *Inn*
Great Strickland, Penrith
CA10 3DF
t (01931) 712238
e stricklandarmspenrith@hotmail.co.uk
w thestricklandarms.co.uk

GREYSTOKE

Stafford House ★★★★ *Hostel*
Greystoke, Penrith
CA11 0TQ
t (01768) 483558
e hazel.knight@btconnect.com
w coast-and-castles.co.uk

HALLBANKGATE

Belted Will Inn ★★★ *Inn*
Hallbankgate, Brampton
CA8 2NJ
t (01697) 746236
e stephenbeltedwill@yahoo.co.uk
w beltedwill.co.uk

HAWKSHEAD

Crosslands Farm ★★★★
Farmhouse
Rusland, Hawkshead, Nr Ulverston, Cumbria
LA12 8JU
t (01229) 860242
e enquiries@crosslandsfarm.co.uk
w crosslandsfarm.co.uk

Hawkshead YHA ★★★ *Hostel*
Esthwaite Lodge, Ambleside
LA22 0QD
t (015394) 436193

Howe Farm Bed & Breakfast
★★★★ *Farmhouse*
Howe Farm, Hawkshead, Ambleside
LA22 0QB
t (015394) 36345
e lisa.woodhouse@btconnect.com
w howefarm.co.uk

Ivy House & Restaurant ★★★★
Guest House
Main Street, Hawkshead, Cumbria
LA22 0NS
t 01539436204
e ivyhousehotel@btconnect.com
w ivyhousehotel.com

Walker Ground Manor ★★★★★
Bed & Breakfast **GOLD AWARD**
Vicarage Lane, Hawkshead
LA22 0PD
t (015394) 36219
e info@walkerground.co.uk
w walkerground.co.uk

HAWKSHEAD HILL

Summer Hill Country House
★★★★ *Guest Accommodation*
GOLD AWARD
Hawkshead Hill, Ambleside
LA22 0PR
t (01539) 436180
e info@summerhillcountryhouse.com
w summerhillcountryhouse.com

Yewfield Vegetarian Guest House
★★★★★ *Guest Accommodation*
SILVER AWARD
Hawkshead Hill, Hawkshead, Ambleside
LA22 0PR
t 01539 436765
e derek.yewfield@btinternet.com
w yewfield.co.uk

HEADS NOOK

Croft House ★★★★★ *Farmhouse*
SILVER AWARD
Newbiggin, Brampton, Carlisle
CA8 9DH
t (01768) 896695
e info@crofthousecumbria.co.uk
w crofthousecumbria.co.uk

String of Horses Inn ★★★ *Inn*
Faugh, Heads Nook, Brampton, Carlisle
CA8 9EG
t (01228) 670297
e info@stringofhorses.com
w stringofhorses.com

HELSINGTON

Helsington Laithes Manor ★★★★
Bed & Breakfast
Helsington, Kendal
LA9 5RJ
t (01539) 741253
e themanor@helsington.uk.com
w helsington.uk.com

HESKET NEWMARKET

Daffodil ★★★★★ *Farmhouse*
SILVER AWARD
Banks Farm, Hesket Newmarket, Penrith
CA7 8HR
t 01697478137
e banksfarm@mac.com
w daffodilbanksfarm.co.uk

Denton House ★★★★ *Guest House*
Hesket Newmarket, Caldbeck
CA7 8JG
t (01697) 478415
e dentonhnm@aol.com
w dentonhouseguesthouse.co.uk

HIGH LORTON

Swinside End Farm ★★★★★
Farmhouse **SILVER AWARD**
Scales, High Lorton, Cockermouth
CA13 9UA
t (01900) 85136
e karen@swinsideendfarm.co.uk
w swinsideendfarm.co.uk

Terrace Farm ★★★★ *Farmhouse*
High Lorton, Cockermouth
CA13 9TX
t (01900) 85278
e catherine@terracefarm.co.uk
w terracefarm.co.uk

HIGH WRAY

High Wray Farm B&B ★★★★
Farmhouse **SILVER AWARD**
High Wray, Ambleside
LA22 0JE
t (015394) 32280
e sheila@highwrayfarm.co.uk
w highwrayfarm.co.uk

INGS

The Hill ★★★★
Guest Accommodation
SILVER AWARD
Ings, Windermere
LA8 9QQ
t (015398) 22217
e thehill@ktdinternet.com
w thehillonline.co.uk

Meadowcroft Country Guest House ★★★★ *Guest House*
Ings, Windermere
LA8 9PY
t (015398) 21171
e info@meadowcroft-guesthouse.com
w meadowcroft-guesthouse.com

The Watermill Inn & Brewery
★★★★ *Inn*
Ings, Windermere
LA8 9PY
t (015398) 21309
e info@watermillinn.co.uk
w watermillinn.co.uk

IRTHINGTON

Newtown Farm ★★★★ *Farmhouse*
Newtown, Irthington, Carlisle
CA6 4NX
t (01697) 72768
e susangrice@tiscali.co.uk
w newtownfarmbedandbreakfast.co.uk

Vallum Barn ★★★★
Bed & Breakfast **SILVER AWARD**
Irthington, Carlisle
CA6 4NN
t (01697) 742478
e vallumbarn@tinyworld.co.uk
w vallumbarn.co.uk

KENDAL

Beech House ★★★★★
Guest House **SILVER AWARD**
40 Greenside, Kendal
LA9 4LD
t (01539) 720385
e stay@beechhouse-kendal.co.uk
w beechhouse-kendal.co.uk

Bridge House
Guest Accommodation
65 Castle Street, Kendal
LA9 7AD
t (015397) 22041
e sheila@bridgehouse-kendal.co.uk
w bridgehouse-kendal.co.uk

The Glen ★★★★ *Guest House*
Oxenholme, Kendal
LA9 7RF
t (01539) 726386
e greenintheglen@btinternet.com
w glen-kendal.co.uk

Hillside Bed & Breakfast ★★★★
Guest Accommodation
4 Beast Banks, Kendal
LA9 4JW
t (015397) 22836
e info@hillside-kendal.co.uk
w hillside-kendal.co.uk

Lyndhurst Guest House ★★★
Guest Accommodation
8 South Road, Kendal
LA9 5QH
t (015397) 23819
e stay@lyndhurst-kendal.co.uk
w lyndhurst-kendal.co.uk

Riversleigh Guest House ★★★
Guest House
49 Milnthorpe Road, Kendal
LA9 5QG
t (01539) 726392

Sonata Guest House ★★★★
Guest House
19 Burneside Road, Kendal
LA9 4RL
t (015397) 732290
e chris@sonataguesthouse.freeserve.co.uk
w sonataguesthouse.co.uk

Summerhow House ★★★★★
Guest Accommodation
Shap Road, Kendal
LA9 6NY
t (015397) 20763
e stay@summerhowbedandbreakfast.co.uk
w summerhowbedandbreakfast.co.uk

Sundial House ★★★
Guest Accommodation
51 Milnthorpe Road, Kendal
LA9 5QG
t (015397) 24468
e info@sundialguesthousekendal.co.uk
w sundialguesthousekendal.co.uk

YHA Kendal ★★★ *Hostel*
118 Highgate, Kendal
LA9 4HE
t 0870 770 5892
e kendal@yha.org.uk
w yha.org.uk/find-accommodation/the-lake-district/hostels/kendal/index.aspx

KESWICK

Abacourt House ★★★★
Guest Accommodation
SILVER AWARD
Abacourt House, 26 Stanger Street Keswick
CA12 5JU
t (01768) 772967
e abacourt.keswick@btinternet.com
w abacourt.co.uk

Acorn House ★★★★ *Guest House*
SILVER AWARD
Ambleside Road, Keswick
CA12 4DL
t (01768) 772553
e info@acornhousehotel.co.uk
w acornhousehotel.co.uk

Allerdale House ★★★★
Guest House **SILVER AWARD**
1 Eskin Street, Keswick
CA12 4DH
t (01768) 773891
e allerdalehouse@btinternet.com
w allerdale-house.co.uk

Amble House Guest House
★★★★ *Guest House*
SILVER AWARD
23 Eskin Street, Keswick
CA12 4DQ
t (01768) 773288
e info@amblehouse.co.uk
w amblehouse.co.uk

The Anchorage Guest House
★★★★ *Guest Accommodation*
14 Ambleside Road, Keswick
CA12 4DL
t (01768) 772813
e info@anchoragekeswick.co.uk
w anchoragekeswick.co.uk

Appletrees ★★★★ *Guest House*
The Heads, Keswick
CA12 5ER
t (01768) 780400
e info@appletreeskeswick.com
w appletreeskeswick.com

North West | Cumbria

h Tree House ★★★
d & Breakfast
nrith Road, Keswick
12 4LJ
t (01768) 772203
e peterredfearn@aol.com
w ashtreehouse.co.uk

ondale Guest House ★★★★
est House
Southey Street, Keswick
12 4EF
t (01768) 772735
e enquiries@avondaleguesthouse.com
w avondaleguesthouse.com

dgers Wood ★★★★
est House SILVER AWARD
Stanger Street, Keswick
12 5JU
t (01768) 772621
e enquiries@badgers-wood.co.uk
w badgers-wood.co.uk

ckside ★★★★ Guest House
Wordsworth Street, Keswick
12 4HU
t (01768) 773093
e info@beckside-keswick.co.uk
w beckside-keswick.co.uk

uestones ★★★★ Guest House
Southey Street, Keswick
12 4EG
t (01768) 774237
e mjr@bluestonesguesthouse.co.uk
w bluestonesguesthouse.co.uk

aemar Guest House ★★★★
est House SILVER AWARD
Eskin Street, Keswick
12 4DQ
t (01768) 773743
e enquiries@braemar-guesthouse.co.uk
w braemar-guesthouse.co.uk

amblewood Cottage Guest ouse ★★★★ Guest House
Greta Street, Keswick
12 4HS
t (01768) 775918
e info@bramblewoodkeswick.com
w bramblewoodkeswick.com

iar Rigg House ★★★★
d & Breakfast SILVER AWARD
undholme Road, Keswick
12 4NL
t 0784 985 9391
e accomm@briarrigghouse.co.uk
w briarrigghouse.co.uk

rookfield ★★★★ Guest House
nrith Road, Keswick
12 4LJ
t (01768) 772867
e info@brookfield-keswick.co.uk
w brookfield-keswick.co.uk

undholme Guest House ★★★★
uest House
he Heads, Keswick
12 5ER
t (01768) 773305
e barbara@brundholme.co.uk
w brundholme.co.uk

urleigh Mead ★★★★
uest House
he Heads, Keswick
12 5ER
t (01768) 775935
e info@burleighmead.co.uk
w burleighmead.co.uk

urnside B&B ★★★★
d & Breakfast SILVER AWARD
nrith Road, Keswick
12 4LJ
t (01768) 772639
e stay@burnside-keswick.co.uk
w burnside-keswick.co.uk/

The Cartwheel ★★★★ Guest House
5 Blencathra Street, Keswick
CA12 4HW
t (01768) 773182
e info@thecartwheel.co.uk
w thecartwheel.co.uk

Castlefell ★★★ Bed & Breakfast
31 The Headlands, Keswick
CA12 5EQ
t (01768) 772849
e castlefell31@tiscali.co.uk
w castlefell.co.uk

Charnwood Guest House ★★★★
Guest House
6 Eskin Street, Keswick
CA12 4DH
t (01768) 774111
e sue.banister@googlemail.com

Cherry Trees Guest House ★★★★
Guest House
16 Eskin Street, Keswick
CA12 4DQ
t (01768) 771048
e info@cherrytrees-keswick.co.uk
w cherrytrees-keswick.co.uk

Cumbria House ★★★★
Guest House
1 Derwentwater Place, Ambleside Road, Keswick
CA12 4DR
t (01768) 773171
e mavisandpatrick@cumbriahouse.co.uk
w cumbriahouse.co.uk

Damson Lodge ★★★★
Bed & Breakfast
Eskin Street, Keswick
CA12 4DQ
t (01768) 775547
e damsonlodge@yahoo.co.uk
w damsonlodge.net

Dolly Waggon ★★★
Guest Accommodation
17 Helvellyn Street, Keswick
CA12 4EN
t (01768) 773593
e info@dollywaggon.co.uk
w dollywaggon.co.uk

Dunsford Guest House ★★★★
Guest House SILVER AWARD
16 Stanger Street, Keswick
CA12 5JU
t (01768) 775059
e enquiries@dunsford.net
w dunsford.net

Easedale House ★★★★
Guest Accommodation
1 Southey Street, Keswick
CA12 4HL
t (01768) 772710
e info@easedalehouse.com
w easedalehouse.com

Eden Green Guest House ★★★★
Guest House
20 Blencathra Street, Keswick
CA12 4HP
t (01768) 772077
e enquiries@edengreenguesthouse.com
w edengreenguesthouse.com

The Edwardene ★★★★
Guest Accommodation
GOLD AWARD
26 Southey Street, Keswick
CA12 4EF
t (01768) 773586
e info@edwardenehotel.com
w edwardenehotel.com

Ellergill Guest House ★★★★
Guest House
22 Stanger Street, Keswick
CA12 5JU
t (01768) 773347
e stay@ellergill.co.uk
w ellergill.com

Fell House ★★★★ Guest House
SILVER AWARD
28 Stanger Street, Keswick
CA12 5JU
t (01768) 772669
e info@fellhouse.co.uk
w fellhouse.co.uk

Glencoe Guest House ★★★★
Guest House
21 Helvellyn Street, Keswick
CA12 4EN
t (01768) 771016
e enquiries@glencoeguesthouse.co.uk
w glencoeguesthouse.co.uk

Glendale Guest House ★★★★
Guest House SILVER AWARD
7 Eskin Street, Keswick
CA12 4DH
t (01768) 773562
e info@glendalekeswick.co.uk
w glendalekeswick.co.uk

Goodwin House Guest House
★★★★ Guest Accommodation
29 Southey Street, Keswick
CA12 4EE
t (01768) 774634
e enquiries@goodwinhouse.co.uk
w goodwinhouse.co.uk

Grange Country House ★★★★★
Guest House SILVER AWARD
Manor Brow, Ambleside Road, Keswick
CA12 4BA
t (01768) 772500
e enquiries@grangekeswick.com
w grangekeswick.com

Grassmoor Guest House ★★★★
Guest House
10 Blencathra Street, Keswick
CA12 4HP
t (01768) 774008
e grassmoorbandb@btinternet.com
w grassmoor-keswick.co.uk

Greystoke House ★★★★
Guest Accommodation
9 Leonard Street, Keswick
CA12 4EL
t (01768) 772603
e info@greystokeguesthouse.co.uk
w greystokeguesthouse.co.uk

Greystones ★★★★
Guest Accommodation
Ambleside Road, Keswick
CA12 4DP
t (01768) 773108
e enquiries@greystoneskeswick.co.uk
w greystoneskeswick.co.uk

Hall Garth ★★★★ Bed & Breakfast
37 Blencathra Street, Keswick
CA12 4HX
t (01768) 772627
e tracyhallgarth@aol.com
w keswickguesthouse.co.uk

Harvington House ★★★
Guest Accommodation
19 Church Street, Keswick
CA12 4DX
t (01768) 775582
e info@harvingtonhouse.co.uk
w harvingtonhouse.co.uk

Hawcliffe House ★★★★
Guest Accommodation
30 Eskin Street, Keswick
CA12 4DG
t (01768) 773250
e diane@hawcliffehouse.co.uk
w hawcliffehouse.co.uk

Hazeldene ★★★★
Guest Accommodation
The Heads, Keswick
CA12 5ER
t (01768) 772106
e info@hazeldene-hotel.co.uk
w hazeldene-hotel.co.uk

Hazelwood Guest House ★★★★
Guest House
Chestnut Hill, Keswick
CA12 4LR
t (01768) 773496
e info@hazelwoodkeswick.com
w hazelwoodkeswick.com

Hedgehog Hill Guesthouse
★★★★ Guest House
18 Blencathra Street, Keswick
CA12 4HP
t (01768) 780654
e keith@hedgehoghill.co.uk
w hedgehoghill.co.uk

Howe Keld ★★★★
Guest Accommodation
GOLD AWARD
5-7 The Heads, Keswick
CA12 5ES
t (01768) 772417
e david@howekeld.co.uk
w howekeld.co.uk

Hunters Way Guest House ★★★★
Guest House
4 Eskin Street, Keswick
CA12 4DH
t (01768) 772324
e huntersway@btconnect.com
w hunterswaykeswick.co.uk

Keswick Park ★★★★
Guest Accommodation
SILVER AWARD
33 Station Road, Keswick
CA12 4NA
t (01768) 772072
e enquiries@keswickparkhotel.com
w keswickparkhotel.com

Keswick YHA ★★★★ Hostel
Station Road, Keswick
CA12 5LH
t (01768) 772484

Lakeland View ★★★★
Bed & Breakfast
13 High Hill, Keswick
CA12 5NY
t (01768) 772555
e lakelandview@aol.com
w lakelandview.net

Lakeside House
Guest Accommodation
40 Lake Road, Keswick
CA12 5DQ
t (01768) 772868
e enquiries@lakesidehouse.co.uk
w lakesidehouse.co.uk

Larry's Lodge ★★★★ Guest House
39 Eskin Street, Keswick
CA12 4DG
t (01768) 773965
e suendave@larryslodge.co.uk
w larryslodge.co.uk

Laurel Bank B&B ★★★★
Guest Accommodation
Penrith Road, Keswick
CA12 4LJ
t (01768) 773006
e info@laurelbankkeswick.co.uk
w laurelbankkeswick.co.uk

Leonard's Field House ★★★★
Guest House
3 Leonard Street, Keswick
CA12 4EJ
t (01768) 774170
e enquiries@leonardsfieldhouse.com
w leonardsfieldhouse.com

Lincoln Guest House ★★★
Guest House
23 Stanger Street, Keswick
CA12 5JX
t (01768) 772597
e info@lincolnguesthouse.com
w lincolnguesthouse.com

North West | Cumbria

Lindisfarne House ★★★★
Guest House
21 Church Street, Keswick
CA12 4DX
t (01768) 773218
e alison230@btinternet.com
w lindisfarnehouse.com

Linnett Hill ★★★★
Guest House
4 Penrith Road, Keswick
CA12 4HF
t (01768) 773109
e info@linnetthillhotel.com
w linnetthillhotel.com

Littlefield ★★★★
Guest Accommodation
32 Eskin Street, Keswick
CA12 4DG
t (01768) 772949
e info@littlefieldguesthouse.co.uk
w littlefieldguesthouse.co.uk

The Lodge in the Vale
Guest Accommodation
Stannah Cross, Thirlmere, Keswick
CA12 4TQ
t 05006 00725
e stay@lakedistrictinns.co.uk
w lakedistrictinn.co.uk

The Lookout ★★★★
Guest Accommodation
SILVER AWARD
Chestnut Hill, Keswick
CA12 4LS
t (01768) 780407
e info@thelookoutkeswick.co.uk
w thelookoutkeswick.co.uk

Lyndhurst ★★★★ *Guest House*
22 Southey Street, Keswick
CA12 4EF
t (01768) 772303
e lyndhurstguesthouse@titanplus.co.uk
w lyndhurstkeswick.co.uk

Lynwood Guest House ★★★★
Guest House SILVER AWARD
12 Ambleside Road, Keswick
CA12 4DL
t (01768) 772081
e info@lynwood-keswick.co.uk
w lynwood-keswick.co.uk

Newlands Fell Guest House
★★★★ *Guest House*
Newlands Valley, Braithwaite, Keswick
CA12 5TS
t (01768) 778477
e kelly.wood8@btinternet.com
w lakedistrict-bandb.co.uk

The Paddock ★★★★ *Guest House*
Wordsworth Street, Keswick
CA12 4HU
t (01768) 772510
e val@thepaddock.info
w thepaddock.info

Parkfield Guest House ★★★★
Guest Accommodation
SILVER AWARD
The Heads, Keswick
CA12 5ES
t (01768) 772328
e enquiries@parkfieldkeswick.co.uk
w parkfield-keswick.co.uk

Pitcairn House ★★★★ *Guest House*
7 Blencathra Street, Keswick
CA12 4HW
t (01768) 772453
e enquiries@pitcairnhouse.co.uk
w pitcairnhouse.co.uk

Ravensworth House ★★★★
Guest Accommodation
SILVER AWARD
29 Station Street, Keswick
CA12 5HH
t (01768) 772476
e info@ravensworth-hotel.co.uk
w ravensworth-hotel.co.uk

Rivendell ★★★★ *Guest House*
23 Helvellyn Street, Keswick
CA12 4EN
t (01768) 773822
e info@rivendellguesthouse.com
w rivendellguesthouse.com

Rooms36 ★★★★ *Guest House*
SILVER AWARD
36 Lake Road, Keswick
CA12 5DQ
t (0800) 056 6401
e andy042195@aol.com
w Rooms36.co.uk

Sandon Guest House ★★★★
Guest House
Southey Street, Keswick
CA12 4EG
t (01768) 773648
e enquiries@sandonguesthouse.com
w sandonguesthouse.com

Seven Oaks ★★★★ *Guest House*
7 Acorn Street, Keswick
CA12 4EA
t (01768) 772088
e enquiries@sevenoaks-keswick.co.uk
w sevenoaks-keswick.co.uk

Shemara Guest House ★★★★
Guest House
27 Bank Street, Keswick
CA12 5JZ
t (01768) 773936
e info@shemara.uk.com
w shemara.uk.com

Skiddaw Grove Country Guest House ★★★★ *Guest House*
Vicarage Hill, Keswick
CA12 5QB
t (01768) 773324
e info@skiddawgrove.co.uk
w skiddawgrove.co.uk

Springs Farm Guesthouse ★★★
Guest House
Springs Farm, Springs Road, Keswick
CA12 4AN
t (01768) 772144
e info@springsfarmcumbria.co.uk
w springsfarmcumbria.co.uk

Squirrel Lodge ★★★★
Guest House
43 Eskin Street, Keswick
CA12 4DG
t (01768) 771189
e enquiries@squirrellodge.co.uk
w squirrellodge.co.uk

Stonegarth Guest House ★★★★
Guest House SILVER AWARD
2 Eskin Street, Keswick
CA12 4DH
t (01768) 772436
e info@stonegarth.com
w stonegarth.com

Swiss Court Guest House ★★★★
Guest House
25 Bank Street, Keswick, Cumbria
CA12 5JZ
t (01687) 72637
e enquiries@swisscourt.co.uk
w swisscourt.co.uk

Tarn Hows ★★★★ *Guest House*
SILVER AWARD
3-5 Eskin Street, Keswick
CA12 4DH
t (01768) 773217
e enquiries@tarnhows.co.uk
w tarnhows.co.uk

Thornleigh Guest House ★★★★
Guest House
23 Bank Street, Keswick
CA12 5JZ
t (01768) 772863
e thornleigh@btinternet.com
w thornleighguesthouse.co.uk

Watendlath Guest House ★★★★
Guest House
15 Acorn Street, Keswick
CA12 4EA
t (01768) 774165
e info@watendlathguesthouse.co.uk
w watendlathguesthouse.co.uk

West View Guest House ★★★★
Guest House
The Heads, Keswick
CA12 5ES
t (01768) 773638
e info@westviewkeswick.co.uk
w westviewkeswick.co.uk

The Winchester ★★★★
Guest Accommodation
58 Blencathra Street, Keswick
CA12 4HT
t (01768) 773664
e dawn@the-winchester.co.uk
w the-winchester.co.uk

Woodside ★★★★ *Guest House*
Penrith Road, Keswick, Cumbria
CA12 4LJ
t (01768) 773522
e info@woodsideguesthouse.co.uk
w woodsideguesthouse.co.uk

KESWICK (5 MILES)

Littletown Farm ★★★ *Farmhouse*
Newlands, Keswick, Cumbria
CA12 5TU
t (01768) 778353
e info@littletownfarm.co.uk
w littletownfarm.co.uk

KESWICK (7.5 MILES)

Lane Head Farm Country Guest House ★★★★
Guest Accommodation
SILVER AWARD
Troutbeck, Nr Keswick, Cumbria
CA11 0SY
t 01768 779220
e info@laneheadfarm.co.uk
w laneheadfarm.co.uk

KIRKBY LONSDALE

Copper Kettle Restaurant & Guest House ★★★ *Guest Accommodation*
3-5 Market Street, Kirkby Lonsdale
LA6 2AU
t (01524) 271714

High Green Farm ★★★★
Farmhouse SILVER AWARD
Middleton-in-Lonsdale, Carnforth, Kirkby Lonsdale, Cumbria
LA6 2NA
t (01524) 276256 Mobile 07920072790
e nora@highgreenfarm.com
w highgreenfarm.com

Ullathorns Farm ★★★★
Farmhouse
Middleton, Kirkby Lonsdale
LA6 2LZ
t (01524) 276214 Mob: 07800990689
e pauline@ullathorns.co.uk
w ullathorns.co.uk

KIRKBY STEPHEN

Kirkby Stephen YHA ★★★ *Hostel*
Market Street, Kirkby Stephen
CA17 4QQ
t (01768) 371793

LAKESIDE

The Knoll Country House
★★★★★ *Guest Accommodation*
GOLD AWARD
Lakeside, Newby Bridge
LA12 8AU
t (015395) 31347
e info@theknoll-lakeside.co.uk
w theknoll-lakeside.co.uk

LANERCOST

Abbey Mill ★★★★ *Bed & Breakfast*
SILVER AWARD
Lanercost, Brampton
CA8 2HG
t (01697) 742746
e tony@abbeymill.me.uk
w abbeymill-lanercost.co.uk

LAZONBY

Bracken Bank Lodge ★★★★
Guest Accommodation
Lazonby, Penrith
CA10 1AX
t (01768) 898241
e info@brackenbank.co.uk
w brackenbank.co.uk

LINDALE

Greenacres Country Guesthouse
★★★★ *Guest House*
Lindale, Grange-over-Sands
LA11 6LP
t (01539) 534578
e greenacres.lindale@googlemail.com
w greenacres-lindale.co.uk

LITTLE LANGDALE

Three Shires Inn ★★★★ *Inn*
Little Langdale, Langdale
LA22 9NZ
t (015394) 37215
e enquiry@threeshiresinn.co.uk
w threeshiresinn.co.uk

LONG MARTON

Broom House ★★★★
Guest Accommodation
SILVER AWARD
Long Marton, Appleby-in-Westmorland
CA16 6JP
t (01768) 361318
e sandra@bland01.freeserve.co.uk
w broomhouseappleby.co.uk

LONGTHWAITE

Borrowdale YHA ★★★★ *Hostel*
Longthwaite, Borrowdale, Keswick
CA12 5XE
t 0870 770 5706
e borrowdale@yha.org.uk
w yha.org.uk/find-accommodation/the-lake-district/hostels/borrowdale/index.aspx

LONGTOWN

Briar Lea Guest House ★★★★
Guest Accommodation
Brampton Road, Longtown, Carlisle
CA6 5TN
t (01228) 791538
e info@briarleahouse.co.uk
w briarleahouse.co.uk

LOUGHRIGG

Langdale YHA ★★ *Hostel*
High Close, Loughrigg, Langdale
LA22 9HJ
t 0870 770 5908
e langdale@yha.org.uk
w yha.org.uk/find-accommodation/the-lake-district/hostels/langdale/index.aspx

LOWESWATER

Askhill Farm ★★★★ *Farmhouse*
Loweswater, Cockermouth
CA13 0SU
t (01946) 861640
e askhillfarm@aol.com
w countrycaravans.co.uk/askhillfarm

North West | Cumbria

LOWICK GREEN

mona Bed & Breakfast ★★★★
d & Breakfast
wick Green, Ulverston, Coniston
12 8DX
t (01229) 885399
e steve@pomonalakedistrict.co.uk
w pomonalakedistrict.co.uk

LOW ROW

nton Hall ★★★★ *Farmhouse*
nton Hall, Low Row, Brampton
8 2JA
t (01697) 746331
e s.brucegormley@btinternet.com
w dentonhallfarm.co.uk

MAULDS MEABURN

eaburn Hill Farmhouse ★★★★
rmhouse SILVER AWARD
aulds Meaburn, Penrith
10 3HN
t (01931) 715168
e kindleysides@btinternet.com
w cumbria-bed-and-breakfast.co.uk

ainlands B&B ★★★ *Farmhouse*
aulds Meaburn, Penrith
10 3HX
t (01768) 351249
e enquire@trainlands.co.uk
w trainlands.co.uk

MILBURN

w Howgill Farm ★★★★
d & Breakfast
w Howgill, Milburn, Appleby-in-
estmorland
10 1TL
t (01768) 361595
e jane@low-howgill.co.uk
w lowhowgill.f9.co.uk

MILNTHORPE

e Cross Keys ★★★★ *Inn*
Park Road, Milnthorpe
7 7AB
t (015395) 62115
e stay@thecrosskeyshotel.co.uk
w thecrosskeyshotel.co.uk

MORLAND

orland House ★★★★
uest Accommodation
orland, Penrith
10 3AZ
t 01931 714989
e enquiries@morlandguesthouse.co.uk
w morlandguesthouse.co.uk

MOSEDALE

osedale End Farm ★★★
Farmhouse
osedale, Penrith, Cumbria
11 0XQ
t (01768) 779605
e enquiries@mosedaleendfarm.co.uk
w mosedaleendfarm.co.uk

MOSSER

osser Heights ★★★★ *Farmhouse*
osser, Cockermouth
13 0SS
t (01900) 822644
e amandavickers1@aol.com

MUNCASTER

Muncaster Coachman's Quarters
★★★ *Guest Accommodation*
uncaster Castle, Muncaster,
avenglass
18 1RQ
t (01229) 717614
e info@muncaster.co.uk
w muncaster.co.uk

Muncaster Country Guest House
★★★★ *Guest House*
Muncaster, Ravenglass
CA18 1RD
t (01229) 717693
e donandsheila@muncastercountryguesthouse.com
w muncastercountryguesthouse.com

NATEBY

The Black Bull ★★★★ *Inn*
Nateby, Kirkby Stephen
CA17 4JP
t (01768) 371588
e enquiries@blackbullnateby.co.uk

NEWBIGGIN

The Old School ★★★★★
Guest House SILVER AWARD
Newbiggin, Stainton, Penrith
CA11 0HT
t (01768) 483709
e info@theold-school.com
w theold-school.com

Tymparon Hall ★★★★ *Farmhouse*
Newbiggin, Penrith
CA11 0HS
t (01768) 483236
e margaret@tymparon.freeserve.co.uk
w tymparon.freeserve.co.uk

NEWBIGGIN-ON-LUNE

Tranna Hill ★★★★
Guest Accommodation
SILVER AWARD
Newbiggin-on-Lune, Kirkby Stephen
CA17 4NY
t (015396) 23227
e enquiries@trannahill.co.uk
w trannahill.co.uk

NEWBY BRIDGE

Old Barn Farm ★★★★
Guest House
Fiddler Hall, Newby Bridge
LA12 8NQ
t (015395) 31842
e peter@oldbarnfarm.com
w oldbarnfarm.com

NEWLANDS

Ellas Crag ★★★★ *Guest House*
SILVER AWARD
Newlands Valley, Keswick
CA12 5TS
t (01768) 778217
e info@ellascrag.co.uk
w ellascrag.co.uk

Gill Brow Farm ★★★ *Farmhouse*
Newlands Valley, Keswick
CA12 5TS
t (01768) 778270
e wilson_gillbrow@hotmail.com
w gillbrow-keswick.co.uk

Keskadale Farm ★★★★
Farmhouse
Newlands, Keswick
CA12 5TS
t (01768) 778544

YHA Hawse End ★★★
Group Hostel
Hawse End Cottage, Portinscale, Keswick
CA12 5UE
t (01768) 772816

ORMSIDE

Slakes Farm ★★★ *Farmhouse*
Milburn, Appleby-in-Westmorland
CA16 6DP
t (01768) 361385
e oakleaves@slakesfarm.co.uk
w slakesfarm.co.uk

ORTON GRANGE

Hazeldean Guest House ★★★
Guest House
Orton Grange, Wigton Road, Carlisle
CA5 6LA
t (01228) 711953
e hazeldean1@btopenworld.com
w smoothhound.co.uk/hotels/hazeldean.html

OUTGATE

High Grassings B&B ★★★★
Bed & Breakfast
Outgate, Ambleside
LA22 0PU
t (015394) 36484
e robparfitt@dial.pipex.com
w highgrassings.com

PARK BROOM

Wallfoot Hotel & Restaurant
★★★ *Guest Accommodation*
Park Broom, Crosby-on-Eden, Carlisle
CA6 4QH
t (01228) 573696
e info@wallfoot.com
w wallfoot.co.uk

PATTERDALE

Deepdale Hall Farmhouse ★★★★
Farmhouse
Deepdale Hall, Patterdale, Ullswater
CA11 0NR
t (01768) 482369
e brown@deepdalehall.co.uk
w deepdalehall.co.uk

Patterdale YHA ★★ *Hostel*
Goldrill House, Penrith
CA11 0NW
t (01768) 482394

PENRITH

Addingham View B&B ★★★★
Bed & Breakfast
Addingham View, Gamblesby, Penrith, Cumbria
CA10 1JA
t (01768) 881477
e addinghamviewbandb@gmail.com
w addinghamviewbandb.co.uk

Bank House ★★★★
Guest Accommodation
Graham Street, Penrith
CA11 9LE
t (01768) 868714
e info@bankhousepenrith.co.uk
w bankhousepenrith.co.uk

Blue Swallow Guest House
★★★★ *Guest House*
11 Victoria Road, Penrith
CA11 8HR
t (01768) 866335
e blueswallow@tiscali.co.uk
w blueswallow.info

Brooklands Guest House ★★★★★
Guest House
2 Portland Place, Penrith, cumbria
CA11 7QN
t (01768) 863595
e enquiries@brooklandsguesthouse.com
w brooklandsguesthouse.com

Caledonia Guest House ★★★★
Guest Accommodation
8 Victoria Road, Penrith
CA11 8HR
t (01768) 864482
e ian.rhind1@virgin.net
w caledoniaguesthouse.co.uk

Glendale Guest House ★★★★
Guest House SILVER AWARD
4 Portland Place, Penrith
CA11 7QN
t (01768) 210061
e glendaleguesthouse@yahoo.co.uk
w glendaleguesthouse.com

Lowthwaite B&B ★★★★
Guest Accommodation
SILVER AWARD
Matterdale, Penrith, Cumbria
CA11 0LE
t 017684 82343
e info@lowthwaiteullswater.com
w lowthwaiteullswater.com

Norcroft Guest House ★★★★
Guest House
Graham Street, Penrith
CA11 9LQ
t (01768) 862365
e info@norcroft-guesthouse.co.uk
w norcroft-guesthouse.co.uk

Stafford House Guest House
★★★★ *Bed & Breakfast*
Greystoke, Penrith
CA11 0TQ
t (01768) 483558
e hazel.knight@btconnect.com
w stafford-house.co.uk

PENTON

Craigburn Farmhouse ★★★★
Farmhouse
Penton, Longtown
CA6 5QP
t (01228) 577214
e louiselawson@hotmail.com
w criagburnfarmhouse.com

PLANTATION BRIDGE

Burrow Hall ★★★★
Bed & Breakfast
Plantation Bridge, Kendal, Staveley
LA8 9JR
t (015398) 21711
e burrow.hall@virgin.net
w burrowhall.co.uk

POOLEY BRIDGE

Elm House ★★★★ *Guest House*
High Street, Pooley Bridge, Ullswater
CA10 2NH
t (01768) 486334
e enquiries@stayullswater.co.uk
w stayullswater.co.uk

Ullswater House ★★★★
Guest House
Ullswater House, Pooley Bridge, Ullswater
CA10 2NN
t (01768) 486292
e ullswaterguesthouse@yahoo.co.uk
w ullswaterguesthouse.co.uk

PORT CARLISLE

Brockelrigg ★★★★★
Bed & Breakfast GOLD AWARD
Port Carlisle, Wigton
CA7 5BU
t (01697) 351953
e mu.atkinson@btopenworld.com
w brockelrigg.co.uk

Hesket House ★★★★
Guest Accommodation
Port Carlisle, Wigton
CA7 5BU
t (01697) 351876
e stay@heskethouse.com
w heskethouse.com

Hope & Anchor ★★★★ *Inn*
Port Carlisle, Carlisle
CA7 5BU
t (01697) 351460
e dougiehill@hotmail.com
w hopeandanchorinn.com

PORTINSCALE

Derwent Bank ★★★★
Guest Accommodation
Derwentwater, Portinscale, Keswick
CA12 5TY
t (020) 8511 1534

North West | Cumbria

Lakeview ★★★★ *Guest House*
SILVER AWARD
Portinscale, Keswick
CA12 5RD
t (01768) 771122
e sandkmuir@aol.com
w lakeviewkeswick.co.uk

The Mount ★★★★ *Guest House*
Portinscale, Keswick
CA12 5RD
t (01768) 773970
e stay@mountkeswick.co.uk
w mountkeswick.co.uk

Powe House ★★★★ *Guest House*
GOLD AWARD
Portinscale, Keswick
CA12 5RW
t (01768) 773611
e andrewandhelen@powehouse.com
w powehouse.com

Rickerby Grange Country House
★★★★ *Guest House*
Portinscale, Keswick
CA12 5RH
t (01768) 772344
e stay@rickerbygrange.co.uk
w rickerbygrange.co.uk

RAVENGLASS

Rosegarth ★★★★ *Guest House*
Main Street, Ravenglass
CA18 1SQ
t (01229) 717275
e info@rose-garth.co.uk
w rose-garth.co.uk

Wayside Guest Accommodation
★★★★ *Guest Accommodation*
SILVER AWARD
Wayside, Whitbeck, Cumbria
LA19 5UP
t 01229718883
e enquiries@waysidehotel.co.uk
w waysidehotel.co.uk

RAVENSTONEDALE

A Corner of Eden ★★★★
Guest Accommodation
GOLD AWARD
Low Stennerskeugh,
Ravenstonedale, Kirkby Stephen
CA17 4LL
t (015396) 23370
e enquiries@acornerofeden.co.uk
w acornerofeden.co.uk

Coldbeck House ★★★★★
Bed & Breakfast **GOLD AWARD**
Ravenstonedale, Kirkby Stephen
CA17 4LW
t (015396) 23407
e belle@coldbeckhouse.co.uk
w coldbeckhouse.co.uk

Westview ★★★★ *Bed & Breakfast*
Ravenstonedale, Kirkby Stephen
CA17 4NG
t (015396) 23415
e enquiries@westview-cumbria.co.uk
w westview-cumbria.co.uk

REDHILLS

The Limes Country Guest House
★★★ *Guest House*
Redhills, Penrith
CA11 0DT
t (01768) 863343
e jdhanton@aol.com
w thelimescountryguesthouse.co.uk

ROUNDTHORN

Roundthorn Country House
★★★★★ *Guest Accommodation*
SILVER AWARD
Beacon Edge, Roundthorn, Penrith
CA11 8SJ
t (01768) 863952
e info@roundthorn.co.uk
w roundthorn.co.uk

ROWELTOWN

Low Luckens Organic Resource Centre ★★★ *Hostel*
Low Luckens, Roweltown, Carlisle
CA6 6LJ
t (01697) 748186
e lowluckensorc@hotmail.com
w lowluckensfarm.co.uk

RYDAL

Cote How Organic Guest House
★★★★ *Guest House* **GOLD AWARD**
Rydal, Ambleside
LA22 9LW
t (01539) 432765
e info@cotehow.co.uk
w cotehow.co.uk

SANDSIDE

Plantation Cottage ★★★★
Bed & Breakfast
Arnside Road, Sandside, Arnside
LA7 7JU
t (01524) 762069
e vicmaxbb@googlemail.com
w plantationcottagearnside.co.uk

SAWREY

Beechmount Country House
★★★★★ *Bed & Breakfast*
GOLD AWARD
Hawkshead, Sawrey
LA22 0JZ
t (015394) 36356
e beechmount@btinternet.com
w beechmountcountryhouse.co.uk

Buckle Yeat Guest House ★★★★
Guest House **SILVER AWARD**
Nr Sawrey, Hawkshead, Ambleside, Cumbria
LA22 0LF
t (01539) 436446 Mob 07703654219
e info@buckle-yeat.co.uk
w buckle-yeat.co.uk

Tower Bank Arms ★★★★ *Inn*
Ambleside, Sawrey
LA22 0LF
t (015394) 36334
e enquiries@towerbankarms.co.uk
w towerbankarms.co.uk

SCOTBY

Willowbeck Lodge ★★★★★
Guest Accommodation
GOLD AWARD
Lambley Bank, Scotby, Carlisle
CA4 8BX
t (01228) 513607
e info@willowbeck-lodge.com
w willowbeck-lodge.com

SEATOLLER

Honister Hause YHA ★★★ *Hostel*
Seatoller, Keswick
CA12 5XN
t (01768) 777267

Seatoller Farm ★★★★ *Farmhouse*
Borrowdale, Keswick
CA12 5XN
t (01768) 777232

SEDBERGH

Dalesman Country Inn ★★★★ *Inn*
Main Street, Sedbergh
LA10 5BN
t (015396) 21183
e info@thedalesman.co.uk
w thedalesman.co.uk

Howgills Bunk Barn ★★★ *Hostel*
Castlehaw Farm, Castlehaw Lane, Sedbergh, Cumbria
LA10 5BA
t (015396) 621990
e cobblesedbergh@yahoo.co.uk
w howgillsbunkbarn.co.uk

SEDGWICK

Thorns Hall ★★★
Guest Accommodation
Thorns Hall, Cautley Road, Sedbergh
LA10 5LE
t (020) 8511 1534

SELSIDE

Low Jock Scar Country Guest House ★★★★ *Guest House*
Selside, Kendal
LA8 9LE
t (015398) 23259
e info@lowjockscar.co.uk
w lowjockscar.co.uk

SETMURTHY

Croft Guesthouse ★★★★
Guest House **SILVER AWARD**
6-8 Challoner Street, Cockermouth
CA13 9QS
t (01900) 827533
e info@croft-guesthouse.com
w croft-guesthouse.com

SHAP

Greyhound Hotel ★★★ *Inn*
Main Street, Shap, Penrith
CA10 3PW
t (01931) 716474
e robertfurber@btconnect.com
w greyhoundshap.co.uk

SIDDICK

Morven Guest House ★★★
Guest Accommodation
Siddick Road, Siddick, Workington
CA14 1LE
t (01900) 602118
e cnelsonmorven@aol.com
w morvenguesthouse.com

SKELWITH BRIDGE

Elterwater Park Country Guest House ★★★★ *Guest House*
Skelwith Bridge, Ambleside, Langdale
LA22 9NP
t (015394) 32227
e enquiries@elterwater.com
w elterwater.com

SKELWITH FOLD

Holmeshead Farm ★★★★
Farmhouse
Skelwith Fold, Ambleside
LA22 0HU
t (015394) 33048
e info@holmesheadfarm.co.uk
w holmesheadfarm.co.uk

STAVELEY

The Eagle & Child Inn ★★★ *Inn*
Kendal Road, Staveley
LA8 9LP
t (015398) 21320
e info@eaglechildinn.co.uk
w eaglechildinn.co.uk

ST BEES

Fleatham House ★★★★★
Guest Accommodation
High Road, St Bees
CA27 0BX
t (01946) 822341
e fleathamhouse@aol.com
w fleathamhouse.com

Stone House Farm ★★★★
Farmhouse
133 Main Street, St Bees
CA27 0DE
t (01946) 822224
e csmith.stonehouse@btopenworld.com
w stonehousefarm.net

TALKIN

Blacksmiths Arms ★★★★ *Inn*
Talkin Village, Brampton
CA8 1LE
t (01697) 73452
e blacksmithsarmstalkin@yahoo.co.uk
w blacksmithstalkin.co.uk

Hullerbank ★★★★
Guest Accommodation
Talkin, Brampton
CA8 1LB
t (01697) 746668
e info@hullerbank.co.uk
w hullerbank.co.uk

TEBAY

Primrose Cottage ★★★★
Bed & Breakfast
Orton Road, Tebay
CA10 3TL
t (015396) 24791
e info@primrosecottagecumbria.co.uk
w primrosecottagecumbria.co.uk

THE GREEN

rooms @ bank house farm
★★★★ *Farmhouse* **SILVER AWARD**
Broadgate, Hallthwaites,
Nr.Broughton-in-Furness, Cumbria
LA18 5JU
t (01229) 777193/07795032163
e karen@wforrester.plus.com
w bank-house-farm.co.uk

THIRLMERE

Barn-Gill House ★★★★ *Farmhouse*
Brotto, Thirlmere, Keswick
CA12 4TN
t (01768) 774391
e jean@keswickfarmholidays.co.uk
w keswickfarmholidays.co.uk

Stybeck Farmhouse ★★★
Farmhouse
Thirlmere, Keswick
CA12 4TN
t (01768) 73232
e stybeckfarm@farming.co.uk
w stybeckfarm.co.uk

THORNTHWAITE

Beckstones Farm Guest House
★★★ *Guest House*
Thornthwaite, Keswick
CA12 5SQ
t (01768) 778510
e enquiries@beckstonesfarm.co.uk
w beckstonesfarm.co.uk

Jenkin Hill Cottage ★★★★
Guest Accommodation
SILVER AWARD
Thornthwaite, Keswick
CA12 5SG
t (01768) 778443
e bookings@jenkinhill.co.uk
w jenkinhill.co.uk

THRELKELD

The Bungalows Country Guest House ★★★★
Guest Accommodation
Sunnyside, Threlkeld, Keswick
CA12 4SD
t (01768) 779679
e paulsunley@msn.com
w thebungalows.co.uk

Horse & Farrier Inn ★★★★ *Inn*
Threlkeld, Keswick
CA12 4SQ
t (01768) 779688
e info@horseandfarrier.com
w horseandfarrier.com

Scales Farm Country Guest House
★★★★ *Guest House*
SILVER AWARD
Scales, Threlkeld, Penrith
CA12 4SY
t (01768) 779660
e scales@scalesfarm.com
w scalesfarm.com

TORVER

The Old Rectory *Guest House*
Torver, Coniston
LA21 8AX
t (015394) 41353
e enquiries@theoldrectoryhotel.com
w theoldrectoryhotel.com

North West | Cumbria

...ilson Arms ★★★ Inn
...orver, Coniston
...A21 8BB
t (015394) 41237
e info@wilsonarms.co.uk

TROUTBECK

...ll Head Farm B&B ★★★★
...rmhouse
...outbeck, Penrith
...A11 0ST
t (01768) 779652
e enquiries@gillheadfarm.co.uk
w gillheadfarm.co.uk

...gh Fold Guest House ★★★★
...uest House SILVER AWARD
...outbeck, Windermere
...A23 1PG
t (015394) 32200
e info@highfoldbedandbreakfast.co.uk
w highfoldbedandbreakfast.co.uk

...he Homestead Lodge ★★★★★
...d & Breakfast SILVER AWARD
...outbeck
...A23 1HF
t 015394 43954 (07747 181424)
e thehomesteadlodge@yahoo.co.uk

...he Troutbeck Inn ★★★★ Inn
...routbeck, Penrith
...A11 0SJ
t (01768) 483635
e info@troutbeckinn.co.uk
w thetroutbeckinn.co.uk

...HA Windermere ★★★ Hostel
...idge Lane, Troutbeck, Windermere
...A23 1LA
t (015394) 43543
e windermere@yha.org.uk
w yha.org.uk/find-accommodation/the-lake-district/hostels/windermere/index.aspx

TROUTBECK BRIDGE

...un Hotel ★★★★ Inn
...routbeck Bridge, Windermere
...A23 1HH
t (015394) 43274
e info@thesunhotel.co.uk
w thesunhotel.co.uk

ULLSWATER

...notts Mill Country Lodge ★★★
...uest House
...atermillock, Ullswater
...A11 0JN
t (01768) 486699
e relax@knottsmill.com
w knottsmill.com

ULVERSTON

...t Marys Mount Manor House
★★★★ Guest Accommodation
...elmont, Ulverston
...A12 7HD
t (01229) 583372
e gerry.bobbett@virgin.net
w stmarysmount.co.uk

...irginia House ★★★★
...uest House
...4 Queen Street, Ulverston
...A12 7AF
t (01229) 584844
e mail@virginia-house.co.uk
w virginia-house.co.uk

UNDERBARROW

...ranquility @ Lab-Bay ★★★★★
...uest Accommodation
SILVER AWARD
...ab-Bay, Garth Row, Underbarrow, ...umbria
...A8 8AY
t 01539 568995
e haven@lakestranquility.co.uk
w lakestranquility.co.uk

Tranthwaite Hall ★★★★
Farmhouse
Underbarrow, Kendal
LA8 8HG
t (015395) 68285
e stay@tranthwaitehall.co.uk
w tranthwaitehall.co.uk

UNDER LOUGHRIGG

Stepping Stones ★★★★
Bed & Breakfast SILVER AWARD
Stepping Stones, Under Loughrigg, Ambleside
LA22 9LN
t (015394) 33552
e info@steppingstonesambleside.com
w steppingstonesambleside.co.uk

WALTON

Low Rigg Farm ★★★★ Farmhouse
Walton, Brampton
CA8 2DX
t (01697) 73233
w lowriggfarm.com

Walton High Rigg ★★★
Farmhouse
Walton, Brampton
CA8 2AZ
t (01697) 72117
e mounsey_highrigg@hotmail.com
w waltonhighrigg.co.uk

WARWICK-ON-EDEN

Warwick Hall ★★★★
Guest Accommodation
Warwick Hall, Warwick-on-Eden, Carlisle
CA4 8PG
t (01228) 561546
e info@warwickhall.org
w warwickhall.org

WASDALE

Wastwater YHA ★★★ Hostel
Wasdale Hall, Wasdale
CA20 1ET
t 0845 371 9350
e wastwater@yha.org.uk
w yha.org.uk/find-accommodation/the-lake-district/hostels/wastwater/index.aspx

WATERHEAD

Ambleside YHA ★★★ Hostel
Waterhead, Ambleside
LA22 0EU
t 0870 770 5908
e ambleside@yha.org.uk
w yha.org.uk/find-accommodation/the-lake-district/hostels/ambleside/index.aspx

WATERMILLOCK

Mellfell House Farm ★★★★
Farmhouse
Watermillock, Penrith, Ullswater
CA11 0LS
t (01768) 486295
e ben@mellfell.co.uk
w mellfell.co.uk

WELTON

Lakelynn ★★★★ Bed & Breakfast
Warnell, Welton, Carlisle
CA5 7HW
t (01697) 476239
e banks181@btinternet.com
w geocities.com/lakelynn.cottage

WETHERAL

Acorn Bank ★★★★★
Guest Accommodation
GOLD AWARD
Wetheral, Carlisle
CA4 8JG
t (01228) 561434
e enquiry@acornbank.co.uk
w acornbank.co.uk

WHITEHAVEN

The Georgian House ★★★★★
Guest Accommodation
9-11 Church Street, Whitehaven
CA28 7AY
t (01946) 696611
e stephanie@thegeorgianhousehotel.net
w thegeorgianhousehotel.net

Grovewood House ★★★★★
Guest Accommodation
SILVER AWARD
Sandwith, Whitehaven, Cumbria
CA28 9UG
t 01946 63482 (07740 465 305)
e elaine@grovewoodhouse.com
w grovewoodhouse.com

Moresby Hall ★★★★★
Guest House GOLD AWARD
Moresby, Whitehaven, Cumbria
CA28 6PJ
t (01946) 696317
e info@moresbyhall.co.uk
w moresbyhall.co.uk

WINDERMERE

1 Park Road ★★★★ Guest House
Cumbria, Windermere
LA23 2AW
t (015394) 42107
e enquiries@1parkroad.com
w 1parkroad.com

All Seasons Guest House ★★★
Guest Accommodation
3 High Street, Windermere
LA23 1AF
t (015394) 48515
e info@allseasonsrest.co.uk
w allseasonsrest.co.uk

Annisgarth B&B ★★★
Bed & Breakfast
48 Craig Walk, Bowness-on-Windermere, Bowness
LA23 2JT
t (015394) 43866
e sharron@annisgarth.com
w annisgarth.co.uk

Applegarth Villa & JR's Restaurant ★★★★
Guest Accommodation
College Road, Windermere
LA23 1BU
t (015394) 43206
e info@lakesapplegarth.co.uk
w lakesapplegarth.co.uk

Archway Guesthouse ★★★★
Guest House
13 College Road, Windermere
LA23 1BU
t (015394) 45613
e stay@archwaywindermere.co.uk
w archwaywindermere.co.uk

Ashleigh Guest House ★★★★
Guest House
11 College Road, Windermere
LA23 1BU
t (015394) 42292
e enquiries@ashleighhouse.com
w ashleighhouse.com

At The White Rose ★★★★
Guest Accommodation
Broad Street, Windermere
LA23 2AB
t (015394) 45180
e whiteroselakes01@tiscali.net
w whiteroselakes.co.uk

Autumn Leaves Guest House ★★★★
Guest House
29 Broad Street, Windermere
LA23 2AB
t (015394) 48410
e info@autumnleavesguesthouse.co.uk
w autumnleavesguesthouse.co.uk

Beaumont House ★★★★★
Guest Accommodation
Holly Road, Windermere
LA23 2AF
t (015394) 447075
e enquiries@lakesbeaumont.com
w lakesbeaumont.com

Beckside Cottage ★★★
Guest Accommodation
4 Park Road, Windermere
LA23 2AW
t (015394) 42069
e info@becksidewindermere.co.uk
w becksidewindermere.co.uk

Beech House ★★★ Guest House
11 Woodland Road, Windermere
LA23 2AE
t (015394) 88985
e info@beech-house.com
w beech-house.com

Beechwood ★★★★
Guest Accommodation
GOLD AWARD
South Craig, Beresford Road, Bowness-on-Windermere, Bowness
LA23 2JF
t (015394) 43403
e enquiries@beechwoodlakes.co.uk
w beechwoodlakes.co.uk

The Boundary ★★★★★
Guest House SILVER AWARD
Lake Road, Windermere
LA23 2EQ
t (015394) 48978
e info@boundaryonline.co.uk
w boundaryonline.com

Bowfell Cottage ★★★
Bed & Breakfast
Middle Entrance Drive, Storrs Park, Bowness-on-Windermere
LA23 3JY
t (01539) 444835
e annetomlinson45@btinternet.com

Braemount House ★★★★
Guest House SILVER AWARD
Sunny Bank Road, Windermere
LA23 2EN
t (01539) 445967
e enquiries@braemount-house.co.uk
w braemount-house.co.uk

Brendan Chase ★★★ Guest House
1 College Road, Windermere
LA23 1BU
t (015394) 45638
e brendanchase@aol.com
w placetostaywindermere.co.uk

Briscoe Lodge Guest House ★★★
Guest House
26 Ellerthwaite Road, Windermere
LA23 2AH
t (015394) 42928
e stay@briscoelodge.co.uk
w briscoelodge.co.uk

Brook House ★★★ Guest House
30 Ellerthwaite Road, Windermere
LA23 2AH
t (01539) 444932
e stay@brookhouselakes.co.uk
w brookhouselakes.co.uk

Clifton House ★★★ Guest House
28 Ellerthwaite Road, Windermere
LA23 2AH
t (015394) 44968
e info@cliftonhse.co.uk
w cliftonhse.co.uk

College House ★★★★ Guest House
15 College Road, Windermere
LA23 1BU
t (015394) 45767
e clghse@aol.com

Crompton House ★★★
Guest House
Lake Road, Windermere
LA23 2EQ
t (015394) 43020

Denecrest ★★★
Guest Accommodation
Woodland Road, Windermere
LA23 2AE
t (015394) 44979
e denecrest@btconnect.com
w denecrest.co.uk

...or key to symbols see page 6   645

North West | Cumbria

Denehurst Guest House ★★★★
Guest House SILVER AWARD
40 Queens Drive, Windermere
LA23 2EL
t (015394) 44710
e denehurst@btconnect.com
w denehurst-guesthouse.co.uk

Dunvegan Guest House ★★★★
Guest Accommodation
Broad Street, Windermere
LA23 2AB
t (015394) 43502
e bryan.twaddle@btinternet.com
w dunveganbedandbreakfast.co.uk

Elim Lodge ★★★ *Guest House*
Biskey Howe Road, Bowness-on-Windermere, Windermere
LA23 2JP
t (015394) 447299
e enquiries@elimlodge.co.uk
w elimlodge.co.uk

Ellerbrook House ★★★★
Guest House
3 Park Avenue, Windermere
LA23 2AR
t (015394) 88014
e information@ellerbrook.co.uk
w ellerbrook.co.uk

Ellerthwaite Lodge ★★★★
Guest Accommodation
SILVER AWARD
New Road, Windermere
LA23 2LA
t (015394) 45115
e info@ellerthwaitelodge.co.uk
w ellerthwaitelodge.com

Fairfield House & Gardens ★★★★
Guest House SILVER AWARD
Brantfell Road, Bowness Bay, Windermere
LA23 3AE
t (01539) 446565
e relax@the-fairfield.co.uk
w the-fairfield.co.uk

Fair Rigg ★★★★ *Guest House*
SILVER AWARD
Ferry View, Bowness-on-Windermere, Windermere
LA23 3JB
t (01539) 443941
e stay@fairrigg.co.uk
w fairrigg.co.uk

Firgarth ★★★★ *Guest House*
Ambleside Road, Windermere
LA23 1EU
t (015394) 46974
e enquiries@firgarth.com
w firgarth.com

Fir Trees ★★★★ *Guest House*
Lake Road, Windermere
LA23 2EQ
t (015394) 442272
e enquiries@fir-trees.co.uk
w fir-trees.co.uk

Glen Wynne ★★★
Guest Accommodation
Broad Street, Windermere
LA23 2AB
t (015394) 43685
e glenwynne@btinternet.com
w glenwynne.co.uk

Greenriggs Guest House ★★★
Guest House
8 Upper Oak Street, Windermere
LA23 2LB
t (015394) 42265
e greenriggs@tiscali.co.uk
w greenriggs.com

Haisthorpe House ★★★★
Guest House
Holly Road, Windermere
LA23 2AF
t (015394) 43445
e enquiries@haisthorpe-house.co.uk
w haisthorpe-house.co.uk

Heatherbank ★★★
Guest Accommodation
13 Birch Street, Windermere
LA23 1EG
t (015394) 46503
e heatherbank@btinternet.com
w heatherbank.com

Hilton House ★★★★ *Guest House*
New Road, Windermere
LA23 2EE
t (015394) 43934
e enquiries@hiltonhouse-guesthouse.co.uk
w hiltonhouse-guesthouse.co.uk

Holly-Wood ★★★★ *Guest House*
Holly Road, Windermere
LA23 2AF
t (01539) 442219
e info@hollywoodguesthouse.co.uk
w hollywoodguesthouse.co.uk

Holly Lodge ★★★★
Guest Accommodation
6 College Road, Windermere
LA23 1BX
t (01539) 443873
e enquiries@hollylodge20.co.uk
w hollylodge20.co.uk

Ivy Bank ★★★★ *Guest House*
SILVER AWARD
Holly Road, Windermere
LA23 2AF
t (015394) 42601
e enquiries@ivy-bank.co.uk
w ivy-bank.co.uk

Ivythwaite Lodge ★★★★
Guest Accommodation
SILVER AWARD
Princes Road, Windermere
LA23 2DD
t (015394) 88914
e enquiries@ivythwaitelodge.co.uk
w ivythwaitelodge.co.uk

Kays Cottage ★★★★ *Guest House*
7 Broad Street, Windermere
LA23 2AB
t (015394) 44146
e rooms@kayscottage.co.uk
w kayscottage.co.uk

Kenilworth Guest House ★★★★
Guest House
Holly Road, Windermere
LA23 2AF
t (015394) 44004
e busby@kenilworth-lake-district.co.uk
w kenilworth-lake-district.co.uk

Kirkwood Guest House ★★★★
Guest House
Prince's Road, Windermere
LA23 2DD
t (015394) 43907
e info@kirkwood51.co.uk
w kirkwood51.co.uk

Lakes Lodge ★★★
Guest Accommodation
1 High Street, Windermere
LA23 1AF
t (015394) 42751
e admin@lakes-hotel.com
w lakes-hotel.com

Lake View Guest House & Coffee Shop ★★★ *Guest Accommodation*
2 Belsfield Terrace, Bowness-on-Windermere, Windermere
LA23 3EQ
t (015394) 47098
e lakeview@dsl.pipex.com
w lakeview-guesthouse.co.uk

Langdale View Guest House
★★★★ *Guest House*
114 Craig Walk, off Helm Road, Bowness-on-Windermere, Cumbria
LA23 3AX
t 01539 444076
e enquiries@langdaleview.co.uk
w langdaleview.co.uk

Latimer House ★★★★
Guest House
Lake Road, Bowness-on-Windermere, Windermere
LA23 2JJ
t (015394) 46888
e enquiries@latimerhouse.co.uk
w latimerhouse.co.uk

Laurel Cottage ★★★★
Guest House
Park Road, Windermere
LA23 2BJ
t (015394) 43053
e info@laurelcottagewindermere.co.uk
w laurelcottagewindermere.co.uk

Lindisfarne Guest House ★★★★
Guest House
Sunny Bank Road, Windermere
LA23 2EN
t (01539) 446295
e enquiries@lindisfarne-house.co.uk
w lindisfarne-house.co.uk

Lingmoor Guesthouse ★★★
Guest House
7 High Street, Windermere
LA23 1AF
t (01539) 444947
e info@lingmoor-guesthouse.co.uk
w lingmoor-guesthouse.co.uk

Lingwood Lodge ★★★★
Guest House SILVER AWARD
Birkett Hill, Bowness-on-Windermere, Windermere
LA23 3EZ
t (01539) 444680
e stay@lingwoodlodge.co.uk
w lingwoodlodge.co.uk

Lonsdale House ★★★★
Guest House SILVER AWARD
Lake Road, Bowness-on-Windermere, Windermere
LA23 2JJ
t (015394) 43348
e info@lonsdale-hotel.co.uk
w lonsdale-hotel.co.uk

Lynwood ★★★★ *Guest House*
Broad Street, Windermere
LA23 2AB
t (015394) 42550
e enquiries@lynwood-guest-house.co.uk
w lynwood-guest-house.co.uk

Meadfoot Guest House ★★★★
Guest Accommodation
New Road, Windermere
LA23 2LA
t (015394) 42610
e queries@meadfoot-guesthouse.co.uk
w meadfoot-guesthouse.co.uk

Millbeck Bed & Breakfast ★★★★
Bed & Breakfast SILVER AWARD
44 Ellerthwaite Road, Windermere
LA23 2BS
t (01539) 445392
e millbeckwindermere@googlemail.com
w themillbeck.co.uk

Montclare ★★★★ *Guest House*
Crag Brow, Bowness-on-Windermere, Cumbria
LA23 3BX
t 01539 442 723
e montclareguesthouse@fsmail.net
w montiesbedandbreakfast.com

Montfort Cottage Guest House
★★★★ *Guest Accommodation*
Princes Road, Windermere
LA23 2DD
t (015394) 45671
e montfortcottage@tiscali.co.uk
w montfortcottage.co.uk

Mylne Bridge House ★★★★
Guest House SILVER AWARD
Brookside, Lake Road, Windermere
LA23 2BX
t (015394) 43314
e stay@mylnebridgehouse.co.uk
w mylnebridgehouse.co.uk

New Hall Bank ★★★★
Guest House
Fallbarrow Road, Bowness-on-Windermere, Windermere
LA23 3DJ
t (01539) 443558
e info@newhallbank.co.uk
w newhallbank.co.uk

Newstead ★★★★★ *Guest House*
New Road, Windermere
LA23 2EE
t (015394) 44485
e info@newstead-guesthouse.co.uk
w newstead-guesthouse.co.uk

Oakfold House ★★★★
Guest House GOLD AWARD
Beresford Road, Bowness
LA23 2JG
t (01539) 443239
e oakfoldhouse@fsmail.net
w oakfoldhouse.co.uk

Oldfield House ★★★★
Guest House SILVER AWARD
Oldfield Road, Windermere
LA23 2BY
t (015394) 88445
e info@oldfieldhouse.co.uk
w oldfieldhouse.co.uk

Orrest Cottage Bed & Breakfast
★★★ *Bed & Breakfast*
17 Church Street, Windermere
LA23 1AQ
t (015394) 88722
e orrestcottage@uwclub.net
w orrestcottage.co.uk

Park Beck ★★★ *Guest House*
3 Park Road, Windermere
LA23 2AW
t (01539) 444025
e parkbeck@supanet.com

Ravenscroft ★★★★
Bed & Breakfast SILVER AWARD
Lake Road, Windermere
LA23 2EQ
t (015394) 47046
e book@lakesguesthouse.co.uk
w lakesguesthouse.co.uk

The Ravensworth ★★★★
Guest House
Ambleside Road, Windermere
LA23 1BA
t (015394) 43747
e info@theravensworth.com
w theravensworth.com

Rayrigg Villa Guest House ★★★
Guest House
Ellerthwaite Square, Windermere
LA23 1DP
t (015394) 88342
e rayriggvilla@etherway.net
w rayriggvilla.co.uk

Rocklea ★★★★ *Guest House*
Brookside, Lake Road, Windermere
LA23 2BX
t (015394) 45326
e info@rocklea.co.uk
w rocklea.co.uk

Rockside Guest House ★★★★
Guest House
25 Church Street, Windermere
LA23 1AQ
t (015394) 45343
e info@rockside-guesthouse.co.uk
w rockside-guesthouse.co.uk

Rosemount ★★★★ *Guest House*
Lake Road, Windermere
LA23 2EQ
t (015394) 43739
e rosemount@live.co.uk
w lakedistrictguesthouse.com

Southview House & Indoor Pool
★★★★ *Guest House*
SILVER AWARD
Cross Street, Windermere
LA23 1AE
t (015394) 42951
e admin@southviewwindermere.co.uk
w southviewwindermere.co.uk

North West | Cumbria/Lancashire

John's Lodge ★★★
Guest Accommodation
ke Road, Windermere
A23 2EQ
t (01539) 443078
e mail@st-johns-lodge.co.uk
w st-johns-lodge.co.uk

ockghyll Cottage ★★★★
ed & Breakfast
yrigg Road, Bowness-on-
indermere, Bowness
A23 1BN
t (015394) 43246
e stay@stockghyllcottage.co.uk
w stockghyllcottage.co.uk

hornbank House ★★★★
uest House
Thornbarrow Road, Windermere
A23 2EW
t (015394) 43724
e enquiries@thornbankwindermere.
co.uk
w thornbankwindermere.co.uk

estbury House ★★★
uest House
7 Broad Street, Windermere
A23 2AB
t (015394) 46839
e stay@windermerebnb.co.uk
w windermerebnb.co.uk

heatlands Lodge ★★★★★
uest Accommodation
ILVER AWARD
ld College Lane, Windermere
A23 1BY
t (015394) 43789
e info@warzecha.plus.com
w wheatlandslodge-windermere.co.
uk

hite Lodge ★★★★ Guest House
ake Road, Bowness-on-
Vindermere, Windermere
A23 2JJ
t (015394) 43624
e enquiries@whitelodgehotel.com
w whitelodgehotel.com

WINSTER

he Brown Horse Inn ★★★★
uest Accommodation
inster, Bowness-on Windermere,
Vindermere
A23 3NR
t (01539) 443443
e steve@thebrownhorseinn.co.uk
w thebrownhorseinn.co.uk

WOODLAND

racelet Hall Farm ★★★
armhouse
oodland, Broughton-in-Furness
A20 6AQ
t (01229) 716276
e bracelet-hall@hotmail.com
w bracelethall.co.uk

WORKINGTON

ld Ginn House Inn ★★★★ Inn
oor Road, Great Clifton,
Vorkington
A14 1TS
t (01900) 64616
e enquiries@oldginnhouse.co.uk
w oldginnhouse.co.uk

Lancashire
ABBEYSTEAD

reenbank Farmhouse ★★★
ed & Breakfast
bbeystead, Lancaster
A2 9BA
t (01524) 792063
e sally@greenbankfarmhouse.co.uk
w greenbankfarmhouse.co.uk

ACCRINGTON

orwood Guest House ★★★★
uest House **SILVER AWARD**
49 Whalley Road, Accrington
B5 5DF
t (01254) 398132
e stuart@norwoodguesthouse.co.uk
w norwoodguesthouse.co.uk

BARNACRE

Kenlis Arms ★★ Inn
Kenlis Road, Barnacre, Preston
PR3 1GD
t (01995) 603307
e andreadjarvis@tiscali.co.uk
w kenlisarmsgarstang.co.uk

BARROWFORD

Merok Bed & Breakfast ★★★★
Bed & Breakfast **SILVER AWARD**
124 Wheatley Lane Road,
Barrowford, Nelson
BB9 6QW
t (01282) 612888
e info@merokguesthouse.co.uk
w merokguesthouse.co.uk

BLACKBURN

Clough Head Farm ★★★★
Bed & Breakfast
Broadhead Road, Turton, Blackburn
BL7 0JN
t (01254) 704758
e ethelhoughton@hotmail.com
w cloughheadfarm.co.uk

BLACKPOOL

Abbey Lodge ★★★★
Guest Accommodation
31 Palatine Road, Blackpool
FY1 4BX
t (01253) 624721
e info@abbeyhotel-blackpool.co.uk
w abbeyhotel-blackpool.co.uk

Abbotsford ★★★
Guest Accommodation
18 Woodfield Road, Blackpool
FY1 6AX
t (01253) 346417
e abbotsford-hotel@btconnect.com
w abbotsfordhotel.net

Adelaide House ★★★
Guest Accommodation
66-68 Adelaide Street, Blackpool
FY1 4LA
t (01253) 625172
e info@adelaidehousehotel.com
w adelaidehousehotel.com

Albany ★★★ Guest House
89 Albert Road, Blackpool
FY1 4PW
t (01253) 622750
e albany.hotel.blackpool@hotmail.
co.uk
w albanyhotelblackpool.co.uk

Albion ★★★ Guest Accommodation
14-16 Vance Road, Blackpool
FY1 4QD
t (01253) 624181
e wayne@albionhotel.fsworld.co.uk
w albionhotelblackpool.com

Alexandra ★★
Guest Accommodation
1 Alexandra Road, Blackpool
FY1 6BU
t (01253) 346139
e bookings@alexandra-blackpool.
co.uk
w alexandra-blackpool.co.uk

The Allendale ★★★ Guest House
104 Albert Road, Blackpool
FY1 4PR
t (01253) 623268
e the-allendale@btconnect.com
w allendalehotelblackpool.co.uk

The Alpha ★★★ Guest House
9 King Edward Avenue, Blackpool
FY2 9TD
t (01253) 354828
e alphablackpool@yahoo.com
w alphablackpool.co.uk

Alviston ★★★
Guest Accommodation
46-48 Charnley Road, Blackpool
FY1 4PF
t (01253) 624772
e alvistonhotel@tiscali.co.uk
w alvistonhotel.com

Amethyst ★★★★
Guest Accommodation
86 Palatine Road, Blackpool
FY1 4BY
t (01253) 622127
e info@amethysthotelblackpool.co.
uk
w amethysthotelblackpool.co.uk

Arabella ★★★ Guest House
102 Albert Road, Blackpool
FY1 4PR
t (01253) 623189
e graham.waters3@virgin.net
w thearabella.co.uk

Ardsley Guest Accommodation
★★★ Guest Accommodation
20 Woodfield Road, Blackpool
FY1 6AX
t (01253) 345419
e christineglass@gmail.com
w ardsleyblackpool.co.uk

Arendale ★★★
Guest Accommodation
23 Gynn Avenue, Blackpool
FY1 2LD
t (01253) 351044
e enquiries@arendalehotel.co.uk
w arendalehotel.co.uk

Argyll ★★ Guest House
53 Hornby Road, Blackpool
FY1 4QJ
t (01253) 624677
e info@argyllhotelblackpool.co.uk
w argyllhotelblackpool.co.uk/

Arncliffe ★★★ Guest House
24 Osborne Road, Blackpool
FY4 1HJ
t (01253) 345209
e josephine.nasbitt@virgin.net

Arthington ★★★★
Guest Accommodation
24 St Chads Road, Blackpool
FY1 6BP
t (01253) 346436
e arthingtonhotel@btinternet.com
w arthingtonhotel.co.uk

The Ascot ★★★
Guest Accommodation
7 Alexandra Road, Blackpool
FY1 6BU
t (01253) 346439
e info@ascothotel.co.uk
w ascothotel.co.uk

Ascot Guest House ★★
Guest House
87 Hornby Road, Blackpool
FY1 4QP
t (01253) 624301
e pwc1952@hotmail.com
w ascotguesthouseblackpool.co.uk

Ash Lea ★★★
Guest Accommodation
49 Reads Avenue, Blackpool
FY1 4DG
t (01253) 624418
e enquiries@ash-lea-hotel.co.uk
w ash-lea-hotel.co.uk

Ashley Victoria ★★★★
Guest Accommodation
17-19 Alexandra Road, Blackpool
FY1 6BU
t (01253) 346641
e admin@blackpoolfamilyaccom
modation.com
w blackpoolfamilyaccommodation.
com

Ash Lodge ★★★ Guest House
131 Hornby Road, Blackpool
FY1 4JG
t (01253) 627637
e admin@ashlodgehotel.co.uk
w ashlodgehotel.co.uk

Aspire ★★★★
Guest Accommodation
51 Albert Road, Blackpool
FY1 4TA
t (01253) 626467
e info@theapire.co.uk
w theaspire.co.uk

Astoria ★★★
Guest Accommodation
118-120 Albert Road, Blackpool
FY1 4PN
t (01253) 621321
e enquiries@astoria-hotel.co.uk
w astoria-hotel.co.uk

The Avenue ★★★★ Guest House
56 Reads Avenue, Blackpool
FY1 4DE
t (01253) 626146
e info@blackpooluk.co.uk
w blackpooluk.co.uk

Avoca ★ Guest House
89 Reads Avenue, Blackpool
FY1 4DG
t (01253) 626579
e avocaguesthouse@fsmail.net
w avocaguesthouseblackpool.co.uk

The Avon ★★★
Guest Accommodation
112 Albert Road, Blackpool
FY1 4PN
t (01253) 290110
e mail@theavonhotel.co.uk
w theavonhotel.co.uk

Babylon ★★★★
Guest Accommodation
8 Banks Street, Blackpool
FY1 1RN
t (01253) 620407
e info@hotelbabylonblackpool.co.
uk
w hotelbabylonblackpool.co.uk

The Bambi ★★★
Guest Accommodation
27 Bright Street, Blackpool
FY4 1BS
t (01253) 343756
e bambihotel@hotmail.com

Bamford House ★★★ Guest House
28 York Street, Blackpool
FY1 5AQ
t (01253) 622433
e info@bamfordhotelblackpool.co.
uk
w bamfordhotelblackpool.co.uk

The Baron ★★★★
Guest Accommodation
296 Promenade, Blackpool
FY1 2EY
t (01253) 622729
e baronhotel@f2s.com
w baron-hotel.co.uk

Beachcomber ★★★★ Guest House
78 Reads Avenue, Blackpool
FY1 4DE
t (01253) 621622
e info@beachcomberhotel.net
w beachcomberhotel.co.uk

Beachwood Guest House ★★★
Guest Accommodation
30 Moore Street, Blackpool
FY4 1DA
t (01253) 401951
e beachwood.guesthouse@virgin.
net
w beachwoodhotel.co.uk

Beauchief ★★★
Guest Accommodation
48 King Edward Avenue, Blackpool
FY2 9TA
t (01253) 353314
e beauchief.hotel@live.co.uk
w thebeauchief.co.uk

The Beaucliffe ★★★
Guest Accommodation
20-22 Holmfield Road, Blackpool
FY2 9TB
t (01253) 351663

Belgrave 21 ★★★ Guest House
21 Barton Avenue, Blackpool
FY1 6AP
t (01253) 346792
e belgrave21@fsmail.net
w belgrave21.co.uk

North West | Lancashire

The Belvedere ★★★
Guest Accommodation
91-93 Albert Road, Blackpool
FY1 4PW
t (01253) 628029
e stay@thebelvedereblackpool.co.uk
w thebelvedereblackpool.co.uk

The Berkswell ★★★
Guest Accommodation
8 Withnell Road, Blackpool
FY4 1HF
t (01253) 341374
e theberkswell@yahoo.com
w berkswellhotel.co.uk

The Berwick ★★★★ *Guest House*
23 King Edward Avenue, North Shore, Blackpool
FY2 9TA
t (01253) 351496
e enquiries@theberwickhotel.co.uk
w theberwickhotel.co.uk

Berwyn ★★★★
Guest Accommodation
1-2 Finchley Road, Blackpool
FY1 2LP
t (01253) 352896
e stay@berwynhotel.co.uk
w berwynhotel.co.uk

The Beverley ★★★
Guest Accommodation
4 Charnley Road, Blackpool
FY1 4PF
t (01253) 623255
e jmorganj@aol.com
w the-beverley-hotel.com

Beverley Dean ★★★ *Guest House*
25 Dean Street, Blackpool
FY4 1AU
t (01253) 344126
e admin@beverleydean.co.uk
w beverleydean.co.uk

The Bianca ★★★ *Guest House*
25 Palatine Road, Blackpool
FY1 4BX
t (01253) 752824
e enquiries@hotelbianca.co.uk
w hotelbianca.co.uk

Blenheim Mount Hotel ★★★
Guest Accommodation
207 Promenade, Blackpool
FY1 5DL
t (01253) 625867
e bmhotel@hotmail.com
w blenheimmounthotel.com

Boltonia ★★★
Guest Accommodation
124-126 Albert Road, Blackpool
FY1 4PN
t (01253) 620248
e info@boltoniahotel.co.uk
w boltoniahotel.co.uk

Bracondale Guest House ★★★★
Guest House
14 Warley Road, Blackpool
FY1 2JU
t (01253) 351650
e bracondale-hotel@btconnect.com
w nosmokingblackpool.co.uk

Branston Lodge ★★★★
Guest Accommodation
64 Withnell Road, Blackpool
FY4 1HE
t (01253) 347391
e info@branstonlodge.co.uk
w branstonlodge.co.uk

Bridges Guest House ★★★
Guest Accommodation
10 General Street, Blackpool
FY1 1RW
t (01253) 294749
e info@bridgesguesthouse.com
w bridgesguesthouse.com

Brincliffe ★★★★
Guest Accommodation
168-170 Queens Promenade, Blackpool
FY2 9JN
t (01253) 351654
e susan@brincliffehotel.co.uk
w brincliffehotel.co.uk

Briny View ★★
Guest Accommodation
2 Woodfield Road, Blackpool
FY1 6AX
t (01253) 346584
e brinyviewhotel@aol.com
w brinyviewhotel.co.uk

The Brioni ★★★
Guest Accommodation
324 Queens Promenade, Blackpool
FY2 9AB
t (01253) 351988
e hamlinheros@aol.com
w brionihotelblackpool.co.uk

Brooklands ★★★
Guest Accommodation
28-30 King Edward Avenue, Blackpool
FY2 9TA
t (01253) 351479
e brooklandhotel@btinternet.com
w brooklands-hotel.com

Brooklyn ★★★ *Guest House*
20 Tyldesley Road, Blackpool
FY1 5DH
t (01253) 623392
e simonsmith285@btinternet.com
w brooklynhotelblackpool.com

Burleigh ★★★
Guest Accommodation
47 Osborne Road, Blackpool
FY4 1HQ
t (01253) 343737
e paulandnett@hotmail.com
w burleighblackpool.com

Caledonia House ★★★
Guest House
83 Hornby Road, Blackpool
FY1 4QP
t (01253) 623059
e caledoniahousemorris@btinternet.com
w caledonia-house.co.uk

California ★★★
Guest Accommodation
90 Hornby Road, Blackpool
FY1 4QS
t (01253) 622481
e daverob05@msn.com
w hotelcaliforniablackpool.co.uk

Camelot House ★★★
Guest Accommodation
24 Crystal Road, Blackpool
FY1 6BS
t (01253) 345636
e camelot.houseblackpool@talktalk.net
w blackpoolcamelot-house.co.uk

Cameo ★★★ *Guest Accommodation*
30 Hornby Road, Blackpool
FY1 4QG
t (01253) 626144
e enquiries@blackpool-cameo.com
w blackpool-cameo.com

The Canberra ★★★ *Guest House*
Palatine Road, Blackpool
FY1 4BX
t (01253) 623812
w canberrahotel.co.uk

Canda ★★★ *Guest House*
34 Vance Road, Blackpool
FY1 4QD
t (01253) 623200
e cliff@candahotel.co.uk
w candahotel.co.uk

Cardoh Lodge ★★★ *Guest House*
21 Hull Road, Blackpool
FY1 4QB
t (01253) 627755
e info@cardohlodge.co.uk
w cardohlodge.co.uk

Carlee ★★★ *Guest Accommodation*
115-117 Park Road, Blackpool
FY1 4ET
t (01253) 628409
e stay@carleehotelblackpool.com
w carleehotelblackpool.com

The Carlton ★★★
Guest Accommodation
64 Albert Road, Blackpool
FY1 4PR
t (01253) 622693
e info@thecarlton.com
w thecarlton.com

Caroldene ★★★
Guest Accommodation
12 Woodfield Road, Blackpool
FY1 6AX
t (01253) 346963
e caroldenehotel2003@yahoo.co.uk
w thecaroldene.yolasite.com

Casablanca ★★★ *Guest House*
84 Hornby Road, Blackpool
FY1 4QS
t (01253) 622574
e jdixon8969@aol.com
w casablancablackpool.co.uk

Cavendish ★★★ *Guest House*
11 Pleasant Street, North Shore, Blackpool, Lancashire
FY1 2JA
t 01253 624575
e roy@cavendishhotel.com
w cavendishhotel.com

Chorlton ★★★
Guest Accommodation
38 Hull Road, Blackpool
FY1 4QB
t (01253) 293668
e info@chorltonhotelblackpool.co.uk
w chorltonhotelblackpool.co.uk

Clarron House Guest House ★★
Guest House
22 Leopold Grove, Blackpool
FY1 4LD
t (01253) 623748
e annodonnell22@aol.com
w clarronhouse.co.uk

Cliff Head Seafront Guest House ★★★ *Guest House*
174 Queens Promenade, Blackpool
FY2 9JN
t (01253) 591086
e mike@cliffhead.com
w cliffhead.com

Clifton House ★★★
Guest Accommodation
38 Bairstow Street, Blackpool
FY1 5BN
t (01253) 621165
e carole.cregan@virgin.net
w cliftonhousehotel.net

Clovelly ★★★★
Guest Accommodation
22 Saint Chads Road, Blackpool
FY1 6BP
t (01253) 346087
e info@clovellyhotel.com
w clovellyhotel.com

Collingwood ★★★★
Guest Accommodation
8-10 Holmfield Road, Blackpool
FY2 9SL
t (01253) 352929
e enquiries@collingwoodhotel.co.uk
w collingwoodhotel.co.uk

Colyndene ★★★
Guest Accommodation
53 Reads Avenue, Blackpool
FY1 4DG
t (01253) 295282
e reception@colyndenehotel.fsnet.co.uk
w blackpool-holidays.com

Come Ye In ★★★ *Guest House*
85 Hornby Road, Blackpool
FY1 4QP
t (01253) 625065
e margery.tracey@virgin.net
w come-ye-in.co.uk

Corona ★★★
Guest Accommodation
18-20 Clifton Drive, Blackpool
FY4 1NX
t (01253) 342586
e coronablackpool@aol.com
w thecoronahotel.com

Courtneys of Gynn Square ★★★
Guest Accommodation
1 Warbreck Hill Road, Blackpool
FY2 9SP
t (01253) 352179
e courtneyshotel@aol.com
w courtneysofgynnsquare.co.uk

The Craimar ★★★
Guest Accommodation
32 Hull Road, Blackpool
FY1 4QB
t (01253) 622185
e thecraimar@sky.com
w craimarhotel.co.uk

Cranstone Guest House ★★★
Guest House
39 Alexandra Road, Blackpool
FY1 6BU
t (01253) 345918
e shirley.hunt1@btopenworld.com
w cranstonehotel.co.uk

Crescent ★★★
Guest Accommodation
70 Hornby Road, Blackpool
FY1 4QJ
t (01253) 624388
e freda.youde@homecall.co.uk
w crescentblackpool.com

The Cresta ★★ *Guest House*
85 Withnell Road, Blackpool
FY4 1HE
t (01253) 343866
e info@crestahotel.co.uk
w crestahotel.co.uk

Crewes Original ★★
Guest Accommodation
203 Promenade, Blackpool
FY1 5DL
t (01253) 625101
e enquiries@crewesoriginal.com
w crewesoriginal.com

Cumbrian Guest House ★★★
Guest House
81 Hornby Road, Blackpool
FY1 4QP
t (01253) 623677
e sheila.lloyd-jones@virgin.net
w blackpool-hotels/cumbrian

David & Wahn's Seaview Guest House ★★★ *Guest House*
10 Nelson Road, Blackpool
FY1 6AS
t (01253) 402316
e seaview-blackpool@live.co.uk
w seaview-blackpool.co.uk

Denely Guest Accommodation ★★★ *Guest House*
15 King Edward Avenue, Blackpool
FY2 9TA
t (01253) 352757
e denely@tesco.net
w denelyhotel.co.uk

Deneside ★★★★
Guest Accommodation
27 Albert Road, Blackpool
FY1 4TA
t (01253) 620703
e booking@denesidehotel.co.uk
w denesidehotel.co.uk

The Derwent ★★★ *Guest House*
42 Palatine Road, Blackpool
FY1 4BY
t (01253) 620004
e chris@derwenthotelblackpool.co.uk
w derwenthotelblackpool.co.uk

Dolphin Guest House ★★★
Guest House
44 Woodfield Road, Blackpool
FY1 6AX
t (01253) 346047
e thedolphin@tiscali.co.uk

North West | Lancashire

The Dragonfly ★★★★
Guest Accommodation
5 Lord Street, Blackpool
FY1 2DA
t (01253) 623204
e queries@dragonflyhotel.com
w dragonflyhotel.com

The Draytonian ★★★
Guest Accommodation
4 Palatine Road, Blackpool
FY1 4BY
t (01253) 628220
e drayhot123@btinternet.com
w centralblackpoolhotel.co.uk

The Dudley ★★★★
Guest Accommodation
2 Alexandra Road, South Shore, Blackpool
FY1 6BU
t (01253) 346827

Dunromin ★★★ Guest House
7 Palatine Road, Blackpool
FY1 4BX
t (01253) 620543
e info@dunrominhotel.co.uk
w dunrominhotel.co.uk

The Edelweiss ★★★
Guest Accommodation
35 St Chads Road, Blackpool
FY1 6BP
t (01253) 341265
e edelweissstchads@aol.com
w edelweisshotel.co.uk

Ellan Vannin ★★★ Guest House
3 Gynn Avenue, Blackpool
FY1 2LD
t (01253) 351784
e blackpoolcoast@googlemail.com
w blackpoolhoteluk.org.uk

Everglades ★★★ Guest House
4 Barton Avenue, Blackpool
FY1 6AP
t (01253) 343093
e info@evergladesblackpool.co.uk
w evergladesblackpool.co.uk

Fairhaven ★★★★
Guest Accommodation
6 Palatine Road, Blackpool
FY1 4BY
t (01253) 628280
e fairhaven-hotel@btconnect.com
w fairhavenhotelblackpool.co.uk

The Fairhaven ★★★★
Guest Accommodation
27/29 Woodfield Road, South Shore, Blackpool
FY1 6AX
t 01253 346261
e liz@fairhavenblackpool.com
w fairhavenblackpool.com

Fairway ★★★
Guest Accommodation
34-36 Hull Road, Blackpool
FY1 4QB
t (01253) 623777
e impulsedh@aol.com
w fairwayhotelblackpool.co.uk

The Fame ★★★
Guest Accommodation
163 Promenade, Blackpool
FY1 6BJ
t (01253) 346615
e info@hotelfame.com
w hotelfame.com

Feng Shui House ★★★★
Guest Accommodation
661 New South Promenade, Blackpool
FY4 1RN
t (01253) 342266
e kate_burns@btconnect.com
w classic-feng-shui.com

Fern Royd ★★★
Guest Accommodation
45 Holmfield Road, Blackpool
FY2 9TE
t (01253) 351066
e fernroyd@btconnect.com
w thefernroyd.co.uk

Fern Villa Hotel ★★★
Guest Accommodation
51 Chapel Street, Blackpool
FY1 5HF
t (01253) 620984
e fern.villa.51@virgin.net
w fernvilla51.co.uk

Four Seasons Blackpool ★★★★★
Guest Accommodation
SILVER AWARD
60 Reads Avenue, Blackpool
FY1 4DE
t (01253) 752171
e mdsewell@fourseasonsblackpool.co.uk
w fourseasonsblackpool.co.uk

The Fylde ★★★★ Backpackers
93 Palatine Road, Blackpool
FY1 4BX
t (01253) 623 735
e enquiries@fyldehotel.com
w fyldehotel.com

Glen Allan ★ Guest House
22 Hornby Road, Blackpool
FY1 4QG
t (01253) 620838
e glenallanhotel@xln.co.uk
w glenallanblackpool.co.uk

Glenburn Guest House ★★★
Guest House
16 Shaw Road, Blackpool
FY1 6HB
t (01253) 347493
e glenburnblackpool@sky.com
w glenburnguesthouse.com

Gleneagles ★★★★
Guest Accommodation
75 Albert Road, Blackpool
FY1 4PW
t (01253) 295266/07818272886
e gleneaglesblackpool@tiscali.co.uk
w gleneagles-hotel.com

Glenholme ★★★
Guest Accommodation
44 Alexandra Road, Blackpool
FY1 6BU
t (01253) 345875
e jamieshelly@hotmail.com

Glenmere ★★★
Guest Accommodation
7 Gynn Avenue, Blackpool
FY1 2LD
t (01253) 351259
e glenmerehotel@aol.com

Glen Stuart ★★ Guest House
71 Palatine Road, Blackpool
FY1 4BX
t (01253) 624706

Glenwalden ★★★
Guest Accommodation
382 North Promenade, Blackpool
FY1 2LB
t (01253) 353332
e glenwalden@btinternet.com
w glenwaldenhotelblackpool.co.uk/

Golden Sands ★★★★ Guest House
20 Gynn Avenue, Blackpool
FY1 2LD
t (01253) 352285
e thegoldensands@hotmail.com
w thegoldensands.co.uk

**Granville Guest Accommodation
★★★** Guest Accommodation
12 Station Road, Blackpool
FY4 1BE
t (01253) 343012
e reservations@granvillehotel.fsnet.co.uk
w granvillehotel.com

The Grenadier ★
Guest Accommodation
20 Springfield Road, Blackpool
FY1 1QL
t (01253) 627729
e enquiries@grenadierhotel.co.uk
w grenadierhotel.co.uk

Grosvenor View ★★★
Guest Accommodation
7 King Edward Avenue, Blackpool
FY2 9TD
t (01253) 352851
e enq@grosvenorviewblackpool.com
w grosvenorviewblackpool.com

Hadley ★★★ Guest Accommodation
225 Promenade, Blackpool
FY1 5DL
t (01253) 621197
e admin@hadley-hotel.com
w hadley-hotel.com

The Happy Return ★★★
Guest Accommodation
17-19 Hull Road, Blackpool
FY1 4QB
t (01253) 622596
e happyreturn@yahoo.com
w happyreturnhotel.co.uk

Hartshead ★★★
Guest Accommodation
17 King Edward Avenue, Blackpool
FY2 9TA
t (01253) 353133
e info@hartshead-hotel.co.uk
w hartshead-hotel.co.uk

Hatton ★★★ Guest Accommodation
10 Banks Street, Blackpool
FY1 1RN
t (01253) 624944
e hattonhotel@hotmail.com
w hattonhotel.co.uk

The Haven Guest House ★★★
Guest Accommodation
11 Alexandra Road, Blackpool
FY1 6BU
t (01253) 346498
e info@haven-guesthouse.com
w haven-guesthouse.com

Heywood House ★★★
Guest Accommodation
30 Rawcliffe Street, Blackpool
FY4 1BZ
t (01253) 344413
e heywoodhousehotel@tiscali.co.uk
w heywoodhousehotelblackpool.co.uk

The Highbank ★★
Guest Accommodation
98-100 Hornby Road, Blackpool
FY1 4QS
t (01253) 624863
e thehighbankhotel@gmail.com
w thehighbankhotel.co.uk

Holme-Lea ★ Guest House
93 Lord Street, Blackpool
FY1 2DJ
t (01253) 625766
w stagandhenhotel.com

Holmsdale ★★★ Guest House
6-8 Pleasant Street, Blackpool
FY1 2JA
t (01253) 621008
e stay@holmsdalehotel-blackpool.com
w holmsdalehotel-blackpool.com

Holmside House ★★★★
Guest House
24 Barton Avenue, Blackpool, Lancs
FY1 6AP
t (01253) 346045
e blackpoolholmsidehouse@talktalk.net
w blackpoolholmsidehouse.co.uk

Homecliffe ★★★★
Guest Accommodation
5-6 Wilton Parade, Blackpool
FY1 2HE
t (01253) 625147
e enquiry@homeclifehotel.com
w homeclifehotel.com

Hornby Villa ★★★
Guest Accommodation
130 Hornby Road, Blackpool
FY1 4QS
t (01253) 624959
e thehornbyvilla@aol.com
w hornbyvillahotel.com

The Hurstmere ★★★
Guest Accommodation
5 Alexandra Road, Blackpool
FY1 6BU
t (01253) 345843
e stay@thehurstmerehotel.com
w thehurstmerehotel.com

The Inglewood ★★★
Guest Accommodation
18 Holmfield Road, Blackpool
FY2 9TB
t (01253) 351668
e enquiries@theinglewoodhotel.com
w theinglewoodhotel.com

Karen Annes Guest House ★★★
Guest House
4 Barton Avenue, Blackpool
FY1 6AP
t (01253) 346719
e enquiries@karenannesguesthouse.co.uk
w karenannesguesthouse.co.uk

Kendal Private Guest Accommodation ★★★
Guest Accommodation
76 Withnell Road, Blackpool
FY4 1HE
t (01253) 348209
e info@icliffsdrivingcourses.com
w the3starkendalatblackpool.com/

The Kimberley ★★★★ Guest House
25 Gynn Avenue, Blackpool
FY1 2LD
t (01253) 352264
e thekimberley@btconnect.com
w kimberleyguesthouse.com

Kimberley House ★★
Guest Accommodation
8 St Chads Road, Blackpool
FY1 6BP
t (01253) 346161
e info@kimberleyhousehotel.com
w kimberleyhousehotel.com

The King Edward ★★★
Guest Accommodation
44 King Edward Avenue, Blackpool
FY2 9TA
t (01253) 352932
e enquiries@kingedwardhotel.co.uk
w kingedwardhotel.co.uk

Kings ★★★ Guest Accommodation
553 New South Promenade, Blackpool
FY4 1NF
t (01253) 341442
e mail@kingshotelblackpool.co.uk
w kingshotelblackpool.co.uk

Kingscliff ★★★★
Guest Accommodation
78 Hornby Road, Blackpool
FY1 4QJ
t (01253) 620200
e kingscliff.blackpool@virgin.net
w kingsclifhotel.co.uk

Kings Court ★★★
Guest Accommodation
34 King Edward Avenue, Blackpool
FY2 9TA
t (01253) 593312
e chris@kingscourthotel.freeserve.co.uk
w blackpoolkingscourthotel.co.uk

Kingsway ★★★ Guest House
68 Charnley Road, Blackpool
FY1 4PF
t (01253) 627696
e kingswayhotel@blueyonder.co.uk
w kingswayhotelblackpool.com

Kirkstall House ★★★
Guest Accommodation
25 Hull Road, Blackpool
FY1 4QB
t (01253) 623077
e rooms@kirkstallhotel.co.uk
w kirkstallhotel.co.uk

North West | Lancashire

Lanayr ★★★ *Guest Accommodation*
73-75 Reads Avenue, Blackpool
FY1 4DG
t (01253) 623302
e lanayrhotel@gmail.com
w lanayrhotel.com

Lancastria ★★★
Guest Accommodation
100 Albert Road, Blackpool
FY1 4PR
t (01253) 624373
e rsburrell@hotmail.com
w lancastriahotel.co.uk

Langroyd ★★★
Guest Accommodation
Station Road, Blackpool
FY4 1EU
t (01253) 342263
e langroyd@tiscali.co.uk
w langroydhotel.co.uk

Langtrys ★★★★★
Guest Accommodation
SILVER AWARD
36 King Edward Avenue, North Shore, Blackpool
FY2 9TA
t (01253) 352031
e info@langtrysblackpool.co.uk
w langtrysblackpool.co.uk

La Tour Hotel ★★★
Guest Accommodation
92-94 Albert Road, Blackpool
FY1 4PR
t 01253 624888
e reservations@latourhotel.co.uk
w latourhotel.co.uk

The Lawton ★★★
Guest Accommodation
58-66 Charnley Road, Blackpool
FY1 4PF
t (01253) 753471
e thelawtonhotel@gmail.com
w thelawtonhotel.co.uk

Leawood ★★★ *Guest House*
72 Hornby Road, Blackpool
FY1 4QJ
t (01253) 627327
e mary.eley@btconnect.com

Llanryan Guest House ★★
Guest Accommodation
37 Reads Avenue, Blackpool
FY1 4DD
t (01253) 628446
e keith@llanryan.co.uk
w llanryan.co.uk

Lynbar Guesthouse ★★★
Guest House
32 Vance Road, Blackpool, Lancashire
FY1 4QD
t (01253) 294504
e enquiries@lynbarhotel.co.uk
w lynbarhotel.co.uk

Lyndene ★★★
Guest Accommodation
18 Cocker Street, Blackpool
FY1 2BY
t (01253) 628317
e thekeans@btconnect.com
w lyndeneblackpool.co.uk

Lyndene Guest House ★★★
Guest House
37 Crystal Road, South Shore, Blackpool
FY1 6BS
t (01253) 346662 mob 07595919972
e geraintgoddard@yahoo.co.uk
w lyndene.org.uk

Lynmoore Guest House ★★★
Guest Accommodation
31 Moore Street, Blackpool
FY4 1DA
t (01253) 349888
e markinblackpool@googlemail.com
w lynmooreblackpool.co.uk

The Mackintosh Guest Accommodation ★★★
Guest Accommodation
5 Gynn Avenue, Blackpool
FY1 2LD
t (01253) 352296
e enquiries@themackintoshblackpool.co.uk
w themackintoshblackpool.co.uk

The Malrow ★★★
Guest Accommodation
79-81 Palatine Road, Blackpool
FY1 4BX
t (01253) 626595
e jayne.brightmore@o2.co.uk
w malrowhotel.co.uk

Manchester House ★★★
Guest Accommodation
77 Withnell Road, Blackpool
FY4 1HE
t (01253) 342637
e manchesterhousehotel@hotmail.com
w hotels-blackpoolpleasurebeach.co.uk

Manor Grove ★★ *Guest House*
24 Leopold Grove, Blackpool
FY1 4LD
t (01253) 625577
e lyndon@evans2000.freeserve.co.uk
w manorgrovehotel.co.uk

The Marina ★★★ *Guest House*
30 Gynn Avenue, Blackpool
FY1 2LD
t (01253) 352833
e robinglockhart@hotmail.com
w smoothhound.co.uk/hotels/marinagh

Marlow Lodge ★★★
Guest Accommodation
76 Station Road, Blackpool
FY4 1EU
t (01253) 341580
e info@marlowlodge.co.uk
w marlowlodge.co.uk

Maxime ★★★
Guest Accommodation
416-418 Promenade, Blackpool
FY1 2LB
t (01253) 351215

The Middleton ★★★
Guest Accommodation
55 Holmfield Road, Blackpool
FY2 9RU
t (01253) 354559
e info@middleton-hotel.co.uk
w middleton-hotel.co.uk

The Montclair ★★★ *Guest House*
95 Albert Road, Blackpool
FY1 4PW
t (01253) 625860
e chrissbowen@aol.com
w hotelmontclair.co.uk

The Morrisy ★★★
Guest Accommodation
17 Dean Street, Blackpool
FY4 1AU
t (01253) 342460
e claze@btopenworld.com
w morrisyhotel.com

Mount ★★★ *Guest Accommodation*
8 Queens Promenade, Blackpool
FY2 9SQ
t (01253) 351454
e mail@mounthotel.co.uk
w mounthotel.co.uk

Myrtle House ★★★
Guest Accommodation
25 Albert Road, Blackpool
FY1 4TA
t (01253) 620002
e myrtlehousehotel@hotmail.co.uk
w myrtlehousehotel.co.uk

New Derby Hotel ★★
Guest Accommodation
35 Chapel Street, Blackpool
FY1 5AW
t (01253) 627970

New Hampshire ★★★
Bed & Breakfast
71 Reads Avenue, Blackpool
FY1 4DG
t (01253) 621024
e info@newhampshireblackpool.co.uk
w newhampshireblackpool.co.uk

Newholme Guest House ★★★
Guest House
2 Wilton Parade, Blackpool
FY1 2HE
t (01253) 624010
e newholmehotel@aol.com
w newholme.biz

New Phildene ★★★★
Guest Accommodation
5-7 St Chads Road, Blackpool
FY1 6BP
t 01253 346141
e info@newphildenehotel.co.uk
w newphildenehotel.co.uk

New Ryton ★★★
Guest Accommodation
14-16 Woodfield Road, Blackpool
FY1 6AX
t (01253) 346228
e info@newrytonhotel.co.uk
w newrytonhotel.co.uk

North Crest ★★★
Guest Accommodation
22 King Edward Avenue, Blackpool
FY2 9TD
t (01253) 355937
e info@northcrestblackpool.co.uk
w northcrestblackpool.co.uk

The Northdene ★★★ *Guest House*
19 Gynn Avenue, Blackpool
FY1 2LD
t (01253) 353005
e phil@tackler.org.uk
w northdene.co.uk

Northfield ★★★
Guest Accommodation
4 Derby Road, Blackpool
FY1 2JF
t (01253) 620923
e info@northfieldhotel.co.uk
w northfieldhotel.co.uk

Norville House ★★★
Guest Accommodation
44 Warbreck Hill Road, Blackpool
FY2 9SU
t (01253) 352714
e norvillehouse@btconnect.com
w norvillehousehotel.co.uk

The Norwood ★★★★
Guest Accommodation
35 Hull Road, Blackpool
FY1 4QB
t (01253) 621118
e norwood35@msn.com
w thenorwood.com

Novello ★★★
Guest Accommodation
11 Hornby Road, Blackpool
FY1 4QG
t (01253) 293474
e enquiry@novellohotel.co.uk
w novellohotel.co.uk

Number One South Beach
★★★★★ *Guest Accommodation*
GOLD AWARD
4 Harrowside West, Blackpool
FY4 1NW
t (01253) 343900
e info@numberonesouthbeach.com
w numberonesouthbeach.com

Number One St Luke's ★★★★★
Bed & Breakfast GOLD AWARD
1 St Lukes Road, Blackpool
FY4 2EL
t (01253) 343901
e info@numberoneblackpool.com
w numberoneblackpool.com

Oban House ★★★
Guest Accommodation
63 Holmfield Road, Blackpool
FY2 9RU
t (01253) 352413
e obanhousehotel@aol.com
w obanhousehotel.co.uk

Octavia Guest House ★★★
Guest Accommodation
21 Bright Street, Blackpool
FY4 1BS
t (01253) 401670
e lisatilly6@hotmail.com
w octaviablackpool.co.uk

The Old Coach House ★★★★
Guest Accommodation
50 Dean Street, Blackpool
FY4 1BP
t (01253) 347657
e info@theoldcoachhouse.co.uk
w theoldcoachhouse.co.uk

Orlando ★★ *Guest House*
50 Alexandra Road, Blackpool
FY1 6BU
t (01253) 345494
e theorlandohotel@tesco.net
w blackpool-orlando.co.uk

Osborne ★★★
Guest Accommodation
31 St Chads Road, Blackpool
FY1 6BP
t (01253) 346093
e stayosborne@tiscali.co.uk
w theosborne.co.uk

The Osprey ★★★ *Guest House*
27 Charnley Road, Blackpool
FY1 4PE
t (01253) 621684
e enquiries@theospreyhotel.co.uk
w theospreyhotel.co.uk

Pembroke ★★★
Guest Accommodation
17 Banks Street, Blackpool
FY1 1RN
t (01253) 625069
e pembroke@xln.co.uk
w pembrokehotelblackpool.com

The Pembroke ★★★★
Guest Accommodation
11 King Edward Avenue, Blackpool
FY2 9TD
t (01253) 351306
e info@neartheprom.com
w neartheprom.com

Pendeen ★ *Guest House*
16 Lonsdale Road, Blackpool
FY1 6EE
t (01253) 343214
e thependeen@googlemail.com
w pendeenhotelblackpool.co.uk

Penrhyn ★★★
Guest Accommodation
38 King Edward Avenue, Blackpool
FY2 9TA
t (01253) 352762
e thepenrhyn@aol.com

The Pilatus ★★★
Guest Accommodation
10 Willshaw Road, Blackpool
FY2 9SH
t (01253) 352470
e debbie@pilatushotel.co.uk
w pilatushotel.co.uk

The Poldhu ★★★
Guest Accommodation
330 Queens Promenade, Blackpool
FY2 9AB
t (01253) 356918
e info@poldhu-hotel.co.uk
w poldhu-hotel.co.uk

Princess ★★★★
Guest Accommodation
18-20 Alexandra Road, Blackpool
FY1 6BU
t (01253) 346641
e info@theprincess-blackpool.co.uk
w theprincess-blackpool.co.uk

The Raffles Guest Accommodation ★★★★
Guest Accommodation
73-77 Hornby Road, Blackpool
FY1 4QJ
t (01253) 294713
e enquiries@raffleshotelblackpool.fsworld.co.uk
w raffleshotelblackpool.co.uk

North West | Lancashire

encliffe ★★★★ *Guest House*
5 Hornby Road, Blackpool
Y1 4QJ
  0800 4320428
e rencliffehotel@aol.com
w rencliffe.co.uk

imini ★★★ *Guest House*
1 Wellington Road, Blackpool
Y1 6AR
t (01253) 346450
e rimini.hotel@hotmail.co.uk
w riminihotelblackpool.co.uk

io Rita ★★★
Guest Accommodation
9 Withnell Road, Blackpool
Y4 1HE
t (01253) 345203
e rioritahotel@btconnect.com
w riorita.co.uk

ockcliffe ★★★
Guest Accommodation
48 Promenade, Blackpool
Y1 1RZ
t (01253) 623476
w rockcliffehotel.co.uk

ockdene ★★★
Guest Accommodation
0 St Chads Road, Blackpool
Y1 6BP
t (01253) 345810
e info@rockdenehotel.co.uk
w rockdenehotel.co.uk

oselea ★★★
Guest Accommodation
7 Albert Road, Blackpool
Y1 4PW
t (01253) 622032
e info@roseleahotel.co.uk
w roseleahotel.com

ossdene House ★★★★
uest Accommodation
ILVER AWARD
2 Gynn Avenue, Blackpool
Y1 2LD
t (01253) 351714
e info@rossdenehouse.com
w rossdenehouse.com

oyal Seabank ★★★
Guest Accommodation
19-223 Promenade, Blackpool
Y1 5DL
t 0845 758 5180
e admin@blackpoolpromotions.com
w blackpoolpromotions.com

Rutland ★★★
Guest Accommodation
30 Promenade, Blackpool
Y1 2JG
t (01253) 622791
e enquiries@rutland-hotel.co.uk
w rutland-hotel.co.uk

The Rutlands ★★★
Guest Accommodation
3 Hornby Road, Blackpool
Y1 4QG
t (01253) 623067
w rutlandshotel.co.uk

Salmar Bed & Breakfast ★★★
Guest Accommodation
38 Albert Road, Blackpool
Y1 4PL
t (01253) 623183
e thesalmar@btconnect.com
w blackpoolseasideaccommodation.com

Sandford Promenade ★★★
Guest Accommodation
353 Promenade, Blackpool
FY1 6BJ
t (01253) 343041
e rbac_mallorca@hotmail.com
w sandfordhotel.co.uk

The Sands ★★★
Guest Accommodation
485 Promenade, Blackpool
FY4 1AZ
t (01253) 349262
e enquiries@thesandshotel.net
w thesandshotel.com

Scott's ★★★ *Guest House*
38 Reads Avenue, Blackpool
FY1 4BP
t (01253) 299659
e holidays@scotts-hotel.co.uk
w scotts-hotel.co.uk

Seabreeze Guest House ★★★★
Guest Accommodation
1 Gynn Avenue, Blackpool
FY1 2LD
t (01253) 351427
e info@vbreezy.co.uk
w vbreezy.co.uk

Shazron Hotel ★★★ *Guest House*
4 Havelock Street, Blackpool
FY1 4BN
t (01253) 620897
e enquiries@shazronhotelblackpool.co.uk
w blackpoolshotel.org

Shepperton Hotel ★★★
Guest Accommodation
74 Station Road, Blackpool
FY4 1HJ
t (01253) 343600

Sheron House ★★★★ *Guest House*
21 Gynn Avenue, Blackpool
FY1 2LD
t (01253) 354614
e sheronhousehotel@btconnect.com
w sheronhouse.co.uk

Shirley Heights ★★
Guest Accommodation
114 Coronation Street, Blackpool
FY1 4QQ
t (01253) 622551
e info@shirleyheights.co.uk
w shirleyheights.co.uk

The Shores ★★★
Guest Accommodation
29-31 Tyldsley Road, Blackpool
FY1 5DH
t (01253) 620064
e theshoreshotel@hotmail.co.uk
w shoreshotelblackpool.com

South Beach Seafront ★★★
Guest Accommodation
365 & 367 Promenade, Blackpool, Lancashire
FY1 6BP
t (01253) 342250
e info@southbeachhotel.co.uk
w southbeachhotel.co.uk

South Lea ★★★ *Guest House*
4 Willshaw Road, Blackpool
FY2 9SH
t (01253) 351940
e info@southlea.co.uk
w southlea.co.uk

The Southview ★★
Guest Accommodation
122 Albert Road, Blackpool
FY1 4PN
t (01253) 624163
e info@thesouthviewhotel.net
w thesouthviewhotel.net

St. Kilda ★★★ *Guest House*
37 Alexandra Road, Blackpool
FY1 6BU
t 01253 346249
e jane37@tiscali.co.uk
w myblackpoolaccommodation.co.uk

Stafford House ★★★
Guest Accommodation
8 Woodfield Road, Blackpool
FY1 6AX
t (01253) 346727
e staffordhousehotel@hotmail.co.uk
w staffordhousehotel.co.uk

St Albans ★★★
Guest Accommodation
355 Promenade, Blackpool
FY1 6BJ
t (01253) 346671
e st.albans355@hotmail.com
w blackpoolstalbanshotel.co.uk

St Elmo ★★★
Guest Accommodation
20-22 Station Road, Blackpool
FY4 1BE
t (01253) 341820
e hotelstelmo@hotmail.co.uk
w hotelstelmo.co.uk

St Ives Blackpool ★★★
Guest Accommodation
10 King George Avenue, Blackpool
FY2 9SN
t (01253) 352122
e enquiries@stiveshotel-blackpool.co.uk
w stiveshotel-blackpool.co.uk

The Strathdon ★★★★
Guest Accommodation
28 St Chads Road, Blackpool
FY1 6BP
t (01253) 343549
e stay@strathdonhotel.com
w strathdonhotel.com

Strathmore ★★★
Guest Accommodation
94 Hornby Road, Blackpool
FY1 4QS
t (01253) 623659
e info@strathmorehotelblackpool.co.uk
w strathmorehotelblackpool.co.uk

Sunny Cliff ★★★★
Guest Accommodation
98 Queens Promenade, Blackpool
FY2 9NS
t (01253) 351155

Sunnydale ★★★
Guest Accommodation
16 King George Avenue, Blackpool
FY2 9SN
t (01253) 351452
e thesunnydalehotel@btopenworld.com
w sunnydalehotelblackpool.co.uk

Sunnymede ★★★
Guest Accommodation
50 King Edward Avenue, Blackpool
FY2 9TA
t (01253) 352877
e enquiries@sunnymedehotel.co.uk
w sunnymedehotel.co.uk

Sunnyside ★★★
Guest Accommodation
84 Osborne Road, Blackpool
FY4 1HQ
t (01253) 343840
e doreenandtrevor@tiscali.co.uk
w thesunnysidehotel.co.uk

Sunset ★★★ *Guest Accommodation*
45 Palatine Road, Blackpool
FY1 4BX
t (01253) 628369
e ruth@sunsethotel.wanadoo.co.uk
w sunsethotel.net

The Sunset Guest House ★★★★
Guest Accommodation
5 Banks Street, Blackpool
FY1 1RN
t (01253) 624949
e thesunsethotel@msn.com
w thesunsethotelblackpool.com/

Surrey House ★★★
Guest Accommodation
9 Northumberland Avenue, Blackpool
FY2 9SB
t (01253) 351743
e coursemanager1@aol.com
w surreyhousehotel.com

Sussex ★★★ *Guest Accommodation*
14-16 Pleasant Street, North Shore, Blackpool
FY1 2JA
t 01253 627824
e sussexhotel.blackpool@virgin.net
w sussexhotelblackpool.com

Tamarind Cove ★★★★
Guest Accommodation
56 Hornby Road, Blackpool
FY1 4QJ
t (01253) 624319

Thornhill ★★★ *Guest House*
14 Wellington Road, Blackpool
FY1 6AR
t (01253) 346496
e gaynor@thornhillhotel.co.uk
w thornhillhotel.co.uk

Tower View ★★★ *Guest House*
31 Bethesda Road, Blackpool
FY1 5DT
t (01253) 620391
e postmaster@blackpooltowerview.co.uk
w blackpooltowerview.co.uk

The Trafalgar ★★★ *Guest House*
106 Albert Road, Blackpool
FY1 4PR
t (01253) 625000
e enquiries@trafalgarhotel.co.uk
w trafalgarhotel.co.uk

Tregenna ★★★
Guest Accommodation
115 Albert Road, Blackpool
FY1 4PW
t (01253) 624151
e enquiries@tregennahotelblackpool.co.uk
w tregennahotelblackpool.co.uk

Tudor Guest House ★★★
Guest Accommodation
30 Crystal Road, Blackpool
FY1 6BS
t (01253) 344345
e tudorhotel@aol.com
w tudorblackpool.co.uk

Tudor House ★★★
Guest Accommodation
37 Woodfield Road, Blackpool
FY1 6AX
t (01253) 346165
e info@tudorhouseblackpool.com
w tudorhouseblackpool.com

Tudor Rose ★★★ *Guest House*
87 Coronation Street, Blackpool
FY1 4PD
t (01253) 292202
e tudorrosehotel@tiscali.co.uk
w tudorrosehotelblackpool.com

Tudor Rose Original ★★★★
Guest House **SILVER AWARD**
5 Withnell Road, Blackpool
FY4 1HF
t (01253) 343485
e tudor_rose@onetel.com
w tudorroseblackpool.com

The Valentine ★★★★
Guest Accommodation
35 Dickson Road, Blackpool
FY1 2AT
t (01253) 622775
e anthony@anthonypalmer.orangehome.co.uk
w valentinehotelblackpool.com

Verdo ★★★ *Guest Accommodation*
50 Osborne Road, Blackpool
FY4 1HQ
t (01253) 343811
e verdohotel@hotmail.com
w verdohotel.com

The Vidella ★★★
Guest Accommodation
80-82 Dickson Road, Blackpool
FY1 2BU
t (01253) 621201
e info@videllahotel.com
w videllahotel.com

The Waterford ★★★★
Guest Accommodation
GOLD AWARD
2 Gynn Avenue, Blackpool
FY1 2LD
t (01253) 351946
e thewaterford@btconnect.com
w thewaterfordblackpool.co.uk

Waverley ★★★
Guest Accommodation
95 Reads Avenue, Blackpool
FY1 4DG
t (01253) 621633
e waverleyrooms@aol.com
w thewaverleyhotel.net

North West | Lancashire

Wellington ★★★
Guest Accommodation
1 Wellington Road, Blackpool
FY1 6AR
t (01253) 343658
e muscroft997@btinternet.com
w wellingtonhotel.info

The Wescoe ★★★ *Guest House*
14 Dean Street, Blackpool
FY4 1AU
t (01253) 342772
e wescoeblackpool@yahoo.com
w thewescoeblackpool.com

Westcliffe ★★★
Guest Accommodation
46 King Edward Avenue, Blackpool
FY2 9TA
t (01253) 352943
e westcliffehotel@aol.com
w westcliffehotel.com

Westdean ★★★
Guest Accommodation
59 Dean Street, Blackpool
FY4 1BP
t (01253) 342904
e westdeanhotel@aol.com
w westdeanhotel.com

Westfield Lodge ★★★
Guest Accommodation
14 Station Road, Blackpool
FY4 1BE
t (01253) 342468
e joycerobinson@btconnect.com
w westfieldhotel.co.uk

White Moon ★★★
Guest Accommodation
35 Reads Avenue, Blackpool
FY1 4DD
t (01253) 624491
e whitemoonhotel@hotmail.com
w whitemoon-hotel.co.uk

White Rose ★★ *Guest House*
29 Reads Avenue, Blackpool
FY1 4DD
t (01253) 292533
e white.rose.blackpool@googlemail.com
w whiterosehotel.net

Wilford Guest House ★★★
Guest Accommodation
55 Station Road, Blackpool
FY4 1EU
t (01253) 344329
e enquiries@wilfordhotel.co.uk
w wilfordhotel.co.uk

The Wilton ★★★
Guest Accommodation
108-112 Dickson Road, Blackpool
FY1 2HF
t (01253) 627763
e wiltonhotel@supanet.com
w wiltonhotel.co.uk

Wimbourne Guest House ★★★
Guest House
10 Moore Street, Blackpool
FY4 1DB
t (01253) 347272
e info@wimborneblackpool.co.uk
w wimbourneblackpool.co.uk

Windsor ★★★★
Guest Accommodation
21 King Edward Avenue, Blackpool
FY2 9TA
t (01253) 353735
e enquiries@windsorblackpool.co.uk
w windsorblackpool.co.uk

Windsor Carlton Guest Accommodation ★★★★
Guest Accommodation
6 Warley Road, Blackpool
FY1 2JU
t (01253) 354924
e info@windsorcarlton.com
w windsorcarlton.com

Windsor Park ★★★
Guest Accommodation
96 Queens Promenade, Blackpool
FY2 9NS
t (01253) 357025
e windsorparkhotel@hotmail.com
w windsorparkhotelblackpool.co.uk

Winterbourne ★
Guest Accommodation
22-30 Clarendon Road, Blackpool
FY1 6EF
t (01253) 342630
e winterbournehotel@sky.com
w thewinterbourne.weebly.com

Woodfield ★★★
Guest Accommodation
31-33 Woodfield Road, Blackpool
FY1 6AX
t (01253) 346304
e bookings@thewoodfieldblackpool.co.uk
w thewoodfieldblackpool.co.uk

Woodleigh ★★★
Guest Accommodation
32 King Edward Avenue, Blackpool
FY2 9TA
t (01253) 593624
e woodleigh.kea@googlemail.com

Wynnstay ★★★ *Guest House*
64 Hornby Road, Blackpool
FY1 4QJ
t (01253) 627601
e enquiries@wynnstayhotel.co.uk
w wynnstayhotel.co.uk

BOLTON

Meadowcroft Barn B&B ★★★★★
Farmhouse GOLD AWARD
Bury Road, Bolton
BL7 0BS
t (01204) 853270
e info@meadowcroftbarn.co.uk
w meadowcroftbarn.co.uk

BOLTON-BY-BOWLAND

Middle Flass Lodge ★★★★
Guest House
Forest Becks Brow, Settle Road, Clitheroe
BB7 4NY
t (01200) 447259
e middleflasslodge@btconnect.com
w middleflasslodge.co.uk

BURNLEY

Grains Barn Farm ★★★★★
Bed & Breakfast SILVER AWARD
Barrowford Road, Fence, Burnley
BB12 9QQ
t (01282) 601320
e stay@grainsbarnfarm.com
w grainsbarnfarm.co.uk

Ormerod ★★★
Guest Accommodation
123 Ormerod Road, Burnley
BB11 3QN
t (01282) 423255

CAPERNWRAY

Capernwray House ★★★★
Guest Accommodation
SILVER AWARD
Borrans Lane, Capernwray, Carnforth
LA6 1AE
t (01524) 732363
e mel@capernwrayhouse.com
w capernwrayhouse.com

CARNFORTH

Chapel Lodge ★★★★
Guest Accommodation
The Chapel, Kirkby Lonsdale Road, Carnforth
LA6 1DS
t (01524) 720660
e jandhammond@supanet.com

Longlands Inn & Restaurant ★★★★ *Inn*
Tewitfield, Carnforth
LA6 1JH
t (01524) 781256
e info@longlandshotel.co.uk
w longlandshotel.co.uk

CHAIGLEY

Rakefoot Farm ★★★★ *Farmhouse*
Thornley Road, Chaigley, Clitheroe
BB7 3LY
t (01995) 61332
e info@rakefootfarm.co.uk
w rakefootfarm.co.uk

CHIPPING

Clark House Farm ★★★★
Farmhouse
Clark House Farm, Chipping, Preston
PR3 2GQ
t (01995) 61209
e fpr@agriplus.net
w clarkhousefarm.com

Town End Farm ★★★
Bed & Breakfast
Longridge Road, Chipping, Forest of Bowland, Lancashire
PR3 2QD
t (01995) 61550
e wendy.foot@virgin.net

CHORLEY

Parr Hall Farm ★★★★
Guest Accommodation
Parr Lane, Eccleston, Chorley, Lancashire
PR7 5SL
t (01257) 451917
e enquiries@parrhallfarm.co.uk
w parrhallfarm.com

CLAUGHTON

Low House Farm, Lancaster ★★★★ *Farmhouse*
Claughton, Lancaster
LA2 9LA
t (01524) 221260
e shirley@lunevalley.freeserve.co.uk
w lowhousefarm.co.uk

CLITHEROE

Alden Cottage - B&B ★★★★
Guest Accommodation
GOLD AWARD
Kemple End, Birdy Brow, Clitheroe
BB7 9QY
t (01254) 826468
e carpenter.aldencottage.f9.co.uk
w aldencottage.co.uk

Angram Green Farmhouse B&B
★★★★ *Farmhouse* SILVER AWARD
Worston, Clitheroe
BB7 1QB
t (01200) 441641
e angela@angramgreenfarm.co.uk
w angramgreenfarm.com

The Bayley Arms ★★★★ *Inn*
Avenue Road, Hurst Green, Clitheroe
BB7 9QB
t (01254) 826478
e sales@bayleyarms.co.uk
w bayleyarms.com

Brooklyn Guest House ★★★★
Guest House
32 Pimlico Road, Clitheroe
BB7 2AH
t (01200) 428268
e information@brooklynguesthouse.com
w brooklynguesthouse.co.uk

Cobden Farm Bed & Breakfast
★★★★ *Farmhouse*
off Whalley Road, Sabden, Clitheroe
BB7 9ED
t (01282) 776285
e enquiries@cobdenfarm.co.uk
w cobdenfarm.co.uk

Foxhill Barn ★★★★
Bed & Breakfast
Great Todber Farm, Howgill Lane, Clitheroe
BB7 4JL
t (01200) 415906
e peter@foxhillbarn.co.uk
w foxhillbarn.co.uk

Mitton Hall ★★★★
Guest Accommodation
Mitton Road, Mitton, Clitheroe
BB7 1PQ
t (01254) 826544
e info@mittonhallhotel.co.uk
w mittonhallhotel.co.uk

Moorhead House Farm ★★
Farmhouse
Thornley Road, Chaigley, Clitheroe
BB7 3LY
t (01995) 61108

Peter Barn Country House ★★★
Bed & Breakfast SILVER AWARD
Cross Lane, Waddington, Clitheroe
BB7 3JH
t (01200) 428585
e jean@peterbarn.co.uk
w peterbarn.co.uk

The Red Pump Inn ★★★★ *Inn*
SILVER AWARD
Clitheroe Road, Bashall Eaves, Clitheroe
BB7 3DA
t (01254) 826227
e info@theredpumpinn.co.uk
w theredpumpinn.co.uk

Rowan Tree ★★★★
Bed & Breakfast
10 Railway View Road, Clitheroe
BB7 2HE
t (01200) 427115
e query@the-rowan-tree.org.uk
w the-rowan-tree.org.uk

The Shireburn Arms Hotel ★★★★
Guest Accommodation
Whalley Road, Hurst Green, Clitheroe
BB7 9QJ
t (01254) 826518
e sales@shireburnarmshotel.com
w shireburnarmshotel.com

York House Bed & Breakfast
★★★★ *Bed & Breakfast*
York House, York Street, Clitheroe
BB7 2DL
t (01200) 429519
e brindle_susan@hotmail.com
w yorkhousebandb.co.uk

COLNE

The Alma Inn ★★★★ *Inn*
Emmott Lane, Colne
BB8 7EG
t (01282) 863447
e reception@thealmainn.com
w thealmainn.com

Blakey Hall Farm ★★★★
Farmhouse SILVER AWARD
Red Lane, Colne
BB8 9TD
t (01282) 863121
e blakeyhall@hotmail.com
w blakeyhallfarm.co.uk

The Crown ★★ *Inn*
94 Albert Road, Colne
BB8 0QD
t (01282) 863580
e crownhotel94@aol.com
w crownhotelcolne.co.uk

North West | Lancashire

are & Hounds Foulridge ★★★
kipton Old Road, Foulridge, Colne
BB8 7PD
t (01282) 864235
e hareandhounds1@hotmail.com

igher Wanless Farm ★★★★
armhouse
ed Lane, Colne
BB8 7JP
t (01282) 865301
e info@stayinlancs.co.uk
w stayinlancs.co.uk

Middle Beardshaw Head Farm
★★★ Guest Accommodation
urnley Road, Trawden, Colne
BB8 8PP
t (01282) 865257
e ursula.mann1940.freeserve.co.uk
w smoothhound.co.uk/a11504.html

ye Flatt Farmhouse ★★★★
ed & Breakfast SILVER AWARD
0 School Lane, Colne
BB8 7JB
t (01282) 871565
e info@rye-flatt.co.uk
w rye-flatt.co.uk

tableCross Bed and Breakfast
★★★ Hostel
Knotts Lane, Colne Pendle,
ancashire
BB8 8AD
t (01282) 863229
e alicermann@aol.com

Wayside Barn Bed & Breakfast
★★★ Bed & Breakfast
reenfield Road, Colne
BB8 9PE
t (01282) 865077
e velma.brads@virgin.net
w waysidebarn.co.uk

CONDER GREEN

The Stork Inn ★★★ Inn
orricks Lane, Conder Green,
ancaster
LA2 0AN
t (01524) 751234
e info@thestorkinn.co.uk
w thestorkinn.co.uk

DUNSOP BRIDGE

Root Farmhouse B&B ★★★★
ed & Breakfast
Dunsop Bridge, Clitheroe
BB7 3BB
t (01200) 448214
e info@roothouse.co.uk
w roothouse.co.uk

Wood End Farm ★★★★
armhouse
Dunsop Bridge, Clitheroe
BB7 3BE
t (01200) 448223

EARBY

Grange Fell ★★★ Bed & Breakfast
kipton Road, Earby, Barnoldswick
BB18 6JL
t (01282) 844991
e info@grangefell.com
w grangefell.com

YHA Earby ★★★ Hostel
9-11 Birch Hall Lane, Earby
BB18 6JX
t (01282) 842349
e earby@yha.org.uk
w yha.org.uk

FORTON

Middle Holly Cottage ★★★★
Guest Accommodation
SILVER AWARD
Middle Holly, Forton
PR3 1AH
t (01524) 792399
e mhcottage@btconnect.com
w middlehollycottage.co.uk

GARSTANG

Broadgate Farm B & B ★★★★
Farmhouse SILVER AWARD
Bleasdale Lane, Bleasdale, Garstang,
Preston
PR3 1UR
t (01995) 602402
e anneclark_71@hotmail.com
w broadgatefarm.co.uk

Guy's Thatched Hamlet & Owd Nell's Tavern ★★★★
Guest Accommodation
Canalside, St Michael's Road,
Bilsborrow, Garstang
PR3 0RS
t (01995) 640010
e info@guysthatchedhamlet.com
w guysthatchedhamlet.com

Little Stubbins Bed & Breakfast
★★★★ Bed & Breakfast
GOLD AWARD
Stubbins Lane, Claughton-on-Brock,
Garstang
PR3 0PL
t (01995) 640376
e littlestubbins@aol.com
w littlestubbins.co.uk

GREAT ECCLESTON

Courtyard Caffé With Rooms
★★★★ Guest Accommodation
SILVER AWARD
The Square, Great Eccleston
PR3 0ZB
t (01995) 672011
e info@courtyardbedandbreakfast.co.uk
w courtyardbedandbreakfast.co.uk

HESKIN

Farmers Arms ★★★ Inn
85 Wood Lane, Heskin, Chorley
PR7 5NP
t (01257) 451276
e info@farmersarms.co.uk
w farmersarms.co.uk

HEYSHAM

Highview ★★★★
Guest Accommodation
235 Heysham Road, Heysham,
Morecambe
LA3 1NN
t (01524) 424991
e wynconway4@tiscali.co.uk

HURST GREEN

The Fold ★★★★ Bed & Breakfast
15 Smithy Row, Hurst Green,
Clitheroe
BB7 9QA
t (01254) 826252
e derek.harwood1@virgin.net

INSKIP

Chesham Hill Farm Bed & Breakfast ★★★ Farmhouse
Pinfold Lane, Inskip, Preston
PR4 0UA
t (01995) 679427
e administrator@cheshamhillfarm.co.uk
w cheshamhillfarm.co.uk

LANCASTER

The Ashton ★★★★★
Guest Accommodation
GOLD AWARD
Well House, Wyresdale Road,
Lancaster
LA1 3JJ
t (01524) 68460
e stay@theashtonlancaster.com
w theashtonlancaster.com

Lancaster Town House ★★★
Guest Accommodation
11-12 Newton Terrace, Caton Road,
Lancaster
LA1 3PB
t (01524) 65527
e hedge-holmes@talk21.com
w lancastertownhouse.co.uk

Old Station House ★★★★
Guest Accommodation
25 Meeting House Lane, Lancaster
LA1 1TX
t (01524) 381060
e oldstationhouse@hotmail.com
w oldstationhouse.enq

The Shakespeare ★★★★
Guest House
96 St Leonardgate, Lancaster
LA1 1NN
t (01524) 841041
e theshakespearelancaster@talktalk.net
w citycoastcountryside.co.uk

Slyne Lodge, Lancaster ★★★★
Inn
92 Main Road, Slyne, Lancaster
LA2 6AZ
t (01524) 825035
e slynelodge@btconnect.com
w slynelodge.co.uk

The Sun Inn ★★★★ Inn
63-65 Church Street, Lancaster
LA1 1ET
t (01524) 66006
e info@thesunhotelandbar.co.uk
w thesunhotelandbar.co.uk

University of Cumbria ★ - ★★
Campus
Bowerham Road, Lancaster
LA1 3JD
t (01524) 384460
e conferences.lancaster@cumbria.ac.uk
w cumbria.ac.uk

Wagon & Horses ★★★★
Guest House
27 St Georges Quay, Lancaster
LA1 1RD
t (01524) 846094
e stay@wagonandhorsespub.co.uk
w wagonandhorsespub.co.uk

LEIGHTON HALL

Grisedale Farm ★★★★ Farmhouse
SILVER AWARD
Leighton, Carnforth
LA5 9ST
t (01524) 734360
e ailsarobinson@btconnect.com
w grisedalefarm.co.uk

LEYLAND

Smithy Lodge Guest House
★★★★ Guest Accommodation
310 Dunkirk Lane, Leyland
PR26 7SN
t (01772) 457650
e enquiries@smithylodge.co.uk
w smithy-lodge.co.uk

LONGRIDGE

The Corporation Arms ★★★★ Inn
Lower Road, Longridge, Preston
PR3 2YJ
t (01772) 782644
e corporationarms@yahoo.co.uk
w corporationarms.co.uk

LYTHAM

The Queens Hotel ★★★ Inn
Central Beach, Lytham
FY8 5LB
t (01253) 737316
e enquiries@the-queens-lytham.co.uk

LYTHAM ST ANNES

The Breverton ★★★
Guest Accommodation
64 Orchard Road, Lytham St Annes
FY8 1PJ
t (01253) 726179
e anna.breverton@tiscali.co.uk

The Carlton ★★★ Guest House
61 South Promenade, St Annes-on-Sea, Lytham St Annes
FY8 1LZ
t (01253) 721036
e carlton.hotel@hotmail.com
w stannescarlton.co.uk

The Claremont ★★★
Guest Accommodation
1 Derbe Road, Lytham St Annes
FY8 1NJ
t (01253) 723488
e info@theclaremont.co.uk
w theclaremont.co.uk

The Fairmile ★★★
Guest Accommodation
9 St Annes Road East, St Annes,
Lytham St Annes
FY8 1TA
t (01253) 728375
w hotellink/lytham/fairmile

Howarth House ★★★★
Guest Accommodation
315 Clifton Drive South, St Annes-on-Sea, Lytham St Annes
FY8 1HN
t (01253) 725622
e enquiries@howarthhouse.co.uk
w howarthhouse.co.uk

The Strathmore ★★★
Guest Accommodation
305 Clifton Drive South, St Annes-on-Sea, Lytham St Annes
FY8 1HN
t (01253) 725478

MELLOR BROOK

Oaklands Country Guest House
★★★★ Guest House
SILVER AWARD
Park Lane, Mellor Brook, Samlesbury
BB2 7PY
t (01254) 814270
e julie@oaklandsguesthouseonline.co.uk
w oaklandsguesthouseonline.co.uk

MORECAMBE

Ashley Guest House ★★★
Guest House
371 Marine Road East, Morecambe
LA4 5AH
t (01524) 412034
e info@ashleyhotel.co.uk
w ashleyhotel.co.uk

The Balmoral ★★★ Guest House
34 Marine Road West, Morecambe
LA3 1BZ
t (01524) 418526
e info@balmoralhotelmorecambe.co.uk
w balmoralhotelmorecambe.co.uk

Berkeley Guest House ★★★
Guest House
39 Promenade West, Morecambe
LA3 1BZ
t (01524) 418201
e donval4144@hotmail.com
w hotelmorecambe.co.uk

Clifton, The ★★★
Guest Accommodation
43-46 Marine Road West,
Morecambe
LA3 1BZ
t (01524) 411573
e info@hotel-clifton.co.uk
w hotel-clifton.co.uk

North West | Lancashire

The Crown Morecambe ★★★★
Guest Accommodation
239 Marine Road Central,
Morecambe
LA4 4BJ
t (01524) 831841
e enquiries@thecrownhotelmorecambe.co.uk
w thecrownhotelmorecambe.co.uk

Sea Crest ★★★
Guest Accommodation
9-13 West End Road, Morecambe
LA4 4DJ
t (01524) 411006
e seacrest-hotel@tiscali.co.uk
w seacrest-hotel.co.uk/seacreasthotel.co.uk

The Townhouse ★★★★
Guest Accommodation
78 Thornton Road, Morecambe
LA4 5PJ
t (01524) 412762
e townhouse@talktalk.net
w townhousemorecambe.co.uk

The Westleigh ★★★ *Guest House*
9 Marine Road West, Morecambe
LA3 1BS
t (01524) 418352
e info@westleighbay.co.uk
w westleighbay.co.uk

Wimslow, The ★★★ *Guest House*
374 Marine Road East, Morecambe
LA4 5AH
t (01524) 417804
e thewimslow@yahoo.co.uk
w thewimslow.co.uk

Yacht Bay View, Morecambe
★★★ *Guest House*
359 Marine Road East, Morecambe
LA4 5AQ
t (01524) 414481
e yachtbayview@hotmail.com
w yachtbay.co.uk

NELSON

Dam Head Barn ★★★★
Guest Accommodation
Dam Head Farm, Nelson
BB9 6NX
t (01282) 617190
e info@damheadbarn.com
w damheadbarn.com

Holmefield Gardens Bed & Breakfast ★★★★ *Bed & Breakfast*
57 Holmefield Gardens, Barrowford, Nelson
BB9 8NW
t (01282) 606984
e jayjay2@talktalk.net

Lovett House Guest House ★★★
Guest House
6 Howard Street, Nelson
BB9 7SZ
t (01282) 697352
e lovetthouse@ntlworld.com
w lovetthouse.co.uk

Thorneyholme Farm Cottage
★★★★ *Guest Accommodation*
SILVER AWARD
Barley New Road, Roughlee, Nelson
BB12 9LH
t (01282) 612452
e thorneyholme@supanet.com
w thorneyholmebandb.co.uk

NEWCHURCH-IN-PENDLE

Old Earth House ★★★★
Bed & Breakfast
33 Newchurch In Pendle, Newchurch Village, Burnley
BB12 9JR
t (01282) 698812
e isolde@healey7809.fsnet.co.uk

ORMSKIRK

The Farm ★★★★ *Farmhouse*
71 Martin Lane, Burscough, Ormskirk
L40 0RT
t (01704) 894889
e freda.neale@ic24.net
w thefarmburscough.co.uk

POULTON-LE-FYLDE

The Shard Riverside Inn ★★★★
Guest Accommodation
Old Bridge Lane, Hambleton, Poulton-le-Fylde
FY6 9BT
t (01253) 700208
e info@shardriversideinn.co.uk
w shardriversideinn.co.uk

PREESALL

Grassendale ★★★ *Bed & Breakfast*
Green Lane, Preesall, Poulton-Le-Fylde
FY6 0NS
t (01253) 812331
e rondeyo@aol.com

PRESTON

Ashdene ★★★
Guest Accommodation
Parkside Lane, Nateby, Preston
PR3 0JA
t (01995) 602676
e ashdene@supanet.com
w ashdenebedandbreakfast.gbr.cc

The Cartford Inn ★★★★ *Inn*
Cartford Lane, Little Eccleston, Preston
PR3 0YP
t (01995) 670166
e info@thecartfordinn.co.uk
w thecartfordinn.co.uk/

Home Barn ★★★★ *Bed & Breakfast*
Hollowforth Lane, Woodplumpton, Preston
PR4 0BD
t 01772 691101
e m.sherdley@sky.com
w homebarngranary.co.uk

New Holly ★★★★ *Inn*
A6 Lancaster Road, Forton, Preston
PR3 0BL
t (01524) 793500
e stay@newholly.co.uk
w newholly.co.uk

Whitestake Farm ★★★★★
Bed & Breakfast SILVER AWARD
Pope Lane, Whitestake, Preston
PR4 4JR
t (01772) 619392
e enquiries@gardenofedenspa.co.uk
w gardenofedenspa.co.uk

Willow Cottage ★★★★
Bed & Breakfast SILVER AWARD
Longton By Pass, Longton, Preston
PR4 4RA
t (01772) 617570
e willow.cottage@btconnect.com
w lancashire-bedandbreakfast.co.uk

Ye Horns Inn ★★★★ *Inn*
Horns Lane, Goosnargh, Preston
PR3 2FJ
t (01772) 865230
e info@yehornsinn.co.uk
w yehornsinn.co.uk

RAWTENSTALL

Middle Carr Farm ★★★★
Bed & Breakfast SILVER AWARD
off Hall Carr Road, Rawtenstall
BB4 6BS
t (01706) 225353
e info@middlecarrfarm.co.uk
w middlecarrfarm.co.uk

RIBCHESTER

Riverside Barn ★★★★★
Bed & Breakfast SILVER AWARD
Riverside, Ribchester, Preston
PR3 3XS
t (01254) 878095
e relax@riversidebarn.co.uk
w riversidebarn.co.uk

ROSSENDALE

Glenvalley Guesthouse ★★★
Guest House
634 Bacup Road, Waterfoot, Rossendale
BB4 7AW
t (01706) 222637
e glenvalleyhouse@sky.com
w glenvalleyguesthouse.co.uk

Number 678 ★★★★ *Guest House*
SILVER AWARD
Burnley Road East, Whitewell Bottom, Rossendale
BB4 9NT
t (01706) 215884
e info@number678.co.uk
w number678.co.uk

The Old White Horse ★★★★
Guest Accommodation
SILVER AWARD
211 Goodshaw Lane, Goodshaw, Rossendale
BB4 8DD
t (01706) 215474
e johnandmaggie54@hotmail.com
w theoldwhitehorse.co.uk

One 3 One Guest House ★★★★
Guest House SILVER AWARD
131 Haslingden Old Road, Rawtenstall, Rossendale
BB4 8RR
t (01706) 600463
e one3oneguesthouse@gmail.com
w one3one.co.uk

Peers Clough Farm ★★★
Guest Accommodation
Peers Clough Road, Lumb, Rossendale
BB4 9NG
t (01706) 210552
e peerscloughfarm@hotmail.com
w peerscloughfarm.co.uk

SABDEN

The Shippon ★★★★
Bed & Breakfast
1 The Barn, Clerk Hill Road, Clitheroe
BB7 9FR
t (01254) 822389

SCORTON

The Priory Inn, Scorton ★★★
Guest Accommodation
The Square, Scorton, Preston
PR3 1AU
t (01524) 791255
e collinsonjulie@aol.com
w theprioryscorton.co.uk

SLAIDBURN

Hark to Bounty Inn ★★★ *Inn*
Townend, Slaidburn, Clitheroe
BB7 3EP
t (01200) 446246
e isobel@harkto-bounty.co.uk
w hark-to-bounty.co.uk

YHA Slaidburn ★★★ *Hostel*
Church Street, Slaidburn, Clitheroe
BB7 3ER
t (01282) 842349
e slaidburn@yha.org.uk
w yha.org.uk

SOWERBY

Tudor Farm ★★★ *Bed & Breakfast*
Sowerby Road, Sowerby
PR3 0TT
t (01995) 679717
e info@tudor-farm.com
w tudor-farm.com

ST ANNES

Tudor House ★★★ *Guest House*
32 St Davids Road South, St Annes
FY8 1TJ
t (01253) 722444
e stay@tudorhouse.uk.com
w tudorhouse.uk.com

TRAWDEN

Oaklands ★★★★ *Bed & Breakfast*
Wycoller Road, Trawden, Colne
BB8 8SY
t (01282) 865893

Parson Lee Farm ★★★ *Farmhouse*
Colne
BB8 8SU
t (01282) 864747
e pathodgson@hotmail.com
w parsonleefarm.co.uk

WADDINGTON

Waddington Arms ★★★★ *Inn*
Clitheroe Road, Waddington, Clitheroe
BB7 3HP
t (01200) 423262
e info@waddingtonarms.co.uk
w waddingtonarms.co.uk

Waddow Hall ★★★
Group Accommodation
Waddington Road, Clitheroe
BB7 3LD
t (01200) 423186
e waddow@girlguiding.org.uk
w girlguiding.org.uk

WHALLEY

The Swan Hotel ★★★★ *Inn*
62 King Street, Whalley, Clitheroe
BB7 9SN
t (01254) 822195
e swanhotel@tiscali.co.uk
w swanhotelwhalley.co.uk

Whalley Abbey ★★★★
Guest Accommodation
The Sands, Whalley, Clitheroe
BB7 9SS
t (01254) 828400
e office@whalleyabbey.org
w whalleyabbey.co.uk

WHITEWELL

The Inn at Whitewell ★★★★★ *Inn*
GOLD AWARD
Dunsop Road, Whitewell, Nr Clitheroe
BB7 3AT
t (01200) 448222
e reception@innatwhitewell.com
w innatwhitewell.com

WHITWORTH

The Red Lion ★★★ *Inn*
Whitworth Square, Whitworth
OL12 8PY
t (01706) 861441
e redlionwhitworth@hotmail.co.uk
w redlionwhitworth.co.uk

WORSTON

The Calf's Head ★★★★
Guest Accommodation
Worston, Clitheroe
BB7 1QA
t (01200) 441218
e info@calfshead.co.uk
w calfshead.co.uk

North West | Greater Manchester/Merseyside

Greater Manchester

ASHTON-UNDER-LYNE

Broadoak Hotel ★★★★ *Inn*
9 Broadoak Road, Ashton-under-Lyne
OL6 8QD
t (0161) 330 2764
e broadoakhotel@googlemail.com
w broadoakhotel.co.uk

Lynwood ★★★★
Guest Accommodation
1 Richmond Street, Ashton-under-Lyne
OL6 7TX
t (0161) 330 5358

BOLTON

Highgrove Guest House ★★★
Guest House
3 Manchester Road, Bolton
BL2 1ES
t (01204) 384928
e thehighgrove@btconnect.com
w highgroveguesthouse.co.uk

Wendover Guest House ★★★
Guest House
303 Chorley New Road, Horwich, Bolton
BL6 6LA
t (01204) 468400
e info@wendoverguesthouse.co.uk
w wendoverguesthouse.co.uk

BURY

Ashbury Guest House ★★★
Guest Accommodation
135 Rochdale Road, Bury
BL9 7BX
t (0161) 762 9623
e glyniswoodall@btinternet.com

Castle Guest House ★★★
Guest Accommodation
7 Wellington Street, Bury
BL8 2AL
t (0161) 797 3396
e alanrusselluk@aol.com
w guesthousebury.co.uk

The Grant Arms Hotel ★★★
Guest Accommodation
Market Place, Ramsbottom, Bury
BL0 9AJ
t (01706) 823354
e reception@thegrantarmshotel.co.uk
w grantarmshotelramsbottom.co.uk/

CHEADLE HULME

Spring Cottage Guest House
★★★ *Guest House*
60 Hulme Hall Road, Cheadle Hulme, Stockport
SK8 6JZ
t (0161) 485 1037
e cottage-spring@hotmail.co.uk

DENSHAW

Cherry Clough Farm House Accommodation ★★★★★
Farmhouse SILVER AWARD
Cherry Clough Farm, Denshaw, Oldham
OL3 5UE
t (01457) 874369
e info@cherryclough.co.uk
w cherryclough.co.uk

FARNWORTH

Fernbank Guest House ★★★★
Bed & Breakfast
51 Rawson Street, Farnworth, Bolton
BL4 7RJ
t (01204) 708832
e bob.dot.sandlan@ntlworld.com
w fernbankguesthouse.com

HALE BARNS

Oaklands Farm ★★★
Bed & Breakfast
Shay Lane, Hale Barns
WA15 8SN
t (0161) 980 4111
e oaklands.farm@yahoo.co.uk
w oaklands.farm.co.uk

HAWKSHAW

Loe Lodge ★★★★★
Guest Accommodation
Redisher Lane, Hawkshaw, Bury
BL8 4HX
t (01204) 888860
e loelodge@btinternet.com
w loelodge.co.uk

LEIGH

The Sporting Lodge Inn ★★★★
Inn
Warrington Road, Leigh
WN7 3XQ
t (01942) 671256
e reservationsgreyhound@sportinglodgeinns.co.uk
w sportinglodgeinns.co.uk

LITTLEBOROUGH

Leighton House B&B ★★★★
Guest House
1 Leighton Avenue, Hollingworth Lake, Rochdale
OL15 0BW
t (01706) 378113
e leightonhouse@aol.com
w smoothound.co.uk/hotels/leightonhouse

Swing Cottage ★★★★
Guest House
31 Lakebank, Hollingworth Lake, Littleborough
OL15 0DQ
t (01706) 379094
e swingcottage@aol.com
w hollingworthlake.com

LOSTOCK

Ingleside House Bed & Breakfast
★★★★ *Bed & Breakfast*
153 Tempest Road, Lostock, Bolton
BL6 4EP
t (01204) 848413
e christine@inglesidehousebb.co.uk
w inglesidehousebb.co.uk

MANCHESTER

Abbey Lodge ★★★
Bed & Breakfast
501 Wilbraham Road, Chorlton, Manchester
M21 0UJ
t (0161) 862 9266
e info@abbey-lodge.co.uk
w abbey-lodge.co.uk

Hatters Hostel ★★ *Hostel*
50 Newton Street, Manchester
M1 2EA
t (0161) 236 9500
e manchester@hattersgroup.com
w hattersgroup.com

Hilton Chambers ★★★ *Hostel*
15 Hilton Street, Manchester
M1 2EA
t (0161) 236 4414
e hilton@hattersgroup.com
w hattersgroup.com/hilton/

Ivy Mount Guest House ★★
Guest Accommodation
35 Half Edge Lane, Eccles, Manchester
M30 9AY
t (0161) 789 1756
e ivymount1@tiscali.co.uk
w ivymountguesthouse.co.uk

Luther King House ★★★
Guest Accommodation
Brighton Grove, Wilmslow Road, Manchester
M14 5JP
t (0161) 224 6404
e reception@lkh.co.uk
w lutherkinghouse.co.uk

Manchester YHA ★★★★ *Hostel*
Potato Wharf, Castlefield, Manchester
M3 4NB
t (0161) 839 9960
e manchester@yha.org.uk
w yhamanchester.org.uk

Monroe's Guest House & Bar ★★
Inn
38 London Road, Manchester
M1 2PF
t (0161) 236 0564

Seasons Guest House ★★★
Guest Accommodation
803 Altrincham Road, Manchester
M23 9AH
t (0161) 945 3232
e seasons803@fsmail.net
w seasonsguesthouse.co.uk

Stay Inn Hotel ★★★
Guest Accommodation
55 Blackfriars Road, Salford, Manchester
M3 7DB
t **(0161) 907 2277**
e info@stayinn.co.uk
w stayinn.co.uk

Victoria Hall ★★★ *Campus*
28 Higher Cambridge Street, Manchester
M15 6AA
t (0161) 908 7000
e manchester.hcs@victoriahall.com
w victoriahall.com

Victoria Hall - Manchester 2 ★★★
Campus
281 Upper Brook Street, Manchester
M13 0FZ
t (0161) 607 8000
e manchester.ubs@victoriahall.com
w victoriahall.com

MIDDLETON

Three Gates Farm B&B ★★★★
Bed & Breakfast
Stakehill Lane, Middleton, Manchester
M24 2RT
t (0161) 653 8314
e info@threegatesfarmbandb.co.uk
w threegatesfarmbandb.co.uk

OLDHAM

Boothstead Farm ★★★★
Guest Accommodation
Rochdale Road, Denshaw, Oldham
OL3 5UE
t (01457) 878622
e boothsteadfarm@tiscali.co.uk

OLD TRAFFORD

Lancashire County Cricket Club & Old Trafford Lodge ★★★
Guest Accommodation
Talbot Road, Old Trafford, Manchester
M16 0PX
t (0161) 874 3333
e lodge@lccc.co.uk
w oldtraffordlodge.co.uk

PRESTWICH

The Church Inn - Bury ★★★ *Inn*
Church Lane, Prestwich, Manchester
M25 1AJ
t (0161) 798 6727
e tom.gribben@virgin.net

ROCHDALE

Fernhill B&B ★★★
Guest Accommodation - Room Only
Fernhill Lane, Rochdale
OL12 6BW
t (01706) 355671
e info@fernhillbreaks.co.uk
w fernhillbreaks.co.uk

Hollingworth Lake B&B ★★★★★
Guest Accommodation
164 Smithy Bridge Road, Littleborough, Rochdale
OL15 0DB
t (01706) 376583
w b-visible.co.uk/businesses/32/hollingworthlakeb+b.htm

Hunters Rest ★★★★ *Inn*
66 Syke Road, Syke, Rochdale
OL12 9TD
t (01706) 646010
e huntersrest@sky.com
w huntersrestrochdale.co.uk

Moss Lodge ★★★★★
Guest Accommodation
SILVER AWARD
Kings Road, Rochdale
OL16 5HW
t (01706) 350555
e info@mosslodgehotel.com
w mosslodgehotel.com

The Villas Residence ★★★★★
Guest House SILVER AWARD
2 Oakenrod Villas, Bury Road, Rochdale
OL11 4EE
t (01706) 525075
e info@the-villas-residence.co.uk
w the-villas-residence.co.uk/

SALE

Belforte House ★★★★
Guest Accommodation
7-9 Broad Road, Sale, Manchester
M33 2AE
t (0161) 973 8779
e belfortehotel@aol.com
w belfortehousehotel.co.uk

Eskdale Lodge ★★★★
Guest Accommodation
35 Harboro Road, Sale
M33 5AN
t (0161) 973 6770
e garvan.smith@eskdalelodge.co.uk
w eskdalelodge.co.uk

STANDISH

The Crown at Worthington ★★★
Inn
Platt Lane, Standish, Wigan
WN1 2XF
t 0800 068 6678
e reservations@thecrownatworthington.co.uk
w thecrownatworthington.co.uk

WESTHOUGHTON

The Mercury ★★ *Inn*
540 Manchester Road, Westhoughton, Bolton
BL5 3JP
t (01942) 810904
e info@themercurybolton.com
w themercurybolton.com

WEST TIMPERLEY

Altrincham Lodge ★★★
Guest Accommodation
350 Manchester Road, West Timperley, Altrincham
WA14 5NH
t (0161) 962 9000
e rooms@altrinchamlodge.co.uk
w altrinchamlodge.co.uk

Merseyside

BIRKENHEAD

Villa Venezia ★★★
Guest Accommodation
14-16 Prenton Road West, Birkenhead, Wirral
CH42 9PN
t (0151) 608 9212
e enquiry@veneziapizzeria.co.uk
w veneziapizzeria.co.uk

North West | Merseyside

GARSTON

Aplin House ★
Guest Accommodation - Room Only
35 Clarendon Road, Garston,
Liverpool
L19 6PJ
t (0151) 427 5047

KNOWSLEY PARK

Knowsley Hall ★★★★★
Guest Accommodation
GOLD AWARD
Knowsley Park, Prescot
L34 4AG
t (0151) 489 4827
e events@knowsley.com
w knowsley.com

LIVERPOOL

Aachen ★★★
Guest Accommodation
89-91 Mount Pleasant, Liverpool
L3 5TB
t (0151) 709 3477
e enquiries@aachenhotel.co.uk
w aachenhotel.co.uk

Beech Mount ★★★★
Guest Accommodation
1-4 Beech Mount, Beech Street,
Liverpool
L7 0HL
t (0151) 264 9189
e reservations@beechmount
executive.co.uk
w beechmountexecutive.co.uk

Blackburne Arms ★★★★
Guest Accommodation - Room Only
24 Catharine Street, Liverpool
L8 7NL
t (0151) 707 1249
e blackburnehotel@btinternet.com

Blackmoor Bed & Breakfast ★★★
Bed & Breakfast
160 Blackmoor Drive, West Derby,
Liverpool
L12 9EF
t (0151) 291 1407
e blackmoorguesthouse@bluey
onder.co.uk

Cocoon @ International Inn ★★★
Hostel
4 South Hunter Street, Off Hardman
Street, Liverpool
L1 9JG
t 0151 7098135
e info@internationalinn.co.uk
w cocoonliverpool.co.uk

Feathers ★★★★
Guest Accommodation
117-125 Mount Pleasant, Liverpool
L3 5TF
t (0151) 709 9655
e feathershotel@feathers.uk.com
w feathers.uk.com

Gateway Lodge ★★★
Guest Accommodation
1 Speke Church Road, Speke,
Liverpool
L24 3TA
t (0151) 284 4801
e info@gatewaylodge.com
w gatewaylodgeuk.com

Greenbank Sports Academy ★★★
Hostel
Greenbank Lane, Liverpool
L17 1AG
t (0151) 280 7757
e tolgun@greenbanksports
academy.co.uk
w greenbanksportsacademy.co.uk

Hatters Hostel ★★ *Hostel*
56-60 Mount Pleasant, Liverpool
L3 5SH
t (0151) 709 5570
e liverpool@hattersgroup.com
w hattersgroup.com

Holmeleigh Guest House ★★★
Guest Accommodation
93 Woodcroft Road, Wavertree,
Liverpool
L15 2HG
t (0151) 734 2216
e info@holmeleigh.com
w holmeleigh.com

International Inn ★★★ *Hostel*
4 South Hunter Street, Liverpool
L1 9JG
t (0151) 709 8135
e info@internationalinn.co.uk
w internationalinn.co.uk

Litherland Park Bed & Breakfast
★★ *Bed & Breakfast*
34 Litherland Park, Litherland,
Liverpool
L21 9HP
t (0151) 928 1085
e bevaharper@yahoo.com

**Liverpool University Roscoe &
Gladstone Hall** ★★ *Campus*
Greenbank Lane, Liverpool
L17 1AH
t (0151) 794 6402
e rgbookings@liv.ac.uk
w liv.ac.uk/conferenceservices/

Lord Nelson ★★
Guest Accommodation
Hotham Street, Liverpool
L3 5PD
t (0151) 709 5161
e reservations@lordnelsonliverpool.
com
w lordnelsonliverpool.com

Marlborough ★★★ *Guest House*
21 Crosby Road South, Waterloo,
Liverpool
L22 1RG
t (0151) 928 7709
e info@marlboroughhoteluk.com
w marlboroughhoteluk.com

O'Tooles Guest House ★★
Guest Accommodation
17 Regent Road, Liverpool
L3 7DS
t (0151) 236 8468
e otooleswinebar@hotmail.com

Real McCoy Guest House ★★
Bed & Breakfast
126 Childwall Park Avenue,
Childwall, Liverpool
L16 0JH
t 07971 161542 / (0151) 722 7116
e ann557@btinternet.com

Royal Chambers ★★
Guest Accommodation - Room Only
29 Prescot Street, Liverpool
L7 8UE
t (0151) 260 6888
e mail@royalchambers.co.uk
w royalchambers.co.uk

The Shamrock B&B ★★
Bed & Breakfast
16 Staplands Road, Broadgreen,
Liverpool
L14 3LL
t (0151) 228 2428
e odonnellkatiep9@aol.com
w shamrockbandb.blogspot.com

Throstles Nest ★★★★
Guest Accommodation
344 Scotland Road, Kirkdale,
Liverpool
L5 5AQ
t (0151) 207 9797
e kvmcmul@aol.com
w throstlesnesthotel.co.uk

Victoria Hall ★★★ *Campus*
29 Hatton Garden, Liverpool
L3 2EZ
t (0151) 907 7000
e liverpool@victoriahall.com
w victoriahall.com

YHA Liverpool International
★★★★ *Hostel*
25 Tabley Street, Liverpool
L1 8EE
t 0845 371 9527
e liverpool@yha.org.uk
w yha.org.uk

PRENTON

Shrewsbury Lodge ★★★
Guest Accommodation
Shrewsbury Lodge Hotel, 31
Shrewsbury Road, Oxton
CH43 2JB
t (0151) 652 4029
e info@shrewsbury-hotel.com
w shrewsbury-hotel.com/
liverpool_hotel.asp

SOUTHPORT

Aaron Guest House ★★★
Guest House
18 Bath Street, Southport
PR9 0DA
t (01704) 530283
e info@theaaron.co.uk
w theaaron.co.uk

Adelphi Guest House ★★★
Guest Accommodation
39 Bold Street, Southport
PR9 0ED
t (01704) 544947
e gromad@aol.com
w adelphihotelsouthport.com

Alexandra & Victoria ★★★★
Guest Accommodation
38 The Promenade, Southport
PR8 1QU
t (01704) 530072
e info@alexandraandvictoriahotel.
com
w alexandraandvictoriahotel.com

Allenby Hotel ★★★
Guest Accommodation
56 Bath Street, Southport
PR9 0DH
t (01704) 532953
e sdblundell@yahoo.co.uk

Ambassador Townhouse ★★★★
SILVER AWARD
13 Bath Street, Southport
PR9 0DP
t (01704) 543998
e rooms@ambassadortownhouse.
com
w ambassadortownhouse.com

Andora ★★★
Guest Accommodation
25 Bath Street, Southport
PR9 0DP
t (01704) 530214
e enquiries@andorahotel.com
w andorahotel.co.uk

Bayona Guest House ★★★
Guest Accommodation
71 Bath Street, Southport
PR9 0DN
t (01704) 543166
e johnandlyn@bayona.freeserve.co.
uk

Braemar ★★★★ *Guest House*
4 Bath Street, Southport
PR9 0DA
t (01704) 535838
e jackiewilbraham@aol.com
w braemarhotelsouthport.com

The Carleton House ★★★★
Guest House
17 Alexandra Road, Southport
PR9 0NB
t (01704) 538035
e enquiries@thecarleton.co.uk

Carlton Lodge ★★★★
Guest Accommodation
43 Bath Street, Southport
PR9 0DP
t (01704) 542290
e christinecoppack@xln.co.uk
w carltonlodgesouthport.co.uk

The Clifton Villa ★★★
Guest Accommodation
6 Bath Street, Southport
PR9 0DA
t (01704) 535780
e sales@cliftonvilla.co.uk
w cliftonvilla.co.uk

Crescent House ★★★
Guest Accommodation
27 Bath Street, Southport
PR9 0DP
t (01704) 530339
e enquiries@crescenthousehotel.co.
uk
w crescenthousehotel.co.uk/index.
htm

Edendale House ★★★
Guest Accommodation
83 Avondale Road North, Southport
PR9 0NE
t (01704) 530718
e edendalehouse@aol.com
w edendalehouse.co.uk

Fairfield House ★★★ *Guest House*
83 The Promenade, Southport
PR9 0JN
t (01704) 530137
e jclulee@toucansurf.com
w fairfieldhotelsouthport.com

Garden Court ★★★
Guest Accommodation
22 Bank Square, Southport
PR9 0DG
t (01704) 530219
e d@gardencourtsouthport.co.uk
w gardencourtsouthport.co.uk

The Heidi ★★★ *Guest House*
43 Bold Street, Southport
PR9 0ED
t (01704) 531273
e claudia@the-heidi.co.uk
w the-heidi.co.uk

Ivydene Guest House ★★★★
Guest House
46 Talbot Street, Southport
PR8 1HS
t (01704) 544760
e book@ivydene-southport.com
w ivydene-southport.com

The Leicester ★★★★
Guest Accommodation
24 Leicester Street, Southport
PR9 0EZ
t (01704) 530049
e lorrain.hennes@btconnect.com
w theleicester.com

Le Maitre ★★★★
Guest Accommodation
69 Bath Street, Southport
PR9 0DN
t (01704) 530394
e enquiries@hotel-lemaitre.co.uk
w hotel-lemaitre.co.uk

Lynwood House ★★★★
Guest House
11a Leicester Street, Southport
PR9 0ER
t (01704) 540794
e info@lynwoodhotel.com
w lynwoodhotel.com

The Norwood Guest House
★★★★ *Guest Accommodation*
62 Bath Street, Southport
PR9 0DH
t (01704) 500536
e thenorwood@aol.com
w thenorwood.com

Penkelie ★★ *Guest Accommodation*
34 Bold Street, Southport
PR9 0ED
t (01704) 538510
e info@penkeliehotel.co.uk
w penkeliehotel.co.uk

North West | Merseyside

andown ★★★
Guest Accommodation
Bath Street, Southport
R9 0DP
t (01704) 530416
e sandownhotel@rapid.southport.co.uk
w sandownhotel-southport.co.uk

andy Brook Farm ★★★
armhouse
yke Cop Road, Scarisbrick,
outhport
R8 5LR
t (01704) 880337
e sandybrookfarm@gmail.com
w sandybrookfarm.co.uk

he Seaview ★★★★
uest Accommodation
Bath Street, Southport
R9 0DA
t (01704) 530874
e enquiries@seaviewsouthport.com
w seaviewsouthport.com

quires ★★ *Guest Accommodation*
3-80 King Street, Southport
R8 1LG
t 07891 038765
e robertcook@live.co.uk
w squireshotel.com

The Stamford ★★★★
Guest Accommodation
17 Bath Street, Southport
PR9 0DP
t (01704) 500836
e booking@thestamfordsouthport.com
w thestamfordsouthport.com

Sunnyside ★★★
Guest Accommodation
47 Bath Street, Southport
PR9 0DP
t (01704) 536521
e info@sunnysidesouthport.co.uk
w sunnysidesouthport.co.uk/index.html

The Victorian ★★★
Guest Accommodation
52 Avondale Road North, Southport
PR9 0NE
t (01704) 530755
e hello@victorianhotel.co.uk
w victorianhotel.co.uk

The Warwick ★★★
Guest Accommodation
39 Bath Street, Southport
PR9 0DP
t (01704) 530707
e contactus@thewarwicksouthport.co.uk
w thewarwicksouthport.co.uk

Waterford ★★★★★
Guest Accommodation
SILVER AWARD
37 Leicester Street, Southport
PR9 0EX
t (01704) 530559
e reception@waterford-hotel.co.uk
w waterford-hotel.co.uk

Windsor Lodge ★★★ *Guest House*
37 Saunders Street, Southport
PR9 0HJ
t (01704) 530070

WALLASEY

Sherwood Guest House ★★★
Guest House
55 Wellington Road, New Brighton, Wirral
CH45 2ND
t (0151) 639 5198
e info@sherwoodguesthouse.com
w sherwoodguesthouse.com

WEST KIRBY

42 Caldy Road ★★★★★
Bed & Breakfast
West Kirby, Wirral
CH48 2HQ
t (0151) 625 8740
e office@warrencott.demon.co.uk
w warrencott.demon.co.uk

At Peel Hey ★★★★ *Guest House*
SILVER AWARD
Frankby Road, Frankby, Nr Liverpool, Wirral
CH48 1PP
t (0151) 677 9077
e enquiries@peelhey.co.uk
w peelhey.co.uk

WIRRAL

21 Park House Guest House
★★★★ *Guest House*
21 Park Road, West Kirby, Wirral
CH48 4DN
t (0151) 625 4665
e enquiries@21parkhouse.co.uk
w 21parkhouse.co.uk

Cheriton Guest House ★★★★
Bed & Breakfast
151 Caldy Road, Caldy, West Kirby
CH48 1LP
t (0151) 625 5271
e cheriton151@hotmail.com
w cheritonguesthouse.co.uk

Mere Brook House ★★★★★
Bed & Breakfast **GOLD AWARD**
Thornton Common Road, Thornton Hough, Wirral
CH63 0LU
t 07713 189949
e lorna@merebrookhouse.co.uk
w merebrookhouse.co.uk

Pendragon House ★★★★
Guest House **SILVER AWARD**
Pendragon House, 1 Bertram Drive, Wirral
CH47 0LG
t (0151) 632 5244
e pendragonhousehoylake@uwclub.net
w pendragonhouseuk.com

OFFICIAL TOURIST BOARD GUIDE

Self Catering 2011
England's quality-assessed holiday homes
New 36th edition. Brighter, better, easier to use.

enjoyEngland.com

Looking for something else?

You can also buy a copy of our popular guide 'Self Catering' including self-catering holiday homes, approved caravan holiday homes, boat accommodation and holiday cottage agencies in England 2011.

Now available in good bookshops and online at **visitbritainshop.com**

£11.99

North East

North East England has the best of both worlds: awe inspiring coastline and breathtaking and diverse countryside. From the stunning Cheviot Hills in Northumberland to the distinctive conical peak of Roseberry Topping in Tees Valley, it is sprinkled with a wealth of stately homes, glorious gardens and more castles than any other area in England.

Wide-open spaces provide a natural adventure playground. Explore Northumberland National Park on foot to appreciate its peaceful valleys and rolling Cheviot Hills, or walk and cycle alongside the mighty Hadrian's Wall. There are two Areas of Outstanding Natural Beauty to explore – the North Pennines, a land of heather covered moors, tumbling rivers, waterfalls and charming stone-built villages and the Northumberland Coast, a stunning backdrop to all sorts of water sports such as Kitesurfing. The Victorian resort town of Saltburn-by-the-Sea and Tynemouth Long Sands both host thriving surfing scenes, while Boulby Cliffs, an invigorating picnic spot, is the highest on England's East Coast.

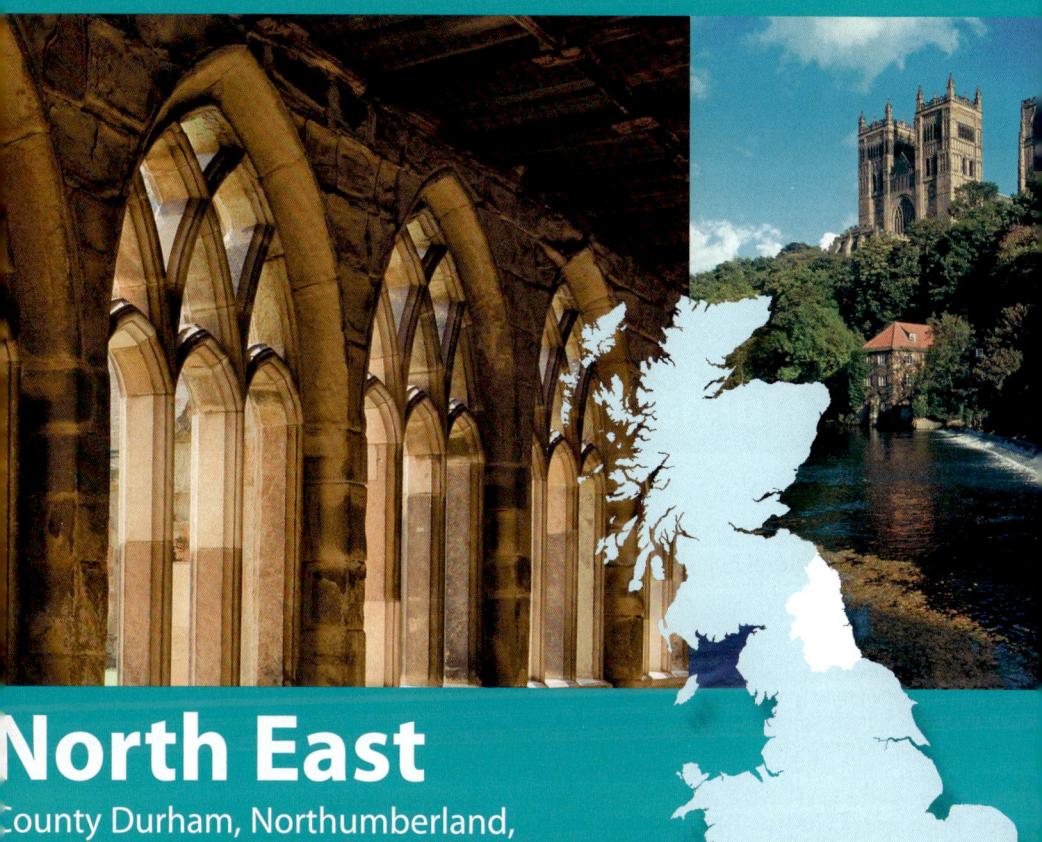

North East

North East

County Durham, Northumberland, Tyne & Wear

660	Counties	666	Where to Eat
663	Where to Go	670	Where to Stay
665	Events		

A 73 mile-long World Heritage Site, Hadrian's Wall was built in AD122 to mark the northern frontier of the Roman Empire. Almost 2000 years later it's still one of the world's most famous landmarks, with eleven fascinating forts and museums along its length.

There's so much to do in the North East where you are guaranteed of a warm welcome.

North East | County Durham

County Durham

This beautiful cathedral city contrasts an amazing history with cosmopolitan cafes and galleries. The surrounding countryside, from the Heritage Coast to the North Pennines Area of Outstanding Natural Beauty, is a walker's paradise.

Barnard Castle

An historic market town. The now ruined castle, an English Heritage property, was named after its 12th century founder, Bernard de Balliol, and was later developed by Richard III. A haven for treasure seekers, the town's many antique shops provide a charming shopping experience. And for food lovers, locally produced specialities can be found at the monthly farmers' market which is held on 'the cobbles' in the Market Place. Nearby, The Bowes Museum is an impressive and charming French-style chateau.

Durham City

A captivating city with winding cobbled streets and a prominent peninsula crowned with the dramatic Cathedral and Castle World Heritage Site – one of the most stunning city panoramas in Europe - Durham is a pleasure to explore and one of the finest cultural and historic destinations in the UK.

There's plenty to see and do: watch the world go by in one of the city centre cafés or shop for gourmet treats, locally produced food or original crafts in an array of shops and markets. Enjoy a moment of reflection in the awe-inspiring cathedral, find city-centre calm at Crook Hall and Gardens or explore the treasures of Durham University's Oriental Museum. Days in Durham are a hard act to follow, but the evenings are also up to the mark. From spellbinding theatre to side-splitting comedy, intimate restaurants to chic café-bars, action films to art house cinema – Durham City has entertainment galore.

Durham Coast

Explore the colourful and dramatic landscape of Durham's Heritage Coast with its beaches, rugged cliffs and imposing headlands. A truly stunning location, the Heritage Coast is recognised internationally for its rare plants and wildlife.

Follow the waymarked path that runs along much of the coast, leading you through a colourful mosaic of grasslands and wildflowers, through areas of natural, historical and geological interest. Enjoy spectacular views along the coastline as the North Sea air blows away the cobwebs.

Durham Dales

The Durham Dales is a peaceful, rich and varied landscape of moors and hills, valleys and meandering rivers, dotted with picturesque villages and market towns and home to the North Pennines Area of Outstanding Natural Beauty.

Spend time in Stanhope, the green and tranquil market town at the heart of the Durham Dales. Whilst in the town, hop aboard the Weardale Railway, built in 1847 to transport limestone, it now transports visitors on scenic trips to Wolsingham. Raby Castle has walled gardens and parkland which is home to herds of fallow and roe deer. Killhope, the North of England Lead Mining Museum, features a huge working water wheel. Visitors can experience the life of mining families and put on hard hats before descending into the mine - an unforgettable experience.

North East | **Northumberland**

Northumberland

Wide open spaces for exhilaration and relaxation, from the glorious coastline to Hadrian's Wall Country and the rolling Cheviot Hills, dotted with historic castles and market towns full of character.

Alnwick

Alnwick originally prospered as a medieval market town, and it still retains many of its cobbled streets, narrow alleys and fine stone buildings which now house a range of specialist shops, family businesses and some of the original coaching inns. Alnwick is home to the magnificent Alnwick Castle, home to the Percy family for seven centuries and boasts beautiful state rooms with Italian Renaissance design, paintings by Canaletto, Van Dyck and Titian and spacious grounds designed by Capability Brown. Nearby Alnwick Garden is one of the most exciting contemporary gardens on earth, which features one of the world's largest treehouses and even a poison garden packed full of rare and dangerous plants.

Berwick upon Tweed

England's most dramatic walled town. Berwick changed hands between England and Scotland 13 times before 1432 when it was captured for the final time by the English. Built in 1558 to safeguard its wealth for good, its impressive town walls were the most expensive building project of the Elizabethan Golden Age. From the top of these walls you can take in some spectacular views over the wide estuary of the River Tweed including Stephenson's famous viaduct bridge, hailed as one of the finest in the world.

Morpeth

Combine the old and the new with a walk around Morpeth's modern Wednesday market - just a stone's throw from the 13th century Chantry that houses the town's Bagpipe Museum and Northumbrian Arts and Craft Gallery. Wander along woodland paths in colourful Carlisle Park, which boasts river boating, tennis courts and bowls. The park also plays host to the wonderful Turner Garden. Celebrating the life of William Turner, the father of English botany who was born and educated in the town. For the best in local produce, experience Morpeth's Farmers Market which takes place on the first Saturday of every month in the historic market place. Within a short distance of Morpeth lie wonderful country estates and gardens such as Wallington House and Belsay Hall, Castle and Gardens. Druridge Bay, with its magnificent seven-mile stretch of golden sand and dunes, is only 20 minutes away by car.

Hexham

Hexham Abbey is the historic centrepiece of the town - built around 675 AD at the direction of St Wilfred. The town also boasts two medieval towers: the 14th century Hexham Old Gaol - the oldest purpose-built prison in England - and a Moot Hall which dates from the 14th or 15th century. Hexham is an ideal base from which to explore some of the area's attractions, including Hadrian's Wall and Kielder Water and Forest Park.

Rothbury

Rothbury is in the centre of Northumberland and is therefore an ideal base for exploring. Close by is the Northumberland Coast Area of Outstanding Natural Beauty and 3 minutes to the Simonside and Cheviot Hills and Northumberland National Park. Walkers and cyclists will love the spectacular countryside. Nearby is Cragside House, former home of the Victorian industrialist Lord Armstrong. The first house to be lit by hydroelectricity, Cragside is also now one of the last strongholds of the Red Squirrel.

661

North East | Tyne & Wear

Tyne & Wear

Vibrant cities and bustling seafront towns; superb shopping and seriously good food; international arts and entertainment for all. Tyne & Wear is a place where you can live life to the full – and relax on miles of award-winning beaches.

Newcastle Gateshead

At its hub is the Quayside, the cultural heart of the city. The skyline is dominated by the iconic Tyne Bridge and the award-winning Gateshead Millennium Bridge, which leads to BALTIC: Centre for Contemporary Art, and The Sage Gateshead international centre for music. Eating out is a treat for all the senses, Newcastle houses the oldest dining room in the UK, Blackfriars, which dates back to the 13th century. There are hundreds more contemporary places to eat too, from laid-back bistros to sophisticated restaurants serving fine local produce with many restaurants having wonderful river or city views. The award-winning Angel of the North sculpture, designed by Antony Gormley, stands just outside Gateshead and welcomes visitors to the city with open wings.

Jesmond

A smart, leafy boutique quarter just ten minutes' walk from Newcastle city centre, Jesmond is renowned for its designer stores and sophisticated cafés and restaurants.

The suburb is flanked by the beautiful Jesmond Dene, a wooded valley and Victorian park. Many tree-lined paths run through the valley, leading past interesting landmarks such as the Eye Bridge and its picturesque weir. Jesmond Dene is spanned by the Armstrong Bridge, which plays host to an artists' market every Sunday.

South Shields

South Shields is a popular coastal town on the South bank of the River Tyne. Beautiful beaches, twisting cliff top paths, exhilarating amusements and miles of natural beauty make it a delight to explore all year round. Journey back to Roman times at Arbeia Roman Fort, learn about Anglo-Saxon history at Bede's World, visit a keeper's cottage at Souter Lighthouse or simply explore beautiful sandy beaches and enjoy traditional seaside fun. All the fun of the fair can be enjoyed at Ocean Beach Pleasure Park.

Sunderland

A city by the sea, offers its visitors a captivating combination of relaxing countryside, beautiful sandy beaches, a lively city centre, fascinating attractions and spectacular events, including the award-winning Sunderland International Airshow. Look out for the Sunderland Museum & Winter Gardens, the National Glass Centre, and the Stadium of Light. Or take a relaxing stroll along the award-winning beaches of Seaburn and Roker.

Whitley Bay & Tynemouth

Just eight miles east of Newcastle, Whitley Bay has Great Britain's seaside resort charm encapsulated in one town. Often referred to as Newcastle's coast, this area boasts three blue flag beaches as well a range of cultural attractions. Fantastic family attractions include Blue Reef Aquarium, Stephenson Railway Museum, Wet 'N' Wild water park and Segedunum – the Roman fort and museum which marks the eastern end of Hadrian's Wall. The coastal town of Whitley Bay has been popular with generations of visitors.

North East | Where to Go

Where to Go

Attractions with this sign participate in the **Visitor Attraction Quality Assurance Scheme** (see page 6) which recognises high standards in all aspects of the visitor experience.

ENTERTAINMENT & CULTURE

BALTIC Centre for Contemporary Art
Gateshead, Tyne and Wear
NE8 3BA
(01914) 781810
www.balticmill.com
Housed in a landmark industrial building on the south bank of the River Tyne in Gateshead, the biggest gallery of its kind in the world - presenting a dynamic, diverse and international programme of contemporary visual art.

Beamish Museum
Beamish, County Durham
DH9 0RG
(01913) 704000
www.beamish.org.uk
Beamish - The Living Museum of the North, is an open air museum vividly recreating life in the North East in the early 1800s and 1900s.

Captain Cook Birthplace Museum
Middlesbrough, Tees Valley
TS7 8AT
(01642) 311211
www.captcook-ne.co.uk
Discover why Captain Cook is the world's most famous navigator and explorer. Find out about life below decks in the 18thC.

Cleveland Ironstone Mining Museum
Saltburn-by-the-Sea, Tees Valley
TS13 4AP
(01287) 642877
www.ironstonemuseum.co.uk
Guided tours which include the underground world of Cleveland's Ironstone Mining past.

Discovery Museum
Newcastle-upon-Tyne,
Tyne and Wear NE1 4JA
(01912) 326789
www.twmuseums.org.uk/discovery
Offers a wide variety of experiences for all the family to enjoy. Explore Newcastle Story, Live Wires, Science Maze and Fashion Works.

DLI Museum and Durham Art Gallery
Durham, County Durham DH1 5TU
(01913) 842214
www.durham.gov.uk/dli
The Museum tells the 200-year story of Durham's famous regiment. Art Gallery has changing exhibition programme. Please ring for free exhibition and events brochure.

Dorman Museum
Middlesbrough, Tees Valley
TS5 6LA
(01642) 813781
www.dormanmuseum.co.uk
With 8 galleries and 3 exhibition spaces, there's something for everyone and plenty of hands-on activities, objects and children's trails. Temporary exhibition galleries and regular holiday events.

Hartlepool Art Gallery
Hartlepool, Tees Valley
TS24 7EQ
(01429) 869706
www.hartlepool.gov.uk
The art gallery has a varied programme of art and craft exhibitions. Former church building also includes the TIC and a bell tower viewing platform looking over Hartlepool.

Hartlepool's Maritime Experience
Hartlepool, Tees Valley TS24 0XZ
(01429) 860077
www.hartlepoolsmaritimeexperience.com
An authentic reconstruction of an 18th Century seaport. Step back in time to a remarkable period in British History. A superb day out for all ages.

Hexham Old Gaol
Hexham, Northumberland
NE46 3NH
(01434) 652349
www.tynedaleheritage.org
Tour the Old Gaol, 1330AD, by glass lift. Meet the gaoler, see a Reiver raid and try on costumes.

Killhope, The North of England Lead Mining Museum
Bishop Auckland, County
Durham DL13 1AR
(01388) 537505
www.killhope.org.uk
The North East's Small Visitor Attraction of the Year and the most complete lead mining site in Great Britain.

Locomotion: The National Railway Museum at Shildon
Shildon, County Durham DL4 1PQ
(01388) 777999
www.locomotion.uk.com
The first National Museum in the North East. View over 60 vehicles, children's play area and interactive displays. Retail and catering available.

663

North East | Where to Go

mima
Middlesbrough, Tees Valley
TS1 2AZ
(01642) 726720
www.visitmima.com
mima showcases an international programme of fine art and applied art from the 1900s to the present day.

Segedunum Roman Fort, Baths and Museum.
Wallsend, Tyne and Wear
NE28 6HR
(01912) 369347
www.twmuseums.org.uk/segedunum
Is the gateway to Hadrian's Wall where you can explore the excavated fort site, visit reconstructions of a Roman bath house, learn about the history of the area in the museum.

Sunderland Museum and Winter Gardens
Sunderland, Tyne and Wear
SR1 1PP
(01915) 532323
www.twmuseums.org.uk/sunderland
Stunning winter gardens, with 1,500 of the world's most exotic flowers, plants and trees.

The Bowes Museum
Barnard Castle, County Durham
DL12 8NP
(01833) 690606
www.thebowesmuseum.org.uk
Houses a collection of outstanding European fine and decorative arts and offers an acclaimed exhibition programme, alongside special events and children's activities.

Woodhorn Museum Archives & Country Park
Ashington, Northumberland
NE63 9YF
(01670) 528080
www.experiencewoodhorn.com
Stunning new architecture and listed colliery buildings set in a country park, house fascinating displays, galleries, interactives and amazing archival treasures. See paintings by the famous Pitmen Painter.

FAMILY FUN

Nature's World
Middlesbrough, Tees Valley
TS5 7YN
(01642) 594895
www.naturesworld.org.uk
The North of England's Pioneering Eco-Experience. Featuring 25 acres of organic gardens, wildlife pond, white garden, shop, tearoom and unique River Tees model. Futuristic Hydroponicum and Eco centre now open powered by renewable energy.

HERITAGE

Alnwick Castle
Alnwick, Northumberland
NE66 1NQ
(01665) 510777
www.alnwickcastle.com
Alnwick Castle is one of Europe's finest. Majestic and imposing, it has a packed daily events programme, fine art treasures, wonderful architecture and children's activities.

Arbeia Roman Fort and Museum
South Shields, Tyne and Wear
NE33 2BB
(01914) 561369
www.twmuseums.org.uk/arbeia
Arbeia is the best reconstruction of a Roman fort in Britain and offers visitors a unique insight into the every day life of the Roman army, from the soldier in his barrack room to the commander in his luxurious house.

Bamburgh Castle
Bamburgh, Northumberland
NE69 7DF
(01668) 214515
www.bamburghcastle.com
A spectacular castle with fantastic coastal views. The stunning Kings Hall and Keep house collections of armour, artwork, porcelain and furniture.

Belsay Hall, Castle and Gardens
Belsay, Northumberland
NE20 0DX
(01661) 881636
www.english-heritage.org.uk/belsay
With so much to see and do, a trip to Belsay is one of the best value family days out in North East England. Stunning gardens, beautiful architecture and magnificent views all in one place.

Durham Castle
Durham, County Durham
DH1 3RW
(01913) 343800
www.durhamcastle.com
Durham Castle is part of the Durham City World Heritage Site. Entrance by guided tour only.

Gateshead Angel of the North
Gateshead, Tyne and Wear
NE9 6AA
(01914) 784222
www.gateshead.gov.uk/leisure and culture/attractions/angel/home.aspx
The Gateshead Angel of the North was designed by Antony Gormley for Gateshead Council. It weighs 200 tons, is 20m high and has a 54m wing span.

George Stephenson's Birthplace
Wylam, Northumberland
NE41 8BP
(01661) 853457
www.nationaltrust.org.uk
Small stone cottage built about 1750. Birthplace in 1781 of inventor George Stephenson. One room open to the public.

Head of Steam Darlington Railway Museum
Darlington, Tees Valley DL3 6ST
(01325) 460532
www.head-of-steam.co.uk
Restored 1842 station housing a collection of exhibits relating to railways in the North East of England, including Stephenson's Locomotion.

Kielder Castle Forest Park Centre
Kielder, Northumberland
NE48 1ER
(01434) 250209
www.forestry.gov.uk/northeastengland
Kielder Castle is the visitor centre for Kielder Forest. Features include forest shop, information centre, tearoom and exhibitions about forestry and conservation. Bike hire available.

National Glass Centre
Sunderland, Tyne and Wear
SR6 0GL
(01915) 155555
www.nationalglasscentre.com
An inspirational visitor experience; enjoy an ever-changing programme of exhibitions, live glass blowing, conference and banqueting and a stunning restaurant overlooking the River Wear.

Ormesby Hall
Middlesbrough, Tees Valley
TS7 9AS
(01642) 324188
www.nationaltrust.org.uk
Beautiful 18thC mansion with impressive contemporary plasterwork, magnificent stable block attributed to Carr of York and model railway exhibition and layout.

Raby Castle
Staindrop, County Durham
DL2 3AH
(01833) 660202
www.rabycastle.com
Medieval Raby Castle, home of Lord Barnard's family since 1626, includes a 200 acre deer park, walled gardens, carriage collection, adventure playground, shop and tearoom.

North East | Where to Go/Events

altburn Miniature ailway
altburn-by-the-Sea, Tees Valley
S10 1SF
(1642) 502863
15" gauge miniature railway running om the seafront to the Valley Gardens nd Woodland Centre.

even Stories, the Centre or Children's Books
ewcastle-upon-Tyne, Tyne and ear NE1 2PQ
345 271 0777
ww.sevenstories.org.uk
even Stories is where our rich heritage f children's books is collected, elebrated and brought to life. With xhibitions, dressing up, storytelling nd crafts, Seven Stories spells the erfect day out for all the family.

ummerhill Visitor Centre
artlepool, Tees Valley TS25 4LL
1429) 284584
ww.sunnysummerhill.com
ummerhill is a 100 acre Country Park n the western edge of Hartlepool that as been transformed for conservation nd outdoor sports.

Warkworth Castle
Warkworth, Northumberland
E65 0UJ
1665) 711423
ww.english-heritage.org.uk/warkworth et in a quaint Northumberland town, nis hill-top fortress and hermitage ffers a fantastic family day out.

Weardale Railway
Stanhope, County Durham
DL13 2YS
(01388) 526203
www.weardale-railway.org.uk
Heritage railway between Wolsingham and Stanhope in beautiful Weardale within the North Pennines Area of Outstanding Natural Beauty.

NATURE & WILDLIFE

Farne Islands
Seahouses, Northumberland
(01665) 721099
Bird reserve holding over 100,000 pairs of breeding birds, of 21 species. Also home to a large colony of grey seals. Boat fees are extra. Boats not operated by National Trust.

Hall Hill Farm
Durham, County Durham
DH7 0TA
(01388) 731333
www.hallhillfarm.co.uk
Award-winning farm attraction set in attractive countryside, see and touch the animals at close quarters. Farm trailer ride, gift shop, tearoom, picnic and play area.

Hamsterley Forest
Bishop Auckland, County Durham DL13 3NL
(01388) 488312
www.forestry.gov.uk/northeastengland
A 5,000 acre mixed woodland open to the public all year. Facilities include a forest drive, woodland walks, cycle routes (hire available) and picnic areas.

High Force Waterfall
Middleton-in-Teesdale, County Durham DL12 0QG
(01833) 640209
www.rabycastle.com/high_force.htm
High Force is the most majestic of the waterfalls on the River Tees. The falls are only a short walk from a bus stop, car park and picnic area.

RSPB Saltholme
Middlesbrough, Tees Valley
TS2 1TT
(01642) 546625
www.rspb.org/saltholme
Saltholme is a fantastic new wildlife experience in the Tees Valley.

WWT Washington Wetland Centre
Washington, Tyne and Wear
NE38 8LE
(01914) 165454
www.wwt.org.uk/visit/washington
Conservation site with 45 hectares of wetland, woodland and wildlife reserve. Home to wildfowl, insects and flora. Lake-side hides, wild bird feeding station, waterside cafe, picnic areas, sustainable garden, playground and events calendar.

OUTDOOR ACTIVITIES

Hadrian's Wall Path National Trail
Hexham, Northumberland
(01912) 691600
www.nationaltrail.co.uk/hadrianswall
84 mile path, providing access to Hadrian's Wall.

Events 2011

llendale Tar Bar'l Ceremony
llendale
ww.northern-pennines.co.uk/ llendale.htm
1 December

rinkburn Music Festival
Morpeth
ww.brinkburnmusic.org/
BC

Kielder Marathon
ielder Water
ww.visitkielder.com/site/kielder- arathon/
BC

Middlesbrough Mela
Middlesbrough
ww.boromela.co.uk/
6-17 July

Middlesbrough Music Live
Middlesbrough
www.middlesbroughmusiclive.co.uk
5 June

Morpeth Northumbrian Gathering
Morpeth
www.northumbriana.org.uk/ gathering/index.htm
TBC

Northumberland County Show
Corbridge
www.northcountyshow.co.uk/
TBC

SIRF and Fringe Festival
www.fringefestival.co.uk/
3-7 August

Take to the Tees featuring Ratrace Stockton
www.rivertees.org.uk/
August

North East | Where to Eat

Where to Eat

The North East England region has great places to eat. The restaurant reviews on these pages are just a small selection from the highly respected *The Good Food Guide 2011*. Please see page 14 for further information on the Guide and details of a Special Offer for our readers.

COUNTY DURHAM

The Oak Tree Inn
Warm welcome and food with flair
Hutton Magna DL11 7HH
(01833) 627371
Modern British | £32

The Rosses' whitewashed country pub is snuggled in a row of terraced cottages, and is run with all the warmth and welcome we hope to find in such establishments. Alastair Ross once worked at the Savoy in London, and brings a sharp seasonal sense and plenty of flair to his modern British repertoire. Start with a salt cod fishcake seasoned with garlic and saffron, before moving on to roast breast of guinea-fowl with confit leg, olive oil mash and rosemary-scented vegetables. Baked vanilla cheesecake with poached plums and pistachio ice cream makes a fitting finale. Good selections of teas, bottled beers and malt whiskies supplement the value conscious wine list, which starts at £12.50.
Chef/s: Alastair Ross. **Open:** Tue to Sun D only 6 to 9 (5 to 8 Sun). **Closed:** Mon, 25 and 27 Dec, 31 Dec, 1 and 2 Jan. **Meals:** alc (main courses £18 to £20). **Service:** not inc. **Details:** major cards accepted. 20 seats. No mobile phones. Music. Car parking.

NORTHUMBERLAND

The Barrasford Arms
Local gastro grub cuts the mustard
Barrasford NE48 4AA
(01434) 681237
www.barrasfordarms.co.uk
Gastropub | £23

With the ruins of Haughton Castle and Hadrian's Wall just a hike away, the Barrasford Arms (circa 1870) isn't short on heritage. It also cuts the mustard as a gastropub with a sound reputation for unfussy food, thanks to Tony Binks' feel for locally sourced ingredients. A warm salad of Northumberland rabbit and black pudding is dressed up with apple and vanilla purée, North Shields halibut is given some Mediterranean warmth with sweet pepper and chorizo stew, and diehards can get stuck in to platefuls of suet-crusted steak, mushroom and ale pie. To finish, rice pudding with damson compote should set you up for some roaming. Corney & Barrow house wines are £13.50.
Chef/s: Tony Binks. **Open:** Tue to Sun L 12 to 2 (3 Sun), Mon to Sat D 6.30 to 9. **Closed:** 26 and 27 Dec, bank hols. **Meals:** alc (main courses £10 to £22). Set L £11.50 (2 courses) to £14.50. Sun L £13.50 (2 courses) to £16. **Service:** not inc. **Details:** major cards accepted. 65 seats. 40 seats outside. Separate bar. Wheelchair access. Music. Children welcome. Car parking.

North East | **Where to Eat**

TYNE & WEAR

Eslington Villa

Stylish starters and fortifying mains

Station Road, Low Fell, Gateshead NE9 6DR
0191) 4876017
www.eslingtonvilla.co.uk
Modern British | £24

Eslington is a late Victorian mansion in a couple of acres of well-maintained gardens. It has smart but informal dining areas in the main house and the conservatory, and a loyal band of regular customers. Andrew Moore cooks a menu of modern brasserie-style dishes, with starters built around the likes of crab fritters with tomato and chilli jam, and vodka-cured trout with beetroot carpaccio. Fortifying main courses may include roast venison loin with cep purée in red wine sauce, or sea bream wrapped in Parma ham with saffron risotto. Chocolate mousse and brandied cherries is a fittingly stylish way to finish. A good modern wine list is well presented, and opens with eight house wines from £16.95 a bottle, £4.25 a glass. **Chef/s:** Andrew Moore. **Open:** Sun to Fri L 12 to 2 (3.30 Sun), Mon to Sat D 7 to 10 (6.30 to 10 Sat). **Closed:** bank hols. **Meals:** Set L £17.50 (2 courses) to £19.50. Set D £20.50 (2 courses) to £24.50. Sun L £19. **Service:** not inc. **Details:** major cards accepted. 80 seats. 20 seats outside. Separate bar. Wheelchair access. Music. Children welcome. Car parking.

Content brought to you by **The Good Food Guide 2011**. Please see page 14 for further details.

North East

Tourist Information Centres

When you arrive at your destination, visit an Official Partner Tourist Information Centre for quality assured help with accommodation and information about local attractions and events, or email your request before you go. To find a Tourist Information Centre by region visit enjoyEngland.com/find-tic.

ALNWICK	2 The Shambles	01665 511333	alnwicktic@alnwick.gov.uk
AMBLE	Queen Street Car Park	01665 712313	amble.tic@northumberland.gov.uk
BARNARD CASTLE	Woodleigh	01833 690909	tourism@teesdale.gov.uk
BELLINGHAM	Station Yard	01434 220616	bellinghamtic@btconnect.com
BERWICK-UPON-TWEED	106 Marygate	01289 330733	berwick.tic@northumberland.gov.uk
BISHOP AUCKLAND	Town Hall Ground Floor	01388 604922	bishopauckland.touristinfo@durham.gov.uk
CORBRIDGE	Hill Street	01434 632815	corbridgetic@btconnect.com
CRASTER	Craster Car Park	01665 576007	crastertic@alnwick.gov.uk
DARLINGTON	13 Horsemarket	01325 388666	tic@darlington.gov.uk
DURHAM	2 Millennium Place	0191 384 3720	touristinfo@durhamcity.gov.uk
GATESHEAD	Central Library	0191 433 8420	tic@gateshead.gov.uk

North East

GATESHEAD	The Sage Gateshead	0191 478 4222	tourism@gateshead.gov.uk
HALTWHISTLE	Railway Station	01434 322002	haltwhistletic@btconnect.com
HARTLEPOOL	Hartlepool Art Gallery	01429 869706	hpooltic@hartlepool.gov.uk
HEXHAM	Wentworth Car Park	01434 652220	hexham.tic@northumberland.gov.uk
MIDDLESBROUGH	(PO Box 69)	01642 729700	middlesbrough_tic@middlesbrough.gov.uk
MORPETH	The Chantry	01670 500700	morpeth.tic@northumberland.gov.uk
NEWCASTLE AIRPORT	Tourist Information Desk	0191 214 4422	niatic@hotmail.com
NEWCASTLE-UPON-TYNE	Newcastle Information Centre	0191 277 8000	tourist.info@newcastle.gov.uk
NORTH SHIELDS	Unit 2	0191 2005895	ticns@northtyneside.gov.uk
ONCE BREWED	Northumberland National Park Centre	01434 344396	tic.oncebrewed@nnpa.org.uk
PETERLEE	4 Upper Yoden Way	0191 586 4450	touristinfo@peterlee.gov.uk
REDCAR	West Terrace	01642 471921	redcar_tic@redcar-cleveland.gov.uk
ROTHBURY	Northumberland National Park Centre	01669 620887	tic.rothbury@nnpa.org.uk
SALTBURN-BY-THE-SEA	3 Station Buildings	01287 622422	saltburn_tic@redcar-cleveland.gov.uk
SEAHOUSES	Seafield Car Park	01665 720884	seahouses.tic@northumberland.gov.uk
SOUTH SHIELDS	South Shields Museum & Gallery	0191 454 6612	museum.tic@southtyneside.gov.uk
SOUTH SHIELDS	Sea Road	0191 455 7411	foreshore.tic@southtyneside.gov.uk
STANHOPE	Durham Dales Centre	01388 527650	durham.dales.centre@durham.gov.uk
STOCKTON-ON-TEES	Stockton Central Library	01642 528130	touristinformation@stockton.gov.uk
SUNDERLAND	50 Fawcett Street	0191 553 2000	tourist.info@sunderland.gov.uk
WHITLEY BAY	Park Road	0191 2008535	ticwb@northtyneside.gov.uk
WOOLER	Wooler TIC, The Cheviot Centre	01668 282123	wooler.tic@northumberland.gov.uk

Regional Contacts and Information

Log on to the North East England website at **www.visitnortheastengland.com** for further information on accommodation, attractions, events and special offers throughout the region. A range of free information is available to download from the website.

North East | Co Durham

Where to Stay

Entries appear alphabetically by town name in each county. A key to symbols appears on page 6. Maps start on page 706. A listing of all Enjoy England assessed accommodation appears at the end of the region.

BEAMISH 3 MILES, Co Durham Map ref 5C2   SAT NAV DH9 9UA

★★★ FARMHOUSE

B&B PER ROOM PER NIGHT
S £40.00
D £60.00

Bushblades Farm
Harperley, Stanley DH9 9UA
t (01207) 232722 e bushbladesfarm@hotmail.com
w bushbladesfarm.co.uk

Georgian Farmhouse with large garden in peaceful setting. Bedrooms en suite with TV, hospitality tray and comfortable chairs Excellent breakfasts. Nearby Beamish Museum, Durham City and A1(M). Ideal base. **directions** Leave A1(M) at Chester-le-Street for Stanley on A693. 0.5 miles after Stanley follow signs for Harperley. Farm on right, 0.5 miles up hill from crossroads. **open** All year except Xmas and New Year **bedrooms** 1 double, 1 twin **bathrooms** 2 en suite **payment** cash, cheques

DARLINGTON, Co Durham Map ref 5C3   SAT NAV DL3 7RN

★★ GUEST HOUSE

B&B PER ROOM PER NIGHT
S £30.00 – £35.00
D £45.00 – £60.00

Trudy's Guesthouse
72 Coniscliffe Road, Darlington DL3 7RN
t (01325) 350918 e trudy_johnson@hotmail.co.uk
w trudysguesthouse.co.uk ONLINE MAP GUEST REVIEWS ONLINE BOOKING

Trudy's Guesthouse is a wonderful place to stay where you will always recieve excellent service and be welcomed as a member of the family. **directions** We are 5 minute walk from Darlington town centre, where you can find a good variety shops, restaurants, bars and leisure centre. **open** All year **bedrooms** 1 single, 2 double, 2 twin, 1 family **bathrooms** 1 en suite, 1 with private bathroom **payment** cash, cheques, euros

Looking for something else?

You can also buy a copy of our popular guide 'Hotels' including country house and town house hotels, metro and budget hotels, serviced apartments, restaurants with rooms and Spas in England 2011. Now available in good bookshops and online at **visitbritainshop.com**

£10.99

North East | Co Durham

DURHAM, Co Durham Map ref 5C2
SAT NAV DH1 2PT

★★ INN

B&B PER ROOM PER NIGHT
S £24.50 – £33.00
D £49.50 – £66.00

EVENING MEAL PER PERSON
£4.50 – £10.95

The Avenue Inn
Avenue Street, High Shincliffe, Durham DH1 2PT
t (0191) 3865954 e info@theavenue.biz

Cosy village inn with eight bedrooms. Real ales and a friendly atmosphere. Traditional home cooked food served 6pm-9pm Monday to Saturday and Sunday Roast served 12pm - 3pm Sundays. **directions** From junction 61 on the A1(M), take A177 (signposted Bowburn) and travel approximately 2miles. Turn right into High Shincliffe and we are on the right. **open** All year **bedrooms** 3 single, 2 double, 2 twin, 1 family **bathrooms** 4 en suite **payment** credit/debit cards, cash, cheques

Room General Leisure

DURHAM, Co Durham Map ref 5C2
SAT NAV DH1 4PS

★★★★ GUEST ACCOMMODATION

B&B PER ROOM PER NIGHT
S £55.00 – £60.00
D £80.00 – £85.00

Castle View Guest House
4 Crossgate, Durham DH1 4PS
t 0191 3868852 e castle_view@hotmail.com
w castle-view.co.uk

Two hundred and fifty year old listed building in the heart of the old city, with woodland and riverside walks and magnificent views of the cathedral and castle. Complimentary parking **directions** From A1(M) take junction 62, follow signs A690 Crook until river crossing. At traffic lights turn left into Crossgate, next to St Margarets Church **open** All year except Xmas and New Year **bedrooms** 1 single, 3 double, 2 twin **bathrooms** 6 en suite **payment** credit/debit cards, cash, cheques

Room General

DURHAM, Co Durham Map ref 5C2
SAT NAV DH1 1QN

★★★★ GUEST ACCOMMODATION **Silver AWARD**

B&B PER ROOM PER NIGHT
S £60.00 – £80.00
D £80.00 – £90.00

Cathedral View Town House
212 Gilesgate, Durham City DH1 1QN
t 0191 3869566 e cathedralview@hotmail.com
w cathedralview.com ONLINE MAP

City centre Georgian Townhouse. Close to Cathedral, Castle, theatre & restaurants. Panoramic views of Cathedral and countryside. Comfortable accommodation. Extensive breakfast. Quality ingredients. Vegetarian & gluten free diets. Complimentary parking. **directions** From A1 take A690 (jct 762). At roundabout (1.5 miles) take fourth exit, passing Woodman Inn. We are on left. **open** All year except Xmas and New Year **bedrooms** 4 double, 2 twin **bathrooms** 6 en suite **payment** credit/debit cards, cash, euros

Room General

DURHAM, Co Durham Map ref 5C2
SAT NAV DH1 3RH

★★★★ GUEST ACCOMMODATION

B&B PER ROOM PER NIGHT
S £26.50 – £36.50
D £48.00 – £68.00

EVENING MEAL PER PERSON
£12.50 – £35.00

Saint Chad's College
18 North Bailey, Durham DH1 3RH
t (0191) 334 3358 f (0191) 334 3371 e chads@durham.ac.uk
w dur.ac.uk/chads/

In the heart of historic Durham, adjacent to the Castle and Cathedral, designated a World Heritage Site. Comfortable and convenient accommodation, friendly service. **directions** Follow the A1(M) until the A690, direct to Durham, through the marketplace towards Cathedral. The college lies opposite the rose window of Durham Cathedral. **open** All year except Xmas **bedrooms** 79 single, 16 double, 50 twin **bathrooms** 34 en suite, 4 with private bathroom **payment** credit/debit cards, cash, cheques

Room General Leisure

or key to symbols see page 6

671

North East | Co Durham

DURHAM, Co Durham Map ref 5C2
SAT NAV DH1 3RW

Durham Castle
Palace Green, Durham DH1 3RW
t (01913) 344106 f (01913) 343801 e durham.castle@durham.ac.uk
w durhamcastle.com

CAMPUS

B&B PER ROOM PER NIGHT
S £28.50 – £39.00

Durham Castle was founded in about 1072 as a Norman fortress; became the ceremonial home of the Prince Bishops of Durham and was the founding college of Durham University. The Castle is home to over 100 students during University terms. Castle tours included for B&B guests.

open University Vacations - Castle closed Summer 2011
bedrooms 133 single, 9 double, 35 twin
bathrooms 10 en suite, 3 with private bathroom
directions From the A1(M) take the exit A690 Durham and follow the road, 2nd major roundabout to the Market Place, follow signs Cathedral & Castle.

General

DURHAM, Co Durham Map ref 5C2
SAT NAV DH1 2NU

Seven Stars Inn
High Street North, Shincliffe, Durham DH1 2NU
t (01913) 848454 f (01913) 741173 e reservations@sevenstarsinn.co.uk
w sevenstarsinn.co.uk LAST MINUTE OFFERS

INN

B&B PER ROOM PER NIGHT
S £55.00 – £75.00
D £70.00 – £95.00
EVENING MEAL PER PERSON
£6.95 – £30.00

Charming old coaching inn, built in 1724, one mile from Durham City. Eight individually decorated rooms, each with en suite shower room, TV and tea-/coffee-making facilities. Excellent reputation for food and real ale. **directions** From A1(M) follow A177 signposted Bowburn and Peterlee. Off at Durham service station. **open** All year
bedrooms 2 single, 4 double, 1 twin, 1 family **bathrooms** 8 en suite **payment** credit/debit cards, cash

Room   General

DURHAM, Co Durham Map ref 5C2
SAT NAV DH1 3RJ

St John's College
3 South Bailey, Durham DH1 3RJ
t (01913) 343877 f (01913) 343501 e s.l.hobson@durham.ac.uk
w durham.ac.uk/st-johns.college

GUEST ACCOMMODATION

B&B PER ROOM PER NIGHT
S £25.00 – £28.00
D £46.00 – £52.00

Located in the heart of Durham City alongside the cathedral, St John's offers accommodation in distinctive, historic buildings with riverside gardens. **directions** Please contact us for directions **open** All year except Xmas and New Year **bedrooms** 36 single, 9 twin **payment** credit/debit cards, cash, cheques

Room   General

672   Official tourist board guide Bed & Breakfa

North East | Co Durham

DURHAM, Co Durham Map ref 5C2
SAT NAV DH1 4RW

The Victorian Town House
2 Victoria Terrace, Durham DH1 4RW
t 05601 459101 **e** stay@durhambedandbreakfast.com
w durhambedandbreakfast.com ONLINE MAP GUEST REVIEWS

B&B PER ROOM PER NIGHT
S £60.00 – £70.00
D £80.00 – £95.00

Victorian terraced family home. Three en suite rooms. City centre, train, bus all five minutes' walk. Private and nearby parking. **directions** 5 minute walk from train station. Turn right at bottom of station approach road. Pass hospital and left on to Western Hill. Turn first right. **open** All year **bedrooms** 1 double, 1 twin, 1 family **bathrooms** 3 en suite **payment** cash, cheques

BREAKFAST AWARD

EDMUNDBYERS, Co Durham Map ref 5B2
SAT NAV DH8 9NL

Punchbowl Inn
Edmundbyers, Consett DH8 9NL
t (01207) 255545 **e** info@thepunchbowlinn.info
w thepunchbowlinn.info ONLINE MAP

B&B PER ROOM PER NIGHT
S £45.00 – £50.00
D £70.00 – £80.00

EVENING MEAL PER PERSON
£10.00 – £30.00

Small, family run village pub/restaurant. Deli, tea room, quality home made food, log fires in winter. Dog friendly. Parking for bicycles. Warm welcome for all. Take away meals available. **directions** 2.5 miles from A68 on B6278 in middle of Edmundbyers. Close to Derwent Reservoir. **open** All year **bedrooms** 1 single, 3 double, 2 twin **bathrooms** 6 en suite **payment** credit/debit cards, cash, cheques

---

FROSTERLEY, Co Durham Map ref 5B2
SAT NAV DL13 2SH

Newlands Hall
Newlands Hall, Frosterley, Nr Bishop Auckland, County Durham DL13 2SH
t (01388) 529233 **e** carol@newlandshall.co.uk
w newlandshall.co.uk ONLINE MAP GUEST REVIEWS ONLINE BOOKING LAST MINUTE OFFERS

B&B PER ROOM PER NIGHT
S £40.00 – £50.00
D £60.00 – £70.00

Traditional farmhouse bed and breakfast in picturesque Weardale, both rooms enjoy southerly views. Newlands Hall is a working Beef and Sheep farm close to Wolsingham and Frosterley. **directions** Please contact us for directions **open** All year except Xmas and New Year **bedrooms** 2 family **bathrooms** 2 en suite **payment** credit/debit cards, cash, cheques

---

NEWTON AYCLIFFE, Co Durham Map ref 5C3
SAT NAV DL5 6NW

2 Main Road
Redworth, Newton Aycliffe, Co. Durham DL5 6NW
t (01388) 772360 **e** anne.dobson@live.co.uk

B&B PER ROOM PER NIGHT
S £35.00
D £60.00

A recently refurbished lovely old family home, with plenty of parking set in a small hamlet close to the motorway, airport and central for all northern tourist areas. **directions** We are set four miles off Junction 58 A1(M) following A68 then A6072 **open** All year except Xmas and New Year **bedrooms** 1 double **bathrooms** 1 en suite **payment** cash, cheques

North East | Co Durham/Northumberland

SPENNYMOOR, Co Durham Map ref 5C2
SAT NAV DL16 7JT

B&B PER ROOM PER NIGHT
S £42.00
D £62.00

Highview Country House
Kirk Merrington, Spennymoor DL16 7JT
t (01388) 811006 f (01388) 811006 e jayne@highviewcountryhouse.co.uk
w **highviewcountryhouse.co.uk** ONLINE MAP ONLINE BOOKING LAST MINUTE OFFERS

Country house in one acre of gardens surrounded by countryside. Peaceful. Safe parking. Situated on the edge of delightful village. Good pubs, newly refurbished rooms. Ten minutes from motorway Durham. **directions** Please contact us for directions **open** All year **bedrooms** 2 single, 4 double, 1 twin, 1 family **bathrooms** 8 en suite **payment** credit/debit cards, cash, cheques

Room   General   Leisure

STOCKTON-ON-TEES, Co Durham Map ref 5C3
SAT NAV TS18 5ER

B&B PER ROOM PER NIGHT
S £45.00
D £59.00
EVENING MEAL PER PERSON
£7.95 – £13.95

The Parkwood Inn
64-66 Darlington Road, Stockton-on-Tees TS18 5ER
t (01642) 587933 e theparkwoodhotel@aol.com
w **theparkwoodhotel.com** GUEST REVIEWS ONLINE BOOKING

A warm friendly welcome awaits you at this family-run inn. The well equipped, comfortable rooms boast ensuite facilities. Meals are professionally prepared and served in the cosy restaurant or conservatory. Popular with locals and Camra pub of the season makes this well worth a visit.

open All year
bedrooms 1 single, 4 double, 1 twin
bathrooms 6 en suite
payment credit/debit cards, cash, cheques

directions Leave A66 at A1327 signed Yarm/Stockton south. Towards Stockton south, 2nd le @ traffic lights into Hartburn Lane. Hotel on the left about 0.75 miles.

Room
General

ALNMOUTH, Northumberland Map ref 5C1
SAT NAV NE66 2RA

B&B PER ROOM PER NIGHT
S £35.00 – £55.00
D £65.00 – £80.00

The Saddle Bed and Breakfast
24-25 Northumberland Street, Alnmouth NE66 2RA
t (01665) 830476 e thesaddlebedandbreakfast@hotmail.com
w **thesaddlebedandbreakfast.co.uk** ONLINE MAP GUEST REVIEWS ONLINE BOOKING LAST MINUTE OFFERS

The Saddle is a small family-run Bed & Breakfast offering cosy accommodation and delicious home-cooked Sunday lunches, in on of the most delightful villages in the heart of beautiful Northumbrian countryside. **directions** In the centre of Alnmouth o the right hand side of the main street just before the church, parking to the rear of hotel **open** All year **bedrooms** 1 single, 3 double, 3 twin, 1 family **bathrooms** 8 en suite, 8 with private bathroom **payment** credit/debit cards, cash, cheques

Room   General   Leisure

North East | Northumberland

ALNMOUTH, Northumberland Map ref 5C1
SAT NAV NE66 3NN

enjoyEngland.com ★★★★ BED & BREAKFAST
enjoyEngland.com Silver Award

B&B PER ROOM PER NIGHT
D £70.00 – £80.00

Beech Lodge
8 Alnwood, Alnmouth NE66 3NN
t (01665) 830709 e beechlodge@hotmail.com
w beechlodge.net ONLINE MAP GUEST REVIEWS

A warm and friendly welcome awaits guests at our spacious, detached, modern bungalow in a quiet woodland setting, close to village shops, pubs and restaurants. Our en suite rooms are decorated and furnished to a high and modern standard. An ideal base for exploring all the wonderful coast and countryside.

open All year except Xmas and New Year
bedrooms 1 double, 1 suite
bathrooms 1 en suite, 1 with private bathroom
payment cash, cheques

directions Take A1068 from Alnwick, to Hipsburn. Take B1338 to Alnmouth, cross bridge, turn right into Alnwood. Last bungalow on left is Beech Lodge.

Room General

ALNWICK, Northumberland Map ref 5C1
SAT NAV NE66 2HJ

enjoyEngland.com ★★★ GUEST ACCOMMODATION

B&B PER ROOM PER NIGHT
S £45.00
D £65.00 – £110.00
EVENING MEAL PER PERSON
£15.00 – £30.00

SPECIAL PROMOTIONS
Stay Mon-Thu get Thursday Half Price. Stay Fri & Sat get Sunday Half Price, Ex Bk Hols Adaptable family rooms.

Alnwick Lodge
West Cawledge Park, Alnwick NE66 2HJ
t (01665) 604363 (01665) 603377 e bookings@alnwicklodge.com
w alnwicklodge.com ONLINE MAP ONLINE BOOKING

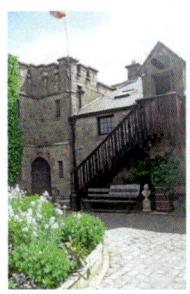

A unique creation AD1650-2007. Alnwick Lodge at West Cawledge Park a combination of history rural charm with an air of sophistication, whilst linked to technology. Fascinating, incomparable accommodation in beautiful Northumberland, 1.5 miles south of Alnwick (A1). For business or pleasure, conferences, functions, parties. Antique galleries, log fires.

open All year
bedrooms 3 single, 6 double, 2 twin, 4 family
bathrooms 15 en suite
payment credit/debit cards, cash, cheques

directions 1 mile south of Alnwick. Direct access from A1 (trunk road) highway signposted to West Cawledge Park (chair on the roof).

BREAKFAST AWARD

Room
General
Leisure

---

or **key to symbols** see page 6

675

North East | Northumberland

ALNWICK, Northumberland Map ref 5C1
SAT NAV NE66 1XU

Greycroft
Croft Place, Alnwick, Northumberland NE66 1XU
t (01665) 602127 e greycroftalnwick@aol.com
w **greycroftalnwick.co.uk** ONLINE MAP GUEST REVIEWS ONLINE BOOKING

B&B PER ROOM PER NIGHT
S £55.00 – £60.00
D £85.00 – £115.00

SPECIAL PROMOTIONS
Stay 3 nights or more and save £5 per person per night off Friday/Saturday rates.

A warm welcome awaits you at Greycroft, a delightful 6 bedroom Victorian guesthouse offering quality guest accommodation. Tastefully furnished. Large walled garden. Guest parking in private road. Conservation area. Two minute walk to Alnwick town centre and a short stroll to Alnwick Castle, The Garden and local amenities.

open All year except Xmas
bedrooms 1 single, 3 double, 1 twin, 1 family
bathrooms 6 en suite
payment credit/debit cards, cash, cheques

directions Opposite the Police Station (very reassuring) off Prudhoe Street.

Room   General   Leisure

ALNWICK, Northumberland Map ref 5C1
SAT NAV NE66 3PG

Hawkhill Farmhouse
Hawkhill, Alnwick, Northumberland NE66 3PG
t (01665) 830380 e stay@hawkhillfarmhouse.com
w **hawkhillfarmhouse.com**

B&B PER ROOM PER NIGHT
S £45.00 – £50.00
D £75.00 – £80.00

Relax in our spacious farmhouse with specactular views. Midway Alnwick and Alnmouth. Secluded parking. Large grounds. Visit Alnwick Castle and Garden, the Farne Islands and Lindisfarne, golf walk, bird watch. **directions** Hawkhill Farmhouse is off the A1068, miles east from Alnwick and the A1 and approx 1.5 miles from Alnmouth rail station. **open** All year except Xmas **bedrooms** 1 double, 2 twin **bathrooms** 3 en suite **payment** cash, cheques

Room   General

ALNWICK, Northumberland Map ref 5C1
SAT NAV NE66 2AJ

Reighamsyde
Alnwick Moor, Alnwick NE66 2AJ
t (01665) 602535 f (01665) 603387 e reighamsyde@aol.com

B&B PER ROOM PER NIGHT
S £40.00 – £60.00
D £55.00 – £70.00

Large detached house within half an acre of beautiful gardens on outskirts of Alnwick with excellent views. 1 min drive from town centre with plenty private off road parking. **directions** From town centre take road to Rothbury at the top of the hill the road levels out we are on the right after phone box. **open** April to October **bedrooms** 2 double, 1 twin **bathrooms** 3 en suite **payment** cash, cheques

Room   General   Leisure

676   Official tourist board guide Bed & Breakfast

North East | Northumberland

ALNWICK, Northumberland Map ref 5C1
SAT NAV NE66 3RX

enjoyEngland.com ★★★★ INN

B&B PER ROOM PER NIGHT
S £45.00
D £75.00 – £95.00

SPECIAL PROMOTIONS
Winter offers 2 nights or more get dinner bed and breakfast for price of bed and breakfast.

Masons Arms Country Inn
Stamford, Rennington, Alnwick NE66 3RX
t (01665) 577275 f (01665) 577894 e bookings@masonsarms.net
w masonsarms.net

A traditional family run country inn, full of period features. Log burning stove in main bar. Local real ales, a good selection of wine and malt whiskies and good, fresh food. Comfortable en suite accommodation. Well positioned for Alnwick and the coast. Licenced for small intimate weddings.

open All year
bedrooms 1 single, 9 double, 2 twin, 1 family, 2 suites
bathrooms 15 en suite
payment credit/debit cards, cash

directions From A1 turn on to B1340 and keep going for approx 4 miles past Rennington.

Room
General
Leisure

AMBLE, Northumberland Map ref 5C1
SAT NAV NE65 0AL

enjoyEngland.com ★★★ GUEST HOUSE

B&B PER ROOM PER NIGHT
S £30.00 – £35.00
D £55.00 – £60.00

Amble Guesthouse
16 Leazes Street, Amble NE65 0AL
t (01665) 714661 e stephmclaughlin@aol.com
w ambleguesthouse.co.uk

A family run 4 bedroom guest house. All rooms en-suite. In picturesque fishing port of Amble. Ten+ golf courses within twelve mile radius. **directions** From main A1 follow signposts to Amble. Will supply more concise details on request by e-mail or phone. **open** All year except Xmas and New Year **bedrooms** 1 single, 1 double, 1 twin, 1 family **bathrooms** 4 en suite **payment** credit/debit cards, cash, cheques

Room   General   Leisure

AMBLE, Northumberland Map ref 5C1
SAT NAV NE65 0AA

enjoyEngland.com ★★★ GUEST HOUSE

B&B PER ROOM PER NIGHT
S £30.00
D £60.00 – £90.00

Harbour Guest House
24 Leazes Street, Amble NE65 0AA
t (01665) 710331 e info@ambleharbourguesthouse.co.uk
w ambleharbourguesthouse.co.uk ONLINE MAP GUEST REVIEWS LAST MINUTE OFFERS

Harbour Guest House is situated next to the harbour within the picturesque coastal town of Amble, all bedrooms ensuite offering comfort and privacy. Local amenities three minutes walk away. **directions** On arrival in Amble follow signs for the harbour which leads you directly to our location. **bedrooms** 1 single, 2 double, 2 twin, 1 family **bathrooms** 6 en suite **payment** credit/debit cards, cash, cheques

Room   General   Leisure

677

North East | Northumberland

BEAL, Northumberland Map ref 5B1
SAT NAV TD15 2PB

B&B PER ROOM PER NIGHT
S £35.00 – £45.00
D £65.00 – £75.00

Brock Mill Farmhouse
Brock Mill, Beal, Berwick-upon-Tweed TD15 2PB
t (01289) 381283 f (01289) 381283 e brockmillfarmhouse@btinternet.com
w holyislandaccommodation.com ONLINE BOOKING

Working farm. Peaceful surroundings. Ideal for touring North Northumberland and Scottish Borders. Quality accommodation with En-suite/suite and private bathrooms new for 2010. Superb English breakfasts or tasty vegetarian alternatives. **directions** About 1.5 miles from A1 at Beal on the Holy Island road. **open** All year except Xmas **bedrooms** 1 single, 1 double, 1 twin, 1 family **bathrooms** 2 en suite, 1 with private bathroom **payment** credit/debit cards, cash, cheques, euros

BERWICK-UPON-TWEED, Northumberland Map ref 5B1
SAT NAV TD15 1DU

B&B PER ROOM PER NIGHT
S £35.00 – £45.00
D £60.00 – £70.00

Alannah House
84 Church Street, Berwick upon Tweed TD15 1DU
t (01289) 307252 e steven@berwick1234.freeserve.co.uk
w alannahhouse.com

Georgian town house, originally married quarters of historic barracks. Situated in town centre with walled garden and residential parking. Close to all amenities. **directions** Enter Berwick town centre, head for town hall turn immediately left behind the hall, 400yds on the right past the police station. **open** All year **bedrooms** 1 double, 1 twin, 1 family **bathrooms** 3 en suite **payment** cash, cheques

BERWICK-UPON-TWEED, Northumberland Map ref 5B1
SAT NAV TD15 1AS

B&B PER ROOM PER NIGHT
S £27.50 – £35.00
D £55.00 – £70.00

Clovelly House
58 West Street, Berwick-upon-Tweed TD15 1AS
t (01289) 302337 e vivroc@clovelly53.freeserve.co.uk
w clovelly53.freeserve.co.uk ONLINE MAP

Clovelly is a centrally situated town house minutes from golf courses and riverside walks, Elizabethan walls, restaurants, shops and Maltings art centre. A high standard of accommodation is offered with many thoughtful little extras and a delicious multi-choice breakfast. Near to Holy Island, Northumberland coast and Border Country.

open All year except Xmas
bedrooms 1 single, 1 double, 1 twin
bathrooms 2 en suite, 1 with private bathroom
payment cash, cheques

directions Clovelly House is situated off the Main Street of Marygate opposite Boots on a small cobbled street running down to the old bridge and river

BREAKFAST AWARD

678 Official tourist board guide Bed & Breakfast

North East | Northumberland

BERWICK-UPON-TWEED, Northumberland   Map ref 5B1
SAT NAV TD15 1PW

Dervaig Guest House
1 North Road, Berwick-upon-Tweed TD15 1PW
t (01289) 302267   **e** jgilmour123@btinternet.com
w dervaigguesthouse.co.uk   LAST MINUTE OFFERS

RATING APPLIED FOR

B&B PER ROOM PER NIGHT
S £30.00 – £35.00
D £60.00 – £75.00

Detached Victorian house in private grounds offering comfortable accommodation. Off road parking & walled gardens. All rooms spacious with en-suite, flat screen TVs & goose & duck down quilts.
directions From all directions enter from North of town. Exit at Morrisons roundabout signposted for town centre. We are 1/2 mile from roundabout. **open** All year **bedrooms** 1 double, 1 twin, 1 family **bathrooms** 3 en suite **payment** cash

Room   General

BERWICK-UPON-TWEED, Northumberland   Map ref 5B1
SAT NAV TD15 2PL

Fenham Farm Coastal Bed & Breakfast
Beal, Berwick-upon-Tweed TD15 2PL
t (01289) 381245   **e** stay@fenhamfarm.co.uk
w fenhamfarm.co.uk   ONLINE MAP   LAST MINUTE OFFERS

GUEST ACCOMMODATION   **Silver AWARD**

B&B PER ROOM PER NIGHT
S £40.00 – £60.00
D £70.00 – £90.00

SPECIAL PROMOTIONS
Special rates for stays of longer than 2 nights. Please contact us for details.

Quality Bed & Breakfast accommodation in converted farm outbuildings on a beautiful coastal spot overlooking the Holy Island of Lindisfarne. 5 en suite bedrooms created with fastidious attention to detail. An ideal base for walkers, cyclists and nature lovers. On St Cuthbert's and St Oswald's Way and Coastal Cycle Route.

open February until November
bedrooms 2 double, 3 twin
bathrooms 5 en suite
payment credit/debit cards, cash, cheques

directions Fenham Farm is on the coast approximately 1.5 miles off the A1, 10 miles south of Berwick upon Tweed and 6 miles north of Belford.

Room
General
Leisure

WALKERS   CYCLISTS

BERWICK-UPON-TWEED, Northumberland   Map ref 5B1
SAT NAV TD15 2XQ

Longridge Towers School
Berwick-upon-Tweed, Northumberland TD15 2XQ
t (01289) 307584   **e** sfleming@lts.org.uk

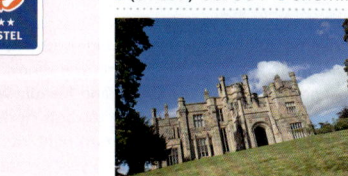

HOSTEL

Longridge Towers is a Victorian building set in 80 acres of beautiful grounds, within easy access of countryside and the coast, ideal group accommodation with excellent indoor and outdoor facilities. **directions** A1 North follow signs for Berwick, at first roundabout go straight on, at next turn left (A698) approx 2 miles, left at Longridge Towers sign. **open** Open Easter and Summer **bedrooms** 11 single, 13 twin **bathrooms** 5 en suite, 2 with private bathroom **payment** cash, cheques

Leisure

WALKERS   CYCLISTS

or key to symbols see page 6

North East | **Northumberland**

BERWICK-UPON-TWEED, Northumberland Map ref 5B1 — SAT NAV TD15 1RP

Marlborough House
133 Main Street, Spittal, Berwick-upon-Tweed, Nortrhumberland TD15 1RP
t (01289) 305293   e seaside133@onetel.com
w marlboroughhouse.info ONLINE MAP GUEST REVIEWS

B&B PER ROOM PER NIGHT
S £40.00 – £45.00
D £60.00 – £70.00

Early Victorian townhouse in stunning seafront setting, overlooking the promenade and beach. Spacious ensuite accommodation, private off road parking. Convenient for public transport, cyclists and walkers welcome. Family rates available. **directions** From North: take A1 Berwick bypass, follow signs for Spittal. From South take 2nd. exit off 1st. roundabout, follow signs for Spittal. Complimentary pickup available. **open** Easter to end of October **bedrooms** 1 family **bathrooms** 1 en suite **payment** cash, cheques

BERWICK-UPON-TWEED, Northumberland Map ref 5B1 — SAT NAV TD15 1UB

Meadow Hill Guest House
Duns Road, Berwick-upon-Tweed TD15 1UB
t (01289) 306325   e christineabart@aol.com
w meadow-hill.co.uk ONLINE MAP ONLINE BOOKING LAST MINUTE OFFERS

B&B PER ROOM PER NIGHT
S £40.00
D £70.00

Family run with spectacular coastal and country views. Comfortable lounge and home-cooked meals. All rooms en suite with tea/coffee facilities. Disabled facilities. Children and pets welcome. **directions** Please contact us for directions **open** All year **bedrooms** 2 double, 2 twin, 1 family **bathrooms** 5 en suite **payment** credit/debit cards, cash, cheques

BERWICK-UPON-TWEED, Northumberland Map ref 5B1 — SAT NAV TD15 2BE

Rob Roy
Dock Road, Tweedmouth, Berwick-upon-Tweed, Northumberland TD15 2BE
t 01289 306428   f 01289 306428   e therobroy@hotmail.co.uk
w robroyberwick.co.uk ONLINE MAP GUEST REVIEWS LAST MINUTE OFFERS

B&B PER ROOM PER NIGHT
S £45.00 – £55.00
D £65.00 – £75.00
EVENING MEAL PER PERSON
£25.00 – £50.00

The Rob Roy proprietors Linda and Ian Woods who have 20 years experience in hospitality welcome you. Set at the mouth of the River Tweed and close to town centre. **directions** Please contact us for directions **open** All year except Xmas **bedrooms** 3 double, 1 twin, 1 family **bathrooms** 5 en suite **payment** credit/debit cards, cash, cheques

CORBRIDGE, Northumberland Map ref 5B2 — SAT NAV NE45 5LW

2 The Crofts
Newcastle Road, Corbridge, Hexham NE45 5LW
t (01434) 633046   e welcome@2thecrofts.co.uk
w 2thecrofts.co.uk GUEST REVIEWS ONLINE BOOKING LAST MINUTE OFFERS

B&B PER ROOM PER NIGHT
S £40.00 – £50.00
D £62.00 – £70.00

Large Victorian terrace on edge of Corbridge with one large double and one twin room, both with en suite shower rooms. Aga-cooked breakfasts, good facilities, quiet position and friendly welcome. **directions** Take the A69 from Newcastle towards Hexham, then the B6530 towards Corbridge. After 2 miles, turn right into The Crofts immediately before the bus stop. **open** All year except Xmas and New Year **bedrooms** 1 double, 1 twin **bathrooms** 2 en suite **payment** cash, cheques

North East | **Northumberland**

CORBRIDGE, Northumberland Map ref 5B2
SAT NAV NE45 5AY

Fellcroft
Station Road, Corbridge NE45 5AY
t (01434) 632384 **e** tove.brown@ukonline.co.uk
w fellcroftbandb.com

B&B PER ROOM PER NIGHT
S £40.00
D £60.00

EVENING MEAL PER PERSON
£15.00

Well-appointed, stone-built Edwardian house with full, private facilities. Quiet country setting, 0.5 miles south of market square. Non-smokers only. Family room (three-four sharing) £70.00. Good for walkers and cyclists. Close public transport. **directions** Southside of village. Follow sign for railway station. **open** All year except Xmas and New Year **bedrooms** 1 twin, 1 family **bathrooms** 1 en suite, 1 with private bathroom **payment** cash, cheques

CORBRIDGE, Northumberland Map ref 5B2
SAT NAV NE45 5LP

The Hayes
Newcastle Road, Corbridge NE45 5LP
t (01434) 632010 **e** camon@onebillinternet.co.uk
w hayes-corbridge.co.uk

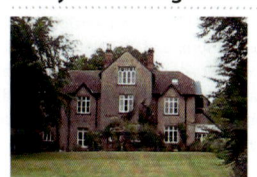

B&B PER ROOM PER NIGHT
S £33.00 – £46.00
D £68.00 – £72.00

Fine country house in lovely setting in historic Corbridge providing family-run well-appointed accommodation. Easy access to Hadrian's Wall, A68 and A69 and Northumbria countryside. **directions** From east: leave A69 at Styford roundabout follow road into Corbridge for 2 mls. From west: pass petrol station, then up hill 0.25mls. **open** All year except Xmas and New Year **bedrooms** 1 single, 1 twin, 2 family **bathrooms** 2 en suite, 2 with private bathroom **payment** credit/debit cards, cash, cheques, euros

CORNHILL-ON-TWEED, Northumberland Map ref 5B1
SAT NAV TD12 4TR

Hay Farm House
Ford and Etal Country Estate, Nr Berwick upon Tweed TD12 4TR
t (01890) 820647 **e** tinahayfarm@tiscali.co.uk
w hayfarm.co.uk ONLINE MAP GUEST REVIEWS ONLINE BOOKING LAST MINUTE OFFERS

B&B PER ROOM PER NIGHT
D £70.00 – £75.00

EVENING MEAL PER PERSON
£16.50 – £19.50

SPECIAL PROMOTIONS
3 for 2 nights bed and breakfast during February, March and April. Based on 2 people sharing. Excluding Easter.

With spectacular views we offer peace, tranquility, comfort, relaxation along with excellent food and surroundings. Close to Berwick upon Tweed midway between vibrant Newcastle upon Tyne and historic Edinburgh. Ideal location for the many attractions of the splendid 'Secret Kingdom' of North Northumberland and the wonderful Scottish Borders.

open February to Mid November
bedrooms 3 double, 1 twin
bathrooms 3 en suite, 1 with private bathroom
payment credit/debit cards, cash, cheques

directions Situated just off the B6354 between Ford and Heatherslaw. Follow the tourist signs to 'Ford and Etal' from the A1 or A697.

BREAKFAST AWARD

North East | **Northumberland**

EAST ORD, Northumberland Map ref 5B1
SAT NAV TD15 2NS

Fairholm
East Ord, Berwick-upon-Tweed TD15 2NS
t (01289) 305370 e bethiawelsh@ukonline.co.uk
w welcometofairholm.com GUEST REVIEWS

B&B PER ROOM PER NIGHT
S £25.00 – £30.00
D £50.00 – £55.00
EVENING MEAL PER PERSON
£8.00 – £10.00

A warm welcome awaits you in this beautiful peaceful village 1.5 miles from Berwick. Cosy bungalow with all facilities and private garden. Close to riverside walk, village pub, garden centre. **directions** Exit into village half way down the Berwick by pass. Very easy to find. **open** All year except Xmas and New Year **bedrooms** 1 double, 1 twin **bathrooms** 1 en suite, 1 with private bathroom **payment** cash, cheques

Room General Leisure

GILSLAND, Northumberland Map ref 5B2
SAT NAV CA8 7DA

Brookside Villa B&B
Gilsland, Brampton CA8 7DA
t (016977) 47300 e brooksidevilla@hotmail.co.uk
w brooksidevilla.com ONLINE MAP GUEST REVIEWS ONLINE BOOKING LAST MINUTE OFFERS

B&B PER ROOM PER NIGHT
S £52.00 – £58.00
D £37.50 – £42.00
EVENING MEAL PER PERSON
£13.50 – £20.00

Brookside Villa B&B at the heart of Hadrian's Wall Country, on the border of Cumbria and the Northumberland National Park. Stylish rooms, excellent service & hospitality, renowned evening meals, honesty bar, local ales. **directions** B6318 west of Gilsland Village. **open** All year **bedrooms** 2 double, 2 twin **bathrooms** 4 en suite **payment** credit/debit cards, cash, cheques, euros

Room General Leisure

GILSLAND, Northumberland Map ref 5B2
SAT NAV CA8 7DA

Tantallon House
Gilsland, Cumbria CA8 7DA
t (016977) 47111 e info@tantallonhouse.co.uk
w tantallonhouse.co.uk ONLINE MAP GUEST REVIEWS

B&B PER ROOM PER NIGHT
S £50.00
D £76.00 – £80.00

A spacious Victorian country house overlooking the longest unbroken stretch of Hadrian's Wall. Three of our four twin/double rooms are south-facing with spectacular views. All have Wi-Fi. **directions** At Bridge Inn pub in Gilsland, take road signposted Birdoswald, take the next left signed for Birdoswald. Tantallon House is 200m on right hand side. **open** All year except Xmas and New Year **bedrooms** 1 double, 3 twin **bathrooms** 2 en suite, 2 with private bathroom **payment** cash, cheques

Room General Leisure

GREENHEAD, Northumberland Map ref 5B2
SAT NAV CA8 7HY

Holmhead Guest House
Holmhead, Hadrian's Wall, Greenhead, Northumberland CA8 7HY
t 016977 47402 e holmhead@forestbarn.com
w bandbhadrianswall.com GUEST REVIEWS ONLINE BOOKING LAST MINUTE OFFERS

B&B PER ROOM PER NIGHT
S £41.00 – £47.50
D £62.00 – £75.00

Built 1800 with Hadrian's Wall stone. Quiet location next to river with beautiful views. Directly on Hadrian's Wall path and Pennine Way. Self catering and camping barn facilities also available. **directions** Greenhead is off the A69, 3 miles west of Haltwhistle. Take lane by tearoom, after 100m turn right and cross bridge. Holmhead is about 1km. **open** All year except Xmas and New Year **bedrooms** 2 double, 2 twin **bathrooms** 4 en suite **payment** credit/debit cards, cash, cheques, euros

Room General Leisure

682 Official tourist board guide Bed & Breakfast

North East | **Northumberland**

HALTWHISTLE, Northumberland Map ref 5B2 — SAT NAV CA8 7HN

enjoyEngland.com
★★★
BED & BREAKFAST

B&B PER ROOM PER NIGHT
S £38.00 – £40.00
D £34.00

Four Wynds Guest House
Longbyre, Greenhead, Nr Haltwhistle, Northumberland CA8 7HN
t (01697) 747972 **e** info@four-wynds-guest-house.co.uk
w four-wynds-guest-house.co.uk ONLINE MAP GUEST REVIEWS ONLINE BOOKING LAST MINUTE OFFERS

Comfort, friendly hospitality, splendid breakfasts and assistance with holiday planning, all await you at Four Wynds. Here in the Heart of Hadrian's Wall country, we have activities, attractions and tranquility. **directions** Situated on the B6318 between Greenhead and Gilsland **open** All year except Xmas **bedrooms** 1 double, 1 twin, 1 family **bathrooms** 3 en suite **payment** credit/debit cards, cash, cheques, euros

Room · General · Leisure

HALTWHISTLE, Northumberland Map ref 5B2 — SAT NAV NE49 9ND

enjoyEngland.com
★★★
BED & BREAKFAST

B&B PER ROOM PER NIGHT
S £65.00 – £105.00
D £70.00 – £140.00
EVENING MEAL PER PERSON
£25.00 – £35.00

Glendale Mews
North Road, Haltwhistle NE49 9ND
t (01434) 320711 **e** philip@glendaleleisure.co.uk
w glendaleleisure.co.uk ONLINE MAP ONLINE BOOKING LAST MINUTE OFFERS

Glendale Mews and cottage are private and secluded, yet offering access to a range of facilities and Hadrian's Wall. The owners are known for the hospitality on offer and the respect for the privacy of their guests. The Mews and Cottage give independence with added on site management support.

open All year
bedrooms 1 twin
bathrooms 1 en suite
payment cash, cheques, euros

directions Please contact us for directions

Room
General
Leisure

HALTWHISTLE, Northumberland Map ref 5B2 — SAT NAV NE49 0AZ

enjoyEngland.com
★★★★
BED & BREAKFAST

B&B PER ROOM PER NIGHT
S £32.00
D £64.00

Hall Meadows
Main Street, Haltwhistle NE49 0AZ
t (01434) 321021 **f** (01434) 321021 **e** richardhumes@tiscali.co.uk
w hallmeadows.co.uk ONLINE MAP GUEST REVIEWS

Built in 1888, a large family house with pleasant garden in the centre of town. Ideally placed for Hadrian's Wall, close to bus and rail connections. A warm welcome awaits. **directions** We are situated in the centre of Haltwhistle, with easy access to all public transport links and major highways. **open** All year except Xmas and New Year **bedrooms** 2 double, 1 twin **bathrooms** 2 en suite **payment** cash, cheques

Room · General · Leisure

key to symbols see page 6   683

North East | Northumberland

HAYDON BRIDGE, Northumberland Map ref 5B2
SAT NAV NE47 6NQ

Grindon Cartshed
Grindon Cartshed, Haydon Bridge, Hexham NE47 6NQ
t (01434) 684273 e cartshed@grindon.force9.co.uk
w grindon-cartshed.co.uk ONLINE MAP GUEST REVIEWS ONLINE BOOKING LAST MINUTE OFFERS

B&B PER ROOM PER NIGHT
S £40.00 – £49.00
D £75.00 – £85.00
EVENING MEAL PER PERSON
£20.00 – £22.00

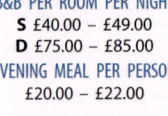

A warm welcome awaits at the beautifully converted cartshed, within walking distance of Hadrian's Wall. Ideal location for touring. Licensed and offering delicious meals prepared from local produce. **directions** Four miles north of Haydon Bridge, 3 miles east of Housesteads, 7 miles west of Chollerford. **open** All year **bedrooms** 1 double, 2 twin **bathrooms** 3 en suite **payment** credit/debit cards, cash, cheques

HAYDON BRIDGE, Northumberland Map ref 5B2
SAT NAV NE47 6BJ

Shaftoe's Guest House
4 Shaftoe Street, Haydon Bridge NE47 6BJ
t (01434) 684664 e bookings@shaftoes.co.uk
w shaftoes.co.uk GUEST REVIEWS ONLINE BOOKING

B&B PER ROOM PER NIGHT
S £49.00 – £65.00
D £70.00 – £100.00

This charming Guest House is located in the heart of Haydon Bridge on the River Tyne. The accommodation provides 21st Century luxury in an idyllic rural setting. **directions** From West on A69 go over bridge. Take first right after bridge. From East on A69 take first left before bridge. Shaftoe's is on right. **open** All year except Xmas **bedrooms** 5 double, 2 twin **bathrooms** 7 en suite **payment** credit/debit cards, cash, cheques

HEDDON-ON-THE-WALL, Northumberland Map ref 5B2
SAT NAV NE15 0EZ

Houghton North Farm Visitor Accommodation
Houghton North Farm, Heddon-on-the-Wall, Northumberland NE15 0EZ
t (01661) 854364 f (01661) 854364 e wjlaws@btconnect.com
w hadrianswallaccommodation.com ONLINE MAP GUEST REVIEWS

B&B PER ROOM PER NIGHT
S £25.00 – £30.00

Comfortable, attractive, luxurious and spacious accommodation in converted barn setting. Bunk-style rooms, some en suite. Self-catering kitchen, luxurious lounge, courtyard. Internet, laundry, parking. Ideally situated on Hadrian's Wall. **directions** Please contact us for directions **open** All year except Xmas and New Year **bedrooms** 1 double, 1 twin **bathrooms** 2 en suite **payment** credit, debit cards, cash, cheques

HEXHAM, Northumberland Map ref 5B2
SAT NAV NE48 3AQ

Hall Barns B&B
Hexham North Road, Simonburn NE48 3AQ
t 01434 681419 e enquiries@hallbarns-simonburn.co.uk
w hallbarns-simonburn.co.uk ONLINE MAP GUEST REVIEWS ONLINE BOOKING LAST MINUTE OFFERS

B&B PER ROOM PER NIGHT
S £50.00 – £70.00
D £70.00 – £90.00
EVENING MEAL PER PERSON
£15.00 – £20.00

Tranquil setting with scenic views near Hadrian's Wall, National Park and historic Corbridge. Garden to relax in and enjoy sunsets or barbecue. Comfortable lounge, log fire, ensuite rooms, hearty breakfast. **directions** From Hexham A6079 Low Brunton crossroads left B6320 4 miles left into Simonburn. **open** All year **bedrooms** 1 double, 2 twin, 1 family **bathrooms** 3 en suite, 1 with private bathroom **payment** cash, cheques

North East | **Northumberland**

HEXHAM, Northumberland Map ref 5B2
SAT NAV NE46 1RS

Loughbrow House
Dipton Mill Road, Hexham NE46 1RS
t (01434) 603351 **e** patriciaclark351@bt.com
w loughbrow.fsnet.co.uk

B&B PER ROOM PER NIGHT
S £40.00 – £45.00
D £80.00 – £90.00

A mansion house built in 1780 set in 9 acres of garden, surrounded by own farm land looking up the North Tyne valley. Situated 1 mile from Hexham. Ample parking. **directions** From Hexham take B6306. After 0.25 miles take right-hand fork, Dipton Mill Road, for further 0.25 miles. Turn into drive gates, house is 0.5 miles. **open** All year except Xmas and New Year **bedrooms** 2 single, 2 double, 2 twin **bathrooms** 3 en suite, 2 with private bathroom **payment** cash, cheques

Room | General | P | Leisure

HEXHAM, Northumberland Map ref 5B2
SAT NAV NE46 1TT

Travellers Rest
Slaley, Hexham, Northumberland NE46 1TT
t (01434) 673231 **f** (01434) 673906 **e** info@travellersrestslaley.com
w travellersrestslaley.com   ONLINE MAP   GUEST REVIEWS   ONLINE BOOKING

B&B PER ROOM PER NIGHT
S £39.00 – £45.00
D £60.00 – £70.00

EVENING MEAL PER PERSON
£10.50 – £16.50

The Travellers Rest offers a warm welcome and high standards of hospitality to all. Fine food and drink can be enjoyed in the bar or in our cosy restaurant and we are open all day.

open All year
bedrooms 2 double, 1 twin
bathrooms 3 en suite
payment credit/debit cards, cash, cheques

directions Please contact us for directions

Room | General | Leisure

INGRAM, Northumberland Map ref 5B1
SAT NAV NE66 4LT

Ingram House
Ingram, Alnwick NE66 4LT
t (01665) 578906 **e** jane_levien@hotmail.com
w ingram-house.com

B&B PER ROOM PER NIGHT
S £40.00 – £50.00
D £60.00 – £70.00

An 18th century farmhouse in the National Park. Hills and beaches easily accessible. Comfortable rooms, and breakfast in family kitchen/dining room. Garden produce, locally sourced food and a warm welcome. **directions** Off A697 10 miles south of Wooler. Take Ingram turning, continue for 3 miles over wrought iron bridge. Follow road to first drive on right. **open** All year except Xmas and New Year **bedrooms** 1 double, 1 twin **bathrooms** 2 en suite **payment** cash, cheques

Room | General | P

North East | Northumberland

KIELDER, Northumberland Map ref 5B1
SAT NAV NE48 1EQ

Twenty Seven B&B and Self Catering Cottage
27 Castle Drive, Kielder NE48 1EQ
t (01284) 250366 **e** twentyseven@staykielder.co.uk
w staykielder.co.uk ONLINE MAP GUEST REVIEWS ONLINE BOOKING LAST MINUTE OFFERS

B&B PER ROOM PER NIGHT
S £38.00 – £45.00
D £76.00

EVENING MEAL PER PERSON
£6.50 – £15.00

Great base to explore Kielder Water & Forest Park. Stay Kielder for home from home comfort. Centrally heated. Delicious breakfasts. Lounge. Laundry. Bike storage. Cyclists, walkers, children & dogs welcome. **directions** See the directions page on our website www.StayKielder.co.uk. or telephone us for a printed copy. **open** All year **bedrooms** 1 family **bathrooms** 1 en suite **payment** cash, cheques

KIELDER WATER, Northumberland Map ref 5B2
SAT NAV NE48 1DD

The Pheasant Inn (by Kielder Water)
Stannersburn, Falstone NE48 1DD
t (01434) 240382 **f** (01434) 240382 **e** stay@thepheasantinn.com
w thepheasantinn.com ONLINE MAP LAST MINUTE OFFERS

B&B PER ROOM PER NIGHT
S £50.00 – £55.00
D £85.00 – £95.00

EVENING MEAL PER PERSON
£8.95 – £15.95

SPECIAL PROMOTIONS
Reduced rates 1 Nov–30 March, DB&B £65pppn.

Full of character and charm, the Pheasant Inn offers comfortable accommodation, a warm welcome and some of the very best home cooking the area has to offer. Set within the Northumberland National Park, the Inn is the perfect retreat where you can relax and enjoy your stay.

open November to March closed Mondays and Tuesdays
bedrooms 4 double, 3 twin, 1 family
bathrooms 8 en suite
payment credit/debit cards, cash, cheques

directions Leave A69 at Acomb junction and travel through Wall, Chollerford, Wark. Turn left over bridge at Bellingham. The establishment is 9 miles up the valley.

MORPETH, Northumberland Map ref 5C2
SAT NAV NE65 8TH

Kington
East Linden, Longhorsley NE65 8TH
t 01670 788554 **e** clivetaylor.services@tiscali.co.uk
w kington-longhorsley.com

B&B PER ROOM PER NIGHT
S £30.00 – £38.00
D £60.00 – £66.00

Kington offers guests extremely comfortable accommodation with their own private suite, a peaceful, rural location (though the A1 is only minutes away) and wonderful breakfasts in a relaxed, homely atmosphere. **directions** 5 miles north of Morpeth, 12 miles south of Alnwick, 1½ miles east of the village of Longhorsley. **open** All year **bedrooms** 1 suite **bathrooms** 1 with private bathroom **payment** cash, cheques

North East | **Northumberland**

NEWBROUGH, Northumberland Map ref 5B2
SAT NAV NE47 5EA

Carr Edge Farm
Newbrough, Hexham, Northumberland NE47 5EA
t (01434) 674788 e stay@carredge.co.uk
w carredge.co.uk

B&B PER ROOM PER NIGHT
S £45.00 – £50.00
D £68.00 – £90.00

Perfect location one mile south of Hadrians Wall, spectacular south facing views in our skilfully converted granary with upstairs guest lounge. We offer traditional farmhouse breakfasts using locally sourced produce. **directions** Leave the A69 follow B6319 to Newbrough. Take road up side of Red Lion. Travel 1½ miles take right fork over cattlegrid to Carr Edge. **open** All year **bedrooms** 1 double, 1 twin, 1 family **bathrooms** 3 en suite **payment** credit/debit cards, cash, cheques

Room   General   Leisure

NEWTON-ON-THE-MOOR, Northumberland Map ref 5C1
SAT NAV NE65 9JY

The Old School
Newton-on-the-Moor, Alnwick NE65 9JY
t (01665) 575717 e info@northumberlandbedandbreakfast.co.uk
w theoldschool.eu ONLINE MAP GUEST REVIEWS ONLINE BOOKING LAST MINUTE OFFERS

B&B PER ROOM PER NIGHT
D £75.00 – £105.00

SPECIAL PROMOTIONS
For 3 nights stay, please refer to the website.

2010 National Bed and Breakfast of the Year (Enjoy England) pictured on front of guide. 5 star Gold Award, 18th Century stone property, in the small conservation village of Newton-on-the-Moor. Near to The Alnwick Garden and Castle. Short walk to village inn, renowned for fine dining and bar meals.

bedrooms 4 double
bathrooms 4 en suite
payment credit/debit cards

directions Please see our website.

BREAKFAST AWARD

Room   General   Leisure

OTTERBURN, Northumberland Map ref 5B1
SAT NAV NE19 1NP

Butterchurn Guest House
Main Street, Otterburn NE19 1NP
t (01830) 520585 e valarieanderson@unicombox.co.uk
w butterchurnguesthouse.co.uk ONLINE MAP ONLINE BOOKING

B&B PER ROOM PER NIGHT
S £30.00 – £40.00
D £65.00 – £70.00

Excellent family-run guest-house, quiet village location, renowned for its welcome, high quality of service. Situated in Northumberland National Park, close to Hadrian's Wall, Kielder Water, Northumbria's coast&castles. **directions** Please refer to website. **open** All year **bedrooms** 4 double, 2 twin, 1 family **bathrooms** 7 en suite **payment** credit/debit cards, cash, cheques

Room   General   Leisure

For key to symbols see page 6

687

North East | Northumberland

POWBURN, Northumberland   Map ref 5B1
SAT NAV NE66 4JD

Low Hedgeley Farm
Powburn, Alnwick NE66 4JD
t (01665) 578815 **e** dianavickers@hotmail.com
w lowhedgeleyfarm.co.uk

B&B PER ROOM PER NIGHT
S £45.00
D £37.50

Grade II Listed farmhouse with extensive grounds. Situated in the Breamish Valley at the foot of the Cheviot Hills. Ideal base for visiting Cragside, and Alnwick Castle and Garden. **directions** Low Hedgeley is located one mile north of Powburn close to the A697 road. **open** All year except Xmas and New Year **bedrooms** 1 double, 1 twin **bathrooms** 1 en suite, 1 with private bathroom **payment** cash, cheques

ROTHBURY, Northumberland   Map ref 5B1
SAT NAV NE65 7TQ

Katerina's Guest House
Katerina's Guest House, Sun Buildings, Rothbury NE65 7TQ
t (01669) 620691 **e** cath@katerinasguesthouse.co.uk
w katerinasguesthouse.co.uk ONLINE BOOKING

B&B PER ROOM PER NIGHT
D £68.00 – £78.00

EVENING MEAL PER PERSON
£14.75 – £24.65

SPECIAL PROMOTIONS
Reduced rates for longer stays all year round.

Situated in lovely country village. Three beautiful en-suite 'fourposter' bedrooms, some with original stone fireplaces/beamed ceilings; all have fridge, TV, superbly stocked teatray (with home-made scones!) and many other little perks for your enjoyment. Central for Cragside, National Park and hills, Alnwick, coast, Hadrian's Wall and Scottish Borders.

open Open 12 months except for holidays and refurbishment.
bedrooms 3 double
bathrooms 3 en suite
payment credit/debit cards, cash, cheques, euros

directions Located in quiet position on Rothbury High Street, c.100 metres west of main shopping area.

BREAKFAST AWARD

SEAHOUSES, Northumberland   Map ref 5C1
SAT NAV NE68 7XW

Kingsway
19-21 King Street, Seahouses NE68 7XW
t (01665) 720621 **e** enquiries@kingsway-guesthouse.co.uk
w kingsway-guesthouse.co.uk ONLINE MAP GUEST REVIEWS

B&B PER ROOM PER NIGHT
D £60.00 – £65.00

1920's detached residence with off street parking, offering warm welcome. Luxury en-suite accommodation including residents conservatory/lounge. Village centre location. Harbour, restaurants and all amenities within 4 minutes walk. **directions** A1 leaving Alnwick bypass onto B1340 signposted Seahouses. On entering Seahouses, passing the golf club Kingsway is situated 300 metres further along on the right. **bedrooms** 2 double, 1 twin **bathrooms** 3 en suite **payment** cash

688   Official tourist board guide Bed & Breakfas

North East | **Northumberland**

SEAHOUSES, Northumberland Map ref 5C1
SAT NAV NE68 7UR

The Lookout Bunkhouse & Wigwams
Springhill Farm, Seahouses NE68 7UR
t (01665) 721820 **e** enquiries@springhill-farm.co.uk
w springhill-farm.co.uk ONLINE MAP GUEST REVIEWS ONLINE BOOKING LAST MINUTE OFFERS

B&B PER ROOM PER NIGHT
S £13.00 – £15.00
BED ONLY PER NIGHT
£10.00 – £12.00

SPECIAL PROMOTIONS
Groups over 12 receive 10% discount School and educationl group discount

The Lookout sleeps 32, located on the AONB Coastal Path and Cycle Route 1 with Seahouses and beach within one mile. The Bunkhouse is perfect for groups, families or independent travellers. Drying room, cycle store, internet, en suite rooms, breakfast/packed lunch upon request, laundry, TV/DVD/iPod dock, and sleeping bag/towel hire.

open All year
bathrooms 8 en suite
payment credit/debit cards, cash, cheques

directions 0.75miles from coastal road between Seahouses 1 mile and Bamburgh 3.5 miles. Market town of Alnwick is 15 miles, Berwick Upon Tweed 25 miles.

STOCKSFIELD, Northumberland Map ref 5B2
SAT NAV NE43 7PY

Locksley, Bed & Breakfast
45 Meadowfield Road, Stocksfield NE43 7PY
t (01661) 844778 **f** (01661) 844778 **e** josie@locksleybedandbreakfast.co.uk
w locksleybedandbreakfast.co.uk

B&B PER ROOM PER NIGHT
S £32.50
D £65.00

Situated in the Tyne Valley, welcoming B&B, large garden, local and home-grown produce served. Well-appointed rooms all en-suite with many extras. Two rooms suitable for guests with limited mobility. Storage and drying facilities for walkers, cyclists and fishermen. Please don't use SatNav if approaching from the West.

open Open all year except New Year
bedrooms 1 double, 1 twin, 1 family
bathrooms 3 en suite
payment credit/debit cards, cash, cheques

directions Leave A695 onto Cadehill Road, continue until road turns 90° left into Meadowfield Road. Over cross roads, Locksley on left quite a long way up.

For **key to symbols** see page 6

689

North East | Northumberland

WALL, Northumberland Map ref 5B2
SAT NAV NE46 4EE

The Hadrian
The Hadrian, Wall Village, Hexham NE46 4EE
t (01434) 681232 **e** david.lindsay13@btinternet.com
w hadrianhotel.com ONLINE MAP

B&B PER ROOM PER NIGHT
S £45.00 – £50.00
D £68.00 – £75.00
EVENING MEAL PER PERSON
£6.25 – £16.75

Attractive 18thC former coaching inn. Excellent bar meals, real ales, open fires and tranquil gardens. Situated close to Hadrian's Wall and near Hexham. **directions** Please contact us for directions **open** All year **bedrooms** 2 double, 4 twin **bathrooms** 4 en suite **payment** credit/debit cards, cash, cheques

Room General

WARK, Northumberland Map ref 5B2
SAT NAV NE48 3LS

The Battlesteads
Wark NE48 3LS
t (01434) 230209 **f** (01434) 230039 **e** info@battlesteads.com
w battlesteads.com ONLINE MAP ONLINE BOOKING LAST MINUTE OFFERS

B&B PER ROOM PER NIGHT
S £60.00
D £95.00 – £125.00
EVENING MEAL PER PERSON
£8.50 – £18.50

SPECIAL PROMOTIONS
Changing offers throughout the year. Please see website.

18thC Inn, formerly a farmhouse, in the heart of rural Northumberland, close to the Roman Wall and Kielder Water. An ideal centre for exploring Border country and for relaxing, walking or cycling. Ground-floor bedrooms available. Excellent restaurant using fresh, local produce. Five cask ales.

open All year
bedrooms 1 single, 7 double, 7 twin, 2 family
bathrooms 17 en suite
payment credit/debit cards, cash, cheques

directions Wark village is on the B6320, 10 miles north of Hexham from A69. Battlesteads is immediately to your left as you enter Wark.

Room General Leisure

WEST WOODBURN, Northumberland Map ref 5B2
SAT NAV NE48 2RX

Bay Horse Inn
The Bay Horse Inn, West Woodburn, Hexham NE48 2RX
t (01434) 270218 **e** enquiry@bayhorseinn.org
w bayhorseinn.org ONLINE BOOKING LAST MINUTE OFFERS

B&B PER ROOM PER NIGHT
S £50.00 – £53.00
D £84.00 – £90.00
EVENING MEAL PER PERSON
£7.95 – £15.00

An 18thC coaching inn nestling on the banks of the River Rede. Personally run, friendly locals. Super food using mostly local produce. Central for Hadrian's Wall, Kielder Water, border towns. **directions** On the side of the A68 scenic route from Corbridge to Scotland. **open** All year **bedrooms** 3 double, 2 twin **bathrooms** 5 en suite **payment** credit/debit cards, cash, cheques

Room General Leisure

690 Official tourist board guide Bed & Breakfast

North East | Northumberland/Tyne and Wear

WOOLER, Northumberland Map ref 5B1
SAT NAV NE71 6DN

Belmont House Bed & Breakfast
Belmont House, 15 Glendale Road, Wooler NE71 6DN
t (01668) 283769   e susan@belmonthouse.org
w belmonthouse.org   ONLINE MAP GUEST REVIEWS ONLINE BOOKING

B&B PER ROOM PER NIGHT
S £45.00 – £50.00
D £65.00 – £70.00

Large Victorian house now run as busy B&B. Wonderful breakfast - all locally sourced, packed lunches. Easy access to pubs, restaurants. **directions** Situated in area of outstanding natural beauty on edge of National Park in the foot of the Cheviot Hills. Easy access to the Heritage Coast **open** All year except Xmas **bedrooms** 1 double, 1 twin **bathrooms** 1 en suite, 1 with private bathroom **payment** cash, cheques

Room | General | Leisure

WOOLER, Northumberland Map ref 5B1
SAT NAV NE71 6EZ

East Horton House
East Horton Farm, Wooler, Northumberland NE71 6EZ
t (01668) 215216   e sed@hazelrigg.fsnet.co.uk
w farmhousebandb.co.uk   ONLINE MAP GUEST REVIEWS LAST MINUTE OFFERS

B&B PER ROOM PER NIGHT
S £40.00
D £70.00

Situated in the most historic and beautiful corner of Northumberland. Stunning views south down the valley towards Alnwick and west to the Cheviot-hills. Recently refurbished to a very high standard. **directions** Please contact us for directions **open** All year except Xmas and New Year **bedrooms** 2 double, 1 twin **bathrooms** 3 en suite **payment** cash, cheques

Room | General | Leisure

WOOLER, Northumberland Map ref 5B1
SAT NAV NE71 6RD

Firwood Country Bed and Breakfast
Middleton Hall, Wooler, Northumberland NE71 6RD
t (01668) 283699   e welcome@firwoodhouse.co.uk
w firwoodhouse.co.uk   ONLINE MAP GUEST REVIEWS

B&B PER ROOM PER NIGHT
D £90.00

Surrounded by stunning scenery, in elevated position, offering peace, tranquility and luxurious accommodation. The ideal centre for exploring Northumberland's countryside and coastline. A warm welcome and hearty breakfast awaits. **directions** From Wooler take Cheviot Street by the Anchor. Follow road until right hand turn to Earle and Middleton Hall. Continue for 1 mile. B&B on right **open** February through to end November **bedrooms** 2 double, 1 twin **bathrooms** 3 en suite **payment** credit/debit cards, cash, cheques

Room | General | Leisure

NEWCASTLE UPON TYNE, Tyne and Wear Map ref 5C2
SAT NAV NE15 8NL

The Keelman's Lodge
Grange Road, Newburn, Newcastle-Upon-Tyne NE15 8NL
t (0191) 2671689   f (01912) 677387   e admin@biglampbrewers.co.uk
w keelmanslodge.co.uk   ONLINE MAP ONLINE BOOKING

B&B PER ROOM PER NIGHT
S £52.45
D £75.40
EVENING MEAL PER PERSON
£5.00 – £15.00

Purpose built accommodation on the edge of the Tyne Riverside Country Park. Sharing its grounds are the Big Lamp Brewery and the Keelman Pub, selling good food and real ale. **directions** Grid reference NZ 160 655. Located close to Newburn Leisure Centre, next to Riverside Country Park. **open** All year **bedrooms** 8 double, 5 twin, 1 family **bathrooms** 14 en suite **payment** credit/debit cards, cash, cheques

Room | General | Leisure

North East | Tyne and Wear

RYTON, Tyne and Wear Map ref 5C2
SAT NAV NE21 4LR

Hedgefield House
Stella Road, Blaydon-on-Tyne NE21 4LR
t (01914) 137373 f (01914) 137373 e david@hedgefieldhouse.co.uk
w hedgefieldhouse.co.uk ONLINE MAP GUEST REVIEWS ONLINE BOOKING LAST MINUTE OFFERS

B&B PER ROOM PER NIGHT
S £25.00 – £60.00
D £55.00 – £90.00

SPECIAL PROMOTIONS
All rooms available as single per request. Weekend promotions on request.

Georgian residence in three acres of wooded gardens. Sauna and gym facilities. Peaceful, yet only minutes from Newcastle city centre, and near Hadrians Wall Trail, Gateshead MetroCentre and A1(M). A warm welcome guaranteed. Historical Link to Alexander Graham Bell.

open All year
bedrooms 3 single, 4 double, 3 twin, 2 family, 1 suite
bathrooms 5 en suite
payment credit/debit cards, cash, cheques

directions From A1(M) take A695 (Blaydon). From Blaydon centre take B6317 (Ryton and Newburn). 1 mile along B6317, on the left.

Room
General
Leisure

TYNEMOUTH, Tyne and Wear Map ref 5C2
SAT NAV NE30 4BX

Martineau Guest House
57 Front Street, Tynemouth, North Shields NE30 4BX
t (01912) 579038 e martineauhouse@gmail.com
w martineau-house.co.uk ONLINE BOOKING LAST MINUTE OFFERS

B&B PER ROOM PER NIGHT
D £70.00 – £90.00

Martineau Guest House is situated in the picturesque village of Tynemouth and is an ideal base for exploring the coastline and countryside of Northumbria or shopping in nearby Newcastle.
directions Off the A1058 turn right at the roundabout, follow the road along the seafront and onto Front Street to the right of the clock. **open** All year **bedrooms** 3 double, 1 twin **bathrooms** 4 en suite **payment** credit/debit cards

Room   General   Leisure

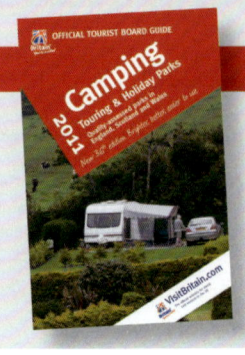

Do you like Camping?
You can also buy a copy of our popular guide 'Camping, Touring & Holiday Parks' including touring parks, camping holidays and holiday parks and villages in Britain 2011.

Now available in good bookshops and online at
visitbritainshop.com

£8.99

North East | Tyne and Wear/Co Durham

WHITLEY BAY, Tyne and Wear Map ref 5C2   SAT NAV NE26 1NX

Sunholme Guest House
53 North Parade, Whitley Bay NE26 1NX
t (01912) 511186   f 0191 2513489   e craw@hotmail.co.uk
w sunholme.co.uk   ONLINE MAP   GUEST REVIEWS

B&B PER ROOM PER NIGHT
S £30.00 – £60.00
D £60.00 – £50.00

SPECIAL PROMOTIONS
Weekend £30 for one night per person B&B £50.00 for two nights B&B

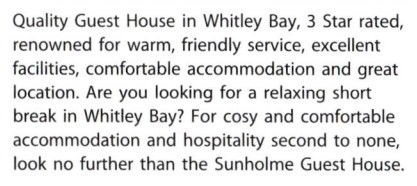

Quality Guest House in Whitley Bay, 3 Star rated, renowned for warm, friendly service, excellent facilities, comfortable accommodation and great location. Are you looking for a relaxing short break in Whitley Bay? For cosy and comfortable accommodation and hospitality second to none, look no further than the Sunholme Guest House.

open All year
bedrooms 2 double, 2 twin, 2 family
bathrooms 3 en suite
payment credit/debit cards, cash

directions www.multimap.com NE26 1NX

Room
General
Leisure

All Assessed Accommodation

Co Durham

BALDERSDALE

Blackton Grange ★★★★
Group Hostel
DL12 9UP
t (01833) 650629
e manager@blacktongrange.com
w blacktongrange.com

BARNARD CASTLE

The Ancient Manor House B&B
★★★ Bed & Breakfast
44 The Bank, Barnard Castle
DL12 8PN
t (01833) 695530
e info@theancientmanorhouse.com
w theancientmanorhouse.com

Crich House Bed & Breakfast
★★★★ Guest Accommodation
SILVER AWARD
Crich House, 94 Galgate, Barnard Castle
DL12 8BJ
t (01833) 630357
e info@crich-house.co.uk
w crich-house.co.uk

Glendale ★★★ Bed & Breakfast
Motherstone, Barnard Castle
DL12 9UH
t (01833) 650384

Greta House ★★★★★
Bed & Breakfast GOLD AWARD
49 Galgate, Barnard Castle
DL12 8ES
t (01833) 631193
e kathchesman@btinternet.com
w gretahouse.co.uk

Homelands ★★★★ Guest House
GOLD AWARD
85 Galgate, Barnard Castle
DL12 8ES
t (01833) 638757
e enquiries@homelandsguesthouse.co.uk
w homelandsguesthouse.co.uk

Langdon Beck YHA ★★★★ Hostel
Forest in Teesdale, Barnard Castle
DL12 0XN
t (01833) 622228
e langdonbeck@yha.org.uk
w yha.org.uk

Lily Hill Farm ★★★★ Farmhouse
Brignall, Barnard Castle
DL12 9SF
t (01833) 627254
e karenerrington@yahoo.com
w lilyhillfarm.co.uk

Mill Riggs Cottage ★★★
Bed & Breakfast
Romaldkirk, Barnard Castle
DL12 9EW
t (01833) 650392

Startforth House Bed & Breakfast
★★★★ Bed & Breakfast
SILVER AWARD
Church Bank, Startforth, Barnard Castle
DL12 9AE
t (01833) 631126
e joan@startforthhouse.co.uk
w startforthhouse.co.uk

Strathmore Lawn East ★★★★
Guest Accommodation
81 Galgate, Barnard Castle
DL12 8ES
t (01833) 637061
e strathmorelawn@aol.com
w strathmorelawneast.co.uk

Vane House ★★★★
Bed & Breakfast
57 Galgate, Barnard Castle
DL12 8EN
t (01833) 631261
e artemisa@btinternet.com

BEAMISH 3 MILES

Bushblades Farm ★★★ Farmhouse
Harperley, Stanley
DH9 9UA
t (01207) 232722
e bushbladesfarm@hotmail.com
w bushbladesfarm.co.uk

BISHOP AUCKLAND

Hamsterley Forest B&B ★★★★
Bed & Breakfast SILVER AWARD
Redford, Hamsterley Forest, Bishop Auckland
DL13 3NL
t (01388) 488420
e jst_ayhope@yahoo.co.uk
w hamsterleyforestbandb.co.uk

BOWBURN

Hillrise Guest House ★★★
Guest Accommodation
13 Durham Road West, Bowburn, Durham
DH6 5AU
t (01913) 770302 / 0191 377 0302
e enquiries@hill-rise.com
w hill-rise.com

BRANCEPETH

Nafferton Farm ★★★★ Farmhouse
Brancepeth, Durham
DH7 8EF
t (01913) 780538
e sndfell@aol.com
w nafferton-farm.co.uk

BURNHOPE

Burnhope Lodge Guest House
★★★ Guest House
1 Wrights Way, Burnhope
DH7 0DL
t (01207) 529596

CASTLESIDE

Bee Cottage Guesthouse ★★★★
Guest House
Castleside, Consett
DH8 9HW
t (01207) 508224
e beecottage68@aol.com
w beecottage.co.uk

CHESTER-LE-STREET

Hollycroft ★★★★ Bed & Breakfast
11 The Parade, Chester-le-Street
DH3 3LR
t (01913) 887088
e staydurham@talktalk.net
w staydurham.co.uk

Low Urpeth Farm ★★★★
Farmhouse SILVER AWARD
Nr Beamish, Chester-le-Street, Durham
DH2 1BD
t 0191 4102901
e stay@lowurpeth.co.uk
w lowurpeth.co.uk

CONSETT

Dene View ★★★★
Guest Accommodation
15 Front Street, Castleside, Consett
DH8 9AR
t (01207) 502925
e catherine@deneview.co.uk
w deneview.co.uk

for key to symbols see page 6   693

North East | Co Durham

Edmundbyers YHA ★★★ *Hostel*
Edmundbyers, Consett
DH8 9NL
t (01912) 812570
e edmundbyers@yha.org.uk
w yha.org.uk

Hownsgill Bunkhouse ★★★ *Hostel*
Hownsgill Farm, Consett
DH8 9AA
t (01207) 503597
e hownsgill_bunkhouse@hotmail.co.uk
w c2cstopoff.co.uk

Wharnley Burn Farm ★★★
Bed & Breakfast
Castleside, Consett
DH8 9AY
t (01207) 508374

CROOK

Dowfold House ★★★★
Bed & Breakfast SILVER AWARD
Low Jobs Hill, Crook
DL15 9AB
t (01388) 762473
e enquiries@dowfoldhouse.co.uk
w dowfoldhouse.co.uk

DALTON PIERCY

The Windmill ★★★★
Guest Accommodation
Dalton Piercy
TS27 3HN
t (01429) 267592
e hartlepool@cameronsbrewery.com
w thewindmillgroup.co.uk

DARLINGTON

The Greenbank ★★★
Guest Accommodation
90 Greenbank Road, Darlington
DL3 6EL
t (01325) 462624
e shell1066@hotmail.co.uk

Harewood Lodge ★★★
Guest House
40 Grange Road, Darlington
DL1 5NP
t (01325) 358152
e harewood.lodge@ntlworld.com
w harewood-lodge.co.uk

Trudy's Guesthouse ★★
Guest House
72 Coniscliffe Road, Darlington
DL3 7RN
t (01325) 350918
e trudy_johnson@hotmail.co.uk
w trudysguesthouse.co.uk

DURHAM

66 Claypath ★★ *Bed & Breakfast*
Durham
DH1 1QT
t (01913) 843193
e richard@66claypath.co.uk
w 66claypath.co.uk

Alum Waters Guest House ★★★★
Bed & Breakfast
Unthank Farmhouse, Alum Waters, Durham
DH7 7JJ
t (01913) 730628
e tony@alumwaters.freeserve.co.uk
w alumwatersgh.co.uk

The Avenue Inn ★★ *Inn*
Avenue Street, High Shincliffe, Durham
DH1 2PT
t (0191) 3865954
e info@theavenue.biz

The Bridge ★★★ *Inn*
40 North Road, Durham
DH1 4SE
t (01913) 868090
e thebridgehotel@fsmail.net
w bridgehoteldurham.co.uk

Broom Farm Guest House ★★★★
Guest House
Front Street, Broompark, Durham
DH7 7QX
t (01913) 864755
e info@broomfarmguesthouse.co.uk
w broomfarmguesthouse.co.uk

Castle View Guest House ★★★★
Guest Accommodation
4 Crossgate, Durham
DH1 4PS
t 0191 3868852
e castle_view@hotmail.com
w castle-view.co.uk

Cathedral View Town House
★★★★ *Guest Accommodation*
SILVER AWARD
212 Gilesgate, Durham City
DH1 1QN
t 0191 3869566
e cathedralview@hotmail.com
w cathedralview.com

The Coach House ★★★★
Guest Accommodation
Stobbilee House, Witton Gilbert, Durham
DH7 6TW
t (01913) 736132
e suzanne@cronin.org.uk
w stobbilee.com

College of St Hild & St Bede
★★★ *Guest Accommodation*
St Hild's Lane, Durham
DH1 1SZ
t (01913) 348568
e p.c.oates@durham.ac.uk
w dur.ac.uk/hild-bede/

Collingwood College ★★★
Guest Accommodation
South Road, Durham
DH1 3LT
t (01913) 345000
e cwd.reception@durham.ac.uk
w dur.ac.uk/collingwood/conferences/

The Court Inn ★★★ *Inn*
Court Lane, Durham
DH1 3AW
t (01913) 847350
w courtinn.co.uk

Cuthberts Rest ★★★
Bed & Breakfast
42 Oswald Court, Durham
DH1 3DJ
t (01913) 840405

Durham Castle ★ *Campus*
Palace Green, Durham
DH1 3RW
t (01913) 344106
e durham.castle@durham.ac.uk
w durhamcastle.com

Durham YHA ★★ *Hostel*
St Chad's College, University of Durham, Durham
DH1 3RH
t (01913) 343358
e chads@durham.ac.uk
w dur.ac.uk

Farnley Tower & Gourmet Spot Restaurant ★★★★
Guest Accommodation
The Avenue, Durham
DH1 4DX
t (01913) 750011
e enquiries@farnley-tower.co.uk
w farnley-tower.co.uk

Garden House ★★★ *Inn*
North Road, Durham
DH1 4NQ
t (01913) 843360
e gardenhousedur@aol.com
w thegardenhousepub.co.uk

Hatfield College ★★
Guest Accommodation
North Bailey, Durham
DH1 3RQ
t (01913) 342633
e hatfield.reception@durham.ac.uk
w dur.ac.uk/hatfield.college

Hatfield College, Melville Building
★★★★ *Guest Accommodation*
North Bailey, Durham
DH1 3RQ
t (01913) 342633
e hatfield.reception@durham.ac.uk
w dur.ac.uk/hatfield.college/conferences_and_events/bed_and_breakfast_accommodation/

The Lambton Hounds Inn ★★★
Inn
Front Street, Pity Me, Durham
DH1 5DE
t (01913) 864742
e info@lambtonhounds.co.uk
w lambtonhounds.co.uk

Moorcroft Bed & Breakfast
★★★★ *Bed & Breakfast*
Moor End, Belmont, Durham
DH1 1BJ
t (01913) 867677
e moorcroft.dur@hotmail.co.uk

Moor End House Bed & Breakfast
★★★★ *Guest House*
7-8 Moor End Terrace, Belmont, Durham
DH1 1BJ
t (01913) 842796
e marybnb@hotmail.com
w moorendurham.co.uk

My Way Guest House ★★★
Bed & Breakfast
West Farm, Broompark Village, Durham
DH7 7RW
t (01913) 750874
e info@mywayguesthouse.co.uk
w mywayguesthouse.co.uk

Prince Bishop Guest House ★★★
Guest House
1 Oxford Terrace, Bowburn, Durham
DH6 5AX
t (01913) 778703
e enquiries@durhamguesthouse.co.uk
w durhamguesthouse.co.uk

Saint Chad's College ★★
Guest Accommodation
18 North Bailey, Durham
DH1 3RH
t (0191) 334 3358
e chads@durham.ac.uk
w dur.ac.uk/chads/

Seven Stars Inn ★★★ *Inn*
High Street North, Shincliffe, Durham
DH1 2NU
t (01913) 848454
e reservations@sevenstarsinn.co.uk
w sevenstarsinn.co.uk

St Aidan's College ★★★
Guest Accommodation
Durham University, Windmill Hill, Durham
DH1 3LJ
t (01913) 345769
e aidans.reception@durham.ac.uk
w dur.ac.uk/st-aidans.college/conferences

St John's College ★★★
Guest Accommodation
3 South Bailey, Durham
DH1 3RJ
t (01913) 343877
e s.l.hobson@durham.ac.uk
w durham.ac.uk/st-johns.college

Ushaw College ★★★ *Campus*
Bearpark, Durham
DH7 9RH
t (01913) 738502
e bookings@ushaw.co.uk
w ushaw.ac.uk

Van Mildert College ★★★
Guest Accommodation
Mill Hill Lane, Durham
DH1 3LH
t (01913) 347100
e van-mildert.college@durham.ac.uk
w dur.ac.uk/van-mildert.college/conference.tourism

Victoria Inn ★★★ *Inn*
86 Hallgarth Street, Durham
DH1 3AS
t (01913) 865269
w victoriainn-durhamcity.co.uk

The Victorian Town House ★★★
Guest Accommodation
GOLD AWARD
2 Victoria Terrace, Durham
DH1 4RW
t 05601 459168
e stay@durhambedandbreakfast.com
w durhambedandbreakfast.com

EASINGTON VILLAGE

Manor House ★★★★
Bed & Breakfast
Southside, Easington Village
SR8 3AX
t (01915) 272141
e danmullaney3009@hotmail.com
w manorhousebandb.net

EASTGATE

Horsley Hall ★★★★★
Guest Accommodation
SILVER AWARD
Eastgate
DL13 2LJ
t (01388) 517239
e info@horsleyhall.co.uk
w horsleyhall.co.uk

Rose Hill Farm ★★★★ *Farmhouse*
SILVER AWARD
Rose Hill, Eastgate
DL13 2LB
t (01388) 517209
e info@rosehillfarmbb.co.uk
w rosehillfarmbb.co.uk

EDMUNDBYERS

Punchbowl Inn ★★★★ *Inn*
SILVER AWARD
Edmundbyers, Consett
DH8 9NL
t (01207) 255545
e info@thepunchbowlinn.info
w thepunchbowlinn.info

FIR TREE

Greenhead Country House ★★★
Guest Accommodation
Green Head, Fir Tree
DL15 8BL
t (01388) 763143
e info@thegreenheadhotel.co.uk
w thegreenheadhotel.co.uk

FROSTERLEY

Newlands Hall ★★★★ *Farmhouse*
Newlands Hall, Frosterley, Nr Bishop Auckland, County Durham
DL13 2SH
t (01388) 529233
e carol@newlandshall.co.uk
w newlandshall.co.uk

GILESGATE

The Shoes ★★★ *Inn*
16 Sunderland Road, Gilesgate
DH1 2JT
t (01913) 844099
e theshoesbbb@btinternet.com
w theshoesbbb.co.uk

GUISBOROUGH

The Fox & Hounds ★★★ *Inn*
Slapewath, Guisborough
TS14 6PX
t (01287) 632964
e info@thefoxandhound.co.uk
w thefoxandhound.co.uk

North East | Co Durham

HAMSTERLEY

ale End ★★★★ *Bed & Breakfast*
SILVER AWARD
amsterley
.13 3PT
t (01388) 488091
e info@dale-endhamsterleybandb.co.uk
w dale-endhamsterleybandb.co.uk

HARTLEPOOL

tonlea Lodge Guest House
★★★ *Guest House*
e Green, Seaton Carew,
artlepool
525 1AT
t (01429) 271289
e enquiries@altonlea.co.uk
w altonlea.co.uk

rafferton Guest House ★★★
uest House
ockton Road, Hartlepool
525 1SL
t (01429) 273875
e julie@braffertonguesthouse.co.uk
w braffertonguesthouse.co.uk

he Douglas ★★★★ *Guest House*
ange Road, Hartlepool
526 8JA
t (01429) 272038
e info@douglas-hotel.co.uk
w douglas-hotel.co.uk

he Norton ★★★ *Guest House*
e Green, Seaton Carew,
artlepool
525 1AR
t (01429) 268317
e sue.russon@hotmail.co.uk
w thenorton.biz

he Oakroyd *Guest Accommodation*
ark Road, Hartlepool
526 9HT
t (01429) 864361
e mandyoakroydhotel@hotmail.com

cean View Guest House ★★★
uest House
e Cliff, Hartlepool
525 1AB
t (01429) 271983
e 2thecliff@tiscali.co.uk
w oceanviewguesthouse.co.uk

he Rothbury ★★★
uest Accommodation
e Cliff, Hartlepool
525 1AP
t (01429) 288419
e rothburyguesthouse.co.uk
w rothburyguesthouse.co.uk

he York House ★★★★
uest Accommodation
35 York Road, Hartlepool
526 9EE
t 0845 500 5566
e info@theyorkhotel.co.uk
w theyorkhotel.co.uk

HASWELL PLOUGH

he Gables ★★★
uest Accommodation
ront Street, Haswell Plough
H6 2EW
t (01915) 262982
e jmgables@aol.com
w the-gables-durham.co.uk

HIGH HESLEDEN

he Ship Inn ★★★★ *Inn*
SILVER AWARD
Main Street, High Hesleden
527 4QD
t (01429) 836453
e sheila@theshipinn.net
w theshipinn.net

MARWOOD

Kirkstone ★★★★ *Bed & Breakfast*
Barnard Castle
DL12 8QS
t (01833) 690497
e clennell6@btinternet.com

MIDDLESBROUGH

Chadwicks Guest House ★★★
Guest House
Clairville Road, Middlesbrough
TS4 2HN
t (01642) 287235
e chadwickguesthouse@hotmail.com
w chadwickguesthouse.com

Sporting Lodge Inn
Middlesbrough ★★★★ *Inn*
Low Lane, Stainton Village,
Middlesbrough
TS17 9LW
t (01642) 578100
e sarah.steed@sportinglodgeinns.co.uk
w sportinglodgeinns.co.uk

MIDDLETON-IN-TEESDALE

Belvedere House ★★★★
Bed & Breakfast
54 Market Place, Middleton-in-Teesdale
DL12 0QH
t (01833) 640884
e belvedere@thecoachhouse.net
w thecoachhouse.net

Brunswick House ★★★★
Guest House **SILVER AWARD**
55 Market Place, Middleton-in-Teesdale
DL12 0QH
t (01833) 640393
e enquiries@brunswickhouse.net
w brunswickhouse.net

The Old Barn ★★★★
Bed & Breakfast
12 Market Place, Middleton-in-Teesdale
DL12 0QG
t (01833) 640258
e lynda@theoldbarn-teesdale.co.uk
w theoldbarn-teesdale.co.uk

NEWFIELD

Malling House ★★★ *Guest House*
1 Oakdale Terrace, Newfield
DH2 2SU
t (01913) 702571
e wendy@kafs.wanadoo.co.uk

NEWTON AYCLIFFE

2 Main Road *Guest Accommodation*
Redworth, Newton Aycliffe, Co. Durham
DL5 6NW
t (01388) 772360
e anne.dobson@live.co.uk

OVINGTON

The Four Alls ★★★ *Inn*
Ovington
DL11 7BP
t (01833) 627302
e john.stroud@virgin.net
w thefouralls-teesdale.co.uk

PETERLEE

The Bell ★★★★ *Guest House*
Sunderland Road, Horden, Peterlee
SR8 4PF
t (01915) 863863
e bar-is.thebell@unicombox.co.uk

QUEBEC

Hamsteels Hall ★★★★ *Farmhouse*
Hamsteels Lane, Quebec
DH7 9RS
t (01207) 520388
e june@hamsteelshall.co.uk
w hamsteelshall.co.uk

REDCAR

A 2 Z Guest House ★★
Guest House
71 Station Road, Redcar
TS10 1RD
t (01642) 775533
e babsredcar@yahoo.co.uk
w a2zguesthouse.co.uk

All Welcome In ★★
Guest Accommodation
81 Queen Street, Redcar
TS10 1BG
t (01642) 484790
e patredcar2004@yahoo.co.uk
w allwelcomein.co.uk

The Central ★★★
Guest Accommodation
44 Queen Street, Redcar
TS10 1BD
t (01642) 482309

Springdale House ★★★★
Bed & Breakfast **SILVER AWARD**
3 Nelson Terrace, Redcar
TS10 1RX
t (01642) 297169
e reservations@springdalehouse.co.uk
w springdalehouse.co.uk

Tudor Lodge ★★
Guest Accommodation
7 Turner Street, Redcar
TS10 1AY
t (01642) 474883
w tudorlodge-redcar.co.uk

RUSHYFORD

Garden House ★★★★
Bed & Breakfast
Windlestone Park, Windlestone, Rushyford
DL17 0LZ
t (01388) 720217
e info@gardenhousedurham.co.uk
w gardenhousedurham.co.uk

SALTBURN-BY-THE-SEA

The Rose Garden ★★★★
Bed & Breakfast
31 Leven Street, Saltburn-by-the-Sea
TS12 1JY
t (01287) 622947
e enquiries@therosegarden.co.uk
w therosegarden.co.uk

Townend Farm B&B ★★★★
Bed & Breakfast **SILVER AWARD**
Whitby Road, Easington, Saltburn-by-the-Sea
TS13 4NE
t (01287) 640444
e info@townendfarm.co.uk
w townendfarm.co.uk

Victorian Guest House ★★★★
Bed & Breakfast
1 Oxford Street, Saltburn-by-the-Sea
TS12 1LG
t (01287) 625237
e susanandstewart@saltburn-accommodation.co.uk
w saltburn-accommodation.co.uk

SEAHAM

Pan Din Thai Accommodation
★★★★ *Guest Accommodation*
4 South Crescent, Seaham
SR7 7HD
t (01915) 812348
e info@pandinthai.co.uk
w pandinthai.co.uk

SEDGEFIELD

Todds House Farm ★★★
Farmhouse
Sedgefield, Stockton-on-Tees
TS21 3EL
t (01740) 620244
e mail@toddshousefarm.co.uk
w toddshousefarm.co.uk

SKELTON-IN-CLEVELAND

Westerland's Guest House ★★
Bed & Breakfast
27 East Parade, Skelton-in-Cleveland
TS12 2BJ
t (01287) 650690

SPENNYMOOR

Highview Country House ★★★★
Guest House
Kirk Merrington, Spennymoor
DL16 7JT
t (01388) 811006
e jayne@highviewcountryhouse.co.uk
w highviewcountryhouse.co.uk

STANHOPE

Parkhead Station ★★★
Guest Accommodation
Stanhope Moor, Stanhope
DL13 2ES
t (01388) 526434
e parkheadstation@aol.com
w parkheadstation.co.uk

STANLEY

Harperley Country House ★★★
Guest Accommodation
Harperley Lane, Harperley, Stanley
DH9 9TY
t (01207) 234011
e stay@harperleycountryhouse.co.uk
w harperleycountryhouse.co.uk

Oak Tree Inn ★★ *Inn*
Front Street, Tantobie, Stanley
DH9 9RF
t (01207) 235445
e paul.boyles@dorbiere.co.uk

South Causey Inn ★★★★ *Inn*
Beamish Burn Road, Stanley
DH9 0LS
t (01207) 235555
e southcausey@hotmail.com
w southcauseyhotel.co.uk

STOCKTON-ON-TEES

Ashton Guest House ★★★
Guest House
88 Yarm Road, Stockton-on-Tees
TS18 3PQ
t (01642) 679044
e ron@theashton.co.uk

The Parkwood Inn ★★★ *Inn*
64-66 Darlington Road, Stockton-on-Tees
TS18 5ER
t (01642) 587933
e theparkwoodhotel@aol.com
w theparkwoodhotel.com

TRIMDON STATION

Polemonium Plantery ★★★★
Bed & Breakfast
28 Sunnyside Terrace, Trimdon Grange, Trimdon Station
TS29 6HF
t (01429) 881529
e bandb@polemonium.co.uk
w polemonium.co.uk

WEST AUCKLAND

The Bridge Inn ★★★ *Inn*
1 Gordon Lane, Ramshaw, West Auckland
DL14 0NS
t (01388) 832509
e thebridgeinnramshaw@hotmail.com
w thebridgeinnramshaw.com

WESTGATE

Lands Farm ★★★★ *Farmhouse*
SILVER AWARD
Westgate
DL13 1SN
t (01388) 517210
e landsfarm@btconnect.com

North East | Northumberland

Northumberland

ACOMB

The Sun Inn ★★★ *Inn*
Main Street, Acomb
NE46 4PW
t (01434) 602934
e info@thesuninnacomb.co.uk
w thesuninn-acomb.co.uk

ALLENDALE

High Keenley Fell Farm ★★★★
Farmhouse
High Keenley Fell Farm, Allendale, Hexham
NE47 9NU
t (01434) 618344
e camaclean@btinternet.com
w highkeenleyfarm.co.uk

Thornley House ★★★★
Bed & Breakfast
Thornley Gate, Allendale
NE47 9NH
t (01434) 683155
e enquiries@thornleyhouse.co.uk
w thornleyhouse.co.uk

ALLERWASH

Allerwash Farmhouse ★★★★★
Bed & Breakfast **GOLD AWARD**
Allerwash, Allerwash
NE47 5AB
t (01434) 674154
e angela@allerwash.co.uk
w allerwash.co.uk

ALNMOUTH

Beech Lodge ★★★★
Bed & Breakfast **SILVER AWARD**
8 Alnwood, Alnmouth
NE66 3NN
t (01665) 830709
e beechlodge@hotmail.com
w beechlodge.net

Hope & Anchor Inn ★★★ *Inn*
44 Northumberland Street, Alnmouth
NE66 2RA
t (01665) 830363
e info@hopeandanchorholidays.co.uk
w hopeandanchorholidays.co.uk

Nether Grange ★★★★
Guest Accommodation
H F Holidays Ltd, Alnmouth
NE66 2RZ
t (020) 8905 9556
e info@hfholidays.co.uk
w hfholidays.co.uk

Red Lion Inn ★★★★ *Inn*
22 Northumberland Street, Alnmouth
NE66 2RJ
t (01665) 830584
e mjmleisure@btconnect.com
w redlionalnmouth.com

The Saddle Bed and Breakfast
★★★ *Guest Accommodation*
24-25 Northumberland Street, Alnmouth
NE66 2RA
t (01665) 830476
e thesaddlebedandbreakfast@hotmail.com
w thesaddlebedandbreakfast.co.uk

Sefton House ★★★★ *Guest House*
15 Argyle Street, Alnmouth
NE66 2SB
t (01665) 833174
e simoneneri@aol.com
w seftonhousealnmouth.com

Westlea ★★★★
Guest Accommodation
SILVER AWARD
29 Riverside Road, Alnmouth
NE66 2SD
t (01665) 830730
e ritaandray77@btinternet.com
w visitalnwick.org.uk/accommodation/bb_westlea.htm

ALNWICK

Alndyke Bed & Breakfast ★★★★
Farmhouse **SILVER AWARD**
Alnmouth Road, Alnwick
NE66 3PB
t (01665) 510252
e laura@alndyke.co.uk
w alndyke.co.uk

Aln House ★★★★
Guest Accommodation
SILVER AWARD
South Road, Alnwick
NE66 2NZ
t (01665) 602265
e enquires@alnhouse.co.uk
w alnhouse.co.uk

Alnwick Lodge ★★★
Guest Accommodation
West Cawledge Park, Alnwick
NE66 2HJ
t (01665) 604363 (01665) 603377
e bookings@alnwicklodge.com
w alnwicklodge.com

Aydon House ★★★
Guest Accommodation
South Road, Alnwick
NE66 2NT
t (01665) 602218
e aydonhouse@yahoo.co.uk
w aydonhouse.co.uk

Bailiffgate Bed & Breakfast ★★★
Guest Accommodation
1 Bailiffgate, Alnwick
NE66 1LZ
t (01665) 602078
e bailiffgate@alnwickaccommodation.com
w alnwickaccommodation.com

Beaconsfield B&B ★★★
Bed & Breakfast
3 Beaconsfield Terrace, Alnwick
NE66 1XB
t (01665) 604912
e enquiries@beaconsfieldbb.co.uk
w beaconsfieldbb.co.uk

Birdsong Cottage Bed & Breakfast
★★★★ *Bed & Breakfast*
SILVER AWARD
Brownieside, Alnwick
NE67 5HW
t (01665) 579362
e stay@birdsongcottage.co.uk
w birdsongcottage.co.uk

Birnam House ★★★★
Bed & Breakfast
Royal Oak Gardens, Alnwick
NE66 2DA
t 07740 652013
e welcome@alnwickholidays.co.uk
w alnwickholidays.co.uk

Callaly Cottage Retreat ★★★★
Bed & Breakfast
Callaly, Alnwick
NE66 4TA
t (01665) 574684
e callalycottage@gmail.com
w callalycottage.com

Castle Gate Guest House ★★★
Bed & Breakfast
23 Bondgate Without, Alnwick
NE66 1PR
t (01665) 602657
e tracy@amfr.co.uk
w castlegatealnwick.co.uk

Castleview B&B ★★★★
Bed & Breakfast
1B Bailiffgate, Alnwick
NE66 1LZ
t (01665) 606227
e enquiries@castleviewalnwick.co.uk
w castleviewalnwick.co.uk

Courtyard Garden ★★★★★
Bed & Breakfast **SILVER AWARD**
10 Prudhoe Street, Alnwick
NE66 1UW
t (01665) 603393
e maureenpeter10@btinternet.com
w courtyardgarden-alnwick.co.uk

Crosshills House ★★★★
Guest House
40 Blakelaw Road, Alnwick
NE66 1BA
t (01665) 602518
e crosshillshouse@hotmail.com
w crosshillshouse.ntb.org.uk/

The Georgian Guest House ★★★
Guest House
3 Hotspur Street, Alnwick
NE66 1QE
t (01665) 602398
e enquiries@georgianguesthouse.co.uk
w georgianguesthouse.co.uk

Green Batt House ★★★
Guest Accommodation
Green Batt, Alnwick
NE66 1TY
t 07985 490327
e gbannex@aol.com

Greycroft ★★★★
Guest Accommodation
SILVER AWARD
Croft Place, Alnwick, Northumberland
NE66 1XU
t (01665) 602127
e greycroftalnwick@aol.com
w greycroftalnwick.co.uk

Hawkhill Farmhouse ★★★★
Farmhouse
Hawkhill, Alnwick, Northumberland
NE66 3PG
t (01665) 830380
e stay@hawkhillfarmhouse.com
w hawkhillfarmhouse.com

Holly Lodge *Guest Accommodation*
The Avenue, Alnwick
NE66 1UL
t (01665) 602743
e hollylodge@live.co.uk
w hollylodgealnwick.co.uk

The Market Tavern ★★ *Inn*
7 Fenkle Street, Alnwick
NE66 1HW
t (01665) 602759
e mandyrussell44@googlemail.com
w themarkettavernalnwick.co.uk

Masons Arms Country Inn ★★★★
Inn
Stamford, Rennington, Alnwick
NE66 3RX
t (01665) 577275
e bookings@masonsarms.net
w masonsarms.net

Norfolk ★★★★ *Guest House*
SILVER AWARD
41 Blakelaw Road, Alnwick
NE66 1BA
t (01665) 602892
w norfolkhouse-alnwick.co.uk

Old Bewick Farmhouse ★★★★★
Bed & Breakfast **GOLD AWARD**
Alnwick
NE66 4DZ
t (01668) 217372
e oldbewickfarmhse@aol.com
w oldbewick.co.uk

Percy Terrace Bed & Breakfast
★★★★ *Bed & Breakfast*
3 Percy Terrace, Alnwick
NE66 1AF
t (01665) 606867
e bookings@alnwick-bedandbreakfast.co.uk
w alnwick-bedandbreakfast.co.uk/

The Queens Head ★★★★ *Inn*
25 Market Street, Alnwick
NE66 1SS
t (01665) 604691
e stay@alnwickqueensheadhotel.co.uk
w alnwickqueensheadhotel.co.uk

Ravensmede Cottage ★★★
Bed & Breakfast
6 Ravensmede Cottage, Alnmouth Road, Alnwick
NE66 2PY
t (01665) 602973
e dcrk@cclark.fsnet.co.uk
w ravensmede-cottage.co.uk

Redfoot Lea Bed & Breakfast
★★★★★ *Bed & Breakfast*
GOLD AWARD
Redfoot Lea, Greensfield Moor Far, Alnwick
NE66 2HH
t (01665) 603891
e info@redfootlea.co.uk
w redfootlea.co.uk

Reighamsyde ★★★★
Bed & Breakfast
Alnwick Moor, Alnwick
NE66 2AJ
t (01665) 602535
e reighamsyde@aol.com

Rooftops ★★★★
Guest Accommodation
SILVER AWARD
14 Blakelaw Road, Alnwick
NE66 1AZ
t (01665) 604201
e rooftops.alnwick@tiscali.co.uk

The Shepherds Rest ★★ *Inn*
Alnwick Moor, Alnwick
NE66 2AH
t (01665) 510809
e robert@raybourn.wanadoo.co.u
w the-shepherds-rest.co.uk

Stamford Farmhouse Bed & Breakfast ★★★ *Farmhouse*
Stamford, Alnwick
NE66 3RY
t 07979 592534
e stamfordfarmhouse@googlemail.com
w northumberlandbedbreakfast.com

Tate House Bed & Breakfast ★★★
Bed & Breakfast
11 Bondgate Without, Alnwick
NE66 1PR
t (01665) 604661
e info@stayinalnwick.co.uk
w stayinalnwick.co.uk

West Acre House ★★★★★
Guest Accommodation
GOLD AWARD
West Acres, Alnwick
NE66 2QA
t (01665) 510374
e info@westacrehouse.co.uk
w westacrehouse.co.uk

ALWINTON

Rose & Thistle ★★★★ *Inn*
Alwinton
NE65 7BQ
t (01669) 650226
e stay@roseandthistlealwinton.co
w roseandthistlealwinton.co.uk

AMBLE

Amble Guesthouse ★★★
Guest House
16 Leazes Street, Amble
NE65 0AL
t (01665) 714661
e stephmclaughlin@aol.com
w ambleguesthouse.co.uk

The Coach House B&B ★★★★
Farmhouse
Hope House Farm, Togston, Amble Northumberland
NE65 0HN
t (01665) 710245
e info@coachhousesuites.co.uk
w coachhousesuites.co.uk

North East | Northumberland

oquetside ★★★★ *Bed & Breakfast*
Broomhill Street, Amble-by-the-a
E65 0AN
t (01665) 710352
w coquetside@talktalk.net

arbour Guest House ★★★
uest House
4 Leazes Street, Amble
E65 0AA
t (01665) 710381
e info@ambleharbourguesthouse.co.uk
w ambleharbourguesthouse.co.uk

o. 20 ★★★ *Bed & Breakfast*
arine House, Marine Road, Amble
E65 0BB
t (01665) 711965
e numbertwenty@hotmail.co.uk
w numbertwenty.com

ANICK

nick Grange Farmhouse B&B
★★★ *Farmhouse*
nick Grange, Anick
E46 4LP
t (01434) 603807
e julie@anickgrange.fsnet.co.uk
w anickgrange.com

BAMBURGH

he Sunningdale ★★★
uest Accommodation
1-23 Lucker Road, Bamburgh
E69 7BS
t (01668) 214134
e enquiries@sunningdale-hotel.com
w sunningdale-hotel.com

BARDON MILL

oach House Bed & Breakfast
★★★ *Bed & Breakfast*
ILVER AWARD
outhview, Tavern House, Bardon
ill
E47 7HZ
t (01434) 344779
e mail@bardonmillcoachhouse.co.uk
w bardonmillcoachhouse.co.uk

ibbs Hill Farm ★★★★ *Farmhouse*
nce Brewed, Bardon Mill
E47 7AP
t (01434) 344030
e val@gibbshillfarm.co.uk
w gibbshillfarm.co.uk

ibbs Hill Farm Hostel ★★★
ostel
ardon Mill
E47 7AP
t (01434) 344030
e val@gibbshillfarm.co.uk
w gibbshillfarm.co.uk

ontcoffer ★★★★★
uest Accommodation
OLD AWARD
ardon Mill
E47 7HZ
t (01434) 344138
e john-dehlia@talk21.com
w montcoffer.co.uk

nce Brewed YHA ★★★ *Hostel*
ilitary Road, Once Brewed
E47 7AN
t (01434) 344360
e oncebrewed@yha.org.uk
w yha.org.uk

trand Cottage Bed & Breakfast
★★★ *Bed & Breakfast*
ain Road (A69), Hadrian's Wall
orridor, Bardon Mill, Hexham
E47 7BH
t (01434) 344643
e stay@strand-cottage.co.uk
w strand-cottage.co.uk

Twice Brewed Inn ★★★ *Inn*
Military Road, Bardon Mill
NE47 7AN
t (01434) 344534
e info@twicebrewedinn.co.uk
w twicebrewedinn.co.uk

Vallum Lodge ★★★★ *Guest House*
SILVER AWARD
Military Road, Twice Brewed
NE47 7AN
t (01434) 344248
e stay@vallum-lodge.co.uk
w vallum-lodge.co.uk

BEADNELL

Beach Court ★★★★★
Guest Accommodation
Harbour Road, Beadnell
NE67 5BJ
t (01665) 720225
e info@beachcourt.com
w beachcourt.com

Low Dover Beadnell Bay ★★★★★
Guest Accommodation
SILVER AWARD
Harbour Road, Beadnell
NE67 5BJ
t (01665) 720291
e enquiries@lowdover.co.uk
w lowdover.co.uk

Shepherds Cottage ★★★★
Guest Accommodation
Beadnell
NE67 5AD
t (01665) 720497
e shepherds.cott@tiscali.co.uk
w shepherdscottagebeadnell.co.uk

BEAL

Brock Mill Farmhouse ★★★★
Guest Accommodation
Brock Mill, Beal, Berwick-upon-Tweed
TD15 2PB
t (01289) 381283
e brockmillfarmhouse@btinternet.com
w holyislandaccommodation.com

BELFORD

Courtyard Cottage at Outchester Manor ★★★★
Guest Accommodation
SILVER AWARD
Outchester Manor, Belford
NE70 7EA
t (01668) 213767
e becssutherland@btinternet.com
w outchestermanor.co.uk

The Farmhouse Guest House
★★★★ *Guest Accommodation*
GOLD AWARD
24 West Street, Belford
NE70 7QE
t (01668) 213083
e farmhouseguesthouse@hotmail.com
w thefarmhouseguesthousebelford.co.uk

Seafields ★★★★ *Bed & Breakfast*
SILVER AWARD
7 Cragside Avenue, Belford
NE70 7NA
t (01668) 213502
e seafields.bryden@tiscali.co.uk
w seafieldsbelford.co.uk

Well House ★★★★ *Bed & Breakfast*
35 High Street, Belford, Northumbland
NE70 7NG
t 01668 219003
e philipn@btinternet.com
w wellhouse-belford.co.uk

BELLINGHAM

Bridgeford Farm ★★★★
Farmhouse
Bellingham
NE48 2HU
t (01434) 220940
e info@bridgefordfarmbandb.co.uk
w bridgefordfarmbandb.co.uk

Lyndale Guest House ★★★★
Guest House
Riverside Walk, Bellingham
NE48 2AW
t (01434) 220361
e lyndaleguesthouse@hotmail.com
w lyndaleguesthouse.co.uk

BERWICK-UPON-TWEED

Alannah House ★★★★
Bed & Breakfast SILVER AWARD
84 Church Street, Berwick upon Tweed
TD15 1DU
t (01289) 307252
e steven@berwick1234.freeserve.co.uk
w alannahhouse.com

Ben More House ★★★
Bed & Breakfast
51 Church Street, Berwick-upon-Tweed
TD15 1EE
t (01289) 309274
e bookings@benmorehouse.com
w benmorehouse.com

Berwick-upon-Tweed Backpackers
★★★★ *Backpackers*
56-58 Bridge Street, Berwick-upon-Tweed
TD15 1AQ
t (01289) 331481
e bkbackpacker@aol.com
w berwickbackpackers.co.uk

Bowsden Bed & Breakfast ★★★★
Bed & Breakfast
West View, Bowsden, Berwick-upon-Tweed
TD15 2TW
t (01289) 388731
e enquiries@bowsdenbedandbreakfast.co.uk
w bowsdenbedandbreakfast.co.uk

Bridge View ★★★★
Guest Accommodation
14 Tweed Street, Berwick-upon-Tweed
TD15 1NG
t (01289) 308098
e lynda@tiscali.co.uk
w bridgeviewberwick.com

Cara House ★★★★
Guest Accommodation
44 Castlegate, Berwick-upon-Tweed
TD15 1JT
t (01289) 302749
e pam@carahouse.co.uk
w carahouse.co.uk

The Cat Inn ★★★ *Inn*
Great North Road, Cheswick
TD15 2RL
t (01289) 387251

Clovelly House ★★★★
Bed & Breakfast SILVER AWARD
58 West Street, Berwick-upon-Tweed
TD15 1AS
t (01289) 302337
e vivroc@clovelly53.freeserve.co.uk
w clovelly53.freeserve.co.uk

Dervaig Guest House *Guest House*
1 North Road, Berwick-upon-Tweed
TD15 1PW
t (01289) 302267
e jgilmour123@btinternet.com
w dervaigguesthouse.co.uk

Elizabethan Townhouse ★★★★
Guest Accommodation
7-8 Sidey Court, Marygate, Berwick-upon-Tweed
TD15 1DR
t (01289) 304-580
e dm27@ethberwick.co.uk
w elizabethan-town-house.co.uk

The Estate House ★★★★
Guest House
Ford, Berwick-upon-Tweed, Northumberland
TD15 2PX
t 01890 820668
e enquiries@theestatehouse.info
w theestatehouse.info

Fenham Farm Coastal Bed & Breakfast ★★★★
Guest Accommodation
SILVER AWARD
Beal, Berwick-upon-Tweed
TD15 2PL
t (01289) 381245
e stay@fenhamfarm.co.uk
w fenhamfarm.co.uk

Four North Road ★★★★
Guest Accommodation
SILVER AWARD
4 North Road, Berwick-upon-Tweed
TD15 1PL
t (01289) 306146
e sandra@thorntonfour.freeserve.co.uk
w fournorthroad.co.uk

Friendly Hound Cottage ★★★★
Bed & Breakfast
Ford Common, Berwick-upon-Tweed
TD15 2QD
t (01289) 388554
e friendlyhound@hotmail.com
w friendlyhoundcottage.co.uk

Granary Guest House ★★★★★
Guest House SILVER AWARD
11 Bridge Street, Berwick-upon-Tweed
TD15 1ES
t (01289) 304403
e pamwaddell@btinternet.com
w granaryguesthouse.co.uk

Ladythorne House ★★★★
Guest House
Ladythorne House, Cheswick, Berwick-upon-Tweed
TD15 2RW
t 01289 387382
e val@ladythorne.wanadoo.co.uk
w ladythorne.wanadoo.co.uk

Longridge Towers School ★★★
Group Hostel
Berwick-upon-Tweed, Northumberland
TD15 2XQ
t (01289) 307584
e sfleming@lts.org.uk

Mansergh House ★★★★
Bed & Breakfast
Church Street, Berwick-upon-Tweed
TD15 1DU
t (01289) 302297
e manserghhouse@btinternet.com
w manserghhouse.co.uk

Marlborough House ★★★★
Bed & Breakfast
133 Main Street, Spittal, Berwick-upon-Tweed, Nortrhumberland
TD15 1RP
t (01289) 305293
e seaside133@onetel.com
w marlboroughhouse.info

Meadow Hill Guest House ★★★★
Guest House
Duns Road, Berwick-upon-Tweed
TD15 1UB
t (01289) 306325
e christineabart@aol.com
w meadow-hill.co.uk

North East | Northumberland

Miranda's Guest House ★★★
Guest House
43 Church Street, Berwick-upon-Tweed
TD15 1EE
t (01289) 306483
e mirandasberwick@aol.com
w mirandasguesthouse.com

No 1 Sallyport ★★★★★
Guest Accommodation
GOLD AWARD
off Bridge Street, Berwick-upon-Tweed
TD15 1EZ
t (01289) 308827
e info@sallyport.co.uk
w sallyport.co.uk

No 4 Ravensdowne ★★★★
Guest Accommodation
SILVER AWARD
4 Ravensdowne, Berwick-upon-Tweed
TD15 1HX
t (01289) 308082
e fourravensdowne@hotmail.co.uk
w 4ravensdowne.co.uk/index.html

Northumbrian House ★★★★
Bed & Breakfast
7 Ravensdowne, Berwick-upon-Tweed
TD15 1HX
t (01289) 309503
e ian.kille@btinternet.com
w 7ravensdowne.co.uk

The Old Vicarage Guest House
★★★★★ *Guest House*
SILVER AWARD
24 Church Road, Berwick-upon-Tweed
TD15 2AN
t (01289) 306909
e stay@oldvicarageberwick.co.uk
w oldvicarageberwick.co.uk

Orkney House ★★ *Guest House*
37 Woolmarket, Berwick-upon-Tweed
TD15 1DH
t (01289) 331710
e orkneyguesthouse@yahoo.co.uk

Parade School Guest House
★★★★ *Guest Accommodation*
SILVER AWARD
61 Church Street, Berwick-upon-Tweed
TD15 1EE
t (01289) 303403
e stay@paradeschoolguesthouse.co.uk
w paradeschoolguesthouse.co.uk/index.htm

Ravensdowne Guest House
★★★★ *Guest Accommodation*
SILVER AWARD
40 Ravensdowne, Berwick-upon-Tweed
TD15 1DQ
t (01289) 306992
e bookings@40ravensdowne.co.uk
w 40ravensdowne.co.uk

Rob Roy ★★★★ *Inn*
Dock Road, Tweedmouth, Berwick-upon-Tweed, Northumberland
TD15 2BE
t 01289 306428
e therobroy@hotmail.co.uk
w robroyberwick.co.uk

Tweed View House ★★★★
Bed & Breakfast
16 Railway Street, Berwick-upon-Tweed
TD15 1NF
t (01289) 302864
w tweedviewhouse.webs.com

The Walls ★★★★★
Bed & Breakfast **SILVER AWARD**
8 Quay Walls, Berwick-upon-Tweed, Northumberland
TD15 1HB
t (01289) 330233
e info@thewallsberwick.com
w thewallsberwick.com

West Coates ★★★★★
Bed & Breakfast **GOLD AWARD**
30 Castle Terrace, Berwick-upon-Tweed
TD15 1NZ
t (01289) 309666
e karenbrownwestcoates@yahoo.com
w westcoates.co.uk

West Sunnyside House ★★★★
Bed & Breakfast **SILVER AWARD**
Berwick-upon-Tweed
TD15 2QH
t (01289) 305387
e kjamieson58@aol.com
w westsunnysidehouse.co.uk

Whyteside House ★★★★
Guest Accommodation
SILVER AWARD
46 Castlegate, Berwick-upon-Tweed
TD15 1JT
t (01289) 331019
e albert.whyte@onetel.net
w secretkingdom.com/whyte/side.htm

BILTON

Bilton Barns Farmhouse ★★★★
Farmhouse **SILVER AWARD**
Bilton
NE66 2TB
t (01665) 830427
e dorothy@biltonbarns.com
w biltonbarns.com

BIRLING

Birling North Cottage ★★★★
Bed & Breakfast **SILVER AWARD**
Birling, Warkworth
NE65 0XS
t (01665) 712276
e candejhowliston@btinternet.com

BLYTH

The Kitty Brewster ★★ *Inn*
469 Cowpen Road, Blyth
NE24 4JF
t (01670) 352732

BOULMER

Boulmer Village B&B ★★★★
Bed & Breakfast **SILVER AWARD**
21 Boulmer Village, Boulmer
NE66 3BS
t (01665) 577262
e hazel_campbell@btopenworld.com

BRUNTON

Brunton House ★★★★
Bed & Breakfast
Brunton, Embleton
NE66 3HQ
t (01665) 589198
e victoriajolliffe@tiscali.co.uk
w bruntonhouse.co.uk

BYRNESS VILLAGE

Forest View ★★★★ *Hostel*
Otterburn Green, Byrness Village
NE19 1TS
t (01830) 520425
e joycetaylor1703@hotmail.co.uk
w yha.org.uk

CHATTON

Chatton Park House Bed & Breakfast ★★★★★ *Bed & Breakfast*
GOLD AWARD
Chatton
NE66 5RA
t (01668) 215507
e enquiries@chattonpark.com
w chattonpark.com

Spylaw Farmhouse B&B ★★★★
Farmhouse **SILVER AWARD**
South Hazelrigg, Chatton
NE66 5RZ
t 07973 703877
e spylaw@btopenworld.com
w spylaw.org.uk

CHOPPINGTON

The Swan at Choppington ★★★
Inn
Choppington
NE62 5TG
t (01670) 826060
e enquiries@theswanchoppington.co.uk
w theswanchoppington.co.uk

CLENNELL

Clennell Hall ★★★★
Guest Accommodation
Rothbury
NE65 7BG
t (01669) 650377
e craig@clennellhallhotel.com
w clennellhallhotel.com

CORBRIDGE

2 The Crofts ★★★★
Bed & Breakfast
Newcastle Road, Corbridge, Hexham
NE45 5LW
t (01434) 633046
e welcome@2thecrofts.co.uk
w 2thecrofts.co.uk

5 Dilston West Cottages ★★★★
Bed & Breakfast
Dilston, Corbridge
NE45 5RL
t (01434) 632464
e liz.nev@hotmail.co.uk
w 5-dilstonwest.com

Broxdale ★★★★ *Bed & Breakfast*
Station Road, Corbridge
NE45 5AY
t (01434) 632492
e mike@broxdale.co.uk

Dilston Mill B&B ★★★★
Bed & Breakfast
Dilston Mill, Corbridge
NE45 5QZ
t (01434) 633493
e susan@dilstonmill.com
w dilstonmill.com

Dyvels Inn ★★★ *Inn*
Station Road, Corbridge
NE45 5AY
t (01434) 633633
e thedyvelsinn@googlemail.com
w dyvelsinn.co.uk

Fellcroft ★★★★ *Bed & Breakfast*
Station Road, Corbridge
NE45 5AY
t (01434) 632384
e tove.brown@ukonline.co.uk
w fellcroftbandb.com

The Hayes ★★★
Guest Accommodation
Newcastle Road, Corbridge
NE45 5LP
t (01434) 632010
e camon@onebillinternet.co.uk
w hayes-corbridge.co.uk

Norgate ★★★★ *Bed & Breakfast*
7 Leazes Terrace, Corbridge
NE45 5HS
t (01434) 633736
e norgatecorbridge@btinternet.com
w norgatecorbridge.co.uk

Priorfield B&B ★★★★
Bed & Breakfast **SILVER AWARD**
Hippingstones Lane, Corbridge
NE45 5JP
t (01434) 633179
e nsteenberg@btinternet.com
w priorfieldbedandbreakfast.co.uk

Prospect House B&B ★★★★
Bed & Breakfast
Ladycutter Lane, Farnley, Corbridge
NE45 5RR
t (01434) 633551
e susanwalne@hotmail.com
w prospecthousebandb.co.uk

The Wheatsheaf ★★★★ *Inn*
St Helens Street, Corbridge
NE45 5HE
t (01434) 632020
e info@wheatsheafhotelcorbridge.co.uk
w wheatsheafhotelcorbridge.co.uk

CORNHILL-ON-TWEED

The Coach House at Crookham
★★★★ *Guest Accommodation*
GOLD AWARD
Crookham
TD12 4TD
t (01890) 820293
e stay@coachhousecrookham.com
w coachhousecrookham.com

Hay Farm House ★★★★
Guest Accommodation
GOLD AWARD
Ford and Etal Country Estate, Nr Berwick upon Tweed
TD12 4TR
t (01890) 820647
e tinahayfarm@tiscali.co.uk
w hayfarm.co.uk

CRASTER

Harbour Lights ★★★★
Bed & Breakfast **SILVER AWARD**
Whin Hill, Craster
NE66 3TP
t (01665) 576062
e info@harbourlights-craster.co.uk
w harbourlights-craster.co.uk

Howick Scar Farmhouse ★★★
Bed & Breakfast
Howick Scar, Craster
NE66 3SU
t (01665) 576665
e howick.scar@virgin.net
w howickscar.co.uk

Old Rectory ★★★★★
Guest Accommodation
SILVER AWARD
Howick, Craster, Alnwick
NE66 3LE
t (01665) 577590
e stay@oldrectoryhowick.co.uk
w oldrectoryhowick.co.uk

Stonecroft ★★★★ *Bed & Breakfast*
GOLD AWARD
Dunstan, Craster, Alnwick
NE66 3SZ
t (01665) 576433
e sally@stonestaff.freeserve.co.uk
w stonecroft-craster.co.uk

DETCHANT

Detchant Farm ★★★★ *Farmhouse*
Detchant
NE70 7PF
t (01668) 213261
e stay@detchantfarm.co.uk
w detchantfarm.co.uk

North East | Northumberland

DUNSTAN VILLAGE

ottage Inn ★★★
Guest Accommodation
unstan Village
E66 3SZ
t (01665) 576658
e enquiries@cottageinnhotel.co.uk
w cottageinnhotel.co.uk

DYKE NEUK

he Dyke Neuk ★★★★ Inn
eldon, Morpeth
E61 3SL
t (01670) 772662
e thedykeneuk@aol.com
w thedykeneuk.co.uk

EASINGTON

asington Farm ★★★★★
armhouse SILVER AWARD
asington, Belford
E70 2NS
t (01668) 213298
e oates925@btinternet.com
w easingtonfarm.co.uk

EAST ORD

airholm ★★★★
uest Accommodation
st Ord, Berwick-upon-Tweed
015 2NS
t (01289) 305370
e bethiawelsh@ukonline.co.uk
w welcometofairholm.com

EGLINGHAM

metree Cottage ★★★★
d & Breakfast
t Eglingham Village, Eglingham
E66 2TX
t (01665) 578322
e viwhillis@aol.com

he Tankerville Arms ★★★★ Inn
ILVER AWARD
t The Village, Eglingham
E66 2TX
t (01665) 578444
e info@tankervillearms.com
w tankervillearms.com

ELLINGHAM

he Pack Horse Inn ★★★ Inn
lingham, Chathill, Northumberland
E67 5HA
t (01665) 589292
e jillybrown777@hotmail.com
w packhorseinn-ellingham.co.uk

EMBLETON

ue Bell Inn ★★★ Inn
T Stead Road, Embleton
E66 3UP
t (01665) 576573

our Winds B&B ★★★
ed & Breakfast
t Woodsteads, Embleton
E66 3XY
t (01665) 576668
e fourwindsbandb@btinternet.com

he Sportsman Inn ★★★ Inn
Sea Lane, Embleton
E66 3XF
t (01665) 576588
e stay@sportsmanhotel.co.uk
w sportsmanhotel.co.uk

FALSTONE

he Blackcock Inn Inn
alstone
E48 1AA
t (01434) 240200
e thebcinn@yahoo.co.uk
w blackcockinn.co.uk

FEATHERSTONE

he Wallace Arms ★★★ Inn
eatherstone
E49 0JF
t (01434) 321872
e duncan@thewallacearms.co.uk
w thewallacearms.co.uk/

FELTON

Eshott Heugh Farm Bed & Breakfast ★★★★ Farmhouse
Felton, Morpeth, Northumberland
NE65 9QH
t (01670) 787061
e carolinejanehogg@mac.com
w eshottheugh.co.uk

River Cottage ★★★★
Bed & Breakfast
Mouldhaugh Farm, Felton
NE65 9NP
t (01670) 787081
e easells@clara.co.uk
w river-cottage-bandb.co.uk

FENWICK

The Manor House ★★★★
Bed & Breakfast SILVER AWARD
7 The Village, Fenwick
TD15 2PQ
t (01289) 381016
e katemoore@homecall.co.uk
w manorhousefenwick.co.uk

FOXTON

Alnmouth Golf Club ★★★
Guest Accommodation
Foxton Hall, Alnmouth
NE66 3BE
t (01665) 830231
e secretary@alnmouthgolfclub.com
w alnmouthgolfclub.com

GILSLAND

Brookside Villa B&B ★★★★
Bed & Breakfast SILVER AWARD
Gilsland, Brampton
CA8 7DA
t (016977) 47300
e brooksidevilla@hotmail.com
w brooksidevilla.com

Samson Inn ★★★
Guest Accommodation
Gilsland
CA8 7DR
t (016977) 747220
e samsoninn@hotmail.co.uk
w samsoninn.co.uk

Tantallon House ★★★★
Bed & Breakfast SILVER AWARD
Gilsland, Cumbria
CA8 7DA
t (016977) 47111
e info@tantallonhouse.co.uk
w tantallonhouse.co.uk

GREAT TOSSON

Tosson Tower Farm B&B ★★★★★
Farmhouse GOLD AWARD
Rothbury
NE65 7NW
t (01669) 620228
e stay@tossontowerfarm.com
w tossontowerfarm.com

GREENHEAD

The Greenhead ★★★ Inn
Brampton
CA8 7HB
t (01697) 747 4111
e daveandsuegreenhead@btconnect.com

Holmhead Guest House ★★★★
Guest Accommodation
Holmhead, Hadrian's Wall, Greenhead, Northumberland
CA8 7HY
t 016977 47402
e holmhead@forestbarn.com
w bandbhadrianswall.com

GUIDEPOST

The Angler's Arms ★★★ Inn
Sheepwash Bank, Choppington
NE62 5NB
t (01670) 822300
e maureen.barry.walker@googlemail.com

GUYZANCE

East House Farm B&B ★★★★
Farmhouse
East House Farm, Guyzance
NE65 9AH
t (01665) 513022
e easthousebandb@tesco.net

HALTWHISTLE

Ashcroft Guest House ★★★★★
Guest House GOLD AWARD
Lanty's Lonnen, Ashcroft, Haltwhistle
NE49 0DA
t (01434) 320213
e info@ashcroftguesthouse.co.uk
w ashcroftguesthouse.co.uk

Burnhead Bed & Breakfast ★★★★ Bed & Breakfast
Cawfields
NE49 9PJ
t (01434) 320841
e enquiries@burnheadbedandbreakfast.co.uk
w burnheadbedandbreakfast.co.uk

Chare Close Bed & Breakfast ★★★★ Bed & Breakfast
Chare Close, Castle Hill, Haltwhistle
NE49 0EE
t (01434) 322789
e chareclose@btinternet.com
w chareclose.com

Four Wynds Guest House ★★★
Bed & Breakfast
Longbyre, Greenhead, Nr Haltwhistle, Northumberland
CA8 7HN
t (01697) 747972
e info@four-wynds-guest-house.co.uk
w four-wynds-guest-house.co.uk

Glendale Mews ★★★
Bed & Breakfast
North Road, Haltwhistle
NE49 9ND
t (01434) 320711
e philip@glendaleleisure.co.uk
w glendaleleisure.co.uk

The Grey Bull ★★★★
Guest Accommodation
Main Street, Haltwhistle
NE49 0DL
t (01434) 321991
e reception@greybullhotel.co.uk
w greybullhotel.co.uk

Hall Meadows ★★★★
Bed & Breakfast
Main Street, Haltwhistle
NE49 0AZ
t (01434) 321021
e richardhumes@tiscali.co.uk
w hallmeadows.co.uk

Kellah Farm B&B ★★★★
Farmhouse SILVER AWARD
Kellah, Haltwhistle
NE49 0JL
t (01434) 320816
e teasdale@ukonline.co.uk
w kellah.co.uk

Manor House Inn ★★★ Inn
Main Street, Haltwhistle
NE49 0BS
t (01434) 322588
e manorhouseinn@orangehome.co.uk

The Mount ★★★ Bed & Breakfast
Comb Hill, Haltwhistle
NE49 9NS
t (01434) 321075
e the-mount@talk21.com
w themountbb.co.uk

SAUGHY RIGG

Saughy Rigg Farm ★★★
Guest House
Twice Brewed
NE49 9PT
t (01434) 344120
e info@saughyrigg.co.uk
w saughyrigg.co.uk

Wydon Farm Bed & Breakfast ★★★★ Farmhouse SILVER AWARD
Wydon Farm, Haltwhistle
NE49 0LG
t (01434) 321702
e stay@wydon-haltwhistle.co.uk
w wydon-haltwhistle.co.uk

HARBOTTLE

Parsonside Bed & Breakfast ★★★★ Bed & Breakfast
Newton Farm, Harbottle
NE65 7DP
t (01669) 650275
e carolyn.graham@harbottle.net

HAYDON BRIDGE

Beggar Bog ★★★★ Farmhouse
Beggar Bog, Housesteads, Haydon Bridge
NE47 6NN
t (01434) 344652
e beggarbog@googlemail.com
w bandb-on-hadrianswall.co.uk

Grindon Cartshed ★★★★
Bed & Breakfast SILVER AWARD
Grindon Cartshed, Haydon Bridge, Hexham
NE47 6NQ
t (01434) 684273
e cartshed@grindon.force9.co.uk
w grindon-cartshed.co.uk

Hadrian Lodge ★★★
Guest Accommodation
Hindshield Moss, North Road, Haydon Bridge
NE47 6NF
t (01434) 684867
e hadrian-lodge@btconnect.com
w hadrianlodge.co.uk

Old Repeater Station ★★★ Hostel
Military Road, Grindon, Haydon Bridge
NE47 6NQ
t (01434) 688668
e les.gibson@tiscali.co.uk
w hadrians-wall-bedandbreakfast.co.uk

The Reading Rooms ★★★★
Bed & Breakfast
2 Church Street, Haydon Bridge
NE47 6JQ
t (01434) 688802
e thereadingrooms@aol.com
w thereadingroomshaydonbridge.co.uk

Shaftoe's Guest House ★★★★
Guest House
4 Shaftoe Street, Haydon Bridge
NE47 6BJ
t (01434) 684664
e bookings@shaftoes.co.uk
w shaftoes.co.uk

HEDDON-ON-THE-WALL

Houghton North Farm Visitor Accommodation ★★★★ Hostel
Houghton North Farm, Heddon-on-the-Wall, Northumberland
NE15 0EZ
t (01661) 854364
e wjlaws@btconnect.com
w hadrianswallaccommodation.com

699

North East | Northumberland

Ironsign Farm B&B ★★★★
Farmhouse **SILVER AWARD**
Military Road, Heddon-on-The-Wall
NE15 0JB
t (01661) 853802
e lowen532@aol.com
w ironsign.co.uk

HEXHAM

Carraw Bed & Breakfast ★★★★
Guest House **GOLD AWARD**
Carraw Farm, Military Road, Hexham
NE46 4DB
t (01434) 689857
e relax@carraw.co.uk
w carraw.co.uk

Crag House B&B ★★★★★
Bed & Breakfast
Crag House, Fallowfield, Hexham
NE46 4HA
t (01434) 681276
e md@fallowfield-alpacas.co.uk
w fallowfield-alpacas.co.uk

Dukesfield Hall Farm ★★★★
Bed & Breakfast
Steel
NE46 1SH
t (01434) 673634
e catherineswallow@btinternet.com
w dukesfieldhall.co.uk

Fairshaw Rigg ★★★★
Bed & Breakfast **SILVER AWARD**
Lowgate, Hexham
NE46 2NW
t (01434) 602630
e kathryn.shrimpton@btinternet.com
w fairshawrigg.co.uk

Hall Barns B&B ★★★★ *Farmhouse*
Hexham North Road, Simonburn
NE48 3AQ
t 01434 681419
e enquiries@hallbarns-simonburn.co.uk
w hallbarns-simonburn.co.uk

High Reins ★★★★ *Bed & Breakfast*
Leazes Lane, Hexham
NE46 3AT
t (01434) 603590
e walton45@hotmail.com
w highreins.co.uk

The Holly Bush Inn ★★★ *Inn*
Hexham
NE48 1PW
t (01434) 240391
e info@hollybushinn.net
w hollybushinn.net

Loughbrow House ★★★★
Guest Accommodation
Dipton Mill Road, Hexham
NE46 1RS
t (01434) 603351
e patriciaclark351@bt.com
w loughbrow.fsnet.co.uk

Station Inn ★★ *Inn*
Station Road, Hexham
NE46 1EZ
t (01434) 603155
e info@stationinnhexham.co.uk
w stationinnhexham.co.uk

Travellers Rest ★★★★ *Inn*
Slaley, Hexham, Northumberland
NE46 1TT
t (01434) 673231
e info@travellersrestslaley.com
w travellersrestslaley.com

Woodley Field ★★★★
Bed & Breakfast
Allendale Road, Hexham
NE46 2NB
t (01434) 601600
e woodleyfield@btinternet.com
w woodleyfield.co.uk

HIGH BUSTON

Old Stables ★★★★
Bed & Breakfast
High Buston
NE66 3QH
t (01665) 833117
e oldstables@mac.com
w oldstables.biz

HOLY ISLAND

The Bungalow ★★★★
Guest Accommodation
SILVER AWARD
Chare Ends, Holy Island, Berwick upon Tweed, Northumberland
TD15 2SE
t (01289) 389308
e bungalow@lindisfarne.org.uk
w lindisfarne.org.uk/bungalow

The Ship ★★★ *Inn*
Marygate, Holy Island
TD15 2SJ
t (01289) 389311
e the_ship_inn@btconnect.com
w theshipinn-holyisland.co.uk

HORNCLIFFE

West Longridge Manor ★★★★★
Bed & Breakfast
Horncliffe, Berwick-upon-Tweed
TD15 2JX
t (01289) 331112
e robert@westlongridge.co.uk
w westlongridge.co.uk

HUMSHAUGH

Greencarts ★★★★ *Farmhouse*
Humshaugh
NE46 4BW
t (01434) 681320
e sandra@greencarts.co.uk
w greencarts.co.uk

INGRAM

Ingram House ★★★★
Bed & Breakfast **SILVER AWARD**
Ingram, Alnwick
NE66 4LT
t (01665) 578906
e jane_levien@hotmail.com
w ingram-house.com

KIELDER

Kielder YHA ★★★★ *Hostel*
Butteryhaugh, Kielder
NE48 1HQ
t 0870 770 5898
e kielder@yha.org.uk
w yha.org.uk

Twenty Seven B&B and Self Catering Cottage ★★
Bed & Breakfast
27 Castle Drive, Kielder
NE48 1EQ
t (01434) 250366
e twentyseven@staykielder.co.uk
w staykielder.co.uk

KIELDER WATER

The Pheasant Inn (by Kielder Water) ★★★★ *Inn* **SILVER AWARD**
Stannersburn, Falstone
NE48 1DD
t (01434) 240382
e stay@thepheasantinn.com
w thepheasantinn.com

KIRKNEWTON

Hethpool House Bed & Breakfast
★★★ *Bed & Breakfast*
Hethpool, Kirknewton
NE71 6TW
t (01668) 216232
e eildon@hethpoolhouse.co.uk
w hethpoolhouse.co.uk

KIRKWHELPINGTON

Cornhills Farmhouse ★★★★
Farmhouse **SILVER AWARD**
Kirkwhelpington
NE19 2RE
t (01830) 540232
e lmt@northumberlandfarmhouse.co.uk
w northumberlandfarmhouse.co.uk

LESBURY

Swallowdale Cottage ★★★★
Bed & Breakfast
Longhoughton Road, Lesbury
NE66 3AT
t (01665) 830389
e swallowdale@fsmail.net
w swallowdale.org.uk

LONGFRAMLINGTON

The Anglers Arms ★★★★ *Inn*
Weldon Bridge, Longframlington
NE65 8AX
t (01665) 570655
e johnyoung@anglersarms.fsnet.co.uk
w anglersarms.com

Coquet Bed & Breakfast ★★★★
Farmhouse **GOLD AWARD**
Elyhaugh Farm, Longframlington
NE65 8BE
t (01665) 570305
e stay@coquetbb.co.uk
w coquetbb.co.uk

Granby Inn & Restaurant ★★★
Inn
Front Street, Longframlington
NE65 8DP
t (01665) 570228
e info@thegranbyinn.co.uk
w thegranbyinn.co.uk

LONGHORSLEY

Thistleyhaugh Farm ★★★★★
Farmhouse **GOLD AWARD**
Thistleyhaugh Farm, Longhorsley, Morpeth, Northumberland
NE65 8RG
t (01665) 570629
e thistleyhaugh@hotmail.com
w thistleyhaugh.co.uk

LONGHOUGHTON

Chestnut Tree House ★★★★
Guest Accommodation
7 Crowlea Road, Longhoughton
NE66 3AN
t (01665) 577153
e janetholtuk@btinternet.com
w chestnuttreeholidays.co.uk

Number One ★★★★
Bed & Breakfast **SILVER AWARD**
1 Springfield, Longhoughton
NE66 3NT
t (01665) 577811
e christine.wilson@numberonespringfield.co.uk
w numberonespringfield.co.uk

Swallows' Rest ★★★★
Bed & Breakfast **GOLD AWARD**
8 The Croft, Longhoughton
NE66 3DD
t (01665) 577425
e stay@swallows-rest.co.uk
w swallows-rest.co.uk

LOWICK

Burn House Bed & Breakfast
★★★★ *Bed & Breakfast*
SILVER AWARD
Lowick Common, Lowick
TD15 2UG
t (01289) 388457
e margaretsoutter@btinternet.com
w burn-house.co.uk

Primrose Cottage ★★★★
Bed & Breakfast **SILVER AWARD**
Main Street, Lowick
TD15 2UA
t (01289) 388900
e info@primrosecottagelowick.co.uk
w primrosecottagelowick.co.uk

MILFIELD

Retlaw Saddlery ★★★★
Bed & Breakfast
Main Road, Milfield
NE71 6JD
t (01668) 216055
e retlawbb@btinternet.com
w retlawsaddlerybedandbreakfast.co.uk

MOHOPE

YHA Ninebanks ★★★★ *Hostel*
Orchard House, Mohope
NE47 8DQ
t (01434) 345288
e ninebanks@yha.org.uk
w yha.ninebanks.org.uk

MORPETH

Castle View B&B ★★★★
Guest House
6 Dacre Street, Morpeth
NE61 1HW
t (01670) 514140
e info@castleviewbedandbreakfas.co.uk
w castleviewbedandbreakfast.co.uk

Cottingburn House B&B ★★★
Bed & Breakfast
40 Bullers Green, Morpeth
NE61 1DE
t (01670) 503195
e enquiries@cottingburnhouse.co.uk
w cottingburnhouse.co.uk

Kington ★★★★ *Bed & Breakfast*
East Linden, Longhorsley
NE65 8TH
t 01670 788554
e clivetaylor.services@tiscali.co.uk
w kington-longhorsley.com

Lansdown House ★★★★
Bed & Breakfast
90 Newgate Street, Morpeth
NE61 1BU
t (01670) 511129
e kitchendiva@gmail.com
w lansdownhouse.co.uk

Morpeth Court ★★★★
Guest Accommodation - Room Only
Castle Bank, Morpeth
NE61 1YJ
t (01670) 517217
e carol_edmundson@hotmail.com
w morpethcourt.com

Morpeth Lodge ★★★
Guest Accommodation
6 Staithes Lane, Morpeth
NE61 1TD
t (01670) 518550
e bookings@morpethlodge.co.uk
w morpethlodge.co.uk

Newminster Cottage ★★★★
Bed & Breakfast
High Stanners, Morpeth
NE61 1QL
t (01670) 503124
e enquiries@newminster-cottage.co.uk
w newminster-cottage.co.uk

Northumberland Cottage ★★★★
Guest House
Chevington Moor, Chevington
NE61 3BA
t (01670) 783339
e info@northumberland-cottage.co.uk
w northumberland-cottage.co.uk

North East | Northumberland

epping Stones B&B ★★★★
uest Accommodation
 Newgate Street, Morpeth
E61 1BX
t (01670) 517869
e steppingstonesbb@aol.com
w steppingstonesbedandbreakfast.co.uk

he Village Inn ★★★ *Inn*
ngframlington, Morpeth
E65 8AD
t (01670) 570268
e steelswheels@hotmail.com
w thevillageinnpub.co.uk

NEWBIGGIN-BY-THE-SEA

aptain's Lodge B&B ★★★★
d & Breakfast
 Haven View, Newbiggin-by-the-
 4 6NR
t (01670) 810082
e captains.lodge@btinternet.com
w captainslodge.co.uk

he Old Ship ★★★ *Inn*
 Front Street, Newbiggin-by-the-
ea
E64 6NJ
t (01670) 817212

ea-ton House ★★ *Bed & Breakfast*
 Seaton Avenue, Newbiggin-by-
e-Sea
E64 6UX
t (01670) 816057
e marybob.dodds@googlemail.com

NEWBROUGH

arr Edge Farm ★★★★ *Farmhouse*
ewbrough, Hexham,
orthumberland
E47 5EA
t (01434) 674788
e stay@carredge.co.uk
w carredge.co.uk

estfield Bed & Breakfast ★★★★
d & Breakfast
ewbrough
E47 5AR
t (01434) 674241
e byhexham@aol.com
w westfieldbandb.co.uk

NEWTON-ON-THE-MOOR

he Old School ★★★★
d & Breakfast **GOLD AWARD**
ewton-on-the-Moor, Alnwick
E65 9JY
t (01665) 575767
e info@northumberlandbedandbreakfast.co.uk
w theoldschool.eu

NORTH SUNDERLAND

he Olde School House ★★★
uest House
 North Lane, North Sunderland
E68 7UQ
t (01665) 720760
e theoldeschoolhouse@hotmail.co.uk
w theoldeschoolhouse.co.uk

ailston House ★★★★
uest Accommodation
ILVER AWARD
33 Main Street, North Sunderland
E68 7TS
t (01665) 720912
e twgrundy@btinternet.com
w railstonhouse.com

pringwood ★★★★
d & Breakfast **SILVER AWARD**
outh Lane, North Sunderland
E68 7UL
t (01665) 720320
e marian@slatehall.freeserve.co.uk
w visitseahouses.co.uk/

Wyndgrove House ★★★★
Guest Accommodation
156 Main Street, North Sunderland
NE68 7UA
t (01665) 722855
e donnathurgood@tiscali.co.uk
w wyndgrove.co.uk

NORTH TOGSTON

Togston Hall Farmhouse ★★★
Farmhouse
North Togston
NE65 0HR
t (01665) 712699
e farmhousebnbleslie@yahoo.co.uk
w togstonhallfarmhouse.net

OAKWOOD

Oakwood Cottage ★★★★
Bed & Breakfast **SILVER AWARD**
Oakwood
NE46 4LE
t (01434) 602013
e sturner@oakwoodcottage.com
w oakwoodcottage.com

OTTERBURN

Butterchurn Guest House ★★★★
Guest House
Main Street, Otterburn
NE19 1NP
t (01830) 520585
e valarieanderson@unicombox.co.uk
w butterchurnguesthouse.co.uk

Dunns Houses Farmhouse Bed & Breakfast ★★★★ *Farmhouse*
Dunns Houses Farm, Otterburn,
Newcastle upon Tyne,
Northumberland
NE19 1LB
t (01830) 520677
e dunnshouses@hotmail.com
w northumberlandfarmholidays.co.uk

OVINGTON

Ovington House Bed & Breakfast ★★★★ *Bed & Breakfast*
SILVER AWARD
Ovington House, Ovington
NE42 6DH
t (01661) 832442
e stay@ovingtonhouse.co.uk
w ovingtonhouse.co.uk

POWBURN

Cheviot View ★★★★
Bed & Breakfast **SILVER AWARD**
Powburn
NE66 4HL
t (01665) 578306
e cheviotview@hotmail.co.uk
w wcheviotview.com

Crawley Farmhouse ★★★
Farmhouse
Powburn
NE66 4JA
t (01665) 578413
e crawleyfarmhouse@hotmail.co.uk

Low Hedgeley Farm ★★★★★
Farmhouse **SILVER AWARD**
Powburn, Alnwick
NE66 4JD
t (01665) 578815
e dianavickers@hotmail.com
w lowhedgeleyfarm.co.uk

RIDING MILL

Low Fotherley Farmhouse Bed & Breakfast ★★★★ *Farmhouse*
Low Fotherley Farm, Riding Mill
NE44 6BB
t (01434) 682377
e hugh@lowfotherley.fsnet.co.uk
w westfarm.freeserve.co.uk

RIDSDALE

The Gun Inn ★★★ *Inn*
Ridsdale
NE48 2TF
t (01434) 270223
e lizasksyou@yahoo.co.uk
w guninn.co.uk

ROTHBURY

Burnfoot Guest House ★★★★
Guest Accommodation
Netherton, Rothbury
NE65 7EY
t 05601 933722
e burnfootghouse@btinternet.com
w burnfoothouse.co.uk

The Haven ★★★★
Guest Accommodation
Back Crofts, Rothbury
NE65 7YA
t (01669) 620577
e the.haven.rothbury@talk21.com
w thehavenrothbury.co.uk

Hillcrest B&B *Guest Accommodation*
Hillcrest House, Rothbury
NE65 7TL
t (01669) 621944
e enquiries@hillcrestnadb.co.uk
w hillcrestbandb.co.uk

Katerina's Guest House ★★★★
Guest House **SILVER AWARD**
Katerina's Guest House, Sun
Buildings, Rothbury
NE65 7TQ
t (01669) 620691
e cath@katerinasguesthouse.co.uk
w katerinasguesthouse.co.uk

Lee Farm ★★★★★ *Farmhouse*
GOLD AWARD
Rothbury
NE65 8JQ
t (01665) 570257
e enqs@leefarm.co.uk
w leefarm.co.uk

Queens Head - Rothbury ★★★
Inn
The Queens Head, Townfoot,
Rothbury, Northumberland
NE65 7SR
t (01669) 620470
e enqs@queensheadrothbury.co.uk
w queensheadrothbury.com

Springfield House ★★★★
Guest House
Townfoot, Rothbury
NE65 7SP
t (01669) 621277
e enquiries@springfieldguesthouse.co.uk
w springfieldguesthouse.co.uk

Wagtail Farm ★★★★ *Farmhouse*
Rothbury
NE65 7PL
t (01669) 620367
e wagtail@tinyworld.co.uk
w wagtailfarm.info

SEAHOUSES

Fairfield B&B ★★★ *Bed & Breakfast*
102 Main Street, Seahouses
NE68 7TP
t (01665) 721736
e fairfield@mypostoffice.co.uk

Gun Rock ★★★★ *Bed & Breakfast*
15 St Aidans, Seahouses
NE68 7SS
t (01665) 721980
e gunrock.oxley@googlemail.com
w gunrockseahouses.co.uk

Holly Trees ★★★★ *Bed & Breakfast*
4 James Street, Seahouses
NE68 7YB
t (01665) 721942
e margaret.tucker@btinternet.com

Kingsway ★★★
Guest Accommodation
19-21 King Street, Seahouses
NE68 7XW
t (01665) 720621
e enquiries@kingsway-guesthouse.co.uk
w kingsway-guesthouse.co.uk

Leeholme ★★★ *Bed & Breakfast*
Leeholme, 93 Main Street,
Seahouses
NE68 7TS
t (01665) 720230
e l.b.evans@btinternet.com

The Lodge ★★★
Guest Accommodation
146 Main Street, North Sunderland,
Seahouses
NE68 7TZ
t (01665) 720158
e thelodge@hotmail.com
w thelodgeseahouses.co.uk

The Lookout Bunkhouse & Wigwams *Hostel*
Springhill Farm, Seahouses
NE68 7UR
t (01665) 721820
e enquiries@springhill-farm.co.uk
w springhill-farm.co.uk

Malabar ★★★★ *Guest House*
20 King Street, Seahouses
NE68 7XP
t (01665) 720531
e malabarenquiries@btinternet.com
w malabar-seahouses.co.uk/

The Olde Ship ★★★★ *Inn*
SILVER AWARD
Main Street, Seahouses
NE68 7RD
t (01665) 720200
e theoldeship@seahouses.co.uk
w seahouses.co.uk

The Old Manse ★★★★
Bed & Breakfast
9 North Lane, Seahouses
NE68 7UQ
t (01665) 720521
e info@theoldemanse.com
w theoldemanse.com

Regal House ★★★★
Bed & Breakfast
6 Regal Close, Seahouses
NE68 7US
t (01665) 720008
e julieashford1@btinternet.com
w regalhouse-seahouses.co.uk

Rowena ★★★
Guest Accommodation
99 Main Street, North Sunderland,
Seahouses
NE68 7TS
t (01665) 721309

Spindrift ★★★★ *Bed & Breakfast*
SILVER AWARD
Kings Field, Seahouses
NE68 7PA
t (01665) 721677
e suewilkinson321@msn.com
w spindrift-seahouses.co.uk

St Cuthbert's House ★★★★★
Guest Accommodation
SILVER AWARD
192 Main Street, North Sunderland,
Seahouses
NE68 7UB
t (01665) 720456
e stay@stcuthbertshouse.com
w stcuthbertshouse.com

SIMONBURN

Simonburn Guest House ★★
Bed & Breakfast
1 The Mains, Simonburn
NE48 3AW
t (01434) 681321
e ann@simonburntearooms.com
w simonburntearooms.com

SLALEY

Forest View B&B ★★
Bed & Breakfast
Main Street, Slaley, Hexham
NE47 0BQ
t (01434) 673486
e moyra@rrca.co.uk

Rye Hill Farm ★★★★ *Farmhouse*
Slaley
NE47 0AH
t (01434) 673259
e info@ryehillfarm.co.uk
w ryehillfarm.co.uk

North East | Northumberland

SPITTAL

Caroline House ★★★
Bed & Breakfast
Main Street, Spittal
TD15 1RD
t (01289) 307595
e carolinehouse@hotmail.com
w carolinehouse.net

The Roxburgh Guest House ★★★
Guest House
117 Main Street, Spittal
TD15 1RP
t (01289) 306266
e roxburghhotel@aol.com
w roxburghguesthouse.co.uk

STANNINGTON

Cheviot View Farmhouse Bed & Breakfast ★★★★ *Farmhouse*
SILVER AWARD
North Shotton Farm, Morpeth
NE61 6EU
t (01670) 789231
e julie.philli@btconnect.com
w cheviotviewfarmhouse.co.uk

STOCKSFIELD

Locksley, Bed & Breakfast ★★★★
Bed & Breakfast GOLD AWARD
45 Meadowfield Road, Stocksfield
NE43 7PY
t (01661) 844778
e josie@locksleybedandbreakfast.co.uk
w locksleybedandbreakfast.co.uk

Old Ridley Hall ★★★
Guest Accommodation
Stocksfield
NE43 7RU
t (01661) 842816
e oldridleyhall@talk21.com

SWARLAND

Swarland Old Hall ★★★★★
Farmhouse GOLD AWARD
Alnwick
NE65 9HU
t (01670) 787642
e proctor@swarlandoldhall.fsnet.co.uk
w swarlandoldhall.co.uk

TARSET

Eals Lodge B&B ★★★★
Bed & Breakfast
Tarset
NE48 1LF
t (01434) 240269
e stay@ealslodgebandb.co.uk

TARSET, BY KEILDER WATER, HEXHAM

Snabdough Farm ★★★★
Farmhouse
Tarset, By Keilder Water, Hexham
NE48 1LB
t (01434) 240239

THORNTON

The Old School House ★★★★
Bed & Breakfast SILVER AWARD
Thornton, Berwick-upon-Tweed
TD15 2LP
t (01289) 382000
e johnburton2@waitrose.com
w oshthornton.co.uk

THROPTON

Farm Cottage Guest House
★★★★★ *Guest House*
GOLD AWARD
Thropton
NE65 7NA
t (01669) 620831
e joan@farmcottageguesthouse.co.uk
w farmcottageguesthouse.co.uk

Lorbottle West Steads ★★★★
Farmhouse
Thropton
NE65 7JT
t (01665) 574672
e info@lorbottle.com
w lorbottle.com

Thropton Demesne Farmhouse B&B ★★★★★ *Guest House*
Thropton
NE65 7LT
t (01669) 620196
e thropton_demesne@yahoo.co.uk
w throptondemesne.co.uk

TILLMOUTH

The Old School House B&B
★★★★★ *Bed & Breakfast*
GOLD AWARD
Tillmouth Park, Tillmouth
TD12 4UT
t (01890) 882463
e noelhodgson@btinternet.com
w tillmouthschoolhouse.co.uk

TWEEDMOUTH

Embleton House B&B ★★
Bed & Breakfast
78 Shielfield Terrace, Tweedmouth,
Berwick-upon-Tweed
TD15 2EE
t (01289) 305000
e aichafagan@hotmail.co.uk

Ford Castle ★★★ *Group Hostel*
Ford Village
TD15 2PX
t (01890) 820257
e fordcastle@northumberland.gov.uk

WALL

The Hadrian ★★★ *Inn*
The Hadrian, Wall Village, Hexham
NE46 4EE
t (01434) 681232
e david.lindsay13@btinternet.com
w hadrianhotel.com

WARDEN

The Boatside Inn ★★★★ *Inn*
Warden
NE46 4SQ
t (01434) 602233
e sales@theboatsideinn.com
w theboatsideinn.com

WARK

The Battlesteads ★★★★ *Inn*
SILVER AWARD
Wark
NE48 3LS
t (01434) 230209
e info@battlesteads.com
w battlesteads.com

WARKWORTH

Beck 'N' Call ★★★★
Bed & Breakfast
Birling West Cottage, Warkworth
NE65 0XS
t (01665) 711653
e beck-n-call@lineone.net
w beck-n-call.co.uk

Fairfield House ★★★★★
Guest House SILVER AWARD
16 Station Road, Warkworth
NE65 0XP
t (01665) 714455
e mandy@fairfield-guesthouse.com
w fairfield-guesthouse.com

Morwick House Bed & Breakfast
★★★★ *Guest Accommodation*
SILVER AWARD
Beal Bank, Warkworth
NE65 0TB
t (01665) 712101
e stay@morwickhouse.co.uk
w morwickhouse.co.uk

Number 28 ★★★★ *Bed & Breakfast*
28 Castle Street, Warkworth
NE65 0UL
t (01665) 712869
e johnross57@aol.com

The Old Manse ★★★★
Bed & Breakfast
20 The Butts, Warkworth
NE65 0SS
t (01665) 710850
e a.coulter1@btinternet.com
w oldmanse.info

Roxbro House ★★★★★
Bed & Breakfast GOLD AWARD
5 Castle Terrace, Warkworth
NE65 0UP
t (01665) 711416
e info@roxbrohouse.co.uk
w roxbrohouse.co.uk

Tower House B&B ★★★★
Bed & Breakfast SILVER AWARD
47 Castle Street, Warkworth
NE65 0UN
t (01665) 714375
e tower.1@tiscali.co.uk
w towerhousebandb.co.uk/

Westrigg Bed & BreakfaSt ★★★★
Bed & Breakfast SILVER AWARD
30 Watershaugh Road, Warkworth
NE65 0TX
t (01665) 711410
e katiemorwick@yahoo.com
w westriggbedandbreakfast.co.uk

WEST WOODBURN

Bay Horse Inn ★★★ *Inn*
The Bay Horse Inn, West Woodburn,
Hexham
NE48 2RX
t (01434) 270218
e enquiry@bayhorseinn.org
w bayhorseinn.org

Yellow House Farm B&B ★★★★
Farmhouse
West Woodburn
NE48 2SB
t (01434) 270070
e avril@yellowhousebandb.com
w yellowhousebandb.co.uk

WHITTONSTALL

The Anchor Inn ★★★★ *Inn*
Whittonstall, Stocksfield
DH8 9JN
t (01207) 561110
e theanchorinnwhittonstall@talktalk.net
w theanchorinnwhittonstall.co.uk

WINGATES

Pele Cottage ★★★★
Bed & Breakfast GOLD AWARD
Wingates, Longhorsley,
Northumberland
NE65 8RW
t (01670) 788320
e jane@pelecottage.co.uk
w pelecottage.co.uk

South Farm ★★★★★ *Farmhouse*
GOLD AWARD
Wingates, Longhorsley
NE65 8RW
t (01670) 788562
e stay@southfarmwingates.co.uk
w southfarmwingates.co.uk

WOOLER

Belmont House Bed & Breakfast
★★★★ *Bed & Breakfast*
Belmont House, 15 Glendale Road,
Wooler
NE71 6DN
t (01668) 283769
e susan@belmonthouse.org
w belmonthouse.org

Cheviot View Bed & Breakfast
★★★★ *Bed & Breakfast*
24 High Street, Wooler
NE71 6BY
t (01668) 281612
e woolercheviotview@btinternet.com
w cheviotview-wooler.co.uk

East Horton House ★★★★★
Bed & Breakfast SILVER AWARD
East Horton Farm, Wooler,
Northumberland
NE71 6EZ
t (01668) 215216
e sed@hazelrigg.fsnet.co.uk
w easthousebandb.co.uk

Firwood Country Bed and Breakfast ★★★★★ *Bed & Breakfa*
GOLD AWARD
Middleton Hall, Wooler,
Northumberland
NE71 6RD
t (01668) 283699
e welcome@firwoodhouse.co.uk
w firwoodhouse.co.uk

The Hemmel Wooler ★★★★
Bed & Breakfast
Way to Wooler Farm, Weetwood
Road, Wooler
NE71 6AQ
t (01668) 283165
e j.staden@btopenworld.com
w thehemmelwooler.co.uk

Millyard House B&B ★★★★
Bed & Breakfast
12 South Road, Wooler
NE71 6NL
t (01668) 282165
e bobsnooks@hotmail.com
w millyardhouse.co.uk

Old Manse ★★★★★
Guest Accommodation
GOLD AWARD
New Road, Chatton, Alnwick
NE66 5PU
t (01668) 215343
e chattonbb@aol.com
w oldmansechatton.co.uk

Rockliffe House ★★★★
Bed & Breakfast SILVER AWARD
6 Glendale Road, Wooler
NE71 6DN
t (01668) 283992
e info@rockliffehouse.co.uk
w rockliffehouse.co.uk

Tilldale House ★★★★
Guest Accommodation
SILVER AWARD
34-40 High Street, Wooler
NE71 6BG
t (01668) 281450
e tilldalehouse@freezone.co.uk
w tilldalehouse.co.uk

Wooler YHA ★★★ *Hostel*
30 Cheviot Street, Wooler
NE71 6LW
t 0870 770 6100
e wooler@yha.org.uk
w yha.org.uk

WYLAM

Wormald House ★★★★
Bed & Breakfast
Main Road, Wylam
NE41 8DN
t (01661) 852529
e angelacraven@btconnect.com
w wormaldhouse.co.uk

North East | Tyne and Wear

Tyne and Wear

BIRTLEY

The Bowes Incline ★★★★ *Inn*
Northside, Birtley, Chester-le-Street
DH3 1RF
t (01914) 102233
e info@bowesinclinehotel.co.uk
w bowesinclinehotel.co.uk

GATESHEAD

Alexandra Guest House ★★★
Guest House
Alexandra Guest House, 377
Alexandra Road, Gateshead
NE8 4HY
t (01914) 781105
w alexandraguesthouses.co.uk

The Bewick ★★★ *Guest House*
The Bewick, 145 Prince Consort
Road, Gateshead
NE8 4DS
t (01914) 771809
e welcome@bewick-hotel.com
w bewick-hotel.com

Park Farm ★★★★
Guest Accommodation
Kibblesworth Lane, Ravensworth,
Gateshead
NE11 0HS
t (01914) 824870
e enquiries@park-farm-hotel.co.uk
w park-farm-hotel.co.uk

Shaftesbury Guest House ★★★
Guest House
Shaftesbury Guest House, 245
Prince Consort Road, Gateshead
NE8 4DT
t (01914) 782544
e shaftesbury.hotel@hotmail.com
w shaftesburyguesthouse.co.uk/

GOSFORTH

The Town House ★★★★
Guest Accommodation
1 West Avenue, Gosforth
NE3 4ES
t (01912) 856812
e bookings@thetownhousehotel.co.uk
w thetownhousehotel.co.uk

JESMOND

The Adelphi ★★★ *Guest House*
8 Fern Avenue, Jesmond
NE2 2QU
t (01912) 813109
e maxine.calvert@yahoo.co.uk
w adelphihotelnewcastle.co.uk

Jesmond Park ★★★
Jesmond Park, 74-76 Queens Road,
Newcastle-upon-Tyne
NE2 2PR
t (01912) 812821
e vh@jespark.fsnet.co.uk
w jesmondpark.com

NEWCASTLE

Victoria Hall *Approved Campus*
Tyron Street, Newcastle
NE2 1XH
t 0845 168 9500
e newcastle@victoriahall.com
w victoriahall.com

NEWCASTLE-UPON-TYNE

The Avenue ★★★ *Guest House*
2 Manor House Road, Newcastle-upon-Tyne
NE2 2LU
t (01912) 811396
e avenue.newcastle@yahoo.co.uk

Backpackers Newcastle *Hostel*
152 Westgate Road, Newcastle-upon-Tyne
NE4 6AQ
t 0776 872 6810
e tonyknox@mobileema.vodafone.net
w backpackersnewcastle.com

Bentleys ★★ *Guest House*
Bentleys, 427 Westgate Road,
Newcastle-upon-Tyne
NE4 8RL
t (01912) 733497
e wendyhaldane@btconnect.com

Brandling Guest House ★★★
Guest House
Brandling Guest House, 4 Brandling
Park, Newcastle-upon-Tyne
NE2 4QA
t (01912) 813175
e johncatto@btconnect.com
w brandlingguesthouse.co.uk

The Brighton ★★
Guest Accommodation
The Brighton, 47-49 Brighton Grove,
Newcastle-upon-Tyne
NE4 5NS
t (01912) 733600
e wendyhaldane@aol.com

**Castle Leazes (Newcastle
University)** ★★ *Campus*
Castle Leazes Halls of Residence,
Spital Tongues, Newcastle-upon-Tyne
NE2 4NY
t (01912) 228362
e clh-hall-secretaries@ncl.ac.uk
w ncl.ac.uk/conferenceteam

The Dene ★★★
Guest Accommodation
The Dene, 38-42 Grosvenor Road,
Newcastle-upon-Tyne
NE2 2RP
t (01912) 811502
e denehotel@ukonline.co.uk

Greenholme ★★★ *Bed & Breakfast*
40 South View, East Denton,
Newcastle-upon-Tyne
NE5 2BP
t (01912) 674828
e info@greenholmeguesthouse.co.uk
w greenholmeguesthouse.co.uk

**Henderson Hall, University of
Newcastle** ★★★ *Campus*
Redhall Drive, Newcastle-upon-Tyne
NE7 7UY
t (01912) 223019
e admin.hh@ncl.ac.uk
w ncl.ac.uk/conferenceteam/henderson-hall.php

Newcastle YHA ★★★ *Hostel*
Newcastle YHA, 107 Jesmond Road,
Newcastle-upon-Tyne
NE2 1NJ
t (01912) 812570
e newcastle@yha.org.uk
w yha.org.uk

Northumbria University ★★★
Campus
Claude Gibb Hall and Camden
Court, University Precinct,
Newcastle-upon-Tyne
NE1 8ST
t (01912) 274717
e rc.conferences@northumbria.ac.uk
w northumbria.ac.uk/conferences

Riding Farm ★★★★ *Farmhouse*
Riding Farm House, Riding Lane,
Beamish Newcastle-upon-Tyne
NE11 0JA
t (01913) 701868
e stay@ridingfarmbedandbreakfast.co.uk
w ridingfarmbedandbreakfast.co.uk

NEWCASTLE UPON TYNE

Albatross ★★ *Backpackers*
Albatross, Backpackers IN!, 51
Grainger Street, Newcastle-upon-Tyne
NE1 5JE
t (0191) 2331330
e info@albatrossnewcastle.co.uk
w albatrossnewcastle.com

Clifton House Hotel ★★★
Guest Accommodation
Clifton House, 46 Clifton Road,
Newcastle-upon-Tyne
NE4 6XH
t (0191) 730407
e cliftonhousehotel@hotmail.com
w cliftonhousehotel.com

The Keelman's Lodge ★★★★
Guest Accommodation
Grange Road, Newburn, Newcastle-Upon-Tyne
NE15 8NL
t (0191) 2671689
e admin@biglampbrewers.co.uk
w keelmanslodge.co.uk

ROWLANDS GILL

Burn View ★★★★ *Bed & Breakfast*
Stirling Lane, Rowlands Gill
NE39 1PR
t (01207) 544014
e burnviewbnb@googlemail.com
w burnview.co.uk

RYTON

Hedgefield House ★★★
Guest Accommodation
Stella Road, Blaydon-on-Tyne
NE21 4LR
t (01914) 137373
e david@hedgefieldhouse.co.uk
w hedgefieldhouse.co.uk

SEABURN

Lemonfield Guesthouse ★★★★
Guest House
Sea Lane, Seaburn
SR6 8EE
t (01915) 293018
e gary@lemonfieldhotel.com
w lemonfieldhotel.com

SOUTH GOSFORTH

**Bowsden Court (Newcastle
University)** ★★★ *Campus*
South Gosforth, Newcastle-upon-Tyne
NE3 1RR
t (01912) 223019
e adminhh@newcastle.ac.uk

SOUTH SHIELDS

Ainsley Guest House ★★★
Guest House
Ainsley Guest House, 59 Ocean
Road, South Shields
NE33 2JJ
t (01914) 543399
e peterntracy@hotmail.com
w ainsleyguesthouse.co.uk

Atlantis Guest House ★★★★
Guest House
Atlantis Guest House, 55 Ocean
Road, South Shields
NE33 2JJ
t (01914) 556070
e hani.gazia@btinternet.com
w atlantisguesthouse.com

Beaches Guest House ★★★
Guest House
Beaches Guest House, 81 Ocean
Road, South Shields
NE33 2JJ
t (01914) 563262
e jdocchar@yahoo.co.uk
w beachesguesthouse.gbr.cc

Beechwood Guest House ★★★
Guest House
119 Ocean Road, South Shields
NE33 2JL
t (01914) 541829
e ask@beechwoodguesthouse.com
w beechwoodguesthouse.com

Britannia Guesthouse ★★★★
Guest House
Britannia Guesthouse, 54/56 Julian
Avenue, South Shields
NE33 2EW
t (01914) 560896
e cbgh56@hotmail.com
w britanniaguesthouse.co.uk

Clifton Guest House Ltd ★★★★
Guest House
Clifton Guest House, 101 Ocean
Road, South Shields
NE33 2JL
t (01914) 551965
e stay@theclifton.co.uk
w theclifton.co.uk/

Elmswood Guest House ★★★
Guest House
77 Ocean Road, South Shields
NE33 2JJ
t (01914) 553783
e info@elmswoodguesthouse.co.uk
w elmswoodguesthouse.co.uk

Forest Guest House ★★★★
Guest House
Forest Guest House, 117 Ocean
Road, South Shields
NE33 2JL
t (01914) 548160
e enquiries@forestguesthouse.com
w forestguesthouse.com

The Magpies Nest ★★★
Guest House
The Magpies Nest, 75 Ocean Road,
South Shields
NE33 2JJ
t (01914) 552361
e info@magpies-nest.co.uk
w magpies-nest.co.uk

Once Upon a Tyne ★★
Guest House
55 Beach Road, South Shields
NE33 2QU
t (01914) 543119
e liveonce@once-tyne.co.uk
w once-tyne.co.uk

Royale Guest House ★★★
Guest House
13 Urfa Terrace, South Shields
NE33 2ES
t (01914) 559085
w royaleguesthouse.net

Saraville Guest House ★★★
Guest House
103 Ocean Road, South Shields
NE33 2JL
t (01914) 541169
e emma@saraville.freeserve.co.uk
w geocities.com/saravillehouse

Seabreeze Guest House ★★★
Guest House
79 Ocean Road, South Shields
NE33 2JJ
t (01914) 558772
e enquiries@seabreeze-guesthouse.co.uk
w seabreeze-guesthouse.co.uk

Seaways Guest House
Guest Accommodation
91 Ocean Road, South Shields
NE33 2JL
t (01914) 271226
e enquiries@seaways-guesthouse.co.uk

SUNDERLAND

Abbey & Areldee Guest House
★★★ *Guest House*
Abbey & Areldee Guest House, 18
Roker Terrace, Sunderland
SR6 9NB
t (01915) 141971
e helen66@fsmail.net

Abingdon Guest House ★★★
Guest House
Abingdon Guest House, 5 St
Georges Terrace, Sunderland
SR6 9LX
t (01915) 140689
e karen@abingdonguesthouse.co.uk
w abingdonguesthouse.co.uk

North East | Tyne and Wear

April Guest House ★★★★
Guest House
April Guest House, 12 St Georges Terrace, Sunderland
SR6 9LX
t (0191) 659550
e hilda@dickinson2772.fslife.com
w aprilguesthouse.com

The Ashborne ★★★ *Guest House*
The Ashborne, 7 St Georges Terrace, Sunderland
SR6 9LX
t (0191) 653997
e ashborneguesthouse@btinternet.com
w ashborne-guesthouse.co.uk

Balmoral Guest House ★★★
Guest House
Balmoral Guest House, 3 Roker Terrace, Sunderland
SR6 9NB
t (0191) 659217
e thebalmoral@supanet.com
w thebalmoral.supanet.com

Belmont Guest House ★★★
Guest House
8 St Georges Terrace, Roker, Sunderland
SR6 9LX
t (0191) 672438
e belmontguesthouse@freedomnames.co.uk
w belmontguesthouse.com

The Chaise Guest House ★★★
Guest House
The Chaise Guest House, 5 Roker Terrace, Sunderland
SR6 9NB
t (0191) 659218
e thechaise@btconnect.com
w activereservations.com/hotel/en/hotels-in-sunderland/ah-116365.html

Felicitations ★★★ *Bed & Breakfast*
Felicitations, 94 Ewesley Road, Sunderland
SR4 7RJ
t (0191) 220960
e felicitations_uk@talk21.com
w felicitations.biz

Mayfield Guesthouse ★★★
Guest House
Mayfield Guesthouse, Sea Lane, Sunderland
SR6 8EE
t (0191) 293345
e enquiries@themayfieldguesthouse.co.uk
w themayfieldguesthouse.co.uk

Queen Vic Hotel ★★★
Guest Accommodation - Room Only
Harbour View, Roker, Sunderland
SR6 0PQ
t (0191) 654732
e thepullman77@yahoo.com

St George's Guest House ★★★
Guest House
6 St Georges Terrace, Sunderland
SR6 9LX
t (0191) 140689
e karen@abingdonguesthouse.co.uk
w abingdonguesthouse.co.uk

Terrace Guest House ★★★
Guest House
2 Roker Terrace, Sunderland
SR6 9NB
t (0191) 650132
e thebalmoral@supanet.com
w thebalmoral.supanet.com

TYNEMOUTH

Martineau Guest House ★★★★
Guest House SILVER AWARD
57 Front Street, Tynemouth, North Shields
NE30 4BX
t (01912) 579038
e martineauhouse@gmail.com
w martineau-house.co.uk

No 61, Guest House & Tea Rooms ★★★★ *Guest House*
No 61, Front Street, Tynemouth
NE30 4BT
t (01912) 573687
e no.61@btconnect.com
w no61.co.uk

WALLSEND

The Dorset Arms ★★★ *Inn*
The Dorset Arms, Dorset Avenue, Wallsend
NE28 8DX
t (01912) 099754
e info@dorsetarmshotel.co.uk
w dorsetarmshotel.co.uk

WASHINGTON

The Victoria Inn ★★★ *Inn*
Oxclose Road, Columbia, Washington
NE38 7DJ
t (01914) 172526
e carling2@aol.com
w victoriainnwashington.com

Ye Olde Cop Shop ★★★★
Guest House
6 The Green, Washington Village
NE38 7AB
t (01914) 165333
e yeoldecopshop@btopenworld.com

WHICKHAM

A1 Summerville Guest House
★★★ *Guest House*
A1 Summerville Guest House, 33 Orchard Road, Whickham
NE16 4TG
t (01914) 883388
e info@a1summerville.co.uk
w a1summerville.co.uk

East Byermoor Guest House
★★★★ *Guest House*
SILVER AWARD
East Byermoor Guest House, Fellside Road, Whickham
NE16 5BD
t (01207) 272687
e stay@eastbyermoor.co.uk
w eastbyermoor.co.uk

WHITLEY BAY

The Avalon Hotel ★★★
Guest Accommodation
26-28 South Parade, Whitley Bay
NE26 2RG
t (01912) 510080
e info@theavalon.co.uk
w theavalon.co.uk

The Cara ★★★ *Guest House*
The Cara, 9 The Links, Whitley Bay
NE26 1PS
t (01912) 530172
e info@caraguesthouse.co.uk
w caraguesthouse.co.uk

The Chedburgh ★★★
Guest Accommodation
12 Esplanade, Whitley Bay
NE26 2AH
t (01912) 530415
e chedburghhotel@aol.com
w chedburgh-hotel.co.uk

Esplanade Lodge ★★★
Guest House
Esplanade, Whitley Bay
NE26 2AA
t (01912) 517557
e esplanadelodge@hotmail.com
w esplanadelodge.co.uk

Lighthouse Guest House ★★
Guest Accommodation
20 North Parade, Whitley Bay
NE26 1PA
t (01912) 522319
e leachgerald@googlemail.com
w lighthouseguesthouse.co.uk

Lindsay Guest House ★★★★
Guest House
Lindsay Guest House, 50 Victoria Avenue, Whitley Bay
NE26 2BA
t (01912) 527341
e info@lindsayguesthouse.co.uk
w lindsayguesthouse.co.uk

Marlborough Hotel ★★★★
Guest Accommodation
20-21 East Parade, Whitley Bay, Tyne and Wear
NE26 1AP
t (01912) 513628
e reception@marlborough-hotel.com
w marlborough-hotel.com

The Northumbria ★★★
Guest Accommodation
The Northumbria, 51-52 Victoria Avenue, Whitley Bay
NE26 2BA
t (01912) 525265
e the.northumbria@btconnect.com
w the-northumbria.co.uk

Oaktree Lodge ★★★★
Guest House SILVER AWARD
15 Esplanade, Whitley Bay
NE26 2AH
t (01912) 528587
e oaktreelodge@aol.com
w oaktree-lodge.co.uk

Sunholme Guest House ★★★
Guest House
53 North Parade, Whitley Bay
NE26 1NX
t (01912) 511186
e craw@hotmail.co.uk
w sunholme.co.uk

York House ★★★★
Guest Accommodation
York House, 106-110 Park Avenue, Whitley Bay
NE26 1DN
t (01912) 528313
e reservations@yorkhousehotel.com
w yorkhousehotel.com

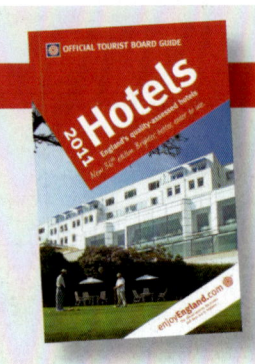

Looking for something else?

You can also buy a copy of our popular guide 'Hotels' including country house and town house hotels, metro and budget hotels, serviced apartments, restaurants with rooms and Spas in England 2011.

Now available in good bookshops and online at
visitbritainshop.com

£10.99

Enjoy England more.

If you're looking for ideas for a weekend break or just planning a day out you can be sure of reliable and inspirational ideas from England's tourist information services. And the best thing is that you can get information on the whole of England from any tourist information provider no matter where you are. Go online and find yours today.

enjoyEngland.com

enjoyEngland
OFFICIAL PARTNER

Map 1

Location Maps

Every place name featured in the regional accommodation sections of this Enjoy England guide has a map reference to help you locate it on the maps which follow. For example, to find Colchester, Essex, which has 'Map ref 3B2', turn to Map 3 and refer to grid square B2.

All place names appearing in the regional sections are shown with orange circles on the maps. This enables you to find other places in your chosen area which may have suitable accommodation – the place index (at the back of this guide) gives page numbers.

Key to regions: South West England

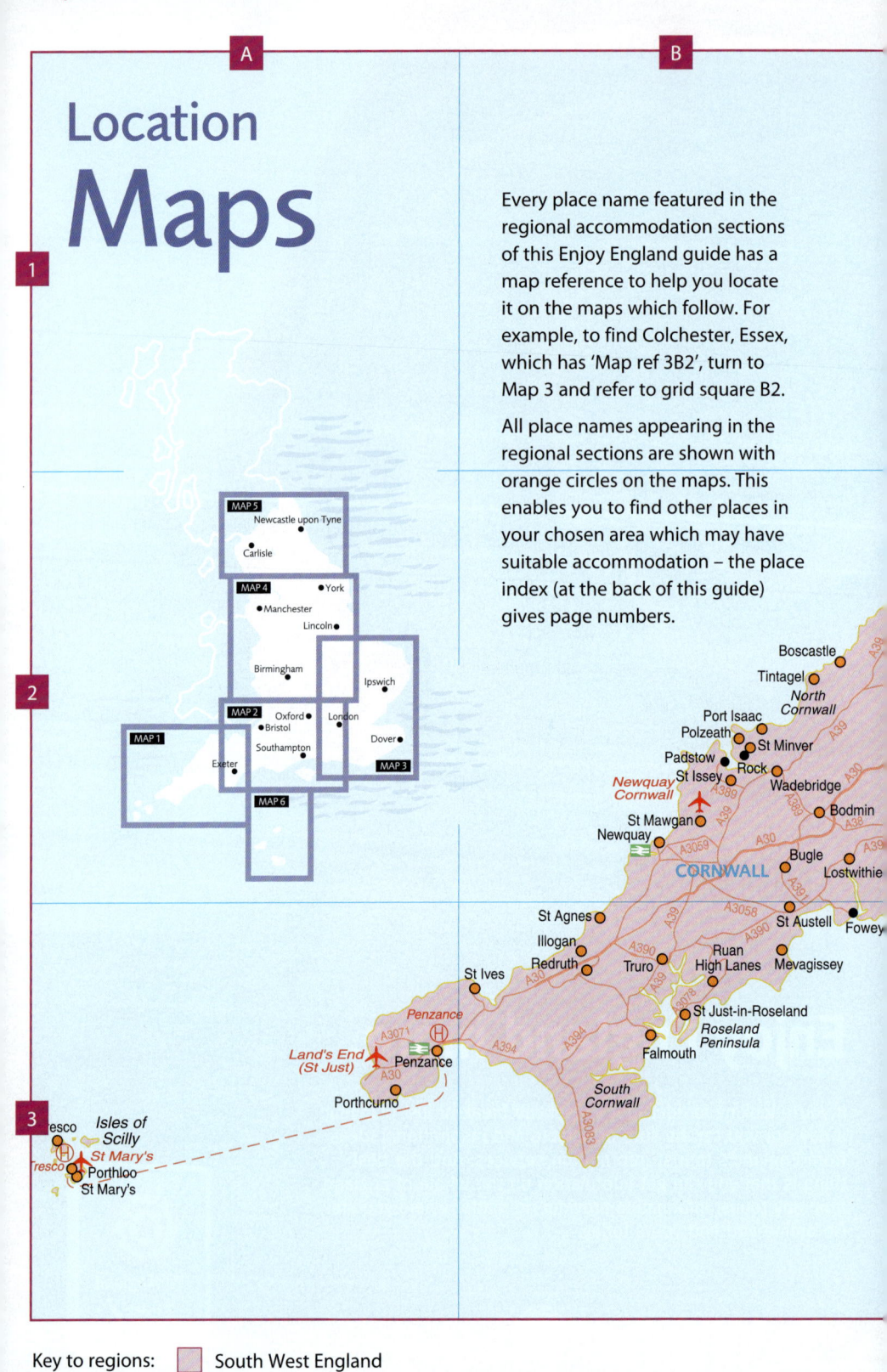

Map 1

Map 2

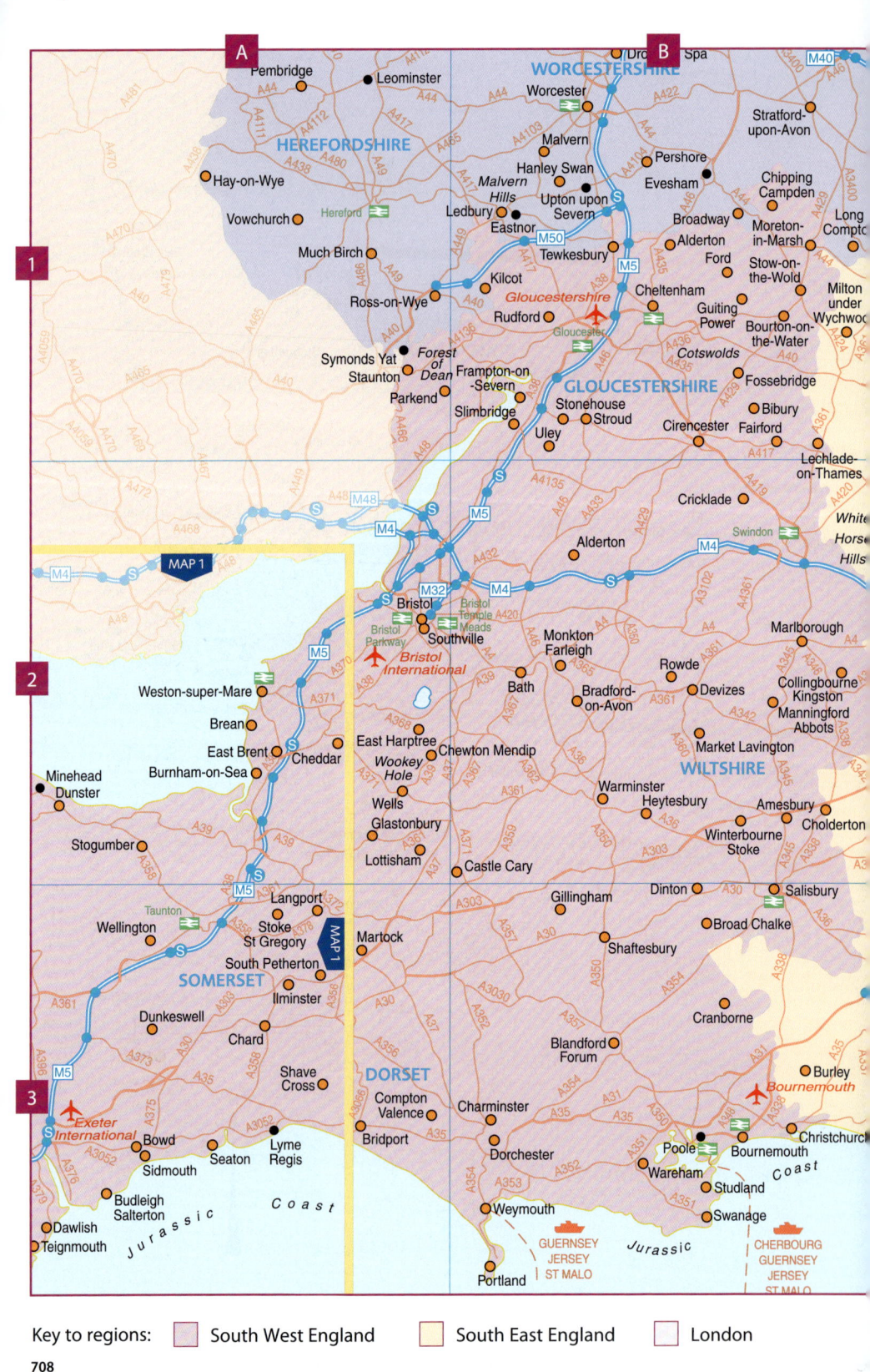

East of England | East Midlands | Heart of England

Orange circles indicate accommodation within the regional sections of this guide

Map 3

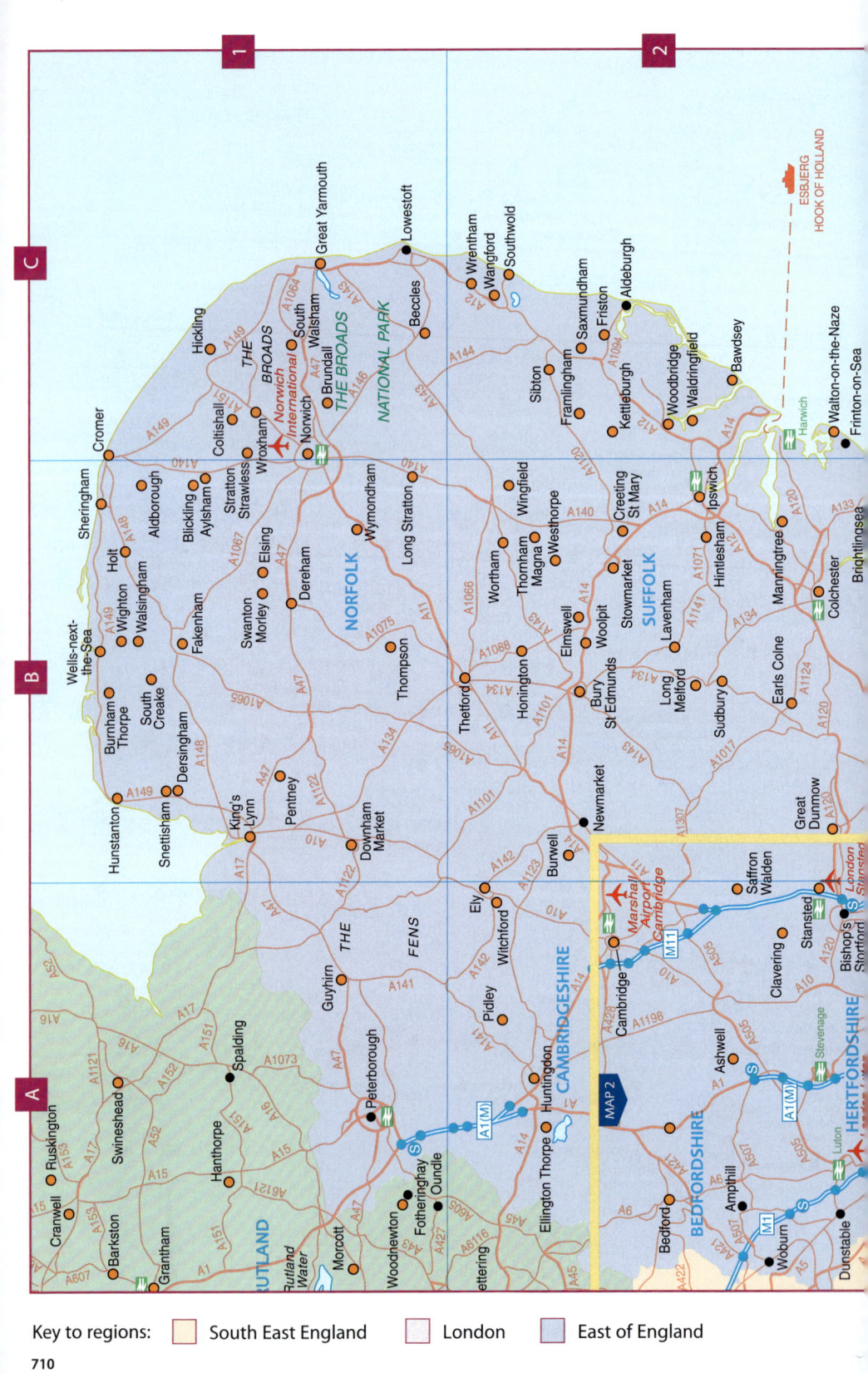

Map 3

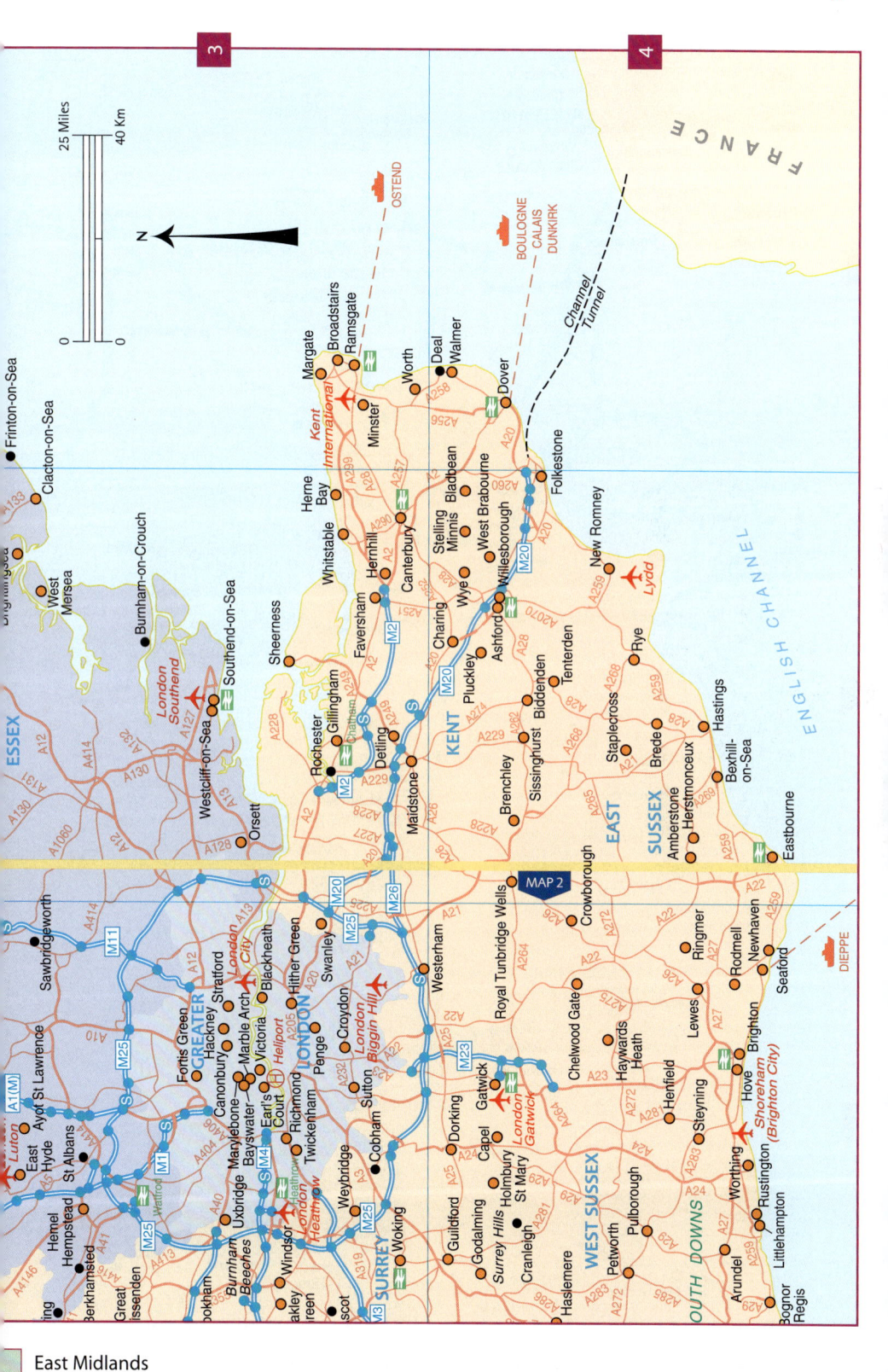

East Midlands

Orange circles indicate accommodation within the regional sections of this guide

711

Map 4

Yorkshire
North West England
North East England

Orange circles indicate accommodation within the regional sections of this guide

Map 5

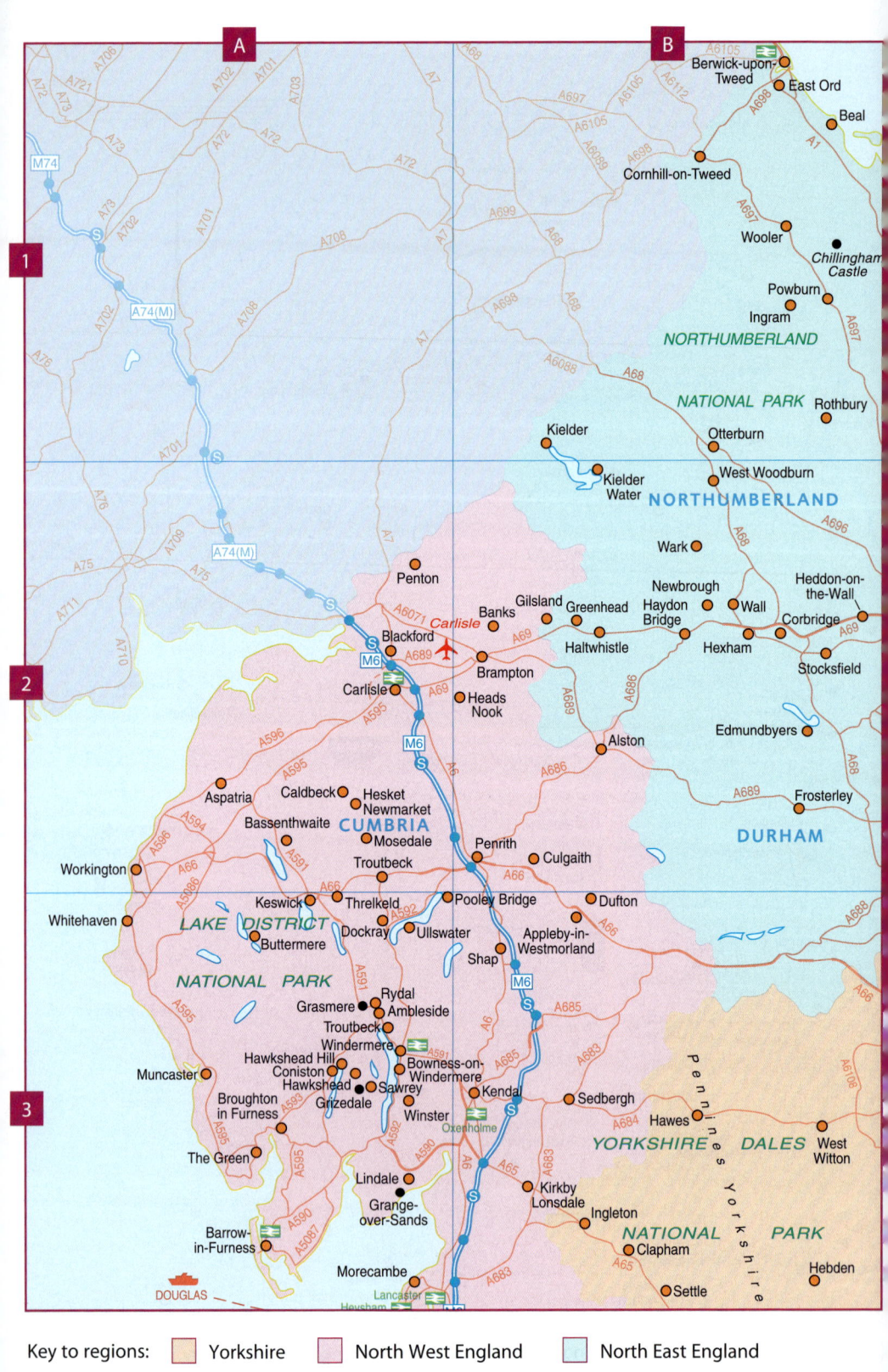

Map 5

Orange circles indicate accommodation within the regional sections of this guide

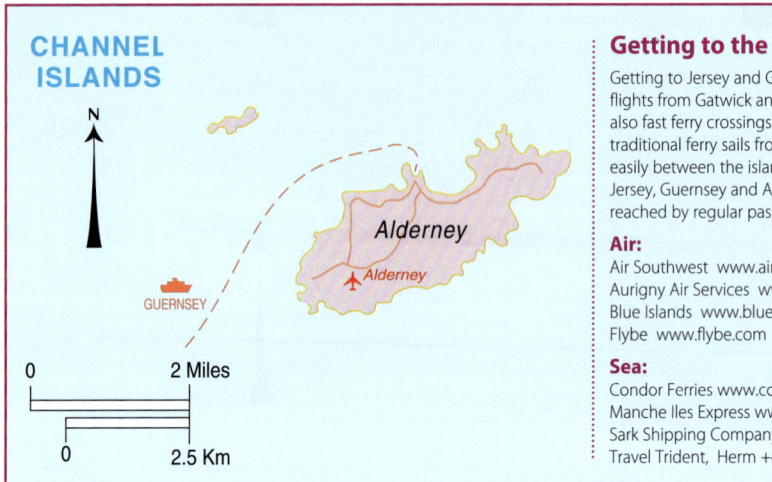

Map 6

CHANNEL ISLANDS

Getting to the Channel Islands

Getting to Jersey and Guernsey is simple, with regular flights from Gatwick and nine other airports. There are also fast ferry crossings from Poole and Weymouth. A traditional ferry sails from Portsmouth. You can travel easily between the islands, flights operate between Jersey, Guernsey and Alderney. Herm and Sark are reached by regular passenger ferries.

Air:
Air Southwest www.airsouthwest.com
Aurigny Air Services www.aurigny.com
Blue Islands www.blueislands.com
Flybe www.flybe.com

Sea:
Condor Ferries www.condorferries.com
Manche Iles Express www.manche-iles-express.com
Sark Shipping Company www.sarkshipping.info
Travel Trident, Herm +44 (0) 1481 721379

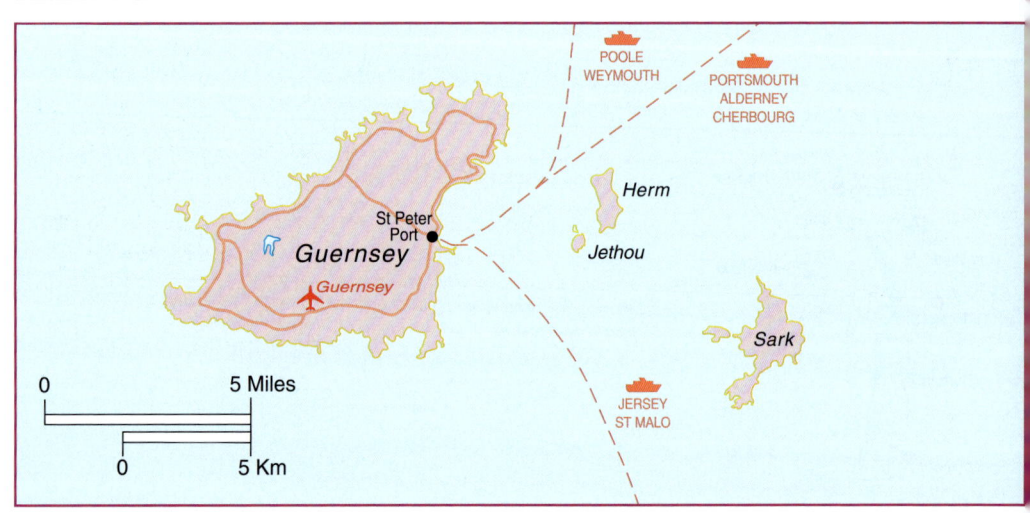

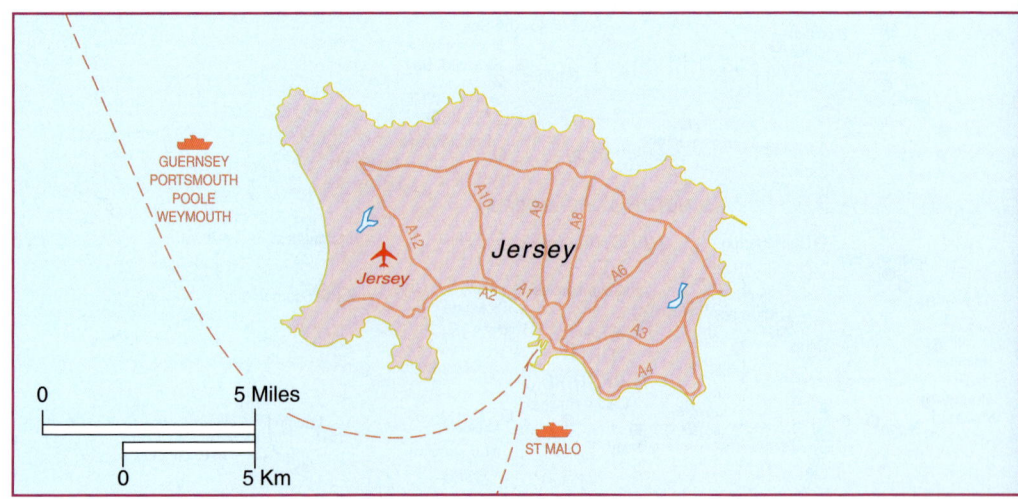

Key to regions: South West England

Orange circles indicate accommodation within the regional sections of this guide

KEY
Motorway
Major Road
Minor Road
Railway
Docklands Light Railway
Canal
Park/open space
Famous buildings & places of interest
Main line Railway Station
Underground Station
Rail Express Link to Airport
Links to City Airport
Launch departure point
Tourist Information Centre
Market
Changing the Guard
Place of Worship
Youth Hostel
MAIDA VALE
ST JOHN'S WOOD
LORD'S CRICKET GROUND MCC and MUSEUM
LONDON CENTRAL MOSQUE AND ISLAMIC CULTURAL CENTRE
BOATING LAKE
Boat Hire
Bandstand
LIBERAL JEWISH SYNAGOGUE
SHERLOCK HOLMES MUSEUM
MARYLEBONE
Marylebone
CHURCH STREET
Warwick Avenue
REGENT'S CANAL WATER BUS - LITTLE VENICE LANDING STAGE
LONDON WATERBUS COMPANY
WESTWAY A40(M)
HARROW ROAD
PADDINGTON
Paddington (Hammersmith & City)
PADDINGTON BASIN
EXPRESS LINK TO HEATHROW
ST MARY'S HOSPITAL
Paddington (Bakerloo & Circle)
Edgware Road (Bakerloo)
Edgware Road (Hammersmith & City and Circle)
Royal Oak
PORCHESTER CENTRE
BAYSWATER
W2
Bayswater
QUEEN'S ICE RINK
NEW WEST END SYNAGOGUE
Queensway
ST SOPHIA GREEK ORTHODOX CATHEDRAL
WEST LONDON SYNAGOGUE
TYBURN CONVENT
Marble Arch
MARBLE ARCH
SPEAKERS' CORNER
Lancaster Gate
BAYSWATER ROAD
Notting Hill Gate
NOTTING HILL GATE
SECOND CHURCH OF CHRIST
THE ELFIN OAK
PRINCESS DIANA MEMORIAL CHILDREN'S PLAYGROUND
KENSINGTON GARDENS
PUMPHOUSE & ITALIAN GARDEN
PETER PAN STATUE
THE LONG WATER
BUCK HILL
QUEEN'S TEMPLE
THE ROUND POND
THE ORANGERY
SUNKEN GARDEN
KENSINGTON PALACE & COURT DRESS COLLECTION
SERPENTINE GALLERY
ALBERT MEMORIAL
HYDE PARK
UPPER PARKLAND
THE PARADE GROUND
BIRD SANCTUARY
LOWER PARKLAND
PARK OFFICE
RANGER'S LODGE & PARK OFFICE
THE SERPENTINE
BOAT HIRE
THE LIDO
CAFETERIA
DIANA MEMORIAL FOUNTAIN
RESTAURANT
ROTTEN ROW
KENSINGTON
W8
KENSINGTON HIGH ST
KENSINGTON ROAD
KENSINGTON GORE
ROYAL COLLEGE OF ART
ROYAL ALBERT HALL
ROYAL GEOGRAPHICAL SOCIETY
ROYAL COLLEGE OF MUSIC
IMPERIAL COLLEGE
South Kensington
SCIENCE MUSEUM
NATURAL HISTORY MUSEUM
VICTORIA AND ALBERT MUSEUM
BROMPTON ORATORY
HOLY TRINITY
KNIGHTSBRIDGE
Knightsbridge
HARRODS
BROMPTON
Gloucester
Mile 0 ¼ ½
Km 0 ¼ ½ ¾ 1
This map is based on information derived from aerial photography and an original field survey conducted by Cosmographics Ltd., 3rd Floor, Gresham House Clarendon Road, Watford, Herts. Map produced by Cosmographics Ltd.
© British Tourist Authority (trading as visitBritain) 2008.

Map 8
London

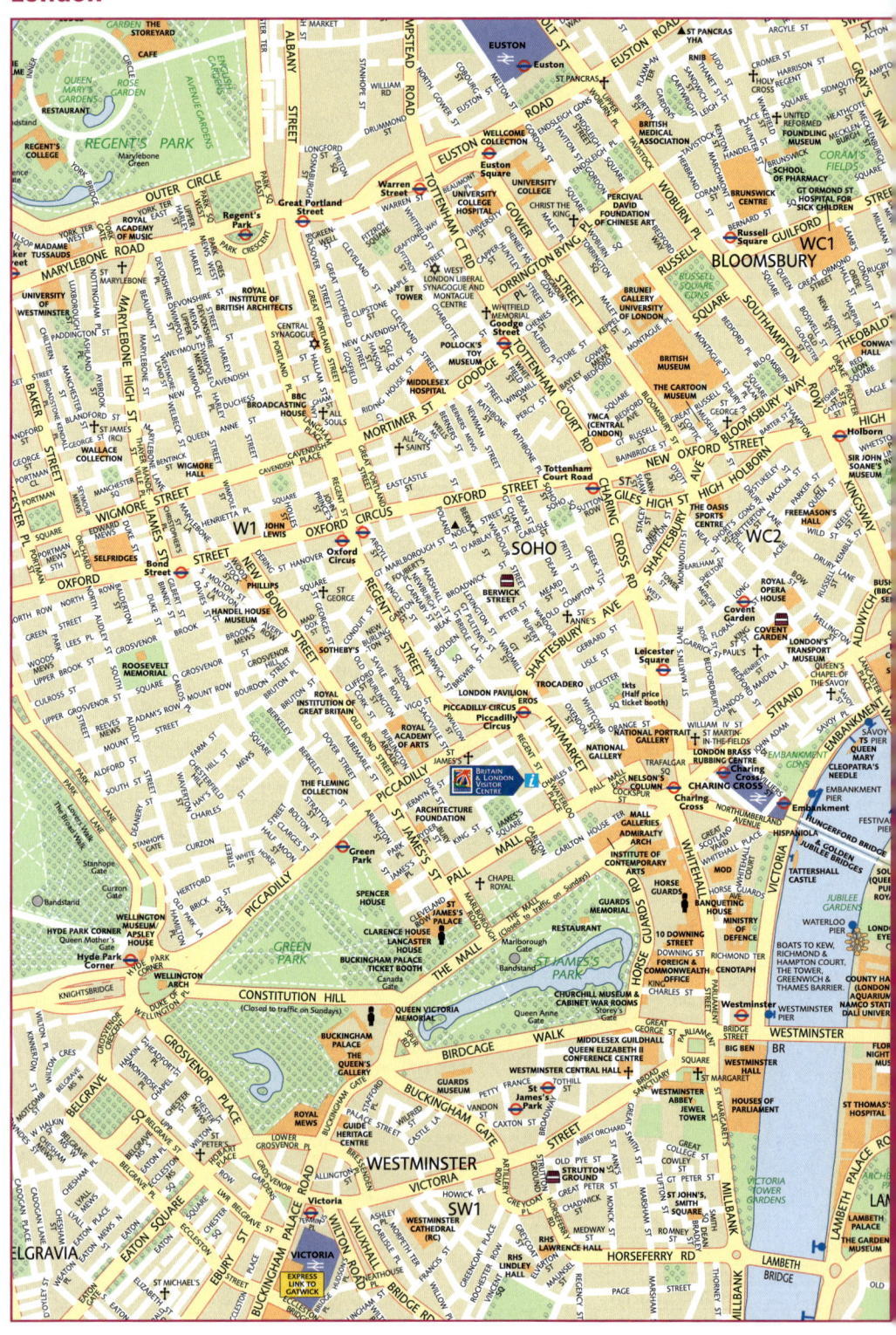

Map 8
London

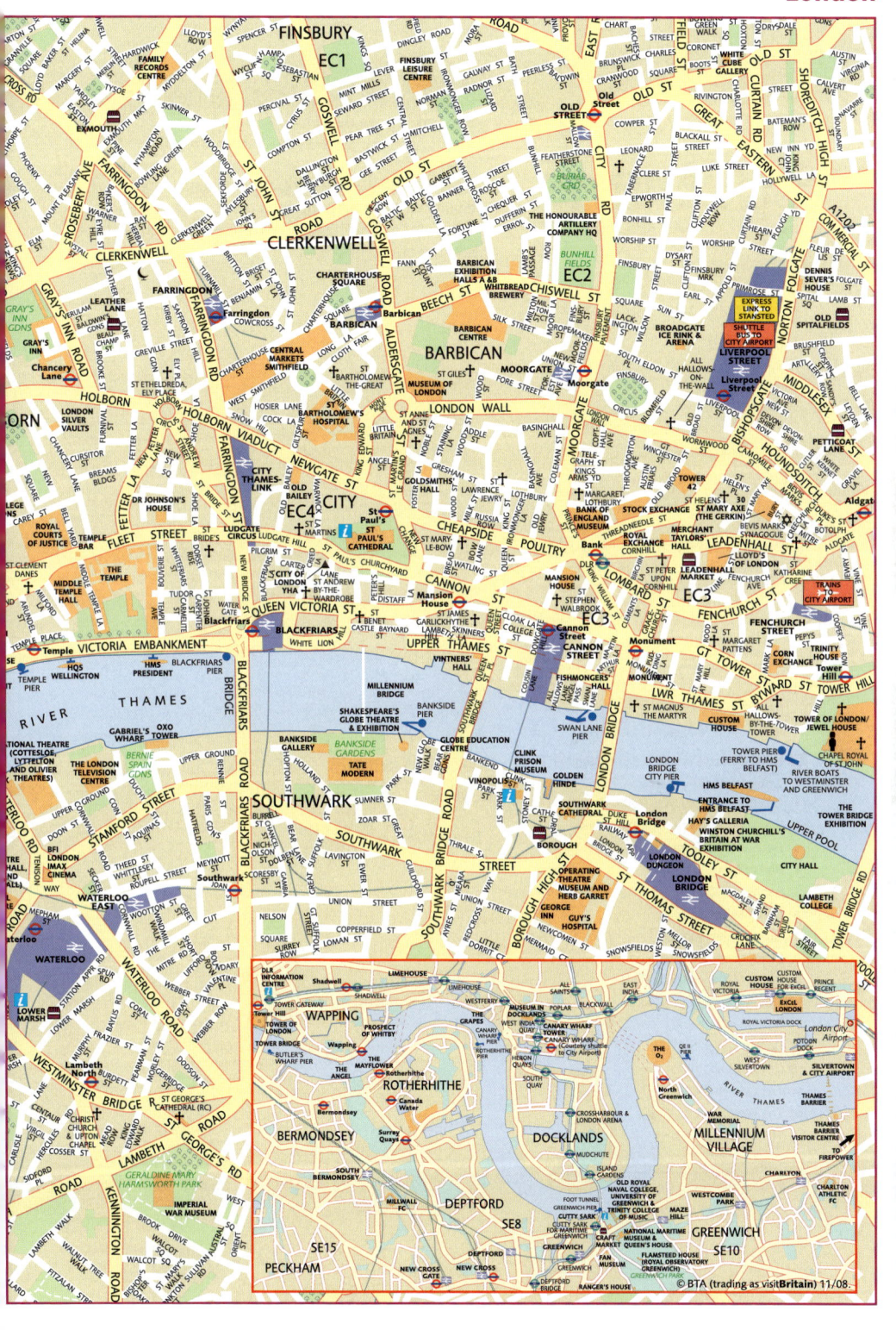

sustrans
JOIN THE MOVEMENT

Here are just some of the most popular long distance routes on the 12,000 mile Sustrans National Cycle Network. To see the Network in it's entirety and to find routes near you, **visit www.sustrans.org.uk**

Sustrans is the UK's leading sustainable transport charity working on practical projects to enable people to choose to travel in ways which benefit their health and the environment.

68 National Cycle Network Route Number

Long Distance Routes
1. Coast & Castles Cycle Route
2. Pennine Cycleway - North Pennines
3. Hadrian's Cycleway
4. Sea to Sea
5. Pennine Cycleway - South Pennines & the Dales
6. Derby to York
7. Hull to Fakenham
8. East of England
9. South Midlands Cycle Route
10. Thames Valley Cycle Route
11. Garden of England
12. Downs & Weald Cycle Route
13. Devon Coast to Coast
14. The Cornish Way
15. The West Country Way
16. The Severn & Thames

Map reproduced from Ordnance Survey material with the permission of Ordnance Survey on behalf of the Controller of Her Majesty's Stationery Office © Crown copyright. Unauthorised reproduction infringes Crown copyright and may lead to prosecution or civil proceedings.
Licence number 100020852 (2009)

Further Information

Advice and information	**723**
About accommodation entries	**726**
Getting around	**728**
Travel information	**732**
Indexes	**734**
National Accessible Scheme Index	734
Gold and Silver Award Winners	738
Walkers and Cyclists Welcome Index	758
Pets and Families Welcome	761
Quick Reference Index	763
Budget Accommodation Index	771
Hostel & Campus Accommodation Index	772
Index by Property Name	773
Index by Place Name	780
Index to Display Advertisers	783

Welcome Pets!

Want to travel with your faithful companion? Look out for accommodation displaying the **Welcome Pets!** sign. Participants in this scheme go out of their way to meet the needs of guests bringing dogs, cats and/or small birds. In addition to providing water and food bowls, torches or nightlights, spare leads and pet washing facilities, they'll buy in food on request, and offer toys, treats and bedding. They'll also have information on pet-friendly attractions, pubs, restaurants and recreation. Of course, not everyone is able to offer suitable facilities for every pet, so do check if there are any restrictions on type, size and number of animals when you book.

Find out more at enjoyEngland.com

Advice and information

Making a reservation
When enquiring about accommodation, make sure you check prices, the quality rating and other important details. You will also need to state your requirements clearly and precisely, for example:

- Arrival and departure dates, with acceptable alternatives if appropriate
- The type of accommodation you need – for example, room with twin beds, en suite bathroom
- The terms you want – for example, bed and breakfast only; dinner and breakfast (where provided)
- The age of any children with you, whether you want them to share your room or be next door, and any other special requirements, such as a cot
- Any particular requirements you may have, such as a special diet, ground-floor room.

Confirmation
Misunderstandings can easily happen over the telephone, so do request a written confirmation, together with details of any terms and conditions.

Deposits
If you make your reservation weeks or months in advance, you will probably be asked for a deposit, which will then be deducted from the final bill when you leave. The amount will vary from establishment to establishment and could be payment in full at peak times.

Payment on arrival
Some establishments ask you to pay for your room on arrival if you have not booked it in advance. This is especially likely to happen if you arrive late and have little or no luggage.

If you are asked to pay on arrival, it is a good idea to see your room first, to make sure it meets your requirements.

Cancellations
Legal contract
When you accept accommodation that is offered to you, by telephone or in writing, you enter a legally binding contract with the proprietor. This means that if you cancel your booking, fail to take up the accommodation or leave early, the proprietor may be entitled to compensation if he or she cannot re-let for all or a good part of the booked period. You will probably forfeit any deposit you have paid, and may well be asked for an additional payment.

At the time of booking you should be advised of what charges would be made in the event of cancelling the accommodation or leaving early. If this is not mentioned, you should ask so that future disputes can be avoided. The proprietor cannot make a claim until after the booked period, and during that time he or she should make every effort to re-let the accommodation. If there is a dispute, it is sensible for both sides to seek legal advice on the matter. If you do have to change your travel plans, it is in your own interests to let the proprietor know in writing as soon as possible, to give them a chance to re-let your accommodation.

And remember, if you book by telephone and are asked for your credit card number, you should check whether the proprietor intends charging your credit card account should you later cancel your reservation. A proprietor should not be able to charge your credit card account with a cancellation fee unless he or she has made this clear at the time of your booking and you have agreed. However, to avoid later disputes, we suggest you check whether this is the intention.

Insurance
A travel or holiday insurance policy will safeguard you if you have to cancel or change your holiday plans both abroad and in the UK. You can arrange a policy quite cheaply through your insurance company or travel agent.

Advice and information

Arriving late
If you know you will be arriving late in the evening, it is a good idea to say so when you book. If you are delayed on your way, a telephone call to say that you will be late would be appreciated.

Service charges and tipping
These days many places levy service charges automatically. If they do, they must clearly say so in their offer of accommodation, at the time of booking. The service charge then becomes part of the legal contract when you accept the offer of accommodation.

If a service charge is levied automatically, there is no need to tip the staff, unless they provide some exceptional service. The usual tip for meals is 10% of the total bill.

Telephone charges
Establishments can set their own charges for telephone calls made through their switchboard or from direct-dial telephones in bedrooms. These charges are often much higher than telephone companies' standard charges (to defray the cost of providing the service).

Comparing costs
It is a condition of the quality assessment schemes that an establishment's unit charges are on display by the telephones or with the room information. It is not always easy to compare these charges with standard rates, so before using a hotel telephone for long-distance calls, you may decide to ask how the charges compare.

Security of valuables
You can deposit your valuables with the proprietor or manager during your stay, and we recommend you do this as a sensible precaution. Make sure you obtain a receipt for them. Some places do not accept articles for safe custody, and in that case it is wisest to keep your valuables with you.

Disclaimer
Some proprietors put up a notice that disclaims liability for property brought on to their premises by a guest. In fact, they can only restrict their liability. By law, a proprietor is liable for the value of the loss or damage to any property (except a car or its contents) of a guest who has engaged overnight accommodation, but if the proprietor has the notice on display, liability is limited to £50 for one article and a total of £100 for any one guest. The notice must be prominently displayed in the reception area or main entrance. These limits do not apply to valuables you have deposited with the proprietor for safekeeping, or to property lost through the default, neglect or wilful act of the proprietor or his staff.

Travelling with pets
Dogs, cats, ferrets and some other pet mammals can be brought into the UK from certain countries without having to undertake six months' quarantine on arrival provided they meet all the rules of the Pet Travel Scheme (PETS).
For full details, visit the PETS website at
w defra.gov.uk/animalh/quarantine/index.htm
or contact the PETS Helpline

t +44 (0)870 241 1710
e quarantine@animalhealth.gsi.gov.uk
Ask for fact sheets which cover dogs and cats, ferrets or domestic rabbits and rodents.

There are no requirements for pets travelling directly between the UK and the Channel Islands. Pets entering Jersey or Guernsey from other countries need to be Pet Travel Scheme compliant and have a valid EU Pet Passport. For more information see jersey.com or visitguernsey.com.

What to expect
The proprietor/management is required to undertake the following:

- To maintain standards of guest care, cleanliness and service appropriate to the type of establishment;

- To describe accurately in any advertisement, brochure or other printed or electronic media, the facilities and services provided;

- To make clear to visitors exactly what is included in all prices quoted for accommodation, including taxes, and any other surcharges. Details of charges for additional services/facilities should also be made clear;

- To give a clear statement of the policy on cancellations to guests at the time of booking, i.e. by telephone, fax, email, as well as information given in a printed format;

- To adhere to and not to exceed prices quoted at the time of booking for accommodation and other services;

- To advise visitors at the time of booking, and subsequently if any change, if the accommodation offered is in an unconnected annexe or similar and to indicate the location of such accommodation and any difference in comfort and/or amenities from accommodation in the establishment;

- To register all guests on arrival;

- To give each visitor on request details of payments due and a receipt, if required;

- To deal promptly and courteously with all enquiries, requests, bookings and correspondence from visitors;

Advice and information

- To ensure complaint handling procedures are in place and that complaints received are investigated promptly and courteously and that the outcome is communicated to the visitor;
- To give due consideration to the requirements of visitors with disabilities and visitors with special needs, and to make suitable provision where applicable;
- To provide public liability insurance or comparable arrangements and to comply with all applicable planning, safety and other statutory requirements;
- To allow a quality ratings assessor reasonable access to the establishment on request, to confirm the Code of Conduct is being observed;
- To welcome all guests courteously and without discrimination in relation to gender, sexual orientation, disability, race, religion or belief.

Comments and complaints

Bed and breakfast accommodation and the law

Places that offer accommodation have legal and statutory responsibilities to their customers, such as providing information about prices, providing adequate fire precautions and safeguarding valuables. They must also describe their accommodation and facilities accurately. All the places featured in this guide have declared that they do fulfil all applicable statutory obligations.

Information

The proprietors themselves supply the descriptions of their establishments and other information for the entries (except quality ratings and awards). The publishers cannot guarantee the accuracy of information in this guide, and accept no responsibility for any error or misrepresentation. All liability for loss, disappointment, negligence or other damage caused by reliance on the information contained in this guide, or in the event of bankruptcy or liquidation or cessation of trade of any company, individual or firm mentioned, is hereby excluded. We strongly recommend that you carefully check prices and other details when you book your accommodation.

Quality signage

All establishments displaying a quality sign have to hold current membership of a quality assessment scheme.
When an establishment is sold, the new owner has to reapply and be reassessed. In some areas the rating may be carried forward in the interim.

Problems

Of course, we hope you will not have cause for complaint, but problems do occur from time to time.

If you are dissatisfied with anything, make your complaint to the management immediately. Then the management can take action at once to investigate the matter and put things right. The longer you leave a complaint, the harder it is to deal with it effectively.

In certain circumstances, the national tourist boards may look into complaints. However, they have no statutory control over establishments or their methods of operating and cannot become involved in legal or contractual matters, nor can they get involved in seeking financial recompense.

If you do have problems that have not been resolved by the proprietor and which you would like to bring to their attention, please write to:

Quality in Tourism
Security House
Ashchurch
Tewkesbury
Gloucestershire
GL20 8NB

At last! A new definitive guide for the disabled traveller.
Whatever their needs, visitors can find everything that they require to enjoy Britain to the full.
Pre-order today...Only £9.99 + p&p
info@openbritain.net | 01603 813740
or visit OPENBRITAIN.NET

To feature your property in the 2011 guide and the website, call 01603 813740 or register online at www.openbritain.net

About the accommodation entries

Entries
All the accommodation featured in this guide has been assessed or has applied for assessment under a quality assessment scheme.

Assessment under the EnjoyEngland Quality Rose scheme automatically entitles establishments to a listing in this guide. Start your search for a place to stay by looking in the 'Where to Stay' sections of this guide where proprietor have paid to have their establishment featured in either a standard entry (includes photograph, description, facilities and prices) or an enhanced entry (photograph(s) and extended details). If you can't find what you're looking for, turn to the listing sections which appear at the back of each region for an even wider choice of accommodation.

Locations
Places to stay are generally listed under the town, city or village where they are located. If a place is in a small village, you may find it listed under a nearby town (provided it is within a seven-mile radius). Within each region, counties run in alphabetical order. Place names are listed alphabetically within each county, along with information on which county that is and their map reference.

Map references
These refer to the colour location maps at the back of the guide. The first figure shown is the map number, the following letter and figure indicate the grid reference on the map. Only place names under which standard or enhanced entries (see above) appear on the maps. Some entries were included just before the guide went to press, so they do not appear on the maps.

Telephone numbers
Telephone numbers are listed below the accommodation address for each entry. Area codes are shown in brackets.

Prices
The prices shown are only a general guide; they were supplied to us by proprietors in summer 2010. Remember, changes may occur after the guide goes to press, so we strongly advise you to check prices when you book your accommodation.

Prices are shown in pounds sterling and include VAT where applicable. Some places also include a service charge in their standard tariff, so check this when you book.

There are many different ways of quoting prices for accommodation. We use a standardised method in the guide to allow you to compare prices. For example, when we show:

Bed and breakfast: the prices shown are per room for overnight accommodation with breakfast. The double room price is for two people. (If a double room is occupied by one person, there is sometimes a reduction in price.)

Evening meal: the prices shown are per person per night.

Some places only provide a continental breakfast in the set price, and you may have to pay extra if you want a full English breakfast.

Checking prices
According to UK law, establishments with at least four bedrooms or eight beds must display their charges in the reception area or entrance. There is no legal requirement for hotels in the Channel Islands to display their prices, but they should make them clear at the time of booking.

In your own interests, do make sure you check prices and what they include.

Children's rates
You will find that many places charge a reduced rate for children, especially if they share a room with their parents. Some places charge the full rate, however, when a child occupies a room which might otherwise have been let to an adult. The upper age limit for reductions for children varies from one accommodation to another, so check this when you book.

About the accommodation entries

Seasonal packages and special promotions
Prices often vary through the year and may be significantly lower outside peak holiday weeks. Many places offer special package rates – fully inclusive weekend breaks, for example – in the autumn, winter and spring. A number of establishments taking an enhanced entry have included any special offers, themed breaks, etc. that are available.

You can get details of other bargain packages that may be available from the establishments themselves, regional tourism organisations or your local Tourist Information Centre (TIC). Your local travel agent may also have information and can help you make reservations.

Bathrooms
Each accommodation entry shows you the number of en suite and private bathrooms available. En suite bathroom means the bath or shower and wc are contained behind the main door of the bedroom. Private bathroom means a bath or shower and wc solely for the occupants of one bedroom, on the same floor, reasonably close and with a key provided. If the availability of a bath, rather than a shower, is important to you, remember to check when you book.

Meals
It is advisable to check availability of meals and set times when making your reservation. Some smaller places may ask you at breakfast whether you want an evening meal. The prices shown in each entry are for bed and breakfast or half board, but many places also offer lunch.

Opening period
If an entry does not indicate an opening period, please check directly with the hotel.

Symbols
The at-a-glance symbols included at the end of each entry show many of the services and facilities available at each establishment. You will find the key to these symbols on page 6.

Smoking
In the UK and the Channel Islands, it is illegal to smoke in enclosed public spaces and places of work. Some establishments may choose to provide designated smoking bedrooms, and may allow smoking in private areas that are not used by any staff. If you wish to smoke, it is advisable to check whether it is allowed when you book.

Alcoholic drinks
Many places listed in the guide are licensed to serve alcohol. The licence may be restricted – to diners only, for example – so you may want to check this when you book. If they have a bar this is shown by the ♇ symbol.

Pets
Many places accept guests with dogs, but we do advise that you check this when you book, and ask if there are any extra charges or rules about exactly where your pet is allowed. The acceptance of dogs is not always extended to cats and it is strongly advised that cat owners contact the establishment well in advance. Some establishments do not accept pets at all. Pets are welcome by arrangement where you see this symbol 🐕.

The quarantine laws have changed, and dogs, cats and ferrets are able to come into Britain and the Channel Islands from over 50 countries. For details of the Pet Travel Scheme (PETS) please turn to page 724.

Payment accepted
The types of payment accepted by an establishment are listed in the payment accepted section. If you plan to pay by card, check that the establishment will take your particular card before you book. Some proprietors will charge you a higher rate if you pay by credit card rather than cash or cheque. The difference is to cover the percentage paid by the proprietor to the credit card company. When you book by telephone, you may be asked for your credit card number as confirmation. But remember, the proprietor may then charge your credit card account if you cancel your booking. See under Cancellations on page 723.

Awaiting confirmation of rating
At the time of going to press some establishments featured in this guide had not yet been assessed for their rating for the year 2011 and so their new rating could not be included. Rating Applied For indicates this.

Property names
Under the Common Standards for assessment, guest accommodation may not include the word 'hotel' in its name. The majority of accommodation in this guide complies with this rule and the national assessing bodies, including VisitBritain, are working towards bringing all guest accommodation in line with this.

Getting around

Travelling in London

London transport
London Underground has 12 lines, each with its own unique colour, so you can easily follow them on the Underground map. Most lines run through central London, and many serve parts of Greater London.

Buses are a quick, convenient way to travel around London, providing plenty of sightseeing opportunities on the way. There are over 6,500 buses in London operating 700 routes every day. You will need to buy a ticket before you board the bus – available from machines at the bus stop – or have a valid Oyster card (see below).

London's National Rail system stretches all over London. Many lines start at the main London railway stations (Paddington, Victoria, Waterloo, Kings Cross) with links to the tube. Trains mainly serve areas outside central London, and travel over ground.

Children usually travel free, or at reduced fare, on all public transport in London.

Oyster cards
Oyster cards can be used to pay fares on all London Underground, buses, Docklands Light Railway and trams; they are generally not valid for National Rail services in London.

Oyster cards are very easy to use – you just touch the card on sensors at stations or on buses and it always charges you the lowest fare available for your journey. You buy credit for your journey and when it runs out you simply top up with more.

Oyster is available to adults only. Children below the age of 11 can accompany adults free of charge. Children between the ages of 11 and 15 should use the standard child travel card. You can get an Oyster card at any underground station, at one of 3,000 Oyster points around London displaying the London Underground sign (usually shops), or from www.visitbritaindirect.com, or https://oyster.tfl.gov.uk/oyster

London congestion charge
The congestion charge is an £8 daily charge to drive in central London at certain times. Check whether the congestion charge is included in the cost of your car when you book. If your car's pick up point is in the congestion-charging zone, the company may pay the charge for the first day of your hire.

Low Emission Zone
The Low Emission Zone is an area covering most of Greater London, within which the most polluting diesel-engine vehicles are required to meet specific emissions standards. If your vehicle does not, you will need to pay a daily charge.

Vehicles affected by the Low Emission Zone are older diesel-engine lorries, buses, coaches, large vans, minibuses and other heavy vehicles such as motor caravans and motorised horse boxes. This includes vehicles registered outside of Great Britain. Cars and motorcycles are not affected by the scheme.

For more information visit www.tfl.gov.uk

Rail and train travel
Britain's rail network covers all main cities and smaller regional towns. Trains on the network are operated by a few large companies running routes from London to stations all over Britain, and smaller companies running routes in regional areas. You can find up-to-the-minute information about routes, fares and train times on National Rail Enquiries (nationalrail.co.uk). For detailed information about routes and services, refer to the train operators' websites (see page 733).

Railway passes
BritRail offers a wide selection of passes and tickets giving you freedom to travel on all National Rail services. Passes can also include sleeper services, city and attraction passes and boat tours. Passes can normally be bought from travel agents outside Britain or by visiting the Britrail website (britrail.com).

Getting around

Bus and coach travel

Public buses
Every city and town in Britain has a local bus service. These services are privatised and run by separate companies. The largest bus companies in Britain are First (www.firstgroup.com/ukbus), Stagecoach (stagecoachbus.com), and Arriva (arrivabus.co.uk), which run buses in most UK towns. Outside London, buses usually travel to and from the town centre or busiest part of town. Most towns have a bus station, where you'll be able to find maps and information about routes. Bus route information may also be posted at bus stops.

Tickets and fares
The cost of a bus ticket normally depends on how far you're travelling. Return fares may be available on some buses, but you usually need to buy a 'single' ticket for each individual journey.

You can buy your ticket when you board a bus, by telling the driver where you are going. One-day and weekly travel cards are available in some towns, and these can be bought from the driver or from an information centre at the bus station. Tickets are valid for each separate journey rather than for a period of time, so if you get off the bus you'll need to buy a new ticket when getting on another bus.

Domestic flights
Flying is a time-saving alternative to road or rail when it comes to travelling around Britain. Domestic flights are fast and frequent and there are 33 airports across Britain operating domestic routes. You will find airports marked on the maps at the front of this guide.

Domestic flight advice
Photo ID is required to travel on domestic flights. It is advisable to bring your passport, as not all airlines will accept other forms of photo identification.

There are very high security measures at all airports in Britain. These include restrictions on items that may be carried in hand luggage. It is important that you check with your airline prior to travel, as these restrictions may vary over time. Make sure you allow adequate time for check-in and boarding.

Cycling
Cycling is a good way to see some of Britain's best scenery and there are many networks of cycling routes. The National Cycle Network offers over 10,000 miles of walking and cycling routes connecting towns and villages, countryside and coast across the UK. For more information and routes see page 720 or visit Sustrans at sustrans.co.uk.

Think green
If you'd rather leave your car behind and travel by 'green transport' when visiting some of the attractions highlighted in this guide you'll be helping to reduce congestion and pollution as well as supporting conservation charities in their commitment to green travel.

The National Trust encourages visits made by non-car travellers. It offers admission discounts or a voucher for the tea room at a selection of its properties if you arrive on foot, cycle or public transport. (You'll need to produce a valid bus or train ticket if travelling by public transport.)

More information about The National Trust's work to encourage car-free days out can be found at nationaltrust.org.uk. Refer to the section entitled Information for Visitors.

OPENBRITAIN.NET

ONE STOP SOLUTION
to accessible places to stay and visit in Britain.

To advertise your property or attraction, contact our friendly staff on 01603 813740 | sales@openbritain.net

Getting around

By car and by train

Distance chart

The distances between towns on the chart below are given to the nearest mile, and are measured along routes based on the quickest travelling time, making maximum use of motorways or dual-carriageway roads. The chart is based upon information supplied by the Automobile Association.

To calculate the distance in kilometres multiply the mileage by 1.6
For example: Brighton to Dover
82 miles x 1.6 =131.2 kilometres

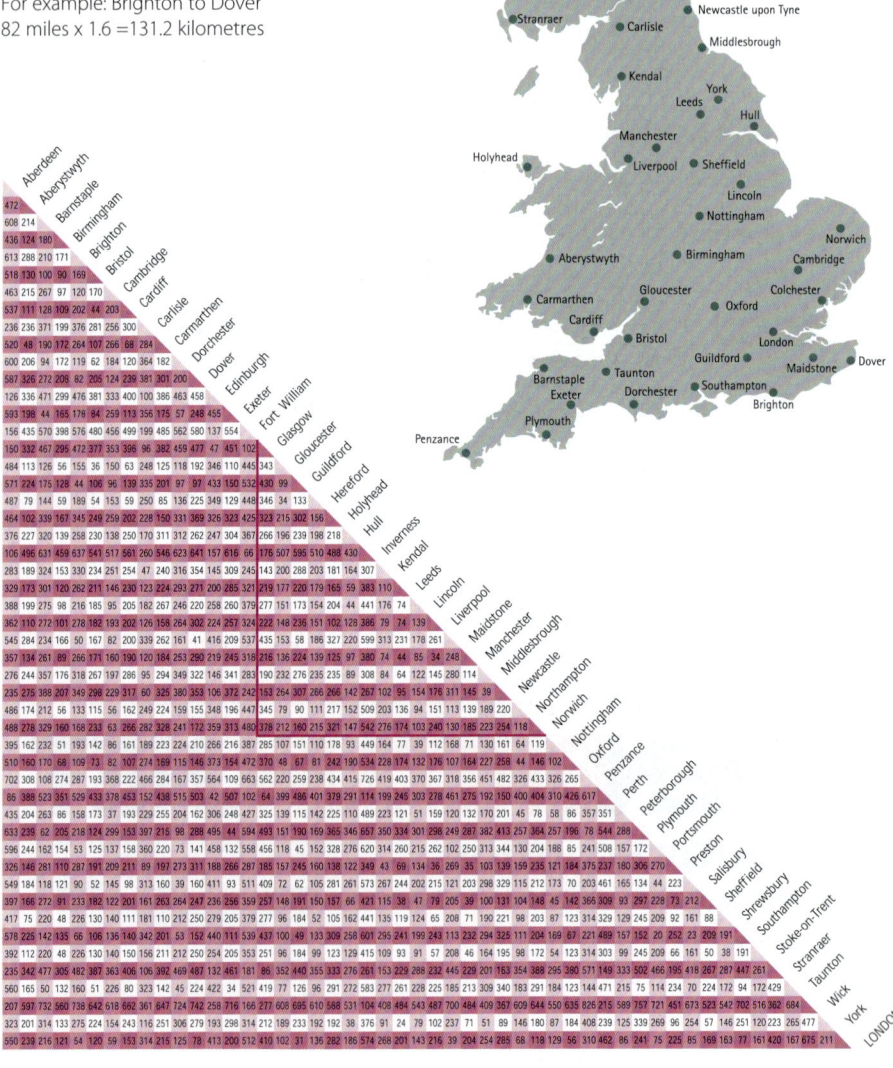

Getting around

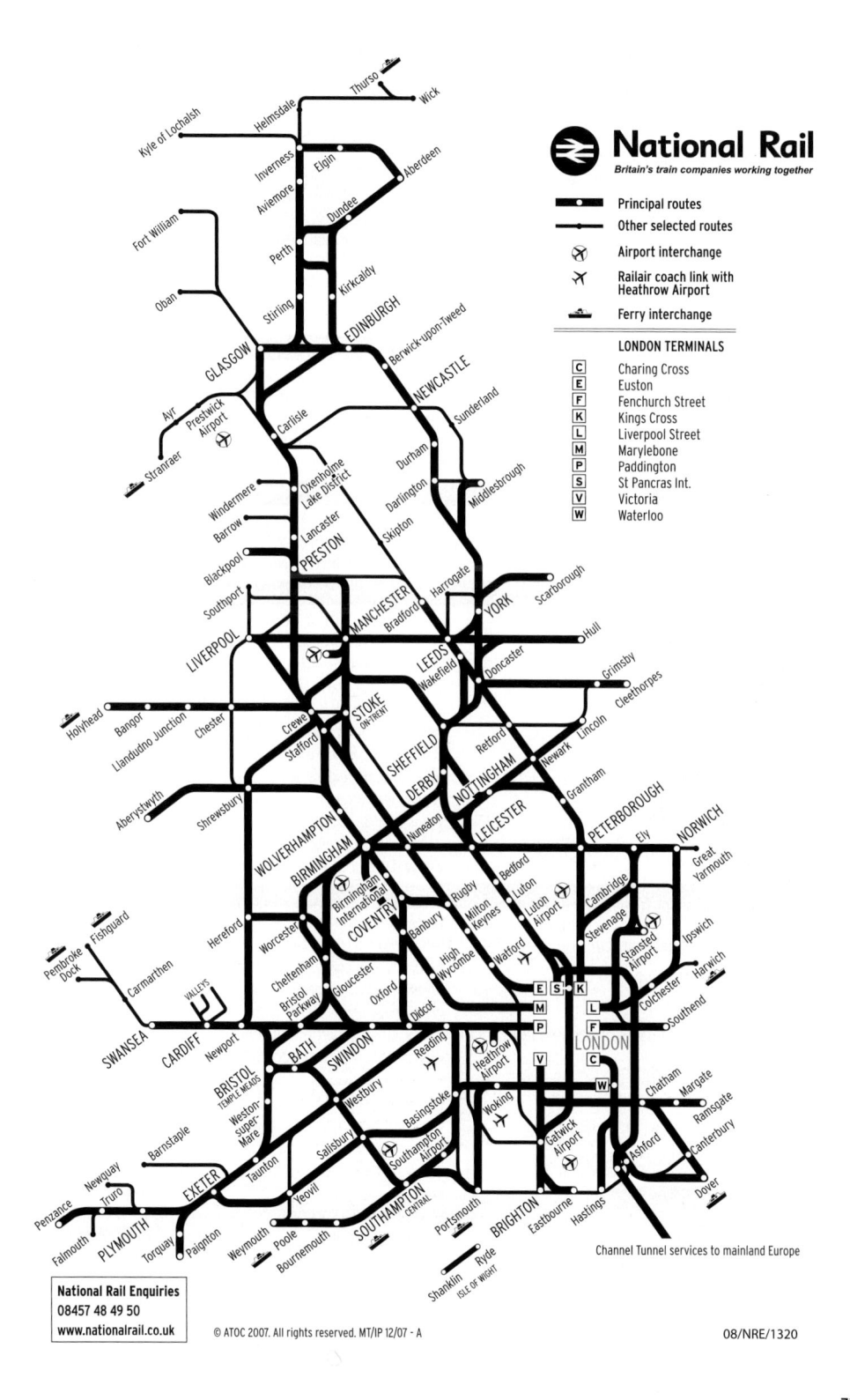

National Rail
Britain's train companies working together

- ━━━ Principal routes
- ─── Other selected routes
- ✈ Airport interchange
- ✈ Railair coach link with Heathrow Airport
- ⛴ Ferry interchange

LONDON TERMINALS
C	Charing Cross
E	Euston
F	Fenchurch Street
K	Kings Cross
L	Liverpool Street
M	Marylebone
P	Paddington
S	St Pancras Int.
V	Victoria
W	Waterloo

Channel Tunnel services to mainland Europe

National Rail Enquiries
08457 48 49 50
www.nationalrail.co.uk

© ATOC 2007. All rights reserved. MT/IP 12/07 - A

08/NRE/1320

Travel information

General travel information
Streetmap	www.streetmap.co.uk	
Transport Direct	www.transportdirect.info	
Transport for London	www.tfl.gov.uk	020 7222 1234
Travel Services	www.departures-arrivals.com	
Traveline	www.traveline.org.uk	0871 200 2233

Bus & coach
Megabus	www.megabus.com	0900 160 0900
National Express	www.nationalexpress.com	08717 818 181
WA Shearings	www.washearings.com	0844 824 6355

Car & car hire
AA	www.theaa.com	0870 600 0371
Green Flag	www.greenflag.co.uk	0845 246 1557
RAC	www.rac.co.uk	0870 572 2722
Alamo	www.alamo.co.uk	0871 384 1086*
Avis	www.avis.co.uk	0844 581 0147*
Budget	www.budget.co.uk	0844 544 3407*
Easycar	www.easycar.com	0871 050 0444
Enterprise	www.enterprise.com	0800 800 227*
Hertz	www.hertz.co.uk	0870 844 8844*
Holiday Autos	www.holidayautos.co.uk	0871 472 5229
National	www.nationalcar.co.uk	0870 400 4581
Thrifty	www.thrifty.co.uk	01494 751500

Air
Air Southwest	www.airsouthwest.com	0870 043 4553
Blue Islands (Channel Islands)	www.blueislands.com	08456 20 2122
BMI	www.flybmi.com	0870 607 0555
BMI Baby	www.bmibaby.com	0905 828 2828*
British Airways	www.ba.com	0844 493 0787
British International (Insles of Scilly to Penzance)	www.islesofscillyhelicopter.com	01736 363871*
Eastern Airways	www.easternairways.com	0870 366 9989
Easyjet	www.easyjet.com	0871 244 2366
Flybe	www.flybe.com	0871 700 2000*
Jet2.com	www.jet2.com	0871 226 1737*
Manx2	www.manx2.com	0871 200 0440*
Ryanair	www.ryanair.com	0871 246 0000
Skybus (Isles of Scilly)	www.islesofscilly-travel.co.uk	0845 710 5555
Thomsonfly	www.thomsonfly.com	0871 231 4787
VLM	www.flyvlm.com	0871 666 5050

Train

National Rail Enquiries	www.nationalrail.co.uk	0845 748 4950
The Trainline	www.trainline.co.uk	0871 244 1545
UK train operating companies	www.rail.co.uk	
Arriva Trains	www.arriva.co.uk	0845 748 4950
c2c	www.c2c-online.co.uk	0845 601 4873
Chiltern Railways	www.chilternrailways.co.uk	0845 600 5165
CrossCountry	www.crosscountrytrains.co.uk	0844 811 0124
East Midlands Trains	www.eastmidlandstrains.co.uk	0845 712 5678
Eurostar	www.eurostar.com	08432 186 186*
First Capital Connect	www.firstcapitalconnect.co.uk	0845 026 4700
First Great Western	www.firstgreatwestern.co.uk	0845 700 0125
Gatwick Express	www.gatwickexpress.com	0845 850 1530
Heathrow Connect	www.heathrowconnect.com	0845 678 6975
Heathrow Express	www.heathrowexpress.com	0845 600 1515
Hull Trains	www.hulltrains.co.uk	0845 071 0222
Island Line	www.islandlinetrains.co.uk	0845 600 0650
London Midlands	www.londonmidland.com	0121 634 2040
Merseyrail	www.merseyrail.org	0151 702 2071
National Express East Anglia	www.nationalexpresseastanglia.com	0845 600 7245
National Express East Coast	www.nationalexpresseastcoast.com	0845 722 5333
Northern Rail	www.northernrail.org	0845 000 0125
ScotRail	www.scotrail.co.uk	0845 601 5929
South Eastern Trains	www.southeasternrailway.co.uk	0845 000 2222
South West Trains	www.southwesttrains.co.uk	0845 600 0650
Southern	www.southernrailway.com	0845 127 2920
Stansted Express	www.stanstedexpress.com	0845 850 0150
Translink	www.nirailways.co.uk	(028) 9066 6630
Transpennine Express	www.tpexpress.co.uk	0845 600 1671
Virgin Trains	www.virgintrains.co.uk	0845 722 2333*

Ferry

Ferry Information	www.sailanddrive.com	
Condor Ferries	www.condorferries.co.uk	0845 609 1024*
Steam Packet Company	www.steam-packet.com	0871 222 1333*
Isles of Scilly Travel	www.islesofscilly-travel.co.uk	0845 710 5555
Red Funnel	www.redfunnel.co.uk	0870 444 8898
Wight Link	www.wightlink.co.uk	0871 376 1000

Phone numbers listed are for general enquiries unless otherwise stated.
* Booking line only

National Accessible Scheme index

Establishments participating in the National Accessible Scheme are listed below - those in colour have a detailed entry in this guide. At the front of the guide you can find information about the scheme. Establishments are listed alphabetically by place name.

Mobility level 1

Abingdon South East	Abbey Guest House ★★★★ SILVER	27
Arnside North West	YHA Arnside ★★★	63
Berwick-upon-Tweed North East	Fenham Farm Coastal Bed & Breakfast ★★★★ SILVER	67
Biddenden South East	Heron Cottage ★★★★	21
Blackpool North West	Holmsdale ★★★	64
Blackpool North West	The Lawton ★★★	65
Blaxhall East of England	Blaxhall YHA ★★★	38
Blyton East Midlands	Blyton (Sunnyside) Ponds ★★★	43
Boscastle South West	The Old Coach House ★★★★ SILVER	12
Boscastle South West	Reddivallen Farm ★★★★★ GOLD	12
Bowness-on-Solway North West	The Old Chapel ★★★	63
Bridgwater South West	Buzzard Heights B&B ★★★	16
Bridlington Yorkshire	Providence Place ★★★★	53
Broseley Heart of England	Coalport YHA ★★★	47
Camelford South West	Pendragon Country House ★★★★★ GOLD	12
Carlisle North West	Bessiestown Farm Country Guesthouse ★★★★★ GOLD	63
Cheddar South West	Cheddar YHA ★★★	16
Cheltenham South West	The Prestbury House ★★★★	15
Cheshunt East of England	YHA Lee Valley Village ★★★★	37
Clapham Yorkshire	New Inn ★★★	50
Claverton Down South West	University of Bath ★★★ - ★★★★	16
Cleethorpes East Midlands	Tudor Terrace Guest House ★★★★	43
Colyton South West	Smallicombe Farm ★★★★ SILVER	14
Congleton North West	Sandhole Farm Bed & Breakfast ★★★★	63
Cropston East Midlands	Horseshoe Cottage Farm ★★★★★ GOLD	41
Dorchester South West	Aquila Heights Guest House ★★★★ SILVER	15
Drewton Yorkshire	Rudstone Walk Country B&B ★★★★	53
East Runton East of England	Incleborough House ★★★★★ GOLD	37
Ellerby Yorkshire	Ellerby Residential Country Inn ★★★★ SILVER	53
Great Snoring East of England	Vine Park Cottage ★★★★ SILVER	37
Hardstoft East Midlands	Whitton Lodge ★★★★	42
Hastings South East	Seaspray Bed and Breakfast ★★★★ SILVER	25
Haydon Bridge North East	Grindon Cartshed ★★★★ SILVER	68
Haydon Bridge North East	Shaftoe's Guest House ★★★★	68
High Cogges South East	Springhill Farm Bed & Breakfast ★★★★	28
High Hesleden North East	The Ship Inn ★★★★ SILVER	69
Hill Brow South East	The Jolly Drover ★★★★ SILVER	28
Hitcham East of England	The White Horse Inn ★★★★	38
Ilam Heart of England	YHA Ilam Hall ★★★★	48

National Accessible Scheme index

Mobility level 1 continued

Location	Establishment	Page
gs North West	Meadowcroft Country Guest House ★★★★	640
rkbymoorside Yorkshire	The Cornmill ★★★★ SILVER	511
eckhampstead South East	Weatherhead Farm ★★★★	265
eominster Heart of England	YHA Leominster ★★★★	477
ghthorne Heart of England	Church Hill Farm B&B ★★★★ SILVER	485
ttle Downham East of England	Wood Fen Lodge ★★★★	370
verpool North West	YHA Liverpool International ★★★★	656
he Lizard South West	Lizard Point Youth Hostel ★★★★	138
ondon SE16 London	YHA London Thameside ★★	308
ondon SW7 London	Meininger City Hostel & Hotel London ★★★★	309
ondon W1 London	YHA London Central ★★★★	309
ongthwaite North West	Borrowdale YHA ★★★★	642
ower Godney South West	Double-Gate Farm ★★★★ GOLD	165
ymington South East	The Nurse's Cottage Restaurant with Rooms ★★★★ GOLD	206
yth Bank Heart of England	Lyth Hill House ★★★★★ GOLD	462
anchester North West	Luther King House ★★★	655
anchester North West	Manchester YHA ★★★★	655
ansfield East Midlands	Sherwood Forest Youth Hostel ★★★★	438
oira East Midlands	YHA National Forest ★★★★	431
undesley East of England	Overcliff Lodge ★★★★	379
ewbrough North East	Carr Edge Farm ★★★★	687
orth Rode North West	Ladderstile Retreat ★★★★★ SILVER	576
orthallerton Yorkshire	Lovesome Hill Farm ★★★★ SILVER	514
xford South East	YHA Oxford ★★★★	282
adstow South West	Arum House Bed & Breakfast ★★★★	133
adstow South West	Woodlands Country House ★★★★★ GOLD	133
arkend South West	Fountain Inn ★★★	100
reston Yorkshire	Little Weghill Farm ★★★★ SILVER	546
ulborough South East	The Labouring Man ★★★★	258
edditch Heart of England	White Hart Inn ★★★	489
ibchester North West	Riverside Barn ★★★★★ SILVER	654
ochdale North West	Fernhill B&B ★★★	655
carborough Yorkshire	The Scarborough Travel & Holiday Lodge ★★★	549
heringham East of England	Sheringham YHA ★★★	380
kegness East Midlands	Chatsworth ★★★	417
outhport North West	Sandy Brook Farm ★★★	632
outhwold East of England	The Plough Inn ★★★★	384
pilsby East Midlands	Red Lion Inn ★★★★	435
t Mary's South West	Isles of Scilly Country Guest House ★★★	137
hrelkeld North West	Scales Farm Country Guest House ★★★★ SILVER	644
orquay South West	Crown Lodge ★★★★	76
ytherington South West	Lighthouse Guest House ★★★★	167
Wells-next-the-Sea East of England	Wells-next-the-Sea YHA ★★★★	381
Wendling East of England	Greenbanks ★★★★	381
West Rudham East of England	Oyster House ★★★★ SILVER	381
Weston-super-Mare South West	Milton Lodge Guest House ★★★★	117
Weston-super-Mare South West	Spreyton Guest House ★★★	168
Whitby Yorkshire	Whitby YHA ★★★★	553
Worksop East Midlands	Browns ★★★★★ GOLD	438

stablishments listed in colour have a detailed entry in this guide   735

National Accessible Scheme index

Mobility level 1 continued

Yelverton South West	Overcombe House ★★★★	8

Mobility level 2

Abingdon South East	Abbey Guest House ★★★★ SILVER	27
Arnside North West	YHA Arnside ★★★	63
Bardon Mill North East	Coach House Bed & Breakfast ★★★★ SILVER	69
Berwick-upon-Tweed North East	Meadow Hill Guest House ★★★★	68
Blaxhall East of England	Blaxhall YHA ★★★	38
Bolton North West	Meadowcroft Barn B&B ★★★★★ GOLD	65
Bridlington Yorkshire	Providence Place ★★★★	53
Brighouse Yorkshire	The Lodge @ Birkby Hall ★★★★ SILVER	53
Carlisle North West	Bessiestown Farm Country Guesthouse ★★★★★ GOLD	63
Cheshunt East of England	YHA Lee Valley Village ★★★★	37
Chichester South East	George Bell House ★★★★★	25
Claverton Down South West	University of Bath ★★★ - ★★★★	16
Colyton South West	Smallicombe Farm ★★★★ SILVER	14
Dorchester South West	Aquila Heights Guest House ★★★★ SILVER	15
East Runton East of England	Incleborough House ★★★★★ GOLD	37
Ellerby Yorkshire	Ellerby Residential Country Inn ★★★★ SILVER	53
Great Snoring East of England	Vine Park Cottage ★★★★ SILVER	37
Hardstoft East Midlands	Whitton Lodge ★★★★	42
Haydon Bridge North East	Grindon Cartshed ★★★★ SILVER	68
Helmsley Yorkshire	Helmsley YHA ★★★★	54
High Hesleden North East	The Ship Inn ★★★★ SILVER	69
Ings North West	Meadowcroft Country Guest House ★★★★	64
Leominster Heart of England	YHA Leominster ★★★★	47
Lockton Yorkshire	YHA Lockton ★★★★	54
Longthwaite North West	Borrowdale YHA ★★★★	64
Lower Godney South West	Double-Gate Farm ★★★★ GOLD	16
Manchester North West	Manchester YHA ★★★★	65
Manningtree East of England	Curlews ★★★★ SILVER	33
Moira East Midlands	YHA National Forest ★★★★	43
Newbrough North East	Carr Edge Farm ★★★★	68
North Rode North West	Ladderstile Retreat ★★★★★ SILVER	57
Northwich North West	Wall Hill Farm Guest House ★★★★★	57
Old Trafford North West	Lancashire County Cricket Club & Old Trafford Lodge ★★★	65
Padstow South West	Woodlands Country House ★★★★★ GOLD	13
Parkend South West	Fountain Inn ★★★	10
Ribchester North West	Riverside Barn ★★★★★ SILVER	65
Sheringham East of England	Sheringham YHA ★★★	38
Southwold East of England	The Plough Inn ★★★★	38
Spilsby East Midlands	Red Lion Inn ★★★★	43
Torquay South West	Crown Lodge ★★★★	7
Tytherington South West	Lighthouse Guest House ★★★★	16
Walton-on-the-Naze East of England	Bufo Villae Guest House ★★★★	34
Wark North East	The Battlesteads ★★★★ SILVER	69
Wells-next-the-Sea East of England	Wells-next-the-Sea YHA ★★★★	38
Wendling East of England	Greenbanks ★★★★	38
Whitby Yorkshire	Whitby YHA ★★★★	55
Worcester Heart of England	The Manor Coach House ★★★★	48

National Accessible Scheme index

Mobility level 2 continued
elverton South West	Overcombe House ★★★★	81

Mobility level 3 Independent
averton Down South West	University of Bath ★★★ - ★★★★	163
arwood Dale Yorkshire	The Grainary ★★★★	541
orsington South West	Half Moon Inn ★★★	164
ongthwaite North West	Borrowdale YHA ★★★★	642
ower Godney South West	Double-Gate Farm ★★★★ GOLD	165
eydon East of England	Newlands Country House ★★★★ SILVER	384
orquay South West	Crown Lodge ★★★★	76

Mobility level 3 Assisted
reat Snoring East of England	Vine Park Cottage ★★★★ SILVER	377
ongthwaite North West	Borrowdale YHA ★★★★	642
ower Godney South West	Double-Gate Farm ★★★★ GOLD	165
andford South West	Ashridge Farm ★★★★	145

Hearing impairment level 1
bingdon South East	Abbey Guest House ★★★★ SILVER	279
ackpool North West	St Elmo ★★★	651
astle Donington East Midlands	Spring Cottage ★★★★	430
ropston East Midlands	Horseshoe Cottage Farm ★★★★★ GOLD	410
astings South East	Seaspray Bed and Breakfast ★★★★ SILVER	254
athern East Midlands	Leys Guest House ★★★	430
orsington South West	Half Moon Inn ★★★	164
ymington South East	The Nurse's Cottage Restaurant with Rooms ★★★★ GOLD	206
ld Trafford North West	Lancashire County Cricket Club & Old Trafford Lodge ★★★	655
hitby Yorkshire	Whitby YHA ★★★★	553

Visual impairment level 1
bingdon South East	Abbey Guest House ★★★★ SILVER	279
iseworth East Midlands	Lady Gate Guest House ★★★★ SILVER	430
astings South East	Seaspray Bed and Breakfast ★★★★ SILVER	254
elmsley Yorkshire	Helmsley YHA ★★★★	542
orsington South West	Half Moon Inn ★★★	164
ymington South East	The Nurse's Cottage Restaurant with Rooms ★★★★ GOLD	206
ld Trafford North West	Lancashire County Cricket Club & Old Trafford Lodge ★★★	655
hitby Yorkshire	Whitby YHA ★★★★	553

stablishments listed in colour have a detailed entry in this guide

Gold and Silver Award winners

Establishments that have achieved a Gold or Silver Award in recognition of exceptional quality are listed below - those in colour have a detailed entry in this guide. Establishments are listed alphabetically by place name within each region.

South West

GOLD AWARD

Amesbury **Anchorage Bed and Breakfast** ★★★★★ 118
Amesbury **The Dovecot** ★★★★★ 168
Ash Mill **Kerscott Farm** ★★★★★ 139
Athelhampton **White Cottage** ★★★★ 149
Axminster **Kerrington House** ★★★★★ 139
Bath **Athole Guest House** ★★★★★ 161
Bath **Lavender House** ★★★★★ 161
Bibury **Cotteswold House** ★★★★ 92
Blandford Forum **Farnham Farm House** ★★★★★ 81
Blisland, Bodmin **Trewint Farm** ★★★★★ 127
Boscastle **Boscastle House** ★★★★★ 127
Boscastle **The Old Rectory** ★★★★★ 128
Boscastle **Orchard Lodge** ★★★★★ 128
Boscastle **Reddivallen Farm** ★★★★★ 128
Boscastle **Valency Bed & Breakfast** ★★★★ 128
Bourton-on-the-Water **Coombe House** ★★★★ 156
Bourton-on-the-Water **Meadow Rise Guest House** ★★★★ 156
Bovey Tracey **Brookfield House** ★★★★★ 139
Bowood **Queenwood Lodge** ★★★★★ 168
Bradford-on-Avon **Clifton House** ★★★★★ 168
Bradpole **Orchard Barn** ★★★★★ 150
Brushford **Three Acres Country House** ★★★★★ 162
Bude **Harefield Cottage** ★★★★ 39
Bude **Heatham Farmhouse** ★★★★ 128
Bude **Shorething** ★★★★ 128
Bude **Willow Tree Cottage** ★★★★ 128
Budleigh Salterton **Heath Close Bed & Breakfast** ★★★★★ 140
Burton Bradstock **Norburton Hall** ★★★★★ 150
Callington **Cadson Manor** ★★★★★ 128
Camelford **Pendragon Country House** ★★★★★ 129
Castle Cary **Clanville Manor B&B** ★★★★ 109
Cheltenham **Beaumont House** ★★★★★ 93
Cheltenham **Butlers** ★★★★ 157
Cheltenham **Hanover House** ★★★★★ 157
Cheriton Fitzpaine **Devon Wine School** ★★★★★ 140
Chipping Campden **Nineveh Farm** ★★★★★ 94

Christchurch **Druid House** ★★★★★ 8
Cirencester **The Leauses** ★★★★ 15
Corfe Mullen **Elms Lodge** ★★★★ 15
Dartmouth **Hill View House** ★★★★ 14
Dawlish **Lammas Park House** ★★★★★ 14
Devizes **Summerhayes** ★★★★★ 17
Dunster **Spears Cross** ★★★★★ 16
East Harptree **Harptree Court** ★★★★★ 11
East Portholland **Caerhays Castle** ★★★★★ 12
Exeter **Larkbeare Grange** ★★★★★ 14
Exeter **Silversprings** ★★★★ 14
Falmouth **Poltair** ★★★★ 12
Gunnislake **Bridge House** ★★★ 13
Harberton **Foales Leigh** ★★★★★ 14
Hartland **Golden Park** ★★★★★ 14
Holsworthy **South Worden B&B** ★★★★★ 14
Langport **Cherry Orchard Cottage** ★★★★★ 16
Launceston **Copper Meadow** ★★★★ 13
Launceston **Primrose Cottage** ★★★★★ 4
Launceston **Wheatley Farm** ★★★★★ 13
Liskeard **Tregondale Manor Farm** ★★★★ 13
Looe **Bucklawren Farm** ★★★★ 4
Lower Godney **Double-Gate Farm** ★★★★ 16
Lynton **Highcliffe House** ★★★★★ 14
Marlborough **Poulton Grange** ★★★★★ 17
Muchelney **The Parsonage** ★★★★★ 16
Padstow **Althea House** ★★★★★ 13
Padstow **Althea Library** ★★★★★ 13
Padstow **Coswarth House Bed & Breakfast** ★★★★★ 13
Padstow **Pendeen House** ★★★★ 13
Padstow **Treann House** ★★★★★ 13
Padstow **Tregudda** ★★★★★ 13
Padstow **Woodlands Country House** ★★★★★ 13
Par **Penarwyn House** ★★★★★ 13
Penzance **Boskenna Home Farm** ★★★★★ 13
Penzance **The Summer House** ★★★★★ 13
Poole **Danecourt Lodge** ★★★★ 15
Poole **Grovefield Manor Guesthouse** ★★★★★ 15
Poole **The Saltings** ★★★★ 15
Port Isaac **Tregellist Farm** ★★★★ 13

738   Official tourist board guide **Bed & Breakfa**

Gold and Silver award index

South West cont.

altash **Lantallack** ★★★★★ 135
eaton **Pebbles** ★★★★ 145
haftesbury **Glebe Farm** ★★★★★ 153
idmouth **Lavenders Blue** ★★★★ 146
t Austell **Anchorage House** ★★★★★ 50
t Austell **Highland Court Lodge** ★★★★★ 50
t Buryan **Downs Barn Farm** ★★★★★ 136
t Issey **Higher Trevorrick Country House** ★★★★★ 51
t Ives **Blue Hayes** ★★★★★ 136
t Ives **The Light House Bed & Breakfast** ★★★★★ 136
t Ives **Salt House** ★★★★★ 136
t Ives **Shun Lee House: Luxury Guest Accommodation** ★★★★★ 136
t Ives **Tradewinds** ★★★★★ 136
t Mawes **The Rosevine** ★★★★★ 137
t Mellion **Pentillie Castle & Estate** ★★★★★ 53
taverton **Kingston House** ★★★★★ 146
toke Fleming **Southfield House** ★★★★ 146
aunton **Fulford Grange** ★★★★★ 167
avistock **Beera Farmhouse** ★★★★ 72
avistock **Burnville Farm** ★★★★★ 146
avistock **Tor Cottage** ★★★★★ 73
eignmouth **Thomas Luny House** ★★★★★ 146
orquay **The Berburry** ★★★★★ 147
orquay **Haldon Priors** ★★★★★ 77
orquay **The Hillcroft** ★★★★ 147
orquay **The Somerville** ★★★★★ 148
Vareham **Bradle Farmhouse** ★★★★ 154
Vaterrow **Handley Farm Accommodation** ★★★★★ 149
Vinchcombe **Postlip Hall Farm** ★★★★ 160

SILVER AWARD

lford **The Coach House** ★★★★ 160
lton Pancras **Whiteways Farmhouse Accommodation** ★★★★ 149
ppledore **West Farm** ★★★★★ 139
shburton **Blackler Barton House** ★★★★★ 57
shcott **Sunnyside** ★★★★ 160
shton Keynes **Wheatleys Farm** ★★★★ 168
xminster **Hedgehog Corner** ★★★★ 139
arnstaple **Huxtable Farm** ★★★★ 139
ath **55a North Road B&B** ★★★★★ 161
ath **Badminton Villa** ★★★★ 161
ath **Fern Cottage Bed & Breakfast** ★★★★ 91
ath **Ravenscroft** ★★★★ 162
ath **Royal Park Guest House** ★★★★ 162
ath **Three Abbey Green** ★★★★ 162
ath **The Villa Magdala** ★★★★★ 162
eckington **Arundel** ★★★★ 162
eckington **Seymours Court** ★★★★ 162
erry Pomeroy **Great Court Farm** ★★★★ 139
ibury **The William Morris Bed & Breakfast** ★★★★ 156
ideford **Bulworthy Cottage** ★★★★ 139

Bideford **The Mount** ★★★★ 139
Bilbrook **The Wayside B&B** ★★★★ 162
Binegar **Mansfield House** ★★★★ 162
Bishops Hull **The Old Mill** ★★★★★ 162
Blackawton **Washwalk Mill** ★★★★ 139
Bledington **Kings Head Inn & Restaurant** ★★★★ 156
Blue Anchor **Camelot House** ★★★★ 162
Blue Anchor **The Langbury** ★★★★ 162
Bodmin **Bedknobs** ★★★★ 38
Bodmin **Bokiddick Farm** ★★★★★ 127
Bodmin **South Tregleath Farm B&B** ★★★★ 127
Boscastle **Home Farm B&B** ★★★★★ 39
Boscastle **Lower Meadows** ★★★★ 127
Boscastle **The Old Coach House** ★★★★ 128
Boscastle **The Old Parsonage** ★★★★★ 128
Bournemouth **Balincourt** ★★★★★ 149
Bournemouth **Cransley** ★★★★ 149
Bournemouth **The Fircliff** ★★★★ 149
Bourton-on-the-Water **Cranbourne House** ★★★★ 156
Bourton-on-the-Water **Holly House** ★★★★ 156
Bourton-on-the-Water **The Ridge Guesthouse** ★★★★ ... 156
Bovey Tracey **Oaklands** ★★★★ 139
Box **Lorne House** ★★★★ 168
Bradford-on-Avon **Great Ashley Farm** ★★★★ 168
Bridestowe **Knole Farm** ★★★★★ 140
Bridgwater **Apple View** ★★★★ 162
Bridgwater **Hill View** ★★★★ 162
Bridport **Britmead House** ★★★★ 150
Bridport **The Gables** ★★★★ 150
Bridport **Gerrards Farm** ★★★★ 150
Bridport **Highway Farm** ★★★★ 150
Bridport **The Roundham House** ★★★★★ 150
Bridport **Wisteria Cottage** ★★★★ 150
Bristol **Westfield House** ★★★★ 156
Britford **Bridge Farm** ★★★★ 169
Brixham **Brookside Guest House** ★★★★★ 140
Brixham **Fair Winds** ★★★★ 140
Broadstone **Honey Lodge** ★★★★ 150
Broadwinsdor **Cross Keys House** ★★★★★ 150
Broughton Gifford **Honeysuckle Cottage** ★★★★ 169
Bryher **Bank Cottage Guest House** ★★★★ 128
Buckland **Burhill Farm** ★★★★★ 156
Bude **Creathorne Farm Bed & Breakfast** ★★★★★ 128
Bude **The Edgcumbe** ★★★★ 128
Bude **Little Haven** ★★★★ 128
Bude **Oak Lodge B&B** ★★★★ 128
Bude **Oketon** ★★★★ 128
Bude **Palms Guest House** ★★★★ 128
Bude **Sunrise Guest House** ★★★★ 128
Bude **Tee-Side** ★★★★ 40
Budleigh Salterton **Hansard House** ★★★★ 60
Burnham-on-Sea **The Warren Guest House** ★★★★ 163
Camelford **Melorne Farmhouse** ★★★★★ 129

Establishments listed in colour have a detailed entry in this guide

739

Gold and Silver award index

South West *cont.*

Entry	Page
Camelford **Warmington House** ★★★★	129
Cannington **Gurney Manor Mill** ★★★★	163
Castle Cary **The Pilgrims at Lovington** ★★★★	163
Cerney Wick **Waverley Cottage B&B** ★★★★	157
Cheltenham **Burlington House** ★★★★	157
Cheltenham **Detmore House** ★★★★	157
Cheltenham **Garden House** ★★★★	157
Cheltenham **Whalley Farm House** ★★★★	157
Cheltenham **Whittington Lodge Farm** ★★★★	157
Cheltenham **The Wyastone Hotel** ★★★★★	157
Chideock **Bay Tree House** ★★★★	150
Child Okeford **Manor Barn Bed & Breakfast** ★★★★★	150
Chippenham **Glebe House** ★★★★	169
Chippenham **King John's Hunting Lodge** ★★★★	169
Chippenham **Lanhill Stables** ★★★★	169
Chippenham **Red Lion** ★★★★	169
Chipping Campden **Arreton House** ★★★★	157
Chipping Campden **Home Farm Bed & Breakfast** ★★★★	157
Chipping Campden **Little Gidding** ★★★★	157
Chipping Campden **Sandalwood House** ★★★★	157
Christchurch **Beechcroft Place** ★★★★	150
Christchurch **Castle Lodge** ★★★★	150
Cirencester **Greensleeves** ★★★★	95
Cirencester **The Old Bungalow Guest House** ★★★★	158
Colyford **Swan Hill House** ★★★★★	140
Colyton **The Old Bakehouse** ★★★★	140
Colyton **Smallicombe Farm** ★★★★	140
Combe Down **Grey Lodge** ★★★★	163
Copplestone **Harebell** ★★★★	140
Corsham **Mead Lodge B&B** ★★★★	169
Corsham **Park Farm Barn** ★★★★	169
Corsham **Pickwick Lodge Farm** ★★★★	169
Crediton **The Lamb Inn** ★★★★	61
Crewkerne **Barn Cottage Bed & Breakfast** ★★★★	163
Cross **The Old Manor House** ★★★★	163
Cullompton **Newcourt Barton** ★★★★	141
Dartmouth **Cladda Bed & Breakfast and Self Catering Apartments** ★★★★	62
Dartmouth **Frogwell Bed & Breakfast** ★★★★	141
Dartmouth **Melverley House** ★★★★	141
Dartmouth **Mounthaven** ★★★★★	141
Dartmouth **Paper Moon Bed & Breakfast** ★★★★	141
Dartmouth **The Victorian House** ★★★★★	141
Dartmouth **Westbourne House** ★★★★★	141
Dawlish **Channel View Guest House** ★★★★	141
Deerhurst **Odda's Barn** ★★★★	158
Devizes **Bramley House** ★★★★	169
Dorchester **Aquila Heights Guest House** ★★★★	151
Dorchester **Bay Tree House B&B** ★★★★	151
Dorchester **Hazel Cottage** ★★★★	151
Dorchester **Westwood House** ★★★★	151
Down Hatherley **Newbridge House Bed & Breakfast** ★★★★★	15
Dulverton **Streamcombe Farm** ★★★★	16
Dulverton **Town Mills** ★★★★	16
Dunster **The Dunster Castle Hotel** ★★★★	16
Dunster **Exmoor House Dunster** ★★★★	16
Dunster **Millstream Cottage** ★★★★	11
East Brent **Burton Row Farmhouse** ★★★★★	11
East Stour **Aysgarth** ★★★★	15
Exeter **Higher Southbrook Farm** ★★★★	14
Exeter **The Old Rectory** ★★★★★	14
Exeter **Rydon Farm** ★★★★	6
Exeter **Strete Ralegh Farm** ★★★★	14
Fairford **Hathaway** ★★★★	15
Falmouth **The Beach House** ★★★★	12
Falmouth **Chellowdene** ★★★★	12
Falmouth **Dolvean House** ★★★★★	12
Falmouth **Hawthorne Dene** ★★★★	12
Falmouth **Highcliffe Guest House** ★★★★	12
Falmouth **Lugo Rock** ★★★★	12
Fowey **Penventinue Manor Farm** ★★★★★	13
Fowey **Terracotta House** ★★★★	13
Fowey **Trehaida** ★★★★	13
Glastonbury **Chalice Hill House** ★★★★	11
Glastonbury **Chestnuts Boutique Bed & Breakfast** ★★★★	16
Glastonbury **Chindit House** ★★★★	16
Glastonbury **Magdalene House B&B** ★★★★	16
Glastonbury **New House Farm** ★★★★	16
Gloucester **Brawn Farm** ★★★★	15
Gloucester **Crickley Court** ★★★★	15
Guiting Power **Foxhill** ★★★★	15
Guiting Power **Guiting Guest House** ★★★★	9
Halse **Rock House** ★★★★	16
Halwell **Orchard House** ★★★★★	14
Helston **Hollow Tree House** ★★★★	13
Helston **Mandeley Guesthouse** ★★★★	13
Helston **New Thatch B&B** ★★★★	13
Helston **Tregaddra Farmhouse B&B** ★★★★	13
Highbridge **Ilex House** ★★★★	16
Holsworthy **Highbre Crest** ★★★★	13
Honiton **Wessington Farm** ★★★★	14
Hooke **Water Meadow House** ★★★★★	15
Iwerne Minster **The Talbot** ★★★★	15
Kenn **Lower Thornton Farm** ★★★★	14
Kimmeridge **Kimmeridge Farmhouse** ★★★★★	15
Kings Stanley **Valley Views** ★★★★	15
Kingsdown **Ashley Wood Farm** ★★★★	17
Lanreath-by-Looe **Bocaddon Farm** ★★★★	13
Launceston **Beechgrove** ★★★★	13
Launceston **Hill Park** ★★★★	13
Launceston **Middle Tremollett** ★★★★	13
Launceston **Rezare Farmhouse** ★★★★	13
Launceston **Stitch Park** ★★★★	13

Gold and Silver award index

South West cont.

eedstown **Little Pengelly - Farmhouse B&B** ★★★★ 131
iskeard **Higher Trevartha Farm** ★★★★ 131
iskeard **Penharget Farm** ★★★★ 131
iskeard **Trecorme Barton** ★★★★ 131
izard **Atlantic House** ★★★★★ 131
ooe **Barclay House** ★★★★ 43
ooe **Dovers House** ★★★★ 131
ooe **The Gulls** ★★★★ 131
ooe **Lesquite Farm B&B** ★★★★ 131
ooe **Little Larnick Farm** ★★★★ 131
ooe **Trenderway Farm** ★★★★★ 44
ooe **The Watermark** ★★★★ 131
ooe **West Kellow Farm** ★★★★ 131
ostwithiel **Hazelmere House** ★★★★ 45
ulworth Cove **Seavale Bed & Breakfast** ★★★★ 151
ydford **Lydford Country House** ★★★★★ 143
yme Regis **Clappentail House** ★★★★★ 152
yme Regis **Devonia Guest House** ★★★★ 152
yme Regis **Hensleigh House** ★★★★ 152
ynmouth **Lorna Doone House** ★★★★ 143
ynton **Denes** ★★★★ 143
ynton **Ingleside** ★★★★ 143
ynton **Kingford House** ★★★★ 143
ynton **Southcliffe** ★★★★ 143
arlborough **Crofton Lodge** ★★★★ 170
arlborough **Mayfield** ★★★★ 124
arlborough **The Old Forge** ★★★★ 170
arlborough **Teal Cottage** ★★★★ 170
arlborough **The White House** ★★★★ 123
evagissey **Corran Farm** ★★★★ 45
evagissey **Portmellon Cove Guest House** ★★★★★ 132
evagissey **Tregorran Guest House** ★★★★ 132
evagissey **Wild Air Guest House** ★★★★ 132
inchinhampton **Forwood Farm** ★★★★ 159
inehead **Glendower House** ★★★★ 165
inehead **Oakfield Guest House** ★★★★★ 165
inehead **The Parks** ★★★★ 165
onkton Combe **Wheelwrights Arms** ★★★★ 165
onkton Farleigh **The Kings Arms** ★★★★ 124
oreton-in-Marsh **Snowshill Hill Estate B&B** ★★★★★ 159
ether Stowey **Castle of Comfort Country House**
★★★★★ 165
ether Stowey **The Old House** ★★★★ 165
ettleton **Fosse Farmhouse** ★★★★ 170
ewent **Three Ashes House** ★★★★ 159
ewquay **The Carlton** ★★★★ 132
ewquay **The Harbour** ★★★★ 132
ewton Abbot **Rock House Bed & Breakfast** ★★★★★ 143
orth Cadbury **Ashlea House** ★★★★ 166
orton St Philip **George Inn** ★★★★ 166
kehampton **Lower Trecott Farm** ★★★★ 143
ld Cleeve **Cedar House** ★★★★ 166

Padstow **50 Church Street** ★★★★ 133
Padstow **Cally Croft** ★★★★★ 133
Padstow **Lellizzick Farm** ★★★★ 133
Padstow **Petrocstowe** ★★★★ 133
Padstow **Symply Padstow** ★★★★ 133
Padstow **Treverbyn House** ★★★★ 133
Padstow **Trewithen Farmhouse** ★★★★ 133
Padstow **West House** ★★★★ 133
Padstow **The White Hart** ★★★★ 133
Paignton **Amber House** ★★★★ 143
Paignton **Blueberry House** ★★★★ 144
Paignton **Roundham Lodge** ★★★★★ 144
Pamington **Pamington Court Farm** ★★★★ 159
Par **An Skyber** ★★★★ 133
Par **Great Pelean Farm** ★★★★ 133
Par **Reynards Rest** ★★★★ 134
Parracombe **Higher Bodley Farm** ★★★★ 144
Payhembury **Yellingham Farm** ★★★★ 144
Penzance **Castallack Farm** ★★★★ 134
Penzance **Chiverton House** ★★★★ 134
Penzance **Kerris Farm** ★★★★ 134
Penzance **Lombard House** ★★★★★ 134
Penzance **Rosevidney Manor** ★★★★★ 134
Penzance **Tregiffian Farm** ★★★★ 134
Penzance **Trelew Farm B&B** ★★★★ 134
Penzance **Tremont** ★★★★ 134
Penzance **Warwick House** ★★★★ 134
Pewsey **Follets B&B** ★★★★ 170
Pilton **Bowermead House** ★★★★★ 166
Polperro **Chyavallon** ★★★★ 134
Poole **Corkers Restaurant & Cafe Bar with Guest Rooms**
★★★★ 152
Poole **Cranborne House** ★★★★ 152
Poole **Foxes B&B** ★★★★★ 152
Poole **Harlequins B&B** ★★★★ 152
Poole **Oakborne** ★★★★ 152
Poole **Pine Ridge** ★★★★ 152
Poole **Viewpoint Guest House** ★★★★ 152
Porlock **Exmoor House** ★★★★★ 166
Porlock **Glen Lodge** ★★★★ 166
Porlock **Rose Bank Guest House** ★★★★ 114
Port Isaac **Westaway** ★★★★★ 135
Porthcurno **Ardensawah Farm** ★★★★ 48
Porthleven **The Copper Kettle** ★★★★ 135
Porthleven **Harbour Inn** ★★★★ 135
Redlynch **Forest Edge Bed & Breakfast** ★★★★ 171
Redruth **Gooneart Cottage** ★★★★ 49
Redruth **Solcett** ★★★★ 135
Relubbus **Rowan Barn** ★★★★ 135
Ringwood **Little Paddock** ★★★★ 153
Rodbourne **The Manor House Bed & Breakfast** ★★★★ .. 171
Salisbury **The Rokeby Guest House** ★★★★ 171
Salisbury **Salisbury Old Mill House** ★★★★ 171
Salisbury **Spire House** ★★★★ 171

stablishments listed in colour have a detailed entry in this guide

741

Gold and Silver award index

South West *cont.*

Salisbury **Walsworth House** ★★★★★	171
Sampford Arundel **Selby House** ★★★★	166
Seaton **Gatcombe Farm** ★★★★	145
Seaton **Holmleigh House Bed & Breakfast** ★★★★	145
Seaton **The Mariners** ★★★★	145
Selsley **Little Owl Cottage** ★★★★	159
Shaftesbury **The Retreat** ★★★★	86
Shave Cross **The Shave Cross Inn** ★★★★★	87
Sherborne **Chetnole Inn** ★★★★	153
Sherborne **Cumberland House** ★★★★	153
Sherborne **Stoneleigh Barn** ★★★★	153
Sidbury **Rose Cottage Guest House** ★★★★	145
Sidmouth **Coombe Bank Guest House** ★★★★	145
Sidmouth **Hollies Guest House** ★★★★	146
Sidmouth **The Longhouse** ★★★★★	146
Sidmouth **Salcombe Close House** ★★★★★	71
Somerton **Lower Farm** ★★★★	166
Somerton **Mill House** ★★★★★	166
St Austell **Beech Tree Guest House** ★★★★	135
St Austell **Hillside House Guest House** ★★★★	136
St Austell **Hunter's Moon** ★★★★	136
St Austell **Lower Barn** ★★★★★	136
St Austell **Pen Star House** ★★★★	136
St Austell **Poltarrow Farmhouse** ★★★★	136
St Austell **Rashleigh Arms** ★★★★	136
St Austell **Tall Ships** ★★★★★	136
St Columb Major **Pennatillie Farm** ★★★★★	136
St Ives **abode** ★★★★★	52
St Ives **Chy an Gwedhen** ★★★★	51
St Ives **Dean Court** ★★★★★	136
St Ives **Sea Breeze** ★★★★	136
St Just-in-Roseland **Roundhouse Barn B&B Holidays** ★★★★★	52
St Mary's **Annet B&B** ★★★★	137
St Mary's **April Cottage** ★★★★	137
St Mary's **Carn Ithen** ★★★★	137
St Mary's **Carntop Guest House** ★★★★	137
St Mary's **Crebinick House** ★★★★	137
St Mary's **Pelistry Cottage** ★★★★	137
St Mary's **Rose Cottage** ★★★★	137
St Mary's **Sylina Guesthouse** ★★★★	137
St Mary's **Tolman House** ★★★★	137
St Neot, Liskeard **Higher Searles Down** ★★★★	138
Staverton **The Sea Trout Inn** ★★★★	146
Stoke Gabriel **Stoke Gabriel Lodgings** ★★★★★	72
Stow-on-the-Wold **Aston House** ★★★★	101
Stow-on-the-Wold **Chure House** ★★★★	102
Stow-on-the-Wold **Number Nine** ★★★★	160
Stow-on-the-Wold **Windy Ridge House** ★★★★★	160
Street **Old Orchard House** ★★★★	166
Stroud **1 Woodchester Lodge** ★★★★	102
Stroud **Pretoria Villa** ★★★★	103
Studland **Shell Bay Cottage** ★★★★	8
Sturminster Newton **Manston Guest House** ★★★★	15
Swanage **A Great Escape Guest House** ★★★★	15
Swanage **Bella Vista** ★★★★	15
Swanage **The Castleton** ★★★★	15
Swanage **Clare House** ★★★★★	8
Swanage **Easter Cottage** ★★★★	15
Swindon **The Village Apartment** ★★★★	17
Sydenham Damerel **Higher Woodley Farm** ★★★★	14
Tarrant Launceston **Launceston Farmhouse** ★★★★★	15
Taunton **Staplegrove Lodge** ★★★★	16
Taunton **Yallands Farmhouse** ★★★★	16
Tavistock **Colcharton Farm** ★★★★	14
Tedburn St Mary **Great Cummins Farm** ★★★★	14
Teignmouth **The Moorings B&B** ★★★★★	14
Tetbury **Lyncombe House B&B** ★★★★	16
Tewkesbury **Gantier** ★★★★	16
Timsbury **Pitfour House** ★★★★★	16
Tintagel **The Avalon** ★★★★★	13
Torquay **The Baytree** ★★★★	14
Torquay **Bentley Lodge** ★★★★	14
Torquay **Carlton Court** ★★★★★	7
Torquay **Cary Arms Hotel & Restaurant** ★★★★★	7
Torquay **The Cleveland** ★★★★	14
Torquay **The Daylesford** ★★★★	14
Torquay **Fairways** ★★★★	14
Torquay **Garway Lodge Guest House** ★★★★	14
Torquay **The Glenross** ★★★★	14
Torquay **Kingston House** ★★★★★	14
Torquay **Lanscombe House** ★★★★	14
Torquay **Villa Marina** ★★★★	7
Torquay **Walnut Lodge** ★★★★	14
Torquay **The Westbank** ★★★★	14
Torquay **The Westgate** ★★★★	14
Totnes **The Elbow Room** ★★★★★	14
Totnes **The Great Grubb B&B** ★★★★	14
Tregony **Tregonan** ★★★★	13
Tresco **The New Inn** ★★★★	5
Ugborough **Hillhead Farm** ★★★★	14
Wadebridge **Brookdale B&B** ★★★★	13
Wadebridge **Cannalidgey Villa Farm** ★★★★	13
Wadebridge **Pawton Stream** ★★★★	13
Wadebridge **Pengelly Farmhouse** ★★★★	13
Washford **Monkscider House** ★★★★	16
Wells **Ashford House** ★★★★	16
West Bay **Beachcroft** ★★★★	15
West Bay **Bridport Arms** ★★★★	15
West Looe **The Old Bridge House** ★★★★	13
West Lulworth **Gatton House** ★★★★	15
Weston-super-Mare **9 The Park** ★★★★★	16
Weston-super-Mare **Orchard House** ★★★★★	16
Weymouth **Chandlers** ★★★★★	15
Weymouth **The Clarence** ★★★★	15

Gold and Silver award index

South West cont.

Weymouth **Corfe Gate House** ★★★★ 154
Weymouth **Glenthorne Castle Cove** ★★★★ 155
Weymouth **Harlequin Guest House Weymouth** ★★★★ 155
Weymouth **The Pebbles** ★★★★ 155
Wheddon Cross **Exmoor House** ★★★★ 168
Wheddon Cross **Little Brendon Hill Farm** ★★★★★ 168
Wheddon Cross **Sundial House** ★★★★ 168
Williton **Arden Cottage** ★★★★ 168
Williton **Stilegate Bed & Breakfast** ★★★★★ 168
Wimborne **Long Lane Farmhouse** ★★★★ 155
Wimborne **The Old George** ★★★★ 155
Winkleigh **Parsonage Farm** ★★★★ 149
Winterbourne Stoke **Scotland Lodge Farm** ★★★★ *127*
Witham Friary **Higher West Barn Farm** ★★★★ 168
Withleigh **Great Bradley Farmhouse** ★★★★ 149
Wiveliscombe **North Down Farm** ★★★★ 168
Woolacombe **Sandunes** ★★★★ 149

South East

GOLD AWARD

Alkham **Alkham Court Farmhouse** ★★★★★ 272
Ansty **Highbridge Mill** ★★★★ 284
Arreton **Arreton Manor** ★★★★★ 270
Arundel **April Cottage** ★★★★ 284
Ash **Molland House B&B** ★★★★★ 272
Aylesford **Wickham Lodge** ★★★★★ 273
Basingstoke **Mallards** ★★★★★ *202*
Benson **Fyfield Manor** ★★★★ 280
Bexhill-on-Sea **The Old Manse** ★★★★★ 285
Bexhill-on-Sea **The Old Vicarage** ★★★★ 285
Bonchurch **Winterbourne Country House** ★★★★★ 270
Bordon **Groomes** ★★★★★ 266
Brighton & Hove **The Twenty One** ★★★★ 286
Brighton **The Cavalaire** ★★★★ 286
Broadstairs **Anchor Lodge** ★★★★ 273
Broadstairs **Burrow House** ★★★★★ 273
Burford **Westview House** ★★★★ 280
Bury **The Barn at Penfolds** ★★★★ 286
Canterbury **Magnolia House** ★★★★★ *219*
Chart Sutton **Chart Hill Cottage** ★★★★ 274
Chatham **College Road B&B** ★★★★★ 274
Deal **Number One B&B** ★★★★ 274
Dorking **Blackbrook House** ★★★★★ *241*
Dover **Hubert House Guesthouse** ★★★★ 275
Earnley **Millstone** ★★★★ 287
Eastbourne **Brayscroft House** ★★★★ *251*
Eastbourne **The New England** ★★★★ 287
Eastbourne **Ocklynge Manor** ★★★★ 287
Egerton **Frasers** ★★★★★ 275
Elsted **The Barn House B&B** ★★★★★ 267
Godalming **Heath House** ★★★★★ 283
Graffham **Withy** ★★★★★ 288

Grafty Green **Foxes Earth Bed & Breakfast** ★★★★ 276
Great Missenden **Rickyard Cottage** ★★★★ *200*
Grendon Underwood **Shakespeare House** ★★★★★ 265
Halland **Tamberry Hall** ★★★★★ 288
Hastings **Black Rock House** ★★★★★ 288
Hastings **Hastings House** ★★★★★ 288
Hastings **Swan House** ★★★★★ *255*
Haywards Heath **Copyhold Hollow Bed & Breakfast**
  ★★★★ *255*
Heathfield **Iwood Bed & Breakfast** ★★★★ 288
Henley-on-Thames **Falaise House** ★★★★★ 281
Kingsdown **The Gardeners Rest** ★★★★★ 276
Kingsley **The Granary** ★★★★ 267
Lamberhurst **Woodpecker Barn** ★★★★★ 289
Letcombe Regis **Brook Barn** ★★★★★ *236*
Lewes **Beechwood B&B** ★★★★★ *256*
Lodsworth **Halfway Bridge Inn** ★★★★★ 289
Lymington **The Nurse's Cottage Restaurant with Rooms**
  ★★★★ *206*
Marsh Green **Starborough Manor** ★★★★★ 277
Milford-on-Sea **The Bay Trees Bed & Breakfast** ★★★★ 267
Minster **Hoo Farmhouse** ★★★★★ 277
Niton **The Enchanted Manor** ★★★★★ 271
Pett **The Lookout** ★★★★ 289
Ripe **Hall Court Farm** ★★★★★ 289
Royal Tunbridge Wells **A & A Studley Cottage** ★★★★ 278
Royal Tunbridge Wells **Alconbury Guest House**
  ★★★★★ 278
Royal Tunbridge Wells **Danehurst House** ★★★★★ 278
Rudgwick **Alliblaster House** ★★★★★ 290
Rudgwick **Linacre Lodge** ★★★★ 284
Rye **Fairacres** ★★★★★ *260*
Rye **Jeake's House** ★★★★★ *260*
Rye **Oaklands** ★★★★★ *261*
Rye **The Rise** ★★★★★ 290
Rye **Saltcote Place** ★★★★★ 290
Rye **Simmons of Rye** ★★★★★ 290
Rye **Strand House** ★★★★ *261*
Rye **Willow Tree House** ★★★★★ 290
Shanklin **Foxhills** ★★★★★ 271
Sidlesham **Landseer House** ★★★★★ 290
Southsea **The Retreat** ★★★★ 269
Staplecross **Woodside Bed & Breakfast** ★★★★★ *262*
Steyning **Nash Manor** ★★★★ 291
Swingfield **The Old Kent Barn** ★★★★★ 278
Tenterden **Barclay Farmhouse** ★★★★★ 278
Tenterden **Brook Farm** ★★★★★ 278
Tenterden **Rosings Bed & Breakfast** ★★★★★ 278
Ventnor **The Hermitage Country House** ★★★★★ 272
Ventnor **The Leconfield** ★★★★★ 272
Whitstable **Victoria Villa** ★★★★ 279
Winchester **Giffard House** ★★★★★ *208*
Winchester **Windy Ridge** ★★★ 270
Woodstock **Hope House** ★★★★★ 283

Establishments listed in colour have a detailed entry in this guide

Gold and Silver award index

South East cont.

Worth **Solley Farm House** ★★★★★ 279
Worthing **Benson's Guest House** ★★★★ 263

SILVER AWARD

Abingdon **Abbey Guest House** ★★★★ 279
Alfriston **Rose Cottage** ★★★★ 284
Alresford **Old Kennetts Cottage** ★★★★ 266
Alton **Boundary House** ★★★★ 266
Alton **St Mary's Hall** ★★★★ 266
Alton **The Threshing Barn** ★★★★★ 266
Alton **Upper Neatham Mill Farm Guest House** ★★★★ 266
Amberley **The Thatched House** ★★★★ 284
Andover **May Cottage** ★★★★ 202
Andover **The Station Hotel** ★★★★ 266
Arundel **Burpham Country House** ★★★★ 284
Arundel **Furzetor** ★★★★ 284
Ascot **Tun Cottage** ★★★★ 263
Ashford **Snap Mill** ★★★★ 273
Aylesbury **Tanamera** ★★★★ 199
Bampton **The Coach House** ★★★★ 279
Banbury **Banbury Cross B&B** ★★★★ 280
Basingstoke **Manor Farm Stables** ★★★★ 266
Battle **Tollgate Farm House** ★★★★ 284
Beaulieu **Dale Farm House** ★★★★ 266
Bethersden **The Old Stables** ★★★★ 273
Bexhill-on-Sea **Albany House** ★★★★ 285
Bexhill-on-Sea **Arden House** ★★★★ 285
Bexhill-on-Sea **Coast B&B** ★★★★ 285
Bexhill-on-Sea **Dunselma** ★★★★ 285
Bexhill-on-Sea **Highwoods Farm B&B** ★★★★★ 285
Biddenden **Whitfield Farm** ★★★★ 273
Bignor **Stane House** ★★★★ 285
Binstead **Newnham Farm** ★★★★★ 270
Binstead **Sillwood Acre** ★★★★ 270
Birdham **Croftside Cottage** ★★★★ 285
Bognor Regis **Willow Rise** ★★★★ 285
Bolney **Broxmead Paddock** ★★★★ 285
Bosham **Good Hope** ★★★★ 285
Bracknell **Holly House** ★★★★ 197
Bramshaw **Wych Green Cottage** ★★★★ 266
Brede **Little Garth Bed & Breakfast** ★★★★ 248
Brenchley **Hononton Cottage** ★★★★★ 217
Brighton & Hove **Lansdowne Guest House** ★★★★ 249
Brighton **brightonwave** ★★★★ 286
Brighton **Kemp Townhouse** ★★★★★ 286
Brighton **Leona House** ★★★★ 286
Brighton **The Neo** ★★★★ 286
Brighton **Sea Breeze** ★★★★ 286
Brighton **Sea Spray** ★★★★ 286
Broad Oak **Hazelhurst** ★★★★ 286
Broadstairs **Aria House Bed & Breakfast** ★★★★ 273
Broadstairs **Cloonlara** ★★★★ 273
Broadstairs **Copperfields Guest House** ★★★★ 273

Broadstairs **The Devonhurst** ★★★★ 27
Broadstairs **East Horndon** ★★★★ 27
Broadstairs **Number 68** ★★★★ 27
Broadstairs **South Lodge Guest House** ★★★★ 27
Broadstairs **Torwood House** ★★★★★ 27
Broadstairs **The Victoria Bed & Breakfast** ★★★★ 27
Broadstairs **Viking Guest House** ★★★★ 27
Burford **Star Cottage** ★★★★ 28
Burgess Hill **St Owens** ★★★★ 28
Burgess Hill **Wellhouse** ★★★★ 28
Bursledon **Heather Gables** ★★★★ 26
Cadnam **Kingsbridge House** ★★★★ 26
Cadnam **Twin Oaks Guest House** ★★★★ 20
Canterbury **Bower Farm House** ★★★★ 27
Canterbury **Yorke Lodge** ★★★★★ 21
Charing **Oak** ★★★★ 22
Charlton **Woodstock House** ★★★★ 28
Chart Sutton **White House Farm** ★★★★ 27
Chelwood Gate **Holly House** ★★★★ 24
Chichester **Anna's** ★★★★ 28
Chichester **The Cottage** ★★★★ 28
Chichester **The Dairy Farm** ★★★★ 28
Chichester **Field View** ★★★★ 28
Chichester **Spooners** ★★★★ 28
Chichester **Stubcroft Farm** ★★★ 28
Chichester **The Studio B&B Birdham** ★★★★ 28
Chiddingly **Hale Farm House** ★★★★ 28
Chieveley **Thatched House B&B** ★★★★ 26
Chieveley **Ye Olde Red Lion** ★★★★ 26
Chipping Norton **Hackers End** ★★★★ 28
Churchill **The Forge** ★★★★ 28
Cold Ash **2 Woodside** ★★★★ 26
Cookham Dean **Riverbank Cottage** ★★★★ 26
Cranbrook **Bargate House** ★★★★ 27
Cranbrook **Beacon Hall House** ★★★★ 27
Cranbrook **Hallwood Farm Oast** ★★★★★ 27
Crowborough **Braemore** ★★★★ 28
Crowborough **Yew House Bed & Breakfast** ★★★★ 25
Dorking **Denbies Farmhouse** ★★★★ 28
Dorking **Stylehurst Farm** ★★★★ 24
Dover **East Lee Guest House** ★★★★ 27
Dover **Maison Dieu Guest House** ★★★★ 22
East Cowes **Crossways House** ★★★★ 27
East Dean **Rubens Barn** ★★★★★ 28
Eastbourne **Albert & Victoria** ★★★★★ 28
Eastbourne **Eastbourne Reymar** ★★★ 25
Eastbourne **The Guesthouse East** ★★★★ 28
Eastbourne **Loriston Guest House** ★★★★★ 28
Eastbourne **Southcroft** ★★★★ 28
Edenbridge **Becketts** ★★★★ 27
Edenbridge **Mowshurst Farm House** ★★★★ 27
Elmsted **Elmsted Court Farm** ★★★★ 27
Ewelme **Fords Farm** ★★★★ 23

Gold and Silver award index

South East cont.

Ewhurst Green **Clouds Bed & Breakfast** ★★★★★ 287
Faversham **Fairlea Bed & Breakfast** ★★★★ 221
Faversham **Gladstone House** ★★★★ 275
Fawley **Walcot Guest House** ★★★★ 267
Fernhurst **Colliers Farm** ★★★★★ 287
Fordingbridge **Cottage Crest** ★★★★★ 267
Forest Row **West Meadows** ★★★★ 287
Gatwick **Southbourne Guest House Gatwick** ★★★★ 254
Godalming **Highview** ★★ 283
Graffham **Little Hoyle** ★★★★ 288
Gravesend **Eastcourt Oast** ★★★ 276
Great Missenden **Lower Bassibones Farm B&B** ★★★★ 265
Greatstone-on-Sea **White Horses Cottage** ★★★★★ 276
Hadlow **Fieldswood Bed & Breakfast** ★★★★ 276
Halnaker **Old Store Guest House** ★★★★ 288
Hampton Poyle **The Bell at Hampton Poyle** ★★★★★ 280
Harpsden **Apple Ash** ★★★★ 280
Haslemere **Langhams Cottage B&B** ★★★★ 283
Hastings **Lavender & Lace** ★★★★ 288
Hastings **Minstrel's Rest** ★★★★ 288
Hastings **Seaspray Bed and Breakfast** ★★★★ 254
Hastings **Summerfields House** ★★★★ 288
Hastings **The White House** ★★★★★ 288
Hawkenbury **The White Cottage** ★★★★ 276
Hayling Island **Copsewood House** ★★★★ 267
Haywards Heath **Oakfield Cottage** ★★★★ 288
Henley-on-Thames **Alushta** ★★★★ 281
Henley-on-Thames **The Baskerville** ★★★★ 235
Henley-on-Thames **Denmark House** ★★★★ 281
Henton **Manor Farm Cottage** ★★★★ 281
Hernhill **Church Oast** ★★★★ 223
High Wycombe **9 Green Road** ★★★★ 265
High Wycombe **Longforgan** ★★★★ 265
High Wycombe **Old Meadows Bed & Breakfast** ★★★★ 265
High Wycombe **Rosling House** ★★★★ 265
Higham **Field View** ★★ 276
Hill Brow **The Jolly Drover** ★★★★ 288
Holton **Home Farm House** ★★★★ 281
Horley **Rosemead Guest House** ★★★★ 284
Horsham **Goffslands Farm B&B** ★★★★ 288
Hove **The Claremont** ★★★★★ 288
Hunston **Spire Cottage** ★★★★ 288
Hurley **Meadow View** ★★★★★ 263
Hurst Green **The Old Courthouse B&B** ★★★★ 288
Hurstpierpoint **Wickham Place** ★★★★ 289
Ibthorpe **Ibthorpe Manor Farm** ★★★★★ 267
Ightham **The Studio At Double Dance** ★★★★ 276
Lavant **West Faldie** ★★★★ 289
Leaveland **Leaveland Court** ★★★★ 276
Leckhampstead **Bow River House** ★★★★★ 263
Lee-on-the-Solent **Leeward House B&B** ★★★★ 267
Lee-on-the-Solent **Milvil Corner** ★★★★★ 267

Lewes **The Blacksmiths Arms** ★★★★ 257
Lewes **Langtons House** ★★★★ 289
Lewes **Millers** ★★★★ 289
Little Compton **The Old School** ★★★★★ 281
Littlehampton **Racing Greens (B&B)** ★★★★ 289
Long Wittenham **Wittas Ham Cottage** ★★★★ 281
Lyminge **Roundwood Hall Bed & Breakfast** ★★★★ 276
Lymington **Britannia House** ★★★★★ 267
Lymington **Ha'penny House** ★★★★★ 205
Lymington **Inglemere B&B** ★★★★ 267
Lyndhurst **Acorns of Lyndhurst** ★★★★ 267
Lyndhurst **Kingswood Cottage** ★★★★ 267
Maidenhead **Sunny Cottage** ★★★★ 263
Maidstone **At Home** ★★ 276
Maidstone **Grove House** ★★★★ 224
Maidstone, Kent **Ash Cottage** ★★★★★ 224
Marden **3 Chainhurst Cottages** ★★★★ 277
Marlow **Granny Anne's** ★★★★ 265
Marlow **Swiss Cottage B&B** ★★★★ 265
Mersham **Stone Green Farm** ★★★★★ 277
Midhurst **Orchard House** ★★★★ 289
Milton Common **Byways** ★★★★ 281
New Milton **Taverners Cottage** ★★★★ 268
Newbury **The Chase Guest House** ★★★★ 264
Newbury **Manor Farm House** ★★★★ 197
Newchurch **Rosemary Cottage** ★★★★ 270
Newick **Holly Lodge** ★★★★ 289
Newport (3 miles) **Freewaters** ★★★★ 211
Nonington **Farthingales Bed & Breakfast** ★★★★ 277
North Moreton **North Moreton House** ★★★★★ 281
Oakley Green **Rainworth House** ★★★★ 198
Old Basing **Millfield House** ★★★★ 268
Olney **Colchester House** ★★★★ 265
Ospringe **The Lodge** ★★★★ 277
Oxford **Broomhill Bed and Breakfast** ★★★★ 237
Oxford **Gables** ★★★★ 281
Oxford **Remont** ★★★★ 282
Oxford **Tilbury Lodge** ★★★★ 282
Pembury **Camden Arms Hotel** ★★★★ 277
Petersfield **Border Cottage** ★★★★ 268
Petersfield **Downsview** ★★★★ 268
Petersfield **Upper Parsonage Farm** ★★★★ 268
Petworth **Brook Barn** ★★★★ 289
Pluckley **Elvey Farm** ★★★★ 226
Portsmouth **Cherry Trees** ★★★★ 207
Portsmouth **Fortitude Cottage** ★★★★ 268
Pulborough **St Cleather** ★★★★ 289
Ringwood **Avonmead House** ★★★★ 268
Ringwood **Moortown Lodge** ★★★★ 268
Ringwood **Torre Avon** ★★★★ 268
Robertsbridge **Slides Farm B&B** ★★★★★ 290
Rochester **Churchfields B&B** ★★ 277
Rochester **The Cottage** ★★★★ 277

Establishments listed in colour have a detailed entry in this guide

745

Gold and Silver award index

South East cont.

Rochester **Orchard Cottage** ★★★★ 277
Rockbourne **Ducks Nest B&B** ★★★★★ 268
Romsey **The Dairy at Packridge Farm** ★★★★ 268
Romsey **The Shoe Inn** ★★★★ 268
Rookley **Kennerley House - B&B** ★★★★ 271
Rustington **Mallondene** ★★★★ 259
Rye **Haydens** ★★★★★ 290
Rye **The Mill House** ★★★★ 290
Rye **Ranters' Rest** ★★★★ 290
Sandford **The Barn** ★★★★ 271
Sandhurst **Lamberden House** ★★★★ 278
Sandown **Copperfield Lodge** ★★★★ 271
Sandown **Treval Guest House** ★★★★ 271
Sandwich **White Rose Lodge** ★★★★ 278
Seaview **1 Cluniac Cottages** ★★★ 271
Seaview **Clover Ridge** ★★★★ 271
Selsey **Keston House** ★★★★ 290
Sevenoaks **Old Timbertop Cottage** ★★★★ 278
Shanklin **Bedford Lodge** ★★★★ 213
Shanklin **The Birkdale** ★★★★ 214
Shanklin **Grange Bank House** ★★★★ 271
Shanklin **The Havelock** ★★★★ 271
Shanklin **Heatherleigh Guest House** ★★★★ 214
Shanklin **The Kenbury** ★★★★ 272
Shanklin **Rosemary B&B** ★★★★ 272
Shanklin **Snowdon House** ★★★★ 272
Shanklin **The St Leonards** ★★★★ 272
Shanklin **Swiss Cottage** ★★★★ 215
Shanklin **Westbury Lodge** ★★★★ 272
Sheerness **Ferry House Inn** ★★★★ 228
Shillingford **Alouette Bed & Breakfast** ★★★★ 282
Shorwell **Westcourt Farm** ★★★★ 272
Singleton **1 Rose Cottage** ★★★★ 290
Sissinghurst **Sissinghurst Castle Farmhouse** ★★★★★ 278
Sittingbourne **Holly House Bed & Breakfast** ★★★★ 278
Sittingbourne **Woodstock Guesthouse** ★★★★ 278
Slaugham **Slaugham Place Farm** ★★★★ 290
Smarden **Hereford Oast** ★★★★ 278
Sonning **The Bull Inn** ★★★★ 264
Southampton **The Avenue Bed & Breakfast** ★★★ 269
Southampton **Pilgrim Inn** ★★★★★ 269
St Leonards-on-Sea **Tower House 1066** ★★★★ 291
St Margarets Bay **Lenox House** ★★★★ 278
St Margaret's Bay **Small Acre** ★★★★ 278
Standlake **The Cottage** ★★★★ 282
Stockbridge **The White Hart Inn** ★★★★ 269
Swanley **Greenacre** ★★★★ 229
Sway **Tiverton** ★★★★ 269
Tenterden **The Tower House** ★★★★★ 278
Totland Bay **The Granville** ★★★★ 272
Totland **Chart House** ★★★★ 272
Tunbridge Wells **Ash Tree Cottage** ★★★★ 278
Tunbridge Wells **The Brick House** ★★★★ 279
Tunbridge Wells **Hazelwood House** ★★★★ 279
Uckfield **Beggars Barn** ★★★★ 291
Uckfield **South Paddock** ★★★★★ 291
Uffington **Norton House** ★★★★ 282
Ventnor **Windsor Carlton** ★★★★ 272
Wadhurst **Church House Bed & Breakfast** ★★★★ 291
Wantage **Regis Guest House** ★★★★ 240
Waterlooville **Fairways** ★★★★ 269
West Chiltington **Old Oaks** ★★★★ 291
West Chiltington **The Old School House** ★★★★★ 291
West Malling **Appledene** ★★★★ 279
Westerham **Old Farmhouse** ★★ 230
Weybridge **The Clock House** ★★★★ 245
Whitstable **Alliston House** ★★★★ 279
Winchester **5 Clifton Terrace** ★★★★ 269
Winchester **Dawn Cottage** ★★★★★ 269
Winchester **Dolphin House Studios** ★★★★ 269
Winchester **Staddle Stones** ★★★★ 270
Windsor **76 Duke Street** ★★★★ 264
Woodstock **Elbie House** ★★★★ 282
Woodstock **Gorselands Hall** ★★★★ 283
Wootton **Grange Farm B&B** ★★★★ 272
Worthing **Edwardian Dreams** ★★★★ 291
Worthing **Merton House** ★★★★ 291
Worthing **The Old Guard House** ★★★★ 291
Yarmouth **Ivy Cottage** ★★★★ 272

London

GOLD AWARD

London SW5 **base2stay Kensington** ★★★★★ 309
London W6 **At Home in London: Westminster Ref 5** ★★ 309
Teddington **Middle Cottage** ★★★★ 310

SILVER AWARD

London **At Home in London: Chiswick Ref 267** ★★★★ ... 311
London SE10 **Captains Retreat** ★★★★ 308
London SW1 **The Lord Milner** ★★★★★ 309
London SW1 **The Windermere** ★★★★ 309

East of England

GOLD AWARD

Aylsham **The Old Pump House** ★★★★★ 343
Beyton **Manorhouse** ★★★★★ 382
Carlton **Moat House Farm** ★★★★ 382
Chorleywood **Ashburton Country House** ★★★★★ 374
Clacton-on-Sea **Pond House** ★★★★ 371
Colchester **Trinity Town House** ★★★★ 338
Coltishall **Seven Acres House** ★★★★★ 345
Dersingham **The Corner House** ★★★★ 376
Dickleburgh **Dickleburgh Hall Country House** ★★★★★ ... 376
Earls Colne **Greenlands Farm** ★★★★ 372
Earsham **Earsham Park Farm** ★★★★ 376
East Rudham **The Close** ★★★★★ 376

Gold and Silver award index

East of England *cont.*

East Runton **Incleborough House** ★★★★★ 376
Edingthorpe **Church Farm Barn** ★★★★★ 376
Elmstead **Pheasant Lodge** ★★★★★ 372
Elmswell **Mulberry Farm** ★★★★ 382
Fakenham **Holly Lodge** ★★★★★ 376
Fakenham **White Rose Lodge** ★★★★★ 376
Framlingham (7 miles) **Flindor Cottage** ★★★★★ 359
Friston **Old School** ★★★★ 360
Haughley **Haughley House** ★★★★★ 383
Helhoughton **Woodfarm House** ★★★★★ 377
Hickling **The Dairy Barns** ★★★★ 347
Hindringham **Field House** ★★★★★ 377
Holt **Byfords** ★★★★★ 378
Hopton **The Old Rectory Hopton** ★★★★★ 383
Hunstanton **The Bays Guest House** ★★★★★ 378
Hunstanton **Burlington House** ★★★★ 378
Hunstanton **Gate Lodge Guest House** ★★★★ 378
Hunstanton **Peacock House** ★★★★ 378
Hunstanton **Rose Fitt House** ★★★★ 378
Ipswich **Sidegate Guesthouse** ★★★★ 383
Kessingland **The Old Rectory** ★★★★★ 383
Lavenham **Lavenham Old Rectory** ★★★★★ 361
Lavenham **Lavenham Priory** ★★★★★ 383
Little Waltham **Channels Lodge** ★★★★ 372
Littleport **Killiney House** ★★★★★ 370
Newmarket **Birdcage Walk** ★★★★ 384
North Lopham **Church Farm House** ★★★★★ 379
Norwich **38 St Giles B&B** ★★★★★ 379
Rougham **Oak Farm Barn** ★★★★ 384
Sheringham **Olivedale Guest House** ★★★★ 380
Snetterton **Holly House Guest House** ★★★★★ 380
Snettisham **Twitchers Retreat** ★★★★ 380
St Osyth **Park Hall Country House** ★★★★★ 373
Stowmarket **Bays Farm** ★★★★★ 363
Stuntney **The Old Hall** ★★★★★ 370
Sutton **The Grove** ★★★★ 370
Swanton Morley **Carricks at Castle Farm** ★★★★★ 354
Thorndon **Moat Farm** ★★★★ 385
Wells-next-the-Sea **Machrimore** ★★★★ 381
Wells-next-the-Sea **The Normans** ★★★★★ 381
Wethersfield **Church Hill House** ★★★★ 374
Weybread **Mill Lane Farm B&B** ★★★★★ 385
Wighton **Meadow View Guest House** ★★★★★ 356
Wymondham **Witch Hazel** ★★★★ 357
Wyton **Magdalene House** ★★★★★ 371

SILVER AWARD

Anstey **Anstey Grove Barn** ★★★★ 374
Ardleigh **Park Cottage** ★★★★ 371
Aylmerton **Driftway Guest House** ★★★★ 375
Badingham **Colston Hall** ★★★★ 381
Barnack **Rowan House** ★★★★ 368
Barnby **Salmon's Leap** ★★★★ 382

Barney **The Old Brick Kilns Guesthouse** ★★★★ 375
Bartlow **Westoe Farm** ★★★★★ 368
Bawburgh **The Old Lodge** ★★★★ 375
Beccles **Eveleigh House B&B** ★★★★ 382
Bedford **Bourne End Farm** ★★★★★ 368
Bildeston **Silwood Barns** ★★★★ 382
Blackheath **Fridaywood Farm** ★★★★ 371
Bolnhurst **Old School House** ★★★★ 368
Brightlingsea **Hurst Green Bed and Breakfast** ★★★★ 336
Brightlingsea **Paxton Dene** ★★★★ 371
Brooke **The Old Vicarage** ★★★★ 375
Brundall **Breckland B&B** ★★★★ 344
Bunwell **The Cottage** ★★★★ 375
Burnham Market **Wood Lodge** ★★★★ 375
Burnham Thorpe **Whitehall Farm** ★★★★ 344
Burnham-on-Crouch **Mangapp Manor** ★★★★ 371
Burnham-on-Crouch **The Railway** ★★★★ 371
Bury St Edmunds (6 miles) **The Old Manse Barn**
★★★★★ 358
Bury St Edmunds **Ounce House** ★★★★★ 382
Bury St Edmunds **Sanctuary B&B** ★★★★ 382
Bury St Edmunds **St Edmunds Guesthouse** ★★★★ 358
Cambridge **Archway House** ★★★★ 368
Cambridge **Avalon** ★★★★ 368
Cambridge **Beech Farm Bed & Breakfast** ★★★★ 368
Cambridge **The Conifers** ★★★★ 368
Cambridge **Harrys Bed & Breakfast** ★★★★ 369
Cambridge **Home From Home** ★★★★ 332
Cambridge **Worth House** ★★★★ 333
Catfield **The Limes** ★★★★ 375
Chedgrave **Little Willows** ★★★★ 375
Cheveley **1eleven Bed & Breakfast** ★★★★ 369
Clacton-on-Sea **Chudleigh** ★★★★ 337
Clavering **Cricketers, The** ★★★★ 337
Clenchwarton **Kismet Lodge Bed & Breakfast** ★★★★ ... 375
Colchester **Charlie Brown's** ★★★★ 371
Cromer **The Old Barn** ★★★★ 376
Cromer **Shrublands Farm Guesthouse** ★★★★ 345
Deopham **Park Farm Bed & Breakfast** ★★★★ 376
Dersingham **Ashdene House** ★★★★ 376
Dersingham **Barn House Bed & Breakfast** ★★★★ 346
Dersingham **The White House** ★★★★ 376
Doddington **Fenview Lodge** ★★★★ 369
Earl Soham **Bridge House** ★★★★ 382
Elmswell **Elmswell Hall B&B** ★★★★ 382
Elmswell **Kiln Farm Guest House** ★★★★ 358
Elveden **Glebe Country House Bed & Breakfast** ★★★★ ... 383
Ely **57 Lynn Road** ★★★★ 369
Ely **96 Lynn Road** ★★★★ 369
Ely **B&B @ 1A** ★★★★ 369
Ely **Bowmount House** ★★★★ 369
Ely **Riverside Inn** ★★★★ 369
Ely **Walnut House** ★★★★ 369
Feering **Old Wills Farm** ★★★★ 372

Establishments listed in colour have a detailed entry in this guide 747

Gold and Silver award index

East of England *cont.*

Felixstowe **Castle Lodge** ★★★★ 383
Felixstowe **The Norfolk Guest House** ★★★★ 383
Fersfield **Strenneth** ★★★★ 376
Fritton **Decoy Barn Bed & Breakfast** ★★★★ 376
Frogmore **Riverside** ★★★★ 374
Gayton **Bridge House** ★★★★ 376
Girton **Finches Bed & Breakfast** ★★★★ 369
Goldhanger **Longwick Farm** ★★★★ 372
Gorefield **The Old Vicarage Bed & Breakfast** ★★★★ 370
Great Barton **The Wallow** ★★★★ 383
Great Easton **The Swan Inn** ★★★★ 372
Great Hormead **Brick House Farm Bed & Breakfast**
★★★★ 374
Great Snoring **Vine Park Cottage** ★★★★ 377
Great Wilbraham **Kettles Cottage** ★★★★ 370
Great Yarmouth **Barnard House** ★★★★ 377
Great Yarmouth **Beaumont House** ★★★★ 377
Great Yarmouth **The Bromley** ★★★★ 377
Great Yarmouth **Merivon Guest House** ★★★★ 347
Great Yarmouth **Saffrons** ★★★★ 377
Great Yarmouth **The Shrewsbury Guest House** ★★★★ 377
Hadleigh **Edge Hall** ★★★★★ 383
Halesworth **Wissett Lodge B&B** ★★★★ 383
Hatfield Heath **Friars Farm** ★★★★ 372
Heacham **Saint Annes Guest House** ★★★★ 377
Hintlesham **College Farm Bed & Breakfast** ★★★★ 360
Hitcham **Box Tree Farm** ★★★★ 383
Horning **The Moorhen** ★★★★ 378
Hoveton **The Vineries Bed & Breakfast** ★★★★ 378
Hunstanton **Belgrave House** ★★★★ 378
Hunstanton **The Burleigh** ★★★★ 378
Hunstanton **Cori House Bed & Breakfast** ★★★★ 378
Hunstanton **Deepdene House** ★★★★ 378
Hunstanton **Glenberis Bed & Breakfast** ★★★★ 378
Hunstanton **The King William IV, Country Inn &
Restaurant** ★★★★ 348
Hunstanton **Kingfisher B&B** ★★★★ 378
Hunstanton **Linksway Country House** ★★★★ 378
Hunstanton **The Lodge** ★★★★ 378
Huntingdon **Cheriton House** ★★★★★ 335
Ingoldisthorpe **Pencob House** ★★★★ 378
Ipswich **Lattice Lodge Guest House** ★★★★ 360
Ipswich **Melverley Heights Guest House** ★★★★ 383
King's Lynn **Fairlight Lodge** ★★★★ 378
Kirby Bedon **Hall Park Bed & Breakfast** ★★★★ 378
Lavenham **Angel Gallery** ★★★★ 383
Lavenham **Guinea House Bed & Breakfast** ★★★★ 383
Leiston **Field End** ★★★★ 384
Little Downham **Bury House Bed & Breakfast** ★★★★ 370
Little Sampford **Bush Farm** ★★★★ 372
Little Snoring **Jex Farm B&B** ★★★★ 379
Littleport **Glebe House** ★★★★ 370

Loddon **Hall Green Farm B&B** ★★★★ 379
Long Melford **High Street Farmhouse** ★★★★ 362
Lowestoft **Britten House** ★★★★★ 384
Lowestoft **Fairways Bed & Breakfast** ★★★★ 384
Lowestoft **The Sandcastle** ★★★★ 384
Ludham **Broadland Bed & Breakfast** ★★★★ 379
Maldon **Home Farm Accommodation** ★★★★ 372
Manningtree **Curlews** ★★★★ 339
Monk Soham **The Firs Farmhouse** ★★★★ 384
Moulton **37 Newmarket Road** ★★★★ 384
Mundesley **The Durdans** ★★★★ 379
Nayland **The Steam Mill House** ★★★★ 384
Neatishead **Regency Guesthouse** ★★★★ 379
Norwich **Arrandale Lodge** ★★★★ 379
Norwich **Beaufort Lodge** ★★★★ 379
Norwich **Catton Old Hall** ★★★★★ 350
Norwich **Gilman Lodge Guest House** ★★★★★ 379
Norwich **The Grove** ★★★★★ 379
Oulton Broad **The Mill House Bed & Breakfast** ★★★★ 384
Oulton **The Courtyard** ★★★★ 384
Pakenham **Fen House Bed & Breakfast** ★★★★ 384
Pentlow **School Barn Farm** ★★★★ 373
Pentney **Little Abbey Farm** ★★★★ 352
Pleshey **Bury Farm** ★★★★ 373
Pulham Market **The Old Bakery** ★★★★★ 380
Renhold **Aldwyck Wood** ★★★★ 368
Reydon **Newlands Country House** ★★★★ 384
RISBY **Brambles Lodge** ★★★★ 384
Roxton **Church Farm** ★★★★ 368
Sandy **Highfield Farm** ★★★★★ 368
Sculthorpe **Manor Farm Bed & Breakfast** ★★★★ 380
Shalford **Lynton House** ★★★ 373
Sheringham **Augusta House** ★★★★ 380
Sheringham **Brook House Bed & Breakfast** ★★★★ 380
Sheringham **Cleat House** ★★★★★ 352
Sheringham **Sheringham View Cottage** ★★★★ 380
Sheringham **Sunrays Bed & Breakfast** ★★★★ 380
Sheringham **Viburnham House Bed & Breakfast**
★★★★ 380
Shotley **Hill House Farm Bed & Breakfast** ★★★★ 384
Sibton **Sibton White Horse Inn** ★★★★ 362
South Walsham **Leeward Bed & Breakfast** ★★★★ 380
South Walsham **Old Hall Farm** ★★★★ 353
Southend-on-Sea **Beaches** ★★★★ 373
Southend-on-Sea **Pier View** ★★★★ 373
Sporle **Corfield House** ★★★★ 380
Sproughton **Finjaro** ★★★★ 384
St Albans **178 London Road** ★★★ 374
St Albans **Fleuchary House** ★★★★ 375
St Cross South Elmham **South Elmham Hall** ★★★★★ 384
Stansted **Chimneys** ★★★★ 373
Stansted **The Cottage** ★★★★ 340
Stansted **White House** ★★★★ 340
Stiffkey **Stiffkey Bed & Breakfast** ★★★★ 380

Gold and Silver award index

East of England *cont.*

Stratton Strawless **Woodmans Farm** ★★★★ 353
Sudbury **St David's Hall** ★★★★ 385
Swaffham Bulbeck **B&B at Martin House** ★★★★ 370
Swaffham **Repton House** ★★★★ 381
Swanton Morley **Frogs Hall Farm** ★★★★★ 381
Takeley **Oak Lodge Bed & Breakfast** ★★★★ 373
Takeley **Pussy Willow** ★★★★ 373
Terrington St John **The White House** ★★★★ 381
Thaxted **Crossways Guesthouse** ★★★★ 373
Thorington **Park Farm** ★★★★ 385
Thornham Magna **Thornham Hall** ★★★★★ 385
Thornham **Rushmeadow** ★★★★ 381
Thurston **The Fox & Hounds** ★★★★ 385
Tunstall **Manor House** ★★★★ 381
Uggeshall **Bankside Bed & Breakfast** ★★★★ 385
Upper Sheringham **Lodge Cottage** ★★★★ 381
Wells-next-the-Sea **Admiral House** ★★★★ 381
Wells-next-the-Sea **Boxwood Guest House** ★★★★ 381
Wells-next-the-Sea **The Globe Inn** ★★★★ 381
West Rudham **Oyster House** ★★★★ 381
West Wickham **Chequer Cottage** ★★★★ 370
Westhorpe **Moat Hill Farm B&B** ★★★★ 365
Wethersfield **The Green** ★★★★ 374
Whepstead **The Old Pear Tree** ★★★★ 385
Wickmere **Pink House Bed & Breakfast** ★★★★ 381
Wimbish **Newdegate House** ★★★★ 374
Wingfield **Gables Farm** ★★★★ 366
Wistow **Pointers Guest House** ★★★★ 371
Woodbridge **2 St Anne's School House** ★★★★ 385
Woodbridge **The Coach House** ★★★★ 385
Woodbridge **Fir Tree Lodge** ★★★★ 385
Woodhurst **Fullards Farm** ★★★★ 371
Wortham **Rookery Farm** ★★★★ 367
Wroxham **Coach House** ★★★★ 381
Yoxford **Chapel Cottage** ★★★★ 385
Yoxford **Sans Souci B&B** ★★★★ 385

East Midlands

GOLD AWARD

Buxton **Grendon Guest House** ★★★★★ 426
Buxton **Southmead** ★★★★ 426
Chapel-en-le-Frith **High Croft Guest House** ★★★★★ 426
Cropston **Horseshoe Cottage Farm** ★★★★★ 410
Edale **Stonecroft Country Guest House** ★★★★ 427
Eyam **Bretton Cottage** ★★★★★ 427
Hathersage **Cannon Croft** ★★★★ 428
Hope **Underleigh House** ★★★★★ 407
Lincoln **Creston Villa Guest House** ★★★★★ 433
Matlock Bath **Sunnybank B&B** ★★★★ 428
Matlock **Sheriff Lodge** ★★★★ 428
Newark **Newark Lodge Guest House** ★★★★★ 438
Newhaven **The Kings at Ivy House** ★★★★★ 428
Nottingham **Greenwood Lodge City Guest House** ★★★★★ 438
Snelston **Oldfield House** ★★★★★ 429
Stamford **Rock Lodge** ★★★★★ 435
Stanton-in-the-Peak **Congreave Farm** ★★★★ 429
Tansley **Silver Ridge** ★★★★★ 409
Towcester **The Old Barn at The Old Mint House** ★★★★ 437
Uppingham **Spanhoe Lodge** ★★★★★ 422
Wirksworth **The Old Lock-Up** ★★★★★ 429
Worksop **Browns** ★★★★★ 438

SILVER AWARD

Alford **Old Mill House** ★★★★ 431
Ashbourne **Shirley Hall** ★★★★ 401
Ashford-in-the-Water **Chy-an-Dour** ★★★★ 425
Ashford-in-the-Water **River Cottage** ★★★★★ 425
Bakewell **Castle Cliffe** ★★★★ 425
Bakewell **Castle Hill Farm House** ★★★★ 401
Bakewell **The Garden Room** ★★★★ 425
Bamford **Pioneer House** ★★★★ 402
Bamford **The Rising Sun** ★★★★ 425
Bamford **Yorkshire Bridge Inn** ★★★★ 403
Barrow-on-Trent **5 Nook Cottages** ★★★★ 425
Bonsall **Cascades Gardens** ★★★★★ 425
Bonsall **Town Head Farmhouse** ★★★★ 426
Brackley **The Old Surgery** ★★★★ 436
Brackley **Two Hoots** ★★★★ 436
Bradley **Holly Meadow Farm** ★★★★ 426
Bradley **Yeldersley Old Hall Farm** ★★★★ 426
Brixworth **Lake House Bed & Breakfast** ★★★★ 436
Buxton **9 Green Lane B&B** ★★★★ 426
Buxton **Devonshire Lodge Guest House** ★★★★ 426
Buxton **Fernydale Farm** ★★★★ 404
Buxton **Grosvenor House** ★★★★ 426
Buxton **Kingscroft Guest House** ★★★★★ 404
Buxton **The Old Manse** ★★★★ 426
Buxton **Roseleigh** ★★★★ 426
Buxton **Stoneridge Guest House** ★★★★ 426
Buxton **Westlands** ★★★★★ 426
Caenby Corner **Ermine Lodge Bed & Breakfast** ★★★★ 432
Calver **The Chequers Inn** ★★★★ 426
Calver **Valley View Guest House** ★★★★ 426
Chapel-en-le-Frith **Rushop Hall B&B** ★★★★ 426
Chesterfield **Anis Louise Guest House** ★★★★ 427
Colsterworth **The Stables** ★★★★ 432
Colsterworth **York House B&B** ★★★★ 432
Conisholme **Wickham House** ★★★★ 432
Cranwell **Byards Leap Lodge** ★★★★ 414
Cressbrook **The Old Hay Barn** ★★★★★ 427
Deeping St Nicholas **St Nicholas House** ★★★★★ 432
Derby **The Lavender Patch** ★★★★★ 406
Derby **Thornhill Lodge Guest House** ★★★★ 427
Digby **Digby Manor Bed & Breakfast** ★★★★ 432
Diseworth **Lady Gate Guest House** ★★★★ 430

Establishments listed in colour have a detailed entry in this guide

749

Gold and Silver award index

East Midlands *cont.*

Donington **Browntoft House** ★★★★ 432
East Barkwith **The Grange** ★★★★ 432
Elton **Hawthorn Cottage** ★★★★★ 427
Eydon **Crockwell Farm** ★★★★ 421
Fairfield **Barms Farm** ★★★★★ 427
Folkingham **The Barn** ★★★★ 432
Grange Mill **Avondale Farm** ★★★★ 427
Grantham **Belvoir Vale Cottage** ★★★★ 432
Great Longstone **The Forge House** ★★★★★ 406
Guilsborough **Coton Lodge** ★★★★★ 436
Hanthorpe **Maycroft Cottage** ★★★★ 415
Hathersage **The Plough Inn** ★★★★ 428
High Peak **Pack Horse Inn** ★★★★ 428
High Peak **Springbank Guest House** ★★★★ 428
Holbeach **Cackle Hill House** ★★★★ 433
Hope **Poachers Arms** ★★★★ 428
Husbands Bosworth **Honeypot Lane Bed & Breakfast**
★★★★ 430
Knaptoft **Bruntingthorpe Farmhouse B&B** ★★★★ 430
Laxton **Crosshill House Bed & Breakfast** ★★★★ 423
Lincoln **Brant House** ★★★★★ 433
Lincoln **Crossfell Bed & Breakfast** ★★★★ 433
Lincoln **The Old Vicarage Bed & Breakfast** ★★★★ 415
Little Casterton **4 Camphill Cottages** ★★★★ 430
Litton **Hall Farm House** ★★★★ 428
Loughborough **Lane End Cottage** ★★★★ 430
Louth **The Old Rectory at Stewton** ★★★★ 433
Louth **The Paddock at Scamblesby** ★★★★ 433
Manton **Broccoli Bottom** ★★★★ 430
Market Rasen **Glebe Farm** ★★★★ 433
Market Rasen **Hoe Hill House** ★★★★ 433
Matlock **Ellen House** ★★★★ 428
Matlock **Riverbank House** ★★★★ 428
Matlock **Robertswood Country House** ★★★★★ 428
Medbourne **Homestead House** ★★★★ 431
Melton Mowbray **Shoby Lodge Farmhouse** ★★★★ 431
Moreton Pinkney **Home Farm** ★★★★ 437
Moulton **The Poplars Hotel** ★★★★ 437
Newark **Bridge House** ★★★★ 438
Newark **The Georgian Townhouse** ★★★★★ 438
Newark **Greystones Guest Accommodation** ★★★★ 438
Newark **The Hollies** ★★★★ 438
Newark **The Old Tavern** ★★★★ 434
North Hykeham **The Gables Guest House** ★★★★ 434
North Kilworth **Old Rectory** ★★★★ 431
Northorpe **Grayingham Lodge** ★★★★★ 416
Norton Disney **Brills Farm** ★★★★ 434
Oakham **17 Northgate** ★★★★ 412
Oakham **Mayfield B&B** ★★★★ 431
Old **Wold Farm** ★★★★ 437
Osbournby **Barn Gallery** ★★★★ 434
Oundle **Rowan House** ★★★★ 437

Ravenshead **Oak House B&B** ★★★★ 43
Retford **Bolham Manor** ★★★★ 43
Saxilby **Orchard Cottage** ★★★★ 43
Scaldwell **The Old House Bed & Breakfast** ★★★★ 43
Shepshed **Grange Courtyard** ★★★★★ 43
Silverstone **Silverstone Guest House** ★★★★ 43
Skegness **The Fountaindale Skegness** ★★★★ 41
Skegness **Stoneleigh** ★★★★ 41
South Cockerington **West View Bed & Breakfast** ★★★★ ... 41
Spalding **White Lodge Guest House** ★★★★★ 43
Spilsby **Spye House** ★★★★ 43
Stamford **Park Farm** ★★★★ 43
Tansley **B&B Yew Tree Cottage** ★★★★ 42
Thornton Curtis **Pine Lodge Bed & Breakfast** ★★★★ ... 43
Thurlby **6 The Pingles** ★★★★ 43
Tideswell **Merman Barn B&B** ★★★★ 42
Towcester **Potcote Bed & Breakfast** ★★★★★ 43
Towcester **Slapton Manor Bed & Breakfast** ★★★★ 42
Wadshelf **Temperance House Farm** ★★★★ 42
Weldon **Thatches on the Green** ★★★★ 43
Weston-on-Trent **The Willows** ★★★★ 42
Winster **Brae Cottage** ★★★★ 42
Witherley **The Old House Bed & Breakfast** ★★★★ 43
Woodhall Spa **Chaplin House** ★★★★ 419
Woodhall Spa **Kirkstead Old Mill Cottage** ★★★★ 419

Heart of England

GOLD AWARD

All Stretton **Jinlye Guest House** ★★★★★ 478
Arley **Tudor Barn** ★★★★ 487
Banbury **Wormleighton Hall** ★★★★ 484
Bewdley **Kateshill House** ★★★★★ 487
Bishops Castle **Magnolia** ★★★★ 478
Bricklehampton **Oaklands Farmhouse** ★★★★★ 487
Broadway **Sheepscombe House** ★★★★ 488
Broadway **Windrush House** ★★★★ 488
Clun **New House Farm** ★★★★★ 479
Eckington **Lower End House** ★★★★★ 488
Hopton Heath **Hopton House** ★★★★★ 480
Ironbridge **The Library House** ★★★★★ 480
Kenilworth **Loweridge Guest House** ★★★★★ 484
Leintwardine **Upper Buckton** ★★★★★ 477
Ludlow **DeGreys** ★★★★★ 461
Lyth Bank **Lyth Hill House** ★★★★★ 462
Mavesyn Ridware **Old Rectory** ★★★★ 483
Mortimer Country **Pear Tree Farm** ★★★★ 477
Pembridge **Lowe Farm B&B** ★★★★ 458
Pershore **Cropvale Farm Bed & Breakfast** ★★★★ 489
Ross-on-Wye **Caradoc Court** ★★★★ 458
Ross-on-Wye **Norton House** ★★★★ 478
Rugeley **Colton House** ★★★★★ 467
Ryelands **Ryelands** ★★★★★ 478
Shilton **Barnacle Hall** ★★★★★ 485

Gold and Silver award index

Heart of England cont.

Shrewsbury **Castlegates House** ★★★★★ 481
Snitterfield **Shakespeare's View** ★★★★★ 485
Stoulton **Sunbrae Bed & Breakfast** ★★★★ 489
Stratford-upon-Avon **Folly Farm Cottage** ★★★★ 470
Stratford-upon-Avon **White-Sails** ★★★★★ 486
Tanworth-in-Arden **Grange Farm** ★★★★ 486
Upton **Uplands House** ★★★★★ 486
Vowchurch **Yew Tree House** ★★★★ 459
Warwick **Park Cottage** ★★★★ 486
Woofferton **Ravenscourt Manor** ★★★★★ 481

SILVER AWARD

All Stretton **Juniper Cottage** ★★★★ 478
Alton **The Warren** ★★★★ 481
Alvechurch **Woodlands Bed & Breakfast** ★★★★ 487
Ashford Bowdler **Orchard House** ★★★★ 478
Aston Munslow **Chadstone** ★★★★★ 478
Barons Cross **Lavender House** ★★★★ 476
Bayston Hill **Chatford House** ★★★★ 478
Bicton **The Isle Estate Bed & Breakfast** ★★★★ 478
Bidford-on-Avon **Buckle House** ★★★★ 484
Bomere Heath **The Old Station** ★★★★ 478
Bridgnorth **Churchdown House** ★★★★★ 479
Bridgnorth **The Croft** ★★★★ 459
Broadway **Lowerfield Farm** ★★★★ 473
Broadway **The Old Stationhouse** ★★★★ 487
Broadway **The Olive Branch Guest House** ★★★★ 488
Broadway **Southwold House** ★★★★ 488
Brobury **Brobury House & Gardens** ★★★★ 476
Brockton **Old Quarry Cottage** ★★★★ 479
Bromsash **Eastview Bed & Breakfast** ★★★★ 476
Bromsgrove **The Durrance** ★★★★ 488
Broseley **Broseley House** ★★★★ 460
Broseley **Rock Dell** ★★★★ 479
Butterton **Coxon Green Farm** ★★★★ 482
Butterton **Stoop House Farm** ★★★★★ 482
Byford **Old Rectory** ★★★★ 476
Chaddesley Corbett **The Brook House** ★★★★ 488
Cheadle **Ley Fields Farm** ★★★★ 482
Church Stretton **Brookfields Guest House** ★★★★★ 479
Church Stretton **Victoria House** ★★★★ 479
Clehonger **The Old Vicarage** ★★★★ 476
Cleobury Mortimer **Woodview B&B** ★★★★★ 479
Clevelode **Severnside Bed & Breakfast** ★★★★ 488
Coalbrookdale **Coalbrookdale Villa Guest House**
★★★★ 479
Coalbrookdale **Springhill B&B** ★★★★ 479
Cradley **The Old Rectory** ★★★★ 476
Cubbington **Mill House** ★★★★ 484
Dawley **Hartfield Guest House** ★★★★ 479
Dorstone **Highfield** ★★★★ 476
The Down **The Down Inn** ★★★★ 481
Eardisland **Lawton Bury Farm B&B** ★★★★ 476

Easthope Wood **Easthope Wood Farm** ★★★★ 479
Eckington **Harrowfields Bed & Breakfast** ★★★★ 488
Eckington **Myrtle Cottage** ★★★★ 488
Ettington **Drybank Farm** ★★★★ 484
Fernhill Heath **Dilmore House** ★★★★ 488
Fernhill Heath **Heathside** ★★★★ 488
Fillongley **Grooms Cottage** ★★★★ 484
Fishmore **Acorn Place** ★★★★ 480
Grendon **Chestnuts Country Guest House** ★★★★ 484
Hadley Heath **The Old Farmhouse** ★★★★★ 488
Hampton-in-Arden **Chelsea Lodge** ★★★★ 487
Hanley Castle **The Chestnuts** ★★★★ 488
Hatton **Shrewley Pools Farm** ★★★★ 484
Hope Bowdler **Sayang House** ★★★★ 480
Ironbridge **The Old Rectory at Broseley** ★★★★★ 480
Kenilworth **Victoria Lodge** ★★★★ 484
Kerne Bridge **Lumleys B&B** ★★★★ 477
Kimbolton **Lower Bache House** ★★★★ 477
Kingsthorne **Pullastone** ★★★★ 477
Lawford Heath **Lawford Hill Farm** ★★★★ 484
Lawley Village **The Stanage** ★★★★ 480
Leamington Spa **The Coach House** ★★★★ 484
Leamington Spa **No 8 Clarendon Crescent** ★★★★ 484
Leintwardine **Lower Buckton Country House** ★★★★ 477
Leintwardine **Walford Court** ★★★★ 477
Lighthorne **Church Hill Farm B&B** ★★★★ 485
Little Stretton **Mynd House** ★★★★ 480
Loxley **Loxley Guest House** ★★★★ 485
Ludlow **Bromley Court** ★★★★ 461
Ludlow **Elm Lodge B&B** ★★★★ 480
Lyonshall **Penrhos Farm** ★★★★ 477
Madeley **The Old Hall Country House** ★★★★★ 483
Malvern **The Brambles** ★★★★ 488
Malvern **Cannara Guest House** ★★★★ 488
Malvern **Clevelands** ★★★ 488
Malvern **Guarlford Grange** ★★★ 488
Malvern **Hidelow House** ★★★★ 475
Malvern **Little Kings Hill** ★★★★ 477
Malvern **The Old Croquet** ★★★★ 489
Malvern **Orchid House** ★★★★ 489
Malvern **Puddle Lane** ★★★ 475
Malvern **Treherne House & The Malvern Retreat**
★★★★ 489
Middleton **Middleton House Farm** ★★★★ 485
Moddershall **Moddershall Oaks Spa Restaurant Suites**
★★★★★ 466
Much Marcle **Little Acre** ★★★★ 478
Orleton **Rosecroft** ★★★★★ 478
Oswestry **Yew Tree House** ★★★★ 462
Pershore **Arbour House** ★★★★ 475
Prestwood **Manor House Farm** ★★★★ 483
Redhill **Brandon Lodge** ★★★★ 478
Salwarpe **Middleton Grange** ★★★★ 489
Shipston-on-Stour **The Howard Arms** ★★★★★ 485

Establishments listed in colour have a detailed entry in this guide

Gold and Silver award index

Heart of England *cont.*

Shrewsbury **Brompton Farmhouse** ★★★★ 463
Shrewsbury **Grove Farm House** ★★★★★ 481
Solihull **Acorn Guest House** ★★★ 472
Stafford **Cedarwood** ★★★★ 483
Stoke-on-Trent **Cedar Tree Cottage** ★★★★ 483
Stottesdon **Hardwicke Farm Bed & Breakfast** ★★★★ 481
Stourport-on-Severn **Victoria Villa Bed & Breakfast** ★★★★ 489
Stratford-upon-Avon **Adelphi Guest House** ★★★★ 485
Stratford-upon-Avon **Ambleside Guest House** ★★★★ 485
Stratford-upon-Avon **Broadlands Guest House** ★★★★ 485
Stratford-upon-Avon **Brook Lodge Guest House** ★★★★ ... 485
Stratford-upon-Avon **Courtland** ★★★★ 485
Stratford-upon-Avon **Penryn Guest House** ★★★★ 486
Stratford-upon-Avon **Victoria Spa Lodge** ★★★★ 486
Stretton-on-Dunsmore **Home Farm** ★★★★ 486
Telford **Old Orleton Inn** ★★★★★ 464
Tewkesbury **Ivydene House Bed & Breakfast** ★★★★★ 489
Upton Warren **Overwood** ★★★★ 489
Upton-upon-Severn **Tiltridge Farm & Vineyard** ★★★★ 489
Warwick **Agincourt Lodge** ★★★★ 471
Warwick **The Seven Stars Guest Accommodation** ★★★★ 486
Warwick **Westham House B&B** ★★★★ 486
Waterhouses **Leehouse Farm** ★★★★ 483
Wetton **The Old Chapel** ★★★★ 483
Wigmore **Abbots Lodge B&B** ★★★★ 478
Wilton **Benhall Farmhouse** ★★★★ 478
Wistanswick **Marsh Farm Bed & Breakfast** ★★★★ 481
Worcester **Hill Farm House** ★★★★ 489

Yorkshire

GOLD AWARD

Addingham **Lumb Beck Farmhouse Bed & Breakfast** ★★★★ 535
Aldfield **Bay Tree Farm** ★★★★ 535
Ampleforth **Daleside** ★★★★★ 535
Ampleforth **Shallowdale House** ★★★★★ 535
Blubberhouses **Scaife Hall Farm** ★★★★ 537
Briggswath **The Lawns** ★★★★★ 538
Brighouse **Elder Lea House** ★★★★★ 538
Burythorpe **Low Penhowe** ★★★★★ 538
Cherry Burton **Burton Mount Country House** ★★★★★ 538
Clapham **Turnerford Fold** ★★★★ 538
Croft-on-Tees **Clow-Beck House** ★★★★★ 538
Cullingworth **Manor Guest House** ★★★★★ 538
Cundall **Cundall Lodge Farm** ★★★★★ 539
Dinnington **Throapham House Bed & Breakfast** ★★★★★ 539
Egton Bridge **Broom House and Whites (Restaurant)** ★★★★ 505
Felliscliffe **Knabbs Ash** ★★★★ 539
Grassington **Grassington Lodge** ★★★★★ 540

Grassington **Yew Tree House** ★★★★ 540
Harrogate **Applewood House** ★★★★ 541
Harrogate **Cold Cotes** ★★★★★ 505
Hawes **Thorney Mire Barn B&B** ★★★★★ 542
Haworth **Ashmount Country House** ★★★★★ 542
Haworth **The Thyme House** ★★★★ 542
Holmfirth **Sunnybank Guesthouse** ★★★★★ 543
Hornsea **Earlham House Guest House** ★★★★ 543
Huddersfield **Castle View Guest House** ★★★★★ 543
Kilham **Kilham Hall Country House** ★★★★★ 510
Leeming Bar **Little Holtby** ★★★★ 513
Levisham **The Moorlands Country House** ★★★★★ 544
Newholm **Beehive Inne** ★★★★ 545
Oldstead **Oldstead Grange** ★★★★★ 546
Patrick Brompton **Mill Close Farm** ★★★★★ 546
Pickering **Number 17 Burgate** ★★★★★ 546
Pickering **The Old Vicarage at Toftly View** ★★★★★ 515
Pockley **West View Cottage** ★★★★ 546
Pontefract **Tower House Executive Guest House** ★★★★★ 546
Redmire **The Old Town Hall Guest House & Tea Room** ★★★★★ 547
Scarborough **The Alexander** ★★★★ 517
Settle **Austwick Hall** ★★★★★ 550
Sharow **Sharow Cross House** ★★★★★ 550
Stape **Flamborough Rigg Cottage** ★★★★★ 551
Stape **High Muffles** ★★★★ 522
Thornton Rust **Thornton Lodge** ★★★★★ 551
Whitby **Dillons of Whitby** ★★★★ 552
Wold Newton **The Wold Cottage** ★★★★★ 553
Worton **Stoney End** ★★★★★ 553
York **Alexander House** ★★★★★ 554
York **Arnot House** ★★★★★ 554
York **Four Seasons** ★★★★★ 555
York **The Hazelwood** ★★★★ 532

SILVER AWARD

Addingham **Beck House Farm** ★★★★ 535
Aldbrough **West Carlton Country Guest House** ★★★★ ... 535
Allerston **Rains Farm Bed & Breakfast** ★★★★ 535
Askrigg **Apothecary's House** ★★★★ 536
Austwick **Wood View** ★★★★ 536
Aysgarth **Cornlee** ★★★★ 536
Aysgarth **Field House** ★★★★ 536
Aysgarth **Heather Cottage Guesthouse** ★★★★ 536
Baildon **Ford House Farm Bed & Breakfast** ★★★★ 536
Bainton **Wolds Village Luxury Guest Accommodation** ★★★★ 536
Barlow **Berewick House** ★★★★ 536
Beckwithshaw **Central House Farm** ★★★★ 536
Bedale **Elmfield House** ★★★★ 499
Bentham **Halsteads Barn** ★★★★★ 536
Bishop Thornton **Bowes Green Farm** ★★★★ 536
Blaxton **Beech Grove Lodge** ★★★★ 536
Bridlington **The Bay Court** ★★★★ 537

752   Official tourist board guide **Bed & Breakfast**

Yorkshire cont.

Bridlington **Number 7 Guest House** ★★★★ 537
Bridlington **Sea View House** ★★★★ 537
Brighouse **The Lodge @ Birkby Hall** ★★★★ 538
Buckden **Nethergill Farm** ★★★★ 538
Carlton Miniott **The Poplars** ★★★★ 538
Chapel-le-Dale **Croft Gate** ★★★★ 538
Colden **Riverdene House** ★★★★ 538
Crayke **Hazelwood Farm Bed & Breakfast** ★★★★ 538
Cropton **High Farm Bed & Breakfast** ★★★★ 538
Easingwold **The Old Vicarage** ★★★★ 539
Ellerby **Ellerby Residential Country Inn** ★★★★ 539
Filey **All Seasons Guesthouse** ★★★★ 539
Filey **The Forge Guest House** ★★★★ 540
Filey **The Seafield** ★★★★ 540
Flaxton **Claxton Hall Cottage Guest House** ★★★★ 540
Giggleswick **Tipperthwaite Barn** ★★★★ 540
Great Ayton *The Kings Head at Newton Under*
Roseberry ★★★★ 505
Great Ayton **Travellers Rest** ★★★★ 540
Harrogate **The Bijou** ★★★★★ 541
Harrogate **Brookfield House** ★★★★★ 541
Harrogate **Franklin View** ★★★★ 541
Harrogate **Park Parade** ★★★★★ 541
Harrogate **Ye Olde Coach House** ★★★★ 541
Hawes **FairView House** ★★★★ 541
Hawes **The Old Dairy Farm** ★★★★★ 542
Hawes *Old Station House* ★★★★ 506
Hawes **Thornsgill House** ★★★★ 542
Haworth **The Old Registry** ★★★★ 542
Hebden Bridge *Holme House* ★★★★★ 508
Hellifield **Chapel Farm B&B** ★★★★ 542
Helmsley **Carlton Lodge** ★★★★ 542
Helmsley **Stilworth House** ★★★★ 542
Hepworth **Uppergate Farm B&B** ★★★★ 542
High Catton **High Catton Grange** ★★★★ 542
Horton-in-Ribblesdale **Broad Croft House** ★★★★ 543
Huddersfield **Elm Crest** ★★★★ 543
Huddersfield **Huddersfield Central Lodge** ★★★★ 543
Huddersfield **Thornes Farm Bed & Breakfast** ★★★★★ 543
Huddersfield **Weirside Bed & Breakfast** ★★★★ 543
Huggate **Greenwick Farm Bed & Breakfast** ★★★★ 543
Hull **Cornerbrook Guest House** ★★★★ 543
Hutton-le-Hole **Burnley House** ★★★★ 543
Ingleton **Riverside Lodge** ★★★★ 543
Ingleton **Thorngarth Country Guest House** ★★★★ 543
Jervaulx **Park House** ★★★★★ 543
Kettlewell **Littlebeck** ★★★★ 543
Kirkbymoorside **Brickfields Farm** ★★★★ 544
Kirkbymoorside *The Cornmill* ★★★★ 511
Knaresborough **Gallon House** ★★★★★ 544
Knaresborough **The Mitre** ★★★★★ 544
Leyburn **Clyde House** ★★★★ 544

Gold and Silver award index

Leyburn **Greenhills** ★★★★ 544
Leyburn **Holmedale Bed & Breakfast** ★★★★ 544
Leyburn **Stow House** ★★★★ 544
Linton **Linton Laithe** ★★★★★ 544
Little Crakehall **Crakehall Watermill** ★★★★ 545
Low Row **The Old Dairy** ★★★★ 545
Low Row **Rowleth End Guest House** ★★★★ 545
Loxley **Barnfield House** ★★★★ 545
Middleham **The Priory** ★★★★ 545
Northallerton **Elmscott** ★★★★ 545
Northallerton *Lovesome Hill Farm* ★★★★ 514
Pateley Bridge **High Green Farm** ★★★★★ 546
Penistone **Cubley Hall Inn** ★★★★ 546
Pickering **Ashfield House Bed & Breakfast** ★★★★ 546
Pickering **Bramwood Guest House** ★★★★ 546
Pickering **Bridge House** ★★★★ 546
Pickering **Cawthorne House** ★★★★ 546
Pickering *Eleven Westgate* ★★★★ 514
Pickering **Grindale House** ★★★★ 546
Pickering *The Hawthornes* ★★★★ 514
Pickering **No 9 luxury B&B** ★★★★ 546
Pickering **Sevenford House** ★★★★ 546
Preston **Little Weghill Farm** ★★★★ 546
Preston-under-Scar **Hawthorn Cottage** ★★★★ 546
Preston-under-Scar **The Old School Barn** ★★★★★ 546
Rathmell **Littlebank Guest House** ★★★★★ 547
Reeth **Cambridge House** ★★★★★ 547
Richmond **Rosedale Bed & Breakfast** ★★★★ 547
Richmond **Victoria House** ★★★★ 547
Richmond **Willance House** ★★★★ 547
Ripon **Lavender House** ★★★★ 547
Ripon **The Old Coach House** ★★★★★ 547
Robin Hoods Bay **Lee-Side** ★★★★ 547
Rosedale East **Ann's Cottage** ★★★★ 547
Saltmarshe **The Dairy Farm** ★★★★ 548
Sawdon **Foxholm B&B** ★★★★ 548
Scarborough **Island House** ★★★★ 548
Scarborough *Killerby Cottage Farm* ★★★★ 518
Scarborough **Raincliffe** ★★★★ 549
Scarborough **Riviera Town House** ★★★★ 549
Scarborough **Sawdon Heights** ★★★★ 549
Scarborough **Scalby Hayes B&B** ★★★★ 549
Scarborough **Tall Storeys** ★★★★ 549
Scarborough **The Waves** ★★★★ 549
Settle **Settle Lodge** ★★★★ 550
Shipton-by-Beningbrough **Wood Farm** ★★★★ 550
Silsden **Pickersgill Manor Farm** ★★★★ 550
Sinnington **Fox & Hounds** ★★★★★ 550
Skeeby **Ewden House** ★★★★ 550
Skeeby **New Skeeby Grange** ★★★★★ 550
Skipsea **Village Farm** ★★★★ 550
Skipton **Chinthurst** ★★★★★ 550
Skipton *Cononley Hall Bed & Breakfast* ★★★★★ 520

Establishments listed in colour have a detailed entry in this guide 753

Gold and Silver award index

Yorkshire *cont.*

Sleights **Hedgefield Guest House** ★★★★ 550
Sleights **Netherby House** ★★★★ 550
Stannington **Loadbrook Cottages B&B** ★★★★ 551
Stannington **Robin Hood Inn** ★★★★ 551
Stape **Rawcliffe House Farm** ★★★★ 551
Stape **Seavy Slack** ★★★★ 551
Stokesley **Willow Cottage** ★★★★ 551
Thirsk **Borrowby Mill Bed & Breakfast** ★★★★ 523
Thoralby **The George Inn** ★★★★ 551
Thoralby **The Old Barn** ★★★★ 551
Thornton Dale **Kirkby House** ★★★★ 551
Thurstonland **Ackroyd House** ★★★★★ 551
Thurstonland **The Old Co-Op** ★★★★★ 551
Todmorden **Kilnhurst Old Hall** ★★★★★ 552
Tollerton **Angel Inn House** ★★★★ 552
Walkington **The Barn House** ★★★★★ 552
Welburn **Welburn Lodge** ★★★★ 552
Wetherby **Linton Close** ★★★★ 552
Wetwang **Life Hill Farm B&B** ★★★★ 552
Whashton **Mount Pleasant Farm** ★★★★ 552
Whashton **Whashton Springs Farm** ★★★★ 552
Whitby **Autumn Leaves** ★★★★ 552
Whitby **Gramarye Suites B&B** ★★★★★ 553
Whitby **Haven Crest** ★★★★ 553
Whitby **The Langley** ★★★★★ 553
Whitby **The Leeway** ★★★★ 553
Whitby **Storrbeck Guest House** ★★★★ 553
Wigglesworth **Cowper Cottage** ★★★★ 553
Wombleton **Rockery Cottage** ★★★★ 553
York **23 Saint Marys guesthouse** ★★★★ 528
York **Abbey Guest House** ★★★★ 553
York **Ascot House** ★★★★ 528
York **Barbican House** ★★★★ 529
York **Beech House** ★★★★ 554
York **Bishops** ★★★★★ 530
York **The Bloomsbury** ★★★★ 554
York **Bowmans Guest House** ★★★★ 554
York **Bronte Guest House** ★★★★ 554
York **Crook Lodge** ★★★★ 554
York **Feversham Lodge** ★★★★ 555
York **Gregory's** ★★★★ 555
York **Holme - Lea - Manor** ★★★★ 555
York **Limes** ★★★★ 532
York **The Manor House** ★★★★ 533
York **St Raphael Guesthouse** ★★★★ 555

North West

GOLD AWARD

Ambleside **Barnes Fell Guest House** ★★★★ 635
Ambleside **Easedale Lodge Guest House** ★★★★ 636
Ambleside **Far Nook** ★★★★ 636
Ambleside **Kingswood 'Bee & Bee'** ★★★★ 636

Ambleside **Riverside** ★★★★ 63
Arnside **Number 43** ★★★★★ 63
Barngates **The Drunken Duck Inn** ★★★★★ 63
Blackpool **Number One South Beach** ★★★★★ 65
Blackpool **Number One St Luke's** ★★★★★ 62
Blackpool **The Waterford** ★★★★ 65
Bolton **Meadowcroft Barn B&B** ★★★★★ 65
Boltongate **Boltongate Old Rectory** ★★★★★ 63
Borrowdale **Hazel Bank Country House** ★★★★★ .. 63
Bowness-on-Windermere **The Cranleigh** ★★★★★ .. 63
Brisco **Crossroads House** ★★★★ 63
Bruera **Churton Heath Farm Bed & Breakfast** ★★★★ ... 57
Burgh-by-Sands **Rosemount Cottage** ★★★★ 63
Carlisle **Bessiestown Farm Country Guesthouse** ★★★★★ 63
Carlisle **Cartref Guest House** ★★★★ 63
Carlisle **Number Thirty One** ★★★★★ 63
Clitheroe **Alden Cottage - B&B** ★★★★ 65
Cockermouth **Graysonside** ★★★★★ 63
Coniston **Yew Tree Farm** ★★★★★ 63
Crosby Ravensworth **Crake Trees Manor** ★★★★ 63
Culgaith **Laurel House** ★★★★ 58
Far Sawrey **West Vale Country House** ★★★★★ 63
Garstang **Little Stubbins Bed & Breakfast** ★★★★ .. 65
Gilsland **The Hill on the Wall** ★★★★★ 58
Grasmere **Heron Beck Guest House** ★★★★ 64
Grasmere **Lake View Country House** ★★★★ 64
Hawkshead Hill **Summer Hill Country House** ★★★★ .. 64
Hawkshead **Walker Ground Manor** ★★★★★ 64
Keswick **The Edwardene** ★★★★ 64
Keswick **Howe Keld** ★★★★ 64
Knowsley Park **Knowsley Hall** ★★★★★ 65
Lakeside **The Knoll Country House** ★★★★★ 64
Lancaster **The Ashton** ★★★★★ 65
Macclesfield **Harrop Fold Farm Bed & Breakfast** ★★★★★ 63
Port Carlisle **Brockelrigg** ★★★★★ 64
Portinscale **Powe House** ★★★★ 64
Ravenstonedale **A Corner of Eden** ★★★★ 64
Ravenstonedale **Coldbeck House** ★★★★★ 64
Rydal **Cote How Organic Guest House** ★★★★ 60
Sawrey **Beechmount Country House** ★★★★★ 64
Scotby **Willowbeck Lodge** ★★★★★ 64
Wetheral **Acorn Bank** ★★★★★ 64
Whitehaven **Moresby Hall** ★★★★★ 60
Whitewell **The Inn at Whitewell** ★★★★★ 62
Windermere **Beechwood** ★★★★ 64
Windermere **Oakfold House** ★★★★ 61
Wirral **Mere Brook House** ★★★★★ 65

SILVER AWARD

Accrington **Norwood Guest House** ★★★★ 64
Ambleside **Amboseli Lodge** ★★★★ 63
Ambleside **Brantfell House** ★★★★ 63
Ambleside **Crow How Country Guest House** ★★★★ ... 63

754 Official tourist board guide **Bed & Breakfast**

Gold and Silver award index

North West cont.

Ambleside **Elder Grove** ★★★★ 579
Ambleside **Fisherbeck** ★★★★ 636
Ambleside **Freshfields Guest House** ★★★★ 636
Ambleside **Glenside** ★★★★ 636
Ambleside **Melrose Guest House** ★★★★ 636
Ambleside **Norwood House** ★★★★ 636
Ambleside **Park House Guest House** ★★★★ 580
Ambleside **Red Bank** ★★★★★ 579
Ambleside **Rysdale Guest House** ★★★★ 636
Ambleside **Waterwheel Guesthouse** ★★★★ 636
Barrow-in-Furness **November House** ★★★★ 637
Barrowford **Merok Bed & Breakfast** ★★★★ 647
Barton **Higher Farm Bed & Breakfast** ★★★★ 574
Bassenthwaite **Highside Farm** ★★★★ 637
Bassenthwaite Lake **Lakeside Country Guest House**
★★★★ 637
Bassenthwaite **Ouse Bridge House** ★★★★ 584
Berrier **Whitbarrow Farm** ★★★★ 637
Blackpool **Four Seasons Blackpool** ★★★★★ 649
Blackpool **Langtrys** ★★★★★ 620
Blackpool **Rossdene House** ★★★★ 651
Blackpool **Tudor Rose Original** ★★★★ 651
Bollington **Red Oaks Farm** ★★★★ 633
Bowness-on-Windermere **Eastbourne Guest House**
★★★★ 637
Bowness-on-Windermere **Storrs Gate House** ★★★★★ 585
Bowness-on-Windermere **The Westbourne** ★★★★ 637
Braithwaite **Hermiston** ★★★★ 637
Brampton **Scarrow Hill Guest House** ★★★★ 585
Brereton **Bagmere Bank Farm Luxury Bed & Breakfast**
★★★★ 633
Burnley **Grains Barn Farm** ★★★★★ 652
Caldbeck **Swaledale Watch** ★★★★ 586
Capernwray **Capernwray House** ★★★★ 652
Carlisle **Courtfield Guest House** ★★★★ 638
Carlisle **Fernlee Guest House** ★★★★ 638
Chester **Buckingham House** ★★★★ 633
Chester **Higher Huxley Hall** ★★★★★ 634
Chester **Manor Farm Bed & Breakfast** ★★★★ 634
Chester **Mitchell's of Chester Guest House** ★★★★★ 576
Chester **Newton Hall Farm Bed & Breakfast** ★★★★ 634
Chester **Roseville Bed & Breakfast** ★★★★★ 634
Clitheroe **Angram Green Farmhouse B&B** ★★★★ 652
Clitheroe **Peter Barn Country House** ★★★★ 652
Clitheroe **The Red Pump Inn** ★★★★ 652
Cockermouth **Rose Cottage** ★★★★ 639
Colby **The Limes** ★★★★ 639
Colne **Blakey Hall Farm** ★★★★ 652
Colne **Rye Flatt Farmhouse** ★★★★ 653
Denshaw **Cherry Clough Farm House Accommodation**
★★★★★ 655
Dufton **Brow Farm Bed & Breakfast** ★★★★ 588
Forton **Middle Holly Cottage** ★★★★ 653

Garstang **Broadgate Farm B & B** ★★★★ 628
Grasmere **Beck Allans Guest House** ★★★★ 639
Grasmere **Dunmail House** ★★★★★ 639
Great Eccleston **Courtyard Caffé With Rooms** ★★★★ 653
The Green **rooms @ bank house farm** ★★★★ 606
Hawkshead Hill **Yewfield Vegetarian Guest House**
★★★★★ 590
Heads Nook **Croft House** ★★★★★ 590
Hesket Newmarket **Daffodil** ★★★★★ 591
High Lorton **Swinside End Farm** ★★★★★ 640
High Wray **High Wray Farm B&B** ★★★★ 640
Holmes Chapel **Padgate Guest House** ★★★★ 634
Ings **The Hill** ★★★★ 640
Irthington **Vallum Barn** ★★★★ 640
Kendal **Beech House** ★★★★★ 592
Kermincham **The Fields Farm** ★★★★ 634
Keswick (7.5 miles) **Lane Head Farm Country Guest
House** ★★★★ 599
Keswick **Abacourt House** ★★★★ 640
Keswick **Acorn House** ★★★★ 640
Keswick **Allerdale House** ★★★★ 640
Keswick **Amble House Guest House** ★★★★ 640
Keswick **Badgers Wood** ★★★★ 594
Keswick **Braemar Guest House** ★★★★ 641
Keswick **Briar Rigg House** ★★★★ 594
Keswick **Burnside B&B** ★★★★ 641
Keswick **Dunsford Guest House** ★★★★ 641
Keswick **Fell House** ★★★★ 641
Keswick **Glendale Guest House** ★★★★ 641
Keswick **Grange Country House** ★★★★★ 641
Keswick **Keswick Park** ★★★★ 641
Keswick **The Lookout** ★★★★ 642
Keswick **Lynwood Guest House** ★★★★ 642
Keswick **Parkfield Guest House** ★★★★ 597
Keswick **Ravensworth House** ★★★★ 642
Keswick **Rooms36** ★★★★ 597
Keswick **Stonegarth Guest House** ★★★★ 642
Keswick **Tarn Hows** ★★★★ 642
Kirkby Lonsdale **High Green Farm** ★★★★ 600
Lanercost **Abbey Mill** ★★★★ 642
Leighton Hall **Grisedale Farm** ★★★★ 653
Long Marton **Broom House** ★★★★ 642
Lower Peover **Moss Farm Bed & Breakfast** ★★★★ 634
Macclesfield **Artizana Suite** ★★★★★ 634
Macclesfield **The Stanley Arms Bed & Breakfast**
★★★★ 635
Maulds Meaburn **Meaburn Hill Farmhouse** ★★★★ 643
Mellor Brook **Oaklands Country Guest House** ★★★★ 653
Nantwich **Coole Hall Farm Bed & Breakfast** ★★★★ 635
Nelson **Thorneyholme Farm Cottage** ★★★★ 654
Newbiggin **The Old School** ★★★★★ 643
Newbiggin-on-Lune **Tranna Hill** ★★★★ 643
Newlands **Ellas Crag** ★★★★ 643
North Rode **Ladderstile Retreat** ★★★★★ 576

Establishments listed in colour have a detailed entry in this guide

Gold and Silver award index

North West cont.

Penrith **Glendale Guest House** ★★★★ 643
Penrith **Lowthwaite B&B** ★★★★ 643
Portinscale **Lakeview** ★★★★ 644
Prestbury **The White House Manor Hotel** ★★★★ 635
Preston **Whitestake Farm** ★★★★★ 654
Preston **Willow Cottage** ★★★★ 654
Ravenglass **Wayside Guest Accommodation** ★★★★ 644
Rawtenstall **Middle Carr Farm** ★★★★ 654
Ribchester **Riverside Barn** ★★★★★ 654
Rochdale **Moss Lodge** ★★★★★ 655
Rochdale **The Villas Residence** ★★★★★ 655
Rossendale **Number 678** ★★★★ 654
Rossendale **The Old White Horse** ★★★★ 654
Rossendale **One 3 One Guest House** ★★★★ 654
Roundthorn **Roundthorn Country House** ★★★★★ 644
Sawrey **Buckle Yeat Guest House** ★★★★ 604
Setmurthy **Croft Guesthouse** ★★★★ 644
Southport **Ambassador Townhouse** ★★★★ 656
Southport **Waterford** ★★★★★ 657
Tarporley **Hill House Farm Bed & Breakfast** ★★★★ 635
Tarvin **Willow Run Bed & Breakfast** ★★★★ 635
Thornthwaite **Jenkin Hill Cottage** ★★★★ 644
Threlkeld **Scales Farm Country Guest House** ★★★★ 644
Troutbeck **High Fold Guest House** ★★★★ 645
Troutbeck **The Homestead Lodge** ★★★★★ 645
Under Loughrigg **Stepping Stones** ★★★★ 645
Underbarrow **Tranquility @ Lab-Bay** ★★★★★ 645
West Kirby **At Peel Hey** ★★★★ 633
Whitehaven **Grovewood House** ★★★★★ 645
Windermere **The Boundary** ★★★★★ 645
Windermere **Braemount House** ★★★★ 645
Windermere **Denehurst Guest House** ★★★★ 646
Windermere **Ellerthwaite Lodge** ★★★★ 646
Windermere **Fair Rigg** ★★★★ 610
Windermere **Fairfield House & Gardens** ★★★★ 609
Windermere **Ivy Bank** ★★★★ 646
Windermere **Ivythwaite Lodge** ★★★★ 646
Windermere **Lingwood Lodge** ★★★★ 611
Windermere **Lonsdale House** ★★★★ 646
Windermere **Millbeck Bed & Breakfast** ★★★★ 646
Windermere **Mylne Bridge House** ★★★★ 646
Windermere **Oldfield House** ★★★★ 646
Windermere **Ravenscroft** ★★★★ 646
Windermere **Southview House & Indoor Pool** ★★★★ 646
Windermere **Wheatlands Lodge** ★★★★★ 647
Wirral **Pendragon House** ★★★★ 657

North East

GOLD AWARD

Allerwash **Allerwash Farmhouse** ★★★★★ 696
Alnwick **Old Bewick Farmhouse** ★★★★★ 696
Alnwick **Redfoot Lea Bed & Breakfast** ★★★★★ 696
Alnwick **West Acre House** ★★★★★ 69
Bardon Mill **Montcoffer** ★★★★★ 69
Barnard Castle **Greta House** ★★★★★ 69
Barnard Castle **Homelands** ★★★★ 69
Belford **The Farmhouse Guest House** ★★★★ 69
Berwick-upon-Tweed **No 1 Sallyport** ★★★★★ 69
Berwick-upon-Tweed **West Coates** ★★★★★ 69
Chatton **Chatton Park House Bed & Breakfast**
★★★★★ 69
Cornhill-on-Tweed **The Coach House at Crookham**
★★★★ 69
Cornhill-on-Tweed **Hay Farm House** ★★★★ 68
Craster **Stonecroft** ★★★★ 69
Durham **The Victorian Town House** ★★★★ 67
Great Tosson **Tosson Tower Farm B&B** ★★★★★ 69
Haltwhistle **Ashcroft Guest House** ★★★★★ 69
Hexham **Carraw Bed & Breakfast** ★★★★ 700
Longframlington **Coquet Bed & Breakfast** ★★★★ 700
Longhorsley **Thistleyhaugh Farm** ★★★★★ 700
Longhoughton **Swallows' Rest** ★★★★ 700
Newton-on-The-Moor **The Old School** ★★★★★ 68
Rothbury **Lee Farm** ★★★★★ 70
Stocksfield **Locksley, Bed & Breakfast** ★★★★ 68
Swarland **Swarland Old Hall** ★★★★★ 70
Thropton **Farm Cottage Guest House** ★★★★★ 70
Tillmouth **The Old School House B&B** ★★★★★ 702
Warkworth **Roxbro House** ★★★★★ 702
Wingates **Pele Cottage** ★★★★ 702
Wingates **South Farm** ★★★★★ 702
Wooler **Firwood Country Bed and Breakfast** ★★★★★ 69
Wooler **Old Manse** ★★★★★ 702

SILVER AWARD

Alnmouth **Beech Lodge** ★★★★ 67
Alnmouth **Westlea** ★★★★ 69
Alnwick **Aln House** ★★★★ 69
Alnwick **Alndyke Bed & Breakfast** ★★★★ 69
Alnwick **Birdsong Cottage Bed & Breakfast** ★★★★ 69
Alnwick **Courtyard Garden** ★★★★★ 69
Alnwick **Greycroft** ★★★★ 67
Alnwick **Norfolk** ★★★★ 69
Alnwick **Rooftops** ★★★★ 69
Bardon Mill **Coach House Bed & Breakfast** ★★★★ 69
Bardon Mill **Vallum Lodge** ★★★★ 69
Barnard Castle **Crich House Bed & Breakfast** ★★★★ 69
Barnard Castle **Startforth House Bed & Breakfast**
★★★★ 69
Beadnell **Low Dover Beadnell Bay** ★★★★★ 69
Belford **Courtyard Cottage at Outchester Manor**
★★★★ 69
Belford **Seafields** ★★★★ 69
Berwick-upon-Tweed **Alannah House** ★★★★ 678
Berwick-upon-Tweed **Clovelly House** ★★★★ 678
Berwick-upon-Tweed **Fenham Farm Coastal Bed &
Breakfast** ★★★★ 679
Berwick-upon-Tweed **Four North Road** ★★★★ 69

Gold and Silver award index

North East *cont.*

Berwick-upon-Tweed **Granary Guest House** ★★★★★ 697
Berwick-upon-Tweed **No 4 Ravensdowne** ★★★★ 698
Berwick-upon-Tweed **The Old Vicarage Guest House** ★★★★★ 698
Berwick-upon-Tweed **Parade School Guest House** ★★★★ 698
Berwick-upon-Tweed **Ravensdowne Guest House** ★★★★ 698
Berwick-upon-Tweed **The Walls** ★★★★★ 698
Berwick-upon-Tweed **West Sunnyside House** ★★★★ 698
Berwick-upon-Tweed **Whyteside House** ★★★★ 698
Bilton **Bilton Barns Farmhouse** ★★★★ 698
Birling **Birling North Cottage** ★★★★ 698
Bishop Auckland **Hamsterley Forest B&B** ★★★★ 693
Boulmer **Boulmer Village B&B** ★★★★ 698
Chatton **Spylaw Farmhouse B&B** ★★★★ 698
Chester-le-Street **Low Urpeth Farm** ★★★★ 693
Corbridge **Priorfield B&B** ★★★★ 698
Craster **Harbour Lights** ★★★★ 698
Craster **Old Rectory** ★★★★★ 698
Crook **Dowfold House** ★★★★ 694
Durham **Cathedral View Town House** ★★★★ 671
Easington **Easington Farm** ★★★★★ 699
Eastgate **Horsley Hall** ★★★★★ 694
Eastgate **Rose Hill Farm** ★★★★ 694
Edmundbyers **Punchbowl Inn** ★★★★ 673
Eglingham **The Tankerville Arms** ★★★★ 699
Fenwick **The Manor House** ★★★★ 699
Gilsland **Brookside Villa B&B** ★★★★ 682
Gilsland **Tantallon House** ★★★★ 682
Haltwhistle **Kellah Farm B&B** ★★★★ 699
Haltwhistle **Wydon Farm Bed & Breakfast** ★★★★ 699
Hamsterley **Dale End** ★★★★ 695
Haydon Bridge **Grindon Cartshed** ★★★★ 684
Heddon-on-the-Wall **Ironsign Farm B&B** ★★★★ 700
Hexham **Fairshaw Rigg** ★★★★ 700

High Hesleden **The Ship Inn** ★★★★ 695
Holy Island **The Bungalow** ★★★★ 700
Ingram **Ingram House** ★★★★ 685
Kielder Water **The Pheasant Inn (by Kielder Water)** ★★★★ 686
Kirkwhelpington **Cornhills Farmhouse** ★★★★ 700
Longhoughton **Number One** ★★★★ 700
Lowick **Burn House Bed & Breakfast** ★★★★ 700
Lowick **Primrose Cottage** ★★★★ 700
Middleton-in-Teesdale **Brunswick House** ★★★★ 695
North Sunderland **Railston House** ★★★★ 701
North Sunderland **Springwood** ★★★★ 701
Oakwood **Oakwood Cottage** ★★★★ 701
Ovington **Ovington House Bed & Breakfast** ★★★★ 701
Powburn **Cheviot View** ★★★★ 701
Powburn **Low Hedgeley Farm** ★★★★★ 688
Redcar **Springdale House** ★★★★ 695
Rothbury **Katerina's Guest House** ★★★★ 688
Saltburn-by-the-Sea **Townend Farm B&B** ★★★★ 695
Seahouses **The Olde Ship** ★★★★ 701
Seahouses **Spindrift** ★★★★ 701
Seahouses **St Cuthbert's House** ★★★★★ 701
Stannington **Cheviot View Farmhouse Bed & Breakfast** ★★★★ 702
Thornton **The Old School House** ★★★★ 702
Tynemouth **Martineau Guest House** ★★★★ 692
Wark **The Battlesteads** ★★★★ 690
Warkworth **Fairfield House** ★★★★★ 702
Warkworth **Morwick House Bed & Breakfast** ★★★★ 702
Warkworth **Tower House B&B** ★★★★ 702
Warkworth **Westrigg Bed & BreakfaSt** ★★★★ 702
Westgate **Lands Farm** ★★★★ 695
Whickham **East Byermoor Guest House** ★★★★ 704
Whitley Bay **Oaktree Lodge** ★★★★ 704
Wooler **East Horton House** ★★★★★ 691
Wooler **Rockliffe House** ★★★★ 702
Wooler **Tilldale House** ★★★★ 702

Establishments listed in colour have a detailed entry in this guide

Walkers and cyclists welcome

Establishments particpating in the Walkers Welcome and Cyclists Welcome schemes provide special facilities and actively encourage these recreations. Accommodation with a detailed entry in this guide is listed below. Place names are listed alphabetically.

Walkers Welcome and Cyclists Welcome

Alderton South West	Arland House ★★★★	118
Amble North East	Harbour Guest House ★★★	67
Ambleside North West	2 Cambridge Villas ★★★★	578
Ambleside North West	Brathay Lodge ★★★★	578
Ambleside North West	Rothay Garth ★★★★	580
Ambleside North West	Wordsworths Guest House ★★★★	58
Ashford South East	Bowl Inn ★★★★	216
Bakewell East Midlands	Castle Hill Farm House ★★★★ SILVER	40
Bamford East Midlands	Pioneer House ★★★★ SILVER	40
Bamford East Midlands	Yorkshire Bridge Inn ★★★★ SILVER	40
Beal North East	Brock Mill Farmhouse ★★★★	678
Beccles East of England	Pinetrees ★★★★	35
Berwick-upon-Tweed North East	Alannah House ★★★★ SILVER	678
Berwick-upon-Tweed North East	Fenham Farm Coastal Bed & Breakfast ★★★★ SILVER	679
Berwick-upon-Tweed North East	Longridge Towers School ★★★	679
Berwick-upon-Tweed North East	Meadow Hill Guest House ★★★★	680
Black Bourton South East	The Vines ★★★★	233
Blickling East of England	Buckinghamshire Arms ★★★★	344
Bodmin South West	Bedknobs ★★★★ SILVER	38
Bognor Regis South East	White Horses Felpham ★★★★	248
Bolton-by-Bowland North West	Middle Flass Lodge ★★★★	626
Bournemouth South West	Ingledene Guest House ★★	82
Bowness-on-Windermere North West	May Cottage B&B ★★★	584
Braunton South West	George Hotel ★★★	58
Brenchley South East	Hononton Cottage ★★★★★ SILVER	217
Bridport South West	The Well ★★★	83
Brighstone South East	Seven Bed & Breakfast ★★★	209
Brighton & Hove South East	Lansdowne Guest House ★★★★ SILVER	249
Broadway Heart of England	Lowerfield Farm ★★★★ SILVER	472
Brundall East of England	Breckland B&B ★★★★ SILVER	344
Bude South West	Harefield Cottage ★★★★ GOLD	39
Burley South East	Wayside Cottage ★★★★	202
Burnley North West	Ormerod ★★★	626
Bury St Edmunds (6 miles) East of England	The Old Manse Barn ★★★★★ SILVER	358
Bury St Edmunds East of England	St Edmunds Guesthouse ★★★★ SILVER	358
Buxton East Midlands	Fernydale Farm ★★★★ SILVER	404
Canterbury South East	Iffin Farmhouse ★★★★	219
Canterbury South East	Kipps Independent Hostel ★★★	218
Castleton East Midlands	Swiss House ★★★★	405
Chipping North West	Town End Farm ★★★	626
Clitheroe North West	Rowan Tree ★★★★	627
Clun Heart of England	The White Horse Inn ★★★	460
Collingbourne Kingston South West	Manor Farm B&B ★★★★	120
Colne North West	The Crown ★★	627
Combe Martin South West	Blair Lodge Guest House ★★★★	60
Coniston North West	Orchard Cottage ★★★★	587

Official tourist board guide **Bed & Breakfast**

Walkers Welcome and Cyclists Welcome continued

Cornhill-on-Tweed North East	Hay Farm House ★★★★ GOLD	681
Cranborne South West	La Fosse at Cranborne ★★★★	85
Cranwell East Midlands	Byards Leap Bed & Breakfast ★★★	413
Cranwell East Midlands	Byards Leap Lodge ★★★★ SILVER	414
Crediton South West	The Lamb Inn ★★★★ SILVER	61
Dalby Yorkshire	South Moor Farm ★★★★	503
Darlington North East	Trudy's Guesthouse ★★	670
Dinton South West	Marshwood Farm B&B ★★★★	122
Dunkeswell South West	The Old Kennels ★★★★	63
Earby North West	Grange Fell ★★★	628
Egton Bridge Yorkshire	Broom House and Whites (Restaurant) ★★★★ GOLD	505
Ellesmere (3 miles) Heart of England	Hordley Hall ★★★★	460
Falmouth South West	Anchor House ★★★	41
Faversham South East	Palace Farm Hostel ★★★	222
Frosterley North East	Newlands Hall ★★★★	673
Gilsland North East	Brookside Villa B&B ★★★★ SILVER	682
Gilsland North East	Tantallon House ★★★★ SILVER	682
Haltwhistle North East	Four Wynds Guest House ★★★	683
Haltwhistle North East	Glendale Mews ★★★	683
Hanthorpe East Midlands	Maycroft Cottage ★★★★ SILVER	415
Hawes Yorkshire	Old Station House ★★★★ SILVER	506
Haworth Yorkshire	Rosebud Cottage Guest House ★★★★	506
Haydon Bridge North East	Grindon Cartshed ★★★★ SILVER	684
Heddon-on-the-Wall North East	Houghton North Farm Visitor Accommodation ★★★★	684
Henley-on-Thames South East	Bank Farm ★★	234
Hesket Newmarket North West	Daffodil ★★★★★ SILVER	591
Hesket Newmarket North West	Denton House ★★★★	592
Hexham North East	Hall Barns B&B ★★★★	684
Hickling East of England	The Dairy Barns ★★★★ GOLD	347
Hope East Midlands	Underleigh House ★★★★★ GOLD	407
Hope East Midlands	Woodbine B&B ★★★	408
Hunstanton East of England	The King William IV, Country Inn & Restaurant ★★★★ SILVER	348
Keswick North West	Briar Rigg House ★★★★ SILVER	594
Keswick North West	Easedale House ★★★★	595
Keswick North West	Laurel Bank B&B ★★★★	596
Keswick North West	Rooms36 ★★★★ SILVER	597
Keswick North West	Sandon Guest House ★★★★	597
Keswick North West	Woodside ★★★★	598
Kingsbridge South West	Ashleigh House ★★★	65
Kirkby Malzeard Yorkshire	Cowscot House ★★★★	511
Kirkbymoorside Yorkshire	The Cornmill ★★★★ SILVER	511
Leicester East Midlands	Wondai B&B ★★★	411
Letcombe Regis South East	Brook Barn ★★★★★ GOLD	236
Lincoln East Midlands	Welbeck Cottage Bed and Breakfast ★★★★	415
Long Compton Heart of England	Butlers Road Farm ★★★	468
Looe South West	Barclay House ★★★★ SILVER	43
Lynton South West	Sinai House	65
Lyth Bank Heart of England	Lyth Hill House ★★★★★ GOLD	461
Maidstone, Kent South East	Ash Cottage ★★★★★ SILVER	224
Market Lavington South West	Green Dragon ★★★	123
Marlborough South West	The White House ★★★★ SILVER	123
Martock South West	The White Hart ★★★	114
Masham Yorkshire	The White Bear Hotel ★★★★★	513
Mumby East Midlands	Brambles ★★★★	416
Newbrough North East	Carr Edge Farm ★★★★	687
Norwich East of England	Becklands ★★★★	350
Norwich East of England	Marsham Arms Inn ★★★★	351
Penrith North West	Stafford House Guest House ★★★★	603
Pershore Heart of England	Arbour House ★★★★ SILVER	475

Establishments listed here have a detailed entry in this guide

Walkers and cyclists welcome

Walkers Welcome and Cyclists Welcome continued

Location	Establishment	Page
Pickering Yorkshire	Eleven Westgate ★★★★ SILVER	514
Pickering Yorkshire	Laurel Bank ★★★	515
Pickering Yorkshire	The Old Vicarage at Toftly View ★★★★★ GOLD	515
Pluckley South East	Elvey Farm ★★★★ SILVER	226
Plymouth South West	Caraneal ★★★★	76
Pooley Bridge North West	Elm House ★★★★	604
Ramsgate South East	Glendevon Guest House ★★★★	226
Robin Hoods Bay Yorkshire	Devon House ★★★	516
Rowde South West	Vine Cottage Bed & Breakfast ★★★★	124
Rydal North West	Cote How Organic Guest House ★★★★ GOLD	604
Rye South East	Fairacres ★★★★★ GOLD	260
Rye South East	Oaklands ★★★★★ GOLD	261
Rye South East	Strand House ★★★★ GOLD	261
Saltburn-by-the-Sea Yorkshire	The Arches ★★★★	517
Sandown South East	The Sandhill ★★★	213
Scorton North West	The Priory Inn, Scorton ★★★	629
Sedbergh North West	Howgills Bunk Barn ★★★	605
Shap North West	Greyhound Hotel ★★★	605
Shrewsbury Heart of England	Brompton Farmhouse ★★★★ SILVER	462
Sibton East of England	Eben-Ezer ★★★★	362
Skipton Yorkshire	Poppy Cottage Guest House ★★★★	521
South Walsham East of England	Old Hall Farm ★★★★ SILVER	353
St Issey South West	Higher Trevorrick Country House ★★★★★ GOLD	51
St Just-in-Roseland South West	Roundhouse Barn B&B Holidays ★★★★★ SILVER	52
Stape Yorkshire	High Muffles ★★★★ GOLD	522
Staplecross South East	Woodside Bed & Breakfast ★★★★★ GOLD	262
Stocksfield North East	Locksley, Bed & Breakfast ★★★★ GOLD	689
Stoke St Gregory South West	Rose & Crown ★★★	115
Stratton Strawless East of England	Woodmans Farm ★★★★ SILVER	353
Swanage South West	Corner Meadow ★★★★	88
Swanage South West	Taunton House ★★★	88
Thirsk Yorkshire	Garbutt Farm ★★★	523
Tissington East Midlands	Bassett Wood Farm ★★★★	409
Torquay South West	Villa Marina ★★★★ SILVER	78
Troutbeck North West	The Troutbeck Inn ★★★★	607
Wainfleet East Midlands	Willow Farm ★★★	418
Waldringfield East of England	Thatched Farm Bed & Breakfast ★★★★	364
Wareham South West	Frome Corner ★★★	89
Wark North East	The Battlesteads ★★★★ SILVER	690
Windermere North West	Brook House ★★★	609
Windermere North West	Langdale View Guest House ★★★★	611
Winster North West	The Brown Horse Inn ★★★★	613
Woodbridge East of England	Grove House Hotel ★★★	366
Woodnewton East Midlands	Bridge Cottage Bed and Breakfast ★★★★	423
Wooler North East	Belmont House Bed & Breakfast ★★★★	691
Wooler North East	Firwood Country Bed and Breakfast ★★★★★ GOLD	691
Yelverton South West	Barnabas House Yelverton ★★★★	80
Yelverton South West	Overcombe House ★★★★	81

Walkers Welcome

Location	Establishment	Page
Bembridge South East	Ivar Cottage Summer House ★★★★	209
Brede South East	Little Garth Bed & Breakfast ★★★★ SILVER	248
Callington South West	Hampton Manor ★★★★	40
Clapham Yorkshire	New Inn ★★★	502
Culham South East	Zouch Farm B&B ★★★★	233
Keswick North West	Appletrees ★★★★	593
Runswick Bay Yorkshire	Runswick Bay ★★★	516
St Ives South West	abode ★★★★★ SILVER	52
Staunton South West	Steep Meadow ★★★★	101

Families and Pets Welcome

Establishments participating in the Families Welcome or Welcome Pets! schemes are listed below. They provide special facilities and actively encourage famlies or guests with pets. Place names are listed alphabetically.

Families and Pets Welcome

Amble North East	Harbour Guest House ★★★	677
Ambleside North West	Brathay Lodge ★★★★	578
Berwick-upon-Tweed North East	Meadow Hill Guest House ★★★★	680
Buxton East Midlands	Fernydale Farm ★★★★ SILVER	404
Dalby Yorkshire	South Moor Farm ★★★★	503
Keswick North West	Rooms36 ★★★★ SILVER	597
Macclesfield North West	Astle Farm East Bed & Breakfast ★★	576
Norwich East of England	Edmar Lodge ★★★	350
Penrith North West	Stafford House Guest House ★★★★	603
Ridlington East Midlands	Post Cottage ★★★★	413
Shap North West	Greyhound Hotel ★★★	605

Families Welcome

Alton Heart of England	Windy Arbour ★★★★	464
Black Bourton South East	The Vines ★★★★	233
Bourton-on-the-Water South West	Chestnuts Bed & Breakfast ★★★★	92
Brede South East	Little Garth Bed & Breakfast ★★★★ SILVER	248
Bury St Edmunds East of England	St Edmunds Guesthouse ★★★★ SILVER	358
Darlington North East	Trudy's Guesthouse ★★	670
Haltwhistle North East	Four Wynds Guest House ★★★	683
Haltwhistle North East	Glendale Mews ★★★	683
Keswick (5 miles) North West	Littletown Farm ★★★	599
Keswick North West	Easedale House ★★★★	595
Keswick North West	Laurel Bank B&B ★★★★	596
Kielder Water North East	The Pheasant Inn (by Kielder Water) ★★★★ SILVER	686
Looe South West	Barclay House ★★★★ SILVER	43
Norwich East of England	Marsham Arms Inn ★★★★	351
Skipton Yorkshire	Poppy Cottage Guest House ★★★★	521
Slimbridge South West	Tudor Arms Lodge and Freehouse ★★★★	100
South Creake East of England	Valentine Studio ★★★★	353
St Ives South West	abode ★★★★★ SILVER	52
Staplecross South East	Woodside Bed & Breakfast ★★★★★ GOLD	262
Stoke Gabriel South West	Stoke Gabriel Lodgings ★★★★★ SILVER	72
Stoke St Gregory South West	Rose & Crown ★★★	115
Winster North West	The Brown Horse Inn ★★★★	613
Woodbridge East of England	Grove House Hotel ★★★	366

Pets Welcome

Adderbury South East	The Bell Inn ★★★	232
Canterbury South East	Hornbeams ★★★★	218
Colne North West	The Crown ★★	627
Ely East of England	The Old School B&B ★★★★	334
Kendal North West	The Glen ★★★★	593
Keswick North West	Woodside ★★★★	598

Establishments listed here have a detailed entry in this guide

Families and pets welcome

🐾 Pets Welcome continued

Kirkby Lonsdale North West	Copper Kettle Restaurant & Guest House ★★★	599
Leicester East Midlands	Wondai B&B ★★★	411
Marlow South East	The Hand & Flowers ★★★★★	201
Minster South East	Durlock Lodge ★★★	225
Mumby East Midlands	Brambles ★★★★	416
Pluckley South East	Elvey Farm ★★★★ SILVER	226
Richmond London	Ivy Cottage ★★★	306
Runswick Bay Yorkshire	Runswick Bay ★★★	516
Seaford South East	The Silverdale ★★★★	262
Sibton East of England	Eben-Ezer ★★★★	362
St Agnes South West	Little Trevellas Farm ★★★	49
St Issey South West	Higher Trevorrick Country House ★★★★★ GOLD	51
St Mawgan South West	Dalswinton House ★★★★	53
Torquay South West	Cary Arms Hotel & Restaurant ★★★★★ SILVER	75
Wainfleet East Midlands	Willow Farm ★★★	418
Windermere North West	Fairfield House & Gardens ★★★★ SILVER	609

762　　　　　　　　　　　　　　　　　　　　　　　　　Official tourist board guide **Bed & Breakfast**

Quick reference index

If you're looking for a specific facility use this index to see at a glance detailed accommodation entries that match your requirement. Establishments are listed alphabetically by place name.

⚑ Indoor pool

Alnwick North East	Alnwick Lodge ★★★	675
Ambleside North West	Elder Grove ★★★★ SILVER	579
Ambleside North West	Red Bank ★★★★★ SILVER	579
Ambleside North West	Smallwood House ★★★★	581
Ambleside North West	Wateredge Inn ★★★★	581
Bognor Regis South East	Selwood Lodge ★★★	247
Bourton-on-the-Water South West	Trevone Bed & Breakfast ★★★	92
Bowness-on-Windermere North West	May Cottage B&B ★★★	584
Bury St Edmunds East of England	St Edmunds Guesthouse ★★★★ SILVER	358
Buxton East Midlands	Kingscroft Guest House ★★★★ SILVER	404
Cadnam South East	Twin Oaks Guest House ★★★★ SILVER	203
Chesterfield East Midlands	Abigail's Guest House ★★★	405
Chipping Campden South West	Manor Farm ★★★★	94
Egton Bridge Yorkshire	Broom House and Whites (Restaurant) ★★★★ GOLD	505
Exeter South West	University of Exeter ★★★★	64
Freshwater South East	The Orchards ★★★★	210
Haltwhistle North East	Four Wynds Guest House ★★★	683
Haltwhistle North East	Glendale Mews ★★★	683
Lewes South East	Beechwood B&B ★★★★★ GOLD	256
Lyth Bank Heart of England	Lyth Hill House ★★★★★ GOLD	462
Malvern Heart of England	Puddle Lane ★★★ SILVER	475
Moddershall Heart of England	Moddershall Oaks Spa Restaurant Suites ★★★★★ SILVER	466
Oakham East Midlands	17 Northgate ★★★★ SILVER	412
Penrith North West	Stafford House Guest House ★★★★	603
Pickering Yorkshire	Eleven Westgate ★★★★ SILVER	514
Pickering Yorkshire	Laurel Bank ★★★	515
Rodmell South East	Garden Cottage ★★★★	259
Rye South East	Old Borough Arms ★★★★	259
Skegness East Midlands	Chatsworth ★★★	417
Southport North West	Crescent House ★★★	632
St Austell South West	Anchorage House ★★★★★ GOLD	50
St Mary's South West	Treboeth Guest House ★★★	56
St Minver / Polzeath South West	Tredower Barton ★★★	53
Stowmarket East of England	Three Bears Cottage ★★★★	364
Torquay South West	Haldon Priors ★★★★★ GOLD	77
Uxbridge London	Oakdene Guest House ★★★	307
Wells South West	Islington Farm ★★★★	116
Weymouth South West	Beaufort Guesthouse ★★★	89
Woking South East	Fenton House ★★★★	245
York Yorkshire	Curzon Lodge & Stable Cottages ★★★★	531

⚑ Outdoor pool

Bath South West	Church Farm Monkton Farleigh ★★★	105
Bath South West	The Hermitage ★★	106
Blandford Forum South West	Farnham Farm House ★★★★★ GOLD	81
Bournemouth South West	Ingledene Guest House ★★	82
Castle Cary South West	Clanville Manor B&B ★★★★ GOLD	109

Establishments listed here have a detailed entry in this guide

763

Quick reference index

✈ Outdoor pool continued

Chelwood Gate South East	Holly House ★★★★ SILVER	249
Detling South East	Wealden Hall ★★★★	220
Devizes South West	Rosemundy Cottage ★★★★	122
Exeter South West	Culm Vale Country House ★★★	63
Exeter South West	University of Exeter ★★★★	64
Haltwhistle North East	Four Wynds Guest House ★★★	683
Kilham Yorkshire	Kilham Hall Country House ★★★★★ GOLD	510
Lewes South East	The Dorset ★★★★	257
Looe South West	Barclay House ★★★★ SILVER	43
Manningford Abbots South West	Huntly's Farmhouse ★★★★	123
Marlborough South West	Mayfield ★★★★ SILVER	124
Okehampton South West	Week Farm ★★★★	67
Penrith North West	Stafford House Guest House ★★★★	603
Porthloo South West	Armeria ★★	56
Scarborough Yorkshire	The Thoresby ★★★	519
Shillingford South East	Marsh House ★★★★	239
Skegness East Midlands	Chatsworth ★★★	417
St Mawgan South West	Dalswinton House ★★★★	53
St Mellion South West	Pentillie Castle & Estate ★★★★★ GOLD	53
Steyning South East	Springwells ★★★	262
Tavistock South West	Tor Cottage ★★★★★ GOLD	73
Torquay South West	Haldon Priors ★★★★★ GOLD	77
Torquay South West	Hotel Cimon ★★★★	77
Tresco South West	The New Inn ★★★★ SILVER	56
Woodhall Spa East Midlands	The Limes ★★★	419

✕ Evening meal by arrangement

Adderbury South East	The Bell Inn ★★★	232
Airton Yorkshire	Lindon House ★★★	498
Aldborough near Cromer East of England	Butterfly Cottage B&B ★★★★	343
Alnwick North East	Alnwick Lodge ★★★	675
Alnwick North East	Masons Arms Country Inn ★★★★	677
Alston North West	Cumberland Inn ★★★	577
Alston North West	The Miners Arms ★★★	578
Alton Heart of England	Fields Farm ★★★★	465
Amble North East	Harbour Guest House ★★★	677
Ambleside North West	Smallwood House ★★★★	581
Ambleside North West	Wateredge Inn ★★★★	581
Appleby-in-Westmorland North West	Bongate House ★★★	582
Ashbourne East Midlands	Peak District Spa ★★★	400
Ashford (5 miles) South East	Dean Court ★★★	216
Ashford South East	Bowl Inn ★★★★	216
Ashwell East of England	Three Tuns Hotel ★★★	342
Aylsham East of England	The Old Pump House ★★★★★ GOLD	343
Ayot St Lawrence East of England	The Brocket Arms ★★★★	342
Bamford East Midlands	Yorkshire Bridge Inn ★★★★ SILVER	403
Bampton South East	Manor Farm Barn B&B	232
Barkston East Midlands	Kelling House ★★★★	413
Bassenthwaite North West	Ouse Bridge House ★★★★ SILVER	584
Bath South West	Fern Cottage Bed & Breakfast ★★★★ SILVER	91
Bath South West	Lamp Post Villa ★★★	106
Bawdsey East of England	Bawdsey Manor ★★★★	357
Bedale Yorkshire	Castle Arms Inn ★★★★	499
Bedford East of England	The Embankment ★★★★	330
Berwick-upon-Tweed North East	Meadow Hill Guest House ★★★★	680
Berwick-upon-Tweed North East	Rob Roy ★★★★	680
Biddenden South East	Heron Cottage ★★★★	217

Quick reference index

✈ Evening meal by arrangement continued

Bishop Wilton Yorkshire	High Belthorpe ★★★		500
Blackpool North West	The Allendale ★★★		614
Blackpool North West	Arabella ★★★		615
Blackpool North West	Argyll ★★		614
Blackpool North West	Ash Lodge ★★★		615
Blackpool North West	Blenheim Mount Hotel ★★★		616
Blackpool North West	Cameo ★★★		616
Blackpool North West	Clovelly ★★★★		617
Blackpool North West	The Dragonfly ★★★★		617
Blackpool North West	Everglades ★★★		617
Blackpool North West	Fairway ★★★		618
Blackpool North West	Fern Royd ★★★		618
Blackpool North West	Holmside House ★★★★		619
Blackpool North West	Homecliffe ★★★★		619
Blackpool North West	Kirkstall House ★★★		620
Blackpool North West	Lynbar Guesthouse ★★★		620
Blackpool North West	Lyndene Guest House ★★★		621
Blackpool North West	Norville House ★★★		621
Blackpool North West	Novello ★★★		621
Blackpool North West	The Raffles Guest Accommodation ★★★★		622
Blackpool North West	Rencliffe ★★★★		623
Blackpool North West	Rio Rita ★★★		623
Blackpool North West	Roselea ★★★		623
Blackpool North West	Sandford Promenade ★★★		624
Blackpool North West	South Beach Seafront ★★★		624
Blackpool North West	The Southview ★★		624
Blackpool North West	Sussex ★★★		625
Blackpool North West	The Valentine ★★★★		625
Bladbean South East	Molehills ★★★★		217
Blandford Forum South West	The Anvil Inn ★★★★		81
Blickling East of England	Buckinghamshire Arms ★★★★		344
Bognor Regis South East	Selwood Lodge ★★★		247
Bolton-by-Bowland North West	Middle Flass Lodge ★★★★		626
Bolventor South West	Jamaica Inn ★★★★		38
Bournemouth South West	Ingledene Guest House ★★		82
Bournemouth South West	Kings Langley ★★★		83
Bowd South West	The Barn & Pinn Cottage Guest House ★★★★		58
Bracknell South East	Elizabeth House ★★★★		196
Bradwell East Midlands	Travellers Rest ★★★		403
Brampton North West	Scarrow Hill Guest House ★★★★ SILVER		585
Braunton South West	George Hotel ★★★		58
Bridgnorth Heart of England	Bulls Head Inn ★★★★		459
Bridlington Yorkshire	Kilburn Guest House ★★★★		501
Brighstone South East	Seven Bed & Breakfast ★★★		209
Brightlingsea East of England	Hurst Green Bed and Breakfast ★★★★ SILVER		336
Bristol South West	The Town & Country Lodge ★★★		93
Broadstairs South East	Bay Tree Broadstairs ★★★★		218
Broadway Heart of England	The Bell at Willersey ★★★★		472
Broadway Heart of England	Lowerfield Farm ★★★★ SILVER		473
Bude South West	Beach House ★★★		39
Bude South West	Harefield Cottage ★★★★ GOLD		39
Bude South West	Surf Haven Guest House ★★★★		40
Bugle South West	The Bugle Inn ★★★		40
Burley South East	Wayside Cottage ★★★★		202
Burnham-on-Sea South West	Royal Clarence Hotel ★★★		108
Buttermere North West	Fish Inn		586
Callington South West	Hampton Manor ★★★★		40

Establishments listed here have a detailed entry in this guide

765

Quick reference index

✕ Evening meal by arrangement continued

Location	Property	Page
Cambridge (12 miles) East of England	Three Hills ★★★★	334
Canterbury South East	Hornbeams ★★★★	218
Canterbury South East	Iffin Farmhouse ★★★★	219
Canterbury South East	Magnolia House ★★★★★ GOLD	219
Carlisle North West	Langleigh House ★★★★	586
Castle Howard Yorkshire	Gate Farm ★★★	501
Chard South West	Hornsbury Mill ★★★★	109
Charing South East	Oak ★★★★ SILVER	220
Charminster South West	The Three Compasses ★★★	84
Cheddar South West	Arundel House ★★★	109
Cheddar South West	Yew Tree Farm ★★★	110
Cheltenham South West	Beaumont House ★★★★★ GOLD	93
Chichester South East	George Bell House ★★★★★	250
Chichester South East	The Nags Head ★★★★	251
Cholderton South West	Parkhouse Motel ★★★★	120
Cirencester South West	Riverside House ★★★★	95
Clapham Yorkshire	New Inn ★★★	502
Clavering East of England	Cricketers, The ★★★★ SILVER	337
Clitheroe North West	Rowan Tree ★★★★	627
Cloughton Yorkshire	Cober Hill ★★★	502
Clun Heart of England	The White Horse Inn ★★★	460
Colne North West	The Crown ★★	627
Combe Martin South West	Blair Lodge Guest House ★★★★	60
Combe Martin South West	Mellstock House ★★★★	61
Compton Valence South West	Manor Farm ★★★★	85
Coniston North West	The Sun, Coniston ★★★★	587
Coniston North West	Yewdale Inn ★★★	587
Corbridge North East	Fellcroft ★★★★	681
Cornhill-on-Tweed North East	Hay Farm House ★★★★ GOLD	681
Coventry Heart of England	Highcroft Guest House ★★★	471
Cranborne South West	La Fosse at Cranborne ★★★★	85
Cranwell East Midlands	Byards Leap Bed & Breakfast ★★★	413
Crediton South West	The Lamb Inn ★★★★ SILVER	61
Creeting St Mary East of England	Creeting House ★★★★	358
Cricklade South West	The Red Lion ★★★★	121
Cropston East Midlands	Horseshoe Cottage Farm ★★★★★ GOLD	410
Crowborough South East	Yew House Bed & Breakfast ★★★★ SILVER	251
Culgaith North West	Laurel House ★★★★ GOLD	588
Dalby Yorkshire	South Moor Farm ★★★★	503
Danby Yorkshire	Fox & Hounds Inn ★★★★	504
Dockray North West	Royal Hotel ★★★★	588
Doncaster Yorkshire	Balmoral Guesthouse ★★★	504
Durham North East	The Avenue Inn ★★	671
Durham North East	Saint Chad's College ★★	671
Durham North East	Seven Stars Inn ★★★	672
Durham North East	St John's College ★★★	672
East Ashling (Chichester 3 miles) South East	Horse & Groom ★★★★	251
East Harptree South West	Harptree Court ★★★★★ GOLD	112
East Ord North East	Fairholm ★★★★	682
Eastbourne South East	Brayscroft House ★★★★ GOLD	251
Eastbourne South East	Eastbourne Reymar ★★★ SILVER	252
Edmundbyers North East	Punchbowl Inn ★★★★ SILVER	673
Egton Bridge Yorkshire	Broom House and Whites (Restaurant) ★★★★ GOLD	505
Elmswell East of England	Kiln Farm Guest House ★★★★ SILVER	358
Ely East of England	The Old School B&B ★★★★	334
Fakenham East of England	Abbott Farm B&B ★★★	346
Falmouth South West	Anchor House ★★★	41

Quick reference index

✕ Evening meal by arrangement continued

Location	Establishment	Page
Fareham South East	Travelrest Solent Gateway ★★★★	204
Ford South West	The Plough Inn ★★★★	96
Fossebridge South West	The Inn at Fossebridge ★★★★	97
Framlingham (7 miles) East of England	Flindor Cottage ★★★★★ GOLD	359
Frampton-on-Severn South West	The Bell Inn ★★★★	97
Freshwater South East	The Orchards ★★★★	210
Frogmore South West	Globe Inn ★★★★	65
Gilsland North East	Brookside Villa B&B ★★★★ SILVER	682
Gilsland North West	Bush Nook Guest House ★★★★	589
Glastonbury South West	Meare Manor ★★★★	113
Grantham East Midlands	The Cedars ★★★★	414
Great Ayton Yorkshire	The Kings Head at Newton Under Roseberry ★★★★ SILVER	505
Great Missenden South East	Rickyard Cottage ★★★★ GOLD	200
Guiting Power South West	Guiting Guest House ★★★★ SILVER	98
Guiting Power South West	The Hollow Bottom ★★★★	98
Guyhirn East of England	Oliver Twist Country Inn ★★★★	335
Haltwhistle North East	Glendale Mews ★★★	683
Harrogate Yorkshire	Cold Cotes ★★★★★ GOLD	505
Haslemere South East	Deerfell ★★★★	243
Haslemere South East	The Wheatsheaf Inn ★★★	244
Hawkshead North West	Crosslands Farm ★★★★	589
Haworth Yorkshire	Old White Lion Hotel ★★★★	507
Hay-on-Wye Heart of England	Rhydspence Inn ★★★★	456
Haydon Bridge North East	Grindon Cartshed ★★★★ SILVER	684
Heads Nook North West	Croft House ★★★★★ SILVER	590
Heads Nook North West	String of Horses Inn ★★★	591
Hebden Bridge Yorkshire	b@r place ★★★★	508
Helmsley Yorkshire	Laskill Grange ★★★★	509
Henley-on-Thames South East	The Baskerville ★★★★ SILVER	235
Hesket Newmarket North West	Daffodil ★★★★★ SILVER	591
Hesket Newmarket North West	Denton House ★★★★	592
Hexham North East	Hall Barns B&B ★★★★	684
Hexham North East	Travellers Rest ★★★★	685
Hickling East of England	The Dairy Barns ★★★★ GOLD	347
Hunstanton East of England	The King William IV, Country Inn & Restaurant ★★★★ SILVER	348
Illogan South West	Sonnier ★★★★	42
Ingleton Yorkshire	New Butts Farm ★★★	509
Keswick (7.5 miles) North West	Lane Head Farm Country Guest House ★★★★ SILVER	599
Kettering East Midlands	Dairy Farm ★★★	421
Kettleburgh East of England	Church Farm ★★★★	361
Kielder North East	Twenty Seven B&B and Self Catering Cottage ★★	686
Kielder Water North East	The Pheasant Inn (by Kielder Water) ★★★★ SILVER	686
Kilham Yorkshire	Kilham Hall Country House ★★★★★ GOLD	510
Kintbury South East	Dundas Arms ★★★	197
Kirkby Lonsdale North West	Copper Kettle Restaurant & Guest House ★★★	599
Kirkbymoorside Yorkshire	The Cornmill ★★★★ SILVER	511
Kirkbymoorside Yorkshire	The Feversham Arms Inn ★★★★	512
Lake South East	Cliff Lodge Guest House ★★★★	210
Langport South West	Orchard Barn ★★★★	114
Langtoft Yorkshire	The Old Mill Hotel & Restaurant ★★★	512
Launceston South West	Primrose Cottage ★★★★★ GOLD	43
Lavenham East of England	Lavenham Old Rectory ★★★★★ GOLD	361
Lea Bridge East Midlands	Pear Tree Farm Guest House ★★★★	408
Lechlade-on-Thames South West	The New Inn hotel ★★★	99
Leeds Yorkshire	Glengarth Guest House ★★★	513
Leintwardine Heart of England	Lower House ★★★★	457
Letcombe Regis South East	Brook Barn ★★★★★ GOLD	236

Establishments listed here have a detailed entry in this guide

Quick reference index

✕ Evening meal by arrangement continued

Lewes South East	The Blacksmiths Arms ★★★★ SILVER	257
Lewes South East	The Dorset ★★★★	257
Lincoln East Midlands	Welbeck Cottage Bed and Breakfast ★★★★	415
Littlehampton South East	Arun View Inn ★★	257
London E15 London	The Railway Tavern ★★★★	301
London E8 London	The Old Ship ★★★★	301
Long Buckby East Midlands	Murcott Mill ★★★★	422
Long Melford East of England	High Street Farmhouse ★★★★ SILVER	362
Looe South West	Barclay House ★★★★ SILVER	43
Lostwithiel South West	Cross Close House B&B ★★★★	44
Loughborough East Midlands	Highbury Guest House ★★★★	411
Ludlow Heart of England	Cecil Guest House ★★★	460
Lymington South East	Gorse Meadow Guest House ★★★★	205
Lymington South East	The Nurse's Cottage Restaurant with Rooms ★★★★ GOLD	206
Malton Yorkshire	Old Lodge Malton ★★★★	513
Manchester North West	Stay Inn Hotel ★★★	630
Manningford Abbots South West	Huntly's Farmhouse ★★★★	123
Margate South East	Hussar ★★★★	225
Market Lavington South West	Green Dragon ★★★	123
Marlborough South West	Mayfield ★★★★ SILVER	124
Marlow South East	The Hand & Flowers ★★★★★	201
Martock South West	The White Hart ★★★★	114
Masham Yorkshire	The White Bear Hotel ★★★★★	513
Mevagissey South West	Tregilgas Farm ★★★★	46
Moddershall Heart of England	Moddershall Oaks Spa Restaurant Suites ★★★★★ SILVER	466
Monkton Farleigh South West	The Kings Arms ★★★★ SILVER	124
Morcott East Midlands	Redoak Bed and Breakfast ★★★	411
Morecambe North West	Sea Crest ★★★	628
Morwenstow South West	The Bush Inn ★★★	46
Mumby East Midlands	Brambles ★★★★	416
Newcastle upon Tyne North East	The Keelman's Lodge ★★★★	691
North Rode North West	Ladderstile Retreat ★★★★★ SILVER	576
Northallerton Yorkshire	Lovesome Hill Farm ★★★★ SILVER	514
Norwich East of England	Marsham Arms Inn ★★★★	351
Oakham East Midlands	Dial House ★★★★	412
Paignton South West	Cliveden Guest House ★★★★	68
Paignton South West	Earlston House ★★★★	69
Parkend South West	Fountain Inn ★★★	100
Pembridge Heart of England	Lowe Farm B&B ★★★★ GOLD	458
Pentney East of England	Little Abbey Farm ★★★★ SILVER	352
Penton North West	Craigburn Farmhouse ★★★★	603
Penzance South West	Cornerways Guest House ★★★	47
Pickering Yorkshire	The Hawthornes ★★★★ SILVER	514
Pidley East of England	Lakeside Lodge Golf Centre ★★★	336
Pluckley South East	Elvey Farm ★★★★ SILVER	226
Polzeath South West	White Heron ★★★★	47
Porlock South West	Rose Bank Guest House ★★★★ SILVER	114
Port Isaac South West	Cornish Arms ★★★	48
Port Isaac South West	Slipway ★★★★	48
Portland South West	Aqua, The ★★★	86
Pulborough South East	The Labouring Man ★★★★	258
Redruth South West	Goonearl Cottage ★★★★ SILVER	49
Richmond London	The Red Cow ★★★	306
Ridlington East Midlands	Post Cottage ★★★★	413
Rothbury North East	Katerina's Guest House ★★★★ SILVER	688
Rudford South West	The Dark Barn ★★★★	100
Rugeley Heart of England	Colton House ★★★★★ GOLD	467

Quick reference index

✗ Evening meal by arrangement continued

Location	Region	Establishment	Page
Runswick Bay	Yorkshire	Firs Guesthouse ★★★★	516
Runswick Bay	Yorkshire	Runswick Bay ★★★	516
Rye	South East	Strand House ★★★★ GOLD	261
Saffron Walden	East of England	Redgates Farmhouse ★★★★	339
Sale	North West	Belforte House ★★★★	630
Sale	North West	Eskdale Lodge ★★★★	630
Sandown	South East	The Sandhill ★★★	213
Scarborough	Yorkshire	The Alexander ★★★★ GOLD	517
Scarborough	Yorkshire	Killerby Cottage Farm ★★★★ SILVER	518
Scarborough	Yorkshire	Robyn's Guest House ★★★★	518
Scarborough	Yorkshire	The Thoresby ★★★	519
Scorton	North West	The Priory Inn, Scorton ★★★	629
Settle	Yorkshire	Maypole Inn ★★★★	520
Shanklin	South East	The Parkway ★★★★	214
Shanklin	South East	Swiss Cottage ★★★★ SILVER	215
Shanklin	South East	Victoria Lodge ★★★★	215
Shap	North West	Greyhound Hotel ★★★	605
Shave Cross	South West	The Shave Cross Inn ★★★★★ SILVER	87
Sheerness	South East	Ferry House Inn ★★★★ SILVER	228
Shifnal	Heart of England	Odfellows Wine Bar ★★★	462
Shrewsbury	Heart of England	Brompton Farmhouse ★★★★ SILVER	463
Sibton	East of England	Sibton White Horse Inn ★★★★ SILVER	362
Sidmouth	South West	Canterbury Guest House ★★★★	71
Skegness	East Midlands	Chatsworth ★★★	417
Skegness	East Midlands	The Fountaindale Skegness ★★★★ SILVER	417
Skegness	East Midlands	Stoneleigh ★★★★ SILVER	417
Skegness	East Midlands	Woodthorpe Guest House ★★★	417
Slimbridge	South West	Tudor Arms Lodge and Freehouse ★★★★	100
Snettisham	East of England	The Queen Victoria ★★★★	353
South Kilvington	Yorkshire	Manor House Cottage ★★★★	521
Southport	North West	Crescent House ★★★	632
St Austell	South West	Anchorage House ★★★★★ GOLD	50
St Austell	South West	The Gables Guest House ★★★★	50
St Austell	South West	Highland Court Lodge ★★★★★ GOLD	50
St Issey	South West	Higher Trevorrick Country House ★★★★★ GOLD	51
St Mawgan	South West	Dalswinton House ★★★★	53
St Mellion	South West	Pentillie Castle & Estate ★★★★★ GOLD	53
Stafford	Heart of England	Wyndale Guest House ★★★	467
Stansted	East of England	White House ★★★★ SILVER	340
Stape	Yorkshire	High Muffles ★★★★ GOLD	522
Staplecross	South East	Woodside Bed & Breakfast ★★★★★ GOLD	262
Staunton	South West	Steep Meadow ★★★★	101
Stockton-on-Tees	North East	The Parkwood Inn ★★★	674
Stogumber	South West	Wick House ★★★★	115
Stoke St Gregory	South West	Rose & Crown ★★★	115
Stratford-upon-Avon	Heart of England	Folly Farm Cottage ★★★★ GOLD	470
Stratford-upon-Avon	Heart of England	Quilt & Croissants ★★★	470
Stroud	South West	1 Woodchester Lodge ★★★★ SILVER	102
Swanton Morley	East of England	Carricks at Castle Farm ★★★★★ GOLD	354
Swineshead	East Midlands	The Wheatsheaf ★★★	418
Tavistock	South West	Beera Farmhouse ★★★★ GOLD	72
Teignmouth	South West	Dresden House ★★★★	73
Telford	Heart of England	Old Orleton Inn ★★★★★ SILVER	464
Tenterden	South East	Collina House ★★★★	229
Thetford	East of England	Colveston Manor ★★★★	354
Thirsk	Yorkshire	Borrowby Mill Bed & Breakfast ★★★★ SILVER	523
Thirsk	Yorkshire	Garbutt Farm ★★★	523

Establishments listed here have a detailed entry in this guide

Quick reference index

✕ Evening meal by arrangement continued

Location	Establishment	Page
Thixendale Yorkshire	The Cross Keys ★★★	524
Thompson East of England	Chequers Inn ★★★★	355
Thornham Magna East of England	The Four Horseshoes ★★★★	364
Thornton Curtis East Midlands	Thornton Hunt Inn ★★★★	418
Threlkeld North West	Horse & Farrier Inn ★★★★	606
Tintagel South West	Mill House ★★★★	53
Torquay South West	Abberley Guest House ★★★	74
Torquay South West	Carlton Court ★★★★★ SILVER	74
Torquay South West	Cary Arms Hotel & Restaurant ★★★★★ SILVER	75
Torquay South West	Coombe Court ★★★★	75
Torquay South West	Crown Lodge ★★★★	76
Torquay South West	Hotel Cimon ★★★★	77
Torquay South West	Mount Edgcombe ★★★★	78
Triangle (Sowerby Bridge) Yorkshire	The Dene ★★★★	524
Troutbeck North West	The Troutbeck Inn ★★★★	607
Tunbridge Wells South East	40 York Road ★★★★	229
Uley South West	The Old Crown Inn ★★★	104
Uppingham East Midlands	Spanhoe Lodge ★★★★★ GOLD	422
Vowchurch Heart of England	Yew Tree House ★★★★ GOLD	459
Wadebridge (4 miles) South West	Tregolls Farm B&B ★★★★	55
Wainfleet East Midlands	Willow Farm ★★★	418
Wakefield Yorkshire	The Bank House Hotel ★★	524
Walkington Yorkshire	The Ferguson Fawsitt Arms ★★★★	525
Wall North East	The Hadrian ★★★	690
Wangford East of England	The Angel Inn ★★★★	365
Wantage South East	Regis Guest House ★★★★ SILVER	240
Wark North East	The Battlesteads ★★★★ SILVER	690
West Down South West	Sunnymeade Country Hotel ★★★	79
West Kirby North West	At Peel Hey ★★★★ SILVER	633
West Mersea East of England	The Victory at Mersea ★★★★	341
West Timperley North West	Altrincham Lodge ★★★	631
West Woodburn North East	Bay Horse Inn ★★★	690
Westhorpe East of England	Moat Hill Farm B&B ★★★★ SILVER	365
Weymouth South West	Beaufort Guesthouse ★★★	89
Weymouth South West	Oaklands Edwardian Guest House ★★★★	90
Whitby Yorkshire	Sneaton Castle Centre ★★★	527
Whitby Yorkshire	Wentworth Guest House ★★★	527
Whitehaven North West	Moresby Hall ★★★★★ GOLD	608
Whitewell North West	The Inn at Whitewell ★★★★★ GOLD	629
Wighton East of England	Meadow View Guest House ★★★★★ GOLD	356
Windermere North West	Bowfell Cottage ★★★	608
Winster North West	The Brown Horse Inn ★★★★	613
Witchford East of England	The Village Inn ★★★	336
Woking South East	Saint Columba's House ★★★	245
Woodbridge East of England	Grove House Hotel ★★★	366
Woodhall Spa East Midlands	Chaplin House ★★★★ SILVER	419
Woodhall Spa East Midlands	Kirkstead Old Mill Cottage ★★★★ SILVER	419
Woodhall Spa East Midlands	Village Limits Country Pub, Restaurant & Motel ★★★★	420
Woodleigh South West	Higher Hendham House ★★★★	79
Woodstock South East	Shepherds Hall ★★★	240
Woolpit East of England	Bull Inn & Restaurant ★★★	366
Worcester Heart of England	Holland House ★★★	476
Workington North West	Old Ginn House Inn ★★★★	613
Worth South East	St Crispin Inn ★★★★	231
Wrentham East of England	Five Bells ★★★	367
Wymondham East of England	Witch Hazel ★★★★ GOLD	357
Yelverton South West	Barnabas House Yelverton ★★★★	80

Quick reference index

✕ Evening meal by arrangement continued

Yelverton South West	Harrabeer Country House ★★★★	80
York Yorkshire	Blakeney House & Restaurant ★★★★	530
York Yorkshire	Blossoms York ★★★	531
York Yorkshire	Heworth Court B&B and Lamplight Restaurant ★★★★	533
York Yorkshire	The Manor House ★★★★ SILVER	533

Budget accommodation

If you're travelling on a budget, the following establishments with a detailed entry in the guide offer accommodation from £25 per person per night or less. This may be for a single room or based on two people sharing a room. These prices are only an indication - please check carefully before confirming a reservation. Establishments are listed alphabetically by place name within each region. See also the index of hostel and campus accommodation on page 772.

South West

Cholderton **Cholderton Stonehenge Youth Hostel** ★★★★	119
Axminster **Graden** ★★★	113
Paignton **Belle Dene Guest House** ★★★★	68
Paignton **Braedene Lodge** ★★★	68
Paignton **Cliveden Guest House** ★★★★	68
Portland **Aqua, The** ★★★	86
Torquay **Crimdon Dene** ★★★★	76

South East

Faversham **Palace Farm Hostel** ★★★	222
Gillingham **The Balmoral** ★★★	222
Lake **Cliff Lodge Guest House** ★★★★	210
Shanklin **Swiss Cottage** ★★★★	215

East of England

Great Yarmouth **The Chimes** ★★★★	347
Great Yarmouth **The Weatherdene** ★★★	347

East Midlands

Ranthorpe **Maycroft Cottage** ★★★★	415
Skegness **Woodthorpe Guest House** ★★★	417

Heart of England

Coventry **Bede Guest House** ★★★	471
Coventry **Highcroft Guest House** ★★★	471

Yorkshire

Bridlington **Kilburn Guest House** ★★★★	501
Scarborough **The Thoresby** ★★★	519

North West

Blackpool **The Allendale** ★★★	614
Blackpool **Arabella** ★★★	615
Blackpool **Argyll** ★★	614
Blackpool **Astoria** ★★★	615
Blackpool **Cameo** ★★★	616
Blackpool **Clovelly** ★★★★	617
Blackpool **Everglades** ★★★	617
Blackpool **Homecliffe** ★★★★	619
Blackpool **Kirkstall House** ★★★	620
Blackpool **Lyndene Guest House** ★★★	621
Blackpool **Novello** ★★★	621
Blackpool **The Shores** ★★★	624
Blackpool **Sunnyside** ★★★	625
Blackpool **Sussex** ★★★	625
Liverpool **Holmeleigh Guest House** ★★★	631
Preesall **Grassendale** ★★★	629

North East

Durham **The Avenue Inn** ★★	671
Seahouses **The Lookout Bunkhouse & Wigwams**	689

Establishments listed here have a detailed entry in this guide

771

Hostel and campus accommodation

The following establishments all have a detailed entry in this guide.

Hostels

Brighton & Hove South East	Kipps Brighton ★★ Hostel	249
Canterbury South East	Kipps Independent Hostel ★★★ Backpackers	218
Cholderton South West	Cholderton Stonehenge Youth Hostel ★★★★ Hostel	119
Faversham South East	Palace Farm Hostel ★★★ Hostel	222
Heddon-on-the-Wall North East	Houghton North Farm Visitor Accommodation ★★★★ Hostel	684
Liverpool North West	Cocoon @ International Inn ★★★ Hostel	631
Seahouses North East	The Lookout Bunkhouse & Wigwams Hostel	689
Sedbergh North West	Howgills Bunk Barn ★★★ Hostel	605

Campus accommodation

Cirencester South West	The Royal Agricultural College ★★★ Campus	96
Durham North East	Durham Castle ★ Campus	672
Exeter South West	University of Exeter ★★★★ Campus	64

So much to see, so little time - how do you choose?

Make the most of your leisure time; look for attractions with the Quality Marque.

VisitEngland operates the Enjoy England Visitor Attraction Quality Assurance Scheme.

Annual assessments by trained impartial assessors test all aspects of the customer experience so you can visit with confidence.

For ideas and inspiration visit
www.enjoyengland.com/attractions

Index by property name

Accommodation with a detailed entry in this guide is listed below.

0 — page

1 The Laurels *Henfield*	256
1 The Spain *Petersfield*	207
1 Woodchester Lodge *Stroud*	102
2 Cambridge Villas *Ambleside*	578
2 Main Road *Newton Aycliffe*	673
2 The Crofts *Corbridge*	680
3 Cambridge Villas *Ambleside*	578
3 Chalk Hill Road B&B *Norwich*	349
12 Christchurch Road *Winchester*	208
17 Northgate *Oakham*	412
23 Saint Marys guesthouse *York*	528
26 Glastonbury Road *Wells*	116
40 York Road *Tunbridge Wells*	229
59A Lee Road *London SE3*	302

A — page

Abberley Guest House *Torquay*	74
Abbots Court Farm *Tewkesbury*	103
Abbott Farm B&B *Fakenham*	346
Abigail's Guest House *Chesterfield*	405
Abinger Guest House *Leicester*	410
abode *St Ives*	52
The Acer Guest House *York*	527
Acorn Guest House *Solihull*	472
Addingham View B&B *Penrith*	602
Agincourt Lodge *Warwick*	471
Alabare House *Salisbury*	125
Alannah House *Berwick-upon-Tweed*	678
Albany Guest House *Bath*	104
The Alexander *Scarborough*	517
Allenbell *Cambridge*	331
The Allendale *Blackpool*	614
Alma Mater Guest House *Milford on Sea*	206
Alnwick Lodge *Alnwick*	675
Alrewas Hayes *Alrewas*	464
Altrincham Lodge *West Timperley*	631
Alverstone B&B *Sheringham*	352
Amble Guesthouse *Amble*	677
Amersham Hill Guest House *High Wycombe*	200
Anchor House *Falmouth*	41
Anchorage Bed and Breakfast *Amesbury*	118
Anchorage House *St Austell*	50
The Angel Inn *Wangford*	365
The Anvil Inn *Blandford Forum*	81
The Apothecary Guest House *Haworth*	507
Apple Tree Guest House *Bath*	104
Appletrees *Keswick*	593
Aqua, The *Portland*	86
Arabella *Blackpool*	615
Arbour House *Pershore*	475
Arch House Bed + Breakfast *Wells-next-the-Sea*	356
The Arches *Saltburn-by-the-Sea*	517
Arden Lodge *Oxford*	237
Ardensawah Farm *Porthcurno*	48
Argyll *Blackpool*	614
Arland House *Alderton*	118
Armeria *Portholo*	56
Arun View Inn *Littlehampton*	257
Arundel House *Cheddar*	109
Ascot House *York*	528
Ash Cottage *Maidstone, Kent*	224
Ash House *Wishaw*	471
Ash Lodge *Blackpool*	615
Ash Tree House *Keswick*	593
Ashberry *York*	529
Ashdale Guest House *Matlock Bath*	409
Ashfields *Chineham*	203
Ashleigh Guest House *Paignton*	67
Ashleigh House *Kingsbridge*	65
Ashley Guest House *Morecambe*	628
Astle Farm East Bed & Breakfast *Macclesfield*	576
Aston House *Stow-on-the-Wold*	101
Astoria *Blackpool*	615
At Peel Hey *West Kirby*	633
Athenaeum Lodge Guest House *Plymouth*	69
Austons Down *Stratford-upon-Avon*	469
Avalon Guest House *Leeds*	512
The Avenue Inn *Durham*	671
Avonlea *Stratford-upon-Avon*	469

B — page

B+B Weymouth *Weymouth*	89
b@r place *Hebden Bridge*	508
Bacchus B&B *Mevagissey*	45
Badgemore Park Golf Club *Badgemore*	232
Badgers Wood *Keswick*	594
The Balmoral *Gillingham*	222
Balmoral Guesthouse *Doncaster*	504
B&B @ Little Gables *Wallingford*	239
B&B in Wantage *Wantage*	239
Bank Farm *Henley-on-Thames*	234
The Bank House Hotel *Wakefield*	524
Bank House *Penrith*	602
Barbara's Bed & Breakfast *Windsor*	198
Barbican House *York*	529
Barclay House *Looe*	43
The Barn & Pinn Cottage Guest House *Bowd*	58
Barn House Bed & Breakfast *Dersingham*	346
Barn House Lodge *Pulborough*	258
Barnabas House Yelverton *Yelverton*	80
Barnsfield *Faversham*	221
Barry House *London W2*	305
Bartles Lodge *Elsing*	346
The Baskerville *Henley-on-Thames*	235
Bassett Wood Farm *Tissington*	409
The Battlesteads *Wark*	690
Bawdsey Manor *Bawdsey*	357
Bay Horse Inn *West Woodburn*	690
Bay Tree Broadstairs *Broadstairs*	218
Bays Farm *Stowmarket*	363
Beach House *Bude*	39
Beaufort Guesthouse *Weymouth*	89
Beaufort House *Sandown*	212
Beaumont Guest House *Seaton*	70
Beaumont House *Cheltenham*	93
Beaumont House *Windermere*	608
Beckford House Bed & Breakfast *Bath*	104
Becklands *Norwich*	350
Bede Guest House *Coventry*	471
Bedford Lodge *Shanklin*	213
Bedknobs *Bodmin*	38
Beech House *Kendal*	592
Beech Lodge *Alnmouth*	675
The Beeches Bed & Breakfast *Dawlish*	62
Beechwood B&B *Lewes*	256
Beera Farmhouse *Tavistock*	72
Belforte House *Sale*	630
The Bell at Willersey *Broadway*	472
The Bell Inn *Adderbury*	232
The Bell Inn *Frampton-on-Severn*	97
Belle Dene Guest House *Paignton*	68
Belmont House Bed & Breakfast *Wooler*	691
Belvoir B & B at Woodside Farm *Nottingham*	424
Benbow *Bosham (Chichester 3 miles)*	248
Benson's Guest House *Worthing*	263
Berkeleys of St James *Plymouth*	69
Berwick Guest House *Sidmouth*	71
Bewdley Hill Guest House *Kidderminster*	474
The Birkdale *Shanklin*	214
Bishops *York*	530
Bissick Old Mill *Truro*	54
Blackbrook House *Dorking*	241
Blacker Barton House *Ashburton*	57
The Blacksmiths Arms *Lewes*	257
Blair Lodge Guest House *Combe Martin*	60
Blakeney House & Restaurant *York*	530
Blands Cliff Lodge *Scarborough*	518
Blaxwell Farm *Salisbury*	125
Blenheim Mount Hotel *Blackpool*	616
Blossoms York *York*	531
Blue Barn Farm *Langwith*	423
Bluebell Lodge *Ledbury*	457
Bollington Hall Farm *Altrincham (3 miles)*	574
Bonehill Farm *Derby*	406
Bongate House *Appleby-in-Westmorland*	582

Establishments listed here have a detailed entry in this guide   773

Index by property name

B continued

Bonninglas Guest House *Meriden* 472
Borrowby Mill Bed & Breakfast *Thirsk* 523
Boundary Farm *Framlingham* 359
Bowfell Cottage *Windermere* 608
Bowl Inn *Ashford* 216
The Bowling Green *Plymouth* 70
Braedene Lodge *Paignton* 68
Braeside Bed & Breakfast *Leamington Spa* 468
Bramble Cottage B&B *Harome* 505
Bramble Cottage *Higham* 407
Brambles *Mumby* 416
Brathay Lodge *Ambleside* 578
Brayscroft House *Eastbourne* 251
Breckland B&B *Brundall* 344
Brecks Cottage B&B *Newark* 424
Brett Farm *Lavenham* 361
Briar Rigg House *Keswick* 594
Bridge Cottage Bed and Breakfast *Woodnewton* 423
Bridge Guest House *Cambridge* 331
Bridge House *Kendal* 592
Brioc *Brixham* 59
Broadacre *New Romney* 225
Broadgate Farm B & B *Garstang* ... 628
Brock Mill Farmhouse *Beal* 678
Brockenhurst *Westward Ho* 79
The Brocket Arms *Ayot St Lawrence* 342
Bromley Court *Ludlow* 461
Brompton Farmhouse *Shrewsbury* 463
Brook Barn *Letcombe Regis* 236
Brook House *Broadway* 472
Brook House *Windermere* 609
Brooklands Guest House *Penrith* 603
Brooklyn Bed & Breakfast *Staithes* 522
Brookside Villa B&B *Gilsland* 682
Broom House and Whites (Restaurant) *Egton Bridge* 505
Broomhill Bed and Breakfast *Oxford* 237
Broomhill *Dorking* 241
Broseley House *Broseley* 460
Brow Farm Bed & Breakfast *Dufton* 588
The Brown Horse Inn *Winster* 613
Bryn Clai *Ringmer* 259
Buckinghamshire Arms *Blickling* 344
Bucklawren Farm *Looe* 44
Buckle Yeat Guest House *Sawrey* ... 604
Bufo Villae Guest House *Walton-on-the-Naze* 341
The Bugle Inn *Bugle* 40
Bull Inn & Restaurant *Woolpit* 366
Bulls Head Inn *Bridgnorth* 459
Bulltown Farmhouse Bed & Breakfast *West Brabourne* 230
Bulmer Farm Bed & Breakfast *Holmbury St Mary* 244
Burcombe Manor *Salisbury* 126
Burleigh Head *Keswick* 594
Burton Row Farmhouse *East Brent* 111
The Bush Inn *Morwenstow* 46
Bush Nook Guest House *Gilsland* ... 589
Bushblades Farm *Beamish 3 miles* 670

Butlers Road Farm *Long Compton* 468
Butterchurn Guest House *Otterburn* 687
Butterfly Cottage B&B *Aldborough near Cromer* 343
Buttermoor Farm *Milton Damerel* ... 66
The Buttery *Oxford* 236
Byards Leap Bed & Breakfast *Cranwell* 413
Byards Leap Lodge *Cranwell* 414

C

Cambrai Lodge *Lechlade-on-Thames* 99
Cambridge Lodge *Huddersfield* 509
Cameo *Blackpool* 616
Canon Grange *Wells* 116
Canterbury Guest House *Sidmouth* 71
Caradoc Court *Ross-on-Wye* 458
Caraneal *Plymouth* 70
Carena House *Canterbury* 218
The Carleton House *Southport* 632
Carlton Court *Torquay* 74
Carr Edge Farm *Newbrough* 687
Carricks at Castle Farm *Swanton Morley* 354
Cary Arms Hotel & Restaurant *Torquay* 75
Castle Arms Inn *Bedale* 499
Castle Hill Farm House *Bakewell* 401
Castle House *Dover* 220
Castle View Guest House *Durham* 671
Castlemont *Aspatria* 582
Caterpillar Cottage *Colchester (5 miles)* 338
Cathedral View Town House *Durham* 671
Catton Old Hall *Norwich* 350
Cecil Guest House *Ludlow* 460
The Cedars *Grantham* 414
Chalice Hill House *Glastonbury* 112
Chaplin House *Woodhall Spa* 419
Charnwood Guest House *Keswick* 595
Chatsworth *Skegness* 417
Chelsea House *Falmouth* 41
Cheltenham Townhouse *Cheltenham* 94
Chequers Inn *Thompson* 355
Cheriton House *Huntingdon* 335
The Cherry Tree Guest House *Eastbourne* 252
Cherry Trees *Portsmouth* 207
Chester Brooklands *Chester* 575
Chestnuts Bed & Breakfast *Bourton-on-the-Water* 92
Chichester Guest House *Newquay* 46
The Chimes *Great Yarmouth* 347
Cholderton Stonehenge Youth Hostel *Cholderton* 119
Chudleigh *Clacton-on-Sea* 337
Church Farm *Kettleburgh* 361
Church Farm Monkton Farleigh *Bath* 105
Church Oast *Hernhill* 223
Chure House *Stow-on-the-Wold* 102
Churton Heath Farm Bed & Breakfast *Bruera* 575
Chy an Gwedhen *St Ives* 51

Chy Vista *Truro* 54
Cladda Bed & Breakfast and Self Catering Apartments *Dartmouth* 62
Clanville Manor B&B *Castle Cary* 109
Clare House *Swanage* 87
Clarence Hotel *Windsor* 199
Cleat House *Sheringham* 352
Cliff Lodge Guest House *Lake* 210
Cliveden Guest House *Paignton* 68
The Clock House *Weybridge* 245
Clock Tower Guest House *Exeter* 63
Cloudlands *Torquay* 74
Clovelly *Blackpool* 617
Clovelly House *Berwick-upon-Tweed* 678
Cober Hill *Cloughton* 502
Cocoon @ International Inn *Liverpool* 631
Cold Cotes *Harrogate* 505
College Farm Bed & Breakfast *Hintlesham* 360
Collina House *Tenterden* 229
Colton House *Rugeley* 467
Colveston Manor *Thetford* 354
Combe Ridge *Godalming* 242
Cononley Hall Bed & Breakfast *Skipton* 520
Coombe Court *Torquay* 75
Copper Beeches *Chewton Mendip* 110
Copper Kettle Restaurant & Guest House *Kirkby Lonsdale* 599
Copper's End Guest House *Lichfield* 466
The Coppice *King's Lynn* 349
Copyhold Hollow Bed & Breakfast *Haywards Heath* 255
Corner Cottage *Alderton* 91
Corner Meadow *Swanage* 88
Cornerways Guest House *Penzance* 47
Cornish Arms *Port Isaac* 48
The Cornmill *Kirkbymoorside* 511
Corran Farm *Mevagissey* 45
Corsham Field Farmhouse *Stow-on-the-Wold* 102
Cote How Organic Guest House *Rydal* 604
Cotswold House *Oxford* 238
The Cottage *Stansted* 340
Cotteswold House *Bibury* 92
Cotton Farm *Chester* 575
Court Croft *Hebden* 508
Cowscot House *Kirkby Malzeard* 511
Craigburn Farmhouse *Penton* 603
Craigleith Lodge *Chester* 576
Creeting House *Creeting St Mary* 358
Cremona B&B *Bournemouth* 82
Crescent House *Southport* 632
Crescent Lodge Guest House *Ripon* 515
Cressbrook Hall *Cressbrook* 406
Crete Down *Folkestone (2 miles)* ... 222
Crich Lane Farm *Wessington* 409
Cricketers, The *Clavering* 337
Crimdon Dene *Torquay* 76
Crockwell Farm *Eydon* 421
The Croft *Bridgnorth* 459
Croft House *Heads Nook* 590
Cross Close House B&B *Lostwithiel* 44
The Cross Keys *Thixendale* 524

Index by property name

C continued — page

Crosshill House Bed & Breakfast *Laxton* 423
Crosslands Farm *Hawkshead* 589
The Crown *Colne* 627
Crown Lodge *Torquay* 76
Culm Vale Country House *Exeter* 63
Cumberland Inn *Alston* 577
Cumbria House *York* 529
Curlews *Manningtree* 339
Curzon Lodge & Stable Cottages *York* 531

D — page

Daffodil *Hesket Newmarket* 591
The Dairy Barns *Hickling* 347
Dairy Farm *Kettering* 421
Dairy Guest House *York* 531
Dalswinton House *St Mawgan* 53
The Dark Barn *Rudford* 100
Dean Court *Ashford (5 miles)* 216
Deerfell *Haslemere* 243
Degembris Farmhouse *Newquay* 46
DeGreys *Ludlow* 461
The Dene *Triangle (Sowerby Bridge)* 524
Denton House *Hesket Newmarket* 592
Dervaig Guest House *Berwick-upon-Tweed* 679
Deverill End *Warminster* 127
Devon House *Robin Hoods Bay* 516
Dial House B&B *Downham Market* 346
Dial House *Oakham* 412
Dippers *Bridport - West Dorset* 84
The Dorset *Lewes* 257
Dove Cottage *Drax* 504
Dove House B&B *Ashbourne (1.25 miles)* 465
Dover *London SW1* 304
The Dragonfly *Blackpool* 617
Dresden House *Teignmouth* 73
Druid House *Christchurch* 84
Dundas Arms *Kintbury* 197
Dunster Farm *Bridport (4 miles)* 83
Durham Castle *Durham* 672
Durlock Lodge *Minster* 225

E — page

Earlston House *Paignton* 69
Easedale House *Keswick* 595
East Horton House *Wooler* 691
East Mount House *Barrow-in-Furness* 583
East View Guest House *Carlisle* 586
Eastbourne Reymar *Eastbourne* 252
Eastgate Guest House *Beverley* 500
Eastmere House B&B *Arundel* 246
Eben-Ezer *Sibton* 362
Edmar Lodge *Norwich* 350
Eedes Cottage *Petworth* 258
Elbury House Bed & Breakfast *Bradford-on-Avon* 119
Elder Grove *Ambleside* 579
Eleven Westgate *Pickering* 514
Elim Lodge *Windermere* 609
Elizabeth House *Bracknell* 196
Ellinbrook House *Hunstanton* 348
Elm House *Pooley Bridge* 604
Elmfield House *Bedale* 499
Elvey Farm *Pluckley* 226
The Embankment *Bedford* 330
Engleton Bed & Breakfast *Falmouth* 41
English Rose *Bexhill-on-Sea* 246
Eskdale Lodge *Sale* 630
Everglades *Blackpool* 617

F — page

Fair Rigg *Windermere* 610
Fairacres *Rye* 260
Fairfield House & Gardens *Windermere* 609
Fairholm *East Ord* 682
Fairlea Bed & Breakfast *Faversham* 221
Fairway *Blackpool* 618
Farnham Farm House *Blandford Forum* 81
Fellcroft *Corbridge* 681
Fenham Farm Coastal Bed & Breakfast *Berwick-upon-Tweed* 679
Fenton House *Woking* 245
The Ferguson Fawsitt Arms *Walkington* 525
Fern Cottage Bed & Breakfast *Bath* 91
Fern Cottage *Ryde* 211
Fern Royd *Blackpool* 618
Ferndale Lodge *Ambleside* 579
Fernlea Cottage Bed & Breakfast *Tattenhall* 577
The Fernside *Sandown* 212
Ferrydale Farm *Buxton* 404
Ferry House Inn *Sheerness* 228
The Feversham Arms Inn *Kirkbymoorside* 512
Fields Farm *Alton* 465
Fifty One *Cambridge* 332
Fir Trees *Windermere* 610
The Firs *Bath* 105
Firs Guesthouse *Runswick Bay* 516
Firs Guesthouse *West Bridgford* 424
Firwood Country Bed and Breakfast *Wooler* 691
Fish Inn *Buttermere* 586
Five Bells *Wrentham* 367
Fleurie House *Torquay* 77
Flindor Cottage *Framlingham (7 miles)* 359
Folly Farm Cottage *Stratford-upon-Avon* 470
Fords Farm *Ewelme* 234
The Forge House *Great Longstone* 406
Forge House *Great Missenden* 200
Fountain Inn *Parkend* 100
The Fountaindale Skegness *Skegness* 417
The Four Horseshoes *Thornham Magna* 364
Four Wynds Guest House *Haltwhistle* 683
Fox & Hounds Inn *Danby* 504
Freewaters *Newport (3 miles)* 211
Frome Corner *Wareham* 89

G — page

Gabber Farm *Plymouth* 70
Gables *Devizes* 121
Gables Farm *Wingfield* 366
The Gables Guest House *St Austell* 50
Gallery 53 *Hastings* 254
Garbutt Farm *Thirsk* 523
Garden Cottage *Rodmell* 259
Gate Farm *Castle Howard* 501
George Bell House *Chichester* 250
George Hotel *Braunton* 58
Giffard House *Winchester* 208
Glebe Farm Bed & Breakfast *Byfield* 420
The Glen *Kendal* 593
Glendale Mews *Haltwhistle* 683
Glendevon Guest House *Ramsgate* 226
Gleneagles *Blackpool* 619
Glengarth Guest House *Leeds* 513
Glenhill Guest House *Worthing* 263
Globe Inn *Frogmore* 65
Golden Lion House *Ashburton* 57
Goldenhayes *New Forest – Brockenhurst* 206
Goonearl Cottage *Redruth* 49
Gorse Meadow Guest House *Lymington* 205
Graden *Ilminster* 113
Graingers Guest Accommodation *Weymouth* 90
The Grange *Exeter* 63
Grange Fell *Earby* 628
The Grange *Gainsborough (4 miles)* 414
Grange Lodge Guest House *York* ... 532
Grassendale *Preesall* 629
Grayingham Lodge *Northorpe* 416
Great Field Farm B&B *Stelling Minnis* 228
Great Oaks *Royal Tunbridge Wells* 226
Great Sloncombe Farm *Moretonhampstead* 66
Great Wooston Farm *Moretonhampstead* 66
Green Dragon *Market Lavington* ... 123
Greenacre *Swanley* 229
Greenacres *Beaworthy* 58
Greenacres Country Guesthouse *Lindale* 601
Greenacres Farmhouse *Long Stratton* 349
Greenbank Farmhouse *Abbeystead* 614
Greenham Hall *Wellington* 115
Greensleeves *Cirencester* 95
Greycroft *Alnwick* 676
Greyhound Hotel *Shap* 605
Griffin Inn *Bath* 105
Grindon Cartshed *Haydon Bridge* ... 684
Grove House Hotel *Woodbridge* 366
Grove House *Maidstone* 224
Guiting Guest House *Guiting Power* 98

H — page

The Hadrian *Wall* 690
Haldon Priors *Torquay* 77
Hall Barns B&B *Hexham* 684
Hall Meadows *Haltwhistle* 683
Hall Paddock *Norwich* 351
Hampton Manor *Callington* 40
The Hand & Flowers *Marlow* 201
Hansard House *Budleigh Salterton* 60

Establishments listed here have a detailed entry in this guide 775

Index by property name

H continued

Ha'penny House *Lymington* 205
Harbour Guest House *Amble* 677
Hardicot Guest House *Walmer* 230
Harefield Cottage *Bude* 39
Harmony House Malvern
  Malvern 474
Harptree Court *East Harptree* 112
Harrabeer Country House
  Yelverton 80
Harvington House *Keswick* 595
Hawcliffe House *Keswick* 596
Hawkenbury Farm Bed & Breakfast
  Royal Tunbridge Wells 227
Hawkhill Farmhouse *Alnwick* 676
The Hawthornes *Pickering* 514
Hay Farm House *Cornhill-on-
  Tweed* 681
The Hayes *Corbridge* 681
Haygarth *Alresford* 201
Hayleys Corner *Bognor Regis* 247
Hazelmere House *Lostwithiel* 45
The Hazelwood *York* 532
Heath Hall Farm *Godalming* 242
Heatherbank *Windermere* 610
Heatherdene B&B *Dibden Purlieu* ... 204
Heatherleigh Guest House
  Shanklin 214
Heathers Guest House *London
  SE6* 303
Hedgefield House *Ryton* 692
The Hermitage *Bath* 106
The Hermitage *Crayke* 503
Heron Cottage *Biddenden* 217
Heworth Court B&B and Lamplight
  Restaurant *York* 533
Hidelow House *Malvern* 475
High Belthorpe *Bishop Wilton* 500
High Green Farm *Kirkby
  Lonsdale* 600
High House Farm *Framlingham* 359
High Muffles *Stape* 522
High Street Farmhouse *Long
  Melford* 362
Highbury Guest House
  Loughborough 411
Highcroft Guest House *Coventry* 471
Higher Farm Bed & Breakfast
  Barton 574
Higher Hendham House
  Woodleigh 79
Higher Manaton *Callington* 41
Higher Trevorrick Country House
  St Issey 51
Highland Court Lodge *St Austell* 50
Highview Country House
  Spennymoor 674
The Hill on the Wall *Gilsland* 589
Hillborough House *Milton-under-
  Wychwood* 236
Hobart Hall Guest House
  Richmond 306
Holland House *Worcester* 476
The Hollow Bottom *Guiting
  Power* 98
Holly House *Bracknell* 197
Holly House *Chelwood Gate* 249
Holly Lodge *Windermere* 610
Holm Oaks *Holt* 348
Holme House *Hebden Bridge* 508
Holmeleigh Guest House
  Liverpool 631

Holmhead Guest House
  Greenhead 682
Holmside House *Blackpool* 619
Home Barn *Preston* 629
Home Farm B&B *Boscastle* 39
Home From Home *Cambridge* 332
Homecliffe *Blackpool* 619
Hononton Cottage *Brenchley* 217
Hordley Hall *Ellesmere (3 miles)* 460
Hornbeams *Canterbury* 218
Hornsbury Mill *Chard* 109
Horse & Farrier Inn *Threlkeld* 606
Horse & Groom *East Ashling
  (Chichester 3 miles)* 251
Horseshoe Cottage Farm
  Cropston 410
Hotel Cimon *Torquay* 77
Houghton North Farm Visitor
  Accommodation *Heddon-on-the-
  Wall* 684
Housley Cottage *Bakewell* 402
Howdale *Scarborough* 518
Howgills Bunk Barn *Sedbergh* 605
Hunters Hall *Dereham* 345
Huntly's Farmhouse *Manningford
  Abbots* 123
Huntsmill Farm B&B *Buckingham* ... 199
Hurst Green Bed and Breakfast
  Brightlingsea 336
Hussar *Margate* 225
Hyde Mill *East Hyde* 331

I

Iffin Farmhouse *Canterbury* 219
Ingledene Guest House
  Bournemouth 82
Ingram House *Ingram* 685
The Inn at Fossebridge
  Fossebridge 97
The Inn at Whitewell *Whitewell* 629
Islington Farm *Wells* 116
Ivar Cottage Summer House
  Bembridge 209
Ivy Cottage *Richmond* 306
The Ivy House *Cirencester* 95

J

Jamaica Inn *Bolventor* 38
Jays Lodge *Orsett* 339
Jeake's House *Rye* 260
Jubilee Guest House *Bognor
  Regis* 247

K

Kandara Guest House *London
  N1* 302
Katerina's Guest House *Rothbury* ... 688
The Keelman's Lodge *Newcastle
  upon Tyne* 691
Kelling House *Barkston* 413
Kia-ora *Chichester* 250
Kilburn Guest House *Bridlington* 501
Kilham Hall Country House
  Kilham 510
Killerby Cottage Farm
  Scarborough 518
Kiln Farm Bed & Breakfast *Lower
  Bourne* 244
Kiln Farm Guest House *Elmswell* ... 358
The Kimberley *Blackpool* 620

The King William IV, Country Inn &
  Restaurant *Hunstanton* 348
Kingfisher Bed & Breakfast *Hanley
  Swan* 474
The Kings Arms *Monkton
  Farleigh* 124
The Kings Head at Newton Under
  Roseberry *Great Ayton* 505
Kings Langley *Bournemouth* 83
Kingscroft Guest House *Buxton* 404
Kingsway Park Guest
  Accommodation *London W2* 305
Kingsway *Seahouses* 688
Kington *Morpeth* 686
Kipps Brighton *Brighton & Hove* 249
Kipps Independent Hostel
  Canterbury 218
Kirkstall House *Blackpool* 620
Kirkstead Old Mill Cottage
  Woodhall Spa 419
Knotts Mill Country Lodge
  Ullswater 607
Knowles Barn *Colchester* 337

L

La Fosse at Cranborne
  Cranborne 85
The Labouring Man *Pulborough* 258
Ladderstile Retreat *North Rode* 576
The Lake *Bonchurch* 209
Lakenham Guest House *Buxton* 404
Lakeside Lodge Golf Centre
  Pidley 336
The Lamb Inn *Crediton* 61
Lamp Post Villa *Bath* 106
Lane Head Farm Country Guest
  House *Keswick (7.5 miles)* 599
Langdale View Guest House
  Windermere 611
Langleigh House *Carlisle* 586
Langtrys *Blackpool* 620
Lansdowne Guest House *Brighton
  & Hove* 249
Lantern House *Cambridge* 332
Larkrise Cottage *Stratford-upon-
  Avon* 469
Laskill Grange *Helmsley* 509
Lattice Lodge Guest House
  Ipswich 360
Laurel Bank B&B *Keswick* 596
Laurel Bank *Pickering* 515
Laurel Cottage *Chelwood Gate,
  East Grinstead* 250
Laurel House *Culgaith* 588
The Lavender Patch *Derby* 406
Lavenham Old Rectory
  Lavenham 361
The Lawn Guest House *Gatwick* 253
Lill Stugan *Lewes* 257
The Limes *Woodhall Spa* 419
Limes *York* 532
Lincoln House - Central *London
  W1* 304
Lindisfarne Guest House *Bath* 106
Lindisfarne Guest House
  Windermere 611
Lindon House *Airton* 498
Lingwood Lodge *Windermere* 611
Little Abbey Farm *Pentney* 352
Little Garth Bed & Breakfast
  Brede 248
Little Holtby *Leeming Bar* 513
Little Orchard *Glastonbury* 113

Index by property name

L continued

Little Trevellas Farm *St Agnes* 49
Littlefield *Keswick* 596
Littlefield Manor *Guildford* 243
Littletown Farm *Keswick (5 miles)* 599
Locking Head Farm *Weston-Super-Mare* 117
Locksley, Bed & Breakfast *Stocksfield* 689
Lodge Farmhouse Bed & Breakfast *Broad Chalke* 119
Longridge Towers School *Berwick-upon-Tweed* 679
The Lookout Bunkhouse & Wigwams *Seahouses* 689
Loughbrow House *Hexham* 685
Lovesome Hill Farm *Northallerton* 514
Low Hall Farm *Broughton in Furness* 585
Low Hedgeley Farm *Powburn* 688
Low Osgoodby Grange *Osgoodby*................................. 514
Lowe Farm B&B *Pembridge*............. 458
Lower Farmhouse Bed & Breakfast *Lottisham* 114
Lower House *Leintwardine*.............. 457
Lowerfield Farm *Broadway* 473
Lyde Hill Farmhouse *Gillingham* 86
Lynbar Guesthouse *Blackpool* 620
Lyndene Guest House *Blackpool* 621
Lypiatt House *Cheltenham*............. 94
Lyth Hill House *Lyth Bank* 462

M

Madison House *Southampton* 207
Magnolia House *Canterbury*............ 219
Maison Dieu Guest House *Dover*.... 221
Mallards *Basingstoke* 202
Mallards *Dunmow*......................... 338
Mallondene *Rustington*.................. 259
Manor Barn House *Norwich* 351
Manor Court Farm Bed & Breakfast *Royal Tunbridge Wells* 227
Manor Farm B&B *Collingbourne Kingston*................................. 120
Manor Farm Barn B&B *Bampton* 232
Manor Farm *Chipping Campden*..... 94
Manor Farm *Compton Valence*....... 85
Manor Farm House *Newbury* 197
Manor Farm *Salisbury* 126
Manor Hill House Guest House *Bromsgrove* 473
Manor House Cottage *South Kilvington*................................. 521
The Manor House *York* 533
Mantle B&B *Wellington*.................. 116
Marble Arch Inn *London W1*........... 305
Marlborough House *Berwick-upon-Tweed*... 680
Marlborough House Guest House *Bath*... 106
Marsh Farm *Hemel Hempstead*....... 343
Marsh House *Shillingford*............... 239
Marsham Arms Inn *Norwich* 351
Marshwood Farm B&B *Dinton*........ 122
Martineau Guest House *Tynemouth*................................. 692
Masons Arms Country Inn *Alnwick*................................... 677
May Cottage *Andover* 202

May Cottage B&B *Bowness-on-Windermere*............................. 584
Maycroft Cottage *Hanthorpe*.......... 415
Mayfield *Marlborough* 124
Maypole Inn *Settle*........................ 520
Meadow Hill Guest House *Berwick-upon-Tweed*............................. 680
The Meadow House B&B *Newmarket (4 miles)*.................... 335
Meadow View Guest House *Wighton*................................... 356
Meadowbank *Ambleside*................. 579
Meare Manor *Glastonbury* 113
Medlars *Yarmouth* 216
Mellstock House *Combe Martin*...... 61
Melrose House *London SE20*.......... 303
Membland Guest House *Bath* 107
Merivon Guest House *Great Yarmouth*................................. 347
Merton Lodge *Stonehouse*............. 101
Middle Flass Lodge *Bolton-by-Bowland* 626
The Middleham *Whitby*................. 526
The Mill House *Telford*.................. 463
Mill House *Tintagel*...................... 53
Mill Lane Lodge *Farnham* 242
Millstream Cottage *Dunster* 111
Milton Lodge Guest House *Weston-super-Mare*..................... 117
The Miners Arms *Alston* 578
Mistral *Wye* 231
Mitchell's of Chester Guest House *Chester* 576
Moat Hill Farm B&B *Westhorpe* 365
Moddershall Oaks Spa Restaurant Suites *Moddershall*..................... 466
Molehills *Bladbean*....................... 217
The Montpelier *Sandown* 212
The Moorings B&B *Southend-on-Sea*.. 340
Moorsands *Croyde* 61
Moresby Hall *Whitehaven*.............. 608
Mosedale End Farm *Mosedale* 601
Mottistone Manor Farmhouse *Brighstone*................................ 209
Mount Edgcombe *Torquay*............ 78
Mount Farm Bed & Breakfast *Blackford*.................................. 584
Mowbray Court *London SW5* 304
Muncaster Coachman's Quarters *Muncaster* 602
Murcott Mill *Long Buckby*.............. 422
The Muswell Hill *London N10*........ 302

N

The Nags Head *Chichester*............. 251
Neatham Barn Self Catering & Bed & Breakfast *Alton* 201
New Butts Farm *Ingleton*............... 509
New Hall Bank *Windermere* 612
New Inn *Clapham*........................ 502
The New Inn hotel *Lechlade-on-Thames*................................... 99
The New Inn *Tresco* 56
Newhaven Lodge *Newhaven* 258
Newlands Hall *Frosterley* 673
Newton Grange *Skipton* 521
Newton House Guest House B&B *Oxford* *Oxford* 238
Nightless Copse *Capel* 240
Nineveh Farm *Chipping Campden*................................. 94

North View Guest House *Honington*................................. 360
Norville House *Blackpool*............... 621
Novello *Blackpool* 621
number 17 *Norwich* 352
Number One St Luke's *Blackpool* ... 622
Nursery Cottage *East Tytherley*...... 204
The Nurse's Cottage Restaurant with Rooms *Lymington* 206

O

Oak *Charing*................................. 220
Oakdene Guest House *Uxbridge*..... 307
Oakfold House *Windermere* 612
Oaklands Edwardian Guest House *Weymouth*................................ 90
Oaklands Guest House *Coniston* 587
Oaklands *Rye* 261
Oakside Farm Bungalow *Launceston*................................ 42
Odfellows Wine Bar *Shifnal* 462
The Old Bakery *Henley-on-Thames*................................... 200
Old Borough Arms *Rye* 259
The Old Coach House *Blackpool* 621
The Old Crown Inn *Uley*................ 104
Old Farm *Moreton-in-Marsh*........... 99
The Old Farmhouse *Newbury*......... 198
Old Farmhouse *Westerham*............ 230
The Old Forge Bed & Breakfast *Pickering (4 miles)* 515
The Old Forge *Haywards Heath* 256
The Old Forge *Totnes* 79
Old Ginn House Inn *Workington* 613
Old Guadaloupe B&B *Eye Kettleby*................................... 410
Old Hall Farm *South Walsham* 353
Old Harbour View *Weymouth* 91
The Old Kennels *Dunkeswell*.......... 63
Old Lodge Malton *Malton* 513
The Old Manse Barn *Bury St Edmunds (6 miles)*....................... 358
The Old Mill Hotel & Restaurant *Langtoft*................................... 512
Old Orleton Inn *Telford* 464
The Old Pump House *Aylsham* 343
The Old Rectory Bed & Breakfast *Salisbury*.................................. 126
Old Rectory Guest House *Chesterfield*................................ 405
The Old School B&B *Ely* 334
Old School *Friston* 360
The Old School *Much Birch* 457
The Old School *Newton-on-The-Moor* 687
The Old Ship *London E8* 301
The Old Stables *Twickenham*......... 307
The Old Star *West Witton* 525
Old Station House *Hawes*.............. 506
The Old Vicarage at Toftly View *Pickering* 515
The Old Vicarage Bed & Breakfast *Lincoln*.................................... 415
Old White Lion Hotel *Haworth*....... 507
The Old Wood *Henley-on-Thames*................................... 234
Oliver Twist Country Inn *Guyhirn* ... 335
onesixtwo *London SE3* 303
Orchard Barn *Langport*................. 114
Orchard Cottage *Coniston* 587
Orchard Dene Cottage *Henley-on-Thames*................................... 235
The Orchards *Freshwater*.............. 210

Establishments listed here have a detailed entry in this guide

777

Index by property name

O continued — page

Ormerod *Burnley* 626
Osterley Lodge *Lake* 211
Ouse Bridge House
   Bassenthwaite 584
Overcombe House *Yelverton* 81

P — page

Palace Farm Hostel *Faversham* 222
Palm Court *York* 534
Park House Guest House
   Ambleside 580
Park House *Oxford* 238
Park View *Exeter* 64
Parkfield Guest House *Keswick* 597
Parkhouse Motel *Cholderton* 120
The Parkway *Shanklin* 214
The Parkwood Inn *Stockton-on-Tees* 674
Parr Hall Farm *Chorley* 627
Peak District Spa *Ashbourne* 400
Pear Tree Farm Guest House *Lea Bridge* 408
Pentillie Castle & Estate *St Mellion* 53
The Pheasant Inn (by Kielder Water) *Kielder Water* 686
Pickwick's Guest House *Oxford* 239
Pinetrees *Beccles* 357
Pioneer House *Bamford* 402
The Plough Inn *Ford* 96
Poplar Hall *Southwold* 363
Poppy Cottage Guest House *Skipton* 521
Post Cottage *Ridlington* 413
Pretoria Villa *Stroud* 103
Primrose Cottage *Launceston* 43
The Priory *Brize Norton* 233
The Priory Inn, Scorton *Scorton* ... 629
Prospect Villa Guest House *Whitby* 526
Pry House Farm B&B *Hawes* 506
Puddle Lane *Malvern* 475
Pulteney House *Bath* 107
Punchbowl Inn *Edmundbyers* 673

Q — page

Quarry Side *Banks* 583
The Queen Victoria *Snettisham* 353
Quilt & Croissants *Stratford-upon-Avon* 470

R — page

Racing Sea Horses *East Wittering* ... 253
The Raffles Guest Accommodation *Blackpool* 622
The Railway Tavern *London E15* 301
Rainworth House *Oakley Green* 198
Rakeway House Farm B&B *Cheadle* 465
Real McCoy Guest House *Liverpool* 631
Red Bank *Ambleside* 579
The Red Cow *Richmond* 306
The Red Lion *Cricklade* 121
Redgates Farmhouse *Saffron Walden* 339
Redoak Bed and Breakfast *Morcott* 411
Regis Guest House *Wantage* 240
Reighamsyde *Alnwick* 676
Rencliffe *Blackpool* 623
The Resting Post *Heytesbury* 123
The Retreat *Shaftesbury* 86
Rhydspence Inn *Hay-on-Wye* 456
Rickyard Cottage *Great Missenden* 200
Rio Rita *Blackpool* 623
Riverside House *Cirencester* 95
Riverside Lodge *Earls Colne* 338
Rob Roy *Berwick-upon-Tweed* 680
The Rob Roy Guest House *Folkestone* 222
Robyn's Guest House *Scarborough* 518
Rock Farm *Doncaster* 504
Rock House B&B *South Petherton* ... 115
Rookery Farm *Wortham* 367
Rooks Nest Farm *Stafford* 467
rooms @ bank house farm *The Green* 606
Rooms36 *Keswick* 597
Rose & Crown *Stoke St Gregory* 115
Rose Bank Guest House *Porlock* 114
Rose House *Westcliff-on-Sea* 341
Rosebud Cottage Guest House *Haworth* 506
Roselea *Blackpool* 623
Rosemundy Cottage *Devizes* 122
Rothay Garth *Ambleside* 580
Rothay House *Ambleside* 580
Roundhouse Barn B&B Holidays *St Just-in-Roseland* 52
Rowan Tree *Clitheroe* 627
The Royal Agricultural College *Cirencester* 96
Royal Clarence Hotel *Burnham-on-Sea* 108
Royal Hotel *Dockray* 588
Runswick Bay *Runswick Bay* 516
Rydon Farm *Exeter* 64

S — page

The Saddle Bed and Breakfast *Alnmouth* 674
Saint Chad's College *Durham* 671
Saint Columba's House *Woking* 245
Salcombe Close House *Sidmouth* ... 71
Sandford Promenade *Blackpool* 624
The Sandhill *Sandown* 213
Sandhurst *Herstmonceux* 256
Sandon Guest House *Keswick* 597
Sandy Brook Farm *Southport* 632
Scarrow Hill Guest House *Brampton* 585
Scotland Lodge Farm *Winterbourne Stoke* 127
Sea Crest *Morecambe* 628
Seahaven *Herne Bay* 223
Seahorses *Freshwater* 210
Seaspray Bed and Breakfast *Hastings* 254
Selwood Lodge *Bognor Regis* 247
Seven Acres House *Coltishall* 345
Seven Bed & Breakfast *Brighstone* 209
Seven Stars Inn *Durham* 672
Shaftoe's Guest House *Haydon Bridge* 684
The Shave Cross Inn *Shave Cross* ... 87
Shell Bay Cottage *Studland* 87
Shepherds Hall *Woodstock* 240
Sherwood Guest House *Wallasey* ... 632
Shirley Hall *Ashbourne* 401
The Shores *Blackpool* 624
Shrublands Farm Guesthouse *Cromer* 345
Sibton White Horse Inn *Sibton* 362
Silver Ridge *Tansley* 409
The Silverdale *Seaford* 262
Sinai House *Lynton* 65
Slapton Manor Bed & Breakfast *Towcester* 422
Slipway *Port Isaac* 48
Smallwood House *Ambleside* 581
Sneaton Castle Centre *Whitby* 527
Sonnier *Illogan* 42
South Beach Seafront *Blackpool* 624
South Moor Farm *Dalby* 503
South View Farm *Exeter* 64
Southampton Guest House *Cambridge* 333
Southbourne Guest House *Gatwick* 254
The Southview *Blackpool* 624
Spanhoe Lodge *Uppingham* 422
The Spinney Country Guesthouse *Barnstaple* 57
Springwells *Steyning* 262
St Crispin Inn *Worth* 231
St Edmunds Guesthouse *Bury St Edmunds* 358
St Felix *Walsingham* 355
St John's College *Durham* 672
St John's Lodge *Windermere* 612
St Margarets Guest House *Sutton* 307
Stafford House Guest House *Penrith* 603
Stay Inn Hotel *Manchester* 630
Steep Meadow *Staunton* 101
Stockghyll Cottage *Windermere* 613
Stoke Gabriel Lodgings *Stoke Gabriel* 72
Stoke House *Guildford* 243
Stone Cottage *Ashbourne* 401
Stone Croft *Barlborough* 403
Stoneleigh *Skegness* 417
Storrs Gate House *Bowness-on-Windermere* 585
Strand House *Rye* 261
String of Horses Inn *Heads Nook* ... 591
Stylehurst Farm *Dorking* 241
The Sun, Coniston *Coniston* 587
Sunholme Guest House *Whitley Bay* 693
Sunnymeade Country Hotel *West Down* 79
Sunnyside *Blackpool* 625
Sunnyside Farm Bed & Breakfast *Ruskington* 416
Surf Haven Guest House *Bude* 40
Surfside Stop Guest House *Newquay* 47
Sussex *Blackpool* 625
Swaledale Watch *Caldbeck* 586
Swan House *Hastings* 255
Swiss Cottage *Shanklin* 215
Swiss Court Guest House *Keswick* 598
Swiss House *Castleton* 405
Sylvern House *Scarborough* 519

T — page

Tanamera *Aylesbury* 199
Tantallon House *Gilsland* 682

Index by property name

T continued

	page
Tarn House Country Inn *Stirton*	523
Taunton House *Swanage*	88
Tee-Side *Bude*	40
Thatched Farm Bed & Breakfast *Waldringfield*	364
The Thoresby *Scarborough*	519
Thornton Hunt Inn *Thornton Curtis*	418
Thorpe Lodge Farm B&B *Ellington Thorpe*	334
Three Bears Cottage *Stowmarket*	364
The Three Compasses *Charminster*	84
Three Hills *Cambridge (12 miles)*	334
Three Tuns Hotel *Ashwell*	342
Threeways House *Daventry*	421
Tidal Court Guest House *West Looe*	55
Tollgate Farm B&B *Sissinghurst*	228
Tor Cottage *Tavistock*	73
Tor Bed & Breakfast *Truro*	54
The Town & Country Lodge *Bristol*	93
Town End Farm *Chipping*	626
Town Pasture Farm *Thirsk*	524
Townhouse Rooms *Truro*	55
Travellers Rest *Bradwell*	403
Travellers Rest *Hexham*	685
Travelrest Solent Gateway *Fareham*	204
Treboeth Guest House *St Mary's*	56
Tredowr Barton *St Minver / Polzeath*	53
Tregilgas Farm *Mevagissey*	46
Tregolls Farm B&B *Wadebridge (4 miles)*	55
Trenderway Farm *Looe*	44
Trenerry House Bed and Breakfast *Southampton*	208
Trenona Farm B&B *Ruan High Lanes*	49
Trevone Bed & Breakfast *Bourton-on-the-Water*	92
Trinity Town House *Colchester*	338
The Troutbeck Inn *Troutbeck*	607
Trudy's Guesthouse *Darlington*	670
Tudor Arms Lodge and Freehouse *Slimbridge*	100
Tudor Cottage *Cambridge*	333
Twenty Seven B&B and Self Catering Cottage *Kielder*	686
Twin Oaks Guest House *Cadnam*	203
Tyburn Guest House *York*	534

U

	page
Ullathorns Farm *Kirkby Lonsdale*	600

Underleigh House *Hope*	407
University of Exeter *Exeter*	64

V

	page
The Valentine *Blackpool*	625
Valentine Studio *South Creake*	353
Valley House *Dartmouth*	62
Venn Farm *Brixton*	59
Verdon Guest House *Stoke-on-Trent*	468
Victoria Lodge *Shanklin*	215
Victoria Park Lodge *Leamington Spa*	468
The Victorian Town House *Durham*	673
The Victory at Mersea *West Mersea*	341
Villa Marina *Torquay*	78
The Village Inn *Witchford*	336
Village Limits Country Pub, Restaurant & Motel *Woodhall Spa*	420
Vine Cottage Bed & Breakfast *Rowde*	124
The Vines *Black Bourton*	233

W

	page
Waiten Hill Farm *Fairford*	96
Waldernheath Country House *Amberstone*	246
Wall Hill Farm Guest House *Northwich*	577
Walton Villa *Bath*	108
Wateredge Inn *Ambleside*	581
Waterside *Cheddar*	110
Wayside Cottage *Burley*	202
Wealden Hall *Detling*	220
The Weatherdene *Great Yarmouth*	347
Week Farm *Okehampton*	67
Welbeck Cottage Bed and Breakfast *Lincoln*	415
The Well *Bridport*	83
Wentworth Guest House *Whitby*	527
West View Bed & Breakfast *South Cockerington*	418
West View Guest House *Keswick*	598
The Wheatsheaf Inn *Haslemere*	244
The Wheatsheaf *Swineshead*	418
Whitburn Guest House *Torquay*	78
The White Bear Hotel *Masham*	513
The White Guest House *Bath*	108
The White Hart *Martock*	114
White Heron *Polzeath*	47
The White Horse Inn *Clun*	460
White Horses Felpham *Bognor Regis*	248

The White House Guest Rooms *Southville*	100
The White House *Marlborough*	123
White House *Stansted*	340
Whitehall Farm *Burnham Thorpe*	344
The Whiteley *Scarborough*	519
Wick House *Stogumber*	115
Willow Farm *Wainfleet*	418
Windy Arbour *Alton*	464
Witch Hazel *Wymondham*	357
Withyland Heights *Kilcot*	456
The Wolds Retreat *Kilnwick Percy*	510
Wondai B&B *Leicester*	411
Woodbine B&B *Hope*	408
Woodhill Bed and Breakfast *Cottingham*	503
Woodmans Farm *Stratton Strawless*	353
Woodside Bed & Breakfast *Staplecross*	262
Woodside Guest House *Teignmouth*	73
Woodside *Keswick*	598
Woodstock Guest House *Croydon*	305
Woodthorpe Guest House *Skegness*	417
Wordsworths Guest House *Ambleside*	582
Worth House *Cambridge*	333
Wroxham Park Lodge Guest House *Wroxham*	356
Wymering Guest House *Penzance*	47
Wyndale Guest House *Stafford*	467

Y

	page
Yellowham Farm *Dorchester*	85
Yew House Bed & Breakfast *Crowborough*	251
Yew Tree Farm *Cheddar*	110
Yew Tree House *Brean*	108
Yew Tree House *Oswestry*	462
Yew Tree House *Vowchurch*	459
Yewdale Inn *Coniston*	587
Yewfield Vegetarian Guest House *Hawkshead Hill*	590
York House *York*	535
Yorke Lodge *Canterbury*	219
Yorkshire Bridge Inn *Bamford*	403

Z

	page
Zouch Farm B&B *Culham*	233

Establishments listed here have a detailed entry in this guide

Index by place name

The following places all have detailed accommodation entries in this guide. If the place where you wish to stay is not shown, the location maps (starting on page 706) will help you to find somewhere to stay in the area.

A

	page
Abbeystead *Lancashire*	614
Adderbury *Oxfordshire*	232
Airton *Yorkshire*	498
Aldborough near Cromer *Norfolk*	343
Alderton *Gloucestershire*	91
Alderton *Wiltshire*	118
Alnmouth *Northumberland*	674
Alnwick *Northumberland*	675
Alresford *Hampshire*	201
Alrewas *Staffordshire*	464
Alston *Cumbria*	577
Alton *Hampshire*	201
Alton *Staffordshire*	464
Altrincham (3 miles) *Cheshire*	574
Amberstone *Sussex*	246
Amble *Northumberland*	677
Ambleside *Cumbria*	578
Amesbury *Wiltshire*	118
Andover *Hampshire*	202
Appleby-in-Westmorland *Cumbria*	582
Arundel *Sussex*	246
Ashbourne (1.25 miles) *Staffordshire*	465
Ashbourne *Derbyshire*	400
Ashburton *Devon*	57
Ashford (5 miles) *Kent*	216
Ashford *Kent*	216
Ashwell *Hertfordshire*	342
Aspatria *Cumbria*	582
Aylesbury *Buckinghamshire*	199
Aylsham *Norfolk*	343
Ayot St Lawrence *Hertfordshire*	342

B

	page
Badgemore *Oxfordshire*	232
Bakewell *Derbyshire*	401
Bamford *Derbyshire*	402
Bampton *Oxfordshire*	232
Banks *Cumbria*	583
Barkston *Lincolnshire*	413
Barlborough *Derbyshire*	403
Barnstaple *Devon*	57
Barrow-in-Furness *Cumbria*	583
Barton *Cheshire*	574
Basingstoke *Hampshire*	202
Bassenthwaite *Cumbria*	584
Bath *Gloucestershire*	91
Bath *Somerset*	104
Bawdsey *Suffolk*	357
Beal *Northumberland*	678
Beamish 3 miles *Co Durham*	670
Beaworthy *Devon*	58
Beccles *Suffolk*	357
Bedale *Yorkshire*	499
Bedford *Bedfordshire*	330
Bembridge *Isle of Wight*	209

Berwick-upon-Tweed *Northumberland* ... 678
Beverley *Yorkshire* ... 500
Bexhill-on-Sea *Sussex* ... 246
Bibury *Gloucestershire* ... 92
Biddenden *Kent* ... 217
Bishop Wilton *Yorkshire* ... 500
Black Bourton *Oxfordshire* ... 233
Blackford *Cumbria* ... 584
Blackpool *Lancashire* ... 614
Bladbean *Kent* ... 217
Blandford Forum *Dorset* ... 81
Blickling *Norfolk* ... 344
Bodmin *Cornwall* ... 38
Bognor Regis *Sussex* ... 247
Bolton-by-Bowland *Lancashire* ... 626
Bolventor *Cornwall* ... 38
Bonchurch *Isle of Wight* ... 209
Boscastle *Cornwall* ... 39
Bosham (Chichester 3 miles) *Sussex* ... 248
Bournemouth *Dorset* ... 82
Bourton-on-the-Water *Gloucestershire* ... 92
Bowd *Devon* ... 58
Bowness-on-Windermere *Cumbria* ... 584
Bracknell *Berkshire* ... 196
Bradford-on-Avon *Wiltshire* ... 119
Bradwell *Derbyshire* ... 403
Brampton *Cumbria* ... 585
Braunton *Devon* ... 58
Brean *Somerset* ... 108
Brede *Sussex* ... 248
Brenchley *Kent* ... 217
Bridgnorth *Shropshire* ... 459
Bridlington *Yorkshire* ... 501
Bridport - West Dorset *Dorset* ... 84
Bridport (4 miles) *Dorset* ... 83
Bridport *Dorset* ... 83
Brighstone *Isle of Wight* ... 209
Brightlingsea *Essex* ... 336
Brighton & Hove *Sussex* ... 249
Bristol *Gloucestershire* ... 93
Brixham *Devon* ... 59
Brixton *Devon* ... 59
Brize Norton *Oxfordshire* ... 233
Broad Chalke *Wiltshire* ... 119
Broadstairs *Kent* ... 218
Broadway *Worcestershire* ... 472
Bromsgrove *Worcestershire* ... 473
Broseley *Shropshire* ... 460
Broughton in Furness *Cumbria* ... 585
Bruera *Cheshire* ... 575
Brundall *Norfolk* ... 344
Buckingham *Buckinghamshire* ... 199
Bude *Cornwall* ... 39
Budleigh Salterton *Devon* ... 60
Bugle *Cornwall* ... 40

Burley *Hampshire* ... 202
Burnham Thorpe *Norfolk* ... 344
Burnham-on-Sea *Somerset* ... 108
Burnley *Lancashire* ... 626
Bury St Edmunds (6 miles) *Suffolk* ... 358
Bury St Edmunds *Suffolk* ... 358
Buttermere *Cumbria* ... 586
Buxton *Derbyshire* ... 404
Byfield *Northamptonshire* ... 420

C

	page
Cadnam *Hampshire*	203
Caldbeck *Cumbria*	586
Callington *Cornwall*	40
Cambridge (12 miles) *Cambridgeshire*	334
Cambridge *Cambridgeshire*	331
Canterbury *Kent*	218
Capel *Surrey*	240
Carlisle *Cumbria*	586
Castle Cary *Somerset*	109
Castle Howard *Yorkshire*	501
Castleton *Derbyshire*	405
Chard *Somerset*	109
Charing *Kent*	220
Charminster *Dorset*	84
Cheadle *Staffordshire*	465
Cheddar *Somerset*	109
Cheltenham *Gloucestershire*	93
Chelwood Gate, East Grinstead *Sussex*	250
Chelwood Gate *Sussex*	249
Chester *Cheshire*	575
Chesterfield *Derbyshire*	405
Chewton Mendip *Somerset*	110
Chichester *Sussex*	250
Chineham *Hampshire*	203
Chipping Campden *Gloucestershire*	94
Chipping *Lancashire*	626
Cholderton *Wiltshire*	119
Chorley *Lancashire*	627
Christchurch *Dorset*	84
Cirencester *Gloucestershire*	95
Clacton-on-Sea *Essex*	337
Clapham *Yorkshire*	502
Clavering *Essex*	337
Clitheroe *Lancashire*	627
Cloughton *Yorkshire*	502
Clun *Shropshire*	460
Colchester (5 miles) *Essex*	338
Colchester *Essex*	337
Collingbourne Kingston *Wiltshire*	120
Colne *Lancashire*	627
Coltishall *Norfolk*	345
Combe Martin *Devon*	60
Compton Valence *Dorset*	85
Coniston *Cumbria*	587

780 Official tourist board guide **Bed & Breakfast**

Index by place name

C continued — page

orbridge *Northumberland* 680
ornhill-on-Tweed
 Northumberland..................... 681
ottingham *Yorkshire*..................... 503
oventry *West Midlands* 471
ranborne *Dorset* 85
ranwell *Lincolnshire*................... 413
rayke *Yorkshire* 503
rediton *Devon* 61
reeting St Mary *Suffolk*............... 358
ressbrook *Derbyshire*................. 406
ricklade *Wiltshire* 121
romer *Norfolk*........................... 345
ropston *Leicestershire & Rutland*... 410
rowborough *Sussex*.................... 251
royde *Devon* 61
roydon *Outer London*................. 305
ulgaith *Cumbria*......................... 588
ulham *Oxfordshire*..................... 233

D — page

alby *Yorkshire* 503
anby *Yorkshire* 504
arlington *Co Durham*................. 670
artmouth *Devon* 62
aventry *Northamptonshire* 421
awlish *Devon* 62
erby *Derbyshire*........................ 406
ereham *Norfolk* 345
ersingham *Norfolk* 346
etling *Kent*............................... 220
evizes *Wiltshire*........................ 121
ibden Purlieu *Hampshire*............ 204
inton *Wiltshire*.......................... 122
ockray *Cumbria* 588
oncaster *Yorkshire* 504
orchester *Dorset*........................ 85
orking *Surrey* 241
over *Kent*................................. 220
ownham Market *Norfolk* 346
rax *Yorkshire* 504
ufton *Cumbria*.......................... 588
unkeswell *Devon* 63
unmow *Essex*........................... 338
unster *Somerset* 111
urham *Co Durham*.................... 671

E — page

arby *Lancashire*........................ 628
arls Colne *Essex* 338
ast Ashling (Chichester 3 miles)
 Sussex................................... 251
ast Brent *Somerset* 111
ast Harptree *Somerset* 112
ast Hyde *Bedfordshire*................ 331
ast Ord *Northumberland* 682
ast Tytherley *Hampshire* 204
ast Wittering *Sussex* 253
astbourne *Sussex* 251
dmundbyers *Co Durham* 673
gton Bridge *Yorkshire*................ 505
llesmere (3 miles) *Shropshire*...... 460
llington Thorpe *Cambridgeshire*... 334
lmswell *Suffolk* 358
lsing *Norfolk*............................ 346
ly *Cambridgeshire*..................... 334
welme *Oxfordshire* 234
xeter *Devon*.............................. 63
ydon *Northamptonshire* 421

Eye Kettleby *Leicestershire & Rutland*........................... 410

F — page

Fairford *Gloucestershire* 96
Fakenham *Norfolk* 346
Falmouth *Cornwall* 41
Fareham *Hampshire* 204
Farnham *Surrey* 242
Faversham *Kent*......................... 221
Folkestone (2 miles) *Kent*............ 222
Folkestone *Kent*......................... 222
Ford *Gloucestershire* 96
Fossebridge *Gloucestershire* 97
Framlingham (7 miles) *Suffolk*...... 359
Framlingham *Suffolk* 359
Frampton-on-Severn
 Gloucestershire........................ 97
Freshwater *Isle of Wight*............. 210
Friston *Suffolk* 360
Frogmore *Devon* 65
Frosterley *Co Durham* 673

G — page

Gainsborough (4 miles)
 Lincolnshire 414
Garstang *Lancashire*................... 628
Gatwick *Sussex*.......................... 253
Gillingham *Dorset*....................... 86
Gillingham *Kent*......................... 222
Gilsland *Cumbria*....................... 589
Gilsland *Northumberland* 682
Glastonbury *Somerset* 112
Godalming *Surrey* 242
Grantham *Lincolnshire*................ 414
Great Ayton *Yorkshire* 505
Great Longstone *Derbyshire*......... 406
Great Missenden
 Buckinghamshire..................... 200
Great Yarmouth *Norfolk* 347
The Green *Cumbria* 606
Greenhead *Northumberland*......... 682
Guildford *Surrey* 243
Guiting Power *Gloucestershire*....... 98
Guyhirn *Cambridgeshire* 335

H — page

Haltwhistle *Northumberland* 683
Hanley Swan *Worcestershire*........ 474
Hanthorpe *Lincolnshire* 415
Harome *Yorkshire* 505
Harrogate *Yorkshire* 505
Haslemere *Surrey*...................... 243
Hastings *Sussex* 254
Hawes *Yorkshire* 506
Hawkshead *Cumbria* 589
Hawkshead Hill *Cumbria* 590
Haworth *Yorkshire* 506
Hay-on-Wye *Herefordshire*........... 456
Haydon Bridge *Northumberland*.... 684
Haywards Heath *Sussex*.............. 255
Heads Nook *Cumbria*.................. 590
Hebden Bridge *Yorkshire*............. 508
Hebden *Yorkshire* 508
Heddon-on-the-Wall
 Northumberland...................... 684
Helmsley *Yorkshire*.................... 509
Hemel Hempstead *Hertfordshire*... 343
Henfield *Sussex* 256
Henley-on-Thames
 Buckinghamshire..................... 200

Henley-on-Thames *Oxfordshire*...... 234
Herne Bay *Kent* 223
Hernhill *Kent*............................. 223
Herstmonceux *Sussex*................. 256
Hesket Newmarket *Cumbria* 591
Hexham *Northumberland*............ 684
Heytesbury *Wiltshire* 123
Hickling *Norfolk*......................... 347
High Wycombe *Buckinghamshire* ... 200
Higham *Derbyshire*.................... 407
Hintlesham *Suffolk*.................... 360
Holmbury St Mary *Surrey* 244
Holt *Norfolk*.............................. 348
Honington *Suffolk*...................... 360
Hope *Derbyshire*....................... 407
Huddersfield *Yorkshire* 509
Hunstanton *Norfolk* 348
Huntingdon *Cambridgeshire* 335

I — page

Illogan *Cornwall* 42
Ilminster *Somerset* 113
Ingleton *Yorkshire*..................... 509
Ingram *Northumberland* 685
Ipswich *Suffolk* 360

K — page

Kendal *Cumbria*......................... 592
Keswick (5 miles) *Cumbria*.......... 599
Keswick (7.5 miles) *Cumbria* 599
Keswick *Cumbria*....................... 593
Kettering *Northamptonshire*......... 421
Kettleburgh *Suffolk* 361
Kidderminster *Worcestershire* 474
Kielder *Northumberland*.............. 686
Kielder Water *Northumberland*...... 686
Kilcot *Gloucestershire*................. 456
Kilham *Yorkshire*....................... 510
Kilnwick Percy *Yorkshire* 510
King's Lynn *Norfolk*................... 349
Kingsbridge *Devon* 65
Kintbury *Berkshire* 197
Kirkby Lonsdale *Cumbria* 599
Kirkby Malzeard *Yorkshire* 511
Kirkbymoorside *Yorkshire*........... 511

L — page

Lake *Isle of Wight*...................... 210
Langport *Somerset*.................... 114
Langtoft *Yorkshire*..................... 512
Langwith *Nottinghamshire*........... 423
Launceston *Cornwall*.................... 42
Lavenham *Suffolk* 361
Laxton *Nottinghamshire* 423
Lea Bridge *Derbyshire* 408
Leamington Spa *Warwickshire* 468
Lechlade-on-Thames
 Gloucestershire........................ 99
Ledbury *Herefordshire* 457
Leeds *Yorkshire* 512
Leeming Bar *Yorkshire*............... 513
Leicester *Leicestershire & Rutland*... 410
Leintwardine *Herefordshire* 457
Letcombe Regis *Oxfordshire*........ 236
Lewes *Sussex*............................ 256
Lichfield *Staffordshire*................. 466
Lincoln *Lincolnshire*.................... 415
Lindale *Cumbria* 601
Littlehampton *Sussex* 257
Liverpool *Merseyside* 631
London E15 *Inner London* 301

Establishments listed here have a detailed entry in this guide   781

Index by place name

L continued | page

London E8 *Inner London* 301
London N1 *Inner London* 302
London N10 *Inner London* 302
London SE20 *Inner London* 303
London SE3 *Inner London* 302
London SE6 *Inner London* 303
London SW1 *Inner London* 304
London SW5 *Inner London* 304
London W1 *Inner London* 304
London W2 *Inner London* 305
Long Buckby *Northamptonshire* 422
Long Compton *Warwickshire* 468
Long Melford *Suffolk* 362
Long Stratton *Norfolk* 349
Looe *Cornwall* 43
Lostwithiel *Cornwall* 44
Lottisham *Somerset* 114
Loughborough *Leicestershire & Rutland* 411
Lower Bourne *Surrey* 244
Ludlow *Shropshire* 460
Lymington *Hampshire* 205
Lynton *Devon* 65
Lyth Bank *Shropshire* 462

M | page

Macclesfield *Cheshire* 576
Maidstone *Kent* 224
Maidstone, Kent *Kent* 224
Malton *Yorkshire* 513
Malvern *Worcestershire* 474
Manchester *Greater Manchester* 630
Manningford Abbots *Wiltshire* 123
Manningtree *Essex* 339
Margate *Kent* 225
Market Lavington *Wiltshire* 123
Marlborough *Wiltshire* 123
Marlow *Buckinghamshire* 201
Martock *Somerset* 114
Masham *Yorkshire* 513
Matlock Bath *Derbyshire* 409
Meriden *West Midlands* 472
Mevagissey *Cornwall* 45
Milford on Sea *Hampshire* 206
Milton Damerel *Devon* 66
Milton-under-Wychwood *Oxfordshire* 236
Minster *Kent* 225
Moddershall *Staffordshire* 466
Monkton Farleigh *Wiltshire* 124
Morcott *Leicestershire & Rutland* 411
Morecambe *Lancashire* 628
Moreton-in-Marsh *Gloucestershire* ... 99
Moretonhampstead *Devon* 66
Morpeth *Northumberland* 686
Morwenstow *Cornwall* 46
Mosedale *Cumbria* 601
Much Birch *Herefordshire* 457
Mumby *Lincolnshire* 416
Muncaster *Cumbria* 602

N | page

New Forest – Brockenhurst *Hampshire* 206
New Romney *Kent* 225
Newark *Nottinghamshire* 424
Newbrough *Northumberland* 687
Newbury *Berkshire* 197
Newcastle upon Tyne *Tyne and Wear* 691

Newhaven *Sussex* 258
Newmarket (4 miles) *Cambridgeshire* 335
Newport (3 miles) *Isle of Wight* 211
Newquay *Cornwall* 46
Newton Aycliffe *Co Durham* 673
Newton-on-The-Moor *Northumberland* 687
North Rode *Cheshire* 576
Northallerton *Yorkshire* 514
Northorpe *Lincolnshire* 416
Northwich *Cheshire* 577
Norwich *Norfolk* 349
Nottingham *Nottinghamshire* 424

O | page

Oakham *Leicestershire & Rutland* ... 412
Oakley Green *Berkshire* 198
Okehampton *Devon* 67
Orsett *Essex* 339
Osgoodby *Yorkshire* 514
Oswestry *Shropshire* 462
Otterburn *Northumberland* 687
Oxford *Oxfordshire* 236

P | page

Paignton *Devon* 67
Parkend *Gloucestershire* 100
Pembridge *Herefordshire* 458
Penrith *Cumbria* 602
Pentney *Norfolk* 352
Penton *Cumbria* 603
Penzance *Cornwall* 47
Pershore *Worcestershire* 475
Petersfield *Hampshire* 207
Petworth *Sussex* 258
Pickering (4 miles) *Yorkshire* 515
Pickering *Yorkshire* 514
Pidley *Cambridgeshire* 336
Pluckley *Kent* 226
Plymouth *Devon* 69
Polzeath *Cornwall* 47
Pooley Bridge *Cumbria* 604
Porlock *Somerset* 114
Port Isaac *Cornwall* 48
Porthcurno *Cornwall* 48
Porthloo *Isles of Scilly* 56
Portland *Dorset* 86
Portsmouth *Hampshire* 207
Powburn *Northumberland* 688
Preesall *Lancashire* 629
Preston *Lancashire* 629
Pulborough *Sussex* 258

R | page

Ramsgate *Kent* 226
Redruth *Cornwall* 49
Richmond *Outer London* 306
Ridlington *Leicestershire & Rutland* 413
Ringmer *Sussex* 259
Ripon *Yorkshire* 515
Robin Hoods Bay *Yorkshire* 516
Rodmell *Sussex* 259
Ross-on-Wye *Herefordshire* 458
Rothbury *Northumberland* 688
Rowde *Wiltshire* 124
Royal Tunbridge Wells *Kent* 226
Ruan High Lanes *Cornwall* 49
Rudford *Gloucestershire* 100
Rugeley *Staffordshire* 467

Runswick Bay *Yorkshire* 516
Ruskington *Lincolnshire* 416
Rustington *Sussex* 259
Rydal *Cumbria* 604
Ryde *Isle of Wight* 211
Rye *Sussex* 259
Ryton *Tyne and Wear* 692

S | page

Saffron Walden *Essex* 339
Sale *Greater Manchester* 630
Salisbury *Wiltshire* 125
Saltburn-by-the-Sea *Yorkshire* 517
Sandown *Isle of Wight* 212
Sawrey *Cumbria* 604
Scarborough *Yorkshire* 517
Scorton *Lancashire* 629
Seaford *Sussex* 262
Seahouses *Northumberland* 688
Seaton *Devon* 70
Sedbergh *Cumbria* 605
Settle *Yorkshire* 520
Shaftesbury *Dorset* 86
Shanklin *Isle of Wight* 213
Shap *Cumbria* 605
Shave Cross *Dorset* 87
Sheerness *Kent* 228
Sheringham *Norfolk* 352
Shifnal *Shropshire* 462
Shillingford *Oxfordshire* 239
Shrewsbury *Shropshire* 463
Sibton *Suffolk* 362
Sidmouth *Devon* 71
Sissinghurst *Kent* 228
Skegness *Lincolnshire* 417
Skipton *Yorkshire* 520
Slimbridge *Gloucestershire* 100
Snettisham *Norfolk* 353
Solihull *West Midlands* 472
South Cockerington *Lincolnshire* ... 418
South Creake *Norfolk* 353
South Kilvington *Yorkshire* 521
South Petherton *Somerset* 115
South Walsham *Norfolk* 353
Southampton *Hampshire* 207
Southend-on-Sea *Essex* 340
Southport *Merseyside* 632
Southville *Gloucestershire* 100
Southwold *Suffolk* 363
Spennymoor *Co Durham* 674
St Agnes *Cornwall* 49
St Austell *Cornwall* 50
St Issey *Cornwall* 51
St Ives *Cornwall* 51
St Just-in-Roseland *Cornwall* 52
St Mary's *Isles of Scilly* 56
St Mawgan *Cornwall* 53
St Mellion *Cornwall* 53
St Minver / Polzeath *Cornwall* 53
Stafford *Staffordshire* 467
Staithes *Yorkshire* 522
Stansted *Essex* 340
Stape *Yorkshire* 522
Staplecross *Sussex* 262
Staunton *Gloucestershire* 101
Stelling Minnis *Kent* 228
Steyning *Sussex* 262
Stirton *Yorkshire* 523
Stocksfield *Northumberland* 689
Stockton-on-Tees *Co Durham* 674
Stogumber *Somerset* 115
Stoke Gabriel *Devon* 72
Stoke St Gregory *Somerset* 115